The New York Times 2009 ALMANAC

Edited by John W. Wright

WITH EDITORS AND REPORTERS OF

The Times

PENGUIN REFERENCE

PENGUIN BOOKS

Published by the Penguin Group
Penguin Group (USA) Inc., 375 Hudson Street, New York, New York 10014, U.S.A.
Penguin Group (Canada), 90 Eglinton Avenue East, Suite 700, Toronto, Ontario, Canada M4P 2Y3 (a division of Pearson Penguin Canada Inc.)
Penguin Books Ltd, 80 Strand, London WC2R 0RL, England
Penguin Ireland, 25 St Stephen's Green, Dublin 2, Ireland (a division of Penguin Books Ltd)
Penguin Group (Australia), 250 Camberwell Road, Camberwell, Victoria 3124, Australia (a division of Pearson Australia Group Pty Ltd)
Penguin Books India Pvt Ltd, 11 Community Centre, Panchsheel Park, New Delhi – 110 017, India
Penguin Group (NZ), 67 Apollo Drive, Rosedale, North Shore 0632, New Zealand (a division of Pearson New Zealand Ltd)
Penguin Books (South Africa) (Pty) Ltd, 24 Sturdee Avenue, Rosebank, Johannesburg 2196, South Africa

Penguin Books Ltd, Registered Offices:
80 Strand, London WC2R 0RL, England

Published in Penguin Books, a member of Penguin Group (USA) Inc. 2008
This edition published 2008

10 9 8 7 6 5 4 3 2 1

Copyright © The New York Times Company, 2008
All rights reserved

ISBN 978-0-14-311457-4
ISSN 1523-7079

Printed in the United States of America
Set in Utopia and Optima
Designed by Virginia Norey

Please direct all comments to:
John W. Wright
The New York Times Almanac
1133 Broadway (1124)
New York, NY 10010

CONTRIBUTORS AND STAFF

General Editor
John W. Wright

Executive Editors
Matt Fisher, Andrea Galyean

Senior Editor
Lisette Johnson

Senior Writers
Ariana Brookes, Bryan Bunch, John Connelly, Grant Flowers, Alan Joyce, David Major, John Major, Allison Paxton Paine, Lincoln Paine, John Rosenthal, Patricia Szczerba, Jenny Tesar

Contributing Editors
Ellen Chodosh, Alice Finer, Glen Gendzel, Kurt Hettler, Deborah Kaple, Jerold Kappes, Michael Kaufman, James McCaffrey, Thomas LaRosa, Mary Quigley, Frederic Riccardi

Researchers and Fact Checkers
Robert L. Spring, Andrew Steinitz, Laura Stickney, Victoria Vine, Julia Ward

Data Entry
Arlene Jacks, Dorothy Green

The New York Times
Cristian L. Edwards, President, News Services; Nancy Lee, Vice President, Business Development; Alex Ward, Editorial Director, Book Development

Correspondents
Lawrence K. Altman, Barry Bearak, Pam Belluck, Alex Berenson, Dan Bilefsky, Ralph Blumenthal, Ethan Bronner, Nick Bunkley, Benedict Carey, Kenneth Chang, Michael Cieply, Nicola Clark, Helene Cooper, Alan Cowell, Karen Crouse, Anthony DePalma, Celia W. Dugger, Ian Fisher, Carlotta Gall, Jeffrey Gettleman, Walter Gibbs, William Glaberson, James Glanz, Peter S. Goodman, Denise Grady, Linda Greenhouse, Danny Hakim, Gardiner Harris, David M. Herszenhorn, Laura M. Holson, Carl Hulse, Andrew Jacobs, Kirk Johnson, David Jolly, David Kocieniewski, Gretel C. Kovach, Clifford Krauss, Stephen Labaton, Clifford J. Levy, Eric Lichtblau, Adam Liptak, Sarah Lyall, Andrew Martin, Salman Masood, Micheline Maynard, Mark Mazzetti, James C. McKinley, Jr., Gretchen Morgenson, Jad Mouawad, Seth Mydans, Steven Lee Myers, Adam Nagourney, Dennis Overbye, Tara Parker-Pope, Richard Perez-Pena, Tilak Pokharel, Lydia Polgreen, Andrew Pollack, Sam Roberts, Simon Romero, Choe Sang-Hun, Susan Saulny, Charles Savage, Michael S. Schmidt, Elaine Sciolino, Scott Shane, Marlise Simons, Jennifer Steinhauer, Sheryl Gay Stolberg, Paul Vitello, Bill Vlasic, Nicholas Wade, Duff Wilson, Jim Yardley

Maps
Steve Hadermeyer, John Papasian

CONTENTS

The 2008 Elections

OBAMA WINS DECISIVELY TO BECOME AMERICA'S FIRST BLACK PRESIDENT

Barack Hussein Obama was elected the 44th president of the United States on Nov. 4, 2008, as voters surged to the polls to elect him as the first black chief executive of the nation.

Mr. Obama, 47, a first-term Democratic senator from Illinois, defeated Senator John McCain of Arizona, 72, a former prisoner of war who was making his second bid for the presidency.

Mr. Obama won a decisive 52 percent of the popular vote, compared to 46 percent for Mr. McCain. The Electoral College vote was sharper, with preliminary results giving Mr. Obama 349 electoral votes to 173 for Mr. McCain. As of Nov. 5, Mr. Obama had won majorities in 28 states and the District of Columbia, with 21 states going to his rival. Missouri was too close to call.

Mr. Obama defeated Mr. McCain in Ohio, a central battleground in American politics, despite a huge effort that brought Mr. McCain and his running mate, Gov. Sarah Palin of Alaska, back there repeatedly. Mr. Obama had lost the state decisively to Senator Hillary Rodham Clinton of New York in the Democratic primary. Mr. Obama also defeated Mr. McCain in Florida, another state that has been at the center of battles between the two parties. That was one of the Republican states Mr. Obama targeted as part of an aggressive effort to expand the political map, taking advantage of his big financial edge over Mr. McCain.

By contrast, Mr. McCain failed to win the two Democratic states that were at the top of his target list: New Hampshire and Pennsylvania. Mr. Obama also held on to Minnesota (the state that played host to the convention that nominated Mr. McCain) as well as Wisconsin, Michigan, and Indiana, which has not voted for a Democrat for President since Lyndon Johnson's landslide in 1964.

Not only did Mr. Obama capture the presidency, but he also led his party to significant gains in Congress. This puts Democrats in control of the House, the Senate and the White House for the first time since 1995, when Bill Clinton was in office.

Democrats picked up at least six seats in the Senate, giving them a clear but not filibuster-proof 56–40 seat majority as the strong anti-Bush surge throughout the country upset such well-known Republicans as Senators Elizabeth Dole of North Carolina and John Sununu of New Hampshire. However, Senator Ted Stevens of Alaska, who only a week before the election had become a convicted felon, won reelection by a narrow margin. Mr. Obama's running mate, Joseph R. Biden Jr. of Delaware, also retained control of his Senate seat, for which Delaware's Democratic governor will appoint a successor.

In the House of Representatives, the Democrats continued to build a strong majority as they gained 18 seats in this election, giving them a margin of 252–173 over the Republicans. Even Christopher Shays of Connecticut—the last House Republican from New England—lost his reelection bid.

In the races for state governors, the Democrats won in seven states (including a strong victory in Missouri for Attorney General Jay Nixon) and the Republicans in four. This is a gain of one state for the Democrats, who now lead in governorships 29 to 21 nationwide.

The news of Mr. Obama's victory came at 11 p.m., Eastern time, when the television networks declared him the victor immediately upon the close of polls in California.

Initial signs were that Mr. Obama and the Democrats had benefited from a huge turnout of voters, particularly among blacks. That group made up 13 percent of the electorate, according to surveys of people leaving the polls, compared with 11 percent in 2006.

Mr. Obama also did strikingly well among Hispanic voters; Mr. McCain did worse among those voters than Mr. Bush did in 2004, suggesting the damage to the Republican Party among Hispanics over the four years in which Republicans have been at the forefront of the crackdown on illegal immigrants.

The election ended what by any definition was one of the longest and most remarkable contests in American political history, drawing unparalleled public interest and potentially record-breaking numbers of voters. Throughout the day, people lined up at the polls for hours—some showing up before dawn—to cast their votes.

Mr. Obama and his expanded Democratic majority on Capitol Hill now face the task of governing the country through a difficult period: the likelihood of a deep and prolonged recession, and two wars. He took note of those circumstances in a victory speech that was notable for its sobriety and its absence of the triumphalism that he might understandably have displayed on a night when he won an Electoral College landslide.

Standing before a crowd of 125,000 people at Grant Park in Chicago, Mr. Obama described his election in historic terms, saying, "If there is anyone out there who still doubts that America is a place where all things are possible, who still wonders if the dream of our founders is alive in our time, who still questions the power of our democracy, tonight is your answer."

—ADAM NAGOURNEY

The 2008 Presidential Election

State (Electoral votes)	REPUBLICAN John McCain/ Sarah Heath Palin		DEMOCRAT Barack Obama/ Joseph R. Biden, Jr.	
	Popular vote	Percent[1]	Popular vote	Percent[1]
Alabama (9)	1,263,541	60%	811,510	39%
Alaska (3)	136,348	62%	80,340	36%
Arizona (10)	1,012,262	54%	850,740	45%
Arkansas (6)	626,562	59%	414,300	39%
California (55)	3,693,865	37%	6,125,805	61%
Colorado (9)	960,865	46%	1,100,491	53%
Connecticut (7)	606,268	39%	942,705	60%
Delaware (3)	151,667	38%	247,386	61%
District of Columbia (3)	14,821	7%	210,403	93%
Florida (27)	3,880,015	48%	4,071,575	51%
Georgia (15)	2,020,680	52%	1,809,884	47%
Hawaii (4)	110,848	27%	298,621	72%
Idaho (4)	400,999	62%	234,769	36%
Illinois (21)	1,970,622	37%	3,265,509	62%
Indiana (11)	1,337,157	49%	1,359,875	50%
Iowa (7)	677,449	45%	818,172	54%
Kansas (6)	683,534	57%	498,081	41%
Kentucky (8)	1,043,264	57%	746,510	41%
Louisiana (9)	1,147,603	59%	780,981	40%
Maine (4)	253,525	40%	365,369	58%
Maryland (10)	870,990	38%	1,406,842	61%
Massachusetts (12)	1,104,003	36%	1,885,922	62%
Michigan (17)	2,044,405	41%	2,867,680	57%
Minnesota (10)	1,275,429	44%	1,573,207	54%
Mississippi (6)	683,952	56%	516,930	43%
Missouri (11)	1,442,613	49%	1,436,745	49%
Montana (3)	230,410	50%	214,581	47%
Nebraska (5)	439,421	57%	315,913	41%
Nevada (5)	411,988	43%	531,884	55%
New Hampshire (4)	273,611	44%	337,620	55%
New Jersey (15)	1,538,946	42%	2,069,640	57%
New Mexico (5)	333,114	42%	452,537	57%
New York (31)	2,557,481	37%	4,332,701	62%
North Carolina (15)	2,089,828	50%	2,101,991	50%
North Dakota (3)	168,523	53%	141,113	45%
Ohio (20)	2,395,130	47%	2,618,612	51%
Oklahoma (7)	959,645	66%	502,286	34%
Oregon (7)	506,498	43%	659,238	55%
Pennsylvania (21)	2,584,088	44%	3,184,778	55%
Rhode Island (4)	152,197	35%	275,028	63%
South Carolina (8)	963,456	54%	796,483	45%
South Dakota (3)	202,999	53%	170,877	45%
Tennessee (11)	1,470,160	57%	1,081,074	42%
Texas (34)	4,464,083	56%	3,518,100	44%
Utah (5)	555,497	63%	301,771	34%
Vermont (3)	86,262	31%	184,644	67%
Virginia (13)	1,635,613	47%	1,791,510	52%
Washington (11)	667,461	41%	938,492	57%
West Virginia (5)	394,277	56%	301,437	43%
Wisconsin (10)	1,250,349	43%	1,631,121	56%
Wyoming (3)	160,639	65%	80,496	33%
Total	**55,904,963**	**46%**	**63,254,279**	**52%**
Electoral Votes	**173**		**349**	

Note: Preliminary results as of Nov. 5, 2008. Only candidates winning at least five percent of the vote are listed. **1.** Percent of total vote reflects votes cast for other candidates not shown here.

State Governors

State, Candidates	Votes[1]	State, Candidates	Votes[1]	State, Candidates	Votes[1]
Delaware		**New Hampshire**		**Vermont**	
Jack Markell (D)	266,858	John Lynch (D)*	418,138	Jim Douglas (R)*	144,465
Bill Lee (R)	126,660	Joe Kenney (R)	163,435	Gaye Symington (D)	56,655
				Anthony Pollina (I)	56,623
Indiana		**North Carolina**			
Mitch Daniels (R)*	1,552,551	Bev Perdue (D)	2,104,082	**Washington**	
Jill Long Thompson (D)	1,072,889	Pat McCrory (R)	1,967,120	Christine Gregoire (D)*	864,302
				Dino Rossi (R)	750,542
Missouri		**North Dakota**			
Jay Nixon (D)	1,675,238	John Hoeven (R)*	234,585	**West Virginia**	
Kenny Hulshof (R)	1,133,751	Tim Mathern (D)	74,173	Joe Manchin (D)	488,835
				Russ Weeks (R)	180,353
Montana		**Utah**			
Brian Schweitzer (D)*	296,138	Jon Huntsman (R)*	682,185		
Roy Brown (R)	147,391	Bob Springmeyer (D)	172,481		

Note: * = Incumbent. Results are as of Nov. 5, 2008. Only candidates winning at least five percent of the vote are listed. **1.** Counts are preliminary, with a majority of precincts reporting.

U.S. Senate

State, Candidates	Votes[1]	State, Candidates	Votes[1]	State, Candidates	Votes[1]
Alabama		**Maine**		**Oklahoma**	
Jeff Sessions (R)*	1,298,580	Susan Collins (R)*	364,754	Jim Inhofe (R) *	763,063
Vivian Figures (D)	746,417	Tom Allen (D)	232,076	Andrew Rice (D)	527,528
Alaska		**Massachusetts**		**Oregon**	
Ted Stevens (R)*	106,351	John Kerry (D)*	1,958,404	Gordon Smith (R)*	532,142
Mark Begich (D)	102,998	Jeff Beatty (R)	922,409	Jeff Merkley (D)	512,834
Arkansas		**Michigan**		**Rhode Island**	
Mark Pryor (D)*	790,518	Carl Levin (D)*	3,028,118	Jack Reed (D)*	295,614
Rebekah Kennedy (G)	205,288	Jack Hoogendyk (R)	1,638,702	Bob Tingle (R)	106,836
Colorado		**Minnesota**[2]		**South Carolina**	
Mark Udall (D)	1,056,531	Norm Coleman (R)*	1,211,403	Lindsey Graham (R)*	999,595
Bob Schaffer (R)	884,506	Al Franken (D)	1,211,089	Bob Conley (D)	734,422
		Dean Barkley (I)	437,376		
Delaware				**South Dakota**	
Joe Biden (D)*	257,484	**Mississippi**		Tim Johnson (D)*	237,815
Christine O'Donnell (R)	140,584	Thad Cochran (R)*	719,611	Joel Dykstra (R)	142,757
		Erik Fleming (D)	446,456		
Georgia				**Tennessee**	
Saxby Chambliss (R)*	1,835,260	**Mississippi**		Lamar Alexander (R)*	1,560,707
Jim Martin (D)	1,723,981	Roger Wicker (R)*	645,877	Robert Tuke (D)	751,270
		Ronnie Musgrove (D)	521,497		
Idaho				**Texas**	
Jim Risch (R)	367,829	**Montana**		John Cornyn (R)*	4,323,205
Larry LaRocco (D)	217,547	Max Baucus (D)*	326,412	Rick Noriega (D)	3,380,842
		Bob Kelleher (R)	121,901		
Illinois				**Virginia**	
Dick Durbin (D)*	3,369,590	**Nebraska**		Mark Warner (D)	2,187,613
Steve Sauerberg (R)	1,461,098	Mike Johanns (R)	439,281	Jim Gilmore (R)	1,174,425
		Scott Kleeb (D)	304,383		
Iowa				**West Virginia**	
Tom Harkin (D)*	930,426	**New Hampshire**		Jay Rockefeller (D)*	444,106
Christopher Reed (R)	556,205	Jeanne Shaheen (D)	314,877	Jay Wolfe (R)	252,763
		John Sununu (R) *	269,835		
Kansas				**Wyoming**	
Pat Roberts (R)*	710,205	**New Jersey**		Mike Enzi (R)*	184,214
Jim Slattery (D)	428,102	Frank Lautenberg (D)*	1,819,948	Chris Rothfuss (D)	58,749
		Dick Zimmer (R)	1,392,896		
Kentucky				**Wyoming**	
Mitch McConnell (R) *	945,067	**New Mexico**		John Barrasso (R)*	178,269
Bruce Lunsford (D)	840,286	Tom Udall (D)	483,100	Nick Carter (D)	64,578
		Steve Pearce (R)	305,839		
Louisiana					
Mary L. Landrieu (D)*	986,411	**North Carolina**			
John Kennedy (R)	866,624	Kay Hagan (D)	2,207,821		
		Elizabeth Dole (R) *	1,855,353		

Note: * = Incumbent. Results are as of Nov. 5, 2008. Only candidates winning at least five percent of the vote are listed. **1.** Counts are preliminary, with a majority of precincts reporting. **2.** Recount pending.

U.S. House of Representatives

State, District, Candidates	Votes[1]
ALABAMA	
1 Jo Bonner (R)*	U
2 Bobby Bright (D)	143,997
Jay Love (R)	142,231
3 Mike Rogers (R)*	150,097
Joshua Segall (D)	130,773
4 Robert Aderholt (R)*	195,419
Nicholas Sparks (D)	65,719
5 Parker Griffith (D)	156,529
Wayne Parker (R)	147,190
6 Spencer Bachus (R)*	U
7 Artur Davis (D)*	U
ALASKA	
1 Don Young (R)*	113,816
Ethan Berkowitz (D)	96,929
ARIZONA	
1 Ann Kirkpatrick (D)	140,879
Sydney Hay (R)	99,332
2 Trent Franks (R)*	165,967
John Thrasher (D)	104,047
3 John Shadegg (R)*	117,439
Bob Lord (D)	92,614
4 Ed Pastor (D)*	71,027
Don Karg (R)	21,165
5 Harry Mitchell (D)*	118,849
David Schweikert (R)	97,569
6 Jeff Flake (R)*	170,303
Rebecca Schneider (D)	96,619
7 Raul Grijalva (D)*	99,906
Joseph Sweeney (R)	52,956
8 Gabrielle Giffords (D)*	147,830
Tim Bee (R)	115,793
ARKANSAS	
1 Marion Berry (D)*	U
2 Vic Snyder (D)*	210,696
Deb McFarland (G)	64,173
3 John Boozman (R)*	214,162[2]
Abel Tomlinson (G)	58,702
4 Mike Ross (D)*	193,299
Joshua Drake (G)	30,951
CALIFORNIA	
1 Mike Thompson (D)*	148,276
Zane Starkewolf (R)	51,415
2 Wally Herger (R)*	129,647
Jeff Morris (D)	96,770
3 Dan Lungren (R)*	117,609
Bill Durston (D)	105,288
4 Tom McClintock (R)	155,771
Charlie Brown (D)	155,320
5 Doris Matsui (D)*	121,805
Paul Smith (R)	34,056
6 Lynn Woolsey (D)*	192,380
Mike Halliwell (R)	65,073
7 George Miller (D)*	128,657
Roger Allen Petersen (R)	37,594
8 Nancy Pelosi (D)*	126,073
Cindy Sheehan (I)	29,951
9 Barbara Lee (D)*	170,966
Charles Hargrave (R)	19,301
10 Ellen Tauscher (D)*	150,233
Nicholas Gerber (R)	70,897
11 Jerry McNerney (D)*	130,078
Dean Andal (R)	105,426
12 Jackie Speier (D)*	138,272
Greg Conlon (R)	34,042
13 Fortney Pete Stark (D)*	120,418
Raymond Chui (R)	37,257
14 Anna Eshoo (D)*	141,623
Ronny Santana (R)	44,902
15 Mike Honda (D)*	128,043
Joyce Stoer Cordi (R)	41,975

State, District, Candidates	Votes[1]
16 Zoe Lofgren (D)*	108,497
Charel Winston (R)	36,561
17 Sam Farr (D)*	109,533[2]
Jeff Taylor (R)	36,486
18 Dennis Cardoza (D)*	U
19 George Radanovich (R)*	U
20 Jim Costa (D)*	71,662
Jim Lopez (R)	25,893
21 Devin Nunes (R)*	105,348
Larry Johnson (D)	48,824
22 Kevin McCarthy (R)*	U
23 Lois Capps (D)*	130,595
Matt Kokkonen (R)	62,832
24 Elton Gallegly (R)*	126,052
Marta Ann Jorgensen (D)	91,289
25 Buck McKeon (R)*	108,940[2]
Jackie Conaway (D)	78,952
26 David Dreier (R)*	97,613[2]
Russ Warner (D)	74,444
27 Brad Sherman (D)*	119,233
Navraj Singh (R)	42,722
28 Howard Berman (D)*	U
29 Adam Schiff (D)*	119,706
Charles Hahn (R)	45,409
30 Henry Waxman (D)*	U
31 Xavier Becerra (D)*	U
32 Hilda Solis (D)*	U
33 Diane Watson (D)*	147,722
David Crowley (R)	20,900
34 Lucille Roybal-Allard (D)*	83,383
Christopher Balding (R)	24,524
35 Maxine Waters (D)*	122,880
Ted Hayes (R)	19,766
36 Jane Harman (D)*	139,712
Brian Gibson (R)	63,408
37 Laura Richardson (D)*	107,565
Nick Dibs (I)	34,842
38 Grace Napolitano (D)*	109,938
Christopher Agrella (I)	24,370
39 Linda Sanchez (D)*	105,734
Diane Lenning (R)	45,557
40 Ed Royce (R)*	109,360
Christina Avalos (D)	64,028
41 Jerry Lewis (R)*	84,842[2]
Tim Prince (D)	52,745
42 Gary Miller (R)*	116,444[2]
Ed Chau (D)	75,478
43 Joe Baca (D)*	62,735[2]
John Roberts (R)	29,413
44 Ken Calvert (R)*	64,599[2]
Bill Hedrick (D)	56,616
45 Mary Bono Mack (R)*	58,529[2]
Julie Bornstein (D)	45,212
46 Dana Rohrabacher (R)*	114,672
Debbie Cook (D)	95,522
47 Loretta Sanchez (D)*	50,102
Rosie Avila (R)	21,029
48 John Campbell (R)*	129,436
Steve Young (D)	95,683
49 Darrell Issa (R)*	82,264[2]
Robert Hamilton (D)	50,342
50 Brian Bilbray (R)*	122,463
Nick Leibham (D)	111,086
51 Bob Filner (D)*	101,824
David Lee Joy (R)	35,856
52 Duncan D. Hunter (R)	117,066
53 Susan Davis (D)*	117,146
Michael Crimmins (R)	46,879
COLORADO	
1 Diana DeGette (D)*	193,502
George Lilly (R)	64,063

State, District, Candidates	Votes[1]
2 Jared Polis (D)	131,570[2]
Scott Starin (R)	81,141
3 John Salazar (D)*	188,842
Wayne Wolf (R)	120,304
4 Betsy Markey (D)	163,155[2]
Marilyn Musgrave (R)*	130,833
5 Doug Lamborn (R)*	174,877
Hal Bidlack (D)	106,618
6 Mike Coffman (R)*	223,873
Hank Eng (D)	146,570
7 Ed Perlmutter (D)*	152,377[2]
John Lerew (R)	88,686
CONNECTICUT	
1 John Larson (D)*	199,223
Joe Visconti (R)	80,446
2 Joe Courtney (D)*	210,786
3 Rosa DeLauro (D)*	194,870[2]
Bo Itshaky (R)	53,677
4 Jim Himes (D)	142,979
Christopher Shays (R)*	135,630
5 Chris Murphy (D)*	170,985
David Cappiello (R)	112,473
DELAWARE	
1 Mike Castle (R)*	235,419
Karen Hartley-Nagle (D)	146,399
FLORIDA	
1 Jeff Miller (R)*	231,372
Jim Bryan (D)	98,304
2 Allen Boyd (D)*	214,577
Mark Mulligan (R)	132,015
3 Corrine Brown (D)*	U
4 Ander Crenshaw (R)*	214,715
Jay McGovern (D)	115,478
5 Ginny Brown-Waite (R)*	264,514
John Russell (D)	167,933
6 Cliff Stearns (R)*	224,367
Tim Cunha (D)	143,769
7 John Mica (R)*	238,081
Faye Armitage (D)	145,908
8 Alan Grayson (D)	172,218
Ric Keller (R)*	158,717
9 Gus Bilirakis (R)*	196,827
Bill Mitchell (D)	112,884
10 Bill Young (R)*	180,101
Bob Hackworth (D)	116,427
11 Kathy Castor (D)*	138,778
Eddie Adams (R)	59,129
12 Adam Putnam (R)*	168,754
Doug Tudor (D)	117,451
13 Vern Buchanan (R)*	177,858
Christine Jennings (D)	121,315
14 Connie Mack (R)*	220,712
Robert Neeld (D)	92,035
15 Bill Posey (R)	191,341
Stephen Blythe (D)	151,031
16 Tom Rooney (R)	207,944
Tim Mahoney (D)*	138,366
17 Kendrick Meek (D)*	U
18 Ileana Ros-Lehtinen (R)*	137,809
Annette Taddeo (D)	100,923
19 Robert Wexler (D)*	186,655
Edward Lynch (R)	76,645
20 Debbie Wasserman Schultz (D)*	192,947
Margaret Hostetter (U)	55,246
21 Lincoln Diaz-Balart (R)*	132,861
Raul L. Martinez (D)	97,184
22 Ron Klein (D)*	158,735
Allen West (R)	130,400
23 Alcee Hastings (D)*	167,526
Marion Thorpe (R)	35,797

State, District, Candidates	Votes[1]
24 Suzanne Kosmas (D)	210,710
Tom Feeney (R)*	151,469
25 Mario Diaz-Balart (R)*	127,059
Joe Garcia (D)	113,495
GEORGIA	
1 Jack Kingston (R)*	165,472
Bill Gillespie (D)	83,065
2 Sanford Bishop (D)*	157,905
Lee Ferrell (R)	71,103
3 Lynn Westmoreland (R)*	222,792
Stephen Camp (D)	115,455
4 Hank Johnson (D)*	U
5 John Lewis (D)*	U
6 Tom Price (R)*	200,292
Bill Jones (D)	91,186
7 John Linder (R)*	197,156
Doug Heckman (D)	123,980
8 Jim Marshall (D)*	156,410
Rick Goddard (R)	116,999
9 Nathan Deal (R)*	216,824
Jeff Scott (D)	70,353
10 Paul Broun (R)*	177,109
Bobby Saxon (D)	114,463
11 Phil Gingrey (R)*	181,742
Bud Gammon (D)	84,794
12 John Barrow (D)*	164,330
John Stone (R)	84,664
13 David Scott (D)*	135,880
Deborah Honeycutt (R)	64,799
HAWAII	
1 Neil Abercrombie (D)*	135,962
Steve Tataii (R)	33,739
2 Mazie Hirono (D)*	157,559
Roger Evans (R)	42,181
IDAHO	
1 Walt Minnick (D)	167,071
Bill Sali (R)*	162,535
2 Mike Simpson (R)*	205,640
Deborah Holmes (D)	83,777
ILLINOIS	
1 Bobby Rush (D)*	188,355[2]
Antoine Members (R)	36,166
2 Jesse Jackson, Jr. (D)*	223,692[2]
Anthony Williams (R)	28,263
3 Daniel Lipinski (D)*	159,751[2]
Michael Hawkins (R)	47,263
4 Luis Gutierrez (D)*	102,287[2]
Daniel Cunningham (R)	14,749
5 Rahm Emanuel (D)*	157,851
Tom Hanson (R)	46,945
6 Peter Roskam (R)*	145,409[2]
Jill Morgenthaler (D)	106,723
7 Danny Davis (D)*	209,800
Steve Miller (R)	37,646
8 Melissa Bean (D)*	143,791
Steve Greenberg (R)	96,512
9 Jan Schakowsky (D)*	164,407[2]
Michael Younan (R)	49,789
10 Mark Kirk (R)*	128,869
Daniel Seals (D)	107,777
11 Debbie Halvorson (D)	182,463
Marty Ozinga (R)	107,725
12 Jerry Costello (D)*	212,913[2]
Timmy Richardson (R)	73,440
13 Judy Biggert (R)*	177,926
Scott Harper (D)	144,936
14 Bill Foster (D)*	180,849
Jim Oberweis (R)	133,959
15 Tim Johnson (R)*	186,785
Steve Cox (D)	104,146
16 Donald Manzullo (R)*	189,511
Robert Abboud (D)	112,287
17 Phil Hare (D)*	U
18 Aaron Schock (R)	180,501
Colleen Callahan (D)	116,429
19 John Shimkus (R)*	201,531
Daniel Davis (D)	104,293
INDIANA	
1 Peter Visclosky (D)*	199,145
Mark Leyva (R)	76,352
2 Joe Donnelly (D)*	187,328
Luke Puckett (R)	84,410
3 Mark Souder (R)*	155,045
Michael Montagano (D)	111,938
4 Steve Buyer (R)*	185,516
Nels Ackerson (D)	123,556
5 Dan Burton (R)*	231,725
Mary Ruley (D)	120,627
6 Mike Pence (R)*	175,381
Barry Welsh (D)	88,110
7 Andre Carson (D)*	169,574
Gabrielle Campo (R)	91,101
8 Brad Ellsworth (D)*	189,047
Greg Goode (R)	102,907
9 Baron Hill (D)*	181,254
Mike Sodrel (R)	121,514
IOWA	
1 Bruce Braley (D)*	180,632
David Hartsuch (R)	100,316
2 Dave Loebsack (D)*	174,876
Mariannette Miller-Meeks (R)	119,108
3 Leonard Boswell (D)*	175,261
Kim Schmett (R)	131,378
4 Tom Latham (R)*	184,537
Becky Greenwald (D)	120,064
5 Steve King (R)*	158,402
Rob Hubler (D)	98,475
KANSAS	
1 Jerry Moran (R)*	208,230
James Bordonaro (D)	33,454
2 Lynn Jenkins (R)	152,432
Nancy Boyda (D)*	137,898
3 Dennis Moore (D)*	197,642
Nick Jordan (R)	139,674
4 Todd Tiahrt (R)*	171,499
Donald Betts (D)	86,703
KENTUCKY	
1 Ed Whitfield (R)*	177,975
Heather Ryan (D)	98,646
2 Brett Guthrie (R)	158,398
David E. Boswell (D)	142,563
3 John Yarmuth (D)*	203,673
Anne Northup (R)	139,446
4 Geoff Davis (R)*	182,485
Michael Kelley (D)	107,048
5 Hal Rogers (R)*	177,571
Jim Holbert (I)	38,505
6 Ben Chandler (D)*	203,756
Jon Larson (R)	111,375
LOUISIANA	
1 Steve Scalise (R)*	189,034
Jim Harlan (D)	98,754
2 Joseph Cao (R)	[3]
TBD (D)	[3]
3 Charlie Melancon (D)*	U
4 TBD (D)	[3]
TBD (R)	[3]
5 Rodney Alexander (R)*	U
6 Bill Cassidy (R)	150,226
Don Cazayoux (D)*	125,716
Michael Jackson (N)	36,133
7 Charles Boustany (R)*	177,150
Don Cravins (D)	98,260
MAINE	
1 Chellie Pingree (D)	162,934
Charlie Summers (R)	129,684
2 Mike Michaud (D)*	177,596
John Frary (R)	86,574
MARYLAND	
1 Frank Kratovil (D)	160,780
Andy Harris (R)	159,787
2 Dutch Ruppersberger (D)*	182,182
Richard Matthews (R)	63,318
3 John Sarbanes (D)*	184,050
Thomas Harris (R)	80,235
4 Donna Edwards (D)*	202,523[2]
Peter James (R)	33,354
5 Steny Hoyer (D)*	210,628[2]
Collins Bailey (R)	72,213
6 Roscoe Bartlett (R)*	176,062
Jennifer Dougherty (D)	116,455
7 Elijah Cummings (D)*	203,519
Michael Hargadon (R)	47,419
8 Chris Van Hollen (D)*	195,552
Steve Hudson (R)	58,323
MICHIGAN	
1 Bart Stupak (D)*	213,174
Tom Casperson (R)	107,319
2 Pete Hoekstra (R)*	215,471
Fred Johnson (D)	119,959
3 Vernon Ehlers (R)*	205,888
Henry Sanchez (D)	119,431
4 Dave Camp (R)*	201,680
Andrew Concannon (D)	115,676
5 Dale Kildee (D)*	206,826
Matt Sawicki (R)	83,105
6 Fred Upton (R)*	183,337
Don Cooney (D)	120,325
7 Mark Schauer (D)	157,189
Tim Walberg (R)*	149,766
8 Mike Rogers (R)*	204,070
Robert Alexander (D)	146,052
9 Gary Peters (D)	178,853
Joe Knollenberg (R)*	150,054
10 Candice Miller (R)*	229,635
Robert Denison (D)	108,306
11 Thad McCotter (R)*	176,767
Joseph Larkin (D)	156,246
12 Sander Levin (D)*	225,070
Bert Copple (R)	74,564
13 Carolyn Cheeks Kilpatrick (D)*	164,204
Edward Gubics (R)	42,174
14 John Conyers (D)*	227,984
Richard Secula (L)	10,736
15 John Dingell (D)*	231,758
John Lynch (R)	81,797
MINNESOTA	
1 Tim Walz (D)*	207,748
Brian Davis (R)	109,242
2 John Kline (R)*	220,926
Steve Sarvi (D)	164,079
3 Erik Paulsen (R)	179,031
Ashwin Madia (D)	150,861
4 Betty McCollum (D)*	216,217
Ed Matthews (R)	98,920
5 Keith Ellison (D)*	227,949
Barb Davis White (R)	70,615
6 Michele Bachmann (R)*	187,808
El Tinklenberg (D)	175,785
7 Collin Peterson (D)*	227,181
Glen Menze (R)	87,051
8 James Oberstar (D)*	240,585
Michael Cummins (R)	114,576
MISSISSIPPI	
1 Travis Childers (D)*	181,398
Greg Davis (R)	146,584
2 Bennie Thompson (D)*	183,179
Richard Cook (R)	93,677
3 Gregg Harper (R)	198,423
Joel Gill (D)	117,188
4 Gene Taylor (D)*	201,389
John McCay (R)	68,548

State, District, Candidates	Votes[1]
MISSOURI	
1 Lacy Clay (D)*	240,813
Robb Cunningham (L)	36,457
2 Todd Akin (R)*	230,976
Bill Haas (D)	131,303
3 Russ Carnahan (D)*	201,732
Chris Sander (R)	92,370
4 Ike Skelton (D)*	199,940
Jeff Parnell (R)	103,421
5 Emanuel Cleaver (D)*	196,481
Jacob Turk (R)	108,801
6 Sam Graves (R)*	196,309
Kay Barnes (D)	121,729
7 Roy Blunt (R)*	218,632
Richard Monroe (D)	90,739
8 Jo Ann Emerson (R)*	198,764
Joe Allen (D)	74,278
9 Blaine Luetkemeyer (R)	160,955
Judy Baker (D)	152,851
MONTANA	
1 Denny Rehberg (R)*	292,426
John Driscoll (D)	144,474
NEBRASKA	
1 Jeff Fortenberry (R)*	181,312
Max Yashirin (D)	75,922
2 Lee Terry (R)*	132,505
Jim Esch (D)	119,917
3 Adrian Smith (R)*	180,568
Jay Stoddard (D)	54,895
NEVADA	
1 Shelley Berkley (D)*	154,227
Kenneth Wegner (R)	64,688
2 Dean Heller (R)*	170,610
Jill Derby (D)	136,313
3 Dina Titus (D)	165,416
Jon Porter (R)*	147,494
NEW HAMPSHIRE	
1 Carol Shea-Porter (D)*	155,997[2]
Jeb Bradley (R)	133,890
2 Paul Hodes (D)*	160,764[2]
Jennifer Horn (R)	115,694
NEW JERSEY	
1 Robert Andrews (D)*	191,062
Dale Glading (R)	70,072
2 Frank LoBiondo (R)*	159,079
David Kurkowski (D)	104,857
3 John Adler (D)	156,114
Chris Myers (R)	146,169
4 Chris Smith (R)*	198,415
Joshua Zeitz (D)	96,976
5 Scott Garrett (R)*	164,594
Dennis Shulman (D)	122,981
6 Frank Pallone (D)*	157,379
Robert McLeod (R)	75,342
7 Leonard Lance (R)	142,004
Linda Stender (D)	116,171
8 Bill Pascrell (D)*	143,096
Roland Straten (R)	58,147
9 Steve Rothman (D)*	140,746
Vincent Micco (R)	65,607
10 Donald Payne (D)*	153,930
Michael Taber (I)	1,564
11 Rodney Frelinghuysen (R)*	174,699
Tom Wyka (D)	103,479
12 Rush Holt (D)*	180,412
Alan Bateman (R)	103,971
13 Albio Sires (D)*	111,002
Joseph Turula (R)	32,310
NEW MEXICO	
1 Martin Heinrich (D)	161,551
Darren White (R)	130,101
2 Harry Teague (D)	113,279
Edward R. Tinsley (R)	91,341
3 Ben R. Lujan (D)	151,113
Daniel East (R)	80,780
NEW YORK	
1 Timothy Bishop (D)*	147,814
Lee Zeldin (R)	107,075
2 Steve Israel (D)*	149,069
Frank Stalzer (R)	75,665
3 Peter King (R)*	161,906
Graham Long (D)	90,179
4 Carolyn McCarthy (D)*	153,320
Jack Martins (R)	87,239
5 Gary Ackerman (D)*	103,033
Elizabeth Berney (R)	40,302
6 Gregory Meeks (D)*	U
7 Joseph Crowley (D)*	108,467
William Britt (R)	19,630
8 Jerrold Nadler (D)*	140,365
Grace Lin (R)	35,822
9 Anthony Weiner (D)*	102,561
Alfred Donohue (Con)	8,608
10 Edolphus Towns (D)*	138,912
Salvatore Grupico (R)	9,319
11 Yvette Clarke (D)*	152,994
Hugh Carr (R)	10,944
12 Nydia Velazquez (D)*	111,381
Allan Romaguera (R)	13,528
13 Michael McMahon (D)	105,128
Robert Straniere (R)	57,530
14 Carolyn Maloney (D)*	156,902
Robert Heim (R)	37,311
15 Charles Rangel (D)*	155,069
Edward Daniels (R)	16,501
16 Jose E. Serrano (D)*	112,204
Ali Mohamed (R)	3,973
17 Eliot Engel (D)*	142,525[2]
Robert Goodman (R)	37,564
18 Nita Lowey (D)*	147,508[2]
Jim Russell (R)	69,924
19 John Hall (D)*	146,756
Kieran Lalor (R)	104,991
20 Kirsten Gillibrand (D)*	175,951
Sandy Treadwell (R)	109,387
21 Paul Tonko (D)	157,158
James Buhrmaster (R)	89,941
22 Maurice Hinchey (D)*	149,912
George Phillips (R)	77,243
23 John McHugh (R)*	129,436
Michael Oot (D)	68,795
24 Michael Arcuri (D)*	116,675
Richard Hanna (R)	110,833
25 Daniel Maffei (D)*	146,411
Dale Sweetland (R)	113,358
26 Christopher Lee (R)	135,118
Alice Kryzan (D)	97,805
27 Brian Higgins (D)*	164,693[2]
Daniel Humiston (R)	51,336
28 Louise Slaughter (D)*	154,325
David Crimmen (R)	43,962
29 Eric Massa (D)	131,646
Randy Kuhl (R)*	127,232
NORTH CAROLINA	
1 G.K. Butterfield (D)*	186,309
Dean Stephens (R)	79,832
2 Bob Etheridge (D)*	196,679
Dan Mansell (R)	92,131
3 Walter Jones (R)*	195,469
Craig Weber (D)	100,558
4 David Price (D)*	263,150
William Lawson (R)	151,668
5 Virginia Foxx (R)*	188,151
Roy Carter (D)	134,566
6 Howard Coble (R)*	219,786
Teresa Sue Bratton (D)	108,312
7 Mike McIntyre (D)*	211,960
Will Breazeale (R)	95,987
8 Larry Kissell (D)	155,096
Robin Hayes (R)*	124,973
9 Sue Myrick (R)*	237,038
Harry Taylor (D)	136,978
10 Patrick McHenry (R)*	171,695
Daniel Johnson (D)	126,594
11 Heath Shuler (D)*	210,270
Carl Mumpower (R)	121,668
12 Mel Watt (D)*	211,906
Ty Cobb (R)	83,906
13 Brad Miller (D)*	209,880
Hugh Webster (R)	106,576
NORTH DAKOTA	
1 Earl Pomeroy (D)*	190,642
Duane Sand (R)	115,797
OHIO	
1 Steve Driehaus (D)	143,146
Steve Chabot (R)*	133,449
2 Jean Schmidt (R)*	143,287
Victoria Wulsin (D)	118,770
3 Mike Turner (R)*	110,261[2]
Jane Mitakides (D)	73,075
4 Jim Jordan (R)*	176,898
Mike Carroll (D)	93,455
5 Bob Latta (R)*	180,751
George Mays (D)	100,012
6 Charlie Wilson (D)*	164,048
Richard Stobbs (R)	87,737
7 Steve Austria (R)	159,265
Sharen Swartz Neuhardt (D)	113,099
8 John Boehner (R)*	163,586[2]
Nicholas von Stein (D)	74,848
9 Marcy Kaptur (D)*	199,569[2]
Bradley Leavitt (R)	69,762
10 Dennis Kucinich (D)*	153,357
Jim Trakas (R)	106,489
11 Marcia Fudge (D)*	204,680
Thomas Pekarek (R)	36,033
12 Pat Tiberi (R)*	252,633
David Robinson (R)	160,303
13 Betty Sutton (D)*	175,921
David Potter (R)	76,513
14 Steven LaTourette (R)*	175,487
Bill O'Neill (D)	116,275
15 Steve Stivers (R)	146,907
Mary Jo Kilroy (D)	134,492
16 John Boccieri (D)	123,849
Kirk Schuring (R)	105,399
17 Tim Ryan (D)*	165,780[2]
Duane Grassell (R)	46,363
18 Zack Space (D)*	154,396
Fred Dailey (R)	103,681
OKLAHOMA	
1 John Sullivan (R)*	193,361
Georgianna Oliver (D)	98,863
2 Dan Boren (D)*	173,075
Raymond Wickson (R)	72,453
3 Frank Lucas (R)*	179,733
Frankie Robbins (D)	60,390
4 Tom Cole (R)*	180,040
Blake Cummings (D)	79,653
5 Mary Fallin (R)*	171,841
Steven Perry (D)	88,961
OREGON	
1 David Wu (D)*	160,893[2]
Joel Haugen (I)	40,271
2 Greg Walden (R)*	183,715[2]
Noah Lemas (D)	69,376
3 Earl Blumenauer (D)*	102,919[2]
Delia Lopez (R)	28,358
4 Peter DeFazio (D)*	170,610[2]
Jaynee Germond (C)	29,732
5 Kurt Schrader (D)	120,597[2]
Mike Erickson (R)	81,757

State, District, Candidates	Votes[1]	State, District, Candidates	Votes[1]	State, District, Candidates	Votes[1]
PENNSYLVANIA		7 Marsha Blackburn (R)*	210,055	2 Jim Matheson (D)*	204,268
1 Robert Brady (D)*	232,642	Randy Morris (D)	96,505	Bill Dew (R)	111,696
Mike Muhammad (R)	23,362	8 John Tanner (D)*	U	3 Jason Chaffetz (R)	171,846
2 Chaka Fattah (D)*	266,077	9 Steve Cohen (D)*	182,849[2]	Bennion Spencer (D)	73,255
Adam Lang (R)	33,070	Jake Ford (I)	9,930	**VERMONT**	
3 Kathy Dahlkemper (D)	141,110	**TEXAS**		1 Peter Welch (D)*	205,986[2]
Phil English (R)*	132,461	1 Louie Gohmert (R)*	183,334	Thomas Hermann (P)	7,100
4 Jason Altmire (D)*	181,206	Roger Owen (I)	25,787	**VIRGINIA**	
Melissa Hart (R)	142,759	2 Ted Poe (R)*	174,492	1 Rob Wittman (R)*	195,470
5 Glenn Thompson (R)	150,036	Craig Wolfe (L)	21,711	Bill Day (D)	140,065
Mark McCracken (D)	108,021	3 Sam Johnson (R)*	169,557	2 Glenn Nye (D)	123,690
6 Jim Gerlach (R)*	174,380	Tom Daley (D)	107,679	Thelma Drake (R)*	115,786
Bob Roggio (D)	160,276	4 Ralph Hall (R)*	206,581	3 Bobby Scott (D)*	U
7 Joe Sestak (D)*	201,684	Glenn Melancon (D)	87,871	4 Randy Forbes (R)*	191,109
W. Craig Williams (R)	137,057	5 Jeb Hensarling (R)*	162,481	Andrea Miller (D)	126,563
8 Patrick Murphy (D)*	197,168	Ken Ashby (L)	31,847	5 Tom Perriello (D)	158,346
Tom Manion (R)	144,732	6 Joe Barton (R)*	173,828	Virgil Goode (R)*	157,785
9 Bill Shuster (R)*	171,636	Ludwig Otto (D)	99,689	6 Bob Goodlatte (R)*	189,096
Tony Barr (D)	97,237	7 John Culberson (R)*	162,205	Sam Rasoul (D)	111,838
10 Christopher Carney (D)*	158,949	Michael Skelly (D)	122,832	7 Eric Cantor (R)*	221,467
Chris Hackett (R)	122,949	8 Kevin Brady (R)*	206,687	Anita Hartke (D)	129,018
11 Paul Kanjorski (D)*	142,585	Kent Hargett (D)	70,575	8 Jim Moran (D)*	200,653
Lou Barletta (R)	133,192	9 Al Green (D)*	143,536	Mark Ellmore (R)	89,099
12 John Murtha (D)*	149,634	Brad Walters (L)	9,734	9 Rick Boucher (D)*	U
William Russell (R)	107,976	10 Michael McCaul (R)*	179,118	10 Frank Wolf (R)*	196,804
13 Allyson Schwartz (D)*	193,144	Larry Joe Doherty (D)	143,388	Judy Feder (D)	122,699
Marina Kats (R)	106,242	11 Mike Conaway (R)*	189,390	11 Gerry Connolly (D)	148,315[2]
14 Mike Doyle (D)*	239,922	John Strohm (L)	25,031	Keith Fimian (R)	126,186
Titus North (G)	22,916	12 Kay Granger (R)*	181,088	**WASHINGTON**	
15 Charles Dent (R)*	180,395	Tracey Smith (D)	81,999	1 Jay Inslee (D)*	121,624[2]
Sam Bennett (D)	127,630	13 Mac Thornberry (R)*	179,653	Larry Ishmael (R)	54,063
16 Joseph Pitts (R)*	167,203	Roger Waun (D)	51,914	2 Rick Larsen (D)*	121,734[2]
Bruce Slater (D)	117,051	14 Ron Paul (R)*	U	Rick Bart (R)	68,144
17 Tim Holden (D)*	189,170	15 Ruben Hinojosa (D)*	107,358	3 Brian Baird (D)*	159,975[2]
Toni Gilhooley (R)	107,359	Eddie Zamora (R)	52,195	Michael Delavar (R)	86,089
18 Tim Murphy (R)*	206,916	16 Silvestre Reyes (D)*	129,944	4 Doc Hastings (R)*	115,205[2]
Steve O'Donnell (D)	116,446	Mette Baker (L)	11,979	George Fearing (R)	70,455
19 Todd Platts (R)*	212,829	17 Chet Edwards (D)*	134,472	5 Cathy McMorris	
Philip Avillo (D)	106,958	Rob Curnock (R)	115,468	Rodgers (R)*	133,223[2]
RHODE ISLAND		18 Sheila Jackson Lee (D)*	148,204	Mark Mays (D)	76,144
1 Patrick Kennedy (D)*	132,079	John Faulk (R)	39,000	6 Norm Dicks (D)*	112,691[2]
Jonathan Scott (R)	45,143	19 Randy Neugebauer (R)*	167,962	Doug Cloud (R)	55,108
2 Jim Langevin (D)*	149,775	Dwight Fullingim (D)	57,824	7 Jim McDermott (D)*	121,137[2]
Mark Zaccaria (R)	64,155	20 Charlie Gonzalez (D)*	127,145	Steve Beren (R)	22,301
SOUTH CAROLINA		Robert Litoff (R)	44,490	8 Dave Reichert (R)*	69,627[2]
1 Henry Brown (R)*	137,394[2]	21 Lamar Smith (R)*	242,756	Darcy Burner (D)	68,746
Linda Ketner (D)	121,902	James Strohm (L)	60,711	9 Adam Smith (D)*	80,703[2]
2 Joe Wilson (R)*	173,814	22 Pete Olson (R)*	161,149	James Postma (R)	41,061
Rob Miller (D)	150,397	Nick Lampson (D)*	138,948	**WEST VIRGINIA**	
3 Gresham Barrett (R)*	186,004	23 Ciro Rodriguez (D)*	133,900	1 Alan Mollohan (D)*	U
Jane Dyer (D)	101,121	Lyle Larson (R)	100,648	2 Shelley Capito (R)*	146,160
4 Bob Inglis (R)*	180,211	24 Kenny Marchant (R)*	151,740	Anne Barth (D)	109,907
Paul Corden (D)	111,141	Tom Love (D)	111,649	3 Nick Rahall (D)*	132,831
5 John Spratt (D)*	185,818	25 Lloyd Doggett (D)*	191,354	Marty Gearheart (R)	65,636
Albert Spencer (R)	111,702	George Morovich (R)	88,553	**WISCONSIN**	
6 Jim Clyburn (D)*	178,715[2]	26 Michael Burgess (R)*	194,849	1 Paul Ryan (R)*	230,973
Nancy Harrelson (R)	86,250	Ken Leach (D)	117,895	Marge Krupp (D)	125,353
SOUTH DAKOTA		27 Solomon Ortiz (D)*	104,698	2 Tammy Baldwin (D)*	274,973
1 Stephanie Herseth		Willie Vaden (R)	69,354	Peter Theron (R)	121,191
Sandlin (D)*	255,974	28 Henry Cuellar (D)*	123,310	3 Ron Kind (D)*	219,849
Chris Lien (R)	122,931	Jim Fish (R)	52,394	Paul Stark (R)	121,168
TENNESSEE		29 Gene Green (D)*	79,581	4 Gwen Moore (D)*	183,795
1 Phil Roe (R)	168,068	Eric Story (R)	25,458	Michael LaForest (I)	25,997
Rob Russell (D)	57,470	30 Eddie Bernice		5 Jim Sensenbrenner (R)*	273,918
2 John Duncan (R)*	223,139	Johnson (D)*	169,860	Robert Raymond (I)	68,820
Bob Scott (D)	62,323	Fred Wood (R)	32,457	6 Tom Petri (R)*	221,812
3 Zach Wamp (R)*	184,787	31 John Carter (R)*	174,669	Roger Kittelson (D)	126,059
Doug Vandagriff (D)	73,030	Brian Ruiz (D)	105,837	7 David Obey (D)*	212,459
4 Lincoln Davis (D)*	146,700	32 Pete Sessions (R)*	116,165	Dan Mielke (R)	136,813
Monty Lankford (R)	94,412	Eric Roberson (D)	82,375	8 Steven Kagen (D)*	191,787
5 Jim Cooper (D)*	180,828	**UTAH**		John Gard (R)	163,575
Gerard Donovan (R)	85,005	1 Rob Bishop (R)*	186,031	**WYOMING**	
6 Bart Gordon (D)*	193,854	Morgan Bowen (D)	87,139	1 Cynthia Lummis (R)	127,809
Chris Baker (I)	66,626			Gary Trauner (D)	103,677

Notes: Results as of Nov. 5, 2008. * = Incumbent. **1.** Counts are preliminary, and reflect at least 95 percent of precincts except where noted. **2.** Count reflects less than 95 percent of precincts. **3.** Not yet decided.

Late Breaking News, October 16-31, 2008

Financial Turmoil Continues As Economy Slows: A Day-by-Day Chronology

Oct. 16 Financial giants Citigroup and Merrill Lynch report new multibillion-dollar losses, marking a complete loss of all profits made by major banks between early 2004 and mid-2007.

The Dow gains 400 points in the final minutes of trading after swinging wildly during the day.

With sales near historic lows, General Motors is considering a merger with Chrysler.

A bankruptcy lawyer for Lehman Brothers reveals that federal prosecutors in Manhattan, Brooklyn and New Jersey have issued subpoenas in an investigation into the collapse of the investment bank.

The price of oil drops below $70 per barrel for the first time in 14 months, prompting OPEC to call an emergency meeting, but raising U.S. consumers' hopes for lower gas and heating oil prices to help boost the economy.

Oct. 18 China declines to provide financial aid to shore up Pakistan's crumbling economy, leaving Pakistani president Asif Ali Zardari with the politically unpopular prospect of having to ask the International Monetary Fund for help.

Oct. 19 Republican and Democratic lawmakers alike are choosing to borrow money and let the already swollen federal deficit rise further in order to pay for both existing and newly allocated budget items. Even as additional emergency funds are needed for the $700 billion bank bailout and a newly proposed stimulus package, unemployment insurance and war expenses are rising and tax revenues are falling.

Oct. 20 After weeks of effort by the world's governments and central banks, a benchmark borrowing rate among banks drops by the largest amount in nine months and the rates on short-term loans are reduced, easing the flow of credit slightly. The Dow rises 413 points (4.7 percent).

Oct. 21 Kirk Kerkorian, one of the biggest single investors in the American auto industry, says that he will sell his stake in Ford Motor Company—a move that raises concerns over the deepening troubles of the Big Three automakers.

Oct. 22 The Dow drops 514 points (5.7 percent) in one day.

Treasury Sec. Henry Paulson says that the Federal Reserve did not have the ability to help Lehman Brothers avoid bankruptcy.

After years of unregulated moneymaking, hedge funds have lost $180 billion during the last three months and investors are quickly pulling out of the once-popular funds.

Oct. 23 As the financial crisis spreads through developing countries worldwide, Western officials weigh coordinated action to stabilize these economies. The I.M.F. says that it is negotiating with several countries to provide emergency loans and is working to arrange a huge credit line that would provide access to foreign capital.

Testifying before a House committee almost three years after stepping down as Federal Reserve chairman, Alan Greenspan admits that he had put too much faith in the self-correcting power of free markets and had failed to anticipate the self-destructive power of wanton lending.

As foreclosures continue to rise, the government says it will help homeowners by insuring against losses on some modified loans.

Oct. 24 Stocks sink worldwide and currencies of developing countries like Brazil, Ukraine and South Korea, and even of some developed countries like Britain, fall as investors turn to the security of the United States dollar and the Japanese yen.

OPEC announces that its members will cut oil output by 1.5 million barrels a day.

Oct. 25 Economists predict that October's job losses will exceed 200,000 and that the current unemployment rate of 6.1 percent is likely to rise, perhaps significantly. In the last two weeks, the list of companies announcing their intention to cut workers has included Merck, Yahoo, General Electric, Xerox, Pratt & Whitney, Goldman Sachs, Whirlpool, Bank of America, Alcoa, Coca-Cola, the Detroit automakers and nearly all the airlines.

Oct. 27 Government officials say that the Bush administration is examining a range of options for providing emergency financial help to spur a merger between General Motors and Chrysler.

Standard & Poor's releases a home price index showing that home prices in 20 cities fell 16.6 percent in August compared with a year ago—the biggest annual drop in the history of the survey.

Oct. 28 *The New York Times* reports that credit card companies wrote off more than $21 billion in bad debt in the first half of 2008 and may lose another $55 billion as an increasing number of consumers are defaulting on payments. Current losses total 5.5 percent of outstanding credit card debt.

The monthly Conference Board survey of consumer confidence shows the lowest reading in the survey's 40-year history and finds that Americans have fewer jobs, smaller incomes and declining home values.

Oct. 29 The Federal Reserve lowers its benchmark interest rate by half a percent—the second rate cut in less than a month—bringing the overnight lending rate to one percent, but warns that "downside risks to growth still remain."

Oct. 30 The Commerce Dept. reports that quarterly consumer spending dropped for the first time in 17 years—personal consumption was down by an annual rate of 3.1 percent—and that the U.S. economy is now shrinking at an annual rate of 0.3 percent.

Oct. 31 The stock market closes higher with a one point gain in the Dow but the month ends as the worst since 1987.

OBITUARIES

Hillerman, Tony, 83, Oklahoma native who left a 17-year newspaper career to write culturally evocative and best-selling detective novels set among the Navajos of his adopted Southwest. Of pulmonary failure, Albuquerque, Oct. 26, 2008.

Terkel, Studs, 96, gregarious and indefatigable author and radio host whose searching interviews with ordinary Americans won him a Pulitzer Prize, chronicled most of the 20th century, and established the oral history as a serious genre. Cause undisclosed, Chicago, Oct. 31, 2008.

U.S. Drops War Crimes Charges For Five Guantanamo Detainees

The Pentagon official in charge of military commissions at the naval base at Guantánamo Bay, Cuba, dismissed war crimes charges on Oct. 21 against five detainees, the latest challenge for the Bush administration's long-troubled system for prosecuting detainees at the base.

All five of the cases had been handled by a prosecutor who stepped down in September, saying there were systemic problems with the fairness of the military prosecutions there.

The dismissed charges included those against a detainee accused in 2002 of plotting to detonate a radioactive "dirty bomb" inside the U.S.

The chief military prosecutor, Col. Lawrence J. Morris, portrayed the dismissals as unexceptional and said he had asked for the dismissals so the files of the former prosecutor, Lt. Col. Darrel Vandeveld, could be reviewed and charges refiled. None of the detainees were to be released.

Senator Stevens Found Guilty Of Failing To Disclose Gifts

Senator Ted Stevens, Alaska's dominant political figure for more than four decades, was found guilty on Oct. 27 by a jury of violating federal ethics laws for failing to report tens of thousands of dollars in gifts and services he had received from friends.

The jury of District of Columbia residents convicted Mr. Stevens, 84, on all seven felony counts he faced in connection with charges that he knowingly failed to list on Senate disclosure forms the receipt of some $250,000 in gifts and services.

In a statement issued after he had left the courthouse, Mr. Stevens, a consistently grim-faced figure, was defiant, calling the verdict "unjust" and urging Alaskans to re-elect him to a seventh full term in the upcoming election.

The 2008 World Series: Phillies Beat Rays, 4-1

In a World Series marked by controversial calls, exciting base running, and torrential rain, the Philadelphia Phillies beat the Tampa Bay Rays four games to one. Phillies starter Cole Hamels opened the series with his fourth straight win of the 2008 postseason; Chase Utley hit a home run in his first World Series at-bat; and third baseman Pedro Feliz made several key defensive plays, including an inning-ending double play with the bases loaded in the third. The Rays won Game 2, 4-2, behind excellent pitching from both James Shields and the bullpen.

In a rain-delayed Game 3, 45-year-old Jamie Moyer pitched a solid 5-4 game for Philadelphia and, in a bizarre ninth inning, Phillies utility player Eric Bruntlett was hit by a pitch, advanced from first to third on a wild pitch and a throwing error, and scored on Pedro Feliz's slow chopper up the third-base line—the first walk-off infield hit in World Series history. The Phillies were up 2-1 despite going only 2 for 33 with runners in scoring position—and both of those hits stayed in the infield. But Philadelphia had four home runs in Game 4, including two by Ryan Howard and one by starter Joe Blanton, the first World Series homer by a pitcher since 1974, and the Phillies won easily, 10-2.

In Game 5, the first five and one-half innings were played in gusting winds and steady rain and the field became saturated. After the Rays tied the score at 2-2 in the top of the sixth, play was suspended. When it resumed 46 hours later, Eric Bruntlett again scored the winning run and the Phillies took the game, 4-3, and the series.

Cole Hamels, the NLCS M.V.P., was also named World Series M.V.P. For the fifth straight year, the series was decided in five games or less; the last time the World Series failed to reach a sixth game for five years was 1912–1916.

The Nobel Prizes, 2008

CHEMISTRY

Osamu Shimomura, 80, (Japan), Marine Biological Laboratory, Woods Hole, Mass. and Boston University; first isolated green fluorescent protein (G.F.P.) from jellyfish. **Martin Chalfie**, 61, (U.S.), Columbia University; pioneered use of G.F.P. as a genetic tag for biological research. **Roger Y. Tsein**, 56, (U.S.), University of California at San Diego; developed additional colors of G.F.P.

ECONOMY

Paul Krugman, 55, (U.S.), Princeton University; "for his analysis of trade patterns and location of economic activity."

LITERATURE

Jean-Marie Gustave Le Clézio, 68, (France); "author of new departures, poetic adventures and sensual ecstasy, explorer of a humanity beyond and below the reigning civilization."

PEACE

Martti Ahtisaari, 71, (Finland) for three decades of work as an international mediator; he has "figured prominently in endeavors to resolve several serious and long-lasting conflicts."

PHYSICS

Yoichiro Nambu, 87, (U.S., b. Japan), Enrico Fermi Institute, Chicago; for his 1960 explanation of how subatomic symmetry might sometimes be "broken" or hidden. **Makoto Kobayashi**, 64, (Japan), High Energy Accelerator Research Organization, Tsukuba, Japan; and **Toshihide Maskawa**, 68, (Japan), Kyoto University; for their 1972 explanations of the origins of spontaneous broken symmetry, which correctly predicted the existence of three families of quarks.

PHYSIOLOGY OR MEDICINE

Françoise Barré-Sinoussi, 61, (France), Institut Pasteur, Paris; and **Luc Montagnier**, 76, (France), World Foundation for AIDS Research and Prevention, Paris; for discovering the human immunodeficiency virus (H.I.V.), which causes AIDS and describing its behavior in the immune system, leading to better prevention efforts and to more effective treatments. **Harald zur Hausen**, 72, (Germany), German Cancer Research Center; for "going against current dogma" to prove that certain strains of human papilloma virus are responsible for most cases of cervical cancer.

THE ALMANAC OF THE YEAR
Chronology of the Year Oct. 1, 2007–Oct. 15, 2008

OCTOBER 2007

1 An Iraqi official and an independent monitoring group report that the number of violent civilian deaths in Iraq fell 29 percent from 2,318 in August to 1,654 in September and the American military reports that service member deaths also declined, from 84 in August, to 63 in September, the lowest monthly total in over a year.

3 North Korea agrees to disable its nuclear facilities by the end of the year, in exchange for 950,000 metric tons of fuel, or its equivalent in monetary aid from China, Russia, South Korea, Japan and the United States.

U.S. government officials say that the Justice Dept. secretly endorsed torture as an interrogation tactic in a 2005 opinion written soon after Alberto Gonzales became Attorney General.

4 Idaho senator Larry Craig says he will not step down from his Senate seat, despite his involvement in an undercover sex sting.

The House approves a bill that brings all U.S. government contractors in the Iraq war zone under American criminal jurisdiction.

5 The State Dept. announces that it will send its own personnel on all Blackwater USA security convoys in and around Baghdad.

President Bush denies Congressional allegations that methods used by the C.I.A. in interrogating high-profile terror suspects, such as head-slapping, waterboarding, and exposure to cold temperatures, are torture.

6 *The New York Times* reports tens of thousands of Medicare recipients have had problems with the private insurers who run the agency's new drug benefit program, including improper termination of coverage for people with HIV and AIDS, failure to follow through with claims and complaints and failure to answer telephone calls from consumers, doctors and drugstores.

7 Following the biggest opium harvest in Afghanistan's history, the U.S. government renews efforts to persuade the Afghan government to spray herbicide on opium poppies, despite earlier opposition from President Hamid Karzai.

The Chicago Marathon is halted for the first time in the race's 30-year history, after hundreds of people fall ill and one dies from unseasonable heat.

8 House Democrats propose a bill that would maintain the broad authority of the National Security Agency in eavesdropping endeavors, despite previous opposition.

British prime minister Gordon Brown announces that he will remove 5,000 British troops from Iraq by the spring of 2008.

9 Two Iraqi women are killed in Baghdad after the car they are driving in is shot at by guards for a private Australian security company.

10 The Marine Corps presses to remove its forces from Iraq and relocate to Afghanistan to take over the leading role in combat there.

United Automobile Workers reach an agreement with Chrysler six hours after 45,000 Chrysler workers began picketing.

11 C.I.A. director Michael Hayden orders an internal inquiry into the work of the C.I.A.'s own inspector general, John L. Helgerson, whose inquiries into the C.I.A.'s detention and interrogation programs have created resentment throughout the agency.

12 New accounts of the Blackwater USA shooting on Sept. 16 given by American soldiers and rooftop witnesses suggest that statements given by Blackwater guards that they were responding to an armed insurgency were false.

13 U.S. intelligence analysts determine that a Syrian site that Israeli forces struck in September was indeed a partially constructed nuclear reactor, as previously suspected, possibly modeled on a North Korean design.

14 Medtronic, the largest U.S. producer of implanted heart devices, urges doctors to stop using its most recent defibrillator because a product defect which has caused hundreds of malfunctions and five deaths.

15 The three largest U.S. banks: Citigroup, JPMorgan Chase and Bank of America, announce plans for a new financing vehicle which would restore consumer confidence and reduce risk of market meltdown by propping up debt markets.

16 House members withdraw support for a Democratic-backed resolution which would condemn the mass killings of Armenians over a century ago as genocide after the Turkish government threatens to reconsider its ties to the U.S.

Defense Sec. Robert Gates presses for a motion to bring all armed security contractors working for the U.S. government under the rule of a single authority, most likely the U.S. Army.

17 The Turkish Parliament votes to send troops into northern Iraq to fight Kurdish rebels, despite U.S. efforts to use Kurdish allies to quell rebel attacks on Turkey through negotiations.

The F.C.C. proposes a plan to relax media ownership rules, including elimination of a rule that forbids a company from owning both a newspaper and a television or radio station in the same city.

18 Two bombs explode in Karachi, Pakistan near a truck carrying the returning former Prime Minister Benazir Bhutto, missing her, but killing over 125 and wounding around 250.

The House upholds a presidential veto on a bill that would provide health insurance to 10 million children nationwide.

19 An F.D.A. advisory panel votes to ban over-the-counter cold remedies for use in children under the age of six.

20 The wait at the U.S.-Mexico border is the longest it's been since the months after 9/11, because of increased scrutiny by border agents practicing for the new rule, effective in January, which will require Americans to show their passport or other proof of citizenry to enter the U.S.

21 Kurdish militants kill twelve Turkish soldiers in an escalation of Turkish-Iraqi tensions.

Wildfires erupt in southern California spreading across 30,000 acres of land, killing one person, injuring four firefighters, and damaging many homes and other buildings.

22 A State Dept. review of its own security practices in Iraq reveal poor communication, coordination and accountability involving armed security companies.

A jury in Texas is not persuaded that the Holy Land Foundation for Relief and Development, a Muslim charity, and five of its backers, were contributing to terrorist funding as charged by the Bush administration.

23 *The New York Times* reports that over the past four years, the amount of money the State Dept. paid to private security and law enforcement contractors increased from $1 billion to $4 billion, though there was no increase in personnel to oversee the contracts.

24 Firefighters are finally able to bring southern California wildfires under control, after they had already burned 500,000 acres and displaced 500,000 residents over four days.

The Bush administration announces a policy of new sanctions against Iran, claiming that the Quds division of the Revolutionary Guards Corps support terrorism.

26 The board at Merrill Lynch begins to consider replacing its C.E.O. due to increasing credit losses at the brokerage firm.

An Army panel overturns the conviction of 28 black soldiers who were convicted of starting a riot on a military base at Puget Sound in 1944.

28 The F.C.C. announces a plan to strike down thousands of contracts that give individual cable companies exclusive rights to provide service to an apartment building.

The Boston Red Sox sweep the World Series, with a 4-3 victory over the Colorado Rockies.

29 *The New York Times* reports that State Dept. investigators offered immunity to Blackwater USA security guards during the inquiry into the September shooting in Iraq, which could seriously complicate efforts to prosecute Blackwater employees involved in the incident.

30 The Supreme Court blocks a lethal injection in Mississippi, moments before it was supposed to occur, signaling their intention to block all executions until they decide a lethal injection case from Kentucky in the spring.

Sec. of State Condoleeza Rice and Defense Sec. Robert M. Gates agree to grant the military control over all State Dept. security convoys in Iraq in response to last month's Blackwater incident.

31 Michael Mukasey, nominee for Attorney General, refuses to declare waterboarding illegal in order to avoid the issue of whether Central Intelligence agents who used the tactic should be prosecuted.

The New York Times reports that Blackwater International has hired a team of bipartisan lawyers, lobbyists and press advisers in order to turn around their public image.

NOVEMBER 2007

1 The Dow Industrial average drops over 360 points after the Fed's announcement that it was reluctant to further reduce rates.

2 Two Democrats on the Senate Judiciary Committee, Charles Schumer of New York and Dianne Feinstein of California, say they will support the confirmation of Michael Mukasey as Attorney General.

3 Pakistani president Gen. Pervez Musharraf declares a state of emergency, suspending the country's constitution and replacing the nation's chief justice, in a move to reassert his waning power in the face of growing opposition. (See "Major News Stories.")

5 Thousands of lawyers demonstrate in Lahore, Pakistan and many are thrown in jail, in the first organized resistance to the emergency rule set in place by General Pervez Musharraf.

6 The House overrides a Bush veto of a water projects measure and approves a $215 billion bill including health, education, labor and veterans programs, despite a threatened veto of the bill.

7 Pat Robertson, conservative Christian broadcaster, backs former New York mayor Rudy Guliani as the 2008 G.O.P. candidate for president.

The Dow drops 360 points and the entire stock market drops three percent, as the dollar sinks to a record low against the euro, at $1.4704 per euro.

8 Ben Bernanke, chairman of the Federal Reserve, announces that worse times are ahead in the economy, and made no signal that the Fed might lower interest rates in the near future.

The Senate confirms Michael Mukasey as Attorney General. (See "Major News Stories.")

9 Around 8,500 police officers lock down the Pakistani city of Rawalpindi, the planned site of a protest against General Pervez Mushrraf's declaration of martial law six days ago.

11 An Iraqi taxi driver is killed by an agent of the private security company DynCorp International, in what witnesses called an unprovoked attack.

Pakistan's president Gen. Pervez Musharraf restores parliamentary elections in early January, but says that they will be held under the current state of emergency rule.

12 At least six Palestinians are killed and over 100 wounded in Gaza in a clash between pro-Western Fatah forces and Hamas during a rally celebrating the third anniversary of the death of Yasir Arafat.

13 Federal agents investigating the Blackwater USA shootings on Sept. 16 in which 17 Iraqi civilians died, find at least 14 of the shootings to be unjustified and in violation of deadly-force rules in effect for security contractors in Iraq.

Ignoring Condoleeza Rice's plea to lift the state of emergency in Pakistan, Gen. Musharraf calls the declaration of martial law throughout the country crucial to fair voting results.

14 John A. Thain, former co-president of Goldman Sachs, is named chief executive at Merrill Lynch, in a move the company hopes will turn the company's failing profits around.

15 A federal appeals court in San Francisco rejects the Bush administration's fuel economy standards for light trucks, voiding the regulations on 2008–2011 model trucks and asking the Transportation Dept. to produce new regulations which take into account the importance of reducing greenhouse gases.

Baseball player Barry Bonds is indicted on five felony charges—four for perjury and one for obstruction of justice—for testifying in 2003 before a federal grand jury that he had never used anabolic steroids or human growth hormones.

16 The U.N. Intergovernmental Panel on Climate Change for the first time specifically names the biggest risks governments take in not responding to global warming, including rising sea levels due to melting ice sheets and the extinction of certain species of animals.

17 *The New York Times* reports that the Bush administration has spent nearly $100 million to help Pakistan's president Gen. Pervez Musharraf secure the country's nuclear program.

18 A new military proposal outlines an intensified effort to enlist tribal leaders on the frontiers of Pakistan to fight Al Qaeda and the Taliban in an effort to counter the increased Al Qaeda militancy in the area.

The U.S. military says that the weekly number of attacks in Iraq has fallen to the lowest level since February 2006.

19 The United Nations acknowledges that it has overestimated the number of global H.I.V. cases, and that there are closer to 33.2 million people infected with the virus, rather than last year's estimate of 39.5 million.

20 Two teams of scientists report that they have created embryonic stem cells out of human skin cells, bypassing the need to make or destroy an embryo.

The first trials to prosecute members of the Khmer Rouge for crimes against humanity begin in Phnom Penh, Cambodia, 28 years after the genocide stopped.

21 According to senior U.S. military officials, Saudi Arabia and Libya—both supposed to be allies in the American war on terror—supplied about 60 percent of the foreign fighters in Iraq during 2007.

22 U.S. army commanders announce that they plan to give remaining combat brigades in Iraq—a quarter of whom are supposed to be leaving by July—an expanded role in training and supporting Iraqi forces.

23 The cruise ship *Explorer* hits an iceberg while sailing the Antarctic; all 154 on board are rescued after escaping on boats.

24 Bush Administration officials say they have scaled back plans for holding regional elections in Iraq, and instead are focusing on more limited but reachable goals.

25 Former Prime Minister Nawaz Sharif arrives home in Pakistan after seven years in exile.

Republican officials announce a plan to recruit wealthy congressional candidates who can finance their own races to offset a lack of G.O.P. funds.

27 At a conference in Annapolis, Md., Israeli and Palestinian leaders commit to negotiating a peace treaty by the end of 2008.

28 The stagehand's union reaches an agreement with the league representing Broadway theater owners and producers, ending a 19-day strike that cost New York City tens of millions of dollars.

The New York Times reports that outstanding commercial and industrial bank loans, and short term loans, dropped nearly nine percent from a peak of $3.3 trillion in August, to $3 trillion by mid-November.

29 The Iraqi government has not yet developed a plan for absorbing the influx of refugees returning to Baghdad, which the U.S. government worries will set off new sectarian violence.

30 Congress reaches a deal on energy legislation that would force American automakers to improve the fuel efficiency of their cars and light trucks, by requiring their vehicles achieve 35 miles per gallon on average, by 2020.

DECEMBER 2007

1 *The New York Times* reports that business lobbyists in Washington are hoping to gain approval on a wide range of rules on health, safety, and labor before Bush's pro-business administration leaves office.

American officials estimate that one-third of the funds meant for rebuilding contracts in Iraq is unaccounted for or stolen.

2 Voters in Venezuela strike down a referendum that would have granted President Hugo Chavéz sweeping new powers.

The New York Times reports that more than two years after Hurricane Katrina, New Orleans is still suffering from an acute housing shortage.

3 American intelligence agencies report that Iran halted its nuclear arms program in 2003, a discovery that directly contradicts a 2005 intelligence judgment which said that Iran had an active secret nuclear arms program.

4 President Bush announces that Iran is still a threat to the United States, despite new evidence that it does not have an active nuclear arms program.

Researchers report that the influenza virus spreads more easily in winter than any other season because the virus is more stable when the air is cold and dry.

5 The Bush Administration and the mortgage industry agree on a plan to freeze interest rates for up to five years for some of the two million homeowners who have recently bought houses with subprime loans.

6 Government officials report that in 2005 the C.I.A. destroyed two videotapes documenting harsh interrogations of two Al Qaeda operatives.

Bush Administration officials say that Pres. Bush has written a letter to North Korean leader Kim Jong-Il offering to normalize relations between the two countries if North Korea fully discloses its nuclear programs and dismantles its nuclear reactor.

7 The C.I.A. and the Justice Dept. both face obstruction-of-justice charges over the destruction of videotapes of interrogations of Al Qaeda operatives.

Budget leaders in Congress are assembling a $500 billion package of unfettered money for the Iraq war for President Bush, in exchange for new spending on domestic programs.

8 *The New York Times* reports that the economies of the largest oil-exporting countries are growing so fast that their need for energy is limiting how much oil they can sell abroad, adding new strain to the global energy market.

9 *The New York Times* reports that delays in the resolution of Social Security disability claims have left hundreds of people in limbo concerning their appeals, some waiting as long as three years for a decision on an appeal.

10 The Supreme Court grants more leeway to federal judges in criminal sentencing, saying that federal district judges should be free to disagree with federal guidelines and have broad discretion in imposing reasonable sentences.

Russian president Vladimir Putin endorses Dmitri Medvedev, a 42-year-old first deputy prime minister and chairman of Russian gas monopoly, Gazprom, as his successor.

11 Two car bombs planted by local Al Qaeda operatives near U.N. offices and an Algerian government building kill at least 26 people in Algiers.

The agency that sets guidelines for federal prison sentences votes to retroactively lighten punishments for crimes related to crack cocaine, a decision that could affect up to 19,500 inmates.

12 Central banks in North America and Europe announce plans to lend billions of dollars to the U.S. banking system as a means of relieving the credit crisis.

The New York Times reports that a major confrontation between the Congolese army and rebel general Laurent Nkunda is threatening to send the Congo back into a new regional conflict.

13 Former Senator George J. Mitchell releases a report that implicates 89 Major League Baseball players in the use of illegal, performance-enhancing drugs.

Investigators report that the failed terrorist attacks in London and Glasgow in June of 2007 were carried out by the group Al Qaeda in Mesopotamia, marking the group's first attacks outside the Middle East.

14 The Justice Dept. asks the House Intelligence Committee to postpone an investigation into the destruction of C.I.A. videotapes from 2005 that show interrogations of two Al Qaeda operatives, due to its own investigation.

The New York Times reports that, due to troop shortages, the Ethiopian government is forcing untrained civilians to fight rebel factions. (See "Major News Stories.")

15 The Bush Administration and NATO, concerned about possible failure in Afghanistan, have begun three comprehensive reviews on U.S. involvement in Iraq.

187 countries, including the U.S., agree to negotiate a new accord on cutting global greenhouse gas emissions.

16 *The New York Times* reports that warriors who fought for the C.I.A. in a secret war against Communists are still hiding in the jungles of Laos, on the run from the Communist Laotian government.

17 Russia delivers nuclear fuel to an Iranian power plant, despite protests from the U.S. government, while Iran announced plans to build a second nuclear power plant.

18 The Federal Reserve proposes a set of restrictions on exotic mortgages and large loans for people with weak credit, in an effort to force mortgage companies to show which mortgages their customers can truly afford.

The New York Times reports that at least four White House lawyers held discussions with the C.I.A. between 2003 and 2005 on whether or not to destroy videotapes of the secret questionings of two Al Qaeda operatives.

19 Congress gives final approval on a bill that will postpone an expansion of the alternative minimum tax for a year, sparing millions of middle-class citizens higher tax bills.

The E.P.A. declines to allow California and 16 other states to declare their own standards on carbon dioxide emissions from automobiles.

21 A study of the panel investigating the 9/11 attacks reveals that the C.I.A. withheld videotapes of interrogations of Al Qaeda operatives from the 9/11 Commission, although it claimed to have "produced or made available for review" everything which was requested.

22 *The New York Times* reports that homeowners around the country are asking county governments to reassess the values of their homes due to falling market prices.

23 American officials concede that there were too few constraints placed on the $5 billon in aid given to Pakistan in order to help bolster the military effort against Al Qaeda, and that the strategy to improve the Pakistani military needs to be revamped.

24 Though the states of California, Illinois, and Pennsylvania all declared they would restructure health care plans in their states during 2007, none will finish the year with health care bills passed or signed.

26 The Equal Employment Opportunity Commission announces that employers can reduce or completely eliminate health benefits for retirees when they become eligible for Medicare at age 65.

27 Benazir Bhutto, former prime minister of Pakistan, is assassinated while leaving a political rally in Rawalpindi, and 20 others are killed and 50 wounded when a car bomb is detonated in her motorcade.

The New York Times reports that, one week before the Iowa caucuses, presidential nominees are spending three times as much on their campaigns as candidates did during the 2004 primaries.

28 The Pakistani government says that it has received information that incriminates Al Qaeda in the assassination of former Prime Minister Benazir Bhutto.

In a surprise move, President Bush vetoes a military policy bill because of a provision that would leave Iraq's new government with billions of dollars in legal claims dating to Saddam Hussein's rule.

29 *The New York Times* reports that Al Qaeda's network in Pakistan has become increasingly filled with homegrown Pakistani militants who seek to destabilize the country.

30 In the wake of Benazir Bhutto's assassination, her 19-year-old son is chosen to succeed her as chairman of Pakistan's largest political party, the Pakistan People's Party.

After a disputed vote in a highly controversial presidential election in Kenya, violence erupts between civilians and government soldiers. (See "Major News Stories.")

31 Nawaz Sharif, formerly exiled opposition leader in Pakistan, calls for President Pervez Musharraf's immediate resignation from power and the formation of a new government of national consensus.

JANUARY 2008

2 Attorney General Michael Mukasey announces that the Justice Dept. will conduct a formal criminal investigation into the destruction of videotapes of C.I.A. interrogations.

A research study finds that delays by hospital staff in treating cardiac arrests contributes to thousands of deaths a year in the U.S.

3 The nomination contest for president begins earlier than ever as Democratic Senator Barack Obama and Republican Mike Huckabee win the Iowa caucuses. (See "Major News Stories.")

4 The Labor Dept. reports that the unemployment rate rose to 5 percent in December, suggesting that the country may be entering a recession.

6 Government officials acknowledge that a secretive American detention center in Afghanistan has not been scaled back as planned and now holds over 600 prisoners in conditions that have prompted complaints from the Red Cross.

7 Pres. Bush concedes that the nation faces "economic challenges" due to rising oil prices, the home mortgage crisis and a weakening job market.

8 American troops in Iraq begin a major offensive to drive Sunni insurgents from strongholds in Diyala Province.

Pres. Bush chastises Iran for committing a "provocative act" by sending boats to confront U.S. warships in the Persian Gulf on January 6.

9 *The New England Journal of Medicine* releases a report that a rare DNA flaw may increase the risk of autism.

10 Colombian rebels release two high profile hostages in a deal with Venezuelan president Hugo Chavez.

U.S. military aircraft drop 40,000 pounds of bombs on suspected militants outside Baghdad.

11 The federal government issues national standards for official identification, setting the stage for a confrontation with several states that have vowed to oppose such measures.

12 The Iraqi government passes a benchmark bill allowing some former officials from Saddam Hussein's party to hold government positions.

14 Pakistani intelligence officials say that they have lost control of militant networks within the country.

The Iraqi defense minister says that his nation will not be able to take full responsibility for its security until 2018.

15 Citigroup, the nation's largest bank, reports a staggering fourth-quarter loss of $9.83 billion and warns that the housing market has still not bottomed out.

After years of debate, the F.D.A. declares that cloned animals are safe to eat, clearing the way for milk and meat from cloned animals to be sold in grocery stores despite protests from some consumer groups.

Former Massachusetts governor Mitt Romney wins the Michigan Republican presidential primary.

16 Researchers at Wake Forest University School of Medicine announce that a test that can predict a man's risk of prostate cancer will be soon available for less than $300.

17 Wall Street stocks plunge three percent on reports of weakness in housing and manufacturing.

A suicide bomber kills 12 people in a mosque in Pakistan.

Rockets from Gaza hit Israel, and Israeli airstrikes kill five Palestinians on the third day of heightened hostilities in the Gaza Strip.

18 Pres. Bush calls for $145 billion in tax relief to spur the economy.

19 *The New York Times* reports that overseas investors purchased a record $414 billion worth of U.S. holdings in 2007, which represents a quarter of all announced deals for the year.

Senator John McCain wins the South Carolina Republican presidential primary and Senator Hillary Clinton wins the Democratic caucus in Nevada, suggesting that neither party has a clear front runner in the nomination process.

21 World stock prices fall sharply amid fears that the U.S. may be in a recession.

22 The Federal Reserve announces the biggest recorded one-day cut in interest rates in an attempt to slow the drop in stock prices.

Jose Padilla is sentenced to 17 years in prison on a terrorism conspiracy conviction.

23 Hamas militants blow up part of the fence dividing Egypt from the Gaza Strip, allowing tens of thousands of Palestinians to cross the border for supplies.

24 Société Générale, one of France's largest banks, announces that it has lost $7.2 billion on unauthorized trades made by a rogue employee.

26 The Kenyan military is deployed to Kenya's Rift Valley to intervene in ethnic violence that has killed more than 650 people and displaced tens of thousands who have fled since the December 30 election.

Senator Barack Obama wins the South Carolina Democratic presidential primary.

28 Pres. Bush delivers his final State of the Union address, which focuses on the Iraq war and his proposed tax rebate.

29 *The New York Times* reports that China is arresting dissidents and human rights advocates as part of a broad crackdown in advance of the Summer Olympics.

30 Democrat John Edwards and Republican Rudy Guiliani drop out of the presidential race in advance of Super Tuesday primaries.

The Federal Reserve cuts short-term interest rates by one half percent and the Senate pushes a $161 billion economic stimulus package.

31 *The New York Times* reports that tensions over oil and revenue sharing are rising between Kurds and the majority Arabs in Iraq.

FEBRUARY 2008

1 Microsoft makes a $44.6 billion hostile bid for Yahoo in an attempt to compete with Google's dominance of online traffic and advertising.

The U.S. Bureau of Labor Statistics reports that the nation's employers cut 17,000 jobs in January, marking the first job decline in four years.

Two women suicide bombers kill dozens of Iraqi citizens in a Baghdad market, renewing fears about a U.S. troop withdrawal.

3 Google offers to help Yahoo fend off a hostile takeover by Microsoft and warns that such a merger would threaten competition.

4 Hundreds of thousands of demonstrators march in Colombia and in major cities across the globe to protest abductions and killings carried out the Columbian F.A.R.C. rebel group.

5 Presidential primary elections and caucuses in 22 states leave Senator John McCain leading the Republican race while Senators Hillary Clinton and Barack Obama are almost tied for the Democratic nomination.

Mike McConnell, the director of national intelligence, tells a Senate panel that Al Qaeda is improving its ability to attack the U.S.

6 Tornadoes blast through five U.S. states, killing at least 55 people and injuring hundreds.

Three days of fighting between government troops and rebels ends in Ndjamena, Chad, leaving bodies in the streets and 20,000 people seeking refuge.

7 The U.S. Senate drops its objections and joins the House in passing a $168 billion package in an attempt to revitalize the national economy.

8 The Nebraska Supreme Court finds that the electric chair constitutes "cruel and unusual punishment," effectively suspending executions in the state, the last to rely solely on electrocution.

A sugar refinery in Port Wentworth, GA explodes, killing four workers and injuring at least 30.

9 Senator Barack Obama wins decisive victories over Senator Hillary Clinton in three states, putting him ahead in the Democratic presidential nomination contest. Despite losses to former Arkansas governor Mike Huckabee, Senator John McCain still leads the Republican race.

The Writer's Guild of America, West reaches a three-year settlement with television and movie producers after a strike by 12,000 screenwriters that began Nov. 5.

10 *The New York Times* reports that the U.S. Army hid the results of an unclassified RAND Corporation study critical of military and White House planning behind the Iraq war.

The U.N. says that thousands of refugees fleeing violence in Darfur are flooding into Chad, despite ongoing unrest there.

11 U.S. military prosecutors announce that they will seek the death penalty for six Guantanamo detainees for their alleged roles in the 9/11 attacks.

The New York Times reports that falling home prices and tighter lending standards are causing a rise in defaults on loans by people with good credit histories.

12 Despite initial concerns about civil liberties, the U.S. Senate votes to broaden governmental spy powers and to give legal protection to phone

companies that cooperated in the Bush Administration's warrantless eavesdropping program.
13 A car bomb in Damascus, Syria, kills Imad Mugniyah, a top Hezbollah commander sought by the U.S. for terrorist attacks that killed hundreds of Americans in the 1980s.

The Iraqi Parliament approves a 2008 budget in addition to measures establishing amnesty and scope of provincial powers.
14 Steve Kazmierczak, a former Northern Illinois University student, opens fire in a lecture hall at the school, killing 5 students and injuring 16 others before fatally shooting himself.
15 Democratic Party officials held private talks seeking to avoid party division over the close nomination race between Senators Hillary Clinton and Barack Obama.
17 The province of Kosovo declares independence from Serbia, leading to celebration by ethnic Albanians and outrage among Serbians and Russians, who failed to convince the U.N. Security Council to nullify the declaration.
18 Pakistani voters overwhelmingly defeat President Musharraf's governing party in parliamentary elections in what is seen as a rejection of his policies and those of the U.S.
19 The party of assassinated Pakistani opposition leader Benazir Bhutto, after winning the most parliamentary seats, says that it will pursue dialogue with Islamic militants and may reverse restrictions on courts and the media imposed under President Musharraf's government.

Fidel Castro, bedridden for 19 months, resigns as head of state in Cuba, leaving his brother Raul Castro in the role pending an official successor.
20 The U.S. Supreme Court finds that makers of medical devices cannot be held liable for personal injury if the F.D.A. approved the device before it was marketed.
21 The Bush Administration and Congress consider proposals to rescue some of the 10.3% of homeowners whose mortgages now exceed the value of their homes.

Serbians protesting Kosovo's independence attack the American Embassy in Belgrade, starting several fires there and looting foreign-owned stores.
22 The U.S. Justice Dept. reveals that its internal ethics office is investigating the legal process that approved C.I.A. waterboarding of Al Qaeda suspects and says that it may disclose a version of the report.
23 *The New York Times* reports that Vladimir Putin's autocratic rule in Russia uses threats, intimidation and suppression of the news media to stifle political dissent even as the Russian economy is improving.
24 High oil prices are forcing rapid inflation in the price of food and basic goods in the Middle East, triggering strikes and demonstrations.
25 Ford Motor Company is pushing workers to accept buyout offers in an attempt to open jobs for lower-wage employees and reduce its financial losses.
26 Oil prices hit a high of $100.88 a barrel, and gas prices are at their highest levels since 1981.

The New York Philharmonic performs a concert in Pyongyang, North Korea, marking the first appearance in the country by an American cultural group.
27 Federal Reserve Chairman Ben Bernanke says that the central bank will consider lowering interest rates even though inflation is rising and the dollar is at a historic low.

A rocket attack by Hamas, the first in nine months, kills an Israeli citizen and reprisal airstrikes from Israel kill at least eight Palestinians.
28 F.D.A. investigators announce "potential deficiencies" at a Chinese drug plant linked to contaminated supplies of the blood thinner Heparin, which led to severe complications in at least 400 Americans and a growing drug recall.

MARCH 2008
1 U.S. military officials say that they will send 100 American trainers to teach counterinsurgency skills to Pakistani soldiers fighting Al Qaeda.

The New York Times reports that Sudan's janjaweed militas and government troops have resumed a series of brutal attacks in Darfur and are burning villages and killing civilians.
2 Vladimir Putin's chosen successor, Dmitri Medvedev, is easily elected as the next president of Russia.
3 Israeli forces withdraw from the northern Gaza Strip after a two-day offensive, triggered by a rocket assault on Israeli cities by Hamas militants, that killed over 100 Palestinians.
4 Senator John McCain wins four primary contests to clinch the G.O.P. presidential nomination, while Senator Hillary Clinton wins major Democratic victories in Ohio and Texas to revive her campaign against Senator Barack Obama.

A study in the *American Journal of Medicine* finds that easily overlooked flat lesions in the colon are both more likely to cause cancer and more common than previously thought.
5 OPEC rebuffs calls from Pres. Bush to increase oil production, citing "mismanagement" of the American economy as a major cause of high oil prices.
6 A gunman kills eight students and wounds at least nine others at a prominent Israeli yeshiva in the first attack inside Jerusalem in four years.
7 The Labor Dept. estimates that the nation lost 63,000 jobs in February and the Federal Reserve announces that it will inject $200 billion into the banking system to ease the worsening credit crisis.
8 Pres. Bush vetoes a bill passed by Congress that would have limited the C.I.A.'s ability to use harsh interrogation tactics on terrorism suspects. (See "Major News Stories.")
9 The leaders of the two major Pakistani political parties agree to reinstate the country's Supreme Court justices, who have been held under house arrest since Nov. 3, and to strip President Musharraf of crucial powers.

The New York Times reports that large Web companies are collecting detailed data about Internet users several hundred times a month in order to target advertising.
10 New York Governor Eliot Spitzer admits that he was a client of a high-end prostitution ring broken up last week by federal authorities. (See "Major News Stories.")

A suicide bomber kills five U.S. soldiers on patrol in Baghdad in the deadliest single attack on troops since the peak of the troop buildup last summer.
11 Stock prices rise as the Federal Reserve offers up to $200 billion in short-term loans to major Wall Street investment banks.

The Pentagon announces that Adm. William Fallon, the commander of American forces in the Middle East who has made public statements at odds with the Bush Administration, is retiring early.
12 Eliot Spitzer resigns as governor of New York.

13 The Bush Administration announces a plan to use state regulators and private industry to better oversee financial markets and mortgage brokers.
14 Ten people are killed in the Tibetan capital, Lhasa, as Buddhist monks and other ethnic Tibetans fight Chinese security forces in the fifth day of demonstrations against Communist rule.

A run on Bear Stearns prompts JPMorgan Chase to offer a secured line of credit, backed by the Federal Reserve Bank of New York, to rescue the investment bank, which has been crippled by mortgage industry losses.
15 A crane collapses into an apartment building on the East Side of Manhattan, killing four people and injuring 13.
16 JPMorgan Chase agrees to buy all of Bear Stearns for $2 per share and to guarantee the obligations of the investment bank using a $30 billion credit line from the Federal Reserve, which agreed to take over the Bear Stearns portfolio.

The Dalai Lama accuses China of waging "cultural genocide" against his followers in Tibet and calls for an international inquiry into violence against protestors there.
17 New York's Lt. Gov. David Paterson is sworn in as governor.
18 A bombing in Iraq kills 43 people near a Shiite shrine, while Vice Pres. Cheney meets with American and Iraqi leaders in Baghdad.
19 The Federal Reserve cuts short-term interest rates for the sixth time in six months, to 2.25 percent, in an attempt to stabilize financial markets.
20 *The New York Times* reports that many states are using an inflated graduation rate for federal reporting requirements and that the real national high school graduation rate is about 70 percent.
21 The State Dept. reveals that employees and contract workers improperly viewed the passport files of the three presidential candidates, Senators Hillary Clinton, John McCain and Barack Obama.
23 A heavy mortar attack on the Green Zone in Baghdad kills 58 Iraqis and four Americans, pushing the number of U.S. military deaths in Iraq to over 4,000.
24 *The New York Times* reports that a peacekeeping mission in Darfur may fail due to bureaucratic delays, stonewalling by Sudan's government and reluctance of international leaders to send troops into active conflict.

Gen. David Petraeus and Ambassador to Iraq Ryan Crocker present plans to Pres. Bush that recommend maintaining troop levels in Iraq through 2008.
25 Heavy fighting between militias and Iraqi forces in two of Iraq's largest cities threatens a long-term truce.
26 *The New York Times* reveals that a lung cancer study conducted by Weill Cornell Medical College and published in 2006 in the *New England Journal of Medicine* was paid for by the cigarette company Liggett Group. (See "Major News Stories.")

AEY Inc., a U.S. company with a federal contract for $300 million to supply arms to Afghanistan's army and police is suspended for selling old and unusable munitions, possible corruption, and dealings with illegal arms traffickers.
27 Thousands of Shiites demonstrate in Baghdad against continuing Iraqi military battles with the Mahdi Army militia.
28 North Korea tests short-range missiles off its western coast, threatens to slow down disabling of its nuclear weapons facilities, and accuses South Korea of sending warships across a disputed border.

The U.S. military conducts airstrikes to aid Iraqi forces in their fight with militias in Basra and Baghdad.
29 Shiite militias maintain control of Basra despite efforts by Iraqi government forces and airstrikes by U.S. military.

Colombian officials release computer files tying the governments of Ecuador and Venezuela to a Columbian rebel group.
30 Iraqi Shiite cleric and milita leader Moktada al-Sadr suspends fighting in Basra and demands concessions from the Iraqi government.

The Congressional Budget Office projects that the number of Americans receiving food stamps will rise to a record 28 million in 2009.
31 Treasury Sec. Henry Paulson presents a plan to overhaul the regulatory structure for the nation's financial system.

APRIL 2008
1 *The New York Times* reports that whistle-blowers have filed lawsuits alleging that insurance companies are overloading the Social Security Administration by forcing disability claimants to also apply for Social Security even when they do not meet the program requirements.

The biggest banks in Germany and Switzerland announce $23 billion in write-downs, adding to the hundreds of billions in losses that financial firms already face.
2 Election results from Zimbabwe show that President Mugabe's party has lost control of the nation's Parliament, but results in the presidential race are still unknown four days after the election. (See "Major News Stories.")
3 A senior Iraqi official says that more than 1,000 Iraqi soldiers and policemen refused to fight in the battle against Shiite militias last week.

Texas law enforcement officials raid a West Texas ranch owned by a polygamist sect and remove 52 girls following an accusation of sexual abuse of a 16-year-old girl. (See "Major News Stories.")
4 A *New York Times/CBS News* poll reports that 81 percent of Americans think the country is "on the wrong track."
5 Pentagon officials express concerns about the mental health of soldiers who would be sent back to Iraq for the long and multiple deployments required to maintain troop levels.

Zimbabwean opposition leader, Morgan Tsvangirai, claims that he defeated President Robert Mugabe in last week's presidential election and that no run-off election is necessary.
6 Fighting breaks out in the Sadr City area of Baghdad as American and Iraqi troops again try to stop militia attacks on the Green Zone.
8 *The New York Times* reports that inflation in Asia is contributing to rising prices on imported products in the United States.

Gen. David Petraeus calls progress in Iraq "fragile and reversible" and recommends that Congress delay any decisions on cutting troop levels until the fall.
9 Over 1,000 commercial air flights are cancelled when the F.A.A. orders a broad round of aircraft inspections because nine American Airlines jets failed checks.

Citing the American housing bust and credit squeeze, the International Monetary Fund cuts its forecast for global economic growth in 2008 and warns that worldwide problems could extend into 2009.

10 Pres. Bush says that the senior U.S. commander in Iraq can have "all the time he needs" before troop levels would be reduced any further.

Millions of Nepalis defy threats of violence and vote in elections that could abolish the monarchy.

11 The government of Zimbabwe issues a ban on political rallies, and arrests the lawyer of the opposition party as dispute over the presidential election continues.

12 *The New York Times* reports that the Iraqi defense minister secretly negotiated an $833 million arms deal with Serbia that sidestepped competitive bidding and anticorruption safeguards and resulted in shoddy goods, revealing the ongoing problems in equipping Iraqi armed forces.

Haitian President René Préval announces an emergency plan to lower the price of rice in an attempt to stop violent protests over food costs. (See "Major News Stories.")

14 *The New York Times* reports that thousands of stores across the country are closing as the tight credit market forces retailing chains to cut back expenses or file for bankruptcy.

A British photographer kidnapped two months ago in Iraq while working for CBS is rescued by Iraqi soldiers in Basra.

Silvio Berlusconi, who lost his position as Italy's prime minister two years ago, wins the job back in a new election.

15 A company of Iraqi soldiers abandons their positions in Sadr City, ignoring pleas from American soldiers to hold the line against Shiite militias.

Pope Benedict XVI arrives in Washington, D.C. on his first official visit to the U.S. (See "Major News Stories.")

The New York Times reports that a bill approved last week by the Senate to help prevent home foreclosures would also provide huge tax breaks to automakers and other industries.

16 The Supreme Court upholds (7–2) Kentucky's method of lethal injection, finding that it does not qualify as "cruel and unusual" punishment.

Dozens of Tibetan protesters storm the Chinese embassy in New Dehli, India in advance of the arrival of the Olympic torch.

Heavy fighting between Israelis and Palestinians kills at least 21 people in Gaza.

17 A suicide bomber in southwestern Afghanistan kills 23 people and wounds at least 31 outside a mosque.

18 A shipment of arms sent from China to Zimbabwe is turned back after South African dock workers refuse to unload the ship and the South Africa's High Court refuses to allow the weapons to be transported across the country, finding that they are likely to be used to repress Zimbabweans.

A Texas judge orders that 416 children who have been taken from a polygamist religious sect be held in protective custody pending further investigation into abuse allegations and that maternal and paternal testing be conducted for all the children. (See "Major News Stories.")

19 The Iraqi army takes control of Basra from the Shiite militia headed by cleric Moktada al-Sadr after air and artillery strikes from American and British forces clear the area.

Election officials in Zimbabwe begin a partial recount of the disputed election results.

20 *The New York Times* reports that more than 1,000 Zimbabweans are fleeing to South Africa every day in an attempt to escape violence by Mugabe loyalists.

21 The F.D.A. announces that contaminated blood thinners from China have been found in drug supplies in 11 countries and a clear link has been established between the contaminant and 81 deaths in the U.S.

Georgia accuses Russia of violating its airspace and using a MiG fighter jet to shoot down an unmanned Georgia reconnaissance drone over the territory of Abkhazia.

22 Senator Hillary Clinton scores a decisive victory over Senator Barack Obama in the Pennsylvania Democratic primary, giving her flagging candidacy a critical boost.

Iraqi Prime Minister Nouri al-Maliki appeals for greater international support for Iraq and asks other Arab nations to send ambassadors to his country.

23 The Pentagon announces a plan to give Gen. David Petraeus command of all military affairs across the Middle East and Central Asia and to replace him in Iraq with Lt. Gen. Raymond Odierno, who spent 15 months as Petraeus's deputy.

Pres. Bush meets privately with King Abdullah of Jordan in advance of a trip to Israel to try to revive the Israeli-Palestinian peace talks.

24 Iraq's largest Sunni bloc agrees to rejoin to Prime Minister Nouri al-Maliki's cabinet after a year-long boycott.

The government reports that new home sales fell 8.5 percent in March to their lowest levels since the housing recession of the 1990s and that the backlog of housing is the largest since 1981.

25 A New York judge finds three police detectives not guilty of criminal charges in the killing of Sean Bell, an unarmed black man shot 50 times on the morning of his wedding in Nov. 2006.

The Chinese government agrees to meet with envoys of the Dalai Lama in an apparent concession to international pressure.

26 *The New York Times* reports that Justice Dept. letters to Congress reveal that C.I.A. agents have been given latitude to legally use interrogation methods that would otherwise be prohibited under the Geneva Convention if they are attempting to prevent a terrorist attack.

Angola follows South Africa in refusing to accept a shipment of Chinese arms bound for Zimbabwe, marking a change in support for Zimbabwe, Angola's onetime ally.

27 8,300 South Korean police officers are dispatched to protect the Olympic torch from South Korean citizens protesting the treatment of North Korean refugees in China.

The Philippine government issues "rice passes" to the country's poorest families in an attempt to deal with food shortages and a doubling in the price of rice.

28 The Supreme Court rules (6–3) that an Indiana law requiring a photo ID for voters is not an unconstitutional burden.

The faction leaders of Zimbabwe's political opposition formally reunite, taking control of Parliament, and ask Pres. Robert Mugabe to concede the presidential election.

29 White House officials warn that the Pakistani government's talks with militant tribes will undermine security along the Afghan border.

30 The Commerce Dept. reports that consumer spending was down dramatically in the first quarter of the year, cutting economic growth to just 0.6 percent, and the Federal Reserve cuts interest rates by one quarter of a percent in an attempt to prevent further declines.

MAY 2008

1 Congress passes a bill banning discrimination by employers and insurance companies based on a person's genetic risk for disease.

2 The Labor Dept. reports that the economy lost another 20,000 jobs in April, the fourth consecutive monthly decline, although the loss was smaller than projected.

Zimbabwe's election authority announces that presidential challenger Morgan Tsvangirai has a lead over President Robert Mugabe but did not win the majority needed to avoid a runoff.

3 Microsoft withdraws its bid for Yahoo after Yahoo rejects Microsoft's higher offer of $47.5 billion.

4 The unbeaten colt Big Brown wins the Kentucky Derby but the second-place finisher, filly Eight Belles, breaks both front ankles and is euthanized on the track.

5 A powerful tropical cyclone called Nargis kills thousands of people and leaves hundreds of thousands of homeless and without food and water in the Irrawaddy Delta region of Myanmar. (See "Major News Stories.")

6 The Chilean government orders an evacuation of people living near the Chaitén volcano in southern Chile after the volcano blasts ash and lava into the air.

7 Hezbollah mobs block roads, shoot at government forces and set fires in Beirut in order to enforce a general strike against the Lebanese government, exacerbating a 17-month-old political crisis in Lebanon.

8 U.N. officials say that the military government of Myanmar is slowing the delivery of relief supplies to the 1.5 million displaced survivors of Cyclone Nargis and warn that conditions are worsening rapidly.

The acting chief of Mexico's federal police is assassinated in response to the government crackdown on organized crime and drug cartels.

9 The State Dept. renews its contract with Blackwater USA, the security firm accused of killing 17 Iraqi civilians in September 2007.

10 Iraqi leaders reach a truce with the militia in the Sadr City neighborhood of Baghdad.

Sudanese forces suppress a bold attack by Darfurian rebels on the capital, Khartoum.

11 Fierce tornadoes across the Midwest kill 23 people in rural Missouri and Oklahoma.

A gun battle in Kashmir between militants and the Indian soldiers leaves seven people dead.

12 A 7.9 magnitude earthquake in southwestern China kills at least 10,000 people and destroys thousands of buildings, including two chemical factories and two large schools. (See "Major News Stories.")

The Lebanese army says that it will use force to end a week of bloody fighting between government supporters and the Hezbollah-led opposition.

13 Seven bombings kill at least 50 people in the Indian city of Jaipur; Indian officials hint that Pakistan is responsible.

A detainee held at the U.S. prison in Guantanamo Bay and who was subjected to aggressive interrogation methods is cleared by the Pentagon of charges that he participated in the terrorist attacks on September 11, 2001.

14 The House approves a five-year, $307 billion farm bill despite a veto threat from Pres. Bush.

The Interior Dept. announces that the polar bear will be added to the list of endangered species due to the effect of climate change on melting sea ice.

Israeli Army strikes kill four Palestinians and wound nine, while a rocket launched from Gaza wounds four Israelis during celebrations in honor of Israel's 60th birthday.

15 The California Supreme Court overturns two state laws that ban gay marriage. (See "Major News Stories.")

16 Pentagon officials say that they are moving forward with plans to build a new 40-acre detention complex in Afghanistan.

A report from the Centers for Disease Control and Prevention finds a pattern of unhygienic practices by health care workers at a Las Vegas endoscopy clinic linked to more than 80 cases of hepatitis C.

17 Thousands of earthquake survivors in China evacuate after the government warns that lakes and rivers blocked by landslides are close to flooding.

Pakistan's ambassador to Afghanistan is freed after being kidnapped three months ago by the Taliban.

18 Violent mob attacks on immigrants in South Africa leave at least 12 people dead and result in over 200 arrests.

A suicide bomber kills 11 people and wounds 22 in a market in Pakistan.

20 Israel and Syria announce that they are engaged in negotiations for a peace treaty.

American Airlines says that it will begin charging $15 to check a bag for passengers flying on discounted fares.

A federal appeals court rules that the design of U.S. currency imposes a burden on the blind.

22 Swiss banking giant UBS says it will issue discounted shares to raise $15 billion in the bank's second round of fundraising since the credit markets began shrinking last year.

23 In Iowa, 270 illegal immigrants arrested in a May 12 raid on a meatpacking plant are sentenced to five months in prison for working with false documents.

25 An earthquake aftershock hits the mountainous Sichuan Province in China, injuring hundreds of people and toppling thousands of buildings.

Colombian FARC rebels confirm that their leader Manuel Marulanda has died, and Colombian president Álvaro Uribe says that FARC leaders have contacted him regarding a possible hostage release.

Gen. Michael Suleiman is elected president of Lebanon in the first part of a power-sharing pact between political parties.

26 The International Atomic Energy Agency reports that Iran's suspected nuclear weapons research remains "a matter of serious concern" and charges that the nation is not cooperating with the agency. (See "Major News Stories.")

27 In two decisions, the Supreme Court rules (7–2 and 6–3) that employees are protected from retaliation when they complain about discrimination in the workplace.

28 New York Gov. David Paterson directs all state agencies to recognize same-sex marriages performed in other jurisdictions.

The newly-elected assembly in Nepal gives Gyanendra, the king of Nepal, 15 days to step down from his throne. (See "Major News Stories.")

29 The Brazilian government releases aerial pictures of an indigenous tribe living in the Amazon basin to prove that the tribe exists and may be in danger from illegal logging.
30 Democratic Party officials agree to seat delegates from Florida and Michigan primaries at the party's August convention, but gives them only half a vote each, settling a dispute about the states' unsanctioned early primary elections.

JUNE 2008

1 Swiss voters defeat a measure that would have legitimized the practice of allowing secret votes by townspeople in deciding whether to grant citizenship to immigrants.

The U.S. military says that 19 Americans died in Iraq in May, the lowest monthly total of American deaths in Iraq since the war began in 2003.
2 A Texas judge orders the release of more than 460 children held in state custody since April after they were seized in a series of raids on a polygamist community. (See "Major News Stories.")

Syria says that it will allow U.N. nuclear inspectors to visit the site of a suspected reactor that Israel bombed last September.

Wachovia Bank fires its chief executive and Washington Mutual strips its chief executive of the chairman's title as both banks struggle.
3 A primary election victory in Montana and a rush of superdelegates clinches the Democratic Presidential nomination for Senator Barack Obama.
5 A Senate committee releases a long-delayed report that concludes that Pres. Bush and his aides exaggerated available intelligence and ignored contrary reports about Iraq's weapons programs and Saddam Hussein's links to Al Qaeda in building the public case for war against Iraq.
6 The F.T.C. opens a formal antitrust investigation of the Intel Corporation.

Two studies find that diabetics who rigorously control their blood sugar levels do not reduce their risk of heart attack or stroke.
7 Senator Hillary Clinton ends her campaign for president and endorses Senator Barack Obama. (See "Major News Stories.")
8 For the first time, gasoline prices reach a national average of $4 a gallon.

American and Asian intelligence analysts say that Al Qaeda support of terrorist groups in Southeast Asia has been significantly weakened since 2005.
9 In a deal with the New York Attorney General, Internet providers Verizon, Sprint, and Time Warner Cable agree to block access to Internet bulletin boards and Web sites nationwide that disseminate child pornography.

Pres. Bush signs an executive order to force federal contractors to use the Homeland Security Dept.'s electronic system to verify the legal immigration status of their workers.
10 Tens of thousands of South Koreans protest in Seoul against imports of American beef, undermining the new presidency of Lee Myung-bak.
11 American air and artillery strikes kill 11 Pakistani paramilitary soldiers during a clash with insurgents on the Afghan border.

The Israeli security cabinet votes to pursue a cease-fire with Palestinian militants in Gaza.
12 The U.S. Supreme Court rebuffs the Bush Administration and rules (5–4) that detainees at Guantánamo Bay can challenge their detentions in federal court. (See "Major News Stories.")

Thunderstorms across the Midwest cause the worst flooding ever seen in Cedar Rapids, sending 8,000 people out of their homes, and a tornado kills four boys at a Boy Scout camp in western Iowa. (See "Major News Stories.")
13 Ireland rejects the Lisbon Treaty, potentially dooming the plan to consolidate the power of the European Union.

A new study says that China has passed the U.S. as the world's leading emitter of carbon dioxide.

Taliban fighters attack a prison in Kandahar, Afghanistan, killing 15 guards and freeing 1,200 prisoners, including 400 Taliban members.
14 International inspectors reveal that a Pakistani nuclear weapons expert may have distributed blueprints for a compact nuclear bomb on the black market.
16 A former Army official says that he was forced out of his job after attempting to impose penalties on military contractor KBR for faulty operations and financial mismanagement.
17 Explosives hidden on a bus kill 51 people and wound 75 in a Baghdad market in an attack that U.S. military blames on a Shiite militia leader.

The rain-swollen Mississippi River breaks through levees in Illinois and Missouri, flooding towns and drowning crops.
19 Congressional leaders agree to expand government wiretapping powers and give legal immunity to the phone companies that cooperated with Pres. Bush's warrantless wiretapping program.

Two executives at failed investment bank Bear Stearns are charged with fraud.

Democratic presidential candidate Senator Barack Obama breaks a campaign pledge and declines public financing.
20 The president of Miami Beach arms dealer AEY Inc. and three others are indicted on conspiracy and fraud charges for selling faulty and illegal ammunition to the Defense Dept.
21 *The New York Times* reports that the U.S. Army has organized an all-Army surveillance unit and other initiatives in Iraq in response to an alleged lack of cooperation from the Air Force in overseas operations.

The leader of the U.N. refugee agency in Somalia is kidnapped in Mogadishu.
22 Typhoon Fengshen in the Philippines kills at least 137 people, displaces tens of thousands, and capsizes a ferry, drowning almost all of the 800 people on board.

Morgan Tsvangirai withdraws from Zimbabwe's presidential runoff election, citing violence from forces backing President Robert Mugabe.
23 Three human rights groups issue a report charging that the U.S. government withheld $54 million meant to provide clean water in Haiti as leverage for political change in the country.
24 U.S. Sugar, the largest country's sugarcane producer, agrees to sell all of its assets to the state of Florida and go out of business in a $1.75 billion deal to restore 187,000 acres of the Everglades.

The Justice Dept. reports that department officials illegally used "political or ideological" factors in recruiting employees. (See "Major News Stories.")
25 The Supreme Court rules (5–4) that the death penalty is an unconstitutional punishment for child rape; the court (5–3) also reduces punitive damages against Exxon Mobil in the Exxon Valdez oil spill from $5 billion to $500 million.

The Taliban claims responsibility for killing 28 members of a Pakistani peace group in South Waziristan.

26 The Supreme Court rejects (5–4) a Washington, D.C. ban on handguns. (See "Major News Stories.")

Pres. Bush announces that he is removing North Korea from the State Dept. list of state sponsors of terrorism. (See "Major News Stories.")

27 *The New York Times* reports that the U.S. and E.U. are nearing agreement on a deal to allow law enforcement and security agencies to trade private information about citizens in the U.S. and Europe.

The Justice Dept. announces that it will pay $4.6 million to settle a lawsuit by Steven J. Hatfill, a scientist who was erroneously suspected of responsibility for the 2001 anthrax letters.

28 Pres. Bush calls for an international arms embargo against Zimbabwe in response to the "sham election" of Robert Mugabe.

29 *The New York Times* reports that policy disputes in Washington have delayed a Pentagon plan to empower Special Operations forces to capture Al Qaeda leaders in Pakistan.

30 Iraq announces that it will opening six key oil fields to more than 30 foreign companies but will delay awarding no bid contracts to Exxon Mobil, Shell, Total, BP and Chevron.

A federal appeals court overturns a Pentagon determination that a Muslim man from China held for more than six years at Guantánamo Bay is an "enemy combatant."

JULY 2008

1 The Catholic Archdiocese of Denver agrees to pay over $5.5 million to settle lawsuits over sexual abuse by priests.

2 Colombian commandos rescue 15 hostages held by FARC rebels. (See "Major News Stories.")

A Congressional committee finds that State Dept. officials violated U.S. policy in allowing a Texas company with ties to Pres. Bush to sign an oil deal with the regional government of Kurdistan.

3 The Bureau of Labor Statistics announces that 62,000 U.S. jobs were lost in June, the sixth consecutive month of job losses.

5 Syrian military police kill nine Islamist inmates during a prison riot outside Damascus.

6 Local officials in eastern Afghanistan say that an American airstrike has killed at least 27 civilians in a wedding party, including the bride.

7 A suicide car bombing in front of the Indian Embassy in Kabul kills 41 people and wounds more than 130, marking a rapid deterioration of security in Afghanistan.

Share prices of Fannie Mae and Freddie Mac, the nation's largest home mortgage buyers, plummet 16 and 18 percent respectively.

8 At a G–8 meeting, the world's richest countries pledge to halve greenhouse gas emissions by 2050, but set no short-term goals for the next decade. (See "Major News Stories.")

American and Czech officials sign a pact allowing the Pentagon to deploy part of an antiballistic missile shield on Czech territory.

9 Three Turkish policeman die when four unidentified assailants open fire on security guards outside the U.S. Consulate in Istanbul.

Iran test-fires nine missiles in war-game maneuvers, including one said to have the range to reach Israel.

11 Czech officials say that the supply of oil from Russia has dropped in the three days since the Czech Republic agreed to host part of a U.S. antiballistic missile shield.

Russia and China block an attempt by the U.N. Security Council to impose sanctions against Zimbabwe.

The F.D.I.C. seizes IndyMac bank, an offshoot of Countrywide Financial and the largest bank to fail since the 1990s.

13 The Treasury Dept. unveils a plan to save mortgage companies Fannie Mae and Freddie Mac with billions of dollars in investments and loans, including a line of credit for up to $300 billion.

St. Louis-based Anheuser-Busch agrees to be sold to Belgian brewer InBev for $52 billion.

Nine American soldiers die in an assault by Taliban insurgents in Afghanistan.

14 Pres. Bush lifts nearly two decades of executive orders banning oil and gas drilling off the U.S. coast, but Congressional bans remain in place.

The International Criminal Court prosecutor requests an arrest warrant for Sudanese president Omar Hassan al-Bashir on charges of genocide, war crimes and crimes against humanity.

15 Congress votes to override Pres. Bush's veto of a bill that would protect doctors from a Medicare pay cut.

16 American forces abandon an outpost in northeastern Afghanistan after a heavy attack by Taliban insurgents.

Five Lebanese prisoners and the bodies of 199 Lebanese and Palestinian combatants are returned to Lebanon from Israel in exchange for the bodies of two Israeli soldiers kidnapped by Hezbollah.

17 The Pentagon acknowledges that shoddy electrical work by private contractors on U.S. military bases in Iraq is widespread and has caused more deaths and injuries than previously revealed.

Pakistani investors set fires in front of the Karachi stock exchange and attack the building to protest falling share prices.

The F.D.A. lifts a warning against raw tomatoes that was implemented in April during the worst food-borne salmonella outbreak in a decade.

18 Pres. Bush agrees to a "general time horizon" for withdrawing U.S. troops in Iraq.

19 International talks on Iran's nuclear ambitions end in deadlock despite the Bush Administration decision to send a senior American official to such talks for the first time.

21 Radovan Karadzic, wanted on war crimes since 1995, is arrested in Serbia. (See "Major News Stories.")

22 The average interest rate for 30-year fixed-rate mortgages rose to the highest level in five years .

23 Orthopedic device maker Zimmer Holdings suspends sales of an artificial hip component after doctors complain that the device is failing.

Hurricane Dolly hits the Rio Grande Valley in Texas with heavy rains, knocking out power for over 80,000 people.

24 The American Embassy in Baghdad announces that it has greatly expanded its visa program for Iraqi employees of the U.S. government.

A barge collides with a tanker near New Orleans, spilling oil that spreads for 100 miles along the Mississippi River to the Gulf of Mexico.

25 The state of California bans the use of trans fats in all restaurants and retail bakeries beginning in 2010.

A Qantas airlines Boeing 747-400 makes a safe emergency landing in Manila after a section of the fuselage bursts open in midair.

26 At least 16 explosions in western India kill 29 people the day after similar blasts hit Bangalore.

27 The Federal Reserve says that commercial loans have dropped by $150 billion since last year, depriving businesses of credit for expansion and hiring.

Two bombs in Istanbul kill 16 people and wound 150 in the worst terrorist attack in Turkey in nearly five years; Kurdish separatist militants are suspected.

28 Ethnic violence and suicide bombers in northern Iraq kill 61 people and injure 238, exacerbating tensions between majority Kurds and ethnic Turkmens.

The Massachusetts Educational Financing Authority says that it will not offer loans for the upcoming academic year due to disruptions in the credit market.

29 The Doha round of world trade talks collapse in Geneva after seven years, due to an impasse between the U.S., China and India over protections for farmers.

A federal grand jury indicts Alaska Senator Ted Stevens on seven felony counts that he failed to disclose gifts from an oil services company; Stevens vows to fight the indictment and continue his re-election campaign.

30 Israeli Prime Minister Ehud Olmert, embroiled in a corruption investigation, announces that he will resign after his party's elections in September.

31 Exxon Mobil reports the best quarterly profit ever for a corporation: $11.68 billion, beating its own record.

A federal judge rules that Pres. Bush's advisers cannot ignore Congressional subpoenas.

Haitian lawmakers end a three-month standoff and ratify Michèle Pierre-Louis as the new prime minister.

AUGUST 2008

1 Pres. Bush signs the sweeping housing bill passed by Congress that gives the Treasury Dept. broad authority to oversee the nation's two largest mortgage companies and allocates funding to rescue homeowners from foreclosure.

G.M. reports a second-quarter loss of $15.5 billion just a week after Ford reported a quarterly loss of $8.7 billion. (See "Major News Stories.")

The F.B.I. says that Army scientist Bruce E. Ivins committed suicide last week after learning that he was to be indicted on murder charges as part of the investigation of the deadly anthrax attacks in 2001. (See "Major News Stories.")

2 The C.D.C. says that the U.S. has significantly under-reported the number of new H.I.V. infections occurring each year and that the actual infection rate is 40 percent higher than previously estimated.

The New York Times reports that an estimated 10,000 to 15,000 people have been displaced by the deepening conflict between American and NATO forces and the Taliban in southern Afghanistan.

3 Eleven mountain climbers are killed due to accidents and falling ice on K2, the world's second highest mountain.

4 Two armed men ambush a military police unit and kill 16 police officers in northwest China.

A federal health care panel advises doctors to stop screening men over 75 for prostate cancer because the testing is doing more harm than good. (See "Major News Stories.")

5 The Government Accountability Office reports that although the Iraqi government will have a 2008 budget surplus of up to $79 billion, Iraq re-

construction costs have been almost entirely paid by American taxpayer money.

Venezuelan president Hugo Chávez issues decrees to expand his powers through measures similar to those rejected last year by voters.

6 A military panel convicts a former driver for Osama bin Laden of one of two war crimes charges in the first military commission trial at Guantánamo Bay. (See "Major News Stories.")

7 Pentagon officials say that Defense Sec. Robert M. Gates is pushing a $20 billion plan to double the size of the Afghan army and restructure the military command of American and NATO forces in response to the growing threat from the Taliban.

8 Russian troops move into South Ossetia, a breakaway region of Georgia, and Russian airplanes attack Georgian targets. (See "Major News Stories.")

The 2008 Summer Olympics open in Beijing, China. (See "Major News Stories.")

9 The conflict between Russia and Georgia intensifies as Russia lands troops in Abkhazia and broadens its bombing campaign across Georgia, striking military facilities near a civilian airport.

The father-in-law of a U.S. Olympic volleyball coach is stabbed to death in Beijing by a Chinese man.

10 Defying international entreaties, Russia expands its attacks on Georgia despite Georgia's withdrawal from South Ossetia and offer of a cease-fire.

Bolivian President Evo Morales easily wins re-election.

Nebraska Beef issues a recall of 1.2 million pounds of beef products just one month after the Dept. of Agriculture ended a previous recall of tainted meat from the same processor.

11 King Abdullah II of Jordan becomes the first Arab head of state to visit Iraq since Saddam Hussein was forced from power.

12 Lawyers for a Hong Kong-born immigrant who died last week in U.S. custody file federal court affidavits charging that the Dept. of Homeland Security failed to provide adequate medical attention to their client.

13 Pres. Bush sends American troops to Georgia to oversee a humanitarian relief mission in a direct challenge to Russia's display of military aggression in the area.

French president Nicolas Sarkozy brokers a peace deal between Russia and Georgia but Russian tanks continue their advance on the Georgian city of Gori.

14 The U.S. and Poland reach a deal to place an American missile defense base on Polish territory.

Nigeria officially transfers the Bakassi Peninsula to Cameroon after 15 years of fighting over the potentially oil-rich area.

15 Nepal's Constituent Assembly elects Maoist leader Pushka Kamal Dahal as prime minister.

Nine people are killed by a truck bomb in the second attack in 24 hours on Shiite pilgrims traveling to Karbala in Iraq.

16 American swimmer Michael Phelps wins his eighth gold medal at the Beijing Olympics, setting a new single Games record. (See "Major News Stories.")

17 Iran reports that it has tested a new rocket capable of carrying a satellite into orbit.

A bomb attack at a mosque in Baghdad kills 14 people including the deputy commander of a local American-backed security force.

Torrential rains cause flooding across Southeast Asia, killing at least 160 people in Vietnam.

18 Pakistani president Gen. Pervez Musharraf resigns. (See "Major News Stories.")

Islamist rebels in the Philippines kill 28 civilians in attacks on several towns.

19 Taliban forces in Afghanistan assault a U.S. base with at least 10 suicide bombers and kill 10 French paratroopers near Kabul in a separate attack by 100 insurgents.

The Dept. of Labor says that prices for goods purchased by American businesses are up nearly 10 percent over last year.

20 A Spanair jet crashes on takeoff in Madrid, killing at least 154 people.

21 Two Taliban suicide bombers kill at least 64 people outside a Pakistani weapons factory.

The U.S. and Iraqi governments agree to a plan to withdraw American troops from Iraqi cities by next June and from the rest of the country by 2011 if conditions remain stable.

22 After two weeks of occupation, Russia withdraws most of its forces from Georgia but maintains strategic checkpoints along major roads.

Six Americans arrested in China for protesting Chinese rule in Tibet are given 10-day detention sentences.

23 Democratic presidential candidate Senator Barack Obama names Delaware Senator Joseph R. Biden Jr. as his running mate.

Afghan president Hamid Karzai says that a U.S. airstrike yesterday killed 95 civilians; U.S. officials refuse to comment.

24 *The New York Times* reports that the Swiss government destroyed evidence that linked the C.I.A. with three Swiss engineers who were involved with black market nuclear weapons smuggling.

25 Israel releases 198 Palestinian prisoners in advance of a visit by U.S. Sec. of State Condoleezza Rice intended to promote peace negotiations.

Sudanese forces open fire on a refugee camp in Darfur, killing dozens and injuring more than 100.

27 Thousands of protestors blockade the prime minister's compound and other government buildings in Thailand. (See "Major News Stories.")

28 Republican presidential candidate Senator John McCain names Alaskan governor Sarah Heath Palin as his running mate.

29 After a dam bursts in Nepal, flood waters spread across northern India, displacing millions of people.

An earthquake in China's Sichuan Province kills at least 32 people and damages more than 258,000 homes.

30 Two million people from Texas to Alabama, including most of the residents of New Orleans, flee the Gulf Coast in advance of Hurricane Gustav.

SEPTEMBER 2008

1 Hurricane Gustav weakens to a tropical storm and passes over Louisiana without inflicting major damage but the mandatory evacuation for New Orleans residents is not immediately lifted.

American military commanders formally return responsibility for Anbar Province to the Iraqi Army and police force.

2 Google releases a free internet browser called Chrome that may compete with Microsoft Explorer.

3 American Special Operations forces attack Al Qaeda militants near the Afghan border in the first publicly acknowledged U.S. ground raid conducted on Pakistani soil.

Pres. Bush proposes a $1 billion aid package for Georgia and Vice Pres. Cheney visits the neighboring state of Azerbaijan in a rebuff to Russia.

5 The Bureau of Labor Statistics reports that U.S. unemployment rate climbed to 6.1% in August, the highest point in five years.

6 Asif Ali Zardari, widower of Benazir Bhutto, is elected president of Pakistan by a wide margin. (See "Major News Stories.")

7 The Treasury Dept. seizes control of Fannie Mae and Freddie Mac in a federal bailout that could cost an estimated $25 billion.

8 Human Rights Watch says that civilian deaths from U.S. and NATO airstrikes in Afghanistan have tripled since 2006 and that the Taliban is endangering civilians by deploying its forces in villages and using civilians as human shields.

9 Fears about the stability of investment bank Lehman Brothers trigger a sell-off that cuts the bank's stock value in half and sends the Standard & Poor index down by 3.4 percent.

Angola's governing party wins the country's first elections since 1992 in a landslide and the leading opposition party peacefully concedes defeat.

10 The Large Hadron Collider, the world's largest and most powerful particle collider, is activated in Geneva. (See "Major News Stories.")

The New York Times reports that Haiti, battered by four recent hurricanes and years of poverty and political bickering, is still partly flooded and largely reliant on foreign relief efforts for food.

11 Zimbabwean president Robert Mugabe and opposition leader Morgan Tsvangirai agree to a power-sharing arrangement brokered by South African president Thabo Mbeki.

12 More than one million residents flee coastal Texas as Hurricane Ike approaches with 110 mile-per-hour winds.

In response to the expulsions of the U.S. ambassadors to Venezuela and Bolivia, the State Dept. announces that it will expel the Venezuelan ambassador to the U.S. and accuses Venezuela's top two intelligence officials of supporting rebel groups.

A commuter train in Los Angeles runs a red signal and crashes into a freight train, killing 25 people. (See ""Major News Stories.")

13 Hurricane Ike floods low-lying areas of Galveston, kills at least four people, and leaves more than three million people without power. (See "Major News Stories.")

14 Brokerage firm Merrill Lynch agrees to sell itself to Bank of America, but Lehman Brothers announces that has failed to find a buyer and will file for bankruptcy.

15 The Dow drops 4.4 percent (504 points) in the biggest decline since 2001.

The Chinese Ministry of Health says that two children have died and 1,250 have been sickened by powdered milk contaminated with melamine.

16 The Federal Reserve agrees to an $85 billion bailout of the insurance giant A.I.G. in the most radical intervention in private business in the central bank's history.

Grenades kill at least seven people and injure more than 100 during Independence Day festivities in Mexico; Mexican authorities suggest that drug cartels are responsible.

17 Credit markets around the world tighten and the cost of borrowing soars as investors sell stocks and buy Treasury bills.

Washington Mutual puts itself up for sale and Wachovia enters merger talks with Morgan Stanley.

Militants detonate car bombs outside the American embassy in Yemen, killing 10 people.
18 Congressional leaders begin talks with the Treasury Dept. and Federal Reserve about a massive bailout for the mortgage industry.

An American soldier in Iraq is held in the shooting deaths of two fellow soldiers.
19 The S.E.C. announces that it will ban short selling on nearly 800 stocks, creating challenges for Wall Street traders, but stock prices rise.
20 The White House proposes a vast bailout of U.S. financial institutions including full authority for the Treasury Dept. to buy up to $700 billion in mortgage-related assets from private firms.

South African president Thabo Mbeki resigns under pressure from his party, the African National Congress.

A truck bomb at a hotel kills at least 40 people in Islamabad, Pakistan.
21 The Federal Reserve announces that investment banks Goldman Sachs and Morgan Stanley will become bank holding companies, subject to much greater regulation.

Ehud Olmert resigns as prime minister of Israel.

Babe Ruth's daughter throws out the first pitch for the New York Yankees' last game at Yankee Stadium, which will be demolished in March.
22 Congressional leaders from both parties express anger at the cost and lack of oversight in the proposed financial bailout.

Taro Aso is selected by Japan's Liberal Democratic Party as the next prime minister.
23 Investor Warren Buffett pledges to invest $5 billion in Goldman Sachs through his firm Berkshire Hathaway.

Myanmar's military government says that it will release 9,002 prisoners, including some high-profile political prisoners.

The Fish and Wildlife Service asks a federal judge to reverse the agency's decision to remove the gray wolf from the Endangered Species list last year.
24 North Korea bars international inspectors from a nuclear complex amid concerns that it is restarting a plutonium reprocessing plant.

Sec. of State Condoleezza Rice meets with her Russian counterpart in an effort to restore relations and to discuss the nuclear ambitions of Iran and North Korea.
25 Washington Mutual is seized by federal regulators and most of it is sold to JPMorgan Chase in the largest bank failure in U.S. history.

U.S. and Pakistani troops exchange fire after the Pakistanis shoot at two American helicopters.
26 The S.E.C. acknowledges that failures in a voluntary supervision program for investment banks have contributed to the global financial crisis; most S.E.C. oversight responsibilities now shift to the Federal Reserve.

The U.S. and Russian navies send ships in pursuit of an arms-laden Ukranian freighter hijacked by Somalian pirates.
27 A car bomb near a Syrian intelligence agency in Damascus kills 17 people.
28 Five bombings kill 27 people and wound 84 in Baghdad, Iraq.

A U.S. military official says that the Army has deployed an advanced radar system on Israeli soil.
29 The House rejects the proposed $700 billion economic bailout plan and the Dow drops 6.8 percent (778 points) in a massive stock sellout.

Federal regulators arrange the sale of Wachovia's bank unit to Citigroup to avert another bank failure.

U.S. warships surround the Ukranian ship *Faina* off the shore of Somalia, where it is held by pirates who have asked for a $20 million ransom.
30 Massachusetts receives federal approval for its landmark universal healthcare plan.

OCTOBER 2008

1 The Senate endorses a revised $700 billion economic bailout plan by a vote of 74-25.
2 Vice-presidential candidates Gov. Sarah Palin and Senator Joseph Biden exchange critiques of each other's positions in a nationally televised debate at Washington University in St. Louis.
3 On the same day that the Labor Dept. reports that the U.S. lost 159,000 jobs in September, the worst month in five years, the House approves the bailout plan and Pres. Bush quickly signs it.
5 European governments scramble to alleviate the growing credit crisis; the German government moves to guarantee all private savings accounts.
6 Stock markets around the world plunge as much as 10 percent as credit markets stay frozen in almost every region.
7 On a day when the U.S. stock market declines by 500 points (5.1 percent), the two presidential candidates debate in Nashville and Senator Barack Obama asserts the need for more government regulation of the financial industry.
9 U.S. officials report that the Treasury Dept. is considering taking ownership stakes in many U.S. banks to help restore confidence in the financial system.

The New York Times says that a draft report by U.S. intelligence agencies found that Afghanistan is in a "downward spiral" and its government is unable to stem the rise in the Taliban's influence.

The Dow plummets 679 points (7.3 percent), falling more than 300 points in the last hour and leaving it below 9,000 for the first time in five years.
10 The U.S. and the governments of the six other richest economies agree to a coordinated plan to rescue the financial industry, and Treasury Sec. Henry Paulsen says the U.S. will infuse cash directly into banks, taking ownership stakes in return.

The Connecticut Supreme Court rules that same-sex couples have a constitutional right to marry. (See "Major News Stories.")
11 The Bush Administration announces that it has removed North Korea from the list of state sponsors of terrorism in an attempt to salvage the nuclear deal. (See "Major News Stories.")
12 In an unprecedented move, the U.S. Treasury assures the Japanese bank, Mitsubishi UFJ, that it will protect the bank's $9 bil. investment in ailing U.S. firm Morgan Stanley.

European governments pledge to inject capital into struggling banks and guarantee some forms of debt that produce positive responses in global markets.
13 In anticipation of a Treasury Dept.'s announcement that it will invest $250 billion in U.S. banks, stock markets rally worldwide; the Dow gains 936 points (11 percent), the largest single-day gain in its history.
14 A *New York Times/CBS News* poll finds that Barack Obama leads John McCain by 53 percent to 39 percent among probable voters.
15 The stock market plunges, giving back over 700 of the 936 points it gained two days ago as new evidence of economic deterioration is revealed.

Senators McCain and Obama debate on national T.V. for the final time with McCain attacking his rival for his tax plan and his ties to a former 1960s radical who bombed the Pentagon.

Major News Stories of 2007-2008

By Correspondents of The New York Times

NATIONAL

In Mortgage Crisis Wake, Widespread Financial Havoc

The financial market woes that began with a germ of a problem—lax home mortgage lending practices—exploded in 2008 into the worst financial crisis in the United States since the Great Depression of the 1930's. Its effects, which by one estimate may wind up costing investors over $1 trillion in losses, reverberated across Main Street, Wall Street and overseas.

Mortgage delinquencies rose throughout the year and foreclosures mounted, badly hurting borrowers nationwide and especially in California, Florida and Arizona. Borrowers hoping to refinance their mortgages found banks less willing to lend because they had recorded billions in losses.

As the losses ballooned, Wall Street was clobbered. After more than 80 years in business, Bear Stearns nearly collapsed in March after investors lost confidence in its operations and financial soundness. The securities firm was absorbed by JPMorgan Chase, at the urging of government regulators in a hastily struck weekend deal that valued the company at $10 a share. The fire-sale price—raised from the original $2 a share offer after strenuous complaints from shareholders —was a far cry from the value of Bear Stearns' stock, which traded as high as $67 a share just weeks earlier, and $170 a year before. A major participant in the mortgage arena as both a trader and seller of securities, Bear Stearns was not allowed to fail after regulators overseeing its books determined that the domino effect of its demise could harm the entire financial system.

Following the Bear debacle, the Federal Reserve Bank of New York began allowing Wall Street banks to finance securities they could not sell at its so-called discount window, an unprecedented development. Previously, only commercial banks overseen by the Fed were able to borrow at the discount window, which the Fed opens to institutions that need short-term funding. But regulators seemed to take the view that investment banks, hobbled by bad loans on their books, needed their help.

In mid-July the Indymac Bank, an aggressive mortgage lender in California with $32 billion in assets, collapsed, sending fears of rising bank failures throughout the market.

"Too big to fail" took on new and urgent meaning in late summer when the Treasury created a taxpayer guarantee to shore up Fannie Mae and Freddie Mac, the nation's two largest mortgage finance companies. Government-sponsored enterprises whose shares are nonetheless held by private investors, the companies were hammered by the mortgage meltdown. Together they back or hold $5.2 trillion in mortgages and clearly they could not be allowed to fail. But Fannie's and Freddie's shareholders lost almost everything as a result of the bailout.

In one extraordinary mid-September weekend, two more venerable Wall Street firms had disappeared. Lehman Brothers, a 158-year-old firm hobbled by soured real estate investments, filed the largest bankruptcy in United States history. Merrill Lynch, an iconic investment name, was acquired by Bank of America in a shotgun marriage arranged by regulators.

The crisis quickly spread to insurance companies. American International Group, once the world's largest insurer, teetered for several days as its own portfolio of mortgage-related securities collapsed. The Fed, which was initially reluctant to get involved, reversed course and agreed on Sept. 16 to an $85 billion bailout of the huge company and loaned an additional $38 billion on Oct. 8.

This failed to calm the turbulence, however, or loosen credit, so a week later, as a possible cratering of the economy seemed to loom, the Bush administration proposed the biggest bailout ever, a $700 billion package that would authorize the government to buy distressed mortgages from banks and other institutions. Many in Congress reacted skeptically to the plan, viewing it as too big a burden on taxpayers and not sufficiently punitive to the financial institutions that created the crisis.

Despite pleas from President Bush and Treasury Secretary Henry M. Paulson, Jr., those reservations led the House of Representatives to reject the plan on Sept. 29 by a margin of 228 to 205. The vote had a seismic effect on the stock market, which fell 778 points. Three days later—with the market fluctuating wildly—the Senate passed the bailout plan after tacking on some additions meant to appease reluctant House members. The plan went back to the House on Friday, Oct. 3, where it passed, 263 to 171, and President Bush signed it within hours.

But the pummeling of the markets, both U.S. and foreign, continued as the crisis went global. Panic spread as foreign and domestic banks refused to lend money and investors fled the markets. The Dow Jones lost 18 percent of its value in the week of Oct. 6-10.

That carnage led to an emergency weekend meeting of international leaders in Washington, where a plan was announced to inject capital directly into banks and to guarantee debt issued by banks. In the United States the injection amounted to $250 billion. The effect was immediate. Monday, Oct. 13, saw one of the biggest one-day rallies in history, with the Dow gaining 936 points, or 11 percent. Two days later, most of those gains were gone.

Amid all of this tumult, banks continued to stagger, and some fell. On Sept. 25, federal regulators seized Washington Mutual, the nation's largest savings and loan, and quickly brokered its sale to JPMorgan Chase for $1.9 billion, averting yet another huge taxpayer bill. Wells Fargo dueled Citigroup for control of Wachovia before acquiring the troubled bank for $11.7 billion in mid-October. Morgan Stanley, after weeks of severe losses, got relief from the giant Japanese bank Mitsubishi UFJ which bought a fifth of Morgan for $9 billion. Even Goldman Sachs, which was initially unscathed by the mortgage crisis, appeared vulnerable until Warren Buffett bought a $5 billion stake.

As retirement investments shrank, businesses closed, jobs evaporated—150,000 in September alone, the ninth consecutive month of losses— mortgage foreclosures mounted and the stock market whipsawed, a wary public could only watch and wait to see what came next.

—GRETCHEN MORGENSON
(See "Late Breaking News.")

Primaries: Hard-Fought, Historic, and Long

The presidential primary races, which dominated the political scene for much of 2008, were both historic and dramatic. For the first time in more than 50 years, the contests for both the Republican and Democratic presidential nominations were wide open, without an incumbent president or vice president on either ballot. And the main contenders for the Democratic nomination were a woman, Senator Hillary Rodham Clinton of New York, and an African-American, Senator Barack Obama of Illinois, who engaged in a tense and very close battle that stretched into June, when Mrs. Clinton finally conceded. Never before had either major party nominated either a woman or an African-American to run for president.

The Republicans chose Sen. John McCain of Arizona, a remarkable resurgence for a candidate whose campaign had all but collapsed a year earlier.

The outcome in both parties was unexpected. Mrs. Clinton entered the Democratic race as the overwhelming favorite. She had what was expected to be a huge financial advantage, the backing of the Washington Democratic establishment and the political expertise that came from the political operation that surrounded Mrs. Clinton and her husband, former president Bill Clinton.

By contrast, Mr. Obama was a first-term United States senator who had not run for national office before. From the start, Mrs. Clinton's aides argued that voters would never rally around someone with so little experience.

But it was clear from the year's first contest— the Iowa caucuses on Jan. 3—that things were not going according to Mrs. Clinton's plan. Her campaign was marked by a number of stumbles, and Mr. Obama, after having shown signs of struggling the previous fall, caught fire after delivering a speech to Iowa Democratic activists at the Jefferson-Jackson dinner that fall. He was exciting new voters and raising money at breakneck speed. Mrs. Clinton not only lost to Mr. Obama in Iowa, but came in third—though by less than a single point—behind John Edwards.

She rebounded to win in New Hampshire as well as Nevada, while Mr. Obama took South Carolina, where Mr. Edwards, the only other remaining candidate, dropped out after a disappointing showing. That ceded the stage to Mrs. Clinton and Mr. Obama going into Super Tuesday, when voting was held in 24 states.

Mrs. Clinton had long expected to nail down the nomination on that day, Feb. 5. But while they arguably split the states, Mr. Obama emerged with a critical lead of 100 delegates. He then went on to win 10 straight states, often by large margins that expanded his delegate lead.

Realizing it would be impossible to achieve the required majority of delegates in the primaries alone, the two began courting so-called superdelegates, elected officials and party leaders who are

sent as uncommitted delegates to the convention. Mr. Obama's supporters argued that superdelegates should in effect join him and ratify the results of the primary votes. Sen. Clinton's supporters argued that their candidate's victories in the big-state primaries of Ohio, Pennsylvania and Texas was evidence that she was the more electable.

On May 7, Mrs. Clinton lost decisively in North Carolina, a state where her campaign had said she could win. Even though she continued to soldier on, her aides—and Mrs. Clinton herself—viewed the fight as over.

On the Republican side, Mike Huckabee, the former governor of Arkansas, won the Iowa caucuses, which was good news for Mr. McCain. It undercut the candidacy of the opponent he had long seen as his main rival for the nomination: Mitt Romney of Massachusetts. (By this point, Rudolph W. Giuliani, the former New York mayor who drew a burst of attention when he entered the race, was quickly fading.)

Mr. McCain was making his second bid for the presidency and had reached this point by an improbable route. The previous summer, his campaign had shown signs of collapsing. It was running out of money and most of the staff was laid off. Mr. McCain focused his scaled-down campaign on New Hampshire, a state which, with its large population of independent voters, had given him a decisive double-digit win against George W. Bush in 2000.

The strategy paid off. Mr. McCain shared a victory that night with Mrs. Clinton in New Hampshire, and he went on to win in South Carolina, a state that he had lost to Mr. Bush in 2000 and where Mr. Romney had made a serious effort for support. From there, Mr. McCain won Florida, defeating Mr. Romney and Mr. Giuliani—who, bowing to reality, quickly pulled out and endorsed Mr. McCain. Mr. Romney waited until after Super Tuesday to withdraw and endorse Mr. McCain.

—ADAM NAGOURNEY

Rulings on Guns, Military Prisoners, Mark High Court Term

The Supreme Court's 2007–2008 term will go down in history for Guantánamo and guns.

In *Boumediene v. Bush*, decided June 12, the court delivered its third straight rebuff of the Bush administration's efforts to sequester the prisoners captured in the "war on terrorism" and housed at the United States naval base at Guantánamo Bay, Cuba from the normal processes of civilian and military justice.

The court ruled that in the Military Commissions Act, enacted in 2006 at the administration's behest in response to the Supreme Court's decision months earlier in *Hamdan v. Rumsfeld*, Congress unconstitutionally stripped the federal courts of jurisdiction to hear claims by the detainees of wrongful imprisonment. The detainees were entitled to file petitions for writs of habeas corpus, challenging their designation as enemy combatants, the court ruled. "The laws and Constitution are designed to survive, and remain in force, in extraordinary times," Justice Anthony M. Kennedy wrote for the 5-to-4 majority.

In a concurring opinion, Justice David H. Souter noted that the court's conclusion was "no bolt out of the blue," but rather was foreshadowed by the first in the series of rulings, *Rasul v. Bush*, in 2004, which held that the Guantánamo property was functionally part of United States territory, where ordinary jurisdictional rules applied. Justices John Paul Stevens, Ruth Bader Ginsburg, and Stephen G. Breyer were the other members of the majority.

Chief Justice John G. Roberts Jr. and Justice Antonin Scalia both wrote dissenting opinions, each opinion also signed by the other and by Justices Clarence Thomas and Samuel A. Alito Jr. "It will almost certainly cause more Americans to be killed," Justice Scalia said of the majority opinion. Chief Justice Roberts deplored what he said was the supplanting of military judgment by "unelected, politically unaccountable judges."

With some 200 petitions for habeas corpus pending, judges of the Federal District Court in Washington began immediate discussions with lawyers for the government and the detainees over how to begin to put the Supreme Court decision into effect.

On June 26, the court opened a new chapter in constitutional law by adopting the long-disputed view that the Second Amendment protects an individual right to own a gun for personal use. The vote, once again, was 5 to 4. The majority was composed of Justice Scalia, who wrote the opinion; Chief Justice Roberts; and Justices Kennedy, Thomas and Alito. The dissenters were Justices Stevens and Breyer, who both wrote dissenting opinions, along with Justices Souter and Ginsburg.

The battle in this case, *District of Columbia v. Heller,* was over what the framers of the Second Amendment intended by its opaque language: "A well regulated militia, being necessary to the security of a free State, the right of the people to keep and bear arms, shall not be infringed." To the majority, the amendment "codified a pre-existing right" to own a gun for private use; preserving the militia was simply one reason the right was deemed important enough to enshrine in the Constitution. The framers did not mean the militia reference to negate the right to keep a loaded gun at home for self-defense, Justice Scalia said. To the dissent, readiness for militia service was the only protected reason for gun ownership, as shown by the contemporary state constitutions that explicitly referred to gun ownership for personal use. The framers did not take that extra step, Justice Stevens observed.

The decision invalidated a Washington gun-control law, the strictest in the country. Justice Scalia's opinion said that "longstanding prohibitions" on the ownership of guns by "felons and the mentally ill" would still be upheld, as would laws against carrying concealed weapons and bringing firearms into "sensitive places" like schools or government buildings. The full extent of permissible regulation remains to be tested, and gun-rights advocates quickly filed new lawsuits for exactly that purpose.

The term began on Oct. 1 and ended on June 26. The court issued only 67 decisions, the fewest since the 1953-54 term. The justices were less sharply divided than in the previous term, with only 11 5-to-4 decisions, compared to 24 such decisions (out of 68) the year before.

Among other important rulings, the court rejected challenges to the most common method of execution by lethal injection (*Baze v. Rees,* a case from Kentucky, decided April 16), and to Indiana's requirement that voters provide photo identification before casting a ballot (*Crawford v. Marion County Election Board,* decided April 28).

—LINDA GREENHOUSE

Trying to Contain Housing Shockwaves

Hoping to stretch a safety net under the nation's tumbling housing market, the Senate on July 26 overwhelmingly approved a huge package of legislation that included a program to save hundreds of thousands of families from losing their homes to foreclosure.

The legislation was the latest in a series of extraordinary interventions this year by the Bush administration, Congress and the Federal Reserve as they sought to limit shockwaves in the housing sector from rippling across the American economy and the world financial system. In the process, the central bank and taxpayers took on what critics warn are incalculable liabilities and risks.

The bill granted the Treasury Department broad authority to safeguard the nation's two mortgage finance giants, Fannie Mae and Freddie Mac, potentially by spending tens of billions of dollars in federal money to prevent the collapse of the companies, which own or guarantee nearly half of the nation's $12 trillion in mortgages.

To accommodate the rescue plan for the mortgage companies, the bill raised the national debt ceiling to $10.6 trillion, an increase of $800 billion and the first time that the limit on the government's credit card has grown to 14 digits.

The Senate, convening for a rare Saturday session as it neared summer recess, approved the bill by a vote of 72 to 13, with 27 Republicans joining all the Democrats in attendance to support it.

The measure then went to President Bush, who signed it, thus sending a reassuring message to the credit markets. Lawmakers in both parties hailed the bill, saying it was crucially needed.

The federal intervention gave the Federal Housing Administration the authority to insure up to $300 billion in refinanced mortgages to help stem a tide of foreclosures.

Analysts, including the Congressional Budget Office, expected less than $100 billion of that authority to be used. The risk to taxpayers is minimal, analysts say, given higher insurance fees that will be charged to recipients of the refinanced loans.

Treasury Secretary Henry M. Paulson Jr., an architect of the rescue plan, said he expected never to use the new authority. And the Congressional Budget Office predicted that any bailout between late July and Dec. 31, 2009, when the authority sunsets, would most likely cost $25 billion or less, and that there was a better-than-even chance of no cost at all.

Critics in Congress who voted against the housing bill warned that the government was taking on too much risk, and that government aid would only reward irresponsibility by corporations and individuals.

The bill was the most aggressive government intervention in the housing market since the 1989 response to the savings and loan crisis and perhaps the boldest attempt to aid troubled borrowers since the creation of the Home Owners' Loan Corporation in 1933 as part of the New Deal.

The bill included $15 billion in housing-related tax incentives, like a $7,500 tax credit for first-time homebuyers and business tax breaks for home builders and other large corporations.

—DAVID M. HERSZENHORN and STEPHEN LABATON

Bush Vetoes Bill on C.I.A. Tactics

President Bush on March 8 further cemented his legacy of fighting for strong executive powers, using his veto to shut down a Congressional effort to limit the Central Intelligence Agency's latitude to subject terrorism suspects to harsh interrogation techniques.

Mr. Bush vetoed a bill that would have explicitly prohibited the agency from using interrogation methods like waterboarding, a technique in which restrained prisoners are threatened with drowning and that has been the subject of intense criticism at home and abroad. Many such techniques are prohibited by the military and law enforcement agencies.

The veto deepened his battle with increasingly assertive Democrats in Congress over issues at the heart of his legacy. As his presidency winds down, Mr. Bush has made it clear he does not intend to bend in this or other confrontations on issues from the war in Iraq to contempt charges against his chief of staff, Joshua B. Bolten, and former counsel, Harriet E. Miers.

Mr. Bush announced the veto in the usual format of his weekly radio address, which is distributed to stations across the country each Saturday. He unflinchingly defended an interrogation program that has prompted critics to accuse him not only of authorizing torture previously but also of refusing to ban it in the future.

Mr. Bush's veto—the ninth of his presidency, but the eighth in the past 10 months with Democrats in control of Congress—underscored his determination to preserve many of the executive prerogatives his administration has claimed in the name of fighting terrorism, and to enshrine them into law.

The bill Mr. Bush vetoed would have limited all American interrogators to techniques allowed in the Army field manual on interrogation, which prohibits physical force against prisoners.

The debate has left the C.I.A. at odds with the Federal Bureau of Investigation and other agencies, whose officials have testified that harsh interrogation methods are either unnecessary or counterproductive. The agency's director, Gen. Michael V. Hayden, issued a statement to employees after Mr. Bush's veto defending the program as legal, saying that the Army field manual did not "exhaust the universe of lawful interrogation techniques."

Democrats, who supported the legislation as part of a larger bill that authorized a vast array of intelligence programs, criticized the veto sharply, but they did not have the votes to override it.

—STEVEN LEE MYERS and MARK MAZZETTI

Senate Approves Bill To Broaden Wiretap Powers

The Senate gave final approval on July 9 to a major expansion of the government's surveillance powers, handing President Bush one more victory in a series of hard-fought clashes with Democrats over national security issues. The president signed the bill the next day.

The measure, approved by a vote of 69 to 28, is the biggest revamping of federal surveillance law in 30 years. It includes a divisive element that Mr. Bush had deemed essential: legal immunity for the phone companies that cooperated in the National Security Agency wiretapping program he approved after the Sept. 11 attacks.

The vote came two and a half years after public disclosure of the wiretapping program set off a fierce national debate over the balance between protecting the country from another terrorist strike and ensuring civil liberties. The final outcome in Congress, which opponents of the surveillance measure had conceded for weeks, seemed almost anticlimactic in contrast.

Even as his political stature waned, Mr. Bush managed to maintain his dominance on national security issues in a Democratic-led Congress. He beat back efforts to cut troops and financing in Iraq, and won important victories on issues like interrogation tactics and military tribunals in the fight against terrorism.

Debate over the surveillance law was the one area where Democrats had held firm in opposition. House Democrats went so far as to allow a temporary surveillance measure to expire in February, leading to a five-month impasse and prompting accusations from Mr. Bush that the nation's defenses against another strike by Al Qaeda had been weakened.

But in the end Mr. Bush won out, as administration officials helped forge a deal between Republican and Democratic leaders that included almost all the major elements the White House wanted. The measure gives the executive branch broader latitude in eavesdropping on people abroad and at home who it believes are tied to terrorism, and it reduces the role of a secret intelligence court in overseeing some operations.

—ERIC LICHTBLAU

Military Panel Convicts Bin Laden Driver

A panel of six military officers on Aug. 6 convicted a former driver for Osama bin Laden of one of two war crimes charges but acquitted him of the other, completing the first military commission trial at Guantánamo Bay, Cuba. It was the first military commission trial conducted by the United States since the aftermath of World War II.

In a setback for the military prosecutors, the commission acquitted the former driver, Salim Ahmed Hamdan, of a conspiracy charge, arguably the more serious of the two charges he faced. At a trial that included references to the landmark Nuremberg war-crimes trials of Nazi leaders in the 1940's, Mr. Hamdan was convicted on a separate charge of providing material support for terrorism. Rejecting a prosecution request for a severe sentence, the panel on the next day sentenced Mr. Hamdan to five and a half years in prison.

The military judge, Capt. Keith J. Allred of the Navy, had already said that he planned to give Mr. Hamdan credit for at least the 61 months he had been held since being charged, out of more than six years in all. The sentence meant that he could complete his punishment by the end of 2008. After that his fate is unclear, because the Bush administration says that it can hold detainees until the end of the war on terror.

The verdict gave both sides grounds for their competing claims. Supporters said the system's fairness was illustrated by the careful verdict, while critics said the trial, which featured secret evidence and closed proceedings, demonstrated the injustice of the Bush administration's military commission

As the verdict was read in an old airport building at the isolated naval station, Mr. Hamdan, a Yemeni who has been in custody since he was detained in Afghanistan in November 2001, stood passively at the defense table. He wore a traditional white headscarf. His head was bent slightly to one side.

Critics have long contended that the military commission system does not meet American standards, partly because it allows hearsay evidence and evidence derived through coercive interrogation methods.

The verdict did not mute the critics. Larry Cox, executive director of Amnesty International USA, "revealed what is common knowledge—the military commissions are fatally flawed and do not adhere to major aspects of the rule of law."

But the military prosecutors said the verdict supported their contentions that Mr. Hamdan was a "career Al Qaeda warrior" who was pledged to protect Mr. bin Laden from the mid-1990s until after the Sept. 11 attacks. The chief military prosecutor, Col. Lawrence J. Morris of the Army, added that the verdict validated the system "as an extraordinarily fair, open and just process that produces a reliable result."

—WILLIAM GLABERSON

Mukasey Approved As Attorney General

The Senate confirmed Michael B. Mukasey as attorney general on Nov. 8, 2007, approving him despite Democratic criticism that he had failed to take an unequivocal stance against the torture of terrorism detainees.

The 53-to-40 vote made Mr. Mukasey, a former federal judge, the third person to head the Justice Department during the tenure of President Bush, placing him in charge of an agency that members of both parties say suffered under the leadership of Alberto R. Gonzales.

Six Democrats joined 46 Republicans and one independent in approving the judge, with his backers praising him as a strong choice to restore morale at the Justice Department and independently oversee federal prosecutions in the final months of the Bush administration.

Thirty-nine Democrats and one Independent opposed him.

They said that Mr. Mukasey's refusal to characterize waterboarding, an interrogation technique that simulates drowning, as illegal torture disqualified him from taking over as the nation's top law enforcement official.

The attorney general's post became vacant in late August 2007, when Mr. Gonzales stepped down. For months, he had faced severe criticism over accusations that political calculations played a part in the department's dismissal of some United States attorneys in 2006 and over his role in shaping the administration's policies on torture and electronic surveillance.

Mr. Mukasey was initially hailed by Democrats as a leader who would bring welcome change to the Justice Department. His nomination had been recommended by Sen. Charles E. Schumer, Democrat of New York, a member of the party leadership familiar with Mr. Mukasey from Mr. Mukasy's service on the bench in New York.

On the first day of his confirmation hearings, Mr. Mukasey said he would resign if directed by the White House to take any action he believed was illegal or violated the Constitution, winning Democratic praise. On the second day of his testimony, Mr. Mukasey sidestepped the question of whether waterboarding was torture and also suggested that the president's Constitutional powers could supersede federal law in some cases.

Those responses stirred strong Democratic opposition, throwing his confirmation into question. Trying to stem the rising opposition, Mr.

Mukasey said that while he personally found the concept of waterboarding repugnant, he could not pass judgment on whether it was illegal because he had not been briefed on administration interrogation techniques.

Republicans hailed Mr. Mukasey and accused Democrats of stalling the nomination and focusing on the torture issue to score political points.
—CARL HULSE

Report Faults Hiring At Justice Department

Senior aides to former Attorney General Alberto R. Gonzales broke Civil Service laws by using politics to guide their hiring decisions, picking less-qualified applicants for important nonpolitical positions, slowing the hiring process at critical times and damaging the department's credibility, an internal report concluded on July 28.

A longtime prosecutor who drew rave reviews from his supervisors was passed over for an important counterterrorism slot because his wife was active in Democratic politics, and a much-less-experienced lawyer with Republican leanings got the job, the report said.

Another prosecutor was rejected for a job in part because she was thought to be a lesbian. And a Republican lawyer received high marks at his job interview because he was found to be sufficiently conservative on the core issues of "god, guns + gays."

The report, prepared by the Justice Department's inspector general and its internal ethics office, centered on the misconduct of a small circle of aides to Mr. Gonzales, including Monica Goodling, a former top adviser to the attorney general, and Kyle Sampson, his former chief of staff. It also found that White House officials were actively involved in some hiring decisions.

According to the report, officials at the White House first developed a method of searching the Internet to glean the political leanings of a candidate and introduced it at a White House seminar called The Thorough Process of Investigation. Justice Department officials then began using the technique to search for key phrases or words in an applicant's background, like "abortion," "homosexual," "Florida recount," or "guns."

The report focused its sharpest criticism on Ms. Goodling, a young lawyer from the Republican National Committee who rose quickly in the department to become a top aide to Mr. Gonzales.

In June, the inspector general, Glenn A. Fine, and the Office of Professional Responsibility released a separate report that found a similar pattern of politicized hiring at the Justice Department in reviewing applications from young lawyers for the honors and intern programs.

The internal report went much further in documenting pervasive evidence of political hiring for some of the department's most senior career positions, including immigration judges, assistant United States attorneys and even senior counterterrorism positions.

On Aug. 12 Attorney General Michael B. Mukasy rejected the idea of bringing criminal charges in the matter, saying he had already taken strong internal steps in response to the "painful" episode.
—ERIC LICHTBLAU

Prosecutor Named In Attorney Firings

Attorney General Michael B. Mukasey on Sept. 29 appointed a federal prosecutor to continue an investigation into the dismissals of nine federal prosecutors in 2006 as an internal Justice Department inquiry concluded that political pressure drove the action against at least three of them.

The internal investigators said that the White House's refusal to cooperate in the high-profile investigation produced significant "gaps" in the understanding of who was to blame and that they did not have enough evidence to justify recommending criminal charges in the affair. Now the task of determining if anyone should be prosecuted will fall to Nora Dannehy, the federal prosecutor in Connecticut.

The 356-page report, prepared by the department's inspector general and its Office of Professional Responsibility, provides the fullest account to date of a scandal that dogged the Bush administration for months in 2007 over accusations that it had politicized the federal justice system by ousting prosecutors seen as disloyal.

It provided particular detail in the dismissal of David C. Iglesias, a former New Mexico prosecutor who was let go at the prodding of Republican leaders in Washington and New Mexico who were dissatisfied with his work in investigating accusations against Democrats. Despite the denials of the Bush administration, the political pressure was "the real reason" for Mr. Iglesias's dismissal, the report said.

The investigators acknowledged, however, that they could not answer some critical questions because the White House refused to turn over internal documents and to allow interviews with some crucial figures.

Investigators interviewed about 90 people in the last year and a half, but three senior administration officials who played a part in crucial phases of the dismissals—Karl Rove, the former political adviser to President Bush; Harriet E. Miers, a former White House counsel; and Monica M. Goodling, a former Justice Department liaison to the White House—refused to be interviewed.

But at the same time, the inquiry rejected accusations that the dismissals of two other prosecutors, in Phoenix and San Diego, were designed to thwart political investigations involving Republicans.

The controversy over the dismissals of nine federal prosecutors led to the resignation of Attorney General Alberto R. Gonzales last September, and the report saves some of its harshest criticism for him. It concludes that Mr. Gonzales was "remarkably unengaged" in an unprecedented process to fire a large number of prosecutors at once, and it says that he, along with his deputy at the time, Paul J. McNulty, "abdicated their responsibility" to ensure the integrity of the process and left it mainly to Mr. Gonzales's chief of staff, D. Kyle Sampson.

—ERIC LICHTBLAU

Raid on Mormon Sect In Texas Sets off Child-Custody Fight

Responding to an accusation of sexual abuse of a 16-year-old girl, Texas enforcement officers and child welfare investigators on April 3 raided a West Texas ranch founded by the convicted polygamist sect leader Warren S. Jeffs.

The raid, in which 468 children were eventually seized, set off one of the biggest child-custody cases in United States history. It tied the Texas child welfare system into knots and became the focus of a national debate over the limits of police power.

The raid came after a call to a domestic violence hot line from a 16-year-old girl who said she had been beaten and raped by her 50-year-old husband.

The 1,700-acre Yearning for Zion Ranch of the Fundamentalist Church of Jesus Christ of Latter-day Saints, a breakaway Mormon sect, is in Eldorado, roughly 160 miles northwest of San Antonio.

The ranch was built in 2003 by followers of Mr. Jeffs, who was sentenced in November 2007 in Utah to 10 years to life in prison for forcing a 14-year-old girl to marry her 19-year-old cousin and to submit to sexual relations against her will.

Mr. Jeffs was in jail in Arizona awaiting trial on separate charges involving the arranged marriages of two teenage girls to older relatives.

Local authorities monitored the compound over the years. But aside from a few traffic tickets, there were no problems with sect members, said Raymond Loomis, the Schleicher County attorney.

The Fundamentalist Church of Jesus Christ of Latter-day Saints—with an estimated 10,000 members in the West—split from the mainstream Mormon Church after church leaders in 1890 repudiated the polygamy prescribed by its founding prophet, Joseph Smith, and excommunicated members practicing plural marriage. The breakaway group continued to teach that a man must have three wives to reach heaven's highest realms.

After the children were taken into custody by child welfare authorities, they were placed in foster homes throughout Texas. Then, on May 23, The Third Court of Appeals, in Austin, ruled unanimously that a district judge had unlawfully allowed the Texas Department of Family and Protective Services to remove the children from their homes on insufficient evidence that they were in immediate danger.

The ruling was upheld by a divided Supreme Court of Texas, which agreed that physical and sexual abuse was unproven.

In early June, the children began going home. A spokeswoman for the protective services department said the investigation into possible sexual abuse would continue. A judge also imposed a lengthy list of caveats pending the conclusion of the investigation, including surprise visits by caseworkers, possible psychiatric evaluations of the children and a ban on travel outside Texas.

Confusion was a constant in the case ever since state officials took the action, prompted, they said, by a call to the hotline by the girl who said she was 16 and had been abused. The girl was never found or identified.

—RALPH BLUMENTHAL, KIRK JOHNSON and GRETEL C. KOVACH

Hurricane Ike Batters Texas

Hurricane Ike barreled across a wide swath of Texas on Sept. 13, deluging the city of Galveston with a wall of water, flooding coastal towns and leaving extensive damage across metropolitan Houston.

With wind gusts approaching 100 miles per hour, the 600-mile-wide Category 2 hurricane peeled sheets of steel off skyscrapers in Houston, smashed bus shelters and blew out windows, sending shattered glass and debris across the nation's fourth-largest city, with a population of 2.2 million.

The storm came ashore on Galveston Island, which in 1900 suffered one of the worst hurricanes to hit the United States. Winds covered the main highway with a layer of boats and debris, shutting it down. Total damage to Galveston was estimated to be more than $10 billion, and officials said they did not expect electricity and natural gas to be restored on the entire island for at least a month. There was concern that the sludge left in homes and on roads as floodwaters receded in the aftermath of the storm posed serious health risks. In Orange, Tex., near the Louisiana coast, the sea rose so rapidly that people were forced to flee to attics and roofs, and the city used trucks to rescue them, local police said.

The authorities said the hurricane could still prove to be the most punishing storm to hit the area since Hurricane Alicia did 25 years ago.

Almost the entire metropolitan area lost power, and authorities said more than three million people were trying to manage in the dark. Utility officials say it could be weeks before power is restored throughout the region.

Refineries were spared the center of the storm, but several major refineries were nonetheless forced to shut down, creating a rise in gasoline prices around the country even while oil prices were dropping on international markets. Overnight, prices rose an average of 5 cents a gallon, to $3.73 for regular gasoline, according to AAA.

More than two million people evacuated coastal areas of Texas and Louisiana before the storm struck. But the authorities estimated that more than 100,000 people throughout the region, including 20,000 in Galveston, had disregarded mandatory evacuation orders.

At least 100,000 homes were inundated by surging waters, while isolated fires broke out around the region when trees and flying objects fell on electrical transformers, causing sparks.

Remnants of the storm reached the Midwest, spurring tornadoes and wind gusts up to 80 miles an hour, and dumping 4 to 10 inches of water on parts of Missouri, Illinois, Indiana and Michigan.
—CLIFFORD KRAUSS and JAMES C. MCKINLEY, JR.

Severe Flooding Hits the Midwest

In early June, much of the Midwest went under water. An especially wet winter and frosty, storm-laden early spring combined to produce some of the most severe flooding ever recorded in parts of Iowa, Indiana, Missouri and Wisconsin.

As the winter slush began to melt in the north of the country's midsection, bands of stationary thunderstorms also began to show up with some regularity, aggravating already swollen rivers and creeks. All the water began to tumble southward, threatening and sometimes inundating town after town along major rivers, triggering large-scale evacuations and breaching levees in some places along the way.

The calamitous weather drew comparisons to great floods that happened along the Mississippi River and its upper tributaries in 1993 and 1927. While the 2008 deluge was not as deadly or massive in scope as those earlier events, the storms and flooding did cause at least 30 deaths in seven states and resulted in many billions of dollars in damage to residences, businesses and agricultural land.

In eastern Iowa, which was hardest hit, the Cedar River crested at more than 31 feet in Cedar Rapids—far higher than it had been during the last significant flood, in 1993, when it reached 19.27 feet. Cedar Rapids alone suffered more than $1 billion in water damage. The flood consumed about 5,400 homes over nine square miles in and around downtown.

Whole towns, such as Palo, Iowa, were destroyed. Others, like Dutchtown, Mo., survived but were completely under water for days. Mass evacuations became commonplace from Wisconsin to Arkansas.

In addition to the flooding, the storms touched off numerous tornadoes. Four Boy Scouts were killed near Blencoe, on the western edge of Iowa, in one of the worst twisters. Countless others caused severe damage across the central states.

In Iowa, damage estimates grew by the week in June as water rushed to more and more areas. In August, the state had tallied some preliminary figures: crops and agricultural infrastructure had suffered nearly $3 billion in damage, $946 million would be needed for housing replacement and repair, and at least $700 million would be necessary to restore public buildings and infrastructure.

The massive flooding revealed weaknesses in levee protections along the upper Mississippi river system. After an enormous flood in 1927, officials designed a standardized system of protection for the lower Mississippi with uniform, federally-maintained levees stretching from Cairo, Ill., south to the Gulf of Mexico.

But the Upper Midwest has no such coordination, and suffered as a result, experts said. The northern states along the Mississippi River rely on a "hodgepodge" of levees, as one Missouri geologist described the situation. Levees maintained by farmers, towns, or local agencies were overwhelmed and overtopped; others developed holes and broke.

Months after the floods, many thousands of people remained displaced from their homes. The area's flooded population was scattered around hotel rooms, temporary apartments and mobile homes financed by housing assistance from the Federal Emergency Management Agency.
—SUSAN SAULNY

Pope Ends U.S. Visit With Yankee Stadium Mass

Before a crowd of nearly 60,000 people at Yankee Stadium, Pope Benedict XVI on April 20 ended his first visit to the United States as leader of the Roman Catholic Church with a reminder to the faithful that "obedience" to the authority of the church, even in a country that prizes individual freedom, is the foundation of their religious faith.

During a six-day visit to Washington and New York, the pope addressed world issues, visited a synagogue and voiced deep shame over the child sexual abuse scandal that has damaged the church's standing in many American dioceses.

At a morning ceremony at ground zero, the pope blessed the World Trade Center site, where more than 2,700 people were killed in the terrorist attack, and prayed for peace.

But at Yankee Stadium on a cool, brilliant Sunday afternoon, with an adoring audience of people waving yellow cloths, one of the colors of the Vatican, Benedict acted chiefly as pastor to America's 65 million Catholics, laying out in simple terms their obligations to a church that represents what he has called the "one church" established on earth by God.

"Authority. Obedience. To be frank, these are not easy words to speak nowadays," the pope said in his homily during the Mass, held on an acre-size platform built over the Yankees infield, "especially in a society which rightly places a high value on personal freedom."

Three years after the death of Pope John Paul II, his popular and charismatic predecessor, the reserved and theologically erudite Pope Benedict XVI gently but unequivocally delineated the source of authority that has since devolved to him, and that he said was integral to the church itself.

Referring to himself, he said, "The presence around this altar of the successor of Peter, his brother bishops and priests, and deacons, men and women religious, and lay faithful from throughout the 50 states of the union, eloquently manifests our communion in the Catholic faith, which comes to us from the apostles."

In a glancing reference to the sexual abuse of children by priests, he said that praying for the kingdom of God "means not losing heart in the face of adversity, resistance and scandal. It means overcoming every separation between faith and life, and countering false gospels of freedom and happiness."

In his writings before and since becoming pope, Benedict has stressed the importance of a strict adherence to orthodoxy, and opposition to a wide array of modern cultural trends, including feminism, gay rights, and demands—especially among American Catholics—for greater democracy and administrative transparency within the church.

After the Mass, waves of excitement followed the path of the pope as he first walked, and then rode in his Popemobile, around the outside track of the field. Surrounded by black-suited Secret Service men, the 81-year-old pontiff moved somewhat haltingly, the papal scepter in his left hand. The crowd roared with all the sustained excitement of spectators at a pennant-clinching game.

—PAUL VITELLO

F.B.I. Says Scientist Acted Alone In Anthrax Killings

The F.B.I. on Aug. 6 outlined a pattern of bizarre and deceptive conduct by Bruce E. Ivins, an Army microbiologist who killed himself a week earlier. It presented a sweeping but circumstantial case that he was solely responsible for mailing the deadly anthrax letters that killed five people in 2001.

After nearly seven years of a troubled investigation, officials of the F.B.I. and the Justice Department declared that the case had been solved. Jeffrey A. Taylor, the United States attorney for the District of Columbia, said the authorities believed "that based on the evidence we had collected, we could prove his guilt to a jury beyond a reasonable doubt."

Some survivors of the attacks and members of Congress said they were persuaded by the evidence against Dr. Ivins, laid out in hundreds of pages of applications for search warrants unsealed for the first time. But some independent scientists, friends and colleagues of Dr. Ivins remained skeptical, noting that officials admitted that more than 100 people had access to the supply of anthrax that matched the powder in the letters.

The skepticism was all the greater because investigators have recently acknowledged that for years they had focused on the wrong man, Steven J. Hatfill, whose career was ruined and who received a settlement of $4.6 million from the Justice Department in June.

The case against Dr. Ivins combined scientific analysis of the mailed anthrax, whose genetic fingerprint investigators linked to a supply in the scientist's laboratory, with a review of his e-mail messages, which showed fury and frustration at problems in his anthrax vaccine research, worsening symptoms of mental illness and language that echoed a phrase in the note sent in the poisoned letters.

In addition, investigators from the F.B.I. and the Postal Inspection Service found records showing that Dr. Ivins had worked late at night in his laboratory at Fort Detrick in Frederick, Md., in the days before the two mailings in September and October 2001.

Investigators also noted that envelopes used in the attacks all had a printing defect indicating that they were sold at only a small number of post offices in Maryland and Virginia in 2001—including in Frederick where Dr. Ivins maintained a box under an assumed name.

An inventory of items taken in the Nov. 1 search included three handguns and a "notebook detailing firearms training."

Searches of Dr. Ivins's house and cars turned up not a spore of anthrax, his lawyers said, and perusal of thousands of his e-mail messages turned up no indication that he planned the crime.

Moreover, months of work uncovered no evidence that Dr. Ivins had traveled to Princeton, N.J., where investigators believe the letters were mailed. The closest connection was that a chapter house of Kappa Kappa Gamma, a sorority with which Dr. Ivins had a long and strange obsession, is near the contaminated Princeton mailbox.

The anthrax investigation began in October 2001 with hundreds of agents working around the clock and many expecting the letters to be linked to Al Qaeda. But investigators concluded early on that a more likely perpetrator was an American biodefense insider, possibly one who wanted to raise public awareness of the bioterrorist threat.

On Sept. 16, F.B.I. Director Robert S. Mueller III, responding to lingering concerns of members of Congress about the handling of the investigation, said he had asked the National Academy of Sciences to convene an expert panel to review the bureau's work on the case.

—SCOTT SHANE and ERIC LICHTBLAU

Sex, Drug Use, Graft Cited In Interior Dept.

As Congress prepared to debate expansion of drilling in taxpayer-owned coastal waters, the Interior Department agency that collects oil and gas royalties was caught up in a wide-ranging ethics scandal—including allegations of financial self-dealing, accepting gifts from energy companies, cocaine use and sexual misconduct.

In three reports delivered to Congress on Sept. 10, the department's inspector general, Earl E. Devaney, found wrongdoing by a dozen current and former employees of the Minerals Management Service, which collects about $10 billion in royalties annually and is one of the government's largest sources of revenue other than taxes. "A culture of ethical failure" pervades the agency, Mr. Devaney wrote in a cover memo.

The reports portray a dysfunctional organization that has been riddled with conflicts of interest, unprofessional behavior and a free-for-all atmosphere for much of the Bush administration's watch.

The highest-ranking official criticized in the reports is Lucy Q. Denett, the former associate director of minerals revenue management, who retired earlier this year as the inquiry was progressing.

The investigations are the latest installment in a series of scathing inquiries into the program's management and competence in recent years. While previous reports have focused on problems the agency had in collecting millions of dollars owed to the Treasury, and hinted at personal misconduct, the new reports went far beyond any previous study in revealing serious concerns with the integrity and behavior of the agency's officials.

In one of the new reports, investigators concluded that Ms. Denett worked with two aides to steer a lucrative consulting contract to one of the aides after he retired, violating competitive procurement rules.

Two other reports focused on "a culture of substance abuse and promiscuity" in the service's royalty-in-kind program. That part of the agency collects about $4 billion a year in oil and gas rather than cash royalties.

Based in suburban Denver and modeled to operate like a private sector energy company, the decade-old royalty-in-kind program sells oil and gas on the open market. Its employees are subject to government ethics rules, such as restrictions on taking gifts from people and companies with whom they conduct official business.

One of the reports says that the officials viewed themselves as exempt from those limits, indulging themselves in the expense-account-fueled world of oil and gas executives.

The report says that eight officials in the royalty program accepted gifts from energy companies whose value exceeded limits set by ethics rules—including golf, ski and paintball outings; meals and drinks; and tickets to a Toby Keith concert, a Houston Texans football game and a Colorado Rockies baseball game.

The investigation also concluded that several of the officials "frequently consumed alcohol at industry functions, had used cocaine and marijuana, and had sexual relationships with oil and gas company representatives."

—CHARLIE SAVAGE

Sen. Kennedy Found To Have Brain Tumor

Senator Edward M. Kennedy, the longtime Massachusetts Democrat and patriarch of the Kennedy family, has a malignant brain tumor, his doctors said on May 21.

Doctors at Massachusetts General Hospital, who were investigating the cause of a seizure that Mr. Kennedy, 76, suffered at his Cape Cod compound, said preliminary results from a biopsy of the brain had revealed that he has a malignant glioma in the left parietal lobe, the upper left part of his brain.

Senator Kennedy successfully underwent surgery on June 2 in Durham, N.C. Mr. Kennedy told his wife, Victoria, immediately after the surgery, "I feel like a million bucks," a spokesman recounted.

Removing the bulk of a tumor improves prognosis in part, Dr. Brian Collins, a radiation oncologist at Georgetown Hospital said, because it tends to let the patient better tolerate chemotherapy and radiation.

On July 9, Mr. Kennedy stirred the normally staid Senate chamber to a rousing ovation and moved many colleagues to tears when he made a surprise appearance in the late afternoon to break a Republican filibuster on a Medicare bill. Then on Aug. 25, he arrived at the Democratic National Convention in a triumphant appearance that provided an emotional start for the event.

—BENEDICT CAREY and PAM BELLUCK

Spitzer Resigns In Sex Scandal

Eliot Spitzer, whose rise to political power as a fierce enforcer of ethics in public life was undone by revelations of his own involvement with prostitutes, resigned on March 12, becoming the first New York governor to leave office amid scandal in nearly a century.

Mr. Spitzer announced that he was stepping down at a grim appearance at his Midtown Manhattan office, less than 48 hours after it emerged that he had been intercepted on a federal wiretap confirming plans to meet a call girl from a high-priced prostitution service in Washington.

With his wife, Silda Wall Spitzer, at his side, Mr. Spitzer, 48, a Democrat, said he would leave political life to concentrate on healing himself and his family.

Though he came into office in January 2007 with a sweeping electoral mandate for change, Mr. Spitzer's time as governor was marked by fierce combat and costly stumbles. He faced a scandal during his first year after members of his staff used the State Police to disseminate damaging information about his chief Republican rival, Joseph L. Bruno, the leader of the State Senate.

Mr. Spitzer's resignation was accompanied by relief, shock and a sense of the surreal. Legislative leaders from both parties voiced condolences to Mr. Spitzer's wife and three daughters and welcomed Lt. Gov. David A. Paterson, the heir to a Harlem political dynasty, who was sworn in as New York's 55th governor, making him the state's first black chief executive.

The son of a wealthy real estate investor, Mr. Spitzer was educated at Princeton and Harvard Law School and was elected New York's attorney general in 1998. He brought some of Wall Street's biggest names to heel and forced banks, insurance companies and brokerage houses to pay defrauded investors huge settlements.

He was reviled on Wall Street. But to millions of Americans who felt swindled in an age when executive salaries and the income gap between rich and middle class were rapidly growing, Mr. Spitzer was viewed as a guardian against corporate excess and was swept into the governor's office in a landslide.

—DAVID KOCIENIEWSKI and DANNY HAKIM

U.S. Prisons Are World's Busiest

The United States has less than 5 percent of the world's population. But it has almost a quarter of the world's prisoners.

Indeed, the United States leads the world in producing prisoners, a reflection of a relatively recent and now entirely distinctive American approach to crime and punishment. Americans are locked up for crimes—from writing bad checks to using drugs—that would rarely produce prison sentences in other countries. And in particular they are kept incarcerated far longer than prisoners in other nations.

Criminologists and legal scholars in other industrialized nations say they are mystified and appalled by the number and length of American prison sentences.

The United States has 2.3 million criminals behind bars, more than any other nation, according to data maintained by the International Center for Prison Studies at King's College London.

China, which is four times more populous than the United States, is a distant second, with 1.6 million people in prison. (That number excludes hundreds of thousands of people held in administrative detention, most of them in China's extrajudicial system of re-education through labor, which often singles out political activists who have not committed crimes.)

The United States comes in first, too, on a more meaningful list from the prison studies center, the one ranked in order of the incarceration rates. It has 751 people in prison or jail for every 100,000 in population. (If you count only adults, one in 100 Americans is locked up.)

The only other major industrialized nation that even comes close is Russia, with 627 prisoners for every 100,000 people

Criminologists and legal experts here and abroad point to a tangle of factors to explain America's extraordinary incarceration rate: higher levels of violent crime, harsher sentencing laws, a legacy of racial turmoil, a special fervor in combating illegal drugs, the American temperament, and the lack of a social safety net. Even democracy plays a role, as judges—many of whom are elected, another American anomaly—yield to populist demands for tough justice.

—ADAM LIPTAK

Two State Courts Overturn Ban On Gay Marriage

The California Supreme Court, striking down two state laws that had limited marriages to unions between a man and a woman, ruled on May 15 that same-sex couples have a constitutional right to marry.

The 4-to-3 decision, drawing on a ruling 60 years ago that struck down a state ban on interracial marriage, would make California the second state, after Massachusetts, to allow same-sex marriages.

The decision was greeted with celebrations at San Francisco City Hall, where thousands of same-sex marriages were thrown out by the courts four years ago.

It was denounced by religious and conservative groups that promised to support an initiative that would amend the California Constitution to ban same-sex marriages and overturn the decision.

Given the historic, cultural, symbolic and constitutional significance of marriage, Chief Justice Ronald M. George wrote for the majority, the state cannot limit its availability to opposite-sex couples.

"In view of the substance and significance of the fundamental constitutional right to form a family relationship," Chief Justice George wrote, "the California Constitution properly must be interpreted to guarantee this basic civil right to all Californians, whether gay or heterosexual, and to same-sex couples as well as to opposite-sex couples."

On Oct. 10 a sharply divided Connecticut Supreme Court struck down the state's civil union law and ruled same-sex couples have a constitutional right to marry. The ruling cannot be appealed and was due to take effect on Oct. 28. Connecticut, California and Massachusetts are the only states to have legalized gay marriages.

—ADAM LIPTAK

Minorities May Become Majority in U.S.

Ethnic and racial minorities will comprise a majority of the nation's population in a little more than a generation, according to new Census Bureau projections, a transformation that is occurring faster than anticipated just a few years ago.

The census calculates that by 2042, Americans who identify themselves as Hispanic, black, Asian, American Indian, Native Hawaiian and Pacific Islander will together outnumber non-Hispanic whites. Four years ago, officials had projected the shift would come in 2050.

The main reason for the accelerating change is significantly higher birthrates among immigrants. Another factor is the influx of foreigners, rising from about 1.3 million annually today to more than 2 million a year by midcentury, according to projections based on current immigration policies.

"No other country has experienced such rapid racial and ethnic change," said Mark Mather, a demographer with the Population Reference Bureau, a research organization in Washington.

The Census Bureau's projections are likely to fuel debates over immigration policy, overpopulation and the changing electorate, and recall earlier eras when the Irish, the Italians and Eastern European Jews were not universally considered as whites.

The latest figures, released in August, are predicated on current and historical trends, which can be thrown awry by several variables, including prospective overhauls of immigration policies and sudden increases in refugees.

"A momentum is built into this as a result of past immigration," said Jeffrey S. Passel, senior demographer at the Pew Hispanic Center. "In the 1970s, '80s and '90s, there were more Hispanic immigrants than births. This decade, there are more births than immigrants. Almost regardless of what you assume about future immigration, the country will be more Hispanic and Asian."

—SAM ROBERTS

Train Collision Kills 25 In L.A.

An engineer who ran a red signal in Los Angeles and crashed head-on into a freight train on Sept. 12 likely caused the nation's deadliest commuter train wreck in nearly four decades, a spokeswoman for the rail line said the following day.

The death toll was 25 from the collision of the northbound Metrolink train carrying about 225 passengers and the freight train in Chatsworth, a mostly residential district in the northwest San Fernando Valley, officials said. More than 130 people were injured.

The crash was the deadliest commuter train accident in the nation since 1972, when 45 people died in Chicago, and the deadliest train crash of any kind since the 1993 Amtrak crash in Mobile, Ala., in which 47 people died.

Many passengers described how their quiet commute was punctured by instant terror and carnage shortly before 4:30 p.m. Passengers flew into one another's laps; nearly severed limbs became tangled together, and blood spilled along the cars' aisles. In some cases, the living were trapped beneath the bodies of the dead.

The impact of the crash was so violent that the Metrolink engine was shoved back into a passenger car, which collapsed on its side. The freight train cars essentially collapsed like an accordion, and the other Metrolink cars were derailed.

The engineer was the only one of five train workers—three on the freight train and two on the commuter railroad—to die in the crash, said Denise Tyrrell, a rail line spokesman. She said the engineer worked for a Metrolink subcontractor.

Ms. Tyrrell said, "Our preliminary investigation shows it was a Metrolink engineer that failed to stop at a red signal and was the probable cause of the accident."

Ms. Tyrrell said her agency's preliminary findings determined that the signal on the track was working properly, and that both trains appeared to be traveling about 40 miles per hour. The conductor of the train, who gives the commands to the engineer, was being interviewed by law enforcement officials, she said.

National Transportation Safety Board officials were far less conclusive. A safety board member, Kitty Higgins, said that while the agency could "absolutely not rule out" human error, it would examine track signals, equipment and many other factors. Three data recorders taken from the two trains, as well as a video recorder from the freight train, would be analyzed, she said.

Federal investigators subsequently discovered that the engineer, Robert M. Sanchez, had been sending text messages on his cell phone seconds before the crash. But the investigators had not determined whether he was sending messages when the train failed to stop for the red signal.

—JENNIFER STEINHAUER and MICHAEL CIEPLY

Steriod Report Ties Baseball Stars To Use

Former Senator George J. Mitchell released a blistering report on Dec. 6, 2007, that tied 89 Major League Baseball players, including Roger Clemens, to the use of illegal, performance-enhancing drugs.

Mr. Clemens, a seven-time Cy Young Award winner, was the most prominent name on a list that included seven other former most valuable players as well as players from all 30 teams. The list included more than a dozen players who have had significant roles with the New York Yankees, and more than a dozen New York Mets, too. It also included 11 players alone from the 2000 Los Angeles Dodgers.

Of all the active players tied to the use of steroids and human growth hormone, which are illegal without a prescription and banned by baseball, only Jason Giambi of the Yankees cooperated with Mr. Mitchell's 20-month investigation. The Toronto Blue Jays' Frank Thomas, widely known for his antisteroids stance, was the only other active player who agreed to talk with Mr. Mitchell's investigators.

Mr. Mitchell's report of about 400 pages was based on interviews with more than 700 people, including 60 former players, and 115,000 pages of documents, including receipts, canceled checks, telephone records and e-mail messages. The key evidence was provided by Kirk Radomski, a former Mets clubhouse attendant, and Brian McNamee, a former trainer for Mr. Clemens and the Yankees pitcher Andy Pettitte, who were also named in the report.

In the report, Mr. McNamee is quoted describing how he injected Mr. Clemens with illegal drugs at least 16 times from 1998 through 2001. Mr. Clemens, 45, adamantly denied the report's accusations of his use of steroids and human growth hormone. In subsequent Congressional hearings in February, Mr. Clemens continued to deny having used the drugs, while Mr. Pettitte, in a statement shortly after the Mitchell report was released, admitted using them.

Mr. Mitchell acknowledged that his report was inhibited by limited cooperation and the absence of subpoena power, and that there was still much about drug use in baseball he did not know. The report was critical of the commissioner's office and the players' union for knowingly tolerating performance-enhancing drugs. It cited many instances where club officials knew about particular steroid use among players and did not report it.

Mr. Mitchell said "baseball's steroids era" started roughly in 1988. It took 15 more years for baseball to start random testing, Mr. Mitchell said. He said that testing had reduced steroid use, but players have switched to human growth hormone, which cannot be detected in urine tests, which baseball's program administers. "Everybody in baseball—commissioners, club officials, the players' association, players—shares responsibility," Mr. Mitchell said.

—DUFF WILSON and MICHAEL S. SCHMIDT

Writers Vote To End Hollywood Strike

Hollywood's writers voted by an overwhelming margin on Feb. 12 to end their bitterly fought strike at the 100-day mark.

The decision to end the strike became all but inevitable after the governing boards of the Writers Guild of America West and the Writers Guild of American East two days' earlier unanimously approved the tentative three-year agreement with the Alliance of Motion Picture and Television Producers, following strong expressions of support at mass meetings on both coasts.

The strike upended the television viewing habits of millions of Americans by shutting down production on most dramas and comedies and forced movie studios to halt some big-budget films. It also dried up the livelihoods of not just the 12,000 guild members but tens of thousands of people who rely on such productions for work.

A running tally by the producers' alliance estimated that the walkout had cost writers about $285 million in lost wages and had cost workers in other film unions nearly $500 million.

The writers' dispute was settled when company executives—notably Peter Chernin, the News Corporation president, and Robert A. Iger, the Walt Disney chief executive—opened talks with Patric M. Verrone, president of the West Coast Guild, David J. Young, the guild's executive director, and John Bowman, who headed the unions' negotiating committee. A crucial break came when the two sides created a provision to deal with what the writers regarded as a make-or-break issue: Web streaming of TV shows after their initial broadcast, which is seen as likely to soon replace the reruns that have paid them tens of thousands of dollars an episode.

The agreement provides the guilds a gain in the payment for digital distribution of entertainment beyond the terms of a recent deal between Hollywood producers and the Directors Guild of America.

—MICHAEL CIEPLY

Detroit Mayor Quits In Scandal

Kwame M. Kilpatrick, the charismatic mayor of Detroit who had been embroiled in legal problems stemming from a sex scandal for most of the year, pleaded guilty to obstruction of justice and resigned his office in early September as part of a deal with prosecutors.

A two-term mayor who brimmed with promise early in his career, Mr. Kilpatrick, 38, had been charged with ten felonies in two criminal cases including perjury and misconduct in office. The charges came after the revelation that the mayor had an extramarital affair with his chief of staff, Christine Beatty, and that he used his power and public money to keep the affair secret.

The affair became public anyway, when The Detroit Free Press published steamy text messages sent from a city-owned pager that detailed much of the romance between Mr. Kilpatrick and Ms. Beatty, who resigned when the affair became public. The text messages and the affair contradicted testimony the two had previously given under oath in a civil trial.

As part of the plea deal, Mr. Kilpatrick also agreed to pay restitution to Detroit, serve 120 days in county jail and give up his law license.

—SUSAN SAULNY

INTERNATIONAL NEWS

A Wary Iraq Sees Drop In Violence

In late March, Iraqi troops were being fought to a standstill by Shiite militias in Basra after Prime Minister Nuri Kamal al-Maliki gambled his political fortunes on a poorly planned assault meant to force out the gunmen who ruled much of the city. But the militias stubbornly held their ground, more than 1,000 members of the inept government forces fled or refused to fight, and it seemed possible that Mr. Maliki's political coalition could crumble.

Two weeks later, after American and British airstrikes had helped induce the radical Shiite cleric Moktada al-Sadr to order his fighters to stand down, Mr. Maliki's fortunes had undergone a striking reversal. The prime minister declared that his forces, now largely in control of Basra, had bested the militias. And he had solidified his standing among members of his fractious political coalition, most of whom loathe and fear Mr. Sadr and the gunmen loyal to him at least as much as Mr. Maliki does.

The Basra fight was in many ways emblematic of a year in which continuing drops in violence across Iraq, along with patchy advances on the political front, were often shadowed by a menacing uncertainty over what was actually responsible for the progress and why negotiations on some critical benchmarks—like laws governing elections and the Iraqi oil industry—dragged on inconclusively into the fall.

The Bush administration made the case that the American troop increase that began in early 2007 was the main reason for the drop in violence, in turn providing an opening for the modest political gains. That increase—the surge, in public-relations shorthand—was presided over by Gen. David H. Petraeus, the top commander in Iraq until September, when he handed the reins to Gen. Ray Odierno.

It will be General Odierno's charge to oversee the withdrawal of 8,000 American troops from Iraq by early next year. But the drawdown will leave about 138,000 troops in the country, still several thousand more than before the surge began in February 2007—a signal that the United States still sees high force levels as critical to maintaining stability.

But others saw a decision by Sunni tribes to join the so-called Awakening Councils and support the government, along with Mr. Sadr's restraint, as far more important factors.

And as the year came to an end, increasing friction between the tribes and the Shiite-led government raised serious questions on how durable the security improvements would prove to be. Anything that depends on the mercurial Sadr is subject to reversal with little notice.

Still, except for a countrywide spike during the Basra operation, violence remained low compared to its peaks during the sectarian bloodletting in 2006 and 2007. Whatever the overall effect of simply bringing more American troops into Iraq, there was wide agreement within the country that General Petraeus's decision to deploy many of those troops in small neighborhood outposts did play an important part in bringing down the violence.

Politically, 2008 began with great promise when the Iraqi parliament passed long-stalled measures that would allow the return of some skilled Baathists who had been banned from government, grant amnesty to certain Iraqi detainees and provide a legal framework for provincial elections.

But as the year wore on, only the amnesty law had much impact. The law on returning Baathists proved difficult to carry out, and after being vetoed and then reinstated, the elections law fell victim to power struggles among the many parties whose fortunes would be influenced by a vote. Mr. Maliki's Dawa party and its allies, for instance, worried that the Sadrists—who had mostly boycotted the last set of provincial elections in 2005— would pick up numerous seats at the expense of the other Shiite parties. The Sadrists even accused Mr. Maliki of launching the Basra assault to weaken them in advance of any elections.

As fall arrived, neither the elections law nor crucial legislation to create a framework for Iraq's oil industry had been passed, despite repeated claims by senior Iraqi and American officials that the differences had been resolved. And on Oct. 1, responsibility for monthly payments to many of the Awakening Councils—often made up of former Sunni insurgents who had agreed to help keep the peace, for a price—passed from the American military to the Iraqi government.

—JAMES GLANZ

For China, Tumult Was The Norm

In China, 2008 was expected to offer a smooth, uneventful prelude to the Beijing Olympics in August—but the year proved anything but smooth. There was a freak winter storm in southern China in late January and early February that stranded millions of migrant workers during the Lunar New Year holiday, knocked out power and water supplies and exposed the weaknesses of China's transportation system.

Then came the violent Tibetan riots that erupted in Lhasa on March 14 and quickly spread to other Tibetan regions of western China. Tibetans and their advocates saw the uprising as an inevitable backlash against years of hard-line government policies, including restrictions on Tibetan religious and cultural expression. Chinese leaders instead accused the Dalai Lama, the exiled Tibetan spiritual leader, of orchestrating the riots in order to "split" China—a charge he flatly denied.

Tibet quickly cast a shadow over the upcoming Olympics as some European leaders announced they would not attend the opening ceremony and advocacy groups intensified their protests. China had organized the longest, most dramatic torch relay in Olympic history, with stops around the globe and even an ascent of Mt. Everest. But large anti-China protests greeted the Olympic flame in London and Paris, sparking a nationalist backlash among Chinese as well as many Chinese living overseas. When the torch reached San Francisco, pro-Tibet advocates and other protesters were met by large crowds of China supporters. San Francisco organizers decided to carry the torch on an abbreviated, unannounced route to avoid a potential confrontation.

The event that ultimately broke the international tension would be the most tragic of the year: the powerful May 12 earthquake in Sichuan Province that killed more than 70,000 people and inspired an unprecedented public response as thousands of ordinary Chinese rushed to the scene to help. International aid poured in as the earthquake devastated one of China's poorest regions. The earthquake also exposed shoddy construction, especially at schools: Thousands of school children were killed beneath collapsed buildings in a tragedy that brought sustained protests by grief-stricken parents.

By Aug. 8, the Olympics finally arrived with a stunning opening ceremony orchestrated by China's most famous film director, Zhang Yimou. The Games went off smoothly and provided a major public relations victory for the ruling Communist Party as foreign visitors were impressed by Beijing's hospitality—and as the Chinese team easily won the most gold medals. But the Games also showed China's harder edges: the authoritarian government had been praised for designating three parks as zones for public protests. Yet none of the people who formally applied for a protest permit were approved, so the zones remained empty. Two elderly women who tried to apply were instead sentenced to two years of labor reeducation, though the sentence was later rescinded.

Then, with the Paralympics still underway in Beijing in September, a major food safety scandal left at least three babies dead and sickened more than 6,200 infants after officials confirmed that they had been exposed to baby formula contaminated with the industrial additive melamine. The scandal exposed serious flaws in the country's rapidly growing dairy industry as well as the failings of a regulatory system that had been overhauled only a year earlier.

Finally, 2008 marked the 30th anniversary of Deng Xiaoping's seminal decision to open China to the outside world and discard Socialist economic for market-driven economic reforms. Deng's Reform and Opening Policy is credited with sparking the astonishing economic progress that has made China a major engine of the world economy—a trend that only continued in 2008. But the anniversary also seemed to mark the end of an era and underscore the uncertainty about what would happen in the next era, as some intellectuals called for new, deeper reforms, especially political reforms, to curb corruption and expand democratic rights.

—JIM YARDLEY

Israeli-Palestinian Peace Talks Bedeviled

Intense diplomatic efforts toward Israeli-Palestinian peace seemed mocked by events on the ground, especially the growing divide between the two halves of the Palestinian political structure, the troubles of Israeli Prime Minister Ehud Olmert and the weakness of the Bush administration, whose waning international esteem made it harder for it to have its way.

There had been street fighting in June 2007 in Gaza between the more secular pro-Western Fatah of Palestinian President Mahmoud Abbas and the Islamist group Hamas. Hamas, which had won parliamentary elections earlier, triumphed. Since Israel, the United States and Europe considered Hamas a terrorist group, they united in an effort to drive it from power through isolation. They closed the borders to Gaza and severely restricted movement of goods and people in and out.

Gaza became a Hamas stronghold supported by Iran, while the West Bank was run by Fatah and backed by the West. Under American patronage, the Israeli government intensified its negotiations with Mr. Abbas in an attempt to reach a peace framework accord before the end of the Bush administration in January 2009. A major Middle East peace conference was held in November in Annapolis, Md. to reinforce this idea and frequent meetings began between Mr. Olmert's aides and Mr. Abbas's.

Meanwhile, Hamas and Fatah did not end their battles. In Gaza, Fatah men were arrested; in the West Bank, Hamas organizations were shut and officials were jailed. Israeli forces continued their pressure on Hamas both in the West Bank and Gaza, killing scores of its militants in frequent raids as well as civilians caught in the crossfire. Hamas, for its part, sponsored the shooting of hundreds of rockets into Israel's southern communities, especially the town of Sderot. Some people were injured and a few were killed. All were terrified.

These developments bedeviled the talks between Israel and the Palestinians of the West Bank but so did other developments. Israel continued to thicken settlements on occupied land despite promising not to do so in the "road map" that was the basis for the Annapolis meeting. And its security measures, consisting of checkpoints, barriers, separate roads for Israeli settlers and a separation barrier, created a sense of caged rage among West Bank Palestinians. For its part, the Palestinian Authority did little to meet its obligation of dismantling violent groups and bringing order to the streets. Each side declared the other to be uninterested in peace.

In Gaza, life behind closed borders with little fuel, closed factories and few consumer goods created a kind of pressure cooker. Hamas tightened its control. Its fighters blew up the metal border fence separating Gaza from Egypt in January and tens of thousands of Palestinians poured into Egypt, stocking up on goods before returning home and thanking Hamas.

Anti-Israel violence, which had declined in the past few years, reappeared in 2008, notably in Jerusalem, carried out by Palestinians with Israeli-issued identity cards permitting them to move freely through the city. In March, a gunman entered a yeshiva, or religious academy, and shot dead eight students, mostly teenagers. Later in the year, on two separate occasions, Jerusalem Palestinians who worked in construction commandeered backhoes, wreaking havoc on city streets. Several people were killed.

Prime Minister Olmert started secret indirect talks with Syria—the first in eight years—over a deal that would give the Golan Heights back to Syria in exchange for peace. He was hoping the Syrians would end their support for Hezbollah in Lebanon and their close alliance with Iran. The Syrians seemed happy to exchange peace for the Golan—and improved relations with Washington —but rejected the other demands. Negotiations continued.

Mr. Olmert found himself engulfed in a set of personal and political scandals that dated from his years as Jerusalem mayor and a government minister. He was investigated for allegedly having taken some $150,000 in cash from an American businessman and for double or triple billing Israeli state organizations for his flights abroad. There were also accusations about a sweetheart deal for a house in Jerusalem.

These troubles came on top of his low poll ratings from his handling of the 2006 Lebanon war, when the Hezbollah militia stood down the vaunted Israeli military in a war many Israelis considered unnecessary and poorly planned, fueling radical sentiments across the Arab world. In July, Mr. Olmert, leader of the centrist Kadima party, announced that there would be a contest for a new leader and that he would step down as prime minister as soon as the winner formed a government. On Sept. 17 the Israeli foreign minister, Tzipi Livni, narrowly won election within Kadima to replace Mr. Olmert, but she was expected to face formidable obstacles in preserving the governing coalition.

—ETHAN BRONNER

Russia's Conflict With Georgia Spurs Rift With West

After years of tension between Russia and its neighbor, the former Soviet republic of Georgia, fighting erupted on Aug. 8, 2008, between the two countries over a separatist enclave that wanted to secede from Georgia.

The conflict lasted less than a week, but it caused the most severe rift between Moscow and the West since the cold war.

The Russians supported the separatist enclave, South Ossetia, while the Georgians had been a close ally of the West since President Mikheil Saakashvili took power in 2004 after the so-called Rose Revolution.

Georgia is a small country with only 4.5 million people, but it is in the Caucasus mountain region at the intersection of Europe and Asia, a strategically vital trade route.

Underlying the conflict was Georgia's desire to join NATO, which Russia fiercely opposed because it said the West was encroaching on Russia's —traditional sphere of influence.

South Ossetia and another enclave, Abkhazia, had broken away from Georgia after the fall of the Soviet Union in 1991. Over the years, Georgia had accused Russia of stirring separatist tensions in order to destabilize Georgia. Russia had responded that the Georgian government mistreated residents of South Ossetia and Abkhazia.

The conflict erupted after a week during which Georgian and South Ossetian forces exchanged sporadic small arms and artillery fire across their border. Then Georgia launched a heavy assault on Tskhinvali, South Ossetia's capital, seeking to reclaim the territory.

Georgia said it moved only because it feared that Russia was beginning its own invasion. Russia denied any such plans, saying that Georgia clearly started the fighting.

Georgian troops entered the disputed enclave, but were repelled by a far larger Russian force that crossed the Russian border to the north.

Routing the Georgians, Russian forces drove well into Georgia, occupying significant swaths of the country. After five days, a ceasefire was brokered by the French president, Nicolas Sarkozy, but Russian troops did not retreat from Georgia for several weeks.

Russia justified its invasion by saying that it had to restore security in the region and protect its citizens. (The Russian government had given Russian passports to many residents of South Ossetia and Abkhazia.)

Still, the invasion drew fierce criticism from Washington and the West. President Bush and European leaders said Russia's newly assertive attitude toward its neighbors was threatening its ties to the West and its revived economy. NATO suspended some cooperation with Russia, though it did not sever relations completely.

Russian leaders, including Prime Minister Vladimir V. Putin, the country's paramount leader, charged that the West had sided with Mr. Saakashvili even though he had provoked the conflict and was unstable.

In the days after the fighting, both sides accused the other of carrying out wartime atrocities and ethnic cleansing.

On Aug. 26, 2008, Russia's president, Dmitri A. Medvedev, formally recognized South Ossetia and Abkhazia as independent nations, intensifying strains with the West.

Georgia's allies, including the United States, declared that Russia was violating international law and that Georgia's territorial integrity had to be respected. No other major country followed Russia's lead and recognized the enclaves.

—CLIFFORD J. LEVY

A New Leader, But Little Calm, In Pakistan

Pakistan plunged into political turmoil and uncertainty when President Pervez Musharraf imposed a state of emergency on Nov. 3, 2007 and suspended the constitution. Fearing that the Supreme Court would not validate his candidacy for a second term, Mr. Musharraf fired the entire court as well as the judges in the high courts. Chief Justice Iftikhar Muhammad Chaudhry was put under house-arrest.

These actions set off a wave of protests across the country as pro-democracy lawyers and civil rights activists joined with opposition political parties. On Nov. 25, former Prime Minister Nawaz Sharif, whose government was toppled by President Musharraf in a bloodless coup in 1999, returned from exile to the cheers of thousands of his supporters in the eastern city of Lahore. Mr. Sharif, a vocal opponent of Musharraf, gave a new impetus to the opposition movement as the president's grip on power became increasingly tenuous.

Under immense pressure—both domestic and international—Mr. Musharraf finally decided to resign as the army chief, the sole source of his immense power. He handed over command to General Ashfaq Pervaiz Kayani, who was heading the country's powerful spy agency, the Inter-Services Intelligence (ISI). At a ceremony held in late November 2007 in Rawalpindi, the garrison city headquarters to the Pakistan military, a visibly emotional Musharraf assumed the role of a civilian president. Many in Pakistan saw it as the beginning of the end of the former general, considered an important ally of the United States in the war against terror.

On Dec. 15, 2007, the state of emergency was lifted. Twelve days later, as the country geared for the general elections, former prime minister and opposition leader Benazir Bhutto was assassinated in a bomb and gun attack in Rawalpindi after she had addressed a political rally. Her death, which the government blamed on the Taliban and Al Qaeda, ignited countrywide protests.

The opposition parties, riding a wave of sympathy and anti-American sentiment, on Feb. 1 dealt a crushing blow to President Musharraf and his ally political party, Pakistan Muslim League, in the general elections. The opposition victory was seen as a rejection of President Musharraf's policies, and he was increasingly castigated as an American stooge.

The parliament elected Yousaf Raza Gilani, a relatively unknown politician belonging to Pakistan Peoples' Party, as the country's new prime minister on March 24. Mr. Sharif's political party, Pakistan Muslim League-Nawaz, joined the cabinet on the condition that the judges deposed by President Musharraf be restored. In early August the ruling coalition announced its plan to impeach President Musharraf and urged him to step down. He announced his resignation on Aug. 18, finally bringing an end to almost a decade of his increasingly unpopular rule.

Asif Ali Zardari, the widower of Benazir Bhutto, who had become the co-chairman of Pakistan Peoples' Party after his wife's assassination, announced his plans to run for the presidency. But the fissures within the ruling coalition widened as Mr. Sharif pulled out of the ruling alliance, accusing Mr. Zardari of reneging on his promise to restore the judges fired by former President Musharraf.

Mr. Zardari, whose past is tainted with allegations of corruption , won the presidential election on Sept. 6 by a thumping majority. He faces daunting challenges: a crippling economy, insurgency by Taliban in the North-West Frontier Province and a divided polity. He was quickly confronted by his first crisis. On Sept. 20 a powerful truck bomb exploded at the Marriott Hotel in Islamabad, killing 53 people and injuring 266.

Relations with the United States also came under strain in September after it was acknowledged for the first time that American ground forces conducted an operation in Pakistan. The U.S. expressed increasing frustration that the militants use the border areas as a refuge to stage attacks against American and NATO soldiers in southern Afghanistan. However, a ground incursion by U.S forces on Sept. 3 was vociferously protested by Pakistani leadership. Adm. Michael Mullen, the chairman of Joint Chiefs of Staff, made a hastily arranged visit to Pakistan in mid-September to defuse the tensions and held meetings with the Pakistani Prime Minister Syed Yousaf Raza Gilani and army chief General Kayani.

—SALMAN MASOOD

Taliban Emboldened In Afghanistan

The Taliban insurgency in Afghanistan showed a growing momentum in 2008, with increasing attacks on foreign and Afghan government forces in more complex operations. They included storming the five-star Serena hotel in Kabul in January, an assassination attempt on President Hamid Karzai at a national parade in April, a jailbreak in the southern town of Kandahar in June that freed hundreds of Taliban and an assault on an American military base in Khost by a wave of 15 suicide bombers in August.

Suicide bomb attacks declined in number but increased in scope, demonstrated by a car bomb blast at the Indian Embassy in Kabul, which killed some 60 people including two Indian diplomats, in July. Insurgents also used truck bombs against military targets in eastern Afghanistan and a bomber on foot at a dog fight in southern Afghanistan who killed up to 100 people, including a large number of local policemen.

American military casualties in Afghanistan since 2001 passed the 500 mark in July, and in June and July the war there accounted for the first time for more casualties than the war in Iraq. June was the second deadliest month for the military in Afghanistan since the war began, with 23 American deaths from hostilities, compared with 22 in Iraq. July was less deadly, with 20 deaths, compared with 6 in Iraq.

The American commander of the NATO-led International Security Assistance Force, Gen. David D. McKiernan, who took over command in June, attributed much of the increased insurgent activity to the lawlessness and freedom of movement militants enjoy in Pakistan's tribal areas bordering Afghanistan since the government of Pakistan began negotiating peace deals with the militants in February. President Bush ordered an additional Marine Corps battalion and an Army brigade to arrive in Afghanistan in early 2009. But in mid-September General McKiernan, calling the military mission short-handed, said that at least three more combat brigades were needed. The total additional troops could exceed 15,000.

In southern Afghanistan, where poppy cultivation remained at record levels even as it declined elsewhere in the country, United Nations officials linked the insurgency to the lucrative drug business. Other militants and criminal groups have joined the insurgency, exploiting the general lawlessness and weak government, in particular followers of the renegade mujahedeen commander Gulbuddin Hekmatyar, who are active in the provinces around the capital Kabul and in the northeast.

Amid the worsening security, Mr. Karzai's popularity was seen to be waning both at home and abroad as he began to look ahead to re-election in 2009. Afghans complained of the worsening security and economic hardship amid growing unemployment and rising food prices. Western governments became increasingly concerned that Mr. Karzai was not up to the job as the government appeared increasingly weak in the face of the Taliban onslaught and failed to move against corrupt officials, druglords and ineffective ministers.

—CARLOTTA GALL

Atomic Monitor Signals Concern Over Iran's Work

The International Atomic Energy Agency, in an unusually blunt and detailed report, said on May 27 that Iran's suspected research into the development of nuclear weapons remained "a matter of serious concern" and that Iran continued to owe the agency "substantial explanations."

The nine-page report accused the Iranians of a willful lack of cooperation, particularly in answering allegations that its nuclear program may be intended more for military use than for energy generation.

Part of the agency's case hinges on 18 documents listed in the report and presented to Iran that, according to Western intelligence agencies, indicate the Iranians have ventured into explosives, uranium processing and a missile warhead design—activities that could be associated with constructing nuclear weapons.

"There are certain parts of their nuclear program where the military seems to have played a role," said one senior official close to the agency, who spoke on the condition of anonymity under normal diplomatic constraints. He added, "We want to understand why."

The atomic energy agency's report highlights the amount of work still to be done before definitive conclusions can be made about the nature of the program, a task that the official associated with the agency said would require months.

Iran's nuclear program has long been a flashpoint, with critics fearing that suggestions that Iran is developing weapons could embolden factions within the Bush administration who have been pushing for a confrontation with Iran.

Iran has dismissed the documents as "forged" or "fabricated," claimed that its experiments and projects had nothing to do with a nuclear weapons program and refused to provide documentation and access to its scientists to support its claims.

The report also makes the allegation that Iran is learning to make more powerful centrifuges that are operating faster and more efficiently, the product of robust research and development that have not been fully disclosed to the agency.

That means that the country may be producing enriched uranium—which can be used to make electricity or to produce bombs—faster than expected at the same time as it replaces its older generation of less reliable centrifuges. Some of the centrifuge components have been produced by Iran's military, said the report, prepared by Mohamed ElBaradei, the director general of the agency, which is the United Nations nuclear monitor.

The report makes no effort to disguise the agency's frustration with Iran's lack of openness. It describes, for example, Iran's installation of new centrifuges, known as the IR-2 and IR-3 (for Iranian second and third generations) and other modifications at its site at Natanz, as "significant, and as such should have been communicated to the agency."

The agency also said that during a visit in April, it was denied access to sites where centrifuge components were being manufactured and where research of uranium enrichment was being conducted.

—ELAINE SCIOLINO

U.S. Declares N. Korea Off Terror List

The Bush administration announced on Oct. 11 that it had removed North Korea from a list of state sponsors of terrorism in a bid to salvage a fragile nuclear deal that seemed on the verge of collapse.

Sean McCormack, the State Department spokesman, said that the United States made the decision after North Korea agreed to resume disabling a plutonium plant and to allow some inspections to verify that it had halted its nuclear program as promised months earlier.

The deal, which the Bush administration had portrayed as a major foreign policy achievement, had begun to slip away in a dispute over the verification program. Just days before the announcement, North Korea barred international inspectors from the plant.

The decision to remove North Korea from the terror list was a dramatic moment for President Bush, who had called the country part of an "axis of evil" and had only reluctantly ordered administration officials to engage in negotiations, saying that the United States had made deals with the nation's leaders before without winning enough concessions. That calculus changed in 2006, when North Korea exploded a nuclear device.

Republican lawmakers, including the presidential nominee, Senator John McCain, expressed concern about the new agreement, complaining that North Korea had yet to demonstrate that it was serious about adhering to its commitment to denuclearize.

Democrats said they welcomed the agreement but noted that it did not go much beyond an agreement President Clinton reached with North Korea in 1994, which the Bush administration, including Secretary of State Condoleezza Rice, criticized as inadequate.

Bush administration officials, trying to head off potential criticism that they were simply seeking a foreign policy victory in their last months, said the agreement was the best the United States could get at this time.

In the most significant part of the accord, North Korea agreed to a verification plan that would allow United States inspectors access to its main declared nuclear compound, at Yongbyon; international inspectors have worked at the site on and off for years. But the deal puts off decisions on the thorniest verification issue: what would happen if international experts suspected the North was hiding other nuclear weapons facilities, particularly those related to uranium enrichment.

The United States wanted the North to agree to inspections at sites that raised suspicions, but North Korea balked. The new agreement calls for United States inspectors to be granted access to such sites "based on mutual consent" with North Korea.

Patricia A. McNerney, one of the State Department negotiators, acknowledged that issue would probably lead to a hornets' nest of problems. "Going into verification with North Korea will not be easy, we know that," she said. "This is the most secret and opaque regime in the world."

There has also been uncertainty over the health of North Korea's leader, Kim Jong-il, who administration officials said had a stroke in August that debilitated him physically and possibly mentally. The Korean Central News Agency reported that Mr. Kim, 66, inspected a military unit on Oct. 11, and state television carried still photographs of him chatting with soldiers.

—HELENE COOPER and CHOE SANG-HUN

Zimbabwe Rivals Sign Power-Sharing Agreement

After more than 28 years of unbroken power, President Robert Mugabe of Zimbabwe signed an agreement with the opposition leader Morgan Tsvangirai on Sept. 15 to divide the responsibilities for running the troubled country.

While many of the pieces of the long-awaited deal remained either unresolved or unannounced, Mr. Tsvangirai said the agreement "sees the return of hope to all our lives."

Despite questions about how the agreement would be implemented after so much acrimony and hostility between the two men, Mr. Mugabe said: "We are committed to the deal. We will do our best."

Opposition supporters at the ceremony at a hotel in the capital of Harare celebrated the signing and were jubilant when Mr. Tsvangirai appeared, hooting and applauding. Among the audience were many opposition workers who had gone into hiding in the run-up to the election in March or been beaten in government-sponsored violence over the last eight years.

Godknows Nyamweda, 36, a local ward councilor here in Harare, rolled up his sleeve to show the scars where he said he had been sliced by a knife.

"I came to make sure my big fishes have not betrayed me and to make sure I'm walking in a free country," he said.

There was still an undercurrent of fear that that the repression could yet return with a vengeance, and some people were afraid to be quoted by name.

The crowd also repeatedly cheered the presence of Botswana's president, Seretse Khama Ian Khama, clapping and chanting, "Khama, Khama, Khama." He had been Mr. Mugabe's harshest critic in the region, refusing to recognize the legitimacy of his election.

Western diplomats were studying the text of the deal to see how power will actually be divided. Western nations are wary of pouring billions of dollars into Zimbabwe for its reconstruction unless they are convinced that Mr. Tsvangirai has the authority he needs to change economic policies they believe have been calamitous for the country.

The arrangement was reached after weeks of negotiations that opened in July. The negotiations followed a season of contentious elections, scarred by bloodletting and intimidation, which the opposition blamed on the government. Mr. Tsvangirai claimed victory in the first round of elections in March. But he boycotted a presidential runoff in June, citing political violence, leaving Mr. Mugabe as the sole candidate.

Despite the violence and bad feelings between the two sides, the sight of Mr. Mugabe, Mr. Tsvangirai and a second opposition leader, Arthur Mutambara, clasping hands beside Thabo Mbeki, the South African president who mediated the deal, prompted some participants to suggest that Zimbabwe's fortunes might have changed after years of autocracy and economic chaos.

—CELIA W. DUGGER and ALAN COWELL

Violence Rocks Kenya After Disputed Election

Kenya exploded into violence after a disputed election on Dec. 27, 2007, plunging one of the most stable, Western-friendly countries in Africa into its deepest turmoil since gaining independence 45 years ago.

More than 1,000 people were killed, an estimated one million displaced and the country's economy, especially its once-thriving tourism industry, was brought to its knees.

The trouble started when allegations surfaced that President Mwai Kibaki had interfered in the vote-tallying process to give himself a narrow, eleventh-hour margin of victory over Raila Odinga, the top opposition leader.

Mr. Odinga's supporters poured into the streets, initially venting their outrage at police officers and government property. But the violence soon took an ethnic tinge, driven by a host of political, economic and long-simmering grievances. Mr. Kibaki is a Kikuyu, the ethnic group that has dominated Kenya since independence in 1963. Mr. Odinga is a Luo, another large ethnic group but one that has long felt marginalized.

Rival ethnic gangs slaughtered each other in the slums ringing Nairobi, the capital. The weapons of choice were clubs, rocks, machetes and fire. For days, coils of black smoke billowed over the iron-roofed shanties.

But the most vicious fighting in the country was in the Rift Valley, the cradle of mankind and home to Kenya's famed wildlife-driven tourist trade. On Jan. 1, a mob of Kalenjins, another historically marginalized ethnic group, burned to death more than a dozen Kikuyus seeking shelter in a church. Many Kalenjins supported Mr. Odinga, and in their fury over the flawed election, Kalenjin gangs drove hundreds of thousands of Kikuyus off their land.

Kikuyus soon took their revenge, massacring Luos and Kalenjins in other Rift Valley towns and sparking a mass exodus of those ethnic groups. Kenya began to violently segregate itself, with people fleeing ethnically-mixed areas for the safety of their ancestral lands. Some violence was spontaneous but much of it was orchestrated by community leaders and even top politicians.

Western diplomats and African officials tried to broker a truce. On Feb. 28, Kofi Annan, former United Nations secretary general, hammered out a deal, in which Mr. Kibaki would remain president but Mr. Odinga would become prime minister.

Most violence subsided after that. But Kenya remained poisonously divided. Many displaced people refused to go home. The country's politicians continued to bicker over who really won the election. And the economy continued to suffer, with tourism projected to be down by 30 percent for the year.

—JEFFREY GETTLEMAN

Mbeki Forced To Quit In South Africa

President Thabo Mbeki of South Africa, the loser in a prolonged power struggle with his rival, Jacob Zuma, agreed on Sept. 20 to resign after the top leaders of his party, the African National Congress, asked him to step down.

The party's decision was a harsh rebuke to Mr. Mbeki, the aloof and scholarly man who succeeded Nelson Mandela, leading the nation to an unprecedented run of economic growth and yet unable to restrain an ever-widening gap between the rich and poor.

Mr. Mbeki had first served the party as an acolyte in the nation's freedom struggle and later for two decades as one of its guiding lights. The power - though not yet the presidency - shifted to Mr. Zuma, an economic populist who promised to loosen the manacles of poverty from the millions still living in shanties.

Kgalema Motlanthe, an A.N.C. party stalwart was appointed acting president several days later. Mr. Zuma was not eligible to be that replacement because he was not yet a member of Parliament. But the A.N.C. enjoys a huge majority in that body, and he is expected to run in parliamentary elections next year and to take over as president after that. The elections are likely to occur some time between February and June.

The events brought to a close a nine-year presidency during which Mr. Mbeki accrued both celebration and disrepute. He became internationally notorious for his views about AIDS, joining maverick scientists in questioning whether a virus was the cause of the illness. He led the resistance to antiretroviral treatment, acting as if the AIDS epidemic were a defamatory plot against Africans and a con job by avaricious pharmaceutical companies. This intransigence, critics say, sent countless thousands to needless deaths.

The resignation was the culmination of seven years of discontent between South Africa's most powerful politicians: Mr. Mbeki and Mr. Zuma, the man he fired in 2005 as his deputy. In December 2007, Mr. Zuma defeated his former boss for the party's leadership in a vote that showed the party deeply split. With that victory, and with the African National Congress dominant in national elections, Mr. Zuma was in line to become president in 2009 when Mr. Mbeki's second term in office expired. But many of Mr. Zuma's supporters, openly despising the president, wanted him gone sooner.

—BARRY BEARAK

Arrest Sought Of Sudan Leader

The prosecutor at the International Criminal Court formally requested an arrest warrant on July 14 for Sudan's president, Omar Hassan al-Bashir, on charges of genocide, war crimes and crimes against humanity committed during the past five years of bloodshed in the Darfur region of his country.

The prosecutor's pursuit of Mr. Bashir introduced new volatility to the already chaotic situation in Darfur. While some diplomats and analysts worried that the move would undermine efforts to negotiate peace and provide aid to the millions displaced by violence, others said it offered new leverage to pressure the Sudanese government to end the conflict in Darfur.

It was the first time the prosecutor of the International Criminal Court had brought genocide charges against anyone. It was also the first time the prosecutor had brought charges against a sitting head of state since the court opened its doors in 2002. Two other presidents, Slobodan Milosevic of Serbia and Charles Taylor of Liberia, were charged by other international war crimes courts, also while they were in office.

Darfur has been a shifting, many-sided conflict, with rebels fighting rebels, government-backed Arab militias killing civilians and one another, freelance bandits attacking aid workers and atrocities committed by all the armed groups.

In announcing the request, the prosecutor, Luis Moreno-Ocampo, said Mr. Bashir had "masterminded and implemented" a plan to destroy three main ethnic groups in Darfur: the Fur, the Masalit and the Zaghawa. Using government soldiers and Arab militias known as janjaweed, the president "purposefully targeted civilians" belonging to these groups, killing 35,000 people "outright" in attacks on towns and villages, he said. In February, thousands fleeing from the attacks in Darfur flooded into neighboring Chad, joining the 240,000 Sudanese refugees already there.

Genocide charges are the gravest any court can bring, and the prosecutor is expected to implicate others at the top of the Sudanese government. But the request for a warrant against Mr. Bashir seemed unlikely to lead to his arrest soon. Mr. Bashir has scoffed at two arrest warrants the court has already issued against two other Sudanese figures, even promoting one of them to minister of humanitarian affairs.

"We will resist this," said Rabie A. Atti, a Sudanese government spokesman. "Everybody in Sudan—the government, the people, even the opposition parties—is against this."

—MARLISE SIMONS, LYDIA POLGREEN and
JEFFREY GETTLEMAN

Somalia Faces Famine Crisis

Somalia—and much of the volatile Horn of Africa—was about the last place on earth that needed a food crisis. Even before commodity prices started shooting up around the globe, civil war, displacement and imperiled aid operations had pushed many people here to the brink of famine.

But with food costs spiraling out of reach and the livestock people live off of dropping dead in the sand, villagers across this sun-blasted landscape say hundreds of people are dying of hunger and thirst.

This is what happens, economists say, when the global food crisis meets local chaos.

United Nations officials have declared Somalia the worst humanitarian disaster in the world. By September, three million people were dependent on emergency food aid, 1.5 million displaced, and aid workers were being hunted down and killed.

There's been a collision of troubles throughout the region: skimpy rainfall; disastrous harvests; soaring food prices; dying livestock; escalating violence; out-of-control inflation; and shrinking food aid because of many of these factors. Jeffrey Sachs, a Columbia economist and top United Nations adviser, described the situation as a "perfect storm."

Somalia has been mired in chaos since the central government collapsed in 1991. But the violence intensified in 2008 with an Islamic insurgency waging relentless attacks against a weak transitional government which is backed up by Ethiopian troops.

"We're getting addicted to anarchy," said Dahabo Abdulleh, a fuel seller in Mogadishu.

The United Nations and donor countries have plowed millions of dollars into the Transitional Federal Government, an entity essentially created by the United Nations, with the idea of bringing order to Somalia from the top down. But many Somali intellectuals and Western academics were pushing an alternative form of government: going local.

"It's the only way viable," said Ali Doy, a Somali analyst who works closely with the United Nations. "Local government is where the actual governance is. It's more realistic, it's more sustainable and it's more secure."

—JEFFREY GETTLEMAN

Kosovo Declares Independence

The province of Kosovo declared independence from Serbia on Feb. 17, sending tens of thousands of ethnic Albanians streaming through the streets of the capital, Pristina, to celebrate what they hoped was the end of a long and bloody struggle for national self-determination.

Kosovo's bid to be recognized as Europe's newest country—after a civil war that killed 10,000 people a decade ago and then years of limbo under United Nations rule—was the latest episode in the dismemberment of the former Yugoslavia, 17 years after its dissolution began.

It brought to a climax a showdown between the West, which argued that Serbia's brutal subjugation of Kosovo's ethnic Albanian majority cost it any right to rule the territory, and the Serbian government and its allies in the Kremlin. They countered that Kosovo's independence is a reckless breach of international law that will spur other secessionist movements across the world.

The United States, Britain, France and Germany were the first to recognize the new nation, while other countries, fearing separatist movements within their own borders, said they would refuse. Russia demanded an emergency meeting of the United Nations Security Council to proclaim the declaration "null and void," but the meeting produced no resolution.

In declaring independence, Kosovo's prime minister, Hashim Thaci, a former leader of the guerrilla force that just over 10 years ago began an armed rebellion against Serbian domination, struck a note of reconciliation. Addressing Parliament in both Albanian and Serbian, he pledged to protect the rights of Kosovo's Serbian minority.

Kosovo, a desperately poor, predominantly Muslim landlocked territory of two million, had been a United Nations protectorate since 1999, policed by 16,000 NATO troops. Its unemployment rate is about 60 percent and average monthly wage is $250.

Electricity is so undependable that lights go out in the capital several times a day. Corruption is rife and human trafficking threatens to entrench a lawless state on Europe's doorstep.

Ethnic Albanians from as far away as the United States poured into Pristina over the weekend, braving freezing temperatures and heavy snow to dance in frenzied jubilation.

In an outpouring of adulation for the United States, the architect of NATO's 1999 bombing campaign against Serbian forces under President Slobodan Milosevic, revelers unfurled giant American flags, carried posters of former President Bill Clinton and chanted, "Thank you, U.S.A." and "God bless America."

That spirit of exaltation contrasted sharply with the despair, anger and disbelief that gripped Serbia and the Serbian enclaves of northern Kosovo. In Belgrade, Serbia's capital, as many as 2,000 angry Serbs converged on the United States Embassy, hurling stones and smashing windows. On Feb. 21 about 100 demonstrators broke into the embassy, which was by then closed for safety reasons, and set part of it on fire.

—DAN BILEFSKY

Karadzic Arrested After Long Hunt

Radovan Karadzic, one of the world's most wanted war criminals for his part in the massacre of nearly 8,000 Muslim men and boys in Srebrenica in 1995, was arrested on July 21 in a raid in Serbia that ended a 13-year hunt.

Serge Brammertz, the prosecutor of the United Nations war crimes tribunal in The Hague, hailed the arrest as an important step in bringing to justice one of the architects of Europe's worst massacre since World War II. Mr. Karadzic, 63, the Bosnian Serb president during the war there between 1992 and 1995, was transferred to The Hague on July 30.

"This is a very important day for the victims who have waited for this arrest for over a decade," Mr. Brammertz said. "It is also an important day for international justice because it clearly demonstrates that nobody is beyond the reach of the law and that sooner or later all fugitives will be brought to justice."

Serbian government officials said Mr. Karadzic was arrested by the Serbian secret police. He was living openly in Belgrade, the capital, disguised as a New Age guru.

Mr. Karadzic, a nationalist hero among Serbian radicals and one of the tribunal's most wanted criminals for more than a decade, was a medical doctor who worked as a psychiatrist in Sarajevo, Bosnia's capital before his political career.

Prosecutors in The Hague and officials of the European Union have long suspected that he was hiding in Serbia, and in recent years have pressed officials in Belgrade to hand him over. The failure to arrest Mr. Karadzic and Ratko Mladic, the still fugitive Bosnian Serb general also indicted on war crimes, has stood as a block to greater Serbian ties to the European Union after the wars in Bosnia and later Kosovo.

Slobodan Milosevic, the former president of Serbia allied with Mr. Karadzic and Mr. Mladic, was arrested in 2001 and put on trial for war crimes in 2002. He died there in 2006 before a verdict was reached.

The arrest of Mr. Karadzic culminated a long and protracted effort by the West to press Serbia to arrest him for the massacres in the southeastern Bosnian town of Srebrenica, in the most heinous crime committed during the Balkan wars.

The arrest was just weeks after a new pro-Western coalition government in Serbia was formed whose overriding goal is to bring Serbia into the European Union, the world's biggest trading bloc. The European Union has made delivering indicted war criminals to The Hague a precondition for Serbia's membership.

—DAN BILEFSKY and MARLISE SIMONS

Richest Nations Pledge To Halve Greenhouse Gas

President Bush and leaders of the world's richest nations pledged on July 8 to "move toward a low-carbon society" by cutting greenhouse gas emissions in half by 2050, the latest step in a long evolution by a president who for years played down the threat of global warming.

The declaration by the Group of 8—the United States, Japan, Germany, Britain, France, Italy, Canada and Russia—was the first time that the Bush White House had publicly backed an explicit long-term target for eliminating the gases that scientists have said are warming the planet. But it failed to set a goal for cutting emissions over the next decade, and drew sharp criticism from environmentalists, who called it a missed opportunity.

On July 9, leaders of developing nations took up the climate change issue and said that they too supported "a long-term global goal for emission reductions," but they were not specific and fell short of supporting the Group of 8 declaration.

In a sense, the Group of 8 document represents an environmental quid pro quo. In exchange for agreeing to the "50 by 2050" language, Mr. Bush got what he has sought as his price for joining an international accord: a statement from the rest of the Group of 8 that developing nations like China and India, which have not accepted mandatory caps on carbon emissions, must be included in any climate change treaty.

European leaders, who have long pressed Mr. Bush to take a more aggressive stance on global warming, said the declaration could enhance efforts to reach a binding agreement to reduce emissions when negotiators meet in Copenhagen in 2009 under United Nations auspices.

"This is a strong signal to citizens around the world," the president of the European Commission, José Manuel Barroso, told reporters. "The science is clear, the economic case for action is stronger than ever. Now we need to go the extra mile to secure an ambitious global deal in Copenhagen."

The leaders of the eight industrialized countries, who gathered on the northern Japanese island of Hokkaido for their annual meeting, spent months debating the language of the communiqué in lower-level talks. Critics said it was short on specifics, and that developed and developing countries would need to make much sharper cuts in emissions to head off the worst effects of global warming.

The statement left unclear, for instance, if the cuts made by 2050 would be pegged to current emissions levels, or 1990 levels, as many advocates had hoped.

A 50 percent cut from current levels would result in a smaller decrease by 2050 than Japan and European nations had envisioned under the Kyoto Protocol, the international climate agreement that the Bush administration rejected after it took office. Kyoto and earlier agreements had set 1990 as the baseline for cuts. The United States emitted about 20 percent more carbon dioxide in 2007 than it did in 1990.

—SHERYL GAY STOLBERG

Gore Shares Nobel For Climate Work

Former Vice President Al Gore was awarded the 2007 Nobel Peace Prize on Oct. 12, 2007, sharing it with the Intergovernmental Panel on Climate Change, a United Nations network of scientists.

The Norwegian Nobel Committee praised both "for their efforts to build up and disseminate greater knowledge about man-made climate change."

The prize was a vindication for Mr. Gore, whose cautionary film about the consequences of climate change, "An Inconvenient Truth," won the 2007 Academy Award for best documentary, even as conservatives in the United States denounced it as alarmist and exaggerated.

The award was also a validation for the United Nations panel, which in its early days was vilified by those who disputed the scientific case for a human role in climate change. In New Delhi, the Indian climatologist who heads the panel, Rajendra K. Pachauri, said that science had won out over skepticism.

In Oslo, Ole Danbolt Mjoes, chairman of the peace committee, was asked whether the award could be seen as criticism of the Bush administration, which did not subscribe to the Kyoto treaty to cap greenhouse gases. He replied that the Nobel was not meant to be a "kick in the leg to anyone"— the Norwegian expression for "kick in the teeth."

In its formal citation, the Nobel committee called Mr. Gore "probably the single individual who has done most to create greater worldwide understanding of the measures that need to be adopted."

—WALTER GIBBS and SARAH LYALL

N. Korea's Leader Said To Be Seriously Ill

Kim Jong-il, North Korea's leader, is seriously ill and is likely to have suffered a stroke in late August, American officials said Sept. 9, raising the prospect of a chaotic power struggle in nuclear-armed North Korea.

Intelligence officials in Washington said that the exact status of Mr. Kim's health was unclear, but that he failed to attend a celebration of the 60th anniversary of the founding of North Korea and that American intelligence agencies believed that he was under the care of doctors in Pyongyang, North Korea's capital.

On Sept. 10, Song Il-ho, a senior North Korean diplomat, denied news reports suggesting Mr. Kim was ill. "We see such reports as not only worthless, but rather as a conspiracy plot," the Kyodo news agency quoted Mr. Song as saying.

Later, the country's No. 2 leader, Kim Yong-nam, said there was "no problem" with Kim Jong-il, Kyodo reported.

Kim Jong-il's health is a topic of intense interest among governments and security experts, especially because Western officials are unclear about who would succeed the man known as the "Dear Leader."

North Korea is one of the world's most isolated and unpredictable states, and a messy transfer of power would focus new attention on the security of its nuclear weapons arsenal.

Mr. Kim had not missed the 10 past military parades staged for major anniversaries, during which columns of armored vehicles and rocket launchers rumbled through Pyongyang's main plaza and legions of goose-stepping soldiers saluted him.

But on Sept. 9, there was only a parade by militia groups in charge of civil defense, and Mr. Kim did not attend.

An American intelligence official, who, like others interviewed for this article, spoke on condition of anonymity because assessments about Mr. Kim's health are classified, said that it did not appear that Mr. Kim's death was imminent. The official said there were no clear indications the North was stepping up preparations for a ransfer of authority. The official would not say whether American intelligence agencies expected Mr. Kim, who is believed to be in his mid-60s, to fully recover.

Earlier in the year, North Korea had agreed to abandon its nuclear weapons programs in return for economic and political rewards from the United States and its allies, a major diplomatic victory for the Bush administration.

But in late August the North Korean government reversed course. Angry that Washington had not removed it from a terrorism list, it said it had stopped disabling its main nuclear complex.

It was unclear whether Mr. Kim ordered the reversal or whether other North Korean officials were making decisions while he was incapacitated.

—MARK MAZZETTI and CHOE SANG-HUN

Putin's Choice Wins Presidency

His election choreographed by the Kremlin, Dmitri A. Medvedev secured a predictably commanding victory on March 2 to become Russia's president.

Though the results were never in doubt, Mr. Medvedev's future role very much is, given that the man who anointed him, President Vladimir V. Putin, intends to remain in the government.

Mr. Medvedev, an unassuming aide to Mr. Putin who has never before held elected office, portrayed himself during a relatively listless campaign as something of a reformer, vowing to crack down on endemic corruption and promote the rule of law.

He also seemed to take a less strident stance toward the West than Mr. Putin. Mr. Medvedev's success at adopting this platform early in his tenure will represent an important indicator of whether Mr. Putin will allow him to be more than a figurehead.

Mr. Putin has pledged to serve as Mr. Medvedev's prime minister, and he has already indicated that he will broaden the responsibilities of that position, which since the Soviet Union's fall has typically been administrative.

The election of Mr. Medvedev, 42, a first deputy prime minister, was the culmination of Mr. Putin's efforts to consolidate control over the government, business and the news media since taking office eight years ago. Vowing to restore stability to Russia after the upheavals of the 1990s, Mr. Putin increasingly used his authority and popularity to create what is in many respects a one-party state. Mr. Putin, who could not run for a third consecutive term under the Constitution, left office with Russia far stronger economically but with far less political pluralism.

—CLIFFORD J. LEVY

Italians Again Turn To Berlusconi

Silvio Berlusconi, the idiosyncratic billionaire who already dominates much of Italy's public life, snatched back political power in elections that ended April 14, heading a center-right coalition that made him prime minister for a third term.

But with a weak economy and frustration high that Italy has lost ground to the rest of Europe, it was unclear whether Italians voted for Mr. Berlusconi out of affection or, as many experts said, as the least bad choice after the nation weathered two years of inaction from the fractured center-left.

Still, Italy now returns to a singular sort of personal politics with Mr. Berlusconi as the unquestioned protagonist.

Mr. Berlusconi, 71, Italy's third-richest man and owner of media and sports businesses, promised immediate action on many of the problems vexing Italians, like the trash crisis in the south that has tarnished the nation's image and the sale of the near-bankrupt national airline, Alitalia.

—IAN FISHER

After Cyclone, Aid Hampered In Myanmar

On the night of May 2, cyclone Nargis roared up the Irrawaddy Delta in Myanmar to the country's largest city, Yangon, with winds of 120 mph and a storm surge of up to 12 feet. According to the United Nations, 2.4 million people were affected and 138,000 were dead or missing. Of the survivors, 800,000 were homeless. It was the worst cyclone to hit Asia since 1991, when 143,000 people died in Bangladesh.

The economic toll was heavy, with damage officially estimated at $4 billion. The United Nations said 42 percent of Myanmar's food stocks were destroyed. Up to 50 percent of water buffalo in the delta were lost, fishing boats were torn from their moorings and rice fields were contaminated with salt water, making recovery difficult. More than 2,000 schools were reported destroyed and many teachers were swept to their deaths. But although 75 percent of health facilities were damaged or destroyed, no major outbreaks of disease were reported in the first three months after the cyclone.

Suspicious of the outside world, the military junta that has ruled Myanmar since 1988 at first barred large-scale relief deliveries. But at a meeting with United Nations Secretary General Ban Ki-moon on May 23, Senior General Than Shwe agreed to let foreign aid workers enter the country "regardless of nationalities." That was followed by a donors meeting in Yangon, organized by the United Nations and the Association of Southeast Asian Nations, at which nearly $50 million was pledged.

In the following months, hundreds of visas were issued to relief workers. But aid agencies said that their movements were hampered by bureaucratic controls and limits on their travel. Myanmar refused assistance from United States and French warships off the coast, but allowed hundreds of deliveries of aid by the United States Air Force.

For the generals, a long-standing political agenda seemed to overshadow the disaster and the junta proceeded on May 10 with a referendum on a constitution that is part of a "road map to democracy." Critics called it a blueprint for continued military domination of the country. The referendum was postponed by two weeks in areas hit by the cyclone. The government said it was approved by 92 percent of the voters.

—SETH MYDANS

Thai Civilians Rule, But Which Ones?

Political uncertainty continued in Thailand throughout 2008 after it returned to civilian rule at the beginning of the year. The generals who ousted Thaksin Shinawatra as prime minister in a coup in September 2006 handed back power to a civilian government after holding a parliamentary election in December 2007. Mr. Thaksin's allies regained power with a party called the People Power Party, and a former Bangkok governor, Samak Sundaravej, was named prime minister.

Mr. Thaksin returned from his self-imposed exile in February. But corruption cases moved forward against him, and on July 31, his wife, Pojaman, was convicted of tax evasion and sentenced to three years in prison. She was granted bail as she appealed the conviction and the couple traveled to Beijing in August to attend the Olympic games. They chose not to return, fleeing to London, where they sought political asylum.

In May, an opposition group called the People's Alliance for Democracy had begun street demonstrations against the government, which it said was a front for Mr. Thaksin. On Aug. 26, thousands of protesters took over the grounds of Government House, which houses the prime minister's office. The People's Alliance, which represents a conservative royalist establishment, pursued parallel goals: the ouster of the pro-Thaksin government and a modification of the democratic system to insure greater representation of professional groups and other established sectors of society.

On Sept. 9, in a case unrelated to the protest, the Constitutional Court found Mr. Samak guilty of violating constitutional provisions against conflict of interest by accepting pay for appearing on televised cooking shows. Mr. Samak was forced to step down and the People Power Party named a brother-in-law of Thaksin, Deputy Prime Minister Somchai Wongsawat, to replace him as new prime minister. Unable to enter the prime minister's office, the Somchai government established its headquarters at the old international airport, Don Muang. The protests continued, and on Oct. 7, antigovernment demonstrators trapped lawmakers inside the Parliament building and fought running battles with police that left one person dead and 400 injured.

—SETH MYDANS

Tibetan Monks Clash With Police

Violence erupted on March 14 in a busy market area of the Tibetan capital, Lhasa, as Buddhist monks and other ethnic Tibetans brawled with Chinese security forces in bloody clashes. Witnesses said angry Tibetan crowds burned shops, cars, military vehicles and at least one tourist bus. State media said at least 10 people died.

The chaotic scene was the most violent confrontation in a series of protests that began several days earlier and represented a major challenge to the ruling Communist Party as it prepared for the Olympic Games in August. By March 15, Chinese armored vehicles were patrolling the center of the city.

Thousands of Buddhists in neighboring India and Nepal took to the streets on March 14 in solidarity. Concerned that the protests might spread elsewhere in China, the authorities moved the military police into other regions with large Tibetan populations.

The Chinese authorities blamed the Dalai Lama, the exiled spiritual leader of Tibet, for the violence and said the government would maintain stability in Lhasa.

The Dalai Lama released a statement calling on both sides to avoid violence. A spokesman for the Dalai Lama called China's accusations "absolutely baseless."

The conflict touched off international criticism of China and prompted protests that dogged the Olympic torch relay in cities around the world, including Seoul, South Korea, the scene of violent skirmishes in late April.

Chinese authorities said that the unrest in Tibet, which was against the ethnic Han Chinese, left 19 people dead and more than 600 wounded, while the Tibetan government in exile said that scores of Tibetans were killed in the ensuing crackdown. On April 29, a Chinese court in Tibet sentenced 30 people to prison terms ranging from three years to life for what the authorities said were their roles in the deadly rioting.

Ethnic friction has long simmered just below the surface in Lhasa. For more than two decades, a steady influx of Chinese migrants has transformed and stratified the city. The protests coincided with the anniversary of a failed 1959 Tibetan uprising against Chinese rule that forced the Dalai Lama to flee to India. Groups that promote Tibetan independence have marked the anniversary with demonstrations around the world.

—JIM YARDLEY and ANDREW JACOBS

Nepal Elects Maoist Leader

The leader of the decade-long Maoist rebellion in Nepal was elected prime minister on Aug. 15 after four months of political wrangling. His victory sets the stage for the former rebels' toughest challenge: how to uplift the lives of 27 million people in one of the poorest countries in the world at a time of soaring food and fuel prices.

The Maoist leader, Pushpa Kamal Dahal—who goes by the nom de guerre Prachanda, "the fierce one" in Nepali—won more than two-thirds of 577 votes cast in the Constituent Assembly on Friday evening.

His election had been expected since April, when the Maoists won a majority in a special assembly elected both to draft a new constitution and to form a government.

For four months, however, Nepali Congress, the nation's oldest party, which has a long list of grievances against the Maoists, blocked their bid to lead a government of national consensus.

The election of the prime minister opened the way to the establishment of a democratic government in Nepal. That would be a milestone in resolving issues remaining after the decade-long civil war, a conflict that claimed the lives of an estimated 13,000 people before it ended with a peace accord in 2006.

The Maoists have already achieved their main goal, ending 239 years of Hindu monarchy. At its first session, in May, a Constituent Assembly declared Nepal a federal republic. The former king, Gyanendra, the world's last Hindu monarch, was forced to vacate the main palace here and live as a commoner.

—TILAK POKHAREL

Fidel Castro Quits, Brother Takes Over

Fidel Castro, bedridden for 19 months, on Feb. 19 gave up the almost unlimited power he had wielded in Cuba for 49 years. He was officially succeeded later in the month by his brother, Raúl, who had been acting predident.

In a letter of resignation read over radio and television programs across the country, the 81-year-old Mr. Castro—who had appeared frail in the few videos released by the Cuban government—was said to be too ill to continue as head of state and would not stand in the way of others who were ready to take over, a sentiment he first expressed in December 2007.

In trying to assess the future, political analysts pointed to signs that the 76-year-old Raul Castro has shown a pragmatic streak. As acting president, he encouraged more debate about Cuba's problems, sponsoring a series of town-hall-style meetings to allow people to speak freely about their economic woes and limits to their rights to travel.

The younger Mr. Castro also has a reputation as a manager who demands results from his cabinet members. Unlike Fidel, who liked to manage every detail of government himself, Raúl delegated authority and held his cabinet ministers accountable.

After decades during which Fidel Castro's grip seemed unbreakable, uncertainties arose in July 2006. Mr. Castro, suffering from an undisclosed abdominal ailment, had emergency surgery and temporarily handed over power to his brother.

In his resignation letter, Mr. Castro said he did not step down earlier to avoid dealing a blow to the Cuban government before the people were ready for a traumatic change "in the middle of the battle" with the United States over control of the Cuba's future.

President Bush, the 10th president to cross swords with Mr. Castro, has tried to tighten the longstanding United States embargo and increase international pressure on Cuba during his time in office, restricting family visits to once every three years and putting a cap on the amount of remittances Cuban-Americans can send to relatives in Cuba.

—ANTHONY DEPALMA

Venezuelan Voters Set Back Chavez

In a contentious referendum, voters in Venezuela in early December 2007 narrowly defeated a proposed overhaul to the constitution that would have granted President Hugo Chávez sweeping new powers.

It was the first major electoral defeat in the nine years of his presidency. Voters rejected the 69 proposed amendments 51 to 49 percent.

The outcome was a stunning development in a country where Mr. Chávez and his supporters control nearly all of the levers of power. Almost immediately after the results were broadcast on state television, Mr. Chávez conceded defeat, describing the results as a "photo finish."

Opposition leaders were ecstatic.

In the weeks before the vote, members of previously splintered opposition movements joined disillusioned Chávez supporters in an attempt to defeat the referendum, which would have abolished term limits, allowed Mr. Chávez to declare states of emergency for unlimited periods and increase the state's role in the economy, among other measures.

The defeat slowed Mr. Chávez's socialist-inspired transformation of the country. Venezuela, once a staunch ally of the United States, has become a leading opponent of the Bush administration's policies in the developing world. It has also taken the most profound leftward turn of any large Latin American nation in decades.

The referendum followed several weeks of street protests and frenetic campaigning over the amendments to the Constitution proposed by Mr. Chávez and his supporters. It capped a year of bold moves by the president, who forged a single Socialist party among his followers, forced a television network critical of the government off the public airwaves, and nationalized oil, telephone and electricity companies.

Mr. Chávez's populist proposals, including an increase in social security benefits for some workers, have been praised even by his critics. But turnout for the referendum in some poor districts was unexpectedly low, indicating that even the president's backers were willing to follow him only so far.

The United States remains the largest buyer of Venezuela's oil despite deteriorating political ties, but that long commercial relationship is starting to change as Mr. Chávez increases exports of oil to China and other countries while gradually selling off the oil refineries owned by Venezuela's government in the United States.

—SIMON ROMERO

Betancourt, 14 Others Rescued in Colombia

Colombian commandos in disguise spirited 15 hostages to freedom on July 2, including Ingrid Betancourt, a French-Colombian politician held for six years, and three American military contractors.

On Colombian television, Ms. Betancourt wept and smiled as she recounted a chain of events that seemed scripted for film, complete with Colombian agents infiltrating guerrilla camps and borrowing Israeli tracking technology to zero in on their target.

Taken captive in 2002 while she campaigned quixotically for the presidency, Ms. Betancourt, over her years as a hostage, became a symbol of suffering, courage and endurance.

The rescue was a major victory in Colombia's struggle with the FARC, a Marxist-inspired insurgency that has been trying to topple the Colombian government for more than four decades.

Colombia's defense minister, Juan Manuel Santos, said the captives, who also included 11 former members of Colombia's security forces, were removed from the jungle by an elite commando unit after Colombian intelligence operatives infiltrated the FARC's seven-member secretariat.

The three Americans, Marc Gonsalves, Keith Stansell and Thomas Howes, were captured in 2003 while working for the Northrop Grumman Corporation after their surveillance plane went down on an antinarcotics mission for the Pentagon.

Ms. Betancourt and the Americans were among more than 40 captives used by the FARC to bargain for political concessions. The rescue came during a period of fragmentation in the FARC after the killing and capture of several senior commanders in recent months. The guerrillas are thought to hold hundreds of other abductees in jungle camps.

—SIMON ROMERO

Olympics in China Make A Splash

The Beijing Olympics was where one American swimmer, Michael Phelps, passed another, Mark Spitz, to become the most decorated athlete in a single Olympic Games. It was a numerologist's dream, with Phelps winning eight golds—one more than Spitz in 1972—at an Olympics that opened on 08/08/08.

The 23-year-old Phelps won his first individual race, the 400-meter individual medley, by a lot (2.32 seconds) and his last individual race, the

100-meter butterfly, by a little (0.01 of a second) and supplanted Spitz with a little help from his teammates, especially Jason Lezak, whose blistering anchor leg sealed the Americans' victory in the 4x100-meter freestyle relay.

Before Phelps dived in for his first race, the Chinese film director Zhang Yimou created a stunning visual splash with an opening ceremony that included 15,000 performers and culminated with the lighting of the caldron by the gymnast Li Ning, a six-time medalist in 1984 who was lifted by wires to the top of the huge stadium as he held aloft the Olympic torch.

Very much up in the air was the age of the six gymnasts on the Chinese women's team that captured the team gold. Documents surfaced that suggested He Kexin, the bronze medalist in the uneven bars, and Yang Yilin, who won two individual bronzes, might be younger than 16, the minimum age to participate in Olympic gymnastics. The International Olympic Committee investigated the athletes' ages and concluded the women were old enough to compete. American women gymnasts, Nastia Liukin and Shawn Johnson combined for nine medals, including one gold apiece.

The Jamaican sprinter Usain Bolt was pure lightning on the track, winning golds in the 100 and 200 meters and the 4-by-100-meter relay, all in world-record time. His unfettered joy, especially toward the end of his 100-meter victory, stood in contrast to the machine-like efficiency of Phelps and the Beijing Games organizers.

The U.S. women's soccer team was rocked by a pre-Games injury to its leading scorer, Abby Wambach, and an opening match loss to Norway. But the team found its footing and won the gold, defeating Brazil 1-0 in extra time in the final.

Brazil also lost the men's volleyball gold to a U.S. squad that played the Olympics with a heavy heart after the father-in-law of its head coach was killed in a random attack at a tourist attraction on the first day of the Games.

Team sports were a gold mine for the United States. Led by N.B.A. stars Kobe Bryant, LeBron James and Dwyane Wade, the men's basketball squad lived up to its Redeem Team nickname, avenging a bronze-medal showing in 2004 with a 118-107 defeat of Spain in the gold-medal game. Lisa Leslie won her fourth consecutive gold medal as the Americans defeated Australia in the women's basketball final.

The United States led the final medal tally with 110, but China finished with 51 golds, the most of any nation at an Olympics in 20 years.

— KAREN CROUSE

BUSINESS AND THE ECONOMY

Job Losses Mount, Reaching 159,000 In September Alone

The American economy lost 159,000 jobs in September, the worst month of retrenchment in five years, the government reported on Oct. 3, amplifying fears that an already painful downturn had entered a more severe stage that could persist well into next year.

Employment has diminished for nine consecutive months, eliminating 760,000 jobs, according to the Labor Department's report. And that did not count the traumatic economic events in mid to late September, as a string of Wall Street institutions collapsed, prompting the $700 billion emergency rescue package approved by Congress.

"It's a dismal report, and the worst thing about it is that it does not reflect the recent seizure that we've seen in the credit markets," said Michael T. Darda, chief economist at MKM Partners, a research and trading firm in Greenwich, Conn. "We've lost jobs in nearly every area of the economy, and this is going to get worse before it gets better because the credit markets have deteriorated basically on a daily basis for the last few weeks."

Few analysts expect the bailout to swiftly reverse the nation's fortunes. Housing prices continue to fall, eroding household wealth just as millions suffer the weight of unmanageable debt. The deteriorating job market has taken paychecks out of the economy, reinforcing a predilection for thrift that has cut sales from car showrooms to hair salons.

Banks should see their balance sheets improve as the government relieves them of disastrous investments, yet they may remain skittish and reluctant to lend.

"At best, the bailout stops a much deeper decline in activity," Mr. Darda said, "but it's not like they're going to do this and all of the sudden the clouds part and the skies are clear."

Only a few weeks earlier, many economists still held hopes that the economy might recover late this year or early next. But with the job market contracting faster, and fear dogging the financial system, the broad assumption has taken hold that 2008 is a lost cause.

"This is an economy in recession, and every dimension of the report confirms that," said Ethan S. Harris, an economist at Barclays Capital. "This has been preceded by a slow-motion recession. Now we're going into the full-speed recession that will last somewhere between three and five quarters."

— PETER S. GOODMAN

A Dizzying Ride For Oil Prices

The wild commodity rollercoaster that kicked off around 2002 showed no signs of slowing in 2008. In fact, this turned out to be one of the most volatile years ever for the energy markets, with oil prices reaching dizzying heights and gasoline topping $4-a-gallon across the United States.

By July, crude oil prices had soared above $145 a barrel in New York—up by an astounding 51 percent from the beginning of the year—but then retreated sharply because of concerns about the state of the American economy and fears of a prolonged economic slowdown.

While most experts warned there was no quick fix to the energy crisis, the shock of record gasoline costs sent Congress into a frenzy of hearings, blaming oil companies, speculators, or the OPEC oil cartel for driving up prices. But in a polarized election year, Washington remained deeply split on how to respond to high energy costs.

The debate also centered on whether to allow oil companies to drill offshore in order to boost domestic supplies. The United States produces a quarter of its oil from the Gulf of Mexico but about 85 percent of the region's coastline is off-limits for exploration. The issue quickly turned into a political football, with Republicans blaming Democrats for opposing more drilling, and Democrats blaming Republicans for blocking other energy-related issues without offshore drilling. In mid-September the House of Representatives approved a measure that would ease the longstanding ban on offshore drilling, but the legislation was derided as too restrictive by many Republicans, and appeared to be facing significant hurdles.

In the absence of a government policy, high prices forced Americans to take matters in their own hands—by driving less and ditching their gas-guzzling trucks and SUVs for more fuel-efficient cars. As a result, gasoline consumption in the United States fell for the second straight year since 1991.

But while oil consumption dropped across the industrialized world, demand continued to grow at a brisk pace in energy-thirsty developing economies, particularly in Asia and the Middle East where energy subsidies shielded most consumers from the real cost of oil.

Because of the risks posed by slowing energy demand, some oil-producing countries voiced their alarm at the rapid price run-up. Saudi Arabia's monarch, King Abdullah, convened a global energy summit in Jeddah to tackle the issue in June. But the hasty meeting produced no agreement on how to bring prices down, let alone what would be a fair price for both producers and consumers.

The elevated price level signaled a deeper problem. Since the turn of the century, oil consumption has grown faster than new energy supplies. Coupled with heightened geopolitical tensions, this mismatch led to a six-fold increase in oil prices in six years.

But energy markets remained exceptionally tight in 2008 as higher prices failed to attract much new energy supplies. Outside of OPEC countries, most producers saw their output drop. Mexico, the second-biggest oil exporter to the United States, had a dramatic collapse in its biggest oil field; Norwegian oil production continued to slow down; and Russia stunned energy experts when its production also started to decline.

Prices remained volatile in the fall, bobbing from $91 to $120 a barrel amid wild swings in the market. But with demand falling in most Western countries and growth weakening in some of Asia's booming economies, the trend was down.

—JAD MOUAWAD

Food Prices Rise Sharply

After decades of abundance and relatively cheap prices, a sharp increase in grain and food prices in 2008 led to widespread rioting in the developing world, a crisis among food banks and global hunger programs, and some instances of starvation.

While grain prices receded midway through the year, they remained historically high, and many experts predicted food prices would remain higher than normal for years to come as supplies catch up with growing demand.

The fallout from the commodity inflation was not as severe in the United States as it was in many parts of the world, particularly ravaged countries like Haiti and Somalia. Nonetheless, when combined with higher gas prices, food inflation strained the budgets of many American consumers, who cut back on everything from eating out at restaurants to buying afternoon lattes.

There was no one reason for the food crisis, but rather a combination of short-term factors and longer-term trends.

Rising incomes in developing countries increased demand for meat and dairy products, and consequently, drove demand for grains to feed livestock. The world's population had been growing at about 1 percent a year, while the growth of agricultural productivity slowed, a problem that many blamed on lack of government investment in crop research.

Demand for biofuels was also blamed for contributing to the food crisis. Often subsidized by governments as a way to reduce reliance on foreign oil, biofuels increased demand for corn, sugar and palm oil, touching off bitter debates about whether it was appropriate to use crops for fuel when food was in short supply.

In addition, droughts in Australia, Russia, Ukraine and South Africa curtailed the grain crop and further drove up prices. As crop prices shot upward, some governments banned exports of commodities like wheat and rice, diminishing the global supply and causing prices to jump even higher.

What was most surprising about the price increases in grains and food was that it came after decades in which both were abundant and relatively cheap, partly a result of government subsidies that encouraged overproduction.

But starting in 2005, grain prices steadily increased and rose significantly in late 2007 and into 2008. From January 2005 through June 2008, corn prices almost tripled, wheat prices increased 127 percent and rice jumped 170 percent.

Overall food prices in the United States increased about 5 percent in 2008, with eggs, milk and bread registering double-digit increases.

For all the misery in the supermarket aisle, American grain farmers were awestruck as corn futures topped $8 a bushel and futures for one variety of wheat climbed to $25 a bushel (even as they complained about high fertilizer and fuel costs.)

"We've lulled the public with cheap food," said Read Smith, a farmer in St. John, Wash. "It's not going to be a steal anymore."

—ANDREW MARTIN

A Rough Road For Automakers

Despite undergoing major revampings in recent years, General Motors and the Ford Motor Company continued to post huge losses. On Aug. 1 G.M. reported a stunning second-quarter loss of $15.5 billion because of a continuing fall in United States sales and charges for job cuts, plant closings and the falling value of trucks and sport utility vehicles.

That followed a loss of $8.7 billion reported the week before by Ford. Overall sales fell by 13 percent in July.

Chrysler, the smallest of the three Detroit auto companies, is privately owned by Cerberus Capital Management and does not report financial results.

The losses stem from a freefall in sales and a shift by consumers away from bigger vehicles that were once G.M.'s and Ford's most profitable products.

G.M. and Ford had expected economic conditions to improve in the second half of 2008, but the fiscal crisis that began in late summer created an even more dismal sales environment. In September, automakers sold fewer than a million new cars and trucks in a single month for the first time since 1993, as a reeling economy scared people

away from showrooms. Nearly every automaker posted double-digit declines. The total was 964,000 vehicles sold, compared to 1.31 million in September 2007.

"There is no question this is an automotive recession," said Erich Merkle, an analyst at the accounting and consulting firm Crowe Horwath in Grand Rapids, Mich.

American automakers have decided to shift production from trucks and sport utility vehicles to smaller, more gas-efficient cars, including hybrids, which are growing in popularity. But it takes time to switch equipment for production.

Compounding Detroit's problems is the move by consumers to small cars and the collapse in sales of pickups and sport utility vehicles that historically provided the bulk of the profits at G.M., Ford and Chrysler.

Ford announced that it would radically shift much of its North American production from trucks to cars, and bring six of its European models to the United States market.

G.M. had already laid plans to make more cars and car-based crossover vehicles, while downsizing its truck production.

But the question facing Detroit is how it can continue to finance its operations and product programs until the market rebounds and its new models hit the showrooms.

"This is almost like evolution, and the survival of the fittest," said Jesse Toprak, chief industry analyst for the automobile research Web site Edmunds.com. "They are on the right path to make fuel-efficient cars, but it's going to take time."

— BILL VLASIC and NICK BUNKLEY

Airlines Cut Back Routes and Flights

When oil prices topped $140 a barrel in summer 2008, leading to record prices for jet fuel, the airline industry began to retrench.

Both the major airlines and the low-fare carriers announced plans to ground aircraft from their fleets, eliminate routes, and in some cases, reduce the frequency of flights to a number of cities.

Although the government and industry analysts had long criticized the carriers for operating too many flights, especially on the east coast, airlines had been reluctant to take such steps because of stiff competition for travelers. But the doubling of jet fuel prices triggered steep losses during 2008, and left them little choice.

By the time the reductions are complete in 2009, analysts predict that the industry will be 10 to 12 percent smaller than it was at the beginning of 2008. It was the biggest decline since 2002, when air traffic dropped significantly amid security fears.

The steps are "going to recalibrate the industry," said Glenn F. Tilton, the chief executive at United.

For passengers, the changes showed up in higher ticket prices and fewer choices of flights. They also began to pay fees for features that used to be included with the price of a ticket. Many airlines started charging passengers to check luggage. JetBlue Airways began selling pillows and blankets, and US Airways even charged $1 for coffee.

Cities like Las Vegas and Orlando, which have long been popular with vacation travelers, lost a number of daily flights. Meanwhile, airlines substituted smaller planes for bigger jets on a number of routes, and even began using medium sized planes like the Boeing 757 on trips overseas.

Many of the industry's aging aircraft are set to disappear. United Airlines announced plans to ground 100 planes, including six big Boeing 747-400 jets that it used on international trips and flights to Hawaii.

American Airlines announced it would ground a number of its McDonnell-Douglas MD-80s, which it has been flying since 1983. Meanwhile, Northwest Airlines said it planned to retire one-quarter of its DC-9 planes, whose average age was about 35 years old.

Even the industry's successful carriers announced plans to cut back. Southwest Airlines, which had added new flights and cities throughout the decade, said it did not expect to add any additional planes in 2009. Virgin America, which started service in 2007, said it would cut about 10 percent of its flights in late 2008.

JetBlue also put off plans to add Embraer and Airbus planes, and said it would keep a lid on its growth, which had averaged 30 percent a year after it began flying in 2000.

"It's time for us to calm it down," said David Barger, the chief executive of JetBlue, echoing a sentiment across the industry.

— MICHELINE MAYNARD

Smartphones Boom As Mini-Computers

When the iPhone from Apple made its debut in 2007, it started nothing less than a cultural revolution among mobile phone users. Consumers who had imagined a phone could only be used to make calls, began to view them as mini-computers that could easily access the Internet, play music and take digital pictures. By 2008, several companies sought to capitalize on the phenomenon, hoping to satiate the mainstream consumer's appetite for new web-savvy devices.

In April Samsung introduced the Instinct which, with a touch screen like the iPhone, was one of the first smartphones to take aim directly at Apple. It was sold in the United States by wireless carrier Sprint Nextel which boasted a fast network. Four months later, Apple came out with an updated iPhone that also promised faster speeds over AT&T's network. But Apple was forced to offer a software upgrade because the phone had trouble connecting to that network. Despite grumblings from consumers, the phone remained popular and analysts predicted sales of 3.5 million by the end of the year.

At the same time, Google, the behemoth Internet search company, created Android, one of the first mainstream open operating systems for mobile phones. The promise for consumers was that, unlike other mobile operating systems, including Apple's, Android could easily be manipulated to suit a user's personal needs. In September Google announced the first phone to be sold with the operating system and a touch screen, made by HTC, a little-known Taiwanese phone maker. Interest was high, but analysts remained skeptical whether it could become the game-changer that the iPhone was.

Later in the year Research in Motion, which made the popular Blackberry devices, planned to offer its own iPhone killer, which had a touch screen and easier access to the Internet.

Not surprisingly, with so many choices, consumers quickly snapped up new models. According to Nielsen Mobile, which tracks mobile phone buying trends, 16.5 percent of new phones purchased in the second quarter of 2008 were smartphones. Prices came down, making them more accessible—as little as $99 for the BlackBerry Pearl.

Women emerged as dominant buyers of smartphones, using them to help manage their families' hectic schedules and keep in touch with friends. By mid-year the number of American women using smartphones more than doubled, to 10.4 million, growing at a faster pace than among men, according to Nielsen. And, in contrast to men, many of these women said they used them primarily for pleasure rather than business.

The increase in smartphones led to a boom in application development—games, maps, information services—which could be downloaded to a mobile phone. Silicon Valley's venture capitalists were more than happy to follow the trend. Investments in mobile phone application development rose 90 percent in the first half of 2008—to $383 million—compared with the second half of 2007, according to Rutberg & Company, a technology research firm based in San Francisco.

—LAURA M. HOLSON

Newspapers Facing Survival Concerns

Doubts about American newpapers' survival turned from a far-off worry to immediate fear in 2008, as the industry suffered its worst period in at least seven decades.

The migration of readers and advertisers from printed paper to the Internet accelerated. At the same time, newspapers were staggered by the economic downturn, higher newsprint and fuel costs, and billions of dollars in debt from recent takeover deals that turned sour.

Newspapers' ad revenue, their primary income, fell more than 20 percent in just two years. Conditions were worse still in Florida, California and Nevada, where a sharp contraction in real estate markets cut real estate advertising in half. Even Internet advertising, which had long been the less lucrative but fast-growing hope of the industry, stopped rising.

Newspaper executives and Wall Street analysts predicted that the economics of the business would continue to worsen for another two years or more, and that a number of newspapers would disappear in that time.

Cost-cutting at most newspapers included significant reductions in the size of the publication and the number of journalists producing it, stoking fears that a diminished product would hasten declining circulation.

The great paradox was that more people read newspapers than ever before. For some major papers, the online audience grew to several times the size of their print readership.

The Tribune Company, publisher of *The Chicago Tribune*, *The Los Angeles Times*, *The Baltimore Sun* and several other papers, emerged as the most prominent example of the industry's turmoil.

The company went private in the final days of 2007, turning control over to Sam Zell, a real estate billionaire. To do that, *Tribune* tripled its debt load, to more than $12 billion, and then struggled to make interest payments at a time of dwindling revenue.

Mr. Zell arrived saying he did not intend to shrink newsrooms or sell newspapers, but quickly reversed himself on both points, sharply cutting staffs and selling *Newsday*, the Long Island daily. He drew attention with off-color remarks and insults, and filled the upper ranks of *Tribune* with people who had no newspaper experience.

The top editor and the publisher of *The Los Angeles Times* were fired, the third turnover in three years for each position. Like his two predecessors, the editor was forced out for resisting more staff cuts. Analysts warned of a risk of serious financial danger to several newspaper companies. Among the most closely watched were MediaNews Group and The McClatchy Company, major chains that spent billions acquiring papers in 2005 and 2006, and were heavily invested in California markets.

The Wall Street Journal was shielded from the worst of the financial pressures by the size and diversity of its new owner, Rupert Murdoch's News Corporation. Mr. Murdoch replaced *The Journal's* top editor while taking steps to overhaul the paper, adding coverage of politics, lifestyles and sports, in what Mr. Murdoch said was a bid to compete directly with *The New York Times.*

—RICHARD PEREZ-PENA

Rogue Trader Lost $7 Billion, Bank Says

A French bank announced on Jan. 24 that it had lost $7.2 billion, not because of complex subprime loans, but the old-fashioned way—because a 31-year-old rogue trader made bad bets on stocks and then, in trying to cover up those losses, dug himself deeper into a hole.

Jerome Kerviel, an unassuming midlevel employee of Société Générale, one of France's largest and most respected banks, managed to evade multiple layers of computer controls and audits for as long as a year, stacking up 4.9 billion euros in losses for the bank.

Unlike many of his high-level trading colleagues, Mr. Kerviel graduated not from one of France's elite universities, but from a business college in Lyon, and worked up the ranks. It was from his perch in the department that deals with auditing the bank's trading that he developed what bank officials described as an "intimate and perverse" knowledge that he used to cover up unauthorized trades.

The fraud appeared to be the largest in history by a rogue trader. Mr. Kerviel, who earned about 100,000 euros ($147,000), made no money personally, but apparently hid the trades by making fake orders to balance each of the genuine orders he placed.

The bank maintained Mr. Kerviel acted alone, but experts wonder how that could be possible, given the checks and balances at financial institutions.

The fraud, carried out over the course of a year, harked back to others that traders managed to inflict on their employers, in particular one carried out by Nick Leeson, a Singapore-based trader, who brought down the venerable British bank Barings in 1995.

—NICOLA CLARK and DAVID JOLLY

SCIENCE & MEDICINE

Overlooked Lesions Tied to Colon Cancer

An easily overlooked type of abnormality in the colon is the most likely type to turn cancerous, and is more common in this country than previously thought, researchers are reporting.

The findings come from a study of colonoscopy, in which a camera-tipped tube is used to examine the lining of the intestine. Generally, doctors search for polyps, abnormal growths that stick out from the lining and can turn into cancer. But another type of growth is much more dangerous, and harder to see because it is flat or depressed and similar in color to healthy tissue.

Japanese researchers became concerned about these flat lesions in the 1980s and 90s, but studies here had mixed results and American doctors tended to think that flat growths were less common and less dangerous in the United States.

The new study, published on March 5 in the Journal of the American Medical Association, suggests otherwise.

Some doctors in this country were already alert to flat lesions, but the findings will pose a challenge to others, because it takes a trained and vigilant eye to see the growths and special techniques to remove them. The results also mean it is especially important that patients take the harsh laxatives that many dread in advance of the test. The flat lesions, hard to find even under the best conditions, will be impossible to see if any waste is left in the bowel.

Colon cancer is the second-leading cause of cancer death in the United States, after lung cancer, with about 154,000 new cases detected and 52,000 deaths a year. It is one of the few cancers that is totally preventable if precancerous growths are found and removed; it can also be cured with surgery alone if found early enough.

People who have just had a colonoscopy should not rush to schedule another one just to look for the flat growths, doctors said. But they emphasized that people should see a doctor any time they have persisting symptoms that could indicate colon cancer, like rectal bleeding or a change in bowel habits—no matter how recently they had a colonoscopy. The test is highly reliable, but not perfect, doctors say.

The study, of 1,819 military veterans, mostly men, found that 9.35 percent had flat lesions, and those lesions were five times as likely as polyps to contain cancerous or precancerous tissue. Depressed or indented lesions were the least common but the most risky. Together, the flat or depressed lesions accounted for only 15 percent of the potentially cancerous growths found in the study, but were involved in half of the cancers. Once the doctors spotted the flat lesions, they sprayed a bluish dye on them to see their outlines better and remove them completely.

— DENISE GRADY

Sex Infections Found In One in Four Teenage Girls

The first national study of four common sexually transmitted diseases among girls and young women has found that one in four are infected with at least one of the diseases, federal health officials reported on March 11.

Nearly half the African-Americans in the study of teenagers ages 14 to 19 were infected with at least one of the diseases monitored in the study—human papillomavirus (HPV), chlamydia, genital herpes and trichomoniasis, a common parasite.

The 50 percent figure compared with 20 percent of white teenagers, health officials and researchers said at a news conference at a scientific meeting in Chicago.

The two most common sexually transmitted diseases, or S.T.D.'s, among all the participants tested were HPV, at 18 percent, and chlamydia, at 4 percent, according to the analysis, part of the National Health and Nutrition Examination Survey.

Each disease can be serious in its own way. HPV, for example, can cause cancer and genital warts.

Among the infected women, 15 percent had more than one of the diseases.

Women may be unaware they are infected. But the diseases, which are infections caused by bacteria, viruses and parasites, can produce acute symptoms like irritating vaginal discharge, painful pelvic inflammatory disease and potentially fatal ectopic pregnancy. The infections can also lead to long-term ailments like infertility and cervical cancer.

The survey tested for specific HPV strains linked to genital warts and cervical cancer.

Officials of the Centers for Disease Control and Prevention said the findings underscored the need to strengthen screening, vaccination and other prevention measures for the diseases, which are among the highest public health priorities.

About 19 million new sexually transmitted infections occur each year among all age groups in the United States.

"High S.T.D. infection rates among young women, particularly young African-American women, are clear signs that we must continue developing ways to reach those most at risk," said Dr. John M. Douglas Jr., who directs the centers' division of S.T.D. prevention.

— LAWRENCE K. ALTMAN

Doubts About Two Drugs Used Against Cholesterol

Two widely prescribed cholesterol-lowering drugs, Vytorin and Zetia, may not work and should be used only as a last resort, a panel of four cardiologists told an audience of more than 5,000 people at a major cardiology conference in Chicago on March 30.

Instead, doctors and patients should rely more heavily on older cholesterol-lowering drugs called statins, which have proven benefits and can be cheaper, the panel said.

Statins include drugs like Lipitor and simvastatin, the generic version of Zocor. But other, lesser-known drugs like the vitamin niacin should also be tried before Vytorin and Zetia, the panel said.

Vytorin and Zetia are among the top-selling drugs in the world, with combined sales of $5 billion last year. About five million people, including four million Americans, take the medicines, which have been heavily advertised to consumers in the United States.

The New England Journal of Medicine made a similar recommendation about the drugs in an editorial published the same day.

The panel and the editorial were timed to coincide with the release of full results from a two-year clinical trial that showed that the drugs did not slow, and might speed up, the growth of fatty plaques in arteries. Those plaques are associated with heart attacks and strokes.

Merck and Schering-Plough, which make Vytorin and Zetia, said that they disagreed with the recommendations. Vytorin and Zetia have been proved to lower cholesterol and are valuable treatments for patients, said Dr. Rick Veltri, vice president of the Schering-Plough Research Institute.

The stakes of the debate are high both medically and financially. The drugs produce about 70 percent of Schering-Plough's profit, analysts say.

Prescriptions for the medicines had already dipped about 15 percent since January, when preliminary results from the trial were disclosed. Still, the drugs are widely used, with about three million prescriptions written each month in the United States alone.

Unlike statins, which block the liver from making cholesterol, Zetia stops the intestine from absorbing cholesterol in food. Vytorin is a single pill that combines Zetia with simvastatin, or Zocor.

Low-density lipoprotein, or LDL, cholesterol, the harmful kind, is a risk factor for heart disease, and so doctors have generally assumed that lowering LDL cholesterol would reduce the risk of heart attacks and strokes.

But proving that a drug actually cuts those risks requires an expensive, multiyear clinical trial involving 10,000 or more patients. Those studies, called outcomes trials, have been conducted for statins, and they have proved that patients taking those drugs have a reduced risk of heart disease. No such outcomes trials exist for Vytorin and Zetia.

— ALEX BERENSON

Star Seen Just Before Unexpectedly Bursting

Far away on the day of Jan. 9, Earth time, a satellite telescope by the name of Swift, which happened to be gazing at the star's galaxy, a smudge of stars 88 million light-years away in the constellation Lynx, recorded an unexpected burst of invisible X-rays 100 billion times as bright as the Sun.

Alicia Soderberg, a Princeton astronomer who had been using the NASA satellite to study the fading remains of a previous supernova explosion, received the startling results of that observation by e-mail while giving a talk in Michigan. Recognizing that this was something extraordinary, she sounded a worldwide alert.

In the following hours and days, as most of the big telescopes on Earth, and the Hubble Space Telescope and the Chandra X-ray Observatory watched from space, the star erupted into cataclysmic explosion known as a supernova, lighting up its galaxy and delighting astronomers who had never been able to catch an exploding star before it exploded.

"We caught the whole thing on tape, so to speak," Dr. Soderberg said in an interview. "I truly won the astronomy lottery. A star in the galaxy exploded right in front of my eyes."

She and 42 colleagues from around the world have now told the tale of this discovery in a paper in Nature. The observations, they say, provide a new window into the process by which the most massive stars end their lives and give astronomers new clues on how to look for these rare events and catch them while they are still in their most explosive, formative stages.

Most supernovas, Dr. Soderberg explained, are discovered and classified by their visible light, but that typically does not happen until the explosion is a month or more old and has brightened enough to be seen over intergalactic distances.

The true fireworks, she said, happen much earlier when a shock wave from the imploding core hits the star's surface, producing so-called breakout light, which lasts only a few minutes.

"The physics of the explosion is encoded in the breakout light," Dr. Soderberg said, adding that the chance that the Swift telescope was observing during those moments was "unfathomable."

— DENNIS OVERBYE

Spacecraft Makes Safe Mars Landing

NASA's Phoenix spacecraft made a safe, flawless landing May 25 on Mars.

During the final, tense minutes of the descent, long stretches of quiet in the mission support room in Pasadena, Calif. were punctuated by cheers and clapping as confirmation of crucial events like the deployment of the parachute were confirmed.

Then, at 7:53 p.m. Eastern time, Richard Kornfeld, the lead communications officer for entry, descent and landing, announced: "Touchdown signal detected."

The mission controllers erupted in cheers and began hugging one another in congratulations. "It was better than we could have possibly wished for," said Barry Goldstein, the project manager for the mission.

At 9:53 p.m., there were more cheers as confirmation came that one more critical event, the unfolding of the solar arrays, had occurred without problem. And then the first pictures arrived: black-and-white images of the solar panels, of one of the lander's footpads and of surrounding terrain, showing the polygonal fractures caused by repeated thawing and freezing.

After being checked out for a few days, the spacecraft began the first up-close investigation of Mars's northern polar region. That area became a prime subject of interest for planetary scientists after NASA's orbiting Odyssey spacecraft discovered in 2002 vast quantities of water ice lying a few inches beneath the surface in the polar regions.

Mars's surface is currently far too cold for life to exist, but in the past, the planet's axis might have periodically tipped over so that its north pole pointed at the sun during summer. That could have warmed the ice into liquid water.

With liquid water comes the possibility of life.

On the Phoenix, a robotic arm with a scoop will dig into the ice layer. Instruments on the spacecraft included a small oven that will heat the scooped-up dirt and ice to 1,800 degrees Fahrenheit. Analyzing the vapors will provide information on the minerals, and that will, in turn, provide clues about whether the ice ever melted and whether this region was habitable.

"'We see Phoenix as a stepping stone to future investigations of Mars," said Peter H. Smith of the University of Arizona, the principal investigator of the mission.

— KENNETH CHANG

Monkeys Think, Moving Artificial Arm as Own

Two monkeys with tiny sensors in their brains have learned to control a mechanical arm with just their thoughts, using it to reach for and grab food and even to adjust for the size and stickiness of morsels when necessary, scientists reported on May 28.

The report, released online by the journal *Nature*, is the most striking demonstration to date of brain-machine interface technology. Scientists expect that technology will eventually allow people with spinal cord injuries and other paralyzing conditions to gain more control over their lives.

The findings suggest that brain-controlled prosthetics, while not practical, are at least technically within reach.

In previous studies, researchers showed that humans who had been paralyzed for years could learn to control a cursor on a computer screen with their brain waves and that nonhuman primates could use their thoughts to move a mechanical arm, a robotic hand or a robot on a treadmill.

The new experiment goes a step further. In it, the monkeys' brains seem to have adopted the mechanical appendage as their own, refining its movement as it interacted with real objects in real time. The monkeys had their own arms gently restrained while they learned to use the added one.

Experts not involved with the study said the findings were likely to accelerate interest in human testing, especially given the need to treat head and spinal injuries in veterans returning from Iraq and Afghanistan.

—BENEDICT CAREY

New Hints Seen That Red Wine May Slow Aging

Red wine may be much more potent than was thought in extending human lifespan, researchers say in a new report that is likely to give impetus to the rapidly growing search for longevity drugs.

The study, made public in early June, is based on dosing mice with resveratrol, an ingredient of some red wines. Some scientists are already taking resveratrol in capsule form, but others believe it is far too early to take the drug, especially using wine as its source, until there is better data on its safety and effectiveness.

The report is part of a new wave of interest in drugs that may enhance longevity. On June 2, Sirtris, a startup founded in 2004 to develop drugs with the same effects as resveratrol, completed its sale to GlaxoSmithKline for $720 million.

Sirtris is seeking to develop drugs that activate protein agents known in people as sirtuins.

Serious scientists have long derided the idea of life-extending elixirs, but the door has now been opened to drugs that exploit an ancient biological survival mechanism, that of switching the body's resources from fertility to tissue maintenance. The improved tissue maintenance seems to extend life by cutting down on the degenerative diseases of aging.

The reflex can be prompted by a faminelike diet, known as caloric restriction, which extends the life of laboratory rodents by up to 30 percent but is far too hard for most people to keep to and in any case has not been proven to work in humans.

Research started nearly 20 years ago by Dr. Leonard Guarente of the Massachusetts Institute of Technology showed recently that the famine-induced switch to tissue preservation might be triggered by activating the body's sirtuins. Dr. David Sinclair of the Harvard Medical School, who is a co-founder of Sirtris and a former student of Dr. Guarente, then found in 2003 that sirtuins could be activated by some natural compounds, including resveratrol, previously known as just an ingredient of certain red wines.

Dr. Sinclair and others have tested resveratrol's effects in mice, mostly at doses far higher than the minuscule amounts in red wine. One of the more spectacular results was obtained last year by Dr. John Auwerx of the Institute of Genetics and Molecular and Cellular Biology in Illkirch, France. He showed that resveratrol could turn couch-potato mice into champion athletes, making them run twice as far on a treadmill before collapsing.

Sirtris, meanwhile, has been testing resveratrol and other drugs that activate sirtuin. These drugs are small molecules, more stable than resveratrol, and can be given in smaller doses. In April, Sirtris reported that its formulation of resveratrol, called SRT501, reduced glucose levels in diabetic patients.

—NICHOLAS WADE

End to Prostate Screening Urged for Elderly Men

In a move that could lead to significant changes in medical care for older men, a national task force on Aug. 4 recommended that doctors stop screening men ages 75 and older for prostate cancer because the search for the disease in this group was causing more harm than good.

The guidelines, issued by the U.S. Preventive Services Task Force, a government-appointed panel of experts, represent an abrupt policy change by an influential panel that had withheld any advice regarding screening for prostate cancer, citing a lack of reliable evidence. Though the task force still has not taken a stand on the value of screening in younger men, the shift is certain to reignite the debate about the appropriateness of prostate cancer screening at any age.

Screening is typically performed with a blood test measuring prostate-specific antigen, or PSA, levels. Widespread PSA testing has led to high rates of detection. Last year, more than 218,000 men learned they had the disease.

Yet various studies suggest the disease is "overdiagnosed"—that is, detected at a point when it most likely would not affect life expectancy—in 29 percent to 44 percent of cases. Prostate cancer often progresses very slowly, and a large number of these cancers discovered through screening will probably never cause symptoms during the patient's lifetime, particularly for men in their 70s and 80s. At the same time, aggressive treatment of prostate cancer can greatly reduce a patient's quality of life, resulting in complications like impotency and incontinence.

"If someone has made it to the age of 75 and they don't have an elevated PSA, the likelihood of them developing clinically significant prostate cancer in the last 10 to 15 years of their life is pretty low," said Dr. Peter C. Albertsen, professor of urology at the University of Connecticut Health Center. "The downside risk begins to outweigh the upside at the age of 75."

—TARA PARKER-POPE

For The Brain, Remembering Is Like Reliving

Scientists have for the first time recorded individual brain cells in the act of summoning a spontaneous memory, revealing not only where a remembered experience is registered but also, in part, how the brain is able to recreate it.

The recordings, taken from the brains of epilepsy patients being prepared for surgery, demonstrate that these spontaneous memories reside in some of the same neurons that fired most furiously when the recalled event had been experienced. Researchers had long theorized as much but until now had only indirect evidence.

Experts said the study had all but closed the case: For the brain, remembering is a lot like doing (at least in the short term, as the research says nothing about more distant memories).

The experiment, reported Sept. 5 in the journal *Science*, is likely to open a new avenue in the investigation of Alzheimer's disease and other forms of dementia, some experts said, as well as help explain how some memories seemingly come out of nowhere. The researchers were even able to identify specific memories in subjects a second or two before the people themselves reported having them.

The new study moved beyond most previous memory research in that it focused not on recognition or recollection of specific symbols but on free recall—whatever popped into people's heads when, in this case, they were asked to remember short film clips they had just seen.

This ability to richly reconstitute past experience often quickly deteriorates in people with Alzheimer's and other forms of dementia, and it is fundamental to so-called episodic memory—the catalog of vignettes that together form our remembered past.

In the study, a team of American and Israeli researchers threaded tiny electrodes into the brains of 13 people with severe epilepsy. The electrode implants are standard procedure in such cases, allowing doctors to pinpoint the location of the mini-storms of brain activity that cause epileptic seizures.

The patients watched a series of 5- to 10-second film clips, some from popular television shows like "Seinfeld" and others depicting animals or landmarks like the Eiffel Tower. The researchers recorded the firing activity of about 100 neurons per person; the recorded neurons were concentrated in and around the hippocampus, a sliver of tissue deep in the brain known to be critical to forming memories.

In each person, the researchers identified single cells that became highly active during some videos and quiet during others. More than half the recorded cells hummed with activity in response to at least one film clip; many of them also responded weakly to others.

After briefly distracting the patients, the researchers then asked them to think about the clips for a minute and to report "what comes to mind." The patients remembered almost all of the clips. And when they recalled a specific one, the same cells that had been active during that clip reignited. In fact, the cells became active a second or two before people were conscious of the memory, which signaled to researchers the memory to come.

Dr. Itzhak Fried, a professor of neurosurgery at the University of California, Los Angeles and the University of Tel Aviv, was the senior author of the study. His co-authors were Hagar Gelbard-Sagiv, Michal Harel and Rafael Malach of the Weizmann Institute of Science in Israel, and Roy Mukamel, of U.C.L.A.

—BENEDICT CAREY

New Particle Collider Revs Up, Shuts Down

Science rode a beam of subatomic particles and a river of Champagne into the future on Sept. 10.

After 14 years of labor, scientists at the CERN laboratory outside Geneva successfully activated the Large Hadron Collider, the world's largest, most powerful particle collider and, at $8 billion, the most expensive scientific experiment to date.

At 4:28 a.m., Eastern time, the scientists announced that a beam of protons had completed its first circuit around the collider's 17-mile-long racetrack, 300 feet underneath the Swiss-French border. They then sent the beam around several more times.

"It's a fantastic moment," said Lyn Evans, who has been the project director of the collider since its inception in 1994. "We can now look forward to a new era of understanding about the origins and evolution of the universe."

Eventually, the collider is expected to accelerate protons to energies of seven trillion electron volts and then smash them together, recreating conditions in the primordial fireball only a trillionth of a second after the Big Bang. Scientists hope the machine will be a sort of Hubble Space Telescope of inner space, allowing them to detect new subatomic particles and forces of nature.

In Batavia, Ill., an ocean away from Geneva, the new collider's activation was watched with rueful excitement here at the Fermi National Accelerator

Laboratory, or Fermilab, which has had the reigning particle collider.

Several dozen physicists, students and onlookers, and three local mayors gathered overnight to watch the dawn of a new high-energy physics. They applauded each milestone as the scientists methodically steered the protons on their course at CERN, the European Organization for Nuclear Research.

Roger Aymar, CERN's director, called the new collider a "discovery machine." The buzz was worldwide. On the blog "Cosmic Variance," Gordon Kane of the University of Michigan called the new collider "a why machine."

Two weeks later, the collider had to be temporarily shut down after an electrical connection between two of the superconducting electromagnets that steer the protons suffered a so-called quench, heating up, melting and leaking helium into the collider tunnel. Liquid helium is used to cool the magnets to superconducting temperatures of only about 3.5 degrees Fahrenheit above absolute zero. Stray heat can cause the magnets to lose their superconductivity with potentially disastrous consequences.

To make repairs, it was necessary to warm the magnets up and then cool them back down again, which takes at least two months, engineers said. That would leave scant time to run the collider before it would have to shut down for the winter in early December to save money on electricity. The Large Hadron Collider will not begin operations again until April 2009.

On Sept. 26, a federal judge in Honolulu dismissed a lawsuit to stop the running of the collider entirely. The action, brought by a retired radiation safety officer in Hawaii and a science writer in Barcelona, claimed the collider could produce a black hole that could have a calamitous effect.

—DENNIS OVERBYE

Researchers' Payments Not Fully Revealed

A world-renowned Harvard child psychiatrist whose work has helped fuel an explosion in the use of powerful antipsychotic medicines in children earned at least $1.6 million in consulting fees from drug makers from 2000 to 2007 but for years did not report much of this income to university officials, according to information given Congressional investigators.

By failing to report income, the psychiatrist, Dr. Joseph Biederman, and a colleague in the psychiatry department at Harvard Medical School, Dr. Timothy E. Wilens, may have violated federal and university research rules designed to police potential conflicts of interest, according to Senator Charles E. Grassley, Republican of Iowa. Some of their research is financed by government grants.

Like Dr. Biederman, Dr. Wilens belatedly reported earning at least $1.6 million from 2000 to 2007, and another Harvard colleague, Dr. Thomas Spencer, reported earning at least $1 million after being pressed by Mr. Grassley's investigators. But even these amended disclosures may understate the researchers' outside income because some entries contradict payment information from drug makers, Mr. Grassley found.

In one example, Dr. Biederman reported no income from Johnson & Johnson for 2001 in a disclosure report filed with the university. When asked to check again, he said he received $3,500. But Johnson & Johnson told Mr. Grassley that it paid him $58,169 in 2001, Mr. Grassley found.

The Harvard group's consulting arrangements with drug makers were already controversial because of the researchers' advocacy of unapproved uses of psychiatric medicines in children.

In an e-mailed statement, Dr. Biederman said, "My interests are solely in the advancement of medical treatment through rigorous and objective study," and he said he took conflict-of-interest policies "very seriously." Drs. Wilens and Spencer said in e-mailed statements that they thought they had complied with conflict-of-interest rules.

John Burklow, a spokesman for the National Institutes of Health, said: "If there have been violations of N.I.H. policy—and if research integrity has been compromised—we will take all the appropriate action within our power to hold those responsible accountable."

The federal grants received by Drs. Biederman and Wilens were administered by Massachusetts General Hospital, which in 2005 won $287 million in such grants. The health institutes could place restrictions on the hospital's grants or even suspend them altogether.

Dr. Biederman is one of the most influential researchers in child psychiatry and is widely admired for focusing the field's attention on its most troubled young patients. His work helped to fuel a controversial 40-fold increase from 1994 to 2003 in the diagnosis of pediatric bipolar disorder, which is characterized by severe mood swings, and a rapid rise in the use of antipsychotic medicines in children. The investigation did not address research quality.

Senator Grassley's inquiry is systematically asking some of the nation's leading researchers to provide their conflict-of-interest disclosures and comparing them with records of actual payments from drug companies. Besides Dr. Biederman, Mr. Grassley questioned Dr. Melissa P. DelBello of the University of Cincinnati, who told university officials that she earned about $100,000 from 2005 to 2007 from eight drug makers. But AstraZeneca alone paid her $238,000 during that period, Mr. Grassley found

Documents provided to the investigators also disclosed that one of the nation's most influential psychiatrists, Dr. Charles B. Nemeroff of Emory University, earned more than $2.8 million in consulting arrangements with drug makers from 2000 to 2007, but that Dr. Nemeroff failed to report at least $1.2 million of that income to his university.

—GARDINER HARRIS and BENEDICT CAREY

Cloning Said to Yield Human Embryos

Scientists at a small biotechnology company said in January that they had used cloning to create human embryos from the skin cells of two men.

The work represents a step toward the promise of creating personalized embryonic stem cells that could be used for medical treatments. Although the embryos grew only to a very early stage, the work could also theoretically be seen as a step toward creating babies that are genetic copies of other people.

Scientists at the company, Stemagen, based in San Diego, said they were the first to use human adult cells to create cloned embryos that advanced to the stage known as a blastocyst, from which embryonic stem cells typically are extracted.

However, the researchers did not derive embryonic stem cells. That left some experts skeptical.

"It's an important step toward the ultimate goal of making patient-specific stem cell lines via nuclear transfer," said Dr. George Q. Daley, a stem cell researcher at Harvard and Children's Hospital Boston, using another term for cloning. But he said skepticism would be erased only when stem cell lines were derived.

Dr. Samuel H. Wood, the chief executive of Stemagen, said the company first wanted to prove it could clone an adult human cell and was now turning to deriving cell lines. "We've at least shown the opening to the cave that has the holy grail," he said. A paper on the work was published online by the journal Stem Cells.

He said Stemagen, which he started with a wealthy friend in 2005, was not interested in creating cloned babies, something that is illegal in places and morally repugnant to many people. Rather it wants to make stem cell lines for research and medical treatments.

—ANDREW POLLACK

Pill for Exercise Without Exertion

For all who have wondered if they could enjoy the benefits of exercise without the pain of exertion, the answer may one day be yes—just take a pill that tricks the muscles into thinking they have been working out furiously.

Researchers at the Salk Institute in San Diego reported that they had found two drugs that did wonders for the athletic endurance of couch potato mice. One drug, known as Aicar, increased the mice's endurance on a treadmill by 44 percent after just four weeks of treatment. A second drug, GW1516, supercharged the mice to a 75 percent increase in endurance but had to be combined with exercise to have any effect.

"It's a little bit like a free lunch without the calories," said Dr. Ronald M. Evans, leader of the Salk group.

The results, Dr. Evans said, seem reasonably likely to apply to people, who control muscle tone with the same underlying genes as do mice. If the drugs work and prove to be safe, they could be useful in a wide range of settings. They should help people who are too frail to exercise and those with health problems like diabetes that are improved with exercise, Dr. Evans said.

In a report in the Aug. 1 issue of the journal Cell, Dr. Evans described the two drugs that successfully activate the muscle-remodeling system in mice, generating more high-endurance Type 1 fiber. The drug GW1516 activates the PPAR-delta protein but the mice must also exercise to show increased endurance. It seems that PPAR-delta switches on one set of genes, and exercise another, and both are needed for endurance.

The chemicals involved are already available, and such muscle-enhancing drugs would also have obvious appeal to athletes seeking to gain an edge in performance. Dr. Evans said athletes often showed up at public lectures he had given and asked him about the drugs.

With money from the Howard Hughes Medical Institute, Dr. Evans has devised a test to detect whether an athlete has taken the drugs and has made it available to the World Anti-Doping Agency, which prepares a list of forbidden substances for the International Olympic Committee. Officials at the antidoping agency confirmed that they were collaborating with Dr. Evans on a test but could not say when they would start using it.

Experts not involved in the study agreed that the drugs held promise for treating disease. Dr. Richard N. Bergman, an expert on obesity and diabetes at the University of Southern California, said the drugs might prove to have serious side effects but, if safe, could become widely used. "It is possible that the couch potato segment of the population might find this to be a good regimen, and of course that is a large number of people."

—NICHOLAS WADE

Discoverers of AIDS, Cancer Viruses Win Nobel

The Nobel Prize in Medicine was awarded on Oct. 6 to three European scientists who had discovered viruses behind two devastating illnesses, AIDS and cervical cancer.

Half of the award will be shared by two French virologists, Françoise Barré-Sinoussi, 61, and Luc A. Montagnier, 76, for discovering H.I.V., the virus that causes AIDS. Conspicuously omitted was Dr. Robert C. Gallo, an American virologist who vied with the French team in a long, often acrimonious dispute over credit for the discovery of H.I.V.

The other half of the $1.4 million award will go to a German physician-scientist, Dr. Harald zur Hausen, 72, for his discovery of H.P.V., or the human papilloma virus. Dr. zur Hausen of the German Cancer Research Center in Heidelberg "went against current dogma" by postulating that the virus caused cervical cancer, said the Karolinska Institute in Stockholm, which selects the medical winners of the prize, formally called the Nobel Prize in Physiology or Medicine.

His discovery led to the development of two vaccines against cervical cancer, the second most common cancer among women. An estimated 250,000 women die of cervical cancer each year, mostly in poor countries.

Since its discovery in 1981, AIDS has rivaled the worst epidemics in history. An estimated 25 million people have died, and 33 million more are living with H.I.V.

In 1983, Dr. Montagnier and Dr. Barré-Sinoussi, a member of his lab at the Pasteur Institute in Paris, published their report of a newly identified virus. The Karolinska Institute said that discovery led to blood tests to detect the infection and to anti-retroviral drugs that can prolong the lives of patients. The tests are now used to screen blood donations, making the blood supply safer for transfusions and blood products.

The viral discovery has also led to an understanding of the natural history of H.I.V. infection in people, which ultimately leads to AIDS and death unless treated.

The link between human papilloma virus and cervical cancer took years to gain acceptance. When Dr. zur Hausen proposed the connection in the 1970s, infection with papilloma virus was thought to cause nothing more serious than common warts. In 1983, he discovered the first H.P.V., type 16, among biopsies of women who had cervical cancer. He went on to show that more than one H.P.V. type could lead to cervical cancer, in part by cloning H.P.V. 16 and another type, 18. Further research has shown that the two H.P.V. types are consistently found in about 70 percent of cervical cancer biopsies throughout the world, the institute said.

—LAWRENCE K. ALTMAN

Obituaries October 15, 2007–October 15, 2008

Adams, Edie, 81, U.S. actress who sang on Broadway as Rosalind Russell's sister, Eileen, in *Wonderful Town* (1953) and as Daisy Mae in *Li'l Abner* (1956, Tony Award), made several movies, and is perhaps best remembered for her come-hither TV commercials for Muriel cigars. Of pneumonia and cancer, Los Angeles, Oct. 15, 2008.

Agee, Philip, 72, C.I.A. operative whose *Inside the Company: CIA Diary* (1975) outlined the quotidian life of an officer as well exposing names and activities of covert operatives, bringing accusations of traitor, though he claimed moral high ground in revealing agency excess. Of peritonitis, Havana, Jan. 7, 2008.

Aoki, Rocky, 69, Japanese restaurateur whose popular Benihana chain featured showy knife-wielding chefs along with the native food they prepared. Of pneumonia, New York, July 10, 2008.

Arnold, Eddy, 89, Tennessee-born singer who brought country style to city stages and studios with many hit records climbing to the top of pop charts, notably "Make the World Go Away" (1965). Cause undisclosed, Nashville, May 8, 2008.

Bavasi, Buzzie (Emil Joseph), 93, baseball executive, mainly with Dodgers, in Brooklyn and Los Angeles, he upheld black player acceptance and free agency, as well opening California to major leagues. Of old age, San Diego, May 1, 2008.

Béjart, Maurice, 80, French choreographer whose company, Ballet of the 20th Century, was applauded by many fans for innovation but assailed by critics for his gaudy pop style. Of heart and kidney disease, Lausanne, Switzerland, Nov. 22, 2007.

Bhutto, Benazir, 54, Pakistan prime minister 1988-90, 1993-96, both times dismissed on corruption allegations, daughter of leading Pakistan politician who was executed by the military; returning from decade-long exile and seeking a third term, she was assassinated, Rawalpindi, Dec. 27, 2007.

Bishop, Joey, 89, Brooklyn-born comedian whose 1950s act impressed Frank Sinatra, leading to nightclub and movie work with the Rat Pack of Las Vegas, and *Ocean's Eleven* fame, and a TV network talk show. Of multiple causes, Newport Beach, Calif., Oct. 17, 2007.

Bolt, Tommy, 92, Hall of Fame golfer who won 15 PGA tournaments 1950-65, including 1958 U.S. Open; his long drives were often overshadowed by a short fuse and his nickname, Thunder Bolt. Of liver failure, Batesville, Ark., Aug. 30, 2008.

Brewer, Teresa, 76, Toledo-born pop singer who chirped her way to the top of the 1950s charts with many peppy records, notably "Music! Music! Music!" and "Ricochet Romance." Of brain disease, New Rochelle, N.Y., Oct. 17, 2007.

Brillstein, Bernie, 77, Manhattan-born movie and TV agent who rose from the William Morris mailroom to Hollywood's Paramount peak; wide-ranging clients included John Belushi, Gilda Radner and the Muppets. Of pulmonary disease, Los Angeles, Aug. 7, 2008.

Britton, Sherry, 89, New Jersey-born burlesque star in 1930s and '40s; after stripping was banned in New York, played in legit musicals, notably as Miss Adelaide in the national company of *Guys and Dolls*. Of natural causes, New York, April 1, 2008.

Buckley, William F. Jr., 82, champion of conservatism who spread his views through all media—TV's *Firing Line*, the right-wing magazine *National Review* and more than 50 books—always with arch wit and grandiloquent rhetoric. Of diabetes and emphysema, Stamford, Conn., Feb. 28, 2008.

Butz, Earl L., 98, U.S. secretary of agriculture 1971-76, forceful in support of reducing farm subsidies and increasing grain shipments to Soviet Union, but forced to resign after making a publicized racist joke. Of natural causes, Kensington, Md., Feb. 2, 2008.

Cachao (Lopez), 89, Havana-born musician who created the mambo in late 1930s by rushing the ending to traditional Cuban dance music, filling dance floors ever since. Of kidney failure, Coral Gables, Fla., March 22, 2008.

Capa, Cornell, 90, Budapest-born photojournalist, he followed his brother, war photographer Robert Capa, into the craft, first for *Life* magazine, then as founder of the International Center of Photography. Cause undisclosed, New York, May 23, 2008.

Caray, Skip, 68, Atlanta Braves announcer, the middle of three generations of baseball voices, equally adept at amusing, irritating and exhilarating fans. Of diabetes and liver failure, Atlanta, Aug. 3, 2008.

Carlin, George, 71, Manhattan-born comic whose 1960s TV popularity morphed into counterculture icon status of 1970s and beyond with witty critiques of hypocrisy in society and its language, notably the famed obscene "Seven Words;" winner of 2008 Mark Twain Humor Prize, awarded posthumously. Of heart failure, Santa Monica, Calif., June 22, 2008.

Charisse, Cyd (Tula Elice Finklea), 86, Texas-born dancer best known for the two top Golden Age musicals, *Singin' in the Rain* (1952) with Gene Kelly and *The Band Wagon* (1953) with Fred Astaire; also danced Garbo's Ninotchka role in *Silk Stockings* (1957). Of a heart attack, Los Angeles, June 17, 2008.

Chinmoy, Sri, 76, Hindu guru from India whose message of ethereal meditation and heavy exercise resonated with thousands of followers including Muhammad Ali and Carl Lewis; made headlines lifting planes and trucks, as well as many world figures such as Nelson Mandela. Of a heart attack, New York, Oct. 11, 2007.

Clarke, Arthur C., 90, British master of science fiction whose vision led to space exploration and satellite communication; best known as author of film and novel *2001: A Space Odyssey* (1968) as well as *Childhood's End* (1953). Of old age, Colombo, Sri Lanka, March 19, 2008.

Collins, Dottie, 84, California-born women's baseball pitcher in World War II league formed in the absence of men at war; also aided in perpetuating history of league, leading to popular movie *A League of Their Own* (1992). After a stroke, Fort Wayne, Ind., Aug. 12, 2008.

Crane, Les, 74, talk-show host who started interviewing celebrities on radio then moved to TV and a national audience that enjoyed his '60s hip rudeness, though network execs did not and soon canceled the show. Cause undisclosed, Greenbrae, Calif., July 13, 2008.

Daniel, Margaret Truman, 83, daughter of Pres. Truman and wife of *New York Times* journalist Clifton Daniel, she made her own mark as author of 32 books, including 23 best-selling mysteries. Cause undisclosed, Chicago, Jan. 29, 2008.

Darman, Richard G., 64, White House adviser to presidents, from Nixon to Bush 41, for whom he served as budget director and led Bush to reverse "no new taxes" pledge. Of leukemia, McLean Va., Jan. 25, 2008.

Darwish, Mahmoud, 67, Palestinian poet whose classical Arab verses celebrated both political protest and personal passion; said to have written Arafat's "guns and olive branch" 1974 U.N. speech. After heart surgery, Houston, Tex., Aug. 9, 2008.

Dassin, Jules, 96, U.S. movie director whose Hollywood films include *Brute Force* (1947) and *The Naked City* (1948); the blacklist sent him to Europe, making *Never on Sunday* (1960) and *Topkapi* (1964) with wife, Melina Mercouri. Cause undisclosed, Athens, March 31, 2008.

Day, Laraine, 87, Hollywood actress best known as Mary Lamont, dedicated nurse in popular *Dr. Kildare* series of 1940s, and for Hitchcock's *Foreign Correspondent* (1940); in 1947 married baseball's Leo Durocher. Of natural causes, Ivins, Utah, Nov. 10, 2007.

DeBakey, Michael, 99, U.S. surgeon renowned worldwide for innovations in bypass operations on millions; pioneer in smoking-cancer link; politically skilled in advising world leaders and making Houston center for research. Of old age, Houston, July 12, 2008.

Diddley, Bo, 79, Mississippi-born Otha Ellas Bates was a founding father of rock 'n' roll who gave the music its pulsing three-pause-two beat, along with the frenzied moves taken up by Elvis. Of heart failure, Archer, Fla., June 2, 2008.

Dith, Pran, 65, Cambodian photojournalist for *The New York Times* whose imprisonment and escape from the Khmer Rouge was the basis of 1984 film *The Killing Fields.* Of pancreatic cancer, New Brunswick, N.J., March 30, 2008.

Elliott, Osborn, 83, Manhattan-born editor of *Newsweek* 1961-69, he moved the magazine away from *Time*-speak into broader coverage of civil rights and women's issues; later served as dean of Columbia Graduate School of Journalism. Of cancer, New York, Sept. 28, 2008.

Fagles, Robert, 74, Philadelphia-born professor who made the classical hat trick with best-selling translations of the *Iliad* (1990), *Odyssey* (1996) and *Aeneid* (2006). Of prostate cancer, Princeton, N.J., March 26, 2008.

Felker, Clay, 82, founding editor of *New York*, the glossy magazine of New Journalism and star writers such as Tom Wolfe and Jimmy Breslin on the highs and lows of the city's cultural life, captured in catchy graphics. Of natural causes, New York, July 1, 2008.

Ferrer, Mel, 90, New Jersey-born actor best known for uncertain heroes he played in *The Brave Bulls* (1951) and *Lili* (1953); directed wife, Audrey Hepburn, in *Green Mansions* (1959). Cause undisclosed, Santa Barbara, Calif., June 2, 2008.

Fields, Freddie, 84, Hollywood powerhouse agent, co-founder of C.M.A., he handled many top movie stars, including Fred Astaire, Judy Garland, Paul Newman and Robert Redford. Of lung cancer, Bevery Hills, Dec. 11, 2007.

Finegan, Bill, 91, Newark-born musician who partnered with Eddie Sauter to form the postwar Sauter-Finegan Orchestra, notable for its unusual sound and classical roots. Of pneumonia, Bridgeport, Conn., June 4, 2008.

Fischer, Bobby, 64, U.S. chess master who made headlines beating Russian Boris Spassky for world championship in 1972 (also in 1992) before becoming a troubled, paranoid recluse who renounced U.S. citizenship. Of kidney failure, Reykjavik, Iceland, Jan. 17, 2008.

Fogelberg, Dan, 56, U.S. singer/composer whose soft-rock hits of the '70s and '80s included "The Power of Gold" and "Leader of the Band," a memorial to his bandleader father. Of prostate cancer, at home in Maine, Dec. 16, 2007.

Fraser, Douglas A., 91, Glasgow-born union leader who served as president of United Automobile Workers 1977-83; promoted concessions to automakers, notably Chrysler, in time of lagging U.S. sales. Of emphysema, Southfield, Mich., Feb. 23, 2008.

Getty, Estelle, 84, Manhattan-born actress best known for playing mothers, from Harvey Fierstein's in *Torch Song Trilogy* (1981) to the lovingly acerbic Sophia Petrillo on TV's *Golden Girls* (1985-92). Of Lewy body dementia, Los Angeles, July 22, 2008.

Giroux, Robert, 94, Farrar, Straus & Giroux editor in chief, he worked with such prestigious authors as T.S. Eliot and George Orwell and then-new writers Robert Lowell, Bernard Malamud, Flannery O'Connor among many others, though he regretted missing out on *The Catcher in the Rye* and *On the Road.* Of natural causes, Sept. 5, 2008.

Giuffre, Jimmy, 86, Dallas-born jazz musician, composer and teacher from 1947 on, best known for smooth clarinet and sax playing in everchanging styles; composed "Four Brothers" hit for Woody Herman band. Of Parkinson's disease, Pittsfield, Mass., April 24, 2008.

Goheen, Robert F., 88, Princeton University president 1957-72; his many campus innovations included coeducation and small classes, as well as large additions of faculty and buildings. Of heart failure, Princeton, N.J. March 31, 2008.

Goulet, Robert, 73, U.S. singer who made a smashing Broadway debut in *Camelot* (1960) as handsome Lancelot, who broke hearts with "If Ever I Would Leave You," then had a long career of recordings and nightclub appearances; won Tony for *The Happy Time* (1968). Of pulmonary fibrosis, Los Angeles, Oct. 30, 2007.

Gray, Simon, 71, British playwright, best known for *Butley* (1971) and *Otherwise Engaged* (1977), in which witty intellectual protagonists face emotional breakdown in a single day; several memoirs such as *The Last Cigarette* (2008) chronicle his real-life troubles. Of lung cancer, London, Aug. 6, 2008.

Greenglass, Ruth, 84, sister-in-law of Ethel Rosenberg, her testimony in the 1950s atomic spy trial led to the guilty verdict and execution of both Julius and Ethel Rosenberg, testimony possibly perjured. Cause undisclosed, New York, April 7, 2008.

Grizzard, George, 79, U.S. actor adept at drama and comedy, notably in two Albee plays: *Who's Afraid of Virginia Woolf* (1962) and 1996 revival of *A Delicate Balance*, winning Tony Award; made Broadway debut in 1955 in *The Desperate Hours.* Of lung cancer, New York, Oct. 2, 2008.

Hagen, Earle, 88, Chicago-born composer of themes for TV shows, including *Dick Van Dyke Show, I Spy*, and most memorably *The Andy Griffith Show*, supplying the loping whistle himself. Of natural causes, Ranch Mirage, Calif., May 26, 2008.

Haider, Jörg, 58, Austrian right-wing politician, governor of Carinthia province, he opposed immigration and European Union policies and lauded past Nazi policies; his party made significant gains against major left parties in September elections. Of auto accident injuries, Klagenfurt, Carinthia, Oct. 11, 2008.

Haines, Connie, 87, Savannah-born pop singer on radio, TV and in nightclubs and movies, she began as a band singer with Tommy Dorsey, alongside up-and-coming vocalists Frank Sinatra and Jo Stafford. Of myasthenia gravis, Clearwater Beach, Fla., Sept. 22, 2008.

Hardwick, Elizabeth, 91, Kentucky-born writer who aspired to the New York intellectual set, becoming one of its leading critics and editors, notably as co-founder and contributor to the influential *New York Review of Books*; persevered in turbulent marriage to poet Robert Lowell 1949-70. Of natural causes, New York, Dec. 2, 2007.

Hartack, Bill, 74, winning jockey–five Kentucky Derbys, three Preakness Stakes, one Belmont Stakes–Hall of Fame 1959 and first to win over $3 million in one year. Of heart disease, Freer, Tex., Nov. 26, 2007.

Hartford, Huntington, 97, A&P heir who came into $90 million and lost $80 million on many schemes such as the 1964 NYC Columbus Circle "lollipop" museum for mediocre art he liked. Of leisurely old age, Bahamas, May 19, 2008.

Hayes, Isaac, 65, Tennessee singer, composer and sometime actor whose Oscar-winning "Theme From Shaft" (1971) epitomized his sexy style of soul music; last acted in *Soul Men* (2008). After an earlier stroke, East Memphis, Tenn., Aug. 10, 2008.

Helms, Jesse, 86, as North Carolina Republican senator 1972-2003 he enjoyed taking tough conservative stands against liberal policies on welfare, civil rights, trade and modern art. Of natural causes, Raleigh, N.C. July 4, 2008.

Herlie, Eileen, 90, Glasgow-born actress; before 32 years as Myrtle Fargate on TV soap *All My Children*, she played Queen Gertrude to the Hamlet of both Laurence Olivier (onscreen, 1948) and Richard Burton (onstage, 1964). Of pneumonia, New York, Oct. 8, 2008

Heston, Charlton, 84, Hollywood actor best known for his towering signature roles—Moses in *The Ten Commandments* (1956), title role in *Ben-Hur* (1959) and Michelangelo in *The Agony and the Ecstasy* (1965); bestowed same authority to presidency of N.R.A., 1998. Of Alzheimer's disease, Beverly Hills, Calif., April 5, 2008.

Hillary, Sir Edmund, 88, New Zealand mountaineer; he and guide Tenzing Norgay were the first to climb Everest's summit, 5.5 miles in the air, May 29, 1953. Cause undisclosed, Auckland, New Zealand, Jan. 11, 2008.

Hinckley, Gordon B., 97, Mormon Church leader since 1995, its 15th president and prophet, he promoted worldwide expansion and openness, modifying the church's logo to make "Jesus Christ" more prominent than "Latter-day Saints." Of natural causes, Salt Lake City, Jan. 27, 2008.

Hoffman, Albert, 102, Swiss chemist whose experiments on rye fungus led to accidental discovery of LSD, potent fuel of the counterculture, a drug he dubbed his "problem child" in 1979 book. Of a heart attack, Basel, April 29, 2008.

Holmes, Tommy, 91, Brooklyn-born outfielder for Boston Braves whose 37-game hitting streak in 1945 broke Rogers Hornsby's N.L. 1922 record of 33; Pete Rose hit in 44 straight games in 1978. Of old age, Boca Raton, Fla., April 14, 2008.

Hua, Guofeng, 87, Chinese party chairman and prime minister for brief period after Mao's death in 1976, he ended the Cultural Revolution and began move toward economic revival before being deposed in 1980. Of old age, Beijing, Aug. 20, 2008.

Hurwicz, Leonid, 90, University of Minnesota economist, co-winner of 2007 Nobel Prize for studies of game theory and the effect of incentives on economic mechanisms. Of kidney failure, Minneapolis, June 24, 2008.

Hyde, Henry J., 83, Illinois Republican congressman (1975-2007) who led House impeachment charges against Pres. Clinton; best known as author of 1976 Hyde Amendment, which denied payment for abortion to Medicaid recipients. After heart surgery, Chicago, Nov. 29, 2007.

Hyland, William, 79, U.S. foreign policy expert who advised Presidents Ford and Carter and Secretary of State Kissinger in 1970s, then served as editor of *Foreign Affairs* in 1980s and '90s. Of aortic aneurysm, Fairfax, Va., March 25, 2008.

Jones, Stephanie Tubbs, 58, Ohio Democrat first elected to House of Representatives in 1998, former chief prosecutor for Cuyahoga County, a liberal voice for health care and mortgage policy reform. Of brain aneurysm rupture, Cleveland, Aug. 20, 2008.

Jordan, Hamilton, 63, Georgia political adviser who engineered Pres. Carter's successful campaign and became his chief aide, often irking Washington insiders. Of cancer, Atlanta, May 20, 2008.

Kelley, Alton, 67, New England native whose artistic skills flowered in partnership with Stanley Mouse in 1960's San Francisco, fusing eclectic imagery and Art Nouveau style into psychedelic posters for the Grateful Dead and defining the look of the counterculture. Of complications from osteoporosis, Petaluma, Calif., June 1, 2008.

Kerr, Deborah, 86, British actress whose proper persona in such films as *Edward, My Son* (1949) and *King Soloman's Mines* (1950) was swept away in the crashing surf as she kissed Burt Lancaster in *From Here to Eternity* (1953), returning to ladylike roles in *The King and I* (1956) and *An Affair to Remember* (1957). Of Parkinson's disease, Suffolk, England, Oct. 17, 2007.

Key, Ted, 95, U.S. cartoonist who in 1943 drew "Hazel," the cheeky maid who ruled the suburban household where she worked, first in *Saturday Evening Post* cartoon, then in 1961 TV show starring Shirley Booth. Of bladder cancer, Tredyffrin Township, Pa., May 3, 2008.

Keyes, Evelyn, 91, Hollywood actress who lost her on-screen fiancé to sister Scarlett O'Hara in *Gone With the Wind* (1939) but didn't let that keep her from marrying many times in real life. Of cancer, Montecito, Calif., July 4, 2008.

Kidd, Michael, 92, Brooklyn-born choreographer for Broadway, winner of five Tony Awards, including *Guys and Dolls* (1951), and Hollywood, notably *The Band Wagon* (1953) and the rousing *Seven Brides for Seven Brothers* (1954). Of cancer, Los Angeles, Dec. 23, 2007.

Knerr, Richard, 82, California co-founder of Wham-O, the company that endowed leisurely America with the Hula Hoop, Frisbee and Super-Ball. After a stroke, Arcadia, Calif., Jan. 14, 2008.

Knievel, Evel, 69, U.S. motorcycle stuntman who attracted millions (and made millions) to watch him fly over fountains, canyons, and car wrecks, as much to see him land safely as to break bones. Of diabetes and lung disease, Clearwater, Fla., Nov. 30, 2007.

Korman, Harvey, 81, Chicago-born actor best known for his many wacky skits on Carol Burnett's TV shows, winning four Emmys and one Golden Globe; roles in Mel Brooks movies include Hedley Lamarr in *Blazing Saddles* (1974). Of aneurysm rupture, Los Angeles, May 29, 2008.

Kornberg, Arthur, 89, Brooklyn-born scientist, co-winner of 1959 Nobel Prize in Medicine for discovery of a DNA enzyme that has led to advances in genetics and development of drugs for cancers and AIDS. Of respiratory failure, Stanford, Calif., Oct. 26, 2007.

Kowalski, Killer (Walter), 81, wrestling warrior on early TV who got his name when he ripped off an opponent's ear; outside the ring he was a gentle giant vegetarian. Of a heart attack, Everett, Mass., Aug. 30, 2008.

Lamb, Willis Jr., 94, U.S scientist was co-winner of 1955 Nobel Prize in Physics for discovery of the "Lamb shift," slight movement in hydrogen atoms due to collisions of virtual particles in what was thought to be empty space. Of gallstone disorder, Tucson, Ariz., May 15, 2008.

Lantos, Tom, 80, California Democratic congressman since 1980; born in Hungary, sole Holocaust survivor to serve in Congress, tenacious champion of human rights. Of esophageal cancer, Bethesda, Md., Feb. 11, 2008.

Lederberg, Joshua, 82, New Jersey-born scientist, co-winner of 1958 Nobel Prize in Medicine for discoveries of genetic and bacterial development, creating the discipline of molecular biology; Rockefeller University president 1978-80; awarded Medal of Freedom 2006. Of pneumonia, New York, Feb. 4, 2008.

Ledger, Heath, 28, heartthrob Australian actor whose supple style promised stardom in *Casanova* and *Brokeback Mountain* (both 2005) and as the Joker in *The Dark Knight* (2008). Of accidental sleep aid overdose, New York, Jan. 22, 2008.

Leigh, Dorian, 91, Texas-born fashion model, considered by many the first supermodel, her image adorned the covers of *Vogue, Harper's Bazaar* and other magazines in the 1940s and '50s; sister of equally famous model Suzy Parker. Of old age, Falls Church, Va., July 7 2008.

Levin, Ira, 78, New York writer of novels and plays that give millions of fans entertaining thrills and chills, notably *Rosemary's Baby* (1967) and *The Stepford Wives* (1972), as well as Broadway hit *Deathtrap* (1978-82). Of natural causes at home, New York, Nov. 12, 2007.

Lorenz, Edward N., 90, M.I.T. meteorologist; forecasting experiments led to development of chaos theory, in which "butterfly's wings in Brazil can set off a tornado in Texas." Of cancer, Cambridge, Mass., April 16, 2008.

Mac, Bernie, 50, Chicago-born comic actor who moved from offbeat clubs to Las Vegas, then to movies and finally to TV for his best work in *The Bernie Mac Show* (2001-06), playing a cranky but softhearted foster dad. Of pneumonia, Chicago, Aug. 9, 2008.

Maharishi Mahesh Yogi, ca. 95, Indian guru who in 1957 set the West on the path of transcendental meditation (TM), now a worldwide organization that became popular in 1968, after the Beatles joined him in the Himalayas. Cause undisclosed, Netherlands, Feb. 5, 2008.

Mailer, Norman, 84, New York literary lion whose 1948 novel, *The Naked and the Dead,* brought celebrity he never shunned—as a writer, opinionated TV talking head, candidate for mayor or movie director; of his 30 books *The Armies of the Night* (1968) and *The Execution's Song* (1979) won Pulitzer Prizes. Of kidney failure, New York, Nov. 10, 2007.

Mann, Abby, 83, Philadelphia-born scriptwriter for film and TV who specialized in social justice themes, most notably Oscar-winning *Judgment at Nuremberg* (1961). Of heart failure, Beverly Hills, Calif., March 25, 2008.

Mann, Delbert, 87, Hollywood director of Oscar-winning *Marty* (1955) started out in TV with hundreds of live broadcasts; his NBC *Heidi* (1968) brought fan outrage when the live show started promptly before the end of a close football game. Of pneumonia, Los Angeles, Nov. 11, 2007.

Martin, Dick, 86, Michigan-born comic; with partner Dan Rowan he socked it to America with *Laugh-In* (1968-73), revolutionizing TV with giddy gags and an array of guest celebrities, including Richard Nixon, being silly. Of respiratory failure, Santa Monica, Calif., May 24, 2008.

McGee, Max, 75, Green Bay Packers receiver who unexpectedly played in first Super Bowl (1967) and caught Bart Starr's pass and scored first Super Bowl touchdown, Packers defeating K.C. Chiefs 35-10. After accidental fall, Deephaven, Minn., Oct. 20. 2007.

McKay, Jim, 86, steady anchor of ABC's *Wide World of Sports* and many Olympics, notably the 1972 Munich Games at which terrorists killed 11 Israelis. Of natural causes, Monkton, Md., June 7, 2008.

Metzenbaum, Howard, 90, Ohio Democratic senator 1976-95, a tenacious, sometimes irritating, voice pro liberal causes and anti big business interests. Of old age, Aventura, Fla., March 12, 2008.

Minghella, Anthony, 54, British film director noted for Oscar winner *The English Patient* (1997) as well as *The Talented Mr. Ripley* (1999); directed *Madama Butterfly* at Metropolitan Opera (2006). After cancer surgery, London, March 18, 2008.

Moiseyev, Igor, 101, Ukrainian-born choreographer; founder of the popular Moiseyev Dance Company, which broke cold war barriers in 1958 when Sol Hurok brought the folk dance troupe to the Metropolitan Opera House and Ed Sullian presented them on TV. Of old age, Moscow, Nov. 2, 2007.

Moore Robin, 82, U.S. writer best known for *The Green Berets* (1965), as well as the official song of the unit, "The Ballad of the Green Berets," and *The French Connection* (1969). Cause undisclosed, Hopkinsville, Ky., Feb. 21, 2008.

Murcer, Bobby, 62, Oklahoma-born baseball All-Star (1971-75) played center field for N.Y. Yankees 1965-83, then became team's enduring broadcast voice. Of brain cancer, Oklahoma City, July 12, 2008.

Muschamp, Herbert, 59, *New York Times* architecture critic 1992-2004, who praised the Post-Modern work of Frank Gehry, Jean Nouvel and others, often in an idiosyncratic and lyrical style. Of lung cancer, New York, Oct. 2, 2008.

Mwanawasa, Levy, 59, Zambia president first elected 2002 and re-elected 2006, he opposed corruption within the struggling land-locked nation as well as the corruption of Pres. Robert Mugabe of Zimbabwe. After a stroke, Paris, Aug. 19, 2008.

Newman, Paul, 83, Cleveland-born actor whose blazing intelligence and blue eyes in 60-plus movies since 1954 brought vitality to a wide range of characters, notably Fast Eddie in *The Hustler* (1961) and *The Color of Money* (1986, Oscar), the willful convict in *Cool Hand Luke* (1967), *Butch Cassidy* (1969), and the gang despot in *Road to Perdition* (2002), his last film; also famed as philanthropist, liberal activist and champion race car driver. Of cancer, Westport, Conn., Sept. 26, 2008.

Oerter, Al, 71, Long Island-born Olympic champion who won gold medal in discus throwing 1956, 1960, 1964, and 1968, a first for consecutive wins in modern games. Of a heart attack, Fort Meyers, Fla., Oct. 1, 2007.

Page, Anita, 98, born in Flushing, Queens, a star of silent films who made the move to talkies with *The Broadway Melody* (1929), the first musical Oscar winner, but then retired at age 23 in 1933. Of old age, Los Angeles, Sept. 6, 2008.

Palade, George, 95, Romanian-born scientist, co-winner 1974 Nobel Prize in Physiology or Medicine "for the creation of modern cell biology" by peering into deep cell structures with the electron microscope; also won Lasker Award and National Medal of Science. Of Parkinson's disease, Del Mar, Calif., Oct. 7, 2008

Pausch, Randy, 47, computer science professor whose "last lecture" cheerfully focused on his impending death and gave comfort and inspiration to millions via the Internet and a best-selling book. Of pancreatic cancer, Chesapeake, Va., July 25, 2008.

Peterson, Oscar, 82, Montreal-born jazz piano master, acclaimed worldwide for his fleet technique and ability to accompany such giants as Louis Armstrong, Ella Fitzgerald and Billie Holiday with grace; recorded many albums, winning eight Grammys, and starred at Jazz at the Philharmonic. Of kidney failure, outside Toronto, Dec. 23, 2007.

Pleshette, Suzanne, 70, Brooklyn-born actress who played Emily Hartley, the dry-witted, dark velvet-voiced wife on TV's *Bob Newhart Show* (1972-78), and the teacher victimized by Hitchcock's *Birds* (1963). Of lung cancer, Los Angeles, Jan. 19, 2008.

Podres, Johnny, 75, Brooklyn Dodgers pitcher who put the stopper on "wait till next year" in 1955 by winning Game 7 and beating Yankees, giving Brooklyn its only World Series championship. Of heart and kidney failure, Queensbury, N.Y., Jan. 13, 2008.

Pollack, Sydney, 73, U.S. director of star-filled films, notably *Tootsie* (1982) with Hoffman and his Oscar-winning *Out of Africa* (1985) with Redford and Streep; also a producer and actor. Of cancer, Los Angeles, May 26, 2008.

Rauschenberg, Robert, 82, Texas-born multimedia artist who found beauty in everyday objects, transforming painting, sculpture, photography and dance, and working with experimentalists such as John Cage and Merce Cunningham. Of heart failure, Captiva Island, Fla., May 12, 2008.

Reynolds, Nick, 75, founding member of the legendary folk group, the Kingston Trio, whose commercial success in the late 50s and early 60s was matched only by the Beatles, and who paved the way for Bob Dylan, Peter, Paul and Mary, and many others. "Tom Dooley," "M.T.A.," and "A Worried Man" were all huge hits. Of acute respiratory disease, San Diego, Oct. 1, 2008.

Rincy, Hal, 75, Seattle-born advertising writer whose folksy words, and sometimes voice, helped sell America on such products as Saturn cars, wine coolers and the "morning again" presidency of Ronald Reagan. Of cancer, San Francisco, March 24, 2008.

Robbe-Grillet, Alain, 85, French novelist and filmmaker best known to U.S. movie buffs for script of *Last Year at Marienbad* (1961); 1963 essay created the "New Novel," rejecting norms of plot and character. Of a heart attack, Paris, Feb. 18, 2008.

Robbins, Irvine, 90, ice cream magnate who put more than good humor into Baskin-Robbins franchise with first 31 then more than 1,000 wild flavors. Of natural causes, Rancho Mirage, Calif., May 5, 2008.

Russell, John, 89, British art critic who championed modern English painters such as Francis Bacon and Lucian Freud in many reviews for *The Sunday Times* of London and *The New York Times.* Of cancer, New York, Aug. 23, 2008.

Russert, Tim, 58, Buffalo-born NBC journalist who took over *Meet the Press* in 1991 and made it into a tough forum politicians sought out at their risk; a devoted family man, he wrote of his father in best-selling *Big Russ & Me.* Of a heart attack at work, Washington, D.C., June 13, 2008.

Saffir, Herbert, 90, New York-born engineer who devised the scale Category 1 to 5, used to describe hurricane force, now familiar on TV to millions in a storm's path; later expanded and now known as Saffir-Simpson scale. After surgery, Miami, Nov. 21, 2007.

Saint Laurent, Yves, 71, French couturier who ruled the fashion world 1958-2002, dressing society women in high style, then the rest of the world in ready to wear, notably pants for all women. Of a brain tumor, Paris, June 1, 2008.

Scheider, Roy, 75, New Jersey-born actor best remembered as the anxious cop in *Jaws* (1975) and an agitated "Bob Fosse" in *All That Jazz* (1979). Of multiple myeloma and staph infection, Little Rock, Ark., Feb. 10, 2008.

Scofield, Paul, 86, British actor, perhaps the finest in second half of 20th century, acclaimed for definitive King Lear and other Shakespeare roles, but best known as Sir Thomas More in *A Man for All Seasons,* onstage, 1960 (Tony), onscreen, 1966 (Oscar). Of leukemia, southern England, March 19, 2008.

Schwartz, Tony, 84, New York radio producer and ad man, best known for TV spot he created for 1964 Johnson presidential campaign—a child pulls petals from a daisy as an ominous voice counts down to an atomic explosion. Of heart disease, New York, June 14, 2008.

Simplot, J.R., 99, Idaho potato farmer who fed World War II troops, then gave postwar America its first edible frozen French fries, mainly through McDonald's, making him a billionaire. Of old age, Boise, Idaho, May 25, 2008.

Smith, Ian, 88, prime minister of Rhodesia, who unilaterally declared independence from Great Britain in 1965 and stubbornly enforced white rule against pressure from the West until forced into negotiations with black leaders in 1978. After a stroke, Cape Town, Nov. 20, 2007.

Snow, Tony, 53, conservative TV and print journalist who became White House press secretary in 2007 and enjoyed contentious back-and-forth with fellow reporters. Of colon cancer, Washington, D.C., July 12, 2008.

Solotaroff, Theodore, 80, New Jersey-born editor who created the influential *New American Review* (1967-77) a paperback anthology of fiction and journalism, introducing such writers as Philip Roth and Conor Cruise O'Brien. Of pneumonia, East Quogue, N.Y., Aug. 8, 2008.

Solzhenitsyn, Aleksandr, 89, Russian literary titan, awarded 1970 Nobel Prize; famed for relentless opposition to Soviet Union with such works as *A Day in the Life of Ivan Denisovich* (1962) and *The Gulag Archipelago* (1973), leading to arrest, deportation and long U.S. exile when he was viewed as anti-Semitic and reactionary in critiques of U.S. democracy and materialism. Of heart disease, Moscow, Aug. 3, 2008.

Stafford, Jo, 90, peerless pop singer of 1940s and '50s adept at standards as well as novelties, from "You Belong to Me" and "Haunted Heart" to a hillbilly "Temptation" with a voice so pitch-perfect her "Darlene Edwards" also sang exactly offkey in comedy records. Of congestive heart failure, Century City, Calif., July 16, 2008.

di Stefano, Giuseppe, 86, Italian tenor who made Metropolitan Opera debut in 1948; applauded for sumptuous voice and style onstage but whose offstage life led to decline by late 1950s; often appeared with Maria Callas. Of head injuries in 2004 attack, Milan, March 3, 2008.

Steinway, Henry Z., 93, born on Park Avenue, the last of his name to run the famous piano manufacturer, which continues to supply concert grands to the world's stages. Of old age, New York, Sept. 18, 2008.

Stockhausen, Karlheinz, 79, German composer of 1950s electronic music, rigorous and abstract; later wrote seven-cycle opera *Light* (1977-2002) fantastic stage works produced at La Scala and Leipzig Opera. Cause undisclosed, Kuerten-Kettenberg, Germany, Dec. 5, 2007.

Suharto, 86, Indonesian president 1965-98; his iron rule brought economic success overshadowed by years of corruption and military repression, leading to chaos and his overthrow. Of multiple organ failure, Jakarta, Jan. 27, 2008.

Teicher, Lou, 83, U.S. classically trained pianist who teamed up with Arthur Ferrante to form a popular duo noted for arrangements of movie themes, including *The Apartment* and *West Side Story*, in more than 150 albums. Of heart failure, Highlands, N.C., Aug. 3, 2008.

Templeton, John, 95, U.S.-born turned British citizen who earned billions in investments and created a foundation to award $1.6 million Templeton Prize for "progress in religion," especially studies of the relationship between science and religion. Of pneumonia, Nassau, Bahamas, July 8, 2008.

Thompson, Hank, 82, Texas-born country music singer/songwriter of 60 million records with 29 Top 10 hits 1948 to 1975, including 1952's No. 1 "The Wild Side of Life," featuring the lyric "I didn't know God made honky-tonk angels." Of lung cancer, Keller, Tex., Nov. 6, 2007.

Tibbets, Paul W. Jr., 92, pilot of the plane, named Enola Gay after his mother, that dropped the atomic bomb on Hiroshima, August 6, 1945; later served in the Strategic Air Command, rising to one-star general. Of natural causes, at home, Columbus, Ohio, Nov. 1, 2007.

Tillion, Germaine, 100, French intellectual who helped found the Resistance and survived a Nazi death camp, she is regarded as a moral sage

for her many works, including books on the Algerian problem and studies of women's issues. Of old age, St.-Mande, France, April 18, 2008.

Turner, Ike, 76, Mississippi Delta-born R&B pioneer remembered as the man who discovered Tina Turner, with whom he maintained an abusive relationship during their successful years. Of emphysema, San Marcos, Calif., Dec. 12, 2007.

Upshaw, Gene, 63, Pro Football Hall of Fame guard who played in three Super Bowls, then served as head of the N.F.L. players union for the last 25 years. Of pancreatic cancer, Lake Tahoe, Calif., Aug. 20, 2008.

Vesco, Robert, 73, Detroit-born financier who became a fugitive in 1971 from U.S. fraud and bribery charges, landing in various Caribbean countries by giving money to political leaders; Cuba welcomed him in 1982, but jailed him in 1996 on fraud charges. Of lung cancer, Havana, Nov. 23, 2007.

Wagoner, Porter, 80, U.S. country music singer/composer who starred on the Grand Ole Opry for more than 50 years and hosted his *Porter Wagoner Show* for 21 years to 3.5 million TV fans; noted for many duets with Dolly Parton. Of lung cancer, Nashville, Oct. 28, 2008.

Wallace, Davis Foster, 46, U.S. writer whose challenging style and searching outlook brought celebrity and cult status, notably for *Infinite Jest* (1996; 1,079 pages), which did not alleviate lifelong depression. A suicide, Claremont, Calif., Sept. 12, 2008.

Watkin, David, 82, British cinematographer whose sumptuous camera work in *Out of Africa* (1985) won an Oscar; other films include *Catch-22* (1970) and *Chariots of Fire* (1981). Of cancer, Brighton, England, Feb. 19, 2008.

Weller, Thomas H., 93, U.S. physician, co-winner of 1954 Nobel Prize in Physiology or Medicine for work on tissue cultures of the polio virus that led to the polio vaccine, as well as other viral vaccines. Of old age, Needham, Mass., Aug. 23, 2008.

Wexler, Jerry, 91, Manhattan-born record producer who renamed "race" music "rhythm and blues" and promoted black music and performers such as Ray Charles and Aretha Franklin. Of congestive heart failure, Sarasota, Fla., Aug. 15, 2008.

Wheeler, John A., 96, Princeton physicist who inspired generations of students, debated with Einstein and Bohr, and shed new light on dead stars, naming them "black holes"; pioneer in development of atomic and nuclear bombs. Of pneumonia, Hightstown, N.J., April 13, 2008.

Whiteley, Frank Jr., 93, horse racing Hall of Fame trainer of champions Tom Rolfe, Forego and, most notably, Ruffian, the ill-starred filly that collapsed at Belmont July 6, 1975. Of old age, Camden S.C., May 2, 2008.

Widmark, Richard, 93, Hollywood actor who burst into stardom playing a psycho killer in *Kiss of Death* (1947), then more than 60 movies, playing wide-ranging villains and heroes, notably in *Night and the City* (1950), *Judgment at Nuremberg* (1961) and *Cheyenne Autumn* (1963). After a bone fracture, Roxbury, Conn., March 24, 2008.

Wright, Richard, 65, understated keyboardist for British art-rock group Pink Floyd, whose moody improvisations and imaginative aural landscapes underscored the group's biggest albums, including *The Dark Side of the Moon* (1973), and *The Wall* (1979), before infighting sent him to a solo career. Of cancer, London, Sept. 15, 2008.

Calendar of the Year

UNDERSTANDING CALENDARS

The day Earth turns at a fairly steady pace about the imaginary line that defines the North and South Poles. This line through the poles is called Earth's *axis*. Each turn about the axis, called a *rotation*, takes slightly less than 24 hours. Since Earth is also traveling around the Sun, however, the time from noon to noon is longer than the time it takes for one rotation—about 3 minutes and 56 seconds longer, or almost exactly 24 hours. The time from noon to noon changes slightly during the year, depending on where Earth is in its path. If you average all the days in a year, the mean time from noon to noon is exactly 24 hours.

The year All the nine planets of the solar system travel in nearly circular paths, called *orbits*, around the Sun. Each trip around the Sun is called a *revolution*. The planets all revolve in the same direction, which can be observed from Earth by noting the position the Sun has among the background stars, which are traditionally grouped into constellations. (Since you can't see the Sun and stars at the same time, you can observe where the Sun rises or sets each day and then note the stars that appear in the same region.) Over the course of a year, the Sun appears to pass through the 12 constellations that make up the zodiac.

Earth's trip around the Sun, reflected in the Sun's trip through the zodiac, takes about 365.25 days. This varies slightly from time to time, so astronomers add or delete a second in some years to keep their records in tune with Earth's motion. (see also "Precession of the equinoxes" below).

Seasons The seasons mark the change in the pattern of daylight over the course of the year. Because the Earth is tilted with respect to its path around the Sun, different parts receive different amounts of sunlight during Earth's annual orbit, the time we know as a year. Between late September (around the 21st) and late March, Earth's Northern Hemisphere is tilted away from the Sun. This period constitutes the fall and winter seasons for the Northern Hemisphere, during which there are fewer than 12 hours of daylight each day. For the rest of the year, spring and summer, the Northern Hemisphere is tilted toward the Sun, and daylight hours constitute more than half of each day. In the Southern Hemisphere, this situation is reversed: spring and summer last from late September to late March, while fall and winter make up the other half of the year.

At the points of transition from long days and short nights to short days and long nights and vice versa, the *equinoxes* occur—the two days of the year when periods of daylight and darkness are equal. The *vernal equinox*, marking the first day of spring, takes place on or around March 21 in the Northern Hemisphere, while the *autumnal equinox*, marking the beginning of fall, is on or around September 21. Officially, summer begins on the day of the longest daytime during the year, about June 21 in the Northern Hemisphere, called the *summer solstice*. The *winter solstice*, about

December 21 in the Northern Hemisphere, has the shortest amount of daylight and the longest night of the year. The word *solstice* means "standing still Sun." These two days are so called because the apparent movement of where the Sun rises or sets reaches its extreme positions on the solstices and then reverses direction.

Precession of the equinoxes Ancient Greek astronomers determined that the direction of Earth's axis is constantly, but very slowly, changing in a regular pattern. The kind of change is similar to the way a spinning top slowly leans one way then another as its axis changes direction. This movement of the Earth is caused by several factors, the most dominant being one called *precession*. The precession of the Earth results from its not being a perfect sphere. Earth's diameter is about 27 miles greater from one side of the equator to the other than it is from one pole to the other. (Earth is oblate, or fat around the middle, as a result of its rotation.)

Picture Earth without considering its revolution. Keep Earth's center in the same place mentally, and think about how the axis changes position during precession. Any point on Earth's axis (except the center of the planet) moves in a slow circle as a result of precession. This movement is so slow that it takes 26,000 years for a point to return to its original spot. In the meantime, the axis gradually changes its position in relation to the stars. While what we call the North Star (officially known as Polaris) is currently positioned above the North Pole about one degree off center, over time the axis will shift, so that about A.D. 15,000 the star Vega will be above the North Pole within about four degrees of that axis. By about A.D. 28,000, Polaris will have returned to its present position.

As the precession continues, one of its effects is to change the times of the year that seasons occur. Our calendar is corrected for this; if it were not, the vernal equinox would, over 13,000 years, shift from around March 21 to about September 21, the date at which the autumnal equinox is now. For this reason, the precession of the Earth is generally known as the precession of the equinoxes.

Although the precession of the equinoxes is slow, it can be easily observed. The year of about 365.25 days is the time it takes from one vernal equinox to the next. Because of the precession of the equinoxes, however, the time it takes the Sun

Solar Phenomena: The Seasons, 2009

Solar phenomenon	Month	Day	Hour	Min
Perigee[1]	Jan.	4	15	—
Vernal equinox	Mar.	20	11	44
Summer solstice	June	21	05	46
Apogee[2]	July	4	02	—
Autumnal equinox	Sept.	22	21	19
Winter solstice	Dec.	21	17	47

Note: Shown in Universal time (UT). To convert to local time, see "Timing Planetary Phenomena." 1. Sun closest to the Earth (91.4 million miles). 2. Sun farthest from the Earth (94.5 million miles).
Source: U.S. Naval Observatory, *Astronomical Phenomena for the Year 2009* (2008).

to appear in the same position with respect to the stars is 20 minutes, 24 seconds longer than the period from one equinox to the next. For this reason, accurate star maps have to specify both the date and the year for which they are intended.

Lunar Calendar

There is some evidence that very early humans (c. 25,000 B.C.) used marks on bone to indicate the passage of time, which they may have measured by the Moon's phases. A calendar for the year can be based upon the Moon's phases, which gives a year of 12 periods from new moon to new moon (hence the word *month*) lasting about 354 days. This is about 11 days shorter than the time it takes Earth to revolve around the Sun. The Chinese, who still use a version of this calendar, resolve the discrepancy by inserting extra months at fixed intervals to bring the lunar and solar years into alignment. The Chinese year is divided into months that are either 29 or 30 days long, since the time from new moon to new moon is approximately 29.5 days. The New Year begins at the first new moon over China between Jan. 21 and Feb. 19, and is celebrated for a four-day period. Each year has both a number and a name. The year 2009, or 4707 in the Chinese era, is the Year of the Ox.

Solar Calendar

The ancient Egyptians were the first people known to have instituted a solar calendar. In actuality, their calendar might be called a stellar calendar, since the year began with the rising of Sirius (the brightest star in the sky) at the same place the Sun rises, which generally happened at the same time the Nile flooded. The Egyptians determined that a year was 365 days, about one-quarter of a day short of the true solar year, so gradually the Egyptian calendar no longer coincided with the seasons. Historical records reveal when the Egyptian calendar and the rising of Sirius coincided, from which astronomers inferred that the Egyptian calendar must have been instituted in either 4241 B.C. or 2773 B.C. The Egyptian calendar had 12 months of 30 days and five days of festival, a system adopted by various early cultures, although some continued to use lunar calendars.

Julian Calendar

In 46 B.C., Julius Caesar realized that various parts of the land controlled by Rome used different calendars, so he asked the astronomer Sosigenes to develop a uniform calendar. Sosigenes proposed that since the year was 365.25 days long (though not exactly), a 365-day calendar be kept with one day added (a leap day) every fourth year. When Caesar introduced the new system, he also added days to the year 46 B.C. to bring the seasons in line with the calendar. With a total of 445 days, 46 B.C. is the longest calendar year on record. A year at that time began in what we call March, and the months were

numbered. *September, October, November,* and *December* derive from this system and mean "seventh," "eighth," "ninth," and "tenth" months respectively.

There was a little further adjustment of the calendar, however, by Augustus Caesar, the first Roman emperor. The name of the fifth month was changed from Quintilis to July to honor Julius Caesar, and Augustus named the sixth month August after himself. So that August would not be shorter than 31-day July, Augustus borrowed a day from February.

Because of the Roman Empire's great sphere of influence, the Julian calendar became the ordinary calendar of Western nations.

Julian Day Count

A year after the Gregorian calendar was first instituted, Joseph Justus Scaliger developed a system of counting days instead of years, which is still used by astronomers. Called the Julian Day Count (after his father Julius Caesar Scaliger), it begins with 1 on Jan. 1, 4713 B.C. On this date, the Julian calendar, the lunar calendar and the Roman tax system (which had its own calendar) all coincided—something that won't happen again until A.D. 3267. Each day within such a 7,980-year period is numbered.

Gregorian Calendar

From at least A.D. 730, it was known that the solar year—measured from vernal equinox to vernal equinox—was somewhat short of 365.25 days. Each century the solar year gets about half a second shorter. In 1990 the solar year was calculated at 365 days, 5 hours, 48 minutes, and 45.5 seconds long, not 365¼ days, which is what the Julian calendar assumes. Because the date of Easter was slipping, Pope Gregory XIII instituted calendar reform in 1582. He proclaimed that the day following Oct. 4 would be Oct. 15, which dropped 10 days from the year. Furthermore, on the advice of astronomer Christoph Clavius, the new calendar would be kept in line by omitting the leap year in century years unless they were divisible by 400. Thus 1900 was not a leap year in the Gregorian calendar, but 2000 was.

Most Roman Catholic countries and some other Western countries adopted the new system, but England did not. Finally, in 1752, England and its colonies adopted the Gregorian calendar, but they had to drop 11 days to fit common Western practice. It was at this time that New Year's Day in England was moved from Mar. 25 to Jan. 1, changing the number of the year for the almost three months affected. Thus George Washington was born according to the Julian calendar on Feb. 11, 1731, but he came to celebrate his birthday on Feb. 22, 1732 according to the Gregorian calendar.

Because the solar year is shortening, astronomers today keep the Gregorian calendar in line by making a one-second adjustment, as needed, usually on Dec. 31 at midnight, whenever the error's accumulation nears one second.

When Did the Third Millennium Begin?

Did the third millennium begin on January 1, 2000, January 1, 2001, or an entirely different day?

The answer depends on how you count your years. If you believe that our calendar began in the year 1, rather than the year 0, then a thousand years did not pass until the end of the year 1000, and the third millennium didn't start until 2001.

But by that logic, the 1990s wouldn't have begun until 1991, and would have included the year

2000. Yet we routinely consider years ending in 0 to be the first year of a decade rather than the last, so why should it be any different for millennia? Also, calendars are an inexact science and plenty of shifting of days, months, and years, have been perpetrated over the years by kings, emperors and popes. The Jewish calendar counted more than 3,700 years before Western calendars counted their first, while the Chinese celebrated the third millennium more than 1,600 years ago.

Perpetual Calendar, 1775–2050

A **perpetual calendar** lets you find the day of the week for any date in any year. Since January 1 may fall on any of the seven days of the week, and may be a leap or non-leap year, 14 different calendars are possible. The number next to each year corresponds to one of the 14 calendars. For example, in 1776, calendar 9 (a leap year in which Jan. 1 fell on a Monday) was used; July 4 of that year was a Thursday. Calendar 12 was used in 2004; Calendar 5 will be used in 2009.

Year	No.	Year	No.	Year	No.	Year	No.	Year	No.	Year	No.	Year	No.
1775	1	1815	1	1855	2	1895	3	1935	3	1975	4	2015	5
1776	9	1816	9	1856	10	1896	11	1936	11	1976	12	2016	13
1777	4	1817	4	1857	5	1897	6	1937	6	1977	7	2017	1
1778	5	1818	5	1858	6	1898	7	1938	7	1978	1	2018	2
1779	6	1819	6	1859	7	1899	1	1939	1	1979	2	2019	3
1780	14	1820	14	1860	8	1900	2	1940	9	1980	10	2020	11
1781	2	1821	2	1861	3	1901	3	1941	4	1981	5	2021	6
1782	3	1822	3	1862	4	1902	4	1942	5	1982	6	2022	7
1783	4	1823	4	1863	5	1903	5	1943	6	1983	7	2023	1
1784	12	1824	12	1864	13	1904	13	1944	14	1984	8	2024	9
1785	7	1825	7	1865	1	1905	1	1945	2	1985	3	2025	4
1786	1	1826	1	1866	2	1906	2	1946	3	1986	4	2026	5
1787	2	1827	2	1867	3	1907	3	1947	4	1987	5	2027	6
1788	10	1828	10	1868	11	1908	11	1948	12	1988	13	2028	14
1789	5	1829	5	1869	6	1909	6	1949	7	1989	1	2029	2
1790	6	1830	6	1870	7	1910	7	1950	1	1990	2	2030	3
1791	7	1831	7	1871	1	1911	1	1951	2	1991	3	2031	4
1792	8	1832	8	1872	9	1912	9	1952	10	1992	11	2032	12
1793	3	1833	3	1873	4	1913	4	1953	5	1993	6	2033	7
1794	4	1834	4	1874	5	1914	5	1954	6	1994	7	2034	1
1795	5	1835	5	1875	6	1915	6	1955	7	1995	1	2035	2
1796	13	1836	13	1876	14	1916	14	1956	8	1996	9	2036	10
1797	1	1837	1	1877	2	1917	2	1957	3	1997	4	2037	5
1798	2	1838	2	1878	3	1918	3	1958	4	1998	5	2038	6
1799	3	1839	3	1879	4	1919	4	1959	5	1999	6	2039	7
1800	4	1840	11	1880	12	1920	12	1960	13	2000	14	2040	8
1801	5	1841	6	1881	7	1921	7	1961	1	2001	2	2041	3
1802	6	1842	7	1882	1	1922	1	1962	2	2002	3	2042	4
1803	7	1843	1	1883	2	1923	2	1963	3	2003	4	2043	5
1804	8	1844	9	1884	10	1924	10	1964	11	2004	12	2044	13
1805	3	1845	4	1885	5	1925	5	1965	6	2005	7	2045	1
1806	4	1846	5	1886	6	1926	6	1966	7	2006	1	2046	2
1807	5	1847	6	1887	7	1927	7	1967	1	2007	2	2047	3
1808	13	1848	14	1888	8	1928	8	1968	9	2008	10	2048	11
1809	1	1849	2	1889	3	1929	3	1969	4	2009	5	2049	6
1810	2	1850	3	1890	4	1930	4	1970	5	2010	6	2050	7
1811	3	1851	4	1891	5	1931	5	1971	6	2011	7		
1812	11	1852	12	1892	13	1932	13	1972	14	2012	8		
1813	6	1853	7	1893	1	1933	1	1973	2	2013	3		
1814	7	1854	1	1894	2	1934	2	1974	3	2014	4		

1

JANUARY · FEBRUARY · MARCH · APRIL · MAY · JUNE · JULY · AUGUST · SEPTEMBER · OCTOBER · NOVEMBER · DECEMBER

2

JANUARY · FEBRUARY · MARCH · APRIL · MAY · JUNE · JULY · AUGUST · SEPTEMBER · OCTOBER · NOVEMBER · DECEMBER

3

JANUARY

S	M	T	W	T	F	S
		1	2	3	4	5
6	7	8	9	10	11	12
13	14	15	16	17	18	19
20	21	22	23	24	25	26
27	28	29	30	31		

FEBRUARY

S	M	T	W	T	F	S
					1	2
3	4	5	6	7	8	9
10	11	12	13	14	15	16
17	18	19	20	21	22	23
24	25	26	27	28		

MARCH

S	M	T	W	T	F	S
					1	2
3	4	5	6	7	8	9
10	11	12	13	14	15	16
17	18	19	20	21	22	23
24	25	26	27	28	29	30
31						

APRIL

S	M	T	W	T	F	S
	1	2	3	4	5	6
7	8	9	10	11	12	13
14	15	16	17	18	19	20
21	22	23	24	25	26	27
28	29	30				

MAY

S	M	T	W	T	F	S
			1	2	3	4
5	6	7	8	9	10	11
12	13	14	15	16	17	18
19	20	21	22	23	24	25
26	27	28	29	30	31	

JUNE

S	M	T	W	T	F	S
						1
2	3	4	5	6	7	8
9	10	11	12	13	14	15
16	17	18	19	20	21	22
23	24	25	26	27	28	29
30						

JULY

S	M	T	W	T	F	S
	1	2	3	4	5	6
7	8	9	10	11	12	13
14	15	16	17	18	19	20
21	22	23	24	25	26	27
28	29	30	31			

AUGUST

S	M	T	W	T	F	S
				1	2	3
4	5	6	7	8	9	10
11	12	13	14	15	16	17
18	19	20	21	22	23	24
25	26	27	28	29	30	31

SEPTEMBER

S	M	T	W	T	F	S
1	2	3	4	5	6	7
8	9	10	11	12	13	14
15	16	17	18	19	20	21
22	23	24	25	26	27	28
29	30					

OCTOBER

S	M	T	W	T	F	S
		1	2	3	4	5
6	7	8	9	10	11	12
13	14	15	16	17	18	19
20	21	22	23	24	25	26
27	28	29	30	31		

NOVEMBER

S	M	T	W	T	F	S
					1	2
3	4	5	6	7	8	9
10	11	12	13	14	15	16
17	18	19	20	21	22	23
24	25	26	27	28	29	30

DECEMBER

S	M	T	W	T	F	S
1	2	3	4	5	6	7
8	9	10	11	12	13	14
15	16	17	18	19	20	21
22	23	24	25	26	27	28
29	30	31				

4

JANUARY

S	M	T	W	T	F	S
			1	2	3	4
5	6	7	8	9	10	11
12	13	14	15	16	17	18
19	20	21	22	23	24	25
26	27	28	29	30	31	

FEBRUARY

S	M	T	W	T	F	S
						1
2	3	4	5	6	7	8
9	10	11	12	13	14	15
16	17	18	19	20	21	22
23	24	25	26	27	28	

MARCH

S	M	T	W	T	F	S
						1
2	3	4	5	6	7	8
9	10	11	12	13	14	15
16	17	18	19	20	21	22
23	24	25	26	27	28	29
30	31					

APRIL

S	M	T	W	T	F	S
		1	2	3	4	5
6	7	8	9	10	11	12
13	14	15	16	17	18	19
20	21	22	23	24	25	26
27	28	29	30			

MAY

S	M	T	W	T	F	S
				1	2	3
4	5	6	7	8	9	10
11	12	13	14	15	16	17
18	19	20	21	22	23	24
25	26	27	28	29	30	31

JUNE

S	M	T	W	T	F	S
1	2	3	4	5	6	7
8	9	10	11	12	13	14
15	16	17	18	19	20	21
22	23	24	25	26	27	28
29	30					

JULY

S	M	T	W	T	F	S
		1	2	3	4	5
6	7	8	9	10	11	12
13	14	15	16	17	18	19
20	21	22	23	24	25	26
27	28	29	30	31		

AUGUST

S	M	T	W	T	F	S
					1	2
3	4	5	6	7	8	9
10	11	12	13	14	15	16
17	18	19	20	21	22	23
24	25	26	27	28	29	30
31						

SEPTEMBER

S	M	T	W	T	F	S
	1	2	3	4	5	6
7	8	9	10	11	12	13
14	15	16	17	18	19	20
21	22	23	24	25	26	27
28	29	30				

OCTOBER

S	M	T	W	T	F	S
			1	2	3	4
5	6	7	8	9	10	11
12	13	14	15	16	17	18
19	20	21	22	23	24	25
26	27	28	29	30	31	

NOVEMBER

S	M	T	W	T	F	S
						1
2	3	4	5	6	7	8
9	10	11	12	13	14	15
16	17	18	19	20	21	22
23	24	25	26	27	28	29
30						

DECEMBER

S	M	T	W	T	F	S
	1	2	3	4	5	6
7	8	9	10	11	12	13
14	15	16	17	18	19	20
21	22	23	24	25	26	27
28	29	30	31			

5

JANUARY

S	M	T	W	T	F	S
				1	2	3
4	5	6	7	8	9	10
11	12	13	14	15	16	17
18	19	20	21	22	23	24
25	26	27	28	29	30	31

FEBRUARY

S	M	T	W	T	F	S
1	2	3	4	5	6	7
8	9	10	11	12	13	14
15	16	17	18	19	20	21
22	23	24	25	26	27	28

MARCH

S	M	T	W	T	F	S
1	2	3	4	5	6	7
8	9	10	11	12	13	14
15	16	17	18	19	20	21
22	23	24	25	26	27	28
29	30	31				

APRIL

S	M	T	W	T	F	S
			1	2	3	4
5	6	7	8	9	10	11
12	13	14	15	16	17	18
19	20	21	22	23	24	25
26	27	28	29	30		

MAY

S	M	T	W	T	F	S
					1	2
3	4	5	6	7	8	9
10	11	12	13	14	15	16
17	18	19	20	21	22	23
24	25	26	27	28	29	30
31						

JUNE

S	M	T	W	T	F	S
	1	2	3	4	5	6
7	8	9	10	11	12	13
14	15	16	17	18	19	20
21	22	23	24	25	26	27
28	29	30				

JULY

S	M	T	W	T	F	S
			1	2	3	4
5	6	7	8	9	10	11
12	13	14	15	16	17	18
19	20	21	22	23	24	25
26	27	28	29	30	31	

AUGUST

S	M	T	W	T	F	S
						1
2	3	4	5	6	7	8
9	10	11	12	13	14	15
16	17	18	19	20	21	22
23	24	25	26	27	28	29
30	31					

SEPTEMBER

S	M	T	W	T	F	S
		1	2	3	4	5
6	7	8	9	10	11	12
13	14	15	16	17	18	19
20	21	22	23	24	25	26
27	28	29	30			

OCTOBER

S	M	T	W	T	F	S
				1	2	3
4	5	6	7	8	9	10
11	12	13	14	15	16	17
18	19	20	21	22	23	24
25	26	27	28	29	30	31

NOVEMBER

S	M	T	W	T	F	S
1	2	3	4	5	6	7
8	9	10	11	12	13	14
15	16	17	18	19	20	21
22	23	24	25	26	27	28
29	30					

DECEMBER

S	M	T	W	T	F	S
		1	2	3	4	5
6	7	8	9	10	11	12
13	14	15	16	17	18	19
20	21	22	23	24	25	26
27	28	29	30	31		

6

JANUARY

S	M	T	W	T	F	S
					1	2
3	4	5	6	7	8	9
10	11	12	13	14	15	16
17	18	19	20	21	22	23
24	25	26	27	28	29	30
31						

FEBRUARY

S	M	T	W	T	F	S
	1	2	3	4	5	6
7	8	9	10	11	12	13
14	15	16	17	18	19	20
21	22	23	24	25	26	27
28						

MARCH

S	M	T	W	T	F	S
	1	2	3	4	5	6
7	8	9	10	11	12	13
14	15	16	17	18	19	20
21	22	23	24	25	26	27
28	29	30	31			

APRIL

S	M	T	W	T	F	S
				1	2	3
4	5	6	7	8	9	10
11	12	13	14	15	16	17
18	19	20	21	22	23	24
25	26	27	28	29	30	

MAY

S	M	T	W	T	F	S
						1
2	3	4	5	6	7	8
9	10	11	12	13	14	15
16	17	18	19	20	21	22
23	24	25	26	27	28	29
30	31					

JUNE

S	M	T	W	T	F	S
		1	2	3	4	5
6	7	8	9	10	11	12
13	14	15	16	17	18	19
20	21	22	23	24	25	26
27	28	29	30			

JULY

S	M	T	W	T	F	S
				1	2	3
4	5	6	7	8	9	10
11	12	13	14	15	16	17
18	19	20	21	22	23	24
25	26	27	28	29	30	31

AUGUST

S	M	T	W	T	F	S
1	2	3	4	5	6	7
8	9	10	11	12	13	14
15	16	17	18	19	20	21
22	23	24	25	26	27	28
29	30	31				

SEPTEMBER

S	M	T	W	T	F	S
			1	2	3	4
5	6	7	8	9	10	11
12	13	14	15	16	17	18
19	20	21	22	23	24	25
26	27	28	29	30		

OCTOBER

S	M	T	W	T	F	S
					1	2
3	4	5	6	7	8	9
10	11	12	13	14	15	16
17	18	19	20	21	22	23
24	25	26	27	28	29	30
31						

NOVEMBER

S	M	T	W	T	F	S
	1	2	3	4	5	6
7	8	9	10	11	12	13
14	15	16	17	18	19	20
21	22	23	24	25	26	27
28	29	30				

DECEMBER

S	M	T	W	T	F	S
			1	2	3	4
5	6	7	8	9	10	11
12	13	14	15	16	17	18
19	20	21	22	23	24	25
26	27	28	29	30	31	

7

JANUARY

S	M	T	W	T	F	S
						1
2	3	4	5	6	7	8
9	10	11	12	13	14	15
16	17	18	19	20	21	22
23	24	25	26	27	28	29
30	31					

FEBRUARY

S	M	T	W	T	F	S
		1	2	3	4	5
6	7	8	9	10	11	12
13	14	15	16	17	18	19
20	21	22	23	24	25	26
27	28					

MARCH

S	M	T	W	T	F	S
		1	2	3	4	5
6	7	8	9	10	11	12
13	14	15	16	17	18	19
20	21	22	23	24	25	26
27	28	29	30	31		

APRIL

S	M	T	W	T	F	S
					1	2
3	4	5	6	7	8	9
10	11	12	13	14	15	16
17	18	19	20	21	22	23
24	25	26	27	28	29	30

MAY

S	M	T	W	T	F	S
1	2	3	4	5	6	7
8	9	10	11	12	13	14
15	16	17	18	19	20	21
22	23	24	25	26	27	28
29	30	31				

JUNE

S	M	T	W	T	F	S
			1	2	3	4
5	6	7	8	9	10	11
12	13	14	15	16	17	18
19	20	21	22	23	24	25
26	27	28	29	30		

JULY

S	M	T	W	T	F	S
					1	2
3	4	5	6	7	8	9
10	11	12	13	14	15	16
17	18	19	20	21	22	23
24	25	26	27	28	29	30
31						

AUGUST

S	M	T	W	T	F	S
	1	2	3	4	5	6
7	8	9	10	11	12	13
14	15	16	17	18	19	20
21	22	23	24	25	26	27
28	29	30	31			

SEPTEMBER

S	M	T	W	T	F	S
				1	2	3
4	5	6	7	8	9	10
11	12	13	14	15	16	17
18	19	20	21	22	23	24
25	26	27	28	29	30	

OCTOBER

S	M	T	W	T	F	S
						1
2	3	4	5	6	7	8
9	10	11	12	13	14	15
16	17	18	19	20	21	22
23	24	25	26	27	28	29
30	31					

NOVEMBER

S	M	T	W	T	F	S
		1	2	3	4	5
6	7	8	9	10	11	12
13	14	15	16	17	18	19
20	21	22	23	24	25	26
27	28	29	30			

DECEMBER

S	M	T	W	T	F	S
				1	2	3
4	5	6	7	8	9	10
11	12	13	14	15	16	17
18	19	20	21	22	23	24
25	26	27	28	29	30	31

8

JANUARY

S	M	T	W	T	F	S
1	2	3	4	5	6	7
8	9	10	11	12	13	14
15	16	17	18	19	20	21
22	23	24	25	26	27	28
29	30	31				

FEBRUARY

S	M	T	W	T	F	S
			1	2	3	4
5	6	7	8	9	10	11
12	13	14	15	16	17	18
19	20	21	22	23	24	25
26	27	28	29			

MARCH

S	M	T	W	T	F	S
				1	2	3
4	5	6	7	8	9	10
11	12	13	14	15	16	17
18	19	20	21	22	23	24
25	26	27	28	29	30	31

APRIL

S	M	T	W	T	F	S
1	2	3	4	5	6	7
8	9	10	11	12	13	14
15	16	17	18	19	20	21
22	23	24	25	26	27	28
29	30					

MAY

S	M	T	W	T	F	S
		1	2	3	4	5
6	7	8	9	10	11	12
13	14	15	16	17	18	19
20	21	22	23	24	25	26
27	28	29	30	31		

JUNE

S	M	T	W	T	F	S
					1	2
3	4	5	6	7	8	9
10	11	12	13	14	15	16
17	18	19	20	21	22	23
24	25	26	27	28	29	30

JULY

S	M	T	W	T	F	S
1	2	3	4	5	6	7
8	9	10	11	12	13	14
15	16	17	18	19	20	21
22	23	24	25	26	27	28
29	30	31				

AUGUST

S	M	T	W	T	F	S
			1	2	3	4
5	6	7	8	9	10	11
12	13	14	15	16	17	18
19	20	21	22	23	24	25
26	27	28	29	30	31	

SEPTEMBER

S	M	T	W	T	F	S
						1
2	3	4	5	6	7	8
9	10	11	12	13	14	15
16	17	18	19	20	21	22
23	24	25	26	27	28	29
30						

OCTOBER

S	M	T	W	T	F	S
	1	2	3	4	5	6
7	8	9	10	11	12	13
14	15	16	17	18	19	20
21	22	23	24	25	26	27
28	29	30	31			

NOVEMBER

S	M	T	W	T	F	S
				1	2	3
4	5	6	7	8	9	10
11	12	13	14	15	16	17
18	19	20	21	22	23	24
25	26	27	28	29	30	

DECEMBER

S	M	T	W	T	F	S
						1
2	3	4	5	6	7	8
9	10	11	12	13	14	15
16	17	18	19	20	21	22
23	24	25	26	27	28	29
30	31					

9

JANUARY
S	M	T	W	T	F	S
		1	2	3	4	5
6	7	8	9	10	11	12
13	14	15	16	17	18	19
20	21	22	23	24	25	26
27	28	29	30	31		

(calendar grids for groups 9–14 follow, each showing the twelve months January–December with day-of-week columns S M T W T F S)

10

JANUARY
FEBRUARY
MARCH
APRIL
MAY
JUNE
JULY
AUGUST
SEPTEMBER
OCTOBER
NOVEMBER
DECEMBER

11

JANUARY
FEBRUARY
MARCH
APRIL
MAY
JUNE
JULY
AUGUST
SEPTEMBER
OCTOBER
NOVEMBER
DECEMBER

12

JANUARY
FEBRUARY
MARCH
APRIL
MAY
JUNE
JULY
AUGUST
SEPTEMBER
OCTOBER
NOVEMBER
DECEMBER

13

JANUARY
FEBRUARY
MARCH
APRIL
MAY
JUNE
JULY
AUGUST
SEPTEMBER
OCTOBER
NOVEMBER
DECEMBER

14

JANUARY
FEBRUARY
MARCH
APRIL
MAY
JUNE
JULY
AUGUST
SEPTEMBER
OCTOBER
NOVEMBER
DECEMBER

HOLIDAYS AND HOLY DAYS

▶ **FEDERAL HOLIDAYS IN THE U.S.**
Congress and the president have designated 10 days as federal holidays. Although these are so widely observed as to be considered "national" holidays, they technically apply only to federal employees and the District of Columbia. It is up to the individual states to designate their own holidays. When a federal holiday falls on a Saturday or a Sunday, it is observed on the preceding Friday or the following Monday.

New Year's Day (January 1)   The observance of the New Year dates back to pre-Christian times when rites were performed to ensure the return of spring.

Martin Luther King, Jr., Day (Third Monday in January)   Before his assassination in 1968, Martin Luther King, Jr., was the foremost civil rights leader of the 1950s and 1960s, and in 1964 he won the Nobel Peace Prize. In 1983, Congress set aside this day to celebrate his life and accomplishments.

Washington's Birthday (Third Monday in February)   Originally celebrated on the actual birthday of America's first president (February 22), this holiday was officially moved in 1971 to the third Monday in February to create a three-day weekend. It is sometimes known as Presidents' Day, because the birthday of Abraham Lincoln (Feb. 12) is so close.

Memorial Day (Last Monday in May)   Memorial Day (also known as Decoration Day) honors soldiers fallen in battle. Dating from the Civil War, it is traditionally marked with parades and memorial services.

Independence Day (Fourth of July)   The most important U.S. holiday, Independence Day commemorates the signing of the Declaration of Independence on July 4, 1776, an event that marked America's birth as a free nation. The holiday was first observed in 1777 and is celebrated with fireworks, parades, and oratory.

Labor Day (First Monday in September)   The idea of Peter J. McGuire, president of the United Brotherhood of Carpenters and Joiners of America, the official observance of a day celebrating the American worker was signed into law on June 28, 1894.

Columbus Day (Second Monday in October)   On Oct. 12, 1492, Christopher Columbus and his crew landed in the Bahama Islands after sailing across the Atlantic. First celebrated in 1792, Columbus Day was not officially recognized until 1909. Its observance is of special national pride to Italian-Americans who claim the Genoese Columbus for their own.

Veterans' Day (November 11)   Armistice Day, which marked the end of World War I on Nov. 11, 1918, was made a legal holiday in 1938. The name

was changed to Veterans' Day in 1954 to honor all of America's veterans.

Thanksgiving (Fourth Thursday in November)   Thanksgiving Day was first observed in Plymouth Colony (Massachusetts) in 1621, the year in which the Pilgrims landed in the New World and gave thanks for their first harvest and for the new land they had colonized. President Lincoln proclaimed Thanksgiving a national holiday in 1863.

Christmas is celebrated December 25.   (See also "Christian Holy Days.")

▶ **U.S. MINOR HOLIDAYS AND OCCASIONS**

April Fool's Day (April 1)   A day for practical jokes, the origins of April Fool's Day are obscure, but it bears some resemblance to an ancient Roman festival honoring the goddess of nature.

Arbor Day (Last Friday in April)   Dedicated to trees and their preservation. Its observance is meant to encourage preservation of the environment. Internationally it is observed on December 22.

Armed Forces Day (Third Saturday in May)   A day to honor of the members of the United States Armed Forces.

Constitution/Citizenship Day (September 17)   First observed by presidential proclamation in 1952, Citizenship Day falls on the same day as the old Constitution Day.

Daylight Saving Time   The idea of moving clocks ahead one hour to capture more daylight on summer evenings dates back to colonial times—Benjamin Franklin first suggested it in a 1784 essay—but it did not become a nationwide practice until the Uniform Time Act of 1966 (effective April of 1967). During World War I, World War II, and the energy crisis of 1973–74, the U.S. adopted daylight saving time all year round to save money on fuel. Daylight saving time is not observed in Hawaii, most of Arizona (except on the Navajo Indian Reservation) or in the territories of American Samoa, Guam, Puerto Rico and the Virgin Islands. Until 2007, daylight saving time began on the first Sunday in April and ended on the last Sunday in October. In 2007, the *Energy Act of 2005* went into effect, and now daylight saving time begins at 2 A.M. on the second Sunday in March and ends at 2 A.M. on the first Sunday in November. Remember to "Spring ahead, Fall back."

Election Day (Tuesday after first Monday in November)   In years evenly divisible by four, presidential elections are held; in years evenly divisible by two, elections for all members of the House of Representatives and for one-third of the members of the Senate are held.

Father's Day (Third Sunday in June)   Father's Day was first observed in West Virginia in 1908, but it was not until 1972 that the president signed a Congressional resolution designating its official observance. Father's Day is a uniquely American institution.

Flag Day (June 14)   The first observance of Flag Day was in 1877, the centenary of the adoption of

Important Dates in the U.S. and Canada, 2009–14

Event	2009	2010	2011	2012	2013	2014
New Year's Day[1]	Jan. 1	Jan. 1	Jan. 1	Jan. 1	Jan. 1	Jan. 1
Martin Luther King Day[1]	Jan. 19	Jan. 18	Jan. 7	Jan. 16	Jan. 21	Jan. 20
Groundhog Day	Feb. 2	Feb. 2	Feb. 2	Feb. 2	Feb. 2	Feb. 2
St. Valentine's Day	Feb. 14	Feb. 14	Feb. 14	Feb. 14	Feb. 14	Feb. 14
Susan B. Anthony Day	Feb. 15	Feb. 15	Feb. 15	Feb. 15	Feb. 15	Feb. 15
Washington's Birthday[1]	Feb. 16	Feb. 15	Feb. 15	Feb. 20	Feb. 18	Feb. 17
Mardi Gras	Feb. 24	Feb. 16	Mar. 8	Feb. 21	Feb. 12	Mar. 4
Daylight Saving begins	Mar. 8	Mar. 14	Mar. 13	Mar. 11	Mar. 10	Mar. 9
St. Patrick's Day	Mar. 17	Mar. 17	Mar. 17	Mar. 17	Mar. 17	Mar. 17
April Fool's Day	Apr. 1	Apr. 1	Apr. 1	Apr. 1	Apr. 1	Apr. 1
Arbor Day	Apr. 24	Apr. 30	Apr. 29	Apr. 27	Apr. 26	Apr. 25
National Teacher Day	May 5	May 4	May 3	May 8	May 7	May 6
Mother's Day	May 10	May 8	May 21	May 13	May 12	May 11
Armed Forces Day	May 16	May 15	May 21	May 19	May 18	May 17
Victoria Day[2]	May 18	May 23	May 23	May 21	May 20	May 19
National Maritime Day	May 22	May 22	May 22	May 22	May 22	May 22
Memorial Day[1]	May 25	May 31	May 30	May 28	May 27	May 26
Flag Day	June 14	June 14	June 14	June 14	June 14	June 14
Father's Day	June 21	June 20	June 19	June 17	June 16	June 15
Canada Day[2]	July 1	July 1	July 1	July 1	July 1	July 1
Independence Day[1]	July 4	July 4	July 4	July 4	July 4	July 4
Labor Day[1, 2]	Sept. 7	Sept. 6	Sept. 5	Sept. 3	Sept. 2	Sept. 1
Constitution/Citizenship Day	Sept. 17	Sept. 17	Sept. 17	Sept. 17	Sept. 17	Sept. 17
Columbus Day[1]	Oct. 12	Oct. 11	Oct. 10	Oct. 8	Oct. 14	Oct. 13
Thanksgiving Day[2] (Can.)	Oct. 12	Oct. 11	Oct. 10	Oct. 8	Oct. 14	Oct. 13
United Nations Day	Oct. 24	Oct. 24	Oct. 24	Oct. 24	Oct. 24	Oct. 24
Halloween	Oct. 31	Oct. 31	Oct. 31	Oct. 31	Oct. 31	Oct. 31
Daylight Saving ends	Nov. 1	Nov. 7	Nov. 6	Nov. 4	Nov. 3	Nov. 2
Election Day (U.S.)	Nov. 3	Nov. 9	Nov. 8	Nov. 6	Nov. 5	Nov. 4
Veterans'(Armistice) Day[1]	Nov. 11	Nov. 11	Nov. 11	Nov. 11	Nov. 11	Nov. 11
Remembrance Day[2]	Nov. 11	Nov. 11	Nov. 11	Nov. 11	Nov. 11	Nov. 11
Thanksgiving Day[1] (U.S.)	Nov. 26	Nov. 25	Nov. 24	Nov. 22	Nov. 28	Nov. 27
Christmas Day[1, 2]	Dec. 25	Dec. 25	Dec. 25	Dec. 25	Dec. 25	Dec. 25
Boxing Day[2]	Dec. 26	Dec. 26	Dec. 26	Dec. 26	Dec. 26	Dec. 26
Kwanzaa[3]	Dec. 26	Dec. 26	Dec. 26	Dec. 26	Dec. 26	Dec. 26
New Year's Eve	Dec. 31	Dec. 31	Dec. 31	Dec. 31	Dec. 31	Dec. 31

Note: 1. Federal holiday in U.S. 2. Federal holiday in Canada. 3. First day of seven-day holiday.

the Flag Resolution, which adopted the design of the American flag flown today. President Truman signed the Flag Day Bill in 1949.

Groundhog Day (February 2) On this day the groundhog peeks out of his burrow to look for his shadow. If he sees his shadow, six weeks of winter will follow; if he doesn't, spring is just around the corner.

Halloween (October 31) All Hallow's Eve (the day before the feast of All Saints in the Christian calendar) began as a pagan custom honoring the dead and a celebration of autumn. The wearing of costumes can be traced back to medieval religious practice in which parishioners dressed as saints and angels and paraded through the churchyard. The modern practice of "trick or treat" is of American origin with no apparent historical basis.

Kwanzaa (or Kwanza) This secular celebration by African-Americans commemorates their African heritage and emphasizes the role of family and community. It begins on Dec. 26 and lasts for seven days; on each day one candle of a candelabrum is lighted. Kwanzaa was developed by Maulana Karenga and was first observed in 1966.

Mother's Day (Second Sunday in May) Conceived by Anne M. Jarvis of Philadelphia, where it was first observed, as a day for children to pay tribute to their mothers, this was declared a national holiday by presidential proclamation in 1914.

National Maritime Day (May 22) Designated by presidential proclamation in 1935, this commemorates the anniversary of the departure of the SS Savannah on the first successful transoceanic voyage of a steam-powered vessel, in 1819. It is also a day of remembrance of merchant mariners who died in defense of their country.

National Teacher Day (Tuesday of first full week in May) This is a day when students and communities around the country honor their teachers and the teaching profession.

St. Patrick's Day (March 17) A day in honor of Ireland's patron saint, St. Patrick's Day is a religious, political and social event rolled into one. In Ireland, St. Patrick is honored by church ceremonies and a three-day period of devotion. In the United States, March 17 is celebrated with parades and the "wearing of the green."

St. Valentine's Day (February 14) Originally an occasion to honor two Christian saints martyred by the Roman Emperor Claudius (214–270), since the Middle Ages St. Valentine's Day has been dedicated to lovers, probably because it is believed to be the day that birds choose their mates.

Susan B. Anthony Day (February 15) Anthony (1820–1906) was one of the first women's rights advocates, working especially for equal suffrage—that is, the right to vote. She was a co-founder and later president of the National Woman Suffrage Association.

United Nations Day (October 24) This commemorates the ratification of the United Nations Charter on this date in 1945 by the five permanent members of the Security Council and a majority of the other Charter signatories.

▶ CHRISTIAN HOLY DAYS

Christmas is the celebration of Christ's birth. The exact date of his birth is unknown, but the date of December 25 was probably chosen because it coincided with the ancient mid-winter celebrations honoring pagan deities. The 12 days of Christmas fall between Christmas and Epiphany (January 6), the day the Wise Men visited the Christ child.

Advent, a religious season that begins on the Sunday nearest Nov. 30 and lasts until Christmas, both celebrates the birth of Jesus and anticipates His second coming. At one time Advent was a solemn season observed by fasting, but this is no longer the case.

Easter is the most important holy day in the Christian religion. It is the celebration of Christ's Resurrection from the dead, which gave Christians the hope of salvation and eternal life. Although Easter is only one day, the full observance of the holy day spans from Septuagesima Sunday (70 days before Easter Sunday), which may fall as early as January, to Pentecost, which can occur as late as June.

Easter always falls on the first Sunday after the first full moon after the vernal equinox on March 21. Thus, Easter can fall no earlier than March 23 (if the first full moon is a Saturday March 22) and no later than April 24 (if the first full moon is a Sunday, April 17).

Mardi Gras (Shrove Tuesday; Fat Tuesday) Originally a day of penance, the last day before the beginning of Lent is now celebrated with feasting and merrymaking.

Ash Wednesday derives its name from the rite of burning the palms carried on the Palm Sunday of the year before and using the ashes to mark worshippers' foreheads with a cross.

Lent, a 40-day period of fasting and penitence beginning on Ash Wednesday and ending on Easter Sunday, Lent is traditionally observed by fasting, performing acts of charity, and by giving up certain pleasures and amusements.

Palm Sunday, the Sunday before Easter, celebrates Jesus' triumphant entry into Jerusalem where palm branches were spread before Him to honor His path.

Holy (Maundy) Thursday, is the anniversary of the Last Supper. The traditional services mark three events that occurred during the week before Jesus was crucified: He washed the feet of His 12 disciples; He instituted the Eucharist (the sacrament of Holy Communion); and He was arrested and imprisoned.

Good Friday marks the day of Christ's Crucifixion. The holy day is observed with fasting, mourning, and penitence.

Holy Saturday is the day that anticipates the Resurrection. In the Catholic church, special vigils are held on Holy Saturday evening.

Easter Sunday marks the day of Christ's Resurrection. Many worshippers celebrate the holy day with sunrise services, a custom believed to be inspired by the example of Mary Magdalene, who went to Christ's tomb "early, while it was yet dark."

Pentecost (literally, "fiftieth day") is the end of the full ecclesiastical observance of Easter. It takes place on the seventh Sunday after Easter Sunday and commemorates the descent of the Holy Spirit upon the Apostles.

The Annunciation This holy day marks the archangel Gabriel's announcement to Mary that she would conceive and give birth to Jesus. It is celebrated by Roman Catholics on March 25; it is not observed by Protestant denominations.

Trinity Sunday The Sunday after Pentecost, this occasion honors the Father, Son and Holy Spirit. It was declared a part of the church calendar in 1334 by Pope John XXII and is observed by Roman Catholics and by some Protestant denominations.

Corpus Christi This feast celebrates the presence of the body (*corpus*) of Christ in the Eucharist. At one time this was the principal feast of the church year, but today it is observed only by Catholic churches. Corpus Christi is celebrated on the Thursday following Trinity Sunday.

All Saints' Day, celebrated on November 1, honors all of the Christian saints. In America, many churches mark the Sunday nearest November 1 as a day to pay tribute to those who have died during the year. All Saints' Day is observed primarily by Roman Catholics.

Holy Days of Obligation are feast days in the Catholic calendar observed by attendance at Mass and rest from unnecessary work. Six holy days of obligation are observed in the United States:

Calendar of Christian Holy Days, 2009–14

Year A.D.	Ash Wednesday	Good Friday	Easter Sunday	Pentecost	Trinity Sunday	Advent
2009	Feb. 25	Apr. 10	Apr. 12	May 31	June 7	Nov. 29
2010	Feb. 17	Apr. 2	Apr. 4	May 23	June 11	Nov. 28
2011	Mar. 9	Apr. 22	Apr. 24	June 12	June 19	Nov. 27
2012	Feb. 22	Apr. 6	Apr. 8	May 27	June 3	Dec. 2
2013	Feb. 13	Mar. 29	Mar. 31	May 19	May 26	Dec. 1
2014	Mar. 5	Apr. 18	Apr. 20	June 8	June 15	Nov. 30

1. Solemnity of Mary, Jan. 1 (formerly, Christ's circumcision, the first shedding of his blood, was commemorated on this day).

2. Ascension (of Jesus to Heaven), 40 days after Easter

3. Assumption of the Blessed Virgin into Heaven, Aug. 15

4. All Saints' Day, Nov. 1

5. Mary's Immaculate Conception (honoring the Mother of God as the only person conceived without original sin), Dec. 8

6. Christmas, Dec. 25

▶ THE JEWISH CALENDAR

The months of the Jewish year are Tishri, Heshvan, Kislev, Tebet, Shebat, Adar, Nisan, Iyar, Sivan, Tammuz, Ab and Elul. The Jewish era dates from the year of the creation (*anno mundii* or A.M.), which is equal to 3761 B.C.), thus 5764 began in 2003 and ends in 2004 of the Gregorian calendar. (Tishri, the first month of the Jewish year, falls in either September or October of the Gregorian calendar.)

Because the Jewish calendar is a blend of solar and lunar calendars, there are intercalated months to keep the lunar and solar years in alignment. (Intercalation is the insertion of an extra day, month, or other unit—February 29 in a leap year, for example—into a calendar). The intercalated month is called Adar Sheni or Veadar—Second Adar.

▶ JEWISH HOLY DAYS

Sabbath is the first and most important Jewish holy day, occurring each week from sundown Friday to sundown Saturday. It is a day of rest and spiritual growth, given to men and women so they will remember the sweetness of freedom and keep it. Sabbath takes precedence over all other observances.

Rosh Hashanah (New Year) held to be the birthday of the world, is also called the Day of Judgment and Remembrance, and the day of the shofar—a ram's horn—which is blown to remind Jews of Abraham's willingness to sacrifice his son Isaac. The holiday takes place on the first and second days of Tishri (in September or October).

Yom Kippur (Day of Atonement) concludes the 10 days of repentance that Rosh Hashanah begins and takes place from sundown on the ninth day of Tishri until sundown on the 10th. The observance begins with the recitation of the most famous passage in the Jewish liturgy—*Kol Nidre*—which nullifies unfulfilled vows made in the past year. The entire day is spent praying and fasting.

Sukkoth (Tabernacles) is a harvest festival celebrated from the 15th through the 22nd of Tishri. Sukkoth also commemorates the journey of the Jewish people through the wilderness to the land of Israel. Jewish families take their meals this week in a roughly constructed *sukkah* (booth)—a reminder of an agricultural society, of the Exodus, and of how precarious and fragile life can be. On the Simchath Torah, the 23rd of Tishri, a congregation finishes reading the last book of the Torah and immediately starts again with the first.

Hanukkah (Chanukah, Feast of Dedication; Festival of Lights) The importance of the eight-day feast, which begins on the 25th day of Kislev, is its commemoration of the first war in human history fought in the cause of religious freedom. The Maccabees vanquished not just the military threat to Judaism, but the internal forces for assimilation into the Hellenistic culture of Israel's rulers. Jews light candles for eight nights to

Calendar of Jewish Holy Days, 5769–75

Year AM	Rosh Hashanah[1]	Yom Kippur	Sukkoth[1]	Hanukkah[1]	Purim	Pesach[1]	Shabuoth[1]
5769	Sept. 30, 2008	Oct. 9, 2008	Oct. 14, 2008	Dec. 21, 2008	Mar. 10, 2009	April 9, 2009	May 29, 2009
5770	Sept. 19, 2009	Sept. 28, 2009	Oct. 3, 2009	Dec. 12, 2009	Feb. 28, 2010	Mar. 30, 2010	May 19, 2010
5771	Sept. 9, 2010	Sept. 18, 2010	Sept. 23, 2010	Dec. 2, 2010	Mar. 20, 2011	Apr. 19, 2011	June 8, 2011
5772	Sept. 29, 2011	Oct. 8, 2011	Oct. 13, 2011	Dec. 21, 2011	Mar. 8, 2012	Apr. 7, 2012	Mar. 27, 2102
5773	Sept. 17, 2012	Sept. 26, 2012	Oct. 1, 2012	Dec. 9, 2012	Feb. 24, 2013	Mar. 26, 2013	May 15, 2013
5774	Sept. 5, 2013	Sept. 14, 2013	Sept. 19, 2013	Nov. 28, 2013	Feb. 14, 2014	Apr. 15, 2014	June 5, 2014
5775	Sept. 24, 2014	Oct. 4, 2014	Oct. 9, 2014	Dec. 17, 2014	Mar. 5, 2015	Apr. 4, 2015	May 24, 2015

Note: The Jewish day begins and ends at sundown. Thus, all holidays begin at sundown of the day preceding the date shown. 1. Multiday holiday; first day of holiday shown. **Source:** B'nai B'rith.

Chinese Years, 1900–2019

The Chinese New Year is the second New Moon after the winter solstice. The Chinese Year 4706 began on February 7, 2008; Chinese Year 4707 begins on January 26, 2009 and ends February 13, 2010.

Year of the Rat	1900	1912	1924	1936	1948	1960	1972	1984	1996	2008
... Ox	1901	1913	1925	1937	1949	1961	1973	1985	1997	2009
... Tiger	1902	1914	1926	1938	1950	1962	1974	1986	1998	2010
... Hare (Rabbit)	1903	1915	1927	1939	1951	1963	1975	1987	1999	2011
... Dragon	1904	1916	1928	1940	1952	1964	1976	1988	2000	2012
... Snake	1905	1917	1929	1941	1953	1965	1977	1989	2001	2013
... Horse	1906	1918	1930	1942	1954	1966	1978	1990	2002	2014
... Sheep (Goat)	1907	1919	1931	1943	1955	1967	1979	1991	2003	2015
... Monkey	1908	1920	1932	1944	1956	1968	1980	1992	2004	2016
... Rooster	1909	1921	1933	1945	1957	1969	1981	1993	2005	2017
... Dog	1910	1922	1934	1946	1958	1970	1982	1994	2006	2018
... Pig	1911	1923	1935	1947	1959	1971	1983	1995	2007	2019

mark a miracle: a day's supply of oil, found in the recaptured Temple, which according to religious myth, burned for eight days.

Purim (Feast of Lots)   set on the 14th day of Adar, is another celebration of survival, noting the events described in the Book of Esther. At Purim, Jews rejoice at Queen Esther's and her cousin Mordecai's defeat of Haman, the Persian King Ahaserus's advisor who plotted to slaughter all the Persian Jews around 400 B.C.

Pesach (Passover)   beginning on the 15th day of Nisan and lasting seven days, commemorates the exodus of the Hebrews from Egypt in about 1300 B.C. The name, Passover, also recalls God's sparing (passing over) the Jewish first-born during the plagues upon the land brought by God through Moses. The holiday is marked by eating only unleavened foods, participating in a *seder*, or special meal, and reading the *Haggadah*, the story of the Hebrews' deliverance from Egypt.

Shabuoth (Feast of Weeks)   is observed on the sixth or seventh day of Sivan. Originally an agricultural festival, Shabuoth is a celebration of the revelation of the Torah at Mt. Sinai, by which God established his covenant with the Jewish people.

▶ THE ISLAMIC CALENDAR
The 12 months of the Islamic year are: Muharram, Safar, Rab'i I, Rab'i II, Jomada I, Jomada II, Rajab, Sha'ban, Ramadan, Shawwal, Dhu al-Qa'dah, Dhu al-Hijja. The Islamic calendar is based on a lunar year of 12 months of 30 and 29 days (alternating every month) and the year is equal to 354 days. It runs in cycles of 30 years, of which the 2nd, 5th, 7th, 10th, 13th, 16th, 18th, 21st, 24th, 26th, and 29th are leap years. Leap years have 355 days, the extra day being added to the last month, Dhu al-Hijja. There are no intercalated months or leap years, so the Islamic year does not keep a constant relationship to the solar year—which dictates the seasons—and months occur about 10 or 11 days earlier than in the year before.

The caliph Abu Bakr adopted A.D. 622, the year of the *hejira* (Mohammed's migration from Mecca to Medina), as the first year of Islam. However, dating of the Muslim era varies throughout the Islamic world. In some countries, the year of the Muslim era is obtained by subtracting 622 from the Gregorian year; 2004 A.D. equals 1382 A.H. (anno hegirae, in the year of the hejira).

Other countries (Saudi Arabia, Yemen, and the principalities of the Persian Gulf) continue to use a purely lunar year. To approximate the Muslim era equivalent of the Gregorian year, subtract 622 (the year of hejira in the Gregorian calendar) from the current year, and multiply the result by 1.031 (days in the year of the Gregorian calendar divided by days in the lunar year): 2005 A.D. = (2005–622) x 1.031 = 1426 A.H. The accompanying calendar uses this method of calculation.

▶ MUSLIM HOLY DAYS
Ramadan   The ninth month of the Islamic calendar, is the Islamic faith's holiest period. To honor the month in which the Koran was revealed, all adult Muslims of sound body and mind fast, eschewing food, water, or even a kiss between the hours of sunrise and sunset. Exempted from the fast are women in menstruation or childbirth bleeding, the chronically ill, or people on a journey, all of whom must make up the fast days at a later date.

Id al-Fitr   This day of feasting is celebrated at the end of Ramadan. To mark the fast's break, worshippers also attend an early morning service, Salat-ul-'Id, at which they give alms in staple foodstuffs or their monetary value.

Id al-Adha   The Feast of Sacrifice takes place on the 10th day of Dhu al-Hijja, the last month of the year and the season of the haj, or pilgrimage. The day begins with a service in the mosques and other places of gathering, and for those who are not pilgrims, continues with the ritual slaughter of a sheep in commemoration of God's ransom of Abraham's son from sacrifice. At least a third of the meat of the animal is to be given in charity.

Fridays   At noontime, Muslims attend mosque or comparable gathering places to say the congregational Friday prayer that ends the week. While Friday is the holy day of the weekly Muslim calendar, it is not a Sabbath comparable to Christian Sundays or Jewish Saturdays, and there are no restrictions on work or other worldly enterprises.

▶ THE HINDU YEAR
The Hindu year consists of 12 months: Caitra, Vaisakha, Jyaistha, Asadha, Sravana, Bhadrapada, Asvina, Karttika, Margasivsa, Pansa, Magha and Phalguna. Calendrically, holidays are of two types, lunar and solar. Solar holidays in the Hindu calendar include:

Mesasamkranti   The beginning of the new astrological year, when the Sun enters the constellation Aries.

Makaraj-Samkranti   The winter solstice, when the sun enters the constellation Capricorn.

Mahavisuva Day   is New Year's Eve.

Calendar of Muslim Holy Days, 2009–13

Year A.H. (A.D.)	New Year's Day 1 Muharram	1 Ramadan	Id al-Fitr, 1 Shawwal	Id al-Adha, 10 Dhu al-Hijja
1430 (2008–09)	Dec. 29, 2008	Aug. 22, 2009	Sept. 20, 2009	Nov. 27, 2009
1431 (2009–10)	Dec. 18, 2009	Aug. 11, 2010	Sept. 10, 2010	Nov. 16, 2010
1432 (2010–11)	Dec. 7, 2010	Aug. 1, 2011	Aug. 30, 2011	Nov. 6, 2011
1433 (2011-12)	Nov. 26, 2011	July 20, 2012	Aug. 19, 2012	Oct. 26, 2012
1434 (2012-13)	Nov. 15, 2012	July 9, 2013	Aug. 8, 2013	Oct. 15, 2013

Note: The Islamic calendar is based on calculation and depends on actual sighting of the moon. Therefore the dates above are estimates. For exact dates, contact your local masjid, organization, or scholar. **Source:** Islamic Shura Council of North America. www.moonsighting.com.

Principal holidays determined by the lunar year are:

Ramanavami   (Caitra 9), celebrates the birth of Rama, in Hindu folklore, the epitome of chivalry, courage and obedience to sacred law. Considered an incarnation of Vishnu, his name is synonymous with God.

Rathayatra   (Asadha 2), the pilgrimage of the chariot festival of Orissa.

Janmastami   (Sravana 8), The birthday of Krishna, an incarnation of the supreme deity, Vishnu, celebrated as a philosopher-king and hero.

Dasahra   (Asvina 7-10), commemorates Rama's victory over the demon Ravana.

Months of the Year

Gregorian	Hebrew	Hindu	Muslim
January	Shebat	Magha	*Muharram*
February	Adar	Phalguna	Safar
March	Nisan	*Caitra*	Rab'i I
April	Iyar	Vaisakha	Rab'i II
May	Sivan	Jyaistha	Jomada I
June	Tammuz	Asadha	Jomada II
July	Ab	Sravana	Rajab
August	Elul	Bhadrapada	Sha'ban
September	*Tishri*	Asvina	Ramadan
October	Heshvan	Karttika	Shawwal
November	Kislev	Margasivsa	Dhu al-Qa'dah
December	Tebet	Pansa	Dhu al-Hijja

Note: The months of the traditional (lunar) Muslim calendar occur at different times every year. Months in *italics* indicate the first month of the year in the respective calendars.

Astrological Calendar

Dates	Sign
January 20-February 18	Aquarius, the water bearer
February 19-March 20	Pisces, the fishes
March 21-April 19	Aries, the ram
April 20-May 20	Taurus, the bull
May 21-June 20	Gemini, the twins
June 21-July 22	Cancer, the crab
July 23-August 22	Leo, the lion
August 23-September 22	Virgo, the virgin
September 23-October 22	Libra, the scales
October 23-November 21	Scorpio, the scorpion
November 22-December 21	Sagittarius, the archer
December 22-January 19	Capricorn, the goat

Birthstones

Month	Stone
January	Garnet
February	Amethyst
March	Aquamarine, Bloodstone
April	Diamond
May	Emerald
June	Alexandrite, Moonstone, Pearl
July	Ruby
August	Peridot, Sardonyx
September	Sapphire
October	Opal, Tourmaline
November	Topaz
December	Turquoise, Lapis Lazuli

Wedding Anniversaries

Anniversary	Type of gift	Anniversary	Type of gift
1st	Paper	14th	Ivory
2nd	Cotton	15th	Crystal
3rd	Leather	20th	China
4th	Fruit, flowers	25th	Silver
5th	Wood	30th	Pearl
6th	Sugar	35th	Coral
7th	Copper, wool	40th	Ruby
8th	Bronze, pottery	45th	Sapphire
9th	Pottery, willow	50th	Gold
10th	Tin	55th	Emerald
11th	Steel	60th	Diamond
12th	Silk, linen	70th	Platinum
13th	Lace		

Laksmipuja   (Asvina 15), honors Laksmi, goddess of good fortune.

Dipavali   (Karttika 15), festival of lights and exchanging of presents.

Mahasivaratri   (Magha 13), which honors the god Shiva, one of the three supreme Hindu gods. Shiva, whose name means "Auspicious One," is a god of both reproduction and destruction.

ASTRONOMICAL EVENTS, 2009

The main astronomical events included in this section are the phases of the Moon, the Moon's perigee (when it is closest to the Earth) and apogee (when it is farthest away), lunar and solar eclipses, and the visibility of the planets.

▶PHASES OF THE MOON

The relative position of the Earth, Moon and Sun affect what, if any, part of the Moon we can see illuminated by the Sun during our night. A *new moon* occurs when the Moon is precisely aligned between the Earth and the Sun, making the Moon invisible from the Earth. When the Moon is at *first quarter* (90° from the Sun relative to the Earth), its sunlit part appears in the shape of a D (in the Southern Hemisphere, a backward D). A *full moon*, when the Moon shows an almost fully illuminated face, occurs when the Moon is 180° around the sky from the Sun. The *last quarter* (or third quarter) occurs when the Moon is again moving toward a position between the Earth and the Sun, and it appears as a backward D (a normal D in the Southern Hemisphere). Intermediate phases are the *crescent moon*—between the new Moon and first quarter, and between the

Phases of the Moon, 2009

New moon				First quarter				Full moon				Last quarter			
Month	d	h	m	Month	d	h	m	Month	d	h	m	Month	d	h	m
				Jan.	4	11	56	Jan.	11	03	27				
Jan.	26	07	55	Feb.	2	23	13	Feb.	9	14	49	Jan.	18	02	46
Feb.	25	01	35	Mar.	4	07	46	Mar.	11	02	38	Feb.	16	21	37
Mar.	26	16	06	Apr.	2	14	34	Apr.	9	14	56	Mar.	18	17	47
Apr.	25	03	23	May	1	20	44	May	9	04	01	Apr.	17	13	36
May	24	12	11	May	31	03	22	June	7	18	12	May	17	07	26
June	22	19	35	June	29	11	28	July	7	09	21	June	15	22	15
July	22	02	35	July	28	22	00	Aug.	6	00	55	July	15	09	53
Aug.	20	10	02	Aug.	27	11	42	Sept.	4	16	03	Aug.	13	18	55
Sept.	18	18	44	Sept.	26	04	50	Oct.	4	06	10	Sept.	12	02	16
Oct.	18	05	33	Oct.	26	00	42	Nov.	2	19	14	Oct.	11	08	56
Nov.	16	19	14	Nov.	24	21	39	Dec.	2	07	30	Nov.	9	15	56
Dec.	16	12	02	Dec.	24	17	36	Dec.	31	19	13	Dec.	9	00	13

Note: Shown in Universal Time (UT). To convert to local time, see "Timing Planetary Phenomena."
Source: U.S. Naval Observatory, *Astronomical Phenomena for the Year 2009* (2008).

last quarter and new Moon; and the *gibbous moon*, occurring between the half and the full Moon. The full cycle from one phase through all the other phases takes about 29.53 days and is called a *lunation*.

▶ **VISIBILITY OF THE PLANETS, 2009**
Mercury can only be seen low in the east before sunrise, or low in the west after sunset (about the time of the beginning or end of twilight). It is visible in the mornings between the following approximate dates: January 27 to March 22, May 28 to July 6, and September 28 to October 23. The planet is brighter at the end of each period (the best conditions in northern latitudes occur in the first half of October, and in southern latitudes from the end of the first week of February to the start of March). It is visible in the evenings between the following approximate dates: January 1 to January 15, April 9 to May 9, July 22 to September 14 and November 22 to December 30. The planet is brighter at the beginning of each period (the best conditions in northern latitudes occur from mid-April to early May and in southern latitudes from mid-August to early September).

Venus is a brilliant object in the evening sky from the beginning of the year until the second half of March, when it becomes too close to the Sun for observation. At the beginning of April it reappears in the morning sky where it stays until the start of December, when it again becomes too close to the sun for observation. Venus is in conjunction with Mars on April 18 and June 19 and with Saturn on October 13.

Mars is too close to the Sun for observation until the start of February when it appears in the morning sky in Sagittarius. Its westward elongation gradually increases as it passes through Capricornus, Aquarius, Pisces, Cetus, into Pisces again, Aries, Taurus, Gemini, Cancer and into Leo, where it can be seen for more than half the night. Mars is in conjunction with Mercury on January 26 and March 1, with Jupiter on February 17 and with Venus on April 18 and June 19.

Jupiter can be seen in the evening sky in Sagittarius at the beginning of January and then passes into Capricornus during the first week of January,

Visibility of the Planets, 2009

Planet	Morning Twilight	Evening Twilight
Venus	Apr. 1–Dec. 1	Jan. 1–Mar. 24
Mars	Feb. 1–Dec. 31	not visible
Jupiter	Feb. 7–Aug. 14	Jan. 1–Jan. 11
		Aug. 14–Dec. 31
Saturn	Jan. 1–Mar. 8	Mar. 8–Aug. 31
	Oct. 6–Dec. 31	

Source: U.S. Naval Observatory, *Astronomical Phenomena for the Year 2009* (2008).

Major Meteor Showers, 2009

Date[1]	Time (UT)	Event	ZHR[2]
Jan. 3	07:55	Quadrantid Shower	120
Apr. 22	05:26	Lyrid Shower	20
May 04	18:41	Eta Aquarid Shower	60
July 27	20:29	Delta Aquarid Shower	20
Aug. 12	12:23	Perseid Shower	90
Oct. 21	04:41	Orionid Shower	20
Nov. 05	05:09	South Taurid Shower	10
Nov. 12	04:25	North Taurid Shower	15
Nov. 17	10:42	Leonid Shower	15
Dec. 13	23:52	Geminid Shower	120
Dec. 22	08:00	Ursid Shower	10

Note: Shown in Universal Time (UT). To convert to local time, see "Timing Planetary Phenomena." 1. Beginning of shower. Periods of showers vary in length, from several days to several weeks. 2. ZHR= Zenithal Hourly Rate, or maximum number of visible meteors per hour under ideal atmospheric conditions. **Source:** Sky Events Calendar, Fred Espenak and Sumit Dutta (NASA's GSFC) www.nasa.gov

remaining in this constellation throughout the year. In the second week of January, it becomes too close to the Sun for observation and reappears in the morning sky in early February. Its westward elongation gradually increases and after mid-May it can be seen for more than half the night. It is at opposition on August 14 when it is visible throughout the night. Its eastward elongation then gradually decreases and from mid-November until the end of the year it can only be seen in the evening sky. Jupiter is in conjunction with Mars on February 17 and with Mercury on February 24.

Saturn rises shortly before midnight at the beginning of the year in Leo and is at opposition on March 8, when it can be seen throughout the night. From mid-June until the end of August it is visible only in the evening sky, and then becomes too close to the Sun for observation. It reappears in the morning sky in Virgo in early October and remains in the morning sky until late December. Saturn is in conjunction with Mercury on August 18 and October 8 and with Venus on October 13.

Uranus is visible from the beginning of the year until mid-February in the evening sky in Aquarius. It then becomes too close to the sun for observation and reappears in early April in the morning sky in Pisces. It is at opposition on September 17. Its eastward elongation gradually decreases and passes into Aquarius once again from early October, remaining in this constellation for the rest of the year. From mid-December it can only be seen in the evening sky.

Neptune is visible from the beginning of the year in the evening sky in Capricornus and remains in this constellation throughout the year. In the fourth week of January it becomes too close to the Sun for observation and reappears in early March in the morning sky. It is at opposition on August 17 and from mid-November can be seen only in the evening sky.

Do not confuse

(1) Jupiter with Mercury in early January and late February and with Mars in mid-February; on all occasions Jupiter is the brighter object. (2) Mercury with Mars from late February to early March and with Saturn in mid-August and in the second week of October; on all occasions Mercury is the brighter object. (3) Venus with Mars from mid-April to the start of May and from early June to early July and with Saturn in mid-October; on all occasions Venus is the brighter object.

▶ TIMING PLANETARY PHENOMENA

The times for astronomical data shown here are expressed in Universal Time (UT) which is the standard time of the Greenwich meridian (0° of longitude) also known as Greenwich mean time (GMT). To convert to local time, determine your longitude and subtract 1 hour for every 15° of longitude west of 0°; or add 1 hour for every 15° of longitude east of 0°.

The first new moon of 2009 occurs Jan. 11 at 0327 hours in UT. The equivalent time in New York (74°W) is 5 hours earlier, or Jan. 10 at 2227 hours (10:27 P.M.); in Chicago (87°W), 6 hours earlier, or Jan. 10 at 9:27 P.M.; in Denver (105°W), 7 hours earlier, or Jan. 10 at 8:27 P.M.; and in San Francisco (122°W), 8 hours earlier, or Jan. 10 at 7:27 P.M. (To obtain the P.M. equivalent of UT times later than 1200, subtract 12.) Note that local times may differ from these standard times, especially in summer when clocks are often advanced by 1 hour.

▶ ECLIPSES
Eclipses of the Moon

A lunar eclipse occurs when the Sun, Earth and Moon are in a straight line and the shadow of the Earth falls on the Moon. There are three kinds of lunar eclipse. A *total eclipse* occurs when the Moon passes completely into the Earth's total umbra, or shadow, so the Sun cannot be seen from the Moon. A *partial eclipse* occurs when only part of the Earth's umbra falls across the Moon

and the Sun is partially visible from some places on the Moon. A *penumbral eclipse* occurs when only the Earth's penumbra (partial shadow) shades the Moon; and from the Moon one's view of the Sun would be only partially blocked by the Earth. It is usually difficult to detect a penumbral eclipse from the Earth.

During 2009, there will be three penumbral eclipses and one partial eclipse of the Moon. (All times shown in universal time (UT). To convert to local time, see *Timing Planetary Phenomena*.)

February 9, 2009 – Penumbral eclipse
Eclipse begins 12:38.46; greatest eclipse 14:38.15; eclipse ends 16:37.40.

This will be the deepest penumbral eclipse of the year, and will be visible in the northern half of the Moon. The best views in western North America will be after mid-eclipse but the full eclipse will be visible only from Alaska, Hawaii, Australia or East Asia.

July 7, 2009 – Penumbral eclipse
Eclipse begins 08:32.48; greatest eclipse 09:38.38; eclipse ends 10:44.27.

This eclipse will be visible from Australia, the Americas, and the Pacific Ocean but is too minor to be seen with the naked eye.

August 6, 2009 – Penumbral eclipse
Eclipse begins 23:01.04; greatest eclipse 00:39.10; eclipse ends 02:17.23.

This eclipse will be visible from Western Asia, Eastern North America, South America, Africa, Europe, and the Atlantic and Indian Oceans but is too minor to be seen with the naked eye.

December 31, 2009 – Partial eclipse
Eclipse begins 18:51.38; greatest eclipse 19:22.41; eclipse ends 19:53.51.

This minor partial eclipse will be visible from Africa, Europe, Asia, extreme Western Australia, and the Indian Ocean.

Eclipses of the Sun

A solar eclipse occurs when the Moon passes between the Earth and the Sun; there are three types. A *total eclipse* occurs when the Moon's shadow completely covers the Sun and the sky turns dark. Total eclipses occur along a narrow path (typically 100-200 miles wide) called the track of totality and last only a few minutes at any point on the track. A *partial eclipse* occurs when the Moon covers only a portion of the Sun. A total eclipse may be only partial in less than optimum viewing locations. An *annular* (ring-shaped) *eclipse* occurs when the Moon is too far from the Earth to completely cover the Sun, so that at the height of the eclipse, a ring of light surrounds the Moon. In 2009, there will be one annular and one total eclipse of the Sun.

January 26, 2009 – Annular Eclipse
Eclipse begins 04:56.37; greatest eclipse 07:58.39; eclipse ends 11:00.41.

This eclipse will be visible across the Indian Ocean and Indonesia. A partial eclipse will be visible from Northwestern Antarctica, Australia, Southern Africa, and Southeast Asia.

July 21-22, 2009 – Total Eclipse
Eclipse begins 23:58.19 on July 21; greatest eclipse 02:35.25; eclipse ends 05:12.25.

This major eclipse will be greatest over the South Pacific. The eclipse will be visible from Asia and the Western Pacific Ocean.

The United States of America shares the North American continent with Canada, Mexico and the Central American nations. The 48 conterminous states lie in a broad land mass from approximately 24°N to 49°N from south to north, and 67°W to 124°W from east to west. It is bordered on the north by Canada, on the south by Mexico and the Gulf of Mexico, on the east by the Atlantic Ocean, and on the west by the Pacific Ocean. The two nonconterminous states of Alaska and Hawaii are located to the northwest on the North American continent, and in the Pacific Ocean Basin approximately 2,400 miles southwest of the state of California, respectively.

▶ POLITICAL-GEOGRAPHIC DIVISIONS

The Bureau of the Census groups the states in a number of divisions and sub-divisions.

Northeast
New England Maine, New Hampshire, Vermont, Massachusetts, Rhode Island, Connecticut.
Middle Atlantic New York, New Jersey, Pennsylvania.

Midwest
East North Central Ohio, Indiana, Illinois, Michigan, Wisconsin.
West North Central Minnesota, Iowa, Missouri, North Dakota, South Dakota, Nebraska, Kansas.

South
South Atlantic Delaware, Maryland, District of Columbia, Virginia, West Virginia, North Carolina, South Carolina, Georgia, Florida.
East South Central Kentucky, Tennessee, Alabama, Mississippi.
West South Central Arkansas, Louisiana, Oklahoma, Texas.

Pacific
Mountain Montana, Idaho, Wyoming, Colorado, New Mexico, Arizona, Utah, Nevada.
Pacific Washington, Oregon, California, Alaska, Hawaii.

▶ PHYSIOGRAPHIC REGIONS

The physiographic regions, or the primary geological features and landforms, of the United States are:

Atlantic and Gulf Coast Plains
These run from the islands of southern New England, Cape Cod, and Long Island, through New Jersey, Delaware, Maryland, Virginia, North Carolina, South Carolina, Georgia, Florida, Alabama, Mississippi, Louisiana, Texas; includes lower Mississippi Valley in Arkansas, Missouri, Tennessee.

Appalachian System
The Appalachian System is divided into five parts:
New England White Mountains (New Hampshire), Green Mountains (Vermont), Champlain Lowland and Hudson Valley (Vermont, New York), Catskill Mountains (New York).
The Piedmont Pennsylvania, Virginia, North Carolina, South Carolina, Georgia, Alabama.
Great Smoky and Blue Ridge Mountains Pennsylvania (Poconos), [discontinuous], Virginia, North Carolina, Georgia.
Ridge and Valley Pennsylvania, West Virginia, Virginia, Kentucky, Tennessee, Alabama.
Appalachian Plateau Pennsylvania, Ohio, West Virginia, Kentucky, Tennessee, Alabama.

Canadian (or Laurentian) Shield
This region covers much of eastern Canada and extends into the U.S. in two places:
Adirondack Mountains New York.
Superior Upland Upper Michigan, Wisconsin, Minnesota.

Central Lowland
The Central Lowland includes most of the U.S. interior, and is divided into four parts:
Interior Lowlands Ohio, Kentucky, Tennessee.
Mississippi Great Lakes Basin Ohio, Indiana, Illinois, Michigan, Wisconsin, Iowa, North Dakota, South Dakota.
Interior Highlands Ozark Mountains: Missouri, Arkansas, Oklahoma; Ouachita Mountains: Arkansas, Oklahoma.
Great Plains North Dakota, South Dakota, Nebraska, Kansas, Oklahoma, Texas, Montana, Wyoming, Colorado, New Mexico.

Cordilleran Province
Rocky Mountains New Mexico, Colorado, Wyoming, Montana.

Intermontane Range
This range is divided into four sections:
Colorado Plateau Colorado, Utah, New Mexico, Arizona (including Grand Canyon).
Basin and Range Plateau Nevada, Utah (including Wasatch Range).
Desert Basin and Range California (including Death Valley), Arizona.
Snake and Columbia River Basins Idaho, Washington, Oregon.

U.S. Geographic Extremes

Because the Aleutian Islands wrap around the Greenwich Meridian, Alaska technically contains both the easternmost and westernmost points in the United States.

Extreme	Contiguous 48 states (Long. or Lat.)	U.S. (Long. or Lat.)[1]
North	Northwest Angle Inlet, Minn. 49° 23′ N	Point Barrow, Alaska, 71° 23′ N
South	Key West, Fla. 24° 33′ N	Ka Lae, Hawaii 18° 55′ N
East	West Quoddy Head, Maine, 66° 57′ W	Pochnoi Point, Alaska, 179° 52′ E
West	Capa Alava, Wash. 124° 44′ W	Amatignak Island, Alaska 179° 09′ W

1. U.S. states only; does not include U.S. territories and possessions. **Source:** U.S. Geological Survey, Elevations and Distances in the United States, online edition. http://mapping.usgs.gov/mac/isb/pubs/booklets/elvadist/elvadist.html.

Pacific Coastlands

This region is divided into four sections, three oriented north-south, the other east-west.

Cascade Mountains and Sierra Nevada Washington, Oregon, California, Nevada.

Puget Sound, Willamette Valley, and Central Valley Washington, Oregon, California.

Coast Ranges Washington, Oregon, California.

Los Angeles Extension Tehachapi Mountains (east-west), San Gabriel Mountains and San Bernardino Mountains.

▶ NATIONAL PARK SYSTEM

The National Park System of the U.S. began in March 1872 with the establishment of the Yellowstone National Park in the Territories of Montana and Wyoming, "as a public park or pleasuring ground for the benefit and enjoyment of the people" and was placed "under exclusive control of the Secretary of the Interior." The founding of Yellowstone began a worldwide national park movement and today more than 100 countries contain some 1,200 national parks or equivalent preserves.

President Woodrow Wilson created the National Park Service as a bureau within the Department of the Interior in 1916, and charged it with protecting the 35 national parks and monuments then in existence. Today, the U.S. National Park System comprises 385 areas covering more than 79 million acres (3 percent of total U.S. area) in 49 states (there are no areas in Delaware), the District of Columbia, Guam, Puerto Rico, Saipan and the Virgin Islands. Additions to the National Park System are generally made through acts of Congress, and national parks can be created only through such acts. But under the Antiquities Act of 1906, the president has authority to proclaim national monuments on lands already under Federal jurisdiction.

The diversity of the parks managed by the National Park Service (NPS) is reflected in the variety of titles given to them. Although the system is best known for its scenic National Parks, more than half the areas of the National Park System preserve places, and commemorate persons, events, and activities important in the nation's history. Brief definitions of each type of park follow, together with the number of areas and total federal acreage. An additional 11 areas such as the White House, the National Mall, etc., totaling nearly 40,000 acres of federal land, are without designation.

National battlefields/battlefield parks/ battlefield site/military parks cover a variety of areas associated with U.S. military history (Antietam National Battlefield, Maryland). (1 battlefield site, 1 acre; 9 military parks, 36,338 acres; 11 battlefields, 12,289 acres; 3 battlefield parks, 8,713 acres)

National capital parks include more than 346 sites (The Ellipse; Lafayette Park) throughout the Washington, D.C., area. (6,482 acres)

National historical parks are areas of greater physical extent and complexity than historic sites (Nez Perce, Idaho). (41; 119,049 acres)

National historic sites include areas of prehistoric and modern historical interest (Tuskegee Institute, Mississippi), archaeological sites, historic structures and the like. Because it is of importance to both the U.S. and Canada, St. Croix Island (28 acres) is designated an International Historic Site. (77; 21,677 acres)

National lakeshores/seashores (Cape Cod NS, Massachusetts; Pictured Rocks NL, Michigan) preserve shoreline areas and offshore islands while providing water-oriented recreation. (4 lakeshores, 145,641 acres; 10 seashores, 479,054 acres)

National memorial designates an area or structure that is commemorative in nature (Mt. Rushmore, South Dakota). (29; 8,081 acres)

National monuments are intended to preserve at least one nationally significant resource (Rainbow Bridge, Utah). They are usually smaller than national parks and lack the diversity of attractions. (75; 2,157,574 acres)

National parks contain a variety of resources and encompass large land and water areas (Grand Canyon, Arizona) to help provide adequate protection of resources. (56; 49,638,564 acres)

National parkways are ribbons of land flanking roadways (Natchez Trace, Mississippi, Alabama and Tennessee) that offer an opportunity for leisurely driving through areas of scenic interest. (4; 163,940 acres)

National preserves serve primarily to protect certain resources (Big Thicket, Texas). Activities like hunting and fishing or mineral extraction may be permitted. (18; 22,027,743 acres)

National recreation areas were originally areas surrounding reservoirs (Lake Mead, Nevada and Arizona), but now include other lands and waters set aside for recreational use. (18; 3,389,572 acres)

National reserves are similar to the preserves, but are administered by state or local authorities (City of Rocks, Idaho). (2; 11,440 acres)

National rivers/wild and scenic riverways preserve ribbons of land bordering freeflowing streams that have not been dammed, channelized, or otherwise altered (Delaware River, Pennsylvania and New Jersey). Activities such as hiking, boating and hunting may be permitted. (5 National Rivers; 312,161 acres; 10 National Wild & Scenic Riverways; 73,892 acres)

National scenic trails are usually long-distance footpaths winding through areas of natural beauty (Appalachian Trail, Maine to Georgia). (3; 166,922 acres)

National wilderness areas are designated under the Wilderness Act of 1964, which provides that "there shall be no commercial enterprise and no permanent road within any wilderness area . . . and (except for emergency uses) no temporary road, no use of motor vehicles, motorized equipment or motorboats, no landing of aircraft, no other form of mechanical transport, and no structure or installation." Wilderness areas are usually part of other larger entities.

In addition to the National Park System, there are three groups of areas that are closely linked in importance and purpose to NPS-managed areas.

U.S. National Parks: Acreage, Visits, and Overnight Stays, 1990–2004

National Park, State	Acres under Federal protection, 2004	Visits ('000s)			Overnight stays ('000s)		
		1990	2000	2004	1990	2000	2004
Acadia, Maine	46,148	2,413	2,469	2,208	223	146	130
Arches, Utah	76,353	621	786	733	58	46	48
Badlands, South Dakota	232,822	1,326	1,106	936	35	54	44
Big Bend, Texas	775,279	257	262	358	215	186	185
Biscayne, Florida	170,955	573	393	478	29	N.A.	N.A.
Black Canyon of the Gunnison, Colo.	30,750	(¹)	192	176	(¹)	14	15
Bryce Canyon, Utah	35,832	863	1,099	987	144	145	133
Canyonlands, Utah	337,570	277	402	372	78	108	94
Capitol Reef, Utah	241,234	562	613	550	48	42	37
Carlsbad Caverns, New Mexico	46,427	747	469	420	(x)	(x)	(x)
Channel Islands, California	79,018	144	483	538	32	101	128
Crater Lake, Oregon	183,223	385	427	417	45	73	74
Cuyahoga Valley, Ohio	19,559	(¹)	3,325	3,306	(¹)	6	6
Death Valley, California-Nevada	3,323,771	(¹)	1,179	765	(¹)	225	181
Denali, Alaska	4,724,790	547	364	404	118	121	123
Dry Tortugas, Florida	61,481	19	84	68	25	41	23
Everglades, Florida	1,398,657	958	995	1,181	128	106	100
Gates of the Arctic, Alaska	7,266,262	1	12	10	5	1	6
Glacier Bay, Alaska	3,223,018	204	385	354	36	44	31
Glacier, Montana	1,013,154	1,987	1,729	2,034	330	309	313
Grand Canyon, Arizona	1,180,862	3,777	4,460	4,326	908	1085	1,220
Grand Teton, Wyoming	307,690	1,588	2,590	2,360	597	532	492
Great Basin, Nevada	77,180	65	81	80	44	32	26
Great Smoky Mountain, Tenn.-N.C.	521,122	8,152	10,176	9,167	463	421	360
Guadalupe Mountains, Texas	86,189	193	199	182	18	20	17
Haleakala, Hawaii	29,110	1,261	1,620	1,455	19	24	13
Hawaii Volcanoes, Hawaii	323,431	1,097	1,515	1,307	112	110	118
Hot Springs, Arkansas	4,932	1,123	1,338	1,419	8	4	6
Isle Royale, Michigan	539,281	23	21	17	56	61	53
Joshua Tree, California	769,175	(¹)	1,234	1,244	(¹)	245	245
Katmai, Alaska	405,432	41	72	56	12	29	7
Kenai Fjords, Alaska	601,839	66	255	244	1	4	3
Kings Canyon, California	461,845	1,063	529	525	302	217	184
Kobuk Valley, Alaska	1,669,912	3	3	5	(x)	(x)	(x)
Lake Clark, Alaska	2,226,807	10	6	5	1	2	2
Lassen Volcanic, California	106,368	461	375	380	113	79	80
Mammoth Cave, Kentucky	52,003	1,925	1,749	1,888	98	89	80
Mesa Verde, Colorado	51,890	611	452	447	159	82	91
Mount Rainier, Washington	235,625	1,327	1,345	1,218	184	196	195
North Cascades, Washington	504,633	456	26	17	97	19	15
Olympic, Washington	913,531	2,795	3,328	3,074	404	506	341
Petrified Forest, Arizona	93,532	845	605	580	1	2	5
Redwood, California	77,726	348	383	392	16	59	13
Rocky Mountain, Colorado	265,461	2,647	3,185	2,782	209	232	187
Saguaro, Arizona	87,526	(¹)	765	651	(¹)	2	2
Sequoia, California	403,875	1,064	839	1,000	345	252	241
Shenandoah, Virginia	198,250	1,772	1,420	1,261	323	284	276
Theodore Roosevelt, North Dakota	69,702	461	432	475	26	28	24
Virgin Island, U.S. Virgin Islands	12,916	665	704	794	173	215	162
Voyageurs, Minnesota	133,121	224	227	249	47	18	22
Wind Cave, South Dakota	28,295	586	669	594	11	10	7
Wrangell-St. Elias, Alaska	7,662,705	36	28	57	3	2	N.A.
Yellowstone, Montana-Wyoming	2,219,789	2,824	2,838	2,868	1,345	1,191	1,207
Yosemite, California	759,530	3,125	3,401	3,281	2,220	1,633	1,614
Zion, Utah	143,073	2,102	2,432	2,677	292	243	271
Total National Parks	**42,055,378**	**54,619**	**66,076**	**63,766**	**10,156**	**9,696**	**9,250**
Total National Parks System²	**79,005,556**	**255,655**	**285,891**	**277,908**	**17,625**	**15,726**	**13,981**

Note: (x) = less than 1,000. Visit and overnight stay data often varies from year to year because of special events such as anniversaries and natural disasters. 1. Area was not a National Park in year shown. 2. Includes National Historic Sites, National Memorials, National Seashores, National Parkways, and other areas under the jurisdiction of the National Park Service. **Source:** U.S. National Park Service Statistical Abstract 2004 (2005).

Affiliated areas (designated by Act of Congress, 1970) are areas in the U.S. and Canada that preserve significant areas outside the National Park System but that rely on NPS assistance.

Wild and Scenic Rivers System (designated by Act of Congress, 1968) preserves undeveloped rivers as free-flowing streams accessible for public use. Wild rivers are free of dams and generally accessible only by trails; scenic rivers

State Parks and Recreation Areas by State, 2004

State	Areas	Total Acreage	Visitors ('000s) Day	Overnight	Total[1]	Revenues ('000s)	Revenues as percent of operating expenses
U.S. Total	5,793	13,825,441	652,875,677	65,982,812	718,858,489	$786,585,753	100%
Alabama	24	49,710	3,259,336	1,137,846	4,397,182	24,094,767	83.9
Alaska	139	3,353,485	3,166,753	835,817	4,002,570	2,155,840	37.4
Arizona	31	60,921	1,636,285	559,632	2,195,917	8,751,133	31.6
Arkansas	50	52,610	9,259,030	545,609	9,804,639	13,690,947	40.1
California	278	1,492,622	75,018,891	7,012,720	82,031,611	73,567,000	26.8
Colorado	114	356,688	11,140,764	1,004,797	12,145,561	17,598,353	65.6
Connecticut	133	203,480	6,278,675	294,706	6,573,381	4,296,678	35.9
Delaware	33	24,366	3,722,646	204,500	3,927,146	7,668,400	32.6
Florida	157	613,701	17,179,032	1,938,912	19,117,944	38,273,069	53.2
Georgia	72	83,809	11,596,127	1,168,737	12,764,864	29,328,362	52.8
Hawaii	68	27,117	9,176,350	44,948	9,221,298	1,772,568	66.3
Idaho	32	45,337	2,415,380	366,892	2,782,272	3,077,900	18.6
Illinois	296	479,175	42,428,543	899,221	43,327,764	6,080,504	12.0
Indiana	33	179,220	15,664,767	2,676,476	18,341,243	35,804,770	100
Iowa	182	63,432	13,928,584	699,844	14,628,428	3,645,510	27.6
Kansas	25	32,900	3,778,818	3,501,902	7,280,720	5,855,702	69.4
Kentucky	50	58,291	6,520,379	1,077,232	7,597,611	53,683,594	62.2
Louisiana	57	41,204	1,105,123	981,612	2,086,735	5,715,217	67.7
Maine	131	98,533	1,958,596	267,666	2,226,262	2,534,705	32.5
Maryland	51	268,176	9,932,541	810,269	10,742,810	14,877,574	39.6
Massachusetts	241	297,517	9,222,251	828,662	10,050,913	5,484,070	17.6
Michigan	103	285,573	15,635,587	4,815,947	20,451,534	32,257,727	62.8
Minnesota	198	221,274	6,932,086	887,580	7,819,666	13,399,000	47.9
Mississippi	28	24,287	2,362,508	765,564	3,128,072	6,869,081	54.3
Missouri	83	140,318	15,900,036	1,146,895	17,046,931	7,514,742	25.5
Montana	396	59,644	1,239,978	245,511	1,485,489	1,877,753	26.8
Nebraska	85	134,681	8,292,993	1,592,635	9,885,628	15,209,533	93.2
Nevada	24	132,524	3,973,730	175,047	4,148,777	2,186,769	23.5
New Hampshire	89	232,006	2,616,425	234,540	2,850,965	7,475,604	87.9
New Jersey	116	388,569	13,662,846	460,663	14,123,509	10,504,357	30.9
New Mexico	31	90,693	1,536,094	2,304,140	3,840,234	3,533,944	18.8
New York	867	1,542,630	49,445,801	4,079,165	53,524,966	79,677,123	48.3
North Carolina	62	174,862	10,972,951	302,166	11,275,117	3,614,408	3.9
North Dakota	30	17,401	880,952	167,578	1,048,530	1,336,285	46.7
Ohio	74	164,406	50,337,984	3,033,017	53,371,001	28,894,665	43.5
Oklahoma	50	71,579	12,676,970	1,408,552	14,085,522	21,586,877	57.8
Oregon	233	99,030	42,731,964	2,412,511	45,144,475	18,784,912	45.4
Pennsylvania	119	290,129	32,978,511	1,713,724	34,692,235	13,704,271	20.1
Rhode Island	74	8,748	2,609,965	461,571	3,071,536	4,276,739	51.9
South Carolina	55	80,734	6,153,127	1,214,244	7,367,371	16,763,173	71.8
South Dakota	129	105,396	8,502,235	714,486	9,216,721	9,403,748	75.1
Tennessee	53	136,403	26,702,434	1,459,147	28,161,581	31,084,502	51.2
Texas	125	601,558	7,342,037	2,373,691	9,715,728	29,399,445	57.2
Utah	52	149,667	4,418,127	1,448,947	5,867,074	8,221,000	35.8
Vermont	103	68,858	315,796	363,818	679,614	6,235,008	95.1
Virginia	38	64,277	5,480,926	644,819	6,125,745	9,626,445	38.1
Washington	252	259,684	38,356,372	2,053,200	40,409,572	18,170,703	39.9
West Virginia	47	195,831	7,177,655	655,437	7,833,092	18,389,666	63.3
Wisconsin	68	132,829	13,366,951	1,600,468	14,967,419	14,977,175	75.8
Wyoming	36	119,266	1,883,765	389,749	2,273,514	1,327,835	16.1

1. Includes overnight visitors.   **Source:** National Association of State Park Directors (Tucson, Ariz.), 2005 Annual Information Exchange.

have relatively primitive shorelines and are largely undeveloped but may be accessible by road.

National Trails System (designated by National Trails System Act of 1968) includes trails in both urban and rural settings for persons of all ages, interests, skills, and physical abilities. The Appalachian Trail and the Pacific Crest were the first two trails designated under the National Trails System. Today, there are more than 800 trails, in every state, Puerto Rico and the District

of Columbia, totaling more than 9,000 miles in length.

▶RIVERS AND LAKES

Major Navigable Waterways of the United States The U.S inland and intracoastal waterway system handles over 500 million tons of traffic each year, carried by a fleet of more than 5,000 towboats and 31,000 barges on over 11,000 miles of primary channels. Ninety percent of these channels have depths of between 9 and 14 feet.

Maintenance and improvement of the waterways—including channel dredging, bridge and levee maintenance, and the construction of canals and locks—are in large measure the responsibility of the U.S. Army Corps of Engineers. The 522-mile New York State Barge Canal System is the only major non-federal waterway in the country.

Mississippi River System

The major inland river transportation network is the Mississippi River and its tributaries. This north-south-oriented system includes the Mississippi River, the Ohio River System, the Illinois Waterway, and the Arkansas and Missouri rivers, among others. In this system there are about 7,000 miles of heavily used, improved navigable channels, 85 percent of which have at least nine-foot navigable channel depths.

Intracoastal Waterways

At its mouth, the Mississippi River is intersected by the Gulf Intracoastal Waterway (GIWW), which parallels the Gulf Coast for 1,180 miles from St. Marks River, Florida, to Brownsville, Texas, at the Mexican border. The GIWW is intersected by a number of river systems in addition to the Mississippi, including the Mobile River, the Apalachicola and the Houston Ship Channel.

This network of major inland and coastal waterways connects some of the largest Gulf Coast ports—New Orleans, La.; Houston, Beaumont and Corpus Christi, Tex.; and Mobile, Ala.—with some of the largest inland ports—St. Louis, Mo.; Pittsburgh, Pa.; Huntington, W. Va.; Cincinnati, Ohio; Memphis, Tenn; and Chicago, Ill. The 40-foot controlling depth of the Mississippi River between the Gulf of Mexico and Baton Rouge allows ocean shipping to join the barge traffic, making this segment especially vital to both the domestic and foreign commerce of the United States.

The Atlantic Intracoastal Waterway provides 1,329 miles of protected channels for commercial and recreational navigation along the Atlantic Coast from Key West, Fla., to Norfolk, Va. Partially protected segments of the waterway continue north from Norfolk along the Delmarva Peninsula, the New Jersey coast and Long Island. Among the major Atlantic Coast ports located along this waterway are Miami, Savannah, Baltimore, Philadelphia and New York/New Jersey.

Pacific Coast

In comparison with the Mississippi River system and the intracoastal waterways of the Atlantic and Gulf coasts, the inland and coastal waterways of the Pacific are few. Shallow draft waterways include the Columbia-Snake Waterway and the Willamette River above Portland, Oreg.; the Sacramento River above Sacramento, Calif.; the San Joaquin River above Stockton, Calif.; and a few short navigable rivers stretching along the Washington and Oregon coasts.

The accompanying table shows the major navigable rivers in the United States, their total length, the distance commercially navigable, the body of water they flow into, and the head of navigation—the upriver point beyond which commercial ships cannot pass—and the states through or by which the rivers pass, from source to mouth.

Great Lakes and St. Lawrence Seaway

The Great Lakes have been crucial to the development of the United States. They were the highways along which people and finished goods moved west, and along which raw materials such as lumber, minerals, and grains were transported to eastern markets. Later, the cities of the Great Lakes, such as Chicago, Duluth, Detroit and Buffalo, became important centers of finance, industry, and trade in their own right. So important was the maritime trade of the Lakes that in the 1890s, Chicago was the fourth-largest port in the world, despite being closed by ice for as many as five months a year.

An early obstacle to Great Lakes navigation was the fact that the lakes are not all at the same elevation: there is a difference of 354 feet between the level of the westernmost Lake Superior and easternmost Lake Ontario, and there is another 246 feet descent from Lake Ontario down the St. Lawrence River where it empties into the Atlantic Ocean. (It is 2,342 miles from Duluth, Minnesota, at the western end of Lake Superior, to the mouth of the St. Lawrence.)

The first canal (1799) was built on the St. Mary's River between Lake Superior and Lake Huron. (Today, there are two Sault Sainte Marie [or Soo] Canals—along the 70-mile river.) In 1825, the United States opened the way between the upper Lakes (all but Lake Ontario) and the Atlantic via the 175-mile Erie Canal between Buffalo, on Lake Erie, and Albany, on the Hudson River north of New York City. Canada followed with the 27-mile Welland Canal (1833) connecting Welland on Lake Erie and St. Catharine's on Lake Ontario.

The most ambitious undertaking was the construction of the St. Lawrence Seaway, a joint Canadian-American effort to open the entire length of the St. Lawrence and the Great Lakes to oceangoing navigation. Started in 1955 and opened to navigation in 1959, the seaway's system of canals and locks allows ships of up to 730 feet in length and 27 feet draft to sail the entire 2,342 miles from the mouth of the St. Lawrence to Duluth, Minn., at the western end of Lake Superior. The seaway also provides hydroelectric power for Canada and the United States.

The Panama Canal

One of the great engineering feats of the world, the 44-mile Panama Canal

The Great Lakes

Lake	Area (sq. mi)	Area (sq. km)	Depth (feet)	Depth (meters)	Height above sea level (feet)	Height above sea level (meters)
Erie	9,940	25,745	210	64	571	174
Huron	23,010	59,596	750	229	577	176
Michigan	22,400	58,016	923	281	577	176
Ontario	7,540	19,529	802	244	246	75
Superior	31,820	82,414	1,333	406	600	183

Source: U.S. Environmental Protection Agency and Environment Canada, The Great Lakes: An Environmental Atlas and Resource Book (1987).

bisects the continents of North and South America, making it possible for ships to sail between the Atlantic and Pacific oceans without rounding the treacherous Cape Horn at the tip of South America. The U.S. government began construction of the canal in 1904, and it was opened to commercial navigation Aug. 15, 1914. For inter-ocean shippers, the savings in distance and time afforded by the canal are enormous. A ship sailing from New York to San Francisco via the Panama Canal travels a distance of 5,264 miles, a savings of more than 7,800 miles—or about 20 days— over the 13,100-mile route around Cape Horn. The minimum depth of the canal is 41 feet, the minimum width 300 feet, and the highest elevation above sea level 85 feet.

The Canal Zone, a 10-mile-wide strip of land around the canal in the Republic of Panama was acquired in 1903 by the United States, who governed it until 1979. The Panama Canal Treaty of 1977 abolished the Canal Zone as an independent political entity, but the canal's maintenance and operation remained the responsibility of the U.S. Panama Canal Commission until 1999, when the Republic of Panama assumed full responsibility.

Land Cover and Use, by State, 1997 (thousands of acres)

| State | Total surface area[1] | Federal land area | Non-Federal land areas | | | | |
			Developed[2]	Rural cropland	Rural pastureland	Rural rangeland	Rural forestland
United States	1,941,827	452,913	104,812	374,690	119,144	402,976	398,409
Alabama	33,424	2,240	2,410	2,919	3,527	68	21,073
Arizona	72,964	30,634	1,675	1,204	67	32,114	4,262
Arkansas	34,037	3,997	1,501	7,582	5,453	73	14,765
California	101,510	48,584	5,687	9,561	1,065	17,457	14,295
Colorado	66,625	24,145	1,706	8,860	1,269	23,855	3,729
Connecticut	3,195	143	897	199	107	—	1,729
Delaware	1,534	321	238	472	23	—	347
Florida	37,534	6,938	5,449	2,719	4,177	3,193	12,255
Georgia	37,741	3,177	4,238	4,661	2,853	—	21,216
Hawaii	4,163	446	186	244	89	946	1,514
Idaho	53,488	34,120	811	5,500	1,253	6,478	3,942
Illinois	36,059	1,252	3,262	23,954	2,525	—	3,631
Indiana	23,158	858	2,356	13,358	1,818	—	3,638
Iowa	36,017	663	1,803	25,262	3,554	—	2,084
Kansas	52,661	1,064	2,882	26,460	2,213	15,179	1,290
Kentucky	25,863	1,815	1,955	5,151	5,613	—	10,440
Louisiana	31,377	5,063	1,693	5,568	2,376	280	13,114
Maine	20,966	1,457	747	419	82	—	17,633
Maryland	7,870	1,832	1,291	1,598	454	—	2,331
Massachusetts	5,339	477	1,549	271	114	—	2,657
Michigan	37,349	4,385	3,764	8,439	2,004	—	16,238
Minnesota	54,010	6,484	2,361	21,328	3,423	—	14,830
Mississippi	30,527	2,632	1,656	5,296	3,699	—	16,019
Missouri	44,614	2,766	2,653	13,710	10,947	98	12,118
Montana	94,110	28,150	881	15,086	3,495	37,016	5,279
Nebraska	49,510	1,139	1,268	19,421	1,976	22,864	799
Nevada	70,763	60,315	416	711	271	8,300	297
New Hampshire	5,941	1,000	642	132	92	—	3,875
New Jersey	5,216	679	1,849	574	109	—	1,625
New Mexico	77,823	26,603	1,325	1,842	207	40,276	4,915
New York	31,361	1,495	3,373	5,375	2,627	—	17,533
North Carolina	33,709	5,284	4,181	5,539	1,980	—	15,678
North Dakota	45,251	2,834	1,152	24,991	1,105	10,551	443
Ohio	26,445	781	3,797	11,504	1,980	—	6,984
Oklahoma	44,738	2,230	1,997	9,709	7,933	13,974	7,254
Oregon	62,161	32,088	1,296	3,800	1,905	9,556	12,295
Pennsylvania	28,995	1,204	4,336	5,245	1,812	—	15,306
Rhode Island	813	154	205	20	24	—	381
South Carolina	19,939	1,857	2,325	2,542	1,182	—	10,958
South Dakota	49,358	3,991	1,035	16,738	2,078	21,764	532
Tennessee	26,974	2,020	2,618	4,566	4,985	—	11,736
Texas	171,052	7,062	8,984	26,762	15,807	95,323	10,627
Utah	54,339	36,079	760	1,676	695	10,720	1,830
Vermont	6,154	659	346	601	342	—	4,118
Virginia	27,087	4,604	2,805	2,879	3,071	—	13,030
Washington	44,035	13,478	2,214	6,689	1,200	5,744	12,666
West Virginia	15,508	1,385	986	848	1,503	—	10,472
Wisconsin	35,920	3,142	2,543	10,537	2,882	—	13,634
Wyoming	62,603	29,184	716	2,171	1,181	27,150	995

Note: U.S. Totals exclude Alaska and the District of Columbia. 1. Includes water area and minor land cover and uses not shown separately. 2. Includes urban and built-up areas in units of 10 acres or greater, and rural transportation areas.
Source: U.S. Department of Agriculture, National Resource and Conservation Service and Iowa State University, Statistical Laboratory, Summary Report, 1997 National Resources Inventory, December, 1999.

Major Navigable Rivers in the U.S.

Ultimate outflow/river	Length (miles)	Navigable length (miles)	Mouth to head of navigation	States/provinces (from source to mouth)
ATLANTIC OCEAN				
St. Lawrence	760	760	Gulf of St. Lawrence to Lake Ontario	N.Y.; Ontario, Quebec (Canada)
Cape Cod Canal	17	17	Sandwich to Buzzards Bay, Mass.	Mass.
Connecticut	407	52	Long Island Sound to Hartford, Conn.	N.H., Vt., Mass., Conn.
Hudson	306	134	New York Bay to Troy Lock, N.Y. New York State Barge Canal links to Lake Erie (353 mi. Troy to Buffalo), and to Lakes Champlain, Ontario, Cayuga, Seneca.	N.Y.
Delaware	367	77	Delaware Bay to Trenton, N.J.	N.Y., Pa., N.J., Del.
Chesapeake and Delaware Canal	14	14	Delaware Bay to Chesapeake Bay	Del., Md.
Potomac	287	101	Chesapeake Bay to Washington, D.C.	Va., Md., D.C.
James	340	87	Chesapeake Bay to Richmond, Va.	Va.
Roanoke	410	112	Atlantic Ocean to Altavista, N.C.	Va., N.C.
Cape Fear	202	111	Atlantic Ocean to Fayetteville, N.C.	N.C.
Savannah	314	181	Atlantic Ocean to Augusta, Ga.	S.C., Ga.
Saint Johns	285	160	Atlantic Ocean to Lake Harney	Fla.
GULF OF MEXICO				
Chattahoochee	436	194	Apalachicola River to Columbus, Ga.	Ga., Ala.
Apalachicola	90	90	Gulf of Mexico to Chattahoochee, Fla.	Fla.
Mobile	45	45	Mobile Bay to confluence of Alabama and Tombigbee rivers	Ala.
Alabama	318	305	Mobile River to Montgomery, Ala.	Ala.
Tombigbee	362	362	Mobile River to Amory, Miss. Linked to Tennessee River by Tennessee-Tombigbee Waterway (253 mi.)	Ala., Miss.
Black Warrior	217	217	Tombigbee River to Birmingham, Ala.	Ala.
Houston Ship Channel	57	57	Galveston Bay to Houston, Tex.	Tex.
Río Grande[1]	1,885	13	Gulf of Mexico to Brownsville, Tex.	Colo., N.Mex., Tex., Mexico
MISSISSIPPI RIVER SYSTEM				
Mississippi	2,348	1,807	Gulf of Mexico to Minneapolis, Minn.,	Minn., Wis., Iowa, Ill., Mo., Ky., Tenn., Ark., Miss., La
EASTERN TRIBUTARIES OF THE MISSISSIPPI				
Illinois	273	273	Mississippi River to Joliet. Also linked to Mississippi by Illinois and Mississippi Canal (La Salle to Rockport); and to Lake Michigan (at Chicago, Calumet, East Chicago Gary) by Illinois Waterway	Ill.
Ohio	981	981	Mississippi River to Pittsburgh, Pa.	Pa., Ohio, W.Va., Ind., Ky., Ill.
Monongahela	129	129	Ohio River to Fairmont, W.Va.	W.Va., Pa.
Allegheny	325	72	Ohio River to East Brady, Pa.	N.Y., Pa.
Kanawha	97	91	Ohio River to Charleston, W.Va.	W.Va.
Kentucky	259	82	Ohio River to Beattyville, Ky.	Ky.
Green	360	103	Ohio River to Bowling Green, Ky.	Ky.
Cumberland	694	387	Ohio River to Burnside, Ky.	Ky., Tenn.
Tennessee	652	648	Ohio River to Knoxville, Tenn.	Tenn., Ala., Miss., Ky.
Yazoo	169	165	Mississippi River to Greenwood, Miss.	Miss.
WESTERN TRIBUTARIES OF THE MISSISSIPPI				
Missouri	2,315	735	Mississippi River to Ponca, Nebr.	Mont., N.Dak., S.Dak., Nebr., Iowa, Kans., Mo.
Arkansas	1,396	448	McClellan-Kerr Arkansas River System from Mississippi River to Catoosa, Okla., incorporates sections of White, Arkansas, Verdigris rivers.	Colo., Kans., Okla., Ark.,
Ouachita[2]	605	351	Mississippi River to Camden, Ark.	Ark., La.
Red	1,018	236	Mississippi River to Shreveport, La.	N.Mex., Tex., Okla., Ark., La.
Atchafalaya[3]	220	220	Atchafalaya Bay to Mississippi River	La.
PACIFIC OCEAN				
San Joaquin	340	103	Sacramento River to Hills Ferry, Calif.	Calif.
Sacramento	374	163	San Francisco Bay to Chico Landing, Calif.	Calif.
Columbia	1,210	285	Pacific Ocean to Pasco, Wash.	British Col. (Can.), Wash., Oreg.
Snake	1,083	192	Columbia River to Johnson Bar Landing,	Wyo., Idaho, Oreg., Wash.
Willamette	294	133	Columbia River to Harrisburg, Oreg.	Oreg.

Note: All distances given in nautical miles except for the Mississippi River and its tributaries: 1 nautical mile = 1.151 statute miles. **1.** In Mexico known as the Río Bravo or Río Bravo del Norte. **2.** Lower 57 miles known as the Black River. **3.** Flows from the Mississippi River to the Gulf of Mexico.
Source: National Oceanic and Atmospheric Administration, *Distances Between United States Ports,* 1987 (1987).

Extreme Elevations of States and Outlying Areas

State	Highest Point Name	Elevation Feet	Elevation Meters	Lowest Point Name	Elevation Feet	Elevation Meters
United States	Mount McKinley, Alaska	20,320	6,198	Death Valley, Calif.	-282	-86
Alabama	Cheaha Mountain	2,405	733	Gulf of Mexico	Sea level	
Alaska	Mount McKinley	20,320	6,198	Pacific Ocean	Sea level	
Arizona	Humphreys Peak	12,633	3,853	Colorado River	70	21
Arkansas	Magazine Mountain	2,753	840	Ouachita River	55	17
California	Mount Whitney	14,494	4,419	Death Valley	-282	-86
Colorado	Mount Elbert	14,433	4,402	Arkansas River	3,315	1,011
Connecticut	Mount Frissell, South slope	2,380	726	Long Island Sound	Sea level	
Delaware	Ebright Rd., New Castle Co.	448	137	Atlantic Ocean	Sea level	
Dist. of Columbia	Tenleytown	410	125	Potomac River	1	0.3
Florida	Sec.30,T6N,R20W, Walton Co.	345	105	Atlantic Ocean	Sea level	
Georgia	Brasstown Bald	4,784	1,459	Atlantic Ocean	Sea level	
Hawaii	Mauna Kea	13,806	4,211	Pacific Ocean	Sea level	
Idaho	Borah Peak	12,662	3,862	Snake River	710	217
Illinois	Charles Mound	1,235	377	Mississippi River	279	85
Indiana	Franklin Township, Wayne Co.	1,257	383	Ohio River	320	98
Iowa	Sec. 29, T100N, R41W Osceola Co.	1,670	509	Mississippi River	480	146
Kansas	Mount Sunflower	4,039	1,232	Verdigris River	679	207
Kentucky	Black Mountain	4,139	1,262	Mississippi River	257	78
Louisiana	Driskill Mountain	535	163	New Orleans	-8	-2
Maine	Mount Katahdin	5,267	1,606	Atlantic Ocean	Sea level	
Maryland	Backbone Mountain	3,360	1,025	Atlantic Ocean	Sea level	
Massachusetts	Mount Greylock	3,487	1,064	Atlantic Ocean	Sea level	
Michigan	Mount Arvon	1,979	604	Lake Erie	571	174
Minnesota	Eagle Mountain, Cook Co.	2,301	702	Lake Superior	600	183
Mississippi	Woodall Mountain	806	246	Gulf of Mexico	Sea level	
Missouri	Taum Sauk Mountain	1,772	540	St. Francis River	230	70
Montana	Granite Peak	12,799	3,904	Kootenai River	1,800	549
Nebraska	Johnson Township, Kimball Co.	5,424	1,653	Missouri River	840	256
Nevada	Boundary Peak	13,140	4,007	Colorado River	479	146
New Hampshire	Mount Washington	6,288	1,918	Atlantic Ocean	Sea level	
New Jersey	High Point	1,803	550	Atlantic Ocean	Sea level	
New Mexico	Wheeler Peak	13,161	4,014	Red Bluff Reservoir	2,842	867
New York	Mount Marcy	5,344	1,630	Atlantic Ocean	Sea level	
North Carolina	Mount Mitchell	6,684	2,039	Atlantic Ocean	Sea level	
North Dakota	White Butte, Slope Co.	3,506	1,069	Red River	750	229
Ohio	Campbell Hill	1,549	472	Ohio River	455	139
Oklahoma	Black Mesa	4,973	1,517	Little River	289	88
Oregon	Mount Hood	11,239	3,428	Pacific Ocean	Sea level	
Pennsylvania	Mount Davis	3,213	980	Delaware River	Sea level	
Rhode Island	Jerimoth Hill	812	248	Atlantic Ocean	Sea level	
South Carolina	Sassafras Mountain	3,560	1,086	Atlantic Ocean	Sea level	
South Dakota	Harney Peak	7,242	2,209	Big Stone Lake	966	295
Tennessee	Clingmans Dome	6,643	2,026	Mississippi River	178	54
Texas	Guadalupe Peak	8,749	2,668	Gulf of Mexico	Sea level	
Utah	Kings Peak	13,528	4,126	Beaverdam Creek	2,000	610
Vermont	Mount Mansfield	4,393	1,340	Lake Champlain	95	29
Virginia	Mount Rogers	5,729	1,747	Atlantic Ocean	Sea level	
Washington	Mount Rainier	14,410	4,395	Pacific Ocean	Sea level	
West Virginia	Spruce Knob	4,861	1,483	Potomac River	240	73
Wisconsin	Timms Hill	1,951	595	Lake Michigan	579	177
Wyoming	Gannett Peak	13,804	4,210	Belle Fourche River	3,099	945
Puerto Rico	Cerro de Punta	4,390	1,339	Atlantic Ocean	Sea level	
Amer. Samoa	Lata Mountain	3,160	964	Pacific Ocean	Sea level	
Guam	Mount Lamlam	1,332	405	Pacific Ocean	Sea level	
Virgin Islands	Crown Mountain	1,556	475	Atlantic Ocean	Sea level	

Note: Sec. denotes section; T, township; R, range; N, north; W, west.
Source: U.S. Geological Survey, Elevations and Distances in the United States (2000).

U.S. History

DOCUMENTS OF U.S. HISTORY

▶THE DECLARATION OF INDEPENDENCE
After a year of war with Britain, American patriots were driven to make the final break in 1776. On June 7, before the Continental Congress in Philadelphia, Richard Henry Lee of Virginia proposed a declaration that the colonies "are, and of right ought to be, free and independent States." A committee of five, headed by Thomas Jefferson, was appointed to draw up the formal Declaration of Independence on June 10. The committee brought its version, mainly the work of Jefferson, back to Congress on June 28. Congress voted unanimously to declare independence on July 2, and after making several changes in the Jefferson committee's draft, they unanimously adopted the Declaration of Independence on July 4. Copies of the Declaration were dispatched to the states for approval. Charles Carroll of Maryland was the last surviving signer of the Declaration when he died on November 14, 1832. The original document is on display today at the National Archives in Washington, D.C.

_____

In Congress, July 4, 1776,
THE UNANIMOUS DECLARATION
OF THE
THIRTEEN UNITED STATES
OF AMERICA,
When in the Course of human events, it becomes necessary for one people to dissolve the political bands which have connected them with another, and to assume among the Powers of the earth, the separate and equal station to which the Laws of Nature and of Nature's God entitle them, a decent respect to the opinions of mankind requires that they should declare the causes which impel them to the separation.

We hold these truths to be self-evident, that all men are created equal, that they are endowed by their Creator with certain unalienable Rights, that among these are Life, Liberty and the pursuit of Happiness. That to secure these rights, Governments are instituted among Men, deriving their just powers from the consent of the governed. That whenever any Form of Government becomes destructive of these ends, it is the Right of the People to alter or to abolish it, and to institute new Government, laying its foundation on such principles and organizing its powers in such form, as to them shall seem most likely to effect their Safety and Happiness. Prudence, indeed, will dictate that governments long established should not be changed for light and transient causes; and accordingly all experience hath shown, that mankind are more disposed to suffer, while evils are sufferable, than to right themselves by abolishing the forms to which they are accustomed. But when a long train of abuses and usurpations, pursuing invariably the same Object evinces a design to reduce them under absolute Despotism, it is their right, it is their duty, to throw off such Government, and to provide new Guards for their future security. Such has been the patient sufferance of these Colonies; and such is now the ne-

cessity which constrains them to alter their former Systems of Government. The history of the present King of Great Britain is a history of repeated injuries and usurpations, all having in direct object the establishment of an absolute Tyranny over these States. To prove this, let Facts be submitted to a candid world.

He has refused his Assent to Laws, the most wholesome and necessary for the public good.

He has forbidden his Governors to pass Laws of immediate and pressing importance, unless suspended in their operation till his Assent should be obtained; and when so suspended, he has utterly neglected to attend to them.

He has refused to pass other Laws for the accommodation of large districts of people, unless those people would relinquish the right of Representation in the Legislature, a right inestimable to them and formidable to tyrants only.

He has called together legislative bodies at places unusual, uncomfortable, and distant from the depository of their Public Records, for the sole purpose of fatiguing them into compliance with his measures.

He has dissolved Representative Houses repeatedly, for opposing with manly firmness his invasions on the rights of the people.

He has refused for a long time, after such dissolutions, to cause others to be elected; whereby the Legislative Powers, incapable of Annihilation, have returned to the People at large for their exercise; the State remaining in the mean time exposed to all the dangers of invasion from without, and convulsions within.

He has endeavoured to prevent the population of these States; for that purpose obstructing the Laws of Naturalization of Foreigners; refusing to pass others to encourage their migration hither, and raising the conditions of new Appropriations of Lands.

He has obstructed the Administration of Justice, by refusing his Assent to Laws for establishing Judiciary Powers.

He has made Judges dependent on his Will alone, for the tenure of their offices, and the amount and payment of their salaries.

He has erected a multitude of New Offices, and sent hither swarms of Officers to harass our People, and eat out their substance.

He has kept among us, in times of peace, Standing Armies without the Consent of our legislature.

He has affected to render the Military independent of and superior to the Civil Power.

He has combined with others to subject us to a jurisdiction foreign to our constitution, and unacknowledged by our laws; giving his Assent to their acts of pretended legislation:

For quartering large bodies of armed troops among us:

For protecting them, by a mock Trial, from Punishment for any Murders which they should commit on the Inhabitants of these States:

For cutting off our Trade with all parts of the world:

For imposing taxes on us without our consent:

For depriving us in many cases, of the benefits of Trial by Jury:

For transporting us beyond Seas to be tried for pretended offences:

For abolishing the free System of English Laws in a neighbouring Province, establishing therein an Arbitrary government, and enlarging its Boundaries so as to render it at once an example and fit Instrument for introducing the same absolute rule into these Colonies:

For taking away our Charters, abolishing our most valuable Laws, and altering fundamentally the forms of our Government:

For suspending our own legislature, and declaring themselves invested with Power to legislate for us in all cases whatsoever.

He has abdicated Government here, by declaring us out of his Protection and waging War against us.

He has plundered our seas, ravaged our Coasts, burnt our towns, and destroyed the lives of our people.

He is at this time transporting large armies of foreign mercenaries to compleat the works of death, desolation and tyranny, already begun with circumstances of Cruelty & perfidy scarcely paralleled in the most barbarous ages, and totally unworthy the Head of a civilized nation.

He has constrained our fellow Citizens taken Captive on the high Seas to bear Arms against their Country, to become the executioners of their friends and Brethren, or to fall themselves by their Hands.

He has excited domestic insurrections amongst us, and has endeavoured to bring on the inhabitants of our frontiers, the merciless Indian Savages, whose known rule of warfare, is an undistinguished destruction of all ages, sexes and conditions.

In every stage of these Oppressions We have Petitioned for Redress in the most humble terms: Our repeated Petitions have been answered only by repeated injury. A prince, whose character is thus marked by every act which may define a Tyrant, is unfit to be the ruler of a free People.

Nor have We been wanting in attention to our British brethren. We have warned them from time to time of attempts by their legislature to extend an unwarrantable jurisdiction over us. We have reminded them of the circumstances of our emigration and settlement here. We have appealed to their native justice and magnanimity, and we have conjured them by the ties of our common kindred to disavow these usurpations, which would inevitably interrupt our connections and correspondence. They too have been deaf to the voice of justice and of consanguinity. We must, therefore, acquiesce in the necessity, which denounces our Separation and hold them, as we hold the rest of mankind, Enemies in War, in Peace Friends.

We, therefore, the Representatives of the United States of America, in General Congress, Assembled, appealing to the Supreme Judge of the world for the rectitude of our intentions, do, in the Name, and by Authority of the good People of these Colonies, solemnly publish and declare, That these United Colonies are, and of Right ought to be Free and Independent States; that they are Absolved from all Allegiance to the British Crown, and that all political connection between them and the State of Great Britain, is and ought to be totally dissolved; and that as Free and Independent States, they have full Power to levy War, conclude Peace, contract Alliances, establish Commerce, and to do all other Acts and Things which Independent States may of right do. And for the support of this Declaration, with a firm reliance on the Protection of Divine Providence, we mutually pledge to each other our Lives, our Fortunes and our sacred Honor.

▶ THE U.S. CONSTITUTION

During and after the Revolution, the United States was governed by the Continental Congress under the Articles of Confederation, which delegated very limited powers to the national government and reserved the rest to the states. Economic chaos, political confusion, and widespread dissatisfaction with the lack of central authority peaked after Shays's Rebellion in 1786. George Washington lent his prestige to the call for a convention to consider a new form of government. Congress endorsed the plan on February 21, 1787, "for the sole and express purpose of revising the Articles of Confederation." All states but Rhode Island sent delegates to the convention, which opened in Philadelphia on May 14. The delegates moved at once to discard the Articles, draw up a new Constitution, and conduct their meetings in secrecy, while Washington presided and James Madison took notes. A long summer of debate and compromise finally produced the document that most of the delegates signed on September 17. Congress ordered the Constitution sent to the states for ratification on September 28, requiring approval by at least nine of them to validate the new charter. Whether the Constitution would be adopted was in doubt until June 21, 1788, when New Hampshire became the ninth state to ratify it. The Constitution went into effect on March 4, 1789. All of the original 13 states eventually ratified the Constitution, ending with Rhode Island on May 29, 1790. The U.S. Constitution is the world's oldest written constitution.

Preamble

We, the People of the United States, in Order to form a more perfect Union, establish Justice, insure domestic Tranquillity, provide for the common defence, promote the general Welfare, and secure the Blessings of Liberty to ourselves and our Posterity, do ordain and establish this Constitution for the United States of America.

Article I

Section 1 All legislative powers herein granted shall be vested in a Congress of the United States, which shall consist of a Senate and House of Representatives.

Section 2 [1] The House of Representatives shall be composed of members chosen every second year by the people of the several States, and the electors in each State shall have the qualifications requisite for electors of the most numerous branch of the State legislature.

[2] No person shall be a Representative who shall not have attained to the age of twenty-five years, and been seven years a citizen of the United States, and who shall not, when elected, be an inhabitant of that State in which he shall be chosen.

[3] Representatives and direct taxes shall be apportioned among the several States which may be included within this Union, according to their respective numbers, which shall be determined by adding to the whole number of free persons, including those bound to service for a term of years, and excluding Indians not taxed, three-fifths of all other persons. The actual enumeration shall be made within three years after the first meeting of the Congress of the United States, and within every subsequent term of ten years, in such manner as they shall by law direct. The number of Representatives shall not exceed one for every thirty thousand, but each State shall have at least one Representative; and until such enumeration shall be made, the State of New Hampshire shall

Signers of the Declaration of Independence

Delegate	State	Born/Died	Delegate	State	Born/Died
Adams, John	Massachusetts	1735–1826	Lynch, Thomas, Jr.	South Carolina	1749–1779
Adams, Samuel	Massachusetts	1722–1803	McKean, Thomas	Delaware	1734–1817
Bartlett, Josiah	New Hampshire	1729–1795	Middleton, Arthur	South Carolina	1742–1787
Braxton, Carter	Virginia	1736–1797	Morris, Lewis	New York	1726–1798
Carroll, Charles	Maryland	1737–1832	Morris, Robert	Pennsylvania	1734–1806
Chase, Samuel	Maryland	1741–1811	Morton, John	Pennsylvania	1724–1777
Clark, Abraham	New Jersey	1726–1794	Nelson, Thomas Jr.	Virginia	1738–1789
Clymer, George	Pennsylvania	1739–1813	Paca, William	Maryland	1740–1799
Ellery, William	Rhode Island	1727–1820	Paine, Robert Treat	Massachusetts	1731–1814
Floyd, William	New York	1734–1821	Penn, John	North Carolina	1741–1788
Franklin, Benjamin	Pennsylvania	1706–1790	Read, George	Delaware	1733–1798
Gerry, Elbridge	Massachusetts	1744–1814	Rodney, Caesar	Delaware	1728–1784
Gwinnett, Button	Georgia	1732–1777	Ross, George	Pennsylvania	1730–1779
Hall, Lyman	Georgia	1724–1790	Rush, Benjamin	Pennsylvania	1745–1813
Hancock, John	Massachusetts	1737–1793	Rutledge, Edward	South Carolina	1749–1800
Harrison, Benjamin	Virginia	1726–1791	Sherman, Roger	Connecticut	1721–1793
Hart, John	New Jersey	?–1779	Smith, James	Pennsylvania	1713–1806
Hewes, Joseph	North Carolina	1730–1779	Stockton, Richard	New Jersey	1730–1781
Heyward, Thomas, Jr.	South Carolina	1746–1809	Stone, Thomas	Maryland	1743–1787
Hooper, William	North Carolina	1742–1790	Taylor, George	Pennsylvania	1716–1781
Hopkins, Stephen	Rhode Island	1707–1785	Thornton, Matthew	New Hampshire	1714–1803
Hopkinson, Francis	New Jersey	1737–1791	Walton, George	Georgia	1741–1804
Huntington, Samuel	Connecticut	1731–1796	Whipple, William	New Hampshire	1730–1785
Jefferson, Thomas	Virginia	1743–1826	Williams, William	Connecticut	1731–1811
Lee, Richard Henry	Virginia	1732–1794	Wilson, James	Pennsylvania	1742–1798
Lee, Francis Lightfoot	Virginia	1734–1797	Witherspoon, John	New Jersey	1723–1794
Lewis, Francis	New York	1713–1803	Wolcott, Oliver	Connecticut	1726–1797
Livingston, Philip	New York	1716–1778	Wythe, George	Virginia	1726–1806

be entitled to choose three; Massachusetts, eight; Rhode Island and Providence Plantations, one; Connecticut, five; New York, six; New Jersey, four; Pennsylvania, eight; Delaware, one; Maryland, six; Virginia, ten; North Carolina, five; South Carolina, five; and Georgia, three.

[4] When vacancies happen in the representation from any State, the executive authority thereof shall issue writs of election to fill such vacancies.

[5] The House of Representatives shall choose their Speaker and other officers, and shall have the sole power of impeachment.

Section 3 [1] The Senate of the United States shall be composed of two Senators from each State, chosen by the legislature thereof for six years; and each Senator shall have one vote.

[2] Immediately after they shall be assembled in consequence of the first election, they shall be divided as equally as may be into three classes. The seats of the Senators of the first class shall be vacated at the expiration of the second year, of the second class at the expiration of the fourth year, and of the third class at the expiration of the sixth year, so that one-third may be chosen every second year; and if vacancies happen by resignation or otherwise during the recess of the legislature of any State, the executive thereof may make temporary appointments until the next meeting of the legislature, which shall then fill such vacancies.

[3] No person shall be a Senator who shall not have attained to the age of thirty years, and been nine years a citizen of the United States, and who shall not, when elected, be an inhabitant of that State for which he shall be chosen.

[4] The Vice-President of the United States shall be President of the Senate, but shall have no vote, unless they be equally divided.

[5] The Senate shall choose their other officers and also a President pro tempore in the absence of the Vice-President, or when he shall exercise the office of President of the United States.

[6] The Senate shall have the sole power to try all impeachments. When sitting for that purpose, they shall be on oath or affirmation. When the President of the United States is tried, the Chief Justice shall preside; and no person shall be convicted without the concurrence of two-thirds of the members present.

[7] Judgment in cases of impeachment shall not extend further than to removal from office, and disqualification to hold and enjoy any office of honor, trust, or profit under the United States; but the party convicted shall, nevertheless, be liable and subject to indictment, trial, judgment, and punishment, according to law.

Section 4 [1] The times, places, and manner of holding elections for Senators and Representatives shall be prescribed in each State by the legislature thereof; but the Congress may at any time by law make or alter such regulations, except as to the places of choosing Senators.

[2] The Congress shall assemble at least once in every year, and such meeting shall be on the first Monday in December, unless they shall by law appoint a different day.

Section 5 [1] Each House shall be the judge of the elections, returns, and qualification of its own members, and a majority of each shall constitute a quorum to do business; but a smaller number may adjourn from day to day, and may be authorized to compel the attendance of absent members, in such manner, and under such penalties, as each House may provide.

[2] Each House may determine the rules of its proceedings, punish its members for disorderly behavior, and with the concurrence of two-thirds, expel a member.

[3] Each House shall keep a journal of its proceedings, and from time to time publish the

same, excepting such parts)as may in their judgment require secrecy, and the yeas and nays of the members of either House on any question shall, at the desire of one-fifth of those present, be entered on the journal.

[4] Neither House, during the session of Congress, shall, without the consent of the other, adjourn for more than three days, nor to any other place than that in which the two Houses shall be sitting.

Section 6 [1] The Senators and Representatives shall receive a compensation for their services, to be ascertained by law and paid out of the Treasury of the United States. They shall, in all cases except treason, felony, and breach of the peace, be privileged from arrest during their attendance at the session of their respective Houses, and in going to and returning from the same; and for any speech or debate in either House they shall not be questioned in any other place.

[2] No Senator or Representative shall, during the time for which he was elected, be appointed to any civil office under the authority of the United States, which shall have been created, or the emoluments whereof shall have been increased during such time; and no person holding any office under the United States shall be a member of either House during his continuance in office.

Section 7 [1] All bills for raising revenue shall originate in the House of Representatives; but the Senate may propose or concur with amendments as on other bills.

[2] Every bill which shall have passed the House of Representatives and the Senate shall, before it becomes a law, be presented to the President of the United States; if he approves he shall sign it, but if not he shall return it, with his objections, to that House in which it shall have originated, who shall enter the objections at large on their journal and proceed to reconsider it. If after such reconsideration two-thirds of that House shall agree to pass the bill, it shall be sent, together with the objections, to the other House, by which it shall likewise be reconsidered, and if approved by two-thirds of that House it shall become a law. But in all such cases the vote of both Houses shall be determined by yeas and nays, and the names of the persons voting for and against the bill shall be entered on the journal of each House respectively. If any bill shall not be returned by the President within ten days (Sundays excepted) after it shall have been presented to him, the same shall be a law, in like manner as if he had signed it, unless the Congress by their adjournment prevent its return, in which case it shall not be a law.

[3] Every order, resolution or vote to which the concurrence of the Senate and House of Representatives may be necessary (except on a question of adjournment) shall be presented to the President of the United States; and before the same shall take effect shall be approved by him, or being disapproved by him, shall be repassed by two-thirds of the Senate and House of Representatives, according to the rules and limitations prescribed in the case of a bill.

Section 8 [1] The Congress shall have power to lay and collect taxes, duties, imposts and excises, to pay the debts and provide for the common defense and general welfare of the United States; but all duties, imposts and excises shall be uniform throughout the United States;

[2] To borrow money on the credit of the United States;

[3] To regulate commerce with foreign nations, and among the several States, and with the Indian tribes;

[4] To establish an uniform rule of naturalization, and uniform laws on the subject of bankruptcies throughout the United States;

[5] To coin money, regulate the value thereof, and of foreign coin, and fix the standard of weights and measures;

[6] To provide for the punishment of counterfeiting the securities and current coin of the United States;

[7] To establish post offices and post roads;

[8] To promote the progress of science and useful arts by securing for limited times to authors and inventors the exclusive right to their respective writings and discoveries;

[9] To constitute tribunals inferior to the Supreme Court;

[10] To define and punish piracies and felonies committed on the high seas and offenses against the law of nations;

[11] To declare war, grant letters of marque and reprisal, and make rules concerning captures on land and water;

[12] To raise and support armies, but no appropriation of money to that use shall be for a longer term than two years;

[13] To provide and maintain a navy;

[14] To make rules for the government and regulation of the land and naval forces;

[15] To provide for calling forth the militia to execute the laws of the Union, suppress insurrections, and repel invasions;

[16] To provide for organizing, arming and disciplining the militia, and for governing such part of them as may be employed in the service of the United States, reserving to the States respectively the appointment of the officers, and the authority of training the militia according to the discipline prescribed by Congress;

[17] To exercise exclusive legislation in all cases whatsoever over such district (not exceeding ten miles square) as may, by cession of particular States and the acceptance of Congress, become the seat of the Government of the United States, and to exercise like authority over all places purchased by the consent of the legislature of the State in which the same shall be, for the erection of forts, magazines, arsenals, dockyards, and other needful buildings;

[18] To make all laws which shall be necessary and proper for carrying into execution the foregoing powers, and all other powers vested by this Constitution in the Government of the United States, or in any department or officer thereof.

Section 9 [1] The migration or importation of such persons as any of the States now existing shall think proper to admit shall not be prohibited by the Congress prior to the year one thousand eight hundred and eight, but a tax or duty may be imposed on such importation, not exceeding ten dollars for each person.

[2] The privilege of the writ of habeas corpus shall not be suspended, unless when in cases of rebellion or invasion the public safety may require it.

[3] No bill of attainder or ex post facto law shall be passed.

[4] No capitation or other direct tax shall be laid, unless in proportion to the census or enumeration hereinbefore directed to be taken.

[5] No tax or duty shall be laid on articles exported from any State.

[6] No preference shall be given by any regulation of commerce or revenue to the ports of one State

over those of another; nor shall vessels bound to or from one State be obliged to enter, clear or pay duties in another.

[7] No money shall be drawn from the Treasury but in consequence of appropriations made by law; and a regular statement and account of the receipts and expenditures of all public money shall be published from time to time.

[8] No title of nobility shall be granted by the United States; and no person holding any office of profit or trust under them shall, without the consent of the Congress, accept of any present, emolument, office, or title of any kind whatever from any king, prince, or foreign state.

Section 10 [1] No State shall enter into any treaty, alliance, or confederation; grant letters of marque and reprisal; coin money, emit bills of credit, make anything but gold and silver coin a tender in payment of debts; pass any bill of attainder, ex post facto law or law impairing the obligation of contracts, or grant any title of nobility.

[2] No State shall, without the consent of the Congress, lay any imposts or duties on imports or exports, except what may be absolutely necessary for executing its inspection laws; and the net produce of all duties and imposts, laid by any State on imports or exports, shall be for the use of the Treasury of the United States; and all such laws shall be subject to the revision and control of the Congress.

[3] No State shall, without the consent of Congress, lay any duty of tonnage, keep troops and ships of war in time of peace, enter into any agreement or compact with another State or with a foreign power, or engage in war, unless actually invaded or in such imminent danger as will not admit of delay.

Article II

Section 1 [1] The executive power shall be vested in a President of the United States of America. He shall hold his office during the term of four years, and together with the Vice-President, chosen for the same term, be elected as follows:

[2] Each State shall appoint, in such manner as the legislature thereof may direct, a number of Electors, equal to the whole number of Senators and Representatives to which the State may be entitled in the Congress; but no Senator or Representative, or person holding an office of trust or profit under the United States shall be appointed an Elector.

[3] The Electors shall meet in their respective States and vote by ballot for two persons, of whom one at least shall not be an inhabitant of the same State with themselves. And they shall make a list of all the persons voted for, and of the number of votes for each; which list they shall sign and certify, and transmit sealed to the seat of government of the United States, directed to the President of the Senate. The President of the Senate shall, in the presence of the Senate and House of Representatives, open all the certificates, and the votes shall then be counted. The person having the greatest number of votes shall be the President, if such number be a majority of the whole number of Electors appointed; and if there be more than one who have such majority, and have an equal number of votes, then the House of Representatives shall immediately choose by ballot one of them for President; and if no person have a majority, then from the five highest on the list the said House shall in like manner choose the President. But in choosing the President the votes shall be taken by States, the representation from each State having one vote; a quorum for this purpose shall consist of a member or members from two-thirds of the States, and a majority of all the States shall be necessary to a choice. In every case, after the choice of the President, the person having the greatest number of votes of the Electors shall be the Vice-President. But if there should remain two or more who have equal votes, the Senate shall choose from them by ballot the Vice-President.

[4] The Congress may determine the time of choosing the Electors and the day on which they shall give their votes, which day shall be the same throughout the United States.

[5] No person except a natural-born citizen, or citizen of the United States at the time of the adoption of this Constitution, shall be eligible to the office of President; neither shall any person be eligible to that office who shall not have attained to the age of thirty-five years, and been fourteen years a resident within the United States.

[6] In case of the removal of the President from office, or of his death, resignation, or inability to discharge the powers and duties of the said office, the same shall devolve on the Vice-President, and the Congress may by law provide for the case of removal, death, resignation, or inability, both of the President and Vice-President, declaring what officer shall then act as President, and such officer shall act accordingly until the disability be removed or a President shall be elected.

[7] The President shall, at stated times, receive for his services a compensation, which shall neither be increased nor diminished during the period for which he shall have been elected, and he shall not receive within that period any other emolument from the United States or any of them.

[8] Before he enter on the execution of his office he shall take the following oath or affirmation: "I do solemnly swear (or affirm) that I will faithfully execute the office of President of the United States, and will to the best of my ability preserve, protect, and defend the Constitution of the United States."

Section 2 [1] The President shall be Commander-in-Chief of the Army and Navy of the United States, and of the militia of the several States when called into the actual service of the United States; he may require the opinion, in writing, of the principal officer in each of the executive departments, upon any subject relating to the duties of their respective offices, and he shall have power to grant reprieves and pardons for offenses against the United States, except in cases of impeachment.

[2] He shall have power, by and with the advice and consent of the Senate, to make treaties, provided two-thirds of the Senators present concur; and he shall nominate, and, by and with the advice and consent of the Senate, shall appoint ambassadors, other public ministers and consuls, judges of the Supreme Court, and all other officers of the United States whose appointments are not herein otherwise provided for, and which shall be established by law; but the Congress may by law vest the appointment of such inferior officers, as they think proper, in the President alone, in the courts of law, or in the heads of departments.

[3] The President shall have power to fill up all vacancies that may happen during the recess of the Senate, by granting commissions which shall expire at the end of their next session.

Section 3 He shall from time to time give to the Congress information of the state of the Union, and recommend to their consideration such measures as he shall judge necessary and expedient; he may, on extraordinary occasions, convene both Houses, or either of them, and in case of disagreement between them with respect to the time of adjournment, he may adjourn them to such time as he shall think proper; he shall receive ambassadors and other public ministers; he shall take care that the laws be faithfully executed, and shall commission all the officers of the United States.

Section 4 The President, Vice-President and all civil officers of the United States shall be removed from office on impeachment for and conviction of treason, bribery, or other high crimes and misdemeanors.

Article III

Section 1 The judicial power of the United States shall be vested in one Supreme Court, and in such inferior courts as the Congress may from time to time ordain and establish. The judges, both of the Supreme and inferior courts, shall hold their offices during good behavior, and shall, at stated times, receive for their services a compensation which shall not be diminished during their continuance in office.

Section 2 [1] The judicial power shall extend to all cases, in law and equity, arising under this Constitution, the laws of the United States, and treaties made, or which shall be made, under their authority; to all cases affecting ambassadors, other public ministers, and consuls; to all cases of admiralty and maritime jurisdiction; to controversies to which the United States shall be a party; to controversies between two or more States; between a State and citizens of another State; between citizens of different States; between citizens of the same State claiming lands under grants of different States, and between a State, or the citizens thereof, and foreign states, citizens, or subjects.

[2] In all cases affecting ambassadors, other public ministers and consuls, and those in which a State shall be party, the Supreme Court shall have original jurisdiction. In all the other cases before mentioned the Supreme Court shall have appellate jurisdiction, both as to law and fact, with such exceptions and under such regulations as the Congress shall make.

[3] The trial of all crimes, except in cases of impeachment, shall be by jury; and such trial shall be held in the State where the said crimes shall have been committed; but when not committed within any State, the trial shall be at such place or places as the Congress may by law have directed.

Section 3 [1] Treason against the United States shall consist only in levying war against them, or in adhering to their enemies, giving them aid and comfort. No person shall be convicted of treason unless on the testimony of two witnesses to the same overt act, or on confession in open court.

[2] The Congress shall have power to declare the punishment of treason, but no attainder of treason shall work corruption of blood or forfeiture except during the life of the person attained.

Article IV

Section 1 Full faith and credit shall be given in each State to the public acts, records, and judicial proceedings of every other State. And the Congress may by general laws prescribe the manner in which such acts, records, and proceedings shall be proved, and the effect thereof.

Section 2 [1] The citizens of each State shall be entitled to all privileges and immunities of citizens in the several States.

[2] A person charged in any State with treason, felony, or other crime, who shall flee from justice, and be found in another State, shall, on demand of the executive authority of the State from which he fled, be delivered up, to be removed to the State having jurisdiction of the crime.

[3] No person held to service or labor in one State, under the laws thereof, escaping into another, shall, in consequence of any law or regulation therein, be discharged from such service or labor, but shall be delivered up on claim to the party to whom such service or labor may be due.

Section 3 [1] New States may be admitted by the Congress into this Union; but no new State shall be formed or erected within the jurisdiction of any other State; nor any State be formed by the junction of two or more States or parts of States, without the consent of the legislatures of the States concerned as well as of the Congress.

[2] The Congress shall have power to dispose of and make all needful rules and regulations respecting the territory or other property belonging to the United States; and nothing in this Constitution shall be so construed as to prejudice any claims of the United States or of any particular State.

Section 4 The United States shall guarantee to every State in this Union a republican form of government, and shall protect each of them against invasion, and on application of the legislature, or of the executive (when the legislature cannot be convened), against domestic violence.

Article V

The Congress, whenever two-thirds of both Houses shall deem it necessary, shall propose amendments to this Constitution, or, on the application of the legislatures of two-thirds of the several States, shall call a convention for proposing amendments, which in either case shall be valid to all intents and purposes as part of this Constitution, when ratified by the legislatures of three-fourths of the several States, or by conventions in three-fourths thereof, as the one or the other mode of ratification may be proposed by the Congress; provided that no amendment which may be made prior to the year one thousand eight hundred and eight shall in any manner affect the first and fourth clauses in the Ninth Section of the First Article; and that no State, without its consent shall be deprived of its equal suffrage in the Senate.

Article VI

[1] All debts contracted and engagements entered into, before the adoption of this Constitution, shall be as valid against the United States under this Constitution as under the Confederation.

[2] This Constitution, and the laws of the United States which shall be made in pursuance thereof, and all treaties made, or which shall be made, under the authority of the United States, shall be the supreme law of the land; and the judges in every State shall be bound thereby, anything in the Constitution or laws of any State to the contrary notwithstanding.

[3] The Senators and Representatives before mentioned and the members of the several State legislatures, and all executive and judicial officers both of the United States and of the several States, shall be bound by oath or affirmation to support

this Constitution; but no religious test shall ever be required as a qualification to any office or public trust under the United States.

Article VII
The ratification of the conventions of nine States shall be sufficient for the establishment of this Constitution between the States so ratifying the same.

Amendments to the Constitution
[The first 10 amendments, known collectively as The Bill of Rights, were adopted in 1791.]

Amendment I
Congress shall make no law respecting an establishment of religion, or prohibiting the free exercise thereof; or abridging the freedom of speech or of the press; or the right of the people peaceably to assemble, and to petition the government for a redress of grievances.

Amendment II
A well-regulated militia being necessary to the security of a free State, the right of the people to keep and bear arms shall not be infringed.

Amendment III
No soldier shall, in time of peace, be quartered in any house without the consent of the owner, nor in time of war, but in a manner to be prescribed by law.

Amendment IV
The right of the people to be secure in their persons, houses, papers, and effects, against unreasonable searches and seizures, shall not be violated, and no warrants shall issue but upon probable cause, supported by oath or affirmation, and particularly describing the place to be searched, and the persons or things to be seized.

Amendment V
No person shall be held to answer for a capital, or otherwise infamous crime, unless on a presentment or indictment of a grand jury, except in cases arising in the land or naval forces, or in the militia, when in actual service in time of war or public danger; nor shall any person be subject for the same offense to be twice put in jeopardy of life or limb; nor shall be compelled in any criminal case to be a witness against himself, nor be deprived of life, liberty or property, without due process of law; nor shall private property be taken for public use without just compensation.

Amendment VI
In all criminal prosecutions, the accused shall enjoy the right to a speedy and public trial, by an impartial jury of the State and district wherein the crime shall have been committed, which district shall have been previously ascertained by law, and to be informed of the nature and cause of the accusation; to be confronted with the witnesses against him; to have compulsory process for obtaining witnesses in his favor, and to have the assistance of counsel for his defense.

Amendment VII
In suits at common law, where the value in controversy shall exceed twenty dollars, the right of trial by jury shall be preserved, and no fact tried by a jury shall be otherwise re-examined in any court of the United States, than according to the rules of the common law.

Amendment VIII
Excessive bail shall not be required, nor excessive fines imposed, nor cruel and unusual punishments inflicted.

Amendment IX
The enumeration in the Constitution of certain rights shall not be construed to deny or disparage others retained by the people.

Amendment X
The powers not delegated to the United States by the Constitution, nor prohibited by it to the States, are reserved to the States respectively, or to the people.

Amendment XI [Adopted Jan. 8, 1798]
The judicial power of the United States shall not be construed to extend to any suit in law or equity, commenced or prosecuted against one of the United States by citizens of another State, or by citizens or subjects of any foreign state.

Amendment XII [Adopted Sept. 25, 1804]
[1] The Electors shall meet in their respective States and vote by ballot for President and Vice-President, one of whom, at least, shall not be an inhabitant of the same State with themselves; they shall name in their ballots the person voted for as President, and in distinct ballots the person voted for as Vice-President, and they shall make distinct lists of all persons voted for as President and of all persons voted for as Vice-President, and of the number of votes for each; which lists they shall sign and certify, and transmit sealed to the seat of the government of the United States, directed to the President of the Senate. The President of the Senate shall, in the presence of the Senate and House of Representatives, open all the certificates and the votes shall then be counted. The person having the greatest number of votes for President shall be the President, if such number be a majority of the whole number of Electors appointed; and if no person have such majority, then from the persons having the highest numbers not exceeding three on the list of those voted for as President, the House of Representatives shall choose immediately, by ballot, the President. But in choosing the President the votes shall be taken by States, the representation from each State having one vote; a quorum for this purpose shall consist of a member or members from two-thirds of the States, and a majority of all the States shall be necessary to a choice. And if the House of Representatives shall not choose a President whenever the right of choice shall devolve upon them, before the fourth day of March next following, then the Vice-President shall act as President, as in the case of the death or other constitutional disability of the President.
[2] The person having the greatest number of votes as Vice-President shall be the Vice-President, if such number be a majority of the whole number of Electors appointed; and if no person have a majority, then from the two highest numbers on the list the Senate shall choose the Vice-President; a quorum for the purpose shall consist of two-thirds of the whole number of Senators, and a majority of the whole number shall be necessary to a choice. But no person constitutionally ineligible to the office of President shall be eligible to that of Vice-President of the United States.

Amendment XIII [Adopted Dec. 18, 1865]
Section 1 Neither slavery nor involuntary servi-

tude, except as a punishment for crime whereof the party shall have been duly convicted, shall exist within the United States, or any place subject to their jurisdiction.

Section 2 Congress shall have power to enforce this article by appropriate legislation.

Amendment XIV [Adopted July 28, 1868]

Section 1 All persons born or naturalized in the United States, and subject to the jurisdiction thereof, are citizens of the United States and of the State wherein they reside. No State shall make or enforce any law which shall abridge the privileges or immunities of citizens of the United States; nor shall any State deprive any person of life, liberty or property, without due process of law; nor deny to any person within its jurisdiction the equal protection of the laws.

Section 2 Representatives shall be apportioned among the several States according to their respective numbers, counting the whole number of persons in each State, excluding Indians not taxed. But when the right to vote at any election for the choice of Electors for President and Vice-President of the United States, Representatives in Congress, the executive and judicial officers of a State, or the members of the legislature thereof, is denied to any of the male inhabitants of such State, being twenty-one years of age, and citizens of the United States, or in any way abridged except for participation in rebellion or other crime, the basis of representation therein shall be reduced in the proportion which the number of such male citizens shall bear to the whole number of male citizens twenty-one years of age in such State.

Section 3 No person shall be a Senator or Representative in Congress, or elector of President and Vice-President, or hold any office, civil or military, under the United States or under any State, who, having previously taken an oath as a member of Congress, or as an officer of the United States, or as a member of any State legislature, or as an executive or judicial officer of any State, to support the Constitution of the United States, shall have engaged in insurrection or rebellion against the same, or given aid or comfort to the enemies thereof. But Congress may, by a vote of two-thirds of each House, remove such disability.

Section 4 The validity of the public debt of the United States, authorized by law, including debts incurred for payment of pensions and bounties for services in suppressing insurrection or rebellion, shall not be questioned. But neither the United States nor any State shall assume or pay any debt or obligation incurred in aid of insurrection or rebellion against the United States, or any claim for the loss or emancipation of any slave; but all such debts, obligations, and claims shall be held illegal and void.

Section 5 The Congress shall have power to enforce, by appropriate legislation, the provisions of this article.

Amendment XV [Adopted Mar. 30, 1870]

Section 1 The right of citizens of the United States to vote shall not be denied or abridged by the United States or by any State on account of race, color, or previous condition of servitude.

Section 2 The Congress shall have power to enforce this article by appropriate legislation.

Amendment XVI [Adopted Feb. 25, 1913]

The Congress shall have power to lay and collect taxes on incomes, from whatever source derived, without apportionment among the several States, and without regard to any census or enumeration.

Amendment XVII [Adopted May 31, 1913]

Section 1 The Senate of the United States shall be composed of two Senators from each State, elected by the people thereof, for six years; and each Senator shall have one vote. The electors in each State shall have the qualifications requisite for electors of the most numerous branch of the State legislatures.

Section 2 When vacancies happen in the representation of any State in the Senate, the executive authority of such State shall issue writs of election to fill such vacancies: Provided, that the legislature of any State may empower the executive thereof to make temporary appointments until the people fill the vacancies by election as the legislature may direct.

Section 3 This amendment shall not be so construed as to affect the election or term of any Senator chosen before it becomes valid as part of the Constitution.

Amendment XVIII [Adopted Jan. 29, 1919]

Section 1 After one year from the ratification of this article the manufacture, sale or transportation of intoxicating liquors within, the importation thereof into, or the exportation thereof from the United States and all territory subject to the jurisdiction thereof, for beverage purposes, is hereby prohibited.

Section 2 The Congress and the several States shall have concurrent power to enforce this article by appropriate legislation.

Section 3 This article shall be inoperative unless it shall have been ratified as an amendment to the Constitution by the legislatures of the several States, as provided in the Constitution, within seven years from the date of the submission hereof to the States by the Congress.

Amendment XIX [Adopted Aug. 26, 1920]

Section 1 The right of citizens of the United States to vote shall not be denied or abridged by the United States or by any State on account of sex.

Section 2 Congress shall have power to enforce this article by appropriate legislation.

Amendment XX [Adopted Feb. 6, 1933]

Section 1 The terms of the President and Vice-President shall end at noon on the 20th day of January, and the terms of Senators and Representatives at noon on the 3d day of January, of the years in which such terms would have ended if this article had not been ratified; and the terms of their successors shall then begin.

Section 2 The Congress shall assemble at least once in every year, and such meeting shall begin at noon on the 3d day of January, unless they shall by law appoint a different day.

Section 3 If, at the time fixed for the beginning of the term of the President, the President-elect shall have died, the Vice-President-elect shall become President. If a President shall not have been chosen before the time fixed for the beginning of his term or if the President-elect shall have failed to qualify, then the Vice-President-elect shall act as President until a President shall have qualified; and the Congress may by law provide for the case wherein neither a President-elect nor a Vice-President-elect shall have qualified, declaring who shall then act as President, or the manner in which one who is to act shall be selected, and such person shall act accordingly until a President or Vice-President shall have qualified.

Section 4 The Congress may by law provide for the case of the death of any of the persons from whom the House of Representatives may choose a President whenever the right of choice shall have devolved upon them, and for the case of death of any of the persons from whom the Senate may choose a Vice-President whenever the right of choice shall have devolved upon them.

Section 5 Sections 1 and 2 shall take effect on the 15th day of October following the ratification of this article.

Section 6 This article shall be inoperative unless it shall have been ratified as an amendment to the Constitution by the legislatures of three-fourths of the several States within seven years from the date of its submission.

Amendment XXI [Adopted Dec. 5, 1933]

Section 1 The eighteenth article of amendment to the Constitution of the United States is hereby repealed.

Section 2 The transportation or importation into any State, territory, or possession of the United States for delivery or use therein of intoxicating liquors, in violation of the laws thereof, is hereby prohibited.

Section 3 This article shall be inoperative unless it shall have been ratified as an amendment to the Constitution by conventions in the several States, as provided in the Constitution, within seven years from the date of the submission hereof to the States by the Congress.

Amendment XXII [Adopted Feb. 26, 1951]

Section 1 No person shall be elected to the office of President more than twice, and no person who has held the office of President, or acted as President, for more than two years of a term to which some other person was elected President shall be elected to the office of President more than once. But this Article shall not apply to any person holding the office of President when this Article was proposed by the Congress, and shall not prevent any person who may be holding the office of President, or acting as President, during the term within which this Article becomes operative from holding the office of President or acting as President during the remainder of such term.

Section 2 This article shall be inoperative unless it shall have been ratified as an amendment to the Constitution by the legislatures of three-fourths of the several States within seven years from the date of its submission to the States by the Congress.

Amendment XXIII [Adopted Apr. 3, 1961]

Section 1 The District constituting the seat of Government of the United States shall appoint in such manner as the Congress may direct:

A number of electors of President and Vice President equal to the whole number of Senators and Representatives in Congress to which the District would be entitled if it were a State, but in no event more than the least populous State; they shall be in addition to those appointed by the States, but they shall be considered, for the purposes of the election of President and Vice-President, to be electors appointed by a State; and they shall meet in the District and perform such duties as provided by the twelfth article of amendment.

Section 2 The Congress shall have power to enforce this article by appropriate legislation.

Amendment XXIV [Adopted Jan. 23, 1964]

Section 1 The right of citizens of the United States to vote in any primary or other election for President or Vice-President, for electors for President or Vice-President, or for Senator or Representative in Congress, shall not be denied or abridged by the United States or any State by reason of failure to pay any poll tax or other tax.

Section 2 The Congress shall have power to enforce this article by appropriate legislation.

Amendment XXV [Adopted Feb. 10, 1967]

Section 1 In case of the removal of the President from office or of his death or resignation, the Vice-President shall become President.

Section 2 Whenever there is a vacancy in the office of the Vice-President, the President shall nominate a Vice-President who shall take office upon confirmation by a majority vote of both Houses of Congress.

Section 3 Whenever the President transmits to the President pro tempore of the Senate and the Speaker of the House of Representatives his written declaration that he is unable to discharge the powers and duties of his office, and until he transmits to them a written declaration to the contrary, such powers and duties shall be discharged by the Vice-President as Acting President.

Section 4 Whenever the Vice-President and a majority of either the principal officers of the executive departments or of such other body as Congress may by law provide, transmit to the President pro tempore of the Senate and the Speaker of the House of Representatives their written declaration that the President is unable to discharge the powers and duties of his office, the Vice-President shall immediately assume the powers and duties of the office as Acting President.

Thereafter, when the President transmits to the President pro tempore of the Senate and the Speaker of the House of Representatives his written declaration that no inability exists, he shall resume the powers and duties of his office unless the Vice-President and a majority of either the principal officers of the executive department or of such other body as Congress may by law provide, transmit within four days to the President pro tempore of the Senate and the Speaker of the House of Representatives their written declaration that the President is unable to discharge the powers and duties of his office. Thereupon Congress shall decide the issue, assembling within forty-eight hours for that purpose if not in session. If the Congress, within twenty-one days after receipt of the latter written declaration, or, if Congress is not in session, within twenty-one days after Congress is required to assemble, determines by two-thirds vote of both Houses that the President is unable to discharge the powers and duties of his office, the Vice-President shall continue to discharge the same as Acting President; otherwise the President shall resume the powers and duties of his office.

Amendment XXVI [Adopted June 30, 1971]

Section 1 The right of citizens of the United States, who are eighteen years of age or older, to vote shall not be denied or abridged by the United States or by any State on account of age.

Section 2 The Congress shall have power to enforce this article by appropriate legislation.

Amendment XXVII [Adopted May 18, 1992]

No law, varying the compensation for the services of the Senators and Representatives, shall take effect until an election of Representatives shall have intervened.

▶THE EMANCIPATION PROCLAMATION

On July 22, 1862, Abraham Lincoln read to his cabinet a preliminary draft of an emancipation proclamation. Secretary of State William Seward suggested that the proclamation not be issued until a military victory had been won. The battle of Antietam gave Lincoln his desired opportunity, and on Sept. 22, he read to his cabinet a second draft of the proclamation. After some changes this was issued as a preliminary proclamation; the formal and definite proclamation came Jan. 1, 1863.

A Proclamation.

Whereas on the 22nd day of September, A.D. 1862, a proclamation was issued by the President of the United States, containing among other things, the following, to wit:

"That on the 1st day of January, A.D. 1863, all persons held as slaves within any State or designated part of a State the people whereof shall then be in rebellion against the United States shall be then, thenceforward, and forever free; and the executive government of the United States, including the military and naval authority thereof, will recognize and maintain the freedom of such persons and will do no act or acts to repress such persons, or any of them, in any efforts they may make for their actual freedom.

"That the executive will on the 1st day of January aforesaid, by proclamation, designate the States and parts of States, if any, in which the people thereof, respectively, shall then be in rebellion against the United States; and the fact that any State or the people thereof shall on that day be in good faith represented in the Congress of the United States by members chosen thereto at elections wherein a majority of the qualified voters of such States shall have participated shall, in the absence of strong countervailing testimony, be deemed conclusive evidence that such State and the people thereof are not then in rebellion against the United States."

Now, therefore, I, Abraham Lincoln, President of the United States, by virtue of the power in me vested as Commander-in-Chief of the Army and Navy of the United States in time of actual armed rebellion against the authority and government of the United States, and as a fit and necessary war measure for suppressing said rebellion, do, on this 1st day of January, A.D. 1863, and in accordance with my purpose so to do, publicly proclaimed for the full period of one hundred days from the first day above mentioned, order and designate as the States and parts of States wherein the people thereof, respectively, are this day in rebellion against the United States the following, to wit:

Arkansas, Texas, Louisiana (except the parishes of St. Bernard, Plaquemines, Jefferson, St. John, St. Charles, St. James, Ascension, Assumption, Terrebonne, Lafourche, St. Mary, St. Martin, and Orleans, including the city of New Orleans), Mississippi, Alabama, Florida, Georgia, South Carolina, North Carolina, and Virginia (except the forty-eight counties designated as West Virginia, and also the counties of Berkeley, Accomac, Northhampton, Elizabeth City, York, Princess Anne, and Norfolk, including the cities of Norfolk and Portsmouth), and which excepted parts are for the present left precisely as if this proclamation were not issued.

And by virtue of the power and for the purpose aforesaid, I do order and declare that all persons held as slaves within said designated States and parts of States are, and henceforward shall be, free; and that the Executive Government of the United States, including the military and naval authorities thereof, will recognize and maintain the freedom of said persons.

And I hereby enjoin upon the people so declared to be free to abstain from all violence, unless in necessary self-defense; and I recommend to them that, in all cases when allowed, they labor faithfully for reasonable wages.

And I further declare and make known that such persons of suitable condition will be received into the armed service of the United States to garrison forts, positions, stations, and other places, and to man vessels of all sorts in said service.

And upon this act, sincerely believed to be an act of justice, warranted by the Constitution upon military necessity, I invoke the considerate judgment of mankind and the gracious favor of Almighty God.

▶THE GETTYSBURG ADDRESS

Abraham Lincoln's most famous and most eloquent words were delivered on Nov. 19, 1863, at the dedication of the cemetery that held the remains of the 45,000 soldiers who fell at the Battle of Gettysburg, a significant Union victory.

"Fourscore and seven years ago our fathers brought forth on this continent, a new nation, conceived in Liberty, and dedicated to the proposition that all men are created equal.

"Now we are engaged in a great civil war, testing whether that nation or any nation so conceived and so dedicated, can long endure. We are met on a great battle-field of that war. We have come to dedicate a portion of that field, as a final resting place for those who here gave their lives that that nation might live. It is altogether fitting and proper that we should do this.

"But, in a larger sense, we can not dedicate—we can not consecrate—we can not hallow—this ground. The brave men, living and dead, who struggled here, have consecrated it, far above our poor power to add or detract. The world will little note, nor long remember what we say here, but it can never forget what they did here. It is for us the living, rather, to be dedicated here to the unfinished work which they who fought here have thus far so nobly advanced. It is rather for us to be here dedicated to the great task remaining before us—that from these honored dead we take increased devotion to that cause for which they gave the last full measure of devotion—that we here highly resolve that these dead shall not have died in vain—that this nation, under God, shall have a new birth of freedom—and that government of the people, by the people, for the people, shall not perish from the earth."

▶PLEDGE OF ALLEGIANCE

The original version of the Pledge of Allegiance appeared in the September 8, 1892, issue of Youth's Companion magazine. Authorship was in dispute between magazine staffers Francis Bellamy and James B. Upham until 1939, when the United States Flag Association declared Bellamy the author, and the Library of Congress concurred in 1957. Congress mandated two wording changes in the original version by substituting "the flag of the United States of America" for "my flag" in 1923, and adding "under God" in 1954. Public schools throughout the United States made the daily Pledge of Allegiance obligatory, and students who refused were expelled until the Supreme Court ruled in West Virginia Board of Education v. Barnette (1943) that the First Amendment protected the "right of silence" as well as freedom of speech.

"I pledge allegiance to the flag of the United States of America, and to the Republic, for which it stands, one nation, under God, indivisible, with liberty and justice for all."

CHRONOLOGY OF U.S. HISTORY

c. 1000 Viking explorer Leif Ericson explores North American coast and founds temporary colony called Vinland.

1492 On first voyage to America, Christopher Columbus lands at San Salvador island in Bahamas.

1493 Pope Alexander VI divides New World between Spain and Portugal.

1497 John Cabot claims Newfoundland for King Henry VII of England.

1499 Florentine merchant Amerigo Vespucci visits New World and begins writing popular accounts of his voyages.

1506 Columbus dies poor and embittered, convinced he found a new route to Asia and refusing to believe he discovered new continent.

1507 German mapmaker Martin Waldseemüller, after reading Vespucci's descriptions of the New World, names it "America" after him.

1513 Juan Ponce de León discovers Florida. Vasco Nuñez de Balboa crosses Panama and sights Pacific Ocean.

1519 Hernán Cortés lands in Mexico.

1520 Ferdinand Magellan, leader of the first expedition to circumnavigate the globe, discovers the South American straits that bear his name. In 1521, he is killed in the Philippines by natives.

1522 Cortés captures Mexico City and conquers Aztec empire.

1524 Giovanni de Verrazano, commissioned by King Francis I of France, discovers New York harbor and Hudson River.

1534 Jacques Cartier of France explores coast of Newfoundland and Gulf of St. Lawrence.

1536 Traveling overland from Gulf of Mexico, Alvar Núñez Cabeza de Vaca reaches Gulf of California.

1539 Fernando de Soto conquers Florida and begins three-year trek across Southeast.

1540 Francisco Vásquez de Coronado explores Southwest, discovering Grand Canyon and introducing horses to North America.

1541 Coronado discovers Mississippi River.

1542 João Rodrígues Cabrilho explores coast of California, missing San Francisco Bay.

1565 Don Pedro Menéndez de Aviles founds first permanent European settlement in North America at St. Augustine, Florida.

1572 Sir Francis Drake of England makes first voyage to America, landing in Panama.

1576 English explorer Martin Frobisher searches for Northwest Passage.

1577 Drake begins voyage of plunder around the world.

1579 Drake lands north of San Francisco Bay and claims region for Queen Elizabeth I.

1584 Sir Walter Raleigh discovers Roanoke Island. He names land Virginia, after Queen Elizabeth.

1585 Raleigh establishes England's first American colony at Roanoke.

1586 Drake evacuates surviving Roanoke settlers.

1587 Raleigh resettles Roanoke with 150 new colonists. Virginia Dare first child of English parents born in America.

1591 Relief expedition returns to the Roanoke colony; all settlers disappeared without trace.

1602 Captain Bartholomew Gosnold, first Englishman to set foot in New England, explores Cape Cod and Martha's Vineyard.

1603 Samuel de Champlain of France explores St. Lawrence Seaway, later founds Quebec.

1607 First permanent English settlement in America established at Jamestown, Virginia. Only 32 of original 105 colonists survive first winter.

1608 Captain John Smith imprisoned by Indians and saved by Pocahontas, daughter of Chief Powhatan.

1609 Henry Hudson sets out in search of Northwest Passage. Champlain sails into Great Lakes.

1611 Hudson cast adrift by mutinous crewmen to die in bay named after him.

1612 First Dutch trading post appears on Manhattan Island.

1616 Smallpox epidemic decimates Indian tribes from Maine to Rhode Island.

1619 Dutch traders bring first African slaves to Virginia for sale. Americans hold first election when Virginia planters vote for House of Burgesses.

1620 Pilgrims and others arrive in Plymouth, Massachusetts, aboard Mayflower. They draw up the Mayflower Compact.

1622 Most of Virginia colony wiped out in an Indian attack.

1624 King James I revokes Virginia's charter and makes it royal colony.

1626 The Dutch colony of New Amsterdam founded on Manhattan Island, bought from Indians for about $24.

1630 John Winthrop sets sail for Massachusetts with 900 Puritans and others, beginning Great Migration to New England.

1632 King Charles I of England grants Lord Baltimore charter to establish colony in Maryland.

1634 Massachusetts adopts representative government. Jean Nicolet of France begins trading with Indians in Wisconsin.

1635 Roger Williams, banished from Massachusetts, founds dissident colony of Rhode Island.

1636 New Englanders massacre hundreds of Indians in Pequot War. Harvard College established.

1638 First Swedish colony founded in Delaware.

1639 "Oath of a Free Man" the first English document printed in America. First public school appears in Dorchester, first post office in Boston, and Connecticut writes first colonial constitution.

1644 Indians make last unsuccessful attempt to expel English settlers from Virginia. First American ship built in Boston.

1647 Margaret Brent of Maryland first American woman to demand right to vote. Massachusetts passes first compulsory education law. First witchcraft execution occurs in Hartford, Conn.

1648 Boston shoemakers and coopers establish first American labor unions.

1651 Parliament passes first Navigation Act regulating colonial trade.

1652 Rhode Island first colony to outlaw slavery. First American coins minted in Boston.

1654 Jacob Barsimon, first American Jew, arrives in New Amsterdam, followed by 23 more Jews from Brazil.

1655 Dutch colonists capture Swedish colony in Delaware. Lady Deborah Moody of Long Island first American woman to vote.

1656 First Quakers arrive in America; imprisoned in Boston, beaten, and deported.

1659 Massachusetts hangs two Quakers on Boston Common.

1660 Parliament forbids Americans to export goods to countries other than England. Massachusetts outlaws celebration of Christmas.

1661 Virginia becomes the first colony to recognize slavery as legal.

1662 Connecticut granted royal charter. Massachusetts appoints official press censors and institutes half-way covenant.

1663 Parliament requires colonial imports from Europe to pass first through England. King Charles II grants charters to Carolina and Rhode Island

1664 New Amsterdam captured by Richard Nicolls, who renames it New York. New Jersey established.

1670 Charles Town, later called Charleston, first permanent settlement in Carolina.

1672 Parliament tightens trade restrictions on colonies and appoints American customs collectors.

1673 French explorers Jacques Marquette and Louis Joliet paddle down Mississippi River to Arkansas. Regular mail service begins between Boston and New York. Dutch forces recapture New York.

1674 Treaty of Westminster restores New York to England. King Louis XIV of France sends Sieur de La Salle to explore Mississippi River.

1675 Thousands die in King Philip's War between New Englanders and five Indian tribes.

1676 Bacon's Rebellion overthrows government of Virginia and burns down Jamestown.

1680 New Hampshire separated from Massachusetts and made royal colony.

1681 King Charles II names William Penn proprietor of Pennsylvania.

1682 Penn founds Philadelphia. Sieur de La Salle claims North American interior for France, naming it Louisiana.

1683 First German-Americans, group of Mennonites, arrive in Philadelphia.

1684 King Charles II revokes Massachusetts charter.

1686 King James II appoints Sir Edmund Andros governor-general of Dominion of New England, dissolving colonial governments.

1688 Quakers publish first anti-slavery tracts in Pennsylvania.

1689 Andros surrenders to Boston mobs and colonial self-government is reestablished. Jacob Leisler seizes power in New York uprising. King William's War begins in America.

1690 Massachusetts issues first colonial paper money. American campaigns against French Canada fail. French and Indians burn Schenectady, N.Y.

1691 Jacob Leisler surrenders and is hanged. Massachusetts rechartered with religious freedom.

1692 Witchcraft hysteria breaks out in Salem, Mass., leading to 20 executions.

1693 College of William and Mary chartered, the second college in America.

1695 New York City organizes public relief for poor and homeless.

1696 Parliament places more commercial restrictions on colonies. American merchants join slave trade.

1697 Treaty of Ryswick ends King William's War.

1701 Antoine de la Mothe Cadillac establishes French outpost at Detroit, Michigan. Yale College founded. Delaware separated from Pennsylvania.

1702 Queen Anne's War breaks out.

1704 Boston News-Letter first regularly published newspaper in America.

1710 German Migration to America begins. British and American forces capture Port Royal, Nova Scotia.

1711 Anglo-American attack on Quebec fails. Tuscarora Indian War breaks out in North Carolina.

1712 Militia quell slave rebellion in New York City. Pennsylvania prohibits importing slaves.

1713 Treaty of Utrecht ends Queen Anne's War.

1716 First American theater built in Williamsburg, Va. Slavery introduced to French Louisiana.

1718 Jean Baptiste le Moyne founds French city of New Orleans.

1721 Sir Robert Walpole loosens colonial trade restrictions with policy of "salutary neglect."

1722 France declares New Orleans capital of Louisiana.

1723 America's first business corporation chartered in Connecticut.

1724 France expels all Jews from Louisiana.

1728 First American synagogue built in New York City.

1729 North and South Carolina receive royal charters.

1731 Benjamin Franklin founds first American library in Philadelphia.

1732 King George II grants charter to Georgia. Only Catholic church in colonial America opens in Philadelphia. Benjamin Franklin begins publishing Poor Richard's Almanac. George Washington born in Virginia.

1733 Parliament passes the Molasses Act, taxing imports from non-British sugar islands.

1734 Beginning of Great Awakening, widespread religious revival.

1735 French begin settling in Illinois.

1737 Boston holds its first public celebration of St. Patrick's Day.

1739 War of Jenkin's Ear begins. South Carolina slaves mount Stono Rebellion. French explorers Pierre and Paul Mallet discover Rocky Mountains.

1741 Danish navigator Vitus Bering, hired by Peter the Great of Russia, explores coast of Alaska. American Magazine, first in colonies, begins publishing in Philadelphia. Slave insurrection panic sweeps New York City.

1742 First sugar cane planted in Louisiana.

1744 King George's War breaks out.

1745 British and Americans capture Fort Louisbourg on Cape Breton Island. French and Indians raid Maine.

1748 Treaty of Aix-la-Chapelle ends King George's War and returns Fort Louisbourg to France.

1751 Parliament forbids New England colonies to issue paper money.

1752 Benjamin Franklin conducts famous kite experiment. Liberty bell is cracked in Philadelphia.

1753 Governor Dinwiddie of Virginia sends George Washington into Ohio country to demand withdrawal of French. First steam engine arrives in America.

1754 Washington skirmishes with French patrol, touching off French and Indian War. Franklin presents Albany Plan of Union for colonies.

1755 Quakers withdraw from Pennsylvania assembly rather than vote for military spending. Washington leads retreat from Battle of the Wilderness.

1758 British and American forces lose Battle of Ticonderoga, but capture Louisbourg and Fort Duquesne. New Jersey sets aside first Indian reservation for Onami tribe.

1759 General Wolfe defeats General Montcalm as British capture Quebec. Both generals fall in battle.

1760 After fall of Montreal, all of New France surrenders to Britain. King George III crowned in England.

1762 King Louis XV of France secretly cedes Louisiana to Spain.

1763 Treaty of Paris ends French and Indian War. France cedes Canada to Britain. King George III prohibits Americans to settle in West. Conspiracy of Pontiac threatens frontier.

1764 Parliament passes Sugar Act and forbids all colonies to issue paper money. French settlers found St. Louis. "Paxton Boys" march on Philadelphia. In Boston, James Otis protests, "no taxation without representation."

1765 Parliament passes Stamp Act (tax on newspapers, legal documents, etc.) and Quartering Act (requiring housing of British soldiers in homes). Sons of Liberty organize resistance and non-importation throughout colonies. Stamp Act Congress meets in New York.

1766 Parliament repeals the Stamp Act, but passes Declaratory Act affirming its right to pass laws binding on colonies. Chief Pontiac makes peace.

1767 Parliament enacts Townshend Duties and suspends New York assembly for resisting Quartering Act.

1768 "Regulators" rebel in North Carolina. Boston riots against Townshend Duties.

1769 Daniel Boone explores Kentucky. Father Junipero Serra founds San Diego, first Spanish mission in California. Gaspar de Portola sails into San Francisco Bay.

1770 Five Americans perish in Boston Massacre (Mar. 5). Parliament repeals Townshend Duties, except tax on tea.

1772 Rhode Island mob burns British revenue ship *Gaspee*. Boston appoints first Committee of Correspondence.

1773 Parliament passes Tea Act, leading to Boston Tea Party (Dec. 16).

1774 Parliament passes "Intolerable Acts" punishing colonists for Tea Party. Boston is occupied by British forces. First Continental Congress meets in Philadelphia.

1775 American Revolution begins with Battle of Lexington and Concord (Apr. 19). Second Continental Congress appoints George Washington as commander of Continental Army. British win Battle of Bunker Hill. First abolition society organized in Pennsylvania.

1776 Tom Paine's *Common Sense* published. Declaration of Independence signed. Congress adopts name, "United States of America." British occupy New York City. Washington crosses Delaware to win Battle of Trenton, N.J.

1777 Americans win battles at Princeton and Saratoga. British occupy Philadelphia. Congress adopts Stars and Stripes flag and endorses Articles of Confederation. Washington's army spends winter at Valley Forge, Pa.

1778 France makes alliance with U.S. and declares war on Britain. When French fleet arrives, British evacuate Philadelphia.

1779 Congress offers to make peace in exchange for independence. British withdraw from New York City.

1780 Pennsylvania first state to abolish slavery. British occupy Charleston, S.C. Washington quells Continental Army mutiny. Benedict Arnold defects to British.

1781 French and American victory at Battle of Yorktown ends the American Revolution. Articles of Confederation take effect. Los Angeles founded by Spanish missionaries.

1782 Parliament votes for peace with U.S. Negotiations in Paris lead to provisional Anglo-American peace treaty. Virginia permits owners to free their slaves. First English Bible printed in America.

1783 Massachusetts, Connecticut, and Rhode Island abolish slavery. Treaty of Paris signed (Sept. 3), officially ending American Revolution. Washington retires to Mount Vernon, Va.

1784 Congress ratifies Treaty of Paris. Spain closes Mississippi River to American trade. First bale of American cotton shipped to Britain.

1785 First state university chartered in Georgia.

1786 Virginia proclaims religious freedom. Shays's Rebellion put down in Massachusetts. Annapolis Convention calls for revising Articles of Confederation. New Jersey abolishes slavery.

1787 Convention in Philadelphia writes Constitution. Congress passes Northwest Ordinance and submits Constitution for state approval.

1788 Constitution ratified by New Hampshire (June 21), the ninth state to do so thereby marking its final approval.

1789 Constitution takes effect (March 4). George Washington wins first presidential election unopposed. Federal government begins meeting in New York City. Congress enacts first Federal tariff.

1790 First antislavery petitions are submitted to Congress. Temporary capital moved to Philadelphia. Pope Pius VI appoints John Carroll first Catholic bishop in U.S. First U.S. census lists population at 3,929,625.

1791 Congress sets up First Bank of the United States and first internal revenue law, a tax on whiskey. Vermont enters union as 14th state. Bill of Rights takes effect. Pres. Washington selects site of new U.S. capital on the Potomac River.

1792 New York stock traders begin meeting under a tree on Wall Street. Pres. Washington is unanimously reelected. Construction begins on White House.

1793 Eli Whitney invents cotton gin. Congress passes first Fugitive Slave Act. Pres. Washington holds first official cabinet meeting and lays cornerstone for Capitol. Britain begins confiscating American ships trading with France.

1794 Pres. Washington defeats Whiskey Rebellion in Pennsylvania. U.S. and Britain sign Jay's Treaty. Ohio Indians defeated at Battle of Fallen Timbers.

1795 Georgia stung by scandal of Yazoo land frauds. Senate ratifies Jay's Treaty with Britain.

1796 Pres. Washington delivers "Farewell Address." France begins to confiscate ships trading with Britain.

1797 France insults American diplomats in XYZ Affair. Spanish begin building Mission San Juan Capistrano in California.

1798 Georgia last state to abolish slave trade. Congress passes Alien and Sedition Acts. U.S. renounces alliance with France as unofficial naval war breaks out.

1799 Russian-American trading company set up in Alaska. New York abolishes slavery.

1800 Library of Congress founded. Convention of 1800 signed, ending quasi-war between U.S. and France. Spain secretly cedes Louisiana to France. Congress begins meeting in Washington.

1801 Election of Thomas Jefferson results in first transfer of executive power between rival parties. Congress takes jurisdiction over District of Columbia. Tripoli pirates declare war on U.S.

1802 U.S. Military Academy established at West Point, N.Y.

1803 Louisiana Purchase from France doubles size of the U.S. Federal outpost founded at Fort Dearborn, Illinois, future site of Chicago.

1804 Lewis and Clark expedition sets out from St. Louis. Alexander Hamilton killed in duel with Aaron Burr.

1805 Barbary War with Tripoli ends.

1806 Congress authorizes construction of Cumberland Road. Noah Webster's first dictionary published.

1807 Britain and France enact blockades in Europe, confiscating American trading ships. British attack USS Chesapeake. Embargo Act forbids all American exports.

1808 Congress declares end to African slave trade.

1809 Embargo Act replaced with Non-Intercourse Act, outlawing exports to Britain and France. First steamboat sea voyage made from New York City to Philadelphia.

1810 Pres. Madison annexes West Florida.

1811 Worst earthquake in U.S. history rocks Ohio-Mississippi valleys. Russians settle at Ft. Ross, California. First Bank of the United States fails to obtain recharter. Gen. William Henry Harrison defeats Indians at Battle of Tippecanoe.

1812 War of 1812 begins by close vote in Congress. New England resists war. British clamp blockade on U.S. ports, capture Detroit, and repel American attack on Canada at Queenstown.

1813 Americans regain Detroit, attack Toronto and Ft. George in Canada, but surrender to British at Beaver Dams, Ontario. Captain Oliver H. Perry wins control of the Great Lakes. British and Indians burn Buffalo, N.Y.

1814 British destroy Fort Oswego, N.Y., and set fire to Washington, D.C. Francis Scott Key writes "The Star Spangled Banner." New Englanders opposed to war meet secretly at Hartford Convention. First textile mill established at Waltham, Mass. Treaty of Ghent ends War of 1812.

1815 General Andrew Jackson routs British at Battle of New Orleans, before news arrives that War of 1812 is over.

1816 Congress charters Second Bank of the U.S.

1817 Rush-Bagot Treaty between Britain and U.S. demilitarizes Great Lakes. New York Stock and Exchange Board organized. Work begins on Erie Canal. Indian attack starts Seminole War in Florida.

1818 Cumberland Road opens. Congress adopts present format for American flag. Canadian boundary dispute with Britain settled.

1819 Panic of 1819 plunges South and West into depression. U.S. obtains Florida from Spain in Adams-Onís Treaty, settling border of Louisiana. Savannah makes first successful trans-Atlantic crossing under steam power.

1820 Missouri Compromise solves crisis over admission of Missouri as slave state. Abolitionists begin colonizing freed slaves to Africa.

1821 First Catholic cathedral in U.S. built in Baltimore.

1822 Denmark Vesey and 36 others executed for organizing rebel slave conspiracy in Charleston, S.C.

1823 Monroe Doctrine, masterminded by Secy. of State John Quincy Adams, announced by Pres. Monroe.

1824 Russia and U.S. settle territorial disputes in Pacific Northwest. First presidential nominating convention held in Utica, N.Y.

1825 John Quincy Adams chosen president in infamous "Corrupt Bargain" with Henry Clay, who becomes Secy. of State. Erie Canal opened. Mexico invites Americans to settle in Texas.

1826 Anti-Mason party organized. John Adams and Thomas Jefferson die on 50th anniversary of Declaration of Independence. Jedediah Smith leads first overland expedition to California.

1827 U.S. and Britain agree to joint occupation of Pacific Northwest.

1828 Congress passes protectionist "Tariff of Abominations" over Southern protests.

1829 Mexico refuses Pres. Jackson's offer to buy Texas.

1830 Webster-Hayne Debate in U.S. Senate reveals sectional tension. Church of Latter-Day Saints (the Mormons) founded by Joseph Smith in Fayette, N.Y. Mexico forbids further American immigration to Texas.

1831 Nat Turner leads bloodiest of all slave rebellions, killing 57 whites in Virginia.

1832 Black Hawk War fought in Illinois and Wisconsin. First nationwide Democratic party convention held in Baltimore. Pres. Jackson vetoes bill to recharter national bank. South Carolina nullifies "Tariff of Abominations."

1833 Massachusetts last state to end tax support for churches. Congress lowers tariff and passes "Force Bill" to pressure South Carolina, which rescinds nullification. American Anti-Slavery Society organized.

1834 Whig party organized by Senators Henry Clay and Daniel Webster in opposition to Pres. Jackson. Anti-abolitionist riots break out in New York and Philadelphia.

1835 Samuel Morse invents telegraph. National debt completely paid off. Pres. Jackson survives first attempt to assassinate a president. Second Seminole War begins in Florida.

1836 Samuel Colt invents revolver. Texas declares independence from Mexico and requests U.S. annexation. Mexican army captures Alamo, but Texans are victorious at San Jacinto.

1837 Panic of 1837 begins lengthy depression.

1838 Joshua Giddings of Ohio is first abolitionist elected to Congress. Trans-Atlantic steamship service established. Congress blocks abolitionist petitions with "Gag Rule."

1839 Abner Doubleday of Cooperstown, N.Y., codifies rules of baseball. Congress outlaws dueling in Washington, D.C.

1840 "Log Cabin Campaign" between William Henry Harrison and Martin Van Buren begins era of mass political participation. Liberty Party founded by abolitionists in Albany, N.Y.

1841 First emigrant train of 48 covered wagons arrives in California. Pres. Harrison dies after month in office. First Japanese immigrant arrives in New Bedford, Mass.

1842 Webster-Ashburton Treaty settles Canada

boundary disputes between U.S. and Britain. U.S. accidentally seizes California, then returns it with apology to Mexico.

1843 End of Second Seminole War. B'Nai B'rith founded in New York. Mormons begin practicing polygamy.

1844 Baptists first church to split North and South over slavery. Samuel Morse sends first telegraph message. James K. Polk, first "Dark horse" candidate, elected President.

1845 "Potato Famine" begins massive Irish immigration. U.S. annexes Texas, over Mexican protests. U.S. Naval Academy opens at Annapolis, Md.

1846 Mexican War begins when U.S. troops are attacked in disputed Texas territory. American settlers in California stage Bear Flag Revolt. Oregon Treaty gives U.S. sole possession of Pacific Northwest up to 49th parallel. First recorded baseball game played in Hoboken, N.J.

1847 Wilmot Proviso, forbidding slavery expansion, passes House and sets off wave of panic in South. General Winfield Scott conquers Mexico City. Brigham Young leads Mormons to Utah. Abraham Lincoln of Illinois arrives in Congress.

1848 Treaty of Guadalupe-Hidalgo ends Mexican War, ceding Southwest to U.S. Revolution of 1848 begins wave of German immigration. New York-Chicago telegraph line completed. Chicago Board of Trade established. Free Soil party organized. Gold discovered in California. First Chinese immigrants arrive in San Francisco. Lucretia Mott and Elizabeth Cady Stanton hold first Women's Rights Convention in Seneca Falls, N.Y.

1849 Gold Rush brings hundreds of thousands to California. Elizabeth Blackwell first American woman to receive medical degree.

1850 Sen. Henry Clay's Compromise of 1850 solves crisis over slavery expansion. Clayton-Bulwer Treaty pledges Anglo-American cooperation in building any Central American canal.

1851 Y.M.C.A. established. Northern mobs resist Fugitive Slave Act. Maine is first state to pass prohibition laws. New York Times founded. Herman Melville's Moby Dick published.

1852 Harriet Beecher Stowe's Uncle Tom's Cabin published.

1853 U.S. buys Gila River valley from Mexico in Gadsden Purchase. Native American, or "Know-Nothing," party founded. Commodore Matthew C. Perry opens trade with Japan.

1854 Congress passes Kansas-Nebraska Act, setting off mass protests across North. Republican Party founded. U.S. threatens to seize Cuba from Spain in Ostend Manifesto.

1855 "Bleeding Kansas" fighting begins as proslavery and anti-slavery settlers hold rival state conventions. First railroad train crosses Mississippi River at Rock Island, Ill., into Davenport, Iowa.

1856 Cong. Preston Brooks of South Carolina beats Sen. Charles Sumner of Massachusetts unconscious on Senate floor. John Brown leads Pottawatomie massacre in Kansas. First Republican national convention in Pittsburgh, Pa., in February.

1857 New York-St. Louis railroad completed. Supreme Court hands down controversial Dred Scott decision protecting slavery. Panic of 1857 sends North into depression.

1858 Lincoln-Douglas Debates dramatize issue of slavery expansion in Illinois race for Senate. First trans-Atlantic telegraph cable laid.

1859 John Brown's raid on Harper's Ferry arse-

nal to launch abolitionist war against slavery ends in his capture and execution. Slave insurrection panic sweeps South. Comstock Silver Lode discovered in Nevada. First producing oil well in U.S. flows in Titusville, Pa.

1860 Democratic Party splits into Northern and Southern wings. South Carolina is first state to secede from Union after victory of Abraham Lincoln. Crittenden Compromise fails to preserve Union. Pony Express begins mail delivery between California and Missouri.

1861 Civil War begins with attack on Ft. Sumter, South Carolina (Apr. 12). Pres. Lincoln calls for 75,000 volunteers to suppress rebellion. Jefferson Davis of Mississippi elected President of Confederate States of America. New York-San Francisco telegraph link completed. Yale awards first American Ph.D. Congress enacts first federal income tax.

1862 Congress issues "greenbacks," subsidizes transcontinental railroad, abolishes slavery in District of Columbia, and passes Homestead Act. Pres. Lincoln issues Emancipation Proclamation after Battle of Antietam, bloodiest of Civil War.

1863 Emancipation Proclamation takes effect (Jan. 1). Union victories at Vicksburg, Miss., and Gettysburg, Pa., signal turning point of Civil War. West Virginia secedes from Virginia and rejoins Union. Hundreds killed in New York City draft riot. Pres. Lincoln proclaims Thanksgiving national holiday.

1864 Pres. Lincoln names General Ulysses S. Grant as commander of Union armies. General William T. Sherman destroys Atlanta and conducts "March to the Sea." Confederate army of General Robert E. Lee crippled in Wilderness Campaign. Cheyenne and Arapaho Indians slaughtered in Sand Creek Massacre in Colorado.

1865 General Lee surrenders to General Grant at Appomattox Court House, Virginia (Apr. 9). Pres. Lincoln assassinated by John Wilkes Booth in Washington, D.C. (Apr. 14). Confederacy dissolved, ending Civil War. Pres. Johnson proclaims amnesty for most rebels. Slavery outlawed by adoption of Thirteenth Amendment. Ku Klux Klan founded in Pulaski, Tenn.

1866 In the struggle over Reconstruction policy, Congress overrides Pres. Johnson's vetoes of Civil Rights Act and New Freedmen's Bureau Bill. Whites riot in New Orleans to protest black suffrage. Grand Army of the Republic organized by Union veterans.

1867 Congress takes control of Reconstruction in the South by passing First Reconstruction Act over Pres. Johnson's veto and Tenure of Office Act. U.S. purchases Alaska from Russia for $7.2 million (2¢ an acre). Farmers organize Patrons of Husbandry, beginning Granger movement.

1868 Pres. Johnson is impeached in the House (Feb. 24), but acquitted in the Senate by a single vote (May 16). U.S. and China sign Burlingame Treaty to allow immigration. Fourteenth Amendment grants equal citizenship and protection to freedmen (July 28). Half a million black votes help elect Gen. Ulysses S. Grant to the presidency. The typewriter invented.

1869 "Hard Money" prevails when Congress passes Public Credit Act, promising repayment of government debts in gold. Transcontinental railroad completed with golden spike between Union Pacific and Central Pacific lines at Promontory Point, Utah (May 10). Jay Gould and James Fisk cause financial panic by trying to corner gold market on "Black Friday" (Sept. 24). Knights of Labor union organized. National Women's Suffrage Association formed in New York. Wyoming Territory grants first U.S. women's suffrage.

1870 Fifteenth Amendment guarantees right to vote for all U.S. citizens, though only Wyoming and Utah territories allow women's suffrage (Mar. 30). Congress passes first Ku Klux Act to enforce Fifteenth Amendment. First black senator and black congressman are elected.

1871 Congress passes second Ku Klux Klan Act to enforce Fourteenth Amendment in the South. New York Times begins exposé of Boss William Marcy Tweed, leading to overthrow of Tammany Hall ring. Most of Chicago destroyed in the Great Fire (Oct. 8-11). Anti-Chinese race riots in Los Angeles.

1872 Crédit Mobilier scandal implicates Vice President Schuyler Colfax and embarrasses Grant administration. Yellowstone National Park created. Susan B. Anthony arrested for leading suffragists to the polls. Montgomery Ward opens for business in Chicago.

1873 Silver withdrawn from money supply in the "Crime of '73." Congressmen raise their own salaries 50 percent, and double president's pay in "Salary Grab" Act. Panic of 1873, triggered by failure of Jay Cooke's banking house, begins depression of 1870s. New York Stock Exchange forced to close for 10 days. Great Bonanza silver lode discovered in Nevada. San Francisco installs first cable cars.

1874 Granger movement begins passing railroad regulations in Midwestern states. Women's Christian Temperance Union founded in Cleveland, Ohio. Greenback Party formed in Indianapolis. Black rioters attack courthouse in Vicksburg, Miss. Chautauqua movement begins bringing educational speakers to rural communities across the country.

1875 Congress passes Specie Resumption Act to reduce money supply by redeeming greenbacks for gold, and Civil Rights Act to guarantee equal rights for freedmen. Whiskey Ring scandal casts further pall on Grant administration. Archbishop John McCloskey of New York first American bishop. Aristides wins first Kentucky Derby at Churchill Downs, Ky.

1876 U.S. awards patent to Alexander Graham Bell for the telephone. Gen. George A. Custer and 265 men are massacred by Sioux at Little Big Horn, S. Dak. (June 25). Democrat Samuel Tilden outpolls Republican Rutherford B. Hayes as presidential election is thrown into the House (Nov. 7). Baseball's National League established. Kappa Alpha opens first fraternity house at Williams College. Central Park in New York completed.

1877 Congress appoints Electoral Commission to solve impasse over disputed 1876 election. House votes 185 to 184 to declare Rutherford Hayes president, three days before his inauguration (Mar. 2). Reconstruction officially ends with withdrawal of federal troops from the South (Apr. 24). Pres. Hayes sends in troops as Great Railroad Strike paralyzes much of the country. Anti-Chinese riots break out in San Francisco.

1878 Sen. A. A. Sargent introduces Women's Suffrage Amendment in Congress (Jan. 10). Greenback-Labor Party formed in Toledo, Ohio. Limited coinage of silver resumes with Bland-Allison Act. American Bar Association organized in Saratoga, N.Y. Edison Electric begins operating in New York City. New Haven, Conn. sets up first commercial telephone network.

1879 U.S. resumes specie payments for greenbacks. F.W. Woolworth opens his first store in

Utica, N.Y. First Church of Christ, Scientist, founded in Boston. Thomas Edison invents light bulb. California adopts state constitution forbidding employment of Chinese labor.

1880 Pres. Hayes declares U.S. must control any Isthmian canal. U.S. and China agree to Chinese Exclusion Treaty. National Farmers' Alliance organized in Chicago. American branch of Salvation Army founded in Philadelphia, Pa. Census lists U.S. population over 50 million for first time (50,155,783).

1881 Pres. Garfield assassinated by Charles Guiteau in Washington, D.C. (July 2—dies Sept. 19). Clara Barton creates American Red Cross. Booker T. Washington founds Tuskegee Institute for black education in Alabama. Russian Jews begin immigrating to U.S. to escape pogroms.

1882 John D. Rockefeller organizes Standard Oil trust, first such combination. Congress passes first Chinese Exclusion Act (May 10), and legislates first immigration restrictions: no paupers, convicts, or mental defectives. Knights of Columbus founded with permission from Roman Catholic Church.

1883 Congress passes Pendleton Act, requiring civil service competition for Federal jobs. Brooklyn Bridge opened in New York. Supreme Court strikes down Civil Rights Act of 1875. New York-Chicago telephone service begins. Ohio River floods devastate Cincinnati. U.S. Navy builds its first steel ships. Railroads agree on Standard Time zones for North America.

1884 "Mugwumps" bolt Republican Party. Statue of Liberty cornerstone laid (Aug. 5). Belva A. Lockwood of Equal Rights Party first woman candidate for president. Grover Cleveland of New York first Democrat elected president since Civil War. Home Insurance Building of Chicago first skyscraper in the world. Moses Fleetwood Walker first black professional baseball player.

1885 Washington Monument completed after 36 years of construction. U.S. Marines land in Panama (Apr. 24). Senate refuses to ratify treaty for building a canal across Nicaragua. Congress outlaws building fences on public lands in the West. Josiah Strong's best-seller Our Country argues for American imperialism.

1886 Knights of Labor rail strike sets off national wave of strikes for eight-hour day. Haymarket Riot in Chicago leads to execution of seven anarchists. Statue of Liberty dedicated (Oct. 28). American Federation of Labor founded in Columbus, Ohio. Indian wars end with capture of Geronimo.

1887 Congress creates Interstate Commerce Commission, first federal regulatory agency, but with weak enforcement powers. Congress distributes reservation land to Indians, also bans opium imports. First electric trolley line built in Richmond, Va. U.S. Navy leases base at Pearl Harbor, Hawaii.

1888 Snow falls for 36 hours in New York, killing 400 people in "Great Blizzard of '88" (Mar. 12). First secret ballot election held in Louisville, Ky. George Eastman markets first Kodak camera. National Geographic Society founded in Washington, D.C. Edward Bellamy's utopian novel, Looking Backward, a sensational best-seller.

1889 Four new states—N.Dak., S.Dak., Mont., Wash.—all admitted in one day (Feb. 22). Oklahoma Land Rush results as former Indian territory is opened for settlement (Apr. 22). Johnstown Flood claims thousands of lives in Pennsylvania (May 31). Kansas passes first antitrust law. Jane Addams founds Hull House in Chicago.

1890   Congress passes Sherman Antitrust Act (July 2) and Sherman Silver Purchase Act. Wyoming admitted as first state with women's suffrage (July 10). Sioux uprising ends at Battle of Wounded Knee (Dec. 29). Yosemite National Park created. Mississippi leads South in disfranchising black voters. Jacob Riis's *How the Other Half Lives* awakens Americans to urban poverty. Navy wins 24-0 in first Army-Navy football game.
1891   New Orleans mob lynches 11 Italian immigrants. People's, or Populist, Party organized in Cincinnati. U.S. and Chile nearly go to war over death of two American sailors in Valparaiso (Oct. 16). Dr. James A. Naismith invents basketball in Springfield, Mass. Thomas Edison patents first American-made motion picture camera.
1892   Populist candidate James B. Weaver of Iowa receives over a million votes for president. Violent strikes break out among steel workers in Homestead, Pa., and silver miners in Coeur d'Alene, Idaho. Chinese immigrants forced to register with Federal government. First gasoline-powered American automobile built in Chicopee, Mass. Boll weevil first appears in Texas.
1893   U.S. gold reserve falls below $100 million (Apr. 21). Panic of 1893, touched off by New York stock market crash (June 27), begins second-worst depression in U.S. history. Congress repeals Sherman Silver Purchase Act (Oct. 30). Mormon Temple dedicated in Salt Lake City, Utah.
1894   Coxey's Army of unemployed march on Washington, D.C. (Apr. 30). U.S. Treasury issues two $50 million bond offerings to shore up dwindling gold reserves. Congress enacts first peacetime Federal income tax, denounced as "socialism, communism, devilism" (Aug. 27). Pullman strike paralyzes railroads across the country.
1895   J.P. Morgan bails out U.S. Treasury, faced with a gold drain. "Silver Democrats" appeal for unlimited silver coinage as way out of depression. Supreme Court rules income tax unconstitutional (May 20). First professional football game played in Latrobe, Pa.
1896   Supreme Court approves segregation (Plessy vs. Ferguson). William Jennings Bryan, "Silver Democrat" of Nebraska, wins nomination with "Cross of Gold" speech. Gold discovered in Klondike, Alaska, defusing the money question (Aug. 16). American athletes win nine of 12 events at first Olympics. Henry Ford builds his first automobile. First American motion pictures appear in theaters. "The Yellow Kid," first comic strip, begins running in *New York World.*
1897   U.S. offers to mediate Cuban rebellion, lodges official complaint against Spanish brutality. "Yellow press" newspapers keep up assault on Spain. First American subway completed in Boston.
1898   After mysterious explosion of battleship *Maine* in Havana (Feb. 15), Spanish-American War breaks out (Apr. 21). Commodore George Dewey destroys Spanish fleet at Manila Bay (May 1); U.S. takes Manila (Aug. 13). After Battle of San Juan Hill (July 1), Spanish garrison at Santiago, Cuba, surrenders (July 17). U.S. takes Cuba, Puerto Rico, Guam, Wake Island, and Philippines from Spain in Treaty of Paris (Dec. 10). Senate agrees to annex Hawaii.
1899   Philippine Revolt against U.S. rule erupts. Sec. of State John Hay issues Open Door notes to European powers and Japan, requesting no spheres of influence in China (Sept. 6). U.S. and Germany agree to partition Samoan Islands. Con-

gress investigates incompetence in War Department, revealed during Spanish-American War.
1900   "Hard Money" triumphs as U.S. returns to single gold standard (Mar. 14). Puerto Rico and Hawaii become U.S. territories (Apr. 12 & Apr. 30). U.S. troops relieve foreign legations under siege in Peking, China, during Boxer Rebellion. Olds Company opens first Detroit auto factory. Carrie Nation leads hatchet-wielding women into Kansas saloons to smash liquor barrels.
1901   J.P. Morgan creates U.S. Steel, first billion-dollar corporation. U.S. retains control over Cuba with Platt Amendment. Pres. McKinley shot by anarchist Leon Czolgosz in Buffalo, N.Y. (Sept. 6—dies Sept. 14). Hay-Pauncefote Treaty secures British approval for a U.S.-built canal in Panama (Nov. 18). First great Texas oil strike made near Beaumont, Tex. Pres. Roosevelt promises to "speak softly and carry a big stick."
1902   End of Philippine Insurrection. Reclamation Act initiates Federal policy of conservation of natural resources (June 17). Congress declares Philippines an unorganized territory whose inhabitants are not U.S. citizens (July 1). First Rose Bowl game played. Pres. Roosevelt helps mediate Pennsylvania coal strike.
1903   Pres. Roosevelt helps Panama gain independence from Colombia, then negotiates treaty to build Panama Canal. Orville and Wilbur Wright conduct first powered flight near Kitty Hawk, N.C. (Dec. 17). The Great Train Robbery, first feature-length motion picture, released. Wisconsin holds first primary elections. Ford Motor Company formed. Boston defeats Pittsburgh in first baseball World Series.
1904   Supreme Court upholds antitrust dissolution of Northern Securities company (Mar. 14). "Roosevelt Corollary" to Monroe Doctrine justifies U.S. intervention to keep other powers out of Western hemisphere. New York state enacts first speed limit: 20 mph Deaf, dumb, and blind, Helen Keller graduates from Radcliffe College.
1905   Supreme Court disallows limits on length of working day. Industrial Workers of the World, a radical labor union, formed in Chicago. Pres. Roosevelt mediates Treaty of Portsmouth, ending Russo-Japanese War. Black leaders hold Niagara Falls Conference, calling for equal rights.
1906   San Francisco destroyed by earthquake and fire (Apr. 18-19). Congress passes Pure Food and Drug Act and Meat Inspection Act. Race riot breaks out in Atlanta (Sept. 22). Japan protests segregation of Asian students in California schools (Oct. 25). Pres. Roosevelt first American to win the Nobel Peace Prize, and first sitting president to leave U.S. on visit to Panama.
1907   Panic of 1907 triggers crash on Wall Street (Mar. 13) and run on banks across the country. Pres. Roosevelt orders exclusion of Japanese laborers (Mar. 14). Congress outlaws corporate contributions to political campaigns. Hundreds killed in coal mine explosions in Monongah, W. Va., and Jacobs Creek, Pa. All-time record 1,285,349 immigrants arrive in one year.
1908   U.S. and Japan conclude "Gentleman's Agreement" limiting immigration. Ford Model T appears on the market (Oct. 1). Root-Takahira Agreement promises U.S. and Japan will respect each other's interests in Pacific. Pres. Roosevelt appoints National Conservation Commission. Federal Bureau of Investigation established. New York City outlaws women smoking in public.
1909   Robert E. Peary plants American flag at North Pole (Apr. 6). Pres. Taft opens 700,000 acres

for settlement in the West. W.E.B. DuBois founds National Association for the Advancement of Colored People (NAACP), advocating racial equality.
1910 Theodore Roosevelt calls for "New Nationalism" in a speech at Ossawatomie, Kans. Los Angeles Times building destroyed by terrorist bomb (Oct. 1). Glacier National Park created. Mann Act cracks down on "white slave" trade. Boy Scouts of America chartered.
1911 Pres. Taft orders U.S. troops to border during Mexican Revolution. Supreme Court upholds antitrust breakups of Standard Oil and American Tobacco. Calbraith P. Rodgers makes first transcontinental airplane flight. U.S. bankers take control of Nicaragua's finances. Steel magnate Andrew Carnegie donates $125 million for philanthropic purposes.
1912 *Titanic* sinks on maiden voyage from England (Apr. 15). Progressive, or "Bull Moose," Party founded by Theodore Roosevelt, who survives an assassination attempt by John Schrank in Milwaukee (Oct. 14). Massachusetts adopts first minimum wage law. U.S. Marines land in Honduras, Cuba, Nicaragua, and Santo Domingo. Textile strike in Lawrence, Mass.
1913 Sixteenth Amendment empowers Federal government to collect income taxes (Feb. 25). Seventeenth Amendment allows for popular election of U.S. senators (May 31). Congress creates Federal Reserve system. Ford Motor Company introduces assembly line. John D. Rockefeller donates $100 million to philanthropic Rockefeller Foundation. Grand Central Station opens in New York City.
1914 Pres. Wilson nearly goes to war with Mexico over arrests of American sailors in Tampico. U.S. Navy shells Vera Cruz and lands Marines in retaliation (Apr. 21). U.S. declares neutrality in World War I (Aug. 4). Congress passes Clayton Act, toughening antitrust standards. Congress proclaims Mother's Day.
1915 The Birth of a Nation, first movie blockbuster. Pres. Wilson strongly protests German sinking of Lusitania with 128 Americans aboard (May 7). U.S. Marines land in Haiti (July 28). Ku Klux Klan revived in Atlanta, Ga. Coast-to-coast long distance telephone service begins.
1916 House-Grey Memorandum warns Germany that refusal to negotiate may bring U.S. into World War I. Gen. John Pershing chases Pancho Villa into Mexico after border raid on Columbus, N.Mex. (Mar. 15). U.S. acquires Virgin Islands from Denmark for $25 million. Jeanette Rankin of Montana first woman elected to Congress. Louis D. Brandeis first Jewish member of Supreme Court. Margaret Sanger opens first birth control clinic in Brooklyn, N.Y. National Park Service created.
1917 Germany resumes unrestricted submarine warfare, leading U.S. to sever diplomatic relations (Feb. 3). Gen. John Pershing withdraws from Mexico. Zimmerman Telegram reveals German overtures to Mexico in case of war (Feb. 24). U.S. merchant ships armed for self-defense against German submarines (Mar. 13). After Pres. Wilson proclaims "the world must be made safe for democracy," Congress declares war on Germany (Apr. 6) and Austria-Hungary (Dec. 7). Prohibition begins as wartime conservation measure.
1918 Pres. Wilson announces U.S. war aims in "Fourteen Points" speech (Jan. 8). U.S. troops join Allied intervention in Russian Revolution (Aug. 2). Congress passes Sedition Act. Over a million U.S. troops participate in month-long Meuse-Argonne

campaign (Sept. 26-Nov. 11). Republicans win control of Congress, a rebuke to Pres. Wilson. Armistice Day ends World War I (Nov. 11) as mass celebrations break out across the country. Pres. Wilson goes to Europe for peace conference. Supreme Court approves draft laws and strikes down child labor laws. Influenza epidemic takes hundreds of thousands American lives.
1919 Eighteenth Amendment establishes Prohibition (Jan. 29). Strike wave sweeps country, triggering "Red Scare." American Communist Party organized in Chicago. Race riots in Washington, D.C., and Chicago. Pres. Wilson suffers incapacitating stroke (Sept. 26). Volstead Act implements national Prohibition enforcement. Senate rejects Versailles Treaty and League of Nations (Nov. 19). Grand Canyon National Park created. New York-Chicago daily airmail service begins.
1920 Attorney General A. Mitchell Palmer stages "Palmer Raids," arresting and deporting thousands of radicals and immigrants. Sacco and Vanzetti are arrested for murder in Braintree, Mass. Supreme Court upholds Prohibition. Nineteenth Amendment establishes women's suffrage (Aug. 26). National League of Women Voters organized. First regular radio broadcasts begin in East Pittsburgh, Pa. Pres. Wilson receives Nobel Peace Prize. U.S. population, more urban than rural for first time, tops 100 million (105,710,620).
1921 Pres. Harding, promising a "return to normalcy," takes office. U.S. negotiates separate peace with Germany, Austria, and Hungary. Ku Klux Klan spreads terror in the South. Jack Dempsey defeats Georges Carpentier in first million-dollar prize fight.
1922 Washington Conference concludes with nine international treaties to limit naval arms race, relax tensions in the Pacific, and protect China. Supreme Court upholds women's suffrage. Lincoln Memorial dedicated in Washington, D.C. (May 30). Pres. Harding vetoes "Bonus Bill" for World War I veterans. Congress passes joint resolution in favor of Jewish homeland in Palestine (Sept. 21). First commercial radio show broadcast in New York.
1923 Last U.S. occupation troops leave Germany (Jan. 10). Senate begins investigating corruption in Veterans Bureau and Teapot Dome oil leases (Oct. 25). Pres. Harding dies mysteriously of "apoplexy" in San Francisco (Aug. 2). Pres. Coolidge's address to Congress, calling for economy in government, first radio broadcast of a presidential speech (Dec. 6). Oklahoma declares martial law to crack down on Ku Klux Klan. Yankee Stadium opens.
1924 Congress provides bonuses for World War I veterans over Pres. Coolidge's veto. Congress passes Immigration Act, imposing strict national quota system. European powers accept Dawes Plan for repayment of war debts and reparations. U.S. Marines withdraw from Santo Domingo. Coast-to-coast air mail service begins.
1925 Tennessee outlaws teaching evolution in school, leading to the Scopes Trial in Dayton, Tenn. (July 10-21). Ku Klux Klan marches on Washington, D.C. (Aug. 8). Nellie Tayloe Ross of Wyoming first woman governor. Florida land boom draws hordes of speculators. Chicago gang wars break out as Al Capone consolidates bootlegging operations.
1926 Treasury Sec. Andrew Mellon's drastic tax cuts approved. Admiral Richard E. Byrd and Floyd Bennett first to fly over North Pole (May 9). Henry

Ford institutes 8-hour day and 5-day work week at Ford Motor Company factories. Hurricane sweeps Florida, killing 372 people. Book of the Month Club founded. U.S. Marines return to Nicaragua.
1927 Charles Lindbergh completes non-stop solo flight from New York to Paris (May 20-21), returns home to huge welcoming crowds. Sacco and Vanzetti executed in Massachusetts, despite international protests. The Jazz Singer with Al Jolson becomes first "talkie" motion picture (Oct. 6). Mississippi River floods causes $300 million damage. Ford Model A unveiled. Mechanical cotton picker invented. New York-London commercial telephone service begins.
1928 U.S. joins fourteen countries in signing Kellogg-Briand Pact for the "outlawry of war" (Aug. 27). Clark Memorandum disavows future U.S. interventions in Latin America. Pres. Coolidge refuses to aid American farmers mired in agricultural depression. Walt Disney creates "Steamboat Willie," first Mickey Mouse cartoon. George Eastman demonstrates color motion picture technology. Republicans promise "a chicken in every pot, a car in every garage."
1929 St. Valentine's Day Massacre claims six lives in Chicago gang wars. Young Plan replaces Dawes Plan for payment of war debts and reparations. Albert B. Fall, former secretary of the Interior, found guilty in Teapot Dome scandal. Stock market crash on "Black Tuesday" (Oct. 29) ushers in Great Depression.
1930 Wave of bank failures sweeps U.S., wiping out millions of savings accounts and leading to private hoarding of gold. U.S., Britain, and Japan sign London Naval Treaty limiting naval arms race (Apr. 22). Hawley-Smoot Tariff raises barriers to world trade, worsening Depression. Congress creates Veteran's Administration (July 3).
1931 World War I veterans are offered "Bonus Loans" to combat Depression. "Star Spangled Banner" becomes national anthem. "Scottsboro Boys" arrested for rape in Alabama. Empire State Building, tallest building in the world, opens in New York City. Pres. Hoover declares moratorium on international debt and reparations payments.
1932 Stimson Doctrine condemns Japanese invasion of China. Congress approves Reconstruction Finance Corporation to help recovery. Norris-LaGuardia act restricts use of injunctions against labor strikes. Franklin D. Roosevelt wins presidential election in a landslide, promising a "New Deal." Stock market drops to 10% of its 1929 value. "Bonus Army" of poor veterans marches on Washington, D.C. Amelia Earhart first woman to fly solo across the Atlantic.
1933 Giuseppe Zangara kills Chicago Mayor Anton J. Cermak in a Miami, Fla., motorcade, narrowly missing president-elect Franklin D. Roosevelt (Feb. 15). Banks are closed for four days by presidential order (Mar. 5). During "Hundred Days" (Mar. 9-June 16), Pres. Roosevelt pushes New Deal through Congress, conducts first "Fireside Chat" on radio, and takes U.S. off gold standard. Prohibition repealed (Mar. 22). U.S. recognizes Soviet Union (Nov. 16). U.S. Marines withdraw from Nicaragua. Frances Perkins, Sec. of Labor, becomes first woman cabinet member.
1934 Dust storms inundate Southwest, driving "Okies" and "Arkies" to California. General strike paralyzes San Francisco (July 16). John Dillinger, public enemy number one, killed by FBI agents (July 22). Sen. Gerald P. Nye of North Dakota begins investigating role of U.S. munitions manufacturers in World War I. U.S. releases Cuba from

Platt Amendment. U.S. troops withdraw from Haiti.
1935 Supreme Court invalidates National Industrial Recovery Act. Pres. Roosevelt pushes more "Second New Deal" legislation through Congress, notably the Wagner Act protecting unions, Social Security Act, and "Soak the Rich" Wealth Tax Act. Sen. Huey P. Long of Louisana assassinated (Sept. 8). Congress of Industrial Organization (CIO) formed (Nov. 9). Congress passes first Neutrality Act. Alcoholics Anonymous founded.
1936 Congress passes second Neutrality Act. France, Britain, and U.S. sign New London Naval Treaty (Mar. 25). U.S. declares neutrality in Spanish Civil War (Aug. 7). CIO auto workers begin sitdown strikes in Flint, Mich. Life magazine begins publishing. Jesse Owens wins four gold medals at "Nazi Olympics" in Berlin.
1937 Congress passes third Neutrality Act. Pres. Roosevelt proposes controversial "court-packing" plan. German dirigible Hindenburg explodes and burns in Lakehurst, N.J. (May 6). Pres. Roosevelt angers isolationists with "Quarantine Speech" (Oct. 5). Japanese planes sink U.S. Navy gunboat Panay in China (Dec. 12). Slow recovery ends abruptly as Depression worsens.
1938 Pres. Roosevelt calls for military buildup. Mexico seizes U.S.-owned oil wells. Rep. Martin Dies of Texas begins House Un-American Activities Committee (HUAC) investigations of Communists and Fascists. Howard Hughes sets record for around-the-world flight in less than four days (July 14). "Invasion from Mars" radio broadcast by Orson Welles causes widespread panic (Oct. 30). Hurricane devastates Atlantic coast, killing 700.
1939 Supreme Court upholds Tennessee Valley Authority. Pan Am begins first regular trans-Atlantic passenger service. U.S. declares neutrality in World War II (Sept. 5). Congress passes fourth Neutrality Act, approving Pres. Roosevelt's request for "cash-and-carry" arms sales to belligerents. First nylon stockings appear on the market.
1940 As World War II engulfs Europe, Pres. Roosevelt announces U.S. move from "neutrality" to "non-belligerency" (June 10). U.S. and Britain conclude Destroyers-for-Bases deal. Congress enacts peacetime draft (Sept. 16) and massive increases in military spending. Over 16 million men register for draft as embargo on strategic exports takes effect. Roosevelt, reelected to an unprecedented third term, calls for U.S. to become "the arsenal of democracy" (Dec. 20).
1941 Congress appropriates $7 billion in Lend-Lease aid to Britain. German submarine sinks merchant ship Robin Moor, first U.S. casualty of war (May 21). Pres. Roosevelt responds by declaring "unlimited national emergency" (May 27), freezing German and Italian assets in U.S. (June 14), and promising aid to Soviet Union (June 24). Pres. Roosevelt freezes Japanese assets in retaliation for invasion of Indochina. U.S. Navy is ordered to "shoot on sight" at German warships. Japanese planes attack Pearl Harbor, Hawaii, killing 2,400 U.S. servicemen and civilians (Dec. 7). U.S. declares war on Japan (Dec. 10) and on Germany and Italy (Dec. 11).
1942 Roosevelt creates War Production Board, calls for mass mobilization, and puts New Deal on hold. U.S. troops land in North Ireland, first to arrive in Europe (Jan. 26). Pres. Roosevelt approves internment of Japanese-Americans for duration of war (Feb. 20). Japanese submarine shells an oil refinery in Santa Barbara, Calif. (Feb. 23). Maj. James H. Doolittle stages carrier-launched bomb-

ing raid on Tokyo (Apr. 18). U.S. armed forces surrender in Philippines (May 6), but win major naval victories over Japan in Coral Sea (May 4-8) and at Midway (June 3-6). U.S. offensive begins in Pacific with invasion of Guadalcanal Island (Aug. 7). First all-U.S. bombing attack launched against German forces at Rouen, France (Aug. 17). Congress approves "Victory Tax" on wartime incomes. Allies land 400,000 men in North Africa (Nov. 7-8). Eight German saboteurs apprehended in New York; six executed. Cocoanut Grove nightclub fire in Boston kills 492.

1943 Congress appropriates $100 billion for war effort. Roosevelt and Churchill demand "unconditional surrender" at Casablanca conference in Morocco. U.S. Marines drive last Japanese from Guadalcanal (Feb. 9). U.S. troops defeated in first battle with Germans at Kasserine Pass, Tunisia (Feb. 20). Pres. Roosevelt declares wage-and-price freeze to stem inflation. U.S. and Britain invade Sicily (July 10) and Italy proper (Sept. 3). Roosevelt and Churchill meet with Chiang Kai-Shek of China in Cairo, Egypt (Nov. 22), and with Josef Stalin of Soviet Union in Teheran, Iran (Dec. 4-6). Gen. Dwight D. Eisenhower named Supreme Commander of Allied forces in Europe.

1944 U.S. and British planes begin around-the-clock bombing of Berlin. Allied forces land at Anzio, Italy (Jan. 22). Congress approves $1.35 billion for United Nations Relief and Reconstruction Agency, first U.S. foreign aid (Mar. 29). Allied forces enter Rome (June 5) as reconquest of Europe begins with D-Day invasion of Normandy (June 6). Allied breakout from Normandy sends German forces reeling across France (July 25). Postwar financial arrangements made at an international conference in Bretton Woods, N.H. (July 1-22). Plans for U.N. made at Dumbarton Oaks conference (Aug. 21-Oct. 7). Gen. Douglas MacArthur begins reconquest of Philippines with landings at Leyte Gulf (Oct. 20). Congress passes Servicemen's Readjustment Act, known as "GI Bill of Rights." Roosevelt wins fourth term.

1945 Roosevelt, Churchill and Stalin meet for last time at Yalta in Soviet Crimea to begin postwar planning (Feb. 4-11). Allied forces cross Rhine River and drive into heart of Germany (Mar. 7). U.S. air raids destroy Tokyo (Mar. 10-11). Pres. Roosevelt dies suddenly of cerebral hemorrhage in Warm Springs, Ga. (Apr. 12). Germany surrenders, ending war in Europe (May 7). Fifty nations sign United Nations Charter (June 26). First atomic explosion occurs in test at Alamagordo, N. Mex. (July 16). Pres. Truman meets with Churchill and Stalin at Potsdam, Germany (July 17-Aug. 2). Atomic bombs dropped on Hiroshima (Aug. 6) and Nagasaki (Aug. 9); Japan surrenders (Aug. 14), ending World War II. Council of Allied Foreign Ministers meets in London, unable to agree on peace treaty (Dec. 16-27). Empire State Building hit by B-25 bomber in heavy fog.

1946 Strike wave sweeps U.S., idling 4.6 million U.S. workers. Congress passes Employment Act, committing Federal government to postwar economic management. Churchill warns Americans about Communist expansion with "Iron Curtain" speech in Fulton, Mo. (Mar. 5). Pres. Truman seizes control of railroads and coal mines during strikes. U.S. presents Baruch Plan for international control of atomic energy, grants independence to Philippines (July 4), and agrees to loan Britain $3.5 billion for postwar reconstruction. Paris Peace Conference ends in failure (July 29-Oct. 15). Congress creates Atomic Energy Commission. U.N. General Assembly begins meeting in New York.

1947 Council of Foreign Ministers meets in Moscow, again unable to agree on peace treaty (Mar. 10-Apr. 24). Pres. Truman announces Truman Doctrine, promising aid to countries threatened by subversion (May 12). Sec. of State George C. Marshall announces Marshall Plan for reconstruction of Europe (June 5). Republican-dominated Congress restricts union organizing with Taft-Hartley Act. House Un-American Activities Committee (HUAC) begins investigating Communism in Hollywood (Oct. 20). Texas City, Tex., wiped out when a ship explodes, killing over 500 people. Jackie Robinson of Brooklyn Dodgers breaks color line in baseball.

1948 Postwar inflation keeps prices rising fast. Congress approves $5.3 billion for Marshall Plan aid to Europe with Foreign Assistance Act. U.S. recognizes new state of Israel (May 14) and admits 205,000 war refugees from Europe. Britain and U.S. begin airlifting supplies into West Berlin after Soviets cut off all traffic into city (June 26). Pres. Truman orders peacetime draft and desegregation of U.S. armed forces. HUAC charges Alger Hiss with spying for Soviet Union. Pres. Truman wins upset reelection victory over New York Gov. Thomas E. Dewey. Idlewild International Airport, world's largest, opens in New York.

1949 Pres. Truman calls for "Fair Deal" domestic programs and "Point Four" foreign aid programs. U.S., Canada, and 10 Western European nations sign treaty that will lead to North Atlantic Treaty Organization (NATO). Berlin Airlift ends when Soviets finally lift blockade (May 12). Pres. Truman announces Soviet atomic bomb test (Sept. 23). Eleven U.S. Communist leaders convicted of conspiring to overthrow government. Steel strike idles half a million workers (Oct. 1-Nov. 11). Lucky Lady II of U.S. Air Force completes first nonstop around-the-world flight.

1950 Sen. Joseph R. McCarthy of Wisconsin issues his first accusations of Communists in government at a speech in Wheeling, W. Va. North Korea invades South Korea, beginning Korean War (June 25). Pres. Truman orders U.S. intervention (June 27), obtains U.N. support (July 7), asks Congress for a $10 billion rearmament program (July 20), and calls up reserves (Aug. 4). Inchon landing begins rout of North Korean invaders (Sept. 15). U.N. troops recapture Seoul (Sept. 26) and invade North Korea (Oct. 7). Congress passes Internal Security Act, requiring registration of Communist organizations, over Pres. Truman's veto (Sept. 23). Puerto Rican nationalists nearly assassinate Pres. Truman in Washington (Nov. 11). After China intervenes in the Korean War, Pres. Truman proclaims a national emergency (Dec. 16).

1951 Gen. Dwight D. Eisenhower comes out of retirement to accept command of Allied forces in Europe (Apr. 4). Julius and Ethel Rosenberg sentenced to death for spying (Apr. 5). Pres. Truman removes Gen. Douglas MacArthur from command in Korea for insubordination (Apr. 11). MacArthur returns to the U.S., greeted by exultant crowds, to deliver address to Congress. Missouri River floods devastate Kansas City, causing over $1 billion in damages (July 11-25). U.S. concludes a mutual defense pact with Australia and New Zealand, and signs a peace treaty with Japan (Sept. 8). Congress passes the Mutual Security Act, providing $7 billion for foreign aid and military cooperation with pro-U.S. nations. CBS transmits first color television broadcast from New York.

1952   Pres. Truman seizes steel mills paralyzed by strikes (Apr. 8). U.S., Britain and France sign a peace treaty with West Germany (May 26). Construction begins on USS Nautilus, first atomic submarine. Supreme Court upholds barring subversives from teaching in schools. Sen. Richard M. Nixon of California, Republican candidate for Vice President, delivers "Checkers Speech" on national television to explain his "secret slush fund." Republicans win control of White House and both houses of Congress for first time since 1928. U.S. announces first successful hydrogen bomb test at Eniwetok Atoll in Marshall Islands (Nov. 16).

1953   Thirteen more Communist leaders are convicted of conspiring to overthrow the government. Julius and Ethel Rosenberg are executed in Ossining, N.Y. (June 19). Pres. Eisenhower lifts wage and price controls, increases U.S. support for French war effort in Indochina, negotiates armistice ending Korean War (June 27). Congress creates Department of Health, Education, and Welfare (Apr. 1). U.S. pledges aid to Spain in exchange for military bases (Sept. 26). Major Chuck Yeager of the U.S. Air Force sets new air speed record in rocket-powered X-1 jet plane.

1954   Sec. of State John Foster Dulles vows "massive retaliation" against Soviet aggression (Jan. 12). Puerto Rican nationalists shoot five Congressmen on the floor of the House of Representatives (Mar. 1). U.S. negotiates the Southeast Asia Treaty Organization (SEATO) security pact (Sept. 8). Supreme Court orders school desegregation in Brown v. Board of Education (May 17). CIA helps overthrow the Arbenz government in Guatemala (June 29). Senate censures Sen. Joseph McCarthy.

1955   Pres. Eisenhower promises to use atomic weapons in case of war and conducts first televised press conference. U.S., Soviet Union, and Allies agree on Austrian peace treaty to end occupation. Supreme Court orders school desegregation to proceed "with all deliberate speed." Interstate Commerce Commission orders desegregation on interstate trains and buses. AFL and CIO labor federations merge to form the AFL-CIO, with 15 million members. Dr. Jonas Salk perfects polio vaccine. Dr. Martin Luther King, Jr., leads bus boycott in Montgomery, Ala.

1956   Pres. Eisenhower refuses to intervene against Soviet invasion of Hungary and exerts pressure on Allies to withdraw from Suez. Congressmen signing Southern Manifesto promise "massive resistance" to school desegregation. Atomic Energy Commission approves commercial nuclear power plants. Congress passes Highway Act, appropriating $32 billion for construction of a vast nationwide road system. TWA and United airliners collide in midair and crash into Grand Canyon, killing 128 people. First transatlantic telephone cable begins operating.

1957   Pres. Eisenhower announces Eisenhower Doctrine, promising aid to any Middle Eastern country threatened by Communism. McClellan Committee begins investigating corruption and racketeering in International Brotherhood of Teamsters union. Sen. J. Strom Thurmond of South Carolina sets all-time filibuster record (24 hours, 27 minutes) with speech against civil rights (Aug. 30). Congress nevertheless approves the first Civil Rights Act since Reconstruction (Sept. 9). Pres. Eisenhower sends troops to Little Rock, Ark., to enforce Federal desegregation order (Sept. 24). First underground atomic test conducted in Nevada (Sept. 19).

1958   In response to Soviet launch of Sputnik, U.S. launches Explorer I, first American satellite; Congress creates National Aeronautics and Space Administration (NASA). Vice President Richard M. Nixon nearly killed by angry mob in Caracas, Venezuela. At request of weak government in Beirut, Pres. Eisenhower orders U.S. Marines to land in Lebanon (July 15). Nuclear submarine Nautilus performs first undersea crossing of North Pole (Aug. 5). Presidential assistant Sherman Adams forced to resign in scandal over accepting favors (Sept. 22).

1959   Fidel Castro's takeover of Cuba begins rapid deterioration of U.S.-Cuba relations (Jan. 1). Alaska becomes 49th state (Jan. 3), and Hawaii becomes 50th state (Aug. 21). Joint U.S.-Canada St. Lawrence Seaway project completed. Congress passes the Landrum-Griffin Act to suppress racketeering in labor unions. Vice Pres. Richard M. Nixon holds impromptu "kitchen debate" in Moscow with Soviet Premier Nikita Khrushchev. Charles Van Doren testifies that his victory on the "$64,000 Question" TV game show was fixed.

1960   U.S. and Japan conclude new security treaty (Jan. 19). Black students stage first sit-in at a Woolworth's lunch counter in Greensboro, N.C. (Feb. 1). U-2 spy plane, with American pilot Francis Gary Powers, is shot down over the Soviet Union (May 1). Congress passes second Civil Rights Act since Reconstruction. Congress investigates "payola" in the radio industry, leading to the arrest of Alan Freed, "father of rock 'n' roll." After Cuba rejects American protests over confiscated property, Pres. Eisenhower imposes trade embargo. John F. Kennedy and Richard M. Nixon hold first televised presidential campaign debates. Kennedy wins election by 0.3 percent of popular vote, closest presidential election since 1884 (Nov. 8).

1961   Pres. Eisenhower breaks diplomatic relations with Cuba, warns Americans to beware of "military-industrial complex." CIA-backed Bay of Pigs invasion fails to overthrow Castro regime in Cuba (Apr. 17). Commander Alan B. Shephard, Jr., U.S. Navy, first American in space on Mercury rocket (May 5). Soviet construction of Berlin Wall creates temporary crisis (Aug. 13). Pres. Kennedy creates Peace Corps and Alliance for Progress. American families advised to build nuclear fallout shelters. "Freedom Rides" civil rights protests broken up by riots in Anniston and Birmingham, Ala. American Medical Association reports link between smoking and heart disease. National Council of Churches endorses birth control for families.

1962   Lt. Col. John H. Glenn, Jr., first American to orbit Earth. Pres. Kennedy convinces steel companies to rescind price increases. U.S. conducts first successful test of sea-launched long-range ballistic missile with nuclear warhead. Pres. Kennedy sends U.S. marshals to protect James H. Meredith, a black student at University of Mississippi. U.S. extends a $100 million emergency loan to the United Nations. Threat of nuclear war during Cuban Missile Crisis averted when Soviet Union agrees to withdraw missiles from Cuba (Oct. 22-28). Rachel Carson's *Silent Spring* draws attention to environmental crisis.

1963   Pres. Kennedy proposes the Medicare program. U.S., Great Britain, and the Soviet Union conclude the Nuclear Test-Ban Treaty outlawing atmospheric testing (July 25). "Hot line" between Washington and Moscow put in place. Civil rights movement reaches a climax with mass demonstrations in Birmingham, Ala., and epic March on

Washington, where Martin Luther King delivers his "I Have a Dream" speech (Aug. 28). Pres. Kennedy is assassinated in Dallas, Tex., by Lee Harvey Oswald (Nov. 22), who is murdered by Jack Ruby (Nov. 24).

1964 Pres. Johnson, taking up Pres. Kennedy's cause, calls for a "War on Poverty." Supreme Court orders states to redraw Congressional boundaries to ensure fair representation. Alaska declared disaster area after major earthquake rocks Anchorage (Mar. 28). Mississippi "Freedom Summer" begins with murder of three civil rights workers (June 22). Pres. Johnson pushes landmark Civil Rights and Economic Opportunity acts through Congress. After alleged North Vietnamese attack on U.S. Navy destroyers, Congress passes Tonkin Gulf Resolution giving Pres. Johnson free hand in Vietnam (Aug. 7). Warren Commission reports there was no conspiracy to assassinate Pres. Kennedy (Sept. 27). The Rev. Martin Luther King Jr. wins Nobel Peace Prize.

1965 Pres. Johnson calls for the "Great Society." Black nationalist Malcolm X is assassinated in New York City (Feb. 21). Pres. Johnson orders U.S. Marines into South Vietnam (Mar. 8) and into Santo Domingo (Apr. 38). U.S. troops authorized to undertake offensive operations in South Vietnam (June 8). Martin Luther King leads civil rights marches from Selma to Montgomery, Ala., and in white neighborhoods of Chicago. Congress approves Medicare (July 30) and Voting Rights Act (Aug. 6). The Watts Riot in Los Angeles leaves 34 dead and over $200 million in damage (Aug. 11-16), accelerating wave of ghetto riots. Tornadoes sweep Midwest, killing 271 and injuring 5,000.

1966 Pres. Johnson orders first B-52 strategic bombing raids on North Vietnam (Apr. 12). Supreme Court rules police must advise suspects of their rights. Cesar Chavez leads United Farm Workers strike and boycott against California grape growers. Stokeley Carmichael of Student Non-Violent Coordinating Committee demands "Black Power." Congress enacts safety standards for automobiles. U.S. troops in Vietnam increase from 215,000 to over 400,000.

1967 Green Bay defeats Kansas City in first ever Super Bowl. Hundreds of thousands of anti-war protesters march on Washington (Apr. 15 & Oct. 21-22). Pres. Johnson announces U.S. troop level will reach 525,000 by end of 1968. Worst race riot in U.S. history erupts in Detroit (July 23), leaving 43 dead, while riot in Newark, N.J., (July 12) kills another 26. Sen. Eugene McCarthy (D-Minn.) announces antiwar candidacy for president (Nov. 30). U.S. agrees to refrain from placing nuclear weapons in space and joins General Agreement on Tariffs and Trade (GATT). Thurgood Marshall becomes first black justice on Supreme Court.

1968 North Korea seizes *USS Pueblo*, holding 82 crewmen hostage (Jan. 23). North Vietnam and Viet Cong launch massive Tet Offensive (Jan. 30). Pres. Johnson makes surprise announcement that he will not seek re-election (Mar. 31). Martin Luther King assassinated by James Earl Ray in Memphis, Tenn. (Apr. 4). Washington-Hanoi peace talks begin in Paris (May 10). After winning California primary, Sen. Robert F. Kennedy of New York murdered by Sirhan Sirhan in Los Angeles (June 5). U.S. signs Nuclear Non-Proliferation Treaty. Democratic Convention in Chicago marred by riots and police violence against antiwar demonstrators. Shirley Chisholm of New York is the first black woman elected to Congress. Apollo VIII completes first moon orbit.

1969 Oil spill off Santa Barbara, Calif., draws attention to need for environmental protection (Feb. 5). Pres. Nixon asks Congress to fund Anti-Ballistic Missile program as "safeguard" for strategic defense. U.S. losses in Vietnam exceed losses in Korean War. Sen. Edward M. Kennedy (D-Mass.) drives off a bridge at Chappaquiddick, Mass., killing Mary Jo Kopechne (July 18). Neil Armstrong and Buzz Aldrin of Apollo XI are first men to walk on the moon (July 20). Hurricane Camille claims over 300 victims in the South. Trial of Chicago Seven begins. Woodstock music festival near Bethel, N.Y., draws 400,000 young fans (Aug. 15-18). Vietnam Moratorium and "March Against Death" antiwar demonstrations draw hundreds of thousands to Washington. U.S. and the Soviet Union begin Strategic Arms Limitation Talks (SALT) in Helsinki, Finland.

1970 Pres. Nixon calls for "Vietnamization" to decrease U.S. involvement in war. U.S. bombing of North Vietnam escalates dramatically; nationwide protests break out when U.S. invades Cambodia (Apr. 29). Four students are killed and nine wounded by National Guard units at Kent State University in Ohio (May 4). Lt. William L. Calley court-martialed for massacre of 102 civilians in My Lai South Vietnam (Nov. 12). Supreme Court upholds new 18-year-old voting age (Dec. 21). Congress creates Environmental Protection Agency, passes Water Quality Improvement Act, Air Quality Control Act, and Occupational Safety and Health Act.

1971 Pres. Nixon proposes federal revenue sharing with states. Charles Manson and three women followers convicted for Tate-LaBianca murders in Los Angeles (Jan. 25). Major earthquake rocks Southern California, killing 64 and injuring over 1,000 (Feb. 9). Supreme Court approves busing to achieve school integration. Indian occupation of Alcatraz Island in San Francisco Bay comes to an end. Prison riot in Attica, N.Y., kills 43 inmates and guards. *The New York Times* begins publishing "Pentagon Papers," top-secret history of Vietnam War (June 13). U.S. devalues dollar (Dec. 18). U.S. troops in Vietnam reach 139,000; U.S. air attacks are heaviest since 1968.

1972 Nixon first president to visit China (Feb. 21-28) and the Soviet Union (May 22-30). Airlines begin screening passengers to prevent hijackings. Congress passes Equal Rights Amendment and submits it to states for ratification. Gov. George Wallace of Alabama shot and seriously wounded by Arthur Bremer while campaigning for president in Laurel, Md. (May 15). Five men arrested for breaking into Democratic National Committee headquarters at the Watergate complex in Washington (June 17). Federal grand jury indicts five burglars and two former White House aides in Watergate break-in (Sept. 15). Pres. Nixon angers farmers with the "Great Grain Robbery," a secret deal to sell wheat at discount to Soviet Union. National Security Advisor Henry Kissinger announces "peace is at hand" in Vietnam in time for Pres. Nixon to carry 49 states in election. U.S. troops in Vietnam fall to 69,000 as Nixon orders resumed bombing of North Vietnam (Dec. 18).

1973 Supreme Court overturns state restrictions on abortions (Roe vs. Wade). U.S. signs Paris peace accords ending Vietnam War (Jan. 27). Indians hold the town of Wounded Knee, S.D. in an armed standoff against Federal Marshals (Feb. 27-May 8). Trial of Watergate burglars reveals conspiracy to conceal White House involvement. Top presidential aides H.R. Haldeman, John Ehrlichman, John Dean, and Attorney General Richard Kleindienst resign amid charges of White House cover-up (Apr. 30). Sen. Sam Ervin of North Carolina chairs Senate investigation of Watergate scandal (May 17–Nov. 15). Pres. Nixon fires Watergate Special Prosecutor Archibald Cox and others in "Saturday Night Massacre" (Oct. 20). Vice President Spiro Agnew resigns after threat of prosecution for tax evasion (Oct. 10). Gasoline prices skyrocket after Arab nations embargo oil exports to U.S. in retaliation for U.S. aid to Israel in Yom Kippur War (Oct. 17). Pres. Nixon turns over first White House tapes, which include mysterious 18 1/2 minute gap (Nov. 26). Gerald R. Ford of Michigan sworn in as first vice president chosen under 25th Amendment (Dec. 6). Indians defy Federal authority in Wounded Knee, S.D.

1974   Arab oil embargo of U.S. lifted (Mar. 18). Supreme Court rules that Pres. Nixon must submit all White House tapes to Special Prosecutor Leon Jaworski (July 24). House Judiciary Committee votes three articles of impeachment (July 24–30). Pres. Nixon releases transcripts of tapes that show he ordered cover-up (Aug. 5). Citing "political" difficulties, Pres. Nixon resigns (Aug. 8), elevating Vice Pres. Ford to presidency (Aug. 9). Pres. Ford shocks nation by pardoning Nixon for all crimes (Sept. 8). Pres. Ford meets with Soviet Premier Leonid Brezhnev in Vladivostock to approve SALT treaty (Nov. 23–24). Newspaper heiress Patty Hearst kidnapped in Berkeley, Calif., by radical Symbionese Liberation Army.

1975   Nixon aides convicted of obstructing justice in Watergate investigation (Jan. 1). Last Americans evacuate Saigon as South Vietnam falls to North Vietnamese invasion (Apr. 30). Cambodia seizes *USS Mayaguez* (May 12), and Pres. Ford orders rescue operation (May 14). Apollo-Soyuz, joint Soviet-American space mission, achieves link-up in space (July 17). Lynette "Squeaky" Fromme and Sarah Jane Moore attempt to assassinate Pres. Ford in separate California incidents (Sept. 5 & Sept. 22). Congress votes to admit women to Army, Navy, and Air Force academies. House Democrats dismantle seniority system. Church Committee discovers CIA helped overthrow Salvador Allende of Chile and plotted to assassinate Fidel Castro of Cuba.

1976   Congress repeatedly overrides Pres. Ford's vetoes of bills providing for jobs, health, education, and welfare programs. Supreme Court upholds death penalty (July 3). Bicentennial of U.S. celebrated coast to coast. Jimmy Carter defeats Pres. Ford as voters hold Ford responsible for pardoning Nixon. Justice Department begins probing South Korean bribery of Congressmen and other officials. Viking I and Viking II space probes land on Mars, transmit scientific data and color photographs back to Earth. "Legionnaire's Disease" breaks out at Philadelphia American Legion convention, killing 29. Hundreds of West Point cadets found to have cheated on exams.

1977   Pres. Carter pardons Vietnam War draft evaders, threatens to reduce foreign aid for countries violating human rights, calls for "moral equivalent of war" in energy conservation, and signs Panama Canal treaty (Sept. 7). U.S. declares 200-mile sovereignty zone in Atlantic and Pacific oceans to exclude foreign fishing vessels. Power blackout sets off arson and looting spree in New York City (July 13–14). Oil begins flowing through the Alaska pipeline. Pres. Carter accuses oil industry of "the biggest rip-off in history" (Oct. 13). ABC mini-series *Roots*, draws 130 million viewers.

1978   Pres. Carter postpones production of neutron bomb. California voters approve Proposition 13, reducing property taxes and setting off a nationwide "taxpayers' revolt." Supreme Court gives limited approval to affirmative action programs, but disallows quotas for college admissions (June 28). In private talks with Anwar Sadat and Menachem Begin, Pres. Carter mediates peace between Egypt and Israel with landmark Camp David Accords (Sept. 17). Nearly one thousand American followers of the Rev. Jim Jones commit mass suicide in Jonestown, Guiana, after cult members murder Rep. Leo Ryan of California and others (Nov. 18). Federal loan guarantees rescue New York City from financial crisis.

1979   U.S. resumes diplomatic relations with China (Jan 1). Worst nuclear accident in U.S. history takes place at Three Mile Island power plant near Harrisburg, Pa. Pres. Carter and Soviet Premier Leonid Brezhnev sign SALT II treaty in Vienna (June 18). The Shah of Iran and Anastasio Somoza of Nicaragua, both U.S.-supported dictators, flee revolutions in their countries. Iranian militants seize U.S. Embassy in Teheran, taking 66 American hostages and demanding return of the Shah from U.S. (Nov. 4). They release 13 hostages, all blacks or women. Pres. Carter deports illegal Iranian students, freezes Iranian assets, and bars oil imports from Iran. Inflation reaches highest level in 33 years as Organization of Petroleum Exporting Countries doubles price of oil.

1980   Canadian embassy officials help six Americans escape from Iran (Jan. 29). In response to Soviet invasion of Afghanistan, Pres. Carter embargoes grain and high technology exports to Soviet Union, approves arms sales to China, and secures U.S. boycott of Olympics in Moscow. Congress grants Pres. Carter's request for Crude Oil Windfall Profits Tax and for resumption of Selective Service draft registration. Pres. Carter's secret rescue mission for American hostages in Iran fails when a U.S. Navy helicopter crashes in desert, killing eight servicemen (Apr. 24). Mt. St. Helens erupts in Washington state, killing 26 people (May 18). Banking and trucking industries deregulated. FBI's "Abscam" operation implicates over 30 public officials, including a senator and seven congressmen, for accepting bribes.

1981   Minutes after Pres. Reagan is sworn in, Iran releases 52 American hostages after 444 days in captivity. Pres. Reagan shot by John Hinckley in Washington (Mar. 30), but makes full recovery. Columbia completes first successful space shuttle mission (Apr. 12–14). Federal air traffic controllers go on strike and lose jobs when Pres. Reagan fires all 13,000 of them. Sandra Day O'Connor unanimously confirmed as first woman justice of Supreme Court. Pres. Reagan lifts grain embargo against Soviet Union, but imposes new sanctions after Poland declares martial law. Congress accepts Pres. Reagan's plans for tax cuts, lower domestic spending, and major defense buildup. U.S. sends military advisors and aid to El Salvador.

1982   Ending 13-year antitrust suit, AT&T agrees to surrender control of local Bell System phone companies in return for expansion into new businesses (Jan. 8). Pres. Reagan calls for "New Federalism," transferring programs to state and local control. Unemployment exceeds 10% for first time since Great Depression, and Federal budget deficit exceeds $100 billion a year for first time ever. After a decade, Equal Rights Amendment fails, falling three states short of ratification.

1983 Congress agrees to bail out the Social Security system, and admits internment of Japanese-Americans during World War II was unjust. Sally Ride is first American woman astronaut, aboard space shuttle Challenger. Pres. Reagan strongly condemns Soviet Union for shooting down Korean airliner with 269 people aboard (Sept. 1). U.S. Marines join peacekeeping force in Beirut, Lebanon, where Muslim terrorists kill 240 of them in suicide bombing (Oct. 23). U.S. invades Grenada to overthrow Cuban-backed regime (Oct. 25). Pres. Reagan calls for large-scale funding of Strategic Defense Initiative, or "Star Wars."

1984 Economic recovery begins as unemployment falls, inflation rate declines, and U.S. dollar soars on international markets. Pres. Reagan orders U.S. Marines out of Lebanon (Feb. 7). The Rev. Jesse Jackson mounts first major challenge by black candidate for major party nomination. Rep. Geraldine Ferraro, (D-N.Y.) becomes first woman to receive major party nomination for vice president. Soviet bloc countries boycott Los Angeles Olympics. Pres. Reagan wins landslide re-election over Democratic challenger Walter Mondale.

1985 Pres. Reagan calls for more tax and budget cuts to sustain economic growth (Feb. 4–6). Despite worldwide protests, Pres. Reagan delivers address at Bitburg cemetery in West Germany, where Nazi SS troops are buried (May 5). Muslim terrorists hijack TWA airliner (June 14), kill one American hostage, then release rest in Beirut (June 30). Palestinian terrorists kill an American hostage aboard hijacked Italian cruise ship Achille Lauro (Oct. 9). Pres. Reagan and Soviet Premier Mikhail Gorbachev hold their first summit meeting in Geneva (Nov. 19–21). Pres. Reagan signs Gramm-Rudman Act, requiring spending cuts if Congress cannot reduce Federal deficit.

1986 Space shuttle Challenger explodes over Florida, killing six astronauts and a civilian passenger (Jan. 28). Investigations reveal NASA relaxed safety regulations to speed up launch date. U.S. Navy repels attack by Libyan forces during maneuvers in Gulf of Sidra (Mar. 24). Pres. Reagan blames Libya for death of two Americans in terrorist bombing of West Berlin disco, then orders retaliatory air raids on Tripoli and Benghazi (Apr. 14). Congress approves sweeping revision of U.S. tax structure. Democrats regain control of Senate. Pres. Reagan denies trading arms for hostages as Iran-Contra scandal breaks (Nov. 19). Wall Street financier Ivan Boesky fined $100 million for illegal insider trading on stock market.

1987 Pres. Reagan submits first trillion-dollar U.S. budget to Congress as national debt mounts steadily. Stock market closes above 2000 for first time in U.S. history. U.S.-Japan trade war erupts. After Pres. Reagan orders U.S. Navy into Persian Gulf to escort Kuwaiti oil tankers, an Iraqi warplane accidentally attacks USS Stark, killing 37 sailors (May 27). Bernhard Goetz acquitted of major charges in New York City "Subway Vigilante" shootings. Stock market crashes a record 508 points in one day, jolting markets around the world (Oct. 16). Third Reagan-Gorbachev summit in Washington produces agreement to dismantle medium-range missiles in Europe (Dec. 8).

1988 After Iran lays mines in Persian Gulf, U.S. Navy warships and planes destroy two Iranian oil platforms and repel Iranian counterattacks (Apr. 18–19). USS Vincennes accidentally shoots down Iranian passenger plane, killing 290 people (July 3). George Bush becomes first sitting vice president elected president since 1836. Terrorist bomb aboard Pan Am Flight 103 kills all 259 aboard, mostly Americans, and 11 on the ground in Lockerbie, Scotland (Dec. 21). Drexel Burnham Lambert agrees to pay all-time record $650 million penalty for securities fraud (Dec. 21).

1989 Exxon Valdez supertanker spills over 11 million gallons of oil off Alaska coast (Mar. 24). House speaker Jim Wright and Democratic majority whip Tony Coelho resign over ethics violations. Supreme Court upholds the right to burn U.S. flag. Pres. Bush signs $300 billion savings-and-loan bailout (Aug. 9). Earthquake, second worst in U.S. history, inflicts $6 billion damage and leaves 62 dead in San Francisco Bay area (Oct. 17). L. Douglas Wilder of Virginia is the first black elected governor (Nov. 7). Pres. Bush sends 24,000 U.S. troops to overthrow the Noriega regime and install a popularly elected government (Dec. 20).

1990 After Iraq invades Kuwait (Aug. 2), U.S. launches Operation Desert Shield: more than 200,000 U.S. troops move into Saudi Arabia. The Navy blockades all oil exports from Iraq and all imports except food. Pres. Bush works with U.N. Security Council to condemn invasion and impose stringent economic sanctions. Bush and Gorbachev meet twice: U.S. agrees to some economic aid, grants U.S.S.R. most favored nation trade status. Pres. Bush breaks campaign pledge of "no new taxes." A major flaw in the $1.5 bil. Hubble Space Telescope is discovered shortly after its deployment. Drexel Burnham Lambert defaults on $100 mil. in loans; Michael Milken, head of junk bond department, is fined $600 mil. and sentenced to jail.

1991 U.S. Operation Desert Storm quickly and decisively drives Iraq's armed forces out of Kuwait. The ground war lasts only 100 hours. Bush and Gorbachev sign first nuclear arms reduction treaty (July 31) as U.S.S.R. continues to crumble. U.S. establishes diplomatic relations with former Soviet republics, Estonia, Latvia, and Lithuania. Unemployment rate rises to highest level in a decade. Interest rates are cut to lowest levels in 20 years. Senate's confirmation of Clarence Thomas's nomination to the Supreme Court is delayed by Anita Hill's luridly detailed charges (Oct. 6) of sexual harassment 10 years earlier. Oliver North and John Poindexter are exonerated in connection with the Iran-contra scandal.

1992 The Americans with Disabilities Act takes efffect, guaranteeing equal access for the disabled (Jan. 26). Pres. Bush and Russian Pres. Boris Yeltsin issue joint statement officially ending the cold war (Feb.1). Riots erupt in Los Angeles after an all-white jury acquits four L.A. police officers of beating Rodney King a black man whose assault by police was captured on videotape (April 29-May 4); more than 50 people are killed, 2,000 injured, and over 7,000 arrested. Federal Reserve cuts discount rate to 3 percent, its lowest rate since 1963, after unemployment skyrockets to 7.8 percent, its highest level since 1983. Bill Clinton defeats Pres. George Bush and billionaire-populist third-party candidate Ross Perot to become the 42nd President. Pres. Bush commits at least 28,000 U.S. troops to protect the delivery of relief supplies to Somalia (Dec. 3). Pres. Bush pardons six Reagan Administration officials for their involvement in the Iran-Contra scandal.

1993 More than 120 nations, including the U.S. and Russia, agree to ban production, stockpiling, and use of all chemical weapons and to destroy them all within 10 years. Family Leave Act guarantees workers up to 12 weeks of unpaid leave for medical emergencies. A car bomb rips through the garage at New York's World Trade Center, killing 7, and injuring 1,000 (Feb. 26). Four federal agents are killed in a gunfight with cult leader David Koresh. After a 51-day standoff, Koresh sets the buildings on fire, killing himself and 86 followers (April 19). "The worst storm of the century" according to the National Weather Service pelts the mid-Atlantic and Northeast with as much as 40 inches of snow, killing at least 104 people. The Supreme Court rules (9-0) that public school systems must permit religious groups to use their buildings after hours if they allow community groups to do so. Law enforcement officials root out a Muslim extremist group plotting to bomb the U.N., federal office buildings, and the Lincoln and Holland tunnels, and to assassinate prominent politicians (June 24). The Supreme Court rules (5-4) that legislative districts drawn to increase black representation can violate the constitutional rights of white voters. Pres. Clinton signs the Brady Bill, requiring background checks before gun purchases. The U.S. and Europe sign the General Agreement of Tariffs and Trade (GATT), substantially reducing tariffs on trade. The Pentagon rules that gays may serve in the military, but may not proclaim their sexual orientation.

1994 Iran-Contra prosecutor Lawrence E. Walsh finds no evidence that Pres. Reagan or Vice Pres. Bush broke the law. All four men on trial for the World Trade Center bombing are found guilty and sentenced to 240 years in prison. Rodney King wins $3.8 mil. in damages for his 1991 beating by the L.A. police. L.A. police charge former football star O.J. Simpson with murdering his ex-wife Nicole Brown and Ron Goldman. Simpson leads police on a bizarre 60-mile low-speed car chase before surrendering (June 17). The dollar dips below 100 Japanese yen, a post-World War II low (June 21). Major league baseball players' strike results in the cancellation of the World Series for the first time ever (Aug. 11). The number of inmates in U.S. prisons tops one million, giving the U.S. the highest incarceration rate in the world. Republicans take control of both Houses of Congress for the first time in 40 years (Nov. 8).

1995 A federal judge issues an injunction against major league baseball owners for unfair labor practices, ending the longest players' strike in sports history. A massive car bomb blows up a Federal building in Oklahoma City, killing 169 people (April 19). The Supreme Court (5-4) overturns term limits on Congressional offices in 23 states. A federal grand jury indicts Timothy J. McVeigh and Terry L. Nichols on charges of blowing up the Oklahoma City Federal Building. Sheik Omar Abdel Rahman and nine militant Muslim followers are convicted of conspiring to blowup the United Nations and assassinate political leaders. A mostly black Los Angeles jury finds O.J. Simpson not guilty of murdering his ex-wife Nicole Brown Simpson and Ron Goldman. (Oct. 3).

1996 Congress votes to return hundreds of thousands of workers to their jobs and to reopen nonessential government offices that had closed for three weeks in the budget impasse. The Hubble Space Telescope returns the first-ever images of Pluto, and pictures showing the existence of more than 50 billion galaxies, or five times the number thought to exist, the Sun is one of 100 billion stars in the Milky Way. Congress approves a vast bill rewriting laws governing the telecommunications industries, deregulating cable television, and increasing competition among local

phone companies. Pres. Clinton signs legislation allowing workers to take their health insurance with them when they change or leave jobs and to restrict insurers' ability to deny policies to workers with preexisting medical conditions. The worst drought since the Dust Bowl era of the 1930's plagues the southwest, bankrupting more than 10,000 farmers. (June 18). TWA Flight 800 explodes in midair over Long Island, NY, killing all 230 aboard (July 17). A pipe bomb blows up in Atlanta during the Olympics, killing one woman and injuring more than 100. Pres. Clinton signs welfare reform legislation, ending more than 60 years of federal cash assistance (July 31). Pres. Clinton signs the Defense of Marriage Act, denying Federal recognition to same-sex marriages.

1997 The Dow Jones Industrial Average breaks 7,000 in Feb., and 8,000 in July. Mergers and acquisitions by major corporations reach record levels. Madeleine Albright becomes the first woman Sec. of State. A civil jury finds O.J. Simpson liable in the killings of his ex-wife and Ronald Goldman and orders Simpson to pay $33.5 million in damages to their families. Comet Hale-Bopp, with its brilliant 31-million-mile tail, makes continuous appearances from March to May. The Supreme Court rules unanimously that a sitting president can be sued for actions outside the scope of his official duties thereby allowing the Paula Jones sexual harassment suit to proceed. Timothy J. McVeigh is found guilty in the 1995 bombing of the Federal building in Oklahoma City that killed 168; he is sentenced to death. A separate jury convicts Terry L. Nichols of conspiracy and manslaughter; he is sentenced to life in prison. The tobacco industry agrees to pay $368.5 bil. over 25 years to compensate states for the cost of smoking-related illnesses. Mars Pathfinder, a robotic spacecraft, arrives on Mars, and sends back panoramic pictures of the landscape. The Hubble Space Telescope returns pictures of a star as bright as 10 million suns. Thirty Wall Street brokerages agree to pay $900 million to end a civil suit contending they conspired for years to fix prices on the Nasdaq stock market.

1998 Bill Clinton becomes the first sitting president to submit as a defendant in civil court when he denies charges that he sexually harassed Paula Jones when he was governor of Arkansas. Under oath, and later in a national television address, Clinton also denies having sexual relations with White House intern Monica Lewinsky. Texas executes a woman, convicted murderer Karla Faye Tucker, for the first time since the Civil War. Astronomers detect a titanic explosion in the outer reaches of the cosmos rivaled only by the Big Bang. The federal government and 20 states file antitrust lawsuits against Microsoft, accusing it of attempting to control access to the Internet. Pictures from the Hubble Space Telescope show the first image of a planet outside our solar system. Scientists break the code of the tuberculosis bacterium, a germ that kills more people in the world than any other infectious agent. Two powerful bombs explode outside the U.S. Embassies in Kenya and Tanzania, killing at least 190 people and wounding nearly 5,000. Pres. Clinton testifies that he had an "inappropriate" relationship with Monica Lewinsky. Pres. Clinton announces a record budget surplus of about $70 bil., the first since 1969. The House of Representatives, strictly along party lines, approves two articles of impeachment against Pres. Clinton: perjury and obstruction of justice (Dec. 19).

1999 The Senate acquits Pres. Clinton on both articles of impeachment (Feb. 12). NATO forces begin dropping bombs on Serbian forces occupying Kosovo (Mar. 24). Astronomers announce the detection of three large planets around a solar-type star, providing the first solid evidence that our solar system is no singular phenomenon (April 15). In the deadliest school massacre in U.S. history, two teenagers at Columbine High School in Littleton, Colo. kill 12 students and one teacher (April 20). The F.C.C. relaxes rules that had prevented a single company from owning multiple radio stations in the same city or from controlling too much of the cable industry. Congress repeals the 1933 Glass-Steagall Act, which had prevented the securities, banking, and insurance industries from expanding into one another's businesses. Thousands of demonstrators wreak havoc on a Seattle meeting of the World Trade Organization, protest the WTO's policies on the environment and international labor. A federal grand jury in New Mexico indicts Wen Ho Lee, a nuclear weapons engineer, on 59 counts of illegally removing highly classified material from the Los Alamos weapons laboratory. Jimmy Carter officially hands over control of the Panama Canal to Panama (Dec. 14).

2000 America Online buys Time Warner for $165 bil. in the biggest merger in history (Jan 10). Four white New York City police officers are acquitted of all charges in the shooting of African immigrant Amadou Diallo (Feb 25). Armed U.S. immigration agents storm a Miami house and remove six-year-old Cuban refugee Elián González so he can be returned to his father in Cuba (Apr 22). Two rival groups of scientists announce they have deciphered the human genome (June 26). The Supreme Court rules that the Boy Scouts of America have a constitutional right to exclude gay members. The U.S. government agrees to drop its entire case against Wen-Ho Lee, the Chinese-American scientist the F.B.I. had accused of stealing nuclear weapons secrets. The independent prosecutor in the Whitewater investigation concludes that there is insufficient evidence to show that Bill or Hillary Clinton committed any crimes (Sept. 20). The *U.S.S Cole*, refueling in Yemen, is rocked by a terrorist bomb, killing 17 sailors (Oct. 12). Hillary Rodham Clinton wins the New York Senate race, becoming the only First Lady ever to hold public office. Despite losing the popular vote, George W. Bush wins a controversial presidential election after a recount in Florida is halted by the U.S. Supreme Court.

2001 Two teams of U.S. scientists report that they have slowed light to a stop and released it again (Jan. 17). F.B.I. agent Robert Hanssen is arrested on charges of spying for Russia (Feb. 20). A federal jury in New York convicts four men of conspiring with Osama bin Laden in the 1988 bombing of U.S. embassies in Kenya and Tanzania (May 29). In the worst terrorist attack in U.S. history, hijackers crash two U.S. airliners into the World Trade Center, destroying both buildings and killing nearly 3,000 people. A third hijacked plane crashes into the Pentagon, and a fourth crashes in western Pennsylvania (Sept. 11). Pres. Bush blames Osama bin Laden, says he wants the Al Qaeda leader captured "dead or alive," calls up 35,000 military reservists, pledges an attack on Afghanistan unless it surrenders bin Laden, and warns of a long campaign against terrorism. Congress passes a $15 billion package to bail out the airlines industry. Pres. Bush orders a freeze on all assets in the U.S. of suspected terrorist groups and individuals (Sept. 24). The U.S. and Great Britain launch a series of air attacks against Afghanistan (Oct. 7). A letter filled with anthrax-laden powder contaminates a Senate office building and leads to 31 anthrax exposures (Oct. 15). An American Airlines jet crashes in New York, killing all 260 people on board (Nov. 12). Pres. Bush signs an executive order allowing foreigners accused of terrorism to be tried in special military tribunals. The Enron Corporation files the largest corporate bankruptcy in U.S. history (Dec. 2). Pres. Bush announces that America has formally withdrawn from the 1972 Antiballistic Missile treaty (Dec. 13). A man on an American Airlines flight is subdued by passengers after he tries to ignite explosives concealed in his shoes (Dec. 22).

2002 The U.S. begins transporting Taliban and Al Qaeda prisoners from Afghanistan to a detention center in Guantánamo Bay, Cuba. Defrocked priest John Geoghan, accused of molesting 130 children over three decades, is sentenced to 10 years in prison; the Boston Archdiocese agrees to pay $10 million to the victims. In his first State of the Union address, Pres. Bush calls Iran, Iraq and North Korea the "axis of evil" (Jan. 23). A federal jury in Houston convicts Arthur Andersen of obstruction of justice for shredding documents and impeding the Enron investigation (Jun. 15). The Supreme Court declares that the Constitution bars the execution of mentally retarded offenders, and that juries, rather than judges, must decide if a convicted murderer should get the death penalty. WorldCom submits the largest bankruptcy filing in U.S. history (Jul. 21). In two 5-4 decisions, the Supreme Court upholds a voucher plan to use public money for religious school tuition, and to permit random drug testing in public schools. (Jun. 27). The Senate votes (77-23) to authorize Pres. Bush to use military force against Iraq (Oct. 10). Republicans regain a majority control in the Senate, giving the G.O.P. control of all three branches of government. The U.S. gives the U.N. a final chance to disarm Iraq through weapons inspections or else face an American-led war invasion (Nov. 6). Congress approves creation of the Department of Homeland Security, expected to employ 170,000. A joint Congressional committee on the Sept. 11 attacks reports that the F.B.I. and C.I.A. did not aggressively pursue leads that might have linked the terrorists to Saudi Arabia (Nov. 22).

2003 Illinois Gov. George Ryan commutes all 167 death sentences in the state to life in prison, citing fundamental questions of fairness in the Illinois capital punishment system (Jan. 11). The space shuttle Columbia breaks up over Texas upon re-entry, killing all seven aboard (Feb. 1). Federal Reserve Chairman Alan Greenspan criticizes Pres. Bush's budget, saying the economy does not need tax cuts, and that the deficits could multiply rapidly (Feb. 11). Millions of demonstrators around the world protest the Bush administration's plans to invade Iraq (Feb. 15). After giving Saddam Hussein 48 hours to quit the country, Pres. Bush orders the invasion of Iraq. Missiles rain on Baghdad, but fail to kill Hussein, who later addresses the nation on television (Mar. 19). As U.S. and British ground troops reach Basra, millions flood the streets of New York and other cities to protest the U.S. invasion (Mar. 22). Pres. Bush flies onto the deck of the U.S.S. Abraham Lincoln to declare "Mission Accomplished" in Iraq. The Supreme Court (5-4) backs affirmative action in a case involving admissions at the University of Michigan; upholds a federal law requiring public libraries to install Internet pornography filters on their computers; and invalidates (6-3) a Texas sodomy law, thus legalizing gay sexual conduct (June 23-24). The White House acknowledges that Pres. Bush relied on less-than-accurate intelligence when he declared that Saddam Hussein tried to purchase uranium from Africa (July 7). The White House projects a $455 billion budget deficit for 2003, the largest in U.S. history. The largest power blackout in American history hits eight Northeastern states and parts of Canada (Aug. 14). Pres. Bush requests $87 billion to reconstruct Iraq and Afghanistan, on top of the $79 billion already spent. Massachusetts's highest court rules that gay couples have the right to marry under the state's Constitution (Nov. 18). Congress approves a Medicare bill that adds prescription drug benefits and expands the role of private health plans (Nov. 25). A Pentagon investigation reveals that a Halliburton subsidiary overcharged the government by $61 million for fuel delivery to Iraq under no-bid contracts (Dec. 11).

2004 *Spirit*, a 400-pound robotic rover, lands on Mars and immediately begins to transmit images; it is soon followed by a second rover, *Opportunity* (Jan. 4). At 115 airports U.S. immigration officers begin fingerprinting and photographing tens of thousands of foreign visitors (Jan. 5). David Kay, who led the American effort to find banned weapons in Iraq, concludes that Iraq had no stockpiles of chemical and biological weapons at the start of the war (Jan. 23). Senior Defense Department officials say that they are planning to keep a large portion of the detainees incarcerated at Guantánamo Bay, Cuba for many years (Feb. 12). Senator John Kerry effectively captures the Democratic nomination (Mar. 2). Pres. Bush's former counterterrorism chief, Richard Clarke, testifies to the Sept. 11 commission that the Bush administration had largely ignored the threat from Al Qaeda prior to the attacks. Officials confirm that Pres. Bush was told in a secret meeting on Aug. 6, 2001, that supporters of Osama bin Laden planned an attack "within the United States" and wanted to hijack airplanes (Apr. 9). Citigroup agrees to pay $2.65 billion to investors who bought stock and bonds in WorldCom before its bankruptcy filing in 2002 (May 10). U.S. legislators are shown hundreds of images of mistreatment of Iraqi prisoners at Abu Ghraib prison (May 12). Hundreds of gay and lesbian couples wed in Massachusetts, the first state to allow same-sex marriages (May 17). A March 2003 legal memo prepared for Defense Secretary Rumsfeld concluded that Pres. Bush was not bound by an international treaty prohibiting torture or by a federal antitorture law because he had the authority as commander in chief to approve any technique needed to protect the nation's security (June 7). The Supreme Court rules that those deemed enemy combatants by the Bush administration must be given the ability to challenge their detention before a judge or other "neutral decision-maker." (June 28). Pres. Bush endorses two main recommendations of the 9/11 commission: to create the post of national intelligence director and to establish a counterterrorism center to coordinate intelligence analysis (Aug. 2). Halliburton is fined $7.5 million for secretly changing accounting practices when Vice President Cheney was its chief executive (Aug. 3). More than 500,000 demonstrators march through New York City on the eve of the Republican convention to protest the war in Iraq and the Bush presidency (Aug. 29). The U.S. death toll in Iraq surpasses 1,000 (Sept. 7). The Food and Drug Administration says that antidepressants appear to lead some children to become suicidal (Sept. 13). Pres. Bush is reelected, defeating Democratic nominee John Kerry with 51 percent of the popular vote (Nov. 2).

2005 The Supreme Court transforms federal criminal sentencing by restoring to judges much of the discretion Congress took away when it put sentencing guidelines in place over two decades ago (Jan. 12). A report from the 9/11 Commission shows that federal aviation officials reviewed dozens of intelligence reports that warned about Osama bin Laden and Al Qaeda (Feb. 9). The Supreme Court decides (5-4) that the Constitution bars capital punishment for crimes committed before the age of 18 (Mar. 1). Chairman of the Federal Reserve Alan Greenspan warns that the federal budget deficits are "unsustainable" (Mar. 2). Former WorldCom chief Bernard J, Ebbers is convicted of a $11 billion securities fraud (Mar. 15). Doctors remove the feeding tube of the brain-damaged woman Terry Schiavo despite efforts by Congress and Pres. Bush to halt the process (Mar. 18). Tens of thousands of demonstrators in Baghdad demand the withdrawal of American troops (Apr. 9). The Defense Intelligence Agency says that North Korea has the technology for arming its missiles with nuclear warheads (Apr. 28). General Motors and Ford Motor Co. lose their investment grade ratings and become junk bonds (May 5). Citigroup agrees to pay $2 billion to investors who accused the bank of aiding Enron in its accounting scandal. J.P. Morgan Chase agrees to pay $2.2 billion to Enron investors. The Supreme Court rules (5-4) that confiscating land for private development in the interest of economic development is an appropriate use of the government's power of eminent domain. The Supreme Court upholds the government display of the Ten Commandments monument in the Texas Capital but rules two Kentucky displays unconstitutional. After a six-month, 85 million-mile journey, NASA's *Deep Impact* spacecraft slams into comet Tempel 1 in an effort to learn more about comets (July 4). *New York Times* reporter Judith Miller is sent to jail for refusing to divulge the name of a confidential source (July 6). Jack Abramoff, a Republican lobbyist linked to the ethics problems of House majority leader Tom DeLay, is indicted in Florida on unrelated charges of fraud in a business deal (Aug. 11). Hurricane Katrina pounds the Gulf Coast, leaving over a million houses without power in Louisiana, Mississippi, and Alabama and flooding much of New Orleans (Aug. 28). Pentagon officials deploy 30,000 troops to the Gulf Coast in the military's largest ever domestic relief effort (Aug. 31). A Texas grand jury indicts majority leader Tom DeLay on a charge of conspiring to violate Texas election laws (Sept. 28). The Senate confirms (78-22) John G. Roberts Jr. as the nation's 17th Chief Justice (Sept. 29). Pres. Bush names Harriet Miers, his White House counsel, to be a justice of the Supreme Court. Less than a month later she withdraws her name after fierce criticism of her abilities, and Samuel J. Alito is nominated in her place. Vice Pres. Cheney's chief-of-staff, I. Lewis Libby Jr. is indicted by a federal jury on felony charges of lying to investigators. Republican Representative, Randy ("Duke") Cunningham resigns from Congress after pleading guilty to taking at least $2.4 mil. in bribes related to defense contracts. Pres.

Bush admits he ordered the National Security Agency to conduct electronic eavesdropping without warrants and says that he will continue to do so. **2006** Rep. Tom DeLay of Texas abandons his effort to remain House majority leader while he is under indictment. The largest study ever to examine the effects of a low-fat diet concludes that it did not reduce heart attacks, strokes, or rates of cancer. Vice Pres. Cheney accidentally shoots a friend in the face during a hunting trip in Texas (Feb. 12). Millions of immigrants and supporters protest in Washington D.C. and in other cities calling on Congress to offer legal status and citizenship to illegal immigrants. The Senate passes $70 bil. in tax cuts mostly for the nation's wealthiest citizens. U.S. drug officials approve a vaccine against cervical cancer. The U.S. Episcopal Church elects a woman as its presiding bishop for the first time. News reports indicate that a secret Bush Administration program gave counterterrorism officials access to financial records of thousands of Americans. The Supreme Court rules that Vermont's limits on campaign spending are unconstitutional. Pres. Bush vetoes a bill supported by his own party to expand federal support for embryonic stem cell research. The Food and Drug Administration approves over-the-counter sales of the morning-after contraceptive pill to women over 18 (Aug. 24). A virulent strain of E-coli linked to pre-packaged spinach from California causes severe illness to over 100 people in 20 states. The Commerce Dept. reports that the U.S. housing market has slowed considerably and is slowing economic growth. A federal audit reveals that the State Dept. agency in charge of $1.4 bil. in reconstruction money for Iraq hid ballooning cost overruns and withheld information from Congress. The Ford Motor Co. cuts output by 20 percent and to offer buyouts to 75,000 workers; later it reports its worst financial results in 14 years. The U.N. Security Council imposes sanctions on North Korea in the wake of that country's first nuclear test. Democrats gain control of both the House and Senate (Nov. 7). Nancy Pelosi of California becomes the first woman to be Speaker of the House. The Iraq Study Group, a bipartisan commission, warns that "the situation in Iraq is grave and deteriorating." Secretary of Defense Donald Rumsfeld resigns and is replaced by former director of itelligence Robert M. Gates (Nov. 8). The FDA lifts a 14-year-old ban on silicone gel breast implants (Nov. 17). Saddam Hussein is hanged in Bahgdad, Iraq (Dec. 30). **2007** Pres. Bush names Lt. General David Petraeus as the top military commander in Iraq and announces a "surge" of 20,000 additional American troops (Jan. 4). Intelligence officials reveal that the Pentagon and C.I.A. have obtained financial records of Americans (Jan. 13). Drew Gilpin Faust becomes the first woman president of Harvard (Feb. 9). A federal appeals court upholds a law stripping federal judges of authority to review foreign prisoners' challenges to their detention at Guantanamo Bay (Feb. 20). Doctors announce that two new AIDS drugs have proved safe and successful in large studies (Feb. 27). Two Army leaders are fired following disclosure of dilapidated buildings and long delays in care for wounded soldiers at Walter Reed Army Medical Center (Mar. 1). F.B.I. Director Robert Mueller concedes that the bureau improperly used the U.S.A. Patriot Act to obtain information about people and businesses (Mar. 9). The Supreme Court rules that the E.P.A. cannot sidestep its au-

thority to regulate heat-trapping gases (Apr. 2). Inquiries by federal investigators and New York's attorney general find widespread corruption in the $85 billion student loan industry, including financial aid directors at Columbia, U.S.C., the Univ. of Texas and at least one Education Dept. official (Apr. 5). The military extends active duty tours in Iraq and Afghanistan from 12 to 15 months (Apr. 11). A 23-year-old student gunman kills 32 people and injures 15 at Virginia Tech before shooting himself (Apr. 16). The Supreme Court upholds the federal Partial Birth Abortion Ban Act; in protest, Justice Ginsberg reads her dissent aloud (Apr. 18). Rupert Murdoch's News Corp. buys Dow Jones & Co., publisher of the *Wall Street Journal*, for $5 bil. Six Muslim men from New Jersey and Philadelphia are arrested and charged with plotting to attack Fort Dix. (May 8) Three American soldiers are captured by insurgents in Iraq, triggering a massive but futile search. (May 13) Congress raises the minimum wage from $5.15 to $7.25 an hour, the first increase in a decade (May 24). An overhaul of federal immigration policy supported by Pres. Bush collapses in the Senate. A federal appeals court rules that the president may not declare civilians, in the U.S. legally, to be "enemy combatants" and hold them indefinitely (June 11). The Supreme Court rules that schools cannot seek integration through measures that take explicit account of a student's race (June 28). The White House admits to giving the C.I.A. approval to resume use of severe interrogation techniques on terrorism suspects held overseas (July 20). An Interstate highway bridge in Minneapolis collapses during rush hour, killing 12 people (Aug. 1). The Senate approves new ethics rules that ban financial gifts from lobbyists and make it harder for lawmakers to exploit their connections when they leave office. A federal jury finds Jose Padilla guilty of terrorism conspiracy charges five years after he was arrested (Aug. 16). Attorney General Alberto Gonzalez resigns after inquiries in Congress and the Justice Dept. find that federal prosecutors across the country were fired for political reasons (Aug. 27). Blackwater USA, a private American security provider, is charged with killing eight Iraqi civilians in Baghdad and is banned by the Iraqi government. The U.S. dollar drops to a new low against the euro (Sept. 20). A Pentagon investigation uncovers a corruption scandal involving $6 billion in military contracts. The Chicago Marathon is halted after hundreds of people fall ill and one dies due to excessive heat (Oct. 7). A Texas jury finds a Muslim charity not guilty of funding terrorists as charged by the Bush Administration (Oct. 22). The Supreme Court blocks a lethal injection in Mississippi and indicates that it will block all executions pending a decision on a Kentucky case (Oct. 30). The Senate confirms Michael B. Mukasey as Attorney General despite Democratic criticism of his stance on torture (Nov. 8). A federal appeals court in San Francisco voids the Bush Administration's fuel economy standards for light trucks because they do not account for the need to reduce greenhouse gases (Nov. 15). The C.I.A. admits that it destroyed videotapes documenting harsh interrogations of two Al Qaeda operatives (Dec. 6). Former Senator George J. Mitchell releases a report that implicates 89 Major League Baseball players in the use of illegal performance-enhancing drugs (Dec. 13). The U.S. and 186 other countries agree to negotiate a new accord on reducing greenhouse gases (Dec. 15). The E.P.A. denies 17 states the right to set their own standards on automobile emissions (Dec. 19).

BIOGRAPHIES OF U.S. PRESIDENTS

1. George Washington (1789–97)

Born in Westmoreland County, Virginia, on Feb. 22, 1732, the first president, with a love for the land, trained as a surveyor in his teens. At age 16 he went to live with his brother Lawrence, who built Mount Vernon. Lawrence died only four years later, leaving his property to George, who went on to become one of Virginia's foremost landowners, ultimately acquiring more than 100,000 acres in Virginia and what is now West Virginia. In 1753 Washington joined the French and Indian War as an officer in the Virginia militia and fought bravely if poorly. The war provided Washington with the beginnings of his anti-British sentiments, exposing him to the arrogance of his British commanders. Upon returning to plantation life, and marrying Martha Custis, in 1759, Washington's resentment of the British was further fueled by their commercial restrictions. With the passage of the Stamp Act of 1765, Washington joined opposition to imperial rule in the Virginia House of Burgesses, becoming ever more active in resisting the British. He went as a delegate to the Continental Congress, which chose him to command the Continental Army when war with Britain broke out in 1775. Washington proved an uncommonly resourceful general, keeping his ragtag army together through years of defeat, retreat, and hard winters to outlast the British and finally prevail at Yorktown in 1781. Here, as in all his life, Washington earned respect for his judgment, dignity, and bearing. Retiring to Mount Vernon after the war, the general quashed suggestions that he assume military dictatorship of the fledgling republic, not wanting to subvert the very principles for which the Americans had fought. But because of his belief in a strong central government, Washington felt compelled to return to public life to salvage his country from the chaotic Articles of Confederation. In 1787 he presided over the Constitutional Convention in Philadelphia, which framed the presidency with him in mind, the only president ever elected unanimously in the electoral college (twice).

Washington's renowned judgment equaled the task of setting presidential precedent, for, as he wrote, "It is devoutly wished on my part, that these precedents may be fixed on true principles." His first act as president was to urge adoption of the Bill of Rights. Other notable achievements included national unity, quelling the Whiskey Rebellion, bolstering the treasury with a national bank, settling Jay's Treaty of commerce with Britain, and maintaining neutrality in the French Revolution. Washington successfully implemented executive power and quieted fears and suspicions of executive tyranny. But he regretted the rivalry between Thomas Jefferson and Alexander Hamilton, which led to the birth of political parties in his own cabinet; Washington feared that allegiance to "factions" would someday eclipse the guiding light of patriotism. After refusing a third term in 1796, Washington in his Farewell Address warned against party spirit, sectionalism, and "entangling alliances" with other nations. He died on Dec. 14, 1799, "first in war, first in peace, and first in the hearts of his countrymen," as his friend Henry Lee eulogized him.

2. John Adams (1797–1801)

A fifth-generation American directly descended from a Mayflower passenger, John Adams was born on Oct. 30, 1735, in Braintree, Massachusetts. At Harvard Adams considered the ministry but turned to law. He joined his cousin Sam Adams as an early opponent of the Stamp Act of 1765, organizing the Sons of Liberty and defending Americans accused of smuggling. Yet he also defended the British soldiers brought to trial for the Boston Massacre in 1770. In the Revolution, Adams persuaded the Continental Congress to commission George Washington as commander in chief, declare independence, and put stars and stripes on the flag. He wrote the Massachusetts state constitution in 1779 and negotiated peace with Britain in 1782. The first vice president, Adams called that position the "most insignificant office that ever the invention of man contrived or his imagination conceived."

Elected president as a Federalist in 1796, Adams retained Washington's cabinet, but Alexander Hamilton turned the party against him for refusing to make war on France. Adams built up the navy and kept the peace, but disaffecting the Federalists and signing the Alien and Sedition Acts (1798) politically weakened "His Rotundity." Adams lost the 1800 election to the increasingly popular Thomas Jefferson. The first president to reside in the White House, Adams lived to be 90, able to see his son John Quincy Adams elected the sixth president in 1824. John Adams died on the same day that Thomas Jefferson did: July 4, 1826, the 50th anniversary of the Declaration of Independence they both signed.

3. Thomas Jefferson (1801–09)

Thomas Jefferson was born on Apr. 13, 1743, in Albemarle County, Virginia, son of a self-made Virginian who died when Jefferson was 14. Jefferson graduated from William and Mary in 1762, began practicing law in 1767, and joined the Virginia House of Burgesses in 1769. With his pen Jefferson sharply criticized British rule, winning a place on Virginia's Committee of Correspondence to keep in touch with patriots in other colonies. His writings amassed great respect, earning him the right, as a delegate to the Continental Congress in 1776, to draft the Declaration of Independence. He then returned to Virginia as wartime governor, narrowly escaping capture when British troops destroyed his home. Congress sent Jefferson to Europe in 1784; he was minister to France during the Constitutional Convention and the early French Revolution, an event that affected him profoundly. As secretary of state under Washington, Jefferson's faith in democracy and states' rights clashed repeatedly with Alexander Hamilton's pursuit of central executive power. Jefferson resigned in 1793 and led opposition to the Federalists, whom Jefferson called "monarchists in principle." As vice president after 1796, Jefferson speeded the Federalists' downfall by secretly authoring the Kentucky Resolutions, critical of the Alien and Sedition Acts.

The House of Representatives chose Jefferson (ironically, with Hamilton's support) over Aaron Burr, whose electoral votes for president equaled his in 1800. "We are all Republicans—we are all Federalists," appealed Jefferson in his inaugural address, easing the transfer of power. In his first term, Jefferson slashed the budget, lowered taxes, reduced the national debt, and sent marines to fight Barbary pirates. Despite some concern over his constitutional authority to make the acquisition, Jefferson's greatest feat was the Louisiana Purchase from France in 1803, which doubled the size of the United States. "The less said about the constitutional difficulties, the better," wrote Jefferson, sending Lewis and Clark to explore the new lands. In his second term, Jefferson's unpopular Embargo Act (1807) was an attempt to avoid war with Britain or France, but it ruined American merchants. Retiring to Monticello in 1809, Jefferson busied himself with inventions and designing the University of Virginia. He died on the 50th anniversary of the Declaration of Independence, July 4, 1826. His broad interests spanned music, science, architecture, agronomy, and the classics, as well as politics and government.

4. James Madison (1809–17)

James Madison was born to a wealthy family on Mar. 16, 1751, in Port Conway, Virginia. A Princeton graduate, Madison attended the first Virginia state convention in 1776, drafting a bill that guaranteed religious liberty. As the youngest member of the Continental Congress in 1780, he led the movement to revise the Articles of Confederation. At the Constitutional Convention in Philadelphia in 1787, Madison's Virginia Plan became the pivot of discussion. Madison, dubbed the Father of the Constitution, tirelessly directed debate and applied his political wisdom. His voluminous notes provide the best record of the convention. Madison helped ratify the Constitution by coauthoring The Federalist (1787–88) with John Jay and Alexander Hamilton. A four-term congressman, Madison drafted the Bill of Rights and cofounded the Democratic-Republican party. In 1794 he married a young and ebullient widow, Dolley Payne Todd, an especially popular first lady. Madison led the opposition to the Federalists' Alien and Sedition Acts with the Virginia Resolutions, arguing the acts were unconstitutional attacks on liberty. Jefferson chose Madison as his secretary of state and later as his successor. Madison easily won the election of 1808. Britain and France preyed on American shipping throughout Madison's first term. Pushed by war hawks in Congress, Madison asked for a declaration of war to defend American rights against British outrages. Reelected despite numerous American defeats in the War of 1812, Madison barely escaped Washington as the British burned the White House. Yet he persisted in "Mr. Madison's War" until the Peace of Ghent (1814) and belated victory at New Orleans (1815) vindicated him. War expenses forced Madison to recharter the national bank and raise the tariff, contrary to his Jeffersonian principles. But by 1817 Madison could retire confident of secure independence, surging nationalism, and the total collapse of his Federalist opponents who had opposed the war. He died on June 28, 1836, having outlived all the Founding Fathers. Madison's presidency pales beside his greatest contributions—the Constitution and the Bill of Rights.

5. James Monroe (1817–25)

The last Revolutionary hero and member of the "Virginia Dynasty" to become president, James Monroe was born on Apr. 28, 1758, in Westmoreland County, Virginia. He left the College of William and Mary to answer the call to arms in 1775. Wounded at Trenton, Monroe fought courageously and rose to lieutenant colonel under Gen. Washington. He learned law as an aide to Thomas Jefferson, who helped Monroe into Congress and

the Senate. Much diplomatic experience followed Monroe's appointment as minister to France in 1794. Governor of Virginia from 1799 to 1802, Monroe returned to Europe to negotiate the Louisiana Purchase and later served in Britain and Spain. James Madison appointed him secretary of state in 1811 and secretary of war in 1814. Chosen to succeed Madison, Monroe won the 1816 election and presided over the Era of Good Feeling, a period marked by minimal sectional or partisan discord. Monroe bought Florida from Spain in 1819, and his popularity survived the Panic of 1819 as well as rancorous debates over the admission of Missouri as a slave state. Monroe toured the nation to jubilant crowds, winning reelection with all but one electoral vote in 1820. John Quincy Adams, his secretary of state, suggested Monroe proclaim American opposition to European encroachment in the Western Hemisphere, which he did in 1823; decades later this became known as the Monroe Doctrine. After retiring, Monroe became a regent of the University of Virginia (1826) and a member of the Virginia constitutional convention of 1829. Because of lack of attention over the years, his private affairs had suffered greatly, and Monroe discovered he was lapsing into bankruptcy. He sold his plantation and died all but penniless on Independence Day, July 4, 1831.

6. John Quincy Adams (1825–29)

The first president's son to become president, John Quincy Adams was born on July 11, 1767, in Braintree, Massachusetts. A true child of the Revolution, Adams watched the Battle of Bunker Hill while holding his mother's hand, and he spent his teens in Europe with his father, John Adams, on diplomatic missions for the new nation. He entered Harvard in 1785, already an experienced diplomat fluent in seven languages. After a brief career as a Boston lawyer, Adams was minister to Holland in 1794 and to Prussia in 1797. As a Federalist, Adams was elected to the Senate in 1803, but after supporting Thomas Jefferson, he had to resign. James Madison made Adams minister to Russia in 1809, in time to witness Napoleon's invasion. Then Adams helped negotiate the Peace of Ghent (1814) before serving as ambassador to England, the second of three Adams generations to hold that post. James Monroe recalled Adams from Europe—where he had spent most of his life—to appoint him secretary of state in 1817, and in that post, Adams purchased Florida from Spain, patched relations with Britain, and conceived the Monroe Doctrine.

Running for president in 1824, Adams was beaten by Andrew Jackson in both popular and electoral votes; but with Henry Clay's support, the House of Representatives chose Adams for president. No one ever became president with less than Adams's 31 percent of the vote, yet he refused to conciliate his foes or even act like a politician. Adams posed above politics and made no effort to deal with Congress or use patronage. Consequently, elaborate plans for internal improvements and national academies came to naught. Adams, like his father, failed to win a second term, as Jackson gained revenge at the polls in 1828. Massachusetts rescued Adams from despair by sending him to Congress in 1830, and "Old Man Eloquent" remained a powerful antislavery leader until he collapsed on the floor of the House at age 80; he died in the Speaker's Room on Feb. 23, 1848. John Quincy Adams, who considered himself a failure as president, worked for the first 11 presidents and numbers among the most important architects of early American foreign policy.

7. Andrew Jackson (1829–37)

Born to Scotch-Irish immigrants in Waxhaw, South Carolina, on Mar. 15, 1767, Andrew Jackson was the first first-generation American to become president, as well as the first president from the western frontier and the first of seven to be born in a log cabin. Orphaned at 15, he was by then already a Revolutionary veteran, a former prisoner of war, and scarred by the saber of a British officer whose boots he refused to clean. Jackson read law and made his way to the Tennessee frontier, marrying Rachel Donelson Robards in 1791. She neglected to divorce her first husband, but Jackson challenged to a duel anyone who questioned his marriage, once even killing a man on the field of honor. Jackson's frontier law practice prospered, and Tennessee elected him its first congressman in 1796. He served only briefly in the Senate; Washington so disgusted the rough-hewn Jackson that he resigned. Back in Tennessee, Jackson became a respected judge and honorary major general of the militia. In the War of 1812, Jackson led troops to victory at the Battle of New Orleans (1815), his men routing British invaders twice their number.

"Old Hickory" was now a national icon, reentering the Senate in 1823 and running for president as a hero above party. Jackson won more popular and electoral votes than anyone in 1824 but lost when the election was thrown into the House and Henry Clay supported John Quincy Adams. Vowing revenge against the politicians, Jackson swept to victory in 1828 as the "people's choice" reform candidate. Jackson's wife died on the eve of his inauguration. As president, Jackson aggrandized the power of his office on behalf of the common man by expanding suffrage, rotating officeholders (the "spoils system"), and economizing in government. Under Jackson the Federal government completely paid off the national debt. Jackson vetoed Federal road-building and banking—yet he asserted Federal authority by ordering troops to South Carolina in the Nullification Crisis of 1832–33. The Whig party arose in opposition to "King Andrew I," especially to his high-handed veto of the national bank, but voters endorsed Jackson's war on privilege by reelecting him in 1832. In his second term, Jackson seized land from the Native Americans, ignoring the Supreme Court, and he recognized Texas in hopes of taking more land from Mexico. He became the first president to ride a train (1833) and to survive an assassination attempt (1835). After placing his friend Martin Van Buren in the White House, Jackson retired to the Hermitage, his plantation in Tennessee. He remained quite influential behind the scenes, persuading the Democrats to discard Van Buren and nominate James K. Polk in 1844. Jackson finally succumbed to dropsy and old wounds on June 8, 1845.

8. Martin Van Buren (1837–41)

The first president to have played no part in the Revolution, Martin Van Buren was born to a Dutch family in Kinderhook, New York, on Dec. 5, 1782. Apprenticed to a lawyer at 14, Van Buren took to law and politics—so well, in fact, that he came to be called the Little Magician. By 1821 staunch party loyalty elevated him to the Senate, where Van Buren led northern supporters of

Andrew Jackson and guided his victory in 1828. Brief service as New York governor ended when Jackson appointed him secretary of state in 1829. Van Buren helped build the Democratic party, and Jackson made him vice president in 1832. As Jackson's heir apparent, Van Buren won the 1836 election, but two months after he took office, the Panic of 1837 launched a severe depression that spoiled his presidency. "Martin Van Ruin" responded by creating the independent treasury system, but his lack of popularity was beyond repair. He made enemies in the North by protecting slavery and in the South by refusing to annex Texas. Though the self-made son of an innkeeper, Van Buren was cast by his opponents as an aristocrat. In 1844 Van Buren lost the Democratic nomination when Jackson abandoned him over the Texas issue. Then, in 1848 Van Buren guaranteed a Democratic defeat by founding the Free Soil party and running for president, which split the decisive New York vote. Van Buren died a Unionist on July 24, 1862, the only president whose life touched both the Revolution and the Civil War.

9. William Henry Harrison (1841)

Son of a signatory of the Declaration of Independence and grandfather of a president, William Henry Harrison was born in Charles City County, Virginia, on Feb. 9, 1773. Campaign legend held that his birthplace was a log cabin, but in fact it was a plantation mansion. Harrison left medical school to join the army and fight Native Americans in the Northwest in 1791. After an illustrious military career, he served in Congress (1816–19), the U.S. Senate (1825–28), and as ambassador to Colombia (1828–29) before falling victim to Andrew Jackson's spoils system. Harrison fit Whig designs of defeating Jacksonians with a war hero of their own and received the Whig nomination to face Martin Van Buren in 1840. Harrison's campaign sidestepped issues to cast him as a plain frontiersman who guzzled hard cider while Van Buren sipped champagne. In the first modern election full of hoopla and hype, "Tippecanoe and Tyler Too"—the Whig slogan—linked Harrison's most famous victory with his obscure running mate. A huge turnout gave Harrison the victory at age 67, the oldest president until Ronald Reagan. Harrison delivered a record 8,500-word inaugural address hatless and coatless on a drizzly winter day. He caught a cold from which he never recovered and succumbed to pneumonia on Apr, 4, 1841. He was the first president to die in the White House—where he lived for only 31 days. His grandson, Benjamin Harrison, was the 23rd president.

10. John Tyler (1841–45)

The first vice president to become president by succession, the first president to see impeachment proposed against him, and the only president to change parties in office, John Tyler was born on Mar. 29, 1790, in Charles City County, Virginia. He was a Virginia legislator, congressman, senator, and governor before the Whigs chose him as William Henry Harrison's running mate in 1840. Though a strict constructionist and states' rights advocate, Tyler earned the Whigs' favor by opposing Andrew Jackson. But as president after Harrison's death, "His Accidency" earned their ire by vetoing, in mid-1842, two tariff bills vital to the Whig party. Eventually, his cabinet resigned and his party expelled him. Outraged members of Congress called for his impeachment. On July 10, 1842, John Minor Botts, a Whig representative from Richmond, Va., proposed the appointment of a special committee to investigate Tyler's conduct in office with an eye toward impeachment. The proposal was defeated on Jan. 10, 1843, by a vote of 127 to 83. This was the first time presidential impeachment proceedings were introduced in Congress. Tyler concluded the Webster-Ashburton Treaty (1842), which adjusted the northeastern boundary of the United States, and the Texas annexation (1845), but without popular or partisan support, he was powerless and decided against running for reelection. A veto on his last day in office became the first ever to be overridden. Tyler died on Jan. 18, 1862, awaiting his seat in the Confederate Congress.

11. James Knox Polk (1845–49)

The first dark-horse president, James Knox Polk was born in Mecklenburg County, North Carolina, on Nov. 2, 1795. A star orator in Tennessee politics, Polk idolized Andrew Jackson. "Young Hickory" took Jackson's old seat in Congress in 1825 and was reelected seven times. Polk was Speaker of the House from 1835 to 1839 and governor of Tennessee until 1841. He lost two bids for reelection, and his political career seemed over when the Democrats nominated him for president in 1844. Polk's name had not even appeared on the first seven ballots, but the deadlocked convention latched onto Polk as a pro-expansion dark horse. In the election he defeated Henry Clay by 1.5 percent of the vote on a platform that ignored slavery. From his inaugural address onward, Polk pursued expansion in the West. In 1846, he bluffed the British into believing the United States would go to war over Oregon, extracting a treaty for it. When Mexico attacked U.S. troops in disputed Texas territory, Polk called it an invasion and got a declaration of war. The ensuing Mexican War (1846–48) won California and the Southwest for the United States in the Treaty of Guadalupe-Hidalgo. Polk declined a second term, having fulfilled the nation's "Manifest Destiny" to span the continent. The last strong president before Abraham Lincoln, Polk added a million square miles to the United States. But the issue of slavery in the new territories split the Democrats and soon the whole country. "The presidency is not a bed of roses," complained Polk, who left the White House totally exhausted and died three months later, on June 15, 1849.

12. Zachary Taylor (1849–50)

Zachary Taylor, the first president to have no previous political experience, was born on Nov. 24, 1784, in Montebello, Virginia. His father was a colonel in the Revolutionary War, and Taylor—along with four brothers—served as a professional soldier for nearly 40 years. After distinguished service against the British and Native Americans, Gen. Taylor's finest hour came during the Mexican War, when he captured Monterrey and smashed Gen. Santa Ana's much larger army at the Battle of Buena Vista (1847). Though Taylor had never held office or even voted, the Whigs eagerly nominated "Old Rough and Ready" for president in 1848; Taylor, like William Henry Harrison, was an apolitical war hero above the slavery controversy. He won the election when the new Free Soil party siphoned off Democratic votes, but Taylor took office with Congress in chaos over the admission of California as a free state. Taylor opposed the Compromise of 1850 and probably would have vetoed it, but he died

suddenly of acute indigestion on July 9, 1850. (A long, hot Fourth of July at Washington Monument ceremonies had no doubt contributed to his weakened state.) Backers of the compromise rejoiced that Taylor's death saved the Union. Taylor was both the last of eight slave owners and the last Whig to be elected president.

13. Millard Fillmore (1850–53)

Born in a log cabin on Jan. 7, 1800, Millard Fillmore was the son of a poor farmer in Locke Township, New York. Apprenticed to a cloth maker in his youth, Fillmore struggled for an education and got a job teaching even though he never attended college. Clerking for a judge taught Fillmore enough law to join the bar at age 23, and he became a prosperous New York attorney. Fillmore entered politics as an Anti-Mason and was a four-term congressman when the Whigs made him Zachary Taylor's vice president in 1848. Dignified good looks were Fillmore's main political asset; he was quite unprepared for the presidency when Taylor died suddenly in 1850. Fillmore delayed civil war another decade by signing the Compromise of 1850, but he lost the nomination in 1852 when the Whigs turned to Gen. Winfield Scott, yet another genial war hero and their last candidate. In 1856 Fillmore ran again for president as candidate of the American, or "Know Nothing," party. Fillmore hoped to unite the country behind anti-Catholicism and nativism, submerging the slavery issue, but he carried only Maryland. Though a Unionist in the Civil War, Fillmore denounced Abraham Lincoln and remained sharply critical of Republicans until his death on Mar. 8, 1874.

14. Franklin Pierce (1853–57)

Son of a Revolutionary War hero, Franklin Pierce was born in Hillsboro, New Hampshire, on Nov. 23, 1804—the first president born in the 19th century. A leader of Jacksonian Democrats in Congress in the 1830s, Pierce had been absent from national politics for a decade when the deadlocked Democratic convention nominated him for president on the 49th ballot in 1852. A dark horse candidate, Pierce won enough southern votes to defeat Gen. Winfield Scott, his Mexican War commander, becoming the youngest president as of that date. Pierce greatly hastened the coming of the Civil War by signing the Kansas-Nebraska Act (1854), which repealed the Missouri Compromise and reopened the dangerous issue of slavery expansion. He continually appeased the South by backing proslavery ruffians in "Bleeding Kansas," encouraging slavery expansionists who coveted Cuba, and buying the land known as the Gadsden Purchase from Mexico for a southern railroad. As a result Pierce's party lost elections to Republicans who charged that "slave power" controlled the White House. In 1856 Pierce became the only elected president to be denied his own party's renomination. During the Civil War, Pierce criticized the Emancipation Proclamation and was nearly lynched by angry New Englanders. He died a forgotten, depressed alcoholic, in Concord, New Hampshire, on Oct. 8, 1869, the only president from New Hampshire.

15. James Buchanan (1857–61)

Considered one of the worst presidents because of his lack of good judgment and moral courage, and also the only bachelor president, James Buchanan was born in Mercersburg, Pennsylvania, on Apr. 23, 1791. A lawyer and veteran of the

War of 1812, Buchanan compiled more than 40 years of public service as legislator and diplomat. The Democrats nominated Buchanan in 1856 largely because he was in England during the Kansas-Nebraska debate and thus remained untainted by either side of the issue. Millard Fillmore's "Know-Nothing" candidacy helped Buchanan defeat John C. Frémont, the first Republican candidate for president. Buchanan favored "popular sovereignty" over slavery in the territories and was the last of the Doughfaces, or northern politicians submissive to the South. Few Americans shared Buchanan's faith that the Supreme Court's Dred Scott decision (1857) would end conflict over slavery expansion "speedily and finally." When it did not, Buchanan tried to close the issue himself by urging that Kansas be admitted as a slave state—an even worse miscalculation. Democrats deserted him, and Republicans won the House in 1858, but Buchanan's vetoes and southern votes in the Senate stalemated the government. He inadvertently helped Abraham Lincoln win in 1860 by refusing to conciliate his own party. The secession crisis paralyzed Buchanan, who denied both the southern right to secede and the Federal government's right to do anything about it; he was relieved to hand Lincoln the reins. Buchanan died on June 1, 1868. On the day before, he predicted that "history will vindicate my memory," but historians continue mainly to denigrate him.

16. Abraham Lincoln (1861–65)

A largely unpopular president until he was assassinated (the first assassinated president), Abraham Lincoln was born in a log cabin in Hodgenville, Kentucky, on Feb. 12, 1809. He accumulated barely a year's total education while growing up, though he did learn to write and developed a fondness for reading. Family moves took him to Indiana and then to Illinois by the time he was 21. At age 19 Lincoln had worked his way down the Mississippi and came away appalled at slavery. He served in the Black Hawk War (1832) before losing an election for the state legislature. A failed storekeeper, Lincoln worked odd jobs while he taught himself law, sometimes walking 20 miles to borrow books. He finally made the state legislature in 1834 as a Whig, and in 1842 married Mary Todd, having canceled their engagement once before.

Elected to Congress in 1846, Lincoln denounced James K. Polk for precipitating the Mexican War. He returned to his Springfield, Ill., law practice after only one term. But the repeal of the Missouri Compromise shocked Lincoln back into politics, and he helped organize the Illinois Republicans. An unsuccessful candidate for the Senate in 1858, Lincoln drew national attention in debates with Stephen A. Douglas, the nation's leading Democrat. Lincoln was rewarded with his party's nomination for president in 1860, the least objectionable candidate among several more prominent Republicans. He defeated three opponents in the election, though his name did not even appear on the ballot in the South. As Southern states left the Union, Lincoln preached conciliation and promised no harm to slavery—but he vowed to crush secession and forced the issue at Ft. Sumter. After early reverses in the Civil War, Lincoln decided slavery had to be abolished altogether to restore the Union, and he issued the Emancipation Proclamation (1862). Lincoln's management of the war was thwarted by incompetent generals, feuding politicians, and his own

inexperience, which matched that of his troops. Yet, like them, Lincoln learned on the job, settling on Ulysses S. Grant as his top general by 1864. The powers of the presidency expanded dramatically under Lincoln, who stretched the Constitution on behalf of the war effort. Lincoln defeated Gen. George McClellan for reelection in 1864, vowing to "bind up the nation's wounds." Before he had the chance, Lincoln was shot on Good Friday, five days after the war's end, by John Wilkes Booth, an arch-Confederate. Lincoln died the next morning, on Apr. 15, 1865. His martyrdom spurred the vengefulness of Reconstruction, ironically against Lincoln's own wishes. Millions of Americans lined the 1,700-mile route of Lincoln's funeral train, their mournful cries resounding all the way back to Illinois. Lincoln's prestige has grown with time, until many have come to regard him as the greatest president.

17. Andrew Johnson (1865–69)

The first president to be impeached, Andrew Johnson was born in Raleigh, North Carolina, on Dec. 29, 1808, the son of a poor laborer. No president could claim humbler origins: Johnson's father died when he was three, his mother worked as a washerwoman, and he never attended a day of school in his life. As a teenager he ran away to Tennessee, opened a successful tailor's shop, and got elected mayor of Greeneville by age 21. A fiery Democratic stump speaker, Johnson's attacks on Whigs and rich planters won him a seat in the state legislature in 1835 and in Congress in 1843, made him governor in 1853, and took him to the Senate in 1857. Alone among 22 southern senators, Johnson stayed loyal to the Union in 1861, though a mob of Virginians nearly lynched him for it. Lincoln appointed Johnson military governor of Tennessee, and he was nominated for vice president on the "National Union" ticket in 1864. Suddenly made president by Lincoln's assassination, Johnson vowed to carry on Lincoln's policy of leniency toward the South, but radical Republican opposition and his own coarse ineptitude led to serious clashes with Congress. Johnson vetoed 29 bills and was overridden 15 times, more than any other president to that time. A former slave owner, Johnson resisted Republican efforts to aid the freedmen. His only victory was the unpopular purchase of Alaska in 1867. Congress systematically stripped him of power until Johnson fought back by removing his disloyal secretary of war, Edwin M. Stanton. Impeached in the House for defying the Tenure of Office Act, Johnson was tried in the Senate and acquitted by a single vote on May 26, 1868. Few presidents were so stymied in office. Tennessee helped vindicate Johnson by making him the only former president elected to the Senate. He died a few months later, on July 31, 1875.

18. Ulysses S. Grant (1869–77)

A better general than president, Ulysses Simpson Grant was born in Point Pleasant, Ohio, on Apr. 27, 1822. Having barely passed West Point's height requirement for entrance, Grant attended the academy and graduated in the middle of his class in 1843. Fifty of Grant's classmates fought with or against him as Civil War generals. He served under Gen. Zachary Taylor in the Mexican War before marrying his sweetheart, Julia Dent, in 1848. Assigned to isolated posts after 1852, Grant grew bored away from his family and reportedly turned to heavy drinking. Finally resigning from the army in 1854, he went to Missouri, only to fail in farming and real estate. When the Civil War began, Grant was working in his younger brother's leather shop in Galena, Ill. He received a commission and rose rapidly to brigadier general. U.S. Grant acquired the nickname Unconditional Surrender for his string of western victories, notably at Vicksburg and Chattanooga in 1863. Once Abraham Lincoln made him supreme commander in 1864, Grant opened a relentless offensive that quickly ended the war. He personally accepted Gen. Robert E. Lee's surrender at Appomattox in 1865. After feuding with Andrew Johnson, Grant joined the Republicans and was elected president in 1868. Grant pressed radical Reconstruction in the South with mixed results. Corruption—notably the Jay Gould (1869), Crédit Mobilier (1872), and Whiskey Ring (1875) scandals—marred Grant's presidency; nevertheless, he easily won reelection in 1872. The Panic of 1873 triggered a deep economic depression that dissuaded Grant from a third term in 1876. Reconsidering in 1880, he sought the Republican nomination again and nearly succeeded. Afterward Grant retired and went bankrupt. To provide for his family, he began writing his memoirs. Developing cancer, Grant valiantly hung on to finish the project, which would earn him some literary fame and his family half a million dollars. He died on July 23, 1885, just four days after completing his autobiography.

19. Rutherford B. Hayes (1877–81)

Rutherford Birchard Hayes was born a frail child on Oct. 4, 1822, in Delaware, Ohio, where he was raised by his mother. After attending Harvard Law School, he set up a successful Cincinnati law practice in 1849. Hayes defended fugitive slaves and helped found the Ohio Republicans. In 1852 he married Lucy Ware Webb, the first college graduate first lady. A decorated Civil War veteran, Hayes was wounded five times and promoted to general. From 1868 to 1876 he served as governor of Ohio. Republicans turned to Hayes as a scandal-free hero in 1876 and nominated him for president. He lost the election to Samuel Tilden of the Democrats, but Republicans in Congress disputed enough state vote totals to connive "Rutherfraud" into office with the support of southern Democrats. Hayes's first acts were to appoint an ex-Confederate to his cabinet and to withdraw Federal troops from the South. He never overcame the resulting stigma of political bargain, and facing a Democratic Congress, Hayes seemed destined for a weak presidency. Yet he put the nation back on the gold standard, put down railroad strikes, reformed the civil service, and banished liquor from the White House before keeping his promise to serve only one term. Hayes viewed the return of prosperity and Republican majorities in Congress as personal triumphs. He worked quietly for charitable causes until his death on Jan. 17, 1893.

20. James A. Garfield (1881)

The last log cabin president, James Abram Garfield was born near Orange, Ohio, on Nov. 19, 1831, and like Rutherford B. Hayes, Garfield was raised by his mother. Garfield graduated from Williams College in 1856, became a classics professor, president of Hiram College, a lawyer, and at age 30 the youngest Union general in the Civil War. Garfield left the battlefield in 1864 to enter Congress, where he remained until the Republicans nominated him for president in 1880, a dark-horse compromise between Grant and James G. Blaine. Garfield defeated Gen. Winfield Scott Hancock of the Democrats by 0.1 percent of the vote in a campaign stressing tariffs. Republicans immediately swarmed to Garfield, demanding patronage for their rival "Stalwart" and "Half-Breed" factions. After only four months in office, Garfield was shot in a train station by Charles J. Guiteau, a disappointed Stalwart office-seeker. Garfield died 80 days later, on Sept. 19, 1881, the second presidential assassination ending the second-shortest presidency. When hordes of Republican hopefuls had besieged the White House begging for jobs, Garfield had exclaimed: "My God! What is there in this place that a man should ever want to get in it?"

21. Chester A. Arthur (1881–85)

Chester Alan Arthur was born a preacher's son on Oct. 5, 1829, in Fairfield, Vermont. He grew up in Vermont and in New York to become an ardent abolitionist like his father. A true machine politician, Arthur worked for Republican candidates in New York and enjoyed several patronage jobs during the Civil War. Ulysses S. Grant appointed him collector of the port of New York in 1871, and Arthur prospered there until 1879, when Rutherford B. Hayes removed him in the name of reform. In 1880 "Half-Breed" Republicans nominated Arthur for vice president in a conciliatory gesture to his "Stalwart" faction. "The office of Vice President is a greater honor than I ever dreamed of attaining," he said. But Arthur acceded to the presidency on Sept. 19, 1881, when another Stalwart assassinated James A. Garfield. Perhaps shamed into supporting civil service reform, Arthur signed the Pendleton Act (1883) and rooted out post office graft. Democrats in Congress thwarted the rest of Arthur's initiatives; Republicans, whose calls for spoils Arthur ignored, denied him renomination in 1884. He lost a Senate race in New York and died two years later, on Nov. 18, 1886. Arthur was the last of three presidents in the single year 1881.

22, 24. Grover Cleveland (1885–89; 1893–97)

The only president to serve two nonconsecutive terms, Stephen Grover Cleveland was a minister's son, born in Caldwell, New Jersey, on Mar. 18, 1837. The family moved to New York, where Cleveland's uncle made him a lawyer. He showed scant interest in politics until Buffalo elected him mayor in 1881, and the next year Cleveland became governor. His war on corrupt Tammany Hall made Cleveland the perfect Democratic reform candidate for president in 1884. During the election campaign, backers of James G. Blaine, the Republican candidate, accused Cleveland of fathering an illegitimate child. He admitted it and won anyway—by 0.3 percent of the vote—but not before the Republicans came up with the immortal campaign chant "Ma! Ma! Where's my Pa? / Gone to the White House, / Ha! Ha! Ha!" The first Democratic president after the Civil War, Cleveland pushed for civil service reform and lower tariffs. In the first White House wedding, Cleveland married Frances Folsom in 1886. Cleveland cast over 300 vetoes—more than twice the combined total of all previous presidents. He cut Civil War pensions, seized 81 million acres of unused land from railroads, and signed the Interstate Commerce Act (1887). Defeated in the 1888 election, Cleveland claimed there was "no happier man in the United States"; yet four years later he won a rematch with Benjamin Harrison. Back in the White House, Cleveland underwent a secret operation to remove his cancerous upper jaw. His tight-money policies did nothing to help the depression after the Panic of 1893. Cleveland sent Federal troops to break up the Pullman strike (1894) and supported William McKinley, a Republican, for president in 1896. "I have tried so hard to do right," Cleveland said on his deathbed on June 24, 1908.

23. Benjamin Harrison (1889–93)

Benjamin Harrison was born on Aug. 20, 1833, at the North Bend, Ohio, farm of his grandfather William Henry Harrison, the ninth president. He took up the law in Indiana before joining the Union Army in 1862. Harrison finished the Civil War a brigadier general and returned to Indiana, where he was a prominent Republican, defeated for governor in 1876 but elected senator in 1881. A colorless compromise candidate for president, Harrison won the 1888 election despite receiving fewer popular votes than Grover Cleveland. Harrison bowed to the "Billion Dollar Congress" of free-spending Republicans who escalated Civil War pensions, transportation subsidies, naval construction, and spoils patronage. The McKinley Tariff, the Sherman Anti-Trust Act, the Sherman Silver Purchase Act (all 1890), and Secretary of State James G. Blaine's vigorous foreign policy were hallmarks of Harrison's administration, which oversaw the admission of six new states. Democrats won back Congress in 1890 and the White House in 1892, when Harrison lost to Cleveland in their rematch. A legal expert, Harrison taught at Stanford University and defended Venezuela in a boundary dispute with Britain before his death, on Mar. 13, 1901. Harrison referred to the White House as "my jail."

25. William McKinley (1897–1901)

The last Civil War veteran to become president, William McKinley was born in Niles, Ohio, on Jan. 29, 1843, son of an iron founder. A college dropout, McKinley was a post office clerk when the Civil War began. He volunteered as a private and mustered out as a 22-year-old major. McKinley studied law and was elected to Congress in 1876. A longtime Republican floor leader, he authored the record-high McKinley Tariff of 1890, before losing his seat that same year. Ohio millionaire Marcus Hanna, McKinley's political manager, engineered two governor's terms for him and funded McKinley's run for the presidency in 1896. William Jennings Bryan opposed him on a free-silver platform, but McKinley's dignified front porch campaign stressed sound money, tariffs, and the "full dinner pail." He won the election with the first popular majority since Grant's reelection. Strongly probusiness, McKinley raised the tariff still higher and reluctantly led the country into the Spanish-American War (1898). By acquiring the Philippines and other islands, the country became a world power under McKinley, who went on to proclaim the open-door policy in China. McKinley defeated Bryan by an even larger margin in 1900 and was enjoying great popularity when anarchist Leon Czolgosz shot him in Buffalo, N.Y. McKinley died two weeks later, on Sept. 14, 1901.

26. Theodore Roosevelt (1901–09)

Theodore Roosevelt was born in New York City on Oct. 27, 1858, the only president born there. A small, sickly child plagued by asthma, Roosevelt overcame a pampered youth to live the "strenuous life:" he boxed, hiked, hunted, rode horses, and climbed the Matterhorn. After graduating Phi Beta Kappa from Harvard in 1880, he attended Columbia Law School and became the youngest member of New York's legislature. Rich men of his day did not consider politics a suitable avocation, but Roosevelt desperately wanted "to be of the governing class." His first wife, Alice Hathaway Lee, died on the same day his mother died in 1884. Roosevelt wrote books and ran a cattle ranch in North Dakota until he married Edith Kermit Carow in 1886 and they moved to Oyster Bay, N.Y. During the Spanish-American War, Roosevelt left a job at the Navy Department in 1898 to lead the Rough Riders volunteer regiment in Cuba, achieving glory in the Battle of San Juan Hill. Elected governor of New York immediately upon returning home, Roosevelt was named William McKinley's running mate, in 1900. Roosevelt learned of McKinley's death while on a mountain-climbing expedition.

The youngest president at 42, "T.R." promised a Square Deal to close the gap between capital and labor. He mounted well-publicized campaigns against big business and successfully arbitrated major strikes. "Teddy's" popularity soared when he humbled billionaire J.P. Morgan in the Northern Securities case, and a record plurality reelected him in 1904. Roosevelt signed progressive laws to regulate railroads, inspect food and drugs, and create more than 150 million acres of national parks and forests. No less vigorous in foreign policy, Roosevelt's corollary to the Monroe Doctrine asserted the country would intervene to prevent European involvement in Latin America. For helping to end the Russo-Japanese War, Roosevelt became the first American to win the Nobel Prize, but he considered the Panama Canal his greatest achievement. Roosevelt kept his pledge not to seek a third term in 1908—but in 1912 he ran against his chosen successor, William Howard Taft. Denied his party's nomination, Roosevelt survived an assassination attempt and won more than four million votes as the Progressive, or Bull Moose, candidate. During World War I, Roosevelt bitterly denounced the neutrality policy of Woodrow Wilson, who then denied Roosevelt's request to lead troops in France. While laying plans for another run at the White House, Roosevelt died suddenly of a cardiac embolism on Jan. 6, 1919. "No president has ever enjoyed himself as much as I have," he once said.

27. William Howard Taft (1909–13)

By far the largest president at over 330 pounds, William Howard Taft was born in Cincinnati, Ohio, on Sept. 15, 1857. He graduated from Yale in 1878, then followed his father into law and Republican politics: "I always had my plate right side up when offices were falling," Taft wrote. William McKinley sent him to govern the Philippines in 1900, and Theodore Roosevelt appointed him secretary of war in 1904. Taft traveled around the world as Roosevelt's personal emissary, becoming T.R.'s chosen successor in 1908. As president, Taft tried to carry on Roosevelt's policies, but he wrecked the Republican party by alienating progressives from conservative "Stand-Patters" over tariff and conservation issues. Taft initiated the income tax and pursued antitrust suits against big business—but generally he sided with wealthy interests. An infuriated Roosevelt challenged Taft unsuccessfully for the Republican nomination in 1912, then outpolled him in the election, giving Woodrow Wilson the victory. With eight electoral votes, Taft suffered the worst-ever defeat for an incumbent president. But the better part of his career lay ahead: Taft, always more comfortable as a jurist, taught law at Yale until he was appointed chief justice of the United States in 1921. He served with distinction, alternating a liberal nationalism in economic affairs with political and social conservatism. Taft died on Mar. 8, 1930. Never nostalgic for the White House, Taft once said, "I don't remember that I ever was president."

28. Woodrow Wilson (1913–21)

Born on Dec. 28, 1856, in Staunton, Virginia, the son of a Presbyterian minister, Thomas Woodrow Wilson grew up in Virginia, Georgia, South Carolina, and North Carolina—the first southern president since Andrew Jackson. Probably dyslexic, Wilson was slow to read; yet he became the most highly educated president. Graduated from Princeton in 1879, Wilson studied law before taking a Ph.D. in political science at Johns Hopkins in 1886. He taught at Bryn Mawr and Wesleyan University before Princeton appointed him professor in 1890. Wilson attracted the attention of Democratic bosses after he was elected Princeton's president in 1902, and they persuaded him to run for New Jersey governor in 1910. A strong progressive, Wilson won easily—and then turned on party bosses by sponsoring anti-machine reforms. In 1912 the Democrats nominated Wilson for president on the 46th ballot, and he won, with Theodore Roosevelt and William Howard Taft splitting the Republican vote.

Wilson's expert knowledge of government and strong party leadership pushed the Underwood Tariff, the Federal Reserve Act, the Federal Trade Commission, and the Clayton Antitrust Act through Congress by 1914. Restoring competition to the monopoly-plagued economy was the goal of Wilson's "New Freedom," until war in Europe made neutrality his top priority. German attacks on Allied ships carrying Americans strained Wilson's commitment, but he was narrowly reelected in 1916 on the slogan "He Kept Us Out of the War." After Germany spurned Wilson's mediation and resumed attacks on Allied shipping, Congress declared war at Wilson's behest in April 1917. World War I would "make the world safe for democracy," Wilson vowed, and he issued "Fourteen Points" for a just peace. After the armistice in November 1918, Wilson became the first president to visit Europe, when he attended the Paris peace conference that produced the Versailles Treaty. Wilson's dream of "peace without vengeance" was frustrated at Versailles, where he compromised away his Fourteen Points to obtain the League of Nations for collective security. In July 1919, Wilson returned home to face hostile Republicans in the Senate, where his treaty languished. On a nationwide speaking tour, Wilson collapsed from exhaustion in Colorado and suffered a paralytic stroke in October 1919. Wilson, all but incapacitated, refused to compromise as the Senate rejected the Versailles Treaty. Wilson's second wife, Edith Bolling Galt, whom he married in 1915, shielded the disabled president from the press and politicians until the end of his term in 1921. Woodrow Wilson died in his sleep on Feb. 3, 1924, frustrated by his own country's refusal to join the League of Nations.

29. Warren G. Harding (1921–23)

The first president born after the Civil War, Warren Gamaliel Harding was born in Blooming Grove, Ohio, which earlier had been named Corsica, on Nov. 2, 1865. He taught, studied law, and sold insurance before following his father into the newspaper business. Marriage to Florence De-Wolfe, a wealthy widow, in 1891 helped finance Harding's paper, the Marion Star. A staunch Republican, Harding's probusiness editorials got him elected state senator and lieutenant governor. Although defeated for governor in 1910, Harding was elected senator four years later. Republicans turned to him in 1920 as a compromise candidate for president, the "best of the second-raters"; his good looks were expected to win over women first-time voters. Elected by an unprecedented 61 percent majority, Harding promised a return to "normalcy" for Americans tired of war and Woodrow Wilson. Harding's administration featured higher tariffs, lower taxes, and immigration restriction—but perhaps most notably, pervasive corruption and incompetence by Harding's crooked appointees. Harding was disturbed by the dishonesty of "my God-damn friends," two of whom committed suicide to avoid prosecution. While visiting San Francisco, Harding died suddenly of an embolism on Aug. 2, 1923. Scandals involving secret love affairs, official graft, and the vast Teapot Dome swindle erupted soon thereafter. Mrs. Harding zealously tracked down Harding's letters and destroyed them, leaving him the most enigmatic president, and certainly one of the worst.

30. Calvin Coolidge (1923–29)

The only president to share the nation's birthday, John Calvin Coolidge was born in Plymouth, Vermont, on July 4, 1872. Descended from a long line of New Englanders, he graduated from Amherst in 1895, practiced law in Massachusetts, and entered Republican politics in 1899. Coolidge rose slowly through a succession of state offices until he was elected governor of Massachusetts in 1918. Acclaimed for crushing the Boston police strike in 1919, Coolidge became the unexpected Republican vice-presidential nominee in 1920. After Warren G. Harding's death while still in office, Coolidge's own father swore him in as the new president. "Silent Cal" was the butt of jokes for his laconic utterances, but his minimalist approach to government fit the public mood, and he restored respectability to the White House, tainted by Harding's corrupt appointees and all-night poker parties. Instead of the whiskey that once flowed freely there, ice water in paper cups was served to visitors. Coolidge, untouched by leftover scandals, won the election in his own right in 1924. Pronouncing that the "business of America is business," he ushered in the heady years of Coolidge Prosperity, as the stock market soared higher and higher. Coolidge ignored foreign affairs and made frugality his trademark, slashing the budget at the expense of farmers and veterans, even driving out a White House cook who could not abide Coolidge's cost cutting. "It's a pretty good idea to get out when they still want you," Coolidge said, surprising the nation at the peak of his success by declining to run again in 1928. A popular president, Coolidge was safely out of politics when the Great Depression arrived. He died on Jan. 5, 1933, on the eve of the New Deal.

31. Herbert Hoover (1929–33)

Born in West Branch, Iowa, on Aug. 10, 1874, Herbert Clark Hoover was the first president from west of the Mississippi. Orphaned at eight and raised by Quaker relatives in Iowa and Oregon, Hoover joined the first graduating class of Stanford University in 1895. He became a world-famous mining engineer and a multimillionaire by age 40. In World War I, Hoover helped rescue Americans stranded in Europe, distributed food supplies to occupied Belgium, and convinced the nation to save food ("Hooverize") for the war effort. Hoover was Woodrow Wilson's economic adviser at Versailles, and he organized relief for famine-struck Russia during the revolution. Joining the Republicans in 1919, Hoover earned prominence as the secretary of commerce in the 1920s and was elected president in 1928—the only electoral victory of his life. He promised a "chicken in every pot," but a few months later, the Wall Street crash brought on the Great Depression. Paralyzed by his conservative instincts, Hoover could not halt the spread of bank failures, bankruptcy, unemployment, and despair. Government should not get involved, he believed, and public relief would ruin American morals—so Hoover called for a balanced budget while promising the return of prosperity. He sent tanks to disperse veterans begging for pensions, and shantytowns across the country were dubbed Hoovervilles. Massively defeated by Franklin D. Roosevelt in 1932, Hoover called the New Deal "socialistic, collectivistic, fascistic and communistic." For decades Americans blamed Hoover for the depression and criticized his hard-hearted refusal to help the needy. Hoover lived another 31 years, the longest postpresidential lifespan, and he salvaged his reputation with more relief work after World War II. In retirement Hoover chaired two bipartisan commissions on government reorganization, issuing many important recommendations for Federal reform. Boulder Dam on the Colorado River was renamed to honor Hoover before he died, at age 90, on Oct. 20, 1964.

32. Franklin D. Roosevelt (1933—45)

The only president elected more than twice, Franklin Delano Roosevelt was born to a wealthy Hyde Park, New York, family on Jan. 30, 1882. He followed his cousin, Theodore Roosevelt, into Harvard and Columbia Law School—but not into the Republican party. F.D.R. was a Democratic state senator, assistant secretary of the navy, and nominee for vice president in 1920. Paralyzed by polio in 1921, Roosevelt learned to walk with braces and canes. As governor of New York after 1928, he pioneered unemployment relief in the Great Depression, earning him the Democratic nomination for president in 1932. Herbert Hoover, brooding and baffled by the depression, posed little challenge to the beaming, magnetic Roosevelt, who won the election by 23 million to 16 million votes. F.D.R. promised vague but bold experimentation ("above all, try something"), and as he took office in the worst inaugural crisis since Abraham Lincoln's, he assured Americans they had "nothing to fear but fear itself." F.D.R.'s first 100 days set a breakneck pace as compliant congressmen approved his New Deal for relief and recovery. Major landmarks were the National Industrial Recovery Act, the Agricultural Adjustment Act, the Tennessee Valley Authority, the Works Progress Administration, the National Labor Relations Act (Wagner Act), and the Social Security Act (1933–35). Though often contradictory and ineffective, the New Deal established the Federal government's responsibility for protecting farmers, workers, and the unemployed while actively regulating the economy to prevent another crash. F.D.R.'s high-profile "fireside chats," public works projects, and Social Security programs overcame despair and restored public confidence in the economy and government.

Reelected by a huge margin in 1936, Roosevelt proved incapable of ending the depression, as he ran afoul of the "nine old men" on the Supreme Court. Almost as many Americans called Roosevelt a Communist as praised him for rescuing the common man. Despite alienating many voters with his court-packing plan and "soak the rich" taxes, F.D.R. won an unprecedented third term in 1940. As war loomed in Europe, F.D.R. used his mastery of public opinion to lead Americans away from isolation, helping Britain with the destroyers-for-bases deal (1940) and Lend-Lease Act (1941) even before Pearl Harbor. World War II then occupied F.D.R.'s full attention as he shelved the New Deal and orchestrated the mammoth war effort. Roosevelt crisscrossed the globe to meet with Allied leaders and kept close personal control of diplomacy and grand strategy. He rallied a powerful sense of national purpose in the war, winning his fourth election in 1944. Together with Winston Churchill and Josef Stalin, F.D.R. planned a postwar peace of UN cooperation. Just after the Yalta Conference, Roosevelt died suddenly of a cerebral hemorrhage on Apr. 12, 1945, days before the war's end. His wife of 40 years, Eleanor Roosevelt, easily the most influential first lady, led her husband's campaign on behalf of disadvantaged Americans and continued it long after his death.

33. Harry S Truman (1945—53)

A plain midwestern farmer and World War I artilleryman, Harry S Truman (the S does not stand for a middle name) was born on May 8, 1884, in Lamar, Missouri. After his Kansas City haberdashery failed, Truman entered politics as a Democrat in the 1920s, and the local Pendergast machine arranged his election to the Senate as a New Dealer in 1934. National attention came to Truman when he headed a congressional committee investigating government waste during World War II. When Franklin D. Roosevelt needed a new vice president in 1944, he chose Truman. After only a few weeks in office, Truman had the presidency thrust upon him by Roosevelt's sudden death in April 1945. "Pray for me, boys," he told his first press conference. Utterly unprepared, Truman did not even know about the atomic bomb project, but he vowed to carry on Roosevelt's policies. Truman proved a remarkably capable chief executive. In his first four months, Truman approved the United Nations, accepted the German surrender, met with Allied leaders at Potsdam, and ordered atomic bombs dropped on Japan. As the Cold War commenced, Truman talked tough with the Soviets, accusing them of breaking agreements and intimidating helpless neighbors. In 1947 he proclaimed the Truman Doctrine, promising U.S. aid to threatened countries, and the Marshall Plan to aid European recovery and contain communism. The next year Truman ordered the Berlin airlift when the Soviets cut off West Berlin, and he promised to help Third World countries with the Point Four program. No less assertive at home, Truman made progress on civil rights, subdued restive unions, and prevented the Republican-controlled Congress from dismantling the New Deal—a specter that he effectively raised to win surprise reelection in 1948. Truman committed the country to the NATO alliance in

1949 and sent troops to South Korea when Communist armies invaded in 1950. But as Congress rejected Truman's ambitious Fair Deal domestic program and the Korean War bogged down, Truman's last years were barren. He had more vetoes overridden than all presidents but Andrew Johnson, and his poll ratings were lower than all but Jimmy Carter's. Truman, who initially raised fears of subversion with his loyalty program, could not quell the Red Scare that swept his party from power in 1952, as Republicans hammered away on the theme that Democrats were "soft on communism." Truman was convinced that he saved the world from communism, prevented World War III, and could have won another term if he chose to run in 1952. "He did his damndest" was the only eulogy Harry Truman desired on his death, on Dec. 26, 1972. Out of favor when he left office, Truman gained rising respect after his death.

34. Dwight D. Eisenhower (1953–61)

The last war hero president, Dwight David Eisenhower was born in Denison, Texas, on Oct. 14, 1890, and grew up poor in Kansas. A military history buff, Eisenhower graduated with the 1915 class of West Point that produced 59 generals. He married Mamie Doud, his wife of 52 years, and spent World War I as a tank-training instructor. Eisenhower, only a major at age 40, rose rapidly during World War II, promoted past 350 senior officers to become commander of U.S. forces in Europe in 1942. By the end of 1944, he was the first U.S. five-star general and Supreme Allied Commander, taking the German surrender in May 1945. By that point a global celebrity, Eisenhower was army chief of staff until 1948, when he resigned to become president of Columbia University. Pres. Truman named him to command NATO forces in 1950, but two years later, Eisenhower retired again to take the Republican nomination and run for president against Adlai E. Stevenson.

"Ike" became perhaps the most popular president in U.S. history, though many questioned his lax work habits, detached management style, and baffling speeches. Prominent millionaires in Eisenhower's cabinet and archconservatives such as Sec. of State John Foster Dulles seemed to have free rein, and Eisenhower acquiesced in Sen. Joe McCarthy's wild charges of subversion. His administration stockpiled atomic weapons and promised "massive retaliation" against Soviet aggression—yet did nothing when the Red Army rolled into Hungary in 1956. Eisenhower did end the Korean War, concluded several alliance agreements, and cut the defense budget. The "Eisenhower Doctrine" promised U.S. aid to Middle Eastern countries fighting communism. When Britain, France, and Israel invaded the Suez Canal in 1956, Eisenhower led UN condemnation and forced them to withdraw, though he sent U.S. Marines into Lebanon two years later. He began heavy U.S. involvement in Vietnam by backing the French and then the puppet Diem regime. At home Eisenhower promised to scale back the government—yet he expanded Social Security; created the Department of Health, Education, and Welfare; and spent billions on public housing and freeways. He pointedly stressed religious devotion. The Supreme Court's *Brown* decision, which Eisenhower deeply regretted, inaugurated the civil rights movement. Eisenhower defeated Stevenson again in 1956, but Soviet domination of space, revolution in Cuba, embarrassment over the Soviets' shooting down of a U.S. spy plane, and his own ill health marred his second term. Eisenhower reluctantly sent paratroopers to enforce desegregation in Little Rock, Ark., in 1957. Democrats controlled Congress for all but two years of Eisenhower's presidency. In retirement Eisenhower approved of U.S. intervention in Vietnam and counseled presidents until his death on Mar. 28, 1969.

35. John F. Kennedy (1961–63)

The youngest man elected president, the only Roman Catholic, and the first born in the 20th century, John Fitzgerald Kennedy was born in Brookline, Massachusetts, on May 29, 1917, to a family of Irish politicos. His father, Joseph P. Kennedy, was ambassador to England and one of the richest men in America. Kennedy attended Dexter and Choate Academies, the London School of Economics, and Princeton before graduating from Harvard in 1940. A patrol boat commander in World War II, Kennedy was decorated for bravery in saving the lives of wounded crew members. Kennedy's father arranged his election to Congress, where he served three undistinguished terms before entering the Senate in 1952. In 1953, he married wealthy socialite Jacqueline Bouvier, and in 1957, he won the Pulitzer Prize for *Profiles in Courage*, a study of principled politicians. In 1960, running on a platform that lambasted Republicans for insufficient anticommunism and "vigor," Kennedy became the first candidate to utilize the presidential primary system to defeat three prominent opponents for the Democratic nomination. In the general election, Kennedy edged sitting vice president Richard M. Nixon by the narrowest of margins: 118,000 votes out of 69 million cast. The campaign was the first to feature televised presidential debates, in which Kennedy's poise, polish, and charisma were an invaluable asset.

During the campaign, Kennedy had pledged a New Frontier, but his social programs languished in Congress. Undaunted, he plunged into foreign affairs, his primary interest. Just after taking office, he approved the disastrous Bay of Pigs invasion, and a year later, he terrified the world by confronting the Soviets over the presence of their missiles in Cuba. He visited the Berlin Wall and expressed solidarity with Germans under the Russian gun. But he also set up the Washington-Moscow hotline, and signed the Nuclear Test Ban Treaty (1963).

Thousands of U.S. troops went to Vietnam as Kennedy escalated the commitment to containing communism. Kennedy vastly increased spending for defense and space programs, vowing to put a man on the Moon. He also engineered a $10 billion tax cut that eventually brought prosperity and increased revenues. As racial unrest spread, Kennedy cautiously supported the civil rights movement, introducing sweeping legislation that would not pass in his lifetime—nor would his plans for aid to education and medical care for the elderly reach fruition before his death. In a Dallas, Tex., motorcade on Nov. 22, 1963, he was fatally shot. Kennedy's alleged assassin, Lee Harvey Oswald, a left-wing ex-marine, was in turn murdered by Jack Ruby two days later. While doubts persisted that Oswald acted alone, Kennedy's martyrdom helped realize his legislative legacy, and subsequent revelation of his many peccadilloes have not tarnished the "Kennedy myth."

36. Lyndon B. Johnson (1963–69)

The eighth vice president to succeed by death of a president, Lyndon Baines Johnson was born on his father's Texas ranch near Stonewall on Aug. 27, 1908. He worked his way through Southwest Texas State Teachers College, taught briefly, then took a job in Washington—where he would live for all but two years until he left the White House. Government fascinated Johnson, and he reveled in making connections, marrying heiress Claudia Alta "Lady Bird" Taylor after a two-month courtship in 1934. An ardent New Dealer, Johnson won election to Congress as a Democrat in 1937. Reelected three times without opposition, Johnson became the first congressman to volunteer for combat in World War II, winning a Silver Star before returning to Washington. In 1948, on his second try, "Landslide Lyndon" was elected to the Senate by just 87 votes. Hard work and Texas oil money made Johnson the youngest Senate majority leader by 1955. A huge man, Johnson's powers of persuasion were legendary, but he failed in his bid for the Democratic nomination for president in 1960. Johnson accepted John F. Kennedy's offer of the vice presidency and campaigned hard in the South to aid their narrow victory. Made president a thousand days later by the tragedy in Dallas, Johnson vowed to continue Kennedy's programs, pushing them through Congress with surprising ease. Notable were the Civil Rights Act outlawing segregation and the Equal Opportunity Act, which declared "war on poverty." After less than a year in office, Johnson defeated Barry Goldwater by the biggest plurality in history.

Now president in his own right, Johnson unveiled plans for a Great Society free from poverty and discrimination and passed the Education Act, Medical Care Act, and the Voting Rights Act in 1965. But Johnson came to grief in Vietnam, where he broke his 1964 campaign promise not to send "American boys to fight Asian wars." Earlier administrations committed the U.S. to defending South Vietnam, but Johnson intervened massively to prove American credibility to allies and enemies alike. Following the Tonkin Gulf incident (1964), Johnson steadily expended American power and lives in Vietnam, but victory, or a means to achieve it, never came within reach—despite the presence of over half a million U.S. troops by 1968. Johnson's presidency unraveled as American losses mounted, antiwar protests grew strident, race riots exploded in inner cities across the nation, and the government developed a credibility gap. Virtually a prisoner of the White House, Johnson faced a war he could neither win nor leave behind and a nation more deeply divided than at any time since the Civil War. In March 1968 Johnson effectively resigned by announcing he would not seek another term. He retired to his sprawling Texas ranch and stayed out of politics until his death, on Jan. 22, 1973.

37. Richard M. Nixon (1969–74)

The only president to resign from office, Richard Milhous Nixon was born in Yorba Linda, California, to a poor Quaker family on Jan. 9, 1913. A graduate of Whittier College and Duke University Law School, Nixon married Thelma "Pat" Ryan in 1940, saw noncombat service in World War II, and rode into Congress on the Republican wave of 1946. He gained fame in the anti-Communist trial of Alger Hiss before entering the Senate in 1950. Dwight D. Eisenhower made Nixon his running mate in 1952, but Nixon was nearly forced to resign for accepting questionable contributions. He appealed for national exoneration in the televised "Checkers" speech. A well-trav-

eled vice president, Nixon almost lost his life to hostile Latin American mobs in 1958, and he waged an impromptu debate in Moscow with Soviet premier Nikita Khrushchev in 1959. Eisenhower's obvious successor in 1960, Nixon narrowly lost the election to John F. Kennedy, and when he lost a California gubernatorial race in 1962, his career seemed over. Yet he practiced law in New York until the Republicans nominated him again in 1968. To a nation riven by the Vietnam War, Nixon promised "law and order," appealing to calm and unity against a background of riots, assassinations, and protest. Nixon defeated Hubert H. Humphrey with the smallest victor's share of the vote since 1912.

Vowing to "bring us together," Nixon tried to thwart the bureaucracy and Democrats in Congress by centralizing executive power. To control inflation, he ordered wage-price controls and devalued the dollar for the first time since the depression. Seeking "peace with honor" in Vietnam, Nixon built up the South Vietnamese army and withdrew U.S. troops—while massively escalating bombing of North Vietnam. Antiwar protests reached fever pitch when the United States invaded Cambodia in 1970. Nixon responded with appeals to the "silent majority," attacks on press freedom, and clandestine harassment of administration critics. High points of his first administration were the Apollo moon landing in 1969, Nixon's path-breaking visit to China in 1972, and the first Strategic Arms Limitation Treaty with the Soviet Union. Twelve days after announcing "peace is at hand" in Vietnam, Nixon was reelected by a landslide, carrying an unprecedented 49 states. During the campaign five burglars were arrested in the Democratic party headquarters, and by early 1973, they were linked to the White House. The ensuing "Watergate" scandal exposed the Nixon administration's rampant corruption, illegality, and deceit. Nixon himself downplayed the scandal as mere politics, but when his aides resigned in disgrace, Nixon's role in ordering an illegal cover-up came to light in the press, courts, and congressional investigations. Nixon evaded taxes, accepted illicit campaign contributions, ordered secret bombings, and harassed opponents with executive agencies, wiretaps, and break-ins. Vice Pres. Spiro T. Agnew resigned in October 1973 for accepting bribes, but Nixon hung on to power, claiming, "I am not a crook," as the House began impeachment proceedings. Subpoenas and Supreme Court orders forced Nixon to release tapes of his White House conversations authorizing the Watergate cover-up. Ultimately, he resigned to avoid impeachment for obstruction of justice, abuse of power, and contempt of Congress. Claiming to have lost his "political base," Nixon announced his resignation on national television on Aug. 9, 1974. He never admitted wrongdoing, though he later conceded errors of judgment. Saved by a blanket pardon from Gerald R. Ford, his second vice president, Nixon retired to California, later moving to New Jersey. He dedicated the remainder of his life to unsullying his name, while becoming a foreign policy adviser to presidents until his death at the age of 81 in 1994.

38. Gerald R. Ford (1974–77)

The only vice president and president never elected to either office, Gerald Rudolph Ford was born in Omaha, Nebraska, on July 14, 1913. An Eagle Scout, he grew up in Michigan and attended the University of Michigan on a football scholarship, playing on the national championship teams of 1932 and 1933. After graduating in 1935, Ford coached football and boxing at Yale while attending law school. In the navy he earned 10 battle stars in the Pacific during World War II. Ford was elected to Congress in 1948 as a Republican. He would be reelected 12 times, never by less than 60 percent. His solid conservative record elevated him to House Republican minority leader by 1965. For supporting Richard M. Nixon, Ford was rewarded with the vice presidency in December 1973, replacing Spiro T. Agnew under the 25th Amendment. Nixon's resignation made Ford the new president on Aug. 9, 1974. When asked at his confirmation hearings if he would ever pardon Nixon, Ford said, "I do not think the public would stand for it." After his inauguration, Ford announced "our long national nightmare is over," but a month later he shocked the nation by giving Nixon a blanket pardon. Ford denied that a deal had been made, but his public standing never recovered. He struggled with huge Democratic majorities in Congress to stem soaring inflation and unemployment, casting 66 vetoes in all. Ford oversaw the final withdrawal from Vietnam and, in the Mayaguez incident, he sent the marines to rescue 39 Americans captured by Cambodia.

Breaking a 1973 pledge, Ford decided to seek reelection, and while campaigning, he survived two assassination attempts by California women. Ford carried four more states than Jimmy Carter in the election but lost by 57 electoral votes. After his defeat, Ford remained involved with Republican politics and advocated for public policy issues including gay rights almost until his death on Dec. 26, 2006 at the age of 93.

39. Jimmy Carter (1977–81)

James Earl Carter, the first deep-southerner elected president in 128 years, was born in Plains, Georgia, on Oct. 1, 1924. He grew up on a farm with no plumbing or electricity but realized his dream of attending the U.S. Naval Academy. Carter graduated in 1946 and married Rosalynn Smith. He joined the submarine fleet and studied nuclear physics, leaving the Navy in 1953 to run the family peanut business. He was elected to the Georgia state senate in 1962. Defeated for governor in 1966, Carter campaigned constantly for the next four years, winning on his second try in 1970. Carter reorganized the government and hired more blacks, declaring that the "time for racial discrimination is over." A month before leaving office in 1974, Carter was the first Democrat to announce his candidacy for president in 1976, again campaigning constantly. "Jimmy Who?" burst into headlines by winning narrow pluralities over nine rivals in early primaries. Carter's grinning, homespun style and earnest vows of honesty ("I will never lie to you") struck a chord with voters after Watergate. Carter won the nomination and defeated incumbent Gerald R. Ford by 2 percent of the vote. Lack of Washington connections helped his candidacy but not his presidency, for Carter never shook his image as the provincial amateur. Democratic majorities in Congress ignored Carter's pleas for tax reform and a long-range energy policy. Transportation deregulation, environmental protection, and new departments of energy and education were Carter's main domestic achievements.

But as federal spending mounted and oil prices doubled, most Americans blamed Carter for runaway inflation. His 20 percent approval rating in August 1979 was the lowest ever recorded. In foreign affairs Carter obtained a Panama Canal treaty, normalized relations with China, and mediated the Camp David peace accords between Israel and Egypt. He moved toward closer relations with the Soviet Union, signing the SALT II treaty in 1979, but the Soviet invasion of Afghanistan led Carter to embargo grain sales to the USSR and to order a boycott of the 1980 Moscow Olympics. The Carter Doctrine announced the United States would defend the Persian Gulf, where ironically, Carter soon met his downfall in the Iran hostage crisis. Early public support for Carter's restraint gradually withered under the glare of relentless media coverage. Carter himself became a hostage of Iran, trapped in the White House as Edward Kennedy nearly deprived him of the Democratic nomination. In April 1980, Carter approved a military rescue mission whose tragic failure reinforced his image of incompetence and weakness, which Republican candidate Ronald Reagan exploited, winning the election in a landslide. Carter left the White House discredited, his informal style ridiculed as inappropriate. However, in later years he won recognition as a trustworthy international negotiator and he was awarded the Nobel Peace Prize in 2002.

40. Ronald Reagan (1981–89)

Ronald Wilson Reagan was born in Tampico, Illinois, on Feb. 6, 1911. Reagan was a radio sports announcer when he made his first movie in 1937. Over 50 more films would follow in Reagan's prolific Hollywood career. In 1940 he married actress Jane Wyman, who divorced him in 1948. During World War II, Reagan made propaganda films for the U.S. Army, and after the war he became president of the Screen Actors Guild. Then a Democrat, Reagan assailed Communists in Hollywood. He married Nancy Davis, another actress, in 1952. As his movie career waned, Reagan espoused conservative causes, switching to the Republican party in 1960. Reagan made a dramatic speech at the end of the 1964 campaign, and despite his total lack of experience he was elected governor of California in 1966. As governor, Reagan broke all promises by raising taxes, increasing spending, and expanding the state government—yet he easily won reelection in 1970. He made unsuccessful runs for the Republican presidential nomination in 1968 and 1976 before winning it in 1980. He swept past Jimmy Carter in the crushing "Reagan Revolution" of 1980, carrying 44 states and making huge Republican gains in Congress.

"Reaganomics" promised to cut taxes and social spending while vastly increasing the defense budget and somehow balancing the budget. Congress was unmoved until Mar. 20, 1981, when a crazed youth named John Hinckley shot Reagan twice in the chest. Reagan's good humor and rapid recovery charmed Americans—especially the press, which had questioned his age and health. Reagan then prevailed over Congress to pass mammoth tax cuts. The national debt began its meteoric rise under Reagan as increases in defense spending outweighed cuts in social programs. By 1986 the U.S. had become a net borrower for the first time since World War I, but falling oil prices slowed inflation and rekindled economic growth, for which Reagan took credit. Calling the Soviet Union an "evil empire," Reagan built up the armed forces, deployed U.S. nuclear missiles in Europe, and began the Strategic Defense Initiative. He sent U.S. Marines to Lebanon, where 240 of them died in a terrorist attack. To halt the spread of communism, Reagan ordered the invasion of Grenada and isolated the Sandinista government of Nicaragua. Reelected in 1984, with the economy booming and his public esteem high, Reagan seemed headed for an even more successful second term. He ordered bombing raids on Libya and met with Soviet leader Mikhail Gorbachev, eventually producing historic arms control agreements. But in 1987 Reagan's invincible popularity finally succumbed to the Iran-Contra scandal: White House staff had secretly sold arms to Iran in hopes of freeing American hostages held in Lebanon, using the profits illegally to fund Contra fighters in Nicaragua. Many top Reagan aides had to resign, but more damaging was the president's apparent loss of control over his own administration.

As the Iran-Contra trials continued in 1990, Reagan was ordered to testify under oath about his role in the scandal; he responded 130 times with "I don't recall" or "I don't remember." In 1995, he revealed he was suffering from Alzheimer's disease, to which he succumbed in 2004.

41. George H. Bush (1989-93)

The first sitting vice president elected president in over 150 years, George Herbert Walker Bush was born in Milton, Massachusetts, on June 12, 1924. His father was former U.S. Senator Prescott Sheldon Bush (R-Conn., 1952-63) As a Navy pilot during World War II, Bush was shot down over the Pacific and rescued at sea. He married Barbara Pierce, a Smith College student, on Jan. 6, 1945, and graduated Phi Beta Kappa in economics from Yale in 1948. Bush spurned an offer from his millionaire father's Wall Street firm to pursue a career in the Texas oil fields that eventually made him a millionaire in his own right.

Running on a conservative anti-Communist and anti-civil rights platform, Bush won the Republican nomination for Senate in 1964 and again in 1970, but lost the general election both times. In between, he was elected to Congress from a wealthy suburban Houston district. Presidents Richard Nixon and Gerald Ford rewarded the Republican party loyalist with appointed offices, including U.S. ambassador to the United Nations (1971), chairman of the Republican National Committee (1973), and director of the C.I.A. (1976). After losing the Republican presidential nomination to Ronald Reagan in 1980, Bush accepted Reagan's offer to join him on the winning ticket.

One of the few members of Reagan's staff to emerge unscathed by the Iran-Contra affair, Bush bested Bob Dole for the Republican nomination in 1988. With Reagan's endorsement, Bush defeated Massachusetts governor Michael S. Dukakis, renewing the Reagan pledge of "no new taxes" and vowing to uphold the Reagan legacy of less government, strong defense, and family values. He declared war on "this scourge" of drugs by creating an office of National Drug Control Policy within the White House. Bush's first official act was to proclaim January 20 as the "National Day of Prayer."

Bush suffered early criticism for lack of leadership, but struck back with major initiatives, including major arms control proposals and two summit meetings with Soviet premier Mikhail Gorbachev. In December 1989, Bush ordered the invasion of Panama, he said, to protect U.S. citizens and overthrow the regime of Gen. Manuel Noriega.

As one eastern bloc country after another opted for democracy in 1989 and 1990, Bush enjoyed the highest public approval rating of any postwar president. This popularity gave him the political leverage to renege on his campaign pledge of "no new taxes." His popularity rose to record levels when he ordered Operation Desert Storm to liberate Kuwait from Iraqi occupation. But it later became apparent that Bush had ordered a cease-fire much too early, allowing Saddam Hussein to retain power in Iraq.

Throughout 1991, as the Soviet Union was crumbling, Bush acted quickly and decisively to support those republics seeking independence and to provide food and medical supplies where needed. He and Gorbachev declared an end to the arms race by signing the first nuclear arms reduction pact in July.

Bush had less success on the domestic front. In spring of 1992, his approval rating dipped below 40 percent, reflecting the deepening economic recession that drove unemployment levels to their highest level in a decade. Bush was challenged first in the primaries and then in the general election by opponents who made the economy the central issue of their campaigns. But unable to get the economy on course, Bush lost to Bill Clinton in a three-way race that saw independent candidate Ross Perot capture nearly 20 percent of the vote. It marked only the 10th time that an incumbent president had been unseated.

42. Bill Clinton (1993-2001)

William Jefferson Clinton was born in tiny Hope, Arkansas, on Aug. 19, 1946. His father, William Jefferson Blythe 3d, was killed before his son was born, leaving his wife, Virginia, to raise their son alone. Four years later, she married Roger Clinton; Bill assumed his stepfather's surname. After graduating from Georgetown University, Bill Clinton went to Oxford University on a Rhodes scholarship and then to Yale Law School, where he met Hillary Rodham, whom he married in 1973.

Clinton was elected Arkansas attorney general in 1976, and two years later became the nation's youngest governor. In 1980 he lost, a victim of the Reagan Republican landslide. But in 1982, Clinton won his old job back, and over the next decade helped Arkansas to transform its economy. He became a leading figure among the so-called New Democrats, who called for welfare reform, smaller government, and other Reagan-like ideas.

In 1992, Clinton emerged as a shaky frontrunner among six Democratic hopefuls for the presidential nomination. Allegations that he had extramarital affairs, dodged the draft during the Vietnam War, and smoked marijuana threatened to derail his campaign. But as the candidate with the most money and the best-articulated campaign strategy—creating more jobs—Clinton was able to stay in the race the longest, fending off all rivals long before the Democratic convention.

In a three-way race against the incumbent George Bush and the billionaire populist Ross Perot, who ran as an independent, Clinton garnered 366 of the 538 electoral votes, despite winning only 43 percent of the popular vote.

Clinton entered office hoping that a Democratic president and a Democratic Congress could untangle the gridlock that had paralyzed Washington for 12 years. But his first act as president, a pledge to end the ban on lesbians and gay men in the armed forces, met with heavy resistance from top military leaders. And his economic stimulus package fell to defeat in the face of a remarkable Republican filibuster in the Senate.

During his second 100 days, he signed the family leave bill, lifted restrictions on abortion counseling at federally funded clinics, and laid the groundwork for the North American Free Trade Agreement. The passage of his first budget—with Vice Pres. Al Gore casting the deciding vote in the Senate—started the nation on the road to recovery from the burden of the enormous deficits created by the Reagan and Bush administrations. In the ensuing economic prosperity, the 5 to 8 percent increase on the tax rates of the wealthiest Americans as well as a surge in capital gains taxes from the booming stock markets generated so much income for the Treasury that deficits turned to surpluses by 1998.

Clinton had several early successes on the foreign policy front, assuring the stability of Russia's government, and negotiating a peace treaty between Israel and the P.L.O. that recognized Palestinian self-rule in Gaza and part of the West Bank.

On the domestic front, however, Clinton found little support for his programs. A complex plan (devised by a committee headed by First Lady Hillary Rodham Clinton) called for guaranteed health coverage to all Americans. But it also promised a huge government bureaucracy that opponents claimed would be less efficient than the post office. The plan was never adopted.

In the 1994 midterm elections, the G.O.P. captured both Houses of Congress for the first time in more than 40 years. New House Speaker Newt Gingrich proclaimed a Republican revolution. In 1995 Republicans in Congress also opened hearings on the Clintons' controversial investment in a land deal known as Whitewater.

As he prepared for a second term, Clinton's approval ratings rebounded. He took centrist positions on issues like abortion and affirmative action, and signed the Republican welfare bill that ended 60-year-old guarantees for poor people. With the stock market soaring, unemployment falling, and inflation firmly in check, Clinton won re-election in 1996 almost effortlessly against Senator Bob Dole.

During Clinton's second term, the Whitewater scandal came back to haunt him in an unexpected way. Failing to uncover anything directly implicating the President or Mrs. Clinton in connection with the land deal, independent counsel Kenneth Starr expanded his inquiry far beyond its original scope and unearthed evidence of an affair between Clinton and a young White House intern, Monica Lewinsky. Clinton emphatically denied the allegation, and then, as the first sitting president ever subpoenaed to testify before a federal grand jury, he lied under oath about the affair. Clinton later admitted that he had had an "inappropriate" relationship with Ms. Lewinsky.

The Republican-controlled House approved two articles of impeachment against Clinton, making him the first president impeached since Andrew Johnson in 1868. The month-long Senate trial was filled with legal wrangling on all sides, but in the end, not even a simple majority could be mustered for either impeachment article.

The day after his acquittal, Clinton sent 4,000 troops to Kosovo as part of a NATO peacekeeping force. After 72 days of air strikes, Serbian Pres. Slobodan Milosevic agreed to withdraw all military forces from Kosovo. On the domestic front, Clinton and the Republican Congress battled over how to spend the first budget surplus since 1969, resulting in a stalemate although some of the money went to paying down the national debt.

Clinton spent much of his final year on a global "farewell tour" trying to shore up his legacy. He successfully shepherded a bill through Congress granting China permanent trade status, but was unable to broker a lasting peace in the Middle East.

43. George W. Bush (2001–2008)

The election of George Walker Bush in 2000 was unusual in several ways. Like John Quincy Adams, the only other son of a president to win the White House, Bush lost the popular vote and, in an unprecedented ruling, the U.S. Supreme Court intervened in the election process, effectively giving him the presidency.

Bush was born on July 6, 1946 in New Haven, Connecticut. His family moved to Texas when he was nearly 2, but in the family tradition, he went back east for prep school (at the exclusive Phillips Andover), and then to Yale University, where he had an undistinguished academic career.

In 1968, at the height of the Vietnam War, Bush entered the Texas National Guard and spent two years learning to fly. His sudden departure from that unit has never been fully explained. In 1973 he attended Harvard Business School, received an M.B.A. in 1975, and returned to Texas to enter the oil business.

After marrying Laura Welch in 1977, he made his first bid for public office, a 1978 campaign for a Congressional seat, which ended in defeat. After the campaign, Bush returned to his oil business, amassing a great personal fortune even though his business steadily lost money. Meanwhile Bush's parents set up a 1985 meeting with evangelist Billy Graham, which ultimately led the younger Bush to give up alcohol and devote himself to a more serious practice of Christianity. In 1989, he joined a family friend in purchasing the Texas Rangers baseball team.

In 1994, Bush challenged Ann Richards, the popular incumbent governor of Texas. Despite his lack of political experience, Bush's downhome style won him the office. Four years later, he became the first Texas governor elected to a second consecutive four-year term. That same year, he and his partners sold the Rangers, with the governor realizing a profit of more than $14 million.

Advisers convinced him that 2000 was the right time to run for president. Before he had even committed to the race, he was the clear favorite in the polls and huge sums of money flowed into his campaign treasury from corporations and wealthy Republicans. Bush lost the New Hampshire primary in a bruising, bitter fight with Senator John McCain of Arizona, but he rebounded to capture 9 of 13 Super Tuesday states, effectively clinching the nomination.

In the general election Bush and Vice Pres. Al Gore both tried to appeal to moderate voters, Bush calling himself a "compassionate conservative," and although Gore unquestionably won the national popular vote, Florida (with its 25 votes in the Electoral College) held the key to the election. After two recounts and the counting of absentee ballots, Bush led in Florida by fewer than 1,000 votes out of six million cast, but allegations of confusing ballots, defective voting machines, faulty absentee ballots from the military, and illegal barring of many voters threw the process into chaos. The race ended on December 12, when the U.S. Supreme Court ordered an end to the recounts, delivering Florida and the White House to Bush.

On his first day in office, Bush moved to block federal aid to foreign groups that offered counseling or any other assistance to women in obtaining abortions. Days later, he announced his commitment to channeling more federal aid to faith-based service organizations. He angered environmentalists, first reneging on a campaign pledge to regulate carbon dioxide emissions by U.S. power plants, then refusing to join the Kyoto accord to prevent global warming, and finally pursuing an energy policy short on conservation and long on drilling for oil and gas.

The terrorist attacks of September 11th, 2001 transformed the Bush presidency. Bush persuaded Congress to give him "all necessary and appropriate force" to respond to the terrorist attacks. He vowed a U.S. military response that would demolish terrorist networks worldwide, and promised to "end" nations that harbored terrorists. Since Afghanistan was known to be bin Laden's chief sponsor, in late October of 2001 the U.S. mounted an invasion. The attack routed the Taliban in less than three months. Bush's popularity ratings rose above 80 percent.

After initially opposing a separate Dept. of Homeland Security as proposed by the Democrats, Bush eventually approved it, creating an enormous new government agency with more than 170,000 employees. Bush also approved the Patriot Act amid overwhelming congressional approval, though civil libertarians strongly criticized it for giving the Justice Dept. unprecedented powers in conducting investigations.

In his Jan. 2002 State of the Union address, Bush shocked the international community by identifying Iran, Iraq and North Korea as "an axis of evil" that threatened the world, even though he offered no evidence that they were involved in the Sept. 11th attacks. Over the next year the administration redefined two centuries of official U.S. policy by declaring it had the right to preemptively attack any nation that posed a threat to its security. Iraq became the first target of that doctrine and by the summer of 2002 Bush was urging the U.N. Security Council to approve military action to remove Saddam Hussein because he was building weapons of mass destruction.

Over the next six months U.N. weapons inspectors sought out these weapons but found none and the U.N. proposed a continuation of inspections. Bush refused and on March 20, 2003 he ordered the world's most powerful military machine to launch a devastating attack. After only three weeks the U.S., with some help from Great Britain, toppled the regime but was now left alone to rebuild a devastated country.

Within months, Bush's approval ratings began to plummet. No weapons of mass destruction were found, evidence showed that the intelligence data had been grossly exaggerated, and U.S. casualties continued to mount even though major combat operations were completed in April of 2003. In spring, 2004, support for the war dropped even more as graphic photos were released showing U.S. soldiers torturing Iraqi detainees at Abu Ghraib prison. Added to this blow of America's deteriorating image was the outcry against the more than 700 Muslim detainees being held at Guantanamo Bay in Cuba, most of them never charged and many subjected to interrogation under harsh conditions.

Domestically, Bush continued to press for deep tax cuts at the highest income levels as a way to stimulate a sluggish economy. As a result, after four years of record budget surpluses under Bill Clinton, the Bush administration ran unprecedented deficits of more than $300 billion annually.

Despite these liabilities Bush was able to win the 2004 election by a small but unchallengable margin against John Kerry, the Democratic candidate and senator from Massachusetts. Kerry was a decorated hero in the Vietnam War while Bush used his family's influence to stay in Texas in the Air National Guard, but polls showed that the president had convinced the people he and his administration would be better able to protect the nation from another terrorist attack. Within a few months of the election, however, as a vicious insurgency in Iraq took an increasing number of U.S. lives (over 1,800 dead, 12,000 seriously wounded) Bush's poll numbers slid below 50 percent by the spring of 2005, and headed toward 40 percent by the summer. Several prominent Republicans in congress began to speak out publicly against the way the war was being managed. On the domestic side Bush's ideas for radically reforming Social Security found few supporters while pork-laden energy and transportation bills gave the lie to stated Republican ideals of fiscal responsibility and small government.

The president suffered another serious blow when a powerful category 5 hurricane called Katrina slammed into the Gulf Coast region, wreaking havoc on parts of Mississippi, Alabama and Louisiana on August 28, 2005. New Orleans was nearly destroyed when two levees on Lake Pontchartrain collapsed, flooding large areas of the city. Hundreds died, tens of thousands were left homeless, and the city's infrastructure was destroyed. The federal government's response was slow and abysmally inefficient. Bush seemed unconcerned but Americans could not fail to notice that hundreds of billions of dollars were going to rebuild Iraq while New Orleans was left to struggle.

But it was the war in Iraq that continued to gnaw away at Bush's standing as he continued throughout 2005–06 to insist the war would be won. Even after huge numbers of Iraqis voted in elections and a constitution was approved, nearly 60 percent of Americans thought the war was a mistake. As congressional elections approached in Nov. 2006 many Republicans were distancing themselves from Bush's position as a vicious insurgency threatened to lead Iraq into civil war. U.S. casualties rose to over 3,000 dead and 20,000 seriously wounded and little or no progress was evident.

The Democrats took control of both houses of Congress in Jan. 2006 and immediately demanded that U.S. troops start to withdraw from Iraq. Bush refused to accept this idea, instead ordering tens of thousands of more troops to quell the growing violence. In 2008, the death toll reached 4,000 with 30,000 wounded. The so-called "surge" in the number of U.S. troops had a positive effect, as did the enlisting of Sunni militias who were paid goodly sums to fight and to reduce sectarian violence. Americans remained confused about the war, for despite dramatically reduced violence, polls still revealed that a large majority of Americans viewed the war as a mistake. Near the end of his term, Bush's approval ratings remained below 30 percent and seemed likely to fall further as the financial system seized up, the economy slowed significantly and oil prices passed $100 a barrel.

Presidential Elections, 1796–2004

George Washington of Virginia ran unopposed for president in 1789 and 1792. He received 69 and 132 electoral votes in those years, respectively. John Adams of Massachusetts was elected vice president in both years, receiving 34 and 77 electoral votes.

1796

Party	Candidate	Popular vote	Percent	Electoral vote
Federalist	John Adams (Mass.)	N.A.	N.A.	71
	and Thomas Pinckney (S.C.)	N.A.	N.A.	59
Democratic-	Thomas Jefferson (Va.)	N.A.	N.A.	68
Republican	and Aaron Burr (N.Y.)	N.A.	N.A.	30

Key Issues Washington set a precedent by refusing to run for a third term. Though the Founders hoped to avoid parties, factions developed around Hamilton and Jefferson during Washington's first term. Hamilton's Federalists supported a strong central government that would play a major role in the national economy and represent the commercial interests of the north. Jefferson's Republicans advocated states' rights and the agrarian interests of the south. Regional Influences Though led by Hamilton, the Federalists nominated the more moderate Adams. Jefferson's strength in the south was balanced by Adams's power in the north. Eleven Federalist electors in New Hampshire failed to vote for Pinckney, their party's vice-presidential nominee, giving the position to Jefferson.

1800

Party	Candidate	Popular vote	Percent	Electoral vote
Democratic-	Thomas Jefferson (Va.)	N.A.	N.A.	73
Republican	and Aaron Burr (N.Y.)	N.A.	N.A.	73
Federalist	John Adams (Mass.)	N.A.	N.A.	65
	and Charles C. Pinckney (S.C.)	N.A.	N.A.	64
Federalist	John Jay (N.Y.)	N.A.	N.A.	1

Key Issues Adams divided the Federalists by keeping the U.S. out of war with France over seizures of American ships by the French. In the meantime the Republicans under Jefferson organized nationally. They accused the Federalists of aristocratic and monarchical leanings, citing large taxes levied to maintain a standing army and navy, the Alien and Sedition Acts seeking to silence the administration's critics, and suppression of the Whiskey Rebellion. Regional Influences The Republicans again carried the South, but also won New York through the efforts of vice-presidential nominee Burr. The election was thrown into the House when Jefferson and Burr received an equal number of electoral votes. With Hamilton's support, Jefferson won the election in the Federalist-dominated House.

1804

Party	Candidate	Popular vote	Percent	Electoral vote
Democratic-	Thomas Jefferson (Va.)	N.A.	N.A.	162
Republican	and George Clinton (N.Y.)	N.A.	N.A.	162
Federalist	Charles C. Pinckney (S.C.)	N.A.	N.A.	14
	and Rufus King (N.Y.)	N.A.	N.A.	14

Key Issues In 1804 Vice President Burr, a northern Republican, joined with a group of northeastern Federalists in a plot to unite New York and New England in a separate nation. The plot was exposed, discrediting the Federalists. Jefferson, already popular for his personal qualities as well as the Louisiana Purchase, swept to an easy victory. Regional Influences Jefferson lost only three states, and even swept all of New England with the exception of Connecticut.

1808

Party	Candidate	Popular vote	Percent	Electoral vote[1]
Democratic-	James Madison (Va.)	N.A.	N.A.	122
Republican	and George Clinton (N.Y.)	N.A.	N.A.	113
Federalist	Charles C. Pinckney (S.C.)	N.A.	N.A.	47
	and Rufus King (N.Y.)	N.A.	N.A.	47

Key Issues Jefferson reinforced the two-term precedent by refusing to run for a third term. Madison, his chosen successor, easily won the Republican nomination and the presidency. Regional Influences Pinckney and the Federalists regained most of the New England votes lost four years earlier and increased their strength in Congress due to commercial opposition to the embargo imposed by Jefferson on the export of American goods to warring European nations.

[1]Clinton received six electoral votes for president. Madison and James Monroe of Virginia both received three electoral votes for vice-president.

1812

Party	Candidate	Popular vote	Percent	Electoral vote
Democratic-	James Madison (Va.)	N.A.	N.A.	128
Republican	and Elbridge Gerry (Mass.)	N.A.	N.A.	131
Federalist	DeWitt Clinton (N.Y.)	N.A.	N.A.	89
	and Jared Ingersoll (Pa.)	N.A.	N.A.	86

Key Issues The election was a referendum on Madison's bid for a declaration of war against Great Britain in response to Britain's attempts to block the sale of southern raw materials in European markets. A vote for Madison was a vote for war, a vote for Clinton a vote for peace. Regional Influences Commercial interests in the northeast opposed war with Great Britain. The original 13 states were evenly split in the election, favoring Madison 90-09. New England, except Vermont, voted for Clinton, as did a majority of the Middle Atlantic states. The South voted unanimously for Madison. But all of the western states voted for Madison and thus for war.

1816

Party	Candidate	Popular vote	Percent	Electoral vote
Democratic-	James Monroe (Va.)	N.A.	N.A.	183
Republican	and D. D. Tompkins (N.Y.)	N.A.	N.A.	183
Federalist	Rufus King (N.Y.)	N.A.	N.A.	34
	and John E. Howard (Md.)	N.A.	N.A.	22

Key Issues Nationalism triumphed after the war with Britain, a time of national and economic growth that saw establishment of an expanded standing army, central bank, Federal tariff and large internal improvements despite opposition from northeastern Federalists. Regional Influences Monroe, Madison's chosen successor, won a landslide victory that seemed to validate Madison's nationalistic program, which called for a stronger standing army, a protective tariff, uniform currency and a nationwide system of roads and canals, including the Cumberland Road. The Federalists won only three states, all in New England.

1820

Party	Candidate	Popular vote	Percent	Electoral vote
Democratic-	James Monroe (Va.)	N.A.	N.A.	231
Republican	and D.D. Tompkins (N.Y.)	N.A.	N.A.	218
Democratic-	John Q. Adams (Mass.)	N.A.	N.A.	1
Republican				

Key Issues The election was held at the height of the "Era of Good Feelings," though sectional differences over slavery earlier in the year led to the Missouri Compromise, which in its final version resulted in the admittance of Missouri as a slave state with the provision that it allow free Negroes of other states to retain their freedom while in Missouri. The Federalists ceased to exist as a functioning party by the time of the election and failed to run a candidate against Monroe. **Regional Influences** Monroe ran unopposed for reelection. One elector from New Hampshire voted for Adams so that only Washington would hold the honor of being elected to the presidency by a unanimous vote.

1824

Party	Candidate	Popular vote	Percent	Electoral vote
Democratic-Republican	John Q. Adams (Mass.)	113,122	30.92	84
Democratic-Republican	Andrew Jackson (Tenn.)	151,271	41.34	99
Democratic-Republican	William H. Crawford (Ga.)	40,876	11.17	41
Democratic-Republican	Henry Clay (Ky.)	47,531	12.99	37
Other		13,053	3.57	—
	Total Vote	365,833		
	Jackson Plurality	38,149		

Key Issues Personalities dominated an election in which all four candidates ran as Democratic-Republicans. Crawford, Monroe's treasury secretary, won the nomination of the party's congressional caucus. But few attended the caucus and most electors were chosen by state legislatures. Crawford later suffered a stroke and was not a serious candidate. John C. Calhoun of South Carolina ran unopposed for vice president. **Regional Influences** Each candidate represented his region: Adams the commercial northeast, Crawford the cotton south, Clay and Jackson the agrarian west. Jackson, a hero of the War of 1812 and battles against Indians, won a clear plurality of the popular vote and was the only candidate with support outside his home region. But no candidate won a majority of the electoral vote and the election was decided in the House, where Speaker Clay's support gave the victory to Adams.

1828

Party	Candidate	Popular vote	Percent	Electoral vote
Democratic-Republican	Andrew Jackson (Tenn.) and John C. Calhoun (S.C.)	642,553	55.97	178 / 171
National-Republican	John Q. Adams (Mass.) and Richard Rush (Pa.)	500,987	43.63	83 / 83
Other		4,568	0.40	—
	Total Vote	1,148,018		
	Jackson Plurality	141,656		

Key Issues Personalities again overshadowed issues. The Jackson campaign catered to popular prejudices, portraying the contest as one between democracy and aristocracy. The Jackson coalition was a forerunner of the modern Democratic Party and reestablished two-party politics in the U.S. **Regional Influences** Jackson won the south and west easily, and appealed to discontented laborers in the north. Adams carried only New England, New Jersey, Maryland and Delaware.

1832

Party	Candidate	Popular vote	Percent	Electoral vote
Democrat	Andrew Jackson (Tenn.) and Martin Van Buren (N.Y.)	701,780	54.23	219 / 189
National-Republican	Henry Clay (Ky.) and John Sergeant (Pa.)	484,205	37.42	49 / 49
Anti-Masonic	William Wirt (Md.) and Amos Ellmaker (Pa.)	100,715	7.78	7 / 7
Independent	John Floyd (Va.) and Henry Lee (Mass.)	—	—	11 / 11
Other		7,273	0.56	—
	Total Vote	1,293,973		
	Jackson Plurality	217,575		

Key Issues The Anti-Masons, the first third-party in American politics, began in opposition to secret societies in particular and privileged groups in general, but were at heart an anti-Jackson party. The two established parties followed the Anti-Masons lead by holding national nominating conventions to select a presidential nominee. While Jackson's opposition to the Bank of the United States was made an issue by the two major par-

ties, the election was more a referendum on Jackson himself. **Regional Influences** Anti-Masonic strength was concentrated in rural sections of New England and the Middle Atlantic states. In those states National-Republicans and Anti-Masons supported the same ticket. With the forces against him divided, Jackson won easily. Clay won only half of the New England states, Wirt won only Vermont. Jackson captured Maine and New Hampshire. In South Carolina, where electors still were chosen by the legislature, nullificationists cast their ballots for Floyd.

1836

Party	Candidate	Popular vote	Percent	Electoral vote
Democrat	Martin Van Buren (N.Y.) and Richard M. Johnson (Ky.)	764,716	50.83	170 / 147
Whig	William Henry Harrison (Ohio)	550,816	36.63	73
Whig	Hugh L. White (Tenn.)	146,107	9.72	26
Whig	Daniel Webster (Mass.)	41,201	2.74	14
	Willie P. Mangum (N.C.)	—	—	11
Other		1,234	0.08	—
	Total Vote	1,503,534		
	Van Buren Plurality	213,360		

Key Issues Jackson's heavy-handed tactics, especially in his successful battle against the national bank, led the National-Republicans to rename themselves Whigs, after the 18th-century British party that tried to lessen the power of the crown. But lacking effective national leadership and divided along sectional lines, the anti-Jackson forces could not agree on a single candidate or platform and instead ran three regional candidates. **Regional Influences** Whig strategy was to throw the election into the House, where they could unite around a single candidate. Webster was to win New England, Harrison the west and Lawson the south. Van Buren, forced on the Democrats by Jackson, foiled the plan by picking up enough states throughout the nation to win by a slim majority. Johnson fell one electoral vote short of a majority for vice president and was selected by the Senate. The South Carolina legislature cast its votes for Mangum.

1840

Party	Candidate	Popular vote	Percent	Electoral vote
Whig	William Henry Harrison (Ohio) and John Tyler (Va.)	1,275,390	52.88	234
Democrat	Martin Van Buren (N.Y.)	1,128,854	46.81	60
Liberty	James G. Birney (N.Y.)	6,797	0.28	—
Other		767	0.03	—
	Total Vote	2,411,808		
	Harrison Plurality	146,536		

Key Issues With the country still reeling from the Panic of 1837, the Democrats were on the defensive. Though differences prevented them from writing a platform, the Whigs rallied around Harrison. In a campaign notable for its absence of issues, the Whigs turned the tables on Jackson's party. Harrison, despite his wealthy origins, was portrayed as the "log-cabin, hard-cider candidate" opposing the allegedly aristocratic Van Buren. The Democrats left the selection of a vice-presidential candidate to each state. **Regional Influences** Van Buren won only seven states, just one outside of the south or west. Harrison was long associated with the west and Tyler was a conservative Southerner and friend of Henry Clay. For the first time, active two-party politics was established across the nation. The 68-year-old Harrison caught a severe cold after delivering a lengthy Inaugural Address in the rain and died one month into his term.

1844

Party	Candidate	Popular vote	Percent	Electoral vote
Democrat	James K. Polk (Tenn.) and George M. Dallas (Pa.)	1,339,494	49.54	170
Whig	Henry Clay (Ky.) and Theodore Frelinghuysen (N.J.)	1,300,004	48.08	105
Abolitionist	James G. Birney (N.Y.)	62,103	2.30	—
Other		2,058	0.08	—
	Total Vote	2,703,659		
	Polk Plurality	39,490		

Key Issues Manifest Destiny, the goal of a U.S. stretching from the Atlantic to the Pacific, was the central issue because of the question of the annexation of Texas. With the election approaching, opponents of slavery lead the Senate to reject a treaty between Texas and the Tyler Administration that would have preserved Texan slavery and made it a U.S. territory. The two leading presidential candidates, Clay and Van Buren, sought to smother the Texas issue by ignoring it. But Polk snatched the Democratic nomination with his clear and vocal advocacy of annexation of Texas and general territorial expansion. **Regional Influences** Expansionism was immensely popular, especially in the south and west, where memories of the depression following 1837 added to the attraction of new, vast, and open public lands. Support for manifest destiny more than made up for anti-slavery sentiment elsewhere and Polk won a narrow plurality but a clear victory.

1848

Party	Candidate	Popular vote	Per- cent	Elec- toral vote
Whig	Zachary Taylor (La.) and Millard Fillmore (N.Y.)	1,361,393	47.28	163
Democrat	Lewis Cass (Mich.) and William O. Butler (Ky.)	1,223,460	42.49	127
Free Soil	Martin Van Buren (N.Y.) and Charles Francis Adams (Mass.)	291,501	10.12	—
Other		2,830	0.10	—
	Total Vote	2,879,184		
	Taylor Plurality	137,933		

Key Issues The Wilmot Proviso, calling for a ban on extension of slavery into territories acquired in the Mexican War, dominated the election. But both major parties evaded the issue. Slavery foes banded together to form the Free Soil Party, which won no electoral votes but drew enough popular support away from the Democrats to throw the election to "Old Rough and Ready," Zachary Taylor, a slave-holder. Taylor died in July 1850. **Regional Influences** Both major parties balanced their tickets with a Northerner and Southerner. Free Soilers were mostly Northern Democrats, anti-slavery Whigs and abolitionists. There was no distinct pattern in the Electoral College following a lackluster campaign. Free Soil strength in New York gave the state and the election to the Whigs.

1852

Party	Candidate	Popular vote	Per- cent	Elec- toral vote
Democrat	Franklin Pierce (N.H.) and William R. D. King (Ala.)	1,607,510	50.84	254
Whig	Winfield Scott (Va.) and William A. Graham (N.C.)	1,386,942	43.87	42
Free Soil	John P. Hale (N.H.) and George Washington Julian (Ind.)	155,210	4.91	—
Other		12,168	0.38	—
	Total Vote	3,161,830		
	Pierce Plurality	220,568		

Key Issues The election was a referendum on the Compromise of 1850, in which Congress voted to admit California as a free state, create the territories of New Mexico and Utah with no restriction on slavery, abolish the slave trade in the District of Columbia, purchase disputed land from Texas on behalf of New Mexico, and toughen the Fugitive Slave Act. The Democrats strongly endorsed the Compromise, but the bitterly divided Whigs only vaguely accepted it. **Regional Influences** The Democrats won a resounding electoral victory, capturing 27 states to the four taken by the Whigs: Massachusetts, Vermont, Kentucky and Tennessee. Free Soilers returned to the Democrats and the Whigs never again were a political force in a nation which believed the slave question was behind it.

1856

Party	Candidate	Popular vote	Per- cent	Elec- toral vote
Democrat	James Buchanan (Pa.) and John C. Breckinridge (Ky.)	1,836,072	45.28	174
Republican	John C. Fremont (Calif.) and William L. Dayton (N.J.)	1,342,345	33.11	114
Whig	Millard Fillmore (N.Y.) and Andrew J. Donelson (Tenn.)	873,053	21.53	8
Other		3,177	0.08	—
	Total Vote	4,054,647		
	Buchanan Plurality	493,727		

Key Issues The Democrats firmly endorsed "popular sovereignty" even though it led to great turmoil in the territory of Kansas. But they chose as their nominee Buchanan, largely because he had been out of the country and was untainted by "Bleeding Kansas" battle, which pitted supporters and foes of slavery trying to organize the territory into a slave or free state. The Republicans, a new party of northern Whigs and Democrats committed to the containment of slavery ran Fremont, a popular general and explorer. **Regional Influences** Fremont carried all but five of the free states. But Buchanan won all of the south in addition to the five northern states and was elected. Fillmore, supported by the Know-Nothings and Whig remnants, only won Maryland but strongly challenged the Democrats in the south.

1860

Party	Candidate	Popular vote	Per- cent	Elec- toral vote
Republican	Abraham Lincoln (Ill.) and Hannibal Hamlin (Maine)	1,865,908	39.82	180
Democrat	Stephen A. Douglas (Ill.) and Herschel V. Johnson (Ga.)	1,380,202	29.46	12
Democrat	John C. Breckinridge (Ky.) and Joseph Lane (Oreg.)	848,019	18.09	72
Constitutional Union	John Bell (Tenn.) and Edward Everett (Mass.)	590,901	12.61	39
and Other		531	0.01	—
	Total Vote	4,685,561		
	Lincoln Plurality	485,706		

Key Issues Sectional differences over slavery came to a head in 1860. The Democrats could not agree on a candidate and split into northern and southern factions. The Northerners backed Douglas and popular sovereignty, the Southerners Breckinridge and Federal protection of slavery in the territories. The Republicans, virtually all Northerners, were a pro-tariff, nationalist party that opposed the extension of slavery but did not seek to overturn it where it already existed. Bell, the candidate of Whigs and Know-Nothings who backed Fillmore in 1856, was a compromise candidate expressing support for preservation of the Union. **Regional Influences** In effect there were two separate contests in 1860 Lincoln versus Douglas in the north, Breckinridge versus Bell in the south. Free states outnumbered slave states and cast half again as many electoral votes. Lincoln won every northern state except New Jersey and, though not even on the ballot in 10 southern states, was elected president. Breckinridge captured 11 of the 15 southern states. The four southern states won by Douglas and Bell were in the upper south.

1864

Party	Candidate	Popular vote	Per- cent	Elec- toral vote
Republican	Abraham Lincoln (Ill.) and Andrew Johnson (Tenn.)	2,218,388	55.02	212
Democrat	George B. McClellan (N.Y.) and George H. Pendleton (Ohio)	1,812,807	44.96	21
	Total Vote	4,031,887		
	Lincoln Plurality	405,581		

Key Issues Lincoln's renomination was not assured. Radical Republicans thought he was not aggressive enough in his conduct of the war or plans for the eventual peace, but moderation ultimately prevailed. The Republicans ran as the Union Party and nominated Johnson, a pro-Union Democrat, for vice president. The Democrats ran a peace campaign, calling the war a failure. But McClellan, a popular general, broke with his party's platform and denied the war was a failure, denouncing members of his party who seemed to advocate peace at any price. He opposed emancipation as a goal of the war. **Regional Influences** Military victories around election time helped the embattled incumbent. Lincoln won a convincing popular and electoral victory with the support of middle-class professionals, farmers, laborers and the strongly pro-Union voters who voted for Bell four years earlier. McClellan was strongest in areas carried by Breckinridge four years before. Eleven Confederate states did not participate in the election.

1868

Party	Candidate	Popular vote	Percent	Electoral vote
Republican	Ulysses S. Grant (Ohio) and Schuyler Colfax (Ind.)	3,013,650	52.66	214
Democrat	Horatio S. Seymour (N.Y.) and Francis P. Blair (Mo.)	2,708,744	47.34	80
Other		46	—	—
	Total Vote	5,722,440		
	Grant Plurality	304,906		

Key Issues The Republicans waved the "bloody shirt" of the war and ran on their program of Radical Reconstruction. While calling for Negro suffrage in the south, the Republicans asserted it was a matter for individual northern states to decide for themselves. Democrats ran against Reconstruction, declaring that the question of Negro suffrage should be decided by individual southern states as well. **Regional Influences** Despite Grant's popularity, the Republicans were just able to win the election. Seymour carried only eight states, though he did well in the states won by Grant. Without black votes in the South, Grant would not have received a majority of the popular vote. The votes of the "unreconstructed" states of Mississippi, Texas and Virginia were not counted.

1872

Party	Candidate	Popular vote	Percent	Electoral vote
Republican	Ulysses S. Grant (Ohio) and Henry Wilson (Mass.)	3,598,235	55.63	286
Liberal Republican/ Democrat	Horace Greeley (N.Y.) and Benjamin Gratz Brown (Mo.)	2,834,761	43.83	
Straight Democrat	Charles O'Conor (N.Y.)	18,602	—	
	Other	16,081	0.25	163
	Total Vote	6,467,679		
	Grant Plurality	763,474		

Key Issues Liberal Republicans broke with Grant over corruption in his administration, high tariffs and continued Radical Reconstruction. They nominated Greeley, editor of the *New York Tribune*. The Democrats endorsed Greeley and the Liberal platform. But the great scandals of the Grant administration were not yet revealed and the Republicans again waved the bloody shirt to victory. **Regional Influences** Greeley carried only two states in the lower South and four border states. He died shortly after the election (Nov. 29, 1872) and his electoral votes went to other candidates: Thomas Hendricks, Indiana, 42; Benjamin Gratz Brown, Missouri, 18; Charles J. Jenkins, Georgia, 2; and David Davis, Illinois, 1.

1876

Party	Candidate	Popular vote	Percent	Electoral vote
Republican	Rutherford B. Hayes (Ohio) and William A. Wheeler (N.Y.)	4,034,311	47.95	185
Democrat	Samuel J. Tilden (N.Y.) and Thomas A. Hendricks (Ind.)	4,288,546	50.97	184
Greenback	Peter Cooper (N.Y.)	75,973	0.90	—
Other		14,271	0.17	—
	Total Vote	8,413,101		
	Tilden Plurality	254,235		

Key Issues The Republicans were in trouble as 1876 approached due to rampant corruption in the Grant administration and the economic depression that followed the Panic of 1873. Hayes, a three-term Ohio governor known for his unassailable integrity, was nominated to run against the favored Democrat, Tilden, a New York reform governor whose reputation was made in opposition to the Tweed political machine. Both men espoused conservative economics. Cooper and the Greenbacks advocated currency expansion. **Regional Influences** As Election Day approached, Tilden could count on winning all of the south except for the three states still controlled by Republican carpetbaggers: South Carolina, Louisiana, and Florida. He seemed assured of victory when those states appeared to go for him along with several northern states, including New York and New Jersey. But Republicans claimed South Carolina, Louisiana and Florida for Hayes, arguing that thousands of blacks who would have voted for Hayes were barred from voting there. Election boards in those Republican-controlled states gave Hayes the needed majority, and thus the election. In the uproar that followed Congress set up an Election Commission to validate the returns. The commission voted strictly along party lines, eight to seven, to give the election to Hayes. Despite charges that Republicans stole the election, Hayes later was inaugurated peaceably after he let it be known that as president he would end military reconstruction by withdrawing Federal troops from the south and that he would restore "efficient local government" to the south.

1880

Party	Candidate	Popular vote	Percent	Electoral vote
Republican	James A. Garfield (Ohio) and Chester A. Arthur (N.Y.)	4,451,158	48.27	214
Democrat	Winfield S. Hancock (Pa.) and William H. English (Ind.)	4,444,260	48.25	155
Greenback	James B. Weaver (Iowa) and Benjamin J. Chambers (Tex.)	305,997	3.32	—
Other		14,005	0.15	—
	Total Vote	9,210,420		
	Garfield Plurality	1,898		

Key Issues With the war and Reconstruction behind, no major issues arose over which the major parties disagreed. The Democrats, the party of secession 20 year earlier, nominated General Hancock to help combat the stigma of treason. Garfield made a protectionist tariff central to his campaign. **Regional Influences** The balance between Republican strength in the Midwest and west and Democratic strength in the south resulted in a plurality of less than 2,000 for Garfield out of more than 9 million votes cast. Four months into his term Garfield was shot by a disappointed office-seeker.

1884

Party	Candidate	Popular vote	Percent	Electoral vote
Democrat	Grover Cleveland (N.Y.) and Thomas A. Hendricks (Ind.)	4,874,621	48.50	219
Republican	James G. Blaine (Maine) and John A. Logan (Ill.)	4,848,936	48.25	182
Greenback	Benjamin F. Butler (Mass.)	175,096	1.74	—
Prohibition	John P. St. John (Kans.)	147,482	1.47	—
Other		3,619	0.04	—
	Total Votes	10,049,754		
	Cleveland Plurality	25,685		

Key Issues The private lives and morals of the candidates were the focus of a campaign notable for mudslinging. Blaine was accused of accepting bribes from a railroad company for whom he obtained a federal grant and Republicans taunted Cleveland for fathering a son out of wedlock. Still, Cleveland, known for his independence and integrity in public life, attracted the votes of many liberal Republicans and reformers unable to stomach Blaine, a Radical Republican leader. **Regional Influences** Cleveland carried all of the southern states as well as the key swing states of Indiana, New Jersey, Connecticut and New York, becoming the first Democrat elected president since the Civil War. Cleveland carried his home state of New York and its 36 electoral votes by less than 1,200 votes.

1888

Party	Candidate	Popular vote	Percent	Electoral vote
Republican	Benjamin Harrison (Ind.) and Levi P. Morton (N.Y.)	5,443,892	47.82	233
Democrat	Grover Cleveland (N.Y.) and Allen G. Thurman (Ohio)	5,534,488	48.62	168
Prohibition	Clinton B. Fisk (N.J.)	249,813	2.19	—
Union Labor	Alson J. Streeter (Ill.)	146,602	1.29	—
Other		8,519	0.07	—
	Total Votes	11,383,320		
	Cleveland Plurality	90,596		

Key Issues Cleveland made tariff reform central to his administration, seeking to lower existing high tariffs. The Republicans campaigned on the need to maintain high wages by keeping a high tariff on imported goods. **Regional Influences** Despite the emphasis on the tariff, Cleveland still carried such manufacturing states as New Jersey and Connecticut as well as most of the south. But though Cleveland won 90,000 more popular votes than Harrison, the Republican carried the pro-tariff swing states of Indiana and New York by slight margins to win the election in the electoral college in one of the most corrupt campaigns in history.

1892

Party	Candidate	Popular vote	Percent	Electoral vote
Democrat	Grover Cleveland (N.Y.) and Adlai E. Stevenson (Ill.)	5,551,883	46.05	277
Republican	Benjamin Harrison (Indiana) and Whitelaw Reid (N.Y.)	5,179,244	42.96	145
Populist	James B. Weaver (Iowa) and James G. Field (Virginia)	1,024,280	8.50	22
Prohibition	John Bidwell (California)	270,770	2.25	—
Other		29,920	0.25	
	Total Votes	12,056,097		
	Cleveland Plurality	372,639		

Key Issues Cleveland and Harrison again fought a battle over the tariff, which the Republicans drastically raised in 1890. Both men were out of touch with the growing agrarian and populist discontent. Weaver, campaigning for free silver, became the first third-party candidate to gain electoral votes since the war. **Regional Influences** Cleveland improved upon his 1884 and 1888 showings to win the most decisive presidential victory in 20 years. This time he carried the swing states of New York, New Jersey, Connecticut and Indiana as well as the traditionally Republican states of Illinois, California and Wisconsin.

1896

Party	Candidate	Popular vote	Percent	Electoral vote
Republican	William McKinley (Ohio) and Garret A. Hobart (N.J.)	7,108,480	51.01	271
Democrat/ Populist	William J. Bryan (Nebr.) and Democrat Arthur Sewall (Me.) and Populist Thomas E. Watson (Ga.)	6,511,495	46.73	176 149
National Democrat	John M. Palmer (Ill.)	133,435	0.96	—
Prohibition	Joshua Levering (Md.)	125,072	0.90	—
Other		57,256	0.41	—
	Total Votes	13,935,738		
	McKinley Plurality	596,985		

Key Issues The Democrats absorbed Populist energies and abandoned the conservatism of Cleveland by nominating Bryan and adopting key elements of the Populist program, especially the call for free silver. The pro-tariff and pro-gold Republicans led by McKinley and Mark Hanna outspent the Democrats by almost 12 to 1. In losing, Bryan amassed more votes than any victorious candidate before him. **Regional Influences** Bryan did not carry a single state north of Virginia or east of Missouri. His hold on the agricultural south and west was broken by Republican victories in Maryland, Delaware,

West Virginia, Kentucky, California and Oregon. Bryan, failing to appeal to labor, carried no industrial or urban states.

1900

Party	Candidate	Popular vote	Percent	Electoral vote
Republican	William McKinley (Ohio) and Theodore Roosevelt (N.Y.)	7,218,039	51.67	292
Democrat	William J. Bryan (Nebr.) and Adlai E. Stevenson (Ill.)	6,358,345	45.51	155
Prohibition	John C. Woolley (Ill.)	209,004	1.50	—
Social Democrat	Eugene V. Debs (Ind.)	86,935	0.62	—
Other		98,147	0.70	—
	Total Vote	13,970,470		
	McKinley Plurality	859,694		

Key Issues Imperialism in the Philippines joined free silver and the tariff as the key issues in a replay of the 1896 election. Bryan tried to unite the silver interests in the west and south with supporters of the gold standard in a coalition against imperialism, which the Democratic platform called the "paramount issue" of the campaign. But voters did not desert McKinley in a time of prosperity. **Regional Influences** Bryan carried only the Solid South and four silver states in the west, and was defeated in the silver states of Kansas, South Dakota, Utah and Wyoming as well as his home state of Nebraska. Both houses of Congress were led by significant Republican majorities.

1904

Party	Candidate	Popular vote	Percent	Electoral vote
Republican	Theodore Roosevelt (N.Y.) and Charles W. Fairbanks (Ind.)	7,626,593	56.41	336
Democrat	Alton B. Parker (N.Y.) and Henry G. Davis (W. Va.)	5,082,898	37.60	140
Socialist	Eugene V. Debs (Ind.)	402,489	2.98	—
Prohibition	Silas C. Swallow (Pa.)	258,596	1.91	—
Other		148,388	1.10	—
	Total Votes	13,518,964		
	Roosevelt Plurality	2,543,695		

Key Issues Roosevelt stole the mantle of reform from the Democrats with his campaigns against the "malefactors of great wealth." The Democrats turned to the right by nominating the lackluster Parker, a judge with close ties to Wall Street. Parker turned his back on Bryan Democrats by renouncing free silver. **Regional Influences** Roosevelt won a landslide victory based largely on his own personality and popularity. The Democrats won only 13 states, none outside the south.

1908

Party	Candidate	Popular vote	Percent	Electoral vote
Republican	William H. Taft (Ohio) and James S. Sherman (N.Y.)	7,662,258	51.58	321
Democrat	William J. Bryan (Nebr.) and John W. Kern (Ind.)	6,406,801	43.05	162
Socialist	Eugene V. Debs (Ind.)	420,380	2.82	—
Prohibition	Eugene W. Chafin (Ill.)	252,821	1.70	—
Other		126,474	0.85	—
	Total Vote	14,882,734		
	Taft Plurality	1,269,457		

Key Issues The immensely popular Roosevelt declined to run. Taft, his secretary of war and handpicked successor, debated Bryan over who was better qualified to complete TR's progressive program. Bryan abandoned silver and courted labor but ran a lackluster losing campaign. **Regional Influences** Bryan again carried the South. But the appeal of Roosevelt's reform programs helped the Republicans to do well in the west and Taft's background as a Yale graduate and Federal jurist enabled him to carry the east as well.

1912

Party	Candidate	Popular vote	Percent	Electoral vote
Democrat	Woodrow Wilson (N.J.) and Thomas Marshall (Ind.)	6,293,152	41.84	435
Progressive	Theodore Roosevelt (N.Y.) and Hiram Johnson (Calif.)	4,119,207	27.39	88
Republican	William H. Taft (Ohio) and James S. Sherman (N.Y.)	3,486,333	23.18	8
Socialist	Eugene V. Debs (Ind.)	900,369	5.99	—
Other		241,902	1.61	—
	Total Vote	15,040,963		
	Wilson Plurality	2,173,945		

Key Issues Taft's conservatism and political ineptitude led Roosevelt to challenge him within the party from the left. Unable to wrest the nomination from Taft, Roosevelt ran a third-party campaign. The election boiled down to a contest between Roosevelt and Wilson and their respective conceptions of progressivism. Roosevelt's "New Nationalism" called for strong Federal regulations to control the trusts and big businesses. Wilson's "New Freedom" sought instead to revive competition through vigorous application of anti-trust laws. The Progressives advocated a broad array of social reforms to be implemented by the Federal government while the Democrats emphasized the primacy of the states in such matters. **Regional Influences** Though he amassed fewer votes than did Bryan in 1908, Wilson took advantage of the split in the Republican ranks to win a decisive plurality of the vote. He did best in traditional Democratic states, but was able to win most traditionally Republican states as well. Roosevelt won only 6 states, including California, which he carried by fewer than 200 votes. Taft carried Utah and Vermont. The Democrats also won control of both houses of Congress, their best overall performance since the Civil War.

1916

Party	Candidate	Popular vote	Percent	Electoral vote
Democrat	Woodrow Wilson (N.J.) and Thomas Marshall (Ind.)	9,126,300	49.24	277
Republican	Charles Evans Hughes (N.Y.) and Charles W. Fairbanks (Ind.)	8,546,789	46.11	254
Socialist	Allen L. Benson (N.Y.)	589,924	3.18	—
Prohibition	James F. Hanly (Ind.)	221,030	1.19	—
Other		50,979	0.28	—
	Total Vote	18,535,022		
	Wilson Plurality	579,511		

Key Issues The campaign was a referendum on Wilson's first term, his program of domestic reform, and his policy toward the war in Europe. He ran a peace campaign with the slogan "He kept us out of war" and attracted the votes of many Bull Moosers. Voters who felt Wilson was either too harsh or too lenient toward Germany tended to vote Republican. Irish-American and German-American extremists, virulently opposed to aiding Great Britain, embarrassed Hughes with their vocal support. A coalition of labor, farmers, reformers, and intellectuals won the election for Wilson. **Regional Influences** Hughes, a former reform governor of New York who left the Supreme Court to challenge Wilson, carried all of the east except New Hampshire and all of the Old Northwest except Ohio. But the South was again solid for the Democrats and so was every state west of the Mississippi except Minnesota, Iowa, South Dakota and Oregon, which Wilson lost by close margins. The electoral vote was the closest since 1876.

1920

Party	Candidate	Popular vote	Percent	Electoral vote
Republican	Warren G. Harding (Ohio) and Calvin Coolidge (Mass.)	16,133,314	60.30	404
Democrat	James M. Cox (Ohio) and Franklin D. Roosevelt (N.Y.)	9,140,884	34.17	127
Socialist	Eugene V. Debs (Ind.)	913,664	3.42	—
Farmer-Labor	Parley P. Christensen (Utah)	264,540	0.99	—
Other		301,384	1.13	—
	Total Vote	26,753,786		
	Harding Plurality	6,992,430		

Key Issues The voters turned against Wilsonian progressivism and internationalism by electing Harding, a vacuous party hack who promised a "return to normalcy" after the turbulent years of domestic reform and world war. The undistinguished Cox ran in support of the League of Nations and little else. **Regional Influences** Harding carried every state outside of the south, except Tennessee. The Republicans added to their majorities in both houses of Congress, regained in 1918.

1924

Party	Candidate	Popular vote	Percent	Electoral vote
Republican	Calvin Coolidge (Mass.) and Charles G. Dawes (Ohio)	15,717,553	54.00	382
Democrat	John W. Davis (N.Y.) and Charles W. Bryan (Nebr.)	8,386,169	28.84	136
Progressive Socialist	Robert M. LaFollette (Wis.) and Burton K. Wheeler (Mont.)	4,814,050	16.56	13
Other		158,187	0.55	—
	Total Vote	29,075,959		
	Coolidge Plurality	7,331,384		

Key Issues The country "kept cool with Coolidge" as the Democrats could not overcome prosperity or themselves. Davis, a conservative Wall Street lawyer, was a compromise nominee selected by a bitterly divided party after 103 ballots. Reformers, labor and farmers flocked to the LaFollette candidacy. **Regional Influences** All 12 of the Democratic states were from the south. LaFollette's 13 electoral votes came from his home of Wisconsin.

1928

Party	Candidate	Popular vote	Percent	Electoral vote
Republican	Herbert C. Hoover (Calif.) and Charles E. Curtis (Kans.)	21,411,911	58.20	444
Democrat	Alfred E. Smith (N.Y.) and Joseph T. Robinson (Ark.)	15,000,185	40.77	87
Socialist	Norman Thomas (N.Y.)	266,453	0.72	—
Worker's	William Z. Foster (Ill.)	48,170	0.13	—
Other		63,565	0.17	—
	Total Vote	36,790,364		
	Hoover Plurality	6,411,806		

Key Issues Booze, bigotry, Tammany and prosperity did in the Democrats. Rural America would not vote for an anti-Prohibition, big-city, Catholic machine politician, despite Smith's success as governor of New York, especially while the Republicans could convincingly cite the success of their economic leadership. **Regional Influences** The solid south was shattered as Hoover Democrats gave Republicans the states of Virginia, North Carolina, Tennessee, Florida and Texas for the first time since Reconstruction. Smith lost his own state and every western and border state. But Smith set the stage for the New Deal coalition with the votes of urban ethnics, he carried the nation's 12 largest cities, all of which had been won by the Republicans four years earlier. The Democrats also won votes in the traditionally Republican west among farmers unsure about prosperity.

1932

Party	Candidate	Popular vote	Percent	Electoral vote
Democrat	Franklin D. Roosevelt (N.Y.) and John Nance Garner (Tex.)	22,825,016	57.42	472
Republican	Herbert C. Hoover (Calif.) and Charles E. Curtis (Kans.)	15,758,397	39.64	59

Socialist	Norman Thomas (N.Y.)	883,990	2.22	—
Communist	William Z. Foster (Ill.)	102,221	0.26	—
Other		179,758	0.45	—
	Total Vote	39,749,382		
	Roosevelt Plurality	7,066,619		

Key Issues The Democrats won by blaming the Republicans for the Great Depression. Roosevelt was the first presidential nominee of a major party to address his nominating convention, pledging to help "the forgotten man at the bottom of the economic pyramid." In a vague and contradictory platform, the Democrats promised to balance the Federal budget by drastically reducing expenses and vowed to spend Federal dollars to attack the nation's economic woes. **Regional Influences** Roosevelt lost only six states, Maine, New Hampshire, Vermont, Connecticut, Delaware and Pennsylvania, carrying all of the agricultural West and South. He put the finishing touches on the New Deal coalition by also improving upon Smith's margins of victory in the nation's big cities.

1936

Party	Candidate	Popular vote	Per- cent	Elec- toral vote
Democrat	Franklin D. Roosevelt (N.Y.) and John Nance Garner (Tex.)	27,747,636	60.79	523
Republican	Alfred M. Landon (Kans.) and Frank Knox (Ill.)	16,679,543	36.54	8
Union	William Lemke (N.Dak.)	892,492	1.96	—
Socialist	Norman Thomas (N.Y.)	187,785	0.41	—
Other		134,847	0.30	—
	Total Vote	45,642,303		
	Roosevelt Plurality	11,068,093		

Key Issues Despite intense opposition to the New Deal, its great public appeal was confirmed in the most one-sided election since 1820 and sweeping victories for the Democrats in Congress. The populist forces of the late Huey Long coalesced around Lemke but failed to gather widespread support. **Regional Influences** Roosevelt carried every state except Maine and Vermont. The New Deal coalition was at its height as every large city voted overwhelmingly for FDR. The middle-class, farmers in the west and south, big-city ethnics, labor and reform intellectuals flocked to the Democrats. Northern Blacks also began to vote heavily Democratic for the first time.

1940

Party	Candidate	Popular vote	Per- cent	Elec- toral vote
Democrat	Franklin D. Roosevelt (N.Y.) and Henry A. Wallace (Iowa)	27,263,448	54.70	449
Republican	Wendell L. Willkie (Ind.) and Charles L. McNary (Oreg.)	22,336,260	44.82	82
Socialist	Norman Thomas (N.Y.)	116,827	0.23	—
Prohibition	Roger W. Babson (Mass.)	58,685	0.12	—
Other		65,223	0.13	—
	Total Vote	49,840,443		
	Roosevelt Plurality	4,927,188		

Key Issues With war raging in Europe the electorate turned its attention from domestic to foreign affairs. The international scene led the Democrats to break with tradition and renominate FDR for a third term. The Republicans turned to businessman and political neophyte Willkie, a charismatic former Democrat. Willkie's internationalism and the pledge of both candidates to keep the U.S. out of the war minimized the role of foreign policy in the campaign. **Regional Influences** Willkie carried only 10 states, mostly in the Midwest. But Roosevelt's percentage of the popular vote was markedly down from 1936.

1944

Party	Candidate	Popular vote	Per- cent	Elec- toral vote
Democrat	Franklin D. Roosevelt (N.Y.) and Harry S Truman (Mo.)	25,611,936	53.39	432

Republican	Thomas E. Dewey (N.Y.) and John W. Bricker (Ohio)	22,013,372	45.89	99
Socialist	Norman Thomas (N.Y.)	79,100	0.16	—
Prohibition	Claude A. Watson (Calif.)	74,733	0.16	—
Other		195,778	0.41	—
	Total Vote	47,974,819		
	Roosevelt Plurality	3,598,564		

Key Issues With both candidates supporting New Deal social legislation and an international organization to maintain the peace after the war, the nation chose to let FDR lead America into the post-war era. Big-city bosses and southern conservatives, with FDR's private support, ousted Wallace from the ticket in favor of Truman. **Regional Influences** Roosevelt won 36 states and the Democrats improved their control over Congress and the nation's statehouses. The Republicans only won a handful of western and New England states.

1948

Party	Candidate	Popular vote	Per- cent	Elec- toral vote
Democrat	Harry S Truman (Mo.) and Alben W. Barkley (Ky.)	24,105,587	49.51	303
Republican	Thomas E. Dewey (N.Y.) and Earl Warren (Calif.)	21,970,017	45.12	189
States' Rights	Strom Thurmond (S.C.) and Fielding L. Wright (Miss.)	1,169,134	2.40	39
Progressive	Henry A. Wallace (Iowa) and Glen H. Taylor (Idaho)	1,157,057	2.38	—
Other		290,647	0.60	—
	Total Vote	48,692,442		
	Truman Plurality	2,135,570		

Key Issues The Republicans were sure of victory after 16 years of Democratic rule and the desertion of the Democrats by conservative Southern Dixiecrats and the ultra-liberal Wallace faction. But Dewey's dour personality and Truman's intense whistle-stop campaign against the "do-nothing, good-for-nothing" Republican 80th Congress resulted in one of the biggest upsets in presidential history. **Regional Influences** Dewey captured all of the Middle Atlantic and New England states, except Massachusetts and Connecticut, along with the Dakotas, Nebraska and Kansas in the Midwest and Oregon in the northwest. Thurmond won South Carolina, Mississippi, Alabama and Louisiana in the Deep South.

1952

Party	Candidate	Popular vote	Per- cent	Elec- toral vote
Republican	Dwight D. Eisenhower (Kans.) and Richard M. Nixon (Calif.)	33,936,137	55.13	442
Democrat	Adlai E. Stevenson (Ill.) and John J. Sparkman (Ala.)	27,314,649	44.38	89
Progressive	Vincent W. Hallinan (Calif.)	140,416	0.23	—
Prohibition	Stuart Hamblen (Calif.)	73,413	0.12	—
Other		86,503	0.14	—
	Total Vote	61,551,118		
	Eisenhower Plurality	6,621,485		

Key Issues Popular war hero Eisenhower swept to victory after uniting the internationalist and isolationist factions of the Republican party. He routed the Democrats by promising to kick out alleged crooks and communists in Washington, wage a more aggressive fight against communists worldwide and "go to Korea," implying that he had a plan to end the war there. **Regional Influences** Stevenson, who appealed to northern liberals as well as southern states' rights Democrats, carried only nine states in the south. The Republicans also won slight majorities in both houses of Congress and were in control of the national government for the first time in 20 years.

1956

Party	Candidate	Popular vote	Per- cent	Elec- toral vote
Republican	Dwight D. Eisenhower (Kans.) and Richard M. Nixon (Calif.)	35,585,247	57.37	457

Party	Candidate	Popular vote	Percent	Electoral vote
Democrat	Adlai E. Stevenson (Ill.) and Estes Kefauver (Tenn.)	26,030,172	41.97	73
Constitution/ States' Rights	T. Coleman Andrews (Va.)	108,055	0.17	—
Socialist-Labor	Eric Hass (New York)	44,300	0.07	—
Other		257,600	0.42	—
	Total Vote	62,025,372		
	Eisenhower Plurality	9,555,073		

Key Issues Eisenhower won an easy victory in a rematch of the 1952 election. His popularity did not translate into victories for his party elsewhere, as Democrats increased their control of Congress, regained in 1954, and their hold on the nation's governorships. **Regional Influences** Winning even more handsomely than he did in 1952, Eisenhower lost only seven southern states.

1960

Party	Candidate	Popular vote	Percent	Electoral vote
Democrat	John F. Kennedy (Mass.) and Lyndon B. Johnson (Tex.)	34,221,344	49.72	303
Republican	Richard M. Nixon (Calif.) and Henry Cabot Lodge (Mass.)	34,106,671	49.55	219
Socialist-Labor	Eric Hass (N.Y.)	47,522	0.07	—
Other		337,175	0.48	15
Unpledged		116,248	0.17	—
	Total Vote	68,828,960		
	Kennedy Plurality	114,673		

Key Issues Kennedy called for the government to play a larger role in stimulating the national economy in order to fund domestic social programs as well as to sustain a defense build-up and keep ahead militarily of the Soviet Union. The election was the first in which there were nationally televised debates between the two candidates. Kennedy's slick television performance played a role in his narrow triumph. **Regional Influences** The Democrats won a thin victory by narrowly defeating the Republicans in the Middle Atlantic states, the Deep South, Illinois and Texas. Nixon carried most of the Midwest, border and western states. Conservative Democratic Senator Harry F. Byrd of Virginia received 15 electoral votes: all eight of Mississippi's 11, six of Alabama's 11, and one of Oklahoma's eight.

1964

Party	Candidate	Popular vote	Percent	Electoral vote
Democrat	Lyndon B. Johnson (Tex.) and Hubert H. Humphrey (Minn.)	43,126,584	61.05	486
Republican	Barry M. Goldwater (Ariz.) and William E. Miller (N.Y.)	27,177,838	38.47	52
Socialist-Labor	Eric Hass (N.Y.)	45,187	0.06	—
Socialist Workers	Clifton DeBerry (N.Y.)	32,701	0.05	—
Other		258,794	0.37	—
	Total Vote	70,641,104		
	Johnson Plurality	15,948,746		

Key Issues Johnson ran for election in his own right on the basis of his Great Society domestic programs. The reactionary Goldwater campaigned against the New Deal and for the bombing of North Vietnam. **Regional Influences** Johnson won all but six states—Goldwater's home state of Arizona and five states in the Deep South—in the biggest popular and electoral landslide since 1936. Forty new Northern Democrats were elected to the House on LBJ's coattails.

1968

Party	Candidate	Popular vote	Percent	Electoral vote
Republican	Richard M. Nixon (Calif.) and Spiro T. Agnew (Md.)	31,785,148	43.42	301
Democrat	Hubert H. Humphrey (Minn.) and Edmund S. Muskie (Maine)	31,274,503	42.72	191
American Independent	George C. Wallace (Ala.) and Curtis LeMay (Ohio)	901,151	13.53	46
Socialist-Labor	Henning A. Blomen (Mass.)	52,591	0.07	—
Other		189,977	0.20	—
	Total Vote	73,203,370		
	Nixon Plurality	510,645		

Key Issues With the country divided over Vietnam, Humphrey failed to emerge from the shadow of the unpopular Johnson, while the previously hawkish Nixon pledged to end the war and hinted that he had a secret plan to do so. Wallace attacked Federal encroachment on states' rights, desegregation, "pointy-headed" intellectuals and the administration's timidity in Vietnam, in an effort to capture blue-collar votes. **Regional Influences** Barely more than 500,000 votes separated Nixon and Humphrey, but the Republican edge in the Electoral College was comfortable and the combined anti-Democratic vote amounted to a repudiation of the Johnson-Humphrey Administration. Humphrey's strength was in the eastern seaboard states. Wallace won five states in the Deep South.

1972

Party	Candidate	Popular vote	Percent	Electoral vote
Republican	Richard M. Nixon (Calif.) and Spiro T. Agnew (Md.)	47,170,179	60.69	520
Democrat	George S. McGovern (S.Dak.) and R. Sargent Shriver (Md.)	29,171,791	37.53	17
American Independent	John G. Schmitz (Calif.)	1,090,673	1.40	—
People's	Benjamin Spock	78,751	0.10	—
Other		216,196	0.28	(1)[1]
	Total Vote	77,727,590		
	Nixon Plurality	17,998,388		

Key Issues Seeking to create a Republican majority by converting Wallace Democrats, Nixon pursued a "Southern strategy" of denouncing busing, the welfare state, the media and intellectuals. McGovern was unable to overcome an image of radicalism furthered by Republican charges that he was the candidate of "acid, abortion, and amnesty." **Regional Influences** The GOP's Southern strategy was aided by an assassination attempt on Wallace that knocked him out of the race. Nixon lost only Massachusetts and the District of Columbia, but Democrats added to their majority in the Senate and maintained control of the House.

[1] The Libertarian slate of John Hospers and Theodora Nathan received 1 electoral vote from a Republican elector in Virginia.

1976

Party	Candidate	Popular vote	Percent	Electoral vote
Democrat	Jimmy Carter (Ga.) and Walter F. Mondale (Minn.)	40,830,763	50.06	297
Republican	Gerald R. Ford (Mich.) and Robert Dole (Kans.)	39,147,793	48.00	240[1]
Independent	Eugene J. McCarthy (Minn.)	756,691	0.93	—
Libertarian	Roger MacBride (Va.)	173,011	0.21	—
Other		647,631	0.79	—
	Total Vote	81,555,889		
	Carter Plurality	1,682,970		

Key Issues In the wake of Watergate, Carter ran a moralistic campaign as a political outsider. Vague on issues, he railed against the Washington bureaucracy and vowed to lead "a government that is as good and honest and decent . . . as filled with love as are the American people." He also promised Americans that he would never lie to them. **Regional Influences** Ford nearly overcame a huge early deficit in the polls. But Carter's background as a southern moderate enabled him to eke out a victory through wins in northern, southern and border states.

[1]Ronald Reagan received one electoral vote from an elector in Washington.

1980

Party	Candidate	Popular vote	Per- cent	Elec- toral vote
Republican	Ronald Reagan (Calif.) and George Bush (Tex.)	43,901,812	50.75	489
Democrat	Jimmy Carter (Ga.) and Walter F. Mondale (Minn.)	35,483,820	41.02	49
Independent	John B. Anderson (Ill.) and Patrick J. Lucey (Wis.)	5,719,722	6.61	—
Libertarian	Edward E. Clark (Calif.)	921,188	1.06	—
Other		486,754	0.56	—
	Total Vote	86,513,296		
	Reagan Plurality	8,417,992		

Key Issues Inflation, an energy shortage, the taking of American hostages by Iran and a strong primary challenge from Edward Kennedy of Massachusetts weakened Carter. Reagan, promising to get government "off the backs fo the American people," pledged to cut taxes, increase defense spending, and balance the federal budget. Anderson, a Republican, ran as an independent to the left of both Carter and Reagan. **Regional Influences** Reagan swept to a landslide win in the Electoral College as Carter carried only six states and Washington, D.C.

1984

Party	Candidate	Popular vote	Per- cent	Elec- toral vote
Republican	Ronald Reagan (Calif.) and George Bush (Tex.)	54,450,603	58.78	525
Democrat	Walter F. Mondale (Minn.) and Geraldine Ferraro (N.Y.)	37,573,671	40.56	13
Libertarian	David Bergland (Calif.)	227,949	0.25	—
Other		570,343	0.61	—
	Total Vote	92,628,458		
	Reagan Plurality	16,876,932		

Key Issues The economy was flying after emerging in late 1983 from the worst economic downturn since the Great Depression. Reagan, whose commercials proclaimed it was "morning in America," ridiculed Mondale as an old-fashioned "tax-and-spend, gloom-and-doom" Democrat. Controversy over her husband's finances blunted Ferraro's appeal as the first woman on a major party ticket. **Regional Influences** Mondale carried only his home state of Minnesota and the District of Columbia as Reagan won the greatest electoral victory in American history and the fifth highest share of the popular vote.

1988

Party	Candidate	Popular vote	Per- cent	Elec- toral vote
Republican	George Bush (Tex.) and J. Danforth Quayle (Ind.)	48,881,011	53.37	426
Democrat	Michael S. Dukakis (Mass.) and Lloyd Bentsen (Tex.)	41,828,350	45.67	111[1]
Libertarian	Ron Paul (Texas)	431,499	0.47	—
New Alliance	Lenora Fulani (New York)	218,159	0.24	—
Other		226,852	0.25	—
	Total Vote	91,585,871		
	Bush Plurality	7,052,661		

Key Issues Trailing Dukakis by 17 points in early summer, Bush made an issue of his opponent's "liberalism," depicting the Massachusetts governor as soft on crime. Bush made a household name out of Willie Horton, a black Massachusetts prison inmate who raped a woman while on a prison furlough. Bush also called Dukakis a card-carrying member of the American Civil Liberties Union and said that he didn't share the same values as the American people. Dukakis' failure to respond to those charges and to shed the "liberal" label until late in the campaign ultimately doomed his candidacy, despite Bush's links to the Iran-Contra scandal and to Panama's drug-running leader, Gen. Mañuel Noriega. **Regional Influences** Dukakis won the District of Columbia and only 10 states including his home state of Massachusettts. Bush easily captured the formerly Democratic "solid South."

[1]Bentsen received one electoral vote for President.

1992

Party	Candidate	Popular vote	Per- cent	Elec- toral vote
Democrat	Bill Clinton (Ark.) and Al Gore (Tenn.)	44,908,233	42.95	370
Republican	George Bush (Tex.) and J. Danforth Quayle (Ind.)	39,102,282	37.40	168
Independent	H. Ross Perot (Tex.) and James H. Stockdale (Calif.)	19,721,433	18.86	—
Other		820,788	0.79	
	Total Vote	104,552,736		
	Clinton Plurality	5,805,951		

Key Issues Bush's approval ratings were sky high as little as 13 months before the election, but a flagging economy and a national debt that wouldn't go away spelled his downfall in a three-way race that saw billionaire Ross Perot capture more votes than any third-party candidate since Theodore Roosevelt in 1912. Excitement for Perot, who entered the race in March, quit in July, and re-entered the campaign in October, brought a record 102 million people to the polls. Clinton ran especially strong among women, who supported his stances in favor of abortion rights and a strong defense of the environment. **Regional Influences** Perot's presence prevented either major party candidate from capturing an outright majority in every state except New York, Maryland, Arkansas (all of which went for Clinton) and Mississippi (which supported Bush). But Clinton won pluralities in 13 states, including delegate-rich California, Pennsylvania and Ohio. The only states with double-digit electoral votes in Bush's column were Florida, Indiana, North Carolina, Texas and Virginia.

1996

Party	Candidate	Popular vote	Per- cent	Elec- toral vote
Democrat	Bill Clinton (Ark.) and Al Gore (Tenn.)	47,402,357	49.24	379
Republican	Bob Dole (Kans.) and Jack Kemp (N.Y.)	39,198,755	40.71	159
Reform	H. Ross Perot and Patrick Choate	8,085,402	8.40	—
Green	Ralph Nader	684,902	0.71	—
Libertarian	Harry Browne	485,798	0.50	—
Other		420,009	0.44	—
	Total Vote	96,277,223		
	Clinton Plurality	8,203,602		

[1]Other includes write-ins and "none of the above."

Key Issues Clinton easily won re-election, campaigning on the strong economy and declining crime rates. Less than half of the voting age population went to the polls, the lowest number since 1924. Among those who did vote, Clinton ran strong with women, Asian-Americans, and Hispanics, and captured about half of the voters who described themselves as Independents. Dole's refusal to contravene his own party's strict stand against abortion hurt him dearly among women, who overwhelmingly chose Clinton. Perot's presence in the race prevented Clinton from winning an outright majority, but was not nearly as influential as it had been four years earlier.

2000

Party	Candidate	Popular vote	Percent	Electoral vote
Republican	George W. Bush (Tex.) and Dick Cheney (Wyo.)	50,455,156	47.87	271
Democrat	Al Gore (Tenn.) and Joe Lieberman (Conn.)	50,992,335	48.38	266[1]
Green	Ralph Nader and Winona LaDuke	2,882,897	2.74	—
Reform	Pat Buchanan and Ezola Foster	448,892	0.42	—
Libertarian	Harry Browne	384,429	0.36	—
Other		232,932	0.23	—
	Total Vote	105,396,641		
	Gore Plurality	537,179		

1. One elector from the District of Columbia abstained.

Key Issues Gore campaigned on the strong economy and budget surplus of the Clinton years, but struggled to distance himself from Clinton's scandals. In debates that centered on social security and health-care, Bush dubbed himself a "compassionate conservative" while Gore was seen as wooden and unapproachable. Ralph Nader drew less than 3 percent of the vote, but Democrats viewed him as a spoiler in a tight race. Gore won the popular vote but the Electoral College results were delayed for a month by a recount in Florida, where Bush appeared to win by fewer than 1,000 votes. On Dec. 12, the U.S. Supreme Court, ruling on a lawsuit by Bush, halted the recount and effectively awarded the presidency to Bush. **Regional Influences** Bush won 30 states, including Texas and the South and all of the Rocky Mountain States except New Mexico. Gore carried 20 states, including most of the Northeast and the West Coast, but lost his home state of Tennessee.

▶ THE ELECTORAL COLLEGE

The Electoral College is the body of electors, chosen by all of the states, that ultimately is responsible for selecting the president of the United States. The Framers did not want the nation's Chief Executive chosen by either the national legislature or the people directly. Instead they set up the Electoral College, under Article II, sections 2 and 3 of the Constitution, to provide for indirect election of the president: "Each State shall appoint, in such manner as the legislature thereof may direct, a number of Electors, equal to the whole number of

2004

Party	Candidate	Popular vote	Percent	Electoral vote
Republican	George W. Bush (Tex.) and Dick Cheney (Wyo.)	62,040,610	50.73	286
Democrat	John Kerry (Mass.) and John Edwards (N.C.)	59,028,444	48.27	252
Independent	Ralph Nader and Peter Miguel Camejo	465,650	0.38	—
Libertarian	Michael Badnarik and Richard Campagna	397,265	0.12	—
	Total Vote	122,352,575		
	Bush Plurality	3,012,166		

Key Issues Despite the lack of military progress in Iraq and Afghanistan, a rising national debt, and a falling approval rating, Bush presented himself as more qualified to manage the "War on Terror" than his opponent, Vietnam War veteran Kerry. Both major parties registered millions of new voters and drove turnout with help from non-profit organizations who sponsored aggressive advertising to appeal to interest groups like Christian conservatives. **Regional Influences** The vote was close across the country but Bush carried a wide swath of 30 states and was especially popular in the South although Ohio proved to be the crucial state for him. Kerry won 20 states including the West Coast, most of the Great Lakes region and the entire Northeast.

Senators and Representatives to which the State may be entitled in the Congress; but no Senator or Representative, or person holding an office of trust or profit under the United States, shall be appointed an Elector."

Electors were supposed to be distinguished, enlightened citizens who would cast a disinterested vote for president. From the start, however, electors have been instruments of partisan passions. At first, most state legislatures were responsible for choosing electors. By 1828, however, all states except South Carolina allowed electors to be chosen by direct popular election. (In South Carolina, the legislature continued to select electors until

Voter Turnout in Presidential Elections, 1928–2004

Year	Total Vote	Voting Age Population		Registered Voters	
		Number	Percent Voting	Number[1]	Percent Voting
1928	36,879,414	71,185,000	51.8%	N.A.	N.A.
1932	39,816,522	75,768,000	52.6	N.A.	N.A.
1936	45,646,817	80,354,000	56.8	N.A.	N.A.
1940	49,815,312	84,728,000	58.8	N.A.	N.A.
1944	48,025,684	95,573,000	56.1	N.A.	N.A.
1948	48,833,680	95,573,000	51.1	N.A.	N.A.
1952	61,551,919	99,929,000	61.6	N.A.	N.A.
1956	62,033,908	104,515,000	59.4	N.A.	N.A.
1960	68,838,204	109,159,000	63.06	N.A.	N.A.
1964	70,644,592	114,090,000	61.92	73,715,818	95.83%
1968	73,211,875	120,328,186	60.84	81,658,180	89.65
1972	77,718,554	140,776,000	55.21	97,328,541	79.85
1976	81,555,789	152,309,190	53.55	105,037,986	77.64
1980	86,515,221	164,597,000	52.56	113,043,734	76.53
1984	92,652,680	174,466,000	53.11	124,150,614	74.63
1988	91,594,693	182,778,000	50.11	126,379,628	72.48
1992	104,405,155	189,529,000	55.09	133,821,178	78.01
1996	96,456,345	196,511,000	49.08	146,211,960	65.97
2000	105,586,274	205,815,000	51.30	156,421,311	67.50
2004	122,295,345	215,694,000	56.70	177,265,030	68.99

Source: Federal Election Commission. www.fec.gov

the Civil War.) When electors began to be selected by popular vote, parties presented slates of candidates for presidential electors who were tacitly pledged to support the party's nominees for president and vice president. This is how the practice began of states voting as a unit. Subsequently, many states passed laws requiring their electors to vote as a bloc. Where it is not required by law, it is customary for all of a state's electors to vote for the candidate receiving a plurality of the popular vote in that state. The names of the candidates for electors may or may not appear on the ballot alongside the names of the candidates to whom they are pledged. Voters really vote for presidential electors, though, even when they seem to be casting a ballot for a presidential candidate.

The presidential electors chosen by the voters in November meet in their state capitals on the first Monday after the second Wednesday in December to cast their vote for president and vice president. The results of this balloting are sent to the president of the U.S. Senate, the directors of the U.S. General Services Administration, the state's secretary of state, and to the judge of the Federal District Court of the district in which the electors gathered. Sealed state ballots are opened and counted at a joint session of Congress on January 6 following the election year.

Originally electors voted for two individuals for president on a single ballot. The winner of a majority of the vote was elected president, and the runner-up vice president. The Framers fully expected there to be many elections in which no candidate would gain a majority of the vote and the president would have to be selected by the House of Representatives, where each state delegation would cast a single vote. But in 1789 and 1792 every elector voted for George Washington. In both years John Adams was the runner-up and, thus, vice president.

Problems inherent in this system became apparent once Washington was no longer a candidate. In 1796, Adams and Thomas Jefferson finished first and second in the balloting and were elected president and vice president, respectively, despite being fierce foes. By 1800, two formal parties had evolved which nominated a single candidate for both president and vice president. A Federalist elector purposely failed to vote for the party's vice presidential nominee, Thomas Pinckney, in order to assure a potential majority for Adams. But overzealous Republican electors all voted for both Jefferson and the party's vice presidential nominee, Aaron Burr. Both men received the same majority of the electoral vote and the election had to be decided by the House, where Jefferson won. This led to adoption of the Twelfth Amendment to

the Constitution, implemented in 1804, which requires electors to cast separate ballots for president and vice president. If no candidate achieves a majority of the electoral vote for vice president, the position is filled by the Senate with each senator casting a single ballot. This has happened only once, when the Senate selected Richard M. Johnson after he fell one electoral vote short of a majority for vice president in 1836.

Today, 270 votes are required to reach a majority in the Electoral College. There have been two elections in which no candidate received a majority of the electoral vote. In 1824, no candidate achieved a majority of the vote, and in 1876, disputed results in several states prevented either Rutherford B. Hayes or Samuel J. Tilden from achieving a majority. John Quincy Adams and Hayes won those contests, respectively. A candidate also can be elected president despite losing the popular vote. This occurred, again in 1824 and 1876, when the House selected Adams and Hayes, though they lost the popular vote to Andrew Jackson and Tilden, respectively; in 1888, when Benjamin Harrison was elected over Grover Cleveland despite receiving a minority of the popular vote; and in 2000, when George W. Bush lost the popular vote by more than 500,000 votes to Al Gore, but won enough states for an Electoral College victory.

▶ THE FEDERAL ELECTION CAMPAIGN ACT

In 1971 Congress passed the Federal Election Campaign Act to deal with various aspects of campaign financing. The law was amended and strengthened in 1974 and 1976, and the Federal Election Commission (FEC) was established to administer the law, which affects candidates for the U.S. House of Representatives, the U.S. Senate, and the presidency. The act requires disclosure of sources and uses of funds for federal elections, provides public financing for presidential elections, and sets limits on campaign contributions. The specific requirements of each of these three parts of the act are detailed below.

Public disclosure Candidates for federal office and the political committees that support them must register and file periodic disclosures of their campaign finance activities with the clerk of the House, the secretary of the Senate, or the FEC. These reports are available to the public within 48 hours of their disclosure. A candidate is defined as one who has raised or spent more than $5,000 in any given year in campaigning for federal office. A political committee, also known as a Polit-

Campaign Contribution Limits

Type of Contribution	Individuals		PACs	
	Old	New	Old	New
Contributions directly to political candidates	$1,000 per election cycle	$2,000 per election cycle	$5,000 per election cycle	$5,000 per election cycle
Hard money contributions to national party committees	$20,000 per year	$25,000 per year	$15,000 per year	$15,000 per year
Soft money contributions to national party committees	UNLIMITED	BANNED	UNLIMITED	BANNED
Contributions to state and local party committees	$5,000 per year	$10,000 per year	$5,000 per year	$5,000 per year
Total contributions	**$25,000 per year**	**$95,000 per cycle**	UNLIMITED	UNLIMITED

Note: The new limits took effect November 6, 2002, pending review by the U.S. Supreme Court, and will be indexed for inflation. An election cycle is two years. **Source:** Federal Election Commission.

ical Action Committee (PAC) is defined as a club, committee, association, or organization that receives contributions or makes expenditures of more than $1,000 to a federal candidate in any calendar year. PACs are subject to different contribution limits than are individuals.

Public financing   Public financing is provided for eligible presidential candidates in primary and general elections, and for national party committees for the nominating conventions. Financing is given in the form of matching payments to primary candidates, public grants to nominees in the general election, and public grants to the national party committees for the conventions. The money for public financing is raised by the Presidential Election Campaign Fund, which collects three dollars from the tax payment of every taxpayer who checks off this box on his or her federal income tax return.

Contribution limits and prohibitions

The Federal Election Campaign Act capped contributions to individual candidates at $1,000 per two-year election cycle, and donations to national political party committees to $20,000 per year. But a 1978 FEC ruling opened a loophole that allowed national political parties to accept unlimited "soft money" contributions from corporations, unions, and individuals, which did not count against the $20,000 limit. In theory, soft money contributions were supposedly limited to general party-building activities, but in practice, these monies were almost always spent in support of specific candidates for office.

After years of failed attempts, Congress in 2002 finally passed a campaign finance reform bill that closed the soft money loophole. The legislation, which took effect after the 2002 elections (subject to review by the Supreme Court) doubled the contribution limit to $2,000 per candidate per election cycle, raised the cap on hard money contributions to national political parties to $25,000 per year, and increased the limit on contributions to state and local political parties (for get-out-the-vote and voter registration efforts) from $5,000 to $10,000 per year. In addition, the law prohibits unions, corporations, and nonprofit groups from paying for so-called "issue ads" advocating the election or defeat of specific candidates within 60 days of a general election and 30 days of a primary. These ads must now be paid for only with regulated hard money.

POLITICAL OFFICE HOLDERS

▶ THE VICE PRESIDENCY

Unlike the office of the president, that of the vice president has sometimes been left vacant after the death of the vice president, or his assumption of higher office on the death of the president. Until adoption of the 25th Amendment to the Constitution in 1967, there was no provision to fill a vacancy in the vice presidency. Under the amendment, the president must name a vice president when the office is vacant, and the nominee must pass a majority vote of approval in both houses of Congress. Gerald Ford, Richard Nixon's choice to replace Spiro Agnew after the latter's resignation in 1973, was the first vice president to gain the office under the amendment. The second was Nel-

son Rockefeller, whom Ford nominated to the position after he became president upon Nixon's resignation the following year. While the 25th Amendment does not supersede the presidential order of succession, it decreases the likelihood of

Vice Presidents of the United States

Name	Party	Tenure	State, birth-death
1. John Adams	Fed.	1789–97	Mass., 1735–1826
2. Thomas Jefferson	D-R	1797–1801	Va., 1743–1826
3. Aaron Burr	D-R	1801–05	N.Y., 1756–1836
4. George Clinton	D-R	1805–13[†]	N.Y., 1739–1812
5. Elbridge Gerry	D-R	1813–17[†]	Mass., 1744–1814
6. Daniel D. Tompkins	D-R	1817–25	N.Y., 1774–1825
7. John C. Calhoun	D-R	1825–33[1]	S.C., 1782–1850
8. Martin Van Buren	D	1833–37	N.Y., 1782–1862
9. Richard M. Johnson	D	1837–41[2]	Ky., 1780–1850
10. John Tyler	Whig	1841[3]	Va., 1790–1862
11. George M. Dallas	D	1845–49	Pa., 1792–1864
12. Millard Fillmore	Whig	1849–50[4]	N.Y., 1800–74
13. William R. King	D	1853–57[†]	Ala., 1786–1853
14. John C. Breckenridge	D	1857–61	Ky., 1821–75
15. Hannibal Hamlin	R	1861–65	Maine, 1809–91
16. Andrew Johnson	R	1865[5]	Tenn., 1808–75
17. Schuyler Colfax	R	1869–73	Ind., 1823–85
18. Henry Wilson	R	1873–77[†]	Mass., 1812–75
19. William A. Wheeler	R	1877–81	N.Y., 1819–87
20. Chester A. Arthur	R	1881[6]	N.Y., 1829–86
21. Thomas A. Hendricks	D	1885[†]	Ind., 1819–85
22. Levi P. Morton	R	1889–93	N.Y., 1824–1920
23. Adlai E. Stevenson	R	1893–97	Ill., 1835–1914
24. Garret A. Hobart	R	1897–1901[†]	N.J., 1844–99
25. Theodore Roosevelt	R	1901[7]	N.Y., 1858–1919
26. Charles W. Fairbanks	R	1905–09	Ind., 1852–1918
27. James S. Sherman	R	1909–13[†]	N.Y., 1855–1912
28. Thomas R. Marshall	D	1913–21	Ind., 1854–1925
29. Calvin Coolidge	R	1921–23[8]	Mass., 1872–1933
30. Charles G. Dawes	R	1925–29	Ill., 1865–1951
31. Charles Curtis	R	1929–33	Kans., 1860–1936
32. John Nance Garner	D	1933–41	Tex., 1868–1967
33. Henry A. Wallace	D	1941–45	Iowa, 1888–1965
34. Harry S Truman	D	1945[9]	Mo., 1884–1972
35. Alben W. Barkley	D	1949–53	Ky., 1877–1956
36. Richard M. Nixon	R	1953–61	Calif., 1913–95
37. Lyndon B. Johnson	D	1961–63[10]	Tex., 1908–73
38. Hubert H. Humphrey	D	1965–69	Minn., 1911–78
39. Spiro T. Agnew	R	1969–73[11]	Md., 1918–96
40. Gerald R. Ford	R	1973–74[12]	Mich., 1913–2006
41. Nelson A. Rockefeller	R	1974–77[13]	N.Y., 1908–79
42. Walter F. Mondale	D	1977–81	Minn., 1928–
43. George H.W. Bush	R	1981–89	Tex., 1924–
44. J. Danforth Quayle	R	1989–93	Ind., 1947–
45. Albert Gore	D	1993–2001	Tenn., 1948–
46. Richard Cheney	R	2001–	Wyo., 1941–

Notes: Fed. = Federalist. D = Democrat. D-R = Democratic-Republican. R = Republican. † = Died in office. 1. Resigned to become senator from South Carolina (1832-43). 2. Voted in by senate after no candidate for vice president gained a majority in the electoral college. 3. Became president after Benjamin Harrison's death. 4. Became president after Zachary Taylor's death. 5. Nominated by Republicans to run with Abraham Lincoln on the Union ticket; became president after Lincoln's assassination. 6. Became president after James Garfield's assassination. 7. Became president after William McKinley's assassination. 8. Became president after Warren Harding's death. 9. Became president after Franklin D. Roosevelt's death. 10. Became president after John F. Kennedy's assassination. 11. Resigned while under investigation for receiving kickbacks as governor of Maryland. 12. First vice president named under terms of the 25th amendment; assumed presidency after Richard Nixon resigned. 13. Named vice president by Ford.

the office's ever falling to the speaker of the House or a sitting cabinet member.

▶ PRESIDENTIAL ORDER OF SUCCESSION

Article II of the Constitution gives to Congress the power to determine the presidential order of succession should both the president and vice president die, become incapacitated or be disqualified from office. The present law, passed in 1947, puts the Speaker of the House first in line to the presidency, followed by the president pro tempore of the Senate. The order of succession then goes through the members of the Cabinet, in the order in which the executive departments were established:

(1) Secretary of State, (2) Secretary of the Treasury, (3) Secretary of Defense, (4) Attorney General, (5) Secretary of the Interior, (6) Secretary of Agriculture, (7) Secretary of Commerce, (8) Secretary of Labor, (9) Secretary of Health and Human Services, (10) Secretary of Housing and Urban Development, (11) Secretary of Transportation, (12) Secretary of Energy, (13) Secretary of Education, (14) Secretary of Veterans' Affairs (15) Secretary of Homeland Security. The following sentence, composed of words using the first letter (or letters) of each cabinet department, is often used as a mnemonic device to remember the order: See The Dog Jump In A Circle; Leave HEr HOuse To ENtertain EDucated Veterans' HOmes. (State, Treasury, Justice, Interior, Agriculture, Commerce, Labor, HEalth and Human Services, HOusing and Urban Development, Transportation, ENergy, EDucation, Veterans Affairs, Homeland Security.)

Until the 1970 legislation removing the Postmaster General from the Cabinet and establishing an independent Postal Service, the Postmaster General was fifth in line to the presidency. The heads of new departments are automatically added to the line of succession as the new departments are created.

A Cabinet member must be a natural-born U.S. citizen and at least 35 years old in order to become acting president. If a Cabinet member next-in-line to fill a presidential vacancy were not yet 35, the presidency would pass to the next Cabinet member in the order of succession who had attained that age.

Cabinet Members

Washington Administration (1789-97)

Secretary of State	Thomas Jefferson	1789-93
	Edmund Randolph	1794-95
	Timothy Pickering	1795-97
Secretary of Treasury	Alexander Hamilton	1789-95
	Oliver Wolcott	1795-97
Secretary of War	Henry Knox	1789-94
	Timothy Pickering	1795
	James McHenry	1796-97
Attorney General	Edmund Randolph	1789-93
	William Bradford	1794-95
	Charles Lee	1795-97
Postmaster General	Samuel Osgood	1789-91
	Timothy Pickering	1791-94
	Joseph Habersham	1795-97

John Adams Administration (1797-1801)

Secretary of State	Timothy Pickering	1797-1800
	John Marshall	1800-1801
Secretary of Treasury	Oliver Wolcott	1797-1800
	Samuel Dexter	1800-1801
Secretary of War	James McHenry	1797-1800
	Samuel Dexter	1800-1801
Attorney General	Charles Lee	1797-1801
Postmaster General	Joseph Habersham	1797-1801
Secretary of Navy	Benjamin Stoddert	1798-1801

Speakers of the U.S. House of Representatives

Name	Party	State	Dates in Office
1. Frederick A.C. Muhlenberg	D-R	Pa.	1789-91
2. Jonathan Trumbull	Fed.	Conn.	1791-93
3. Frederick A. C. Muhlenberg	D-R	Pa.	1793-95
4. Jonathan Dayton	Fed.	N.J.	1795-97
5. George Dent	Fed.	Md.	1797-99
6. Theodore Sedgwick	Fed.	Mass.	1799-1801
7. Nathaniel Macon	D-R	N.C.	1801-07
8. Joseph B. Varnum	D-R	Mass.	1807-11
9. Henry Clay	D-R	Ky.	1811-14
10. Langdon Cheves	D-R	S.C.	1814-15
11. Henry Clay	D-R	Ky.	1815-20
12. John W. Taylor	D-R	N.Y.	1820-21
13. Philip Barbour	D-R	Va.	1821-23
14. Henry Clay	D-R	Ky.	1823-25
15. John W. Taylor	D-R	N.Y.	1825-27
16. Andrew Stevenson	D	Va.	1827-34
17. John Bell	D	Tenn.	1834-35
18. James K. Polk	D	Tenn.	1835-39
19. Robert M.T. Hunter	NP	Va.	1839-41
20. John White	Whig	Ky.	1841-43
21. John W. Jones	D	Va.	1843-45
22. John W. Davis	D	Ind.	1845-47
23. Robert C. Winthrop	Whig	Mass.	1847-49
24. Howell Cobb	D	Ga.	1849-51
25. Linn Boyd	D	Ky.	1851-55
26. Nathaniel Banks	R	Mass.	1855-57
27. James L. Orr	D	S.C.	1857-59
28. William Pennington	Whig	N.J.	1859-61
29. Galusha A. Grow	R	Pa.	1861-63
30. Schuyler Colfax	R	Ind.	1863-69
31. James G. Blaine	R	Maine	1869-75
32. Michael C. Kerr	D	Ind.	1875-76
33. Samuel J. Randall	D	Pa.	1876-81
34. J. Warren Keifer	R	Ohio	1881-83
35. John G. Carlisle	D	Ky.	1883-89
36. Thomas B. Reed	R	Maine	1889-91
37. Charles F. Crisp	D	Ga.	1891-95
38. Thomas B. Reed	R	Maine	1895-99
39. David B. Henderson	R	Iowa	1899-1903
40. Joseph G. Cannon	R	Ill.	1903-11
41. Champ Clark	D	Mo.	1911-19
42. Frederick H. Gillett	R	Mass.	1919-25
43. Nicholas Longworth	R	Ohio	1925-31
44. John Nance Garner	D	Tex.	1931-33
45. Henry T. Rainey	D	Ill.	1933-34
46. Joseph W. Byrns	D	Tenn.	1935-36
47. William B. Bankhead	D	Ala.	1936-39
48. Sam Rayburn	D	Tex.	1940-46
49. Joseph W. Martin Jr.	R	Mass.	1947-49
50. Sam Rayburn	D	Tex.	1949-52
51. Joseph W. Martin Jr.	R	Mass.	1953-54
52. Sam Rayburn	D	Tex.	1955-61
53. John W. McCormack	D	Mass.	1962-71
54. Carl B. Albert	D	Okla.	1971-76
55. Thomas P. O'Neill Jr.	D	Mass.	1977-87
56. James C. Wright Jr.	D	Tex.	1987-89
57. Thomas S. Foley	D	Wash.	1989-95
58. Newt Gingrich	R	Ga.	1995-99
59. J. Dennis Hastert	R	Ill.	1999-2006
60. Nancy Pelosi	D	Calif.	2006-

Notes: D = Democrat. Fed. = Federalist. R = Republican.

Jefferson Administration (1801–09)

Secretary of State	James Madison	1801–09
Secretary of Treasury	Samuel Dexter	1801
	Albert Gallatin	1801–09
Secretary of War	Henry Dearborn	1801–09
Attorney General	Levi Lincoln	1801–05
	Robert Smith	1805
	John Breckinridge	1805–06
	Caesar Rodney	1807–09
Postmaster General	Joseph Habersham	1801
	Gideon Granger	1801–09
Secretary of Navy	Robert Smith	1801–09

Madison Administration (1809–17)

Secretary of State	Robert Smith	1809–11
	James Monroe	1811–17
Secretary of Treasury	Albert Gallatin	1809–13
	George Campbell	1814
	Alexander Dallas	1814–16
	William Crawford	1816–17
Secretary of War	William Eustis	1809–13
	John Armstrong	1813–14
	James Monroe	1814–15
	William Crawford	1815–17
Attorney General	Caesar Rodney	1809–11
	William Pinkney	1811–14
	Richard Rush	1814–17
Postmaster General	Gideon Granger	1809–14
	Return Meigs	1814–17
Secretary of Navy	Paul Hamilton	1809–13
	William Jones	1813–14
	Benjamin Crowninshield	1814–17

Monroe Administration (1817–25)

Secretary of State	John Quincy Adams	1817–25
Secretary of Treasury	William Crawford	1817–25
Secretary of War	George Graham	1817
	John C. Calhoun	1817–25
Attorney General	Richard Rush	1817
	William Wirt	1817–25
Postmaster General	Return Meigs	1817–23
	John McLean	1823–25
Secretary of Navy	Benjamin Crowninshield	1817–18
	Smith Thompson	1818–23
	Samuel Southard	1823–25

John Quincy Adams Administration (1825–29)

Secretary of State	Henry Clay	1825–25
Secretary of Treasury	Richard Rush	1825–25
Secretary of War	James Barbour	1825–29
	Peter Porter	1828–29
Attorney General	William Wirt	1825–29
Postmaster General	John McLean	1825–29
Secretary of Navy	Samuel Southard	1825–29

Jackson Administration (1829–37)

Secretary of State	Martin Van Buren	1829–33
	Edward Livingston	1831–33
	Louis McLane	1833–34
	John Forsyth	1834–37
Secretary of Treasury	Samuel Ingham	1829–31
	Louis McLane	1831–33
	William Duane	1833
	Roger B. Taney	1833–34
	Levi Woodbury	1834–37
Secretary of War	John H. Eaton	1829–31
	Lewis Cass	1831–37
	Benjamin Butler	1837
Attorney General	John M. Berrien	1829–31
	Roger B. Taney	1831–33

	Benjamin Butler	1833–37
Postmaster General	William Barry	1829–35
	Amos Kendall	1835–37
Secretary of Navy	John Branch	1829–31
	Levi Woodbury	1831–34
	Mahlon Dickerson	1834–37

Van Buren Administration (1837–41)

Secretary of State	John Forsyth	1837–41
Secretary of Treasury	Levi Woodbury	1837–41
Secretary of War	Joel Poinsett	1837–41
Attorney General	Benjamin Butler	1837–38
	Felix Grundy	1838–40
	Henry D. Gilpin	1840–41
Postmaster General	Amos Kendall	1837–40
	John M. Niles	1840–41
Secretary of Navy	Mahlon Dickerson	1837–38
	James Paulding	1838–41

William Harrison Administration (1841)

Secretary of State	Daniel Webster	1841
Secretary of Treasury	Thomas Ewing	1841
Secretary of War	John Bell	1841
Attorney General	John J. Crittenden	1841
Postmaster General	Francis Granger	1841
Secretary of Navy	George Badger	1841

Tyler Administration (1841–45)

Secretary of State	Daniel Webster	1841–43
	Hugh S. Legaré	1843
	Abel P. Upshur	1843–44
	John C. Calhoun	1844–45
Secretary of Treasury	Thomas Ewing	1841
	Walter Forward	1841–43
	John C. Spencer	1843–44
	George Bibb	1844–45
Secretary of War	John Bell	1841
	John C. Spencer	1841–43
	James M. Porter	1843–44
	William Wilkins	1844–45
Attorney General	John J. Crittenden	1841
	Hugh S. Legaré	1841–43
	John Nelson	1843–45
Postmaster General	Francis Granger	1841
	Charles Wickliffe	1841
Secretary of Navy	George Badger	1841
	Abel P. Upshur	1841
	David Henshaw	1843–44
	Thomas Gilmer	1844
	John Y. Mason	1844–45

Polk Administration (1845–49)

Secretary of State	James Buchanan	1845–49
Secretary of Treasury	Robert J. Walker	1845–49
Secretary of War	William L. Marcy	1845–49
Attorney General	John Y. Mason	1845–46
	Nathan Clifford	1846–48
	Isaac Toucey	1848–49
Postmaster General	Cave Johnson	1845–49
Secretary of Navy	George Bancroft	1845–46
	John Y. Mason	1846–49

Taylor Administration (1849–50)

Secretary of State	John M. Clayton	1849–50
Secretary of Treasury	William Meredith	1849–50
Secretary of War	George Crawford	1849–50
Attorney General	Reverdy Johnson	1849–50
Postmaster General	Jacob Collamer	1849–50
Secretary of Navy	William Preston	1849–50
Secretary of Interior	Thomas Ewing	1849–50

Fillmore Administration (1850–53)

Secretary of State	Daniel Webster	1850–52
	Edward Everett	1852–53
Secretary of Treasury	Thomas Corwin	1850–53
Secretary of War	Charles Conrad	1850–53
Attorney General	John J. Crittenden	1850–53
Postmaster General	Nathan Hall	1850–52
	Sam D. Hubbard	1852–53
Secretary of Navy	William A. Graham	1852–53
	John P. Kennedy	1852–53
Secretary of Interior	Thomas McKennan	1850
	Alexander Stuart	1850–53

Pierce Administration (1853–57)

Secretary of State	William L. Marcy	1853–57
Secretary of Treasury	James Guthrie	1853–57
Secretary of War	Jefferson Davis	1853–57
Attorney General	Caleb Cushing	1853–57
Postmaster General	James Campbell	1853–57
Secretary of Navy	James C. Dobbin	1853–57
Secretary of Interior	Robert McClelland	1853–57

Buchanan Administration (1857–61)

Secretary of State	Lewis Cass	1857–60
	Jeremiah S. Black	1860–61
Secretary of Treasury	Howell Cobb	1857–60
	Philip Thomas	1860–61
	John A. Dix	1861
Secretary of War	John B. Floyd	1857–61
	Joseph Holt	1861
Attorney General	Jeremiah S. Black	1857–60
	Edwin M. Stanton	1860–61
Postmaster General	Aaron W. Brown	1857–59
	Joseph Holt	1859–61
	Horatio King	1861
Secretary of Navy	Isaac Toucey	1857–61
Secretary of Interior	Jacob Thompson	1857–61

Lincoln Administration (1861–65)

Secretary of State	William H. Seward	1861–65
Secretary of Treasury	Salmon P. Chase	1861–65
	William P. Fessenden	1864–65
	Hugh McCulloch	1865
Secretary of War	Simon Cameron	1861–62
	Edwin M. Stanton	1862–65
Attorney General	Edward Bates	1861–64
	James Speed	1864–65
Postmaster General	Horatio King	1861
	Montgomery Blair	1861–64
	William Dennison	1864–65
Secretary of Navy	Gideon Welles	1861–65
Secretary of Interior	Caleb B. Smith	1861–63
	John P. Usher	1863–65

Andrew Johnson Administration (1865–69)

Secretary of State	William H. Seward	1865–69
Secretary of Treasury	Hugh McCulloch	1865–69
Secretary of War	Edwin M. Stanton	1865–67
	Ulysses S. Grant	1867–68
	Lorenzo Thomas	1868
	John M. Schofield	1868–69
Attorney General	James Speed	1865–66
	Henry Stanbery	1866–68
	William M. Evarts	1868–69
Postmaster General	William Dennison	1865–66
	Alexander Randall	1866–69
Secretary of Navy	Gideon Welles	1865–69
Secretary of Interior	John P. Usher	1865
	James Harlan	1865–66
	Orville H. Browning	1866–69

Grant Administration (1869–77)

Secretary of State	Elihu B. Washburne	1869
	Hamilton Fish	1869–77
Secretary of Treasury	George S. Boutwell	1869–73
	William Richardson	1873–74
	Benjamin Bristow	1874–76
	Lot M. Morrill	1876–77
Secretary of War	John A. Rawlins	1869
	William T. Sherman	1869
	William W. Belknap	1869–76
	Alphonso Taft	1876
	James D. Cameron	1876–77
Attorney General	Ebenezer Hoar	1869–70
	Amos T. Ackerman	1870–71
	G. H. Williams	1871–75
	Edwards Pierrepont	1875–76
	Alphonso Taft	1876–77
Postmaster General	John A. J. Creswell	1869–74
	James W. Marshall	1874
	Marshall Jewell	1874–76
	James N. Tyner	1876–77
Secretary of Navy	Adolph E. Borie	1869
	George M. Robeson	1869–77
Secretary of Interior	Jacob D. Cox	1869–70
	Columbus Delano	1870–75
	Zachariah Chandler	1875–77

Hayes Administration (1877–81)

Secretary of State	William M. Evarts	1877–81
Secretary of Treasury	John Sherman	1877–81
Secretary of War	George W. McCrary	1877–79
	Alex Ramsey	1879–81
Attorney General	Charles Devens	1877–81
Postmaster General	David M. Key	1877–80
	Horace Maynard	1880–81
Secretary of Navy	Richard W. Thompson	1877–80
	Nathan Goff, Jr.	1881
Secretary of Interior	Carl Schurz	1877–81

Garfield Administration (1881)

Secretary of State	James G. Blaine	1881
Secretary of Treasury	William Windom	1881
Secretary of War	Robert T. Lincoln	1881
Attorney General	Wayne MacVeagh	1881
Postmaster General	Thomas L. James	1881
Secretary of Navy	William H. Hunt	1881
Secretary of Interior	Samuel J. Kirkwood	1881

Arthur Administration (1881–85)

Secretary of State	F. T. Frelinghuysen	1881–85
Secretary of Treasury	Charles J. Folger	1881–84
	Walter Q. Gresham	1884
	Hugh McCulloch	1884–85
Secretary of War	Robert T. Lincoln	1881–85
Attorney General	Benjamin H. Brewster	1881–85
Postmaster General	Timothy O. Howe	1881–83
	Walter Q. Gresham	1883–84
	Frank Hatton	1884–85
Secretary of Navy	William H. Hunt	1881–82
	William E. Chandler	1882–85
Secretary of Interior	Samuel J. Kirkwood	1881–82
	Henry M. Teller	1882–85

Cleveland Administration (1885–89)

Secretary of State	Thomas F. Bayard	1885–89
Secretary of Treasury	Daniel Manning	1885–87
	Charles S. Fairchild	1887–89
Secretary of War	William C. Endicott	1885–89
Attorney General	Augustus H. Garland	1885–89
Postmaster General	William F. Vilas	1885–88
	Don M. Dickinson	1888–89

Secretary of Navy	William C. Whitney	1885–89
Secretary of Interior	Lucius Q. C. Lamar	1885–88
	William F. Vilas	1888–89
Secretary of Agriculture	Norman J. Colman	1889

Benjamin Harrison Administration (1889–93)

Secretary of State	James G. Blaine	1889–92
	John W. Foster	1892–93
Secretary of Treasury	William Windom	1889–91
	Charles Foster	1891–93
Secretary of War	Redfield Proctor	1889–91
	Stephen B. Elkins	1891–93
Attorney General	William H. H. Miller	1889–91
Postmaster General	John Wanamaker	1889–93
Secretary of Navy	Benjamin F. Tracy	1889–93
Secretary of Interior	John W. Noble	1889–93
Secretary of Agriculture	Jeremiah M. Rusk	1889–93

Cleveland Administration (1893–97)

Secretary of State	Walter Q. Gresham	1893–95
	Richard Olney	1895–97
Secretary of Treasury	John G. Carlisle	1893–97
Secretary of War	Daniel S. Lamont	1893–97
Attorney General	Richard Olney	1893–95
	James Harmon	1895–97
Postmaster General	Wilson S. Bissell	1893–95
	William L. Wilson	1895–95
Secretary of Navy	Hilary A. Herbert	1893–97
Secretary of Interior	Hoke Smith	1893–96
	David R. Francis	1896–97
Secretary of Agriculture	Julius S. Morton	1893–97

McKinley Administration (1897–1901)

Secretary of State	John Sherman	1897–98
	William R. Day	1898
	John Hay	1898–1901
Secretary of Treasury	Lyman J. Gage	1897–1901
Secretary of War	Russell A. Alger	1897–99
	Elihu Root	1899–1901
Attorney General	Joseph McKenna	1897–98
	John W. Griggs	1898–1901
	Philander C. Knox	1901
Postmaster General	James A. Gary	1897–98
	Charles E. Smith	1898–1901
Secretary of Navy	John D. Long	1897–1901
Secretary of Interior	Cornelius N. Bliss	1897–99
	Ethan A. Hitchcock	1899–1901
Secretary of Agriculture	James Wilson	1897–1901

Theodore Roosevelt Administration (1901–09)

Secretary of State	John Hay	1901–05
	Elihu Root	1905–09
	Robert Bacon	1909
Secretary of Treasury	Lyman J. Gage	1901–02
	Leslie M. Shaw	1902–07
	George B. Cortelyou	1907–09
Secretary of War	Elihu Root	1901–04
	William H. Taft	1904–08
	Luke E. Wright	1908–09
Attorney General	Philander C. Knox	1901–04
	William H. Moody	1904–06
	Charles J. Bonaparte	1906–09
Postmaster General	Charles E. Smith	1901–02
	Henry C. Payne	1902–04
	Robert J. Wynne	1904–05
	George B. Cortelyou	1905–07
	George von L. Meyer	1907–09
Secretary of Navy	John D. Long	1901–02
	William H. Moody	1902–04
	Paul Morton	1904–05
	Charles J. Bonaparte	1905–06

	Victor H. Metcalf	1906–08
	Truman H. Newberry	1908–09
Secretary of Interior	Ethan A. Hitchcock	1901–07
	James R. Garfield	1907–09
Secretary of Agriculture	James Wilson	1901–09
Secretary of Labor and Commerce	George B. Cortelyou	1903–04
	Victor H. Metcalf	1904–06
	Oscar S. Straus	1906–09
	Charles Nagel	1909

Taft Administration (1909–13)

Secretary of State	Philander C. Knox	1909–13
Secretary of Treasury	Franklin MacVeagh	1909–13
Secretary of War	Jacob M. Dickinson	1909–11
	Henry L. Stimson	1911–13
Attorney General	George W. Wickersham	1909–13
Postmaster General	Frank H. Hitchcock	1909–13
Secretary of Navy	George von L. Meyer	1909–13
Secretary of Interior	Richard A. Ballinger	1909–11
	Walter Fisher	1911–13
Secretary of Agriculture	James Wilson	1909–13
Secretary of Labor and Commerce	Charles Nagel	1909–13

Wilson Administration (1913–21)

Secretary of State	William J. Bryan	1913–15
	Robert Lansing	1915–20
	Bainbridge Colby	1920–21
Secretary of Treasury	William G. McAdoo	1913–18
	Carter Glass	1918–20
	David F. Houston	1920–21
Secretary of War	Lindley M. Garrison	1913–16
	Newton D. Baker	1916–21
Attorney General	James C. McReynolds	1913–14
	Thomas W. Gregory	1914–19
	A. Mitchell Palmer	1919–21
Postmaster General	Albert S. Burleson	1913–21
Secretary of Navy	Josephus Daniels	1913–21
Secretary of Interior	Franklin K. Lane	1913–20
	John B. Payne	1920–21
Secretary of Agriculture	David F. Houston	1913–20
	Edwin T. Meredith	1920–21
Secretary of Commerce	William C. Redfield	1913–19
Secretary of Labor	William B. Wilson	1913–21

Harding Administration (1921–23)

Secretary of State	Charles E. Hughes	1921–23
Secretary of Treasury	Andrew Mellon	1921–23
Secretary of War	John W. Weeks	1921–23
Attorney General	Harry M. Daugherty	1921–23
Postmaster General	Will H. Hays	1921–22
	Hubert Work	1922–23
	Harry S. New	1923
Secretary of Navy	Edwin Denby	1921–23
Secretary of Interior	Albert B. Fall	1921–23
	Hubert Work	1923
Secretary of Agriculture	Henry C. Wallace	1921–23
Secretary of Commerce	Herbert C. Hoover	1921–23
Secretary of Labor	James J. Davis	1921–23

Coolidge Administration (1923–29)

Secretary of State	Charles E. Hughes	1923–25
	Frank B. Kellogg	1925–29
Secretary of Treasury	John W. Weeks	1923–25
	Dwight F. Davis	1925–29
Attorney General	Henry M. Daugherty	1923–24
	Harlan F. Stone	1923–25
	John G. Sargent	1925–29
Postmaster General	Harry S. New	1923–29
Secretary of Navy	Edwin Denby	1923–24
	Curtis D. Wilbur	1924–29

Secretary of Interior	Hubert Work	1923–28
	Roy O. West	1928–29
Secretary of Agriculture	Henry C. Wallace	1923–24
	Howard M. Gore	1924–25
	William M. Jardine	1925–29
Secretary of Commerce	Herbert C. Hoover	1923–28
	William F. Whiting	1928–29
Secretary of Labor	James J. Davis	1923–29

Hoover Administration (1929–33)

Secretary of State	Henry L. Stimson	1929–33
Secretary of Treasury	Andrew Mellon	1929–32
	Ogden L. Mills	1932–33
Secretary of War	James W. Good	1929
	Patrick J. Hurley	1929–33
Attorney General	William D. Mitchell	1929–33
Postmaster General	Walter F. Brown	1929–33
Secretary of Navy	Charles F. Adams	1929–33
Secretary of Interior	Ray L. Wilbur	1929–33
Secretary of Agriculture	Arthur M. Hyde	1929–33
Secretary of Commerce	Robert P. Lamont	1929–32
	Roy D. Chapin	1932–33
Secretary of Labor	James J. Davis	1929–30
	William N. Doak	1930–33

Franklin D. Roosevelt Administration (1933–45)

Secretary of State	Cordell Hull	1933–44
	Edward R. Stettinius, Jr.	1944–45
Secretary of Treasury	William H. Woodin	1933–34
	Henry Morgenthau, Jr.	1934–45
Secretary of War	George H. Dern	1933–36
	Henry A. Woodring	1936–40
	Henry L. Stimson	1940–45
Attorney General	Homer S. Cummings	1933–39
	Frank Murphy	1939–40
	Robert H. Jackson	1940–41
	Francis Biddle	1941–45
Postmaster General	James A. Farley	1933–40
	Frank C. Walker	1940–45
Secretary of Navy	Claude A. Swanson	1933–40
	Charles Edison	1940
	Frank Knox	1940–44
	James V. Forrestal	1944–45
Secretary of Interior	Harold L. Ickes	1933–45
Secretary of Agriculture	Henry A. Wallace	1933–40
	Claude R. Wickard	1940–45
Secretary of Commerce	Daniel C. Roper	1933–39
	Harry L. Hopkins	1939–40
	Jesse Jones	1940–45
	Henry A. Wallace	1945
Secretary of Labor	Frances Perkins	1933–45

Truman Administration (1945–53)

Secretary of State	Edward R. Stettinius, Jr.	1945
	James F. Byrnes	1945–47
	George C. Marshall	1947–49
	Dean G. Acheson	1949–53
Secretary of Treasury	Fred M. Vinson	1945–46
	John W. Snyder	1946–53
Secretary of War	Robert P. Patterson	1945–47
	Kenneth C. Royall	1947
Attorney General	Tom C. Clark	1945–49
	J. Howard McGrath	1949–52
	James P. McGranery	1952–53
Postmaster General	Frank C. Walker	1945
	Robert E. Hannegan	1945–47
	Jesse M. Donaldson	1947–53
Secretary of Navy	James V. Forrestal	1945–47
Secretary of Interior	Harold L. Ickes	1945–46
	Julius A. Krug	1946–49
	Oscar L. Chapman	1949–53
Secretary of Agriculture	Clinton P. Anderson	1945–48

	Charles F. Brannan	1948–53
Secretary of Commerce	Henry A. Wallace	1945–46
	W. Averell Harriman	1946–48
	Charles W. Sawyer	1948–53
Secretary of Labor	Lewis B. Schwellenbach	1945–48
	Maurice J. Tobin	1948–53
Secretary of Defense	James V. Forrestal	1947–49
	Louis A. Johnson	1949–50
	George C. Marshall	1950–51
	Robert A. Lovett	1951–53

Eisenhower Administration (1953–61)

Secretary of State	John Foster Dulles	1953–59
	Christian A. Herter	1959–61
Secretary of Treasury	George M. Humphrey	1953–57
	Robert B. Anderson	1957–61
Attorney General	Herbert Brownell, Jr.	1953–58
	William P. Rogers	1958–61
Postmaster General	Arthur E. Summerfield	1953–61
Secretary of Interior	Douglas McKay	1953–56
	Fred A. Seaton	1956–61
Secretary of Agriculture	Ezra T. Benson	1953–61
Secretary of Commerce	Sinclair Weeks	1953–58
	Lewis L. Strauss	1958–59
	Frederick H. Mueller	1959–61
Secretary of Labor	Martin P. Durkin	1953
	James P. Mitchell	1953–61
Secretary of Defense	Charles E. Wilson	1953–57
	Neil H. McElroy	1957–59
	Thomas S. Gates, Jr.	1959–61
Secretary of Health, Education, and Welfare	Oveta Culp Hobby	1953–55
	Marion B. Folsom	1955–58
	Arthur S. Flemming	1958–61

Kennedy Administration (1961–63)

Secretary of State	Dean Rusk	1961–63
Secretary of Treasury	C. Douglas Dillon	1961–63
Attorney General	Robert F. Kennedy	1961–63
Postmaster General	J. Edward Day	1961–63
	John A. Gronouski	1963
Secretary of Interior	Stewart L. Udall	1961–63
Secretary of Agriculture	Orville L. Freeman	1961–63
Secretary of Commerce	Luther H. Hodges	1961–63
Secretary of Labor	Arthur J. Goldberg	1961–62
	W. Willard Wirtz	1962–63
Secretary of Defense	Robert S. McNamara	1961–63
Secretary of Health, Education, and Welfare	Abraham A. Ribicoff	1961–62
	Anthony J. Celebrezze	1962–63

Lyndon Johnson Administration (1963–69)

Secretary of State	Dean Rusk	1963–69
Secretary of Treasury	C. Douglas Dillon	1963–65
	Henry H. Fowler	1965–69
Attorney General	Robert F. Kennedy	1963–64
	Nicholas Katzenbach	1965–66
	Ramsey Clark	1967–69
Postmaster General	John A. Gronouski	1963–65
	Lawrence F. O'Brien	1965–68
	Marvin Watson	1968–69
Secretary of Interior	Stewart L. Udall	1963–69
Secretary of Agriculture	Orville L. Freeman	1963–69
Secretary of Commerce	Luther H. Hodges	1963–64
	John T. Connor	1964–67
	Alexander B. Trowbridge	1967–68
	Cyrus R. Smith	1968–69
Secretary of Labor	W. Willard Wirtz	1963–69
Secretary of Defense	Robert F. McNamara	1963–68
	Clark Clifford	1968–69
Secretary of Health, Education, and Welfare	Anthony J. Celebrezze	1963–65
	John W. Gardner	1965–68
	Wilbur J. Cohen	1968–69
Secretary of Housing & Urban Development	Robert C. Weaver	1966–69
	Robert C. Wood	1969

Secretary of Transportation	Alan S. Boyd	1967–69

Nixon Administration (1969–74)

Secretary of State	William P. Rogers	1969–73
	Henry A. Kissinger	1973–74
Secretary of Treasury	David M. Kennedy	1969–70
	John B. Connally	1971–72
	George P. Shultz	1972–74
	William E. Simon	1974
Attorney General	John N. Mitchell	1969–72
	Richard G. Kleindienst	1973–73
	Elliot L. Richardson	1973
	William B. Saxbe	1973–74
Postmaster General	Winton M. Blount	1969–71
Secretary of Interior	Walter J. Hickel	1969–70
	Rogers Morton	1971–74
Secretary of Agriculture	Clifford M. Hardin	1969–71
	Earl L. Butz	1971–74
Secretary of Commerce	Maurice H. Stans	1969–72
	Peter G. Peterson	1972–73
	Frederick B. Dent	1973–74
Secretary of Labor	George P. Shultz	1969–70
	James D. Hodgson	1970–73
	Peter J. Brennan	1973–74
Secretary of Defense	Melvin R. Laird	1969–73
	Elliot L. Richardson	1973
	James R. Schlesinger	1973–74
Secretary of Health, Education, and Welfare	Robert H. Finch	1969–70
	Elliot L. Richardson	1970–73
	Caspar W. Weinberger	1973–74
Secretary of Housing & Urban Development	George Romney	1969–73
	James T. Lyon	1973–74
Secretary of Transportation	John A. Volpe	1969–73
	Claude S. Brinegar	1973–74

Ford Administration (1974–77)

Secretary of State	Henry A. Kissinger	1974–77
Secretary of Treasury	William E. Simon	1974–77
Attorney General	William Saxbe	1974–75
	Edward Levi	1975–77
Secretary of Interior	Rogers Morton	1974–75
	Stanley K. Hathaway	1975
	Thomas Kleppe	1975–77
Secretary of Agriculture	Earl L. Butz	1974–76
	John A. Knebel	1976–77
Secretary of Commerce	Frederick B. Dent	1974–75
	Rogers Morton	1975–76
	Elliot L. Richardson	1976–77
Secretary of Labor	Peter J. Brennan	1974–75
	John T. Dunlop	1975–76
	W. J. Usery	1976–77
Secretary of Defense	James R. Schlesinger	1974–75
	Donald Rumsfeld	1975–77
Secretary of Health, Education, and Welfare	Caspar Weinberger	1974–75
	Forrest D. Mathews	1975–77
Secretary of Housing & Urban Development	James T. Lynn	1974–75
	Carla A. Hills	1975–77
Secretary of Transportation	William T. Coleman	1975–77

Carter Administration (1977–81)

Secretary of State	Cyrus R. Vance	1977–80
	Edmund Muskie	1980–81
Secretary of Treasury	W. Michael Blumenthal	1977–79
	G. William Miller	1979–81
Attorney General	Griffin Bell	1977–79
	Benjamin R. Civiletti	1979–81
Secretary of Interior	Cecil D. Andrus	1977–81
Secretary of Agriculture	Robert Bergland	1977–81
Secretary of Commerce	Juanita M. Kreps	1977–79
	Philip M. Klutznick	1979–81
Secretary of Labor	F. Ray Marshall	1977–81

Secretary of Defense	Harold Brown	1977–81
Secretary of Health, Education, and Welfare	Joseph A. Califano	1977–79
	Patricia R. Harris	1979–80
Secretary of Health & Human Services[1]	Patricia R. Harris	1980–81
Secretary of Housing & Urban Development	Patricia R. Harris	1977–79
	Moon Landrieu	1979–81
Secretary of Transportation	Brock Adams	1977–79
	Neil E. Goldschmidt	1979–81
Secretary of Energy	James R. Schlesinger	1977–79
	Charles W. Duncan	1979–81
Secretary of Education[1]	Shirley M. Hufstedler	1980–81

1. The Dept. of Health, Education, and Welfare was split into the Dept. of Education and the Dept. of Health and Human Services on May 4, 1980.

Reagan Administration (1981–89)

Secretary of State	Alexander M. Haig	1981–82
	George P. Shultz	1982–89
Secretary of Treasury	Donald Regan	1981–85
	James A. Baker, III	1985–89
Secretary of Defense	Caspar Weinberger	1981–87
	Frank Carlucci	1987–89
Attorney General	William F. Smith	1981–85
	Edwin A. Meese, III	1985–88
	Richard L. Thornburgh	1988–89
Secretary of Interior	James Watt	1981–83
	William P. Clark, Jr.	1983–85
	Donald P. Hodel	1985–89
Secretary of Agriculture	John Block	1981–86
	Richard E. Lyng	1986–89
Secretary of Commerce	Malcolm Baldrige	1981–87
	C. William Verity Jr	1987–89
Secretary of Labor	Raymond Donovan	1981–85
	William E. Brock	1985–89
Secretary of Health & Human Services	Richard Schweiker	1981–83
	Margaret Heckler	1983–85
	Otis R. Bowen	1985–89
Secretary of Housing & Urban Development	Samuel Pierce	1981–89
Secretary of Transportation	Drew Lewis	1981–83
	Elizabeth Dole	1983–89
Secretary of Energy	James Edwards	1981–82
	Donald P. Hodel	1982–85
	John S. Herrington	1985–89
Secretary of Education	Terrel H. Bell	1981–85
	William J. Bennett	1985–89

George Bush Administration (1989–93)

Secretary of State	James A. Baker III	1989–92
	Lawrence Eagleburger	1992–93
Secretary of Treasury	Nicholas F. Brady	1989–93
Secretary of Defense	Dick Cheney	1989–93
Attorney General	Richard L. Thornburgh	1989–91
	William P. Barr	1991–93
Secretary of Interior	Manuel Lujan	1989–93
Secretary of Agriculture	Clayton K. Yeutter	1989–91
	Edward Madigan	1991–93
Secretary of Commerce	Robert A. Mosbacher	1989–91
	Barbara Franklin	1991–93
Secretary of Labor	Elizabeth Hanford Dole	1989–90
	Lynn Martin	1990–93
Secretary of Health & Human Services	Louis Sullivan	1989–93
Secretary of Housing & Urban Development	Jack F. Kemp	1989–93
Secretary of Transportation	Samuel K. Skinner	1989–91
	Andrew Card	1991–93
Secretary of Energy	James D. Watkins	1989–93
Secretary of Education	Lauro D. Cavazos	1989–90
	Lamar Alexander	1990–93
Secretary of Veterans' Affairs	Edward J. Derwinski	1989–92
	Anthony J. Principi	1992–93

Clinton Administration (1993–2001)

Secretary of State	Warren M. Christopher	1993–97
	Madeleine K. Albright	1997–2001
Secretary of Treasury	Lloyd Bentsen	1993–94
	Robert E. Rubin	1994–99
	Lawrence H. Summers	1999–2001
Secretary of Defense	Les Aspin	1993–94
	William Perry	1994–97
	William S. Cohen	1997–2001
Attorney General	Janet Reno	1993–2001
Secretary of Interior	Bruce Babbitt	1993–2001
Secretary of Agriculture	Mike Espy	1993–94
	Dan Glickman	1995–2001
Secretary of Commerce	Ronald H. Brown	1993–96
	Mickey Kantor	1996–97
	William M. Daley	1997–2000
	Norman Y. Mineta	2000–2001
Secretary of Labor	Robert B. Reich	1993–97
	Alexis M. Herman	1997–2001
Secretary of Health & Human Services	Donna E. Shalala	1993–2001
Secretary of Housing & Urban Development	Henry G. Cisneros	1993–97
	Andrew M. Cuomo	1997–2001
Secretary of Transportation	Federico F. Peña	1993–97
	Rodney E. Slater	1997–2001
Secretary of Energy	Hazel O'Leary	1993–97
	Federico F. Peña	1997–98
	Bill Richardson	1998–2001
Secretary of Education	Richard W. Riley	1993–2001
Secretary of Veterans' Affairs	Jesse Brown	1993–97
	Hershel Gober, acting	1997–98
	Togo D. West Jr.	1998–99
	Hershel Gober, acting	1999–2001

George W. Bush Administration (2001–)

Secretary of State	Colin Powell	2001–05
	Condoleezza Rice	2005–
Secretary of Treasury	Paul O'Neill	2001–02
	John Snow	2003–06
	Henry M. Paulson, Jr.	2006–
Secretary of Defense	Donald Rumsfeld	2001–06
	Robert M. Gates	2006–
Attorney General	John Ashcroft	2001–05
	Alberto Gonzales	2005–07
	Michael Mukasey	2007–
Secretary of Interior	Gale Norton	2001–06
	Dirk Kempthorne	2006–
Secretary of Agriculture	Ann Veneman	2001–05
	Michael Johanns	2005–07
	Ed Schafer	2008–
Secretary of Commerce	Donald Evans	2001–05
	Carlos Gutierrez	2005–
Secretary of Labor	Elaine Chao	2001–
Secretary of Health & Human Services	Tommy Thompson	2001–05
	Michael Leavitt	2005–
Secretary of Housing & Urban Development	Mel Martinez	2001–04
	Alphonso Jackson	2004–08
	Steve Preston	2008–
Secretary of Transportation	Norman Mineta	2001–06
	Mary Peters	2006–
Secretary of Energy	Spencer Abraham	2001–05
	Samuel Bodman	2005–
Secretary of Education	Rod Paige	2001–05
	Margaret Spellings	2005–
Secretary of Veterans' Affairs	Anthony Principi	2001–05
	Jim Nicholson	2005–07
	James Peake	2007–
Secretary of Homeland Security	Tom Ridge	2002–05
	Michael Chertoff	2005–

THE U.S. SUPREME COURT

▶IMPORTANT SUPREME COURT DECISIONS

Marbury v. Madison (1803) The Court struck down a law "repugnant to the constitution" for the first time and set the precedent for judicial review of acts of Congress. In a politically ingenious ruling on the Judiciary Act of 1789, Chief Justice John Marshall asserted the Supreme Court's power "to say what the law is," while avoiding a confrontation with President Thomas Jefferson. Not until the *Dred Scott* case of 1857 would another Federal law be ruled unconstitutional.

Fletcher v. Peck (1810) The Court ruled that Georgia could not deprive land speculators of their title, even though the previous owners had obtained the land from the state through fraud and bribery. Arising from the infamous Yazoo land frauds of 1795, this decision followed the Constitution's obligation of contracts clause and was the first time the Court invalidated a state law.

Dartmouth College v. Woodward (1819) The Court encouraged business investment with this decision by treating corporate charters as fully protected contracts. Not even the state legislatures that originally granted them could tamper with charters to private corporations, unless they retained the power to do so. Dartmouth College remained a private institution despite New Hampshire's attempt to take it over. This decision, which opened the way for abuse of corporate privileges, would later be modified in the *Charles River Bridge* (1837) and *Munn v. Illinois* (1877) cases.

McCulloch v. Maryland (1819) "Broad," as opposed to "strict," construction of the Constitution received high court approval in Chief Justice John Marshall's opinion upholding the constitutionality of the national bank against a Maryland challenge. This ruling enhanced Federal governmental authority by liberally interpreting the power of Congress to make laws "necessary and proper" for its specified powers. At a time when states were trying to tax the Bank of the United States out of existence, this decision also forbade such state interference with the Federal government. "The power to tax," Marshall wrote, "involves the power to destroy."

Cohens v. Virginia (1821) With this ruling, the Court reiterated its power to hear appeals from state courts, and affirmed the national supremacy of Federal judicial power. Virginia's conviction of the Cohens for selling lottery tickets in violation of state law was upheld, but so too was the Cohens' right to appeal to the Court, which Virginia had challenged. Critics of judicial "consolidationism" were reminded of the Court's comprehensive powers as the ultimate appellate court for all Americans.

Gibbons v. Ogden (1824) In a dispute arising from a New York ferry monopoly, the Court ruled that states could not restrain interstate commerce in any way, and that congressional power to regulate interstate commerce "does not stop at the jurisdictional lines of the several states." The decision helped prevent interstate trade wars, quite common under the Articles of Confederation, from breaking out under the Constitution. Chief Justice Marshall's opinion also confirmed the broad potential power of the Constitution's commerce clause.

Charles River Bridge v. Warren Bridge (1837) A key decision for economic development, this case arose when state-chartered proprietors of a Boston toll bridge objected that a new state-chartered bridge across the Charles River would put them out of business. Chief Justice Roger B. Taney, in his first constitutional ruling, held that state charters implied no vested rights and that ambiguities must be construed in favor of the public, which would benefit from the new toll-free bridge. This decision balanced private property rights against the public welfare.

Dred Scott v. Sanford (1857) Dred Scott, a Missouri slave, sued for his liberty after his owner took him into free territory. The Court ruled that Congress could not bar slavery in the territories. Scott remained a slave because the Missouri Compromise of 1820, prohibiting slavery from part of the Louisiana Purchase, violated the Fifth Amendment by depriving slave owners of their right to enjoy property without due process of law. Scott himself could not even sue, for he was held to be property, not a citizen. This decision sharpened sectional conflict by sweeping away legal barriers to the expansion of slavery.

Ex Parte Milligan (1866) President Abraham Lincoln's suspension of some civil liberties during the Civil War was attacked in this decision, which upheld the right of *habeas corpus*. The Court ruled that the president could not hold military tribunals in areas remote from battle and where civil courts were open and functioning. Milligan's conviction by such a Civil War tribunal in Indianapolis, was overturned. The Constitution, admonished the Court, applies "at all times, and under all circumstances."

Slaughter-House Cases (1873) In its first ruling on the Fourteenth Amendment, the Court held that Louisiana's grant of a butcher monopoly did not violate the privileges and immunities of competitors, nor deny them equal protection of the laws, nor deprive them of property without due process. Only a few rights deriving from "Federal citizenship" were subject to Federal protection, while states still protected most civil and property rights. Federal protection of civil rights, even for former slaves, was very narrowly interpreted in this ruling. But this decision broadly upheld business regulation by states until *Santa Clara Co. v. Southern Pacific Railroad Co.* (1886) applied the Fourteenth Amendment to defense of corporate property rights.

Munn v. Illinois (1877) This decision, in one of the "Granger Cases," enabled states to regulate private property in the public interest when the public had an interest in that property. The Court held that Illinois laws setting maximum rates for grain storage did not violate the Fourteenth Amendment's ban on deprivation of property without due process of law, and did not restrain interstate commerce. But for the next half century, the Court imposed the burden of proof on the states for their regulatory laws.

Civil Rights Cases (1883) Racial equality was postponed 80 years by this decision, which struck down the Civil Rights Act of 1875 and allowed for private segregation. The Fourteenth Amendment's guarantee of equal protection, the Court ruled, applied against state action—but not against private individuals, whose discrimination unaided by the states was beyond Federal control. Segregation of public facilities was approved soon afterward in *Plessy v. Ferguson* (1896).

United States v. E.C. Knight Co. (1895) The first ruling on the Sherman Antitrust Act of 1890, this decision curtailed Federal regulation of monopolies by placing national manufacturers beyond the reach of the Constitution's commerce clause. Only the actual interstate commerce of monopolies, not their production activities, was subject to Federal control. The Court's distinction between production and commerce impeded Federal regulation of manufacturing until *National Labor Relations Board v. Jones & Laughlin Steel Corp.* (1937).

Plessy v. Ferguson (1896) The "separate but equal" doctrine supporting public segregation by law received the Court's approval in this ruling, which originated with segregated railroad cars in Louisiana. The Court held that as long as equal accommodations were provided, segregation was not discrimination and did not deprive blacks of equal protection of the laws under the Fourteenth Amendment. This decision was overturned in *Brown v. Board of Education* (1954).

Lochner v. New York (1905) This decision struck down a New York law placing limits on maximum working hours for bakers. The law violated the Fourteenth Amendment by restricting individual "freedom of contract" to buy and sell labor, and was an excessive use of state police power, the Court held. The ruling was soon modified in *Muller v. Oregon* (1908), which approved state-regulated limits on women's labor after the Court used sociological and economic data to consider the health and morals of women workers.

Standard Oil Co. of New Jersey v. United States (1911) Federal efforts to break up monopolies under the Sherman Antitrust Act had to follow the "rule of reason," according to this ruling. Only those combinations in restraint of trade which were contrary to the public interest, and therefore unreasonable, were illegal. Although the Taft administration's prosecution of Standard Oil was upheld, breaking up one of the nation's leading monopolies, further antitrust suits were impaired by this decision, which facilitated the 1920's merger movement.

Schenk v. United States (1919) The Court unanimously held that World War I limits on freedom of speech did not violate the First Amendment—if the speech in question represented a "clear and present danger." That famous doctrine of Justice Oliver Wendell Holmes, which approved the arrest of a draft resister for handing out pamphlets to soldiers in wartime, became an important standard for interpreting the First Amendment. But in subsequent cases of this period, the Court added that the mere "bad tendency" of speech to cause danger could be grounds for censorship.

Schechter Poultry Corp. v. United States (1935) At the height of its assault on the New Deal, the Court struck down the National Industrial Recovery Act in the famous "Sick Chicken Case." The NIRA was found to delegate excessive legislative regulatory powers to

Chief Justices of the United States

Chief Justice	Tenure[1]	Appointed by
John Jay	1789–1795	George Washington
John Rutledge[3]	1795	George Washington
Oliver Ellsworth	1796–1800	George Washington
John Marshall[4]	1801–35	John Adams
Roger B. Taney	1836–64	Andrew Jackson
Salmon P. Chase	1864–73	Abraham Lincoln
Morrison R. Waite	1874–88	Ulysses S. Grant
Melville W. Fuller	1888–1910	Grover Cleveland
Edward D. White	1910–21	William Howard Taft
William Howard Taft[5]	1921–30	Warren G. Harding
Charles Evans Hughes[2]	1930–41	Herbert Hoover
Harlan F. Stone[2]	1941–46	Franklin D. Roosevelt
Fred M. Vinson	1946–53	Harry S Truman
Earl Warren	1953–69	Dwight D. Eisenhower
Warren E. Burger	1969–86	Richard M. Nixon
William H. Rehnquist[2]	1986–2005	Ronald Reagan
John G. Roberts, Jr.	2005–	George W. Bush

1. Dates are for tenure as Chief Justice. For complete tenure on Supreme Court, see "Supreme Court Justices." 2. Served one term, but appointment not confirmed by Senate. 3. Served one term, but appointment not confirmed by Senate. 4. Longest tenure as Chief Justice. 5. Formerly served as 27th president of the United States.

Justices of the Supreme Court of the United States, 1789–2008

Name	Tenure	Appointed by	Name	Tenure	Appointed by
Alito, Samuel A., Jr.	2006–	George W. Bush	Livingston, H. Brockholst	1806–23	Thomas Jefferson
Baldwin, Henry	1830–44	Andrew Jackson			
Barbour, Philip P.	1836–41	Andrew Jackson	Lurton, Horace H.	1910–14	William Howard Taft
Black, Hugo L.	1937–71	Franklin D. Roosevelt	Marshall, John[1]	1801–35	John Adams
Blackmun, Harry A.	1970–94	Richard M. Nixon	Marshall, Thurgood	1967–92	Lyndon B. Johnson
Blair, John	1789–96	George Washington	Matthews, Stanley	1881–89	James A. Garfield
Blatchford, Samuel	1882–93	Chester A. Arthur	McKenna, Joseph	1898–1925	William McKinley
Bradley, Joseph P.	1870–92	Ulysses S. Grant	McKinley, John	1837–52	Martin Van Buren
Brandeis, Louis D.	1916–39	Woodrow Wilson	McLean, John	1829–61	Andrew Jackson
Brennan, William J., Jr.	1956–90	Dwight D. Eisenhower	McReynolds, James C.	1914–41	Woodrow Wilson
Brewer, David J.	1889–1910	Benjamin Harrison	Miller, Samuel F.	1862–90	Abraham Lincoln
Breyer, Stephen G.	1994–	Bill Clinton	Minton, Sherman	1949–56	Harry S Truman
Brown, Henry B.	1890–1906	Benjamin Harrison	Moody, William H.	1906–10	Theodore Roosevelt
Burger, Warren E.[1]	1969–87	Richard M. Nixon	Moore, Alfred	1799–1804	John Adams
Burton, Harold H.	1945–58	Harry S Truman	Murphy, Frank	1940–49	Franklin D. Roosevelt
Butler, Pierce	1922–39	Warren G. Harding	Nelson, Samuel	1845–72	John Tyler
Byrnes, James F.	1941–42	Franklin D. Roosevelt	O'Connor, Sandra Day	1981–2005	Ronald Reagan
Campbell, John A.	1853–61	Franklin Pierce	Paterson, William	1793–1806	George Washington
Cardozo, Benjamin N.	1932–38	Herbert Hoover	Peckham, Rufus W.	1895–1910	Grover Cleveland
Catron, John	1837–65	Martin Van Buren	Pitney, Mahlon	1912–22	William Howard Taft
Chase, Salmon P.[1]	1864–73	Abraham Lincoln	Powell, Lewis F., Jr.	1972–87	Richard M. Nixon
Chase, Samuel	1796–1811	George Washington	Reed, Stanley F.	1938–57	Franklin D. Roosevelt
Clark, Tom C.	1949–67	Harry S Truman	Rehnquist, William H.[1]	1972–2005	Richard M. Nixon
Clarke, John H.	1916–22	Woodrow Wilson	Roberts, John G., Jr.	2005–	George W. Bush
Clifford, Nathan	1858–81	James J. Buchanan	Roberts, Owen J.	1930–45	Herbert Hoover
Curtis, Benjamin R.	1851–57	Millard Fillmore	Rutledge, John[1]	1789–91	George Washington
Cushing, William	1789–1810	George Washington		1795	George Washington
Daniel, Peter V.	1841–60	Martin Van Buren	Rutledge, Wiley B.	1943–49	Franklin D. Roosevelt
Davis, David	1862–77	Abraham Lincoln	Sanford, Edward T.	1923–30	Warren G. Harding
Day, William R.	1903–22	Theodore Roosevelt	Scalia, Antonin	1986–	Ronald Reagan
Douglas, William O.[2]	1939–75	Franklin D. Roosevelt	Shiras, George	1892–1903	Benjamin Harrison
Duval, Gabriel	1811–36	James Madison	Souter, David H.	1990–	George Bush
Ellsworth, Oliver[1]	1796–1800	George Washington	Stevens, John Paul	1975–	Gerald R. Ford
Field, Stephen J.	1863–97	Abraham Lincoln	Stewart, Potter	1959–81	Dwight D. Eisenhower
Fortas, Abe	1965–69	Lyndon B. Johnson	Stone, Harlan F.[1]	1925–46	Calvin Coolidge
Frankfurter, Felix	1939–62	Franklin D. Roosevelt	Story, Joseph	1811–45	James Madison
Fuller, Melville W.[1]	1888–1910	Grover Cleveland	Strong, William	1870–80	Ulysses S. Grant
Ginsburg, Ruth Bader	1993–	Bill Clinton	Sutherland, George	1922–38	Warren G. Harding
Goldberg, Arthur J.	1962–65	John F. Kennedy	Swayne, Noah H.	1862–81	Abraham Lincoln
Gray, Horace	1881–1902	Chester A. Arthur	Taft, William Howard[1,5]	1921–30	Warren G. Harding
Grier, Robert C.	1846–70	James K. Polk	Taney, Roger B.[1]	1836–64	Andrew Jackson
Harlan, John Marshall	1877–1911	Rutherford B. Hayes	Thomas, Clarence	1991–	George Bush
Harlan, John Marshall[3]	1955–71	Dwight D. Eisenhower	Thompson, Smith	1823–43	James Monroe
Harrison, Robert H.	1789–90	George Washington	Todd, Thomas	1807–26	Thomas Jefferson
Holmes, Oliver Wendell	1902–32	Theodore Roosevelt	Trimble, Robert	1826–28	John Quincy Adams
Hughes, Charles Evans[1,4]	1910–16	William Howard Taft	Van Devanter, Willis	1910–37	William Howard Taft
	1930–41	Herbert Hoover	Vinson, Fred M.[1]	1946–53	Harry S Truman
Hunt, Ward	1872–82	Ulysses S. Grant	Waite, Morrison R.[1]	1874–88	Ulysses S. Grant
Iredell, James	1790–99	George Washington	Warren, Earl[1]	1953–69	Dwight D. Eisenhower
Jackson, Howell E.	1893–95	Benjamin Harrison	Washington, Bushrod	1798–1829	John Adams
Jackson, Robert H.	1941–54	Franklin D. Roosevelt	Wayne, James M.	1835–67	Andrew Jackson
Jay, John[1]	1789–95	George Washington	White, Byron R.	1962–93	John F. Kennedy
Johnson, Thomas	1791–93	George Washington	White, Edward D.[1]	1894–1921	Grover Cleveland
Johnson, William	1804–34	Thomas Jefferson	Whittaker, Charles E.	1957–62	Dwight D. Eisenhower
Kennedy, Anthony M.	1987–	Ronald Reagan	Wilson, James	1789–98	George Washington
Lamar, Joseph R.	1911–16	William Howard Taft	Woodbury, Levi	1845–51	James K. Polk
Lamar, Lucius Q. C.	1888–93	Grover Cleveland	Woods, William B.	1880–87	Rutherford B. Hayes

Note: Dates reflect complete tenure on the Supreme Court, including tenure as Chief Justice. 1. See "Chief Justices of the United States" for dates of tenure and appointment as Chief Justice. 2. Longest-serving justice. 3. The two Harlans were grandfather and grandson. 4. Stepped down as Associate Justice to run for president in 1916; later appointed Chief Justice. 5. Formerly served as 27th U.S. president.

the executive without constitutional authority, and to regulate commerce within states in violation of the commerce clause. Schechter's kosher chicken supply house in New York did not have to abide by the NIRA's rigid industry codes, the Court ruled.

National Labor Relations Board v. Jones & Laughlin Steel Corp. (1937)
Under pressure from the public and President Franklin D. Roosevelt, the Court abruptly reversed itself and began approving New Deal legislation. In this case, laws protecting unions and barring "unfair labor practices" were upheld by the "stream of commerce" doctrine that employers who sold their goods and obtained their raw materials through interstate commerce were subject to Federal regulation. This ruling overturned *U.S. v. E.C. Knight Co.* (1895) and became the basis for the expansive understanding of the commerce power.

West Virginia Board of Education v. Barnette (1943)
The Court reversed its earlier ruling in *Minersville School District v. Gobitis* (1940), which had required Jehovah's Witnesses to salute the flag in school. In this case, also brought against a Jehovah's Witness, the Court recognized that refusing to salute the flag did not violate anyone's rights, and that the First Amendment protected the "right of silence" as well as freedom of speech.

Korematsu v. United States (1944)
President Franklin D. Roosevelt's Executive Order No. 9066, which approved the West Coast evacuation and internment of 120,000 Japanese-Americans during World War II, was upheld on the grounds of "military necessity" in this ruling. The Court was reluctant to interfere with executive authority in time of national emergency. But in *Ex parte Endo* (1944), the Court held that persons of proven loyalty should not be interned. In August 1988, Congress made a formal apology to former internees and appropriated $1.25 billion in compensation for the 60,000 survivors.

Dennis v. United States (1951)
At the height of the postwar "Red Scare," the Court upheld the conviction of 11 American Communist leaders under the Smith Act of 1940, which made it a crime to belong to organizations teaching or advocating the violent overthrow of the government. The "clear and present danger" doctrine could be disregarded, the Court held, if "the gravity of the 'evil,' discounted by its improbability, justifies such invasion of free speech as is necessary to avoid the evil." Over 100 Communists were indicted as a result, effectively destroying the Communist Party as a political force.

Youngstown Sheet and Tube Co. v. Sawyer (1952)
During the Korean War, when President Harry S Truman seized steel plants to keep them operating despite a strike, the Court held that his action was an unconstitutional usurpation of legislative authority. Only an act of Congress, not the president's inherent executive powers or military powers as commander-in-chief, could justify such a sizeable confiscation of property, even in wartime.

Brown v. Board of Education of Topeka (1954)
Chief Justice Earl Warren led the Court unanimously to decide that segregated schools violated the equal protection clause of the Fourteenth Amendment. The "separate but equal" doctrine of *Plessy v. Ferguson* (1896) was overruled after a series of cases dating back to *Missouri ex. rel. Gaines v. Canada* (1938) had already limited it. "Separate educational facilities are inherently unequal," held the Court. Efforts to desegregate southern schools after the *Brown* decision met with massive resistance for many years.

Baker v. Carr (1962)
Overrepresentation of rural districts in state legislatures, which effectively disfranchised millions of voters, led the Court to abandon its traditional non-interference in drawing legislative boundaries. Tennessee citizens deprived of full representation by "arbitrary and capricious" malapportionment were denied equal protection under

the Fourteenth Amendment, ruled the Court. All states eventually reapportioned their legislatures in conformance with the "one man, one vote" doctrine of *Reynolds v. Sims* (1964).

Gideon v. Wainwright (1963)
Reversing an earlier ruling in *Betts v. Brady* (1942), the Court held that the Sixth Amendment guaranteed access to qualified counsel, which was "fundamental to a fair trial." Gideon was entitled to a retrial because Florida failed to provide him with an attorney. After this decision, states were required to furnish public defenders for indigent defendants in felony cases. In *Argersinger v. Hamlin* (1972), the ruling was extended to all cases that might result in imprisonment.

Heart of Atlanta Motel, Inc. v. United States (1964)
The Court upheld Title II of the Civil Rights Act of 1964, outlawing private discrimination in public accommodations, as a legitimate exertion of Federal power over interstate commerce. Congress had "ample power" to forbid racial discrimination in facilities that affected commerce by serving interstate travelers. The Heart of Atlanta Motel was located on two interstate highways, so the Court could sidestep the *Civil Rights Cases* (1883) protection of private discrimination to overrule it.

Griswold v. Connecticut (1965)
In striking down an 1879 Connecticut law against the use of contraceptives, the Court established a "right to privacy" that was implied by, though not specifically enumerated in the First, Third, Fourth, Fifth, Ninth, and Fourteenth Amendments. The case is most notable for laying the groundwork for other legal challenges invoking this newfound right to privacy. Foremost among them is the 1973 *Roe v. Wade* decision allowing women to choose abortion.

South Carolina v. Katzenbach (1966)
Federal intervention on behalf of voting rights was upheld in this decision. South Carolina sued the Attorney General, contending that the 1965 Voting Rights Act encroached on the reserved powers of the states, treated the states unequally, and violated separation of powers. Chief Justice Warren ruled that the Fifteenth Amendment gave Congress broad powers to "use any rational means to effectuate the constitutional prohibition of racial discrimination in voting." After this decision, blacks registered and voted in massive numbers in the South.

Miranda v. Arizona (1966)
Expanding upon *Gideon v. Wainwright* (1963) and *Escobedo v. Illinois* (1964), the Court set forth stringent interrogation procedures for criminal suspects to protect their Fifth Amendment freedom from self-incrimination. Miranda's confession to kidnapping and rape was obtained without counsel and without his having been advised of his right to silence, so it was ruled inadmissible as evidence. This decision obliged police to advise suspects of their rights upon taking them into custody.

New York Times Co. v. United States (1971)
When the *New York Times* and the *Washington Post* published the top-secret "Pentagon Papers" in 1971, revealing government duplicity in the Vietnam War, the Nixon administration obtained an injunction against the *Times* on grounds of national security. But in a brief *per curiam* opinion, the Court observed that in this case, the government had not met the "heavy burden of showing justification" for "prior restraint" on freedom of the press.

Roe v. Wade (1973)
In a controversial ruling, the Court held that state laws restricting abortion were an unconstitutional invasion of a woman's right to privacy. Only in the last trimester of pregnancy, when the fetus achieved viability outside the womb, might states regulate abortion—except when the life or health of the mother was at stake. In *Planned Parenthood of Central Missouri v. Danforth* (1976), the Court added that wives did not need their husbands' consent to obtain abortions. However, in *Gonzales v.*

Carhart (2007), a more conservative Court for the first time upheld a prohibition on a specific form of abortion when it reversed lower court rulings that had found the 2003 federal Partial-Birth Abortion Ban Act to be unconstitutional because it did not provide a broad exception for the health of the mother.

United States v. Nixon (1974) In a unanimous ruling, the Court held that the secret White House recordings of President Richard M. Nixon's conversations with aides were subject to subpoena in the Watergate coverup trial. Nixon's claim to "executive privilege" was rejected as invalid because military and national security issues were not at stake, and Chief Justice Warren Burger cited *Marbury v. Madison* (1803) to assert the Court's primacy in constitutional issues. Once the tapes were released, documenting Nixon's obstruction of justice, the president resigned to avoid impeachment.

University of California Regents v. Bakke (1978) Twice refused admission to medical school, Bakke sued the University of California for giving "affirmative action" preference to less-qualified black applicants. In an ambiguous 5-4 ruling, the Court agreed that Bakke's right to equal protection had been denied, that he should be admitted, and that affirmative action quotas should be discarded. But at the same time, the Court recognized race as "a factor" in admissions and hiring decisions. Affirmative action could continue as long as rigid quotas did not constitute, in effect, "reverse discrimination."

Immigration and Naturalization Service v. Chadha (1983) The legislative veto, contained in hundreds of Federal statutes since 1932, was disallowed in this decision. Congress exceeded its constitutional powers when it blocked the Attorney General's suspension of a deportation order for Jagdish Rai Chadha, a Kenyan student who overstayed his visa. The Court held that the Immigration and Nationality Act's legislative veto provision violated the constitutional separation of powers. Chief Justice Warren Burger recognized that Congress would prefer to delegate authority to the executive branch and reserve the right to veto administrative regulations, but "we have not found a better way to preserve freedom" than the separation of powers.

Bush v. Gore (2000) For the first time ever, the Court decided a presidential election. With Florida's decisive 25 electoral votes in the balance, Vice Pres. Al Gore filed suit in state court to begin a recount of ballots in several counties where machines were unable to determine the voter's selection. Texas Gov. George W. Bush appealed the decision to the Supreme Court, which ruled that because there were no uniform standards for how to conduct a recount, doing so would violate the Fourteenth Amendment's guarantee of equal protection. The highly controversial 5-4 decision ended the recount 36 days after Election Day, and with it, Gore's chance of winning the presidency.

Lawrence v. Texas (2003) In overturning a Texas law against sodomy, the Court explicitly reversed *Bowers v. Hardwick* (1986). The majority opinion in Lawrence echoed Justice John Paul Stevens' dissent in *Bowers*, with its broad interpretation of due process rights. "The liberty protected by the Constitution allows homosexual persons the right to choose to enter upon relationships in the confines of their homes and their own private lives." The fact that 12 states repealed sodomy laws after Bowers was further evidence that "Bowers was not correct when it was decided, is not correct today, and is hereby overruled."

Hamdi v. Rumsfeld (2004) In a case that maintained judicial authority over a wartime executive, the Court ruled that the president could not deny defendants access to American courts simply by labeling them "enemy combatants." Declaring that "a state of war is not a blank check for the president," the Court said the government had deprived Yaser Esam Hamdi, an American citizen seized in Afghanistan, of his due process rights. In two companion cases, the Court ruled that non-citizens seized during military operations could not be held without access to U.S. courts.

Kelo v. City of New London (2005) This eminent domain case was brought against New London, Connecticut by its residents. The city planned to turn a faded residential neighborhood into a multi-use complex, but the owners of 15 of the houses scheduled for demolition rejected the city's compensation offer and filed suit. Taking private property for "public use" traditionally referred to highway projects and utility right-of-ways, but the Court ruled that "public use" should be understood as "public purpose," and that the city's plan for economic rejuvenation fell under that heading. The 5-4 decision upholding the plan was met with strenuous objections from politicians and the public.

Hamdan v. Rumsfeld (2006) In a 5-3 decision, the Court blocked President Bush's plan to try Guantanamo Bay detainees before the military commission he established without Congressional approval in 2001. Salim Ahmed Hamdan, a Yemini detainee captured in Afghanistan in 2001, brought to Guantanamo in 2002, and charged with conspiracy to commit terrorism in 2004, would have been the first tried before the commission. The Court ruled that the commission's procedures violated the Uniform Code of Military Justice and the Geneva Conventions by permitting a defendant to be barred from his trial and denied access to evidence presented against him.

Massachusetts v. Environmental Protection Agency (2007) Twelve states, two cities and several interest groups filed suit against the Environmental Protection Agency (E.P.A.) in an attempt to force the agency to regulate carbon dioxide emissions, which the Bush Administration had declined to do, citing a lack of regulatory authority. This 5-4 decision found that the Clean Air Act gives the agency that authority and obligation and the court ordered the E.P.A. to either implement such regulations or justify its refusal to do so. The most significant aspect of the decision may be the court's conclusion that sovereign states have "standing to sue" the federal government.

Parents Involved in Community Schools v. Seattle School District No. 1 (2007) Combining two affirmative action cases, the court invalidated school integration plans adopted by Seattle and Louisville, Ky. school systems, finding that they violated the 14th Amendment guarantee of equal protection. While the plans differed, both were similar to those in hundreds of school districts around the country that seek to maintain school diversity by using race as a deciding factor in granting school assignment or transfer requests. Although the minority found that such plans were consistent with *Brown v. Board of Education*, Chief Justice Roberts, writing for the 5-4 majority, said, "The way to stop discrimination on the basis of race is to stop discriminating on the basis of race."

Boumediene v. Bush (2008) In 2004, the Court ruled (*Rasul v. Bush*) that foreign detainees who were being held without charges outside U.S. territory were entitled to challenge their detentions through habeas corpus. Lakhdar Boumediene, an Algerian held since 2001 on suspicion of planning an attack on the U.S. embassy in Bosnia, and 36 other Guantanamo Bay detainees then filed a joint habeas corpus petition. But, in 2005, Congress passed the Detainee Treatment Act, which stripped federal courts of the power to hear such cases, and instead gave the D.C. Court of Appeals sole jurisdiction to review decisions of the military tribunals overseeing such detainees. In a 5-4 decision that brought strong words from the minority and politicians, the court majority declared these provisions unconstitutional, holding that habeas corpus does apply to aliens imprisoned at Guantanamo and that a military tribunal with only a limited appeal is not an adequate substitution for a writ in a federal court.

The Federal Government

In their desire to create a government based on an elaborate system of "checks and balances," the Founding Fathers divided the sources of power into three separate and distinct branches of government—the legislative, the judicial, and the executive. The fundamental purpose, organization, and workings of these three branches are set down in the first three articles of the Constitution. Despite the passing of more than two centuries, the creation of dozens of departments, agencies, and commissions, the ongoing employment of almost 2.7 million civilian workers, and the presence of a standing peacetime military force of some 1.5 million, this structure remains essentially unchanged.

Below is a list of every major body within the Federal Government. Wherever possible, a Web home page is included. Every entry mentions the date each entity was founded and summarizes its official function. (The primary source of this information is the National Archives and Records Administration, Office of the Federal Register, *U.S. Government Manual*.)

THE JUDICIAL BRANCH

▶**SUPREME COURT OF THE UNITED STATES**
United States Supreme Court Building, 1 First St. NE, Washington, DC 20543. (202) 479-3000. *www.supremecourtus.gov*. Created by the Judiciary Act of September 24, 1789 in accordance with Article III, section 1 of the Constitution. Composed of the chief justice and a number of associate justices to be fixed by Congress. Justices (including the chief justice) are chosen by the president with the advice and consent of the Senate and have lifetime tenure. Court terms begin the first Monday of October and usually end on the preceding day the next year. In recent years, the Court has seen the size of its docket more than double (from 4,212 cases in 1970 to more than 10,000 in 2007), but it has heard fewer and fewer of these cases (see the accompanying table).

▶**LOWER COURTS**
U.S. Courts of Appeals
These intermediate appellate courts were created by an act on March 3, 1891, to relieve the Supreme Court of having to reconsider all trials originally decided by federal courts. Decisions of these courts are final except when law provides for direct review by the Supreme Court. Each of the 50 states is assigned to one of the 11 judicial circuits that compose the Court of Appeals system.

District of Columbia Circuit: Washington, D.C.
First Circuit: Maine, Massachusetts, New Hampshire, Rhode Island, Puerto Rico
Second Circuit: Connecticut, New York, Vermont
Third Circuit: Delaware, New Jersey, Pennsylvania, Virgin Islands

The Supreme Court, 2007-08

Name	Appointed by	Born	Law school
John G. Roberts, Jr. Chief Justice	Bush, 2005	1955	Harvard
John Paul Stevens	Ford, 1975	1920	Northwestern
Antonin Scalia	Reagan, 1986	1936	Harvard
Anthony M. Kennedy	Reagan, 1987	1936	Harvard
David H. Souter	Bush, 1990	1939	Harvard
Clarence Thomas	Bush, 1991	1948	Yale
Ruth Bader Ginsburg	Clinton, 1993	1933	Columbia
Stephen G. Breyer	Clinton, 1994	1938	Harvard
Samuel A. Alito, Jr.	Bush, 2006	1950	Yale

Cases Before U.S. Supreme Court, U.S. Courts of Appeals, and U.S. District Courts, 1970–2007

Status	1970	1980	1990	1995	2000	2005	2007
U.S. Supreme Court							
Total cases on docket	4,212	5,144	6,316	7,565	8,445	8,588	10,256
Cases argued	151	154	125	90	83	87	78
Number of signed opinions	109	123	112	75	79	85	74
U.S. Courts of Appeals							
Cases commenced	11,662	23,200	40,898	49,671	54,967	68,473	58,410
Cases terminated	10,699	20,887	38,520	50,085	56,512	61,975	62,846
Cases disposed of[1]	6,139	10,607	21,006	28,187	27,516	29,913	31,717
Median months to final disposition[2]	8.2	8.9	10.1	10.5	11.6	11.8	12.2
U.S. District Courts							
Civil cases commenced[3]	87,300	168,800	217,900	239,013	259,517	253,273	257,507
Trials[3,4]	8,000	10,100	9,200	7,700	5,780	5,294	5,600
Percent reaching trial	10.0%	6.5%	4.3%	3.4%	2.2%	2.0%	2.2%
Criminal cases commenced[3,5]	38,100	28,000	46,500	44,200	62,745	69,575	68,413
Defendants disposed of	36,400	36,600	56,500	55,300	75,071	86,000	88,014
Not convicted	8,200	8,000	9,800	9,000	8,035	8,661	9,153
Convicted	28,200	28,600	46,700	46,300	67,036	73,616	78,861

Note: Data are for the 12 months ending on September 30 of year shown. **1.** Terminated on the merits after hearing or submission. Beginning 1980, data not comparable with earlier years due to changes in criteria. **2.** Prior to 1985, the figure is from filing of complete record to final disposition; beginning 1985, figure is from filing notice of appeal to final disposition. **3.** Figures rounded in source. **4.** A trial is defined as a contested proceeding (other than a hearing on a motion) before either court or jury in which evidence is introduced and final judgment sought. **5.** Excludes transfers. **Source:** Administrative Office of the U.S. Courts. Judicial Business of the United States Courts, 2008.

Fourth Circuit: Maryland, North Carolina, South Carolina, Virginia, West Virginia
Fifth Circuit: Louisiana, Mississippi, Texas
Sixth Circuit: Kentucky, Michigan, Ohio, Tennessee
Seventh Circuit: Illinois, Indiana, Wisconsin
Eighth Circuit: Arkansas, Iowa, Minnesota, Missouri, Nebraska, North Dakota, South Dakota
Ninth Circuit: Alaska, Arizona, California, Guam, Hawaii, Idaho, Montana, Nevada, Northern Mariana Islands, Oregon, Washington
Tenth Circuit: Colorado, Kansas, New Mexico, Oklahoma, Utah, Wyoming
Eleventh Circuit: Alabama, Florida, Georgia
Federal Circuit: nationwide

U.S. District Courts   These are trial courts of general federal jurisdiction. There are 89 courts in the 50 states, including at least one in each state and the District of Columbia. Each court has from 2 to 28 federal district judgeships, depending on the amount of work within the territory. Overall, there are 645 permanent district judges in the 50 states, 15 in the District of Columbia and seven in Puerto Rico. Usually one judge is required to decide a case, but in some limited cases it is required that three judges be called together to comprise the court.

Administrative Office of the U.S. Courts   One Columbus Circle NE, Washington, DC 20544. (202) 502-2600.   *www.uscourts.gov*. Created by act of Aug. 7, 1939 as a support agency for federal courts except the Supreme Court. Administers courts, supervises probation office, and oversees administration of bankruptcy courts, magistrate offices, and public defender's offices.

Federal Judicial Center   Thurgood Marshall Federal Judiciary Building, One Columbus Circle NE, Washington, DC 20002-8003. (202) 502-4000. *www.fjc.gov*. Created by act of Dec. 20, 1967. Its mission is to further the development and adoption of improved judicial administration in U.S. courts. The Chief Justice of the Supreme Court is the permanent chairman of the center's Board of Directors.

United States Sentencing Commission   Suite 2-500, South Lobby, One Columbus Circle NE, Washington, DC 20002-8002. (202) 502-4500. *www.ussc.gov*. Created by the Sentencing Reform Act of 1984. Establishes sentencing guidelines (including forms and severity of punishment) for federal offenses.

THE LEGISLATIVE BRANCH

Architect of the Capitol   U.S. Capitol, Washington, DC 20515. (202) 228-1793. *www.aoc.gov*. First Architect appointed in 1793 by President Washington. Permanent authority for care of Capitol established by Act of August 15, 1876. Responsible for care and maintenance of Capitol building and grounds, Library of Congress buildings, U.S. Supreme Court building and U.S. Botanic Garden. Operates Senate and House restaurants. Maintains, operates, and cares for House and Senate office buildings. Plans future construction, renovation, reconstruction, and alterations to existing buildings.

U.S. Botanic Garden   Director's Office: 245 First Street SW, Washington, DC 20024. (202) 226-8333. *www.usbg.gov*. Conservatory: Maryland Avenue-First to Second Streets SW; Washington, D.C. 20024. Plant Hotline: (202) 226-4785. Created in 1820. Collects, cultivates, and grows vegetable and plant matter of this and other countries for exhibition and display. Provides study materials on vegetable and plant matter for students, botanists, horticulturists, floriculturists, and garden clubs.

Government Accountability Office (GAO)   441 G Street NW Washington, DC 20548. (202) 512-3000. *www.gao.gov*. Created in 1921 by Budget and Accounting Act. Provides legal, accounting, auditing, and claims settlement services for Congress. Facilitates more efficient government operations.

Government Printing Office (GPO)   732 North Capitol Street NW, Washington, DC 20401. (202) 512-0000. *www.gpo.gov*. Created June 23, 1860 by Congressional Joint Resolution 25. Provides printing and binding services for Congress and the departments and establishments of the Federal Government. Furnishes blank paper, ink, and supplies to all agencies. Prepares and distributes catalogs and government publications.

Library of Congress   101 Independence Ave. SE Washington, DC 20540. (202) 707-5000. *www.loc.gov*. Created by law of April 24, 1800. Librarian appointed by the President. Buys books necessary for use by Congress and/or other governmental agencies. National library of the United States. Develops and maintains national book classification systems such as the Library of Congress and Dewey Decimal systems. Maintains and publishes The National Union Catalogs.

Congressional Budget Office (CBO)   Ford House Office Building, Fourth Floor, Second and D Streets SW, Washington, DC 20515. (202) 226-2600. *www.cbo.gov*. Created by Congressional Budget Act of 1974. Provides basic budget data to Congress. Analyzes and evaluates fiscal and budgetary policy options to Congress. Publishes annual report on the budget.

How A Bill Becomes Law

Usually bills are raised in any of the various committees of the Senate or House of Representatives. If the bill is supported by a majority of the committee, it is brought to the floor of the house in which it originated, and voted upon. If it gains majority support in the full Senate or House, the other house of Congress votes on it. If the bill is passed in both the Senate and House, it is sent to the President, who may either sign it, veto it, or not act on it.

If the president signs it or refuses to act within 10 days and the Congress is still in session, the bill becomes law. If the president vetoes it, it is returned to the Senate and the House for another vote; a two-thirds majority in each house is then required to overturn the presidential veto. However, if the president refuses to act on a bill and Congress adjourns before the end of the 10-day period, the legislation is dead. This is known as a *pocket veto*.

Occasionally, bills are raised on the floor of the Senate or the House, in which case the first step of committee voting is avoided and the legislation process begins with the full Senate or House Vote. All other processes remain the same.

How to Contact Your Senator or Representative

To contact any senator, call (202) 224-3121. More information about the Senate is available on the Internet at *www.senate.gov*. To reach a Represen- tative, call (202) 225-3121. More information about the House is available on the Internet at *www.house.gov.*

The 110th Congress of the United States

The upper house of the U.S. Congress, the Senate, is composed of 100 members: two from each state. Members are elected to six-year terms. One-third of the Senate faces re-election every two years. Senators must have been U.S. citizens for at least nine years and must be at least 30 years old. In the table below, the senior senator is listed first.

The lower house of government is known as the House of Representatives, and is composed of 435 members. The number of representatives from each state is determined by population every 10 years; every state is entitled to at least one representative. The entire House faces re-election every two years. Representatives must have been U.S. citizens for at least seven years and must be at least 25 years old.

In addition to state representatives, there are delegates from the District of Columbia, American Samoa, Guam, and the Virgin Islands, and a resident commissioner from Puerto Rico. They may take part in floor debates, but they may not vote.

Senate Offices

President	Dick Cheney (R-Wyoming)
President Pro Tem	Robert Byrd (D-West Virginia)
Majority Leader	Harry Reid (D-Nevada)
Majority Whip	Richard Durbin (D-Illinois)
Minority Leader	Mitch McConnell (R-Kentucky)
Minority Whip	John Kyl (R-Arizona)

House Offices

Speaker	Nancy Pelosi (D-California)
Majority Leader	Steny Hoyer (D-Maryland)
Majority Whip	James E. Clyburn (D-S. Carolina)
Minority Leader	John Boehner (R-Ohio)
Minority Whip	Roy Blunt (R-Missouri)

U.S. Senators 2008

Alabama
Richard C. Shelby (R)
*Jeff Sessions (R)

Alaska
*Ted Stevens (R)
Lisa Murkowski (R)

Arizona
John McCain (R)
Jon Kyl (R)

Arkansas
Blanche Lincoln (D)
*Mark Pryor (D)

California
Dianne Feinstein (D)
Barbara Boxer (D)

Colorado
*Wayne A. Allard (R)
Ken Salazar (D)

Connecticut
Christopher Dodd (D)
Joseph I. Lieberman (I)

Delaware
*Joseph R. Biden Jr. (D)
Thomas R. Carper (D)

Florida
Bill Nelson (D)
Mel Martinez (R)

Georgia
*Saxby Chambliss (R)
Johnny Isakson (R)

Hawaii
Daniel K. Inouye (D)
Daniel K. Akaka (D)

Idaho
*Larry E. Craig (R)
Mike Crapo (R)

Illinois
*Richard J. Durbin (D)
Barack Obama (D)

Indiana
Richard G. Lugar (R)
Evan Bayh (D)

Iowa
Chuck Grassley (R)
*Tom Harkin (D)

Kansas
*Pat Roberts (R)
Sam Brownback (R)

Kentucky
*Mitch McConnell (R)
Jim Bunning (R)

Louisiana
*Mary Landrieu (D)
David Vitter (R)

Maine
Olympia J. Snowe (R)
*Susan Collins (R)

Maryland
Barbara A. Mikulski (D)
Benjamin L. Cardin (D

Massachusetts
Edward M. Kennedy (D)
*John F. Kerry (D)

Michigan
*Carl Levin (D)
Debbie Stabenow (D)

Minnesota
*Norm Coleman (R)
Amy Klobuchar (D)

Mississippi
*Thad Cochran (R)
Roger Wicker (R)

Missouri
Christopher S. Bond (R)
Claire McCaskill (D)

Montana
*Max Baucus (D)
Jon Tester (D)

Nebraska
*Chuck Hagel (R)
Benjamin E. Nelson (D)

Nevada
Harry Reid (D)
John Ensign (R)

New Hampshire
Judd Gregg (R)
*John Sununu (R)

New Jersey
*Frank Lautenberg (D)
Robert Menendez (D)

New Mexico
*Pete V. Domenici (R)
Jeff Bingaman (D)

New York
Charles Schumer (D)
Hillary Rodham
  Clinton (D)

North Carolina
*Elizabeth Dole (R)
Richard Burr (R)

North Dakota
Kent Conrad (D)
Byron L. Dorgan (D)

Ohio
George Voinovich (R)
Sherrod Brown (D)

Oklahoma
*James Inhofe (R)
Tom Coburn (R)

Oregon
Ron Wyden (D)
*Gordon Smith (R)

Pennsylvania
Arlen Specter (R)
Robert P. Casey Jr. (D)

Rhode Island
*Jack Reed (D)
Sheldon Whitehouse (D)

South Carolina
*Lindsey Graham (R)
Jim DeMint (R)

South Dakota
*Tim Johnson (D)
John Thune (R)

Tennessee
*Lamar Alexander (R)
Bob Corker (R)

Texas
Kay Bailey
  Hutchison (R)
*John Cornyn (R)

Utah
Orrin G. Hatch (R)
Robert F. Bennett (R)

Vermont
Patrick J. Leahy (D)
Bernard Sanders (I)

Virginia
*John W. Warner (R)
Jim Webb (D)

Washington
Patty Murray (D)
Maria Cantwell (D)

West Virginia
Robert C. Byrd (D)
*John D.
  Rockefeller IV (D)

Wisconsin
Herb Kohl (D)
Russell D. Feingold (D)

Wyoming
*Michael Enzi (R)
John Barrasso (R)

Note: The senior senator is listed first. * = Seat up for re-election in 2008. See Part I: *The Almanac of the Year* for complete results.

Congressional Reapportionment, 2000–02

As a result of population shifts reported in the 2000 Census, a total of eight states gained representatives (four of them gained two), while 10 states lost representatives (two states lost two each). States cannot have fewer than one representative, so even though North Dakota experienced a much lower growth rate than New York, it could not lose its sole member of Congress, whereas New York lost two representatives. The table below shows states gaining and losing representation. States were reapportioned prior to the November, 2002 elections, and the reapportionment took effect in January, 2003.

States Gaining Representatives

Arizona	+2	California	+1
Florida	+2	Colorado	+1
Georgia	+2	Nevada	+1
Texas	+2	North Carolina	+1

Source: U.S. Census Bureau.

States Losing Representatives

New York	-2	Michigan	-1
Pennsylvania	-2	Mississippi	-1
Connecticut	-1	Ohio	-1
Illinois	-1	Oklahoma	-1
Indiana	-1	Wisconsin	-1

THE EXECUTIVE BRANCH

►EXECUTIVE OFFICE OF THE PRESIDENT

White House Office 1600 Pennsylvania Ave. NW, Washington, D.C. 20500 (202) 456-1414. *www.whitehouse.gov.* Serves president in performance of duties incident to his office. Maintains communication with Congress, individual members of Congress, heads of executive agencies, media, and public.

Office of the Vice President of the United States Eisenhower Executive Office Building, Washington, D.C. 20501. (202) 456-2326. *www.whitehouse.gov/vicepresident.* Vice president participates in cabinet meetings, serves as president of Senate, and is, by statute, a member of National Security Council and board of regents of the Smithsonian Institution; empowered to succeed to presidency pursuant to Article II and the 20th and 25th amendments to the Constitution.

Council of Economic Advisers 1800 G St. NW; Washington, D.C. 20502. (202) 395-5084. *www.whitehouse.gov/cea.* Created by Employment Act of 1946. Council's three members—appointed by president—analyze the various segments of the economy, appraise and assess existing economic programs, recommend new economic programs, and assist in preparation President's economic reports to Congress.

Council on Environmental Quality 722 Jackson Place NW, Washington D.C. 20503. (202) 395-5750. *www.whitehouse.gov/ceq.* Eisenhower Executive Office Building, Room 360, Washington D.C. 20501. (202) 456-6224. Created by National Environmental Policy Act of 1969. Recommends national policies to improve quality of environment. Analyzes environmental changes and trends. Assesses and evaluates existing environmental programs. Assists president in compiling annual environmental quality report to Congress.

National Security Council (NSC) Eisenhower Executive Office Building, Washington D.C. 20504. (202) 456-1414. *www.whitehouse.gov/nsc.* Created by National Security Act of 1947. Chaired by president. Members include vice president and secretaries of state and defense. Chairman of Joint Chiefs of Staff is statutory military adviser; CIA director is intelligence adviser. Advises president on integration of domestic, foreign, and military policies relating to national security.

Office of Administration Eisenhower Executive Office Building, 725 17th St. NW, Washington, D.C. 20503. (202) 456-2861. *www.whitehouse. gov/oa.* Created Dec. 12, 1977 by Reorganization Plan No. 1. Provides administrative services to all units within executive office including, upon request, those in direct support of president.

Office of Management and Budget (OMB) 725 17th St. NW, Washington, D.C. 20503. (202) 395-3080. *www.whitehouse.gov/omb.* Created July 1, 1970. Assists president in reviewing and assessing efficiency of structure and management of executive branch. Expands interagency cooperation. Assists president in preparing government's budget and fiscal program. Supervises, controls, and administers the budget. Coordinates departmental advice and makes recommendations to president based on this advice. Plans, conducts, and promotes evaluation efforts to help president assess program objectives, performance, and efficiency. Keeps president informed of work planned and performed by the various government agencies.

Office of National Drug Control Policy 750 17th St. NW, Washington, D.C., 20503. (202) 395-6700. Drug Policy Information Clearinghouse: 800-666-3332. *www.whitehousedrugpolicy.gov.* Created by National Narcotics Leadership Act of 1988. Coordinates Federal, state and local efforts to control illegal drug abuse and devises national strategies to ensure that national anti-drug activities are carried out effectively.

Office of Policy Development Eisenhower Executive Office Building, Washington, D.C. 20502. Composed of the **Domestic Policy Council** (202) 456-5594; *www.whitehouse.gov/dpc,* **National Economic Council** (202) 456-2800, and **Office of National AIDS Policy** (202) 456-7320, Council on Environmental Quality, Office of National Drug Control Policy, Office of Faith Based Initiatives, and USA Freedom Corps, which are responsible for advising and assisting the president in the formulation, coordination, and implementation of domestic and economic policy.

Office of Science and Technology Policy Eisenhower Executive Office Building, Washington, D.C. 20502. (202) 395-7347. *www.ostp.gov.* Created May 11, 1976. Serves as source of scientific, engineering, and technological analysis and expertise for president with respect to public policy in areas of economy, national security, health, foreign relations, and environment. Appraises sale, quality and effectiveness of U.S. efforts in science and technology.

Office of the U.S. Trade Representative

600 17th St. NW, Washington, D.C. 20508. (202) 395-7360. *www.ustr.gov.* Created as Office of the Special Representative for Trade Negotiations, Jan. 15, 1963. Congress made it agency of executive office under Trade Act of 1974. Sets and administers overall trade policy. Representative is chief U.S. representative for all activities of the General Agreement on Tariffs and Trade (GATT) and at discussions, meetings, and negotiations in most conferences in which trade and commodity are issues.

▶DEPARTMENT OF AGRICULTURE (USDA)

1400 Independence Ave. SW, Washington, D.C. 20250. (202) 720-2791. *www.usda.gov.* Created May 15, 1862; incorporated into cabinet, Feb. 8, 1889. Improves and maintains farm income, develops agricultural markets abroad, curbs poverty, hunger, and malnutrition. Through inspection and grading services, safeguard standards of quality in the nation's food supply. The dept. was re-

---

The Cabinet

The president is the administrative head of the executive branch of the Federal Government. A creation of custom and tradition dating back to George Washington's administration, the cabinet functions at the pleasure of the president. Its purpose is to advise the president on any subject on which he requests information. The cabinet is composed of the heads of the 15 executive departments and certain other executive officials to whom the president accords cabinet rank. In the Bush Administration, cabinet-level rank has been accorded to the officials listed below (as of September 30, 2008).

President George W. Bush
Vice President Richard B. Cheney

Office	Officer
Secretary of State	Condoleezza Rice
Secretary of the Treasury	Henry M. Paulson, Jr.
Secretary of Defense	Robert M. Gates
Attorney General (Dept. of Justice)	Michael Mukasey
Secretary of the Interior	Dirk Kempthorne
Secretary of Agriculture	Ed Schafer
Secretary of Commerce	Carlos Gutierrez
Secretary of Labor	Elaine Chao
Secretary of Health and Human Services	Michael O. Leavitt
Secretary of Housing and Urban Development	Steve Preston
Secretary of Transportation	Mary E. Peters
Secretary of Energy	Samuel W. Bodman
Secretary of Education	Margaret Spellings
Secretary of Veterans Affairs	James Peake
Secretary of Homeland Security	Michael Chertoff
White House Chief of Staff	Joshua B. Bolten
Administrator, Environmental Protection Agency	Stephen Johnson
Director, Office of Management and Budget	Jim Nussle
U.S. Trade Representative	Susan Schwab
Director, Office of National Drug Control Policy	John Walters

Source: White House Press Office

---

organized in 1994 into seven program or mission areas: *Rural Development, Marketing & Regulatory Programs, Food Safety, Food Nutrition & Consumer Services, Farm & Foreign Agriculture Services, Research Education & Economics,* and *Natural Resources & Environment.* Each program area may be further divided into more specific agencies, such as the Rural Housing Service or the Food Safety and Inspection Service.

▶DEPARTMENT OF COMMERCE

1401 Constitution Ave. NW, Washington, D.C. 20230. (202) 482-2000. *www.commerce.gov.* Created Feb. 14, 1903 as part of Dept. of Commerce and Labor. Redesignated Dept. of Commerce Mar. 4, 1913. Promotes international trade, economic growth, and technological advancement through encouragement of competitive free-enterprise system, prevention of unfair trade, granting of patents, promotion of tourism and assistance in the growth of minority businesses. The department is divided into 12 operating units; only the major agencies are described in detail below.

Bureau of the Census *www.census.gov.* Created Mar. 6, 1902 by act of Congress. Collects, tabulates, and publishes census statistics about America, its people, and its economy. Statistics are used by Congress, president, and public to aid development and evaluation of public policy. Population and housing censuses are performed every 10 years. Censuses of agriculture, state and local governments, manufacturers, mineral industries, distributive trades, and construction and transportation industries are performed every five years. Special censuses are performed on demand from state and local governments.

Economic Development Administration (EDA) *www.eda.gov.* Created by Public Works and Economic Development Act of 1965. Promotes new jobs, protects existing jobs, and stimulates job growth in areas where unemployment is high or incomes are low.

International Trade Administration (ITA) *www.ita.doc.gov.* Created Jan. 2, 1980. Promotes world trade and strengthens U.S. position in relation to world trade and investment.

Minority Business Development Agency (MBDA) *www.mbda.gov.* Created Nov. 1, 1979. Promotes minority business. Ensures effective, equitable, and competitive participation by minority business in free enterprise system.

National Oceanic and Atmospheric Administration (NOAA) *www.noaa.gov.* Created Oct. 3, 1970. Investigates and maps oceans of world. Discovers, utilizes, and conserves living resources of oceans. Monitors and predicts conditions of atmosphere, sun, and oceans; warns against deterioration of these conditions arising from natural and manmade events and circumstances. Provides weather reports and forecasts. Forecasts floods, hurricanes and other weather-related natural disasters.

National Institute of Standards and Technology (NIST) *www.nist.gov.* Created by Congress in 1901 and expanded in 2007 by America COMPETES Act. Promotes U.S. innovation and industrial competitiveness by conducting research, advising on standards and advancing technology.

▶DEPARTMENT OF DEFENSE (DOD)

The Pentagon, Washington, D.C. 20301-1155. (703) 545-6700. *www.defenselink.mil.* Created by National Security Act Amendments of 1949. Provides necessary military forces to deter war and protect security of the country. The three armed forces departments and the Organization of the Joint Chiefs of Staff make up the military side of the Defense Dept. (Additional information can be found in "National Defense.")

Organization of the Joint Chiefs of Staff

Consists of Chairman of Joint Chiefs of Staff, the chiefs of staff of the three armed forces departments, and the Commandant of the Marine Corps. Advises and assists president and secretary of defense on most military issues. Assists president and secretary of defense in planning, direction, and allocation of strategic resources. Compares strengths and capabilities of American forces with those of potential adversaries.

Department of the Air Force *www.af.mil.*
Created Sept. 18, 1947 by National Security Act of 1947. Works in conjunction with other armed forces to protect peace and security of the U.S. Focuses on air missions and protecting American interests from invasion by air.

Department of the Army *www.army.mil.* U.S. Army created June 14, 1775 by Continental Congress. Dept. of the Army created by National Security Act of 1947. Organizes, trains, and equips active and reserve forces to protect peace, security, welfare, and defense of the U.S. Mission focuses on land operations and maneuvers.

Department of the Navy *www.navy.mil.* U.S. Navy created Oct. 13, 1775, by Continental Congress. Dept. of the Navy created Apr. 30, 1798. Encompasses Marine Corps. Protects U.S. from attack by sea and maintains freedom of the seas.

▶DEPARTMENT OF EDUCATION
400 Maryland Ave. SW, Washington, D.C. 20202. (800) USA-LEARN. *www.ed.gov.* Created Oct. 17, 1979, by Dept. of Education Organization Act. Establishes policy for, administers, and coordinates almost all federal assistance to education.

▶DEPARTMENT OF ENERGY (DOE)
1000 Independence Ave. SW, Washington, D.C. 20585. (202) 586-5000. *www.energy.gov.* Created Oct. 1, 1977, by Dept. of Energy Organization Act. Coordinates and administrates energy functions of Federal Government, including research and development of energy technology, marketing federal power, energy conservation, nuclear weapons and energy regulation.

▶DEPARTMENT OF HEALTH AND HUMAN SERVICES (HHS)
200 Independence Ave. SW, Washington, D.C. 20201. (202) 619-0257. *www.hhs.gov.* Created Apr. 11, 1953, as Dept. of Health, Education, and Welfare. Re-designated Dept. of Health and Human Services Oct. 17, 1979, by Dept. of Education Organization Act. Advises president in formulation of public policy regarding health, welfare, and income and security programs. The department is divided into 12 major administrations and agencies; only the major agencies are described in detail below.

Administration for Children and Families (ACF) *www.acf.hhs.gov.* Created April 15, 1991. Administers child welfare services, foster care and child care programs, the Head Start Program, and other family preservation and support services.

Centers for Disease Control and Prevention (CDC) *www.cdc.gov.* Reorganized, Nov. 9, 1995. Responsible for protecting the public health by preventing and controlling diseases.

Centers for Medicare and Medicaid Services (CMS) *www.cms.hhs.gov.* Formerly Health Care Financing Administration; reorganized June 14, 2001. Oversees Medicare and Medicaid Health Insurance and grant programs. (See "Social Insurance Programs" for additional information).

Food and Drug Administration (FDA) *www.fda.gov.* Created by Agriculture Appropriation Act of 1931; reorganized into HHS Dept. Nov. 9, 1995. It protects the health of the nation against impure and unsafe foods, drugs, cosmetics and other hazards.

National Institutes of Health (NIH) *www.nih.gov.* Reorganized, Nov. 1995. The principal biomedical research agency of the Federal Government, its mission is to employ science in the pursuit of knowledge to improve human health conditions.

Substance Abuse and Mental Health Services Administration *www.samhsa.gov.* Disseminates accurate and up-to-date information on and provides leadership in the prevention and treatment of addictive and mental disorders.

▶DEPARTMENT OF HOMELAND SECURITY
Washington, D.C. 20528. (202) 282-8000. *www.dhs.gov.* Created Jan. 24, 2003 by the Homeland Security Act of 2002. Aims to protect the nation against terrorist attacks while allowing for the free flow of people, goods, and commerce. Provides public services such as natural disaster assistance and citizenship services. The Department continues to change as agencies from other departments are incorporated into it. Major agencies are described below.

Federal Emergency Management Agency (FEMA) 500 C St. SW, Washington, D.C. 20472. (202) 646-4600. *www.fema.gov.* Created Mar. 31, 1979. Transferred to Dept. of Homeland Security Jan. 24, 2003. Provides single point of accountability for all federal emergency preparedness, mitigation, and response activities. Facilitates most efficient use of resources in cases of natural or man-made emergencies.

U.S. Citizenship and Immigration Services (USCIS) *www.uscis.gov.* Created Mar. 3, 1891. Transferred to Dept. of Homeland Security March 1, 2003. Controls immigration into U.S. by facilitating entry to qualified persons and denying admission to unqualified aliens. Deports illegal aliens already in U.S. Encourages and facilitates naturalization and citizenship.

United States Coast Guard *www.uscg.mil.* Created Jan. 28, 1915 as a merger of Revenue Cutter Service and U.S. Lifesaving Service. Moved to Dept. of Transportation Apr. 1, 1967. Transferred to Dept. of Homeland Security in 2003. The Coast Guard is at all times a branch of armed forces and a service with Dept. of Homeland Security except when operating as part of Navy during war. Primary maritime law enforcement agency for U.S. Suppresses drug smuggling and trafficking. Licenses marine vessels. Administers and inspects violations of safety standards for design, construction, equipment and maintenance of commercial marine vessels and offshore structures in U.S. waters. Provides search and rescue functions for saving lives and property in U.S. waters. Operates ice-breaking vessels to facilitate marine transportation.

United States Customs and Border Protection *www.cbp.gov.* Created Mar. 3, 1927 as Bureau of

Customs. Re-designated Customs Service Apr. 4, 1973. Renamed and transferred to Dept. of Homeland Security, Jan. 24, 2003. Priority mission of keeping terrorists and weapons out of the U.S. Responsible for securing and facilitating trade and travel, enforcing customs treaties, collecting customs duties, excise taxes, fees and penalties on imports. Supresses illegal trade; quarantines animals, plants and food. Enforces U.S. regulations including immigration, copyright, trademark, patent and drug laws. Includes border patrol.

United States Secret Service   *www.secretservice.gov.* Protects president and vice president (and president-elect and vice president-elect) of U.S. and their families. Protects former presidents and their spouses until their death. Protects distinguished foreign visitors and U.S. officials abroad at direction of president. Detects and apprehends counterfeiters. Suppresses forgery of government securities and documents.

Transportation   Security   Administration *www.tsa.gov.* Formed by the Aviation and Transportation Security Act on Nov. 19, 2001. Transferred to Dept. of Homeland Security in 2003. Protects U.S. transportation systems, screens cargo and passengers for weapons and provides transportation law enforcement.

▶**DEPARTMENT OF HOUSING AND URBAN DEVELOPMENT (HUD)**
451 Seventh St. SW, Washington, D.C. 20410. (202) 708-1112. *www.hud.gov.* Created Nov. 9, 1965, by Dept. of Housing and Urban Development Act. Administers mortgage programs to help families become homeowners. Fosters construction of new housing and renovation of existing rental housing. Provides aid for low-income families who cannot afford their rent. Enacts programs to prevent housing discrimination. Encourages strong private sector housing industry.

▶**DEPARTMENT OF THE INTERIOR**
1849 C St. NW, Washington, D.C. 20240. (202) 208-3171. *www.doi.gov.* Created Mar. 3, 1849. Principal U.S. conservation agency. Directs use and conservation of public lands and natural resources; administers over 500 million acres of Federal land and has trust responsibilities for approximately 50 million acres, mostly Indian reservations. Prescribes use of land and water resources, fish and wildlife, national parks and historic places, and mineral resources; aids in preservation of American Indian reservation communities.

United States Fish and Wildlife Service *www.fws.gov.* Conserves and protects fish and wildlife and their habitats. Assesses environmental impact of pesticides, thermal pollution, hydroelectric dams and nuclear power sites.

National Park Service   *www.nps.gov.* Created Aug. 25, 1916. Administers, protects, and maintains diverse system of national parks, monuments, historic areas and recreation areas; encourages understanding of the historic value of these sites through lectures, tours and exhibits.

U.S. Geological Survey   *www.usgs.gov.* Created Mar. 3, 1879. Identifies and classifies land, water, energy, and mineral resources. Investigates potential hazards such as earthquakes and volcanoes. Conducts topographic mapping.

Bureau of Indian Affairs   (*The BIA website and mail servers are temporarily unavailable due to the Cobell Litigation, a suit brought against the*

DOI in 1996 and ongoing as of May 31, 2008. Some information is available at www.doi.gov/bureauindian-affairs.html or call BIA public affairs: 202-208-3710.) Created 1824 as part of Dept. of War. Transferred to Dept. of Interior in 1849. Trains American Indian and Alaska native peoples to manage their own affairs under trust relationship to Federal Government. Facilitates public and private aid to advancement of these peoples.

Bureau   of   Land   Management   (BLM)
www.blm.gov. Created July 16, 1946, by consolidation of the General Land Office and the Grazing Service. Manages 270 million acres of public lands primarily in Far West and in Alaska. Responsible for managing and conserving resources in these lands, including timber, oil, gas, hard minerals and wildlife habitats.

▶**DEPARTMENT OF JUSTICE**
950 Pennsylvania Ave. NW, Washington, D.C. 20530. (202) 514-2000. *www.usdoj.gov.* Created June 22, 1870. Enforces the law in the public interest. Ensures fair competition in free enterprise system; enforces drug, immigration, and naturalization laws; conducts all Supreme Court suits in which U.S. is party or is concerned. Advises president on legal matters.

Federal   Bureau   of   Investigation   (FBI)
www.fbi.gov. Created 1908. Principal investigative bureau of Justice Dept. Investigates violations of Federal law. Areas of primary concern are organized crime (including drug trafficking), terrorism, white-collar crime, and foreign counterintelligence.

Bureau of Alcohol, Tobacco, Firearms, and Explosives *www.atf.gov.* Created July 1, 1972. Transferred to Dept. of Justice in 2003. Enforces and administers laws regulating production, use, distribution, and sale of alcohol and tobacco products, firearms, and explosives. A principal law enforcement agency within the Dept. of Justice.

Bureau of Prisons   *www.bop.gov.* Created 1930. Imprisons and rehabilitates criminals convicted of Federal crimes and sentenced to federal prison.

United States Marshals Service *www.usdoj.gov/marshals.* Provides security and support to federal court system. Apprehends federal fugitives. Ensures safety of federal witnesses. Executes court orders and arrest warrants. Maintains custody, manages, and sells property seized from criminals.

Drug Enforcement Administration   (DEA)
www.dea.gov. Created July 1973. Investigates interstate drug-trafficking. Enforces Government regulations regarding manufacture, distribution, sale and dispensing of controlled substances.

▶**DEPARTMENT OF LABOR**
200 Constitution Ave NW, Washington, D.C. 20210. (202) 693-5000. *www.dol.gov.* Created Mar. 4, 1913. Improves welfare and working conditions of wage earners. Guarantees minimum wages and overtime pay as well as unemployment insurance and   workers'   compensation. Prevents employment discrimination. Protects pension rights. Provides for job training programs. Pays special attention to labor-related needs of minority workers, old and young, women and disabled people.

Employee Benefits Security Administration (EBSA) *www.dol.gov/ebsa.* (Formerly Pension and Welfare Benefits Administration. Created

Sept. 2, 1974, by Employment Retirement Income Security Act of 1974 (ERISA). Requires private pension and welfare plan administrators to give participants summaries of pension and welfare plans. Keeps summaries on file. Regulates financial operations of pension and welfare plans.

Employment and Training Administration (ETA) www.doleta.gov.
Provides employment security through unemployment insurance, worker dislocation programs and federal-state employment service system. Trains or retrains and finds employment for disadvantaged workers through Job Training Partnership Act (JTPA).

Occupational Safety and Health Administration (OSHA) www.osha.gov.
Created 1970 by Occupational Safety and Health Act. Promotes safety and health standards in workplace. Issues regulations, conducts investigations, issues citations, and proposes penalties for violations of health standards and regulations.

Bureau of Labor Statistics (BLS) www.bls.gov.
Data-gathering agency. Collects, processes, interprets, and distributes data involving employment, unemployment, wages, family income and expenditures, worker's compensation, industrial relations, productivity and technological change.

Veterans' Employment and Training Service (VETS) www.dol.gov/vets.
Maximizes training and employment opportunities for veterans and disabled. Ensures that legislation involving veterans is carried out by local public employment services and by private enterprise.

▶DEPARTMENT OF STATE
2201 C Street NW; Washington, D.C. 20520. (202) 647-4000. www.state.gov. Created July 27, 1789, as Dept. of Foreign Affairs. Renamed Dept. of State Sept. 15, 1789. Advises president on foreign policy. Formulates and executes policy to protect and defend American interests overseas. Negotiates treaties and agreements with foreign countries. Oversees and administers overseas information and cultural programs, including Voice of America and Fulbright scholarship program.

United States Mission to the United Nations
Represents U.S. at U.N.. Carries out U.S. foreign policy as it relates to U.N.

Foreign Service
Maintains relations with more than 140 nations around world. Reports to State Dept. on developments relating to safety and welfare of U.S., its citizens, and their interests. Ambassadors to each country are personal representatives of the president and have full responsibility for carrying out U.S. foreign policy within the country. Ambassadors negotiate agreements between host country and U.S., explain and administer U.S. foreign policy, and maintain relations with government and public of host country.

▶DEPARTMENT OF TRANSPORTATION
400 Seventh St. SW, Washington, D.C. 20590. (202) 366-4000. www.dot.gov. Created Oct. 15, 1966. Establishes nation's comprehensive transportation policy. Major administrations are responsible for highway planning, development, and construction; urban mass transit; railroads; aviation; and the safety of waterways, ports, highways, and oil and gas pipelines.

Federal Aviation Administration (FAA) www.faa.gov.
Created 1958 by Federal Aviation Act. Included in Dept. of Transportation in 1967. Regulates air commerce in effort to promote safety and secure national defense interests. Directs use of navigable U.S. airspace. Develops and operates system of air traffic control for both civil and military aircraft. Regulates aircraft noise.

Federal Highway Administration (FHWA) www.fhwa.dot.gov.
Included in Dept. of Transportation in 1967 by Dept. of Transportation Act. Promotes highway safety. Provides aid for construction and maintenance of state and Federal highway systems.

Federal Railroad Administration (FRA) www.fra.dot.gov.
Created by Dept. of Transportation Act of 1966. Administers and enforces railroad safety regulations such as track maintenance, inspection and equipment standards, and operating practices. Administers federal grants to Amtrak.

National Highway Traffic Safety Administration www.nhtsa.dot.gov.
Created by Highway Safety Act of 1970. Research and development programs are aimed at reducing number of highway collisions, reducing severity of injuries and economic loss involved in highway accidents, and reducing fatalities resulting from highway crashes.

Federal Transit Administration www.fta.dot.gov.
Created July 1, 1968. Improves equipment and methods used in urban mass transit. Encourages planning of cost-effective mass transit systems. Provides economic and technical assistance for mass transit programs.

Maritime Administration (MARAD) www.marad.dot.gov.
Created May 24, 1950. Included in Dept. of Transportation Aug. 6, 1981, by Maritime Act of 1981. Constructs or supervises construction of U.S. flag merchant ships for federal government. Generates business for U.S. ships. Develops ports and facilities for maritime transport.

Saint Lawrence Seaway Development Corporation www.seaway.dot.gov.
Created May 13, 1954. Owns, develops, maintains, and operates St. Lawrence Seaway between Montreal and Lake Erie within territorial limits of U.S. Provides safe and efficient waterway for maritime commerce.

Research and Innovative Technology Administration www.rita.dot.gov.
Created Nov. 30, 2004. Conducts research on innovative technologies, including intelligent transportation, provides education and training in education fields. Bureau of Transportation Statistics (www.bts.gov) compiles statistics and other information on U.S. transportation systems.

▶DEPARTMENT OF THE TREASURY
1500 Pennsylvania Ave. NW, Washington, D.C. 20220. (202) 622-2000. www.treas.gov. Created Sept. 2, 1789. Formulates and recommends economic, financial, tax, and fiscal policies. Acts as financial agent for U.S. Government. Manufactures coins and currency.

Alcohol and Tobacco Tax and Trade Bureau www.ttb.gov.
Created Jan, 24, 2003. Collects alcohol, tobacco, firearms and ammunition excise taxes. Ensures that regulated products comply with federal requirements for labeling, advertising and marketing.

Bureau of Engraving and Printing www.moneyfactory.gov.
Created July 11, 1862. De-

signs, prints, and finishes Federal Reserve notes, U.S. postage stamps, identification cards, and Treasury securities. Inhibits counterfeiting of these documents.

Internal Revenue Service (IRS) *www.irs.gov.* Created July 1, 1862. Administers and enforces internal revenue laws except those relating to alcohol, tobacco, firearms and explosives. Determines, assesses, and collects federal tax revenues from public. Encourages, assesses, and enforces compliance with tax laws.

United States Mint *www.usmint.gov.* Mint of the United States created Apr. 2, 1792. Bureau of the Mint created Feb. 12, 1873. Renamed United States Mint Jan. 9, 1984. Manufactures and distributes coins for circulation through Federal Reserve Banks. Mints foreign coins. Processes gold and silver bullion. Manufactures national medals, proof coin sets, and commemorative coins for sale to public.

Bureau of the Public Debt *www.publicdebt. treas.gov.* Created June 30, 1940. Manages public debt. Offers public debt securities. Audits retired securities and interest coupons. Maintains accounting control over public debt receipts and expenditures, securities, and interest costs. Adjudicates claims of lost, stolen or destroyed securities.

Office of Thrift Supervision (OTS) 1700 G St., NW, Washington, D.C. 20552. (202) 906-6000. *www.ots.treas.gov.* Created by the Financial Institutions Reform, Recovery and Enforcement Act, Aug. 9, 1989. Established by Congress as part of a reorganization of the thrift regulatory structure, the OTS has authority to charter federal thrift institutions, and to serve as the primary regulator of

Money Men

The first U.S. paper money was printed in 1862. Until then, state banks printed their own notes, but there were no federal bills. The Secretary of the Treasury selects the designs shown on United States currency and coinage. In 1862, Treasury Secretary Salmon Chase put his face on the first U.S. notes in an attempt to further his political ambitions. To this day, he remains on the front of the $10,000 bill, though it is no longer in circulation.

Federal law prohibits portraits of living persons from appearing on government securities. Therefore, the portraits on our currency notes and coins are of deceased persons whose places in history are well-known.

Note	Portrait, Importance
$ 1	George Washington, 1st President
$ 2	Thomas Jefferson, 3rd President
$ 5	Abraham Lincoln, 16th President
$ 10	Alexander Hamilton, 1st Sec. of Treasury
$ 20	Andrew Jackson, 7th President
$ 50	Ulysses Grant, 18th President
$100	Ben Franklin, Statesman
$500[1]	William McKinley, 25th President
$1,000[1]	Grover Cleveland, 22nd/24th President
$5,000[1]	James Madison, 4th President
$10,000[1]	Salmon Chase, Sec. of Treasury in 1862
$100,000[2]	Woodrow Wilson, 28th President

1. No longer in circulation. 2. This note never appeared in general circulation, and was only used in transactions between Federal Reserve Banks. **Source:** U.S. Bureau of Engraving and Printing. www.moneyfactory.com.

federal- and state-chartered thrifts belonging to the Savings Association Insurance Fund (SAIF).

▶DEPARTMENT OF VETERANS AFFAIRS

810 Vermont Ave. NW, Washington, D.C. 20420. (202) 273-4800. *www.va.gov.* Created by Dept. of Veterans Affairs Act of 1988; predecessor Veterans Administration created 1930. Administers benefit programs for veterans and their families, including military-related death or disability compensation, pensions, education and rehabilitation, home loan guaranty, medical care programs, and the National Cemetery System.

Veterans Health Administration 877-222-8387 *www.va.gov/health* Provides hospital, nursing home and outpatient care to eligible veterans. Operates over 100 medical centers, nearly 400 outpatient clinics, over 100 nursing home care units and many Vietnam Veteran Outreach Centers.

Veterans Benefits Administration 800-827-1000 *www.vba.gov* Has responsibility for claims for disability compensation and pension, specially adapted housing and automobiles, special clothing allowances, and emergency officers' retirement pay, survivors' claims for death compensation, dependency and indemnity compensation, burial and plot allowance claims, and reimbursement for headstones.

▶INDEPENDENT ESTABLISHMENTS & GOVERNMENT CORPORATIONS

African Development Foundation 1400 Eye St. NW, Suite 1000, Washington, D.C. 20005. (202) 673-3916. *www.adf.gov.* Created in 1984 by African Development Foundation Act. Nonprofit Government corporation. Through grants, loans, and loan guarantees, aids self-help efforts by poor people in African countries.

AMTRAK (National Railroad Passenger Corporation) 60 Massachusetts Ave. NE, Washington, D.C. 20002. (202) 906-3000. *www.amtrak.com.* Created by Rail Passenger Service Act of 1970 as a for-profit corporation. Develops, operates, and improves inter-city rail passenger service to create national rail transportation system.

Central Intelligence Agency (CIA) Washington, D.C. 20505. (703) 482-0623. *www.cia.gov.* Created by National Security Act of 1947. Under direction of president and National Security Council. Advises NSC on intelligence matters of national security. Collects, evaluates, and disseminates intelligence information relating to national security and to drug production and trafficking. Collects, produces and disseminates counterintelligence and foreign intelligence here (in conjunction with FBI) and abroad. Conducts special activities as directed by president. Protects security of its activities, information, and personnel by necessary and appropriate means.

Commodity Futures Trading Commission (CFTC) 1155 21st St. NW, Washington, D.C. 20581. (202) 418-5000. *www.cftc.gov.* Created May 14, 1973 by Commodity Futures Act of 1973. Regulates trading on the 11 U.S. futures exchanges. Regulates activities of commodity exchange members, public brokerage houses, commodity trading advisers and other related employees.

Consumer Product Safety Commission (CPSC) East-West Towers, 4330 East-West Highway, Bethesda, Md. 20814. *www.cpsc.gov.* (301)

504-7923. Created May 14, 1973 by Consumer Product Safety Act. Protects public from unreasonable risk of injury from consumer products. Develops, enforces, and evaluates safety standards for consumer products.

Corporation for National Community Service
1201 New York Ave. NW, Washington, D.C. 20525. (202) 606-5000. *www.nationalservice.org*. Created by National and Community Service Act of 1993. Incorporates programs previously administered by ACTION. Administers agencies such as SeniorCorps, AmeriCorps and AmeriCorps VISTA, which encourage and provide national and community service by volunteers, schools, and retired and senior volunteers.

Defense Nuclear Facilities Safety Board
625 Indiana Ave. NW, Suite 700, Washington, D.C. 20004. (202) 694-7000. *www.dnfsb.gov*. Created by Atomic Energy Act of 1954; established as independent agency Sept. 29, 1988. Reviews and evaluates standards for defense nuclear facilities of the Department of Energy. Investigates practices that may imperil public health and safety.

Environmental Protection Agency (EPA)
1200 Pennsylvania Avenue NW., Washington, D.C. 20460-0001. (202) 260-2090. *www.epa.gov*. Created Dec. 2, 1970. Protects and enhances environment. Controls and reduces pollution of air and water. Regulates solid-waste disposal and use of pesticides, radiation and toxic substances.

Equal Employment Opportunity Commission (EEOC)
1801 L St. NW, Washington, D.C. 20507. (202) 663-4900. *www.eeoc.gov*. Created July 2, 1965, by Title VII of Civil Rights Act of 1964. Protects against discrimination based on race, color, handicap, religion, sex, age and national origin in hiring, promoting, firing, wages, testing, training, apprenticeship and all other terms and conditions of employment.

Export-Import Bank of the United States
811 Vermont Ave. NW, Washington, D.C. 20571. (800) 565-EXIM. *www.exim.gov*. Created Feb. 2, 1934. Facilitates and aids exports of U.S. goods and services through loans, loan guarantees and insurance to exporters and private banks.

Farm Credit Administration
1501 Farm Credit Drive, McLean, VA 22102-5090. (703) 883-4056. *www.fca.gov*. Created by Farm Credit Act of 1971. Regulates and examines programs, banks, associations, and organizations of the Farm Credit System, which provides credit to farmers, ranchers, producers of farm products, rural home owners, and associations and organizations of farmers, ranchers, and farm-equipment producers.

Federal Communications Commission (FCC)
445 12th St. SW, Washington, D.C. 20554. (888) 225-5322. *www.fcc.gov*. Created by Communications Act of 1934. Regulates interstate and foreign communications by radio, television, wire, satellite, and cable. Oversees development of broadcast services and the rapid, efficient provision of telephone and telegraph services at reasonable rates.

Federal Deposit Insurance Corporation (FDIC)
550 17th St. NW, Washington, D.C. 20429. (877) 275-3342. *www.fdic.gov*. Created June 16, 1933, by Federal Reserve Act. Protects money supply by insuring deposits in and reviewing operations of state-chartered banks that are not members of the Federal Reserve System. Assumed responsibility for insuring savings and loan institutions formerly insured by defunct Federal Savings and Loan Insurance Corp. (FSLIC) in 1989.

Federal Election Commission (FEC)
999 E St. NW, Washington, D.C. 20463. (800) 424-9530. *www.fec.gov*. Created by Federal Election Campaign Act of 1971. Provides public funding for presidential elections. Ensures public disclosure of campaign finance activities. Administers and enforces contribution and spending limits for Federal elections. (See also "U.S. Presidential Elections.")

Federal Housing Finance Board
1625 Eye St. 4th Floor, Washington, D.C. 20006. (202) 408-2500. *www.fhfb.gov*. Created August 9, 1989. Responsible for the administration and enforcement of the Federal Home Loan Bank Act, ensuring that banks carry out their housing finance and community investment mission.

Federal Labor Relations Authority (FLRA)
1400 K St. NW, Suite 250, Washington, D.C. 20424. (202) 218-7000. *www.flra.gov*. Created Jan. 1, 1979. Protects rights of federal employees to organize, bargain collectively, and participate in labor organizations. Oversees rights and obligations of federal employees and the labor organizations that represent them.

Federal Maritime Commission
800 North Capitol St. NW, Washington, D.C. 20573-0001. (202) 523-5707. *www.fmc.gov*. Created August 12, 1961. Regulates waterborne foreign commerce, insures that U.S. international trade is open to all nations on fair and equitable terms, and protects against unauthorized, concerted activity in U.S. waterborne commerce.

Federal Mediation and Conciliation Service
2100 K. St. NW, Washington, D.C. 20427. (202) 606-8100. *www.fmcs.gov*. Created in 1947 by Labor Management Relations Act. Promotes development of stable labor management relations. Prevents or minimizes work stoppages by helping to settle disputes and by advocating collective bargaining, mediation, and arbitration.

Federal Reserve System
20th St. and Constitution Ave. NW, Washington, D.C. 20551. (202) 452-3000. *www.federalreserve.gov*. Created Dec. 23, 1913, by Federal Reserve Act. Central Bank of U.S. Administers and creates national credit and monetary policy. Regulates money supply. Maintains soundness of banking industry. (See also the section on "The U.S. Economy").

Federal Trade Commission (FTC)
600 Pennsylvania Ave. NW, Washington, D.C. 20580. (202) 326-2222. *www.ftc.gov*. Created in 1914 by Federal Trade Commission Act and Clayton Act. Maintains free and fair competition in free enterprise system. Breaks up monopolies. Seeks to prevent corruption, restraints on trade, unfair trade practices and identity theft.

General Services Administration (GSA)
1800 F St. NW, Washington, D.C. 20405. (202) 501-0705. *www.gsa.gov*. Created July 1, 1949, by Federal Property and Administrative Services Act of 1949. Establishes policy for and manages Government property and records, construction of buildings, distribution of supplies, and other government services.

Inter-American Foundation
901 North Stuart St., 10th Fl., Arlington, VA 22203. (703) 306-4301. *www.iaf.gov*. Created by Congress in 1969. Sup-

ports social and economic development in Latin America and Caribbean. Makes grants to self-help organizations for the poor.

National Aeronautics and Space Administration (NASA) 300 E Street SW, Washington, D.C. 20546. (202) 358-0000. *www.nasa.gov*. Created by National Aeronautics and Space Act of 1958. Develops, constructs, tests, and operates vehicles for in-flight research within and outside Earth's atmosphere. Disseminates information about space exploration and agency's activities.

National Archives and Records Administration (NARA) 8601 Adelphi Rd., College Park, Md. 20740-6001. (866) 272-6272. *www.archives.gov*. Created Oct. 19, 1984. Establishes policy for managing records of U.S. government and making them available to public. Maintains 14 regional archives and 17 federal records centers, as well as 12 presidential libraries or collections.

National Capital Planning Commission Suite 500, 401 Ninth St. NW, Washington, D.C. 20004. (202) 482-7200. *www.ncpc.gov*. Created as a park planning agency by act of June 6, 1924. Serves as the central planning agency for development activities for federal lands in the National Capital region in and around Washington.

National Credit Union Administration (NCUA) 1775 Duke St., Alexandria, VA 22314-3428. (703) 518-6300. *www.ncua.gov*. Created Mar. 10, 1970. Charters, insures, supervises and examines federal credit unions. Administers National Credit Union Share Insurance Fund. Supplies emergency loans to credit unions through Central Liquidity Facility.

National Foundation on the Arts and the Humanities 1100 Pennsylvania Ave. NW, Washington, D.C. 20506. Created in 1965. Its three divisions encourage and support national progress in humanities and arts. The *National Endowment for the Arts (NEA)* (202-682-5400; *www.arts.gov*) fosters professional excellence in arts. The *National Endowment for the Humanities (NEH)* (202-606-8400; *www.neh.gov*) is an independent grant-making agency that supports research, education, and public programs in the humanities. The *Institute of Museum and Library Services* (1800 M St, 9th Fl, Washington DC 20036; *www.imls.gov*; 202-653-4657) assists museums and libraries in maintaining, increasing, and improving services to the public.

National Labor Relations Board (NLRB) 1099 14th Street NW, Washington, D.C. 20570. (202) 273-1000. *www.nlrb.gov*. Created by National Labor Relations Act of 1935 (also known as Wagner Act). Administers Federal labor law. Safeguards employees' right to organize, conducts elections to determine whether workers want unions as their bargaining representative, and prevents or remedies unfair labor practices.

National Mediation Board 1301 K Street NW, Suite 250 East, Washington, D.C. 20572. (202) 692-5050. *www.nmb.gov*. Created June 21, 1934, by amendment to Railway Labor Act. Resolves and investigates representation disputes in railroad and airline industries that could interrupt flow of commerce and endanger national economy.

National Science Foundation (NSF) 4201 Wilson Blvd., Arlington, VA 22230. (703) 292-5111; *www.nsf.gov*. Created by National Science Foundation Act of 1950. Promotes progress of science

and engineering through support of research and education programs.

National Transportation Safety Board (NTSB) 490 L'Enfant Plaza SW, Washington, D.C. 20594. (202) 314-6000. *www.ntsb.gov*. Created Apr. 1, 1975, by Independent Safety Board Act of 1974. Ensures safe operation of all types of transportation in U.S. Investigates accidents, conducts studies, and makes policy recommendations to government agencies, transportation industry and others.

Nuclear Regulatory Commission (NRC) Washington, D.C. 20555-0001. (301) 415-7000. *www.nrc.gov*. Created by Energy Reorganization Act of 1974. Licenses and regulates uses of civilian nuclear energy to protect public health and environment. Sets licensing regulations, issues licenses for, and inspects construction, ownership, and operation of nuclear reactors and other nuclear materials.

Office of Personnel Management (OPM) 1900 E St. NW, Washington, D.C. 20415. (202) 606-1800. *www.opm.gov*. Created Jan. 1, 1979. Recruits, examines, trains, and promotes people for Government jobs, regardless of race, religion, sex, political influence and other nonmerit factors. Provides direct benefits, including health and life insurance, to employees and to retired employees and their survivors.

Overseas Private Investment Corporation (OPIC) 1100 New York Ave. NW, Washington, D.C. 20527. (202) 336-8400. *www.opic.gov*. Established as an independent agency in 1998. Promotes economic growth in developing countries by encouraging U.S. private investment in those nations.

Office of Special Counsel Suite 218, 1730 M Street NW., Washington, D.C. 20036-4505. (202) 254-3600. *www.osc.gov*. Created Jan. 1, 1979. Investigates allegations of certain activities prohibited by civil service laws, rules, or regulations before the Merit Sysems Protection Board. Protects whistleblowers from reprisals by their employers or former employers.

Peace Corps 1111 20th St. NW, Washington, D.C. 20526. (800) 424-8580. *www.peacecorps.gov*. Created by Peace Corps Act of 1961. Promotes world peace and friendship. Helps people of other countries develop manpower by bringing U.S. volunteers abroad to participate in public works programs. Emphasis placed on helping the poorest areas of countries served by the Peace Corps.

Pension Benefit Guaranty Corporation (PBGC) 1200 K St. NW, Washington, D.C. 20005. (800) 400-4272. *www.pbgc.gov*. Created Sept. 2, 1974, by Title IV of Employee Retirement Income Security Act of 1974. Guarantees payment of non-forfeitable pension benefits in covered private sector defined benefit pension plans.

Postal Regulatory Commission 901 New York Avenue SW, Washington, D.C. 20268-0001. (202) 789-6800. *www.prc.gov*. Created Aug. 12, 1970, by Postal Reorganization Act. Recommends changes in postal rates, fees, services, programs, studies and mail classification schedules. Hears complaints about postal rates, services, and fees.

Securities and Exchange Commission (SEC) 100 F Street NE, Washington, D.C. 20549. (202) 942-8088. *www.sec.gov*. Created July 2, 1934 by Securities Exchange Act of 1934. Provides fullest possible disclosure to the public of securities sales, operations, and registrations. Protects public against malpractice in securities and financial markets.

Selective Service System   National Headquarters, Arlington, VA 22209-2425. (703) 605-4000. www.sss.gov. Created June 24, 1948, by Military Selective Service Act. Requires registration, and maintains list of males age 18-26 eligible to serve in armed forces in case of national security emergency.

Small Business Administration (SBA)   409 Third St. SW, Washington, D.C. 20416. (202) 205-6600. www.sba.gov. Created by Small Business Act of 1953. Aids, counsels, makes loans to and protects interests of small businesses; ensures that they receive a fair amount of government purchases and contracts.

Social Security Administration   6401 Security Blvd., Baltimore, MD 21235. (800) 772-1213. www.ssa.gov. Created July 16, 1946; made independent agency by Social Security Independence Act of 1994. Manages the nation's social insurance program, consisting of retirement, survivors, and disability insurance programs, commonly known as Social Security. Administers Supplemental Security Income program for the aged, blind, and disabled. Studies poverty and recommends solutions. Assigns Social Security numbers to all U.S. workers.

Tennessee Valley Authority (TVA)   400 West Summit Hill Dr., Knoxville, TN 37902. (865) 632-2101. www.tva.gov. Created May 18, 1933. Government-owned corporation. Conducts resource development programs for advancement of growth in Tennessee Valley region. Controls floods, develops navigation, produces electric

power, develops fertilizer, improves recreation, and develops forestry and wildlife.

United States Agency for International Development (AID)   Ronald Reagan Bldg., Washington, DC 20523-1000. (202) 712-4810. www.usaid.gov. Established as independent agency in 1998. Administers foreign economic and humanitarian assistance programs in the developing world, Central and Eastern Europe, and the countries of the former Soviet Union.

United States Commission on Civil Rights   624 Ninth St. NW, Washington, D.C. 20425. (202) 376-7700. www.usccr.gov. Created by Civil Rights Act of 1957. Collects and studies information on discrimination based on race, color, religion, age, sex, handicap or national origin. Assures equal protection in voting rights and enforcement of civil rights laws. Promotes equal opportunity in education, employment, and housing.

United States International Trade Commission   500 E St. SW, Washington, D.C. 20436. (202) 205-2000. www.usitc.gov. Created Sept. 8, 1916. Furnishes studies, reports, and recommendations regarding international trade and tariffs to president, Congress, and other government agencies.

United States Postal Service   475 L'Enfant Plaza SW, Washington, D.C. 20260-0010. (202) 268-2000. www.usps.gov. Created Aug. 12, 1970, by Postal Reorganization Act. Provides mail processing and delivery service to individuals and businesses in U.S. Protects mail from loss or theft and apprehends violators of postal laws.

FEDERAL EMPLOYEES AND BUDGET

▶ FEDERAL JOBS AND SALARIES

As of September 30, 2007, there were 1,713,961 full-time non-postal federal civilian employees. Nearly 97 percent of the federal civilian workforce was employed in the United States; 17,836 (0.7 percent) worked in U.S. territories, and 68,841 (2.6 percent) worked in foreign countries. The majority of government employees worked in metropolitan statistical areas (MSAs), led by the Washington, D.C. MSA, with 333,090, or 12.3 percent of the total.

Four executive departments accounted for more than 62 percent of the federal civilian workforce. The Department of Defense employed 659,000 civilians (35.9 percent of the total), Veterans Affairs employed 230,000 (12.5 percent), Homeland Security 148,000 (8.0 percent), and the Treasury 108,000 (5.8 percent).

Federal government civilian employees are paid according to a number of different systems: the General Schedule (GS), Federal Wage Systems, and other acts and administratively determined systems. Overall, the average salary for full-time civilian government employees was $68,233. Employees under the General Schedule on average earned more than those on Federal Wage Systems ($66,085 to $47,502), but not as much as employees covered by other acts and administrative determinations, who averaged $82,204. Average salaries by major geographic areas were: United

States, $68,496; Washington, D.C. area, $90,415; foreign countries, $58,107; and U.S. territories, $58,107.

White-Collar Employees General Schedule   The number of white-collar employees decreased over the last three years, from to 1,244,413 in 2004 to 1,234,205 in 2007.

The Federal Government: Employees and Budget, 1901–2008

| Year | Number of employees[1] | Budget (millions) | | |
		Receipts	Outlays	Surplus or deficit (-)
1901	239,476	$588	$525	$63
1910	388,708	676	694	−18
1920	655,265	6,649	6,358	291
1930	601,319	4,058	3,320	738
1940	1,042,420	6,548	9,468	−2,920
1945	3,816,310	45,159	92,712	−47,553
1950	1,960,708	39,443	42,562	−3,119
1960	2,398,704	92,492	92,191	301
1970	2,984,574	192,807	195,649	−2,842
1980	2,875,866	517,112	590,941	−73,830
1990	3,128,261	1,031,969	1,253,165	−221,195
2000	2,702,258	2,025,457	1,789,216	236,241
2005	2,701,920	2,153,859	2,472,205	−318,346
2006	2,700,716	2,407,254	2,655,435	−248,181
2007	2,698,989	2,568,239	2,730,241	−162,002
2008[2]	N.A.	2,521,175	2,931,222	−410,047

1. Paid civilians only. 2. Projected. **Source:** Office of Management and Budget, *Budget of the United States Government, FY 2009.*

There are 15 grades broadly defined in terms of responsibility, difficulty, and qualifications; within each grade there are 10 steps. Within-grade advancement occurs on a fixed schedule, though employees demonstrating "high-quality performance" can receive "quality step increases." In all, General Schedule employees make up more than three-quarters of all civilians employed by the government.

Veterans Affairs   The pay system of the Department of Veterans Affairs covered 254,033 employees, including 11,377 physicians with an average salary of $176,449; 513 optometrists ($87,091); and 1,555 physician's assistants ($85,776).

Executive Schedule (EX) and Senior Executive Service (SES)   The very top executives in the executive branch are paid under a system known as the Executive Schedule (EX).

Broadly speaking, the five Executive Schedule levels include the following job titles: level I, cabinet members; level II, deputy secretaries of major departments; level III, presidential advisors, chief administrators of major independent agencies, and under secretaries; level IV, assistant secretaries, deputy under secretaries, and general counsels in executive departments; and level V, deputy assistant secretaries, administrators, commissioners, and directors. The Executive Schedule covers approximately 450 employees each year: the average salary in 2007 was $151,411. The Senior Executive Service (SES) covers most managerial and policy positions in the executive branch that do not require Senate confirmation. In 2007, there were

Salaries of Federal Officials, 2008

To prevent themselves from having to vote publicly on raising their own pay, Congress in 1999 passed a law that gives legislators an automatic annual cost of living increase unless they actively vote against such a raise. Salaries in the judicial branch are pegged to those in Congress, so whenever legislators get a raise, so does the judiciary. All of the salaries printed below are expected to increase by approximately 2.8 percent in 2009.

Branch/Official	2008 Salary
Executive Branch	
President	$400,000
Vice President	221,100
Legislative Branch	
Senate	
President pro tempore	$188,100
Majority and minority leaders	188,100
Senators	169,300
House of Representatives	
Speaker of the House	$217,400
Minority and majority leaders	188,100
Representatives	169,300
Judicial Branch	
Chief Justice	$217,400
Associate justices	208,100
Circuit judges	179,500
District judges	169,300

Source: Congressional Research Service: CRS Report for Congress, February 5, 2008.

Federal Government Pay Systems, 2008

Grade	Employees[1]	Salary Range[2]
General Schedule		
GS-1	270	$17,046 - 21,324
GS-2	955	19,165 - 24,115
GS-3	8,445	20,911 - 27,184
GS-4	45,327	23,475 - 30,522
GS-5	100,984	26,264 - 34,139
GS-6	81,255	29,276 - 38,060
GS-7	130,828	32,534 - 42,290
GS-8	51,413	36,030 - 46,839
GS-9	123,437	39,795 - 51,738
GS-10	16,975	43,824 - 56,973
GS-11	180,333	48,148 - 62,593
GS-12	207,566	57,709 - 75,025
GS-13	174,575	68,625 - 89,217
GS-14	80,205	81,093 - 105,420
GS-15	41,845	95,390 - 124,010
Total	**1,244,413**	
Senior Level (SL)		
Total	**578**	$114,468 - 149,000
Executive Schedule (EX)		
Level I	21	$186,600
Level II	289	168,000
Level III	107	154,600
Level IV	35	145,400
Level V	18	136,200
Total	**470**	
Senior Executive Service (SES)		
Total	**7,038**	$114,468 - 172,200

Note: 1. As of March 31, 2004, the latest year available. 2. Effective Jan. 2008.
Source: U.S. Office of Personnel Management, 2008.

U.S. Federal Employment, 1992–2007

Description	1992	2000	2005	2007
Executive branch civilian employment[1]	**2,226,778**	**1,778,138**	**1,872,200**	**1,831,574**
U.S. Postal Service[2]	792,049	860,777	764,210	801,641
Military personnel on active duty[3]	1,847,600	1,426,338	1,430,104	1,429,988
Department of Defense	1,808,131	1,384,338	1,389,394	1,382,260
Department of Homeland Security (Coast Guard)	39,469	36,157	40,710	41,478
Total executive branch employment	**4,866,427**	**4,065,253**	**4,066,514**	**4,063,203**
Legislative branch	38,509	31,157	30,816	31,185
Judicial branch	27,987	32,186	34,064	33,558
Total federal employment	**4,932,923**	**4,128,596**	**4,131,394**	**4,127,946**

Note: 1.Excludes Postal Service employees. 2. Includes Postal Rate Commission. 3. Excludes reserve components.
Source: Office of Management and Budget, *Budget of the United States Government, FY 2009.*

Government Employment and Population, 1962–2007

	Government employment					
Fiscal year	Federal executive branch[1] ('000s)	Total Federal personnel ('000s)	State and local governments ('000s)	All governmental units ('000s)	Executive branch employment as a percent of all governmental units[1]	Executive branch employment per 1,000 population[1]
1962	2,485	5,354	6,549	11,903	20.9%	13.3
1965	2,496	5,215	7,696	12,911	19.3	12.8
1970[2]	2,944	6,085	9,822	15,907	18.5	14.4
1975	2,848	5,061	11,937	16,998	16.8	13.2
1980[2]	2,821	4,965	13,375	18,340	15.4	12.4
1985	3,008	5,256	13,519	18,775	16.0	12.6
1990[2]	3,067	5,234	15,219	20,453	15.0	12.3
1995	2,858	4,475	16,484	20,959	13.6	10.7
2000[2]	2,639	4,129	17,925	22,054	12.0	9.4
2005	2,636	4,138	19,078	23,216	11.4	8.9
2006	2,637	4,133	19,284	23,417	11.3	8.8
2007	2,636	4,127	19,538	23,665	11.1	8.7

Notes: 1. Civilian employment only, including full-time permanent, temporary, part-time, and intermittent employees in the executive branch, including the Postal Service, and beginning in 1970, includes various disadvantaged worker-trainee programs. 2. Includes temporary employees in the decennial census. Source: Office of Management and Budget, *Budget of the United States Government, FY 2009.*

Federal Government Employment and Outlays, by Branch and Agency, 1990–2008

Agency	Employment 2007[1]	Outlays (millions of dollars)			
		1990	2000	2007	2008[2]
Legislative branch	31,185	$2,241	$2,911	$4,308	$4,586
Judicial branch	33,558	1,646	4,086	6,006	6,161
Executive branch[3]	1,831,600	—	—	—	—
Executive Office of the President	N.A.	158	283	2,956	2,079
Department of Agriculture	94,800	46,012	75,663	84,437	94,764
Department of Commerce	36,300	3,734	7,807	6,476	8,151
Department of Defense[4] (military functions)	658,800	289,755	281,223	529,875	583,057
Department of Defense (civil functions)	21,200	21,692	32,864	51,031	56,278
Department of Education	4,100	22,972	33,900	66,372	68,046
Department of Energy	14,600	12,084	15,010	20,116	23.209
Department of Health and Human Services	58,500	175,531	382,626	672,035	709,381
Department of Homeland Security	148,100	N.A.	N.A.	39,172	42,340
Dept. of Housing and Urban Development	9,500	20,167	30,828	45,561	52,269
Department of the Interior	67,400	5,825	8,029	10,490	11,081
Department of Justice	105,000	6,507	20,064	23,349	25,026
Department of Labor	15,900	25,215	31,876	47,544	49,652
Department of State	30,100	4,802	6,850	13,747	18,892
Department of Transportation	53,400	28,650	45,965	61,697	68,662
Department of the Treasury	107,700	255,172	390,677	490,605	520,163
Department of Veterans Affairs	230,400	28,998	47,087	72,820	86,643
Environmental Protection Agency	17,000	5,108	7,238	8,258	7,541
General Services Administration	11,900	–93	28	31	357
National Aeronautics & Space Administration (NASA)	18,200	12,429	13,442	15,861	17,318
Office of Personnel Management	4,600	31,949	48,660	58,450	64,173
Small Business Administration	4,400	692	–421	1,175	530
Social Security Administration (off-budget)	61,700	244,998	396,169	566,846	596,528
Totals[5, 6]	1,832,800	$1,253,198	$1,788,773	$2,730,241	$2,931,222

Notes: Outlays are the measure of Government spending--payments to liquidate obligations (other than the repayment of debt), net of cash, and offsetting collections. Outlays are generally recorded on a cash basis, but also include many cash-equivalent transactions and interest accrued on public issues of the public debt. 1. Employment figures exclude developmental positions under the Worker-Trainee Opportunity Program; participants in the Cooperative Education Program; disadvantaged summer and part-time workers under such Office of Personnel Management programs as Summer Aides, stay-in-school, and junior fellowship; and certain statutory exemptions. Figures for executive branch rounded at source. 2. Estimate. 3. Civilian employment. 4. By law (10 U.S.C. Chapter 4, section 140b) the Department of Defense is exempt from full-time equivalent employment controls. Data shown are estimated. 5. Employment totals do not include FDIC or U.S. Postal Service. 6. Outlay totals do not account for undistributed offsetting receipts.
Source: Office of Management and Budget, *Budget of the United States Government, FY 2009.*

7,465 employees covered by SES, an increase from 7,055 in 2006; salaries averaged $153,588.

Special rates   If the government has difficulty recruiting and retaining qualified personnel in occupations with higher competitive market rates, it can establish special salary rates for such occupations. The number of white-collar employees receiving special-rate salaries varies from year to year. As locality pay amounts have increased and some agencies have established banded pay systems, the number of Federal employees receiving special rates has declined. In 2007, about 74,000 employees were on special rates.

Blue-Collar Employees

As of September 30, 2007, the federal government employed 188,212 workers (11 percent of the civilian government workforce) in blue-collar (trades and labor) occupations. The vast majority of these

The Congressional Budget Process

On or before	Action to be completed
First Monday in February	President submits his budget.
	Congressional committees have six weeks to submit views and estimates to Budget Committees.
February 15	Congressional Budget Office submits report to budget committees.
April 1	Senate budget committee reports concurrent resolution on the budget.
April 15	Congress completes action on concurrent resolution on the budget.
May 15	Annual appropriation bills may be considered in the House.
June 10	House Appropriations Committee reports last annual appropriations bill.
June 15	Congress completes action on reconciliation legislation.
June 30	House completes action on annual appropriation bills.
October 1	Fiscal year begins.

Note: 1. A concurrent resolution sets levels for new budget authority and outlays, direct loan obligations, primary loan guarantee commitments, the amount by which Federal revenues should be increased or decreased, the budget surplus or deficit, the public debt, and so on. **Source:** Committee on Ways and Means, U.S. House of Representatives, *Overview of Entitlement Programs*, (annual).

employees, 137,011, worked in the United States, mostly for the Defense Department (72.8 percent). The Department of Veterans Affairs employed 25,073 blue-collar workers (13.3 percent of the total). Blue-collar pay rates are governed by federal Wage Systems and determined on a prevailing rate basis by pay locality. The worldwide average salary for the blue-collar workforce in 2007 was $47,702. Salaries were highest in the United States (where they averaged $47,853) and lowest in U.S. territories (where they averaged just $35,360). Blue-collar salaries averaged $52,175 in the Washington D.C. metropolitan area, but only $40,188 in foreign countries.

▶DEFICITS AND THE FEDERAL DEBT

After 30 years of annual budget deficits, the federal government recorded four consecutive years of surpluses from 1998-2001, a feat not seen since before the Depression. Yet even these surpluses did little to dent the immense federal debt incurred over the past 40 years; they didn't even equal the net interest payments on this huge debt. Since 2002, the government has returned to running annual budget deficits, sending the gross federal debt spiraling to more than $9.4 trillion, or 10 times what it was in 1980. (See "U.S. Economy" for an explanation of the difference between deficits and the debt.)

▶GLOSSARY OF FEDERAL BUDGET TERMS

Budget authority   The term budget authority means the authority provided by law to incur financial obligations that result in immediate or future outlays involving government funds or to collect offsetting receipts.

Budget deficit/surplus   A budget deficit occurs when government outlays exceed government receipts; a surplus occurs when receipts exceed outlays. The record budget surplus was $236.4 billion (in 2000); the record deficit is the $412.7 billion recorded in 2004.

Fiscal year   The federal government's fiscal year begins Oct. 1 and ends Sept. 30 of the next calendar year; so, FY 2009 began Oct. 1, 2008, and ends Sept. 30, 2009.

Intergovernmental expenditure/revenue   Amounts paid to or received from other governments either in the form of shared revenues and grants-in-aid, as reimbursements for performance of general government activities or for specific services such

Federal Government Receipts by Source, 1934-2008 (billions of dollars)

Year	Individual income taxes	Corporation income taxes[1]	Social insurance & retirement receipts	Excise taxes	Other[2]	Total
1934	$0.4	$0.3	(3)	$1.4	$0.8	$3.0
1940	0.9	1.2	$1.8	2.0	0.7	6.5
1950	15.8	10.4	4.3	7.6	1.4	39.4
1960	40.7	21.5	14.7	11.7	3.9	92.5
1970	90.4	32.8	44.3	15.7	9.5	192.8
1980	244.1	64.6	157.8	24.3	26.3	517.1
1990	466.9	93.5	380.0	35.3	56.2	1,032.0
2000	1,004.5	207.3	652.9	68.9	92.0	2,025.5
2005	927.2	278.3	794.1	73.1	81.1	2,153.9
2007	1,163.5	370.2	869.6	65.1	99.8	2,568.2
2008[4]	1,219.7	345.3	910.1	68.8	-22.8	2,521.2

Notes: 1. Beginning in 1990 includes trust fund receipts for the hazardous substance Superfund. 2. Includes estate and gift taxes, customs duties and fees, federal reserve deposits, and other. 3. Less than $100 million. 4. Estimate.
Source: Office of Management and Budget, *Budget of the United States Government, FY 2009*.

as care of prisoners for the paying government, or in lieu of taxes.

Off-budget/on-budget Some presentations in the federal budget distinguish on-budget totals from off-budget totals. On-budget totals reflect the transactions of all federal government entities except those excluded from the budget totals by law, the two Social Security trust funds (old-age and survivors insurance and the federal disability insurance trust funds), and the Postal Service fund. Off-budget totals reflect the transactions of government entities excluded from the on-budget totals by law.

Offsetting collections Offsetting collections are collections from the public that result from business-type or market-oriented activities and collections; examples include proceeds from the sale of electric power by the Tennessee Valley Authority, voluntary medical insurance premiums paid to the supplementary medical insurance trust fund, and the sale of postage stamps.

Outlays by Budget Enforcement Act Category, 1970–2008 (billions)

Category	1970	1980	1990	2000	2005	2007	2008[1]
Total Outlays	**$195.6**	**$590.9**	**$1,253.2**	**$1,789.18**	**$2,472.2**	**$2,730.2**	**$2,931.2**
Discretionary outlays	120.3	276.3	500.6	614.8	968.5	1,042.1	1,136.5
National defense	81.9	134.6	300.1	295.0	493.6	549.2	603.7
Non-defense	38.3	141.7	200.4	319.9	474.8	493.0	532.8
Mandatory outlays	61.0	262.1	568.2	951.4	1,319.8	1,688.1	1,794.7
Social Security	29.6	117.1	246.5	406.0	518.7	581.4	610.4
Deposit Insurance	−0.5	−0.4	57.9	−3.1	−1.4	−1.5	−1.9
Means-tested entitlements[2]	10.1	45.0	94.1	232.6	350.9	366.6	394.2
Other	30.4	120.4	206.4	358.4	516.7	586.7	635.9
Undistributed offsetting receipts[3]	−8.6	−19.9	−36.7	−42.6	−65.2	−82.2	−87.7
Net interest	14.4	52.5	184.4	222.9	184.0	237.1	243.9

Notes: **1.** Estimate. **2.** Includes Medicaid, food stamps, family support assistance (AFDC), supplemental security income (SSI), child nutrition programs, earned income tax credits, and veterans' pensions. **3.** Includes asset sales.
Source: Office of Management and Budget, *Budget of the United States Government, FY 2009.*

Budget Outlays and Percent Distribution, by Function, 1970–2008

Function	1970	1980	1990	2000	2007	2008[1]
			MILLIONS OF DOLLARS			
National defense	**$81,692**	**$133,995**	**$299,331**	**$294,394**	**$552,568**	**$607,263**
Human resources	**75,349**	**313,374**	**619,329**	**1,115,665**	**1,758,490**	**1,864,535**
Education, training, employment & social services	8,634	31,843	38,755	53,789	91,676	93,389
Health	5,907	23,169	57,716	154,533	266,432	284,499
Medicare	6,213	32,090	98,102	197,113	375,407	396,333
Income Security	15,655	86,540	147,076	253,724	365,975	388,440
Social Security	30,270	118,547	248,623	409,423	586,153	615,256
Veterans benefits & services	8,669	21,185	29,058	47,083	72,847	86,618
Physical resources	**15,574**	**65,985**	**126,039**	**84,954**	**133,872**	**153,784**
Energy	997	10,156	3,341	−761	−860	3,005
Natural resources & environment	3,065	13,858	17,080	25,031	31,772	35,549
Commerce and housing credit	2,112	9,390	67,600	3,208	488	7,361
Transportation	7,008	21,329	29,485	46,853	72,905	80,268
Community and regional development	2,392	11,252	8,498	10,623	29,567	27,601
Net interest	**14,380**	**52,538**	**184,380**	**222,949**	**237,109**	**243,947**
Other functions	**17,286**	**44,996**	**60,734**	**113,835**	**130,440**	**149,435**
International affairs	4,330	12,714	13,764	17,216	28,510	34,826
General science, space, & technology	4,511	5,832	14,444	18,633	25,566	27,631
Agriculture	5,166	8,839	11,958	36,459	17,663	20,967
Administration of justice	959	4,584	9,993	28,499	41,244	46,202
General government	2,320	13,028	10,575	13,028	17,457	19,809
Total[2]	**$195,649**	**$590,947**	**$1,253,198**	**$1,789,216**	**$2,730,241**	**$2,931,222**
			AS PERCENTAGE OF TOTAL			
National defense	41.8%	22.7%	23.9%	16.5%	20.2%	20.7%
Human resources	38.5	53.0	49.4	62.4	64.4	63.6
Physical resources	8.0	11.2	10.1	4.7	4.9	5.2
Net interest	7.4	8.9	14.7	12.5	8.7	8.3
Other functions	8.8	7.6	4.8	6.4	4.8	5.1

Note: **1.** Includes undistributed offsetting receipts not shown separately.
Source: Office of Management and Budget, *Budget of the United States Government, FY 2009.*

Outlays Budget outlays are expenditures and net lending of funds under budget authority during the fiscal year. They constitute the spending side of the budget and are compared to receipts in calculating the budget surplus or deficit.

Receipts Budget receipts constitute the income side of the budget and are composed almost entirely of taxes or other compulsory payments to the government. They are compared to outlays in calculating the budget surplus or deficit.

Trust fund In the federal budget, a trust fund means only that the law requires that funds must be accounted for separately and used only for specified purposes. The largest trust funds are those for civil service and military retirement, Social Security, Medicare and unemployment insurance. These are financed largely by Social Security taxes and contributions and payments from the general fund. There are also major trust funds for transportation and bank deposit insurance which are financed by user charges.

User charges These are charges for services rendered, collected in the form of taxes, such as highway excise taxes to fund the highway trust fund.

Federal Government Finances, 1990–2008 (in millions of dollars)

Category	1990	2000	2007	2008[1]
RECEIPTS, TOTAL	**$1,031,969**	**$2,025,218**	**$2,568,239**	**$2,521,175**
Individual income taxes, total	**466,884**	**1,004,462**	**1,163,472**	**1,219,661**
Corporation income taxes, total	**93,507**	**207,289**	**370,243**	**345,336**
Social insurance and retirement receipts, total	**380,047**	**652,852**	**869,607**	**910,125**
Employment and general retirement:	**353,891**	**620,451**	**824,258**	**862,023**
Old-age and survivors insurance (Off-budget)	255,031	411,677	542,901	566,104
Disability insurance (Off-budget)	26,625	68,907	92,188	96,111
Hospital insurance	68,556	135,529	184,908	195,453
Railroad retirement:	2,292	4,338	4,261	4,355
Unemployment insurance:	21,635	27,640	41,091	43,382
Other retirement:	4,522	4,761	4,258	4,720
Federal employees' retirement—employee share	4,405	4,691	4,207	4,695
Non-Federal employees retirement[2]	117	70	51	25
Excise taxes, total	**35,345**	**68,865**	**65,069**	**68,835**
Federal funds, total	15,591	22,692	11,076	14,825
Alcohol taxes	5,695	8,140	8,648	8,819
Tobacco taxes	4,081	7,221	7,556	7,622
Telephone taxes	2,995	5,670	−2,125	586
Transportation fuels taxes	—	819	−3,291	−4,261
Other Federal fund excise taxes	2,460	717	288	2,059
Trust funds, total	19,754	46,173	53,993	54,010
Highway	13,867	34,972	39,361	39,203
Airport and airway	3,700	9,739	11,468	11,871
Aquatic resources	218	342	581	561
Black lung disability insurance	665	518	639	638
Inland waterway	63	101	91	89
Vaccine injury compensation	159	133	241	218
Leaking underground storage tank	122	184	226	197
Estate and gift taxes, total	**11,500**	**29,010**	**26,044**	**26,757**
Customs duties, total	**16,707**	**19,914**	**26,010**	**29,208**
Miscellaneous receipts, total	**27,978**	**42,826**	**47,794**	**−78,747**
OUTLAYS, TOTAL	**$1,253,116**	**$1,789,067**	**$2,730,241**	**$2,931,222**
National defense, total	**299,331**	**294,495**	**552,568**	**607,263**
Department of Defense—Military, total	289,704	281,161	529,845	583,054
Military Personnel	75,622	75,950	128,826	137,401
Operation and Maintenance	88,294	105,812	216,631	225,062
Procurement	80,972	51,696	99,647	130,477
Research, Development, Test, and Evaluation	37,454	37,602	73,136	74,735
Military Construction	5,080	5,109	7,899	10,241
Family Housing	3,501	3,413	3,473	4,290
Other	−1,218	1,579	233	848
Atomic energy defense activities	8,988	12,138	17,050	17,775
Defense-related activities	639	1,196	5,673	6,434
International affairs, total	13,764	17,216	28,510	34,826
International development and humanitarian assistance	5,498	6,518	15,542	14,253
International security assistance	8,652	6,387	7,982	9,025
Conduct of foreign affairs	3,050	4,709	8,389	12,202
Foreign information and exchange activities	1,103	817	1,220	1,252
International financial programs	−4,539	−1,215	−4,623	−1,906
General science, space and technology, total	**14,443**	**18,633**	**25,566**	**27,631**
General science and basic research	2,834	6,206	10,308	10,907
Space flight, research, and supporting activities	11,609	12,427	15,258	16,724
Energy, total	**3,341**	**−761**	**−860**	**3,005**
Energy supply	1,976	−1,818	−1,991	865

Category	1990	2000	2007	2008[1]
Energy conservation	$365	$666	$580	$924
Emergency energy preparedness	442	162	195	776
Energy information, policy, and regulation	558	229	356	440
Natural resources and environment, total	**17,080**	**25,031**	**31,772**	**35,549**
Water resources	4,401	5,081	5,099	8,749
Conservation and land management	4,030	6,762	9,646	9,735
Recreational resources	1,400	2,558	2,983	3,377
Pollution control and abatement	5,170	7,402	8,426	7,771
Other natural resources	2,080	3,228	5,618	5,917
Agriculture, total	**11,806**	**36,459**	**17,663**	**20,967**
Farm income stabilization	9,717	33,446	13,094	16,305
Agricultural research and services	2,089	3,013	4,569	4,662
Commerce and housing credit, total	**67,600**	**3,208**	**488**	**7,361**
Mortgage credit	3,845	–3,335	–4,986	325
Postal Service	2,116	2,129	–3,161	–4,556
Deposit insurance	57,891	–3,053	–1,492	–1,941
Other advancement of commerce	3,748	7,467	10,127	13,533
Transportation, total	**29,485**	**46,853**	**72,905**	**80,268**
Ground transportation	18,954	31,697	46,818	53,090
Air transportation	7,234	10,571	18,096	18,132
Water transportation	3,151	4,394	7,695	8,484
Other transportation	146	191	296	562
Community and regional development, total	**8,531**	**10,623**	**29,567**	**27,601**
Community development	3,530	5,480	11,834	12,688
Area and regional development	2,902	2,538	2,514	2,890
Disaster relief and insurance	2,098	2,605	15,219	12,023
Education, training, employment, and social services, total	**37,176**	**53,754**	**91,676**	**93,389**
Elementary, secondary, and vocational education	9,918	20,578	38,430	39,788
Higher education	11,107	10,116	24,637	24,475
Research and general education aids	1,577	2,532	3,170	3,230
Training and employment	5,619	6,772	7,080	7,096
Other labor services	810	1,199	1,635	1,600
Social services	8,145	12,557	16,724	17,200
Health, total	**57,716**	**154,533**	**266,432**	**284,499**
Health care services	47,642	136,230	233,928	251,834
Health research and training	8,611	15,979	29,279	29,518
Consumer and occupational health and safety	1,462	2,324	3,225	3,147
Medicare, total	**98,102**	**197,113**	**375,407**	**396,333**
Income security, total	**148,655**	**253,575**	**365,975**	**388,440**
General retirement and disability insurance (excluding social security)	5,148	5,189	7,829	7,923
Federal employee retirement and disability	52,037	77,152	103,916	109,086
Unemployment compensation	18,889	23,012	35,107	37,333
Housing assistance	15,891	28,800	39,715	41,041
Food and nutrition assistance	23,964	32,483	54,458	60,269
Other income security	32,725	86,939	124,950	132,788
Social security, total	**248,623**	**409,423**	**586,153**	**615,256**
Veterans benefits and services, total	**29,058**	**47,083**	**72,847**	**86,618**
Income security for veterans	15,566	25,461	35,684	42,466
Veterans education, training and rehabilitation	395	1,430	2,713	2,907
Hospital and medical care for veterans	12,107	19,477	32,294	37,810
Veterans housing	633	364	–868	–403
Other veterans benefits and services	356	351	3,024	3,838
Administration of justice, total	**10,185**	**28,501**	**41,244**	**46,202**
Federal law enforcement activities	4,840	12,123	19,617	24,926
Federal litigative and judicial activities	3,577	7,762	10,954	10,953
Federal correctional activities	1,291	3,707	6,328	6,229
Criminal justice assistance	477	4,909	4,345	4,094
General government, total	**10,490**	**12,960**	**17,457**	**19,809**
Legislative functions	1,759	2,223	3,541	3,553
Executive direction and management	160	456	490	499
Central fiscal operations	5,826	8,285	10,300	10,393
General property and records management	–32	–29	291	736
Central personnel management	184	184	–1	261
General purpose fiscal assistance	2,161	2,084	3,543	4,026
Other general government	792	2,241	1,636	1,698
Deductions for offsetting receipts	–361	–2,484	–2,343	–1,357
Net interest, total	**184,347**	**222,949**	**237,109**	**243,947**

Notes: 1. Estimate. 2. Represents employer and employee contributions to the civil service retirement and disability fund for covered employees of Government-sponsored, privately owned enterprises and the District of Columbia municipal government.
Source: Office of Management and Budget, *Budget of the United States Government, FY 2009.*

Federal Government Dollar, Fiscal Year 2008

Revenues: $2,521 billion

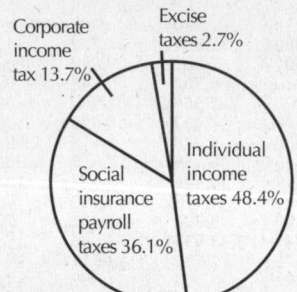

Corporate income tax 13.7%

Excise taxes 2.7%

Individual income taxes 48.4%

Social insurance payroll taxes 36.1%

Outlays: $2,931 billion

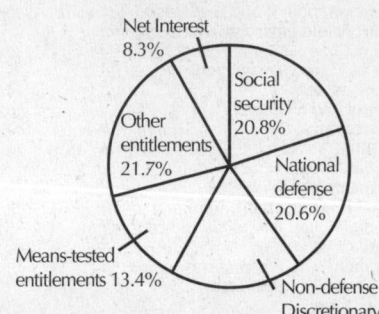

Net Interest 8.3%

Social security 20.8%

Other entitlements 21.7%

National defense 20.6%

Means-tested entitlements 13.4%

Non-defense Discretionary 18.2%

Federal Budget Outlays for National Defense Functions, 1962–2008 (millions of dollars)

Function	1962	1970	1980	1990	2000	2007	2008[1]
Military personnel	$16,331	$29,032	$40,897	$75,622	$75,950	$128,826	$137,401
Percent of defense budget	31.2%	35.4%	30.5%	25.2%	25.8%	23.3%	22.6%
Operations & maintenance	$11,594	$21,609	$44,788	$88,294	$105,812	$216,631	$225,062
Procurement	14,532	21,584	29,021	80,972	51,696	99,647	130,477
Research, development, test and evaluation	6,319	7,166	13,127	37,454	37,602	73,136	74,735
Military construction	1,347	1,168	2,450	5,080	5,109	7,899	10,241
Family housing	259	614	1,680	3,501	3,413	3,473	4,290
Other	−271	−1,050	−1,050	−1,218	1,478	233	848
Total outlays[2]	$52,345	$81,692	$133,995	$299,331	$294,394	$552,568	$607,263

Notes: 1. Estimate. 2. Includes atomic energy defense activities and other defense-related activities not shown separately.
Source: Office of Management and Budget, *Budget of the United States Government, FY 2009.*

NATIONAL DEFENSE

In 2007, the United States spent over half a trillion dollars to keep 1.4 million people in active military service and to build and maintain the greatest arsenal of weapons ever known.

Since the end of World War II, a large percentage of people and material have been committed to regions around the world that the government has determined are vital to U.S. interests. Between 1961 and 1980, the defense budget averaged around $200 billion annually (in 1982 constant dollars)—even during the Vietnam War. In 1981, however, the Reagan administration began a massive defense buildup that swelled successive defense budgets to unprecedented peacetime levels and in the process helped to quadruple the annual federal deficit in less than five years.

When the cold war ended, the defense budget started to recede from its previous high of $303 billion in 1989. But since 1998, the amount spent on the military has been increasing steadily every year, to its present all-time high. The operations in Afghanistan (2001-) and Iraq (2003-) have caused the defense budget to double since 1998. In the 2008 budget, more than one fifth of all Federal Outlays were slated for National Defense.

The defense establishment The earliest precursor to the Department of Defense was the War Department, established by Congress in 1789; a separate Navy Department was created in 1798. These were merged under the National Security Act of 1947 and subsequent amendments. By 1949 the secretary of defense was established as the principal assistant to the president on defense matters in charge of the Defense Department.

The Department of Defense (DoD) is a cabinet-level organization responsible for providing the military forces needed to deter war and protect the security of the United States. The major elements of these forces are the Army, Navy, Air Force, and Marine Corps. Under the president, who is also the commander-in-chief, the secretary of defense exercises direction, authority and control over the Department of Defense, which includes the three military departments, the Joint Chiefs of Staff and Joint Staff, nine unified commands, 15 defense agencies, and seven DoD field activities.

The four armed services are subordinate to the military departments, which are responsible for recruiting, training and equipping their forces. The Marine Corps is the second armed service in the Department of the Navy. (A fifth armed service, the U.S. Coast Guard, joined the Department of Homeland Security in 2003.)

Chain of command Operational command of U.S. combat forces is assigned to the nation's unified and specified commands. The chain of command runs from the president to the secretary of defense, through the Joint Chiefs of Staff, to the commanders-in-chief of the unified and specified commands. The four service secretaries are not part of this chain of command. A *unified command* is composed of forces from two or more services, has a broad and continuing mission and is normally organized on a geographical basis.

►U.S. ARMY
In peacetime, the primary mission of the continental U.S. armies is to train reserves and national guard, plan for mobilization, and coordinate domestic emergency relief efforts. The largest unit is a numbered *army*, such as the Fifth Army. (In time of war, two or three armies may be

brought under a single command in an *army group*.) An *army* is made up of two or more corps plus a headquarters (HQ) unit; a *corps* is made up of two to five divisions and an HQ.

There are 10 active and 8 reserve divisions in the U.S. Army combat forces. The *division* is a self-sufficient force, typically consisting of three *brigades* (each comprising three to five battalions) and various combat support elements. A *brigade* is made up of two or more regiments or battalions; a *regiment*, of subordinate units such as battalions, companies or squadrons; a *battalion*, of four or more companies; a *company* of several platoons; and a *platoon* of four squads. A *squad* consists of about 10 soldiers.

►U.S. MARINE CORPS
Marine Corps organization emphasizes the close integration of air-ground operations for service

Chairmen of the Joint Chiefs of Staff, 1949-2008

General of the Army Omar N. Bradley, USA	1949–53
Adm. Arthur W. Radford, USN	1953–57
Gen. Nathan F. Twining, USAF	1957–60
Gen. Lyman L. Lemnitzer, USA	1960–62
Gen. Maxwell D. Taylor, USA	1962–64
Gen. Earle G. Wheeler, USA	1964–70
Adm. Thomas H. Moorer, USN	1970–74
Gen. George S. Brown, USAF	1974–78
Gen. David C. Jones, USAF	1978–82
Gen. John W. Vessey Jr., USA	1982–85
Adm. William J. Crowe, USN	1985–89
Gen. Colin L. Powell, USA	1989–93
Gen. John Shalikashvili, USA	1993–97
Gen. H. Hugh Shelton, USA	1997–2001
Gen. Richard B. Myers, USAF	2001-05
Gen. Peter Pace, USMC	2005 07
Adm. Michael Mullen, USN	2007-present

Defense Establishment Employees, 2007-08

Branch	Active Duty[1]			Civilian employees[2]
	Officers	Enlisted	Total	
Army	85,275	435,081	524,681	229,881
Navy	50,965	276,265	331,566	176,922
Marine Corps	19,862	169,684	189,546	—
Air Force	64,198	259,691	328,202	152,584
Total DoD	220,300	1,140,721	1,373,995	675,450

1. As of April 30, 2008. Includes Academy Cadets and Midshipmen, not shown separately. 2. As of April, 2008. Marine Corps Civilian personnel are included under Navy. Total civilian employees includes other Defense Dept. organizations not shown separately.
Source: U.S. Dept. of Defense, *DOD Personnel and Military Casualty Statistics*; www.defenselink.mil.

Military Personnel on Active Duty, 1789–2007

Year/War	Total	Year/War	Total	Year/War	Total	Year/War	Total
1789	718	Civil War (1861-65)		World War II (1941-46)		1975	2,128,120
1795	5,296	*1861*	*217,112*	*1941*	*1,801,101*	1980	2,050,627
1801	7,108	*1862*	*673,124*	*1942*	*3,858,791*	1985	2,151,032
1810	11,554	*1863*	*960,061*	*1943*	*9,044,745*		
		1864	*1,031,724*	*1944*	*11,451,719*	Operation Desert Storm	
War of 1812 (1812-15)		*1865*	*1,062,848*	*1945*	*12,123,455*	(1990-91)	
1812	*12,631*	*1870*	*50,348*	*1946*	*3,030,088*	*1990*	*2,043,705*
1813	*25,152*	*1880*	*37,894*			*1991*	*1,985,555*
1814	*46,858*	*1890*	*38,666*	Korean Conflict (1950-53)			
1815	*40,885*			*1950*	*1,460,261*	1995	1,518,224
		Spanish-American War		*1951*	*3,249,455*	2000	1,384,338
1820	15,113	(1898)		*1952*	*3,635,912*		
1830	11,942	*1898*	*235,785*	*1953*	*3,555,067*	Operation Enduring	
1840	21,616					Freedom (2001-)	
		1900	139,344	1960	2,476,435	*2001*	*1,385,116*
Mexican War (1846-48)		1915	174,112			*2002*	*1,411,600*
1846	*39,165*			Vietnam Conflict (1964-73)			
1847	*57,761*	World War I (1917-18)		*1964*	*2,687,409*	Operation Iraqi Freedom	
1848	*60,308*	*1917*	*643,833*	*1965*	*2,655,389*	(2003-)	
		1918	*2,897,167*	*1966*	*3,094,058*	*2003*	*1,434,377*
1850	20,824			*1967*	*3,376,880*	*2004*	*1,426,836*
1860	27,958	1919	1,172,602	*1968*	*3,547,902*	*2005*	*1,389,394*
		1920	343,302	*1969*	*3,460,162*	*2006*	*1,384,960*
		1930	255,648	*1970*	*3,066,294*	*2007*	*1,367,426*
		1940	458,365				

Note: Figures in italics are wartime years. Totals exclude Coast Guard.
Source: Bureau of the Census, *Statistical History of the U.S.* (1976) and U.S. Dept. of Defense, unpublished statistics.

with the U.S. fleet and for the conduct of land operations essential to the prosecution of a naval campaign. All Marines serve "at the pleasure of the president," and the Corps's mission includes "performing such other duties as the President may direct."

The smallest tactical unit of Marine Corps infantry is the *fire team*, which consists of 4 Marines. A *squad* is made up of three fire teams, and there are three squads to a *platoon*, three platoons to a *company*, three companies to a *battalion*, three battalions to a *regiment*, three regiments to a *brigade*, and three brigades to a *division*.

These components are organized into three basic organizational structures called *Marine air-ground task forces*, or MAGTFs. The largest—about 47,500 personnel—is the *Marine Expeditionary Force* (MEF), which consists of a Marine air wing (330 planes), a Marine division, and a force service support group. The *Marine Expeditionary Brigade* (MEB) consists of a Marine air group (150 planes), a regimental landing group and a brigade service support group—about 15,000 personnel. The smallest and most responsive Marine force, the *Marine Expeditionary Unit* (MEU), consists of about 2,500 personnel and is made up of a helicopter squadron, a battalion landing team, and a unit service support group. MEUs are sea-based, can be airlifted and they are equipped and trained to be self-sustaining in the field for up to 15 days.

▶ U.S. NAVY

The ships of the U.S. Navy are organized into the Pacific Fleet, the Atlantic Fleet, and U.S. Naval Forces Europe. These are composed of numbered fleets which consist of *carrier battle groups, battleship surface action groups* and one or more *underway replenishment groups*. Smaller subdivisions of naval forces are the *flotilla* consisting of two or more squadrons; a *squadron*, of two or more divisions; and a *division*, normally made up of four ships.

A naval *task force* designates a collection of ships under a single command designed to accomplish a particular tactical or strategic purpose. An *amphibious squadron* consists of amphibious assault ships, amphibious transport docks, dock landing ships and tank landing ships, and transports troops, and equipment necessary for an assault landing from the sea.

U.S. Service and Casualties in Major Wars and Conflicts

War or conflict	Number serving	Battle deaths	Other deaths	Wounds not mortal	War or conflict	Number serving	Battle deaths	Other deaths	Wounds not mortal
Revolutionary War (1775–83)					**Korean Conflict (1950–53)**				
Army	N.A.	4,044	N.A.	6,004	Army	2,834,000	27,709	806	77,596
Navy	N.A.	342	N.A.	114	Navy	1,177,000	468	939	1,576
Marines	N.A.	49	N.A.	70	Marines	424,000	4,267	1,261	23,744
Total	N.A.	4,435	N.A.	6,188	Air Force	1,285,000	1,302	243	368
War of 1812 (1812–15)					Total	5,720,000	33,746	3,249	103,284
Army	N.A.	1,950	N.A.	4,000					
Navy	N.A.	265	N.A.	439	**Vietnam Conflict (1964–73)**				
Marines	N.A.	45	N.A.	66	Army	4,368,000	30,905	7,275	96,802
Total	286,730	2,260	N.A.	4,505	Navy	1,842,000	1,631	925	4,178
Mexican War (1846–48)					Marines	794,000	13,081	1,754	51,392
Army	N.A.	1,721	11,550	4,102	Air Force	1,740,000	1,738	842	931
Navy	N.A.	1	N.A.	3	Total	8,744,000	47,355	10,796	153,303
Marines	N.A.	11	N.A.	47					
Total	78,718	1,733	11,550	4,152	**Operation Desert Storm (1990–91)[3]**				
Civil War (1861–65)[1]					Army	782,000	98	126	354
Army	2,128,948	138,154	221,374	280,040	Navy	669,000	5	50	12
Navy	84,415[2]	2,112	2,411	1,710	Marines	213,000	24	44	92
Marines	N.A.	148	312	131	Air Force	561,000	20	15	9
Total	2,213,363	140,414	224,097	281,881	Total	2,225,000	147	235	467
Spanish-American War (1898)									
Army	280,564	369	2,061	1,594	**Operation Enduring Freedom (Oct. 2001–)[4]**				
Navy	22,875	10	0	47	Army	19,700	264	135	1,791
Marines	3,321	6	0	21	Navy[5]	800	19	15	22
Total	306,760	385	2,061	1,662	Marines	400	15	29	147
World War I (1917–1918)					Air Force	4,800	12	19	82
Army	4,057,101	50,510	55,868	193,663	Total	25,700	310	198	2,042
Navy	599,051	431	6,856	819					
Marines	78,839	2,461	390	9,520	**Operation Iraqi Freedom (March 2003–)[4]**				
Total	4,734,991	53,402	63,114	204,002	Army	125,800	2,396	552	20,710
World War II (1941–46)					Navy[5]	21,300	63	32	620
Army	11,260,000	234,874	83,400	565,861	Marines	26,900	836	151	8,462
Navy	4,183,466	36,950	25,664	37,778	Air Force	22,600	28	18	390
Marines	669,100	19,733	4,778	67,207	Total	196,600	3,323	753	30,182
Total	16,112,566	291,557	113,842	670,846					

Note: N.A. = not available. Prior to World War I, dates are approximate. Actual period covered for World War I: Apr. 6, 1917-Nov. 11, 1918; World War II: Dec. 7, 1941-Dec. 31, 1946; Korea: June 25, 1950-July 27, 1953; Vietnam: Aug. 4, 1964-Jan. 27, 1973. **1.** Union Forces only; authoritative statistics for Confederate forces not available. Estimates of the number who served range from 600,000 to 1.5 million. The Final Report of the Provost Marshal General, 1863-1866 indicated 133,821 Confederate deaths (74,524 battle and 59,297 other) based upon incomplete returns. In addition, an estimated 26,000-31,000 Confederate prisoners died in prisons. **2.** Includes Navy and Marines. **3.** DMDC, Sept. 9, 1991. Deployment figures changed continuously throughout the operation and have since, and have depended on, among other things, the timely reporting and posting of data. **4.** Service and casualties as of May 31, 2008. **5.** Navy figures include Coast Guard. **Source:** U.S. Dept. of Defense, *Personnel and Military Casualty Statistics.* www.defenselink.mil

▶**U.S. COAST GUARD**
A successor to the Revenue Marine established in 1790, the primary function of the Coast Guard is to enforce federal maritime law. For most of its history, the Coast Guard served as part of the Department of Transportation during peacetime and as part of the Navy during wartime. On January 24, 2003, the Coast Guard became part of the newly created Department of Homeland Security, though it may still operate as an element of the Defense Department in the event of war or at the President's direction.

▶**U.S. AIR FORCE**
The Air Force is organized into a number of commands. Within commands concerned with the strategic or tactical operation of aircraft, the primary subdivisions are indicated by the term air force prefaced by a number, as the Eighth Air Force. Such an *air force* is comprised of wings; a *wing* consists of two or more groups or

U.S. Armed Forces Worldwide, 2007

Region/Area	Army	Navy	Marine Corps	Air Force	Total
United States and Territories[1]	**445,608**	**223,564**	**139,213**	**271,214**	**1,079,599**
Continental United States	405,616	114,978	107,790	251,139	879,523
Alaska	11,681	44	30	7,776	19,531
Hawaii	20,328	5,569	6,286	4,838	37,021
Guam	41	1,061	7	1,781	2,890
Puerto Rico	52	46	49	21	168
Transients	7,889	9,489	25,048	5,655	48,081
Afloat	0	92,377	0	0	92,377
Europe[1]	**48,116**	**5,831**	**886**	**31,029**	**85,862**
Belgium[2]	693	102	26	471	1,292
Germany[2]	42,023	277	319	14,536	57,155
Greece[2]	9	290	16	54	369
Greenland[2]	0	0	0	131	131
Italy[2]	3,183	2,422	52	4,044	9,701
Netherlands[2]	301	22	13	247	583
Portugal[2]	27	28	7	767	829
Serbia (includes Kosovo)	1,300	0	3	40	1,343
Spain[2]	93	704	163	304	1,264
Turkey[2]	63	9	15	1,499	1,586
United Kingdom[2]	334	436	82	8,803	9,655
Afloat	0	1,492	0	0	1,492
Former Soviet Union[1]	**39**	**4**	**93**	**13**	**149**
East Asia and Pacific[1]	**20,434**	**14,806**	**14,591**	**20,802**	**70,633**
Australia	27	26	20	65	138
China (includes Hong Kong)	10	8	32	14	64
Japan	2,483	3,734	14,226	12,721	33,164
Korea, Republic of	17,798	227	108	7,943	26,076
Philippines	16	4	119	9	148
Singapore	8	84	14	16	122
Thailand	41	9	31	23	104
Afloat	0	10,707	0	0	10,707
North Africa, Near East, South Asia[1]	**587**	**1,912**	**2,696**	**489**	**5,684**
Bahrain	23	1,258	136	25	1,442
Diego Garcia	0	213	0	41	254
Egypt	195	5	24	37	261
Saudi Arabia	126	27	31	73	257
United Arab Emirates	3	6	18	62	89
Afloat	0	382	2,282	0	2,664
Sub-Saharan Africa[1]	**516**	**1,007**	**640**	**337**	**2,500**
Djibouti	450	970	450	320	2,190
Western Hemisphere[1]	**706**	**588**	**337**	**362**	**1,993**
Canada	7	44	7	85	143
Colombia	67	4	27	8	106
Cuba (Guantanamo)	337	449	131	0	917
Honduras	186	2	8	192	388
Afloat	0	12	0	0	12
Total–Foreign Countries	**72,460**	**110,163**	**47,129**	**58,875**	**288,627**
Total–Worldwide	**518,068**	**333,727**	**186,342**	**330,089**	**1,368,226**
Ashore	518,068	222,227	184,060	330,089	1,254,444
Afloat	0	111,500	2,282	0	113,782
DEPLOYMENTS					
Operation Enduring Freedom[3,5]	19,700	800	400	4,800	25,700
Operation Iraqi Freedom[4,5]	125,800	21,300	26,900	22,600	196,600

Note: As of Dec. 31, 2007. **1.** Includes other countries not shown separately. **2.** Member of NATO Europe. **3.** Total personnel (including Reserve/National Guard) deployed in and around Afghanistan. **4.** Total personnel (including Reserve/National Guard) deployed in and around Iraq. **5.** Number rounded in source. Source: U.S. Dept. of Defense. *Military Personnel Statistics.* www.defenselink.mil

squadrons; a *group* consists of two or more squadrons; and a *squadron* is made up of two or more flights. A *flight* is the basic tactical unit and consists of four or more planes.

▶**SPECIAL OPERATIONS FORCES (SOF)**

A unified command whose elements are drawn from the four major services, the special operations forces are designated to achieve military objectives of a limited and specific nature. Among the various elements of the SOF are: *Army* special forces; Rangers; psychological operations, civil affairs, and special operations aviation units; *Navy* SEAL and SEAL delivery vehicle teams; and *Air Force* Twenty-third Air Force special operations force.

▶**RESERVE FORCES**

The United States has always relied on reserve forces that can be called to active duty or mobilized to deal with emergencies beyond the capacities of active forces. The reserve forces constitute the ini-

Top 10 Defense Contractors, 2006–07

2007 Rank, Company (2006 rank)	Awards (billions)	
	2006	2007
1. Lockheed Martin Corp. (1)	$27.0	$27.9
2. Boeing Company (2)	19.9	22.5
3. Northrop Grumman Corp. (3)	13.4	14.7
4. General Dynamics Corp. (4)	12.1	14.6
5. Raytheon Company (5)	9.8	11.2
6. BAE Systems, PLC (6)	6.1	9.2
7. L-3 Communications Holding Inc. (9)	5.0	6.0
8. United Technologies Corp. (10)	4.6	5.3
9. KBR, Inc. (7)	6.0	4.8
10. SAIC, Inc. (11)	3.2	3.6

Source: Federal Procurement Data System, www.USAspending.gov

Major Weapon Systems and Combat Forces, 1980–2001

Weapon or force	1980	1990	1999	2000	2001
STRATEGIC (NUCLEAR) FORCES					
Land-based ICBMs					
Minuteman	1,000	950	500	500	500
Peacekeeper	0	50	50	50	50
Heavy bombers[1]					
B-52	241	154	56	56	56
B-1	0	90	74	80	82
B-2 (stealth bomber)	0	0	13	16	16
Submarine-Launched Ballistic Missiles[2]					
Poseidon (C-3 and C-4)[3]	336	368	0	0	0
Trident (C-4 and D-5)	0	216	432	432	432
GENERAL PURPOSE FORCES					
Active land forces					
Army divisions	16	18	10	10	10
Marine Corps divisions	3	3	3	3	3
Army Separate brigades[4]	8	8	3	3	3
Army Special Forces groups	2	5	7	7	7
Army Ranger regiment	0	1	1	1	1
Active tactical air forces (PAA/squadrons)					
Air Force attack and fighter aircraft	1,608/74	1,722/76	936/49	936/47	906/45
Navy attack and fighter aircraft	696/60	622/57	432/36	432/36	432/36
Marine Corps attack and fighter aircraft	329/25	334/24	308/21	308/21	308/21
Naval forces					
Strategic forces ships	48	39	18	18	18
Battle forces ships	384	412	256	259	259
Support forces ships	41	65	25	25	25
Reserve forces ships	6	31	18	16	15
Total battle forces deployable	479	547	317	318	317
Coastal defense, mine warfare, and other	52	19	22	22	22
AIRLIFT AND SEALIFT FORCES					
Intertheater airlift (PMAI)[5]					
C-5	70	109	104	104	104
C-141	234	234	136	104	88
KC-10	0	57	54	54	54
C-17	0	0	37	46	58
Intratheater airlift (PMAI)[5]					
C-1306	482	460	425	425	418
Sealift ships[7]					
Tankers, active	21	28	10	10	10
Cargo, active	23	40	49	52	57
Ready Reserve Force (RRF)	24	96	87	87	87

Note: PMAI = primary mission aircraft inventory. **1.** Excludes backup and attrition reserve aircraft. **2.** Number operational. **3.** C-3 missiles were removed from Poseidon submarines in September of 1992. **4.** Includes the Eskimo scout group and the armored cavalry regiments. **5.** Excludes development/test and training aircraft. **6.** Excludes Dept. of Navy aircraft. **7.** Includes fast sealift ships, afloat pre-positioned force ships, and common user (charter) ships. **Source:** U.S. Dept. of Defense, *Defense Almanac.* www.defenselink.mil

tial and primary augmentation of active forces in any emergency requiring rapid expansion of those forces.

There are seven reserve components: Army National Guard, Army Reserve, Naval Reserve, Marine Corps Reserve, Air National Guard, Air Force Reserve, and Coast Guard Reserve. All National Guard and Reserve personnel are assigned to one of three categories: the Ready Reserve, the Standby Reserve, or the Retired Reserve. All National Guard members are in the Ready Reserve.

The Ready Reserve consists of the Selected Reserve, the Individual Ready Reserve, and the Inactive National Guard. All are subject to orders for active duty in time of war or national emergency.

In addition, members of the Selected Reserve may be ordered to active duty under implementation of the presidential call-up authority, under which the president can activate up to 200,000 members of the Selected Reserve involuntarily, for operational missions, for not more than 90 days, without declaring a national emergency.

Minorities in Uniform, 2000

Service	Black Americans Number	Black Americans Percent	Hispanic Americans Number	Hispanic Americans Percent	Other[1] Number	Other[1] Percent	Total Number	Total Percent
Officers, Total	18,309	8.5%	8,269	3.8%	11,150	5.2%	37,728	17.5%
Army	9,162	12.0	3,105	4.1	4,075	5.3	16,342	21.4
Navy	3,524	6.7	2,732	5.2	2,653	5.0	8,909	16.9
Marines	1,341	7.5	914	5.1	599	3.3	2,854	15.9
Air Force	4,282	6.3	1,518	2.2	3,823	5.6	9,623	14.1
Enlisted, Total	254,509	22.3%	99,297	8.7%	73,888	6.5%	427,694	37.5%
Army	115,240	29.2	34,232	8.7	26,388	6.7	175,860	44.6
Navy	62,974	20.3	29,630	9.5	27,568	8.9	120,172	38.7
Marines	25,023	16.4	20,174	13.2	7,185	4.7	52,382	34.4
Air Force	51,272	18.2	15,261	5.4	12,747	4.5	79,280	28.1
DoD Total	272,818	20.1%	107,566	7.9%	85,038	6.3%	465,422	34.4%

Note: As of September 5, 2000. 1. Includes Native Americans, Alaskan Natives, and Pacific Islanders.
Source: U.S. Dept. of Defense, *Defense 2000*. www.defenselink.mil

Guard and Reserve Forces, 2007

Status	Army National Guard	Army Reserve	Naval Reserve	Marine Corps Reserve	Air National Guard	Air Force Reserve	Total DoD	Coast Guard Reserve
Selected Reserve								
Officers	37,495	35,990	15,727	3,326	14,025	16,346	122,909	1,316
Enlisted	315,212	153,892	54,206	35,231	92,229	54,800	705,570	6,461
Total	352,707	189,882	69,933	38,557	106,254	71,146	828,479	7,777
Individual Ready Reserve/Inactive National Guard								
Officers	274	9,311	11,506	3,164	—	13,224	37,479	124
Enlisted	2,011	67,237	46,982	59,066	—	36,182	211,478	3,250
Total	2,285	76,548	58,488	62,230	—	49,406	248,957	3,374
Total Ready Reserve								
Officers	37,769	45,301	27,233	6,490	14,025	29,570	160,388	1,440
Enlisted	317,223	221,129	101,188	94,297	92,229	90,982	917,048	9,711
Total	354,992	266,430	128,421	100,787	106,254	120,552	1,077,436	11,151

Note: As of September 30, 2007.
Source: U.S. Dept. of Defense, *Guard and Reserve Summary Strength Report, Sept. 2007*

Women in Uniform: Female Active Duty Military Personnel 1945-2007

Year	Total DoD	Army Officers	Army Enlisted	Navy Officers	Navy Enlisted	Marine Corps. Officers	Marine Corps. Enlisted	Air Force Officers	Air Force Enlisted
1945	266,256	62,775	93,095	19,188	72,833	809	17,556	N.A.	N.A.
1950	22,069	4,431	6,551	2,447	2,746	45	535	1,532	3,782
1960	31,550	4,263	8,279	2,711	5,360	123	1,488	3,675	5,651
1970	41,479	5,248	11,476	2,888	5,795	299	2,119	4,667	8,987
1980	171,418	7,609	61,729	4,877	30,103	487	6,219	8,493	51,901
1990	227,018	12,404	71,217	7,808	52,099	677	8,679	13,331	60,803
2000	202,601	10,814	62,889	7,846	43,760	932	9,530	11,819	55,011
2007	198,490	12,963	58,120	7,617	41,252	1,135	10,572	11,835	52,595

Source: U.S. Dept. of Defense, *Military Personnel Statistics*, Sept. 2007, www.defenselink.mil

►NUCLEAR FORCES

Nuclear forces are classified as either strategic or nonstrategic. The strategic triad—a cornerstone of post–World War II U.S. defense—is composed of land-based missile forces, including intercontinental ballistic missiles (ICBMs); submarine-launched ballistic missiles (SLBMs); and manned aircraft of the strategic bomber force. Nonstrategic nuclear weapons are shorter-range weapons that can be deployed on the battlefield and include sea-launched cruise missiles, artillery-fired atomic projectiles, and dual-capable (conventional and nuclear) aircraft.

Department of Defense Contract Awards, Payroll, and Civilian and Military Personnel by State, Fiscal 2006

State	Payroll[1] ('000s)	Contract awards[2] ('000s)	Personnel Military	Civilian	Total
Alabama	$3,503,330	$6,953,772	9,742	22,312	32,054
Alaska	1,639,960	1,655,627	20,363	4,894	25,257
Arizona	2,655,501	9,695,948	21,997	9,047	31,044
Arkansas	1,080,151	881,346	4,905	3,977	8,882
California	15,269,710	32,126,109	149,481	55,709	205,190
Colorado	3,210,364	4,127,154	29,932	10,907	40,839
Connecticut	757,759	7,780,823	6,594	2,388	8,982
Delaware	419,848	124,776	3,297	1,564	4,861
District of Columbia	2,561,181	4,066,784	12,351	14,634	26,985
Florida	8,863,769	10,706,644	58,100	26,072	84,172
Georgia	7,409,373	5,515,093	68,928	32,862	101,790
Hawaii	4,064,063	1,963,468	45,366	17,079	62,445
Idaho	541,290	168,321	4,042	1,522	5,564
Illinois	2,838,406	3,273,844	24,536	13,617	38,153
Indiana	1,360,874	4,627,372	805	9,281	10,086
Iowa	444,967	944,483	390	1,582	1,972
Kansas	1,827,165	1,705,691	17,645	6,577	24,222
Kentucky	2,959,047	5,394,692	38,799	9,170	47,969
Louisiana	1,734,325	5,154,128	15,069	6,212	21,281
Maine	827,224	1,019,801	2,096	6,445	8,541
Maryland	5,333,575	10,244,137	29,626	30,749	60,375
Massachusetts	1,097,587	9,077,395	2,175	6,491	8,666
Michigan	1,307,212	3,897,649	1,073	8,147	9,220
Minnesota	761,594	1,525,731	729	2,522	3,251
Mississippi	1,702,149	5,477,261	10,158	8,630	18,788
Missouri	2,432,471	9,392,852	16,241	9,483	25,724
Montana	407,142	247,146	3,589	1,358	4,947
Nebraska	960,998	718,281	6,784	3,774	10,558
Nevada	1,145,774	750,415	9,127	2,178	11,305
New Hampshire	324,356	1,105,518	912	1,069	1,981
New Jersey	2,004,030	6,151,133	6,293	13,959	20,252
New Mexico	1,465,574	1,074,568	10,834	6,863	17,697
New York	2,668,950	8,020,492	26,240	11,145	37,385
North Carolina	7,131,669	2,690,120	102,845	17,447	120,292
North Dakota	500,849	240,478	7,013	1,853	8,866
Ohio	3,030,082	5,980,221	6,845	21,789	28,634
Oklahoma	3,259,656	2,069,823	25,064	21,539	46,603
Oregon	760,465	562,475	558	3,241	3,799
Pennsylvania	3,077,484	7,514,783	2,979	25,266	28,245
Rhode Island	677,943	430,736	2,403	4,213	6,616
South Carolina	3,430,778	2,197,034	38,090	9,640	47,730
South Dakota	357,662	371,727	3,150	1,237	4,387
Tennessee	1,519,720	2,865,761	2,441	5,334	7,775
Texas	11,908,183	27,101,956	119,176	41,462	160,638
Utah	1,739,346	2,303,676	5,188	15,081	20,269
Vermont	168,378	829,033	70	608	678
Virginia	16,692,841	29,246,034	128,515	81,342	209,857
Washington	5,652,251	4,765,782	49,887	24,501	74,388
West Virginia	383,624	392,274	373	1,745	2,118
Wisconsin	680,804	2,165,274	449	2,695	3,144
Wyoming	306,051	161,156	3,043	1,002	4,045
Total U.S.	$146,857,505	$257,456,798	1,156,308	642,214	1,798,522

Notes: 1. Payroll estimates cover active duty military and direct hire civilian personnel, including Army Corps of Engineers. 2. Military awards for supplies, services and construction; expenditures relating to awards may extend over several years. Net value of contracts of over $25,000 for work in each state; the state in which the prime contractor is located is not necessarily the state in which the subcontracted work is done. **Source:** U.S. Dept. of Defense, *Statistical Information Analysis Division Work Force Publications, DoD Personnel and Procurement Statistics.* www.defenselink.mil.

Military Active Duty Monthly Basic Pay Table, 2008

| Pay Grade | Army Rank | Years of Service | | | |
		over 2	over 10	over 20	over 26
	Commissioned Officers				
0-10	General, Admiral	N.A.	N.A.	$14,137	$15,017
0-9	Lieut. General, Vice-Admiral	N.A.	N.A.	12,365	13,249
0-8	Maj. General, Rear Admiral	$9,035	$10,005	11,715	12,004
0-7	Brig. General, Commodore	7,607	8,592	10,594	10,648
0-6	Colonel, Captain	5,919	6,639	8,466	9,352
0-5	Lt. Colonel, Commander	5,060	6,113	7,409	7,631
0-4	Major, Lt. Commander	4,487	5,799	6,471	6,471
0-3	Captain, Lieutenant	3,863	5,157	5,543	5,543
0-2	1st Lieutenant, Lieut. (J.G.)	3,353	4,074	4,074	4,074
0-1	2nd Lieutenant, Ensign	2,660	3,215	3,215	3,215
	Warrant Officers				
W-5	Chief Warrant Officer	N.A.	N.A.	$6,261	$7,078
W-4	Chief Warrant Officer	$3,788	$4,555	5,682	6,431
W-3	Chief Warrant Officer	3,350	4,255	5,219	5,641
W-2	Chief Warrant Officer	3,115	3,868	4,579	4,750
W-1	Warrant Officer	2,766	3,563	4,316	4,316
	Enlisted Personnel				
E-9	Sgt. Major, Master C.P.O.	N.A.	$4,255	$4,991	$5,706
E-8	Master Sgt., Senior C.P.O.	N.A.	3,637	4,307	4,870
E-7	Sgt.1st Class, Chief Petty Officer	$2,642	3,263	3,845	4,351
E-6	Staff Sgt., Petty Officer 1st Class	2,304	2,930	3,243	3,243
E-5	Sergeant, Petty Officer 2d Class	2,047	2,705	2,722	2,722
E-4	Corporal, Petty Officer 3d Class	1,849	2,135	2,135	2,135
E-3	Private First Class, Seaman	1,687	1,790	1,790	1,790
E-2	Private, Seaman	1,510	1,510	1,510	1,510
E-1	Recruit, Seaman Recruit[1]	1,347	1,347	1,347	1,347

Note: Effective Jan. 1, 2008. Numbers rounded to nearest dollar. N.A.: Not Applicable 1. Applicable to E-1 with 4 or more months of active duty. Basic pay for an E-1 with less than 4 months of active duty is $1,245.90. Source: U.S. Department of Defense.

SOCIAL INSURANCE PROGRAMS

In order to provide a "safety net" for the disadvantaged, the elderly, and the disabled, the federal government administers a range of social insurance and social assistance programs. Many of these programs are administered by the Social Security Administration, which became an independent government agency in 1995. But many cabinet-level departments, other independent government agencies, and state government human services agencies also run programs such as food stamps (Dept. of Agriculture), public housing (Dept. of Housing and Urban Development), and programs for veterans (Dept. of Veterans Affairs).

Social insurance programs were not developed all at once to fulfill a specific agenda of national need. Rather they are a hodgepodge of legislation passed (and often altered) over the years to meet the needs of particular groups of citizens at particular times. In what the government calls "social insurance programs," certain risks—injury, disability, unemployment, old age, and death—are lumped together. "Premiums," usually in the form of a payroll tax, are paid by employees and/or their employers. The benefit is paid, regardless of other financial resources (other than earnings), when one of those "risks" occurs.

▶ SOCIAL SECURITY
The Depression proved that the traditional support systems—the family, private charities, and local government—failed in nationwide economic hard times. Many old people had exhausted their savings and were destitute; in fact, during the Depression less than 10 percent of the aged left estates large enough to be probated. This led to the enactment of one of the most comprehensive pieces of legislation ever passed by Congress, the Social Security Act.

Signed into law by Franklin Roosevelt on August 14, 1935, the Social Security Act established two social insurance programs: a federal system of old-age benefits for retired workers in commerce and industry and a federal-state system of unemployment insurance. The law also provided for federal matching grants-in-aid to states to help them assist the needy aged, the blind, and children. Today, in the words of former Social Security Commissioner Dorcas R. Hardy, it is "the most complex government program that God and Congress ever created."

The first payments of monthly benefits were made in 1940. Major changes in the scope of Social Security were made in 1956, when the program was broadened through the addition of disability insurance; in 1965, through the addition of Medicare and Medicaid; in 1970, when the black lung program was developed to provide benefits to coal miners (and their survivors) who suffer from pneumoconiosis (black lung disease); in 1972, when Congress authorized provisions for cost-of-living increases; and in 1974, when Social Security insurance was taken over by the Social Security Administration. In 1983, amendments provided for the taxing of up to one-half of benefits for certain upper-income beneficiaries.

Workers and their employers each contribute an equal amount to the Social Security program to pay for retirement, disability, and Medicare benefits. This is sometimes referred to as the "payroll tax." The tax money collected is placed in a trust fund, which can be used only to pay Social Security benefits and expenses

Since 1990, the Federal Insurance Contributions Act (FICA) has mandated that 15.3 percent be deducted from each worker's paycheck. Half of that amount (7.65 percent) is paid by the employer; the other half is paid by the employee. Self-employed workers, who are both employee and employer, pay both shares, or a total of 15.3

SOCIAL SERVICE PROGRAMS INFORMATION

Information about social service programs can be obtained from the following government agencies:

Black lung program Office of Workers Compensation Programs, U.S. Dept. of Labor. (800) 638-7072. **www.dol.gov.**

Food Stamps Food and Nutrition Service, U.S. Dept. of Agriculture. (800) 221-5689. **www.fns.usda.gov/fsp.**

Head Start Administration for Children and Families, U.S. Dept. of Health and Human Services. (202)-205-9336. **www.acf.dhhs.gov**

Medicaid Centers for Medicare & Medicaid Services, U.S. Dept. of Health and Human Services. (877) 267-2323. **http://cms.hhs.gov.**

Medicare (HI) Health Care Financing Administration, U.S. Dept. of Health and Human Services. (877) 267-2323. **www.medicare.gov.**

Social Security (OASDI) Social Security Administration. (800) 772-1213. **www.ssa.gov.**

Special nutrition programs Food and Nutrition Service, U.S. Dept. of Agriculture. (703) 305-2052. **www.fns.usda.gov.**

Supplemental Security Income (SSI) Social Security Administration. (800) 772-1213. **www.ssa.gov.**

Temporary Assistance to Needy Families (TANF) This program replaced the Aid to Families and Dependent Children (AFDC) program under the Welfare Reform Act of 1996. Administration for Children and Families, U.S. Dept. of Health and Human Services. (202) 401-9200. **www.acf.dhhs.gov.**

Temporary disability insurance Office of Workers Compensation Programs, U.S. Dept. of Labor. (866) 487-2365. **www.dol.gov/ esa/owcp_org.htm**

Unemployment insurance Office of Workers Compensation Programs, U.S. Dept. of Labor. (866) 487-2365. **www.dol.gov/esa/owcp_org.htm**

Veterans' benefits U.S. Dept. of Veterans Affairs. (800) 827-1000. **www.va.gov**

---

percent. Earnings above a certain amount ($102,000 in 2008) are not subject to the deduction for Social Security, but they are subject to Medicare taxes (1.45 percent each for employer and employee; 2.9 percent for the self-employed).

Old Age, Survivors and Disability Insurance (OASDI)

This is the program most people mean when they refer to "social security." It has three basic principles: 1) benefits are related to earnings from covered work; 2) benefits are paid regardless of additional income from savings, pensions, and other private retirement accounts; and 3) universal compulsory coverage assures a base of economic security.

The addition of disability insurance in 1956 broadened the program's scope, and in 1972 Congress authorized provisions for cost-of-living increases. The 1983 amendments improved the program's financial footing by raising the self-employment tax rate, and by taxing up to one-half of benefits for certain upper-income beneficiaries.

Old Age From the program's inception, workers became eligible for benefits upon turning 65. But in 2003, the retirement age started increasing by two months each year (See the accompanying table). People born between 1943 and 1954 must wait until age 66 to retire with full benefits, while the minimum retirement age for people born after January 1, 1960 is 67. Anybody can still retire as early as age 62, but doing so brings with it a significant reduction (as much as 30 percent) in annual benefits. See the accompanying table for approximate monthly retired, disabled and survivor benefits.

The Retirement Age Is Going Up

For many years, workers became eligible for Social Security benefits upon turning 65. But in 2003, the retirement age started increasing by two months each year. You should still apply for Medicare benefits upon turning 65, regardless of when you were born.

Year of birth	Full retirement age	Year of birth	Full retirement age
1937 or earlier	65 years	1943-54	66 years
		1956	66 & 4 months
1938	65 & 2 months	1957	66 & 6 months
1939	65 & 4 months	1958	66 & 8 months
1940	65 & 6 months	1959	66 & 10 months
1941	65 & 8 months	1960 or later	67 years
1942	65 & 10 months		

Source: Social Security Administration.

OASDI Beneficiaries and Benefit Payments, 2007

Type of Beneficiaries	Number ('000s)	Monthly rate (millions)	Average monthly benefit
Retired workers	31,525	$34,001	$1,079
Dependents of retired workers	2,925	1,558	1,070
Survivors of deceased workers[1]	6,495	5,990	646-1,040
Disabled workers	7,101	7,131	1,004
Dependents of disabled workers[1]	1,819	539	565
Total monthly beneficiaries	**49,865**	**$49,218**	**N.A.**

Note: OASDI = old-age, survivors and disability insurance. 1. Benefits vary depending on relationship to beneficiary. Range of benefits shown. **Source:** Social Security Administration, *Fact Sheet on OASDI*, Dec. 31, 2007.

To receive Social Security benefits, you must have worked for 10 years in a job in which you contributed to the fund. Your Social Security benefit is not directly dependent on the number of years you worked. Rather it is based on your average earnings over your working lifetime. The average recipient receives benefits equivalent to 42 percent of an average working year's earnings. But because Social Security is designed to benefit low-income workers, people in upper-income tax brackets generally receive a lower percentage of their working year's earnings when they collect their benefits.

You can still earn money while collecting Social Security. In 2008, recipients under full retirement age may earn up to $13,560 ($1,130 per month)

before their benefits are reduced; after that amount, $1 is withheld for every $2 earned. In the year they reach the full retirement age, recipients may earn up to $36,120; after that, benefits are reduced $1 for every $3 earned. After recipients reach the full retirement age, there is no limit to the amount of money they may earn while collecting Social Security benefits.

Disability   If you become disabled, you are eligible for additional benefits after six months. Disabled is defined as having a physical or mental impairment that permanently prevents you from doing any substantial work. For 2008, "substantial" meant work that brought in more than $940 a month ($1,570 if you're blind). See the accompanying table for examples of disability benefits.

Approximate Annual Retirement, Disability, and Survivor Benefits

Worker's age, 2008	Beneficiaries	Worker's lifetime average annual earnings level			
		$20,000	$40,000	$60,000	$97,500 or more
Retirement Benefits[1]					
25	Retired worker only	$11,556	$17,952	$23,280	$28,908
35	Retired worker only	11,556	17,952	23,280	28,908
45	Retired worker only	11,556	17,952	23,280	29,028
55	Retired worker only	11,556	17,952	23,280	28,944
65	Retired worker only	10,764	16,728	21,672	26,328
Disability Benefits[2]					
25	Disabled worker only	$7,992	$11,052	$14,100	$27,984
35	Disabled worker only	9,984	15,024	20,064	27,960
45	Disabled worker only	10,848	16,752	21,996	27,912
55	Disabled worker only	11,208	17,472	22,500	27,600
Survivor benefits[3,4]					
25	1 child only	$6,216	$8,736	$11,256	$21,048
	Spouse and 1 child	12,432	17,472	22,512	42,096
	Spouse and 2 children	12,444	18,396	27,528	49,116
35	1 child only	7,778	11,880	15,972	21,072
	Spouse and 1 child	15,576	23,760	31,944	42,144
	Spouse and 2 children	15,588	29,652	37,272	49,188
45	1 child only	8,196	12,696	16,584	20,952
	Spouse and 1 child	16,392	25,392	33,168	41,904
	Spouse and 2 children	16,452	31,104	38,712	48,888
60	Spouse only	7,980	12,420	16,032	19,308
	1 Child only	8,364	13,020	16,824	20,256
	Spouse and 2 children	17,040	31,692	39,252	47,280

Note: The worker's lifetime average annual earnings level reflects the average amount earned over a lifetime of work. Actual benefits depend on the pattern of past and future earnings. 1. If worker retires at the normal retirement age. 2. For workers who became disabled in 2008. 3. For workers who died in 2008; benefits are based on 2007 earnings. 4. Spouse is assumed to be the same age as the worker. Spouse may qualify for a higher retirement benefit based on his or her own work record. **Source:** Social Security Administration, *Illustrative Benefits for Retired Workers, Disabled Workers, and Survivors.* www.ssa.gov/OACT/NOTES/ran4/index.html

Medicare: Recipients and Benefits, 1966-2007

	Enrollment (in thousands)							Average Yearly Benefit		
	Hospital Insurance (Part A)			Supplemental Medical Insurance						
						Part B		Part D			
Year	Total	Aged	Disabled	Total	Aged	Disabled	Total	Part A	Part B	Part D
1966	19,082	19,082	N.A.	17,736	17,736	N.A.	—	N.A.	N.A.	—
1970	20,104	20,361	N.A.	19,496	19,584	N.A.	—	$255	$101	—
1975	24,481	22,472	2,168	23,744	21,945	1,959	—	462	180	—
1980	28,002	25,104	2,963	27,278	24,680	2,719	—	895	390	—
1985	30,621	27,683	2,907	29,869	27,311	2,678	—	1,554	768	—
1990	33,747	30,464	3,255	32,567	29,686	2,943	—	1,963	1,304	—
1995	37,175	32,742	4,393	35,641	31,742	3,942	—	3,130	1,823	—
2000	39,257	33,833	5,367	37,335	32,590	4,770	—	3,272	2,381	—
2005	42,181	35,400	6,700	39,968	33,700	5,900	1,841	4,268	3,759	—
2007[1]	43,769	36,800	7,200	40,914	34,600	6,400	30,874	4,573	4,312	$1,575

1. Estimated. **Source:** Centers for Medicare and Medicaid Services, *2008 Trustees Report.* www.cms.hhs.gov/statistics/nhe

Survivors   Additional benefits are also paid to the survivors of workers who would have been eligible for Social Security. Widows and widowers over the age of 50, children under the age of 18 (or 19 if they're still in high school), and certain other survivors each receive amounts ranging from 71.5 to 100 percent of what the deceased worker would have received from Social Security. There is, however, a per-family benefit limit, usually equal to 150-180 percent of the worker's benefit rate.

Medicare

The Social Security Amendments of 1965 established two contributory health insurance programs designed to provide assistance for medical expenses for the aged and disabled. The first is a compulsory program of hospital insurance (HI), which provides basic protection against the costs of inpatient hospital services and related post-hospital care, including home health services, part-time nursing care, and physical therapy. This is commonly referred to as Part A. Persons reaching full retirement age without qualifying for HI may voluntarily enroll by paying a monthly premium. In 2008, the premium was $233 per month for people who had contributed to Medicare for 30-39 quarters (7.5-10 years), or $423 for those who had worked fewer than 30 quarters. HI pays all hospital bills for 60 days after the patient pays a deductible ($1,024 in 2008). After 60 days, the patient is responsible for a daily co-payment. In 2008, the co-payment was $256 for days 61–90, $512 per day for days 91–150, and the entire bill after 150 days. For nursing homes, the first 20 days have no deductible, but $128 a day thereafter, up to 100 days.

As with OASDI, hospital insurance is financed by the 7.65 percent tax on earnings (FICA) deducted from employee paychecks: 6.2 percent is for OASDI and 1.45 percent is for Medicare.

The second health program is supplementary medical insurance (SMI), a voluntary program in which enrolled individuals pay a monthly premium. The program's coverage includes physician's and surgeon's services, outpatient services, laboratory tests, ambulance services, surgical dressings, home health services, and comprehensive outpatient services. The premium in 2008 was $96.40 per month. After the patient has paid the deductible ($135), SMI pays for 80 percent of covered services.

In the past, supplementary medical insurance was synonymous with the term Part B. But beginning in 2004, an additional program, known as Part D, was added to SMI, allowing anyone eligible for Medicare to obtain prescription drug discount cards. Thus, Part B and Part D are the two portions of SMI, with separate accounting systems to prevent one from financing the other. The drug cards, which offer discounts on brand-name and generic drugs, are offered by private health care companies, which may charge no more than $30 for them. Part D carries a deductible ($275 in 2008), then covers 75 percent of costs up to an initial limit ($2,510 in 2008). The beneficiary pays 100% of all costs between the initial limit and an out-of-pocket maximum ($4,050 in 2008).

Some private companies also contract with Medicare to offer Medicare+Choice ("Medicare plus Choice") health plans, which offer a choice of managed care plans or private fee-for-service

Supplemental Security Insurance Beneficiaries and Benefits, 1975–2006

| | Beneficiaries | | | | Benefits (thousands) | | |
| | | | State Supplement | | | | |
Year	Total[1]	Federal SSI	Federally administered	State administered	Total	Federal SSI	State supplementation[2]
Total							
1975	4,359,625	3,893,419	1,684,018	303,391	$ 5,716,0	$ 4,313.5	$ 1,402.5
1990	4,888,180	4,412,131	2,058,273	285,530	16,133.0	12,893.8	3,239.2
2000	6,685,169	6,319,907	2,480,637	682,867	30,671.7	27,290.2	3,381.5
2005	7,113,879	6,818,944	2,242,112	294,935	37,235.8	33,058.1	4,177.8
2006	7,235,583	6,938,690	1,971,686	296,893	34,995.7	31,308.0	3,687.7
Aged							
1975	2,333,685	2,024,765	843,917	184,679	$ 2,516.5	$ 1,843.0	$ 673.5
1990	1,484,160	1,256,623	649,530	115,890	3,559.4	2,521.4	1,038.0
2000	1,327,567	1,186,309	622,668	144,644	4,540.0	3,597.5	942.5
2005	1,214,296	1,112,779	584,787	101,517	4,964.6	3,836.6	1,128.0
2006	1,211,656	1,108,925	487,844	102,731	4,535.3	3,519.2	1,016.1
Blind							
1975	75,315	68,375	31,376	4,933	$ 127.2	$ 92.4	$ 34.8
1990	84,109	74,781	40,334	3,042	328.9	238.4	90.5
2000	79,295	72,931	35,940	4,645	385.9	312.2	73.7
2005	75,039	69,637	31,346	5,402	414.1	330.6	83.6
2006	73,418	68,165	25,404	5,253	363.0	291.3	71.6
Disabled							
1975	11,950,625	1,800,279	808,725	113,504	$ 3,072.3	$ 2,378.1	$ 694.2
1990	3,319,911	3,080,727	1,368,409	166,598	12,244.6	10,134.0	2,110.6
2000	5,270,126	5,060,667	1,822,029	325,916	25,745.7	23,380.5	2,365.2
2005	5,824,544	5,636,528	1,625,979	188,016	31,857.1	28,890.8	2,966.2
2006	5,950,509	5,761,600	1,458,438	188,909	30,097.4	27,497.5	2,749.8

Note: 1. Total beneficiaries includes some people who receive both Federal SSI and a state supplement. 2. Federally administered only.
Source: *Social Security Bulletin, Supplemental Security Record.* www.ssa.gov/policy/docs/statcomps/supplement/2007/7a.html#table7.a1

plans. These are often referred to as Part C. Both plans generally offer extra benefits (prescription drugs, eye exams, extra hospital days) in addition to basic Medicare benefits and may reduce out-of-pocket costs, but doctor choice is usually limited in comparison to Medicare.

Supplemental Security Income (SSI)
In 1974, Congress replaced the federal-state programs for needy aged (over 65 years old), blind, and disabled people with a single Federal Supplementary Security Income program. SSI eligibility depends on whether you work and in what state you live. In addition, SSI recipients may have no more than $2,000 in assets ($3,000 for married couples), though houses and cars are not usually counted as assets in this equation. The qualifying standards for disability benefits are the same as those used for the Social Security disability insurance program. More than 7 million people received SSI benefits in 2007. The basic monthly federal benefit is the same in all states: in 2008, it was $637 for one person and $956 for a couple. States have the option of supplementing Federal SSI under their own programs administered. Nearly 2.3 million persons received state supplements in 2006.

Black Lung Program
Established by the Federal Coal Mine Health and Safety Act of 1969, this provides monthly cash benefits to coal miners who are totally disabled because of "black lung" disease (pneumoconiosis) and to survivors of miners who die from this disease. Benefits are paid mostly out of a trust fund financed by an excise tax on coal. The monthly benefit in 2008 ranged from $599 for a single recipient to $1,197 for a recipient with three or more dependents. The number of beneficiaries continues to decline as older beneficiaries are dying in greater numbers than new claimants are entering the program. Claims in 2006 numbered 40,018, totaling $312.5 million in benefits. That's down significantly from 1985, when 294,846 people were receiving $1 billion in benefits.

Social Security Information
While Social Security benefits are automatic for all people who hold a Social Security card and who are eligible for programs, the Social Security Administration (SSA) recommends that workers check the agency's records of their earnings every three to five years. If their records are not accurate—the SSA says that 1 percent of eligible wages are not credited to workers' records—your benefits could be lower than you deserve.

To find out what your earnings are, pick up a Personal Earnings and Benefit Estimate Statement (PEBES). This, as well as free booklets detailing eligibility requirements and benefit payments, is available at any of the more than 1,300 local Social Security offices nationwide. They are also available by calling 1-800-772-1213, or on the Internet at *www.ssa.gov.*

▶OTHER INCOME SUPPORT PROGRAMS
Welfare
The Social Security Act of 1935 included a provision authorizing Aid to Families with Dependent Children (AFDC), commonly known as "welfare." Benefits were limited to families with children under 18. But in the much-ballyhooed 1996 welfare reform effort, the federal government ended more than 60 years of guaranteed assistance to the needy, and replaced it with a system of block grants to the states, who could use the money to enact their own welfare programs. The Temporary Assistance to Needy Families (TANF) Block Grant replaced AFDC on July 1, 1997. TANF gives states broad discretion to determine eligibility and benefit levels. However, families may not receive benefits for longer than 60 months, unwed teenage parents must stay in school and live at home, and people convicted of drug-related felonies are banned from receiving TANF or Food Stamp benefits. In addition, non-working adults must participate in community service within two months of receiving benefits, and must find work within two years. Parents with children under age 1 are exempt from the work requirements (under age 6 if child care is not available).

Welfare reform has succeeded in reducing the number of people receiving government assistance. The number of people receiving welfare benefits has dropped steadily from the all-time high of 14.4 million in March, 1994. The ethnic make-up of welfare recipients has also changed. White families made up 38 percent of all welfare families in 1990, but only 33 percent in 2006. Over the same period, the percentage of welfare families that were black declined from 40 percent to 36 percent, while the percentage of Hispanic families increased from 16.6 percent to 26 percent. Among welfare recipients, the employment rate has also increased dramatically, from 11 percent in 1996 to 22 percent in 2006.

Medicaid
Enacted jointly with Medicare in 1965, Medicaid provides federal matching funds to states to help pay the cost of medical care and services for low-income persons. Payments are made to suppliers of the care and service. To be eligible for matching funds, a state Medicaid program must cover all persons who receive assistance under TANF. (Most SSI recipients are also covered.) In 2006, 61 million aged, blind, disabled or poor persons with families received Medicaid benefits at a total cost to state and federal governments of $309 billion. Medicaid may also pay the premiums for supplementary medical insurance and the deductible and co-insurance cost of hospital insurance. Medicaid also covers some medical services that Medicare does not.

Welfare Beneficiaries and Benefits, 1970–2007

| Year | Average monthly beneficiaries ('000s) | | | Average monthly benefit per family |
	Total	Families	Children	
1970	7,429	1,909	5,494	$178
1975	11,067	3,269	7,821	208
1980	10,597	3,574	7,220	269
1985	10,813	3,692	7,165	329
1990	11,460	3,974	7,755	389
1995	13,652	4,876	9,274	377
2000	5,943	2,216	4,370	388
2003	4,965	2,032	3,730	392
2005	4,471	1,895	3,405	370
2007	3,964	1,692	3,045	N.A.

Note: "Welfare" refers to the Aid to Families with Dependent Children (AFDC) program through 1996; in 1997, AFDC was renamed Temporary Assistance to Needy Families (TANF), and many more restrictions were added. **Source:** Administration for Children and Families, Office of Family Assistance, Caseload Data, Total Number of Recipients 2007.

Food Stamps

By providing eligible applicants with coupons to buy food, this program enables families in need to purchase a nutritionally adequate diet. In general, a household is considered eligible if it has less than $2,000 in liquid assets ($3,000 if one person in the home is 60 or over), or if 30 percent of its countable cash income is insufficient to purchase an adequate low-cost diet as defined by the U.S. Department of Agriculture (USDA) "Thrifty Food Plan." States delegate varying degrees of authority to counties and cities, but the federal government finances 100 percent of the state-issued food benefits and part of the state's administrative costs.

In 2004, the Food and Nutrition Service replaced the system of paper food coupons with Electronic Benefit Transfer (EBT) cards, which act like a bank debit card. The cards are encoded with a magnetic stripe and a password, to reduce food stamp fraud, and can be replaced if lost or stolen. Government surveys show that participants like the cards because they reduce the stigma associated with using food stamps; merchants prefer it because they get paid faster; and state officials say the program is simpler to administer.

Special nutrition programs

The USDA administers a number of programs designed to help safeguard the health and well-be-

Federal Food Assistance Programs, 1970–2007

Program	1970	1980	1990	2000	2004	2005	2007
Participants (millions)							
Food stamps	4.3	21.1	20.0	17.2	23.9	25.7	26.5
National school lunch program[1]	22.4	26.6	24.1	27.3	29.0	29.6	30.5
School breakfast[1]	0.5	3.6	4.1	7.6	8.9	9.4	10.1
Women-infants-children[2]	N.A.	1.9	4.5	7.2	7.9	8.0	8.3
Child and adult care[3]	0.1	0.7	1.5	2.7	3.0	3.1	3.2
Federal cost (millions)							
Food stamps	$550	$8,721	$14,186	$14,983	$24,619	$28,566	$33,204
National school lunch program[1]	300	2,279	3,214	5,494	6,663	7,055	7,706
School breakfast[1]	11	288	596	1,393	1,776	1,927	2,164
Women-infants-children[2]	N.A.	584	1,637	2,853	3,562	3,603	3,887
Child and adult care[3]	6	207	719	1,500	1,812	1,904	2,024

Notes: 1. Average monthly participation during school year. Covers public and private elementary and secondary schools and residential child care institutions. Costs do not include the value of USDA donated commodities. 2. WIC serves pregnant and postpartum women, infants, and children up to age five. 3. Provides year-round subsidies to feed preschool children in child care centers and family day care programs. Certain care centers serving disabled or elderly adults also receive meal subsidies.
Source: U.S. Dept. of Agriculture, Annual Summary of Food and Nutrition Service Programs. (www.fns.usda.gov/pd/annual.htm).

Medicaid Recipients and Vendor Payments 1975–2005

Year	Aged	Blind/Disabled[1]	Dependent children under 21	Adults in families with dependent children	Other/ Unknown	Total
Recipients (thousands)						
1975	3,615	2,464	9,598	4,529	1,800	22,007
1980	3,440	2,911	9,333	4,877	1,499	21,605
1985	3,061	3,017	9,757	5,518	1,214	21,814
1990	3,202	3,718	11,220	6,010	1,105	25,255
1995	4,119	5,859	17,164	7,604	1,537	36,282
2000	4,289	7,479	21,086	10,543	862	42,886
2003	4,041	7,669	23,992	11,679	4,591	51,971
2005	4,396	8,210	26,337	12,529	6,171	57,643
Payments (millions of dollars)						
1975	$4,358	$3,145	$2,186	$2,062	$492	$12,242
1980	8,739	7,621	3,123	3,231	596	23,311
1985	14,096	13,452	4,414	4,746	798	37,508
1990	21,508	24,403	9,100	8,590	1,257	64,859
1995	36,527	49,418	17,976	13,511	2,708	120,141
2000	44,560	72,772	23,490	17,671	9,948	168,442
2003	55,271	102,014	35,079	26,689	14,153	233,206
2005	63,358	119,647	42,012	32,385	18,167	275,569
Average payment (dollars)						
1975	$1,205	$1,296	$228	$455	$273	$556
1980	2,540	2,659	335	663	398	1,079
1985	4,605	4,496	452	860	658	1,719
1990	6,717	6,595	811	1,429	1,138	2,568
1995	8,868	8,422	1,047	1,777	1,762	3,311
2000	10,388	9,729	1,114	1,676	11,536	3,928
2003	13,677	13,303	1,462	2,285	3,083	4,487
2005	14,413	14,574	1,595	2,585	2,944	4,781

Note: Figures are in current dollars. A small number of recipients are in more than one category. 1. Figures for blind were combined with those for the disabled in 1997. Source: Social Security Administration, Annual Statistical Supplement, 2007.

ing of the nation's children by assisting the states in providing adequate meals to all children at a moderate cost. The programs include the National School Lunch Program, the School Breakfast Program, the Summer Food Service Program, the Child Care Food Program, the Special Milk Program, and the Special Supplemental Food Program for Women, Infants, and Children (WIC) Program. The nutrition program for the elderly requires no income test, but preference is given to those with the greatest need.

Housing subsidies

The federal government has traditionally provided housing aid directly to lower-income households in the form of rental and mortgage-interest subsidies. The primary purposes are to improve housing quality and to reduce housing costs for lower-income households. Other goals include promoting residential construction, expanding housing opportunities for disadvantaged groups and groups with special housing needs, promoting neighborhood preservation and revitalization, increasing homeownership, and empowering the poor to become homeowners.

Most housing aid is targeted to very-low-income renters through two basic types of rental assistance programs. Project-based aid is typically tied to projects specifically produced for lower-income households through new construction or substantial renovation. Almost all project-based aid is provided through production-oriented programs, including the public-housing program, the section 8 new construction and substantial rehabilitation program, and the section 236 mortgage-interest-subsidy program (administered by the Department of Housing and Urban Development), and the section 515 mortgage-interest-subsidy program administered by the Farmers Home Administration.

Household-based subsidies permit renters to choose from standard housing units in the existing private housing stock. Rental assistance programs generally reduce tenants' rent payments to 30 percent of their income, with the government paying the balance of the contract rents.

The federal government also assists some lower- and moderate-income households in becoming homeowners by making long-term commitments to reduce their mortgage interest. These generally reduce mortgage payments, property taxes and insurance costs to a fixed percentage of income, ranging from 20 percent to 28 percent.

Housing for the homeless

HUD funding for homeless programs is made available to state and local governments, Indian tribes, and nonprofit organizations. The specific programs are the Emergency Shelter Grants (ESG) Program, the Supportive Housing Demonstration Program, the Shelter-Plus-Care Homeless Rental Housing Assistance, and the HUD-Owned Single Property Disposition Program.

Head Start

Head Start provides services to children of low-income families up to the age of five. Its goals are to improve the social competence, learning skills, and health and nutrition status of low-income children so that they can begin school on an equal footing with their more advantaged peers. Services include cognitive and language development, medical, dental, and mental health services (including screening and immunizations), and nutritional and social services. Parental involvement includes volunteer participation and employment of parents as Head Start staff.

At least 90 percent of Head Start children come from families with incomes at or below the poverty line, and at least 10 percent of enrollment slots in each state must be available to disabled children. Just under a million children annually are served in Head Start programs, at a total federal cost of $6.9 billion, or an average cost of $7,326 per child. The program has served more than 25 million children since it began in 1965. Since 1980, the demographic served by Head Start has become younger, less black, and more Hispanic. Five-year-olds made up 21 percent of the Head Start population in 1980; in 2007 they constituted only 3 percent. Meanwhile, three-year-olds increased from 24 to 36 percent over the same period. In 1980, 19 percent of Head Start children were Hispanic, in 2007, 35 percent were Hispanic; black Head Start children declined from 42 to 30 percent over the same period.

Head Start Participation and Funding, 1966–2007

Year	Enrollment	Appropriations
1966	733,000	$ 198,900,000
1970	477,400	325,700,000
1980	376,300	735,000,000
1990	540,930	1,552,000,000
1995	750,696	3,534,128,000
2000	857,664	5,267,000,000
2004	905,851	6,773,909,000
2005	906,993	6,843,114,000
2007	908,412	6,888,571,000

Source: U.S. Dept of Health and Human Services, Administration for Children and Families. www.acf.hhs.gov.

U.S. Weighted Average Poverty Thresholds by Family Size, 1960–2007

Year	Maximum yearly family income						
	1 person	2 people	3 people	4 people	5 people	6 people	7 people
1960	$1,490	$1,924	$2,359	$3,022	$3,560	$4,002	$4,921[1]
1970	1,954	2,525	3,099	3,968	4,680	5,260	6,468[1]
1980	4,190	5,363	6,565	8,414	9,966	11,269	12,761
1990	6,652	8,509	10,419	13,359	15,792	17,839	20,241
2000	8,791	11,235	13,740	17,604	20,815	23,533	26,750
2004	9,645	12,334	15,067	19,307	22,831	25,788	29,236
2005	9,973	12,755	15,577	19,971	23,613	26,683	30,249
2007	10,587	13,542	16,537	21,201	25,076	28,345	32,094

Note: 1. Seven or more people. **Source:** U.S. Bureau of the Census, 2008.

Poverty income guidelines

The poverty income guidelines are used to determine whether a person or family is eligible for assistance under a particular federal program. The poverty threshold is established each year by increasing the previous year's threshold by the change in the Consumer Price Index. The original poverty threshold was devised in 1960 and was equal to three times the amount of money to buy the cheapest "nutritionally adequate" diet as dictated by the Department of Agriculture.

Unemployment Compensation

The Social Security Act provided an inducement to states to enact unemployment insurance laws, and by 1937 all 48 states, the territories of Alaska and Hawaii, and the District of Columbia had passed such laws. All contributions collected under state laws are deposited in the unemployment trust fund of the U.S. Treasury, but each state maintains a separate account. A state may withdraw money from its account only to pay benefits. Each state has major responsibility for the content and development of its unemployment insurance law. Nationwide, Unemployment covers about 134 million workers.

Workers must be ready, able and willing to work and must be registered for work at a state public employment office. A worker's benefit is based on his or her employment in covered work over a prior performance period. No state can deny benefit to a claimant if he or she refuses to accept a new job under substandard labor conditions or where he or she would be required to join a company union.

In 2007, 16.9 million people made initial unemployment claims and 2.7 million exhausted their compensation. The average weekly benefit was $288 and the average duration of benefit was 15.2 weeks, making the average total benefit $4,243. The weekly benefit varies from state to state, but the general formula is designed to compensate for between 50 percent and 70 percent of average weekly pretax wage, up to a state-determined minimum.

Workers' compensation

Social insurance began in the United States with worker's compensation. A law covering federal civilian employees was passed in 1908; the first state compensation law to be held constitutional was enacted in 1911. These laws made industry responsible for the compensation of workers (or their survivors) injured or killed while on the job. A worker incurring an occupational injury is compensated regardless of fault or blame in the accident. A separate federal program enacted in 1969 protects coal miners (see "Black lung program" above).

Workers' compensation is almost exclusively financed by employers on the principle that the cost of work-related accidents is part of the expense of production. Every state except Texas mandates coverage under workers' compensation for private employees. Certain categories of workers, usually domestic, agricultural, and casual laborers, are often exempted from this requirement. Employers can use private insurance companies or can qualify as self-insurers. Workers' compensation covered more than 130 million workers in 2006; total payments on workers' behalf was $0.99 per $100 of covered wages at a cost to employers of $1.58 per $100 of covered wages. The cash benefit for temporary total disability, permanent, total or partial disability, or death of a breadwinner is usually about two-thirds of weekly earnings at the time of the accident. Most state laws pay temporary disability benefits for as long as the disability lasts and the condition has not been stabilized to the point where no further improvement can result from medical treatment. Total benefit payments under workers' compensation programs in 2006 were $54.7 billion, a 1.5 percent decline from $55.5 billion in 2005.

Permanent partial disability compensation

for specific, or "schedule" injuries (for clearly measurable matters) is generally subject to different (usually lower) dollar maximums and is determined without regard to loss of earning power. Compensation for "nonschedule" injuries (injuries to head, back, nervous system) is the difference between wages before and after impairment. Death benefits are related to earnings and graduated by the number of dependents. Medical benefits are furnished without limit as to time or amount for accidental injuries. Temporary Disability Insurance provides coverage against the risk of lost wages due to short-term nonoccupational disability. The Federal Unemployment Tax Act permits states where employees make contributions under the unemployment insurance program to use some or all of those contributions for disability benefits. It is estimated that about two-thirds of the nation's wage and salary earners in private employment have some protection through various voluntary and governmental group arrangements. In general the benefit amount for a week is intended to replace at least half the weekly wage loss for a maximum of 26 to 39 weeks per year.

▶VETERANS' BENEFITS

The tradition of veterans' benefits dates to the 18th century, when the Continental Congress provided disability pensions for veterans of the Revolutionary War. Today, the Department of Veterans Affairs (DVA) offers a range of services and benefits to eligible veterans, their dependents, and their survivors.

The total number of veterans has been decreasing in recent years, from about 29.5 million in 1975 to 24 million in 2007. Nearly 75 percent of veterans served during a war or official period of conflict. The number of veterans age 65 or older is increasing very rapidly, and the use and cost of medical care are expected to grow more rapidly in the near future than those of other veterans' ben-

Unemployment Insurance Compensation, 1975–2007				
Year	Total initial claims ('000s)	Total exhaustions ('000s)	Average weekly benefit per recipient	Average duration of benefits (in weeks)	Average total benefit per recipient
1975	24,843	4,195	$70.23	15.7	$1,103
1980	25,370	3,072	99.59	14.9	1,485
1985	20,634	2,572	128.11	14.3	1,827
1990	20,183	2,323	161.20	13.5	2,171
1995	18,553	2,662	187.04	14.8	2,759
2000	15,633	2,144	221.01	13.7	3,028
2003	20,986	4,417	261.67	16.4	4,291
2004	17,958	3,532	262.50	16.1	4,226
2005	17,053	2,856	266.62	15.3	4,079
2007	16,934	2,670	287.71	15.2	4,243

Source: U.S. Dept. of Labor. www.workforcesecurity.doleta.gov

efits and services. Compensation and pension caseloads are decreasing steadily due to beneficiary deaths, terminations for excess incomes, and age limitation for dependents. The number of trainees under the Montgomery GI bill will increase as more veterans become eligible.

Veterans who have incurred injuries or illness while in service are entitled to service-connected compensation. The amounts are determined by disability ratings. Death compensation or dependency and indemnity compensation is paid to survivors of veterans who died as a result of service-connected causes.

War veterans who have become permanently and totally disabled from non-service-connected causes, and to survivors of war veterans may receive means-tested veterans' pensions. Benefits are based on family size, and the pensions provide a floor of income.

Medical programs The V.A. operates 155 hospital centers, 135 nursing homes, 45 residential rehab treatment programs, and more than 872 community-based ambulatory care and outpatient clinics. In 2006, the V.A. treated almost 5.5 million people. The V.A. extends free priority care to service-connected disabled veterans, to veterans in special categories, and to needy non-service-connected veterans. As facilities and other resources permit, the V.A. provides care to non-service-connected veterans with incomes that exceed the mandatory care income limits. Since 1979, the V.A. has also operated Vet Centers, which provide psychological counseling for war-related trauma and other social services to more than 2 million veterans and their families. There were 209 such centers in 2006; they served more than 130,000 veterans who made over one million visits.

Housing and loan programs Since 1944, when the Montgomery GI bill began helping veterans buy homes, the V.A. has guaranteed more than 18 million loans totaling $911 billion; in fiscal 2006, the V.A. guaranteed 135,151 loans totaling $23.5 billion. The maximum guaranty is as follows: 50 percent of the loan amount for loans of $45,000 or less; for loans between $45,001 and $144,000, a minimum of $22,500 and a maximum of 40 percent of the loan up to $36,000; and a maximum guaranty of 25 percent of loans over $144,000, up to $60,000.

Other veterans' programs The GI Bill has also provided education and training programs to more than 21.8 million veterans since 1944, at a total cost of more than $75.6 billion. Contributions are required, and veterans can receive a basic educational benefit of up to $1,101 per month for 36 months while in an educational program.

The Veterans Job Training Act program provides payments to defray training costs of employers who hire certain veterans of the Korean conflict or Vietnam era who have been unemployed for long periods of time.

Veterans Benefits and Services: Outlays and Recipients, 1975–2006

Fiscal year	Compensation and pensions	Readjustment, education, job training	Medical programs	Housing loans
Outlays (millions)				
1975	$ 7,860	$4,593	$3,665	N.A.
1980	11,688	2,342	6,515	N.A.
1985	14,714	1,059	9,547	N.A.
1990	15,241	278	12,134	N.A.
1995	18,966	1,124	15,981	N.A.
2000	21,500	N.A.	19,326	$23,300
2006	34,400	N.A.	N.A.	$23,500
Recipients ('000s)				
1975	4,855	2,804	1,985	290
1980	4,646	1,232	2,671	297
1985	4,005	491	2,963	179
1990	3,614	329	3,018	196
1995	3,332	476	2,859	263
2000	2,700	279	3,817	200
2006	3,600	332	5,500	135

Source: *Facts About the Department of Veterans Affairs* (1975-2007).

THE INTERNAL REVENUE SERVICE

Founded in 1862, the Internal Revenue Service (I.R.S.) is the office of the Department of the Treasury charged with collecting federal taxes. The Constitution empowers Congress to levy excise taxes and—in emergencies—to raise direct taxes. Congress's right to levy taxes on the income of individuals and corporations was contested throughout the 19th century, but that authority was written into the Constitution with the passage of the 16th Amendment in 1913. Today, the source of most of the federal government's revenues are the individual income tax, corporate income tax, excise taxes, estate taxes, and gift taxes. The I.R.S. is responsible for these taxes as well as for collecting employee and employer payments for social insurance and retirement insurance (see "Social Insurance Programs").

In 1998, Congress enacted a major overhaul of the I.R.S. in hopes of transforming the agency from a menacing symbol of government authority into a resource for taxpayers trying to cope with the increasingly bewildering tax code. The legislation established an outside board with broad authority to supervise the I.R.S.'s operations, and perhaps more important, shifted the burden of proof in tax dispute cases to the I.R.S. (previously, taxpayers had to prove their innocence). Initial reaction to the legislation was overwhelmingly favorable, but tax experts correctly predicted the law would give scofflaws greater incentive to cheat on their taxes. Property seizures dropped by 98 percent between 1997 and 1999, garnishments of bank accounts and paychecks were a quarter of their level two years earlier, and tax liens, which insure that back taxes are paid when properties are sold, were down by 67 percent.

The most damaging change was the anti-harassment section of the legislation, which tax collectors say has thwarted them from collecting taxes from delinquent filers. Several I.R.S. agents said they no longer pursued outstanding tax bills vigorously because they feared losing their jobs under the anti-harassment policy. In 1998, the I.R.S. gave up on collecting back taxes from just 98 taxpayers; in 2000, the agency wrote off $2.5 billion in back taxes owed by more than 650,000 delinquent taxpayers.

The decline in aggressive pursuit of tax cheats actually began even before the new law went into effect. In 1996, the I.R.S. audited 2.13 million of the 155 million tax returns filed, a rate of 1.4 percent. In 2007, the agency examined just 1.6 million of the 179 million returns filed, a rate of 0.9 percent. The I.R.S. audited just under 2 million individual returns in 1996; that number dropped to 1.4 million in 2007. The agency also eased up on corporate tax filings. It audited 69,650 corporate returns (2.7 percent) in 1996; but less than half as many (30,004 or 1.3%) in 2007.

The shift can also be seen in the number of I.R.S. employees, which has declined from an all-

Tax Returns Processed, 1990–2007

	Number of returns ('000s)				
Type of return	1990	1995	2000	2005	2007
Income Taxes					
Individual income tax (Form 1040 series)	112,492	116,298	127,590	132,845	138,896
Individual estimated tax (Form 1040ES)	38,188	35,475	39,230	28,669	29,996
Fiduciary estate and trust (Form 1041 series)	2,702	3,187	3,530	3,684	3,718
Fiduciary estate and trust estimated tax	651	583	892	503	780
Partnership (Form 1065)	1,741	1,572	2,048	2,665	3,097
Corporation (Forms 1120 series, 1066)	4,311	4,781	5,458	6,128	6,607
Estate tax (Forms 706, 706NA)	59	83	121	66	50
Gift tax (Form 709)	146	215	305	277	253
Employment taxes (Forms 94X series, CT-1, 1042)	28,914	29,006	28,911	30,872	30,740
Tax-exempt organizations (Forms 990 series, 4720, 5227)	484	560	707	815	901
Excise taxes (Forms 720, 730, 2290, 11C)	840	787	916	1,064	907
Supplemental documents (1040X, 2688, 4868, 7004, 1041A)	10,170	11,937	15,260	19,090	19,496
Total tax returns	201,715	205,747	226,130	226,677	235,438

Source: Internal Revenue Service, *2007 Data Book* (2008).

Tax Rate Schedules, 2008

Taxable income	What you pay
Single Individual	
$0-$8,025	10% of sum over $0
$8,025–$32,550	$802.50 + 15% of sum over $8,025
$32,550- $78,850	$4,481.25 + 25% of sum over $32,550
$78,850-$164,550	$16,056.25 + 28% of sum over $78,850
$164,550- $357,000	$40,052.25 + 33% of sum over $164,550
over $357,000	$103,791.75 + 35% of sum over $357,700
Married individuals filing jointly, or qualifying widow(er)	
$0- $16,050	10% of sum over $0
$16,050–$65,100	$1,605 + 15% of sum over $16,050
$65,100- $131,450	$8,962.50 + 25% of sum over $65,100
$131,450- $200,300	$25,550 + 28% of sum over $131,450
$200,300- $357,700	$44,828 + 33% of sum over $200,300
over $357,700	$96,770 + 35% of sum over $357,700
Married, Filing Separate Return	
$0- $8,025	10% of sum over $0
$8,025–$32,550	$802.50 + 15% of sum over $8,025
$32,550- $65,725	$4,481.25 + 25% of sum over $32,550
$65,725- $100,150	$12,775 + 28% of sum over $65,725
$100,150- $178,850	$22,414 + 33% of sum over $100,150
over $178,850	$48,385 + 35% of sum over $178,850
Heads of Households	
$0- $11,450	10% of sum over $0
$11,450–$43,650	$1,145 + 15% of sum over $11,450
$43,650- $112,650	$5,975 + 25% of sum over $43,650
$112,650- $182,400	$23,225 + 28% of sum over $112,650
$182,400- $357,700	$42,755 + 33% of sum over $182,400
over $357,700	$100,604 + 35% of sum over $357,700

Source: Internal Revenue Service, *Internal Revenue Bulletin, Rev. Proc. 2007-66*, Nov. 5, 2007.

time high of 115,628 in 1996 to just 92,033 in 2007, even as the returns filed has increased. The agency has gotten leaner by putting greater emphasis on auditing the taxpayers with the highest incomes. In 2007 it examined 30 percent of the 12,584 returns filed by corporations with total revenues of $250 million or more, resulting in $24 billion in additional taxes and penalties, or almost $7 million per audit. The other closely monitored group of tax returns is from estates valued at $5 million or more. There were 8,038 such returns filed in 2007; the I.R.S. examined 19.9 percent of them, resulting in $850 million in additional taxes.

▶ TAX CHANGES

In 2003, President Bush signed the Jobs and Growth Tax Relief Reconciliation Act, lowering three of the top four income tax rates (35 percent, 30 percent, and 27 percent) by two full percentage points, and the highest rate (38.6 percent) by 3.6 percentage points. The Act also expanded the 15 percent rate bracket for married taxpayers to twice that of single filers; increased the maximum taxable income subject to the lowest (10 percent) tax rate; and increased the maximum child tax credit from $600 to $1,000.

▶ PRINCIPAL DEDUCTIONS

Taxes: Taxpayers who pay a state and/or local tax may deduct this amount from their federal tax payment. In addition, in Alabama, Iowa, Louisiana, Missouri, Oklahoma, Oregon and Utah, taxpayers may deduct their federal income tax before calculating their state tax payments.

Personal exemptions: Taxpayers are allowed to claim personal exemptions for the taxpayer and each dependent claimed in filing income tax. Congress determines the amount (since 1990, pegged to the inflation rate) allowable for deductions on personal and other exemptions. Because the personal exemption is the same for a single person as for a married couple, the tax schedule effectively dissuades people from getting married. For several years, politicians have discussed elim-

Returns Filed and Examined, and Additional Taxes and Penalties, 2007

Type of return	Total returns filed, 2007[1]	Total returns examined	Percent examined	Recommended additional taxes Total (000's)	Average per return[2]
All returns, total	**179,419,771**	**1,550,922**	**0.9%**	**$44,370,539**	**$77,493**
Individual, total[4]	**134,542,879**	**1,384,563**	**1.0**	**15,705,155**	**20,419**
Nonbusiness, income under $200,000	76,729,589	297,545	0.4	1,184,446	9,521
Schedule E, income under $200,000	14,158,305	165,137	1.2	759,884	6,992
with EIC, receipts under $25,000	21,613,857	400,206	1.9	1,264,786	4,815
with EIC, receipts over $25,000	1,404,507	135,850	9.7	501,977	6,359
Business, receipts under $25,000	10,356,000	134,329	1.3	1,154,236	4,836
Business, receipts $25,000-$100,000	3,076,877	62,876	2.0	569,858	6,320
Business, receipts $100,000-$200,000	912,280	56,327	6.2	1,610,565	24,582
Business, receipts over $200,000	698,893	13,049	1.9	192,777	15,959
Farm returns	1,528,390	5,705	0.4	41,207	9,206
Nonbusiness, income $200,000-$1 mil.	2,482,382	48,944	2.0	1,298,718	27,583
Business, income $200,000-$1 mil.	1,121,182	32,779	2.9	875,821	20,880
Income over $1 mil.	339,138	31,382	9.3	6,250,049	258,836
International returns	121,479	434	0.4	831	3,979
Corporation, total except Form 1120S	**2,256,485**	**30,004**	**1.3%**	**$25,741,487**	**$918,350**
No balance sheet	402,915	2,186	0.5	194,092	112,699
Under $250,000	1,183,402	9,038	0.8	204,223	24,936
$250,000-$1 mil.	372,953	4,836	1.3	111,598	23,816
$1 mil-$ 5 mil.	181,442	3,032	1.7	135,273	46,422
$5 mil-$10 mil.	30,432	928	3.0	48,704	54,927
$10 mil-$50 mil.	29,869	4,473	15.0	396,970	79,880
$50 mil-$100 mil.	7,057	801	11.4	85,295	110,949
$100 mil-$250 mil.	7,847	946	12.1	319,619	349,517
$250 mil. and over[4]	12,584	3,764	27.2	24,140,565	6,968,985
Form 1120F	27,984	340	1.2	105,148	357,646
Fiduciary	3,751,386	4,544	0.1	149,075	117,911
Estate, total	**59,978**	**4,616**	**7.7%**	**$1,147,801**	**$248,657**
Gross estate under $5 mil.	51,940	3,017	5.8	297,267	98,531
Gross estate $5 mil. and over	8,038	1,599	19.9	850,534	531,916
Gift	**264,315**	**1,490**	**0.6%**	**$230,833**	**$154,921**
Employment	**30,803,939**	**56,738**	**0.2**	**907,852**	**18,504**
Excise	**896,462**	**36,018**	**4.0**	**235,841**	**6,805**
Miscellaneous taxable[3]	N.A.	1,460	N.A.	252,495	175,101
Partnerships	**2,934,597**	**12,195**	**0.4**	**N.A.**	**N.A.**
S-Corporations (Form 1120S)	**3,909,730**	**17,657**	**0.5**	**N.A.**	**N.A.**

Note: Totals may not add due to rounding. 1. Calendar year. 2. Includes only returns reviewed by revenue agents. Additional taxes and penalties were recovered through reviews of individual returns by tax auditors and service centers. 3. Includes returns examined for taxpayers claiming an Earned Income Tax Credit and for those with total positive income of $1 million or more. 4. Estimated average per return. **Source:** Internal Revenue Service, *2007 Data Book* (2008).

inating the so-called marriage tax penalty, but to date have not remedied this situation.

Interest expenses: The most common interest deduction is on home mortgages, thus making the cost of owning a home more affordable to most Americans. Although politically very popular, the mortgage deduction is what experts call an "upside-down" subsidy because the more a taxpayer earns, the greater the tax cut yielded. In recent years, 20 percent of the tax savings from home mortgage interest has gone to taxpayers earning more than $200,000.

Medical expenses: Although almost all medical expenses are deductible, it is difficult to take a deduction because your combined expenses for the year must total 7.5 percent of your adjusted gross income. So, for someone with an adjusted gross income of $25,000, medical expenses would have to exceed $1,875 not covered by any medical insurance.

▶ELECTRONIC FILING

The number of people filing their tax returns electronically has jumped dramatically in the 1990s. Just over 4 million individuals filed electronically in 1990; by 1993, that number had tripled to 12.3 million; in 2007, 87 million returns (more than half of all individual returns) were filed electronically.

▶CHECK BOXES

More than 15 million people check the little box authorizing the I.R.S. to send $3 from their tax to the Presidential Election Campaign Fund. A total of $50.1 million went to that fund in Fiscal Year 2006. Checking the box does not increase the amount of tax owed or reduce the size of any refund.

Internal Revenue Collections, Costs, and Tax Per Capita, 1960–2007

Fiscal year	Collections ('000s)	Cost of collecting $100	Tax per capita
1960	$91,774,803	$ 0.40	$ 508
1965	114,434,634	0.52	589
1970	195,722,096	0.45	955
1975	293,822,726	0.54	1,376
1980	519,375,273	0.44	2,276
1985	742,871,541	0.48	3,099
1990	1,056,365,652	0.52	4,208
1995	1,375,731,835	0.54	5,144
2000	2,096,916,925	0.39	7,404
2003	1,952,929,045	0.48	6,691
2004	2,018,502,103	0.48	6,849
2005	2,268,895,122	0.46	7,620
2006	2,518,680,230	0.42	8,379
2007[1]	2,691,537,557	0.40	8,871

Note: In current dollars. 1. Preliminary. **Source:** Internal Revenue Service, *2007 Data Book* (2008).

Internal Revenue Collections, 2007

Type of return	Gross collections	Refunds[1]	Net collections Amount	Net collections Percent of total
Corporation income taxes	$395,535,825	$27,054,347	$368,481,478	15.4%
Individual income taxes[2]	1,366,241,437	248,641,454	1,117,599,983	46.6
Employment taxes, total	849,732,729	11,690,664	838,042,065	35.0
Estate and gift taxes	26,977,953	969,331	26,008,622	1.1
Excise taxes	53,049,612	6,890,764	46,158,848	2.0
Grand total	**$2,691,537,557**	**$295,246,560**	**$2,396,290,997**	**100.0%**

Note: 1. Excludes excise taxes paid to the Customs Service and Bureau of Alcohol, Tobacco and Firearms. Does not include interest paid on refunds. 2. Includes Presidential Election Campaign Fund contributions of $50.1 million. **Source:** Internal Revenue Service, *2007 Data Book* (2008).

I.R.S. Collections by Principal Sources, 1961–2007 (thousands of dollars)

Year	Total Internal Revenue collections	Corporate income & profits tax	Individual income tax	Employment taxes	Estate and gift taxes	Excise taxes
1961	$94,401,086	$21,764,940	$46,153,001	$12,502,451	$ 1,916,392	$12,064,302
1970	195,722,096	35,036,983	103,651,585	37,449,188	3,680,076	15,904,264
1980	519,375,273	72,379,610	287,547,782	128,330,480	6,498,381	24,619,021
1990	1,056,365,652	110,016,539	540,228,408	367,219,321	11,761,939	27,139,445
1995	1,375,731,835	174,422,173	675,779,337	465,405,305	15,144,394	44,980,627
1998	1,769,408,739	213,270,011	928,065,856	557,799,193	24,630,962	45,642,716
1999	1,904,151,888	216,324,889	1,002,185,765	598,669,865	28,385,607	58,585,763
2000	2,096,916,925	235,654,894	1,137,077,702	639,651,814	29,721,620	54,810,895
2003	1,952,929,045	194,146,298	987,208,878	695,975,801	22,826,908	32,771,160
2004	2,018,502,103	230,619,359	990,248,760	717,247,296	25,579,462	54,807,225
2005	2,268,895,122	307,094,837	1,107,500,994	771,441,662	25,605,531	57,252,098
2006	2,518,680,230	380,924,573	1,236,259,371	814,819,218	28,687,525	57,989,543
2007	2,691,537,557	395,535,825	1,366,241,437	849,732,729	26,977,953	53,049,612

Note: In current dollars. **Source:** Internal Revenue Service, *2007 Data Book* (2008).).

THE U.S. POSTAL SERVICE

With more than 757,000 employees moving more than 200 billion pieces of mail annually, the U.S. Postal Service provides one of the most vital government services. What most people don't realize is that it's done at a cost to the consumer significantly less than in any other industrial nation, and that for first-class mail, the on-time delivery rate is still over 95 percent for local mail and 90 percent for cross-country.

First established by the Continental Congress in 1775, the Postal Service was made part of the federal system in the Constitution and the office of postmaster general established in George Washington's very first cabinet. In 1969, however, in response to vociferous complaints of mismanagement, waste, unreliable service and staggering financial losses, the Nixon administration reorganized the service as an independent establishment within the executive branch. The Postal Service Act of 1969 removed the postmaster general from the cabinet and created a self-supporting postal corporation owned by the federal government and vested power in an 11-member Board of Governors, nine of whom are appointed by the president with the consent of the Senate; these in turn appoint the postmaster general who serves as the CEO of the postal service; the 11th member of the board is chosen by the other 10 and serves as deputy postmaster general.

Finally, the 1969 law established an independent Postal Rate Commission of five members, appointed by the president, to recommend postal rates and classifications for adoption by the Board of Governors. Under this agreement, the Postal Service turned a profit five times in the early 1980s. But between 1989 and 1994, the Postal Service lost money every year.

In 2007, the Postal Service delivered a near record 212 billion pieces of mail; it delivers more mail each day than Federal Express delivers all year. It owns or leases 34,318 facilities ranging from 60 square feet to 34 acres under one roof. If the Postal Service were privately held, its $75 billion in 2007 revenues would have ranked it among the top companies in the world.

International Postage Rates

Weight up to	Canada	Mexico	Other countries[1]
Airmail letters			
up to 1.0 ounces	$0.72	$0.72	$0.94
1-2 ounces	.96	1.27	1.74
2-3 ounces	1.20	1.82	2.80
3-4 ounces	1.70	2.63	3.60
4-8 ounces	2.66	4.83	6.80
1/2 -1 pound	4.56	7.83	10.10
1-2 pounds	8.63	13.83	16.70
Postcards	$0.72	$0.72	$0.94

Note: 1. Rates for weights not shown maybe higher in some countries, but lower in Micronesia and the Marshall Islands.
Source: U.S. Postal Service. www.usps.gov

Domestic Postage Rates

Type of Mail	Rate
Postcards	$0.27
Letters	
up to 1 ounce	$0.42
1-2 ounces	0.59
2-3 ounces	0.76
3-3.5 ounces	0.93
over 3.5 ounces	**Use flat rate sizes**
Flats	
up to 1 ounce	$0.83
1-2 ounces	1.00
2-3 ounces	1.17
3-4 ounces	1.34
4-5 ounces	1.51
5-6 ounces	1.68
6-7 ounces	1.85
8-9 ounces	2.19
10-11 ounces	2.36
over 13 ounces	**Use Priority Mail**

Priority mail provides two-day delivery to all major parts of the U.S. For packages over one pound, rates depend on the zone; the greater the distance, the greater the cost.

up to 1 pound	$4.80
1-2 pounds	4.80-8.25
2-3 pounds	5.20-11.50
3-4 pounds	5.80-14.25
4-5 pounds	6.45-16.80
5-10 pounds	7.05-27.55
10-20 pounds	9.35-37.05
21-70 pounds	12.80-103.10

Express mail is an overnight and second-day delivery service. A flat rate of $16.50 is charged, regardless of weight, for matter sent in a USPS flat-rate envelope. Cheaper rates apply for Express Mail sent from one post office to another.

up to 1/2 pound	$12.60-19.50
1/2 pound-1 pound	14.55-23.40
1-2 pounds	15.70-25.65
4-5 pounds	17.95-33.10
9-10 pounds	27.80-51.70
11-70 pounds	32.00-239.55

Parcel Post is a zone-based class of mail for sending books, circulars, catalogs, other printed matter, and merchandise-weighing not more than 70 pounds. The cheapest rate, for a machine-sorted package up to one pound, is $3.67; the maximum rate is $16.27 for a 35-pound package sent to zone 8. Oversized parcels (more than 35 pounds or 108 inches in combined length and girth) are charged additional fees and priced by weight and distance.

Pickups The post office will pick up priority mail and express mail packages with the correct postage. The fee is $14.25 (per pickup, not per package). Call 1-800-222-1811.
Source: U.S. Postal Service. www.usps.gov

Postage rates If you know the weight of a package, you can determine the amount of postage you will need before going to the post office. Point your browser to http://postcalc.usps.gov.

Because the price of stamps tends to rise with the rate of inflation, the Post Office in 2007 introduced the Forever Stamp. It costs whatever the current rate is for first class postage, but is valid forever. No additional postage is required even if the price of stamps goes up.

Semipostal Stamps Semipostal stamps are First Class Mail postage stamps that are issued and sold by the Postal Service at a price above the First Class Mail single-piece first-ounce rate to raise funds for designated causes. The Breast Cancer Awareness stamp, the first semipostal stamp, was introduced in 1998 and, by the end of 2007,

had raised $59.5 million for breast cancer research.

ZIP Codes There are about 42,000 separate ZIP codes in the U.S.; the number is constantly changing. A national ZIP code directory is available in every post office. Directory assistance telephone operators can provide ZIP code information, and there is also a ZIP code lookup at www.usps.gov.

Volume and Revenue of Mail by Type, 1990–2007

Type of Service	Millions of pieces				Revenues (millions)	
	1990	2000	2005	2007	2000	2007
First-class	89,269	103,526	98,071	95,898	$35,516	$37,564
Standard mail	63,725	90,057	100,942	103,516	15,193	20,779
Priority mail	518	1,222	888	897	4,837	5,233
Package mervices	663	1,128	1,166	1,163	1,912	2,306
Periodicals	10,682	10,365	9,070	8,796	2,171	2,188
Express mail	59	71	56	55	996	951
International air	632	1,021	829	833[1]	1,477	2,036
International economy	166	79	22	N.A.	180	N.A.
Mailgrams	14	4	0.8	N.A.	1	N.A.
U.S. Postal Service	538	363	621	1,008	N.A.	N.A.
Free for the blind	35	47	76	69	N.A.	N.A.
Total mail	**166,301**	**207,882**	**211,743**	**212,234**	**$62,284**	**$74,973[2]**

1. Includes all international mail. 2. Includes investment income and other revenue not listed separately. **Source**: U.S. Postal Service, *2007 Annual Report*.

Postal Abbreviations for States and Territories

State	Abb.	State	Abb.
Alabama	AL	Nevada	NV
Alaska	AK	New Hampshire	NH
Arizona	AZ	New Jersey	NJ
Arkansas	AR	New Mexico	NM
California	CA	New York	NY
Colorado	CO	North Carolina	NC
Connecticut	CT	North Dakota	ND
Delaware	DE	Ohio	OH
District of	DC	Oklahoma	OK
Columbia		Oregon	OR
Florida	FL	Pennsylvania	PA
Georgia	GA	Rhode Island	RI
Hawaii	HI	South Carolina	SC
Idaho	ID	South Dakota	SD
Illinois	IL	Tennessee	TN
Indiana	IN	Texas	TX
Iowa	IA	Utah	UT
Kansas	KS	Vermont	VT
Kentucky	KY	Virginia	VA
Louisiana	LA	Washington	WA
Maine	ME	West Virginia	WV
Maryland	MD	Wisconsin	WI
Massachusetts	MA	Wyoming	WY
Michigan	MI	American Samoa	AS
Minnesota	MN	Guam	GU
Mississippi	MS	Northern Mariana	CM
Missouri	MO	Islands	
Montana	MT	Puerto Rico	PR
Nebraska	NE	Virgin Islands	VI

Postal Service Employees and Offices, 1990–2007

Category	1990	2007
Employees		
Headquarters (Washington, D.C.)	2,291	2,856
Field support units	5,691	4,527
Inspection services (field)	4,259	2,991
Area offices	N.A.	1,281
Postmasters	26,995	25,285
Supervisors, managers	43,458	32,635
Professional, administrative, and technical personnel	9,793	8,058
Clerks	290,380	204,145
Nurses	286	160
Mail Handlers	51,123	57,882
City delivery carriers	236,081	222,132
Motor vehicle operators	7,308	8,726
Rural delivery carriers (full-time)	42,252	67,584
Building and equipment maintenance personnel	33,323	39,948
Vehicle maintenance personnel	4,874	5,405
Total career employees	**760,668**	**684,762**
Non-career employees (casuals)	26,829	22,078
Offices, stations and branches	**40,067**	**36,826**
Post offices	28,959	27,276
Classified stations and branches	5,008	4,887
Contract stations and branches	4,397	3,131
Community post offices	1,703	895

Source: U.S. Postal Service, *2007 Annual Report*.

States, Territories, and Possessions

This section, a compilation of history and statistics about the 50 United States, the District of Columbia, and U.S. territories and possessions, includes a brief history of each state and territory; its official motto and other emblems; a summary of geographic, demographic, and economic facts; and a list of prominent natives, places, and dates.

Statistical sources include the U.S. Census Bureau's 2000 decennial census and *The Statistical Abstract* (annual); the Council of State Government's *Book of the States* and *State Elective Officials and the Legislatures*; and the Bureau of Economic Analysis' *Survey of Current Business*.

The headings for demographic statistics in the paragraphs on People and Language conform to U.S. Census Bureau usage, except that "Black" is used as short for Black or African American, "Indian" is used for American Indian and Alaska Native, and "Pacific Islander" is used for Native Hawaiian and other Pacific Islander. Note that Hispanics may be of any race.

U.S. Resident Population, by State, 1990-2000

State	Population ('000s)		Change 1990 to 2000	
	2000 Census	1990 Census	Number	Percent
United States	281,422	248,710	32,712	13.2%
Alabama	4,447	4,041	407	10.1
Alaska	627	550	77	14.0
Arizona	5,131	3,665	1,465	40.0
Arkansas	2,673	2,351	323	13.7
California	33,872	29,760	4,112	13.8
Colorado	4,301	3,294	1,007	30.6
Connecticut	3,406	3,287	118	3.6
Delaware	784	666	117	17.6
Dist. of Columbia	572	607	-35	-5.7
Florida	15,982	12,938	3,044	23.5
Georgia	8,186	6,478	1,708	26.4
Hawaii	1,212	1,108	103	9.3
Idaho	1,294	1,007	287	28.5
Illinois	12,419	11,431	989	8.6
Indiana	6,080	5,544	536	9.7
Iowa	2,926	2,777	150	5.4
Kansas	2,688	2,478	211	8.5
Kentucky	4,042	3,685	356	9.7
Louisiana	4,469	4,220	249	5.9
Maine	1,275	1,228	47	3.8
Maryland	5,296	4,781	515	10.8
Massachusetts	6,349	6,016	333	5.5
Michigan	9,938	9,295	643	6.9
Minnesota	4,919	4,375	544	12.4
Mississippi	2,845	2,573	271	10.5
Missouri	5,595	5,117	478	9.3
Montana	902	799	103	12.9
Nebraska	1,711	1,578	133	8.4
Nevada	1,998	1,202	796	66.3
New Hampshire	1,236	1,109	127	11.4
New Jersey	8,414	7,730	684	8.9
New Mexico	1,819	1,515	304	20.1
New York	18,976	17,990	986	5.5
North Carolina	8,049	6,629	1,421	21.4
North Dakota	642	639	3	0.5
Ohio	11,353	10,847	506	4.7
Oklahoma	3,451	3,146	305	9.7
Oregon	3,421	2,842	579	20.4
Pennsylvania	12,281	11,882	399	3.4
Rhode Island	1,048	1,003	45	4.5
South Carolina	4,012	3,487	525	15.1
South Dakota	755	696	59	8.5
Tennessee	5,689	4,877	812	16.7
Texas	20,852	16,987	3,865	22.8
Utah	2,233	1,723	510	29.6
Vermont	609	563	46	8.2
Virginia	7,079	6,187	891	14.4
Washington	5,894	4,867	1,027	21.1
West Virginia	1,808	1,793	15	0.8
Wisconsin	5,364	4,892	472	9.6
Wyoming	494	454	40	8.9

Note: Includes armed forces residing in each state.
Source: U.S. Bureau of the Census, 2001. www.census.gov

►ALABAMA

The memory of the Native American presence is particularly strong in Alabama. Trade with the Northeast via the Ohio River valley began during the Burial Mound Period (1000 B.C.–A.D. 700) and continued until European contact. Meso-American influence is evident in the agrarian Mississippian culture that followed. Pressured by white settlers in the early 19th century, the Creeks warred against the U.S. government until defeated by General Andrew Jackson.

The cradle of the Confederacy during the Civil War, Alabama was at stage center in the civil rights movement of the 1950s and 1960s. Although cotton is still a major crop, the northern part of the state around Birmingham is a major industrial area with abundant coal, iron ore, limestone, and electricity from the TVA. Increasingly urban—70 percent of the population lived in rural areas 50 years ago, compared with less than 40 percent today—Alabama's economy is progressing slowly, although it still ranks near last in taxes and in money spent on education.

Name Probably after Alabama tribe. **Nickname** Yellowhammer State, Heart of Dixie. **Capital** Montgomery. **Entered union** Dec. 14, 1819 (22nd). **Motto** "We dare defend our rights."
Emblems **Bird** Yellowhammer. **Dance** Square dance. **Game bird** Wild turkey. **Fish** Tarpon. **Fossil** *Basilosaurus oetoides*. **Mineral** Hematite. **Nut** Pecan. **Song** "Alabama." **Stone** Marble. **Tree** Southern (longleaf) pine.
Land **Total area** 52,419 sq. mi. (30th), incl. 1,675 sq. mi. inland water. **Borders** Tenn., Ga., Fla., Gulf of Mexico, Miss. **Rivers** Alabama, Chattahoochee, Mobile, Tennessee, Tennessee-Tombigbee Waterway, Tensaw, Tombigbee. **Lakes** Guntersville, Pickwick, Wheeler, Wilson (all formed by Tennessee Valley Authority [TVA]); Dannelly Res., Martin, Lewis Smith, Weiss. **Mountains** Cumberland, Lookout, Raccoon, Sand.
Elected officials Gov. Bob Riley (R, term exp. 2010). Lt. Gov. Jim Folsom, J (D). Sec. State Beth Chapman (R). Atty. Gen. Troy King (R).
People (July 2007 est.) 4,627,851 (23rd). Race/Hispanic Origin: White 71.0%. Black 26.5%. Indian 0.5%. Asian 1.0%. Two or more races 1.0%. Hispanic 2.7%.
Cities (2006) Birmingham 229,424. Montgomery 201,998. Mobile 192,830. Huntsville 168,132. Tuscaloosa 83,052. Hoover 68,707. Dothan 64,053. Decatur 55,778. Auburn 51,906. Gadsden 37,291.

Business Gross State Product, 2005: $149.8 bil. (25th). **Leading Sectors of GSP (2001):** Services 18.10%; Manufacturing 17.80%; Government 15.8%. *Fortune 500* **Companies (2007):** 1.

Famous natives Hank Aaron, baseball player. Tallulah Bankhead, actress. William B. Bankhead, politician. Charles Barkley, basketball player. Hugo L. Black, jurist. Wernher von Braun (b. Germany), rocket scientist. Nat "King" Cole, singer. Red Eagle (William Weatherfield), Creek leader. W.C. Handy, musician. Frank M. Johnson, Jr., jurist. Helen Keller, author. Coretta Scott King, reformer. Harper Lee, author. Joe Louis, boxer. Jesse Owens, runner. Condoleeza Rice, secretary of state. Leroy Robert "Satchell" Paige, baseball player. Walker Percy, author. George Wallace, politician. Hank Williams, singer. Tammy Wynette, singer.

Noteworthy places Alabama Deep Sea Fishing Rodeo, Dauphin Island. Alabama Space and Rocket Center, U.S. Space Camp, Huntsville. Battleship USS *Alabama*, Mobile. Birmingham Museum of Art. First White House of the Confederacy, Montgomery. Horseshoe Bend Natl. Military Park. Mound State Monument Archaeological Museum, Moundville. Museum of Natural History, Univ. Alabama, Tuscaloosa. Point Clear (resort). Russell Cave Natl. Monument. Tuskegee Institute.

Memorable events Humans first inhabit Russell Cave c. 6000 B.C. Temple Mound culture flourishes around Moundville, A.D. 1200–1500. First Europeans in Mobile Bay 1519. Hernando de Soto's battle with Tuscaloosa possibly bloodiest encounter ever between Europeans and Native Americans in U.S. 1540. Spanish at Mobile Bay 1599. Pierre Le Moyne, sieur d'Iberville, establishes first permanent colony at Mobile 1711. Treaty of Paris gives Mobile to Britain 1763. U.S. control recognized 1783. Chickasaws, Choctaws, and Cherokees cede lands to U.S. 1805. First Baptist Church established 1808. Gen. Andrew Jackson defeats Creek Indian Confederacy at Horseshoe Bend 1814. Cotton principal cash crop 1820's. Beginning of coal and iron mining and steel manufacturing 1850's. Alabama secedes from Union; first capital of Confederate States of America at Montgomery 1861. Battle of Mobile Bay 1864. Readmitted to Union 1868. Booker T. Washington founds Tuskegee Institute 1881. Destruction of cotton crops by boll weevils leads to diversification of rural economy 1915. Tennessee Valley Authority enacted by Congress 1933. Montgomery bus boycott 1955. Freedom march from Selma to Montgomery 1965.

Tourist information (800) ALABAMA. www.alabama.gov.

▶ALASKA

One-fifth the size of the entire lower 48 states, Alaska is a vast, geographically varied wilderness. The coast from the Bering Sea to the Arctic was originally inhabited by Eskimos and Aleuts, while inland and to the south were Athapascans and people of the Northwest Indian culture. Russian fur traders in the 1740's were the first Europeans to recognize the region's commercial potential, and the Russian Orthodox faith is still found in the old territorial capital of Sitka (New Archangel).

Russia sold Alaska to the United States in 1867 for $7.2 million—2 cents an acre—and Alaska experienced successive booms in furs, fishing and whaling, and gold. Discovery of oil on the North Slope near Prudhoe Bay in 1968 and completion of an 800-mile trans-Alaska pipeline a decade later made oil production the centerpiece of the state's economy in the 1980's. Although the population has grown by more than 10 percent during the 1990's, the number of people per square mile remains below 1.5. In recent years, tourism based on the state's extraordinary beauty has grown substantially and now many Alaskans oppose proposed oil exploration at the Arctic National Wildlife Refuge. The memory of the *Exxon Valdez*

Population Density of U.S. States, 1980–2000

State	Population per square mile		
	1980	1990	2000
U.S. Total	64.1	70.4	79.6
Alabama	76.7	79.6	87.6
Alaska	0.7	1.0	1.1
Arizona	23.9	32.3	45.2
Arkansas	43.9	45.1	51.3
California	151.7	191.0	217.2
Colorado	27.9	31.8	41.5
Connecticut	641.4	678.5	702.9
Delaware	304.0	340.8	401.1
Dist. of Columbia	10,397.9	9,884.4	9,316.4
Florida	180.7	239.9	296.4
Georgia	94.3	111.8	141.4
Hawaii	150.2	172.5	188.6
Idaho	11.4	12.2	15.6
Illinois	205.6	205.6	223.4
Indiana	153.1	154.6	169.5
Iowa	52.1	49.7	52.4
Kansas	28.9	30.3	32.9
Kentucky	92.1	92.8	101.7
Louisiana	96.5	96.9	102.6
Maine	36.5	39.8	41.3
Maryland	431.4	489.1	541.9
Massachusetts	732.0	767.6	809.8
Michigan	163.0	163.6	175.0
Minnesota	51.2	55.0	61.8
Mississippi	53.7	54.9	60.6
Missouri	71.4	74.3	81.2
Montana	5.4	5.5	6.2
Nebraska	20.4	20.5	22.3
Nevada	7.3	10.9	18.2
New Hampshire	102.6	123.7	137.8
New Jersey	992.7	1,044.3	1,134.4
New Mexico	10.7	12.5	15.0
New York	371.8	381.0	401.9
North Carolina	120.7	136.1	165.2
North Dakota	9.5	9.3	9.3
Ohio	263.7	264.9	277.3
Oklahoma	44.1	45.8	50.3
Oregon	27.4	29.6	35.6
Pennsylvania	264.7	265.1	274.0
Rhode Island	906.4	960.3	1,003.2
South Carolina	103.6	115.8	133.2
South Dakota	9.1	9.2	9.9
Tennessee	111.4	118.3	138.0
Texas	54.3	64.9	79.6
Utah	17.8	21.0	27.2
Vermont	55.3	60.8	65.8
Virginia	135.0	156.3	178.8
Washington	62.1	73.1	88.6
West Virginia	81.0	74.5	75.1
Wisconsin	86.6	90.1	98.8
Wyoming	4.8	4.7	5.1

Note: Persons per square mile for all years calculated on the basis of land area data from the 1990 census.

Source: U.S. Bureau of the Census, 2002. www.census.gov.

oil spill into Prince William Sound in 1989 has had a powerful effect.

Name From Aleut *alaska* and Eskimo *alakshak*, both meaning "mainland." **Nickname** "The Last Frontier." **Capital** Juneau. **Entered union** Jan. 3, 1959 (49th). **Motto** "North to the future."
Emblems **Bird** Willow ptarmigan. **Fish** King salmon. **Flower** Forget-me-not. **Gem** Jade. **Marine mammal** Bowhead whale. **Mineral** Gold. **Song** "Alaska's Flag." **Sport** Mushing (dog-team racing). **Tree** Sitka spruce.
Land Total area 663,267 sq. mi (1st), incl. 91,316 sq. mi. inland water. **Borders** Arctic Ocean (Chukchi Sea, Beaufort Sea), Yukon, British Columbia, Pacific Ocean, Bering Strait. **Rivers** Colville, Porcupine, Noatak, Yukon, Susitna, Copper, Kobuk, Koyukuk, Kuskokwim, Tanana. **Mountains** Alaska Range (Mt. McKinley 20,320 ft., highest in North America), Aleutian Range, Brooks Range, Kuskokwim, St. Elias. **Other notable features** Aleutian Islands, Alexander Archipelago, Kodiak Island, Nunivak Island, Point Barrow (71°23′N), Pribilof Islands, Seward Peninsula, St. Lawrence Island.
Elected officials Gov. Sarah Palin (R). Lt. Gov. Sean Parnell (R). Atty. Gen. Talis J. Colberg (R).
People (July 2007 est.) 683,478 (47th). Race/Hispanic Origin: White 70.8%. Black 4.1%. Indian 15.2%. Asian 4.6%. Pacific Islander 0.6%. Other 1.6%. Two or more races 4.7%. Hispanic 5.9%.
Cities (2006) Anchorage 278,700. Juneau 30,737. Fairbanks 31,142. Wasilla 9,236. Sitka 8,920. Ketchikan 7,446. Kenai 7,533. Kodiak 6,259. Bethel 6,356.
Business Gross State Product, 2005: $39.9 bil. (45th). **Leading Sectors of GSP (2001):** Mining 19.56%; Government 19.50%; Oil and gas extraction 17.12%. *Fortune 500* **Companies (2007):** 0.
Famous natives Aleksandr Baranov (b. Russia), first governor of Russian America. Vitus Bering (b. Denmark), explorer. Ernest Gruening (b. N.Y.), governor. Carl Ben Eielson, bush pilot. Walter Hickel (b. Kans.), governor.
Noteworthy places Aniakchak Natl. Monument. Bering Land Bridge Natl. Preserve. Cape Krusenstern Natl. Monument. Denali Natl. Park (formerly Mt. McKinley Natl. Park). Gates of the Arctic Natl. Park. Glacier Bay Natl. Park. Katmai Natl. Park (Valley of Ten Thousand Smokes). Kenai Fjords Natl. Park. Klondike Gold Rush Natl. Hist. Park. Kobuk Valley Natl. Park. Lake Clark Natl. Park. Little Diomede Island—2.5 mi. from Big Diomede Island (Russia). Sitka Natl. Hist. Park. St. Michael's Cathedral, Sitka. Wrangell–St. Elias Natl. Park.
Memorable events Earliest migration from Asia to Americas across Bering Sea land bridge, c. 15,000 years ago. Alaska inhabited by Tlingits, Tinnehs, Aleuts, and Eskimos. Peter the Great sponsors expedition to find land opposite Siberia 1728. Bering expedition lands near Mt. Elias; begins Pacific Northwest fur trade with Europe and Asia 1741. Russians establish first European settlement at Three Saints Bay 1784. Russian-American Company chartered 1799. Baranov's massacre of Tlingits at Sitka 1802. Gold discovered at Stikine Creek (1861), Juneau (1880), Fortymile Creek (1886), Nome (1898), Fairbanks (1903). Russians sell Alaska to U.S. for $7.2 million 1867. First salmon cannery established 1878. First oil well drilled at Cook's Inlet 1896. Japanese occupy Agattu, Attu, and Kiska islands 1942–43. Alaskans vote for statehood 1946. Statehood 1959. Earthquake destroys Anchorage, Northwest Panhandle, and Cook Inlet; tsunami wipes out Valdez; coast sinks 32 ft. at Kodiak and Seward and rises 16 ft. at Cordova 1964. Oil discovered on North Slope 1968. Alaska Native Claims Settlement Act gives Alaska's Native Americans 44 million acres for native landholdings 1971. Completion of 789-mi. pipeline to Valdez 1977. Population growth of 32.8% highest in U.S. 1980–86. *Exxon Valdez* spills 10 million gallons of oil into Prince William Sound off Valdez — worst oil spill in U.S. history 1989.
Tourist information (907) 929-2200.
www.travelalaska.com

▶ARIZONA

The Hopi village of Oraibi is the oldest continuously inhabited town in the United States, and today vast tracts of Arizona are reserved for Apaches, Hopis, Navajos, Papagos and other Native Americans. Last of the 48 conterminous states admitted to the union, Arizona was sparsely settled until the advent of air conditioning in the postwar years made it habitable and a popular destination for retirees. More recently, there has been a boom in manufacturing and light industry, and in the last decade, population growth has been among the highest in the nation. Mexican-Americans are an important political force.

As in most southwestern states, water scarcity is a major problem. Arizona draws 2.8 million acre-feet of water from the Colorado River, whose water it shares with 5 other states and Mexico.

Name Probably from the Pima or Papago for "place of small springs." **Nickname** Grand Canyon State. **Capital** Phoenix. **Entered union** Feb. 14, 1912 (48th). **Motto** *Ditat deus* (God enriches).
Emblems **Bird** Cactus wren. **Flower** Blossom of the saguaro cactus. **Gemstone** Turquoise. **Official neck wear** Bolo tie. **Songs** "Arizona March Song," "Arizona." **Tree** Palo verde.
Land Total area 113,998 sq. mi. (6th), incl. 364 sq. mi. inland water. **Borders** Utah, Colo., N.Mex., Sonora, Baja California Norte, Calif., Nev. **Rivers** Colorado, Gila, Little Colorado, Salt, Zuni. **Lakes** Havasu, Mead, Mohave, Powell, Roosevelt, San Carlos. **Mountains** Black, Gila, Hualpai, Mohawk, San Francisco Peaks (Humphreys Peak 12,633 ft.). **Other notable features** Grand Canyon, Kaibab Plateau, Painted and Sonoran Deserts, Petrified Forest.
Elected officials Gov. Janet Napolitano (D). Atty. Gen. Terry Goddard (D). Sec. State Janice Brewer (R).
People (July 2007 est.) 6,338,755 (16th). Race/Hispanic Origin: White 87.0%. Black 4.0%. Indian 4.7%. Asian 2.5%. Pacific Islander 0.2%. Two or more races 1.7%. Hispanic 29.6%.
Cities (2006) Phoenix 1,512,986. Tucson 518,956. Mesa 447,541. Glendale 246,531. Chandler 240,595. Scottsdale 231,127. Gilbert 191,517. Tempe 169,712. Peoria 142,024. Yuma 87,423.
Business Gross State Product, 2006: $216.5 bil. (20th). **Leading Sectors of GSP (2001):** Services 21.46%; Finance, insurance, and real estate 19.53%; Manufacturing 13.51%. *Fortune 500* **Companies (2007):** 4.
Famous natives Bruce Babbitt, politician. Cesar Chavez, labor leader. Cochise, Apache chief. Andrew Ellicott Douglass (b. Vt.), dendrochronologist. Wyatt Earp (b. Ill.), lawman. Barry Goldwater, politician. Goyathlay (Geronimo), Apache chieftain. Carl Hayden, congressman. Eusebio Kino (b. Italy), missionary. Sandra Day O'Connor, jurist. William H. Rehnquist, jurist. Marty Robbins, singer. Linda Ronstadt, singer. Kerri Strug, gymnast. Morris Udall, politician.
Noteworthy Places Canyon de Chelly Natl. Monument. Casa Grande Ruins Natl. Monument.

Chiricahua Natl. Monument. Ft. Bowie. Grand Canyon Natl. Park. Heard Museum, Phoenix. London Bridge, Lake Havasu City. Montezuma Castle Natl. Monument. Navajo Natl. Monument. Organ Pipe Cactus Natl. Monument. Painted Desert. Petrified Forest Natl. Park. Pipe Spring Natl. Monument. Saguaro Natl. Monument. Slot canyons, Upper and Lower Antelope Canyons, near Page. Sunset Crater Natl. Monument. Taliesin West, near Scottsdale. Tonto Natl. Monument. Tumacacori Natl. Monument. Tuzigoot Natl. Monument. Walnut Canyon Natl. Monument. Wupatki Natl. Monument.

Memorable events   Apaches and Navajos absorb Pueblos c. A.D. 1000. Alvar Núñez Cabeza de Vaca, first Spanish explorer 1536. Marcos de Niza 1539. Ruled as part of New Spain 1598–1821. First missionaries among Hopis 1638. Tubac first European settlement 1752. Tucson founded 1776. Apaches wipe out settlements under Mexican control, except Tucson 1821. Northern part ceded to U.S. following Mexican War 1848. Area south of Gila River to U.S. after Gadsden Purchase 1853. Territory 1863. Southern Pacific Railroad reaches Tucson 1880. Apaches subjugated 1886. Congress refuses to grant statehood 1906. Roosevelt Dam and Reservoir built on Salt River 1911. Native Americans given right to vote 1948. Glen Canyon Dam built on Colorado River 1964. Population growth of 24.3 percent is second highest in U.S., 1990–97.

Tourist information   (888) 520-3434.
www.az.gov

▶**ARKANSAS**
First inhabited by bluff dwellers 10,000 years ago, the Boston and Ouachita mountains of western Arkansas are the only mountains between the Appalachians and the Rockies. By the time of the Hernando De Soto expedition of 1541, Arkansas was inhabited by a variety of peoples: the agrarian Quapaws to the south, the Caddo to the west and south, the Osage to the north, and the Chickasaw and Choctaw in the northeast. The Arkansas Post, the first permanent settlement in the Mississippi Valley, became the pillar of the French claim to the region that became the Louisiana Purchase.

Not fully part of the deep south, and cut off geographically from the Midwest, Arkansas has developed slowly. Although cotton was a mainstay of the economy and Arkansas joined the Confederacy during the Civil War, it was the first southern state to have integrated public colleges after World War II, a fact overshadowed by Gov. Orville Faubus's resistance to the integration of the Little Rock public schools. In recent years, Arkansas has attracted manufacturing and industry, but has one of the highest rural populations and ranks low in services, income, and education attainment.

Name From term for Quapaw tribe given by other Indians. **Nickname** Land of Opportunity. **Capital** Little Rock. **Entered union** June 15, 1836 (25th). **Motto** *Regnat populus* (Let the people rule). **Emblems**   **Bird** Mockingbird. **Flower** Apple blossom. **Gem** Diamond. **Song** "Arkansas." **Tree** Pine. **Land**   **Total area** 53,179 sq. mi (29th), incl. 1,110 sq. mi. inland water. **Borders** Mo., Tenn., Miss., La., Tex., Okla. **Rivers** Arkansas, Mississippi, Ouachita, Red, St. Francis, White. **Lakes** Beaver, Bull Shoals, Chicot, Dardanelle, Greers Ferry, Greeson, Norfolk, Ouachita. **Mountains** Ozark Mts.
Elected officials   Gov. Mike Beebe (D). Lt. Gov. Bill Halter (R). Sec. State Charlie Daniels (D). Atty. Gen. Dustin McDaniel (D).

People   (July 2007 est.) 2,834,797 (32nd). Race/Hispanic Origin: White 80.9%. Black 15.8%. Indian 0.8%. Asian 1.1%. Pacific Islander 0.1%. Two or more races 1.3%. Hispanic 5.3%.
Cities   (2006) Little Rock 184,422. Fort Smith 83,461. Fayetteville 68,726. Springdale 63,082. Jonesboro 60,489. North Little Rock 58,896. Conway 55,334. Rogers 52,181. Pine Bluff 51,758. Hot Springs 38,468.
Business   **Gross State Product, 2005:** $86.8 bil. (34th). **Leading Sectors of GSP (2001):** Manufacturing 19.34%; Services 16.95%; Government 13.07%. *Fortune 500* Companies (2007): 5.
Famous natives   Maya Angelou, author. Linda Bloodworth-Thomason, television writer. Glen Campbell, singer. Hattie W. Caraway, first woman senator. Johnny Cash, singer. Eldridge Cleaver, author. Bill Clinton, U.S. president. William Fulbright (b. Mo.), politician. John Grisham, author. Alan Ladd, actor. Douglas MacArthur, general. Brooks Robinson, baseball player. Winthrop Rockefeller (b. N.Y.), politician/philanthropist. Edward Durrell Stone, architect. Billy Bob Thornton, actor. C. Vann Woodward, historian.
Noteworthy places   Arkansas Post Natl. Monument (first permanent French settlement in lower Mississippi Valley). Buffalo Natl. River. Clinton Presidential Library. Crater of Diamonds State Park, Murfreesboro. Eureka Springs. Ft. Smith Natl. Hist. Site. Hot Springs Natl. Park. Pea Ridge Natl. Military Park.
Memorable Events   Bluff-dwellers present c. A.D. 500, followed by mound-building cultures. Hernando de Soto explores for Spain 1541. Jacques Marquette and Louis Jolliet explore for France 1673. René-Robert de La Salle meets Quapaws 1682. Henri de Tonti founds Arkansas Post on Arkansas River 1686. Ceded from France to Spain 1782; to France 1800; to U.S. 1803. Territory 1819. Admitted to Union as slave state, under terms of 1820 Missouri Compromise, 1836. Secedes from Union 1861. Fall of Little Rock to Union army 1863. Readmitted to Union 1868. Bauxite discovered 1887. Oil production begins 1920's. Federal troops called to Little Rock to ensure high school desegregation 1957. Winthrop Rockefeller (b. N.Y.) first Republican governor since Reconstruction 1966. McClellan-Kerr Arkansas River Navigation System links Arkansas and Oklahoma to Mississippi River system 1971. Governor Bill Clinton Elected U.S. President 1992.
Tourist information   (800) NATURAL.
www.arkansas.com.

▶**CALIFORNIA**
Before the arrival of Europeans, no area of comparable size in North America was home to a greater variety of languages and cultures than what is now California, and today the state's population is more diverse than that of any other. In 2001, non-Hispanic whites became a minority of California's population and demographers project that the majority of Californians will be Hispanic by 2040.

The largest state by population since the 1960s, California gained seven Congressional representatives in the 1990 Census redistricting, and one more in 2000. By some estimates, California is the sixth largest economic power in the world.

Despite its economic strength, rugged terrain and dramatic vistas, California has problems. The state's position as a leader in agriculture masks an alarming lack of water. It draws 4.5 to over 5 million acre-feet annually from the Colorado River, mostly for irrigating the Imperial Valley—a desert when settlers crossed it 150 years ago. Almost the entire flow of the San Joaquin River is similarly diverted for the Central Valley. This leaves less and less water for citizens, whose numbers have leaped from 15 million in 1960 to over 36 million today. In 2008, the governor declared official drought conditions in the state.

The threat of earthquakes is a constant concern for California, which has suffered eight major earthquakes and dozens of smaller ones since 1900. The 1906 quake destroyed San Francisco, and the Loma Prieta earthquake in 1989 killed 67 people and left 48,000 homeless. The 1994 Northridge quake killed 60 people, injured 7,000 and left 20,000 more homeless, destroyed freeway overpasses and caused over $13 billion in damages.

Name Probably from mythical island in García Ordoñez de Montalvo's 16th-century romance, *The Deeds of Esplandián*. **Nickname** Golden State. **Capital** Sacramento. **Entered union** Sept. 9, 1850 (31st). **Motto** *"Eureka"* (I have found it). **Emblems** **Animal** California grizzly bear (extinct). **Bird** California valley quail. **Fish** California golden trout. **Flower** Golden poppy. **Fossil** California saber-toothed cat. **Gemstone** Benitoite. **Insect** California dog-face butterfly. **Marine mammal** California gray whale. **Mineral** Gold. **Reptile** California desert tortoise. **Rock** Serpentine. **Song** "I Love You, California." **Tree** California redwood. **Land** Total area 163,696 sq. mi (3rd), incl. 7,736 sq. mi. inland water. **Borders** Oreg., Nev., Ariz., Baja California Norte, Pacific Ocean. **Rivers** American, Colorado, Colorado River Aqueduct, Eel, Friant-Kern Canal, Klamath, Russian, Sacramento, Salinas, San Joaquin. **Lakes** Clear, Goose, Honey, Mono, Owens, Salton Sea, Shasta, Tahoe. **Mountains** Coast Ranges, Klamath, Lassen Peak, Sierra Nevada (Mt. Whitney 14,494 ft.). **Other notable features** Catalina Islands, Death Valley (282 ft. below sea level), San Francisco Bay, San Joaquin Valley.

Elected officials Gov. Arnold Schwarzenegger (R). Lt. Gov. John Garamendi (D) Sec. State Debra Bowen (D). Atty. Gen. Edmund G. Brown, Jr. (D).

People (July, 2007 est.) 36,553,215 (1st). Race/Hispanic Origin: White 76.8%. Black 6.7%. Indian 1.2%. Asian 12.4%. Pacific Islander 0.4%. Two or more races 2.5%. Hispanic 36.2%.

Cities (2006) Los Angeles 3,849,378. San Diego 1,256,951. San Jose 929,936. San Francisco 744,041. Long Beach 472,494. Fresno 466,714. Sacramento 453,781. Oakland 397,067. Santa Ana 340,024. Anaheim 334,425.

Business Gross State Product, 2005: $1,621.8 bil. (1st). **Leading Sectors of GSP (2001):** Services 23.99%; Finance, insurance, and real estate 23.36%; Real estate 16.21%. *Fortune 500* **Companies (2007):** 52.

Famous natives Ansel Adams, photographer. Dave Brubeck, musician. Luther Burbank (b. Mass.), horticulturist. John Cage, composer. Joe DiMaggio, baseball player. Robert Frost, poet. Ernest and Julio Gallo (b. Italy), vintners. Pancho Gonzales, tennis player. Samuel Ichiye Hayakawa, politician/educator. William Randolph Hearst, publisher. Steve Jobs, computer scientist. Billie Jean King, tennis player. Allen Lockheed, aviator. Jack London, author. Paul Masson (b. France), vintner. Marilyn Monroe, actress. John Muir (b. Scotland), naturalist. Richard M. Nixon, U.S. president. John Northrop, aviator. Adlai Stevenson, politician. John Steinbeck, author. Levi Strauss (b. Germany), clothier. Edward Teller (b. Hungary), nuclear physicist. Shirley Temple, actress. Earl Warren, politician/jurist.

Noteworthy places Big Sur, Monterey. Cabrillo Natl. Monument. California Academy of Sciences, San Francisco. California Palace of the Legion of Honor, San Francisco. Channel Islands Natl. Park. Devils Postpile Natl. Monument. Death Valley Natl. Monument. Disneyland. Fine Arts Museum of San Francisco. Fishermen's Wharf, San Francisco. Hollywood. Huntington Library and Botanical Gardens, San Marino. J. Paul Getty Museum, Malibu. Joshua Tree Natl. Monument. Kings Canyon Natl. Park. Lassen Volcanic Natl. Park. Lava Beds Natl. Monument. Los Angeles Co. Museum of Art. Muir Woods Natl. Monument. Mt. Palomar Observatory. Natl. Maritime Museum, San Francisco. Natural History Museum, Los Angeles. Natural History Museum of San Diego. Norton Simon Museum of Art at Pasadena. Pinnacles Natl. Monument. Redwood Natl. Park. Rosicrucian Egyptian Museum, San José. San Diego Museum of Art. San Diego Museum of Man. San Diego Zoo. San Francisco Museum of Modern Art. Sequoia Natl. Park. Southwest Museum (Casa de Adobe), Los Angeles. Yosemite Natl. Park.

Memorable events João Rodrigues Cabrilho lands at San Diego Bay 1542. Francis Drake lands north of San Francisco Bay 1579. Junípero Serra founds missions at San Diego (1769), Monterey (1770), San Luis Obispo (1772), and San Juan Capistrano (1776). California declares allegiance to independent Mexico 1821. First wagon train from Missouri 1841. Gold discovered north of Los Angeles 1842. California declares itself independent republic 1846. Gold found at John Sutter's mill; nine days later, by Treaty of Guadalupe Hidalgo, Mexico cedes California to U.S. 1848. Announcement of gold discovery brings 80,000 'Forty-niners. Gold rush peaks 1852. Transcontine immigration of Chinese laborers 1882, 1892, and 1902; Act repealed 1943. San Francisco earthquake kills 452, destroys 28,000 buildings 1906. Webb Alien Land Law prohibits Japanese from holding land 1913. Los Angeles has one car for every three people, twice national average, 1925. Dust Bowl immigrants 1930. Hollywood produces bulk of movies for U.S. theaters, which number more than banks 1940. Most populous state 1963. Proposition 13 limits property tax 1978. Loma Prieta earthquake registers 7.1 on Richter scale — second most powerful in U.S. history; 67 dead, 48,000 homeless, and $10 billion in property damage 1989. Riots in Los Angeles kill 60 and cause $1 billion in damage 1992.

Tourist information (800) TO-CALIF. www.visitcalifornia.com

►COLORADO

The native peoples of Colorado were the Plains Indians (Arapahoe and Cheyenne) to the east and Great Basin Indians (Utes) to the west. This pre-Columbian division of the land is reflected today in Colorado's economy, which is a mix of agriculture and technology in the east and mining and ski tourism in the mountains. During the oil price shocks of the 1970s, shale-oil production on the Western Slope created a boom comparable to Colorado's silver and lead boom in the late 19th century. Strong job growth and an outdoor lifestyle has attracted many young people since the early 1990s; while the population has increased, the percentage of people over 65 has fallen to one of the lowest in the nation. While a state of great natural beauty, Colorado's high-altitude almost doubles the effect of auto emissions. Economic development largely means resource

extraction and requires more and more water, whose limited supply poses a great challenge. **Name** From Spanish for the color red. **Nickname** Centennial State. **Capital** Denver. **Entered union** Aug. 1, 1876 (38th). **Motto** *Nil sine numine* (Nothing without providence).
Emblems **Animal** Rocky Mountain bighorn sheep. **Bird** Lark bunting. **Flower** Rocky Mountain Columbine. **Gem** Aquamarine. **Song** "Where the Columbines Grow." **Tree** Colorado blue spruce.
Land **Total area** 104,094 sq. mi (8th), incl. 376 sq. mi. inland water. **Borders** Wyo., Nebr., Kans., N.Mex., Ariz., Utah. **Rivers** Arkansas, Colorado, Green, Platte, Rio Grande. **Lakes** Blue Mesa, Dillon, Granby. **Mountains** Front Range, Laramie, Sangre de Cristo, San Juan, Sawatch Range (Mt. Elbert 14,443 ft.).
Elected officials Gov. Bill Ritter (D). Lt. Gov. Barbara O'Brien (D). Sec. Mike Coffman (R). Atty. Gen. John Suthers (R).
People (July, 2007 est.) 4,861,515 (22nd). Race/ Hispanic Origin: White 89.9%. Black 4.2%. Indian 1.2%. Asian 2.7%. Pacific Islander 0.1%. Two or more races 1.9%. Hispanic 19.9%.
Cities (2006) Denver 566,974. Colorado Springs 372,437. Aurora 303,582. Lakewood 140,024. Fort Collins 129,467. Thornton 109,155. Westminster 105,753. Arvada 104,830. Pueblo 103,730. Centennial 98,270.
Business **Gross State Product, 2005:** $216.1 bil. (20th). **Leading Sectors of GSP (2001):** Services 24.09%; Finance, insurance, and real estate 18.31%; Government 11.82%. ***Fortune 500* Companies (2007):** 12.
Famous natives Charlie Bent (b. Va.), trapper. "Unsinkable" Molly Brown, *Titanic* survivor. Scott Carpenter, astronaut. Lon Chaney, actor. Jack Dempsey, boxer. Mamie Eisenhower, first lady. Douglas Fairbanks, actor. Horace Greeley, journalist. Scott Hamilton, ice skater. Anne Parrish, novelist. Lowell Thomas, journalist. Byron R. White, jurist.
Noteworthy Places Black Canyon of the Gunnison National Park. Buffalo Bill grave site, Evergreen. Central City Opera House. Colorado Springs Fine Arts Center. Denver Art Museum. Denver Mint. Denver Museum of Natural History. Dinosaur Natl. Monument. Florissant Fossil Beds Natl. Monument. Garden of the Gods, Colorado Springs. Great Sand Dunes Natl. Monument. Hovenweep Natl. Monument. Mesa Verde Natl. Park. Molly Brown House, Denver. Pikes Peak. Red Rocks Amphitheater. Rocky Mountain Natl. Park, Aspen. Rocky Mountain Natl. Park. U.S. Air Force Academy, Colorado Springs. U.S. Olympic Headquarters, Colorado Springs. Yucca House Natl. Monument.
Memorable events Anasazi build cliff dwellings near Mesa Verde through 1200s. Arapahos and Cheyennes settle area after 13th century. France abandons claims 1763. Juan de Uribarri explores area 1786. Spain restores area to France 1801. To United States as part of Louisiana Purchase 1803. Zebulon Pike explores for United States 1806. Kit Carson and other scouts explore and trade with Native Americans 1810s–20s. Native Americans form alliance at Brent's Fork 1840. John Frémont's explorations 1842–53. Present territorial limits after Mexican War 1848. First permanent settlement at San Luis 1851. Gold found west of Denver—"Pikes Peak or Bust"—1858. Mineral springs bring first tourists 1861. Homestead Act encourages farming 1862. U.S. Army kills 400 Cheyenne at Sand Creek Massacre 1864. Utes and Cheyennes fight white settlement through 1870s. John Wesley Powell and nine

others navigate Colorado River from the Green River branch in Wyoming to the end of Grand Canyon in Arizona 1869. Railroad link to Denver 1870. Silver and lead discoveries 1875. Uranium discovered near Grand Junction 1946. U.S. Air Force Academy founded Denver 1954; to Colorado Springs 1958. Shale oil boom on Western Slope 1974 and 1979. Accumulation of nuclear waste threatens suspension of operations at Rocky Flats 1988.
Tourist information   (800) COLORADO. **www.colorado.gov**

▶ CONNECTICUT

Called the "arsenal of the nation" during the Revolution, Connecticut remained in modern times the leader among the 50 states in defense-contract dollars per capita. In the late 20th century, this caused a serious dislocation in the economy as the nation downsizes its military capabilities. Still, with eleven *Fortune* 500 companies (including major insurance companies), and easy access to New York City, Connecticut remains the state with the country's highest per capita income.

Severe budget deficits in 1991 forced passage of a state income tax and helped to reveal the disparities in wealth between the very rich suburbs and the decaying industrial cities such as Bridgeport. As the economy was retooled, population growth slowed and the state has recently lost population.

Name From Mahican word meaning "beside the long tidal river." **Nicknames** Constitution State, Nutmeg State. **Capital** Hartford. **Entered union** Jan. 9, 1788 (5th). **Motto** *Qui transtulit sustinet* (He who transplanted still sustains).
Emblems **Animal** Sperm whale. **Bird** American robin. **Flower** Mountain laurel. **Hero** Nathan Hale. **Insect** European praying mantis. **Mineral** Garnet. **Ship** USS *Nautilus*. **Song** "Yankee Doodle." **Tree** White oak.
Land **Total area** 5,543 sq. mi (48th), incl. 699 sq. mi. inland water **Borders** Mass., R.I., Long Island Sound, N.Y. **Rivers** Connecticut, Housatonic, Mianus, Naugatuck, Thames. **Lakes** Bantam, Barkhamstead, Candlewood, Waramaug. **Other notable features** Berkshire Hills, Long Island Sound.
Elected officials Gov. M. Jodi Rell (R, term exp. 2007). Lt. Gov. Michael Fedele (R). Sec. State Susan Bysiewicz (D). Atty. Gen. Richard Blumenthal (D).
People (July 2007 est.) 3,502,309 (29th). Race/ Hispanic Origin: White 84.5%. Black 10.3%. Indian 0.4%. Asian 3.4%. Pacific Islander 0.1%. Two or more races 1.4%. Hispanic 11.5%.
Cities (2006) Bridgeport 137,912. Hartford 124,512. New Haven 124,001. Stamford 119,261. Waterbury 107,251. Norwalk 84,187. Danbury 79,285. New Britain 70,746. Bristol 61,161. Meriden 59,439.
Business **Gross State Product, 2005:** $194.5 bil. (23rd). **Leading Sectors of GSP (2001):** Finance, insurance, and real estate 30.97%; Services 21.46%; Real estate 15.82%. ***Fortune 500* Companies (2007):** 11.
Famous natives Benedict Arnold, traitor. P.T. Barnum, showman. Lyman Beecher, theologian. John Brown, abolitionist. Samuel Colt, inventor. Jonathan Edwards, theologian. Charles Goodyear, inventor. Nathan Hale, patriot. Katharine Hepburn, actress. Charles Ives, composer. J.P. Morgan, financier. Ralph Nader, consumer advocate. Frederick Law Olmsted, landscape architect. Harriet Beecher Stowe, author. John Trumbell, artist. Noah Webster, lexicographer. Eli Whitney, inventor.

Noteworthy places Charles Ives Center, Danbury. Eugene O'Neill Memorial Theater Center, Waterford. Gilette Castle. Housatonic State Park. Mark Twain House, Hartford. Mystic Marinelife Aquarium. Mystic Seaport. Norwalk Maritime Center. U.S. Coast Guard Academy. USS *Nautilus*, New London. Wadsworth Atheneum, Hartford. Whitney Museum of Modern Art, Stamford. Yale Center for British Art, New Haven. Yale University, New Haven.

Memorable events Adriaen Block claims for Dutch 1614. First English settlement in Windsor 1633. Royal charter of 1662 hidden in Charter Oak 1687. *Hartford Courant*, oldest continuously published newspaper in U.S., first published 1764. Samuel Colt develops six-shooter 1835. Horace Wells uses first anesthesia 1844. Elias Howe invents sewing machine 1845. U.S. Coast Guard Academy founded New London 1876. First woman governor elected in her own right, Ella T. Grasso, 1974.

Tourist information   (800) CT-BOUND.
www.ctvisit.com

▶ **DELAWARE**

The du Pont family has enjoyed a political and economic prominence in Delaware unmatched in the history of the other 49 states. Seven generations ago E.I. du Pont de Nemours and Co. was founded as a gunpowder mill, then grew into a monopoly, and in the wake of World War I, diversified into today's giant, with interests in banking, media, and real estate. Only half the size of Los Angeles County, Delaware was called the Company State by Ralph Nader's "raiders" in 1973. Its liberal incorporation laws has led more than half the Fortune 500 companies to incorporate there. (A total of more than 170,000 corporations are incorporated in Delaware). It was one of the few states to prosper even during the recessions of the early 1980s and early 1990s.

Name For Thomas West, Lord De La Warre, colonial governor of Virginia. **Nicknames** First State, Diamond State. **Capital** Dover. **Entered union** Dec. 7, 1787 (1st). **Motto** "Liberty and Independence."

Emblems **Bird** Blue hen chicken. **Fish** Weakfish. **Flower** Peach blossom. **Insect** Ladybug. **Rock** Sillimanite. **Song** "Our Delaware." **Tree** American holly.

Land Total area 2,489 sq. mi (49th), incl. 536 sq. mi. inland water. **Borders** Pa., N.J., Atlantic Ocean, Md. **Rivers** Chesapeake & Delaware Canal, Delaware, Nanticoke.

Elected officials Gov. Ruth Ann Minner (D, term exp. 2008). Lt. Gov. John Carney (D). Sec. State Harriet Smith Windsor (D). Atty. Gen. Beau Biden (D).

People (July 2007 est.) 864,764 (45th). Race/Hispanic Origin: White 74.5%. Black 20.9%. Indian 0.4%. Asian 2.8%. Pacific Islander 0.1%. Two or more races 1.4%. Hispanic 6.5%.

Cities (2006) Wilmington 72,664. Dover 32,135. Newark 28,547. Milford 6,732. Seaford 6,699. Middletown 6,161. Elsmere 5,800. Smyrna 5,679. New Castle 4,862. Georgetown 4,643.

Business Gross State Product, 2005: $54.4 bil. (38th). **Leading Sectors of GSP (2001):** Finance, insurance, and real estate 43.14%; Depository and nondepository institutions 30.64%. *Fortune 500* **Companies (2007): 1.**

Famous natives Valerie Bertinelli, actress. John Dickinson (b. Md.), Penman of the Revolution. Eleuthère I. du Pont, manufacturer. Pierre S. ("Pete") du Pont, politician. Morgan Edwards, founder of Brown University (R.I.). Thomas Mac-

donough, navy officer. Howard Pyle, illustrator. Edward R. Squibb, physician/manufacturer. Christopher Ward, historian.

Noteworthy places Brandywine Zoo, Wilmington. Delaware Art Museum, Wilmington. Delaware State Museum, Dover. Dover Downs International Speedway. Grand Opera House, Wilmington. Hagley Museum, Wilmington. Kalmar Nykel Sailing Ship, Cape May. Rehoboth Beach.

Memorable events Dutch arrive 1631. Swedes establish first permanent settlement at Wilmington 1638. Captured by Dutch 1655. To England 1664. Part of territory granted to William Penn 1682. Breaks off from Pennsylvania; first to ratify Constitution 1787. E.I. du Pont de Nemours Co. founded 1802. Railroad connects Wilmington to Philadelphia and Baltimore 1838. Though slave state, sides with Union during Civil War 1861–65. Delaware last state to abolish whipping post (last used 1952) 1972.

Tourist information   (800) 2-VISIT-DE.
www.visitdelaware.com

▶ **DISTRICT OF COLUMBIA**

Chosen as the site for the nation's capital by George Washington, Washington, D.C., was built on land ceded by Maryland and Virginia. Although under Federal jurisdiction, the District has petitioned for statehood as New Columbia. In 1961, the 23rd Amendment granted citizens of D.C. the right to vote in Presidential elections for the first time, and 10 years later Congress gave the District one nonvoting delegate to the House of Representatives. In recent years, the District has protested its lack of full representation and issues license unofficial motto "Taxation Without Representation." D.C.'s largest employer is the federal government, and printing is the largest industry. Pres. John F. Kennedy called it a city of "Southern efficiency and Northern charm," but the city has become a leading patron of the arts. However, the problems of any large city are exacerbated by the transience of D.C.'s government workers. As the seat of the U.S. Government, D.C. attracts more than 17 million visitors annually.

Name After Christopher Columbus; Columbia was commonly used for the United States before 1800. **Nickname** None. **Capital** Washington. **Became capital** Dec. 1, 1800. **Motto** *Justitia omnibus* (Justice for all).

Emblems **Bird** Wood thrush. **Flower** American beauty rose. **Tree** Scarlet oak.

Land Total area 68 sq. mi., incl. 7 sq. mi. inland water. **Borders** Md., Va. **Rivers** Anacostia, Potomac.

Elected officials Mayor Adrian Fenty (D, term exp. 2010).

People (July 2007 est.) 588,292 (N.A.) Race/Hispanic Origin: White 39.4%. Black 55.2%. Indian 0.4%. Asian 3.4%. Pacific Islander 0.1%. Two or more races 1.6%. Hispanic 8.3%.

Business Gross State Product, 2005: $82.8 bil. (N.A.). **Leading Sectors of GSP (2001):** Services 37.65%; Government 35.18%; Federal civilian employment 30.07%. *Fortune 500* **Companies (2007): 2.**

Famous natives Edward Albee, playwright. Carl Bernstein, journalist. John Foster Dulles, politician. Duke Ellington, composer. J. Edgar Hoover, FBI director. Marjorie Kinnan Rawlings, novelist. John Philip Sousa, composer.

Noteworthy places The Capitol. Chesapeake & Ohio Canal Natl. Hist. Park. Corcoran Gallery of Art. Dumbarton Oaks. FDR Memorial. Folger Shakespeare Library. Freer Gallery of Art. Hirshhorn Museum. Jefferson Memorial. Kennedy Center. Korean War Veterans Memorial. Library of Congress. Lincoln Memorial. Natl. Air and Space Museum. Natl. Gallery of Art. Natl. Museum of African Art. Natl. Museum of American Art. Natl. Museum of American History. Natl. Museum of American Indian. Natl. Museum of Natural History. Natl. Portrait Gallery. Naval Observatory. Navy Memorial Museum. Renwick Gallery. Smithsonian Institution. Vietnam Veterans Memorial. Washington Monument. Washington Zoo. White House. Woodrow Wilson House.

Memorable events Originally part of Maryland. Congress approves plan to secure land for seat of Federal Government, no more than 10 miles square, on land in Virginia and Maryland 1787. George Washington commissions Pierre Charles l'Enfant to lay out city 1791. Government moves 1800. British sail up the Potomac and burn capital 1814. Virginia reclaims its half of District 1846. President Abrahâm Lincoln assassinated 1865. Coxey's Army marches on Washington 1894. The Bonus Army—17,000 veterans—marches on Washington 1932. Led by Martin Luther King, Jr., 200,000 march for Civil Rights 1963. 100,000 protest Vietnam War 1971. Democratic party headquarters at Watergate burglarized by men linked to President Richard M. Nixon's reelection effort 1972. Congress grants limited self-rule; mayor and city council elected 1975.

Tourist information (202) 789-7000. www.washington.org

▶ FLORIDA

A vast network of swamps, rivers, and lakes, much of Florida is barely above sea level. Florida is home to Disney World, Cypress Gardens, the wealth-laden resort of Palm Beach, the *National Enquirer*, and the Okefenokee Swamp. The pleasant climate and proximity to the Caribbean and Latin America have attracted tourists, retirees (almost 19 percent of the population is over 65) and immigrants. Over the last two decades, it has been one of the fastest-growing states, but growth has brought attendant increases in drug trafficking, racial disturbances, and environmental damage to such wildlife as the crocodile, alligator, and the Florida panther.

Name By Juan Ponce de León for Pascua Florida (Easter festival of the flowers). **Nickname** Sunshine State. **Capital** Tallahassee. **Entered union** Mar. 3, 1845 (27th). **Motto** "In God We Trust." **Poet laureate** Dr. Edmund Skellings.

Emblems **Animal** Florida panther. **Beverage** Orange juice. **Bird** Mockingbird. **Flower** Orange blossom. **Freshwater fish** Florida largemouth bass. **Gem** Moonstone. **Marine mammals** Dolphin, manatee. **Saltwater fish** Atlantic sailfish. **Shell** Horse conch. **Song** "Old Folks at Home" ("Swanee River"). **Stone** Agatized coral. **Tree** Sabal palmetto palm.

Land **Total area** 65,755 sq. mi (22nd), incl. 11,828 sq. mi. inland water. **Borders** Ga., Atlantic Ocean, Gulf of Mexico, Ala. **Rivers** Apalachicola, Caloosahatchee, Indian, Kissimmee, Perdido, St. Johns, St. Mary's, Suwanee, Withlacoochee. **Lakes** Apopka, George, Okeechobee, Seminole. **Other notable features** Everglades, Florida Keys, Okefenokee Swamp.

Elected officials Gov. Charlie Crist (R). Lt. Gov. Jeff Kottkamp (R). Sec. State Kurt Browning (D). Atty. Gen. Bill McCollum (R).

People (July 2007 est.) 18,251,243 (4th). Race/Hispanic Origin: White 80.0%. Black 15.9%. Indian 0.5%. Asian 2.3%. Pacific Islander 0.1%. Two or more races 1.3%. Hispanic 20.6%.

Cities (2006) Jacksonville 794,555. Miami 404,048. Tampa 332,888. St. Petersburg 248,098. Orlando 220,186. Hialeah 217,141. Fort Lauderdale 185,804. Tallahassee 159,012. Cape Coral 151,389. Pembroke Pines 150,064.

Business **Gross State Product, 2005:** $674.4 bil. (4th). **Leading Sectors of GSP (2001):** Services 25.62%; Finance, insurance, and real estate 22.08%; Real estate 14.52%. *Fortune 500* **Companies (2007):** 12.

Famous natives Mary Bethune, educator/reformer. Faye Dunaway, actress. Chris Evert, tennis player. Zora Neale Hurston, writer. James Weldon Johnson, lawyer/novelist. Osceola, Seminole chief. Sidney Poitier, actor. A. Philip Randolph, labor leader. Edmund Kirby Smith, Confederate general. Joseph Warren "Vinegar Joe" Stillwell, army officer. Ben Vereen, actor/singer.

Noteworthy places Biscayne Natl. Park. Castillo de San Marcos, St. Augustine. Everglades Natl. Park. Florida State Museum, Gainesville. Ft. Jefferson Natl. Monument. Ft. Matanzas Natl. Monument. Kennedy Space Center, Cape Canaveral. Ringling Museum, Sarasota. St. Augustine. Walt Disney World/EPCOT Center, Orlando.

Memorable events Juan Ponce de León claims Florida for Spain 1513. French stake claim for Florida 1562; build Ft. Caroline 1564. Pedro Menéndez de Avilés founds St. Augustine, first permanent European settlement in U.S. 1565. Spain cedes Florida to United States 1819. Seminole War 1835–42. State secedes from Union 1861. Readmitted 1868. Carl Fisher begins to develop Miami Beach as resort 1912. Florida's first paper mill opens expanding forest industry 1931. More than 100,000 Cuban refugees enter United States, most through Florida, during Mariel boat lift 1980. Army Corps of Engineers announce plans to let Kissimmee River, canalized in 1971, return to natural course to Lake Okeechobee; the largest back-to-nature project ever undertaken in U.S. 1990. Hurricane Andrew causes $10 billion in damage to South Florida 1992. Voting irregularities in Florida during the Presidential election lead to U.S. Supreme Court intervention 2000.

Tourist information (888) 735-2872. www.visitflorida.com

▶ GEORGIA

Georgia is diverse in its terrain, embracing the woods of the Blue Ridge Mountains to the north and the alligators of the Okefenokee Swamp in the south. Though two-thirds of the population are urban dwellers, Georgia's farms rank at or near the top in poultry production and are leading producers of pecans, cattle, hogs, and peanuts. Atlanta, the largest city in the South, elected Andrew Young the first black member of the U.S. Congress and Maynard Jackson the first black mayor from the South since Reconstruction. Today divisions linger in Georgia, the cities favoring a progressive stance and the rural areas clinging to some of the ways of the Old South. Some of those divisions came to a peaceful resolution in early 2001, when the state redesigned its flag to reduce the size and prominence of the Confederate cross.

Name For King George II of England 1732. **Nicknames** Empire State of the South, Peach State. **Capital** Atlanta. **Entered union** Jan. 2, 1788 (4th). **Motto** "Wisdom, justice, moderation."

Emblems **Bird** Brown thrasher. **Fish** Largemouth bass. **Flower** Cherokee rose. **Fossil** Shark tooth. **Gem** Quartz. **Insect** Honeybee. **Songs** "Georgia," "Georgia on My Mind." **Tree** Live oak. **Wildflower** Azalea.

Land Total area 59,425 sq. mi (24th), incl. 1,519 sq. mi. inland water. **Borders** Tenn., N.C., S.C., Atlantic Ocean, Fla., Ala. **Rivers** Altamaha, Apalachicola, Chattahoochee, Flint, Ocmulgee, Oconee, Savannah, Suwanee. **Lakes** Clark Hill, Harding, Hartwell, Seminole, Sidney Lanier, Sinclair, Walter F. George, West Point Lake. **Other notable features** Blue Ridge Mountains (Mount Enotah 4,784 ft.), Okefenokee Swamp.

Elected officials Gov. Sonny Perdue (R, term exp. 2011). Lt. Gov. Casey Cagle (R). Sec. State Karen Handel (R). Atty. Gen. Thurbert E. Baker (D).

People (July 2007 est.) 9,544,750 (9th). Race/Hispanic Origin: White 65.6%. Black 30.0%. Indian 0.3%. Asian 2.8%. Pacific Islander 0.1%. Two or more races 1.2%. Hispanic 2.8%.

Cities (2006) Atlanta 486,411. Augusta 189,366. Columbus 188,660. Savannah 127,889. Athens 111,580. Macon 93,665. Roswell 87,802. Sandy Springs 85,771. Albany 75,335. Marietta 63,152.

Business Gross State Product, 2005: $364.3 bil. (10th). **Leading Sectors of GSP (2001):** Services 20.38%; Finance, insurance, and real estate 16.33%; Manufacturing 14.50%. *Fortune 500* **Companies (2007):** 15.

Famous natives James Brown, singer. Erskine Caldwell, author. James Earl ("Jimmy") Carter, U.S. president. Ray Charles, musician. Ty Cobb, baseball player. James Dickey, poet. Martin Luther King, Jr., minister/reformer. Sidney Lanier, author. Little Richard, musician. Carson McCullers, author. Alexander McGillivray, Creek chief. Margaret Mitchell, author. Elijah Muhammad, religious leader. Flannery O'Connor, author. Burt Reynolds, actor. Jackie Robinson, baseball player. Tomochichi, Yamacraw chief. Ted Turner (b. Ohio), businessman. Joanne Woodward, actress.

Noteworthy places Chickamauga and Chattanooga Natl. Military Park. Confederate Memorial, Stone Mountain. Ft. Frederica Natl. Monument. Ft. Pulaski Natl. Monument. High Museum of Art, Atlanta. Martin Luther King Natl. Hist. Site, Atlanta. Ocmulgee Natl. Monument. Okefenokee Swamp. Savannah Historic District.

Memorable events Hernando de Soto explores region 1540. Cotton gin invented 1793. Georgia expels Cherokee Indian tribes on Trail of Tears 1832–38. Secedes from Union 1860. Gen. William T. Sherman's 60,000 troops cut 60-mi. swath and burn Atlanta to the ground in their "march to the sea" 1864. Formula for Coca-Cola developed by chemist in search of hangover cure 1886. Cyclone kills 1,000 in Charleston, S.C., and Savannah 1893. Franklin D. Roosevelt dies at the Little White House, Warm Springs 1945. First state to give vote to 18-year-olds 1948. Emory University designated to receive $100-million gift from Robert W. Woodruff 1979. Dept. of Justice rules that state's process for electing superior court judges violates 1965 Voting Rights Act 1990. Summer Olympics held in Atlanta 1996.

Tourist information (800) VISIT-GA. www.exploregeorgia.org

►HAWAII

What the air conditioner did for the Sunbelt, the jetliner has done for Hawaii. Affordable air travel has made Hawaii one of the country's most popular vacation and honeymoon spots in the five decades since it entered the Union. Tourism is Hawaii's key industry, attracting more than 6.5 million visitors to the state each year. Recent economic problems in Japan have had a negative effect on Hawaii's tourism numbers, and the state economy has suffered greatly as a result. Thousands of miles from both California and mainland Asia, Hawaii was originally peopled by Polynesian seafarers around A.D. 500 and has the richest ethnic mix of any state, with the lowest percentage of whites and highest percentages of Asians. It was partly fear of this diversity that stalled its statehood. A link between the United States and Asia, Hawaii is the center of U.S. defense in the Pacific and is home to 100,000 veterans, three-quarters of them veterans of Vietnam. Hawaii produces large quantities of pineapples and sugar cane, and efforts are under way to harness thermal electric power from Mauna Loa volcano.

Name Of unknown origin, perhaps from Hawaii Loa, traditional discoverer of islands, or from Hawaiki, the traditional Polynesian homeland. **Nicknames** Aloha State, Paradise of the Pacific. **Capital** Honolulu. **Entered union** Aug. 21, 1959 (50th). **Motto** *Ua mau ke ea o ka aina i ke pono* (The life of the land is perpetuated in righteousness). **Emblems** **Bird** Nene (Hawaiian goose). **Fish** Humuhumunukunukuapuaa (reef triggerfish). **Flower** Pua aloalo (hibiscus). **Song** "Hawaii Ponoi." **Tree** Kukui (candlenut).

Land Total area 10,931 sq. mi (43rd), incl. 4,508 sq. mi. inland water. Surrounded by Pacific Ocean. **Rivers** Kaukonahua Stream, Wailuku Stream. **Lakes** Halulu, Kolekole, Salt Lake, Waiia Res. **Other notable features** Pearl Harbor. Hualalai, Kilauea, Mauna Kea (13,796 ft.), and Mauna Loa volcanoes. **Main islands** Hawaii, Kauai, Lanai, Maui, Molokai, Oahu.

Elected officials Gov. Linda Lingle (R, term exp. 2006). Lt. Gov/Sec. State, James Aiona, Jr. (R). Atty. Gen. Mark Bennett (R).

People (July 2007 est.) 1,283,388 (42nd). Race/Hispanic Origin: White 29.1%. Black 2.9%. Indian 0.5%. Asian 39.9%. Pacific Islander 8.9%. Two or more races 18.6%. Hispanic 8.2%.

Cities (2006) Honolulu 377,357. (2000) Hilo 40,759. Kailua 36,513. Kaneohe 34,970. Waipahu 33,108. Pearl City 30,976. Waimalu 29,371. Mililani Town 28,608. Kahului 20,146. Kihei 16,749. (The Census Bureau does not update counts for Hawaiian cities other than Honolulu between decennial censuses because most are not incorporated.)

Business Gross State Product, 2005: $53.7 bil. (40th). **Leading Sectors of GSP (2001):** Finance, insurance, and real estate 23.01%; Services 22.92%; Government 21.51%. *Fortune 500* **Companies (2007):** 0.

Famous natives Bernice P. Bishop, philanthropist. Sanford B. Dole, statehood advocate. Charlotte (b. Ohio) and Luther Halsey Gulick, Camp Fire Girls founders. Don Ho, singer. Daniel J. Inouye, politician. Duke Kahanamoku, swimmer. Victoria Kaiulani, last heiress presumptive to Hawaiian throne. Kamehameha I, king. Kamehameha III, king. Liliuokalani, queen. Bette Midler, singer.

Noteworthy places Bernice P. Bishop Museum, Honolulu. Diamond Head. Haleakala Natl. Park, Maui. Hawaii Volcanoes Natl. Park (Kilauea and Mauna Loa), Hawaii. Iolani Palace, Honolulu. Kaloko-Honokohau Natl. Hist. Park, Molokai. Natl. Cemetery of the Pacific and USS *Arizona* Memorial. Polynesian Cultural Center, Laiea. Pu'uhonua o Honaunau Natl. Hist. Park, Hawaii.

Memorable events Polynesians first arrive 6th century. Second wave of Polynesians arrive 10th century. Captain James Cook first European to visit islands 1778; killed on Hawaii 1779. Sugar production begins 1835. Land reform ends feudal system 1848. Monarchy rule ends in revolution

1893. Becomes U.S. Territory 1900. Japanese attack Pearl Harbor 1941. Statehood 1959.
Tourist information (800) GOHAWAII. www.gohawaii.com

▶**IDAHO**
Home to some of the most isolated and rugged country in the United States, Idaho's diversified economy has traditionally been based on lumber and potatoes (more than 13 billion pounds in 1993). In the 1980s these were augmented by a number of small high-tech industries fleeing the high cost of business in California. During the 1990s the population grew rapidly (20 percent by 1997).
Name Means "gem of the mountains." **Nickname** Gem State. **Capital** Boise. **Entered union** July 3, 1890 (43rd). **Motto** *Esto perpetua* (May it last forever).
Emblems **Bird** Mountain bluebird. **Flower** Syringa. **Gem** Star garnet. **Horse** Appaloosa. **Song** "Here We Have Idaho." **Tree** Western white pine.
Land **Total area** 83,570 sq. mi (14th), incl. 823 sq. mi. inland water. **Borders** British Columbia, Mont., Wyo., Utah, Nev., Oreg., Wash. **Rivers** Bear, Clearwater, Payette, Salmon, Snake. **Lakes** American Falls Res., Coeur d'Alene, Pend Oreille. **Mountains** Bitterroot Range, Centennial, Clearwater, Salmon River, Sawtooth Range (Castle Peak 11,820 ft.), Wasatch Range. **Other notable features** Grand Canyon of the Snake River.
Elected officials Gov. Butch Otter (R). Lt. Gov. Jim Risch (R). Sec. State Ben Ysursa (R). Atty. Gen. Lawrence Wasden (R).
People (July 2007 est.) 1,499,402 (39th). Race/Hispanic Origin: White 94.8%. Black 0.9%. Indian 1.4%. Asian 1.2%. Pacific Islander 0.1%. Two or more races 1.6%. Hispanic 9.8%.
Cities (2006) Boise City 198,638. Nampa 76,587. Meridian 59,832. Pocatello 53,932. Idaho Falls 52,786. Coeur d'Alene 41,328. Twin Falls 40,380. Caldwell 37,056. Lewiston 31,293. Rexburg 26,657.
Business **Gross State Product, 2005:** $47.2 bil. (42nd). **Leading Sectors of GSP (2001):** Services 17.98%; Manufacturing 17.80%; Government 14.08%. *Fortune 500* **Companies (2007):** 2.
Famous natives Joseph, Nez Percé chief. Ezra Taft Benson, politician. Gutzon Borglum, sculptor. Frank Church, politician. Ezra Pound, poet. Harmon Killebrew, baseball player. Jerry Kramer, football player. Sacagawea (Bird Woman), Shoshone interpreter. Lana Turner, actress.
Noteworthy places Craters of the Moons Natl. Monument. Hell's Canyon Natl. Recreation Area. Nez Percé Natl. Hist. Park. Sawtooth Natl. Recreation Area. Sun Valley ski resort. Yellowstone Natl. Park.
Memorable events Lewis and Clark expedition 1805. Becomes part of U.S. when Idaho Treaty concluded with Britain 1846. Gold Rush 1860. Nez Percé War 1877. Statehood 1890. World's first breeder reactor built at Idaho Falls, 1951. Snake River opened to navigation, linking Lewiston to Pacific Ocean at Astoria, Oregon 1975. New Teton River Dam collapses as it is being filled for first time; 10 dead, $400 million in damage 1976.
Tourist information (800) 635-7820. www.idaho.gov

▶**ILLINOIS**
The Illinois economy is enormously productive and diverse. While Chicago is a leader in world finance and trade, the southern part of the state has rich farmlands (the state is second to Iowa in corn and soybean exports) and mineral deposits (both coal and gas—there are especially rich coal deposits in the southeast region around Cairo, known as Little Egypt). Manufacturing centers on Chicago, Rockford—the state's second-largest city—and Springfield, the capital. Chicago is also a major transportation hub with extensive rail networks, an international port serving ships from both the Atlantic and Gulf of Mexico, and the largest airport in the country.
Name Corruption of *iliniwek* ("tribe of the superior men"), natives of region at time of earliest French explorations. **Nickname** Prairie State. **Capital** Springfield. **Entered union** Dec. 3, 1818 (21st). **Motto** "State sovereignty—national unity." **Slogan** "Land of Lincoln."
Emblems **Animal** White-tailed deer. **Bird** Cardinal. **Flower** Violet. **Insect** Monarch butterfly. **Mineral** Fluorite. **Song** "Illinois." **Tree** White oak.
Land **Total area** 57,914 sq. mi (25th), incl. 2,331 sq. mi. inland water. **Borders** Wis., Lake Michigan, Ind., Ky., Mo., Iowa. **Rivers** Fox, Illinois, Illinois Waterway, Kankakee, Kaskaskia, Mississippi, Ohio, Rock, Vermillion, Wabash. **Lakes** Carlyle, Crab Orchard. **Other notable features** Charles Mound (1,235 ft.), Little Egypt.
Elected officials Gov. Rod Blagojevich (D, term exp. 2011). Lt. Gov. Pat Quinn (D). Sec. State Jesse White (D). Atty. Gen. Lisa Madigan (D).
People (July 2007 est.) 12,852,548 (5th). Race/Hispanic Origin: White 79.2%. Black 15.0%. Indian 0.3%. Asian 4.3%. Pacific Islander 0.1%. Two or more races 1.2%. Hispanic 14.9%.
Cities (2006) Chicago 2,833,321. Aurora 170,617. Rockford 155,138. Naperville 142,901. Joliet 142,702. Springfield 116,482. Peoria 113,107. Elgin 101,903. Waukegan 92,066. Cicero 81,823.
Business **Gross State Product, 2005:** $560.2 bil. (5th). **Leading Sectors of GSP (2001):** Services 22.73%; Finance, insurance, and real estate 22.10%; Manufacturing 14.37%. *Fortune 500* **Companies (2007):** 33.
Famous natives Jane Addams, reformer (Nobel Peace Prize, 1930). Ernie Banks, baseball player. Saul Bellow, author (Nobel Prize, 1976). Harry A. Blackmun, jurist. Ray Bradbury, author. Gwendolyn Brooks, poet. William Jennings Bryan, politician. Edgar Rice Burroughs, novelist. St. Frances Xavier Cabrini (b. Italy). Clarence Darrow, lawyer. Miles Davis, musician. John Dos Passos, novelist. Enrico Fermi (b. Italy), nuclear physicist (Nobel Prize, 1938). Robert Louis ("Bob") Fosse, choreographer. Milton Friedman, economist (Nobel Prize, 1976). Benny Goodman, musician. Ernest Hemingway, novelist. Charlton Heston, actor. William Holden, actor. Abraham Lincoln, U.S. President (b. Kentucky). Vachel Lindsay, poet. Archibald MacLeish, poet. Ludwig Mies van der Rohe (b. Germany), architect. Charles W. Post, cereal manufacturer. Ronald Reagan, U.S. president. Carl Sandburg, poet. Albert G. Spalding, merchant. John Paul Stevens, jurist. Gloria Swanson, actress.
Noteworthy places Art Institute of Chicago. Crab Orchard Wildlife Refuge. Dickson Mounds Museum, Lewistown. Field Museum of Natural History, Chicago. Ft. Chartres. Ft. Kaskaskia. Ft. Massac. Frank Lloyd Wright Historic District, Oak Park. Illinois State Museum, Springfield. Lincoln Home Natl. Hist. Park, Springfield. Mormon Settlement, Nauvoo. Morton Arboretum, Lisle. Museum of Science and Industry, Chicago. Shawnee Natl. Forest. Starved Rock State Park.

Memorable events French missionaries Jacques Marquette and Louis Jolliet explore Illinois 1673. Cahokia first European settlement 1699. Territory to England after French and Indian War 1763. Chicago founded by Jean-Baptiste Point du Sable 1779. Illinois and Michigan Canal links Lake Michigan and Mississippi River 1848. Lincoln-Douglas Debates at Springfield 1860. Half of Chicago destroyed by great fire 1871. Terrorist bombing kills nine and wounds 130 in Haymarket affair, Chicago 1886. Columbia Exposition, Chicago 1893. First successful nuclear chain reaction created at University of Chicago 1942. Argonne National Lab develops first nuclear power generating system in U.S. 1957. Riots at Democratic National Convention in Chicago 1968. Sears Tower, world's tallest building at time (1,454 ft.), completed in Chicago 1973. Mississippi and Illinois rivers flood causing $1.5 billion in damage 1993. **Tourist information** (800) 2-CONNECT. www.enjoyillinois.com

▶**INDIANA**
Indiana is strong in both farms and manufacturing. Its southern half has large coal deposits and produces most of the limestone quarried in the United States. To the north the fertile land helps make Indiana one of the primary farm-belt states. Indiana is also very much a part of the industrial Midwest, where unemployment is always a threat, especially in the heavily industrial areas of Gary and Indianapolis (the latter of which developed into a center for high-tech industries through the 1980s and 1990s). These geographic divisions have parallels in the political history of the state, which during the Civil War was Union in the north and Confederate in the south.

Name For the land of Indians by early settlers, who found many distinct tribes living in region. **Nickname** Hoosier State. **Capital** Indianapolis. **Entered union** Dec. 11, 1816 (19th). **Motto** "The Crossroads of America."
Emblems **Bird** Cardinal. **Flower** Peony. **Poem** "Indiana." **Song** "On the Banks of the Wabash, Far Away." **Stone** Indiana limestone. **Tree** Tulip tree.
Land Total area 36,418 sq. mi (38th), incl. 551 sq. mi. inland water. **Borders** Lake Michigan, Mich., Ohio, Ky., Ill. **Rivers** Kankakee, Ohio, Tippecanoe, Wabash, White, Whitewater. **Lakes** Freeman, Shafer.
Elected officials Gov. Mitch Daniels (R, term exp. 2009). Lt. Gov. Becky Skillman (R). Sec. State Todd Rokita (R). Atty. Gen. Stephen Carter (D).
People (July 2007 est.) 6,345,289 (14th). Race/Hispanic Origin: White 88.1%. Black 9.0%. Indian 0.3%. Asian 1.4%. Two or more races 1.1%. Hispanic 5.0%.
Cities (2006) Indianapolis 785,597. Fort Wayne 248,637. Evansville 115,738. South Bend 104,905. Gary 97,715. Hammond 78,292. Bloomington 69,247. Muncie 65,287. Fishers 61,840. Lafayette 61,244.
Business Gross State Product, 2005: $238.6 bil. (16th). **Leading Sectors of GSP (2001):** Manufacturing 27.19%; Durable Goods 18.94%; Services 18.06%. *Fortune 500* Companies (2007): 5.
Famous natives Larry Bird, basketball player. Hoagy Carmichael, composer. Eugene V. Debs, politician/organizer. Theodore Dreiser, author. Benjamin Harrison, U.S. president. Jimmy Hoffa, union leader. Michael Jackson, singer. David Letterman, comedian. Carole Lombard, actress. Cole Porter, composer. Ernie Pyle, journalist. Knute Rockne (b. Norway), football coach. Paul Samuelson, economist (Nobel Prize, 1960). Booth Tarkington, author. Kurt Vonnegut, author. Wendell L. Willkie, politician. Wilbur Wright, aviator.
Noteworthy places Ernie Pyle birthplace, Dana. George Rogers Clark Natl. Hist. Park, Vincennes. Benjamin Harrison home, Indianapolis. Hoosier Natl. Forest. Indiana Dunes Natl. Lakeshore. Indianapolis Motor Speedway and Museum. Indianapolis Museum of Art. New Harmony village. Notre Dame Univ., South Bend. Old state capital, Corydon. Wilbur Wright State Memorial, Millville. Wyandotte Cave. Tippecanoe sites.
Memorable events Mound Builders present c. A.D. 1000. René-Robert Cavelier de La Salle explores for French 1679–87. French near Vincennes from c. 1700. French cede territory to British 1763. Gen. Ambrose Clark captures Ft. Vincennes 1779. Territory ceded to U.S. 1783; included in Northwest Territory 1787. Miamis defeat U.S. twice in 1790. Gen. Anthony Wayne defeats Miamis at Battle of Fallen Timbers 1794. Territory included in Indiana Territory 1800. Gen. William Henry Harrison defeats Tecumseh's Indian Confederation at Tippecanoe 1811. Statehood 1816. Studebaker wagon company founded in South Bend 1852. U.S. Steel establishes mill at company-built town of Gary 1906. First Indianapolis 500 run 1911. Only a dozen companies producing cars, down from a pre-World War I peak of 375, 1920. Studebaker, last Indiana-based car maker, closes 1963. **Tourist information** (888) ENJOYIN. www.in.gov/enjoyindana.com

▶**IOWA**
Iowa lies between the two great rivers of the central United States, the Mississippi and the Missouri, with a quarter of the nation's richest and deepest topsoil. Iowa's farmers lead the country in the production of corn, and Iowa is also a big producer of hogs, cattle, and other livestock. With about 75 percent of Iowans employed in agriculture-related industries and 90 percent of the land farmed, Iowa can be deeply affected by natural disasters such as droughts and floods. Yet more than 100 *Fortune 500* Companies have production facilities in this farm state. Industrial production has risen since World War II. Iowans send abroad a quarter of the food they produce.

Name For Iowa tribe. **Nickname** Hawkeye State. **Capital** Des Moines. **Entered union** Dec. 28, 1846 (29th). **Motto** "Our liberties we prize and our rights we will maintain."
Emblems **Bird** Eastern goldfinch. **Flower** Wild rose. **Song** "The Song of Iowa." **Stone** Geode. **Tree** Oak.
Land Total area 56,272 sq. mi (26th), incl. 402 sq. mi. inland water. **Borders** Minn., Wis., Ill., Mo., Nebr., S.Dak. **Rivers** Big Sioux, Des Moines, Mississippi, Missouri. **Lakes** Okoboji, Rathburn Res., Red Rock, Saylorville Res., Spirit, Storm. **Other notable features** Ocheyedan Mound (1,675 ft.).
Elected officials Gov. Chet Culver (D, term exp. 2011). Lt. Gov. Patty Judge (D). Sec. State Michael Mauro (D). Atty. Gen. Thomas J. Miller (D).
People (July 2007 est.) 2,988,046 (30th). Race/Hispanic Origin: White 94.4%. Black 2.6%. Indian 0.4%. Asian 1.6%. Two or more races 1.0%. Hispanic 4.0%.
Cities (2006) Des Moines 193,886. Cedar Rapids 124,417. Davenport 99,514. Sioux City 83,262. Waterloo 65,998. Iowa City 62,649. Council Bluffs 60,271. Dubuque 57,696. West Des Moines 53,945. Ames 51,557.

Business   **Gross State Product, 2005:** $114.3 bil. (30th). **Leading Sectors of GSP (2001):** Manufacturing 21.02%; Services 17.82%; Finance, insurance, and real estate 16.05%. *Fortune 500* **Companies (2007):** 1.

Famous natives   Norman E. Borlaug, agronomist (Nobel Peace Prize, 1970). William F. "Buffalo Bill" Cody, scout/showman. George Gallup, pollster. Josiah B. Grinnell (b. Vt.), abolitionist. Herbert Hoover, U.S. president. Harry L. Hopkins, politician. John L. Lewis, labor leader. John R. Mott, religious leader. Billy Sunday, baseball player/evangelist. John Wayne, actor. Meredith Wilson, composer. Grant Wood, painter.

Noteworthy places   Amana Colonies. Davenport Art Gallery. Des Moines Art Center. Effigy Mounds Natl. Monument, Marquette. Ft. Dodge Hist. Museum. Herbert Hoover birthplace and library, West Branch. Natl. Rivers Hall of Fame, Dubuque. Putnam Museum, Davenport.

Memorable events   Mound Builders present c. A.D. 1000. Jacques Marquette and Louis Jolliet claim land for France 1673. Part of Louisiana Purchase 1803. Part of Missouri Territory 1812–21. Black Hawk Wars 1832, 1834–37. First permanent settlement at Dubuque 1833. Organized as Iowa Territory (incl. parts of Minnesota, North Dakota, and South Dakota) 1838. Statehood 1846. Capital moved from Iowa City to Des Moines 1857. Fifty percent of Iowa's farms foreclosed during depression 1929–35. Iowa's urban population exceeds rural for first time 1960. Population loss of 7.9 percent in the 1980s. Floods cause $2.2 billion in damage 1993 and struck again in 2008.

Tourist information   (800) 345-IOWA. www.traveliowa.com

▶KANSAS

Kansas burst on the American scene as the territory called Bleeding Kansas, seething with conflict over the spread of slavery. Victorious New England abolitionists imprinted the state with the Puritan ethic. They were early supporters of prohibition, partly to discourage foreign newcomers. Kansas suffered enormously during the Great Depression and "Dust Bowl" days of the 1930's but rebounded strongly during the war. Wichita's aircraft industries, vital to the war effort, helped the Kansas economy to remain strong in the postwar years as family farming declined dramatically. Today Kansas remains a primary producer of wheat, cattle, and other agricultural products. Its manufacturing base still includes extensive aircraft industries, and it leads the states in the production of helium. The geographic center of the lower 48 U.S. states is near Lebanon.

Name   For Kansa or Kaw, "people of the south wind." **Nickname** Sunflower State. **Capital** Topeka. **Entered union** Jan. 29, 1861 (34th). **Motto** *Ad astra per aspera* (To the stars through adversity).

Emblems   **Animal** American buffalo. **Bird** Western meadowlark. **Flower** Wild native sunflower. **March** "The Kansas March." **Song** "Home on the Range."

Land   **Total area** 82,277 sq. mi (15th), incl. 462 sq. mi. inland water. **Borders** Nebr., Mo., Okla., Colo. **Rivers** Arkansas, Kansas, Missouri, Republican, Saline, Smoky Hill, Solomon. **Lakes** Kanapolis, Malvern, Perry, Pomona, Tuttle Creek, Waconda. **Other notable features** Flint Hills.

Elected officials   Gov. Kathleen Sebelius (D, term exp. 2010). Lt. Gov. Mark Parkinson (D). Sec. State Ron Thornburgh (R). Atty. Gen. Stephen Six (D).

People   (July 2007 est.) 2,775,997 (33rd). Race/Hispanic Origin: White 88.9%. Black 6.1%. Indian 1.0%. Asian 2.2%. Pacific Islander 0.1%. Two or more races 1.8%. Hispanic 8.8%.

Cities   (2004) Wichita 357,698. Overland Park 166,722. Kansas City 143,801. Topeka 122,113. Olathe 114,662. Lawrence 88,605. Shawnee 59,252. Manhattan 50,737. Salina 46,140. Lenexa 44,520.

Business   **Gross State Product, 2005:** $105.4 bil. (32nd). **Leading Sectors of GSP (2001):** Services 17.81%; Manufacturing 16.12%; Government 13.77%. *Fortune 500* **Companies (2007):** 1.

Famous natives   "Buffalo Bill" Cody. Walter Chrysler, carmaker. Robert Dole, politician. Amelia Earhart, aviator. Dwight David Eisenhower (b. Tex.), general/U.S. president. Dennis Hopper, actor. William Inge, playwright. Nancy Landon Kassebaum, politician. Alf Landon, politician. Edgar Lee Masters, poet. James Naismith, inventor of basketball. Carrie Nation (b. Ky.), prohibitionist. Charlie "Bird" Parker, musician. Damon Runyon, writer. Gale Sayers, football player. William Allen White, the Sage of Emporia, editor.

Noteworthy places   Agricultural Hall of Fame, Kansas City. Dodge City. Eisenhower Center, Abilene. Ft. Larned. Ft. Leavenworth. Ft. Riley. Ft. Scott. John Brown's Cabin, Osawatomie. Kansas Cosmosphere and Space Discovery Center, Hutchinson. Kansas State Historical Society Museum, Topeka. Wichita Art Museum.

Memorable events   First major expedition to region under Francisco Vásquez de Coronado 1540–41. La Salle claims territory including Kansas for France 1682. Part of Louisiana Purchase 1803. Area visited by Meriwether Lewis and George Rogers Clark (1803), Zebulon Pike (1806), and Stephen H. Long (1819). Santa Fe Trail crosses Kansas 1821. Fts. Leavenworth (1827), Scott (1842), and Riley (1853) established to protect pioneers on Santa Fe and Oregon trails. Organized as Territory by Kansas-Nebraska Act 1854, which repealed Missouri Compromise of 1820. "Bleeding Kansas" scene of free vs. slave rivalry 1854–56. Statehood 1861. Introduction of winter wheat makes Kansas leading U.S. wheat producer 1870. Airplane manufacturing starts in Wichita 1919. World-famous Menninger Foundation for mental health founded 1919. "Dust Bowl" drought drives thousands of farmers off the land, especially in western Kansas, 1934–35. Murder of Clutter family by Richard E. Hickock and Perry E. Smith at Holcomb (later the subject of Truman Capote's *In Cold Blood*) 1959.

Tourist information   (800) 252-6727. www.travelks.org

▶KENTUCKY, COMMONWEALTH OF

First pioneered by English immigrants in the mid-17th century, Kentucky's golden age as a choice frontier destination in the early 1800s was brought to an end by the Civil War. During the Civil War, the Bluegrass gentry supported the Confederacy, while the Appalachian backwoodsmen enlisted in the Union Army. Many took advantage of their uniforms to settle old accounts, and the social order was often threatened before the turn of the century. Though the state is known today for its bourbon and horse breeding, many Kentuckians make their living from the land as tobacco farmers or coal miners. The Appalachian part of the state in the east delivers about 20 percent of the nation's coal, but its economic problems remain acute, despite vast expenditures during the "war on poverty."

Name Corruption of the Iroquois *kenta-ke* (meadow land) or Wyandot *kuh-ten-tah-teh* (land of tomorrow). **Nickname** Bluegrass State. **Capital** Frankfort. **Entered union** June 1, 1792 (15th). **Motto** "United we stand, divided we fall." **Emblems   Bird** Cardinal. **Colors** Blue and gold. **Fish** Bass. **Flower** Goldenrod. **Song** "My Old Kentucky Home." **Tree** Tulip poplar. **Wild animal** Gray squirrel.
Land   Total area 40,409 sq. mi (37th), incl. 681 sq. mi. inland water. **Borders** Ind., Ohio, W.Va., Va., Tenn., Mo., Ill. **Rivers** Cumberland, Kentucky, Licking, Ohio, Tennessee. **Lakes** Barkley, Barren River Res., Dewey, Grayson Res., Laurel Res., Nolin Res., Rough Res. **Mountains** Appalachian (Black Mt. 4,145 ft.), Cumberland. **Other notable features** Tennessee Valley.
Elected officials   Gov. Steve Beshear (D, term exp. 2011). Lt. Gov. Daniel Mongiardo (D). Sec. State Trey Grayson (R). Atty. Gen. Jack Conway (D).
People   (July 2007 est.) 4,241,474 (26th). Race/Hispanic Origin: White 90.0%. Black 7.7%. Indian 0.2%. Asian 1.0%. Two or more races 1.0%. Hispanic 2.2%.
Cities   (2006) Louisville 554,496. Lexington 270,789. Owensboro 55,525. Bowling Green 53,176. Covington 42,797. Richmond 31,431. Hopkinsville 27,415. Henderson 27,915. Frankfort 27,077. Florence 26,929.
Business   Gross State Product, 2005: $140.4 bil. (27th). **Leading Sectors of GSP (2001):** Manufacturing 25.19%; Services 16.70%; Durable Goods 15.79%. *Fortune 500* **Companies (2007):** 6.
Famous natives   Muhammad Ali, boxer. Alben W. Barkley, politician. Daniel Boone (b. Pa.), frontiersman. Louis D. Brandeis, jurist. Kit Carson, frontiersman. Henry Clay, politician. Jefferson Davis, president of Confederate States of America. D.W. Griffith, director. John Marshall Harlan, jurist. Abraham Lincoln, U.S. president. Col. Harland Sanders, entrepreneur. Frederick M. Vinson, jurist. Robert Penn Warren, author.
Noteworthy places   Abraham Lincoln birthplace, Hodgenville. Churchill Downs, Louisville. George S. Patton, Jr. Military Museum, Fort Knox. J.B. Speed Art Museum, Louisville. Land Between the Lakes Natl. Rec. Area. Mammoth Cave Natl. Park. My Old Kentucky Home, Bardstown. Old Ft. Harrod State Park.
Memorable events   English enter territory through Cumberland Gap 1750. Territory included in area ceded by French 1763. Daniel Boone leads expeditions into region 1769. First settlement Harrodsburg 1774. Daniel Boone blazes Wilderness Trail through Cumberland Gap, establishes Ft. Boonesborough 1775. Organized as a county of Virginia 1776. British support Indian resistance ("Dark and Bloody Wars") until George Rogers Clark captures British forts in Indiana and Illinois 1778. Included as part of United States after Revolution 1783. Virginia approves separate statehood, achieved 1792. First steamboat reaches Louisville from New Orleans 1815. Invaded by Confederate armies 1862. Kentucky Derby first run at Louisville 1875. State has highest per capita income of southern states 1900; ranks last among all 48 states in per capita income 1940. Farm population decreases by 76%, and total number of farms by 53%, 1945–80.
Tourist information   (800) 225-TRIP or (800) 255-PARK.
www.kytourism.com

▶ LOUISIANA

European influences and ethnic diversity distinguish Louisiana from the rest of the nation. When Louisiana entered the Union in 1812, it brought with it a French legal system and a bilingualism that still survive. African-Americans, Cajuns and Creoles have contributed to its distinctive music and cuisine. The state has rich farmland, more oil and gas reserves than any other state but Texas, and in New Orleans an international port that serves the most extensive river system in North America.

The "devil's bargain" with the petrochemical industry struck by charismatic populist governor Huey Long (assassinated in 1935) brought needed jobs to the state. But the environmental impact of 100 loosely regulated petrochemical plants on the Mississippi River between New Orleans and Baton Rouge is being assessed only now. The state's reliance on the petroleum industry led to massive unemployment after a drop in oil prices in the 1980s. Tourism, especially in New Orleans, helped to diversify the economy, but the devastating hurricanes of 2005 created new challenges.
Name For King Louis XIV. **Nickname** Pelican State. **Capital** Baton Rouge. **Entered union** Apr. 30, 1812 (18th). **Motto** "Union, justice, confidence."
Emblems   Bird Eastern brown pelican. **Colors** Gold, white, and blue. **Crustacean** Crawfish. **Dog** Catahoula leopard. **Flower** Magnolia. **Fossil** Petrified palmwood. **Gem** Agate. **Insect** Honeybee. **Songs** "Give Me Louisiana," "You Are My Sunshine." **Tree** Bald cypress.
Land   Total area 51,840 sq. mi (31st), incl. 8,278 sq. mi. inland water. **Borders** Ark., Miss., Gulf of Mexico, Tex. **Rivers** Atchafalaya, Mississippi, Ouachita, Pearl, Red, Sabine. **Lakes** Bistineau, Borgne, Caddo, Catahoula, Grand, Maurepas, Pontchartrain, Salvador, White. **Other notable features** Bayou Barataria, Bayou Bodcau, Bayou D'Arbonne, Driskill Mt. (535 ft.).
Elected officials   Gov. Bobby Jindal (R, term exp. 2012). Lt. Gov. Mitch Landrieu (D). Sec. State Jay Dardenne (R). Atty. Gen. Buddy Caldwell (D).
People   (July 2007 est.) 4,293,204 (25th). Race/Hispanic Origin: White 65.1%. Black 31.9%. Indian 0.6%. Asian 1.4%. Two or more races 0.9%. Hispanic 3.2%.
Cities ·(2006) Baton Rouge 229,553. New Orleans 223,388. Shreveport 200,199. Metairie 130,000. Lafayette 114,214. Lake Charles 70,224. Kenner 66,592. Bossier City 61,306. Monroe 51,555. Alexandria 45,836.
Business   Gross State Product, 2005: $166.3 bil. (24th). **Leading Sectors of GSP (2001):** Mining 28.11%; Oil and gas extraction 18.77%; Services 16.82%. *Fortune 500* **Companies (2007):** 3.
Famous natives   Louis "Satchmo" Armstrong, jazz musician. Pierre Beauregard, Confederate general. Terry Bradshaw, football player. Braxton Bragg, Confederate general. Truman Capote, author. Clyde Cessna, aviator. Michael DeBakey, surgeon. Fats Domino, singer. Lillian Hellman, author. Mahalia Jackson, singer. Jean Baptiste Le Moyne, sieur de Bienville (b. Canada), founded New Orleans. Jerry Lee Lewis, singer. Huey P. Long, senator. Ferdinand Joseph La Menthe "Jelly Roll" Morton, musician. Leonidas K. Polk, clergyman/Confederate general. Henry Miller Shreve (b. NJ), riverboat captain. Edward D. White, Jr., jurist.
Noteworthy places   Avery Island. Cabildo, New Orleans. French Quarter, New Orleans. Garden District, New Orleans. Hodges Gardens, Natchitoches. Jean Lafitte Natl. Hist. Park, Chalmette. Kent House Museum, Alexandria. Longfellow-Evangeline State Commemorative Area, St.

Martinsville. Louisiana Maritime Museum, Baton Rouge. New Orleans Museum of Art.

Memorable events Area first visited by Alonso Alvarez de Piñeda 1519. Claimed by René-Robert Cavelier de La Salle for France 1682. New Orleans founded 1718. French crown colony 1731. Four thousand Acadians (Cajuns) from Nova Scotia forcibly transported by British to Louisiana and settled in Bayou Teche 1755. Lands west of Mississippi given to Spain for help in French and Indian War 1763. Lands east of Mississippi ceded to Britain 1763. Same lands retroceded to France 1800. Jefferson negotiates Louisiana Purchase; U.S. acquires 885,000 sq. mi. for $15 million 1803. Statehood 1812. Andrew Jackson beats British at Battle of New Orleans 1815. State secedes 1861. Surrenders to Union forces 1862. Readmitted to Union 1868. Petroleum discovered 1901. Huey "The Kingfish" Long elected to Senate 1928; assassinated 1935. Racial designation law of 1970 repealed 1983. New Orleans flooded by Hurricane Katrina 2005.

Tourist information   (800) 33-GUMBO.
www.louisianatravel.com

►MAINE

Down-Easters—the original Puritans and the later French Canadians—are distinct from the New Englanders of Maine's economically stronger sister states. Their land, especially the coast, is rugged, and the living everywhere is hard. The first state to see the sunrise, Maine borders only one other state, and it preserves much of its historic isolation. More than half of the state is still unincorporated territory. Lumbering, fishing, shipbuilding and potato farming are still practiced as traditional occupations. The 18th century brought canneries, textile and shoe factories but most of those jobs have gone abroad. Maine's economy now combines light industry with tourism and the modern Maine entrepreneur—sometimes an out-of-stater—develops small businesses in keeping with Maine's independent spirit.

   Name Either for Maine in France or to distinguish mainland from islands in the Gulf of Maine. **Nickname** Pine Tree State. **Capital** Augusta. **Entered union** Mar. 15, 1820 (23rd). **Motto** *Dirigo* (I lead). **Emblems Animal** Moose. **Bird** Chickadee. **Fish** Landlocked salmon. **Flower** White pinecone and tassel. **Insect** Honeybee. **Mineral** Tourmaline. **Song** "State of Maine Song." **Tree** Eastern white pine.
Land   Total area 35,385 sq. mi (39th), incl. 4,523 sq. mi. inland water. **Borders** Quebec, New Brunswick, Atlantic Ocean; N.H. **Rivers** Allagash, Androscoggin, Aroostock, Kennebec, Machias, Penobscot, Piscataqua, Salmon Falls, St. John. **Lakes** Chamberlain, Chesuncook, Grand, Moosehead, Rangeley, Sebago. **Other notable features** Mt. Katahdin (5,268 ft.), Mt. Desert Island, Penobscot Bay.
Elected officials Gov. John Baldacci (D, term exp. 2010). Sec. State Matthew Dunlap (D). Atty. Gen. G. Steven Rowe (D).
People (July 2007 est.) 1,317,207 (40th). Race/ Hispanic Origin: White 96.5%. Black 1.0%. Indian 0.6%. Asian 0.9%. Two or more races 1.0%. Hispanic 1.2%.
Cities (2006) Portland 63,011. Lewiston 35,734. Bangor 31,008. South Portland 23,784. Auburn 23,156. Biddeford 21,889. Augusta 18,560. Saco 18,289. Westbrook 16,201. Waterville 15,639.
Business   Gross State Product, 2005: $45.1bil. (43rd). **Leading Sectors of GSP (2001):** Services 21.28%; Finance, insurance, and real estate 19.21%; Government 14.41%. *Fortune 500* Companies **(2007):** 1.

Famous natives L.L. Bean, entrepreneur. Cyrus H.K. Curtis, publisher. Hannibal Hamlin, politician. Sarah Orne Jewett, novelist. Henry Wadsworth Longfellow, poet. Stephen King, novelist. Sir Hiram and Hudson Maxim, inventors. Edna St. Vincent Millay, poet. Edmund S. Muskie, politician. John Knowles Paine, composer. Kenneth Roberts, novelist. Edward Arlington Robinson, poet. Nelson Rockefeller, politician. Marguerite Yourcenar (b. France), author.

Noteworthy places Acadia National Park, Mt. Desert Island. Allagash National Wilderness Waterway. Boothbay Railway Museum. Campobello-Longfellow House, Portland. Maine Maritime Museum, Bath. Portland Art Museum Roosevelt-Campobello Intl. Park, Campobello Island. St. Croix Island Natl. Monument.

Memorable events Vikings explore coast c. A.D. 1000. Bartholomew Gosnold sails along coast 1602. French settlers at St. Croix River 1604. Included in grant to Plymouth Company 1606. Monhegan Island and Saco settled 1622. Annexed to Massachusetts Colony 1652. French attack northern territory intermittently through 1713. Statehood 1820. Border with Canada settled 1842. First state prohibition law enacted 1851. Penobscot and Passamaquoddy tribes file claim against state for $300 million compensation for land seized in violation of 1790 Indian Non-Intercourse Act, 1972; settled for $81.5 million 1980.

Tourist information   (888) 624-6345.
www.visitmaine.com

►MARYLAND

Maryland wraps like a fishhook from the Atlantic Ocean around the fish-rich Chesapeake Bay and into the Cumberland Mountains in the northwest. Baltimore—full of urban problems but newly redeveloped with urban homesteading and shopsteading—holds the center. The suburbs of Baltimore and Washington seem far removed from the Delmarva (Delaware, Maryland, Virginia) peninsula with its watermen hanging on to an older way of life. Terrain, cultures, and history are a border state's mix of North and South. Founded as a haven for Catholics, Maryland's population is still 20 percent Catholic.

   Name For Henrietta Maria, queen consort of Charles I. **Nicknames** Old Line State, Free State. **Capital** Annapolis. **Entered union** Apr. 28, 1788 (7th). **Motto** *Fatti maschii, parole femine* (Manly deeds, womanly words).
Emblems   Bird Baltimore oriole. **Dog** Chesapeake Bay retriever. **Fish** Rockfish. **Flower** Black-eyed Susan. **Fossil** *Ecphora quadricostata* (extinct snail). **Insect** Baltimore checkerspot butterfly. **Song** "Maryland, My Maryland." **Sport** Jousting. **Tree** White oak.
Land   Total area 12,407 sq. mi (42nd), incl. 2,633 sq. mi. inland water. **Borders** Pa., Del., Atlantic Ocean, Va., D.C., W.Va. **Rivers** Chester, Choptank, Nanticoke, Patapsco, Patuxent, Pocomoke, Potomac, Susquehanna. **Other notable features** Allegheny Mts., Blue Ridge Mts., Chesapeake Bay.
Elected officials Gov. Martin O'Malley (D, term exp. 2011). Lt. Gov. Anthony G. Brown (D). Sec. State John McDonough (D). Atty. Gen. Doug Gansler (D).
People (July 2007 est.) 5,618,344 (19th). Race/ Hispanic Origin: White 63.6%. Black 29.5%. Indian 0.3%. Asian 5.0%. Pacific Islander 0.1%. Two or more races 1.6%. Hispanic 6.3%.
Cities (2006) Baltimore 651,154. Columbia 88,254. Silver Spring 76,540. Dundalk 62,306.

Wheaton-Glenmont 60,500. Ellicott City 56,397. Germantown 55,419. Bethesda 55,277. Frederick 52,816. Gaithersburg 52,455.

Business **Gross State Product, 2005:** $244.9 bil. (15th). **Leading Sectors of GSP (2001):** Services 24.89%; Finance, insurance, and real estate 21.55%; Government 17.58%. *Fortune 500* **Companies (2007):** 6.

Famous natives Russell Baker, journalist. Benjamin Banneker, surveyor. Eubie Blake, pianist. Rachel Carson, biologist/author. Stephen Decatur, navy officer. Frederick Douglass, abolitionist. Billie Holiday, singer. Johns Hopkins, financier/philanthropist. Francis Scott Key, lawyer/poet. Thurgood Marshall, jurist. H.L. Mencken, writer. Charles Willson Peale, artist. William Pinckney, statesman. James Rouse, urban planner. Babe Ruth, baseball player. Upton Sinclair, author. Roger B. Taney, jurist. Harriet Tubman, abolitionist. John Waters, filmmaker.

Noteworthy places Aberdeen Proving Ground. Antietam Natl. Battlefield, Sharpsburg. Assateague Island Natl. Seashore. Natl. Aquarium in Baltimore. Baltimore Museum of Art. Baltimore Museum of Industry. Calvert Marine Museum, Solomons. Chesapeake & Ohio Canal Natl. Hist. Park. Chesapeake Bay Maritime Museum, St. Michaels. Ft. McHenry Natl. Monument, Baltimore. Harpers Ferry Natl. Hist. Park. Liberty ship *John W. Brown*, Baltimore. Peabody Institute, Baltimore. St. Marys City. State House, Annapolis. U.S. Naval Academy, Annapolis. USS *Constellation*, Baltimore. Walters Art Gallery, Baltimore.

Memorable events John Smith explores area 1608. William Claiborne sets up trading post on Kent Island 1631. Land granted to Cecilius Calvert, Lord Baltimore, 1632. Leonard Calvert and 200 Roman Catholic settlers land on Blakistone Island 1634. Mason Dixon Line establishes northern boundary of state 1763–67; later identified as boundary between slave and nonslave states. Francis Scott Key composes "The Star Spangled Banner" after British fail to take Ft. McHenry 1814. U.S. Naval Academy founded Annapolis 1845. State under federal military control during Civil War 1861–65. First state to adopt income tax 1938. Alabama Gov. George C. Wallace shot while campaigning in Democratic presidential primary 1972.

Tourist Information   (800) MD-IS-FUN. **www.mdisfun.org.**

▶**MASSACHUSETTS, COMMONWEALTH OF**

Massachusetts is rich in the history of the early American republic. The Boston Tea Party, the "shot heard round the world" from Lexington and Concord, and the Battle of Bunker Hill are American folklore. So is the feast of Thanksgiving, first celebrated by the Puritans at Plymouth. Fishing, trade, textiles and leather industries were the backbone of Massachusetts's 19th-century economy. In the 1980s, Boston's Route 128 became the East Coast counterpart to California's Silicon Valley, with some of the nation's most advanced computer and electronic research and manufacturing. The state's "economic miracle" of the 1980s ended abruptly, and Massachusetts endured a severe downturn during the recession of the early 1990s. It recently rebounded, along with most of the nation.

A staple of the Massachusetts scene is education, in which the state is a national leader. Boston alone boasts such institutions as Harvard University (founded 1636), M.I.T., Northeastern, Brandeis, Boston University, Boston College, Wellesley and Tufts. To the west are the University of Massachusetts, Amherst, Williams, Smith and Mt. Holyoke.

Name For Massachuset tribe, whose name means "at or about the great hill." **Nickname** Bay State. **Capital** Boston. **Entered union** Feb. 6, 1788 (6th). **Motto** *Ense petit placidam sub libertate quietem* (By the sword we seek peace, but peace only under liberty).

Emblems **Beverage** Cranberry juice. **Bird** Chickadee. **Dog** Boston terrier. **Fish** Cod. **Flower** Mayflower. **Gem** Rhodonite. **Insect** Ladybug. **Mineral** Babingtonite. **Song** "All Hail to Massachusetts." **Tree** American elm.

Land Total area 10,555 sq. mi (44th), incl. 2,715 sq. mi. inland water. **Borders** Vt., N.H., Atlantic Ocean, R.I., Conn., N.Y. **Rivers** Cape Cod Canal, Connecticut, Merrimack, Taunton. **Other notable features** Buzzard's Bay, Cape Ann, Cape Cod, Cape Cod Bay, Connecticut Valley, Elizabeth Islands, Martha's Vineyard, Monomoy Island, Nantucket Island.

Elected officials Gov. Deval Patrick (D). Lt. Gov. Tim Murray (D). Sec. of Commonwealth William Francis Galvin (D). Atty. Gen. Martha Coakley (D).

People (July 2007 est.) 6,449,755 (14th). Race/Hispanic Origin: White 86.5%. Black 6.9%. Indian 0.3%. Asian 4.9%. Pacific Islander 0.1%. Two or more races 1.3%. Hispanic 8.2%.

Cities (2006) Boston 590,763. Worcester 175,454. Springfield 151,176. Lowell 103,229. Cambridge 101,365. Brockton 94,191. New Bedford 92,538. Fall River 91,474. Quincy 91,058. Lynn 87,991.

Business **Gross State Product, 2005:** $328.5 bil. (13th). **Leading Sectors of GSP (2001):** Services 27.76%; Finance, insurance, and real estate 25.67%; Real estate 14.48%. *Fortune 500* **Companies (2007):** 10.

Famous natives John Adams, U.S. president. John Quincy Adams, U.S. president. Samuel Adams, patriot. Horatio Alger, clergyman/author. Susan B. Anthony, suffragette. Clara Barton, nurse. Leonard Bernstein, composer. George Herbert Walker Bush, U.S. president. John ("Johnny Appleseed") Chapman, pioneer. Richard Cardinal Cushing, prelate. Bette Davis, actress. Emily Dickinson, poet. Ralph Waldo Emerson, author. Marshall Field, merchant. R. Buckminster Fuller, inventor/engineer. John Hancock, patriot. Oliver Wendell Holmes, jurist. Winslow Homer, painter. John F. Kennedy, U.S. president. Jack Kerouac, author. Cotton Mather, theologian. Samuel Eliot Morison, historian. Samuel Morse, inventor. Thomas P. "Tip" O'Neill, congressman. Edgar Allan Poe, poet/author. Paul Revere patriot/silversmith. Louis Sullivan, architect. Henry David Thoreau, author.

Noteworthy places Addison Gallery of American Art, Andover. Arnold Arboretum, Boston. Arthur M. Sackler Museum, Cambridge. Berkshires Museum, Pittsfield. Boston Museum of Fine Arts. Boston Natl. Hist. Park (incl. Bunker Hill, Charlestown Navy Yard, Old North Church). Busch-Reisinger Museum, Cambridge. Cape Cod Natl. Seashore. Clark Art Institute, Williamsburg. Fogg Art Museum, Boston. Gardner Art Museum, Boston. Hancock Shaker Village. Kennedy Presidential Library, Boston. Lowell Natl. Hist. Park. Minute Man Natl. Hist. Park, Lexington and Concord. Nantucket Hist. Society. Old Sturbridge Village. Peabody Museum, Salem. Plimoth Plantation, Plymouth. Tanglewood Music Festival, Lenox. *U.S.S. Constitution* ("Old Ironsides"), Charlestown. Walden Pond. Woods Hole Oceanographic Institute. Worcester Art Museum.

Memorable events Pilgrims land at Plymouth 1620. First Thanksgiving celebrated 1621. Harvard College founded 1636. Region acquires province of Maine 1652. Colonists battle Wampanoags in King Philip's War 1655–56. Boston Massacre 1770. Boston Tea Party protests taxation 1773. Battles at Lexington, Concord, and Bunker Hill 1775. Shays's Rebellion 1785–86. Maine becomes a separate state 1820. Massachusetts receives influx of Irish immigrants fleeing famine 1845. Textile workers' strike at Lawrence brings International Workers of the World (IWW) to prominence in East 1912. Cape Cod Canal completed 1914. International protest follows trial and execution of anarchists Nicola Sacco and Bartolomeo Vanzetti for robbery and murder 1920; names cleared by governor's proclamation 1970. Eleven robbers steal $2.7 million from Brink's North Terminal Garage 1950. Martha's Vineyard and Nantucket symbolically vote to secede from state 1973. **Tourist information** (800) 227-MASS. **www.massvacation.com**

▶MICHIGAN

The automobile is the commodity with which Michigan is identified, and it is the home of General Motors and Ford, the nation's two largest automakers. More than 50 percent of Michiganders live in the southeastern corner of the state, where the car industry flourishes. In the Upper Peninsula, across the Straits of Mackinac, lumber and copper have been the principal commodities from the 19th century, and the northern part of the Lower Peninsula boasts rich farmland. Michigan includes parts of four of the five Great Lakes, and it has more coastline than any state except Alaska. Michigan has an outstanding reputation in higher education, and the University of Michigan at Ann Arbor and Michigan State are helping to foster the state's high-tech industries. But Michigan's reliance on auto manufacturing makes it vulnerable to economic downturns, as well as the general contraction of the American industry.

Name From the Fox *mesikami*, "large lake." **Nicknames** Wolverine State, Lake State. **Capital** Lansing. **Entered union** Jan. 26, 1837 (26th). **Motto** *Si quaeris peninsulam amoenam circumspice* (If you are looking for a beautiful peninsula, look around you). **Emblems** **Bird** Robin. **Fish** Trout. **Flower** Apple blossom. **Gem** Chlorastrolite. **Insect** Dragonfly. **Song** "Michigan, My Michigan." **Stone** Petoskey stone. **Tree** White pine. **Land** **Total area** 96,716 sq. mi (11th), incl. 39,912 sq. mi. inland water. **Borders** Lake Superior, Ontario, Lake Huron, Lake Erie, Ohio, Ind., Lake Michigan, Wisc. **Rivers** Brule, Detroit, Kalamazoo, Menominee, Montreal, Muskegon, St. Joseph, St. Mary's. **Lakes** Burt, Higgins, Houghton, Huron, Manistique, Michigan, Mullett, St. Clair, Superior. **Other notable features** Isle Royale, Mt. Curwood (1,980 ft.), Saginaw Bay, Traverse Bay, Whitefish Bay. **Elected officials** Gov. Jennifer Granholm (D, term exp. 2011). Lt. Gov. John Cherry, Jr.(D). Sec. State Terri Lynn Land (R). Atty. Gen. Mike Cox (R). **People** (July 2007 est.) 10,071,822 (8th). Race/Hispanic Origin: White 81.2%. Black 14.3%. Indian 0.6%. Asian 2.4%. Two or more races 1.5%. Hispanic 4.0%. **Cities** (2006) Detroit 871,121. Grand Rapids 193,083. Warren 134,589. Sterling Heights 127,991. Flint 117,068. Lansing 114,276. Ann Arbor 113,206. Clinton 93,781. Livonia 96,736. Dearborn 92,382. **Business** **Gross State Product, 2005:** $377.9 bil.

(9th). **Leading Sectors of GSP (2001):** Manufacturing 23.07%; Services 20.72%; Durable goods 17.40%. *Fortune 500* **Companies (2007):** 22. **Famous natives** French explorers in region 1634. Jacques Marquette settles Sault Ste. Marie 1668. Detroit founded as French military post 1701. Region ceded to England 1763; to United States 1783. Included in Northwest Territory but British maintain control until 1796. Michigan Territory 1805. First steamboat on Great Lakes reaches Detroit 1818. Statehood 1837. First state to outlaw capital punishment 1846. Republican party organized at Jackson 1854. Canals at Sault Ste. Marie link Lakes Superior and Huron 1855. Ransom E. Olds and Henry Ford, working independently, develop gasoline-powered car 1896. United Auto Workers first to use sit-down strike successfully in contract negotiations 1935. Race riot, one of the worst in U.S. history, leaves 43 dead and $200 million in damages in Detroit 1967. Congress authorizes $1.5 billion in federal loan guarantees to bail out Chrysler Corp. 1979. **Tourist information** (888) 784-7328. **www.michigan.org**

▶MINNESOTA

A land of at least 10,000 lakes, Minnesota is a magnet for those who love the outdoors. It is also home to the largest Scandinavian populations in the United States. Originally exploited for its wealth of lumber and iron—the Mesabi Range still produces much of the nation's iron ore—Minnesota also has highly developed agribusinesses (especially dairy products), manufacturing and transportation industries. Minneapolis and St. Paul are at the north end of the Mississippi River system, and Duluth at the westernmost point of Lake Superior is the largest U.S. inland port. Minnesota has one of the best state school systems.

Name From the Sioux *minisota*, "sky-tinted waters." **Nicknames** North Star State, Gopher State, Land of 10,000 Lakes. **Capital** St. Paul. **Entered union** May 11, 1858 (32rd). **Motto** *L'étoile du nord* (Star of the north). **Emblems** **Bird** Common loon. **Beverage** Milk. **Fish** Walleye. **Flower** Pink and white lady's-slipper. **Gem** Lake Superior agate. **Grain** Wild rice. **Mushroom** Morel, or sponge mushroom. **Song** "Hail, Minnesota!." **Tree** Red pine. **Land** **Total area** 86,939 sq. mi (12th), incl. 7,329 sq. mi. inland water. **Borders** Manitoba, Ontario,

Lake Superior, Wisc., Iowa, S.Dak., N.Dak. **Rivers** Minnesota, Mississippi, Red River of the North, St. Croix. **Lakes** Itasca, Lake of the Woods, Leech, Mille Lacs, Red, Winnibigoshish. **Other notable features** Mesabi Range.

Elected officials Gov. Tim Pawlenty (R, term exp. 2011). Lt. Gov. Carol Molnau (R). Sec. State Mark Ritchie (D). Atty. Gen. Lori Swanson (D).

People (July 2007 est.) 5,197,621 (21st). Race/Hispanic Origin: White 89.3%. Black 4.5%. Indian 1.2%. Asian 3.5%. Pacific Islander 0.1%. Two or more races 1.5%. Hispanic 4.0%.

Cities (2006) Minneapolis 372,833. St. Paul 273,535. Rochester 96,975. Duluth 84,167. Bloomington 80,869. Plymouth 70,102. Brooklyn Park 69,942. Eagan 66,228. Coon Rapids 63,736. Burnsville 62,207.

Business Gross State Product, 2005: $233.0 bil. (17th). **Leading Sectors of GSP (2001):** Services 21.58%; Finance, insurance, and real estate 19.33%; Manufacturing 15.85%. *Fortune 500* **Companies (2007):** 20.

Famous natives Warren Burger, jurist. Bob Dylan, musician. F. Scott Fitzgerald, novelist. Judy Garland, actress. J. Paul Getty, businessman. Garrison Keillor, humorist. Sinclair Lewis, author (Nobel Prize, 1930). Paul Manship, sculptor. William and Charles Mayo, surgeons. Eugene McCarthy, politician. Walter F. Mondale, politician. Charles Schulz, cartoonist. Richard W. Sears, merchant.

Noteworthy places Boundary Waters Canoe Area. Grand Portage Natl. Monument. International Falls. Lake Itasca State Park (headwaters of Mississippi). Mall of America. Mayo Clinic, Rochester. Minneapolis Institute of Arts. Minnehaha Falls, Minneapolis. Minnesota Zoo, Apple Valley. Paul Bunyanland, Brainerd. Pipestone Natl. Monument. Tyrone Guthrie Theater, Minneapolis. Voyageurs Natl. Park. Walker Art Center, Minneapolis.

Memorable events Pierre Esprit Radisson and Médard Chouart des Groselliers visit area 1654–60. René-Robert de La Salle and Louis Hennepin explore upper Mississippi 1680. Daniel Greysolon, sieur de Duluth, claims region for France 1679. Area east of Mississippi to Britain 1763; to United States 1783. Western region of state as part of Louisiana Purchase 1803. Britain cedes northern strip to United States 1818. Ft. Snelling built 1820. Northern border settled by Ashburton Treaty 1842. Minnesota Territory created 1849. Statehood 1858. Sioux driven from state after uprising led by Chief Little Crow 1862. Iron ore deposits discovered in Mesabi Range 1890. Democratic party merges with Farmer-Labor party 1944. Interstate bridge collapses, killing 13 and injuring 145 in Minneapolis, 2007.

Tourist information (800) 657-3700. **www.exploreminnesota.com**

▶**MISSISSIPPI**
Mississippi's rank as the poorest state in the nation can be traced to the Civil War. Before the Civil War, Mississippi was the fifth-wealthiest state in the nation but the war cost the state 30,000 men. Plantation owners who survived the war were virtually bankrupted by the emancipation of the slaves, and Union troops under Sherman and others left widespread destruction in their wake. The increasingly harsh race-laws passed around 1900 also cost the state in the emigration of almost half a million (75 percent blacks, 25 percent whites) in the 1940s. Compounding all this was the fact that until World War II, Mississippi had virtually no urban center such as Jackson to at-

tract or sustain major industry. In race relations particularly, Mississippi has made vast improvements, and there have been substantial gains in education and the attraction of out-of-state companies, especially light industry.

Name From the Ojibwa *misi sipi*, "great river." **Nickname** Magnolia State. **Capital** Jackson. **Entered union** Dec. 10, 1817 (20th). **Motto** *Virtute et armis* (By virtue and arms).

Emblems Beverage Milk. **Bird** Mockingbird. **Fish** Largemouth or black bass. **Flower** Magnolia. **Fossil** Prehistoric whale. **Insect** Honeybee. **Mammal** White-tailed deer. **Song** "Go, Mississippi." **Stone** Petrified wood. **Tree** Magnolia. **Waterfowl** Wood duck. **Water mammal** Porpoise.

Land Total area 48,430 sq. mi (32nd), incl. 1,523 sq. mi. inland water. **Borders** Tenn., Ala., Gulf of Mexico, La., Ark. **Rivers** Big Black, Mississippi, Pearl, Tennessee, Yazoo. **Lakes** Arkabutla, Grenada, Ross Barnett Res., Sardis. **Other notable features** Pontotoc Ridge.

Elected officials Gov. Haley Barbour (R, term exp. 2012). Lt. Gov. Phil Bryant (R). Sec. State Delbert Hosemann (R). Atty. Gen. Jim Hood (D).

People (July 2007 est.) 2,918,785 (31st). Race/Hispanic Origin: White 60.7%. Black 37.2%. Indian 0.5%. Asian 0.8%. Two or more races 0.8%. Hispanic 2.1%.

Cities (2006) Jackson 176,614. Gulfport 64,316. Hattiesburg 48,012. Biloxi 44,342. Southaven 41,295. Meridian 38,200. Greenville 37,801. Tupelo 35,930. Olive Branch 29,861. Clinton 26,212.

Business Gross State Product, 2005: $81.3 bil. (35th). **Leading Sectors of GSP (2001):** Services 17.95%; Manufacturing 17.94%; Government 17.15%. *Fortune 500* **Companies (2007):** 0.

Famous natives Medgar Evers, civil rights leader. William Faulkner, novelist. Shelby Foote, historian. Jim Henson, puppeteer. B.B. King, musician. Elvis Presley, singer. Leontyne Price, opera singer. Jerry Rice, football player. John C. Stennis, politician. Conway Twitty, singer. Muddy Waters, musician. Eudora Welty, novelist. Ben Ames Williams, novelist. Tennessee Williams, playwright. Richard Wright, author.

Noteworthy places Delta Blues Museum, Clarksdale. Natchez Trace Natl. Parkway. Seafood Industry Museum, Biloxi. Tupelo Natl. Battlefield. Vicksburg Natl. Military Park.

Memorable events Hernando de Soto's expedition travels through Mississippi 1540–41. René-Robert Cavelier de La Salle claims Mississippi valley for France 1682. Pierre Le Moyne, sieur d'Iberville builds Ft. Maurepas on Biloxi Bay 1699. Natchez (Ft. Rosalie) established 1716. France cedes territory to Britain 1763. Mississippi Territory (including presentday Alabama) created 1798. Statehood (Natchez first capital) 1817. Secedes from Union; Jefferson Davis becomes president of Confederacy 1861. Siege of Vicksburg 1863. Petroleum discovered 1939. Gov. Ross R. Barnett found guilty of contempt in preventing desegregation of University of Mississippi; James H. Meredith first black enrolled at University of Mississippi 1962. Civil rights leader Medgar Evers assassinated in Jackson and buried in Arlington National Cemetery 1963. White civil rights workers James Cheney, Andrew Goodman, and Michael Schwener killed 1964.

Tourist information (800) SEE-MISS. **www.visitmississippi.org.**

▶**MISSOURI**
Missouri is remarkable for the number and variety of its neighbors—southern states (Arkansas,

Kentucky, and Tennessee), midwestern states (Illinois and Iowa), and Plains states (Oklahoma, Nebraska, and Kansas). For Missouri, geography was destiny. Still one of the country's most important inland ports, St. Louis was founded at the confluence of the Missouri and Mississippi rivers and became the gateway to the West; and Independence (now part of metropolitan Kansas City) got its start provisioning wagons for the Oregon and Santa Fe trails. The Pony Express from St. Joseph to Sacramento began in 1860, and the first attempt at airmail service was tried in St. Louis in 1911. While farming and livestock are still important to the state's economy, manufacturing, and services are now the biggest sectors.

Name From the Iliniwek *missouri*, "owner of big canoes." **Nickname** Show Me State. **Capital** Jefferson City. **Entered union** Aug. 10, 1821 (24th). **Motto** *Salus populi suprema lex esto* (The welfare of the people shall be the supreme law).
Emblems Bird Bluebird. **Flower** Hawthorne. **Insect** Honeybee. **Mineral** Galena. **Rock** Mozarkite. **Song** "Missouri Waltz." **Tree** Dogwood.
Land Total area 69,704 sq. mi. (21st), incl. 818 sq. mi. inland water. **Borders** Iowa, Ill., Ky., Tenn., Ark., Okla., Kans., Nebr. **Rivers** Des Moines, Mississippi, Missouri, Osage, St. Francis. **Lakes** Bull Shoals, Clearwater, Lake of the Ozarks, Lake of the Woods, Table, Wappapella. **Other notable features** Ozark Mts. (Taum Sauk Mt. 1,772 ft.).
Elected officials Gov. Matthew Blunt (R, term exp. 2009). Lt. Gov. Peter Kinder (R). Sec. State Robin Carnahan (D). Atty. Gen. Jay Nixon (D).
People (July 2007 est.) 5,878,415 (18th). Race/Hispanic Origin: White 85.1%. Black 11.5%. Indian 0.5%. Asian 1.5%. Pacific Islander 0.1%. Two or more races 1.4%. Hispanic 3.0%.
Cities (2006) Kansas City 447,306. St. Louis 347,181. Springfield 150,797. Independence 109,400. Columbia 94,428. Lee's Summit 81,913. St. Joseph 72,651. O'Fallon 72,477. St. Charles 63,009. St. Peters 54,839.
Business Gross State Product, 2005: $216.1bil. (22nd). **Leading Sectors of GSP (2001):** Services 21.29%; Manufacturing 16.77%; Finance, insurance, and real estate 16.34%. *Fortune 500* Companies (2007): 10.
Famous natives Thomas Hart Benton, painter. Yogi Berra, baseball player. George Caleb Bingham (b. Va.), painter. Omar Bradley, general. Adolphus Busch (b. Germany), brewer. George Washington Carver, botanist. Walter Cronkite, journalist. Walt Disney, film producer. T.S. Eliot, poet. Walker Evans, photographer. Langston Hughes, poet. Jesse James, outlaw. Marianne Moore, poet. Reinhold Niebuhr, theologian. J.C. Penny, businessman. John J. "Black Jack" Pershing, soldier. Joseph Pulitzer (b. Hungary), publisher. Ginger Rogers, dancer. Casey Stengel, baseball player. Virgil Thompson, composer. Harry S Truman, U.S. president. Mark Twain, writer. Tom Watson, golfer. Shelley Winters, actress.
Noteworthy places Churchill Memorial, Gateway Arch, St. Louis. George Washington Carver Natl. Monument, Diamond. Harry S Truman Library, Independence. Mark Twain Area, Hannibal. Nelson-Atkins Museum of Art, Kansas City. Pony Express Museum, St. Joseph. St. Louis Art Museum. Wilson's Creek Natl. Battlefield. Cahokia Mounds State Historic Site, near St. Louis.
Memorable events French miners and hunters settle at Ste. Genevieve 1735. Pierre Laclade settles St. Louis 1765. New Madrid earthquakes (8.6 on Richter scale) rock buildings as far away as Baltimore 1811-12. Statehood 1821. Missouri legislature split over secesssion: minority party adopts secession ordinance; Missouri admitted to Confederacy; majority party remains loyal to Union 1861. Jesse James killed by fellow gang member at St. Joseph 1882. Lake of the Ozarks formed after completion of Bagnell Dam on Missouri River 1931. Winston Churchill delivers "iron curtain" speech at Fulton 1952. Gateway Arch, 630 ft. high, opens at St. Louis 1964. St. Louis population declines 53 percent 1950–90. Floods cause $3 billion in damage 1993.
Tourist information (800) 877-1234. **www.visitmo.com**

▶**MONTANA**
Mountains account for only the western two-fifths of "Big Sky Country," where copper mining, lumber and tourism are the chief industries. The eastern portion of the state is part of the Great Plains, devoted to agriculture and ranching. For many years Montana was in the grip of the Anaconda Copper Mining Company, which virtually owned the state government and took most of its profits out of the state. After Anaconda's demise in the 1970's, Montana developed some of the most stringent environmental laws in the West. In recent years, many famous Hollywood stars, as well as media mogul Ted Turner, have bought large tracts of land in western Montana.

Name From Spanish *montaña*, "mountainous." **Nicknames** Treasure State, Big Sky Country. **Capital** Helena. **Entered union** Nov. 8, 1889 (41st). **Motto** *Oro y plata* (Gold and silver).
Emblems Bird Western meadowlark. **Fish** Blackspotted cutthroat trout. **Flower** Bitterroot. **Gems** Yogo sapphire, Montana agate. **Grass** Bluebunch wheatgrass. **Song** "Montana." **State ballad** "Montana Melody." **Tree** Ponderosa pine.
Land Total area 147,042 sq. mi (4th), incl. 1,490 sq. mi. inland water. **Borders** British Columbia, Alberta, Saskatchewan, N.Dak., S.Dak., Wyo., Idaho. **Rivers** Kootenai, Milk, Missouri, Musselshell, Powder, Yellowstone. **Lakes** Bighorn, Canyon Ferry, Elwell, Flathead, Ft. Peck. **Mountains** Absaroka Range, Beartooth Range (Granite Peak 12,799 ft.), Big Belt, Bitterroot Range, Centennial, Crazy, Lewis Range, Little Belt. **Other notable features** Continental Divide, Missoula Valley.
Elected officials Gov. Brian Schweitzer (D, term exp. 2009). Lt. Gov. John Bohlinger (D). Sec. State Brad Johnson (R). Atty. Gen. Mike McGrath (D).
People (July 2007 est.) 957,861 (44th). Race/Hispanic Origin: White 90.6%. Black 0.6%. Indian 6.3%. Asian 0.7%. Pacific Islander 0.1%. Two or more races 1.7%. Hispanic 2.8%.
Cities (2006) Billings 100,148. Missoula 64,081. Great Falls 56,215. Bozeman 35,061. Butte-Silver Bow 32,110. Helena 27,885. Kalispell 19,432. (2004) Havre 9,460.
Business Gross State Product, 2005: $29.9 bil. (47th). **Leading Sectors of GSP (2001):** Services 21.22%; Government 17.12%; Finance, insurance, and real estate 14.14%. *Fortune 500* Companies (2007): 0.
Famous natives Gary Cooper, actor. Marcus Daly (b. Ireland), mine owner. Chet Huntley, journalist. Myrna Loy, actress. Mike Mansfield (b. N.Y.), politician/diplomat. Jeanette Rankin, politician/reformer. Charles M. Russell, artist.
Noteworthy places Big Hole Natl. Battlefield. Bob Marshall Wilderness. Charles M. Russell Museum, Great Falls. Custer Battlefield Natl. Monument. Ft. Union Trading Post Natl. Hist. Site. Lewis and Clark Caverns State Park. Museum of the

Plains Indian, Browning. Natl. Bison Range. Waterton-Glacier International Peace Park. World Museum of Mining, Butte. Yellowstone Natl. Park. **Memorable events** French explorers and trappers visit region 1740s. Large part of state in Louisiana Purchase 1803. Lewis and Clark expedition 1805–6. Ft. Benton first permanent settlement 1846. Western part of state included in Washington Territory 1853 and 1859; eastern part in Nebraska (1854) and Dakota (1861) territories. Gold discovered at Bannack (1862) and Alder Gulch (1863). Organized as Montana Territory 1864. Dakota and Cheyenne defeat U.S. troops under Gen. William Armstrong Custer at Battle of Little Bighorn 1876. Under Chief Joseph, Nez Percé beat U.S. Army at Big Hole Basin 1877. Marcus Daly discovers copper near Butte 1880's. Statehood 1889. Homesteaders enter state 1909. Ft. Peck Dam completed 1940. Anaconda Copper Mining, dominant in Montana industry and politics since 1915, closes mining operations at Butte 1983. Elizabeth Prophet (Guru Ma) convinces 3,000 disciples of the Church Universal and Triumphant to await nuclear cataclysm in underground shelters in Paradise Valley while state bureaucrats worried over sewage facilities 1990. **Tourist information** (800) VISIT-MT, (800) 548-3390. www.visitmt.com

▶**NEBRASKA**

Although set aside as Indian territory in 1834 and made off-limits to white settlement, thousands of whites crossed the region along the Independence, Mormon and Oregon trails. Eventually Congress opened the land to settlement, which accelerated after the Homestead Act of 1862 and the coming of the railroads. The newcomers took up ranching and farming under hard conditions. The winter of 1886–87 killed thousands of cattle and drove many large-scale ranchers into bankruptcy, while the dust bowl of the 1930s spurred a mass exodus. Significant industry did not develop until World War II, when many war-related industries and army airfields moved to the center of the country. Nebraska is among the leading agricultural states, especially in the production of corn for grain and livestock. A state constitutional amendment passed in 1982 prevents the sale of farmlands and ranch lands from being sold to anyone other than a Nebraska family farm corporation.

Name From the Oto *nebrathka*, "flat water." **Nickname** Cornhusker State. **Capital** Lincoln. **Entered union** Mar. 1, 1867 (37th). **Motto** "Equality before the law." **Emblems** **Bird** Western meadowlark. **Flower** Goldenrod. **Fossil** Mammoth. **Gem** Blue agate. **Grass** Little blue stem. **Insect** Honeybee. **Mammal** White-tailed deer. **Rock** Prairie agate. **Soil** Soils of the Holdrege series. **Song** "Beautiful Nebraska." **Tree** Western cottonwood.
Land Total area 77,354 sq. mi (16th), incl. 481 sq. mi. inland water. **Borders** S.Dak., Iowa, Mo., Kans., Colo., Wyo. **Rivers** Missouri, North Platte, Republican, South Platte. **Lakes** Harlan Co. Res., Lewis and Clark Lake. **Other notable features** Pine Ridge, Sand Hills.
Elected officials Lt. Gov. Dave Heineman (R, term exp. 2010). Lt. Gov. Rick Sheehy (R). Sec. State John A. Gale (R). Atty. Gen. Jon Bruning (R).
People (July 2007 est.) 1,774,571 (38th). Race/Hispanic Origin: White 91.6%. Black 4.4%. Indian 1.0%. Asian 1.7%. Pacific Islander 0.1%. Two or more races 1.2%. Hispanic 7.5%.
Cities (2006) Omaha 419,545. Lincoln 241,167. Bellevue 47,594. Grand Island 44,632. Kearney

29,385. Fremont 25,417. Norfolk 23,896. North Platte 24,386. Hastings 25,144. Columbus 21,414. **Business** Gross State Product, 2005: $70.3 bil. (36th). **Leading Sectors of GSP (2001):** Services 20.25%; Finance, insurance, and real estate 15.77%; Government 14.40%. *Fortune 500* Companies (2007): 5.
Famous natives Fred Astaire, dancer. Marlon Brando, actor. William Jennings Bryan, politician. Johnny Carson (b. Iowa), comedian. Willa Cather (b. Va.), author. Loren Eiseley, anthropologist. The Rev. Edward J. Flanagan (b. Ireland), reformer. Henry Fonda, actor. Rollin Kirby, cartoonist. Melvin Laird, politician. Harold Lloyd, actor. Mahpiua Luta (Red Cloud), Oglala Sioux chief. Malcolm X, religious leader. Roscoe Pound, educator.
Noteworthy places Agate Fossil Beds Natl. Monument. Arbor Lodge State Park, Nebraska City. Boys Town, Omaha. Buffalo Bill Ranch State Hist. Park. Chimney Rock Hist. Site. Homestead Natl. Monument, Beatrice. Oregon Trail. Pioneer Village, Minden. Scotts Bluff Natl. Monument. Strategic Air and Space Museum, Ashland. Stuhr Museum of the Prairie Pioneer, Grand Island.
Memorable events Acquired as part of Louisiana Purchase 1803. Separate territory created by Kansas-Nebraska Act 1854. Size reduced after creation of Colorado and Dakota territories 1861. Statehood 1867. To encourage tree planting, becomes first state to observe Arbor Day 1872. Adopts unicameral legislature 1937. Oil discovered 1939. Population peaks at 1,605,000 1984–85. **Tourist information** (877) NEBRASKA. www.visitnebraska.org

▶**NEVADA**

Set in the Great Basin desert, Nevada is one of the most barren places in North America, and the state receives less rainfall than any other. First explored by Europeans in 1776, it was 75 years before anyone thought of establishing a town in the area, and it did not last a decade. Miners came to Nevada early, but the discovery of the Comstock Lode in 1859 brought thousands. To add free-state Congressional votes, Nevada was hustled into the Union in 1864, three years before its boundaries were settled. That boom was over by the 1870s, and it took more gold and silver strikes in the early 1900s, as well as the discovery of copper, to get the economy rolling again. The mainstay of the economy since World War II has been the gambling industry, which generates virtually half of all tax revenues. Since the 1990s, Nevada has been the fastest growing state in the union, with skyrocketing tourism fueling much of the growth.

Name From Spanish, meaning "snow-covered sierra." **Nicknames** Sagebrush State, Silver State. **Capital** Carson City. **Entered union** Oct. 31, 1864 (36th). **Motto** "All for our country." **Emblems** **Animal** Desert bighorn sheep. **Bird** Mountain bluebird. **Flower** Sagebrush. **Fossil** Icthyosaur. **Grass** Indian ricegrass. **Metal** Silver. **Song** "Home Means Nevada." **Tree** Single-leaf piñon. **Land** Total area 110,561 sq. mi (7th), incl. 735 sq. mi. inland water. **Borders** Oreg., Idaho, Utah, Ariz., Calif. **Rivers** Colorado, Humboldt. **Lakes** Pyramid, Walker, Winnemucca. **Other notable features** Black Rock Desert, Carson Sink, Humboldt Salt Marsh, Mojave Desert.
Elected officials Gov. Jim Gibbons (R, term exp. 2011). Lt. Gov. Brian Krolicki (R). Sec. State Ross Miller (D). Atty. Gen. Catherine Cortez Masto (D).
People (July 2007 est.) 2,565,382 (35th). Race/Hispanic Origin: White 81.4%. Black 8.0%. Indian 1.4%. Asian 6.1%. Pacific Islander 0.5%. Two or

more races 2.6%. Hispanic 25.1%.
Cities (2006) Las Vegas 552,539. Henderson 240,614. Reno 210,255. North Las Vegas 197,567. Sunrise Manor 191,858. Paradise 186,370. Spring Valley 172,110. Enterprise 119,100. Sparks 83,959. Carson City 55,289.
Business Gross State Product, 2005: $110.5 bil. (31st). **Leading Sectors of GSP (2001):** Services 31.82%; Finance, insurance, and real estate 18.76%; Hotels and other lodging places 14.31%. *Fortune 500* **Companies (2007):** 2.
Famous natives Andre Agassi, tennis player. Walter Van Tilburg Clark (b. Me.), author. Sarah Winnemucca Hopkins, interpeter/teacher. John William MacKay, miner. William Morris Stewart (b. N.Y.), lawyer/senator.
Noteworthy places Death Valley Natl. Monument. Las Vegas. Lehman Caves Natl. Monument. Valley of the Fire State Park, Overton.
Memorable events Francisco Tomás Garcés explores area 1775–76. Jedediah Smith, trader, crosses region 1826–27. Old Spanish Trail (1830) and California Trail (1833) cross region. John Frémont explores area 1843–45. To United States after Mexican War 1846. Genoa, first settlement in Nevada, founded as Mormon Station 1849. Gold of Comstock Lode discovered 1859. Organized as separate territory 1861. Statehood 1864. Nevada legalizes gambling 1931. Hoover Dam built on Colorado River 1935. Nuclear tests begun at Yucca Flats 1951. Population grows more than 550 percent 1950–88, and 25 percent in 1990s.
Tourist information (800) NEVADA8.
www.travelnevada.com

▶ **NEW HAMPSHIRE**
New Hampshire has a disproportionate influence on presidential elections because by state law its primary must fall at least one week before any other state's (though Iowa's caucuses can come earlier). Through independence the mainstays of the economy were fishing, trade and farming. Boston proved more suitable for trade, and New Hampshire's stubborn land was outproduced by the more fertile valleys to the south and west. The state's economy receded until the beginning of the Industrial Revolution, when there was tremendous growth in textile-producing mill towns in the Merrimack River Valley. The mills began to close after World War I, and the economy faltered again. Improvement came as high-tech firms from Boston sought refuge in New Hampshire's favorable tax climate. The state's economy was pummeled by the severe New England recession in the early 1990's, but has rebounded since.
Name For English county of Hampshire. **Nickname** Granite State. **Capital** Concord. **Entered union** June 21, 1788 (9th). **Motto** "Live free or die."
Emblems Amphibian Spotted newt. **Bird** Purple finch. **Flower** Purple lilac. **Gem** Smoke quartz. **Insect** Ladybug. **Mineral** Beryl. **Song** "Old New Hampshire." **Tree** White birch.
Land Total area 9,350 sq. mi (46th), incl. 382 sq. mi. inland water. **Borders** Quebec, Maine, Atlantic Ocean, Mass., Vt. **Rivers** Connecticut, Merrimack, Piscataqua, Saco, Salmon Falls. **Lakes** First Connecticut, Francis, Newfound, Ossipee, Sunapee, Winnipesaukee. **Other notable features** Isles of Shoals, White Mts. (Mt. Washington 6,288 ft., highest peak in Northeast).
Elected officials Gov. John Lynch (D, term exp. 2009). Sec. State William Gardner (D). Atty. Gen. Kelly Ayotte.

People (July 2007 est.) 1,315,828 (41st). Race/Hispanic Origin: White 95.6%. Black 1.2%. Indian 0.3%. Asian 1.9%. Two or more races 1.0%. Hispanic 2.5%.
Cities (2006) Manchester 109,497. Nashua 87,157. Concord 42,378. Derry 34,103. Rochester 30,117. Salem 29,580. Dover 28,422. Merrimack 26,613. Londonderry 24,879. Hudson 24,729.
Business Gross State Product, 2005: $55.7 bil. (39th). **Leading Sectors of GSP (2001):** Finance, insurance, and real estate 24.99%; Services 21.57%; Manufacturing 16.13%. *Fortune 500* **Companies (2007):** 0.
Famous natives Salmon P. Chase, jurist. Ralph Adams Cram, architect. Mary Baker Eddy, founder, Church of Christ, Scientist. Daniel Chester French, sculptor. Horace Greeley, journalist. Sarah Buell Hale, author. Franklin Pierce, U.S. president. Augustus Saint-Gaudens (b. Ireland), sculptor. Alan Shepard, astronaut. Daniel Webster, politician. Eleazar Wheelock (b. Conn.), Dartmouth founder.
Noteworthy places Currier Gallery of Art, Manchester. The Flume (gorge). Franconia Notch. Isles of Shoals. Lake Winnipesaukee. Mt. Washington. Shaker Village, Canterbury. St. Gaudens Natl. Hist. Site. Strawberry Bank. White Mountains Natl. Forest.
Memorable events Martin Pring sails along coast 1603. Champlain explores area 1604. John Smith visits Isles of Shoals 1614. Included in king's grant to John Mason and Sir Ferdinando Gorges 1622. First settlers at Little Harbor, near Portsmouth 1623. Made separate royal province 1679, though under Massachusetts governor 1699–1741. Rogers's Rangers halt Indian raids 1759. New Hampshire patriots seize British fort at Portsmouth and drive out Royal governor 1775. Province relinquishes claims to New Connecticut (Vermont) 1782. First textile mill built 1803. Treaty of Portsmouth ends Russo-Japanese War 1905. Bretton Woods conference leads to establishment of International Monetary Fund 1944. First state to adopt lottery to support public education 1963.
Tourist information (800) FUN-IN-NH.
www.visitnh.gov

▶ **NEW JERSEY**
With the entire state population classified as living in metro areas, New Jersey is the most densely populated state, 15 times the national average, and its public schools are among the very best in the nation. Pharmaceuticals and chemicals are New Jersey's leading products, but the next most important industry is tourism, because of its beautiful ocean beaches, many lovely lakes, and because of the money tourists spend at the gaming tables of Atlantic City. What earns New Jersey its nick-name, the Garden State, is its extensive small-scale agriculture, which produces tomatoes, dairy products, asparagus, blueberries, corn and poultry.
New Jersey lies on a plain between Philadelphia and New York City, two larger neighbors that have overshadowed New Jersey on the national scene since colonial days. Yet during the Revolution, more than 100 battles were fought on New Jersey soil, and today the overwhelming majority of containerized shipping in the Port of New York and New Jersey is shipped from New Jersey terminals. Per capita income is always among the top five in the nation.
Name After English Channel Island of Jersey. **Nickname** Garden State. **Capital** Trenton. **En-**

tered union Dec. 18, 1787 (3rd). **Motto** "Liberty and prosperity."

Emblems **Animal** Horse. **Bird** Eastern goldfinch. **Flower** Violet. **Insect** Honeybee. **Memorial tree** Dogwood. **Tree** Red oak.

Land **Total area** 8,721 sq. mi (47th), incl. 1,304 sq. mi. inland water. **Borders** N.Y., Atlantic Ocean, Del., Pa. **Rivers** Delaware, Hackensack, Hudson, Passaic. **Lakes** Greenwood, Hopatcong, Round Valley Res., Spruce Run. **Other notable features** Delaware Water Gap, Kittatinny Mts., Palisades, Pine Barrens, Ramapo Mts.

Elected officials Gov. Jon S. Corzine (D, term exp. 2010). Sec. State Nina Mitchell Wells (D). Atty. Gen. Anne Milgram (D).

People (July 2007 est.) 8,685,920 (11th). Race/ Hispanic Origin: White 76.3%. Black 14.5%. Indian 0.3%. Asian 7.5%. Pacific Islander 0.1%. Two or more races 1.3%. Hispanic 15.9%.

Cities (2006) Newark 281,402. Jersey City 241,789. Paterson 148,708. Elizabeth 126,179. Edison 99,523. Toms River 93,500. Trenton 83,923. Clifton 79,606. Camden 79,318. Brick Township 78,232.

Business **Gross State Product, 2005:** $430.8 bil. (8th). **Leading Sectors of GSP (2001):** Finance, insurance, and real estate 24.66%; Services 22.85%; Real estate 15.71%. *Fortune 500* **Companies (2007):** 24.

Famous natives Buzz Aldrin, astronaut. Count Basie, jazz musician. William J. Brennan, jurist. Aaron Burr, politician. Grover Cleveland, U.S. president. James Fenimore Cooper, novelist/historian. Stephen Crane, author. Thomas Edison, inventor. Albert Einstein (b. Germany), nuclear physicist. Waldo Frank, author. Joyce Kilmer, poet. Jerry Lewis, actor. Jack Nicholson, actor. Zebulon Pike, explorer. Molly Pitcher, Revolutionary War heroine. Paul Robeson, actor/singer. Walter Schirra, astronaut. Frank Sinatra, singer. Bruce Springsteen, the boss. Alfred Stieglitz, photographer. Meryl Streep, actress. Aaron Montgomery Ward, merchant. William Carlos Williams, poet. Woodrow Wilson (b. Va.), U.S. president.

Noteworthy places Atlantic City. Cape May Historic District. Edison Natl. Hist. Site, West Orange. Lakehurst Naval Air Station. Liberty State Park, Jersey City. Morristown Natl. Hist. Park. Newark Museum. Palisades Interstate Park. Pine Barrens wilderness area. Princeton University. Walt Whitman House, Camden.

Memorable events Giovanni de Verrazano explores 1524. Hudson explores up Hudson River 1609. Dutch settlers establish Ft. Nassau 1623. New Jersey taken over by British and organized as colony under Sir George Carteret 1665. Major battles of Revolution at Trenton (1776), Princeton (1777), and Monmouth (1778). Women given vote at Elizabethtown 1800. Voting rights restricted to men 1807. Adopts state constitution 1844. Passenger ship *Morro Castle* burns off Asbury Park; 134 die 1934. Dirigible *Hindenburg* explodes while mooring at Lakehurst; 36 die 1937. New Jersey Turnpike linking New York City and Philadelphia opens 1952. Five days of race riots in Newark leave 26 dead 1967. Gambling legalized in Atlantic City 1978. State enacts strictest gun legislation in United States 1990.

Tourist information (800) VISITNJ. www.visitnj.org

▶**NEW MEXICO**

The development problem of the western states is shared by New Mexico, which of all states has the smallest percentage of its area covered by water.

Rich in other resources, it is the uranium capital of the world. The state mineral tax brings in a large percentage of state revenues, some of which goes into permanent endowments. Distribution of wealth in New Mexico remains uneven, but Hispanics, who tend to register as Democrats, vote in roughly the same ways as Anglos. A higher percentage of Native Americans live in New Mexico than in any other state.

Today, mining's influence on the state economy has waned in favor of service industry jobs. Despite the enormous governmental investment in research at Los Alamos, where the atom bomb was born, the highly classified nature of this work limits the development of related industry.

Name By Spanish explorers after Mexico. **Nickname** Land of Enchantment. **Capital** Santa Fe. **Entered union** Jan. 6, 1912 (47th). **Motto** *Crescit eundo* (It grows as it goes).

Emblems **Animal** Black bear. **Bird** Roadrunner (chaparral bird). **Fish** Cutthroat trout. **Flower** Yucca. **Fossil** *Coelphysis* dinosaur. **Gem** Turquoise. **Songs** "O, Fair New Mexico," "Así es Nuevo Mejico." **Tree** Piñon. **Vegetables** Frijole, chili.

Land **Total area** 121,589 sq. mi (5th), incl. 234 sq. mi. inland water. **Borders** Colo., Okla., Tex., Chihuahua, Ariz. **Rivers** Gila, Pecos, Rio Grande, Zuni. **Lakes** Conchas Res., Eagle Nest, Elephant Butte Res., Navajo Res., Ute Res. **Mountains** Chuska, Guadalupe, Sacramento, San Andres, Sangre de Cristo. **Other notable features** Carlsbad Caverns, Continental Divide, Staked Plain.

Elected officials Gov. Bill Richardson (D, term exp. 2011). Lt. Gov. Diane Denish (D). Sec. State Mary Herrera (D). Atty. Gen. Gary King (D).

People (July 2007 est.) 1,969,915 (36th). Race/ Hispanic Origin: White 84.5%. Black 2.8%. Indian 9.5%. Asian 1.4%. Pacific Islander 0.1%. Two or more races 1.7%. Hispanic 44.4%.

Cities (2006) Albuquerque 504,949. Las Cruces 86,268. Santa Fe 72,056. Rio Rancho 71,607. Roswell 45,582. Farmington 43,573. South Valley 40,500. Alamogordo 36,069. Clovis 33,258. Hobbs 29,292.

Business **Gross State Product, 2005:** $69.3 bil. (37th). **Leading Sectors of GSP (2001):** Services 18.30%; Government 18.05%; Manufacturing 13.61%. *Fortune 500* **Companies (2007):** 0.

Famous natives William "Billy the Kid" Bonney (b. N.Y.), outlaw. Peter Hurd, artist. Archbishop Jean Baptiste Lamy (b. France), missionary. Georgia O'Keeffe (b. Wis.), artist. Popé, Tewa Pueblo chief. Harrison Schmitt, astronaut.

Noteworthy places Aztec Ruins Natl. Monument. Bandelier Natl. Monument. Capulin Mt. Natl. Monument. Carlsbad Caverns Natl. Park. Chaco Culture Natl. Hist. Park. El Morro Natl. Monument. Ft. Union Natl. Monument. Gila Cliff Dwellings Natl. Monument. Museum of New Mexico, Santa Fe. Pecos Mission. Salinas Mission. Santa Fe Opera. Wheelwright Museum of the American Indian, Santa Fe. White Sands Natl. Monument.

Memorable events Marcos de Niza enters Zuni country 1539. Juan de Oñate establishes first Spanish settlement on Rio Grande near Espanola 1598. Santa Fe founded; becomes capital of New Mexico 1710. Santa Fe Trail from Independence, Missouri, completed; Mexico secedes from Spain 1821. Manuel Armijo suppresses revolt against Mexican rule (1837); defeats invasion from Republic of Texas (1841). Land annexed by United States after Mexican-American War 1848. Organized as territory with Arizona and part of Colorado 1850. Lincoln County War pits cattlemen

against merchants 1878–81. Statehood; 17 killed in raid by Pancho Villa 1912. Los Alamos selected as first research and development facility for nuclear weapons 1942. First atom bomb exploded at Alamagordo Air Base 1945.
Tourist information   (800) 545-2040.
www.newmexico.org.

▶**NEW YORK**
New York's greatest and most inviting asset has always been its strategic location and long arteries into the hinterland. New York Bay is one of the great natural harbors of the world, and the broad Hudson River is one of the most fortunately placed. After the opening of the Erie Canal between the Hudson and Lake Erie in 1825, New York City became the trading center for the Midwest as well as the Hudson Valley and the Atlantic Coast. Buffalo also experienced a boom, becoming a major Great Lakes industrial port. New York is still the first state in number of manufacturing establishments and employees. Wall Street alone employs half a million people.

Although New York's population grew by nearly half a million people between 1980 and 1990, its relatively slow rate of growth resulted in a loss of three Congressional seats—an indication of the change in the state's political clout. As its place among the 50 states has fallen by some measures, New York City's worldwide importance in business, culture and communications has risen.
Name For Duke of York, later James II, of England. **Nickname** Empire State. **Capital** Albany. **Entered union** July 26, 1788 (11th). **Motto** *Excelsior* (Higher).
Emblems   Animal Beaver. **Beverage** Milk. **Bird** Bluebird. **Fish** Brook or speckled trout. **Flower** Rose. **Fossil** Prehistoric crab (*Eurypterus remipes*). **Fruit** Apple. **Gem** Garnet. **Song** "I Love New York." **Tree** Sugar maple.
Land   Total area 54,556 sq. mi (27th), incl. 7,342 sq. mi. inland water. **Borders** Lake Ontario, Ontario, Quebec, Vt., Mass., Conn., Atlantic Ocean, N.J., Pa., Lake Erie. **Rivers** Allegheny, Delaware, Genesee, Hudson, Mohawk, New York State Barge Canal, Niagara, St. Lawrence, Susquehanna. **Lakes** Cayuga, Champlain, Chautauqua, Erie, George, Oneida, Ontario, Seneca. **Mountains** Adirondack (Mt. Marcy 5,344 ft.), Allegheny, Berkshire Hills, Catskill, Kittatinny, Ramapo. **Other notable features** Hudson Valley, Mohawk Valley, Niagara Falls, Palisades, Thousand Islands.
Elected officials   Gov. David Paterson (D, term exp. 2010). Acting Lt. Gov. Joseph Bruno (R). Sec. State Lorriane Cortes-Vazquez (D). Atty. Gen. Andrew M. Cuomo (D).
People   (July 2007 est.) 19,297,729 (3rd). Race/Hispanic Origin: White 73.6%. Black, 17.3%. Indian 0.5%. Asian 6.9%. Pacific Islander 0.1%. Two or more races 1.5%. Hispanic 16.4%.
Cities   (2006) New York 8,214,426. Buffalo 276,059. Rochester 208,123. Yonkers 197,852. Syracuse 140,658. Albany 93,963. Cheektowaga 80,700. New Rochelle 73,446. Mount Vernon 68,395. Schenectady 61,560.
Business   Gross State Product, 2005: $963.5 bil. (2nd). **Leading Sectors of GSP (2001):** Finance, insurance, and real estate 34.23%; Services 23.01%; Real Estate 14.10%. *Fortune 500* **Companies (2007):** 57.
Famous natives   Woody Allen, director. John Jacob Astor (b. Germany), merchant. Humphrey Bogart, actor. George Burns, actor. Aaron Copland, composer. Agnes de Mille, choreographer.

George Eastman, camera inventor. Millard Fillmore, U.S. president. Lou Gehrig, baseball player. George Gershwin, composer. Julia Ward Howe, reformer. Washington Irving, author. Henry James, author. Vince Lombardi, football coach. Groucho Marx, comedian. Herman Melville, author. Ogden Nash, poet/humorist. Eugene O'Neill, playwright. Otetiani "Red Jacket", Seneca chief. Channing E. Phillips, minister/reformer. John D. Rockefeller, industrialist. Norman Rockwell, illustrator. Richard Rodgers, composer. Franklin Delano Roosevelt, U.S. president. Theodore Roosevelt, U.S. president. Jonas Salk, physician. Elizabeth Ann Seton, first American saint. Elizabeth Cady Stanton, suffragette. James Johnson Sweeney, art critic. Martin Van Buren, U.S. president. Mae West, actress. E.B. White, author. Walt Whitman, poet.
Noteworthy places   Albright-Knox Gallery of American Art, Buffalo. American Merchant Marine Museum, Kings Point. Baseball Hall of Fame, Cooperstown. Bear Mt. State Park. Buffalo Museum of Science. Corning Glass Center, Corning. Erie Canal Museum, Syracuse. Farmers' Museum, Cooperstown. Fenimore House, Cooperstown. Franklin D. Roosevelt Natl. Hist. Site, Hyde Park. Ft. Stanwix Natl. Monument, Rome. Ft. Ticonderoga. Hudson Valley. Mohawk Valley. Niagara Falls. Palisades Interstate Park. Saratoga Natl. Hist. Park. Vanderbilt Museum, Hyde Park. U.S. Military Academy, West Point. Women's Rights Natl. Hist. Park, Seneca Falls. **New York City** American Academy of Arts & Sciences. American Museum of Natural History. Bronx Zoo. Brooklyn Botanical Garden. Brooklyn Museum. Cathedral of St. John the Divine. Cooper-Hewitt Museum. Federal Hall. Fraunces Tavern. Frick Collection. Guggenheim Museum. Hispanic Society of America. Jewish Museum. Lincoln Center for the Performing Arts. Metropolitan Museum of Art. Museum of Modern Art. Museum of the American Indian. N.Y. Public Library. Coney Island. N.Y. Stock Exchange. Rockefeller Center. South Street Seaport Museum. Statue of Liberty. United Nations.
Memorable events   Giovanni de Verrazano sails into New York Bay 1524. Samuel de Champlain sails down the St. Lawrence River 1603. Henry Hudson sails up Hudson River 1609. Dutch establish Ft. Orange (Albany) 1614. Peter Minuit buys Manhattan Island and founds colony of New Amsterdam 1625. British take New Amsterdam and name it New York 1664. Ethan Allen takes Ft. Ticonderoga 1775. George Washington inaugurated president New York City 1789. U.S. Military Academy founded West Point 1802. Erie Canal opened 1825. Statue of Liberty dedicated 1886. New York City includes Manhattan, Bronx, Queens, Brooklyn, and Staten Island 1898. President William McKinley assassinated in Buffalo 1901. UN headquarters established at New York City 1945. St. Lawrence Seaway opened 1959. One-fourth of New York City below poverty level 1984. Terrorist attack destroys World Trade Center in New York City, killing 3,000 people 2001. Governor Eliot Spitzer resigns after federal investigation 2008.
Tourist information   (800) CALL-NYS.
www.iloveny.com

▶**NORTH CAROLINA**
At the time of the Revolution, tobacco and rice plantations dominated the economy of the eastern part of the state, which in turn dominated the legislature. Next to last to ratify the Constitution, North Carolina was the last Southern state to secede from the Union. The Civil War cost North Carolina dearly; reconstruction was short-lived,

and blacks were effectively disenfranchised again by the turn of the century. Since World War II, the state has grown increasingly prosperous, especially in the "academic triangle" that encloses the University of North Carolina at Chapel Hill, Duke, and North Carolina State. The traditional industries of textiles, furniture, and tobacco still lead, partly because of diversification within them. North Carolina benefits from the general Sunbelt boom and from an influx of foreign capital; it maintains a healthy manufacturing sector, and has enjoyed steady economic growth in the 1990's.

Name For King Charles I (*Carolus* is Latin for Charles). **Nicknames** Tarheel State, Old North State. **Capital** Raleigh. **Entered union** Nov. 21, 1789 (12th). **Motto** *Esse quam videri* (To be rather than to seem).

Emblems **Bird** Cardinal. **Fish** Channel bass. **Flower** Dogwood. **Insect** Honeybee. **Precious stone** Emerald. **Reptile** Eastern box turtle. **Rock** Granite. **Shell** Scotch bonnet. **Song** "The Old North State." **Tree** Pine.

Land **Total area** 53,819 sq. mi (28th), incl. 5,108 sq. mi. inland water. **Borders** Va., Atlantic Ocean, S.C., Tenn., Georgia. **Rivers** Pee Dee, Roanoke, Yadkin. **Lakes** Buggs Island, High Rock, Mattamuskeet, Norman, Waccamaw. **Mountains** Black, Blue Ridge, Great Smoky, Unaka. **Other notable features** Great Dismal Swamp, Mount Mitchell, Outer Banks, Pamlico Sound.

Elected officials Gov. Michael F. Easley (D, term exp. 2009). Lt. Gov. Beverly Eaves Purdue (D). Sec. State Elaine Marshall (D). Atty. Gen. Roy Cooper (D).

People (July 2007 est.) 9,061,032 (10th). Race/Hispanic Origin: White 74%. Black 21.7%. Indian 1.2%. Asian 1.9%. Pacific Islander 0.1%. Two or more races 1.1%. Hispanic 7.0%.

Cities (2006) Charlotte 630,478. Raleigh 356,321. Greensboro 236,865. Durham 209,000. Winston-Salem 196,990. Fayetteville 168,033. Cary 112,414. High Point 97,796. Wilmington 95,944. Asheville 72,789.

Business **Gross State Product, 2005:** $344.6 bil. (12th). **Leading Sectors of GSP (2001):** Manufacturing 21.38%; Finance, insurance, and real estate 18.98%; Services 17.41%. *Fortune 500* **Companies (2007):** 14.

Famous natives Benjamin Newton Duke and James Buchanan Duke, industrialists/philanthropists. Richard J. Gatling, inventor. Billy Graham, minister. Andy Griffith, actor. O. Henry, writer. Andrew Johnson, U.S. president. William Rufus King, politician. Charles Kuralt, journalist. Meadowlark Lemon, athlete. Dolley Madison, First Lady. Thelonius Monk, musician. Edward R. Murrow, journalist. James Knox Polk, U.S. president. Moses Waddell, Confederate general. Thomas Wolfe, author.

Noteworthy places Bennett Place. Blue Ridge Natl. Parkway. Cape Hatteras and Cape Lookout Natl. Seashore. Carl Sandburg home, Hendersonville. Ft. Raleigh. Great Smoky Mountains Natl. Park. Great Smoky Mountains Natl. Hist. Park. Guilford Courthouse Natl. Military Park. Mint Museum, Charlotte. Moores Creek Natl. Battlefield. North Carolina Maritime Museum, Beaufort. North Carolina Museum of Art, Raleigh. Roanoke Island. Wright Brothers Natl. Memorial, Kitty Hawk.

Memorable events Part of Carolina grant given to eight noblemen by Charles II 1663. Culpepper's Rebellion in reaction to unfair tax collection policies 1677. Tuscarora lose war against European immigrants 1713. Proprietors sell rights to Crown; becomes royal province 1729. Mecklenburg Declaration (1775), forerunner of Declaration of Independence. Becomes first colony to sanction explicitly declaration of independence from Britain in Apr. 1776. Gen. Charles Cornwallis wins Battle of Guilford Courthouse, but British lose control of colony 1781. Ratifies Constitution 1789. Gives up claims to western territories, now part of Tennessee 1790. Establishes first state university system in United States 1829. Cherokees driven out of North Carolina to Oklahoma 1838. Secedes 1861. Readmitted to Union 1868. American Tobacco Company founded 1890. Wright brothers launch first successful airplane at Kitty Hawk 1903. Confrontation between Ku Klux Klan and anti-Klan demonstrators leaves five dead; 12 Klansmen charged with first-degree murder 1979.

Tourist information (800) VISIT-NC. www.visitnc.com

▶ **NORTH DAKOTA**

The first permanent settlers in North Dakota were Scots-Canadians who settled at Pembina on the Red River near the Canadian border, and who traded primarily with Winnipeg and St. Paul. The arrival of the Northern Pacific Railway in 1872 created a surge of huge farms, many of which were wiped out by drought and harsh winters in the 1880s. There followed a huge influx of Norwegians and Germans whose influence is still very apparent today. North Dakota's economy is heavily agricultural and leads the nation in production of wheat. Farming is centered in the fertile Red River of the North Valley, with livestock throughout the rest of the state.

Name For northern section of Dakota territory; *dakota* is Sioux word for "allies." **Nicknames** Sioux State, Peace Garden State, Flickertail State. **Capital** Bismarck. **Entered union** Nov. 2, 1889 (39th). **Motto** "Liberty and union, now and forever, one and inseparable."

Emblems **Beverage** Milk. **Bird** Western meadowlark. **Fish** Northern pike. **Flower** Wild prairie rose. **Fossil** Teredo petrified wood. **Grass** Western wheatgrass. **March** "Spirit of North Dakota." **Song** "North Dakota Hymn." **Tree** American elm.

Land **Total area** 70,700 sq. mi (19th), incl. 1,724 sq. mi. inland water. **Borders** Saskatchewan, Manitoba, Minn., S.Dak., Mont. **Rivers** Missouri, Red River of the North. **Lakes** Ashtabula, Devils, Oahe, Sakakawea. **Other notable features** Geographical center of North America, Missouri Plateau, Red River Valley, Rolling Drift Prairie.

Elected officials Gov. John Hoeven (R, term exp. 2008). Lt. Gov. John Dalrymple (R). Sec. State Alvin A. Jaeger (R). Atty. Gen. Wayne Stenehjem (R).

People (July 2007 est.) 639,715 (48th). Race/Hispanic Origin: White 91.6%. Black 1.0%. Indian 5.4%. Asian 0.8%. Pacific Islander 1.1%. Two or more races 1.2%. Hispanic 1.9%.

Cities (2006) Fargo 90,056. Bismarck 58,333. Grand Forks 50,372. Minot 34,745. West Fargo 21,508. Jamestown 14,680. Mandan 17,449. Dickinson 15,636. Williston 12,303. Wahpeton 7,907.

Business **Gross State Product, 2005:** $24.2 bil. (49th). **Leading Sectors of GSP (2001):** Services 19.27%; Government 15.60%; Finance, insurance, and real estate 14.58%. *Fortune 500* **Companies (2007):** 0.

Famous natives Angie Dickinson, actress. John Bernard Flannagan, sculptor. Louis L'Amour, novelist. Peggy Lee, singer. Roger Maris, baseball player. Eric Sevareid, broadcaster. Vihjalmur Ste-

fansson (b. Canada), ethnologist. Lawrence Welk, entertainer.
Noteworthy places Arrowwood Natl. Wildlife Refuge. Dinosaur Museum, Dickinson. Ft. Abraham Lincoln State Park. Ft. Union Trading Post Natl. Hist. Site. International Peace Garden. Knife River Indian Villages Natl. Hist. Site. Theodore Roosevelt Natl. Park, the Badlands.
Memorable events Pierre Gaultier de Varennes, sieur de Vérendrye first European to visit area 1738. United States acquires half of territory in Louisiana Purchase 1803. Meriwether Lewis and William Clark expedition builds Ft. Mandan 1804–5. First permanent settlement at Pembina 1812. Britain cedes western half of state to United States 1818. Missouri River steamboats reach territory 1838. First railroad arrives 1873. Statehood 1889. First state to hold presidential primary 1912. Garrison Dam completed forming Lake Sakakawea; gambling (blackjack) legalized 1981. Red River floods, devastating agriculture, 1997.
Tourist information (800) HELLO-ND.
www.ndtourism.com.

▶OHIO

The first settlements in Ohio were Marietta, in 1788, and Cincinnati in 1789, on the Ohio River, but significant migration into the state didn't occur until after the War of 1812. Shipping flourished in the 1820s and 1830s thanks to a network of canals connecting the Ohio and Lake Erie. Since 1959 the St. Lawrence Seaway has helped keep Ohio among the top five exporting states. Heavy industry also flourished in the northern cities that had access to coal and iron ore from the Lake Superior region. The 1870s saw the development of a manufacturing base that later became an integral part of the automotive industry. Although Ohio's economy has traditionally been well balanced between agriculture, industry, mining, and trade, the recession of the early 1980s weakened manufacturing, triggered flight from the industrial cities, and saw a dramatic shift to a service economy and to high-tech industry.

Name From the Iroquois *oheo*, "beautiful." **Nickname** Buckeye State. **Capital** Columbus. **Entered union** Mar. 1, 1803 (17th). **Motto** "With God, all things are possible."
Emblems **Beverage** Tomato juice. **Bird** Cardinal. **Flower** Scarlet carnation. **Gem** Ohio flint. **Insect** Ladybug. **Song** "Beautiful Ohio." **Tree** Buckeye.
Land **Total area** 44,825 sq. mi (34th), incl. 3,877 sq. mi. inland water. **Borders** Mich., Lake Erie, Pa., W.Va., Ky., Ind. **Rivers** Cuyahoga, Maumee, Miami, Muskingum, Ohio, Sandusky, Scioto. **Lakes** Berlin Res., Dillon Res., Erie, Mosquito Res., St. Mary's.
Elected officials Gov. Ted Strickland (D, term exp. 2011). Lt. Gov. Lee Fisher (D). Sec. State. Jennifer Brunner (D). Atty. Gen. Nancy H. Rogers (R).
People (July 2007 est.) 11,466,917 (7th). Race/Hispanic Origin: White 84.9%. Black 12.0%. Indian 0.2%. Asian 1.6%. Two or more races 1.3%. Hispanic 2.5%.
Cities (2006) Columbus 733,203. Cleveland 444,313. Cincinnati 332,252. Toledo 298,446. Akron 209,704. Dayton 156,771. Youngstown 81,520. Parma 80,009. Canton 78,924. Lorain 70,592.
Business **Gross State Product, 2005:** $442.4 bil. (7th). **Leading Sectors of GSP (2001):** Manufacturing 21.30%; Services 19.61%; Finance, insurance, and real estate 17.78%. *Fortune 500* **Companies (2007):** 28.
Famous natives Sherwood Anderson, writer. Neil Armstrong, astronaut. George Bellows, artist.

Ambrose Bierce, author. George Armstrong Custer, army officer. Paul Laurence Dunbar, poet. Thomas A. Edison, inventor. James A. Garfield, U.S. president. John Glenn, astronaut/politician. Ulysses S. Grant, U.S. president/general. Zane Grey, author. Warren G. Harding, U.S. president. Benjamin Harrison, U.S. president. Rutherford B. Hayes, U.S. president. Bob Hope, entertainer. William McKinley, U.S. president. Annie Oakley, markswoman. Ransom Eli Olds, carmaker. Eddie Rickenbacker, pilot. William Sherman, army officer. William Howard Taft, U.S. president/chief justice. Art Tatum, pianist. Tecumseh, Shawnee chief. James Thurber, humorist. Orville Wright, airplane inventor.
Noteworthy places Air Force Museum, Dayton. National Underground Railroad Freedom Center, Cincinnati. Cleveland Museum of Art. Cleveland Museum of Natural History. Columbus Museum of Art. Great Lakes Historical Society Museum, Vermilion. Cincinnati Museum of Natural History. Mound City Group Natl. Monument, Chillicothe. Neil Armstrong Air and Space Museum, Wapakoneta. Ohio River Museum, Marietta. Pro Football Hall of Fame, Canton. Rock and Roll Hall of Fame, Cleveland. Toledo Museum of Art.
Memorable events Hopewell Mound-Builders present throughout state prior to arrival of Miamis, Shawnees, Wyandots, and Delawares. Conflicting claims by France, Virginia, Connecticut, and New York 1609–1786. René-Roger Cavelier de La Salle visits region 1669–70. To Britain 1763. To United States after 1783. Becomes part of Northwest Territory 1787. First settlement at Marietta 1788. Gen. "Mad" Anthony Wayne beats Tecumseh at Battle of Fallen Timbers 1794. Enters Union 1803. Harrison beats Tecumseh at Battle of Tippecanoe 1811. Oliver Hazard Perry beats British fleet at Battle of Put-in-Bay 1813. Ohio and Erie Canal completed 1832. Dayton flood kills 400 in Miami River Valley; damage put at $100 million 1913. Carl B. Stokes elected mayor of Cleveland, first black mayor of major U.S. city 1967. Four students protesting Vietnam War killed by National Guard at Kent State University 1970.
Tourist information (800) BUCKEYE.
www.discoverohio.com

▶OKLAHOMA

French trappers entered the region of Oklahoma in the 1700s. In 1830 the land was designated the Indian Country, set aside for members of the Cherokees, Chickasaw, Choctaw, Creek, and Seminole deported from the southeast by the Indian Removal Act of 1830. These "Five Civilized Tribes," among others, fared well until the Civil War. They supported the Confederacy (some were actually slave-holders), and in 1868 Col. George Armstrong Custer led a massacre of Cheyenne at the Battle of the Washita. Twenty years later the government abrogated its treaty commitments and opened the territory to settlement. Today the state has a distinctly southern character. The region bordering the Red River is known as "Little Dixie," and as many as two-thirds of all Oklahomans consider themselves born-again Christians.

Oklahoma has a diversified economy. The state led the country in oil and gas production through the 1920s. Agriculture was hit heavily by the dust bowl of the 1930s, and thousands of "Okies" fled west. While agriculture and petroleum are still vital to the economy, manufacturing is increasingly important. The state is crossed by two of the country's longest rivers. The Arkansas links Catoosa (near Tulsa) to the Gulf of Mexico and the Mississippi

River system; but the Red River is not navigable in Oklahoma, and dissolved salts make it useless for agriculture, industry or residential purposes.

Name From the Choctaw *okla humma*, "land of the red people." **Nickname** Sooner State. **Capital** Oklahoma City. **Entered union** Nov. 16, 1907 (46th). **Motto** *Labor omnia vincit* (Work overcomes all obstacles).

Emblems   Animal American buffalo. **Bird** Scissor-tailed flycatcher. **Colors** Green and white. **Fish** White bass. **Floral emblem** Mistletoe. **Grass** Indian grass. **Poem** "Howdy Folks." **Reptile** Collared lizard (mountain boomer). **Song** "Oklahoma!" **Stone** Barite rose (rose rock). **Tree** Redbud. **Waltz** "Oklahoma Wind."

Land   Total area 69,898 sq. mi (20th), incl. 1,231 sq. mi. inland water. **Borders** Kans., Mo., Ark., Tex., N.Mex., Colo. **Rivers** Arkansas, Canadian, Cimarron, Red. **Lakes** Canton, Lake o' the Cherokees, Oologah, Texoma. **Other notable features** Ouachita Mts., Ozark Plateau, Staked Plain, Wichita Mts.

Elected officials   Gov. Brad Henry (D, term exp. 2010). Lt. Gov. Jari Askins (D). Sec. State M. Susan Savage (D). Atty. Gen. Drew Edmondson (D).

People   (July 2007 est.) 3,617,316 (28th). Race/Hispanic Origin: White 78.3%. Black 7.9%. Indian 7.9%. Asian 1.7%. Pacific Islander 0.1%. Two or more races 4.0%. Hispanic 7.2%.

Cities   (2006) Oklahoma City 537,734. Tulsa 382,872. Norman 102,827. Broken Arrow 88,314. Lawton 87,540. Edmond 76,644. Midwest City 55,161. Moore 49,277. Enid 46,514. Stillwater 44,818.

Business   Gross State Product, 2005: $120.5 bil. (29th). **Leading Sectors of GSP (2001):** Services 18.73%; Government 16.81%; Manufacturing 13.89%. *Fortune 500* **Companies (2007):** 4.

Famous natives   Ralph Ellison, author. Woody Guthrie, reformer/musician. Patrick J. Hurley, diplomat. Karl Jansky, electrical engineer. Mickey Mantle, baseball player. Wiley Post, aviator. Tony Randall, actor. Oral Roberts, evangelist. Will Rogers, humorist. Maria Tallchief, ballerina. Jim Thorpe, athlete.

Noteworthy places   American Indian Hall of Fame, Anadarko. Chisholm Trail Museum, Kingfisher. Ft. Gibson Stockade, Muskogee. Natl. Cowboy Hall of Fame, Oklahoma City. Ouachita Natl. Forest. Pioneer Woman Museum, Ponca City. Wildlife Heritage Center Museum, Antlers. Will Rogers Memorial, Claremore.

Memorable events   Francisco Vásquez de Coronado expedition in territory 1541, Except for panhandle, becomes part of Louisiana purchase 1803. Region made Indian Territory (not organized) in 1830 and becomes home of "Five Civilized Tribes"—Cherokee, Choctaw, Chickasaw, Creek, and Seminole—after they left the southeast on Trail of Tears 1828–46. United States acquires panhandle with annexation of Texas 1845. Territory opened to homesteaders 1889. Commercial oil well at Bartlesville 1897. Indian Territory and Oklahoma Territory merged and granted statehood 1907. Gov. John C. Walton impeached after declaring martial law to quell violence 1923. McClellan-Kerr Arkansas River Navigation system links Oklahoma to Mississippi, making Catoosa (Tulsa) major inland port 1971. Timothy McVeigh blows up Federal Building in Oklahoma City, killing 168 people 1995.

Tourist information   (800) 652-6552. **www.travelok.com**

▶OREGON

Although the Lewis and Clark expedition reached the mouth of the Columbia River in 1805, interest in the area was kindled by the Hudson's Bay Company and later by Jason Lee, a Methodist minister who settled near Salem in 1834. After the decline of the fur trade, lumbering became the most important industry in Oregon. Though lumbering and related industries are still leading employers—the state is the leading grower of Christmas trees—Oregon has benefited from the arrival of smaller computer and electronics firms leaving California in search of a more favorable business climate. Traditionally progressive, it is one of most active states in the environmental protection movement. Only one-third of the population is affiliated with an organized religion.

Name Unknown origin, first applied to Columbia River. **Nickname** Beaver State. **Capital** Salem. **Entered union** Feb. 14, 1859 (33rd). **Motto** "She flies with her own wings." **Poet laureate** William E. Stafford.

Emblems   Animal Beaver. **Bird** Western meadowlark. **Dance** Square dance. **Fish** Chinook salmon. **Flower** Oregon grape. **Insect** Swallowtail butterfly. **Song** "Oregon, My Oregon." **Stone** Thunderegg. **Tree** Douglas fir.

Land   Total area 98,381 sq. mi (9th), incl. 2,384 sq. mi. inland water. **Borders** Wash., Idaho, Nev., Calif., Pacific Ocean. **Rivers** Columbia, Snake, Willamette. **Mountains** Cascade Range, Coast Range, Klamath. **Other notable features** Willamette Valley.

Elected officials   Gov. Ted Kulongoski (D, term exp. 2011). Sec. State Bill Bradbury (D). Atty. Gen. Hardy Myers (D).

People   (July 2007 est.) 3,747,455 (27th). Race/Hispanic Origin: White 90.3%. Black 2.0%. Indian 1.4%. Asian 3.7%. Pacific Islander 0.3%. Other 4.2%. Two or more races 2.4%. Hispanic 10.6%.

Cities   (2006) Portland 537,081. Salem 152,239. Eugene 146,356. Gresham 97,105. Beaverton 89,643. Hillsboro 87,732. Bend 71,892. Medford 71,138. Springfield 55,848. Corvallis 49,807.

Business   Gross State Product, 2005: $145.4 bil. (26th). **Leading Sectors of GSP (2001):** Manufacturing 25.50%; Durable Goods 22.00%; Services 18.20%. *Fortune 500* **Companies (2007):** 1.

Famous natives   Beverly Cleary, author. Inmut-too-yah-lat-lat (Joseph), Nez Percé chief. Matt Groening, cartoonist. Ursula LeGuin (b. Calif.), author. Edwin Markham, poet. Dr. John McLoughlin, fur trader, "Father of Oregon". Linus Pauling, chemist. John Reed, author. William Simon U'Ren (b. Wis.), lawyer/reformer.

Noteworthy places   Bonneville Dam, Columbia River. Columbia River Gorge. Columbia River Museum, Astoria. Crater Lakes Natl. Park. Ft. Clatsop Natl. Monument. Hells Canyon. High Desert Museum, Bend. John Day Fossil Beds Natl. Monument. Mt. Hood. Oregon Caves Natl. Monument. Oregon Dunes Natl. Recreation Area. Point Perpetua. Timberline Lodge.

Memorable events   Sir Francis Drake turns away from fogbound coast of Pacific Northwest 1578. Capt. James Cook visits 1778. Mouth of Columbia River explored by Capt. Robert Gray, who claims region for U.S. 1792. Meriwether Lewis and George Rogers Clark expedition arrives at mouth of Columbia 1805. Claims to Oregon Territory, from California border to Alaska and east to Montana and Wyoming, relinquished by Spain (1819), Russia (1825), and Britain (1846). First settlers arrive Willamette Valley 1843. Organized as territory

1848. Statehood 1859. Railroad arrives 1883. Bonneville Dam completed 1937. Following severe rain and snow that claim 40 lives, Oregon declared disaster area 1964. First state to enact "bottle law" 1972. Snake River opened to navigation, linking Astoria to Lewiston, Idaho, 1975.
Tourist information　(800) 547-7842.
www.traveloregon.com

▶ PENNSYLVANIA, COMMONWEALTH OF

William Penn and his Quakers encouraged settlement and religious tolerance, and Pennsylvania was the first state to abolish slavery. In the late colonial period, Philadelphia was the cultural capital of the colonies. The first Continental Congress convened there in 1774, and it was for a decade the U.S. capital. With access to both the Great Lakes and to the Atlantic, Pennsylvanians took a lead in opening up the Midwest. Its resources include large coal deposits—which contribute to its iron-making capabilities—lumber, textiles, and leather. Leadership in these sectors lasted well into the 20th century, when Pennsylvania lost ground to Sunbelt states. As in many states, there has been growth in tourist and service industries, though machinery production and trade continue to expand significantly.

Name For Adm. William Penn, father of William Penn, founder of commonwealth. **Nickname** Keystone State. **Capital** Harrisburg. **Entered union** Dec. 12, 1787 (2nd). **Motto** "Virtue, liberty and independence."
Emblems　**Animal** White-tailed deer. **Beautification and conservation plant** Penngift crown vetch. **Beverage** Milk. **Bird** Ruffed grouse. **Dog** Great Dane. **Fish** Brook trout. **Flower** Mountain laurel. **Insect** Firefly. **Tree** Hemlock.
Land　**Total area** 46,055 sq. mi. (33rd), incl. 1,239 sq. mi. inland water. **Borders** N.Y., N.J., Del., Md., W.Va., Ohio, Lake Erie. **Rivers** Allegheny, Delaware, Juniata, Monongahela, Ohio, Schuylkill, Susquehanna. **Lakes** Allegheny Res., Erie, Pymatuning Res., Shenango Res. **Mountains** Allegheny, Kittatinny, Laurel Hills, Pocono.
Elected officials　Gov. Edward Rendell (D, term exp. 2011). Lt. Gov. Catherine Baker Knoll (D). Sec. Commonwealth Pedro Cortes (D). Atty. Gen. Tom Corbett (R).
People　(July 2007 est.) 12,432,792 (6th). Race/Hispanic Origin: White 85.6%. Black 10.8%. Indian 0.2%. Asian 2.4%. Two or more races 1.0%. Hispanic 4.5%.
Cities　(2006) Philadelphia 1,448,394. Pittsburgh 312,819. Allentown 107,294. Erie 102,036. Reading 81,183. Scranton 72,861. Bethlehem 72,704. Lancaster 54,779. Levittown 53,500. Harrisburg 47,164.
Business　**Gross State Product, 2005:** $487.2 bil. (6th). **Leading Sectors of GSP (2001):** Services 23.65%; Finance, insurance, and real estate 19.42%; Manufacturing 16.72%. *Fortune 500* **Companies (2007):** 25.
Famous natives　Louisa May Alcott, author. Maxwell Anderson, playwright. James Buchanan, U.S. president. Alexander Calder, sculptor. Andrew Carnegie (b. Scotland), industrialist/philanthropist. Mary Cassatt, painter. Wilt Chamberlain, basketball player. Bill Cosby, comedian/philanthropist. Stephen Foster, songwriter. Benjamin Franklin (b. Mass.), inventor/statesman. Robert Fulton, inventor. Milton S. Hershey, chocolatier. George C. Marshall, statesman. Andrew W. Mellon, financier/philanthropist. Robert E. Peary, explorer. Betsy Ross, patriot. Andy

Warhol, artist. Johnny Weismuller, swimmer/actor. Benjamin West, painter.
Noteworthy places　Academy of Natural Sciences, Philadelphia. Carnegie Institute, Pittsburgh. Delaware Water Gap Natl. Recreation Area. Ft. Necessity Natl. Battlefield. Franklin Institute, Philadelphia. Gettysburg Battlefield. Hugh Moore Hist. Park and Museums, Easton. Independence Natl. Hist. Park, Philadelphia. Liberty Bell, Carpenters Hall, Philadelphia. Pennsylvania Academy of Fine Arts, Philadelphia. Pennsylvania Dutch Country. Philadelphia Museum of Art. Pine Creek Gorge. Rodin Museum, Philadelphia. Valley Forge Natl. Hist. Park.
Memorable events　Cornelis Jacobssen sails into Delaware Bay 1614. Swedes settle at Tinicum Island 1643. Charles II grants proprietary charter to William Penn 1681. First U.S. hospital established, in Philadelphia, 1751. Mason-Dixon Line establishes southern boundary of state 1763–67—later boundary between slave and nonslave states. Declaration of Independence (1776) and Constitution (1787) signed in Philadelphia. Becomes first state to abolish slavery 1780. Bank of North America becomes first bank chartered in United States 1781. Philadelphia capital of United States 1790–1800. First iron furnace in U.S. 1792. First oil well in the world driven near Titusville 1859. Battle of Gettysburg turning point in Civil War; Lincoln's Gettysburg Address 1863. Centennial Exhibition at Philadelphia 1876. Johnstown flood—worst in U.S. history—kills 2,200 people 1889. Pinkerton detectives kill 12 strikers at Homestead steel works near Pittsburgh 1892. Twenty coal miners killed during strike for eight-hour day and other concessions 1897. More than 500 injured during three-day race riot in Philadelphia 1964. Partial meltdown at Three Mile Island forces closure of nuclear reactor 1979. Storage tank spills 713,000 gallons diesel fuel into Monongahela River, disrupting water supplies in Pennsylvania, West Virginia, and Ohio 1988.
Tourist information　(800) VISIT-PA. www.visitpa.com.

▶ RHODE ISLAND AND PROVIDENCE PLANTATIONS

Giovanni de Verrazano was the first European to record visiting the area of Narragansett Bay, the prominent inlet that almost splits the eastern third of the state from the rest. The first settlers were followers of Roger Williams, who left the restrictive religious atmosphere of the Puritan Massachusetts Bay Colony to found Providence in 1636. Rhode Island is the site of the first U.S. Baptist church, at Providence, and at Newport the first Quaker meetinghouse and the first synagogue. It was the last of the 13 original colonies to ratify the Constitution, the centralized federalism of which many Rhode Islanders objected to. The development of 19th-century Rhode Island was influenced by immigration and the Industrial Revolution; the state's leading manufacturers are still silver, jewelry and textiles. Although it ranks 43rd in population, Rhode Island is second in population density (behind New Jersey) at 948 people per square mile.

Name For Rhode Island in Narragansett Bay, named in turn for Mediterranean island of Rhodes. **Nicknames** Ocean State, Little Rhody. **Capital** Providence. **Entered union** May 29, 1790 (13th). **Motto** "Hope."

Emblems **Bird** Rhode Island red. **Flower** Violet. **Mineral** Bowenite. **Rock** Cumberlandite. **Song** "Rhode Island's It for Me." **Tree** Red maple. **Land** Total area 1,545 sq. mi (50th), incl. 500 sq. mi. inland water. **Borders** Mass., Atlantic Ocean, Conn. **Rivers** Blackstone, Pawcatuck, Providence, Sakonnet. **Other notable features** Block Island, Narragansett Bay, Aquidneck Island.

Elected officials Gov. Donald Carcieri (R, term exp. 2011). Lt. Gov. Elizabeth Roberts (D). Sec. State A. Ralph Mollis (D). Atty. Gen. Patrick Lynch (D).

People (July 2007 est.) 1,057,832 (43rd). Race/ Hispanic Origin: White 88.7%. Black 6.3%. Indian 0.6%. Asian 2.8%. Pacific Islander 0.1%. Two or more races 1.5%. Hispanic 11.2%.

Cities (2006) Providence 175,255. Warwick 85,925. Cranston 81,479. Pawtucket 72,998. East Providence 49,123. Woonsocket 43,940. North Providence 32,993. West Warwick 29,564. Bristol 24,498. Newport 24,409.

Business Gross State Product, 2005: $43.8 bil. (44th). **Leading Sectors of GSP (2001):** Finance, insurance, and real estate 29.60%; Services 21.52%; Real estate 14.35%. *Fortune 500* Companies (2007): 2.

Famous natives George M. Cohan, actor/ producer. Nathanael Greene, army officer. Galway Kinell, poet. Metacomet (King Philip), Wampanoag chief. Oliver H. Perry and Matthew C. Perry, naval officers. Gilbert Stuart, portraitist.

Noteworthy places Brown University, Providence. First Baptist Church in North America (1638), Providence. Hoffenreffer Museum of Anthropology, Bristol. John Carter Brown Library, Providence. Rhode Island School of Design, Providence. Nathanael Greene homestead, Coventry. Museum of Yachting, Newport. Newport mansions. Tennis Hall of Fame, Newport. Touro Synagogue (oldest extant in North America), Newport.

Memorable events Roger Williams, expelled from Massachusetts Bay Colony, settles in Providence 1636. Other religious exiles settle in Portsmouth (1638), Newport (1639), and Warwick (1642). King Philip's War 1675–76. First Quaker meetinghouse in North America founded 1699. First colony to renounce allegiance to Britain 1776. Last colony to ratify Constitution 1790. Dorr's Rebellion achieves liberalization of state constitution, which had remained unchanged since 1663, 1842. America's Cup Race held in Newport for first time 1930. Newport Bridge across Narragansett Bay completed 1969. *Australia II* first non-U.S. boat to win America's Cup in 132 years 1983.

Tourist information (800) 556-2484. www.visitrhodeisland.com

▶SOUTH CAROLINA

South Carolina's early economy was based on rice—its plantations worked by slaves—though tobacco later played a major role. As was true in North Carolina, many settlers made their way into the back country where they eked out a living as tenant farmers. During the Revolution, Ft. Charlotte was the first British installation to fall to Colonial troops, and at the outbreak of the Civil War, Ft. Sumter was the first Union installation to fall to Confederate forces. While agriculture remained a staple of the state's economy through the close of the 19th century, textile manufacture took over in the early 20th century. The postwar era has seen the rapid expansion of the chemical and paper industries, as well as large-scale development of the Atlantic Coast ports of Charleston, Georgetown, and Port Royal.

Name For King Charles II (Carolus is Latin for Charles). **Nickname** Palmetto State. **Capital** Columbia. **Entered union** May 23, 1788 (8th). **Motto** *Animis opibusque parati* (Prepared in mind and deed); *Dum spiro spero* (While I breathe I hope). **Poet laureate** Helen von Kolnitz Hyer.

Emblems **Animal** White-tailed deer. **Beverage** Milk. **Bird** Carolina wren. **Dance** Shag. **Dog** Boykin spaniel. **Fish** Striped bass. **Flower** Yellow jessamine. **Fruit** Peach. **Shell** Lettered olive. **Song** "Carolina." **Stone** Blue granite. **Tree** Palmetto. **Wild game bird** Wild turkey.

Land Total area 32,020 sq. mi (40th), incl. 1,911 sq. mi. inland water. **Borders** N.C., Atlantic Ocean, Ga. **Rivers** Catawba, Congaree, Edisto, Pee Dee, Savannah, Tugalos, Wateree. **Lakes** Greenwood, Hartwell, Keowee, Marion, Murray, Santee Res., Wylie. **Other notable features** Blue Ridge Mts., Congaree Swamp, Sea Islands.

Elected officials Gov. Mark Sanford (R, term exp. 2011). Lt. Gov. Andre Bauer (R). Sec. State J. Mark Hammond (R). Atty. Gen. Henry McMaster (R).

People (July 2007 est.) 4,407,409 (24th). Race/ Hispanic Origin: White 68.6%. Black 28.7%. Indian 0.4%. Asian 1.2%. Pacific Islander 0.1%. Two or more races 1.0%. Hispanic 3.8%.

Cities (2006) Columbia 119,961. Charleston 107,845. North Charleston 87,482. Rock Hill 61,620. Mount Pleasant 59,113. Greenville 57,428. Summerville 41,575. Sumter 39,159. Spartanburg 38,561. Hilton Head Island 33,838.

Business Gross State Product, 2005: $139.8 bil. (28th). **Leading Sectors of GSP (2001):** Manufacturing 20.07%; Services 17.00%; Government 15.54%. *Fortune 500* Companies (2007): 1.

Famous natives James Brown, singer. James F. Byrnes, politician/jurist. John C. Calhoun, politician. Joe Frazier, boxer. Dizzy Gillespie, musician. Althea Gibson, athlete. DuBose Heyward, author. Andrew Jackson, U.S. president. Jasper Johns. artist. Eartha Kitt, singer. James Longstreet, army officer. Francis Marion, army officer/politician. Charles C. Pinckney and Thomas Pinckney, diplomats. Edward Rutledge and John Rutledge, politicians. Strom Thurmond, politician.

Noteworthy places Charleston Museum (1773, oldest in United States). Congaree Swamp Natl. Monument. Cowpens Natl. Battlefield. Ft. Moultrie, Ft. Johnson, and Ft. Sumter Natl. Monument, Charleston. Hilton Head Island. Kings Mountain Natl. Military Park. Ninety-Six Natl. Hist. Site, Greenwood. Patriots Point Maritime Museum, Charleston. Sea Islands. Spoleto Music Festival, Charleston.

Memorable events Spanish visit 1521. French Huguenots at Port Royal 1562. Included in Carolina grant by Charles II 1663. Charleston founded 1680. Becomes royal province 1729. Ratifies Constitution 1787. *Best Friend of Charleston,* first American steam locomotive built for passenger use 1833. First state to secede from Union Dec. 20, 1860. Confederate forces attack Ft. Sumter Apr. 12, 1861. Secession repealed 1865. Readmitted to Union 1868. Cyclone kills 1,000 in Savannah, Georgia, and Charleston 1893. Savannah River nuclear plant begins production near Aiken 1951; closed for safety reasons 1988. Hurricane Hugo kills 24 and causes $700 million in damages 1989. BMW opens plant in Spartanburg 1994.

Tourist information (803) 734-1700. www.discoversouthcarolina.com

▶ SOUTH DAKOTA

The United States did not organize the Dakota Territory until 1861, and even then interest in the region was scant until gold was discovered in 1874. The majority of those who remained after the gold rush turned to cattle ranching, which was a mainstay of the economy through the first half of the 20th century. The manufacturing base was developed after four major dams were built on the Missouri River in the 1930s. They provided hydroelectric power and increased irrigation along the Missouri, which cuts the state in half. Concerned especially over the abrogation of 19th-century treaties, the American Indian Movement (AIM) took over the courthouse at Wounded Knee for 10 weeks in 1973. While U.S. courts have found in favor of the Sioux in several cases concerning the earlier treaties, many maintain that the settlements were insufficient.

Name For southern section of Dakota territory; *dakota* is Sioux word for "allies." **Nicknames** Coyote State, Sunshine State. **Capital** Pierre. **Entered union** Nov. 2, 1889 (40th). **Motto** "Under God the people rule."
Emblems Animal Coyote. **Bird** Chinese ringnecked pheasant. **Fish** Walleye. **Flower** Pasque .
Land Total area 77,116 sq. mi (17th), incl. 1,232 sq. mi. inland water. **Borders** N.Dak., Minn., Iowa, Nebr., Wyo., Mont. **Rivers** Cheyenne, James, Missouri, Moreau, White. **Lakes** Belle Fourche Res., Big Stone, Traverse. **Other notable features** Badlands, Black Hills (Harney Peak 7,242 ft.).
Elected officials Gov. M. Michael Rounds (R, term exp. 2011). Lt. Gov. Dennis Daugaard (R). Sec. State Chris Nelson (R). Atty. Gen. Larry Long (R).
People (July 2007 est.) 796,214 (46th). Race/ Hispanic Origin: White 88.4%. Black 1.1%. Indian 8.3%. Asian 0.8%. Pacific Islander 0.1%. Two or more races 1.4%. Hispanic 2.3%.
Cities (2006) Sioux Falls 142,396. Rapid City 62,715. Aberdeen 24,071. Watertown 20,526. Brookings 18,802. Mitchell 14,887. Pierre 14,095. Yankton 13,767. Huron 10,909. Vermillion 9,862.
Business Gross State Product, 2004: $31.1 bil. (46th). **Leading Sectors of GSP (2001):** Finance, insurance, and real estate 22.07%; Services 17.32%; Depository and nondepository 13.94%. *Fortune 500* **Companies (2007):** 0.
Famous natives Tom Brokaw, journalist. Martha "Calamity" Jane Burk (b. Mo.), frontierswoman. Alvin Hansen, economist. Hubert H. Humphrey, politician. Ernest O. Lawrence, physicist (Nobel Prize, 1939). George McGovern, politician. Ta-sunko-witko (Crazy Horse), Oglala Sioux chief. Tatanka Iyotake (Sitting Bull), Sioux chief.
Noteworthy places Badlands Natl. Park. Crazy Horse State Memorial, Custer. Custer State Park. Ft. Sisseton. Geographical center of the United States. Jewel Cave Natl. Monument. Mount Rushmore. Natl. Memorial. Wind Cave Natl. Park.
Memorable events French visit region 1742–43. To United States in Louisiana Purchase 1803. Ft. Pierre first permanent settlement 1817. Part of Dakota Territory 1861. Gold discovered in Black Hills 1874. Divided from North Dakota; statehood 1889. U.S. troops massacre Sioux at Battle of Wounded Knee 1890.
Tourist information (800) SDAKOTA.
www.travelsd.com

▶ TENNESSEE

First claimed by Virginia and later by North Carolina, Tennessee had its first great pioneer in Daniel Boone, who traversed the region in the 1760s. Political attitudes in the 18th century were shaped by the land, with the cotton and tobacco growers in the fertile western part of the state favoring slavery and the backwoods people of the eastern hills opposed to it. The Cherokees were removed to Oklahoma by the federal government in the 1830s. The state was captured by Union troops in 1862 and put under the governorship of Andrew Johnson, later a U.S. president.

Its economy was radically altered in the 1930s and 1940s by the creation of the Tennessee Valley Authority, which provided abundant energy for industry, and to a lesser extent by the location of the government's first uranium enrichment facility at Oak Ridge during World War II. The state's leading industries are textiles, food processing, and chemicals, and there is considerable lead and coal mining in the east.

Name For Tenase, principal village of Cherokees. **Nickname** Volunteer State. **Capital** Nashville. **Entered union** June 1, 1796 (16th). **Motto** "Agriculture and commerce." **Slogan** "Tennessee—America at its best." **Poet laureate** Richard M. ("Pek") Gunn.
Emblems Animal Raccoon. **Bird** Mockingbird. **Folk dance** Square dance. **Cultivated flower** Iris. **Gem** Tennessee pearl. **Insects** Ladybug, firefly. **Poem** "Oh Tennessee, My Tennessee." **Public school song** "My Tennessee." **Rock** Limestone agate. **Songs** "When It's Iris Time in Tennessee," "The Tennessee Waltz," "My Homeland, Tennessee," "Rocky Top." **Tree** Tulip poplar. **Wildflower** Passion flower.
Land Total area 42,143 sq. mi (36th), incl. 926 sq. mi. inland water. **Borders** Ky., Va., N.C., Ga., Ala., Miss., Ark., Mo. **Rivers** Clinch, Cumberland, Mississippi, Tennessee. **Lakes** Boone, Center Hill, Cherokee, Dale Hollow, Douglass, J. Percy Priest, Watauga. **Other notable features** Cumberland Mts., Great Smoky Mts., Tennessee Valley, Unaka Mts.
Elected officials Gov. Phil Bredesen (D, term exp. 2011). Lt. Gov. Ron Ramsey (R). Sec. State Riley C. Darnell (D). Atty. Gen. Robert Cooper (D).
People (July 2007 est.) 6,156,719 (17th). Race/ Hispanic Origin: White 80.4%. Black 16.9%. Indian 0.3%. Asian 1.3%. Pacific Islander 0.1%. Two or more races 1.0%. Hispanic 3.5%.
Cities (2006) Memphis 670,902. Nashville 552,120. Knoxville 182,337. Chattanooga 155,190. Clarksville 113,175. Murfreesboro 92,559. Jackson 62,711. Johnson City 59,866. Franklin 55,870. Bartlett 46,932.
Business Gross State Product, 2005: $226.5 bil. (18th). **Leading Sectors of GSP (2001):** Services 21.73%; Manufacturing 18.72%; Finance, insurance, and real estate 15.09%. *Fortune 500* **Companies (2007):** 9.
Famous natives James Agee, author. Davy Crockett, frontiersman. David Farragut, naval officer. Aretha Franklin, singer. Morgan Freeman, actor. Al Gore, (b. Washington, D.C.), politician. Cordell Hull, statesman (Nobel Peace Prize, 1945). Dolly Parton, singer. Sikawyi (Sequoya), Cherokee scholar. Alvin York, soldier.
Noteworthy places American Museum of Science and Energy, Oak Ridge. Andrew Johnson Natl. Hist. Site, Greenville. Chickamauga and Chattanooga Natl. Military Park. Cumberland Natl. Hist. Park. Ft. Donelson Natl. Military Park. Graceland, Memphis. Grand Old Opry, Nashville. Great Smoky Mountains Natl. Park. The Hermitage (Andrew Jackson home), Nashville. Lookout Mountain, Chattanooga. Dollyworld,

Gatlinburg. The Parthenon, Nashville. Shiloh Natl. Mil. Park, Pittsburgh Landing. Stones River Natl. Battlefield, Murfreesboro.

Memorable events De Soto expedition passes through region 1540. French claim territory as part of Louisiana; English claim territory as part of Carolina grant 1663. French claim given up after French and Indian War 1763. State of Franklin established in what is now eastern Tennessee 1784–87. Organized as Territory South of the Ohio 1790. Statehood 1796. Secedes from Union 1861. Battles of Shiloh (1862), Chattanooga (1863), Stones River (1863), and Nashville (1864). Readmitted to Union 1866. Clarence Darrow defends John T. Scopes for violating ban on teaching evolution in public schools; loses case 1925. Congress creates Tennessee Valley Authority 1933. First operational nuclear reactor at Oak Ridge 1943. Martin Luther King assassinated at Memphis 1968. World's Fair held in Knoxville 1982.

Tourist information   (800) 836-6200.
www.tnvacation.com

▶TEXAS

The land that is Texas today was originally part of Spain's holdings in Mexico. After Mexico won independence, the new government invited U.S. citizens to settle there. After many clashes between the Mexican and Anglo cultures, Texas broke away and for 10 years was an independent country before becoming a state in 1845. Modern Texas was made by oil, discovered at Spindletop in 1901, and the state's economy has been tied to the oil market ever since. After World War II, the Texas economy soared, bringing both prosperity and an unprecedented population boom. With the oil glut of the early 1980s, growth came to a halt, causing a drastic realignment of economic priorities. Unemployment jumped more than 20 percent during the 1980s, and remained higher than the national average in 1990, a year that saw many bank failures. The economy has been forced to diversify; currently the petroleum industry accounts for only 7 percent of state revenues, down from 25 percent a decade before. Texas has enormous resources ranging from cotton, cattle and timber to aerospace, computers and electronics. The largest of the 48 conterminous states, Texas's image as a state of wide-open spaces is understandable, but fully 80 percent of its people live in metropolitan areas, and Dallas, Houston and San Antonio are among the nation's 10 largest cities. Thirty-six percent of the population is Hispanic; the majority of those are Mexican-American.

Name From the Caddo *tavshas*, "friends." **Nickname** Lone Star State. **Capital** Austin. **Entered union** Dec. 29, 1845 (28th). **Motto** "Friendship." **Emblems Bird** Mockingbird. **Dish** Chili. **Flower** Bluebonnet. **Gem** Topaz. **Grass** Sideoats grama. **Songs** "Texas, Our Texas," "The Eyes of Texas." **Stone** Palmwood. **Tree** Pecan.

Land Total area 268,581 sq. mi (2nd), incl. 6,784 sq. mi. inland water. **Borders** Okla., Ark., La., Gulf of Mexico, Tamaulipas, Coahuila, Chihuahua, N.Mex. **Rivers** Brazos, Colorado, Natchez, Red, Rio Grande, Sabine, Trinity. **Lakes** Sam Rayburn Res., Texoma, Toledo Bend Res. **Other notable features** Balcones Escarpment, Diablo Sierra, Edwards Plateau, Guadalupe Mts., Staked Plain, Stockton Plateau.

Elected officials   Gov. Rick Perry (R, term exp. 2011). Lt. Gov. David Dewhurst (R). Sec. State Phil Wilson (R). Atty. Gen. Greg Abbott (R).

People (July 2007 est.) 23,904,380 (2nd). Race/ Hispanic Origin: White 82.6%. Black 12%. Indian 0.7%. Asian 3.4%. Pacific Islander 0.1%. Two or more races 1.2%. Hispanic 36%.

Cities (2006) Houston 2,144,491. San Antonio 1,296,682. Dallas 1,232,940. Austin 709,893. Fort Worth 653,320. El Paso 609,415. Arlington 367,197. Corpus Christi 285,267. Plano 255,009. Garland 217,963.

Business Gross State Product, 2004: $982.4 bil. (2nd). **Leading Sectors of GSP (2001):** Services 20.48%; Finance, insurance, and real estate 15.48%; Manufacturing 12.27%. **Fortune 500 Companies (2007):** 56.

Famous natives Lance Armstrong, cyclist. Stephen Austin (b. Va.), pioneer. James "Jim" Bowie (b. Ky.), army officer. Carol Burnett, comedian. J. Frank Dobie, folklorist. Dwight D. Eisenhower, U.S. president/general. Samuel Houston (b. Va.), president Republic of Texas/governor State of Texas. Howard Hughes, industrialist/aviator. Lyndon Baines Johnson, U.S. president. Janis Joplin, singer. Barbara Jordan, politician. Audie Murphy, soldier/actor. Chester Nimitz, navy officer. Katherine Anne Porter, author. Samuel T. Rayburn, politician. Mildred "Babe" Didrikson Zaharias, athlete.

Noteworthy places The Alamo, San Antonio. Alibates Flint Quarries Natl. Monument. Big Bend Natl. Park. Ft. Davis. Galveston Historical Foundation. Guadalupe Mountains Natl. Park. Houston Museum of Fine Arts. Lyndon B. Johnson Natl. Hist. Park, Johnson City. Lyndon B. Johnson Space Center, Houston. Old Stone Ft., Nacogdoches. Padre Island Natl. Seashore. San Antonio Missions Natl. Hist. Park. Texas Ranger Museum, Waco.

Memorable events Alonzo Alvarez de Piñeda sails along coast 1519. Estevanico blazes trail through West Texas 1539. Spanish establish settlement at Ysleta near El Paso 1682. René-Robert Cavalier de La Salle attempts to found colony on Matagorda Bay, establishing claim to region for France 1685. Effective Spanish occupation 1715. United States acquires French claim to region with Louisiana Purchase 1803. United States relinquishes claim to Spain 1819. Americans move into region in early 19th century. Mexico, of which Texas is a province, wins independence from Spain 1821. Declaration of Independence from Mexico; Santa Anna victor at Battle of the Alamo; Sam Houston victor at Battle of San Jacinto; founding of Republic of Texas 1836. Texas granted statehood by United States 1845. Secedes from Union 1861; readmitted 1870. Hurricane kills 6,000 at Galveston 1900. NASA Space Center opens at Houston 1962. Pres. Kennedy assassinated at Dallas 1963. Price of oil plunges during 1980s, crippling state economy.

Tourist information   (800) 888-8TEX.
www.traveltex.com

▶UTAH

In the middle of the Great Basin between the Rocky Mountains and the Sierra Nevada, Utah was an arid and uninviting region. After Joseph Smith, the founder of the Church of Jesus Christ of Latter-day Saints (Mormons), was shot in Illinois, Brigham Young led his people west, ultimately to the Salt Lake Valley in 1847. The chief obstacle to statehood was polygamy, which the church eventually renounced. There was an influx of non-Mormons after the discovery of silver in 1863, but Mormons still comprise two-thirds of the state's population, and the state remains conservative in outlook. Although the federal government is a major employer, government policy has lately been challenged by increased concern over the issues of chemical weapons testing, the MX missile, and disposal of nuclear waste from the Rocky Mountain Arsenal in neighboring Colorado.

Name For Ute Indians. **Nicknames** Beehive State, Mormon State. **Capital** Salt Lake City. **Entered Union** Jan. 4, 1896 (45th). **Motto:** "Industry."

Emblems **Animal** Elk. **Bird** California Gull. **Emblem** Beehive **Fish** Rainbow Trout **Flower** Sego lily. **Gem** Topaz. **Song** "Utah, We Love Thee." **Tree** Blue spruce.

Land Total area 84,899 sq. mi (13th), incl. 2,755 sq. mi. inland water. **Borders** Idaho, Wyo., Colo., Ariz., Nev. **Rivers** Bear, Colorado, Green, Sevier. **Lakes** Bear, Great Salt, Utah. **Mountains** La Sal, Uinta (Kings Peak 13,528 ft.) Wasatch Range. **Other notable features** Great Salt Lake Desert (Bonneville Salt Flats), Kaibab Plateau.

Elected officials Gov. Jon Huntsman, Jr. (R, term exp. 2009). Lt. Gov. Gary R. Herbert (R). Atty. Gen. Mark Shurtleff (R).

People (July 2007 est.) 2,645,330 (34th). Race/Hispanic Origin: White 93.2%. Black 1.2%. Indian 1.3%. Asian 2.0%. Pacific Islander 0.7%. Two or more races 1.6%. Hispanic 11.6%.

Cities (2006) Salt Lake City 178,858. West Valley City 119,841. Provo 113,984. West Jordan 94,309. Sandy 94,203. Orem 90,857. Ogden 78,086. St. George 67,614. Layton 62,716. Taylorsville 58,048.

Business Gross State Product, 2005: $89.8 bil. (33rd). **Leading Sectors of GSP (2001):** Services 20.59%; Finance, insurance, and real estate 20.08%; Government 14.65%. *Fortune 500* Companies (2007): 1.

Famous natives Maud Adams, actress. John Moses Browning, inventor. Philo Farnsworth, engineer. Merlin Olsen, football player/actor. Ivy Baker Priest, U.S. treasurer. Brigham Young (b. Vt.), religious leader. Loretta Young, actress.

Noteworthy places Arches Natl. Park. Bryce Canyon Natl. Park. Canyonlands Natl. Park. Capitol Reef Natl. Park. Cedar Breaks Natl. Monument. Dinosaur Natl. Monument. Flaming Gorge Dam Natl. Monument. Grand Staircase-Escalante Natl. Monument. Great Salt Lake. Lake Powell Natl. Monument. Monument Valley. Mormon Tabernacle, Salt Lake City. Natural Bridges Natl. Monument. Promontory Point. Rainbow Bridge Natl. Monument. Temple Square, Salt Lake City. Timpanogas Cave Natl. Monument. Zion Natl. Park.

Memorable events First visited probably by explorers from Coronado expedition 1540. Silvestre Vélez de Escalante and Francisco Atanasio Dominguez explore for Spain 1776. James Bridger discovers Great Salt Lake 1824. Led by Brigham Young, Mormons reach Great Salt Lake 1847. United States acquires Utah region from Mexico 1848. Mormons organize state of Deseret 1849; Congress refuses to recognize and instead organizes Territory of Utah 1850. Silver discovered at Little Cottonwood Canyon 1868. First transcontinental railroad completed with driving of golden spike at Promontory Point 1869. Mormon church renounces polygamy 1890, paving way to statehood 1896. Uranium discovered near Moab 1952. Winter Olympics held in Salt Lake City 2002.

Tourist Information (800) 200-1160. www.utah.com

▶VERMONT

Originally claimed by both New Hampshire and New York, Vermont's independence was asserted by Ethan Allen. His Green Mountain Boys rid the state of New Yorkers in 1770, fought well against the British in the Revolution, and declared the independent republic of New Connecticut in 1777. Allen was eventually overthrown, and Vermont joined the Union in 1791.

Vermont traditionally has strong ties to Canada, and there was an influx of French-Canadians as Vermont began to develop its manufacturing base in the mid-19th century. Vermont's politics have always been characterized by tolerance and progressivism. As New Connecticut, it abolished slavery and allowed universal male suffrage. Vermont's environmental concerns focus on acid rain and the degree to which development (especially by the tourist industry) should infringe on the state's remaining unspoiled land.

Name From French *vert mont*, "green mountain." **Nickname** Green Mountain State. **Capital** Montpelier. **Entered Union** Mar. 4, 1791 (14th). **Motto** "Freedom and unity."

Emblems **Animal** Morgan horse. **Beverage** Milk. **Bird** Hermit thrush. **Cold-Water Fish** Brook trout. **Flower** Red Clover. **Insect** Honeybee. **Song** "These Green Mountains" **Tree** Sugar Maple. **Warm-Water Fish** Walleye pike.

Land Total Area 9,614 sq. mi (45th), incl. 365 sq. mi. inland water. **Borders** Quebec, N.H., Mass., N.Y. **Rivers** Connecticut, Lamoille, Otter Creek, Poultney, White, Winooski. **Lakes** Bomoseen, Champlain, Memphremagog, Willoughby. **Other Notable Features** Grand Isle, Green Mts. (Mt. Mansfield 4,393 ft.), Taconic Mts.

Elected officials Gov. James H. Douglas (R, term exp. 2009). Lt. Gov. Brian Dubie (R). Sec. State Deborah Markowitz (D). Atty. Gen. William H. Sorrell (D).

People (July 2007 est.) 621,254 (49th). Race/Hispanic Origin: White 96.5%. Black 0.8%. Indian 0.4%. Asian 1.2%. Two or more races 1.1%. Hispanic 1.3%.

Cities (2006) Burlington 38,358. Essex 19,264. Colchester 17,180. South Burlington 17,014. Rutland 16,964. Bennington 15,349. Brattleboro 11,741. Hartford 10,829. Milton 10,347. Barre 9,038.

Business Gross State Product, 2005: $23.1bil. (50th). **Leading Sectors of GSP (2001):** Services 22.88%; Finance, insurance, and real estate 18.41%; Manufacturing 15.66%. *Fortune 500* Companies (2007): 0.

Famous natives Ethan Allen (b. Conn.), army officer. Chester A. Arthur, U.S. President. Calvin Coolidge, U.S. president. John Deere, industrialist. George Dewey, naval officer. John Dewey, philosopher. Stephen Douglas, politician. James Fisk, financier. Robert Frost (b. Calif.), poet. Rudy Vallee, singer.

Noteworthy places Bennington Battleground/Monument. Billings Farm and Museum, Woodstock. Calvin Coolidge Homestead, Plymouth. Maple Grove Maple Museum, Rock of Ages Tourist Center, Graniteville. Shelburne Museum. St. Johnsbury. Vermont Marble Exhibit, Proctor.

Memorable events Samuel de Champlain explores for France 1609. First French settlement at Ste. Anne 1666. First English settlers build Ft. Drummer near Brattleboro 1724. Bennington settled 1761. Ethan Allen organizes Green Mountain Boys 1764. Green Mountain Boys capture Ft. Ticonderoga and Ft. Crown Point 1775. Gen. John

Stark defeats British general John Burgoyne near Bennington; constitution abolishes slavery and grants universal male suffrage 1777. Claims to area relinquished by Massachusetts (1781), New Hampshire (1782), and New York (1790). First state admitted after original 13 1791. MacDonough defeats British Lake Champlain fleet 1814. Canal between Hudson River and Lake Champlain gives Vermont direct access to port of New York 1823. Confederate soldiers steal $400,000 from St. Albans bank 1864. State recognizes "civil unions" giving gay and lesbian couples virtually all the benefits of marriage 2000.
Tourist Information (800) VERMONT. www.vermontvacation.com

▶**VIRGINIA, COMMONWEALTH OF**
The first successful English settlement in America was at Jamestown in 1607. The differences between the Virginia colonists and those of Massachusetts were pronounced, and the commercial southern planter class shared little of their New England counterparts' religious zeal. Virginia bred its own strain of independence, and it was the fiery Patrick Henry who heralded the American Revolution with the cry "Give me liberty or give me death." Seven of the first 12 presidents were from Virginia. With an economy very dependent on labor-intensive tobacco in the mid-19th century, Virginia seceded from the Union over the slavery issue, despite the misgivings of many, including Robert E. Lee. After the war Virginia developed an increasingly diversified industrial and manufacturing base that survives today, with food products, tobacco, and chemicals leading the way. Despite the dramatic decline of the American merchant marine, Virginia's shipbuilding industry in Newport News flourished in the 1980s, thanks to the Pentagon's commitment to a 600-ship navy. Norfolk is also one of the country's leading commercial ports.
Name For Elizabeth I, called Virgin Queen. **Nicknames** Old Dominion, Mother of Presidents, Mother of States. **Capital** Richmond. **Entered union** June 25, 1788 (10th). **Motto** *Sic semper tyrannis* (Thus always to tyrants).
Emblems **Beverage** Milk. **Bird** Cardinal. **Dog** Foxhound. **Flower** Dogwood. **Shell** Oyster. **Song** "Carry Me Back to Old Virginia." **Tree** Dogwood.
Land **Total area** 42,774 sq. mi (35th), incl. 3,180 sq. mi. inland water. **Borders** Md., D.C., Atlantic Ocean, N.C., Tenn., Ky., W.Va. **Rivers** James, Potomac, Rappahannock, Roanoke, Shenandoah, York. **Lakes** Buggs Island, Claytor, Gaston, Leesville. **Mountains** Allegheny, Blue Ridge, Cumberland, Unaka. **Other notable features** Great Dismal Swamp, Shenandoah Valley.
Elected officials Gov. Tim Kaine (D, term exp. 2011). Lt. Gov. William Bolling (R). Sec. Commonwealth Katherine Hanley (D). Atty. Gen. Robert McDonnell (R).
People (July 2007 est.) 7,712,091 (12th). Race/Hispanic Origin: White 73.2%. Black 19.9%. Indian 0.4%. Asian 4.8%. Pacific Islander 0.1%. Two or more races 1.6%. Hispanic 6.6%.
Cities (2006) Virginia Beach 435,619. Norfolk 229,112. Chesapeake 220,560. Arlington 199,776. Richmond 192,913. Newport News 178,281. Hampton 145,017. Alexandria 136,974. Portsmouth 101,377. Roanoke 91,552.
Business **Gross State Product, 2005:** $352.7 bil. (11th). **Leading Sectors of GSP (2001):** Services 23.63%; Finance, insurance, and real estate

18.97%; Government 17.67%. *Fortune 500* Companies (2007): 17.
Famous natives Arthur Ashe, tennis player. Richard E. Byrd, explorer/aviator. William Clark, explorer. Jerry Falwell, evangelist. William Henry Harrison, U.S. president. Patrick Henry, Revolutionary patriot. Thomas Jefferson, U.S. president. Joseph E. Johnston, Confederate general. John Paul Jones (b. Scotland), navy officer. Robert E. Lee, Confederate general. Meriwether Lewis, explorer. James Madison, U.S. president. John Marshall, jurist. Cyrus Hall McCormick, inventor. James Monroe, U.S. president. Walter Reed, doctor. Pat Robertson, evangelist/politician. Bill "Bojangles" Robinson, dancer. George C. Scott, actor. Thomas Sumter, army officer. Zachary Taylor, U.S. president. John Tyler, U.S. president. Booker T. Washington, educator. George Washington, U.S. president. Woodrow Wilson, U.S. president.
Noteworthy places Appomattox Courthouse Natl. Hist. Park. Arlington Natl. Cemetery. Booker T. Washington Natl. Monument, Roanoke. Colonial Natl. Hist. Park (incl. Jamestown, Yorktown & Williamsburg). Fredricksburg and Spotsylvania Natl. Military Park. George Washington birthplace, Frederick Co. Harpers Ferry Natl. Hist. Site. The Mariners' Museum, Newport News. Monticello, Charlottesville. Mount Vernon. Petersburg Natl. Battlefield. Robert E. Lee Memorial, Lexington. Shenandoah Natl. Park. Virginia Beach. Virginia Museum of Fine Arts. Wolf Trap Farm for the Performing Arts, Reston.
Memorable events John Smith founds Jamestown, first permanent settlement in North America, 1607. John Rolfe marries Pocahontas, daughter of Powhatan, leader of so-called Powhatan Confederacy 1614. First English women arrive at Jamestown; House of Burgesses established 1619. Northampton Declaration first resistance to taxation without representation 1653. College of William and Mary founded 1693. First state to establish Committee of Correspondence 1773. American Revolution ends with Charles Cornwallis's surrender to George Washington at Yorktown 1781. Nat Turner's slave revolt 1831. State secedes from Union 1861. Civil War ends with Robert E. Lee's surrender to Ulysses S. Grant at Appomattox Courthouse 1865. Readmitted to Union 1870. Norfolk Naval Base founded 1917. John D. Rockefeller, Jr. restores Colonial Williamsburg 1926. E. Claiborne Robins donates $50 million to University of Richmond 1969. Douglas Wilder becomes nation's first black governor 1989.
Tourist information (800) VISIT-VA. www.virginia.org

▶**WASHINGTON**
The northwest corner of the continental U.S. was originally the locus of a rich Native American culture noted today primarily for its ornately carved canoes and totem poles. In 1792, Boston merchant Capt. Robert Gray began a trade in sea otter pelts; but the first permanent settlers in the region did not establish themselves for almost 50 years. Agriculture and lumbering were, and remain, mainstays of the state's economy—the farming regions in the east, rich in dairy products, fruit and wheat, and the lumber industry in the western part of the state rely heavily on exports to the Far East. This geographic split reflects the weather patterns: eastern Washington rarely gets more than 10 inches of rain in a year, while on the Pacific coast almost 40 inches is the average.

Since World War I, Puget Sound has been a center of heavy industry and shipbuilding, and 60 percent of the population is concentrated in the region. Boeing maintains one of the country's largest airplane-manufacturing plants in the Seattle-Tacoma area, and Microsoft, the world's leading software company, is located in Redmond. The industrial work force was open to progressive and sometimes radical unionism, and the International Workers of the World (Wobblies) had their national headquarters at Seattle. Before statehood the territorial government pioneered women's suffrage, but Congress declared the women's right to vote unconstitutional.

Name For George Washington. **Nickname** Evergreen State. **Capital** Olympia. **Entered union** Nov. 11, 1889 (42nd). **Motto** *Alki* (By and by).
Emblems Bird Willow goldfinch. **Fish** Steelhead trout. **Flower** Coast rhododendron. **Gem** Petrified wood. **Song** "Washington, My Home." **Tree** Western hemlock.
Land Total area 71,300 sq. mi (18th), incl. 4,756 sq. mi. inland water. **Borders** British Columbia, Idaho, Oreg., Pacific Ocean. **Rivers** Chehalis, Columbia, Pend Oreille, Snake, Yakima. **Lakes** Baker, Bank, Chelan, Franklin D. Roosevelt, Ross, Rufus Woods. **Mountains** Cascade Range, Coast Range, Kettle River Range, Olympic. **Other notable features** Puget Sound, San Juan Islands, Strait of Juan de Fuca.
Elected officials Gov. Christine Gregoire (D, term exp. 2009). Lt. Gov. Brad Owen (D). Sec. State Sam Reed (D). Atty. Gen. Rob McKenna (R).
People (July 2007 est.) 6,468,424 (13th). Race/Hispanic Origin: White 84.6%. Black 3.6%. Indian 1.6%. Asian 6.7%. Pacific Islander 0.5%. Two or more races 3.0%. Hispanic 9.4%.
Cities (2006) Seattle 582,454. Spokane 198,081. Tacoma 196,532. Vancouver 158,855. Bellevue 118,186. Everett 98,514. Federal Way 84,166. Kent 83,501. Yakima 82,805. Bellingham 75,150.
Business Gross State Product, 2005: $268.5 bil. (14th). **Leading Sectors of GSP (2001):** Services 23.38%; Finance, insurance, and real estate 18.41%; Government 13.82%. *Fortune 500* **Companies (2007):** 10.
Famous natives Harry L. "Bing" Crosby, singer. Merce Cunningham, choreographer. Bill Gates, businessman. Jimi Hendrix, guitarist. Henry M. "Scoop" Jackson, politician. Robert Joffrey, choreographer. Gary Larson, cartoonist. Edward R. Murrow, reporter (b. North Carolina). Theodore Roethke (b. Mich.), poet. Marcus Whitman (b. N.Y.), missionary/pioneer.
Noteworthy places Grand Coulee Dam. Klondike Gold Rush Natl. Hist. Park, Seattle. Mount Rainier Natl. Park. Mount Saint Helens Natl. Monument. North Cascades Natl. Park. Olympic Natl. Park. San Juan Islands Natl. Hist. Park. Seattle Art Museum. Space Needle, Seattle.
Memorable events Sir Francis Drake skirts coast of Pacific Northwest 1579. Juan de Fuca sails into straits now bearing his name. Bruno de Heceta lands at Hoh River 1775. Capt. James Cook arrives 1778. Capt. Robert Gray discovers mouth of Columbia River, which he names for his ship; George Vancouver explores Puget Sound 1792. Lewis and Clark expedition winters at Columbia River 1805. Marcus Whitman, Protestant Mission Board, settles near Walla Walla 1836. Territorial status 1853. Northern Pacific railroad reaches Puget Sound 1883. Alaska-Yukon-Pacific Exposition at Seattle 1909. Grand Coulee Dam, largest concrete hydroelectric dam in United States, completed

1941. Hanford works atomic energy plant opens 1943. Upholding treaty provisions from Washinton's days as a territory, a decision awards Native Americans half the catch of Northwest salmon and steelhead 1974. Mt. Saint Helens erupts, killing 61, 1980. Washington Public Power Supply System (known as "whoops") defaults on $8.25 billion bond issue 1983.
Tourist information (800) 544-1800.
www.experiencewa.com

▶ WEST VIRGINIA

When Virginia seceded in 1861, its western counties reorganized and in 1863 were admitted to the Union as a separate state. Despite the rugged terrain, through which transportation has always been difficult, farming remained the backbone of the economy until the close of the 19th century, when coal mining and other extractive industries developed. After World War II, the manufacturing base developed to include steel and chemical manufacturing. Even with vast natural resources, West Virginia has long been one of the poorest states in the union. Population losses since the 1950's have been pronounced, and the 8 percent loss between 1980 and 1990 was the highest in the country. There is low participation in the workforce by women and educational achievement is well below the national average.

Name for western part of Virginia. **Nickname** Mountain State. **Capital** Charleston. **Entered union** June 20, 1863 (35th). **Motto** *Montani semper liberi* (Mountaineers are always free).
Emblems Animal Black bear. **Bird** Cardinal. **Colors** Old gold and blue. **Fish** Brook trout. **Flower** *Rhododendron maximum* (big laurel). **Fruit** Apple. **Songs** "The West Virginia Hills," "West Virginia, My Home Sweet Home," "This Is My West Virginia." **Tree** Sugar maple.
Land Total area 24,230 sq. mi (41st), incl. 152 sq. mi. inland water. **Borders** Ohio, Pa., Md., Va., Ky. **Rivers** Big Sandy, Guayandotte, Kanawha, Little Kanawha, Monongahela, Ohio, Potomac. **Lakes** Summersville Dam. **Mountains** Allegheny, Blue Ridge, Cumberland.
Elected officials Gov. Joe Manchin III (D, term exp. 2009). Sec. State Betty Ireland (R). Atty. Gen. Darrell V. McGraw (D).
People (July 2007 est.) 1,812,035 (37th). Race/Hispanic Origin: White 94.6%. Black 3.5%. Indian 0.2%. Asian 0.7%. Two or more races 0.9%. Hispanic 1.1%.
Cities (2006) Charleston 50,846. Huntington 49,007. Parkersburg 31,755. Wheeling 29,330. Morgantown 28,654. Weirton 19,250. Fairmont 19,145. Beckley 16,828. Clarksburg 16,459. Martinsburg 16,392.
Business Gross State Product, 2005: $53.8 bil. (41st). **Leading Sectors of GSP (2000):** Services 18.26%; Government 16.07%; Manufacturing 15.99%. *Fortune 500* **Companies (2007):** 0.
Famous natives Newton D. Baker, politician. Pearl Buck, novelist (Nobel Prize, 1938). John W. Davis, politician. Dwight Whitney Morrow, lawyer/diplomat. Michael Owens, manufacturer. Walter Reuther, labor leader. Cyrus Vance, statesman. Jerry West, basketball player. Charles "Chuck" Yeager, pilot.
Noteworthy places Cass Scenic Railroad. Harpers Ferry Natl. Hist. Park. Monongahela Natl. Forest. New River Gorge Bridge. Science and Cultural Center, Charleston.
Memorable events First permanent settlement by Morgan Morgan at Mill Creek 1731. Coal

discovered on Coal River 1742. Wheeling Convention repudiates act of secession; forms new state of Kanahwa 1861. Enters Union as West Virginia 1863. Population peaks at 2.5 million 1950. Unemployment jumps 8.6% to 18.0%, highest in nation, 1980–83.

Tourist information (800) CALL-WVA. www.wvtourism.com

▶ WISCONSIN

The indigenous people of the region had a largely agricultural economy, but the fur trade drew Europeans into the region. Native resistance to white settlement was strong and not overcome until the Black Hawk Wars of 1832. In the early 19th century, German, Scandinavian, and Dutch farmers migrated to the region in large numbers. Many social welfare policies now common to the nation as a whole—including aid to dependent children, workmen's compensation, and old-age assistance—were pioneered in Wisconsin. Although manufacturing accounts for the lion's share of Wisconsin's profits, agriculture is extremely important, and the state is the nation's leading producer of dairy products. There are major shipping facilities at Superior, Green Bay, and Milwaukee.

Name From the Ojibwa *wishkonsing*, "place of the bearer." **Nickname** Badger State. **Capital** Madison. **Entered union** May 29, 1848 (30th). **Motto** "Forward."
Emblems **Animal** Badger. **Bird** Robin. **Domestic animal** Dairy cow. **Fish** Muskellunge. **Flower** Wood violet. **Insect** Honeybee. **Mineral** Galena. **Rock** Red granite. **Soil** Antigo silt loam. **Song** "On, Wisconsin!" **Symbol of peace** Mourning dove. **Tree** Sugar maple. **Wildlife animal** White-tailed deer.
Land **Total area** 65,498 sq. mi (23rd), incl. 11,188 sq. mi. inland water. **Borders** Minn., Lake Superior, Mich., Lake Michigan, Ill., Iowa. **Rivers** Black, Chippewa, Menominee, Mississippi, St. Croix, Wisconsin. **Lakes** Chippewa, Du Bay, Mendota, Michigan, Superior, Winnebago. **Other notable features** Apostle Islands, Door Peninsula, Green Bay.
Elected officials Gov. Jim Doyle (D, term exp. 2011). Lt. Gov. Barbara Lawton (D). Sec. State Douglas La Follette (D). Atty. Gen. J.B. Van Hollen (R).
People (July, 2007 est.) 5,601,640 (20th). Race/Hispanic Origin: White 89.9%. Black 6.0%. Indian 0.9%. Asian 2.0%. Two or more races 1.1%. Hispanic 4.9%.
Cities (2006) Milwaukee 578,887. Madison 221,551. Green Bay 101,203. Kenosha 95,240. Racine 79,392. Appleton 70,217. Waukesha 67,658. Oshkosh 63,485. Eau Claire 62,570. Janesville 61,962.
Business **Gross State Product, 2005:** $217.5 bil. (21st). **Leading Sectors of GSP (2001):** Manufacturing 25.38%; Services 18.21%; Finance, insurance, and real estate 15.81%. *Fortune 500* **Companies (2007):** 9.
Famous natives King Camp Gillette, inventor/businessman. Eric Heiden, speed skater. Harry Houdini (b. Hungary), magician. Robert La Follette, politician. Liberace (Wladziu Valentino), pianist. Alfred Lunt, actor. Joseph R. McCarthy, politician. Spencer Tracy, actor. Thorstein Veblen, economist. Orson Welles, director. Laura Ingalls Wilder, novelist. Thornton Wilder, author. Frank Lloyd Wright, architect.
Noteworthy places Apostle Island Natl. Lakeshore. Chequamegon Natl. Forest. Circus World Museum, Baraboo. Door County Peninsula. Ice Age Natl. Scientific Reserve. Little House Wayside, Pepin. Manitowoc Maritime Museum. Mil-

waukee Art Museum. Milwaukee Public Museum. Nicolet Natl. Forest. Old Wade House and Carriage Museum, Greenbush. Old World Wisconsin, Eagle. Villa Louis, Prairie du Chien. Wisconsin Dells.
Memorable events Jean Nicolet lands at Green Bay 1634. French establish mission and trading post near Ashland 1634. British take control of region 1763. Land ceded to United States 1787, but U.S. control not established until after War of 1812. Becomes independent Territory 1836. Statehood 1848. More than 800 die in forest fire near Peshtigo 1871. First hydroelectric plant completed at Appleton 1882. Ringling Brothers circus formed at Baraboo 1884. First state to enact income tax 1911. Milwaukee transfers more than 11,000 students between city and surburban schools 1986.

Tourist information (800) 372-2737. www.travelwisconsin.com

▶ WYOMING

Tens of thousands of migrants traveled through the region along the Oregon Trail, but few settled the land until Ft. Laramie was built in 1834. Territorial status came in 1869. Wyoming was the first state to give the vote to women, and in 1925 Nellie Tayloe Ross became the first woman governor following the death of her husband. Cattle ranching is the traditional mainstay of the economy. The state ranks second in uranium output, petroleum and coal production have become increasingly important. Wyoming is best known for its natural wonders. Yellowstone National Park—the site of Old Faithful—is the oldest and largest national park in the country. Following a decade-long mining boom in the 1970s and 1980s, Wyoming's population declined, and it has fallen behind even Alaska in total population. Although the population has increased in the 1990s, there are still no more than five people per square mile.

Name From the Delaware *maugh-wau-wa-ma*, "large plains" or "mountains and valleys alternating." **Nickname** Equality State. **Capital** Cheyenne. **Entered union** July 10, 1890 (44th). **Motto** "Equal rights."
Emblems **Bird** Meadowlark. **Flower** Indian paintbrush. **Gem** Jade. **Song** "Wyoming." **Tree** Cottonwood.
Land **Total area** 97,814 sq. mi (10th), incl. 713 sq. mi. inland water. **Borders** Mont., S.Dak., Nebr., Colo., Utah, Idaho. **Rivers** Bighorn, Green, North Platte, Powder, Snake, Yellowstone. **Lakes** Bighorn, Yellowstone. **Mountains** Absaroka, Bighorn, Black Hills, Laramie, Owl Creek, Teton Range, Wind River Range, Wyoming Range.
Elected officials Gov. Dave Freudenthal (D). Sec. State Max Maxfield (R). Atty. Gen. Bruce Salzburg (D).
People (July 2007 est.) 522,830 (50th). Race/Hispanic Origin: White 94.1%. Black 1.2%. Indian 2.5%. Asian 0.7%. Pacific Islander 0.1%. Two or more races 1.4%. Hispanic 7.3%.
Cities (2006) Cheyenne 55,314. Casper 52,089. Laramie 25,688. Gillette 23,899. Rock Springs 19,324. Sheridan 16,429. Green River 11,933. Evanston 11,567. Riverton 9,728. Cody 9,217.
Business **Gross State Product, 2005:** $27.4 bil. (48th). **Leading Sectors of GSP (2001):** Mining 24.35%; Transportation & utilities 13.61%; Government 13.42%. *Fortune 500* **Companies (2007):** 0.
Famous natives James Bridger (b. Va.), pioneer. J.C. Penney, businessman. Jackson Pollock, painter. Nellie Tayloe Ross (b. Mo.), politician.

Noteworthy places Bighorn Canyon Natl. Rec. Area. Buffalo Bill Museum, Cody. Devil's Tower Natl. Monument. Ft. Bridger State Park. Ft. Laramie Natl. Hist. Site. Fossil Butte Natl. Monument. Grand Teton Natl. Park. Medicine Wheel Natl. Hist. Landmark, near Lovell. Natl. Elk Refuge. Yellowstone Natl. Park (Old Faithful).

Memorable events Part of Louisiana Territory claimed for France 1682. Pierre Gaultier de Varennes, sieur de Vérendrye explores region for France 1743. Region to United States with Louisiana Purchase 1803. John Colter crosses area of Yellowstone 1807–08. Indian Wars follow massacre of army detachments 1854 and 1866. Wyoming Territory organized 1868. Women's suffrage adopted permanently (first instance in United States); Union Pacific railroad crosses state 1869. Yellowstone, world's first national park, opens 1872. White mob kills 28 Chinese miners and burns Chinatown in Rock Springs 1885. Statehood 1890. Nellie Tayloe Ross first woman governor 1925. First Intercontinental Ballistic Missile (ICBM) base opens near Cheyenne 1951. Fires consume 1.6 million acres of forest in and around Yellowstone Park 1988.

Tourist information   (800) CALL-WYO.
www.wyomingtourism.org

The Most Livable States, 2007

2007 Rank/State	2006 Rank	Change
1. New Hampshire	1	0
2. Minnesota	2	0
3. Wyoming	6	3
4. Utah	11	7
5. New Jersey	5	0
6. Iowa	3	-3
7. Vermont	4	-3
8. Massachusetts	7	-1
9. South Dakota	13	4
10. Connecticut	10	0
11. Nebraska	9	-2
12. Virginia	8	-4
13. North Dakota	12	-1
14. Idaho	18	4
15. Maryland	16	1
16. Maine	17	1
17. Kansas	15	-2
18. Colorado	20	2
19. Hawaii	22	3
20. Wisconsin	14	-6
21. Delaware	18	-3
22. Montana	21	-1
23. Oregon	33	10
24. Alaska	23	-1
25. Nevada	24	-1
26. Illinois	28	2
27. Florida	31	4
28. Rhode Island	26	-2
29. New York	32	3
30. California	34	4
31. Washington	25	-6
32. Arizona	29	-3
33. Pennsylvania	30	-3
34. Missouri	27	-7
35. Indiana	36	1
36. Ohio	37	1
37. New Mexico	41	4
38. Michigan	35	-3
39. Texas	41	2
40. Oklahoma	43	3
41. Georgia	38	-3
42. Alabama	39	-3
42. North Carolina	40	-2
44. Tennessee	45	1
45. West Virginia	44	-1
46. South Carolina	46	0
47. Kentucky	47	0
48. Arkansas	48	0
49. Louisiana	50	1
50. Mississippi	49	-1

Note: Ratings based on average of several statistics, including crime, education, and access to health care. **Source:** Morgan Quinto Press, *State & City Ranking Publications*, 2007. www.morganquitno.com

The Healthiest States, 2007

2007 Rank/State	2006 Rank	Change
1. Vermont	1	0
2. Minnesota	3	1
3. Massachusetts	6	3
4. Maine	4	0
5. New Hampshire	2	-3
6. Nebraska	7	1
7. Iowa	5	-2
8. Utah	8	0
9. Hawaii	10	1
10. Kansas	12	2
11. Rhode Island	13	2
12. North Dakota	11	-1
13. Connecticut	9	-4
14. Washington	20	6
15. Wisconsin	14	-1
16. New Jersey	16	0
17. Oregon	15	-2
18. Virginia	21	3
19. California	19	0
20. Ohio	24	4
21. Michigan	23	2
22. South Dakota	17	-5
23. Pennsylvania	29	6
24. Idaho	18	-6
25. West Virginia	22	-3
26. Montana	27	1
27. New York	31	4
28. Colorado	32	4
29. Kentucky	26	-3
30. Wyoming	25	-5
31. North Carolina	30	-1
32. Illinois	33	1
33. Indiana	28	-5
34. Missouri	34	0
35. Maryland	35	0
36. Alaska	39	3
37. Arkansas	36	-1
38. Tennessee	38	0
39. Delaware	37	-2
40. Alabama	42	2
41. Oklahoma	45	4
42. Arizona	40	-2
43. Texas	46	3
44. Georgia	44	0
45. South Carolina	42	-3
46. Florida	41	-5
47. Nevada	47	0
48. Mississippi	50	2
49. New Mexico	49	0
50. Louisiana	48	-2

Note: Ratings based on average of several statistics. **Source:** Morgan Quinto Press, *State & City Ranking Publications*, 2007. www.morganquitno.com

Composition of State Legislatures, 2008

State or other jurisdiction	Senate Demo-crats	Senate Repub-licans	Senate Total	House Demo-crats	House Repub-licans	House Total
Alabama	**22**	13	35	**62**	43	105
Alaska	9	**11**	20	17	**23**	40
Arizona	13	**17**	30	27	**33**	60
Arkansas	**27**	8	35	**75**	25	100
California	**25**	15	40	**48**	32	80
Colorado	**20**	15	35	**40**	25	65
Connecticut	**23**	13	36	**107**	44	151
Delaware	**13**	8	21	19	**22**	41
Florida	14	**26**	40	42	**77**	120[2]
Georgia	22	**34**	56	73	**107**	180
Hawaii	**21**	4	25	**44**	7	51
Idaho	7	**28**	35	19	**51**	70
Illinois	**37**	27	59	**67**	51	118
Indiana	17	**33**	50	**51**	49	100
Iowa	**30**	20	50	**53**	47	100
Kansas	10	**30**	40	47	**78**	125
Kentucky	15	**22**	38[1]	**63**	36	100[2]
Louisiana	**23**	16	39	**53**	50	105[1]
Maine	**18**	17	35	**90**	59	151[1]
Maryland	**33**	14	47	**104**	37	141
Massachusetts	**35**	5	40	**141**	19	160
Michigan	17	**21**	38	**58**	52	110
Minnesota	**45**	22	67	**85**	45	134[1]
Mississippi	**27**	25	52	**75**	47	122
Missouri	14	**20**	34	71	**92**	163
Montana	26	**26**	50	49	**50**	100[1]
Nebraska	Nonpartisan			49	Unicameral	
Nevada	10	**11**	21	**27**	15	42
New Hampshire	**14**	10	24	**236**	159	400[1,2]
New Jersey	**23**	17	40	**48**	32	80
New Mexico	**24**	18	42	**42**	28	70
New York	30	**32**	62	**108**	42	150
North Carolina	**31**	19	50	**68**	52	120
North Dakota	21	**26**	47	33	**61**	94
Ohio	12	**21**	33	46	**53**	99
Oklahoma	24	**24**	48	44	**57**	101
Oregon	**18**	11	30[1]	**31**	29	60
Pennsylvania	21	**29**	50	**102**	101	203
Rhode Island	**32**	5	38[2]	**61**	13	75[1]
South Carolina	19	**27**	46	51	**72**	124[2]
South Dakota	15	**20**	35	20	**50**	70
Tennessee	16	16	33[1]	**53**	46	99
Texas	11	**20**	31	71	**79**	150
Utah	8	**21**	29	20	**55**	75
Vermont	**23**	7	30	**93**	49	150[1]
Virginia	**21**	19	40	45	**53**	100[1]
Washington	**32**	17	49	**63**	35	98
West Virginia	**23**	11	34	**72**	28	100
Wisconsin	**18**	15	33	47	**52**	99
Wyoming	7	**23**	30	17	**43**	60
Dist./Columbia[3]	**11**	1	13[1]	Unicameral		
Amer. Samoa	Nonpartisan	18		Nonpartisan		21
Guam	7	**8**	15	Unicameral		
No. Mariana Isl.	N.A.	N.A.	9	N.A.	N.A.	18
Puerto Rico	9	**17**	27[1]	17	**33**	51[1]
U.S. Virgin Isl.	**9**	0	15[1]	Unicameral		

Note: As of 2008. Numbers in bold indicates the party in the majority. 1. Includes one or more Independent or other third-party legislator. 2. Includes one or more vacancy. 3. Council of the District of Columbia. **Source:** National Conference of State Legislatures, 2008.

Salaries of Major State Administrative Officials, 2004

State	Governor	Lieutenant governor	Secretary of state	Attorney general
Alabama	$96,361	$45,360	$71,500	$163,429
Alaska	85,776	80,040	([1])	91,200
Arizona	95,000	([2])	70,000	90,000
Arkansas	75,296	36,392	47,060	62,746
California	175,000	131,250	123,750	148,750
Colorado	90,000	68,500	68,500	80,000
Connecticut	150,000	110,000	110,000	110,000
Delaware	114,000	62,400	106,000	116,700
Florida	120,171	115,112	116,056	118,957
Georgia	127,303	83,148	112,776	125,871
Hawaii	94,780	90,041	([1])	85,302
Idaho	98,500	26,750	82,500	91,500
Illinois	150,691	115,235	132,963	132,963
Indiana	95,000	76,000	66,000	79,400
Iowa	107,482	76,698	87,990	105,430
Kansas	98,331	111,523	76,389	76,389
Kentucky	125,130	91,075	91,075	91,075
Louisiana	94,532	85,000	85,000	85,000
Maine	70,000	([3])	N.A.	78,062
Maryland	135,000	112,500	78,750	112,500
Massachusetts	135,000	120,000	120,000	122,500
Michigan	177,000	123,900	124,900	124,900
Minnesota	120,311	78,196	90,222	114,297
Mississippi	122,160	60,000	90,000	108,960
Missouri	120,087	77,184	96,455	104,332
Montana	93,089	66,724	72,085	81,919
Nebraska	85,000	60,000	65,000	75,000
Nevada	117,000	50,000	80,000	110,000
New Hampshire	100,690	([3])	65,540	85,753
New Jersey	157,000	([3])	137,165	137,165
New Mexico	110,000	85,000	85,000	95,000
New York	179,000	151,500	120,800	151,500
North Carolina	118,430	104,523	104,523	104,523
North Dakota	85,506	66,380	68,108	74,668
Ohio	126,485	73,715	90,725	93,434
Oklahoma	110,298	85,500	90,000	103,109
Oregon	93,600	([2])	72,000	77,200
Pennsylvania	144,416	121,309	103,980	120,154
Rhode Island	105,194	88,584	88,584	94,121
South Carolina	106,078	46,545	92,007	92,007
South Dakota	95,389	12,635	64,812	80,995
Tennessee	85,000	49,500	131,124	121,728
Texas	115,345	97,200	117,546	92,217
Utah	100,680	78,200	([1])	84,600
Vermont	127,456	54,080	80,808	96,752
Virginia	124,855	36,321	131,370	110,667
Washington	139,087	72,705	89,004	126,443
West Virginia	90,000	([3])	65,000	80,000
Wisconsin	122,406	69,579	62,549	127,868
Wyoming	130,000	([2])	110,000	89,067

Note: The current governor and lieutenant governor of Massachusetts waive their salaries. 1. Lieutenant governor also serves as secretary of state. 2. Secretary of state also serves as lieutenant governor. 3. No lieutenant governor. Speaker or President of the Senate are next in line of succession.
Source: Council of State Governments, *The Book of the States*, 2004.

Summary of State Government Finances, 1995–2003

Item	Amount (millions) 1995	2003	Item	Amount (millions) 1995	2003
TOTAL REVENUES	**$903,756**	**$1,295,658**	General expenditure	$733,503	$1,163,968
General revenue	739,016	1,112,349	Intergovernmental expenditure	240,978	382,196
Intergovernmental revenue	215,558	361,617	Direct expenditure	492,525	781,772
Taxes	399,148	548,990	**General expenditures, by function:**		
General sales	222,934	184,596	Education	249,670	411,094
Individual income tax	125,610	181,932	Public welfare	194,854	314,406
Corporate income tax	29,075	28,384	Hospitals	29,139	38,395
Other taxes	21,528	38,382	Health	30,865	50,221
Current charges	64,774	106,356	Highways	57,374	85,726
Miscellaneous general revenue	59,536	95,384	Police protection	6,451	11,144
Utility revenue	3,845	12,517	Correction	26,069	39,188
Liquor store revenue	3,073	4,517	Natural resources	12,534	18,577
Insurance trust revenue	157,821	166,273	Parks and recreation	3,403	5,844
			Government administration	26,078	43,909
TOTAL EXPENDITURES	**$836,894**	**$1,359,048**	Interest on general debt	24,485	31,294
Intergovernmental expenditure	240,978	382,196	Other and unallocable	72,648	114,170
Direct expenditure	595,916	976,851	Utility expenditure	7,586	22,404
Current operation	396,035	656,989	Liquor store expenditure	2,522	3,696
Capital outlay	57,829	91,942	Insurance trust expenditure	93,282	168,978
Insurance benefits and repayments	93,282	168,978			
Assistance and subsidies	23,511	25,900	**Debt at end of fiscal year**	**$427,239**	**$697,929**
Interest on debt	25,259	33,039			
Exhibit: Salaries and wages	125,432	183,385	**Cash and security holdings**	**$1,388,527**	**$2,594,215**

Source: U.S. Bureau of the Census, Governments Division, *State Government Finances.*

State Government Individual Income Taxes, 2005

State	Taxable income rate range	Taxable income brackets Lowest: amount under	Highest: amount over	State	Taxable income rate range	Taxable income brackets Lowest: amount under	Highest: amount over
Alabama[1,2]	2.0-5.0%	$ 500	$ 3,000	Missouri[1,2]	1.5-6.0%	$ 1,000	$ 9,000
Arizona	2.87-5.04	10,000	150,000	Montana[1]	2.0-11.0	2,300	13,900
Arkansas	1.0-7.0	3,999	28,500	Nebraska	2.56-6.84	2,400	26,500
California	1.0-9.3	6,147	40,346	New Hampshire	5.0% on dividend and interest income over $2,400		
Colorado	4.63% on modified federal tax liability						
Connecticut	3.0-5.0	10,000	10,000	New Jersey	1.4-6.37	20,000	500,000
Delaware	2.2-5.95	5,000	60,000	New Mexico	1.7-8.2	5,500	16,000
District of Columbia	5.0-9.3	10,000	30,000	New York[2]	4.0-7.7	8,000	500,000
Georgia	1.0-6.0	750	7,000	North Carolina	6.0-8.25	12,750	120,000
Hawaii	1.4-8.25	2,000	40,000	North Dakota	2.1-5.54	29,050	319,100
Idaho[2]	1.6-7.8	1,129	22,577	Ohio[2]	0.743-7.5	5,000	200,000
Illinois	3.0% of taxable net income			Oklahoma[1]	0.5-7.0	1,000	10,000
Indiana[2]	3.4% of federal adjusted gross income			Oregon[1,2]	5.0-9.0	2,650	6,550
Iowa[1]	0.36-8.98	1,242	55,890	Pennsylvania[2]	3.07% on taxable income		
Kansas	3.5-6.45	15,000	30,000	Rhode Island	25.0% Federal tax liability		
Kentucky	2.0-6.0	3,000	8,000	South Carolina	2.5-7.0	2,460	12,300
Louisiana[1]	2.0-6.0	12,500	25,000	Tennessee	6.0% on interest and dividend income		
Maine	2.0-8.5	4,350	17,350	Utah[1]	2.3-7.0	863	4,313
Maryland[2]	2.0-4.75	1,000	3,000	Vermont	3.6-9.5	29,900	326,450
Massachusetts	5.3% of taxable income			Virginia	2.0-5.75	3,000	17,000
Michigan[2]	4.0% of federal adjusted gross income			West Virginia	3.0-6.5	10,000	60,000
Minnesota	5.35-7.85	19,890	65,350	Wisconsin	4.6-6.75	8,840	132,580
Mississippi	3.0-5.0	5,000	10,000				

Note: Rates and brackets shown are for single taxpayers as of January 1, 2005. Brackets for married taxpayers filing jointly are usually double those shown. Alaska, Florida, Nevada, South Dakota, Texas, Washington, and Wyoming have no state income tax. 1. State with a provision that allows the taxpayer to deduct fully the federal income tax payment. 2. States in which one or more local governments levy a local income tax. **Source:** Government of the District of Columbia, Dept. of Finance and Revenue, *Tax Rates and Tax Burdens in the District of Columbia: A Nationwide Comparison* (August, 2005).

U.S. TERRITORIES AND POSSESSIONS

The United States administers a number of overseas territories and commonwealth states under a variety of circumstances. The provisions of the Northwest Ordinance of 1787 established the system under which territories of the United States can achieve statehood. In order to elect a territorial legislature and send a nonvoting delegate to Congress, a territory must contain 5,000 inhabitants of voting age; it is eligible for statehood when the population numbers 60,000.

►AMERICAN SAMOA
Territory of American Samoa
Geography Location: seven islands (Tutuila, Ta'u, Olosega, Ofu, Aunun, Rose, Swain's) in southern central Pacific Ocean. **Boundaries:** Hawaii about 2,300 mi. (3,700 km) to NNE, Cook Islands to E, Tonga to SW, Western Samoa to W. **Total area:** 76.1 sq. mi. (199 sq km). **Coastline:** 72 mi. (116 km). **Comparative area:** slightly larger than Washington, D.C. **Land use:** 10% arable land; 15% permanent crops; 75% other. **Major cities:** (2000 census) Nu'uuli 5,154. Pago Pago (capital) 4,278. Leone 3,568.

People Population: 57,496 (July 2008 est.) **Nationality:** noun—American Samoan(s); adjective—American Samoan. **Ethnic groups:** Pacific Islander 91.6%. Asian 2.8%. White 1.1%. Two or more races 4.2%. Other 0.3%. **Languages:** Samoan (closely related to Hawaiian and other Polynesian languages) and English; most people are bilingual. **Religions:** 50% Christian Congregationalist, 20% Roman Catholic, 30% mostly Protestant denominations and other.

Government Type: unincorporated and unorganized territory of U.S. Constitution: ratified 1966, in effect 1967. **National holiday:** Flag Day, Apr. 17 (1900). **Heads of Government:** Togiola T.A. Tulafono, Governor (since April, 2003). **Structure:** executive—governor is popularly elected to four-year term and exercises authority under direction of U.S. Secretary of Interior; legislative—bicameral legislature (Fono) with 18 member Senate chosen by county councils to serve four-year terms and House of Representatives with 20 members popularly elected to serve two-year terms, plus a nonvoting delegate from Swain's Island; judicial—High Court with chief justice and associate justices appointed by U.S. Secretary of Interior.

Economy Monetary unit: U.S. dollar. **Budget:** (1996-97 est.) income: $121 mil.; expend.: 127 mil. **GDP:** $510.1 mil. (2003); $5,800 per capita (2005). **Chief crops:** bananas, coconuts, vegetables, taro, breadfruit, yams, copra, pineapples, papayas. **Natural resources:** pumice and pumicite. **Major industries:** tuna canneries, handicrafts. **Labor force:** 17,630 (2005) 34% agriculture, 33% industry, 33% services. 29.8% unemployment rate (2004 est.). **Exports:** $415.6 mil. (2004); 93% canned tuna. **Imports:** $308.8 mil. (2004); 56% material for canneries, 8% food, 7% petroleum products, 6% machinery and parts. **Major trading partners:** (2006) *exports:* Indonesia 28.2%, India 22.3 %, Australia 15.3%, Japan 11.2%, New Zealand 7.1%. *imports:* Australia 66%, Samoa 13.8%, New Zealand 10.8%.

American Samoa consists of seven islands between 14° and 15°S, and 168° and 171°W. It was first peopled by Polynesians in the first millennium B.C. The first European to visit the islands was Louis Antoine de Bougainville, who came in 1768 and called them "The Islands of the Navigators," in recognition of the islanders' seamanship. American whalers and missionaries began visiting the islands in the 1830s, and the United States secured trading privileges by treaty in 1878. In 1889, the United States, Britain, and Germany established tripartite control of the islands. The High Chiefs of Tutuila ceded the islands of Tutuila and Aunun to the United States in 1900, and the High Chiefs of the Manu'a islands ceded those of, Tau, Ofu, Olosega, and Rose in 1904. Swain's Island became part of American Samoa in 1925. The islands have been administered by Department of Interior since 1951.

►BAKER AND HOWLAND ISLANDS
About 1,600 mi. (2,575 km) southwest of Hawaii and 1,000 miles west of Jarvis Island are Baker Is land (0°14'N, 176°28'W) and Howland Island (0°48'N, 176°38'W, 40 miles north of Baker). Discovered in 1842, the two coral atolls were worked for guano until about 1890. Great Britain claimed them in 1889, but the U.S. made them territories in 1935 and sent colonists to them. With an area about of about 1 sq. mi. each, neither is inhabited today. Both are unincorporated territories administered by the U.S. Fish and Wildlife Service as part of the Pacific/Remote Islands National Wildlife Refuge.

►GUAM
Territory of Guam
Geography Location: southernmost and largest of Mariana Islands in western North Pacific Ocean; Agaña 13°28'N, 144°47'E. **Boundaries:** Tokyo, Japan about 1,350 mi. (2,170 km) to N, Honolulu, Hawaii 3,300 mi. (5,955 km) to ENE; Federated States of Micronesia to S, Philippines to W across Philippine Sea. **Total area:** 209 sq. mi. (541 sq km). **Coastline:** 78 mi. (125.5 km). **Comparative area:** Three times size of Washington, D.C. **Land use:** 3.64% arable land; 18.18% permanent crops; 78.18% other. **Major cities:** (2000 census) Tamunig 10,833; Mangilao 7,794; Yigo 6,391; Astumbo 5,207; Hagatna (or Agaña) (capital) 1,112.

People Population: 175,877 (July 2008 est.) **Nationality:** noun—Guamanian(s); adjective—Guamanian. **Ethnic groups:** Chamorro 37.1% Filipino 26.3%. Other Pacific Islander 11.3%. White 6.9%. Other Asian 6.3%. Other or mixed 12.1%. **Languages:** English, Chamorro, Philippine, other Asian. **Religions:** 85% Roman Catholic, 15% other.

Government Type: organized, unincorporated territory of U.S. Constitution: Organic Act of Aug. 1, 1950. **National holiday:** Guam Discovery Day, first Monday in Mar. (1521) **Heads of Government:** Felix Camacho, governor (since Nov. 2002). **Structure:** executive—governor elected to 4-year term; legislative—unicameral; Senate has 15 members elected for 2-year terms; judicial—U.S. District Court, Guam Superior Court.

Economy Monetary unit: U.S. dollar. **Budget:** (2002) revenues: $319.6 mil.; expend.: $427.8 mil. **GDP:** $2.5 bil., $15,000 per capita (2005 est.). **Chief crops:** fruits, copra, vegetables, eggs; relatively undeveloped with most food imported.

Livestock: poultry, pigs, cows. **Natural resources:** fishing (largely undeveloped), tourism (especially from Japan). **Major industries:** U.S. military, tourism, construction, transshipment services, concrete products, printing and publishing, food processing, textiles. **Labor force:** 62,050 (2002 est.); 26% agriculture, 10% industry, 64% service. (2004) **Exports:** $45 mil. (f.o.b., 2004) mostly transshipments of refined petroleum products, construction materials, fish, food and beverage products. **Imports:** $701 mil. (f.o.b. 2004); petroleum and petroleum products; food, manufactured goods. **Major trading partners:** (2006) *exports:* Japan 67.2%, Singapore 11.6%, U.K. 4.8%; *imports:* Singapore 50%, South Korea 21.4%, Japan 14%, Hong Kong 4.6%.

Guam was inhabited by Chamorros from the Malay Peninsula as early as 1500 B.C. The first European to stop at Guam was Ferdinand Magellan in 1521. Spanish colonization began with the arrival of Jesuit missionaries in 1668. By 1700 pestilence and insurrection had reduced the Chamorro population from 50,000 to about 2,000. Guam was ceded to the United States in 1899. In 1941 it was occupied by Japan—the only inhabited territory of the U.S. to be seized by enemy forces during World War II. It was retaken by the Americans in 1944. Though unincorporated, the Congressionally approved Guam Organic Act provides for a republican form of government with executive, legislative, and judicial branches.

Guam receives major financial assistance from the U.S. federal government and Guamanians pay no federal income or excise taxes.

The U.S. plans to shift 8,000 marines to Guam from Okinawa over the next decade.

▶ JARVIS ISLAND, KINGMAN REEF, AND PALMYRA ATOLL

Jarvis Island (0°23'S, 160°02'W, about 1,510 mi. S of Hawaii), Kingman Reef (6°24'N, 162°22'W, about 1,070 mi. SSW of Hawaii), and Palmyra Atoll (5°52'N, 162°05'W, about 1,100 mi. SSW of Hawaii) in the Line Island group.

Discovered in 1798, Kingman Reef (0.4 sq. mi.; 1 sq km) was annexed by the U.S. in 1922, and used as an aviation station during the 1930s. Discovered in 1802, Palmyra Atoll consists of about 50 islets with a combined area of four square miles. It was annexed by the Kingdom of Hawaii in 1862, by Great Britain in 1889, and claimed by the U.S. in 1912. Privately owned, it is administered by the Department of the Navy, as is Kingman Reef. Jarvis Island was claimed by the U.S. in 1857, annexed by Great Britain in 1889, and reclaimed by the U.S. in 1935. Its rich guano deposits were worked by U.S. and British companies in the late 19th century.

▶ JOHNSTON ATOLL

GEOGRAPHY Location: Johnston Island and Sand Island (uninhabited) in central Pacific Ocean. **Boundaries:** Honolulu, Hawaii about 825 mi. (1,330 km) to ENE, Marshall Islands to SW. **Total area:** 1.1 sq. mi. (2.8 sq km). **Coastline:** 6.21 mi. (10 km). **Comparative area:** about 4.7 times size of The Mall in Washington, D.C. **Land use:** 0% arable land; 0% permanent crops; 0% meadows and pastures; 0% forest and woodland; 100% other. **Major cities:** none.

People Population: 970 (Jan. 2001), all U.S. government personnel and contractors.

Government Type: unincorporated territory of U.S.

Johnston Atoll (16°45N, 169°32'W) , 820 miles SW of Hawaii includes Johnston, Hikina, and Akan Islands, with a total area of 1.1 square miles. Claimed by the U.S. in 1858, Johnston Atoll is manned and administered by the U.S. Defense Special Weapons Agency and managed jointly as a National Wildlife Refuge by the DSWA and the Fish and Wildlife Service.

▶ MIDWAY ISLANDS

Geography Location: Sand Island and Eastern Island in northern Pacific Ocean; 28°15'N, 177°22'W. **Boundaries:** Honolulu, Hawaii about 1,460 mi. (2,350 km) to SE, Hawaiian Islands to SW. **Total area:** 2.0 sq. mi. (5.2 sq km). **Coastline:** 9.3 mi. (15.0 km). **Comparative area:** about nine times size of The Mall in Washington, D.C. **Land use:** 0% arable land; 0% permanent crops; 100% other. **Major cities:** none.

People Population: 40 U.S. Fish and Wildlife Service personnel and contractors (July 2008 est.). No indigenous population. **Nationality:** noun— Midway Islander(s); adjective—Midway Island. **Languages:** English.

Government Type: unincorporated territory of U.S.

Economy Monetary unit: U.S. dollar. **Major industries:** support of National Wildlife Refuge activities.

Midway Atoll consists of Eastern Island and Sand Island. Although they are part of the Leeward Islands—the westernmost islands of the Hawaiian chain—they are not part of the state of Hawaii. They were the site of the Battle of Midway, June 1942, a turning point in the Pacific theater of World War II. The islands continued to serve as a naval station until 1993; since 1996, they have been managed by the U.S. Fish and Wildlife Service as a National Wlidlife Refuge open to the public for snorkeling, scuba diving, and sportfishing.

▶ NAVASSA

Located in the Caribbean between the islands of Jamaica and Haiti and 100 mi. (160km) south of the U.S. Naval Base at Guantánamo, Cuba, Navassa was claimed by the U.S. in 1857. It is uninhabited. A lighthouse built in 1917 was shut down by the U.S. Coast Guard in 1996. The island, which is about 2 sq. mi. (5.2 sq km), was designated a National Wildlife Refuge in 1999 and is administered by the Fish and Wildlife Service.

▶ NORTHERN MARIANA ISLANDS
Commonwealth of the Northern Mariana Islands (CNMI)

GEOGRAPHY Location: Fourteen major islands (including Saipan, Rota, and Tinian) in western central Pacific Ocean. Saipan 15°12'N, 145°44'E. **Boundaries:** Japan to N; Honolulu, Hawaii about 3,500 mi. (5,635 km) to E; Guam to SW; Philippines to W across Philippine Sea. **Total area:** 184 sq. mi. (477 sq km). **Coastline:** 921 mi. (1482 km). **Comparative area:** slightly more than 2.5 times size of Washington, D.C. **Land use:** 13% arable land, 4.35% permanent crops, 82.61% other. **Major cities:** (2000 census) Saipan (capital) 61,502.

People Population: 86,616 (July 2008 est.) **Nationality:** U.S. citizens. **Ethnic groups:** Asian 56.3%. Pacific Islander 36.3%. White 1.8%. Other and mixed 5.6%. **Languages:** Philippine languages, Chinese, Chamorro, English. 86 percent speak a language other than English at home. **Religions:** Christian (Roman Catholic majority); some traditional beliefs and taboos.

Government Type: Self-governing commonwealth associated with U.S. **Constitution:** Covenant Agreement effective Nov. 3, 1986. **National holiday:** Commonwealth Day, Jan. 8. **Heads of Government:** Benigno Fitial, governor (since January, 2006). **Structure:** executive—governor elected by popular vote; legislative—bicameral legislature (nine-member Senate elected for four-year term, 20-member House of Representatives elected for two-year term; judiciary—U.S. District Court, Commonwealth Supreme Court, Superior Court.

Economy Monetary unit: U.S. dollar. **Budget:** (FY 2001/02) *revenues:* $193 mil. *expend:* 223 mil. **GDP:** $900 mil., $12,500 per capita (2000). **Chief crops:** coconuts, fruits, vegetables. **Livestock:** cattle. **Natural resources:** arable land, fish. **Major industries:** tourism, construction, light industry, handicrafts. **Labor force:** 44,470 total indigenous labor force, 2,699 unemployed, 28,717 foreign workers (2000). **Exports:** $N.A. garments. **Imports:** $214.4 (2001) food, construction equipment and materials, petroleum products. **Major trading partners:** U.S., Japan.

Running north from the island of Guam across a 600-mile-long archipelago in the Pacific Island group known as Micronesia, the islands of the Northern Marianas (CNMI) were originally settled by Pacific argonauts as early as 1500 B.C. Ferdinand Magellan landed at Saipan in 1521, introducing Western culture to the region. The Spanish took control of the archipelago in 1565 and ruled until 1898, when Germany took over the islands. After World War I, the League of Nations mandated the Marianas to Japan, who developed extensive sugar processing works on Saipan. Allied forces took the Marianas in 1944.

In 1947, the islands were included in the United Nations Trust Territory of the Pacific and placed under U.S. administration. In 1976, the CNMI adopted its own constitution. A mutually approved Covenant to Establish a Commonwealth was implemented by the Marianas and the United States in 1986. The Northern Marianas are subject to provisions of U.S. law, except regarding customs, minimum wages, immigration, and taxation. The people are, as a rule, U.S. citizens. The CNMI benefits from substantially from United States assistance and from duty and quota exemptions for garments produced by 17,500 workers—most of whom are Chinese.

▶ PUERTO RICO
Commonwealth of Puerto Rico

GEOGRAPHY Location: Large island of Puerto Rico, together with Vieques, Culebra, and many smaller islands, in northeastern Caribbean Sea. 18°15'N, 66°30'W **Boundaries:** Atlantic Ocean to N, Virgin Islands to E, Caribbean Sea to S, Dominican Republic 50 mi. (80 km) to W. **Total land area:** 3,459 sq. mi. (8,959 sq km). **Coastline:** 311 mi. (501 km). **Comparative area:** slightly less than three times size of Rhode Island. **Land use:** 3.69% arable land, 5.59% permanent crops, 90.72% other. **Major cities:** (2000 Census) San Juan (capital) 421,958, Bayamón 203,499, Carolina 168,164, Ponce 155,038, Caguas 88,680.

People Population: 3,958,128 (July 2008 est.). **Nationality:** noun—Puerto Rican(s); adjective—Puerto Rican. **Ethnic groups:** White (mostly Hispanic) 80.5%. Black 8%. Native American 0.4%. Asian 0.2%. Other and mixed 10.9%. **Languages:** Spanish (official), English. **Religions:** 85% Roman Catholic, 15% Protestant denominations and other.

Government Type: commonwealth associated with U.S. **Constitution:** effective July 25, 1952. **National holiday:** U.S. Independence Day, July 4. Puerto Rico Constitution Day, July 25. **Heads of Government:** Gov. Aníbal Acevedo Vilá (since 2005). **Structure:** executive—governor elected by direct vote to four-year term; legislative—bicameral legislature (Senate with 29 members, House of Representatives with 51 members, all elected by popular vote to four-year terms); judiciary—Supreme Court appointed by governor.

Economy Monetary unit: U.S. dollar. **Budget:** (2007 est.) *income:* $6.7 bil.; *expend.:* $9.6 bil. **GDP:** $77.4 bil., $19,600 per capita (2007 est.). **Chief crops:** sugarcane, coffee, pineapples, plantains, bananas (imports a large share of food needs). **Livestock:** cattle, chickens. **Natural resources:** copper, nickel; potential for crude oil. **Major industries:** manufacturing of pharmaceuticals, electronics, apparel, food products, instruments, tourism. **Labor force:** 1.3 mil. (2000); agriculture 3%, industry 20%, services 77%. Unemployment rate 12%. **Exports:** $46.9 bil. (f.o.b. 2001); pharmaceuticals, electronics, apparel, canned tuna, rum, beverage concentrates, medical equipment, tourism. **Imports:** $29.1 bil. (c.i.f. 2001); chemicals, machinery and equipment, clothing, food, fish, petroleum products. **Major trading partners:** (2006) *exports:* U.S. 90.3%, U.K. 1.6%, Dominican Republic 1.4%, Netherlands 1.4%; *imports:* U.S. 55%, Ireland 23.7%, Japan 5.4%.

Puerto Rico was initially peopled by the Igneri and Taíno tribes. The island's first European visitor was Christopher Columbus, who landed on the island in 1493. In 1508, Juan Ponce de León led the first settlers to San Juan, and by 1514 the Taíno population had dropped from an estimated 30,000 to 4,000. In the 17th and 18th centuries, Puerto Rico was invaded by both English and Danish forces, and though San Juan was captured or burned several times, the Spanish maintained control.

The Spanish constitution granted Puerto Ricans citizenship in 1812, but a revolution was put down in 1868. Spain granted Puerto Rico self-government in 1897 but this was repealed when sovereignty was transferred to the U.S. after the Spanish-American War. Despite early attempts to Americanize Puerto Rico, including an effort to make English the official language and granting citizenship in 1917, the Popular Democratic Party, founded in 1938, brought about a change in political status from that of a U.S. colony to an autonomous commonwealth in 1952.

Governed under the Puerto Rican Federal Relations Act and a constitution modeled on that of the U.S., Puerto Rico is nonetheless an autonomous political entity in voluntary association with the U.S. Despite dramatic increases in industrial development since the 1950's, Puerto Rico suffered from net outward migration until 1988.

Puerto Ricans remain almost equally divided between those who favor statehood and those who favor maintaining commonwealth status, with those seeking independence constituting a vocal but small minority. The statehood-minded argue that limited citizenship is disadvantageous since it allows them to be drafted into the U.S. military but they cannot vote in national elections. The other side fears the burden of full U.S. taxes. In the most recent balloting on the issue, held December 13, 1998, 50.2 percent of Puerto Ricans voted for "none of the above," an option that maintained Puerto Rico's commonwealth status; 46.5 percent voted for statehood, while 2.5 percent preferred independence.

▶ VIRGIN ISLANDS
Virgin Islands of the United States
GEOGRAPHY Location: three main inhabited islands (St. Croix, St. Thomas and St. John) and about 50 smaller islands, mostly uninhabited, in northeastern Caribbean Sea. 18°20′N, 64°50′W. **Boundaries:** British Virgin Islands to N, Netherlands Antilles to E, Caribbean Sea to S, Puerto Rico about 40 mi. (64 km) to W. **Total area:** 136 sq. mi. (352 sq km). **Coastline:** 117 mi. (188 km). **Comparative area:** twice the size of Washington, D.C. **Land use:** 5.71% arable land. 2.86% permanent crops. 91.43% other. **Major cities:** (2000 census) Charlotte Amalie (capital) 11,004; Christiansted 2,637.

People Population: 108,210 (July 2008 est.) **Nationality:** noun—Virgin Islander(s); adjective—Virgin Islander. **Ethnic groups:** 74% West Indian (45% born in Virgin Islands, 29% born elsewhere in West Indies), 13% U.S. mainland, 5% Puerto Rican, 8% other; Black 76.2%. White 13.1%. Asian 1.1% Other and mixed 9.6%. **Languages:** English (official), Spanish, Creole. **Religions:** 42% Baptist, 34% Roman Catholic, 17% Episcopalian, 7% other.

Government Type: organized, unincorporated territory of U.S. **Constitution:** Revised Organic Act of July 22, 1954 serves as constitution. **National holiday:** Transfer Day (from Denmark to U.S.), Mar. 27 (1917) **Heads of Government:** John DeJohngh, governor (since Jan. 2007). **Structure:** executive—governor elected to four-year term; unicameral legislature—senate with 15 members elected to two-year terms; judiciary—U.S. district court under Third Circuit jurisdiction, Superior Court of the Virgin Islands—judges appointed by governor for 10-year terms.

Economy Monetary unit: U.S. dollar. **Budget:** (2003) *income:* $560 mil.; *expend.:* N.A. **GDP:** $1.6 bil., $14,500 per capita (2004). **Chief crops:** fruit, vegetables, sorghum. **Livestock:** Senepol cattle. **Natural resources:** sun, sand, sea, surf. **Major industries:** tourism, petroleum refining, watch assembly, rum distilling, construction, pharmaceuticals, textiles, electronics. **Labor force:** 43,980 (2004); 1% agriculture. 19% industry. 80% services. 6.2% unemployment rate. (2004) **Exports:** $4.23 bil; refined petroleum products to U.S. **Imports:** $4.6 bil.; 82% crude petroleum, foodstuffs. **Major trading partners:** *exports:* U.S., Puerto Rico; *imports:* U.S., Puerto Rico.

The Virgin Islands of the United States (USVI) consists of more than 50 islands located about 40 miles east of Puerto Rico, and about 1,730 east-southeast of Miami. Excavations have revealed evidence of human habitation in the Virgin Islands from as early as A.D. 100. By 1493, when Christopher Columbus landed in the islands—which he named for the virgin martyr St. Ursula—they were inhabited by Carib Indians who were driven out by the Spanish in 1555.

In 1672, St. Thomas was settled by the Danish West India Company. The Danes laid claim to St. John in 1683 and purchased St. Croix from the French in 1773. The United States purchased the Virgin Islands from Denmark for $25 million in 1917, and they were made a territory under the jurisdiction of the Navy. U.S. citizenship was granted in 1927, and the Department of the Interior assumed administration of the islands in 1931. The first governor elected by popular vote was installed in 1970, and an independent constitution was voted down by the electorate 1979.

The primary industry is tourism, which accounts for 70 percent of GDP and employs 70 percent of the work force. International business and financial services are increasingly important.

▶ WAKE ISLANDS
GEOGRAPHY Location: three islands (Wake, Wilkes, and Peale) in North Pacific Ocean; Wake 19°17′N, 166°39′E. **Boundaries:** Honolulu, Hawaii 2,3000 mi. (3,700 km) to E, Marshall Islands to S, Guam about 1,280 mi. (2,060 km) to W. **Total area:** 2.5 sq. mi. (6.5 sq km). **Coastline:** 12 mi. (19.3 km) **Comparative area:** about 11 times size of the Mall in Washington, D.C. **Land use:** 0% arable land; 0% permanent crops; 100% other. **Major cities:** none.

People Population: no indigenous inhabitants; temporary population of military personnel and 75 civilian contractors (July 2008).

Government Type: territory of U.S., administered by Dept. of the Interior with U.S. Air Force.

The Wake Island group was first discovered by British captain William Wake in 1796. It was chartered by Capt. Charles Wilkes' surveying expedition, which was accompanied by a naturalist named Peale. Annexed by the United States in 1898, Wake became a civil aviation station in the 1930's, and was captured by the Japanese in December 1941. It was retaken in 1944. Formerly an important commercial aviation base, it is now used only by some commercial cargo planes for refueling and for emergency landings.

Resident Population of U.S. Territories, 1960–2020 (in thousands)							
Territory	1960	1970	1980	1990	2000	2010[1]	2020[1]
Puerto Rico	2,358	2,7122	3,210	3,537	3,916	4,088	4,196
Guam	67	86	107	134	155	184	211
Virgin Islands	33	63	100	104	121	133	144
American Samoa	20	27	32	47	65	81	95
Northern Mariana Islands	9	12	17	44	72	99	123

1. Projected. **Source:** U.S. Census Bureau, International Data Base.

Cities and Counties in the U.S.

Included here is basic information about population change, cost of living, and government finances in major U.S. cities, metropolitan statistical areas and counties. In addition, there are brief descriptions of the 50 largest cities—from Albuquerque to Virginia Beach. Statistical sources include the U.S. Census Bureau's decennial census, *City Government Finances*, *County Government Finances*, and the *Statistical Abstract of the United States* (all annual publications).

▶ FORMS OF LOCAL GOVERNMENT

In addition to the one federal and 50 state governments, the Bureau of the Census recognizes five basic types of organized local government. In addition to these, which are authorized in state constitutions and statutes, some local governments operate under a "home-rule charter" the form and organization of which are specified by locally approved charters rather than by general or special state law. The number of local governments and officials continues to climb even as the size of the federal bureaucracy shrinks. In 2007, there were a total of 89,527 state and local governments compared with 87,453 just 10 years earlier.

Counties

County governments are established to provide general government; and include those governments designated as boroughs in Alaska, parishes in Louisiana, and counties in the other states. In 2007, there were 3,033 county governments; the most common forms are:

Council-commission A county government without a chief executive but with an elected governing body that shares administrative responsibility with officials elected or appointed to specific positions.

Council-administrator A county government with an elected governing body responsible for overall policy, and an appointed administrator (sometimes called a county manager, county commissioner, or county judge) responsible for administration. The powers of the administrator under this form of government may vary widely.

Council-elected executive A county government with an elected governing body and an elected chief executive—sometimes called a president or a chairperson of the board. The powers of the executive under this form of government may vary widely.

Municipalities

Municipal governments are established to provide general government for a specific concentration of population in a defined area and include those governments designated as cities, villages, boroughs (except in Alaska), and towns (except in the six New England states, Minnesota, New York and Wisconsin). In 2007, there were 19,492 municipal governments; the most common forms are:

Mayor-council A municipal government with an elected mayor and an elected council or other governing body. In some mayor-council municipalities, the mayor is the chief executive, with broad powers. In some other mayor-council cities, the mayor has limited powers.

Council-manager A municipal government with an elected council or other governing body responsible for overall policy, and an appointed manager responsible for administration. The council may select a chairperson from among their own number who may be designated as the mayor.

Commission A municipal government with an elected board of commissioners responsible for overall policy. Each commissioner is responsible for administration of one or more departments of the municipal government. The board may select a chairperson from among their own number who may be designated as the mayor.

Towns

Township governments are established to provide general government for areas defined without regard to population concentration and include those governments designated as towns in Connecticut, Maine (including organized plantations), Massachusetts, Minnesota, New Hampshire (including organized locations), New York, Rhode Island, Vermont, and Wisconsin, and townships in other states. In 2007, there were 16,519 township governments; the most common forms are:

Town meeting A township government in which an annual town meeting of resident voters makes basic policy. An elected board (often called "a board of selectmen" or "township supervisors") is responsible for day-to-day administration of the township.

Representative town meeting A township government in which a town meeting composed of elected representatives of the resident voters makes basic policy. This form of government is usually found in more populous towns or townships. An elected board (often called "a board of selectmen" or "township supervisors") is responsible for day-to-day administration of the township.

School districts

School district governments are organized local entities providing public elementary, secondary and/or higher education which, under state law, have sufficient administrative and fiscal autonomy to qualify as separate governments. Excludes "dependent public school systems" of county, township or state governments. In 2007, there were 13,051 school district governments.

Special district governments

All organized local entities other than the four categories listed above, authorized by state law to provide only one or a limited number of designated functions, and with sufficient administrative and fiscal autonomy to qualify as separate governments; known by a variety of titles, including districts, authorities, boards, commissions, etc., as specified in the state legislation. In 2007, there were 37,381 special district governments.

Source: U.S. Bureau of the Census.

THE 50 LARGEST CITIES, 2007

Between 1990 and 2000, the westward movement of the U.S. population again revealed its strength as four cities in the so-called Rust Belt (Buffalo, Cincinnati, Pittsburgh and Toledo) fell from the list of the 50 largest cities in the U.S. They were replaced by Colorado Springs, Las Vegas, Mesa, Ariz. and Wichita, Kansas. By 2006, Witchita had been replaced by Arlington, Texas, and St. Louis had been bumped by Louisville.

Among the largest cities in the U.S., however, no city came close to Las Vegas in terms of population growth. Between 1990 and 2000, its population increased from 258,295 to 478,434, leapfrogging more than 30 cities in going from the 63rd largest city to the 32nd.

Following are brief descriptions of the 50 largest cities in the U.S. according to the most recent data available from the Census Bureau. They are set forth in alphabetical order. Several tables showing the growth of major cities in America follow this section. See also the section on Metropolitan Statistical Areas (MSAs) later in this chapter.

▶ALBUQUERQUE, NEW MEXICO
Seventy million years ago, earthquakes and volcanoes pushed the land that is now Albuquerque above the sea, forming the Rio Grande Valley and a ring of mountain ranges. Even today, the 10,000-foot-high Sandia Mountains are rising slowly and the Rio Grande Valley continues gradually to deepen. During the Ice Age, Sandia Man roamed the area hunting mastodon and buffalo, and some 3,000 years ago, the Anasazi built stone and adobe cities which still stand. The 1530s marked the arrival of Spanish conquistadors and missionaries.

Founded as a Spanish Villa in 1706, when 35 families moved to the land along the Rio Grande, Albuquerque was named by Don Francisco Cuervo y Valdez in honor of the Duke of Albuquerque, King Phillip's Viceroy of New Spain. Indian raids arrested the villa's expansion, and 100 years after its founding, its population numbered a mere 2,200. Benefitting from their proximity to the Santa Fe Trail, the people farmed, raised cattle, marketed wool and adobe for building, and ran trading posts, military supply depots, saloons, hotels, and mercantile businesses. The introduction of the railroad in 1880 spurred Albuquerque's growth, and the 1940 population of 35,000 has since grown more than tenfold.

Today, Albuquerque occupies a central position along the Rio Grande Research Corridor, which stretches from Los Alamos to Las Cruces, and is home to the University of New Mexico and such major high-tech installments as GTE Communications, UNISYS, GE, and Sandia National Laboratories. Albuquerque's cultural and historical attractions include the Albuquerque Museum, the Indian Pueblo Culture Center, the Maxwell Museum of Anthropology, the National Atomic Museum, and Petroglyph National Monument.
Population 518,271 (2007). Rank: 34th. Race/Hispanic Origin (2000): White 71.6%. Black 3.1%. Indian 3.9%. Asian 2.2%. Pacific Islander 0.1%. Other 14.8%. Two or more races 4.3%. Hispanic 39.9%.
Location: 35°05'N, 106°47'W. County: Bernalillo.
Terrain and climate Elev.: 5,300 ft. Area: 127.2 sq. mi. (329.4 sq km). Avg. daily min. temp.: Jan.: 22.3°F/-5.3°C; avg. daily max. July: 92.8°F/33.7°C. Avg. annual: rainfall, 8.12"; snowfall, 11"; clear days, 71; precipitation days, 135.
Government Form: mayor and council. Mayor: Martin Chavez. (505) 768-3000. www.cabq.gov
Visitor info: (505) 842-9918 or (800) 284-2282. www.cabq.gov

▶ARLINGTON, TEXAS
Nestled squarely between Dallas and Fort Worth, Arlington traces its roots back a century and a half to a small frontier outpost set up in the 1840s at Marrow Bone Spring near Johnson Station. Authorized by Texas Republic President Sam Houston, it served as a dividing line between white settlers and a collection of Native American tribes driven to the area by American westward expansion. In 1877 it was named Arlington after the Virginia estate of Confederate commander Robert E. Lee.

Arlington developed into an agricultural center where Old West mentalities took shootouts to the streets. The city had as many as five working cotton gins at one time and became a major distribution point for cotton as well as hay, oats, and corn. The town was also famed for its mineral water, which was bottled and sold and from which medicinal crystals were produced.

Population increased steadily throughout the 19th century, and until pari-mutuel betting was made illegal in Texas in 1937, racetrack Arlington Downs drew thousands of visitors every year. By the mid-20th century, industrialization had taken over the city and with the construction of a General Motors Assembly plant in 1951, the population skyrocketed again. To accommodate the recreational needs of the booming population, Lake Arlington was developed in 1957, and Six Flags Over Texas opened in 1961. In 1972, the city became home to the Texas Rangers who play at the Arlington Stadium. There are two universities (University of Texas at Arlington and Tarrant County College Southeast Campus), and the public is served by four independent school districts. It is expected that the Dallas Cowboys will move to Arlington in 2009, and the Super Bowl XLV in 2011 is expected to be held at the new stadium.
Population 371,038 (2007). Rank: 50th. Race/Hispanic Origin (2000): White 68.9%. Black 9.3%. Indian 0.3%. Asian 8.6%. Other 8.3%. Two or more races 4.3%. Hispanic 18.6%.
Location: 32°43'N, 97°8'W. County: Tarrant.
Terrain and climate Elev.: 598 ft. Area: 99.5 sq. mi. (257.7 sq km). Avg. daily min. temp.: Jan.: 43.5°F/6.39°C; avg. daily max. July: 84.5°F/29.2°C. Avg. annual: rainfall, 34.73"; clear days, 135; precipitation days, 77.
Government Form: mayor and council. Mayor: Robert Cluck. (817) 459-6122.
www.arlingtontx.gov
Visitor info: (866) 656-3866 www.arlington.org

▶ATLANTA, GEORGIA
Atlanta, the capital and largest city of Georgia, lies at the base of the Blue Ridge Mountains, near the Chattahoochee River. First settled in 1836, the area became the terminus for the Georgia Railroad in 1845 and took the name Atlanta. The population grew to 15,000 by 1861, and during the Civil War, Atlanta became a strategic Confederate depot and collection point for recruits, establishing it as one of the most important cities of the Confederacy and making it a vital objective during Gen. William Tecumseh Sherman's infamous "March to the Sea" in 1864. After two months of bitter battle, Sherman took the city on Sept. 1 and burned most of it to the ground. After the war, the

ravaged city was rebuilt; it became the state capital in 1868.

The leading city of the "New South," Atlanta is the chief commercial hub of the southeastern United States. Atlanta is nicknamed the "City Without Limits" because there are no major rivers, mountains, or coastlines to retard its burgeoning growth into the ever-expanding suburbs. Several *Fortune* 500 Companies have their headquarters in Atlanta (including Coca-Cola and United Parcel Service) as do CNN and the U.S. Centers for Disease Control. Hartsfield Atlanta International (the major hub for Delta Airlines) is the world's busiest airport, giving rise to the saying, "whether you're going to heaven or hell, you still have to change planes in Atlanta."

The city is also an important educational and cultural center, home to more than 30 institutions of higher learning, including Georgia Tech, Emory University, and Morehouse and Spelman Colleges. The Jimmy Carter Presidential Library is here, as is the grave of the Rev. Martin Luther King Jr.

The 1996 Summer Olympics thrust Atlanta into the international spotlight, and helped fuel the city's economic future. The Olympiad added hundreds of thousands of jobs (most of them permanent) and an estimated $500 million in construction to Atlanta's economy. It also brought Centennial Olympic Park and Turner Field to the downtown landscape.

Population   517,145 (2007). Rank: 33rd. Race/ Hispanic Origin (2000): White 33.2%. Black 61.4%. Indian 0.2%. Asian 1.9%. Other 2.0%. Two or more races 1.2%. Hispanic 4.5%.
Location: 33°50'N, 84°24'W. County: Fulton.
Terrain and climate   Elev.: 1,034 ft. Area: 131.2 sq. mi. (339.80 sq km). Avg. daily min. temp.: Jan.: 32.6°F/0.3°C; avg. daily max. July: 87.9°F/31°C. Avg. annual: rainfall, 48.61"; snowfall, 2"; clear days, 108; precipitation days, 116.
Government Form: mayor and council. Mayor: Shirley Franklin. (404) 330-6100.
www.atlantaga.gov
Visitor info: (800) ATLANTA. www.atlanta.net

▶ **AUSTIN, TEXAS**
Austin, the capital of Texas, lies about 80 miles northeast of San Antonio on the banks of the Colorado River. First inhabited by nomadic Indian tribes, the area had as its first permanent European settler Jacob Harrell, in 1835, who established the town of Waterloo. In 1839, it was chosen as the site of the Texas Republic's capital and was renamed after Stephen F. Austin, who brought the first Anglo settlers to Texas in the 1820s. After 1845, when Texas gained admission into the Union, Austin began to flourish, and by 1930 it had grown into a major regional center with a population of 75,000.

Originally a business and distribution center serving the farmers of the Blackland Prairies to the east, Austin's farmers produce cotton, maize, corn, livestock, and poultry. Traditional industries such as meat packing, canning, and furniture manufacturing have been outstripped by the high-tech companies that have helped to nearly double the population since 1970. The city's economic landscape has for decades been defined by the state government (responsible for 131,000 jobs, or one-fourth of Austin's workforce). The University of Texas, founded in 1881 in Austin, boasts the highest endowment of any U.S. university—a legacy of the Texas oil fields. As the University developed into a first-class institution (with 50,000 students) feeding the city's cultural and economic

life, and with the influx of electronics and computer companies, Austin has prospered into a metropolis of national, even worldwide, scope.

In recent years, the university's academic excellence and Austin's reputation for liberalism and progressivism (coffeehouses are more common here than cowboy hats) have attracted both the arts and high-tech companies such as Dell Computer, Motorola, 3M, IBM, and Texas Instruments.

Population   743,074 (2007). Rank: 16th. Race/ Hispanic Origin (2000): White 65.4%. Black 10.0%. Indian 0.6%. Asian 4.7%. Pacific Islander 0.1%. Other 16.2%. Two or more races 3.0%. Hispanic 30.5%.
Location: 30°20'N, 97°45'W. Counties: Travis, Williamson
Terrain and climate   Elev.: 570 ft. Area: 232 sq. mi. (600.9 sq km). Avg. daily min. temp.: Jan.: 38.8°F/3.8°C; avg. daily max. July: 95.4°F/35.2°C. Avg. annual: rainfall, 31.50"; snowfall, 1"; clear days, 115; precipitation days, 82.
Government Form: council and manager. Mayor: Will Wynn. (512) 974-2250.
www.ci.austin.tx.us
Visitor info: (866) GO-AUSTIN.
www.austintexas.org

▶ **BALTIMORE, MARYLAND**
One of America's most active seaports since Colonial days and chartered in 1729 as a major conduit of tobacco exportation, Baltimore was named after the founder of the colony of Maryland, George Calvert, Lord Baltimore. By the time of the Revolutionary War, it earned fame as an important commercial and maritime center, and ships sailing from Baltimore plied their trade with northern Europe, the Mediterranean and the Caribbean. Chartered as a city in 1797, Baltimore's commercial activity began to surge, spurred by its burgeoning iron and copper industries, its proximity to the nation's capital, and the arrival of the Baltimore and Ohio Railroad, which developed links to the Midwest. However, the deep, divisive passions of the Civil War stunted growth and it would take years before the city recovered.

A fire in 1904 destroyed almost every building in the downtown area, providing impetus for needed revitalization. The two world wars renewed demands for Baltimore's port facilities and fostered development of a solid heavy industrial base. After World War II, however, the city's infrastructure aged and decayed. Today, Baltimore remains a large port and industrial city with one of the largest steel plants in the world (Bethlehem Steel's Sparrow Point works). Much of the city has been rebuilt through urban renewal efforts, including the nationally acclaimed Inner Harbor Project, and Oriole Park at Camden Yards. The population seems to have stabilized after a loss of almost 20 percent in 1960.

Among the city's historic sites is Fort McHenry, where Francis Scott Key wrote "The Star-Spangled Banner." Baltimore is home to St. Mary's Seminary and University (1791), Johns Hopkins University (1876), and the University of Baltimore (1925), among other noted institutions of higher learning.
Population   637,455 (2007). Rank: 20th. Race/ Hispanic Origin (2000): White 31.6%. Black 64.3%. Indian 0.3%. Asian 1.5%. Other 0.7%. Two or more races 1.5%. Hispanic 1.7%.
Location: 39°18'N, 76°37'W. County: independent city within Baltimore County.
Terrain and climate   Elev.: 155 ft. Area: 80.3 sq. mi. (208 sq km). Avg. daily min. temp.: Jan.: 24.3°F/-4.2°C; avg. daily max. July: 87.1°F/30.6°C.

Avg. annual: rainfall, 43.39"; snowfall, 22"; clear days, 106; precipitation days, 112.
Government Form: mayor and council. Mayor: Sheila Dixon. (410) 396-3835.
www.baltimorecity.gov
Visitor info: (877) BALTIMORE.
www.baltimore.org

▶BOSTON, MASSACHUSETTS

Named for the English port from which many Puritan immigrants to America came, Boston was first settled in 1630 under the leadership of John Winthrop. As the capital of the Massachusetts Bay Colony, it quickly became the cultural and mercantile capital of the New England colonies. Bostonians never wholly embraced British authority, and they provided the earliest challenges to British rule in their reaction to the Stamp Act (1765) and the Boston Tea Party (1773). The colonists killed in the Boston Massacre (1770) were the first to fall in the years immediately preceding the American Revolution.

With the end of the Revolution, Boston merchants found themselves shut out of English ports by prohibitive tariffs, and in their quest for new markets for American goods opened American trade to the Orient and India. In the 19th century, Boston benefitted early from the industrial revolution, and from several waves of immigration, particularly blacks from the southern states, and Irish and Italians from Europe.

Although Boston's preeminence in trade and industry did not survive the 19th century, it continues to be a major center for banking and financial services. Since World War II, its suburbs have flourished as a center of research and development and of the computer industry—Route 128 was the East Coast's answer to California's Silicon Valley during the 1980s—spurring investment in downtown Boston. As the gateway to New England and the birthplace of the Revolution, Boston is also a center for tourism.

Perhaps most important to its identity is Boston's wealth of educational, cultural, and religious tolerance. Harvard University (across the Charles River in Cambridge, 1636) is the country's oldest, and Roxbury Latin (1645) the country's oldest privately endowed secondary school. Today Boston is home to more than 30 colleges and universities, as well as to some of the finest cultural institutions in the country, including the American Academy of Arts and Sciences (1780), the Massachusetts Historical Society (1791), the Boston Athenaeum (1807), the Boston Public Library (the nation's first, 1854), the Boston Museum of Fine Arts (1870), and the Boston Symphony (1881). Boston is also home to three major medical schools and 27 hospitals including the world famous Massachusetts General and Brigham and Women's.
Population 599,351 (2007). Rank: 23rd. Race/Hispanic Origin (2000): White 54.5%. Black 25.3%. Indian 0.4%. Asian 7.5%. Pacific Islander 0.1%. Other 7.8%. Two or more races 4.4%. Hispanic 14.4%.
Location: 42°20'N, 71°05'W. County: Suffolk.
Terrain and climate Elev.: 10 ft. Area: 47.2 sq. mi. (122.2 sq km). Avg. daily min. temp.: Jan.: 22.8°F/-5.1°C; avg. daily max. July: 81.8°F/27.6°C. Avg. annual: rainfall, 43.81"; snowfall, 42"; clear days, 99; precipitation days, 128.
Government Form: mayor and council. Mayor: Thomas M. Menino. (617) 635-4500.
www.cityofboston.gov
Visitor info: (888) SEE-BOSTON.
www.bostonusa.com

▶CHARLOTTE, NORTH CAROLINA

An area of lush green foothills lying at the southernmost tip of the Carolina Piedmont, Charlotte has long been a crossroads city and an important distribution point for the surrounding farmlands. About 250 years ago, Scotch-Irish settlers retracing old Catawba Indian trading routes established a settlement where the paths crossed, and in 1762 it was named Charlotte, after the new bride of King George III. Remembering Gen. Cornwallis's reference to Charlotte as a "hornet's nest" while his army briefly occupied it during the American Revolution, the city adopted the symbol as its emblem.

The discovery of a 17-pound gold nugget in 1799 triggered a gold rush, and although the mines dotting the landscape boosted business, the California gold rush in the mid-1800's lured away prospectors, putting Charlotte on its future course as a top cotton producer. A leading city of the Confederacy in the Civil War, Charlotte hosted the last full meeting of the Confederate cabinet in 1865. The Queen City's second population surge has occurred over the past 20 years. Charlotte is one of the country's largest banking centers, with Bank of America making its headquarters there. Charlotte is also the home of Duke Energy, one of the largest electric utilities in the United States, and the teachers' pension fund TIAA-CREF.

Recently, the city's economic base has diversified beyond the production of chemicals, foodstuffs, machinery, metals, and textiles, and matured into a major center of world trade and technology, with more than 160 multinational companies engaging in such businesses as microelectronics, insurance, machining and biomedical supplies. North Carolina's status as a right-to-work state has given Charlotte the country's second-lowest unionization rate (less than 4 percent). Located at the intersection of Interstates I-77 and I-85, Charlotte is a key distribution hub, equidistant from the northwestern, midwestern, and southern Florida markets. The Carolina Panthers and the Charlotte Motor Speedway, are both sources of the city's legendary civic pride and boosterism.
Population 671,588 (2007). Rank: 19th. Race/Hispanic Origin (2000): White 58.3%. Black 32.7%. Indian 0.3%. Asian 3.4%. Pacific Islander 0.1%. Other 3.6%. Two or more races 1.7%. Hispanic 7.4%.
Location: 35°16'N, 80°46'W. County: Mecklenburg.
Terrain and climate Elev.: 665 ft. Area: 152.1 sq. mi. (393.9 sq km). Avg. daily min. temp.: Jan.: 30.7°F/-0.7°C; avg. daily max. July: 88.3°F/31.2°C. Avg. annual: rainfall, 43.16"; snowfall, 6"; clear days, 111; precipitation days, 111.
Government Form: council and manager. Mayor: Patrick McCrory. (704) 336-2241.
www.charmeck.org
Visitor Info: (704) 334-2282 or (800) 722-1994.
www.charlottesgotalot.com

▶CHICAGO, ILLINOIS

Chicago extends roughly 26 miles along the southwestern shoreline of Lake Michigan. The city has historically been a major transportation hub and gateway to the Great Plains, and continues to be one today with major air, rail, and highway hubs. Nineteen trunk-line railroad routes converge at Chicago, linking it with every major U.S. and Canadian city. The city has three major airports, including O'Hare, the second-busiest in the nation. It is also the terminus for major interstate highways running east-west and north-south.

Historically, Chicago's rise parallels the growth of the American republic to the west. Chicago was first settled in 1779, when Jean Baptiste Point de Sable built a house on the site. In 1803, federal troops built a stockade named Fort Dearborn, but by 1830 only 12 families had settled in the area. In the 1830s, however, the population grew rapidly as Americans spread westward, and the city of Chicago was incorporated in 1837 with a population of 4,170. Chicago then began to grow into a bustling Great Lakes port, connected to the Mississippi via a system of rivers and canals.

Chicago has maintained its strategic importance despite changes in transportation technology and remains today a prosperous city. Over the years, Chicago has been noted as a hotbed of labor reform, the center of violent organized crime gang wars during the prohibition era, and a prime example of the good and the bad of American city machine politics. But despite its checkered past, it has grown into the wealthiest and most vibrant city in the Midwest with hardly a sign of the rust belt malaise plaguing many of its sister cities. Chicago has grown into a financial center with three of the nation's four largest futures exchanges and the world's largest listed stock options exchange.

Chicago also far outstrips other midwestern cities in cultural, entertainment, recreational and commercial facilities. Major attractions include the Museum of Science and Industry, the Field Museum of Natural History, the Chicago Historical Society, the Lincoln Park Zoo, the Chicago Lyric Opera Company, the Chicago Symphony Orchestra and the Chicago Art Institute. Downtown Chicago currently has three of the tallest manmade structures in the world—the Sears Tower (1,454 ft. high), the John Hancock Building (1,127 ft.) and the Amoco Building (1,136 ft.). It is also home to the world's tallest apartment complex, the 70-story Lake Point Tower and the world's largest commercial building, the Merchandise Mart.

Population 2,836,658 (2007). Rank: 3rd. Race/ Hispanic Origin (2000): White 42.0%. Black 36.8%. Indian 0.4%. Asian 4.3%. Pacific Islander 0.1%. Other 13.6%. Two or more races 2.9%. Hispanic 26.0%.
Location: 41°53'N, 87°40'W. County: Cook.
Terrain and climate Elev.: 623 ft. Area: 228.1 sq. mi. (590.8 sq km). Avg. daily min. temp.: Jan.: 13.6°F/-10.2°C; avg. daily max. July: 83.3°F/28.5°C. Avg. annual: rainfall, 33.34"; snowfall, 40"; clear days, 94; precipitation days, 123.
Government Form: mayor and council. Mayor: Richard M. Daley. (312) 744-3300.
www.cityofchicago.org
Visitor info: (877) CHICAGO or (312) 567-8500.
www.choosechicago.com

▶CLEVELAND, OHIO

The heart of the largest metropolitan area in Ohio, Cleveland was founded in 1796 and named after Moses Cleaveland, a surveyor with the Connecticut Land Company, which administered the state of Connecticut's lingering claim on 3.5 million acres of what is now Ohio (the Western Reserve). A frontier village at the mouth of the Cuyahoga River on Lake Erie, Cleveland was transformed into the business and manufacturing center of northern Ohio by the opening of the Erie Canal in 1825, and the Ohio and Erie Canal, which linked Cleveland with Portsmouth on the Ohio River. When the Soo Locks opened Lake Superior to trade with the Lower Lakes in 1855, Cleveland became a major shipping center for ore, lumber, copper, coal and farm produce.

During the Civil War, the city's iron ore and coal deposits were mined for steel production and commercial activity increased to meet the Union's increased demands for heavy machinery, railroad equipment and ships. In the postwar years, Cleveland's mills and factories expanded even further to satisfy the increased needs of the new cities and farms springing up in the wake of westward migration.

Although heavy manufacturing still employs about 20 percent of the city's workforce, the national trend toward a service economy had a severe impact on the local economy, and the population of the Cleveland metropolitan area declined from a high of 2.8 million in 1970 to only 1.8 million today. Nonetheless, Cleveland is still home to many large industrial companies. There are also many medical and industrial research firms, most notably the world-famous Cleveland Clinic and NASA's Lewis Research Center.

Cleveland's industrial strength manifests itself in its flourishing cultural institutions, including the Cleveland Play House, the oldest repertory house in the nation, the world-famous Cleveland Orchestra, the Cleveland Institute of Art, the Cleveland Museum of Natural History, Western Reserve Historical Society, the Cleveland Health Museum, the Allen Memorial Medical Library and the Cleveland Zoo.

Population 438,042 (2007). Rank: 40th. Race/ Hispanic Origin (2000): White 41.5%. Black 51.0%. Indian 0.3%. Asian 1.3%. Other 3.6%. Two or more races 2.2%. Hispanic 7.3%.
Location: 41°28'N, 81°43'W. County: Cuyahoga.
Terrain and climate Elev.: 805 ft. Area: 79 sq. mi. (204.6 sq km). Avg. daily min. temp.: Jan.: 18.5°F/-7.5°C; avg. daily max. July: 81.7°F/27.6°C. Avg. annual: rainfall, 35.40"; snowfall, 52"; clear days, 70; precipitation days, 156.
Government Form: mayor and council. Mayor: Frank G. Jackson. (216) 664-3990.
www.city.cleveland.oh.us
Visitor info: (800) 321-1004 or (216) 875-6600.
www.positivelycleveland.com

▶COLORADO SPRINGS, COLORADO

Colorado's second-largest city lies on the eastern edge of the Rocky Mountains, some 60 miles south of Denver. Most of Colorado Springs is nestled among rolling hills with views of the 14,110–foot Pikes Peak to the west. General William Jackson Palmer was the first to recognize the area's natural beauty when he founded the city in 1871. In its early years, it was popular with Europeans, especially Britons, and the city acquired the nickname Little London.

The city's first big boom came during the 1890s, when gold was discovered in nearby Cripple Creek in 1891. The gold rush ended in 1917, when the U.S. began coining money with silver. Since the beginning of World War II, the military has been a major presence in Colorado Springs, beginning with the establishment of Fort Carson in 1942 and continuing with the location of the Air Force Academy, several Air Force bases and the North American Aerospace Defense Command (NORAD) over the years since then.

The city's manufacturing base experienced record growth during the 1960s and 70s due to Colorado Springs' low cost of living and sunny weather patterns (the city has 129 clear days a year and receives less snow than Denver or Minneapolis). Semiconductors, electronic equipment, computers and plastics are among the major manufacturing industries.

Leading an expansion of the service industry in the Pikes Peak region, the United States Olympic Committee has its headquarters in Colorado Springs, as well as its Olympic Training Center, the world's premier multi-sport training facility.

Colorado Springs also prides itself on its extremely clean air. According to local officials, the city's pollen counts are among the lowest in the country, providing relief to people suffering from asthma, nasal allergies, and other respiratory ailments.

Population   376,427 (2007). Rank: 47th. Race/ Hispanic Origin (2000): White 80.7%. Black 6.6%. Indian 0.9%. Asian 2.8%. Pacific Islander 0.2%. Other 5.0%. Two or more races 3.9%. Hispanic 12.0%.

Location: 38°48'N, 104°42'W. County: El Paso. **Terrain and climate**   Elev. 6,145 ft. Area 183.2 sq. mi. (474.5 sq km). Avg. daily min. temp.: Jan.: 16.1°F/−8.8°C; avg. daily max. July: 86.5°F/30.3°C. Avg. annual: rainfall, 16.24"; snowfall, 51"; clear days, 129; precipitation days, 98.

Government   Form: council and manager. Mayor: Lionel Rivera. (719) 385-5986. www.springsgov.com **Visitor info:**   (877) 745-3773. www.experiencecoloradosprings.com

▶ COLUMBUS, OHIO

The Ohio legislature designated a site along the banks of the Scioto River in the center of the state as the capital in 1812, and named it Columbus in honor of the famous explorer of the New World. From the first, the city exploited its status as the seat of government and its prime location in the middle of the nation's growing network of roads, canals and highways. Incorporated in 1834, Columbus became a thriving hub of agricultural trade.

Between 1850 and 1900, its population grew from 17,800 to over 100,000. Because of the many carriage factories, in the 19th century Columbus was known as the "Buggy Capital of the World." Five railroads passed through the city, so banks soon began to spring up, making Columbus a financial center for the surrounding farm counties.

As in the 19th century, Columbus's modern economy is built on government, agriculture, local finance, and education. In 1950, to counter the trend of suburbanization, the city developed a policy of annexation of surrounding communities. Because it is less reliant on heavy industry than other midwestern cities, it has weathered the decline of the rust belt better than most and it remains a bustling metropolis. In the 1980s, the city realized the creation of more than $780 million in new development and about 100,000 new jobs.

The Ohio State University, one of the nation's largest universities, opened as the Ohio Agricultural and Mechanical College in 1870, and the city today has a rich academic community that includes the Ohio Dominican College (whose origins date to 1868), the Columbus College of Art and Design and the Ohio Institute of Technology. Business leaders and politicians have joined in an effort to make the city a center for the arts, refurbishing three theaters and building a complex of three more.

Population   747,755 (2007). Rank: 15th. Race/ Hispanic Origin (2000): White 67.9%. Black 24.5%. Indian 0.3%. Asian 3.4%. Pacific Islander 0.1%. Other 1.2%. Two or more races 2.6%. Hispanic 2.5%.

Location: 39°57'N, 83°01'W. Counties: Fairfield, Franklin. **Terrain and climate**   Elev.: 833 ft. Area: 186.8

sq. mi. (483.8 sq km). Avg. daily min. temp.: Jan.: 19.4°F/−7°C; avg. daily max. July: 84.4°F/29.1°C. Avg. annual: rainfall, 36.97"; snowfall, 28"; clear days, 75; precipitation days, 136.

Government   Form: mayor and council. Mayor: Michael B. Coleman. (614) 645-7671. www.cityofcolumbus.org **Visitor info:**   (866) EXP-COLS or (614) 221-6623. www.experiencecolumbus.com

▶ DALLAS, TEXAS

First settled in 1841 by John Neely Bryan, a Tennessee trader and lawyer, Dallas stretches about 30 miles east of Forth Worth on the Trinity River. Named in 1846 after James K. Polk's vice president, George Mifflin Dallas, it was chartered as a city in 1871. Though it grew substantially with the arrival of railroads in 1872, the population numbered a mere 92,000 in 1910.

Located in the heart of the northern Texas oil belt, Dallas today thrives on a diverse economic base, which, in addition to oil and natural gas, includes production of brick clay and the raw materials for Portland cement, and cotton, grains, fruits, beef, dairy cattle, hogs, sheep and poultry from the farms that surround the city. One of the largest inland cotton markets, and a leading distributor of farm goods and machinery, Dallas also serves as the southwest's banking center with major banks, insurance companies, and the Federal Reserve Bank for the Eleventh District. Key manufacturing industries include aerospace, electronics, transportation equipment, machinery, food and related products, and apparel. Among its leading high-tech employers are Texas Instruments and Electronic Data Systems.

Some of Dallas' distinguished universities are Southern Methodist, Southwestern Medical School of the University of Texas, the Dallas Theological Seminary and Graduate School of Theology, and the Baylor University Schools of Dentistry and Nursing. The Dallas Symphony Orchestra, the Dallas Theater Center, the Dallas Civic Opera, the Dallas Historical Society Museum in the Texas Hall of State, and the Dallas Garden Center, contribute to the city's rich cultural life. Fair Park, the site of the annual State Fair of Texas, remains the most widely attended state fair in the country.

Population   1,240,499 (2007). Rank: 9th. Race/ Hispanic Origin (2000): White 50.8%. Black 25.9%. Indian 0.5%. Asian 2.7%. Other 17.2%. Two or more races 2.7%. Hispanic 35.6%.

Location: 32°50'N, 96°50'W. Counties: Collin, Dallas, Denton, Kaufman, Rockwall. **Terrain and climate**   Elev.: 596 ft. Area: 331.4 sq. mi. (858.3 sq km). Avg. daily min. temp.: Jan.: 33.9°F/1°C; avg. daily max. July: 97.8°F/36.5°C. Avg. annual: rainfall, 34.16"; snowfall, 3"; clear days, 138; precipitation days, 79.

Government   Form: council and manager. Mayor: Tom Leppert. (214) 670-4054. www.dallascityhall.com **Visitor info:**   (800) CDALLAS or (214) 571-1000. www.visitdallas.com

▶ DENVER, COLORADO

Denver was born during the great "Pikes Peak or Bust" gold rush of 1859 when small flakes of placer gold were found where the South Platte River meets Cherry Creek. In its first few years, the city survived a flood, several major fires, attacks from native Americans, and an invasion by Confederate soldiers during the Civil War. With the discovery of more gold in the Rocky Mountains, Denver became a boom town. Saloons, gambling halls, and wagon trains lined the mud-filled streets and just about every outlaw, desperado, and lawman in the West made at least one visit to the city. The turn of the century brought respectability and the wealth of the mountains was poured into parks, fountains, tree-lined streets, and elaborate mansions.

During the oil crisis of the late 1970s and early 80s, Denver experienced a second boom when it became a corporate center for oil-from-shale companies working the Western Slope of the Rockies. Then one of the fastest-growing cities in the United States, in 1983, it doubled its office space as part of a five-year building campaign that added 16 skyscrapers, a $76 million pedestrian mall, and an $80 million performing arts center. Expansion was slowed by the energy glut of the mid-1980s, but it has rebounded dramatically in the 1990s and the population grew by close to 10,000 per year in the first few years of the 1990s.

In 1993, the Colorado Rockies baseball team drew more than four million fans to a converted football stadium. And in 1995, after countless setbacks stemming from problems with its automated baggage system, the much-heralded Denver International Airport finally opened its doors, thus completing the final chapter of a vastly overbudget boondoggle.

Denver's population is among the youngest in the nation, and the youthful flavor of the city is very evident. Denver leads the nation in movie attendance and has more sporting goods stores per resident than any city in the world. The city's 205 parks are so active that a speed limit was instituted—for bicycles.

Population 588,349 (2007). Rank: 26th. Race/Hispanic Origin (2000): White 65.3%. Black 11.1%. Indian 1.3%. Asian 2.8%. Pacific Islander 0.1%. Other 15.6%. Two or more races 3.7%. Hispanic 31.7%.
Location: 39°45'N, 105°00'W. County: Denver.
Terrain and climate Elev.: 5,280 ft. Area: 106.8 sq. mi. (276.6 sq km). Avg. daily min. temp.: Jan.: 15.9°F/-8.9°C; avg. daily max. July: 88°F/31°C. Avg. annual: rainfall, 15.31"; snowfall, 60"; clear days, 115; precipitation days, 88.
Government Form: mayor and council. Mayor: John Hickenlooper. (720) 913-1311.
www.denvergov.org
Visitor info: (800) 233-6837.
www.denver.org

▶DETROIT, MICHIGAN

Founded in 1701 by Antoine de La Mothe, sieur de Cadillac, Detroit lies on the Detroit River between Lake Erie and Lake Huron. Named Fort Pontchartrain-du-Détroit (of the strait), the oldest permanent settlement on the Great Lakes flourished as a trading post for trappers, under French control (to 1760), then British (to 1796) and then American.

The first steamboat reached Detroit from Buffalo in 1818, but it was the easy access to eastern markets via the Erie Canal in 1825 that allowed Detroit to exploit the abundant natural resources in the Michigan peninsula and fostered its emergence as a modern industrial giant in the post-Civil War years. Tenth among cities in the value of its manufactures by 1899, Detroit's main exports included iron ore, copper, lead, salt, and fish. The development of the automotive industry, which eventually became centered in Detroit, propelled Detroit to number three by the 1920s. While Detroit is the home of General Motors, Chrysler, and Ford, recently the automotive industry has been as much a curse as a blessing, for every setback to any of the "Big Three" is felt throughout the Motor City.

Despite the fact that it still ranks high in industrial manufacturing, Detroit has been plagued by urban decline. The relatively low standard of living among the predominantly black inhabitants ignited riots in the 1940s and 1960s, and the city's crime rate is today among the highest in the nation. However, it was Detroit blacks who gave rise to one of the most sensational expressions of popular culture in the 1960s. Founded in 1960, the Tamla Motown label propelled the Jackson 5, the Supremes, and Stevie Wonder—among others—to world renown, and in the process created one of the largest black-owned businesses in the country.

The city's rich and diverse cultural institutions include the Detroit Institute of Arts (which contains one of the largest collections of American art in the world in addition to extensive European holdings), the Detroit Symphony, the Cranbrook Academy of Art, and the 1,000-acre Belle Isle Park, situated on an island in the Detroit River and featuring beaches, a yacht basin, a zoo, an aquarium, and a botanical gardens. In 2000, Detroit became the first U.S. city to see its population drop below one million.

Population 916,952 (2007). Rank: 11th. Race/Hispanic Origin (2000): White 12.3%. Black 81.6%. Indian 0.3%. Asian 1.0%. Other 2.5%. Two or more races 2.3%. Hispanic 5.0%.
Location: 42°23'N, 83°05'W. County: Wayne.
Terrain and climate Elev.: 581 ft. Area: 135.6 sq. mi. (351.2 sq km). Avg. daily min. temp.: Jan.: 16.1°F/-8.8°C; avg. daily max. July: 83.1°F/28.3°C. Avg. annual: rainfall, 30.97"; snowfall, 39"; clear days, 75; precipitation days, 133.
Government Form: mayor and council. Mayor: Kenneth Cockrel, Jr. (313) 224-3400.
www.detroitmi.gov
Visitor info: (800) DETROIT or (313) 202-1800.
www.visitdetroit.com

▶EL PASO, TEXAS

The largest Texas city bordering Mexico, El Paso sits in the western part of the state on the northern bank of the Rio Grande across from Juarez. A major port of entry, with the biggest commercial and manufacturing base in the area, the city encompasses a region of mines, oil fields, livestock ranches, and farms (principal crops: pecans, fruit, cotton, alfalfa, onions, lettuce, chiles). Important industries include metals smelting and refining, oil and gas refining, textiles, meat packing, and food processing. The city is also home to the University of Texas, at El Paso.

In 1536, Alvar Núñez Cabeza de Vaca crossed the Rio Grande, becoming the first European to set foot in the area, but settlement did not follow until 1659, with the establishment of both El Paso del Norte on the southern bank of the Rio Grande, and the Mission of Guadalupe. In 1682, settlers from New Mexico founded Ysleta, an area within the current city limits of El Paso, but permanent settlement did not begin until the arrival of Juan Maria Ponce de Leon in 1827. Incorporated as a city in 1873, El Paso grew into a major industrial center with the introduction of the railroads in 1881.

El Paso's access to sources of cheap labor complemented its mining, refining, and agricultural activities and helped build the city's manufacturing base. In recent years, however, the movement of manufacturing back to Mexico, where labor costs are far less, has created some concern for that portion of the economy. El Paso's proximity to Juarez, Mexico, makes it a vibrant tourist haven, and its pleasant climate, combined with its position on the immigration route from Latin America, have made El Paso one of the fastest-growing cities in the U.S. El Paso also has the highest percentage of citizens with Hispanic ancestry of any American city, more than 3 out of 4.

Population 606,913 (2007). Rank: 21st. Race/Hispanic Origin (2000): White 73.3%. Black 3.1%. Indian 0.8%. Asian 1.1%. Pacific Islander 0.1%. Other 18.2%. Two or more races 3.4%. Hispanic 76.6%.

Location: 31°50'N, 106°30'W. County: El Paso.

Terrain and climate Elev.: 3,700 ft. Area: 239.7 sq. mi. (620.8 sq km). Avg. daily min. temp.: Jan.: 30.4°F/-0.8°C; avg. daily max. July: 95.3°F/35.1°C. Avg. annual: rainfall, 7.82"; snowfall, 5"; clear days, 194; precipitation days, 45.

Government Form: council and manager. Mayor: John Cook. (915) 541-4145.

www.elpasotexas.gov

Visitor info: (800) 351-6024 or (915) 534-0601. www.visitelpaso.com

▶ FORT WORTH, TEXAS

Named in 1849 after Gen. William J. Worth, commander of the U.S. Army in Texas, Forth Worth originally served to protect settlers from Indian attacks. It grew slowly mainly as a stopover on the cattle drives along the Chisholm Trail until the Texas and Pacific Railroad reached the city in 1871. Stockyards sprang up, making Fort Worth a conduit of cattle shipping, and with the building of a grain elevator, it developed into a milling center as well. By the turn of the century, it had also emerged as a flourishing meat packing market. Oil was discovered in 1917, bringing prosperity and transforming the city into a major refining center with a dozen operating facilities. The two world wars introduced military installations (particularly airfields) to the area. Fort Worth is the sixth largest city in Texas, boasting the state's three finest art museums and a network of parks with total acreage second only to Chicago's.

Population 681,818 (2007). Rank: 17th. Race/Hispanic Origin (2000): White 59.7%. Black 20.3%. Indian 0.6%. Asian 2.6%. Pacific Islander 0.1%. Other 14.0%. Two or more races 2.7%. Hispanic 29.8%.

Location 32°45'N, 97°25'W. County: Tarrant.

Terrain and climate Elev.: 670 ft. Area: 258.5 sq. mi. (670.3 sq km). Avg. daily min. temp.: Jan.: 33.9°F/1°C; avg. daily max. July: 97.8°F/36.5°C. Avg. annual: rainfall, 29.45"; snowfall, 1.4"; clear days, 137; precipitation days, 78.

Government Form: council and manager. Mayor: Michael J. Moncrief. (817) 392-6118.

www.fortworthgov.org

Visitor info: (800) 433-5747 or (817) 336-8791. www.fortworth.com

▶ FRESNO, CALIFORNIA

Fresno grew up around a train station established in 1872 for what became the Southern Pacific Railway. The city was incorporated in 1874. With the introduction of irrigation to the fertile San Joaquin Valley in the 1880's, the small city thrived at the center of a healthy agricultural economy. Today Fresno County is the number one producer of agricultural products in the nation—and the world—and averages more than $2 billion a year in the production and processing of 200 commercial crops, including grapes (for raisins and wine), melon, cotton, alfalfa, barley, grains, cattle, sheep, and poultry.

Fresno's population grew 63 percent between 1980 and 1990, and in the 1980s it was the ninth fastest growing city in the United States and by far the fastest growing of the nation's 50 largest cities.

Located in central California, Fresno—the name is Spanish for ash tree—is a gateway to the Sierra Nevadas, and it is less than 90 minutes from three national parks—Kings Canyon (55 miles), Sequoia (85 miles) and Yosemite (92 miles). Among the attractions to be found within the city limits are the Fresno Art Museum, the Fresno Zoo, the Kearney Mansion Museum (restored home of Theo Kearney, "Raisin King of California"), the Fresno Metropolitan Museum, and the Discovery Center. There are also 10 colleges and universities including a campus of California State University and Fresno City College.

Population 470,508 (2007). Rank: 35th. Race/Hispanic Origin (2000): White 50.2%. Black 8.4%. Indian 1.6%. Asian 11.2%. Pacific Islander 0.1%. Other 23.4%. Two or more races 5.2%. Hispanic 39.9%.

Location 36°47'N, 119°50'W. County: Fresno.

Terrain and climate Elev. 328 ft.; Area: 99.4 sq. mi. (257 sq. km). Avg. daily min. temp. Jan.: 37.4°/3°C; avg. daily max. July: 98°.7F/37°C. Avg. annual rainfall: 10"; snowfall 0"; clear days: 200; precipitation days: 44.

Government Form: council and manager. Mayor: Alan Autry. (559) 621-8000.

www.fresno.gov

Visitor info: (800) 788-0836 or (559) 445-8300. www.fresnocvb.org

▶ HONOLULU, HAWAII

First visited by Europeans in 1794, Honolulu, meaning "sheltered harbor," has attracted droves of visitors ever since. Situated on Oahu Island, it benefits from a large bay fully protected by coral reefs and its large port facilities. Because of its hospitable climate, the beaches of Waikiki, its majestic mountains, and exotic locale, tourism is Honolulu's major industry; several million visitors come annually, mainly from the U.S. mainland and the Far East, particularly from Japan.

The defense industry is the second mainstay of Honolulu's economy, as the U.S. has long maintained major installations around the island, including the naval base at Pearl Harbor, Hickam Air Force Base, and the U.S. Army's Schofield Barracks and Fort Shafter. Honolulu also serves as the center for Hawaii's export crops—sugar, pineapple, and molasses—and is the principal port for the import of much of the island state's necessities.

Population 375,571 (2007). Rank: 49th. Race/Hispanic Origin (2000): White 19.7%. Black 1.6%. Indian 0.2%. Asian 55.9%. Pacific Islander 6.8%. Other 0.9%. Two or more races 14.9%. Hispanic 4.4%.

Location: 21°19'N, 157°52'W. County: Honolulu.

Terrain and climate Elev.: 15 ft. Area: 25.3 sq. mi. (65.52 sq. km). Avg. daily min. temp. Jan.: 65.3°F/18.5°C; avg. daily max. July: 87.1°F/30.6°C. Avg. annual rainfall: 23.47"; snowfall: 0"; clear days: 90; precipitation days: 102.

Government Form: mayor and council. Mayor: Mufi Hannemann. (808) 523-4141.

www.co.honolulu.hi.us

Visitor info: (877) 525-OAHU. www.visit-oahu.com

▶ HOUSTON, TEXAS

On August 30, 1836, brothers August C. and John K. Allen founded this city and named it after Sam Houston, the first president of the Republic of Texas. The Allens paid just over $1.40 per share for 6,642 acres of land near the headwaters of Buffalo Bayou about 50 miles inland from the Gulf of Mexico. Houston's proximity to Stephen Austin's central Texas colonies gave it great potential as a marketing and distribution site. Incorporated in 1837, the city served as capital of the Republic of Texas until 1840. When the first railroad in Texas began operating out of Houston in 1853, the city developed into a major agricultural center while the discovery of oil in southeast Texas at Spindletop in 1901, and the opening of the man-made Houston Ship Channel in 1914, stimulated petroleum refining and metal fabricating. During World War II, petrochemical production began on a large scale, and with the building of NASA's $761 million complex in the early 1960's (now known as the Johnson Space Center), Houston took center stage as the main player in manned spacecraft.

A major corporate and international business center—more than a dozen *Fortune* 500 companies are based here—present-day Houston has successfully limited its dependence on the energy economy. The Port of Houston is the eighth largest in the world in terms of tonnage handled; the city is also home to four of the nation's 10 major liquid gas pipelines. The presence of the Texas Medical Center also makes Houston a vital U.S. center for the practice and progress of modern high-tech medicine. The Center's 39 institutions occupy in excess of 550 acres and employ more than 50,000 workers. Houston's total health employment exceeds 100,000.

Population   2,208,180 (2007). Rank: 4th. Race/Hispanic Origin (2000): White 49.3%. Black 25.3%. Indian 0.4%. Asian 5.3%. Pacific Islander 0.1%. Other 16.5%. Two or more races 3.1%. Hispanic 37.4%.

Location: 29°50'N, 95°20'W. Counties: Fort Bend, Harris, Montgomery.

Terrain and climate   Elev.: 49 ft. Area: 572.7 sq. mi. (1,483.3 sq km). Avg. daily min. temp.: Jan.: 40.8°F/4.8°C; avg. daily max. July: 93.6°F/34.2°C. Avg. annual rainfall: 44.77"; snowfall: 0"; clear days: 94; precipitation days: 107.

Government   Form: mayor and council. Mayor: Bill White. (832) 393-1000.

www.houstontx.gov
Visitor info: (800) 4HOUSTON.
www.visithoustontexas.com

▶ INDIANAPOLIS, INDIANA

Indianapolis, the capital of Indiana and a major commercial center in the country's heartland, is intersected by more highways than any other in the nation, earning it the name, the "Crossroads of America." Fifty percent of America's population is within a day's drive of the city, a geographic asset that makes it a focal point of transportation and manufacturing.

The first European-American settlement, established in 1820 where Fall Creek meets the White River, was chosen as the location of Indiana's capital in 1825. The state government created jobs triggering an expanding population that further swelled with the routing of the National Road (U.S. 40) in 1830. Development mushroomed in 1839 with the building of the Central Canal on the White River, providing a vital transportation link and the necessary water power to run factories, sawmills, and paper mills. Maintenance of the canal, however, proved impossible, and the town declined until the introduction of the railroad. By 1853, railroad lines fed into Indianapolis from every corner of the nation and at one point, nearly 200 trains passed through daily. At the turn of the century, Indianapolis had emerged as a sophisticated city with sidewalks and streetcars. The city's economy prospered during the early stages of the automotive industry,

producing more than 50 types of car—including the Duesenberg, the Marmon, and the Stutz—before Detroit gained ascendancy.

Having survived the decline in heavy industry and the flight of the affluent to the suburbs, Indianapolis remains a hub of manufacturing and transportation, with a bustling wheat, soybean, and livestock market. Key industries include electronics, metal fabrication, pharmaceuticals, and transportation equipment. Downtown Indianapolis has enjoyed a renaissance with the construction of a convention center, the Hoosier Dome, Market Square Arena, and the refurbishment of Union Station. But the city's premier attraction remains the Indianapolis 500, the annual Memorial Day weekend auto race, first held in 1911.

Population   795,458 (2007). Rank: 13th. Race/Hispanic Origin (2000): White 69.3%. Black 25.3%. Indian 0.3%. Asian 1.4%. Pacific Islander 0.0%. Other 2.0%. Two or more races 1.6%. Hispanic 3.9%.

Location   39°42'N, 86°10'W. County: Marion.

Terrain and climate   Elev.: 808 ft. Area: 352 sq. mi. (911.7 sq km). Avg. daily min. temp.: Jan.: 17.8°F/ 7.8°C; avg. daily max. July: 85.2°F/29.5°C. Avg. annual rainfall: 39.12"; snowfall: 21"; clear days: 90; precipitation days: 122.

Government   Form: mayor and council. Mayor: Gregory A. Ballard. (317) 327-3601.

www.indygov.org
Visitor info: 1-800-323-INDY.
 www.indy.org

▶ JACKSONVILLE, FLORIDA

The first Europeans to visit the area were French Huguenots who in 1564 established a colony at Fort Caroline on the Saint Johns River in northeast Florida. The Spanish destroyed the fort in the following year. Permanent settlement began in 1816, and in 1822 Jacksonville was laid out and named for then Maj. Gen. Andrew Jackson, who had led the U.S. campaign to take Florida from the Spanish. Growth was slow until after the Civil War. After World War II, several large naval bases were located here and by 1960 the population was over 200,000. In 1968, the population jumped to more than 500,000 when it was consolidated with Duval County, and Jacksonville became one of the largest cities by area in the U.S.

Florida's largest city, Jacksonville is a major regional center for commerce, industry, finance, and medicine. After years of improvements on its harbor, 25 miles west from the mouth of the Saint Johns, it has grown into a major port of entry and it is the primary distribution center for the region. Jacksonville has also emerged as a leading resort with extensive recreational and convention facilities. Among its amenities are the Haydon Burns Library, the Cummer Gallery of Art, the Jacksonville Art Museum, the Jacksonville Zoological Park, the Saint Johns River Park, and Fort Caroline National Memorial, site of the first European colony in Florida. Among its leading educational institutions are Jacksonville University and the University of Northern Florida.

Population   805,605 (2007). Rank: 12th. Race/Hispanic Origin (2000): White 64.5%. Black 29.0%. Indian 0.3%. Asian 2.8%. Pacific Islander 0.1%. Other 1.3%. Two or more races 2.0%. Hispanic 4.2%.

Location: 30°15'N, 81°38'W. County: Duval.

Terrain and climate   Elev.: 31 ft. Area: 840 sq. mi. (1,967.6 sq km). Avg. daily min. temp.: Jan.: 41.7°F/ 5.4°C; avg. daily max. July: 90.7°F/29.5°C. Avg. annual rainfall: 52.77"; snowfall: 0"; clear

days: 98; precipitation days: 116.
Government Form: mayor and council.
Mayor: John Peyton. (904) 630-1776.
www.coj.net
Visitor info: 1(800)733-2668 or (904)798-9111.
www.visitjacksonville.com

▶KANSAS CITY, MISSOURI

Kansas City was begun as a trading outpost by the French fur trader François Chouteau in 1821. In 1833, the town of Westport was founded nearby, and in 1850 the City of Kansas received its first charter. (Its name was changed to Kansas City in 1889.)

Situated at the confluence of the Kansas and Missouri rivers, Kansas City prospered early on as a river port and as the terminus of the Santa Fe and Oregon trails. With the arrival of the railroad in 1866, Kansas City's status as a major commercial hub was assured. Thanks to its central location and the development of excellent and diversified transportation and storage facilities, Kansas City is one of the nation's key markets for agricultural and livestock products, as well as for the distribution of heavy agricultural machinery. The Kansas City Board of Trade is one of the largest grain and commodities trading markets in the world. Other major industries are greeting card publishing, telecommunications, and high-tech manufacturing, especially instrument landing systems for airplanes. Kansas City is also home to the 10th Federal Reserve Bank.

An early oasis of culture in the midst of an unsettled, untamed prairie (the city once boasted two opera houses), Kansas City remains a mecca of the arts, with cultural offerings like the Kansas City Art Institute, the Nelson Atkins Museum of Art, the Kansas City Symphony, the Lyric Opera, and the Missouri Repertory Theatre. The city's beginnings are preserved in the Lone Jack Civil War Museum and Missouri Town 1855, and it is the site of the annual American Royal Livestock, Horse Show, and Rodeo, held as part of the annual convention of the Future Farmers of America. Among its institutes of higher learning are Rockhurst College (1916), the University of Missouri-Kansas City, and the DeVry Institute of Technology.
Population 450,375 (2007). Rank: 39th. Race/Hispanic Origin (2000): White 60.7%. Black 31.2%. Indian 0.5%. Asian 1.9%. Pacific Islander 0.1%. Other 3.2%. Two or more races 2.4%. Hispanic 6.9%.
Location: 39°07'N, 94°38'W. Counties: Cass, Clay, Jackson, and Platte.
Terrain and climate Elev.: 744 ft. Area: 316.4 sq. mi. (819.5 sq km). Avg. daily min. temp.: Jan.: 17.2°F/-8.2°C; avg. daily max. July: 88.5°F/31.3°C. Avg. annual rainfall: 29.27"; snowfall: 5.9"; clear days: 132; precipitation days: 97.
Government Form: council and manager. Mayor: Mark Funkhouser. (816) 513-3500.
www.kcmo.org
Visitor info: (800) 767-7700.
www.visitkc.com

▶LAS VEGAS, NEVADA

Las Vegas was originally settled by Mormons in 1855, but its modern history began in 1931, when Nevada legalized gambling and liberalized marriage and divorce laws. From then until 1978 (when Atlantic City re-opened its casinos), Las Vegas prospered while it enjoyed a monopoly on casino gambling in the U.S. Since 1980, it has been one of America's fastest-growing cities, more than doubling in size between 1980 and 1996. There were 164,674 people living in Las Vegas in

1980; by 1996 the city's population had climbed to 376,906. Since the 2000 Census the city's population has passed the 500,000 mark.

To be sure, gambling has fueled this growth—gaming revenues topped $6 billion in 1997—but the city's expansion has come even as dozens of other cities across the country have legalized casino gambling on riverboats, at Native American reservations, or even in the French Quarter of New Orleans. Las Vegas has thrived because of a mix of gambling, nightlife, shopping, and an unequivocal commitment to excess. Since 1993, five major resorts have been torn down, only to make way for newer, bigger properties. The nation's 10 largest hotels (including the 5,000-room MGM Grand) are all here. Over the past decade, the city has built hotels replicating New York City, Paris, Venice (complete with canals through the desert landscape), and the pyramids of Egypt.

More than 30 million visitors (including 3 million conventioneers) travel to Las Vegas each year. With all this tourism have come tens of thousands of new jobs and new housing (an average of 578 new homes per month). Because the city is laid out in a desert, there are few geographical barriers to limit urban expansion, except the availability of drinking water. The city is beginning to confront problems of urban sprawl such as traffic, air pollution, and distribution of resources such as schools and water.
Population 558,880 (2007). Rank: 28th. Race/Hispanic Origin (2000): White 69.9%. Black 10.4%. Indian 0.7%. Asian 4.8%. Pacific Islander 0.4%. Other 9.7%. Two or more races 4.1%. Hispanic 23.6%.
Location: 36° 05'N, 115°10'W. County: Clark.
Terrain and climate Elev.: 2,162 ft. Area: 83.3 sq. mi. (215.7 sq km). Avg. daily min. temp.: Jan.: 33.6°F/0.9°C; avg. daily max. July: 105.9°F/41.1°C. Avg. annual rainfall: 4"; snowfall: 1"; clear days: 211; precipitation days: 26.
Government Form: Council and manager. Mayor: Oscar B. Goodman. (702) 229-6241.
www.lasvegasnevada.gov
Visitor info: (877) VISIT-LV or (702) 892-0711.
www.visitlasvegas.com

▶LONG BEACH, CALIFORNIA

Originally the site of a native American trading camp, by the end of the 18th century the area of what is now Long Beach was part of the Spanish Ranchos Los Alamitos and Cerritos. In 1881, William E. Willmore began development of the land as a resort (which he named for himself). When first incorporated in 1888, the town was named Long Beach after its 8.5 miles of Pacific beachfront. Content to remain a resort community, Long Beach saw its fortunes rewritten in 1921 when extensive petroleum deposits were discovered at Signal Hill. Today, industry is a major presence in Long Beach—especially ship repair, transportation, oil refining, and marine research; in addition, the Navy maintains a large base and dry dock.

Among the cultural and recreational attractions Long Beach boasts are its own Museum of Art, the Terrace Theater, home of the Long Beach Symphony Orchestra, and the Long Beach Community Playhouse. Popular tourist attractions include Los Cerritos (a Spanish adobe house which dates to 1844), the Aquarium of the Pacific, and the magnificent ocean liner *Queen Mary* which today serves as a floating maritime museum, convention center, and hotel. Long Beach is also the site of a Formula 1 Grand Prix every

spring. Disneyland is in nearby Anaheim.
Population: 466,520 (2007). Rank: 36th. Race/Hispanic Origin (2000): White 45.2%. Black 14.9%. Indian 0.8%. Asian 12.0%. Pacific Islander 1.2%. Other 20.6%. Two or more races 5.3%. Hispanic 35.8%.
Location: 33°46′N, 118°10′W. County: Los Angeles.
Terrain and climate Elev.: 35 ft. Area: 49.8 sq. mi. (129 sq km). Avg. daily min. temp.: Jan.: 44.3°F/6.8°C; avg. daily max. July: 83°F/28.3°C. Avg. annual rainfall: 12″; snowfall: 0″; clear days: 143; precipitation days: 35.
Government Form: council and manager. Mayor: Bob Foster. (562) 570-6801.
www.longbeach.gov
Visitor info: (800) 452-7829 or (562) 436-3645.
www.visitlongbeach.com

▶ LOS ANGELES, CALIFORNIA

In pre-Spanish days, the area of Los Angeles was inhabited by approximately 4,000 Indians representing some 30 tribes. The village of Yang-na, with a population of 300, was located in what is now downtown Los Angeles, in the vicinity of Alameda and Commercial Streets. In October of 1542, João Rodrigues Cabrilho, a Portuguese explorer in the employ of Spain, became the first European to set foot on Los Angeles soil, but 200 years passed before a land expedition under the command of Gaspar de Portola crossed the territory on the way from Monterey to San Diego, in 1769.

The establishment of the Mission of San Gabriel (destined to become the largest of the Franciscan Missions) followed and in 1781, the Spanish Governor Felipe Neve founded the city of El Pueblo de Nuestra Señora de los Angeles de Porciuncula ("The Village of Our Lady of the Angels") as part of a plan to colonize California. Spanish rule continued until 1822 when Spain relinquished her holdings in western America, prompting California to pledge her allegiance to the Mexican empire. With the Treaty of Guadalupe Hidalgo (1848) the U.S. acquired all of California from Mexico and in 1850 Los Angeles was incorporated as a city. Introduction of the Southern Pacific Railroad in 1876 sparked a 12-year land boom, promoting the city's growth. By 1892, Los Angeles thrived as a center of oil production and in 1899 work began on the largest man-made deep-water facility in the world. Emerging as the motion picture capital of the world by 1910, industry accelerated in the 1920s and today L.A. ranks as one of the three great industrial cities in the country.

A thriving metropolis, Los Angeles boasts one of the finest highway systems in the world, handling about 6 million cars registered in its five-county area—a car for every two people, the highest ratio in the world. Three transcontinental railway systems terminate in L.A., about 40 certified air carriers fly to all parts of the world, its harbors have 46 miles of waterfront, and the city has the largest trucking center in the west. L.A. remains the world's movie mecca, teeming with studios, stars, and the starstruck.

Los Angelenos live with daily problems of smog, traffic jams, spectacular traffic accidents, and the ever-present threats of mud slides, fires, floods, high winds, and earthquakes. But the year-round sunshine, and the number of beaches and mountain areas, all within an easy drive, tend to ameliorate one's anxiety.
Population 3,834,340 (2007). Rank: 2nd. Race/Hispanic Origin (2000): White 46.9%. Black 11.2%. Indian 0.8%. Asian 10.0%. Pacific Islander 0.2%. Other 25.7%. Two or more races 5.2%. Hispanic

46.5%.
Location: 34°00′N, 118°10′W. County: Los Angeles.
Terrain and climate Elev.: 104 ft. Area: 465.9 sq. mi. (1206.7 sq km). Avg. daily min. temp.: Jan.: 47.3°F/8.5°C; avg. daily max. July: 75.3°F/24°C. Avg. annual rainfall: 14.85″; snowfall: 0″; clear days: 143; precipitation days: 35.
Government Form: mayor and council. Mayor: Antonio Villaraigosa. (213) 978-0600.
www.lacity.org
Visitor info: (800) 228-2452 or (213) 624-7300.
www.discoverlosangeles.com

▶ LOUISVILLE, KENTUCKY

Known as "the Gateway to the South," Louisville lies mainly on a long low flood plain along a bend of the Ohio River across from the towns of New Albany and Jeffersonville, Indiana, at a series of rapids known as the Falls of the Ohio. The first permanent settlement on the site of present-day Louisville was established in June 1778. In 1780 the Commonwealth of Virginia, of which Kentucky was then still a part, approved the town charter of Louisville, named after Louis XVI of France in gratitude for his support of the American Revolution. Louisville was established as the seat of Jefferson County and became an incorporated city in 1828. The completion of a canal in 1830 greatly increased the importance of Louisville as a center of commercial shipping. Despite being a slave state, Kentucky stayed in the Union throughout the Civil War, and Louisville was the base from which major operations in the west were carried out. The first Kentucky Derby was run in 1875 at the Louisville Jockey Club, officially renamed Churchill Downs in 1937.

Louisville has twice been hit by major tornadoes. On March 27, 1890, an F4 twister took about 100 lives and destroyed much of downtown. Another F4 tornado struck in 1974, destroying hundreds of houses, but this time there were only two fatalities. In late winter, 1937, a great flood submerged 70 percent of the city and forced the evacuation of 175,000 people.

The Ohio River is less important commercially than it used to be, but Louisville remains a major shipping center. Louisville became one of the 50 largest cities when it merged with Jefferson County in 2003. Three Interstate highways pass through the city, and its airport is an international hub for United Parcel Service (UPS). Louisville's major industries include tobacco and motor vehicles, and it is the home of the Louisville "Slugger" and to several leading producers of bourbon. The city is also home to the University of Louisville which enrolls 22,000 students and houses one of the most prestigious medical research facilities in the country which developed the first self-contained artificial heart transplant in 2001, and the first cervical cancer vaccine in 2006.
Population 557,789 (2007). Rank: 29th. Race/Hispanic Origin (2000): White 62.9%. Black 33.0%. Indian 0.2%. Asian 1.4%. Pacific Islander N.A. Other 0.7%. Two or more races 1.7%. Hispanic 1.9%.
Location: 38°13′N, 85°44′W. County: Jefferson.
Terrain and climate Elev.: 462 ft. Area: 385 sq. mi. (997 sq km). Avg. daily min. temp.: Jan.: 33°F/-0.5°C; avg. daily max. July: 78.4°F/25.8°C. Avg. annual rainfall: 44.53″; snowfall: 16.4″; clear days: 95; precipitation days: 125.
Government Form: mayor and council. Mayor: Jerry Abramson. (502) 574-2003.
www.louisvilleky.gov
Visitor info: (800) 626-5646 or (502) 584-2121.
www.gotolouisville.com

▶MEMPHIS, TENNESSEE

The first settlers in the area of Memphis arrived on the bluffs overlooking the Mississippi River more than 1,000 years ago. The Chickasaw forcibly displaced these people and then lived there for eight centuries until 1838, when the U.S. government scattered the entire tribe to Oklahoma and parts further west so its citizens could develop the land. The Spanish explorer Hernando de Soto first set eyes on the bluffs in 1541. Other explorers passed through over the next century and in 1739 the French built Fort Assumption. The French, Spanish, and the Chickasaw fought over the land for the balance of the 18th century until it became a part of the U.S. in 1797. The area's original American owners, Gen. James Winchester, Judge John Overton, and Gen. Andrew Jackson (who later sold his share and went on to become President), established the town in 1819, and named it Memphis, after the ancient Egyptian city on the Nile.

Riverboatmen gave young Memphis a reputation for brawls and bawdiness, while mosquitoes gave it a history of yellow fever epidemics, which in the 1880s claimed more than half the city's population and jeopardized its charter. A sewage system, the first of its kind, helped finally conquer the epidemic. Between the river traffic and cotton crops, the city prospered, attracting Irish and German immigrants, and by the 20th century was on its way to becoming the unofficial capital of the mid-south. Elvis Presley, who expanded the city's rhythm and blues tradition to become the world's first rock-and-roll idol, remains the city's most enduring contribution to popular culture. In 1991, the Lorraine Motel, where civil rights leader Dr. Martin Luther King Jr. was assassinated in 1968, was opened as the National Civil Rights Museum. In recent years the city's central location has helped it to attract major corporations, most notably FedEx and Northwest Airlines.

Population 674,028 (2007). Rank: 18th. Race/Hispanic Origin (2000): White 34.4%. Black 61.4%. Indian 0.2%. Asian 1.5%. Pacific Islander 0.0%. Other 1.5%. Two or more races 1.0%. Hispanic 3.0%.
Location: 35°07'N, 90°00'W. County: Shelby.
Terrain and climate Elev.: 307 ft. Area: 264.1 sq. mi. (684 sq km). Avg. daily min. temp.: Jan.: 30.9°F/-0.6°C; avg. daily max. July: 91.5°F/33°C. Avg. annual rainfall: 51.57"; snowfall: 6"; clear days: 118; precipitation days: 106.
Government Form: mayor and council. Mayor: Willie W. Herenton. (901) 576-6007.
www.cityofmemphis.org
Visitor info: (901) 543-5300.
www.memphistravel.com

▶MESA, ARIZONA

Just 15 miles east of Phoenix is Mesa, a one-time suburb that has quickly climbed onto the list of the nation's largest cities. Arizona's third largest city grew by 24.5 percent between 1990 and 1998. There are solid reasons for Mesa's growth: low costs of doing business; a reasonable tax structure; a skilled and well-educated workforce; low crime rate; superior schools; affordable housing; and an abundant water supply. Founded in 1878 and incorporated in 1883, Mesa is the Spanish word for "table top," describing a flat-topped, raised area. The first settlers built homes and farms on a mesa above the surrounding area.

Population 452,933 (2007). Rank: 38th. Race/Hispanic Origin (2000): White 81.7%. Black 2.5%. Indian 1.7%. Asian 1.5%. Pacific Islander 0.2%. Other 9.7%. Two or more races 2.8%. Hispanic 19.7%.

Location: 33°N, 112°W. County: Maricopa.
Terrain and climate Elev.: 1,241 ft. Area: 124.62 sq. mi. Avg. daily min temp.: Jan.: 35.6°F/2°C; avg. daily max. July: 104.3°F/40.16°C. Avg. annual: rainfall, 7.52"; snowfall, 0"; clear days, 320; precipitation days, 45.
Government Form: council and manager. Mayor: Scott Smith. (480) 644-2388.
www.ci.mesa.az.us
Visitor info: (800) 283-6372 or (480) 827-4700.
www.visitmesa.com

▶MIAMI, FLORIDA

Miami, the most southerly major city in the continental U.S., sits about two degrees north of the Tropic of Cancer, a location that has made it a long-standing resort haven. Miami in the 1980's also thrived as a major hub of commerce and as a population center for Latin American immigrants, particularly those arriving from Cuba, whose ambition and business acumen contributed to the city's prosperity. While tourists still generate more than 60 percent of the area's economic activity, many other areas of enterprise, such as construction, light industry, and agriculture (limes, tomatoes, avocados, mangoes, and beans) have flourished.

Miami (whose name is thought to derive from the Indian mayami, meaning "big water"), dates back to the 16th century when Native Americans occupied the southern part of Florida. Fort Dallas, built near the mouth of the Miami River in 1836 as a base of war against the Seminoles, became the first permanent European-American settlement. The building of the Florida East Coast Railroad, coinciding with Miami's incorporation as a city in 1896 (population 343), offered ready access to the area. Resort hotels quickly cropped up and Miami, along with the rest of Florida, enjoyed great success. In 1926, a severe hurricane submerged much of its land under water, abruptly ending Miami's prosperity, but the city managed to steadily grow by draining and developing swampland. After World War II, new resorts rose up, and Miami thrived both as a haven for older retirees and a refuge for a substantial number of Cubans fleeing Castro's repressive regime. In 2000, the city attracted national media attention when Elian Gonzalez, a five-year-old Cuban refugee became the center of a custody battle between Cuba and the U.S. when he survived a raft crossing from Cuba to Florida, but his mother did not.

As the U.S. city closest to Central and South America, Miami bills itself as the "Gateway of the Americas." Foreign banking has expanded rapidly.
Population 409,719 (2007). Rank: 43rd. Race/Hispanic Origin (2000): White 66.6%. Black 22.3%. Indian 0.2%. Asian 0.7%. Other 5.4%. Two or more races 4.7%. Hispanic 65.8%.
Location: 25°45'N, 80°15'W. County: Dade.
Terrain and climate Elev.: 12 ft. Area: 34.3 sq. mi. (88.8 sq km). Avg. daily min. temp.: Jan.: 59.2°F/15.1°C; avg. daily max. July: 88.7°F/31.5°C. Avg. annual rainfall: 57.55"; snowfall: 0"; clear days: 76; precipitation days: 129.
Government Form: council and manager. Mayor: Manuel A. Diaz. (305) 250-5300.
www.miamigov.com
Visitor info: (800) 933-8448 or (305) 539-3000.
www.miamiandbeaches.com

▶MILWAUKEE, WISCONSIN

During the 1670s the French explorers Jacques Marquette and Louis Joliet were the first Europeans to visit the site of present-day Milwaukee, an area on the western shore of Lake Michigan at the confluence of the Menomonee and Kinnickinnic Rivers. In 1795, Jacques Vieau of the North West Company established a trading post and in 1818, Solomon Laurent Juneau, the first permanent settler, founded Milwaukee (from the Indian term millioke, meaning "beautiful land"). From the 1840s on, large numbers of German immigrants came to the city, making up over 60 percent of the 1850 population; today, an estimated one-third of the city's residents are of German descent.

A flourishing agricultural center, Milwaukee had by the Civil War become the largest wheat market in the world. Its industrial base expanded after the war and by 1940 the city ranked fourth in manufacturing among U.S. cities. Still one of the most vigorous producers of durable goods, especially automotive parts, construction and road building equipment, diesel and gasoline engines, tractors, and outboard motors, Milwaukee also emerged as a major meat-packing center. Reflecting its German heritage, the city developed a thriving brewing industry with several of the largest beer-producing companies in the U.S. (though almost all have since disappeared). A major Great Lakes and international port, Milwaukee handles several international steamship lines.

Population 602,191 (2007). Rank: 22nd. Race/Hispanic Origin (2000): White 50.0%. Black 37.3%. Indian 0.9%. Asian 2.9%. Pacific Islander 0.1%. Other 6.1%. Two or more races 2.7%. Hispanic 12.0%.

Location: 43°09'N, 87°58'W. County: Milwaukee.

Terrain and climate Elev.: 581 ft. Area: 95.8 sq. mi. (248.1 sq km). Avg. daily min. temp.: Jan.: 11.3°F/-11.5°C; avg. daily max. July: 79.8°F/26.5°C. Avg. annual rainfall: 30.94"; snowfall: 45"; clear days: 96; precipitation days: 122.

Government Form: mayor and council. Mayor: Tom Barrett. (414) 286-2200.
www.ci.mil.wi.us
Visitor info: (800) 554-1448 or (414) 273-7222.
www.milwaukee.org

▶MINNEAPOLIS, MINNESOTA

With an average annual temperature of 45° F, Minneapolis is the second coldest city in the U.S. But despite its arctic winters, it is one of the most desirable cities in the U.S. It sits astride the Mississippi River, near the headwaters of the Minnesota River, about 350 miles northwest of Chicago. While it is the largest commercial metropolis in the north between Milwaukee and Seattle, no single industry dominates, although many large computer and electronics companies make Minneapolis their home. A regional banking center and the site of the Federal Reserve Bank for the Ninth District, Minneapolis has the world's largest cash grain exchange, the world's four largest wheat-flour-milling companies, and provides the upper Midwest with truck, barge, and air transport.

In 1682 Father Louis Hennepin, the French priest who explored the Mississippi, was the first European to set eyes on the Falls of St. Anthony, the future site of Minneapolis. Unsettled until Fort Snelling was built in 1819 to protect the fur traders from the Sioux and Chippewa, the town of St. Anthony began growing up on one side of the Mississippi and a second settlement sprang up on the other. The two were consolidated in 1872; the new name was a hybrid of the Indian word minne, meaning "water," and the Greek word for "city," polis. Minneapolis blossomed on the basis of its flour and lumber milling. By century's end, the forests to the north had been depleted, but flour milling continues as a thriving industry to this day.

Long considered a center of progressive political and social thinking, it is a mecca of education and culture. Minneapolis contains the main campus of the University of Minnesota, and boasts the Minnesota Orchestra and the Minneapolis Institute of the Arts. A haven for outdoor enthusiasts, the park system numbers 153 parks encompassing 6,000 acres, and with 12 lakes within its city limits, Minneapolis has 10 percent of its surface covered by water. Despite all this, the city lost one fifth of its population to suburban areas in the last half of the 20th century.

Population 377,392 (2007). Rank: 46th. Race/Hispanic Origin (2000): White 65.1%. Black 18.0%. Indian 2.2%. Asian 6.1%. Pacific Islander 0.1%. Other 4.1%. Two or more races 4.4%. Hispanic 7.6%.

Location: 44°58'N, 93°20'W. County: Hennepin.

Terrain and climate Elev.: 828 ft. Area: 55.1 sq. mi. (142.7 sq km). Avg. daily min. temp.: Jan.: 2.4°F/-16.4°C; avg. daily max. July: 83.4°F/28.5°C. Avg. annual rainfall: 26.36"; snowfall: 46"; clear days: 100; precipitation days: 113.

Government Form: mayor and council. Mayor: R.T. Rybak. (612) 673-2100.
www.ci.minneapolis.mn.us
Visitor info: (888) 676-6757.
www.minneapolis.org

▶NASHVILLE, TENNESSEE

In the winter of 1779–80, settlers from North Carolina, led by James Robertson, arrived at a place on the Cumberland River called Big Salt Lick, and built forts on both sides of the river, one of which they named Nashborough, after Gen. Francis Nash of the Revolutionary Army. Adopting the name Nashville in 1784, the settlement was chartered as a city in 1806, became state capital in 1843, and prospered until the Civil War as the northern terminus of the Natchez Trace, a 500-mile road to Natchez, Mississippi. The site of one of the war's last major battles in December 1864, the city underwent a long period of rebuilding and by the end of the century, the population reached 81,000. The city continued to grow, doubling in population by World War II, and has experienced even greater expansion since that time.

While best known as a major center of both the recording and music-publishing industries, Nashville enjoys a widely diversified economic foundation and serves as a distribution and marketing point for the upper southern region of the U.S. Several religious organizations and their publishing operations are headquartered here, and the city is home to more than a dozen institutions of higher learning, including Vanderbilt University, Fisk University, and Tennessee State University. With a growing base of manufacturing, especially in the automotive sector, and with the insurance and banking industries firmly entrenched, Nashville leaders project a prosperous future. As home of the Grand Ole Opry, Nashville has also developed into a regional tourist and convention attraction. A full-scale replica of the Greek temple the Parthenon is a noted site.

Population 590,807 (2007). Rank: 25th. Race/Hispanic Origin (2000): White 67.0%. Black 25.9%. Indian 0.3%. Asian 2.3%. Pacific Islander 0.1%. Other 2.4%. Two or more races 2.0%. Hispanic 4.6%.

Location: 36°12'N, 86°46'W. County: Davidson.

Terrain and climate Elev.: 605 ft. Area: 479.5 sq. mi. (1241.9 sq km). Avg. daily min. temp.: Jan.: 27.8°F/-2.3°C; avg. daily max. July: 89.8°F/32.1°C. Avg. annual rainfall: 48.49"; snowfall: 10.7"; clear days: 103; precipitation days: 119.

Government Form: mayor and council. Mayor: Karl Dean. (615) 862-6000.
www.nashville.org
Visitor info: (800) 657-6910.
www.visitmusiccity.com

► **NEW YORK CITY, NEW YORK**

Even before the arrival of Europeans in North America, the waters that today make New York one of the world's foremost ports—and the foremost city in the United States—were the scene of lively trade between the predominant Algonquian tribes in the region. The city's modern history dates to 1524 when the Florentine explorer, Giovanni de Verrazano, sailed into New York Bay. In 1609, Henry Hudson, an English navigator sailing for the Dutch East India Company, explored the river that bears his name today. In 1625, the Dutch West India Company purchased Manhattan and established Nieuw Amsterdam, which quickly became a profitable trading post. Dutch settlers soon expanded beyond the original colony settling Breukelen, Nieuw Harlem, Bronck, and Staaten Eylandt. Taken by the British in 1664 (the Dutch briefly regained control in 1673-74), and renamed for the Duke of York, the town continued to prosper.

As resentment of British authority grew, New York became a seat of colonial discontent, participating in actions against the Stamp Act (1763) and tea tax (1773). But after the Battle of Long Island and Washington's retreat in August 1776, the British held New York through the end of the war. Yet Washington was inaugurated president at Federal Hall (today the site of the second Federal Reserve Bank) on Wall Street, and from 1789-90 New York was the nation's capital.

Industry and trade expanded dramatically after the opening of the Erie Canal from Troy (150 miles up the Hudson River) and Buffalo (350 miles west of Troy) gave New York direct access to the raw materials and the markets of the Great Lakes states. In the mid-19th century, New York became the primary port of immigration to the U.S. and many of the millions of immigrants who came to America carved out distinctly ethnic neighborhoods throughout the city in a patchwork that survives to the present.

In 1898, an act of the state legislature created "Greater New York," and today New York's population is greater than that of Los Angeles and Chicago (the second and third largest cities in the country) combined. Even if they were separate cities, four of New York boroughs would rank in the top 10—Brooklyn fourth (2.3 million), Queens fifth (1.9 million), Manhattan eighth (1.5 million), and the Bronx ninth (1.2 million).

New York's attractions are seemingly innumerable—enough to draw more than 17 million visitors annually—but they include 150 museums, 400 art galleries, dozens of Broadway theaters, and scores of concert halls, clubs, and dance halls. In addition, there are close to 1,000 landmark buildings, more than 50 landmark interiors, and more than 50 historic districts. (A list of attractions can be found under "New York State.") The city leads the nation in the arts, fashion, advertising, banking and financial services, publishing, broadcasting, and certain service industries; it is also the home of the General Assembly of the United Nations. There are 87 colleges and universities here, including Columbia University, New York University, Long Island University, Brooklyn College, Fordham University, the Pratt Institute of Technology, the Juilliard School, and the School of Visual Arts. Manufactured goods include apparel, chemicals, metal products, and printing.

New York City was the site of the worst terrorist attack in U.S. history on Sept. 11, 2001, when two hijacked commercial jets crashed into the twin towers of the World Trade Center, causing the complete collapse of both buildings and killing more than 2,800 people.

Population 8,274,527 (2007). Rank: 1st. Race/Hispanic Origin (2000): White 44.7%. Black 26.6%. Indian 0.5%. Asian 9.8%. Pacific Islander 0.1%. Other 13.4%. Two or more races 4.9%. Hispanic 27.0%.
Location: 40°45'N, 74°00'W. Counties: Bronx, Kings, New York, Queens, and Richmond.
Terrain and climate Elev.: 87 ft. Area: 301.5 sq. mi. (780.9 sq km). Avg. daily min. temp.: Jan.: 25.6°F/-3.5°C; avg. daily max. July: 85.3°F/29.6°C. Avg. annual rainfall: 44.12"; snowfall: 29"; clear days: 107; precipitation days: 121.
Government Form: mayor and council. Mayor: Michael R. Bloomberg. (212) 639-9675.
www.nyc.gov
Visitor info: (212) 484-1200.
www.nycvisit.com

► **OAKLAND, CALIFORNIA**

The first European-American to settle present-day Oakland was Dom Luis Maria Peralta, who established the 44,000-acre settlement called Rancho San Antonio in 1820. Its first real growth began with the establishment of ferry service to San Francisco in 1852, though the ferry's importance was overshadowed by Oakland's selection as the western terminus of the first transcontinental railroad in 1869. The city remained in the economic shadow of its more sophisticated neighbor across the Bay until the San Francisco earthquake of 1906 drove 100,000-150,000 people to Oakland for shelter. An estimated 65,000 of these are thought to have settled there permanently, providing an impetus for a long period of growth as an international port and industrial center.

A major commercial and cultural center with a container port ranked 10th in the world, Oakland is also the major northern hub of the California freeway system, which is integrated into the Bay Area Rapid Transit (BART) system. It has also become the premier biotechnology center in the region, and it is home to regional and international headquarters for firms in finance, medicine, telecommunications, international trade, and heavy industry.

Long a primarily industrial urban center, Oakland has pumped hundreds of millions of dollars into development of its downtown area and the Jack London waterfront—named for the author who spent his youth on the Oakland docks. Oakland embraces a racially and culturally diverse populace. Oakland sustained heavy damage in the 1989 Loma Prieta earthquake. Two years later, almost to the day, the second worst fire in California history leveled more than 1,000 buildings in the Oakland Hills neighborhood, killing 14 people and inflicting more than $1.5 billion in damage.
Population 401,489 (2007). Rank: 44th. Race/Hispanic Origin (2000): White 31.3%. Black 35.7%. Indian 0.7%. Asian 15.2%. Pacific Islander 0.5%. Other 11.7%. Two or more races 5.0%. Hispanic 21.9%.
Location: 37°50'N, 122°18'W. County: Alameda.
Terrain and climate Elev.: 42 ft. Area: 53.9 sq. mi. (139.6 sq km). Avg. daily min. temp.: Jan.: 43.4°F/6.3°C; avg. daily max. July: 70.6°F/29.6°C. Avg. annual rainfall: 18.03"; snowfall: N.A.; clear days: N.A; precipitation days: N.A.

Government Form: council and manager. Mayor: Ron Dellums. (510) 238-3141.
www.oaklandnet.com
Visitor info: (510) 839-9000.
www.oaklandcvb.com

▶ OKLAHOMA CITY, OKLAHOMA

Oklahoma City quite literally sprang up during the Great Land Rush of 1889 and, by presidential proclamation, opened for European-American settlement officially on April 22 of that year. At day's end, approximately 10,000 settlers had moved in—the greatest one-day non-annexation population increase in the history of cities. Oklahoma became a state in 1907 and Oklahoma City its capital in 1910, by which time the population had swelled to about 64,000. Since then, it has become Oklahoma's largest city, its leading commercial center, and home to the National Cowboy Hall of Fame.

Oklahoma City's economy, based on oil and livestock, thrives on petroleum production, meat processing, and the breeding of stocker and feeder cattle. The city hosts a flourishing printing and publishing industry and manufactures a diversity of products including automobiles, electronic equipment, computers, communications switches, and oil well supplies. As a vital banking center serving the central and western regions of the state, Oklahoma City boasts a Federal Reserve branch bank. However, Oklahoma City reportedly sparked the "go-go" banking syndrome that characterized the 1970s oil boom, when Penn Square Bank's ill-advised oil patch loans nearly devastated the U.S. banking system.

Oklahoma City was the site of one of the deadliest terrorist bombings in U.S. history on April 19, 1995, when a 5,000-pound car bomb ripped a huge hole in the Alfred Murrah Federal Building, killing 169 people, including 15 children in a day care center within the building.
Population 547,274 (2007). Rank: 31st. Race/ Hispanic Origin (2000): White 68.4%. Black 15.4%. Indian 3.5%. Asian 3.5%. Pacific Islander 0.1%. Other 5.3%. Two or more races 3.9%. Hispanic 10.1%.
Location: 35°25'N, 97°30'W. Counties: Canadian, Cleveland, McClain, Oklahoma.
Terrain and climate Elev.: 1,304 ft. Area: 604 sq. mi. (1,564.4 sq km). Avg. daily min. temp.: Jan.: 25.2°F/-3.7°C; avg. daily max. July: 93.5°F/34.1°C. Avg. annual: rainfall, 30.89"; snowfall, 9"; clear days, 141; precipitation days, 81.
Government Form: council and manager. Mayor: Mick Cornett. (405) 297-2424.
www.okc.gov
Visitor info: (800) 225-5652 or (405) 297-8912.
www.okccvb.org

▶ OMAHA, NEBRASKA

Permanent settlement in what is now Omaha began with a fur-trading post established shortly after the Lewis and Clark expedition passed through the area in 1804. In 1820, the government built Ft. Atkinson, and the surrounding community became a major stop on both the Mormon and the Lewis and Clark trails, and was incorporated as a city in 1854. After strong lobbying by citizens of Council Bluffs, Iowa, just across the Missouri River to the east, Omaha (the name means "above all others on the stream") became the eastern terminus of the Union-Pacific transcontinental railroad, the country's first, in 1869. Within six years, the population grew to 39,000 and by the turn of the century, it had passed the 100,000 mark.

As a major transportation hub of the Midwest—Omaha today boasts seven major railroads and the recently expanded Port of Omaha services a dozen barge lines—the city became a major distribution center for meat and grain, living up to its motto "We feed the world" (ConAgra is based here). Its major food products include pasta, potato chips, coffee, pancake mixes, frozen dinners, and Omaha steaks. With dozens of *Fortune* 500 manufacturing operations, and a healthy publishing industry (roughly one out of every four manufacturers is either a publisher or printer), Omaha's diversified economy also has strong roots in insurance (Mutual of Omaha), communications, direct mail/telemarketing, and sophisticated medical facilities are centered at the medical schools of Creighton University and the University of Nebraska. Since 1989 employment in the metro area has grown by 15 percent, while the unemployment rate, one of the lowest in the nation, has been less than 3 percent for several years.

Among its performing arts institutions are the Omaha Symphony, Opera/Omaha, the Omaha Ballet, the Orpheum Theater, and the Omaha Community Playhouse. Museums and historic sites include the Boys Town Hall of Fame, the Henry Doorly Zoo and Aquarium, the Great Plains Black Museum, the historic ships *U.S.S. Hazard* and *U.S.S. Marlin*, and the Old Market, a mixed-use National Historic District on the Missouri River.
Population 424,482 (2007). Rank: 42nd. Race/ Hispanic Origin (2000): White 78.4%. Black 13.3%. Indian 0.7%. Asian 1.7%. Pacific Islander 0.1%. Other 3.9%. Two or more races 1.9%. Hispanic 7.5%.
Location: 41°15'N, 95°55'W. County: Douglas.
Terrain and climate Elev.: 982 ft. Area: 99.3 sq. mi. (257.2 sq km). Avg. daily min. temp.: Jan.: 10.2°F/-12.1°C; avg. daily max. July: 88.5°F/31.3°C. Avg. annual rainfall: 30.34"; snowfall: 32"; clear days: 113; precipitation days: 99.
Government Form: mayor and council. Mayor: Mike Fahey. (402) 444-5000.
www.ci.omaha.ne.us
Visitor info: (866) YES-OMAHA or (402) 444-4660.
www.visitomaha.com

▶ PHILADELPHIA, PENNSYLVANIA

In 1632, a small contingent of Swedes and Finns came to the land where the Schuylkill River meets the Delaware and founded New Sweden. In 1655, Peter Stuyvesant seized New Sweden for the Dutch, inciting conflict with the British until the Dutch relinquished their rights to the territory in 1673. Nine years later, William Penn established a town between the Schuylkill and the Delaware Rivers, named it Philadelphia, "the city of brotherly love," and in two years it evolved into an active settlement of about 2,500 people, most of them Quakers.

In the mid-1700s, Benjamin Franklin began shaping the destiny of Philadelphia by presiding over the founding of the University of Pennsylvania, the Pennsylvania Hospital, and a fire insurance company (the last two were firsts for the young nation). Under his guidance, Philadelphia became the premier colonial city for the arts and the home of many famous educators, scientists, mathematicians, authors, and painters. In addition, a total of 17 libraries were founded at this time. The meeting place of the Continental Congress and the site of the signing of the Declaration of Independence, Philadelphia was the nation's capital from 1790 to 1800, when the federal government moved permanently to Washington, D.C.

Throughout the 19th century, the influx first of Irish and German, then Jewish, Italian, Polish, and Slavic immigrants from Europe, and blacks

from the South, helped build the city's industrial base. Today, Philadelphia ranks high among U.S. cities in oil refining; other principal industries are electrical machinery, automobile and truck bodies, petrochemicals, metalworking, and scientific instruments. But many other businesses have left the city and unemployment and poverty have taken a heavy toll in recent years. Since 1990, the city has lost almost 7 percent of its population.
Population 1,449,634 (2007). Rank: 6th. Race/Hispanic Origin (2000): White 45.0%. Black 43.2%. Indian 0.3%. Asian 4.5%. Other 4.8%. Two or more races 2.2%. Hispanic 8.5%.
Location: 40°00'N, 75°10'W. County: Philadelphia.
Terrain and climate Elev.: 28 ft. Area: 136 sq. mi. (352.2 sq km). Avg. daily min. temp.: Jan.: 23.8°F/-4.5°C; avg. daily max. July: 86.1°F/30°C. Avg. annual rainfall: 41.42"; snowfall: 20"; clear days: 92; precipitation days: 116.
Government Form: mayor and council.
Mayor: Michael Nutter. (215) 686-2181.
www.phila.gov
Visitor info: (800) 537-7676 or (215) 599-0776.
www.gophila.com

▶ PHOENIX, ARIZONA

Arizona's capital and its largest city sits in the Salt River Valley in a former desert that has become a prosperous agricultural area because of a network of irrigated dams located northeast of the city. Long a resort area owing to its mild climate, Phoenix has recently emerged as a lively commercial and agricultural center as well. A flourishing high-tech haven attracting businesses engaged in electronics, communications, and research and development, the city also has a strong manufacturing base that includes airplane parts, electronic equipment, agricultural chemicals, radios, air conditioners, and leather goods. Among its agricultural products are lettuce, melons, vegetables, grapefruit, oranges, lemons, and olives.

While Phoenix benefits from modern irrigation efforts, the Hohokam Indian people dug the area's first irrigation ditches in the 3rd century, B.C. and developed an extensive network of canals that lasted until their culture's decline in A.D. 1400. The area was not resettled until 1864, when a hay camp was established to supply Camp McDowell 30 miles away. Jack Swilling and "Lord Darrell" Dupa rebuilt the old Indian irrigation ditches in 1867, and named the site Phoenix, after the mythical bird that rose from its own ashes. The settlement grew as a trading post, was incorporated as a city in 1881, became capital of the territory in 1889 and the state capital when Arizona was admitted to the Union in 1912.

With the westward exodus from the snowbelt states, and the perfecting of air conditioning to make the summer heat bearable, the small 1950s resort city of 106,818 people has since swelled to be the fifth largest city in the U.S. In the 1980s, Phoenix's population grew 24.5 percent from 789,704 to just under a million. Growth between 1990 and 2000 was even faster (34 percent).
Population 1,552,259 (2007). Rank: 5th. Race/Hispanic Origin (2000): White 71.1%. Black 5.1%. Indian 2.0%. Asian 2.0%. Pacific Islander 0.1%. Other 16.4%. Two or more races 3.3%. Hispanic 34.1%.
Location: 33°30'N, 112°04'W. County: Maricopa.
Terrain and climate Elev.: 1,117 ft. Area: 375 sq. mi. (971.3 sq km). Avg. daily min. temp.: Jan.: 44.4°F/6.8°C; avg. daily max. July: 107.5°F/41°C. Avg. annual rainfall: 7.11"; snowfall: 0"; clear days: 214; precipitation days: 34.
Government Form: council and manager.

Mayor: Phil Gordon. (602) 262-7111.
www.phoenix.gov
Visitor info: (877) CALL-PHX or (602) 254-6500.
www.visitphoenix.com

▶ PORTLAND, OREGON

Portland's renowned beauty is a result of its unique natural setting, which offers a view of the Cascade Mountains and Mt. Hood to the east, Mt. Adams to the northeast, and Mt. St. Helens and Mt. Rainier to the north. Eleven bridges span the Willamette River, which divides the city into east and west sections.

Indian traders traveling between Oregon City and Vancouver carved out an acre of land by the Willamette River 12 miles north of Oregon City, which became known as The Clearing. In 1884 William Overton claimed the 640 acres surrounding the area, which he then sold to Asa Lovejoy and Francis W. Pettygrove, who set out to build a city. Winning a coin toss, Pettygrove named the city-to-be after his hometown in Maine.

As a vital port of entry (the coast's only freshwater port) with a large inland harbor, Portland is a leader in the shipping of lumber, flour, and grain, and has blossomed into Oregon's largest city. Main industries also include paper and pulp, mining, high-technology equipment, and aerospace. Portland enjoys a flourishing arts community and its residents partake of the beaches and ski slopes within easy driving distance.
Population 550,396 (2007). Rank: 30th. Race/Hispanic Origin (2000): White 77.9%. Black 6.6%. Indian 1.1%. Asian 6.3%. Pacific Islander 0.4%. Other 3.5%. Two or more races 4.1%. Hispanic 6.8%.
Location: 45°35'N, 122°40'W. Counties: Clackamas, Multnomah, Washington.
Terrain and climate Elev.: 39 ft. Area: 113.9 sq. mi. (295 sq km). Avg. daily min. temp.: Jan.: 33.5°F/0.8°C; avg. daily max. July: 79.5°F/26.3°C. Avg. annual rainfall: 37.39"; snowfall: 7"; clear days: 69; precipitation days: 152.
Government Form: commission.
Mayor: Tom Potter 503-823-4120.
www.portlandonline.com
Visitor info: (800) 962-3700 or (503) 275-9750.
www.travelportland.com

▶ RALEIGH, NORTH CAROLINA

An early planned community, Raleigh was created as North Carolina's capital and is now the second largest city in the state. Never a major manufacturing area, Raleigh has instead become a retail, educational and cultural center, with well-regarded public schools, the land-grant North Carolina State University, two women's colleges and two historically black colleges.

In the 1760's, tavernkeeper Isaac Hunter began serving travelers along North Carolina's main north-south road in an area of the Piedmont region that became known as Wake Crossroads. Nearby landowner Joel Lane convinced the colony to form a new county in 1770 with the crossroads as the seat. After the American Revolution, the State of North Carolina chose centrally-located Wake County as the site for a legislative capital and purchased 1,000 acres from Lane in 1792, naming the new city in honor of the explorer Sir Walter Raleigh.

During the Civil War, a training camp outside Raleigh held more than 5,000 Confederate soldiers. However, Raleigh survived the war with little harm and was quietly surrendered to Union General William T. Sherman in 1865.

In recent decades, Raleigh's mild four-season climate, excellent educational systems, and the

Research Triangle Park, located between Raleigh and Durham, have drawn high-tech and biotech businesses and research organizations. While it has become a popular retirement area, the city's gracious old architecture, natural beauty, and good jobs also attract many young workers and population has grown dramatically from 207,951 in 1990 to more than 375,000 today.

Population 375,806 (2007). Rank 48th. Race/Hispanic Origin (2000): White 63.3%. Black 27.8%. Indian 0.4%. Asian 3.4%. Other 3.2%. Two or more races 1.9%. Hispanic 7.0%.
Location: 35°77'N, 78°65'W. County: Wake, Durham.
Terrain and climate Elev.: 298 ft. Area: 114.6 sq. mi. (296.8 sq km). Avg. daily min. temp.: Jan.: 29.6°F/1.3°C; avg. daily max. July: 89.1°F/31.7°C. Avg. annual rainfall: 43.05"; snowfall: 7.6"; clear days: 215; precipitation days: 113.
Government Form: council and manager. Mayor: Charles Meeker. (919) 830-3050.
www.raleigh-nc.org
Visitor info: (800)849-8499 or (919)834-5900
www.visitraleigh.com

▶ **SACRAMENTO, CALIFORNIA**
The capital of California and its seventh largest city, Sacramento sits 75 miles northeast of San Francisco at the confluence of the American and Sacramento rivers. A wholesale and retail center for the surrounding rich farmland, the city includes among its main commercial enterprises food processing and canning, and one of the world's largest almond-shelling plants.

Receiving a land grant from the Mexican government in 1839, Swiss-American John Augustus Sutter founded a colony called New Helvetia, and when Fort Sutter was constructed in 1844, it became one of California's chief trading posts. Established soon after the discovery of gold in 1848, Sacramento grew to 7,000 residents by 1850, became state capital in 1854, and in 1863 was incorporated as a city.

The "Gateway to the Goldfields," "Old Sacramento" became a pivotal point of commerce in the 1860s, connected to the mining towns by the American River, and transporting produce from the farms and orchards lining the banks of the Sacramento River. Sailors stopping in San Francisco visited Sacramento to replenish their stocks of fresh produce and to entertain themselves in the saloons and gambling halls. The wealthy lived in great mansions by the river and the cobblestone streets, gaslights, and wood sidewalks imbued the town with a touch of civility. Today's Sacramento, appreciated for its subtle, quiet charms, boasts 120 parks, hiking and biking trails along the American River Parkway, a large collection of art galleries, two symphony orchestras, ballet, theater and opera companies, and a number of jazz clubs and coffee houses.

Population 460,242 (2007). Rank 37th. Race/Hispanic Origin (2000): White 48.3%. Black 15.5%. Indian 1.3%. Asian 16.6%. Pacific Islander 0.9%. Other 11.0%. Two or more races 6.4%. Hispanic 21.6%.
Location: 38°33'N, 121°30'W. County: Sacramento.
Terrain and climate Elev.: 25 ft. Area: 97.3 sq. mi. (252 sq km). Avg. daily min. temp.: Jan.: 37.9°F/3.2°C; avg. daily max. July: 93.3°F/34°C. Avg. annual rainfall: 17.87"; snowfall: 0.1"; clear days: 193; precipitation days: 57.
Government Form: council and manager. Mayor: Heather Fargo. (916) 808-5300.
www.cityofsacramento.org
Visitor info: (800) 292-2334.

www.sacramentocvb.org

▶ **SAN ANTONIO, TEXAS**
San Antonio, the third-largest city in Texas, lies in the state's south-central region at the edge of the Gulf Coastal Plain 140 miles from the Gulf of Mexico. Its economy thrives on agriculture, livestock, and the activity of the wholesale traders who dominate the commerce of southwestern Texas and northern Mexico. It is also a regional leader in biotechnology. Adding further stimulus to the economy are five major military installations—Fort Sam Houston, Randolph Air Force Base, Kelly Air Force Base, Lackland Air Force Base, and Brooks Air Force Base. The military contributes approximately $3 billion annually to the area economy.

The founding of the mission of San Antonio de Valero (later known as the Alamo) and the Presidio of San Antonio in 1718 represented the area's first permanent settlement. When 56 settlers from the Canary Islands joined the original coterie of ranchmen, missionaries, and soldiers, they formed the first municipal organization in Texas, called the villa of San Fernando de Bexar, which became a city in 1809, and suffered under Mexican rule until the battle of San Jacinto in 1836. With the influx of American pioneers and German immigrants (following Texas's statehood in 1845), the population grew to over 96,000 by 1910, and has since increased nearly tenfold. By 1998 it had reached 1.1 million, up 22 percent since 1990.

Today San Antonio is a popular haven for vacationers, with over 10 million visitors per year. San Antonio's attractions include the Alamo and its four sister missions, the Riverwalk along the San Antonio River, Breckenridge Park (home of one of America's largest zoos), Sea World of Texas; La Villita, the Tower of the Americas, and the Spanish Governor's Palace.

Population 1,328,984 (2007). Rank: 7th. Race/Hispanic Origin (2000): White 67.7%. Black 6.8%. Indian 0.8%. Asian 1.6%. Pacific Islander 0.1%. Other 19.3%. Two or more races 3.7%. Hispanic 58.7%.
Location: 29°30'N, 98°30'W. County: Bexar.
Terrain and climate Elev.: 701 ft. Area: 304.5 sq. mi. (788.7 sq km). Avg. daily min. temp.: Jan.: 39°F/3.8°C; avg. daily max. July: 96.3°F/35.7°C. Avg. annual rainfall: 29.13"; snowfall: 0.5"; clear days: 110; precipitation days: 81.
Government Form: council and manager. Mayor: Phil Hardberger. (210) 207-7060.
www.sanantonio.gov
Visitor info: (800) 447-3372 or (210) 270-6700.
www.sanantoniovisit.com

▶ **SAN DIEGO, CALIFORNIA**
Sixty years after João Rodrigues Cabrilho first sailed into San Diego Bay, Sebastian Vizcaino embarked from Spain with three ships to explore the coast of California, and in November 1602 anchored on the lee of what is now known as Point Loma. When he finished charting the bay two days later, he changed its original name, San Miguel, to San Diego, in honor of the saint San Diego de Alcalal de Henares, In 1769, Father Junipero Serra established California's first mission, the Mission San Diego de Alcala.

Compared to its sister cities to the north—Los Angeles and San Francisco—San Diego developed slowly, despite its large and hospitable harbor. In 1887, the city became the southern terminus for the Santa Fe Railroad, but floods soon washed out the tracks and trackbeds, and the railroad was rebuilt to terminate in L.A. which had a new man-made harbor. This put San Diego at an almost insurmountable disadvantage. With its industrial development stunted, San Diego welcomed the establishment of a U.S. Navy base during World War I; since then, about a quarter of the Navy's seagoing vessels and roughly 20 percent of the Marine Corps' forces have been located there. Jonas Salk's work on polio and the emergence of the University of California at San Diego have earned the city the reputation as a premier biomedical research center, luring billions of dollars in development and research grants.

San Diego, a picturesque city with many tourist attractions, enjoys an average of 350 days of sunshine, enticing both residents and visitors to its 70 beaches and the parks, resorts, and health spas lining its great bay. Coronado Island is a popular attraction. Balboa Park, host to international expositions in 1915 and 1935, contains the San Diego Zoo, one of the finest in the nation. The pleasure boats berthed at the city's numerous yacht clubs offer a curious contrast to the naval warships moored nearby. San Diego was the site of the 1992 America's Cup yacht races.

Population 1,266,731 (2007). Rank: 8th. Race/Hispanic Origin (2000): White 60.2%. Black 7.9%. Indian 0.6%. Asian 13.6%. Pacific Islander 0.5%. Other 12.4%. Two or more races 4.8%. Hispanic 25.4%.
Location: 32°43'N, 117°10'W. County: San Diego.
Terrain and climate Elev.: 13 ft. Area: 329 sq. mi. (852.1 sq km). Avg. daily min. temp.: Jan.: 48.4°F/9.1°C; avg. daily max. July: 75.6°F/24.2°C. Avg. annual rainfall: 9.32"; snowfall: 0"; clear days: 150; precipitation days: 41.
Government Form: council and manager. Mayor: Jerry Sanders. (619) 236-6330.
www.sandiego.gov
Visitor info: (619) 236-1212.
www.sandiego.org

▶ SAN FRANCISCO, CALIFORNIA

Located near the Golden Gate, the strait between San Francisco Bay and the Pacific Ocean, fogbound San Francisco hid from some of the greatest European navigators to explore the West Coast. João Rodrigues Cabrilho discovered the Farrallon Islands just off the coast in 1542 and Sir Francis Drake landed a few miles north of the Golden Gate in 1579. Yet it was another 200 years before Don Gasper de Portola sailed into the Bay, followed six years later by Don Juan Manuel Ayala who established a town and mission.

Neither the Spanish nor (after 1821) the Mexican governments were very keen on capitalizing on San Francisco's temperate and strategic location, and when Captain John Montgomery raised the American flag there on July 9, 1846, the community consisted of only 840 people. The discovery of gold at Sutter's mill in 1848, and the gold rush of 1849—which brought 40,000 of the hopeful to California, most by ship—catapulted San Francisco onto the world map, and the following year it was incorporated as a city.

San Francisco continued to prosper as a major transportation and industrial center, but in 1906 an earthquake registering 8.6 on the Richter scale claimed 452 lives, 28,000 buildings, and losses totalling approximately $350 million. San Francisco rose from the ashes to become a thriving, multifaceted, cosmopolitan city and one of the country's leaders in world trade. Another major earthquake, measuring 7.1 on the Richter scale, struck on Oct. 17, 1989, causing extensive damage and 67 deaths in the region, but did not devastate the city as thoroughly as the 1906 tremor.

San Francisco today is a port of call for more than 40 steamship lines which import approximately $25 billion worth of goods from more than 300 ports around the world. A major international financial center, it is the headquarters of three of the nation's largest banks, the 12th Federal Reserve District, and the Pacific Stock Exchange. There are also more than 650 insurance companies, and the city is a haven for venture capitalists and entrepreneurs: more than 90 percent of its businesses have fewer than 25 employees. There are also several U.S. military installations in the area.

Well known for its spirit of individualism, San Francisco was a haven for the beat movement of the 1950s, and the capital of the hippie movement of the 1960s was the Haight-Ashbury district. Its more traditional arts institutions include the San Francisco Ballet, the San Francisco Opera, the San Francisco Symphony, and the American Conservatory Theater. Among its leading educational institutions are the University of San Francisco, the Heald Institute of Technology, the University of California, the San Francisco Art Institute, the San Francisco Conservatory of Music, and the San Francisco College of Mortuary Science. Among its many museums are the National Maritime Historic Park, the Fine Arts Museum, and the California Palace of the Legion of Honor. Other attractions include its historic cable cars (first used in 1873), Chinatown, and Fisherman's Wharf.

Population 764,976 (2007). Rank: 14th. Race/Hispanic Origin (2000): White 49.7%. Black 7.8%. Indian 0.4%. Asian 30.8%. Pacific Islander 0.5%. Other 6.5%. Two or more races 4.3%. Hispanic 14.1%.
Location: 37°47'N, 122°30'W. County: San Francisco.
Terrain and climate Elev.: 155 ft. Area: 46.4 sq. mi. (120.2 sq km). Avg. daily min. temp.: Jan.: 41.5°F/5.2°C; avg. daily max. July: 71°F/21°C. Avg. annual rainfall: 19.71"; snowfall: 0"; clear days: 162; precipitation days: 67.
Government Form: mayor and council. Mayor: Gavin Newsom. (415) 554-6141.
www.ci.sf.ca.us
Visitor info: (415) 391-2000.
www.onlyinsanfrancisco.com

▶ SAN JOSE, CALIFORNIA

Located at the southern end of San Francisco Bay, about 45 miles south of San Francisco, San Jose was the first non-religious European community founded in California. Pueblo de San Jose de Guadalupe was settled in 1777 by enterprising farmers who sought to make themselves and the region independent of Mexico and the Spanish mission network for their supplies. Fruit and olive trees, hides, tallow, livestock, grain, and lively retail activity all contributed to San Jose's early prosperity, and it was the first state capital (1849–52).

San Jose remained an agricultural center until World War II, when industry and technology began to expand. The rapid growth of innovative industry over the last 20 years, taking its lead from research and development begun at nearby Stanford University in the 1930s, changed the area dramatically. With the revolution in high technology, Santa Clara County became known as Silicon Valley, excelling in the production of information systems, personal computers, peripherals, and fostering a burgeoning semi-conductor industry. At the same time, financial services, real estate, construction, and retail industries all flourished.

More than 2,600 high-tech companies employing 250,000 people are located in San Jose, and one-third of the labor force works in manufacturing, a very high proportion in post-industrial America. Santa Clara County has the highest median family income in California, and median housing prices in San Jose are perennially among the highest in the nation.

Population   939,899 (2007). Rank: 10th. Race/Hispanic Origin (2000): White 47.5%. Black 3.5%. Indian 0.8%. Asian 26.9%. Pacific Islander 0.4%. Other 15.9%. Two or more races 5.0%. Hispanic 30.2%.

Location: 37°20'N, 121°53'W. County: Santa Clara.

Terrain and climate   Elev.: 65 ft. Area: 169.2 sq. mi. (438.2 sq km). Avg. daily min. temp.: Jan.: 41.1°F/5°C; avg. daily max.: July: 81.5°F/27.5°C. Avg. annual rainfall: 13.06"; snowfall: 0"; clear days: N.A.; precipitation days: N.A.

Government   Form: council and manager. Mayor: Chuck Reed. (408) 535-4800.

www.sanjoseca.gov

Visitor info: (800) SAN JOSE. **www.sanjose.org**

▶SEATTLE, WASHINGTON

Located on the protected waters of Puget Sound, Seattle was the first European-American settlement established in the Pacific Northwest north of the Columbia River. Starting out at Alki Point in 1851, the settlers moved to what is now known as Pioneer Square. Befriended by the Suquamish Chief Sealth (Seattle is a loose approximation of his name), the people turned to lumber harvesting and log milling, which formed the backbone of the city's economy.

With the completion of the Great Northern Railway in 1893 and the Alaska gold rush of 1897, when Seattle became "the Gateway to the Klondike," the city was transformed into a metropolis of merchants and entrepreneurs. Even as gold fever abated, and despite a devastating fire in 1899, the city prospered as a major port to the Orient and as an industrial center. In 1909 Seattle was the site of the Alaska-Yukon-Pacific Exposition. The completion of the Panama Canal in 1914 brought even more business to the already bustling port. Two years later, a small company began building two-seater biplanes; in time the little company became Boeing, the world's largest producer of commercial planes, and the largest employer (more than 80,000 people) in the Seattle area. In 2001, the company stunned the Emerald City by announcing that it was moving its corporate headquarters (and 500 jobs) to Chicago.

Endowed with spectacular natural beauty, with the broad expanse of Puget Sound before it, and the snow-capped peaks of the Cascade Mountains and Mt. Rainier visible to the south and east, the Seattle area offers a wide variety of outdoor activities, from skiing and hiking to fishing and boating. A second international exposition, the Seattle World's Fair in 1962, helped establish the city's reputation as a center of technology, trade, industry, and tourism. In 1974 Bill Gates and Paul Allen founded Microsoft and Seattle has since been seen as the hub of the computer world. The leading cultural programs are put on by the Seattle Symphony Orchestra, the Seattle Opera Association, and the Seattle Repertory Theater. Other attractions include the Seattle Art Museum, Pioneer Square, Pike Place Market, the historic ships on Lake Union, and Woodland Park and Zoo, as well as the many events at the 74-acre Seattle Convention Center, whose buildings (including the famed Space Needle), and park-like grounds and fountains are legacies of the World's Fair. Among the 20 universities and colleges in the area are the University of Washington and Seattle Pacific University.

Population   594,210 (2007). Rank: 24th. Race/Hispanic Origin (2000): White 70.1%. Black 8.4%. Indian 1.0%. Asian 13.1%. Pacific Islander 0.5%. Other 2.4%. Two or more races 4.5%. Hispanic 5.3%.

Location: 47°41'N, 122°15'W. County: King.

Terrain and climate   Elev.: 450 ft. Area: 83.6 sq. mi. (216.5 sq km). Avg. daily min. temp.: Jan.: 34.3°F/1.2°C; avg. daily max.: July: 75.2°F/24°C. Avg. annual rainfall: 38.85"; snowfall: 15"; clear days: 57; precipitation days: 160.

Government   Form: mayor and council. Mayor: Greg Nickels. (206) 684-4000.

www.seattle.gov

Visitor info: (206) 461-5840. **www.seeseattle.org**

▶TUCSON, ARIZONA

The first European to travel through the area that is now Tucson was the Jesuit missionary Eusebio Kino, in 1692. In 1700 the mission of San Xavier del Bac was established among the Papago Indians nearby. It was not until 1776, however, that the Spanish established a permanent settlement, taking its name from the Papago *Stjukshon* (or *Chuk Shon*), meaning "village of the dark spring at the foot of the mountain." Tucson remained under Spanish and Mexican control until acquired by the U.S. government as part of the Gadsden Purchase in 1853. During the Civil War it was under Confederate control, but from 1867 to 1877 it was the territorial capital.

Despite the arrival of the Southern Pacific railroad in 1880 and the discovery of extensive copper deposits in southern Arizona, neither the city's location nor its natural resources much stimulated its economy. It was best known as a winter and health resort, and as a commercial hub for the surrounding agricultural and mining industries. In 1950, the population was only 45,500.

The last half-century has seen a dramatic change. One of the many beneficiaries of the exodus from the industrial states to the Sunbelt, Tucson's population has grown almost tenfold in that period, and in the last decade Tucson added 20,000 manufacturing jobs. Surrounded by a wealth of natural beauty, the city is still appealing to retirees and tourists, as is reflected in the many golf courses, ranches, and resorts in and around Tucson. It is ringed by four mountain ranges: the Rincon, Santa Catalina, Tucson, and Santa Rita. Other natural wonders include Sabino Canyon (which has the only year-round stream in the region), the Saguaro National Monument (a preserve for Saguaro cacti), and Tucson Mountain Park, home of the Arizona-Sonora Desert Museum. The University of Arizona is located in Tucson, and the Davis-Monthan Air Force Base and Kitts Peak Observatory are nearby.

Population   525,529 (2007). Rank: 32nd. Race/Hispanic Origin (2000): White 70.2%. Black 4.3%. Indian 2.3%. Asian 2.5%. Pacific Islander 0.2%. Other 16.8%. Two or more races 3.8%. Hispanic 35.7%.

Location: 32°14'N, 110°59'W. County: Pima.

Terrain and climate   Elev.: 2,584 ft. Area: 125 sq. mi. (324.8 sq km). Avg. daily min. temp.: Jan.: 38.1°F/3.3°C; avg. daily max.: July: 98.5°F/3.3°C. Avg. annual rainfall: 11.14"; snowfall: 2"; clear days: 198; precipitation days: 50.

Government   Form: council and manager. Mayor: Bob Walkup. (520) 791-4201.

www.tucsonaz.gov

Visitor info: (888) 2TUCSON. **www.visittucson.org**

►TULSA, OKLAHOMA

Tulsa was first settled by Indian nations forced out of the South Atlantic States by the Indian Removal Act of 1830. The name they chose for their new home was Tulsey Town, a corruption of *Tullahassee*, meaning "old town." The name Tulsa was made official with the establishment of a post office in 1879. In 1900, Tulsa's population numbered less than 2,000, but the discovery of extensive oil fields at the turn of the century, beginning with the Glenn Pool and Red Fork strikes, started Tulsa on the way from a small Indian settlement to a sizable metropolis. By 1907, its population had increased to 7,298, and by 1920 it was 10 times that. Soon Tulsa was "the Oil Capital of the World."

While still heavily involved in the oil and gas industry—it remains the home of about 500 oil-related companies—modern Tulsa is a far more diverse city than its old oil patch origins. Among Tulsa's top employers are regional, national and international firms involved in aviation and aerospace, energy, computer technology, insurance, telecommunications, health care, and electronic equipment. The Port of Catoosa, which opened in 1972 after the completion of the 445-mile Arkansas-Mississippi Waterway, is a major inland port which provides Tulsa with a direct link to the Mississippi River system and the Gulf of Mexico.

While growing in business, Tulsa has preserved the cultural heritage of its early oil barons and workers as well as that of its original Indian settlers. Thomas Gilcrease, a Creek Indian, became a millionaire with the Glenn Pool oil strike, and founded the Thomas Gilcrease Institute of American History and Art, devoted to the American Indian. The Tulsa Opera Company was founded in the early 1900s, and along with the city's philharmonic, ballet, and theaters, it gives Tulsa just cause to lay claim to being the cultural capital of Oklahoma. Tulsans also honor their roots through rodeos and regional music festivals. In addition, representatives of the state's 65 Indian tribes gather in Tulsa each summer for their annual powwow. Among Tulsa's universities are the University of Tulsa and Oral Roberts University.

Population 384,037 (2007). Rank: 45th. Race/ Hispanic Origin (2000): White 70.1%. Black 15.5%. Indian 4.7%. Asian 1.8%. Pacific Islander 0.1%. Other 3.5%. Two or more races 4.4%. Hispanic 7.2%.
Location: 36°10'N, 96°00'W. Counties: Osage, Tulsa.
Terrain and climate Elev.: 676 ft. Area: 186.1 sq. mi. (482 sq km). Avg. daily min. temp.: Jan.: 24.8°F/-4°C; avg. daily max. July: 93.9°F/34.3°C. Avg. annual rainfall: 38.77"; snowfall: 9"; clear days: 127; precipitation days: 90.
Government Form: mayor and council. Mayor: Kathryn L. Taylor. (918) 596-7700.
www.cityoftulsa.org
Visitor info: (918) 560-0263.
www.visittulsa.com

►VIRGINIA BEACH, VIRGINIA

Throughout much of its history—from the landing of the Jamestown colonists at Point Henry in 1607—Virginia Beach was overshadowed by its northern neighbor, Norfolk, which was long the home of many shipping and naval enterprises at the mouth of Chesapeake Bay. But Virginia Beach has seen remarkable change in the last two decades.

In 1970, Virginia Beach's population was 172,000, only slightly more than half that of Norfolk. By 1990, it had grown 128 percent, to 393,000, and surpassing Norfolk as the state's largest city, a distinction it still holds today, though growth cooled to a 8.2 percent between 1990 and 2000. Local initiative accounts for most of this growth: in the same period Norfolk's population fell 10 percent. A dominant presence is the U.S. Navy, which has three bases—Oceana Naval Air Station, Little Creek Naval Amphibious Base, and the Dam Neck Fleet Training Center—and which together with the U.S. Army's Fort Story employs 36,000 military and civilian personnel.

With 38 miles of Atlantic shoreline, 28 miles of public beaches, and the Seashore State Park— 2,700 acres of shady upland woods, cypress swamps, and Spanish moss—the city continues to depend on tourism as a major factor in its economy, attracting 2.5 million visitors a year. The city's main industries, which include marine and engineering services, construction, communications, and electronics, occupy 10 industrial/business parks, including four built by the Virginia Beach Development Authority.

Among Virginia Beach's outstanding historic and recreational attractions are the Virginia Marine Science Museum, the Adam Thoroughgood House (c. 1680, one of the oldest brick houses in North America), the Old Cape Henry Lighthouse, authorized by the first Congress in 1790, and the statue of Admiral Compte de Grasse whose defeat of the British at the Battle of the Virginia Capes brought about the defeat of Gen. Cornwallis at Yorktown and the end of the American Revolution in 1781.
Population 434,743 (2007). Rank: 41st. Race/ Hispanic Origin (2000): White 71.4%. Black 19.0%. Indian 0.4%. Asian 4.9%. Pacific Islander 0.1%. Other 1.5%. Two or more races 2.7%. Hispanic 4.2%.
Location: 36°54'N, 75°58'W. County: independent city.
Terrain and climate Elev.: 12 ft. Area: 225.9 sq. mi. (585.1 sq km). Avg. daily min. temp.: Jan.: 31.7°F/-0.1°C; avg. daily max. July: 86.9°F/30.5°C. Avg. annual rainfall: 45.22"; snowfall: 7"; clear days: 110; precipitation days: 115.
Government Form: council and manager. Mayor: Meyera E. Oberndorf. (757) 385-4581.
www.vbgov.com
Visitor info: (800) VA-BEACH.
www.vbfun.com

►WASHINGTON, D.C.

[*For description, see District of Columbia entry in "States, Territories, and Possessions."*]
Population 588,292 (2007). Rank: 27th. Race/ Hispanic Origin (2000): White 30.8%. Black 60.0%. Indian 0.3%. Asian 2.7%. Pacific Islander 0.1%. Other 3.8%. Two or more races 2.4%. Hispanic 7.9%.
Location: 38°52'N, 77°00'W. County: independent city.
Terrain and climate Elev.: 30 ft. Area: 62.7 sq. mi. (162.4 sq km). Avg. daily min. temp.: Jan.: 27.5°F/-2.5°C; avg. daily max. July: 87.9°F/31°C. Avg. annual rainfall: 39"; snowfall: 16"; clear days: 101; precipitation days: 111.
Government Form: mayor and council. Mayor: Adrian Fenty. (202) 727-6263.
www.dc.gov
Visitor info: (202) 789-7000.
www.washington.org

CITIES IN AMERICA

The number of large U.S. cities continues to grow. The 2000 Census recorded 243 cities with populations over 100,000, up from 199 such places in 1990.

The number of very large cities also continues to grow. In 1990, the only cities with more than a million residents were New York, Los Angeles, Chicago, Houston, Philadelphia, Detroit, Dallas and San Diego. In the 2000 Census, Detroit's population dropped below a million (mostly from flight to the suburbs), but Phoenix, and San Antonio topped a million.

New York, the nation's largest city, grew by 685,000 people between censuses, with most of that growth coming in the latter half of the decade. Meanwhile, Los Angeles, which declined in population early in the decade, grew by an overall 479,000 people.

Major U.S. Cities: Population, Population Change, Population Density, and Land Area, 1970–2000

| City (Rank, 2000) | Population ('000s) | | | | Percent change | Population per sq. mi. | Land area (sq.mi.) |
	1970	1980	1990	2000	1990-2000	1990	1990
Abilene, Texas (197)	90	98	107	116	8.7%	1,035	103.1
Akron, Ohio (82)	275	237	223	217	-2.7	3,586	62.2
Albuquerque, N.Mex. (35)	245	332	385	449	16.6	2,909	132.2
Alexandria, Va. (170)	111	103	111	128	15.4	7,267	15.3
Allentown, Pa. (219)	110	104	105	107	1.5	5,949	17.7
Amarillo, Texas (120)	127	149	158	174	10.2	1,793	87.9
Anaheim, Calif. (56)	166	219	266	328	23.1	6,014	44.3
Anchorage , Alaska[1] (66)	48	174	226	260	15.0	133	1,697.7
Ann Arbor, Mich. (199)	100	108	110	114	4.0	4,231	25.9
Arlington, Texas (54)	90	160	262	333	27.2	2,814	93.0
Arvada, Colo. (235)	N.A.	N.A.	89	102	14.5	N.A.	N.A.
Athens-Clarke County, Ga.[1] (237)	N.A.	N.A.	46	101	121.9	N.A.	N.A.
Atlanta, Ga. (40)	495	425	394	416	5.7	2,990	131.8
Augusta-Richmond County, Ga.[1] (91)	N.A.	N.A.	45	200	347.5	N.A.	N.A.
Aurora, Colo. (62)	75	159	222	276	24.4	1,676	132.5
Aurora, Ill. (151)	N.A.	N.A.	100	143	43.6	N.A.	N.A.
Austin, Texas (16)	254	346	466	657	41.0	2,138	217.8
Bakersfield, Calif. (70)	70	106	175	247	41.3	1,904	91.8
Baltimore, Md. (17)	905	787	736	651	-11.5	9,108	80.8
Baton Rouge, La. (75)	166	220	220	228	3.8	2,969	74.0
Bayamon, Puerto Rico (86)	N.A.	N.A.	202	203	0.7	N.A.	N.A.
Beaumont, Texas (200)	118	118	114	114	-0.4	1,427	80.1
Bellevue, Wash. (210)	N.A.	N.A.	87	110	26.1	N.A.	N.A.
Berkeley, Calif. (231)	114	103	103	103	0.0	9,783	10.5
Birmingham, Ala. (72)	301	284	266	243	-8.7	1,791	148.5
Boise City, Idaho (108)	75	102	126	186	47.8	2,726	46.1
Boston, Mass. (20)	641	563	574	589	2.6	11,860	48.4
Bridgeport, Conn. (156)	157	143	142	140	-1.5	8,855	16.0
Brownsville, Texas (155)	N.A.	N.A.	99	140	41.2	N.A.	N.A.
Buffalo, N.Y. (59)	463	358	328	293	-10.8	8,083	40.6
Burbank, Calif. (243)	N.A.	N.A.	94	100	7.1	N.A.	N.A.
Cambridge, Mass. (238)	N.A.	N.A.	96	101	5.8	N.A.	N.A.
Cape Coral, Fla. (234)	N.A.	N.A.	75	102	36.4	N.A.	N.A.
Carolina , Puerto Rico (125)	N.A.	N.A.	162	168	3.5	N.A.	N.A.
Carrollton, Texas (209)	N.A.	N.A.	82	110	33.4	N.A.	N.A.
Cedar Rapids, Iowa (185)	111	110	109	121	11.0	2,033	53.5
Chandler, Ariz. (116)	N.A.	N.A.	91	177	95.0	N.A.	N.A.
Charlotte, N.C. (26)	241	315	396	541	36.6	2,272	174.3
Chattanooga, Tenn. (132)	120	170	152	156	2.0	1,288	118.4
Chesapeake, Va. (93)	90	114	152	199	31.1	446	340.7
Chicago, Ill. (3)	3,369	3,005	2,784	2,896	4.0	12,251	227.2
Chula Vista, Calif. (122)	68	84	135	174	28.4	4,661	29.0
Cincinnati, Ohio (55)	454	385	364	331	-9.0	4,717	77.2
Clarksville, Tenn. (228)	N.A.	N.A.	75	103	37.0	N.A.	N.A.
Clearwater, Fla. (212)	N.A.	N.A.	99	109	10.1	N.A.	N.A.
Cleveland, Ohio (33)	751	574	506	478	-5.4	6,565	77.0
Colorado Springs, Colo. (49)	136	215	281	361	28.4	1,535	183.2
Columbia, S.C. (195)	114	101	98	116	18.6	884	117.1
Columbus, Ga. [1] (106)	155	169	179	186	3.9	827	216.1
Columbus, Ohio (15)	540	565	633	711	12.4	3,315	190.9
Concord, Calif. (181)	85	104	111	122	9.4	3,773	29.5
Coral Springs, Fla. (190)	N.A.	N.A.	79	118	48.0	N.A.	N.A.
Corona, Calif. (174)	N.A.	N.A.	76	125	64.2	N.A.	N.A.
Corpus Christi, Texas (61)	205	232	257	277	7.8	1,907	135.0

City (Rank, 2000)	Population ('000s) 1970	1980	1990	2000	Percent change 1990-2000	Population per sq. mi. 1990	Land area (sq.mi.) 1990
Costa Mesa, Calif. (213)	N.A.	N.A.	96	109	12.8%	N.A.	N.A.
Dallas, Texas (8)	844	905	1,007	1,189	18.0	2,943	342.4
Daly City, Calif. (227)	N.A.	N.A.	92	104	12.3	N.A.	N.A.
Dayton, Ohio (126)	243	194	182	166	-8.7	3,310	55.0
Denver, Colo.[1] (25)	515	493	468	555	18.6	3,051	153.3
Des Moines, Iowa (95)	201	191	193	199	2.8	2,567	75.3
Detroit, Mich. (10)	1,514	1,203	1,028	951	-7.5	7,410	138.7
Downey, Calif. (216)	N.A.	N.A.	91	107	17.4	N.A.	N.A.
Durham, N.C. (105)	95	101	137	187	36.9	1,972	69.3
El Monte, Calif. (196)	70	79	106	116	9.2	11,175	9.5
El Paso, Texas (23)	322	425	515	564	9.4	2,100	245.4
Elizabeth, N.J. (186)	113	106	110	121	9.6	8,929	12.3
Erie, Pa. (226)	129	119	109	104	-4.6	4,944	22.0
Escondido, Calif. (164)	37	64	109	134	22.9	3,048	35.6
Eugene, Oreg. (160)	79	106	113	138	22.4	2,962	38.0
Evansville, Ind. (182)	139	130	126	122	-3.7	3,102	40.7
Fayetteville, N.C. (184)	N.A.	N.A.	76	121	59.9	N.A.	N.A.
Flint, Mich. (175)	193	160	141	125	-11.2	4,161	33.8
Fontana, Calif. (167)	N.A.	N.A.	88	129	47.3	N.A.	N.A.
Fort Collins, Colo. (189)	N.A.	N.A.	88	119	35.2	N.A.	N.A.
Fort Lauderdale, Fla. (134)	140	153	149	152	2.0	4,753	31.4
Fort Wayne, Ind. (85)	178	172	173	206	18.9	2,762	62.7
Fort Worth, Texas (27)	393	385	448	535	19.5	1,592	281.1
Fremont, Calif. (87)	101	132	173	203	17.3	2,250	77.0
Fresno, Calif. (37)	166	217	354	428	20.7	3,573	99.1
Fullerton, Calif. (173)	86	102	114	126	10.4	5,160	22.1
Garden Grove, Calif. (127)	121	123	143	165	15.5	7,974	17.9
Garland, Texas (83)	81	139	181	216	19.4	3,150	57.4
Gary, Ind. (230)	175	152	117	103	-11.9	2,322	50.2
Gilbert town, Ariz. (208)	N.A.	N.A.	29	110	275.8	N.A.	N.A.
Glendale, Ariz. (81)	36	97	148	219	47.7	2,837	52.2
Glendale, Calif. (100)	133	139	180	195	8.3	5,882	30.6
Grand Prairie, Texas (172)	N.A.	N.A.	100	127	27.9	N.A.	N.A.
Grand Rapids, Mich. (96)	198	182	189	198	4.6	4,273	44.3
Green Bay, Wisc. (233)	N.A.	N.A.	96	102	6.1	N.A.	N.A.
Greensboro, N.C. (78)	144	156	184	224	22.0	2,304	79.8
Hampton, Va. (147)	121	123	134	146	9.5	2,583	51.8
Hartford, Conn. (183)	158	136	140	122	-13.0	8,077	17.3
Hayward, Calif. (154)	93	94	111	140	25.6	2,560	43.5
Henderson, Nevada (118)	N.A.	N.A.	65	175	170.1	N.A.	N.A.
Hialeah, Fla. (76)	102	145	188	226	20.4	9,772	19.2
Hollywood, Fla. (157)	107	121	122	139	14.5	4,464	27.3
Honolulu, Hawaii[2] (47)	325	365	365	372	1.7	4,400	85.7
Houston, Texas (4)	1,234	1,595	1,631	1,954	19.8	3,021	539.9
Huntington Beach, Calif. (103)	116	171	182	190	4.4	6,871	26.4
Huntsville, Ala. (130)	139	143	160	158	-1.0	973	164.4
Independence, Mo. (202)	112	112	112	113	0.9	1,436	78.2
Indianapolis , Ind. (12)	737	701	742	792	6.7	2,022	361.7
Inglewood, Calif. (204)	90	94	110	113	2.7	11,952	9.2
Irvine, Calif. (150)	(3)	62	110	143	29.7	2,607	42.3
Irving, Texas (102)	97	110	155	192	23.6	2,293	67.6
Jackson, Miss. (111)	154	203	197	184	-6.3	1,804	109.0
Jacksonville, Fla. (14)	504	541	635	736	15.8	837	758.7
Jersey City, N.J. (73)	260	224	229	240	5.0	15,337	14.9
Joliet, Ill. (221)	N.A.	N.A.	77	106	38.2	N.A.	N.A.
Kansas City, Kans. (146)	168	161	150	147	-1.9	1,390	107.8
Kansas City, Mo. (36)	507	448	435	442	1.5	1,397	311.5
Knoxville, Tenn. (119)	175	175	165	174	5.3	2,135	77.2
Lafayette, La. (207)	N.A.	N.A.	94	110	16.7	N.A.	N.A.
Lakewood, Colo. (148)	93	114	126	144	14.0	3,100	40.8
Lancaster, Calif. (188)	N.A.	N.A.	97	119	22.0	N.A.	N.A.
Lansing, Mich. (187)	131	130	127	119	-6.4	3,755	33.9
Laredo, Texas (117)	69	91	123	177	43.7	3,739	32.9
Las Vegas, Nevada (32)	126	165	258	478	85.2	3,100	83.3
Lexington-Fayette, Ky. (65)	108	204	225	261	15.6	792	284.5
Lincoln, Neb. (77)	150	172	192	226	17.5	3,033	63.3
Little Rock, Ark. (112)	132	159	176	183	4.2	1,709	102.9
Livonia, Mich. (242)	110	105	101	101	-0.3	2,823	35.7
Long Beach, Calif. (34)	359	361	429	462	7.5	8,586	50.0
Los Angeles, Calif. (2)	2,812	2,969	3,485	3,695	6.0	7,426	469.3
Louisville, Ky. (67)	362	299	269	256	-4.8	4,341	62.1
Lowell, Mass. (222)	94	92	103	105	1.7	7,506	13.8

City (Rank, 2000)	Population ('000s)				Percent change	Population per sq. mi.	Land area (sq.mi.)
	1970	1980	1990	2000	1990-2000	1990	1990
Lubbock, Texas (92)	149	174	186	200	7.2%	1,789	104.1
Madison, Wisc. (84)	172	171	191	208	8.8	3,300	57.8
Manchester, N.H. (218)	N.A.	N.A.	100	107	7.5	N.A.	N.A.
McAllen, Texas (220)	N.A.	N.A.	84	106	26.7	N.A.	N.A.
Memphis, Tenn. (18)	624	646	610	650	6.5	2,384	256.0
Mesa, Ariz. (43)	63	152	288	396	37.6	2,653	108.6
Mesquite, Texas (176)	55	67	101	125	22.7	2,369	42.8
Miami, Fla. (48)	335	347	359	362	1.1	10,074	35.6
Milwaukee, Wisc. (19)	717	636	628	597	-5.0	6,537	96.1
Minneapolis, Minn. (46)	434	371	368	383	3.9	6,706	54.9
Mobile, Ala. (94)	190	200	196	199	1.3	1,663	118.0
Modesto, Calif. (104)	62	107	165	189	14.6	5,458	30.2
Montgomery, Ala. (89)	133	178	187	202	7.7	1,389	135.0
Moreno Valley, Calif. (152)	(3)	(3)	119	142	19.9	2,418	49.1
Naperville, Ill. (169)	N.A.	N.A.	85	128	50.4	N.A.	N.A.
Nashville-Davidson, Tenn.[1] (22)	426	456	511	570	11.6	1,032	473.3
New Haven, Conn. (179)	138	126	130	124	-5.2	6,922	18.9
New Orleans, La. (31)	593	558	497	485	-2.5	2,751	180.7
New York, N.Y. (1)	7,896	7,072	7,323	8,008	9.4	23,701	309.0
Newark, N.J. (64)	382	329	275	274	-0.6	11,554	23.8
Newport News, Va. (115)	130	145	170	180	5.9	2,510	68.3
Norfolk, Va. (74)	308	267	261	234	-10.3	4,856	53.8
North Las Vegas, Nevada (198)	N.A.	N.A.	48	115	142.1	N.A.	N.A.
Norwalk, Calif. (229)	N.A.	N.A.	94	103	9.6	N.A.	N.A.
Oakland, Calif. (42)	362	339	372	399	7.3	6,640	56.1
Oceanside, Calif. (128)	40	77	128	161	25.4	3,164	40.5
Oklahoma City, Okla. (29)	368	404	445	506	13.8	731	608.2
Omaha, Neb. (45)	347	314	336	390	16.1	3,336	100.7
Ontario, Calif. (131)	64	89	133	158	18.6	3,624	36.8
Orange, Calif. (168)	77	91	111	129	16.4	4,741	23.3
Orlando, Fla. (107)	99	128	165	186	12.9	2,448	67.3
Overland Park, Kans. (143)	78	82	112	149	33.4	2,007	55.7
Oxnard, Calif. (124)	71	108	142	170	19.8	5,843	24.4
Palmdale, Calif. (194)	N.A.	N.A.	69	117	69.5	N.A.	N.A.
Pasadena, Calif. (163)	113	118	132	134	1.8	5,724	23.0
Pasadena, Texas (153)	90	113	119	142	18.7	2,726	43.8
Paterson, N.J. (142)	145	138	141	149	5.9	16,693	8.4
Pembroke Pines, Fla. (161)	N.A.	N.A.	65	137	110.0	N.A.	N.A.
Peoria, Ariz. (214)	N.A.	N.A.	51	108	114.1	N.A.	N.A.
Peoria, Ill. (203)	127	124	114	113	-0.5	2,776	40.9
Philadelphia, Pa. [1] (5)	1,949	1,688	1,586	1,518	-4.3	11,734	135.1
Phoenix, Ariz. (6)	584	790	983	1,321	34.3	2,342	419.9
Pittsburgh, Pa. (53)	520	424	370	335	-9.5	6,649	55.6
Plano, Texas (79)	18	72	129	222	72.5	1,929	66.3
Pomona, Calif. (141)	87	93	132	149	13.5	5,770	22.8
Ponce, Puerto Rico (133)	N.A.	N.A.	159	155	-2.6	N.A.	N.A.
Portland, Oreg. (28)	380	368	437	529	21.0	3,508	124.7
Portsmouth, Va. (241)	111	105	104	101	-3.2	3,139	33.1
Providence, R.I. (121)	179	157	161	174	8.0	8,707	18.5
Provo, Utah (223)	N.A.	N.A.	87	105	21.1	N.A.	N.A.
Pueblo, Colo. (236)	N.A.	N.A.	99	102	3.5	N.A.	N.A.
Raleigh, N.C. (63)	123	150	208	276	32.8	2,395	88.1
Rancho Cucamonga, Calif. (171)	(3)	55	101	128	26.0	2,682	37.8
Reno, Nevada (114)	73	101	134	180	34.8	2,328	57.5
Richmond, Va. (97)	249	219	203	198	-2.6	3,374	60.1
Riverside, Calif. (68)	140	171	227	255	12.7	2,916	77.7
Rochester, N.Y. (80)	295	242	232	220	-5.1	6,435	35.8
Rockford, Ill. (140)	147	140	139	150	7.7	3,110	45.0
Sacramento, Calif. (41)	257	276	369	407	10.2	3,836	96.3
Salem, Oreg. (162)	69	89	108	137	27.0	2,595	41.5
Salinas, Calif. (138)	59	80	109	151	38.9	5,839	18.6
Salt Lake City, Utah (113)	176	163	160	182	13.6	1,467	109.0
San Antonio, Texas (9)	654	786	936	1,145	22.3	2,810	333.0
San Bernardino, Calif. (110)	107	119	164	185	12.9	2,980	55.1
San Diego, Calif. (7)	697	876	1,111	1,223	10.2	3,428	324.0
San Francisco, Calif. [1] (13)	716	679	724	777	7.3	15,502	46.7
San Jose, Calif. (11)	460	629	782	895	14.4	4,568	171.3
San Juan , Puerto Rico (39)	N.A.	N.A.	427	422	-1.1	N.A.	N.A.
Santa Ana, Calif. (52)	156	204	294	338	15.1	10,842	27.1
Santa Clara, Calif. (232)	N.A.	N.A.	94	102	9.3	N.A.	N.A.
Santa Clarita, Calif. (137)	(3)	(3)	111	151	36.6	2,733	40.5
Santa Rosa, Calif. (144)	50	83	113	148	30.3	3,362	33.7

City (Rank, 2000)	Population ('000s)				Percent change 1990-2000	Population per sq. mi. 1990	Land area (sq.mi.) 1990
	1970	1980	1990	2000			
Savannah, Ga. (166)	118	142	138	132	-4.4%	2,204	62.6
Scottsdale, Ariz. (88)	68	89	130	203	55.8	706	184.4
Seattle, Wash. (24)	531	494	516	563	9.1	6,154	83.9
Shreveport, La. (90)	182	206	199	200	0.8	2,013	98.6
Simi Valley, Calif. (206)	60	78	100	111	11.1	3,034	33.0
Sioux Falls, S.D. (178)	72	81	101	124	23.0	2,236	45.1
South Bend, Ind. (215)	126	110	106	108	2.2	2,897	36.4
Spokane, Wash. (99)	171	171	177	196	10.4	3,169	55.9
Springfield, Ill. (205)	92	100	105	111	5.9	2,474	42.5
Springfield, Mass. (135)	164	152	157	152	-3.1	4,890	32.1
Springfield, Mo. (136)	120	133	140	152	7.9	2,068	68.0
St. Louis, Mo. (50)	622	453	397	348	-12.2	6,405	61.9
St. Paul, Minn. (60)	310	270	272	287	5.5	5,157	52.8
St. Petersburg, Fla. (69)	216	239	239	248	4.0	4,059	59.2
Stamford, Conn. (191)	109	102	108	117	8.4	2,865	37.7
Sterling Heights, Mich. (177)	61	109	118	124	5.7	3,215	36.6
Stockton, Calif. (71)	110	150	211	244	15.6	4,013	52.6
Sunnyvale, Calif. (165)	96	107	117	132	12.4	5,353	21.9
Syracuse, N.Y. (145)	197	170	164	147	-10.1	6,528	25.1
Tacoma, Wash. (101)	154	159	177	194	9.6	3,677	48.1
Tallahassee, Fla. (139)	73	82	125	151	20.7	1,972	63.3
Tampa, Fla. (58)	278	272	280	303	8.4	2,577	108.7
Tempe, Ariz. (129)	64	107	142	159	11.8	3,590	39.5
Thousand Oaks, Calif. (192)	36	77	104	117	12.1	2,104	49.6
Toledo, Ohio (57)	383	355	333	314	-5.8	4,132	80.6
Topeka, Kans. (180)	125	119	120	122	2.1	2,173	55.2
Torrance, Calif. (159)	135	130	133	138	3.6	6,487	20.5
Tucson, Ariz. (30)	263	331	405	487	20.1	2,594	156.3
Tulsa, Okla. (44)	330	361	367	393	7.0	2,001	183.5
Vallejo, Calif. (193)	72	80	109	117	6.9	3,613	30.2
Vancouver, Wash. (149)	N.A.	N.A.	46	144	209.5	N.A.	N.A.
Ventura, Calif. (240)	N.A.	N.A.	93	101	9.0	N.A.	N.A.
Virginia Beach, Va. (38)	172	262	393	425	8.2	1,583	248.3
Waco, Texas (201)	95	101	104	114	9.8	1,367	75.8
Warren, Mich. (158)	179	161	145	138	-4.6	4,226	34.3
Washington, D.C. (21)	757	638	607	572	-5.7	9,883	61.4
Waterbury, Conn. (217)	108	103	109	107	-1.6	3,815	28.6
West Covina, Calif. (224)	N.A.	N.A.	96	105	9.4	N.A.	N.A.
West Valley City, Utah (211)	N.A.	N.A.	87	109	25.2	N.A.	N.A.
Westminster, Colo. (239)	N.A.	N.A.	75	101	35.3	N.A.	N.A.
Wichita Falls, Texas (225)	N.A.	N.A.	96	104	8.2	N.A.	N.A.
Wichita, Kans. (51)	277	280	304	344	13.2	2,640	115.1
Winston-Salem, N.C. (109)	134	132	143	186	29.5	2,018	71.1
Worcester, Mass. (123)	177	162	170	173	1.7	4,520	37.6
Yonkers, N.Y. (98)	204	195	188	196	4.3	10,403	18.1

Notes: Cities over 100,000 population. 1. Represents the portion of a consolidated city not within one or more separately incorporated areas. 2. Data represent the census designated place of Honolulu, as delineated by the State of Hawaii.
Source: U.S. Bureau of the Census, Statistical Abstract of the United States 1990 and 2000, and Release (2001).

Historical Rankings, Top 10 Cities

	1910		1960		2007
City	Population	City	Population	City	Population
New York	4,766,883	New York	7,781,984	New York	8,274,527
Chicago	2,185,283	Chicago	3,550,404	Los Angeles	3,834,340
Philadelphia	1,549,008	Los Angeles	2,479,015	Chicago	2,836,658
St. Louis	687,029	Philadelphia	2,002,512	Houston	2,208,180
Boston	670,585	Detroit	1,670,144	Phoenix	1,552,259
Cleveland	560,663	Baltimore	939,024	Philadelphia	1,449,634
Baltimore	558,485	Houston	938,219	San Antonio	1,328,984
Pittsburgh	533,905	Cleveland	876,050	San Diego	1,266,731
Detroit	465,766	Washington, D.C.	763,956	Dallas	1,240,499
Buffalo, N.Y.	423,715	St. Louis	750,026	San Jose, Calif.	939,899

Source: U.S. Bureau of the Census.

Resident Population of Major U.S Cities by Race and Hispanic Origin, 2000

Geographic area	Total population	Black	American Indian	Asian	Native Hawaiian	Some other race	Two or more races	Hispanic or Latino (any race)
Abilene, Texas	115,930	8.8%	0.6%	1.3%	0.1%	8.7%	2.4%	19.4%
Akron, Ohio	217,074	28.5	0.3	1.5	—	0.4	2.1	1.2
Albuquerque, N. Mex.	448,607	3.1	3.9	2.2	0.1	14.8	4.3	39.9
Alexandria, Va.	128,283	22.5	0.3	5.7	0.1	7.4	4.3	14.7
Allentown, Pa.	106,632	7.8	0.3	2.3	0.1	13.4	3.6	24.4
Amarillo, Texas	173,627	6.0	0.8	2.1	—	11.3	2.3	21.9
Anaheim, Calif.	328,014	2.7	0.9	12.0	0.4	24.2	5.0	46.8
Anchorage, Alaska	260,283	5.8	7.3	5.5	0.9	2.2	6.0	5.7
Ann Arbor, Mich.	114,024	8.8	0.3	11.9	—	1.2	3.1	3.3
Arlington, Texas	332,969	13.7	0.5	6.0	0.1	8.9	2.9	18.3
Arlington, Va.	189,453	9.3	0.3	8.6	0.1	8.3	4.3	18.6
Arvada, Colo.	102,153	0.7	0.7	2.2	0.1	3.1	2.3	9.8
Athens, Ga.	101,489	27.3	0.2	3.1	—	3.1	1.4	6.3
Atlanta, Ga.	416,474	61.4	0.2	1.9	—	2.0	1.2	4.5
Augusta, Ga.	199,775	49.8	0.3	1.5	0.1	1.0	1.8	2.8
Aurora, Colo.	276,393	13.4	0.8	4.4	0.2	8.1	4.2	19.8
Aurora, Ill.	142,990	11.1	0.4	3.1	—	14.5	2.9	32.6
Austin, Texas	656,562	10.0	0.6	4.7	0.1	16.2	3.0	30.5
Bakersfield, Calif.	247,057	9.2	1.4	4.3	0.1	18.7	4.4	32.5
Baltimore, Md.	651,154	64.3	0.3	1.5	—	0.7	1.5	1.7
Baton Rouge, La.	227,818	50.0	0.2	2.6	—	0.5	1.0	1.7
Beaumont, Texas	113,866	45.8	0.2	2.5	—	3.5	1.5	7.9
Bellevue, Wash.	109,569	2.0	0.3	17.4	0.2	2.5	3.2	5.3
Berkeley, Calif.	102,743	13.6	0.5	16.4	0.1	4.6	5.6	9.7
Birmingham, Ala.	242,820	73.5	0.2	0.8	—	0.6	0.8	1.6
Boise City, Idaho	185,787	0.8	0.7	2.1	0.2	1.7	2.4	4.5
Boston, Mass.	589,141	25.3	0.4	7.5	0.1	7.8	4.4	14.4
Bridgeport, Conn.	139,529	30.8	0.5	3.3	0.1	14.8	5.6	31.9
Brownsville, Texas	139,722	0.4	0.4	0.5	—	14.7	2.3	91.3
Buffalo, N.Y.	292,648	37.2	0.8	1.4	—	3.7	2.5	7.5
Burbank, Calif.	100,316	2.1	0.5	9.2	0.1	9.9	6.0	24.9
Cambridge, Mass.	101,355	11.9	0.3	11.9	0.1	3.2	4.6	7.4
Cape Coral, Fla.	102,286	2.0	0.3	0.9	0.1	2.2	1.6	8.3
Carrollton, Texas	109,576	6.3	0.5	10.9	0.1	7.7	2.7	19.5
Cedar Rapids, Iowa	120,758	3.7	0.3	1.8	0.1	0.6	1.8	1.7
Chandler, Ariz.	176,581	3.5	1.2	4.2	0.1	10.8	3.0	21.0
Charlotte, N.C.	540,828	32.7	0.3	3.4	0.1	3.6	1.7	7.4
Chattanooga, Tenn.	155,554	36.1	0.3	1.5	0.1	1.0	1.3	2.1
Chesapeake, Va.	199,184	28.5	0.4	1.8	0.1	0.7	1.6	2.0
Chicago, Ill.	2,896,016	36.8	0.4	4.3	0.1	13.6	2.9	26.0
Chula Vista, Calif.	173,556	4.6	0.8	11.0	0.6	22.1	5.8	49.6
Cincinnati, Ohio	331,285	42.9	0.2	1.5	—	0.6	1.7	1.3
Clarksville, Tenn.	103,455	23.2	0.5	2.2	0.3	2.6	3.3	6.0
Clearwater, Fla.	108,787	9.8	0.3	1.6	0.1	2.5	1.8	9.0
Cleveland, Ohio	478,403	51.0	0.3	1.3	—	3.6	2.2	7.3
Colorado Springs, Colo.	360,890	6.6	0.9	2.8	0.2	5.0	3.9	12.0
Columbia, S.C.	116,278	46.0	0.3	1.7	0.1	1.4	1.4	3.0
Columbus, Ga.	186,291	43.7	0.4	1.5	0.1	1.9	1.9	4.5
Columbus, Ohio	711,470	24.5	0.3	3.4	0.1	1.2	2.6	2.5
Concord, Calif.	121,780	3.0	0.8	9.4	0.5	9.7	5.9	21.8
Coral Springs, Fla.	117,549	9.2	0.2	3.5	0.1	3.0	2.5	15.5
Corona, Calif.	124,966	6.4	0.9	7.5	0.3	17.5	5.3	35.7
Corpus Christi, Texas	277,454	4.7	0.6	1.3	0.1	18.6	3.1	54.3
Costa Mesa, Calif.	108,724	1.4	0.8	6.9	0.6	16.6	4.3	31.8
Dallas, Texas	1,188,580	25.9	0.5	2.7	—	17.2	2.7	35.6
Daly City, Calif.	103,621	4.6	0.4	50.7	0.9	11.3	6.2	22.3
Dayton, Ohio	166,179	43.1	0.3	0.6	—	0.7	1.8	1.6
Denver, Colo.	554,636	11.1	1.3	2.8	0.1	15.6	3.7	31.7
Des Moines, Iowa	198,682	8.1	0.4	3.5	—	3.5	2.2	6.6
Detroit, Mich.	951,270	81.6	0.3	1.0	—	2.5	2.3	5.0
Downey, Calif.	107,323	3.8	0.9	7.7	0.2	29.1	4.9	57.9
Durham, N.C.	187,035	43.8	0.3	3.6	—	4.7	1.9	8.6
East Los Angeles, Calif.	124,283	0.4	1.3	0.8	0.1	54.0	4.2	96.8
El Monte, Calif.	115,965	0.8	1.4	18.5	0.1	39.3	4.3	72.4
El Paso, Texas	563,662	3.1	0.8	1.1	0.1	18.2	3.4	76.6
Elizabeth, N.J.	120,568	20.0	0.5	2.3	—	15.5	5.9	49.5
Erie, Pa.	103,717	14.2	0.2	0.7	—	1.9	2.3	4.4
Escondido, Calif.	133,559	2.3	1.2	4.5	0.2	19.2	4.8	38.7

Geographic area	Total population	Black	American Indian	Asian	Native Hawaiian	Some other race	Two or more races	Hispanic or Latino (any race)
Eugene, Oreg.	137,893	1.3%	0.9%	3.6%	0.2%	2.2%	3.7%	5.0%
Evansville, Ind.	121,582	10.9	0.2	0.7	—	0.5	1.4	1.1
Fayetteville, N.C.	121,015	42.4	1.1	2.2	0.2	2.5	2.8	5.7
Flint, Mich.	124,943	53.3	0.6	0.4	—	1.1	3.1	3.0
Fontana, Calif.	128,929	11.8	1.1	4.4	0.3	31.9	5.4	57.7
Fort Collins, Colo.	118,652	1.0	0.6	2.5	0.1	3.6	2.5	8.8
Fort Lauderdale, Fla.	152,397	28.9	0.2	1.0	—	1.8	3.8	9.5
Fort Wayne, Ind.	205,727	17.4	0.4	1.6	—	2.9	2.3	5.8
Fort Worth, Texas	534,694	20.3	0.6	2.6	0.1	14.0	2.7	29.8
Fremont, Calif.	203,413	3.1	0.5	37.0	0.4	5.5	5.8	13.5
Fresno, Calif.	427,652	8.4	1.6	11.2	0.1	23.4	5.2	39.9
Fullerton, Calif.	126,003	2.3	0.7	16.1	0.2	14.8	4.0	30.2
Garden Grove, Calif.	165,196	1.3	0.8	30.9	0.7	15.4	4.1	32.5
Garland, Texas	215,768	11.9	0.6	7.3	0.1	12.0	2.9	25.6
Gary, Ind.	102,746	84.0	0.2	0.1	—	2.0	1.7	4.9
Gilbert, Ariz.	109,697	2.4	0.6	3.6	0.1	4.8	2.8	11.9
Glendale, Ariz.	218,812	4.7	1.5	2.7	0.1	12.0	3.5	24.8
Glendale, Calif.	194,973	1.3	0.3	16.1	0.1	8.6	10.1	19.7
Grand Prairie, Texas	127,427	13.5	0.8	4.4	0.1	15.9	3.3	33.0
Grand Rapids, Mich.	197,800	20.4	0.7	1.6	0.1	6.6	3.2	13.1
Green Bay, Wisc.	102,313	1.4	3.3	3.8	—	3.7	2.0	7.1
Greensboro, N.C.	223,891	37.4	0.4	2.8	—	2.1	1.7	4.4
Hampton, Va.	146,437	44.7	0.4	1.8	0.1	1.0	2.4	2.8
Hartford, Conn.	121,578	38.1	0.5	1.6	0.1	26.5	5.4	40.5
Hayward, Calif.	140,030	11.0	0.8	19.0	1.9	16.8	7.5	34.2
Henderson, Nevada	175,381	3.8	0.7	4.0	0.4	3.2	3.5	10.7
Hialeah, Fla.	226,419	2.4	0.1	0.4	—	5.5	3.6	90.3
Hollywood, Fla.	139,357	12.1	0.3	2.0	0.1	4.0	3.3	22.5
Honolulu, Hawaii	371,657	1.6	0.2	55.9	6.8	0.9	14.9	4.4
Houston, Texas	1,953,631	25.3	0.4	5.3	0.1	16.5	3.1	37.4
Huntington Beach, Calif.	189,594	0.8	0.6	9.3	0.2	5.8	3.9	14.7
Huntsville, Ala.	158,216	30.2	0.5	2.2	0.1	0.7	1.8	2.0
Independence, Mo.	113,288	2.6	0.6	0.7	0.5	1.4	2.3	3.7
Indianapolis, Ind.	791,926	25.3	0.3	1.4	—	2.0	1.6	3.9
Inglewood, Calif.	112,580	47.1	0.7	1.1	0.4	27.4	4.2	46.0
Irvine, Calif.	143,072	1.4	0.2	29.8	0.1	2.5	4.8	7.4
Irving, Texas	191,615	10.2	0.6	8.2	0.1	13.4	3.2	31.2
Jackson, Miss.	184,256	70.6	0.1	0.6	—	0.2	0.7	0.8
Jacksonville, Fla.	735,617	29.0	0.3	2.8	0.1	1.3	2.0	4.2
Jersey City, N.J.	240,055	28.3	0.4	16.2	0.1	15.1	5.8	28.3
Joliet, Ill.	106,221	18.2	0.3	1.1	—	9.0	2.1	18.4
Kansas City, Kans.	146,866	30.1	0.8	1.7	—	8.6	3.0	16.8
Kansas City, Mo.	441,545	31.2	0.5	1.9	0.1	3.2	2.4	6.9
Knoxville, Tenn.	173,890	16.2	0.3	1.5	—	0.7	1.6	1.6
Lafayette, La.	110,257	28.5	0.2	1.4	—	0.6	1.0	1.9
Lakewood, Colo.	144,126	1.5	1.1	2.7	0.1	4.9	2.6	14.5
Lancaster, Calif.	118,718	16.0	1.0	3.8	0.2	11.1	5.0	24.1
Lansing, Mich.	119,128	21.9	0.8	2.8	0.1	4.5	4.6	10.0
Laredo, Texas	176,576	0.4	0.4	0.5	—	13.9	2.5	94.1
Las Vegas, Nevada	478,434	10.4	0.7	4.8	0.4	9.7	4.1	23.6
Lexington-Fayette, Ky.	260,512	13.5	0.2	2.5	—	1.2	1.6	3.3
Lincoln, Neb.	225,581	3.1	0.7	3.1	0.1	1.8	2.0	3.6
Little Rock, Ark.	183,133	40.4	0.3	1.7	—	1.3	1.3	2.7
Livonia, Mich.	100,545	0.9	0.2	1.9	—	0.3	1.1	1.7
Long Beach, Calif.	461,522	14.9	0.8	12.0	1.2	20.6	5.3	35.8
Los Angeles, Calif.	3,694,820	11.2	0.8	10.0	0.2	25.7	5.2	46.5
Louisville, Ky.	256,231	33.0	0.2	1.4	—	0.7	1.7	1.9
Lowell, Mass.	105,167	4.2	0.2	16.5	—	6.5	3.9	14.0
Lubbock, Texas	199,564	8.7	0.6	1.5	—	14.3	2.0	27.5
Madison, Wisc.	208,054	5.8	0.4	5.8	—	1.7	2.3	4.1
Manchester, N.H.	107,006	2.1	0.3	2.3	—	1.8	1.7	4.6
McAllen, Texas	106,414	0.6	0.4	1.9	—	15.8	2.7	80.3
Memphis, Tenn.	650,100	61.4	0.2	1.5	—	1.5	1.0	3.0
Mesa, Ariz.	396,375	2.5	1.7	1.5	0.2	9.7	2.8	19.7
Mesquite, Texas	124,523	13.3	0.6	3.7	0.1	6.4	2.3	15.7
Metairie, La.	146,136	6.8	0.3	2.8	—	1.9	1.7	7.3
Miami, Fla.	362,470	22.3	0.2	0.7	—	5.4	4.7	65.8
Milwaukee, Wisc.	596,974	37.3	0.9	2.9	0.1	6.1	2.7	12.0
Minneapolis, Minn.	382,618	18.0	2.2	6.1	0.1	4.1	4.4	7.6
Mobile, Ala.	198,915	46.3	0.2	1.5	—	0.5	1.0	1.4
Modesto, Calif.	188,856	4.0	1.2	6.0	0.5	12.7	5.9	25.6

Geographic area	Total population	Black	American Indian	Asian	Native Hawaiian	Some other race	Two or more races	Hispanic or Latino (any race)
Montgomery, Ala.	201,568	49.6%	0.2%	1.1%	—%	0.4%	1.0%	1.2%
Moreno Valley, Calif.	142,381	19.9	0.9	5.9	0.5	20.1	5.8	38.4
Naperville, Ill.	128,358	3.0	0.1	9.6	—	0.8	1.2	3.2
Nashville-Davidson, Tenn..	569,891	25.9	0.3	2.3	0.1	2.4	2.0	4.6
New Haven, Conn.	123,626	37.4	0.4	3.9	0.1	10.9	3.9	21.4
New Orleans, La.	484,674	67.3	0.2	2.3	—	0.9	1.3	3.1
New York, N.Y.	8,008,278	26.6	0.5	9.8	0.1	13.4	4.9	27.0
Bronx borough	1,332,650	35.6	0.9	3.0	0.1	24.7.	5.8	48.4
Brooklyn borough	2,465,326	36.4	0.4	7.5	0.1	10.1	4.3	19.8
Manhattan borough	1,537,195	17.4	0.5	9.4	0.1	14.1	4.1	27.2
Queens borough	2,229,379	20.0	0.5	17.6	0.1	11.7	6.1	25.0
Staten Island borough	443,728	9.7	0.2	5.7	—	4.1	2.7	12.1
Newark, N.J.	273,546	53.5	0.4	1.2	—	14.0	4.4	29.5
Newport News, Va.	180,150	39.1	0.4	2.3	0.1	1.8	2.8	4.2
Norfolk, Va.	234,403	44.1	0.5	2.8	0.1	1.7	2.5	3.8
North Las Vegas, Nevada	115,488	19.0	0.8	3.2	0.5	15.8	4.7	37.6
Norwalk, Calif.	103,298	4.6	1.2	11.5	0.4	32.7	4.7	62.9
Oakland, Calif.	399,484	35.7	0.7	15.2	0.5	11.7	5.0	21.9
Oceanside, Calif.	161,029	6.3	0.9	5.5	1.3	14.5	5.2	30.2
Oklahoma City, Okla.	506,132	15.4	3.5	3.5	0.1	5.3	3.9	10.1
Omaha, Neb.	390,007	13.3	0.7	1.7	0.1	3.9	1.9	7.5
Ontario, Calif.	158,007	7.5	1.1	3.9	0.4	34.1	5.3	59.9
Orange, Calif.	128,821	1.6	0.8	9.3	0.2	13.8	3.8	32.2
Orlando, Fla.	185,951	26.9	0.3	2.7	0.1	5.4	3.5	17.5
Overland Park, Kans.	149,080	2.5	0.3	3.8	—	1.2	1.4	3.8
Oxnard, Calif.	170,358	3.8	1.3	7.4	0.4	40.4	4.7	66.2
Palmdale, Calif.	116,670	14.5	1.0	3.8	0.2	20.4	5.2	37.7
Paradise, Nevada	186,070	6.6	0.8	6.5	0.6	8.4	4.7	23.5
Pasadena, Calif.	133,936	14.4	0.7	10.0	0.1	16.0	5.4	33.4
Pasadena, Texas	141,674	1.6	0.7	1.8	—	21.3	3.1	48.2
Paterson, N.J.	149,222	32.9	0.6	1.9	0.1	27.6	6.2	50.1
Pembroke Pines, Fla.	137,427	13.3	0.2	3.8	—	3.7	3.5	28.2
Peoria, Ariz.	108,364	2.8	0.7	1.9	0.1	7.1	2.5	15.4
Peoria, Ill.	112,936	24.8	0.2	2.3	—	1.2	2.2	2.5
Philadelphia, Pa.	1,517,550	43.2	0.3	4.5	—	4.8	2.2	8.5
Phoenix, Ariz.	1,321,045	5.1	2.0	2.0	0.1	16.4	3.3	34.1
Pittsburgh, Pa.	334,563	27.1	0.2	2.7	—	0.7	1.6	1.3
Plano, Texas	222,030	5.0	0.4	10.2	—	3.9	2.3	10.1
Pomona, Calif.	149,473	9.6	1.3	7.2	0.2	34.9	5.0	64.5
Portland, Oreg.	529,121	6.6	1.1	6.3	0.4	3.5	4.1	6.8
Portsmouth, Va.	100,565	50.6	0.5	0.8	0.1	0.6	1.6	1.7
Providence, R.I.	173,618	14.5	1.1	6.0	0.2	17.6	6.1	30.0
Provo, Utah	105,166	0.5	0.8	1.8	0.8	5.1	2.4	10.5
Pueblo, Colo.	102,121	2.4	1.7	0.7	0.1	15.2	3.7	44.1
Raleigh, N.C.	276,093	27.8	0.4	3.4	—	3.2	1.9	7.0
Rancho Cucamonga, Calif.	127,743	7.9	0.7	6.0	0.3	13.3	5.4	27.8
Reno, Nevada	180,480	2.6	1.3	5.3	0.6	9.3	3.6	19.2
Richmond, Va.	197,790	57.2	0.2	1.2	0.1	1.5	1.5	2.6
Riverside, Calif.	255,166	7.4	1.1	5.7	0.4	21.0	5.1	38.1
Rochester, N.Y.	219,773	38.5	0.5	2.2	—	6.6	3.8	12.8
Rockford, Ill.	150,115	17.4	0.3	2.2	—	4.8	2.5	10.2
Sacramento, Calif.	407,018	15.5	1.3	16.6	0.9	11.0	6.4	21.6
Salem, Oreg.	136,924	1.3	1.5	2.4	0.5	7.9	3.4	14.6
Salinas, Calif.	151,060	3.3	1.3	6.2	0.3	38.7	5.1	64.1
Salt Lake City, Utah	181,743	1.9	1.3	3.6	1.9	8.5	3.5	18.8
San Antonio, Texas	1,144,646	6.8	0.8	1.6	0.1	19.3	3.7	58.7
San Bernardino, Calif.	185,401	16.4	1.4	4.2	0.4	27.1	5.3	47.5
San Diego, Calif.	1,223,400	7.9	0.6	13.6	0.5	12.4	4.8	25.4
San Francisco, Calif.	776,733	7.8	0.4	30.8	0.5	6.5	4.3	14.1
San Jose, Calif.	894,943	3.5	0.8	26.9	0.4	15.9	5.0	30.2
Santa Ana, Calif.	337,977	1.7	1.2	8.8	0.3	40.6	4.6	76.1
Santa Clara, Calif.	102,361	2.3	0.5	29.3	0.4	6.9	5.0	16.0
Santa Clarita, Calif.	151,088	2.1	0.6	5.2	0.1	8.5	3.9	20.5
Santa Rosa, Calif.	147,595	2.2	1.4	3.8	0.3	10.3	4.4	19.2
Savannah, Ga.	131,510	57.1	0.2	1.5	0.1	0.9	1.3	2.2
Scottsdale, Ariz.	202,705	1.2	0.6	2.0	—	2.3	1.7	7.0
Seattle, Wash.	563,374	8.4	1.0	13.1	0.5	2.4	4.5	5.3
Shreveport, La.	200,145	50.8	0.3	0.8	—	0.4	1.0	1.6
Simi Valley, Calif.	111,351	1.3	0.7	6.3	0.1	6.5	3.7	16.8
Sioux Falls, S. Dak.	123,975	1.8	2.1	1.2	0.1	1.2	1.7	2.5
South Bend, Ind.	107,789	24.6	0.4	1.2	0.1	4.9	2.8	8.5

Geographic area	Total population	Black	American Indian	Asian	Native Hawaiian	Some other race	Two or more races	Hispanic or Latino (any race)
Spokane, Wash.	195,629	2.1%	1.8%	2.2%	0.2%	0.9%	3.4%	3.0%
Spring Valley, Nevada	117,390	5.3	0.6	11.2	0.5	5.1	4.7	13.8
Springfield, Ill.	111,454	15.3	0.2	1.5	—	0.5	1.5	1.2
Springfield, Mass.	152,082	21.0	0.4	1.9	0.1	16.4	4.0	27.2
Springfield, Mo.	151,580	3.3	0.8	1.4	0.1	0.9	2.0	2.3
St. Louis, Mo.	348,189	51.2	0.3	2.0	—	0.8	1.9	2.0
St. Paul, Minn.	287,151	11.7	1.1	12.4	0.1	3.8	3.9	7.9
St. Petersburg, Fla.	248,232	22.4	0.3	2.7	0.1	1.1	2.2	4.2
Stamford, Conn.	117,083	15.4	0.2	5.0	—	6.5	3.1	16.8
Sterling Heights, Mich.	124,471	1.3	0.2	4.9	—	0.3	2.5	1.3
Stockton, Calif.	243,771	11.2	1.1	19.9	0.4	17.3	6.8	32.5
Sunnyvale, Calif.	131,760	2.2	0.5	32.3	0.3	7.2	4.3	15.5
Sunrise Manor, Nevada	156,120	12.9	1.0	5.4	0.5	10.1	4.7	26.0
Syracuse, N.Y.	147,306	25.3	1.1	3.4	—	2.2	3.6	5.3
Tacoma, Wash.	193,556	11.2	2.0	7.6	0.9	2.9	6.3	6.9
Tallahassee, Fla.	150,624	34.2	0.2	2.4	0.1	1.0	1.7	4.2
Tampa, Fla.	303,447	26.1	0.4	2.2	0.1	4.2	2.9	19.3
Tempe, Ariz.	158,625	3.7	2.0	4.7	0.3	8.5	3.3	17.9
Thousand Oaks, Calif.	117,005	1.1	0.5	5.9	0.1	4.5	2.8	13.1
Toledo, Ohio	313,619	23.5	0.3	1.0	—	2.3	2.6	5.5
Topeka, Kans.	122,377	11.7	1.3	1.1	—	4.1	3.3	8.9
Torrance, Calif.	137,946	2.2	0.4	28.6	0.3	4.6	4.7	12.8
Tucson, Ariz.	486,699	4.3	2.3	2.5	0.2	16.8	3.8	35.7
Tulsa, Okla.	393,049	15.5	4.7	1.8	0.1	3.5	4.4	7.2
Vallejo, Calif.	116,760	23.7	0.7	24.2	1.1	7.9	6.6	15.9
Vancouver, Wash.	143,560	2.5	1.0	4.5	0.5	2.9	3.8	6.3
Ventura, Calif.	100,916	1.4	1.2	3.0	0.2	11.1	4.3	24.3
Virginia Beach, Va.	425,257	19.0	0.4	4.9	0.1	1.5	2.7	4.2
Waco, Texas	113,726	22.6	0.5	1.4	0.1	12.4	2.3	23.6
Warren, Mich.	138,247	2.7	0.4	3.1	—	0.3	2.2	1.4
Washington, D.C.	572,059	60.0	0.3	2.7	0.1	3.8	2.4	7.9
Waterbury, Conn.	107,271	16.3	0.4	1.5	0.1	10.9	3.7	21.8
West Covina, Calif.	105,080	6.4	0.8	22.7	0.2	21.2	4.9	45.7
West Valley City, Utah	108,896	1.1	1.2	4.3	2.9	8.7	3.5	18.5
Westminster, Colo.	100,940	1.2	0.7	5.5	0.1	5.5	2.8	15.2
Wichita Falls, Texas	104,197	12.4	0.9	2.2	0.1	6.4	3.0	14.0
Wichita, Kans.	344,284	11.4	1.2	4.0	0.1	5.1	3.1	9.6
Winston-Salem, N.C.	185,776	37.1	0.3	1.1	—	4.3	1.6	8.6
Worcester, Mass.	172,648	6.9	0.4	4.9	0.1	7.2	3.4	15.1
Yonkers, N.Y	196,086	16.6	0.4	4.9	—	13.4	4.4	25.9

Note: Black includes African-American. Native American includes Alaska Native. Native Hawaiian Includes other Pacific Islander. Cities with populations over 100,000 as of April 1, 2000. **Source:** U.S. Bureau of the Census.

Population Change in the 75 Largest U.S. Cities, 1980–2000

City (2000 Rank)	Population			Percent change, 1980–2000	Change, 1990–2000	
	1980	1990	2000		Number	Percent
Albuquerque, N. Mex (35)	332,920	384,736	448,607	15.6%	63,871	16.6%
Anaheim, Calif. (56)	219,494	266,406	328,014	21.4	61,608	23.1
Anchorage, Alaska (66)	174,731	226,338	260,283	29.5	33,945	15.0
Arlington, Texas (54)	160,113	261,721	332,969	63.5	71,248	27.2
Atlanta, Ga. (40)	425,022	394,017	416,474	-7.3	22,457	5.7
Aurora, Colo. (62)	158,588	222,103	276,393	40.1	54,290	24.4
Austin, Texas (16)	345,890	465,622	656,562	34.6	190,940	41.0
Bakersfield, Calif. (70)	N.A.	174,820	247,057	N.A.	72,237	41.3
Baltimore, Md. (17)	786,741	736,014	651,154	-6.4	-84,860	-11.5
Baton Rouge, La. (75)	220,394	219,531	227,818	-0.4	8,287	3.8
Birmingham, Ala. (72)	284,413	265,968	242,820	-6.5	-23,148	-8.7
Boston, Mass. (20)	562,994	574,283	589,141	2.0	14,858	2.6
Buffalo, N.Y (59)	357,870	328,123	292,648	-8.3	-35,475	-10.8
Charlotte, N.C (26)	315,474	395,934	540,828	25.5	144,894	36.6
Chicago, Ill. (3)	3,005,072	2,783,726	2,896,016	-7.4	112,290	4.0
Cincinnati, Ohio (55)	385,409	364,040	331,285	-5.5	-32,755	-9.0
Cleveland, Ohio (33)	573,822	505,616	478,403	-11.9	-27,213	-5.4
Colorado Springs, Colo. (49)	215,105	281,140	360,890	30.7	79,750	28.4
Columbus, Ohio (15)	565,021	632,910	711,470	12.0	78,560	12.4

City (2000 Rank)	Population 1980	Population 1990	Population 2000	Percent change, 1980–2000	Change, 1990–2000 Number	Change, 1990–2000 Percent
Corpus Christi, Texas (61)	232,134	257,453	277,454	10.9%	20,001	7.8%
Dallas, Texas (8)	904,599	1,006,877	1,188,580	11.3	181,703	18.0
Denver, Colo. (25)	492,686	467,610	554,636	-5.1	87,026	18.6
Detroit, Mich. (10)	1,203,368	1,027,974	951,270	-14.6	-76,704	-7.5
El Paso, Texas (23)	425,259	515,342	563,662	21.2	48,320	9.4
Fort Worth, Texas (27)	385,164	447,619	534,694	16.2	87,075	19.5
Fresno, Calif. (37)	217,491	354,202	427,652	62.9	73,450	20.7
Honolulu, Hawaii. (47)	365,048	365,272	371,657	0.1	6,385	1.7
Houston, Texas (4)	1,595,138	1,630,553	1,953,631	2.2	323,078	19.8
Indianapolis, Ind. (12)	711,539	741,952	791,926	4.3	49,974	6.7
Jacksonville, Fla. (14)	571,003	635,230	735,617	17.9	100,387	15.8
Jersey City, N.J. (73)	223,532	228,537	240,055	2.2	11,518	5.0
Kansas City, Mo. (36)	448,028	435,146	441,545	-2.9	6,399	1.5
Las Vegas, Nev. (32)	164,674	258,295	478,434	56.9	220,139	85.2
Lexington-Fayette, Ky. (65)	204,165	225,366	260,512	10.4	35,146	15.6
Long Beach, Calif. (34)	361,498	429,433	461,522	18.8	32,089	7.5
Los Angeles, Calif. (2)	2,968,528	3,485,557	3,694,820	17.4	209,422	6.0
Louisville, Ky. (67)	298,694	269,063	256,231	-9.9	-12,832	-4.8
Memphis, Tenn. (18)	646,174	610,337	650,100	-5.5	39,763	6.5
Mesa, Ariz. (43)	152,404	288,091	396,375	89.0	108,284	37.6
Miami, Fla. (48)	346,681	358,548	362,470	3.4	3,922	1.1
Milwaukee, Wis. (19)	636,297	628,088	596,974	-1.3	-31,114	-5.0
Minneapolis, Minn. (46)	370,951	368,383	382,618	-0.7	14,235	3.9
Nashville, Tenn. (22)	477,811	510,784	569,891	6.9	59,107	11.6
New Orleans, La. (31)	557,927	496,938	484,674	-10.9	-12,264	-2.5
New York, N.Y. (1)	7,071,639	7,322,564	8,008,278	3.5	685,714	9.4
Newark, N.J. (64)	329,248	275,221	273,546	-16.4	-1,675	-0.6
Norfolk, Va. (74)	266,979	261,229	234,403	-2.2	-26,826	-10.3
Oakland, Calif. (42)	339,337	372,242	399,484	9.7	27,242	7.3
Oklahoma City, Okla. (29)	404,014	444,719	506,132	10.1	61,413	13.8
Omaha, Nebr. (45)	313,939	335,795	390,007	7.0	54,212	16.1
Philadelphia, Pa. (5)	1,688,210	1,585,577	1,517,550	-6.1	-68,027	-4.3
Phoenix, Ariz. (6)	789,704	983,403	1,321,045	24.5	337,642	34.3
Pittsburgh, Pa. (53)	423,959	369,879	334,563	-12.8	-35,316	-9.5
Portland, Oreg. (28)	368,148	437,319	529,121	18.8	91,802	21.0
Raleigh, N.C. (63)	150,255	207,951	276,093	38.4	68,142	32.8
Riverside, Calif. (68)	170,591	226,505	255,166	32.8	28,661	12.7
Sacramento, Calif. (41)	275,741	369,365	407,018	34.0	37,653	10.2
San Antonio, Texas (9)	785,940	935,933	1,144,646	19.1	208,713	22.3
San Diego, Calif. (7)	875,538	1,110,549	1,223,400	26.8	112,851	10.2
San Francisco, Calif. (13)	678,974	723,959	776,733	6.6	52,774	7.3
San Jose, Calif. (11)	629,400	782,248	894,943	24.3	112,695	14.4
San Juan, Puerto Rico (39)	N.A.	426,832	421,958	N.A.	-4,874	-1.1
Santa Ana, Calif. (52)	204,023	293,742	337,977	44.0	44,235	15.1
Seattle, Wash. (24)	493,846	516,259	563,374	4.5	47,115	9.1
St. Louis, Mo. (50)	452,801	396,685	348,189	-12.4	-48,496	-12.2
St. Paul, Minn. (60)	270,320	272,235	287,151	0.7	14,916	5.5
St. Petersburg, Fla. (69)	238,647	238,629	248,232	-0.0	9,603	4.0
Stockton, Calif. (71)	148,283	210,943	243,771	42.3	32,828	15.6
Tampa, Fla. (58)	271,577	280,015	303,447	3.1	23,432	8.4
Toledo, Ohio (57)	354,635	332,943	313,619	-6.1	-19,324	-5.8
Tucson, Ariz. (30)	330,537	405,390	486,699	22.6	81,309	20.1
Tulsa, Okla. (44)	360,919	367,302	393,049	1.8	25,747	7.0
Virginia Beach, Va. (38)	262,199	393,069	425,257	49.9	32,188	8.2
Washington, D.C. (21)	638,432	606,900	572,059	-4.9	-34,841	-5.7
Wichita, Kans. (51)	279,838	304,011	344,284	8.6	40,273	13.2

Source: U.S. Bureau of the Census, 2000.

Population of the 50 Largest Cities, 1950–2000

2000 Rank, City	1950	1960	1970[1]	1980[1]	1990	2000	Population change, 1990–2000
1. New York, N.Y.	7,891,957	7,781,984	7,896,000	7,072,000	7,322,564	8,008,278	685,714
2. Los Angeles, Calif.	1,970,358	2,479,015	2,812,000	2,969,000	3,485,557	3,694,820	209,422
3. Chicago, Ill.	3,620,962	3,550,404	3,369,000	3,005,000	2,783,726	2,896,016	112,290
4. Houston, Texas	596,163	938,219	1,234,000	1,595,000	1,630,864	1,953,631	323,078
5. Philadelphia, Pa.	2,071,605	2,002,512	1,949,000	1,688,000	1,585,577	1,517,550	-68,027
6. Phoenix, Ariz.	(2)	439,170	584,000	790,000	984,309	1,321,045	337,642
7. San Diego, Calif.	334,387	573,224	697,000	876,000	1,110,623	1,223,400	112,851
8. Dallas, Texas	434,462	679,684	844,000	905,000	1,007,618	1,188,580	181,703
9. San Antonio, Texas	408,442	587,718	654,000	786,000	935,393	1,144,646	208,713
10. Detroit, Mich.	1,849,568	1,670,144	1,514,000	1,203,000	1,027,974	951,270	-76,704
11. San Jose, Calif.	(2)	(2)	460,000	629,000	782,224	894,943	112,695
12. Indianapolis, Ind.[3]	427,173	476,258	737,000	701,000	731,278	791,926	49,974
13. San Francisco, Calif.	775,357	742,855	716,000	679,000	723,959	776,733	52,774
14. Jacksonville, Fla.[3]	204,517	(2)	504,000	541,000	635,230	735,617	100,387
15. Columbus, Ohio	375,901	471,316	540,000	565,000	632,945	711,470	78,560
16. Austin, Texas	(2)	(2)	254,000	346,000	472,020	656,562	190,940
17. Baltimore, Md.	949,708	939,024	905,000	787,000	736,014	651,154	-84,860
18. Memphis, Tenn.	396,000	497,524	624,000	646,000	618,652	650,100	39,763
19. Milwaukee, Wisc.	637,392	741,324	717,000	636,000	628,088	596,974	-31,114
20. Boston, Mass.	801,444	697,197	641,000	563,000	574,283	589,141	14,858
21. Washington, D.C.	802,178	763,956	757,000	638,000	606,900	572,059	-34,841
22. Nashville, Tenn.[3]	(2)	(2)	426,000	456,000	488,366	569,891	59,107
23. El Paso, Texas	(2)	276,687	322,000	425,000	515,342	563,662	48,320
24. Seattle, Wash.	467,591	557,087	531,000	494,000	516,259	563,374	47,115
25. Denver, Colo.	415,786	493,887	515,000	493,000	467,610	554,636	87,026
26. Charlotte, N.C.	(2)	(2)	241,000	315,000	419,558	540,828	144,894
27. Fort Worth, Texas	278,778	356,268	393,000	385,000	447,619	534,694	87,075
28. Portland, Oreg.	373,628	372,676	380,000	368,000	485,975	529,121	91,802
29. Oklahoma City, Okla.	243,504	324,253	368,000	404,000	444,724	506,132	61,413
30. Tucson, Ariz.	(2)	(2)	263,000	331,000	415,444	486,699	81,309
31. New Orleans, La.	570,445	627,525	593,000	558,000	496,938	484,674	-12,264
32. Las Vegas, Nev.	(2)	(2)	(2)	(2)	258,295	478,434	220,139
33. Cleveland, Ohio	914,808	876,050	751,000	574,000	505,616	478,403	-27,213
34. Long Beach, Calif.	250,767	344,168	359,000	361,000	429,321	461,522	32,089
35. Albuquerque, N. Mex.	(2)	(2)	245,000	332,000	384,619	448,607	63,871
36. Kansas City, Mo.	456,622	475,539	507,000	448,000	434,829	441,545	6,399
37. Fresno, Calif.	(2)	(2)	166,000	217,000	354,091	427,652	73,450
38. Virginia Beach, Va.	(2)	(2)	172,000	262,000	393,089	425,257	32,188
39. Atlanta, Ga.	332,314	487,455	495,000	425,000	394,017	416,474	22,457
40. Sacramento, Calif.	(2)	(2)	257,000	276,000	369,365	407,018	37,653
41. Oakland, Calif.	384,575	367,548	362,000	339,000	372,242	399,484	27,472
42. Mesa, Ariz.	(2)	(2)	(2)	(2)	288,091	396,375	108,284
43. Tulsa, Okla.	(2)	261,685	330,000	361,000	367,302	393,049	25,747
44. Omaha, Neb.	251,117	301,598	347,000	314,000	335,795	390,007	54,212
45. Minneapolis, Minn.	521,718	482,872	434,000	371,000	368,383	382,618	14,235
46. Honolulu, Hawaii[4]	248,034	294,194	325,000	365,000	365,272	371,657	6,385
47. Miami, Fla.	249,276	291,688	335,000	347,000	358,548	362,470	3,922
48. Colorado Springs, Colo.	(2)	(2)	(2)	(2)	281,140	360,890	79,750
49. St. Louis, Mo.	856,796	750,026	622,000	453,000	396,685	348,189	-48,496
50. Wichita, Kans.	(2)	(2)	(2)	279,838	304,011	344,284	40,273

Notes: 1. Figure rounded in source. 2. City was not one of the 50 largest that year. 3. City is part of a consolidated city-county government; populations of the other incorporated places in the county have been excluded from the population totals shown here. 4. Not incorporated as a city, but recognized for census purposes as large urban places. Honolulu CDP is coextensive with Honolulu Judicial District within the City and County of Honolulu. **Source:** U.S. Bureau of the Census, 2001

25 Fastest-Growing Major Cities in the U.S., 1990–2000

2000 Rank, City	Population		Change, 1990–2000		Overall rank, 2000
	1990	2000	Number	Percent	
1. Augusta, Ga.	44,639	199,775	155,136	347.5%	91
2. Gilbert, Ariz.	29,188	109,697	80,509	275.8	208
3. Vancouver, Wash.	46,380	143,560	97,180	209.5	149
4. Henderson, Nev.	64,942	175,381	110,439	170.1	118
5. North Las Vegas, Nev.	47,707	115,488	67,781	142.1	198
6. Athens, Ga.	45,734	101,489	55,755	121.9	237
7. Peoria, Ariz.	50,618	108,364	57,746	114.1	214
8. Pembroke Pines, Fla.	65,452	137,427	71,975	110.0	161
9. Chandler, Ariz.	90,533	176,581	86,048	95.0	116
10. Las Vegas, Nevada	258,295	478,434	220,139	85.2	32
11. Plano, Texas	128,713	222,030	93,317	72.5	79
12. Palmdale, Calif.	68,842	116,670	47,828	69.5	194
13. Corona, Calif.	76,095	124,966	48,871	64.2	174
14. Fayetteville, N.C.	75,695	121,015	45,320	59.9	184
15. Scottsdale, Ariz.	130,069	202,705	72,636	55.8	88
16. Naperville, Ill.	85,351	128,358	43,007	50.4	169
17. Coral Springs, Fla.	79,443	117,549	38,106	48.0	190
18. Boise City, Idaho	125,738	185,787	60,049	47.8	108
19. Glendale, Ariz.	148,134	218,812	70,678	47.7	81
20. Fontana, Calif.	87,535	128,929	41,394	47.3	167
21. Laredo, Texas	122,899	176,576	53,677	43.7	117
22. Aurora, Ill.	99,581	142,990	43,409	43.6	151
23. Bakersfield, Calif.	174,820	247,057	72,237	41.3	70
24. Brownsville, Texas	98,962	139,722	40,760	41.2	155
25. Austin, Texas	465,622	656,562	190,940	41.0	16

Note: Cities over 100,000 population.   **Source:** U.S. Bureau of the Census.

25 Fastest-Declining Major U.S. Cities, 1990–2000

2000 Rank, City	Population		Change, 1990–2000		Overall rank, 2000
	1990	2000	Number	Percent	
1. Hartford, Conn.	139,739	121,578	-18,161	-13.0%	183
2. St. Louis, Miss.	396,685	348,189	-48,496	-12.2	50
3. Gary, Ind.	116,646	102,746	-13,900	-11.9	230
4. Baltimore, Md.	736,014	651,154	-84,860	-11.5	17
5. Flint, Mich.	140,761	124,943	-15,818	-11.2	175
6. Buffalo, N.Y.	328,123	292,648	-35,475	-10.8	59
7. Norfolk, Va.	261,229	234,403	-26,826	-10.3	74
8. Syracuse, N.Y.	163,860	147,306	-16,554	-10.1	145
9. Pittsburgh, Penn.	369,879	334,563	-35,316	-9.5	53
10. Cincinnati, Ohio	364,040	331,285	-32,755	-9.0	55
11. Dayton, Ohio	182,044	166,179	-15,865	-8.7	126
12. Birmingham, Ala.	265,968	242,820	-23,148	-8.7	72
13. Detroit, Mich.	1,027,974	951,270	-76,704	-7.5	10
14. Lansing, Mich.	127,321	119,128	-8,193	-6.4	187
15. Jackson, Miss.	196,637	184,256	-12,381	-6.3	111
16. Toledo, Ohio	332,943	313,619	-19,324	-5.8	57
17. Washington, D.C.	606,900	572,059	-34,841	-5.7	21
18. Cleveland, Ohio	505,616	478,403	-27,213	-5.4	33
19. New Haven, Conn.	130,474	123,626	-6,848	-5.2	179
20. Rochester, N.Y.	231,636	219,773	-11,863	-5.1	80
21. Milwaukee, Wis.	628,088	596,974	-31,114	-5.0	19
22. Louisville, Ky.	269,063	256,231	-12,832	-4.8	67
23. Erie, Penn.	108,718	103,717	-5,001	-4.6	226
24. Warren, Mich.	144,864	138,247	-6,617	-4.6	158
25. Savannah, Ga.	137,560	131,510	-6,050	-4.4	166

Note: Cities over 100,000 population in 1990.   **Source:** U.S. Bureau of the Census.

CITY FINANCES

▶TAX BURDENS AND PROGRESSIVITY IN MAJOR U.S. CITIES

Tax rates differ widely not only from state to state and city to city, but also from one income level to another. Any tax system in which the percentage of taxes paid rises with the income level is said to be *progressive*. A system where the percentage tax burden is the same at all income levels is said to be *proportional*. And a system in which the percentage of taxes paid decreases as income rises is said to be *regressive*. Because progressivity is measured as the ratio of one tax rate to another, progressivity does not necessarily reflect the actual tax burden.

Several factors contribute to the progressivity of a tax system. A graduated individual income tax

Estimated Burden of State & Local Taxes by Income Level in Selected Cities, 2006

City	$25,000 Percent[1]	Amount	$50,000 Percent[1]	Amount	$75,000 Percent[1]	Amount	$100,000 Percent[1]	Amount
Albuquerque, N. Mex.	9.8%	$2,457	7.5%	$3,742	7.8%	$5,828	7.6%	$7,564
Anchorage, Alaska	8.9	2,230	4.6	2,318	3.8	2,817	3.2	3,189
Atlanta, Ga.	12.9	3,228	9.7	4,857	10.4	7,764	10.2	10,181
Baltimore, Md.	8.9	2,216	10.1	5,040	10.3	7,731	10.2	10,172
Billings, Mont.	7.3	1,833	6.6	3,321	7.4	5,574	7.6	7,585
Birmingham, Ala.	13.0	3,248	7.4	3,716	8.0	6,012	7.7	7,746
Boise City, Idaho	9.3	2,318	7.4	3,720	8.5	6,353	8.7	8,735
Boston, Mass.	12.5	3,113	11.0	5,489	10.3	7,698	9.5	9,503
Bridgeport, Conn.	12.8	3,196	22.3	11,132	20.4	15,313	18.5	18,506
Burlington, Vt.	9.2	2,300	11.1	5,529	10.2	7,679	9.9	9,871
Charleston, W.Va.	12.0	3,001	7.7	3,853	8.6	6,468	8.6	8,610
Charlotte, N.C.	12.2	3,044	8.6	4,317	9.4	7,066	9.5	9,481
Cheyenne, Wyo.	9.5	2,370	4.4	2,198	4.4	3,298	3.9	3,931
Chicago, Ill.	13.1	3,269	11.0	5,496	9.9	7,453	8.8	8,848
Columbia, S.C.	11.6	2,890	7.0	3,520	9.3	6,955	9.2	9,232
Columbus, Ohio	12.4	3,112	10.1	5,061	10.2	7,621	10.0	10,025
Denver, Colo.	11.3	2,836	7.0	3,524	7.6	5,728	7.5	7,458
Des Moines, Iowa	10.2	2,557	9.8	4,883	10.2	7,679	10.2	10,225
Detroit, Mich.	13.8	3,443	11.3	5,639	10.9	8,140	10.2	10,242
Fargo, N. Dak.	7.9	1,983	6.3	3,170	6.1	4,597	6.1	6,099
Honolulu, Hawaii	12.4	3,094	5.8	2,919	7.1	5,305	7.5	7,524
Houston, Tex.	9.9	2,465	6.4	3,204	6.1	4,608	5.3	5,329
Indianapolis, Ind.	12.3	3,082	11.4	5,707	10.6	7,971	10.1	10,096
Jackson, Miss.	10.9	2,715	8.7	4,359	9.5	7,112	9.2	9,188
Jacksonville, Fla.	9.8	2,439	4.6	2,308	4.6	3,419	4.1	4,091
Kansas City, Mo.	12.7	3,174	8.5	4,270	9.3	7,003	8.9	8,868
Las Vegas, Nev.	9.8	2,451	6.3	3,174	5.5	4,150	4.8	4,792
Little Rock, Ark.	12.4	3,092	7.9	3,948	8.9	6,710	8.9	8,883
Los Angeles, Calif.	10.8	2,703	9.9	4,950	10.0	7,532	9.7	9,653
Louisville, Ky.	12.9	3,233	9.5	4,772	10.0	7,470	9.9	9,889
Manchester, N.H.	9.5	2,364	12.9	6,454	10.2	7,654	8.6	8,556
Memphis, Tenn.	10.8	2,705	6.0	3,012	5.8	4,344	4.9	4,924
Milwaukee, Wis.	9.1	2,272	9.7	4,837	9.4	7,083	9.3	9,345
Minneapolis, Minn.	11.4	2,843	9.0	4,495	9.1	6,813	8.9	8,900
New Orleans, La.	11.1	2,769	7.1	3,540	7.9	5,934	7.7	7,748
New York, N.Y.	11.5	2,871	9.1	4,562	10.2	7,673	10.6	10,580
Newark, N.J.	11.0	2,742	13.0	6,517	11.0	8,244	9.3	9,290
Oklahoma City, Okla.	12.7	3,183	7.1	3,565	8.6	6,446	8.5	8,547
Omaha, Nebr.	10.1	2,519	8.7	4,337	9.3	6,979	9.2	9,225
Philadelphia, Pa.	16.5	4,118	13.7	6,839	12.6	9,446	11.8	11,754
Phoenix, Ariz.	11.6	2,904	6.7	3,338	6.8	5,120	6.6	6,575
Portland, Maine	9.8	2,459	8.6	4,319	9.8	7,378	10.1	10,120
Portland, Oreg.	12.1	3,028	8.4	4,214	9.1	6,841	9.5	9,532
Providence, R.I.	11.2	2,793	12.8	6,423	12.0	9,013	11.0	11,044
Salt Lake City, Utah	11.9	2,977	7.8	3,923	8.5	6,364	8.3	8,322
Seattle, Wash.	11.4	2,843	8.5	4,257	7.7	5,789	6.2	6,157
Sioux Falls, S.Dak.	9.2	2,312	5.2	2,597	4.9	3,682	4.3	4,257
Virginia Beach, Va.	11.2	2,794	7.7	3,834	8.4	6,269	8.1	8,149
Washington, D.C.	12.2	3,045	8.1	4,052	9.3	6,986	9.5	9,482
Wichita, Kans.	10.2	2,549	6.7	3,335	8.0	6,031	8.4	8,358
Wilmington, Del.	9.4	2,349	7.9	3,967	8.0	5,970	8.0	7,975
51 city average[2]	11.1%	$2,775	8.7%	$4,364	8.9%	$6,649	8.5%	$8,517

Notes: Tax burdens computed for a family of three. The four major taxes compared are the individual income tax, real property taxes on residential property, general sales and use taxes, and various automobile taxes, including the gasoline tax, registration fees, excise taxes, and personal property taxes. 1. Percentage of income. 2. Average of the largest city in each state plus the District of Columbia.
Source: Government of the District of Columbia, Dept. of Finance and Revenue, *Tax Rates and Tax Burdens in the District of Columbia: A Nationwide Comparison* (2007).

rate combined with exemptions and credits to lessen the regressiveness of the property tax will increase the progressivity of a tax system. Progressivity can be lessened by a lack of an individual income tax as well as by reliance on regressive taxes such as the sales tax and certain automobile taxes. The upper and lower income levels chosen for comparison also affect progressiveness.

The Cost of Living Index in Selected U.S. Cities, 2008

Urban area	Composite index (100%)	Grocery items (12%)	Housing (30%)	Utilities (10%)	Trans- portation (11%)	Health care (4%)	Misc. goods & services (33%)
Atlanta, Ga.	97.6	96.4	94.0	90.3	105.0	103.6	100.3
Austin, Tx.	94.7	93.4	83.8	93.0	98.7	96.2	104.1
Baltimore, Md.	120.6	105.5	156.8	123.7	106.7	104.6	99.2
Boston, Mass.	134.0	121.6	160.5	130.4	108.5	136.2	123.8
Charlotte, N.C.	94.7	101.2	79.9	94.5	99.6	111.3	102.0
Chicago, Ill.	111.5	107.9	129.0	118.0	109.2	103.3	96.9
Cincinnati, Ohio	91.6	87.9	82.8	104.0	99.1	91.3	94.9
Cleveland, Ohio	95.1	100.5	84.5	101.0	101.7	104.0	97.7
Columbus, Ohio	98.6	100.7	97.9	101.3	103.3	105.6	95.4
Dallas, Texas	91.9	100.6	72.1	99.1	100.6	103.0	100.0
Denver, Colo.	105.1	104.7	111.4	103.4	92.8	104.0	104.2
Detroit, Mich.	97.6	94.3	99.1	105.6	99.4	96.8	94.6
Fort Worth, Texas	87.2	91.4	68.2	110.3	94.7	91.2	92.8
Houston, Texas	90.3	82.8	76.2	95.9	98.2	101.1	100.3
Indianapolis, Ind.	94.2	93.7	94.5	88.4	102.6	99.9	92.4
Kansas City, Mo.-Ks.	96.1	90.5	88.8	105.4	99.2	98.0	100.7
Las Vegas, Nev.	110.6	99.0	136.7	99.5	101.4	104.7	98.3
Los Angeles-Long Beach, Calif.	150.3	111.4	256.5	96.9	111.0	108.9	102.8
Memphis, Tenn.	89.0	93.0	75.7	84.6	93.6	98.8	98.3
Miami/Dade County, Fla.	117.8	105.1	144.4	100.1	107.7	107.4	108.4
Milwaukee, Wisc.	100.2	92.6	104.8	104.2	99.8	111.5	96.3
Minneapolis, Minn.	109.3	124.4	117.7	105.4	96.8	104.2	101.8
New York (Manhattan), N.Y.	218.8	141.0	404.9	150.1	124.8	129.1	142.0
Oakland, Calif.	150.1	133.9	228.4	86.8	111.5	121.3	120.6
Orlando, Fla.	102.1	106.5	93.5	102.1	105.5	95.2	108.1
Philadelphia, Pa.	122.6	126.5	140.6	118.5	105.2	108.6	113.3
Phoenix, Ariz.	101.6	103.8	101.0	94.7	98.7	99.0	104.7
Pittsburgh, Pa.	91.3	97.8	80.5	102.4	104.9	84.3	91.6
Portland, Oreg.	119.9	108.2	138.9	101.3	109.4	105.5	117.9
Providence, R.I.	122.5	112.5	134.1	132.0	103.7	125.8	118.7
San Antonio, Texas	88.7	83.7	78.2	83.7	97.3	98.3	97.7
San Diego, Calif.	139.4	112.7	216.5	94.6	109.6	114.1	106.0
San Francisco, Calif.	173.6	131.4	292.7	96.6	114.5	118.6	131.1
San Jose, Calif.	154.3	140.8	246.0	100.3	113.1	117.8	110.5
Seattle, Wash.	121.5	115.1	148.7	88.8	108.0	119.1	113.7
St. Louis, Mo.	90.0	99.0	78.3	96.9	95.9	95.9	92.4
Tampa, Fla.	99.1	98.5	89.8	103.0	105.3	92.9	105.4
Virginia Beach, Va.	109.5	102.6	122.7	98.0	104.8	104.0	105.7
Washington, D.C.	138.0	107.4	218.2	102.4	105.9	108.6	101.7

Note: Metropolitan areas with more than 1.5 million population. Percentage figures in parentheses show relative weight of component indexes used in calculating composite index. Figures are from first quarter 2008. **Source:** The Council for Community and Economic Research (C2ER) *ACCRA Cost of Living Index*, www.coli.org.

Cities, by Population Size, 1960–2000

Population size	Number of Cities				Population (mil.)				Percent of Total			
	1960	1980	1990	2000	1960	1980	1990	2000	1960	1980	1990	2000
Total	18,088	19,097	19,262	19,452	115.9	140.3	152.9	173.5	100%	100%	100%	100%
1 million +	5	6	8	9	17.5	17.5	20.0	22.9	15.1	12.5	13.0	13.2
500,000- 1 million	16	16	15	20	11.1	10.9	10.1	12.9	9.6	7.8	6.6	7.4
250,000- 500,000	30	33	41	37	10.8	11.8	14.2	13.3	9.3	8.4	9.3	7.7
100,000- 250,000	79	114	131	172	11.4	16.6	19.1	25.5	9.8	11.8	12.5	14.7
50,000- 100,000	180	250	309	363	12.5	17.6	21.2	24.9	10.8	12.3	13.9	14.3
25,000- 50,000	366	526	567	644	12.7	18.4	20.0	22.6	11.0	13.1	13.0	13.0
10,000- 25,000	978	1,260	1,290	1,435	15.1	19.8	20.3	22.6	13.1	14.1	13.3	13.0
<10,000	16,434	16,892	16,901	16,772	24.9	28.0	28.2	28.7	21.5	20.0	18.4	16.6

Source: U.S. Bureau of the Census, *Statistical Abstract of the United States* (annual).

METROPOLITAN STATISTICAL AREAS (MSAs)

Because population patterns don't conform strictly to city boundaries, statisticians have devised a way of measuring city populations to include people who live around an urban area but whose address is outside the city limits. Known as Metropolitan Statistical Areas (or MSAs), these measures give a much more accurate reflection of how many people actually live in the area than do city population figures. For example, the city of Boston is relatively small: just 589,000 people lived in Boston proper, according to the 2000 Census, making it the 20th-largest city in America. But the Boston metropolitan area, which includes suburbs ranging from Rhode Island to New Hampshire, is the seventh-largest in the country, with a total population of 7.4 million within an hour's commute of the Hub. On the other hand, the population of San Diego proper was more than 1.2 million in 2000, making it the seventh-largest city in the U.S., but the entire San Diego metro area was only 2.8 million, or 17th-largest in the country.

The United States Office of Management and Budget (OMB) first defined metropolitan areas in 1949, subsequently changed the designation to "standard metropolitan area," "standard metropolitan statistical area," and finally "metropolitan statistical area" in 1983.

Defining MSAS, CMSAs, and PMSAs

Currently, the OMB distinguishes between MSAs, consolidated metropolitan statistical areas (CMSAs), and primary metropolitan statistical areas (PMSAs).

Metropolitan Statistical Areas (MSAs) are defined as an area that includes at least one city with 50,000 or more inhabitants, or a Census Bureau-defined urbanized area (of at least 50,000 inhabitants) and a total metropolitan population of at least 100,000. An MSA includes the county in which the central city is located plus any adjacent counties in which at least 50 percent of the population lives in the urbanized area. Additional "outlying counties" are included in the MSA if they meet specified requirements of commuting to the central counties and other selected requirements of metropolitan character (such as population density and percent urban). In New England, MSAs are defined in terms of cities and towns rather than counties.

Consolidated Metropolitan Statistical Areas (CMSAs) are defined as MSAs with populations of one million or more that also contain separate component areas that can each be identified as smaller urban areas, or *Primary Metropolitan Statistical Areas (PMSAs)*. For example, the New York CMSA includes the Primary MSAs of Nassau and Suffolk Counties on Long Island, Bergen and Passaic Counties in Northern New Jersey, and Bridgeport and Milford Counties in Connecticut. PMSAs, like the CMSAs that contain them, are composed of entire counties, except in New England where they are composed of cities and towns.

The 2000 Census counted 280 MSAs in the U.S (down from 284 in 1990), including 20 CMSAs. Although MSAs take up only about 16 percent of the country's land area, they are home to more than 75 percent of all Americans.

According to the 2000 Census, the U.S. population living in all metropolitan areas totaled 229,192,836, an increase of more than 36 million people (19.3 percent) since 1990. That's a significant increase over the previous decade, when MSAs grew by only 11.6 percent. The 1950 Census indicated that there were 14 metropolitan areas of at least one million population; these areas had a combined population of about 45 million people, or less than 30 percent of the national total. By the 1990 Census, the number of MSAs with a million people had grown to 39, with a combined population of 124.8 million people, or 50.2 percent of the U.S. total. By 2000, there were an even 50 MSAs with more than a million people, with a total population of 164.0 million people, or 58.2 percent of the national total.

Population of Metropolitan Statistical Areas, 2000–07

Metropolitan Statistical Area	Population 2000	Population 2007	Change 2000–07 Number	Change 2000–07 Percent	Rank 2000	Rank 2007
Abilene, TX	160,241	159,343	-898	-0.6%	230	245
Akron, OH	694,960	699,356	4,396	0.6	67	71
Albany, GA	157,866	164,069	6,203	3.9	233	234
Albany-Schenectady-Troy, NY	825,875	825,875	27,843	3.3	56	57
Albuquerque, NM	729,653	835,120	105,467	14.5	65	60
Alexandria, LA	145,035	145,035	4,802	3.3	252	255
Allentown-Bethlehem-Easton, PA-NJ	740,394	803,844	63,450	8.6	64	62
Altoona, PA	129,144	125,527	-3,617	-2.8	276	297
Amarillo, TX	226,522	242,240	15,718	6.9	179	181
Ames, IA	79,981	84,752	4,771	6.0	355	354
Anchorage, AK	319,605	362,340	42,734	13.4	143	137
Anderson, IN	133,358	131,312	-2,046	-1.5	268	284
Anderson, SC	165,740	179,981	14,241	8.6	224	225
Ann Arbor, MI	322,770	350,003	27,233	8.4	140	141
Anniston-Oxford, AL	112,243	113,103	860	0.8	305	319
Appleton, WI	201,722	218,026	16,304	8.1	191	195
Asheville, NC	369,172	404,320	35,149	9.5	124	122
Athens-Clarke County, GA	166,079	187,405	21,326	12.8	223	218
Atlanta-Sandy Springs-Marietta, GA	4,248,012	5,278,904	1,030,892	24.3	11	9
Atlantic City, NJ	252,552	270,644	18,092	7.2	165	165
Auburn-Opelika, AL	115,092	130,516	15,392	13.4	297	287
Augusta-Richmond County, GA-SC	499,653	528,519	28,866	5.8	89	95
Austin-Round Rock, TX	1,249,763	1,598,161	348,413	27.9	40	37
Bakersfield, CA	661,655	790,710	129,055	19.5	70	64

Metropolitan Statistical Area	Population 2000	2007	Change 2000–07 Number	Percent	Rank 2000	2007
Baltimore-Towson, MD	2,552,994	2,668,056	115,060	4.5%	19	20
Bangor, ME	144,919	148,784	3,865	2.7	253	259
Barnstable Town, MA	222,230	222,175	-55	>0.1	184	192
Baton Rouge, LA	705,967	770,037	64,289	9.1	66	67
Battle Creek, MI	137,985	136,615	-1,370	-1.0	265	276
Bay City, MI	110,157	107,517	-2,640	-2.4	310	328
Beaumont-Port Arthur, TX	385,090	376,241	-8,849	-2.3	117	131
Bellingham, WA	166,823	192,999	26,173	15.7	222	212
Bend, OR	115,367	154,028	38,661	33.5	296	250
Billings, MT	138,904	149,657	10,753	7.7	264	256
Binghamton, NY	252,320	246,426	-5,894	-2.3	166	177
Birmingham-Hoover, AL	1,051,305	1,108,210	56,909	5.4	48	47
Bismarck, ND	94,719	103,242	8,523	9.0	342	335
Blacksburg-Christiansburg-Radford, VA	151,324	157,614	6,290	4.2	242	247
Bloomington, IN	175,506	183,733	8,227	4.7	211	220
Bloomington-Normal, IL	150,435	164,209	13,776	9.2	244	232
Boise City-Nampa, ID	464,840	587,689	122,849	26.4	97	86
Boston-Cambridge-Quincy, MA-NH	4,392,340	4,482,857	90,517	2.1	10	10
Boulder, CO	269,787	290,262	20,493	7.6	159	157
Bowling Green, KY	104,166	116,001	11,835	11.4	324	312
Bremerton-Silverdale, WA	231,969	236,732	4,763	2.1	177	183
Bridgeport-Stamford-Norwalk, CT	882,567	895,015	12,448	1.4	51	56
Brownsville-Harlingen, TX	335,227	387,210	51,983	15.5	137	128
Brunswick, GA	93,044	101,792	8,748	9.4	343	337
Buffalo-Niagara Falls, NY	1,170,109	1,128,183	-41,926	-3.6	42	46
Burlington, NC	130,794	145,360	14,560	11.1	272	266
Burlington-South Burlington, VT	198,889	207,361	8,472	4.3	193	197
Canton-Massillon, OH	406,968	407,180	212	0.1	110	120
Cape Coral-Fort Myers, FL	440,888	590,564	149,676	33.9	103	85
Carson City, NV	52,457	54,939	2,482	4.7	362	363
Casper, WY	66,533	71,750	5,217	7.8	360	361
Cedar Rapids, IA	237,230	252,784	15,554	6.6	174	174
Champaign-Urbana, IL	210,279	220,923	10,644	5.1	187	193
Charleston, WV	309,632	303,950	-5,682	-1.8	147	151
Charleston-North Charleston, SC	548,972	630,100	81,128	14.8	85	81
Charlotte-Gastonia-Concord, NC-SC	1,330,403	1,651,568	321,129	24.1	37	35
Charlottesville, VA	174,021	192,779	18,758	10.8	215	213
Chattanooga, TN-GA	476,513	514,568	38,055	8.0	94	97
Cheyenne, WY	81,607	86,353	4,746	5.8	353	353
Chicago-Naperville-Joliet, IL-IN-WI	9,098,615	9,524,673	426,058	4.7	3	3
Chico, CA	203,171	218,779	15,608	7.7	190	194
Cincinnati-Middletown, OH-KY-IN	2,009,673	2,133,678	124,024	6.2	24	24
Clarksville, TN-KY	232,043	261,816	29,773	12.8	176	169
Cleveland, TN	104,003	111,121	7,118	6.8	325	323
Cleveland-Elyria-Mentor, OH	2,945,698	2,096,471	-51,539	-2.4	23	25
Coeur d'Alene, ID	108,685	134,442	25,757	23.7	315	278
College Station-Bryan, TX	184,885	203,371	18,486	10.0	204	201
Colorado Springs, CO	537,484	609,096	71,608	13.3	86	83
Columbia, MO	145,666	162,314	16,648	11.4	251	239
Columbia, SC	647,253	716,030	68,777	10.6	73	69
Columbus, GA-AL	281,768	282,756	1,020	0.4	154	161
Columbus, IN	71,435	74,750	3,315	4.6	359	359
Columbus, OH	1,612,841	1,754,337	141,493	8.8	31	32
Corpus Christi, TX	403,280	414,376	11,096	2.8	111	115
Corvallis, OR	78,139	81,428	3,289	4.2	357	356
Cumberland, MD-WV	102,008	99,316	-2,692	-2.6	333	342
Dallas-Fort Worth-Arlington, TX	5,161,518	6,145,037	983,517	19.1	5	4
Dalton, GA	120,061	134,043	13,982	11.6	289	280
Danville, IL	83,924	81,191	-2,733	-3.3	350	357
Danville, VA	110,156	105,773	-4,383	-4.0	311	331
Davenport-Moline-Rock Island, IA-IL	376,052	376,160	108	<0.1	121	132
Dayton, OH	848,157	835,537	-12,616	-1.5	54	59
Decatur, AL	145,867	149,279	3,412	2.3	250	257
Decatur, IL	114,706	108,732	-5,974	-5.2	299	326
Deltona-Daytona Beach-Ormond Beach, FL	443,340	500,413	57,070	12.9	101	100
Denver-Aurora, CO	2,179,320	2,464,866	285,524	13.1	22	21
Des Moines-West Des Moines, IA	481,398	546,599	68,201	13.5	93	91
Detroit-Warren-Livonia, MI	4,452,557	4,467,592	15,033	0.3	9	11
Dothan, AL	130,861	139,499	8,638	6.6	271	273
Dover, DE	126,700	152,255	25,555	20.2	279	253
Dubuque, IA	89,156	92,359	3,203	3.6	348	349
Duluth, MN-WI	275,486	274,308	-1,178	-0.4	156	164
Durham, NC	423,800	479,624	55,830	13.2	105	103
Eau Claire, WI	148,337	157,808	9,471	6.4	246	246

Metropolitan Statistical Area	Population		Change 2000–07		Rank	
	2000	2007	Number	Percent	2000	2007
El Centro, CA	142,361	161,867	19,506	13.7%	258	241
Elizabethtown, KY	107,543	111,610	4,067	3.8	319	322
Elkhart-Goshen, IN	182,791	197,942	15,151	8.3	205	208
Elmira, NY	91,070	88,015	-3,055	-3.4	345	351
El Paso, TX	679,622	734,669	55,047	8.1	69	68
Erie, PA	280,843	279,092	-1,751	-0.6	155	162
Eugene-Springfield, OR	322,977	343,591	20,614	6.4	139	144
Evansville, IN-KY	342,816	349,717	6,901	2.0	133	142
Fairbanks, AK	82,840	97,484	14,644	17.7	352	345
Fargo, ND-MN	174,367	192,417	18,050	10.4	214	214
Farmington, NM	113,801	122,427	8,626	7.6	300	300
Fayetteville, NC	336,608	348,940	12,330	3.7	136	143
Fayetteville-Springdale-Rogers, AR-MO	347,045	435,714	88,669	25.5	130	110
Flagstaff, AZ	116,320	127,450	11,130	9.6	294	294
Flint, MI	436,148	434,715	-1,433	-0.3	104	111
Florence, SC	193,155	198,719	5,564	2.9	198	206
Florence-Muscle Shoals, AL	142,950	143,149	199	0.1	257	269
Fond du Lac, WI	97,296	99,124	1,828	1.9	339	343
Fort Collins-Loveland, CO	251,494	287,574	36,080	14.3	167	159
Fort Smith, AR-OK	273,171	289,693	16,522	6.0	158	158
Fort Walton Beach-Crestview-Destin, FL	170,497	181,499	11,002	6.5	217	222
Fort Wayne, IN	390,154	410,070	19,914	5.1	116	117
Fresno, CA	799,407	899,348	99,941	12.5	58	55
Gadsden, AL	103,460	103,217	-242	-0.2	328	336
Gainesville, FL	232,392	257,099	24,707	10.6	175	172
Gainesville, GA	139,315	180,175	40,860	29.3	262	224
Glens Falls, NY	124,345	128,886	4,541	3.7	281	292
Goldsboro, NC	113,329	113,590	261	0.2	301	317
Grand Forks, ND-MN	97,478	97,691	213	0.2	338	344
Grand Junction, CO	116,935	139,082	22,147	18.9	293	274
Grand Rapids-Wyoming, MI	740,482	776,742	36,260	4.9	63	66
Great Falls, MT	80,357	81,775	1,418	1.8	354	355
Greeley, CO	180,861	243,759	62,893	34.8	208	179
Green Bay, WI	282,497	301,131	18,634	6.6	153	153
Greensboro-High Point, NC	643,446	698,497	55,050	8.6	74	72
Greenville, NC	152,693	172,473	19,780	13.0	238	228
Greenville-Mauldin-Easley, SC	559,922	613,828	53,906	9.6	84	82
Gulfport-Biloxi, MS	246,190	231,523	-14,667	-6.0	171	186
Hagerstown-Martinsburg, MD-WV	222,771	261,198	38,427	17.2	181	170
Hanford-Corcoran, CA	129,461	148,875	19,414	15.0	274	258
Harrisburg-Carlisle, PA	509,074	528,892	19,811	3.9	87	94
Harrisonburg, VA	108,169	117,563	9,394	8.7	317	308
Hartford-West Hartford-East Hartford, CT	1,148,618	1,189,113	40,495	3.5	44	45
Hattiesburg, MS	123,812	138,144	14,332	11.6	284	275
Hickory-Lenoir-Morganton, NC	341,819	360,471	18,651	5.5	135	138
Hinesville-Fort Stewart, GA	71,914	71,803	-111	-0.2	358	360
Holland-Grand Haven, MI	238,314	259,206	20,892	8.8	173	171
Honolulu, HI	876,156	905,601	29,445	3.4	52	54
Hot Springs, AR	88,066	96,371	8,303	9.4	349	347
Houma-Bayou Cane-Thibodaux, LA	194,477	201,137	6,660	3.4	195	203
Houston-Sugar Land-Baytown, TX	4,715,402	5,628,101	912,699	19.4	8	6
Huntington-Ashland, WV-KY-OH	288,650	284,026	-4,624	-1.6	151	160
Huntsville, AL	342,627	386,632	44,005	12.8	134	130
Idaho Falls, ID	101,677	119,396	17,719	17.4	334	305
Indianapolis-Carmel, IN	1,525,104	1,695,037	169,933	11.1	34	33
Iowa City, IA	131,676	147,038	15,362	11.7	270	261
Ithaca, NY	96,502	101,055	4,553	4.7	340	339
Jackson, MI	158,422	163,006	4,584	2.9	232	237
Jackson, MS	497,197	534,047	36,850	7.4	90	93
Jackson, TN	107,365	112,660	5,295	4.9	320	320
Jacksonville, FL	1,122,750	1,300,823	178,073	15.9	45	40
Jacksonville, NC	150,355	162,745	12,390	8.2	245	238
Janesville, WI	152,307	159,623	7,316	4.8	240	243
Jefferson City, MO	140,052	145,686	5,632	4.0	261	263
Johnson City, TN	181,607	193,554	11,947	6.6	206	211
Johnstown, PA	152,598	144,995	-7,603	-5.0	239	267
Jonesboro, AR	107,762	116,402	8,640	8.0	318	310
Joplin, MO	157,322	171,278	13,956	8.9	234	230
Kalamazoo-Portage, MI	314,866	323,264	8,398	2.7	146	148
Kankakee-Bradley, IL	103,833	110,705	6,872	6.6	326	324
Kansas City, MO-KS	1,836,420	1,985,429	149,000	8.1	26	29
Kennewick-Richland-Pasco, WA	191,825	228,992	37,167	19.4	201	188
Killeen-Temple-Fort Hood, TX	330,712	370,008	39,296	11.9	138	134

Metropolitan Statistical Area	Population 2000	2007	Change 2000-07 Number	Percent	Rank 2000	2007
Kingsport-Bristol-Bristol, TN-VA	298,484	303,686	5,202	1.7%	149	152
Kingston, NY	177,749	181,860	4,111	2.3	210	221
Knoxville, TN	616,080	681,525	65,445	10.6	76	75
Kokomo, IN	101,541	99,845	-1,696	-1.7	335	341
La Crosse, WI-MN	126,838	130,926	4,088	3.2	278	286
Lafayette, IN	178,541	192,161	13,620	7.6	209	215
Lafayette, LA	238,906	256,494	17,588	7.4	172	173
Lake Charles, LA	193,565	191,926	-1,639	-0.8	197	216
Lakeland, FL	483,924	194,944	39,912	25.7	236	210
Lancaster, PA	470,635	574,746	90,822	18.8	92	87
Lansing-East Lansing, MI	447,822	498,465	27,807	5.9	96	101
Laredo, TX	193,117	456,440	8,618	1.9	99	106
Las Cruces, NM	174,682	233,152	40,035	20.7	199	184
Las Vegas-Paradise, NV	1,375,738	1,836,333	460,798	33.5	36	30
Lawrence, KS	99,965	113,488	13,526	13.5	336	318
Lawton, OK	114,996	113,811	-1,185	-1.0	298	315
Lebanon, PA	120,327	127,889	7,562	6.3	288	293
Lewiston, ID-WA	57,961	60,043	2,082	3.6	361	362
Lewiston-Auburn, ME	103,793	106,815	3,022	2.9	327	330
Lexington-Fayette, KY	408,326	447,173	38,847	9.5	109	109
Lima, OH	108,473	105,233	-3,240	-3.0	316	333
Lincoln, NE	266,787	292,219	25,432	9.5	160	156
Little Rock-North Little Rock, AR	610,520	666,401	55,883	9.2	77	78
Logan, UT-ID	102,720	121,090	18,370	17.9	331	302
Longview, TX	194,042	203,611	9,569	4.9	196	200
Longview, WA	92,948	100,467	7,519	8.1	344	340
Los Angeles-Long Beach-Santa Ana, CA	12,365,619	12,875,587	509,964	4.1	2	2
Louisville-Jefferson County, KY-IN	1,162,409	1,233,735	71,326	6.1	43	42
Lubbock, TX	249,700	267,211	17,511	7.0	169	167
Lynchburg, VA	228,616	243,580	14,964	6.5	178	180
Macon, GA	222,385	229,846	7,461	3.4	183	187
Madera, CA	123,109	146,513	23,404	19.0	285	262
Madison, WI	501,773	555,626	53,853	10.7	88	89
Manchester-Nashua, NH	380,843	402,302	21,459	5.6	119	124
Mansfield, OH	128,852	125,679	-3,173	-2.5	277	296
McAllen-Edinburg-Mission, TX	569,463	710,514	141,051	24.8	81	70
Medford, OR	181,323	199,295	18,020	9.9	207	204
Memphis, TN-MS-AR	1,205,194	1,280,533	75,339	6.3	41	41
Merced, CA	210,554	245,514	34,960	16.6	186	178
Miami-Fort Lauderdale-Miami Beach, FL	5,007,988	5,413,212	405,224	8.1	6	7
Michigan City-La Porte, IN	110,106	109,787	-319	-0.3	312	325
Midland, TX	116,009	126,408	10,399	9.0	295	295
Milwaukee-Waukesha-West Allis, WI	1,500,744	1,544,398	43,654	2.9	35	38
Minneapolis-Bloomington, MN-WI	2,968,817	3,208,212	239,395	8.1	16	16
Missoula, MT	95,802	105,650	9,848	10.3	341	332
Mobile, AL	399,843	404,406	4,563	1.1	113	121
Modesto, CA	446,997	511,263	64,269	14.4	100	99
Monroe, LA	170,053	172,275	2,222	1.3	219	229
Monroe, MI	145,945	153,608	7,663	5.3	249	251
Montgomery, AL	346,530	365,962	19,436	5.6	131	135
Morgantown, WV	111,200	117,770	6,570	5.9	307	307
Morristown, TN	123,081	134,596	11,515	9.4	286	277
Mount Vernon-Anacortes, WA	102,982	116,397	13,418	13.0	330	311
Muncie, IN	118,769	115,419	-3,350	-2.8	292	313
Muskegon-Norton Shores, MI	170,200	174,386	4,186	2.5	218	227
Myrtle Beach-North Myrtle Beach, SC	196,629	249,925	53,265	27.1	194	176
Napa, CA	124,308	132,565	8,286	6.7	282	282
Naples-Marco Island, FL	251,377	315,839	64,462	25.6	168	150
Nashville-Davidson-Murfreesboro, TN	1,311,789	1,521,437	209,648	16.0	39	39
New Haven-Milford, CT	824,008	845,494	21,486	2.6	57	58
New Orleans-Metairie-Kenner, LA	1,316,512	1,030,363	-286,149	-21.7	38	51
New York-Northern NJ-Long Island, NY-NJ	18,323,382	18,815,988	492,606	2.7	1	1
Niles-Benton Harbor, MI	162,455	159,589	-2,866	-1.8	229	244
Norwich-New London, CT	259,106	267,376	8,270	3.2	161	166
Ocala, FL	258,916	324,857	65,941	25.5	162	147
Ocean City, NJ	102,326	96,422	-5,904	-5.8	332	346
Odessa, TX	121,123	129,570	8,447	7.0	287	291
Ogden-Clearfield, UT	442,656	518,349	75,693	17.1	102	96
Oklahoma City, OK	1,095,421	1,192,989	97,568	8.9	47	44
Olympia, WA	207,355	238,555	31,200	15.0	189	182
Omaha-Council Bluffs, NE-IA	767,140	829,890	62,750	8.2	60	61
Orlando-Kissimmee, FL	1,644,563	2,032,496	387,933	23.6	30	27
Oshkosh-Neenah, WI	156,763	162,154	5,391	3.4	235	240

Metropolitan Statistical Area	Population 2000	2007	Change 2000–07 Number	Percent	Rank 2000	2007
Owensboro, KY	109,875	112,104	2,229	2.0%	313	321
Oxnard-Thousand Oaks-Ventura, CA	753,195	798,364	45,169	6.0	61	63
Palm Bay-Melbourne-Titusville, FL	476,230	536,161	59,931	12.6	95	92
Palm Coast, FL	49,832	88,397	38,565	77.4	363	350
Panama City-Lynn Haven, FL	148,218	163,984	15,766	10.6	247	235
Parkersburg-Marietta-Vienna, WV-OH	164,624	160,656	-3,968	-2.4	225	242
Pascagoula, MS	150,564	152,035	1,471	1.0	243	254
Pensacola-Ferry Pass-Brent, FL	412,153	453,451	41,298	10.0	108	108
Peoria, IL	366,875	371,206	4,331	1.2	127	133
Philadelphia-Wilmington, PA-NJ-DE-MD	5,687,141	5,827,962	140,817	2.5	4	5
Phoenix-Mesa-Scottsdale, AZ	3,251,876	4,179,427	927,551	28.5	14	13
Pine Bluff, AR	107,345	101,484	-5,861	-5.5	321	338
Pittsburgh, PA	2,431,085	2,355,712	-75,375	-3.1	20	22
Pittsfield, MA	134,953	129,798	-5,155	-3.8	267	290
Pocatello, ID	83,103	87,609	4,506	5.4	351	352
Portland-South Portland-Biddeford, ME	487,568	513,102	25,536	5.2	91	98
Portland-Vancouver-Beaverton, OR-WA	1,927,881	2,175,113	247,232	12.8	25	23
Port St. Lucie-Fort Pierce, FL	319,426	400,121	80,695	25.3	144	126
Poughkeepsie-Newburgh-Middletown, NY	621,517	669,915	48,398	7.8	75	77
Prescott, AZ	167,517	212,635	45,118	26.9	220	196
Providence-New Bedford-Fall River, RI-MA	1,582,997	1,600,856	17,859	1.1	32	36
Provo-Orem, UT	376,778	493,306	116,528	30.9	120	102
Pueblo, CO	141,472	154,538	13,066	9.2	260	249
Punta Gorda, FL	141,627	152,814	11,187	7.9	259	252
Racine, WI	188,831	195,099	6,268	3.3	202	209
Raleigh-Cary, NC	797,025	1,047,629	250,623	31.4	59	49
Rapid City, SD	112,818	120,279	7,461	6.6	303	303
Reading, PA	373,661	401,955	28,317	7.6	123	125
Redding, CA	163,256	179,427	16,171	9.9	228	226
Reno-Sparks, NV	342,885	410,272	67,387	19.7	132	116
Richmond, VA	1,096,957	1,212,977	116,022	10.6	46	43
Riverside-San Bernardino-Ontario, CA	3,254,821	4,081,371	826,554	25.4	13	14
Roanoke, VA	288,254	296,532	8,278	2.9	152	154
Rochester, MN	163,618	181,082	17,464	10.7	227	223
Rochester, NY	1,037,833	1,030,495	-7,338	-0.7	49	50
Rockford, IL	320,204	352,290	32,086	10.0	142	140
Rocky Mount, NC	142,991	145,596	2,605	1.8	256	264
Rome, GA	90,565	95,618	5,053	5.6	346	348
Sacramento-Arden-Arcade-Roseville, CA	1,796,857	2,091,120	294,263	16.4	27	26
Saginaw-Saginaw Township North, MI	210,042	202,268	-7,774	-3.7	188	202
St. Cloud, MN	167,396	185,555	18,161	10.8	221	219
St. George, UT	90,354	133,791	43,437	48.1	347	281
St. Joseph, MO-KS	123,820	123,339	-481	-0.4	283	298
St. Louis, MO-IL	2,698,672	2,803,707	105,035	3.9	18	18
Salem, OR	347,218	386,714	39,496	11.4	129	129
Salinas, CA	401,764	407,637	5,873	1.5	112	119
Salisbury, MD	109,392	119,616	10,225	9.3	314	304
Salt Lake City, UT	968,883	1,099,973	131,090	13.5	50	48
San Angelo, TX	105,781	108,085	2,034	2.2	322	327
San Antonio, TX	1,711,716	1,990,675	278,954	16.3	29	28
San Diego-Carlsbad-San Marcos, CA	2,813,833	2,974,859	161,026	5.7	17	17
Sandusky, OH	79,551	77,323	-2,228	-2.8	356	358
San Francisco-Oakland-Fremont, CA	4,123,742	4,203,898	80,151	1.9	12	12
San Jose-Sunnyvale-Santa Clara, CA	1,735,819	1,803,643	67,824	3.9	28	31
San Luis Obispo-Paso Robles, CA	246,681	262,436	15,755	6.4	170	168
Santa Barbara-Santa Maria-Goleta, CA	399,347	404,197	4,850	1.2	114	123
Santa Cruz-Watsonville, CA	255,600	251,747	-3,853	-1.5	163	175
Santa Fe, NM	129,287	142,955	13,668	10.6	275	270
Santa Rosa-Petaluma, CA	458,614	464,435	5,819	1.3	98	104
Sarasota-Bradenton-Venice, FL	589,963	687,181	97,218	16.5	79	73
Savannah, GA	293,299	329,329	36,030	12.3	150	146
Scranton-Wilkes-Barre, PA	560,627	549,430	-11,197	-2.0	83	90
Seattle-Tacoma-Bellevue, WA	3,043,885	3,309,347	265,462	8.7	15	15
Sebastian-Vero Beach, FL	112,947	131,837	18,890	16.7	302	283
Sheboygan, WI	112,656	114,504	1,848	1.6	304	314
Sherman-Denison, TX	110,595	118,675	8,080	7.3	309	306
Shreveport-Bossier City, LA	375,968	387,583	11,615	3.1	122	127
Sioux City, IA-NE-SD	143,053	142,794	-259	-0.2	255	271
Sioux Falls, SD	187,093	227,171	40,078	21.4	203	191
South Bend-Mishawaka, IN-MI	316,661	316,639	-22	<0.1	145	149
Spartanburg, SC	253,782	275,534	21,752	8.6	164	163
Spokane, WA	417,938	456,175	38,236	9.1	107	107
Springfield, IL	201,440	206,588	5,148	2.6	192	198

Metropolitan Statistical Area	Population 2000	Population 2007	Change 2000–07 Number	Change 2000–07 Percent	Rank 2000	Rank 2007
Springfield, MA	680,014	682,657	2,643	0.4%	68	74
Springfield, MO	368,374	420,020	51,646	14.0	125	114
Springfield, OH	144,741	140,477	-4,261	-2.9	254	272
State College, PA	135,758	144,658	8,900	6.6	266	268
Stockton, CA	563,598	670,990	107,394	19.1	82	76
Sumter, SC	104,636	103,943	-693	-0.7	323	334
Syracuse, NY	650,154	645,293	-4,861	-0.7	72	80
Tallahassee, FL	320,304	352,319	32,015	10.0	141	139
Tampa-St. Petersburg-Clearwater, FL	2,396,013	2,723,949	327,936	13.7	21	19
Terre Haute, IN	170,954	169,346	-1,608	-0.9	216	231
Texarkana, TX-Texarkana, AR	129,749	134,215	4,466	3.4	273	279
Toledo, OH	659,184	650,955	-8,229	-1.2	71	79
Topeka, KS	224,551	228,692	4,141	1.8	180	189
Trenton-Ewing, NJ	350,761	365,449	14,688	4.2	128	136
Tucson, AZ	843,746	967,089	123,343	14.6	55	52
Tulsa, OK	859,530	905,755	46,225	5.4	53	53
Tuscaloosa, AL	193,106	205,218	12,112	6.3	200	199
Tyler, TX	174,706	198,705	23,999	13.7	212	207
Utica-Rome, NY	299,896	294,862	-5,034	-1.7	148	155
Valdosta, GA	119,566	130,170	10,604	8.9	291	288
Vallejo-Fairfield, CA	394,513	408,599	14,057	3.6	115	118
Victoria, TX	111,666	113,797	2,131	1.9	306	316
Vineland-Millville-Bridgeton, NJ	146,438	155,544	9,110	6.2	248	248
Virginia Beach-Newport News, VA-NC	1,576,917	1,658,754	81,837	5.2	33	34
Visalia-Porterville, CA	368,021	421,553	53,532	14.5	126	112
Waco, TX	213,513	228,123	14,604	6.8	185	190
Warner Robins, GA	110,765	131,016	20,251	18.3	308	285
Washington-Alexandria, DC-VA-MD-WV	4,796,180	5,306,565	510,502	10.6	7	8
Waterloo-Cedar Falls, IA	163,707	163,329	-378	-0.2	226	236
Wausau, WI	125,834	129,958	4,124	3.3	280	289
Weirton-Steubenville, WV-OH	132,008	122,580	-9,428	-7.1	269	299
Wenatchee, WA	99,219	107,170	7,951	8.0	337	329
Wheeling, WV-OH	153,178	145,454	-7,724	-5.0	237	265
Wichita, KS	571,168	596,452	25,281	4.4	80	84
Wichita Falls, TX	151,524	148,148	-3,376	-2.2	241	260
Williamsport, PA	120,048	116,811	-3,237	-2.7	290	309
Wilmington, NC	274,550	339,511	64,961	23.7	157	145
Winchester, VA-WV	102,997	121,190	18,193	17.7	329	301
Winston-Salem, NC	421,934	463,159	41,199	9.8	106	105
Worcester, MA	749,973	781,352	31,379	4.2	62	65
Yakima, WA	222,578	233,062	10,484	4.7	182	185
York-Hanover, PA	381,751	421,049	39,298	10.3	118	113
Youngstown-Warren-Boardman, OH-PA	602,964	570,704	-32,260	-5.4	78	88
Yuba City, CA	139,149	164,138	24,989	18.0	263	233
Yuma, AZ	160,026	190,557	30,531	19.1	231	217

Source: U.S. Bureau of the Census, *Cumulative Estimates of Population Change for Micropolitan Statistical Areas and Rankings: April 1, 2000 to July 1, 2007.*

Population of U.S. Metropolitan Areas by Race and Hispanic Origin, 2000

Metropolitan area	Total	White	Black	Indian/ Alaska Native	Asian	Pacific Islander	Other	Two or more races	Hispanic[1]
Abilene, Texas MSA	126,555	80.6%	6.7%	0.6%	1.2%	0.1%	8.3%	2.4%	17.6%
Albany, Ga. MSA	120,822	46.9	51.0	0.2	0.6	0.0	0.5	0.7	1.3
Albany–Schenectady–Troy, N.Y. MSA	875,583	89.4	6.1	0.2	1.8	0.0	0.9	1.5	2.7
Albuquerque, N.Mex. MSA	712,738	69.6	2.5	5.6	1.7	0.1	16.3	4.2	41.6
Alexandria, La. MSA	126,337	66.5	30.4	0.7	0.9	0.0	0.4	1.0	1.4
Allentown–Bethlehem– Easton, Pa. MSA	637,958	89.8	3.0	0.2	1.6	0.0	3.9	1.5	7.9
Altoona, Pa. MSA	129,144	97.6	1.2	0.1	0.4	0.0	0.1	0.6	0.5
Amarillo, Texas MSA	217,858	79.1	5.9	0.8	1.8	0.0	10.3	2.1	19.6
Anchorage, Alaska MSA	260,283	72.2	5.8	7.3	5.5	0.9	2.2	6.0	5.7
Anniston, Ala. MSA	112,249	78.9	18.5	0.4	0.6	0.1	0.6	1.0	1.6
Appleton–Oshkosh– Neenah, Wis. MSA	358,365	94.6	0.8	0.9	2.0	0.0	0.7	0.9	1.9
Asheville, N.C. MSA	225,965	89.8	6.9	0.4	0.6	0.0	1.1	1.2	2.7
Athens, Ga. MSA	153,444	73.2	20.5	0.2	2.4	0.0	2.5	1.2	5.1
Atlanta, Ga. MSA	4,112,198	63.0	28.9	0.3	3.3	0.0	2.8	1.7	6.5
Auburn–Opelika, Ala. MSA	115,092	74.1	22.7	0.2	1.6	0.0	0.5	0.9	1.4
Augusta–Aiken, Ga.–S.C. MSA	477,441	61.5	34.4	0.3	1.5	0.1	0.9	1.5	2.4
Austin–San Marcos, Texas MSA	1,249,763	72.5	8.0	0.6	3.5	0.1	12.8	2.6	26.2
Bakersfield, Calif. MSA	661,645	61.6	6.0	1.5	3.4	0.1	23.2	4.1	38.4
Bangor, Maine MSA	90,864	95.6	0.7	1.3	1.0	0.0	0.3	1.1	0.7
Barnstable–Yarmouth, Mass. MSA	162,582	94.4	1.7	0.6	0.6	0.0	1.1	1.6	1.3
Baton Rouge, La. MSA	602,894	64.9	31.9	0.2	1.5	0.0	0.5	0.9	1.8
Beaumont–Port Arthur, Texas MSA	385,090	68.2	24.8	0.4	2.1	0.0	3.1	1.4	8.0
Bellingham, Wash. MSA	166,814	88.4	0.7	2.8	2.8	0.1	2.5	2.7	5.2
Benton Harbor, Mich. MSA	162,453	79.7	15.9	0.4	1.1	0.0	1.1	1.6	3.0
Billings, Mont. MSA	129,352	92.8	0.4	3.1	0.5	0.0	1.3	1.9	3.7
Biloxi–Gulfport– Pascagoula, Miss.MSA	363,988	76.0	19.3	0.4	2.0	0.1	0.8	1.4	2.3
Binghamton, N.Y. MSA	252,320	92.6	2.7	0.2	2.3	0.0	0.7	1.5	1.8
Birmingham, Ala. MSA	921,106	67.3	30.1	0.3	0.8	0.0	0.7	0.8	1.8
Bismarck, N.Dak. MSA	94,719	95.2	0.2	3.0	0.4	0.0	0.2	0.9	0.7
Bloomington, Ind. MSA	120,563	90.8	3.0	0.3	3.4	0.0	0.9	1.6	1.9
Bloomington–Normal, Ill. MSA	150,433	89.2	6.2	0.2	2.1	0.0	1.0	1.4	2.5
Boise City, Idaho MSA	432,345	89.9	0.5	0.7	1.5	0.1	4.9	2.4	8.8
Boston–Worcester–Lawrence, Mass.–N.H.–Maine–Conn. CMSA	5,819,100	85.1	5.1	0.2	4.0	0.0	3.3	2.2	6.2
Boston, MA–NH PMSA	3,406,829	82.5	7.0	0.2	4.9	0.0	3.0	2.4	5.9
Brockton, MA PMSA	255,459	82.4	7.6	0.2	1.3	0.0	5.0	3.5	3.7
Fitchburg–Leominster, MA PMSA	142,284	89.5	2.6	0.2	2.3	0.0	3.4	2.0	8.3
Lawrence, MA–NH PMSA	396,230	85.6	1.7	0.3	2.1	0.0	8.1	2.1	14.0
Lowell, MA–NH PMSA	301,686	85.9	1.9	0.2	7.6	0.0	2.5	2.0	5.7
Manchester, NH PMSA	198,378	94.4	1.3	0.3	1.7	0.0	1.1	1.3	3.0
Nashua, NH PMSA	190,949	93.4	1.3	0.2	2.4	0.0	1.5	1.1	3.4
New Bedford, MA PMSA	175,198	85.9	2.7	0.4	0.7	0.0	6.4	3.8	5.9
Portsmouth–Rochester, NH–ME PMSA	240,698	96.5	0.7	0.2	1.3	0.0	0.3	1.0	1.0
Worcester, MA–CT PMSA	511,389	88.7	3.0	0.3	3.0	0.0	3.2	1.9	7.1
Brownsville–Harlingen– San Benito, Texas MSA	335,227	80.3	0.5	0.4	0.5	0.0	16.0	2.3	84.3
Bryan–College Station, Texas MSA	152,415	74.5	10.7	0.4	4.0	0.1	8.4	2.0	17.9
Buffalo–Niagara Falls, N.Y. MSA	1,170,111	83.8	11.7	0.7	1.3	0.0	1.2	1.3	2.9
Burlington, Vt. MSA	169,391	95.2	0.8	0.5	1.8	0.0	0.3	1.4	1.0
Canton–Massillon, Ohio MSA	406,934	90.8	6.7	0.2	0.5	0.0	0.3	1.4	0.9
Casper, Wyo. MSA	66,533	94.2	0.8	1.0	0.4	0.0	1.9	1.7	4.9
Cedar Rapids, Iowa MSA	191,701	93.9	2.6	0.2	1.4	0.0	0.5	1.4	1.4
Champaign–Urbana, Ill. MSA	179,669	78.8	11.2	0.2	6.5	0.0	1.3	2.0	2.9
Charleston–North Charleston, S.C. MSA	549,033	65.1	30.8	0.4	1.3	0.1	1.0	1.3	2.4
Charleston, W.Va. MSA	251,662	92.0	5.7	0.2	0.8	0.0	0.2	1.1	0.6
Charlotte–Gastonia–Rock Hill, N.C.–S.C. MSA	1,499,293	73.6	20.5	0.4	1.9	0.0	2.3	1.2	5.1
Charlottesville, Va. MSA	159,576	80.6	14.0	0.2	2.9	0.0	0.8	1.5	2.2
Chattanooga, Tenn.–Ga. MSA	465,161	82.8	14.2	0.3	1.0	0.0	0.6	1.0	1.5
Cheyenne, Wyo. MSA	81,607	88.9	2.6	0.8	1.0	0.1	4.0	2.6	10.9
Chicago–Gary–Kenosha, Ill.–Ind.–Wis. CMSA	9,157,540	66.8	18.6	0.3	4.2	0.0	7.7	2.2	16.4
Chicago, IL PMSA	8,272,768	65.8	18.9	0.3	4.6	0.0	8.2	2.3	17.1
Gary, IN PMSA	631,362	73.4	19.7	0.3	0.8	0.0	4.1	1.7	10.5

Metropolitan area	Total	White	Black	Indian/ Alaska Native	Asian	Pacific Islander	Other	Two or more races	Hispanic[1]
Kankakee, IL PMSA	103,833	79.9%	15.5%	0.2%	0.7%	0.0%	2.4%	1.4%	4.8%
Kenosha, WI PMSA	149,577	88.4	5.1	0.4	0.9	0.0	3.3	1.9	7.2
Chico–Paradise, Calif. MSA	203,171	84.5	1.4	1.9	3.3	0.1	4.8	3.9	10.5
Cincinnati–Hamilton, Ohio–Ky.– Ind. CMSA	1,979,202	85.3	11.7	0.2	1.2	0.0	0.5	1.1	1.1
Cincinnati, OH–KY–IN PMSA	1,646,395	84.1	13.0	0.2	1.2	0.0	0.4	1.1	1.1
Hamilton–Middletown, OH PMSA	332,807	91.2	5.3	0.2	1.5	0.0	0.6	1.1	1.4
Clarksville–Hopkinsville, Tenn.–Ky. MSA	207,033	72.0	20.8	0.5	1.5	0.2	2.2	2.7	5.0
Cleveland–Akron, Ohio CMSA	2,945,831	79.0	16.8	0.2	1.3	0.0	1.2	1.5	2.7
Akron, OH PMSA	694,960	85.9	11.0	0.2	1.3	0.0	0.3	1.3	0.8
Cleveland–Lorain– Elyria, OH PMSA	2,250,871	76.9	18.5	0.2	1.4	0.0	1.4	1.6	3.3
Colorado Springs, Colo. MSA	516,929	81.2	6.5	0.9	2.5	0.2	4.7	3.9	11.3
Columbia, Mo. MSA	135,454	85.4	8.5	0.4	3.0	0.0	0.7	1.9	1.8
Columbia, S.C. MSA	536,691	63.9	32.1	0.3	1.4	0.1	1.0	1.2	2.4
Columbus, Ga.–Ala. MSA	274,624	54.4	40.4	0.4	1.3	0.1	1.7	1.7	4.0
Columbus, Ohio MSA	1,540,157	81.3	13.4	0.3	2.4	0.0	0.8	1.9	1.8
Corpus Christi, Texas MSA	380,783	72.9	4.0	0.6	1.1	0.1	18.2	3.1	54.7
Corvallis, Oreg. MSA	78,153	89.2	0.8	0.8	4.5	0.2	1.9	2.6	4.7
Cumberland, Md.–W.Va. MSA	102,008	93.9	4.6	0.1	0.4	0.0	0.2	0.8	0.7
Dallas–Fort Worth, Texas CMSA	5,221,801	69.5	13.8	0.6	3.7	0.1	9.9	2.4	21.5
Dallas, TX PMSA	3,519,176	67.2	15.1	0.6	4.0	0.1	10.7	2.4	23.0
Fort Worth–Arlington, TX PMSA	1,702,625	74.3	11.2	0.6	3.2	0.1	8.3	2.4	18.2
Danville, Va. MSA	110,156	65.7	32.6	0.2	0.4	0.0	0.4	0.7	1.2
Davenport–Moline–Rock Island, Iowa–Ill. MSA	359,062	88.4	6.0	0.3	1.2	0.0	2.5	1.7	5.8
Dayton–Springfield, Ohio MSA	950,558	82.3	14.2	0.2	1.2	0.0	0.5	1.5	1.2
Daytona Beach, Fla. MSA	493,175	86.2	9.2	0.3	1.0	0.0	1.7	1.4	6.4
Decatur, Ala. MSA	145,867	83.3	11.7	1.8	0.4	0.1	1.0	1.7	2.8
Decatur, Ill. MSA	114,706	83.5	14.1	0.2	0.6	0.0	0.3	1.4	1.0
Denver–Boulder–Greeley, Colo. CMSA	2,581,506	80.6	4.6	0.9	2.8	0.1	8.1	2.9	18.5
Boulder–Longmont, CO PMSA	291,288	88.5	0.9	0.6	3.1	0.1	4.7	2.2	10.5
Denver, CO PMSA	2,109,282	79.4	5.5	0.9	3.0	0.1	8.1	3.0	18.8
Greeley, CO PMSA	180,936	81.7	0.6	0.9	0.8	0.1	13.3	2.7	27.0
Des Moines, Iowa MSA	456,022	89.8	4.1	0.2	2.3	0.1	2.1	1.5	4.2
Detroit–Ann Arbor–Flint, Mich. CMSA	5,456,428	73.4	21.1	0.4	2.4	0.0	1.1	2.1	2.9
Ann Arbor, MI PMSA	578,736	85.3	7.3	0.4	3.7	0.0	1.2	2.0	3.1
Detroit, MI PMSA	4,441,551	71.2	22.9	0.3	2.3	0.0	1.1	2.1	2.9
Flint, MI PMSA	436,141	75.3	20.4	0.6	0.8	0.0	0.8	2.2	2.3
Dothan, Ala. MSA	137,916	73.5	23.1	0.5	0.8	0.1	0.7	1.4	2.0
Dover, Del. MSA	126,697	73.5	20.7	0.6	1.7	0.0	1.3	2.2	3.2
Dubuque, Iowa MSA	89,143	97.1	0.9	0.1	0.6	0.1	0.5	0.8	1.2
Duluth–Superior, Minn.–Wis. MSA	243,815	94.9	0.8	2.0	0.7	0.0	0.2	1.4	0.8
Eau Claire, Wis. MSA	148,337	96.0	0.4	0.5	1.9	0.0	0.3	0.9	0.8
El Paso, Texas MSA	679,622	73.9	3.1	0.8	1.0	0.1	17.9	3.2	78.2
Elkhart–Goshen, Ind. MSA	182,791	86.4	5.2	0.3	0.9	0.0	5.4	1.8	8.9
Elmira, N.Y. MSA	91,070	91.0	5.8	0.2	0.8	0.0	0.7	1.4	1.8
Enid, Okla. MSA	57,813	88.7	3.3	2.1	0.8	0.5	2.0	2.6	4.1
Erie, Pa. MSA	280,843	90.9	6.1	0.2	0.7	0.0	0.9	1.2	2.2
Eugene–Springfield, Oreg. MSA	322,959	90.6	0.8	1.1	2.0	0.2	1.9	3.3	4.6
Evansville–Henderson, Ind.–Ky. MSA	296,195	91.8	6.1	0.2	0.6	0.0	0.3	0.9	0.9
Fargo–Moorhead, N.Dak.– Minn. MSA	174,367	94.8	0.7	1.2	1.1	0.0	0.8	1.3	1.9
Fayetteville, N.C. MSA	302,963	55.2	34.9	1.5	1.9	0.3	3.1	3.1	6.9
Fayetteville–Springdale–Rogers, Ark. MSA	311,121	89.4	1.3	1.4	1.3	0.3	4.2	2.0	8.5
Flagstaff, Ariz.–Utah MSA	122,366	64.7	1.0	27.2	0.8	0.1	4.0	2.3	10.5
Florence, Ala. MSA	142,950	85.7	12.5	0.3	0.3	0.0	0.4	0.8	1.1
Florence, S.C. MSA	125,761	58.7	39.3	0.2	0.7	0.0	0.4	0.7	1.1
Fort Collins–Loveland, Colo. MSA	251,494	91.4	0.7	0.7	1.6	0.1	3.4	2.2	8.3
Fort Myers–Cape Coral, Fla. MSA	440,888	87.7	6.6	0.3	0.8	0.0	3.1	1.6	9.5
Fort Pierce–Port St. Lucie, Fla. MSA	319,426	83.4	11.4	0.3	0.8	0.1	2.5	1.5	7.9
Fort Smith, Ark.–Okla. MSA	207,290	82.2	4.0	5.1	2.3	0.0	2.6	3.8	4.9
Fort Walton Beach, Fla. MSA	170,498	83.4	9.1	0.6	2.5	0.1	1.3	3.0	4.3
Fort Wayne, Ind. MSA	502,141	88.1	7.5	0.3	1.0	0.0	1.6	1.4	3.3
Fresno, Calif. MSA	922,516	55.4	5.1	1.7	7.1	0.1	25.7	4.8	44.0
Gadsden, Ala. MSA	103,459	82.9	14.7	0.3	0.4	0.0	0.7	0.9	1.7
Gainesville, Fla. MSA	217,955	73.5	19.3	0.2	3.5	0.0	1.4	2.0	5.7

Metropolitan area	Total	White	Black	Indian/ Alaska Native	Asian	Pacific Islander	Other	Two or more races	Hispanic[1]
Glens Falls, N.Y. MSA	124,345	96.2%	1.8%	0.2%	0.4%	0.0%	0.5%	0.8%	1.5%
Goldsboro, N.C. MSA	113,329	61.3	33.0	0.4	1.0	0.0	3.1	1.3	4.9
Grand Forks, N.Dak.–Minn. MSA	97,478	93.4	1.0	2.0	0.8	0.1	1.3	1.5	2.9
Grand Junction, Colo. MSA	116,255	92.3	0.5	0.9	0.5	0.1	3.7	2.0	10.0
Grand Rapids–Muskegon– Holland, Mich. MSA	1,088,514	85.7	7.3	0.5	1.6	0.0	3.0	1.9	6.3
Great Falls, Mont. MSA	80,357	90.7	1.1	4.2	0.8	0.1	0.7	2.4	2.4
Green Bay, Wis. MSA	226,778	91.1	1.2	2.3	2.2	0.0	1.9	1.3	3.8
Greensboro–Winston-Salem– High Point, N.C. MSA	1,251,509	74.4	20.2	0.4	1.4	0.0	2.4	1.2	5.0
Greenville, N.C. MSA	133,798	62.1	33.6	0.3	1.1	0.0	1.8	1.1	3.2
Greenville–Spartanburg– Anderson, S.C. MSA	962,441	79.0	17.5	0.2	1.2	0.0	1.1	1.0	2.7
Harrisburg–Lebanon– Carlisle, Pa. MSA	629,401	87.8	7.8	0.1	1.5	0.0	1.4	1.3	3.1
Hartford, Conn. MSA	1,183,110	80.7	9.5	0.2	2.2	0.0	5.2	2.1	9.6
Hattiesburg, Miss.MSA	111,674	71.7	26.3	0.2	0.7	0.0	0.4	0.7	1.2
Hickory–Morganton–Lenoir, N.C. MSA	341,851	87.5	6.9	0.2	2.3	0.1	2.0	1.0	4.0
Honolulu, Hawaii MSA	876,156	21.3	2.4	0.2	46.0	8.9	1.3	19.9	6.7
Houma, La. MSA	194,477	78.1	15.4	3.9	0.7	0.0	0.6	1.2	1.5
Houston–Galveston–Brazoria, Texas CMSA	4,669,571	62.6	16.9	0.4	4.9	0.1	12.4	2.7	28.9
Brazoria, TX PMSA	241,767	77.1	8.5	0.5	2.0	0.0	9.6	2.2	22.8
Galveston–Texas City, TX PMSA	250,158	72.7	15.4	0.5	2.1	0.0	7.2	2.1	18.0
Houston, TX PMSA	4,177,646	61.1	17.5	0.4	5.2	0.1	12.9	2.8	29.9
Huntington–Ashland, W.Va.– Ky.–Ohio MSA	315,538	96.2	2.2	0.2	0.4	0.0	0.1	0.8	0.7
Huntsville, Ala. MSA	342,376	74.3	21.0	0.7	1.6	0.1	0.7	1.7	2.0
Indianapolis, Ind. MSA	1,607,486	82.1	13.9	0.2	1.2	0.0	1.3	1.3	2.7
Iowa City, Iowa MSA	111,006	90.1	2.9	0.3	4.1	0.0	1.0	1.5	2.5
Jackson, Mich. MSA	158,422	88.5	7.9	0.4	0.5	0.0	0.8	1.7	2.2
Jackson, Miss.MSA	440,801	52.6	45.6	0.1	0.7	0.0	0.3	0.6	1.0
Jackson, Tenn. MSA	107,377	68.5	29.2	0.2	0.6	0.0	0.6	0.9	1.6
Jacksonville, Fla. MSA	1,100,491	72.6	21.7	0.3	2.3	0.1	1.2	1.8	3.8
Jacksonville, N.C. MSA	150,355	72.1	18.5	0.7	1.7	0.2	3.6	3.2	7.2
Jamestown, N.Y. MSA	139,750	94.0	2.2	0.4	0.4	0.0	1.7	1.2	4.2
Janesville–Beloit, Wis. MSA	152,307	91.0	4.6	0.3	0.8	0.0	1.8	1.5	3.9
Johnson City–Kingsport–Bristol, Tenn.–Va. MSA	480,091	96.2	2.1	0.2	0.4	0.0	0.3	0.7	0.9
Johnstown, Pa. MSA	232,621	96.3	2.4	0.1	0.3	0.0	0.3	0.6	0.8
Jonesboro, Ark. MSA	82,148	89.3	7.8	0.3	0.6	0.0	0.9	1.1	2.1
Joplin, Mo. MSA	157,322	92.8	1.2	1.6	0.6	0.1	1.4	2.2	3.0
Kalamazoo–Battle Creek, Mich. MSA	452,851	84.9	9.3	0.6	1.4	0.0	1.6	2.1	3.6
Kansas City, Mo.–Kans. MSA	1,776,062	80.8	12.8	0.5	1.6	0.1	2.3	2.0	5.2
Killeen–Temple, Texas MSA	312,952	63.9	20.8	0.8	2.4	0.5	8.0	3.8	15.7
Knoxville, Tenn. MSA	687,249	91.3	5.8	0.3	1.0	0.0	0.5	1.1	1.3
Kokomo, Ind. MSA	101,541	91.1	5.5	0.3	0.9	0.0	0.8	1.4	1.9
La Crosse, Wis.–Minn. MSA	126,838	94.8	0.8	0.4	2.7	0.0	0.2	0.9	0.9
Lafayette, La. MSA	385,647	69.7	28.2	0.2	0.7	0.0	0.4	0.8	1.3
Lafayette, Ind. MSA	182,821	89.9	2.1	0.3	3.7	0.0	2.8	1.3	5.6
Lake Charles, La. MSA	183,577	73.6	24.0	0.3	0.6	0.0	0.4	1.0	1.3
Lakeland–Winter Haven, Fla. MSA	483,924	79.6	13.5	0.4	0.9	0.0	3.8	1.7	9.5
Lancaster, Pa. MSA	470,658	91.5	2.8	0.1	1.4	0.0	2.9	1.3	5.7
Lansing–East Lansing, Mich. MSA	447,728	84.4	8.1	0.5	2.6	0.0	1.9	2.4	4.7
Laredo, Texas MSA	193,117	82.2	0.4	0.5	0.4	0.0	14.0	2.5	94.3
Las Cruces, N.Mex. MSA	174,682	67.8	1.6	1.5	0.8	0.1	24.7	3.6	63.4
Las Vegas, Nev.–Ariz. MSA	1,563,282	73.8	8.1	1.0	4.7	0.4	8.0	4.0	20.6
Lawrence, Kans. MSA	99,962	86.1	4.2	2.6	3.1	0.1	1.2	2.7	3.3
Lawton, Okla. MSA	114,996	65.2	19.0	5.1	2.1	0.4	3.5	4.7	8.4
Lewiston–Auburn, Maine MSA	90,830	96.8	0.7	0.3	0.6	0.0	0.3	1.3	1.0
Lexington, Ky. MSA	479,198	86.4	9.5	0.2	1.6	0.0	1.0	1.3	2.5
Lima, Ohio MSA	155,084	88.9	8.6	0.2	0.5	0.0	0.5	1.3	1.2
Lincoln, Nebr. MSA	250,291	90.1	2.8	0.6	2.9	0.1	1.7	1.9	3.4
Little Rock–North Little Rock, Ark. MSA	583,845	74.5	21.9	0.4	1.0	0.0	0.9	1.3	2.1
Longview–Marshall, Texas MSA	208,780	74.6	19.5	0.5	0.5	0.0	3.6	1.3	7.1
Los Angeles–Riverside–Orange County, Calif. CMSA	16,373,645	55.1	7.6	0.9	10.4	0.3	21.0	4.7	40.3
Los Angeles–Long Beach, Calif. PMSA	9,519,338	48.7	9.8	0.8	11.9	0.3	23.5	4.9	44.6

Metropolitan area	Total	White	Black	Indian/ Alaska Native	Asian	Pacific Islander	Other	Two or more races	Hispanic[1]
Orange County, Calif. PMSA	2,846,289	64.8%	1.7%	0.7%	13.6%	0.3%	14.8%	4.1%	30.8%
Riverside–San Bernardino, Calif. PMSA	3,254,821	62.1	7.7	1.2	4.2	0.3	19.8	4.7	37.8
Ventura, CA PMSA	753,197	69.9	1.9	0.9	5.3	0.2	17.7	3.9	33.4
Louisville, Ky.–Ind. MSA	1,025,598	82.8	13.9	0.2	1.1	0.0	0.6	1.3	1.6
Lubbock, Texas MSA	242,628	74.3	7.7	0.6	1.3	0.0	14.1	2.0	27.5
Lynchburg, Va. MSA	214,911	79.6	17.9	0.3	0.7	0.0	0.4	1.0	1.0
Macon, Ga. MSA	322,549	59.2	37.5	0.2	1.1	0.0	0.7	1.1	2.1
Madison, Wis. MSA	426,526	89.0	4.0	0.3	3.5	0.0	1.4	1.8	3.4
Mansfield, Ohio MSA	175,818	90.8	7.1	0.2	0.5	0.0	0.3	1.1	0.9
McAllen–Edinburg–Mission, Texas MSA	569,463	77.7	0.5	0.4	0.6	0.0	18.6	2.1	88.3
Medford–Ashland, Oreg. MSA	181,269	91.6	0.4	1.1	0.9	0.2	2.9	2.9	6.7
Melbourne–Titusville–Palm Bay, Fla. MSA	476,230	86.8	8.4	0.4	1.5	0.1	1.1	1.8	4.6
Memphis, Tenn.–Ark.–Miss.MSA	1,135,614	52.9	43.4	0.2	1.4	0.0	1.1	1.0	2.4
Merced, Calif. MSA	210,554	56.2	3.8	1.2	6.8	0.2	26.1	5.7	45.3
Miami–Fort Lauderdale, Fla. CMSA	3,876,380	70.1	20.4	0.2	1.8	0.0	3.9	3.6	40.3
Fort Lauderdale, FL PMSA	1,623,018	70.6	20.5	0.2	2.3	0.1	3.0	3.4	16.7
Miami, FL PMSA	2,253,362	69.7	20.3	0.2	1.4	0.0	4.6	3.8	57.3
Milwaukee–Racine, Wis. CMSA	1,689,572	77.8	15.1	0.5	1.9	0.0	3.0	1.7	6.5
Milwaukee–Waukesha, WI PMSA	1,500,741	77.1	15.7	0.5	2.1	0.0	2.9	1.7	6.3
Racine, WI PMSA	188,831	83.0	10.5	0.4	0.7	0.0	3.7	1.7	7.9
Minneapolis–St. Paul, Minn.– Wis. MSA	2,968,806	86.1	5.3	0.7	4.1	0.0	1.6	2.1	3.3
Missoula, Mont. MSA	95,802	94.0	0.3	2.3	1.0	0.1	0.4	1.9	1.6
Mobile, Ala. MSA	540,258	69.3	27.4	0.6	1.1	0.0	0.4	1.0	1.4
Modesto, Calif. MSA	446,997	69.3	2.6	1.3	4.2	0.3	16.8	5.4	31.7
Monroe, La. MSA	147,250	64.5	33.6	0.2	0.6	0.0	0.3	0.7	1.2
Montgomery, Ala. MSA	333,055	58.6	38.9	0.3	0.8	0.0	0.4	1.0	1.2
Muncie, Ind. MSA	118,769	90.7	6.7	0.2	0.7	0.1	0.5	1.1	1.1
Myrtle Beach, S.C. MSA	196,629	81.0	15.5	0.4	0.8	0.1	1.2	1.1	2.6
Naples, Fla. MSA	251,377	86.1	4.5	0.3	0.6	0.1	6.2	2.2	19.6
Nashville, Tenn. MSA	1,231,311	79.4	15.6	0.3	1.6	0.0	1.6	1.4	3.3
New London–Norwich, Conn.–R.I. MSA	293,566	88.0	4.7	0.9	1.9	0.1	1.8	2.5	4.7
New Orleans, La. MSA	1,337,726	57.3	37.5	0.4	2.1	0.0	1.2	1.4	4.4
New York–Northern New Jersey– Long Island, N.Y.–N.J.– Conn.–Pa. CMSA	21,199,865	64.1	17.2	0.3	6.8	0.0	8.2	3.4	18.2
Bergen–Passaic, NJ PMSA	1,373,167	72.7	8.1	0.3	8.2	0.0	7.9	2.9	17.3
Bridgeport, CT PMSA	459,479	78.1	11.5	0.2	2.3	0.0	5.3	2.5	12.4
Danbury, CT PMSA	217,980	88.6	3.0	0.2	3.2	0.0	3.0	2.0	7.0
Dutchess County, NY PMSA	280,150	83.7	9.3	0.2	2.5	0.0	2.4	1.9	6.4
Jersey City, NJ PMSA	608,975	55.6	13.5	0.4	9.4	0.1	15.5	5.6	39.8
Middlesex–Somerset– Hunterdon, NJ PMSA	1,169,641	73.9	8.0	0.2	11.2	0.0	4.4	2.2	11.2
Monmouth–Ocean, NJ PMSA	1,126,217	88.3	5.8	0.1	2.7	0.0	1.5	1.5	5.7
Nassau–Suffolk, NY PMSA	2,753,913	82.0	8.5	0.2	3.6	0.0	3.6	2.1	10.3
New Haven–Meriden, CT PMSA	542,149	77.4	13.1	0.2	2.7	0.0	4.3	2.1	9.8
New York, NY PMSA	9,314,235	48.8	24.6	0.5	9.1	0.1	12.3	4.6	25.1
Newark, NJ PMSA	2,032,989	65.9	22.3	0.2	4.0	0.0	4.9	2.7	13.3
Newburgh, NY–PA PMSA	387,669	84.8	7.5	0.3	1.4	0.0	3.8	2.1	10.8
Stamford–Norwalk, CT PMSA	353,556	81.0	9.2	0.1	3.9	0.0	3.5	2.2	10.8
Trenton, NJ PMSA	350,761	68.5	19.8	0.2	4.9	0.1	4.3	2.2	9.7
Waterbury, CT PMSA	228,984	82.2	8.3	0.3	1.3	0.0	5.5	2.3	11.5
Norfolk–Virginia Beach– Newport News, Va.–N.C. MSA	1,569,541	62.5	30.9	0.4	2.7	0.1	1.2	2.2	3.1
Ocala, Fla. MSA	258,916	84.2	11.5	0.4	0.7	0.0	1.7	1.4	6.0
Odessa–Midland, Texas MSA	237,132	75.5	5.8	0.7	0.8	0.0	14.8	2.4	35.8
Oklahoma City, Okla. MSA	1,083,346	75.7	10.6	4.2	2.5	0.1	3.2	3.9	6.7
Omaha, Nebr.–Iowa MSA	716,998	85.2	8.3	0.5	1.5	0.1	2.7	1.7	5.5
Orlando, Fla. MSA	1,644,561	75.0	13.9	0.3	2.7	0.1	5.1	2.9	16.5
Owensboro, Ky. MSA	91,545	93.7	4.3	0.1	0.4	0.0	0.4	0.9	0.9
Panama City, Fla. MSA	148,217	84.2	10.6	0.8	1.7	0.1	0.7	1.9	2.4
Parkersburg–Marietta, W.Va.– Ohio MSA	151,237	97.3	1.0	0.2	0.5	0.0	0.1	0.8	0.6
Pensacola, Fla. MSA	412,153	77.6	16.5	0.9	2.0	0.1	0.8	2.1	2.6
Peoria–Pekin, Ill. MSA	347,387	88.0	8.9	0.2	1.1	0.0	0.6	1.2	1.6

Metropolitan area	Total	White	Black	Indian/ Alaska Native	Asian	Pacific Islander	Other	Two or more races	Hispanic[1]
Philadelphia–Wilmington– Atlantic City, Pa.–N.J.–Del.– Md. CMSA	6,188,463	72.5%	19.6%	0.2%	3.2%	0.0%	2.7%	1.7%	5.6%
Atlantic–Cape May, NJ PMSA	354,878	75.0	14.0	0.2	3.8	0.0	4.7	2.2	9.6
Philadelphia, PA–NJ PMSA	5,100,931	72.1	20.1	0.2	3.4	0.0	2.5	1.6	5.1
Vineland–Millville–Bridgeton, NJ PMSA	146,438	65.9	20.2	1.0	1.0	0.1	9.1	2.9	19.0
Wilmington–Newark, DE–MD PMSA	586,216	76.1	17.8	0.2	2.3	0.0	2.0	1.6	4.7
Phoenix–Mesa, Ariz. MSA	3,251,876	77.0	3.7	2.2	2.1	0.1	12.1	2.9	25.1
Pine Bluff, Ark. MSA	84,278	48.5	49.6	0.2	0.7	0.0	0.3	0.8	1.0
Pittsburgh, Pa. MSA	2,358,695	89.5	8.1	0.1	1.1	0.0	0.3	0.9	0.7
Pittsfield, Mass. MSA	84,699	94.8	2.3	0.1	0.9	0.0	0.6	1.2	1.7
Pocatello, Idaho MSA	75,565	91.3	0.6	2.9	1.0	0.2	2.1	2.0	4.7
Portland, Maine MSA	243,537	95.8	1.0	0.3	1.4	0.0	0.3	1.1	0.9
Portland–Salem, Oreg.– Wash. CMSA	2,265,223	84.3	2.4	1.0	4.1	0.3	4.6	3.3	8.7
Portland–Vancouver, OR– WA PMSA	1,918,009	84.5	2.7	0.9	4.6	0.3	3.8	3.3	7.4
Salem, OR PMSA	347,214	83.0	0.8	1.5	1.6	0.3	9.5	3.2	15.6
Providence–Fall River–Warwick, R.I.–Mass. MSA	1,188,613	86.2	4.0	0.4	2.2	0.0	4.5	2.6	7.9
Provo–Orem, Utah MSA	368,536	92.4	0.3	0.6	1.1	0.6	3.2	1.9	7.0
Pueblo, Colo. MSA	141,472	79.5	1.9	1.6	0.7	0.1	12.9	3.4	38.0
Punta Gorda, Fla. MSA	141,627	92.6	4.4	0.2	0.9	0.0	0.8	1.1	3.3
Raleigh–Durham–Chapel Hill, N.C. MSA	1,187,941	69.4	22.7	0.4	2.9	0.0	3.1	1.6	6.1
Rapid City, S.Dak. MSA	88,565	86.7	0.9	8.1	0.9	0.1	0.7	2.7	2.6
Reading, Pa. MSA	373,638	88.2	3.7	0.2	1.0	0.0	5.4	1.5	9.7
Redding, Calif. MSA	163,256	89.3	0.8	2.8	1.9	0.1	1.7	3.5	5.5
Reno, Nev. MSA	339,486	80.4	2.1	1.8	4.3	0.5	7.7	3.3	16.6
Richland–Kennewick–Pasco, Wash. MSA	191,822	80.0	1.3	0.8	2.1	0.1	12.7	3.1	21.3
Richmond–Petersburg, Va. MSA	996,512	64.9	30.2	0.4	2.1	0.0	1.1	1.3	2.3
Roanoke, Va. MSA	235,932	83.9	13.0	0.2	1.2	0.0	0.5	1.2	1.1
Rochester, Minn. MSA	124,277	90.3	2.7	0.3	4.3	0.0	0.9	1.5	2.4
Rochester, N.Y. MSA	1,098,201	84.0	10.3	0.3	1.8	0.0	1.9	1.7	4.3
Rockford, Ill. MSA	371,236	85.1	8.1	0.3	1.4	0.0	3.4	1.7	7.4
Rocky Mount, N.C. MSA	143,026	53.4	43.1	0.4	0.4	0.0	1.9	0.8	3.1
Sacramento–Yolo, Calif. CMSA	1,796,857	70.0	7.1	1.1	9.0	0.5	7.2	5.2	15.5
Sacramento, CA PMSA	1,628,197	70.2	7.7	1.1	8.9	0.5	6.5	5.2	14.4
Yolo, CA PMSA	168,660	67.7	2.0	1.2	9.9	0.3	13.8	5.2	25.9
Saginaw–Bay City–Midland, Mich. MSA	403,070	84.8	10.3	0.4	0.9	0.0	1.9	1.7	4.9
St. Cloud, Minn. MSA	167,392	96.0	0.8	0.3	1.5	0.0	0.4	0.8	1.3
St. Joseph, Mo. MSA	102,490	93.6	3.7	0.4	0.4	0.0	0.6	1.2	2.2
St. Louis, Mo.–Ill. MSA	2,603,607	78.3	18.3	0.2	1.4	0.0	0.5	1.2	1.5
Salinas, Calif. MSA	401,762	55.9	3.7	1.0	6.0	0.4	27.8	5.0	46.8
Salt Lake City–Ogden, Utah MSA	1,333,914	87.6	1.1	0.8	2.2	0.9	5.0	2.4	10.8
San Angelo, Texas MSA	104,010	79.1	4.1	0.7	0.9	0.1	12.8	2.4	30.7
San Antonio, Texas MSA	1,592,383	70.6	6.6	0.8	1.5	0.1	16.9	3.5	51.2
San Diego, Calif. MSA	2,813,833	66.5	5.7	0.9	8.9	0.5	12.8	4.7	26.7
San Francisco–Oakland– San Jose, Calif. CMSA	7,039,362	58.7	7.3	0.7	18.4	0.5	9.5	4.9	19.7
Oakland, CA PMSA	2,392,557	55.4	12.7	0.6	16.7	0.5	8.6	5.4	18.5
San Francisco, CA PMSA	1,731,183	58.6	5.3	0.4	22.7	0.8	7.7	4.5	16.8
San Jose, CA PMSA	1,682,585	53.8	2.8	0.7	25.6	0.3	12.1	4.7	24.0
Santa Cruz–Watsonville, CA PMSA	255,602	75.1	1.0	1.0	3.4	0.1	15.0	4.4	26.8
Santa Rosa, CA PMSA	458,614	81.6	1.4	1.2	3.1	0.2	8.4	4.1	17.3
Vallejo–Fairfield–Napa, CA PMSA	518,821	62.0	11.7	0.8	10.4	0.6	8.7	5.8	19.1
San Luis Obispo–Atascadero– Paso Robles, Calif. MSA	246,681	84.6	2.0	0.9	2.7	0.1	6.2	3.4	16.3
Santa Barbara–Santa Maria– Lompoc, Calif. MSA	399,347	72.7	2.3	1.2	4.1	0.2	15.2	4.3	34.2
Santa Fe, N.Mex. MSA	147,635	75.6	0.6	2.8	1.2	0.1	15.9	3.9	44.4
Sarasota–Bradenton, Fla. MSA	589,959	89.8	6.0	0.2	0.8	0.0	1.9	1.2	6.6
Savannah, Ga. MSA	293,000	61.2	34.9	0.3	1.5	0.1	0.8	1.3	2.2
Scranton–Wilkes-Barre– Hazleton, Pa. MSA	624,776	96.8	1.4	0.1	0.6	0.0	0.4	0.6	1.2
Seattle–Tacoma–Bremerton, Wash. CMSA	3,554,760	79.3	4.7	1.2	7.9	0.6	2.2	4.2	5.2

Metropolitan area	Total	White	Black	Indian/ Alaska Native	Asian	Pacific Islander	Other	Two or more races	Hispanic[1]
Bremerton, WA PMSA	231,969	84.3%	2.9%	1.6%	4.4%	0.8%	1.4%	4.6%	4.1%
Olympia, WA PMSA	207,355	85.7	2.4	1.5	4.4	0.5	1.7	3.9	4.5
Seattle–Bellevue–Everett, WA PMSA	2,414,616	78.6	4.4	1.0	9.4	0.5	2.4	3.9	5.2
Tacoma, WA PMSA	700,820	78.4	7.0	1.4	5.1	0.8	2.2	5.1	5.5
Sharon, Pa. MSA	120,293	93.1	5.3	0.1	0.4	0.0	0.2	0.9	0.7
Sheboygan, Wis. MSA	112,646	92.7	1.1	0.4	3.3	0.0	1.5	1.1	3.4
Sherman–Denison, Texas MSA	110,595	87.2	5.9	1.3	0.6	0.0	2.9	2.1	6.8
Shreveport–Bossier City, La. MSA	392,302	59.7	37.4	0.4	0.8	0.0	0.5	1.1	1.8
Sioux City, Iowa–Nebr. MSA	124,130	86.1	1.8	1.7	2.5	0.0	5.8	2.1	11.3
Sioux Falls, S.Dak. MSA	172,412	93.7	1.4	1.7	0.9	0.0	0.9	1.4	1.9
South Bend, Ind. MSA	265,559	82.4	11.5	0.4	1.3	0.1	2.5	2.0	4.7
Spokane, Wash. MSA	417,939	91.4	1.6	1.4	1.9	0.2	0.8	2.8	2.8
Springfield, Ill. MSA	201,437	88.1	9.1	0.2	1.0	0.0	0.4	1.2	1.0
Springfield, Mo. MSA	325,721	94.4	1.8	0.6	0.9	0.1	0.6	1.6	1.7
Springfield, Mass. MSA	591,932	81.6	6.7	0.2	1.9	0.1	7.2	2.2	12.5
State College, Pa. MSA	135,758	91.4	2.6	0.1	4.0	0.1	0.7	1.1	1.7
Steubenville–Weirton, Ohio– W.Va. MSA	132,008	94.5	3.9	0.2	0.3	0.0	0.2	0.9	0.6
Stockton–Lodi, Calif. MSA	563,598	58.1	6.7	1.1	11.4	0.3	16.3	6.0	30.5
Sumter, S.C. MSA	104,646	50.1	46.7	0.3	0.9	0.1	0.8	1.2	1.8
Syracuse, N.Y. MSA	732,117	88.9	6.5	0.7	1.5	0.0	0.8	1.6	2.1
Tallahassee, Fla. MSA	284,539	62.0	33.6	0.3	1.6	0.0	1.1	1.4	3.9
Tampa–St. Petersburg– Clearwater, Fla. MSA	2,395,997	82.9	10.2	0.3	1.9	0.1	2.7	2.0	10.4
Terre Haute, Ind. MSA	149,192	92.9	4.4	0.3	0.9	0.0	0.3	1.2	1.0
Texarkana, Texas–Texarkana, Ark. MSA	129,749	73.5	23.3	0.6	0.4	0.0	0.9	1.2	3.6
Toledo, Ohio MSA	618,203	82.1	12.8	0.3	1.1	0.0	1.8	1.9	4.4
Topeka, Kans. MSA	169,871	82.9	9.0	1.2	1.0	0.0	3.2	2.7	7.3
Tucson, Ariz. MSA	843,746	75.1	3.0	3.2	2.0	0.1	13.3	3.2	29.3
Tulsa, Okla. MSA	803,235	76.0	8.8	6.9	1.2	0.0	2.1	4.8	4.8
Tuscaloosa, Ala. MSA	164,875	68.1	29.3	0.2	0.9	0.0	0.6	0.8	1.3
Tyler, Texas MSA	174,706	72.6	19.1	0.4	0.7	0.0	5.7	1.4	11.2
Utica–Rome, N.Y. MSA	299,896	91.8	4.6	0.2	1.0	0.0	0.9	1.4	2.7
Victoria, Texas MSA	84,088	74.2	6.3	0.5	0.8	0.0	15.9	2.2	39.2
Visalia–Tulare–Porterville, Calif. MSA	368,021	58.1	1.6	1.6	3.3	0.1	30.8	4.6	50.8
Waco, Texas MSA	213,517	72.2	15.2	0.5	1.1	0.0	9.2	1.8	17.9
Washington–Baltimore, D.C.– Md.–W.Va. CMSA	7,608,070	63.0	26.2	0.3	5.3	0.1	2.7	2.4	6.4
Baltimore, MD PMSA	2,552,994	67.3	27.4	0.3	2.7	0.0	0.7	1.5	2.0
Hagerstown, MD PMSA	131,923	89.7	7.8	0.2	0.8	0.0	0.5	1.0	1.2
Washington, DC–MD–VA– WV PMSA	4,923,153	60.1	26.0	0.3	6.7	0.1	3.9	2.9	8.8
Waterloo–Cedar Falls, Iowa MSA	128,012	88.4	8.0	0.2	1.0	0.0	0.9	1.5	1.8
Wausau, Wis. MSA	125,834	93.8	0.3	0.3	4.5	0.0	0.3	0.7	0.8
West Palm Beach–Boca Raton, Fla. MSA	1,131,184	79.1	13.8	0.2	1.5	0.1	3.0	2.4	12.4
Wheeling, W.Va.–Ohio MSA	153,172	95.6	2.9	0.1	0.4	0.0	0.1	0.8	0.5
Wichita, Kans. MSA	545,220	81.8	7.8	1.1	2.9	0.1	3.8	2.6	7.4
Wichita Falls, Texas MSA	140,518	79.8	9.6	0.9	1.7	0.1	5.3	2.6	11.8
Williamsport, Pa. MSA	120,044	93.9	4.3	0.2	0.4	0.0	0.3	0.9	0.7
Wilmington, N.C. MSA	233,450	80.7	16.2	0.5	0.7	0.1	1.0	1.0	2.2
Yakima, Wash. MSA	222,581	65.6	1.0	4.5	1.0	0.1	24.4	3.5	35.9
York, Pa. MSA	381,751	92.8	3.7	0.2	0.9	0.0	1.4	1.1	3.0
Youngstown–Warren, Ohio MSA	594,746	87.4	10.3	0.2	0.4	0.0	0.6	1.2	1.8
Yuba City, Calif. MSA	139,149	68.9	2.5	2.0	9.6	0.2	11.7	5.2	20.1
Yuma, Ariz. MSA	160,026	68.3	2.2	1.6	0.9	0.1	23.6	3.2	50.5
Aguadilla, PR MSA	146,424	87.1	3.9	0.2	0.1	0.0	5.8	2.8	98.8
Mayag,ez, PR MSA	253,347	85.7	4.4	0.3	0.2	0.0	4.9	4.6	99.1
Ponce, PR MSA	361,094	83.4	5.4	0.3	0.1	0.0	5.8	4.9	99.2
San Juan–Caguas–Arecibo, PR CMSA	2,450,292	78.2	9.5	0.4	0.3	0.0	7.3	4.4	98.6
Arecibo, PR PMSA	174,300	89.9	3.4	0.2	0.1	0.0	3.8	2.7	99.2
Caguas, PR PMSA	308,365	83.5	5.8	0.3	0.1	0.0	7.3	2.9	99.2
San Juan–Bayamon, PR PMSA	1,967,627	76.3	10.6	0.4	0.3	0.0	7.6	4.7	98.5

Notes: MSA= metropolitan statistical area. CMSA= consolidated metropolitan statistical area. 1. Hispanic persons may be of any race.
Source: U.S Bureau of the Census, Press Release CB91-229

Population Change in the Top 100 Metropolitan Statistical Areas, 1990–2000

Since the 1990 Census, the Census Bureau has changed the boundaries of several dozen metropolitan statistical areas (MSAs), merging some areas and separating others. As a result, population statistics before and after 1990 are not directly comparable for more than 75 MSAs.

Rank, Metropolitan Statistical Area	Population 1990	Population 2000	Change, 1990–2000 Number	Change, 1990–2000 Percent
1. New York–Northern New Jersey–Long Island, N.Y.–N.J.–Conn.–Pa. CMSA	19,549,649	21,199,865	1,650,216	8.4%
2. Los Angeles–Riverside–Orange County, Calif. CMSA	14,531,529	16,373,645	1,842,116	12.7
3. Chicago–Gary–Kenosha, Ill.–Ind.–Wisc. CMSA	8,239,820	9,157,540	917,720	11.1
4. Washington–Baltimore, D.C.–Md.–Va.–WV CMSA	6,727,050	7,608,070	881,020	13.1
5. San Francisco–Oakland–San Jose, Calif. CMSA	6,253,311	7,039,362	786,051	12.6
6. Philadelphia–Wilmington–Atlantic City, Pa.–N.J.–Del.–Md. CMSA	5,892,937	6,188,463	295,526	5.0
7. Boston–Worcester–Lawrence, Mass.–N.H.–Maine–Conn. CMSA	5,455,403	5,819,100	363,697	6.7
8. Detroit–Ann Arbor–Flint, Mich. CMSA	5,187,171	5,456,428	269,257	5.2
9. Dallas–Fort Worth, Texas CMSA	4,037,282	5,221,801	1,184,519	29.3
10. Houston–Galveston–Brazoria, Texas CMSA	3,731,131	4,669,571	938,440	25.2
11. Atlanta, Ga. MSA	2,959,950	4,112,198	1,152,248	38.9
12. Miami–Fort Lauderdale, Fla. CMSA	3,192,582	3,876,380	683,798	21.4
13. Seattle–Tacoma–Bremerton, Wash. CMSA	2,970,328	3,554,760	584,432	19.7
14. Phoenix–Mesa, Ariz. MSA	2,238,480	3,251,876	1,013,396	45.3
15. Minneapolis–St. Paul, Minn.–Wisc. MSA	2,538,834	2,968,806	429,972	16.9
16. Cleveland–Akron, Ohio CMSA	2,859,644	2,945,831	86,187	3.0
17. San Diego, Calif. MSA	2,498,016	2,813,833	315,817	12.6
18. St. Louis, Mo.–Ill. MSA	2,492,525	2,603,607	111,082	4.5
19. Denver–Boulder–Greeley, Colo. CMSA	1,980,140	2,581,506	601,366	30.4
20. San Juan–Caguas–Arecibo, Puerto Rico CMSA	2,270,808	2,450,292	179,484	7.9
21. Tampa–St. Petersburg–Clearwater, Fla. MSA	2,067,959	2,395,997	328,038	15.9
22. Pittsburgh, Pa. MSA	2,394,811	2,358,695	-36,116	-1.5
23. Portland–Salem, Oreg.–Wash. CMSA	1,793,476	2,265,223	471,747	26.3
24. Cincinnati–Hamilton, Ohio–KY–Ind. CMSA	1,817,571	1,979,202	161,631	8.9
25. Sacramento–Yolo, Calif. CMSA	1,481,102	1,796,857	315,755	21.3
26. Kansas City, Mo.–Kans. MSA	1,582,875	1,776,062	193,187	12.2
27. Milwaukee–Racine, Wisc. CMSA	1,607,183	1,689,572	82,389	5.1
28. Orlando, Fla. MSA	1,224,852	1,644,561	419,709	34.3
29. Indianapolis, Ind. MSA	1,380,491	1,607,486	226,995	16.4
30. San Antonio, Texas MSA	1,324,749	1,592,383	267,634	20.2
31. Norfolk–Virginia Beach–Newport News, Va.–N.C. MSA	1,443,244	1,569,541	126,297	8.8
32. Las Vegas, Nev.–Ariz. MSA	852,737	1,563,282	710,545	83.3
33. Columbus, Ohio MSA	1,345,450	1,540,157	194,707	14.5
34. Charlotte–Gastonia–Rock Hill, N.C.–S.C. MSA	1,162,093	1,499,293	337,200	29.0
35. New Orleans, La. MSA	1,285,270	1,337,726	52,456	4.1
36. Salt Lake City–Ogden, Utah MSA	1,072,227	1,333,914	261,687	24.4
37. Greensboro–Winston-Salem–High Point, N.C. MSA	1,050,304	1,251,509	201,205	19.2
38. Austin–San Marcos, Texas MSA	846,227	1,249,763	403,536	47.7
39. Nashville, Tenn. MSA	985,026	1,231,311	246,285	25.0
40. Providence–Fall River–Warwick, R.I.–Mass. MSA	1,134,350	1,188,613	54,263	4.8
41. Raleigh–Durham–Chapel Hill, N.C. MSA	855,545	1,187,941	332,396	38.9
42. Hartford, Conn. MSA	1,157,585	1,183,110	25,525	2.2
43. Buffalo–Niagara Falls, N.Y. MSA	1,189,288	1,170,111	-19,177	-1.6
44. Memphis, Tenn.–Ark.–Miss. MSA	1,007,306	1,135,614	128,308	12.7
45. West Palm Beach–Boca Raton, Fla. MSA	863,518	1,131,184	267,666	31.0
46. Jacksonville, Fla. MSA	906,727	1,100,491	193,764	21.4
47. Rochester, N.Y. MSA	1,062,470	1,098,201	35,731	3.4
48. Grand Rapids–Muskegon–Holland, Mich. MSA	937,891	1,088,514	150,623	16.1
49. Oklahoma City, Okla. MSA	958,839	1,083,346	124,507	13.0
50. Louisville, Ky.–Ind. MSA	948,829	1,025,598	76,769	8.1
51. Richmond–Petersburg, Va. MSA	865,640	996,512	130,872	15.1
52. Greenville–Spartanburg–Anderson, S.C. MSA	830,563	962,441	131,878	15.9
53. Dayton–Springfield, Ohio MSA	951,270	950,558	-712	-0.1
54. Fresno, Calif. MSA	755,580	922,516	166,936	22.1
55. Birmingham, Ala. MSA	840,140	921,106	80,966	9.6
56. Honolulu, Hawaii MSA	836,231	876,156	39,925	4.8
57. Albany–Schenectady–Troy, N.Y. MSA	861,424	875,583	14,159	1.6
58. Tucson, Ariz. MSA	666,880	843,746	176,866	26.5
59. Tulsa, Okla. MSA	708,954	803,235	94,281	13.3
60. Syracuse, N.Y. MSA	742,177	732,117	-10,060	-1.4
61. Omaha, Neb.–Iowa MSA	639,580	716,998	77,418	12.1
62. Albuquerque, New Mex. MSA	589,131	712,738	123,607	21.0
63. Knoxville, Tenn. MSA	585,960	687,249	101,289	17.3

Rank, Metropolitan Statistical Area	Population		Change, 1990–2000	
	1990	2000	Number	Percent
64. El Paso, Texas MSA	591,610	679,622	88,012	14.9%
65. Bakersfield, Calif. MSA	543,477	661,645	118,168	21.7
66. Allentown–Bethlehem–Easton, Pa. MSA	595,081	637,958	42,877	7.2
67. Harrisburg–Lebanon–Carlisle, Pa. MSA	587,986	629,401	41,415	7.0
68. Scranton–Wilkes-Barre–Hazleton, Pa. MSA	638,466	624,776	-13,690	-2.1
69. Toledo, Ohio MSA	614,128	618,203	4,075	0.7
70. Baton Rouge, LA MSA	528,264	602,894	74,630	14.1
71. Youngstown–Warren, Ohio MSA	600,895	594,746	-6,149	-1.0
72. Springfield, Mass. MSA	587,884	591,932	4,048	0.7
73. Sarasota–Bradenton, Fla. MSA	489,483	589,959	100,476	20.5
74. Little Rock–North Little Rock, Ark. MSA	513,117	583,845	70,728	13.8
75. McAllen–Edinburg–Mission, Texas MSA	383,545	569,463	185,918	48.5
76. Stockton–Lodi, Calif. MSA	480,628	563,598	82,970	17.3
77. Charleston–North Charleston, S.C. MSA	506,875	549,033	42,158	8.3
78. Wichita, Kans. MSA	485,270	545,220	59,950	12.4
79. Mobile, Ala. MSA	476,923	540,258	63,335	13.3
80. Columbia, S.C. MSA	453,331	536,691	83,360	18.4
81. Colorado Springs, Colo. MSA	397,014	516,929	119,915	30.2
82. Fort Wayne, Ind. MSA	456,281	502,141	45,860	10.1
83. Daytona Beach, Fla. MSA	399,413	493,175	93,762	23.5
84. Lakeland–Winter Haven, Fla. MSA	405,382	483,924	78,542	19.4
85. Johnson City–Kingsport–Bristol, Tenn.–Va. MSA	436,047	480,091	44,044	10.1
86. Lexington, Ky. MSA	405,936	479,198	73,262	18.0
87. Augusta–Aiken, Ga.–S.C. MSA	415,184	477,441	62,257	15.0
88. Melbourne–Titusville–Palm Bay, Fla. MSA	398,978	476,230	77,252	19.4
89. Lancaster, Pa. MSA	422,822	470,658	47,836	11.3
90. Chattanooga, Tenn.–Ga. MSA	424,347	465,161	40,814	9.6
91. Des Moines, Iowa MSA	392,928	456,022	63,094	16.1
92. Kalamazoo–Battle Creek, Mich. MSA	429,453	452,851	23,398	5.4
93. Lansing–East Lansing, Mich. MSA	432,674	447,728	15,054	3.5
94. Modesto, Calif. MSA	370,522	446,997	76,475	20.6
95. Fort Myers–Cape Coral, Fla. MSA	335,113	440,888	105,775	31.6
96. Jackson, Miss. MSA	395,396	440,801	45,405	11.5
97. Boise City, Idaho MSA	295,851	432,345	136,494	46.1
98. Madison, Wisc. MSA	367,085	426,526	59,441	16.2
99. Spokane, Wash. MSA	361,364	417,939	56,575	15.7
100. Pensacola, Fla. MSA	344,406	412,153	67,747	19.7

Note: CMSA = consolidated metropolitan statistical area; MSA = metropolitan statistical area. For component areas see "Population of Metropolitan Statistical Areas, 1990-2000." **Source:** U.S. Bureau of the Census, 2001.

Fastest Growing and Declining Metropolitan Statistical Areas, 1990–2000

Rank, Metropolitan Statistical Area	Population		Change, 1990–2000	
	1990	2000	Number	Percent
FASTEST GROWING				
1. Las Vegas, Nev.-Ariz. MSA	852,737	1,563,282	710,545	83.3%
2. Naples, Fla. MSA	152,099	251,377	99,278	65.3
3. Yuma, Ariz. MSA	106,895	160,026	53,131	49.7
4. McAllen–Edinburg–Mission, Texas MSA	383,545	569,463	185,918	48.5
5. Austin–San Marcos, Texas MSA	846,227	1,249,763	403,536	47.7
6. Fayetteville–Springdale–Rogers, Ark. MSA	210,908	311,121	100,213	47.5
7. Boise City, Idaho MSA	295,851	432,345	136,494	46.1
8. Phoenix–Mesa, Ariz. MSA	2,238,480	3,251,876	1,013,396	45.3
9. Laredo, Texas MSA	133,239	193,117	59,878	44.9
10. Provo–Orem, Utah MSA	263,590	368,536	104,946	39.8
FASTEST DECLINING				
1. Steubenville–Weirton, Ohio–W.Va. MSA	142,523	132,008	-10,515	-7.4%
2. Grand Forks, N.Dak.,–Minn. MSA	103,181	97,478	-5,703	-5.5
3. Utica–Rome, N.Y. MSA	316,633	299,896	-16,737	-5.3
4. Binghamton, N.Y. MSA	264,497	252,320	-12,177	-4.6
5. Pittsfield, Mass. MSA	88,695	84,699	-3,996	-4.5
6. Elmira, N.Y. MSA	95,195	91,070	-4,125	-4.3
7. Alexandria, La. MSA	131,556	126,337	-5,219	-4.0
8. Wheeling, W.Va.–Ohio MSA	159,301	153,172	-6,129	-3.8
9. Johnstown, Pa. MSA	241,247	232,621	-8,626	-3.6
10. Anniston, Ala. MSA	116,034	112,249	-3,785	-3.3

Note: For component areas see "Population of Metropolitan Statistical Areas, 1990-2000." **Source:** U.S. Bureau of the Census.

COUNTIES IN AMERICA

In 2001 there were 3,141 counties in the United States. While only 50 percent of Americans live in cities, almost every American lives in a county. Counties were originally the creation of state governments, which saw them as the local arm of state authority, with special responsibility for rural areas. Counties were intended more for the administrative convenience of the state than to meet the immediate needs of county residents and were not designed to have the intimate relationship with, or understanding of, the needs of localities theoretically characteristic of municipalities. But most states have loosened the reins on county governments in recent years, giving them more authority to meet the needs of population centers that have pushed beyond municipal limits. (Note that in Louisiana, counties are called parishes, and in Alaska and New York City, they are known as boroughs.)

Like cities and metropolitan areas, the fastest-growing counties are in the southern and western United States. Seven of the 10 fastest-growing counties in 2000 were in Colorado or Georgia; the other three were in Virginia, Utah and Idaho.

The counties with the largest numerical increase in population between 1990 and 2000 are all in the western U.S.: Maricopa County, Ariz. (950,048), Los Angeles County, Calif. (656,174), Clark County, Nevada (634,306), Harris County, Texas (582,379), and Orange County, Calif. (435,733).

In addition, most of the counties with greatest growth are those in or around major metropolitan areas. Colorado's Douglas and Elbert Counties, which border both the Denver and Colorado Springs metropolitan areas, ranked 1 and 3 in population growth between 1990 and 2000. Both more than doubled over that period. Forsyth County, Ga. (within the Atlanta metropolitan area) was the second-fastest-growing county, increasing by 123.2 percent.

The 50 Largest Counties, 1990–2000

Rank, 2000/County	Population, 1990	Population, 2000	Change, 1990-2000	Percent Change
1. Los Angeles County, Calif.	8,863,164	9,519,338	656,174	7.4%
2. Cook County, Ill.	5,105,067	5,376,741	271,674	5.3
3. Harris County, Texas	2,818,199	3,400,578	582,379	20.7
4. Maricopa County, Ariz.	2,122,101	3,072,149	950,048	44.8
5. Orange County, Calif.	2,410,556	2,846,289	435,733	18.1
6. San Diego County, Calif.	2,498,016	2,813,833	315,817	12.6
7. Kings County, N.Y.	2,300,664	2,465,326	164,662	7.2
8. Miami-Dade County, Fla.	1,937,094	2,253,362	316,268	16.3
9. Queens County, N.Y.	1,951,598	2,229,379	277,781	14.2
10. Dallas County, Texas	1,852,810	2,218,899	366,089	19.8
11. Wayne County, Mich.	2,111,687	2,061,162	-50,525	-2.4
12. King County, Wash.	1,507,319	1,737,034	229,715	15.2
13. San Bernardino County, Calif.	1,418,380	1,709,434	291,054	20.5
14. Santa Clara County, Calif.	1,497,577	1,682,585	185,008	12.4
15. Broward County, Fla.	1,255,488	1,623,018	367,530	29.3
16. Riverside County, Calif.	1,170,413	1,545,387	374,974	32.0
17. New York County, N.Y.	1,487,536	1,537,195	49,659	3.3
18. Philadelphia County, Pa.	1,585,577	1,517,550	-68,027	-4.3
19. Middlesex County, Mass.	1,398,468	1,465,396	66,928	4.8
20. Tarrant County, Texas	1,170,103	1,446,219	276,116	23.6
21. Alameda County, Calif.	1,279,182	1,443,741	164,559	12.9
22. Suffolk County, N.Y.	1,321,864	1,419,369	97,505	7.4
23. Cuyahoga County, Ohio	1,412,140	1,393,978	-18,162	-1.3
24. Bexar County, Texas	1,185,394	1,392,931	207,537	17.5
25. Clark County, Nev.	741,459	1,375,765	634,306	85.5
26. Nassau County, N.Y.	1,287,348	1,334,544	47,196	3.7
27. Bronx County, N.Y.	1,203,789	1,332,650	128,861	10.7
28. Allegheny County, Pa.	1,336,449	1,281,666	-54,783	-4.1
29. Sacramento County, Calif.	1,041,219	1,223,499	182,280	17.5
30. Oakland County, Mich.	1,083,592	1,194,156	110,564	10.2
31. Palm Beach County, Fla.	863,518	1,131,184	267,666	31.0
32. Hennepin County, Minn.	1,032,431	1,116,200	83,769	8.1
33. Franklin County, Ohio	961,437	1,068,978	107,541	11.2
34. St. Louis County, Mo.	993,529	1,016,315	22,786	2.3
35. Hillsborough County, Fla.	834,054	998,948	164,894	19.8
36. Fairfax County, Va.	818,584	969,749	151,165	18.5
37. Erie County, N.Y.	968,532	950,265	-18,267	-1.9
38. Contra Costa County, Calif.	803,732	948,816	145,084	18.1
39. Milwaukee County, Wis.	959,275	940,164	-19,111	-2.0
40. Westchester County, N.Y.	874,866	923,459	48,593	5.6
41. Pinellas County, Fla.	851,659	921,482	69,823	8.2
42. DuPage County, Ill.	781,666	904,161	122,495	15.7
43. Salt Lake County, Utah	725,956	898,387	172,431	23.8
44. Shelby County, Tenn.	826,330	897,472	71,142	8.6
45. Orange County, Fla.	677,491	896,344	218,853	32.3
46. Bergen County, N.J.	825,380	884,118	58,738	7.1
47. Fairfield County, Conn.	827,645	882,567	54,922	6.6
48. Honolulu County, Hawaii	836,231	876,156	39,925	4.8
49. Montgomery County, Md.	757,027	873,341	116,314	15.4
50. Marion County, Ind.	797,159	860,454	63,295	7.9

Source: U.S. Bureau of the Census release, 1991.

The 75 Largest Counties, 2000–07

Rank, 2007/County	April 1, 2000	July 1, 2007	Change 2000–07	Percent change
1. Los Angeles County, CA	9,519,330	9,878,554	359,224	3.8%
2. Cook County, IL	5,376,822	5,285,107	-91,715	-1.7
3. Harris County, TX	3,400,578	3,935,855	535,277	15.7
4. Maricopa County, AZ	3,072,161	3,880,181	808,020	26.3
5. Orange County, CA	2,846,293	2,997,033	150,740	5.3
6. San Diego County, CA	2,813,833	2,974,859	161,026	5.7
7. Kings County, NY	2,465,525	2,528,050	62,525	2.5
8. Miami-Dade County, FL	2,253,779	2,387,170	133,391	5.9
9. Dallas County, TX	2,218,786	2,366,511	147,725	6.7
10. Queens County, NY	2,229,379	2,270,338	40,959	1.8
11. Riverside County, CA	1,545,374	2,073,571	528,197	34.2
12. San Bernardino County, CA	1,709,443	2,007,800	298,357	17.5
13. Wayne County, MI	2,061,162	1,985,101	-76,061	-3.7
14. King County, WA	1,737,043	1,859,284	122,241	7.0
15. Clark County, NV	1,375,535	1,836,333	460,798	33.5
16. Broward County, FL	1,623,018	1,759,591	136,573	8.4
17. Santa Clara County, CA	1,682,585	1,748,976	66,391	3.9
18. Tarrant County, TX	1,446,225	1,717,435	271,210	18.8
19. New York County, NY	1,537,372	1,620,867	83,495	5.4
20. Bexar County, TX	1,392,931	1,594,493	201,562	14.5
21. Middlesex County, MA	1,466,394	1,473,416	7,022	0.5
22. Alameda County, CA	1,443,746	1,464,202	20,456	1.4
23. Suffolk County, NY	1,419,369	1,453,229	33,860	2.4
24. Philadelphia County, PA	1,517,550	1,449,634	-67,916	-4.5
25. Sacramento County, CA	1,223,499	1,386,667	163,168	13.3
26. Bronx County, NY	1,332,650	1,373,659	41,009	3.1
27. Nassau County, NY	1,334,544	1,306,533	-28,011	-2.1
28. Cuyahoga County, OH	1,393,845	1,295,958	-97,887	-7.0
29. Palm Beach County, FL	1,131,191	1,266,451	135,260	12.0
30. Allegheny County, PA	1,281,666	1,219,210	-62,456	-4.9
31. Oakland County, MI	1,194,156	1,206,089	11,933	1.0
32. Hillsborough County, FL	998,948	1,174,727	175,779	17.6
33. Hennepin County, MN	1,116,039	1,136,599	20,560	1.8
34. Franklin County, OH	1,068,869	1,118,107	49,238	4.6
35. Orange County, FL	896,346	1,066,113	169,769	18.9
36. Contra Costa County, CA	948,816	1,019,640	70,824	7.5
37. Fairfax County, VA	969,677	1,010,241	40,564	4.2
38. Salt Lake County, UT	898,412	1,009,518	111,106	12.4
39. St. Louis County, MO	1,016,300	995,118	-21,182	-2.1
40. Fulton County, GA	815,835	992,137	176,302	21.6
41. Travis County, TX	812,284	974,365	162,081	20.0
42. Pima County, AZ	843,746	967,089	123,343	14.6
43. Westchester County, NY	923,459	951,325	27,866	3.0
44. Milwaukee County, WI	940,164	951,252	11,088	1.2
45. Montgomery County, MD	873,341	930,813	57,472	6.6
44. DuPage County, IL	904,152	929,192	25,040	2.8
46. Pinellas County, FL	921,495	917,437	-4,058	-0.4
47. Erie County, NY	950,265	913,338	-36,927	-3.9
49. Shelby County, TN	897,472	910,100	12,628	1.4
50. Honolulu County, HI	876,156	905,601	29,445	3.4
51. Fresno County, CA	799,407	899,348	99,941	12.5
52. Bergen County, NJ	884,118	895,744	11,626	1.3
53. Fairfield County, CT	882,567	895,015	12,448	1.4
54. Hartford County, CT	857,183	876,824	19,641	2.3
55. Marion County, IN	860,454	876,804	16,350	1.9
56. Mecklenburg County, NC	695,372	867,067	171,697	24.7
57. Duval County, FL	778,866	849,159	70,293	9.0
58. New Haven County, CT	824,008	845,494	21,486	2.6
59. Hamilton County, OH	845,303	842,369	-2,934	-0.3
60. Wake County, NC	627,846	832,970	205,124	32.7
61. Macomb County, MI	788,149	831,077	42,928	5.4
62. Prince George's County, MD	801,515	828,770	27,255	3.4
63. Ventura County, CA	753,195	798,364	45,169	6.0
64. Kern County, CA	661,645	790,710	129,055	19.5
65. Baltimore County, MD	754,292	788,994	34,702	4.6
66. Middlesex County, NJ	750,167	788,629	38,462	5.1
67. Worcester County, MA	749,973	781,352	31,379	4.2
68. Gwinnett County, GA	588,448	776,380	187,932	31.9
69. Montgomery County, PA	748,987	776,172	27,185	3.6
70. Essex County, NJ	792,305	776,087	-16,218	-2.0
71. Pierce County, WA	700,818	773,165	72,347	10.3
72. San Francisco County, CA	776,733	764,976	-11,757	-1.5
73. De Kalb County, GA	666,043	737,093	71,050	10.7
74. El Paso County, TX	679,622	734,669	55,047	8.1
75. Essex County, MA	723,419	733,101	9,682	1.3

Source: U.S. Bureau of the Census, *Cumulative Estimates of Population Change and County Rankings: April 1, 2000 to July 1, 2007*

The American People Today

The United States is the third most populous nation in the world, ranking behind only China and India. The population increased 7.2 percent from 2000 to 2007; it was estimated at 301,621,157 in 2007 and by July 2008 at 304,461,810. There were just under 250 million in 1990; the U.S. population has increased by more than 100 million since 1960, and has doubled since 1950.

The single most noteworthy characteristic of the U.S. population continues to be the "baby boom generation," the 75 million people born between 1946 and 1964. During these years the crude birth rate soared to as high as 24 live births per 1,000 population (compared to 20 or so in the years before World War II). Fertility rates, too, which had stood at about 75 live births per 1,000 women aged 15-44, jumped to as high as 121. As a result the population grew at an annual rate of between 1.4 percent and 1.8 percent.

The baby boom produced a generation of Americans much more populous than any other; the result has been that this generation attracts a great deal of attention as it passes through statistical age categories. Demographers sometimes refer to baby boomers, somewhat inelegantly perhaps, as the "pig in the python" in order to explain how this group has continued to distort the normal contours of the general body of the population. During the 1950's, their numbers required great capital outlays for new schools, and in the 1960's, for expanding colleges and universities. In the 1970's, they jammed the labor market causing higher unemployment rates, but helped the economy by increasing consumption and expanding the housing market.

The most troubling aspect of the 2000 Census is its stark revelation that the American population is very rapidly growing older. In 1970, 9.8 percent of the population was 65 or over; by 2000, 12.6 percent were. In 2030, the Census Bureau projects that fully 20 percent of Americans will 65 or over.

The impact of this change on the Social Security system cannot be taken seriously enough. In 2013, the first baby boomers turn 67 (the aging of the population has forced a deferral of the traditional retirement age from 65), and will begin collecting Social Security instead of paying into the fund. Ordinarily, this wouldn't be a remarkable fact. But the generation that followed the baby boom—the so-called baby bust generation, also known as generation X—was unusually small. By 1968 the population growth rate had sunk to 1.0 percent; the birth rate to fewer than 18 live births per 1,000 population, and fertility rates to about 85 live births per woman 15-44. As a result, the ratio of people working and paying into Social Security to those receiving payments will shrink dramatically. Today, that ratio is only 3.5-1, but by 2030 it will be closer to 2-1.

In the pages that follow, we have attempted to create a statistical portrait of the population. Note that the Census Bureau updates some information more often than every 10 years with annual population estimates.

THE CENSUS

Article I, section 2 of the U.S. Constitution requires Congress to undertake a census of the population every 10 years for the purpose of apportioning seats in the House of Representatives. Today the decennial census is also used to apportion federal and state funds totalling as much as $100 billion a year, so it is vitally important to local governments and individuals throughout the country. City and county planners, health care administrators, as well as the entire marketing and advertising industries are all strongly dependent on census data for their day-to-day operations. So it's not surprising that the 2000 census, officially taken on April 1, was the largest undertaking of its kind in our history.

▶ HIGHLIGHTS OF THE 2000 CENSUS

Population growth   The resident U.S. population grew from 248.7 million people in 1990 to 281.4 million in 2000. For the first time in the 20th century, every state gained population. The total increase (32.7 million) is the largest numerical increase ever between censuses, though by percentage of total population (13.1), it still ranks below the 28 million person jump caused by the baby boom between 1950 and 1960 (an 18.5 percent increase), and far below the 35.1 percent increase between 1790 and 1800.

State and regional growth   The greatest growth occurred in the West and South. The five fastest-growing states were all in the West: Nevada (which grew an astounding 66.3 percent since 1990), Arizona (40.0 percent), Colorado (30.6 percent), Utah (29.6 percent), and Idaho (28.5 percent). Overall, the West grew by 10.4 million people to a total of 63.2 million, or an increase of 19.7 percent. The South increased by 14.8 million, or 17.3 percent. Georgia was the fastest-growing state in the South, increasing by 26.4 percent.

The Midwest grew by 7.9 percent, while the Northeast experienced 5.5 percent growth. Minnesota, up 12.4 percent, was the fastest-growing state in the Midwest, while New Hampshire, which also grew by 12.4 percent, led the Northeast. The state with the lowest population growth was North Dakota, which increased only 0.5 percent. Still, that's a turnaround for the Peace Garden State, which lost 13,917 people between 1980 and 1990.

The center of U.S. population—the exact spot where an imaginary map of the U.S. would balance perfectly if all 281 million residents were of equal weight—was approximately 2.8 miles east of a town called Edgar Springs, Mo. This point is approximately 12.1 miles south and 32.5 miles west of Steelville, Mo., which was the 1990 center of population.

U.S. Resident Population and Population Change by State, 1990–2000

State	1990 Population	Rank	2000 Population	Rank	Change, 1990–2000 Number	Percent
United States	248,709,873	—	281,421,906	—	32,712,033	13.2%
Alabama	4,040,587	(22)	4,447,100	(23)	406,513	10.1
Alaska	550,043	(49)	626,932	(48)	76,889	14.0
Arizona	3,665,228	(24)	5,130,632	(20)	1,465,404	40.0
Arkansas	2,350,725	(33)	2,673,400	(33)	322,675	13.7
California	29,760,021	(1)	33,871,648	(1)	4,111,627	13.8
Colorado	3,294,394	(26)	4,301,261	(24)	1,006,867	30.6
Connecticut	3,287,116	(27)	3,405,565	(29)	118,449	3.6
Delaware	666,168	(46)	783,600	(45)	117,432	17.6
District of Columbia[1]	606,900	—	572,059	—	-34,841	-5.7
Florida	12,937,926	(4)	15,982,378	(4)	3,044,452	23.5
Georgia	6,478,216	(11)	8,186,453	(10)	1,708,237	26.4
Hawaii	1,108,229	(41)	1,211,537	(42)	103,308	9.3
Idaho	1,006,749	(42)	1,293,953	(39)	287,204	28.5
Illinois	11,430,602	(6)	12,419,293	(5)	988,691	8.6
Indiana	5,544,159	(14)	6,080,485	(14)	536,326	9.7
Iowa	2,776,755	(30)	2,926,324	(30)	149,569	5.4
Kansas	2,477,574	(32)	2,688,418	(32)	210,844	8.5
Kentucky	3,685,296	(23)	4,041,769	(25)	356,473	9.7
Louisiana	4,219,973	(21)	4,468,976	(22)	249,003	5.9
Maine	1,227,928	(38)	1,274,923	(40)	46,995	3.8
Maryland	4,781,468	(19)	5,296,486	(19)	515,018	10.8
Massachusetts	6,016,425	(13)	6,349,097	(13)	332,672	5.5
Michigan	9,295,297	(8)	9,938,444	(8)	643,147	6.9
Minnesota	4,375,099	(20)	4,919,479	(21)	544,380	12.4
Mississippi	2,573,216	(31)	2,844,658	(31)	271,442	10.5
Missouri	5,117,073	(15)	5,595,211	(17)	478,138	9.3
Montana	799,065	(44)	902,195	(44)	103,130	12.9
Nebraska	1,578,385	(36)	1,711,263	(38)	132,878	8.4
Nevada	1,201,833	(39)	1,998,257	(35)	796,424	66.3
New Hampshire	1,109,252	(40)	1,235,786	(41)	126,534	11.4
New Jersey	7,730,188	(9)	8,414,350	(9)	684,162	8.9
New Mexico	1,515,069	(37)	1,819,046	(36)	303,977	20.1
New York	17,990,455	(2)	18,976,457	(3)	986,002	5.5
North Carolina	6,628,637	(10)	8,049,313	(11)	1,420,676	21.4
North Dakota	638,800	(47)	642,200	(47)	3,400	0.5
Ohio	10,847,115	(7)	11,353,140	(7)	506,025	4.7
Oklahoma	3,145,585	(28)	3,450,654	(27)	305,069	9.7
Oregon	2,842,321	(29)	3,421,399	(28)	579,078	20.4
Pennsylvania	11,881,643	(5)	12,281,054	(6)	399,411	3.4
Rhode Island	1,003,464	(43)	1,048,319	(43)	44,855	4.5
South Carolina	3,486,703	(25)	4,012,012	(26)	525,309	15.1
South Dakota	696,004	(45)	754,844	(46)	58,840	8.5
Tennessee	4,877,185	(17)	5,689,283	(16)	812,098	16.7
Texas	16,986,510	(3)	20,851,820	(2)	3,865,310	22.8
Utah	1,722,850	(35)	2,233,169	(34)	510,319	29.6
Vermont	562,758	(48)	608,827	(49)	46,069	8.2
Virginia	6,187,358	(12)	7,078,515	(12)	891,157	14.4
Washington	4,866,692	(18)	5,894,121	(15)	1,027,429	21.1
West Virginia	1,793,477	(34)	1,808,344	(37)	14,867	0.8
Wisconsin	4,891,769	(16)	5,363,675	(18)	471,906	9.6
Wyoming	453,588	(50)	493,782	(50)	40,194	8.9

1. If the District of Columbia were included with the states, it would have ranked 48th in 1990 and 49th in 2000.
Source: U.S. Bureau of the Census, 2001.

Congressional representation Because each state's number of representatives in Congress is based on its population, the population shift to the South and West brought with it a corresponding shift in representation. A total of eight states gained representatives (four of them gained two), while 10 states lost representatives (two states lost two each). States cannot have fewer than one representative, so even though North Dakota experienced a much lower growth rate than New York, it did not lose its sole member of Congress, whereas New York lost two representatives.

Gainers		Losers	
Arizona	+2	New York	-2
Florida	+2	Pennsylvania	-2
Georgia	+2	Connecticut	-1
Texas	+2	Illinois	-1
California	+1	Indiana	-1
Colorado	+1	Michigan	-1
Nevada	+1	Mississippi	-1
Norh Carolina	+1	Ohio	-1
		Oklahoma	-1
		Wisconsin	-1

State, Urban, and Rural Percentage of Land Area and Population, 1990–2000

State	Sq. miles	Land area, 2000 Urban	Rural	Population 1990 Urban	Rural	2000 Urban	Rural
U.S. total	3,620,501	2.5%	97.5%	75.2%	24.8%	79.0%	21.0%
Alabama	50,753	6.3	93.7	60.4	39.6	55.4	44.5
Alaska	570,374	0.2	99.8	67.5	32.5	65.6	34.4
Arizona	113,609	2.5	97.5	87.5	12.5	88.2	11.8
Arkansas	52,079	2.2	97.8	53.5	46.5	52.5	47.5
California	156,062	6.0	94.0	92.6	7.4	94.4	5.6
Colorado	103,729	1.7	98.3	82.4	17.6	84.5	15.5
Connecticut	4,844	32.1	67.9	79.1	20.9	87.7	12.3
Delaware	1,978	14.1	85.9	73.0	27.0	80.1	19.9
District of Columbia	61.4	100.0	0.0	100.0	0.0	100.0	0
Florida	59,120	21.8	78.2	84.8	15.2	89.3	10.7
Georgia	58,051	6.3	93.7	63.2	36.8	71.6	28.4
Hawaii	6,425	4.1	95.9	89.0	11.0	91.5	8.5
Idaho	82,752	2.8	97.2	57.4	42.6	66.4	33.5
Illinois	55,588	7.4	92.6	84.6	15.4	87.8	12.2
Indiana	36,097	5.8	94.2	64.9	35.1	70.8	29.2
Iowa	57,853	1.9	98.1	60.6	39.4	61.1	38.9
Kansas	81,822	1.4	98.6	69.1	30.9	71.4	28.6
Kentucky	39,733	3.5	98.1	51.8	48.2	55.8	44.2
Louisiana	43,026	3.7	96.3	68.1	31.9	72.6	27.4
Maine	30,685	1.6	98.4	44.6	55.4	40.2	59.8
Maryland	9,833	17.5	82.5	81.3	18.7	86.1	13.9
Massachusetts	7,839	38.9	61.1	84.3	15.7	91.4	8.6
Michigan	56,804	6.3	93.7	70.5	29.5	74.7	25.3
Minnesota	79,617	2.3	97.7	69.9	30.1	70.9	29.1
Mississippi	46,918	2.5	97.5	47.1	52.9	48.8	51.2
Missouri	68,898	3.2	96.8	68.7	31.3	69.4	30.6
Montana	145,556	0.2	99.8	52.5	47.5	54.1	45.9
Nebraska	76,878	0.6	99.4	66.1	33.9	69.8	30.3
Nevada	109,806	0.8	99.2	88.3	11.7	91.5	8.5
New Hampshire	8,970	5.2	94.8	51.0	49.0	59.3	40.7
New Jersey	7,419	32.1	67.9	89.4	10.6	94.4	5.6
New Mexico	121,577	0.4	99.6	73.0	27.0	75.0	25.1
New York	47,224	11.6	88.4	84.3	15.7	87.5	12.5
North Carolina	48,715	6.6	93.4	50.4	49.6	60.2	39.8
North Dakota	68,994	0.3	99.7	53.3	46.7	55.9	44.1
Ohio	40,953	10.9	89.1	74.1	25.9	77.4	22.6
Oklahoma	68,680	2.7	97.3	67.7	32.3	65.3	34.7
Oregon	95,997	1.0	99.0	70.5	29.5	78.7	21.3
Pennsylvania	44,820	8.7	91.3	68.9	31.1	77.1	22.9
Rhode Island	1,045	50.5	49.5	86.0	14.0	90.9	9.1
South Carolina	30,111	4.7	93.4	54.6	45.4	60.5	39.5
South Dakota	75,898	0.3	99.7	50.0	50.0	51.9	48.1
Tennessee	41,219	6.6	93.4	60.9	39.1	63.6	36.4
Texas	261,914	3.4	96.6	80.3	19.7	82.5	17.5
Utah	82,168	1.1	98.9	87.0	13.0	88.2	11.8
Vermont	1,149	2.5	97.5	32.2	67.8	38.2	61.7
Virginia	39,598	6.3	93.7	69.4	30.6	73.0	27.0
Washington	66,581	3.3	96.7	76.4	23.6	82.0	18.0
West Virginia	24,664	1.8	98.2	36.1	63.9	46.1	54.0
Wisconsin	138,971	1.5	98.5	65.7	34.3	68.3	31.7
Wyoming	97,105	0.5	99.5	65.0	35.0	65.1	34.8

Source: U.S. Bureau of the Census, 2002.

Since 1960, California's representatives have increased from 38 to 53, Florida's have more than doubled from 12 to 25, and Texas's have grown from 23 to 32. Over the same period, New York lost a total of 12 representatives while Illinois has lost 5.

Urban and rural population growth Since the 1920 census, more than one half of all Americans have lived in an urban area, which can be loosely defined as a place of 2,500 or more inhabitants. During the 1990's, the population of urban areas grew by 35 million people, from 187.1 to 222.3 million people, an increase of 19 percent. By 2000, the proportion of the U.S. population living in urban areas reached 79.0 percent, up from 75.2 percent in 1990. California and New Jersey had the highest proportion of urban population, at 94.4 percent each. In comparison, the country's rural population shrank by 2.6 percent, from 61.7 million in 1990 to 59.1 million in 2000. Vermont had the highest rural percentage of population: 61.7 percent, down from 67.8 percent in 1990.

U.S. Population by State, 1790–1990

State	1790	1800	1810	1820	1830	1840	1850
Total U.S.	3,929,214	5,308,483	7,239,881	9,638,453	12,860,702	17,063,353	23,191,876
Alabama	—	1,250	9,046	127,901	309,527	590,756	771,623
Alaska	—	—	—	—	—	—	—
Arizona	—	—	—	—	—	—	—
Arkansas	—	—	1,062	14,273	30,388	97,574	209,897
California	—	—	—	—	—	—	92,597
Colorado	—	—	—	—	—	—	—
Connecticut	237,946	251,002	261,942	275,248	297,675	309,978	370,792
Delaware	59,096	64,273	72,674	72,749	76,748	78,085	91,532
District of Columbia	—	8,144	15,471	23,336	30,261	33,745	51,687
Florida	—	—	—	—	34,730	54,477	87,445
Georgia	82,548	162,686	252,433	340,989	516,823	691,392	906,185
Hawaii	—	—	—	—	—	—	—
Idaho	—	—	—	—	—	—	—
Illinois	—	—	12,282	55,211	157,445	476,183	851,470
Indiana	—	5,641	24,520	147,178	343,031	685,866	988,416
Iowa	—	—	—	—	—	43,112	192,214
Kansas	—	—	—	—	—	—	—
Kentucky	73,677	220,955	406,511	564,317	687,917	779,828	982,405
Louisiana	—	—	76,556	153,407	215,739	352,411	517,762
Maine	96,540	151,719	228,705	298,335	399,455	501,793	583,169
Maryland	319,728	341,548	380,546	407,350	447,040	470,019	583,034
Massachusetts	378,787	422,845	472,040	523,287	610,408	737,699	994,514
Michigan	—	—	4,762	8,896	31,369	212,267	397,654
Minnesota	—	—	—	—	—	—	6,077
Mississippi	—	7,600	31,306	75,448	136,621	375,651	606,526
Missouri	—	—	19,783	66,586	140,455	383,702	682,044
Montana	—	—	—	—	—	—	—
Nebraska	—	—	—	—	—	—	—
Nevada	—	—	—	—	—	—	—
New Hampshire	141,885	183,858	214,460	244,161	269,328	284,574	317,976
New Jersey	184,139	211,149	245,562	277,575	320,823	373,306	489,555
New Mexico	—	—	—	—	—	—	61,547
New York	340,120	589,051	959,049	1,372,812	1,918,608	2,428,921	3,097,394
North Carolina	393,751	478,103	555,500	638,829	737,987	753,419	869,039
North Dakota	—	—	—	—	—	—	—
Ohio	—	45,365	230,760	581,434	937,903	1,519,467	1,980,329
Oklahoma	—	—	—	—	—	—	—
Oregon	—	—	—	—	—	—	12,093
Pennsylvania	434,373	602,365	810,091	1,049,458	1,348,233	1,724,033	2,311,786
Rhode Island	68,825	69,122	76,931	83,059	97,199	108,830	147,545
South Carolina	249,073	345,591	415,115	502,741	581,185	594,398	668,507
South Dakota	—	—	—	—	—	—	—
Tennessee	35,691	105,602	261,727	422,832	681,904	829,210	1,002,717
Texas	—	—	—	—	—	—	212,592
Utah	—	—	—	—	—	—	11,380
Vermont	85,425	154,465	217,895	235,981	280,652	291,948	314,120
Virginia[2]	747,610	880,200	974,600	1,065,366	1,211,405	1,239,797	1,421,661
Washington	—	—	—	—	—	—	1,201
West Virginia	—	—	—	—	—	—	—
Wisconsin	—	—	—	—	—	30,945	305,391
Wyoming	—	—	—	—	—	—	—

Population growth in metropolitan areas

The 2000 census revealed that more than 80 percent of all U.S. residents (226.0 million) lived in metropolitan areas, while just under 30 percent (84.1 million) lived in metro areas of 5 million people or more. Areas with populations between 2.0 million and 5.0 million grew the fastest: they increased by a total of 20 percent. Metro areas with more than 1 million but fewer than 2 million people grew by 17.7 percent. Nonmetropolitan areas grew slowest: a total of 10.2 percent between 1990 and 2000. That's better than the previous decade, however, when nonmetropolitan areas grew by only 3.9 percent.

The 10 fastest-growing metropolitan areas were all in the South or the West. Las Vegas, which leaped from 852,737 to 1.5 million, grew by an astounding 83.3 percent. Naples, Fla. was second, with 65.3 percent growth. Yuma, Ariz. (49.7), McAllen-Edinburg Mission, Texas (48.5) and Austin-San Marcos, Texas (47.7) rounded out the top five.

Race and Hispanic origin

Since 1960, each Census has approached the issue of race in slightly different ways. The most important change for the 2000 Census was the ability of respondents to classify themselves as members of more than one race. In previous censuses, someone who was part black and part white had to choose one race or the other on Census forms. For the 2000 Census, however, people with more than

State	1860	1870	1880	1890	1900	1910	1920
Total U.S.	31,443,321	38,558,371	50,189,209	62,979,766	76,212,168	92,228,496	106,021,537
Alabama	964,201	996,992	1,262,505	1,513,401	1,828,697	2,138,093	2,348,174
Alaska	—	—	33,426	32,052	63,592	64,356	55,036
Arizona	—	9,658	40,440	88,243	122,931	204,354	334,162
Arkansas	435,450	484,471	802,525	1,128,211	1,311,564	1,574,449	1,752,204
California	379,994	560,247	864,694	1,213,396	1,485,053	2,377,549	3,426,861
Colorado	34,277	39,864	194,327	413,249	539,700	799,024	939,629
Connecticut	460,147	537,454	622,700	746,258	908,420	1,114,756	1,380,631
Delaware	112,216	125,015	146,608	168,493	184,735	202,322	223,003
District of Columbia	75,080	131,700	177,624	230,392	278,718	331,069	437,571
Florida	140,424	187,748	269,493	391,422	528,542	752,619	968,470
Georgia	1,057,286	1,184,109	1,542,180	1,837,353	2,216,331	2,609,121	2,895,832
Hawaii	—	—	—	—	154,001	191,874	255,881
Idaho	—	14,999	32,610	88,548	161,772	325,594	431,866
Illinois	1,711,951	2,539,891	3,077,871	3,826,352	4,821,550	5,638,591	6,485,280
Indiana	1,350,428	1,680,637	1,978,301	2,192,404	2,516,462	2,700,876	2,930,390
Iowa	674,913	1,194,020	1,624,615	1,912,297	2,231,853	2,224,771	2,404,021
Kansas	107,206	364,399	996,096	1,428,108	1,470,495	1,690,949	1,769,257
Kentucky	1,155,684	1,321,011	1,648,690	1,858,635	2,147,174	2,289,905	2,416,630
Louisiana	708,002	726,915	939,946	1,118,588	1,381,625	1,656,388	1,798,509
Maine	628,279	626,915	648,936	661,086	694,466	742,371	768,014
Maryland	687,049	780,894	934,943	1,042,390	1,188,044	1,295,346	1,449,661
Massachusetts	1,231,066	1,457,351	1,783,085	2,238,947	2,805,346	3,366,416	3,852,356
Michigan	749,113	1,184,059	1,636,937	2,093,890	2,420,982	2,810,173	3,668,412
Minnesota	172,023	439,706	780,773	1,310,283	1,751,394	2,075,708	2,387,125
Mississippi	791,305	827,922	1,131,597	1,289,600	1,551,270	1,797,114	1,790,618
Missouri	1,182,012	1,721,295	2,168,380	2,679,185	3,106,665	3,293,335	3,404,055
Montana	—	20,595	39,159	142,924	243,329	376,053	548,889
Nebraska	28,841	122,993	452,402	1,062,656	1,066,300	1,192,214	1,296,372
Nevada	6,857	42,491	62,266	47,355	42,335	81,875	77,407
New Hampshire	326,073	318,300	346,991	376,530	411,588	430,572	443,083
New Jersey	672,035	906,096	1,131,116	1,444,933	1,883,669	2,537,167	3,155,900
New Mexico	93,516	91,874	119,565	160,282	195,310	327,301	360,350
New York	3,880,735	4,382,759	5,082,871	6,003,174	7,268,894	9,113,614	10,385,227
North Carolina	992,622	1,071,361	1,399,750	1,617,949	1,893,810	2,206,287	2,559,123
North Dakota	—	2,405	36,909	190,983	319,146	577,056	646,872
Ohio	2,339,511	2,665,260	3,198,062	3,672,329	4,157,545	4,767,121	5,759,394
Oklahoma	—	—	—	258,657	790,371	1,657,155	2,028,283
Oregon	52,465	90,923	174,768	317,704	413,536	672,765	783,389
Pennsylvania	2,906,215	3,521,951	4,282,891	5,258,113	6,302,115	7,665,111	8,720,017
Rhode Island	174,620	217,353	276,531	345,506	428,556	542,610	604,397
South Carolina	703,708	705,606	995,577	1,151,149	1,340,316	1,515,400	1,683,724
South Dakota	4,837	11,776	98,268	348,600	401,570	583,888	636,547
Tennessee	1,109,801	1,258,520	1,542,359	1,767,518	2,020,616	2,184,789	2,337,885
Texas	604,215	818,579	1,591,749	2,235,527	3,048,710	3,896,542	4,663,228
Utah	40,273	86,786	143,963	210,779	276,749	373,351	449,396
Vermont	315,098	330,551	332,286	332,422	343,641	355,956	352,428
Virginia[2]	1,596,318	1,225,163	1,512,565	1,655,980	1,854,184	2,061,612	2,309,187
Washington	11,594	23,955	75,116	357,232	518,103	1,141,990	1,356,621
West Virginia	—	442,014	618,457	762,794	958,800	1,221,119	1,463,701
Wisconsin	775,881	1,054,670	1,315,497	1,693,330	2,069,042	2,333,860	2,632,067
Wyoming	—	9,118	20,789	62,555	92,531	145,965	194,402

one race in their heritage were permitted to identify all their racial backgrounds. More than 6.8 million people identified themselves as being of more than one race. Because it is impossible to know how people of more than one race identified themselves in the past, racial data from the 2000 Census is not strictly comparable with those from previous censuses.

The United States remains overwhelmingly white, though less so than in the past. There were 211 million white people in the U.S. in 2000, and 5 million more who were white and at least one other race. The white-only population was 75.1 percent of the total U.S. population in 2000, down from 80.3 percent 10 years earlier. In 1970, the white population of the U.S. was 87.5 percent of the total.

The black-only population was 34.7 million in 2000, up from just under 30 million in 1990. An-

other 1.8 million people were black and at least one other race. The black-only population is 12.3 percent of the total, up slightly from 12.1 in 1990 and 11.1 percent in 1970.

The Asian population increased from 6.9 million in 1990 to 10.2 million (Asian-only) in 2000. Another 1.6 million people considered themselves Asian and at least one other race. The Asian-only population represented 3.6 percent of the total, up from 2.8 in 1990. For 2000, the Census Bureau separated out Native Hawaiian and other Pacific Islander from the Asian population for the first time.

People of Hispanic origin may be of any race. Hispanics or Latinos continue to be the fastest-growing segment of the population, primarily because of immigration and high birth rates. The Hispanic or Latino population grew 53 percent between 1980 and 1990 and another 58 percent

State	1930	1940	1950	1960	1970	1980[1]	1990
Total U.S.	123,202,624	132,164,569	151,325,798	179,323,175	203,302,031	226,542,203	248,709,873
Alabama	2,646,248	2,832,961	3,061,743	3,266,740	3,444,354	3,894,025	4,040,587
Alaska	59,278	72,524	128,643	226,167	302,583	401,851	550,043
Arizona	435,573	499,261	749,587	1,302,161	1,775,399	2,716,546	3,665,228
Arkansas	1,854,482	1,949,387	1,909,511	1,786,272	1,923,322	2,286,357	2,350,725
California	5,677,251	6,907,387	10,586,223	15,717,204	19,971,069	23,667,764	29,760,021
Colorado	1,035,791	1,123,296	1,325,089	1,753,947	2,209,596	2,889,735	3,294,394
Connecticut	1,606,903	1,709,242	2,007,280	2,535,234	3,032,217	3,107,564	3,287,116
Delaware	238,380	266,505	318,085	446,292	548,104	594,338	666,168
District of Columbia	486,869	663,091	802,178	763,956	756,668	638,432	606,900
Florida	1,468,211	1,897,414	2,771,305	4,951,560	6,791,418	9,746,961	12,937,926
Georgia	2,908,506	3,123,723	3,444,578	3,943,116	4,587,930	5,462,982	6,478,216
Hawaii	368,300	422,770	499,794	632,772	769,913	964,691	1,108,229
Idaho	445,032	524,873	588,637	667,191	713,015	944,127	1,006,749
Illinois	7,630,654	7,897,241	8,712,176	10,081,158	11,110,285	11,427,409	11,430,602
Indiana	3,238,503	3,427,796	3,934,224	4,662,498	5,195,392	5,490,214	5,544,159
Iowa	2,470,939	2,538,268	2,621,073	2,757,537	2,825,368	2,913,808	2,776,755
Kansas	1,880,999	1,801,028	1,905,299	2,178,611	2,249,071	2,364,236	2,477,574
Kentucky	2,614,589	2,845,627	2,944,806	3,038,156	3,220,711	3,660,324	3,685,296
Louisiana	2,101,593	2,363,880	2,683,516	3,257,022	3,644,637	4,206,116	4,219,973
Maine	797,423	847,226	913,774	969,265	993,722	1,125,043	1,227,928
Maryland	1,631,526	1,821,244	2,343,001	3,100,689	3,923,897	4,216,933	4,781,468
Massachusetts	4,249,614	4,316,721	4,690,514	5,148,578	5,689,170	5,737,093	6,016,425
Michigan	4,842,325	5,256,106	6,371,766	7,823,194	8,881,826	9,262,044	9,295,297
Minnesota	2,563,953	2,792,300	2,982,483	3,413,864	3,806,103	4,075,970	4,375,099
Mississippi	2,009,821	2,183,796	2,178,914	2,178,141	2,216,994	2,520,770	2,573,216
Missouri	3,629,367	3,784,664	3,954,653	4,319,813	4,677,623	4,916,762	5,117,073
Montana	537,606	559,456	591,024	674,767	694,409	786,690	799,065
Nebraska	1,377,963	1,315,834	1,325,510	1,411,330	1,485,333	1,569,825	1,578,385
Nevada	91,058	110,247	160,083	285,278	488,738	800,508	1,201,833
New Hampshire	465,293	491,524	533,242	606,921	737,681	920,610	1,109,252
New Jersey	4,041,334	4,160,165	4,835,329	6,066,782	7,171,112	7,365,011	7,730,188
New Mexico	423,317	531,818	681,187	951,023	1,017,055	1,303,302	1,515,069
New York	12,588,066	13,479,142	14,830,192	16,782,304	18,241,391	17,558,165	17,990,455
North Carolina	3,170,276	3,571,623	4,061,929	4,556,155	5,084,411	5,880,095	6,628,637
North Dakota	680,845	641,935	619,636	632,446	617,792	652,717	638,800
Ohio	6,646,697	6,907,612	7,946,627	9,706,397	10,657,423	10,797,603	10,847,115
Oklahoma	2,396,040	2,336,434	2,233,351	2,328,284	2,559,463	3,025,487	3,145,585
Oregon	953,786	1,089,684	1,521,341	1,760,687	2,091,533	2,633,156	2,842,321
Pennsylvania	9,631,350	9,900,180	10,498,012	11,319,366	11,800,766	11,864,720	11,881,643
Rhode Island	687,497	713,346	791,896	859,488	949,723	947,154	1,003,464
South Carolina	1,738,765	1,899,804	2,117,027	2,382,594	2,590,713	3,120,729	3,486,703
South Dakota	692,849	642,961	652,740	680,514	666,257	690,768	696,004
Tennessee	2,616,556	2,915,841	3,291,718	3,567,089	3,926,018	4,591,023	4,877,185
Texas	5,824,715	6,414,824	7,711,194	9,579,677	11,198,655	14,225,513	16,986,510
Utah	507,847	550,310	688,862	890,627	1,059,273	1,461,037	1,722,850
Vermont	359,611	359,231	377,747	389,881	444,732	511,456	562,758
Virginia	2,421,851	2,677,773	3,318,680	3,966,949	4,651,448	5,346,797	6,187,358
Washington	1,563,396	1,736,191	2,378,963	2,853,214	3,413,244	4,132,353	4,866,692
West Virginia	1,729,205	1,901,974	2,005,552	1,860,421	1,744,237	1,950,186	1,793,477
Wisconsin	2,939,006	3,137,587	3,434,575	3,951,777	4,417,821	4,705,642	4,891,769
Wyoming	225,565	250,742	290,529	330,066	332,416	469,557	453,588

Note: Excludes military and overseas population. Wherever possible, 1980 state boundaries are used in calculating populations of regions, areas, and territories prior to their statehoods. 1. 1980 figures are revised estimates issued by the Census Bureau in 1987. 2. The figures for Virginia through 1860 are from the 1960 census; in the 1980 summary, the Census Bureau gave separate figures for West Virginia between 1790 and 1860, even though it did not become a state until 1863. Since the result diminishes Virginia's population by over 300,000 in 1850 and 1860, a crucial period, we decided to keep the earlier breakdowns. **Sources:** U.S. Bureau of the Census, 1980 Census of Population: U.S. Summary, Number of Inhabitants (1981), and Release (1990).

between 1990 and 2000. Hispanics now make up 12.5 percent of the U.S. population, up from 9.0 percent in 1990 and 6.4 percent in 1980.

Undercounting the U.S. population in the 1990 and 2000 Censuses

The Census Bureau estimates it undercounted the original 1990 Census by about 1.6 percent nationwide. The Bureau concluded that it failed to enumerate 8 million people, and double-counted about 4 million others. That's a net difference of

just over 4 million people, or a little more than the population within the Los Angeles city limits.

To prevent this problem in the 2000 Census, the Bureau planned to use statistical sampling methods to enumerate the hardest-to-count 10 percent of the population, and to conduct a follow-up survey of 750,000 households, which would point out inaccuracies in the initial count. But because census numbers are used to apportion Congressional districts and because blacks and Hispanics (who tend to vote Democratic) made up a significant

Portrait of the U.S. Population, April 1, 2000

Characteristic	Number	Percent
Total population	**281,421,906**	**100.0%**
SEX		
Male	138,053,563	49.1
Female	143,368,343	50.9
AGE		
Under 18 years	6,042,435	2.1
18 years and over	209,128,094	74.3
21 years and over	196,899,193	70.0
65 years and over	34,991,753	12.4
Median age	35.3	—
RACE		
One race, total	274,595,678	97.6
White only	211,460,626	75.1
Black only	34,658,190	12.3
American Indian and Alaska Native only	2,475,956	0.9
Asian only	10,242,998	3.6
Native Hawaiian and other Pacific Islander only	398,835	0.1
Other race	15,359,073	5.5
Two or more races, total	6,826,228	2.4
Hispanic or Latino (of any race)	35,305,818	12.5
HOUSEHOLD TYPE		
Total households	**105,480,101**	**100.0%**
Family households (families)	71,787,347	68.1
With own children under 18 years	34,588,368	32.8
Married-couple family	54,493,232	51.7
With own children under 18 years	24,835,505	23.5
Female householder[1]	12,900,103	12.2
With own children under 18 years	7,561,874	7.2
Nonfamily households	33,692,754	31.9
Householder living alone	27,230,075	25.8
65 years and over	9,722,857	9.2
Average household size (people)	2.59	—
Average family size (people)	3.14	—
HOUSING OCCUPANCY		
Total housing units	**115,904,641**	**100.0%**
Occupied housing units	105,480,101	91.0
Vacant housing units	10,424,540	9.0
For seasonal, recreational or occasional use	3,578,718	3.1
Homeowner vacancy rate (percent)		1.7
Rental vacancy rate (percent)		6.8
HOUSING TENURE		
Occupied housing units	**105,480,101**	**100.0%**
Owner-occupied	69,815,753	66.2
Renter-occupied	35,664,348	33.8

Note: 1. No husband present. Source: U.S. Bureau of the Census, 2001

U.S. Population by Region, 1990–2000

Region	1990 Census	2000 Census
United States	**248,790,925**	**281,421,906**
Northeast	**50,828,313**	**53,594,378**
New England	13,206,943	13,922,517
Middle Atlantic	37,621,370	39,671,861
Midwest	**59,669,320**	**64,392,776**
East North Central	42,009,114	45,155,037
West North Central	17,660,206	19,237,739
South	**85,455,793**	**100,236,820**
South Atlantic	43,571,473	51,769,160
East South Central	15,179,959	17,022,810
West South Central	26,704,361	31,444,850
West	**52,837,499**	**63,197,932**
Mountain	13,658,794	18,172,295
Pacific	39,178,705	45,025,637

Source: U.S. Census Bureau.

Population Growth by Region, 1790–2000 (in thousands)

Year	Northeast	Midwest[1]	South[2]	West
1790	1,968	N.A.	1,961	N.A.
1800	2,636	51	2,622	N.A.
1810	3,487	292	3,461	N.A.
1820	4,360	859	4,419	N.A.
1830	5,542	1,610	5,708	N.A.
1840	6,761	3,352	6,951	N.A.
1850	8,627	5,404	8,983	179
1860	10,594	9,097	11,133	619
1870	12,299	12,981	12,288	991
1880	14,507	17,364	16,517	1,801
1890	17,407	22,410	20,028	3,134
1900	21,047	26,333	24,524	4,309
1910	25,869	29,889	29,389	7,082
1920	29,662	34,020	33,126	9,214
1930	34,427	38,594	37,858	12,324
1940	35,977	40,143	41,666	14,379
1950	39,478	44,461	47,197	20,190
1960	44,678	51,619	54,973	28,053
1970	49,041	56,572	62,795	34,804
1980	49,135	58,866	75,372	43,172
1990	50,809	59,669	85,446	52,786
2000	53,594	64,393	100,237	63,198

Note: 1. Called North Central prior to 1980. 2. Includes black slave population through 1860.
Source: U.S. Bureau of Census, *The Statistical History of the U.S.* (1976) and 2000 Census of the U.S. www.census.gov.

jected the Clinton administration's appeal of the decision.

As a result, the Census Bureau had to spend an additional $1.7 billion (over the $5 billion budgeted) to count each and every person in 2000, even those who didn't want to cooperate with pollsters; because of this additional cost, the size of the follow-up survey had to be cut to 314,000 interviews. By comparing this survey with results from traditional census-taking methods, the Census Bureau estimated in early 2001 that at least 6.4 million people were not counted in the 2000 census and at least 3.1 million were counted twice. The undercount rate of aproximately 1.2 percent was better than the 1.6 percent undercount in 1990, but controversy over the uncounted millions continued throughout 2001. In March 2001, the Census Bureau announced that it would recommend the use of unadjusted numbers for re-

portion of the 1990 undercount, Republicans in Congress challenged the plan, fearing that an accurate count of the country's minorities would erode GOP numbers. In August 1998 a federal court struck down the use of sampling, saying it violated 1957 and 1976 federal laws governing the census, and in July 1999 the Supreme Court re-

U.S. Population, Population Density, and Area of Residence, 1790–2000

Year	Total population	Percent increase	Population per square mile	Percent urban	Percent rural
1790	3,929,214	N.A.	4.5	5.1%	94.9%
1800	5,308,483	35.1%	6.1	6.1	93.9
1810	7,239,881	36.4	4.3	7.3	92.7
1820	9,638,453	33.1	5.5	7.2	92.8
1830	12,866,020	33.5	7.4	8.8	91.2
1840	17,069,453	32.7	9.8	10.8	89.2
1850	23,191,876	35.9	7.9	15.3	84.7
1860	31,443,321	35.6	10.6	19.8	80.2
1870	39,818,449	26.6	13.4	25.7	74.3
1880	50,155,783	26.0	16.9	28.2	71.8
1890	62,947,714	25.5	21.2	35.1	64.9
1900	75,994,575	20.7	25.6	39.6	60.4
1910	91,972,266	21.0	31.0	45.6	54.4
1920	105,710,620	14.9	35.6	51.2	48.8
1930	122,775,046	16.1	41.2	56.1	43.9
1940	131,669,275	7.2	44.2	56.5	43.5
1950	150,697,361	14.5	50.7	64.0	36.0
1960	179,323,175	18.5	50.6	69.9	30.1
1970	203,302,031	13.4	57.4	73.5	26.5
1980	226,542,199	11.4	64.0	73.7	26.3
1990	248,718,302	9.8	70.3	75.2	24.8
2000	281,421,906	13.1	79.6	79.0	21.0

Note: Figures for 1980, 1990, and 2000 Censuses have been revised since publication. Source: U.S. Bureau of Census, *The Statistical History of the U.S.* (1976); *The Statistical Abstract of the United States* (annual).

drawing Congressional districts; several large cities planned to sue for the release of detailed data about regional and local undercounts, and debates over the use of adjusted census figures for allocation of other federal and state resources continued throughout the year.
Source: U.S. Bureau of the Census Executive Steering Committee for Accuracy and Coverage Evaluation Policy; www.census.gov.

U.S. POPULATION BY RACE AND HISPANIC ORIGIN

It is important to note that the Census Bureau's classification of the population by race, in its words, "reflects common usage not an attempt to define biological stock." Only since 1960, however, have the Census Bureau's race figures been based on self-identification, and only since 1980 has the Bureau reported statistics on Native Americans, Asians and persons of Hispanic origin.

The people of the United States are predominantly white, accounting for an estimated 80.1 percent of the total population in 2006—continuing a downward trend from 84.1 percent in the 1990 census and 81.1 in 2000. This dominance has been true since colonial days, although even then the indigenous peoples and the African slaves were significant racial minorities. In fact as slave labor became essential to the Southern economy so many slaves were brought here that just before the Civil War blacks constituted 15 percent of the U.S. population.

After the war, the proportion of whites rapidly increased as millions of immigrants from northern Europe settled throughout the country. The relentless movement of the population westward deprived the Native Americans of their lands and—with the assistance of several bloody wars—helped to reduce their numbers to a small fraction of what they were estimated to have been only a century before.

The black population, which represented between 9 and 12 percent of the total for many decades, remained the only significant minority group until the 1960's, when a surge of new immigrants from Puerto Rico, Mexico and Cuba made the Hispanic presence felt. So rapid and strong an impression did these groups make that the Census Bureau created a new population category, "Hispanic Origin." Since some Hispanics are black, some white, and still others Indian, this designation has nothing to do with race.

During the 1970's and 1980's, the arrival of several million Asians again caused a noticeable change in the composition of the population. The 1990 census was the first one to include a separate category for Asians and Pacific Islanders; in previous years, they had been included together with American Indians, Aleuts and Eskimos in the "other races" grouping.

The 2000 Census took an even more expansive approach. For the first time, it allowed people to identify themselves by more than one race. Although the vast majority of Americans (97.6 percent) still consider themselves of one race, a total of 6.8 million people said they were members of two or more races (2.4 percent). The most common mix was white and American Indian or Alaska Native; just over a million people identified themselves as such. Another 868,395 said they were a mix of white and Asian, and 784,764 said they were white and black or African-American. Another 2.2 million people said they were white and some other race. A total of 410,285 people identified themselves as members of three races, 38,408 said they were of four races, 8,637 were of five races, and 823 people were of six races.

The 2000 Census was also the first to separate out "Native Hawaiian and Other Pacific Islander" from the Asian category. This new category includes people who indicated their races as Guamanian, Chamorro, Samoan, Tahitian, Mariana Islander or Chuukese. The 2000 Census also included an "Other race" category, which includes people who did not identify their race, or who wrote in races such as Moroccan, South African or Belizean. This category also includes people who wrote in a Hispanic origin (e.g. Mexican, Cuban) instead of a race.

As a result of the expanded race categories, data from the 2000 Census is not directly comparable with information from previous censuses. Wherever possible, we have tried to provide two sets of race statistics for 2000: a) those who consider themselves members only of the race (i.e. white only or black only) and b) the aforementioned members of the race plus those who consider themselves members of the race and at least one other race as well

(i.e. white and Asian, or black and Native American). We have also tried to provide more recent population estimates where they are available.

▶THE BLACK POPULATION

Ever since the Founding Fathers reached their famous "compromise" declaring a slave the equivalent of three-fifths of a person, the black population has had a less-than-equal standing in relation to the majority of Americans. Over the last two centuries, the struggle for equality, even in a nation pledged to that ideal, has proven long, hard, and in many cases, intractable, as so many contemporary facts and figures in this book make all too evident. From higher infant mortality rates and poverty rates to lower life expectancy and family income levels, the black population continues to suffer the effects of two centuries of slavery and one of institutionalized segregation.

Resident Population of the U.S., by Race and Hispanic Origin, 1990–2000

The 2000 Census was the first to allow people to identify themselves as of more than one race. In the table below, the fourth and fifth columns include people who described themeselves only as the race shown. The last two columns includes all of those people, as well as people who described themselves as the race indicated, in addition to at

least one other race. For example, 10.2 million Americans described themeselves as Asian alone, but an additional 1.7 million described themselves as part Asian and part some other race. Thus, a total of 11.9 million people may be considered at least partly Asian. Note that persons of Hispanic origin may be of any race.

Race/ Hispanic origin	1990 Number	1990 Percent	2000 Race shown only	2000 Percent	2000 Race shown alone or in combination with other race(s)	2000 Percent
Total population	248,709,873	100.0%	281,421,906	100.0%	281,421,906	100.0%
White	199,686,070	80.3	211,460,626	75.1	216,930,975	77.1
Black (African-American)	29,986,060	12.1	34,658,190	12.3	36,419,434	12.9
American Indian and Alaska Native	1,959,234	0.8	2,475,956	0.9	4,119,301	1.5
Asian	6,908,638	2.8	10,242,998	3.6	11,898,828	4.2
Native Hawaiian and other Pacific Islander	365,024	0.1	398,835	0.1	874,414	0.3
Other race	9,804,847	3.9	15,359,073	5.5	18,521,486	6.6
Two or more races	N.A.	N.A.	6,826,228	2.4	N.A.	N.A.
Hispanic origin[1]	22,354,059	9.0	35,305,818	12.5	35,305,818	12.5

Note: 1. Persons of Hispanic origin may be of any race. **Source:** U.S. Bureau of the Census.

Change in the Resident Population, by Race and Hispanic Origin, 1980–2000

Race/ Hispanic origin	Change, 1980–90 Number	Change, 1980–90 Percent change	Change, 1990–2000 Number (race only)	Change, 1990–2000 Percent change	Change, 1990–2000 Race alone or in combination with other race(s)	Change, 1990–2000 Percent change
Total population	22,164,068	9.8%	32,713,033	13.2%	32,713,033	13.2%
White	11,314,448	6.0	11,774,556	5.9	17,244,905	8.6
Black (African-American)	3,491,035	13.2	4,672,130	15.6	6,433,374	21.5
American Indian and Alaska Native	538,834	37.9	516,722	26.4	2,160,067	110.3
Asian	3,773,223	107.8	3,334,360	18.3	4,990,190	72.2
Native Hawaiian and other Pacific Islander	(1)	(1)	33,811	9.3	509,390	139.5
Other race	N.A.	N.A.	5,554,226	56.6	8,716,639	88.9
Hispanic origin[2]	7,745,386	53.0	12,951,759	57.9	12,951,759	57.9

Note: 1. Native Hawaiian and other Pacific Islander included with Asian from 1980–90. 2. Persons of Hispanic origin may be of any race. **Source:** U.S. Bureau of the Census.

According to 2007 population estimates, 38,756,452 Americans identify themselves as black only. They represented 12.8 percent of all Americans. An additional 1,987,680 consider themselves black and at least one other race (most often white), making a total of 40,744,132 people (13.5 pecent of the population) at least partly black. The black-only population grew by 15.6 percent between the censuses of 1990 and 2000, significantly faster than the overall population, which increased only by 13.2

percent. The number of people who are black or partly black increased even faster: 6.4 million, or 21.5 percent from 1990-2000.

Most black Americans (53.5 percent of the black-only population) continue to live in the South, where they made up 19.5 percent of the population in 2004. Blacks constituted 12.9 percent of the population in the Northeast, 10.7 percent in the Midwest, and just 5.5 percent in the West (up from 4.9 in 2000). The black population of the U.S.

Resident Population of States by Race and Hispanic Origin, 2007

State	Total population	White	Black or African American	American Indian & Alaska Native	Asian	Native Hawaiian	Two or more races	Hispanic or Latino origin
				One race only				
United States	301,621,157	80.0%	12.8%	1.0%	4.4%	0.2%	2.0%	15.1%
Alabama	4,627,851	71.0	26.5	0.5	1.0	0.0	1.0	2.7
Alaska	683,478	70.8	4.1	15.2	4.6	0.6	8.1	5.9
Arizona	6,338,755	87.0	4.0	4.7	2.5	0.2	2.4	29.6
Arkansas	2,834,797	80.9	15.8	0.8	1.1	0.1	1.6	5.3
California	36,553,215	76.8	6.7	1.2	12.4	0.4	3.3	36.2
Colorado	4,861,515	89.9	4.2	1.2	2.7	0.1	2.6	19.9
Connecticut	3,502,309	84.5	10.3	0.4	3.4	0.1	1.8	11.5
Delaware	864,764	74.5	20.9	0.4	2.8	0.1	1.4	6.5
District of Columbia	588,292	39.4	55.2	0.4	3.4	0.1	1.5	8.3
Florida	18,251,243	80.0	15.9	0.5	2.3	0.1	1.8	20.6
Georgia	9,544,750	65.6	30.0	0.3	2.8	0.1	1.3	7.8
Hawaii	1,283,388	29.1	2.9	0.5	39.9	8.9	21.5	8.2
Idaho	1,499,402	94.8	0.9	1.4	1.2	0.1	2.1	9.8
Illinois	12,852,548	79.2	15.0	0.3	4.3	0.1	1.6	14.9
Indiana	6,345,548	88.1	9.0	0.3	1.4	0.0	1.4	5.0
Iowa	2,988,046	94.4	2.6	0.4	1.6	0.0	1.4	4.0
Kansas	2,775,997	88.9	6.1	1.0	2.2	0.1	2.5	8.8
Kentucky	4,241,474	90.0	7.7	0.2	1.0	0.0	1.2	2.2
Louisiana	4,293,204	65.1	31.9	0.6	1.4	0.0	1.0	3.2
Maine	1,317,207	96.5	1.0	0.6	0.9	0.0	1.4	1.2
Maryland	5,618,344	63.6	29.5	0.3	5.0	0.1	1.9	6.3
Massachusetts	6,449,755	86.5	6.9	0.3	4.9	0.1	1.7	8.2
Michigan	10,071,822	81.2	14.3	0.6	2.4	0.0	1.8	4.0
Minnesota	5,197,621	89.3	4.5	1.2	3.5	0.1	1.6	4.0
Mississippi	2,918,785	60.7	37.2	0.5	0.8	0.0	0.7	2.1
Missouri	5,878,415	85.1	11.5	0.5	1.5	0.1	1.8	3.0
Montana	957,861	90.6	0.6	6.3	0.7	0.1	2.0	2.8
Nebraska	1,774,571	91.6	4.4	1.0	1.7	0.1	1.5	7.5
Nevada	2,565,382	81.4	8.0	1.4	6.1	0.5	3.2	25.1
New Hampshire	1,315,828	95.6	1.2	0.3	1.9	0.0	0.8	2.5
New Jersey	8,685,920	76.3	14.5	0.3	7.5	0.1	1.5	15.9
New Mexico	1,969,915	84.5	2.8	9.5	1.4	0.1	3.2	44.4
New York	19,297,729	73.6	14.5	0.5	6.9	0.1	1.7	16.4
North Carolina	9,061,032	74.0	21.7	1.2	1.9	0.1	1.4	7.0
North Dakota	639,715	91.6	1.0	5.4	0.8	0.1	1.3	1.9
Ohio	11,466,917	84.9	12.0	0.2	1.6	0.0	1.5	2.5
Oklahoma	3,617,316	78.3	7.9	7.9	1.7	0.1	6.1	7.2
Oregon	3,747,455	90.3	2.0	1.4	3.7	0.3	3.0	10.6
Pennsylvania	12,432,792	85.6	10.8	0.2	2.4	0.0	1.2	4.5
Rhode Island	1,057,832	88.7	6.3	0.6	2.8	0.1	2.2	11.2
South Carolina	4,407,709	68.6	28.7	0.4	1.2	0.1	1.3	3.8
South Dakota	796,214	88.4	1.1	8.3	0.8	0.1	1.6	2.3
Tennessee	6,156,719	80.4	16.9	0.3	1.3	0.1	1.2	3.5
Texas	23,904,380	82.6	12.0	0.7	3.4	0.1	1.8	36.0
Utah	2,645,330	93.2	1.2	1.3	2.0	0.7	1.8	11.6
Vermont	621,254	96.5	0.8	0.4	1.2	0.0	1.3	1.3
Virginia	7,712,091	73.2	19.9	0.4	4.8	0.1	1.9	6.6
Washington	6,468,424	84.6	3.6	1.6	6.7	0.5	3.3	9.4
West Virginia	1,812,035	94.6	3.5	0.2	0.7	0.1	1.1	1.1
Wisconsin	5,601,640	89.9	6.0	0.9	2.0	0.0	1.3	4.9
Wyoming	522,830	94.1	1.2	2.5	0.7	0.1	1.8	7.3

Note: Persons of Hispanic origin may be of any race. **Source:** U.S. Census Bureau.

remains highly concentrated. The 10 states with the largest number of blacks (see the accompanying table) had 59 percent of all blacks in America (but only 51 percent of the total U.S. population). Blacks constituted more than 50 percent of the population in 90 counties; all of these counties were in the South and all of them were nonmetropolitan counties (with the exceptions of Baltimore City and Prince George's County, Md.; Orleans Parish, La.; Shelby County, Tn.; and Clayton and DeKalb Counties, Ga.). New York and Chicago alone accounted for 8 percent of the total black population. Among places with 100,000 or more in population, Gary, Ind. had the highest percentage of blacks, with 84 percent, followed by Detroit, Mich., which was 83 percent black.

Significant differences between the races also exist in other demographic categories, most notably in the high rates of divorce and single-motherhood for blacks. Compared to other single mothers, blacks are the least likely to be divorced (17 percent) and most likely to never be married (65 percent). In 2006, less than half (45 percent) of all black families were married-couple families, compared with 81 percent of all non-Hispanic white families. (See also "The U.S. Economy" for information about black employment, income, wealth and poverty.)

▶THE HISPANIC POPULATION
The term Hispanic refers to people of Spanish or Latin American origin. American Hispanics are of diverse backgrounds. The vast majority trace their roots to Mexico (64 percent), and then Cuba, Dominican Republic, and El Salvador with roughly 3 percent each. A mere 0.3 percent of Hispanic-Americans are from Spain. (These figures do not include Puerto Ricans living in Puerto Rico, which is a U.S. territory, but for which a separate census is issued. In recent years, the flow of Puerto Ricans to U.S. cities has been reversed, with more Puerto Ricans emigrating from the mainland to the island than the other way around.)

Contrary to popular opinion, Spanish-speaking countries are not culturally homogeneous, but varied and complex. They incorporate Spanish and other European influences, as well as Indian and African traits. In the Caribbean area, Panama, and the coasts of Venezuela, Colombia, Ecuador and sections of Peru, African culture has left a strong legacy. In Mexico, most of Central America and the Andean countries, diverse Indian cultures have had a major impact. Latin-American society varies greatly according to social class and vast differences exist between urban and rural areas. Since American Hispanics come from different countries and social backgrounds, they do not compose a uniform, cohesive population group.

U.S. Hispanics are of many races. In some areas, intermingling has made it impossible to distinguish one race from another, but in others, races are clearly defined. In Argentina, for example, there is a white majority of 85 percent—mostly of Italian,

Ten States With Largest Black Populations, 2007

| Rank, State | Black only | | Black only or in combination with other race(s) | |
	Number	Percent	Number	Percent
1. New York	3,347,282	17.3%	3,520,002	18.2%
2. Florida	2,896,282	15.9	3,009,773	16.5
3. Texas	2,857,111	12.0	2,971,494	12.4
4. Georgia	2,864,431	30.0	2,923,725	30.6
5. California	2,450,444	6.7	2,718,070	7.4
6. North Carolina	1,967,156	21.7	2,021,579	22.3
7. Illinois	1,926,515	15.0	1,999,258	15.6
8. Maryland	1,655,231	29.5	1,705,996	30.4
9. Virginia	1,537,603	19.9	1,599,430	20.7
10. Louisiana	1,442,470	14.3	1,517,854	15.1

Note: States ranked by Black-only population. **Source:** U.S. Bureau of the Census.

Ten States with Highest Percentage of Black Population, 2007

| Rank, State | Total Population | Black only | | Black only or in combination with other race(s) | |
		Number	Percent	Number	Percent
1. Mississippi	2,918,785	1,086,584	37.2%	1,098,181	37.6%
2. Louisiana	4,293,204	1,369,250	31.9	1,388,217	32.7
3. Georgia	9,544,750	2,864,431	30.0	2,923,725	30.6
4. Maryland	5,618,344	1,655,231	29.5	1,705,996	30.4
5. South Carolina	4,407,709	1,266,225	28.7	1,289,010	29.2
6. Alabama	4,627,851	1,224,496	26.5	1,242,344	26.8
7. North Carolina	9,061,032	1,967,156	21.7	2,021,579	22.3
8. Delaware	864,764	180,474	20.9	187,929	21.7
9. Virginia	7,712,091	1,537,603	19.9	1,599,430	20.7
10. New York	19,297,729	3,347,282	17.3	3,520,002	18.2

Note: States ranked by Black-only population. **Source:** U.S. Bureau of the Census.

Black Population of the U.S., 1790-2007

Year	Number ('000s)	Percent of total population	Year	Number ('000s)	Percent of total population	Year	Number ('000s)	Percent of total population
1790	757	19.3%	1920	10,463	9.9%	1995	33,116	12.6%
1800	1,002	18.9	1930	11,891	9.7	1998	34,427	12.7
1850	3,639	15.7	1940	12,866	9.8	1999	34,862	12.8
1860	4,442	14.1	1950	15,042	10.0	2000[2]	36,419	12.9
1870	4,880	12.7	1960[1]	18,872	10.5	2002[2]	38,248	13.3
1880	6,581	13.1	1970	22,581	11.1	2004[2]	39,204	13.4
1890	7,489	11.9	1980	26,683	11.8	2005[2]	39,718	13.4
1900	8,834	11.6	1985	28,994	12.1	2006[2]	40,241	13.4
1910	9,828	10.7	1990	30,517	12.3	2007[2]	40,744	13.5

Note: Decennial census figures are as of April 1. Figures for 1998 & 2001-06 are as of July 1. 1. Includes Alaska and Hawaii for first time. 2. Figures are only for "Black only or in combination of other race" after 2000.
Source: U.S. Bureau of the Census, *The Black Population 2000.* (2001); Annual Population Estimates (2008)

Black Population in the Largest U.S. Cities, 2000

City	Total Population Rank	Total Population Number	Black-only population Rank	Black-only population Number	Black-only population Percent black	Black only or in combination with other race(s) population Rank	Black only or in combination with other race(s) population Number	Black only or in combination with other race(s) population Percent black
New York, N.Y.	1	8,008,278	1	2,129,762	26.6%	1	2,274,049	28.4%
Los Angeles, Calif.	2	3,694,820	7	415,195	11.2	6	444,635	12.0
Chicago, Ill.	3	2,896,016	2	1,065,009	36.8	2	1,084,221	37.4
Houston, Texas	4	1,953,631	5	494,496	25.3	5	505,101	25.9
Philadelphia, Pa.	5	1,517,550	4	655,824	43.2	4	672,162	44.3
Phoenix, Ariz.	6	1,321,045	60	67,416	5.1	53	76,065	5.8
San Diego, Calif.	7	1,223,400	36	96,216	7.9	32	109,470	8.9
Dallas, Texas	8	1,188,580	11	307,957	25.9	11	314,678	26.5
San Antonio, Texas	9	1,144,646	48	78,120	6.8	45	84,250	7.4
Detroit, Mich.	10	951,270	3	775,772	81.6	3	787,687	82.8
Baltimore, Md.	17	651,154	6	418,951	64.3	7	424,449	65.2
Memphis, Tenn.	18	650,100	8	399,208	61.4	8	402,367	61.9
Washington, D.C.	21	572,059	9	343,312	60.0	9	350,455	61.3
New Orleans, La.	31	484,674	10	325,947	67.3	10	329,171	67.9

Source: U.S. Bureau of Census, *The Black Population 2000* (2001).

Black Population of Metropolitan Areas, 2000

Metropolitan Areas with Largest Black Population	Percent	Number
1. New York–Northern New Jersey–Long Island, NY–NJ–CT–PA CMSA	17.2%	3,646,377
2. Washington–Baltimore, DC–MD–VA–WV CMSA	26.2	1,993,314
3. Chicago–Gary–Kenosha, IL–IN–WI CMSA	18.6	1,703,302
4. Los Angeles–Riverside–Orange County, CA CMSA	7.6	1,244,397
5. Philadelphia–Wilmington–Atlantic City, PA–NJ–DE–MD CMSA	19.6	1,212,939
6. Atlanta, GA MSA	28.9	1,188,425
7. Detroit–Ann Arbor–Flint, MI CMSA	21.1	1,151,306
8. Miami–Fort Lauderdale, FL CMSA	20.4	790,782
9. Houston–Galveston–Brazoria, TX CMSA	16.9	789,158
10. Dallas–Fort Worth, TX CMSA	13.8	720,609

Metropolitan Areas with Highest Percentage Black Population	Percent	Number
1. Albany, GA MSA	51.0%	61,619
2. Pine Bluff, AR MSA	49.6	41,802
3. Sumter, SC MSA	46.7	48,870
4. Jackson, MS MSA	45.6	201,005
5. Memphis, TN–AR–MS MSA	43.4	492,856
6. Rocky Mount, NC MSA	43.1	61,644
7. Columbus, GA–AL MSA	40.4	110,948
8. Florence, SC MSA	39.3	49,424
9. Montgomery, AL MSA	38.9	129,558
10. New Orleans, LA MSA	37.5	501,647

Note: Figures are for people identifying their race as black only; data on people identifying themselves as black and one or more other races is not available. Source: U.S. Bureau of the Census.

German or English extraction. Cuba, the Dominican Republic, Panama, Venezuela, and the coastal areas of Colombia, Ecuador and Peru all have significant black populations. In Bolivia, about one-half of the population is Indian and a third is mestizo (of mixed white and Indian ancestry). Both Peru and Cuba have concentrations of persons of Chinese ancestry, and Peru has a growing Japanese population. In Mexico, birthplace of the majority of most Hispanic-Americans, about 55 percent of the population is mestizo, 30 percent is Indian, and 15 percent is white.

Despite their diversity, the Hispanic peoples are united by many factors, among them language, religion, customs, and attitudes toward self, family and society. In the United States, these factors vary in importance according to the degree to which an individual has assimilated into the mainstream. For example, although language has traditionally been an important unifying factor, large numbers of second-generation Hispanics are English-dominant. About 85 percent of U.S. Hispanics speak English. Although the Spanish language continues to exert a strong emotional pull among U.S. Hispanics, it is difficult to assess to what extent Spanish will remain a unifying force among future generations.

Growth of the Hispanic population The Hispanic population is the fastest-growing segment of the U.S. population. Between 1980 and 2006, the number of Hispanics nearly tripled, from 14.6 million to 43.2 million, according to the Census Bureau. According to numbers from the 2000 Census, the Hispanic population for the first time outnumbered the black-alone population (35.3 million to 34.7 million), although blacks alone or in combination with other races outnumbered Hispanics by just over one million. By July 2005, however, the total number of Hispanics of any race had increased to 42.7 million, finally exceeding the number of blacks alone or in combination with other races,

and officially becoming the largest minority population in the United States. Hispanics currently represent almost 15 percent of the U.S. population.

The Hispanic population increased by 57.9 percent overall between 1990 and 2000. Mexicans increased by 52.9 percent, Puerto Ricans increased by 24.9 percent, and Cubans increased by 18.9 percent. The "other Hispanic" category, which includes people from Spain, people from all other Spanish-speaking countries in Latin America, and people who did not specify a detailed origin beyond "Hispanic," was the fastest-growing group of Hispanics, increasing by 96.9 percent.

The rapid growth of the Hispanic population is due primarily to immigration. For example, the number of people of Mexican background living in the U.S. more than doubled between 1980 and 1990, due in large part to the Immigration and Reform Control Act of 1986, which allowed immigrants living illegally in the United States to obtain legal U.S. citizenship. By 2003, 44.6 percent of the Hispanic population in the United States was foreign born. (See the section on immigration later in this chapter.) Hispanics also have higher fertility rates than do the non-Hispanic population. In 2006, the overall fertility rate per 100,000 women ages 15-44 was 66.7, but for Hispanic women, it was 99.1. Mexican-American women had the highest fertility rates of all: 116.6 births per 100,000 women aged 15-44, or approximately double the rate for Cuban-American women.

Half of all Hispanics lived in one of two states in 2000: California and Texas. Hispanics represented 24.3 percent of the population in the West; they constituted more than 25 percent of the populations of Arizona, California, New Mexico and Texas. Mexicans were the biggest component of Hispanic populations in the South and West, but there were fewer than half a million Mexicans in the Northeast. The majority of Hispanics in the Northeast were of Puerto Rican origin. Over a million Puerto Ricans lived in New York alone; another half million lived in

Hispanic Population of Metropolitan Areas, 2000

Metropolitan Areas with Largest Hispanic Population	Percent	Number
1. Los Angeles–Riverside–Orange County, CA CMSA	40.3%	6,598,578
2. New York–Northern New Jersey–Long Island, NY–NJ–CT–PA CMSA	18.2	3,858,375
3. Miami–Fort Lauderdale, FL CMSA	40.3	1,562,181
4. Chicago–Gary–Kenosha, IL–IN–WI CMSA	16.4	1,501,836
5. San Francisco–Oakland–San Jose, CA CMSA	19.7	1,386,754
6. Houston–Galveston–Brazoria, TX CMSA	28.9	1,349,506
7. Dallas–Fort Worth, TX CMSA	21.5	1,122,687
8. Phoenix–Mesa, AZ MSA	25.1	816,220
9. San Antonio, TX MSA	51.2	815,300
10. San Diego, CA MSA	26.7	751,293

Metropolitan Areas with Highest Percentage Hispanic Population	Percent	Number
1. Laredo, TX MSA	94.3%	182,109
2. McAllen–Edinburg–Mission, TX MSA	88.3	502,835
3. Brownsville–Harlingen–San Benito, TX MSA	84.3	282,596
4. El Paso, TX MSA	78.2	531,464
5. Las Cruces, NM MSA	63.4	110,748
6. Corpus Christi, TX MSA	54.7	208,288
7. San Antonio, TX MSA	51.2	815,300
8. Visalia–Tulare–Porterville, CA MSA	50.8	186,954
9. Yuma, AZ MSA	50.5	80,813
10. Salinas, CA MSA	46.8	188,024

Source: U.S. Bureau of the Census.

Hispanic Population in the Largest U.S. Cities, 2000

City	Total Population Rank	Total Population Number	Hispanic population Rank	Hispanic population Number	Percent Hispanic
New York, N.Y.	1	8,008,278	1	2,160,554	27.0%
Los Angeles, Calif.	2	3,694,820	2	1,719,073	46.5
Chicago, Ill.	3	2,896,016	3	753,644	26.0
Houston, Texas	4	1,953,631	4	730,865	37.4
Philadelphia, Pa.	5	1,517,550	24	128,928	8.5
Phoenix, Ariz.	6	1,321,045	6	449,972	34.1
San Diego, Calif.	7	1,223,400	9	310,752	25.4
Dallas, Texas	8	1,188,580	8	422,587	35.6
San Antonio, Texas	9	1,144,646	5	671,394	58.7
Detroit, Mich.	10	951,270	72	47,167	5.0
El Paso, Texas	23	563,662	7	431,875	76.6
San Jose, Calif.	11	894,943	10	269,989	30.2

Source: U.S. Bureau of Census, *The Hispanic Population 2000* (2001).

Resident Hispanic Population by Region and Origin, 2000

	Total, U.S. Number	Northeast Number	Northeast Percent	Midwest Number	Midwest Percent	South Number	South Percent	West Number	West Percent
All Hispanics	35,305,818	5,254,087	14.9%	3,124,532	8.8%	11,586,696	32.8%	15,340,503	43.4%
Mexican	20,640,711	479,169	2.3	2,200,196	10.7	6,548,081	31.7	11,413,265	55.3
Puerto Rican	3,406,178	2,074,574	60.9	325,363	9.6	759,305	22.3	246,936	7.2
Cuban	1,241,685	168,959	13.6	45,305	3.6	921,427	74.2	105,994	8.5
Other Hispanic	10,017,244	2,531,385	25.3	553,668	5.5	3,357,883	33.5	3,574,308	35.7

Source: U.S. Bureau of the Census, *The Hispanic Population 2000* (2001).

New Jersey and Connecticut. The vast majority of Cubans (67 percent) lived in Florida, where they represented 5.2 percent of the entire state population. The heaviest concentration of Hispanics in the U.S. is the area of East Los Angeles, Calif., where 120,307 of the 124,283 residents (96.8 percent) are Hispanic. Laredo, Texas, is close behind, with a population that is 94.1 percent Hispanic.

▶**THE ASIAN AND NATIVE HAWAIIAN/ OTHER PACIFIC ISLANDER POPULATION**

In 1970 the Census Bureau counted about 1.5 million Asians and Pacific Islanders living in the U.S. By the 1980 census that figure had more than doubled to 3.4 million, thanks in large part to the more than 400,000 Southeast Asian refugees who came to America between 1975-80 under the Refugee Resettlement Program. By the 1990 Census, their numbers had doubled yet again, with Koreans and Vietnamese responsible for the majority of the increase.

The 2000 Census was the first to consider Native Hawaiians and Other Pacific Islanders (Guamanians, Chamorros and Samoans) separately from Asians. In 2007, a total of 1,019,301 people identified themselves as at least partly Native Hawaiian. Almost half of Native Hawaiians (482,212) were also members of at least one other race. The majority, however (537,089), identified themselves as Native Hawaiian and Other Pacific Islander alone. The city with the largest number of Native Hawaiians was Honolulu, both alone (21,485, or 5.9 percent of the city population) or in combination with other races (58,102, or 15.9 percent).

Contrast that with the Asian population: 15,165,186 people said they were Asian or partly Asian in 2007. Of these, 13,366,154 (88.1 percent)

States With Largest Hispanic Population, 2006

State	Hispanic population	Total population	Percentage Hispanic
1. California	13,074,156	36,547,549	35.9%
2. Texas	8,385,139	23,507,783	35.7
3. Florida	3,646,499	18,089,888	20.2
4. New York	3,139,456	19,306,183	16.3
5. Illinois	1,886,933	12,831,970	14.7
6. Arizona	1,803,378	6,166,318	29.2
7. New Jersey	1,364,696	8,724,560	15.6
9. Colorado	934,413	4,753,377	19.7
8. New Mexico	860,688	1,954,599	44.0
10. Georgia	703,246	9,363,941	7.5

Note: Ranked by number of Hispanics. Nevada, which is 24.4 percent Hispanic, has a total of 610,052 Hispanics. Source: U.S. Bureau of the Census.

said they were Asian only, while only 1,799,032 were Asian and another race. Chinese are still the largest group of Asians in the U.S., followed closely by Filipinos and Japanese.

▶**THE AMERICAN INDIAN AND ALASKA NATIVE POPULATION**

This race was known as the American Indian, Eskimo, and Aleut population for the 1990 Census, which reported a total of 1,959,234 American Indians living in the United States (of these, 85,698 were Eskimos and Aleuts, a.k.a. Alaska Natives). After the 2000 Census, the definition was changed to encompass anyone having origins in any of the native peoples of North and South America, and who maintain community or tribal attachment. According to population estimates for 2007, 2,938,436 people identify themselves as American Indian or Alaska Native only, and another 1,598,421 identify as this race and at least one other race. That makes for a total of 4,536,857 people who consider themselves at least partly American Indian or Alaska Native.

Not surprisingly, the state with the greatest percentage of American Indians and Alaska natives is Alaska, where people of this race constitute 15.2 percent of the population. New Mexico is second, with 10.3 percent, followed by South Dakota (9 per-

cent) and Oklahoma (7.8 percent). The state with the most American Indians and Alaska Natives is California (423,238). Arizona is second, with 297,422, Oklahoma is third, with 285,764, and New Mexico is fourth, with 186,256. Washington, which had 102,940 Native Americans and Alaska Natives in 1990, saw this population drop to 93,301 for the 2000 Census, but because of the revised defintion, the number climbed to 105,515 in 2007. Meanwhile, the American Indian and Alaska Native population of Texas grew from 118,362 in 2000 to 170,835 in 2007. In 2000, almost half of all American Indians

States With Largest American Indian or Alaska Native Population, 2007

Rank, State	Total Population	American Indian or Alaska Native only		American Indian or Alaska Native only or in combination with other race(s)	
		Number	Percent	Number	Percent
1. California	36,553,215	423,238	1.2%	689,120	1.9%
2. Arizona	6,338,755	297,422	4.7	335,381	5.3
3. Oklahoma	3,617,316	285,764	7.9	393,500	10.9
4. New Mexico	1,969,915	186,256	9.5	203,047	10.3
5. Texas	23,904,380	170,835	0.7	277,368	1.2
6. North Carolina	9,061,032	111,853	1.2	146,108	1.6
7. New York	19,297,729	106,132	0.5	189,601	1.0
8. Washington	6,468,424	105,515	1.6	166,026	2.6
9. Alaska	683,478	103,690	15.2	121,560	17.8
10. Florida	18,251,243	83,667	0.5	157,302	0.9

Note: Ranked by American Indian or Alaska Native-only population. Source: U.S. Bureau of the Census.

Ten Cities With Largest Asian Population, 2000

Rank, State	Total Population	Asian only		Asian only or in combination with other race(s)	
		Number	Percent	Number	Percent
1. New York City	8,008,278	787,047	9.8%	872,777	10.9%
2. Los Angeles	3,694,820	369,254	10.0	407,444	11.0
3. San Jose	894,943	240,375	26.9	257,571	28.8
4. San Francisco	776,733	239,565	30.8	253,477	32.6
5. Honolulu	371,657	207,588	55.9	251,686	67.7
6. San Diego	1,223,400	166,968	13.6	189,413	15.5
7. Chicago	2,896,016	125,974	4.3	140,517	4.9
8. Houston	1,953,631	103,694	5.3	114,140	5.8
9. Fremont, Ca.	203,413	75,165	37.0	80,979	39.8
10. Seattle	563,374	73,910	13.1	84,649	15.0

Source: Ranked by number of Asian-only population. Seattle ranks 9th when states are ranked by number of Asians-only or Asians in combination with other races. Source: U.S. Bureau of the Census, Census 2000.

Ten States With Largest Asian Population, 2007

Rank, State	Total Population	Asian only		Asian only or in combination with other race(s)	
		Number	Percent	Number	Percent
1. California	36,553,215	4,544,182	12.4%	5,008,379	13.7%
2. New York	19,297,729	1,338,924	6.9	1,443,367	7.5
3. Texas	23,904,380	814,454	3.4	915,201	3.8
4. New Jersey	8,685,920	651,787	7.5	695,118	8.0
5. Illinois	12,852,548	549,043	4.3	602,374	4.7
6. Hawaii	1,283,388	511,919	39.9	705,106	54.9
7. Washington	6,468,424	430,862	6.7	517,057	8.0
8. Florida	18,251,243	411,726	2.3	494,925	2.7
9. Virginia	7,712,091	371,405	4.8	422,802	5.5
10. Massachusetts	6,449,755	315,114	4.9	341,781	5.3

Source: Ranked by number of Asian-only population. Source: U.S. Bureau of the Census.

and Alaska Natives (1.2 million) reported living in the West. Only 162,558 American Indians and Alaska Natives live in the Northeast.

There are 561 federally recognized Indian tribes in the U.S. and 554 federally identified areas associated with them, including reservations, which the federal government recognizes as territory in which American Indian tribes have jurisdiction, and "trust lands," which are held in trust by the federal government but consist of property associated with a particular tribe or reservation. The Bureau of Indian Affairs counted 304 reservations in 2006, down from

314 in 1997. Of the 2.4 million people who identified their race as American Indian or Alaska Native alone in the 2000 Census, the two tribes with the largest populations by far were the Cherokee (281,069) and the Navajo (269,202), followed at some distance by Canadian and Latin American Indians (108,802) and the Sioux (108,272) and Chippewa (105,907) tribes. 103,174 people identified themselves as American Indian alone without specifying a tribe.

U.S. POPULATION BY AGE AND SEX

▶ THE POPULATION BY AGE

With birth rates and fertility rates declining rapidly since 1965 it should come as no surprise that the average age of the U.S. population has been increasing almost as quickly. It will continue to rise for the foreseeable future in part because of the aging members of the baby boom generation.

During the Baby Boom years of the 1950's and 1960's, the median age of the population actually declined, the only time it has done so. Since then, however, the steady decline in the percentage of young people, especially those under 18 years of age, (from 34.1 percent in 1970 to 25.1 percent in 2003) combined with the increase of those between 25 and 44 (they were 23.6 percent of the population in 1970, and 29.0 percent in 2003) has driven the median age from 28.0 in 1970 to 34.1 in 2000. A five-year increase in 20 years is unprecedented in U.S. history, but what's more revealing is that we will most likely duplicate that feat over the next 20 years. By 2007, the median age of the U.S. population had already increased to 36.6.

The other major factor in the so-called "graying of America" is the increased life expectancy for older

people. In 1950, the over-65 population totaled 7 percent of all Americans and numbered 9 million. In 2005, 36.8 million Americans (12.4 percent of the population) were over 65; this represents a 40.6 percent increase since 1980 and a more than 1,000 percent increase since 1900.

As the population ages, 65 no longer seems old to most people. Especially when millions more people are living past the age of 80. There were 7 million people 80 or older in 1990, 3 million age 85 or older, nearly a million 90 years or older, and 36,000 people over the age of 100. By 2003, there were 4.7 million age 85 or more.

Over the first decade of the 21st century, the over-65 population will grow another 13-14 percent—but between 2010 and 2030 the over-65 population will nearly double as the baby boom generation finally becomes senior citizens. In the year 2030, an estimated 20 percent of the population, or 70 million Americans, will be 65 years old or older.

Florida, and to a lesser degree, Pennsylvania, have long had the highest concentrations of retirees, but in the 1990's, several states saw dramatic growth in their over-65 population. Nevada's senior population grew by 55 percent between 1990 and 2000, while Alaska's increased 49 percent and Arizona's jumped 29 percent. Hawaii experienced 27 percent growth, Utah saw a 22 percent increase, and Colorado and New Mexico both had increases of 21 percent.

Number of Persons and Percent of Total Population, by Age Group, 1960–2050 (numbers in thousands)

Age in Years	1960	1970	1980	1990	2000	2010	2050
Under 5	20,341	17,166	16,458	18,765	19,176	20,099	26,914
percent	11.3%	8.4%	7.2%	7.5%	6.8%	6.7%	6.7%
5-13	32,965	36,672	31,095	31,839	37,025	35,321	47,582
percent	18.2	17.9	13.7	12.8	13.2	11.8	11.8
14-17	11,219	15,924	16,142	13,345	16,093	16,681	21,252
percent	6.2	7.8	7.1	5.4	5.7	5.6	5.3
18-24	16,128	24,712	30,350	26,961	27,143	30,163	36,804
percent	8.9	12.1	13.3	10.8	9.6	10.1	9.1
25-34	22,919	25,323	37,626	43,174	39,891	38,851	50,458
percent	12.7	12.3	16.5	17.4	14.2	13.0	12.5
35-44	24,221	23,150	25,868	37,444	45,149	39,443	49,588
percent	13.4	11.3	11.4	15.1	16.0	13.2	12.3
45-64	36,203	41,999	44,515	46,178	61,902	81,590	89,089
percent	20.0	20.5	19.5	18.6	22.0	27.2	22.1
65 & over	16,675	20,107	25,704	31,084	34,992	39,715	81,999
percent	9.2	9.8	11.3	12.5	12.4	13.2	20.3
85 & over	940	1,430	2,269	3,022	4,240	5,786	19,352
percent	0.5	0.7	1.0	1.2	1.5	1.9	4.8
100 & over	3	5	15	N.A.	N.A.	129	1,095
percent	—	—	—	—	—	—	0.3
Total U.S. population	180,671	205,052	227,757	248,791	281,422	299,862	403,687
Median age	29.4	27.9	30.0	32.8	35.3	37.4	38.8

Note: Figures for 2010 and after are the projections the Census Bureau calls the "middle" or "most likely" series.   Source: U.S. Bureau of the Census, *Projections of the Population of the U.S., by Age, Sex, and Race: 1995 to 2050* (2002).

Resident Population of States, by Age, 2008

	Total	Under 5 Years	5–13 Years	15–44 Years	45–64 Years	65 Years+	85 Years+
United States	301,621,157	20,724,125	35,970,646	126,258,301	76,586,836	37,887,958	5,512,298
Alabama	4,627,851	308,234	552,768	1,880,794	1,195,948	625,756	82,025
Alaska	683,478	51,311	86,484	305,521	181,778	47,935	4,543
Arizona	6,338,755	499,581	808,864	2,643,240	1,477,188	820,391	112,761
Arkansas	2,834,797	198,977	341,733	1,142,505	715,742	397,108	56,752
California	36,553,215	2,660,386	4,524,590	16,168,220	8,660,887	4,003,593	584,500
Colorado	4,861,515	349,902	578,343	2,117,997	1,257,630	492,685	64,753
Connecticut	3,502,309	210,985	408,419	1,405,040	956,322	472,284	77,772
Delaware	864,764	58,869	98,827	352,395	225,239	117,678	15,333
D.C.	588,292	36,215	51,486	286,375	138,196	69,741	10,676
Florida	18,251,243	1,148,213	1,948,094	7,145,922	4,681,530	3,098,364	493,778
Georgia	9,544,750	737,422	1,232,840	4,170,565	2,321,991	942,832	118,022
Hawaii	1,283,388	86,690	132,775	530,971	332,840	183,994	29,401
Idaho	1,499,402	118,630	198,599	618,043	367,055	174,946	24,673
Illinois	12,852,548	891,315	1,571,044	5,468,375	3,191,959	1,548,781	233,526
Indiana	6,345,289	437,494	782,990	2,618,075	1,621,442	795,441	114,665
Iowa	2,988,046	195,916	346,318	1,189,655	776,627	438,448	77,381
Kansas	2,775,997	196,138	340,593	1,139,351	701,097	360,216	60,712
Kentucky	4,241,474	278,330	493,320	1,750,555	1,113,258	549,504	71,744
Louisiana	4,293,204	298,157	528,804	1,796,052	1,086,231	522,334	68,613
Maine	1,317,207	70,744	136,239	506,071	391,934	194,986	27,927
Maryland	5,618,344	376,745	656,153	2,356,479	1,488,360	661,809	89,349
Massachusetts	6,449,755	376,848	705,820	2,704,289	1,718,777	858,939	139,754
Michigan	10,071,822	633,017	1,208,248	4,125,853	2,678,986	1,280,152	181,746
Minnesota	5,197,621	353,901	609,464	2,162,376	1,363,876	636,216	104,864
Mississippi	2,918,785	219,282	371,898	1,201,310	717,666	364,614	50,676
Missouri	5,878,415	393,177	694,082	2,394,801	1,526,015	788,371	118,030
Montana	957,861	59,117	105,806	372,057	274,454	133,578	19,841
Nebraska	1,774,571	129,796	214,286	724,029	445,327	236,648	40,075
Nevada	2,565,382	194,651	322,007	1,084,975	642,528	285,654	29,868
New Hampshire	1,315,828	75,125	147,182	529,293	380,187	165,742	23,948
New Jersey	8,685,920	556,673	1,018,458	3,553,989	2,302,420	1,134,636	169,186
New Mexico	1,969,915	144,945	239,790	811,493	495,340	250,235	33,895
New York	19,297,729	1,196,688	2,140,741	8,157,719	4,996,316	2,546,405	384,636
North Carolina	9,061,032	637,664	1,083,026	3,790,795	2,324,127	1,103,413	142,606
North Dakota	639,715	39,988	68,116	265,672	164,395	93,285	17,450
Ohio	11,466,917	736,416	1,356,032	4,626,512	3,046,263	1,545,085	221,823
Oklahoma	3,617,316	261,146	434,227	1,486,285	906,297	480,140	68,255
Oregon	3,747,455	236,390	422,519	1,531,782	1,019,057	488,936	73,204
Pennsylvania	12,432,792	730,061	1,361,476	4,912,978	3,370,799	1,889,660	302,279
Rhode Island	1,057,832	61,397	113,646	442,015	279,928	146,847	25,355
South Carolina	4,407,709	296,302	513,914	1,807,236	1,156,945	573,098	72,499
South Dakota	796,214	56,450	94,216	315,274	205,586	113,555	20,088
Tennessee	6,156,719	409,580	722,690	2,536,939	1,611,762	793,117	102,277
Texas	23,904,380	1,988,979	3,212,978	10,461,002	5,494,877	2,394,157	318,320
Utah	2,645,330	255,708	395,605	1,201,809	517,603	233,982	31,032
Vermont	621,254	32,435	64,053	245,938	186,217	84,425	12,071
Virginia	7,712,091	518,410	887,448	3,290,941	2,002,959	909,522	117,152
Washington	6,468,424	423,096	748,431	2,719,418	1,730,987	757,852	111,429
West Virginia	1,812,035	104,452	190,114	703,856	510,704	280,666	37,425
Wisconsin	5,601,640	356,287	645,297	2,294,430	1,492,009	736,301	115,036
Wyoming	522,830	35,890	59,793	210,974	145,175	63,901	8,572
Puerto Rico	3,941,459	245,188	515,463	1,662,480	935,710	521,983	62,568

Source: Population Division, U.S. Census Bureau, (as of July 1, 2007)

►THE POPULATION BY SEX

The Census Bureau estimates that in 2006, there were 44.7 million men and 52.3 million women 18 years and over who had never married or who were currently widowed, separated, or divorced -a ratio of 85 unmarried men per 100 unmarried women. The popular interpretation of these figures—that there is a shortage of eligible men—fails to consider that women are more likely to live longer (and so be counted among the widowed) and less likely to remarry after a divorce. In fact, the surplus of women can be entirely attributed to the fact that there are over 6 million more widows

than widowers over the age of 65. But during the peak marrying ages, unmarried men actually outnumber unmarried women: among persons between the ages of 18 and 24 there were 117 unmarried men for every 100 unmarried women; in the 25-to-34 age group, there were 120 men for every 100 women. It's not until the 35-to-44 group that the reversal begins (99 unmarried men for every 100 available women). In the 45-to-64 age group, there are 76 unmarried men for every 100 available women, and among the 65-and-over there is a dramatic change, with only 35 unmarried men for every 100 unmarried women.

Growth of the Over-65 Population, 1900–2050

Year	Population 65 and over		Population 85 and over	
	Number ('000s)	Percent of total population	Number ('000s)	Percent of total population
1900	3,099	4.1%	N.A.	N.A.
1910	3,986	4.3	N.A.	N.A.
1920	4,929	4.7	N.A.	N.A.
1930	6,705	5.5	N.A.	N.A.
1940	9,031	6.9	N.A.	N.A.
1950	12,397	8.1	N.A.	N.A.
1960	16,675	9.2	940	0.5%
1970	20,107	9.8	1,430	0.7
1980	25,549	11.3	2,269	1.0
1990	31,242	12.5	3,080	1.2
2000	34,992	12.4	4,240	1.5
2010	40,244	13.0	6,123	2.0
2020	54,632	16.3	7,269	2.2
2030	71,453	19.7	9,603	2.6
2040	80,050	20.4	15,409	3.9
2050	86,706	20.7	20,861	5.0

Note: Prior to 1960, the Census Bureau did not count persons over 85 separately. Figures for 2010 through 2050 are Census Bureau projections based on their "most likely" series of estimates.
Source: U.S. Bureau of the Census, *Resident Population Projections by Sex and Age: 2005 to 2050.*

VITAL STATISTICS

The National Center for Health Statistics does a month-by-month tracking of four sets of numbers, which both it and the Census Bureau refer to as "vital": births, deaths, marriages, and divorces.

Births   An estimated 4.27 million babies were born in the U.S. in 2006, up from 4.06 million in 2000. The crude birth rate (the number of live births per 1,000 total population) increased slightly to 14.3, and the fertility rate (the number of births per 1,000 women aged 15-44) was 66.7.

Deaths   An estimated 2.42 million people died in 2006, only slightly higher that the 2.40 million in 2000. The crude death rate held steady at 8.1 per 1,000 population. In 1910, by comparison, the death rate was 14.7. (For infant mortality figures and for more specific information about death rates by cause see the section, "Health and Medicine.")

In 2006 there were 1.85 million more births than deaths; this figure is called the *natural increase,* meaning the growth in population without immigration (which accounted for over 1,200,000 people in 2006).

Marriages   An estimated 2.16 million couples married during 2006, markedly down from 2.35 in 2001; the marriage rate of 7.3 per 1,000 people was the lowest rate recorded in over 40 years. In addition to getting married in fewer numbers, people are getting married at a later age. In 1960, for example, about 40 percent of all 19-year-old women were married, but by 2006 only 4.8 percent were. Also in 1960, about 92 percent of all women were married before they reached age 30, but by 2006 only 51 percent were. In 2006, 28.7 percent of 30–34-year-olds were never married, up dramatically from less than 6 percent in 1970.

Characteristics of Persons 65 or Older, 2006

Characteristic	Total	Male	Female
Total (millions)	35.5	15.2	20.3
Percent distribution			
Marital status:			
Never married	3.6%	3.8%	3.6%
Married	57.8	75.0	44.9
Spouse present	54.7	71.9	41.9
Spouse absent	3.0	3.1	3.0
Widowed	29.9	13.1	42.4
Divorced	8.7	8.1	9.1
Educational attainment:			
Less than ninth grade	13.0%	13.0%	12.9%
Completed grades 9–12 but no diploma	11.9	11.0	12.5
High school graduate	36.7	32.9	39.5
Some college/associate deg.	19.0	17.4	20.2
Bachelor's/advanced deg.	19.5	25.6	14.9
Labor force participation:			
Employed	15.0%	19.8%	11.4%
Unemployed	0.4	0.6	0.3
Not in labor force	84.6	79.7	88.3
Percent below poverty level	10.1	7.3	12.3

Note: 1. Excludes those living in unrelated subfamilies. Source: U.S. Bureau of the Census, *Statistical Abstract of the United States* (annual).

Divorces   The National Center for Health Statistics stopped publishing cumulative numbers of divorces in 2000 because six states no longer report divorce statistics. The latest available year for which data is available is 1998, when an estimated 1.13 million divorces were granted, down slightly from the previous year. The divorce rate per 1,000 population was 3.6 in 2006, its lowest rate in more than 30 years. The divorce rate peaked in 1979 at 5.3 per 1,000 population. (In that year there were 22.8 divorced women for every 1,000 married women, up from 9.2 in 1960. While the divorce rate has declined,

U.S. Population by Sex: Totals and Ratio of Males to Females, 1920–2006

Year	Male ('000s)	Female ('000s)	Males per 100 females			
			All ages	14-24	25-44	65+
1920	53,900	51,810	104.0	97.3	105.1	101.3
1930	62,137	60,638	102.5	98.4	101.8	100.5
1940	66,062	65,608	100.7	98.9	98.5	95.5
1950	74,833	75,864	98.6	98.2	96.4	89.6
1960	88,331	90,992	97.1	98.7	95.7	82.8
1970	98,926	104,309	94.8	98.7	95.5	72.1
1980	110,053	116,493	94.5	101.9	97.4	67.6
1990	122,049	127,875	95.1	104.6	98.9	67.2
2000	138,054	143,368	96.3	105.1	100.2	70.0
2004	144,537	149,118	96.9	105.8	101.4	71.7
2006	147,512	151,886	97.1	106.0	101.8	72.5

Source: U.S. Bureau of the Census, *Statistical Abstract of the United States* (annual).

Births and Deaths in the U.S., 1910–2006

Year	Live births ('000s)	Birth rate[1]	Deaths[2] ('000s)	Death rate[1]
1910	2,777	30.1	N.A.	14.7
1920	2,950	27.7	N.A.	13.0
1930	2,618	21.3	N.A.	11.3
1940	2,559	19.4	1,417	10.8
1950	3,632	24.1	1,452	9.6
1955	4,097	25.0	1,529	9.3
1960	4,258	23.7	1,712	9.5
1965	3,760	19.5	1,828	9.4
1970	3,731	18.4	1,921	9.5
1975	3,144	14.6	1,893	8.8
1980	3,612	15.9	1,990	8.8
1985	3,761	15.8	2,086	8.8
1990	4,158	16.7	2,148	8.6
1995	3,892	14.8	2,309	8.8
1998	3,946	14.6	2,331	8.6
1999	3,965	14.5	2,396	8.8
2000	4,059	14.7	2,403	8.7
2001	4,026	14.1	2,418	8.5
2002	4,022	13.9	2,438	8.5
2003	4,093	14.0	2,423	8.3
2004	4,121	14.0	2,393	8.1
2005	4,138	14.0	2,421	8.2
2006	4,269	14.3	2,416	8.1

Note: 1. Per 1,000 total population. 2. Excludes fetal deaths.
Source: U.S. National Center for Health Statistics, *Vital Statistics of the United States* (annual).

Marriages and Divorces in the U.S., 1920–2006

Year	Marriages ('000s)	Rate per 1,000 population	Divorces ('000s)	Rate per 1,000 population
1920	1,274	12.0	171	1.6
1930	1,127	9.2	196	1.6
1940	1,596	12.1	264	2.0
1950	1,667	11.1	385	2.6
1955	1,531	9.3	377	2.3
1960	1,523	8.5	393	2.2
1965	1,800	9.3	479	2.5
1970	2,163	10.6	708	3.5
1975	2,153	10.0	1,036	4.8
1980	2,390	10.0	1,036	4.8
1985	2,413	10.1	1,190	5.0
1990	2,448	9.8	1,175	4.7
1995	2,336	8.9	1,169	4.4
1997	2,384	8.9	1,163	4.3
1998	2,244	8.4	1,135	4.2
1999	2,358	8.6	N.A.	4.1[1]
2000	2,329	8.5	N.A.	4.2[1]
2001	2,327	8.4	N.A.	4.0[1]
2002	2,254	7.7	N.A.	4.0[2]
2003	2,187	7.5	N.A.	3.8[2]
2004	2,178	7.4	N.A.	3.7[3]
2005	2,203	7.7	N.A.	3.6[4]
2006	2,160	7.3[5]	N.A.	3.6[4]

Note: 1. Divorce rates exclude CA, CO, IN, and LA. 2. Divorce rates exclude CA, HI, IN, LA, and OK. 3. Divorce rates exclude CA, GA, HI, IN, and LA. 4. Divorce rates exclude CA, GA, HI, IN, LA, and MN. 5. Marriage rate excludes LA. Source: U.S. National Center for Health Statistics, *Vital Statistics of the United States* (annual)

the ratio of divorced persons to married persons (with spouse present) has skyrocketed. Between 1970 and 2001, the proportion nearly quadrupled, from 47 divorced per 1,000 married to 180 per 1,000. For blacks, the rise was even greater, going from 83 per 1,000 to 330 per 1,000 in the same period.

In 2006, there were 22.8 million currently divorced persons in the U.S., more than 10 percent of the total adult population over 18. There are more divorced women (13.1 million) than men (9.7 million) because women are less likely to remarry.

A 2001 study by the National Center for Health Statistics revealed that 43 percent of all first marriages end in separation or divorce within 15 years. One in five ends in the first five years, and one in three ends within 10 years. The report also showed a link between the age of the bride and the duration of a marriage. Fifty-nine percent of first marriages involving women under 18 ended in separation or divorce within 15 years, compared with 36 percent of marriages where the bride was 20 or older.

▶**FERTILITY RATES OF AMERICAN WOMEN**
Population experts predict future trends by studying many factors including the crude birth rate (see "Vital Statistics") and the all-important fertility rates. The *general fertility rate* measures the ratio of live births to the total number of women aged 15 to 44. (Until 1990, the Census Bureau had reported based on the number of women 18 to 44, thus projecting a higher fertility rate but discounting the high number of teenage pregnancies.)

The *total fertility rate* is the number of births 1,000 women aged 10 to 50 would have in their lifetimes if, at each year of age, they experienced the birth rates occurring to women of that age in the specified calendar year. The total fertility rate is sometimes defined in the popular media as the number of *likely* births one woman will have in her lifetime; they do this by dividing by 1,000.

The total fertility rate is most helpful in measuring long-term trends, especially in determining whether or not the nation is sustaining a level of reproduction necessary for maintaining current population levels. That level, generally regarded as 2,100 per 1,000 women, was not achieved in the U.S. from 1971 through 1999, but by 2002 the figure had climbed to 2,013 and was almost steady at 2,101 in 2006.

Fertility rates in 2006 were highest among women in their 20s. The fertility rate for women 20-24 was 105.9, for women 25-29 it was 116.8. American Indian women (62.8) had slightly higher fertility rates overall than non-Hispanic white women (59.5), Asian or Pacific Islander women (67.2), or black women (70.6). Women of Hispanic origin had an overall fertility rate of 101.5.

One clear indication that women are having children much later in life is the increasing fertility rate of women over 35. In 2006, the rate for women 35-39 was 47.3, more than double the rate in 1978.

▶WOMEN AND CHILDBEARING: CURRENT TRENDS

Childless women An increasing number of women are choosing not to have children at all. In 2006, 20 percent of women ages 40-44 had no children - double the level of 30 years ago. For women with advanced degrees, the rate is 27 percent.

Unmarried mothers According to the National Center for Health Statistics, 1.5 million births in 2006 were to unmarried women, which represented 38.5 percent of all births, and was up significantly from 33.2 percent of all births in 2000. The percentage of births to unmarried women increased for all races and ethnicities, but was highest among blacks (70.7 percent) and Native Americans (64.6) and lowest among Asians (16.3). Of these unmarried mothers, 60.8 percent were under 24 years old.

Births and Birth Rates in the U.S., by Age, Race and Hispanic Origin, 2006

	All races	White, Non-Hispanic	Black Non-Hispanic	American Indian[1]	Asian/Pacific Islander	Hispanic[2]
BIRTHS						
Total, by mothers ages 10-54	**4,265,996**	**2,309,833**	**617,220**	**47,494**	**239,829**	**1,039,051**
10-14	6,405	1,270	2,470	122	71	2,455
15-19	435,427	169,837	103,692	8,222	7,672	145,651
20-24	1,080,507	528,596	198,718	16,388	31,535	303,443
25-29	1,182,187	665,889	153,639	12,127	66,562	280,630
30-34	950,472	567,103	95,804	6,752	82,614	194,590
35-39	498,566	309,130	49,893	3,120	42,290	91,562
40-44	105,476	63,546	12,270	722	8,525	19,697
45-54	6,956	4,461	733	41	560	1,022
BIRTH RATES						
Total, by mothers ages 10-54	**68.5**	**59.5**	**70.6**	**62.8**	**67.2**	**101.5**
10-14	0.6	0.2	1.6	0.9	0.2	1.3
15-19	41.9	26.6	63.7	54.7	16.7	83.0
20-24	105.9	83.4	133.1	114.9	62.5	177.0
25-29	116.8	109.2	107.1	97.2	107.8	152.4
30-34	97.7	98.1	72.6	61.5	116.5	108.4
35-39	47.3	46.3	36.0	28.2	62.8	55.6
40-44	9.4	8.4	8.3	6.1	14.1	13.3
45-54[3]	0.6	0.6	0.5	0.4	1.0	0.8

Notes: Figures are preliminary. **1.** Includes births to Aleuts and Eskimos. **2.** Hispanic persons may be of any race. **3.** The birth rate is computed by relating the number of births to women aged 45-54 years to women aged 45-49 years; most of the births in this group are to women aged 45-49. **Source:** U.S. National Center for Health Statistics, *National Vital Statistics Report (2007)*.

Women and Childbearing in the U.S, by Age, 1976-2006

Characteristic	1976	1980	1990	1995	2000	2006
Total number of women, 18-44 years old ('000s)	**41,618**	**45,652**	**58,381**	**60,225**	**60,133**	**55,930[1]**
Births per 1,000 women						
All women 15-44 years old	67.2	68.4	70.9	65.6	67.6	68.5
15-19 years	N.A.	53.0	59.9	56.8	48.7	41.9
20-24 years	93.2	115.1	116.5	109.8	112.5	105.9
25-29 years	104.8	112.9	120.2	112.2	121.7	116.8
30-34 years	56.4	61.9	80.8	82.5	94.2	97.7
35-39 years	22.6	19.8	31.7	34.3	40.3	47.3
40-44 years	6.5	3.9	5.5	6.6	7.9	9.4

Source: U.S. National Center for Health Statistics, *National Vital Statistics Reports (2007)*. **1.** From U.S. Census Bureau.

Percent of Population Never Married, by Age and Sex, 1960–2006

Age	1960	1970	1980	1990	2000	2006
MEN						
Total: 15 and over	**23.2%**	**28.1%**	**29.6%**	**29.9%**	**31.3%**	**32.8%**
15-17	98.8	99.4	99.4	99.8	98.7	98.9
18	94.6	95.1	97.4	98.5	98.2	97.8
19	87.1	89.9	90.9	95.3	(1)	(1)
20-24	53.1	54.7	68.8	79.3	83.7	86.7
25-29	20.8	19.1	33.1	45.2	51.7	57.4
30-34	11.9	9.4	15.9	27.0	30.1	33.4
35-39	8.8	7.2	7.8	14.7	20.3	23.3
40-44	7.3	6.3	7.1	10.5	15.7	18.5
45-54	7.4	7.5	6.1	6.3	9.4	12.4
55-64	8.0	7.8	5.3	5.8	5.5	6.9
65 and over	7.7	7.5	4.9	4.2	4.2	3.8
WOMEN						
Total: 15 and over	**17.3%**	**22.1%**	**22.5%**	**22.8%**	**25.1%**	**26.2%**
15-17	93.2	97.3	97.0	98.5	97.9	98.6
18	75.6	82.0	88.0	92.0	93.0	94.7
19	59.7	68.8	77.6	88.7	(1)	(1)
20-24	28.4	35.8	50.2	62.8	72.8	75.3
25-29	10.5	10.5	20.9	31.1	38.9	43.1
30-34	6.9	6.2	9.5	16.4	21.9	24.0
35-39	6.1	5.4	6.2	10.4	14.3	16.7
40-44	6.1	4.9	4.8	8.0	11.8	13.1
45-54	7.0	4.9	4.7	5.0	8.6	10.3
55-64	8.0	6.8	4.5	3.9	4.9	6.5
65 and over	8.5	7.7	5.9	4.9	3.6	3.6

Note: 1. Population aged 18-19 included under 18. **Source:** U.S. Bureau of the Census, *Children's Living Arrangements and Characteristics* (March 2002); *America's Families and Living Arrangements 2006.* www.census.gov.

Marital Status by Race and Hispanic Origin, 1970–2006 (in thousands)

Year and Race	Total Adults	Never married Number	Never married Percent	Married Number	Married Percent	Widowed Number	Widowed Percent	Divorced Number	Divorced Percent	Separated Number	Separated Percent
All Races											
1970	132,507	21,443	16.2%	94,999	71.7%	11,784	8.9%	4,282	3.2%	N.A.	N.A.
1980	159,528	32,342	20.3	104,564	65.5	12,734	8.0	9,886	6.2	N.A.	N.A.
1990	181,849	40,361	22.2	112,552	61.9	13,810	7.6	15,125	8.3	N.A.	N.A.
2000	201,762	48,213	23.9	115,655	57.3	13,655	6.8	19,828	9.8	4,412	2.2%
2006	233,039	68,515	29.4	122,840	52.7	13,914	6.0	22,806	9.8	4,963	2.1
White											
1970	118,179	18,444	15.6	85,784	72.6	10,280	8.7	3,671	3.1	N.A.	N.A.
1980	139,480	26,405	18.9	93,800	67.2	10,938	7.8	8,338	6.0	N.A.	N.A.
1990	155,454	31,633	20.3	99,450	64.0	11,730	7.5	12,640	8.1	N.A.	N.A.
2000	168,140	36,017	21.4	101,159	60.2	11,529	6.9	16,507	9.8	2,928	1.7
2006[1]	192,630	51,988	27.0	106,703	55.4	11,659	6.1	18,893	9.8	3,386	1.8
Black											
1970	12,972	2,668	20.6	8,310	64.1	1,427	11.0	567	4.4	N.A.	N.A.
1980	16,638	5,070	30.5	8,545	51.4	1,627	9.8	1,396	8.4	N.A.	N.A.
1990	20,320	7,141	35.1	9,302	45.8	1,730	8.5	2,146	10.6	N.A.	N.A.
2000	24,016	9,451	39.4	8,818	36.7	1,692	7.0	2,765	11.5	1,290	5.4
2006[1]	28,554	12,964	45.4	9,214	32.3	1,790	6.3	3,198	11.2	1,388	4.9
Hispanic											
1970	5,066	943	18.6	3,637	71.8	286	5.6	200	3.9	N.A.	N.A.
1980	7,888	1,901	24.1	5,176	65.6	350	4.4	460	5.8	N.A.	N.A.
1990	13,560	3,694	27.2	8,365	61.7	548	4.0	952	7.0	N.A.	N.A.
2000	21,109	5,907	28.0	11,864	56.2	881	4.2	1,619	7.7	838	4.0
2006[1]	30,613	10,765	35.2	15,530	50.7	1,007	3.3	2,246	7.3	1,065	3.5
Asian and Pacific Islander											
2000	7,859	2,241	28.5	4,792	61.0	332	4.2	360	4.6	135	1.7
2006[1]	10,832	3,416	31.5	6,853	58.7	403	3.7	517	4.8	144	1.3

Note: Only those people 15 years old and over are included. Hispanic persons may be of any race. 1. Alone or in combination with other races. **Source:** U.S. Bureau of the Census, *Children's Living Arrangements and Characteristics* (March 2004); *America's Families and Living Arrangements 2006* (2007). www.census.gov.

Births to teenagers Births to teenage mothers, most of whom are unmarried, have generally been declining in recent years. In 2006, there were 441,832 births to mothers under 20, down from 469,000 in 2000 but up slightly from 421,315 in 2005. The birth rate for women aged 15-19 hit a 20-year high of 62.1 in 1991, but has declined almost every year after that, to a record low of 40.5 in 2005, although it was up to 41.9 in 2006.

New mothers in the labor force Due to economic necessity and career goals, fewer than half of all mothers are stay-at-home parents. In June 2006, 56 percent of women who had a child in the last year were in the labor force. That's up significantly from 38 percent in 1980. 68.1 percent of all mothers with children under 18 were in the labor force in 2005, up from 47.4 percent in 1975.

▶ADOPTION

Between 1973 and 1994, the percent of never-married women who had ever adopted a child declined from 2.1 percent to 1.3 percent, but climbed to 1.5 in 2002, according to National Surveys of Family Growth. The National Center for Health Statistics attributed the drop to several factors, including the legalization of abortion in 1973 and the new reproductive technologies that have reduced the number of unwanted pregnancies. Almost all of the decrease since 1973 has come in unrelated children; the percent of women adopting related (by blood or otherwise) children has held steady and 12.6 percent of all

women have lived with and cared for a child to whom they did not give birth.

Twice as many men as women had ever adopted a child — 2.3 percent compared to 1.1 percent overall — probably because men are more likely than women to adopt their stepchildren.

In 2002, there were 28.3 million currently married women between the ages of 18 and 44. Of these, 35.2 percent had considered adoption, 4.4 percent had taken steps toward adoption, and 566,000 were currently looking to adopt a child. Infertility leads many women to choose adoption: over a quarter of women ages 40-44 who had ever used infertility services had adopted a child.

Perhaps the greatest shifts have come in the number and origin of children available for adoption. Before 1973, never-married women under the age of 45 relinquished 8.7 percent of their children for adoption. In 1995, they gave up less than 1 percent. This drop has resulted in an increase in foreign adoptions and adoptions across race.

Of those looking to adopt, 94.6 percent of white women and 92.7 percent of black women said that they would prefer or accept a child of another race. According to a U.S. Census Bureau Special Report, of the 2.1 million adopted children in the U.S. in 2000, 12.5 percent, or 257,792, were foreign-born. Almost half of these foreign-born adopted children were born in Asia, with Korea as the largest single source of foreign-born adoptees — about 57,000 in 2000.

Marital Status of the Population by Sex and Age, 2006 (numbers in thousands)

Sex and Age	Total	Never married Number	Never married Percent	Married Number	Married Percent	Widowed Number	Widowed Percent	Divorced Number	Divorced Percent	Separated Number	Separated Percent
MALE											
Total 15+	113,073	37,086	32.8%	61,624	54.5%	2,624	2.3%	9,679	8.6%	2,059	1.8%
15-17	6,817	6,741	98.9	25	0.3	1	N.A.	25	0.4	25	0.4
18-19	3,795	3,701	97.8	62	1.6	2	N.A.	2	N.A.	21	0.5
20-24	10,305	8,931	86.7	1,208	11.7	13	0.1	80	0.8	74	0.7
25-29	10,185	5,843	57.4	3,848	37.8	9	N.A.	312	3.1	173	1.7
30-34	9,639	3,223	33.4	5,815	59.1	12	0.1	555	5.8	187	1.9
35-39	10,305	2,396	23.3	6,689	64.9	21	0.2	973	9.4	225	2.2
40-44	11,039	2,045	18.5	7,286	66.0	62	0.6	1,356	12.3	289	2.6
45-49	11,041	1,530	13.9	7,550	68.4	84	0.8	1,555	14.1	321	2.9
50-54	9,916	1,064	10.7	6,881	69.3	112	1.1	1,582	16.0	278	2.8
55-64	14,856	1,030	6.9	11,231	75.6	323	2.2	2,005	13.5	266	1.8
65-74	8,518	350	4.1	6,530	76.7	621	7.3	867	10.2	151	1.8
75-84	5,330	177	3.3	3,846	72.2	936	17.6	325	6.1	46	0.9
85+	1,327	46	3.5	804	60.6	429	32.4	43	3.2	4	0.3
FEMALE											
Total 15+	119,966	31,429	26.2%	61,217	51.0%	11,290	9.4%	13,127	10.9%	2,904	2.4%
15-17	6,523	6,435	98.6	32	0.5	6	0.1	24	0.4	27	0.4
18-19	3,766	3,565	94.7	160	4.2	5	0.1	13	0.3	24	0.6
20-24	10,075	7,589	75.3	2,171	21.5	17	0.2	152	1.5	146	1.4
25-29	9,953	4,289	43.1	4,820	48.4	43	0.4	526	5.3	276	2.8
30-34	9,700	2,327	24.0	6,206	64.0	52	0.5	778	8.0	337	3.5
35-39	10,450	1,741	16.7	6,877	65.8	114	1.1	1,334	12.8	384	3.7
40-44	11,295	1,476	13.1	7,437	65.8	201	1.8	1,764	15.6	418	3.7
45-49	11,464	1,299	11.3	7,595	66.3	281	2.5	1,916	16.7	371	3.2
50-54	10,354	947	9.1	6,762	65.3	421	4.1	1,901	18.4	323	3.1
55-64	16,100	1,041	6.5	10,264	63.8	1,540	9.6	2,868	17.8	387	2.4
65-74	10,022	391	3.9	5,623	56.1	2,631	26.3	1,235	12.3	142	1.4
75-84	7,629	247	3.2	2,807	36.8	3,989	52.3	531	7.0	56	0.7
85+	2,636	83	3.1	463	17.6	1,990	75.5	87	3.3	13	0.5

Note: Totals may not add up due to independent rounding.
Source: U.S. Bureau of the Census, www.census.gov.

Fertility Rates of U.S. Women, 1930-2006

Year	General fertility rate	Total fertility rate	Year	General fertility rate	Total fertility rate
1930	89.2	2,600	1994	66.7	2,002
1935	77.2	2,250	1995	65.6	1,978
1940	79.9	2,301	1996	65.3	1,976
1945	85.9	2,491	1997	65.0	1,971
1950	106.2	3,091	1998	65.6	1,999
1955	118.3	3,574	1999	65.9	2,007
1960	118.0	3,654	2000	67.5	2,056
1965	96.6	2,928	2001	66.9	2,034
1970	87.9	2,480	2002	64.8	2,013
1975	66.0	1,774	2003	65.8	N.A.
1980	68.4	1,840	2004	66.4	2,045
1985	66.3	1,840	2005	66.7	2,054
1990	70.9	2,081	2006	68.5	2,101

Source: U.S. National Center for Health Statistics, *National Vital Statistics Reports*.

Median Age at First Marriage, by Sex, 1890-2006

Year	Male	Female	Year	Male	Female
1890	26.1	22.0	1994	26.7	24.5
1900	25.9	21.9	1995	26.9	24.5
1910	25.1	21.6	1996	27.1	24.8
1920	24.6	21.2	1997	26.8	25.0
1930	24.3	21.3	1998	26.7	25.0
1940	24.3	21.5	1999	26.9	25.1
1950	22.8	20.3	2000	26.8	25.1
1960	22.8	20.3	2001	26.9	25.1
1970	23.2	20.8	2002	26.9	25.3
1980	24.7	22.0	2003	27.1	25.3
1990	26.1	23.9	2004	27.4	25.3
1991	26.3	24.1	2005	27.1	25.3
1993	26.5	24.5	2006	27.5	25.5

Source: U.S. Bureau of the Census, *America's Families and Living Arrangements 2005* (2006). www.census.gov.

Black-White Married Couples in the U.S., 1960-2006 (thousands)

Year	Total married couples	Total black-white couples	Husband black, wife white	Wife black, husband white
1960	40,491	51	25	26
1970	44,598	65	41	24
1980	49,714	167	122	45
1990	53,256	211	150	61
1995	54,937	328	206	122
1998	55,305	330	210	120
1999	55,849	364	240	124
2000	56,497	363	268	95
2002	57,919	395	279	116
2004	59,064	413	287	126
2006	59,528	403	286	117

Source: U.S. Bureau of the Census, *America's Families and Living Arrangements 2000* (2001); *Statistical Abstract of the United States, 2008*. www.census.gov.

Divorced Persons per 1,000 Married Persons by Sex and Race 1960-2006

Sex/year	All races	White	Black	Hispanic[1]
Both sexes:				
1960	35	33	62	N.A.
1970	47	44	83	61
1980	100	92	203	98
1990	142	133	282	129
2000	175	166	330	145
2003	185	177	339	142
2006	186	176	349	145
Male:				
1960	28	27	45	N.A.
1970	35	32	62	40
1980	79	74	149	64
1990	118	112	208	103
2000	151	145	257	120
2003	153	151	238	122
2006	157	152	256	113
Female:				
1960	42	38	78	N.A.
1970	60	56	104	81
1980	120	110	258	132
1990	166	153	358	155
2000	200	187	406	168
2003	216	204	444	163
2006	214	201	445	178

Note: Persons 18 years and over. Per 1,000 married persons with spouse present. 1. Persons of Hispanic origin may be of any race.
Source: U.S. Bureau of the Census, *Children's Living Arrangements and Characteristics* (March 2002); *America's Families and Living Arrangements 2006 (2007)*. www.census.gov

Percent of First Marriages Ending in Separation or Divorce, by Length of Marriage and Age of Wife, 2000

Length of Marriage (years)	Percent ending in separation or divorce				
		Wife's age at first marriage			
	Total	Under 18	18-19	20-24	25 and over
1	3%	4%	4%	2%	2%
2	7	10	9	6	5
3	12	17	15	10	8
4	16	23	20	14	11
5	20	29	24	17	15
6	23	34	28	19	17
7	26	39	32	22	19
8	29	42	35	25	20
9	31	45	37	27	22
10	33	48	40	29	24
11	35	49	42	31	26
12	38	52	44	33	29
13	39	54	46	33	30
14	41	57	47	35	31
15+	43	59	49	36	35

Source: National Center for Health Statistics, *Advance Data: First Marriage Dissolution, Divorce, and Remarriage: United States*, May 31, 2001.

HOUSEHOLDS AND FAMILIES

Since the very first census in 1790, the federal government has not only attempted to count every individual, it has also tried to determine where those individuals live and with whom. While the definition of *household* has changed somewhat over the years, it has remained a central element in understanding the basic structure of American society. Since 1970, changes in the size and composition of the household unit have revealed the extent of social change more clearly than any other measure. Note that data on households and families is from the Census Bureau's annual Current Population Survey, not from the decennial census.

▶HOUSEHOLDS

Virtually all Americans are part of a household. As of March 2000, the Census Bureau determined that 274 million persons belonged to a household, even if that household consisted of only one person. A small number of people in institutions or in unique group living arrangements do not belong to households. According to the official Census Bureau definition, a household consists of all persons who occupy a housing unit. A house, an apartment or other group of rooms, or a single room, is regarded as a housing unit when it is occupied or intended for occupancy as separate living quarters; that is when the occupants do not live and eat with any other persons in the structure and there is direct access from the outside or through a common hall.

There are two major categories of households identified by the Census Bureau: family and nonfamily. A family or family household requires the presence of at least two persons, the householder (i.e. the person in whose name the housing unit is owned or rented) and one or more additional family members related to the householder through birth, adoption or marriage. A nonfamily household consists of a householder who either lives alone or exclusively with persons who are not related to the householder. Since 1970 the rapid growth of nonfamily households has led to a continuous increase in the number of households and a fall in the average number of persons in each.

In 2006, there were 114.4 million households in the U.S., the largest number ever, with an average of 2.57 persons in each, unchanged since 2003. The overall trend since the 1970's has been towards larger households; in that decade the number of households increased by more than 20 percent and over 17.3 million units, nearly double the growth of the 1940's and 1950's and over 60 percent more than the relatively explosive 1960's. The most significant change helping to ignite this surge was the unprecedented increase in the number of nonfamily households, which grew by 77.7 percent in the 1970's and 28.4 percent during the 1980's.

Several factors help to account for this change, including the rapid rise in the divorce rate, as well as an increase in the number of young single people living on their own and deciding to postpone marriage. In 2006, 30.5 million people, or more than 26% of all households, lived alone—a considerable increase even since the 2000 Census figure of 26.7 million. The number of people living alone grew 59 percent during the 1970's, 21 percent during the 1980's, but only 16 percent from 1990 to 2000.

In 2006, an additional 5.01 million unmarried-couple households were another large segment of the nonfamily population. Unmarried couples made up only a small percentage of all U.S. couples, but their numbers have continued to skyrocket since their sudden appearance on the American social landscape during the 1970's. There were only 523,000 unmarried couples living together in 1970, but their numbers had tripled to 1.6 million in 1980. A growing number of unmarried couples (1.9 million in 2006) have children under 18 years old in their households. This doesn't necessarily mean more children are being born out of wedlock, however, since this category includes children from previous marriages living with an un-remarried parent. As currently defined by the Census Bureau, an unmarried-couple household is two persons of the opposite sex who share living quarters. Although a close personal relationship is implied, other types—including tenancy—are included. But no more than two unrelated adults are present in an unmarried-couple household although children under age 18 may be present.

In 2000, there were 594,391 same-sex unmarried partner households in the United States. That's less than 1 percent of total households, but in some metropolitan areas the percentage is significantly

U.S. Households, Number and Size, 1940–2006

Year	Number of households ('000s)	Average number per household		
		All ages	Under 18 years	18 years and older
1940	34,949	3.67	1.14	2.53
1950	43,544	3.37	1.06	2.31
1960[1]	52,799	3.33	1.21	2.12
1970	63,401	3.14	1.09	2.05
1980	80,776	2.76	0.79	1.97
1990	93,347	2.63	0.69	1.94
1995	98,990	2.65	0.71	1.93
1997	101,018	2.64	0.71	1.93
1998	102,528	2.62	0.70	1.92
1999	103,874	2.61	0.69	1.92
2000	104,705	2.62	0.69	1.93
2006	114,384	2.57	0.65	1.92

Note: 1. Alaska and Hawaii included for first time. **Source:** U.S. Bureau of the Census, *The Statistical History of the U.S.* (1976); *America's Families and Living Arrangements: 2006* (2007).

Unmarried Couple Households, 1960–2006

Year	Total	Without children under 15	With children under 15
1960	439,000	242,000	197,000
1970	523,000	327,000	196,000
1980	1,589,000	1,159,000	431,000
1990	2,856,000	1,966,000	891,000
1995	3,668,000	2,349,000	1,319,000
1997	4,130,000	2,660,000	1,470,000
1998	4,236,000	2,716,000	1,520,000
1999	4,486,000	2,981,000	1,505,000
2000	4,736,000	3,061,000	1,675,000
2006	5,012,000	3,041,000[1]	1,971,000[1]

Note: 1. 2006 figures for children under 18. Figures may not add to total due to rounding. **Source:** *America's Families and Living Arrangements: 2006* (2007).

higher; in San Francisco same-sex unmarried partners constitute 2.7 percent of all households. Over 85 percent of same-sex households are in metropolitan areas.

Despite all the attention given to the growth of nonfamily households, the fact remains that the overwhelming majority of Americans live in some kind of family situation. This is not to say that the size and structure of the family hasn't undergone major revamping in recent decades but rather to emphasize its inherent strength as the basic social unit despite the presence of powerful forces for change.

▶**FAMILIES**

In 2006 there were 77.4 million families in the U.S., up from 51.6 million in 1970. But the 21st- century American family bears less and less resemblance to the 20th-century family. Perhaps the greatest change is the drop in the percentage of nuclear families: married couples with their own children. These types of households represented 45 percent of the total in 1960; in 2000, they dropped below 25 for the first time (23.5 percent). Market researchers who once assumed the family consisted of four members now base their assumptions on families of three, re-

flecting a steady, dramatic decline in the average family size, from 3.58 in 1970 to 3.13 in 2006. These numbers indicate a growing number of families opting not to have children. They constituted 44.1 percent of all families in 1970, but since 1990, they have outnumbered families with children. In 2006, 35.6 million families had children under 18, compared to 41.8 million without children.

More important, perhaps, the proportion of married-couple families declined from 86.8 percent of all family households in 1970 to 75.1 percent in 2006, while the number of family households headed by females with no husbands present climbed from 5.5 million, or 10.7 percent of all family households in 1970, to 14.1 million, or 18.2 percent in 2006. (A startling 45.3 percent of black families were headed by single women in 2006, up from 28.0 percent in 1970, but down from 47.2 percent in 2000.)

A related development, recently turned into a political issue by those advocating "family values," has been the rising number of single-parent situations. 24.8 percent of families with children under 18 were headed by a single parent in 2006, up from only 13 percent in 1970. The vast majority of these single-parent families were headed by women. The number of households headed by never-married women

Households and Families: Growth and Change, 1960–2006

Type of unit	1960	1970	1980	1990	2000	2006	% Change 2000-2006
All Households	**52,799**	**63,401**	**80,776**	**93,347**	**104,705**	**114,384**	**9.2%**
Average size	3.33	3.14	2.76	2.63	2.62	2.57	—
Families	**45,111**	**51,586**	**59,550**	**66,090**	**72,025**	**77,402**	**7.5%**
Average size	3.67	3.58	3.29	3.17	3.17	3.13	—
Married couple	39,329	44,755	49,112	52,317	55,311	58,179	5.2
Male householder[1]	1,275	1,239	1,733	2,884	4,028	5,130	27.4
Female householder[1]	4,507	5,591	8,705	10,890	12,687	14,093	11.1
Unrelated subfamilies	**207**	**130**	**360**	**534**	**571**	**504**	**-11.7%**
Married couple	75	27	20	68	37	36	N.A.[2]
Father-child[1]	47	11	36	45	57	59	N.A.[2]
Mother-child[1]	85	91	304	421	477	409	-14.3
Related subfamilies	**1,514**	**1,150**	**1,150**	**2,403**	**2,983**	**3,265**	**9.5%**
Married couple	871	617	582	871	1,149	1,312	14.2
Father-child[1]	115	48	54	153	201	347	72.6
Mother-child[1]	528	484	512	1,378	1,633	1,606	-2.0
Nonfamily households	**7,895**	**11,945**	**21,226**	**27,257**	**32,680**	**36,982**	**13.2%**
Male householder	2,716	4,063	8,807	11,606	14,641	16,753	14.4
Female householder	5,179	7,882	12,419	15,651	18,039	20,230	12.1
One person	6,896	10,851	18,296	22,999	26,724	30,497[3]	14.1

Notes: 1. No spouse present. 2. Not shown; base less than 75,000. 3. from American Community Survey.
Source: U.S. Bureau of the Census, *America's Families and Living Arrangements 2006* (2007).

Families: Number, Average Size and Percent Distribution by Number of Children, 1970–2006

Year	Number of families ('000s)	Average size of family	Percent distribution by number of own children under 18				
			None	1	2	3	4 or more
1970	51,586	3.58	44.1%	18.2%	17.4%	10.6%	9.8%
1980	59,550	3.29	47.9	20.9	19.3	7.8	4.1
1985	62,706	3.23	50.4	20.9	18.6	7.2	3.0
1990	66,090	3.17	51.1	20.5	18.5	7.0	2.8
1995	69,305	3.19	50.5	20.3	19.1	7.3	2.8
1997	70,241	3.19	50.6	20.4	18.9	7.3	2.8
1999	71,535	3.18	51.6	20.0	18.3	7.3	2.8
2000	72,025	3.17	50.4	21.5	18.5	6.9	2.8
2005	76,858	3.13	47.1	19.6	17.9	7.0[1]	2.6
2006[2]	77,402	3.13	53.0	20.0	18.0	9.0[1]	N.A.

Notes: 1. Represents percentage for 3 or more children. 2. Numbers rounded in source. Source: U.S. Bureau of the Census, *America's Families and Living Arrangements 2006*. www.census.gov.

Living Arrangements of Children Under 18, by Race, 1970–2006

Arrangement	1970 Number ('000s)	1970 Percent	1990 Number ('000s)	1990 Percent	2000 Number ('000s)	2000 Percent	2006 Number ('000s)	2006 Percent
All children								
Children under 18	69,162	100.0%	64,137	100.0%	72,012	100.0%	73,664	100.0%
Living with:								
Two parents	58,939	85.2	46,503	72.5	49,795	69.1	49,661	67.4
One Parent	8,199	11.9	15,867	24.7	19,220	26.7	20,619	28.0
Mother only	7,452	10.8	13,874	21.6	16,162	22.4	17,161	23.3
Father only	748	1.1	1,993	3.1	3,058	4.2	3,458	4.7
Other relatives	1,547	2.2	1,421	2.2	2,160	3.0	2,419	3.3
Nonrelatives only	477	0.7	346	0.5	837	1.2	964	1.3
White children								
Children under 18	58,791	100.0%	51,390	100.0%	56,455	100.0%	58,567	100.0%
Living with:								
Two parents	52,624	89.5	40,593	79.0	42,497	75.3	42,906	73.3
One Parent	5,110	8.7	9,869	19.2	12,192	21.6	13,513	23.1
Mother only	4,581	7.8	8,321	16.2	9,765	17.3	10,772	18.4
Father only	528	0.9	1,549	3.0	2,427	4.3	2,741	4.7
Other relatives	695	1.2	708	1.4	1,132	2.0	1,451	2.4
Nonrelatives only	362	0.6	220	0.4	634	1.1	697	1.2
Black children								
Children under 18	9,422	100.0%	10,018	100.0%	11,412	100.0%	12,261	100.0%
Living with:								
Two parents	5,508	58.5	3,781	37.7	4,286	37.6	4,338	35.4
One Parent	2,995	31.8	5,484	54.7	6,080	53.3	6.807	55.5
Mother only	2,783	29.5	5,132	51.2	5,596	49.0	6,199	50.6
Father only	213	2.3	353	3.5	484	4.2	608	5.0
Other relatives	822	8.7	655	6.5	879	7.7	876	7.1
Nonrelatives only	97	1.0	98	1.0	167	1.5	239	1.9
Hispanic children								
Children under 18	4,006	100.0%	7,174	100.0%	11,613	100.0%	14,697	100.0%
Living with:								
Two parents	3,111	77.7	4,789	66.8	7,561	65.1	9,686	65.9
One Parent	N.A.	N.A.	2,154	30.0	3,425	29.5	4,277	29.1
Mother only	N.A.	N.A.	1,943	27.1	2,919	25.4	3,674	25.0
Father only	N.A.	N.A.	211	2.9	506	4.4	603	4.1
Other relatives	N.A.	N.A.	177	2.5	431	3.7	531	3.6
Nonrelatives only	N.A.	N.A.	54	0.8	196	1.7	203	1.4

Note: Hispanic children may be of any race. Excludes persons under 18 years who were maintaining households or family groups and spouses. **Source:** U.S. Bureau of the Census, *America's Families and Living Arrangements 2006* (2007).

with children continues to grow. There were 248,000 such households in 1970; in 2006, there were 4.9 million of them, almost the same as the number headed by divorced women with children.

According to the Census Bureau, the period between 1990 and 2000 saw a general stabilizing of these trends; in the past 10 years, the percentage of married couple families and single-parent families has remained fairly constant. The one startling change was the growth of single-parent homes headed by fathers. In 2006, they numbered 2.5 million, up from 1.8 million in 1998.

Another important though less vital sign of change is the growth in the number of so-called *subfamilies*. These are families who live in a household and are either related or not to the householder; the Census Bureau describes a *related subfamily* as a married couple with or without children, or one parent with one or more single (never married) children under 18, living in a household and related to the person who maintains the household. They are not counted in the total number of families. Related subfamilies have nearly tripled since 1980 and now stand at nearly 3 million.

An *unrelated subfamily* is a group of two persons or more who are related to one another by birth, marriage or adoption, but who are not related to the householder. Unrelated subfamilies numbered 483,000 in 2006.

▶SINGLE PARENTS AND GROWN CHILDREN LIVING AT HOME

Among the social changes that have taken place over the last 20 years, two of the most revealing are where children live, and how soon young people start to live on their own. Since 1970, the percentage of children under 18 living with only one parent has more than doubled. In 2006, 28 percent lived with only one parent, as compared to just under 12 percent in 1970 (4.6 percent lived with neither parent). This increase reflects not only a higher divorce rate, but a also an increase in the number of children born to unwed mothers, especially among blacks. The numbers of households headed by unmarried black women and divorced black women were equal in 1970. In 2006, never-married black mother households outnumbered black households headed by divorced or separated black mothers by almost two to one. In 2006, 55.5 percent of black children, 23.1 percent of white children, and 29 percent of Hispanic children under the age of 18 lived with one parent only, usually the mother. Older children are living with their parents longer than they used to - due in part to delayed marriage and rising housing costs. In 1970, 8 percent of 25-34 year olds lived with their parents, by 1996 that number increased to nearly 12.3 percent. In 2004, almost a third of single men ages 18-34 (31.7 percent) lived in their parents' homes. However, most of this group (78.3 percent) were under 25. Because they marry younger and, even single, are more likely to own their own home, women were less likely to live at home with their parents. Only 25.2% of women ages 18-34 were living with their parents in 2004, and 86.6 percent of women ages 25-29 had moved out of their parents' homes.

▶LIVING WITH GRANDPARENTS

In 2006, the Census Bureau estimated that 3.73 million (5.0 percent of the nation's 73.7 million) children under age 18 lived in the home of their grandparents. This is up from 3.2 percent in 1970 and 3.6 percent in 1980, but down from the all-time high of 5.7 percent in 1996. Of those children, 60.2 percent had at least one parent in the household. Black children were more likely (10 percent) to live in a household with a grandparent present, compared with 5.5 percent of Hispanic children, 3 percent non-Hispanic white, and 4 percent Asian/Pacific Islanders.

HOUSING

According to the Census Bureau, there were 111.6 million occupied housing units in the U.S. in 2007, the latest year for which data are available. Of these units, 75.1 million (67.3 percent) were occupied by homeowners, while the remaining 36.5 million (32.7 percent) were occupied by renters.

Housing units The U.S. Department of Housing and Urban Development conducts the American Housing Survey every two years. In 2005, the last year for which data is available, traditional houses were still the vast majority. Nearly two of every three occupied homes (77.7 million) were detached single unit structures. Mobile homes or trailers, numbering 8.6 million, are not included in those totals. Another 7.0 million were attached single-unit structures such as a brownstone or row house. Cooperatives and condominiums, totalling more than 7.4 million, are counted separately since they may include any number of dwellings.

Size of housing units Although the typical American family is growing smaller, the typical American house is growing larger. The median

Characteristics of Occupied Housing Units 1995-2005

Characteristic	1995 Units ('000)	1995 Percent of units	1999 Units ('000)	1999 Percent of units	2003 Units ('000)	2003 Percent of units	2005 Units ('000)	2005 Percent of units
Total occupied units	97,693	100.0%	102,803	100.0%	120,777	100.0%	124,377	100.0%
Owner occupied	63,544	65	68,796	66.9	72,238	59.8	74,931	60.2
Renter occupied	34,150	35	31,007	30.2	33,604	27.8	33,940	27.3
Units in structure								
Single, detached	60,826	62.30%	64,536	62.80%	74,916	62.0%	77,703	62.5%
Single, attached	5,545	5.7	6,963	6.8	7,227	6.0	7,046	5.7
2 to 4	9,299	9.5	8,572	8.3	9,965	8.3	10,071	8.1
5 to 9	4,803	4.9	4,847	4.7	6,012	5.0	6,073	4.9
10 to 19	4,342	4.4	4,416	4.3	5,433	4.5	5,696	4.6
20 to 49	3,244	3.3	3,343	3.2	3,964	3.3	4,402	3.5
50 or more	3,470	3.6	3,341	3.2	4,289	3.6	4,757	3.8
Mobile home or trailer	6,164	6.3	6,785	6.6	8,971	7.4	8,630	6.9
Median Size								
Size of unit (sq. ft.)	1,732	N.A.	1,730	N.A.	1,708	N.A.	1,795	N.A.
Size of lot (acres)	0.43	N.A.	0.34	N.A.	0.35	N.A.	0.38	N.A
Number of bedrooms								
One	11,777	12.1%	11,986	11.70%	14,389	11.9%	11,857	9.5%
Two	29,146	29.8	29,166	28.4	34,810	28.8	28,218	22.7
Three	40,302	41.2	43,103	41.9	48,819	40.4	46,137	37.1
Four or more	15,421	15.8	17,689	17.2	21,543	17.8	21,830	17.6
Number of bathrooms								
None	465	0.50%	676	0.70%	642	0.53%	554	0.45%
One	43,777	44.8	42,838	41.7	48,264	40.0	39,920	32.1
One and a half	14,780	15.1	16,189	15.8	17,626	14.6	15,878	12.8
Two or more	38,671	39.6	43,100	41.9	52,625	43.6	52,520	42.2
Median age (years)	28	N.A.	31	N.A.	32	N.A.	34	N.A.
Mortgage status[1]								
None, owned free and clear	24,518	38.60%	25,604	37.22%	25,020	20.7%	24,776	19.9%
One mortgage	34,730	54.7	28,960	42.1	33,429	27.7	33,409	26.9
Two mortgages	4,244	6.7	6,884	10.0	8,127	6.7	10,877	8.7
Three or more mortgages	52	0.1	415	0.6	855	0.7	1,164	0.93
Median years remaining	20	N.A.	20	N.A.	22	N.A.	24	N.A.
Median amount outstanding	$48,466	N.A.	$63,939	N.A.	$82,010	N.A.	$92,607	N.A.

Note: 1. In this category, figures are perecentages of owner-occupied units only, which represent approximately two-thirds of all occupied units. Not all homeowners reported their mortgage status. **Source:** U.S. Bureau of the Census, *American Housing Surveys* 1995, 1999, 2003 and 2005.

size of all single, detached one-family houses (including mobile homes) was 1,795 square feet in 2005, up from 1,737 in 2001; for owner-occupied houses, the figure was 1,858 square feet, also up from 1,798 in 2001. About 27 percent of single houses (21 million) had more than 2,500 square feet, and 9.6 percent (7.4 million) had less than 1,000 square feet. The majority of houses in 2005 (64.6 percent) had between 4 and 7 rooms; most houses (54.6 percent) had 3 or more bedrooms, and 42.2 percent had two or more bathrooms.

Homeownership Rates, 1890–2007

Year	Homeownership rate	Year	Homeownership rate
1890	47.8%	1990	64.2%
1900	46.7	1995	64.7
1910	45.9	1997	65.7
1920	45.6	1998	66.3
1930	47.8	1999	66.8
1940	43.6	2000	67.4
1950	55.0	2001	67.8
1960	61.9	2004	69.0
1970	62.9	2005	68.9
1980	64.4	2007	68.1

Note: Figures from 1890-1990 are from the decennial census, which counts every home. Figures from 1995-2007 are from the Census Bureau's annual *Housing Vacancy Survey*, which uses statistical samples. **Source:** U.S. Census Bureau.

Equipment and fuel More houses had air conditioning (78.4 percent) than a dishwasher (55.1 percent), a washing machine (71.8 percent), or clothes dryer (69.2 percent). Natural gas was the fuel of choice for most houses: it heated 50.3 percent of houses. Electricity heated 27.5 percent, while 7.5 percent of houses had oil furnaces. Oil is most popular in the Northeast, where it is used to heat 36.1 percent of all houses; outside the Northeast, fewer than 2 percent of houses use oil heat. Gas heats 68.1 percent of the houses in the West and and 79.8 percent of the houses in the Midwest. Electricity heats 54.9 percent of houses in the South. Over 352,000 households reported using alternative energy in 2005.

Growth of housing In 2005, the median age of all housing structures in the U.S. was 32 years (i.e. built in 1973). Only 7.9 million units built before 1919 were still in use. This reflects the extraordinary growth of the housing industry during the 1970's and 80's, when 35.8 million of extant units were built. By comparison, only 17.9 million of the housing units still in use were built between 1920 and 1950.

Home ownership Home ownership rates, while still high, have begun to decline from the record levels earlier in the decade. More than two thirds of householders (68.1 percent) owned their

Homeownership Rates in the U.S. by Age, Race, and Hispanic Origin, 1982–2007

Characteristic	1982	1985	1990	1995	1999	2000	2004	2007
U.S., total	**64.8%**	**63.9%**	**63.9%**	**64.7%**	**66.8%**	**67.4%**	**69.0%**	**68.1%**
By age								
Under 25	19.3	17.2	15.7	15.9	19.9	21.7	25.2	24.8%
Under 35	41.2	39.9	38.5	38.6	39.7	40.8	43.1	41.7
35 to 44	70.0	68.1	66.3	65.2	67.2	67.9	69.2	67.8
45 to 54	77.4	75.9	75.2	75.2	76.0	76.5	77.2	75.4
55 to 64	80.0	79.5	79.3	79.5	81.0	80.3	81.7	80.6
65 and over	74.4	74.8	76.3	78.1	80.1	80.4	81.1	80.4
By race and origin								
White	N.A.	N.A.	N.A.	68.7	70.5	71.1	72.8	72.0%
Black	N.A.	N.A.	N.A.	42.7	46.3	47.2	49.1	47.2
Asian or Pacific Islander	N.A.	N.A.	N.A.	50.8	53.1	52.8	59.8	60.0
Hispanic (all races)	N.A.	N.A.	N.A.	42.0	45.5	46.3	48.1	49.7

Source: U.S. Bureau of the Census, *2001 Housing Vacancy Survey*, 2002; *Housing Vacancies and Homeownership Annual Statistics*, 2007 (2008).

Average Sales Prices of New One-Family Houses, by Region, 1965–2007

Year	Northeast	Midwest	South	West	United States Amount	United States Annual percent increase
1965	$22,900	$22,800	$18,900	$23,200	$21,500	N.A.
1970	32,800	28,000	24,000	26,900	26,600	N.A.
1975	47,000	43,400	39,600	44,300	42,600	N.A.
1980	80,300	74,400	69,100	89,400	76,400	6.4%
1985	121,900	95,400	88,900	111,800	100,800	3.3
1990	190,500	133,000	123,500	180,600	149,800	0.7
1995	216,600	157,200	142,000	169,800	158,700	2.7
1998	240,100	179,200	159,700	200,500	181,900	3.2
2000	274,800	199,300	179,000	238,900	207,000	5.8
2002	301,300	209,800	197,500	276,500	228,700	7.3
2004	366,100	240,800	232,800	340,000	274,500	11.4
2005[1]	397,000	249,800	232,800	388,700	297,000	8.2
2006[1]	428,300	257,100	257,700	405,900	305,900	3.0
2007[1]	437,700	256,800	269,800	403,700	313,600	2.5

Note: Figures are in current dollars. **Source:** U.S. Bureau of the Census, *Median and Average Sales Price of New Houses Sold by Region* (2008). 1. Starting in 2005, the Sales Price and Price per Square Foot ranges for new one-family homes were updated to better reflect current economic conditions.

homes in 2007, which was up from 63.9 percent in 1990 but down from the high of 69 percent in 2004. Among those under 25, homeownership held steady from 2006 rates at 24.8 percent after climbing from 14.8 percent in 1993. Rates held at 81.5 percent for those ages 60-64, but fell from 2006 levels for all other age groups. Homeownership rates for the population over 75 was 78.7 percent, down from 80.6 percent in 2002, but well above historical rates, reflecting the relative independence of elderly people today.

The steady decline in homeownership since 2004 is a reversal of an increase that began in the late 1980's.

In 2007, married-couple families had the highest rates of homeownership (83.8 percent) while families with only a female head-of-household had the lowest (49.9 percent). However, among people without families, women were far more likely than men to own their own homes, with the rate for single women (59.1 percent) well above that for single men (50.2 percent). Homeownership rates fell across the country but remained highest in the Midwest (71.9 percent) and South (70.1 percent) and lowest in the Northeast (65.0 percent) and West (63.5 percent).

Housing costs According to the National Association of Realtors, the median sales price of an

Existing One-Family Houses Sold and Median Sales Price, by Region, 1970–2007

	Houses Sold ('000s)				Median Sales Price				
Year	United States	Northeast	Midwest	South	West	United States	Northeast	Midwest	South	West
1970	1,612	251	501	568	292	$23,000	$25,700	$20,100	$20,100	$24,300
1975	2,476	370	701	862	543	35,300	39,300	30,100	30,100	39,600
1980	2,973	403	806	1,092	672	62,200	60,800	51,900	51,900	89,300
1985	3,134	561	806	1,063	704	75,500	88,900	58,900	58,900	95,400
1990	3,219	458	809	1,193	759	92,000	126,400	75,300	75,300	129,600
1995	3,888	547	945	1,433	964	110,500	126,700	94,800	94,800	141,000
1998	4,970	662	1,130	1,868	1,309	128,400	135,900	114,300	114,300	164,800
1999	5,205	656	1,148	2,015	1,386	133,300	139,000	119,600	119,600	173,900
2000	5,152	643	1,119	2,015	1,376	139,000	139,400	123,600	128,300	183,000
2002	5,566	656	1,217	2,203	1,490	158,100	164,300	136,000	147,300	215,400
2004	6,779	1,113	1,550	2,542	1,574	195,400	243,800	154,600	170,400	286,400
2005	7,075	1,170	1,587	2,703	1,615	219,600	271,300	170,600	181,700	335,300
2007	5,652	1,006	1,327	2,235	1,084	217,900	288,100	161,400	178,800	342,500

Source: National Association of Realtors, *Existing Home Sales* (June 2008).

Median Sales Prices of Existing Single-Family Homes for Selected Metropolitan Areas, 1985–2007

Metropolitan area	1985	1995	2000	2005	2007
Atlanta, Ga.	$66,200[1]	$ 97,500	$131,200	$167,200	$172,000
Baltimore, Md.	72,600	111,300	153,000	265,300	286,100
Boston, Mass.	134,200	179,000	314,200	413,200	395,600
Chicago, Ill.	81,100	147,900	171,800	264,200	276,600
Cincinnati, Ohio-Ky.-In.	60,200	100,400	126,700	145,900	140,800
Cleveland, Ohio	64,400	104,700	N.A.	138,900	130,000
Dallas, Tex.	94,000	96,400	122,500	147,600	150,900
Denver, Colo.	84,300	127,300	196,800	247,100	245,400
Detroit, Mich.	51,700	98,200	N.A.	134,500	140,300
Honolulu, Hawaii	N.A.	349,000	295,000	590,000	643,500
Houston, Tex.	78,600	79,200	116,100	143,000	152,500
Kansas City, Mo.-Kans.	61,400	91,700	127,400	156,700	153,300
Las Vegas, Nev.	N.A.	113,500	137,400	304,700	297,700
Los Angeles area, Calif.	125,200	179,900	215,900	529,000	589,200
Miami, Fla.	80,500	107,100	144,600	370,100	365,500
Milwaukee, Wis.	67,500	114,700	140,700	215,700	223,400
Minneapolis-St. Paul, Minn.-Wis.	75,200	106,800	151,400	234,800	225,200
New Orleans, La.	N.A.	87,000	112,000	159,200	160,300
New York City area, N.Y. - N.J.	134,000	169,700	230,200	445,200	469,700
Philadelphia, Pa-N.J.	74,000	118,700	125,200	215,300	234,900
Phoenix, Ariz.	74,800	96,800	134,400	247,400	257,400
Pittsburgh, Pa.	N.A.	82,100	93,600	116,100	120,700
St. Louis, Mo.-Ill.	65,700	87,700	108,400	141,000	145,400
San Diego, Calif.	107,400	171,600	269,400	604,300	588,700
San Francisco Bay Area, Calif.	145,100	254,400	454,600	715,700	805,400
Seattle, Wash.	N.A.	159,000	230,100	316,800	386,900
Tampa-St. Petersburg-Clearwater, Fla.	58,400	78,300	110,800	205,300	214,900
Washington, D.C.-Md.-Va.	97,100	156,500	182,600	425,800	430,800
U.S. average	N.A.	$112,900	$139,000	$219,600	$217,900

Note: 1. Figure is for 1984.   Source: National Association of Realtors, *Home Sales* (June 2008).

existing single-family home in 2007 was $217,000, down 1.8 percent from the 2006 median of $221,000. Prices in continued to climb in some areas, including San Francisco Bay, which was again the most expensive place to buy a home: the median price was $836,800 in San Jose and $805,400 in San Francisco-Oakland, compared to $775,000 and $752,800 respectively in 2006. That outpaced even still-elevated markets in Honolulu ($643,500), Los Angeles ($589,200), San Diego ($588,700) and White Plains NY ($540,300). Prices in Washington, D.C. ($430,800) and Boston ($395,600) fell slightly.

But the biggest losses came in the South, such as in Tampa, where the median was down 6.1 percent to $214,900, and Midwestern markets like Detroit, which fell 7.5 percent to $140,300. Of the 30 largest cities in the country, Indianapolis had by far the lowest median housing price at only $120,500 in 2007. One third of home sales in 2007 were second homes, with 12 percent intended for vacation use (with a median sales price of $195,000) and 21 percent purchased as investment properties ($150,000).

Fair Market Monthly Rents for Existing Housing for Selected Metropolitan Areas, 2002 vs. 2008

Metropolitan area	2002			2008		
	1 bedroom	2 bedrooms	3 bedrooms	1 bedroom	2 bedrooms	3 bedrooms
Albuquerque, N.M	$505	$632	$871	$602	$760	$1,107
Atlanta, Ga.	720	839	1,119	741	824	1,003
Austin-San Marcos, Tex.	645	858	1,192	766	935	1,272
Baltimore, Md.	542	661	875	844	1,013	1,301
Boston, Mass.	782	979	1,223	1,153	1,353	1,618
Charlotte-Gastonia-Rock Hill, N.C.	585	659	869	667	740	932
Chicago, Ill.	711	848	1,060	840	944	1,154
Cincinnati, Ohio	416	557	746	560	726	972
Cleveland-Lorain-Elyria, Ohio	555	687	874	602	725	929
Colorado Springs, Colo.	486	647	902	631	797	1,137
Columbus, Ohio	471	605	768	568	718	903
Dallas, Tex.	647	830	1,146	718	871	1,156
Denver, Colo.	625	832	1,154	692	876	1,244
Detroit, Mich.	598	723	904	673	805	963
El Paso, Tex.	451	534	739	476	567	813
Fort Lauderdale, Fla.	609	754	1,049	1,016	1,221	1,689
Fort Worth-Arlington, Tex.	521	675	943	699	861	1,168
Fresno, Calif.	433	517	720	682	805	1,171
Honolulu, Hawaii	713	839	1,134	1,348	1,630	2,377
Houston, Tex.	529	684	954	702	852	1,136
Indianapolis, Ind.	465	559	700	611	726	939
Jacksonville, Fla.	530	638	843	701	816	1,024
Kansas City, Mo.	526	633	875	657	754	1,020
Las Vegas, Nev.	636	757	1,054	843	996	1,382
Los Angeles-Long Beach, Calif.	618	782	1,055	1,041	1,300	1,746
Memphis, Tenn.-Ark.-Miss.	462	542	753	669	743	990
Miami, Fla.	616	768	1,054	853	1,035	1,324
Milwaukee-Waukeshau, Wis.	504	633	794	665	795	1,002
Minneapolis-St. Paul, Minn.	580	742	1,004	699	848	1,110
Nashville, Tenn.	520	641	873	629	723	938
New Orleans, La.	423	527	717	846	990	1,271
New York, N.Y[1]	836	949	1,187	1,185	1,318	1,621
Oakland, Calif.	921	1,155	1,583	1,046	1,239	1,680
Oklahoma City, Okla.	422	547	760	528	641	865
Philadelphia, Pa.	657	812	1,016	781	932	1,116
Phoenix-Mesa, Ariz.	544	683	950	715	862	1,256
Pittsburgh, Pa.	476	574	719	557	666	828
Portland-Vancouver, Oreg.-Wash.	592	730	1,015	655	757	1,102
Sacramento, Calif.	547	685	950	805	982	1,417
Saint Louis, Mo.	429	556	724	572	711	916
Salt Lake City, Utah	550	698	971	625	754	1,061
San Antonio, Tex.	461	596	829	632	780	1,006
San Diego, Calif.	716	896	1,247	1,117	1,355	1,976
San Francisco, Calif.	1,154	1,459	2,001	1,272	1,592	2,125
San Jose, Calif.	1,199	1,481	2,030	1,076	1,293	1,859
Seattle-Bellevue-Everett, Wash.	639	809	1,123	783	942	1,331
Tampa-St. Petersburg, Fla.	557	690	917	730	883	1,119
Tucson, Ariz.	470	625	869	588	769	1,110
Tulsa, Okla.	427	559	778	545	666	880
Washington, D.C.-Md.-Va.	773	907	1,236	1,168	1,324	1,708
West Palm Beach-Boca Raton, Fla.	628	777	1,032	1,006	1,188	1,680

Note: Figures are projections made in the year prior to date shown. 1. Figures include areas outside Manhattan. Source: U.S. Dept. of Housing and Urban Development, Office of the Federal Housing Commissioner, *Fair Market Rents*, effective October 1, 2007.

Average monthly mortgage payments for all homeowners rose from $1,212 in 1998 to $1,240 in 1999 but fell again to $1,040 in 2005. These payments represented roughly 30 percent of owners's incomes, about the same as 2004, but up from 24 percent in 1976. Payments were higher among repeat buyers, but first-time buyers paid a larger percentage of their incomes toward their mortgages. Low interest rates were responsible for the popularity of fixed-rate mortgages, in which the consumer locks into a monthly payment for the life of the loan. Fixed-rate mortgages were the choice of 90 percent of mortgage buyers in 2005, up from 55 percent as recently as 1995.

Adjustable rate mortgages, in which the monthly payment changes based on the prevailing national interest rates, usually feature lower interest rates for the first several years, and higher rates toward the end of the loan. They were responsible for 5.9 percent of all mortgages in 2005, down from the high of 36.2 percent in 1995.

The average mortgage length was 28.5 years for first-time home buyers and 27.3 years for repeat buyers. Both numbers are down slightly from the year before. Meanwhile, the average down payment as a percentage of the purchase price continues to decline. In 1976, 26.9 percent of buyers put 10 percent or less down on a home purchase. In 1998, that number quintupled to 50.7 percent. The average down payment was 19.5 percent, down from 25.2 percent in 1976.

Renting In 2007, approximately almost a third of occupied housing was rented, with median rent of $1,017 per month. Rental vacancies were highest in the South (12.3 percent) and Midwest (11 percent) and lowest in the West and Northeast (6.7 and 7 percent, respectively).

Moving In 2006, approximately 48 million people, or 16 percent of the population over one year old, lived in a different home than they did the year before. One third of these moved within the same city or town; 21 percent moved to a different county in the same state; 16 percent moved between states; and 4 percent moved to the U.S. from another country.

Housing and the poor Despite the economic growth of recent years, the housing problems of the poor have grown worse. A shortage of affordable apartments has existed across the nation for several years, forcing 4.4 million poor families to pay more than half their income on rent. Between 2000 and 2005, the population spending over 30 percent of their income on housing increased 10 percent or more in 15 states. In 2007, 13 percent of Americans lived below the poverty line.

The major reasons for this development are stagnating wages for the unskilled, rising real estate values, and the government's failure to supply enough subsidized housing. The number of new subsidized units fell to 70,000 a year during the Reagan-Bush years, down from 260,000 during the Carter administration. When the Republicans took over Congress in 1995, the government actually stopped expanding the pool of subsidized housing for the first time in modern history.

About 15 million households currently qualify for federal housing assistance, but only 4.5 million families get it. Of those, about one-third live in conventional housing projects, while the rest receive subsidies that allow them to live in private housing. In each case, the tenants contribute 30 percent of their income toward the rent and the government provides the rest.

The recent subprime mortgage crisis led to almost 2 million foreclosures in 2007, a 149 percent increase from 2005. One result is that surveys by the National League of Cities and the National Coalition for the Homeless both found that two thirds of U.S. cities reported an increased number of homeless persons in their communities.

▶ THE HOMELESS

Although homeless people have become a common sight in almost every community, their plight is always surrounded by some kind of controversy, one that is fueled by a wide range of opinions, some based on fact and others on stereotypes. The often shrill debate about just who the homeless are and what can or should be done for them has been hampered by a lack of reliable information on everything from the causes of homelessness to the actual number of people living on the streets or in shelters.

The number of homeless Because homelessness is a temporary circumstance, it is nearly impossible to measure the number of homeless. In 1990, the Census Bureau made the first comprehensive federal effort to count the homeless, and identified a total of 228,621 homeless persons on the night of March 21-22, but most studies since then have suggested that the number is much higher.

In 1996, the Department of Housing and Urban Development (HUD) counted 470,000 homeless, but suggested that this only represented a quarter of

Sheltered Homeless, Impoverished, and General U.S. Households, 2005

Household Type	% of Sheltered Homeless Population	% of U.S. Poverty Population	% of U.S. Population
Persons not living with children	65.7%	44.8%	51.7%
Adult male	47.4	19.8	25.7
Adult female	15.6	25.0	26.0
Adult, gender unknown	1.3	0.0	0.0
Unaccompanied youth[1]	1.4	—	0.1
Persons living with children	34.4%	53.9%	48.0%
Adult, with child(ren)	13.0	20.4	22.5
Child, with adult(s)	21.2	33.5	25.5
Household member, age unknown	0.2	0.0	0.0

Note: 1. If children under age 18 are present in a household with no adults, they are identified as unaccompanied youth. This includes parents under age 18. **Source:** *U.S. Census Bureau 2006 Summary* (2007).

all homeless. In January 2007, a one-night count found 671,888 homeless persons nationwide, one third of which were families. This number was down from 759,101 in January 2006, but some of the decline may be due to a change in reporting methods. Only 58 percent of these persons were in shelters, the rest were sleeping on the street or in another place not intended for human habitation. Homeless families were more likely to be in a shelter (72 percent) than were individuals (50 percent). 18 percent of the total were chronically homeless.

In 2000, the Urban Institute estimated that about 1.8 percent of all families spent at least one night in a homeless shelter each year, but this number is much higher (9 percent) for poor families. Between October 2006 and September 2007, almost 1.59 million Americans used a homeless shelter. Most of these homeless (84 percent) were in emergency shelters rather than transitional housing. 35 percent of were black, 21 percent were children (half of whom are younger than five), 65 percent of the adults were men, 11 percent were veterans and at least a quarter were disabled.

In 2006, the president of the National Center on Family Homelessness estimated that one out of every three homeless children has a diagnosable psychiatric disorder, such as post-traumatic stress, and nine out of ten homeless mothers have been victimized.

The vast majority (76 percent) of the homeless are in major cities rather than in suburban or rural areas. In 2005, the metropolitan areas of Los Angeles (60,289) and New York (28,290) had by far the most homeless people. The next biggest concentration of homeless were in Detroit (14,827), Las Vegas (12,198) and Houston (12,005).

Federal funding The federal government programs to assist the homeless are grouped under what is now known as the McKinney-Vento Act, which became law in July 1987. The act includes 16 different provisions for emergency shelter, food, health care, mental health care, housing, educational programs, job training and other community services. Federal agencies providing services specifically for the homeless include the Federal Emergency Management Agency, and Departments of Agriculture, Education, Health and Human Services, Housing and Urban Development, Labor and Veterans' Affairs. An additional 34 programs, ranging from Medicaid and the Supplemental Security Income program to the Public and Indian housing program and the Ryan White CARE Act, provide general assistance to low-income people, including the homeless. Despite $1 billion of federal funding in 2006 for the McKinney program, states and cities still foot the major part of the bill for care of the homeless.

As of 2006, HUD, along with several advocacy groups nationwide, are funding new initiatives that place homeless persons in apartments of their own. Known as the "housing first" approach, the idea was first pioneered in New York during the 1990s. Despite the high costs of living in metropolitan areas where homelessness is most severe, officials of the program have found that they can provide housing and most medical services for $15,000 a year per person. Federal funding has increased more than $1 billion for such programs because of their success — in Philadelphia, street-dwellers have declined 60 percent from 2001-06, in San Francisco, chronic homelessness has decreased 28 percent from 2004-06, in Dallas 26 percent, and in Raleigh-Durham 15 percent. Over 200 American cities currently participate in the campaign with ambitious 10-year plans to end chronic homelessness.

IMMIGRATION

Over the last four centuries the mingling of peoples from all parts of the world has been a vital element in the formation of the United States both as a land of opportunity and in its emergence as a world power. In one relatively brief period between 1880 and 1920 the massive influx of more than 20 million European immigrants provided the continuous labor supply necessary to transform the nation from an agricultural society to an industrialized one with extraordinary rapidity.

Over the next 40 years, however, the flow of immigration slowed dramatically as the government decided to close the doors to most foreign groups. Motivated at first by a disconcerting kind of nativism, the nation's anti-immigration sentiments were later bolstered by the Great Depression and the need to provide work for those already living here. World War II and the subsequent national readjustment limited immigration for several decades.

Since 1960 a steadily increasing number of immigrants—both legal and illegal—has had a very noticeable impact on both the size and ethnic composition of the American population. The startling upsurge in the number of Asians and Hispanic immigrants during the 1970's, 80's, and 90's has been caused by a variety of factors from wars and political upheaval to the mundane fact of geographical proximity in the case of Mexico. In 2005, 1.12 million persons obtained legal perma-

---

The Statue of Liberty

The Statue of Liberty was conceived and designed by Frédéric-Auguste Bartholdi (with Gustave Eiffel's help) and given to the U.S. by the French government in honor of the centennial of American independence in 1876. Funded by subscriptions from the French people, it was dedicated by President Grover Cleveland in 1886 and became a national monument in 1924.

Measuring 151 feet (46 m) to the top of her torch, Miss Liberty still stands guard over the entrance to New York harbor, the inscription on its base a poignant reminder of the vision Americans once had of their country:

Give me your tired, your poor,
Your huddled masses yearning to breathe free,
The wretched refuse of your teeming shore,
Send these, the homeless, tempest-tost to me:
I lift my lamp beside the golden door.

U.S. Immigration and Rate by Decade, 1820–2000

Period	Total immigrants	Rate per 1,000 U.S. population
1820-30	151,824	1.2
1831-40	599,125	3.9
1841-50	1,713,251	8.4
1851-60	2,598,214	9.3
1861-70	2,314,824	6.4
1871-80	2,812,191	6.2
1881-90	5,246,613	9.2
1891-1900	3,687,564	5.3
1901-10	8,795,386	10.4
1911-20	5,735,811	5.7
1921-30	4,107,209	3.5
1931-40	528,431	0.4
1941-50	1,035,039	0.7
1951-60	2,515,479	1.5
1961-70	3,321,677	1.7
1971-80	4,493,314	2.1
1981-90	7,338,062	2.9
1991-2000[1]	9,095,417	3.2
Total 1820-2000	66,089,431	N.A.

Notes: 1. Includes more than 2 million aliens adjusting under the legalization provisions of the Immigration and Control Act (IRCA) of 1986. **Source:** U.S. Dept. of Homeland Security, *2000 Statistical Yearbook of the Immigration and Naturalization Service* (2002).

nent resident status, and well over half are from those two ethnic backgrounds.

In 1998, total immigration hit a 10-year low of 660,477. In 2003, legal immigration hit a five-year low of 703,542 after exceeding one million in 2001 and 2002. The rate has steadily risen since then, however, and there is much political debate to the future of immigration policies.

With the dramatic decline in its birth rates and fertility rates, the U.S. might very well begin to experience negative population growth by the year 2030; by 2020 immigration will add more popula-

Immigration as a Percentage of Total Population Growth, 1901–2000

Period	Percent	Period	Percent
1901-10	39.6%	1950-54	10.6%
1911-20	17.7	1955-59	10.7
1921-30	15.0	1960-64	12.5
1931-34	-0.1	1965-69	19.7
1935-39	3.2	1970-80	19.4
1940-44	7.4	1981-90	32.8
1945-49	10.2	1991-2000	27.8

Source: U.S. Dept. of Homeland Security, *2000 Statistical Yearbook of the Immigration and Naturalization Service* (2000).

Foreign-Born Population by Region of Birth, 1850–2006

Year	Total population	Foreign-born population	percent	Europe	Asia	Africa	Oceania	Latin America	North America
1850[1]	23,191,876	2,244,602	9.7%	2,031,867	1,135	551	588	20,773	147,711
1860[1]	31,443,321	4,138,697	13.2	3,807,062	36,796	526	2,140	38,315	249,970
1870	38,558,371	5,567,229	14.4	4,941,049	64,565	2,657	4,028	57,871	493,467
1880	50,155,783	6,679,943	13.3	5,751,823	107,630	2,204	6,859	90,073	717,286
1890	62,622,250	9,249,547	14.8	8,030,347	113,383	2,207	9,353	107,307	980,938
1900	75,994,575	10,341,276	13.6	8,881,548	120,248	2,538	8,820	137,458	1,179,922
1910	91,972,266	13,515,886	14.7	11,810,115	191,484	3,992	11,450	279,514	1,209,717
1920	105,710,620	13,920,692	13.2	11,916,048	237,950	16,126	14,626	588,843	1,138,174
1930	122,775,046	14,204,149	11.6	11,784,010	275,665	18,326	17,343	791,840	1,310,369
1940	131,669,275	11,594,896	8.8	N.A.	N.A.	N.A.	N.A.	N.A.	N.A.
1950	150,216,110	10,347,395	6.9	N.A.	N.A.	N.A.	N.A.	N.A.	N.A.
1960	179,325,671	9,738,091	5.4	7,256,311	490,996	35,355	34,730	908,309	952,500
1970	203,210,158	9,619,302	4.7	5,740,891	824,887	80,143	41,258	1,803,970	812,421
1980	226,545,805	14,079,906	6.2	5,149,572	2,539,777	199,723	77,577	4,372,487	853,427
1990	248,709,873	19,767,316	7.9	4,350,403	4,979,037	363,819	104,145	8,407,837	753,917
2000[2]	274,087,000	28,379,000	10.4	4,355,000	7,246,000	N.A.	N.A.	14,407,000	N.A.
2007	298,754,819	37,547,315	12.5	4,993,135	10,052,929	1,375,676	181,987	20,088,292	855,2961.

Notes: **1.** In 1850 and 1860, information on nativity was not collected for slaves. The data in the table assume, as was done in 1870 census reports, that all slaves in 1850 and 1860 were native, even though 0.2 percent were foreign-born. **2.** Numbers for 2000 rounded at source. **Source:** U.S. Bureau of the Census, *American Community Survey* (2007).

Percent of Immigrants Admitted by Region, 1951–2006

Region	Total, 1951-2000	1951-60	1961-70	1971-80	1981-90	1991-2000	2006
Europe	20.0%	52.7%	33.8%	17.8%	10.4%	14.9%	13.3%
Asia	28.8	6.1	12.9	35.3	37.3	30.7	26.8
Africa	2.4	5.6	8.7	1.8	2.4	3.9	3.6
Oceania	N.A.	0.5	0.8	0.9	0.6	0.6	0.5
America[1]	47.8	39.6	51.7	44.1	49.3	49.3	55.8
Caribbean	11.9	4.9	14.2	16.5	11.9	10.8	8.9
Central America	4.8	1.8	3.1	3.0	6.4	5.8	37.8
Other North America[1]	24.7	26.9	26.1	18.0	24.7	26.8	0.0
South America	6.2	3.6	7.8	6.6	6.3	5.9	6.8

Note: Data are for fiscal years. 1. Includes more than 2 million illegal immigrants from Mexico granted permanent legal residence under the 1986 Immigration Reform & Control Act. **Source:** U.S. Dept. of Homeland Security, *2006 Yearbook of Immigration Statistics* (2007).

Top 20 Countries of Birth for U.S. Immigrants, and Major Categories of Admission, 2006

Country of birth	Total immigrants[1]	Percent of total	Category of admission				
			Relative preferences	Occupational preferences	Immediate relatives	Refugees and asylees	Other[2]
All countries	1,266,264	100.0%	222,229	159,081	580,483	216,454	88,017
Mexico	173,753	13.7	62,998	8,864	94,663	491	6,737
China, People's Republic	87,345	6.9	16,573	9,484	33,773	27,454	61
Philippines	74,607	5.9	16,020	23,733	34,354	272	228
India	61,369	4.8	14,525	17,169	22,608	6,841	226
Cuba	45,614	3.6	1,447	18	2,792	40,985	372
Colombia	43,151	3.4	3,828	3,242	23,330	12,591	160
Dominican Republic	38,069	3.0	17,563	385	19,957	(1)	(1)
El Salvador	31,783	2.5	6,003	1,964	7,519	(1)	15,418
Vietnam	30,695	2.4	12,781	56	15,129	1,832	797
Jamaica	24,976	1.9	6,218	873	17,827	16	42
Korea	24,386	1.9	2,412	10,886	11,040	14	34
Guatemala	24,146	1.9	2,702	1,304	9,144	1,559	9,437
Haiti	22,228	1.8	3,624	194	8,937	6,101	3,372
Peru	21,718	1.7	2,790	2,305	13,536	1,644	1,443
Canada	18,207	1.4	714	6,382	10,762	63	286
Brazil	17,910	1.4	464	5,553	11,399	235	259
Ecuador	17,490	1.4	3,095	3,990	9,931	234	210
Pakistan	17,418	1.4	3,777	3,136	7,966	2,408	131
United Kingdom	17,207	1.4	671	6,409	9,893	47	187
Ukraine	17,142	1.4	289	754	5,076	5,934	5,089

Notes: 1. Data withheld to limit disclosure. 2. Includes Diversity. Source: U.S. Dept of Homeland Security, *2006 Yearbook of Immigration Statistics* (2007).

Top 10 States and Metropolitan Areas of Intended Residence for U.S. Immigrants, 1995–2006

	Immigrants					
	1995		2000		2006	
Rank, 2006 and State	Number	Percent of total	Number	Percent of total	Number	Percent of total
1. California	166,482	N.A.	217,753	25.6%	264,677	20.9%
2. New York	128,406	N.A.	106,061	12.5	180,165	14.2
3. Florida	62,023	N.A.	98,391	11.6	155,996	12.3
4. Texas	49,963	N.A.	63,840	7.5	89,037	7.0
5. New Jersey	65,934	N.A.	40,013	4.7	50,303	5.2
6. Illinois	33,898	N.A.	36,180	4.3	52,459	4.1
7. Virginia	16,319	N.A.	20,087	2.4	38,488	3.0
8. Massachusetts	20,523	N.A.	23,483	2.8	35,560	2.8
9. Georgia	N.A.	N.A.	14,707	N.A.	32,202	2.5
10. Maryland	15,055	N.A.	17,705	2.1	30,204	2.3

Rank, 2006 and Metropolitan area	Number	Percent of total	Number	Percent of total	Number	Percent of total
1. New York, N.Y.	111,687	15.5%	85,867	12.3%	224,444	17.7%
2. Los Angeles-Long Beach, Calif.	54,669	7.6	70,644	9.1	120,880	9.5
3. Miami, Fla.	30,935	4.3	47,404	4.4	98,922	7.8
4. Washington D.C.-MD-Va.	25,717	3.6	29,394	3.9	54,556	4.3
5. Chicago, Ill.	31,730	4.4	32,300	4.7	49,755	3.9
6. San Francisco-Oakland, Calif.	N.A.	N.A.	32,236	3.8	38,350	3.0
7. Houston, Tex.	14,379	2.0	17,429	2.0	31,557	2.5
8. Boston-Lawrence-Lowell, Mass.	16,750	2.3	16,469	2.0	28,473	2.2
9. Dallas-Ft. Worth, Tex.	N.A.	N.A.	19,643	2.3	26,654	2.1
10. Atlanta-Marietta, Geo.	N.A.	N.A.	11,660	1.4	25,270	2.0

Source: U.S. Dept. of Homeland Security, *2006 Yearbook of Immigration Statistics* (2007).

Immigration to the U.S. by Country of Last Residence, 1820–2006

Since 1820, Germany has sent more immigrants to the U.S. than has any other country, but Mexico is gaining fast. More than 7 million people immigrated to the U.S. from Mexico between 1820 and 2006, almost 5 million since 1980. In 2006, 13.4 percent of all immigrants came from Mexico, but recent years have also seen a surge in immigrants from Asia, especially from the Philippines, China and India. This table ranks the top 10 nations by the total number of U.S. immigrants since 1820.

Country	1820–2006 Number	Percent of total	1981–90 Number	Percent of total	1991–2000 Number	Percent of total
All countries	72,066,614	100.0%	7,338,062	100.0%	9,095,417	100.0%
Germany	7,258,224	10.1	91,961	1.2	92,606	1.0
Mexico	7,144,904	9.9	1,655,843	22.6	2,249,421	24.7
Italy	5,450,468	7.6	67,254	1.0	62,722	1.0
United Kingdom	5,373,423	7.5	159,173	2.2	151,866	2.0
Ireland	4,790,377	6.6	31,969	0.4	56,950	1.0
Canada	4,643,377	6.4	156,938	2.1	191,987	2.0
Russia[2]	4,190,569	5.8	57,677	0.8	462,874	5.1
Austria[1]	1,856,240	2.6	18,340	0.2	15,500	0.2
Philippines	1,832,691	2.5	548,764	7.5	503,945	5.5
Hungary[1]	1,683,827	2.3	6,545	0.1	9,382	0.1

Note: 1. Austria and Hungary not counted separately for all years. 2. Includes former Soviet Union. **Source:** U.S. Dept. of Homeland Security, *2006 Yearbook of Immigration Statistics* (2007).

Estimated Number of U.S. Immigrants, by Region and Selected Country of Last Residence, 1820–2006

Region/country	Total 1820–2005	2006	Region/country	Total 1820–2005	2006
EUROPE	39,176,930	169,197	Philippines	1,761,557	71,134
Austria[1]	1,854,939	1,301	Turkey	468,797	6,433
Belgium	221,955	891	Vietnam	809,704	29,705
Czechoslovakia[2]	162,795	2,844	Other Asia	2,299,171	108,234
Denmark	379,129	738			
France	846,936	4,945	AMERICAS	19,533,562	548,848
Germany	7,247,953	10,271	Canada & Newfoundland	4,619,464	23,913
Greece	735,356	1,544	Mexico	6,974,855	170,046
Hungary[1]	1,682,137	1,690	Caribbean	4,052,572	144,480
Ireland	4,788,339	2,038	Cuba	988,608	44,248
Italy	5,447,062	3,406	Dominican Republic	964,657	37,997
Netherlands	395,935	1,928	Haiti	490,489	21,628
Norway[3]	790,231	532	Jamaica	660,400	24,538
Poland	828,486	16,705	Other Caribbean	948,418	16,069
Portugal	527,065	1,439	Central America	1,643,655	74,258
Romania	275,823	6,753	El Salvador	626,535	31,259
Russia[6]	4,130,809	59,760	Guatemala	317,462	23,687
Spain	312,665	2,387	South America	2,133,429	136,149
Sweden[3]	1,304,738	1,579	Argentina	178,214	7,239
Switzerland	377,901	1,199	Colombia	509,096	42,024
United Kingdom	5,353,439	19,984	Ecuador	276,687	17,625
Yugoslavia[4]	290,895	11,066	Other South America	1,169,432	69,261
Other Europe	1,222,342	16,197	Other America	109,587	N.A.
ASIA	10,113,486	411,795	AFRICA	963,872	112,108
China[5]	1,252,005	83,628	Egypt	142,839	13,163
Hong Kong	468,045	4,514	Ethiopia	92,858	13,395
India	1,127,109	58,072			
Iran	262,675	9,829	OCEANIA	291,841	8,001
Israel	203,225	6,667			
Japan	573,281	9,107	Not specified	720,659	16,315
Korea	887,917	24,472	All countries	70,800,350	1,266,264

Notes: Because of changes in boundaries and government, figures for many countries, especially those in Asia, are not available for all years or were not reported separately for all years, and are therefore not strictly comparable throughout. Data for many countries are included with countries to which they belonged prior to World War I. 1. Data for Austria and Hungary not reported separately for all years. Total does not include 846,076 immigrants whose country of last residence is listed as Austria-Hungary, including 4,569 in 2005. 2. No data available for Czechoslovakia until 1920. 3. Data for Norway and Sweden not reported separately until 1871. Total does not include 60,255 immigrants whose country of last residence is listed as Norway-Sweden. 4. Since 1922, includes immigrants from the Serb, Croat, and Slovene Kingdom. 5. Beginning in 1957, China includes Taiwan. 6. From 1991- present, the data refer to the Russian Federation: Armenia, Azerbaijan, Belarus, Georgia, Kazakhstan, Kyrgtzstan, Moldova, Russia, Tajikistan, Ukraine, and Uzbekistan. **Source:** U.S. Dept. of Homeland Security, *2006 Yearbook of Immigration Statistics* (2007).

tion than natural increase will. According to the Office of Population Research at Princeton University, the U.S. will need 464,000 immigrants each year over the next century just to keep total population in 2100 at the same size as in 1980.

▶ELIGIBILITY

Prior to 1875 anyone from any foreign country could enter the U.S. freely and take up permanent residence here. Over the next 60 years, however, Congress passed laws restricting immigration on the basis of morality (no prostitutes or convicts), race (the Chinese Exclusion Act of 1882 was the

first), and national origin (Immigrants from Southern and Central Europe as well as Asia were severely limited during the 1920's). In 1952 Congress passed the Immigration and Nationality Act, which reaffirmed national origin as the central criterion for eligibility and in 1965, the Hart-Cellar Immigration Act established a preferential system for skilled workers and relatives of U.S. citizens, but restricted the total number of immigrants to 270,000 each year. However, the number of exceptions to this limit was far greater even than the 270,000 limit. An average of more than 700,000 immigrants legally entered the U.S. each year dur-

Foreign-Born Population by State, 1990-2006

	1990			2006		
	Total population	Foreign-born population	Percent foreign-born	Total population	Foreign-born population	Percent foreign-born
United States	248,709,873	19,767,316	7.9%	299,398,485	37,547,789	12.5%
Alabama	4,040,587	43,533	1.1	4,599,030	130,049	2.8
Alaska	550,043	24,814	4.5	670,053	47,066	7.0
Arizona	3,665,228	278,205	7.6	6,166,318	929,083	15.1
Arkansas	2,350,725	24,867	1.1	2,810,872	107,346	3.8
California	29,760,021	6,458,825	21.7	36,457,549	9,902,067	27.2
Colorado	3,294,394	142,434	4.3	4,753,377	489,496	10.3
Connecticut	3,287,116	279,383	8.5	3,504,809	452,358	12.9
Delaware	666,168	22,275	3.3	853,476	68,722	8.1
District of Columbia	606,900	58,887	9.7	581,530	73,820	12.7
Florida	12,937,926	1,662,601	12.9	18,089,889	3,425,634	18.9
Georgia	6,478,216	173,126	2.7	9,363,941	859,590	9.2
Hawaii	1,108,229	162,704	14.7	1,285,498	210,162	16.3
Idaho	1,006,749	28,905	2.9	1,466,465	82,040	5.6
Illinois	11,430,602	952,272	8.3	12,831,970	1,773,600	13.8
Indiana	5,544,159	94,263	1.7	6,313,520	263,607	4.2
Iowa	2,776,755	43,316	1.6	2,982,085	112,299	3.8
Kansas	2,477,574	62,840	2.5	2,764,075	176,394	6.3
Kentucky	3,685,296	34,119	0.9	4,206,074	111,724	2.7
Louisiana	4,219,973	87,407	2.1	4,287,768	125,204	2.9
Maine	1,227,928	36,296	3.0	1,321,574	41,956	3.2
Maryland	4,781,468	313,494	6.6	5,615,727	683,157	12.2
Massachusetts	6,016,425	573,733	9.5	6,437,193	908,271	14.1
Michigan	9,295,297	355,393	3.8	10,095,643	598,651	5.9
Minnesota	4,375,099	113,039	2.6	5,167,101	339,236	6.6
Mississippi	2,573,216	20,383	0.8	2,910,540	51,044	1.8
Missouri	5,117,073	83,633	1.6	5,842,713	339,236	3.3
Montana	799,065	13,779	1.7	944,632	17,512	1.9
Nebraska	1,578,385	28,198	1.8	1,768,331	99,500	5.6
Nevada	1,201,833	104,828	8.7	2,495,529	475,914	19.1
New Hampshire	1,109,252	41,193	3.7	1,314,895	71,200	5.4
New Jersey	7,730,188	966,610	12.5	8,724,560	1,754,253	20.1
New Mexico	1,515,069	80,514	5.3	1,954,599	197,251	10.1
New York	17,990,455	2,851,861	15.9	19,306,183	4,178,962	21.6
North Carolina	6,628,637	115,077	1.7	8,856,505	614,198	6.9
North Dakota	638,800	9,388	1.5	635,867	13,378	2.1
Ohio	10,847,115	259,673	2.4	11,478,006	412,352	3.6
Oklahoma	3,145,585	65,489	2.1	3,579,212	175,987	4.9
Oregon	2,842,321	139,307	4.9	3,700,758	359,867	9.7
Pennsylvania	11,881,643	369,316	3.1	12,440,621	636,567	5.1
Rhode Island	1,003,464	95,088	9.5	1,067,610	134,390	12.6
South Carolina	3,486,703	49,964	1.4	4,321,249	176,018	4.1
South Dakota	696,004	7,731	1.1	781,919	16,852	2.2
Tennessee	4,877,185	59,114	1.2	6,038,803	236,516	3.9
Texas	16,986,510	1,524,436	9.0	23,507,783	3,740,667	15.9
Utah	1,722,850	58,600	3.4	2,550,063	210,500	8.3
Vermont	562,758	17,544	3.1	623,908	24,182	3.9
Virginia	6,187,358	311,809	5.0	7,642,884	773,785	10.1
Washington	4,866,692	322,144	6.6	6,395,798	793,789	12.4
West Virginia	1,793,477	15,712	0.9	1,818,470	21,948	1.2
Wisconsin	4,891,769	121,547	2.5	5,556,506	245,006	4.4
Wyoming	453,588	7,647	1.7	515,004	13,929	2.7

Source: Migration Policy Institute; U.S. Bureau of the Census, *American Community Survey 2006* (2007).

ing the 1980's (not counting illegal aliens naturalized under provisions of the 1986 Immigration Reform and Control Act).

In 1992, the 270,000 limit was replaced with a sliding cap that is even less restrictive than previous immigration laws. The 1990 Immigration Act limited the total number of immigrants to 700,000 from 1992 to 1995, and to 675,000 thereafter. The act increased the number of openings for immigrants with valuable employment skills from 54,000 to 140,000 each year, and reserved 55,000 openings each year for immigrants from under-

Selected Characteristics of Foreign-Born Population, 2006

The foreign-born population of the United States consists of naturalized citizens and more recent immigrants who have not obtained citizenship. As the following table illustrates, the foreign-born population is heavily represented in the West (19.1 percent of the population in the West was not born here) and the Northeast (13.7 percent) and lowest in the Midwest (5.9 percent). Note that race data for foreign-born residents has not been updated since 2000. See the accompanying table for race data.

		Foreign-born population			
Characteristic	Total U.S. population ('000s)	Total number ('000s)	As percent of U.S. population	Naturalized citizens ('000s)	Not citizens ('000s)
Total Population	299,398	35,659	12.1%	13,884	21,775
Age					
under 5 years	20,363	319	1.6%	43	276
5 to 14 years	40,277	1,769	4.4	223	1,545
15 to 24 years	41,309	4,365	1.1	905	3,460
25 to 34 years	39,481	7,952	20.1	1,740	6,212
35 to 44 years	43,121	7,935	18.4	3,035	4,899
45 to 54 years	42,797	5,733	13.4	2,927	2,807
55 to 64 years	30,980	3,644	11.8	2,204	1,439
65 to 74 years	18,554	2,224	12.0	1,516	708
75 to 84 years	12,962	1,345	10.4	1,011	334
85 years and over	3,989	374	9.3	279	95
Sex					
Male	144,188	18,010	12.5%	6,593	11,417
Female	149,647	17,649	11.8	7,291	10,358
Educational Attainment[1]					
Not a high school graduate	27,896	9,327	33.4%	2,714	6,613
High school graduate or some college	110,269	11,756	10.7	5,649	6,107
Bachelors degree	35,153	5,045	14.4	2,752	2,293
Advanced degree	18,567	3,078	16.6	1,598	1,480
Economic Status					
Employed	151,428	22,225	14.7%	N.A.	N.A.
Unemployed	7,001	923	13.2	N.A.	N.A.
At or below poverty[2]	31,080	5,870	18.9	1,441	4,429
Region of Residence					
Northeast	54,741	8,202	15.0%	4,086	4,116
Midwest	66,218	4,242	6.4	1,838	2,404
South	109,084	11,375	10.4	4,209	7,167
West	69,356	13,729	19.8	5,635	8,094

Notes: 1. Persons aged 25 and over. 2. data from 2005. **Source:** U.S. Bureau of the Census, *American Community Survey, 2006.*

Foreign-Born Population by Sex and Race, 1990-2006

Characteristic	1990[1]	1995	2000	2006
Total	19,846,000	22,978,000	28,379,000	35,659,000
Percent of U.S. population	8.0%	8.7%	10.4%	12.1%
By sex				
Male	9,737,000	11,173,000	14,200,000	18,903,957
Female	10,109,000	11805,000	14,179,000	18,643,832
By race				
White	13,428,000	14,930,000	14,100,000	17,002,305
Black	1,705,000	2117,000	2,200,000	2,925,804
American Indian, Eskimo, Aleut	86,000	120,000	N.A.	131,552
Asian and Pacific Islander	4,627,000	5,811,000	6,700,000	8,804,809
Hispanic Origin[2]	7,997,000	9,532,000	12,800,000	17,715,095

Notes: 1. Figures are from the April 1990 Census. All other figures are as of July 1 of the year shown. 2. People of Hispanic origin may be of any race. **Source:** U.S. Bureau of the Census, *Foreign-Born Resident Population Estimates of the U.S.* (2006).

represented countries. In addition, the new law introduced a sliding scale for admitting family-sponsored immigrants. As in previous years, there is no limit to the number of immediate family members admitted each year. However, beginning in 1995, the number of immediate family members admitted in the previous year is subtracted from 480,000 to determine the number of family-sponsored immigrants eligible for admission. The family-sponsored limit may not go below 226,000 in any year, however.

▶ THE FOREIGN-BORN POPULATION

An increase in the number of immigrants since the 1970's has helped to reshape the makeup of American society. The percentage of the population that was born outside this country continues to increase. In 2006, according to the Census Bureau, 37.5 million U.S. residents (12.1 percent of the to-

Foreign-Born Population by Place of Birth, 2000

Place of Birth	Number	Percent	Place of Birth	Number	Percent
All Foreign-born persons	**28,379,000**	**100.00%**	**North America**	**13,300,000**	**46.87%**
			Canada	678,000	2.39
Europe	**4,355,000**	**15.35%**	Caribbean, total	2,813,000	9.91
Austria	65,000	0.23	Bahamas	13,000	0.05
Belgium	17,000	0.06	Barbados	54,000	0.19
Czechoslovakia	71,000	0.25	Cuba	952,000	3.35
Denmark	8,000	0.03	Dominican Republic	692,000	2.44
Finland	19,000	0.07	Grenada	42,000	0.15
France	127,000	0.45	Haiti	385,000	1.36
Germany	653,000	2.30	Jamaica	411,000	1.45
Greece	136,000	0.48	Trinidad/Tobago	173,000	0.61
Hungary	87,000	0.31	Other Caribbean	91,000	0.32
Ireland	202,000	0.71	Central America, total	9,789,000	34.49
Italy	451,000	1.59	Belize	59,000	0.21
Latvia	11,000	0.04	Costa Rica	77,000	0.27
Lithuania	39,000	0.14	El Salvador	765,000	2.70
Netherlands	93,000	0.33	Guatemala	327,000	1.15
Norway	18,000	0.06	Honduras	250,000	0.88
Poland	445,000	1.57	Mexico	7,841,000	27.63
Portugal	206,000	0.73	Nicaragua	245,000	0.86
Romania	99,000	0.35	Panama	69,000	0.24
Spain	80,000	0.28	Other Central America	157,000	0.55
Sweden	49,000	0.17	Other North America	20,000	0.07
Switzerland	29,000	0.10			
United Kingdom	613,000	2.16			
Yugoslavia	123,000	0.43	**South America**	**1,876,000**	**6.62%**
Other Europe	714,000	2.52	Argentina	89,000	0.31
			Bolivia	44,000	0.16
Soviet Union / Russia	**624,000**	**2.20%**	Brazil	160,000	0.56
			Chile	83,000	0.29
Asia	**7,246,000**	**25.53%**	Colombia	435,000	1.53
Afghanistan	27,000	0.10	Ecuador	281,000	0.99
Cambodia	122,000	0.43	Guyana	202,000	0.71
China	871,000	3.07	Peru	328,000	1.16
Hong Kong	195,000	0.69	Uruguay	73,000	0.26
India	1,007,000	3.55	Venezuela	126,000	0.44
Indonesia	53,000	0.19	Other South America	55,000	0.19
Iran	306,000	1.08			
Iraq	81,000	0.29	**Africa**	**701,000**	**2.47%**
Israel	82,000	0.29	Egypt	126,000	0.44
Japan	274,000	0.97	Ethiopia	68,000	0.24
Jordan	39,000	0.14	Ghana	80,000	0.28
Korea (South)	701,000	2.47	Kenya	28,000	0.10
Laos	74,000	0.26	Morocco	38,000	0.13
Lebanon	127,000	0.45	Nigeria	87,000	0.31
Malaysia	43,000	0.15	South Africa	69,000	0.24
Myanmar	35,000	0.12	Other Africa	205,000	0.72
Pakistan	197,000	0.69			
Philippines	1,222,000	4.31	**Oceania**	**147,000**	**0.52%**
Saudi Arabia	20,000	0.07	Australia	36,000	0.13
Syria	45,000	0.16	Fiji	33,000	0.12
Taiwan	325,000	1.15	New Zealand	20,000	0.07
Thailand	147,000	0.52	Other Oceania	11,682	0.04
Turkey	97,000	0.34			
Vietnam	863,000	3.04	**Not reported**	**916,046**	**3.23%**
Other Asia	293,000	1.03			

Note: The foreign-born population includes 1,864,285 persons who were born abroad of American parents. Numbers are rounded at source. **Source:** U.S. Bureau of the Census, 2000.

tal population) were foreign-born. The last time the figure was higher was in 1920, when 13.2 percent of the population was born in another country. More than half of the foreign-born population in America came from Latin America (20 million); of these, the majority (11.5 million) listed Mexico as their birthplace. Another 26.8 percent of the foreign-born population was from Asia. The remainder was divided between Europe (13.3 percent) and other regions (6.4 percent).

Many foreign-born residents come to the U.S. and stay. In 2006, naturalized citizens constituted almost 42 percent of the foreign-born population. More than 78 percent of foreign-born people who arrived before 1980 are now U.S. citizens. The percentage is 57.9 for foreign-born persons arriving during the 1980's, 32.5 percent for immigrants arriving during the 1990's, and 7.2 percent for those immigrating since 2000.

SEX IN AMERICA

Pollsters scrutinize every angle of American life, including what goes on beyond closed bedroom doors. The research ranges from the statistical— the survey done by the National Center for Health Statistics—to the anecdotal, such as reader polls taken by popular magazines. Here's a summary of the two most serious studies, one conducted by the federal government, the other by a leading university.

▶ WOMEN AND SEX

The National Survey of Family Growth is conducted periodically by the National Center for Health Statistics, with a national sample of women aged 15 to 44 years old. The most recent comprehensive report, issued in December 2005, used data compiled in 2002. Questions concerned marriage and sexual activity, as well as several other aspects of family life and reproductive health. Some findings from the report:

• 85 percent of all married women had pre-marital intercourse; only 15 percent of women waited until marriage to have sex for the first time.

• 56 percent of women aged 20-44 had their first intercourse by age 18, up from 52 percent in 1997; 75 percent were sexually experienced by age 20.

• Nearly 13 percent of women aged 20-24 had sex before age 15; the median age at first intercourse for these women was 16.6 years old.

• 31 percent of women had ever had an unintended birth; poor women and non-Hispanic black women were most likely to have had an unplanned birth.

• 22.6 percent of women aged 18-44 reported having nonvoluntary intercourse at some time in their lives; more than one-fourth of these women were under 15 when they were forced to have sex.

• 47 percent of unmarried women reported having just one sexual partner in the past year; 10.3 percent had two partners, and 32.5 percent said they had no partners. But over their lifetimes, women of all marital statuses reported many

more sexual partners. More than half (55.2 percent) of all women had three or more sexual partners in their lifetimes.

• 61.9 percent of women age 15-44 currently use contraceptives; the remaining 38.1 percent are divided among women who are pregnant, seeking to have children, or abstinent. Only 7.4 percent of women admitted having unprotected sex. Among women using contraceptives, the pill (30.6 percent) was the most popular method, followed by female sterilization (27.0 percent) and the condom (18 percent). Women under the age of 30 were most likely to use the pill.

▶ SEX PARTNERS AND FREQUENCY OF INTERCOURSE

The National Opinion Research Center at the University of Chicago (NORC) periodically conducts a study of the sexual behavior of adults. The Center interviews a nationwide representative sample of about 1,500 adults to collect accurate data on a wide range of topics dealing with sex. Here are some of the survey's primary findings.

Cohabitation   As premarital sex becomes more commonplace and the average age at first marriage grows older, the number of couples liv-

Homosexuality in the U.S., 1998-2000

	1998		2000	
Category	Men	Women	Men	Women
Total	**3.3%**	**2.3%**	**3.3%**	**2.6%**
By race				
Whites	2.7	2.1	3.1	2.7
Blacks	5.3	1.8	5.4	2.5
By age				
18-29	3.5	2.6	N.A.	N.A.
30-39	3.6	2.1	N.A.	N.A.
40-49	2.8	2.5	N.A.	N.A.
50-59	2.4	0.8	N.A.	N.A.
60-69	1.9	1.4	N.A.	N.A.
70 and over	1.7	0.5	N.A.	N.A.
By education				
Postgraduate degree	3.2	3.3	3.0	4.4
College graduate	3.6	1.7	4.6	2.6
Some college	2.4	2.7	3.1	3.0
High school graduate	2.6	1.8	3.1	2.2
Less than high school	3.1	2.5	3.3	3.3
By household income				
Less than $10,000	6.1	3.2	7.2	4.4
$10,000-19,999	4.6	2.5	4.5	3.0
$20,000-29,999	4.0	2.8	4.0	3.3
$30,000-39,999	2.2	1.8	2.6	3.5
$40,000-59,999	2.7	1.4	3.4	1.8
$60,000 or more	1.1	1.6	1.8	2.2
Refused to specify	2.7	1.7	3.5	2.0
By church attendance				
Rarely	2.7	3.4	3.5	4.3
Occasionally	2.5	1.3	3.0	1.9
Regularly	3.0	1.3	3.7	1.5

Note: Refers to individuals reporting a same-gender sexual experience within the last 12 months as a percentage of sexually active adults.   **Source:** National Opinion Research Center NORC) *General Social Survey*, 1998, 2000.

ing together out of wedlock continues to spiral. Just over 1.1 percent of all couples were living together in 1960; in 1997 (the latest year for which data are available), the rate was 7.0 percent. In 1988, 23.4 percent of married couples had lived together before marrying; by 1994, 28.0 percent had. Cohabiting was most popular among younger couples: 11.0 percent of people 18-29 were cohabiting in 2002, and in 1998, 43.7 percent had cohabited with their current spouse before marriage. The exact same percentage of 30-39-year-olds cohabited before marriage in 1998, but only 8.5 percent of the people in this age group were currently cohabiting in 2002.

Extramarital sex Numbers regarding sex out of wedlock are usually unreliable, since most people are reluctant to admit their affairs to interviewers. The percentage of currently married people admitting to extramarital sex within the last year (3.0 percent in 2002) has fluctuated very little since 1988. More people were willing to admit having an affair at one point in their lives. In 1991, 14.6 percent of people who had ever been married admitted having at least one affair while married; in 2002, 17.7 percent said they had had extramarital sex. These figures are much higher than the one-year numbers because they include married people as well as those who are separated and divorced, perhaps as a result of one of these affairs. Men (4.3 percent in the last year, and 21.8 percent ever) were more likely than women (1.9 percent 14.7 respectively) to admit extramarital activity.

Gender of sex partners For the same reasons, many people are also reluctant to admit homosexual behavior. The percentage of sexually active adults admitting to homosexual behavior within the last year has remained steady at between 2 and 3.5 percent since 1988, but the actual number is probably somewhat higher. In 2002, a smaller percentage (1.6 percent of women and 0.4 percent of men) of people claim to have had sex with partners of both genders. Men who attend church regularly (3.2 percent) were as likely to have had a same sex partner than those who attended church occasionally (3.2 percent). Among those who attended church rarely, 3.7 admitted to having a same sex partner.

Number of sex partners The average number of sex partners per person has remained fairly constant over the past few years. A majority of adults have had only one sexual partner in the past five years, and more than two-thirds had only one partner in the past year. Adults in 2006 had an average of 1.18 partners in the last 12 months, and 2.72 partners in the past five years.

Frequency of sexual intercourse Americans had intercourse an average of 56.9 times a year in 2006. That's down from 63.9 times a year in 2002, but not significantly different than data from surveys dating back to 1989. Not surprisingly, married people aged 18-29 had the most sex—96.3 times a year (or almost twice a week); unmarried people over 70 had the least sex: an average of 3.4 times annually in 2006. Just over 19 percent of adults had no sex at all in 2006, 20.9 percent of women and 13.4 percent of men.

Frequency of Sexual Intercourse by Age, Race and Marital Status 2000-2006

Mean number of times per year

| Marital Status | All Adults | By Race | | By Age | | | | | |
		White	Black	18-29	30-39	40-49	50-59	60-69	70+
2000, Total	**62.5**	**61.2**	**70.8**	N.A.	N.A.	N.A.	N.A.	N.A.	N.A.
Married	N.A.	N.A.	N.A.	99.3	84.2	71.7	54.8	30.7	16.9
Unmarried	N.A.	N.A.	N.A.	75.2	67.6	48.9	34.1	13.1	3.6
2002, Total	**63.9**	**61.2**	**65.6**	N.A.	N.A.	N.A.	N.A.	N.A.	N.A.
Married	N.A.	N.A.	N.A.	110.2	86.2	70.6	54.5	33.4	17.6
Unmarried	N.A.	N.A.	N.A.	74.0	67.8	47.1	31.3	16.3	3.3
2004, Total	**59.6**	**58.2**	**71.2**	N.A.	N.A.	N.A.	N.A.	N.A.	N.A.
Married	N.A.	N.A.	N.A.	102.9	90.6	65.9	38.6	27.4	16.0
Unmarried	N.A.	N.A.	N.A.	77.4	73.3	52.7	21.1	18.1	3.7
2006, Total	**56.9**	**55.8**	**65.1**	N.A.	N.A.	N.A.	N.A.	N.A.	N.A.
Married	N.A.	N.A.	N.A.	96.3	78.9	70.0	45.2	33.6	9.6
Unmarried	N.A.	N.A.	N.A.	77.5	71.9	51.7	29.8	16.7	3.4

Source: National Opinion Research Center (NORC) *General Social Survey,* 2000, 2002, 2004, 2006.

Number of Sexual Partners, 2000-2006

Number of sexual partners

Year	None	1	2	3	4	5–9	10+	Mean
				Last 12 months				
2000	18.2%	69.2%	5.9%	2.2%	1.5%	1.4%	0.5%	1.14
2002	18.8	67.8	6.4	3.1	1.7	1.3	0.7	1.32
2004	15.7	72.2	5.5	2.8	1.6	1.5	0.6	1.21
2006	19.8	68.3	5.4	2.6	1.5	1.7	0.8	1.18
				Last five years				
2000	11.3%	58.1%	9.9%	6.4%	4.3%	6.0%	3.3%	2.74
2002	12.1	56.5	9.1	6.3	5.0	7.0	3.9	2.81
2004	10.1	61.0	10.4	5.0	4.9	5.3	3.3	2.77
2006	12.0	59.2	9.3	6.2	4.0	5.5	4.0	2.72

Source: National Opinion Research Center (NORC) *General Social Surveys,* 2000-2006.

Agriculture

In recent years, U.S. agriculture has become an integral part of the global economy. American farmers currently produce 38.6 percent of the world's corn, 37.8 percent of its soybeans, and 8.3 percent of its wheat. Much of this they export to all parts of the world, but especially to Asia and Latin America. In 1990, U.S. agricultural exports totaled $39.5 billion, but by 2006, exports topped $70 billion. 27.2 percent of that total was in grains and feeds; 19.1 percent was in animals and animal products.

This is a far cry from the small nation of "embattled farmers" who launched the American Revolution. In the early years of the Republic, agriculture, while vital (involving 95 percent of the population), remained relatively small-scale and in economic terms primitive, with the exception of large plantations in the South devoted to cotton, tobacco and rice. The Civil War brought higher food prices and increased mechanization throughout the farming industry. It also led to federal legislation aimed at encouraging farming; the Homestead Act of 1862 and the Morrill Land Grant College Act were especially important. The decision to build a transcontinental rail system—undertaken by private enterprise abetted by government grants—opened up large areas of the Great Plains to farming, and the railroad companies recruited immigrants to buy and farm the land the government had given the companies.

In the early 20th century, machinery gradually replaced animal power. World War I stimulated agriculture, but the stimulus led to overproduction, which, with the coming of peace, depressed prices and land values. This decline both contributed to and was intensified by the Great Depression, one of the most paralyzing aspects of which was a near total cessation of world agricultural trade. The plight of farmers during the 1930s prompted considerable government remedies, including various forms of credit, price supports, rural electrification, and serious efforts at soil conservation. World War II again gave impetus to agriculture.

After the war, new machinery, new chemicals, and hybrid crops, more resistant to weather and biological enemies significantly increased crop yields. By the end of the 1940s, the United States had become the world's largest single producer of wheat, corn, and soybeans. One byproduct of this success was the creation of huge surpluses. U.S. agriculture proved a potent force in the world economy and in foreign policy, and in 1954, Public Law 480 provided for the export of surplus grains to poorer nations both to prevent starvation and stimulate economic development, and to alleviate the pressures on the domestic agriculture sector caused by the surpluses.

Since 1960, the number of American farms has declined as small units lose out to huge agribusinesses owned by corporations. Between 1980 and

Percent of U.S. Agricultural Exports by Region and Selected Nation, 1990–2006

Category	1990	1995	2000	2006
Total agricultural exports (billions)	$39.5	$56.2	$51.2	$70.9
Percent by region and nation				
Asia	40.2%	45.7%	38.8%	36.3%
Japan	20.6	19.8	18.1	11.9
Korea, South	6.7	6.7	5.0	4.0
Taiwan	4.2	4.6	3.9	3.5
China	2.1	4.7	3.3	9.5
Hong Kong	1.8	2.7	2.5	N.A.
Western Europe	20.0	16.4	13.7	12.3
European Union	18.4	15.5	12.7	10.3
Latin America	13.0	14.3	20.8	21.2
Mexico	6.5	6.3	12.5	15.3
Canada	10.7	10.3	14.9	16.8
Africa	4.7	5.0	4.5	4.3

Source: U.S. Bureau of the Census, *Statistical Abstract of the United States* (2008)

U.S. Farms, Acreage and Population, 1850–2006

Year	Farms ('000s)	Acreage Total ('000s)	Avg. per farm	Percent of U.S.	Farm Population Total ('000s)	Percent of U.S.
1850	1,449	293,561	203	15.6%	—	—
1860	2,044	407,213	199	21.4	—	—
1870	2,660	407,735	153	21.4	—	—
1880	4,009	536,082	134	28.2	21,973	43.8%
1890	4,565	623,219	137	32.7	24,771	42.3
1900	5,740	841,202	147	37.0	29,835	41.9
1910	6,406	881,431	139	38.8	32,077	34.9
1920	6,518	958,677	149	42.2	31,974	30.1
1930	6,546	990,112	157	43.6	30,529	24.9
1940	6,350	1,065,114	175	46.8	30,547	23.2
1950	5,648	1,202,019	213	51.1	23,048	15.3
1960	3,963	1,176,646	297	49.5	15,635	8.7
1970	2,949	1,102,371	374	47.0	9,712	4.8
1980	2,440	1,038,885	426	44.8	6,051	2.7
1990	2,146	986,850	460	42.7	4,801	1.9
1995	2,196	962,515	438	N.A.	N.A.	N.A.
2000	2,167	945,080	436	N.A.	N.A.	N.A.
2006	2,090	932,430	445	N.A.	N.A.	N.A.

Note: Acreage figures after 1980 rounded in source. 1. Figure for 1959. 2. Figure for 1969. **Source:** U.S. Bureau of the Census, *Statistical History of the United States* (1970); *Statistical Abstract of the United States*; National Agricultural Statistics Service; U.S. Dept. of Agriculture, *2008 Agricultural Statistics*.

2006, the number of farms fell from 2.44 million to 2.09 million, (a decline of 14 percent) while average acreage per farm rose from 426 to 445. Overall, the total land area devoted to farming dropped from 1.04 billion acres to 932 million, a decline of 11 percent. Meanwhile, improved technology has made farming less labor intensive, so the total farm population has also declined precipitously. The last data available showed that the farm population had fallen to less than 2 percent of the total population, down from 42 percent at the turn of the century, and 15 percent in 1950.

The surpluses created by expanded and more efficient production required governments to prop up prices, often at the consumer's expense. In 1996, a Republican-led Congress pushed through the "Freedom to Farm" law, which was intended to remove price subsidies on most major crops. But in 2002, just as the program was to become fully effective, President George W. Bush signed legislation that instead raised farm subsidies to $190 billion, an increase of $83 billion. The majority of the subsidy did not go to individual family farms, but to giant agribusinesses, continuing the trend of consolidation in the farming industry. In 2008, Congress passed a controversial farm subsidy bill that increased spending by nearly $20 billion.

The worldwide nature of agricultural progress—the "green revolution"—has increased competition for markets, in some cases hurting farmers who depend upon exporting a large share of their crop.

Farms—Number and Acreage, by State, 1980–2006

State	Number of Farms ('000s)				Acreage (millions)				Acreage per farm			
	1980	1990	2000	2006	1980	1990	2000	2006	1980	1990	2000	2006
U.S. total	2,440	2,146	2,172	2,090	1,039	987	943	932	426	460	434	446
Alabama	59	47	47	43	12	10	9	9	207	215	191	200
Alaska	1	1	1	1	2	1	1	1	3,378	1,707	1,586	1,406
Arizona	8	8	11	10	38	36	27	26	5,080	4,641	3,560	2,610
Arkansas	59	47	48	47	17	16	15	14	280	330	304	308
California	81	85	83	76	34	31	26	26	417	382	318	346
Colorado	27	27	30	31	36	33	32	31	1,358	1,249	1,071	1,000
Connecticut	4	4	4	4	(z)	(z)	(z)	(z)	117	108	92	86
Delaware	4	3	3	2	1	1	1	1	186	207	223	224
Florida	39	41	44	41	11	11	10	10	344	266	234	244
Georgia	48	50	49	49	13	11	11	11	254	260	222	220
Hawaii	4	5	6	6	2	2	1	1	458	357	262	236
Idaho	24	22	25	25	15	14	12	12	623	628	486	472
Illinois	107	83	77	72	29	28	28	27	269	342	355	377
Indiana	87	68	63	59	17	16	16	15	193	240	242	254
Iowa	119	104	94	89	34	34	33	32	284	322	345	356
Kansas	75	69	64	65	48	48	48	47	644	694	742	738
Kentucky	102	93	90	84	15	14	14	14	143	152	151	163
Louisiana	37	32	29	27	10	9	8	8	273	278	275	291
Maine	8	7	7	7	2	1	1	1	195	201	187	192
Maryland	18	15	12	12	3	2	2	2	157	148	169	170
Massachusetts	6	6	6	6	1	1	1	1	116	100	93	85
Michigan	65	54	52	53	11	11	10	10	175	200	200	191
Minnesota	104	89	81	79	30	30	29	27	291	337	362	346
Mississippi	55	40	43	42	15	13	11	11	265	325	258	262
Missouri	120	108	109	105	31	30	30	30	261	281	275	287
Montana	24	25	28	28	62	61	57	60	2,601	2,449	2,054	2,139
Nebraska	65	37	54	48	48	47	46	46	734	826	859	960
Nevada	3	3	3	3	9	9	7	6	3,100	3,560	2,267	2,100
New Hampshire	3	3	3	3	1	(z)	(z)	(z)	160	163	135	132
New Jersey	9	8	10	10	1	1	1	1	109	107	86	81
New Mexico	14	14	15	18	47	45	44	45	3,467	3,296	2,895	2,543
New York	47	39	38	35	9	8	8	8	200	218	203	214
North Carolina	93	62	57	48	12	10	9	9	126	156	161	183
North Dakota	40	34	30	30	42	41	39	39	1,043	1,209	1,300	1,300
Ohio	95	83	79	76	16	16	15	14	171	188	186	187
Oklahoma	72	70	85	83	35	33	34	34	481	471	400	406
Oregon	35	37	40	39	18	18	17	17	517	488	430	435
Pennsylvania	62	53	59	58	9	8	8	8	145	153	131	131
Rhode Island	1	1	1	1	(z)	(z)	(z)	(z)	87	95	86	71
South Carolina	34	25	24	25	6	5	5	5	188	208	200	197
South Dakota	39	35	32	31	45	44	44	44	1,169	1266	1,354	1,396
Tennessee	96	87	88	82	14	12	12	11	142	139	130	139
Texas	196	196	228	230	138	132	131	130	705	673	575	564
Utah	14	13	16	15	12	11	12	12	919	856	748	768
Vermont	8	7	7	6	2	1	1	1	226	222	200	197
Virginia	58	46	49	47	10	9	9	9	169	193	178	182
Washington	38	37	37	34	16	16	16	15	429	432	393	444
West Virginia	22	21	21	21	4	4	4	4	191	180	176	170
Wisconsin	93	80	78	76	19	16	16	15	200	220	210	201
Wyoming	9	9	9	9	35	35	35	34	3,846	3,899	3,761	3,780

Note: 1. Fewer than 500,000 acres.   Source: U.S. Dept. of Agriculture, *2008 Agricultural Statistics*.

Nevertheless, the U.S. continues to export agricultural products worth more than $70 billion a year, most of the total (over 36 percent) to Asia. The 1997–98 financial crisis there drove down the price of all major commodities, and led to a decline in farm exports. Today's farmers face a difficult future. Record crops from 1996 to 1998 also pushed prices down, in some cases as low as during the Depression. Severe drought in the Southwest and part of the Southeast during 2000 also caused hardship. As a result, government subsidies rose from $7.3 billion in 1996 to $23.1 billion in 2000; they have since fallen to $13.4 billion in 2006. Further consolidation in the industry threatens to force even more family farmers from the business, and to continue the trend of agribusinesses swallowing up land once individually owned and farmed.

U.S. Agricultural Exports: Principal Commodities by Value and Percentage of Agriculture Exports, 1980–2006

Category	1980 Value (billions)	1980 Percent	1990 Value (billions)	1990 Percent	2000 Value (billions)	2000 Percent	2006 Value (billions)	2006 Percent
Total agricultural exports	$41.2	100.0%	$39.5	100.0%	$50.7	100.0%	$68.7	100%
Commodities								
Grains and feeds	$19.1	46.4%	$14.4	36.5%	$13.8	27.2%	$18.4	26.7%
Oilseeds and products	9.4	22.8	5.7	14.4	8.4	16.6	10.6	15.4
Animals and animal products	3.8	9.2	6.7	16.9	11.5	22.7	13.1	19.0
Cotton	2.9	7.0	2.8	7.0	1.8	3.6	4.6	6.6
Tobacco, unmanufactured	1.3	3.3	1.4	3.6	1.2	2.4	1.0	1.4
Fruits and preparations	1.3	3.3	2.4	6.0	3.4	6.7	3.7[1]	5.3[1]
Vegetables and preparations	1.2	2.9	2.2	5.6	4.4	8.7	3.8	5.5
Nuts and preparations	0.8	1.9	1.0	2.5	1.2	2.4	3.1[1]	4.5[1]
Other	1.5	3.6	2.9	7.3	5.0	9.9	10.4	15.1

Note: Figures might not round due to independent rounding. 1. In 2003, the categories "fruits and preparations" and "nuts and preparations" were combined. **Source:** U.S. Dept. of Agriculture, *Agricultural Outlook*, July 2004.

U.S. Production of Leading Farm Products as Percent of World Total, 1995–2006

Product	U.S. production (millions of metric tons) 1995	1999	2000	2006	As percent of world total 1995	1999	2000	2006
Total production								
Corn	188.0	240.0	251.9	282.3	36.5%	39.6%	42.7%	40.6%
Wheat	59.0	63.0	60.6	57.3	11.0	10.7	10.4	9.2
Soybeans	59.0	72.0	75.1	83.4	47.4	45.3	42.7	38.2
Cotton[1]	17.9	17.0	17.2	23.9	22.9	16.3	19.4	20.9
Rice, milled	5.6	6.6	5.9	7.1	1.5	1.6	1.5	1.7
Amount exported								
Corn	52.7	49.4	48.3	56.2	72.4%	67.5%	63.2%	70.0%
Wheat	33.7	29.5	28.0	27.4	33.9	26.2	26.9	24.1
Soybeans	23.1	26.5	27.1	25.8	72.4	57.2	50.4	40.1
Cotton[1]	7.7	6.8	6.7	18.0	27.9	24.9	25.5	40.3
Rice, milled	3.1	2.6	2.5	3.7	14.8	10.4	10.2	13.3

Note: 1. Millions of bales. **Source:** U.S. Dept. of Agriculture, *2007 Agricultural Statistics*.

Top Agricultural States by Farm Marketings, 2006

Rank, State	Total farm marketings (millions)	Crops (millions)	Livestock & products (millions)	Principal commodities
1. California	$31,706	$23,252	$7,615	Dairy products, greenhouse, grapes, lettuce
2. Texas	16,355	5,693	10,661	Cattle, cotton, greenhouse, broilers
3. Iowa	14,621	6,674	7,947	Corn, hogs, soybeans, cattle
4. Nebraska	11,470	3,924	7,545	Cattle, corn, soybeans, hogs
5. Kansas	9,975	3,106	6,868	Cattle, wheat, corn, soybeans
6. Minnesota	9,300	4,338	4,962	Corn, soybeans, hogs, dairy products
7. Illinois	8,846	6,858	1,988	Corn, soybeans, hogs, cattle
8. North Carolina	8,264	2,662	5,601	Hogs, broilers, greenhouse, tobacco
9. Florida	7,760	6,306	1,453	Greenhouse, oranges, sugarcane, tomatoes
10. Wisconsin	6,758	1,745	5,014	Dairy products, cattle, corn, greenhouse

Source: U.S. Dept. of Agriculture, Economic Research Service.

Crime and Punishment

▶ SERIOUS CRIME

Serious crime is the Justice Department's measure of the total number of violent crimes (murder, rape, robbery, and assault) plus property crimes (burglary, larceny/theft, motor vehicle theft, and arson). The number of serious crimes in the U.S. fell from an all-time high of close to 15 million in 1991 to just over 11.6 million in 2000, and has hovered between 11 and 12 million since then.

The number of violent crimes peaked at 1.93 million in 1992 and steadily declined over the next decade. But while the overall number of crimes continues to decline, violent crimes have inched back up since 2004. The number of murders, robberies, and assaults reported to police all increased in 2006 but fell again in 2007. However, these figures are still far below what they were from 1990-94, when more than 23,000 people were murdered each year. Guns remain the weapon of choice, used in about two-thirds of all homicides and in nearly half of robberies; handguns alone account for half of all murders.

Property crime reached its all-time high in 1991, at 12.96 million total offenses reported to police. It has continued to decrease since then, to just under 10 million. The number of burglaries is declining even faster, from close to 4 million in 1980 to just under 2.2 million in 2007.

A strong economy and a thriving job market were major reasons for the steadily declining number of serious crimes throughout the last 20 years, especially the crimes of robbery, burglary, and motor vehicle theft, which have experienced some of the biggest drops. Better policing techniques and an aging population help to explain the decline in the violent crime rate. The increase in violent crime over the past two years has been blamed on everything from video games to methamphetamines, but police say the biggest factor has been easy access to guns by people willing to use them to settle disputes. Aggravated assault with a gun is one of the fastest-growing categories of crime.

The number of forcible rapes is up nearly 70 percent since 1975, though much of this significant jump may be the result of more women reporting this crime to police. The 90,427 rapes reported in 2007 were down from the 1992 high of 109,066, and follow a decline from 95,089 in 2004.

The crime rate Raw numbers of crime do not necessarily tell the whole story. To account for population growth, criminologists use the crime rate per 100,000 population to compare statistics from different years. Because the population continues to grow, the rate of crime (or the likelihood that you would become a victim of crime) declines if the total number of crimes stays the same or grows slower than the population. While the number of crimes is down slightly, the violent crime rate has dropped 36 percent since 1990, and the overall crime rate has fallen by a third.

The murder rate in 2007 was 5.6 per 100,000 population, up slightly from 2004, but down significantly from 1990, when it was 9.4. Violent crime overall increased from 463.2 per 100,000 residents in 2004 to 466.9 in 2007; that's still down from 506.5 in 2000. The property crime rate continues to fall, from over 5,000 in 1990 to a new low of 3,263.5 per 100,000 residents in 2007.

Serious Crime in the U.S., 1980-2007

Crime	1980	1990	2000	2007	Crime percent change		
					2yrs	5yrs	10yrs
Number of Offenses Reported to Police							
Violent crime	1,344,520	1,820,127	1,425,486	1,408,337	-0.7%	+1.8%	-8.2%
Murder	23,040	23,438	15,586	16,929	-0.6	+2.4	-0.3
Forcible rape	82,990	102,555	90,178	90,427	-2.5	-3.7	-2.9
Robbery	565,840	639,271	408,016	445,125	-0.5	+7.5	-0.5
Aggravated assault	672,650	1,054,863	911,706	855,856	-0.6	-0.4	-12.4
Property crime	12,063,700	12,655,486	10,182,584	9,843,481	-1.4	-5.7	-10.1
Burglary	3,795,200	3,073,909	2,050,992	2,179,140	-0.2	+1.1	-6.6
Larceny/theft	7,136,900	7,945,670	6,971,590	6,568,572	-0.6	-6.5	-11.0
Motor vehicle theft	1,131,700	1,635,907	1,160,002	1,095,769	-8.1	-13.1	-11.8
Total serious crimes	13,408,300	14,475,613	11,608,070	11,251,818			
					Rate percent change		
Rate per 100,000 inhabitants					2yrs	5yrs	10yrs
Violent crime	596.6	729.6	506.5	466.9	-1.4%	-1.9%	-17.7%
Murder	10.2	9.4	5.5	5.6	-1.3	-1.3	-10.6
Forcible rape	36.8	41.1	32.0	30.0	-3.2	-7.1	-13.0
Robbery	251.1	256.3	145.0	147.6	-1.2	+3.6	-10.8
Aggravated assault	298.5	422.9	324.0	283.8	-1.3	-3.9	-12.4
Property crime	5,353.3	5,073.1	3,618.3	3,263.5	-2.1	-9.1	-10.1
Burglary	1,684.1	1,232.2	728.8	722.5	-0.9	+1.1	-6.6
Larceny/theft	3,167.0	3,185.1	2,477.3	2,177.8	-1.3	-9.9	-20.2
Motor vehicle theft	502.2	655.8	412.2	363.3	-8.8	-16.2	-21.0
Total serious crimes	5,950.0	5,802.7	4,124.8	3,730.4			

Note: Totals may not add up due to independent rounding.
Source: Federal Bureau of Investigation, *Uniform Crime Reports: Crime in the United States 2007.*

Serious Crime by 100,000 Population by State, 2006

State	All	Murder	Forcible rape	Robbery	Aggravated Assault	All	Burglary	Larceny/ theft	Motor theft
				Violent crime rate			Property crime rate		
Alabama	425.2	8.3	35.9	153.5	227.6	3,936.1	969.1	2,644.3	322.7
Alaska	688.0	5.4	76.0	90.3	516.4	3,604.9	617.3	2,610.2	377.4
Arizona	501.4	7.5	31.5	149.6	312.7	4,627.9	925.3	2,813.1	889.5
Arkansas	551.6	7.3	46.5	98.4	399.4	3,967.5	1,139.9	2,562.1	265.5
California	532.5	6.8	25.3	194.7	305.7	3,170.9	676.0	1,829.1	665.7
Colorado	391.6	3.3	43.7	80.7	264.0	3,451.3	682.1	2,331.8	437.5
Connecticut	280.8	3.1	18.1	121.0	138.6	2,504.1	419.3	1,788.4	296.4
Delaware	681.6	4.9	46.9	203.3	426.5	3,417.9	725.2	2,362.8	329.9
D.C.	1,508.4	29.1	31.8	658.4	789.1	4,653.8	659.5	2,735.4	1258.9
Florida	712.0	6.2	35.8	188.8	481.2	3,986.1	944.6	2,619.0	422.5
Georgia	471.0	6.4	23.2	165.6	275.8	3,889.2	909.0	2,519.3	460.9
Hawaii	281.2	1.6	27.6	88.9	163.0	4,230.4	677.5	2,949.1	603.9
Idaho	247.2	2.5	40.0	20.5	184.2	2,418.8	513.2	1,740.0	165.6
Illinois[1]	541.6	6.1	31.8	185.3	318.4	3,019.6	602.1	2,124.2	293.3
Indiana	314.8	5.8	29.1	114.7	165.2	3,502.4	731.3	2,424.8	346.3
Iowa	283.5	1.8	27.8	43.5	210.4	2,802.7	604.2	2,030.7	167.9
Kansas	425.0	4.6	44.8	67.9	307.7	3,750.2	723.3	2,712.0	314.9
Kentucky	263.0	4.0	30.8	86.2	142.0	2,544.5	644.8	1,679.9	219.8
Louisiana	697.8	12.4	36.4	133.6	515.4	3,993.7	1,049.2	2,579.7	364.8
Maine	115.5	1.7	25.7	29.1	59.0	2,518.7	512.9	1,904.3	101.4
Maryland	678.6	9.7	21.0	256.0	392.0	3,480.9	667.0	2,270.4	543.5
Massachusetts	447.0	2.9	27.1	125.0	292.1	2,391.0	546.5	1,565.4	279.0
Michigan	562.4	7.1	52.2	140.7	362.4	3,212.8	753.9	1,963.5	495.4
Minnesota	312.0	2.4	31.8	105.1	172.6	3,079.5	583.9	2,236.6	258.9
Mississippi	298.6	7.7	34.4	107.1	149.5	3,208.8	935.9	1,986.1	286.8
Missouri	545.6	6.3	30.2	129.9	379.3	3,826.5	764.1	2,627.0	435.3
Montana	253.7	1.8	28.5	17.4	206.1	2,687.5	310.7	2,191.8	185.0
Nebraska	281.8	2.8	31.0	63.8	184.1	3,340.7	534.5	2,521.3	284.9
Nevada	741.6	9.0	43.2	281.6	407.8	4,088.8	994.6	2,013.8	1080.4
New Hampshire	138.7	1.0	26.2	32.2	79.4	1,874.1	331.4	1,434.5	108.1
New Jersey	351.6	4.9	14.2	153.1	179.4	2,291.9	452.0	1,556.5	283.4
New Mexico	643.2	6.8	56.0	107.7	472.8	3,937.2	1,069.7	2,395.5	472.0
New York	434.9	4.8	16.4	178.6	235.1	2,052.7	355.1	1,531.1	166.4
North Carolina	475.6	6.1	28.2	152.2	289.1	4,120.8	1,212.7	2,567.9	340.2
North Dakota	127.9	1.3	30.4	11.3	84.9	2,000.3	376.3	1,464.8	159.2
Ohio	350.3	4.7	39.6	166.8	139.2	3,678.6	909.8	2,442.8	326.1
Oklahoma	497.4	5.8	41.6	87.5	362.5	3,604.2	960.5	2,270.5	373.2
Oregon	280.3	2.3	32.3	72.7	173.0	3,672.1	645.2	2,636.1	390.7
Pennsylvania	439.4	5.9	27.3	168.6	237.6	2,443.5	463.2	1,742.9	237.4
Rhode Island	227.5	2.6	26.7	68.8	129.4	2,586.9	507.2	1,744.2	335.5
South Carolina	765.5	8.3	40.8	136.5	579.9	4,242.3	989.8	2,873.0	379.6
South Dakota	171.4	1.2	43.0	15.2	112.0	1,619.6	338.9	1,188.9	91.8
Tennessee	760.2	6.8	35.5	184.3	533.7	4,128.3	1040.9	2,713.2	374.1
Texas	516.3	5.9	35.6	158.5	316.4	4,081.5	917.3	2,758.2	405.9
Utah	224.4	1.8	34.1	48.8	139.7	3,516.4	576.5	2,614.5	325.4
Vermont	136.6	1.9	24.0	17.6	93.0	2,304.7	528.9	1,681.8	93.9
Virginia	282.2	5.2	23.4	101.4	152.1	2,478.2	417.6	1,866.8	193.8
Washington	345.9	3.0	42.9	100.1	199.8	4,480.0	911.6	2,850.7	717.6
West Virginia	279.7	4.1	21.4	46.9	207.3	2,621.5	634.1	1,771.8	215.6
Wisconsin	284.0	3.0	20.4	100.2	160.6	2,817.8	485.8	2,079.5	252.5
Wyoming	239.6	1.7	27.2	14.0	196.7	2,980.6	450.5	2,379.4	150.7
U.S.	473.5	5.7	30.9	149.4	287.5	3,334.5	729.4	2,206.8	398.4

Note: 1. Illinois - Since complete data were not available from Illinois for 1993-2006, the estimation method used differs from the standard procedure. Since the 1985-2006 forcible rape figures were not in accordance with national UCR guidelines, forcible rape totals for Illinois were estimated using national rates per 100,000 population in the eight population groups and assigning them proportionally to the State.
Source: Federal Bureau of Investigation, *Uniform Crime Reports*, prepared by the National Archive of Criminal Justice Data.

The largest states, of course, had the most numbers of crimes. But the rate of crime was by far the greatest in Arizona (5,129.3 serious crimes per 100,000 residents,), South Carolina (5,007.8), and Tennessee (4,888.5). Meanwhile, New York, supposedly one of the most dangerous states, had 2,487.6 crimes per 100,000 residents, significantly below the national average. The safest state is South Dakota, with just 1,791 crimes per 100,000 residents; the most dangerous place to live, remains the nation's capital, with 6,162.2

Serious Crime Per 100,000 Population, by Metropolitan Area, 2005

| Metropolitan area | All serious crime[1] | Violent crime | | | | Total violent crime[1] | Total property crime[1] |
		Murder	Forcible rape	Robbery	Aggravated assault		
25 HIGHEST CRIME RATES							
Hot Springs, Ark.	8,265.1	663.2	8.6	55.9	111.8	486.9	7,601.9
Myrtle Beach-Conway, S.C.	7,722.5	860.5	13.1	52.6	187.2	607.5	6,862.0
Mount Vernon-Anacortes, Wash.	7,683.4	214.1	2.7	53.3	46.2	111.9	7,469.3
Yakima, Wash.	7,346.9	329.5	9.5	56.0	94.7	169.3	7,017.4
Memphis, Tenn.	7,282.6	1,196.8	13.9	45.3	389.8	747.9	6,085.8
Florence, S.C.	7,019.8	1,286.4	8.0	51.0	222.6	1,004.8	5,733.4
Corpus Christi, Texas	6,897.8	601.7	2.9	68.7	129.4	400.7	6,296.1
Macon, Ga.	6,682.3	501.6	11.9	32.8	166.3	290.5	6,180.7
Little Rock-N. Little Rock, Ark.	6,630.7	863.5	8.9	47.6	197.3	609.7	5,767.2
Jackson, Tenn.	6,596.8	989.0	7.2	62.0	174.3	745.5	5,607.8
Fairbanks, Alaska	6,517.5	960.1	6.2	147.7	200.0	606.2	5,557.4
Stockton, Calif.	6,496.8	909.4	8.6	27.7	267.5	605.6	5,587.4
Springfield, Ohio	6,472.0	440.9	6.3	60.3	211.7	162.6	6,031.1
Lubbock, Texas	6,414.2	904.5	5.3	47.7	123.3	728.1	5,509.7
Longview, Wash.	6,403.6	315.9	3.1	67.7	56.4	188.7	6,087.7
Pine Bluff, Ark.	6,318.0	799.9	19.6	49.6	206.8	523.9	5,518.1
Laredo, Texas	6,270.1	502.5	10.3	31.8	113.4	347.0	5,767.6
Miami-Miami Beach, Fla.	6,248.4	989.1	7.1	32.2	305.6	644.3	5,259.3
Wichita Falls, Texas	6,247.3	523.8	5.3	31.9	163.7	322.8	5,723.5
Pueblo, Colo.	6,158.2	483.4	8.5	15.8	110.3	348.8	5,674.8
Fayetteville, N.C.	6,142.2	581.8	6.5	25.5	184.1	365.7	5,560.4
Waco, Texas	6,075.7	552.0	6.2	52.2	128.3	365.3	5,523.7
Modesto, Calif.	6,032.0	614.0	6.0	25.7	132.2	450.1	5,418.0
Seattle-Bellevue-Everett, Wash.	6,025.9	363.0	2.9	37.2	126.2	196.8	5,359.1
Columbus, Ga.	5,890.7	422.1	9.4	13.6	177.2	221.9	5,468.6
25 LOWEST CRIME RATES							
Harrisonburg, Va.	1,676.8	1.8	22.1	33.7	60.2	117.8	1,559.0
Rockingham-Strafford Counties, N.H.	1,717.3	1.2	33.6	19.3	63.8	117.9	1,599.4
Nassau-Suffolk Counties, N.Y.	1,881.9	2.0	7.4	83.7	108.6	201.7	1,680.2
Logan, Utah	1,922.0	1.8	30.0	6.2	29.1	67.1	1,854.9
Fond du Lac, Wisc.	1,950.6	0.0	9.1	11.1	105.9	126.1	1,824.5
Wheeling, W.Va.	2,013.5	0.7	23.4	30.7	121.7	176.5	1,837.0
Elizabethtown, Ky.	2,020.4	0.9	26.3	45.3	88.0	160.5	1,859.9
Wausau, Wisc.	2,029.4	0.0	24.2	22.6	102.1	148.8	1,880.6
Edison, N.J.	2,048.1	1.1	10.6	60.2	100.5	172.4	1,875.7
Holland-Grand Haven, Mich.	2,101.3	0.8	78.8	15.0	99.8	194.4	1,906.9
State College, Pa.	2,108.9	0.7	14.2	12.1	81.0	108.0	2,000.9
Cambridge, Mass.	2,143.8	0.9	14.3	69.3	155.3	239.8	1,904.0
Rochester, Minn.	2,147.8	0.0	35.2	42.6	103.4	181.3	1,966.5
Poughkeepsie-Newburgh-Middletown, N.Y.	2,154.4	2.0	23.0	85.0	164.3	274.3	1,880.1
Manchester-Nashua, N.H.	2,189.8	1.7	30.4	49.8	71.9	153.8	2,036.0
Lynchburg, Va.	2,204.8	4.2	22.5	45.4	130.1	202.2	2,002.6
Appleton, Wisc.	2,254.0	0.9	17.7	9.8	83.1	111.6	2,142.4
Erie, Pa.	2,274.4	2.8	41.4	87.3	129.0	260.5	2,013.9
Kingston, N.Y.	2,287.4	1.6	36.3	59.3	215.9	313.1	1,974.3
Bismarck, N.D.	2,312.8	0.0	19.3	11.2	79.4	109.9	2,202.9
Oshkosh-Neenah, Wisc.	2,313.0	0.6	17.5	13.1	159.6	190.9	2,122.1
Williamsport, Pa.	2,325.6	3.4	24.4	63.1	102.7	193.7	2,131.9
Oxnard-Thousand Oaks-Ventura, Calif.	2,342.5	4.0	18.2	90.8	146.5	259.4	2,083.1
Worcester, Mass.	2,378.8	1.2	40.3	76.4	256.5	374.4	2,004.4
Lancaster, Pa.	2,395.5	1.2	17.4	65.1	88.5	172.2	2,223.3

Note: 1. Serious crimes are violent crimes (offenses of murder, forcible rape, robbery, and aggravated assault) and property crimes (offenses of burglary, larceny-theft, and motor vehicle theft). Data are not included for the property crime of arson.
Source: Federal Bureau of Investigation, *Uniform Crime Reports: Crime in the United States 2005.*

serious crimes per 100,000 residents, nearly double the national average. By metropolitan area, Hot Springs, Ark. (8,265.1), Myrtle Beach, N.C. (7,722.5), and Mount Vernon, Wash. (7,683.4) topped the list of dangerous metro areas in 2005. Pine Bluff, Ark. was the murder capital of the United States in 2005, with 19.6 homicides per 100,000 residents. The rate in New York City was 5.0. The safest city in the country was Harrisonburg, Va., where there were just 1,676.8 serious crimes per 100,000 residents (see the accompanying table).

Violent crime in other nations Although many reports and news stories have emphasized the continuing decline of serious crime, it is helpful to keep in mind that the U.S. remains far and away the most violent industrialized nation. In 1999, the Bureau of Justice Statistics released a detailed comparison of crime rates in the U.S and England. Although violent crime was increasing in England while it was decreasing in the U.S., the rates of murder, rape, and robbery were still significantly higher in this country than in the U.K. The U.S. murder rate was six times as high as England's, the number of rapes per 100,000 population three times as high, and the robbery rate 40 percent higher. It

is interesting to note, however, that the rate of assault was 13 percent higher in England, while the rates for burglary and motor vehicle theft were about double U.S. rates.

Homicide, Guns, and Young People Murders by youthful offenders have followed the same downward trend evidenced in the population at large, but still remain alarmingly high. The rate of homicides by 14- to 17-year-olds dropped from an all-time high of 31.3 per 100,000 in 1993 to about 9.3 murders per 100,000 population in 2005. Similarly, the homicide rate for 18-24-year-olds was 26.5 per 100,000 in 2005, down from highs of more than 40 in 1991 and 1993, but still considerably higher than the 22 in 1985. Over the period 1976-2005, the number of nongun homicides by offenders aged 14-24

Crimes per 100,000 Population in Select Metropolitan Areas, 1995–2005

Metropolitan area	All serious crimes[1]			Violent crimes[1]		
	1995	2003	2005	1995	2003	2005
Albuquerque, N. Mex.	7,521.9	5,717.8	5,753.3	879.4	815.3	838.9
Anchorage, Alaska	7,220.9	5,227.2	5,029.8	990.1	678.9	753.7
Atlanta-Sandy Springs-Marietta, Ga.	N.A.	N.A.	4,607.2	N.A.	N.A.	4,115.2
Boston-Cambridge-Quincy, Mass.	N.A.	N.A.	2,628.1	N.A.	N.A.	2,229.9
Charlotte-Gastonia-Concord, N.C.	N.A.	N.A.	6,008.3	N.A.	N.A.	5,170.6
Cincinnati-Middletown, Ohio	N.A.	N.A.	4,042.8	N.A.	N.A.	3,675.9
Dallas-Fort Worth-Arlington, Texas	6,571.5	5,668.5	5,278.5	819.2	582.0	550.8
Denver, Colo.	5,591.3	4,757.8	4,902.0	513.4	390.5	444.3
El Paso, Texas	6,623.4	4,052.2	3,511.4	802.0	553.4	408.9
Fresno, Calif.	8,566.2	5,634.4	5,439.8	1,189.0	599.4	638.8
Honolulu, Hawaii	7,627.8	5,623.8	4,948.0	327.4	287.9	282.9
Houston-Baytown-Sugar Land, Tex.	5,633.8	5,097.1	4,933.1	856.1	738.5	712.6
Jacksonville, Fla.	7,557.8	5,318.3	5,253.8	1,168.6	754.8	741.9
Las Vegas-Paradise, Nev.	7,408.6	5,255.1	5,288.0	1,085.9	694.5	674.9
Los Angeles-Long Beach, Calif.	6,141.8	3,675.4	3,328.3	1,422.6	721.3	575.5
Miami, Fla.	12,319.2	5,843.2	5,293.0	1,886.3	813.1	784.5
Milwaukee-Waukesha-Wisc.	N.A.	N.A.	3,979.4	N.A.	N.A.	457.9
Minneapolis-St. Paul, Minn.	5,287.2	3,780.1	N.A.	489.9	327.4	N.A.
New Orleans, La.	8,210.5	4,981.2	N.A.	1,334.5	660.4	N.A.
New York, N.Y.	5,669.5	2,651.7	2,429.1	1,392.8	483.3	453.4
Oklahoma City, Okla.	7,905.8	6,449.4	5,878.1	808.5	563.7	532.7
Omaha, Nebr.-Iowa	5,602.6	5,256.0	4,606.2	623.7	446.7	430.4
Orlando, Fla.	7,123.5	5,297.9	5,135.4	1,007.0	758.9	821.4
Philadelphia-Camden-Wilmington, N.Y.-N.J.-Pa.	N.A.	3,446.0	3,360.4	N.A.	609.4	626.5
Phoenix-Mesa, Ariz.	8,808.5	6,359.1	5,749.0	765.0	506.5	513.0
Pittsburgh, Pa.	N.A.	2,767.3	2,794.3	N.A.	359.5	360.5
Portland-Vancouver, Oreg.	6,738.1	5,321.1	4,734.9	726.9	361.0	327.3
Riverside-San Bernardino, Calif.	6,409.2	4,234.9	4,165.4	945.5	544.3	481.8
Salt Lake City-Ogden, Utah	7,200.3	5,940.5	5,619.5	411.4	363.1	332.3
San Antonio, Texas	6,697.4	6,200.9	5,861.5	484.3	485.0	514.6
San Diego, Calif.	5,030.5	3,767.0	3,777.2	794.5	476.9	469.3
San Francisco, Calif.	5,833.8	4,596.1	4,432.3	884.3	537.7	555.6
San Jose, Calif.	4,244.6	2,785.6	2,964.1	614.5	317.1	316.2
Seattle-Bellevue-Everett, Wash.	N.A.	5,458.4	5,753.5	N.A.	409.7	405.4
Tampa-St. Petersburg, Fla.	7,127.8	5,772.2	4,912.7	1,120.4	863.8	749.7
Tucson, Ariz.	9,769.5	7,699.9	5,879.5	877.2	639.0	649.7
Tulsa, Okla.	5,386.7	5,129.2	4,861.9	737.8	633.7	701.4
Virginia Beach, Va.	N.A.	N.A.	4,153.3	N.A.	N.A.	3,683.0
Washington D.C.	N.A.	N.A.	3,518.2	N.A.	N.A.	3,036.2
West Palm Beach-Boca Raton, Fla.	N.A.	N.A.	4,960.1	N.A.	N.A.	4,290.7

1. Serious crimes are violent crimes (offenses of murder, forcible rape, robbery, and aggravated assault) and property crimes (offenses of burglary, larceny-theft, and motor vehicle theft). Data are not included for the property crime of arson.
Source: Federal Bureau of Investigation, *Uniform Crime Reports: Crime in the United States 2005.*

has declined slightly, while the number of murders involving guns has increased by nearly 50 percent. By comparison, the number of gun homicides by offenders over the age of 25 has actually declined by more than 2,500 since 1976.

▶CRIME VICTIMS

Crime victimization statistics are a second mea-

sure of the so-called crime rate. Unlike reported crime statistics, which are based on reports to law enforcement authorities, crime victimization statistics are based on Bureau of Justice Statistics interviews with a sampling of people about their personal experience with crime. (The BJS does not ask about or keep statistics on homicides because it is impossible to question the victim.) In

Criminal Victimization Rates, 1992-2006

Crime	Victimizations ('000s)				Victimization rate per 1,000 persons			
	1992	2000	2005	2006	1992	2000	2005	2006
All crimes[1]	42,834	25,893	23,441	25,078	N.A.	N.A.	N.A.	N.A.
Violent crimes[1]	10,249	6,323	5,174	6,095	49.0	27.9	21.2	24.6
Simple assault	6,053	4,038	3,305	3,756	28.9	17.8	13.5	15.2
Aggravated assault	2,317	1,293	1,052	1,355	11.1	5.7	4.3	5.5
Robbery	1,272	732	625	712	6.1	3.2	2.6	2.9
Rape/sexual assault	607	261	192	272	2.9	1.2	0.8	1.1
Personal theft[2]	369	274	227	174	1.8	1.2	0.9	0.7
Property crime	32,217	19,297	18,040	18,809	325.3	178.1	154.0	159.5
Property thefts	24,579	14,916	13,606	14,275	248.2	137.7	116.2	121.0
Household burglary	5,803	3,444	3,456	3,540	58.6	31.8	29.5	30.0
Motor vehicle theft	1,835	937	978	994	18.5	8.6	8.4	8.4

Note: Rates per 1,000 people ages 12 or older. 1. The National Crime Victimization Survey cannot measure murder because it is impossible to question the victim. 2. Includes pocket picking, purse snatching, and attempted purse snatching.
Source: Bureau of Justice Statistics Bulletin, *Criminal Victimization 2006.*

Rates of Violent Crime and Personal Theft Victimization, by Sex, Age, Race, Hispanic Origin, Income and Marital Status, 2005

Characteristic	Total	Crimes of violence[1]			Theft
		Rape/Sexual assault	Robbery	Assault	
By sex					
Male	26.3	0.1	3.8	21.5	0.8
Female	18.1	1.4	1.4	14.3	1.0
By age					
12-15	45.3	1.2	3.5	39.3	1.3
16-19	45.8	3.2	7.0	33.9	1.6
20-24	48.4	1.1	5.5	40.3	1.5
25-34	24.6	0.7	3.1	19.9	1.0
35-49	18.4	0.6	1.9	15.0	1.0
50-64	12.0	0.6	1.4	9.3	0.6
65+	2.8	0.0	0.6	1.9	0.4
By race					
White only	20.9	0.6	2.2	17.2	0.9
Black only	28.7	1.8	4.6	20.6	1.7
One other race only	14.1	0.5	3.0	10.4	0.2
By Hispanic origin					
Hispanic	26.0	1.1	4.0	19.9	1.0
Non-Hispanic	21.5	0.7	2.4	17.5	0.9
By family income					
Less than $7,500	40.9	2.2	5.6	29.9	3.2
$ 7,500-$14,999	28.1	0.6	4.9	21.0	1.6
$15,000-$24,999	31.2	1.4	3.5	25.2	1.1
$25,000-$34,999	27.1	1.7	2.8	21.6	1.0
$35,000-$49,999	23.6	0.9	2.5	19.0	1.1
$50,000-$74,999	21.7	0.5	1.8	18.8	0.6
$75,000 or more	17.4	0.6	2.1	13.7	1.0
By marital status					
Never married	39.0	1.4	4.8	31.2	1.5
Married	10.8	0.2	1.0	9.0	0.5
Divorced/separated	32.8	1.5	3.8	26.4	1.1
Widowed	6.9	0.8	1.4	4.0	0.8

Note: Rates per 1,000 people ages 12 or older. Some figures based on 10 or fewer sample cases. 1. The National Crime Victimization Survey cannot measure murder because it is impossible to question the victim.
Source: Bureau of Justice Statistics Bulletin, *Criminal Victimization 2005.*

most years, these different statistical methods have reported similar trends in criminal activity in the U.S.

As the accompanying table shows, the victims of most kinds of crime are most likely to be black, young, poor, urban, single, and except for rape and domestic violence, male. In 2005, people with family incomes of less than $7,500 were the most likely to be victimized by crime, especially violent crime. In general, the poorer a person is, the more likely he or she is to be the victim of a crime. And while senior citizens often feel most vulnerable to crime, it is teenagers who are most likely to be victimized by all kinds of crime. Children 12-19 years old are almost 20 times as likely to be the victims of violent crime as people over the age of 65.

▶ LAW ENFORCEMENT

In 2006, there were 683,396 sworn police officers in the United States (up from 675,734 the year before) and an additional 303,729 civilians employed in police departments. This translates into 3.0 full-time police officers for every 1,000 residents. In cities with more than 250,000 residents, the ratio averaged 3.8 law enforcement employees per 1,000 residents. In cities with populations between 10,000 and 249,999 the ratio averaged 2.4. In suburban areas (including cities with fewer than 50,000 residents) the average was 3.8.

Overall, civilians made up 30 percent of the law enforcement workforce in 2006. In cities, civilians comprised 23.2 percent of the workforce; in suburban and rural areas, they made up approximately 40 percent. Northeastern states have the greatest number of sworn officers (2.7 officers per 1,000 inhabitants); the West has the fewest (1.7). By sex, 88.2 percent of sworn officers nationally and in cities collectively are male, but civilian police employees are overwhelmingly female (61.6 percent on average).

Arrests Nationwide, law enforcement agencies made an estimated 10.5 million arrests in 2006 for all criminal infractions except traffic violations, representing a rate of 4,832.5 arrests per 100,000 population, up slightly from the year before. Among cities, those with populations over 250,000 had the highest rate of arrests, 5,480.4 per 100,000 population; those with populations from 25,000–49,999 had the lowest rate (4,685.9). The arrest rate was highest in the South (5,406.8 per

Arrests in the U.S., 1984–2006

Offense	1984	1989	Total arrests 2000	2005	2006	Rate per 100,000 in 2006
Violent crime	400,877	619,230	415,573	445,846	448,612	207.0
Murder	15,126	16,701	8,709	10,335	9,815	4.5
Forcible rape	28,565	26,561	17,914	18,733	17,792	8.2
Robbery	115,522	137,811	72,320	85,309	93,527	43.2
Aggravated assault	241,664	438,157	316,630	331,469	327,478	151.1
Property crime	1,431,812	1,620,704	1,080,797	1,195,560	1,136,602	524.5
Burglary	338,737	292,315	189,343	220,391	222,192	102.5
Larceny/theft	981,812	1,164,371	782,082	854,856	801,633	370.0
Motor vehicle theft	96,975	149,053	98,697	108,301	100,775	46.5
Arson	14,288	14,965	10,675	12,012	12,002	5.5
All serious crimes	1,832,689	2,239,934	1,496,370	1,641,406	1,585,214	731.5
Other crimes	6,995,758	9,167,354	7,627,058	8,725,666	8,886,713	4,101.0
Total arrests	8,828,447	11,407,288	9,123,428	10,367,072	10,471,387	4,832.5

Note: Statistics are based on a survey of more than 10,000 law enforcement agencies representing more than 200 million inhabitants. The number of agencies surveyed and the populations they represent changes from year to year.
Source: Federal Bureau of Investigation, *Uniform Crime Reports: Crime in the United States 2005*.

Arrests by Race, 2006

Offense	Total arrests Total	White	Black	Am. Indian	Asian	Percent distribution White	Black	Am. Indian	Asian
All arrests	10,437,620	7,270,214	2,924,724	130,589	112,093	69.7%	28.0%	1.3%	1.1%
Violent crime	446,957	261,553	175,712	4,865	4,827	58.5	39.3	1.1	1.1
Murder	9,801	4,595	4,990	110	106	46.9	50.9	1.1	1.1
Forcible rape	17,042	11,122	5,536	195	189	65.3	32.5	1.1	1.1
Robbery	93,393	39,419	52,541	611	822	42.2	56.3	0.7	0.9
Aggravated assault	326,721	206,417	112,645	3,949	3,710	63.2	34.5	1.2	1.1
Property crime	1,133,299	773,213	333,342	12,594	14,150	68.2	29.4	1.1	1.2
Burglary	221,732	152,965	64,655	2,123	1,989	69.0	29.2	1.0	0.9
Larceny-theft	798,983	548,057	230,980	9,377	10,569	68.6	28.9	1.2	1.3
Motor vehicle theft	100,612	63,090	35,116	978	1,428	62.7	34.9	1.0	1.4
Arson	11,972	9,101	2,591	116	164	76.0	21.6	1.0	1.4
Other arrests	8,857,364	6,235,448	2,415,670	113,130	93,116	70.4	27.3	1.3	1.1

Source: Federal Breau of Investigation, *Uniform Crime Reports: Crime in the United States 2006*.

Arrests and Convictions for Crimes Committed in the U.S., 2002

As the following table demonstrates, the number of police and the number of prisons have very little effect on the number of crimes committed because people who commit crimes have very little expectation of getting caught. Except for murder, most felonies rarely even result in an arrest, and result in a conviction even more infrequently. These statistics indicate neither a shortage of police nor leniency by judges, but simply the difficulty of solving a crime after it has been committed and proving who did it.

Offense	Number of crimes reported to police	Number of adults arrested	Arrests as percent of number of crimes	Number of felony convictions	Convictions as percent of number arrested	Convictions as percent of number of crimes
Murder[1]	16,204	12,799	79.0	8,990	70.2%	55.5%
Rape	95,136	23,564	24.8	10,980	46.6	11.5
Robbery	420,637	81,340	19.3	38,430	47.2	9.1
Aggravated assault	894,348	410,892	45.9	95,600	23.3	10.7
Burglary	2,151,875	201,804	9.4	100,640	49.9	4.7
Motor vehicle theft	1,246,096	103,664	8.3	18,530	17.9	1.5
Drug trafficking	N.A.	266,465	N.A.	212,810	79.9	N.A.

Note: 1. Includes non-negligent manslaughter. **Source:** Bureau of Justice Statistics Bulletin, *Felony Sentences in State Courts, 2002* (December, 2004).

100,000) and lowest in the Northeast (3,901.2). The greatest number of arrests were for drug abuse (1.4 million), driving under the influence of drugs or alcohol (1.0 million), simple assault (953,000) and larceny or theft (802,000).

By age, 4.5 percent of all people arrested nationwide in 2006 were under 15; 15.5 percent were under 18. By sex, 76.3 percent of all those arrested were males. Of serious crime arrests, females were most often arrested for larceny/theft. By race, 69.7 percent of all those arrested were white, 28 percent were black.

▶ CORRECTIONS

The United States has more people in prison (as well as more people in prison per capita) than any other Western industrialized nation. In 2006, the Bureau of Justice Statistics reported a record 1.56 million inmates in federal and state prisons. The prison population rose 2.8 percent during 2006. Since 1980 the incarceration rate (the number of sentenced inmates per 100,000 residents) has risen from 139 to 496. Put another way, one of every 136 U.S. residents was behind bars.

The states with the highest incarceration rates were all in the South. Louisiana led the way with 835 prisoners per 100,000 residents, followed by Texas (687) and Mississippi (661). The lowest rates were found in Maine (141), Rhode Island (195), and New Hampshire (200). During 2006, Alaska reported the largest increase in its prison population (9.4 percent), followed by Vermont (8.3 percent) and Georgia (8.1 percent). The states with the largest declines were Missouri (down 2.9 percent), Louisiana (down 1.8 percent), and Maine (down 1.8 percent).

Prison and race African Americans have made up the majority of the increase in the prison and jail population. Between 1990 (the last year in which white prisoners outnumbered blacks) and 2006, the number of blacks behind bars in prisons or jails jumped from 360,000 to 836,800. Meanwhile, the white prison population grew from 370,900 in 1990 to 718,100 in 2006. Black males have the highest incarceration rates (3,145 per 100,000 residents in 2005) while white females have the lowest (45 per 100,000 residents). Put another way, about 3.5 percent of all black males are in prison. By age, incarceration rates peak between 25 and 35. More than 8 percent of black men aged 25-29 are in prison.

Jails and prisons Although the terms tend to be used synonymously, "jails" and "prisons" differ in the types of inmates they house, their locations, their physical size and their programs. Jails are locally administered facilities that house inmates after arraignment, prisoners serving terms of less than one year, and prisoners who cannot be housed in state prisons due to overcrowding.

Prisons are administered by either state or federal government authority. Typically they hold convicted offenders sentenced to terms of confinement for more than one year. They tend to be located away from dense population centers, and they are usually larger than jails and have more rehabilitation programs.

Costs of prisons According to the Census Bureau's Government Finance Annual, total U.S. expenditures for adult correctional facilities was $65.0 billion in 2005. According to the Bureau of Justice statistics, the average cost in state prisons per inmate was $57.92 per day in 2000.

Total U.S. prison capital costs increased from $538 million in 1980 to $2.8 billion in 2000. Operating costs surged from $3.1 billion in 1980 to $31.4 billion in 2000. In California, where more than 20 new prisons were built during this period, expenditures on prisons rose from $336 million to $4 billion, with capital expenditures increasing by over 1,400 percent (in constant dollars). In Texas, capital expenditures rose over 1,500 percent.

Probation and Parole When an offender is convicted, the primary sentencing alternatives are incarceration or probation. Once imprisoned, the offender may become eligible for parole, a form of conditional release. The explosion in the prison population has understandably led to a corresponding increase in the number of prisoners released on probation or parole. At the end of 2006, according to the Bureau of Justice Statistics, a record 7.2 million people (3.2 percent of all U.S. adult residents, or 1 in every 32 adults) were under "correctional supervision" in the United States: in jail, in prison, on probation or on parole. More than half this population (4.2 million) were on probation; another 798,202 were on parole.

Recidivism In 2002 the Bureau of Justice Statistics released a study of recidivism among 272,111 inmates (from 15 different states) who were released in 1994. The study found that 67.5 percent were rearrested within 3 years; 46.9 percent were reconvicted for a new crime; 25.9 percent were resentenced to prison for a new crime; and 51.8 percent were back in prison within three years for either a new prison sentence or a violation of their original release. Prisoners with the highest rates of recidivism included those convicted of possessing or selling stolen property (77.4 percent), car thieves (78.8 percent), and larcenists (74.6 percent); prisoners with the lowest rates included those in prison for homicide (40.7 percent), sexual assault (41.4 percent), and rape (46.0 percent). Overall recidivism was up from 1983, when an earlier study estimated rearrests at 62.5 percent.

The Innocence Project The Innocence Project is a non-profit legal clinic and criminal justice resource center that uses post-conviction DNA testing to exonerate people wrongly convicted of serious crimes like rape and murder. More than 200 people have been exonerated through DNA evidence since the Project's inception in 1992 (another five men were exonerated before 1992 using DNA evidence). The Innocence Project was founded by civil rights attorneys Barry C. Scheck and Peter J. Neufeld and was originally housed at the Benjamin N. Cardozo School of Law at Yeshiva University. Each year roughly 20 Cardozo law students work with the staff attorneys and co-directors to exonerate the innocent and prevent future wrongful convictions.

▶ CAPITAL PUNISHMENT

The United States is the only Western industrialized nation that allows capital punishment. In the period 1930–2005, 4,863 executions were carried

Prisoners in the U.S. by System, Sex and Race, 1980-2005

| | By system | | | By sex, race, and Hispanic origin[1] | | | | | |
| | | | | Male | | | Female | | |
Year	Total	Federal	State	White	Black	Hispanic	White	Black	Hispanic
Number									
1980	329,821	24,363	305,458	159,500	140,600	N.A.	5,900	6,300	N.A.
1990	773,919	65,526	708,393	350,700	340,300	N.A.	20,200	19,700	N.A.
1995	1,125,874	100,250	1,025,624	487,400	509,800	N.A.	30,500	31,900	N.A.
2000	1,391,892	145,416	1,245,845	436,500	572,900	206,900	34,500	37,400	10,000
2003	1,468,601	173,059	1,295,542	454,300	586,300	251,900	39,100	35,000	16,200
2004	1,497,100	180,328	1,316,772	449,300	551,300	260,600	42,500	32,100	15,000
2005	1,525,924	187,618	1,338,306	459,700	547,200	279,000	45,800	29,900	15,900
Rate (Prisoners per 100,000 resident population)									
1980	139	9	130	168	1,111	N.A.	6	45	N.A.
1990	292	20	272	338	2,234	N.A.	19	117	N.A.
1995	411	32	379	449	3,095	N.A.	27	176	N.A.
2000	469	44	425	449	3,457	1,220	34	205	60
2003	482	52	430	465	3,405	1,231	38	185	84
2004	486	54	432	463	3,218	1,220	42	170	75
2005	491	56	435	471	3,145	1,244	45	156	76

Note: Prisoners sentenced to more than one year. N/A = not available. 1. Prisoners of other races not shown.
Source Bureau of Justice Statistics Bulletin, *Prisoners in 2005* (2006).

Jail Population, 1985-2006

Age and sex	1985	1990	1995	2000	2004	2005	2006
Number of inmates at midyear	**256,615**	**405,320**	**507,044**	**621,149**	**713,990**	**747,529**	**766,010**
Adults	254,986	403,019	499,300	613,534	706,907	740,770	759,906
Male	235,909	365,821	448,000	543,120	619,908	646,807	661,329
Female	19,077	37,198	51,300	70,414	86,999	93,963	98,577
Juveniles	**1,629**	**2,301**	**7,800**	**7,615**	**7,083**	**6,759**	**6,104**
Held as adults	—	—	5,900	6,126	6,159	5,750	4,836
Held as juveniles	1,629	2,301	1,800	1,489	924	1,009	1,268
Average daily population	**265,010**	**408,075**	**509,828**	**618,319**	**706,242**	**733,442**	**755,896**

Note: As of June 30 of each year. The average daily population is the sum of the number of inmates in a jail each day for a year, divided by 365. Juveniles are persons defined by state statute as being under a certain age, usually 18, and subject initially to juvenile court authority even if tried as adults. In 1994, the definition was changed to include all persons under age 18.
Source: Bureau of Justice Statistics, *Prison and Jail Inmates at Midyear 2006* (2007).

Number of Inmate Under Jurisdiction of State or Federal Correctional Authorities, Year-end 2000, 2005, and 2006

	2000	2005	2006	Change 2000-05		Change 2005-06		Incarceration rate, 2006[b]
				Avg. annual change	Percent change[a]	Annual change	Percent change	
U.S. total	1,331,278	1,462,866	1,502,179	26,318	1.9%	39,313	2.7%	501
Federal	125,044	166,173	173,533	8,226	6.6	7,360	4.4	58
State	1,206,234	1,296,693	1,328,646	18,092	1.5	31,953	2.5	445
Northeast	**166,632**	**162,383**	**166,078**	**-850**	**-0.5%**	**3,695**	**2.3%**	**303**
Connecticut[c]	13,155	13,121	13,746	-7	-0.1	625	4.8	392
Maine	1,635	1,905	1,997	54	3.1	92	4.8	151
Massachusetts[d]	9,479	9,081	9,472	-80	-0.9	391	4.3	243
New Hampshire	2,257	2,520	2,737	53	2.2	217	8.6	207
New Jersey[e]	29,784	27,359	27,371	-485	-1.7	12	0.0	313
New York	70,199	62,485	62,974	-1,543	-2.3	489	0.8	326
Pennsylvania	36,844	42,345	43,998	1,100	2.8	1,653	3.9	353
Rhode Island[c]	1,966	2,025	2,149	12	0.6	124	6.1	202
Vermont[c]	1,313	1,542	1,634	46	3.3	92	6.0	262
Midwest	**236,458**	**253,662**	**259,610**	**3,441**	**1.4%**	**5,948**	**2.3%**	**391**
Illinois[e]	45,281	44,919	45,106	-72	-0.2	187	0.4	350
Indiana	19,811	24,416	26,055	921	4.3	1,639	6.7	411
Iowa[e,f]	7,955	8,737	8,838	156	1.9	101	1.2	296
Kansas[e]	8,344	9,068	8,816	145	1.7	-252	-2.8	318
Michigan	47,718	49,546	51,577	366	0.8	2,031	4.1	511
Minnesota	6,238	9,281	9,108	609	8.3	173	1.9	176
Missouri[e]	27,519	30,803	30,146	657	2.3	-657	-2.1	514
Nebraska	3,816	4,330	4,204	103	2.6	-126	-2.9	237
North Dakota	994	1,327	1,363	67	5.9	36	2.7	214
Ohio[e]	45,833	45,854	49,166	4	0.0	3,312	7.2	428
South Dakota	2,613	3,454	3,350	168	5.7	-104	-3.0	426
Wisconsin	20,336	21,927	21,881	318	1.5	-46	-0.2	393
South	**538,997**	**584,301**	**597,828**	**9,061**	**1.7%**	**13,527**	**2.3%**	**547**
Alabama	26,034	27,003	27,526	194	0.7	523	1.9	595
Arkansas	11,851	13,383	13,713	306	2.5	330	2.5	485
Delaware[c]	3,937	3,972	4,195	7	0.2	223	5.6	488
D.C.[g]	5,008	—	—	—	—	—	—	—
Florida	71,318	89,766	92,874	3,690	4.7	3,108	3.5	509
Georgia[f]	44,141	48,741	52,781	920	2.0	4,040	8.3	558
Kentucky	14,919	19,215	19,514	859	5.2	299	1.6	462
Louisiana	35,207	36,083	36,376	175	0.5	293	0.8	846
Maryland	22,490	22,143	22,316	-69	-0.3	173	0.8	396
Mississippi	19,239	19,335	19,219	19	0.1	-116	-0.6	658
North Carolina	27,043	31,522	32,219	896	3.1	697	2.2	360
Oklahoma[e]	23,181	24,414	23,889	247	1.0	-525	-2.2	664
South Carolina	21,017	22,464	22,861	289	1.3	397	1.8	525
Tennessee[e]	22,166	26,369	25,745	841	3.5	-624	-2.4	423
Texas	158,008	159,255	162,193	249	0.2	2,938	1.8	683
Virginia	29,643	35,344	36,688	1,140	3.6	1,344	3.8	477
West Virginia	3,795	5,292	5,719	299	6.9	427	8.1	314
West	**264,147**	**296,347**	**305,130**	**6,440**	**2.3%**	**8,783**	**3.0%**	**437**
Alaska[c]	2,128	2,781	3,116	131	5.5	335	12.0	462
Arizona[f]	25,412	31,411	31,830	1,200	4.3	419	1.3	509
California	160,412	168,982	173,942	1,714	1.0	4,960	2.9	475
Colorado[e]	16,833	21,456	22,481	925	5.0	1,025	4.8	469
Hawaii[c]	3,553	4,422	4,373	174	4.5	-49	-1.1	338
Idaho	5,535	6,818	7,124	257	4.3	306	4.5	480
Montana	3,105	3,509	3,547	81	2.5	38	1.1	374
Nevada	10,063	11,644	12,753	316	3.0	1,109	9.5	503
New Mexico	4,666	6,292	6,361	325	6.2	69	1.1	323
Oregon	10,553	13,390	13,667	567	4.9	277	2.1	367
Utah	5,541	6,275	6,339	147	2.5	64	1.0	246
Washington	14,666	17,320	17,483	531	3.4	163	0.9	271
Wyoming	1,680	2,047	2,114	73	-4.0	67	3.3	408

Note: Sentenced prisoner is defined as a prisoner sentenced to more than 1 year. **a.** Average annual percentage increase. **b.** The number of prisoners with a sentence of more than 1 year per 100,000 U.S. residents. **c.** Prisons and jails form one integrated system. Data include total jail and prison population. **d.** The incarceration rate includes an estimated 6,200 inmates sentenced to more than 1 year, but held in local jails or houses of corrections. **e.** Includes some inmates sentenced to 1 year or less. **f.** Population figures based on custody counts. **g.** D.C. prisoners were transferred to the Federal Bureau of Prisons in 2001.
Source: Bureau of Justice Statistcs, *Prisoners in 2006* (2007).

Lifetime Likelihood of Going to Prison by Age, Sex, Race and Hispanic Origin

One of every 20 people in the U.S. (5.1 percent) will serve time in a prison during their lifetime, according to a March, 1997, BJS report, if 1991 incarceration rates do not change dramatically. Men (9.0 percent) are much more likely than women (1.1 percent) to be incarcerated in prison at least once during their life, and black men (28.5 percent) are six times as likely as white men (4.4 percent) to be imprisoned. Sixteen percent of Hispanic men are likely to be imprisoned.

Category	Percent expected to go to prison at some time, by age[1]						
	Birth	20	25	30	35	40	45
Total	5.1%	4.5%	3.1%	2.1%	1.4%	0.9%	0.6%
By Sex							
Male	9.0	7.9	5.5	3.7	2.5	1.6	1.0
Female	1.1	1.0	0.8	0.6	0.3	0.2	0.1
By Race/Hispanic origin							
White (non-Hispanic)	2.5%	2.3%	1.7%	1.2%	0.9%	0.6%	0.4%
Male	4.4	4.1	3.0	2.1	1.5	1.1	0.8
Female	0.5	0.5	0.4	0.3	0.2	0.1	0.1
Black (non-Hispanic)	16.2	14.1	9.6	6.0	3.6	2.0	1.2
Male	28.5	25.3	17.3	10.8	6.5	3.6	2.1
Female	3.6	3.5	2.8	1.9	1.1	0.6	0.4
Hispanic	9.4	8.7	6.4	4.9	3.8	2.3	1.6
Male	16.0	14.8	11.1	8.6	6.8	4.3	3.0
Female	1.5	1.5	1.2	0.9	0.6	0.4	0.2

1. Among those not previously incarcerated.
Source: Bureau of Justice Statistics *Lifetime Likelihood of Going to State or Federal Prison*, March, 1997.

out under state or federal authority. The majority of those (3,859) occurred in the years before the Supreme Court ruled capital punishment unconstitutional in 1972. The Court reinstated the death penalty in 1976; since then, an additional 1,044 executions have been carried out; all but nine were males. Another 3,228 prisoners were on death row at the end of 2006 (all of whom had been convicted of murder); 79 prisoners were removed from death row in 2005, while 115 were sentenced to death.

The 53 prisoners executed in 2006 had been on death row an average of 12 years and one month, or twice as long as those executed in 1984. Because capital cases move so deliberately through the court system, it is more expensive to sentence a prisoner to death than to life in prison. A positive aspect of this long delay is that it allows some death row prisoners to prove their innocence before they face the death chamber. According to the Death Penalty Information Center in Washington, D.C., 129 prisoners have been released from death row in 25 states since 1973 because they were improperly convicted or because evidence of their innocence was discovered after they were sentenced to death. The greatest number of exonerations came in 2003, when 12 inmates were released from death row.

Eighteen states have carried out 100 or more executions since 1930. Since the death penalty was reinstated in 1976, Texas has executed far more prisoners (413) than any other state. The Lone Star State executed 26 prisoners in 2007 alone; no other state executed more than 3. Fourteen states and the District of Columbia currently do not authorize the death penalty for any crime: Alaska, Hawaii, Iowa, Maine, Massachusetts, Michigan, Minnesota, North Dakota, New Jersey, New York, Rhode Island, Vermont, West Virginia, and Wisconsin. In Maine, Minnesota, and Wisconsin, there has been no death penalty statute in force

Prisoners Executed by Race, 1930–2005

Year	Total	White	Black	Other
1930–39	1,667	827	816	24
1940–49	1,284	490	781	13
1950–59	717	336	376	5
1960–67	191	98	93	0
Total, 1930–67	**3,859**	**1,751**	**2,066**	**42**
1977–79	3	3	0	0
1980–89	117	68	49	0
1990–99	478	303	164	11
2000	85	49	35	1
2001	66	48	17	1
2002	71	53	18	1
2003	65	44	20	0
2004	59	39	19	1
2005	60	41	19	0
Total, 1977–2005	**1,044**	**651**	**341**	**15**
Total, 1930–2005	**4,863**	**2,399**	**2,407**	**57**

Note: Executions under civil authority only. Does not include 160 executions carried out under military authority since 1930. There were no executions carried out between 1968 and 1977.
Source: Bureau of Justice Statistics, *Sourcebook of Criminal Justice Statistics*, and *Capital Punishment 2005* (2006).

since 1930, and Alaska and Hawaii have never had death penalty statutes. The death penalty was either abolished or declared unconstitutional in Michigan (1963), Iowa and West Virginia (1965), the District of Columbia (1973), Rhode Island (1979), Massachusetts (1984), New York (2004) and New Jersey (2007). Kansas abolished the death penalty in 1973, but restored it in July, 1994. And South Dakota abolished the death penalty in 1915, restored it in 1939, abolished it again 1977, and restored it again 1979.

Race and and capital punishment Historically, blacks have been more likely to be executed than

Prisoners Executed by System, 1930–2006

System	Number executed Since 1930	Number executed Since 1977	Number executed In 2006	Removed from death row, in 2006	Sentenced to death in 2006	On death row in 2006[1]	Minimum age authorized for execution
Alabama	169	34	4	12	12	189	16
Alaska	0	0	0	0	0	0	—
Arizona	60	22	0	6	8	109	none
Arkansas	145	27	1	1	2	38	14
California[2]	304	12	2	12	23	646	18
Colorado	48	1	0	1	0	2	18
Connecticut	22	1	1	0	1	7	18
Delaware	26	14	1	0	0	16	16
District of Columbia	40	0	0	0	0	0	—
Federal system	36	3	0	1	6	37	18
Florida[2]	230	60	1	9	15	372	17
Georgia[2]	405	39	3	3	3	107	17
Hawaii	0	0	0	0	0	0	—
Idaho[2]	4	1	0	4	0	18	none
Illinois	102	12	0	0	1	7	18
Indiana	57	16	5	3	1	20	18
Iowa	18	0	0	0	0	0	—
Kansas[3]	15	0	0	0	0	0	18
Kentucky[2]	105	2	0	0	1	36	16
Louisiana[2]	160	27	0	8	4	83	none
Maine	0	0	0	0	0	0	—
Maryland	73	5	1	0	0	7	18
Massachusetts	27	0	0	0	0	0	—
Michigan	0	0	0	0	0	0	—
Minnesota	0	0	0	0	0	0	—
Mississippi[2]	161	7	1	3	2	68	16
Missouri	128	66	5	2	2	46	16
Montana[2]	8	2	0	0	0	4	18
Nebraska	7	3	0	0	2	10	18
Nevada	40	11	0	2	1	82	18
New Hampshire	1	0	0	0	0	0	17
New Jersey[2]	74	0	0	1	0	10	18
New Mexico	9	1	0	0	0	2	18
New York[4]	329	0	0	1	0	1	18
North Carolina	302	39	5	7	6	174	17
North Dakota	0	0	0	0	0	0	—
Ohio	191	19	4	4	5	199	18
Oklahoma	139	79	4	7	5	86	16
Oregon	21	2	0	0	1	31	18
Pennsylvania	155	3	0	9	7	218	none
Rhode Island	0	0	0	0	0	0	—
South Carolina	197	35	3	3	3	68	none
South Dakota[2]	1	0	0	0	0	4	18
Tennessee	94	1	0	0	2	103	18
Texas	652	355	19	32	14	411	17
Utah	19	6	0	1	0	9	14
Vermont	4	0	0	0	0	0	—
Virginia	186	94	0	2	1	22	14
Washington	51	4	0	0	0	10	18
West Virginia	40	0	0	0	0	0	—
Wisconsin	0	0	0	0	0	0	—
Wyoming	8	1	0	0	0	2	18
Total U.S.	4,863	944	60	134	128	3,254	—

Note: Removed from death row includes only prisoners removed for reasons other than execution. 1. As of December 31. 2. State authorizes capital punishment for selected crimes other than murder. 3. Death penalty restored in 1994; no executions yet carried out. 4. Death penalty restored in 1995; no executions yet carried out.
Source: Bureau of Justice Statistics Bulletin, *Capital Punishment 2006* (2007).

whites in proportion both to the general population and to the prison population. In the 1940s, for example, blacks made up less than 10 percent of the population, but more than 60 percent of prisoners executed were black. Since 1930, equal numbers of blacks (2,407) and whites (2,399) have been executed, though nearly twice as many whites (609) have been executed since 1977 as blacks (359). But while the race of the defendant has been shown to influence whether he receives a death sentence, the race of the victim plays an even larger role. Murderers of white people were far more likely to be charged with a capital crime than those who killed blacks. Since 1977, nearly four of every five victims of an executed prisoner have been white.

Economy and Business

THE U.S. ECONOMY

(For more on the financial crisis of 2008, see "Major News Stories.")

▶**GROSS NATIONAL PRODUCT AND GROSS DOMESTIC PRODUCT**

The goal of an economic system is to transform resources into final products by business enterprises for consumption by society. This includes manufacturing goods such as cars, bread, furniture and so on, and providing services such as health care, education and motion pictures. The most commonly used measures associated with this goal are Gross National Product (G.N.P.) and Gross Domestic Product (G.D.P.). G.N.P. is the total national output of goods and services valued at market prices. G.N.P. in this broad context measures the output attributable to the factors of production—labor and property—supplied by a country's residents. G.N.P. differs from "national income" mainly in that G.N.P. includes allowances for depreciation and for indirect business taxes (sales and property taxes). G.D.P. is the measure of the output of production attributable to all factors of production (labor and property) physically located within a country. G.D.P., therefore, excludes net property income from abroad (such as the earnings of U.S. nationals working overseas), which is included in the G.N.P.

The word *final* serves to exclude intermediate goods sold to producers and used to make finished products eventually sold to consumers in the market. Auto parts such as batteries and tires are examples of intermediate goods and are included in G.N.P. or G.D.P. only through the price of a car when it is sold. G.N.P. and G.D.P., in terms of expenditure categories, comprise purchases of goods and services by consumers and government, gross private domestic investment (or business purchases), and net exports.

The assessment of G.N.P. and G.D.P. in current dollars is referred to as a nominal measure. Nominal measures may be misleading because G.N.P. and G.D.P. can appear to rise as average prices rise with inflation. An alternative method is to evaluate G.N.P. and G.D.P. by measuring the value of goods and services using constant prices for a given year; the government currently uses 2000 as the base year. Assessments based on constant prices are referred to as real measures because they indicate the change in quantity of output produced by the economy.

▶**DEFINITIONS OF OUTPUT, INCOME, AND EXPENDITURE TERMS**

Capital consumption adjustment Used for corporations, nonfarm sole proprietorships and

G.D.P. in Current and Constant (2000) Dollars, 1960–2007 (billions)

Item	1960	1970	1980	1990	2000	2006	2007
CURRENT DOLLARS							
Gross domestic product (G.D.P.)	$526.4	$1,038.5	$2,789.5	$5,803.1	$9,817.0	$13,194.7	$13,841.3
Personal consumption expenditures	331.7	648.5	1,757.1	3,839.9	6,739.4	9,224.5	9,734.2
Durable goods	43.3	85.0	214.2	474.2	863.3	1,048.9	1,078.2
Nondurable goods	152.8	272.0	696.1	1,249.9	1,947.2	2,688.0	2,833.2
Services	135.6	291.5	846.9	2,115.9	3,928.8	5,487.6	5,822.8
Gross private domestic investment	78.9	152.4	479.3	861.0	1,735.5	2,209.2	2,125.4
Fixed investment	75.7	150.4	485.6	846.4	1,679.0	2,162.5	2,122.4
Change in private inventories	3.2	2.0	-6.3	14.5	56.5	46.7	2.9
Net exports of goods and services	4.2	4.0	-13.1	-78.0	-379.5	-762.0	-708.0
Exports	27.0	59.7	280.8	552.4	1,096.3	1,467.6	1,643.0
Imports	22.8	55.8	293.8	630.3	1,475.8	2,229.6	2,351.0
Government consumption	111.6	233.8	566.2	1,180.2	1,721.6	2,523.0	2,689.8
Federal	64.1	113.5	243.8	508.3	578.8	932.5	976.0
National defense	53.4	87.6	168.0	374.0	370.3	624.3	660.1
State and local	47.5	120.3	322.4	671.9	1,142.8	1,590.5	1,713.8
CONSTANT (2000) DOLLARS							
Gross domestic product (G.D.P.)	$2,501.8	$3,771.9	$5,161.7	$7,112.5	$9,817.0	$11,319.4	$11,566.8
Personal consumption expenditures	1,597.4	2,451.9	3,374.1	4,770.3	6,739.4	8,044.1	8,277.8
Gross private domestic investment	266.6	427.1	645.3	895.1	1,735.5	1,919.5	1,825.5
Net exports of goods and services	—	—	—	-54.7	-379.5	-624.5	-555.6
Exports	90.6	161.4	323.5	552.5	1,096.3	1,304.1	1,409.9
Imports	103.3	213.4	310.9	607.1	1,475.8	1,928.6	1,965.4
Government consumption	715.4	1,012.9	1,115.4	1,530.0	1,721.6	1,981.4	2,021.6

Source: U.S. Bureau of Economic Analysis, *National Income and Product Accounts of the United States.* www.bea.gov

partnerships, this is the difference between capital consumption claimed on income tax returns and capital consumption allowances measured at straight-line depreciation, consistent service lives, and replacement cost. The tax return data are valued at historical costs and reflect changes over time in service lives and depreciation patterns as permitted by tax regulations.

Consumer expenditure Consumer expenditure statistics presented in the accompanying tables are arrived at from the findings of the Consumer Expenditure Survey program, designed to provide a continuous flow of data on the buying habits of American consumers, necessary for future revisions of the Consumer Price Index. One group of 5,000 consumers in 85 urban areas around the country keeps diaries of expenditures on small, frequently purchased items, such as food and beverages, tobacco, housekeeping supplies, nonprescription drugs, and personal care products and services. Another 5,000 consumers are interviewed quarterly for information about large expenditures, such as those for property, automobiles and major appliances, or expenditures occurring on a fairly regular basis, such as rent, utilities and insurance premiums.

Disposable personal income is that income after personal tax and nontax payments; this is the income available to persons for spending and saving. Personal tax and nontax payments are tax payments (except personal contributions for social insurance, net of refunds) by persons that are not chargeable to business expense, and also include certain personal payments to general government that are treated like taxes. Personal taxes include income, estate, gift, and personal property taxes and motor vehicle licenses. Nontax payments include passport fees, fines and penalties, donations, and tuitions and fees paid to schools and hospitals operated mainly by government.

Family income The term *family* refers to a group of two or more persons related by birth, marriage or adoption who reside together; all such persons are considered as members of one family. Family income refers to the sum of all income of the family members.

Gross domestic product (G.D.P.) see "Gross National Product and Gross Domestic Product," above.

Gross national product (G.N.P.) see "Gross National Product and Gross Domestic Product," above.

Gross state product (G.S.P.) is the gross market value of the goods and services attributable to labor and property located in a state. It is the state counterpart of the nation's G.D.P.

Household income A household includes related family members and all unrelated persons, if any—such as lodgers, foster children, wards or employees—who share a house, an apartment or a single room when it is occupied or intended for occupancy as separate living quarters by that household; that is, when the members of the household do not live and eat with any other persons in the structure and there is direct access from the outside or through a common hall. Household income, therefore, is the sum of all income of household members. The *householder* (which replaced the term *head of household* beginning with the 1980 Current Population Survey) is the person in whose name the home is owned or rented. In the case of joint ownership, one per-

National Income by Industry, 1998–2007 (billions)

Industry	1998	2000	2002	2005	2006	2007
National income, Total	**$7,661.4**	**$8,687.4**	**$9,013.5**	**$10,128.8**	**$11,791.8**	**$12,368.1**
Domestic industries	$7,640.1	$8,648.5	$8,982.9	$10,052.6	$11,733.8	$12,272.3
Private industries	6,724.6	7,642.8	7,854.7	8,791.1	10,352.1	10,820.3
Agriculture, forestry, fishing, and hunting	78.5	70.1	65.9	95.7	87.0	112.0
Mining	72.6	93.8	81.4	124.1	199.2	200.8
Utilities	138.6	144.3	143.8	161.6	193.7	210.5
Construction	366.6	440.6	470.8	523.6	621.3	540.2
Manufacturing	1,112.1	1,228.5	1,071.6	1,214.2	1,421.6	1,472.5
Durable goods	672.5	744.0	613.8	678.6	777.6	824.3
Nondurable goods	439.5	484.5	457.8	535.7	644.0	648.2
Wholesale trade	505.4	563.8	553.4	631.9	721.6	758.2
Retail trade	591.1	665.3	710.1	764.3	864.9	905.9
Transportation and warehousing	235.3	261.2	250.3	290.7	348.2	368.3
Information	273.7	308.3	307.3	361.8	432.6	460.2
Finance, insurance, real estate, rental, and leasing	1,328.5	1,529.3	1,644.7	1,780.4	2,127.6	2,216.4
Professional and business services[1]	975.1	1,146.6	1,211.2	1,336.4	1,630.3	1,766.9
Educational services, health care, and social assistance	582.7	664.6	777.0	880.1	994.5	1,060.9
Arts, entertainment, recreation, accommodation, and food service	267.9	310.5	330.3	369.4	425.8	449.0
Other services, except government	196.6	215.8	237.1	256.8	283.8	298.5
Government	**$915.5**	**$1,005.7**	**$1,128.2**	**$1,261.5**	**$1,381.6**	**$1,452.1**
Rest of the world	**$21.3**	**$38.9**	**$30.6**	**$76.2**	**$58.0**	**$95.7**

Note: Figures do not include capital consumption adjustment. **1.** Professional, scientific, and technical services; management of companies and enterprises; and administrative and waste management services.
Source: U.S. Bureau of Economic Analysis, *National Income and Product Accounts of the United States.* www.bea.gov

son in each household is designated as the householder for statistical purposes.

Inventory valuation adjustment This represents the difference between the book value of inventories used in production and the cost of replacing them.

Mean vs. median income Mean (or average) income refers to the sum of all incomes of a group divided by the number of incomes in that group. Median income is the middle income when they are arranged in order of size—that is, there are the same number of incomes above and below the median. For example, consider incomes of $2,000, $3,000, $4,000, $15,000 and $95,000: the mean income is the sum of these divided by five, or $23,800; the median income is $4,000.

Money income This refers to income received (exclusive of certain money receipts such as capital gains) before payments for such things as personal income taxes, Social Security, union dues, and Medicare deductions. Money income does not include income in the form of noncash benefits such as food stamps, health benefits and subsidized housing; rent-free housing and goods produced and consumed on farms; or the use of business transportation and facilities, full or partial payments by business for retirement programs, medical and educational expenses, and so on. These elements should be considered when comparing income levels. None of the aggregate income concepts (G.N.P., national income, or personal income) is exactly comparable with money income, although personal income is the closest.

National income, the aggregate of labor and property earnings derived from the current production of goods and services, is the sum of employee compensation, proprietors' income, rental income, corporate profits and net interest. It measures the total factor costs of the goods and services produced by the economy. Income is measured before deduction of taxes.

Personal income is the current income received by persons from all sources minus their personal contributions for social insurance. *Persons* include individuals (including owners

National Income, by Type of Income, 1960-2007 (billions of current dollars)

Type of Income	1960	1970	1980	1990	2000	2006	2007
National income	$474.9	$930.9	$2,439.3	$5,089.1	$8,795.2	$11,655.6	$12,270.9
Compensation of employees	296.4	617.2	1,651.8	3,338.2	5,782.7	7,448.3	7,812.3
Wages and salaries	272.9	551.6	1,377.6	2,754.0	4,829.2	6,025.7	6,355.7
Government	49.2	117.2	261.5	517.7	774.7	1,020.6	1,075.2
Other	223.7	434.3	1,116.2	2,236.3	4,054.5	5,005.1	5,280.5
Supplements to wages & salaries	23.6	65.7	274.2	584.2	953.4	1,422.6	1,456.6
Employer contributions to pension and insurance funds	14.3	41.8	185.2	377.8	609.9	970.7	991.9
Employer contributions to government social insurance	9.3	23.8	88.9	206.5	343.5	451.8	464.7
Proprietors' income[1,2]	**50.8**	**78.4**	**174.1**	**380.6**	**728.4**	**1,006.7**	**1,056.2**
Farm	10.5	12.7	11.3	31.9	22.7	19.4	44.0
Nonfarm	40.3	65.7	162.8	348.7	705.7	987.4	1,012.2
Rental income of persons[1]	**17.1**	**21.4**	**30.0**	**50.7**	**150.3**	**54.5**	**40.0**
Corporate profits[1,2]	**53.8**	**83.6**	**201.1**	**437.8**	**817.9**	**1,553.7**	**1,642.4**
Taxes on corporate income	22.8	34.8	87.2	145.4	265.2	453.9	450.4
Profits after tax[1,2]	31.0	48.9	113.9	292.4	552.7	1,099.8	1,192.0
Net dividends	13.4	24.3	64.1	169.1	377.9	698.9	788.7
Undistributed profits[1,2]	17.6	24.6	49.9	123.3	174.8	400.9	403.4
Net interest and miscellaneous	**10.6**	**39.1**	**181.8**	**442.2**	**559.0**	**598.5**	**664.4**
Inventory valuation adjustment	-0.2	-6.6	-42.1	-12.9	-14.1	-36.3	-6.8
Capital consumption adjustment	2.3	9.2	-10.2	41.2	58.6	-215.8	125.5

Notes: 1. With capital consumption adjustment. 2. With inventory valuation adjustment.
Source: U.S. Bureau of Economic Analysis, *National Income and Product Accounts of the United States.* www.bea.gov

Percent Distribution of National Income, by Type, 1960-2007

Type of income	1960	1970	1980	1990	2000	2006	2007
National income, total	100.0%	100.0%	100.0%	100.0%	100.0%	100.0%	100.0%
Compensation of employees	**62.4**	**66.3**	**67.7**	**65.6**	**65.8**	**63.9**	**64.4**
Wages and salaries	57.5	59.2	56.5	54.1	54.9	51.7	52.2
Supplements to wages & salaries	5.0	7.1	11.2	11.5	10.8	12.2	12.2
Proprietors' income[1]	**10.7**	**8.4**	**7.1**	**7.5**	**8.3**	**8.6**	**8.5**
Farm	2.2	1.4	0.5	0.6	0.3	0.2	0.3
Non-farm	8.5	7.1	6.7	6.8	8.0	8.5	8.2
Rental income of persons[2]	**3.6**	**2.3**	**1.2**	**1.0**	**1.7**	**0.5**	**0.5**
Corporate profits[1]	**11.3**	**9.0**	**8.2**	**8.6**	**9.3**	**13.3**	**13.0**
Profits before tax	4.8	3.7	3.6	2.9	3.0	3.9	3.8
Profits after tax	6.5	5.2	4.7	5.8	6.3	9.4	9.2
Net interest	**2.2**	**4.2**	**7.4**	**8.7**	**6.4**	**5.1**	**4.9**

Notes: 1. With inventory valuation and capital consumption adjustments (not shown separately). 2. With capital consumption adjustment (not shown separately). **Source:** U.S. Bureau of the Census, based on data from U.S. Bureau of Economic Analysis, *National Income and Product Accounts of the United States.* www.bea.gov

of unincorporated firms), nonprofit institutions serving individuals, private trust funds and private noninsured welfare funds. Personal income includes transfers (payments not resulting from current production) from government and business, such as Social Security benefits and public assistance, but excludes transfers among persons. Also included are certain nonmonetary types of income: estimated net rental value to owner-occupants of their homes, the value of services furnished without payment by financial intermediaries, and food and fuel produced and consumed on farms.

Poverty level is an estimate of the income necessary to purchase what society defines as a minimally acceptable standard of living. Families and unrelated individuals are classified as being above or below the poverty level according to their money income as a group and the number of people in the group (e.g. in 2007, a family of four with income less than $21,027 lived below the poverty level). Classification is based on the poverty index originated by the Social Security Administration in 1964 and revised in 1969 and 1980. The poverty index is based solely on money in-

Per Capita Personal Income by State, 1970–2007

State	Personal income (rank)				
	1970	1980	1990	2000	2007
Alabama	$2,957 (49)	$ 7,836 (48)	$15,723 (43)	$23,767 (45)	$32,404 (43)
Alaska	5,263 (1)	14,866 (1)	22,804 (7)	29,869 (16)	40,352 (16)
Arizona	3,835 (27)	9,524 (29)	17,005 (36)	25,653 (38)	33,029 (41)
Arkansas	2,828 (50)	7,524 (50)	14,460 (50)	21,926 (49)	30,060 (49)
California	4,810 (8)	11,951 (4)	21,638 (9)	32,462 (9)	41,571 (8)
Colorado	4,048 (18)	10,746 (14)	19,575 (19)	33,361 (8)	41,042 (11)
Connecticut	5,078 (3)	12,357 (2)	26,504 (1)	41,492 (1)	54,117 (2)
Delaware	4,597 (9)	10,748 (13)	21,421 (10)	30,869 (14)	40,608 (13)
District of Columbia	4,973 (4)	12,291 (3)	26,473 (2)	40,403 (2)	61,092 (1)
Florida	4,004 (20)	9,933 (24)	19,564 (20)	28,508 (21)	38,444 (21)
Georgia	3,378 (39)	8,420 (39)	17,603 (30)	27,987 (27)	33,457 (39)
Hawaii	5,094 (2)	11,443 (8)	22,186 (8)	28,435 (23)	39,239 (19)
Idaho	3,520 (35)	8,648 (36)	15,724 (42)	24,077 (43)	31,197 (45)
Illinois	4,570 (10)	11,005 (11)	20,824 (11)	32,186 (10)	40,322 (17)
Indiana	3,782 (31)	9,374 (31)	17,491 (31)	27,133 (32)	33,616 (38)
Iowa	3,865 (25)	9,585 (28)	17,389 (33)	26,556 (34)	35,023 (28)
Kansas	3,818 (28)	9,953 (23)	18,085 (23)	27,691 (28)	36,768 (23)
Kentucky	3,166 (45)	8,178 (44)	15,437 (45)	24,412 (41)	31,111 (47)
Louisiana	3,090 (47)	8,777 (35)	15,173 (46)	23,081 (46)	34,756 (32)
Maine	3,411 (37)	8,347 (40)	17,376 (34)	25,973 (36)	33,722 (36)
Maryland	4,558 (11)	11,187 (9)	22,852 (6)	34,261 (6)	46,021 (6)
Massachusetts	4,483 (12)	10,602 (15)	23,043 (5)	37,750 (4)	49,082 (4)
Michigan	4,198 (13)	10,314 (16)	18,922 (21)	29,554 (18)	35,086 (27)
Minnesota	4,039 (19)	10,256 (17)	19,891 (16)	32,014 (11)	41,034 (12)
Mississippi	2,617 (51)	7,007 (51)	13,089 (51)	21,007 (51)	28,845 (51)
Missouri	3,850 (26)	9,324 (32)	17,627 (29)	27,242 (31)	34,389 (33)
Montana	3,611 (34)	9,058 (34)	15,448 (44)	22,933 (47)	32,458 (42)
Nebraska	3,792 (29)	9,160 (33)	17,983 (27)	27,624 (30)	36,471 (25)
Nevada	4,936 (5)	11,700 (7)	20,346 (14)	30,433 (15)	40,480 (14)
New Hampshire	3,886 (24)	9,850 (26)	20,512 (12)	33,399 (7)	41,512 (9)
New Jersey	4,821 (7)	11,707 (6)	24,572 (3)	38,372 (3)	49,194 (3)
New Mexico	3,188 (43)	8,346 (41)	14,924 (47)	22,143 (48)	31,474 (44)
New York	4,874 (6)	11,015 (10)	23,523 (4)	34,901 (5)	47,385 (5)
North Carolina	3,267 (40)	8,195 (43)	17,246 (35)	27,064 (33)	33,636 (37)
North Dakota	3,230 (42)	7,907 (47)	15,943 (40)	25,103 (39)	34,846 (30)
Ohio	4,086 (16)	10,046 (22)	18,743 (22)	28,206 (25)	34,874 (29)
Oklahoma	3,475 (36)	9,506 (30)	16,187 (38)	24,409 (42)	34,153 (34)
Oregon	3,924 (22)	10,113 (19)	18,010 (25)	28,096 (26)	34,784 (31)
Pennsylvania	4,071 (17)	10,085 (21)	19,687 (18)	29,696 (17)	38,788 (20)
Rhode Island	4,104 (15)	9,677 (27)	20,006 (15)	29,213 (19)	39,463 (18)
South Carolina	3,051 (48)	7,743 (49)	15,894 (41)	24,423 (40)	31,013 (48)
South Dakota	3,265 (41)	8,073 (46)	16,172 (39)	25,721 (37)	33,905 (35)
Tennessee	3,170 (44)	8,259 (42)	16,692 (37)	26,095 (35)	33,280 (40)
Texas	3,633 (32)	9,880 (25)	17,421 (32)	28,314 (24)	37,187 (22)
Utah	3,389 (38)	8,501 (38)	14,913 (48)	23,864 (44)	31,189 (46)
Vermont	3,617 (33)	8,613 (37)	17,876 (28)	27,681 (29)	36,670 (24)
Virginia	3,789 (30)	10,144 (18)	20,449 (13)	31,083 (13)	41,347 (10)
Washington	4,191 (14)	10,832 (12)	19,865 (17)	31,777 (12)	40,414 (15)
West Virginia	3,108 (46)	8,118 (45)	14,493 (49)	21,904 (50)	29,537 (50)
Wisconsin	3,979 (21)	10,107 (20)	18,072 (24)	28,570 (20)	36,047 (26)
Wyoming	3,904 (23)	11,718 (5)	18,002 (26)	28,469 (22)	43,226 (7)
U.S. average	$4,085	$10,114	$19,477	$29,845	$38,611

Source: Bureau of Economic Analysis, *Survey of Current Business*, (monthly). www.bea.gov.

come and does not reflect the fact that many low-income persons receive noncash benefits such as food stamps, Medicaid and public housing. The poverty thresholds are updated every year to reflect changes in the Consumer Price Index.

Private domestic investment This consists of (1) non-residential fixed investment, i.e., firms' purchases of capital goods such as plants and equipment; (2) residential fixed investment (the building of single- and multi-family housing units); and (3) the change in business inventories, which are stocks on hand of raw materials and finished goods.

Per Capita Personal Income by Metropolitan Area, 1970–2007

Metropolitan Statistical Area (ranked by 2007 income)	1970	1980	1990	2000	2007
United States	**$4,085**	**$10,114**	**$19,477**	**$29,845**	**$38,632**
Metropolitan portion	4,307	10,640	20,526	31,474	40,536
Non-metropolitan portion	3,145	7,923	14,673	22,028	28,991
Highest per capita income, 2007					
1. Bridgeport-Stamford-Norwalk, Conn.	$6,085	$15,068	$34,300	$58,986	$80,192
2. Naples-Marco Island, Fla.	5,348	12,239	27,120	39,402	61,788
3. San Francisco-Oakland-Fremont, Calif.	5,562	14,092	27,082	48,343	61,337
4. San Jose-Sunnyvale-Santa Clara, Calif.	4,969	13,486	25,867	53,415	58,716
5. Sebastian-Vero Beach, Fla.	4,030	11,311	25,207	37,110	58,144
6. Washington-Arlington-Alexandria, D.C.-Va-. Md.-W.Va	5,192	12,928	26,839	40,672	54,211
7. Boston-Cambridge-Quincy, Mass.	4,698	11,044	24,702	41,436	53,763
8. New York-Northern New Jersey-Long Island, N.Y.-N.J.-Pa.	5,247	12,040	26,314	39,915	53,423
9. Boulder, Colo.	4,292	11,546	22,072	40,362	52,438
10. Trenton-Ewing, N.J.	4,832	12,066	26,048	39,455	52,388
11. Midland, Texas	4,639	14,616	22,610	35,417	52,294
12. Napa, Calif.	4,552	11,549	23,090	37,818	50,817
13. Seattle-Tacoma-Bellevue, Wash.	4,529	11,990	22,595	37,746	48,499
14. Sarasota-Bradenton-Venice, Fla.	4,412	11,533	24,257	35,474	48,498
15. Barnstable, Mass.	4,609	10,875	23,135	35,746	48,468
16. Santa Cruz-Watsonville, Calif.	4,379	11,345	21,813	39,149	47,923
17. Hartford-West Hartford-East Hartford, Conn.	4,913	11,955	25,196	36,981	47,641
18. Casper, Wyoming	4,605	14,313	21,732	33,902	47,354
19. Reno-Sparks, Nev.	5,280	13,293	23,015	36,022	46,734
20. Minneapolis-St. Paul-Bloomington, Minn.	4,652	11,768	22,728	36,838	46,458
21. Denver-Aurora, Colo.	4,543	12,019	21,835	37,848	46,439
22. Houston-Sugar Land-Baytown, Texas	4,172	12,219	20,350	34,047	46,235
23. New Orleans-Metairie-Kenner, La.	3,679	9,911	17,469	26,304	46,188
24. Santa Barbara-Santa Maria-Goleta, Calif.	4,829	12,517	22,656	32,297	46,120
25. Santa Rosa-Petaluma, Calif.	4,493	11,527	22,419	36,437	45,766
Lowest per capita income, 2007	**1970**	**1980**	**1990**	**2000**	**2007**
1. McAllen-Edinburg-Mission, Texas	$1,937	$5,297	$9,282	$13,576	$18,320
2. Brownsville-Harlingen, Texas	2,156	5,694	9,853	14,913	19,636
3. Laredo, Texas	2,244	5,418	9,406	15,069	21,103
4. Yuma, Ariz.	3,445	8,154	13,764	16,509	22,772
5. Provo-Orem, Utah	2,716	6,698	12,035	19,605	23,720
6. Madera, Calif.	3,714	10,575	14,890	18,317	23,726
7. Merced, Calif.	3,808	9,493	15,176	19,531	23,864
8. El Centro, Calif.	3,850	9,450	16,018	17,752	24,065
9. Logan, Utah	2,745	7,192	12,952	18,749	24,170
10. Hanford-Corcoran, Calif.	3,568	11,016	13,280	16,312	24,226
11. Lake Havasu City-Kingman, Ariz.	3,776	8,005	14,859	18,610	24,324
12. St. George, Utah	2,861	6,846	12,532	19,203	24,951
13. Hinesville-Fort Stewart, Ga.	2,759	6,132	10,094	16,638	25,066
14. Las Cruces, N.Mex.	2,999	6,864	12,611	17,830	25,351
15. Visalia-Porterville, Calif.	3,630	9,338	14,785	19,567	25,351
16. Morristown, Tenn.	2,620	6,499	14,080	21,215	25,446
17. Blacksburg-Christiansburg-Radford, Va.	2,876	7,174	13,629	20,097	26,260
18. Auburn-Opelika, Ala.	2,650	7,309	14,066	20,233	26,411
19. Pine Bluff, Ark.	2,697	7,318	13,166	19,071	26,469
20. El Paso, Texas	2,980	6,498	12,284	18,562	26,556
21. Valdosta, Ga.	2,970	6,734	13,888	20,751	26,582
22. Albany, Ga.	2,761	7,089	14,157	21,370	26,597
23. Greeley, Colo.	3,578	8,428	15,705	25,044	26,771
24. College Station-Bryan, Texas	2,794	7,130	12,963	19,802	26,790
25. Pocatello, Idaho	3,400	8,763	14,396	20,819	26,881

Note: Figures in 2007 dollars. **Source:** U.S. Bureau of Economic Analysis, *Survey of Current Business.* www.bea.gov

►ECONOMIC INDICATORS

All market economies regularly go through cycles of recession—when output declines and unemployment rises—and expansion—when output and employment rise. These "business cycles" are one of the most important factors determining the socioeconomic conditions in any society. Although economists still have very little idea what actually causes recessions and what leads the economy to begin expanding again, they have had some success in predicting business cycles. Economic forecasting is the science of making these predictions. It is especially useful to be able to predict recessions sufficiently far in advance so that governments can take actions to stimulate the economy and reduce the severity of these downturns.

Per Capita Personal Income by County, 2006

Rank/County	Per capita income 2006	Percent of national average
Highest per capita income		
1. New York, New York	$110,292	300.4%
2. Teton, Wyoming	103,852	282.9
3. Pitkin, Colorado	86,122	234.6
4. Marin, California	86,062	234.4
5. Loving, Texas	83,569	227.6
6. Fairfield, Connecticut	74,281	202.3
7. Westchester, New York	70,519	192.1
8. San Francisco, California	69,942	190.5
9. Morris, New Jersey	67,788	184.6
10. Somerset, New Jersey	67,196	183.0
11. San Mateo, California	66,839	182.1
12. Alexandria City, Virginia	65,141	177.4
13. Fairfax, Fairfax City, Falls Church, Virginia	64,698	176.2
14. Hunterdon, New Jersey	64,094	174.6
15. Arlington, Virginia	63,827	173.8
16. Montgomery, Maryland	63,753	173.6
17. Nassau, New York	62,278	169.6
18. Bergen, New Jersey	61,264	166.9
19. St. Bernard, Louisiana	61,201	166.7
20. Blaine, Idaho	59,939	163.3
21. Orleans, Louisiana	59,449	161.9
22. Montgomery, Pennsylvania	58,451	159.2
23. Norfolk, Massachusetts	58,357	159.0
24. District of Columbia	57,746	157.3
25. Summit, Utah	57,725	157.2
Lowest per capita income		
1. Loup, Nebraska	$ 9,140	24.9%
2. Ziebach, South Dakota	11,381	31.0
3. Buffalo, South Dakota	12,471	34.0
4. Starr, Texas	12,971	35.3
5. Slope, North Dakota	13,885	37.8
6. Grant, Nebraska	14,158	38.6
7. Zavala, Texas	14,607	39.8
8. Todd, South Dakota	15,066	41.0
9. Madison, Idaho	15,166	41.3
10. Maverick, Texas	15,667	42.7
11. Shannon, South Dakota	15,759	42.9
12. Lafayette, Florida	15,791	43.0
13. Hancock, Tennessee	15,795	43.0
14. Jackson, South Dakota	15,846	43.2
15. Jackson, Kentucky	16,034	43.7
16. Elliott, Kentucky	16,439	44.8
17. Jefferson, Mississippi	16,518	45.0
18. Presidio, Texas	16,534	45.0
19. San Juan, Utah	16,569	45.1
20. Zapata, Texas	16,598	45.2
21. Hamilton, Florida	16,614	45.3
22. Wade Hampton, Alaska	16,677	45.4
23. Crowley, Colorado	16,859	45.9
24. Union, Florida	16,950	46.2
25. Hudspeth, Texas	17,007	46.3

Source: U.S. Bureau of Economic Analysis, *Survey of Current Business.* www.bea.gov

Percent of Persons Below Poverty Level, by State, 1980–2007

State	1980	1990	2000	2007
United States	13.0%	13.5%	11.3%	12.5%
Alabama	21.2	19.2	13.3	14.5
Alaska	9.6	11.4	7.6	7.6
Arizona	12.8	13.7	11.7	14.3
Arkansas	21.5	19.6	16.5	13.8
California	11.0	13.9	12.7	12.7
Colorado	8.6	13.7	9.8	9.8
Connecticut	8.3	6.0	7.7	8.9
Delaware	11.8	6.9	8.4	9.3
District of Columbia	20.9	21.1	15.2	18.0
Florida	16.7	14.4	11.0	12.5
Georgia	13.9	15.8	12.1	13.6
Hawaii	8.5	11.0	8.9	7.5
Idaho	14.7	14.9	12.5	9.9
Illinois	12.3	13.7	10.7	10.0
Indiana	11.8	13.0	8.5	11.8
Iowa	10.8	10.4	8.3	8.9
Kansas	9.4	10.3	8.0	11.7
Kentucky	19.3	17.3	12.6	15.5
Louisiana	20.3	23.6	17.2	16.1
Maine	14.6	13.1	10.1	10.9
Maryland	9.5	9.9	7.4	8.8
Massachusetts	9.5	10.7	9.8	11.2
Michigan	12.9	14.3	9.9	10.8
Minnesota	8.7	12.0	5.7	9.3
Mississippi	24.3	25.7	14.9	22.6
Missouri	13.0	13.4	9.2	12.8
Montana	13.2	16.3	14.1	13.0
Nebraska	13.0	10.3	8.6	9.9
Nevada	8.3	9.8	8.8	9.7
New Hampshire	7.0	6.3	4.5	5.8
New Jersey	9.0	9.2	7.3	8.7
New Mexico	20.6	20.9	17.5	14.0
New York	13.8	14.3	13.9	14.5
North Carolina	15.0	13.0	12.5	15.5
North Dakota	15.5	13.7	10.4	9.3
Ohio	9.8	11.5	10.0	12.8
Oklahoma	13.9	15.6	14.9	13.4
Oregon	11.5	9.2	10.9	12.8
Pennsylvania	9.8	11.0	8.6	10.4
Rhode Island	10.7	7.5	10.2	9.5
South Carolina	16.8	16.2	11.1	14.1
South Dakota	18.8	13.3	10.7	9.4
Tennessee	19.6	16.9	13.5	14.8
Texas	15.7	15.9	15.5	16.5
Utah	10.0	8.2	7.6	9.6
Vermont	12.0	10.9	10.0	9.9
Virginia	12.4	11.1	8.3	8.6
Washington	12.7	8.9	10.8	10.2
West Virginia	15.2	18.1	14.7	14.8
Wisconsin	8.5	9.3	9.3	11.0
Wyoming	10.4	11.0	10.8	10.9

Source: U.S. Bureau of the Census, *Poverty Status by State: 2007* www.census.gov

Per Capita Money Income, by Race and Hispanic Origin, 1970–2007

Year	Current dollars					Constant (2007) dollars				
	All races	White	Black	Asian	Hispanic	All races	White	Black	Asian	Hispanic
1970	$3,177	$3,354	$1,869	N.A.	N.A.	$15,139	$15,983	$8,906	N.A.	N.A.
1980	7,787	8,23	4,804	N.A.	$4,865	18,656	19,724	11,509	N.A.	$11,655
1990	14,387	15,265	9,017	N.A.	8,424	22,125	23,476	13,867	N.A.	12,955
1995	17,227	18,304	10,982	$16,567	9,300	23,273	24,727	14,836	$22,381	12,564
2000	22,346	23,582	14,796	23,350	12,651	26,905	28,394	17,815	28,114	15,232
2005	25,036	26,496	16,874	27,331	14,483	26,590	28,141	17,922	29,028	15,382
2006	26,352	27,821	17,902	30,474	15,421	27,100	28,610	18,410	31,339	15,858
2007	26,804	28,325	18,428	29,901	15,603	26,804	28,325	18,428	29,901	15,603

Note: Beginning in 2002, figures for each racial category include those who identified themselves as belonging to that race alone. Asian includes Pacific Islander from 1970-2001. Hispanic persons may be of any race. Total includes other races not shown separately.
Source: U.S. Bureau of the Census, *Current Population Survey*. www.census.gov.

Median Income of Families by Race and Hispanic Origin, 1980–2007

Year	Current dollars					Constant (2007) dollars				
	All races	White	Black	Asian	Hispanic	All races	White	Black	Asian	Hispanic
1980	$21,023	$21,904	$12,674	N.A.	$14,716	$50,366	$52,477	$30,364	N.A.	$35,256
1990	35,353	36,915	21,423	$42,246	23,431	54,369	56,771	32,946	$64,969	36,034
2000	50,732	53,029	33,676	62,617	34,442	61,083	63,849	40,547	75,393	41,469
2005	56,194	59,317	35,464	68,957	37,867	59,683	63,000	37,666	73,238	40,218
2006	58,407	61,280	38,269	74,612	40,000	60,064	63,018	39,355	76,729	41,135
2007	61,355	64,427	40,143	76,606	40,566	61,355	64,427	40,143	77,133	40,566

Note: Beginning in 2002, figures for each racial category include those who identified themselves as belonging to that race alone. Asian includes Pacific Islander from 1990-2001. Hispanic persons may be of any race. Total includes other races not shown separately.
Source: U.S. Bureau of the Census, Current Population Survey. www.census.gov.

Persons Below Poverty Level, by Race, 1960–2007

Year	Number below poverty level (millions)					Percent below poverty level				
	All races	White	Black	Asian	Hispanic	All races	White	Black	Asian	Hispanic
1960	39.9	28.3	N.A.	N.A.	N.A.	22.2%	17.8%	N.A.	N.A.	N.A.
1970	25.4	17.5	7.5	N.A.	N.A.	12.6	9.9	33.5%	N.A.	N.A.
1980	29.3	19.7	8.6	N.A.	3.5	13.0	10.2	32.5	N.A.	25.7%
1990	33.6	22.3	9.8	0.9	6.0	13.5	10.7	31.9	12.2%	28.1
2000	31.6	21.6	8.0	1.3	7.7	11.3	9.5	22.5	9.9	21.5
2005	37.0	24.9	9.2	1.4	9.4	12.6	10.6	24.9	11.1	21.8
2006	36.5	24.4	9.0	1.4	9.2	12.3	10.3	24.3	10.3	20.6
2007	37.3	25.1	9.2	1.3	9.9	12.5	10.5	24.5	10.2	21.5

Note: Beginning in 2002, figures for each racial category include those who identified themselves as belonging to that race alone. Asian includes Pacific Islander from 1960-2001. Hispanic persons may be of any race. Total includes other races not shown separately.
Source: U.S. Bureau of the Census, *Poverty in the United States 2006* (2007).

Economic indicators track developments in areas of the economy that are thought to be crucial to the future health of the economy, just as a barometer measures changes in air pressure that are crucial to changes in the weather. The development of economic indicators began around World War I but suffered a setback when the early forecasters failed to predict the Great Depression in 1929. During the depression the government asked a private research group, the National Bureau of Economic Research, to develop a set of measures that would help predict changes in business cycles. The group devised a list of measures based on analyses of previous business cycles. Since then, the list has been revised several times to reflect changes in the way the economy is structured.

Leading Indicators

There are currently 10 leading economic indicators, representing a broad spectrum of economic activity. These indicators are said to "lead" because their numbers change months in advance of a change in the general level of economic activity. They are as follows:

1. Average length of workweek of production workers in manufacturing.

2. Average weekly state unemployment insurance claims.

3. New orders for consumer goods and materials (in constant dollars).

4. Vendor performance (percent of companies receiving slower deliveries from suppliers).

5. Contracts and orders for plant and equipment (in constant dollars).

6. Index of new private housing units authorized by local building permits.

7. Index of stock prices, i.e., of 500 common stocks (Standard and Poor's 500).

8. Money supply-M2 in constant dollars. (See "Money and Banking" section.)

9. Interest rate spread.
10. Index of consumer expectations.

This composite of leading economic indicators is published by the U.S. Department of Commerce, Bureau of Economic Analysis. The composite has a noteworthy record: since 1948 it has accurately predicted every downturn and upswing in the economy. One major reason for this success is that many of the indicators represent commitments to economic activity in the coming months. The average lead for the index is 9.5 months at business cycle peaks (indicating the end of a business cycle expansion and the beginning of a recession) and 4.5 months at business cycle troughs (indicating the end of a business cycle recession and the beginning of an expansion).

Coincident and Lagging Indicators

In addition to the leading economic indicators, two other sets of measures are used to track business cycles and the state of the economy. One set includes the coincident indicators, which measure how well the economy is doing at that moment (roughly, within three months of the business cycle turning points). These include the number of employees on nonagricultural payrolls; manufacturing and trade sales (in constant dollars); index of industrial production; and personal income less transfer payments (in constant dollars). The second set includes lagging economic indicators. These are the ratio of consumer installment credit outstanding to personal income; commercial and industrial loans outstanding (in constant dollars); the average prime interest rate charged by banks; the ratio of manufacturing and trade inventories to sales (in constant dollars); the average duration of unemployment in weeks (inverted); the change in index of labor cost per unit of output in manufacturing; and the change in the Consumer Price Index for services per unit labor costs. At business cycle peaks, the average lag of the index is 4.5 months, and at business cycle troughs 8.5 months. It seems reasonable to wonder what use there is for an indicator that tells you where you have already been. But in fact that is exactly their use: they provide another way of measuring whether turning points in the business cycle truly have occurred.

The government produces a wide variety of economic indicators in addition to those discussed here for use in tracking more specific aspects of the economy, such as labor or capital markets.

The Employment Cost Index (ECI)

The ECI measures the *rate of change* in total employee compensation (wages, salaries, employer cost for employee benefits) in nonfarm private industry and in state and local governments. Provided quarterly by the Bureau of Labor Statistics, the ECI has become one of the most closely watched indexes because any significant rise could signal an inflationary trend. The ECI grew annually by 4 to 5 percent in the late 1980's, but fell below 3 percent in the 1990s. ECI growth hovered between 3 and 4 percent in 2006-07.

▶ PRICES AND INFLATION
Inflation

Inflation is a sustained rise in the general price level in the economy. It affects the level and timing of spending in the economy since it indicates the extent to which income will cover the purchase of a consumer's basket of goods (food, clothes, entertainment, medical services, housing, gasoline, and so on). For example, if a consumer is considering purchasing a television and inflation is high (that is, prices are rising rapidly), he or she will buy the television as soon as possible since savings may not cover the cost a month or a year from now. Inflation is closely watched to determine wage contracts and Social Security benefits that contain cost-of-living adjustment clauses. If wage contracts cover a long period of time and inflation is rapid, consumers' standard of living will fall in the interim before new contracts can be negotiated. Savings will tend to fall as consumers store their wealth in the form of commodities.

The cause of inflation is often described as "too much money chasing too few goods," brought about by the money supply rising rapidly or production of goods falling behind demand for them. Inflation may be due to (1) cost-push factors—that is, if the cost of inputs such as labor, raw materials,

Composite Index of Economic Indicators, 1960–2008 (1996=100)

Year	Leading indicators	Coincident indicators	Lagging indicators
1960	72.7	37.2	82.2
1970	83.1	53.1	96.9
1980	88.0	70.8	100.4
1990	97.8	88.1	101.7
2000	106.4	114.2	103.4
2001	109.4	116.6	107.7
2002	112.2	115.4	102.6
2003	111.2	115.5	99.2
2004	115.0	115.8	98.2
2000	106.4	114.2	103.4
2005	115.6	119.6	98.6
2006	140.1	121.7	122.8
2007	138.5	123.3	127.6
2008	135.8	125.2	130.7

Note: As of January of each year.
Source: The Conference Board. www.conference-board.org.

Employment Cost Index (ECI) 1985–2007 (December 2005 =100)

Year	Civilian workers	Private industry workers	State and local government workers
1985	48.3	48.5	47.1
1990	59.8	59.4	61.4
1995	70.6	70.3	71.9
2000	83.6	83.8	82.7
2001[1]	87.2	87.5	86.1
2002	90.1	90.2	89.6
2003	93.5	93.8	92.7
2004	97.0	97.3	95.9
2005	100.1	100.1	99.8
2006	103.4	103.3	103.9
2007	106.8	106.4	108.1

Note: Figures are as of December of each year and are not seasonally adjusted. Excludes farm, household, and federal government workers. 1. Indexes before 2001 are not directly comparable because the BLS switched from the Standard Industrial Classification (SIC) System to the North American Industry Classification System (NAICS). Source: U.S. Bureau of Labor Statistics, Employment Cost Index, (quarterly).

or other intermediate goods rises, the cost of the final product also rises; or (2) demand-pull factors—that is, if the demand for goods and services rises above the full employment level, wages rise as employers compete for labor, and the general price level of goods and services rises.

Consumer Price Index

Often referred to as the "cost of living index," the Consumer Price Index is the most commonly used measure of inflation. The index measures the average change in prices relative to an arbitrary base year of a common bundle of goods and services bought by the average consumer on a regular basis. The Bureau of Labor Statistics publishes two CPI's: (1) CPI-U for All Urban Consumers, which includes wage earners and clerical workers; professional, managerial, and technical workers; the self-employed; short-term workers; the unemployed; retirees and others not in the labor force—altogether covering 80 percent of the population—and (2) CPI-W for Urban Wage Earners and Clerical Workers, covering 32 percent of the population. Prices (including direct taxes) are collected from over 57,000 housing units and 19,000 establishments in 85 areas across the country. In calculating the index number, based on 100,000 price quotes a month, larger weights are assigned to goods that represent larger proportions of consumer expenditure. The index costs $26 million a year to produce and requires 40 economists and analysts tracking price changes in 365 categories.

Producer Price Index

The Producer Price Index measures average changes in prices received by producers of all commodities, at all stages of processing, produced in the United States. Prices used in constructing the index are collected from sellers and generally apply to the first significant large-volume commercial transaction for each commodity—i.e., the manufacturer's or other producer's selling price or the selling price on an organized exchange or at a central market. The weights used in the index represent the total net selling value of commodities produced or processed in the country. Values are f.o.b. (free on board) at the production point and are exclusive of excise taxes.

Implicit Price Deflator

The implicit price deflator (also called the G.D.P. deflator) is derived from the ratio of current-to-constant dollar G.D.P. (multiplied by 100) and measures the value of current production in current prices relative to the value of the same goods and services in prices for the base year. For example, in 2007, G.D.P. in current dollars was $13,841.3 billion and G.D.P. in constant (2000) dollars was $11,566.8 billion. Therefore, the GDP deflator for 2007 was (13,841.3 ÷ 11,566.8) x 100, or 119.7, which is simply a comparison between 2000 and 2007 prices. It is a weighted average of the detailed price indexes used in the deflation of GDP, but the indexes are combined using weights that reflect the composition of G.D.P. in each period. Thus changes in the implicit price deflator reflect not only changes in prices, but also changes in the composition of G.D.P.

▶MONEY AND BANKING
Federal Reserve System

The government's interest in monitoring and controlling the banking industry and managing the money supply led to the Federal Reserve Act of 1913. The act created the Federal Reserve System (or the "Fed," as it is popularly known), the nation's central bank. There are 12 regional Fed banks located in major cities throughout the country (Boston, New York, Philadelphia, Cleveland, Richmond, Atlanta, Chicago, St. Louis, Minneapolis, Kansas City, Dallas and San Francisco). Commercial banks within each region select a majority of the directors who run each regional Fed bank. The president of the United States appoints a board of governors for the whole system, and the board is responsible for coordinating policies across the system. But the regional Feds play an important role in shaping those policies by representing regional interests and decentralizing the decision-making process.

The Fed has three main policy tools for managing the overall economy. First, it controls the *reserve requirements* at all depository institutions. These requirements determine what percentage of a bank's deposits must be held in reserve in the form of either deposits with Federal Reserve banks or vault cash. Raising the reserve requirements reduces the amount of loans available to borrowers and helps slow down the economy.

A more frequently used instrument is *the discount rate*, the interest rate the Federal Reserve banks charge their commercial bank customers to borrow money. The Fed is known as the lender of last resort because of its responsibility to lend to banks in need, and it thus maintains the stability of the banking system. Raising the discount rate generally leads the commercial banks to raise

Consumer Price Index (CPI-U) 1915–2007 (1982-84 = 100)

Year	Consumer Price Index	Year	Consumer Price Index	Year	Consumer Price Index
1915	10.1	1955	26.8	1995	152.4
1920	20.0	1960	29.6	2000	172.2
1925	17.5	1965	31.5	2002	179.9
1930	16.7	1970	38.8	2003	184.0
1935	13.7	1975	53.8	2004	188.9
1940	14.0	1980	82.4	2005	195.3
1945	18.0	1985	107.6	2006	201.6
1950	24.1	1990	130.7	2007	207.3

Source: U.S. Bureau of Labor Statistics. www.bls.gov/cpi/home.htm

Purchasing Power of the Dollar, 1950–2007

Year	Annual average as measured by:		Year	Annual average as measured by:	
	Producer prices	Consumer prices		Producer prices	Consumer Prices
1950	$3.546	$4.151	1990	$0.839	$0.766
1955	3.279	3.732	1995	0.782	0.656
1960	2.994	3.373	2000	0.725	0.581
1965	2.933	3.166	2003	0.698	0.544
1970	2.545	2.574	2004	0.673	0.530
1975	1.718	1.859	2005	0.642	0.512
1980	1.136	1.215	2006	0.623	0.496
1985	0.955	0.928	2007[1]	0.600	0.482

Note: 1. Producer prices data are preliminary. Source: U.S. Bureau of Economic Analysis, *Survey of Current Business* (monthly).

Consumer Price Indexes for Selected Metropolitan Statistical Areas, 2007 (1982–84 = 100)

Area	All items	Apparel	Education and comm-unication	Food and beverages	Housing	Medical care	Rec-reation	Transpor-tation
U.S. City average	207.3	119.0	119.6	203.3	209.6	351.1	111.4	184.7
Anchorage, Alaska	181.2	123.4	107.3	184.2	163.5	367.0	116.7	180.7
Atlanta, Ga.	200.0	124.1	110.1	207.5	197.4	318.4	115.9	178.1
Boston-Brockton-Nashua, Mass.-N.H.	227.4	136.3	121.9	213.5	232.9	481.9	116.4	175.7
Chicago-Gary-Kenosha Ill.-Ind.-Wisc.	204.8	94.0	126.8	200.3	212.8	348.4	109.0	175.8
Cincinnati-Hamilton, Ohio-Ky.-Ind.	193.9	122.3	117.3	181.0	181.9	367.8	118.1	182.2
Cleveland-Akron, Ohio	196.0	107.2	110.2	204.0	188.7	321.1	107.4	190.0
Dallas-Ft. Worth, Tex.	193.2	127.1	126.9	205.4	176.1	316.8	114.6	186.0
Denver-Boulder-Greeley, Colo.	202.0	99.4	110.4	192.2	188.7	402.9	124.2	219.4
Detroit-Ann Arbor-Flint, Mich.	200.1	107.2	127.8	189.1	189.8	350.5	119.5	204.5
Honolulu, Hawaii	219.5	104.1	114.0	204.9	238.4	N.A.	102.6	205.0
Houston-Galveston-Brazoria, Tex.	183.8	153.5	106.0	186.1	170.2	329.0	109.2	167.2
Kansas City, Mo.-Kans.	194.5	109.5	114.8	198.3	188.2	301.0	113.7	180.2
Los Angeles-Riverside-Orange County, Calif.	217.3	104.4	120.6	211.2	236.9	340.0	114.3	183.2
Miami-Ft. Lauderdale, Fla.	212.4	155.3	113.5	211.0	216.6	330.5	111.8	189.7
Milwaukee-Racine, Wisc.	194.1	114.3	120.8	205.0	190.7	331.0	104.1	178.0
Minneapolis-St. Paul, Minn.-Wisc.	201.2	129.2	122.9	218.5	183.7	366.7	115.3	187.4
New York-Northern New Jersey-Long Island, NY-NJ-Conn.-Pa.	226.9	111.5	125.1	210.9	246.3	359.9	114.3	190.5
Philadelphia-Wilmington-Atlantic City Pa.-N.J.-Del.-Md.	216.7	99.6	120.4	196.1	226.1	403.2	117.4	185.0
Phoenix-Mesa, Ariz.	115.3	116.8	113.0	118.9	115.3	126.3	103.1	113.0
Pittsburgh, Pa.	201.5	141.2	124.8	199.5	206.2	338.3	106.4	160.9
Portland-Salem, Oreg.-Wash.	208.6	120.4	106.0	187.9	202.8	378.6	112.2	209.4
San Diego, Calif.	233.3	123.4	115.8	212.0	261.0	N.A.	137.1	193.2
San Francisco-Oakland-San Jose, Calif.	216.0	107.2	126.9	215.3	238.1	353.2	103.7	166.6
Seattle-Tacoma-Bremerton, Wash.	215.7	134.7	118.6	215.1	225.5	329.4	94.7	197.8
St. Louis, Mo.-Ill.	193.2	124.7	124.0	195.8	185.1	343.9	119.2	178.5
Tampa-St. Petersburg-Clearwater, Fla.	184.3	140.7	106.1	178.8	183.4	294.4	114.2	173.8
Washington-Baltimore, D.C.-Md.-Va.-W.Va.	133.5	92.7	125.0	130.6	143.0	133.8	115.9	128.3

Note: Figures are not seasonally adjusted. The base period for Education and Communication and for Recreation is December 1997 = 100 in all cities. Except where otherwise indicated, the base period for Phoenix-Mesa is December 2001 = 100; for Tampa-St. Petersburg it is 1987 = 100; and for Washington-Baltimore it is November 1996 = 100.
Source: U.S. Bureau of Labor Statistics, *Monthly Labor Review* and *CPI Detailed Report* (Jan. issues). www.bls.gov/cpi/home.htm.

the interest rates they charge their customers. This raises the costs of borrowing in the private sector and slows the economy. (Cutting the discount rate does the reverse and stimulates the economy.)

Most important, the Fed can also control the level of bank reserves through *open market operations*; that is, the direct sale on purchase of Treasury securities and other government debt instruments. When the Fed sells securities, it takes money from the buyer and holds it in its reserves, reducing the money supply; when it buys these instruments, it pays for them by taking money from its reserves, which then goes into circulation, increasing the money supply.

Controlling the money supply through open market operations is certainly the most common and, many would argue, the most important function of the Fed. The money supply shapes interest rates, through the supply and demand of money. Because the Fed is constantly involved in these open market operations (in order to keep the size of the money supply in proportion with a growing economy, for example), adjustments can be made subtly.

In addition, the Federal Reserve regulates banks through the Federal Deposit Insurance Corporation, (F.D.I.C.) influences foreign-currency exchange rates through the sale or purchase of foreign currencies, and coordinates international financial policy.

The money supply Money provides a medium of exchange as well as a way to store value. Traditionally, currency (paper money and coins) served that role exclusively. But over time, new financial instruments have developed that serve at least some of the functions of money. Checking accounts serve exactly the same role as currency, and to an extent, so do money market funds and other instruments.

The Fed uses three different measures of the money supply, which include different monetary instruments:

Producer Price Indexes for Selected Commodities, 1970–2007 (1982=100)

Commodity group	1970	1980	1990	2000	2004	2005	2006	2007
All commodities	**38.1**	**89.8**	**116.3**	**132.7**	**146.7**	**157.4**	**164.7**	**172.6**
Farm products	45.8	102.9	95.1	99.5	123.3	118.5	117.0	143.4
Processed foods and feeds	44.6	95.9	103.5	133.1	151.2	153.1	153.8	165.1
Industrial commodities	**35.2**	**88.0**	**115.8**	**134.8**	**147.6**	**160.2**	**168.8**	**175.1**
Textile products and apparel	52.4	89.7	114.9	121.4	121.0	122.8	124.5	125.8
Hides, skins, leather and related products	42.0	94.7	141.7	151.5	164.5	165.4	168.4	173.6
Fuels, related products, power	15.3	82.8	82.2	103.5	126.9	156.4	166.7	177.6
Chemicals and allied products	35.0	89.0	123.6	151.0	174.4	192.0	205.8	214.8
Rubber and plastic products	44.9	90.1	113.6	125.5	133.8	143.8	153.8	155.0
Lumber and wood products	39.9	101.5	129.7	178.2	195.6	196.5	194.4	192.4
Pulp, paper, and allied products	37.5	86.3	141.3	183.7	195.7	202.6	209.8	216.9
Metals and metal products	38.7	95.0	123.0	128.1	149.6	160.8	181.6	193.5
Machinery and equipment	40.0	86.0	120.7	124.0	122.1	123.7	126.2	127.3
Furniture & household durables	51.9	90.7	119.1	132.6	135.1	139.4	142.6	144.7
Nonmetallic mineral products	35.3	88.4	114.7	142.5	153.2	164.2	179.9	186.2
Transportation equipment	41.9	82.9	121.5	143.8	148.6	151.0	152.6	155.0

Source: U.S. Bureau of Labor Statistics, *Producer Price Indexes*, monthly and annual.

Federal Reserve Bank, Discount Rates, 1914–2008

Year	Range	Year	Range	Year	Range	Year	Range
1914	6.0-5.0%	1942	1.0-0.5%	1970	6.0-5.5%	1998	5.00-4.50%
1915	5.0-4.0	1943	0.5	1971	5.5-4.5	1999	4.5-5.0
1916	4.0-3.0	1944	0.5	1972	4.5	2000	5.0-6.0
1917	3-3.5.0	1945	0.5	1973	4.5-7.5	2001	6.0-1.25
1918	3.5-4.0	1946	0.5-1.0	1974	7.5-8.0-7.75	2002	1.25-0.75
1919	4.0-4.75	1947	1.0	1975	7.75-6.0	2003[2]	2.25-2.00
1920	4.75-7.0	1948	1.0-1.5	1976	6.6-5.25	2004	2.00-3.25
1921	7.0-4.5	1949	1.5	1977	5.25-6.0	Feb. 2, 2005	3.50
1922	4.5-4.0	1950	1.5-1.75	1978	6.0-9.5	Mar. 22, 2005	3.75
1923	4.0-4.5	1951	1.75	1979	9.5-12.0	May 3, 2005	4.00
1924	4.5-3.0	1952	1.75	1980[1]	12.0-10.0-13.0	June 30, 2005	4.25
1925	3.0-3.5	1953	1.75-2.0	1981[1]	13.0-14.0-12.0	Aug. 9, 2005	4.50
1926	3.5-4.0	1954	2.0-1.5	1982	12.0-8.5	Sept. 20, 2005	4.75
1927	4.0-3.50	1955	1.5-2.5	1983	8.5	Nov. 1, 2005	5.00
1928	3.50-5.0	1956	2.5-3.0	1984	8.5-9.0-8.0	Dec. 13, 2005	5.25
1929	5.0-6.0-4.5	1957	3.0-3.5-3.0	1985	8.0-7.5	Jan. 31, 2006	5.50
1930	4.5-2.0	1958	3.0-1.75-2.5	1986	7.5-5.5	Mar. 28, 2006	5.75
1931	2.0-1.5-3.5	1959	2.5-4.0	1987	5.5-6.0	May 10, 2006	6.00
1932	3.5-2.5	1960	4.0-3.0	1988	6.0-6.5	June 29, 2006	6.25
1933	2.5-3.2-2.0	1961	3.0	1989	6.5-7.0	Aug. 17, 2007	5.75
1934	2.0-1.5	1962	3.0	1990	7.0-6.5	Sept. 18, 2007	5.25
1935	1.5	1963	3.0-3.5	1991	6.5-3.5	Oct. 31, 2007	5.00
1936	1.5-1.0	1964	3.5-4.0	1992	3.5-3.0	Dec. 11, 2007	4.75
1937	1.0	1965	4.0-4.5	1993	3.00	Jan. 22, 2008	4.00
1938	1.0	1966	4.5	1994	3.0-4.75	Jan. 30, 2008	3.50
1939	1.0	1967	4.5-4.0-4.5	1995	4.75-5.25	Mar. 18, 2008	2.50
1940	1.0	1968	4.5-5.5	1996	5.00	April 30, 2008[3]	2.25
1941	1.0	1969	5.5-6.0	1997	5.00		

Note: 1. The discount rates for 1980 and 1981 do not include the surcharge applied to frequent borrowings by large institutions. The surcharge reached 3% in 1980 and 4% in 1981, and was eliminated in November 1981. **2.** The discount rate applied to short term adjustment credit until Jan. 9, 2003, when it was changed to primary credit, in an effort to eliminate the incentive for institutions to borrow for the purpose of exploiting the positive spread of money market rates over the discount rate. **3.** Latest rate in effect as of July 21, 2008. **Source:** Board of Governors of the Federal Reserve System, *Federal Reserve Bulletin*, monthly, and *Annual Statistical Digest*.

M1 is the original and most commonly reported measure of the money supply, which embraces currency and coins, demand deposits, traveler's checks, and other checkable deposits.

M2 is M1 plus money-market accounts, and savings and small time-deposits.

M3 is M2 plus money-market mutual-fund balances held by financial institutions, term repurchase agreements and term Eurodollars, and large time-deposits.The Federal Reserve discontinued publishing M3 statistics in 2006.

The U.S. Banking System

Commercial banks are the largest financial institutions in the country and are the principal vehicles for exchanging money. The nation's first commercial bank was the Bank of America (now

First Pennsylvania Bank), established in Philadelphia in 1782. Commercial banks hold about two-thirds of the nation's money deposits. Savings and loans, the next-largest source of deposits, hold about half as much.

There are approximately 10,000 commercial banks in the country. They may be chartered either by the federal government or by individual states. While banks themselves may not operate across states, they may be owned by holding companies that can operate interstate, if state laws permit.

Commercial banks can make loans to individuals and to commercial operations, establish checking or demand deposits, maintain "trust" departments that make investments for customers, and perform a variety of other functions such as issuing credit cards. Until the deregulation of the 1980's, commercial banks were the only ones permitted to issue checking accounts. Regulations that developed after bank failures in the Great Depression still keep these banks out of the investment business—largely to protect depositors and the solvency of banks from potential effects of bad investments. But deregulation of the banking industry in the 1980's is blurring many of these distinctions. In particular, investment companies are now permitted to issue demand deposits and to compete with banks in other areas as well. (As a result these companies are sometimes referred to as nonbanks.)

Bank failures are especially serious problems because of the domino effect they may have on other financial institutions and businesses. Banks, and indeed all depository institutions, ultimately fail when many of their loans go bad and cannot be repaid. But even before that happens, depositors may get nervous about the security of their accounts and withdraw them all at once—a "run on the bank." Because banks loan out deposits and hold in reserve only a small percentage of the value of those deposits, banks experiencing a run would have to call in some of their loans (mainly those already due), putting sudden pressure on many commercial borrowers and causing some to fail. In addition the withdrawal of deposits and of loans reduces the money supply sharply. This process was an important cause of the Great Depression. Following the banking failures during the depression (2,293 banks failed in 1931, and 4,000 banks failed in 1933), the Federal Deposit Insurance Corporation (F.D.I.C.) was created in 1933 to protect the accounts of depositors and, more important, to help prevent bank failures. The F.D.I.C. charges banks a premium to pay for this coverage. The corporation is designed to prevent runs on banks by insuring deposits and lending to banks to prevent the need to call in loans.

But banks still fail because of bad loans. Between 1945 and 1980, U.S. banks failed at the rate of about six per year. Since then, hundreds of

The Money Supply, 1970–2007 (billions of dollars)

Item	1970	1980	1990	2000	2005	2006	2007
M1, total	**$214**	**$408**	**$825**	**$1,088**	**$1,375**	**$1,367**	**$1,364**
Currency[1]	49	115	246	531	724	749	759
Travelers' checks[2]	1	3	8	8	7	7	6
Demand deposits[3]	165	261	277	310	325	306	293
Other checkable deposits[4]	(z)	28	294	238	319	305	306
M2, total	**$628**	**$1,600**	**$3,278**	**$4,931**	**$6,692**	**$7,063**	**$7,447**
M1	214	408	825	1,088	1,375	1,367	1,364
Non-M1 components in M2	414	1,192	2,453	3,844	5,317	5,669	6,083
Money market funds, retail	(z)	64	357	921	700	799	976
Savings deposits (including money market deposit accounts)	261	400	923	1,878	3,622	3,699	3,890
Commercial banks	99	186	582	1,424	2,772	2,906	3,035
Thrift institutions	162	215	342	454	850	793	855
Small time deposits[5]	151	729	1,173	1,045	996	1,170	1,217
Commercial banks	79	286	611	700	645	758	815
Thrift institutions	72	442	563	345	351	412	402
M3, total	**$677**	**$1,996**	**$4,153**	**$7,120**	**$10,155**	**(9)**	**(9)**
M2	628	1,600	3,278	4,931	6,66976	(9)	(9)
Non-M1 components in M3	49	396	875	2,186	3,479	(9)	(9)
Large time deposits[6]	45	260	480	836	1,354	(9)	(9)
Commercial banks[7]	44	215	358	734	1,123	(9)	(9)
Thrift institutions	1	45	121	102	231	(9)	(9)
Repurchase agreements[8]	4	58	151	364	564	(9)	(9)
Eurodollars[8]	(z)	61	103	195	424	(9)	(9)
Money market funds, institution only	(z)	16	140	788	1,137	(9)	(9)

Note: As of December of year shown. Adjusted seasonally. Figures may not add up because of independent rounding. z = less than $500 million. **1.** Currency outside U.S. Treasury, Federal Reserve Banks, and the vaults of depository institutions. **2.** Outstanding amount of non-bank issuers. **3.** At commercial banks and foreign-related institutions. **4.** Consists of negotiable order of withdrawal (NOW) and automatic transfer service (ATS) accounts at all depository institutions, credit union share draft balances and demand deposits at thrift institutions. **5.** Issued in amounts of less than $100,000. Includes retail repurchase agreements. Excludes individual retirement accounts (IRAs) and Keogh accounts. **6.** Issued in amounts of $100,000 or more. Excludes those booked at international banking facilities. **7.** Excludes those held by money market mutual funds, depository institutions, U.S. Government, foreign banks, and official institutions. **8.** Excludes those held by depository institutions and money market mutual funds. **9.** The Federal Reserve discontinued publishing M3 statistics in 2006. **Source:** Board of Governors of the Federal Reserve System, *Federal Reserve Bulletin*, monthly, and *Money Stock, Liquid Assets, and Debt Measures*, Federal Reserve Statistical Release H.6, weekly.

banks have failed each year. Most of these failures occurred in agricultural states where the failure of farms led to defaults on loans; more than half of all bank failures can be attributed to agriculture loans. Fraud also played an important role, especially in Tennessee, where more than 30 banks have failed since 1982. When a bank fails, the F.D.I.C. pays off each depositor and then sells the bank's assets. Sometimes the F.D.I.C. arranges for another bank's acquisition of the failed bank by subsidizing the sale. (For more on the 2008 financial tumoil, see "Major News Stories.")

Thrifts are depository institutions including savings and loans (S&Ls), savings banks, and

Consumer Credit Outstanding, 1980–2007 (billions of dollars)

Year	Total	Revolving[1]	Other[2]
1980	$ 349.4	$ 55.1	$ 294.3
1985	593.2	124.7	468.5
1990	789.1	238.6	550.5
1995	1,095.8	443.1	652.7
2000	1,704.3	676.9	1,027.4
2003	2,006.6	759.3	1,247.3
2004	2,191.3	800.0	1,391.3
2005	2,284.9	825.0	1,459.9
2006	2,387.5	875.4	1,512.1
2007	2,524.3	941.4	1,582.8

Note: 1. Consists mainly of outstanding balances on credit card accounts, but also includes borrowing under check credit and overdraft plans, and unsecured personal lines of credit. 2. Includes automobile loans and all other loans not included in revolving credit, such as loans for mobile homes, trailers or vacations. noninstallment credit.
Source: Board of Governors of the Federal Reserve System, Federal Reserve Bulletin (monthly). www.federalreserve.gov.

credit unions. The largest and most important thrifts are the S&Ls, which were created to provide home mortgages for borrowers and long-term savings deposits for individual investors. Until recently, thrifts were prohibited from engaging in riskier loans—including most commercial loans—and issuing checking deposits, and a ceiling was placed on the rate of interest they could pay depositors. Congress lifted the ceiling on interest payments to depositors in 1980 and in 1982 allowed the S&Ls to issue commercial loans and to invest directly in real estate developments. Unwise investment in these areas by many thrifts was a major cause of the savings and loan debacle of the late 1980's and early 1990's.

The Federal Home Loan Bank System was established in 1932 to serve some of the same functions for S&Ls that the Federal Reserve provides for banks. It has now been succeeded by the Office of Thrift Supervision (O.T.S.), which identifies institutions that may be financially distressed or likely to fail. All federally chartered S&Ls are regulated by the system (and must have the word *Federal* in their name). Less than half the thrifts are federally chartered, however; the rest are chartered by states, although most of these have joined the system as well. The F.S.L.I.C. (Federal Savings and Loan Insurance Corporation) insured deposits at member S&Ls until 1989, when it became insolvent and was dismantled.

Credit unions are employer-sponsored cooperative organizations that provide consumer and mortgage credit to their members. Employers often arrange for payroll-deduction savings plans through the credit union. Perhaps in response to the high rates charged by commercial banks for maintaining checking accounts, the number of people joining credit unions has jumped dramat-

Assets and Deposits of FDIC/BIF-Insured Banks, 2006–07

| | | 2006 | | | 2007 | |
| | | Assets | Deposits | | Assets | Deposits |
Charter class	Banks	(millions)	(millions)	Banks	(millions)	(millions)
All banks	8,680	$11,860,042	$7,825,219	8,533	$13,038,765	$8,414,336
Commercial banks	7,401	10,090,145	6,731,420	7,282	11,176,096	7,308,856
National banks	1,715	6,829,026	4,336,544	1,632	7,782,387	4,858,844
State banks	5,686	3,261,120	2,394,875	5,650	3,393,709	2,450,012
Savings banks	1,279	1,769,896	1,093,800	1,251	1,862,669	1,105,500
Federal charter	760	1,450,127	867,769	754	1,544,834	840,848
State charter	519	319,770	226,031	497	317,835	221,883

Note: As of Dec. 31 of each year. Source: Federal Deposit Insurance Corp., Statistics on Banking, (interactive).

Assets and Deposits of Deposit-Taking Institutions, 2007

Type of institution	Number of institutions	Percent share	Assets (millions)	Percent share	Deposits (millions)	Percent share
Commercial banks	7,282	41.7%	$11,176,096	73.0%	$7,308,856	73.6%
Savings banks[1]	1,251	7.2	1,862,669	12.2	1,105,500	11.1
Savings & Loans (thrifts)[2]	826	4.7	1,510,000	9.9	891,000	9.0
Credit unions[3]	8,101	46.4	753,463	4.9	632,399	6.4
Total	**17,460**	**100.0%**	**$15,302,228**	**100.0%**	**$9,937,755**	**100.0%**

Note: 1. Includes Federal and State-chartered Savings institutions. 2. Includes only thrifts regulated by the Office of Thrift Supervision. 3. Credit union deposits refer to total savings. Sources: Federal Deposit Insurance Corp, Statistics on Banking (interactive); Office of Thrift Supervision. OTS Fact Book; National Credit Union Association, 2007 Year-End Statistics.

Top 100 U.S. Banking Companies, 2007

Rank, Bank, City	Assets (millions)	Rank, Bank, City	Assets (millions)
1. Citigroup Inc., New York	$2,187,631	52. City National Corp., Beverly Hills, Calif.	$15,894
2. Bank of America Corp., Charlotte	1,720,688	53. *Flagstar Bancorp Inc., Troy, Mich.	15,757
3. JPMorgan Chase & Co., New York	1,562,147	54. *B.F. Saul Real Estate Investment Trust,	15,301
4. Wachovia Corp., Charlotte	782,896	Chevy Chase, Md.	
5. Wells Fargo & Co., San Francisco	575,442	55. FBOP Corp., Oak Park, Ill.	14,969
6. MetLife Inc., New York	558,563	56. *Charles Schwab Corp., San Francisco	14,763
7. *Washington Mutual Inc., Seattle	327,206	57. *BankUnited Financial Corp.,	14,416
8. U.S. Bancorp, Minneapolis	237,615	Coral Gables, Fla.	
9. Bank of New York Mellon Corp., New York	197,839	58. New York Private Bank and Trust Corp., New York	14,358
10. SunTrust Banks Inc., Atlanta	179,574	59. South Financial Group Inc.,	13,872
11. Capital One Financial Corp., McLean, Va.	150,590	Greenville, S.C.	
		60. Cullen/Frost Bankers Inc., San Antonio	13,646
12. National City Corp., Cleveland	150,384	61. Citizens Republic Bancorp Inc.,	13,524
13. State Street Corp., Boston	142,937	Flint, Mich.	
14. Regions Financial Corp., Birmingham, Ala.	141,044	62. *Downey Financial Corp., Newport Beach, Calif.	13,409
15. PNC Financial Services Group Inc., Pittsburgh	138,976	63. BancorpSouth Inc., Tupelo, Miss.	13,204
		64. Susquehanna Bancshares Inc., Lititz, Pa.	13,078
16. BB&T Corp., Winston-Salem, N.C.	132,618	65. Valley National Bancorp, Wayne, N.J.	12,749
17. *Countrywide Financial Corp., Calabasas, Calif.	121,055	66. Sterling Financial Corp., Spokane, Wash.	12,151
		67. *People's United Financial Inc.,	12,113
18. Fifth Third Bancorp, Cincinnati	110,962	Bridgeport, Conn.	
19. KeyCorp, Cleveland	99,567	68. East West Bancorp Inc., Pasadena, Calif.	11,852
20. *Sovereign Bancorp Inc., Philadelphia	84,701	69. UCBH Holdings Inc., San Francisco	11,804
21. Northern Trust Corp., Chicago	67,611	70. Wilmington Trust Corp., Wilmington, Del.	11,623
22. M&T Bank Corp., Buffalo	64,876	71. International Bancshares Corp.,	11,167
23. Comerica Inc., Dallas	62,757	Laredo, Tex.	
24. Marshall & Ilsley Corp., Milwaukee	59,857	72. Whitney Holding Corp., New Orleans	11,030
25. Huntington Bancshares Inc., Columbus, Ohio	54,629	73. First Banks Inc., Clayton, Mo.	10,883
		74. *Washington Federal Inc., Seattle	10,577
26. Zions Bancorp., Salt Lake City	52,947	75. Bank of Hawaii Corp., Honolulu	10,473
27. *E-Trade Financial Corp., New York	51,751	76. *Third Federal Savings and Loan Assn.,	10,442
28. Popular Inc., Hato Rey, Puerto Rico	44,411	Cleveland	
29. *Hudson City Bancorp Inc., Paramus, N.J.	44,142	77. FirstMerit Corp., Akron	10,408
30. *Merrill Lynch and Co. Inc. New York	37,832	78. Cathay General Bancorp, Los Angeles	10,403
31. First Horizon National Corp. Memphis	37,017	79. Arvest Bank Group Inc., Bentonville, Ark.	9,731
32. Synovus Financial Corp., Columbus, Ga.	33,018	80. Franklin Resources Inc., San Mateo, Calif.	9,627
33. *IndyMac Bancorp Inc., Pasadena, Calif.	32,514	81. Wintrust Financial Corp., Lake Forest, Ill.	9,369
34. New York Community Bancorp Inc., Westbury, N.Y.	30,600	82. UMB Financial Corp., Kansas City, Mo.	9,343
		83. Doral GP Ltd., San Juan, Puerto Rico	9,263
35. *USAA Bancorp, San Antonio	30,220	84. Trustmark Corp., Jackson, Miss.	8,967
36. Colonial BancGroup Inc., Montgomery, Ala.	25,971	85. Corus Bankshares Inc., Chicago	8,927
		86. FirstBank, Lakewood, Colo.	8,690
37. *American Express Co., New York	25,040	87. Central Bancompany Inc.,	8,502
38. *Astoria Financial Corp., Lake Success, N.Y.	21,735	Jefferson City, Mo.	
		88. Umpqua Holdings Corp., Portland, Ore.	8,353
39. Associated Banc-Corp, Green Bay, Wis.	21,592	89. NewAlliance Bancshares Inc.,	8,227
40. BOK Financial Corp., Tulsa, Okla.	20,903	New Haven, Conn.	
41. W Holding Co. Inc., Mayaguez, Puerto Rico	18,002	90. United Community Banks Inc., Blairsville, Ga.	8,207
42. Webster Financial Corp., Waterbury, Conn.	17,208	91. First Midwest Bancorp Inc., Itasca, Ill.	8,096
		92. *First Niagara Financial Group Inc.,	8,082
43. First BanCorp., San Juan, Puerto Rico	17,187	Lockport, N.Y.	
44. *AmTrust Financial Corp., Cleveland	16,938	93. R and G Financial Corp., Hato Rey, Puerto Rico	8,011
45. *Guaranty Financial Group Inc., Austin, Tex.	16,674	94. United Bankshares Inc., Charleston, W.Va.	7,995
46. First Citizens Bancshares Inc., Raleigh, N.C.	16,230	95. *Capitol Federal Savings Bank MHC, Topeka, Kan.	7,968
47. Commerce Bancshares Inc., Kansas City, Mo.	16,212	96. Old National Bancorp, Evansville, Ind.	7,848
		97. MB Financial Inc., Chicago	7,835
48. TCF Financial Corp. Wayzata,, Minn.	16,068	98. Apple Financial Holdings Inc., New York	7,444
49. *Lehman Brothers Holdings Inc., New York	16,050	99. Pacific Capital Bancorp, Santa Barbara, Calif.	7,387
50. Fulton Financial Corp., Lancaster, Pa.	15,923	100. Bremer Financial Corp., St. Paul, Minn.	7,250
51. *State Farm Bank, Bloomington, Ill.	15,898		

Note: The financial upheaval of 2008 resulted in the merger or dissolution of many of these companies. Institutions preceded by * are thrifts. **Source:** © 2008 *American Banker*, April 15, 2008. Reprinted by permission.

ically in recent years, from 61.4 million members in 1992 to 86.8 million in 2007.

Mortgage loans

Mortgages are loans backed by buildings—either private dwellings or commercial buildings. Until the 1970s, virtually all mortgages had fixed-interest payments and 30-year terms. With the escalation of interest rates beginning in the late 1970s, however, several alternative arrangements have developed. For example, in order to reduce the interest payments, many borrowers repay their loans in 15 years. Others use a *variable* or *adjustable rate mortgage* in which the interest rate varies with market rates. Some mortgages that hold payments down in the first few years and then increase them rapidly for the remaining term of the mortgage are known as balloon mortgages.

Mortgage crisis

In the first decade of the 20th century, lenders became ever more creative with mortgages, tempting less-than-ideal buyers with extra-low initial or "teaser" rates that soared in later years, or "interest-only" loans in which the homeowner never paid back the principal. These mortgage products allowed higher-risk (or "sub-prime") borrowers to get in on the real estate boom that was sweeping the U.S. at the time. They were a sound investment as long as property values continued to increase. But when the housing bubble started to burst in 2006 and 2007, many homeowners found they couldn't keep up with the escalating payments, didn't have any assets that would allow them to refinance, and owed more than the declining value of their homes.

Defaults and foreclosures turned subdivisions into ghost-towns almost overnight. But homeowners weren't the only ones affected. The banks that lent them the money suffered nearly $400 billion in losses on bad loans. And because lenders usually disperse risk by selling their mortgages to third parties, the credit crisis quickly spread to other financial markets throughout 2007 and 2008. One of the biggest casualties of the sub-prime mortgage crisis was Bear Stearns, which had invested heavily in mortgage-backed securities. The investment bank's stock was valued at a high of $171.52 in January of 2007, but by March, 2008, it had plummeted so far that the government, fearing complete default, arranged for JP Morgan Chase to buy out Bear Stearns for $10 a share. By mid-2008 the growing crisis resulted in the dissolution of several additional banks. (For more on the 2008 financial upheaval, see "Major News Stories.")

Money Instruments

Treasury bills,

also called T-bills, are securities sold by the U.S. Treasury in denominations of $10,000 that mature at various dates, but all in less than one year. Treasury bills pay an interest rate that is adjusted by the Treasury according to supply and demand. The Treasury bill rate is thought to have the highest risk-free rate of return among all investments.

Federal funds

are the reserves the Fed requires depository institutions such as commercial banks to hold on deposit at their regional Federal Reserve Bank as protection against withdrawals. Banks and other depository institutions can loan reserves in excess of those required by the Fed to each other. These Fed Fund loans can provide institutions with large amounts of liquid assets on very short notice, and most loans are for no more than one day.

Certificates of deposit (CDs)

Customers who make these deposits at commercial banks or thrift institutions receive a certificate describing the maturity date of the deposit (e.g., a five-year CD). CDs guarantee a rate of return for as long as 10 years into the future. In addition, the fact that they can be purchased at local banks also makes them easy to secure. These factors make them appealing to the general public. The interest paid on CDs is set by the market and is generally the same across large institutions. Smaller institutions often offer higher rates to attract depositors.

Money Market Interest Rates and Mortgage Rates, 1970-2007

Type	1970	1980	1990	2000	2005	2006	2007
Federal funds, effective rate	7.18%	13.35%	8.10%	6.24%	3.22%	4.97%	5.02%
Prime rate charged by banks	7.91	15.26	10.01	9.23	6.19	7.96	8.05
Eurodollar deposits, 3-month	8.52	14.03	8.16	6.45	3.51	5.19	5.32
Large negotiable CDs, 3-month, secondary market	7.56	13.07	8.15	6.46	3.51	5.16	5.27
Federal Reserve discount rate[1]	5.50	10.00	6.50	5.00	3.25	5.25	4.75
	-6.00	-13.00	-7.00	-6.00	-5.25	-6.25	-6.25
Taxable money market funds[2]	N.A.	12.68	7.82	5.89	2.66	4.51	4.70
Tax-exempt money market funds[2]	N.A.	N.A.	5.45	3.54	1.87	2.90	3.13
U.S. Government securities:							
3-month Treasury bill[3]	6.39%	11.39%	7.50%	5.82%	3.15%	4.73%	4.36%
6-month Treasury bill[3]	6.51	11.32	7.46	5.90	3.39	4.81	4.44
1-year Treasury bill[3]	6.48	10.85	7.35	5.78	N.A.	N.A.	N.A.
Home mortgages							
New home mortgage yields[4]	N.A.	12.70%	10.05%	7.52%	5.94%	6.60%	6.40%
Conventional, 15-year fixed[3]	N.A.	N.A.	9.73	7.76	5.50	6.13	6.11
Conventional, 30-year fixed[3]	N.A.	N.A.	9.97	8.08	5.93	6.47	6.40

Note: 1. Federal Reserve Bank of New York, low and high. The discount rate for 1980 does not include the 3% surcharge applied to frequent borrowings by large institutions. **2.** 12-month return for Dec. 31 of year shown. **3.** Annual averages. **4.** Effective rate (in the primary market) on conventional mortgages, reflecting fees and charges as well as contract rate and assumed, on the average, repayment after 10 years. **Source:** Except as noted, Board of Governors of the Federal Reserve System, *Federal Reserve Bulletin,* monthly.

Money-market accounts Customers pool their money into a fund that then purchases short-term debt such as Treasury bills and commercial paper in order to earn a high rate of return while maintaining liquidity (i.e., being able to convert assets quickly into cash). Customers typically can write checks on their money-market accounts, which are processed through cooperating banks, but checks generally have to be in large denominations—greater than $250—to prevent customers from using them as demand deposit accounts.

Capital Instruments

Stock, or equity, the most important source of capital for firms, represents a claim on the assets or equity of a business as well as on its earnings. See the chapter on U.S. Business later in this section.

Treasury bonds, or notes, have longer-term dates of maturity, from one to 10 years, than do Treasury bills. They are sold by the Treasury in denominations of $1,000 and are the principal means of funding government borrowing and the national debt. The interest on these bonds is paid out regularly. *Thirty-year Treasury Bonds,* commonly called the Long Bond, are also sold by the Treasury; their yield is watched closely because it forms the basis for all other interest rates, including mortgage-backed securities and fixed rates. Bond prices are determined by the relative number of investors willing to buy and sell them on the open market. Their decisions are in turn based on expectations about inflation. When the Federal Reserve announces that it will not change interest rates, indicating its belief that inflation will remain steady, more investors are willing to buy long-term investments, so bond prices rise, but result in a lower yield. When the economy heats up, however—that is, with increased business activity employing more workers—inflation is expected to rise, resulting in fewer investors willing to buy long-term instruments, and bond prices will fall as yields and other interest rates rise.

Other government securities Some agencies of the government that are involved in lending are permitted to sell securities in order to raise funds. The most important of these is the Federal National Mortgage Association—FNMA, or "Fanny Mae." It buys and sells mortgages insured by the federal government and stabilizes the market for those mortgages in the process.

Municipal bonds are issued by state and local governments to raise funds, usually to provide public works and other facilities. The federal government is prohibited by the Constitution from interfering in the ability of state and local governments to raise revenue, so income from municipal bonds is not subject to federal taxes. So-called revenue bonds are paid for by user fees—for example, tolls collected on a parkway are used to pay for the bonds used to build it. General-obligation bonds are paid for through general taxes. Municipal bonds tend to be very safe, although there have been occasions on which some state and local governments have had to take extraordinary actions to avoid default—most notably, New York City in 1975, which received a federal loan and sold new bonds to its municipal employee unions in order to avoid default.

▶ GOVERNMENT DEBT

One of the most debated economic issues since the 1980's has been the importance of the government's budget deficit. The government raises most of its resources through taxes, but it can also raise money by borrowing. The government borrows by selling bonds (Treasury bonds and savings bonds, for example) which have increasingly been purchased by investors outside the U.S. The bonds raise money now but must be repaid in the future through revenues from taxes. The *budget deficit* in any year indicates the difference between what the government takes in through taxes and other forms of revenues, and the expenditures it makes. The deficit therefore suggests how much the government needed to borrow to fill that gap. The total amount of present and past borrowing, plus interest, constitutes the total *national debt.*

Governments routinely borrow to pay for long-term projects that will give benefits to the community into the future. It can be argued that because much of the benefit from projects such as highways and other public works will be enjoyed by the next generation of taxpayers, they should also bear much of the cost. And they can do that by paying off the government debt (paying the premiums on the government bonds) through taxes in the future. Controversy arises when the government

Bonds Yields, 1970–2007							
Type	1970	1980	1990	2000	2005	2006	2007
U.S. Treasury, constant maturities:[1,2]							
1-year	N.A.	12.00%	7.89%	6.11%	3.62%	4.94%	4.53%
5-year	7.38%	11.45	8.37	6.16	4.05	4.75	4.43
10-year	7.35	11.43	8.55	6.03	4.29	4.80	4.63
State and local govt. bonds, Aaa	6.12	7.86	6.96	5.58	4.28	4.15	4.13
State and local govt. bonds, Baa	6.75	9.02	7.30	6.19	4.86	4.71	4.59
Municipal (Bond Buyer, 20 bonds)	6.35	8.55	7.27	5.71	4.40	4.40	4.40
High-grade municipal bonds (Standard & Poor's)	6.51	8.51	7.25	5.77	4.29	4.42	4.42
Corporate Aaa seasoned	8.04	11.94	9.32	7.62	5.23	5.59	5.56
Corporate Baa seasoned	9.11	13.67	10.36	8.37	6.06	6.48	6.48
Corporate seasoned, all industries	8.51	12.75	9.77	7.98	5.57	5.98	6.01

Note: 1. Yields on the more actively traded issues adjusted to constant maturities by the U.S. Treasury. **2.** Through 1990, yields are based on closing bid prices quoted by at least five dealers. Yields since 2000 are based on closing indicative prices quoted by secondary market participants. **Sources:** Board of Governors of the Federal Reserve System, *Federal Reserve Bulletin,* monthly; U.S. Council of Economic Advisors, *Economic Indicators,* monthly (high-grade bonds); Moody's Investors Service (corporate bonds).

borrows to pay for its more routine expenditures. One justification for such borrowing is that it can be used to manage business cycles in the economy: in other words, during recessions, the government can borrow in order to increase expenditures and expand the economy without raising taxes, which would slow it down.

When the total amount of government debt becomes large, some economists believe that it damages the economy in the following ways. First the fact that the government is selling large amounts of debt means that it is competing for limited investor dollars with private borrowers, driving up the cost of borrowing, and making it harder for private sector businesses to make investments for future growth. Second, the future taxes needed to pay off large amounts of government debt may place a serious drain on the future economy, again diverting resources from investment in the private sector. Politicians are concerned because debt payments must be funded from tax revenues so they must either raise taxes or reduce government spending in other areas (e.g. in defense, or in entitlement programs).

The debate over debt really turns on how much is "too much." Between 1935 and 1981 the only two significant increases in the deficit occurred during World War II and certain years of the Vietnam War, when deficits were about $25 billion. Between 1981 and 1989, however, the Reagan administration consistently ran annual deficits averaging $167 billion and increased the nation's total outstanding gross debt from just over $1 trillion to over $2.6 trillion.

The strong economy and prudent government accounting allowed the Clinton administration to wipe out the annual deficit in 1998 and post four straight years of surpluses (a feat not achieved since before the Depression). The total national debt, on the other hand, never decreased because the interest payments on the debt were higher even than the record-level surpluses. In 2002, George W. Bush's tax cut turned a $126 billion annual surplus into a $158 billion deficit over a single year, and pushed the total federal debt over the $6 trillion mark. The deficit set an all time high of $413 billion in 2004. The annual deficit declined from 2004-07, but is expected to return to $410 billion for 2008. Meanwhile, the total national debt continues to skyrocket, reaching an estimated $10 trillion in 2008.

▶ THE LABOR FORCE
Labor Force Participation Rate

The Labor Force Participation Rate (LFPR), often referred to simply as the labor force, is that proportion of the population that is either employed or actively seeking employment. It represents the supply of labor available to the economy. The LFPR is lower for young people because many are in school, and for older people because many have retired. It is highest for married men and for women who are heads of households.

Women in the work force One of the most important developments in the labor force has been the sharp increase in the LFPR of women, which has virtually doubled since the early 1960's. With higher levels of education than ever before, most women now opt for careers in the labor force rather than homemaking. Women are having fewer children, and are having them later in life, after they have started to establish their careers, and are returning to work sooner after childbirth. Furthermore, women are continuing to make inroads into professions like law and medicine that have previously been dominated by men.

Women joined the labor force at an astounding rate between 1960 and 1990. Just under 38 percent of women worked in 1960; in 1990, 57 percent did.

Deficits and the Debt, 1940–2008 (billions of dollars)

Year	Total receipts	Total outlays	Surplus or Deficit	Gross Federal Debt	Debt held by the public	Net interest paid[1] Total	Net interest paid[1] As percent of federal outlays
1940	$ 6.5	$ 9.5	$ -2.9	$ 50.7	$ 42.7	$ 1.0	9.5%
1945	45.2	92.7	-47.6	260.1	235.2	3.1	3.4
1950	39.4	42.6	-3.1	256.9	219.0	4.8	11.4
1955	65.5	68.4	-3.0	274.4	226.6	4.9	7.6
1960	92.5	92.2	0.3	290.5	236.8	6.9	8.5
1965	116.8	118.2	-1.4	322.3	260.8	8.6	8.1
1970	192.8	195.6	-2.8	380.9	283.2	14.4	7.9
1975	279.1	332.3	-53.2	541.9	394.7	23.2	7.5
1980	517.1	590.9	-73.8	909.0	711.9	52.5	10.6
1985	734.1	946.4	-212.3	1,817.4	1,507.3	129.5	16.2
1990	1,032.0	1,253.2	-221.2	3,206.3	2,411.6	184.3	16.1
1995	1,351.8	1,515.8	-164.0	4,920.6	3,604.8	232.1	15.8
1998	1,721.8	1,652.6	69.2	5,478.2	3,721.1	241.1	15.1
2000	2,025.5	1,789.2	236.2	5,628.7	3,409.8	223.0	12.0
2001	1,991.4	1,863.2	128.2	5,769.9	3,319.6	206.2	11.1
2002	1,853.4	2,011.2	-157.8	6,198.4	3,540.4	171.0	8.5
2003	1,782.5	2,160.1	-377.6	6,760.0	3,913.4	153.1	7.1
2004	1,880.3	2,293.0	-412.7	7,354.7	4,295.5	160.2	7.0
2005	2,153.9	2,472.2	-318.3	7,905.3	4,592.2	184.0	7.4
2006	2,407.3	2,655.4	-248.2	8,451.4	4,829.0	226.6	8.5
2007	2,568.2	2,730.2	-162.0	8,950.7	5,035.1	237.1	8.5
2008[2]	2,521.2	1,931.2	-410.0	9,654.4	5,428.6	143.9	7.5

Note: For fiscal years ending in year shown. Public debt excludes debt held by Federal Government accounts. 1. Net interest is interest paid on debt held by the public. 2. Estimate. **Source:** *Budget of the United States Government, Fiscal Year 2009* (2008).

The percentage of women in the labor force has declined slightly since 2000 and stood at 59.3 percent in 2007. The percentage of men in the labor force continues to drop, from 83.3 percent in 1960 to 73.2 percent in 2007.

Unemployment rate   One of the most closely watched labor force statistics is the unemployment rate, which in 1997 fell below 5 percent for the first time in 30 years. It dropped all the way to 3.9 percent in April, 2000, before climbing slowly back over 6 percent in 2003. It held steady at 4.6 percent in 2007. Contrary to popular opinion, the unemployment rate is only an indirect measure of the people without jobs, since it only measures the number of active (within the last four weeks) job seekers as a proportion of the total labor force. So the unemployment rate may rise as new job seekers enter the labor force. Every spring, for example, it rises slightly as school graduates enter the labor force and look for jobs. The rate may also fall as workers retire or otherwise leave the labor force. And when the economy is in a prolonged recession, the unemployment rate may actually drop slightly because some of the job seekers may give up trying to find a job and withdraw from the labor force.

The unemployment rate over time for the United States is a measure associated with identifying periods of expansion and recession. It reached a peak of 9.6 percent during the 1982–83 recession. The relatively high periods of unemployment beginning in the mid-1970s are in part due to the expansion of the labor force as the baby boom generation left school and began looking for work. Unemployment rates for women have paralleled those for men since 1990.

Hispanics   People of Hispanic origin constitute the fastest-growing population group in the labor force, in large part due to immigration, with Mexicans making up the largest share. The proportion of Hispanic women working—historically, these women were more likely to stay at home—has boosted Hispanic participation in the labor force. But a doubling of the Hispanic population in the U.S. since 1980 has been responsible for most of the growth. In 2007, Hispanic workers made up 14.1 percent of the labor force, up from 1995, when they were just 9.3 percent. Overall, Hispanic workers earn only three-quarters as much as the average for all workers.   Hispanics also have a higher unemployment rate, though not as high as the rate for blacks.

Productivity   measures how much output an economy or organization can generate from a given amount of input. Higher levels of productivity suggest greater efficiency—i.e. doing more with the same amount of resources, just as an efficient or economical car goes farther on a gallon of gasoline. Increases in productivity, as the result of better tools or improved methods, provide the main mechanism for increasing output in an economy and ultimately for raising standards of living. Productivity is usually measured in terms of labor—such as output per worker or output per hour of labor—not only because labor is the most

Occupations with Greatest Percentage of Women, Blacks, and Hispanics, 2007

Occupation	Number ('000s)	Percent women
Dental hygienists	156	99.2%
Speech-language pathologists	122	98.0
Preschool & kindergarten teachers	667	97.3
Secretaries and administrative assistants	3,401	96.7
Dental assistants	275	96.3
Child care workers	1,341	94.6
Licensed practical and licensed vocational nurses	533	93.2
Medical records and health information technicians	83	93.0
Receptionists & information clerks	1,441	93.0
Hairdressers, hairstylists, and cosmetologists	778	92.9

Occupation	Number ('000s)	Percent black
Postal service mail sorters, processors, and processing machine operators	84	37.0%
Nursing, psychiatric, and home health aides	1,879	33.6
Security guards and gaming surveillance officers	891	28.3
Barbers	102	27.3
Bus drivers	578	26.8
Residential advisors	64	26.6
Mail clerks and mail machine operators, except postal service	123	25.7
Miscellaneous health technologists and technicians	124	25.7
Postal service clerks	172	24.8
Taxi drivers and chauffeurs	333	24.3

Occupation	Number ('000s)	Percent Hispanic
Plasterers and stucco masons	82	65.3%
Drywall installers, ceiling tile installers, and tapers	232	53.6
Pressers, textile, garment, and related materials	59	52.3
Cement masons, concrete finishers, and terrazzo workers	112	52.1
Graders and sorters of agricultural products	81	50.2
Miscellaneous agricultural workers	683	45.9
Roofers	269	45.1
Construction laborers	1,771	44.6
Grounds maintenance workers	1,332	44.4
Carpet, floor, and tile installers and finishers	258	43.3

Source: U.S. Department of Labor, Bureau of Labor Statistics, *Employment and Earnings* January issues.

Unemployment Rate, 1947–2007

Year	Percent unemployed	Year	Percent unemployed	Year	Percent unemployed
1947	3.9%	1980	7.1%	2001	4.7%
1950	5.3	1985	7.2	2002	5.8
1955	4.4	1990	5.6	2003	6.0
1960	5.5	1995	5.6	2004	5.5
1965	4.5	1998	4.5	2005	5.1
1970	4.9	1999	4.2	2006	4.6
1975	8.5	2000	4.0	2007	4.6

Source: U.S. Department of Labor, Bureau of Labor Statistics, *Employment and Earnings* January issues.

Employment Status of the Population by Sex, Race, and Hispanic Origin 1960-2007 (numbers in thousands)

Year	Civilian noninstitutional population[1]	Total	Percent of population	Number employed	Employment/ population ratio[2]	Percent unemployed
			Total			
1960	117,245	69,628	59.4%	65,778	56.1%	5.5%
1970	137,085	82,771	60.4	78,678	57.4	4.9
1980	167,745	106,940	63.8	99,303	59.2	7.1
1990	188,049	124,787	66.4	117,914	62.7	5.5
1995[3]	198,584	132,304	66.6	124,900	62.9	5.6
2000	212,577	142,583	67.1	136,891	64.4	4.0
2005	226,082	149,320	66.0	141,730	62.7	5.1
2006	228,815	151,428	66.2	144,427	63.1	4.6
2007	231,867	153,124	66.0	146,047	63.0	4.6
			Male			
1960	55,662	46,388	83.3%	43,904	78.9%	5.4%
1970	64,304	51,228	79.7	48,990	76.2	4.4
1980	79,398	61,453	77.4	57,186	72.0	6.9
1990	89,650	68,234	76.1	64,435	71.9	5.6
1995[3]	95,178	71,360	75.0	67,377	70.8	5.6
2000	101,964	76,280	74.8	73,305	71.9	3.9
2005	109,151	80,033	73.3	74,319	69.6	5.1
2006	110,605	81,255	73.5	77,502	70.1	4.6
2007	112,173	82,136	73.2	18,254	69.8	4.7
			Female			
1960	61,582	23,240	37.7%	21,874	35.5%	5.9%
1970	72,782	31,543	43.3	29,688	40.8	5.9
1980	88,348	45,487	51.5	42,117	47.7	7.4
1990	98,399	56,554	57.5	53,479	54.3	5.4
1995[3]	103,406	60,944	58.9	57,523	55.6	5.6
2000	110,613	66,303	59.9	63,586	57.5	4.1
2005	116,931	69,288	59.3	65,757	56.2	5.1
2006	118,210	70,173	59.4	66,925	56.6	4.6
2007	119,694	70,988	59.3	67,792	56.6	4.5
			White			
1975	134,790	82,831	61.5%	76,411	56.7%	7.8%
1980	146,122	93,600	64.1	87,715	60.0	6.3
1990	160,415	107,177	66.8	102,087	63.6	4.7
1995[3]	166,914	111,950	67.1	106,490	63.8	4.9
2000	176,220	118,545	67.3	114,424	64.9	3.5
2005	184,446	122,299	66.3	116,949	63.4	4.4
2006	186,264	123,834	66.5	118,833	63.8	4.0
2007	188,253	124,935	66.4	119,792	63.6	4.1
			Black			
1975	15,751	9,263	58.8%	7,894	50.1%	14.8%
1980	17,824	10,865	61.0	9,313	52.2	14.3
1990	21,300	13,493	63.3	11,966	56.2	11.3
1995[3]	23,246	14,817	63.7	13,279	57.1	10.4
2000	24,902	16,397	65.8	15,156	60.9	7.6
2005	26,517	17,013	64.2	15,313	57.7	10.0
2006	27,007	17,314	64.1	15,765	58.4	8.9
2007	27,485	17,496	63.7	16,051	58.4	8.3
			Hispanic[4]			
1975	N.A.	N.A.	N.A.	N.A.	N.A.	N.A.
1980	9,598	6,146	64.0%	5,527	57.6%	10.1%
1990	14,297	9,576	67.0	8,808	61.6	8.0
1995[3]	18,629	12,267	65.8	11,127	59.7	9.3
2000	23,938	16,689	69.7	15,735	65.7	5.7
2005	29,133	19,824	68.0	18,632	64.0	6.0
2006	30,103	20,694	68.7	19,613	65.2	5.2
2007	31,383	21,602	68.8	20,382	64.9	5.6

Note: 1. Age 16 and over. 2. Civilians employed as a percent of the civilian noninstitutional population. 3. Data after 1995 are not directly comparable with data for previous years because of a major redesign of the Current Population Survey questionnaire and collection methodology and the introduction of 1990 census-based population controls, adjusted for the estimated undercount. 4. Hispanic persons may be of any race. **Source:** U.S. Bureau of Labor Statistics, *Employment and Earnings*, January issues.

important resource but also because it is one of the easiest to measure.

Wages vary not only among the different professions but also between sexes and regions of the country. For example, women in year-round, full-time executive, administrative, and managerial positions have a median yearly income of only 61 percent of the median income for men in the same occupation group. This percentage is higher in the field of laborers, precision production, craft, and repair; but for all major occupation groups reported by the U.S. Bureau of the Census, women receive only a fraction of that received by

Average Earnings of Year-Round Full-Time Workers by Age and Educational Attainment, 2006

Age and Sex	All workers	Less than 9th grade	Some high school	High school graduate	Some college	Associate degree	Bachelor's degree or more
Male, total	**$57,791**	**$26,789**	**$31,434**	**$42,466**	**$48,431**	**$51,485**	**$88,843**
18 - 24 years old	26,170	19,361	20,918	24,974	26,957	29,698	38,275
25 - 34 years old	46,181	23,453	29,347	37,181	41,073	42,357	67,195
35 - 44 years old	63,247	29,302	31,018	45,316	53,080	58,759	95,002
45 - 54 years old	67,635	28,988	35,615	49,199	56,320	57,363	101,763
55 - 64 years old	65,956	29,913	41,136	47,741	56,120	51,978	92,223
65 years and over	58,565	26,062	32,810	42,766	51,091	48,347	85,106
Female, total	**$41,518**	**$20,499**	**$23,351**	**$29,410**	**$35,916**	**$40,463**	**$59,052**
18 - 24 years old	23,462	N.A.	17,514	20,427	21,822	26,638	32,865
25 - 34 years old	38,581	18,180	21,955	26,299	32,853	38,857	50,341
35 - 44 years old	44,183	21,152	24,637	30,769	37,323	41,892	63,427
45 - 54 years old	45,332	21,633	24,304	31,984	39,785	44,191	65,001
55 - 64 years old	43,870	19,681	25,078	31,015	40,749	39,477	64,054
65 years and over	38,629	N.A.	27,948	29,170	43,082	37,079	58,288

Note: High school graduate category includes equivalency.
Source: U.S. Bureau of the Census, *Current Population Reports.* www.census.gov/hhes/www/income/histinc/p32.html

Average Hourly and Weekly Earnings in Current and Constant (1982) Dollars, By Private Industry Group, 1970-2007

Average hourly and weekly wages (in current dollars) have increased by about 50 percent since 1990, but as the following table illustrates, when inflation is accounted for, real earnings (in constant dollars) have actually decreased since 1970.

Constant (1982)[1] dollars	1970	1980	1990	2000	2004	2005	2006	2007
Average hourly earnings	**$8.46**	**$7.99**	**$7.66**	**$8.04**	**$8.24**	**$8.18**	**$8.24**	**$8.32**
Average weekly earnings	**$313**	**$281**	**$262**	**$276**	**$278**	**$276**	**$279**	**$282**

Current dollars	1970	1980	1990	2000	2004	2005	2006	2007
Average hourly earnings	**$3.40**	**$6.84**	**$10.19**	**$14.02**	**$15.69**	**$16.13**	**$16.76**	**$17.42**
Natural resources and mining	3.77	8.97	13.40	16.55	18.07	18.72	19.90	20.96
Construction	4.74	9.37	13.42	17.48	19.23	19.46	20.02	20.95
Manufacturing	3.23	7.15	10.78	14.32	16.15	16.56	16.81	17.26
Trade, transportation, and public utilities	3.65	7.04	9.83	13.31	14.58	14.92	15.39	15.79
Information	5.25	9.47	13.40	19.07	21.40	22.06	23.23	23.94
Financial activities	3.07	5.82	9.99	14.98	17.52	17.94	18.80	19.64
Professional & business services	4.04	7.22	11.14	15.52	17.48	18.08	19.13	20.13
Education and health services	2.88	5.93	10.00	13.95	16.15	16.71	17.38	18.11
Leisure and hospitality	1.78	3.89	5.88	8.32	9.15	9.38	9.75	10.41
Average weekly earnings	**$126**	**$241**	**$349**	**$481**	**$529**	**$544**	**$568**	**$590**
Natural resources and mining	166	403	603	735	804	854	908	962
Construction	179	351	513	686	736	751	781	816
Manufacturing	129	284	436	591	658	673	691	711
Trade, transportation, and public utilities	137	246	332	450	488	498	514	526
Information	195	344	480	701	777	805	850	874
Financial activities	112	210	355	537	623	645	672	705
Professional & business services	145	248	381	535	598	619	662	700
Education and health services	97	190	319	449	524	545	565	590
Leisure and hospitality	53	105	152	217	234	241	250	265

Note: Averages include other services not shown separately. **1.** Earnings in current dollars divided by the Consumer Price Index on a 1982 base. **Source:** U.S. Bureau of Labor Statistics, *Employment and Earnings,* monthly.

their male counterparts. This may be due, in part, to the fact that women enter and leave the work force more times throughout their lives than do men and spend a smaller percentage of their lives economically active.

Another factor influencing the discrepancy between men's and women's wages is the concentration of women in occupations that pay less. As the accompanying table demonstrates, women make up the vast majority of child care workers and receptionists, two poorly paid positions.

Minimum wage in the nation was first enacted by the state of Massachusetts in 1912, covered only women, and was designed to shorten hours and raise pay in the covered industries. The nationwide minimum wage was established in 1938, and has grown in both dollar value and the types of employees it covers since then (see the accompanying table). Some states may estab-

Federal Minimum Wage Rates, 1938–2009

The Fair Labor Standards Act of 1938 set a minimum wage of 25 cents per hour for employees engaged in interstate commerce or in the production of goods for interstate commerce. Over the years, the government has expanded the numbers of workers covered by the federal minimums (waiters and workers under age 20 in their first three months of work, for example, may be paid less than minimum wage) and has increased the minimum amount. But, as this table shows, the increases have not always kept up with inflation.

Effective date	Hourly minimum (current dollars)	Purchasing power in constant (=1996) dollars
Oct. 24, 1938	$0.25	$2.78
Oct. 24, 1939	0.30	3.39
Oct. 24, 1945	0.40	3.49
Jan. 25, 1950	0.75	4.88
Mar. 1, 1956	1.00	5.77
Sept. 3, 1961	1.15[1]	6.03
Sept. 3, 1961	1.25	6.41
Feb. 1, 1967	1.40[2]	6.58
Feb. 1, 1968	1.60	7.21
May 1, 1974	2.00	6.37
Jan. 1, 1975	2.10	6.12
Jan. 1, 1976	2.30	6.34
Jan. 1, 1978	2.65	6.38
Jan. 1, 1979	2.90	6.27
Jan. 1, 1980	3.10	5.90
Jan. 1, 1981	3.35	5.78
Apr. 1, 1990	3.50	4.56
Apr. 1, 1991	4.25	4.90
Oct. 1, 1996	4.75	4.75
Sept. 1, 1997	5.15	3.90
July 26, 2007	5.85	4.43
July 24, 2008[3]	6.55	4.78
July 24, 2009[3]	7.25	5.30

Note: Purchasing power is based on the CPI-U Consumer Price Index. **1.** A lower rate of $1.00 per hour was extended to employees in large retail and service enterprises as well as to local transit, construction, and gas service station employees. This rate was increased to $1.15 in 1964, and put on par with the higher rate on Sept. 3, 1965. **2.** A lower rate of $1.00 was extended to state and local government employees of hospitals, nursing homes, and schools, and to laundries, dry cleaners, and large hotels, motels, restaurants, and farms. This rate continued to lag behind the rate guaranteed other workers until 1977 (1978 for farm workers). **3.** As calculated in 2008 using the Consumer Price Index. **Source:** U.S. Department of Labor.

lish minimum wages higher than the federal minimum.

Unions are organizations of workers who engage in collective bargaining with employers for higher wages, better working conditions, and increased benefits. **Industrial unions** represent workers of a particular firm or industry, such as autoworkers and steelworkers, while **craft unions,** represent employees with a specific skill, such as pilots and musicians.

In the United States, unions are organized at three levels: (1) local unions, which administer labor contracts, serving individual members, employers, and in some cases, establishments directly; (2) national unions, which coordinate agreements across local unions and conduct collective bargaining negotiations with industry employers; and (3) labor federations or voluntary associations of national unions, which settle disputes between national unions, lobby for favorable labor legislation, and engage in public relations In 1955, the American Federation of Labor merged with the Congress of Industrial Organizations, to form the AFL-CIO, which was for 50 years the only labor federation in the country. But in 2005, several unions, including the Teamsters, Service Employees International Union, the United Food and Commercial Workers, and several others representing a total of more than 6 million workers, disaffiliated from the AFL-CIO to start the rival Change to Win coalition.

Many workers choose not to unionize because of the potential costs involved in membership, such as dues, lost pay during strikes, and possible retribution by employers. Union membership nationwide has declined steadily since 1954, when 25.4 percent of the total labor force was unionized. Even as recently as 1983, more than 20 percent of the workforce was unionized. In 2003, less

Work Stoppages, 1947–2007

Year	Number of work stoppages of 1,000 or more workers[1]	Total number of workers involved[2] ('000s)	Days idle Number[3] ('000s)	Days idle Percent of estimated working time[4]
1947	270	1,629	25,720	N.A.
1950	424	1,698	30,390	0.26%
1955	363	2,055	21,180	0.16
1960	222	896	13,260	0.09
1965	268	999	15,140	0.10
1970	381	2,468	52,761	0.29
1975	235	965	17,563	0.09
1980	187	795	20,844	0.09
1985	54	324	7,079	0.03
1990	44	185	5,926	0.02
1995	31	192	5,771	0.02
2000	39	394	20,419	0.06
2004	17	171	3,344	0.01
2005	22	100	1,736	0.01
2006	20	70	2,688	0.01
2007	21	189	1,268	0.01

Note: Excludes work stoppages lasting less than 1 day. **1.** Beginning in year indicated. **2.** Workers counted more than once if involved in more than one stoppage during the year. **3.** Resulting from all stoppages in effect in a year, including those that began in an earlier year. **4.** Agricultural and government employees are included in the total working time; private household, forestry and fishery employees are excluded. **Source:** U.S. Bureau of Labor Statistics, *Compensation and Conditions,* monthly.

than 13 percent of the workforce belonged to unions. Notable examples of membership decline are among steelworkers, garment workers, and oil, chemical and atomic workers, which each fell by about 50 percent during 1979-90. Virtually all of these losses are due to the loss of jobs in unionized firms. Several factors may have contributed to this decline, such as changes in technology that displace workers; "downsizing," in which firms lay off large numbers of employees to keep the company's stock prices high; and "outsourcing," in which firms hire cheaper labor overseas to do jobs formerly performed by unionized workers in the United States.

U.S. Membership in AFL-CIO Affiliated Unions, 1979–2001

Labor organization	1979	1985	1995	2000	2001
Total[1]	N.A.	N.A.	12,986,453	12,869,540	13,223,316
Actors and Artists	75,000	100,000	75,893	69,000	69,000
Air Line Pilots	N.A.	N.A.	N.A.	43,633	46,048
Automobile, Aerospace and Agriculture (UAW)	N.A.	974,000	760,038	742,409	731,396
Bakery, Confectionery and Tobacco	131,000	115,000	95,186.	108,250	103,939
Boilermakers	129,000	110,000	42,802	39,540	39,452
Bricklayers	106,000	95,000	84,000	63,784	62,275
Carpenters and Joiners	626,000	609,000	354,306	N.A.	N.A.
Communications Workers (CWA)	485,000	524,000	490,482	627,080	625,192
Electrical Workers (IBEW)	825,000	791,000	673,117	663,602	676,611
Electronic, Electrical, and Salaried	243,000	198,000	136,502	N.A.	N.A.
Engineers, Operating	313,000	330,000	295,833	281,167	280,000
Firefighters	150,000	142,000	151,000	175,000	193,750
Flight Attendants	N.A.	N.A.	31,776	40,671	42,657
Food and Commercial Workers (UFCW)	1,123,000	989,000	1,009,523	1,140,884	1,129,688
Garment Workers (ILGWU)	314,000	210,000	N.A.	N.A.	N.A.
Glass, Molders, Pottery, and Plastics	50,000	72,000	69,000	57,466	53,684
Government Employees (AFGE)	236,000	199,000	157,100	191,260	196,902
Graphic Communications	171,000	141,000	95,580	88,772	71,351
Hotel and Restaurant Employees	373,000	327,000	232,160	234,509	240,938
Ironworkers	146,000	140,000	80,485	86,294	90,546
Laborers	475,000	383,000	330,694	301,591	310,468
Letter Carriers (NALC)	151,000	186,000	210,000	210,000	210,000
Longshoreman's Association	63,000	65,000	60,595	61,601	61,997
Machinists and Aerospace (IAM)	688,000	520,000	431,619	458,008	446,078
Mine Workers	N.A.	N.A.	75,021	75,250	70,125
Needletrades, Industrial and Textile Employees	308,000	228,000	244,783	208,232	206,801
Nurses, United American	N.A.	N.A.	N.A.	N.A.	100,000
Office and Professional Employees	83,000	90,000	82,987	95,760	106,134
Oil, Chemical, Atomic Workers (OCAW)	146,000	108,000	82,080	N.A.	N.A.
Painters	160,000	133,000	90,000	102,044	101,617
Paper, Chemical and Energy Workers	262,000	232,000	235,302	262,816	283,916
Plumbing and Pipefitting	228,000	226,000	219,800	219,800	219,800
Postal Workers	245,000	232,000	265,757	275,915	266,002
Retail, Wholesale, Department Store	122,000	106,000	73,133	N.A.	N.A.
Rubber, Cork, Linoleum, Plastic	158,000	106,000	N.A.	N.A.	N.A.
School Employees Assocation, California	N.A.	N.A.	N.A.	N.A.	129,000
Seafarers	84,000	80,000	80,250	80,250	80,250
Service Employees (SEIU)[2]	537,000	688,000	1,077,854	1,261,276	1,281,770
Sheet Metal Workers	120,000	108,000	103,042	93,000	93,000
Stage Employees, Moving Picture Machine Operators	50,000	50,000	50,900	55,788	57,150
State, County, Municipal (AFSCME)[2]	889,000	997,000	1,210,949	1,249,306	1,265,894
Steelworkers	964,000	572,000	516,880	450,436	438,908
Teachers (AFT)	423,000	470,000	631,529	822,191	893,453
Teamsters	N.A.	N.A.	1,286,371	1,226,300	1,217,880
Transit Union	94,000	94,000	96,340	108,117	112,142
Transport Workers	85,000	85,000	75,000	75,000	88,750
Transportation Union, United	121,000	52,000	59,575	90,725	92,300

Note: Membership figures based on average per capita paid membership to the AFL-CIO for the 12 months ending in June of the year shown. Figures reflect all mergers that have occurred since 1999. 1. Includes other AFL-CIO affiliated unions, not shown separately. 2. Figures for 1979 and 1985 exclude Hospital and Health Care Employees which merged with these unions in 1989.
Source: American Federation of Labor and Congress of Industrial Organizations, Report of the AFL-CIO Executive Council (annual).

Metropolitan Areas with Greatest Projected Job Growth, 2007–30

MOST JOBS ADDED	Number of jobs ('000s)		Jobs added
Rank, Metropolitan statistical area	2007	2030	2007-30 ('000s)
1. Atlanta-Sandy Springs-Marietta, Ga.	3,194,050	6,050,160	2,856,110
2. Dallas-Fort Worth-Arlington, Texas	3,840,290	6,520,970	2,680,680
3. Los Angeles-Long Beach-Santa Ana, Calif.	7,911,080	10,394,060	2,483,520
4. Phoenix-Mesa-Scottsdale, Ariz.	2,431,580	4,672,830	2,241,250
5. Houston-Baytown-Sugar Land, Texas	3,270,130	5,293,310	2,023,180
6. Washington D.C.-Arlington-Alexandria, Va.	3,924,240	5,838,460	1,914,220
7. Miami-Ft. Lauderdale-Miami Beach, Fla.	3,316,900	5,179,450	1,862,550
8. Las Vegas-Paradise, Nevada	1,197,360	2,993,510	1,796,150
9. Denver-Aurora, Colo.	1,700,780	3,142,000	1,441,530
10. Orlando, Fla.	1,351,460	2,665,330	1,313,870
11. Riverside-San Bernardino-Ontario, Calif.	1,810,910	2,035,890	1,224,980
12. Tampa-St. Petersburg-Clearwater, Fla.	1,681,350	2,805,130	1,123,780
13. San Diego-Carlsbad-San Marcos, Calif.	1,982,210	3,048,620	1,066,410
14. Austin-Round Rock, Texas	1,015,070	2,068,170	1,053,100
15. Minneapolis-St. Paul-Bloomington, Minn.	2,323,110	3,357,040	1,033,930
16. Seattle-Tacoma-Bellevue, Wash	2,216,050	3,223,110	1,007,060
17. Chicago-Naperville-Joliet, Ill.	5,665,770	6,670,410	1,004,640
18. New York-No. New Jersey-Long Island, N.Y.	10,667,980	11,527,760	859,780
19. Sacramento-Arden-Arcade-Roseville, Calif.	1,269,800	2,110,480	840,680
20. Portland-Vancouver-Beaverton, Oreg-Wash.	1,364,890	2,073,930	709,040
21. San Francisco-Oakland-Fremont, Calif.	2,814,580	3,523,370	708,790
22. Baltimore-Towson, Md.	1,693,050	2,288,790	595,740
23. Nashville-Davidson-Murfreesboro, Tenn.	1,036,790	1,598,170	561,380
24. Boston-Cambridge-Quincy, Mass.	3,105,340	3,647,500	542,160
25. Salt Lake City, Utah	787,100	1,279,740	492,640
26. Kansas City, Mo.	1,307,110	1,793,550	486,440
27. San Antonio, Texs	1,114,330	1,598,520	484,190
28. Philadelphia-Camden, N.J.-Wilmington, Del.	3,445,680	3,916,480	470,800
29. Indianapolis, Ind.	1,129,810	1,576,060	446,250
30. Charlotte-Gastonia-Concord, N.C.-S.C.	1,039,960	1,479,130	439,170
Total 30 MSA's	**79,608,760**	**115,372,780**	**35,761,020**

FASTEST JOB GROWTH	Number of jobs ('000s)		Annual percent
Rank, Metropolitan statistical area	2007	2030	increase, 2007-30
1. St. George, Utah	73,550	222,750	4.94%
2. Palm Coast, Fla.	27,830	79,210	4.64
3. Las Vegas-Paradise, Nevada	1,197,360	2,993,510	4.06
4. Naples-Marco Island, Fla.	205,920	511,280	4.03
5. Lake Havasu City - Kingman, Ariz.	77,350	183,860	3.84
6. Punta Gorda, Fla.	71,500	162,490	3.63
7. Cape Coral-Fort Myers, Fla.	321,800	707,380	3.48
8. Prescott, Ariz.	93,270	197,630	3.32
9. Bend, Oreg.	101,610	211,150	3.23
10. Austin-Round Rock, Texas	1,015,070	2,068,170	3.14
11. Orlando-Kissimmee, Fla.	1,351,460	2,068,170	3.00
12. Phoenix-Mesa-Scottsdale, Ariz.	2,431,580	4,672,830	2.88
13. Port St. Lucie-Fort Pierce, Fla.	199,600	379,100	2.83
14. Atlanta-Sandy Springs-Marietta, Ga.	3,194,050	6,050,160	2.82
15. McAllen-Edinburg-Pharr, Texas	289,080	546,070	2.80
16. Sarasota-Bradenton-Venice, Fla.	428,210	808,770	2.80
17. Carson City, Nevada	45,750	85,690	2.77
18. Ocala, Fla.	145,660	270,100	2.72
19. Denver-Aurora, Colo.	1,700,780	3,142,310	2.70
20. Fort Collins-Loveland, Colo.	197,160	364,240	2.70
21. Coeur D'alene, Idaho	77,850	143,070	2.68
22. Provo-Orem, Utah	248,690	451,250	2.62
23. Hinesville-Fort Stewart, Ga.	41,390	73,850	2.55
24. Fayetteville-Springdale-Rogers, Ark.	269,610	476,820	2.51
25. Myrtle Beach-Conway, S.C.	151,640	264,880	2.45
26. Flagstaff, Ariz	85,230	148,800	2.45
27. Reno-Sparks, Nevada	290,350	499,370	2.39
28. Sebastian-Vero Beach, Fla.	71,510	122,670	2.37
29. Santa Fe, N.Mex.	94,810	161,660	2.35
30. Boise City-Nampa, Idaho	368,930	628,520	2.34
U.S. Total	**180,289,680**	**244,975,230**	

Source: NPA Data Services, Inc., *Regional Economic Growth in the U.S. Projections for 2007-30* (2008).

U.S. BUSINESS

The Office of Management and Budget (O.M.B.) classifies the entire national economy into industries, based on principal product or activity. There are nine industrial divisions, which are further classified into groups and subgroups. For example, under "manufacturing" would fall "food and kindred products," and beneath that, "meat-packing plants." The nine industrial divisions listed in the O.M.B.'s Standard Industry Classification (SIC) are agriculture, forestry and fishing; mining; construction; manufacturing; transportation and public utilities; finance, insurance and real estate; wholesale trade; retail trade; and services. In 2005, 7.5 million establishments employed 116 million workers with payrolls totaling $4.5 trillion.

Services and Manufacturing

Another way to view the economy is to divide it into manufacturing industries, producing tangible goods such as cars, shoes and furniture, and service industries, whose products are intangible, such as entertainment, tourism and banking. The manufacturing industries are further broken down into those that produce durable goods— that is, goods that are consumed over time, such as cars and houses—and nondurable goods that are consumed in the short run (food and soap). Services have played an increasingly important role in the economy, partly because companies in the manufacturing sector increasingly contract out services such as transportation, accounting, marketing and communications, previously performed in-house.

The service sector, which includes government, is responsible for approximately 80 percent of U.S. employment. Seven of the 10 fastest-growing industries over the next 10 years are service industries. They include health services, computer and data processing services, and child day care services.

Financing Business

When an individual or a group of individuals decides to start a new company, they need money to rent or buy office space and equipment and to pay workers. Since there is a time lag between the day a business opens and the day a business sells its first good or service, funds must be borrowed from a bank or other financial institution or from individual investors to meet costs before revenues are generated. Additional funds may be needed throughout the life of the business to finance research and development of a new product or service or for the construction of new factories. Financing can take many forms, from short-term bank loans, commercial paper, or trade credit to long-term stocks and bonds.

Short-term Financing *Trade credit*, the largest category of short-term financing, is an arrangement between a company and its suppliers, whereby materials and supplies are delivered to the company with a promise to pay the invoice, plus interest, usually within a specified number of weeks. *Commercial bank lending* may take the form of a single loan with repayment in a lump sum or in installments over the life of the loan, or it may be a line of credit up to a maximum the

Number of Business Establishments with Employees and Payroll, by Major Group, 2003

Major group	Number of establishments	Number of employees	Annual payroll ('000s)
Total	7,499,702	116,317,003	$4,482,722,481
Forestry, fishing, hunting, and agricultural support	24,102	168,744	5,095,741
Forestry & logging	11,048	69,541	2,266,199
Fishing, hunting & trapping	2,415	7,202	313,554
Mining	24,696	497,272	30,823,272
Oil and gas extraction	7,390	85,562	7,743,489
Mining, except oil and gas	7,130	196,940	10,892,679
Support activities for mining	10,176	214,770	12,187,104
Utilities	17,326	633,106	46,292,766
Construction	787,672	6,781,327	292,519,343
Construction of buildings	243,567	1,613,063	76,179,574
Heavy and civil engineering construction	50,827	908,222	47,153,128
Specialty trade contractors	493,278	4,260,042	169,186,641
Manufacturing	333,460	13,667,337	600,696,305
Food	25,785	1,469,730	48,474,315
Beverage & tobacco products	3,516	154,233	7,263,140
Textile mills	3,411	208,968	6,518,199
Textile product mills	6,891	163,675	4,648,814
Apparel	11,165	243,416	5,607,118
Leather & allied products	1,414	40,551	1,253,700
Wood products	16,707	555,942	18,232,348
Paper	5,273	453,966	21,560,403
Printing & related support activities	34,385	657,759	25,059,720
Petroleum & coal products	2,362	101,505	8,201,183
Chemicals	13,220	810,368	49,209,739
Plastics & rubber products	14,707	902,109	33,391,197
Nonmetallic mineral products	16,908	469,151	19,691,409
Primary metals	5,362	450,811	22,108,497
Fabricated metal products	59,053	1,519,845	60,693,213

Major group	Number of establishments	Number of employees	Annual payroll ('000s)
Machinery	26,723	1,107,285	$ 52,652,677
Computer & electronic products	14,741	1,058,992	65,601,082
Electrical equipment, appliances, & components	6,201	426,822	17,885,134
Transportation equipment	12,694	1,636,111	86,006,495
Furniture & related products	21,563	547,859	17,560,322
Wholesale trade	**429,823**	**5,968,929**	**308,918,023**
Durable goods	245,898	3,365,466	185,347,677
Nondurable goods	132,897	2,289,266	109,507,833
Wholesale electronic markets	51,028	314,197	14,062,513
Retail trade	**1,123,207**	**15,338,672**	**348,047,012**
Motor vehicle & parts dealers	128,585	1,947,916	73,347,475
Furniture & home furnishings stores	66,396	575,629	15,258,877
Electronics & appliance stores	50,176	469,248	12,148,882
Building material and garden equipment stores	87,118	1,262,662	35,761,327
Food & beverage stores	153,355	2,937,918	52,958,681
Health & personal care stores	84,886	1,037,354	25,491,609
Gasoline stations	117,189	908,818	14,574,165
Clothing & clothing accessories stores	150,580	1,555,928	25,001,470
Sporting goods, hobby, book, & music stores	61,352	631,095	9,748,522
General merchandise stores	45,925	2,670,710	50,231,639
Nonstore retailers	49,688	521,491	18,889,132
Transportation & warehousing	**211,150**	**4,168,016**	**154,375,938**
Air transportation	5,715	486,355	24,222,703
Water transportation	1,946	65,483	3,731,909
Truck transportation	117,224	1,478,299	54,774,508
Transit & ground passenger transportation	17,266	406,709	8,520,810
Pipeline transportation	2,681	38,053	2,901,766
Scenic & sightseeing transportation	2,752	24,156	717,091
Support activities for transportation	36,221	543,666	21,831,345
Couriers & messengers	13,862	547,255	17,531,674
Warehousing & storage	13,483	578,040	20,144,132
Information	**141,290**	**3,402,599**	**203,129,725**
Publishing industries (except Internet)	31,538	1,032,273	67,094,229
Motion picture & sound recording industries	23,579	314,396	14,040,450
Broadcasting (except Internet)	10,342	287,038	17,354,082
Internet publishing & broadcasting	2,343	36,145	2,686,805
Telecommunications	49,431	1,226,536	69,687,071
Internet service providers, web search portals	20,142	452,159	30,292,120
Finance & insurance	**476,806**	**6,431,837**	**446,739,512**
Credit intermediation & related activities	214,062	3,201,715	172,455,610
Securities intermediation & related activities	82,117	860,384	131,960,503
Insurance carriers & related activities	177,214	2,323,045	138,389,496
Funds, trusts, & other financial vehicles	3,320	26,757	2,696,871
Real estate & rental & leasing	**370,651**	**2,144,077**	**81,790,239**
Real estate	302,453	1,480,040	59,673,918
Rental & leasing services	65,860	634,901	19,870,212
Professional, scientific, & technical services	826,101	7,689,366	456,455,965
Management of companies & enterprises	47,593	2,856,418	243,267,191
Administrative, support, and waste management	**369,507**	**9,280,282**	**255,399,069**
Administrative and support services	350,208	8,946,939	241,700,336
Waste management and remediation	19,299	333,343	13,698,733
Educational services	**80,486**	**2,879,374**	**82,522,976**
Health care & social assistance	**746,600**	**16,025,147**	**589,654,273**
Ambulatory health care services	519,578	5,422,574	251,443,187
Hospitals	7,081	5,321,600	228,608,351
Nursing & residential care facilities	72,103	2,959,571	66,661,534
Social assistance	147,838	2,321,402	42,941,201
Arts, entertainment, & recreation	**121,777**	**1,936,484**	**52,935,670**
Performing arts and spectator sports	41,675	412,146	24,073,756
Museums and historical sites	6,980	120,908	3,174,529
Amusement, gambling, and recreation industries	73,122	1,403,430	25,687,385
Accommodation and food services	603,435	11,025,909	156,041,233
Accommodation	62,502	1,854,499	41,832,778
Food services and drinking places	540,933	9,171,410	114,208,455
Other services (except public administration)	**740,034**	**5,390,954**	**127,480,612**
Repair & maintenance	228,341	1,294,783	39,521,789
Personal & laundry services	209,875	1,337,443	26,395,287
Religious, grantmaking, civic, & professional organizations	301,818	2,758,728	61,563,536
Unclassified establishments	**23,986**	**31,153**	**537,616**

Note: Excludes most government employees, railroad employees, and self-employed persons. Totals include other categories not shown separately. **Source:** U.S. Bureau of the Census, *County Business Patterns 2005* (2007).

bank will allow the company to overdraw on its account. *Commercial paper* is a promissory note of a well-established firm sold primarily to other business firms, with repayments made in two to six months. The only problem with commercial paper is that its resources are limited to the liquidity that corporations have at any given time for lending to other firms.

Intermediate-term financing,

with a time frame of one to 15 years, may take the form of lease financing, whereby a company rents, rather than buys, the assets it uses; conditional sales contracts, by which equipment is bought over a period of time (the seller continues to have title of ownership until payment is completed); or term loans or business credit supplied by commercial banks and life insurance companies, repaid by amortization payments over the life of the loan (one to 15 years).

Long-term financing

The issuance of stocks and bonds constitute the long-term source of finance for firms. *Bonds* are debt instruments (IOUs issued by a company to the bondholder) that obligate the firm to pay interest at specific times. Alternatively firms can raise money by issuing preferred and common stocks. Unlike bonds, *stocks* entitle the holder to share in ownership and profits made by the firm through dividends paid out for the entire period the investor owns the stock. However, if the business has low profits or limited funds, bondholders are paid first, preferred stockholders next, and common stockholders last.

▶ WALL STREET

The U.S. stock market, commonly known as Wall Street, began in the late 18th century as a merchant-organized public auction in stocks and government bonds for the purpose of financing the government and expanding business and trade. At that time, brokers handed over securities to auctioneers who sold securities to the highest bidder. Today, while the form of the stock exchange has changed dramatically, the purpose remains the same.

The most commonly cited index of Wall Street's performance is the Dow Jones Industrial average (see "Glossary of Financial Terms"). From the

Dow's inception in 1896 until the early 1980's, the 1,000 mark was considered the benchmark of a bull market. During that period, the Dow passed the 1,000 mark for the first time in 1972 and remained above that level until 1976. These days, the benchmark of a bull market is closer to 11,000. The Dow reached that lofty level in 1999, but fell back below 8,000 in 2002 as companies like Enron, WorldCom, Tyco, Adelphia and others were forced to admit they had illegally inflated their profits. The Dow crested 14,000 in the summer of 2007 and remained near all-time highs until the crisis of mid-2008. (See "Major News Stories.")

The Dow's vicissitudes are of greater concern to larger numbers of people these days because many more people are invested in the stock market. The unprecedented growth of the 1990s, combined with easier access to trading due to on-line brokerages, attracted hundreds of thousands of new investors to the stock market. Today, more than half of all American households own stocks, either directly or through pension plans or mutual funds (see related table). That's up from 31.7 percent in 1989 and 19 percent in 1983.

There are three major stock and bond markets in the U.S., all located in New York City. The growth of all three markets has been staggering. A total of 19.7 billion shares were traded on all three exchanges in 1980; today, nearly a trillion shares are traded annually.

New York Stock Exchange (NYSE)

The oldest exchange in the country was formally founded in 1817, when fewer than 100 shares were traded each day. In 2007, nearly 700 billion shares were

NYSE Group Shares Traded, 2004-07

The New York Stock Exchange merged with ARCA in 2004. Figures are not directly comparable with those from before 2004.

Year	Number of trades (millions)	Shares traded (millions)	Dollar volume of shares traded (millions)
2004	728	471,580	$14,402,000
2005	919	516,743	17,857,000
2006	1,271	588,133	21,790,000
2007	2,333	698,646	29,908,880

Source: New York Stock Exchange, *Facts and Figures*, www.nyse.com.

NYSE Listed Stocks, 1924-2004

Year	Shares outstanding (millions)	Market value (millions)	Average price[1]
1924	433	$27,072	$62.45
1945	1,592	73,765	46.33
1950	2,353	93,807	39.86
1960	6,458	306,967	47.53
1970	16,065	636,380	39.61
1980	33,709	1,242,803	36.87
1985	52,427	1,950,332	37.20
1990	90,732	2,819,778	33.40
1995	154,719	6,012,971	38.86
2000	313,937	12,372,304	42.14
2001	341,509	11,713,707	34.11
2002	349,908	9,603,327	28.39
2003	359,660	12,157,862	33.80
2004	382,745	13,562,265	35.43

Note: 1. This average cannot be used as an index of price trend owing to changes in shares listed caused by new listing, suspensions, stock splits, and stock dividends.
Source: New York Stock Exchange, NYSE *Facts and Figures*, 2005.

NYSE: Daily Shares Traded, 1900-2004 (in thousands)

Year	Daily Average	Record High	Record Low
1900	505	1,627	89
1910	601	1,656	111
1920	828	2,008	227
1930	2,959	8,279	1,090
1940	751	3,940	130
1950	1,980	4,859	1,061
1960	3,042	7,077	2,184
1970	11,564	21,345	6,660
1980	44,871	84,297	16,132
1990	156,777	292,364	56,853
2000	1,041,578	1,560,808	403,254
2002	1,441,015	2,812,919	462,000
2003	1,398,404	1,886,074	359,769
2004	1,457,000	2,690,200	508,800

Source: New York Stock Exchange, *Facts and Figures*, 2005.

traded on the New York Stock Exchange. The growth in the value of those stocks has been equally impressive. The market value of all stocks traded on the NYSE doubled between 1987 and 1993, and then more than doubled again between 1993 and 2000, when it reached a staggering $12.3 trillion. The dollar volume of shares traded doubled again between 2004 ($14.4 trillion) and 2007 ($29.9 trillion).

NASDAQ The National Association of Securities Dealers Automated Quotations was founded in 1971 and was the first to use computers and high-technology telecommunications to trade— and to monitor the trading of—millions of securities daily. Today, all the major stock markets have followed suit.

The American Stock Exchange (AMEX) The American Stock Exchange, also in downtown New York, is known as the stock market for the small investor and small companies because the stocks of organizations that do not meet the listing and size requirements of the NYSE are typically traded there. For years, the Amex was known as the "New York Curb Exchange" because its trading was conducted on the street outside the office buildings of many brokers. The exchange moved indoors in 1921. In 1998, the NASDAQ stock market bought the American Stock Exchange bringing the NASDAQ's advanced technology to the Amex's trading floor, but the two exchanges continue to operate as separate entities.

Online trading Internet, or online brokerages allow people to trade stocks directly without a broker for commissions as low as $5 per trade. The popularity of online accounts has encouraged investors to make more trades, and to buy and sell more quickly to take advantage of short-term changes in market prices. Online trading has also sparked the creation of the day trader: an investor who buys and sells thousands of shares in hundreds of different stocks each day.

Mutual funds, in which investors pool their funds to purchase a variety of securities rather than investing in a single stock or bond, date back to 1924 in the U.S., but few Americans were aware of them until their popularity surged in the 1980's. In 2007, according to the Investment Company Institute, 44 percent of all American households owned some kind of mutual funds, up from less

Milestones in the Dow Jones Industrial Average

Date	Average	Date	Average
Jan. 12, 1906	100	Feb. 13, 1997	7,000
Sept. 1, 1929	381	July 16, 1997	8,000
March 12, 1956	500	April 6, 1998	9,000
Nov. 14, 1972	1,000	March 16, 1999	10,000
Jan. 8, 1987	2,000	May 3, 1999	11,000
Feb. 23, 1995	4,000	Oct. 18, 2006	12,000
Nov. 21, 1995	5,000	April 25, 2007	13,000
Oct. 14, 1996	6,000	July 17, 2007	14,000

Source: Dow Jones.

Components of the Dow Jones Industrial Average, 2008

The Dow Jones Industrial Average is composed of 30 stocks that collectively reflect the performance of the entire market. There are no rules for admission, but the components of the Dow are typically the largest publicly traded companies in the country. The list is maintained and reviewed by the editors of the Wall Street Journal. For the sake of continuity, changes to the roster are infrequent. The last major revision—the first in nearly four years, came in February, 2008, when Bank of America and Chevron replaced Altria and Honeywell. The 30 stocks in the Dow are listed in alphabetical order below.

3M Co.	Hewlett-Packard Co.
Alcoa Inc.	Home Depot Inc.
American Express Co.	Intel Corp.
American International.	I.B.M. Corp.
Group Inc	Johnson & Johnson
AT&T Inc.	JPMorgan Chase & Co.
Bank of America Corp.	McDonald's Corp.
Boeing Co.	Merck & Co. Inc.
Caterpillar Inc.	Microsoft Corp.
Chevron Corp.	Pfizer Inc.
Citigroup Inc.	Procter & Gamble Co.
Coca-Cola Co.	United Technologies Corp.
E.I. DuPont de Nemours	Verizon
Exxon Mobil Corp.	Communications Inc.
General Electric Co.	Wal-Mart Stores Inc.
General Motors Corp.	Walt Disney Co.

Source: Dow Jones.

Top U.S. Mutual Fund Managers, 2006-07, by Assets

	Assets (billions)	
Rank, Fund Manager	2006	2007
1. Fidelity Investments	$1,171,487	$1,375,170
2. Vanguard Group	1,085,969	1,239,383
3. Capital Research and Management	1,080,687	1,278,267
4. MFS Investment Management	101,177	103,446
5. Putnam Funds	120,320	108,840
6. Dimensional Fund Advisors Inc.	90,188	109,029
7. Hartford Mutual Funds	103,332	114,801
8. John Hancock Financial Services	108,245	119,971
9. Janus	94,060	122,696
10. Deutsche Asset Management	120,555	124,502
11. AIM Investments	117,223	129,688
12. Prudential Mutual Funds	117,717	135,103
13. Wells Fargo	124,716	147,518
14. Dodge & Cox	136,514	159,634
15. PIMCO Funds	185,328	205,185
16. Goldman Sachs & Co.	133,856	205,630
17. Legg Mason	205,906	215,827
18. TIAA-CREF	213,846	231,356
19. Schwab Funds	205,395	234,987
20. Morgan Stanley	230,643	242,378
21. OppenheimerFunds/ MassMutual	226,280	244,721
22. T. Rowe Price	208,981	250,203
23. Federated Investors	206,133	252,868
24. Bank of New York/Dreyfus Corporation	176,745	256,785
25. Columbia Mgmt. Group	243,080	298,835

Note: Figures are as of Dec. 31 of each year.
Source: Investment Company Institute.

than 6 percent in 1980. Total assets of all mutual funds reached an all-time high of $12 trillion in 2007, or 10 times the amount invested in 1990 ($1.1 trillion). More money is invested in mutual funds today than in any other financial institution, more even than commercial banks, which held a total of $11.2 trillion in assets in 2007, according to the Federal Deposit Insurance Corporation (F.D.I.C.).

There are four kinds of mutual funds: stock (or equity), bond, hybrid, and money market. Funds can consist of stocks, bonds, gold, government securities or other assets. The share price of a mutual fund, called the *net asset value (NAV)*, is the market value of all the fund's securities, minus expenses, divided by the total number of shares outstanding, and rises or falls based on the performance of the securities in which the fund is invested. Each fund employs a professional fund manager, who chooses a diverse range of securities, so that a drop in the value of one security will

not cause a shock to the entire portfolio. As securities prices rise or fall, the fund manager may seek to change the composition of the fund's portfolio. Like securities, but unlike investments offered by banks, mutual funds are not insured by the FDIC or any other government agency.

There were 8,029 different mutual funds in 2007, more than twice the number in 1992, representing the full spectrum of investment objectives. *Aggressive growth funds* seek the maximum capital growth but also carry the greatest risk, because the stocks they invest in are very volatile. *Income-equity funds* forgo high growth rates in favor of a constant stream of income from stocks with a history of steady dividends. *Bond funds*, which invest in corporate bonds and government-issued securities, are generally more conservative than stock funds. *Hybrid funds* invest in both stocks and bonds. *Money market funds* are called short-term funds because they invest in securities that mature in a year or less, such as Treasury bills,

Assets of IRA Plans by Type of Investment, 1990–2007

Year	Total (billions)	Bank and thrift deposits[1]		Life insurance companies		Mutual funds		Securities[2]	
		Amount (billions)	Percent of total	Amount (billions)	Percent of total	Amount (billions)	Percent of total	Amount (billions)	Percent of total
1990	$ 637	$266	41.8%	$ 40	6.3%	$ 139	21.8%	$ 191	30.0%
1995	1,288	261	20.3	81	6.3	470	36.5	477	37.0
2000	2,629	250	9.5	203	7.7	1,231	46.8	945	36.0
2005[3]	3,652	278	7.6	308	8.4	1,663	45.5	1,403	38.4
2006[3]	4,220	313	7.4	318	7.5	1,975	46.8	1,614	38.2
2007[3]	4,747	340	7.2	336	7.1	2,241	47.2	1,831	38.6

Note: 1. Includes Keogh deposits. 2. Stocks, bonds, CDs sold by brokers, and other investments held in brokerage accounts. 3. Estimate. **Source:** Investment Company Institute, *Investment Company Fact Book* (2008).

Number of Funds, Accounts, and Total Assets of Mutual Funds, 1970–2007

Year	Total	Equity	Type of Fund		Money market	
			Hybrid[1]	Bond & Income[1]	Taxable	Tax exempt
Number of Funds						
1970	361	323	N.A.	38	—	—
1980	564	288	N.A.	170	96	10
1990	3,079	1,099	193	1,046	506	235
2000	8,155	4,385	523	2,208	703	336
2005	7,975	4,586	505	2,013	595	276
2006	8,118	4,769	508	1,993	575	273
2007	8,029	4,767	488	1,967	548	259
Number of Accounts (millions)						
1970	10.7	N.A.	N.A.	N.A.	—	—
1980	12.1	5.8	N.A.	1.5	4.8	—
1990	61.9	22.2	3.2	13.6	21.6	1.4
2000	244.7	163.9	13.1	19.6	45.5	2.7
2005	275.5	188.0	21.2	29.4	34.0	2.8
2006	288.6	200.0	22.0	29.5	34.0	3.1
2007	299.0	207.6	22.3	30.2	35.4	3.5
Total Net Assets (billions)						
1970	$47.6	$45.1	N.A.	$2.5	—	—
1980	134.8	44.4	N.A.	14.0	$74.5	$1.9
1990	1,065.2	239.5	$36.1	291.3	414.7	83.6
2000	6,964.6	3,961.9	346.3	811.2	1,607.2	238.0
2005	8,904.8	4,939.8	567.3	1,357.2	1,706.5	334.0
2006	10,412.5	5,910.5	653.2	1,494.4	1,988.0	366.4
2007	12,021.0	6,521.4	713.4	1,679.0	2,642.1	465.1

1. Bond and Income Funds were divided into Bond Funds and Hybrid Funds beginning in 1984. Data from before 1984 in all categories is not directly comparable to later years.   **Source:** Investment Company Institute, *Investment Company Fact Book* (2008).

CDs, and commercial paper. Many money market funds offer tax-exempt income (though their rate of return is often lower than taxable money market funds). *Special funds* meet the needs of specific investors by investing only in certain segments of financial markets (e.g. biotechnology, telecommunications, small-companies) or by pegging the fund's net asset value to one of several economic indexes (hence the name index fund). *Global equity funds* invest in the stock markets of other countries.

By far the largest segment of the mutual fund industry has been stock or equity funds. Assets of equity funds in 2007 totaled $6.5 trillion, more than half of all mutual fund assets. Money market funds, with $4.1 trillion in assets, were the next-most popular, followed by bond and income funds ($1.7 trillion in assets).

Mergers and Acquisitions

Beginning in the 1980's and 1990's, a growing number of companies have sought to increase their power in the new global marketplace by buying rival companies or by merging with one. Because fierce competition tends to drive down prices, making profitability more difficult, and because one company needs fewer employees than two, the reasons for the current merger mania are obviously compelling. An additional incentive is that the CEOs who broker these deals also make huge cash profits on the mergers.

▶ GLOSSARY OF FINANCIAL TERMS

Arbitrage　Simultaneous purchase and sale of a commodity or currency in at least two markets where price discrepancies exist. The arbitrageur makes a profit by buying an asset with a low price in one market and selling it in another market where the asset carries a higher price.

Bear/bull　A bear is a speculator who expects prices to fall and sells stocks or bonds in order to buy them later at a lower price. A bull expects prices to rise and therefore buys now for resale later. Thus, a bearish (bullish) market is one in which prices are generally falling (rising).

Blue chip stock　A stock that is considered a safe investment, with a low yield and a high price per share, issued by companies that are well known and have a history of good management and increasing profit levels.

Bond　A debt obligation that requires the issuer to pay a fixed sum of money annually until maturity (interest payments) and then, at maturity, a fixed sum of money to repay the initial amount borrowed (principal). (See *Corporate Bonds*.)

Capital gain　An increase in the market value of an asset above the price originally paid for it, realized when the asset is sold.

Capital loss　A decrease in the market value of an asset below the price originally paid for it, realized when the asset is sold.

Common stock/equity　A piece of paper that entitles the owner to a share of the firm's profits and a share of the voting power in shareholder elections. In other words, a shareholder is part owner of the firm. If he owns 50 percent of the issued shares of common stock (when no preferred stock is issued), he owns 50 percent of the company, and will receive 50 percent of profits paid out in dividends. Over 40 million Americans invest in common stocks.

Convertible bond　A debt instrument which carries an option for the holder to convert it into a specified amount of company stock.

Corporate bonds　Debt obligations that require the corporation to pay a fixed sum of money an-

Mergers and Acquisitions Worldwide, 1990–2007

Year	Number of deals	Total value (millions)
1990	10,002	$　422,360.2
1995	19,712	927,432.8
2000	38,753	3,406,206.5
2001	30,193	1,694,422.1
2002	26,514	1,212,443.8
2003	28,899	1,379,013.2
2004	31,633	1,912,224.3
2005	33,844	2,745,580.0
2006	38,674	3,614,611.3
2007	43,368	4,483,204.7

Source: Securities Data Company.

Largest Mergers and Acquisitions in World History

Acquiring Company (Country)	Acquired Company (Country)	Date effective	Value (millions)
1. Vodafone AirTouch PLC (U.K.)	Mannesmann (Germany)	June 19, 2000	$202,785
2. America Online Inc. (U.S.)	Time Warner (U.S.)	Jan. 12, 2001	181,569
3. Shareholders	Philip Morris Int'l Inc.	Mar. 28, 2008	112,955
4. RFS Holdings BV	ABN-AMRO Holding NV	Nov. 2, 2007	98,189
5. A.T.&T. Inc. (U.S.)	BellSouth Corp. (U.S.)	Dec. 29, 2006	89,432
6. Pfizer Inc. (U.S.)	Warner-Lambert Co. (U.S.)	June 19, 2000	88,771
7. Exxon Corp., (U.S.)	Mobil Corp., (U.S.)	Nov. 30, 1999	85,126
8. Royal Dutch Petroleum Co. (Neth.)	Shell Transport and Trading Co. (U.K.)	Aug. 9, 2005	80,305
9. GlaxoWellcome PLC (U.K)	SmithKline Beecham PLC (U.K.)	Dec. 27, 2000	78,775
10. Travelers Group (U.S.)	Citicorp (U.S.)	Oct. 8, 1998	72,558
11. Comcast Corp., (U.S.)	AT&T Broadband & Internet Svcs. (U.S.)	Nov. 18, 2002	72,041
12. Bell Atlantic Corp., (U.S.)	GTE Corp., (U.S.)	June 30, 2000	71,324
13. SBC Communications Inc. (U.S.)	Ameritech Corp., (U.S.)	Oct. 8, 1999	70,395
14. AT&T Corp., (U.S.)	Tele-Communications Inc. (U.S.)	Mar. 9, 1999	69,896
15. Vodafone Group PLC (U.K.)	AirTouch Communications (U.S.)	June 30, 1999	65,763
16. Sanofi-Synthelabo SA (France)	Aventis SA (France)	Aug. 20, 2004	65,657
17. NationsBank Corp., (U.S.)	BankAmerica Corp., (U.S.)	Sept. 30, 1998	61,633
18. Shareholders	Kraft Foods Inc.	Mar. 30, 2007	61,454
19. Pfizer Inc. (U.S.)	Pharmacia Corp., (U.S.)	April 15, 2003	60,704
20. Shareholders	Nortel Networks Corp.	May 1, 2000	59,974

Note: As of June 1, 2008. Does not include mergers resulting from the 2008 financial crisis. **Source:** Securities Data Company.

Securities Industry Revenues and Expenses, 1980–2006 (millions)

Type	1980	1990	1995	2000	2004	2005	2006
Revenues, total	**$19,829**	**$71,356**	**$143,414**	**$349,493**	**$242,930**	**$332,501**	**$458,464**
Commissions	6,777	12,032	23,215	54,107	47,569	46,803	49,671
Trading/investment gains	5,091	15,746	28,963	70,778	30,669	30,681	55,193
Underwriting profits	1,571	3,728	8,865	18,718	19,099	19,878	23,623
Margin interest	2,151	3,179	6,470	24,547	6,984	13,270	23,690
Mutual fund sales	278	3,242	7,434	19,395	18,550	20,699	23,346
Other	3,960	33,428	68,468	161,949	120,058	201,170	282,941
Expenses, total	**$16,668**	**$70,566**	**$132,089**	**$310,390**	**$219,741**	**$311,317**	**$419,896**
Interest expense	3,876	28,093	56,877	131,877	59,726	140,240	226,146
Compensation	7,619	22,931	41,541	95,206	83,480	88,813	103,382
Commissions/clearance paid	1,055	2,959	5,700	15,523	17,375	18,645	21,980
Other	4,119	16,583	27,970	67,784	59,160	63,168	68,388
Net income, pretax	**$3,160**	**$790**	**$11,325**	**$39,103**	**$23,189**	**$21,184**	**$38,567**

Source: U.S. Securities and Exchange Commission, *2007 Annual Report* (2008).

nually until maturity (interest payments) and then, at maturity, a fixed sum of money to repay the initial amount borrowed (principal). Bonds carry no claim to ownership and therefore pay no dividends, but payments to bondholders take priority over payments to stockholders.

Debentures Debt securities issued by a company that pay a fixed interest rate, in order to raise finance for commercial or industrial operations.

Divestiture The sales by a company of a product line, subsidiary or division. The number of divestitures sold peaked in 1986, with a total of 1,316, for a record total price of $65.2 billion.

Dividends Payments made to common and preferred stockholders out of a firm's profits either in the form of cash or additional shares.

Dow Jones Industrial Average Dating back to 1893, this index of 30 blue chip stocks in industry traded on the New York Stock Exchange (and determined by the editors of the *Wall Street Journal*) is the most widely cited indicator of how the stock market is doing.

Establishment A physical place of business activity such as a factory, assembly plant, retail store, warehouse, etc. where goods are made, stored or processed, or where services are performed.

Eurocurrency Currency of the major industrial and financial countries held in the banks of major financial and industrial countries for the purpose of lending and borrowing. Most loans are for up to one year and are used for payments of deficits. Eurodollars are U.S. dollars held in foreign banks.

Firm A business organization that owns and/or operates one or more establishments. Also called a company, enterprise or business venture. Firms can be of three types: 1) sole proprietorships—firms owned directly by one person; 2) partnerships—firms whose ownership is shared by a fixed number of proprietors; and 3) corporations—firms created by a government charter, granting them greater accessibility to financial capital through the selling of common or preferred stock, greater accessibility to debt capital through the selling of bonds, and limited liability in the event of bankruptcy.

Futures market/forward market A market in which commodities or securities are bought and sold at prices fixed now, for delivery at specified future date. Futures are traded on the American Stock Exchange; the Chicago Board of Trade; Chicago Board Options Exchange; Chicago Mer-

Top 25 Securities Firms by Capital, 2004–07

2007 Rank/Firm	2004	2007
1. Merrill Lynch & Co.[1]	$115,452	$224,251
2. Morgan Stanley[1]	90,467	162,134
3. Goldman Sachs Group,[1,2]	79,114	158,628
4. Lehman Brothers Holdings[1,2]	58,013	113,247
5. Citigroup Global Markets	59,634	78,428
6. Bear Stearns Companies[1,2]	36,901	66,699
7. Credit Suisse (USA), Inc.[1]	33,741	57,902
8. UBS Securities LLC	10,505	15,817
9. Deutsche Bank Securities Inc.	7,068	11,612
10. J.P. Morgan Securities Inc.	5,747	9,972
11. Charles Schwab Corporation[2]	5,233	5,396
12. Wachovia Capital Markets	1,794	4,381
13. UBS Financial Services Inc.	3,057	4,318
14. TD Ameritrade Holding Corp.	2,742	3,456
15. E*TRADE Brokerage Holdings	N.A.	3,029
16. Jefferies Group, Inc.[2]	1,282	3,000
17. RBS Greenwich Capital	1,283	2,977
18. Fidelity Brokerage	1,924	2,611
19. Wachovia Securities, LLC	2,765	2,434
20. Nomura Securities Intl. Inc.	1,656	2,083
21. A.G. Edwards, Inc.	1,738	2,055
22. Pershing LLC	N.A.	1,668
23. Raymond James Financial, Inc.	N.A.	1,644
24. CIBC World Markets Corp.	1,515	1,636
25. ABN-AMRO Incorporated	1,695	1,489

Note: Data as of January 1 of year shown, except as noted.
1. Data as of Nov. 30 of previous year. 2. Firm's capital is the sum of long-term borrowings and ownership equity.
Source: Securities Industry Association.

cantile Exchange; Chicago Rice and Cotton Exchange; Commodity Exchange, New York (COMEX); Kansas City Board of Trade; MidAmerica Commodity Exchange, Chicago; Minneapolis Grain Exchange; New York Coffee, Sugar, and Coca Exchange (including the Citrus Associates); New York Cotton Exchange; New York Futures Exchange; and New York Mercantile Exchange; New York Stock Exchange; Pacific Stock Exchange, Los Angeles and San Francisco; and Philadelphia Stock Exchange.

Greenmail Analogous to blackmail, greenmail is the practice of purchasing enough shares in a firm or trading company to threaten a takeover, thereby forcing the owners to buy them back at a higher rate in order to retain control of the business.

Individual Retirement Account (IRA) An account set up by individual investors to hold and invest funds until retirement. Under a traditional IRA, which was established as an alternative for people not eligible for employee-sponsored pension plans, individuals may contribute up to $2,000 pre-tax per year to a tax-deferred retirement account. In 1997, Congress established the Roth IRA, which allows individuals to contribute $2,000 post-tax to a retirement account on which earnings are tax free forever in most cases.

Inital Public Offfering (IPO) A company's first sale of stock to the public (also known as "going public.") An IPO generates working capital in exchange for equity. A well-publicized IPO can drive up the stock price, making millionaires of company insiders who already own stock or options. For this reason, it is often difficult for outsiders to purchase shares in an IPO at the public offering price.

Insider trading Illegal trading in the stock market based on information that has not been made public, and which is intended to remain confidential—for example, information that a small company is about to become part of a national corporation. The penalties paid by individuals and corporations for such activities in recent years have reached into the hundreds of millions of dollars. Drexel Burnham Lambert, Inc., was fined $650 million to settle six charges of securities law violations; and investor Ivan Boesky was fined $100 million and imprisoned for his insider trading activities.

Junk bond/high-yield bond Bonds with a rating below investment grade (at or below Ba1 by Moody's Investors Service, at or below BB+ by Standard & Poor's), or unrated. Issuers of junk bonds are usually small companies that in the past have been limited to borrowing from banks to raise capital for corporate growth. Although the major ratings services consider junk bonds risky (hence their name), they have a historically low default rate—only 1.5 percent between the mid-1970's and mid-1980's. The junk market grew considerably in the 1980's, and by 1987 accounted for over 25 percent of the value of all corporate bonds outstanding.

Leveraged buyout The purchase of a company by one of its employee groups (usually upper management) or a large shareholder with borrowed funds, usually using the company's assets as security for the loans. Leveraged buy-outs have been used to combat hostile takeover bids.

Mutual fund A pool of financial assets in which investors may buy shares and get the benefits (or share the losses) depending on the performance of the collective securities. Shares are sold publicly and can be redeemed at any time. Funds can consist of stocks, bonds, gold, government securities or other assets, and their names are descriptive of their primary purpose; for example, bonds funds, equity-fund portfolios, income funds, money market-mutual funds, and municipal funds. (See the section on mutual funds earlier in this chapter; see also "Money Market Accounts" in "Money and Banking.")

Option A contract to buy or sell commodities or securities within a given time period at a fixed price. For stocks, this period is usually three months. A contract to sell is a *put option* (or put); to buy, a *call option* (or call) and one to buy or sell is a *double option*. A buyer (seller) will gain if the trading price rises (falls) by more than the cost of entering into the contract. Options are traded on the same exchanges as futures contracts (see *Futures market*).

Over-the-counter (OTC) stock A security not listed on an exchange that is traded between two individuals. The name stems from the 18th-century practice of merchants selling stocks over the counter in their own shops directly to investors without the use of stockbrokers or auctioneers.

Pension fund An arrangement whereby private or public-sector employers, unions, and—as in the case of individual retirement accounts (IRAs) and Keogh plans—individuals contribute to a fund from which money is paid out to the employees, union members, or contributors (or their dependents) upon death, disability or retirement. Contributions can be based on a percentage of salary or corporate profits; in some cases employees may make voluntary or mandatory contributions to the fund. Pension fund assets are usually held in the form of securities or property with a preference for long-term assets.

Preferred stock Similar to common stock, except that owners of preferred stock have no voting rights, and preferred stock holders are paid their dividends at a fixed rate, before common stockholders receive any dividends.

Rating An agency evaluation of the quality of a debt instrument or a company issuing debt. Standard & Poor's and Moody's Investment Service are the two major credit ratings agencies in the U.S. The ratings measure the safety of interest and principal payments of bonds. S&P bond ratings are, from most to least secure: AAA, AA, A, BBB, BB, B, CCC, CC, C. Moody's ratings are: Aaa, Aa, A, Baa, Ba, B, Caa, Ca, C.

Russell Indexes These measure the performance of the largest U.S.-headquartered companies, based on total market capitalization. The Russell 3,000 Index measures the 3,000 largest U.S.-based companies (their total market capitalization represents approximately 98 percent of the investable U.S. equity market). The Russell 1,000 measures the largest 1,000 of these companies. The Russell 2,000 measures the smallest 2,000 companies in the Russell 3,000.

Securities Financial assets (usually long-term), such as equities/stocks and debentures/bonds; may also refer to shorter-term assets such as U.S. Treasury bills.

Venture Capital Investments, 1990–2007

Year	Total amount invested (millions)	Total number of companies invested in	Average investment per company (millions)
1990	$2,914	1,143	$2.55
1995	7,868	1,483	5.31
1998	20,906	2,909	7.19
1999	53,532	4,347	12.31
2000	105,035	7,905	13.29
2002	21,681	2,582	7.12
2003	19,729	2,926	6.74
2004	22,488	3,082	7.30
2005	23,038	3,146	7.32
2006	26,592	3,647	7.29
2007	30,515	3,914	7.80

Source: Pricewaterhouse Coopers, *MoneyTree Report 2008*.
www.pwcmoneytree.com.

Securities and Exchange Commission (SEC) U.S. government agency that regulates the securities industry by requiring registration of brokers, dealers, and stock exchanges. The SEC also reviews the financial position of companies issuing securities for public sale, and investigates illegal activities such as insider trading.

Standard & Poor's 500 Composite Stock Price Index (S&P 500) A widely used measure of the movement of the U.S. stock market. The S&P 500 was introduced in 1957 and is one of 12 leading economic indicators used by the U.S. Commerce Department. The 500 issues include 400 industrial, 40 utility, 20 transportation and 40 financial companies—primarily those listed on the New York Stock Exchange (NYSE). The index is considered to be value-weighted because each stock is weighted according to its market value. As of December 31, 1987, the market value of issues tracked by the S&P 500 was equal to approximately 70 percent of the value of all publicly traded U.S. equities. Its value is calculated on a total return basis with dividends reinvested.

Stock exchange A market in which securities (other than bills and similar short-term instruments) issued by central and local government bodies, and public companies are traded (e.g., the New York Stock Exchange, the American Stock Exchange, the London Stock Exchange). Only members of a stock exchange may deal on it, and membership and arrangements for trading are strictly regulated. Stock exchanges in the United States are the American Stock Exchange (New York); Boston Stock Exchange; Cincinnati Stock Exchange; Intermountain Stock Exchange (Salt Lake City); Midwest Stock Exchange (Chicago); New York Stock Exchange; Pacific Stock Exchange (Los Angeles, San Francisco); Philadelphia Stock Exchange; and Spokane Stock Exchange.

Stock market An institution where stocks and shares are traded, existing in all advanced Western countries. Stock markets enable companies to more easily raise equity or loan capital from the public since investors can quickly realize their holdings because of the stock exchange share quotation. In other words, there is a ready market. The principal overseas stock markets are located in Amsterdam, Brussels, Frankfurt, Hong Kong, Johannesburg, London, Milan, Paris, Singapore, Stockholm, Sydney, Tokyo, Toronto and Zurich.

Stockbroker An individual who acts as an adviser and an agent (working on commission), to buy and sell stocks on behalf of a client on a particular stock exchange where the stockbroker is a member.

Venture capital Funds made available to start-up businesses that have excellent growth potential, but are unable to obtain more traditional methods of business financing. Also known as risk capital because these investments have a high risk and a high reward.

Wilshire 5000 Index The broadest measure of the U.S. stock market, containing some 5,000 issues including all publicly traded U.S. stocks for which daily pricing is available (i.e., includes all Amex, NYSE and OTC stocks).

Yield The annual return on a security, as a percentage of its current market price. A stock's dividend yield is the annual dividend divided by its current stock price.

▶ BIG BUSINESS: THE *FORTUNE* 500

The ultimate measure of success in the business world is inclusion on *Fortune* magazine's annual list of the 500 biggest companies in America. In recent years, the global trend toward mega-mergers creating monolithic organizations has raised the bar for admission to this select circle. Since 2005, Wal-Mart and Exxon Mobil have each posted more than $300 billion in annual revenues. In 2007, the top 14 companies on the Fortune 500 all had revenues of over $100 billion.

The accompanying tables list the top 100 companies of the *Fortune* 500 by revenues, the top three companies in several performance categories, and the top companies by industry.

▶ SMALL BUSINESS

Small businesses account for 98 percent of the 5.65 million employer firms in the United States today. Nearly half of the small businesses in America had fewer than four employees. Small businesses create the vast majority of the net new jobs in America every year. Businesses with 100 employees or fewer employed 36 percent of the 114 million employees working for U.S. employer firms, according to the Census Bureau in 2000; 55.2 percent worked in businesses with fewer than 1,000 employees. According to the Small Business Administration, two-thirds of small businesses survive at least two years, and just over half make it four years. About three-quarters of

---

Fortune 500 Performance Leaders, 2007

Profits	Millions of dollars	Return on Revenues	Percent
1. Exxon Mobil (2)	$40,610	1. Charles Schwab (402)	39.7%
2. General Electric (6)	22,208	2. Qualcomm (297)	37.2
3. Chevron (3)	18,688	3. Corning (417)	36.7

Market Value	Millions of dollars	Return to Investors, 1 year	Percent
1. Exxon Mobil (2)	$455,929	1. Mosaic (422)	341.7%
2. General Electric (6)	365,582	2. AK Steel Holding (351)	173.6
3. Microsoft (44)	259,758	3. Owens-Illinois (314)	168.3

Employees	Number	Return to Investors, 10 years	Percent
1. Wal-Mart Stores (1)	2,055,000	1. Apple (103)	50.7%
2. United Parcel Service (46)	425,300	2. NVR (464)	37.4
3. McDonald's (106)	390,000	3. Frontier Oil (462)	36.3

Note: Numbers in parentheses reflect overall *Fortune* 500 rank.

The Top U.S. Companies, by Industry and *Fortune* 1,000 Rank, 2007

Industry, Company, Rank	Revenues (millions)
Aerospace and Defense	
Boeing (27)	$66,387
United Technologies (42)	54,759
Lockheed Martin (57)	41,682
Airlines	
AMR (109)	22,935
UAL (124)	20,143
Delta Air Lines (129)	19,154
Apparel	
Nike (153)	16,326
VF (335)	7,416
Liz Claiborne (479)	4,824
Beverages	
Coca-Cola (83)	28,857
Coca Cola Enterprises (118)	20,936
Anheuser-Busch (149)	16,686
Chemicals	
Dow Chemical (42)	53,513
DuPont (81)	30,653
PPG Industries (217)	12,299
Commercial Banks	
Citigroup (8)	159,229
Bank of America Corp. (9)	119,190
JPMorgan Chase (12)	116,353
Computer Software	
Microsoft (44)	51,122
Oracle (137)	17,996
Symantec (461)	5,199
Computers, Office Equipment	
Hewlett-Packard (14)	104,286
Dell (34)	61,133
Apple (103)	24,006
Diversified Financials	
General Electric (6)	176,656
Fannie Mae (53)	43,355
Freddie Mac (54)	43,104
Electronics	
Emerson Electric (111)	22,572
Whirlpool (127)	19,451
Rockwell Automation (450)	5,345
Energy	
Constellation Energy (117)	21,193
ONEOK (192)	13,477
American Electric Power (196)	13,380
Engineering, Construction	
Fluor (148)	16,691
KBR (284)	9,194
Jacobs Engineering (308)	8,474
Entertainment	
Time Warner (49)	46,615
Walt Disney (67)	35,882
News Corp. (84)	28,655
Food Products (Consumer)	
PepsiCo (59)	39,474
Kraft Foods (63)	37,241
Sara Lee (203)	13,179
Food & Drug Stores	
CVS/Caremark (24)	76,330
Kroger (26)	70,235
Walgreen (40)	53,762
Food Production	
Archer Daniels Midland (52)	44,018
Tyson Foods (88)	26,900
Smithfield Foods (222)	11,933

Industry, Company, Rank	Revenues (millions)
Food Services	
McDonald's (106)	$23,231
Yum Brands (253)	10,416
Starbucks (277)	9,412
Forest & Paper Products	
International Paper (114)	22,284
Weyerhaeuser (147)	16,871
Boise Cascade (445)	3,414
General Merchandisers	
Wal-Mart Stores (1)	378,799
Target (31)	63,367
Sears Holdings (45)	50,703
Health Care	
UnitedHealth Group (25)	75,431
Wellpoint (33)	61,134
Aetna (85)	27,600
Hotels, Casinos & Resorts	
Marriott International (197)	13,342
Harrah's (244)	10,825
MGM Mirage (323)	7,820
Household & Personal Products	
Procter & Gamble (23)	76,476
Kimberly-Clark (136)	18,266
Colgate-Palmolive (186)	13,790
Industrial & Farm Equipment	
Caterpillar (50)	44,958
Deere (102)	24,082
Illinois Tool Works (155)	16,279
Information Technology Services	
International Business Machines (15)	98,786
Electronic Data Systems (115)	22,135
Computer Sciences (170)	14,857
Insurance	
Berkshire Hathaway (11)	118,245
American Intl. Grp (13)	110,064
State Farm Insurance (32)	61,612
Mail, Package, Freight Delivery	
United Parcel Service (46)	49,692
FedEx (68)	35,214
Metals	
Alcoa (80)	30,748
United States Steel (146)	16,873
Nucor (151)	16,593
Mining, Crude Oil Production	
Occidental Petroleum (123)	20,206
Freeport McMoRan Copper & Gold (140)	17,876
Anadarko Petroleum (159)	15,916
Motor Vehicles & Parts	
General Motors (4)	182,347
Ford Motor (7)	172,468
Johnson Controls (72)	34,678
Network Communications	
Motorola (65)	36,622
Cisco Systems (71)	34,922
Qualcomm (297)	8,871
Oil and Gas Equipment	
Halliburton (167)	15,264
Baker Hughes (252)	10,428
National Oilwell Varco (268)	9,789

Industry, Company, Rank	Revenues (millions)
Petroleum Refining	
Exxon Mobil (2)	$372,824
Chevron (3)	210,783
ConocoPhillips (5)	178,558
Pharmaceuticals	
Johnson & Johnson (35)	61,095
Pfizer (47)	48,418
Abbott Laboratories (96)	25,914
Publishing, Printing	
R. R. Donnelley & Sons (229)	11,587
Gannett (332)	7,480
McGraw-Hill (362)	6,772
Railroads	
Union Pacific (154)	16,283
Burlington Northern Santa Fe (160)	15,802
CSX (261)	10,030
Real Estate	
ProLogis (387)	6,217
CB Richard Ellis Group (404)	6,036
Realogy (414)	5,967
Savings Institutions	
Washington Mutual (97)	25,531
Sovereign Bancorp (469)	5,011
Hudson City Bancorp (860)	2,135
Securities	
Goldman Sachs Group (20)	87,968
Morgan Stanley (21)	87,879
Merrill Lynch (30)	64,217
Semiconductors	
Intel (60)	38,334
Texas Instruments (185)	13,835
Jabil Circuit (219)	12,291
Specialty Retailers	
Home Depot (22)	84,740
Costco Wholesale (29)	64,400
Lowe's (48)	48,283
Telecommunications	
AT&T (10)	118,928
Verizon (17)	93,775
Sprint Nextel (58)	40,146
Tobacco	
Altria Group (61)	38,051
Reynolds American (290)	9,023
Universal (683)	2,937
Utilities	
Exelon (131)	18,925
Dominion Resources (161)	15,790
Southern (166)	15,353
Waste Management	
Waste Management (199)	13,310
Allied Waste Industries (400)	6,118
Republic Services (647)	3,176
Wholesalers: Food and Grocery	
Sysco (70)	35,042
CHS (145)	17,216
Performance Food Group (384)	6,305
Wholesalers: Health Care	
McKesson (18)	93,574
Cardinal Health (19)	88,364
AmerisourceBergen (28)	66,074

Source: *Fortune* magazine, 2008. Reprinted by permission.

Fortune 100 Largest U.S. Corporations, 2007

Rank	Company (2006 Rank)	Revenues (millions)	Rank	Company (200 Rank)	Revenues (millions)
1.	Wal-Mart Stores (1)	$378,799.0	51.	Medco Health Solutions (54)	$44,506.2
2.	Exxon Mobil (2)	372,824.0	52.	Archer Daniels Midland (59)	44,018.0
3.	Chevron (4)	210,783.0	53.	Fannie Mae (N.A.)	43,355.0
4.	General Motors (3)	182,347.0	54.	Freddie Mac (50)	43,104.0
5.	ConocoPhillips (5)	178,558.0	55.	Safeway (56)	42,286.0
6.	General Electric (6)	176,656.0	56.	Sunoco (60)	42,101.0
7.	Ford Motor (7)	172,468.0	57.	Lockheed Martin (57)	41,862.0
8.	Citigroup (8)	159,229.0	58.	Sprint Nextel (53)	40,146.0
9.	Bank of America Corp. (9)	119,190.0	59.	PepsiCo (63)	39,474.0
10.	AT&T (27)	118,928.0	60.	Intel (62)	38,334.0
11.	Berkshire Hathaway (12)	118,245.0	61.	Altria Group (23)	38,051.0
12.	JPMorgan Chase & Co. (11)	116,353.0	62.	Supervalu (117)	37,406.0
13.	American International Group (10)	110,064.0	63.	Kraft Foods (N.A.)	37,241.0
14.	Hewlett-Packard (14)	104,286.0	64.	Allstate (61)	36,769.0
15.	International Business Machines (15)	98,786.0	65.	Motorola (52)	36,622.0
16.	Valero Energy (16)	96,758.0	66.	Best Buy (72)	35,934.0
17.	Verizon Communications (13)	93,775.0	67.	Walt Disney (64)	35,882.0
18.	McKesson (18)	93,574.0	68.	FedEx (68)	35,214.0
19.	Cardinal Health (19)	88,363.9	69.	Ingram Micro (70)	35,047.1
20.	Goldman Sachs Group (24)	87,968.0	70.	Sysco (65)	35,042.1
21.	Morgan Stanley (20)	87,879.0	71.	Cisco Systems (77)	34,922.0
22.	Home Depot (17)	84,740.0	72.	Johnson Controls (67)	34,678.0
23.	Procter & Gamble (25)	76,476.0	73.	Honeywell Intl. (69)	34,589.0
24.	CVS/Caremark (51)	76,329.5	74.	Prudential Financial (66)	34,401.0
25.	United Health Group (21)	75,431.0	75.	American Express (79)	32,316.0
26.	Kroger (26)	70,234.7	76.	Northrop Grumman (73)	32,032.0
27.	Boeing (28)	66,387.0	77.	Hess (75)	31,924.0
28.	AmerisourceBergen (29)	66,074.3	78.	GMAC (N.A.)	31,490.0
29.	Costco Wholesale (32)	64,400.2	79.	Comcast (84)	30,895.0
30.	Merrill Lynch (22)	64,217.0	80.	Alcoa (71)	30,748.0
31.	Target (33)	63,367.0	81.	DuPont (74)	30,653.0
32.	State Farm Insurance Cos (31)	61,611.6	82.	New York Life Insurance (78)	29,279.6
33.	Wellpoint (35)	61,134.3	83.	Coca-Cola (94)	28,857.0
34.	Dell (34)	61,133.0	84.	News Corp. (88)	28,655.0
35.	Johnson & Johnson (36)	61,095.0	85.	Aetna (85)	27,599.6
36.	Marathon Oil (30)	60,044.0	86.	TIAA-CREF (80)	27,526.0
37.	Lehman Brothers Holdings (47)	59,003.0	87.	General Dynamics (92)	27,294.0
38.	Wachovia Corp. (46)	55,528.0	88.	Tyson Foods (86)	26,900.0
39.	United Technologies (42)	54,759.0	89.	HCA (87)	26,858.0
40.	Walgreen (44)	53,762.0	90.	Enterprise GP Holdings (177)	26,713.8
41.	Wells Fargo (41)	53,593.0	91.	Macy's (76)	26,340.0
42.	Dow Chemical (40)	53,513.0	92.	Delphi (83)	26,160.0
43.	MetLife (37)	53,150.0	93.	Travelers Cos. (89)	26,017.0
44.	Microsoft (49)	51,122.0	94.	Liberty Mutual Insurance Group (95)	25,961.0
45.	Sears Holdings (38)	50,703.0	95.	Hartford Financial Services (82)	25,916.0
46.	United Parcel Service (43)	49,692.0	96.	Abbott Laboratories (102)	25,914.2
47.	Pfizer (39)	48,418.0	97.	Washington Mutual (81)	25,531.0
48.	Lowe's (45)	48,283.0	98.	Humana (110)	25,290.0
49.	Time Warner (48)	46,615.0	99.	Mass. Mutual Life Insurance (90)	25,268.2
50.	Caterpillar (55)	44,958.0	100.	3M (97)	24,462.0

Source: *Fortune* magazine, 2008. Reprinted by permission.

new business owners are still employed in a salaried job when they start their own business; 60 percent of new businesses start at home.

Franchising, a century-old tradition, continues to grow in popularity. The Department of Commerce estimates that franchising accounts for more than half of all sales in the U.S. The benefits to the franchisor are enormous: expansion with little or no risk, royalties and licensing revenue from the franchisee, and an initial franchise fee (usually around $25,000). The benefits to the franchisee are less obvious, but may include name recognition, a national advertising campaign, and training and financial assistance from the parent company. Although tales of self-made millionaires abound in franchising circles, far greater numbers of franchisees go bankrupt. As the accompanying table demonstrates, opening a franchised business is no simple proposition, often requiring hundreds of thousands (or even millions) of dollars in start-up costs.

Top 50 Franchises, by Number of Franchises, 2007

Rank, Franchise	Business	Number of franchises	Startup costs[1]	Franchise fees
1. 7-Eleven Inc.	Convenience stores	30,642	varies	varies
2. Subway	Submarine sandwiches & salads	27,929	$76,100-227,800	$15,000
3. Kumon Math & Reading Centers	Supplemental education	25,916	30,400-110,300	1,000
4. McDonald's	Hamburgers, chicken, salads	23,099	506,000-1.6 million	45,000
5. Jani-King	Commercial cleaning	12,699	11,300-34,100	8,600-16,300+
6. KFC Corp.	Chicken	11,071	1.1-1.7 million	25,000
7. Curves	Women's fitness and weight-loss centers	10,454	31,400-53,500	24,900-44,900
8. Pizza Hut	Pizza	9,981	1.1-1.7 million	25,000
9. Century 21 Real Estate	Real estate	8,380	11,800-522,800	up to 25,000
10. Domino's Pizza	Pizza and breadsticks	7,902	118,500-460,300	25,000
11. Dunkin' Donuts	Donuts & baked goods	7,376	varies	40,000-80,000
12. Jazzercise Inc.	Dance/exercise classes	7,191	2,990-33,100	500-1,000
13. Jan-Pro Franchising Int'l. Inc.	Commercial cleaning	7,032	3,300-49,900	2,800-44,000
14. RE/MAX Int'l. Inc.	Real estate	6,973	35,000-191,000	12,500-25,000
15. UPS Store	Postal, business, and communications services	5,899	170,800-279,400	29,950
16. Baskin-Robbins	Ice cream, frozen yogurt	5,835	156,900-560,400	20,000-30,000
17. Jackson Hewitt Tax Service	Tax preparation services	5,778	48,600-91,800	up to 25,000
18. Dairy Queen	Soft-serve dairy products	5,688	655,000-1.3 million	25,000-35,000
19. Choice Hotels International	Hotels, inns, suites, and resorts	5,471	2.3-12.6 million	7,500-60,000
20. Quizno's Sub	Sandwiches, soups, and salads	5,200	29,100-323,900	10,000-25,000
21. ServiceMaster Clean	Commercial and residential cleaning	4,596	21,100-111,100	16,900-45,000
22. Taco Bell	Quick-service Mexican restaurants	4,571	1.7 million	45,000
23. Ace Hardware Corp.	Hardware & home improvement stores	4,457	236,000-1.1 million	5,000
24. Chem-Dry	Carpet, draper, and upholstery cleaning	4,285	25,300-213,600	12,950-34,900
25. Snap-On Tools	Professional tools and equipment	4,264	19,800-276,400	7,500
26. CleanNet USA Inc.	Commercial cleaning	3,861	3,900-35,600	2,950-32,000
27. Circle K	Convenience stores	3,841	648,000	15,000
28. InterContinental Hotels Group	Hotels	3,289	varies	varies
29. Coldwell Banker Real Estate	Real estate	3,218	23,500-490,500	13,000-25,000
30. ERA Franchise Systems	Real estate	2,930	427,000-205,900	up to 20,000
31. am/pm Mini Market	Convenience stores/ gas stations	2,702	2.5-6.4 million	70,000
32. Sonic Drive-in Restaurants	Drive-in restaurants	2,656	820,000-2.3 million	45,000
33. Great Clips Inc.	Hair salons	2,600	106,900-197,700	25,000
34. Arby's	Sandwiches, chicken and salads	2,522	336,500-2.4 million	25,000/37,500
35. Midas	Auto repair & maintenance	2,496	243,000-329,700	20,000
36. Liberty Tax Service	Income tax preparation	2,329	33,800-63,900	17,000-34,000
37. Papa John's International	Pizza	2,073	250,000	25,000
38. Super 8 Motels Inc.	Economy motels	2,054	278,900-2.9 million	varies
39. GNC Franchising Inc.	Vitamin & nutrition stores	2,050	132,700-182,000	40,000/30,000
40. Novus Auto Glass	Windshield repair and replacement	2,026	14,900-190,000	7,500
41. Jiffy Lube Int'l. Inc.	Fast oil change	1,950	214,000-273,000	35,000
42. Days Inn Worldwide	Hotels & inns	1,862	394,700-5.7 million	varies
43. Merle Norman Cosmetics	Cosmetics studios	1,840	30,400-166,100	0
44. WSI Internet	Internet services	1,823	58,400-163,200	49,700-147,000
45. Popeye's Chicken & Biscuits	New Orleans-style fried chicken	1,817	658,000-971,000	30,000
46. Bonus Building Care	Commercial cleaning	1,774	7,800-13,400	6,500
47. Matco Tools	Tools	1,481	79,000-182,000	0
48. Cold Stone Creamery	Ice cream & Italian sorbet	1,414	292,400-438,980	42,000
49. Hampton Inns & Suites	Midprice hotels	1,413	3.6-10.8 million	50,000+
50. Fantastic Sam's	Full-service hair salons	1,398	100,500-230,100	25,000-35,000

Note: Does not include franchises owned by the company. **1.** Includes franchise fees.
Source: *Entrepreneur* (Jan. 2008). Reprinted by permission.

ADVERTISING

Few facts and figures reveal the extraordinary growth of the mass-consumption society as vividly as those dealing with the advertising business. In 1950, as the postwar economy began to heat up, American business spent $5.7 billion to advertise its goods and services; by 1960 that figure would double, and then almost double again by 1970. Between 1970 and 1990, as the Baby Boom generation entered the marketplace and the economy expanded, advertising expenditures grew at a spiraling rate, topping $100 billion in 1986. That rate of growth has not been sustained, but advertising spending continued to reach new highs every year until 2000. The industry suffered its worst decline in more than a decade in 2001, when total expenditures fell 6.5 percent, from $243 to $231 billion. The decline was short-lived: expenditures rose again through 2006, when they reached another all-time high of $281 billion. In 2007, they fell slightly to $279 billion.

More than half of all advertising dollars are spent to place ads in newspapers or magazines or to run commercials on radio and television. Meanwhile, although the Internet is the fastest-growing source of advertising dollars, it still represents only a tiny fraction of all advertising dollars spent. Companies continue to spend far more dollars for listings in the Yellow Pages as they do on pop-up ads.

The biggest advertisers are the nation's largest manufacturers of automobiles, food, soft drinks, tobacco and beer. Most advertising dollars are filtered through about 13,000 advertising agencies, which mainly create the ads and buy the space or time from the media. The agency business has undergone a dramatic restructuring recently, as many of the largest agencies, most of them with worldwide connections, have merged to form enormous corporations. The largest such mega-corporation is the New York-based Omnicom Group, followed by the London-based WPP Group. These two parent groups owned 6 of the top 10 U.S. ad agencies in 2007 (see the accompanying table).

Advertising Expenditures in the U.S., 1776–2007 (in millions)

Year	Amount[1]	Year	Amount[1]	Year	Amount[1]
1776	$ 0.2	1909	$1,000	2000	$243,680
1800	1	1915	1,100	2001	231,300
1820	3	1940	2,110	2002	236,875
1840	7	1950	5,700	2003	245,477
1850	12	1960	11,960	2004	263,766
1860	22	1970	19,550	2005	271,074
1867	40	1980	54,780	2006	281,653
1880	175	1985	94,750	2007	279,612
1890	300	1990	128,640		
1900	450	1995	160,930		

Source: *Advertising Age*. 1. These are estimated figures of the monies spent on placing advertising in all media; the costs of producing the advertising are not included.

Total U.S. Advertising Volume by Medium and Category, 2006–07

	2006		2007		Percent change
	Expenditures (millions)	Share of total	Expenditures (millions)	Share of total	2006-07
BY MEDIUM					
Magazines, total	**$17,363**	**6.2%**	**$17,890**	**6.4%**	**3.1%**
National magazines	13,168	4.7	13,787	4.9	4.7
Business to business magazines	4,195	1.5	4,111	1.5	-2.0
Newspapers, total	**46,555**	**16.5**	**42,133**	**15.1**	**-9.5**
National newspapers	7,084	2.5	6,609	2.4	-6.7
Local newspapers	39,47	14.0	35,524	12.7	-10.0
Broadcast TV, total	**46,880**	**16.6**	**44,521**	**15.9**	**-5.1**
Network TV	16,676	5.9	16,643	5.9	-0.2
Spot TV	26,513	9.4	24,549	8.8	-7.4
Syndicated TV	3,691	1.3	3,329	1.2	-9.8
Cable TV networks	19,320	6.9	20,614	7.4	6.7
Radio, total	**19,643**	**7.0**	**19,152**	**6.9**	**-2.5**
Network radio	798	0.3	830	0.3	4.0
National spot radio	3,642	1.3	3,423	1.2	-6.0
Local radio	15,203	5.4	14,899	5.3	-2.0
Outdoor	**6,731**	**2.4**	**7,202**	**2.6**	**7.0**
Direct mail	**58,642**	**20.8**	**60,225**	**21.5**	**2.7**
Internet	**9,100**	**3.2**	**10,529**	**3.8**	**15.7**
TOTAL U.S. SPENDING	**$281,653**	**100%**	**$279,612**	**100%**	**-0.7%**
BY CATEGORY					
Retail	$19,103	N.A.	$18,702	12.4%	-2.1%
Automotive	19,808	N.A.	18,540	12.3	-6.4
Telecommunications	11,041	N.A.	10,909	7.3	-1.2
Medicine & remedies	9,187	N.A.	9,298	6.2	1.2
Financial services	8,697	N.A.	9,219	6.1	6.0
General services	8,636	N.A.	8,930	5.9	3.4
Food, beverages, candy	7,200	N.A.	7,459	5.0	3.6
Personal care	5,728	N.A.	6,307	4.2	10.1
Airlines, hotels, car rental, travel	5,436	N.A.	5,414	3.6	-0.4
Movies, recorded video & music	5,381	N.A.	5,408	3.6	0.5

Note: Total includes miscellaneous other amounts not shown separately. Network TV includes Fox; Syndicated TV includes UPN and WB. Source: Prepared for *Advertising Age* by Universal McCann's Robert J. Coen. www.adage.com.

Top 25 U.S. Advertising Agencies, by Gross Domestic Income, 2006-07

U.S. Rank /Agency, Headquarters (Parent Company)	U.S. Revenues (millions) 2006	2007	Percent change, 2006-07	Worldwide revenues (millions) 2006	2007
1. BBDO Worldwide, New York (Omnicom)	$584.7	$628.0	7.4%	$1,680	$1,899
2. DraftFCB, Chicago/New York (Interpublic)	496.1	518.9	4.6	941	991
3. McCann Erickson Worldwide, New York (Interpublic)	443.4	490.0	10.5	1,479	1,619
4. Epsilon/Purple, Irving, Texas (Alliance Data Systems)	232.0	360.0	55.2	232	370
5. Rapp Collins Worldwide, New York (Omnicom)	306.0	351.9	15.0	517	602
6. Digitas, Boston (Publicis)	257.0	345.0	34.2	257	364
7. OgilvyOne Worldwide, New York (WPP)	297.8	338.5	13.7	604	690
8. JWT, New York (WPP)	303.3	315.5	4.0	1,140	1,237
9. Y&R, New York (WPP)	280.0	307.0	9.6	820	907
10. MindShare Worldwide, New York (WPP)	277.8	302.4	8.9	687	734
11. Avenue A/Razorfish, Seattle (Microsoft Corp.)	235.4	299.3	27.1	268	368
12. Carlson Marketing, Minneapolis (Carlson)	282.0	299.0	6.0	390	413
13. OMD Worldwide, New York (Omnicom)	290.1	298.8	3.0	790	859
14. Wunderman, New York (WPP)	264.0	295.0	11.7	615	720
15. DDB Worldwide, New York (Omnicom)	277.9	290.8	4.6	1,264	1,432
16. Starcom USA, Chicago (Publicis)	227.9	259.0	13.6	228	259
17. Ogilvy & Mather Worldwide, New York (WPP)	250.0	255.0	2.0	770	812
18. Grey, New York (WPP)	235.7	249.8	6.0	605	645
19. Mediaedge:cia, New York (WPP)	196.7	242.9	23.5	539	641
20. Campbell-Ewald, Warren, Mich. (Interpublic)	230.0	239.2	4.0	230	239
21. Zenith Media USA, New York (Publicis)	188.5	215.0	14.1	189	215
22. TBWA Worldwide, New York (Omnicom)	199.0	208.2	4.6	1,135	1,292
23. MediaVest USA, New York (Publicis)	167.1	200.0	19.7	167	200
24. Saatchi & Saatchi, New York (Publicis)	171.7	193.1	12.5	542	603
25. Leo Burnett Worldwide, Chicago (Publicis)	204.8	190.7	-6.9	751	717

Note: Revenues are estimated by Advertising Age and do not include non-advertising specialty and subsidiary shops.
Source: *Advertising Age* (May 5, 2008); reprinted by permission of Crain Communications, Inc. www.adage.com.

The 100 Leading U.S. Advertisers, 1991-2007

2007 Rank, Company (2006 rank)	Total spending (millions) 1991	1995	2000	2006	2007
1. Procter & Gamble Co. (1)	$1,166.4	$1,507.4	$2,363.5	$4,883.7	$5,230.1
2. AT&T (2)	391.7	675.2	1,415.7	3,344.5	3,207.3
3. Verizon Communications (5)	N.A.	N.A.	1,612.9	2,791.9	3,016.1
4. General Motors Corp. (3)	1,056.5	1,499.6	3,934.8	3,296.1	3,010.1
5. Time Warner (4)	311.3	543.0	1,770.1	3,073.7	2,962.1
6. Ford Motor Co. (6)	517.7	891.8	2,345.2	2,576.6	2,525.2
7. GlaxoSmithKline (7)	83.3	173.2	1,126.4	2,504.0	2,456.9
8. Johnson & Johnson (8)	371.1	601.3	1,601.2	2,401.4	2,408.8
9. Walt Disney Co. (9)	257.3	777.8	1,757.5	2,300.5	2,293.3
10. Unilever (10)	371.4	442.7	1,453.6	2,099.5	2,245.8
11. Sprint Nextel Corp. (15)	N.A.	213.9	1,227.3	1,775.9	1,903.2
12. General Electric Co. (12)	N.A.	N.A.	1,310.1	1,916.8	1,791.3
13. Toyota Motor Corp. (14)	442.5	513.4	1,273.9	1,850.3	1,757.9
14. DaimlerChrysler (13)	414.8	954.7	1,984.0	1,886.4	1,739.4
15. Sony Corp. (11)	262.8	431.0	1,030.0	2,001.3	1,736.8
16. L'Oreal (17)	N.A.	N.A.	987.1	1,458.0	1,632.3
17. Sears Holdings Corp. (16)	462.3	557.8	1,455.4	1,650.8	1,627.8
18. Kraft Foods (18)	1,110.4	1,397.7	2,602.9	1,426.7	1,508.0
19. Bank of America Corp. (31)	N.A.	N.A	N.A	1,140.6	1,491.3
20. Nissan Motor Co. (19)	212.0	367.7	813.8	1,407.4	1,422.9
21. Macy's (21)	111.4	407.6	1,127.6	1,362.9	1,389.7
22. Anheuser-Busch Cos. (23)	327.9	320.5	707.6	1,279.1	1,354.1
23. Honda Motor Co. (22)	242.5	388.8	1,035.0	1,351.2	1,326.5
24. Viacom (41)	N.A.	N.A.	1,220.9	1,010.5	1,309.9
25. Berkshire Hathaway (27)	N.A.	N.A.	455.8	1,194.3	1,308.3
26. PepsiCo (23)	542.0	730.2	2,100.7	1,323.8	1,308.3
27. Nestle (25)	307.6	490.1	637.7	1,255.8	1,260.3
28. Pfizer (42)	N.A.	N.A.	2,265.3	1,006.5	1,252.9
29. News Corp. (20)	358.6	275.9	923.2	1,400.4	1,210.4
30. Target Corp. (29)	N.A.	N.A.	826.7	1,161.4	1,186.2
31. J.C. Penney Co. (28)	105.2	273.9	1,011.2	1,162.7	1,161.8
32. McDonald's Corp. (34)	87.4	586.4	1,273.9	1,083.9	1,150.1

2007 Rank, Company (2006 rank)	Total spending (millions)				
	1991	1995	2000	2006	2007
33. Citigroup (26)	N.A.	N.A.	N.A.	$1,224.1	$1,135.3
34. U.S. Government (32)	$123.4	$219.9	$1,246.3	1,133.4	1,121.9
35. Home Depot (33)	N.A.	96.6	651.6	1,119.6	1,119.6
36. Wal-Mart Stores (35)	76.7	143.2	497.8	1,073.7	1,102.5
37. Schering-Plough Corp. (48)	95.9	104.0	510.5	883.6	1,092.0
38. Wyeth (37)	N.A.	N.A.	N.A.	1,051.3	1,078.3
39. JPMorgan Chase & Co. (30)	N.A.	N.A.	N.A.	1,156.5	1,073.9
40. American Express Co. (46)	156.2	210.4	538.2	929.3	1,050.0
41. Yum Brands (38)	N.A.	N.A.	N.A.	1,039.9	1,004.4
42. Microsoft Corp. (47)	N.A.	147.7	854.8	913.7	959.5
43. Estee Lauder Cos. (39)	N.A.	N.A.	717.3	1,031.4	956.1
44. General Mills (45)	419.1	367.7	639.2	937.2	955.2
45. Kellogg Co. (56)	381.3	488.2	455.4	765.2	871.5
46. Bayer (59)	55.8	160.5	648.9	683.4	860.8
47. Dell (43)	N.A.	N.A.	429.5	984.0	843.4
48. Kohl's Corp. (55)	N.A.	N.A.	231.7	766.0	836.7
49. Deutsche Telekom (52)	N.A.	N.A.	N.A.	815.2	831.3
50. IAC/InterActiveCorp (54)	N.A.	N.A.	N.A.	792.4	806.1
51. Bristol-Myers Squibb Co. (58)	184.0	219.4	1,190.7	690.6	796.3
52. Hewlett-Packard Co. (51)	N.A.	N.A.	791.4	828.9	786.6
53. Coca-Cola Co. (57)	218.8	238.2	894.9	755.1	776.0
54. Eli Lilly & Co. (70)	N.A.	N.A.	N.A.	511.1	774.2
55. Lowe's Cos. (50)	N.A.	N.A.	206.7	838.8	757.1
56. Capital One Financial Corp. (49)	N.A	N.A	N.A	864.9	757.0
57. Merck & Co. (40)	129.5	199.0	983.9	1,024.2	751.8
58. Mars Inc. (61)	128.2	210.1	670.8	660.1	715.9
59. Nike (62)	109.5	146.3	613.5	654.2	702.9
60. AstraZeneca (36)	N.A.	N.A.	N.A.	1,066.5	697.4
61. Comcast Corp. (63)	N.A.	N.A.	N.A.	628.5	692.6
62. Clorox Co. (60)	127.8	157.8	397.1	660.1	683.2
63. Campbell Soup Co. (69)	109.5	169.0	331.2	559.3	670.3
64. Novartis (44)	N.A.	N.A.	573.9	950.8	665.6
65. Hyundai Motor Co. (53)	N.A.	N.A.	N.A.	809.0	650.9
66. Reckitt Benckiser (77)	N.A.	N.A.	289.2	471.6	601.3
67. Best Buy Co. (67)	N.A.	94.0	446.7	572.2	598.3
68. SC Johnson (64)	93.1	115.6	464.8	621.3	591.9
69. Visa (66)	N.A.	N.A.	427.3	580.5	580.6
70. IBM Corp. (68)	387.4	490.6	1189.0	571.4	558.7
71. Allstate Corp. (74)	N.A.	N.A.	N.A.	500.8	536.8
72. Kroger Co. (71)	N.A.	N.A.	551.2	508.3	506.3
73. Boehringer Ingelheim (171)	N.A.	N.A.	N.A.	191.8	505.3
74. FMR Corp. (Fidelity) (102)	N.A.	N.A.	N.A.	334.1	499.0
75. Sanofi-Aventis (75)	N.A.	N.A.	N.A.	490.8	493.1
76. Apple (89)	N.A.	N.A.	N.A.	383.7	491.8
77. MasterCard (73)	N.A.	N.A.	311.1	500.9	488.7
78. eBay (79)	N.A.	N.A.	N.A.	453.3	487.5
79. Safeway (72)	N.A.	N.A.	397.7	507.7	473.7
80. Progressive Corp. (94)	N.A.	N.A.	N.A.	368.2	459.7
81. Washington Mutual (81)	N.A.	N.A.	N.A.	443.0	445.0
82. State Farm Mutual Auto Insurance Co. (97)	N.A.	N.A.	N.A.	360.7	431.2
83. Doctor's Associates (83)	N.A.	N.A.	N.A.	425.5	425.7
84. Mattel (85)	63.8	184.5	451.4	415.8	424.6
85. Coty (JAB Investments) (103)	N.A.	N.A.	N.A.	331.6	421.2
86. SABMiller (84)	N.A.	N.A.	N.A.	422.8	419.7
87. Diageo (90)	N.A.	N.A.	1,112.1	382.6	414.4
88. Circuit City Stores (86)	N.A.	N.A.	N.A.	410.9	401.8
89. Wendy's International (82)	61.1	179.4	296.3	435.2	404.8
90. Gap Inc. (76)	N.A.	N.A.	449.6	489.4	394.2
91. ConAgra Foods (118)	N.A.	N.A.	578.5	298.2	384.9
92. Molson Coors Brewing Co. (87)	N.A.	N.A.	444.2	406.0	382.8
93. Energizer Holdings (96)	N.A.	N.A.	N.A.	361.9	375.4
94. Philips Electronics (110)	N.A.	N.A.	N.A.	309.8	365.0
95. Burger King Holdings (99)	N.A.	N.A.	N.A.	357.0	364.0
96. Alltel Corp. (93)	N.A.	N.A.	N.A.	368.4	363.8
97. Metro-Goldwyn-Mayer (152)	N.A.	N.A.	N.A.	228.3	363.2
98. DirecTV Group (98)	N.A.	N.A.	N.A.	359.7	356.4
99. Wells Fargo & Co. (88)	N.A.	N.A.	N.A.	393.7	355.7
100. Walgreen Co. (112)	N.A.	N.A.	N.A.	306.4	355.4

Note: The top 100 companies are not the same each year. **Source:** *Advertising Age*, 100 Leading National Advertisers, 2008.

Education

The American people's unwavering commitment to public education dates back more than 150 years. Fueled by a demand for literacy from two different creeds, one described in the Bible, the other in the Declaration of Independence, the American system of education grew to be an essential element in our faith that this nation was uniquely the land of opportunity.

Today that belief has evolved into what is called equality of opportunity, and this vital idea has helped to create a school system whose size, scope and ambitions are unrivalled by any Western democracy. Nearly 74 million students and 5 million faculty, from elementary to college levels, are directly involved in education. The cost of this undertaking is, of course, staggering: more than half a trillion dollars annually—over $8,000 per student in 2005—or 7.4 percent of the gross domestic product (G.D.P.), virtually all of it for public education. The portion of G.D.P. spent on education rose rapidly between 1959 and 1969, declined in the 1970s as enrollment in elementary and secondary schools fell, and began rising steadily again in 1984. Since 1990, it has remained relatively stable. And while some complain bitterly about the quality of the results, or about overt waste, mismanagement and even fraud, no one any longer questions the essential role of education in American life today.

▶ PUBLIC ELEMENTARY AND SECONDARY SCHOOLS

Expenditures on public elementary and secondary schools have been increasing faster than inflation in almost every year since figures were first kept in 1900. The exception was the period between 1978 and 1982, when inflation outpaced increases in expenditures. Total expenditures for public elementary and secondary schools topped $550 billion in 2006–07, almost double what they were in 1996–97; on the basis of fall enrollment, expenditures per student were $8,701 in 2005. The accompanying table shows that even after adjusting for inflation, the amount spent to educate each student at public elementary and secondary schools continues to skyrocket.

In 1979, a historic shift occurred in the source of money to operate the American public school system. That was the year the state share of revenues rose above the local share for the first time. The federal share for elementary and secondary schools has always been relatively small.

Enrollment in public elementary schools declined dramatically from 1970 to 1985 (from 32.6 million to 27.0 million) as the number of young people decreased. That trend evidenced itself in secondary school populations between 1980 and 1990. Since 1990, however, populations of both elementary and secondary school populations have generally risen. For the fall of 2007, the U.S. Depart-

Revenues for Public Elementary and Secondary Schools, 1920–2006

School year	Total revenues (thousands)	Percentage		
		Federal	State	Local[1]
1919–20	$970	0.3%	16.5%	83.2%
1929–30	2,089	0.4	16.9	82.7
1939–40	2,261	1.8	30.3	68.0
1949–50	5,437	2.9	39.8	57.3
1959–60	14,747	4.4	39.1	56.5
1969–70	40,267	8.0	39.9	52.1
1979–80	96,881	9.8	46.8	43.4
1989–90	208,548	6.1	47.3	46.6
1995–96	287,703	6.6	47.5	45.9
1997–98	325,976	6.8	48.4	44.8
1999–2000	372,943	7.3	49.5	43.2
2001–2002	419,502	7.9	49.2	42.9
2002–2003	440,112	8.5	48.7	42.8
2003–2004	462,016	9.1	47.1	43.9
2005–2006	520,644	9.1	46.5	44.4

Notes: 1. Includes a relatively small amount from nongovernmental sources (gifts and tuition and transportation fees from patrons). These sources accounted for 2.5 percent of total revenues in 1997–98. **Source:** U.S. Dept. of Education, National Center for Education Statistics, Digest of Education Statistics, 2007.

Education Expenditures, 1950–2007

School year	All educational institutions		Elementary and Secondary schools			Colleges and Universities	
	Total expenditures (millions)	As percentage of GDP	Public			Public (millions)	Private (millions)
			Total (millions)	Per pupil (constant dollars)[1]	Private (millions)		
1949–50	$ 8,911	3.3%	$ 5,838	$1,738	$ 411	$ 1,430	$ 1,233
1959–60	23,860	4.7	15,613	2,668	1,100	3,904	3,244
1969–70	68,459	6.9	40,683	4,147	2,500	16,234	9,041
1979–80	165,627	6.5	95,962	5,255	7,200	41,434	21,031
1989–90	381,525	7.0	212,770	7,262	18,200	96,387	54,169
1995–96	508,523	6.9	293,646	8,299	24,400	119,525	70,952
1997–98	570,471	6.9	334,315	8,787	27,300	132,846	76,010
1999–2000	649,322	7.0	381,838	9,442	30,700	152,325	84,459
2001–02	752,780	7.4	435,364	10,046	36,700	183,436	97,280
2002–03	795,568	7.6	454,907	10,161	37,900	196,891	105,871
2003–04	829,913	7.6	473,863	10,286	39,300	205,069	111,682
2004–05	878,300	7.5	495,800	N/A	41,100	218,300	123,100
2005–06	921,800	7.4	515,600	N/A	42,700	229,900	133,600
2006–07	972,000	7.4	553,000	N/A	46,000	239,000	134,000

Notes: 1. Expenditure per pupil in fall enrollment, as measured in constant (2005-06) dollars, based on the Consumer Price Index. **Source:** U.S. Dept. of Education, National Center for Education Statistics, Digest of Education Statistics, 2007.

Number of Schools and Teachers in the U.S., Fall, 2006

School type	Schools			Teachers		
	Total	Public	Private	Total	Public[3]	Private
Elementary and secondary	**124,110**	**95,726**	**28,384**	**3,351,362**	**3,090,513**	**440,850**
Elementary	82,995	65,758	17,797	1,931,638	1,716,961	214,677
Secondary	25,476	22,782	2,694	1,219,007	1,150,663	68,334
Combined	13,931	5,437	8,494	380,719	222,889	157,830
Other schools	1,749	1,749	N.A.	N.A.	N.A.	N.A.
Colleges and universities[1]	**6,412**	**2,047**	**4,365**	**1,290,426**	**841,188**	**449,238**
4-year colleges[2]	2,530	634	1,896	916,996	486,691	430,305
2-year colleges[2]	1,706	1,086	620	373,430	354,497	18,933

Note: 1. Totals include non-degree granting institutions. 2. Title IV degree-granting only. 3. Public teacher figures are for 2004. **Source:** U.S. Dept. of Education, National Center for Education Statistics, Digest of Education Statistics, 2006.

School Enrollment, 1970–2007 (millions of students)

	Elementary (K-8)		Type of school Secondary (9-12)		Higher education		
Year	Public	Private	Public	Private	Public	Private	Total
1970	32.6	4.1	13.3	1.3	6.4	2.2	**59.9**
1975	30.5	3.7	14.3	1.3	8.8	2.4	**61.0**
1980	27.6	4.0	13.2	1.3	9.5	2.6	**58.3**
1985	27.0	4.2	12.4	1.4	9.5	2.8	**57.2**
1990	29.9	4.1[1]	11.3	1.2[1]	10.8	3.0	**60.3**
1995	32.3	4.4	12.5	1.3	11.1	3.2	**64.8**
1997	33.1	4.6	13.1	1.2	11.2	3.3	**66.5**
1998	33.3	4.7[1]	13.2	1.2[1]	11.1	3.4	**67.0**
1999	33.5	4.8	13.4	1.3	11.3	3.5	**67.7**
2000	33.7	4.9	13.5	1.3	11.8	3.6	**69.7**
2005	33.8	4.7	14.9	1.4	13.0	4.1	**72.7**
2006	33.9	4.8	15.0	1.4	13.4	4.1	**72.7**
2007	34.6	4.8	15.1	1.4	13.5	4.5	**73.9**

Note: Totals may not add up due to independent rounding.
Source: U.S. Dept. of Education, National Center for Education Statistics, Digest of Education Statistics, 2007.

ment of Education predicted a public elementary school population of 49.6 million; public secondary school enrollment reached 16.4 million. These numbers suggest that baby boomers started a baby boom of their own, often called the "boomlet", who started high school in the early 2000s.

Teachers have more than kept pace with the growth in the number of students. There were over 3.6 million elementary and secondary school teachers in 2007, more than double the number in 1955. The number of secondary school teachers has remained at about one million since 1975, while the number of public elementary school teachers has risen consistently every year since 1982, when they numbered 1.2 million. A more telling statistic, though, is pupil-teacher ratios. Despite constant complaints about overcrowded inner-city classrooms, the average number of pupils supervised by each teacher has declined dramatically in the past 30 years. It was projected that each public school teacher was responsible for 15.4 students in 2007, down from 16.8 in 1997. Each private school teacher was responsible for 13.2 students in 2007, down from 15.2 in 1997.

According to the American Federation of Teachers, during the 2005-06 year (the most recent year for which data is available) the average teacher salary was $49,026, while the average salary of a first-year teacher was $31,753. Those are increases of 2.2 percent and 3.1 percent, respectively, over the prior year, and after adjusting for inflation, a teacher's average salary is slightly higher than 1972 levels ($40,350). Since 1995, teacher salaries have increased faster than inflation. Teachers, perhaps because their salaries come from tax revenues, earn significantly less than other college graduates. A 2002 survey by the organization found that teachers earn 58 percent as much as engineers, 61 percent of a computer analyst's paycheck, and 82 percent of what an accountant makes. The AFT asserts that in order to make teacher pay competitive with other professions, teachers will need a 30 percent raise by the end of the decade.

Nursery schools have increased dramatically in popularity since 1965, when 27.1 percent of 3-to-5-year-olds were enrolled in a kindergarten or pre-kindergarten program. That percentage has increased gradually ever since, reaching a high of 65.8 percent in 1999. (In 2006, it was 56 percent.) The percentage of youngsters attending full-time nursery school has also risen. Only 17 percent of pre-primary students were in full-time programs in 1970; in 2000, 51.8 percent were full-time enrollees. Most nursery school students were in private schools, while most kindergarten students were enrolled in public schools.

School districts declined drastically between 1930, when there were 119,000 of them, and 1984, when there were a mere 15,695. Numbers since 1985 are not directly comparable with earlier years, but school districts have continued

How the States Rank in Public Education, 2005–2006

State	Enrollment	Rank	Expenditures per pupil[2]	Rank	Average teacher salary	Rank
U.S.	48,727,536[1]	—	$9,100	—	$49,026[1]	—
Alabama	738,450	23	7,706	42	40,347	44
Alaska	133,437	45	10,171	13	53,553	13
Arizona	1,010,094[1]	15	5,585	50	44,672[1]	24
Arkansas	453,209	34	8,402	30	42,768	32
California	6,309,689	1	8,486	29	59,825	1
Colorado	780,708	22	8,861	24	44,439	25
Connecticut	576,772	28	12,436	6	59,304	2
D.C.	61,484	51	15,508	1	59,000[1]	3
Delaware	120,938	46	12,036	7	54,264	11
Florida	2,669,565	4	7,762	41	43,302	29
Georgia	1,598,461	9	8,534	27	48,300	18
Hawaii	182,767	42	9,879	18	49,292	16
Idaho	261,907	39	7,042	46	41,150[1]	38
Illinois	2,111,312	5	9,456	21	58,686	4
Indiana	1,034,399	13	8,935	23	47,255	19
Iowa	483,482	32	7,807	39	41,083	39
Kansas	467,201	33	8,373	32	41,467	37
Kentucky	641,913	26	8,300	34	42,592	33
Louisiana	654,146	25	8,519	28	40,029	45
Maine	199,118[1]	41	11,285	9	40,737	40
Maryland	865,836	20	9,771	19	54,333	10
Massachusetts	971,909	16	12,596	4	56,369	7
Michigan	1,741,737[1]	8	9,880	17	54,739	8
Minnesota	835,588[1]	21	9,675	20	48,489[1]	17
Mississippi	494,038	30	7,215	45	40,576	41
Missouri	899,997	18	7,840	38	40,462	42
Montana	145,416	44	8,361	33	39,832[1]	47
Nebraska	285,549	37	7,900	37	40,382	43
Nevada	413,252	35	6,755	49	44,426	26
New Hampshire	205,567	40	10,206	12	45,263	23
New Jersey	1,394,779	10	13,781	2	58,156[1]	5
New Mexico	326,859	36	8,622	26	41,637	36
New York	2,815,504[1]	3	13,551	3	57,354[1]	6
North Carolina	1,376,530	11	7,675	43	43,922	27
North Dakota	97,120	48	7,807	40	37,764	50
Ohio	1,862,880	6	10,034	14	50,314[1]	14
Oklahoma	634,468	27	6,944	48	38,772	48
Oregon	559,254	29	8,649	25	50,044	15
Pennsylvania	1,830,684	7	10,711	11	54,027[1]	12
Rhode Island	161,237[1]	43	11,089	10	54,730[1]	9
South Carolina	694,155	24	8,377	31	43,011	31
South Dakota	120,682	47	7,911	36	34,709	51
Tennessee	939,571	17	6,979	47	42,537	34
Texas	4,505,572	2	7,547	44	41,744	35
Utah	484,623	31	5,347	51	40,007	46
Vermont	94,600	49	12,475	5	46,622[1]	20
Virginia	1,214,737	12	9,275	22	43,823[1]	28
Washington	1,033,489	14	7,958	35	46,326	22
West Virginia	279,788	38	9,886	16	38,284	49
Wisconsin	875,174	19	9,965	15	46,390[1]	21
Wyoming	83,705	50	11,596	8	43,255	30

Notes: 1. Data estimated by NEA.   2. Data from NEA estimates for all states except CA.
Source: National Education Association, *Rankings & Estimates*, 2005–2006 (2007).

to decline. There were 14,166 public school districts in 2005-06, down from 14,205 in 2004-05. The greatest number of school districts had between 1,000 and 2,499 students in them, but school districts with 25,000 students or more were responsible for educating nearly one-third of public school students.

▶ PRIVATE SCHOOLS
The U.S. Department of Education updates its data on private schools less frequently than it does for public institutions. The 2006-07 school year is the latest year for which data is available for private elementary and secondary schools.

Schools and enrollment There were 28,996 private schools engaged in educating 5,057,520 students. Of these schools, 16,812 were elementary schools (responsible for educating 2,551,196 students), 2,927 were secondary schools (859,453 students), and 9,257 offered instruction in all 12 grades (1,646,871 students). Most private schools were religiously affiliated. One-fourth, or 7,634 schools, were affiliated with the Catholic Church; 14,445 were affiliated with other religious groups.

6,916 private schools were nonsectarian, nearly half the number of nonsectarian schools in 2003-2004.

Tuition Average tuition for private school students was $6,600 per year in 2003-04, but that average is kept low by the large number of parochial schools offering free or low-cost private education. The average cost of all nonsectarian private schools (elementary and secondary) was $13,419, and more than half of such schools charge at least $7,500 per year in tuition. Average tuition for non-

sectarian secondary schools was $17,413 per year, almost twice as much than a decade ago.

Teachers There were 479,775 full-time private school teachers in the 2005-06 school year. In 2004, the average teacher salary in private schools was $34,700, a fraction of the $47,700 earned by public school teachers. Male teachers earned substantially more than their female counterparts in both public and private schools, but the difference was most pronounced in private schools, where male compensation ($40,800) was 20 percent greater than female salaries ($32,800).

Catholic Schools, Pupils & Teachers, 1960–2008

Year	Schools	Pupils	Total	Religious	Lay
			Teachers		
Elementary schools					
1960	10,501	4,373,000	108,000	79,000	29,000
1970	9,362	3,355,000	112,000	52,000	60,000
1980	8,043	2,269,000	97,000	25,000	72,000
1990	7,291	1,883,906	91,039	10,837	80,202
1995	6,979	1,990,784	116,494	10,564	105,930
2000	6,923	2,013,084	109,404	6,862	102,542
2005	6,574	1,779,638	107,764	4,686	103,078
2007	6,288	1,682,412	107,682	4,097	103,585
2008	6,165	1,633,535	107,217	3,825	103,392
Secondary schools					
1960	2,392	880,000	44,000	33,000	11,000
1970	1,981	1,008,000	55,000	29,000	26,000
1980	1,516	837,000	49,000	14,000	35,000
1990	1,296	591,533	40,159	6,579	33,580
1995	1,238	614,571	46,599	6,193	40,406
2000	1,221	639,954	47,730	4,149	43,581
2005	1,225	640,952	52,389	3,304	49,085
2007	1,210	638,239	51,453	2,967	48,486
2008	1,213	637,378	52,858	2,769	50,089

Source: National Catholic Educational Association.

Average SAT and ACT Scores by Group, 1987–2008

Group	1987	1990	1997	2000	2008[2]	Total test-takers, class of 2008
			Composite scores			
SAT Scores						
American Indian, Alaskan Native	934	934	963	963	976	9,595
Asian American, Pacific Islander	1,020	1,029	1,060	1,064	1,094	151,235
Black	839	847	860	860	856	174,383
Mexican-American	912	917	913	913	917	70,661
Puerto Rican	868	872	899	907	909	21,953
Other Hispanic	926	923	927	928	916	97,589
White	1,038	1,034	1,054	1,058	1,065	858,561
Men	1,035	1,026	1,040	1,040	1,008	704,226
Women	983	989	998	1,002	963	812,764
National average[1]	**1,008**	**1,001**	**1,017**	**1,019**	**1,017**	**1,518,859**
ACT Scores						
American Indian, Alaskan Native	17.5	18.0	19.0	19.0	19.0	14,380
Asian American, Pacific Islander	21.9	21.7	21.8	21.7	22.9	51,368
Black	16.6	17.0	17.1	17.0	16.9	178,417
Mexican-American	18.1	18.3	18.5	18.6	N.A.	N.A.
Other Hispanic	19.3	19.3	19.6	19.5	18.7	114,697
White	21.3	21.2	21.7	21.8	22.1	895,588
Men	21.2	21.0	21.2	21.2	21.2	625,887
Women	20.1	20.3	20.9	20.9	21.0	764,282
National average[1]	**20.6**	**20.6**	**21.0**	**21.0**	**21.2**	**1,421,941**

1. Includes students of other ethnicities and students who did not identify their gender or their ethnicity. 2. Composite score does not include the 2008 SAT writing section. **Source:** The College Board, American College Testing Program.

Race and ethnicity Private schools are traditionally white enclaves; three-quarters of students were white in the 2005-06 school year. Yet the enrollment of minority students in private schools continues to rise. In 2005-06, total black enrollment was up to 9.5 percent, and Hispanic to 9.2 percent. Catholic schools had a total minority population of 25.9 percent, and 12.6 percent of private school students were Hispanic.

Student-teacher ratios Students in private schools continue to get more teacher attention than do students in public schools. The average teacher in public elementary and secondary schools was responsible for 15.5 students, compared to 13.4 students for private school teachers in 2006-07.

Average Cost of 4-Year Colleges in Current and Constant Dollars, 1971–2008 (tuition and fees)

The cost of a college education continues to skyrocket. Tuition and fees in 2007–08 were more than three times what they were as recently as 1985–86, and nearly ten times what they were in 1976–77.

In constant dollars (which negates the effect of inflation), the cost of college has nearly doubled since 1985-86. That's a departure from the trend during the 1970s, when the real cost of college actually decreased several times, and never reached $8,000.

Tuition and fees are in addition to room and board charges at most 4-year colleges (unless students commute). Room and board charges averaged $7,404 at public colleges, and $8,595 at private colleges, pushing the total cost of a private college education to $35,374 a year.

According to a 2002 study by the Public Interest Research Group, the percentage of students who went into debt to finance their educations rose from 42 percent in 1992 to 64 percent in 2000. By 2004, more than two-thirds of students graduated with college loans. The average debt of graduating seniors was $16,928 in 2000, and up to $19,200 in

Tuition and fees

	Current dollars		Constant dollars	
Year	Private	Public	Private	Public
1976–77	$2,272	$433	$7,940	$1,933
1980–81	3,617	804	7,679	1,707
1985–86	6,121	1,318	10,344	2,227
1990–91	9,340	1,908	12,826	2,620
1991–92	9,812	2,107	13,056	2,804
1992–93	10,448	2,334	13,481	3,012
1993–94	11,007	2,535	13,844	3,188
1994–95	11,719	2,705	14,328	3,307
1995–96	12,216	2,811	14,541	3,346
1996–97	12,994	2,975	15,038	3,443
1997–98	13,785	3,111	15,674	3,537
1998–99	14,709	3,247	16,454	3,632
1999–2000	15,518	3,362	16,876	3,656
2000–01	16,233	3,487	17,050	3,662
2001–02	17,272	3,725	17,825	3,844
2002–03	18,273	4,081	18,779	4,155
2003–04	19,710	4,694	19,710	4,694
2004–05	20,082	5,132	20,082	5,132
2005–06	21,235	5,491	21,235	5,491
2006–07	22,218	5,836	22,218	5,836
2007–08	23,712	6,185	23,712	6,185

Source: The College Board, *Trends in College Pricing, 2007*

▶COLLEGE ENTRANCE EXAMINATION SCORES

SATs (Scholastic Assessment Tests) purportedly measure verbal and mathematical reasoning abilities. These tests are administered by the College Board, a nonprofit organization that provides tests and many other educational services for students, schools and colleges.

In March 2005, the College Board revised the SAT: the analogies section was replaced with short reading sections, and a written essay section was added for the first time. The class of 2006 was the first to take the new version. In addition, the math portion of the test covers concepts taught in advanced high school algebra courses.

The test is scored on a range from 400 to 2200, with average scores usually around 900. Male students consistently outscore females on the SAT, and whites and Asians typically score about 100 points higher than all other ethnic groups, and about 200 points higher than blacks. In response to criticisms of racial and gender bias, the College Board rewrote the SAT in 1994 to make it a test of aptitude, rather than of knowledge or test-taking techniques. The new test had more open-ended questions, which the College Board claimed made the test uncoachable. But scores on the new test

Most Popular Majors Among Incoming Freshmen, 1990–2007

	Percentage		
Major	1990	2000	2007
Arts and Humanities, total	N.A.	N.A.	12.8%
Art, fine and applied	2.0%	2.5%	2.5
English	1.0	1.7	1.9
Journalism	N.A.	1.7	1.8
Biological Science, total	N.A.	N.A.	8.6
General biology	1.8	3.6	4.7
Business, total	N.A.	N.A.	17.7
Accounting	5.3	2.3	2.6
Business administration	5.5	4.1	3.6
Finance	N.A.	1.7	2.2
Marketing	2.5	2.7	2.9
Management	4.0	3.3	3.9
Education, total	N.A.	N.A.	9.2
Elementary education	5.1	5.6	4.0
Secondary education	1.9	2.5	2.3
Engineering, total	N.A.	N.A.	7.5
Electrical engineering	2.5	2.0	1.2
Mechanical engineering	2.0	1.9	1.9
Physical Science, total	N.A.	N.A.	3.2
Professional, total	N.A.	N.A.	14.5
Premedicine, predental, preveterinary	3.2	4.4	4.2
Nursing	4.2	2.1	4.2
Therapy	2.3	1.9	2.3
Social Science, total	N.A.	N.A.	11.1
Political science	3.0	2.8	3.4
Psychology	4.2	4.8	4.7
Technical, total	N.A.	N.A.	1.0
Other fields, total	N.A.	N.A.	14.2
Communications	2.3	2.7	N.A.
Computer science	1.7	3.7	N.A.

Note: Totals include other categories not shown separately.
Source: Higher Education Research Institute, University of California, Los Angeles, *The American Freshman: National Norms for Fall,* 2008.

suffered from the same gender and ethnicity gaps as the old test.

In 2002, the College Board published figures showing that scores generally reflect income levels (students from the poorest homes scored lowest; those from the wealthiest homes scored highest).

ACTs are administered by the American College Testing Program, a nonprofit educational organization headquartered in Iowa City, Iowa. Its use is more popular than the SAT in states west of the Mississippi River. The ACT composite score is the average of four tests that measure academic

Educational Attainment by State, 2006

State	Persons over 25 ('000s)	Completed 4 years high school or more	Completed 4 years college or more
Alabama	3,009	82.1%	20.8%
Alaska	405	92.0	27.7
Arizona	3,821	83.1	24.5
Arkansas	1,822	82.5	19.0
California	22,710	80.8	29.8
Colorado	3,034	90.0	36.4
Connecticut	2,380	88.4	36.0
Delaware	570	86.0	26.2
Dist. of Columbia	369	83.3	49.1
Florida	12,282	86.7	27.2
Georgia	5,708	84.2	28.1
Hawaii	873	88.7	32.3
Idaho	927	88.9	25.1
Illinois	8,094	87.6	31.2
Indiana	3,956	88.2	21.9
Iowa	1,937	90.4	24.7
Kansas	1,707	90.2	31.6
Kentucky	2,658	79.9	20.2
Louisiana	2,593	79.7	21.2
Maine	905	89.3	26.9
Maryland	3,681	87.2	35.7
Massachusetts	4,243	89.9	40.4
Michigan	6,534	89.7	26.1
Minnesota	3,386	93.0	33.5
Mississippi	1,821	81.1	21.1
Missouri	3,792	87.1	24.3
Montana	628	91.4	25.1
Nebraska	1,161	91.0	27.2
Nevada	1,579	85.6	20.8
New Hampshire	893	91.6	32.1
New Jersey	5,788	86.7	35.6
New Mexico	1,232	81.8	26.7
New York	12,693	85.1	32.2
North Carolina	5,666	84.2	25.6
North Dakota	419	88.7	28.7
Ohio	7,467	88.1	23.3
Oklahoma	2,283	87.5	22.9
Oregon	2,415	89.7	28.3
Pennsylvania	8,266	87.5	26.6
Rhode Island	694	84.0	30.9
South Carolina	2,759	83.1	22.6
South Dakota	498	89.9	25.3
Tennessee	3,869	80.7	22.0
Texas	14,190	78.7	25.5
Utah	1,433	91.2	27.0
Vermont	420	91.0	34.0
Virginia	4,923	86.5	32.1
Washington	4,145	91.1	31.4
West Virginia	1,254	81.5	15.9
Wisconsin	3,652	91.1	24.6
Wyoming	339	91.1	20.8

Source: U.S. Bureau of the Census, *Current Population Survey,* 2006 (2007).

abilities in English, mathematics, social studies and natural sciences. Although similar numbers of students take each test, the ACT draws less criticism than the SAT, even though both tests evidence similar racial and gender biases.

▶ HIGHER EDUCATION

The accompanying figures give a startling picture of just how the coming of age of the baby boom generation transformed U.S. higher education. In just one decade (the 1960s) the number of undergraduate degrees conferred more than doubled, while the number of doctorates actually tripled. These extraordinary changes were matched in kind by dramatic shifts in what students wanted to study: during the late 1960s, for example, the number of degrees in sociology and psychology jumped by more than 15,000 each in just a few years (1966–1970), while interest in business soared during the 1980s. That trend reversed in the 1990s, as the need for social workers and other health and human service professionals has expanded.

College enrollment Between 1980 and 1992, college enrollment increased about 20 percent, from just over 12 million to a record 14.5 million. Since then, enrollment has increased only to approximately 17.9 million in 2007, even though the traditional college-age population has dropped. This is projected to rise to 19 million by 2011. Much of the growth in college enrollment was fueled by increases in older students, women and minorities on campus. Women have outnumbered men on college campuses since 1979, when there were just under 6 million of each in institutions of higher education. Since then, male enrollment has increased only to 7.5 million, while female enrollment has leapt to 10.1 million. Minorities, especially Hispanics and Asians, have increased from 15.7 percent of the campus population in 1976 to 28.2 percent in 2000, the latest year for which statistics are available. The percentage of blacks on campus fluctuated for many years, but began increasing again in 1990. In 2000, non-Hispanic blacks made up 11.3 percent of college students, up from 9.3 percent in 1990.

▶ EDUCATIONAL ATTAINMENT

In 2007, approximately 87 percent of all adults over age 25 had completed high school, and more than a quarter of American adults had a bachelor's degree or more. It's not surprising that those numbers were both much lower in 1940, when only 24 percent of adults who graduated from high school and college degrees belonged to fewer than 5 percent of the population. But even as recently as 1980, only 69 percent of adults over 25 had a high school diploma and only 17 percent had graduated from college. (See the accompanying table.)

The greatest proof of the importance of education is the correlation between years of schooling and higher salaries. In 2006, the median annual income for men with bachelor's degrees was $60,910 per year and $45,410 for women, compared with $37,030 for men and $26,740 for women with only high school diplomas. At the extreme ends of the spectrum, men with doctorates had a median income of $100,000 ($70,520 for women) while men who failed to graduate from high school measured at only $27,650 (women at $20,130).

Number Of Degrees Conferred in U.S. by Type, 1950–2009

Year	All degrees[1]	Associate's	Bachelor's	First professional	Master's	Doctorate
1949–50	496,661	N.A.	432,058[2]	[2]	58,183	6,420
1959–60	476,704	N.A.	392,440[2]	[2]	74,435	9,829
1969-70	1,065,098	206,023	792,317	34,578	208,291	29,912
1979-80	1,330,244	400,910	929,417	70,131	298,081	32,615
1989-90	1,485,004	455,102	1,051,344	70,988	324,301	38,371
1997-98	1,739,178	558,555	1,184,406	78,598	430,164	46,010
1999-2000	1,819,796	564,933	1,237,875	80,057	457,056	44,808
2002-03	1,987,982	632,912	1,348,503	80,810	512,645	46,024
2003-04	2,089,902	665,301	1,399,542	83,042	558,940	48,378
2004-05	2,110,200	696,660	1,416,000	85,000	562,000	47,200
2006-07	2,228,900	686,000	1,448,000	87,400	603,000	50,500
2007-08[3]	3,018,600	699,000	1,544,000	89,300	631,000	55,300
2008-09[3]	3,092,800	714,000	1,585,000	91,000	647,000	55,800

Note: Does not include associate of arts (A.A.); more than 500,000 of these have been given since 1992. 1. Degrees are: medical doctor, law, dentistry, optometry, podiatry, pharmacy, theology, chiropractic, and veterinary medicine. 2. Prior to 1961, bachelor's and first professional degrees were listed together. 3. Projected. **Source:** U.S. Dept. of Education, National Center for Education Statistics, Digest of Education Statistics, (2007).

Educational Attainment of the Population 25+ Years, 1940–2007

	Completed 4 years of high school or more			Completed 4 years of college or more		
Year	Both Sexes	Male	Female	Both Sexes	Male	Female
1940	24.5%	22.7%	26.3%	4.6%	5.5%	3.8%
1950	34.3	32.6	36.0	6.2	7.3	5.2
1959	43.7	42.2	45.2	8.1	10.3	6.0
1970	55.2	55.0	55.4	11.0	14.1	8.2
1980	68.6	69.1	68.1	17.0	20.8	13.5
1991	78.4	78.5	78.3	21.4	24.3	18.8
1995	81.7	81.7	81.6	23.0	26.0	20.2
2000	84.1	84.2	84.0	25.6	27.8	23.6
2003	84.6	84.1	85.0	27.2	28.9	25.7
2005	85.2	84.8	85.4	27.7	29.4	26.1
2006	85.5	85.0	85.9	28.0	29.2	26.9
2007	87.0	84.9	89.1	29.6	26.3	33.0

Source: Bureau of the Census, Current Population Survey: Educational Attainment in the United States, March 2007 (2008).

Educational Attainment of the Population, Ages 18 and Over, 2007

Characteristic	Number of people	Highest Level of Attainment			
		None	High school	Some college	Bachelor's degree
All persons	222,723,000	0.4%	31.5%	19.0%	17.5%
Sex:					
Male	107,843,000	0.4	31.7	18.4	17.1
Female	114,880,000	0.4	31.3	19.6	17.8
Race and Hispanic origin:					
White	181,414,000	0.3	31.4	19.0	17.8
Black	25,991,000	0.4	36.3	20.7	11.6
Asian	8,552,000	1.5	24.0	15.8	35.6
Hispanic origin[1]	29,637,000	1.5	29.3	14.9	8.3
Age groups:					
25 to 29 years	20,666,000	0.3	29.3	19.1	23.3
30 to 34 years	19,202,000	0.2	27.9	17.1	22.2
35 to 39 years	20,907,000	0.2	28.7	15.9	22.8
40 to 44 years	21,856,000	0.2	30.6	16.8	21.6
45 to 49 years	22,643,000	0.3	32.7	16.9	19.5
50 to 54 years	20,819,000	0.4	31.5	17.3	19.0
55 to 59 years	18,221,000	0.5	29.6	18.3	19.1
60 to 64 years	13,970,000	0.5	32.4	17.2	16.1
65 to 69 years	10,629,000	0.6	36.6	15.6	12.3
70 to 74 years	8,369,000	0.7	36.9	14.2	12.2
75 years or older	17,037,000	1.1	38.1	13.2	9.8

Note: 1. People of Hispanic origin may be of any race. **Source:** Bureau of the Census, Current Population Survey: Educational Attainment in the United States, March 2007 (2008).

U.S. Energy

►ENERGY PRODUCTION AND CONSUMPTION

Energy is usually measured in millions or larger quantities of British thermal units (Btu). One Btu is approximately equal to the energy released in burning a wooden match. An engine burning eight gallons of gasoline releases one million (10^6) Btu. One quadrillion (10^{15}) Btu is the equivalent of the energy released from an engine burning eight billion gallons of gasoline.

Total U.S. energy production was 71.71 quadrillion Btu in 2007. Natural gas and coal each accounted for more than one-quarter of domestic energy production. Fossil fuels, which also include crude oil, accounted for nearly 80 percent of all energy production, down from 95 percent as recently as 1970. Nuclear energy (11.7 percent) and renewable energy forms like solar energy and wind power (9.2 percent) have made up the difference.

U.S. energy consumption hit an all-time high of 101.6 quadrillion Btu in 2006. Since the U.S. consumes more energy than it produces, it must import the difference.

Despite increasing prices for all forms of energy, American consumers continue to be lavish in their use, opting for convenience over energy efficiency at nearly every turn. The average home size increased by more than 500 square feet between 1973 and 1997 (bringing with it an attendant increase in heating costs), and is now packed with many more energy-sucking appliances than ever before, including whirlpool tubs, microwave ovens, toaster-ovens, washer-dryers, and central air-conditioning. In addition, Americans are driving bigger, less-efficient cars and trucks, and are driving them more total miles each year, thus consuming more gas than ever before.

Petroleum continues to be the energy of choice among U.S. consumers. It accounted for nearly 40 percent of all U.S. energy consumption in 2007, compared to 23.3 percent for natural gas and 22.4 percent for coal. Consumption of nuclear energy has grown steadily from nearly zero in 1960 to 8.23 quadrillion Btu in 2006. Renewable energy consumption grew similarly, from 1.66 quadrillion Btu, in 1960, to more than 7 quadrillion Btu in 1997; since then, it has fallen back to 6.7 quadrillion Btu in 2007.

There are, however, federal initiatives to increase biodiesel production, especially ethanol, mandated by the Energy Policy Act of 2005. According to the Renewable Fuels Association, there were 168 operating in 2008 at a total capacity of 9.96 billion gallons per year, with another 36 refineries under construction. Currently, nearly half of all gasoline in the United States is blended with ethanol.

As a result, the cost for farmland, especially in the midwest, is skyrocketing. In Iowa, where more corn is grown and more ethanol produced than in any other state, land costs increased by 10 percent in 2007. The federal government gives a 51-cent-tax credit per gallon to ethanol producers, and maintains a 54-cent-a-gallon tariff on ethanol imported from Brazil.

The relationship between total energy consumption and real gross domestic product (GDP) is a primary indicator of the energy intensity of the

U.S. Energy Overview, 1960–2007

Activity and energy source	(Quadrillion Btu)							As percent of total, 2007
	1960	1970	1980	1990	2000	2006	2007[1]	
Production, Total	**41.49**	**63.50**	**67.24**	**70.84**	**71.22**	**71.03**	**71.71**	**100.0%**
Coal	10.82	14.61	18.60	22.46	22.62	23.79	23.48	32.7
Natural gas (dry)	12.66	21.67	19.91	18.36	19.66	19.02	19.82	27.6
Crude oil[2]	14.93	20.40	18.25	15.57	12.36	10.88	10.80	15.1
Natural gas plant liquids	1.46	2.51	2.25	2.17	2.61	2.35	2.40	3.3
Nuclear electric power	0.01	0.24	2.74	6.16	7.86	8.21	8.42	11.7
Renewable energy[3]	1.61	4.08	5.49	6.14	6.16	6.79	6.80	9.2
Imports, Total	**4.23**	**8.39**	**15.97**	**18.95**	**28.97**	**34.49**	**35.00**	**100.0%**
Natural gas	0.16	0.85	1.01	1.55	3.87	4.25	4.72	13.5
Petroleum[4]	4.00	7.47	14.66	17.12	24.53	29.03	28.70	82.0
Other[5]	0.07	0.07	0.31	0.29	0.58	1.21	1.58	4.5
Exports, Total	**1.48**	**2.66**	**3.72**	**4.87**	**4.01**	**4.93**	**5.36**	**100.0%**
Coal	1.02	1.94	2.42	2.77	1.53	1.26	1.51	28.2
Petroleum	0.43	0.55	1.16	1.82	2.15	2.78	2.93	54.7
Other[6]	0.03	0.18	0.14	0.27	0.33	0.88	0.92	16.8
Consumption, Total	**43.80**	**67.86**	**78.44**	**84.34**	**98.90**	**99.80**	**101.60**	**100.0%**
Coal	9.84	12.26	15.42	19.25	22.58	22.60	22.77	22.4
Natural gas	12.39	21.79	20.39	19.30	23.92	22.40	23.64	23.3
Petroleum products[7]	19.92	29.52	34.20	33.55	38.40	39.80	39.82	39.2
Nuclear electric power	0.01	0.24	2.74	6.16	7.86	8.20	8.42	8.3
Renewable energy[3]	1.66	4.10	5.71	6.25	6.16	6.80	6.83	6.7

Notes: Sum of components may not equal 100 percent due to independent rounding. 1. Preliminary. 2. Includes lease condensate. 3. Includes hydroelectric power, geothermal energy, solar energy, wind energy, and biofuels such as wood waste, landfill gases, fish oils, and other waste. 4. Includes imports of crude oil for the Strategic Petroleum Reserve, which began in 1977. 5. Includes coal, coal coke, and electricity. 6. Includes natural gas, coal coke, and petroleum products. 7. Petroleum products supplied include natural gas plant liquids and crude oil burned as fuel. **Source:** U.S. Dept. of Energy, *Annual Energy Review 2007* (2008).

economy. In 1949, the country used 19,570 Btu of energy per dollar of GDP (measured in constant 2000 dollars). Since then, energy consumption has more than tripled, but increases in energy efficiency, conservation, and the expansion of the service sector of the economy have propelled GDP sixfold. As a result, energy consumption now totals only 8,750 Btu per dollar of GDP, or approximately half what it was in 1949. In other words, the country is using much more energy, but literally getting twice as much bang for its buck.

A second indicator is per capita consumption, which rose from 215 million Btu per capita in 1949 to a record 360 million Btu in 1978. Efforts at conservation persuaded people to decrease their consumption to 314 million Btu in 1983, but per capita use has rebounded since then, to 337 mil-

lion Btu in 2007. Alaska and Louisiana were the biggest per capita consumers of energy in 2004. Hawaii and Arizona used the least energy per capita because so few houses need to be heated. *(For information about energy consumption and production worldwide, see Part III: World Energy).*

▶FOSSIL FUELS
Petroleum

Since 1958 the United States has consumed more energy than it produces; the difference has been met with energy imports. Net imports of energy (primarily petroleum) grew rapidly through 1973, when they totaled 13 quadrillion Btu, or 20 percent of consumption.

Despite the Arab oil embargo of 1973–74 and increases in the price of crude oil, petroleum net imports continued to grow, reaching a peak of nearly 19 quadrillion Btu in 1977. That year, U.S. dependence on petroleum net imports peaked at 47 percent of consumption. In 1985, petroleum net imports dropped to 9 quadrillion Btu and U.S. dependence on foreign oil fell to 27 percent of consumption, its lowest level since 1972.

But a drop in the worldwide price of oil ($12.52 per barrel in 1998, its lowest level in more than two decades) inhibited domestic production and caused U.S. reliance on imports to spring back. Oil prices spiked to $28.26 per barrel in 2000, retreated to $22.95 in 2001, and rebounded to $28.50 in 2003. On August 30, 2005, after Hurricane Katrina hit the Gulf coast, the price of oil skyrocketed to an all-time high of $70.85 a barrel, and continued to rise thereafter, crossing the $100.00 mark in January 2008 and holding near $134.00 a barrel through summer 2008. Saudi Arabia, Venezuela, Canada and Mexico are the U.S.'s primary suppliers of foreign oil; each exports more than 1.3 million barrels of oil per day to the U.S.

In June 2006, oil from Canada arrived to Cushing, Okla., a key hub for distribution in the U.S. In 2005, Canada provided 16.1 percent of U.S. oil imports, but this figure is bound to increase as six new pipelines are scheduled to open by 2011, helping to replace oil from less reliable sources.

U.S. Energy Consumption, Total and Per Capita, 1950–2007

Year	Total energy consumption (billion Btu)	Per capita consumption (billion Btu)
1950	34,630,000	.229
1955	40,240,000	.244
1960	45,120,000	.252
1965	54,016,000	.279
1970	67,858,000	.334
1975	72,040,000	.334
1980	78,435,000	.346
1985	76,705,000	.322
1990	84,567,000	.340
1995	91,501,000	.343
2000	98,900,000	.351
2005	100,157,000	.340
2006	100,747,000	.334
2007	101,600,000	.337

Note: 1. Preliminary. **Source:** U.S. Dept. of Energy, *Annual Energy Review 2007* (2008).

U.S. Fuel Consumption by Type and End-Use Sector, 1950–2007 (quadrillion Btu)

Year	Residential	Commercial	Industrial	Transportation	Electric utilities	Total
Petroleum						
1950	1.340	0.862	3.951	6.690	0.472	13.315
1960	2.265	1.228	5.747	10.126	0.553	19.919
1970	2.755	1.551	7.787	15.310	2.117	29.520
1980	1.748	1.287	9.525	19.008	2.634	34.202
1990	1.407	0.953	8.278	21.625	1.289	33.552
2000	1.563	0.756	9.120	25.820	1.144	38.403
2007[1]	1.283	0.631	9.523	27.719	0.660	39.816
Natural Gas						
1950	1.240	0.401	3.546	0.130	0.651	5.968
1960	3.212	1.056	5.973	0.359	1.785	12.385
1970	4.987	2.473	9.536	0.745	4.054	21.795
1980	4.866	2.674	8.395	0.650	3.810	20.395
1990	4.523	2.701	8.502	0.680	3.332	19.738
2000	5.126	3.265	9.535	0.672	5.316	23.914
2007[1]	4.842	3.083	7.999	0.667	7.046	23.667
Coal						
1950	1.261	1.542	5.781	1.564	2.199	12.347
1960	0.585	0.407	4.543	0.075	4.228	9.838
1970	0.209	0.165	4.656	0.007	7.227	12.264
1980	0.031	0.115	3.155	[2]	12.123	12.123
1990	0.031	0.124	2.756	[2]	16.261	16.261
2000	0.011	0.092	2.256	[2]	20.220	22.579
2007[1]	0.006	0.065	1.861	[2]	20.835	22.767

Notes: 1. Preliminary. 2. Small quantities consumed by transportation sector are included in industrial column. **Source:** U.S. Dept. of Energy, *Annual Energy Review 2007* (2008).

Natural gas

Once considered a useless byproduct of oil well drilling (it was simply burned off at the site), natural gas is today the primary source of energy for space heating in 56 million U.S. households. U.S. natural gas trade was limited to the border countries of Mexico and Canada until shipping natural gas in liquefied form emerged as an alternative to pipelines. In 1969, the first shipments of liquefied natural gas (LNG) were sent to Japan, and U.S. imports from Algeria began the following year. In 2007, U.S. net imports of natural gas by all routes totaled 4.72 quadrillion Btu (almost all of it from Canada).

Coal

Since World War II coal has been the major U.S. energy export. Throughout most of the 1960s and 1970s, U.S. exports of coal increased, peaking at 112 million short tons in 1981. Exports have dropped steadily since 1991, when they totaled 109 million short tons; in 2006, exports were 49.6 million short tons, or less than half the 1991 total. Canada is the largest market for U.S. coal, importing close to 15 million tons in 2006. Japan, which imported more than 25 million short tons as recently as 1982, imported less than 2 million short tons from the U.S. in 2006.

Electric utilities are the primary domestic consumers of coal. Their consumption grew from 17 percent of the total in 1949 to 92 percent in 2006. Over the same period, consumption in all other sectors declined, most dramatically in the transportation sector, due primarily to railroads switching from coal to petroleum-driven trains. Transportation sector consumption, which topped 70 million short tons in 1949, has totaled fewer than 50,000 short tons every year since 1975. Consumption by the residential and commercial sector has also declined steadily, from a high of 117 million short tons in 1949 to 4.2 million short tons in 2006.

▶ THE STRATEGIC PETROLEUM RESERVE

In an attempt to minimize the wild fluctuations in prices caused by the Arab oil embargoes of the 1970s, the U.S. in 1977 created the Strategic Petroleum Reserve, which permitted the storage of 580 million barrels of oil. The reserve proved useful in preventing additional oil price hikes during the Iraqi invasion of Kuwait in 1990.

The reserve can also be used as an emergency supply of oil in case of a disaster such as Hurricane Katrina (2005), which shut down production and refining in the Gulf of Mexico for weeks. In 1985, the reserve held enough oil to provide a normal level of petroleum to the U.S. for 115 days in the absence of any other petroleum imports. Since then, however, the reserve has dwindled to 56 days of oil.

▶ ELECTRICITY

Net generation of electricity by electric utilities topped 2.5 trillion megawatthours (mWh) in 2006. Coal continued to fuel more than half the generation, accounting for 1.5 trillion mWh, while natural gas contributed 272 billion mWh. Petroleum-fired generation was responsible for 41 billion mWh, while nuclear-based generation was 458 billion mWh in 2006. Hydroelectric generation rebounded from an all-time low of 166 billion mWh in 2001 to 633 billion mWh in 2006.

The weighted average real price (based on 2000 dollars) of electricity to all sectors in 2004 was 6.99 cents per kWh, 30 percent below the price in 1982, but about the same as in 1974. But although prices of other major energy sources increased significantly during the same period, electricity remained by far the most expensive source of energy on a Btu basis.

▶ NUCLEAR POWER

The number of nuclear power plants in operation in the U.S. skyrocketed from 18 in 1970 to 112 in 1990, and net nuclear generation of electricity jumped from 21.8 to 577 billion kWh. Since 1990, three new plants have opened and 10 have closed, but generation nonetheless increased to 787 billion kWh. More than three-quarters of the 105 nuclear power plants in the U.S. are located east of the Mississippi River. The U.S. has the highest number of reactors of any country in the world, but far fewer (105) than the 236 that were in the stages of planning, construction or operation as recently as 1975.

Several factors have contributed to the decline in the number of planned nuclear units, but nuclear plant operators have been able to increase their generation of electricity steadily without increasing the number of reactors. Nuclear plants ran at 90.5 percent of capacity in 2004, up from 66.0 percent in 1990 and 56.3 percent in 1980.

In 2007, an energy bill passed through the Senate at the urging of the nuclear power industry could make builders of new nuclear plants eligible for tens of billions of dollars in government loans. In late 2007, the Nuclear Regulatory Commission anticipated 12 applications to build nuclear-power reactors at seven different sites. Plans for another 15 reactors are expected in 2008.

A setback for the industry has been the increased public opposition to nuclear power plants because of concerns about their safety and the disposal of spent nuclear fuel. These were heightened

U.S. Petroleum Prices Per Gallon 1995-2007

Year	Unleaded Gasoline			Heating Oil	Diesel Fuel	Consumer Grade Propane
	Regular	Midgrade	Premium			
1995	$0.72	$0.80	$0.89	$0.87	$0.64	$0.77
1996	0.81	0.89	0.96	0.99	0.78	0.89
1997	0.80	0.88	0.96	0.98	0.71	0.88
1998	0.62	0.71	0.79	0.85	0.56	0.77
1999	0.73	0.81	0.88	0.88	0.65	0.78
2000	1.06	1.15	1.22	1.31	1.01	1.05
2001	1.00	1.09	1.15	1.25	0.91	1.09
2002	0.92	1.00	1.08	1.13	0.84	0.96
2003	1.11	1.20	1.28	1.36	1.01	1.15
2004	1.40	1.48	1.58	1.55	1.32	1.31
2005	1.81	1.88	1.99	2.05	1.89	1.53
2006	2.10	2.18	2.30	2.37	2.17	1.73
2007[1]	2.31	2.41	2.53	2.59	2.35	1.89

Note: Unadjusted prices. Prices reflect price paid at time of transaction. 1. Preliminary. **Source:** U.S. Dept. of Energy, *Annual Energy Review* 2007 (2008).

in the wake of the 1979 accident at Three Mile Island near Harrisburg, Penn., and the far more devastating one at Chernobyl in Ukraine in 1986.

▶ ENERGY TRADING

Deregulation in the energy industry has led in the past decade to the the development of energy trading companies, large corporations that buy and sell power much like any other commodity. Because of an accounting procedure known as "mark-to-market," energy trading can produce huge paper profits overnight, even though it may take as much as 20 years for the revenues from these trades to appear, and fattens the company's debt load in the meantime. This arcane structure allowed energy traders at Enron to create fictitious trades that boosted profits even more (and triggered performance bonuses for top executives) before they were found out in the summer of 2002.

Primary Energy Production by Source, 1949–2007 (Billion Btu)

Year	Coal	Natural Gas (Dry)	Crude Oil	NGPL	Nuclear electric	Hydro-electric	Geo-thermal	Solar	Wind	Biomass	Total
1950	14,060	6,233	11,447	823	[1]	1,415	N.A.	N.A.	N.A.	1,549	35,540
1955	12,370	9,345	14,410	1,240	[1]	1,360	N.A.	N.A.	N.A.	1,424	40,148
1960	10,817	12,656	14,935	1,461	6	1,608	1	N.A.	N.A.	1,320	42,804
1965	13,055	15,775	16,521	1,883	43	2,059	4	N.A.	N.A.	1,335	50,676
1970	14,607	21,666	20,401	2,512	239	2,634	11	N.A.	N.A.	1,431	63,501
1975	14,989	19,640	17,729	2,374	1,900	3,155	70	N.A.	N.A.	1,499	61,357
1980	18,598	19,908	18,249	2,254	2,739	2,900	110	N.A.	N.A.	2,476	67,232
1985	19,325	16,980	18,992	2,241	4,076	2,970	198	[1]	[1]	3,016	67,799
1990	22,488	18,326	15,571	2,175	6,104	3,046	336	60	29	2,735	70,870
1995	22,130	19,082	13,887	2,442	7,075	3,205	294	70	33	3,107	71,319
2000	22,735	19,662	12,358	2,611	7,862	2,811	317	66	57	3,010	71,490
2005	23,185	18,574	10,963	2,334	8,160	2,703	343	66	178	3,141	69,647
2006	23,790	18,993	10,801	2,356	8,214	2,869	343	72	264	3,324	71,025
2007[2]	23,480	19,817	10,802	2,400	8,415	2,463	353	80	319	3,584	71,713

Notes: 1. Less than 0.5 billion kilowatthours. 2. Preliminary estimates. **Source:** U.S. Dept. of Energy, *Annual Energy Review 2007* (2008).

U.S. Commercial Nuclear Plants, 2008

There are 105 operable nuclear reactors in 31 states. The following table lists the states, with the total number of reactors in each, the names of the individual units and their location.

Alabama = 5
Browns Ferry 1, 2 & 3, Decatur
Joseph M. Farley 1 & 2, Dothan
Arizona = 3
Palo Verde 1, 2 & 3, Wintersburg
Arkansas = 2
Arkansas Nuclear 1 & 2, Russellville
California = 4
Diablo Canyon 1 & 2, Avila Beach
San Onofre 2 & 3, San Clemente
Connecticticut = 2
Millstone 2 & 3, Waterford
Florida = 5
Crystal River 3, Red Level
St. Lucie 1 & 2, Ft. Pierce
Turkey Point 3 & 4, Florida City
Georgia = 4
Hatch 1 & 2, Baxley
Vogtle 1 & 2, Waynesboro
Illinois = 11
Braidwood 1 & 2, Braidwood
Byron 1 & 2, Rockfort
Clinton 1, Clinton
Dresden 2 & 3, Morris
La Salle 1 & 2, Seneca
Quad Cities 1 & 2, Cordova
Iowa = 1
Duane Arnold, Cedar Rapids
Kansas = 1
Wolf Creek, Burlington
Louisiana = 2
River Bend 1, St. Francisville
Waterford 3, Taft

Maryland = 2
Calvert Cliffs 1 & 2, Lusby
Massachusetts = 1
Pilgrim 1, Plymouth
Michigan = 4
Donald C. Cook 1 & 2, Benton Harbor
Fermi 2, Newport
Palisades, South Haven
Minnesota = 3
Monticello, Monticello
Prairie Island 1 & 2, Red Wing
Mississippi = 1
Grand Gulf 1, Port Gibson
Missouri = 1
Callaway 1, Fulton
Nebraska = 2
Cooper, Brownville
Fort Calhoun 1, Fort Calhoun
New Hampshire = 1
Seabrook 1, Seabrook
New Jersey = 4
Hope Creek 1, Hope Creek
Oyster Creek 1, Forked River
Salem 1 & 2, Wilmington
New York = 6
Indian Point 2 & 3, Buchanan
Fitzpatrick 1, Oswego
Nine Mile Point 1 & 2, Oswego
Robert E. Ginna, Rochester
North Carolina = 5
Brunswick 1 & 2, Southport

McGuire 1 & 2, Cowens Ford Dam
Shearon Harris 1, New Hill
Ohio = 3
Davis-Besse 1, Oak Harbor
Fermi 2, Toledo
Perry 1, North Perry
Pennsylvania = 9
Beaver Valley 1 & 2, McCandless
Limerick 1 & 2, Pottstown
Peach Bottom 2 & 3, Lancaster
Susquehanna 1 & 2, Berwick
Three Mile Island 1, Middletown
South Carolina = 7
Catawba 1 & 2, Rock Hill
H.B. Robinson 2, Hartsville
Oconee 1, 2 & 3, Seneca
Summer 1, Jenkinsville
Tennessee = 3
Sequoyah 1 & 2, Daisy
Watts Bar 1, Spring City
Texas = 4
Comanche Peak 1&2, Glen Rose
South Texas 1 & 2, Bay City
Vermont = 1
Vermont Yankee 1, Vernon
Virginia = 4
North Anna 1 & 2, Mineral
Surry 1 & 2, Surry
Washington = 1
Columbia Generative Station, Richland
Wisconsin = 3
Kewaunee, Carlton
Point Beach 1 & 2, Two Creeks

Note: As of September 1, 2008. **Source:** U.S. Nuclear Regulatory Commission, *Information Digest.* www.nrc.gov

U.S. Health and Medicine

Milestones in the History of Medicine

B.C.

c. 2700 Chinese emperor Shen Nung develops principles of herbal medicine and acupuncture.

c. 1700 The Code of Hammurabi, king of Babylon, comprises regulations concerning physicians, including what they may treat and what their fees should be.

c. 1500 The Ebers Papyrus describes many remedies used in Ancient Egypt to treat dental ailments.

c. 400 Hippocrates of Cos (Greek: c. 460–c. 377), teacher and medical practitioner known as Father of Medicine, writes Hippocratic Oath, which sets ethical standards still followed by physicians throughout the world.

c. 300 Herophilus (Greek: c. 355–280) pioneers dissection of human body and founds first school of anatomy.

A.D.

c. 20 Aulus Cornelius Celsus (Roman: first cent.) writes first-known medical textbook.

c. 100 Romans develop a public medical service and appoint physicians to provide medical help to poor.

c. 180 Galen (Greek: c. 130–c. 201) writes *Methodus Medendo*, which summarizes medical knowledge of ancient times. Galen's views on human physiology and disease would influence medical thought for more than 1,500 years.

c. 450 Susruta (Indian) notes relationship of malaria to mosquitoes and of bubonic plague to rats.

c. 900 Rhazes (Persian: c. 865–923/35) is first to describe smallpox and establish criteria for diagnosing and treating it.

1030 Ibn Sina (Avicenna; Persian: 980–1037) publishes *Canon of Medicine*, which becomes leading medical encyclopedia for centuries.

c. 1270–80 Spectacles are introduced by Venetian glassmakers.

1403 Venice imposes world's first quarantine of infected areas as safeguard against Black Death (bubonic plague).

1543 Andreas Vesalius (Flemish: 1514–64) publishes first accurate anatomy text and establishes foundations of modern anatomy.

1597 Gaspare Tagliacozzi (Italian) publishes first textbook of plastic surgery and revives operation of rhinoplasty (nose surgery).

1601 Sir James Lancaster (English: c. 1554–1618) writes that lemon juice helps prevent scurvy.

1628 William Harvey (English: 1578–1657) describes functions of the heart and how blood circulates throughout the body.

1658 Jan Swammerdam (Dutch: 1637–80) discerns red blood cells.

1670 Thomas Willis (English: 1621–75) rediscovers connection between sugar in urine and diabetes (known in antiquity by Greeks, Chinese, and Indians).

1751 Pennsylvania Hospital, first general hospital in U.S., founded in Philadelphia by Quakers.

1761 Leopold Auenbrugger von Auenbrugg (Australian: 1722–1809) discovers that fluid in chest cavity and other health problems can be detected by tapping gently on the chest.

Giovanni B. Morgagni (Italian: 1682–1771) establishes modern pathological anatomy with publication of *On the Seats and Causes of Disease*.

1796 Edward Jenner (English: 1749–1823) develops smallpox vaccine from cowpox serum.

1816 René T.H. Laënnec (French: 1781–1826) invents stethoscope and introduces auscultation (monitoring sounds made by internal organs).

1818 James Blundel (English) performs first successful human blood transfusion.

1831 Samuel Guthrie (American: 1782–1848) discovers chloroform.

1839 Horace Hayden (American: 1769–1844) and Chapin Harris (1806–60) found world's first dental school, Baltimore College of Dental Surgery.

1842 Crawford Long (American: 1815–78) removes tumor from patient inhaling ether—first known operation under general anesthesia; publishes his findings in 1849, three years after William Morton (American: 1819–68) demonstrates effectiveness of ether as anesthetic.

1850 Hermann Helmholtz (German: 1821–94) invents ophthalmoscope, instrument used to examine interior of the eye.

1855 Manuel Garcia (Spanish: 1805–1906) invents modern laryngoscope, used to inspect the throat, especially the larynx and vocal cords.

1863 International Red Cross established at Geneva, Switzerland.

1865 Joseph Lister (English: 1827–1912) introduces use of disinfectants to reduce infection.

Louis Pasteur (French: 1822–95) shows that spoilage of wine can be prevented by partial heat-sterilization; this process, called pasteurization, soon applied to milk and other foods.

1866 Sir Thomas C. Allbutt (English: 1836–1925) invents clinical thermometer.

1868 Carl Wunderlich (German: 1815–77) establishes that fever is a symptom, not a disease, and introduces use of thermometer for taking body temperature.

1879 Wilhelm Wundt (German: 1832–1920) founds the first laboratory for psychology.

1881 Pasteur produces vaccine that successfully prevents anthrax.

1890 Emil von Behring (German: 1854–1917) and Shibasaburo Kitasato (Japanese: 1852–1931) independently discover antitoxins.

1892 Dmitri Ivanovski (Russian: 1864–1920) discovers filterable viruses (viruses tiny enough to pass through fine filters previously believed to trap all living organisms).

1893 Felix Hoffmann (German: 1868–1946) develops a process for production of acetylsalicylic acid, the form of aspirin used today.

1895 Wilhelm Röntgen (German: 1845–1923) discovers X rays.

1900 Sigmund Freud (Austrian: 1856–1939), founder of psychoanalysis, publishes *The Interpretations of Dreams*.

Karl Landsteiner (Austrian-American: 1868–1943) discovers three blood groups, later named A, B, and O; fourth group, to be named AB, discovered in 1902.

Walter Reed (American: 1851–1902) establishes that yellow fever virus is transmitted by mosquitoes.

1901 Jokichi Takamine (Japanese-American: 1854–1922) isolates adrenaline, first hormone to be isolated.

1902   Eugene Opie (American: 1873-1971) establishes that diabetes results from destruction of specific portions of pancreatic tissue.

1905   Albert Einhorn (Austrian: 1856-1917) synthesizes procaine (novocaine), which becomes the most widely used dental anesthetic.

1906   August von Wassermann (German: 1866-1925) develops blood test for syphilis.

1910   Marie Curie (French: 1867–1934) isolates pure radium metal, which came to be used to treat cancer.

1913   Béla Schick (Hungarian-American: 1877-1967) perfects test for determining susceptibility to diphtheria.

1915   Death certificates come into general use in U.S.

Margaret Sanger (American: 1883–1966) founds the National Birth Control League, which in 1942 becomes Planned Parenthood.

1918   Francis Benedict (American: 1870–1957) devises basal metabolism test for measuring rate at which metabolism (total of all chemical reactions) occurs in the body.

1921   Sir Frederick G. Banting (Canadian: 1891–1941) and Charles H. Best (1899–1978) extract insulin from the pancreas.

1928   Sir Alexander Fleming (Scottish: 1881–1955) discovers penicillin, a substance in the mold *Penicillium notatum* that kills certain bacteria.

1929   Hans Berger (German: 1873–1941) publishes his results of the first electroencephalograms (EEGs) of humans.

1935   Gerhard Domagk (German: 1895–1964) announces discovery of Prontosil (sulfonamidecrysoidin), the first useful sulfa drug.

1937   First blood bank is established, at Cook County Hospital in Chicago.

Alton Ochsner (American: 1896–1981) and Michael De Bakey (1908–2008) suggest that cigarette smoking is cause of lung cancer.

1943   Willem Kolff (Dutch-American: 1911–) develops first kidney dialysis machine.

1944   Canadians Oswald Avery (1877–1955), Colin MacLeod (1909–72), and Maclyn McCarty (1911–2005) prove that DNA (deoxyribonucleic acid) is blueprint of heredity that determines how an organism develops.

First eye bank, Eye-Bank for Sight Restoration, founded in New York.

Albert Schatz (American: 1921–2005) and Selman Waksman (American: 1888–1973) isolate streptomycin, an antibiotic effective against bacterium that causes tuberculosis.

1945   Alfred Blalock (American: 1899–1964) introduces first operation to enable blue, or cyanotic, babies to survive (cyanosis, caused by poor circulatory flow or other problems, results in diminished oxygen in blood, causing bluish discoloration of the skin).

1947   Chloromycetin, developed by Parke-Davis researchers, is used to treat typhus patients; first use of "broadspectrum" antibiotic.

1948   Philip S. Hench (American: 1896–1965) and Edward C. Kendall (1886–1972) synthesize cortisone and use it to treat arthritis victims.

1952   Jonas Salk (American: 1914–95) develops first vaccine against polio.

1953   John H. Gibbon, Jr. (American: 1903–73) uses heart-lung machine he invented in successful open-heart operation.

1954   Surgeons led by Joseph Murray (American: 1919-) perform first successful kidney transplant.

1957   Alick Isaacs (Scottish: 1921–67) and Jean Lindenmann (Swiss) discover interferon, a protein that interferes with viral reproduction.

1958   Wilson Greatbatch (American: 1919–) invents the implantable artificial pacemaker.

1961   Scientists at Bell Laboratories (Americans) announce first continuously operating laser, a tool having many surgical uses.

1963   Thomas Starzl (American: 1926–) performs first human liver transplant operation.

1964   James Hardy (American: 1918–2003) performs first human lung transplant.

1965   Medicare and Medicaid are established, guaranteeing medical insurance coverage for the aged and the poor.

1966   Americans Paul Parkman (1932-) and Harry Meyer (1928–2001) develop vaccine for rubella (German measles).

Insulin synthesized independently by U.S. and Chinese scientists—first hormone to be synthesized.

1967   Christiaan Barnard (South African: 1922–2001) performs world's first heart transplant.

Rene Favaloro (Argentinian: 1923–2000) performs first successful coronary bypass operation.

First modern hospice founded in London.

1969   Denton Cooley (American: 1920–) implants first temporary artificial heart in human being.

1972   Computerized axial tomography (CAT scan) is introduced in Great Britain.

1977   Scientists at Genentech Corporation (Americans) induce bacteria to make human-brain hormone somatostatin—first human chemical produced by recombinant-DNA techniques.

The first known human cases of cyclospora infection are diagnosed.

1978   First "test tube baby" (person conceived outside human body) is born, in England.

1981   Scientists identify acquired immune deficiency syndrome (AIDS) for the first time.

Surgeons at University of California at San Francisco perform first successful operation on a fetus.

1982   A team led by William DeVries (American: 1943–) performs first complete replacement of human heart with artificial heart.

1983   Luc Montagnier (French: 1932–) discovers virus believed to cause AIDS.

1984   First baby produced from frozen embryo is born, in Melbourne, Australia.

1990   R. Michael Blaese, W. French Anderson, and Kenneth W. Culver (Americans) develop procedure to infuse genetically engineered blood cells for treatment of immune system disorder—first gene therapy used in a human.

1993   The U.S. Environmental Protection Agency concludes that environmental tobacco smoke ("secondhand smoke") is a lung carcinogen and causes respiratory problems for infants and young children.

1996   British scientists announce the possibility that a new form of Creutzfeldt-Jakob disease is transmitted to humans through the meat of cattle infected with bovine spongiform encephalopathy ("mad cow disease").

1999   Surgeons at Vanderbilt University Medical Center perform first successful brain surgery on a fetus.

2000   Scientists announce they have deciphered most of the human genetic code; by 2003, more than 99 percent is decoded.

2001   U.S. surgeons implant the first self-contained artificial heart.

2003   A new viral infection called SARS (severe acute respiratory syndrome) arises in China.

2004   The F.D.A. concludes that antidepressants can cause some young people to become suicidal.

2006   Gardasil, the first vaccine to target the viruses responsible for most cervical cancers, is approved for sale.

▶QUALITY OF HEALTH

Americans are living longer, healthier lives than ever before, yet many of the health problems they face could be avoided or alleviated with appropriate prevention or treatment. With this in mind, government health officials have three broad goals: increasing the span of healthy life, reducing health disparities, and achieving access to preventive services for everyone.

Health quality varies significantly by economic level, age group, and geographic region. Among the most persistent disparities are disease, injury, disability and mortality rates for various racial and ethnic groups. These disparities are especially stark between white and black Americans. For example:

- A white baby can expect to live 78.3 years; a black baby, 73.1 years (2004 data).
- The prevalence of obesity is 49.6 percent among black adult females aged 20 to 74, 31.3 percent among white adult females (1999-2002).
- Blacks have almost twice the risk of first strokes than whites (2001).
- The age-adjusted death rate for prostate cancer for black men is almost 2.4 times that for white men (2003).
- The prevalence of AIDS cases per 100,000 population is 54.1 among blacks, 5.9 among whites (2005).
- Gonorrhea cases per 100,000 population is 626.4 among blacks, 35.2 among whites (2005).
- The infant mortality rate is 5.7 per 1,000 live births for whites, 13.6 for blacks (2004).
- Pregnancy-related deaths per 100,000 live births for black women are 3.5 times higher than for white women (2003).
- The average risk of death for blacks is about 33 percent higher than for whites (2003).
- Black Medicare beneficiaries are more than twice as likely as whites to report they can't afford prescription medications (2003).

A growing body of evidence indicates that race, discrimination, and economic and cultural factors influence the care that people receive and, consequently, their health.

▶HEALTH CARE EXPENDITURES

National health care spending was nearly $1.9 trillion in 2004. It increased to 16 percent of gross domestic product (GDP)—the largest share of GDP on record and leading the rest of the industrialized world by a wide margin. The upward trend is predicted to continue: a 2006 report from the Centers for Medicare & Medicaid Services projected that by 2015 health care spending will be over $4.0 trillion and 20 percent of GDP.

The 2004 health expenditures amounted to $6,280 per person, up from $2,737 in 1990—and only $143 in 1960—yet many Americans are missing out. According to the 2005 National Health Interview Survey, about 7 percent of persons (21.7 million) delayed medical care during the year prior to the survey because of worry about costs; another 5 percent (15.2 million) did not receive needed care because they could not afford it. Persons whose health was assessed as fair or poor were four to five times as likely as persons whose health was assessed as excellent or very good to delay or not receive needed medical care because of costs.

A variety of factors contribute to the high costs of health care, including:

1. Use of sophisticated, expensive medical equipment.

2. New, higher priced prescription drugs and increased consumer demand induced by drug manufacturers' advertising.

3. Excessive and arguably unnecessary procedures, including duplication of tests and use of technologies that yield similar results.

4. Increasing elderly population, which use medical care more intensely than younger people.

5. Increasing number of accidents and other incidents that require emergency medical services.

6. Labor intensiveness and earnings growth for health care professionals and executives.

7. Malpractice insurance.

8. Administrative waste.

9. Fraud.

National Expenditures for Health Care, 1960–2006

Category	1960	1970	1980	1990	1997	2000	2005	2006
Total expenditures (billions)	$27.5	$74.9	$253.4	$714.0	$1,125.3	$1,353.6	$1,973.3	$2,105.5
Private[1]	20.7	46.8	147.0	427.3	614.1	757.0	1,076.6	1,135.2
Public	6.8	28.1	106.3	286.7	511.3	596.6	896.8	970.3
Federal	2.9	17.7	71.6	193.9	364.9	417.6	639.1	704.9
State and local	3.9	10.4	34.8	92.8	146.3	179.0	257.7	265.4
Total expenditures per capita	$148	$356	$1,100	$2,813	$4,104	$4,790	$6,649	$7,026
Private[1]	111	222	638	1,684	2,239	2,679	3,627	3,788
Public	36	134	462	1,130	1,864	2,111	3,022	3,238
Federal	15	84	311	764	1,331	1,478	2,153	2,352
State and local	21	49	151	366	534	634	868	886
Total expenditures	100.0%	100.0%	100.0%	100.0%	100.0%	100.0%	100.0%	100.0%
Private[1]	75.3	62.4	58.0	59.8	54.6	55.9	54.6	53.9
Public	24.7	37.6	42.0	40.2	45.4	44.1	45.4	46.1
Federal	10.4	23.7	28.2	27.1	32.4	30.8	32.4	33.5
State and local	14.3	13.9	13.7	13.0	13.0	13.2	13.1	12.6
Health care expenditures as percent of GDP	5.2%	7.2%	9.1%	12.3%	13.6%	13.8%	15.9%	16.0%

Note: Figures may not add to totals because of rounding. **1.** Includes out-of-pocket expenses, private health insurance and other funds.
Source: Centers for Medicare & Medicaid Services, office of the Actuary, National Health Statistics Group; U.S. Dept. of Commerce, Bureau of Economic Analysis; and U.S. Bureau of the Census.

Prescription Drugs

A major component of personal health-care expenditures is prescription drugs, which topped $200 billion in 2005. Diverse reasons account for the rising expenditures. These include the increasing incidence of chronic conditions such as diabetes, arthritis, and elevated cholesterol, due to an aging population but also to factors such as the growing number of overweight Americans. Doctors are treating chronic illnesses more aggressively than in the past. New medicines are typically more expensive than older ones or than generic drugs, and they are heavily marketed to both consumers and doctors. Managed-care health plans cover more of the costs of prescription drugs than traditional health insurance, making it easy for patients to afford medicines.

In the second half of 2006, growth in prices for prescription drugs fell, mainly due to price cuts in the generic side of the market. For instance, several large retailers introduced low-cost generic-drug programs. Also, two widely prescribed drugs, Zocor and Zoloft, lost their patent protection.

Health Care Spending by Category, 2006

Category	Amount (billions)	Change 2005–06
Hospital care	$648.2	7.0%
Physician's services	447.6	5.9
Dental services	91.5	5.7
Other professional services	58.9	4.9
Other personal health care	62.2	9.5
Prescription drugs	216.7	8.5
Durable medical equipment	23.7	2.3
Other medical products	35.6	3.5
Nursing-home care	124.9	3.5
Home health care	52.7	9.9
Administration and net cost of private health insurance	145.4	8.8
Government public health activities	58.7	4.3
Research	41.8	2.9
Construction	97.6	9.5
Total	**$2,105.5**	**6.7%**

Source: Centers for Medicare & Medicaid Services, Office of the Actuary, National Health Statistics Group.

Health Expenditures as Percent of G.D.P. for Selected Countries, 1970–2005

Nation	1970	1980	1990	2000	2005
United States	6.9%	8.7%	11.9%	13.3%	15.2%
Switzerland	5.6	7.6	8.5	20.9	11.4
Germany	6.2	8.7	8.7	10.6	10.7
Austria	5.3	7.6	7.1	7.5	10.2
Greece	6.1	6.6	7.4	9.9	10.1
Canada	7.0	7.1	9.0	8.9	9.7
Iceland	4.7	6.2	8.0	9.3	9.5
Norway	4.4	6.9	7.7	8.5	9.0
Italy	5.1	7.0	8.0	8.1	8.9
New Zealand	5.1	5.9	6.9	7.8	8.9
Ireland	5.1	8.4	6.1	6.2	8.2
Spain	3.6	5.4	6.7	7.4	8.2
United Kingdom	4.5	5.6	6.0	7.3	8.2
Finland	5.6	6.4	7.8	6.6	7.5

Source: World Health Organization, *World Health Statistics 2008.*

The National Institute for Health Care Management Research and Educational Foundation reported that the 50 best-selling drugs in 2001 accounted for 44.4 percent of total outpatient retail drug sales. The remaining 9,482 drugs accounted for 55.6 percent. The year's top-selling drug was Pfizer's cholesterol reducer Lipitor (atorvastatin), with $4.5 billion in retail sales.

Hospital Care

In 2003, spending for hospital care reached $515.9 billion, marking the fifth consecutive year of accelerated growth. The resurgence in hospital spending reflects growing demands for services, rising compensation, and the increased ability of hospitals to negotiate higher prices from private payers.

In 2002, the average adult stay in community hospitals (excluding federal hospitals, psychiatric institutions, and long-term hospitals) was 5.7 days. The average costs to the hospital were $1,290 per day and $7,355 per stay. In contrast, the average stay in 1980 was 7.6 days; average costs were $245 per day and $1,851 per stay.

The average age and age distribution of inpatients has also changed dramatically. According to the National Center for Health Statistics, the average age of patients in 1970 was 40.7 years, with 20 percent of all inpatients age 65 or older. In 2002, the average age had increased to 52.1 years with 38 percent of inpatients 65 or older. During the same period, the percent of inpatients under age 15 declined from 13 to 8 percent and inpatients 15 to 44 declined from 43 to 32 percent. Advances in anesthesia and pain relief, the development of minimally invasive procedures, the growing availability of ambulatory surgery, and efforts to contain health-care costs contributed to the shift of care from inpatient to outpatient settings. Technological advances in cardiac surgery resulted in increased hospitalization of elderly patients for cardiovascular procedures.

Paying for Health Care

Most medical care is paid for in one of three ways:
1. By patients; according to the U.S. Dept. of Health and Human Services, an estimated 14 percent of the nation's personal health care costs in 2002 were paid directly by patients.
2. By a private insurance plan; employers, employees and individuals funded 35 percent of all health care spending in 2002.
3. As a public charge, which means that the government—and, ultimately, the taxpayer—pays the bill. In 2002, 46 percent ($713.4 billion) of personal health care costs were paid for by federal, state, and local governments. Medicare and Medicaid accounted for 73 percent of public sector expenditures. Workers compensation, Department of Defense and Department of Veterans Affairs programs, and other programs made up the rest.

Health insurance   There are five basic types of insurance:
1. Hospital expense insurance—pays costs of hospital room, X-rays, medicines, etc.
2. Surgical expense insurance—pays costs of an operation.
3. Medical expense insurance—pays for visits to a physician's office.

4. Major medical expense insurance—pays costs associated with extended sickness or injury.

5. Disability income insurance—pays a benefit when the person is unable to work because of illness or injury.

Federal insurance plans   Two government health programs, Medicare and Medicaid, financed $516 billion in health care services in 2002, one-third of the nation's total health care bill. (The remaining federal health spending covers military and veterans' health care.)

Medicare is a federal health insurance plan for people age 65 and older, certain disabled people, and people with kidney failure. Medicaid is a health care program for poor people. It is funded jointly by federal and state agencies. (See also Part II: "Social Insurance Programs.")

In 2006, Medicare had over 43 million beneficiaries. Traditionally, Medicare consisted of two parts: Hospital Insurance, also known as Part A, and Supplementary Medicare Insurance, also known as Part B. A third, managed care part, Medicare Advantage (formerly Medicare+Choice), was established in 1997; almost 6 million Medicare beneficiaries were enrolled in 2006.

In 2006 a new Medicare prescription drug benefit, called Part D, was established. Medicare beneficiaries who choose to enroll in the program have some of their prescription drug costs subsidized by the federal government.

Managed care (HMOs, PPOs)   A managed health care plan provides comprehensive health care coverage to enrolled members on a prepaid basis; that is, insurance and health care delivery are integrated within one system. The objective is to control costs, assure access to effective treatments, and eliminate inappropriate and duplicative services.

HMO patients generally must use their HMO's physicians in order to be reimbursed. Preferred provider organizations (PPOs), a modified version of HMOs, permit enrollees to use non-plan providers (physicians and hospitals). However, patients who use services outside their PPO must pay a financial penalty.

In 2003, about 112.9 million people belonged to PPOs. HMO enrollment, which had reached a high of about 81 million in 1999, declined to 71.8 million by 2003 due largely to concerns about access to health care and demands for a choice in choosing physicians. Enrollment varied significantly from state to state—from lows in Alaska

(0.0%), North Dakota (0.4%), and Mississippi (0.8%) to highs in California (48.5%), Massachusetts (38.7%), and Connecticut (37.8%).

Nursing-Home Care
The approximately 17,000 nursing homes in the United States have some 1.6 million residents, about 91 percent of who are age 65 or older. Typically, residents are white (85%), female (72%), widowed (57%), and 85 or older (46%).

Americans spent $800 million on nursing-home care in 1960, $42 billion in 1970, $17.7 billion in 1980, and $52.7 billion in 1990. By 2001, the figure had reached $98.9 billion. State and federal governments pay more than 70 percent of the cost. Out-of-pocket payments, including personal savings and Social Security benefits, cover most of the rest.

According to a 2007 survey from MetLife Mature Market Institute, the average cost of a nursing home stay was $213 per day for a private room, $189 for a semiprivate room. There were large variations from one metropolitan area to another. The costliest metropolitan area surveyed was

Nursing Home Residents Age 65 and Older, 2004

Characteristic	Number	Rate per 1,000 population
Total	**1,317,300**	**36.3**
65-74 years	174,100	9.4
75-84 years	468,700	36.1
85 years and over	674,500	138.8
Male	**336,900**	**22.2**
65-74 years	75,400	8.9
75-84 years	140,900	27.0
85 years and over	120,600	80.0
Female	**980,400**	**46.4**
65-74 years	98,800	9.8
75-84 years	327,800	42.3
85 years and over	553,900	165.2
White	**1,148,900**	**36.2**
65-74 years	134,200	8.5
75-84 years	405,800	35.2
85 years and over	608,900	139.4
Black	**145,400**	**47.7**
65-74 years	34,500	20.2
75-84 years	54,600	55.5
85 years and over	56,300	160.7

Source: Centers for Disease Control and Prevention, National Center for Health Statistics, *National Nursing Home Survey*, 2004.

Hospital Facilities and Their Use, 1946–2003

Year	Number of hospitals	Number of beds ('000s)	Admissions ('000s)[1]	Average stay (days)	Outpatient visits ('000s)
1946	6,125	1,436	15,675	9.1	N.A.
1950	6,788	1,456	18,483	8.1	N.A.
1960	6,876	1,658	25,027	7.6	N.A.
1970	7,123	1,616	31,759	8.2	181,370
1975	7,156	1,466	36,157	7.7	254,844
1980	6,965	1,365	38,892	7.6	262,951
1985	6,872	1,318	36,304	7.1	282,140
1990	6,649	1,213	33,774	7.3	368,184
1995	6,291	1,081	33,282	6.5	483,195
2000	5,810	984	34,891	5.8	592,673
2002	5,794	976	36,326	5.7	640,515
2003	5,764	965	36,611	N.A.	N.A.

Note: N.A.= Not Available. **1.** Total nonfederal short-term general and other special hospitals   **Source:** American Hospital Association, *Hospital Statistics* (annual).

Stamford, Conn., at $372 per day for a private room; Baton Rouge, Louisiana was the lowest at $123 per day. (Alaska as a whole was highest, at $510 per day.)

The Uninsured

Some 43.6 million Americans (14.8% of the population) did not have health insurance in 2006, with percentages ranging from 7.7 percent in Michigan to 23.8 percent in Texas. Among chil-

dren under 18, approximately 11.2 percent were uninsured, a decrease from 13.9 percent in 1997. Lack of insurance was much more common among people with low incomes. Also, non-citizen immigrants were far more likely to be uninsured than native-born citizens, mainly because they were less likely to be offered health insurance by their employers.

Health Care Quality by State

The federal Agency for Healthcare Research and Quality (AHRQ) annually releases *State Snapshots*, which helps people understand the status of health care quality in each of the 50 states plus the District of Columbia. The snapshots are based on 129 quality measures, each of which evaluates a different segment of health care performance. In a subset of 15 "State Rankings for Selected Measures," specific state strengths are highlighted. In the report released in June 2007, New York, for example, ranked best for its low suicide rate. Montana ranked first for pneumonia vaccinations for seniors. Utah ranked first for its low colorectal cancer death rate.

For overall health care, the best-performing states were Wisconsin (score: 65.76), Minnesota (62.77), New Hampshire (62.36), Maine (62.35), and Rhode Island (61.67). Obviously, no state was good at everything, and the report points out areas in which states need improvement. Some

People With and Without Health Insurance Coverage, by State, 2006

State	People with coverage ('000s)	People without coverage ('000s)	Percent of people without coverage
United States	249,829	46,995	15.8%
Alabama	3,843	689	15.2
Alaska	550	109	16.5
Arizona	4,958	1,311	20.9
Arkansas	2,237	521	18.9
California	29,417	6,791	18.8
Colorado	3,977	826	17.2
Connecticut	3,137	325	9.4
Delaware	757	105	12.1
District of Columbia	503	66	1
Florida	14,233	3,828	21.2
Georgia	7,688	1,659	17.7
Hawaii	1,144	110	8.8
Idaho	1,248	227	15.4
Illinois	10,867	1,776	14.0
Indiana	5,590	748	11.8
Iowa	2,612	307	10.5
Kansas	2,387	335	12.3
Kentucky	3,467	639	15.6
Louisiana	3,291	921	21.9
Maine	1,192	122	9.3
Maryland	4,836	776	13.8
Massachusetts	5,678	657	10.4
Michigan	8,928	1,043	10.5
Minnesota	4,675	475	9.2
Mississippi	2,292	600	20.8
Missouri	5,028	772	13.3
Montana	772	160	17.1
Nebraska	1,549	217	12.3
Nevada	2,039	496	19.6
New Hampshire	1,159	150	11.5
New Jersey	7,319	1,341	15.5
New Mexico	1,498	445	22.9
New York	16,378	2,662	14.0
North Carolina	7,266	1,585	15.3
North Dakota	541	75	12.2
Ohio	10,181	1,138	10.1
Oklahoma	2,831	661	18.9
Oregon	3,051	665	17.9
Pennsylvania	11,108	1,237	10.0
Rhode Island	963	91	8.6
South Carolina	3,553	672	15.9
South Dakota	679	91	11.8
Tennessee	5,111	809	13.7
Texas	17,533	5,704	24.5
Utah	2,094	442	17.4
Vermont	557	63	1
Virginia	6,532	1,006	13.3
Washington	5,572	746	11.8
West Virginia	1,570	245	13.5
Wisconsin	4,995	481	8.8
Wyoming	441	75	14.6

1. Base less than 75,000. **Source:** U.S. Bureau of the Census, *Current Population Survey, 2007 Annual Social and Economic Supplement.*

Uninsured Americans, 2006

Category	Number('000s)	Percent of total population
Total	**44,995**	**15.8%**
Age		
Under 18	8,661	11.7
18-24	8,323	29.3
25-34	10,713	26.9
35-44	8,018	18.8
45-64	10,738	14.2
65 and older	541	1.5
Race/Ethnicity		
White[1]	21,162	10.8
Black[1]	7,652	20.5
Hispanic[2]	15,296	34.1
Asian[1]	2,045	15.5
Citizenship		
Native-born	34,380	13.2
Foreign-born	12,615	33.8
Naturalized citizen	2,384	16.4
Non-citizen	10,231	45.0
Region		
Northeast	6,648	12.3
Northwest	7,458	11.4
South	20,486	19.0
West	12,403	17.9
Annual household income		
Under $25,000	13,933	24.9
$25,000-$49,999	15,319	21.1
$50,000-$74,999	8,459	14.4
$75,000 or more	9,283	8.5

1. Non-Hispanic. 2. Of any race. **Source:** U.S. Bureau of the Census, *Current Population Survey, 2007 Annual Social and Economic Supplement.*

shortcomings are widespread. On average, for example, states reported that only about 59 percent of adult surgery patients insured by Medicare received appropriate timing of antibiotics. Only 54 percent of men over 50 reported they ever had had a flexible sigmoidoscopy or colonoscopy. Only 54 percent of Medicare managed care patients said their health providers always listened carefully, explained things clearly, showed respect for what they had to say, and spent enough time with them.

▶SURGERY

Increases in the number of surgical operations during recent years have been accompanied by dramatic changes in the rates of some procedures. An example is the incidence of cesarean sections—surgical incisions through the abdomen and uterus for removal of a baby, performed when normal vaginal delivery is deemed hazardous for the mother or child. Cesareans accounted for 30.2 percent of all live births in 2005—the highest rate ever in the United States and over five times the rate in 1970 (5.5 percent).

The frequency of certain procedures varies according to age, but, surprisingly, there may also be variations from one geographical region to another. For example, in 2004, when the national rate of cesarean delivery was 29.1 percent, state rates ranged from lows of 20.4 in Utah and 20.9 in Alaska to highs of 34.9 in New Jersey and 33.3 in West Virginia. A survey by Dartmouth Medical Schools researchers released in 1996 also noted disparities in the treatment of choice. For example, they found that a person in Kingsport, Tennessee, with a herniated disk was seven times as likely to have back surgery as one in Provo, Utah.

Organ Transplantation

Transplant surgery is more successful than ever, thanks to improved surgical techniques, a better understanding of the body's immune system, and

Cardiovascular Procedures in the U.S., 2005

Operation	Sex		Age			
	Male	Female	Under 15	15–44	45–64	65 plus
Total procedures	**4,062**	**2,927**	**200**	**655**	**2,524**	**3,609**
Cardiac catheterization	808	513	11	104	548	659
Angioplasty	874	397	—	69	563	639
Bypass	335	145	—	15	188	266
Endarterectomy	62	42	—	—	21	82
Pacemaker	93	87	—	—	19	155
Valve replacement	57	49	—	8	34	59
Defibrillator implants	67	24	—	7	34	50
Open heart surgery[1]	453	245	25	42	255	377

Note: Estimated figures; numbers in '000s. Breakdowns not available for some procedures, causing entries for some categories not to add up to the total. Does not include outpatient and other nonhospitalized procedures. **1.** Includes valves, bypass, and "other" open heart procedures. **Source:** American Heart Association, *Heart Disease and Stroke Statistics*, 2008 Update.

Common Operations and Procedures, 2005

Type of procedure	Total	Males	Females
All procedures[1]	**44,950,000**	**17,991,000**	**26,959,000**
Endoscopy of large or small intestine	1,620,000	703,000	917,000
Cesarean section	1,262,000	—	1,262,000
Repair of lacerations due to giving birth	1,259,000	—	1,259,000
Cardiac catheterization	1,209,000	742,000	467,000
Respiratory system operations	1,118,000	617,000	501,000
Reduction of fracture	1,045,000	483,000	563,000
Diagnostic ultrasound	884,000	411,000	473,000
CAT scan	811,000	378,000	434,000
Insertion of coronary artery stent	620,000	429,000	192,000
Hemodialysis	593,000	311,000	282,000
Hysterectomy	575,000	—	575,000
Knee replacement (total)	534,000	184,000	349,000
Coronary artery bypass	466,000	321,000	144,000
Removal of one or both ovaries	434,000	—	434,000
Gall bladder removal	398,000	143,000	256,000
Pacemaker insertion, removal or replacement	384,000	200,000	184,000
Destruction or closing off of fallopian tubes	346,000	—	346,000
Spinal tap	343,000	168,000	175,000
Appendectomy	341,000	178,000	163,000
Nose, mouth, pharynx operations	302,000	181,000	121,000
Spinal disc operation	294,000	148,000	146,000
Cancer chemotherapy	209,000	116,000	93,000
Prostatectomy	155,000	155,000	—

Note: Discharges of inpatients from non-Federal hospitals. Excludes newborn infants. **1.** Includes operations not shown separately. **Source:** U.S. Dept. of Health and Human Services, National Center for Health Statistics, *2005 National Hospital Discharge Survey* (July 12, 2007).

the development of drugs that combat rejection of implanted organs. Kidney transplants, for instance, enjoy a high rate of success and are much less expensive—and much more convenient—than maintaining a patient on dialysis. Unfortunately, a scarcity of donor organs keeps thousands of patients waiting, sometimes in vain. The number of donors has increased, but not as rapidly as the waiting list. As of August 30, 2007, 97,067 patients were on the national patient waiting list for organ transplants. Every 90 minutes someone on the list dies before they can receive the organs they need.

In addition to organs, tissues—cornea, bone, and skin—can be transplanted. In fact, corneal transplants are the most frequently performed

transplant surgery. According to the Eye Bank Association, more than 550,000 such operations have been performed since 1961, with a success rate averaging better than 90 percent. As with organs, the need for tissues frequently exceeds the supply.

There are 50 independent and 8 hospital organ procurement programs in the United States. According to the United Network for Organ Sharing (UNOS), 258 medical institutions were licensed to operate organ transplant programs as of mid-2004. These can be separated into organ-specific programs, including:

247 kidney transplants
134 heart transplants
140 pancreas transplants
124 liver transplants
59 heart-lung transplants
68 lung transplants
46 intestine transplants
45 pancreas islet cell transplants

Number and Survival Rates of Transplant Operations, 2006

Organ	Year first performed	Number (2006)	Survival rates[1]
Heart	1967	2,192	87.9%
Heart-lung	1982	31	70.3
Intestine	1990	175	83.8
Kidney	1954	17,090	96.1
Cadaver	—	10,659	—
Living donor	—	6,431	—
Kidney-pancreas	1966	924	94.7
Liver	1963	6,650	86.8
Cadaver	—	6,362	—
Living donor	—	288	—
Lung	1963	1,405	82.2
Cadaver	—	1,401	—
Living donor	—	4	—
Pancreas	1966	463	96.9

1. One-year adult patient survival rates for operations from January 2004 through June 2006, except for heart, lung and heart-lung, which are for July 2003 through December 2005.
Source: United Network for Organ Sharing.

Abortion

The deliberate termination of a pregnancy before the fetus is capable of living outside the womb has generally been legal in the United States since 1973, when the Supreme Court ruled (in *Roe v. Wade*) that abortion cannot be prohibited during the first three months of pregnancy. During most years from 1973 through 1984, the ratio of abortions to live births increased, peaking at 364 per 1,000 live births in 1984.

According to a report released by the Centers for Disease Control and Prevention (CDC) in 2006, women who obtained abortions in 2003 were predominantly 24 years of age or younger, white, and unmarried. Slightly more than half were obtaining an abortion for the first time. Over 60 percent of the abortions were performed during the first eight weeks of gestation; 88.2 percent were performed in the first 12 weeks.

Reported Abortions, 1972–2004

Category	1972	1980	1990	1995	2000	2004
NUMBER OF ABORTIONS						
Reported Abortions	586,760	1,297,606	1,429,577	1,210,883	857,475[1]	839,226[1]
Number per 1,000 live births	180	359	345	311	245	238
PERCENT OF TOTAL						
Race						
White	77.0%	69.9%	64.8%	59.5%	56.6%	54.1%
Black[2]	23.0	30.1	31.8	35.0	36.3	38.2
Other	—	—	3.3	5.4	7.1	7.7
Marital Status						
Married	29.7%	23.1%	21.7%	19.7%	18.7%	17.2%
Unmarried	70.3	76.9	78.3	80.3	81.3	82.8
Age						
Under 20	32.6%	29.2%	22.4%	20.1%	18.8%	17.4%
20-24	32.5	35.5	33.2	32.5	32.8	32.8
25 or older	34.9	35.3	44.4	47.4	48.4	49.5
Weeks of gestation						
Up to 8	34.0%	51.7%	51.6%	54.0%	58.1%	61.4%
9-10	30.7	26.2	25.3	23.1	19.8	17.6
11-12	17.5	12.2	11.8	10.9	10.2	9.3
13-15	8.4	5.1	6.4	6.3	6.2	6.3
16-20	8.2	3.9	4.0	4.3	4.3	4.0
21 or more	1.2	0.9	1.0	1.4	1.4	1.4

1. Acutal numbers may vary because not all states report data. 2. 1972 and 1980 include other nonwhite groups.
Source: U.S. Dept of Health and Human Services, Centers for Disease Control and Prevention, *Morbidity and Mortality Weekly Reports.*

▶DISEASE

Five of the most common categories of disease are:
1. Hereditary diseases—transferred from parent to child by genes. Examples: hemophilia, Down's syndrome, cystic fibrosis, sickle cell anemia, Tay-Sachs disease.
2. Deficiency diseases—caused by lack of vitamins or other essential nutrients. Examples: scurvy, pellagra, rickets, beriberi.
3. Infectious diseases—caused by viruses, bacteria, fungi, and other organisms and transferred from person to person. Examples: common cold, influenza, chicken pox, measles, tuberculosis, AIDS.
4. Diseases caused by chemical and physical agents such as radiation, smoke, drugs, and poisons. Examples: allergies, asbestosis, bysinosis, lead poisoning.
5. Degenerative diseases—resulting from natural aging processes. In some cases, cancer and high blood pressure are degenerative diseases.

Heart Disease

Cardiovascular diseases (diseases of the heart and blood vessels) are America's number one killer. One in three Americans—an estimated 79.4 million people—have one or more types of cardiovascular disease. During 2004 these diseases claimed 871,517 lives, or 36.3 percent of all U.S. deaths—an average of one every 36 seconds.

Death rates vary according to age, sex, race, even geographical location. Rates increase with age and are higher among men than among women. For both sexes, death rates are significantly higher among blacks than among whites.

In 2003, Minnesota had the lowest age-adjusted death rate from cardiovascular disease (221.2 per 100,000 population) followed by Hawaii, New Mexico, Colorado, and Utah. Mississippi had the highest rate (405.9) followed by Oklahoma, Alabama, Tennessee, and West Virginia.

The good news is that the death rates from cardiovascular disease have declined dramatically,

Reported Cases of Common Infectious Diseases, 1950–2006

Disease	1950	1960	1970	1980	1990	2000	2006
Brucellosis (undulant fever)	3,510	751	213	183	85	63	121
Cholera	N.A.	N.A.	N.A.	9	6	2	9
Legionnellosis	N.A.	N.A.	N.A.	N.A.	1,370	1,127	2,834
Leprosy (Hansen's disease)	44	54	129	223	198	64	66
Malaria	2,184	72	3,051	2,062	1,292	1,560	1,474
Meningococcal infections	3,788	2,259	2,505	2,840	2,451	2,256	1,194
Mumps	N.A.	N.A.	104,953	8,576	5,292	338	6,584
Pertussis (whooping cough)	120,718	14,809	4,249	1,730	4,570	7,867	15,632
Plague[1]	N.A.	2	13	18	2	6	17
Poliomyelitis	33,300	3,190	33	9	6	0	0
Psittacosis	26	113	35	124	113	11	21
Rabies, in animals	7,901	3,567	3,224	6,421	4,826	6,934	5,534
Rabies, in humans	18	2	3	0	1	2	3
Rubella (German measles)	N.A.	N.A.	56,552	3,904	1,125	176	11
Tetanus	486	368	148	95	64	26	41
Toxic shock syndrome	N.A.	N.A.	N.A.	N.A.	322	125	101
Trichinosis	327	160	109	131	129	15	15
Tuberculosis[2]	121,742	55,494	37,137	27,749	25,701	15,976	13,779
Typhoid fever	2,484	816	346	510	552	317	353
Venereal diseases							
Gonorrhea	286,746	258,933	600,072	1,004,029	690,042	357,570	358,966
Syphilis[3]	23,939	16,145	21,982	27,204	50,578	5,978	9,756

1. Plague: disease caused by the bite of fleas infected with the bacterium Yersinia pestis. 2. Data after 1970 not comparable to prior years because of changes in reporting criteria effective in 1975. 3. Primary and secondary syphilis cases. **Sources:** U.S. Dept. of Health and Human Services, Centers for Disease Control and Prevention, *Morbidity and Mortality Weekly Reports.*

Heart Disease Death Rates, 1950–2003 (per 100,000 population)

Age	1950[1]	1960[1]	1970	1980	1990	1995	2000	2003
All ages								
Age adjusted	307.2	286.2	253.6	202.2	152.0	138.3	257.6	232.3
Crude	355.5	369.0	362.0	336.0	289.5	280.7	252.6	235.6
Under 1 year	3.5	6.6	13.1	22.8	20.1	17.1	13.0	11.0
1-4 years	1.3	1.3	1.7	2.6	1.9	1.6	1.2	1.2
5-14 years	2.1	1.3	0.8	0.9	0.9	0.8	0.7	0.6
15-24 years	6.8	4.0	3.0	2.9	2.5	2.9	2.6	2.7
25-34 years	19.4	15.6	11.4	8.3	7.6	8.5	7.4	8.2
35-44 years	86.4	74.6	66.7	44.6	31.4	32.0	29.2	30.7
45-54 years	308.6	271.8	238.4	180.2	120.5	111.0	94.2	92.5
55-64 years	808.1	737.9	652.3	494.1	367.3	322.9	261.2	233.2
65-74 years	1,839.8	1,740.5	1,558.2	1,218.6	894.3	799.9	665.6	585.0
75-84 years	4,310.1	4,089.4	3,683.8	2,993.1	2,295.7	2,064.7	1,780.3	1,611.1
85 and older	9,150.6	9,317.8	7,891.3	7,777.1	6,739.9	6,484.1	5,926.1	5,278.4

Note: Comparability between years is affected by changes in coding of the cause of death. 1. Includes deaths of nonresidents of the U.S. **Source:** U.S. Dept. of Health and Human Services, Center for Health Statistics.

falling 9.2 percent from 1991 to 2001. This is due in part to improved drug treatments and other medical advancements. For instance, from 1979 to 2001, the number of cardiovascular operations and procedures increased 417 percent. Another factor has been improved personal health habits: people have stopped smoking, lowered the fat content of their diets, and taken other steps that reduce the risks of cardiovascular disease.

Evidence suggests that further significant reductions in deaths from heart disease could be achieved through aggressive treatment of high cholesterol. In 2001, a U.S. government panel recommended that some 36 million Americans are candidates for cholesterol-lowering drugs and about 65 million should be on cholesterol-lowering diets.

Heart attacks A heart attack, or coronary event, occurs when the blood supply to the heart muscles is blocked. An uncomfortable pressure, fullness, squeezing, or pain in the center of the chest that lasts for two minutes or more may be a sign of a heart attack. Sweating, dizziness, nausea, fainting, or shortness of breath may also occur. Some 1.2 million people suffer heart attacks annually. According to the American Heart Association, about 700,000 of these are first attacks and 500,000 are recurrent attacks. Over 40 percent of the people who experience a heart attack in a given year will die from it. Among survivors, many develop congestive heart failure, which can leave the heart unable to pump blood effectively.

The American Heart Association estimates that 516,000 bypass operations were performed on 305,000 patients in 2001; 46.3 percent of the procedures were performed on people under age 65. In this operation a blood vessel from elsewhere in the body is used to reroute blood around a blocked coronary artery. The purpose: to reduce the person's risk of a heart attack.

Strokes Each year, approximately 700,000 Americans suffer a stroke. The good news is that from 1994 to 2004 the stroke death rate fell 20.4 percent, and the actual number of stroke deaths declined 6.7 percent. However, stroke remains a leading cause of serious long-term disability. A stroke occurs when the blood supply to the brain is blocked, usually by a clot. The primary signal of a stroke is a sudden, temporary weakness or numbness of the face, arm, or leg on one side of the body. Other signals include temporary loss of speech, difficulty in speaking or understanding speech, temporary vision problems (particularly in one eye), unsteadiness, or unexplained dizziness.

Cancer
The nation's second leading cause of death is a group of diseases characterized by the unrestrained growth of cells. It afflicts people of all ages and races, although about 76 percent of all cancers are diagnosed at ages 55 and above. Cancers vary greatly in cause, symptoms, response to treatment, and possibility of cure.

A U.S. male has a little less than a 1 in 2 risk of developing invasive cancer at some time during his life; a female's risk is a little more than 1 in 3. The incidence of cancer varies from state to state. Between 1999 and 2003, the highest cancer death rates occurred in the District of Columbia (299.1 deaths per 100,000 males and 187.8 per 100,000 females). The lowest cancer death rates were in Utah (182.2, 124.1) and Hawaii (192.5, 122.7).

Cancer survival rates The National Cancer Institute estimates that approximately 10.5 million Americans alive in 2003 had a history of cancer. Chances of surviving cancer have steadily improved. In the 1930s, about one in four U.S. cancer patients survived at least five years after diagnosis. In contrast, more than six out of 10 who get cancer this year will be alive five years after diagnosis.
Survival depends on many factors. Two of the most important are the site of the tumor and how much the cancer has spread before treatment is begun. Lifestyle choices are also important. The American Cancer Society estimated that more than some 168,000 cancer deaths in 2007 would be caused by tobacco use, and that about one-third of all cancer deaths are related to nutrition, physical inactivity, obesity, and other lifestyle choices.

5-Year Survival Rates for Cancer, by Race and Site, 1975–2003

Cancer Site	Whites			Blacks		
	1975-77	1984-86	1996-2003	1975-77	1984-86	1996-2003
All sites	51%	55%	67%	40%	41%	57%
Brain	23	28	34	27	33	37
Breast (females)	76	80	90	62	65	78
Cervix	71	70	74	65	58	66
Colon	52	60	66	46	50	55
Leukemia	36	43	51	34	34	40
Liver	4	6	10	2	5	7
Lung (and bronchus)	13	14	16	12	11	13
Ovary	37	39	45	43	41	38
Pancreas	3	3	5	2	5	5
Prostate	70	77	99	61	66	95
Rectum	49	58	66	45	46	58
Stomach	15	18	22	16	20	24
Testis	83	93	96	82	87	88
Thyroid	93	94	97	91	90	94
Urinary bladder	75	79	81	51	61	65
Uterus	71	70	74	65	58	66

Note: Rates are an average of cases diagnosed in years shown. **Source:** U.S. Dept. of Health and Human Services, National Cancer Institute; published in American Cancer Society, *Cancer Facts and Figures 2008*.

Cancer death incidence and rates After increasing steadily for most of the century, cancer incidence and death rates for all cancers combined and for most of the top 10 cancer sites declined beginning in 1992. Overall incidence rates decreased an average of 0.5 percent per year from 1991 to 2001. From 1993 to 2001, overall cancer death rates declined by 1.1 percent per year. Death rates decreased for 11 of the top 15 cancers in men, and 8 of the top 15 cancers in women. Improved detection and treatment, coupled with healthier lifestyles, are believed to account for the declining rates.

The American Cancer Society estimated that about 559,650 Americans would die of cancer in 2007—more than 1,500 people a day. Lung cancer is the leading cause of cancer deaths, killing an estimated 89,510 men and 70,880 women in 2007. Among women, breast cancer is the second most common killer, though if detected early and treated properly, it has a very high cure rate. Among men, prostate cancer causes the second greatest number of deaths. It, too, has a high survival rate if discovered while still localized within the general region of the prostate.

Cancer warning signs Early detection is the key in fighting cancer. See your doctor if one of the following symptoms lasts longer than two weeks.
1. Unusual bleeding or discharge.
2. A sore that does not heal.
3. A change in a wart or mole.
4. A lump or thickening in the breast or elsewhere.
5. A change in bowel or bladder habits.
6. Nagging cough or hoarseness.
7. Indigestion or difficulty in swallowing.

HIV/AIDS

Following the discovery of acquired immune deficiency syndrome (AIDS) in 1981, the disease spread rapidly around the world. In the United States, sharp rises in new infections with human immunodeficiency virus (HIV), which causes AIDS, were recorded throughout the 1980's and into the early 1990's. The number of deaths also jumped annually, reaching almost 50,000 in 1995. The introduction of powerful drugs around that time showed significant success in controlling progression of HIV and AIDS, so that the number of yearly deaths declined to an average of around 17,600 in the years 2001-2005. Still, the rate of HIV infection remained stubbornly high, leveling off at about 40,000 new cases a year. Since 1981, AIDS has been diagnosed in more than a million Americans. Of these over 550,000 have died.

HIV is spread through contact with infected body fluids such as blood and semen. Infected people may harbor the virus within their bodies for several years or even longer before developing symptoms of AIDS. Though symptomless, they still can infect others. By 2005, an estimated 640,000 people in the United States were living with HIV/AIDS.

No cure for HIV/AIDS is known. Medical experts stress that preventive measures, including

Estimated New Cancer Cases and Deaths by Site and Sex, 2008

Site	New cases			Deaths		
	Total	Male	Female	Total	Male	Female
All Sites	**1,437,480**	**745,180**	**692,000**	**565,650**	**294,120**	**271,530**
Skin[1]	67,720	38,150	29,570	11,200	7,360	3,840
Oral	35,310	25,310	10,000	7,590	5,210	2,380
Lung, bronchus, and other respiratory	232,270	127,880	104,390	166,280	94,210	72,070
Breast	184,450	1,990	182,450	40,930	450	40,480
Esophagus	16,470	12,970	3,500	14,280	11,250	3,030
Stomach	21,500	13,190	8,310	10,880	6,450	4,430
Small intestine	6,110	3,200	2,910	1,110	580	530
Colon, rectum, and anus	153,880	79,270	74,610	50,640	24,510	26,130
Liver and bile passages	30,890	19,690	11,200	21,750	13,820	7,930
Pancreas	37,680	18,770	18,910	34,290	17,500	16,790
Other digestive organs	4,760	1,470	3,290	2,180	740	1,440
Urinary (bladder, kidney, etc.)	125,490	85,870	39,620	27,810	18,430	9,380
Leukemia	44,270	25,180	19,090	21,710	12,460	9,250
Lymphoma	74,340	39,850	34,490	20,510	10,490	10,020
Myeloma	19,920	11,190	8,730	10,690	5,640	5,050
Bone and joints	2,380	1,270	1,110	1,470	820	650
Endocrine system	39,510	10,030	29,480	2,430	1,110	1,320
Eye	2,390	1,340	1,050	240	130	110
Brain, other nervous system	21,810	11,780	10,030	13,070	7,420	5,650
Ovary	21,650	—	21,650	15,520	—	15,520
Uterus	51,170	—	51,170	11,340	—	11,340
Other genital, female	5,670	—	5,670	1,630	—	1,630
Prostate	186,320	186,320	—	28,660	29,660	—
Testis	8,090	8,090	—	380	380	—
Other genital, male	1,250	1,250	—	290	290	—
All other plus unspecified sites[2]	41,880	21,120	20,760	48,770	26,210	22,560

Note: Except for urinary bladder, figures for invasive cancer only. Carcinoma in situ of the female breast accounts for about 67,770 new cases annually and melanoma carcinoma in situ accounts for about 54,020 cases annually. **1.** Melanoma and other nonepithelial skin cancers only; higher curable basal cell and squamous cell skin cancers account for more than one million new cases annually. **2.** More deaths than cases suggests lack of specificity in recording underlying causes of death on death certificate. **Source:** American Cancer Society, *Cancer Facts & Figures*, 2008.

sex education, condom distribution, and needle-exchange programs for drug addicts, need to be emphasized. They also fear that the new AIDS drugs are making people complacent and careless about their sexual behavior. In 2004, the first HIV test that uses saliva rather than blood and provides results in 20 minutes was approved. Public health officials hoped the test would result in wider and more frequent testing. No cure for HIV infection or AIDS is known.

(See also "World Health" for information on AIDS worldwide.)

AIDS patients. People at highest risk for HIV include men who have sex with men, injecting drug users, persons who received a transfusion or who were tissue transplant recipients before March 1985, heterosexual partners of infected persons, children born to infected mothers, and persons with mucous membrane or through-the-skin exposure to blood or body fluids of infected persons (e.g., health care workers). Men who have sex with men make up the largest group of AIDS cases. The proportion of women with AIDS increased steadily, accounting for 26.6 percent of adult-adolescent cases diagnosed in 2005. Beginning in 1996, blacks outnumbered whites in new AIDS diagnoses. In 2005, there were 20,187 newly diagnosed cases among blacks (54.1 per 100,000 population) and 11,780 among whites (5.9).

Individuals most at risk are those with venereal disease and multiple sex partners. Evidence suggests that sexually transmitted diseases that cause genital ulcers, such as herpes and syphilis, are especially dangerous because they cause breaks in the skin through which HIV can enter. People with these diseases are three to five times more likely than usual to get HIV if they have sex with an HIV-infected person.

An encouraging change in the 1990's was the steep reduction in mother-to-fetus transmission of HIV. This resulted from the use of zidovudine (ZDV), taken by the pregnant woman beginning as early as the 14th week of

AIDS Cases 2006 and Cumulative

	Diagnoses		Deaths	
	2006	Cumulative[1]	2006	Cumulative[1]
Totals[2]	37,852	1,014,797	14,627	565,927
Age				
Birth to 13	38	9,156	13	4,889
13-19	474	6,704	49	1,380
20-29	5,092	153,324	567	52,387
30-39	10,751	411,103	2,467	212,097
40-49	12,926	277,738	5,522	176,964
50-59	5,758	92,097	3,823	69,378
60-64	955	17,303	771	14,315
64 & older	835	15,074	805	14,393
Race/Ethnicity				
White[3]	10,929	394,024	3,860	239,529
Black[3]	17,960	409,982	7,426	218,392
Hispanic	6,907	161,505	2,425	80,690
Asian/ Pacific Islander	519	7,951	114	3,426
American Indian/ Alaska Native	155	3,345	66	1,693

Note: Estimated. **1.** From the beginning of the epidemic through 2006. **2.** Includes persons of unknown race or multiple races and persons whose age at diagnosis is unknown. **3.** Not Hispanic. Source: U.S. Dept. of Health and Human Services, Centers for Disease Control and Prevention, *HIV/AIDS Surveillance Report,* Vol. 18, Revised April 1, 2008.

Adults and Adolescents With AIDS, 2005

	Males		Females		Total	
Exposure category	Cases	Percent	Cases	Percent	Cases	Percent
Male-to-male sexual contact	416,232	54.0	—	—	416,232	44.0
Intravenous (IV) drug abuse	159,676	21.0	65,534	36.0	225,210	24.0
Male-to-male sexual contact and IV drug abuse	62,940	8.0	—	—	62,940	7.0
Heterosexual contact	46,533	6.0	79,872	44.0	126,405	13.0
Other[1]	79,427	11.0	36,363	20.0	115,791	13.0
Total[2]	764,805	100%	181,769	100%	946,578	100%

Note: Cases with more than one risk factor other than the combinations listed are tabulated only in the category listed first. **1.** Includes hemophilia/coagulation disorder, receipt of contaminated blood, and patients whose mode of exposure to HIV is unknown. **2.** Due to rounding, category totals may not total 100%. **Source:** U.S. Dept. of Health and Human Services, Centers for Disease Control and Prevention, *HIV/AIDS Surveillance Reports,* Revised Edition, June 2007.

AIDS in the Cities, 2006

City	Number of cases	City	Number of cases	City	Number of cases
New York, N.Y.	162,731	Ft. Lauderdale, Fla.	16,674	Boston, Mass.	8,542
Los Angeles, Calif.	51,348	Dallas, Texas	16,075	Detroit, Mich.	8,325
San Francisco, Calif.	30,654	San Diego, Calif.	12,995	Nassau–Suffolk, N.Y.	8,251
Miami, Fla.	30,215	Tampa–St.		Seattle, Wash.	8,179
Washington, D.C.	28,648	Petersburg, Fla.	11,286	Phoenix, Ariz.	7,490
Chicago, Ill.	28,548	West Palm Beach, Fla.	9,915	Denver, Colo.	6,921
Houston, Texas	25,993	Oakland, Calif.	9,594	Santa Anna, Calif.	6,898
Philadelphia, Pa.	22,362	New Orleans, La.	8,902	Edison, N.J.	6,848
Atlanta, Ga.	22,024	Orlando, Fla.	8,745	Jacksonville, Fla.	6,095
Baltimore, Md.	20,570	Riverside–San Bernardino,		St. Louis, Mo.	6,005
Newark, N.J.	20,253	Calif.	8,628		

Note: Metropolitan statistical areas. For example, the Atlanta area includes Sandy Springs and Marietta. **Source:** U.S. Dept. of Health and Human Services, Centers for Disease Control and Prevention, *HIV/AIDS Surveillance Report,* Vol. 18, revised April 1, 2008.

pregnancy and continuing until labor; at birth, the baby takes ZDV for six weeks. In 2002, there were 90 reported cases of AIDS transmission from mothers to newborns, bringing the total to 8,629 since the epidemic began.

The overwhelming majority of AIDS cases are found in large cities and metropolitan areas. Through 2002, metropolitan areas in the United States and Puerto Rico with 500,000 or more population accounted for 719,566 of the 857,516 reported AIDS cases (83.9 percent).

Sexually Transmitted Diseases

The United States has the highest rates of sexually transmitted diseases (STDs) in the industrialized world, some 50 to 100 times higher than in other industrial nations. An estimated 15.3 million new cases of STDs are reported each year in the United States; roughly half of these cases are incurable. STDs are difficult to track, in part because many infected people, though able to infect others, do not have symptoms and remain undiagnosed. Even diagnosed cases frequently remain unreported and uncounted.

The most prevalent STD in the United States, infecting some 45 million people, is genital herpes, caused by a virus. It is followed by human papillomaviruses (HPV), which cause genital warts and cervical cancers; chlamydia, caused by a bacterium; trichomoniasis, caused by a protozoan; gonorrhea, caused by a bacterium; and syphilis, caused by a bacterium. People with these STDs have a significantly increased risk of becoming infected with HIV, in part because they may have open sores that provide the virus with an easy route of entry to the body.

Viral Hepatitis

Several viruses are responsible for viral hepatitis, a sometimes-fatal disease that attacks the liver. In the United States almost all cases are accounted for by hepatitis viruses A, B, C, D, and E—particularly the first three.

Hepatitis A is spread primarily by fecal contamination of food and water and through person-to-person contact. Data suggest that one-third of Americans have evidence of past infection (i.e., they demonstrate immunity). Since 1995, vaccines have been available for prevention of infection in people age two and older, and disease incidence has declined dramatically.

Hepatitis B is generally transmitted via contact with the blood of an infected person during sex, during birth, or through contaminated needles and syringes. People at high risk include intravenous drug users who share needles, homosexual men, and heterosexuals with multiple partners. An estimated 1.25 million people in the United States are believed to be chronic carriers of hepatitis B, capable of transmitting the virus to others. Approximately half of those infected are Asians or Pacific Islanders, most of whom became infected before arriving in the country. Chronic carriers are at high risk of developing cirrhosis or liver cancer; each year about 4,000 to 5,000 hepatitis B patients die of these illnesses. Vaccines are available for all age groups, and have markedly cut the number of new infections.

Hepatitis C is a major cause of cirrhosis and the leading reason for liver transplants in the United States. It also is believed to be responsible for much of the recent increase in liver cancer. The main risk factors of infection are injecting drugs and having sex with an infected person. An estimated 2.7 million persons are chronically infected, making hepatitis C the most common chronic blood-borne infection in the nation. Therapies often are ineffective or cause serious side effects, and no vaccine is available.

Diabetes

Diabetes mellitus is a group of diseases characterized by high blood sugar levels that result from the body's inability to make or use the hormone insulin. Diabetes can lead to debilitating and life-threatening complications including blindness,

Percentage of Overweight Children and Adolescents, 1971–2004

Age	Years of Surveys					
	1971 –74	1976 –80	1988 –94	1999 –2000	2001 –02	2003 –04
2-5	5.0%	5.0%	7.2%	10.3%	10.6%	13.9%
6-11	4.0	6.5	11.3	15.1	16.3	18.8
12-19	6.1	5.0	10.5	14.8	16.7	17.4

Note: Excludes young women who were pregnant.
Source: National Health and Nutrition Examination Surveys.

Death Rates (per 100,000 population) by Sex and Race, 1940–2005

Year	Total	All races		Whites		Black	
		Male	Female	Male	Female	Male	Female
1940	1,076.4	1,197.4	954.6	1,162.2	919.4	N.A.	N.A.
1950	963.8	1,106.1	823.5	1,089.5	803.3	N.A.	N.A.
1960	954.7	1,104.5	809.2	1,098.5	800.9	1,181.7	905.0
1970	945.3	1,090.3	807.8	1,086.7	812.6	1,186.6	829.2
1980	878.3	976.9	785.3	983.3	806.1	1,034.1	733.3
1985	876.9	948.6	809.1	963.6	840.1	989.3	734.2
1990	863.8	918.4	812.0	930.9	846.9	1,008.0	747.9
1995	880.0	914.1	847.3	932.1	891.3	980.7	759.0
2000	854.0	853.0	855.0	887.8	912.3	834.1	733.0
2002	848.9	847.8	849.9	885.9	909.5	814.6	723.3
2005	825.9	827.2	824.6	864.5	882.8	799.2	703.9

Note: Death rates are based on population estimates prepared by the U.S. Bureau of the Census.
Source: U.S. Dept. of Health and Human Services, National Center for Health Statistics. *National Vital Statistics Reports.*

memory problems, kidney disease, heart disease, nerve damage, and amputations.

The most common type is type 2 diabetes, which usually develops because the body fails to use insulin properly. It occurs in people who are overweight; other risk factors include high cholesterol, high blood pressure, ethnicity, and a family history of diabetes. Treatment includes a healthy diet, weight loss, and regular exercise. Many patients require daily insulin injections.

In 2003-2004, about 16 percent of U.S. children and adolescents were overweight—about double the number of two decades ago. At the same time, 66 percent of adults were overweight. This has led to increasing numbers of people with type 2 diabetes. According to the American Diabetes Association, an estimated 20.8 million Americans—7.0 percent of the population—have diabetes. In addition, 54 million people have pre-diabetes.

Alzheimer's disease

Alzheimer's disease is a progressive degenerative condition characterized by forgetfulness in early stages and, as the disease progresses, increasingly severe debilitating symptoms that create demanding care-giving needs. More than 5 million Americans, most of them elderly, now have Alzheimer's disease. It caused 65,824 deaths in 2004, making it

Leading Causes of Death, 1970–2005

Cause of death	Deaths in 2004	Death rate per 100,000				
		1970	1980	1990	2000	2005
All causes	2,397,615	945.3	878.3	863.8	854.0	825.9
Heart diseases	652,486	362.0	336.0	289.5	252.6	220.0
Cancer	553,888	162.8	183.9	203.3	196.5	188.7
Cerebrovascular diseases	150,074	101.9	75.1	57.9	59.6	48.4
Chronic lower respiratory diseases	121,987	15.2	24.7	34.9	43.4	44.2
Accidents	112,012	56.4	46.7	37.3	34.8	39.7
Diabetes mellitus	73,138	18.9	15.4	19.5	24.6	25.3
Alzheimer's disease	59,664	30.9	24.1	31.3	23.2	24.2
Pneumonia and influenza	65,965	N.A.	N.A.	N.A.	17.6	21.3
Kidney diseases	42,480	4.4	7.4	8.3	13.2	14.8
Septicemia	33,373	1.7	4.2	7.9	11.1	11.5
Suicide	32,439	11.6	11.9	12.4	10.4	11.0
Liver disease and cirrhosis	27,013	15.5	13.5	10.2	9.4	9.3
Hypertension	23,076	N.A.	N.A.	N.A.	6.4	8.4
Parkinson's disease	17,989	N.A.	N.A.	N.A.	N.A.	6.6
Homicide and legal intervention	17,357	8.3	10.7	10.2	6.0	6.1

Note: Causes of death are classified by the International Classification of Diseases, which has been revised periodically, resulting in new cause-of-death titles and breaks in comparability of cause-of-death statistics. **Source:** U.S. Dept. of Health and Human Services, National Center for Health Statistics, *National Vital Statistics Reports.*

Deaths and Death Rates, 2006

Age	Total deaths	Rate per 100,000 population		
		Both sexes	Male	Female
All ages	2,448,017	825.9	827.2	824.6
Under 1 year	28,440	692.5	762.3	619.4
1-4 years	4,756	29.4	33.4	25.1
5-9 years	2,837	14.5	15.6	13.4
10-14 years	3,765	18.1	21.5	14.4
15-19 years	13,703	65.1	91.6	37.2
20-24 years	20,531	97.6	143.9	48.2
25-29 years	19,568	97.5	138.7	54.4
30-34 years	22,357	111.4	148.1	73.7
35-39 years	31,420	149.6	189.4	109.3
40-44 years	53,365	233.4	292.7	174.7
45-49 years	79,383	353.1	443.7	264.6
50-54 years	104,147	520.8	666.0	381.6
55-59 years	127,478	734.6	925.7	554.3
60-64 years	147,823	1,126.9	1,410.0	887.9
65-69 years	172,236	1,700.0	2,084.2	1,364.7
70-74 years	226,119	2,657.6	3,267.0	2,164.0
75-79 years	307,888	4,154.0	5,103.4	3,464.7
80-84 years	378,777	6,712.9	8,147.4	5,822.0
85 and older	703,169	13,798.6	14,889.4	13,297.7
Not stated	255	—	—	—

Note: Preliminary data.   **Source:** U.S. Dept. of Health and Human Services, National Center for Health Statistics. *National Vital Statistics Reports* (April 24, 2008).

the seventh-leading cause of death. Many more women than men die from Alzheimer's, but this mainly reflects the larger number of women alive at older ages. Death rates are much higher for whites than blacks, but the risk of acquiring Alzheimer's is higher for blacks than whites.

▶DEATH

In 2004, a total of 2,397,615 deaths were registered in the United States, 50,673 fewer than in 2003. The age-adjusted death rate, which takes into account changes and variations in the age composition of the population, reached a record low of 800.8 per 100,000 population, 3.8 percent lower than the 2003 rate.

Mortality for Hispanics is somewhat under stated because of underreporting of Hispanic origin on death certificates, by an estimated 5 percent. However, in 2004, the age-adjusted death rate was 27.9 percent lower for Hispanics than for non-Hispanics. Various hypotheses have been proposed to explain Hispanics' favorable mortality outcomes.

Males experience higher age-adjusted death rates than females, with black males having significantly higher rates than white males. Age-adjusted death rates for 2004 were: white females, 666.9 deaths per 100,000 population; black females, 855.3; white males, 936.9; and black males, 1,269.4.

Socioeconomic disparities in death rates also exist. A 1998 report from University of Michigan researchers said that adults in the lowest income group (less than $10,000 annual income) were 3.2 times more likely to die compared with those in the highest income bracket ($30,000 or more). Middle income adults ($10,000-$29,999) were 2.3 times as likely to die as those in the high-income group. Possible factors for higher death rates among the poor include depression, social isolation, a lack of optimism, low self-esteem, chronic stress, and inequality in health-care delivery.

Causes of Death

For the purposes of national mortality statistics, every death is attributed to one underlying condition. The 15 leading cases of death in 2002 accounted for 83 percent of all deaths in the United States. During the 20th century the leading causes of death changed significantly. In 1900, infectious diseases took many lives; indeed, the leading causes of death were (1) pneumonia and influenza and (2) tuberculosis. By century's end, heart disease and cancer headed the list.

Suicide

Each year, more than 30,000 Americans kill themselves—about one person every 20 minutes. In addition, about 130,000 individuals are hospitalized following suicide attempts and 115,000 are treated in emergency departments and released. Although women report attempting suicide during their lifetime about three times as often as men, men are four times more likely to succeed at it. In 2004, 25,566 men and 6,873 females committed suicide.

Suicide is the eleventh-leading cause of death of all Americans but the third-leading cause for young people age 10-24. Depression, drug abuse, and a history of impulsive, aggressive, or antisocial behavior appear to be associated with suicide in young people.

Rates are generally higher than the national average in the western states and lower in the eastern and midwestern states. For 2004, the highest rates were reported for Alaska (23.6 per 100,000 population), Montana (18.9), Nevada (18.8), New Mexico (18.7), and Wyoming (17.4). The lowest were for the District of Columbia (6.0), New York (6.2), Massachusetts (6.6), New Jersey (6.9), and Rhode Island (7.9).

The majority of Americans who commit suicide shoot themselves (55 percent in 2001). Other common methods are hanging, strangulation or suffocation, and poisons.

Changes in Leading Causes of Death, 1900–2005

Cause of death	Death rate (per 100,000 population)
1900: All causes	**1,719.1**
Pneumonia and influenza	202.2
Tuberculosis	194.4
Diarrhea, enteritis, and ulceration of the intestines	142.7
1920: All causes	**1,298.9**
Pneumonia and influenza	207.3
Heart disease	159.6
Tuberculosis	113.1
1940: All causes	**1,076.4**
Heart disease	291.3
Cancer	120.0
Cerebrovascular disease	90.8
1960: All causes	**954.7**
Heart disease	369.0
Cancer	149.2
Cerebrovascular disease	108.0
1980: All causes	**878.3**
Heart disease	336.0
Cancer	183.9
Cerebrovascular disease	75.1
2000: All causes	**854.0**
Heart disease	252.6
Cancer	196.5
Cerebrovascular disease	59.6
2005: All cases	**825.9**
Heart disease	220.0
Cancer	188.7
Cerebrovascular disease	48.4

Source: U.S. Dept. of Health and Human Services, National Center for Health Statistics.

Suicide in the U.S., 1960–2005

	Rate per 100,000 population					
Age	1960	1970	1980	1990	2000	2005
All ages[1]	**12.5**	**13.1**	**12.2**	**12.5**	**10.4**	**11.0**
0 - 4	—	—	—	—	—	—
5-14	0.3	0.3	0.4	0.8	0.7	0.7
15-24	5.2	8.8	12.3	13.2	10.2	10.0
25-34	10.0	14.1	16.0	15.2	12.0	12.4
35-44	14.2	16.9	15.4	15.3	14.5	14.9
45-54	20.7	20.0	15.9	14.8	14.4	16.5
55-64	23.7	21.4	15.9	16.0	12.1	13.9
65-74	23.0	20.8	16.9	17.9	12.5	12.6
75-84	27.9	21.2	19.1	24.9	17.6	16.9
85 & older	26.0	19.0	19.2	22.2	19.6	16.9

1. Age-adjusted. **Source:** U.S. Dept. of Health and Human Services, National Center for Health Statistics. *National Vital Statistics Reports.*

Unintentional Deaths due to Injury, in U.S., 2005

Type	Number of deaths[1]	0–4	5–14	15–24	25–44	45–64	65–74	75+
All accidents	117,809	2,747	2,415	15,753	30,916	29,192	8,632	28,097
Transport[2]	48,441	793	1,547	11,288	14,933	12,019	3,353	4,497
Poisoning	23,618	41	51	2,484	11,115	8,990	435	496
Falls	19,656	50	32	236	902	3,534	2,319	13,483
Drowning	3,582	557	253	649	882	758	193	272
Fires and burns	3,197	238	222	168	558	895	390	722
Firearms	789	23	52	203	244	175	44	48
All other[3]	18,526	1,045	258	725	2,282	6,005	1,898	8,579

Age group (years)

1. Figures for age groups not stated are included in this column but not distributed among age groups. 2. Motor vehicles, pedestrians, airplanes, etc. 3. Machinery, cuts, overexertion, excessive cold, unspecified, etc. **Source:** U.S. Department of Health and Human Services, *National Vital Statistics Reports*, April 24, 2008.

Estimated Number of Injuries in U.S. From Selected Products, 2006

Product group	Estimated injuries
Stairs, ramps, landings, floors	2,329,829
Beds, mattresses, pillows	553,091
Basketball	529,837
Doors, windows, glass panels	496,073
Bicycles, accessories	490,434
Chairs, sofas, sofa beds	473,733
Football	460,210
Bathroom structures and fixtures	331,033
Household containers (cans, bottles, jars)	301,273
ATVs, mopeds, minibikes	275,123
Baseball, softball	274,867
Exercise, exercise equipment	269,249
Ladders, stools	237,030
Clothing	222,007
Playground equipment	221,777
Toys	213,171
Soccer	186,544
Swimming pools, equipment	164,607
Home workshop manual tools	131,742
Carpets, rugs	127,017
Skateboards	125,713
Fences	110,011
Trampolines	109,522
Skiing and snowboarding	96,119
Nursery equipment	86,573
Lawn mowers	78,740
Drug poisoning, children under 5	71,418
Horseback riding	70,915
Television sets and stands	61,356
Hand garden tools	39,827
Razors, shavers, razor blades	38,773
Refrigerators, freezers	38,651

Notes: These national estimates are based on injuries treated in hospital emergency rooms participating in the National Electronic Injury Surveillance System. Patients said their injuries were related to the products; this does not necessarily mean the products caused the injuries. **Source:** Consumer Product Safety Commission, National Electronic Injury Surveillance System, *Consumer Product Safety Review*, Summer 2007.

Accidental Deaths in the U.S., 1910–2005 (per 100,000 population)

Year	Death rate	Year	Death rate	Year	Death rate
1910	84.4	1950	60.3	1990	36.9
1920	71.2	1960	52.1	1995	35.5
1930	80.5	1970	56.2	2000	34.0
1940	73.4	1980	46.5	2005	39.7

Source: U.S. Dept. of Health and Human Services, National Center for Health Statistics.

Life Expectancy in U.S., 1950–2004

Year	All races Male	All races Female	Whites Male	Whites Female	Blacks Male	Blacks Female
At birth						
1950[1]	65.6	71.1	66.5	72.2	58.9	62.7
1960[1]	66.6	73.1	67.4	74.1	60.7	65.9
1970	67.1	74.7	68.0	75.6	60.0	68.3
1980	70.0	77.4	70.7	78.1	63.8	72.5
1990	71.8	78.8	72.7	79.4	64.5	73.6
1995	72.5	78.9	73.4	79.6	65.2	73.9
2000	74.3	79.7	74.9	80.1	68.3	75.2
2004	75.2	80.4	75.7	80.8	69.5	76.3
At age 65 (years remaining)						
1950[1]	12.8	15.0	12.8	15.1	12.9	14.9
1960[1]	12.8	15.8	12.9	15.9	12.7	15.1
1970	13.1	17.0	13.1	17.1	12.5	15.7
1980	14.1	18.3	14.2	18.4	13.0	16.8
1990	15.1	18.9	15.2	19.1	13.2	17.2
1995	15.6	18.9	15.7	19.1	13.6	17.1
2000	16.3	19.2	16.3	19.2	14.6	17.5
2004	17.1	20.0	17.2	20.0	15.2	18.6

1. Includes deaths of persons who were not residents of the 50 states and the District of Columbia. **Source:** U.S. Dept. of Health and Human Services, National Center for Health Statistics, *Health United States 2000, National Vital Statistics Reports*.

Many experts believe that suicide statistics are grimmer than reported. They contend that numerous suicides are categorized as accidents or other deaths to spare families.

▶ACCIDENTS

Every 10 minutes, two people are killed and about 370 suffer a disabling injury in accidents in the United States. Accidents are the nation's fifth most common cause of death. But for people between the ages of 1 and 44, accidents are the leading cause of death.

The accident death rate has declined significantly from the 1912 rate of 82.5 deaths per 100,000 population. In 1992 it reached a record low of 34.0. In 2004 the rate was 38.1, or a total of 112,012 accidental deaths, according to the U.S. Department of Health and Human Services. Accident rates vary significantly from one place to another. The highest accidental death rates in 2004 were in New Mexico (65.6), Mississippi (59.5), and West Virginia (58.7). The lowest were in Massachusetts (19.6), New York (22.6), and Rhode Island (24.2).

Motor Vehicle Deaths

Since the nation's first motor vehicle death (reportedly in New York City on September 13, 1899) some 2.9 million people have died in motor vehicle accidents. Over the years, however, the numbers of deaths per 100,000 population and per 100,000 registered vehicles have declined drastically. For example, there were 3,100 motor vehicle deaths in 1912, when the number of registered vehicles totaled only 950,000. In 2006, there were 42,642 fatalities, but registered vehicles had risen to more than 246 million. The motor vehicle death rate in 2005 was 1.45 deaths per 100 million vehicle miles. This ranged from a low of 0.8 deaths in Massachusetts to a high of 2.6 deaths in Montana.

Data suggest that safety belts, air bags, bicycle and motorcycle helmets, child safety seats, strict drunk-driving laws, and speed limits save thousands of lives each year. More than 6.3 million police-reported motor vehicle crashes occurred in 2002. Almost one-third of these crashes resulted in

Average Remaining Life Expectancy in U.S. (in years)

Age in 2004	All races M	F	White M	F	Black M	F	Age in 2004	All races M	F	White M	F	Black M	F
At birth	75.2	80.4	75.7	80.8	69.5	76.3	50	28.8	32.7	29.1	32.9	25.1	30.1
1	74.7	79.9	75.2	80.2	69.6	76.3	51	28.0	31.8	28.2	32.0	24.4	29.3
2	73.8	78.9	74.2	79.2	68.6	75.3	52	27.2	30.9	27.4	31.1	23.6	28.5
3	72.8	77.9	73.2	78.2	67.7	74.3	53	26.3	30.0	26.5	30.2	22.9	27.6
4	71.8	76.9	72.2	77.3	66.7	73.4	54	25.5	29.1	25.7	29.3	22.2	26.8
5	70.8	76.0	71.3	76.3	65.7	72.4	55	24.7	28.3	24.9	28.4	21.5	26.0
6	69.8	75.0	70.3	75.3	64.7	71.4	56	23.9	27.4	24.1	27.5	20.8	25.3
7	68.9	74.0	69.3	74.3	63.8	70.4	57	23.1	26.5	23.3	26.6	20.1	24.5
8	67.9	73.0	68.3	73.3	62.8	69.4	58	22.3	25.7	22.7	25.8	19.7	23.7
9	66.9	72.0	67.3	72.3	61.8	68.4	59	21.5	24.8	21.7	24.9	18.8	22.9
10	65.9	71.0	66.3	71.3	60.8	67.5	60	20.8	24.0	20.9	24.1	18.2	22.2
11	64.9	70.0	65.3	70.3	59.8	66.5	61	20.0	23.2	20.1	23.2	17.5	21.4
12	63.9	69.0	64.3	69.3	58.8	65.5	62	19.3	22.4	19.3	22.4	16.9	20.7
13	62.9	68.0	63.3	68.3	57.8	64.5	63	18.5	21.6	18.6	21.6	16.3	20.0
14	61.9	67.0	62.4	67.3	56.9	63.5	64	17.8	20.9	17.9	20.8	15.7	19.3
15	61.0	66.1	61.4	66.4	55.9	62.5	65	17.1	20.0	17.2	20.0	15.2	18.6
16	60.0	65.1	60.4	65.4	54.9	61.5	66	16.4	19.2	16.4	19.2	14.6	17.9
17	59.0	64.1	59.5	64.4	54.0	60.6	67	15.7	18.4	15.7	18.5	14.0	17.2
18	58.1	63.1	58.5	63.4	53.0	59.6	68	15.0	17.7	15.1	17.7	13.5	16.6
19	57.2	62.2	57.6	62.5	52.1	58.6	69	14.4	16.9	14.4	17.0	12.9	15.9
20	56.2	61.2	56.6	61.5	51.2	57.7	70	13.7	16.2	13.7	16.2	12.4	15.3
21	55.3	60.2	55.7	60.5	50.3	56.7	71	13.1	15.5	13.1	15.5	11.9	14.6
22	54.4	59.2	54.8	59.5	49.4	55.7	72	12.5	14.8	12.5	14.8	11.4	14.0
23	53.4	58.3	53.8	58.6	48.5	54.8	73	11.9	14.4	11.9	14.1	10.9	13.4
24	52.5	57.3	52.9	57.6	47.6	53.8	74	11.3	13.5	11.3	13.4	10.4	12.8
25	51.6	56.3	52.0	56.6	46.7	52.8	75	10.7	12.8	10.7	12.8	9.9	12.2
26	50.7	55.4	51.1	55.7	45.8	51.9	76	10.2	12.2	10.1	12.1	9.5	11.7
27	49.7	54.4	50.1	54.7	44.9	50.9	77	9.6	11.5	9.6	11.5	9.1	11.2
28	48.8	53.4	49.2	53.7	44.0	50.0	78	9.1	10.9	9.1	10.9	8.7	10.6
29	47.9	52.4	48.2	52.7	43.2	49.0	79	8.6	10.3	8.6	10.3	8.3	10.1
30	46.9	51.5	47.3	51.8	42.3	48.1	80	8.2	9.8	8.1	9.7	8.0	9.6
31	46.0	50.5	46.3	50.8	41.4	47.1	81	7.7	9.2	7.6	9.1	7.6	9.2
32	45.1	49.5	45.4	49.8	40.5	46.2	82	7.3	8.7	7.2	8.6	7.3	8.7
33	44.1	48.6	44.5	48.8	39.6	45.2	83	6.9	8.2	6.8	8.1	6.9	8.3
34	43.2	47.6	43.5	47.9	38.7	44.3	84	6.5	7.7	6.4	7.6	6.6	7.9
35	42.2	46.7	42.6	46.9	37.8	43.4	85	6.1	7.2	6.0	7.1	6.3	7.5
36	41.3	45.7	41.6	46.0	36.9	42.4	86	5.7	6.8	5.6	6.7	6.0	7.1
37	40.4	44.7	40.7	45.0	36.0	41.5	87	5.4	6.3	5.3	6.3	5.7	6.7
38	39.5	43.8	39.8	44.0	36.1	40.6	88	5.0	5.9	4.9	5.9	5.4	6.3
39	38.5	42.8	38.9	43.1	34.2	39.7	89	4.7	5.6	4.6	5.5	5.1	6.0
40	37.6	41.9	37.9	42.1	33.4	38.8	90	4.4	5.2	4.3	5.1	4.9	5.7
41	36.7	40.9	37.0	41.2	32.5	37.9	91	4.2	4.9	4.1	4.8	4.6	5.4
42	35.8	40.0	36.1	40.2	31.6	37.0	92	3.9	4.5	3.8	4.4	4.4	5.1
43	34.9	39.1	35.2	39.2	30.8	36.1	93	3.7	4.2	3.6	4.1	4.2	4.8
44	34.0	38.2	34.3	38.4	29.9	35.2	94	3.4	3.9	3.3	3.9	4.0	4.5
45	33.1	37.2	33.4	37.4	29.1	34.3	95	3.2	3.7	3.1	3.6	3.8	4.3
46	32.3	36.3	32.5	36.5	28.3	33.5	96	3.0	3.4	2.9	3.3	3.6	4.0
47	31.4	35.4	31.7	35.6	27.5	32.6	97	2.8	3.2	2.7	3.1	3.4	3.8
48	30.5	34.5	30.8	34.7	26.7	31.8	98	2.6	3.0	2.6	2.9	3.2	3.6
49	29.7	33.6	29.9	33.8	25.9	30.9	99	2.5	2.8	2.4	2.7	3.1	3.4
							100+	2.3	2.6	2.2	2.5	2.9	3.2

Note: Based on an individual's age in 2004. For example, a white male age 25 in 2004 would be expected to live 52 more years, or to about 77 years old. A female born in 2004 would be expected to live to more than 80 years of age. **Source:** U.S. Dept. Health and Human Services, National Center for Health Statistics, *National Vital Statistics Reports*, December 28, 2007.

an injury, with less than one percent of total crashes (38,309) resulting in a death.

- More than half of the fatal crashes occur on roads with posted speed limits of 55 miles per hour or higher (2005 data).

- 58 percent of fatal crashes involve only one vehicle (2005 data).

- 39 percent of fatal crashes involve alcohol. For fatal crashes occurring from midnight to 3 a.m., 76 percent involve alcohol (2005).

►LIFE EXPECTANCY

Life expectancy figures represent the average number of years that infants are expected to live. Life expectancy has improved steadily over the years, due largely to a decline in deaths during childhood. The development of drugs to combat

U.S. Infant Mortality Rate, 1940–2005 (per 1,000 live births)

Year	All races	White	Black
1940	47.0	43.2	72.9
1950	29.2	26.8	43.9
1960	26.0	22.9	44.3
1970	20.0	17.8	32.6
1980	12.6	11.0	21.4
1990	9.2	7.6	18.0
1995	7.6	6.3	15.1
2000	6.9	5.7	14.0
2005	6.9	5.7	13.7

Source: U.S. Dept. Health and Human Services, National Center for Health Statistics, *Monthly Vital Statistics Reports, National Vital Statistics Report,* April 24, 2008.

Childhood Vaccines: Recommended Immunization Schedule, 2007

Age	Vaccines
Birth	Hepatitis B
2 months	Hepatitis B, polio, rotavirus, diphtheria, tetanus, pertussis (DTaP), haemophilus B (Hib), pneumonia and other pneumococcal bacteria (PVC)
4 months	Rotavirus, Polio, DTaP, Hib, PVC
6 months	Rotavirus, DTaP, Hib, PVC
6-18 months	Hepatitis B, polio
6 months-18 years	Influenza (yearly)
12-15 months	Hib; measles, mumps, rubella (MMR#1); chicken pox, PVC
12-23 months	Hepatitis A series
15-18 months	DTaP
4-6 years	Polio, DtaP, MMR#2
11-12 years	DTaP, human papillomavirus (HPV, 3 doses, females only), meningococcal (MCV4)

Note: It generally takes several doses of each vaccine for full protection. In some cases, there is a range of acceptable ages for vaccination. For example, the third dose of hepatitis B vaccine may be given between 6 and 18 months of age. Children who have not been vaccinated against Hepatitis B in infancy may begin the series during any childhood visit. For additional information, contact your physician.
Sources: American Academy of Pediatrics; American Academy of Family Physicians; and U.S. Dept. of Health and Human Services, Centers for Disease Control and Prevention.

infectious diseases, plus improved nutrition and better environmental sanitation, have all played major roles in combating early deaths.

In 2004, the average length of life in the U.S. was 77.8 years. Whites were expected to outlive blacks by more than five years: 77.8 years versus 72.5 years. Homicides, killings in police confrontations, auto accidents, AIDS, tuberculosis, and several other diseases have had a disproportionate impact on black people's life expectancy rates in recent years.

►INFANT MORTALITY

In 2004, there were 27,936 reported deaths of infants age one year or younger. The most commonly used index for measuring the risk of dying during the first year of life are infant mortality rates, which are calculated by dividing the number of infant deaths by the number of live births registered for the same period. The 2004 rate of 6.8 infant deaths per 1,000 live births was lower than the 7.0 rate recorded in 2002.

The rate among white infants was less than half that of black infants: 5.7 infant deaths per 1,000 live births for whites in 2004, versus 13.8 per 1,000 for blacks. The reasons for this discrepancy are not clear, although an important factor is believed to be the quality of medical care received by people of different socioeconomic groups. For example, studies have shown that adequate prenatal care is strongly associated with higher infant birth weight and survival. Many black mothers, who are far more likely to be poor than white mothers, do not have access to proper prenatal care. Poor nutrition, alcohol and drug abuse, and other social factors also play significant roles.

Disproportionate poverty among minority groups is not the whole story, however. Studies have shown that even black infants born to college-educated mothers had nearly twice the mortality rate of comparable white infants.

The leading cause of infant mortality, congenital malformations and chromosomal abnormalities, accounted for 20.1 percent of all infant deaths in 2004. Disorders related to short gestation and low birth weight, the second leading cause of infant deaths, accounted for 16.6 percent.

(See also "World Health" for infant mortality rates in other nations.)

►SUBSTANCE ABUSE
Illicit Drugs

The 2005 National Survey on Drug Use and Health obtained information on nine categories of illicit drug use: marijuana, cocaine, heroin, hallucinogens, inhalants, and the nonmedical use of prescription-type pain relievers, tranquilizers, stimulants, and sedatives. The survey estimated that 19.7 million Americans age 12 or older were current users, meaning they had used an illicit drug in the month prior to interview. Usage varied by age group: 9.9 percent of people age 12-17 used an illicit drug in the previous month, 20.1 percent of people age 18-25, and 5.8 percent of people age 26 or older.

Of growing concern has been the rising abuse of prescription drugs, specifically pain relievers, tranquilizers, stimulants, and sedatives. Based on data from 2002 to 2004 surveys, an annual average of 11.3 million persons age 12 or older were using prescription pain relievers nonmedically in the previous year compared with an annual average of 25.5 million past-year users of marijuana.

Marijuana is the most commonly used illegal drug, used by 75 percent of current U.S. drug users; approximately 55 percent of current illicit drug users consume no drugs other than marijuana. It is made from the leaves and flowering tops of the hemp plant, *Cannabis sativa*, which contains psychoactive substances called cannabinoids. The primary psychoactive ingredient in marijuana and hashish (a resin exuded from the flowering tops) is tetrahydrocannabinol, or THC. The amount of each cannabinoid varies markedly from one plant to another depending on climate, soil, and other factors.

Marijuana is typically prepared as a tobacco-like mixture that is smoked in hand-rolled cigarettes or in pipes. It typically produces a feeling of well-being, relaxation, and sleepiness. It also interferes with coordination and mental abilities. For instance, it distorts judgment and reaction time, which can be particularly dangerous when a user drives a car. However, there has never been a verified case of someone dying of an overdose.

Possession or sale of marijuana has been illegal in the United States since 1937. Nonetheless, marijuana has legitimate medical uses. A significant body of evidence shows that marijuana combats nausea and weight loss in cancer and AIDS patients. It also helps reduce pressure within the eyes of glaucoma patients.

A study commissioned by the federal government confirmed in 1999 that marijuana has medical uses and that there is no evidence that giving the drug to sick people would increase illicit use in the general population. Since 1996, twelve states have legalized medical marijuana use. However, the federal government—despite allowing medical uses of cocaine and morphine—continues to prosecute those who cultivate and distribute marijuana for medical purposes and prohibits doctors from recommending medical marijuana.

Cocaine is made from the leaves of the coca plant, a shrub native to South America. In the late 1800's and early 1900's, before its dangers were recognized, cocaine was used by doctors as an anesthetic because of its effectiveness in depressing nerve endings. It has since been replaced by less toxic, non-addictive anesthetics.

Cocaine causes a short-lived euphoria. It also suppresses appetite, interferes with sleep, and increases heart rate and blood pressure. Even small doses have been linked to heart attacks and cerebral hemorrhages. Repeated usage is required to maintain a "high." Abusers who try to abstain often experience a tremendous craving for the drug—a hallmark of addiction.

As of 2005, more than 33.6 million Americans age 12 or older (13.8 percent of that population) had used cocaine at least once in their lifetime. Almost 8 million (3.3 percent) reported lifetime use of crack, a form of cocaine that can be smoked. However, only 1 percent had used any form of cocaine within the previous month.

Methamphetamine, popularly called meth, is a powerfully addictive stimulant chemically related to amphetamine but much more potent. It is legally available, via prescriptions that cannot be refilled, for obesity and certain neurological disorders. It is also used illegally to lose weight or maintain alertness, or for recreational purposes. It can be taken orally or by snorting, injection, or smoking. It impairs brain function, increases heart rate and blood pressure, and can lead to convulsions, cardiovascular collapse, and death. The street drug is often referred to as "meth" or "speed." Methamphetamine hydrochloride, consisting of clear crystals, is pop-

Lifetime Experience With Illicit Drugs, 2006

Age	Used in lifetime	Used in past year	Used in past month
Total[1]	**45.4%**	**14.5%**	**8.3%**
By Age			
12-17	27.6	19.6	9.8
18-25	59.0	34.4	19.8
26 and older	45.5	10.4	6.1
By Sex			
Male	50.3	17.4	10.5
Female	40.9	11.8	6.2
By Race/Ethnicity			
White[2]	49.0	14.8	8.5
Black[2]	42.9	16.4	9.8
Hispanic	35.0	13.1	6.9
Asian	23.7	8.9	3.6

Note: Includes marijuana, cocaine, heroin, hallucinogens, inhalants, or prescription-type psychotherapeutic drugs (stimulants, sedatives, tranquilizers, and analgesics) for nonmedical purposes. 1. Age 12 and older. 2. Non-Hispanic. **Source:** U.S. Dept. of Health and Human Services, Substance Abuse and Mental Health Services Administration, *2005 National Survey on Drug Use and Health,* (Sept. 2007).

Drug Use by U.S. High School Seniors, 1975–2006

Drug	1975	1980	1985	1990	1995	2000	2005	2006
Alcohol	68.2%	72.0%	65.9%	57.1%	51.3%	50.0%	47.0%	45.3%
Cigarettes	36.7	30.5	30.1	29.4	33.5	31.4	23.2	21.6
Marijuana	27.1	33.7	25.7	14.0	21.2	21.6	19.8	18.3
LSD	2.3	2.3	4.4	1.9	4.0	1.6	0.7	0.6
Cocaine	1.9	5.2	6.7	1.9	1.8	2.1	2.3	2.5
Heroin	0.4	0.2	0.3	0.2	0.6	0.7	0.5	0.4
Methamphetamine	—	—	—	—	—	1.9	0.9	0.9

Note: Drug use during the 30 days preceding the survey.   Source: U.S. Dept. of Health and Human Services, National Institute on Drug Abuse, *Monitoring the Future Study.*

Alcohol Use in U.S., 2005

Characteristic	Total[1]	By Age		26 and older
		12-17	18-25	
Total	51.8%	16.5%	60.9%	55.1%
Race/Ethnicity				
White[2]	56.5	18.5	67.9	59.2
Black[2]	40.8	11.6	47.9	44.7
Hispanic or Latino	42.6	16.7	50.5	45.7
Asian	38.1	7.0	47.4	40.6
Sex				
Male	58.1	15.9	66.3	62.7
Female	45.9	17.2	55.4	48.0
Adult Education				
Less than high school	N.A.	N.A.	46.3	34.5
High school graduate	N.A.	N.A.	55.8	49.2
Some college	N.A.	N.A.	68.8	59.2
College graduate	N.A.	N.A.	78.0	68.7
Current Employment				
Full-time	N.A.	N.A.	66.7	62.7
Part-time	N.A.	N.A.	61.6	57.1
Unemployed	N.A.	N.A.	56.9	56.3
Other[3]	N.A.	N.A.	47.4	39.6

Notes: Percentages reporting use of alcohol in the previous month. N.A.=Not Applicable. 1. Age 12 and older. 2. Non-Hispanic. 3. Includes retired, disabled, homemaker, student, etc. Source: U.S. Dept. of Health and Human Services, Substance Abuse and Mental Health Services Administration, *2005 National Survey on Drug Use and Health* (Sept. 2006).

U.S. Alcohol Consumption, 1940–2005 (gallons of ethanol, per capita)

Year	Beer	Wine	Spirits	All beverages
1940	0.73	0.16	0.67	1.56
1950	1.04	0.23	0.77	2.04
1960	0.99	0.22	0.86	2.07
1970	1.14	0.27	1.11	2.52
1980	1.38	0.34	1.04	2.76
1990	1.34	0.33	0.77	2.45
1995	1.23	0.29	0.63	2.15
1998	1.25	0.31	0.63	2.19
2000	1.22	0.31	0.65	2.18
2004	1.21	0.35	0.68	2.23
2005	1.19	0.36	0.70	2.24

Note: Based on population age 15 and older prior to 1970 and on population age 14 and older thereafter.
Source: U.S. Dept. of Health and Human Services, National Institute on Alcohol Abuse and Alcoholism (updated Nov. 2007).

ularly referred to as "ice" or "crystal." As of 2005, some 10.4 million Americans age 12 and older had tried methamphetamine at least once in their lifetimes.

Heroin is a synthetic compound derived from morphine, which is extracted from the seed pods of certain varieties of poppy plants. Highly addictive, it comes in various forms, but most illicit heroin comes in powder form in colors ranging from white to dark brown. In 2005, an estimated 379,000 Americans age 12 or older used heroin, including 108,000 who used it for the first time.

Ecstasy, a synthetic drug with both stimulant and hallucinogenic properties, came onto the scene in the 1990's. Also known as MDMA, an acronym of its lengthy scientific name, it is available in pill form, with pills often embossed with smiley faces, shamrocks, and other enticing designs. Its popularity among young adults grew dramatically until 2001, then began to decline. For example, according to the Monitoring the Future study, the proportion of 12th graders reporting use of ecstasy in the prior 12 months rose from 5.6 percent in 1999 to 9.2 percent in 2001, then fell to 4.5 percent in 2003.

Initially associated with dance venues such as raves, ecstasy now is being used in a variety of settings. However, a growing body of evidence indicates that its use can lead to severe overheating and dehydration, as well as stroke, heart attack, and neurological damage.

Alcohol

Consumption of alcohol constitutes the nation's most common drug abuse problem. According to the Centers for Disease Control and Prevention, excessive alcohol use is responsible for more than 75,000 deaths annually. For exam-

ple, according to the National Highway Traffic Safety Administration, 17,013 people were killed in alcohol-related crashes in 2003. Additionally, alcohol is implicated in the three top causes of teen deaths: accidents, homicide, and suicide.

The 2005 National Survey on Drug Use and Health reported that 51.8 percent of Americans age 12 or older currently used alcohol (defined as any use in the previous month); 22.7 percent engaged in binge drinking (defined as five or more drinks on at least one occasion in the past month. The rate of past month alcohol use was lower in the South (47.8%) than in the Northeast (55.0), Midwest (55.0), or West (52.5).

According to the National Institute of Alcohol Abuse and Alcoholism (NIAAA), men are heavier drinkers than women, and much more likely to be binge drinkers. Younger people drink more than older people. Annual per capita consumption of alcoholic beverages was 2.23 gallons of ethanol in 2004. Consumption was highest in New Hampshire (4.07 gallons), the District of Columbia (3.93), and Nevada (3.66). It was lowest in Utah (1.28), Oklahoma (1.53), and West Virginia (1.75).

Tobacco

Smoking is the leading cause of preventable death in the United States, causing approximately 440,000 premature deaths annually and an estimated $157.7 billion in annual health-related economic losses. The good news is that smoking has fallen to its lowest level in recent memory. The decline is attributed to growing appreciation of the link between smoking and health problems; the increased cost of cigarettes, mostly because of tax increases; the growing number of smoking restrictions in public places; and decreasing social acceptability of smoking.

The percentage of adults who smoke decreased dramatically after 1964, the year the U.S. surgeon general first warned about the link between smoking and health problems such as cancer and heart disease. At that time, 40 percent of the adult population were smokers; in 2006, approximately 20.8 percent smoked. The percentage of high school students who reported current cigarette use increased significantly from 1991 to 1997 (27.5 to 36.4 percent), then decreased dramatically from 1997 to 2003 (36.4 to 21.9 percent—the lowest level since the Centers for Disease Control and Prevention began keeping track in 1975) before climbing slightly to 22.3 in 2004. Surveys indicate that more than 90 percent of adults who are regular smokers began smoking while they were teenagers and that 32 percent of young people who become regular smokers will die of a smoking-related disorder.

Health effects The U.S. surgeon general's report, The Health Consequences of Smoking, released in May 2004, concluded that smoking harms nearly every organ of the body, causing many diseases and reducing the health of smokers in general. Smoking cigarettes with lower machine-measured yields of tar and nicotine provides no clear benefit to health. However, quitting smoking has immediate as well as long-term benefits, reducing risks for diseases caused by smoking and improving health in general.

The effects of smoking include:
- Shortened life span. Each year, some 440,000 Americans—and about 4.9 million people worldwide—die prematurely as a result of smoking
- Cancer of the lungs, mouth, esophagus, stomach, bladder, kidney, pancreas, and cervix. Smoking accounts for at least 30 percent of all cancer deaths in the United States each year, including 87 percent of lung cancer deaths.
- Cardiovascular disease, including heart attack, stroke, aneurysm, and the peripheral vascular disease. Smoking weakens the heart's ability to pump blood, promotes clot formation, and damages the inner lining of blood vessels.
- Pulmonary illness, including emphysema, pneumonia, and chronic bronchitis. Annually, more than 80,000 Americans die from non-cancerous chronic lung diseases linked to smoking.
- Fetal and infant mortality. Smoking and secondhand smoke contribute to spontaneous abortions, stillbirths, and sudden infant death syndrome (SIDS). Also, infants of smokers are 74 percent more likely to be of low birth weight than are infants born to mothers who do not smoke.
- Oral health problems. Tobacco, particularly spit tobacco, causes serious oral problems, including cancer of the mouth and gum, periodontitis, and tooth loss.
- Environmental smoking risks. Nonsmokers who are exposed to the tobacco smoke of other people are at increased risk for various diseases. Exposure to secondhand smoke is responsible for approximately 3,000 lung cancer deaths annually among nonsmokers and 150,000 to 300,000 cases of lower respiratory tract infections such as bronchitis and pneumonia in children up to 18 months old. It also doubles a person's risk of heart disease.

U.S. Cigarette Consumption, 1900–2006

Year	Cigarettes (billions)	Per capita[1]	Year	Cigarettes (billions)	Per capita[1]
1900	2.5	54	1960	484.4	4,171
1910	8.6	151	1970	536.5	3,985
1920	44.6	665	1980	631.5	3,849
1930	119.3	1,485	1990	525.0	2,817
1940	181.9	1,976	2000	430.0	2,092
1950	369.8	3,552	2006	372.0	1,691[2]

1. Among persons age 18 and older. 2. Preliminary. **Source:** U.S. Dept. of Health and Human Services, Centers for Disease Control and Prevention; USDA, Economic Research Service.

Teenage Tobacco Use, 1991–2007

Category	1991	1997	2001	2007
Sex				
Male	27.6%	37.7%	29.2%	21.3%
Female	27.3	34.7	27.7	18.7
Race/Ethnicity				
White[1]	30.9	39.7	31.9	23.2
Black[1]	12.6	22.7	14.7	11.6
Hispanic	25.3	34.0	26.6	16.7
High school grade				
9	23.2	33.4	23.0	14.3
10	25.2	35.3	26.9	19.6
11	31.6	36.6	29.8	21.6
12	30.1	39.6	35.2	26.5

Note: Smoked cigarettes within 30 days preceding the survey.
1. Non-Hispanic. **Source:** U.S. Dept. of Health and Human Services, Centers for Disease Control and Prevention, *Morbidity and Mortality Weekly Report*, June 27, 2008.

Adult Cigarette Smokers in the U.S., 2005

Year	Men	Women	Total
Total	23.9%	18.1%	20.9%
Age			
18-24	28.0	20.7	24.4
25-44	26.8	21.4	24.1
45-64	25.2	18.8	21.9
65 and older	8.9	8.3	8.6
Race/Ethnicity			
White[1]	24.0	20.0	21.9
Black[1]	26.7	17.3	21.5
Hispanic	21.1	11.1	16.2
American Indian/ Alaska Native[1]	37.5	26.8	32.0
Asian	20.6	6.1	13.3
Education[2]			
8 years or less	21.0	13.4	17.1
9-11 years	36.8	29.0	32.6
High school graduate	28.8	20.7	24.6
Undergraduate degree	11.9	9.6	10.7
Graduate degree	6.9	7.4	7.1

1. Non-Hispanic. 2. Among those age 25 and older.
Source: U.S. Dept. of Health and Human Services, Centers for Disease Control and Prevention, *Morbidity and Mortality Weekly Report*, October 27, 2006.

The Media

THE PRINT MEDIA

▶**NEWSPAPERS**

The first American newspaper was a three-page publication called *Publick Occurrences, Both Foreign and Domestick*, printed in 1690 and immediately suppressed by the Massachussetts government. Despite this setback, a number of newspapers, led by James Franklin's *New England Courant*, slowly emerged, and by 1775, the 2.5 million colonists were served by 48 small weekly newspapers.

In 1783, the *Pennsylvania Evening Post*, which had been the first paper to print the Declaration of Independence, expanded from three printings a week to become the country's first daily newspaper. By 1800 there were 20 dailies and more than 1,000 small-town and frontier weeklies. Most of the dailies, filled with political and business news, were aimed at educated, affluent readers, but rising literacy created an opportunity for cheap, mass-circulation papers. The *New York Sun* started in 1833 and was sold on the street for just one cent. Other "penny presses" copied the *Sun's* approach and the graphic crime stories, vivid anecdotes and soft features drove their circulations far higher than those of the more staid presses.

During and after the Civil War, innovations like the transatlantic cable, the telephone, electric lights, typewriters, web-fed presses, and typesetting machines made reporting and printing cheaper and easier. In 1900 the number of daily newspapers peaked at 2,326, but readership continued to increase, due in part to the popularity of Sunday editions, to a high of 62,324 in 1990, even as the number of newspapers began to decline.

Newspapers today

The total number of daily newspapers was down to 1,411 in 2007. The continuing decline is partly because of radio, television and the Internet, but also

because of newspaper competition and mergers. A century ago, most major cities had at least two newspapers, but today fewer than 50 cities have more than one and, in 12 of those cities, the competing newspapers have actually combined all operations except for the editorial staffs. Nationwide, newsroom jobs have dropped to 52,600, a loss of 3,800 full-time employees since 2000.

Newspapers have become volatile business investments, losing 42% of their value from 2005-07, and some family-owned newspapers, like the Los Angeles *Times* and the *Wall Street Journal*, have been sold to conglomerates. Six companies—Gannett, McClatchy Co., Tribune Co., Advance Publications Inc., The New York Times Co., and NewsCorp—now account for almost half of all newspaper circulation.

Newspaper revenue from advertising fell to $42.2 million in 2007 for print advertising, and $45.4 for print and online advertising combined, an 8% drop from the peak combined total of $49.4 in 2005. Online newspaper advertising revenues reached a high of $3.2 million, a 16% increase over $2.7 million in 2006. Retail advertising has remained relatively stable since 2000, hovering around $21 million per year, but classified advertising has dropped from $19.6 million in 2000 to just $14.2 million in 2007.

Of the 1,411 daily newspapers published in the U.S. in 2007, most have circulations well under 50,000; 88 have circulations between 50,000 and 100,000; and 102 have a daily circulation of more than 100,000. *USA Today*, with almost 2.3 million readers, is the most widely read U.S newspaper, but worldwide more than half of the 532 million newspapers sold each day in 2007 were in Asia. The newspaper with the largest circulation is Japan's *Yomiuri Shimbun*, with more than 14 million readers, and its rival, the *Asahi Shimbun*, read by more than 12 million people each day.

While worldwide newspaper circulation rose 2.6 percent in 2007, U.S. papers lost 3 percent of their circulation since 2006, with evening dailies falling over 10 percent compared to a 2 percent loss for morning dailies. Daily circulation revenue for U.S. newspapers dropped to $52.3 million in

Daily Newspapers, Number and Circulation, 1900–2006

Year	Total Number of Daily papers	Total Daily circulation ('000s)	Morning Number of papers	Morning Daily circulation ('000s)	Evening Number of papers	Evening Daily circulation ('000s)	Sunday Number of papers	Sunday Daily circulation ('000s)
1900	2,226	15,102	—	—	—	—	—	—
1920	2,042	27,791	437	—	1,605	—	522	17,084
1930	1,942	39,589	388	—	1,554	—	521	26,413
1940	1,878	41,132	380	16,114	1,498	25,008	525	32,371
1950	1,772	53,829	322	21,266	1,450	32,563	549	46,582
1960	1,763	58,882	312	24,029	1,459	34,853	563	47,699
1970	1,748	62,108	334	25,934	1,429	36,174	586	49,217
1980	1,745	62,202	387	29,414	1,388	32,787	735	54,672
1990	1,611	62,324	559	41,308	1,084	21,015	863	62,634
1995	1,533	58,193	656	44,310	891	13,883	888	61,529
2000	1,480	55,773	766	46,772	727	9,000	917	59,421
2002	1,457	55,186	777	46,617	692	8,569	913	58,780
2004	1,457	54,626	814	46,887	653	7,738	915	57,754
2006	1,437	52,329	833	45,441	614	6,888	907	53,179

Note: All-day newspapers are listed in both morning and evening columns, but are counted only once in the total. **Source:** Newspaper Association of America.

Top U.S. Daily and Sunday Newspapers by Circulation, 2008

Rank	Newspaper	Average daily paid circulation		Rank	Newspaper	Average Sunday paid circulation
1.	USA Today	2,284,219		1.	The New York Times	1,476,400
2.	The Wall Street Journal	2,069,463		2.	Los Angeles Times	1,101,981
3.	The New York Times	1,077,256		3.	Chicago Tribune	898,703
4.	Los Angeles Times	773,884		4.	The Washington Post	890,163
5.	The Daily News (New York City)	703,137		5.	The Daily News (New York City)	704,157
6.	New York Post	702,488		6.	Houston Chronicle	632,797
7.	The Washington Post	673,180		7.	Philadelphia Inquirer	630,665
8.	Chicago Tribune	541,663		8.	Detroit Free Press	606,374
9.	Houston Chronicle	494,131		9.	The Denver Post / Rocky Mountain News	600,026
10.	Arizona Republic	413,332		10.	Star Tribune (Minneapolis)	534,750
11.	Newsday (Long Island, NY)	379,613		11.	The Boston Globe	525,959
12.	San Francisco Chronicle	370,345		12.	Dallas Morning News	520,215
13.	Dallas Morning News	368,313		13.	Arizona Republic	515,523
14.	The Boston Globe	350,605		14.	The Star-Ledger (Newark)	500,382
15.	The Star-Ledger (Newark)	345,130		15.	Atlanta Journal-Constitution	497,149
16.	The Philadelphia Inquirer	330,622		16.	Newsday (Long Island, NY)	441,728
17.	The Plain Dealer (Cleveland)	336,939		17.	The St. Petersburg Times	432,779
18.	Atlanta Journal-Constitution	350,157		18.	The Plain Dealer (Cleveland)	428,090
19.	Minneapolis Star Tribune	358,887		19.	San Francisco Chronicle	424,603
20.	St. Petersburg Times	305,854		20.	The St. Louis Post-Dispatch	414,564
21.	Chicago Sun-Times	382,796		21.	The Seattle Times Post–Intelligencer	409,231
22.	Detroit Free Press	345,861		22.	New York Post	401,315
23.	The Oregonian (Portland, Ore.)	310,803		23.	Milwaukee Journal Sentinel	384,539
24.	San Diego Union-Tribune	304,334		24.	Baltimore Sun	372,970
25.	Sacramento Bee	273,609		25.	The Oregonian (Portland, Ore.)	361,988
26.	Indianapolis Star	258,696		26.	The San Diego Union-Tribune	355,537
27.	St. Louis Post-Dispatch	276,588		27.	Kansas City Star	345,332
28.	Kansas City Star	254,793		28.	Columbus Dispatch	334,422
29.	Orange County (CA) Register	287,204		29.	Orlando Sentinel	332,030
30.	Miami Herald	279,878		30.	Pittsburgh Post-Gazette	331,053
31.	San Jose Mercury News	228,880		31.	The Indianapolis Star	324,349
32.	The Baltimore Sun	236,172		32.	San Antonio Express-News	315,959
33.	The Orlando Sentinel	221,826		33.	The Orange County (CA) Register	311,982
34.	San Antonio Express–News	223,846		34.	Miami Herald	311,245
35.	The Denver Post	255,935		35.	The Sacramento Bee	307,480
36.	Rocky Mountain News (Denver)	255,675		36.	South Florida Sun-Sentinel (Ft. Lauderdale)	303,399
37.	The Seattle Times	212,691		37.	Fort Worth Star-Telegram	289,974
38.	Tampa Tribune	220,277		38.	Tampa Tribune & Times	283,784
39.	South Florida Sun-Sentinel (Ft. Lauderdale)	235,154		39.	Cincinnati Enquirer	279,825
40.	Milwaukee Journal Sentinel	230,781		40.	Arkansas Democrat-Gazette (Little Rock)	274,494
41.	The Courier-Journal (Louisville, KY)	210,081		41.	Charlotte Observer	264,170
42.	The Pittsburgh Post-Gazette	212,075		42.	Oklahoma City Oklahoman	262,150
43.	Cincinnati Enquirer	212,369		43.	Buffalo News	260,445
44.	The Charlotte Observer	210,616		44.	The Courier-Journal (Louisville, KY)	258,778
45.	Fort Worth Star Telegram	207,045		45.	St. Paul Pioneer Press	252,055
46.	Oklahoma City Oklahoman	201,771		46.	San Jose Mercury News	251,851
47.	The Columbus Dispatch	199,524		47.	Chicago Sun-Times	247,469
48.	St. Paul Pioneer Press	191,768		48.	Hartford Courant	237,933
49.	Detroit News	188,171		49.	Des Moines Sunday Register	222,122
50.	Boston Herald	182,350		50.	Omaha World-Herald	219,795

Note: Average daily and Sunday circulation based on six-month period ending March 31, 2008.
Source: Audit Bureau of Circulations, 2008

2007. The percentage of Americans who read a daily newspaper fell in 2007 to 48 percent of adults, down from 54.1 percent in 2003 and well below the high of 62.4 percent in 1990. Sunday edition readership is traditionally higher, but was 55.4 percent in 2007, compared to 68.2 percent in 1998. Newspaper readership remains highest among people with the most education, the highest income, and the greatest job responsibilities. The average reader is over 55 years old, and only 19 percent of 18 to 34-year-olds read newspapers at all.

Newspapers tomorrow

Facing increasing competition from Internet-based news sites for readers and advertisers, U.S. newspapers have struggled to establish an online presence. According to a report by the Carnegie Corporation, 39 percent of Americans under 35-years-old planned to get news from the Internet, compared to 8 percent who planned to read a newspaper. Most newspapers in the U.S. (including the top 100 in circulation) now have Web sites, and nearly one in three Internet users (44 million people) read at least one of these online editions.

However, news-based Web sites with no print affiliation have been very successful at drawing readers with commentary and other features that traditional newspapers shun. The *Huffington Post* outranks all but six newspaper websites in visitor counts and, in 2007, *Talking Points Memo* became the first Web-only publication to win a major journalism prize, the George Polk Award.

Weekly Newspapers in the U.S., 1960–2005

Year	Number of newspapers[1]	Average circulation	Total weekly circulation	Year	Number of newspapers[1]	Average circulation	Total weekly circulation
1960	8,174	2,566	20,974,338	1990	7,606	6,958	52,919,846
1965	8,061	3,106	25,036,031	1995[2]	8,453	9,425	79,668,266
1970	7,612	3,660	27,857,332	2000[2]	6,579	7,295	47,990,892
1975	7,612	4,715	35,892,409	2004[2]	6,692	7,444	49,814,806
1980	7,954	5,324	42,347,512	2005[2]	6,659	7,319	49,541,617
1985	7,704	6,359	48,988,801				

Notes: 1. Any newspaper published less than four times a week. 2. 1995 and later not comparable to prior years due to change in information collection procedures. **Source:** Newspaper Association of America.

Top 100 U.S. Magazines by Circulation, 2007

Rank Magazine	Average paid circulation per issue	Percent change 2006–07	Rank Magazine	Average paid circulation per issue	Percent change 2006–07
1. AARP The Magazine	24,204,313	4.1%	51. VFW Magazine	1,577,616	–2.2%
2. AARP Bulletin	23,567,607	4.2	52. Fitness	1,569,467	1.1
3. Reader's Digest	9,684,759	–4.1	53. Field & Stream	1,534,969	10.0
4. Better Homes and Gardens	7,681,722	0.7	54. Home & Away	1,484,885	–0.6
5. National Geographic	5,051,999	–0.4	55. Every Day with Rachel Ray	1,483,516	60.8
6. Good Housekeeping	4,686,152	0.2	56. Woman's World	1,481,949	–3.1
7. Family Circle	3,967,065	–0.8	57. Self	1,478,892	–0.7
8. Woman's Day	3,924,195	–2.2	58. Cosmo Girl!	1,451,222	2.0
9. Ladies' Home Journal	3,918,472	–5.3	59. Rolling Stone	1,445,493	–0.2
10. AAA Westways	3,764,966	0.8	60. Ebony	1,429,691	0.1
11. People	3,676,499	–2.9	61. First For Women	1,425,193	–3.4
12. Prevention	3,390,084	2.0	62. Golf Magazine	1,419,133	2.0
13. Time	3,374,505	–17.3	63. Star Magazine	1,411,057	–7.7
14. TV Guide	3,276,474	–6.4	64. Popular Science	1,379,637	2.5
15. Sports Illustrated	3,231,969	0.7	65. Health	1,369,471	0.6
16. Taste of Home[2]	3,163,669	N.A.	66. Bon Appetit	1,367,673	1.3
17. Newsweek	3,124,059	–0.2	67. Stuff	1,362,245	6.0
18. Cosmopolitan	2,909,332	–0.9	68. American Rifleman	1,347,288	0.4
19. Via Magazine	2,832,721	0.9	69. Weight Watchers	1,312,180	1.6
20. Southern Living	2,807,269	–0.5	70. Car and Driver	1,308,150	0.0
21. Playboy	2,790,300	–7.5	71. In Touch Weekly	1,290,769	5.0
22. Maxim	2,558,475	0.7	72. Country Home	1,288,721	1.9
23. AAA Going Places	2,551,164	0.9	73. Vogue	1,287,561	0.0
24. American Legion	2,550,056	1.0	74. More	1,260,136	7.5
25. O, The Oprah Magazine	2,420,940	2.6	75. Popular Mechanics	1,232,138	0.9
26. AAA Living	2,409,958	–0.9	76. Sunset	1,231,467	–16.9
27. Guideposts	2,374,212	0.3	77. Scholastic Parent & Child[1]	1,230,653	1.3
28. Redbook	2,318,456	–3.0	78. Boys' Life	1,170,659	–4.1
29. Glamour	2,308,048	1.4	79. Family Handyman	1,170,394	–0.6
30. AAA World[2]	2,121,699	0.7	80. Lucky	1,160,165	4.1
31. Parents	2,100,786	0.8	81. Vanity Fair	1,157,653	–5.7
32. ESPN The Magazine	2,075,672	2.9	82. Motor Trend	1,126,326	1.0
33. Seventeen	2,066,825	2.1	83. Essence	1,087,720	–0.2
34. Smithsonian	2,044,654	0.4	84. Allure	1,078,405	–4.4
35. U.S. News & World Report	2,036,185	0.0	85. The New Yorker	1,065,893	0.1
36. Martha Stewart Living	2,013,957	0.6	86. Elle	1,063,878	0.6
37. Real Simple	1,979,956	1.5	87. National Enquirer	1,033,271	–8.9
38. Money	1,921,436	–1.4	88. Cottage Living	1,012,985	9.7
39. US Weekly	1,905,030	7.4	89. Scouting	1,010,332	0.3
40. Parenting	1,901,790	0.3	90. Marie Claire	984,643	2.7
41. Men's Health	1,810,810	–1.1	91. Teen Vogue	981,246	–0.8
42. Entertainment Weekly	1,804,797	0.4	92. Travel + Leisure	978,303	0.2
43. FamilyFun	1,802,012	–3.1	93. House & Garden[1]	976,443	6.9
44. Endless Vacation[2]	1,782,403	0.5	94. Elks Magazine[1]	975,307	–2.6
45. Cooking Light	1,775,950	2.7	95. This Old House	966,100	0.1
46. In Style	1,752,261	–0.9	96. Gourmet	963,222	–2.8
47. Shape	1,738,829	2.0	97. Traditional Home	961,757	–1.9
48. Golf Digest	1,648,856	1.1	98. Midwest Living	953,175	1.1
49. Country Living	1,639,182	–1.0	99. Outdoor Life	946,955	14.1
50. Remedy	1,604,878	39.8	100. Food & Wine	940,983	–1.4
			Total Top 100	**245,274,376**	**1.9%**

Notes: 1. First half figures only. 2. Second half figures only.　**Source:** Magazine Publishers of America, 2008.

Top 50 U.S. Magazines by Advertising Revenues, 2006-07

Rank, Magazine	Advertising revenues	Percent change 2006-07	Rank, Magazine	Advertising revenues	Percent change 2006-07
1. People	$979,760,812	12.3%	26. New York Magazine	$227,382,026	16.3%
2. Better Homes & Gardens	857,593,385	10.4	27. The New Yorker	226,152,740	10.6
3. Sports Illustrated	681,768,075	10.3	28. Redbook	226,010,828	13.1
4. Time	540,390,066	–18.3	29. Rolling Stone	223,298,997	0.5
5. Good Housekeeping	527,874,148	6.1	30. Parents	223,242,922	10.0
6. Newsweek	474,512,372	–1.8	31. Car and Driver	219,934,948	7.3
7. Vogue	419,036,800	10.0	32. Shape Magazine	216,993,257	21.0
8. Family Circle	406,256,973	17.0	33. TV Guide	212,595,267	33.5
9. Cosmopolitan	405,881,697	10.5	34. GQ	212,542,269	11.8
10. Woman's Day	398,466,220	–4.6	35. Harper's Bazaar	209,954,250	26.8
11. In Style	397,182,207	–3.1	36. Maxim	207,744,826	7.6
12. Forbes	369,343,727	7.9	37. Southern Living	205,662,950	–0.9
13. Glamour	365,550,912	18.2	38. Martha Stewart Living	202,926,833	24.0
14. Ladies' Home Journal	356,393,316	0.0	39. Star	195,111,994	26.8
15. ESPN Magazine	318,286,253	18.2	40. Bride's	188,891,043	–1.0
16. Reader's Digest	312,579,834	8.0	41. Golf Magazine	188,157,982	7.6
17. O, The Oprah Magazine	311,608,429	8.4	42. Self	187,916,925	14.5
18. Vanity Fair	311,025,731	23.0	43. Conde Nast Traveler	187,566,052	22.0
19. US Weekly	309,921,951	12.2	44. Allure	185,986,908	15.9
20. Real Simple	304,785,393	22.8	45. Lucky	183,673,893	6.7
21. Elle	292,880,302	13.0	46. Motor Trend	181,343,379	6.5
22. Business Week	270,460,663	–12.9	47. Men's Health	178,099,101	19.4
23. US News & World Report	270,186,387	1.0	48. AARP-The Magazine	176,723,187	6.3
24. Fortune	269,446,328	–10.5	49. W	176,544,099	16.8
25. Entertainment Weekly	230,317,855	–6.5	50. Golf Digest	176,255,644	3.3

Source: Magazine Publishers of America, *Publishers Information Bureau Publications Ranked by Revenue, Jan. - Dec. 2007*

►MAGAZINES

Consumer magazines range from the very specialized (*Fly Fisherman*) to the general interest (*People*) and are sold either by subscription or through retail stores. Some (*Audubon*) published by membership groups, are also distributed to members. The Audit Bureau of Circulations monitors the sales of about 500 of the most popular consumer magazines. Trade publications are magazines focused on a particular area of business (e.g. trucking, restaurants, computers).

Top 20 U.S. Newspaper Web sites by Unique Visitors, 2007

Rank, Newspaper	Unique Visitors each month[1]
1. New York Times	13,857,000
2. Washington Post	11,682,000
3. USA Today	9,186,000
4. Wall Street Journal	8,337,000
5. Los Angeles Times	4,992,000
6. Boston Globe	3,798,000
7. San Francisco Chronicle	3,653,000
8. Chicago Tribune	3,316,000
9. New York Post	2,895,000
10. Seattle Times Post-Intelligencer	2,838,000
11. Houston Chronicle	2,520,000
12. Atlanta Journal Constitution	2,448,000
13. Orlando Sentinel	2,153,000
14. Arizona Republic	2,150,000
15. Newsday (Long Island, NY)	2,065,000
16. New York Daily News	1,979,000
17. San Diego Union Tribune	1,643,000
18. Philadelphia Inquirer	1,620,000
19. Dallas Morning News	1,530,000
20. Pittsburgh Post Gazette	1,461,000

Note: 1: Six-month average Mar.-Aug. 2007.
Source: Nielsen/Net Ratings.

About 2,700 trade publications are sold either by subscription or distributed free.

Most magazines make money through both circulation sales and advertising. The most financially successful magazines are not necessarily the largest sellers, because they may command high advertising fees. *Vogue*, for example, ranked 7th in advertising revenue for 2007, but was 73rd in circulation. Total magazine revenues for 2007 were almost $27.5 billion.

►BOOKS

Book sales in the United States held steady in 2007, according to figures released by the Book Industry Study Group, which monitors the reading habits of American households. The number of books sold was almost unchanged from the 2006 high of 2.3 billion, but the dollar volume of book sales was up 4 percent, indicating that the average price of books increased slightly.

Ironically, it is the computer, predicted by many to be the book industry's death knell, which has been responsible for the overall increase in book production since 1990. Computers not only reduce publishers' production costs, but they have also made possible the "superstore" in which computer indexes keep track of so many titles. Use of new print-on-demand capabilities for small and major publishers grew from 21,936 titles in 2006 to 134,773 in 2007, and electronic readers are now emerging as a viable sales method.

Steadily rising levels of educational attainment over recent decades—more than 87 percent of the population over 25 had finished high school in 2007 compared with 68.6 percent in 1980, while more than 29 percent had finished college, compared with 17 percent in 1980—has created a growing audience for the printed word. It has also fueled a corresponding increase in the number of libraries in the U.S. Since 1980, the number of libraries has increased by more than 8 percent.

Number and Value of U.S. Books Sold, 1990–2007 (in millions)

Type of publication and market area	Publishers' units			Domestic consumer expenditures		
	1990	2000	2007[1]	1990	2000	2007[1]
TYPE OF PUBLICATION						
Trade	730.7	1,156.1	2,272.7	$6,497.8	$11,583.2	$26,391.1
Adult trade	420.4	564.4	838.8	4,776.8	8,124.2	16,842.6
Juvenile trade	310.3	278.8	900.9	1,721.0	3,459.0	6,423.8
Mass market paperback	488.8	421.2	541.8	1,775.4	2,934.7	3,125.4
Book clubs	110.6	111.5	223.7	704.7	1,753.0	2213.1
Mail order publications	142.6	67.9	64.3	751.7	576.5	1148.3
Religious	137.7	133.4	274.5	1,361.9	2,782.7	4981.7
Professional	148.6	187.3	285.6	2,956.8	6,340.1	12,104.0
University press	15.8	18.4	28.7	284.1	541.4	683.6
Elementary and high school	218.7	151.9	178.4	1,947.9	4,373.3	5,713.4
College	149.7	82.8	77.9	2,319.0	4,265.2	6,750.6
Subscription reference	1.1	1.2	N.A.	443.6	986.1	1,132.3
All books	**2,144.3**	**2,331.6**	**2,295.0**	**$19,042.9**	**$36,136.2**	**$56,625.1**
MARKET AREA						
Domestic (total)	2,005.0	2,218.5	2,591.6	$19,042.9	$22,981.8	$56,625.1
General retailers	1,009.8	1,387.9	1,120.8	8,465.4	8,091.0	19,577.3
Colleges	254.6	220.3	283.1	3,403.2	3,980.7	10,434.9
Libraries and institutions	88.4	107.9	146.2	1,591.8	2,249.5	5,133.5
Schools and school libraries	244.1	198.3	214.8	2,365.0	4,314.6	6,674.0
Direct to consumers	304.1	272.0	125.2	2,901.0	4,097.9	4,373.1
Other	104.1	115.1	150.1	316.5	248.0	805.6
Export	139.4	220.9	171.2	—	—	—
Total	**2,144.3**	**2,461.9**	**3,126.8**	**—**	**—**	**—**

Note: Includes all titles released by publishers in the United States, and imports that appear under the imprint of American publishers. Multi-volume sets are counted as one unit. School libraries included with schools. Does not include standardized tests. Data from 2007 includes sales for small publishers ($50 million and below in annual revenue) and is not directly comparable with previous years. **1.** Estimated. **Source:** Book Industry Study Group, Inc., *Book Industry TRENDS 2008*, reprinted by permission.

Best Selling Books in America, 1917–2007

Year	Fiction Title, Author	Nonfiction Title, Author
1917	*Mr. Britling Sees It Through,* H.G. Wells	*Rhymes of A Red Cross Man,* Robert W. Service
1918	*The U.P. Trail,* Zane Grey	*Rhymes of A Red Cross Man,* Robert W. Service
1919	*The Four Horsemen of the Apocalypse,* V. Blasco Iañez	*The Education of Henry Adams,* Henry Adams
1920	*The Man of the Forest,* Zane Grey	*Now It Can Be Told,* Philip Gibbs
1921	*Main Street,* Sinclair Lewis	*The Outline of History,* H.G. Wells
1922	*If Winter Comes,* A.S.M. Hitchinson	*The Outline of History,* H.G. Wells
1923	*Black Oxen,* Gertrude Atherton	*Etiquette,* Emily Post
1924	*So Big,* Edna Ferber	*Diet and Health,* Lulu Hunt Peters
1925	*Soundings,* A. Hamilton Gibbs	*Diet and Health,* Lulu Hunt Peters
1926	*The Private Life of Helen of Troy,* John Erskine	*The Man Nobody Knows,* Bruce Barton
1927	*Elmer Gantry,* Sinclair Lewis	*The Story of Philosophy,* Will Durant
1928	*The Bridge on San Luis Rey,* Thornton Wilder	*Disraeli,* Andre Maurois
1929	*All Quiet on the Western Front,* Erich Maria Remarque	*The Art of Thinking,* Ernest Dimmet
1930	*Cimarron,* Edna Ferber	*The Story of San Michele,* Axel Munthe
1931	*The Good Earth,* Pearl S. Buck	*Education of a Princess,* Grand Duchess Marie
1932	*The Good Earth,* Pearl S. Buck	*The Epic of America,* James Truslow Adams
1933	*Anthony Adverse,* Hervey Allen	*Life Begins at Forty,* Walter Pitkin
1934	*Anthony Adverse,* Hervey Allen	*While Rome Burns,* Alexander Woollcott
1935	*Green Light,* Lloyd C. Douglas	*North to the Orient,* Anne Morrow Lindbergh
1936	*Gone With the Wind,* Margaret Mitchell	*Man the Unknown,* Alexis Carrel
1937	*Gone With the Wind,* Margaret Mitchell	*How to Win Friends and Influence People,* Dale Carnegie
1938	*The Yearling,* Marjorie Kinnan Rawlings	*The Importance of Living,* Lin Yutang
1939	*The Grapes of Wrath,* John Steinbeck	*Days of Our Years,* Piere von Paaseen
1940	*How Green Was My Valley,* Richard Llewellyn	*I Married Adventure,* Osa Johnson
1941	*The Keys of the Kingdom,* A.J. Cronin	*Berlin Diary,* William C. Shirer
1942	*The Song of Bernadette,* Franz Werfel	*See Here, Private Hargrove,* Marion Hargrove
1943	*The Robe,* Lloyd C. Douglas	*Under Cover,* John Roy Carlson
1944	*Strange Fruit,* Lillian Smith	*I Never Left Home,* Bob Hope
1945	*Forever Amber,* Kathleen Winsor	*Brave Men,* Ernie Pyle
1946	*The King's General,* Daphne du Maurier	*The Egg and I,* Betty MacDonald
1947	*The Miracle of the Bells,* Russell Janney	*Peace of Mind,* Joshua L. Liebman

Year	Fiction Title, Author	Nonfiction Title, Author
1948	*The Big Fisherman*, Lloyd C. Douglas	*Crusade in Europe*, Dwight D. Eisenhower
1949	*The Egyptian*, Mika Waltari	*White Collar Zoo*, Clare Barnes, Jr.
1950	*The Cardinal*, Henry Morton Robinson	*Betty Crocker's Picture Cookbook*
1951	*From Here to Eternity*, James Jones	*Look Younger, Live Longer*, Gayelord Hauser
1952	*The Silver Chalice*, Thomas B.Costain	*The Holy Bible: Revised Standard Version*
1953	*The Robe*, Lloyd C. Douglas	*The Holy Bible: Revised Standard Version*
1954	*Not As A Stranger*, Morton Thompson	*The Holy Bible: Revised Standard Version*
1955	*Marjorie Morningstar*, Herman Wouk	*Gift from the Sea*, Anne Morrow Lindbergh
1956	*Don't Go Near the Water*, William Brinkley	*Arthritis and Common Sense*, Dan Dale Alexander
1957	*By Love Possessed*, James Gould Cozzens	*Kids Say the Darndest Things!*, Art Linkletter
1958	*Doctor Zhivago*, Boris Pasternak	*Kids Say the Darndest Things!*, Art Linkletter
1959	*Exodus*, Leon Uris	*'Twixt Twelve and Twenty*, Pat Boone
1960	*Advise and Consent*, Allen Drury	*Folk Medicine*, D.C. Jarvis
1961	*The Agony and the Ecstasy*, Irving Stone	*The New English Bible: The New Testament*
1962	*Ship of Fools*, Katherine Anne Porter	*Calories Don't Count*, Dr. Herman Taller
1963	*The Shoes of the Fisherman*, Morris L. West	*Happiness Is a Warm Puppy*, Charles M. Schulz
1964	*The Spy Who Came in From the Cold*, John le Carré	*Four Days*, American Heritage
1965	*The Source*, James A. Michener	*How To Be a Jewish Mother*, Dan Greenburg
1966	*Valley of the Dolls*, Jacqueline Susann	*How to Avoid Probate*, Norman F. Dacey
1967	*The Arrangement*, Elia Kazan	*Death of a President*, William Manchester
1968	*Airport*, Arthur Hailey	*Better Homes & Gardens New Cook Book*
1969	*Portnoy's Complaint*, Philip Roth	*American Heritage Dictionary of the English Language*, ed. William Morris
1970	*Love Story*, Erich Segal	*Everything You Wanted to Know About Sex but Were Afraid to Ask*, David Reuben, M.D.
1971	*Wheels*, Arthur Hailey	*The Sensuous Man*, "M."
1972	*Jonathan Livingston Seagull*, Richard Bach	*The Living Bible*, Kenneth Taylor
1973	*Jonathan Livingston Seagull*, Richard Bach	*The Living Bible*, Kenneth Taylor
1974	*Centennial*, James A. Michener	*The Total Woman*, Marabel Morgan
1975	*Ragtime*, E. L. Doctorow	*Angels: God's Secret Agents*, Billy Graham
1976	*Trinity*, Leon Uris	*The Final Days*, Bob Woodward, Carl Bernstein
1977	*The Silmarillion*, J.R.R. Tolkien	*Roots*, Alex Haley
1978	*Chesapeake*, James A. Michener	*If Life is a Bowl of Cherries—What Am I Doing in the Pits?* Erma Bombeck
1979	*The Matarese Circle*, Robert Ludlum	*Aunt Erma's Cope Book*, Erma Bombeck
1980	*The Covenant*, James Michener	*Crisis Investing*, Douglas R. Casey
1981	*Noble House*, James Clavell	*The Beverly Hills Diet*, Judy Mazel
1982	*E.T. The Extra-Terrestrial Storybook*	*Jane Fonda's Workout Book*, Jane Fonda with William Kotzwinkle
1983	*Return of the Jedi Storybook*, Joan D. Vinge	*In Search of Excellence*, Thomas J. Peters, Robert H. Waterman Jr.
1984	*The Talisman*, Stephen King, Peter Straub	*Iacocca: An Autobiography*, Lee Iacocca with William Novak
1985	*The Mammoth Hunters*, Jean M.Auel	*Iacocca: An Autobiography*, Lee Iacocca with William Novak
1986	*It*, Stephen King	*Fatherhood*, Bill Cosby
1987	*The Tommyknockers*, Stephen King	*Time Flies*, Bill Cosby
1988	*The Cardinal of the Kremlin*,Tom Clancy	*The Eight-Week Cholesterol Diet*, Robert Kowalski
1989	*Clear and Present Danger*, Tom Clancy	*All I Really Need to Know I Learned in Kindergarten*, Robert Fulghum
1990	*The Plains of Passage*, Jean Auel	*A Life on the Road*, Charles Kuralt
1991	*Scarlett*, Alexandra Ripley	*Me: The Stories of My Life*, Katharine Hepburn
1992	*Dolores Claiborne*, Stephen King	*The Way Things Ought to Be*, Rush Limbaugh
1993	*The Bridges of Madison County*, Robert James Waller	*See, I Told You So*, Rush Limbaugh
1994	*The Chamber*, John Grisham	*In the Kitchen with Rosie*, Rosie Daley
1995	*The Rainmaker*, John Grisham	*Men are From Mars, Women are From Venus*, John Gray
1996	*The Runaway Jury*, John Grisham	*Make the Connection*, Oprah Winfrey & Bob Greene
1997	*The Partner*, John Grisham	*Angela's Ashes*, Frank McCourt
1998	*The Street Lawyer*, John Grisham	*The Nine Steps to Financial Freedom*, Suze Orman
1999	*The Testament*, John Grisham	*Tuesdays with Morrie*, Mitch Albom
2000	*The Brethren*, John Grisham	*Who Moved My Cheese?* Spencer Johnson
2001	*Desecration*, Jerry B. Jenkins and Tim LaHaye	*The Prayer of Jabez*, Bruce Wilkinson
2002	*The Summons*, John Grisham	*Self Matters*, Phillip C. McGraw
2003	*The Da Vinci Code*, Dan Brown	*The Purpose-Driven Life*, Rick Warren
2004	*The Da Vinci Code*, Dan Brown	*The South Beach Diet*, Arthur Agatston
2005	*The Broker*, John Grisham	*Natural Cures "They" Don't Want You to Know About*, Kevin Trudeau
2006	*For One More Day*, Mitch Albom	*The Innocent Man*, John Grisham
2007	*A Thousand Splendid Suns*, Khaled Hosseini	*The Secret*, Rhonda Byrne

Sources: Alice Payne Hackett, *70 Years of Best Sellers; Publishers Weekly.*

New Books and Editions Published, by Subject, 1990–2007

Subject	1990	2000	2007[1]	Subject	1990	2000	2007[1]
Agriculture	514	1,073	1,298	Literature	2,049	3,371	9,796
Arts	1,262	4,980	9,423	Medicine	3,014	6,234	10,720
Biography	1,957	3,899	10,615	Music	289	1,582	3,407
Business	1,191	4,068	7,651	Personal Finance	N.A.	N.A.	538
Computers	N.A.	N.A.	5,709	Philosophy,	1,688	5,556	12,635
Cookery	N.A.	N.A.	2,673	Psychology			
Education	1,039	3,378	7,335	Poetry, Drama	874	2,479	10,258
Fiction	5,764	14,617	50,071	Religion	2,285	6,206	18,956
General works	1,760	1,318	2,346	Science	2,742	8,464	12,872
History	2,248	7,931	14,764	Sociology,	7,042	14,908	24,596
Home economics	758	2,513	1,682	Economics			
Juvenile	5,172	8,690	30,063	Sports, Recreation	978	3,483	6,363
Language	649	2,536	4,846	Technology	2,092	8,582	6,858
Law	896	3,070	5,380	Travel	495	3,170	5,793
				Total	46,748	122,108	276,649

Note: Comprises new books (published for the first time), and new editions. Includes mass-market paperbacks. Excludes government publications, books sold only by subscription, dissertations, periodicals, quarterlies, and pamphlets under 49 pages. 1. Projected. **Note on Methodology:** Beginning in 2006, Bowker changed methodology to include ISBNs without prices, as well as new book bindings. The total counts for 2007 cannot be compared directly with previous years. **Source:** R.R. Bowker Co., *The Bowker Annual Library and Book Trade Almanac,* copyright 2004 Reed Elsevier Inc. Used with the permission of R.R. Bowker, a business unit of Reed Elsevier Inc., and R.R. Bowker *New Book Titles and Editions, 2002-2007.*

The American Library Association's 10 Most Frequently Challenged Books of 2000–2005

Rank, Title, Author

1. Harry Potter series, J.K. Rowling
2. *The Chocolate War,* Robert Cormier
3. Alice series, Phyllis Reynolds Naylor
4. *Of Mice and Men,* John Steinbeck
5. *I Know Why the Caged Bird Sings,* Maya Angelou

6. *Fallen Angels,* Walter Dean Myers
7. *It's Perfectly Normal,* Robie Harris
8. Scary Stories series, Alvin Schwartz
9. Captain Underpants series, Dav Pilkey
10. *Forever,* Judy Blume

The American Library Association's 10 Most Frequently Challenged Books of 2007

Rank, Title, Author

1. *And Tango Makes Three,* Justin Richardson and Peter Parnell
2. *The Chocolate War,* Robert Cormier
3. *Olive's Ocean,* Kevin Henkes
4. *The Golden Compass,* Philip Pullman
5. *The Adventures of Huckleberry Finn,* Mark Twain
6. *The Color Purple,* Alice Walker
7. *TTYL,* Lauren Myracle
8. *I Know Why the Caged Bird Sings,* Maya Angelou
9. *It's Perfectly Normal,* Robie Harris
10. *The Perks of Being a Wallflower,* Stephen Chbosky

Source: American Library Association.

Number of Libraries in U.S. and Canada by Type, 1980–2000

Type of Library	1980	1990	1999	2000
Public	8,717	9,060	9,837	9,480
Branches of public libraries	5,936	5,833	6,376	6,957
Special	7,649	9,051	9,691	9,948
Medical	1,674	1,861	1,906	1,955
Religious	913	946	1,001	767
Law	417	647	1,136	1,172
Academic	4,591	4,593	4,723	3,491
Junior college	1,191	1,233	1,274	1,148
Colleges, universities	3,400	3,360	3,449	2,251
Departmental	1,489	1,454	1,467	1,454
Law, medical, religious	269	501	493	418
Government	1,260	1,735	1,874	1,411
Armed forces	485	489	352	341
Total, U.S.	28,638	30,761	33,108	31,628
Total, U.S. and Canada	31,564	34,613	37,039	35,261

Source: R.R. Bowker Co., *The Bowker Annual: Library and Book Trade Almanac.* (2001). Used with the permission of R.R. Bowker ® a Unit of Cahners Business Information.

THE ELECTRONIC MEDIA

► TELEVISION

Few people doubt the pervasiveness of television's influence on America. Once a symbol of luxury, the color television set has found its way into almost every home in America, and a great majority of American households have two or more televisions. According to Nielsen Media Research, which monitors television viewership, at least one of these televisions was on in each household for 8 hours 11 minutes during the 2004-2005 television season. That's two hours and 10 minutes more than in 1971, when the average was just 6 hours 1 minute. Average daily viewing per person is still much higher than 1970s levels. Women over the age of 18 watched longest; they averaged 4 hours 37 minutes per day, down 7 minutes from the year before, while men over 18 watched for 4 hours 1 minute, down 5 minutes from 1999-2000. Children aged 12-17 watched an average of 3 hours 17 minutes, up 11 minutes from a year ago. Viewing by children 2-11 has dropped from 3 hours 49 minutes in 1984-85 to three hours and 10 minutes in 2000-2001.

Top 50 Single Shows in TV History, by Rating

Rank, Program	Date	Network	Rating	Share
1. M*A*S*H Special (Last episode)	2/28/83	CBS	60.2%	77%
2. Dallas (Who Shot J.R.?)	11/21/80	CBS	53.3	76
3. Roots, part 8	1/30/77	ABC	51.1	71
4. Super Bowl XVI (San Francisco/Cincinnati)	1/24/82	CBS	49.1	73
5. Super Bowl XVII (Washington/Miami)	1/30/83	NBC	48.6	69
6. XVII Winter Olympics (Figure skating round 1)	2/23/94	CBS	48.5	64
7. Super Bowl XX (Chicago/New England)	1/26/86	NBC	48.3	70
8. Gone With the Wind, part 1	11/7/76	NBC	47.7	65
9. Gone With the Wind, part 2	11/8/76	NBC	47.4	64
10. Super Bowl XII (Dallas/Denver)	1/15/78	CBS	47.2	67
11. Super Bowl XIII (Pittsburgh/Dallas)	1/21/79	NBC	47.1	74
12. Bob Hope Christmas Show	1/15/70	NBC	46.6	64
13. Super Bowl XVIII (L.A. Raiders/Washington)	1/22/84	CBS	46.4	71
14. Super Bowl XIX (San Francisco/Miami)	1/20/85	ABC	46.4	63
15. Super Bowl XIV (Pittsburgh/L.A. Rams)	1/20/80	CBS	46.3	67
16. Super Bowl XXX (Dallas/Pittsburgh)	1/28/96	NBC	46.0	68
17. ABC Theater "The Day After"	1/20/83	ABC	46.0	62
18. The Fugitive	8/29/67	ABC	45.9	72
19. Roots, part 6	1/28/77	ABC	45.9	66
20. Super Bowl XXI (N.Y. Giants/Denver)	1/25/87	CBS	45.8	66
21. Roots, part 5	1/27/77	ABC	45.7	71
22. Super Bowl XXVIII (Dallas/Buffalo)	1/30/94	NBC	45.5	66
23. Cheers (Last episode)	5/20/93	NBC	45.5	64
24. The Ed Sullivan Show	2/9/64	CBS	45.3	60
25. Super Bowl XXVII (Dallas/Buffalo)	1/31/93	NBC	45.1	66
26. Bob Hope Christmas Show	1/14/71	NBC	45.0	61
27. Roots, part 3	1/25/77	ABC	44.8	68
28. Super Bowl XXXII (Denver/Green Bay)	1/25/98	NBC	44.5	67
29. Super Bowl XI (Oakland/Minnesota)	1/9/77	NBC	44.4	73
30. Super Bowl XV (Oakland/Philadelphia)	1/25/81	NBC	44.4	63
31. Super Bowl VI (Dallas/Miami)	1/16/72	CBS	44.2	74
32. XVII Winter Olympics (Figure skating finals)	2/25/94	CBS	44.1	64
33. Roots, part 2	1/24/77	ABC	44.1	62
34. The Beverly Hillbillies	1/8/64	CBS	44.0	65
35. Roots, part 4	1/26/77	ABC	43.8	66
36. The Ed Sullivan Show (with the Beatles)	2/16/64	CBS	43.8	60
37. Super Bowl XXIII (San Francisco/Cincinnati)	1/22/89	NBC	43.5	68
38. Academy Awards	4/7/70	ABC	43.4	78
39. Super Bowl XXXI (Green Bay/New England)	1/26/97	FOX	43.3	65
40. Super Bowl XXXIV (St. Louis/Tennessee)	1/30/00	ABC	43.3	63
41. The Thorn Birds, part 3	3/29/83	ABC	43.2	62
42. The Thorn Birds, part 4	3/30/83	ABC	43.1	62
43. NFC Championship game (San Francisco/Dallas)	1/10/82	CBS	42.9	62
44. The Beverly Hillbillies	1/15/64	CBS	42.8	62
45. Super Bowl VII (Miami/Washington)	1/14/73	NBC	42.7	72
46. Super Bowl XLI (Indianapolis/Chicago)	2/4/07	CBS	42.6	N.A.
47. The Thorn Birds, part 2	3/28/83	ABC	42.5	59
48. Super Bowl IX (Pittsburgh/Minnesota)	1/12/75	NBC	42.4	72
49. The Beverly Hillbillies	2/26/64	CBS	42.4	60
50. Super Bowl X (Pittsburgh/Dallas)	1/18/76	CBS	42.3	78

Note: As of August 2007. Does not include programs broadcast on more than one network, e.g. the Apollo moon landing or programs under 30 minutes scheduled duration. **Rating** is the number of people watching as a percentage of all television owners. **Share** is the number watching as a percentage of people with their TVs on at that particular time.   **Source:** Nielsen Media Research.

▶ CABLE TELEVISION

Cable television was originally designed as a means of improving TV reception in some rural areas. In the 1960s, operators realized that viewers were willing to pay for commercial-free programming, but their efforts to capitalize on the idea were hampered by stringent Federal Communications Commission restrictions. Not until 1975, when RCA put its first communications satellite into operation, did the industry really bloom. Under the name Home Box Office, the company started to transmit programming that could be received by independent operators around the country and then relayed to subscribers at minimal cost. When a federal appeals court dismissed most of the FCC's regulations in 1977, the door was opened for the development of what is now a multibillion-dollar industry.

In three decades, cable has changed the television broadcasting landscape, drawing more than one-

Top 10 TV Shows of 2007

Rank, Program (Network)	Avg. rating
1. American Idol- Wed. (Fox)	17.3
2. American Idol- Tues. (Fox)	16.8
3. Dancing With the Stars- Mon. (ABC)	13.2
4. Dancing With the Stars- Results (ABC)	12.2
5. NBC Sunday Night Football	10.2
6. CSI (CBS)	10.1
7. Grey's Anatomy-Thu. (ABC)	9.2
7. Samantha Who? (ABC)	9.2
9. House (Fox)	9.0
10. CSI: Miami (CBS)	8.9

Note: From Jan. 1, 2007—Dec. 2, 2007. Regularly scheduled programs. Includes Live and Same Day timeshifted viewing. **Rating** is the percentage of all television owners watching that program. **Source:** Nielsen Media Research.

Top 5 Single Telecasts of 2007

Rank, Program (Network)	Date	Avg. rating
1. Super Bowl XLI (CBS)	2/4/07	42.6
2. Super Bowl XLI Post Game (CBS)	2/4/07	28.1
3. Academy Awards (ABC)	2/25/07	23.6
4. American Idol- Wed. (Fox)	1/16/07	20.3
5. American Idol- Tues. (Fox)	1/17/07	20.1

Note: From Jan. 1—Dec. 2, 2007. Telecasts over 5 minutes. Includes Live and Same Day timeshifted viewing. **Source:** Nielsen Media Research.

Longest-Running National Network Series of All Time

Program	Seasons	Years[1]
60 Minutes	39	1968-
Walt Disney	33	1954-90
The Ed Sullivan Show	24	1948-71
Gunsmoke	20	1955-75
The Red Skelton Show	20	1951-71
Meet the Press	18	1947-65[2]
What's My Line?	18	1950-67
I've Got a Secret	17	1952-76
Lassie	17	1954-71
The Lawrence Welk Show	17	1955-71

Note: Includes prime-time (6-11 p.m.) shows only; sports broadcasts and movie series are not included. 1. Dates reflect the first and last broadcasts of each show. Programs did not necessarily run continuously throughout this period. 2. Ceased broadcasting in prime-time in 1965, though still on the air.

Viewing Shares of Free and Cable TV Networks, 2001–2006

	01–02	02–03	03–04	04–05	05-06
TOTAL DAY					
Pay Cable	6%	6%	6%	6%	5%
Basic Cable	49	51	53	54	62
Public	3	3	3	3	2
Independents	4	4	4	5	2
Network Affiliates	46	44	43	42	41
PRIMETIME					
Pay Cable	6%	6%	6%	5%	4%
Basic Cable	48	50	52	52	60
Public	3	3	3	3	2
Independents	4	4	5	6	2
Network Affiliates	51	50	49	50	50

Note: Due to multiset use and independent roundings, totals add up to more than 100. **Source:** Nielsen Media Research.

Top 16 Cable Television Networks, 2008

Network	Estimated Subscribers (millions)	Launch date	Content
The Discovery Channel	98.0	1985	Nonfiction, nature, science
TNT (Turner Network Television)	98.0	1988	Movies, sports, and original programming
ESPN	97.8	1979	Sports events and sports news
Cable News Network (CNN)	97.5	1980	24-hour news, special interest reports
USA Network	97.5	1980	Sports, family entertainment
Lifetime Television	97.3	1984	Programming aimed at women
Nickelodeon/Nick at Nite	97.3	1979	Programming for kids
TBS Superstation	97.3	1976	Movies, sports, and original programming
Weather Channel	97.3	1982	Weather, news, talk
TLC The Learning Channel	97.3	1980	Original programming, family entertainment
ABC Family	97.0	2001	Original movies, series, and specials
ESPN 2	97.0	1993	Sports events and sports news
C-Span	96.5	1979	Coverage of Congress, judiciary, and public affairs
HGTV	96.5	1994	Home, garden and lifestyle programming
Food Network	96.3	1993	Food, travel, and lifestyle programming
MTV	96.3	1981	Music television aimed at young adults

Source: National Cable & Telecommunications Association, 2008.

third of the total television viewing audiences away from broadcast channels. As a result, the fractured total television audience means that no single program will likely ever reach the kind of viewership numbers achieved during the 1960s and 70s, when viewers had only three or four choices. A case in point: the final episode of *Friends* in 2004, was one of the most anticipated shows in a decade, but it didn't attract even as many viewers as regular episodes of *The Beverly Hillbillies.*

The number of basic cable subscribers is currently increasing by about a half million per year (pay cable has grown at a more rapid rate of several million per year). But despite deregulation and increased competition from direct satellite providers, the average basic cable bill has continued to increase, from $7.69 in 1980 to $42.76 in 2007. The number of digital cable subscribers has also increased, from 1.5 million in 1998 to over 37 million in 2007, and the number of cable modem subscribers has increased from 500,000 to 35.6 million including commercial customers. The nation's two largest cable providers are Comcast Cable Communications (24.1 million subscribers) and Time Warner Cable (13.3 million subscribers).

Top 5 Pay-Cable Services, 2004–05

Rank/Network	Subscribers	Content
1. The Disney Channel[1]	85,000,000	Movies, cartoons
2. Showtime/The Movie Channel	39,500,000	Movies, variety, comedy, sports
3. HBO/Cinemax	39,000,000	Movies, variety, sports, documentaries
4. Encore	24,500,000	On-demand movies
5. Starz!	14,000,000	Movies

Note: **1.** Disney is a basic cable service on some cable systems.
Source: National Cable Television Association, *Cable Developments 2005.*

Basic and Pay Cable TV Systems and Subscribers, 1952–2007

Year	Number of of systems	Basic cable		Pay cable	
		Subscribers	Percent of U.S. TV households	Subscribers	Percent of households with cable
1952	70	14,000	0.1%	N.A.	N.A.
1955	400	150,000	0.5	N.A.	N.A.
1960	640	650,000	1.4	N.A.	N.A.
1970	2,490	3,900,000	6.7	N.A.	N.A.
1980	4,225	17,671,490	22.6	9,144,000	50.6
1990	9,575	54,871,330	59.0	39,900,000	77.1
2000	10,400	69,297,290	67.8	48,300,000	71.5
2004	N.A.	73,575,460	67.1	51,500,000	70.0
2005	8,875	72,965,820	66.8	50,100,000	68.7
2006	7,926	65,500,000	59.2	51,800,000	N.A.
2007	6,635	65,100,000	58.0	53,100,000	N.A.

Sources: National Cable & Telecommunications Association, 2008; Nielsen Media Research.

Video and Audio: Sales & Penetration in U.S. Homes, 1990–2008

Product	Sales (000s of units)				Percent of U.S. homes			
	1990	2000	2004	2008[1]	1990	2000	2004	2008[1]
Video								
Analog color TV	20,384	24,175	19,934	0	96%	98%	98%	98%
Digital TV set[2]	N.A.	1,117	10,706	31,807	N.A.	N.A.	12	50
TV/VCR combination	424	4,964	1,463	N.A.	N.A.	18	30	N.A.
VCR[3]	11,986	35,117	2,267	6	68	93	91	70
TV/DVD combination	N.A.	0	979	1,769	N.A.	N.A.	N.A.	N.A.
DVD player	N.A.	8,499	19,990	20,913	N.A.	5	70	84
Camcorder[4]	2,962	5,848	5,559	6,106	10	36	54	48
Direct Satellite Receiver	330	4,250	16,250	13,788	2	16	25	29
Audio								
Home Radio	21,585	19,976	14,902	9,044	99%	98%	98%	98%
Home Theater-in-a-Box	N.A.	1,157	4,701	3,620	N.A.	23	32	36
Compact disc player[5]	9,155	54,776	37,470	N.A.	23	74	80	N.A.
Compact audio system	2,447	11,455	6,874	3,164	N.A.	42	44	37
MP3 Players	N.A.	587	7,126	48,473	N.A.	2	11	45

Notes: **1.** Estimate. **2.** Includes direct-view and projection digital TVs with integrated decoders and stand-alone digital TV displays. Household penetration figures do not include digital projection sets. **3.** Includes mono and stereo decks, but not machines that play but do not record. Does not include TV/VCR combinations. **4.** Includes digital camcorders. **5.** Sales represent total CD players; market penetration represents home CD players.
Source: *U.S. Consumer Electronics Sales & Forecasts,* 2008, Consumer Electronics Association.

Commercial AM & FM Radio Stations by Primary Format, 2007

Format	2007[1]	Format	2007[1]	Format	2007[1]
Religion[2]	2,151	Sports	574	R&B Adult/Oldies	39
Country	2,049	Classic Hits	505	Easy Listening	27
News/Talk	2,025	Top 40	496	Format not available	9
Adult Contemporary[3]	1,512	Adult Standards	379	Stations off the air	140
Rock[4]	1,322	Classical	176		
Spanish	917	R&B	160	**Total stations**	**14,856**
Oldies	738	Ethnic	132		
Variety	672	Jazz	151		
Gospel (Black, Southern)	625	Pre-Teen	57		

Source: M Street Corporation, 2008.

Note: **1.** As of Dec. 2007. **2.** Inc. Teaching, Variety, Contemporary Christian. **3.** Inc. Hot, Soft, Urban, Modern. **4.** Inc. Classic, Modern, Alternative.

▶ RADIO

According to the Radio Advertising Bureau, 98 percent of all U.S. households own at least one radio. Of Americans over age 12, 95.3 percent listen to radio for an average of 3 hours and 20 minutes each workday.

▶ THE RECORDING INDUSTRY

The total U.S. dollar value of all music sold in 2007 was $10.3 billion, a 16.3 percent decrease from the high in 2004. CD sales dropped to a ten year low of $7.5 billion, down 20.5 percent from 2006. Music video sales rose slightly to $485 million but couldn't offset continuing declines in sales of cassettes, LPs, and Super Audio CDs.

Fewer than 100,000 CDs were sold in 1983, the first year they were available, but the format overtook LPs by 1988, and topped cassette sales in 1992. In 2005, CDs accounted for over 90 percent of all music sales and revived the entire music industry, which in the late 1970s and early 80s was worried about losing young consumers to movies and videogames.

Internet Music Sales and File-Sharing

Industry concerns surfaced again in the late 1990s, as the popularity of online file-sharing services grew. Napster, the most prominent of these services, was forced to stop the process known as peer-to-peer (P2P) file sharing in 2000 because of a lawsuit brought by the music industry. In 2002 some major record labels responded to the ongoing music piracy by making more of their music legally available online, despite fears that such a move would cannibalize more profitable CD sales.

The most successful service has been Apple Computer's iTunes, which sold 10 million song downloads (for an average 99 cents each) in its first four months of operation in 2003, and by 2005 had sold more than 500 million. P2P services remain active, but lawsuits filed by the music industry against hundreds of file sharers (many of them young children), as well as a 2005 Supreme Court decision against two prominent file-sharing software companies, appear to have had a chilling effect on Internet music-sharing. Instead, legal digital downloads have become an important revenue stream for the faltering recording industry, generating over $1.26 billion in 2007.

Sales by Category

The sales of different types of music are in almost as constant a flux as the music types themselves. The category defined as rock accounted for nearly half of all music sales in 1987; in 2007, it was less than a third. Pop, Rap, R & B, and Country have made up the difference. For many years, the single largest group of recorded music consumers (as a percentage of total dollar value) was teenagers (buyers aged 15-19). But the high price of music and Internet music-sharing sites have cut into record sales among younger consumers. Since 1999, buyers over 45 have accounted for about 25

U.S. Radio Stations and Radio Sales, 1946–2001

Year	Radio stations on air[1]	Unit sales to dealers[2]
1946	961	N.A.
1950	2,773	N.A.
1955	3,211	7,327
1960	4,133	18,031
1965	5,249	31,689
1970	6,760	34,049
1975	7,744	25,276
1980	8,566	27,104
1985	10,359	21,575
1990	10,788	21,585
1995	11,834	17,051
1998	12,641	18,734
1999	12,641	19,899
2000	N.A.	19,976
2001[3]	13,058	17,200

Notes: 1. Includes AM and FM, commercial and noncommercial. 2. Includes table, clock, and portable—but not car—radios. 3. Estimate Source: M Street Corporation, 2001; Consumer Electronics Association, *U.S. Consumer Electronics Sales & Forecasts,* (2002).

Top-Selling Digital Albums of 2007

Title	Artist	Copies Sold
It Won't Be Soon Before Long	Maroon 5	252,000
Back to Black	Amy Winehouse	241,000
Graduation	Kayne West	237,000
Coco	Colbie Caillat	207,000
Daughtry	Daughtry	205,000
Minutes to Midnight	Linkin Park	189,000
High School Musical 2	Soundtrack	176,000
Timbaland Presents Shock Value	Timbaland	151,000
Continuum	John Mayer	137,000
Futuresex/Love Sounds	Justin Timberlake	137,000

Source: Nielsen SoundScan, 2008

Top-Selling Albums of 2007

Title	Artist	Copies Sold
Noel	Josh Groban	3,699,000
High School Musical 2	Soundtrack	2,957,000
Long Road Out of Eden	Eagles	2,608,000
As I Am	Alicia Keys	2,543,000
Daughtry	Daughtry	2,497,000
Hannah Montana 2	Soundtrack	2,489,000
Minutes to Midnight	Linkin Park	2,099,000
Dutchess	Fergie	2,064,000
Taylor Swift	Taylor Swift	1,951,000
Graduation	Kayne West	1,892,000

Source: Nielsen SoundScan, 2008

U.S. Recorded Music Sales by Genre, Format, and Age Group, 1987–2007

Characteristic	1987	1990	1995	2000	2004	2005	2007
Genre							
Rock	45.5%	36.1%	33.5%	24.8%	23.9%	31.5%	32.4%
Pop	13.5	13.7	10.1	11.0	10.0	8.1	10.7
Rap/Hip Hop	3.8	8.5	6.7	12.9	12.1	13.3	10.8
R&B/Urban[1]	9.0	11.6	11.3	9.7	11.3	10.2	11.8
Country	10.6	9.6	16.7	10.7	13.0	12.5	11.5
Religious/Gospel[2]	2.9	2.5	3.1	4.8	6.0	5.3	3.9
Jazz	3.8	4.8	3.0	2.9	2.7	1.8	2.6
Classical	3.9	3.1	2.9	2.7	2.0	2.4	2.3
Other[3]	6.2	8.8	10.1	11.0	8.9	8.5	11.5
Format							
CDs (full length)	11.5%	31.1%	65.0%	89.3%	90.3%	87.0%	82.6%
Cassettes (full length)	62.5	54.7	25.1	4.9	1.7	1.1	0.3
Singles (all types)	5.7	8.7	7.5	2.5	2.4	2.7	2.4
Videos/Video DVDs	N.A.	N.A.	0.9	0.8	1.0	0.7	0.4
DVD Audio	N.A.	N.A.	N.A.	N.A.	1.7	0.8	1.2
Digital Download	N.A.	N.A.	N.A.	N.A.	0.9	5.7	11.2
LPs	20.1	4.7	0.5	0.5	0.9	0.7	0.7
SACD	N.A.	N.A.	N.A.	N.A.	0.8	1.2	0.6
Age group							
10-14	7.3%	7.6%	8.0%	8.9%	9.4%	8.6%	11.5%
15-19	24.2	18.3	17.1	12.9	11.9	11.9	12.3
20-24	19.1	16.5	15.3	12.5	9.2	12.7	11.3
25-29	14.5	14.6	12.3	10.6	10.0	12.1	9.2
30-34	10.8	13.2	12.1	9.8	10.4	11.3	11.3
35-39	8.2	10.2	10.8	10.6	10.7	8.8	11.9
40-44	4.8	7.8	7.5	9.6	10.9	9.2	7.9
45+	10.7	11.1	16.1	23.8	26.4	25.5	24.8

Notes: Figures represent a percentage of that year's total U.S. dollar sales. **1.** Includes R&B, blues, dance, disco, funk, fusion, Motown, reggae, soul. **2.** Includes Christian, Gospel, Inspirational, Religious, and Spiritual. **3.** Includes soundtracks, children's music, and other categories not shown separately. Totals may not add to 100 percent due to "Don't Know/No Answer" Responses. **Source:** Recording Industry Association of America, *Consumer Profile.*

percent of annual music purchases, compared with just 11 to 13 percent by 15-19-year-olds. Women made over half of the music purchases in the U.S. in 2007. The recording industry saw promise in online sales of digital downloads of music that accounted for 11.2 percent of 2007 music sales, up from just 0.5 percent in 2002.

A decision in 1996 by Wal-Mart stores to restrict albums with controversial lyrics caused consternation among record executives because of discount stores' increasing influence on the industry's bottom line. In 1989, 71.7 percent of all recorded music was sold in record stores, while 15.6 percent was sold in "other stores," which includes discount and consumer electronic stores. In 2007, record stores accounted for less than one-third of all music purchases (31.1 percent), while "other stores" made up 29.7 percent. In many remote areas, the local Wal-Mart is the only place to buy recorded music, forcing many top musical acts to release special versions of their albums with bowdlerized lyrics. However, music purchases via the Internet grew from 0.3 percent in 1997 to 10.9 percent in 2007, and digital downloads accounted for another 12.2 percent, providing important new outlets.

Individual Record Sales

Up until 1958, the term **gold** album simply meant a hit album. But in that year, the Recording Industry Association of America codified the term to mean a record that had reached $1 million in sales. (Separate levels were established for singles, which have since been amended). The cast album from *Oklahoma!* was the first gold album. By 1975, inflation had diluted the importance of the award, so the RIAA also required gold records to sell at least 500,000 copies. The following year, it introduced the **platinum** record, awarded to albums that sell at least 1 million copies. The Eagles' *Their Greatest Hits 1971 1975* was the first platinum album, and is to date, the largest-selling album of all time, with 29 million copies sold. **Multi-platinum** awards go to albums selling more than 2 million copies. In 1999, the RIAA introduced the **diamond** award, for singles or records with U.S. sales of 10 million or more. As of December 2007, more than 100 titles had qualified for the award, in genres ranging from pop, R&B, and rock to rap, country, and instrumental. The Beatles have the most diamond records (five).

▶ VIDEO

Video Cassette Recorders (VCRs)

In 20 years, the video cassette recorder (VCR) went from a curiosity to a luxury to an appliance found in more than 90 percent of American homes, but it is now losing out to DVDs and VCR ownership is down to 79 percent of homes.

DVD (Digital Video Disc) Players are the fastest-growing consumer electronics product in history, with 2007 sales of 21.2 million units, up from 20 million the previous year. DVDs resemble CDs, but are capable of storing an entire feature-length film as well as additional features such as deleted scenes or the director's running commentary on the film. The average wholesale price for a DVD is $15 to $20; they are more durable than VHS tapes and take up much less space.

DVD sales overtook videocassette sales in 2004, and the steady drop in price for DVD players (an average of $72 in 2007) has increased their presence in American homes (87 percent, up from 25 percent in 2002). In light of this change, video rental and retail stores have shifted to DVDs, much as CDs supplanted vinyl albums and cassette tapes in the 1980s.

Personal Video Recorders (PVRs),
also known as Digital Video Recorders (DVRs) have been touted by many as the next big thing in home entertainment: an estimated 3.2 million

Top Rental DVDs 2007

Rank, Title	Rental Revenue (in millions)
1. *Rush Hour 3*	$71.2
2. *The Bourne Ultimatum*	69.7
3. *The Kingdom*	66.4
4. *Superbad*	64.3
5. *Live Free or Die Hard*	57.2
6. *The Simpsons Movie*	56.7
7. *Night at the Museum*	55.3
8. *Harry Potter and the Order of the Phoenix*	54.1
9. *Shrek the Third*	51.8
10. *The Heartbreak Kid*	51.2

Note: Rental revenue for each film is calculated its cumulative revenue before it drops from the weekly top 50 rental charts.
Source: Home Media Retailing.

Top Selling DVDs 2007

Rank, Title	Distributor
1. *Happy Feet*	Warner Home Video
2. *Transformers*	Paramount
3. *300*	Warner Home Video
4. *Night at the Museum*	20th Century Fox Home Ent.
5. *The Departed*	Warner Home Video
6. *Ratatouille*	Disney/Buena Vista Home Video
7. *Casino Royale*	Sony Pictures Home Ent.
8. *Shrek The Third*	Paramount
9. *Wild Hogs*	Disney/Buena Vista Home Video
10. *The Pursuit of Happyness*	Sony Pictures Home Ent.

Note: Data from Jan. 1, 2007—Nov. 18, 2007. Based on aggregate unit sales. Does not include sales from Wal-Mart.
Source: Nielsen VideoScan.

were sold in 2005, up from only 336,000 in 2001, and the consumer electronics association projects that sales will double in 2006. Prices have also fallen from an average of $429 per unit in 2001 to less than $250 in 2005.

PVRs perform the same basic function as VCRs—recording television shows—but instead of recording on removable videocassettes, a PVR uses an internal computer hard drive, generally 40 or 80 gigabytes, capable of holding up to 80 hours or more of television programming. Other features, depending on the model of PVR, include the ability to pause and rewind live TV and the ability to automatically record of future programs based on specific criteria (for example, every new episode of a particular sitcom). Tivo Inc. is the most recognized name in the market, but cable companies have moved quickly to capitalize on the growing popularity of PVRs; most cable providers now offer proprietary cable boxes with integrated PVR functionality.

▶ FILM

The motion picture industry grossed more than $9.6 billion in 2007, but a relatively small number of people are involved in this endeavor: only 357,300 in 2007. The various studios produce about 600 films per year; they submit most of these films to the Motion Picture Association of America for ratings and wide release in theaters. Over half of these movies (59 percent in 2007) receive an R rating. Most of the rest receive a PG or PG-13 rating. Only 3 percent of 2007 movies were G-rated, and even fewer (less than 1 percent) received an NC-17 or X-rating. (In 2007 PG and PG-13 films accounted for 80 percent of the top 20 grossing films.) Because many theaters refuse to show NC-17 movies, producers are loath to release a film with an NC-17 label. While the number of theaters has fallen recently, the number of movie screens has nearly doubled since 1985. Single-screen theaters made up 28 percent of all movie theaters in 2007; miniplexes accounted for 37 percent. There were 1,617 multiplexes (8-15 screens) and 616 megaplexes (16 or more screens). The number of megaplaxes grew in 2007, up 4.2 percent from 2006 and 6 new single screen theaters were added.

U.S. Film Box-Office Receipts, Screens, Admissions, and Admission Charges, 1926–2007 (in current dollars)

Year	Box office receipts (millions)	Movie Screens			Annual admissions		Average admission charge	Number of $20 million hits
		Indoor	Drive-in	Digital	Total (millions)	Per person		
1926	$720.0	N.A.	N.A.	N.A.	2,600	N.A.	N.A.	N.A.
1930	732.0	N.A.	N.A.	N.A.	4,680	N.A.	N.A.	N.A.
1935	566.0	N.A.	N.A.	N.A.	3,900	N.A.	$0.24	N.A.
1940	735.0	N.A.	N.A.	N.A.	4,160	N.A.	0.24	N.A.
1950	1,376.0	N.A.	N.A.	N.A.	3,120	N.A.	0.53	N.A.
1960	951.0	N.A.	N.A.	N.A.	2,080	N.A.	0.69	N.A.
1970[1]	1,162.0	10,335	3,720	N.A.	920	N.A.	1.55	N.A.
1980	2,748.5	14,029	3,561	N.A.	1,022	4.5	2.69	N.A.
1990[2]	5,021.8	22,774	915	N.A.	1,189	4.8	4.23	N.A.
1995	5,493.5	26,958	847	N.A.	1,263	4.8	4.35	N.A.
2000	7,661.0	36,679	717	31	1,421	5.2	5.39	16
2005	8,991.2	37,092	648	324	1,402	5.9	6.41	N.A.
2007	9,629.0	38,159	635	4,632	1,470	6.0	6.88	N.A.

Notes: 1. Theater figures are for 1971. 2. Beginning in 1990, admission totals and average prices are supplied by the National Association of Theater Owners and are not strictly comparable with data from previous years, which are based on the U.S. Department of Commerce's Consumer Price Index. Source: U.S. Dept. of Commerce; *Film Daily Yearbook;* Motion Picture Association of America, *2005 U.S. Economic Review,* National Association of Theatre Owners.

20 Top-Grossing Feature Films, 2007

Rank, Film	Distributor	Gross
1. *Spiderman 3*	Sony	$336,530,303
2. *Shrek the Third*	Paramount/Dreamworks	322,719,944
3. *Transformers*	Paramount/Dreamworks	319,246,193
4. *Pirates of the Caribbean: At World's End*	Walt Disney	309,420,425
5. *Harry Potter and the Order of the Phoenix*	Warner Bros.	292,004,738
6. *I Am Legend*	Warner Bros.	256,393,010
7. *The Bourne Ultimatum*	Universal	227,471,070
8. *National Treasure: Book of Secrets*	Walt Disney	219,548,127
9. *Alvin and the Chipmunks*	Fox	217,292,442
10. *300*	Warner Bros.	210,614,939
11. *Ratatouille*	Walt Disney	206,445,654
12. *The Simpsons Movie*	Fox	183,135,014
13. *Wild Hogs*	Buena Vista	168,273,550
14. *Knocked Up*	Universal	148,768,917
15. *Juno*	Fox Searchlight	143,448,146
16. *Rush Hour 3*	New Line	140,125,968
17. *Live Free or Die Hard*	Fox	134,529,403
18. *Fantastic Four: Rise of the Silver Surfer*	Fox	131,921,738
19. *American Gangster*	Universal	130,164,645
20. *Enchanted*	Walt Disney	127,807,262

Source: Exhibitor Relations Co., Inc.

Most Popular Films, By Decade

Title (Year)	Director	Rental (millions)	Title (Year)	Director	Rental (millions)
Pre-1930			**1970–79**		
The Birth of a Nation (1915)	D.W. Griffith	$10.0	*Star Wars* (1977)	G. Lucas	$193.8
The Big Parade (1925)	K. Vidor	5.5	*Jaws* (1975)	S. Spielberg	129.6
The Singing Fool (1928)	L. Bacon	4.0	*Grease* (1978)	R. Kleiser	96.3
			The Exorcist (1973)	W. Friedkin	89.0
1930–39			*The Godfather* (1972)	F. F. Coppola	86.3
Gone With the Wind (1939)	V. Fleming	$77.6			
Snow White and the Seven Dwarfs (1937)	(Animated)	62.8	**1980–89**		
King Kong (1933)	M. Cooper	5.0	*E.T.—The Extra-Terrestrial* (1982)	S. Spielberg	$228.2
The Wizard of Oz (1939)	V. Fleming	4.5	*Return of the Jedi* (1983)	R. Marquand	168.2
San Francisco (1936)	W.S. Van Dyke	4.0	*Batman* (1989)	T. Burton	150.5
			The Empire Strikes Back (1980)	J. Kershner	141.7
1940–49[1]			*Ghostbusters* (1984)	I. Reitman	132.7
Cinderella (1949)	(Animated)	$38.5	*Raiders of the Lost Ark* (1981)	S. Spielberg	115.6
Pinocchio (1940)	(Animated)	32.9	*Indiana Jones and the Last Crusade* (1989)	S. Spielberg	115.5
Song of the South (1946)	H. Foster/ W. Jackson	29.2	*Indiana Jones and the Temple of Doom* (1984)	S. Spielberg	109.0
Fantasia (1940)	(Animated)	28.5	*Beverly Hills Cop* (1984)	M. Brest	108.0
Bambi (1942)	(Animated)	28.4	*Back to the Future* (1985)	R. Zemeckis	105.5
1950–59			**1990–99**		
The Ten Commandments (1956)	C.B. DeMille	$43.0	*Titanic* (1997)	J. Cameron	$600.8
Lady and the Tramp (1955)	(Animated)	40.2	*Star Wars: Episode One -The Phantom Menace* (1999)	G. Lucas	431.1
Ben-Hur (1959)	W. Wyler	36.7	*Jurassic Park* (1993)	S. Spielberg	357.1
Around the World in 80 Days (1956)	M. Anderson	23.1	*Forrest Gump* (1994)	R. Zemeckis	329.7
Sleeping Beauty (1959)	(Animated)	21.5	*The Lion King* (1993)	R. Allers/R. Minkoff	312.9
			Independence Day (1996)	R. Emmerich	306.2
1960–69			*The Sixth Sense* (1999)	M. Shyamalan	293.5
The Sound of Music (1965)	R. Wise	$80.0	*Home Alone* (1990)	C. Columbus	285.7
Doctor Zhivago (1965)	D. Lean	61.0	*Men in Black* (1997)	B. Sonnenfeld	250.7
Butch Cassidy and the Sundance Kid (1969)	G.R. Hill	46.0	*Toy Story 2* (1999)	A. Brannon	245.8
Mary Poppins (1964)	R. Stevenson	45.0			
The Graduate (1968)	M. Nichols	44.1			

Note: Films from the 1990s are ranked according to their gross box office receipts. Films for previous decades are ranked according to film rentals, the portion of a film's box-office receipts paid by theater owners to the film's distribution company for renting the film. Figures include the U.S. and Canada. **1.** All films listed for this decade were made by Disney studios and have been rereleased on a regular basis ever since. Their dominance on this chart is partly due to the fact that they are continually generating revenue.
Sources: *Variety,* Exhibitor Relations Co., Inc.

Top-Grossing Movies of All Time

Because of inflation and periodic re-releases, it is nearly impossible to compare the successes of films from different eras. What is simpler to compare is the number of people who went to see a film, regardless of when it was released, and regardless of how much they paid for their ticket. To arrive at this number, the Exhibitor Relations Co. divides domestic gross receipts by the average ticket prices for the year(s) in which the film was released. The estimated number of admissions is then multiplied by the current average ticket price to give an idea of what each film's domestic gross would be if it were released today. It is admittedly an imperfect measure, but it makes it quite clear that despite its $600 million unadjusted gross, *Titanic* will have to be re-released several times to match the success of *Gone With the Wind*, which has made only $200 million over the years, but has been seen by 70 million more people.

Rank, Film, (Year of Release)	Estimated admissions	Inflation-adjusted domestic gross
1. *Gone With the Wind* (1939)[1]	202,044,600	$1,390,000,000
2. *Star Wars* (1977)[1]	178,119,600	1,225,462,000
3. *The Sound of Music* (1965)[1]	142,415,400[2]	979,817,000
4. *E.T. The Extra-Terrestrial* (1982)[1]	141,854,300	975,957,000
5. *The Ten Commandments* (1956)	131,000,000[2]	901,280,000
6. *Titanic* (1997)	128,345,900	883,019,000
7. *Jaws* (1975)[1]	128,078,800	881,182,000
8. *Doctor Zhivago* (1965)[1]	124,135,500	854,051,000
9. *The Exorcist* (1973)	110,568,700	760,712,000
10. *Snow White and the Seven Dwarfs* (1937)[1]	109,000,000[2]	749,920,000

Note: As of May 2008. 1. Includes re-issues; ticket price used to calculate admissions is an average of ticket prices charged throughout the film's theatrical runs. 2. Gross estimated from the film rental, which is approximately 50 percent of the gross.
Source: Exhibitor Relations Co., Inc.

Movie Budgets

The cost of making movies has escalated dramatically in recent years. In 1988, the average price tag of a motion picture was $18.1 million. Today, that's just half of the average marketing budget for a feature film. Rising actors' salaries, increased demand for special effects, and other spiraling costs drove the average cost of making a movie to a whopping $106.6 million in 2007. In addition to production costs, studios spent an average of $35.9 million on advertising and publicity in 2007, more than twice what they spent in 1993 ($14.1 million).

▶COMPUTER AND VIDEO GAMES

The computer and video game industry showed dramatic growth in recent years, shooting from sales of $3.7 billion in 1996 to $18.8 billion in 2007. Sales of computer games were nearly 1 billion in 2007, down from $1.2 billion in 2001, but video game sales rose. Much of the increase has been in video game consoles, which reached $5.12 billion in 2007.

The stereotypical computer and video game player is a young male, but in 2004 women constituted 43 percent of the PC and console game-playing population, and the average age of a computer or video game player was 33 years old. Among video game players, the best-selling game genres were action (30.1 percent) and sports (17.3 percent); computer gamers spent their money on strategy games (30.8 percent) and children's titles (19.8 percent).

One of the fastest-growing segments of the computer and video game industry is online gaming. Microsoft claims over 10 million subscribers to its Xbox Live service, which allows owners of the Xbox video game console to compete with other gamers over the Internet. Massively Multiplayer Online Role Playing Games (MMORPGs) are also booming in the PC segment; the top-selling World of Warcraft, developed by Blizzard Entertainment, boasted 10 million subscribers worldwide (2.5 million of them in North America) as of January 2008.

Top-Selling Computer & Video Games, 2007

VIDEO GAMES

Rank, Title	Publisher
1. Halo 3	Microsoft
2. Wii Play w/Remote	Nintendo
3. Call of Duty 4: Modern Warfare	Activision
4. Guitar Hero 3: Legends of Rock	Activision
5. Super Mario Galaxy	Nintendo
6. Pokemon Diamond Version	Nintendo
7. Madden NFL 08	Electronic Arts
8. Guitar Hero 2	Activision
9. Assassin's Creed	Ubisoft
10. Wii Mario Party 8	Nintendo

COMPUTER GAMES

Rank, Title	Publisher
1. World of Warcraft: Burning Crusade Expansion Pack	Vivendi Universal
2. World of Warcraft	Vivendi Universal
3. The Sims 2: Seasons Expansion Pack	Electronic Arts
4. Call of Duty 4: Modern Warfare	Activision
5. Sim City 4 Deluxe	Electronic Arts
6. The Sims 2	Electronic Arts
7. Command & Conquer 3: Tiberium Wars	Electronic Arts
8. The Sims 2: Bon Voyage Expansion Pack	Electronic Arts
9. MS Age of Empires III	Microsoft
10. The Sims 2: Pets Expansion Pack	Electronic Arts

Note: Ranked by units sold in 2007.
Source: The NPD Group/ Retail Tracking Service.

Religion in America

▶RELIGIOUS AFFILIATION

According to a 2001 survey by the City University of New York Graduate Center, roughly 76.5 percent of the American population described themselves as Christian, 3.7 percent as having another religion, and 14.1 percent as having no religion specified (the last category encompasses Atheism, Agnosticism, Humanism, Secularism, and none).

Because the U.S. Census Bureau does not ask questions about religious affiliation, all of these numbers can be regarded as educated approximations at best. Each year, the *Yearbook of American and Canadian Churches* asks more than 200 Christian religious bodies "How many members does your organization have?" The answers to these questions, which necessarily vary from denomination to denomination, are reflected in the accompanying table, which arranges Christian churches by their size and family. Denominations listed in the same family nearly always share common historical roots and some principal doctrines, but they should not be assumed to be similar in belief or practice. Denominations with 80,000 or more members are shown separately within their families.

The following are brief descriptions of each of the Christian denominational families and of major non-Christian faiths in the United States. Information is taken from the *Yearbook of American and Canadian Churches* and *The Atlas of Religion*, published by the University of California Press. *(For information about religion internationally, see Part III: World Religions.)*

▶CHRISTIANITY
Roman Catholic Church

The Roman Catholic Church is the largest single Christian denomination in the United States. It claims nearly 37 percent of all religiously affiliated people—23 percent of the total population. Worldwide, there are over one billion Roman Catholics (see "World Religions").

Many U.S. Catholics—descendants of immigrants from Ireland, Germany, Poland, Italy, and France—are concentrated in the Northeast and the industrial Midwest. Hispanic-Americans in Florida and the Southwest are also predominantly Catholic.

The church is hierarchically organized. Bishops, who administer church affairs in a given region, are appointed by higher authority. The world leader of the Roman church is the pope, who directs the church from Vatican City in Rome.

Priests are male and in most parts of the church must be and remain unmarried. Orders of nuns and monks provide many educational and charitable services. Many local churches operate parochial elementary schools. Regional bodies and religious orders operate high schools and help administer many seminaries and church-related colleges. In recent years the number of applicants for the priesthood and for religious orders has sharply decreased, even as membership in the church has continued to increase.

Catholic leaders have taken strong stands on many contemporary issues. The National Conference of Catholic Bishops has taken relatively liberal positions on efforts to bring about world peace and economic justice. In areas of personal conduct, the church is more conservative. It leads the campaign to outlaw abortion and opposes artificial means of birth control.

Baptist Churches

The Baptist family of churches is the largest Protestant family in the United States. Baptists trace their theological roots back to radical reformers in Europe in the 1500s, but the number of Baptists in the world was tiny until the 1800s, when Baptist faith and practice became predominant in the American South (both for whites and for blacks). Baptists are still most heavily represented in the southern and border states.

Local Baptist congregations have great independence, determining many of their own policies. At the same time, these churches share many practices. They agree that the rite of baptism should be administered only to those who have reached an age of independent judgment. Consequently, children are baptized no earlier than the age of six or seven, often by total immersion in the baptismal water. A Baptist child is not counted as a member until after baptism, which means that small children are not included in the membership totals reported above.

Most Baptists take a strong stand on the authority of the Bible, and many (though not all) believe that it should be interpreted literally. Baptists have traditionally been strong supporters of separation of church and state. Many Baptist denominations have mounted energetic missionary campaigns to bring the Christian message to people around the world.

The Southern Baptist Convention, a predominantly white church, is the largest Protestant denomination in the United States, but but has experienced division within its membership in recent years. The split, involving a moderate minority, was sparked by reluctance to accept the increasingly conservative church leadership's insistence that the Bible be interpreted literally and that women submit to their husbands and be barred from serving as pastors. As of September 2002, conventions had been organized by liberal and moderate Baptists to compete with mainstream state conventions in Missouri, Texas and Virginia.

The two National Baptist Conventions and the Progressive National Baptist Convention are predominantly black churches. Together they account for the religious affiliation of more blacks than any other family of churches.

Methodist Churches

Methodist churches trace their origins to John Wesley (1703-91), a minister in the Church of England who sought to bring a new sense of warmth and commitment to individuals' religious life. He urged his followers to set aside regular times to study the Bible and pray together. Wesley's opponents laughingly called his followers Methodists because of their discipline and seriousness. Wesley himself remained in the Church of England his whole life, but his followers began to develop independent organizations, both in England and the United States.

On the American frontier, Methodist "circuit riders" traveled from settlement to settlement, preaching and marrying, baptizing and burying members of pioneer families. Methodism grew with astonishing swiftness. By 1820 it was the largest religious family in the United States, and it remained the largest Protestant family until the 1920s.

The United Methodist Church accounts for nearly two-thirds of the Methodist family's total membership. This denomination is made up of not only traditional Methodists but also several churches of German origin whose beliefs and spirit accorded well with Methodism. The two "African" churches and the Christian Methodist Church are predominantly black churches, and they account for nearly all of the remaining third of the Methodist group.

Lutheran Churches

Lutherans trace their churches back to the German reformer Martin Luther (1483-1546). Luther sought to reform the doctrine and practice of the Roman Christian Church in Europe. He complained about corruption among the clergy and advocated worship in the language of the people rather than in Latin. He also came to favor a married, rather than a celibate, clergy. The Church of Rome considered Luther disloyal and eventually drove him out. He then helped establish independent churches in northern Germany.

Immigrants from Germany and Scandinavia brought the Lutheran faith to North America, concentrating first in Pennsylvania. Later immigrants settled in the upper Midwest. By 1900 scores of small Lutheran church bodies were divided from one another by language, theology, and degree of assimilation into American society. The Evangelical Lutheran Church in America represents a uniting of many of those earlier churches. The Lutheran Church-Missouri Synod, a national church despite its name, is more conservative theologically.

In July 2000, the Evangelical Lutheran Church announced a historic alliance with the Episcopal Church. The alliance, "Called to Common Mission," could play a significant role in helping both churches stem declines in membership.

Pentecostal Churches

The Pentecostal churches share a belief that God grants believers special spiritual gifts—especially the experience called "speaking in tongues," a common feature of Pentecostal services.

Pentecostal churches trace their origin to the day of Pentecost, described in the biblical book of Acts, when early Christians received ecstatic or mystical powers. Modern Pentecostalism began in the early 1900s, when members of some Holiness churches received the gift of tongues (see "Holiness Churches").

Pentecostal congregations tend to be small. They may meet in storefronts or in rented quarters on upper floors. Yet the Pentecostal faith, with its immediacy and emotional power, is perhaps the fastest-growing in the nation, attracting thousands of new adherents each year. In addition, Pentecostal beliefs have had an impact on Roman Catholic, Lutheran, Episcopal, and other denominations. These denominations report a growth among adherents of "charismatic renewal," a movement based on spiritual gifts.

The two Churches of God in Christ and the United Pentecostal Church are predominantly black denominations. The Assemblies of God is the largest predominantly white denomination. Many Pentecostal organizations are regional or purely local. Because of this loose organization, there are likely to be thousands of Pentecostal believers not counted here because their local congregations are not affiliated with a regional or national group.

Reformed Churches

Reformed churches trace their descent to the French-Swiss reformer John Calvin (1509-64). These churches were especially significant in the early settlement of the present-day United States. The Pilgrims and Puritans who settled in New England established the Congregational church, which is a main component of today's United Church of Christ. New York was settled by the Dutch, who established the present-day Reformed Church in America. Later, immigrants of Scottish and Scotch-Irish descent established a strong Presbyterian church. Presbyterians differed from Congregationalists in matters of church governance but shared many points of theology and practice.

Reformed church buildings are generally simple and sparsely adorned. Similarly, worship in these churches is austere and simple. Reformed churches generally value a well-educated clergy. In the past they helped found Harvard, Yale, and Princeton. Direct ties to these universities have ended, but Reformed organizations still support many colleges.

The Presbyterian Church (USA) is the result of several mergers between smaller Presbyterian churches that had been separated by regional and doctrinal differences. The United Church of Christ includes, in addition to Congregational churches, descendants of German Reformed churches and of the Evangelical and Reformed Church (also of German descent). The Reformed Church in America and the Christian Reformed Church are both of Dutch descent.

Orthodox Churches

The first great schism in the Christian church occurred in A.D.1054 between the Western church, centered at Rome, and the Eastern church, centered at Constantinople (present-day Istanbul). In 1054 Eastern Christianity was predominant in Greece and the Middle East, and missionaries had already introduced the faith in Russia. The Russian church celebrated its 1,000th anniversary in 1988. Immigrants from these countries brought Orthodox churches to the United States.

The two largest Orthodox churches in the U.S. today are Greek and Russian, respectively. The next largest represent Armenians and Syrians. Together these four churches have more than 80 percent of the Orthodox membership.

Orthodox churches are organized hierarchically. Archbishops and bishops possess special spiritual authority and administer church affairs. Religious observances tend to be solemn and elaborate. Ancient liturgies in the ancient languages have been carefully preserved. Orthodox clergy are male, and in most churches they are allowed to marry. Because of differences in calculating feast days, Easter and other movable feasts may occur on different dates in the Orthodox Church than in the Western churches.

In the U.S., many Orthodox churches have served as cultural centers for immigrants seeking to preserve their own ethnic heritage. At the same time, however, many denominations are active members of ecumenical groups such as the National Council of Churches.

Latter-day Saints (Mormons)

The Church of Jesus Christ of Latter-day Saints, known popularly as the Mormon church, was "established anew," according to Mormon doctrine, on Apr. 6, 1830, by a 19th-century American prophet named Joseph Smith (1805-44). Smith, who grew up in western New York State, reported direct revelations from God. The Book of Mormon, which Smith said he translated, tells of a visit by the resurrected Jesus Christ to pre-Columbian America.

Smith assembled a community of believers that settled first in western New York and later in Ohio, Missouri, and Illinois. Wherever they went, the Mormons aroused the antagonism of neighboring non-Mormons, in part because Mormons allowed men to take more than one wife. Persecution peaked with the murder of Smith himself in 1844.

The next great leader of the church was Brigham Young (1801-77), who led the majority of Mormons westward to settle in the then-uninhabited basin by the Great Salt Lake. There the church grew and prospered. To this day, the majority of religiously affiliated people in Utah are Mormons. There are also many adherents in surrounding states, especially Colorado and Idaho.

Most of the church's 12 million-plus members live in the United States, but the Mormons' legendary missionary work goes on around the globe. Since about 1900, the church has encouraged converts to stay in their own countries and organize congregations there. The National Council of Churches reports that in 2002 the Church of Jesus Christ of Latter-day Saints became the fifth largest church in the U.S., displacing the Evangelical Lutheran Church in America.

The Reorganized Church is the largest of the groups that did not make the trek to the Great Salt Lake. Its headquarters are in Independence, Missouri, which Smith had designated as the site of a great future temple. Members of the Reorganized Church do not consider themselves Mormons.

Christian Churches and Churches of Christ

This family of churches traces its origins to a great religious awakening in 1800 on the Pennsylvania and Kentucky frontiers. Discouraged by sectarian competition among Methodists, Presbyterians, and others, leaders of the revival did not seek to form a denomination but to reestablish a single nondenominational Christian church. In time they became a denomination themselves.

In the 1870s the Churches of Christ and the Christian Church (Disciples) split over questions of using musical instruments in worship and over the issue of centralizing some church functions. The Churches of Christ opposed both instrumental music and national organization. The Disciples allowed instrumental music and established a central missionary board to coordinate mission work. They are ecumenically minded and have a long history of cooperation and discussion with other denominations.

The third group, the Christian churches and Churches of Christ, split from the Disciples in the 1920s–30s. They allow instrumental music but are theologically more conservative than the Disciples.

Episcopal Family of Churches

The Episcopal churches are descendants of the Church of England, which was established as a separate church by King Henry VIII in 1534. Churches descending from the English church make up the worldwide Anglican Communion. The American church takes its name from the word *bishop*, which suggests its hierarchical organization.

In colonial times the Church of England was established in the southern colonies and had some influence in the middle colonies, but was not welcome in New England, where Reformed churches were predominant. During the American Revolution, most Church of England members and clergy remained loyal to England. Thousands migrated to Canada. Those who remained were under suspicion, and some were persecuted. The church almost ceased to function.

After the Revolution, a small group of Anglicans loyal to the United States gradually revived the church. It never grew as rapidly as the Methodist and Baptist families, but it did gain considerable influence. Especially in eastern cities, many families of wealth and power were Episcopalian.

The Episcopal Church accommodates a wide spectrum of belief and practice. It is usually considered Protestant and shares much with other Protestant denominations, yet its worship services retain much of pre-Reformation Catholic tradition. One wing of the church retains a strong emphasis on the church's Catholic heritage. In July 2000, the Episcopal Church announced an alliance with the Evangelical Lutheran Church.

Holiness Churches

The Holiness churches grew from a religious revival in the late 1800s, primarily in Methodist congregations. The originators of the movement objected to the excessive bureaucracy of established denominations and sought to refocus attention on the need for deep personal change. They placed great emphasis on the teachings of Methodism's founder, John Wesley, that those who are saved may aspire to the gift of complete sanctification, or holiness.

Around 1900, groups of especially intense Holiness worshipers began experiencing further "gifts of the Spirit." From these experiences grew the first Pentecostal churches with their emphasis on speaking in tongues. Many who began as adherents of Holiness churches became Pentacostalists. The Holiness churches rejected Pentecostal worship as extremist.

Jehovah's Witnesses

Jehovah's Witnesses are a remarkably active and dynamic sect, visible to most from street-corner or door-to-door encounters. They were founded by Charles Taze Russell (1852–1916) in western Pennsylvania in the 1870s. The Witnesses preach a slightly unorthodox form of the Christian message and look intently for the end of the present world. They claim three million members worldwide, of whom about a quarter live in the U.S.

Church of Christ, Scientist

Christian Scientists, as adherents are often known, follow the teaching of Mary Baker Eddy (1821–1910), who founded the church in 1879 in Boston and wrote *Science and Health with a Key to the Scriptures*, which remains a major sourcebook for the church. Christian Science asserts that sickness and other adversities exist only in the mind and that disciplined spiritual thinking can correct them. Thus, Christian Scientists refuse most or all medical treatment. Christian Science practitioners help adherents deal with illness but do not serve as clergy. The church operates many reading rooms open to the public.

The Adventist Family of Churches

Adventist churches sprang up in the U.S. in the 1840s with a wave of concern about prophecies of the end of the world. Adventists anticipate and prepare for the world's end and the second coming of Jesus Christ. The largest Adventist group, the Seventh-day Adventists, is one of the most dynamic religious groups in the world today, claiming a worldwide membership of 14 million and a growth rate of more than one million annually. As their name suggests, they worship on Saturday rather than Sunday. They operate parochial schools, colleges, medical schools, and hospitals.

The Salvation Army

The Salvation Army is familiar to outsiders through its work among the homeless and the poor and its fund-raising on the streets, especially before Christmas. The church, which originated in England in 1865, is organized in quasi-military style, and many of its members devote their lives to its service.

Roman Rite Churches

The Roman Rite churches are those that have split from the Roman Catholic Church in recent times but have maintained many of its rituals and doctrines. The Polish church was established in Scranton, Pennsylvania, in the 1890s by church leaders of Polish descent. The Old Catholic churches had their origin in Europe after 1870.

Mennonite Churches

Mennonites trace their roots to a small group of Christians after 1530 who sought a reformation even more radical than those advocated by Lutherans and Calvinists. They were called Mennonites after Menno Simons (1469-1561), one of their early leaders. Their most distinctive practice is adult baptism, offered only to those who have made a decision to follow Christ's teachings.

Because they would not swear oaths and would not bear arms in the service of their temporal leaders, Mennonites were severely persecuted. Small bands were scattered to many corners of the world. Some settled in Pennsylvania beginning in the late 1600s. In the 1870s other groups arrived from Russia. The largest concentration of the world's nearly 1.3 million Mennonites is in Africa (532,000). There are almost 500,000 adherents in North America. In recent years, Mennonites have become well-known for their world relief work.

The Amish are groups with Mennonite beliefs who seek to remain quite aloof from the surrounding culture. The Old Order Amish, centered in

Christian Churches in the United States by Size and Family

Family/Denomination	Local congregations	Total clergy	Total membership
Total Christian Churches	**330,742**	**600,025**	**156,702,658**
Roman Catholic Church	**18,992**	**42,271**	**69,135,254**
Baptist Churches	**76,615**	**123,249**	**28,293,420**
Southern Baptist Convention	43,669	136,664	17,144,002
National Baptist Convention, USA Inc.	9,000	N.A.	5,000,000
National Baptist Convention of America	N.A.	N.A.	2,500,000
Progressive National Baptist Convention Inc.	2,000	N.A.	2,500,000
National Missionary Baptist Convention of America	N.A.	N.A.	2,500,000
American Baptist Churches in the USA	5,740	7,524	1,396,700
Baptist Bible Fellowship International	4,500	N.A.	1,200,000
Baptist Missionary Association of America	1,270	1,500	232,350
National Association of Free Will Baptists	2,425	3,959	198,924
Conservative Baptist Association of America	1,200	2,100	200,000
Baptist General Conference	902	N.A.	145,148
General Association of Regular Baptist Churches	842	N.A.	132,900
Other (8 denominations)	5,067	4,509	1,137,980
Methodist Churches	**48,481**	**72,962**	**12,842,296**
United Methodist Church	34,660	45,149	8,075,010
African Methodist Episcopal Church	4,174	14,428	2,500,000
African Methodist Episcopal Zion Church	3,260	4,063	1,215,508
Christian Methodist Episcopal Church	3,320	3,424.	850,000
Wesleyan Church	1,626	3,341	116,151
Other (6 denominations)	1,441	2,557	85,627
Pentecostal Churches	**49,785**	**111,896**	**11,540,890**
Church of God in Christ	15,300	33,593	5,499,875
Assemblies of God	12,298	33,553	1,612,336
Pentecostal Assemblies of the World	1,750	4,500	1,500,000
Church of God (Cleveland, Tenn.)	6,587	10,458	1,013,488
International Church of the Foursquare Gospel	1,888	7,254	251,614
Full Gospel Fellowship of Churches and Ministers Intl.	902	2,887	412,000
International Pentecostal Holiness Church	1,990	3,949	244,184
Pentecostal Church of God	1,170	2,870	40,000
Other (14 denominations)	7,900	12,832	967,393
Lutheran Churches	**18,728**	**29,036**	**5,913,309**
Evangelical Lutheran Church in America	10,549	17,665	3,636,948
Lutheran Church-Missouri Synod	6,144	8,502	1,870,659
Wisconsin Evangelical Lutheran Synod	1,263	1,844	313,553
Other (9 denominations)	772	1,025	92,149
Latter-day Saints Churches	**14,052**	**63,468**	**5,279,005**
Church of Jesus Christ of Latter-day Saints	12,753	42,786	5,095,959
Community of Christ	1,236	20,420	180,339
Church of Jesus Christ (Bickertonites)	63	262	2,707
Orthodox (Eastern) Churches	**2,780**	**3,917**	**4,447,270**
Orthodox Church in America	737	905	970,000
Greek Orthodox Archdiocese of North & South America	566	840	1,500,000
Armenian Apostolic Church of America, Diocese of America	72	70	414,000
Coptic Orthodox Church	100	145	100,000
Armenian Apostolic Church of America	35	48	360,000
Other (14 denominations)	1,270	1,909	1,103,270
Churches of Christ	**24,356**	**23,547**	**2,799,970**
Churches of Christ	15,000	16,350	1,265,844
Christian Churches and Churches of Christ	5,579	N.A.	1,071,616
Christian Church (Disciples of Christ)	3,777	7,197	462,510
Presbyterian Churches	**13,969**	**26,988**	**2,780,153**
Presbyterian Church (USA)	10,960	21,312	2,313,662
Presbyterian Church in America	1,534	3,287	260,919
Cumberland Presbyterian Church	759	858	81,464
Other (4 denominations)	716	1,531	124,108

Family/Denomination	Local congregations	Total clergy	Total membership
Episcopal Church	**7,200**	**15,870**	**1,834,530**
Reformed Churches	**7,696**	**14,011**	**1,648,258**
United Church of Christ	5,567	10,231	1,224,297
Reformed Church in America	894	1,838	164,697
Christian Reformed Church in North America	776	1,340	187,060
Other (5 denominations)	459	602	72,204
Jehovah's Witnesses	**12,384**	**N.A.**	**1,046,006**
Adventist Churches	**5,388**	**6,101**	**1,022,193**
Seventh-Day Adventists	4,750	5,210	964,811
Other (3 denominations)	638	891	57,382
Church of the Nazarene	**5,225**	**9,355**	**630,150**
Salvation Army	**1,316**	**5,256**	**422,543**
Mennonite Churches	**3,140**	**8,368**	**362,822**
Mennonite Church	913	2,561	109,315
General Conference of Mennonite Brethren Churches	368	N.A.	82,130
Old Order Amish Church	898	3,617	80,820
Other (8 denominations)	961	2,190	90,557
Christian and Missionary Alliance	**2,004**	**3,019**	**201,009**
Churches of God	**4,341**	**6,194**	**347,895**
Church of God (Anderson, Ind.)	2,240	6,064	252,419
Other (2 denominations)	2,101	130	95,476
International Council of Community Churches	**150**	**374**	**108,806**
Evangelical Free Church of America	**1,420**	**2,733**	**130,000**
Brethren Churches	**1,945**	**3,382**	**219,599**
Church of the Brethren	1,068	1,838	128,820
Other (5 denominations)	877	1,544	90,779
Friends (Quaker) Churches	**2,848**	**355**	**212,701**
Religious Society of Friends (Conservative)	1,200	N.A.	104,000
Other (4 denominations)	1,640	355	108,701
Christian Congregation	**1,496**	**1,575**	**122,181**
Christian Brethren	**1,150**	**600**	**86,000**
Unitarian Universalist Assoc. of Congregations	**1,010**	**171**	**214,738**
Evangelical Covenant Church	**775**	**1,512**	**117,962**
Moravian Church in America	**92**	**170**	**18,529**
Other Christian Churches (20 denominations)	**36,306**	**50,192**	**2,617,853**

Note: Congregation, clergy and membership totals (in bold) do not include figures for denominations not reporting. **Source:** *2007 Yearbook of American and Canadian Churches.* Copyright ©National Council of the Churches of Christ in the U.S.A. Editor Eileen W. Lindner. www.ncccusa.org. Reprinted by permission.

Christian Denominations in the U.S.

The 30 largest churches in the U.S. (by membership) comprise almost 90 percent of all Christian church membership. But because not all churches report membership figures to the *Yearbook of American and Canadian Churches* every year, these figures must be considered an approximation at best.

Denomination	Membership, 2005	Percent of total	Denomination	Membership, 2005	Percent of total
Roman Catholic Church	69,135,254	44.12%	**American Baptist Churches in the U.S.A.**	1,396,700	0.89%
Southern Baptist Convention	16,270,315	10.38			
The United Methodist Church	8,075,010	5.15	**Churches of Christ**	1,265,844	0.81
Church of God in Christ	5,499,875	3.51	**United Church of Christ**	1,224,297	0.78
Church of Jesus Christ of Latter-day Saints	5,095,959	3.25	**African Methodist Episcopal Zion Church**	1,215,508	0.78
National Baptist Convention, U.S.A., Inc.	5,000,000	3.19	**Baptist Bible Fellowship International**	1,200,000	0.77
Evangelical Lutheran Church in America	3,636,948	2.32	**Christian Churches and Churches of Christ**	1,071,616	0.68
National Missionary Baptist Convention of America	2,500,000	1.60	**Jehovah's Witnesses**	1,046,006	0.67
Progressive National Baptist Convention (U.S.A.)	2,500,000 2,313,662	1.60 1.48	**Church of God (Cleveland, Tenn.)**	1,013,488	0.65
The Lutheran Church - Missouri Synod	1,870,659	1.19	**Orthodox Church in America**	970,000	0.62
African Methodist Episcopal Church	1,857,186	1.19	**Seventh-day Adventists**	964,811	0.62
Episcopal Church	1,834,530	1.17	**Christian Methodist Baptist Convention, Inc.**	850,000	0.54
Assemblies of God	1,612,336	1.03	**Church of the Nazarene**	630,150	0.40
Greek Orthodox Archdiocese of North and South America	1,500,000	0.96	**Christian Church (Disciples of Christ)**	462,510	0.30
Pentecostal Assemblies of the World	1,500,000	0.96	**Full Gospel Fellowship of Churches and Ministers Intl.**	412,000	0.26

Source: *2007 Yearbook of American and Canadian Churches.* Copyright ©National Council of the Churches of Christ in the U.S.A. Editor Eileen W. Lindner. www.ncccusa.org. Reprinted by permission.

Pennsylvania, wear "plain" clothing and still drive horses and buggies rather than automobiles.

Churches of the Brethren
The Brethren, founded as a dissenting group in Germany in the early 1700s, immigrated to Pennsylvania in the 1720s to escape persecution. There they have remained. Brethren share many doctrinal points with their neighbors, the Mennonites. They practice adult baptism, refuse to swear oaths, and will not serve as combatants in war. The various Brethren denominations agree in basic theology but differ on less significant matters of interpretation.

Unitarian Universalist Association
Unitarianism was an outgrowth of New England Congregationalism in the late 1700s and early 1800s. Unitarians asserted God's unity and repudiated the doctrine of the Trinity. They also interpreted other Christian beliefs in a liberal, figurative manner. Universalism was a separate movement emphasizing the availability of God's care to all people, not only to a small chosen group. In 1961 Unitarian and Universalist organizations merged.

Friends (Quaker) Churches
Known popularly as Quakers, the Friends were established by the English religious mystic George Fox (1624–91) in the mid-1600s. They were persecuted in England for refusing to take oaths or to serve as combatants in war. Under the protection of William Penn (1644–1718), many settled in Pennsylvania. According to Fox, they were called Quakers because they were admonished to "tremble at the word of the Lord." In Pennsylvania the Quakers set themselves apart, dressing plainly and avoiding worldly amusements. In Philadelphia they became influential business people.

The most distinctive doctrine of the Friends is that of the Inner Light, the spark of God in each individual. Friends have avoided setting up formal church structures, and many groups have no clergy. Friends have organized remarkable world relief and peace organizations, by which they are perhaps best known to outsiders.

Other Christian Churches
Among the other denominations reported by the *Yearbook of American and Canadian Churches*, there is a wide variety of religious belief and practice. Many of the groups are radically congregational, making generalizations risky. Other groups are heterodox offshoots from the Pentecostal family. In many cases they depend on a single strong leader. The smallest denominations listed may actually be a single local congregation that reports as a separate church body.

Among the miscellaneous groups are spiritualist and other "New Age" groups. Some of these mix spiritualism with Christianity; others may not consider themselves Christian in any sense.

▶JUDAISM
Judaism is the largest non-Christian religious family in the United States. Jewish organizations and the Pew Forum on Religion and Public Life report that there are 5.2 million American Jews. Of these, roughly 4 million are religiously affiliated. The remaining million consider their Judaism to be more ethnic or cultural than religious.

As descendants of the Jews of biblical times, Jews worship one God and follow the religious precepts in the Hebrew scriptures, the writings called the Old Testament by Christians. Jews recognize Jesus as a religious teacher but do not acknowledge him as the Messiah or Son of God. Jews still await the coming of the Messiah as foretold by the prophets.

A handful of Jews arrived in North America in the 1600s. In the 1800s, Jews from Germany arrived with other immigrants. Then between 1890 and 1920, several million Jews arrived from eastern Europe, fleeing persecution and hard times in Russia and Poland. In the 1930s and 1940s, Jews reached America as refugees from the Nazi extermination campaigns. The slaughter of some six million Jews by the Germans, called the Holocaust, is one of two central facts of modern Jewish experience. The second is the establishment of Israel as an independent state in 1948. Today more Jews live in Israel than in any other country except the U.S.

There are three main branches of religious Judaism in the U.S. today: Orthodox, Reform, and Conservative. Orthodox Judaism is by far the most rigorous and smallest of the three branches, with an estimated 500,000 adherents. Orthodox Jews may keep entirely separate kitchens for milk and meat, refuse to operate electric and mechanical devices on the Sabbath, and often attend temple services or hold prayer sessions every day. Orthodox services are conducted in Hebrew, and require men and women to pray separately, even when not in temple. Many orthodox communities, especially self-contained communities such as the Hasidic Jews (located mainly in New York), impose strict dress codes, dictating not only the clothes, but also the hairstyles of their members.

Reform Judaism is the least strict branch. It flowered in the U.S. in the late 1800s, especially among immigrants from Germany. Reform Jews do not generally wear yarmulkes, don't usually observe the kosher dietary laws, and conduct their religious services primarily in English (though most of the prayers are recited in Hebrew). About 1.13 million Jews are affiliated with Reform temples.

Conservative Judaism rose in response to the Reform movement. It sought to preserve more of the ancient observances of the old orthodoxy, but without losing touch with American culture and behavior. As a middle road between Reform and Orthodox Judaism, Conservative Judaism has gained many adherents. About two million Jews are affiliated with Conservative institutions.

▶ISLAM
The Islamic faith, whose followers are called Muslims, is one of the three great theistic world religions, along with Judaism and Christianity. The first sizable group of Muslims arrived in the U.S. from Lebanon in the early 1900s. Later waves of immigration have brought Pakistanis, Indians, Arabs, and Iranians, among others.

There are about 1,600 mosques in the U.S. but membership estimates vary greatly, in part because many Muslims are new immigrants or recent converts. Some Muslim groups claim as many as six or seven million American Muslims; but recent surveys by the U.S. Census and the Pew Forum on Religion and Public Life have yielded estimates between one and two million. Regardless of overall numbers, most Muslims are in cities in the Northeast and industrial Midwest. Observances may vary from one center to another, depending on the nationality of its adherents and their length of residence in the United States. In general, recent immigrants are more conservative and follow Islamic ritual and custom more closely.

▶BUDDHIST CHURCHES OF AMERICA
The Buddhist Churches of America is the oldest and largest U.S. Buddhist group. It represents the Jodo Shinshu sect of Buddhism, and many of its members are of Japanese descent. There are many other Buddhist organizations in the U.S., and there may be as many as three million additional Americans who subscribe to Buddhist tenets.

Transportation

Americans spend well over $1 trillion annually on transportation products and services. Transportation expenditures (which include personal and governmental spending on motor vehicles and parts, gasoline and oil, airfares, and public transportation) accounted for 10.6 percent of gross domestic product in 2006, almost as much as what the country spent on food, and much more than it spent on education. In 2005, the United States recorded over 5.5 trillion passenger miles of travel and over 4.5 trillion ton-miles of freight traffic. More than 250 million vehicles (most of them cars) were involved in domestic transportation in 2006, using nearly 200 billion gallons of fuel, and causing almost 45,000 fatalities.

The government has traditionally played a leading role in the development of the nation's transportation infrastructure. Technological, economic,

Passenger Miles and Ton-Miles of Freight, by Mode of Transportation, 1980–2005 (numbers in millions)

Mode of transport	1980	1990	2000	2002	2005
Passenger miles, total[1]	2,653,510	2,846,130	3,345,986	3,383,225	5,523,307
Air carrier[2]	204,368	345,873	516,129	482,310	583,689
General aviation, intercity	14,700	13,000	15,200	N.A.	N.A.
Highway, total	2,653,510	3,561,209	4,304,270	4,667,038	4,884,557
Passenger car and motorcycle	2,024,246	2,293,815	2,555,973	2,632,520	2,683,822
Other 2-axle, 4-tire vehicles	520,774	999,754	1,467,664	1,674,792	1,836,988
Truck	108,491	146,242	205,520	214,603	222,836
Transit	39,854	41,143	47,666	48,324	49,680
Amtrak/Inter-city rail	4,503	6,057	5,498	5,468	5,381
Ton-miles of freight, total	2,989,000	3,621,943	4,328,642	4,409,000	4,537,921
Air[3]	4,528	10,420	15,810	13,837	15,731
Trucks	555,000	848,779	1,192,825	1,245,542	1,293,326
Railroad	918,958	1,064,408	1,546,319	1,605,532	1,733,777
Water transport	921,836	833,544	645,799	612,081	591,276
Oil pipeline	588,200	584,100	577,000	586,000	572,000

Note: For 1980, "Ton-miles Air" was "Air carrier"; "Ton-miles trucks" was "Intercity trucks"; "Ton-miles railroad" was "Class 1 Rail." Figures for 1990-2002 have been adjusted. 1. Includes mileage not shown separately. 2. Domestic, all services. 3. Includes revenue ton-miles, U.S. and foreign mail, and express. **Source:** U.S. Dept. of Transportation, *National Transportation Statistics 2007* (2008).

Number of Vehicles in the U.S., 1970–2005

Mode of Transport	1970	1980	1990	2000	2005
Air, total[6]	134,422	205,305	204,083	225,588	232,577
Air carrier, certificated, all services[6]	2,679	3,808	6,083	8,055	8,225
General aviation[6]	131,743	211,045	198,000	217,533	224,352
Highway, total[1]	111,242,295	161,490,159	193,057,376	225,821,241	247,421,120
Passenger car & motorcycle	92,067,655	127,294,783	137,959,958	137,967,488	142,211,521
Other 2-axle 4-tire vehicle	14,210,591	27,875,934	48,274,555	79,084,979	95,336,839
Truck, total	4,586,487	5,790,473	6,195,876	8,022,649	8,481,999
Intercity bus	377,562	528,789	626,987	746,125	807,053
Local transit, total[2,6]	61,298	75,388	92,961	131,493	150,998
Motor bus[6]	49,700	59,411	58,714	75,013	82,027
Light rail[6]	1,262	1,013	913	1,577	1,645
Heavy rail[6]	9,286	9,641	10,419	10,591	11,110
Trolley bus[6]	1,050	823	832	951	615
Commuter rail[6]	—	4,500	4,415	5,073	6,392
Demand response[6]	—	—	16,471	33,080	41,958
Other[6]	—	—	1,197	5,208	7,251
Rail, total[3]	1,450,998	1,198,755	679,918	582,454	499,068
Class I Freight cars	1,423,921	1,168,114	658,902	560,154	474,839
Class I Locomotives	27,077	28,094	18,835	20,028	22,779
Amtrak[4]	—	2,547	2,181	2,272	1,444
Water transport, total[6]	5,155,716	8,817,509	11,036,334	12,823,951	12,983,799
Non self-propelled vessels[6]	19,337	31,662	31,209	33,152	32,052
Self-propelled vessels[6]	6,455	7,126	8,236	8,202	8,976
Oceangoing ships[5]	1,579	864	636	454	357
Recreational boats	5,128,345	8,777,857	10,996,253	12,782,143	12,942,414

Notes: 1. Registered vehicles. 2. Prior to 1984, excludes most rural and smaller transit systems. 3. Does not include non-Class I freight cars or shippers' freight cars. 4. Includes passenger cars and locomotives. 5. Vessels 1,000 gross tons and over. 6. Figures for 2005 are preliminary. **Source:** U.S. Dept. of Transportation, *National Transportation Statistics 2007* (2008).

and demographic changes all shape the government's priorities. In the 19th and early 20th centuries, for instance, the government made enormous direct and indirect contributions to the development of the nation's railroads. Today, the government spends vastly more on highways and aviation than on mass transit, railroad transportation or water transportation.

▶PASSENGER TRAVEL

In order to compare the costs of different modes of transportation, statisticians calculate the price for one passenger to travel one mile. For modes of transportation that carry large numbers of passengers at once, these numbers are remarkably similar. It costs about 13 cents for a coach passenger to travel one mile by plane, 18 cents by commuter rail, 27 cents by Amtrak, and 13 by inter-city bus. By comparison, the average cost of operating a car in 2005 (including variable costs for gas and oil, maintenance and tires, and fixed costs for insurance, registration, depreciation and finance charges) was 54.1 cents per mile (up from 51 cents in 2000, largely due to rising gas prices). The average fare in 2005 was $106 for an airline seat, $4.08 for commuter rail, and $51 for a ride on Amtrak; in 2002, it was $30 for an inter-city bus ticket. Most of these fares have tripled since 1980, though airfares have risen less than 20 percent.

▶TRANSPORTATION SAFETY

Because they kill large numbers of people at once, plane crashes attract much more attention than do automobile accidents. But over the course of a year, air travel accounts for only a tiny percentage of transportation fatalities; in a typical year, more people die in boating accidents than in aviation mishaps. Between 2002 and 2006, the nation's major commercial carriers experienced a grand total of 108 fatalities; smaller commuter airlines were responsible for 4 deaths over this period. The combined total of this five-year period is still less than the number of people killed each day in automobile accidents in 2006.

Almost 95 percent of transportation fatalities and 99 percent of transportation injuries are a re-

World Motor Vehicle Production, 2006

Country	Passenger cars	Commercial vehicles	Total vehicles
Australia	297,986	29,750	327,736
Belgium	881,929	36,127	918,056
Brazil	2,092,003	519,031	2,611,034
Canada	1,389,536	1,181,830	2,571,366
China	3,869,494	3,410,232	7,279,726
Czech Rep.	849,999	4,908	854,907
France	2,728,196	446,064	3,174,260
Germany	5,398,508	421,106	5,819,614
India	1,185,544	772,211	1,957,755
Italy	892,502	319,092	1,211,594
Japan	9,756,515	1,727,718	11,484,233
Mexico	1,097,619	947,899	2,045,518
Netherlands	87,332	72,122	159,454
Poland	608,919	106,310	715,299
Portugal	143,478	83,847	227,325
Russia	1,173,624	327,898	1,501,522
South Africa	334,482	253,237	587,719
South Korea	2,298,474	1,541,628	3,840,102
Spain	2,078,639	698,796	2,777,435
Sweden	288,583	38,759	327,342
Taiwan	211,306	91,923	303,229
Turkey	545,682	441,898	987,580
U.K.	1,442,085	207,707	1,649,792
U.S.	4,366,996	6,893,281	11,260,277
Total[1]	46,511,648	22,049,239	68,560,887

Note: North America excludes buses. 1. Includes other countries not shown separately. **Source:** Ward's Communications, *Ward's Motor Vehicle Facts & Figures, 2007.*

Traffic Deaths by Selected Country, 1995–2005

Country	Deaths per 100,000 registered vehicles		
	1995	2000	2005
Austria	27.7	22.0	17.1
Belgium	30.5	27.1	19.4
Canada	20.1	16.9	15.4
China	N.A.	530.0	N.A
Denmark	28.9	22.3	12.6
Finland	20.2	18.0	13.6
France	27.8	22.3	14.7
Germany	21.7	17.9	10.8
Hungary	N.A.	51.1	38.7
Italy	19.8	18.9	N.A.
Japan	16.0	12.4	10.7
Netherlands	21.2	16.1	9.0
Norway	14.8	14.7	8.8
Poland	175.3	53.1	35.6
Portugal	61.1	39.2	22.5
Spain	N.A.	29.4	17.4
Sweden	13.1	13.5	9.5
Switzerland	19.6	15.4	9.5
Turkey	148.6	84.1	54.8
U.K.	13.5	14.8	9.2
U.S.	21.5	19.5	18.2

Note: Data vary significantly between countries both definitionally and quantitatively. **Source:** Ward's Communications, *Ward's Motor Vehicle Facts & Figures, 2007.*

World Motor Vehicle Production, 1950–2006 (numbers in thousands)

Year	United States	Canada	Europe	Japan	Other	World total	U.S. share of total
1950	8,006	388	1,991	32	160	10,577	75.7%
1960	7,905	398	6,837	482	866	16,488	47.9
1970	8,284	1,160	13,049	5,289	1,637	29,419	28.2
1980	8,010	1,324	15,496	11,043	2,692	38,565	20.8
1990	9,783	1,928	18,866	13,487	4,496	48,554	20.1
1995	11,985	2,408	17,045	10,196	8,349	49,983	24.0
2000	12,771	2,962	17,161	10,145	14,490	57,528	22.2
2002	12,280	2,629	17,295	10,258	16,511	44,064	27.9
2004	11,960	2,712	17,723	10,512	21,056	49,291	24.3
2006	11,260	2,571	21,744	11,484	21,501	68,561	23.1

Source: Ward's Communications, *Ward's Motor Vehicle Facts & Figures, 2007.*

sult of automobile accidents. In 2006, there were 5,973,000 automobile accidents, resulting in 2,604,648 injuries (down from 3.1 million in 2001) and 42,642 fatalities. In 2005, the number of deaths had risen to 43,443. Despite safety improvements to the production of automobiles, wider highway lanes, better lighting and lower speed limits, the annual number of automobile accidents, injuries and fatalities have not changed much since 1970. But over the same period, the number of miles traveled has more than doubled (from 1 trillion miles in 1970 to nearly 3 trillion in 2006), indicating that Americans are driving many more miles without having any more accidents.

Something that has changed, though, is the number of accidents involving light trucks (including minivans and sport-utility vehicles). In 2003, crashes between light trucks and passenger cars resulted in 4,901 fatalities and 470,000 injuries—more than any other category of vehicular accident. In such a crash, car occupants are 4 times more likely to be killed than light truck occupants.

Another change is the number of people killed in accidents involving drunk drivers. In 1985, 23,167 people, or 53 percent of the total, died in alcohol-related auto accidents. In 2006, the total number of fatalities was about the same, but only 17,602, or 41 percent, involved a drunk driver. The number of non-motorists (pedestrians and cyclists) killed in auto accidents also decreased between 1985 and 2006, from 7,782 to 5,849.

▶MOTOR VEHICLES

Although the accompanying table would suggest that the average fuel efficiency of U.S. cars is on the rise, the statistics mask the explosion in the number of light trucks, minivans, and sport utility vehicles favored by so many American drivers of the 1990's. These vehicles get much poorer gas mileage than most cars, but because they are classified as trucks, they are not held to the same fuel efficiency standards as cars. In 1980, over 80 percent of all new vehicles were cars (9.1 million), with an average fuel efficiency of 23 miles per gallon. In comparison, there were only 2.2 million new trucks, which got 18 miles per gallon. Although gas-guzzling light trucks still commanded 52.8 percent of the market in 2006, sales fell 2.6 percent from 2005 to 16.9 million units. (Light truck sales totaled roughly nine million in 2001.) On the opposite end of the spectrum, hybrid sales totaled 205,749 in 2005, which, although it was nearly a 250 percent increase from 2004, still comprised only 1.2 percent of total vehicles sold.

World Motor Vehicle Registrations, 1960–2005

Year	Registrations ('000s)			Population per car
	Cars	Trucks and buses	Total vehicles	
1960	98,317	28,637	126,955	29
1970	193,516	52,852	246,368	18
1980	320,539	90,573	411,113	14
1985	374,727	112,816	487,544	13
1990	444,900	138,082	582,982	12
1995	477,010	169,749	646,759	12
2000	547,147	203,274	750,420	11
2001	561,687	206,218	767,905	11
2002	576,278	210,918	787,196	10
2005	617,172	245,248	862,420	10

Source: Ward's Communications, *Ward's Motor Vehicle Facts & Figures, 2007.*

U.S. Retail Sales of Passenger Cars by Size and Country of Origin, 1983–2006

Category	1983	1990	1995	2000	2006
By size					
Small	38.8%	32.8%	27.1%	28.1%	32.4%
Middle	40.6	44.8	48.5	47.8	41.6
Large	10.7	9.4	10.8	7.0	8.6
Luxury	9.9	13.0	13.6	17.1	16.4
By origin					
U.S.	74.0%	74.2%	82.6%	77.2%	69.9%
Imports	26.0	25.8	17.4	22.8	30.1
Japan	20.9	18.5	11.4	9.8	14.8
Germany	3.0	2.9	2.4	5.8	7.2
Other	2.0	4.4	3.6	7.2	8.1

Source: Ward's Communications, *Ward's Motor Vehicle Facts & Figures, 2007.*

U.S. Motor Vehicle Sales and Registrations, 1900–2006

Year	Factory sales			Motor vehicle registrations[1]
	Passenger cars	Trucks and buses	Total	
1900	4,192	—	4,192	8,000
1910	181,000	6,000	187,000	468,500
1920	1,905,560	321,789	2,227,349	9,239,161
1930	2,787,456	575,364	3,362,820	26,749,853
1940	3,717,385	754,901	4,472,286	32,453,233
1950	6,665,863	1,337,193	8,003,056	49,161,691
1960	6,674,796	1,194,475	7,869,271	73,857,768
1970	6,546,817	1,692,440	8,239,257	108,418,197
1980	6,400,026	1,667,283	8,067,309	155,796,219
1990	6,049,749	3,725,205	9,774,954	188,655,462
1995	6,309,836	5,713,469	12,023,305	201,530,021
1999	5,427,746	6,699,113	12,126,859	216,308,623
2000	5,504,385	7,022,478	12,526,863	213,299,313
2001	4,884,313	6,223,586	11,107,899	216,682,937
2003	N.A.	7,143,429	N.A.	N.A.
2006	7,781,000	9,268,000	17,049,000	237,697,097[2]

Notes: 1. Data exclude military vehicles as well as farm trucks registered at a nominal fee in certain states and restricted to use in the vicinity of owners' farms; in 1995, there were 60,490 such trucks. 2. Figure is for 2005. **Source:** Ward's Communications, *Ward's Motor Vehicle Facts & Figures, 2007.*

The popularity of larger vehicles, which up until 1999 were allowed to produce up to three times as much pollution per mile as standard cars, has had serious implications for the environment. To remedy that situation, the Clinton administration in 1999 announced that minivans, pickup trucks, and sport utility vehicles would be subject to the same pollution standards as ordinary cars. In 2002, the Bush administration proposed a 7 percent improvement in the fuel economy of these vehicles by 2007. As of Aug. 2006, SUVs got on average 17 miles to the gallon (mpg), but 2007 mod-

U.S. Motor Vehicle Registrations, 2006 and Insurance Costs by State, 2005

State	Automobiles[1]	Buses	Trucks	Total motor vehicles	Average expenditure per insured vehicle
United States	135,399,945	821,959	107,943,782	244,165,686	$829.17
Alabama	1,795,596	9,082	2,825,636	4,630,314	678.01
Alaska	242,487	2,706	429,901	675,094	961.72
Arizona	2,189,979	4,961	1,987,392	4,182,332	926.33
Arkansas	958,640	8,201	1,027,414	1,994,255	693.31
California	19,835,554	56,814	13,289,690	33,182,058	844.50
Colorado	858,967	5,829	943,027	1,807,823	827.47
Connecticut	1,999,809	10,492	1,041,651	3,051,952	990.52
Delaware	432,509	2,167	378,512	813,188	1,027.65
District of Columbia	168,916	2,889	47,300	219,105	1,181.77
Florida	7,425,148	48,929	8,899,488	16,373,565	1,063.36
Georgia	4,141,179	21,343	4,123,932	8,286,454	783.69
Hawaii	538,581	5,671	464,288	1,008,540	842.78
Idaho	541,487	3,767	729,861	1,275,115	582.99
Illinois	5,947,468	18,036	3,910,742	9,876,246	742.65
Indiana	2,694,901	31,974	2,228,559	4,955,434	657.35
Iowa	1,744,519	8,429	1,593,003	3,345,951	555.04
Kansas	872,878	3,918	1,512,396	2,389,192	590.29
Kentucky	1,969,142	14,249	1,574,731	3,558,122	749.62
Louisiana	1,950,372	22,102	1,900,270	3,872,744	1,076.09
Maine	581,797	3,399	486,680	1,071,876	643.50
Maryland	2,656,597	12,155	1,819,645	4,488,397	944.73
Massachusetts	3,310,725	11,207	2,063,283	5,385,215	1,112.73
Michigan	4,765,547	26,248	3,362,440	8,154,235	930.79
Minnesota	2,512,491	17,610	2,174,813	4,704,914	791.47
Mississippi	1,118,200	9,521	869,860	1,997,581	744.84
Missouri	2,715,297	11,485	2,230,390	4,957,172	685.49
Montana	447,446	2,503	616,613	1,066,562	685.01
Nebraska	832,511	6,995	893,627	1,733,133	620.60
Nevada	679,828	1,923	684,806	1,366,557	982.56
New Hampshire	585,455	1,873	472,635	1,059,963	791.71
New Jersey	3,692,966	23,827	2,241,195	5,957,988	1,183.54
New Mexico	699,312	3,552	877,956	1,580,820	727.35
New York	8,528,457	70,015	2,685,424	11,283,896	1,122.45
North Carolina	3,659,926	33,720	2,607,790	6,301,436	602.20
North Dakota	345,502	2,587	364,080	712,169	554.30
Ohio	6,438,988	44,484	4,345,371	10,828,843	668.93
Oklahoma	1,606,517	18,634	1,576,680	3,201,831	677.53
Oregon	1,427,597	14,822	1,538,960	2,981,379	736.67
Pennsylvania	5,842,819	38,029	4,013,315	9,894,163	849.14
Rhode Island	508,389	1,726	295,433	805,548	1,059.13
South Carolina	1,964,994	18,078	1,470,771	3,453,843	752.56
South Dakota	375,760	2,644	465,580	843,984	565.23
Tennessee	2,878,136	19,979	2,193,213	5,091,328	658.60
Texas	8,805,316	90,173	8,642,899	17,538,388	844.87
Utah	1,079,455	1,308	1,155,325	2,236,088	705.56
Vermont	309,972	1,745	275,951	587,668	698.74
Virginia	4,031,355	18,264	2,586,357	6,635,976	697.86
Washington	3,087,818	11,665	2,590,014	5,689,497	840.17
West Virginia	734,599	2,794	703,706	1,441,099	856.53
Wisconsin	2,639,984	14,347	2,317,130	4,971,461	615.33
Wyoming	228,057	3,088	414,047	645,192	639.05

Note: Motor vehicle registration figures are for 2006. Insurance expenditures are for 2005. Total includes privately owned vehicles and federal, state, and municipal vehicles; does not include vehicles owned by the military services. Farm trucks, registered at a nominal fee and restricted to use on farms, are not included. 1 Includes taxicabs. **Sources:** U.S. Dept. of Transportation, *Highway Statistics 2007* (2008); National Association of Insurance Commissioners, *2004/05 Auto Insurance Database Report* (2007).

els were required to get 22.2 mpg and 2008 models were required to get 22.5.

Traffic

According to the Census Bureau, 90 percent of Americans have access to a motor vehicle, and half of the nation's households have two or more vehicles. In 2006, nearly 87 percent of all U.S. workers drove to work: 76 percent drove alone; only 10.7 percent were in car pools, down from 12 percent in 2000. The remaining workers used mass transportation (4.3 percent); walked (2.9), worked at home (3.9), or used bicycles, motorcycles, or some other transportation (2.0). The average commute was 24.4 minutes in 2004, down from 25.5 minutes in 2000. Nationally, only 2 percent of Americans faced an extreme commute (90 minutes or more) in 2003. New York topped this list for longest average commute for workers by state (30.4 minutes), and South Dakota boasted the shortest (15.2 minutes).

It's no wonder, then, that traffic jams are routine. According to the Texas Transportation Institute's 2005 Mobility Study, congestion caused 3.7 billion hours of travel delay nationally and wasted 2.3 billion gallons of fuel—a total cost of $63 billion. The average rush hour driver in the 85 urban areas studied spent 47 hours stuck in traffic in 2003, up from 16 hours a year in 1982. Not surprisingly, delays were longest in Los Angeles, where drivers lost 93 hours per year to congestion. San Francisco was second, with 72 hours lost annually, followed by Washington D.C. with 69.

▶ AVIATION

U.S. airlines made a modest $3 billion profit in 2006, ending a five-year string of losses that followed the September 11, 2001 terrorist attacks, which pushed the already shaky industry to the edge of financial ruin. A $15 billion bailout by the

U.S. Roads and Streets, 1904–2007

Year	Mileage ('000s)			
	State control[1]	County & local control	Total[2]	Percent paved
1904	—	—	2,351	N.A.
1921	203	2,957	3,160	N.A.
1930	324	2,935	3,259	N.A.
1940	551	2,666	3,287	N.A.
1950	609	2,623	3,313	23.5%
1960	694	2,725	3,546	34.7
1970	755	2,762	3,731	44.5
1980	848	2,764	3,860	53.7
1990	798	2,889	3,867	58.4
1995	803	2,937	3,912	60.8
2000	775	3,058	3,950	63.4
2007	783	3,121	4,017[3]	65.2

Note: Some years contain estimates by the Federal Highway Administration. 1. Reflects state highway agency roadways prior to 1980. Includes state park, state toll, and other state agency roadways beginning in 1980. 2. After 1930, includes mileage in federal parks, forests, and reservations not part of the state and local highway system and not shown separately. 3. Includes mileage controlled by Federal Agency and other jurisdictions. **Source:** U.S. Department of Transportation, *Highway Statistics Summary to 1995* and *Highway Statistics 2007.*

Top-Selling Passenger Cars and Trucks in the U.S., 2005–06

2006 rank, Cars (2005 rank)	Units sold, 2006	Units sold, 2005
1. Toyota Camry (1)	448,445	431,703
2. Toyota Corolla/Matrix (3)	387,388	341,290
3. Honda Accord (2)	354,441	369,293
4. Honda Civic (4)	316,638	308,415
5. Chevrolet Impala (6)	289,868	246,481
6. Nissan Altima (5)	232,457	255,371
7. Chevrolet Cobalt (7)	211,449	212,667
8. Ford Focus (10)	177,006	184,825
9. Ford Taurus (9)	174,803	196,919
10. Ford Mustang (11)	166,530	160,975
11. Chevrolet Malibu (8)	163,853	203,503
12. Pontiac G6 (14)	157,644	124,844
13. Hyundai Sonata (13)	149,513	130,365
14. Chrysler 300 Series (12)	143,647	144,048
15. Ford Fusion (x)	142,502	N.A.
16. BMW 3 Series (x)	120,180	N.A.
17. Nissan Sentra (16)	117,922	119,489
18. Dodge Charger (x)	114,201	N.A.
19. Pontiac Grand Prix (15)	108,634	122,398
20. Toyota Prius (20)	106,971	107,897

LIGHT TRUCKS	Units sold, 2006	Units sold, 2005
1. Ford F-Series (1)	744,996	854,878
2. Chevrolet Silverado (2)	636,069	705,980
3. Dodge Ram Pickup (3)	364,177	400,543
4. Dodge Caravan (7)	211,140	226,771
5. GMC Sierra (6)	210,736	229,488
6. Ford Econoline (10)	180,457	179,543
7. Ford Explorer (5)	179,229	239,788
8. Toyota Tacoma (12)	178,351	168,831
9. Honda Odyssey (11)	177,919	174,275
10. Chevrolet TrailBlazer (4)	174,797	244,150

Note: (x)=Not ranked in 2005. **Source:** Ward's Communications, *Ward's Motor Vehicle Facts & Figures, 2007.*

Fuel Efficiency of U.S. Passenger Cars and Trucks, 1955–2004

Since 1980, the federal government has required car manufacturers to maintain a corporate average fuel efficiency (CAFE). Since 1985, the CAFE standard for cars has been 27.5 mpg, which automakers have exceeded by curtailing production of station wagons and full-size sedans. The CAFE standard for light trucks, minivans and sport utility vehicles, however, is much lower (20.7 mpg), yet the average new light truck has rarely attained even this lower level of fuel efficiency.

Model Year	All passenger cars	Average New Vehicle		
		Passenger cars[1]	Light trucks	Average vehicle
1955	14.5 mpg	16.0 mpg	—	—
1960	14.3	15.5	—	—
1965	14.3	15.4	—	—
1990	13.5	14.1	—	—
1975	13.5	15.1	—	—
1990	16.0	22.6	18.5 mpg	21.4 mpg
1985	17.5	26.3	20.7	24.0
1990	20.3	26.9	20.8	23.9
1995	21.1	27.7	20.5	23.8
1997	21.5	27.8	20.6	23.3
1998	21.6	28.1	21.1	23.3
1999	21.4	28.3	20.9	23.3
2000	22.0	28.5	21.2	N.A.
2006	22.4	30.4	22.5	N.A.

Note: Calculated on the basis of 55% city and 45% highway miles sales weighted average. 1. Domestic vehicles only. **Source:** U.S. Dept. of Transportation, *National Transportation Statistics 2006* (2007).

federal government (a $5 bil. giveaway and $10 bil. in guaranteed federal loans) prevented an industry collapse, but most airlines remain in dire straits. U.S. Airways received a $900 million federal loan guarantee after emerging from bankruptcy in 2003 and merged with America West Airlines in 2005. The federal government's denial of a $1.8 billion loan guarantee to United Airlines forced the airline to seek bankruptcy protection in 2002, and even American Airlines, the country's largest air carrier, teetered on the verge of bankruptcy in 2003.

After posting record profits of $5.6 billion in 1999, and $2.6 billion in 2000, the airline industry lost an astonishing $7.7 billion in 2001 and over $11 billion in 2002. American Airlines alone

posted a net loss of $3.51 billion in 2002—the largest single annual loss in airline history. The precipitous decline in passengers after September 11, 2001, was responsible for the vast majority

Top 25 Domestic Airline Routes, 2006

	Cities		Passengers
Rank	inbound	outbound	('000s)
1.	Fort Lauderdale	New York	3,783
2.	New York	Orlando	3,576
3.	Chicago	New York	3,292
4.	Atlanta	New York	2,654
5.	Los Angeles	New York	2,642
6.	West Palm Beach	New York	1,980
7.	Boston	New York	1,867
8.	Las Vegas	New York	1,786
9.	New York	Tampa	1,776
10.	New York	San Francisco	1,767
11.	Miami	New York	1,735
12.	Honolulu	Kahului, Maui	1,677
13.	New York	Washington, D.C.	1,672
14.	Chicago	Las Vegas	1,617
15.	New York	San Juan	1,589
16.	Dallas/Fort Worth	Houston	1,580
17.	Chicago	Los Angeles	1,565
18.	Dallas/Fort Worth	New York	1,459
19.	Chicago	Orlando	1,438
20.	Chicago	Phoenix	1,386
21.	Chicago	Washington, D.C.	1,345
22.	Las Vegas	Los Angeles	1,330
23.	Atlanta	Washington, D.C.	1,289
24.	Orlando	Philadelphia	1,262
25.	Chicago	Dallas/Fort Worth	1,261

Source: Air Transport Association of America, *2007 Economic Report* (2008).

On-time Performance and Mishandled Baggage, 1987–2008, by Major U.S. Airlines

Airline	Percent of Flights Arriving On-Time		Mishandled bags per 1,000
	2008[1]	1987-2008	2008[1]
Alaska	77.8%	75.6%	4.52
American	58.8	78.2	6.06
Continental	67.4	78.3	4.33
Delta	72.9	77.6	4.66
Northwest	67.6	79.0	3.98
Southwest	76.3	81.9	4.24
United	59.3	75.9	5.86
US Airways	76.3	78.1	4.65

1. 12 months ending June, 2008. **Source:** Federal Aviation Administration, Office of Aviation Enforcement and Proceedings, *Air Travel Consumer Report*, (August, 2008). www.dot.gov/airconsumer/

Top U.S. Airlines, 2006

Rank	Passengers ('000s)	Rank	Revenue Passenger Miles (millions)[1]	Rank	Cargo: Freight Ton Miles (millions)[2]
1. American	98,142	1. American	139,392	1. FedEx	10,543
2. Southwest	96,276	2. United	117,247	2. UPS	6,270
3. Delta	73,524	3. Delta	98,769	3. Atlas/Polar	5,342
4. United	69,265	4. Northwest	76,251	4. Northwest	2,269
5. US Airways	57,659	5. Continental	72,588	5. American	2,231
6. Northwest	54,837	6. Southwest	67,691	6. United	2,048
7. Continental	46,738	7. US Airways	60,895	7. Delta	1,239
8. AirTran	20,033	8. JetBlue	23,310	8. Kalitta	1,190
9. Sky West	19,496	9. Alaska	17,814	9. Continental	1,006
10. American Eagle	18,765	10. AirTran	13,798	10. Evergreen Int'l.	840
11. Jet Blue	18,507	11. ExpressJet	10,296	11. Southern	784
12. ExpressJet	17,962	12. SkyWest	9,497	12. Gemini	761
13. Alaska	17,148	13. American Eagle	8,420	13. World	745
14. Mesa	13,316	14. Frontier	8,317	14. ABX	571
15. Atlantic Southeast	11,814	15. Hawaiian	6,832	15. Tradewinds	412
16. Comair	10,590	16. Atlantic Southeast	6,276	16. US Airways	356
17. Pinnacle	9,018	17. Mesa	6,078	17. Focus	343
18. Frontier	8,895	18. Comair	5,287	18. Omni	328
19. Horizon	6,859	19. Spirit	4,569	19. Cargo 360	312
20. Chautauqua	6,780	20. Pinnacle	4,304	20. ASTAR	289
21. Hawaiian	6,157	21. ATA	4,064	21. Air Transport Int'l.	259
22. Air Wisconsin	5,790	22. Midwest	3,829	22. Centurion	189
23. PSA	5,153	23. Continental Micronesia	2,944	23. Florida West	179
24. Spirit	4,447	24. Chautauqua	2,822	24. Southwest	171
25. Midwest	3,870	25. Horizon Air	2,692	25. Express.Net	140

Notes: Carriers certificated under section 401, Federal Aviation Act. Figures for American include the former TWA. 1. One paying passenger traveling 1 mile generates 1 revenue passenger mile. 2. One ton of freight traveling 1 mile generates 1 freight-ton mile. **Source:** Air Transport Association of America, *2007 Economic Report* (2008).

of that loss. Revenue passenger miles (one passenger traveling one mile) declined a record 5.9 percent in 2001. International passenger revenue fell even further, by 7.1 percent.

With the decline in air traffic came a sharp reduction in the number of airport delays. In 2000, 78.9 percent of flights departed on time, and 77.0 percent arrived on time. In 2002, those numbers improved to 82.1 percent and 81.0 percent respectively. New York's La Guardia, which was the worst airport for delays in 2000 (only 57.1 of flights arrived on-time) boosted its on-time arrival rate to 73.3 percent in 2002. But by 2008, increased air travel pushed on-time arrivals down to 57.5 percent nationwide.

Some carriers managed to escape much of the recent turmoil. Once regarded as just a regional airline, Southwest flew 96,276 passengers in 2006,

On-time Arrival Rates at Major U.S. Airports, 1995–2008

Airport	Ontime Arrival Rate			Airport	Ontime Arrival Rate		
	1995	2000	2008		1995	2000	2008
Atlanta/Hartsfield Intl.	74.6%	74.9%	76.1%	New York/La Guardia Intl.	80.6%	57.1%	57.5%
Baltimore-Washington Intl.	N.A.	74.9	78.6	Newark Liberty Intl.	75.3	69.2	60.4
Boston/Logan International	74.3	65.5	72.9	Orlando International	77.3	74.0	75.7
Charlotte/Douglas Intl.	81.7	78.1	76.9	Oakland International	N.A.	N.A.	74.0
Chicago/Midway	N.A.	N.A.	77.3	Philadelphia International	79.8	66.7	72.0
Chicago/O'Hare Intl.	79.0	63.2	61.2	Phoenix/Sky Harbor Intl.	79.1	71.2	79.0
Cincinnati/Northern Ky. Intl.	82.3	79.8	76.6	Pittsburgh International	81.0	76.4	71.0
Dallas-Fort Worth Intl.	80.7	78.0	70.6	Portland (Oreg.) Intl.	N.A.	71.9	75.3
Denver International[1]	81.2	68.2	75.7	Salt Lake City International	78.1	76.8	80.9
Detroit Metropolitan	81.5	79.0	75.9	San Diego/Lindbergh Field	77.8	70.8	74.6
Fort Lauderdale Intl.	N.A.	N.A.	73.4	San Francisco Internationa	71.2	60.8	65.3
Houston Intercontinental	81.2	79.3	76.2	Seattle/Tacoma International	75.0	67.7	73.6
Las Vegas/McCarran Intl.	79.2	70.5	74.9	St.Louis/Lambert Intl.	75.9	77.6	73.3
Los Angeles International	70.8	66.6	72.7	Tampa International	75.9	73.4	76.1
Miami International	76.1	73.9	68.3	Washington Dulles Intl.	N.A.	N.A.	71.5
Minneapolis/St. Paul Intl.	81.7	79.5	75.8	Washington National	79.8	76.2	75.8
New York/Kennedy Intl.	73.1	71.9	70.2	**U.S. Average[2]**	**78.0%**	**71.9%**	**69.7%**

1. Data for 1995 refers to Stapleton Airport. 2. Average of major U.S. airports only. **Source:** Federal Aviation Administration, Office of Aviation Enforcement and Proceedings, *Air Travel Consumer Report,* Feb. 2008. www.dot.gov/airconsumer

World's Busiest Airports, 2007

	PASSENGERS				CARGO		
City (Airport code)		Passengers	% change, 2006–07	City (Airport code)		Metric tons	% change, 2006–07
1. Atlanta (ATL)		89,379,287	5.3%	**1.** Memphis (MEM)		3,840,491	4.0%
2. Chicago (ORD)		76,177,855	-0.1	**2.** Hong Kong (HKG)		3,773,964	4.5
3. London (LHR)		68,068,304	0.8	**3.** Anchorage (ANC)[1]		2,825,511	0.6
4. Tokyo (HND)		66,823,414	1.1	**4.** Shanghai (PVG)		2,559,310	18.0
5. Los Angeles (LAX)		61,896,075	1.4	**5.** Seoul Incheon (ICN)		2,555,580	9.4
6. Paris (CDG)		59,922,177	5.4	**6.** Paris (CDG)		2,297,896	7.9
7. Dallas/Fort Worth (DFW)		59,786,476	-0.7	**7.** Tokyo (NRT)		2,254,421	-1.2
8. Frankfurt/Main (FRA)		54,161,856	2.6	**8.** Frankfurt/Main (FRA)		2,127,646	8.4
9. Beijing (PEK)		53,583,664	10.1	**9.** Louisville (SDF)		2,078,947	4.8
10. Madrid (MAD)		52,122,702	13.9	**10.** Miami (MIA)		1,922,985	5.1
11. Denver (DEN)		49,863,352	5.4	**11.** Singapore (SIN)		1,918,159	-0.7
12. Amsterdam (AMS)		47,794,994	3.8	**12.** Los Angeles (LAX)		1,884,317	-1.2
13. New York (JFK)		47,716,941	11.9	**13.** Dubai (DBX)		1,668,505	11.0
14. Hong Kong (HKG)		47,042,419	7.3	**14.** Amsterdam (AMS)		1,651,385	5.4
15. Las Vegas (LAS)		46,961,011	3.2	**15.** New York (JFK)		1,607,050	-1.9
16. Houston (IAH)		42,998,040	1.1	**16.** Taipei (TPE)		1,605,681	-5.5
17. Phoenix (PHX)		42,184,515	1.8	**17.** Chicago (ORD)		1,533,606	-1.6
18. Bangkok (BKK)		41,210,081	-3.7	**18.** London (LHR)		1,395,905	3.9
19. Singapore (SIN)		36,701,556	4.8	**19.** Bangkok (BKK)		1,220,001	3.2
20. Orlando (MCO)		36,480,416	5.3	**20.** Beijing (PEK)		1,192,553	15.9
21. Newark (EWR)		36,367,240	2.1	**21.** Indianapolis (IND)		998,675	1.1
22. Detriot (DTW)		35,983,478	0.0	**22.** Newark (EWR)		963,794	-0.6
23. San Francisco (SFO)		35,792,707	6.6	**23.** Luxembourg (LUX)		856,741	13.8
24. Tokyo (NRT)		35,478,146	1.4	**24.** Tokyo (HND)		852,454	1.8
25. London (LGW)		35,218,374	3.1	**25.** Osaka (KIX)		845,976	0.5
26. Minneapolis (MSP)		35,157,322	-1.3	**26.** Brussels (BRU)		747,434	11.3
27. Dubai (DXB)		34,348,110	19.3	**27.** Dallas/Fort Worth (DFW)		724,140	-4.1
28. Munich (MUC)		33,959,422	10.4	**28.** Atlanta (ATL)		724,140	-3.5
29. Miami (MIA)		33,740,416	3.7	**29.** Cologne (CGN)		710,244	2.8
30. Charlotte, NC (CLT)		33,165,688	11.7	**30.** Guangzhou (CAN)		694,923	6.4

Source: Airports Association Council International, *Worldwide Airport Traffic Report—Calendar Year 2007* (2008). www.airports.org

more than any carrier except American. One reason for Southwest's success is its focus on domestic routes, which produce an average of 13 cents per passenger mile, as compared with 11.85 cents for international flights. Southwest also flies only one kind of aircraft, meaning that all of its mechanics know how to fix all of its planes. Upstart airline JetBlue has also been a consistently strong performer, though it has suffered along with the majors since fuel prices starting climbing in 2005.

With more than 89 million people passing through its terminals each year, Hartsfield Atlanta International Airport remained the busiest airport in the world in 2006. Nationwide, a record 744 million air passengers flew in 2006, suggesting that Americans have recovered from their unwillingness to fly. Air cargo, however, never suffered such a drop and continues to climb. Tennessee's Memphis International, home of Federal Express, logged more than 3.8 million metric tons of cargo in 2007, up 4.0 percent from the year before.

World's Top Tourist Destinations 2006

2006 Rank/ Destination	International Arrivals (millions)		Pct. Change 05/06
	2006	2005	
1. France	79.1	76.0	4.2
2. Spain	58.5	55.6	4.5
3. United States	51.1	49.4	3.8
4. China	49.6	46.8	6.0
5. Italy	41.1	36.5	12.4
6. United Kingdom	30.7	28.0	9.3
7. Germany	23.6	21.5	9.6
8. Mexico	21.4	21.9	-2.6
9. Austria	20.3	20.0	1.3
10. Russian Federation	20.2	19.9	1.3

Note: Preliminary. Excludes same-day visitors but includes people who pass through a country for one or more nights en route to another country. Source: World Tourism Organization, Tourism Highlights 2006 (2008).

Tourists in the U.S., by Country of Origin, 1997–2007

2007 Rank/ Country	Arrivals in U.S.		
	1997	2002	2007
1. Canada	15,127,000	12,968,000	17,761,000
2. Mexico	8,433,000	9,807,000	14,333,000
3. U. K.	3,720,979	3,816,736	4,497,858
4. Japan	5,367,578	3,627,264	3,531,489
5. Germany	1,994,296	1,189,856	1,524,151
6. France	978,327	734,260	997,506
7. South Korea	746,550	638,697	806,175
8. Australia	500,615	407,130	669,536
9. Brazil	940,698	405,094	639,431
10. Italy	580,261	406,160	567,045
11. India	173,327	257,271	567,045
12. Spain	382,024	269,250	516,471
13. Netherlands	473,420	384,367	506,852
14. Ireland	217,278	259,687	491,055
15. Venezuela	487,981	395,913	458,678
16. China	209,609	225,565	397,405
17. Colombia	317,736	321,439	389,752
18. Sweden	292,424	204,156	337,474
19. Israel	260,052	263,097	313,077
20. Taiwan	442,780	288,032	311,020
World Total	47,754,476	41,891,707	55,986,277

Source: U.S. Department of Commerce, International Trade Administration, Office of Travel and Tourism Industries.

Select Destinations for U.S. Tourists, 1997–2007

2007 Rank/ Destination	U.S. tourist arrivals		
	1997	2002	2007
1. Mexico	17,909,000	18,501,000	19,453,000
2. Canada	13,401,000	16,167,000	13,371,000
3. U.K.	3,570,000	3,229,000	3,777,000
4. Italy	1,471,000	1,661,000	3,123,000
5. France	2,098,000	2,223,000	2,217,000
6. Germany	1,796,000	1,591,000	1,936,000
7. Japan	1,082,000	1,287,000	1,718,000
8. Bahamas[1]	1,017,000	796,000	1,538,000
9. Jamaica	1,341,000	983,000	1,530,000
10. China	1,147,000	725,000	1,374,000
11. Spain	714,000	866,000	1,093,000
12. India	368,000	398,000	999,000
13. Hong Kong	671,000	749,000	968,000
14. Netherlands	822,000	866,000	937,000
15. Ireland	411,000	562,000	749,000
16. Taiwan	562,000	632,000	687,000
17. Brazil	498,000	491,000	687,000
18. South Korea	649,000	608,000	687,000
19. Switzerland	671,000	562,000	656,000
20. Australia	454,000	562,000	593,000
21. Colombia	325,000	304,000	562,000
22. Greece	433,000	328,000	562,000
23. Israel	303,000	117,000	500,000
24. Thailand	303,000	398,000	468,000
25. Aruba	N.A.	N.A.	422,000
Total[2]	52,735,000	58,065,000	64,052,000

Notes: Data rounded in source. Includes only countries having a sample size of 400 or more. 1. 2007 figures from 2006. 2. Includes destinations not shown separately. Source: U.S. Department of Commerce, International Trade Adminstration, Office of Travel and Tourism Industries.

Most Popular U.S. Destinations for Overseas Travelers, 2000 & 2007

2007 Rank/ Destination	Overseas Visitors	
	2000	2007
1. New York City, NY.	5,714,000	7,646,000
2. Los Angeles, CA	3,533,000	2,652,000
3. Miami, FL	2,934,000	2,341,000
4. San Francisco, CA	2,831,000	2,270,000
5. Orlando, FL	3,013,000	2,055,000
6. Las Vegas, NV	2,260,000	1,720,000
7. Honolulu, HI	2,234,000	1,553,000
8. Washington, DC	1,481,000	1,195,000
9. Chicago, IL	1,351,000	1,147,000
10. Boston, MA	1,325,000	1,075,000
Total overseas visitors[1]	25,975,000	23,892,277

Note: Excludes visitors from Canada and Mexico. 1. Includes other destinations not shown separately. Source: U.S. Department of Commerce, International Trade Administration, Office of Travel and Tourism Industries.

Commuter and Rapid Rail Systems in the U.S., 2001

System	Passenger trips ('000s)	Passenger miles ('000s)	Stations	Route miles	Vehicles operated
Commuter Rail					
New York, Long Island RR	101,923.0	2,126,874.9	124	638.2	954
Chicago RTA-Metra	72,121.8	1,577,183.7	227	940.4	995
New York, Metro North	72,919.6	2,185,376.0	108	545.7	772
Newark, New Jersey Transit	63,970.7	1,357,374.5	167	1,091.4	733
Boston MBTA	36,992.6	784,413.0	121	710.0	376
Philadelphia SEPTA	30,781.9	388,882.7	177	449.2	291
Los Angeles, SCRRA	7,398.0	274,625.4	49	770.0	134
Indiana, NICTD	3,771.6	105,584.9	18	179.8	58
Rapid or Heavy Rail					
New York City TA	1,740,326.1	8,273,784.3	468	493.8	4,985
Washington Metro Area TA	235,731.7	1,362,866.3	83	206.6	628
Chicago RTA-CTA	181,692.2	1,009,234.0	144	206.3	988
Boston, MBTA	137,234.0	502,501.9	53	76.3	320
San Francisco, BART	103,919.4	1,263,667.8	39	190.1	507
Philadelphia, SEPTA	87,344.1	392,693.4	76	76.1	308
Atlanta, MARTA	82,388.6	563,016.8	38	96.0	186
New York, PATH	78,901.3	338,386.7	13	25.0	288
Los Angeles MTA-Metro	31,191.5	126,460.7	16	31.9	70
Miami/Dade Co. TA	13,735.3	107,648.8	21	42.2	86
Baltimore MTA	13,585.2	62,457.4	14	29.4	66
New Jersey/Port Authority TA	10,038.4	88,781.5	13	31.5	96
Cleveland RTA	8,232.2	61,606.8	18	38.2	28
New York, Staten Island MTA	3,968.0	24,985.1	23	28.6	44

Note: Rapid rail includes subways, elevated trains, and metros. BART = Bay Area Rapid Transit Authority; MBTA = Metropolitan Boston Transit Authority; PATH = Port Authority Trans Hudson; SCRRA = Southern California Railroad Authority; SEPTA = Southeastern Pennsylvania Transit Authority. **Source:** Federal Transit Administration, *2001 National Transit Database, Transit Summaries and Trends.*

U.S. Railroads: Mileage and Accident Rates, 2001–07

Railroad	2001			2007[1]		
	Train-miles operated	Accidents		Train-miles operated	Accidents	
		Total	Per million train miles		Total	Per million train miles
Amtrak (National Railroad Passenger Corp.)	38,575,104	149	3.86	39,547,096	84	2.12
Burlington Northern Santa Fe	162,943,990	606	3.72	193,504,107	589	3.04
Canadian National Railway[2]	15,908,962	81	5.09	20,412,545	89	4.36
Canadian Pacific Railway[3]	8,292,477	30	3.62	11,525,436	29	2.52
CSX Transportation	108,619,574	362	3.33	109,015,883	315	2.89
Kansas City Southern Railway Co.	7,659,908	92	12.01	11,393,344	90	7.90
Norfolk Southern Corp.	89,950,834	226	2.51	102,362,845	241	2.35
Union Pacific Railroad Co.	172,712,098	896	5.19	194,228,915	715	3.68

Note: **1.** Preliminary. **2.** Figures for 2001 include only Grand Trunk Western R.R. and Illinois Central R.R.; figures for 2007 include all Canadian National R.R. lines in the U.S. **3.** Figures for 2001 include only Soo Line R.R. subsidiaries; figures for 2007 include all Canadian Pacific R.R. lines in the U.S. **Source:** U.S. Dept. of Transportation, Federal Railroad Administration, *Railroad Safety Statistics 2007* (Aug. 2008).

Amtrak Operating Statistics, 1985–2007

Category	1985	1990	1995	2000	2007
Ridership					
Passengers (millions)	21	22	21	23	26
Passenger miles (millions)	4,582	6,057	5,545	5,498	5,654
Passenger-Train Cars					
Operating fleet (active units)	1,854	1,863	1,722	1,894	N.A.
Average age (years)	14	20	22	19	22[1]
Train-miles operated (millions)	30	33	32	35	37
On-time performance	**81%**	**76%**	**76%**	**78%**	**69%**
Short Distance (<400 miles)	82	82	81	81	66
Long Distance (400+ miles)	78	53	57	56	40
Financial					
Revenues (millions)	$ 825	$1,308	$1,490	$2,111	$2,153
Expenses (millions)	1,600	2,012	2,257	2,876	3,180

Note: **1.** Figure from 2006. **Source:** *Amtrak FY2007 Annual Report, Monthly Performance Report,* (June 2008). www.amtrak.com

▶ THE DAWN OF CIVILIZATION (c. 3000–1500 B.C.)

The transition from pre-historic Neolithic culture to civilization seems to have involved in every case two things combined: the establishment of settled agricultural communities instead of no-madic food-gathering communities and, in those settled communities, the development of urban centers with literate religious and social hierar-chies in control of irrigation projects. The first condition is found (independently, so far as is now known) in at least four centers: Mexico and Central America; the great bend of the Niger River in Africa; the Yellow River valley in China; and in Mesopotamia (the "land between the waters" of the Tigris and Euphrates Rivers). Priority in time belongs to Mesopotamia. And there also the sec-ond condition of civilization, the urban center, first emerged.

Mesopotamia

The 600-mile-long plain of the Tigris and Eu-phrates valleys stretching to the Persian Gulf is the site of earliest civilization. The city-state of Sumer gives its name to this first flowering which blos-somed about 3000 B.C. Each of the cities was a sa-cred temple city, the realm of a god whose regent on earth was the priest-king. To the Sumerians we owe: the calendar, the invention of writing (cuneiform), the plow, the potter's wheel and wheeled carts, boats using sails, and a host of other "firsts."

The separate and frequently warring city-states such as Lagash, Nippur, and Ur fell under the con-trol of the more northerly *Empire of Akkad* whose greatest king was Sargon (c. 2250 B.C.) which in turn fell under the sway of the *Babylonian Empire* whose king Hammurabi (c. 1750 B.C.) conquered all of Mesopotamia and who is credited with the first known Code of Laws. Shortly before 1500 B.C. this empire fell under the domination of the more barbarous *Kassites* whose advantage lay in the use of horse-and-chariot manned by bowmen.

Egypt

The great valley of the Nile, a thin stream travers-ing the eastern Sahara desert, had given birth by about 3000 B.C. to no urban centers but to a net-work of farming villages whose population was of urban density. The legendary founder of Egypt was Menes whose conquest of Lower (i.e., north-ern) Egypt established the *Old Kingdom* (c. 3000–2200 B.C.). Political unification, quite differ-ent from the pattern of Sumer, permitted a rapid assimilation of Sumerian technology while the desert meant relative freedom from invasion. The pharaohs did not rule by permission of the gods, but were divine beings themselves; the building of their colossal tombs, the pyramids, were great re-ligious works directed by the unitary state. The most famous is the Great Pyramid of Cheops at Gizeh (c. 2500 B.C.)

The older diversity of the valley reasserted itself during a century of dissolution and division called the *First Intermediate Period*, after which the tra-ditions of Menes asserted themselves in the *Mid-dle Kingdom* (c. 2100–1800 B.C.). Architecture and sculpture were consciously restorationist, modeled after the Old Kingdom, though temple architec-ture testifies to the importance of various priest-hoods. In literature, it was Egypt's "classical age."

But this age ended with the invasion from Syria-Palestine of the barbarian charioteers known as Hyksos who ruled during the *Second Intermediate Period* (c. 1800–1600 B.C.). But the Eighteenth Dy-nasty, with its capital at Thebes, at last managed to drive out the Hyksos and re-establish royal au-thority throughout the valley, thereby initiating the *New Kingdom* (c. 1600–1100 B.C.).

Other Significant Centers

The *Indus Valley*, stretching from Tibet to the Ara-bian Sea, had become by about 3000 B.C. another locus of settled agriculture with obvious Sumer-ian influence. Innumerable small villages but only two cities have been excavated and the ancient Indian script remains a mystery to scholars. This Indian civilization flourished from about 2500 to about 1500 B.C. until it was conquered by Aryan tribesmen also utilizing chariots and arrows.

About the year 2000 B.C. three centers of civi-lization influenced by Mesopotamia and Egypt began to develop: the *Canaanites* in Syria and Palestine, the *Hittites* in Asia Minor, and the *Mi-noan civilization* on the island of Crete. It is not clear whether Minos was a name or, like "pharaoh" a title, but it was his palace, the Labyrinth, which dominated the trading city of Knossos, center of an elegant "sea empire" whose ships were in contact with Italy, Egypt, Asia Minor and mainland Greece. Yet by about 1500 B.C. Mi-noan trade was in decline and not long after a Greek prince was ruling at Knossos.

In China around 1875 B.C., the millet-based agricultural villages of the North China Plain gave rise to the semi-legendary Xia Dynasty, which ushered in the Bronze Age in East Asia. The Xia were overthrown around 1550 B.C. by Tang the Vic-torious, who established the Shang Dynasty, which endured for five hundred years. The Shang Dynasty is noted for its sophisticated bronze ves-sels, used in worship of the royal ancestors, and for oracle bones inscribed with an early form of Chinese script asking questions of the gods. Shang culture was enriched after around 1350 B.C. by new technologies from western Eurasia, in-cluding the chariot, the cultivation of wheat, and sheep-raising.

▶ THE SPREAD OF CIVILIZATION (c. 1500–500 B.C.)

The impact of the chariot warriors from the steppes of Eurasia, a huge stretch of grassland stretching from the Black Sea almost to the Pacific Ocean, altered the earliest civilizations in differ-ent ways and to different degrees—least in the Near East, most in India. In the millennium from about 1500 to about 500 B.C., the area of civilized life continued to spread as the civilizations took on their classic form in the "heroic age" of the an-cient world.

Egypt

Almost immediately after the hated Hyksos had been expelled from Egypt proper, the pharaohs of the *New Kingdom* (1570–1065 B.C.)—preeminently Thutmose III (c. 1500–1447 B.C.) and his regent queen Hatshepsut (d. 1468 B.C.)—created an empire in Palestine and Syria in which local princes ruled their peoples while Egyptian bureaucrats and garrison commanders oversaw imperial interests, especially the tribute payments. Egyptian control southward along the Nile into the Sudan and Nubia was also reestablished. The empire functioned well until ruled by a pharaoh whose interests lay elsewhere.

The pharaoh Amenhotep IV (ruled c. 1372–1354 B.C.) changed his name to Akhenaton and led a movement after 1370 B.C. to obliterate the name and memory of all the Egyptian gods save for the sun-god Aton (and his incarnation on earth, the pharaoh). This almost-monotheistic revolution absorbed the attention of the monarchy to such an extent that it helped the empire to crumble and the dynasty to be overthrown. A rigid traditionalism accompanied the painful recovery of the empire. Tutankhamen (whose famous tomb was discovered in 1922) was Akhenaton's son-in law; his name shows the return of the god Amon and the eclipse of Aton. But by 1200 B.C. a series of invasions brought the Egyptians to withdraw from the empire to defend the Nile Valley, a withdrawal complete by about 1100.

The *Post-Empire Period* (1065-525 B.C.) saw Egypt's survival in a cultural and religious sense; but the state grew disunified and finally fell victim to conquests by the Assyrians (671 B.C.) and the Persians (525 B.C.).

Mesopotamia and Persia

The Kassite conquest of the First Babylonian Empire led to no great revolution since the conquerors adopted the culture and political structure of the conquered. To the north, the Assyrians were left under native rulers, then took advantage of a series of barbarian incursions against the Kassites to gain their independence in the *First Assyrian Empire* (c. 1150–728 B.C.). The Assyrians were fierce warriors, and they fell upon the south of Mesopotamia, upon Syria and Palestine, and even, briefly, Egypt, and they established the *Second Assyrian Empire* (728–612 B.C.).

The destruction of the great Assyrian capital of Nineveh (612 B.C.) was the work of the mobile strike force of the cavalry of the Medes who proceeded to conquer the Assyrian territory east of the Tigris as well as Armenia and eastern Iran, forming the short-lived *Median Empire* (625–559 B.C.). Assyria's fall permitted the *Second Babylonian Empire* (625–538 B.C.) to arise in Mesopotamia.

Both fell victim to the *Persian Empire* (559–331 B.C.). Cyrus the Great (550–533 B.C.) overturned his Median overlord (559 B.C.), conquered King Croesus of Lydia in Asia Minor (546 B.C.) and overthrew King Nebuchadnezzar III of Babylon (538 B.C.). It was his son who conquered Egypt and his grandson Darius I (521–485 B.C.)who brought the empire to its greatest extent, expanding eastward beyond the Indus by 519 B.C. Dividing his empire into 20 "satrapies" (administrative offices), Darius improved communications by building good roads and was farsighted enough to commence the construction of a Mediterranean war fleet.

Under this Persian dynasty's patronage, the religious doctrines of Zoroaster (c. 628–c. 551 B.C.) spread through its immense empire. Zoroaster taught a dualist doctrine of a cosmic struggle between the god Ahuramazda, the good god of light, truth and peace, and Ahriman, the evil god of darkness, lies, and discord. It was to prove one of the most profoundly influential teachings in the history of the world.

Israel and Judah

Amidst the ebb and flow of empire emerged the people of Israel. Tracing their origin to the ancient city of Ur in Mesopotamia and the covenant between their patriarch Abraham and their god Yahweh, they migrated to Canaan sometime after 1900 B.C. Entering Egypt, probably in the Hyksos period, they dwelt in the Egyptian delta until about 1280 B.C. when, against strong resistance from the pharaoh, Moses led the Hebrews out of Egypt into the desert of Sinai where, according to the Old Testament, they became Yahweh's chosen people in the Sinai covenant. Shortly before 1200 B.C. they occupied Canaan during the decline of Egyptian power there.

The religious league of clans was transformed into the *Kingdom of Israel* (c. 1020–922 B.C.) which flourished under the kings Saul (1028–1013 B.C.), David (1013–973 B.C.), and Solomon (973–933 B.C.) in the interstices of the great powers. But after the death of Solomon, the kingdom divided into Israel in the north and Judah in the south. The northern kingdom fell to the Assyrians under Sargon II (722–705 B.C.) in 721 B.C. Judah held on until the Second Babylonian Empire under Nebuchadnezzar II (c. 605–562 B.C.)destroyed the capital Jerusalem in 587 B.C.

While ethnic Israel fell, the spiritual Israel was preserved through the work of *the prophets*, especially Isaiah (c. 700 B.C.), Jeremiah (c. 600 B.C.) and the second Isaiah (c. 540) who taught an uncompromising monotheism: Yahweh not the god of the Jews alone, but the one God of mankind.

With the establishment of the Persian Empire, the Jews were permitted (538 B.C.) to return to Palestine and to build the second Temple, there to live under the great code of law, the *Torah*.

Greece

The Minoan culture of Crete had been in contact with the Greek mainland before 1650 B.C. The people of Greece (called Achaeans) had arranged themselves in small principalities of which Mycenae, located on the Greek mainland of the Peleponnesian peninsula, had pre-eminence. Adopting the courtly style of the life of Minoans and the war chariots of the Hyksos, the Achaeans expanded their settlements and with Cretan decline became heirs of Minoan trade with Egypt and Syria. This is the culture pictured for us in the epics of Homer's (c. 800 B.C.), *The Odyssey* and *The Iliad*.

About 1100 B.C., a second wave of Greek-speaking Dorians invaded from the north and the Achaeans were forced to migrate to the islands and the coast of Asia Minor. In defeat they performed their greatest work: the preservation of Mycenaean (and therefore also Minoan) traditions both socially and in the Homeric epics. Through these great poems the enterprise against Troy became the living symbol of the unity of the Greeks, the mythology of Mycenae provided a common religious background for local cults, and the language of the Achaeans became the norm for the whole Greek world.

By about 750 B.C. the Greek world had recovered. Colonies spread westward to Italy and Sicily and eastward to the northern Aegean and the Black Seas. The lyric poetry of Archilochus (c. 700 B.C.) and Sappho (c. 600 B.C.) flourished. The first philosophers (Thales, Heraclitus, Parmenides), later called the pre-Socratics, commenced their speculations on nature and the order of the universe; to this philosophy, the Pythagoreans added mathematical genius. And the characteristic unit of the city-state, the *polis* was created.

The greatest of these city-states were Athens and Sparta. *Sparta* emerged in 716 B.C. as conqueror of about 3,200 square miles of territory; by about 610 B.C. Sparta already had the formidable military organization based on strict education for citizenship to inculcate the "savage valor" that Spartans so esteemed. And by 540 B.C. Sparta had formed the Peloponnesian League, uniting all but two of the city-states of the peninsula.

The polis of *Athens* was, like other Greek cities, dominated by its aristocratic families. The grievous problem of increasing slavery for debt led the Athenian leaders to turn over power to Solon, a wealthy merchant and poet, descended from the old kings. Taking office in 594, he cancelled all debts, abolished debt-slavery, encouraged both agriculture and industry, and opened the assembly to all free men. But Athens remained divided among its landed wealth, its trading class and the poor peasants, the latter led by the nobleman Peisistratus who established a dictatorship in the name of the poor (546–528 B.C.). But its democratic constitution was not in place until it was imposed, in 508 B.C., by the aristocrat Cleisthenes.

India

The charioteers who invaded the civilization of the Indus valley called themselves Aryans, a word meaning "noble" in their Sanskrit language. Those they conquered were called Sudras, "slaves." The Aryans settled in villages along the Indus, organized in tribal principalities about which almost nothing is known. Over the half-millennium from about 800 B.C. to about 300 B.C. they moved south along the coast and east across the peninsula to the delta of the Ganges River. There, once the lush jungle vegetation was cleared (using the new tools of the iron age), rice could be cultivated in the rich soil, a food supply sufficient for a very dense and stable population.

Religiously, this is the classic age of Hinduism. The ancient *Vedas*, hymns to the gods, date back to about 1000 B.C.—though not written down until much later. The *Brahmanas* are a body of instructions for rituals, evidence of the rise of an important priestly body, composed over the years 800–600 B.C. Lastly, about 600 B.C. appeared the *Upanishads* with their stress on asceticism and mysticism.

Embodied in this classic religious literature are the germs of the later "caste" system, for they envision four *varnas* or castes: priests (brahmans), warriors (kshatriyas), peasants and artisans (vaisyas), and slaves (sudras).

China

The late Shang period, known for the extravagance of its royal burials, declined into misrule; the dynasty was overthrown around 1055 B.C. by the ruler of the state of Zhou, which controlled the Wei River Valley in northwestern China. The Duke of Zhou, regent for the third Zhou king, established a sort of feudal system in which the territory of China was parcelled out in small states governed by Zhou clansmen and supporters. These states gradually grew larger at the expense of the Zhou royal domain. The Zhou capital was forcibly moved eastwards from Chang'an (now Xi'an) to Luoyang around 770 B.C. but the Zhou kings continued to lose both territory and political authority. Zhou rule broke down altogether during the Warring States Period (c. 480–221 B.C.), when a handful of large feudal states swallowed up their smaller neighbors.

The principal states of northern China were known collectively as *zhongguo*, the "middle kingdoms"; the Chinese, isolated from the high cultures of western Eurasia and India, imagined their culture to be at the center of the world, surrounded by zones of ever-increasing barbarism. In this view, the Chinese ruler governed "all under heaven" by authority of the Mandate of Heaven (*tian ming*). This theory held that a dynastic founder, because of his own virtue, attracted the cosmic force of heaven itself in his support, bequeathing heaven's mandate to his descendants so long as they cherished the principle of virtuous rule. This poltical theory, which assumed that exhausted and corrupt dynasties would eventually be overthrown by righteous rebellions, was a force for renewal and long-term stability throughout Chinese history.

Confucius (c. 551–479 B.C.), China's first philosopher, sought a remedy for the political turmoil of his time in an attempted revival of the golden age of the Duke of Zhou. Thwarted in his search for a ruler who would put his ideas into practice, Confucius became a teacher whose disciples perpetuated his prescription for good government. Confucius looked to a natural aristocracy of virtue, rather than an hereditary elite, for social leadership; this led centuries later to the Chinese innovation of government by means of a professional civil service recruited through competitive examination. The Taoists, rivals of the Confucian school (and supposedly founded by Laozi, of whose life nothing is known) rejected government altogether in favor of individual self-cultivation.

The Warring States Period was an era of cultural brilliance in philosophy, technology, and the arts, a prelude to China's first great imperial age.

▶ THE GROWTH OF WORLD EMPIRES (c. 500 B.C.–A.D. 500)

The millennium after 500 B.C. had as its most characteristic development the conquest of the earliest centers of civilization by certain small nations or tribes—Persians, Macedonians, Romans, Mauryans—on their peripheries. Territories of immense extent (the whole world as they knew it) were organized by these smaller nations, although without any attempt to integrate the conquered peoples into their own cultures. Rarely constructed according to any deliberate plan, these world empires grew up haphazardly.

Significant too was the extraordinary clustering in one generation (at about 500 B.C.) of Pythagoras and Heraclitus, the second Isaiah, Confucius, and the Buddha. And yet more so was the fourth century B.C. eruption of philosophic thought with Plato and Aristotle. Finally, at the middle of the millennium, appeared Jesus Christ.

The Persian Empire and the Greeks

The Persian Wars (499–479 B.C.) began with a failed revolt of the Greek cities of coastal Asia Minor against the Persian Empire (of which they had become a part in 546 B.C.). To punish the mainland Greek allies of the rebels, the city-states of Athens and Eretria, the Persian Empire made war on Greece, but unsuccessfully. From a Persian point of view the Athenian and Spartan victories were only a border issue of minor import; but to the Greeks, the battles of Marathon, Salamis, Plataea and Mycale were inspiring symbols of the superiority of their ideals of liberty and free citizenship over the servitude of Eastern despotism, with the unity of Athens and Sparta embodying what had been prefigured in the united Greek enterprise against Troy. The historian Herodotus first told this story.

Under the leadership of Pericles (d. 429 B.C.) Athens transformed its naval league into an Athenian Empire, thus allowing Sparta to appear the defender of Greek liberties. The former allies, with their leagues, entered their death-struggle, the *Peloponnesian War* (431–404 B.C.) in which the Spartans won a crushing victory. The saga was told by the second great Greek historian, Thucydides (c. 460–400 B.C.) Spartan hegemony in Greece lasted only until 387 B.C. when a league of Greek cities with Persian assistance imposed a settlement which made all Greek poleis autonomous (and therefore weak) except for those in Asia under Persian rule. It was all but the end of the golden age of Greece.

But in just over a century the Greeks had created tragedy (Aeschylus, Sophocles, Euripides), philosophy (Socrates, Plato, Aristotle), history (Herodotus, Thucydides), and the imperishable glory of their monumental architecture (the Parthenon, the Acropolis) and the sculpture of Myron and Phidias.

The Macedonian Empire

Brooding above the disunited Greek city-states lay the small but militarily powerful kingdom of Macedon, militaristic but greatly influenced by Greek civilization. King Philip (356–330 B.C.), having conquered Illyria and Thrace on the northern Aegean, intervened in Greece and forced the formation of a Hellenic League which with Macedon began war against Persia (336 B.C.). No sooner had war began than Philip was assassinated, a death which occasioned the revolt of the Greek cities he dominated. But his son and successor, Alexander the Great (336–323 B.C.) ruthlessly crushed the revolt and plunged into Asia; after his great victory in the battle of Issus (333 B.C.) over Darius III of Persia, Alexander declared himself successor to the last Persian emperor under the title King of Asia, continuing rule through the satrapies after the final defeat of the Persians in 330 B.C. In the meantime he added Egypt to his conquests (331 B.C.) and founded the great city of Alexandria. He pushed on into Bactria (modern Uzbekistan) and then to the Indus Valley beyond which his soldiers would not go. When he died of a fever in Babylon in 323 B.C. he had assembled in but a dozen years the largest empire the world had known; but his premature death meant the division of the empire among the *Diadochi* (Alexander's generals who claimed the succession) who battled for half a century before stabilizing into fragments, each a formidable military monarchy: descendants of Antigonus ruled Macedonia, those of Ptolemy Egypt, those of Seleucus most of Asia. The fringes, the western Mediterranean and India, were left to their own development.

Rome: From Republic to Empire

About the midpoint of the western side of the 650-mile long peninsula of Italy the primitive, devout, peasant community of Rome overturned their Etruscan rulers and established a republic shortly before the year 500 B.C. as the Greek golden age was just beginning. A century of patient expansion against neighboring tribes in central Italy was undone in 390 B.C. when Celts (or Gauls) from the Po Valley plundered and burnt the city. But the Romans commenced anew and within three generations had brought under their sway all of the peninsula except the Greek cities (Magna Graecia) in the south; and these they added by 272 B.C., just at the time the Diodochi were stabilizing their sectors of Alexander's empire.

The move into southern Italy involved Rome in a struggle with Carthage. Originally a Canaanite colony, the city of Carthage in north Africa had established a necklace of commercial colonies along the Mediterranean coast from Sicily across North Africa and Spain to the mouth of the valley of the Rhone, commanding the western seas. In a prodigious struggle called the *Punic Wars* (264–146 B.C.), during which Rome itself was almost brought to ruin by Hannibal (247–183 B.C.), the Romans utterly vanquished Carthage.

After the Second Punic War (218–201 B.C.) Rome became embroiled in the east as Pergamum, Rhodes and Athens appealed for help against the Diodochi. With the war against Macedon (100–196 B.C.) Rome's eastward expansions began. One by one, Greece, Macedonia, Asia Minor, Syria, Palestine, Egypt, and the whole north African coast came under Roman rule by 62 B.C. making the Mediterranean Sea truly what the Romans called *mare nostrum:* our sea.

But Asia did not beckon; rather the Romans embarked on that extraordinary experiment in the west, the conquest of Gaul by Julius Caesar (100–44 B.C.) in which almost 100 small Celtic principalities were brought into the civilization of the Roman Mediterranean. In time Gaul would lead to Britain (A.D. 43–84), while eastern defense considerations would lead to the annexation of Armenia, Mesopotamia and Assyria (A.D. 114–16). At its greatest extent, the Roman Empire stretched from the North Sea to the Sahara Desert, from the highlands of Scotland to the Persian Gulf.

But in winning their empire, the Romans lost their republic, with its freely elected assemblies and magistrates and its famous "council of elders," the Senate. The tremendous population losses in the Second Punic War, the increase in the slave population with every conquest, the transformation from a peasant agriculture to huge *latifundia* (plantations), the rise of a class of financiers (the *equites*), the rivalry of military commanders, the involvement of the military in politics—all conspired to strangle the old republican institutions. In the century from 298 B.C. to 133 B.C., the rivalry for power among demagogues and generals—the Gracchi brothers, Marius, Sulla, the triumvirate of Pompey, Caesar and Crassus, the dictatorship of Caesar, the second triumvirate of Lepidus, Octavian, and Antony—meant endless civil war leading to the final victory of the revolutionary adventurer Octavian who, renamed Augustus, initiated imperial rule in Rome itself and the *Pax Romana*, 200 years of peace in the Roman imperial orbit (27 B.C.–A.D. 180).

Christianity and the Roman Empire

More impressive than the military aspect of the work of Rome was the spread of the Mediterranean civic tradition into continental Europe: colonies of veterans such as Cologne, legionary headquarters such as York, imitated the old Italian, Greek, Phoenician and Syrian cities as well as the numerous foundations of Alexander. The empire became a network of administrative departments centered on cities with central power at Rome; with the external forms of civic life came economic prosperity and the intellectual culture of the Hellenized Roman civilization.

It was in this world that Christ and Christianity were born. In the reign of Augustus Jesus of Nazareth was born (c. 4 B.C.) and in the reign of Tiberius he died, crucified as a criminal (c. A.D. 30). His closest followers affirmed to his resurrection from the dead and his ascent to the one he always called "My Father" and they eagerly preached the "good news" (gospel) that God himself had become man and died for man's sins. This preaching and their communion in their liturgies were the focal points of the early Christians, as the Romans called them. Considering themselves the "second Israel" they nonetheless broke with the synagogue and through missionaries like Paul, Barnabas, and Timothy preached to the Gentiles. While numerically few, they spread through the cities of the Roman world: from Palestine to Syria, Anatolia and Greece, to Africa and Italy; in the second century to Gaul, Germany, Yugoslavia and Spain.

Because they met in secret societies and because they reused to worship the Roman imperial gods, the Christians were persecuted by Roman magistrates; after A.D. 110, adherence to Christianity became a capital offense. Yet the church continued to spread, not only among the poor and outcast but among the nobles and the philosophers (like Justin the Martyr who perished in A.D. 165). These Christians viewed the Pax Romana as providential.

When after the death of the Stoic emperor Marcus Aurelius (A.D. 180) the empire fell into civil war, economic decline, the exhaustion of civic life through excessive taxation and centralized government control, the frontiers became unsafe as well: for after A.D. 226 a revived Persian Empire grew aggressive in the east while great confederations of tribes (Goths, Vandals, Allemani, Franks) arose on the Rhine and Danube Rivers. The emperor Diocletian (284–305) attempted to stem the decline with a political and military reorganization; but it was the emperor Constantine (312–37) who saw that much more was needed.

He attempted to provide a new internal principal of spiritual unity to the Roman Empire through Christianity. His "new Rome" of Constantinople was a Christian city from the start; from persecution to toleration to favored position to state religion–such was the changed estate of the Catholic Church in less than one century. But it had become the religion of a state far gone in decline. Visigothic troops sacked Rome in 410 (for the first time in 800 years) then carved out a realm in southern Gaul and Spain by 450. Vandals tore north Africa away from Rome (429–39). Franks reached the Loire by 486. Saxons, Angles and Jutes ended the Roman province of Britain. Disintegration in the west seemed complete, under the impact of the so-called *Barbarian Invasions*.

Meanwhile in the Roman east, imperial control remained intact but the subject peoples asserted their nationality in religious, not political, forms, adopting one or another of the heresies that flourished after the formal definition of Christian orthodoxy at the Council of Chalcedon (450); that Christ was truly God and truly man.

India and Southeast Asia

The India that the armies of Alexander entered was a complex welter of tribal principalities and republics, of which a certain primacy attached to the kingdom of Magadha in the Ganges valley ruled by the Nanda dynasty. Resistance to the Macedonians was strongest among the Brahman caste: the Kshatriya princes proved more practical and accommodating. After the last Macedonian satrap left India in 317 B.C. Chandragupta Maurya, who has met Alexander, attacked and conquered Magadha with the aid of northwestern tribes, exterminating the house of Nanda and commencing the *Mauryan Empire* (317–184 B.C.). Married to a Macedonian princess, Chandragupta subdued the Indus valley as well and gained recognition from the Diadochus, Seleucus Nicator. By the reign of his grandson Asoka (269–232 B.C.), central and most of southern India had been added to the empire which extended north to the foothills of the Himalayas and west to the eastern reaches of Afghanistan.

Asoka was known as *the Buddhist Emperor*, personally devout and publicly the protector and propagator of the religion of the *Buddha*. Like Asoka, prince Siddhartha Gautama (563–483 B.C.) was not Brahman but Kshatriya; enlightenment came when he realized that desire is the source of all suffering and that salvation therefore means escape from existence into *nirvana* (or nothingness) through rightful living. (Buddha, in Sanskrit, is a title meaning "the enlightened one.") He founded no church but disciples lived in communities following his "eightfold path" to holiness. It was these communities that Asoka fostered and patronized. The more sternly ascetical *Jainism,* founded by Mahavira (probably a contemporary of the Buddha) had spread without political support amongst an elite; its characteristic doctrines were the eternity of everything that is, even matter, and the attainment of nirvana after nine reincarnations.

After the death of Asoka (233 B.C.) the Mauryan Empire began to crumble into its constituent parts, the last emperor being assassinated by one of his generals in 184 B.C. One of the successor states was the Graeco-Indian kingdom in the north and north-west founded by a general of the Diodoch king of Bactria; another was the Kushan Empire of the first and second centuries A.D., which proved to be the route by which Buddhism expanded into central Asia.

A second Chandragupta was the founder of the last great Indian imperial regime, the *Gupta Empire* (320–535 A.D.) which at its greatest extent stretched across the subcontinent from the mouth of the Indus to the mouth of the Ganges. The source of its unity was a revived Hinduism whose brahmans provided advisors to the emperors and drew up the great codes of Hindu law which articulated the structures of the caste system. It was the age also of the revival of the Sanskrit language both in the drama of Kalidasa (c. 400–55) and in the final composition of the epic poems Mahabharata and Ramayana. The Gupta period was the golden age of Indian science, especially astronomy, and mathematics, to which we owe the decimal system and the invention of the number zero. The sway of the classic Indian civilization was spread far beyond the political borders of the Gupta realm by traders and missionaries to Burma, Thailand, and Indo-China, to the Malay peninsula and beyond into Indonesia. The shores of the Bay of Bengal and of the South China Sea thus became a kind of "greater India", as the Diodoch kingdoms had become a "greater Greece."

The Chinese Empire

In 246 B.C. the cavalry troops of the far western state of Qin, hardened by years of warfare with the barbarian nomads of the steppe, hurtled eastward to conquer and subjugate, one by one, all of the other feudal principalities in a quarter century of war that brought the period of the "warring states" to an abrupt halt. On this territorial basis arose the first *Chinese Empire* under the *Qin Dynasty* (221–206 B.C.) Qin Shihuangdi ("The First Emperor of Qin") proved more than just a conqueror: he oversaw the completion of the Great Wall along the edge of Inner Mongolia and provided a structure of government for the empire by dividing the land into regions of administration and war, governed by deputies responsible to himself alone. The old nobility he destroyed by land confiscations; the Confucian schools he closed, executing many prominent scholars, cowing the rest into submission. And while a weakling successor proved unable to stem rebellion and met his death by assassination (206 B.C.) the structure of imperial rule inaugurated by the Qin would endure for over two thousand years.

A rebel leader named Liu Bang emerged victorious in the confused and bloody uprisings that brought the Qin Dynasty to an end. Liu proclaimed himself emperor of the Han Dynasty, which was to endure (with a brief interregnum under the usurper Wang Mang) for four centuries, from 206 B.C. to A.D. 220. The Han founder retained the imperial structure of Qin rule, while moderating its punitive harshness; he opened the way for renewed Confucian participation in government. The greatest Han ruler, Emperor Wu (r. 140–87 B.C.) instituted the practice of choosing officials on the basis of learning and merit. He brought the rich ricelands of the Yangtze River Valley firmly under imperial control, and also greatly extended the boundaries of the empire, conquering south to the South China Sea, southwest to the borders of Burma and Tibet, northeast to northern Korea, and westward to the deserts of Central Asia. He pacified the northern frontier, defeating the Xiongnu tribes whose descendants the Huns would later invade Europe. In an early arms race, the powerful laminated compound bow and cavalry tactics of the northern nomads were countered by Chinese infantry armed with mass-produced crossbows—a refinement of a weapon of Southeast Asian origin. At this time trade increased along the Silk Route, a network of caravan trails that, through many intermediaries, brought Chinese silk to the Roman Empire and warhorses from Central Asia to China.

The "dynastic cycle" completed its course in the last decades of the Han period, when court corruption, peasant uprisings, and military insurrections led to the overthrow of the last Han emperor in A.D. 220. There followed the Three Kingdoms Period (220–265), when rival states tries without success to reunite the empire, and the period of the Northern and Southern Dynasties (265–589), when northern China was frequently ruled by short-lived dynasties of invaders from the steppes, and southern China was fragmented into equally short-lived and ineffectual kingdoms. During this period of disunion Buddhism, which had entered China via Central Asia in late Han times, began to establish itself as one of China's major religions. Especially successful were sects of Mahayana ("Greater Vehicle") Buddhism, which promised salvation to the faithful through the mediation of saints called *bodhisattvas*.

Japan and Korea

Around 300 B.C., invaders from northeastern Asia had invaded Japan via the Korean Peninsula. These invaders, equipped with horses, bronze weapons, and the wealth produced by rice agriculture, displaced the ancient Jomon culture of the original inhabitants of Japan. This bronze-age Yayoi civilization, which also shows evidence of influence from Austronesian culture via Taiwan and Okinawa, laid the foundations for the subsequent Japanese empire. But for several centuries Japan was fragmented into small states ruled by military clans (uji), with those associated with the Shinto shrines at Izumo and Ise claiming some degree of primacy.

In Korea, the decline of the Chinese colony at Lolang led to the establishment of indigenous kingdoms; three of these—Silla, Paekche, and Koguryo—predominated during the period 313-668 A.D. Chinese cultural influence, via Korea, helped to transform the Japanese petty states into a centralized kingdom by the 5th century A.D.

▶ EUROPE'S "DARK AGE" AND THE IMPACT OF ISLAM (A.D. 500–1000)

The seventh-century eruption of Islam with its compact secular-religious civilization and its characteristic institution of the *jihad* (holy war), both rooted in the sacred writings of the Koran, created an empire stretching from the Iberian Peninsula to the Indus Valley but influencing events in far-off Ghana as well. It also provoked in response the formation of eastern and western Christendom.

Untouched by these developments, China underwent another dynastic cycle—one in which Chinese civilization spread to Korea and Japan. And in utter isolation, without iron or even the wheel, civilizations in Central America began.

The Roman Empire and Europe's "Dark Age"

The lapse of direct Roman rule in the west did not imply "the fall of the Roman Empire", for the Germanic barbarians lived in a "greater Rome" whose heir and representative was the Catholic Church while in the east Roman rule continued with enough vigor to experience a great revival under the emperor Justinian (527–65). Maintaining a rough alliance with the Christian Franks in Gaul under their *Merovingian* dynasty, Justinian's armies recovered the western provinces: Vandal Africa, Ostrogothic Italy and the Mediterranean sector of Visigothic Spain. Meanwhile his jurists codified and preserved the whole body of *Roman law* since the days of the republic. And under imperial patronage there grew up a magnificent cluster of churches whose pinnacle was the Hagia Sophia ·in Constantinople, constructed in 537.

But the cost was very great: the treasury was beggared and the eastern frontiers neglected so that the west might be rewon. After Justinian's death the empire had neither treasure nor troops enough to save Italy from new invaders, the Lombards. The city of Ravenna on its marshes kept its link with Constantinople and Rome itself was saved, principally through the work of the pope, Gregory the Great. In the 14 years of his papacy (590–604) he not only organized the defense of the city but oversaw the work of converting Visigothic Spain and began the restoration of Christianity in faraway Britain through the mission of St. Augustine to Kent. In this evangelizing effort Gregory relied upon the monks who followed the *Rule* of St. Benedict (480–547) who brought moderation and a Roman sense of order to the *monasticism* of the west. In a chaotic world, Benedict's *Rule* provided a uniform way of life for monks living as a community, including vows of poverty, chastity, and obedience, regular and frequent hours of prayer, study of the Bible, and manual work.

The empire, which barely held on in the east against Persia, met catastrophe at the hands of the armies of Islam (see next section). In half a dozen years (636–42) Syria, Egypt and Libya fell away; in a second wave of invasions (696–711) the rest of north Africa and Spain were lost as well; Frankish Gaul was only just saved by the cavalry of Charles Martel in the battle of Tours (732). The Mediterranean seemed on its way toward becoming a Moslem lake.

Two successor states to the old Roman empire emerged. In the east lay the empire proper, but now usually called the *Byzantine Empire* (610–1453). Its wealth and power were based in Asia Minor, its unity dependent upon three factors: Orthodox Christianity (slowly drifting away from Roman Catholicism until the final break with Rome in 1054); Hellenistic culture and the Greek language; and Roman law and administration. Missionary ventures carried Christianity and Byzantine influence to the Serbs and Croats in the Balkans, to the Moravians and Slovaks north of the Danube, and even as far as Kievian Rus, all in the ninth and tenth centuries.

In the west there arose the *Carolingian Empire* (751–888). The son of Charles Martel, Pepin III, cooperated with St. Boniface to reform the Frankish Church in close relation with Rome, deposed (with papal approval) the last Merovingian shadow-king, and was himself anointed king in 751. Before his death in 768 Pepin had made Frankish sovereignty felt southward to the Pyrenees and the Mediterranean. His son Charlemagne (768–814) conquered Lombardy, absorbed Bavaria, expanded into Saxony and beyond the Pyrenees, bringing under his sway an area equal in size to the old Roman Empire in the west. At the same time, to foster missionary endeavors, he ordered the creation of cathedral and monastic schools, drawing heavily for his scholars on Northumbria, the small English kingdom where Celtic and Roman monastic traditions had intermingled. The pinnacle of his work came on Christmas Day in the year 800 when in the city of Rome he was acclaimed and crowned as Roman Emperor, by the pope.

But with his death disintegration began. By 843 his grandsons divided his realm in three parts with a middle kingdom of the emperor Lothair separating the kingdoms of the East and West Franks (the nuclei of Germany and France yet to be). These realms faced deadly peril on all sides: Viking corsairs from the north (who also ravaged the British Isles and established commercial bases between the Baltic and Byzantium), Moslem pirates attacking from the south, and, just as these threats had abated, the fierce horsemen of the Hungarians, about the year 900. The family of the Carolingians proved unable to lead any effective resistance; that arose among the nobles of the empire who, inspired by the example of King Alfred the Great of Wessex (849–901) against the Danes in England, defended their people but demanded in return their obedience and support. This was the origin of that pattern of decentralized authority and allegiance known as *feudalism*. Not that monarchy died, but the medieval kings became "firsts amongst equals": Henry the Fowler (919–36) began the *Saxon Dynasty* of German kings while his son Otto I also assumed (962) the title of Emperor; and Hugh Capet in 987 began the *Capetian Dynasty* of France which ruled into the 19th century.

The aftermath of this terrible dark age was the creation of the new Christian monarchies on the fringe of the older Carolingian world: the restoration of the Empire in 962, replacing Charlemagne's empire, which barbarian tribes had destroyed; the consolidation and conversion of the Scandinavian monarchies about 990; the establishment of an independent and Catholic Poland (966) the already mentioned conversion of Kievian Rus (988) under St. Vladimir; and the founding in 1001 of a Catholic Hungarian kingdom under St. Stephen (997–1038).

The Islamic World

To the Roman Empire, the Arabs were a frontier annoyance, no menace as was Sassanid Persia; yet it was out of the Arabian Desert that the whirlwind of Islam arose. Its founder, Mohammed (or Muhammad) (570–632) was a religious prophet whose revelations came from God; these revelations form the heart of the Moslem sacred book, the *Koran*. Utter simplicity of doctrine (a stern monotheism and a focus on the world to come) and of moral code ("hard against the infidels, merciful among themselves") combine with an elaborate ceremonial (the strict fast of Ramadan, prayer five times daily, the Meccan pilgrimage). Driven out of Mecca to Yathrib (now Medina), Mohammed and his followers formed a religious and political community which, after eight years of desert warfare, returned to capture Mecca (630).

Within two years of Mohammed's death the armies of Islam were marching. From the Romans they wrested Syria, Mesopotamia, Egypt and Libya (636–46); the Persians they conquered outright (637–49). Not until 661 was the vexed question of the succession settled when the old tribal aristocracy triumphed over the family of the prophet and established *Umayyad Dynasty* (661–750) of caliphs ("successors") ruling not from Medina but from Damascus and utilizing the old Persian and Roman bureaucracies. For almost half a century Islam lay quiescent; then, with the conversion of the Berbers, Byzantine Africa was swept away (696) as was Visigothic Spain (711). In the same year a Moslem commander established himself in the lower Indus Valley.

A series of revolts protesting the purely Arabic dominance of the Umayyads led to the establishment of a new dynasty of caliphs, the *Abbasid Dynasty* (750–1258), descended from a cousin of Mohammed. Arab by descent, the Abbasids nonetheless moved the capital to the new city of Baghdad in Mesopotamia where Persian influence came to predominate in politics as in literature while the Islamic scientific and mathematical flowering owed as much to Gupta India and ancient Greece as to archaic Babylonian astral speculations, especially the decimal system of numeration and the use of the zero.

The Umayyads had not been totally overturned; Spain followed their rule when the rest of the empire turned to the house of Abbas; after about 800 there were independent Moslem states in Morocco, Tunis, and eastern Persia; and by about 875 in Egypt and Turkestan. Before the year 1000 the caliphs had lost almost all their political power, becoming largely a focus of religious unity, relying even then on the *ulema*, adepts of Islamic law and lore. To this day, ultimate authority in many Islamic states has remained with the religious leaders.

India and Africa on the Fringe of Islam

After the fall of the Gupta Dynasty in 535, India reverted to its older pattern of a large number of tribal principalities. The White Huns, whose incursion had overturned Gupta power, coexisted with the Hindu princes who knew them as *Rajputs* and established a feudal state across north India east of the Indus valley, the kingdom of Rajputana. The Sind (or lower Indus) was already in Moslem hands after 711. By the ninth century Buddhism had all but disappeared from India, absorbed into Hinduism; one exception was in the state of the Pala kings who ruled Bengal and Magadha into the 12th century. Buddhism remained influential in "greater India": in the small kingdoms of Burma, in the kingdom of Dvaravati in Siam, in Sri Lanka, and in the Sumatran state of Srivishaya under its Sailendra dynasty.

At the other extremity of the caliphate, Moslem traders from Morocco were in contact with the *Kingdom of Ancient Ghana* by about the year 800. Camel caravans crossed the Sahara to the grasslands between the upper Niger and Senegal rivers bearing salt and goods from the Mediterranean basin. There the king of Ghana supplied gold and ivory brought north from the southern reaches of the "shoulder" of Africa. Extracting import and export taxes and monopolizing the gold supply, the kings of Ghana exercised a kind of imperial control over the trading cities of the region, growing wealthy and powerful. Yet by 1076 the caliphs in Morocco were able to conquer the region.

At the opposite side of Africa, Moslem Arabs crossed the Red Sea and annexed the Somali coast (c. 1050) from the ancient Christian kingdom of Ethiopia.

China: Tang and Song Dynasties

Three centuries of disunion in China came to an end with the establishment of the *Sui Dynasty* in 589. Like the Qin, the Sui was a short-lived dynasty that paved the way for a long-enduring one. Extravagant expenditures on construction of the Grand Canal linking Hangzhou and Chang'an (a distance of over 1000 miles), a disastrous attempt to conquer Korea, and a Turkish invasion of northwestern China doomed the Sui. It was replaced in 618 by the *Tang Dynasty*, one of the most glorious eras in all of Chinese history. Buddhism flourished, as did poetry and the fine arts; Tang Chang'an was the largest and most cosmopolitan city in the world by around 700. But in 751 Chinese troops on the westernmost frontier were defeated by an Arab army in the Battle of Talas, and the Tang abandoned much of Central Asia; in 755, China's greatest general, An Lushan, rebelled against the throne. The rebellion was defeated, but the empire never recovered fully. An imperial persecution of Buddhism in the 840s, during which the wealth of many temples was confiscated, signaled the rise of Neo-Confucianism, reinvigorating China's oldest philosophical tradition. But with the imperial house in disarray, the Tang collapsed in 907.

After five decades of inconclusive attempts to restore central rule, the *Song Dynasty* was founded in 960, and endured until 1279. But the Song never had firm control of northern China. The northeast was controlled by the *Liao Dynasty* in the hands of the non-Chinese Khitan people (whose name gives us the world Cathay). They were replaced in the early 12th century by the *Jurchen Jin Dynasty*, which in 1127 conquered all of northern China, sending the Song emperors south to a new capital at Hangzhou. Although the Song were politically weak this was nevertheless a time of cultural brilliance, when Chinese landscape painting was perfected, poetry flourished, and urban life (rich with the wealth of overseas trade) attained new heights of sophistication. With the old northern aristocratic clans destroyed by the downfall of Tang and subsequent centuries of barbarian rule, the Song state was run by a surprisingly modern bureaucratic government recruited from a prosperous and well educated rural gentry.

Japan and Korea

In Korea, the state of Silla in 562 put an end to Japanese attempts to carve out colonial enclaves on the peninsula, and then, with Tang support, turned its attention to defeating its rivals Paekche and Koguryo. This process was completed by 670, and Silla grew prosperous with Tang support and cultural influence. But Silla in turn was defeated in 935 by the small western state of Koryo, which established a dynasty ruling all of Korea until 1392. Relatively isolated from Song influence by the intervening states of Liao, and later Jin, the Koryo state became culturally more independent of China.

In Japan, *the Yamato clan*, which had gradually pressed its claim to recognition as an imperial dynasty on the Chinese model, was firmly established on the throne by the fifth century A.D. Buddhism came to Japan in the following century, along with such continental innovations as the use of Chinese script to write (phonetically) the very different Japanese language. In 589 Prince Shotoku issued a 17-article "constitution" establishing imperial support for Buddhism and enjoining all aristocrats to respect the imperial throne. The throne thereupon came under the influence of the powerful *Soga clan* until 645; a restoration movement emphasized emulation of the Chinese model of government. But the principle of appointment to office on the basis of merit never caught on in Japan, which continued to be ruled by an hereditary aristocracy.

Japan's first permanent capital city was founded at Nara in 710; by 750 the city was wholly dominated by its rich and powerful Buddhist temples. In response the emperors moved the capital to the new city of Heian-kyo (now Kyoto) in 794; the emperors remained there for over a thousand years. Both Nara and Heian-kyo were built on a grid plan, modeled after Tang Chang'an; Heian-kyo especially boasted a glittering cultural life, supported by agrarian wealth from the provinces. The powerful *Fujiwara clan* gained control of the country's political life through the expedient of making sure that every emperor married a Fujiwara daughter, and abdicated the throne for a life of monastic retirement shortly after producing an heir; the head of the Fujiwara clan thus was always the father-in-law of one emperor and the legal guardian of the heir-apparent.

The Classic Age of Mayan Culture
Splendid archaeological remains wrapped in chronological obscurity give tantalizing hints of culture in central America before the year 1000. Sometime around 2500 B.C. (but perhaps a millennium earlier) the hybrid maize (or Indian corn) was developed on present-day Mexico's Gulf coast. Permanent agricultural settlements, stretching from Mexico's central plateau to the Guatemalan highlands, seem to date from about 1500 B.C. But it was not until the period A.D. 300–900 that Central America attained approximately the cultural level of ancient Mesopotamia. From Guatemala to the Yucatàn the Mayans developed temples, ritual calendars and a system of writing as yet not deciphered. Similarly, in the Mexican Plateau, there grew up a culture associated with the great city of Teotihuacan. Both seem to have been "empires" of city-states, but except for Teotihuacan itself the sites were not really cities, rather religious centers surrounded by agricultural hamlets. The Mexican development seems to have been cut short by invasions about A.D. 900, probably by the Toltecs. The abandonment about the same time of the Mayan temple sites may have been the result of drought, deforestation, and other environmental factors.

▶ THE MUSLIMS, THE TURKS, AND THE RISE OF THE CHRISTIAN WEST (A.D. 1000–1500)
The four major centers of civilization that had been established by the year 1000—European Christendom, the Islamic world, India and China—all underwent tremendous challenges from confederations of warlike Turkish and Mongol tribes in the next 500 years. Of all the developments the most significant for world history proved to be the maturation of western Christendom which had already commenced, before the period closed, its expansion to the Americas, to Africa and to southern Asia as well.

Expansion of the Muslim World: Asia and Africa
The *Abbasid* dynasty of caliphs of Baghdad had long employed Turkish auxiliaries (rather as the Romans had used German tribes) in their Near Eastern armies; one such army, under their chieftain Mohammed of Ghazni, moved out of Afghanistan into the Punjab about the year 1000

and by 1030 established a Muslim dynasty there. Over the next 200 years they spread their conquests over the Rajputs eastward into the plain of the Ganges, establishing their capital at Delhi about the year 1200. The rich Hindu temples were plundered and, as "heathen," destroyed by these Muslim Turks. Under the sultan (="ruler") Âla-ud-din (1296–1316) most of the subcontinent was brought under one rule for the first time since Asoka.

Unable to break the caste tradition, the ruling Turks became yet another caste, a minority of warrior-aristocrats extracting heavy taxes but relying upon the Hindu princes for administration. Though the Hindu temples had been destroyed, the Turks had to permit a practical tolerance for a now less sacerdotal Hinduism. After the death of Âla-ud-din his empire dissolved into a medley of warring kingdoms ruled by Muslim generals or Hindu princes over whom the sultans at Delhi exercised greater or lesser control.

In the "greater India" of Southeast Asia, Islamic influence expanded through trade and Chinese influence through trade and warfare. In Burma, the Buddhist kingdom founded by Anawrata in 1044 was destroyed by the Mongol armies of Kublai Khan in 1287 and the land was divided into a number of small principalities. Dvaravati Siam (briefly annexed to Cambodia in the 11th century) was overrun by Thai tribesmen from China in the 13th century; by 1350 a Thai kingdom of Siam had established its capital at Ayutthaya, which was to remain its capital until the end of the 18th century. Over the next century, Siam subdued the independent kingdom of Cambodia to the east and expanded against Burma as well. In the archipelago of Indonesia and curving north into the Philippines, Muslim traders and missionaries had established 20 Islamic states by the year 1500. The Hindu aristocracy of Java took refuge on the island of Bali, which still preserves elements of pre-Islamic Indonesian culture.

Muslim expansion occurred in western Africa as well. The conquest of ancient Ghana by Muslim Berbers in 1076 (who had conquered Morocco as well 20 years earlier) led to no new empire but a series of successor states. One of these, Kangaba, had by the 13th century established another trading state of immense size, the *Kingdom of Mali* which stretched, in the 14th century, from the Atlantic coast eastward beyond Gao on the Niger. Under king Mansa Musa (c. 1312–37) Islam spread through the western savanna, the king himself making a pilgrimage to Mecca in 1324. Further east, the king of the Songhay people on the great bend of the Niger had already converted to Islam in the 11th century; thus, when the dominance of Mali was replaced in the 15th century by the *Kingdom of Songhay*, Islam dominated not only the northern coast of Africa but almost the entire belt of savanna south of the Sahara as well.

It was also in this period, but obscurely and beyond the range of Islam, that African tribes (speaking various languages of the Bantu family) continued their long migrations. In the previous period (c. 600-900) they had moved out of the Cameroon highlands east to the Great Lakes; from there they migrated in two streams: southwest to the Congo basin, and south to the savanna of modern Zambia. Now in the period from about 1000 to about 1500, they occupied Kenya and Tanzania on the east and the lands south to the edge of the Kalahari desert.

Transformation of the Muslim World: The Turks

No sooner had Mohammed of Ghazni established Turkish rule in the Punjab than two brothers of the Seljuk clan revolted and took Afghanistan (1037), then expanded into Persia and Mesopotamia (by 1055). After the battle of Manzikert (1071) they took most of Asia Minor from Byzantium. When Syria was added (1084) the *Seljuk Empire* (1037–1243) stretched from Egypt to India. During the 12th century, in the aftermath of the First Crusade (1096–99), their empire became a jumble of small emirates ruled by Seljuk princes or their generals. What brought the Seljuks low was the sudden appearance in the 1240s of the Mongols in the Near East; though menacing to both Muslims and Christians, Mongols power proved ephemeral and the true heirs of the Seljuks proved to be another clan of Turks, the Ottomans. In 1326 they drove Byzantine forces entirely out of Asia Minor, thus beginning the *Ottoman Empire* (1326–1920). By century's end they controlled all of Asia Minor and the Balkans as far north as Bosnia. Half a century later (1453) they took Constantinople, turning Hagia Sophia into a mosque in their re-named capital of Istanbul.

Eastern Christendom Submerged: Mongols and Turks

The 11th century was the apogee of the *Eastern Roman Empire* (Byzantium) as it conquered the Christian kingdom of Bulgaria (1018) and made Serbia a client state in the west, while to the east Armenia and the Crimea were annexed (1022). But by mid-century the Normans, descendants of Vikings who settled in the French province of Normandy, were establishing themselves in Byzantine Italy (and Muslim Sicily), and the battle of Manzikert (1071) proved a catastrophe from which the Empire never recovered, losing both its granary and its military recruiting ground to the Turks in a single blow. Although the first three crusades (1096–1192) were initially successful in wresting the Holy Land from Islam, the subsequent organization of the territory in the French pattern of small squabbling and isolated feudal statelets rendered them impotent and hence of only marginal help to Byzantium. The Fourth Crusade (1202–04) was a disaster, for the crusaders took Constantinople, establishing what is called the *Latin Empire* (1204–61). In 1261, Michael Palaeologus (1261–82) restored a rump Byzantium along the shores of the Aegean and it was against this state that the Ottoman Turks expanded. The doom of Constantinople brought Turkish power right to the borders of Hungary, with the Balkans absorbed into the Ottoman Empire for 450 years.

In the northeast it was not the Turks but the Mongols whose arrival transformed Christendom. Hungary, Poland and Kievian Rus were weakened by dynastic struggles from the 11th century on, yet maintained their independence of the Holy Roman Empire to the west and the Turkish Cumans in the east. But the uniting of the Mongol federation under Genghis Khan (1206-27) created a power great enough to strike at China, the Near East, and Europe at the same time; by his death his realm extended from Korea to the borders of Persia and Rus. A decade later Mongol armies under Genghis Khan's grandson Batu (d. 1255) fell upon Europe (1237–40) attacking beyond Russia into Poland and Hungary and the lands of the German knights on the Baltic; but with the death of the Khan, the Mongols retreated. Still the "Golden Horde," an independent Mongol Khanate organized by Batu on the lower Volga River, ruled all of south Russia and reduced the north Russian principalities to vassal status.

Not until the late 15th century was the prince of Moscow sufficiently established to refuse tribute money to the Empire. His marriage to the niece of the last Byzantine emperor established the claim of Ivan III to imperial succession as he took the title "czar" (= Caesar or emperor) and his conquest of the principality of Novgorod (1478) established a large Russian state northeast of Poland. Poland had attained its status as the largest state in Christendom with the marriage (1386) of its queen Jadwiga (1384–99) to the Grand Duke Jagiello of Lithuania; in the 15th century the Jagellon Dynasty (1386–1572) controlled the entire region between the Baltic and Black Seas. But thereby it was exposed to a four-fold danger: from Ottomans to the south, Germans to the west, Swedes to the north and Russians to the northeast.

The Rise of Western Christendom

For 600 years out of the ruins of the western Roman Empire and the anarchy of barbarian invasions, Western Christendom slowly emerged, the process essentially completed with the conversion to Christianity of the Scandinavians, the Poles and the Magyars (950–1050). It was not a society associated with a great empire (for the Carolingian Empire had fallen in the ninth century) but with the feudal states of France and the tribal duchies of Germany. Its unity, such as it was, was religious and cultural as well as political.

Whether the leadership of this society should fall to the popes or the Holy Roman Emperors was settled in the 11th century in the *Investiture Struggle* in which the papacy emerged victorious. From Pope Gregory VII (1073–85) to Boniface VIII (1294–1303) the papacy gave the lead to western Christendom often in alliance with reforming monastic leaders. In the 12th and 13th centuries the characteristic architecture and sculpture of medieval Europe (*Romanesque* and *Gothic*) spread across Europe under Church patronage while the Leagues of the Peace and the Crusades attempted to limit and channel to constructive use the warrior ethos of the feudal nobles.

Beginning in 11th century Italy and 12th century Netherlands, the commune movement, in which all the inhabitants of a town bound themselves by oath to obey their magistrates, keep the peace, and defend their liberties, revived town life and created the medieval city as a confederation of self-governing guilds. *Guilds* were associations of craftsmen of one trade or merchants bound together for mutual aid. In the west the fairs of Champagne and Burgundy provided ground for the re-establishment of trade while in the Mediterranean, the Italian cities (especially Venice and Genoa) linked the west with Byzantium and the Muslim Near East.

In these towns arose the great universities (Paris, Bologna, Salerno, Oxford) where Greek and Arab learning met with the Christian traditions of the Carolingian schools; the insights of Aristotle re-thought in Christian terms issued into the legal, philosophic, theological and scientific work of *scholasticism*, the work of men like Albertus Magnus, Thomas Aquinas, Bonaventure, Roger Bacon, and Duns Scotus—all members also of the new religious orders, Franciscans (St. Francis, 1182–1226) and Dominicans (St. Dominic, 1170–1221), which arose in the towns of the 13th century. Committed to evangelical poverty and combating heresy, they played a role in university life as well.

Late in the 12th century in Spain and Italy, in the 13th in Germany, England and France, in the 14th and 15th in Hungary, Poland and Scandinavia, the custom arose for monarchs to call the elected representatives of the towns to meet with prelates and nobles to render advice; such was the origin of *parliaments*.

The development of these social and cultural and religious institutions was accompanied by the expansion of western Christendom. One aspect was internal with the clearing of forests and the cultivation of new farmland able to support an increased population. The other was external, not so much the ephemeral Kingdom of Jerusalem (1099-1162) or Latin Empire of Constantinople (1204–61) as the reconquest of Spain from the Muslims (1085–1492), the conquest of Prussia and Livonia by the Teutonic Knights (1229–1466) and the conversion of Lithuania (1386 and after.)

The most significant check to population growth was the *Black Death*, an outbreak of bubonic plague that swept over Europe (1347–51), wiping out perhaps 25 million, a third of the population. The loose unity of western Christendom began to alter in the 14th century in significant ways. First of all, the universality of the papacy seemed compromised when seven popes in succession (1305–78) preferred to reside at Avignon rather than Rome, in too close an association with the kings of France; then, after the return to Rome arose that series of disputed elections to the papacy which is called the *Great Schism* (1378–1417); and third, with the end of the schism, the popes became more and more involved in the politics of Renaissance Italy.

Meanwhile, while theories of sovereignty derived from the study of Roman law exalted the authorities of kings, royal powers disastrously declined due to chronic feudal violence: the "age of princes" in Germany (1273-1493), the Hundred Years' War in England and France (1337–1453), and the dynastic Wars of the Roses in England (1455–85). Out of the turmoil arose the "new monarchies" of more unified states: the Tudors in England (1485), the Valois and in France (1328–1529), and in Spain the Spanish branch of the Habsburgs (1504–1700).

In the Italy of the 14th and 15th centuries, increasingly the plaything of the new monarchies, there began that great cultural transformation known as the *Renaissance*. Humanists like Petrarch (1304–74), and Boccaccio (1313–75) sought a revival of Latin antiquity, both pagan (Cicero, Virgil, Tacitus) and Christian (Augustine and the other Church fathers), in an educational movement that sought to unite the values of Hellenism with Christianity. At the same time artists, studying Roman architecture and Hellenistic sculpture on the one hand and the new sciences of anatomy and perspective on the other, created a new world of beauty. In painting, Botticelli and da Vinci, in architecture Brunelleschi (1377–1446), in sculpture Ghiberti (1378–1455) and Donatello (1386–1466)—these represent the output of the city of Florence alone.

Building on medieval foundations and new navigational discoveries (magnetic compasses, the astolabe, the quadrant), the Portuguese monarchy pioneered the exploration of the African coast; the Gulf of Guinea was reached by 1470, the Cape of Good Hope by 1487, and India itself by 1498. The Spanish monarchs sponsored the western route of Columbus whose four voyages (1492–1504) brought Europeans to the shores of the Caribbean (which he mistook for Japan and the Malay Peninsula). Finally, before the period closed, the new Tudor monarchy of England financed the more northerly westward explorations of the Cabots who reached Newfoundland and New England in 1497 and 1498. Like the humanists, by seeking a very old world, the explorers found something very new as well.

The Americas

The New World which Columbus discovered was dominated by two great empires. In Mexico, the Toltecs established an empire with its capital in the magnificent temple city of Tula; it included most of the old Mayan realm (c. 900–1200). But the 12th and 13th centuries saw a series of incursions of barbarian nomadic hunters from the south known collectively as Chichimecs whose armed might destroyed the Toltec civilization. In time, one of these tribes, the Aztecs, established a capital at Tenochtitlan and over the century from about 1360 to about 1470 conquered neighboring peoples and constructed the sanguinary *Aztec Empire* (c. 1360–1520). The king Montezuma I (died c. 1470) was a ruthless conqueror but a great builder as well, transforming the capital into a magnificent city of stone. By 1500 the Aztecs had reached Guatemala. For the subject peoples war and subjections were evil enough; worse was the Aztec worship of the sun god who required for his nourishment human blood.

Stretching thousands of miles along the west coast of South America lay the empire of the Incas with their capital at Cuzco. Unlike the military Aztec empire of subject states paying tribute including the blood tax, the *Inca Empire* was a centralized bureaucratic state which engaged in social engineering as well as road and bridge building and irrigation projects. Begun about 1200, the empire attained its greatest size under Huayna Capac (c. 1493–1527).

China and East Asia (1200–1500)

Genghis Khan (b. 1162–1227), leader of the Mongol federation, wished to unite all of the nomadic peoples of the Asian steppes under his rule. The Mongol conquest of northern China, ruled by Jurchen tribesmen from Manchuria, was completed by Genghis Khan's successors in 1234. The Mongols then turned their attention to Korea, which they conquered in 1231–36, and to the Chinese Song Dynasty in the Yangtze River Valley. The Song defended their territory vigorously, while the Mongols were slowed down as their horsemen learned to cope with wet ricefields and rivers defended by heavily armed ships; but in 1271 Kubilai Khan (b. 1215–94) proclaimed himself emperor of the *Yuan Dynasty* of China, and in 1279 the last Song emperor capitulated. During his reign Kubilai Khan tried twice to invade Japan; his fleets were stopped by *kamikaze*, "divine winds," i.e. typhoons. An attempt to conquer Java also met with only limited and temporary success.

In China the Mongols were seen as an alien occupying power; their habit of using foreign, Persian speaking tax-collectors made them especially hated. The successors to Kubilai Khan were mediocre rulers; in 1368 a Chinese nativist rebellion led by a charismatic ex-Buddhist monk named Zhu Yuanzhang succeeded in overthrowing the Mongols and establishing the *Ming Dynasty* (1368–1644). The early Ming emperors were vigorous and forward-looking; they rebuilt the Great Wall, re-routed the Grand Canal to terminate near Beijing, built a new southern capital at Nanjing, and sent maritime expeditions on missions of exploration and diplomacy throughout the South China Sea and the Indian Ocean to the east coast of Africa. These expeditions, under Admiral Zheng He, were however abruptly terminated in 1433, criticized by the conservative Confucian bureaucracy as a waste of money and resources. Thus the Chinese missed by only three decades the chance to confront the Portuguese as rival maritime powers in the Indian Ocean.

In Korea, the *Koryo Dynasty* did not long outlast the rule of their Mongol patrons. The last Koryo king in 1388 sent his best general, Yi Songgye (famous for his victories over Japanese pirates), to invade China to try to overthrow the Ming Dynasty on behalf of the Mongols. General Yi instead turned back at the border, overthrew the Koryo king, and established his own dynasty, the *Kingdom of Choson*, which soon proclaimed its support for the Ming emperors. The third Choson (or Yi Dynasty) ruler, King Sejong (r. 1418–1450) was Korea's greatest sovereign, a patron of art, science and technology during whose reign Korean scholars and craftsmen perfected printing with moveable metal type, invented a syllabic script to write vernacular Korean, and equipped Seoul with what was, for a time, the best astronomical observatory in the world. The Choson monarchs tolerated Buddhism, promoted Confucianism, ruled through a very conservative aristocracy, and remained on the throne until 1910.

In Japan, the Fujiwara-dominated aristocrats of Heian-kyo ignored the rise of a provincial warrior aristocracy in the provinces until it was too late. The Fujiwaras were ousted by the western Taira clan in 1160; they in turn were defeated by Minamoto no Yoritomo at the naval battle of Dan-no-Ura in 1185. Yoritomo then took the hereditary title of *shogun* ("generalissimo"), and established a military capital at Kamakura, leaving the emperors to reign but not rule in Heian-kyo. The Minamoto were shunted aside by their own hereditary retainers, the *Hojo Clan*, in 1229. A crisis was precipitated in 1331 by Emperor Daigo II, who refused to abdicate on command of the shogun, and attempted to institute direct imperial rule. In 1333 another general, Ashikaga Takauji, helped Daigo II overthrow the Hojo, but Ashikaga then promptly proclaimed himself shogun, moved the military capital to the Muromachi district of Kyoto, and put the emperors firmly in their place once again. The *Muromachi* shogunate endured until 1568, though with little military power; the shoguns were better known as patrons of Zen Buddhism, Noh theater, and the tea ceremony. With the waning of central authority, Japanese merchants were more free to establish domestic and overseas trade routes (and to engage in piracy on the China coast), leading to economic prosperity amidst political instability.

▶ THE EXPANSION OF THE WEST AND THE ENDURANCE OF THE EAST (1500–1650)

During this period, the great empires of Asia—Ottoman Turkey, Safavid Persia, Mogul India and Ming China—remained intact and even expanded, but the dynamic power and movement of this extraordinary age were driven by the emerging nation-states of Europe. Despite severe internal divisions both religious (the Reformation) and national, which led to incessant warfare among all of them, the major powers managed to dominate the sea lanes of the globe and control the coasts and islands of Africa, southern Asia, and the Americas.

The Near East: Ottoman Empire and Safavid Persia

Under their sultans Selim I the Grim (1512–20) and Suleiman I the Magnificent (1520–66) the Ottoman Turks added Syria and Egypt to their domains, then from their fortress at Belgrade launched an invasion of Hungary which climaxed at the battle of Mohacs (1526), where over 20,000 Christian soldiers were slain and three-quarters of the realm fell under Turkish rule either directly or through Ottoman client princes of Transylvania. The Turks moved on to besiege Vienna (1529), halting the campaign because of troubles with Persia. On the seas Turkish fleets added Yemen and Aden on the Persian Gulf and Tripoli, Algeria, and Tunis on the southern shores of the Mediterranean.

But Suleiman's successor was Selim II (the Sot), the first in a series of weak sultans who came to the throne between 1566–1718 as a result of that perennial weakness of Muslim dynasties, harem intrigues of wives and eunuchs, and of the specifically Ottoman problem, the "praetorian guard" of Janissaries. In 1571, the Holy League (the Papacy, Venice, Tuscany and Spain) triumphed over the Turkish navy in the battle of Lepanto, though dissolution of the League after the victory meant that the Ottoman fleet could still raid almost at will through the Mediterranean.

Persia saw the revival of a native Iranian dynasty under the *Safavid Dynasty* (1501–1736). Its founder Shah Ismail seized power from the White Sheep Turks in 1501 and successfully defended Persia from Ottoman expansion into Mesopotamia, a work continued under his son and successor (1514–55). After the reign of the dynasty's greatest representative, Abbas I the Great (1587–1629), there began a period of harem intrigues which greatly weakened the dynasty. The Turks succeeded in taking Baghdad (1638).

Christian trading presence in Persia began with the Portuguese establishment at Hormuz in 1507; by 1622 the Portuguese were turned out by Abbas, English merchants supplanting them.

Mogul India and the Portuguese Spice Trade

In 1526, a descendent of Genghis Khan attacked the sultan at Delhi and established his dominance east of the Indus. Though a Turk, because of the long association of his family with the Mongols, his empire came to be called the *Mogul Empire* (1526–1857). Babur (b. 1483–1530), the founder then expanded east to the borders of Bengal. Although his son lost almost all Babur had conquered, his grandson Akbar (1556–1605), contemporary of Philip II of Spain and Elizabeth of England, restored Babur's realm and expanded it further until it included all of India north of the Deccan Plateau. Vigorous in warfare, gracious in victory, wise in administration, tolerant in religion, Akbar's empire knew peace and prosperity. Most of the Deccan was added in the reign of his grandson Shah Jahan (1628–58), who also built the Taj Mahal.

It seems almost miraculous that Portugal, a tiny state on the edge of the Atlantic, should create a seaborne empire dominating the Indian Ocean, but that is what Portugal did in the 16th century. In 1497, Vasco da Gama (c. 1469–1524) began a journey that took him around Africa's Cape of Good Hope and across the Indian Ocean to Calicut where he encountered the great riches of India's spice trade. After da Gama's second voyage (1502), the Muslim state of Gujerat, allied with Mameluke Egypt, declared a *jihad* against the Portuguese, but at Diu, the Portuguese won a complete victory (1508). The Portuguese viceroy organized the building of a "rosary" of over a dozen forts stretching form Hormuz on the Persian Gulf through Goa to Malacca on the Malay Peninsula. Thus the Portuguese could monopolize the carrying trade in the Indian Ocean as well as divert the spice trade around Africa. And from Malacca they established trading posts in the Spice Islands (Moluccas), China and Japan. This network provided the route for Christian missionaries as well.

But it proved all too much for Portugal. The English and the Dutch had established their East India Companies in 1600 and 1602 and in the 17th century the Dutch, piecemeal, took the place of the Portuguese by war and diplomacy. One portent for the future: by 1639 the English were at Madras.

East Asia: China, Korea, Japan

The late Ming emperors were great patrons of culture, but mediocre rulers. The former Chinese protectorate of Annam, while maintaining its mandarin culture, became independent, the first true monarchy of Vietnam. In 1557 the Portuguese established a trading colony at Macao (due to revert to Chinese rule in 1999). The danger to China from Mongolia, from where Altan Khan (1543–83) raided almost annually across the Great Wall, was kept in check by adroit Ming diplomacy, and further allayed by the Mongol acceptance of Tibetan religious authority; with the spread of Lamaism, monasteries absorbed surplus sons who might otherwise have become warriors. But danger lurked in the lands north of Korea, where descendants of the 12th-century Jurched rulers of the *Jin Dynasty* were forming a new tribal confederation of people who would become known as *Manchus*. Their chieftain Nurhachi took the title of emperor; his son brought all of Mongolia under his rule, overran Korea in 1627, and took the Ming northeastern outpost of Mukden in 1636.

Domestically in China, a combination of rising imperial expenditures and increasing land tax evasion by the rural gentry eventually destabilized even so rich an empire as the Ming. Factionalism and eunuch intrigues in the capital weakened the dynasty further; popular rebellions broke out and were not thoroughly suppressed. In desperation, the last Ming emperor invited a Manchu army to Beijing to expell a rebel band that had seized the city. Having expelled the rebels, the Manchus refused to leave. The Ming emperor hanged himself, and the Manchus proclaimed the founding of the *Qing Dynasty*

(1644–1911). Ming resistance in southern China was quashed by 1661; all Chinese men were required to braid their hair in a queue as a sign of submission.

During the last decades of the Ming, China began to feel the first effects of European influence. The Jesuit missionary Matteo Ricci reached Macao in 1582 and Beijing in 1601. Adapting himself to local custom, he became an accomplished Confucian scholar and used that guise as a means of introducing to China such things as the astrolabe, the weight-driven clock, prisms, and the Mercator map of the world. For a brief time Christianity became a vogue among some members of the mandarin class, but imperial disapproval (exacerbated by factional disputes among the Christian missionary orders) discouraged conversions. Under Qing rule the Jesuits were prohibited from preaching, but allowed to remain in China for their technical skills in astronomy, mathematics, painting, and cannon-founding.

In Korea, the *Choson Dynasty* was badly shaken by a destructive invasion (1592–98) from Japan under the leadership of the shogun Toyotomi Hideyoshi. The invasion was finally repelled with Chinese aid, but Korea suffered long-term economic and social damage. Conquered by the Manchus in 1627, the Koreans had no difficulty in transferring their loyalty from the Ming to the Qing; Choson remained a loyal vassal of China, and isolated from the rest of the world, until the late 19th century.

Japan borrowed the old Chinese term "Warring States Period" to describe the century from 1467 to 1568, when Muromachi rule dissolved in a welter of mutually hostile feudal domains. Order was gradually restored after 1568 by three remarkable generals: Oda Nobunaga, who was the first Japanese general to use firearms extensively in battle; Toyotomi Hideyoshi, a peasant who rose to rule Japan, only to squander his resources in a fruitless invasion of Korea; and Tokugawa Ieyasu, who defeated Hideyoshi's army at the Battle of Sekigahara in 1600 and established the Tokugawa shogunate, military rulers of Japan until 1868. The Tokugawa period is sometimes known as the *Edo Period*, after its capital (now Tokyo).

Japan readily absorbed European influence in the 16th century. The Portuguese arrived as traders in 1543; another Jesuit, Francis Xavier (1506–52) began his mission to the Japanese in 1549. Within three decades the number of Catholic converts, including some members of the high military aristocracy, reached 150,000. Thereafter Hideyoshi began to suppress Christianity as a foreign threat, banishing Portuguese missionaries in 1587. The Tokugawa shoguns persecuted Christianity even more fiercely, executing thousands after 1612 and driving the church underground after the Christian Shimbara Uprising of 1637–38 ended in an appalling slaughter. Thereafter no foreigners were allowed in Japan except for a small number of Dutch traders, who were rigorously confined to an island in Nagasaki harbor.

Africa's Time of Troubles (1500–1650)

The Portuguese sea route to the east diverted attention from the earlier trading contacts with Africa where Portuguese traders brought cotton goods and metal manufactures to exchange for ivory and gold as far as the delta of the Niger river, and where, further south, at the mouth of the Congo, a Bantu-speaking Christian state developed after 1483. And the new world of the Americas, the Spanish Caribbean and Portuguese Brazil, provided a large market for traffic in human beings: the *slave trade* which the Portuguese monopolized until the Dutch drove them out of the Gold Coast in 1642. African slavery, once the result of tribal warfare, now became its cause. First the Portuguese, then the Dutch and, after 1562, the English encouraged tributary states along the west coast to provide them with workers for new world plantations.

The trading *Kingdom of Songhay* which had reached its greatest extent under Askia Mohammed and Askia Dawud in the 16th century was smashed by a Moroccan invasion in 1591. The fall of Songhay brought decline further east to the *Kingdom of Kanem (Bornu)* in the savanna surrounding Lake Chad after 1617. The paradoxical result was the decline of Islamic influence for with the destruction of the Muslim towns the old caravan routes across the Sahara dwindled to a trickle. Further south, the Portuguese established themselves on the west and east coasts in *Angola* (1574) and Mozambique (1508) and after 1628 reduced to vassal status the *Kingdom of the Makaranga* which stretched from the Zambesi to the Limpopo with its capital at Great Zimbabwe. At Africa's southern tip the Dutch established themselves, founding Capetown in 1652.

The Americas: Europe's New Provinces

The Treaty of Tordesillas (1494) between Spain and Portugal divided the world by a line 370 leagues west of the Azores, establishing monopolies for Spain westward and Portugal eastward of the line, approximately 45 degrees west longitude. Thus Brazil, not discovered until 1500, accidentally, by Pedro Cabral (c. 1467–c. 1520) on a voyage to India, became Portuguese territory. But the new world seemed a dead end: the shores of the Caribbean were clearly not the islands and coasts of Asia, the Spanish westward route to the Indies bumped up against an apparently interminable barrier, the Americas.

What altered the picture entirely were the events of 1519–22. In 1520, Ferdinand Magellan (c. 1480-1521) sailed around the southern tip of South America, bringing the Spanish to the Philippines and the Moluccas across the Pacific. Then in 1521, the *conquistador* (conqueror) Hernando Cortez's (1485–1547) brutally subdued the Aztec Empire in 1521. When Francisco Pizarro (1476–1541) toppled the Inca Empire in 1534, Spain acquired a stupendous world empire the wealth of whose silver mines dwarfed the riches of the Indies.

Organized into two vice-royalties, the *Spanish Empire* granted *encomiendas* or plantations to the conquerors; although enslavement of the Indians was forbidden, the Spanish reduced them to serf-like status and forced them to work for their new lords. Christian missions were immediately established with such success that over 20 bishoprics had been created by the mid-16th century. Five universities were flourishing by the middle of the 17th century.

France also sent exploratory ventures to America led by Giovanni da Verrazano (1524) and Jacques Cartier (1534); but it was not until the 17th century that a permanent settlement was established by Samuel de Champlain (1567–1635) who founded New France (1608)

with a capital at Quebec. Missions began in 1615 but the process of christianizing the Indians met with no such success as did the Spanish endeavor although Jesuits were involved here. Jean de Brébeuf's conversion of the Huron tribe only exposed them the more to the Iroquois savagery who undid his work and that of Isaac Jogues among the Mohawks. The establishment of Montreal made that more westward site the focus of the fur trade on which the economy of New France was based. Earlier the French began colonizing the Lesser Antilles, right on the fringe of the Spanish Empire and by 1656 had colonized a dozen.

England's Queen Elizabeth (1558–1603) limited herself to encouraging courtiers like Sir Humphrey Gilbert and Sir Walter Raleigh in their ill-fated attempts at early settlement (Roanoke I., 1585) and pirates and slave traders like Sir Francis Drake and Sir John Hawkins in their plundering Spanish ships. Not until the Stuart Dynasty (1603–49) did English settlement begin in earnest. Through grants to commercial companies and individual proprietors, the English established colonies from the Chesapeake to Maine broken only by the Swedes on the lower Delaware River and the Dutch in the Hudson Valley. The Chesapeake became the center of a thriving agricultural region based upon tobacco, while New England flourished as a haven for the English Calvinists known as Puritans.

Europe in the Age of the Reformation

The Europe whose sea-borne enterprise established the first truly worldwide empires was a civilization menaced from without by the Ottoman Turks and divided within both by dynastic-national rivalries and the sundering of Christian unity by the *Reformation*. For many years, leading members of the church had cried out for reform of the clergy, who often led scandalous lives amidst great wealth and who sold God's forgiveness (indulgences) for cash. But not even the powerful voices of the Dutch humanist Desiderius Erasmus (1466–1536) or the English statesman Sir Thomas More (1478–1535) had any impact.

In 1517, the call of the Augustinian monk Martin Luther (1483-1546) for a cleansing of the Church on the basis of his doctrine of "salvation by faith alone" (with its implication of the worthlessness of the priesthood and the sacramental system) swept across northern Germany from the Rhine to the Memel; the adherence of the Scandinavian monarchies to the new faith made the Baltic almost a Lutheran lake. The English king Henry VIII (1509–47), while anti-Lutheran, severed his realm from the Catholic Church after 1532. But what secured Protestantism's hold in Europe was the work of John Calvin (1509–64) who, from 1541 until his death, made Geneva a theocratic state and directed the spread of Calvinism to France, the Low Countries and the British Isles.

The attempts of the Holy Roman Emperor Charles V (1519–56) to halt the spread of Lutheranism were hampered by his need to defend the West against the Ottoman Turks (and thus not offend the Lutheran princes) and to maintain his dynastic territories against the kings of France who allied with the Turks against him. For he ruled the Netherlands and Spain in addition to holding the office of Emperor. At his abdication he willed the Empire to his brother Ferdinand along with Habsburg holdings in central Europe; Spain with its empire, both in the new world and Europe (Netherlands, Burgundy, Milan and Naples), he willed to his son Philip II (1556–98).

Philip faced rebellion in the Netherlands, where by the end of his reign the northern provinces had all but won their independence while the southern provinces were held. His Armada (1588) against England met disaster, thereby confirming Queen Elizabeth's rule and the triumph of Protestantism in both England and Scotland. France was given over to the Wars of Religion (1562–98) in which Philip ineffectively intervened on the Catholic side against the Calvinists; the upshot was victory for the Calvinist claimant Henry IV (1589–1610) who, however, turned Catholic but issued the Edict of Nantes (1598) granting French Calvinists ("Huguenots") equal rights, even to the extent of maintaining their own armies.

Philip II considered himself the Catholic champion and it was during his reign that the Catholic *Counter-Reformation* made its greatest strides, not politically but ecclesiastically. Spanish religious leadership came from the new Jesuit Order founded in 1540 by Ignatius Loyola (1491–1556), a fertile source of missionaries, preachers, scholars and schoolmasters, and from the great mystic theologians Theresa of Avila and John of the Cross. Institutionally the *Council of Trent* (1545–63), while not healing the breach with the Protestants, managed to reform the most gratuitous abuses in the Church and provide a clear and authoritative expression of Catholic belief that would last for four centuries.

The uneasy balance between the opposing forces at the start of the 17th century broke down, provoking a time of great crisis. Germany and the Empire were devastated by the Thirty Years' War (1618–48) in which the triumph of the Catholic Habsburgs was prevented by the interventions of Lutheran Sweden and Catholic France personified by King Gustavus Adolphus of Lutheran Sweden and Cardinal Richelieu of France. Britain was shaken by the struggle between Anglicans and Puritans religiously, between the Stuart kings and Parliament politically, the climax coming in the English Civil Wars (1642–49) where the Puritan victory entailed the beheading of King Charles I and the establishment of a military dictatorship under Oliver Cromwell (1649–58).

In eastern Europe there was instability as well. After the long reign of Ivan IV the Terrible (1533–84) in which the entire Volga came under Russian rule and expansion began beyond the Ural Mountains, Russia underwent its "time of troubles." The nobles ("boyars") whose power he thought he had broken rose again to prominence under his weaker son Theodore and confusion as to the succession permitted Polish penetration deep into Russia until the national assembly in 1613 elected Michael Romanov, founder of the *Romanov Dynasty* (1613–1917). In Poland, under Sigismund II (1548–72), the spread of the Reformation was checked and Lithuania was united with Poland into a single state (1569). But Sigismund was the last of the Jagellonian dynasty and at his death the monarchy became in fact what it had always been in theory, elective and thus increasingly the plaything of other great powers. From 1587 to 1648 two members of the Catholic branch of Sweden's royal family, the Vasas, ruled in Poland. Their interventions in Swedish affairs and in Russia during the time of trouble made significant enemies for Poland.

It was a Polish priest, Copernicus (1473–1543) who stands at the beginning of the *Scientific Revolution*, overturning the ancient cosmology of Ptolemy for the heliocentric theory. Expanded by the work of the Dane Tycho Brahe (1546–1601) and his scientific heir, the German Johannes Kepler (1571–1630), the movement reached its first climax in the system of the Italian Galileo (1564–1642), the greatest scientist of the age.

It was also the age of the great flowering of the vernacular literatures of Europe, especially in epic poetry and the drama: in England, Spenser and Shakespeare; in Italy, Ariosto and Tasso; in Spain, Cervantes, Lope de Vega, and Calderon; in Portugal, Camoens. Ironically, this turbulent age also saw the magnificent flowering of painting and sculpture from the universal genius of Michelangelo (1475–1564), the sculptor Bernini (1598–1680), and the painters Raphael, Titian (c. 1490–1576), El Greco (c. 1541–1614), Velasquez (1599–1660), Rubens (1577–1640), and Rembrandt (1606–69).

▶EXPANSION OF THE EUROPEAN WORLD HEGEMONY (1650–1815)

The period in Europe was characterized by the predominance of France, absolutist at the start, revolutionary at the close—a dominance that was as much cultural as it was political. In the western hemisphere, the age saw the maturing of the colonial extensions of western civilization, with the British dominating the north and the Spanish the south. In Africa and the Middle East, western influence grew primarily through trade, principally British controlled. And in the great land mass of Eurasia, two huge empires grew, those of Russia and China.

Europe in Enlightenment and Revolution

The religious wars of the previous period had a double effect: the boundaries of religious division between Catholic and Protestant Europe solidified and there grew up, especially in northwest Europe, men whom the French called *politiques*, seeking peace beyond the reach of religious controversy and division. Parallel with the rise of the politique mentality there had arisen the philosophical movement known as *rationalism*, which sought to reconstruct philosophy on the basis of "clear and distinct ideas" (Rene Descartes, 1596–1650). Then came the climax of the scientific revolution in the achievement of Isaac Newton (1642–1727), whose *Principia Mathematica* (1687) united the key ideas of inertia, gravitation, and centrifugal force.

These three streams flowed together in the movement known as the *Enlightenment*, whose publicists, called "philosophes," skeptical of all things except reason (and reason understood as the application to all matters of the method of Newton), called all authority into question save their own and subjected all traditional institutions, including the Church, to the corrosive solvents of their argument and mockery.

The man who gave his name to the *Age of Louis XIV* (1661–1715) was no philosopher but an absolute monarch whose court at Versailles became the model for sovereigns across Europe, establishing a French cultural dominance more significant than her political power. Not that the latter was insignificant: in a series of four wars the "Sun King" expanded France's frontiers to the Rhine and his Bourbon dynasty to the throne of Spain. It took alliances of almost all Europe to limit him even to this, alliances organized principally by the Dutch stadtholder William of Orange who conspired as well with the Protestant English aristocracy to overturn their Catholic king James II, the second of the Stuarts restored after the Cromwellian dictatorship, and install him as William III of England. This event is known as the "Glorious Revolution" and it turned England essentially into an aristocratic republic dominated by Parliament.

Louis XIV's revocation of the Edict of Nantes (1685) forced the Protestant Huguenots to leave France for Holland, Britain, and Prussia, where they became industrious businessmen and artisans; through their dominance of publishing, they laid the basis for the spread of the Enlightenment.

In eastern Europe the age of Louis XIV was principally the story of the decline of Polish and Ottoman power and the rise to dominance of Prussia and Russia in the Baltic region and the new *Habsburg Empire* in the southeast. With the Spanish Habsburgs sliding toward extinction and the Holy Roman Empire rendered ghostly by the Thirty Years' War, the Austrian Habsburgs drove the Ottomans out of Croatia and Hungary (1699) and added Galicia from helpless Poland (1772). Meanwhile, the War of the Spanish Succession (1702–13) which established the Bourbons on the throne of Spain also detached from Spain its holdings in the Netherlands (roughly modern Belgium) and Italy (Milan and Tuscany), awarding both to the Austrian Habsburgs. This unwieldy dynastic empire, so diverse as to lack even a name, is usually called the *Austrian Empire*, though that title was not taken until 1804. The heart of Catholic Baroque culture in art and architecture and music, Austria became in the reign of Joseph II (1765–80) the seat of an enlightened despotism as well.

More an army than a state, Brandenburg excelled in switching alliances: Frederick William the Great Elector gained sovereignty in the Duchy of Prussia from Poland (1660), and his son a royal title there from the Emperor (1701); thus the *Hohenzollern* dynasty's holdings are usually called *Prussia*. Under Frederick II the Great (1740–86), friend and patron of Voltaire, Prussia snatched Silesia from the Habsburgs (1748). Participating in the partitions of Poland (1772,1793,1795) the Hohenzollerns again doubled the size of their dynastic holdings.

Fought on three continents, the Seven Years' War (1756–63) was the first truly world war. In the European theater the alliances (Great Britain and Prussia against France, Austria and Russia) fought to a draw; the war was won overseas: in North America and in India the British drove out the French and established their hegemony. But in attempting to organize their new and gigantic North American holdings (the "new imperial system") Great Britain provoked into rebellion her old coastal colonies whose independence as the United States of America was recognized in the Peace of Paris (1783). (For North American developments afterward, see Part II: U.S. History.)

The French Revolution

A war for independence rather than, as its common name implies, a revolution, the American experience was an odd model for the tumultuous upheaval known as the *French Revolution*. France was the most prosperous state in Europe, but the long series of wars since 1660 combined with the clergy's and the aristocracy's exemption from taxation impoverished the monarchy. As a way out of the impasse, Louis XVI resurrected the old medieval Estates General (1789) but the representatives transformed themselves into a constitutional convention called the National Assembly. After abolishing serfdom, setting the peasants free, they remodeled the French state into a constitutional monarchy. But they also confiscated Church lands, dissolved the monasteries, and attempted to make the Church a department of the state, complete with elected bishops. This tore many devout Catholics away from the revolutionary cause.

The universal appeal of the French Revolution to so many people across Europe frightened the monarchs and encouraged the National Assembly to declare war on them all. The new mass armies of the French, fired by ideology and national pride, were a juggernaut against the old-fangled monarchical armies. At home, the war emergency and a revolt in a pro-royalist area (Vendee) against the newly declared republic were used to justify a Committee of Public Safety led by George Danton (1759–94) and Maximilien Robespierre (1758–94) and its *Reign of Terror* (1793–94); it's first victims were the royal family, including Louis XVI and his wife, Marie Antoinette. The rule of the Directory (1795–99) that followed was overturned by its general, the Corsican adventurer and military genius Napoleon Bonaparte (1769–1821), who established a popular and military dictatorship (1799) first disguised as a republic, then under the name *French Empire* (1804–15).

Several coalitions of nations were formed to stop Napoleon, but he defeated all of them. Coalition after coalition broke up in defeat. At its peak, the Empire dominated all of Europe from the English Channel to the Ottoman Empire by incorporation into the Empire, or as satellites, or as allies. But a popular uprising in Spain, supported by Britain, and the failure of Napoleon's invasion of Russia (1812) began the breakup of his Empire. By 1814 the anti-French nationalisms that conquest had evoked and the recovery of the monarchs' courage brought Napoleon down and, when he returned in 1815, produced his final defeat at Waterloo (1815) at the hands of the first Duke of Wellington (1769–1852).

Scarcely noticed, another and perhaps more powerful revolution was already under way before the period ended. Enlightened British landowners were enclosing the commons (the village lands tenant farmers used to graze cattle) and developing new crops while inventors were creating the machinery (the spinning jenny, the waterframe, and the steam engine) which would provide the basis in the following period for the *Industrial Revolution*.

Europe Overseas: The Americas and Africa

Between the crises of the Cromwellian period (1643–60) and the Glorious Revolution (1688) the Stuart kings of England fostered new proprietary grants in the Hudson Valley, in Pennsylvania, and in the Carolinas. Thereafter the North American colonies became habituated to self-government under their elected assemblies in a period of "salutary neglect" by the home government. Legally colonies, they were in fact mature provinces of Britain overseas. When after the Seven Years' War the government attempted to limit settlement beyond the Appalachians, to tax the colonists for the costs of the enlarged British holdings, and to extend toleration to Catholics in Canada, the colonial resistance led to war and to independence.

The Spanish new world colonies, with new viceroyalties of New Granada (1717) (roughly modern Venezuela, Colombia, and Ecuador) and La Plata (1776) (Bolivia, Paraguay, Uruguay, and Argentina) remained essentially Indian states governed paternalistically by *Yo, el rey*—the king, in whose name all regulations were sent to the viceroys. After about 1650 Indian population grew rapidly. While rule remained in the hands of "peninsulares" from the home country and, to a lesser degree, in those of the "creoles," colonists of Spanish descent, in the towns, the Indians' chief contact with Spanish culture was in the Church, whose missionaries and bishops provided a spiritual elite. Of special note were the Jesuit "reductions" on the upper Parana: self-governing, communistic Catholic Indian republics which fell victim to European politics and Brazilian incursions. Brazil by 1800 had a population larger than Portugal's.

To the viceroyalty of New Spain (Mexico) was attached the Philippines. No one was sure where in the Pacific lay the treaty line of 1494 so that while the Philippines were in fact on the Portuguese side, it was Spain that claimed them in 1565, founding Manila in 1571 which became the western terminus for the famous Manila galleons bearing Mexican silver. Through the whole period coasting voyages of English, Dutch and Spanish mariners discovered the islands of the South Pacific: the Carolines, the Marshalls, Tasmania, New Zealand and Australia; but no settlements disturbed the hunting and gathering culture of the Stone Age people who inhabited them.

It was otherwise in Africa where the slave trade continued until the end of the period, peaking in the 1780s but with demand dropping decade by decade thereafter. And in the early years of the 19th century Britain, Denmark and the United States abolished the trade, Britain actively but not always effectively blocking the trade along the African coast. In west Africa, there was an Islamic revival in the savanna as the *Fulbe people*, over the century after 1670, spread eastward toward Lake Chad in a series of *jihads* against *Hausa* cities. In south Africa, the *Zulu* nation, utilizing trained infantry units armed with spears established a small empire in the late 1700s over their neighbors who still relied on the hurling of javelins; while the Dutch at the southern tip, with its Mediterranean climate and its few Khoikhoi (Hottentots), built a Dutch-speaking, Calvinist, multiracial colony which by 1815 had a population of about 80,000. The pioneering "trekboers" beyond the Cape found their expansion limited by the Xhosa people and when the colony passed from the Dutch to the British (1814), British governors attempted to halt the expansion in the name of peace. Finally, on the east coast trade reached inland as far as Lake Victoria, initiated by the Nyamwezi people of Tanzania but falling after 1800 into the hands of the trade network of Oman, an ally of Britain.

Two Eurasian Empires: Russian and Ottoman

In one aspect the development of the Russian Empire was an eastward expansion of Europe, in another it was the creation of a stupendous Oriental state menacing Europe. Russian pioneers had already reached the Pacific by 1637; expansion into Central Asia brought the Russians up against Chinese expansion westward into the same region, peace being established in 1689 by the Treaty of Nerchinsk which set the common boundary along the peaks of the Stanovoi Mountains, the Russians evacuating a fort they had constructed on the Amur. This shifted Russian interests to the northeast, leading eventually to Russian settlements in Canada and California (1805–1912).

A certain important but superficial "westernizing" of Russia took place under Peter the Great (1689–1725) who in a "revolution from above" autocratically imposed upon his land Western modes in manufacturing, in political administration, in military techniques, in court manners and even in dress. Russia had already taken the eastern Ukraine including Kiev from Poland (1667), then the portion (1681) that their allies the Ottomans had won in that war. Peter's attempts to gain Azov—the warm-water port on the Black Sea that would provide access to the Mediterranean—from the Ottoman Empire proved ineffectual. But in the Great Northern War (1700-21) he proved more successful against Sweden, establishing Russia on the Baltic and founding a new capital at St. Petersburg.

Under Catherine II the Great (1762–96), another "enlightened despot" favored by Voltaire, Russia fought a war with the Ottoman Empire. The Treaty of Kuchuk Kainarji (1774) established Russia in the Crimea along the north of the Black Sea, granted navigation rights to Russia in Turkish waters, including the Straits into the Mediterranean, and provided a legal basis for Russia to intervene to protect Orthodox Christians in the provinces of Moldavia and Walachia—i.e. most of what Peter the Great wanted. Catherine also participated in the partitions of Poland (1772, 1793, 1795), which obliterated that ancient Christian state.

In a third stage of expansion Russia took Finland (1809) from Sweden and Bessarabia (1812) from the Ottomans during the Napoleonic Wars. After the invasion of Russia (1812) the czar Alexander I participated in the great coalition that at last brought Napoleon down. In 1815 Russian troops were participating in the occupation of Paris and the Polish Kingdom that emerged from the post-war settlement had Alexander as its king.

The Russian ascendancy was paralleled by Ottoman decline. Of the dozen sultans who ruled between 1648 and 1839 only Selim III (1789–1807) was a man of intelligence and vigor. The period began with misleading signs of strength, as the Turks took Podolia from Poland (1672) and advanced against the Habsburgs, climaxing in the siege of Vienna (1683). The failure of the siege proved a real turning point, the beginning of a long slow sag in Ottoman fortunes that made it by the 19th century "the sick man of Europe." Facing war after war against Austria and Russia (often in tandem) in the west and Persia in the east, the Empire yielded territory, strained its already chaotic finances, and developed a defensive mentality. Its domestic power waned as well as frontier garrisons meant for defense had to be used to suppress rebellions and endemic banditry.

The year after the siege of Vienna was lifted, the Austrians were victorious in the second Battle of Mohacs (1684) which reversed that of 1526, a victory confirmed by the Battle of Zenta (1697): Hungary and Croatia fell away. After the Treaty of Kuchuk Kainarji (1774), the Black Sea was no longer a Turkish lake and Russian ships sailed freely through Ottoman waters. Egypt, temporarily independent in 1769, gained its autonomy in 1805 while Serbia became the first Christian Balkan state to gain autonomy. Even Arabia, the original homeland of Islam, slipped from Ottoman rule as the Saud clan provided the political and economic support necessary for *Wahhabism* which sought a return to the primitive theocracy of the Prophet himself.

The Growth of British Influence in the Middle East and India

With the Portuguese control of the spice route in disarray and the Dutch diverted toward the Spice Islands, British commercial interests grew ascendant in India. Bombay became the headquarters of the *East Indian Company* (1661) from which Calcutta was founded (1690). But not uncontested: the French founded their East India Company in 1664 and established a trading post at Pondichery in 1674.

The Safavid Persian Empire with which the British East India Company had established trade in 1616 entered after 1664 a decline like that which had earlier begun in the Ottoman realm.

In the long reign of Mogul emperor Aurangzeb (1659–1707) the empire had reached its greatest territorial extent, principally through conquests in the Deccan plateau in south-central India. But within the empire his rule was weak as local governors grew increasingly independent. The Maratha people, under their raja Sivadi, established an independent Hindu state against which the emperor waged inconclusive war until his death, and the religious order of Sikhs (blending Hindu and Muslim beliefs) became under Govind Singh a military order.

After Aurangzeb's death Mogul decline became precipitous. Afghanistan became independent in 1709 then invaded Persia (1722) its leader, Mir Mohammed, becoming shah in 1725. With the death of the last Safavid in 1736 the general Nadir Shah reestablished rule over Afghanistan and even invaded India (1738). But all proved ephemeral. With his death Persia came under the rule of the *Zand Dynasty* (1750–94), then the *Kajar Dynasty* (1794-1925) under whom Great Britain gained the right by treaty (1814) to negate any Persian treaty contrary to her interests. The Afghans (1809) became British allies, bound to assist Britain were Persia or France to attack India.

In India during the 18th century the Maratha state became the dominant Indian body, collecting taxes (1720) in Southern India. Nadir Shah's invasion (1738) wrested the north and west from the Moguls. In the turmoil, the European companies began forming private armies of Indian troops ("sepoys") under European officers. After the War of the Austrian Succession (1746–48) French forces ruled virtually the entire south. But in the Indian theater of the Seven Years' War

(1756–63) Robert Clive (1725–74) roundly defeated the French; the Treaty of Paris left but a few holdings to the French. In the aftermath, the East India Company gained from the *nawab* (viceroy) of Bengal landowner status over Calcutta, then pensioned off the *nawab* and ruled Bengal directly (1764).

During this struggle the Afghans invaded from the northeast establishing their rule over the Maratha and Sikhs (1761–62). Faced with the two foreign powers most Indian princes gravitated towards the British, a movement not halted by Parliament's India Act (1784) which brought the Company under government control and prohibited it from interfering in Indian affairs or from engaging in war. Still, between 1786 and 1813, the Company's governors-general began a judicial system, gained control over the foreign affairs of most southern principalities in return for British protection, and entered into the treaties with Persia and Afghanistan already mentioned.

In reality, there was no British empire. The Company ruled directly only certain territories whose princes could not secure peace and order and established treaty obligations with other princes—there were no missionaries, no conversions—not even British law: an odd combination of feelings of superiority with respect for Indian culture led to a hands-off policy. And to the Hindus, the British were but another caste.

Chinese Expansion, Japanese Isolation (1650–1800)

The Manchu emperors of China adapted themselves rapidly to the ancient system of empire government, maintaining the examination system for the bureaucracy (though sometimes doubling officials, one Manchu, one Chinese). So serene and sensible (and non-theological) did the Manchu state appear to the European mind that it almost rivaled England in their fantasies.

Taiwan was annexed in 1683, Tibet gradually brought under Chinese control (1705-51) with the emperor controlling succession of the Dalai Lamas. But the great expansion was into central Asia, settled diplomatically with the Russians in 1689 to China's advantage. All this was the work of Kang Xi, the contemporary of Louis XIV.

Under Qian Long, who ruled from 1736-95, Burma had to recognize Chinese overlordship (1769) as did Nepal (1792). Burma had only recently been re-united (1753) and that with British assistance to Alaungpaya, so the relationships became an avenue of British influence. At the same time Annam, largely Chinese in culture and recognizing its overlordship, nonetheless permitted Catholic missions which met with surprising success especially after Gia Long emerged as emperor in 1802.

The whole period was for China one of expansion, not only territorially. In agriculture new crops from the Americas (maize and yams) provided a larger and more diversified food supply, though by the end of the period population was pressing up against its limits. Trade with Europe and with Japan, carried in Portuguese ships, was based upon Chinese exports of tea, silk and porcelain, the latter increasingly produced on a mass basis in imperial and private kilns. But China showed little interest in the outside world. The late 19th-century mission of the British diplomat Lord George MacCartney was met with total indifference. The papacy's finding (1715) that reverence shown toward Confucius or toward one's ancestors was incompatible with Catholic belief led to the ban of Catholic missionaries in 1720.

In Japan the splendid isolation of the Tokugawa period continued. But the internal peace that they enforced left the samurai warriors functionless, increasingly dissolute and in debt to the thriving merchant class. The heyday of the latter in the *Genroku Period* (1688-1704) led to a flourishing of Japanese literature free of Chinese influence: the development of haiku poetry, and of the Kabuki drama. Late in the period there were signs of restiveness against the Tokugawa not only from the great clans excluded from power but from the imperial family as well, both merging patriotic feeling and imperial loyalty with the increasing vogue of the Shinto religion, both worried about the danger of the Westerners to Japan's isolated development.

▶ TRIUMPH AND TRAGEDY OF WESTERN CIVILIZATION (1815–1945)

With the defeat of Napoleon in 1815, Europe entered 100 years of peace, the ending of serfdom, the extraordinary development of industrial capitalism, the spread of liberal and democratic institutions, and the apogee of her world-wide imperial influence. But then ensued 30 years of tumultuous upheaval: two world wars, waged with new weapons of mass destruction, flanking the subjection of most of Europe to grim totalitarian domination. At the end Europe lay broken and prostrate, its fate and the fate of the world in the hands of the two atomic superpowers, liberal-democratic America and Communist Russia.

Europe: The Rise of Nationalism

After a quarter-century of exhausting warfare the conservative monarchs and statesmen of Britain, Austria, Prussia and Russia made a generous peace with France, restoring the Bourbon dynasty but hedging her borders with an enlarged Netherlands to the north, the Prussians on the Rhine and the Habsburgs in northern Italy. To maintain the peace they established the Concert of Europe, a series of international conferences (to which France was soon admitted) to regulate European affairs, initiating the longest sustained general European peace since Rome's Antonine emperors in the second century A.D. Fearing revolution as the source of war and so a threat to themselves, they suppressed liberal and nationalist organizations and sent troops into Italy and Spain to prop up their tottering monarchies; but Britain, supporting the U.S. prevented any intervention against the revolts in Latin America. With the devolution of the Ottoman Empire in the Balkans, the powers supported an independent Greece (1829) and autonomy for Serbia, Moldavia and Walachia. Similarly, liberal revolts in Belgium and France (1830) led not to suppression but to independence for the first and a change of dynasty for the second; in the same year, however, Russia crushed a Polish revolt and absorbed that state into her empire. Britain herself, carried out a liberal reform of her constitution (1832) abolishing "rotten" or underpopulated boroughs and expanding the electorate by 50 percent, especially in the new manufacturing centers. Britain was also the first major power to abolish slavery (1833).

The year 1848 saw a remarkable series of liberal and nationalist revolts in virtually all the capitals of the German and Italian principalities and of the Habsburg realms. Yet all proved stillborn, and the armies remained loyal to their sovereigns. Still they had lasting effects, as serfdom was abolished throughout central Europe. The liberal route to national unity, which combined political goals (representative government) with nationalist ones seemed discredited; and the 1848 revolt in Paris led to the establishment of a brief Second Republic, then, in a revival of Bonapartism, a *Second Empire* (1852-70) under Napoleon III (Louis Napoleon Bonaparte, 1808-73).

His assistance was essential in aiding Piedmont's conquests of all the Italian states save Venice and Rome; the *Kingdom of Italy* was proclaimed in 1861 and by 1870 it included Venice and Rome as well. The latter two it gained as an ally of Otto von Bismarck's (1815-98) Prussia, which in a series of three brief wars incorporated all of non-Habsburg Germany into the *German Empire*, proclaimed in 1871. The third of those wars (the Franco-Prussian war), took Alsace and Lorraine from France, toppled Napoleon III, and led to the formation of France's *Third Republic* (1871–1940). The second, which had excluded Austria from German affairs, led that empire to its own reform, the establishment in 1867 of the "Dual Monarchy" of *Austria-Hungary*.

In one decade the map of Europe had been transformed, its most powerful state the new Germany which, with rapid industrialization, became stronger still in the years which led up to the World War I.

Europe: Two World Wars, 1914–45

Bismarck attempted to keep France isolated. He encouraged her colonial expansion to compensate for her diminished status in Europe and in the hope that imperial rivalry with Britain would keep those western states apart. He hoped for similar results from Russian and British rivalry in Persia and Afghanistan. And he formed the Triple Alliance of Germany, Austria-Hungary, and Italy.

But France and Russia allied in 1894 and a decade later, after settling colonial issues that had nearly brought them to war, France and Britain came too a "friendly understanding." The triangle was completed in 1907 when Britain and Russia established spheres of influence in Persia. Bismarck's diplomacy was undone by Kaiser Wilhelm II's (r. 1888–1918) aggressive foreign policy and a naval arms race with Britain.

Not in the colonies but in the Balkans events moved beyond any statesman's ability. In the disintegration of Ottoman power there, Serbia, Romania and Montenegro became independent in 1878 and Bulgaria in 1908. The powers consistently checked Russian advances there while the influence of Austria-Hungary grew. Struggling for territory from the Ottomans and from each other, the Balkan states fought a series of three wars in 1912, 1913 and 1914. It was the third one, which began with the assassination of the Archduke Francis Ferdinand in Sarajevo by a Serbian nationalist that expanded into the catastrophe of World War I.

Outside Europe fighting was slight: German holdings in the Pacific and Africa were taken by British and French imperial forces; Russian and British forces engaged the Ottomans in Mesopotamia and Armenia; and western-backed Arab revolts further weakened Ottoman strength. But in Belgium and northern France developed the horror of four years of trench warfare and on the gigantic eastern front immense armies clashed but without resolution until 1917, when the Bolsheviks, led by Vladimir I. Lenin (1870-1924), took Russia out of the war after their revolution (Nov. 6, 1917) toppled the Provisional Government that had succeeded the czarist collapse. But Russia's withdrawal in the east was balanced in the west by the American entry that same year, provoked by Germany's resumption of unrestricted submarine warfare in a futile attempt to escape the noose of Britain's naval blockade. The fighting at last ended November 11, 1918.

Besides its immense cost to blood (over eight million died in battle and six million civilians perished) and treasure, the war overturned the old European state system as four empires collapsed and were partitioned. Germany, under the Versailles Treaty (1919) emerged as the Weimar Republic with small territorial losses to France and to a resurrected Poland but burdened with the war guilt clauses and the immense financial reparations they were meant to justify. Russia lost all her western gains since Peter the Great, retreating eastward into the cruel experiment of Communist Revolution. Austria-Hungary disappeared utterly, two republics maintaining the names at least of those once great states. And by 1923 in Asia Minor a one-party Turkish Republic emerged under Mustafa Kemal Ataturk (1818-1938).

The successor states in eastern Europe, readily adopted the parliamentary government of the victorious western Allies which, in the years after 1848, had steadily democratized the franchise. But most contained substantial ethnic minorities whose rivalries poisoned parliamentary life; tariff barriers which arose everywhere fragmented the old common markets of the empires they replaced, protecting inefficient industry; in agriculture depression was chronic.

To the east brooded the reduced but still vast Soviet Union. The death of Lenin in 1924 led to the dictatorship of Joseph Stalin (1879-1953) who oversaw the murderous collectivization of agriculture and the forced industrialization of the Five Year Plans, then purged the party and the army and the secret police of all but his own men. Millions died.

Western and central Europe seemed sheltered from these grim developments by the "cordon sanitaire" of the new states of east-central Europe. After a period of post-war adjustment, prosperity returned to the western democracies, especially in Germany whose adherence to the Locarno Treaties (1925) presaged enduring peace. Yet in Italy whose wartime sacrifices seemed unrewarded by territorial gains and whose economy did not recover but rather seemed to dissolve into the chaos of political violence. In 1922 Benito Mussolini (1883-1945) came to power as his fascist movement promised a halfway house between liberal individualism and communist class war, stressing a belligerent nationalism with a corporative economy. In fact it was little more than bombast.

But with the collapse of the world economy after 1929, the social and ethnic divisions of the successor states, their boundary grievances, and the real or imagined fear of communist revolution, most of Europe outside the monarchies of the north and west turned to right-wing authoritarian regimes which, though often called "fascist," resembled Italy less than they did Latin America. The very different and very grievous case was Germany where after 1933 Adolf Hitler (1889-1945) established the Nazi dictatorship in the heart of Europe.

The western democracies dithered, deluded themselves, and sought peace through appeasement (not that they had much alternative, unprepared as they were for military action) as Hitler, bent on overturning the Versailles settlement, successfully re-militarized the Rhineland (1936) and absorbed Austria (the Anschluss) and the ethnically German parts of Czechoslovakia (1938) then turned the remainder of Czechoslovakia into a satellite, took the city of Memel from Lithuania, and began demands on Poland (1939). In August 1939, Germany and Russia agreed to partition Poland yet again and with Hitler's invasion in September began World War II.

It was, until 1941, a European war with nonstop totalitarian triumphs; by June of 1940, when France fell, all of Europe outside Britain was neutral or an ally or a satellite of Germany. But in June of 1941 Hitler invaded Russia and in December Hitler's ally, Japan, attacked the U.S. in Hawaii. Japanese dominion reached as far as Burma in 1942, while German armies penetrated as far east as Stalingrad. Nevertheless, the grand alliance of Britain and the U.S. with the U.S.S.R. caused Nazi Germany to fight a two-front war, which ultimately spelled utter defeat in May of 1945—but not before Germany killed six million Jews during the Holocaust. Three months later, atomic bomb attacks on Hiroshima and Nagasaki, by the U.S., hastened Japan's surrender. The United States and the Soviet Union, with Great Britain a very junior partner, bestrode the globe. The European Age in world history was at an end.

The Troubled Independence of Latin America

The impact of the Napoleonic wars upon Europe's trans-Atlantic provinces (and the newly independent United States as well) was profound. For one thing, Haiti's success in maintaining its independence, gained in 1794, against Napoleon's attempt to reconquer it led to his abandonment of any scheme for a New World empire: Louisiana was therefore sold to the United States. For another, placing his brother Joseph on the throne of Spain (1808) threw Spanish America into confusion: which king to obey? Juntas loyal to the Bourbon king Ferdinand VII, led by creoles such as Simon Bolivar (1783-1830) and Jose San Martin (1778-1850), resisted French rule at first, then turned against the absolutism of the restored Ferdinand in whose name they had first risen up. In colony after colony the juntas' armies fought for and won their independence: La Plata (1810), Chile (1818), New Granada (1819), Peru (1821). In separate and more complicated developments, Mexico and Brazil followed in 1822.

The *Monroe Doctrine* (1823) of the United States, instigated and given force by Great Britain, shielded the new states from Spanish repression. But nothing could shield them from the effects of their own inexperience in politics (an effect of Spanish imperial centralization) or from boundary disputes (for New World boundaries too were purely Spanish creations) or from the internal struggles of local leader (*caudillos*) seeking autonomy within the new republics. Thus independence was followed by a long period of wars, civil wars, insurrections and coups.

When the trade links with Spain were cut, the new states found a welcome from Great Britain for their products. British investment fostered mining and industrial development; American investment entered late in the 19th century. The development in the 1880s of adequate methods of refrigeration on steamships meant that beef could join wheat and sugar and coffee as exports. The needs of the Allies in World War I for massive increases in raw materials brought a great increase in trade; large-scale post-war investment from the U.S. both in industry and in plantation agriculture helped economic growth but with serious decline after 1929 in the rate of growth.

This expansion brought social tension through the growth of both a middle class and agricultural and industrial working classes, adding new elements to the older political instability. In the 1930s governments in Mexico and Argentina respectively followed the "popular front" or "corporate state" models of Europe but these were usually but trappings for a new breed of *caudillo*. In the Caribbean, the interests of the United States predominated whether as "policeman" or, as after 1934, "good neighbor."

European Empires in Africa

For 60 years after the Napoleonic wars, Europeans evinced only small interest in Africa. Liberal economic thought supported free trade rather than empire. Trading forts dotted the west African coasts while steamboats penetrated only somewhat further inland and missionaries began evangelization on a small scale. "Cash crop" agriculture was no European imposition: the profits from nuts and palm products, especially oil for lighting and machine lubrication, were enough encouragement to African kings and chiefs, especially with the drying up of the trade in slaves. In the south, the expansion of the Zulu nation after 1818 led to disruptions lasting into the 1850s while amongst the Boers in the south, the British ban on slavery provoked the Great Trek of some 10,000 settlers into the high veld, (or grassy plateau) depopulating the old Cape Colony except for some new British settlers. On the east coast the sultan of Oman moved his capital to Zanzibar the better to control his network of trade in cloves and slaves; the latter brought increasing British estrangement from their protege. Along the Mediterranean coast, the Ottoman Empire was nominally sovereign though rule in fact was exercised by local beys and sultans who gladly countenanced piracy; this provoked the French in 1830 to occupy Algiers and a few coastal cities.

About 1880 a group of French projects—a railways scheme at Dakar, new trading posts on the Ivory Coast and north of the Congo river—alarmed the other powers into the witless "scramble for Africa" which brought Britain and Portugal and eventually even Germany into a contest to annex territory, principally to prevent the others from doing the same and gaining some unknown benefit. The Congress of Berlin (1885) sought to put some order into the competition and in 15 years the entire continent had been divided up, save for the colony of freed American slaves in Liberia and the ancient Christian empire of Ethiopia. Colonial theorists gained the ear of western governments for grand schemes of great belts of territory, the French to stretch from Dakar to the Red Sea, the British from Capetown to Cairo—all just after the construction of the Suez Canal (1859–69) had rendered such imaginings nugatory. Of great interest was the discovery of deposits of gold and diamonds in the republic of Transvaal which led to Britain's conquest of the Boer republics in the Boer War (1889–1901) and

her formation (1910) of the Union of South Africa, which through elections Boers soon governed.

There was something illusory about it all: tiny armies setting up the national flag, treaties signed with hundreds of tribal chiefs who lacked authority, boundary lines drawn on maps in European capitals. But European administration did bring some measure of peace, some road and rail construction, some schools and hospitals, some westernizing of tribal leaders. The last would provide a certain leadership class in the independence movements after World War II which dismantled the empires even faster than they had been thrown together before World War I.

Europe's Asian Domination and the Rise of Japan

If Africa experienced European claims of sovereignty with only hints of the reality, Asia underwent the reverse as British rule was established in India, Burma and Malaya, Holland's in Indonesia, America's in the islands of the South Pacific (Hawaii, Samoa, and later the Philippines) and France's in Indochina. Two new provinces of Western civilization grew in Australia and New Zealand. China underwent yet another cycle of imperial decline but with the new element of the presence of the "southern barbarians" (the Europeans) and the aggressive designs of a suddenly modernized Japan.

Three 19th-century wars mark the decline of China's power and prestige. Her attempts to maintain Canton as the sole port for western trade and to end Britain's sale of opium led to the Opium War (1841–42) and a thorough British victory. The Treaty of Nanking opened four further cities to trade and ended the "tribute system," Westerners now accepted as China's equals, with a uniform tariff of 5 percent on trade; in addition Hong Kong was ceded to the United Kingdom. In the aftermath of the war, in 1844 and 1845, the United States gained the right of "extraterritoriality" (exemption from Chinese law) for its citizens, soon extended to all the western states, and the French gained toleration for Catholic Christianity, soon extended to Protestant Christians as well.

The social and economic dislocations caused by the Opium War in south China culminated in the *Taiping Rebellion* (1851–64), led by Hong Xiuquan, a failed examination candidate who, having read some Christian missionary pamphlets, imagined himself to be the younger brother of Jesus Christ. A charismatic figure, he raised a huge army and seized much of southern and central China, including the city of Nanjing. To put down the rebellion the Qing emperor resorted to the very dangerous expedient of allowing provincial governors-general to raise their own military units; these were effective but would prove destabilizing in the future. Some Western military assistance helped keep the Taipings away from the trading port of Shanghai.

At the same time China experienced three other major rebellions: Muslim uprisings in the northwest and in Yunnan Province in the southwest, and the millenarian Nian Rebellion in the north-central plains. Total loss of life from these rebellions exceeded 20 million; the dynasty itself barely survived. In 1858, in the midst of this turmoil, the British provoked a small affray called the Arrow War, settled by the Treaty of Tientsin in 1860. The cost was the opening of yet another 11 ports, the legalization of the opium trade, and the collection of China's customs by Great Britain. Sir Robert Hart became, equivalently, China's finance minister through the years 1863–1908.

Japan's attempt to gain concessions like those of the Western powers and to challenge Chinese control over the Manchu tributary state of Korea led to the Sino-Japanese War (1894-95): China had to cede Taiwan and certain mainland territories to Japan and recognize the independence of Korea, a prelude to that kingdom's incorporation into Japan in 1910.

Meanwhile in Indochina the French ignored Manchu protests and established protectorates over Annam (1883) and, right on China's border, Tonkin (1893).

After an unsuccessful attempt in 1898 to reform the imperial government, followed by the abortive, anti-Western Boxer Rebellion (1900) discontent with the feebleness of the Manchu government led to the *Chinese Revolution* (1911). The new Chinese Republic's president, General Yuan Shih-k'ai, might have established yet another new dynasty but his death in 1916 permitted the republic to continue, at least in form. But in reality it was the return of feudal anarchy, this time with modern weapons and mass political organizations. Dr. Sun Yat-sen's party, the Kuo Min Tang (KMT), came after his death under the control of his brother-in-law, Chiang Kai-shek, the warlord who controlled south China and whose armies conquered the north in 1927. But the expelling of the Communists from the KMT in 1927 led to a failed series of Communist uprisings and their retreat to the northwest in *The Long March* In their new stronghold at Yan'an, Mao Zedong (1893–1976) emerged as the party leader and Chiang's chief rival. Their struggle was submerged in the 1930's by the need to oppose Japanese dominance; Japan in 1931–32 occupied Manchuria as a protectorate and invaded China in 1937. The great powers, especially America, kept up the illusion that China was a great power with Chiang its ruler, an illusion blown to pieces within four years after the end of World War II.

Japan's rise to great power status was rooted in an extraordinary adaptability. After the American Commodore Matthew Perry forced the opening of Japan to western trade in 1853 and 1854 patriotic sentiment, anti-foreign and pro-imperial, grew until in 1867, young patriots at the court of the emperor Mutsuhito felt strong enough to end the shogunate and restore imperial control. From his reigning name, Meiji, we speak of the *Meiji Restoration*. During his long rule until 1912, Japan embarked on a course of furious imitation of western ways, as earlier they had imitated the Chinese; western science, technology, industry and arms became the basis for attaining the goal of "wealthy land, strong army." The imitation reached the extent of inventing (1884) a Japanese peerage so that there might be an upper house on the British model when the Meiji Constitution (1889) established a Diet.

But it was the military (and industrial) aspects, not the political, that showed most rapid advance, providing the basis for triumphs over China (1895) and much more surprisingly Russia (1905), the takeover of some German holdings in the Pacific during World War I, and the incursions against China in the 1930s. The parliamentarianism of the West was repudiated in the reign of Mutsuhito's grandson Hirohito after 1926 as military cliques and gangs came to control the government became the order of the day. The attack on Hawaii in December 1941 was designed to cripple the American Pacific fleet, protection for the invasion of southeast Asia, which brought Japanese forces by mid-1942 to occupy the American Philippines, the Dutch East Indies, British Hong Kong, Malaya, Singapore and Burma while French Indochina and independent Thailand collaborated. By August 1945, however, this whole proud bubble had burst and Japan itself was occupied by American forces.

In India the British kept up the fiction of Mogul rule but proceeded to act more and more like a sovereign power: commencing the repair of the Mogul system of canals (1818) and later building roads and irrigation projects; replacing Persian as the language of law courts with English in the higher courts and local tongues in local courts; founding schools whose curriculum was European and whose language of instruction was English; suppressing, in the 1830s, the funerary suicide of widows, banditry, and murder.

In the 1840s warfare in Afghanistan, in the Sind and against the Sikhs made Britain a true imperial power, the ruling authority in India, protecting Indian princes from aggression, annexing territory when princely families died out. After the *Great Mutiny* (1857–58) of the sepoys, Britain banished the last of the Moguls. Twenty years later came the symbolic climax, the proclamation (1877) of Queen Victoria as *Empress of India*.

But at the same time the British were establishing executive and legislative councils with Indians represented and courts with Indian justices sitting on the bench. And between the world wars, in which Indian troops fought loyally and with valor on the British side, the Indian National Congress, first established in 1885, came increasingly under the influence of Mahatma Gandhi. His campaigns of civil disobedience in 1921 and in 1930, presaged the post-war demands that would signal the end of British rule.

More enduring than British India or British rule in Singapore (1819) or Burma (1886) as vehicles of European influence was Australia, a convict colony founded in 1788 which was gradually transformed by generous land grants into the Commonwealth of Australia (1901) and New Zealand where assisted immigration after 1840 and land grants brought dominion status by 1907.

▶ THE COLD WAR AND AFTER (1945–PRESENT)

The wartime alliance of Great Britain, France, the United States, and the Soviet Union was one of expediency rather than long-term mutual interest; suspicion and misunderstandings characterized the alliance even during the war. Soon after the war, hostility and divergent interests between the United States and its Western allies, on the one hand, and the Soviet Union, on the other, led to the Cold War, a period of international danger, distrust, and nuclear standoff, during which direct armed conflict was avoided, but wars fought indirectly by proxy nations and movements were endemic.

As the only major power to emerge from World War II with its population, infrastructure, and economy largely intact, the United States saw itself as the leader of the entire postwar world. Its goals, backed by a monopoly on nuclear weapons, included the rapid reconstruction of Western Europe, the fostering of independent and democratic countries in Eastern Europe, rendering Japan harmless in East

Asia, encouraging democratic reform in Nationalist China, and promoting peaceful decolonization in Asia and Africa. The United Nations, organized under American leadership in 1945, was to be the vehicle for a postwar *pax Americana*.

The Soviet Union, devastated by the war, its industrial base and agricultural economy in a shambles, reeling from military and civilian casualties that probably exceeded 20 million dead, sought on the other hand to insulate itself behind a band of submissive neighbors, vowing never again to suffer the kind of invasion that Germany had mounted against the U.S.S.R. during the war. The Soviet Union also determined to make a concerted effort to match the U.S. in production of nuclear weapons and delivery systems; the resulting arms race eventually resulted in the production of enough nuclear weapons by the two powers to obliterate the entire population of the world. (Beginning in the 1960s, a series of agreements between the US and the U.S.S.R. succeeded in limiting the testing and production of nuclear weapons, and greatly reducing their numbers.)

Sharply differing visions of a desirable postwar world set the stage for a prolonged conflict between America and the Soviet Union. In Europe, the Soviet Union's interpretation of the wartime Yalta agreements enabled it to move rapidly to depose fledgling democratic governments in the Eastern European countries under Soviet Occupation; as early as 1946 Winston Churchill warned that an "Iron Curtain" was being drawn around a Soviet zone in Eastern Europe. Soviet power was made credible with the rapid development of atomic weapons. Pro-U.S.S.R. communist governments were in place in Poland, Czechoslovakia, Hungary, Yugoslavia, Bulgaria, and Romania by 1947. Austria and Finland accepted a neutral status highly deferential to the Soviet Union; communist movements in Italy, Greece and Turkey were defeated with American and British support.

The United States moved rapidly, especially after the development of the Marshall Plan aid program in 1948, to rebuild the economic and political stability of Western Europe in part to counter Soviet expansionism. A Soviet attempt to blockade the Western occupied zone of Berlin was met with the Berlin Airlift, which preserved a Western presence in the city; thereafter West and East Germany became for the balance of the Cold War in effect two separate and mutually hostile states. The Berlin Wall was built in 1961 to stem a tide of illegal migration from East to West Germany; its fall in 1989 marked the end of the Cold War. Meanwhile the North Atlantic Treaty Organization (NATO) was founded under American leadership in 1949 as a Soviet-containment strategy; it was countered by the organization of the Eastern-bloc Warsaw Pact in 1955. Later popular anti-Soviet uprisings in Hungary (1956), Czechoslovakia (1968), and Poland (1981) were ruthlessly suppressed.

Part of the European price for bowing to American leadership was American acquiescence in the postwar reconstitution of the old colonial empires of Britain, France, the Netherlands, and others. These colonial empires were gradually relinquished during the course of the Cold War, sometimes peacefully, as with the British African colonies, sometimes after bloody nationalist uprisings, as in Portuguese Africa and the French colonies of Algeria and Vietnam. The United

States tended to step into the power-vacuum of the post-colonial world, in large part to forestall Soviet influence. The hysteria of McCarthyism in the early 1950s ushered in a long period of reflexive anti-communism that led America to support a series of corrupt, unpopular and repressive—but anti-communist—regimes in various parts of the Third World.

In Asia, the simmering conflict between Communist and Nationalist forces in China broke out into open civil war by 1946, despite American efforts at mediation. With only grudging material support from the U.S.S.R., Chinese Communists under the leadership of Mao Zedong (1893-1976) defeated the far larger and better equipped Nationalists, whose corruption, ineptitude, and bourgeois orientation proved no match for the simple Communist slogan, "Land to the tiller." The Nationalists retreated to Taiwan in 1948-49, and Mao proclaimed the founding of the People's Republic of China in Beijing on October 1, 1949. A break between the U.S.S.R. and the People's Republic of China in the late 1950s, over both geopolitical and ideological issues, did not alter American policy assumptions of a monolithic international communism until the U.S.-Chinese rapprochement of 1973 under the leadership of Pres. Richard M. Nixon.

In Korea, divided after the war into separate occupation zones, a Soviet-backed government led by the veteran communist Kim Il-sung rapidly took control in the north, whereas in the south an inept and ill-prepared American occupation squandered the opportunity for democratic development, and eventually backed the corrupt right-wing movement of Singman Rhee. When North Korean troops invaded the south on June 25, 1950, the United States successfully obtained United Nations backing to rescue the south; the Korean War ensued, fought to a bloody standoff over the next three years.

The "loss" of China and the Korean war transformed American policy in Japan, which was suddenly seen as the anchor of a democratic and capitalist pro-American security zone surrounding communist Asia. India and Pakistan were similarly wooed by Britain and America. Elsewhere in Asia, communist-inspired uprisings in Malaysia and the Philippines were defeated, while an indigenous anti-communist backlash led to the slaughter of tens of thousands of people in Indonesia in 1965. But it was Vietnam that would prove to be the Asian battleground of the Cold War. After the French withdrawal in 1954, America felt impelled to step in to halt what seemed to be a clear case of international communist subversion of a friendly country; the results were devastating to all concerned, and in retrospect the Vietnamese communist movement seems certainly not to have been merely a cat's-paw for the Soviet Union and Communist China.

In Latin America, the 1959 triumph of Fidel Castro's Cuban revolution struck the American government as an unacceptable provocation on its own doorstep. The failed Bay of Pigs invasion of anti-Castro partisans trained by the CIA was a humiliation for American policy (1961). In 1954 the Russians had exploded a hydrogen bomb, and in 1957 Sputnik proclaimed the success of Soviet rocketry; the 1960 U.S. presidential election was held in an atmosphere of fear of Russian nuclear missiles. In 1962 the Cuban Missile Crisis was the most potentially deadly confrontation of the entire Cold War. Emboldened by success in that face-off, America intervened militarily to counter what it regarded as communist subversion in Guatemala, El Salvador, Nicaragua, Grenada, and elsewhere in Latin America.

In Africa, both the US and the USSR supported client states in the post-colonial period; America had some success in preserving the unity of the Congo (Zaire) and Nigeria, though at the cost of supporting kleptocratic regimes; the Soviet Union maintained an African presence in Angola and Mozambique (both garrisoned with Cuban troops), among other places.

The Middle East was an area of strong Soviet initiatives throughout the Cold War. With Israel seen as a creature of the United States, its Arab neighbors readily accepted Soviet aid and advice. Britain's inept and humiliating loss of the Suez Canal to Egypt in 1956 bolstered Nasser's socialist regime there, already friendly to Russia for aid in building the Aswan High Dam. Iraq, Syria, and Libya became anti-Israeli Soviet clients, while the U.S. sought support among the more conservative Arab monarchies. Further east, the CIA-sponsored overthrow of the democratic Mossadegh regime in 1953 led to the return to power of the shah; in 1979 his unpopular and autocratic government fell to a fundamentalist Islamic revolution. The subsequent Iran-Iraq war led the U.S. into the anomalous position of supporting the former Soviet client, Iraq's Saddam Hussein.

America's strategy throughout the Cold War had been to use its economic power to intimidate the Soviet bloc militarily and tempt the uncommitted nations of the world commercially. In this sense, the dramatic images of Neil Armstrong walking on the moon on July 20, 1969 were a key element in American Cold War propaganda. Conversely, the image of Americans hastily evacuating Saigon at the end of the Vietnam War were devastating to American interests because it seemed to show American impotence in the face of communist-inspired nationalism, even if the reality of the situation was, of course, much more complicated.

The anti-Soviet rhetoric of Pres. Ronald Reagan in the 1980s seemed like a throwback to the Cold War paranoia of the 1950s, but it seems to have hastened the Cold War's end. With a restless population and a crumbling economy, Russia found itself unable to sustain the military expenditures needed to keep pace with the U.S. in Cold War competition around the world. With the domestic softening of policy of Mikahil Gorbachev's *glasnost* and *perestroika* in the mid-80's, people in Poland, East Germany, Czechoslovakia, and elsewhere in Eastern Europe, and also in the Baltic states, rapidly overthrew their governments and threw out Soviet troops. The fall of the Berlin Wall meant in effect the fall of international communism, and the end of the Cold War.

There was fallout, to be sure, in the Persian Gulf War (1990-91), in the turmoil of the ex-Soviet republics, in the struggle of Africa to emerge from the era of Cold War patronage and great-power rivalry. But in the end the Cold War did not seem to amount to much. For all its espionage and paranoia, all the arms races and space races, all the proxy wars in unhappy countries throughout the world, the Cold War passed away with only a whimper, an historical episode that had outlived its day. The U.S. emerged as the only superpower both militarily and economically. The challenges for the future were how to maintain peace around the world, helping poorer nations find prosperity, and still remaining faithful to its ideal of self-determination for all peoples of the world.

In the ensuing years, the U.S. response to these critical problems has centered on efforts to strengthen the world economy and to do so on its own terms by maintaining an overwhelming military dominance. Despite the absence of any serious threat from a large power or a coalition of smaller ones, American military budgets continued to exceed $250 billion a year, sufficient to maintain an advanced weaponry program and to keep 1.5 million men and women on active duty. Russia still had nuclear weapons but its military was in disarray and its economy keeps hovering on the edge of collapse. Only China had a larger military force than the U.S., but it lacked anything like America's air, sea, and nuclear power.

Since 1990, China has been the focal point of U.S. foreign policy and economic strategy. Despite the Chinese government's overt acts of repression and manifest evidence of serious human rights abuses, Presidents Bush and Clinton both aggressively pursued an economic alliance that has benefited both countries. Tens of billions of dollars were invested in China in the 1990s and, not surprisingly, China became the chief supplier of low-cost consumer goods and other items to the U.S. In 1997, China sent exports worth $62 billion to the U.S. but imported only $13 billion. By 2003 China's exports to the U.S. ad soared to $152 bil. and China held over $600 bil. in U.S. treasuries (debt).

During the 1990s, the U.S. and its allies promulgated the idea that democracy and economic freedom are inseparable ideals that only market economy rules can bring to fruition. A central element in this creed is free trade, and the U.S. has led the fight to end tariffs and other barriers by helping to establish the World Trade Organization to develop international rules and policies for trade. The W.T.O. grew quickly to 148 nations including China. So successful was the U.S. effort to spur free trade that it's imports far exceeded exports creating a trade deficit that made the future worrisome to many economists. In 1994, the North American Free Trade Agreement ended all trade barriers for Canada, Mexico, and the U.S. In Europe, the European Union moved nations closer to economic integration by regulating trade and in 2002 establishing a single currency—the euro—that would quickly rival the dollar. By 2005 the E.U. had grown to embrace 25 nations and over 400 million people.

Politically the early years of the 21st century were driven by the terrorist attacks of Sept. 11, 2001 against New York's World Trade Center, which killed nearly 3,000 people. Symbolically the Arab-led Muslim terrorist group, Al-Qaeda had struck a serious blow against the West but in 2002 it was driven underground by a fierce U.S. attack on its headquarters in Afghanistan. The world applauded this response but then strangely President George W. Bush began to link events of 9-11 to Iraq's Saddam Hussein—left in power after his defeat in 1991 by Bush's father—who was accused of possessing weapons of mass destruction capable of attacking the U.S. Despite pleas from around the world the U.S. invaded Iraq in 2003, and quickly subdued the country. Very poor planning by the U.S. Pentagon, an unexpectedly serious insurgency, and increased violence between rival Muslim groups, led to more than 4,000 U.S. deaths and 30,000 seriously wounded by 2008.

Rulers of the World

EMPERORS OF ROME 27 B.C.–A.D. 491

Augustus   27 B.C.–14 A.D.
Tiberius   14–37
Caligula   37–41
Claudius   41–54
Nero   54–68
Galba   68–69
Otho   69
Vitellius   69
Vespasian   69–79
Titus   79–81
Domitian   81–96
Nerva   96–98
Trajan   98–117
Hadrian   117–38
Antoninus Pius   138–61
Marcus Aurelius (co-emperor with Lucius Verus)   161–69
Marcus Aurelius alone   169–77
Marcus Aurelius (co-emperor with Commodus)   177–80
Comodus alone   180–92
Pertinax   193
Didius Julianus   193

Septimius Severus   193–98
Carcalla (co-emperor with Geta)   211–12
Caracalla alone   212–17
Macrinus   217–18
Heliogabalus   218–22
Severus Alexander   222–35
Maximinus   235–38
Gordian I (co-emperor with Gordian II)   238
Pupienus Maximus (co-emperor with Balbinus)   238
Gordian III   238–44
Philip ("The Arab")   244–49
Decius   249–51
Hostilianus   251
Gallus   251–53
Aemilianus   253
Valerian (co-emperor with Gallienus)   253–60
Gallienus alone   253–68
Claudius II ("Gothicus")   268–70
Aurelian   270–75
Tacitus   275–76
Florianus   276
Probus   276–82
Carus   282–83
Carinus (co-emperor with Numerianus)   283–84
Carinus alone   284–85

Between 270 and 283, there were seven emperors, all chosen by the army. Carus was killed in battle, and Numerianus died on the march. The other five were murderd by their soldiers. In an attempt to end the chaos of the "barracks emperors," Diocletian attempted to establish an orderly succession in the East and West halves of the Empire, the emperor in the East being the senior emperor. Dicocletian and Maximian both abdicated in 305,

although Maximian was recalled in 306. Subsequently, the succession became disputed in both East and West, and between 305 and 474 there were 39 claimants to the imperial title, five of whom ruled both the East and the West, most notably Constantine (324–37). With the demise of the last emperor in the West (476), the eastern emperor, Zeno, reunited the imperial office in one person.

East	Constantine I 312–37	West
Diocletian 284–305		Maximian 286–308
Galerius 305–11		Constantius I 305–306
Licinius 311–24		Severus 306–307
		Maximin 307–13
Constantius II 337–61		Constantine II 337–40
		Constans 340–50
	Constantius II 350–61	
	Julian 361–63	
	Jovian 363–64	
Valens 364–78		Valentinian I 364–75
Theodosius I 378–92		Gratian 375–83
		Valentinian II 385–92
	Theodosius I 392–95	
Arcadius 395–408		Honorius1 395–423
Theodosius II 408–50		Valentinian III 425–55
Marcian 450–57		Petronius Maximus 455
Leo I 457–74		Avitus 455–56
Leo II 474		Marjorian 457–61
Zeno 474–91		Libius Severus 461–65
		Anthemius 467–72
		Olybrius 472–73
		Glycerius 473–74
		Julius Nepos 474–75
		Romulus Augustus 475–76

Note: Names in **bold italics** ruled in both the East and the West. These lists are designed to make history neater than it was, so they do not reflect the turmoil of the fourth and fifth centuries, when usurpers and pretenders were numerous.
1. Stilicho was regent until 408.

DYNASTIES OF EUROPE

▶THE CAROLINGIANS (751-887)

The first Carolingian king of the Franks was Pepin the Short who usurped the title from the Merovingian line in 751.Taking their dynastic name from Pepin's father, Charles (Carolus) Martel, the Carolingians divided their realm among surviving sons. It was in this family that the papacy revived the Roman imperial title in the year 800. The lists below cover only the major figures and ignore brief reigns and minor claimants.

Pepin the Short, King   751-68
Charlemagne and Carloman   768-71
Charlemagne, King   771-814
Charlemagne, Emperor   800-814
Louis the Pious, Emperor   814-40

West Franks
Charles the Bald   843-77 (Emperor 875-77)
Louis II, the Stammerer   077-079
Louis III   879-82
Carloman   879-84

Lotharingia
Lothair, Emperor   840-55
Louis II, Emperor   855-75
Charles, King of Provence   855-63
Lothair II, King of Lorraine   855-69

East Franks
Louis the German   843-76
Carloman   876-80
Louis   876-82
Charles the Fat   882-87, Emperor (881-87)

▶HOLY ROMAN EMPIRE (962-1806)

The Holy Roman Empire refers to the second medieval "revival" of the Roman Empire in the West, in the year 962. Though drained of most of its power after 1250 and virtually all of its power after 1648, the Empire endured until 1806 when it was abolished by the Emperor Francis II (though he had no power to do so) who thereafter ruled as Francis I of the Austrian Empire which had been founded in 1804. Whatever the power of the Emperor, the title was the most prestigious in all of Europe. Normally the king of Germany was emperor once he was crowned by the pope; in 1356 the Golden Bull established a seven-member electoral college to choose the Emperor but from the 15th century on it was traditional for the electors to choose the Habsburg candidate.

Saxon Dynasty

The dukes of Saxony were most able in combatting the Hungarian menace in the 10th century and thus were chosen kings of Germany. The first was Henry the Fowler (919-936). His son Otto was the first Holy Roman Emperor.

Otto I, King   936, **Emperor**   962-73
Otto II   973-83
Otto III   983-1002
Henry II   1002-24

Franconian (or Salian) Dynasty

When Henry II died without heirs, Conrad of Franconia (a great-great grandson of Otto I) secured the succession. The dynasty intervened in

Rome to reform the papacy, perhaps too successfully, for the popes contended with the emperors for the leadership of the Christian world in the Investiture Controversy (1076-1122). Both the imperial office and the kingship of Germany were greatly weakened by the papal victory.

Conrad II   1024-39
Henry III   1039-56
Henry IV   1056-1106
Henry V   1106-25
Lothair II   1125-37

Hohenstaufen Dynasty

The Hohenstaufen of Swabia were nephews of Henry V but the Church tended to support candidates of the Guelph (also known as Welf) family of Saxony and Bavaria. The struggle of these families and the involvement of the papacy fatally weakened the empire ushering in the "Age of the Princes" in Germany and the "Great Interregnum" in the Empire.

Conrad III   1138-52
Frederick I "Barbarossa"   1152-90
Henry VI   1190-97
Philip of Swabia   1198-1208
Otto IV (Guelph) (anti-king)   1198-1208
Otto IV   1208-12
Frederick II   1212-50
Conrad IV   1250-54
Interregnum   1254-73

When kingship and the imperial office were restored in 1273 the princes refused to establish any one dynasty; for a century and a half candidates from four families were elected.

Rudolf I (Habsburg)   1273-91
Adolf (Nassau)   1292-98
Albert I (Habsburg)   1298-1308
Henry VII (Luxemburg)   1308-13
Louis IV (Wittelsbach)   1314-46
Charles IV (Luxemburg)   1346-78
Wenceslas (Luxemburg)   1378-1400
Rupert (Wittelsbach)   1400-1410
Sigismund (Luxemburg)   1410-37

The Habsburgs

The House of Habsburg (the name is a contraction of the name of their castle, Habichtsburg, in Switzerland) was the most illustrious of the European dynasties. From the 15th century they became hereditary rulers of the Empire and through a series of brilliant marriages gained, by inheritance, the Netherlands, the Spanish kingdoms and Spain's empire in the New World, and Hungary and Bohemia. (From the reign of Francis I, the official family name is Habsburg-Lorraine.)

Albert II   1440-93
Frederick III   1440-93
Maximilian I   1493-1519
Charles V   1519-56
Ferdinand I   1556-64
Maximilian II   1564-76
Rudolf II   1576-1612
Matthias   1612-19
Ferdinand II   1619-37
Ferdinand III   1637-57
Leopold I   1658-1705
Joseph I   1705-11
Charles VI   1711-40
Interregnum   1740-42
Charles VII   1742-45
Francis I   1745-65
Joseph II   1765-90
Leopold II   1790-92
Francis II   1792-1806

▶DYNASTIES OF FRANCE (987–1848)

In 987 the West Frankish nobles elected as their king Hugh Capet. His descendants ruled France continuously until the French Revolution and again from 1814 until 1848. The direct line died out in 1328, and the collateral *Valois* branch of the Capetian family succeeded. The Valois ruled with difficulty, as the Hundred Years' War (1337–1453) blighted the beginning and the Wars of Religion (1562–98) the end of their rule. The last three Valois produced no male heirs so the throne passed to the victor in the Wars of Religion, Henry of Navarre (a distant cousin in the male line of Louis IX), who began the reign of the *Bourbon* branch of the Capetians. (After 1700, the Bourbon family became, with many interruptions, kings of Spain.)

Direct Capetians

Hugh Capet   987–96
Robert II the Pious   996–1031
Henry I   1031–60
Philip I   1060–1108
Louis VI   1108–37
Louis VII   1137–80
Philip II Augustus   1180–1223
Louis VIII   1223–26
Louis IX   1226–70
Philip III   1270–85
Philip IV   1285–1314
Louis X   1314–16
John I the Posthumous   1316
Philip V   1316–22
Charles IV   1322–28

Valois Branch

Philip VI   1328–50
John   1350–64
Charles V   1364–80
Charles VI   1380–1422
Charles VII   1422–61
Louis XI   1461–83
Charles VIII   1483–98
Louis XII (Valois-Orléans)   1498–1515
Francis I (Valois-Angoulême)   1515–47
Henry II   1547–59
Francis II   1559–60
Charles IX   1560–74
Henry III   1574–89

Bourbon Branch

Henry IV   1589–1610
Louis XIII   1610–43
Louis XIV   1643–1715
Louis XV   1715–74
Louis XVI   1774–92
French Revolution and Napoleon
   1792–1814

Restored Bourbons

Louis XVIII   1814–24
Charles X   1824–30
Louis Philippe (Bourbon-Orléans)
   1830–48

▶DYNASTIES OF ENGLAND (871–PRESENT)

Saxons

With the end of Roman rule, seven Germanic kingdoms emerged in England. The leader of the resistance to the Vikings was Alfred the Great of Wessex (871–99) who began a reconquest of the island and is considered the first true king of England; his dynasty, with interruptions, continued until the Norman Conquest in 1066.

Alfred the Great   871–99
Edward the Elder   899–924
Aethelstan   924–39
Edmund   939–46
Eadred   946–55
Eadwig   955–59
Edgar   959–75
Edward   975–78
Aethelred "the Unready"   978–1016
Edmund Ironside   1016
Canute   (of   Denmark,   by   conquest)
   1016–35
Harold Harefoot   1035–40
Hardicanute (of Denmark)   1040–42
Edward the Confessor   1042–66
Harold Godwinson   1066

Normans

Duke William of Normandy, a cousin of Edward the Confessor, made good his claim to the throne by conquest, bringing with him highly organized Continental feudalism and the French tongue, which so enriched the English language.

William the Conqueror   1066–87
William II   1087–1100
Henry I   1100–1135
Stephen   1135–54

Angevins (Plantagenets)

The grandson of Henry I was Henry of Anjou, who, by marrying the heiress Eleanor of Aquitaine, assembled for his family the greatest feudal state in 12th century Europe. In 1154 he established his family on the throne of England as well; the direct line continued until 1399, when Richard II was deposed and killed by his first cousin, who then ruled as Henry IV and established the *Lancastrian Dynasty*. Another branch of the family, with a stronger claim than the usurping Lancastrians, contested the succession in the War of the Roses and after 1461 ruled briefly as the *Yorkist Dynasty*.

Henry II   1154–89
Richard I   1189–99
John I   1199–1216
Henry III   1216–72
Edward I   1272–1307
Edward II   1307–27
Edward III   1327–77
Richard II   1377–99

Lancastrian Kings

Henry IV   1399–1413
Henry V   1413–22
Henry VI   1422–61

Yorkist Kings

Edward IV   1461–83
Edward V   1483
Richard III   1483–85

Tudors

An obscure Welsh family and adherents of the Lancastrian line, the Tudors became champions of the faction supporting them. Richard III died in battle at Bosworth Field against Henry Tudor, who usurped the throne, ruling as Henry VII and founding the dynasty that brought the Reformation to England.

Henry VII   1485–1509
Henry VIII   1509–47
Edward VI   1547–53
Mary I   1553–58
Elizabeth I   1558–1603

Stuarts

Elizabeth never married and had no heirs, so the Tudor line died with her. Rule passed to Elizabeth's cousin, James VI of Scotland who ruled in England as James I. Serious troubles with the Puritans and Parliament twice turned the Stuarts from the throne: Charles I was beheaded and James II was betrayed by his daughters and the husband of one, William of Orange.

James I   1603–25
Charles I   1625–49
Interregnum—Oliver Cromwell   1649–58
                    Richard Cromwell   1658–59
Charles II   1660–85
James II   1685–88
William III and Mary II   1689–94
William III alone   1694–1702
Anne   1702–14

Hanoverians and Windsors

Queen Anne had 17 children but died without leaving an heir. Geneological and religious considerations (Anne's brother "James III," the Catholic pretender, was still alive) brought to the throne the German House of Hanover. After the reign of Victoria, the family is Saxe-Coburg-Gotha but in 1917, for political reasons, George V changed the name to Windsor.

George I   1714–27
George II   1727–60
George III   1760–1820
George IV   1820–30
William IV   1830–37
Victoria   1837–1901
Edward VII   1901–10
George V   1910–36
Edward VIII   1936
George VI   1936–52
Elizabeth II   1952–present

▶DYNASTIES OF SPAIN (1506–PRESENT)

Until 1808 there was no kingdom called Spain but a number of separate kingdoms of which Castile and Aragon were only the principal ones. With the deaths of Isabella, then Ferdinand, the crowns passed to their grandson, the Habsburg Charles of Ghent; in the Empire he was Charles V, in the Spanish kingdoms Charles I. His *Habsburg Dynasty* ruled until 1700, when the line died out and was replaced by the *Bourbon Dynasty*, which has ruled with numerous interruptions until the present day.

Habsburgs

Charles I (Holy Roman Emperor as Charles V)   1506–56
Philip II   1556–98
Philip III   1598–1621
Philip IV   1621–65
Charles II   1665–1700

Bourbons

Philip V   1700–1746
Ferdinand VI   1746–59
Charles III   1759–88
Charles IV   1788–1808
Joseph Bonaparte   1808–13

Ferdinand VII   1814–33
Isabella II   1833–68
Interregnum   1868–70
Amadeo   1870–73
Republic   1873–75
Alphonso XII   1875–85
Alphonso XIII   1886–1931
Republic   1931–36
Civil War   1936–39
Franco regime   1939–75
Juan Carlos   1975–present

▶AUSTRIAN HABSBURGS (1792–1918)

When Charles V retired, his worldwide empire was divided into two parts, one Spanish, one Austrian. The Austrian branch always supplied the Holy Roman Emperors except during the reign of Maria Theresa (1740–80) when Charles Albert of Bavaria, then her husband and son held the imperial title. In 1804 Emperor Francis II proclaimed an Austrian Empire, which he ruled as Francis I; two years later he abolished the Holy Roman Empire.

Francis II & I   1792–1835
Ferdinand I   1835–48
Francis Joseph   1848–1916
Charles I   1916–18

▶HOHENZOLLERN DYNASTY (1640–1918)

For centuries the Hohenzollern were electors of Brandenburg in northeastern Germany. In 1701, with permission of the emperor, they took the royal titles King in Prussia. (Prussia was a duchy of Poland, which the family inherited in 1618.) In 1871 they added the title German Emperor. Both titles disappeared with Germany's loss in World War I.

Frederick William, the Great Elector   1640–88
Frederick III, Elector of Brandenburg   1688–1701
Frederick I, King of Prussia   1701–13
Frederick William I   1713–40
Frederick II   1740–86
Frederick William II   1786–97
Frederick William III   1797–1840
Frederick William IV   1840–61
William I (German Emperor after 1871)   1861–88
Frederick III   1888
William II   1888–1918

▶ROMANOV DYNASTY (1613–1917)

At the end of Russia's "time of troubles" early in the 17th century, the national assembly elected Michael Romanov as czar in 1613. The dynasty died out in 1762, when at the death of czarina Elizabeth, her nephew Peter III briefly succeeded. His family ruled until the Russian Revolution. Their name was Holstein-Gottorp but ruled under the name Romanov.

Michael   1613–45
Alexius   1645–76
Theodore III   1676–82
Ivan V and Peter I   1682–89
Peter I, the Great, alone   1689–1725
Catherine I   1725–27
Peter II   1727–30
Anna   1730–40
Ivan VI   1740–41
Elizabeth   1741–62
Peter III   1762
Catherine II the Great   1762–96
Paul   1796–1801
Alexander I   1801–25

Nicholas I   1825–55
Alexander II   1855–81
Alexander III   1881–94
Nicholas II   1894–1917

▶ **HOUSE OF SAVOY-CARIGNANO (1861–1946)**
The dukes of Savoy ruled in a personal union Piedmont, Nice, and Sardinia until 1831, when the line died out and a distant cousin, Charles Albert came to the throne. It was his son, Victor Emmanuel II of Savoy whose armies conquered the rest of Italy over the years 1858–71 and who was proclaimed King of Italy in 1861. The dynasty fell with the end of the Second World War.
Victor Emmanuel II   1861–78
Humbert I   1878–1900
Victor Emmanuel III   1900–46
Humbert II   1946

THE DYNASTIES AND EMPERORS OF CHINA

Dates for the Xia and Shang Dynasties, and for the beginning of the Zhou Dynasty, are uncertain. Rulers of these three dynasties were known as kings (*wang*); only a few notable individuals are listed below. The title "emperor" (*huangdi*) was instituted with the Qin Dynasty. As is customary, names of emperors prior to A.D. 1368 are given in the form of their posthumous "temple names" (*miaohao*); names of emperors for the Ming and Qing Dynasties are given as their reign-title names (*nianhao*).

Xia Dynasty   c. 1875–1550 B.C.
Yü the Great (legendary?)   c. 1875–1850 B.C.
King Jie   c. 1560–1550 B.C.

Shang Dynasty   c. 1550–1055 B.C.
Tang the Victorious   c. 1550–1500 B.C.
King Zhou   c. 1070–1055 B.C.

Zhou Dynasty   c. 1055–256 B.C.
Western Zhou Period   c. 1055–771 B.C.
King Wen (pre-conquest)   c. 1060–1055 B.C.
King Wu   c. 1055–1048 B.C.
Duke of Zhou, regent for
King Cheng   c. 1048–1011 B.C.
Era of the Spring and Autumn Annals   722–481 B.C.
Warring States Period   481–256 B.C.

Qin Dynasty   221–206 B.C.
Shihuangdi   221–209 B.C.
Erhuangdi   209–207 B.C.

Han Dynasty   206 B.C.–A.D. 220
Western or Former Han   206 B.C.–A.D. 9
Gaozu   206–195 B.C.
Huidi   195–188 B.C.
Gaohou (Empress Lü)   188–180 B.C.
Wendi   180–157 B.C.
Jingdi   157–141 B.C.
Wudi   141–87 B.C.
Zhaodi   87–74 B.C.

Xuandi   74–48 B.C.
Yuandi   48–33 B.C.
Chengdi   33–7 B.C.
Aidi   7–1 B.C.
Pingdi   1 B.C. –A.D. 6
Wang Mang (usurper)   A.D. 9–23
Eastern or Latter Han   A.D. 23–220
Guangwudi   25–57
Mingdi   57–75
Zhangdi   75–88
Hedi   88–105
Shangdi   105
Andi   106–25
Shaodi   125
Shundi   125–44
Chongdi   144–45
Zhidi   145–46
Huandi   146–68
Lingdi   168–89
Shaodi   189
Xiandi   189–220

Period of Disunion
The fall of the Han Dynasty ushered in a period of 369 years of disunion during which no dynasty succeeded in bringing all of China under its control This period is divided into the brief Three Kingdoms Period and the longer Period of Northern and Southern Dynasties, of which only the three most important dynasties are listed below.

Three Kingdoms   220–65
Kingdom of Shu Han   220–64
Kingdom of Wei   220–65
Kingdom of Wu   220–65

Period of Northern and Southern Dynasties   265–589
Western Jin Dynasty   265–317
Eastern Jin Dynasty   317–419
Northern Wei Dynasty   424–535

Sui Dynasty   589–618
Wendi   589–604
Yangdi   604–17
Gongdi   617–18

Tang Dynasty   618–907
Gaozu   618–26
Taizong   626–49
Gaozong   649–83
Zhongzong   683–84
Ruizong   684–90
Wuhou   690–705
Zhongzong   705–10
Ruizong   710–12
Xuanzong   712–56
Suzong   756–62
Taizong   762–79
Dezong   779–805
Shunzong   805
Xianzong   805–20
Muzong   820–24
Jingzong   824–26
Wenzong   826–40
Wuzong   840–46
Xuanzong   846–59
Yizong   859–73
Xizong   873–88
Zhaozong   888–904
Jingzong   904–7

Five Dynasties   907–60

Song Dynasty   960–1279
Northern Song   960–1127
Taizu   960–76
Taizong   976–97
Zhenzong   997–1022
Renzong   1022–63
Yingzong   1063–67
Shenzong   1067–85
Zhezong   1085–1100
Huizong   1100–1125
Qinzong   1125–27
Southern Song   1127–1279
Gaozong   1127–62
Xiaozong   1162–89
Guangzong   1189–94
Ningzong   1194–1224
Lizong   1224–64
Duzong   1264–74
Gongzong   1274–76
Duanzong   1276–79

Yuan (Mongol) Dynasty   1279–1368
Shizu (Kubilai Khan)   1260–94
Chengzong (Temür)   1294–1307
Wuzong (Khaishan)   1307–11
Renzong (Buyantu)   1311–20
Yingzong (Sudhipela)   1320–23
Taiding (Yesen-Temür)   1323–28
Mingzong (Asikipa)   1328

Wenzong (Tog-Temür)   1328–33
Xunzong (Toghon-Temür)   1333–68

Ming Dynasty   1368–1644
Hongwu   1368–98
Jianwen   1398–1402
Yongle   1402–24
Hongxi   1424–25
Xuande   1425–35
Zhengtong   1435–49
Jingtai   1449–57
Tianshun   1457–64
Chenghua   1464–87
Hongzhi   1487–1505
Zhengde   1505–21
Jiaqing   1521–66
Wanli   1572–1620
Taichang   1620
Tianzhi   1620–27
Chongzhen   1627–44

Qing Dynasty   1644–1911
Shunzhi   1644–61
Kangxi   1661–1722
Yongzheng   1722–35
Qianlong   1735–96
Jiaqing   1796–1820
Daoguang   1820–50
Xianfeng   1850–61
Tongzhi   1861–75
Guangxu   1875–1908
Puyi   1908–11

CHRONOLOGICAL LISTING OF THE POPES

Peter, Apostle   d. c. 64
Linus   c.66–c.78
Anacletus   c.79–c.91
Clement I   c.91–c.101
Evaristus   c.100–c.109
Alexander I   c.109–c.116
Sixtus I   c.116–c.125
Telesphorus   c.125–c.136
Hyginus   c.138–c.142
Pius I   c.142–c.155
Anicetus   c.155–c.166
Soter   c.166–c.174
Eleutherius, or Eleutherus
   c.174–89
Victor I   189–98
Zephyrinus   198/9–217
Callistus I (often Calixtus)
   217–22
Hippolytus (antipope)   217–35
Urban I   222–30
Pontian   230–35
Anterus   235–36
Fabian   236–50
Cornelius   251–53
Novatian (antipope)   251–58
Lucius I   253–54
Stephen I   254–57
Sixtus II   257–58
Dionysius   260–68
Felix I   269–74
Eutychian   275–83
Gaius, or Caius   283–96
Marcellinus   296–304?
Marcellus I   306–8
Eusebius   310
Miltiades, or Melchiades
   311–31
Silvester I   314–35
Mark   336

Julius I   337–52
Liberius   352–66
Felix II (antipope)[1]   355–65
Damasus I   366–84
Ursinus (antipope)   366–67
Siricius   384–99
Anastasius I   399–401
Innocent I   401–17
Zosimus   417–18
Eulalius (antipope)   418–19
Boniface I   418–22
Celestine I   422–32
Sixtus (Xystus) III   432–40
Leo I   440–61
Hilarus   461–68
Simplicius   468–83
Felix III[1]   483–92
Gelasius I   492–96
Anastasius II   496–98
Symmachus   498–514
Lawrence (antipope)   498–99,
   501–6
Hormisdas   514–23
John I   523–26
Felix III[1]   526–30
Dioscorus (antipope)   530
Boniface II   530–32
John II   533–35
Agapitus I   535–36
Silverius   536–37
Vigilius   537–55
Pelagius I   556–61
John III   561–74
Benedict I   575–79
Pelagius II   579–90
Gregory I   590–604
Sabinian   604–6
Boniface III   607
Boniface IV   608–15

Deusdedit (later Adeodatus I)
   615–18
Boniface V   619–25
Honorius I   625–38
Severinus   640
John IV   640–42
Theodore I   642–49
Martin I   649–53
Eugene I   654–57
Vitalian   657–72
Adeodatus II   672–76
Donus   676–78
Agatho   678–81
Leo II   682–83
Benedict II   684–85
John V   685–86
Conon   686–87
Theodore (antipope)   687
Paschal (antipope)   687
Sergius I   687–701
John VI   701–5
John VII   705–7
Sisinnius   708
Gregory II   715–31
Gregory III   731–41
Zacharias   741–52
Stephen (II)[2]   752
Stephen II (III)[2]   752–57
Paul I   757–67
Constantine (antipope)   767–68
Philip (antipope)   768
Stephen III (IV)[2]   768–72
Hadrian I   772–95
Leo III   795–816
Stephen IV (V)[2]   816–17
Paschal I   817–24
Eugene II   824–27
Valentine   827
Gregory IV   827–44

John (antipope)   844
Sergius II   844–47
Leo IV   847–55
Benedict III   855–58
*Anastasius Bibliothecarius
  (antipope)*   855
Nicholas I   858–67
Hadrian II   867–72
John VIII   872–82
Marinus I   882–84
Hadrian III   884–85
Stephen V (VI)[2]   885–91
Formosus   891–96
Boniface VI   896
Stephen VI (VII)[2]   896–97
Romanus   897
Theodore II   897
John IX   898–900
Benedict IV   900–903
Leo V   903
Christopher (antipope)   903–4
Sergius III   904–11
Anastasius III   911–13
Lando   913–14
John X   914–28
Leo VI   928
Stephen VII (VIII)[2]   928–31
John XI   931–36?
Leo VII   936–39
Stephen VIII (IX)[2]   939–42
Marinus II   942–46
Agapitus II   946–55
John XII   955–64
Leo VIII   963–65
Benedict V   964
John XIII   965–72
Benedict VI   973–74
Boniface VII (antipope)   974,
  984–85
Benedict VII   974–83
John XIV   983–84
John XV   985–96
Gregory V   996–99
John XVI (antipope)   997–98
Silvester II   999–1003
John XVII   1003
John XVIII   1003–1009
Sergius IV   1009–12
Benedict VIII   1012–24
Gregory (VI) (antipope)   1012
John XIX   1024–32
Benedict IX   1032–44, 1045,
  1047–48
Silvester III   1045
Gregory VI   1045–46
Clement II   1046–47
Damasus II   1048
Leo IX   1049–54
Victor II   1055–57
Stephen IX (X)[2]   1057–58
Benedict X (antipope)
  1058–59
Nicholas II   1058–61
Alexander II   1061–73
Honorius (II) (antipope)
  1061–64
Gregory VII   1073–85
Clement III (antipope)   1080,
  1084–1100
Victor III   1086–87

Urban II   1088–99
Paschal II   1099–1118
Theoderic (antipope)
  1100–1101
Albert or Adalbert (antipope)
  1101
Silvester IV (antipope)
  1105–11
Gelasius II   1118–19
Gregory (VIII) (antipope)
  1118–21
Callistus II   1119–24
Celestine (II)   1124
Honorius II   1124–30
Innocent II   1130–43
Anacletus II (antipope)
  1130–38
Victor IV (antipope)   1138
Celestine II   1143–44
Lucius II   1144–45
Eugene III   1145–53
Anastasius IV   1153–54
Hadrian IV   1154–59
Alexander III   1159–81
Victor IV (antipope)[3]   1159–64
Paschal III (antipope)   1164–68
Callistus (III) (antipope)
  1168–78
Innocent (III) (antipope)
  1179–80
Lucius III   1181–85
Urban III   1185–87
Gregory VIII   1187
Clement III   1187–91
Celestine III   1191–98
Innocent III   1198–1216
Honorius III   1216–27
Gregory IX   1227–41
Celestine IV   1241
Innocent IV   1243–54
Alexander IV   1254–61
Urban IV   1261–64
Clement IV   1265–68
Gregory X   1271–76
Innocent V   1276
Hadrian V   1276
John XXI   1276–77
Nicholas III   1277–80
Martin IV   1281–85
Honorius IV   1285–87
Nicholas IV   1288–92
Celestine V   1294
Boniface VIII   1294–1303
Benedict XI   1303–4
Clement V   1305–14
John XXII   1316–34
Nicholas (V) (antipope)
  1328–30
Benedict XII   1334–42
Clement VI   1342–52
Innocent VI   1352–62
Urban V   1362–70
Gregory XI   1370–78
Urban VI   1378–89
Clement (VII) (antipope)
  1378–94
Boniface IX   1389–1404
Benedict (XIII) (antipope)
  1394–1417
Innocent VII   1404–6

Gregory XII   1406–15
Alexander V (antipope)
  1409–10
John (XXIII) (antipope)
  1410–15
Martin V   1417–31
Clement (VIII) (antipope)
  1423–29
Benedict (XIV) (antipope)
  1425–?
Eugene IV   1431–47
Felix V (antipope)   1439–49
Nicholas V   1447–55
Callistus III   1455–58
Pius II   1458–64
Paul II   1464–71
Sixtus IV   1471–84
Innocent VIII   1484–92
Alexander VI   1492–1503
Pius III   1503
Julius II   1503–13
Leo X   1513–21
Hadrian VI   1522–23
Clement VII   1523–34
Paul III   1534–49
Julius III   1550–55
Marcellus II   1555
Paul IV   1555–59
Pius IV   1559–65
Pius V   1566–72
Gregory XIII   1572–85
Sixtus V   1585–90
Urban VII   1590
Gregory XIV   1590–91
Innocent IX   1591
Clement VIII   1592–1605
Leo XI   1605
Paul V   1605–21
Gregory XV   1621–23
Urban VIII   1623–44
Innocent X   1644–55
Alexander VII   1655–67
Clement IX   1667–69
Clement X   1670–76
Innocent XI   1676–89
Alexander VIII   1689–91
Innocent XII   1691–1700
Clement XI   1700–21
Innocent XIII   1721–24
Benedict XIII   1724–30
Clement XII   1730–40
Benedict XIV   1740–58
Clement XIII   1758–69
Clement XIV   1769–74
Pius VI   1775–99
Pius VII   1800–23
Leo XII   1823–29
Pius VIII   1829–30
Gregory XVI   1831–46
Pius IX   1846–78
Leo XIII   1878–1903
Pius X   1903–14
Benedict XV   1914–22
Pius XI   1922–39
Pius XII   1939–58
John XXIII   1958–63
Paul VI   1963–78
John Paul I   1978
John Paul II   1978–2005
Benedict XVI   2005–present

Note: Antipopes, *listed in italics*, were appointed in opposition to the one canonically chosen by the college of cardinals, usually by a prince, king, or emperor. 1. Because Felix II was an antipope, subsequent Felixes were sometime misnumbered. 2. Although elected and installed as pope, Stephen (II) died before his consecration. Though the Vatican's *Annuario Pontifico* has excluded him from the official list of popes since 1961, subsequent Stephens have a dual numbering. 3. He should have been Victor V, but he used Victor IV because the previous Victor IV's tenure (1138) as antipope was largely ignored.

World Geography

▶GLOSSARY OF GEOGRAPHICAL WORDS AND TERMS

(Note: See also Part IV: Science and Technology, Composition of the Earth)

Altitude The height of a place or thing, usually measured from sea level or the surface of the land.

Archipelago A cluster of islands.

Arctic Circle An imaginary line drawn along approximately latitude 66° 30'N. The climate north of the Arctic Circle is very cold, and relatively few people live there.

Atmosphere The mass of air that extends outward from the surface of the earth into space. The atmosphere is divided into four layers: the troposphere, in which temperature decreases as altitude increases; the stratosphere, in which temperature is constant, then increases; the mesosphere, in which it decreases; and the thermosphere, in which it increases again.

Atoll A coral reef that partially or completely surrounds a lagoon.

Basin A portion of land that is lower than the surrounding area. Basins are created when vertical movement causes the earth's crust to warp. Also, the area drained by a river and its tributaries.

Bay Part of an ocean, sea, or other body of water which extends inland. Bays are generally smaller than gulfs.

Bight A bay formed by a bend in the coastline.

Caldera A huge crater formed when the top of a volcano collapses or is exploded away.

Canyon A narrow, deep valley with steep sides. Many canyons have a river on their floor.

Climate General weather conditions over a long period. (See "Climates of the World".)

Continent A large unbroken land mass, distinguished from an island or peninsula. The seven continents are North America, South America, Europe, Asia, Africa, Australia, and Antarctica, though Europe and Asia are a continuous land mass divided along the spine of the Ural Mountains running south from the Arctic Ocean.

Continental drift theory The theory, proposed in 1915 by Alfred Wegener, that all of the continents used to be joined in one supercontinent, Pangaea. Some 200 million years ago Pangaea began to break up, and the continents drifted through the oceans to their present locations. The continental drift theory has now largely been replaced by the *plate tectonics theory*. (See "Earth Sciences".)

Continental shelf The edge of a continent covered by shallow ocean water, up to about 100 fathoms (600 feet), beyond which is the continental slope, which decends to the deep-sea plain, about 13,000-20,000 feet (4,000-6,000 m).

Cove A small and sheltered bay or inlet. Also, a small valley in a mountain.

Crater The bowl-shaped depression at the top of a volcano. Also, the depression made when a meteorite hits the earth. (See also *caldera*.)

Delta A triangular-shaped piece of land formed by sediment at the mouth of a river.

Desert (See "The Great Deserts".)

Dune A hill or ridge of sand that has been deposited by wind.

Equator An imaginary line circling earth halfway between the poles. The equator is at latitude 0°.

Equinox The two times during the year (on or about March 21 and September 23) when the sun's rays strike the equator vertically. At equinox, day and night are the same length everywhere in the world. (See also *Solstice*.)

Erosion The gradual wearing away of the surface of the land. For example, soil is eroded by wind and water; rock is eroded by freezing and thawing.

Estuary A valley at the mouth of a river where fresh water and sea water mix. Estuaries are created either when the land sinks or when the sea level rises, and are generally shaped like a funnel.

Fjord A long, narrow inlet of the ocean with steeply sloping sides.

Floodplain Flat, low-lying land along either side of a river that is subject to flooding.

Geyser A jet of hot water or steam periodically thrown up by a hot spring.

Glacier A large mass of slowly moving ice. Glaciers are formed on land when snow is compacted and recrystallizes.

Gorge An especially narrow and steep-walled canyon.

Gulf Part of an ocean or sea that extends inland. Gulfs are generally larger than bays.

Hemisphere One half of the Earth's surface, however it is divided. For example, the Northern Hemisphere lies north of the equator; the Southern Hemisphere, south of the equator. By convention, the Eastern Hemisphere consists of the continents of Europe, Asia, and Africa; the Western Hemisphere, of North America and South America.

Inlet An indentation in the shore of a sea or an ocean or in the bank of a river. Also, a narrow waterway which connects a lagoon to a larger body of water or which passes between two peninsulas.

Island A land mass completely surrounded by water.

Isthmus A narrow strip of land that connects two larger land masses.

Lagoon A shallow pool or pond completely or almost completely separated from the sea.

Lake A body of water, often of considerable size, surrounded by land.

Latitude and Longitude Latitude is the angle (measured in degrees, minutes, and seconds) between a point on the Earth's surface north or south of the equator, the center of the Earth, and the equator (0°0'0 latitude). Longitude is the angle between a point on the Earth's surface, the center of the Earth, and the prime meridian (0°0'0 longitude). There are 90° of latitude between the equator and each of the poles (shown on a globe as parallel horizontal lines). There are 360° of longitude (shown as vertical lines) divided into 180° east and west of the prime meridian (180°E and 180°W are thus the same). Since 1884, Greenwich, England (near London), has been universally recognized as the point through which the prime meridien passes. A degree (°) is 1/360 of a circle, a minute (') 1/60 of a degree, and a second (") 1/60 of a minute.

Lava   Magma which reaches the surface of the Earth and from which most of the gases have escaped. (See *Magma, Volcano*.)

Leeward   The direction or side sheltered from the wind. (See *Windward*.)

Magma   Molten rock that lies deep within the earth. In a volcanic eruption, magma bursts through the outer surface of the Earth's crust. (See *Lava, Volcano*.)

Mountain   Land that rises above its surroundings. Mountains are higher than hills. Older mountain ranges, like the Appalachians, are rounded because they are old and worn down; younger ranges, like the Andes or the Himalayas, have jagged peaks because they are still rising.

North Pole   The northernmost point of the Earth's axis, at latitude 90°N. From this point, the only direction is south. It is entirely surrounded by water, and usually covered by ice. The first successful expedition to the North Pole—there is some doubt as to whether they actually reached the pole—was led by by Adm. Robert E. Peary, Apr. 6, 1909.

Ocean   (See "Oceans of the World".)

Peninsula   A portion of land surrounded by water on three sides.

Plain   A large portion of level or rolling land which is treeless.

Plate tectonics theory   The theory, first proposed in 1968, that Earth's crust is made up of 20 sections or plates, each of which consists of continental and ocean crust. The plates shift, moving continents, changing the size and shape of oceans, causing earthquakes, and creating volcanos and mountains. The plate tectonics theory has largely replaced the *continental drift theory*.

Plateau   A portion of land, generally large and with a level surface, which is sharply elevated above the surrounding land. Plateaus are created when vertical movement causes the Earth's crust to warp.

Pond   A small body of water surrounded by land.

Prairie   Level or rolling land generally covered with grasses, with few trees.

Rain shadow   An area on the leeward side of a mountain range which receives little rainfall.

River   A large stream.

Sahel   The Arabic word for shore, the Sahel is a dry region separating the Sahara from tropical West Central Africa running from Senegal to Sudan. The meager rainfall (4–8 inches per year) supports limited crops and grazing.

Savanna   A portion of land in the tropics or subtropics with only scattered trees but whose grasses can survive with scant rainfall.

Sea   A large body of saltwater, generally considered smaller than an ocean.

Solstice   The time when the sun's rays strike vertically the Tropic of Cancer or the Tropic of Capricorn. At solstice, the daylight hours reach their maximum or minimum. In the Northern Hemisphere, for example, summer solstice occurs on or about June 22; that is the longest day of the year and signals the beginning of summer. The winter solstice occurs on or about December 22; that is the shortest day of the year and signals the beginning of winter. In the Southern Hemisphere, the longest and shortest days of the year occur on December 22 and June 22, respectively. (See also *Equinox*.)

Sound   A body of water that separates an island from the mainland, or that connects two oceans, seas, or other bodies of water. Sounds are generally long and narrow.

South Pole   The southernmost point of the Earth's axis, at 90°S. First reached by Norwegian explorer Roald Admundsen in 1911, the South Pole lies in the South Polar region.

Steppe   A portion of land with little rainfall, extreme temperature variations, and drought-resistant vegetation.

Strait   A narrow body of water that connects two large bodies of water.

Stream   Any body of running water that flows on or under the surface of the Earth. Brooks and creeks are small streams; rivers are large streams.

Swamp   A portion of wet, waterlogged, or flooded land.

Tide   The rise and fall of the surface of the ocean and of bays, gulfs, and other bodies of water connected to the ocean. Tides are caused by the gravitational pull of the moon, which passes over the same meridian of the Earth about once every 24 hours and 50 minutes. The length of time between successive high (or low) tides is about 12 hours and 25 minutes.

World Land Area and Population by Selected Region

| Region | Land Area | | | Population | | | |
	Square miles	Square kilometers	Percent of world total	Total ('000s)	Percent of world total	Per square mile	Per square kilometer
World total[1]	57,308,738	148,429,000	100.0%	6,068,511	100.0%	99.5	38.4
Africa	11,608,156	30,065,000	20.3	805,243	13.3	69.4	40.9
Antarctica	5,404,000	14,000,000	9.4	(2)	(2)	(2)	(2)
Asia	17,212,041	44,579,000	30.0	3,688,072	60.8	214.3	82.7
Australia	2,967,966	7,687,000	5.2	19,164	0.3	6.5	2.5
Europe	3,837,082	9,938,000	6.7	728,981	12.0	190.0	73.4
North America	9,365,290	24,256,000	16.3	480,545	8.0	51.3	19.8
South America	6,879,952	17,819,000	12.0	346,504	5.7	50.4	19.4

Notes: 1. Land only. Includes small islands not shown separately. **2.** Antarctica has no indigenous population.
Sources: *National Geographic Atlas of the World* (1995); U.S. Census Bureau, mid-year 2000 population estimates.

Tributary A stream or river that flows into a larger stream or river.

Tropic of Cancer Latitude 23½°N, which marks the northernmost limit of the sun's vertical rays. The area between the Tropic of Cancer and the Tropic of Capricorn is known as the tropics.

Tropic of Capricorn Latitude 23½°S, the southernmost limit of the sun's vertical rays.

Tundra An area of treeless plain near or above the Arctic Circle. Tundra subsoil is permanently frozen, but the soil thaws enough to support the growth of mosses, lichens, and some small flowering shrubs.

Valley A long and sometimes narrow depression on the surface of the earth, usually between two mountain ridges or ranges.

Volcano A mountain formed by lava and/or other materials which have burst forth from deep within the Earth. (See *Caldera, Lava, Magma.*)

Windward The direction or side facing the wind.

▶THE OCEANS OF THE WORLD

The water of the world's oceans covers more than 70 percent of the world's surface. While for most of the 20th century the so-called World Ocean was divided into the Pacific, Atlantic, Indian and Arctic Oceans, a decision by the International Hydrographic Organization in 2000 delimited a fifth ocean, the Southern Ocean, extending from 60 degrees south latitude to the coast of Antarctica. Other large bodies of water such as the Caribbean Sea, the Gulf of Mexico, Hudson Bay, the Mediterranean and Black Seas, and the South China Sea are termed marginal seas. The International Hydrographic Organization identifies 66 seas, gulfs, bays, bights, straits, channels, and passages, many of which are further subdivided. For instance, the Mediterranean Sea is divided into western and eastern basins, and the western basin is subdivided into the Strait of Gibraltar, Aboran Sea, Balearic Sea, Ligurian Sea, Tyrrhenian Sea, Ionian Sea, Adriatic Sea, and Aegean Sea. The table (below) gives the area and maximum depths of the world's major oceans and selected marginal seas.

▶THE GREAT DESERTS OF THE WORLD

To many people, the word *desert* brings to mind images of shifting sand dunes, scorching sun,

The Oceans of the World

Ocean	Area ('000s sq. km.)	Coastline (km.)	Deepest point	Comparative area
Arctic	14,056	45,389	4,665 m (Fram Basin)	1.5 times size of U.S.
Atlantic	76,762	111,866	8,605 m (Milwaukee Deep, Puerto Rico Trench)	More than 6.5 times size of U.S.
Indian	68,556	66,526	7,258 m (Java Trench)	5.5 times size of U.S.
Pacific	155,557	135,663	10,924 m (Challenger Deep, Mariana Trench)	15 times size of U.S.; approx. 28% of global surface (more than total world land area)
Southern	20,327	17,968	7,235 m (South Sandwich Trench)	More than 2 times size of U.S.

The Continents: Highest and Lowest Elevations

Continent	Highest point	Location	Feet above sea level	Meters above sea level
Africa	Mt. Kilimanjaro	Tanzania	19,340	5,895
Antarctica	Vinson Massif	Ellsworth Mts.	16,066	4,897
Asia	Mt. Everest	Nepal-China	29,028	8,848
Australia	Mt. Kosciusko	New South Wales	7,310	2,228
Europe	Mt. Elbrus	Russia	18,510	5,642
North America	Mt. McKinley	U.S. (Alaska)	20,320	6,194
South America	Mt. Aconcagua	Argentina	22,834	6,960

Continent	Lowest point	Location	Feet below sea level	Meters below sea level
Africa	Lake Assal	Djibouti	512	156
Antarctica	ice covered	—	8,327	2,538
Asia	Dead Sea	Israel-Jordan	1,339	408
Australia	Lake Eyre	South Australia	52	16
Europe	Caspian Sea	Russia, Kazakhstan	92	28
North America	Death Valley	U.S. (California)	282	86
South America	Valdes Peninsula	Argentina	131	40

Source: *National Geographic Atlas of the World* (1995).

Great Deserts of the World

Desert	Location	Approximate size	
		Sq. mi.	Sq. km.
An Nafud[1]	N Saudi Arabia	40,000	103,600
Arabian	Arabian Peninsula	900,000	2,330,000
Atacama	N Chile	70,000	181,300
Australian	Australia	600,000	1,554,000
Black Rock	NW Nevada	1,000	2,600
Chihuahuan	Texas, New Mexico, Arizona; Mexico	140,000	362,600
Dasht-e-Kavir	Central Iran	30,000	77,600
Dasht-e-Lut	E Iran	20,000	51,800
Death Valley	E California; SW Nevada	3,000	7,800
Gibson[2]	W Australia	120,000	310,800
Gobi	Mongolia; China	500,000	1,295,000
Great Sandy[2]	NW Australia	150,000	338,500
Great Victoria[2]	SW Australia	150,000	338,500
Kalahari	S Africa	225,000	582,800
Kara Kum (Turkestan)	Turkmenistan	120,000	310,800
Kyzyl Kum	Uzbekistan	100,000	259,000
Libyan[3]	Libya; SW Egypt; Sudan	450,000	1,165,500
Mojave	S California, W Arizona	15,000	38,900
Namib	Namibia	52,000	135,000
Negev	S Israel	4,700	12,200
Nubian[3]	NE Sudan	100,000	259,000
Painted Desert	N Arizona	5,000	12,950
Rub al-Khali (Empty Quarter)[1]	S Saudi Arabia	250,000	647,500
Sahara	N Africa	3,500,000	9,065,000
Simpson[2]	Central Australia	40,000	103,600
Sonoran	SW Arizona; SE California; NW Mexico	70,000	181,300
Syrian[1]	N Saudi Arabia; E Jordan; S Syria; W Iraq	100,000	259,000
Taklimakan	Xinjiang Uygur Autonomous Region, China	140,000	362,600
Thar (Great Indian)	NW India; Pakistan	100,000	259,000

1. Part of Great Arabian Desert. 2. Part of Great Australian Desert. 3. Part of Sahara Desert.

and occasional lush oases. But there are actually many kinds of deserts, because a desert is simply an area that receives little precipitation and has little plant cover. Thus polar areas can be considered deserts, for their precipitation is locked into ice and snow. So are places like the Taklimakan in China, which lies in a rain shadow on the leeward side of mountain ranges, and the Atacama, which is near cold ocean currents that cool the air and prevent the formation of rain clouds. But most deserts are found in the tropics, where giant high-pressure cells keep rain from forming. Some deserts are indeed flat and sandy, but others are solid rock, loose pebbles, or even mountain plateaus. One of the many fascinating characteristics of deserts is their strangely shaped rock formations, created by wind-whipped sand.

Altogether, arid lands cover about a fifth of the Earth's total land surface—a third if semi-arid areas are also included. About a billion people live in arid and semiarid areas, and more than 100 countries are facing problems associated with expanding deserts.

Uses of the desert Even the hot, sandy tropical deserts are not necessarily, as their name implies, deserted. Traders, herders, and farmers have called the desert home for thousands of years. Settlements have grown up around oases or in irrigated areas, from ancient times to the present. Deserts are important to historians, archaeologists, paleontologists, and other scientists, for the relics of the past that are preserved there. Dinosaur eggs have been found in the Gobi Desert, for instance, and whole cities are said to lie buried beneath the Taklimakan Desert.

Deserts are also important for extractive industries. The Negev was the site of the fabled King Solomon's mines. In the 19th century, borax was mined in Death Valley. Petroleum is found in the Sahara and in the deserts of the Arabian Peninsula. The Atacama is famed for its deposits of nitrate and copper. The Rub al-Khali, or Empty Quarter of Saudi Arabia, is thought to contain deposits of limestone and gravel—but no one is certain because it has never been fully explored.

Desert extremes
- The Sahara is the largest desert, with an area greater than the contiguous United States.
- The driest place on earth is in the Atacama Desert of Chile, where no rainfall at all was recorded between 1570 and 1971.
- The highest temperature ever recorded— 136°F (58°C)—was at Al-Aziziya, in the Libyan Desert, but the Dalol, Denakil Depression in Ethiopia is consistently the hottest place on

The World's Highest Mountain Peaks

Mountain peak	Range	Location	Height Feet	Meters
Everest	Himalayas	Nepal-China	29,028	8,848
K2 (Godwin Austen)	Karakoram	Kashmir	28,250	8,611
Kanchenjunga	Himalayas	Nepal-India	28,208	8,598
Lhotse I	Himalayas	Nepal-China	27,923	8,511
Makalu I	Himalayas	Nepal-China	27,824	8,481
Lhotse II	Himalayas	Nepal-China	27,560	8,400
Dhaulagiri	Himalayas	Nepal	26,810	8,172
Manaslu I	Himalayas	Nepal	26,760	8,156
Cho Oyu	Himalayas	Nepal-China	26,750	8,153
Nanga Parbat	Himalayas	Kashmir	26,660	8,126
Annapurna	Himalayas	Nepal	26,504	8,078
Gasherbrum	Karakoram	Kashmir	26,470	8,068
Broad	Karakoram	Kashmir	26,400	8,047
Gosainthan	Himalayas	China	26,287	8,012
Annapurna II	Himalayas	Nepal	26,041	7,937
Gyachung Kang	Himalayas	Nepal-China	25,910	7,897
Disteghil Sar	Himalayas	Kashmir	25,858	7,882
Himalchuli	Himalayas	Nepal	25,801	7,864
Nuptse	Himalayas	Nepal-China	25,726	7,841
Masherbrum	Karakoram	Kashmir	25,660	7,821
Nanda Devi	Himalayas	India	25,645	7,817
Rakaposhi	Karakoram	Kashmir	25,550	7,788
Kanjut Sar	Karakoram	Kashmir	25,461	7,761
Kamet	Himalayas	India-China	25,447	7,756
Namcha Barwa	Himalayas	China	25,445	7,756
Kua-la-man-ta-t'a (Gurla Mandhata)	Himalayas	China	25,355	7,728
Wu-lu-k'o-mu-shih (Ulugh Muztagh)	Kunlun	China	25,340	7,724
Kung-ko-erh (Kungur)	Mu-ssu-t'a-ko-a-t'e (Muztagh Ata)	China	25,325	7,719
Tirich Mir	Hindu Kush	Pakistan	25,230	7,690
Saser Kangri	Karakoram	Kashmir	25,172	7,672
Makalu II	Himalayas	Nepal-China	25,120	7,657
Minya Konka (Gonggashan)	Daxue Shan	China	24,900	7,590
Kula Kangri	Himalayas	Bhutan-China	24,784	7,554
Chang-tzu	Himalayas	Nepal-China	24,780	7,553
Mu-ssu-t'a-ko-a-t'e (Muztagh Ata)	Mu-ssu-t'a-ko-a-t'e (Muztagh Ata)	China	24,757	7,546
Skyang Kangri	Himalayas	Kashmir	24,750	7,544
Communism Peak	Pamirs	Tajikistan	24,590	7,495
Jongsong Peak	Himalayas	Nepal-India	24,472	7,459
Pobeda Peak	Tien Shan	Kyrgyzstan-China	24,406	7,439
Sia Kangri	Himalayas	Kashmir	24,350	7,422
Haramosh Peak	Karakoram	Kashmir	24,270	7,397
Istoro Nal	Hindu Kush	Pakistan	24,240	7,388
Tent Peak	Himalayas	Nepal-India	24,165	7,365
Chomo Lhari	Himalayas	Bhutan-China	24,040	7,327
Chamlang	Himalayas	Nepal	24,012	7,319
Kabru	Himalayas	Nepal-India	24,002	7,316
Alung Gangri	Himalayas	China	24,000	7,315
Baltoro Kangri	Himalayas	Kashmir	23,990	7,312
Muztagh Ata	Kunlun	China	23,890	7,282
Mana	Himalayas	India	23,860	7,273
Baruntse	Himalayas	Nepal	23,688	7,220
Nepal Peak	Himalayas	Nepal-India	23,500	7,163
Amne Machin	Kunlun	China	23,490	7,160
Gauri Sankar	Himalayas	Nepal-China	23,440	7,145
Badrinath	Himalayas	India	23,420	7,138
Nunkun	Himalayas	Kashmir	23,410	7,135
Lenin Peak	Pamirs	Tajikistan	23,405	7,134
Pyramid	Himalayas	Nepal-India	23,400	7,132

Mountain peak	Range	Location	Height	
			Feet	Meters
Api	Himalayas	Nepal	23,399	7,132
Pauhunri	Himalayas	India-China	23,385	7,128
Trisul	Himalayas	India	23,360	7,120
Korzhenevski Peak	Pamirs	Tajikistan	23,310	7,105
Kangto	Himalayas	India-China	23,260	7,090
Nyainqentanglha	Nyainqentanglha Shan	China	23,255	7,088
Trisuli	Himalayas	India	23,210	7,074
Dunagiri	Himalayas	India	23,184	7,066
Revolution Peak	Pamirs	Tajikistan	22,880	6,974
Aconcagua	Andes	Argentina	22,834	6,960
Ojos del Salado	Andes	Argentina-Chile	22,572	6,880
Bonete	Andes	Argentina	22,546	6,872
Tupungato	Andes	Argentina-Chile	22,310	6,800
Moscow Peak	Pamirs	Tajikistan	22,260	6,785
Pissis	Andes	Argentina	22,241	6,779
Mercedario	Andes	Argentina	22,211	6,770
Huascaran	Andes	Peru	22,205	6,768
Llullaillaco	Andes	Argentina-Chile	22,057	6,723
El Libertador	Andes	Argentina	22,047	6,720
Cachi	Andes	Argentina	22,047	6,720
Kailas	Himalayas	China	22,027	6,714
Incahuasi	Andes	Argentina-Chile	21,720	6,620
Yerupaja	Andes	Peru	21,709	6,617
Kurumda	Pamirs	Tajikistan	21,686	6,610
Galan	Andes	Argentina	21,654	6,600
El Muerto	Andes	Argentina-Chile	21,457	6,540
Sajama	Andes	Bolivia	21,391	6,520
Nacimiento	Andes	Argentina	21,302	6,493
Illimani	Andes	Bolivia	21,201	6,462
Coropuna	Andes	Peru	21,083	6,426
Laudo	Andes	Argentina	20,997	6,400
Ancohuma	Andes	Bolivia	20,958	6,388
Ausangate	Andes	Peru	20,945	6,384
Toro	Andes	Argentina-Chile	20,932	6,380
Illampu	Andes	Bolivia	20,873	6,362
Tres Cruces	Andes	Argentina-Chile	20,853	6,356
Huandoy	Andes	Peru	20,852	6,356
Parinacota	Andes	Bolivia-Chile	20,768	6,330
Tortolas	Andes	Argentina-Chile	20,745	6,323
Ampato	Andes	Peru	20,702	6,310
El Condor	Andes	Argentina	20,669	6,300
Salcantay	Andes	Peru	20,574	6,271
Chimborazo	Andes	Ecuador	20,561	6,267
Huancarhuas	Andes	Peru	20,531	6,258
Famatina[1]	Andes	Argentina	20,505	6,250
Pumasillo	Andes	Peru	20,492	6,246
Solo	Andes	Argentina	20,492	6,246
Polleras	Andes	Argentina	20,456	6,235
Pular	Andes	Chile	20,423	6,225
Chani	Andes	Argentina	20,341	6,200
McKinley	Alaska	U.S. (Alaska)	20,320	6,194
Aucanquilcha	Andes	Chile	20,295	6,186
Juncal	Andes	Argentina-Chile	20,276	6,180
Negro	Andes	Argentina	20,184	6,152
Quela	Andes	Argentina	20,128	6,135
Condoriri	Andes	Bolivia	20,095	6,125
Palermo	Andes	Argentina	20,079	6,120
Solimana	Andes	Peru	20,068	6,117
San Juan	Andes	Argentina-Chile	20,049	6,111
(Sierra) Nevada	Andes	Argentina-Chile	20,023	6,103
Antofalla	Andes	Argentina	20,013	6,100
Marmolejo	Andes	Argentina-Chile	20,013	6,100

1. Formerly General Manuel Belgrano.

Major Natural Lakes of the World

Lake	Surface area Sq. mi.	Sq. km.	Location	Maximum depth Feet	Meters	Elevation Feet	Meters
Caspian Sea[1]	143,240	370,992	Russia, Kazakhstan, Azerbaijan, Turkmenistan, Iran	3,363	1,025	-92	-28
Superior	31,700	82,103	Ontario, Canada; Mich., Wis., Minn.	1,333	406	600	183
Victoria	26,820	69,464	Uganda, Kenya, Tanzania	279	85	3,720	1,134
Aral Sea[1]	24,904	64,501	Uzbekistan, Kazakhstan	220	67	174	53
Huron	23,000	59,570	Ontario, Can.; Mich.	750	229	576	176
Michigan	22,300	57,757	Mich., Ind., Ill., Wis.	923	281	579	176
Tanganyika	12,350	31,987	Burundi, Tanzania, Zambia, Zaire	4,800	1,463	2,543	775
Baikal	12,160	31,494	Russia	5,315	1,620	1,493	455
Great Bear	12,028	31,153	Northwest Terr., Canada	1,356	413	512	156
Nyasa (Malawi)	11,150	28,879	Tanzania, Mozambique, Malawi	2,280	695	1,550	472
Great Slave	11,030	28,568	Northwest Terr., Canada	2,015	614	513	156
Erie	9,910	25,667	Ontario, Canada; N.Y., Pa., Ohio, Mich.	210	64	570	174
Winnipeg	9,417	24,390	Manitoba, Canada	92	28	713	217
Ontario	7,540	19,529	Ontario, Canada; N.Y.	802	244	245	75
Balkhash[1]	7,115[2]	18,428[2]	Kazakhstan	87	27	1,115	340
Ladoga	6,835	17,703	Russia	755	230	13	4
Chad	6,300	16,317	Chad, Nigeria, Niger	24	7	787	240
Maracaibo[3]	5,200	13,468	Venezuela	197	60	sea level	
Patos[3]	3,920	10,153	Brazil	15	5	([4])	([4])
Onega	3,720	9,635	Russia	394	120	108	33
Titicaca	3,200	8,288	Bolivia, Peru	990	302	12,500	3,810
Nicaragua	3,150	8,159	Nicaragua	230	70	102	31
Mai-Ndombe	3,100	8,029[2]	Zaire	36	11	1,116	340
Athabasca	3,064	7,936	Saskatchewan, Alberta, Canada	407	124	700	213
Eyre[1]	2,970[2]	7,692[2]	Australia	4	1	-52	-16
Reindeer	2,568	6,651	Saskatchewan, Manitoba, Canada	720	219	1,106	337
Tonle Sap	2,500[2]	6,475[2]	Cambodia	39	12	([4])	([4])
Rudolf[1]	2,473	6,405	Kenya, Ethiopia	720	219	1,230	375
Issyk-Kul[1]	2,355	6,099	Kyrghyzstan	2,303	702	5,279	1,609
Torrens[1]	2,230[2]	5,776[2]	Australia	0.5	0.2	92	28
Albert	2,160	5,594	Uganda, Zaire	168	51	2,030	619
Vanern	2,156	5,54	Sweden	325	99	144	44
Nettilling	2,140	5,543	Baffin Island, Canada	([4])	([4])	95	29
Winnipegosis	2,075	5,374	Manitoba, Canada	39	12	830	253
Bangweulu	1,930	4,999	Zambia	5	2	3,500	1,067
Nipigon	1,872	4,848	Ontario, Canada	541	165	1,050	320
Gairdner[1]	1,840[2]	4,763[2]	Australia	0.5	0.2	112	34
Urmia[1]	1,815[2]	4,701[2]	Iran	49	15	4,180	1,274
Manitoba	1,800	4,662	Manitoba, Canada	92	28	813	248
Kyoga	1,710	4,429	Uganda	26	8	4	4
Khanka	1,700	4,403	China, Russia	33	10	4	4
Lake of the Woods	1,695	4,390	Ontario, Manitoba, Canada; Minn.	55	17	1,060	323
Great Salt[1]	1,680	4,351	Utah	48	15	4,200	1,280
Mweru	1,680	4,351	Zambia, Zaire	10	3	3,008	917
Peipus	1,660	4,299	Estonia, Russia	41	12	98	30
Koko Nor (Tsing Hai)	1,650	4,274	China	125	38	10,515	3,205
Dubawnt	1,600	4,144	Northwest Terr., Canada	([4])	([4])	774	236
Tung-t'ing Hu	1,430[2]	3,704[2]	China	([4])	([4])	36	11
Van Golu[1]	1,420	3,678	Turkey	82	25	5,643	1,720
Tana	1,390	3,600	Ethiopia	30	9	6,003	1,830

1. Saltwater. A lake is a body of water surrounded by land. The Caspian Sea is thus a lake. It was called a sea by the Romans because of its salty water. **2.** Subject to large seasonal variation in surface area. **3.** Lagoon. **4.** No information available.   **Source:** U.S. Department of Commerce, National Oceanic and Atmospheric Administration, *Principal Rivers and Lakes of the World* (1982).

Major Rivers of the World, by Length

River	Length		Source	Outflow
	Miles	Km		
Nile	4,145	6,673	Tributaries of Lake Victoria, E. Africa	Mediterranean Sea
Amazon	4,000	6,440	Andes Mts., Peru	Atlantic Ocean
Mississippi-Missouri	3,740[1]	6,021[1]	Confluence of Jefferson, Madison, and Galatin R., Montana	Gulf of Mexico
Changjiang (Yangtze)	3,720	5,989	Kunlun Mts., China	China Sea
Yenisei-Angara	3,650[2]	5,877[2]	Lake Baikal, Russia	Kara Sea (Arctic Ocean)
Amur-Argun	3,590[2]	5,780[2]	Khingan Mts., China	Tatar Strait
Ob-Irtysh	3,360[2]	5,410[2]	Altai Mts., China	Gulf of Ob (Arctic Ocean)
Plata-Parana	3,030[2]	4,878[2]	Confluence of the Paranaiba and Grande rivers, Brazil	Atlantic Ocean
Huang He (Yellow)	2,903	4,674	Kunlun Mts., China	Gulf of Chihli (Yellow Sea)
Congo (Zaire)	2,900	4,669	Confluence of the Luapula and Lualaba rivers, Zaire	Atlantic Ocean
Lena	2,730	4,395	Baikal Mts., Russia	Laptev Sea (Arctic Ocean)
MacKenzie	2,635[2]	4,242[2]	Headwaters of Finlay Rivers, British Columbia, Canada	Beaufort Sea (Arctic Ocean)
Mekong	2,600	4,186	T'ang-ku-la Mts., Tibet	South China Sea
Niger	2,600	4,186	Guinea	Gulf of Guinea
Missouri	2,315	3,725	Confluence of Jefferson, Madison, and Montana Galatin rivers, Montana	Mississippi River
Mississippi	2,348[3]	3,780[3]	Lake Itasca, northwestern Minnesota	Gulf of Mexico
Murray-Darling	2,330	3,751	Great Dividing Range, Australia	Indian Ocean
Volga	2,290	3,687	Valdai Hills, Russia	Caspian Sea
Madeira	2,013	3,241	Confluence of the Mamore and Beni rivers, Bolivia/Brazil	Amazon River
Sao Francisco	1,988	3,201	Minas Gerais State, Brazil	Atlantic Ocean
Yukon	1,979	3,186	Confluence of Lewes and Pelly rivers, Yukon Territory, Canada	Bering Sea
Rio Grande	1,885	3,035	San Juan Mts., southwestern Colorado	Gulf of Mexico
Purus	1,860	2,995	Andes Mts., Peru	Amazon River
Tunguska, Lower	1,860	2,995	North of Lake Baikal, Russia	Yenesei River
Indus	1,800	2,898	Himalayas, Tibet	Arabian Sea
Danube	1,776	2,859	Confluence of Breg and Brigach rivers, Germany	Black Sea
Brahmaputra	1,770	2,850	Himalayas, Tibet	Ganges River
Salween	1,750	2,818	Tibetan Plateau, Tibet	Bay of Bengal
Para-Tocantins	1,710[2]	2,753[2]	Goias State, Brazil	Atlantic Ocean
Zambezi	1,700	2,737	Northwestern Zambia	Mozambique Channel
Paraguay	1,610	2,592	Mato Grosso State, Brazil	Parana River
Kolyma	1,320	2,130	Kolyma Mts., Russia	Arctic Ocean
Nelson-Saskatchewan	1,600	2,576	Rocky Mts., Canada	Hudson Bay
Orinoco	1,600	2,576	Sierra Parima Mts., Venezuela	Atlantic Ocean
Amu Darya	1,578	2,541	Pamir Mts., Uzbekistan/Turkmenistan	Aral Sea
Ural	1,575	2,536	Ural Mountains, Russia	Caspian Sea
Ganges	1,560	2,512	Himalayas, India	Bay of Bengal
Euphrates	1,510	2,431	Confluence of the Murat Nehri and Kara Su rivers, Turkey	Shatt-al-Arab
Arkansas	1,450	2,335	Central Colorado	Mississippi River
Colorado	1,450	2,335	Northern Colorado	Gulf of California
Dneiper	1,420	2,286	Valdai Hills, Russia	Black Sea
Atchafalaya-Red	1,400	2,254	Eastern New Mexico	Gulf of Mexico
Syr Darya	1,370	2,206	Tien Shan, China/Kyrghzstan	Aral Sea
Kasai	1,338	2,154	Central Angola	Congo (Zaire) River
Irrawaddy	1,300	2,093	Confluence of Mali and Nmai rivers, Myanmar	Bay of Bengal
Ohio-Allegheny	1,300	2,093	Pennsylvania	Mississippi River
Orange	1,300	2,093	Lesotho	Atlantic Ocean
Columbia	1,243	2,001	Columbia Lake, British Columbia, Canada	Pacific Ocean
Tigris	1,180	1,900	Eastern Turkey	Shatt-al-Arab
Rhine	820	1,320	Confluence of Hinterrhein and Vorderrhein rivers, Switzerland	North Sea
St. Lawrence	800	1,288	Lake Ontario	Gulf of St. Lawrence

Notes: 1. From the mouth of the Mississippi, up the Missouri to the Red Rock River in Montana. 2. Includes the length of tributaries that are part of the main trunk stream. 3. From the mouth of the Mississippi, up to its source in Minnesota. Source: U.S. Dept. of Commerce, National Oceanic and Atmospheric Administration, *Principal Rivers and Lakes of the World* (1982).

World's 25 Largest Capacity Reservoirs

	Capacity (mil.)			
Rank, Reservoir	Cubic yards[1]	Cubic meters[1]	River or basin and location	Year completed
1. Owen Falls[2]	3,537,000	2,700,000	Lake Victoria/Nile, Uganda	1954
2. Kariba	236,586	180,600	Zambezi, Zimbabwe/Zambia	1959
3. Bratsk	221,744	169,270	Angara, Russia	1964
4. Aswan High	211,765	162,000	Nile, Egypt	1970
5. Akosombo	196,078	150,000	Volta, Ghana	1965
6. Daniel Johnson	185,826	141,852	Manicouagan, Quebec	1968
7. Guri	176,470	135,000	Caroni, Venezuela	1986
8. Krasnoyarsk	96,023	73,300	Yenesei, Russia	1967
9. W.A.C. Bennett	92,105	70,309	Peace, British Columbia	1967
10. Zeya	89,604	68,400	Zeya, Russia	1978
11. Cabora Bassa	82,530	63,000	Zambezi, Mozambique	1974
12. La Grande 2	80,847	61,715	La Grande, Quebec	1978
13. La Grande 3	78,626	60,020	La Grande, Quebec	1981
14. Ust-Ilim	77,683	59,300	Angara, Russia	1977
15. Boguchany	76,242	58,200	Angara, Russia	1989
16. Volga-V.I. Lenin (Kuibyshev)	75,980	58,000	Volga, Russia	1955
17. Caniapiscau	70,478	53,800	Caniapiscau, Quebec, Canada	1981
18. Bukhtarma	65,238	49,800	Irtysh, Russia	1960
19. Atatürk	63,797	48,700	Euphrates, Turkey	1990
20. Irkutsk	60,260	46,000	Angara, Russia	1956
21. Tucurul	64,753	49,536	Tocantins, Brazil	1984
22. Lower Kama	58,858	45,000	Kama, Russia	1987
23. Vilyui	47,029	35,900	Vilyui, Russia	1967
24. Sanmenxia	46,374	35,400	Huanghe (Yellow River), China	1960
25. Wuluwati	45,359	34,700	Kalakashi, China	1999

Note: Uncompleted reservoirs are not officially ranked. 1. One cubic yard equals 0.765 cubic meters. 2. Capacity includes Lake Victoria, a large natural lake. Source: International Committee on Large Dams (1998).

World's 25 Largest Volume Dams

	Volume ('000s)			
Rank, Reservoir	Cubic yards[1]	Cubic meters[1]	River or basin and location	Year completed
1. New Cornelia Tailings	274,026	209,500	Ten Mile Wash, Arizona	1973
2. Tarbela	159,210	121,720	Indus, Pakistan	1976
3. Fort Peck	125,628	96,049	Missouri, Montana	1937
4. Lower Usuma	121,644	93,000	Usuma, Nigeria	1990
5. Atatürk	110,522	84,500	Euphrates, Turkey	1990
6. Yacyreta-Apipe	105,944	81,000	Corrientes Province, Argentina	1998
7. Guri (Raul Leoni)	102,014	78,000	Caroni, Venezuela	1986
8. Rogun	98,750	75,500	Vakhsh River, Tajikistan	1985
9. Oahe	92,000	70,339	Missouri, South Dakota	1958
10. Mangla	85,872	65,651	Jhelum, Pakistan	1967
11. Gardiner	85,592	65,440	South Saskatchewan, Saskatchewan	1968
12. Afsluitdijk	82,927	63,400	Zuider Zee, Netherlands	1932
13. Oroville	78,008	59,639	Feather, California	1968
14. San Luis	77,770	59,405	San Luis, California	1967
15. Nurek	75,861	58,000	Vakhsh, Tajikistan	1980
16. Garrison	66,500	50,843	Missouri, North Dakota	1956
17. Cochiti	62,850	48,052	Grande, New Mexico	1975
18. Tabqua (Thawra)	60,168	46,000	Euphrates, Syria	1976
19. W.A.C. Bennett	57,201	43,733	Peace, Canada	1967
20. Tucurui	56,242	43,000	Tocantins, Brazil	1984
20. Aswan, High	56,242	43,000	Nile, Egypt	1970
22. Kiev	56,034	42,841	Dnieper, Ukraine	1964
23. Dantiwada	53,680	41,040	Banas, India	1965
24. Saratov	52,843	40,400	Volga, Russia	1967
25. Mission Tailings 2	52,435	40,088	Twin Buttes, Arizona	1973

Note: Volume refers to amount of material (earth, concrete, etc.) used in construction of dam. Tailings dams are formed from waste ore (tailings) from mining. Uncompleted reservoirs are not officially ranked. 1. One cubic meter equals 1.31 cubic yards.
Source: Department of the Interior, Bureau of Reclamation.

Earth, with an annual average temperature of 93°F (34 °C)
- The lowest point in the world—1,339 feet (408 m) below sea level—is on the shores of the Dead Sea in the Negev Desert.
- The lowest point in the Western Hemisphere—282 feet (86 meters) below sea level—is in Death Valley, California.

▶MAJOR ISLANDS AND ISLAND GROUPS

Admiralty Is.: see *Bismarck Archipelago*.

Åland Is. (Ahvenanmaa): 60°N, 20°E. Finnish archipelago of more than 6,000 islands between Finland and Sweden.

Aleutian Is.: 51°-55°N, 163°W-166°E. Chain between Pacific Ocean and Bering Sea stretching 2,700 km: Unimak, Fox Is., Andreanof Is., Rat Is. and Near Is. (Alaska) and Komandorskiye Ostrova (Russia).

Andaman and Nicobar Is.: 12°N, 93°E. Union Territory of India comprising some 300 islands in two major archipelagos stretching 725 km north-south in the Bay of Bengal off the coast of Myanmar.

Anglesey: 53°N, 4°W. Irish Sea island off Wales.

Anticosti: 50°N, 63°W. Canadian island in Gulf of St. Lawrence.

Antigua and Barbuda: 17°N, 62°W. Two-island Caribbean country.

Antilles. Name for the Caribbean islands from Cuba to Trinidad and Tobago, but not including the Bahamas. *Greater Antilles:* Cuba, Jamaica, Hispaniola, and Puerto Rico. *Lesser Antilles:* Leeward Is. Virgin Is., Antigua and Barbuda, and Dominica. *Windward Is.:* Martinique, St. Lucia, St. Vincent, Grenada, Barbados, Trinidad and Tobago, and Aruba.

Aran Is.: 53°N, 10°W. Three islands—Inishmore, Inishmaan and Inisheer—off western Ireland.

Aruba: 12°N, 70°W. Dutch Caribbean island 30 km N of Venezuela.

Ascension: 7°S, 14°W. Island of the British Crown Colony of St. Helena about 1,100 km northwest of St. Helena, 2,250 km east of Brazil and 2,500 km west of Africa

Auckland Is.: 51°S, 166°E. Group about 300 km south of New Zealand.

Azores/Açores: 37°-40°N, 25°-31°W. Portuguese Atlantic group 1,400 km west of Portugal: Faial, Flores, São Miguel; first settled in 1430s.

Baffin: 68°N, 70°W. Largest Canadian Arctic island, on Davis Strait opposite Greenland.

Bahamas: 21°-27°N, 71°-79°W. Chain of 2,700 islands and cays stretching 800 km southeast of Florida; shared by Bahamas, Turks, Caicos (British); Columbus's first American landfall in 1492.

Bahrain: Persian Gulf island 25 km off coast of Saudi Arabia; probable site of ancient Dilmun.

Balearic Is.: 39°N, 3°E. Sixteen Spanish Mediterranean islands: incl. Majorca, Minorca and Ibiza.

Bali: 9°S, 115°E. Predominantly Hindu Indonesian island east of Java.

Banks: 73°N, 121°W. Westernmost large Canadian Arctic island, on Beaufort Sea.

Bear: see *Spitsbergen*.

Barbados: 13°N, 60°W. Island nation about 150 km east of southern Antilles.

Bermuda: 32°N, 65°W. British dependency of 138 coral islands, 20 inhabited, 900 km east of North Carolina.

Bikini: see *Marshall Is.*

Bismarck Archipelago: 5°S, 150°E. Papua New Guinea archipelago: Admiralty Is., New Britain and New Ireland; formerly a German colony.

Block: 41°N, 72°W. Island between Long Island Sound and Atlantic Ocean, 15 km off Rhode Island.

Borneo: 0°N/S, 114°E. Large equatorial Southeast Asian island shared by Indonesia, Malaya and Brunei.

British Isles: Group off Northwest Europe: Great Britain, Ireland, Man, Wight, Hebrides, Shetlands, Orkneys and Anglesey.

Canary Is.: 28°N, 16°W. Spanish archipelago of seven islands 100 km west of Morocco: incl. Tenerife, Gomera, Gran Canaria, Fuertaventura, Lanzarote. Inhabited since antiquity (Latin: *Fortunatae Insulae*); colonized by the Spanish in 1400s.

Cape Verde Is.: 15°-17°N, 23°-25°W. Ten-island nation 500 km west of Senegal: incl. São Tiago, Fogo. Settled by Portuguese in 15th century.

Capri: 41°N, 14°E. Italian island in Bay of Naples.

Caroline Is.: 5°-10°N, 130°-166°E. Micronesian group of more than 600 islands: Belau (Palau), Kusaie, Ponape, Satawal, Truk and Yap.

Cayman Is.: 20°N, 81°W. British dependency of 3 main islands 240 km south of Cuba.

Chagos Archipelago: 6°S, 72°E. Part of the British Indian Ocean Territory 600 km south of the Maldives. Diego Garcia has been a U.K./U.S. military base since the 1970's when its 1,500 inhabitants—the descendents of slaves—were deported.

Channel/Santa Barbara Is.: 34°N, 120°W. Eight-island group off Los Angeles.

Channel Is.: 49°N, 2°W. Group in English Channel near France: Jersey, Guernsey, Alderney and Sark. They are dependent territories of the English Crown, as successor to William the Conqueror, Duke of Normandy, but not part of the U.K.

Chatham Is.: 44°S, 176°W. Polynesian group 860 km east of New Zealand from where they were settled around 1500.

Chincha Is.: 14°S, 76°W. Group of three Peruvian islands; important source of guano before synthetic fertilizers.

Christmas: 10°S, 106°E. Australian dependency 360 km south of Java.

Cocos/Keeling Is.: 12°S, 97°E. Australian archipelago of 27 coral atolls 2,800 km northwest of Perth, settled in 19th century.

Comoros: 12°S, 44°E. Indian Ocean nation of three islands about 325 km east of Mozambique.

Cook Is.: 8°-23°S, 156°-167°W. Group of 15 islands 3,200 km northeast of New Zealand: Rarotonga.

Corsica: 42°N, 9°E. French Mediterranean island; birthplace of Napoleon Bonaparte.

Crete: 41°N, 97°E.

Cuba: 21°N, 80°W. Northernmost Caribbean island, 1,250 km east-west; largest of 1,200 islands in Cuban archipelago.

Cyclades/Kikládhes: 37°N, 25°E. Greek Aegean archipelago of about 220 islands; so-called because they encircle sacred island of Delos.

Cyprus: 35°N, 33°E.

Delos: see *Cyclades*.

Devil's: 5°N, 52°W. Island off French Guiana; used as penal colony until 1938.

Diego Garcia: see *Chagos Archipelago*.

Dodecanese/Sporádhes: 36°N, 27°E. Greek Aegean archipelago of 12 islands, including Samos, Kos and Ródhos.

Dominica: 16°N, 61°W. Caribbean island nation.

The World's Largest Islands

Island	Location	Flags	Area	
			Sq. mi.	Sq. km.
Greenland	N. Atlantic Ocean	Denmark	840,000	2,175,600
New Guinea	S. Pacific Ocean	Indonesia, Papua New Guinea	306,000	792,540
Borneo	Pacific Ocean	Indonesia, Malaysia, Brunei	280,100	725,459
Madagascar	Indian Ocean	Madagascar	226,658	587,044
Baffin	Arctic Ocean	Canada	195,928	507,454
Sumatra	Indian Ocean	Indonesia	165,000	427,350
Honshu	N. Pacific Ocean	Japan	87,805	227,415
Great Britain	N. Atlantic Ocean	United Kingdom	84,200	218,078
Victoria	Arctic Ocean	Canada	83,896	217,291
Ellesmere	Arctic Ocean	Canada	75,767	196,237
Celebes	Pacific Ocean	Indonesia	69,000	178,710
South Island	S. Pacific Ocean	New Zealand	58,305	151,010
Java	S. Pacific Ocean	Indonesia	48,900	126,651
Cuba	Caribbean Sea	Cuba	44,218	114,525
North Island	S. Pacific Ocean	New Zealand	44,035	114,051
Newfoundland	N. Atlantic Ocean	Canada	42,030	108,858
Luzon	N. Pacific Ocean	Philippines	40,880	105,879
Iceland	N. Atlantic Ocean	Iceland	39,769	103,002
Mindanao	N. Pacific Ocean	Philippines	36,775	95,247
Novaya Zemlya	Arctic Ocean	Russia	35,000	90,650
Ireland	N. Atlantic Ocean	Irish Republic, United Kingdom	32,599	84,431
Hokkaido	N. Pacific Ocean	Japan	30,144	78,073
Hispaniola	Caribbean Sea	Haiti, Dominican Republic	29,530	76,483
Sakhalin	N. Pacific Ocean	Russia	29,500	76,405
Banks	Arctic Ocean	Canada	27,033	70,015
Tasmania	S. Pacific Ocean	Australia	26,178	67,801
Sri Lanka	Indian Ocean	Sri Lanka	25,332	65,610
Devon	Arctic Ocean	Canada	21,331	55,247

Easter Island/Isla de Pascua/Rapa Nui: 27°07'S, 109°22'W. The most remote island on Earth, Rapa Nui is the eastern tip of Polynesia, about 3,700 km west of Chile, which administers it, and 1,600 km east of Pitcairn Island. Settled by Marquesans around the fourth century, it is famous for its thousand carved statues, some 10 meters tall.

Elba: 43°N, 10°E. Italian island where Napoleon was briefly exiled.

Ellesmere Island, Nunavut Territory: 79°N, 82°W. Cape Columbia (83°08'N) is the northernmost point in Canada; part of Queen Elizabeth group.

Faeroe Is.: 62°N, 7°W. Group of 18 islands about 118 km north-south, 320 km north of the Shetlands and halfway between Norway and Iceland; settled in 7th century they are an autonomous part of Denmark.

Falkland Is./Islas Malvinas: 51°-53°S, 57°-62°W. British Crown Colony of 340 islands about 600 km east of Argentina. Claimed by French sailors from St. Mâlo (hence Malvinas), contested by Spanish, settled by English. An Argentine invasion in 1982 failed.

Faylakah: 29°N, 48°E. Persian Gulf island off Kuwait.

Fernando de Noronha: 4°S, 32°W. Atlantic island about 500 km east of Brazil.

Fernando Po: 3°S, 9°E. Former name for Bioko, Equatorial Guinea.

Fiji Is.: 16°-19°S, 178°W-177°E. Pacific nation of about 330 islands, a third inhabited, about 1,770 km north of New Zealand.

Florida Keys: 24°-25°N, 80°-82°W. Chain of coral islands running 240 km west from tip of Florida: Key Largo, Islamorada, Key West and Dry Tortugas.

Frisian Is.: 53°-55°N, 5°-8°E. Chain of North Sea islands, 18 inhabited, off The Netherlands, Germany, and Denmark: Rømø, Sylt, Terschelling, Vlieland and Texel.

Galápagos: 1°S, 91°W. Archipelago of 60 volcanic islands about 430 km across and 1,000 km west of Ecuador; known for its diverse flora and fauna and Charles Darwin's research there in 1835.

Gotland: 57°N, 18°E. Swedish Baltic island, thought to be the homeland of the Goths.

Great Britain: 54°N, 3°W. Principal island of British Isles; includes England, Scotland and Wales.

Greenland: 70°N, 40°W. Large North Atlantic island, settled about 2500 B.C.; first visited by Europeans around 1000.

Guadalcanal: see *Solomon Is.*

Guam: see *Mariana Is.*

Guernsey: see *Channel Is.*

Hainan: 19°N, 109°E. Chinese island between South China Sea and Gulf of Tonkin.

Hawaiian Is.: 19°-28°N, 155°-178°W. Polynesian chain comprising eight large and 124 smaller islands stretching 2,400 km from Hawaii to Midway and Kure. Settled in 8th century from the Marquesas. U.S. state: Hawaii, Maui, Lauai, Molokai, Oahu, Kaui and Nihau.

Hebrides/Western Isles: 57°N, 7°W. Islands off the west coast of Scotland. Inner Hebrides: Skye, Mull and Islay; 210-km-long Outer Hebrides: Lewis, North Uist and South Uist.

Hispaniola: 19°N, 71°W. Caribbean island divided between Haiti and Dominican Republic.

Hokkaido: 43°N, 143°E. Northernmost of main Japanese islands.

Hong Kong: 22°N, 114°E. Chinese island at mouth of Pearl River, 145 km southeast of Guangzhou (Canton).

Honshu: 36°N, 136°E. Largest of main Japanese islands; cities include Tokyo.

Ibiza: see *Balearic Is.*

Iceland: 65°N, 18°W. North Atlantic island 900 km west of Norway, settled in 9th century.

Indonesia: From the Greek meaning Indian islands, the name applies to the archipelagic nation of 18,108 islands: Sumatra, Java, Sulawesi, Bali, Malaku Is., and parts of Borneo, Timor and New Guinea.

Ionian Is.: 39°N, 21°E. Greek Adriatic archipelago of seven islands: Kerkira (Corfu), Kefallinia, Zákinthos and Odysseus's Itháki.

Ireland: 53°N, 8°W. Second largest island in British Isles; divided between Republic of Ireland and Northern Ireland (which is still part of the U.K.).

Iwo Jima: see *Volcano Is.*

Jamaica: 18°N, 75°W. Caribbean island nation about 175 km south of Cuba.

Jan Mayen: 71°N, 8°W. Norwegian island 400 km east of Greenland.

Japanese islands: see *Hokkaido, Honshu, Kyushu, Shikoku, Ryukyu Is., Tsushima* and *Volcano Is.*

Java: 7°S, 110°E. Indonesian island east of Sumatra.

Jersey: see *Channel Is.*

Juan Fernandez Is.: 33°S, 80°W. Three-island group 650 km west of Chile. Alexander Selkirk, model for Daniel Defoe's Robinson Crusoe, was marooned on Más a Tierra 1705–09.

Kerguelen/Desolation Is.: 49°-50°S, 69°-71°E. French Indian Ocean territory of 300 islands and islets, including Crozet Is., about 4,500 km southeast of South Africa.

Komandorskiye Ostrova: 55°N, 167°E. Russian group at western tip of Aleutians.

Krakatoa: 6°S, 105°E. Volcanic Indonesian island west of Java.

Kuril Is.: 44°-51°N, 146°-155°E. Chain of some 56 islands stretching about 1,200 km between Japan and Russia.

Kyushu: 33°N, 131°E. Southernmost of main Japanese islands.

Lakshadweep/Laccadive Is.: 8°-12°N, 71°-74°E. Indian archipelago of 12 atolls, 250 km west of India.

Leeward Is.: see *Antilles.*

Line Is.: 6°N-11°S, 162°-152°W. Group of islands straddling the Equator (Line) south of Hawaii and belonging variously to the U.S., Great Britain and Kiribati.

Lofoten Is.: 69°N, 15°E. Northern Norwegian archipelago.

Long Island: 41°N, 73°W. New York island, 190 km long, between Atlantic Ocean and Long Island Sound.

Luzon: see *Philippines.*

Madagascar: 20°S, 47°E. Indian Ocean island, about 400 km east of Mozambique.

Madeira: 33°N, 17°W. Portuguese Atlantic archipelago of four main islands about 500 km west of Morocco: incl. Madeira, Porto Santo; discovered in 15th century.

Madeleine, Iles de la: 47°N, 61°W. Canadian group in Gulf of St. Lawrence.

Majorca: see *Balearic Is.*

Maldive Is.: 7°N-1°S, 73°E. Country of 26 archipelagos stretching 823 km north-south about 670 km

southwest of Sri Lanka; about 750 km southwest of India.

Malta: 36°N, 14°E. Strategic island nation in central Mediterranean south of Sicily.

Maluku (Moluccas)/Spice Is.: 2°N-8°S, 124°-131°E: Indonesian archipelago; in the 16th century, sole source of cloves, nutmeg and mace, and a major goal of European merchants.

Man, Isle of: 54°N, 4°W. Irish Sea crown dependency of Great Britain.

Manhattan: 41°N, 74°W. New York island between the Hudson River and Long Island Sound.

Manitoulin: 46°N, 83°W. Canadian island in Lake Huron.

Mariana Is.: 13°-20°N, 146°E. Micronesian archipelago 2,400 km east of the Philippines comprising Commonwealth of the Northern Mariana Is. (Saipan, 15°N, 146°E), and Guam (13°N, 144°E).

Marquesas Is.: 7°-10°S, 138°-141°W. French Polynesian archipelago of 12 islands about 1,200 km northeast of Tahiti.

Marshall Is.: 5°-15°N, 161°-172°E. Micronesian group of 34 atolls and islands including Ratak and Ralik chains. Bikini was a nuclear test site in the 1940-50s.

Martha's Vineyard: 41°N, 71°W. Massachusetts island south of Cape Cod.

Martinique: 15°N, 61°W. French Caribbean island.

Matsu (26°N, 120°E) and **Quemoy** (24°N, 118°E): Chinese coastal islands about 250 km apart; administered and garrisoned by Taiwan since 1950.

Mauritius: 20°S, 58°E. Indian Ocean island 800 km east of Madagascar. Part of Mascarene Archipelago, with Réunion.

Melanesia: From the Greek meaning black islands; Pacific islands south of Micronesia and west of Polynesia—including New Guinea, the Solomons, New Hebrides and Fiji.

Micronesia: From the Greek meaning small islands; Pacific islands north of the Equator between Hawaii and the Philippines.

Midway: 28°N, 177°W.

Mindanao: see *Philippines.*

Nantucket, Massachusetts: 41°N, 70°W. Massachusetts island south of Cape Cod. Major 19th-century whaling port.

Nauru: 1°S, 167°E. Island nation 2,300 km northeast of Sydney, Australia.

New Caledonia: 18°-22°S, 163-168°E. Pacific island that forms, with Loyalty Is., French overseas territory.

New Guinea: 5°S, 140°E. Largest island in Melanesia, shared by Indonesia and Papua New Guinea.

Newfoundland: 48°N, 56°W. Large Canadian Atlantic island south of Labrador.

Novaya Zemlya: 74°N, 57°E. New Land; Russian archipelago comprising two main islands, 960 km long, between Barents and Kara Seas.

Novosibirskiye Ostrova: 75°N, 142°E. New Siberian Is.; Russian group between Laptev and East Siberian Seas.

Okinawa: see *Ryukyu Is.*

Orkney Is.: 59°N, 3°W. Group of more than 20 islands, 85 km north-south, 10 km north of Scotland.

Outer Banks, North Carolina: 35°N, 76°W. Barrier islands—Roanoke, Pea, Bodie, Hatteras, Ocracoke and Portsmouth—stretching 145 km north-south off North Carolina between the Atlantic Ocean and Albemarle and Pamlico Sounds.

Ouessant, Ile d' (Ushant): 48°N, 5°W. Atlantic island off northwest France at entrance to English Channel.

Paracel Is.: 17°N, 112°E. South China Sea group about 400 km east of Vietnam; also claimed by China and Taiwan.

Philippines: Southeast Asian nation of more than 7,000 islands: Luzon, Samar, Palawan, Mindanao, Sulu Archipelago, Zamboanga.

Pitcairn: 25°S, 130°W. British colony (with Ducie, Henderson and Oeno Is.) halfway between Tahiti and Easter Island. HMS *Bounty* mutineers arrived in 1790.

Polynesia: From the Greek meaning many islands; Pacific islands within a triangle drawn between Hawaii, New Zealand and Easter Island.

Pribilof Is.: 57°N, 170°W. Alaskan Bering Sea group.

Prince Edward: 46°N, 63°W. Canadian island province in Gulf of St. Lawrence and connected to Nova Scotia by bridge.

Puerto Rico: 18°N, 66°W. Easternmost and fourth largest of Greater Antilles.

Qeshm: 26°N, 56°E. Iranian island in Strait of Hormuz at the mouth of the Persian Gulf.

Queen Charlotte Is.: 51°N, 129°W. Canadian group off British Columbia.

Queen Elizabeth Is.: 74°-82°N, 60°-125°W. Northernmost Canadian Arctic archipelago: Ellesmere Is., Parry Group and Sverdrup Group.

Quemoy: see *Matsu and Quemoy.*

Réunion: 21°S, 56°E. French Indian Ocean island 690 km east of Madagsacar; part of Mascarene Archipelago, with Mauritius.

Ryukyu Is.: 24°-31°N, 123°-131°E. Japanese chain stretching 1,000 km between Taiwan and Kyushu. Okinawa was a major World War II battleground.

Saipan: see *Mariana Is.*

St. Helena: 15°S, 6°W. British Atlantic island where Napoleon was exiled and died.

St. Lawrence Is.: 64°N, 171°W. Alaskan Bering Sea island south of Bering Strait.

St. Lucia: 14°N, 61°W. Second largest of Windward Is.

St. Pierre & Miquelon: 47°N, 56°W. French Atlantic islands southwest of Newfoundland, Canada.

Sakhalin: 51°N, 143°E. Russian island, 950 km long, between Sea of Japan and Sea of Okhostk.

Samoa Is.: 13°-14°S, 168°-173°W. Pacific group divided between Western Samoa and American Samoa.

Sandwich Islands: Former name of the Hawaiian Islands.

Sardinia: 40°N, 9°E. Italian island in western Mediterranean.

Severnaya Zemlya: 80°N, 98°E. Russian group (four main islands) discovered in 1913, between Kara and Laptev Seas.

Seychelles: 4°-5°S, 56°E. Indian Ocean republic of 115 islands extending 1,200 km northeast-southwest about 1,600 km east of Kenya.

Shetland Is.: 61°N, 1°W. British group of about 100 islands 80 km northeast of the Orkneys.

Shikoku: 33°N, 133°E. Smallest of four main Japanese islands.

Sicily: 37°N, 14°E. Italian island in central Mediterranean.

Singapore: 1°N, 104°E. Island nation off tip of Malay Peninsula at east end of Strait of Malacca.

Skye: see *Hebrides/Western Isles.*

Society Is.: 16°-18°S, 148°-154°W. French Polynesian archipelago, 750-km long, including Tahiti; settled around 500 B.C.

Socotra: 13°N, 54°E. Yemeni Indian Ocean island about 250 km northeast of Somalia.

Solomon Is.: 156°-171°E, 5°-13°S. Melanesian archipelago of about 1,000 islands stretching 1,400 km southeast from New Guinea. Guadalcanal was major World War II battleground.

South Georgia Is.: 54°S, 37°W; and South Sandwich Is.: 56°S, 26°W. British dependent territory 1,500 km east of the Falklands.

South Orkney Is.: 61°S, 44°-46°W. British group about 1,440 km southeast of South America.

South Shetland Is.: 61°-64°S, 54°-63°W. Four-group island, 540-km long, about 120 km north of the Antarctic Peninsula.

Spice Islands: See *Maluku.*

Spitsbergen: 79°N, 20°E: Norwegian Atlantic island; forms, with Bear Island (74°N, 19°E), dependency of Svalbard.

Spratly Is.: 9°N, 112°E. South China Sea archipelago about 500 km southeast of Vietnam; also claimed by China, Taiwan, Malaysia and the Philippines.

Sulawesi (Celebes): 2°S, 121°E. Indonesian island between Borneo and Maluku Is.

Sulu Archipelago: 5°-7°N, 120°-122°E. Philippine archipelago of about 900 islands between Celebes and Sulu Seas.

Sumatra: 0°, 100°E. Largest and westernmost island in Indonesia.

Taiwan: 23°N, 121°E. South China Sea island about 130 km east of mainland China.

Tasmania: 43°S, 17°E. Indian Ocean island 500 km south of southeast Australia; Australian state.

Tierra del Fuego: 54°S, 69°W. Island shared by Chile and Argentina between the Atlantic and Pacific Oceans; separated from South America by Strait of Magellan, and north of Cape Horn (55°59'S, 67°16'W).

Tongan (Friendly) Is.: 15°-23°S, 173°-177°W. Polynesian country of 171 islands (36 inhabited) stretching 1,000 km north-south about 2,000 km northeast of New Zealand.

Trinidad, Isla: 39°S, 62°W. Brazilian island 1,200 east of Brazil.

Trinidad and Tobago: 10°N, 61°W. Caribbean nation group off Venezuela.

Tristan da Cunha: 37°S, 12°W. British Atlantic group about 2,800 km east southeast of South Africa.

Tsushima: 34°N, 129°E. Japanese island in Korean (or Tsushima) Strait.

Tuamotu Archipelago: 14°-23°S, 134°-149°W. French Polynesian chain of 80 islands, 1,700 km long, east of Tahiti.

Vancouver: 50°N, 126°W. Largest island on west coast of Canada; part of British Columbia.

Vanuatu (New Hebrides): 13°-20°S, 166°-170°E. Melanesian island nation, 900 km long.

Victoria: 71°N, 114°W. Canadian Arctic island.

Volcano Is. (Kazan-Retto): 25°N, 141°E. Japanese group of three islands 1,100 km southwest of Tokyo. Iwo Jima was a major World War II battleground.

Wake Is.: 19°N, 177°E. U.S. Pacific atoll, 1,900 km west of Midway: Wilkes, Wake and Peale Islands.

Wight, Isle of: 51°N, 1°W. British English-Channel island off Portsmouth and Southampton.

Windward Is.: see *Antilles.*

Wrangel Island (Ostrov Vrangelia): 71°N, 180°E/W. Russian island in East Siberian Sea.

▶THE POLAR REGIONS

Antarctica
• **GEOGRAPHY Location:** continent mostly south of Antarctic Circle at 90°S. **Boundaries:** None. Bordered by South Atlantic, Indian and South Pacific oceans. **Total land area:** about 5,404,000 sq. mi. (14,000,000 sq km). **Coastline:** 11,165 mi. (17,968 km). **Comparative area:** twice the size of Australia. **Land use:** 98% continental ice sheet; 2% barren rock. **Natural Resources:** None presently exploited. Iron ore, chromium, copper, gold, nickel, platinum, and other minerals, as well as coal and

The 50 Tallest Buildings in the World

The two towers of New York City's World Trade Center were, until their destruction by a terrorist plane attack on Sept. 11, 2001, the fifth- and sixth-tallest buildings in the world, at 1,368 and 1,362 feet. In July 2007, the Burj Dubai Tower in U.A.E. became the tallest building in the world and by January 2008 stood, still incomplete, at 688 m (2,257 ft.) tall.

Rank, Building	City	Height Meters	Feet	Floors	Year
1. Taipei 101	Taipei, Taiwan	509 m	1,671 ft	101	2004
2. Petronas Tower 1	Kuala Lumpur, Malaysia	452 m	1,483 ft	88	1998
3. Petronas Tower 2	Kuala Lumpur, Malaysia	452 m	1,483 ft	88	1998
4. Sears Tower	Chicago	442 m	1,451 ft	108	1974
5. Jin Mao Tower	Shanghai, China	421 m	1,380 ft	88	1998
6. Two International Finance	Hong Kong	415 m	1,362 ft	88	2003
7. CITIC Plaza	Guangzhou, China	391 m	1,283 ft	80	1997
8. Shun Hing Square	Shenzhen, China	384 m	1,260 ft	69	1996
9. Empire State Building	New York City	381 m	1,250 ft	102	1931
10. Central Plaza	Hong Kong	374 m	1,227 ft	78	1992
11. Bank of China Tower	Hong Kong	367 m	1,205 ft	70	1990
12. Emirates Office Tower	Dubai, U.A.E.	355 m	1,163 ft	54	2000
13. Tuntex Sky Tower	Kaohsiung, Taiwan	348 m	1,140 ft	85	1997
14. Aon Center	Chicago	346 m	1,136 ft	83	1973
15. The Center	Hong Kong	346 m	1,135 ft	73	1998
16. John Hancock Center	Chicago	344 m	1,127 ft	100	1969
17. Shimao International Plaza	Shanghai, China	333 m	1,093 ft	60	2006
18. Minsheng Bank Building	Wuhan, China	331 m	1,087 ft	68	2006
19. Ryugyong Hotel	Pyongyang, North Korea	330 m	1,083 ft	105	1992
20. Q1 Tower	Gold Coast City, Australia	323 m	1,058 ft	78	2005
21. Burj Al Arab	Dubai, U.A.E.	321 m	1,053 ft	60	1999
22. Chrysler Building	New York City	319 m	1,046 ft	77	1930
23. Nina Tower I	Hong Kong	319 m	1,046 ft	80	2006
24. Bank of America Plaza	Atlanta	312 m	1,023 ft	55	1992
25. US Bank Tower	Los Angeles	310 m	1,018 ft	73	1989
26. Menara Telekom	Kuala Lumpur, Malaysia	310 m	1,017 ft	55	2001
27. Jumeirah Emirates Towers	Dubai, U.A.E.	309 m	1,014 ft	56	2000
28. AT&T Corporate Center	Chicago	307 m	1,007 ft	60	1989
29. JPMorganChase Tower	Houston	305 m	1,002 ft	75	1982
30. Baiyoke Tower II	Bangkok, Thailand	304 m	997 ft	85	1997
31. Two Prudential Plaza	Chicago	303 m	995 ft	64	1990
32. Wells Fargo Plaza	Houston	302 m	992 ft	71	1983
33. Kingdom Centre	Riyadh, Saudi Arabia	302 m	992 ft	41	2002
34. First Canadian Place	Toronto, Canada	298 m	978 ft	72	1976
35. Eureka Tower	Melbourne, Australia	297 m	975 ft	91	2006
36. Yokohama Landmark Tower	Yokohama, Japan	296 m	972 ft	70	1993
37. 311 South Wacker Drive	Chicago	293 m	961 ft	65	1990
38. SEG Plaza	Shenzhen, China	292 m	957 ft	70	2000
39. American International	New York City	290 m	952 ft	66	1932
40. Key Tower	Cleveland	289 m	947 ft	57	1991
41. Plaza 66	Shanghai, China	288 m	945 ft	66	2001
42. One Liberty Place	Philadelphia	288 m	945 ft	61	1987
43. Columbia Center	Seattle	285 m	937 ft	76	1985
44. Tomorrow Square	Shanghai, China	285 m	934 ft	55	2003
45. Chongqing World Trade Center	Chongqing, China	283 m	929 ft	60	2005
46. Cheung Kong Centre	Hong Kong	283 m	928 ft	62	1999
47. The Trump Building	New York City	283 m	927 ft	70	1930
48. Bank of America Plaza	Dallas	281 m	921 ft	72	1985
49. Bright Start Tower	Dubai, U.A.E.	280 m	919 ft	60	2007
50. Republic Plaza	Singapore	280 m	919 ft	66	1996

Note: Building height measured from sidewalk to structural top, and does not include antennae or poles. **Source:** Emporis © 2006 hydrocarbons have been found in small uncommercial qualities. **Temperature:** Varies with location and altitude. East Antarctica is coldest; Antarctic Peninsula in the west is mildest; mean annual temperature of the interior regions is -57°C (-71°F); mean temperatures at the coastal McMurdo station range from -28°C (-18°F) in August to -3°C (27°F) in January. **Major cities:** none.

● **THE LAND** Some 200 million years ago Antarctica was joined to South America, Africa, India and Australia as one large continent. Geological changes caused the breakup into separate continents. Studies indicate that Antarctica once had a tropical environment, but that its present ice form is at least 20 million years old. Approximately 98 percent of the continent is covered by ice; contains about 90 percent of the world's ice and 70 percent of the fresh water. Elevations average from 6,600 ft. to 13,200 ft. (2,000-4,000 m); mountain ranges up to 16,066 ft. (4,897 m) high. Ice-free coastal areas include parts of southern Victoria Land, Wilkes Land and Ross Island. The Antarctic ice sheet averages 7,090 ft. (2,160 m) in depth and is 15,670 ft. (4,776 m) deep at its thickest point. Altitude at the South Pole is about 9,800 ft. (3,000 m).

● **LAND/SEA LIFE:** Land life includes bacteria, lichens, mosses, two kinds of flowering plants in the ice-free areas, penguins and some flying birds. Sea life includes several types of seals and whales many of which were hunted to near extinction but are now protected by international conventions.

● **EXPLORATION:** British Captain James Cook circumnavigated the continent without sighting land in 1772–75. U.S. Capt. John Davis made the first known landing on the continent on Feb. 7, 1821. In 1908 the U.K. became the first nation to claim a slice of the continent, subsequently followed by claims from New Zealand (1923), France (1924), Australia (1933), Norway (1939), Chile (1940) and Argentina (1943). The U.S. and Russia have never claimed any Antarctica territory. Claims made by other nations are not recognized by other countries nor by the U.N.

In 1911 Capt. Robert F. Scott and Roald Amundsen of Norway began a race to the pole. Amundsen's party arrived at the South Pole on December 14, 1911 while Scott located the pole on January 18, 1912.

● **SCIENTIFIC RESEARCH:** The greatest scientific study ever conducted in Antarctica occurred in 1957–58 when 67 nations participated in the International Geophysical Year (IGY). Twelve countries established more than 50 stations to study the effects of the continent's huge ice mass on global weather, the oceans, the aurora australis and the ionosphere. During the late 1980s research was focused on the study of the ozone depletion in the stratosphere—called the ozone hole—which allows high levels of potentially harmful ultraviolet radiation to reach the earth's surface.

In 1998, 18 different countries maintained 42 research stations year-round. Argentina and the former Soviet Union each had six, the U.K. maintained five, Australia, Chile, South Africa and the U.S. kept three, China and Japan each had two, and Brazil, Finland, France, Germany, India, South Korea, New Zealand, Poland, and Uruguay each had one.

● **PEOPLE Population:** No indigenous inhabitants. Staffing of research stations varies seasonally; Summer (January) popuation: approximately 4,415; Winter (July) population: approximately 1,046

● **GOVERNMENT Antarctica Treaty:** Signed in 1959 by the 12 IGY nations (in force as of June 23, 1961), it establishes a legal framework for the management of Antarctica. The treaty was renewed in 1991 in Madrid, where 24 countries, including the United States, signed a protocol to ban mineral and oil exploration for 50 years and to provide wildlife protection. The treaty states that the area is to be used for peaceful purposes only and military activity such as weapons testing is prohibited; calls for freedom of scientific investigation and cooperation and a free exchange of information and personnel; nuclear explosions or disposal of radioactive wastes is forbidden; and, treaty-state observers have free access, including aerial observation, to any area and may inspect all stations, installations and equipment.

At the Treaty's 17th meeting in November, 1992, there were 26 consultative (voting) members and 15 acceding (non-voting) members. The 26 consultative members include the seven countries that claim part of Antarctica as national territory (Argentina, Australia, Chile, France, New Zealand, Norway, and the U.K.) as well as 15 nonclaimant nations. The claimant nations all signed the Antarctica Treaty in 1959; the 15 non-claimant nations (followed by the year they signed the treaty) are Belgium (1959), Brazil (1983), China (1985), Ecuador (1990), Finland (1989), Germany (1981), India (1983), Italy (1987), Japan (1959), South Korea (1989), Netherlands (1990), Peru (1989), Poland (1977), South Africa (1959), Spain (1988), Sweden (1988), Uruguay (1985), the U.S. (1959), and Russia (1959). The nonvoting members (and their year of accession) are Austria (1987), Bulgaria (1978), Canada (1988), Colombia (1988), Cuba (1984), Czechoslovakia (1962), Denmark (1965), Greece (1987), Guatemala (1991), Hungary (1984), North Korea (1987), Papua New Guinea (1981), Romania (1971), Slovakia (1993), Switzerland (1990), and Ukraine (1992).

The Arctic

● **GEOGRAPHY Location:** The Arctic Regions comprise all the lands north of the Arctic Circle—66°30′N—including the northern reaches of Asia, Europe, and North America, the Arctic Ocean, and its islands. In terms of climate, geography, and culture this demarcation is relatively insignificant, but within the Arctic Circle there is at least one 24-hour period during which the sun never sets (summer solstice), and one in which it never rises (winter solstice). The Arctic Ocean is the fourth largest after the Pacific, Atlantic and Indian; its primary marginal seas are Baffin Bay, the Barents Sea, the Beaufort Sea, the Chukchi Sea, the East Siberian Sea, the Greenland Sea, Hudson Bay, Hudson Strait, the Kara Sea, and the Laptev Sea. Some oceanographers consider the Arctic Ocean to be a marginal sea of the Atlantic Ocean. **Boundaries:** None. **Total area:** The Arctic Ocean is 5,440,000 sq. mi. (14,090,000 sq km). The main island groups are the Canadian Arctic Archipelago (550,000 sq. mi.; 1,424,483 sq km), Greenland (840,000 sq.

mi.; 2,175,590 sq km), Novaya Zemlya (31,000 sq. mi.; 80,290 sq km), and Svalbard (24,000 sq. mi.; 62,160 sq km). **Coastline:** 17,525 sq. mi. (45,389 km). **Comparative area:** The Arctic Ocean is about 1.5 times the size of the United States. **Land use:** The central surface is covered by a perennial drifting polar ice cap which averages about 3 meters thick, although pressure ridges may be three times that size. It drifts in a clockwise pattern in the Beaufort Gyral Stream, but exhibits nearly straight-line movement from the New Siberian Islands (Russia) to the Denmark Strait (between Greenland and Iceland). The ice pack is surrounded by open seas during the summer, but more than doubles in size during the winter and extends to the encircling land masses; the ocean floor is about 50 percent continental shelf (the highest percentage of any ocean) with the remainder a central basin interrupted by three submarine ridges (the Alpha Cordillera, Nansen Cordillera, and Lomonsov Ridge). The maximum depth is 17,881 ft. (5,450 m) in the Fram Basin. **Natural resources:** In the Arctic Ocean there are sand and gravel aggregates, placer deposits, polymetallic nodules, oil and gas fields, fish, and marine mammals (seals and whales). **Climate:** The dominant fact of life is the frigid conditions: persistent cold and relatively modest annual temperature ranges; winters characterized by continuous darkness, cold and stable weather conditions and clear skies; summers characterized by continuous daylight, damp and foggy weather, and weak cyclones with rain or snow. Between 60°N and 75°N there is seasonal freezing, while north of 75°N there is permanent ice. In North America, temperatures during the colder months average -25°F (-31°C), while Siberia is somewhat colder at -35°F (-37°C). **Environment:** Endangered marine species include walruses and whales; ice islands occasionally break away from northern Ellesmere Island; icebergs calved from western Greenland and extreme northeastern Canada; maximum snow cover in March or April is about 20-50 cm over the frozen ocean and lasts about 10 months; permafrost in islands; virtually icelocked from October to June; fragile ecosystem slow to change and slow to recover from disruptions or damage.

● **PEOPLE Population** Ethnologists distinguish three native cultural areas—the Western Arctic, including Eskimo peoples (from the east coast of Greenland to Alaska) and Aleuts; Paleo-Siberian, including the Chukchi and Eskimos of Eastern Asia; and Eurasian Arctic, including some Chukchi, Yakut, Nenets, and Lapps. Today, however, the vast majority of the people living and working within the Arctic Circle are non-native peoples in industry or scientific enterprises.

● **GOVERNMENT** Governments with territory north of the Arctic Circle are Canada, the United States, Russia, Finland, Sweden, Norway, and Denmark (Greenland). Svalbard is the focus of a maritime boundary dispute between Norway and Russia.

● **ECONOMY** While there is a fair amount of economic activity in the continental portions of the Arctic—principally extractive industries in Siberia, northern Canada, and Alaska's North Slope—conditions in the numerous Arctic islands all but prevent significant development there. Norwegian and Russian miners extract about 1 million tons of coal per year from mines on Svalbard, and in Greenland there are large deposits of cryolite, lead, and other minerals, but only lead can be mined economically. Economic activity in the Arctic Ocean is limited to the exploitation of natural resources including crude oil, natural gas, fishing and sealing.

● **COMMUNICATIONS Ports:** Churchill (Canada), Murmansk (Russia), Prudhoe Bay (U.S.). **Telecommunications:** No submarine cables. **Transportation:** There is a sparse network of air, ocean, river, and land routes. The Arctic provides the shortest marine link between the extremes of eastern and western Russia. The two major waterways are the Northwest Passage, in North America, and the Northern Sea Route, in Asia, but ships are subject to superstructure icing from October to May. The U.S. and Russia operate floating research stations. Access to the Arctic Ocean from the Pacific Ocean is through the Bering Strait; from the Atlantic, through the Davis Strait (between Canada and Greenland), the Denmark Strait (between Greenland and Iceland), or the Norwegian Sea (between Iceland and Norway).

Climate and Weather

▶ CLIMATES OF THE WORLD

Knowing the similarities and differences between climates in various parts of the world helps us understand many things about our planet: why people live where they do; how they make their living; the problems and potentials of their land. Climates are very complex, however, and no climatic classification is ideal. The most commonly used classification was developed more than 50 years ago by a German climatologist, Wladimir Koppen. The Koppen system uses temperature and precipitation as the major criteria for grouping climates. Boundaries between climatic zones are determined by the limits of where certain plants grow. The five major climatic zones are known by the capital letters **A**, **B**, **C**, **D**, and **E**; each major zone

has subzones. High-altitude areas are sometimes shown with the letter **H** because their climates are so complex that small maps cannot show all the detail.

(Note: In the following chart, **R** stands for the annual rainfall in centimeters; **T** is the average annual temperature in degrees Celsius.)

A Humid tropical climates. The average temperature of every month is 64° F (18°C) or higher. There is no winter.

Af *Rain forest.* The driest month has at least 2.4 inches (6 cm) of rain. The Amazon Basin is an example of an **Af** climate.

Am *Monsoon.* Similar to **Af** but with a short dry season. The amount of rainfall in the driest month is less than 2.4 inches (6 cm) but equal to or greater than 10 - (R/25). The southwestern coast of India is an example of an **Am** climate.

Aw *Savanna.* There is a well-defined dry season in the winter. The amount of rainfall in the driest month is less than 10 - (R/25). The Brazilian Highlands are a large area with an **Aw** climate.

As (Rare) There is a well-defined dry season in the summer.

B Dry climates. Annual rainfall is less than annual potential evaporation. The boundary between dry areas and humid areas is R < 2T + 28 when at least 70% of the rainfall occurs in the warmer six months; R < 2T when at least 70 percent of the rainfall occurs in the cooler six months; or R < 2T + 14 when neither half of the year receives at least 70 percent of the total annual rainfall.

BS *Steppe.* The boundary between steppe and desert is half of the dry/humid boundary. Steppes border many of the world's large deserts.

BSh *Low-latitude steppe.* The average annual temperature is at least 64° F (18° C).

BSk *Mid-latitude steppe.* The average annual temperature is less than 64° F (18° C).

BW *Desert.* The boundary between desert and steppe is half of the dry/humid boundary. The Sahara Desert is the largest area with a **BW** climate.

BWh *Low-latitude desert.* The average annual temperature is at least 64° F (18° C).

BWk *Mid-latitude desert.* The average annual temperature is less than 64° F (18° C).

C Subtropical climates. The average temperature of the coldest month is between 64° F (18° C) and 27° F (-3° C). These are mainly humid mid-latitude areas with mild winters. The principal natural vegetation is broad-leafed forest.

Cw (Rare) The wettest month occurs in summer and has at least ten times as much rainfall as the driest month in winter. **Cw** zones are mainly areas of evergreen forest in mountainous **Aw** zones.

Cs *Dry summer.* The wettest month occurs in winter and has at least three times as much rainfall as the driest month in summer. Less than 1.5 inches (4 cm) of rain falls during the driest summer month.

Csa *Warm, dry summer.* The average temperature of the warmest month is more than 72° F (22° C), and for at least four months the average temperature is more than 50° F (10° C). Italy and other Mediterranean countries have a **Csa** climate.

Csb *Cool, dry summer.* In no month is the average temperature more than 72° F (22° C), but for at least four months the average temperature is more than 50° F (10° C). **Csb** climates are found near San Francisco, California; on the coast near Santiago, Chile; and in Portugal.

Cf *Humid summer.* Areas that cannot meet the criteria for **Cw** and **Cs**.

Cfa *Humid, warm summer.* The average temperature of the warmest month is more than 72° F (22° C), and for at least four months the average temperature is more than 50° F (10° C). Much of the eastern United States is in a **Cfa** zone.

Cfb *Marine west coast.* In no month is the average temperature more than 72° F (22° C), but for at least four months the average temperature is more than 50° F (10° C). Great Britain, New Zealand, and the west coast of Alaska are all examples of **Cfb** climates.

D Continental climates. The average temperature of the warmest month is more than 50° F (10° C), and the average temperature of the coldest month is 27° F (-3° C) or below. Forests are the principal natural vegetation.

Dfa *Humid, warm summer.* All seasons have some precipitation. The average temperature of the warmest month is more than 72° F (22° C), and for at least four months the average temperature is more than 50° F (10° C). The northern Great Plains of the United States have a **Dfa** climate.

Dwa *Humid, warm summer.* The wettest month occurs in summer and has at least ten times as much rainfall as the driest month in winter. The average temperature of the warmest month is more than 72° F (22° C), and for at least four months the average temperature is more than 50° F (10° C). The land around the northern part of the Yellow Sea has a **Dwa** climate.

Dfb *Humid, cool summer.* All seasons have some precipitation. In no month is the average temperature more than 72° F (22° C), but for at least four months the average temperature is more than 50° F (10° C). A large **Dfb** area stretches from eastern Europe into Asia.

Dwb *Humid, cool summer.* The wettest month occurs in summer and has at least ten times as much rainfall as the driest month in winter. In no month is the average temperature more than 72° F (22° C), but for at least four months the average temperature is more than 50° F (10° C). Much of the area between Manchuria and the Sea of Okhotsk has a **Dwb** climate.

Dfc *Subpolar.* All seasons have some precipitation. For one to three months, the average temperature is 50° (10° C) or more. A huge **Dfc** area is in Siberia and adjacent parts of the Soviet Union.

E Polar climates. The average temperature of the warmest month is less than 50° F (10° C). There is no summer, and no trees grow.

ET *Tundra.* The average temperature of the warmest month is less than 50° F (10° C) but more than 32° F (0° C). Vast areas of northern North America, Europe, and Asia lie in the **ET** climate zone.

EF *Ice cap.* The average temperature of the warmest 8 month is 32° F (0° C) or less. The **EF** climate is found at the North and South Poles and in interior Greenland.

▶WEATHER EXTREMES

Hottest: Dalol Danakil Depression, Ethiopia. Average annual temperature: 35°C/95°F.

Coldest: Plateau Station, Antarctica. Average annual temperature: -56.7°C/-71.7°F.

Wettest: Mawsynram, Assam, India. Average annual rainfall: 11.873 m/38.925 ft.

Driest: Atacama Desert, Chile. Average annual rainfall: too small to measure.

▶EL NINO AND LA NINA

The two ends of a natural, very complex climatic balancing act, caused by the interaction between the surface layers of the tropical Pacific Ocean and the atmosphere above it, with winds and planetary-scale ocean waves shipping the changing conditions from one side of the ocean to the other.

The sheer size and breadth of the Pacific allow El Niños and La Niñas time to develop and to have widespread effects. During La Niñas, tropical ocean temperatures become colder in the eastern and central Pacific regions and warmer in the west; tradewinds are stronger and normally wet regions become drier. During El Niños the shift is exactly the opposite: weaker tradewinds, colder tropical water in the west and warmer water in the east off the coast of South America, and much more rain in dry areas—and more frequent and more intense hurricanes in the eastern Pacific. These systemic changes also noticeably affect winters in the continental U.S.: La Niñas bring warmer than normal winters to the Southeast and colder than normal to the Northwest, while El Niños generally cause warmer winters in the North Central states and colder winters in the Southeast and Southwest.

Fishermen off the coasts of Peru, Ecuador and Colombia first noticed and named El Niño for the tendency of its very warm waters to arrive around Christmastime. Before the 1982–83 El Niño, scientists had no ability to forecast these massive weather changes, and, despite great advances in the field, still missed the rapid onset, the great magnitude and sudden demise of the 1997–98 El Niño. Yet once forecasters had some of the data, they were able to predict six months in advance the unusual 1997–98 winter in the U.S. season and government, business and individuals were better prepared for disaster. La Niñas often (but not always) occur after El Niños. Typically, La Niñas occur less frequently than El Niños, which occur irregularly every 2-7 years (1976–77, 1982–83, 1986–87, 1991–94, 1997–98) and last 12–18 months. In between these extremes is normal weather.

So far, researchers have been unable to link El Niños-La Niñas to sunspots or volcanic eruptions.

Scientists are studying the compelling question of whether there is a relationship between El Niños-La Niñas and the greenhouse effect. And there is still considerable disagreement and contending theories about exactly what constitutes these phenomena, what their effects are and what role they play in Earth's complex climate and ecology.

▶GLOSSARY OF WEATHER WORDS

Air mass   A large body of air that, at a given elevation, has about the same temperature and humidity throughout.

Barometric pressure   The weight of a column of air at a particular place is determined by measuring the height of a column of mercury under a vacuum. The instrument for making such a measurement is called a barometer. At sea level, the standard barometric pressure is 29.92 inches (76 cm). In the International System, air pressure is measured in bars or in kiloPascals. A bar is slightly less than the standard air pressure at sea level, and a kiloPascal is one-hundredth of a bar. At any location, however, barometric pressure is affected by changes in temperature, humidity, or elevation. When the barometric pressure is falling, the air pressure is decreasing, usually a sign of a storm. When the barometer is rising, fairer weather is on its way.

Climate   General weather conditions over a long period of time.

Cold front   The place where cold air that is advancing meets warm air that is retreating before it. This kind of weather not only lowers temperature as it passes but also causes high winds and may cause thunderstorms.

Determining the Wind-Chill Factor

Sometimes called a wind-chill index, this is a measure of the cooling power of air movement and low temperature on the human body. Because heat passes directly from a warm body to the cooler air surrounding it—a process known as convection—wind produces a continuing source of cooler air and a chilling effect that is equivalent to a lower temperature. The effect on a warm day

is pleasant, but as temperatures approach freezing, wind chill is not only unpleasant, but can be dangerous. As the table below shows, a temperature of 5°F combined with a breeze of 20 mph produces a wind-chill temperature of -15°F—a temperature at which frostbite occurs much sooner than at 5°F. Wind speeds above 45 mph have little additional cooling effect.

Actual Temperature	5 mph	10 mph	15 mph	Wind speed 20 mph	25 mph	30 mph	35 mph	40 mph	45 mph
35°F	31°F	27°F	25°F	24°F	23°F	22°F	21°F	20°F	19°F
30°F	25	21	19	17	16	15	14	13	12
25°F	19	15	13	11	9	8	7	6	5
20°F	13	9	6	4	3	1	0	-1	-2
15°F	7	3	0	-2	-4	-5	-7	-8	-9
10°F	1	-4	-7	-9	-11	-12	-14	-15	-16
5°F	-5	-10	-13	-15	-17	-19	-21	-22	-23
0°F	-11	-16	-19	-22	-24	-26	-27	-29	-30
–5°F	-16	-22	-26	-29	-31	-33	-34	-36	-37
–10°F	-22	-28	-32	-35	-37	-39	-41	-43	-44
–15°F	-28	-35	-39	-42	-44	-46	-48	-50	-51
–20°F	-34	-41	-45	-48	-51	-53	-55	-57	-58
–25°F	-40	-47	-51	-55	-58	-60	-62	-64	-65
–30°F	-46	-53	-58	-61	-64	-67	-69	-71	-72
–35°F	-52	-59	-64	-68	-71	-73	-76	-78	-79
–40°F	-57	-66	-71	-74	-78	-80	-82	-84	-86
–45°F	-63	-72	-77	-81	-84	-87	-89	-91	-93

Source: National Oceanic and Atmospheric Administration (2000), www.noaa.gov.

Cyclone A region of low atmospheric pressure (see Depression). Severe cyclones are known as hurricanes, tropical cyclones, and typhoons.

Degree-days A degree-day is one degree of deviation of the daily mean temperature from a given norm, usually 65°F. Cooling degree-days are the number of degrees Fahrenheit by which the mean temperature exceeds 65°F, while heating degree-days are the number of degrees the mean temperature is below 65°F. During a year, keeping track of the total number of degree days for each day is used to keep track of cooling or heating needs. For example, oil companies use heating degree-days to estimate how much oil their customers have used and when they might need a refill.

Depression Any region of low air pressure. In temperate regions over land, the typical depression is a *low*. The often more powerful depression occurring over tropical waters is called a *tropical depression*. If the air pressure in a tropical depression continues to fall, it becomes a tropical storm, or, lower still, a *hurricane*.

Dew point The temperature at which dew (drops of water) begins to form as air cools. Air can hold only a certain amount of water vapor at a given temperature. When the temperature falls, excess water vapor must turn into a liquid.

Worst Hurricanes in U.S. History

Measuring the cost of hurricanes is an imperfect science, primarily because of the difficulty in determining which damages are directly attributable to a particular storm. The following table ranks hurricanes by the amount of insured losses they caused. Insured losses are the amount claimed by property owners against their insurance policies. It is impossible to calculate the costs incurred by those without insurance. Even after discounting inflation, most of the costliest hurricanes have come within the past 30 years, as more people have built large homes close to shore—and in harm's way. Improved meteorology and organized evacuations, however, have greatly reduced loss of human life. Until Katrina in 2005, the 25 deadliest hurricanes in U.S. history had all occurred before 1975.

Hurricanes are commonly described by their top wind speed, but their strength is measured in units of atmospheric pressure called Millibars—the strongest storms have the lowest pressure. The most intense hurricane was an unnamed storm that hit the Florida Keys in 1935 with winds greater than 155 mph and minimum pressure of 892 Millibars. By comparison, the two costliest hurricanes—Katrina and Andrew—had minimum pressures of 909 and 920 Millibars, respectively.

COSTLIEST HURRICANES

Rank, Hurricane (year)	Location of primary damage	Insured losses (billions)[1]	Deaths
1. Katrina (2005)	Louisiana, Mississipi	$84.6	1,500
2. Andrew (1992)	Florida, Louisiana	48.1	26
3. Wilma (2005)	Florida	21.5	5
4. Charley (2004)	Florida	16.3	10
5. Ivan (2004)	Florida, Alabama	15.5	25
6. Hugo (1989)	South Carolina	13.5	26
7. Agnes (1972)	Florida, NE states	12.4	122
8. Betsy (1965)	Florida, Louisiana	11.9	75
9. Rita (2005)	Louisiana, Texas, Florida	11.8	7
10. Camille (1969)	Miss., Louisiana, Virginia	9.8	256

DEADLIEST HURRICANES

Rank, Hurricane (year)	Deaths[2]
1. Galveston, Texas (1900)	8,000
2. Lake Okeechobee, Fla. (1928)	2,500
3. Katrina–La,. Miss., Ga. (2005)	1,500
4. Cheniere, La. (1893)	1,400
5. Sea Islands, S.C., Ga. (1893)	1,000
6. S. Carolina/Georgia (1881)	700
7. Audrey–SW La., N. Texas (1957)	416
8. Florida Keys (1935)	408
9. Last Island, La. (1856)	400
10. Florida, Miss., Ala. (1926)	372

Notes: Official figures for Hurricane Ike (2008, Fl, LA, TX) were not available at press time. Insured losses were estimated at 12 billion and the death toll at 51 as of Sept. 23, 2008. 1. Estimate, adjusted to 2006 dollars. 2. U.S. deaths directly attributable to storm (estimated). **Source:** National Oceanic and Atmospheric Administration, National Hurricane Center. www.nhc.noaa.gov.

Worst Tornadoes in U.S. History

COSTLIEST TORNADOES

Rank, Location	Date	Damages (millions)[1]
1. Topeka, Kansas	June 8, 1966	$1,600
2. Lubbock, Texas	May 11, 1970	1,336
3. Oklahoma City, Okla.	May 3, 1999	1,244
4. Xenia, Ohio	April 3, 1974	1,051
5. Omaha, Neb.	May 6, 1975	966
6. Wichita Falls, Texas	Apr. 10, 1979	793
7. Grand Island, Neb.	June 3, 1980	717
8. Windsor Locks, Conn.	Oct. 3, 1979	714
9. St. Louis, Mo.	May 27, 1896	491
10. Oklahoma City, Okla.	May 8, 2003	417

DEADLIEST TORNADOES

Rank, Location	Date	Deaths
1. Missouri-Illinois-Indiana	Mar. 18, 1925	695
2. Natchez, Miss.	May 6, 1840	317
3. St. Louis, Mo.- E. St. Louis, Ill.	May 27, 1896	255
4. Tupelo, Miss.	April 5, 1936	216
5. Gainesville, Ga.	April 6, 1936	203
6. Woodward, Okla.	April 9, 1947	181
7. Louisiana-Mississippi	April 24, 1908	143
8. New Richmond, Wisc.	June 12, 1899	117
9. Flint, Mich.	June 8, 1953	115
10. Goliad, Texas	May 18, 1902	114
10. Waco, Texas	May 11, 1953	114

Note: 1. In constant (2007) dollars. **Source:** National Oceanic and Atmospheric Administration, National Severe Storms Laboratory. www.nssl.noaa.gov

El Niño (see pp. 477-78)

Front The boundary between two different air masses.

High An air mass characterized by higher-than-normal air pressure; usually this is a fair-weather system. Some highs are typically found in the same place each year, such as the one that occurs over Bermuda in most summers.

Hurricane A huge tropical rainstorm with winds that swirl rapidly around a calm, dry central eye. To be classified a hurricane, a tropical storm must have wind speeds of more than 74 mph (119 km/hr). The average hurricane is 375 miles (600 km) in diameter and extends up 40,000 feet (12,000 m) above the surface of the ocean. The eye averages 12.5 miles (20 km) in diameter. When a hurricane hits land, its fierce winds and floods can do great damage. On average five hurricanes each year threaten the eastern and southern United States.

Jet stream A strong river or two of high winds in the upper atmosphere (but below the stratosphere) that travels from west to east at between 75 and 150 mph (120-240 km/hr), most often in the middle latitudes. Discovered by American bomber pilots in World War II, it is now known to have significant effects on weather.

La Niña (see pp. 477-78)

Low An air mass characterized by lower-than-normal air pressure; usually this is the heart of a storm system. Some lows are found in the same region most of the year, such as the low in the Pacific just off the coast of Alaska.

Mean temperature Technically, this should be the average of all temperatures during the day. Sometimes it is the average of 24 temperatures taken once each hour, but most often the mean temperature is simply the average of the high and low for the day.

Monsoon A wind system in which the prevailing direction of the wind reverses itself from season to season. Southeast Asia is the most typical monsoon region. The summer (southwest) monsoon, characterized by hot, moist air and heavy rains lasts from April to September. The winter (northeast) monsoon lasts from October to March and is characterized by cool, dry air.

Occluded front When a cold front overtakes a warm front, the denser cold air flows under the less dense warm air.

Prevailing winds Throughout the world, winds follow regular patterns. In some places winds are so light and infrequent as to scarcely exist, such as in the doldrums along the equator and in the horse latitudes near latitude 30° north and south. In other places the winds tend to come from a particular direction and are called prevailing winds.

Rain shadow An area on the leeward side of a mountain range that receives little rainfall.

Relative humidity The amount of moisture (water vapor) in the air compared with the total amount it can hold expressed as a percent. Warm air can hold more water vapor than cold air, so a relative humidity of 75 percent on a warm summer day is moister than a relative humidity of 75 percent on a cool winter day. However, because evaporation is greater on warm days, the relative humidity is generally higher in summer than in winter.

Secondary cold front A cold front that sometimes forms behind another cold front and that is often even colder than the first front.

Secondary depression A low that forms to the south or east of a low that is a storm center.

Squall line A line of instability that often precedes a cold front, marked by wind gusts and often by heavy rain.

Stationary front A front that stays in the same place.

Storm surge The rise in water levels in the ocean or a large lake that comes from a combination of wind and low pressure during a storm, especially pronounced during a hurricane.

Temperature-humidity index A number derived from a formula relating temperature and humidity to discomfort. When it is 75, many are uncomfortable, while at 80 or above, almost everybody is uncomfortable. Temperatures are less comfortable at high humidities because cooling by sweating is less efficient.

Temperature inversion A layer of warm air on top of a layer of cooler surface air. Such layering, usually occurring at night, can prevent air pollutants near the surface from rising into the upper air. A long-lasting inversion, especially in industrial areas, can cause an excessive concentration of pollutants to accumulate in the surrounding air.

Tornado A small and short-lived but very severe windstorm. Tornadoes are whirling columns of air that reach down from a cloud, and they often accompany thunderstorms, rain, and hail. With wind speeds up to 300 mph (480 km/hr), tornadoes can do tremendous damage. The diameter of the average tornado is between 500 and 2,000 feet (150-600 m). The average tornado moves along the ground at 28 mph (45 km/hr) and has a path that is 16 miles (26 km) long. In the United States, some 750 tornadoes are reported every year, most frequently between April and June.

Tropical storm A storm that forms over the ocean in the tropics and often moves onto land, where it loses strength. Technically, a storm is designated a tropical storm only when winds are between 39 and 73 miles per hour. If winds become greater, a tropical storm becomes a hurricane.

Trough A low that is long, rather than nearly circular.

Typhoon A hurricane formed in the western Pacific Ocean.

Warm front The boundary of a moving warm air mass.

Weather The condition of the atmosphere—temperature, rain, and wind, for example—in a particular place. A climate is defined by weather conditions over a long period of time.

Wind Any current of air, measured on land in miles per hour, and at sea in knots. The direction of a given wind is determined from the point of the compass from which it blows (e.g., northeast, south). In various regions of the world, names are given to seasonal winds of particular quality. Among these are the *bora*, a cold usually dry north/northeast wind along the eastern Adriatic; *brickfielder*, a hot north wind of southeastern Australia; *buran*, a cold, violent north/northeast wind of Siberia and Central Asia, common in winter; *chinook*, a dry winter or spring wind which blows down the eastern slopes of the Rocky Mountains often warm enough to melt the snow;

harmattan, a hot, dry north wind in West Africa which cools as it evaporates the moist air of the coast; *mistral,* a cold, strong north/northwest wind of the western Mediterranean with a surface strength of 60 km/hour, frequent in winter; *pampero,* a sudden, cold south or west wind in Argentina and Uruguay frequent in summer; *Santa Ana* a hot, dry wind that blows from the north or cast in Southern California; *sirocco,* a hot south wind of North Africa and southern Italy; *southerly burster,* a cold, violent south wind of southeastern Australia; *williwaw,* a violent squall that blows in the Strait of Magellan (South America); and *zonda,* a hot, dry north wind of Argentina and Uruguay.

Beaufort Wind Scale

In 1806 Adm. Francis Beaufort devised a scale for recording wind force at sea based on the effect of the wind on a full-rigged ship. In 1838, this scale was adopted by the British Admiralty, and in 1874 it was adopted for international use. It is now the chief scale for specifying the force of the wind and is used in all parts of the world, both on land and at sea. Originally, there were no specific wind speeds corresponding to various force numbers on the Beaufort Wind Scale. Since 1946, wind speed has been determined according to measurements made by an anemometer (a device for measuring wind) at 10m (30 ft) above the ground.

Force	Description of wind	Mean wind speed in knots[1]	Specification for use on land and at sea
Force 0	Calm	Less than 1	Calm, smoke rises vertically. Sea like a mirror.
Force 1	Light air	1-3	Direction of wind shown by smoke drift, but not by wind vanes. Ripples with appearance of scales are formed, but without foam crests.
Force 2	Light breeze	4-6	Wind felt on face; leaves rustle; ordinary vane moved by wind. Small wavelets, still short but more pronounced; crests have a glassy appearance and do not break.
Force 3	Gentle breeze	7-10	Leaves and small twigs in constant motion; wind extends light flag. Large wavelets; crests begin to break; foam of glassy appearance; perhaps scattered white horses.
Force 4	Moderate breeze	11-16	Raises dust and loose paper; small branches are moved. Small waves becoming longer; fairly frequent white horses.
Force 5	Fresh breeze	17-21	Small trees in leaf begin to sway; crested wavelets form on inland waters. Moderate waves, taking a more pronounced long form; many white horses are formed (chance of some spray).
Force 6	Strong breeze	22-27	Large branches In motion; whistling heard in telegraph wires; umbrellas used with difficulty. Large waves begin to form; the white foam crests are more extensive everywhere (probably some spray).
Force 7	Moderate gale, near gale	28-33	Whole trees in motion; inconvenience felt when walking against wind. Sea heaps up and white foam from breaking waves begins to be blown in streaks along the direction of the wind.
Force 8	Fresh gale, gale	34-40	Breaks twigs off trees; generally impedes progress. Moderately high waves of greater length; edges of crests begin to break into spindrift; foam is blown in well-marked streaks.
Force 9	Strong gale	41-47	Slight structural damage occurs (chimney pots and slate removed). High waves; dense streaks of foam; crests of waves begin to topple, tumble and roll over.
Force 10	Whole gale, storm	48-55	Seldom experienced inland; trees uprooted; considerable structural damage occurs. Very high waves with long overhanging crests; the resulting foam, in great patches, is blown in dense white streaks; the sea takes a white appearance; the tumbling of the sea becomes heavy and shock like; visibility affected.
Force 11	Storm, violent storm	56-63	Very rarely experienced; accompanied by widespread damage. Exceptionally high waves at sea (medium-sized ships might be lost to view behind the waves); the sea is completely covered with white patches of foam; visibility affected.
Force 12+	Hurricane[2]	64 and above	The air is filled with foam and spray; sea completely white with driving spray; visibility very seriously affected.

Notes: 1. Nautical miles-per-hour; 1 nautical mile = 1.151 statute miles. 2. Force 13: 72-80 knots; force 14: 81-89; force 15: 90-99; force 16: 100-108; force 17: 109-118. **Sources:** Smithsonian Institution, *Smithsonian Meteorological Tables* (1966); Hydrographer of the Navy (U.K.), *Ocean Passages for the World* (1977).

Climate of Selected U.S. Cities

The first line following each city lists the normal daily high temperatures for each month (in degrees Fahrenheit); the second line lists the normal monthly precipitation inches (rain, snow, and melted ice).

	Jan.	Feb.	Mar.	Apr.	May	June	July	Aug.	Sept.	Oct.	Nov.	Dec.
Atlanta,	51.9°	56.8°	65.0°	72.9°	80.0°	86.5°	89.4°	87.9°	82.3°	72.9°	63.3°	54.6°
Georgia	5.02	4.68	5.38	3.62	3.95	3.63	5.12	3.67	4.09	3.11	4.10	3.82
Baltimore,	41.2°	44.8°	53.9°	64.5°	73.9°	82.7°	87.2°	85.1°	78.2°	67.0°	56.3°	46.0°
Maryland	3.47	3.02	3.93	3.00	3.89	3.43	3.85	3.74	3.98	3.16	3.12	3.35
Boston,	36.5°	38.7°	46.3°	56.1°	66.7°	76.6°	82.2°	80.1°	72.5°	61.8°	51.8°	41.7°
Massachusetts	3.92	3.30	3.85	3.60	3.24	3.22	3.06	3.37	3.47	3.79	3.98	3.73
Charlotte,	51.3°	55.9°	64.1°	72.8°	79.7°	86.6°	90.1°	88.4°	82.3°	72.6°	62.8°	54.0°
North Carolina	4.00	3.55	4.39	2.95	3.66	3.42	3.79	3.72	3.83	3.66	3.36	3.18
Chicago,	29.6°	34.7°	46.1°	58.0°	69.9°	79.2°	83.5°	81.2°	73.9°	62.1°	47.1°	34.4°
Illinois	1.75	1.63	2.65	3.68	3.38	3.63	3.63	3.51	3.27	2.71	3.01	2.43
Cleveland,	32.6°	35.8°	46.1°	57.3°	68.6°	77.4°	81.4°	79.2°	72.3°	60.8°	48.7°	37.4°
Ohio	2.48	2.29	2.94	3.37	3.50	3.89	3.52	3.69	3.77	2.73	3.38	3.14
Columbus,	36.2°	40.5°	51.7°	62.9°	73.3°	81.6°	85.3°	83.8°	77.1°	65.4°	52.4°	41.0°
Ohio	2.53	2.20	2.89	3.25	3.88	4.07	4.61	3.72	2.92	2.31	3.19	2.93
Dallas-Fort Worth,	54.1°	60.1°	68.3°	75.9°	83.2°	91.1°	95.4°	94.8°	87.7°	77.9°	65.1°	56.5°
Texas	1.90	2.37	3.06	3.20	5.15	3.23	2.12	2.03	2.42	4.11	2.57	2.57
Denver,	43.2°	47.2°	53.7°	60.9°	70.5°	82.1°	88.0°	86.0°	77.4°	66.0°	51.5°	44.1°
Colorado	0.51	0.49	1.28	1.93	2.32	1.56	2.16	1.82	1.14	0.99	0.98	0.63
Detroit,	31.1°	34.4°	45.2°	57.8°	70.2°	79.0°	83.4°	81.4°	73.7°	61.2°	47.8°	35.9°
Michigan	1.91	1.88	2.52	3.05	3.05	3.55	3.16	3.10	3.27	2.23	2.66	2.51
El Paso,	57.2°	63.4°	70.2°	78.1°	86.7°	95.3°	94.5°	92.0°	87.1°	77.9°	65.5°	57.4°
Texas	0.45	0.39	0.26	0.23	0.38	0.87	1.49	1.75	1.61	0.81	0.42	0.77
Gainesville,	66.2°	69.3°	75.1°	80.4°	86.5°	89.9°	90.9°	90.1°	87.4°	81.0°	74.4°	68.1°
Florida	3.51	3.39	4.26	2.86	3.23	6.78	6.10	6.63	4.37	2.50	2.17	2.56
Honolulu,	80.4°	80.7°	81.7°	83.1°	84.9°	86.9°	87.8°	88.9°	88.9°	87.2°	84.3°	81.7°
Hawaii	2.73	2.35	1.89	1.11	0.78	0.43	0.50	0.46	0.74	2.18	2.26	2.85
Houston,	62.3°	66.5°	73.3°	79.1°	85.5°	90.7°	93.6°	93.5°	89.3°	82.0°	72.0°	64.6°
Texas	3.68	2.98	3.36	3.60	5.15	5.35	3.18	3.83	4.33	4.50	4.19	3.69
Indianapolis,	34.5°	39.9°	51.4°	62.9°	73.5°	82.1°	85.6°	83.7°	77.4°	65.6°	51.6°	39.2°
Indiana	2.48	2.41	3.44	3.61	4.35	4.13	4.42	3.82	2.88	2.76	3.61	3.03
Jacksonville,	64.2°	67.3°	73.4°	78.6°	84.3°	88.7°	90.8°	89.4°	86.1°	79.1°	72.5°	65.8°
Florida	3.69	3.15	3.93	3.14	3.48	5.37	5.97	6.87	7.90	3.86	2.34	2.64
Kansas City,	36.0°	42.6°	54.4°	65.2°	74.6°	83.9°	88.8°	87.1°	79.0°	67.6°	52.0°	40.0°
Missouri	1.15	1.31	2.44	3.38	5.39	4.44	4.42	3.54	4.64	3.33	2.30	1.64
Las Vegas,	57.1°	63.0°	69.5°	78.1°	87.8°	98.9°	104.1°	101.8°	93.8°	80.8°	66.0°	57.3°
Nevada	0.59	0.69	0.59	0.15	0.24	0.08	0.44	0.45	0.31	0.24	0.31	0.40
Los Angeles,	68.1°	69.6°	69.8°	73.1°	74.5°	79.5°	83.8°	84.8°	83.3°	79.0°	73.2°	68.7°
California	3.33	3.68	3.14	0.83	0.31	0.06	0.01	0.13	0.32	0.37	1.05	1.91
Memphis,	48.6°	54.4°	63.3°	72.4°	80.4°	88.5°	92.1°	91.2°	85.3°	75.1°	62.1°	52.2°
Tennessee	4.24	4.31	5.58	5.79	5.15	4.30	4.22	3.00	3.31	3.31	5.76	5.68
Miami,	76.5°	77.7°	80.7°	83.8°	87.2°	89.5°	90.9°	90.6°	89.0°	85.4°	81.2°	77.5°
Florida	1.88	2.07	2.56	3.36	5.52	8.54	5.79	8.63	8.38	6.19	3.43	2.18
Milwaukee,	28.0°	32.5°	42.6°	53.9°	66.0°	76.3°	81.1°	79.1°	71.9°	60.2°	45.7°	33.1°
Wisconsin	1.85	1.65	2.59	3.78	3.06	3.56	3.58	4.03	3.30	2.49	2.70	2.22
Minneapolis-St. Paul,	21.9°	28.4°	40.6°	57.0°	70.1°	79.0°	83.3°	80.4°	71.1°	58.4°	40.1°	26.4°
Minnesota	1.04	0.79	1.86	2.31	3.24	4.34	4.04	4.05	2.69	2.11	1.94	1.00
New Orleans,	61.8°	65.3°	72.1°	78.0°	84.8°	89.4°	91.1°	91.0°	87.1°	79.7°	71.0°	64.5°
Louisiana	5.87	5.47	5.24	5.02	4.62	6.83	6.20	6.15	5.55	3.05	5.09	5.07
New York City,	38.0°	41.0°	49.8°	60.7°	70.9°	79.0°	84.2°	82.4°	74.7°	63.5°	53.1°	42.9°
New York	4.13	3.15	4.37	4.28	4.69	3.84	4.62	4.22	4.23	3.85	4.36	3.95
Oklahoma City,	47.1°	53.5°	62.5°	71.2°	78.9°	87.2°	93.1°	92.5°	84.1°	73.4°	59.6°	49.8°
Oklahoma	1.28	1.56	2.90	3.00	5.44	4.63	2.94	2.48	3.98	3.64	2.11	1.89
Philadelphia,	39.0°	42.1°	51.3°	62.0°	72.1°	80.6°	85.5°	84.0°	76.7°	65.7°	54.8°	44.2°
Pennsylvania	3.52	2.74	3.81	3.49	3.88	3.29	4.39	3.82	3.88	2.75	3.16	3.31
Phoenix,	65.0°	69.4°	74.3°	83.0°	91.9°	102.0°	104.2°	102.4°	97.4°	86.4°	73.3°	65.0°
Arizona	0.83	0.77	1.07	0.25	0.16	0.09	0.99	0.94	0.75	0.79	0.73	0.92
Pittsburgh,	35.1°	38.8°	49.5°	60.7°	70.8°	79.1°	82.7°	81.1°	74.2°	62.5°	50.5°	39.8°
Pennsylvania	2.70	2.37	3.17	3.01	3.80	4.12	3.96	3.38	3.21	2.25	3.02	2.86
Portland,	45.6°	50.3°	55.7°	60.5°	66.7°	72.7°	79.3°	79.7°	74.6°	63.3°	51.8°	45.4°
Oregon	5.07	4.18	3.71	2.64	2.38	1.59	0.72	0.93	1.65	2.88	5.61	5.71
Salt Lake City,	37.0°	43.4°	52.8°	60.9°	70.6°	82.2°	90.6°	88.7°	77.6°	64.0°	48.7°	38.0°
Utah	1.37	1.33	1.91	2.02	2.09	0.77	0.72	0.76	1.33	1.57	1.40	1.23
San Antonio,	62.1°	67.1°	74.3°	80.4°	86.0°	91.4°	94.6°	94.7°	90.0°	82.0°	71.4°	64.0°
Texas	1.66	1.75	1.89	2.60	4.72	4.30	2.03	2.57	3.00	3.86	2.58	1.96
San Francisco,	58.1°	61.4°	62.5°	64.5°	65.4°	67.7°	68.2°	69.2°	71.3°	70.4°	64.1°	58.6°
California	4.72	4.15	3.40	1.25	0.54	0.13	0.04	0.09	0.28	1.19	3.31	3.18
Seattle,	46.9°	50.5°	54.5°	59.3°	64.9°	69.5°	74.5°	74.9°	69.9°	60.3°	51.5°	46.5°
Washington	5.24	4.09	3.92	2.75	2.03	1.55	0.93	1.16	1.61	3.24	5.67	6.06
St. Louis,	37.9°	44.3°	55.4°	66.7°	76.5°	85.3°	89.8°	87.9°	80.1°	68.3°	53.8°	42.0°
Missouri	2.14	2.28	3.60	3.69	4.11	3.76	3.90	2.98	2.96	2.76	3.71	2.86
Washington,	41.4°	45.5°	55.0°	65.9°	74.6°	82.8°	87.4°	85.9°	78.9°	67.7°	56.5°	45.9°
D.C.	3.05	2.77	3.55	3.22	4.22	4.07	3.57	3.78	3.82	3.37	3.31	3.07

Source U.S. Department of Commerce, National Oceanic and Atmospheric Administration, *Climatic Averages and Extremes for U.S. Cities* (2003).

Climate of Selected World Cities

Average low and high temperatures for selected months in degrees Fahrenheit. Precipitation is the average monthly amount in inches of rainfall equivalent.

City	January Temp. Max.	January Temp. Min.	January Avg. precip.	April Temp. Max.	April Temp. Min.	April Avg. precip.	July Temp. Max.	July Temp. Min.	July Avg. precip.	October Temp. Max.	October Temp. Min.	October Avg. precip.
Accra, Ghana	87°	73°	0.6	88°	76°	3.2	81°	73°	1.8	85°	74°	2.5
Amsterdam, Netherlands	40	34	2.0	52	43	4.6	69	59	2.6	56	48	2.8
Athens, Greece	54	42	2.2	67	52	0.8	90	72	0.2	74	60	1.7
Auckland, New Zealand	73	60	3.1	67	56	3.8	56	46	5.7	63	52	4.0
Baghdad, Iraq	60	39	0.9	85	57	0.5	110	76	t	92	61	0.1
Bangkok, Thailand	89	67	0.2	95	78	2.3	90	76	6.9	88	76	9.9
Beirut, Lebanon	62	51	7.5	72	58	2.2	87	73	t	81	69	2.0
Berlin, Germany	35	26	1.9	55	38	1.7	74	55	3.1	55	41	1.7
Bogotá, Colombia	67	48	2.3	67	51	5.8	64	50	2.0	66	50	6.3
Bombay, India	88	62	0.1	93	74	t	88	75	24.3	93	73	2.5
Budapest, Hungary	35	26	1.5	62	44	2.0	82	61	2.0	61	45	2.1
Buenos Aires, Argentina	85	63	3.1	72	53	3.5	57	42	2.2	69	50	3.4
Cairo, Egypt	65	47	0.2	83	57	0.1	96	70	0.0	86	65	t
Calcutta, India	80	55	0.4	97	76	1.7	90	79	12.8	89	74	4.5
Cape Town, South Africa	78	60	0.6	72	53	1.9	63	45	3.5	70	52	1.2
Caracas, Venezuela	75	56	0.9	81	60	1.3	78	61	4.3	79	61	4.3
Casablanca, Morocco	63	45	2.1	69	52	1.4	79	65	0.0	76	58	1.5
Copenhagen, Denmark	36	29	1.6	50	37	1.7	72	55	2.2	53	42	2.1
Dakha, Bangladesh	77	56	0.3	92	74	5.4	89	79	13.0	88	75	5.3
Dakar, Senegal	79	64	t	81	65	t	88	76	3.5	89	76	1.5
Dublin, Ireland	47	35	2.7	54	38	1.9	67	51	2.8	57	43	2.7
Geneva, Switzerland	39	29	1.9	58	41	2.5	77	58	2.9	58	44	3.8
Hanoi, Vietnam	68	58	0.8	80	70	3.6	92	79	11.9	84	72	3.5
Hong Kong	64	56	1.3	75	67	5.4	87	78	15.0	81	73	4.5
Istanbul, Turkey	45	36	3.7	61	45	1.9	81	65	1.7	67	54	3.8
Jakarta, Indonesia	84	74	11.8	87	75	5.8	87	73	2.5	87	74	4.4
Jerusalem, Israel	55	41	5.1	73	50	0.9	87	63	0.0	81	59	0.3
Kabul, Afghanistan	36	18	1.3	66	43	3.3	92	61	0.1	73	42	0.4
Karachi, Pakistan	77	55	0.5	90	73	0.1	91	81	3.2	91	72	0.1
Kinshasa, Congo, Dem. Rep.	87	70	5.3	89	71	7.7	81	64	0.1	88	70	4.7
Lagos, Nigeria	88	74	1.1	89	77	5.9	83	74	11.0	85	74	8.1
Lima, Peru	82	66	0.1	80	63	t	67	57	0.3	71	58	0.1
Lisbon, Portugal	56	46	3.3	64	52	2.4	79	63	0.2	69	57	3.1
London, United Kingdom	44	35	2.0	56	40	1.8	73	55	2.0	58	44	2.3
Madrid, Spain	47	33	1.1	64	44	1.7	87	62	0.4	66	48	1.9
Manila, Philippines	86	69	0.9	93	73	1.3	88	75	17.0	88	74	7.6
Melbourne, Australia	78	57	1.9	68	51	2.3	56	42	1.9	67	48	2.6
Mexico City, Mexico	66	42	0.2	78	52	0.7	74	54	4.5	70	50	1.6
Montreal, Canada	21	6	3.8	50	33	2.6	78	61	3.7	54	40	3.4
Moscow, Russia	21	9	1.5	47	31	1.9	76	55	3.0	46	34	2.7
Nairobi, Kenya	77	54	1.5	75	58	8.3	69	51	0.6	76	55	2.1
New Delhi, India	71	43	0.9	97	68	0.3	95	80	7.1	93	64	0.4
Osaka, Japan	47	32	1.7	65	47	5.2	87	73	5.9	72	55	5.1
Oslo, Norway	30	20	1.7	50	34	1.6	73	56	2.9	49	37	2.9
Paris, France	42	32	1.5	60	41	1.7	76	55	2.1	59	44	2.2
Prague, Czechoslovakia	34	25	0.9	55	40	1.5	74	58	2.6	54	44	1.2
Rio de Janeiro, Brazil	84	73	4.9	80	69	4.2	75	63	1.6	77	66	3.1
Riyadh, Saudi Arabia	70	46	0.1	89	64	0.1	107	78	0.0	94	61	0.0
Rome, Italy	54	39	3.3	68	46	2.0	88	64	0.4	73	53	4.3
Santiago, Chile	85	53	0.1	74	45	0.5	59	37	3.0	72	45	0.6
São Paulo, Brazil	77	63	8.8	73	59	2.2	66	53	1.5	68	57	4.6
Seoul, South Korea	32	15	1.2	62	41	3.0	84	70	14.8	67	45	1.6
Shanghai, China	47	32	1.9	67	49	3.6	91	75	5.8	75	56	2.9
Singapore	86	73	9.9	88	75	7.4	88	75	6.7	87	74	8.2
Stockholm, Sweden	31	23	1.5	45	32	1.5	70	55	2.8	48	39	2.1
St. Petersburg, Russia	23	12	1.0	45	31	1.0	71	57	2.5	45	37	1.8
Sydney, Australia	78	65	3.5	71	58	5.3	60	46	4.6	71	56	2.8
Tahiti, French Polynesia	89	72	13.2	89	72	6.8	86	68	2.6	87	70	3.4
Taipei, Taiwan	66	53	3.8	77	64	5.3	92	76	8.8	80	68	5.5
Tehran, Iran	45	27	1.8	71	49	1.4	99	72	0.1	76	53	0.3
Tokyo, Japan	47	29	1.9	63	46	5.3	83	70	5.6	69	55	8.2
Toronto, Canada	30	16	2.7	50	34	2.5	79	59	3.0	56	40	2.4
Vienna, Austria	34	26	1.5	57	41	2.0	75	59	3.0	55	44	2.0
Warsaw, Poland	30	21	1.2	54	38	1.5	75	56	3.0	54	41	1.7

t= trace. **Source:** U.S. Department of Commerce, National Oceanic and Atmospheric Administration, *Climates of the World* (1991).

World Population

The United Nations Population Fund estimates that in 2008 world population reached 6.8 billion people; 1.2 billion in developed countries and 5.5 billion in the developing regions. The UN estimates that world population will reach 7.3 billion in 2015, eight billion in 2025 and 9.3 billion in 2050.

World population growth rate has fallen from its peak of two percent per year to around 1.2 percent today. Of the 78 million people added to the world each year since 2000, 95 percent live in developing regions of Africa, Asia and Latin America. Six countries contribute half of the annual population increase: India for 21 percent; China for 12 percent; Pakistan for five percent; Bangladesh, Nigeria and the United States for four percent each.

In 2008 the world has two billionaire countries: China at 1.3 billion people and India at 1.2 billion. The United States has the third largest population with 309 million people, followed by Indonesia with 234 million and Brazil with 194 million people.

The U.N. estimates that by 2050 India will have a population of 1.66 billion which will be larger than all the more developed countries combined, that is, all the countries of Europe, including Russia, Australia, New Zealand, Japan, Canada and the

United States. It is also projected that by 2050 India will have a larger population than China, which will have 1.41 billion.

▶WORLD POPULATION TRENDS

Four factors are impacting future world population: birth and death rates, ageing of the population, AIDS and migration. While birth rates continue to decline and couples in developing regions have three children on average, the total population continues to increase with 78 million persons added in 2008. However, population is increasing and decreasing in different regions of the world. Europe has significant population declines and several countries in Africa and the Caribbean are also projected to have less people in 2050. European population is estimated at 731.1 million in 2008 and is projected to decline to 664.2 million by 2050, a loss of 66.9 million people. All European countries have declining population except for Albania, France, Ireland, Macedonia, Netherlands, Norway, and the United Kingdom. Russia is calculated to have the greatest decline over this time period, 347 million people or 24.3 percent of its population. From 2007 to 2050 the number of people living in Japan is expected to decline by 25.5 million or 19.9 percent of its people. Ukraine will decline by 15.3 million or 33 percent, and Germany by 8.5 million for 10.3 percent of its population. Bulgaria is expected to loose 2.7 million people but that translates into 35.2 percent of its population. In less developed regions, Guyana is expected to reduce its population by 35.4 percent or 261 million people, Georgia will lose 28.7 percent or 1.3 million people, Armenia will decline by

Years to Reach Population Milestones

Milestone	Year Reached	Years to Reach	Milestone	Year Reached	Years to Reach
1 billion	1804	N.A.	6 billion	1999	12
2 billion	1927	123	7 billion	2012[1]	13
3 billion	1960	33	8 billion	2026[1]	14
4 billion	1974	14	9 billion	2043[1]	17
5 billion	1987	13			

Note: 1. Projected. **Source:** U.S. Census Bureau, *World Population Profile:* 1998 (1999).

World Vital Events per Time Unit, 2008

Time unit	Births	Deaths	Natural Increase
Year	135,330,281	55,205,782	80,124,499
Month	11,277,523	4,600,482	6,677,042
Day	369,755	150,835	218,919
Hour	15,406	6,285	9,122
Minute	257	105	152
Second	4.3	1.7	2.5

Source: U.S Bureau of the Census, *International Data Base* (2008).

Distribution of the World's Population, 1950–2050

Area	1950	2000	2050[1]
More developed regions	32.3%	19.7%	12.7%
Less developed regions	67.7	80.3	87.3
Africa	8.8	13.1	21.5
Asia	55.5	60.6	58.2
Latin America and the Caribbean	6.6	8.6	8.6
Europe	21.8	12.0	6.5
Northern America	6.8	5.2	4.7
Oceania	0.5	0.5	0.5
Total world population (millions)	2,519	6,057	9,322

Note: 1. Based on the U.N.'s medium population projections.
Source: U. S. Bureau of the Census, *World Population Prospects: The 2000 Revision Highlights* (2001).

World Births, Deaths and Population Growth, 2007

Characteristic	World	Developed	Developing
Population	6,706,992,932	1,219,190,903	5,487,802,029
Births	135,330,281	13,420,906	121,909,375
Deaths	55,205,782	12,662,252	42,543,530
Natural increase	80,224,499	758,654	79,365,845
Births per 1,000 population	20.2	11.0	22.2
Deaths per 1,000 population	8.2	10.4	7.8
Rate of natural increase (percent)	1.2%	0.06%	1.4%

Source: U.S. Bureau of the Census, *International Data Base* (2008).

544 million people or 18.1 percent, and South Korea will lose 5.9 million or 12.2 percent of their population.

The world's life expectancy now averages 67.2 years and by 2050 the UN estimates that it will reach 75.4 years. However, life expectancy for 2005-2010 varies from an average of 76.5 years in developed nations to 65.4 years in less developed countries, to 54.6 years in the least developed areas. Longevity, declining birth rates and AIDS are now changing the average median age and the traditional proportion between the old and the young. Median age is the age at which 50 percent of the population is older and 50 percent are younger than that age. The world's median age increased from 23.9 years in 1950 to 28 years in 2005 and is estimated to reach 38.1 years in 2050. The proportion of youth less than 15 years of age was 34 percent of total population in 1950, 30 percent in 2000, and will reduce to 21 percent in 2050. The proportion of people over the age of 60 was eight percent in 1950, ten percent in 1999 and is expected to reach 21 percent in 2050.

Countries with Declining Population Estimates, 2005–50 (in thousands)

Country	2005	2050	Decrease	Percent
Russia	142,499	107,832	34,667	-24.3%
Japan	127,967	102,511	25,455	-19.9
Ukraine	46,205	30,937	15,268	-33.0
Germany	82,599	74,088	8,512	-10.3
Poland	38,082	30,260	7,822	-20.5
South Korea	48,224	42,327	5,897	-12.2
Romania	21,438	15,928	5,509	-25.7
Italy	58,877	54,610	4,267	-7.2
Belarus	9,689	6,960	2,729	-28.2
Bulgaria	7,639	4,949	2,690	-35.2
Hungary	10,030	8,459	1,570	-15.7
Czech Republic	10,186	8,825	1,361	-13.4
Cuba	11,268	9,911	1,357	-12.0
Georgia	4,395	3,134	1,261	-28.7
Moldova	3,794	2,883	910	-24.0
Croatia	4,555	3,692	864	-19.0
Bosnia & Herzegovina	3,935	3,160	775	-19.7
Lithuania	3,390	2,654	736	-21.7
Slovakia	5,390	4,664	726	-13.5

Source: United Nations Department of Economic and Social Affairs, Population Division, *World Population Prospects: The 2006 Revision Highlights* (2007).

Countries with Oldest and Youngest Populations, 2005 and 2050

Country	Median age, 2005	Country	Median age, 2050
Oldest Population			
1. Japan	42.9	1. China, Macao	55.5
2. Germany	42.1	2. Japan	54.9
3. Italy	42.0	3. South Korea	54.9
4. Finland	40.9	4. Singapore	53.7
5. Bulgaria	40.8	5. Martinique	53.0
6. Croatia	40.6	6. Poland	52.4
7. Belgium	40.3	7. Bulgaria	52.3
8. Sweden	40.2	8. Slovenia	52.2
9. Slovenia	40.2	9. China, Hong Kong	52.1
10. Switzerland	40.1	10. Cuba	52.1
Youngest Population			
1. Uganda	15.3	1. Burundi	20.8
2. Mali	16.0	2. Niger	21.1
3. Niger	16.0	3. Liberia	21.2
4. Guinea-Bissau	16.2	4. Guinea-Bissau	21.5
5. Congo, Dem.	16.3	5. Congo, Dem.	22.5
6. Malawi	16.4	6. Afghanistan	23.0
7. Afghanistan	16.4	7. Angola	23.2
8. Liberia	16.4	8. Uganda	23.3
9. Angola	16.6	9. Sierra Leone	24.0
10. Yemen	16.7	10. Chad	24.3
World	**28.0**	**World**	**38.1**

Source: United Nations Population Division, *World Population Prospects: The 2006 Revision Highlights* (2007).

World's Largest Countries, by Population, 2007–25

Rank, Country	2007 Population	Rank	2015 Population	Rank	2025 Population
1. China	1,329,000,000	1	1,402,321,000	1	1,445,100,000
2. India	1,169,000,000	2	1,246,351,000	2	1,369,284,000
3. United States	306,000,000	3	329,669,000	3	358,030,000
4. Indonesia	232,000,000	4	250,428,000	4	270,113,000
5. Brazil	192,000,000	6	201,970,000	6	216,372,000
6. Pakistan	164,000,000	5	204,465,000	5	249,766,000
7. Bangladesh	159,000,000	9	133,429,000	10	124,428,000
8. Nigeria	148,000,000	7	181,428,000	7	208,268,000
9. Russian Federation	142,000,000	8	161,726,000	8	192,115,000
10. Japan	128,000,000	10	127,224,000	11	123,444,000
11. Mexico	107,000,000	11	119,618,000	9	129,866,000
12. Philippines	88,000,000	13	94,742,000	14	104,649,000
13. Vietnam	87,000,000	12	96,338,000	13	108,589,000
14. Ethiopia	83,000,000	16	82,497,000	18	81,959,000
15. Germany	83,000,000	14	93,845,000	12	116,006,000
16. Egypt	75,000,000	15	89,996,000	15	103,165,000
17. Turkey	75,000,000	17	82,150,000	17	88,995,000
18. Iran	71,000,000	18	81,422,000	16	90,927,000
19. Thailand	64,000,000	19	69,585,000	19	73,869,000
20. Congo, Dem Rep	63,000,000	20	62,841,000	20	64,165,000

Source: United Nations Department of Economic and Social Affairs, Population Division, *World Population Prospects: The 2004 Revision Highlights* (2005) and *World Population Prospects: The 2006 Revision Highlights* (2007).

In 2005, Japan had the oldest median age population, 42.9 years, followed by Germany at 42.1 years, Italy at 42 years and Finland 40.9 years. In contrast, Uganda had the youngest median age population, 15.5 years. The US median age was 30 in 1950, rose to 36 in 2005 and is expected to be 41.1 in 2050. Average population age in Niger and Mali was 16, followed by Guinea-Bissau at 16.2 years and the Democratic Republic of the Congo at 16.3 years. By 2050 Japan and South Korea will have the world's oldest median age population, 54.9 years, followed by Singapore at 53.7, Poland at 52.4 and Bulgaria at 52.3 years. Burundi will have the youngest average at 20.8 years, followed by Niger at 21.1, Liberia at 21.2 and Guinea-Bissau at 21.5 years.

The United Nations Population Division identified 53 countries as having populations highly affected by HIV/AIDS: 38 in Sub-Saharan Africa, five in Asia, eight in Latin America and the Caribbean, one in Europe and one in North America. The UN estimates that the population of these 53 countries in 2050 will be 479 million less than it would have been without AIDS.

▶URBANIZATION

The United Nations estimates that 3.2 billion people or 49 percent of the world's population lived in urban areas in 2005, and is expected to rise to 4.9 billion or 60 percent by 2030. In 2008 half of the world's population is expected to be living in cities. The world's urban population reached one billion in 1960, two billion in 1985, and three billion in 2002 and is projected to attain four billion in 2017 and 4.9 billion in 2030.

Population growth will be rapid in urban areas, averaging 2.2 percent per year from 2005 to 2030. In 2005, developing countries had 43 percent of their people living in urban areas and this is projected to increase to 56 percent by 2030. In 2005, developing areas had 2.3 billion urban people which is expected to reach 3.9 billion by 2030.

In contrast, the urban population of the more developed regions is expected to increase very slowly, from 0.9 billion in 2005 to one billion in 2030 for an annual growth rate of about 0.5 percent. The more developed countries were 74 percent urban in 2005 and this is expected to increase to 81 percent by 2030.

In 2005 the majority of the world's urban dwellers lived in Asia (1.6 billon), Europe (0.5 billion), Latin America and the Caribbean (0.4 billion), Africa (0.3 billion), Northern America (0.3 billion) and Oceania (0.02 billion). In terms of percentage of their populations, Europe, Latin America and the Caribbean, Northern America and Oceania had 70 percent of their people living in cities. Africa was 38.3 percent and Asia was 39.8 percent urbanized in the same year and is expected to be 50.7 percent and 54.1 percent urbanized, respectively.

In 2005, China, India and the United States had the largest numbers of urban dwellers in the world and the largest number of rural residents lived in India (0.8 billion), China (0.8 billion) and Indonesia (0.1 billion). It is anticipated that the rural population in developing countries will reach its peak of 3.1 billion people in 2020 and will then start to decline slowly.

In 2005 the majority of urban dwellers of almost every country lived in small and medium-sized cities. Almost all of the world's expected population growth in the next 25 years will be in medium-sized cities in developing countries, that is, cities that have less than 500,000 people. These cities will contain 53.4 percent of the people in de-

Population of Areas with 10 Million or more Inhabitants, 1975–2015

1975		2000		2005		2015	
1. Tokyo	26.6	1. Tokyo	34.4	1. Tokyo	35.2	1. Toyko	35.5
2. New York-Newark	15.9	2. Mexico City	18.1	2. Mexico City	19.4	2. Mumbai	21.9
3. Mexico City	10.7	3. New York-Newark	17.8	3. New York-Newark	18.7	3. Mexico City	21.6
		4. São Paulo	17.1	4. São Paulo	18.3	4. São Paulo	20.5
		5. Mumbai	16.1	5. Mumbai	18.2	5. New York-Newark	19.9
		6. Shanghai	13.2	6. Delhi	15.0	6. Delhi	18.6
		7. Kolkata	13.1	7. Shanghai	14.5	7. Shanghai	17.2
		8. Delhi	12.4	8. Kolkata	14.3	8. Kolkata	17.0
		9. Buenos Aires	11.8	9. Jakarta	13.2	9. Khaka	16.8
		10. Los Angeles-Long Beach	11.8	10. Buenos Aires	12.6	10. Jakarta	16.8
		11. Osaka-Kobe	11.2	11. Dhaka	12.4	11. Lagos	16.1
		12. Jakarta	11.1	12. Los Angeles-Long Beach	12.3	12. Karachi	15.2
		13. Rio de Janeiro	10.8	13. Karachi	11.6	13. Buenos Aires	13.4
		14. Cairo	10.4	14. Rio de Janeiro	11.5	14. Cairo	13.1
		15. Dhaka	10.2	15. Osaka-Kobe	11.3	15. Los Angeles-Long Beach-	13.1
		16. Moscow	10.1	16. Cairo	11.1	16. Manila	12.9
		17. Karachi	10.0	17. Lagos	10.9	17. Beijing	12.9
		18. Manila	10.0	18. Beijing	10.7	18. Rio de Janeiro	12.8
				19. Manila	10.7	19. Osaka-Kobe	11.3
				20. Moscow	10.7	20. Istanbul	11.2
						21. Moscow	11.0
						22. Guangzhou Guangdong	10.4

Note: An urban area is a central city or central cities, and the surrounding urbanized areas, also called a metropolitan area.
Sources: United Nations Department of Economic and Social Affairs, Population Division, *World Urbanization Prospects: The 2005 Revision* (2007).

veloped regions and 50.7 percent in developing countries.

In 2005, mega-cities held 9.3 percent of the world's urban population and by 2015 these large urban centers will hold 9.4 percent of the of the world's city dwellers. In 2005, the world's largest city was Tokyo with 35.2 million people, followed by Mexico City with 19.4 million, New York-Newark with 18.7 million, São Paulo with 18.3 million, and Mumbai (Bombay) with 18.2 million people. In 2015, Tokyo will still be the world's largest urban agglomeration with 35.5 million people, followed by Mumbai (Bombay) with 21.9 million, Mexico City with 21.6 million, São Paulo with 20.5 million, and New York-Newark with 19.9 million residents.

Today almost half of humanity lives in cities and by 2030 three out of five people will reside in urban areas. The UN projects that cities with 10 million or more people will increase from 20 in 2005 to 22 in 2015, with 17 being in developing countries.

Nations with Highest and Lowest Fertility Rates, 2008

HIGHEST RATES		LOWEST RATES	
Country	Fertility rate per woman	Country	Fertility rate per woman
Niger	7.16	China, Hong Kong	0.96
Guinea-Bissau	7.04	Belarus	1.20
Afghanistan	7.03	South Korea	1.21
Burundi	6.79	Ukraine	1.21
Liberia	6.69	Poland	1.22
Congo, Dem. Rep.	6.70	Bosnia and	1.23
Timor-Leste	6.53	Herzegovina	
Mali	6.46	Czech Republic	1.24
Sierra Leone	6.44	Slovakia	1.25
Uganda	6.42	Lithuania	1.26
		Singapore	1.26

Source: United Nations Population Fund (UNFPA), *The State of World Population 2008* (2008).

Population Indicators by Region and Nation

Region/Country	Population estimate ('000s) 2008	2050	Birth rate per 1,000, 2003	Death rate per 1,000, 2003	Life expectancy, 2005-10	Percent urban, 2008	Fertility rate per woman 2008
World Total	6,749,700	9,191,300	20	9	67	50%	2.54%
More Developed Regions	1,226,300	1,245,200	11	10	76	75	1.6
Less Developed Regions	5,523,400	7,946,000	23	9	63	44	2.7
Least Developed Countries	823,800	1,742,000	15	50	27	28	4.6
Africa	987,000	1,997,900	36	14	49	39	4.6
Arab States	335,000	598,500	—	—	68	56	3.4
Asia	4,075,400	5,265,900	19	8	67	41	2.3
Europe	731,100	664,200	10	11	74	72	1.4
Latin America and the Caribbean	579,400	769,200	21	6	71	79	2.4
Northern America	339,800	438,000	14	8	77	82	2.0
Oceania	34,700	48,700	17	7	74	71	2.3
Afghanistan	28,200	79,400	41	17	44	24	7.0
Albania	3,190	3,700	15	5	76	47	2.0
Algeria	34,400	49,600	22	5	72	65	2.4
Angola	17,500	44,600	46	26	43	57	6.4
Argentina	39,900	51,400	17	8	75	92	2.2
Armenia	3,000	2,500	13	10	72	64	1.4
Australia	21,000	28,000	13	7	81	89	1.8
Austria	8,400	8,500	9	9	80	67	1.4
Azerbaijan	8,500	9,400	19	10	68	52	1.8
Bahrain	753	1,155	19	4	76	97	2.3
Bangladesh	161,300	254,100	30	9	64	27	2.8
Belarus	9,600	7,000	10	14	69	73	1.2
Belgium	10,500	10,600	11	10	79	97	1.7
Belize	288	442	31	6	76	49	2.9
Benin	9,300	22,500	43	14	57	41	5.4
Bhutan	700	900	35	14	66	35	2.2
Bolivia	9,700	14,900	26	8	66	66	3.5
Bosnia and Herzegovina	3,935	3,600	13	8	75	47	1.2
Botswana	1,900	2,700	26	31	51	60	2.9
Brazil	194,200	254,100	18	6	72	86	2.2
Brunei Darussalam	390	681	20	3	77	74	2.3
Bulgaria	7,639	5,300	10	14	73	71	1.3
Burkina Faso	15,200	37,500	45	19	52	20	6.0
Burundi	8,900	28,300	40	18	50	10	6.8
Cambodia	14,700	25,100	27	9	60	22	3.1
Cameroon	18,900	33,100	35	15	50	57	4.3
Canada	33,200	42,800	11	8	81	80	1.5
Central African Republic	4,400	7,600	36	20	45	39	4.5
Chad	11,100	29,400	47	16	51	27	6.2
Chile	16,800	20,700	16	6	79	88	1.9

Region/Country	Population estimate ('000s)		Birth rate per 1,000, 2003	Death rate per 1,000, 2003	Life expec- tancy, 2005-10	Percent urban, 2008	Fertility rate per woman 2008
	2008	2050					
China	1,336,300	1,408,800	13	7	73	43	1.7
Colombia	46,700	61,900	22	6	73	74	2.2
Congo, Dem. Rep. of	64,700	186,800	45	15	47	34	6.7
Congo, Republic of	3,800	7,600	29	14	55	61	4.4
Costa Rica	4,500	6,400	19	4	79	63	2.1
Croatia	4,555	3,600	13	11	76	57	1.4
Cuba	11,300	9,900	12	7	78	76	1.5
Czech Republic	10,186	8,600	9	11	77	73	1.2
Denmark	5,442	5,300	12	11	78	87	1.8
Djibouti	833	1,547	41	20	55	87	4.0
Dominican Republic	9,900	14,000	24	7	72	69	2.8
Ecuador	13,500	18,000	25	5	75	66	2.6
Egypt	76,800	121,200	24	5	71	43	2.9
El Salvador	7,000	10,000	28	6	72	61	2.7
Eritrea	5,000	11,500	39	13	58	21	5.0
Estonia	1,335	700	9	13	71	69	1.5
Ethiopia	85,200	183,400	40	20	53	17	5.2
Fiji	839	934	23	6	69	52	2.8
Finland	5,277	4,900	11	10	79	63	1.8
France	61,900	68,300	13	9	81	77	1.9
Gabon	1,400	2,100	37	11	57	85	3.0
Gambia	1,800	3,600	41	12	59	57	4.7
Georgia	4,400	3,100	12	15	71	53	1.4
Germany	82,500	74,100	9	10	79	74	1.4
Ghana	23,900	41,900	26	11	60	50	3.8
Greece	11,147	9,800	10	10	80	61	1.3
Guatemala	13,700	27,500	35	7	70	49	4.1
Guinea	9,600	22,700	43	16	56	34	5.4
Guinea-Bissau	1,700	5,300	38	17	46	30	7.0
Guyana	738	488	18	9	67	28	2.3
Haiti	9,800	15,300	34	13	61	47	3.5
Honduras	7,200	12,100	32	6	70	48	3.3
Hong Kong SAR, China	7,300	9,000	11	6	82	100	1.0
Hungary	10,030	7,600	10	13	73	68	1.3
Iceland	301	370	14	7	82	93	2.1
India	1,186,200	1,658,300	23	8	65	29	2.8
Indonesia	234,300	296,900	21	6	71	69	2.2
Iran	72,200	100,200	17	6	71	68	2.0
Iraq	29,500	61,900	34	6	60	67	4.2
Ireland	4,301	5,000	14	8	79	61	2.0
Israel	7,000	10,500	19	6	81	92	2.7
Italy	58,877	44,900	9	10	81	68	1.4
Ivory Coast	19,600	34,700	40	18	48	49	4.4
Jamaica	2,700	2,800	17	5	73	53	2.4
Japan	127,900	102,500	10	9	83	66	1.3
Jordan	6,100	10,100	24	3	73	78	3.1
Kazakhstan	15,500	17,300	18	11	67	58	2.3
Kenya	38,600	84,800	29	16	54	22	4.9
Korea, North	23,900	24,700	18	7	67	63	1.9
Korea, South	48,400	42,300	13	6	79	81	1.2
Kuwait	2,900	5,200	22	2	78	98	2.2
Kyrgyzstan	5,400	6,600	26	9	66	36	2.5
Laos	6,000	11,400	37	12	64	31	3.2
Latvia	2,277	1,300	9	15	73	68	1.3
Lebanon	4,100	5,200	20	6	72	87	2.2
Lesotho	2,000	2,000	27	25	43	25	3.3
Liberia	3,900	12,500	45	18	46	60	6.8
Libya	6,300	9,700	27	3	74	78	2.7
Lithuania	3,390	2,500	10	13	73	67	1.3
Luxembourg	467	721	12	8	79	83	1.7
Macedonia	2,038	2,200	13	8	74	67	1.4
Madagascar	20,200	44,500	42	12	59	29	4.7
Malawi	14,300	31,900	45	23	48	19	5.6
Malaysia	27,000	39,600	24	5	74	70	2.6
Maldives	306	682	37	8	69	31	2.6
Mali	12,700	34,200	48	19	55	32	6.5
Malta	407	428	13	8	79	96	1.4
Mauritania	3,200	6,400	42	13	64	41	4.3
Mauritius	1,300	1,400	16	7	73	42	1.9
Mexico	107,800	132,300	22	5	76	77	2.2

Region/Country	Population estimate ('000s) 2008	Population estimate ('000s) 2050	Birth rate per 1,000, 2003	Death rate per 1,000, 2003	Life expectancy, 2005-10	Percent urban, 2008	Fertility rate per woman 2008
Moldova	3,800	2,900	14	13	69	42	1.4
Mongolia	2,700	3,400	21	7	67	57	1.9
Montenegro	600	600	—	—	75	—	1.8
Morocco	31,600	42,600	23	6	71	56	2.4
Mozambique	21,800	39,100	37	23	42	37	5.0
Myanmar	49,200	58,700	19	12	62	33	2.0
Namibia	2,100	3,000	34	19	53	37	3.2
Nepal	28,800	51,900	32	10	64	17	3.2
Netherlands	16,500	17,200	12	9	80	82	1.7
New Zealand	4,200	5,200	14	8	80	87	2.0
Nicaragua	5,700	8,200	26	5	73	57	2.7
Niger	14,700	53,200	50	22	57	16	7.2
Nigeria	151,500	288,700	39	14	47	48	5.3
Norway	4,698	4,900	12	10	80	77	1.8
Oman	2,700	4,600	38	4	76	72	3.0
Pakistan	167,902	292,200	30	9	66	36	3.5
Panama	3,400	5,100	21	6	76	73	2.6
Papua New Guinea	6,500	11,200	31	8	57	12	3.7
Paraguay	6,200	9,900	30	5	72	60	3.0
Peru	28,200	39,000	23	6	71	71	2.5
Philippines	89,700	140,500	26	6	72	65	3.2
Poland	38,082	33,000	11	10	76	61	1.2
Portugal	10,700	10,000	12	10	78	59	1.5
Puerto Rico	4,000	4,400	14	8	79	98	1.8
Qatar	841	1,330	16	4	76	96	2.7
Romania	21,438	18,100	11	12	73	54	1.3
Russian Federation	141,800	107,800	10	14	66	73	1.3
Rwanda	10,000	22,600	40	22	46	18	5.9
Saudi Arabia	25,300	45,000	37	6	73	82	3.3
Senegal	12,700	25,300	36	11	63	42	4.6
Serbia	9,900	9,600	—	—	74	52	1.8
Sierra Leone	6,000	13,500	44	21	43	38	6.4
Singapore	4,500	5,000	13	4	80	100	1.3
Slovakia	5,390	4,900	10	10	75	56	1.3
Slovenia	2,000	1,700	9	10	78	48	1.3
Somalia	9,000	21,100	46	18	48	37	6.0
South Africa	48,800	55,600	19	18	49	61	2.6
Spain	44,600	46,400	10	9	81	77	1.4
Sri Lanka	19,400	18,700	16	6	72	15	1.9
Sudan	39,400	73,000	36	10	59	43	4.2
Suriname	458	429	19	7	70	75	2.4
Swaziland	1,100	1,400	29	21	40	25	3.4
Sweden	9,119	8,700	11	10	81	85	1.8
Switzerland	7,500	8,400	10	8	82	73	1.4
Syria	20,400	34,900	30	5	74	54	3.0
Tajikistan	6,800	10,800	33	8	67	26	3.3
Tanzania	41,500	85,100	40	17	53	25	5.1
Thailand	64,300	67,400	16	7	71	33	1.9
Timor-Liste	1,200	3,500	28	6	61	27	6.5
Togo	6,800	14,100	35	12	58	42	4.7
Trinidad and Tobago	1,300	1,300	13	9	70	13	1.6
Tunisia	10,400	13,200	17	5	74	67	1.9
Turkey	75,800	98,900	18	6	72	69	2.1
Turkmenistan	5,000	6,800	28	9	63	49	2.5
Uganda	31,900	92,900	47	17	52	13	6.4
Ukraine	45,900	30,900	10	16	68	68	1.2
United Arab Emirates	4,500	8,500	18	4	79	78	2.3
United Kingdom	60,769	66,200	11	10	79	90	1.8
United States	308,800	402,400	14	8	78	82	2.0
Uruguay	3,400	3,600	17	9	76	92	2.1
Uzbekistan	27,800	38,400	26	8	67	37	2.5
Vanuatu	226	375	24	8	70	24	3.7
Venezuela	28,100	42,000	20	5	74	93	2.5
Vietnam	88,500	120,000	20	6	74	31	2.1
Yemen	23,100	58,000	43	9	63	28	5.4
Zambia	12,200	22,900	40	24	42	35	5.1
Zimbabwe	13,500	19,100	30	22	42	37	3.1

Note: Totals may not add because of rounding numbers. Data for small countries or areas, generally those with population of 200,000 or less in 2005, are not given in this table. Source: United Nations Population Division, *World Population Prospects: The 2006 Revision Highlights* (2007), United Nations Population Fund (UNFPA), *The State of World Population 2008* (2008) U.S. Bureau of the Census, *International Data Base*, (2002) and (2004).

▶FERTILITY

Across the world, women continue having fewer children. The United Nations estimates world fertility per woman dropped from 4.47 in 1970-1975 to 2.54 births in 2008. In developed regions fertility rates dropped from an average of 2.13 per woman in 1970-1975 to 1.60 births in 2008. Fertility in less developed regions dropped from an average of 5.41 births per woman to 2.73 in this same time period.

Replacement level fertility represents the point at which each couple has only the number of births required to replace themselves in the population. The replacement level fertility rate is usually 2.1 births per woman. Most countries in Europe and North America have fertility rates at or below that level. In 2008, Hong Kong, SAR China had the lowest fertility rate of 0.96 and Niger had the highest birth rate at 7.16 births per woman.

The United Nations reports that fertility rates are declining in sub-Sahara Africa, South-central Asia and the Middle East, where fertility levels have been very high for decades. From 1970-1975 to 2008 China's fertility rate dropped from 4.86 children per woman to 1.73 children, India went from 5.26 to 2.78 births, Indonesia from 5.30 to 2.16, Iran from 6.40 to 2.02, and Nicaragua from 6.79 to 2.72 fertility rate.

Mongolia, South Korea, Tunisia and Kuwait, made the greatest fertility rate reductions from 1970-1975 to 2008. Mongolia's fertility rate went from 7.33 to 1.86, South Korea's from 4.28 to 1.20, Tunisia's from 6.21 to 1.91 and Kuwait's from 6.90 to 2.17.

By 2008 all countries in the developed regions had fertility levels below 2.1 children per woman, and 12 countries had levels below 1.3, with Belarus, Ukraine, and Poland having the lowest fertility levels.

These reductions in family size are largely due to contraceptive use. The UN estimates that 18 million couples reached their childbearing years each year during the 1990s. Almost all research studies indicate that couples the world over want fewer children. Thirty years ago less than 10 percent of couples in the developing world had access to family planning. Today 60 percent of those couples have access, causing family size to drop from an average of six children during the 1960s to less than three today.

▶GLOSSARY OF DEMOGRAPHIC TERMS

Birth rate The average annual number of births during a year per 1,000 population at midyear; also known as the crude birth rate.

Contraception Deliberate use of methods to prevent conception or pregnancy. Contraception is an important portion of family planning.

Death rate The average annual number of deaths during a year per 1,000 population at mid-year; also known as the crude death rate.

Growth rate The average annual percent change in the population, resulting from a surplus (or deficit) of births over deaths and the balance of migrants entering and leaving a country. The rate may be positive or negative; also known as population growth rate or average annual rate of growth.

Infant mortality rate The number of deaths to infants under one year of age in a given year per 1,000 live births occurring in the same year.

Least developed countries Defined by the United Nations as the countries with the poorest living standards. In 2001, the UN counted 49 countries, most of them landlocked, among the least developed.

Less developed countries Defined by the U.N. as countries with poorer people than in more developed countries, with economies based on agricultural production, with low GNPs, and lacking in advanced technologies. Approximately 77 countries, including those in Africa, Latin America, and the Caribbean, Asia (except Japan) and regions of Melanesia, Micronesia and Polynesia, are considered less developed.

More developed countries The U.N. defines developed countries as industrialized nations with a high gross national product (GNP), high per capita GNP, and advanced science and technology. Approximately 45 countries including those in Europe, North America, Japan, Australia, and New Zealand, are considered developed.

Projections Data on population and vital rates derived for future years based on statistics from population censuses, vital registration system or sample surveys pertaining to the recent past, and on assumptions about future trends.

Vital rates Birth rates and death rates.

World Health

The World Health Organization (W.H.O.), a specialized agency of the United Nations, is the global intergovernmental directing and coordinating authority for international health work. Headquartered in Geneva, Switzerland, W.H.O. gathers health statistics, sets international health standards, provides assistance to individual countries when invited, and issues publications. Most of the information here is from the World Health Organization. (For information on the U.S. see the section Health and Medicine in Part II.)

W.H.O. estimates that in 2005 over 13 million people died of heart attacks or strokes. Over 80 percent of these deaths were in low and middle income countries, and men and women were equally affected. At least 171 million people worldwide have diabetes and this number is expected to more than double by 2030 to 366 million.

Eighty percent of premature heart attacks and strokes are preventable. A healthy diet, regular physical activity, and not using tobacco products not only reduce the chance of a heart attack or stroke, but will also help prevent most type 2 diabetes and chronic respiratory disorders, and certain types of cancer.

A balanced diet is crucial to a healthy heart and vascular system. A healthy diet includes plenty of fruits and vegetables, whole grains, lean meat, fish and pulses, and restricted salt and sugar intake. Up to 2.7 million lives could be saved each year by increased fruit and vegetable consumption. At least thirty minutes of regular physical activity every day helps to maintain cardiovascular fitness and helps lower blood pressure, reduce body fat, improve glucose metabolism, and reduce osteoporosis and falls among older people.

▶ THE GLOBAL SITUATION

The newest potential global pandemic is from Avian influenza. The W.H.O. defines Avian influenza, or bird flu, as a contagious disease of animals caused by viruses that normally infect only birds and, less commonly, pigs. Avian influenza viruses are highly species-specific, but have, on rare occasions, crossed the species barrier to infect humans. Scientists report that some migratory birds are now directly spreading the H5N1 virus in its highly pathogenic form and can pass the virus to domestic chickens and other animals. Further spread to new areas is expected.

From mid-December 2003 through early February 2004, poultry outbreaks caused by the H5N1 virus were reported in eight Asian nations (listed in order of reporting): South Korea, Viet Nam, Japan, Thailand, Cambodia, Laos, Indonesia and China. Most of these countries had never before experienced an outbreak of highly pathogenic avian influenza. In early August 2004, Malaysia reported its first outbreak of H5N1 in poultry; Russia reported its first outbreak in late July 2005; reports of disease in adjacent parts of Kazakhstan followed in early August. Deaths of wild birds from highly pathogenic H5N1 were reported in both countries, as well as Mongolia. In October 2005, H5N1 was confirmed in poultry in Turkey and Romania.

The spread of H5N1 throughout poultry populations poses two main risks for human health. The first risk is of direct infection when the virus passes from poultry to humans, resulting in very severe disease. Currently more than half of those infected with the virus have died. The second risk, of even greater concern, is that the virus—if given enough opportunity—will change into a form that is highly infectious for humans and spread easily from person to person. Such a change could mark the start of a global outbreak (a pandemic).

As of July 2006 the W.H.O. estimates that more than 130 people have died of bird flu since late 2003. Most deaths were in East Asia, but cases of the virus were also found in Europe, Africa, and South and Central Asia. Vietnam has reported 42 deaths from bird flu, none since the institution og a culling and vaccination policy in 2006. In May 2006 Indonesia reported a number of deaths which the W.H.O. believes were the result of human-to-human transmission. In early July 2006 Indonesia reported its fortieth bird flu death, apparently from contact with an infected chicken.

Outbreaks in wild and domestic birds are under investigation around the world.

Global Health Risk Factors

Many of the world's health risks today concern consumption—either too little in poor countries, or too much in richer societies. Around the world, people are changing their patterns of consumption, particularly of food, alcohol and tobacco. These changes are causing a shift in health risks for billions of people, especially in middle- and low-income countries. In addition, infectious disease control and reduced fertility are creating a shift from young societies to societies with increasing numbers of middle-aged and elderly people, which brings larger health burdens.

In poor countries, 170 million children are underweight; over three million of these children die each year as a result. In contrast, there are more than one billion adults worldwide who are overweight and at least 300 million who are clinically obese. Among these, about half a million people in North America and Western Europe die each year from obesity-related diseases. And the number of young people who are overweight is causing growing alarm.

Poverty and lack of nutritious food make underweight a massive health problem that is the leading cause of disease among hundreds of millions of the world's poorest people and a major cause of premature death, especially among children. While all ages are at risk, underweight is most prevalent among children under five years of age. the W.H.O. estimates that approximately 27 percent of children under five are underweight. This caused an estimated 3.4 million child deaths in 2000, including about 1.8 million in Africa and 1.2 million in Asia. Underweight is a contributing factor in 60 percent of all child deaths in developing countries.

Overweight and obesity, a problem largely in wealthy societies, leads to increases in blood pres-

Infant Mortality Rates by Region, 2008

Region	Infant mortality rate (per 1,000 live births)
World	**49**
More developed regions	7
Less developed regions	54
Least developed countries	87
Africa	86
Asia	43
Arab States	50
Europe	8
Latin America and Caribbean	21
North America	6
Oceania	27
Former USSR	21

Source: United Nations Population Fund (UNFPA), *The State of World Population 2008* (2008).

Nations with Highest and Lowest Infant Mortality Rates, 2005–10

Country	Infant Mortality Rate[1]	Country	Infant Mortality Rate[1]
Highest rates		**Lowest rates**	
Sierra Leone	277	Czech Rep.	4
Afghanistan	235	Finland	4
Angola	229	Hong Kong, China	4
Liberia	203	Japan	4
Mali	198	Norway	4
Congo, Dem. Rep.	195	Singapore	4
Guinea Bissau	193	Sweden	4
Somalia	191	Australia	5
Chad	188	Austria	5
Niger	186	Belgium	5
Nigeria	186	France	5
Rwanda	186	Germany	5
Ivory Coast	183	South Korea	5
Burkina Baso	180	Spain	5
		Switzerland	5

Note: 1. Rate per 1,000 live births. **Source:** United Nations Population Fund (UNFPA), *The State of World Population 2008* (2008).

Killer Diseases, 2002

Cause	Estimated deaths	Percent of total
Cardiovascular diseases	16,733,000	29.3%
Ischaemic heart disease	7,208,000	12.6
Cerebrovascular disease	5,509,000	9.7
Cancer	7,121,000	12.5
Trachae/bronchus/lung	1,243,000	2.2
Stomach	850,000	1.5
Liver	618,000	1.1
Colon/rectum	622,000	1.1
Beast	477,000	0.8
Esophagus	446,000	0.8
Mouth/oropharynx	318,000	0.6
Respiratory infections	3,963,000	6.9
Lower respiratory infections	3,884,000	6.8
Respiratory diseases[1]	3,702,000	6.5
HIV/AIDS	2,777,000	4.9
Perinatal conditions	2,462,000	4.3
Diarrheal diseases	1,798,000	3.2
Tuberculosis	1,566,000	2.7
Malaria	1,272,000	2.2
Childhood diseases	1,124,000	2.0
Neuropsychiatric disorders	1,112,000	1.9

Note: 1. Includes chronic obstructive pulmonary disease, asthma, and other respiratory diseases. **Source:** World Health Organization, *The World Health Report 2004.*

Leading Worldwide Causes of Death, 2002

Cause	Estimated deaths (millions)	Percent of total
World total deaths	**57.0**	**100.0%**
Communicable diseases, maternal and perinatal conditions and nutritional deficiencies	18.3	32.1
Infectious and parasitic diseases	11.0	19.3
Respiratory infections	4.0	6.9
Noncommunicable conditions	33.5	58.8
Cardiovascular diseases	16.7	29.3
Cancers	7.1	12.5
Injuries	5.0	9.1
Respiratory diseases	3.7	6.5
Digestive diseases	2.0	3.5

Source: World Health Organization, *The World Health Report 2004.*

sure, high cholesterol levels and increased resistance to insulin. They raise the risk of coronary heart disease, stroke, diabetes and many forms of cancer. Obesity is killing about 220,000 men and women a year in the United States and Canada, and about 320,000 in 20 countries of Western Europe.

These noncommunicable diseases, which are currently responsible for 60 percent of world deaths, are related to changes in global dietary patterns, such as increased consumption of processed fatty, salty and sugary foods, and a large drop in physical activity. Physical inactivity causes about 15 percent of some cancers, diabetes and heart disease.

Missing nutrients are causing millions of people to suffer ill health and premature death. Iodine deficiency is the single most common preventable cause of mental retardation and brain damage. Over 2.2 billion people are at risk for iodine deficiency and over a billion have some degree of goiter.

Iron is needed by all tissues of the body for ba-

sic cellular functions and is important in muscle, brain and red blood cells. Iron deficiency is a major cause of anemia and affects two billion people. In total, iron deficiency causes 0.8 million (1.5 percent) deaths worldwide.

Vitamin A is needed for proper eye health, vision and immune function. Vitamin A deficiency is the leading cause of acquired blindness in children. Approximately 21 percent of all children under five years of age and women of reproductive age are at highest risk. In total, about 0.8 million (1.4 percent) deaths worldwide result from vitamin A deficiency.

Zinc deficiency can be indicated by short stature, hypogonadism, impaired immune function, skin disorders, cognitive dysfunction and anorexia. The W.H.O. estimates that about one-third of the world's population is zinc deficient. In total, 0.8 million (1.4 percent) of deaths worldwide are attributable to zinc deficiency.

Aging Populations Globally

The United Nations estimates that in 2006, there were 688 million people over the age of 60 and that by 2050 that number could increase to two billion. In 2050, for the first time in human history, the world will have more persons over 60 than under 15. The largest number of older persons live in Asia (54 percent); Europe has the next largest share (24 percent). In developed countries, persons over 60 are expected to increase from 20 percent of the population today to 33 percent by 2050. In less developed regions, 8 percent of people are were 60 years old or older in 2000; by 2050, that percentage is estimated to increase to 20 percent.

In 2008 the median age for the world was 26 years, a number that is expected to increase to 36 by 2050. Yemen has the youngest median age, 15 years, and Japan has the oldest, 41 years. In 2050, Niger will have the youngest median age, 20 years, and Spain will have the oldest, at 55 years.

▶TOBACCO USE: A GLOBAL HEALTH PROBLEM

The World Health Organization estimates that tobacco is the second major cause of death in the world and is currently responsible for the death of one in 10 adults worldwide (about 5 million deaths each year). If current smoking patterns continue, tobacco will cause 10 million deaths each year by 2020. About one-third of the adult male population smokes and smoking related-diseases kill one in 10 adults globally. About 15 billion cigarettes are sold daily, over 10 million every minute. Approximately 80,000 to 100,000 children start to smoke every day, about half of whom live in Asia.

Smoking is increasing in developing countries and declining in the developed nations. The highest smoking rate is in East Asia and the Pacific, where nearly two-thirds of men smoke. China is the world's largest tobacco producer; about 67 percent of the men smoke, and 4 percent of the women. About 3,000 people die each day in China from smoking, and it is estimated that smoking will kill about a third of all Chinese men under 30 today. In Cambodia 67 percent of men in urban areas smoke and 86 percent of men in rural areas. Half the men in Japan and Malaysia are smokers.

Half of long-term smokers will die from tobacco. Smoking is the single largest preventable cause of disease and premature death. It is a prime factor in heart disease, stroke and chronic lung disease. It can cause cancer of the lungs, larynx, esophagus, mouth, and bladder, and contributes to cancer of the cervix, pancreas and kidneys. Smoking is related to at least a quarter of all deaths from heart disease and about three-quarters of the world's chronic bronchitis.

Current World Health Indicators, by Nation

Country	Life expectancy at birth (years) 1970	Life expectancy at birth (years) 2005-10	Daily calorie supply, 1997	Infant mortality per 1,000 births[1] 2008	Population with access to: Improved water, 2004	Population with access to: Improved sanitation, 2004	Population with access to: Essential drugs, 1999
Afghanistan	37	44	1,523	156	39%	34%	—%
Albania	67	76	2,523	19	96	91	60
Algeria	53	72	3,020	30	85	92	95
Angola	37	43	1,983	131	53	31	20
Argentina	67	75	3,136	13	96	91	70
Armenia	—	72	2,147	29	92	83	40
Australia	71	81	3,001	4	100	100	100
Austria	70	80	3,343	4	100	100	100
Azerbaijan	—	68	2,139	72	77	54	66
Bahamas	65	74	2,443	13	97	100	80
Bahrain	62	76	—	11	—	—	100
Bangladesh	45	64	2,105	51	74	39	65
Barbados	69	77	3,207	11	100	100	100
Belarus	—	69	3,101	9	100	84	70
Belgium	71	79	3,543	4	100	100	99
Belize	—	76	2,862	16	91	47	80
Benin	44	57	2,415	97	67	33	77
Bhutan	42	66	—	44	62	70	85
Bolivia	46	66	2,170	45	85	46	70
Bosnia & Herzegovina	—	75	—	12	97	95	—
Botswana	50	51	2,272	46	95	42	90
Brazil	59	72	2,938	23	90	75	40
Brunei Darussalam	—	77	2,331	5	—	—	99
Bulgaria	70	73	2,756	12	99	99	88
Burkina Faso	40	52	2,137	104	61	13	60
Burundi	45	50	1,708	99	79	36	20
Cambodia	42	60	1,974	62	41	17	30
Cameroon	49	50	2,175	87	66	51	66
Canada	73	81	3,056	5	100	100	100
Cape Verde	56	77	3,135	24	80	43	80
Central African	42	45	1,938	96	75	27	50
Chad	38	51	1,972	119	42	9	46
Chile	62	79	2,810	7	95	91	88
China	59	73	2,844	23	77	44	85
Colombia	59	73	2,800	19	93	86	88
Comoros	48	66	1,824	48	86	33	90
Congo, Rep. of	51	55	2,107	70	58	27	—
Congo, Dem. Rep.	—	52	1,815	113	46	30	—
Costa Rica	67	79	2,822	10	97	92	100
Croatia	—	76	2,458	6	100	100	100
Cuba	70	78	2,357	5	91	98	92
Cyprus	71	79	3,102	6	100	100	100
Czech Republic	69	77	3,177	4	100	98	88
Denmark	73	78	3,808	4	100	100	99
Djibouti	40	55	1,920	84	73	82	80
Dominican Republic	59	72	2,316	29	95	78	66
East Timor	—	61	—	67	58	36	—
Ecuador	58	75	2,592	21	94	89	40
Egypt	51	71	3,289	29	98	70	88
El Salvador	58	72	2,515	21	84	62	80
Equatorial Guinea	40	52	—	91	43	53	44
Eritrea	—	58	1,585	55	60	9	57
Estonia	—	71	3,004	7	100	97	100
Ethiopia	43	53	1,845	86	22	13	66
Fiji	64	69	3,038	19	47	72	100
Finland	70	79	2,916	4	100	100	98
France	72	81	3,551	4	100	—	99
Gabon	44	57	2,517	53	88	36	30
Gambia	36	59	2,332	74	82	53	90
Georgia	—	71	2,184	39	82	94	30
Germany	71	79	3,330	4	100	100	100
Ghana	49	60	2,560	56	75	18	44
Greece	72	80	3,575	7	—	—	100
Guatemala	53	70	2,191	29	95	86	50
Guinea	36	56	2,099	102	50	18	93
Guinea-Bissau	36	46	2,381	112	59	35	44

Country	Life expectancy at birth (years)		Daily calorie supply 1997	Infant mortality per 1,000 births 2008	Population with access to:		
	1970	2005-10			Improved water, 2004	Improved sanitation, 2004	Essential drugs, 1999
Guyana	65	67	2,392	43	83%	70%	—%
Haiti	48	61	1,855	48	54	30	30
Honduras	53	70	2,368	28	87	69	40
Hong Kong, SAR, China	—	82	3,282	4	—	—	—
Hungary	70	73	3,402	7	99	95	100
Iceland	74	82	3,104	3	100	100	100
India	48	65	2,415	54	86	33	35
Indonesia	47	71	2,930	26	77	55	80
Iran	55	71	2,824	30	94	—	85
Iraq	55	60	2,252	79	81	79	70
Ireland	71	79	3,636	5	—	—	99
Israel	71	81	3,272	5	100	—	99
Italy	72	81	3,504	5	—	—	99
Ivory Coast	—	48	2,421	116	69	21	80
Jamaica	67	73	2,575	13	93	80	95
Japan	72	83	2,905	3	100	100	100
Jordan	55	73	2,681	19	97	93	100
Kazakhstan	—	67	3,007	24	86	72	66
Kenya	50	54	1,971	64	61	43	36
Kiribati	—	56	—	60	65	40	—
Korea, South	60	79	3,336	4	92	—	99
Korea, North	—	67	2,834	48	100	59	—
Kuwait	66	78	3,075	8	—	—	99
Kyrgyzstan	—	66	2,489	53	77	59	66
Laos	40	64	2,143	50	51	30	66
Latvia	—	73	2,861	10	99	78	90
Lebanon	—	72	3,279	22	100	98	88
Lesotho	49	43	2,209	64	79	37	80
Liberia	47	46	1,640	131	61	27	30
Libya	52	74	3,132	18	711	97	100
Lithuania	—	73	2,805	8	—	—	88
Luxembourg	70	79	—	4	100	100	99
Macedonia	—	74	2,336	15	—	—	66
Madagascar	45	59	2,001	65	46	32	65
Malawi	40	48	2,097	88	73	61	44
Malaysia	62	74	2,899	9	99	94	70
Maldives	—	69	2,495	33	83	59	50
Mali	40	55	2,027	128	50	46	60
Malta	70	79	3,417	6	100	—	100
Mauritania	39	64	2,653	63	53	34	66
Mauritius	62	73	2,952	14	100	94	100
Mexico	62	76	3,137	16	97	79	92
Micronesia	—	69	—	34	94	28	—
Moldova	—	69	2,562	16	92	68	66
Monaco	—	63	2,985	58	100	100	41
Mongolia	60	67	2,098	39	62	59	60
Morocco	52	71	3,244	30	81	73	66
Mozambique	41	42	1,799	95	43	32	50
Myanmar	51	62	2,752	65	78	77	60
Namibia	48	53	2,168	41	87	25	80
Nepal	42	64	2,339	53	90	35	20
Netherlands	74	80	3,259	5	100	100	100
New Zealand	72	80	3,405	5	971	—	100
Nicaragua	54	73	2,328	21	79	47	46
Niger	38	57	2,116	109	46	13	66
Nigeria	44	47	2,609	109	48	44	10
Norway	74	80	3,350	3	100	100	100
Oman	45	76	—	12	801	831	90
Pakistan	48	66	2,408	67	91	59	65
Panama	66	76	2,556	18	90	73	80
Papua New Guinea	47	57	2,253	60	39	44	90
Paraguay	65	72	2,485	32	86	80	44
Peru	54	71	2,310	21	83	63	60
Philippines	57	72	2,356	23	85	72	66
Poland	70	76	3,344	7	—	—	88
Portugal	—	78	3,658	5	—	—	100
Qatar	61	76	—	8	100	100	99
Romania	69	73	2,943	15	57	—	85

Country	Life expectancy at birth (years) 1970	2005-10	Daily caloric supply, 1997	Infant mortality per 1,000 births 2008	Improved water, 2004	Improved sanitation, 2004	Essential drugs, 1999
Russian Fed.	—	66	2,704	16	97%	87%	66%
Rwanda	48	46	2,142	112	74	42	44
Samoa	—	72	—	22	88	100	100
São Tomé & Principe	—	66	2,156	72	79	25	—
Saudi Arabia	52	73	2,735	19	901	—	99
Senegal	43	63	2,394	65	76	57	66
Serbia	—	74	—	12	932	872	—
Seychelles	—	71	2,424	12	88	—	—
Sierra Leone	34	43	2,002	160	57	39	44
Singapore	68	80	—	3	100	100	100
Slovakia	—	75	3,030	7	100	99	100
Slovenia	—	78	3,117	5	—	—	100
Solomon Islands	40	64	2,103	54	70	31	—
Somalia	—	48	1,505	115	29	26	18
South Africa	53	49	2,933	45	88	65	80
Spain	72	81	3,295	4	100	100	100
Sri Lanka	64	72	2,240	11	79	91	95
St. Kitts & Nevis	—	70	2,263	30	99	95	—
St. Lucia	62	74	2,822	13	98	89	—
St. Vincent and The Grenadines	63	71	2,434	23	—	—	—
Sudan	—	59	2,391	64	70	34	15
Suriname	64	70	2,578	28	92	94	100
Swaziland	46	40	2,529	70	62	48	100
Sweden	75	81	3,160	3	100	100	99
Switzerland	73	82	3,280	4	100	100	100
Syria	56	74	3,339	16	93	90	80
Tajikistan	—	67	2,129	59	59	51	44
Tanzania	45	53	2,028	71	62	47	66
Thailand	58	71	2,334	10	99	99	95
Togo	45	58	2,155	88	52	35	70
Tonga	—	73	—	19	100	96	—
Trinidad and Tobago	66	70	2,751	12	91	100	77
Tunisia	54	74	3,250	19	93	85	51
Turkey	57	72	3,568	27	96	88	99
Turkmenistan	—	63	2,563	74	72	62	66
Uganda	47	52	2,110	76	60	43	70
Ukraine	—	68	2,753	13	96	96	66
United Arab Emirates	61	79	3,366	8	100	98	99
United Kingdom	72	79	3,237	5	100	—	99
United States	71	78	3,642	6	100	100	99
Uruguay	—	76	2,830	13	100	100	66
Uzbekistan	—	67	2,550	55	82	67	66
Vanuatu	—	70	2,624	28	60	50	—
Venezuela	65	74	2,398	17	83	68	90
Vietnam	—	74	2,502	19	85	61	85
Yemen	42	63	2,041	58	67	43	50
Zambia	47	42	1,939	92	58	55	66
Zimbabwe	51	44	2,083	57	81	53	70

Source: United Nations Population Fund (UNFPA), *The State of World Population 2008*, (2008), United Nations Department for Economic and Social Affairs, Population Division, *World Population Prospects: The 2006 Revision Highlights* (2007); UN Department for Economic and Social Information and Policy Analysis, chart: *World Population 1996;* United Nations Development Programme, *Human Development Report 2001* (2001; World Health Organization (WHO) and United Nations Children's Fund (UNICEF), *Drinking Water and Sanitation Coverage, 1990 and 2004* (2006).

▶CIRCULATORY DISEASES

According to the World Health Organization, diseases of the heart and circulatory system (cardiovascular and cerebrovascular diseases) such as heart attacks and stroke kill over 17 million people worldwide and account for 29.2 percent of the total number of deaths each year. Additional millions are disabled, frequently in their prime years. Worldwide, heart disease accounts for 6.5 million deaths and strokes kill another 5.1 million. But in developing countries, strokes kill twice as many people as heart disease.

Coronary heart disease became an epidemic in North America, Europe and Australasia in the early 1900s, peaked in the 1960s and early 1970s, and has since declined dramatically—by over 50 percent in some countries. The world's highest rates are now in eastern and central Europe.

In developed countries, almost half of all deaths—5 out of 12 million each year—are due to circulatory diseases. As the developing nations adopt Western lifestyles, these diseases are increasing rapidly; they now account for about 25 percent of all deaths.

Decades of research show that an unhealthy lifestyle, beginning in childhood, is the main cause of coronary heart disease. The major risk factors are high blood pressure, cigarette-smoking, poor dietary habits (especially the intake of saturated fat), elevated blood cholesterol, lack of physical activity, obesity and diabetes. Lack of physical activity is the most common risk factor in industrialized countries.

►CANCER

The World Health Organization estimates that in 2007 cancer was the leading cause of death worldwide causing 7.9 million deaths or about 13% of all deaths. The main types of cancer deaths are: lung (1.4 million deaths/year); stomach (866,000 deaths); liver (653,000 deaths); colon (677,000 deaths); breast (548,000 deaths).

The most frequent types of cancer worldwide (in order of the number of global deaths) differ in men and women: Among men—lung, stomach, liver, colorectal, oesophagus and prostate; Among women—breast, lung, stomach, colorectal and cervical.

About 30% of cancer deaths can be prevented. Tobacco use is the single most important risk factor for cancer. The incidence of cancer rises dramatically with age, due to an increase in risk factors and the fact that cellular repair mechanisms are less effective with age.

Tobacco use, alcohol use, low fruit and vegetable diet, and infections from hepatitis B, hepatitis C and the human papilloma viruses are leading risk factors for cancer in low- and middle-income countries. Cervical cancer, which is caused by HPV, is a leading cause of cancer death among women in low-income countries. In high-income countries, tobacco use, alcohol use, and being overweight or obese are primary causes of cancer. Other risk factors include low physical activity, unsafe sex, urban air pollution and indoor smoke from household use of solid fuels.

Prevention strategies include increase avoidance of the risk factors listed above, vaccination against human papilloma virus (HPV) and hepatitis B virus (HBV) infection, control of occupational hazards and reduction of exposure to sunlight.

Deaths from cancer worldwide are projected to continue rising, with an estimated 12 million deaths in 2030.

►MATERNAL DEATHS WORLDWIDE

Approximately 510,000 women die around the world each year from pregnancy-related causes, according to the World Health Organization. In parts of some developing countries, the chance of a woman dying this way is 100 times greater than in the industrialized countries.

The five major causes of maternal death are: hemorrhage (25 percent), indirect causes (19 percent), sepsis or postpartum infection (15 percent), hypertensive disorders of pregnancy and eclampsia (13 percent), and unsafe abortion (13 percent). About 70,000 women die each year from unsafe abortion—600 in developed countries and 69,000 in less developed countries—and an unknown but much larger number suffer infection, injury and trauma. There are an estimated 20 million unsafe abortions each year, 90 percent of them in developing countries.

Women who do not have adequate family planning materials and services have unwanted pregnancies and bear too many children, or they have children when they are too young or too old, or have children too close together. Virtually all studies report that most women would prefer using contraceptives and resort to abortion as a last resort.

►DEATHS OF CHILDREN

Of the 136 million births each year, 3.3 million babies are stillborn, more than four million die within 28 days of birth, and 6.6 million die before the age of five. The leading cause of neonatal deaths are preterm birth, severe infection, and birth asphyxia. Once an infant has survived the first year, childhood diseases, AIDS, malaria and other health hazards need to be surmounted. The leading single cause of childhood deaths is acute respiratory infection which takes more than two million young lives annually, followed by diarrhoeal diseases which take 1.8 million young lives. Malaria claims 853,000 children, 395,000 die from measles, HIV/AIDS 321,000.

In 2000, 42 countries accounted for 90 percent of all childhood deaths. Children in these countries often suffer from Vitamin A deficiency and lack access to antibiotics, clean drinking water, and sanitary living conditions. The majority of the 10.6 million childhood deaths can be prevented with proper health care.

►GLOBAL SEX FACTS

According to the World Health Organization, sexual intercourse occurs more than 100 million times a day around the world, resulting in approximately 910,000 conceptions and 350,000 cases of sexually transmitted diseases.

The W.H.O. estimates that 1,440 women die each day (an average of one a minute) because of complications during pregnancy or childbirth. About 150,000 unwanted pregnancies each day end in abortion.

The number of people using contraception in developing countries has increased sharply in recent years, from 31 million in the 1960–65 period to 381 million during 1985–90. Women in developing countries had, on average, 6.1 children in the years 1965–70, but the figure declined to 3.9 in 1985–90.

►SEXUALLY TRANSMITTED DISEASES (STDs)

In 2002, some 180,000 people died of sexually transmitted diseases other than HIV, including 152,000 from syphilis, 9,000 from chlamydia and 1,000 from gonorrhea. There are an estimated 333 million new cases of STDs each year. STDs are most frequent in young people aged 15 to 24. Women contract STDs five times more often than men. Almost two-thirds of all cases of infertility are due to STDs. W.H.O. estimates that in 1995, there were 150 million cases of STDs in adults in southern/southeastern Asia, 65 million cases in sub-Saharan Africa, 36 million in Latin America and the Caribbean, and 14 million in North America.

►AIDS WORLDWIDE

The Joint United Nations Programme on HIV/AIDS (UNAIDS) and the World Health Organization estimated that at the end of 2005, approximately 38.6 million people worldwide were living with HIV/AIDS, two-thirds of them in sub-Saharan Africa. During 2005, an estimated 4.1 million people were newly infected with HIV and 2.8 million people died from AIDS. UNAIDS now calculates that 2.8 million people aged 50 and older were living with HIV in 2005. The proportion of people who have become infected with HIV appears to have peaked in the late 1990s and is now stabilized even though there is an increase in several countries. This favorable trend is related to changes in behavior, prevention programs and antiretroviral drugs reaching more people.

Since the first clinical evidence of HIV/AIDS was reported in 1981, more than 65 million people have been infected with HIV and over 25 million people have died of AIDS. Sub-Saharan Africa has just over 10 percent of the world's population, but 64 percent of all people living with AIDS—some 25.5 million.

Across sub-Saharan Africa 6.4 percent of adults aged 15 to 49 have HIV. In 2005, about 2.7 million people in the region became newly infected, while 2 million died of AIDS. South Africa now has the world's second largest number of people infected with HIV/AIDS, 5.5 million adults and children, 18.8 percent of their population, and the virus shows no evidence of decline. The highest concentration of HIV/AIDS cases: 33.4 percent of the adult population is in Swaziland; Botswana has a 24.1 percent infection rate, Zimbabwe 20.1 percent, and Zambia 17 percent. Only Kenya and Zimbabwe and urban areas of Burkina Faso show a decline in HIV infections. The

global HIV/AIDS epicenter remains in the countries of southern Africa where about 43 percent of children under 15 and 52 percent of all women over the age of 15 are infected.

A growing number of people across sub-Saharan Africa, 810,000 in 2005, are now receiving antiretroviral drugs, but this is only 17 percent of the 4.7 million people who need this therapy. In Uganda 56 percent of adults are receiving these life extending drugs, 8 percent in Zimbabwe, 21 percent in South Africa and 27 percent in Zambia.

At the end of 2005, some 8.3 million people across Asia were living with HIV, more than two-thirds of them, 5.7 million people, in India, which now makes India home to more people infected with HIV than any other country. In Asia an estimated 930,000 people were newly infected in 2005, 180,000 children had HIV and 600,000 people died from AIDS. There were 650,000 people living with HIV in China in 2005, 580,000 in Thailand, and 360,000 in Myanmar (Burma). Some 180,000 people received antiretrovi-

HIV Estimates By Region, 2005

Region	Adults and children living with HIV	Number of women living with HIV	Adult prevalence[1]	Adults/children newly infected with HIV	Adult and child deaths due to AIDS
Sub-Saharan Africa	24,500,000	13,300,000	7.0%	2,700,000	2,000,000
Asia	8,300,000	2,300,000	0.4	930,000	600,000
South/South-east Asia	7,600,000	2,200,000	0.6	890,000	560,000
Latin America	1,600,000	480,000	0.5	140,000	59,000
Eastern Europe and Central Asia	1,500,000	420,000	0.8	220,000	53,000
North America	1,300,000	190,000	0.6	44,000	16,000
Western Europe	720,000	220,000	0.3	44,000	12,000
North Africa and Middle East	440,000	190,000	0.2	92,000	37,000
Caribbean	330,000	210,000	1.6	37,000	27,000
Oceania	78,000	35,100	0.3	7,200	3,400
TOTALS	**38,600,000**	**17,587,100**	**1.0**	**4,100,000**	**2,800,700**

1. The proportion of adults (15 to 49 years of age) living with HIV/AIDS in 2004, using 2004 population numbers **Source:** Joint United Nations Programme on HIV/AIDS (UNAIDS) and World Health Organization, *2006 Report on the Global AIDS Epidemic,* 2005.

Nations with Highest HIV Infected Populations, 2005

Region	Adults and children living with HIV	Adults living with HIV	Number of women living with HIV	Adult prevalence	Antiretroviral therapy among infected adults	Adult and child deaths due to AIDS
India	5,700,000	5,600,000	1,600,000	0.9%	7.0%	475,000
South Africa	5,500,000	5,300,000	3,100,000	18.8	21.0	320,000
Nigeria	2,900,000	2,600,000	1,600,000	3.9	7.0	220,000
Mozambique	1,800,000	1,600,000	976,000	16.1	9.0	140,000
Zimbabwe	1,700,000	1,500,000	890,000	20.1	8.0	180,000
Ethiopia1	1,500,000	1,400,000	770,000	4.4	7.0	120,000
Tanzania	1,400,000	1,300,000	710,000	6.5	7.0	160,000
Kenya	1,300,000	1,200,000	740,000	6.1	19.7	140,000
Zambia	1,100,000	1,000,000	570,000	17.0	27.0	98,000
Congo, Dem. Rep.	1,000,000	890,000	520,000	3.2	4.0	90,000
Uganda	1,000,000	900,000	520,000	6.7	56.0	91,000
Russia	940,000	940,000	210,000	1.1	NA	NA
Ivory Coast	750,000	680,000	400,000	7.1	17.0	65,000
China	650,000	650,000	180,000	0.1	NA	31,000
Brazil	620,000	610,000	220,000	0.5	NA	14,000
Thailand	580,000	560,000	220,000	1.4	60.0	21,000
Cameroon	510,000	470,000	290,000	5.4	22.0	46,000
Ukraine	410,000	410,000	200,000	1.4	NA	22,000
Botswana	270,000	260,000	140,000	24.1	85.0	18,000
Lesotho	270,000	250,000	150,000	23.2	14.0	23,000

Note: UNAIDS/WHO defines living orphans as living children under age 15 in 2001, who have lost at least one parent to AIDS.
Source: Joint United Nations Programme on HIV/AIDS (UNAIDS) and World Health Organization, Global HIV/AIDS & STD Surveillance, *Epi fact sheets by country,* 2005 updates.

ral drugs in Asia in 2005, with Thailand providing antiretroviral drugs to 60 percent of the people who need them. Across Asia about one in six people or 16 percent who need the antiretroviral drugs are receiving them.

HIV/AIDS continues to expand across eastern Europe and central Asia. Some 220,000 people were newly infected with HIV in 2005, bringing the total infections for the region to 1.5 million. An estimated 53,000 adults and children died from AIDS in 2005. Most people with HIV in eastern Europe are in the Ukraine and Russia. Only 21,000 of the 160,000 who need antiretroviral drugs are receiving them.

In the Caribbean HIV infection rates have decreased in urban areas of the Bahamas and Haiti, to about 3 percent. Infection rates in the Dominican Republic and Barbados appear to have leveled off, and antiretroviral treatments is reducing AIDS-related deaths. Overall, 23 percent of persons needing the antiretroviral drugs are receiving them.

In Latin America 140,000 people were newly infected with HIV in 2005, raising the total to 1.6 million across the region. Brazil has 620,000 infected people, 0.5 percent of the population. Belize and Honduras, much smaller countries, have infection rates of more than 1.5 percent. Antiretroviral treatment has increased in Argentina, Brazil, Chile, Costa Rica, Mexico, Panama, Uruguay and Venezuela, but the poorest countries in Central America and the Andean region are facing affordability limitations.

Infection rates in the Middle East and North Africa are less than 0.1 percent, but infections are increasing in Algeria, Iran, Libya and Morocco. Some 64,000 people were newly infected in the region in 2005, bringing the total number of people living with HIV to 440,000. Sudan accounts for 350,000 of these cases. Only 5 percent of the estimated 75,000 people needing antiretroviral therapy were receiving it at the end of 2005.

HIV rates remain low across Oceania, 78,000 infected people. Australia's epidemic is continuing and Papua New Guinea accounts for 90 percent of all HIV infections in the region, outside of Australia and New Zealand. Statistics on antiretroviral therapy for the region are not published by UNAIDS.

Between 2001 and 2005, the number of people getting antiretroviral treatment in poorer countries increased from 240,000 to 1.3 million. However, antiretroviral drugs still reach only one in five people who need them. Costs and inadequate delivery systems are still large problems.

From 2000 to 2005, funding for all aspects of HIV/AIDS programs increased. Funding for development of preventive vaccines rose from $327 million to $630 million during this period. Resources from public and philanthropic sectors in microbicide research and development rose from $65 million in 2001 to $163 million in 2005. Funding for AIDS work in poorer countries reached $8.3 billion in 2005, and is expected to reach $8.9 billion in 2006 and $10 billion in 2007, but this funding will still be far short of the estimated $14.9 billion needed in 2006 and $18.1 billion needed in 2007.

(For more detailed information on AIDS in the United States, see Health and Medicine in Part II.)

World Religions

In 1996, 4.7 billion, or an estimated 80 percent of the world's population, identified themselves as adherents of one religion or another. Four religions—Christianity, Islam, Hinduism and Buddhism— claim 4.2 billion adherents, or 72 percent of the world's population, Approximately 19 percent of the world's people are atheist or nonreligious.

This section describes the major religions of the world, their basic tenets, scriptures, schools and sects, and their history. (Additional details may be found in the section Religion in America.)

▶JUDAISM

Origins Judaism is the oldest of the world's three major monotheistic religions and a forerunner of Christianity and Islam. The Hebrew Bible recounts the story of the world and mankind from the creation, through the flood, and the work of the patriarch Abraham who brought his people from Mesopotamia to Canaan—the Promised Land. His descendants were enslaved in Egypt until Moses led them out of captivity. During the exodus, Moses received from God the Ten Commandments that form the bedrock of Jewish law. Jewish custom and law further evolved from the 10th century B.C. and the conquest of Canaan to the destruction of Jerusalem by the Romans in A.D. 70.

Scripture The sacred scripture of the Hebrew Bible, or Masorah, consists of 24 books. (The Christian Old Testament divides the same text into 39 books.) The *Torah*, or Law, was composed between the 10th and 5th centuries B.C. These five books—Genesis, Exodus, Leviticus, Numbers and Deuteronomy—are also known by their Greek name, *Pentateuch*. The later history of Israel and the divided kingdom is told in two separate but overlapping traditions known as the Prophets (13th-6th centuries B.C.) and the Writings (11th-2nd centuries B.C.). The Hebrew Bible is also known by the Greek name *Septuagint* (seventy), a reference to the number of authors engaged in its translation from Hebrew to Greek in the 3rd century B.C. In addition to scripture, there is a rich ancient tradition of rabbinical commentary called the *Talmud*, a huge compilation of the Oral Law and the accepted authority for Orthodox Jews. First codified around A.D. 200, the Talmudic tradition continued through the centuries and constitutes not only commentary on the law (*Halakah*), but also stories from the Bible and parables, legends, etc. (*Haggadah*) illustrating religious principles.

Beliefs Central to Jewish belief is the idea of a single God—Yahweh—who made a covenant (i.e. an agreement or contract) with His chosen people that He would protect them and provide for them if they swore Him love and obedience. Yahweh shapes history (the end of which is the kingdom of God) and imposes His will upon mankind; He saves, and He judges. The people of *Israel* have a unique relationship with God affirmed on the one hand by His covenant, and on the other, by His law. While Yahweh the creator guides human destiny, the humanity of mankind is defined by the ability of individuals to make ethical choices in keeping with His law. The failure to act according to His law— that is, to know God—is sin, and a basic tenet of Jewish faith is that sin is a willful act; so, too, is turning, or returning, to God.

The book of Isaiah (8th century B.C.) brings to the fore a messianic tradition identifying a future Israel under a divine ruler descended from the house of David as a restoration of paradise and the attainment of salvation.

Practice Jews worship in synagogues in congregations led by a rabbi—a teacher or master. The Sabbath is observed from sunset Friday to sunset

Saturday; worship consists of readings from scripture, prayer, and singing. The most important holidays in the Jewish calendar are Rosh Hashanah (New Year), Yom Kippur (Day of Atonement), Hanukah (Festival of Lights), and Pesach (Passover). (See Part I: Holidays and Holy Days.)

Schools and sects   There are three main branches of modern Judaism. Orthodox Jews rigorously observe Jewish law, ritual and custom. Reform Judaism professes a more liberal interpretation of Jewish doctrine and ritual, and is especially prevalent in the United States. Conservative Judaism combines elements of doctrinal reform with more traditional observance. Hasidism is today a branch of Orthodox Judaism with origins in a mystical movement in 18th-century Poland that stressed prayer over studying the Torah. Hasidim are very strict observers of the Jewish religious laws.

History   The Bible recounts the history of the Jewish people from the creation, through the flood and the covenant of the rainbow, the patriarchs Abraham, Isaac and Jacob, and the story of the tribe of Israel in Egypt. The foundation of Jewish faith began with the exodus from Egypt, and the transmission of the Ten Commandments (the Decalogue) from God to his people through Moses, probably sometime between 1450 and 1290 B.C. The people of Israel conquered and settled in Canaan—the promised land—and were ruled by a succession of judges. The monarchical period under Samuel and David dates to the 11th and 10th centuries B.C. Israel and Judah continued under separate rulers until the fall of Israel in 722 B.C. Judah was conquered by Babylonians, and the Temple of David in Jerusalem was destroyed in 586 B.C. at the start of the Babylonian captivity, which also marks the start of the Jewish Diaspora, or dispersal. Exile lasted until 538 B.C., and the Second Temple was dedicated in 516 B.C. Under Seleucid rule the Maccabees successfully resisted efforts to suppress Judaism (168-142 B.C.). Under Roman rule (63 B.C.—A.D. 135), there were several revolts, the first of which resulted in the destruction of the Second Temple (A.D. 70). It was at around this time that Christianity began to diverge sharply from its Jewish sectarian origins.

The early Middle Ages saw the rise of the Talmudic tradition. Following the rise of Islam, Judaism evolved into two distinct strains, the Sephardim, centered in Spain, and the Ashkenazim, found mainly in France and Germany. Organized persecution of European Jewry began with their expulsion from France (1306) and Spain (1492), and culminated in the Nazi regime in Germany's attempt to eradicate all Jews during the Holocaust (1933-45). The Jewish enlightenment (*Haskala*) in 18th-century Germany gave rise to Reform Judaism and Conservative Judaism (1845). The nationalistic Zionist movement, a reaction to extreme anti-Semitism, led eventually to the birth of the State of Israel in 1948. Though Israel is a secular republic, religious parties play an active role in politics.

Geography and numbers   There are an estimated 15 million Jews in 134 countries, the overwhelming majority of whom live in the United States (5.8 million) and Israel (4.3 million). There are an estimated 2.4 million Jews in Europe.

▶ CHRISTIANITY

Origins   Christianity is based on the acts and sayings of Jesus of Nazareth as related by his followers and apostles. Jesus was born a Jew in Bethlehem in about 4 B.C., but details of his life before about 26–28 A.D. are obscure. In his early 30s, Jesus was baptized by John the Baptist, whose ministry prophesied the coming judgment of God, and who recognized Jesus as the Messiah (Greek for the Christ, or anointed one). Jesus' ministry, chiefly among the poor and dispossessed, lasted only a few years before he was crucified by Roman authorities. According to Christian belief, Jesus rose from the dead three days after his crucifixion, and 40 days later he ascended to heaven to sit at the right hand of God.

Scripture   The Bible consists of the Old Testament (the Hebrew Bible), originally written in Hebrew and Aramaic, and the New Testament (first written in Greek in the first century), which relates the life and teachings of Jesus and his early followers. A 3rd-century translation of the Bible into Latin is called the Vulgate. The central portion of the New Testament consists of the Four Gospels (each attributed to one of Christ's earliest followers: Matthew, Mark, Luke, and John). While each tells the story of Jesus' life and death, they differ in details, with Luke and John providing more stories and greater emphasis on Christ's divinity. The story of the spread of Christianity in the first century is told in the Acts of the Apostles and the epistles (letters) of St. Paul. The Roman Catholic canon also includes 15 books found in the Greek Septuagint but not in the Hebrew Bible. The Orthodox Church accepts four of these Apocryphal books; Protestants accept none.

Beliefs   Christian belief is rooted in three basic ideas: incarnation—Christ was the human embodiment of God; atonement—mankind was reconciled to God through the agency of Christ; and the Trinity—the belief that the one God has three natures, God the Father, God the Son (Jesus), and God the Holy Spirit.

Practice   Central to the practice of most Christians are the seven sacraments: baptism, confirmation, holy matrimony, holy orders, sacrament of the sick, reconciliation (confession), and the Eucharist, (or communion), the sacramental offering and consumption of bread and wine representing the body and blood of Christ. Christians are organized into congregations and worship in churches led by priests or ministers who administer the sacraments. Most denominations designate Sunday as the sabbath and the day for special observance and worship.

Schools and sects   Christianity has three major branches: Eastern Orthodoxy, Roman Catholicism, and Protestantism. The division between Eastern Orthodoxy and Roman Catholicism came in 1054. In the 16th century, reform-minded priests broke with Rome and there emerged a number of distinct denominations known collectively as Protestantism.

The hierarchical authority of the Catholic Church starts with the pope, and includes cardinals, bishops, and priests, all celibate men. In addition there are a number of Catholic lay and priestly orders for men and/or women.

The Eastern Orthodox Church embraces a number of national or regional churches. The laity are invested with more authority than are Catholics, and the bishop of Constantinople, titular head of the eastern church, is regarded as first among equals.

Protestant denominations number in the hundreds. There is no single governing authority for all of them. (See Part II: Religion in America for a summary of the major sects.)

History   At the time of his death, Jesus had a small handful of followers among Jews. His teachings were not widely accepted among the larger Jewish community, however, and his disciples preached to non-Jewish gentiles throughout the Roman Empire. Jesus' teachings were gathered in a collection of books known as the Gospel, or New Testament. Christians were widely persecuted until the Emperor Constantine legalized the religion in 313; in

380 Christianity became the official religion of the Roman Empire. Christianity also reached northern Ethiopia.

Disputes over theological issues such as the nature of the Trinity and the person of Christ were resolved at a series of ecumenical councils. In 1054 the Eastern and Western churches split over differences of theology, politics, geography and language. The papacy in Rome acquired the nature of a civil authority and within the Western church ascetic, spiritual traditions competed with secular ones. In the 16th century, papal authority was challenged by such reform-minded priests as Martin Luther and John Calvin, abetted by England's King Henry VIII, who transferred authority over the church in England from the pope to himself. Sectarian wars engulfed Europe for more than a century as Catholics and Protestants vied for temporal and spiritual power.

European explorers and colonists spread Christianity to the Americas, Asia and Africa. The Spanish and Portuguese brought Catholicism to Latin America, while North America became a haven for Protestant denominations from northern Europe. Since the mid-1800s, Protestant and Catholic evangelists have carried out energetic missionary programs to Africa and East Asia.

Geography and numbers   Christianity is the most populous and most widespread religion in the world, with almost 2 billion adherents in 260 countries. Europe is home to more than 555 million Christians (76 percent of the region's population), but Latin America has proportionally the highest number of Christian adherents—93 percent of the population. There are more Christians in Africa (360 million, or 48 percent of the population) and Asia (303 million) than in North America (255 million).

▶ISLAM

Origins   The precepts of Islam were revealed through Mohammed, the last of a line of prophets including Abraham, Moses and Jesus. Mohammed was born about 570 at Mecca (in western Saudi Arabia) and died in 632 in the nearby city of Medina.
Scripture   The Koran (recitation) consists of 114 chapters. The text is the infallible word of God as revealed to Mohammed and transcribed by his followers over the course of 23 years.
Beliefs   Islam is a monotheistic religion with explicit links to Judaism and Christianity. The Koran's narrative includes stories of Abraham and Isaac, and Moses and the Ten Commandments. Unlike Jews, who trace their descent from Abraham through Isaac, the son of Sarah, Muslims trace their decent through Ishmael, Abraham's son by Hagar. The Koran recounts the virgin birth of Jesus, but does not accept his divinity.

The word Islam comes from the Arabic root s-l-m, meaning peace and submission, and a hallmark of Islam is obedience to God.
Practice   A Muslim's relations with God are regulated by the Five Pillars of Islam: the Shahadah, or profession of faith—There is no God but God, and Mohammed is his prophet; public and collective prayer five times daily; charity to the poor; fasting during the holy month of Ramadan; and pilgrimage to Mecca, the most holy place in the Muslim world, at least once in one's lifetime.

Islam has strict dietary laws and prohibitions against promiscuity, theft, gambling and lying. Muslims worship in mosques led by imams. The principal weekly worship is on Friday at midday.
Schools and sects   The overwhelming majority of Muslims are Sunnites, or traditionalists (83 percent, or 934 million people). Shi'ites, or partisans, represent another 16 percent (180 million) and smaller sects make up the rest. The Shi'ite/Sunnite schism reflects differences about who should have succeeded Mohammed. Shi'ites follow somewhat different rites than Sunnites, and recognize additional holy days and places.
History   Mohammed was born in Arabia in about 570 A.D. Raised by his uncle, at the age of 25 he became a trader, and later married his employer, the widow Khadija. In 610, an angel descended on Mohammed and ordered him to proclaim the word of God. Rebuked in Mecca, in 622 he was invited to Medina to help bring order to the city. He accepted on the condition that the citizens worship Allah—the one God—and accept the precepts of Islam. This move—the hegira—is the year from which the Muslim calendar dates. Eight years later Mohammed returned to Mecca, and by the time of his death in 632, most Arabs were Muslims.

Under a succession of secular and theocratic caliphates, Islam swept east and west from Arabia. Muslims reached the Indus River in 713, and their advance in France was only stopped in 733 at the Battle of Tours; Muslims remained in Spain until 1492. Islamic armies captured the Byzantine capital of Constantinople in 1453, and controlled much of southeastern Europe until the 19th century. In the east, Muslims swept through India at the end of the 10th century and reached the East Indies in the 15th century.

The arts, architecture and technology flourished in the golden age of Islam and Islamic learning and culture was responsible for the transmission of much of classical philosophy and science to the West.

From the 18th to 20th centuries, traditionally Islamic countries came under Western cultural and political influence. In the 20th century, some traditionally Islamic countries like Turkey opted for a secular state; others such as Saudi Arabia and Iran came under strict fundamentalist rule.
Geography and numbers   With 1.3 billion adherents in 184 countries, Islam is the second largest religion in the world. It is the dominant religion throughout the Middle East, North Africa, Central Asia, Afghanistan, Pakistan, and Indonesia, the country with the largest number of adherents (172 million people). There are 104 million Muslims in India—11 percent of that country's population.

▶HINDUISM

Origins   Hinduism is a complex of polytheistic religion and philosophy that evolved from Vedism, an ancient Indian religion of Indo-European origin dating from the second millennium B.C.
Scripture   Different Hindu sects rely on different holy texts, but common to the majority are the Vedic texts called the Upanishads. The Svetasvatara Upanishad describes Siva, the creator, preserver and destroyer of the universe. Sources for Hindu mythology include the Mahabharata, Ramayana (concerning Rama, the incarnation of the great god Vishnu), and the Puaranas. The Bhagavad Gita (Lord's song, a part of the Mahabharata), is a dialogue between Krishna (another incarnation of the god Vishnu) and Prince Arjuna in which are described the three paths to union with God.
Beliefs   Hinduism is rooted in the belief that individuals should connect their selves (Atman) with Brahman, or Godhead, the spiritual source of the tangible universe. Hindus also believe in reincarnation—samsara—one's subsequent status being dependent on one's actions (karma) and duties (dharma) in this life. The cycle of reincarnation is broken when one attains liberation (moksha) from the finite world through self-discovery—the union of self with the Godhead, or Atman-Brahman. There are four paths to union with Brahman: jnana yoga, based on knowledge; bhakti yoga, based on service to God; karma yoga, based on work for God (as opposed to oneself); and raja yoga, based on psychophysical exercise.

Hinduism has three primary theistic traditions revolving around the cults of anthropomorphic gods. Vishnu is a loving god incarnated as Krishna; Siva is a god at once protective and destructive; and Brahma is creator. Saktism is a form of worship dedicated to the female consorts of Vishnu and Siva.

Hindus have a deep respect for all living things; the most revered animal is the cow.

Practice Hindu worship is largely an individual and family matter. Hindu temples are devoted to a particular god or group of gods. Worship in temples or before domestic shrines includes prayers and offerings to an image of the god. Such rituals are intended to bring the worshipper and the god closer together.

Hindu pilgrimage sites include seven sacred cities, among others, where thousands or even millions of Hindus worship at annual festivals. Some of the most famous temples are on the banks of the Ganges River, which is sacred to Hindus, in northern India. Important festival days include Dipavali, festival of lights, sacred to Lakshmi, goddess of prosperity; holi, a spring festival; and Dashara, a harvest festival.

Individuals follow a code of moral and religious conduct called *dharma*. Traditional Hinduism observes complex societal divisions into four primary (and thousands of subsidiary) castes defined by occupation and social standing: *brahmins:* leaders, philosophers, artists and their families; *kshatriyas:* princes, soldiers and administrators; *vaishyas:* merchants and landowners; and *shudras*, or laborers. Beyond the caste system are untouchables, or outcasts. India's modern constitution outlawed the caste system.

Schools and sects Hinduism comprises myriad religious cults and various schools of philosophy. The principle of religious toleration is reflected in the Hindu belief that Christianity, Islam and other religions offer alternative paths to the same goal. Among the more prominent modes of belief are *yoga* and *tantrism*, both of which evolved in both Hinduism and Buddhism, and *bhakti*. *Tantrism* emphasizes meditation and ritual involving mystical diagrams (mandalas) and chants (mantras) as a means to enlightenment. *Yoga* emphasizes an eightfold path to enlightenment through physical and mental training. *Bhakti* focuses on the primacy of love for a deity.

History Hinduism is the oldest of the world's great religions. Originating in India, it spread to Nepal and southeast Asia. The oldest Hindu writings are actually Vedic texts brought by Aryan invaders in the second millennium B.C. To the Vedic concept of future life, Hinduism attached the ideas of karma, reincarnation and ultimately release from the cycle of life, death and rebirth. Following the rise of rival religions such as Buddhism and Jainism in the 6th century B.C., ritual sacrifice to Vedic deities overseen by priests gave way to polytheistic worship intended to unite the worshipper with the god worshipped.

The classical period of Hinduism dates from the 6th century B.C. to the 10th century A.D., when the major theistic sects emerged and many of the classic works of Hinduism were composed, including the epic *Mahabharata* and *Ramayana* and a variety of works that discuss the duties of caste, advice to rulers, the attainment of pleasure and the attainment of liberation, or moksha. Hindu princes successfully resisted Muslim encroachment from the West until the 10th century. The Muslim ascendancy was coupled with the rise of *bhakti*, a devotional Hinduism that stresses love for the deity, and the adoption of vernacular languages for worship rather than Sanskrit.

Since the 18th century there have been several movements to strip Hinduism of its polytheistic practices, and in this century, great emphasis has been laid on Hindu prescriptions for non-violence and social equality, especially as practiced by the founder of modern India, Mahatma Gandhi.

Geography and numbers Hinduism has an estimated 793 million adherents worldwide. With deep roots in India, and lacking a missionary tradition, it is found almost nowhere outside of India and neighboring countries except in expatriate Indian communities.

▶ BUDDHISM

Origins Buddhism was established by the followers of Siddhartha Gautama (ca. 563-483 B.C.), who was born into a kshatriya caste Hindu family in present-day Nepal. At the age of 29, he left his wife and young son in search of enlightenment. This he attained, according to tradition, while sitting under a bodhi tree near Patna. After 49 days of rapture, and withstanding the temptations of the devil Mara, Buddha—the enlightened one—inspired an order of monks and went forth to preach his philosophy of enlightenment for 45 years before passing into nirvana, in which ideas and consciousness cease to be.

Scripture Of primary importance to all Buddhists is the *Tipitaka* (Three baskets), a record of the Buddha's teachings set down set down by Buddha's early followers after his death. These tell the story of his life (Buddha), his laws (Dharma) for personal conduct, and the guidelines for the monastic order (Sangha). There is a large body of other writings peculiar to individual sects and schools. The Buddhist canon continued to evolve over many centuries.

Beliefs Buddhists share with Hinduism a belief in the cycle of reincarnation and that this cycle could be broken. Buddha's teachings are predicated on the Four Noble Truths. Life is impermanent and fundamentally produces suffering, or *dukkha*, perpetuated due to the endless cycle of life, death, and rebirth. This suffering results from the pursuit of mortal desires. Desire can be overcome by attaining *nirvana*. *Nirvana* can be reached by adhering to the Eightfold Path. This path, or Middle Way, consists of right belief, thought, speech, action, livelihood, effort, mindfulness and concentration. These are the backbone of Buddhist ethics.

Practice A hallmark of Buddhist practice is the monastic order, to which monks withdraw from the everyday world and live austere lives of meditation either for a few years or for a lifetime. Mendicants also live on alms contributed by lay Buddhists. In certain sects, adolescents spend time in a monastery as part of a rite of passage into adulthood.

Buddhist temples are primarily for individual meditation, and collective rituals play a smaller part in the life of a Buddhist than in the lives of Jews, Christians and Muslims, or even of Hindus.

Schools and sects There are three main sects in Buddhism. Theravada (or Hinayana) Buddhism, which predominates today in Sri Lanka, Myanmar and Thailand, adheres most closely to the tenets of the early Buddhist sects. In this tradition, attainment of nirvana for oneself is the goal. Mahayana Buddhism, which became the larger sect, spread along the Silk Road from India to China and East Asia. This includes the worship of Buddha and Buddhist saints (*bodhisattvas*). Stressing compassion for others, *boddhisatvas*—literally wisdom beings—withhold themselves from attaining nirvana in order to help others attain enlightenment. In Zen Buddhism, a sect of Mahayana, adherents strive for enlightenment through mental conditioning and meditation. The third sect of Tantric Buddhism (Vajrayana), most common in Tibet and Mongolia, attempts to identify the initiate with a visualized deity. The Tantric canon includes esoteric texts, and meditation engages both the mind and the senses with the use of *mantras* (chants), *mudras* (hand gestures) and *mandalas* (visible icons of the universe). The spiritual and temporal leader of Tibetan Buddhists is the Dalai Lama.

History Following Buddha's death, his *sutras* (sermons) and *vinaya* (regulations) were written down by his disciples. Originally, Buddhist mendicants taught for nine months and held retreats during the monsoon. These retreats led to the establishment of monasteries and the rise of differing interpretations of Buddha's teaching. The Mahayana school more easily absorbs (and is absorbed by) different cultures. It received its greatest impetus in India from the Buddhist emperor Ashoka (272-232 B.C.), who sent missionaries to Ceylon, Southeast Asia and China, from where it was carried to Korea and Japan in the 6th century A.D.

The 7th century saw the rise of Zen Buddhism in China and Japan, and of Tantric Buddhism in Tibet. Chinese Buddhism reached its height in the 9th century during the T'ang Dynasty, when it was partially suppressed. Buddhism flourished in Japan until the 19th century, when Shintoism gained imperial favor.

Buddhism lost its influence in India beginning in the 8th century, partly through absorption of its ideas into Hinduism, and partly because of the rise of Islam. By the 13th century, Buddhism was all but extinct there.

Geography and numbers There are an estimated 350 million people in 92 countries who adhere to Buddhist beliefs and practices. Mahayana Buddhists account for about 53 percent (185 million) of all Buddhists, mostly in Japan, Korea and China; Theravada Buddhists account for 35 percent (124 million), in Southeast Asia and Sri Lanka. Lamaist Buddhists account for about 6 percent (21 million) in Tibet and Mongolia. Buddhist practice in Tibet is under threat from the Chinese government.

▶**OTHER ORGANIZED RELIGIONS**

Baha'i Founded by Baha'Ullah (glory of God) in Iran in 1844, Baha'i teaches that the revealed religions of the world are in agreement and that the respective prophet-founders of each revealed the will of God for a particular time and place in history. There are approximately 6 million members of the Baha'i faith; the center of the Baha'i faith is in Haifa, Israel. A major temple in Wilmette, Illinois, attracts many visitors.

Chinese folk religions Chinese folk religions consist of a blend of ancient ancestor worship with elements of Buddhism, Confucianism, and Taoism. Taoism is a philosophy or religion based on the teachings of Lao-tzu, another great teacher of Confucian times. The vast majority of the world's 215 to 220 million adherents of Chinese folk religions live in China; the remainder live in scattered Chinese settlements around the world.

Confucianism As much a code of ethical conduct as a religion, Confucianism takes its name from the 6th-century B.C. scholar and civil servant Kung Fu-Tzu (Confucius), whose *Analects* prescribe the proper conduct for life. His impact on China has been enormous, and at times his cult has attained the status of a quasi-official religion. There are about 5 million Confucianists in the world; most of them live in South Korea.

Jainism Jainism is a polytheistic religion established in India by Vardhamana in the 6th century B.C. Its primary features are a belief in the perfection of the soul and in non-injury to living creatures. Almost all of the world's 5 million Jainists live in India.

New Religion This term applies to a variety of more or less organized religious systems that have grown up, primarily in East Asia, since the turn of the century. These religions are characterized by a synthesis of indigenous folk religion with various major Asian traditions (Hinduism, Buddhism, Confucianism and/or Taoism) overlaid with modern Western philosophy. There are more than 100 million people professing adherence to these religions, the majority of them in the Philippines, Indonesia, and Japan.

Parsiism This religion has its roots in Zoroastrianism, an ancient Iranian religion whose central focus is the struggle between good and evil. Its monotheistic tendencies are thought to have influenced the development of Judaism and Christianity. Parsis emigrated to India between the 10th and 15th centuries, and prospered as merchants, especially in Bombay.

Shintoism Evolved from ancient Japanese religious traditions, Shintoism became a state religion under the Meijis in the 19th century. Although some sacred Shinto (literally way of the gods) texts date from the 8th century, none is considered authoritative. There are three strains of Shinto practice: State Shinto, Shrine Shinto, and Folk Shinto.

Sikhism The Sikh religion was founded by Guru Nanak in the early 16th century. A hybrid of Hindu and Islamic beliefs, it advocates a search for eternal truth and, while believing in reincarnation, rejects the notion of divine incarnation. It was led by a succession of ten gurus, the last of whom declared himself the last human guru. Sikhs now follow the sacred text known as Guru Granth Singh, or Collection of Sacred Wisdom. There are almost 19 million Sikhs in the world; almost all of them live in the Punjab region of India.

▶**NONRELIGIOUS AND ATHEISTS**

An estimated 887 million people (15 percent of the world's population) profess no religion, are agnostic or are indifferent to religion. Another 222 million people (4 percent) are declared atheists who do not believe in God. More than three-quarters (852 million) of these nonreligious and atheists live in China, where religious observance is sharply curtailed by the government. An estimated 12 percent of people in Europe are nonreligious, compared with 9.8 percent in Oceania, 7.2 percent in North America, and 3.3 percent in Latin America.

▶**CHRONOLOGY OF WORLD RELIGION**
B.C.

3000 Earliest elements of Hinduism develop in India.

c. 2500 Egyptian pyramids at Giza completed.

c. 1500 Aryan peoples invade India; bring additional elements of Hinduism.

c. 1290 Moses leads Israelites out of Egypt.

1010–922 Reigns of Hebrew kings David and Solomon. A great temple built at Jerusalem.

740 Hebrew prophet Isaiah flourishes.

628 Traditional birth date of Zoroaster, religious teacher in Persia. Followers today are Parsees in India.

587 Babylonians destroy Hebrew temple at Jerusalem and take many Hebrews as slaves. Fifty years later, Hebrews are freed and begin to rebuild temple.

560 Birth of Siddartha Gautama in northern India; later known as Buddha. Dies c. 480. His teachings, on which Buddhism is based, gain many followers in India, later spread to Southeast Asia.

551 Birth of Chinese teacher Confucius. Dies c. 479.

200 Mahayana Buddhism begins to spread in China and Japan.

4 Birth of Jesus Christ. The Western calendar dates from the supposed year of his birth.

A.D.

30 Death and resurrection of Jesus Christ.

66–70 Jewish revolt against Romans ends in destruction of second temple and scattering of Jews (a.k.a. The First Diaspora).

175 Apostles' Creed, a brief statement of Christian beliefs, formulated.

303–12 In final organized program of persecution, Romans kill estimated 500,000 Christians.

313 The emperor Constantine decrees toleration for Christianity in Roman Empire. In 325, he calls synod of Nicaea, which formulates Nicene Creed. By end of 300s, Christianity is official religion of empire.

354 Birth of St. Augustine, influential Christian teacher, in North Africa. Dies 430.

451 Council of Chalcedon (fourth ecumenical council) formulates long-held Christian understanding of Christ, the union in one person of two distinct natures, human and divine.

570 Muhammad, founder of Islam, born in Mecca (now in Saudi Arabia). Dies in 632 in nearby city of Medina.

600+ Tantrism, a Hindu school, grows up, emphasizing special rituals as means of enlightenment; uses mystical diagrams (mandalas) and chants (mantras).

650+ Islam enters India, gains many converts.

700+ Development in China of Zen, a school of Buddhism, which later attracted particular attention in the modern Western world.

711–715 Muslim Arabs settle in Spain.

800 Roman Empire revived in the West with the coronation of Charlemagne as emperor on Christmas Day, in St. Peter's in Rome.

988 Christianity reaches Russia through missionaries from eastern churches.

1054 Eastern (or Orthodox) and Western (or Roman) churches go separate ways after disputes about doctrine and authority.

1096 Christians in Europe go on first Crusade to take Holy Land from Muslims. Seven other major Crusades pursued between 1100 and 1300. Christian warriors temporarily occupy Jerusalem and other cities, but soon lose them again to Muslims.

1216 Pope Innocent III approves formation of Franciscans and Dominicans.

1227 Thomas Aquinas, great Christian theologian, born in Italy.

1300+ Bhakti, a Hindu sect, develops emphasizing primacy of love for a deity and using love between humans as illustration; rejects caste, ritual, and creeds, and emphasizes need for sincerity.

1309 The papacy moves from Rome to Avignon, France, where it remains until 1377 (The Babylonian Captivity of the Church).

1377 English theologian and religious reformer John Wycliffe accused of heresy by Pope Gregory XI for attacks on worldliness of the church.

1378–1417 The Great Western Schism, during which first two, then three, claimants sought recognition as pope.

1415 Excommunication and execution of Czech religious leader Jan Hus, who protested sale of indulgences and other papal excesses, sets off Hussite Wars, which end with Compactata of Prague.

1453 Ottoman Turks (Muslims) conquer capital of Eastern Roman Empire, Constantinople. Turks push westward into Europe.

1454 Johannes Gutenberg prints first Bible with moveable type.

1469 Birth of Nanak, founder of Sikhism, in Punjab region of India.

1492 Muslims overthrown in Spain; Spanish Inquisition begins.

1517 Martin Luther, a German priest, posts 95 theses on cathedral door, questioning church teachings. Luther refuses to recant; is excommunicated from Catholic church. With cooperation of north German princes, he forms new Protestant churches. This begins Reformation, which ultimately divides European Christianity into two warring camps.

1534 King Henry VIII of England denies power of pope over church in England and establishes Church of England responsible to monarch. New church gradually adopts Protestant beliefs but maintains many practices of earlier Catholic era.

1536 John Calvin, a young French scholar, publishes *Institutes of the Christian Religion*, and becomes second major leader of Protestant Christianity; helping to create Presbyterian and other Reformed churches.

1540 Ignatius Loyola, a Spaniard, establishes the Jesuits (Society of Jesus) with papal approval. This order becomes powerful instrument of Catholic church in disputes with Protestants, in missionary efforts around world, and in education.

1545–63 Council of Trent makes major reforms in Catholic church and defines disagreements with Protestants. Its work begins Catholic Reformation, or Counter-Reformation.

1598 In the Edict of Nantes, Henry IV proclaims peaceful coexistence of Catholics and Calvinists in France. Revoked in 1685 by Louis XIV.

1618–48 Thirty Years War, caused in part by Protestant-Catholic hatreds, decimates central Europe. Calvinist leaders in England overthrow monarchy and execute king in civil war (1642-49). Monarchy is restored in 1660.

1620 Pilgrims, a small group of English Calvinists, establish colony at Plymouth in North America to escape persecution in England.

1683 Muslim Turks defeated near Vienna, Austria, in their last attempt to establish foothold in western Europe.

1734 The Great Awakening, a religious revival, sweeps New England, begun by prominent Massachusetts preacher Jonathan Edwards. English evangelist George Whitefield tours American colonies beginning in 1738, preaching to outdoor gatherings.

1738 Christian conversion experienced by brothers John and Charles Wesley in England. They begin evangelical activities, leading to development of independent Methodist church.

1789 U.S. Constitution guarantees separation of church and state.

1792 Second Awakening sweeps new United States, lasting more than 20 years. Revivals in Kentucky in 1800 result in formation of new denominations, ancestors of Disciples of Christ, Churches of Christ, and Christian churches.

1830 American Joseph Smith has religious visions that lead him to organize the Church of Jesus Christ of the Latter-Day Saints (Mormons).

1844 Baha'i established in Iran.

1869–79 Vatican Council I, convened by Pope Pius IX, declares that teachings of pope in matters of faith and morals are infallible.

1875 Mary Baker Eddy publishes *Science and Health with Key to the Scriptures* in Boston; it becomes basis of Church of Christ, Scientist.

1900 First documented modern Pentecostal experience—worshipers speak in unknown tongues during prayer meeting in Kansas. Within 20 years, Pentecostal churches form major new Christian denomination.

1935–45 Nazi government in Germany carries out destruction of estimated six million European Jews. This event known as the Holocaust.

1945–46 Compulsory adherence to Shintoism ended in Japan; Emperor Hirohito disavows his divinity to Japanese people.

1947 U.N. approves creation of the new state of Israel in Middle East for settlement by Jews.

1948 World Council of Churches established at huge assembly in Amsterdam. This ecumenical organization supported by many Protestant, Anglican, and Orthodox denominations. Headquarters are in Geneva, Switzerland.

1962–65 Vatican Council II, convened by Pope John XXIII, announces many liberalizing changes in Roman Catholic liturgy and practice; supports cautious involvement in ecumenical discussions with other Christians.

1978 Karol Josef Wojtyla, archbishop of Krakow, Poland, elected to papacy as John Paul II, the first non-Italian pope since Hadrian VI in 1523.

1988 For the first time, a woman is elected to a bishopric in U.S. Episcopal church.

1991 Religious freedom granted in U.S.S.R.

The Books of the Bible

The first five books of the Bible are known as the Torah (to teach in Hebrew) in the Jewish faith. Roman Catholic canon recognizes additional deuterocanonical books, as well as additional parts of other books. Together, they are known as the Apocrypha. They are listed in *italics* following the Old Testament.

Old Testament	Job	Zephaniah	*Second Maccabees*	Philippians
Genesis	Psalms	Haggai	*First Esdras*	Colossians
Exodus	Proverbs	Zechariah	*The Prayer of Manasseh*	First Thessalonians
Leviticus	Ecclesiastes	Malachi	*Psalm 151*	Second
Numbers	Song of Solomon	***The Apocrypha***	*Third Maccabees*	Thessalonians
Deuteronomy	Isaiah	*Tobit*	*Second Esdras*	First Timothy
Joshua	Jeremiah	*Judith*	*Fourth Maccabees*	Second Timothy
Judges	Lamentations	*Additions to Esther*	**New Testament**	Titus
Ruth	Ezekiel	*Wisdom of Solomon*	Matthew	Philemon
First Samuel	Daniel	*Ecclesisasticus (Sirach)*	Mark	Hebrews
Second Samuel	Hosea	*Baruch*	Luke	James
First Kings	Joel	*The Letter of Jeremiah*	John	First Peter
Second Kings	Amos	*The Prayer of Azariah*	Acts	Second Peter
First Chronicles	Obadiah	*and the Song of the*	Romans	First John
Second Chronicles	Jonah	*Three Young Men*	First Corinthians	Second John
Ezra	Micah	*Susanna*	Second Corinthians	Third John
Nehemiah	Nahum	*Bel and the Dragon*	Galatians	Jude
Esther	Habakuk	*First Maccabees*	Ephesians	Revelation

The Ten Commandments

Significant differences exist among the Protestant, Catholic, and Jewish versions of the Ten Commandments, both in wording and in numbering. Even within the King James Bible, the Commandments are presented twice, first in Exodus and later in Deuteronomy. The Exodus version (Exodus 20: 2-17) is the most familiar, and is reprinted here from the King James Version. Numbers refer to commandment numbers, not Biblical verses.

1 I am the Lord thy God, which have brought thee out of the land of Egypt, out of the house of bondage.

2 Thou shalt have no other gods before me.

Thou shalt not make unto thee any graven image, or any likeness of any thing that is in heaven above, or that is in the earth beneath, or that is in the water under the earth:

Thou shalt not bow down thyself to them, nor serve them: for I the Lord thy God am a jealous God, visiting the iniquity of the fathers upon the children unto the third and fourth generation of them that hate me;

And showing mercy unto thousands of them that love me and keep my commandments.

3 Thou shalt not take the name of the Lord thy God in vain; for the Lord will not hold him guiltless that taketh his name in vain.

4 Remember the sabbath day, to keep it holy.

Six days shalt thou labor, and do all thy work:

But the seventh day is the sabbath of the Lord thy God: in it thou shalt not do any work, thou, nor thy son, nor thy daughter, thy manservant, nor thy maidservant, nor thy cattle, nor thy stranger that is within thy gates:

For in six days the Lord made heaven and earth, the sea, and all that in them is, and rested the seventh day: wherefore the Lord blessed the sabbath day, and hallowed it.

5 Honor thy father and thy mother: that thy days may be long upon the land which the Lord thy God giveth thee.

6 Thou shalt not kill.

7 Thou shalt not commit adultery.

8 Thou shalt not steal.

9 Thou shalt not bear false witness against thy neighbor.

10 Thou shalt not covet thy neighbor's house, thou shalt not covet thy neighbor's wife, nor his manservant, nor his maidservant, nor his ox, nor his ass, nor any thing that is thy neighbor's.

The Koran

The sacred book of Islam was revealed by God to the prophet Mohammed over his life at Mecca and Medina. Its various versions were reconciled in the 7th century by Uthman, the third Caliph. It is divided into 114 chapters of verses, with chapters appearing in size order from longest to shortest, rather than in chronological order.

The Seven Deadly Sins

1 Pride
2 Envy
3 Anger
4 Sloth
5 Greed
6 Gluttony
7 Lust

Major Languages of the World

There are approximately 100 languages designated as official by national governments around the world. These run the gamut from Chinese and English—with hundreds of millions of speakers worldwide—to local languages whose speakers may number only in the tens of thousands.

Chinese This is the mother tongue of more than one billion people. Although spoken dialects of Chinese are not mutually intelligible, they share the same writing system—Chinese characters, or *hanzi*—and two people can speak different dialects and still be able to read each other's writing. This is possible because *hanzi* characters represent words independently of their pronunciation (just as Arabic numerals can represent the words for numbers in any language), and also because written Chinese has diverged less from a common standard than have the various spoken dialects.

Based on the dialect spoken in northern China around Beijing, Mandarin is an official language in China, Taiwan, and Singapore, where it is the primary language of more than 800 million people. The other principal dialects are Cantonese (or *Yue*), spoken in southern China and Hong Kong; *Wu*, spoken in Shanghai and nearby provinces in eastern China; *Min*, found in southeastern China, Taiwan and Malaysia; and *Xiang, Kan*, and *Hakka*, all spoken in southeastern China and Taiwan. Chinese is also an official language of the U.N.

English Although there are fewer native speakers of English than of Chinese, English is by far the most commonly found language outside of China. Some estimates suggest that as many as one-third of the world's people can speak English—which means four billion people can't. From the island kingdom in northwest Europe, the language spread throughout the British Empire to the Americas, Africa, India and Oceania. Today, 58 countries and the U.N. designate English as an official language, and these countries account for more than 460 million speakers. The main concentrations of English speakers are the United States (258 million), United Kingdom (57 million), Philippines (37 million), India (31 million), Canada (18 million), Australia (17 million) and Nigeria (16 million).

Hindi Spoken by an estimated 430 million people in India alone, Hindi is one of that country's two official languages, the other being English. There are significant numbers (relative to the local population) of Hindi speakers in Trinidad, Guyana, South Africa, Mauritius and other countries with large Indian expatriate communities.

Spanish Carried by Spanish conquistadors from Europe to the Americas and Asia, Spanish is now an official language of 21 nations, territories and colonies in which it is the mother tongue of more than 300 million people. By far the greatest number of Spanish speakers live in Mexico (85 million), followed by Colombia (35 million), Argentina (34 million), Spain (29 million) and Venezuela (21 million). Although the United States does not recognize an official language per se, the U.S. ranks sixth in the number of people who consider Spanish a first language with 20 million. Spanish is also an official language of the U.N.

Arabic Twenty-five countries around the world have adopted Arabic as an official language, more than any other language but English and French. These 25 countries alone represent nearly 200 million Arabic speakers. Arabic is also the language of the Koran—and thus, for many Muslims, of God. For this reason, it is the second language of many Indians, Indonesians, Iranians and other inhabitants of largely Muslim countries. Arabic is also an official language of the U.N.

Portuguese The transmission of Portuguese paralleled that of Spanish, but today it is used as an official language in only seven countries outside of Portugal (where there are a scant 10 million speakers): five in Africa, one in Latin America, and one in Macau, a special administrative region of China. Of the 168 million native Portuguese speakers worldwide, the vast majority of them live in Brazil (154 million). In Angola, there are just over 4 million.

Russian There are an estimated 130 million people who claim Russian as their mother tongue in the two countries where it is an official language, Russia (127 million) and Belarus (3 million). There are still significant numbers of people claiming Russian as a first language in the former republics of the Soviet Union, especially Ukraine (17 million) and Kazakhstan (8 million), Uzbekistan (2.5 million), and Kyrgyzstan and Moldova (1 million each). Russian is an official language of the U.N.

Japanese The official language of only one country, Japanese is spoken by more than 125 million. The most significant Japanese-speaking minorities outside of Japan are found in Brazil (600,000 people) and the United States (490,000). Modern Japanese employs four writing systems: *kanji* (adapted from the Chinese *hanzi*), *hiragana, katakana* and *romaji*.

Bengali The official language of Bangladesh, where it is the mother tongue of more than 120 million people, Bengali is also the first language of an estimated 72 million Indians, chiefly the state of West Bengal.

German An official language of six European countries (Germany, Austria, Switzerland, Luxembourg, Liechtenstein, and Belgium), German is spoken by more than 117 million in those countries. There are also significant German-speaking minorities in Eastern Europe (500,000 in Poland and 350,000 in Russia), Brazil (870,000) and the United States (1.8 million).

French Although there are fewer speakers of French than of other languages—fewer than 100 million people claim it is as a first language worldwide—its significance stems from the fact that it is an official language of 32 countries—more than any other language except English—and of the U.N. (These countries account for 88 million native speakers of French.) The most important in terms of numbers are France (55 million), Canada (7 million), Ivory Coast (Côte d'Ivoire) (5 million). Democratic Republic of the Congo, Belgium, Cameroon, Niger, Madagascar and Switzerland also have more than 1 million each claiming French as a first language.

Malay Variants and dialects of Malay are used as an official language in Indonesia (where it is known as *Bahasa Indonesia*), Malaysia (*Bahasa Nalaysia*), and Singapore and Brunei (*Bahasa Melayu*). Although these four countries have a combined population of more than 220 million people, Malay is not the mother tongue of the majority in any of them. A mere 33 million people claim Malay as their first language. In Indonesia, Malay runs a distant third to Javanese (78 million speakers) and Sundanese (31 million).

World Energy

The world's primary energy sources in 2007 were crude oil and natural gas liquids, natural gas, coal, and electricity from hydroelectric and nuclear power. In order to compare the energy produced by different sources, energy is measured in British thermal units (Btu). Energy production and consumption worldwide increased drastically during the 1980s, but their growth slowed somewhat in the 1990's. Petroleum production and consumption continues to increase, but whereas petroleum once constituted almost half the world's energy, it now accounts for less than 40 percent. Natural gas and nuclear power have made up most of the difference.

Petroleum World production of petroleum (which includes crude oil and natural gas plant liquids) was 84.4 million barrels per day in 2007. The United States, Russia and Saudi Arabia are the world's largest producers of petroleum; the three countries together account for nearly one-third of the world's petroleum production.

Consumption of petroleum has kept pace with the increase in production. But the United States is by far the biggest consumer. In 2007, the U.S. consumes 20.7 million barrels of petroleum per day, more than one-fourth the world's total. That's more than double the amount the U.S. produces each

World Primary Energy Production, by Source, 1980–2005 (quadrillion Btu)

Source	1980	1985	1990	1995	2000	2005
Petroleum[1]	133.14	121.20	136.22	141.83	156.46	169.28
Dry Natural Gas	54.73	64.22	75.90	80.26	91.32	105.33
Coal	71.31	82.29	91.02	88.52	90.41	122.25
Hydroelectric	17.90	20.42	22.35	25.34	26.99	28.00
Nuclear Electric	7.58	15.30	20.36	23.26	25.66	27.47
Geothermal, Solar, Wind, Wood and Waste	0.47	0.82	1.70	2.17	3.01	4.29
Total	**287.59**	**307.26**	**349.83**	**363.93**	**396.26**	**460.13**

Note: Totals may not add up due to rounding. **1.** Includes natural gas plant liquids. **Source:** Energy Information Administration, *International Energy Annual, 2005* (2007).

World Energy Production, by Region, 1980–2007

Region	1980	1985	1990	1995	2000	2005	2007[1]
Petroleum[2] (thousand barrels/day)	**63,987**	**59,172**	**66,425**	**70,271**	**77,762**	**84,582**	**84,439**
North America	14,754	16,068	14,709	14,928	15,267	15,197	15,382
Central & South America	3,848	3,916	4,703	6,055	7,326	7,244	7,244
Western Europe	3,047	4,637	4,818	6,872	7,145	6,093	5,426
Eurasia	11,991	11,935	11,300	7,135	8,191	11,768	12,603
Middle East	19,024	11,001	17,449	20,420	23,479	25,559	24,582
Africa	6,229	5,614	6,708	7,357	8,039	10,265	10,741
Asia & Oceania	5,092	5,999	6,736	7,501	8,313	8,453	8,458
Dry Natural Gas (trillion cubic feet)	**53.35**	**62.39**	**73.71**	**78.11**	**88.42**	**101.52**	**N.A.**
North America	23.06	20.50	22.56	25.16	26.97	26.13	27.86
Central & South America	1.23	1.76	2.01	2.58	3.43	4.86	N.A.
Western Europe	9.14	9.19	8.60	9.86	10.98	11.42	N.A.
Eurasia	15.37	22.71	28.78	24.88	25.43	28.79	N.A.
Middle East	1.42	2.38	3.72	4.99	7.57	11.21	N.A.
Africa	0.69	1.86	2.46	3.01	4.44	6.11	N.A.
Asia & Oceania	2.49	4.00	5.58	7.64	9.60	13.00	N.A.
Coal (million short tons)	**4,188.0**	**4,895.5**	**5,353.9**	**5,105.0**	**4,949.5**	**6,492.1**	**7,036.3**
North America	874.2	957.5	1,113.0	1,125.9	1,162.4	1,217.8	1,233.6
Central & South America	12.1	20.5	32.9	40.1	58.8	80.6	91.9
Western Europe	1,334.6	1,463.4	1,332.4	959.7	832.0	805.5	814.2
Eurasia	789.7	800.7	881.8	481.6	443.1	502.4	537.2
Middle East	1.0	1.4	1.2	1.3	1.4	1.5	1.4
Africa	138.0	197.3	201.1	234.9	255.8	276.2	288.7
Asia & Oceania	1,038.5	1,454.9	1,791.5	2,261.5	2,196.0	3,608.0	4,069.1
Electric power[3] (billion kWh)	**8,026.9**	**9,477.1**	**11,322.7**	**12,624.6**	**14,619.2**	**17,350.6**	**N.A.**
North America	2,721.6	3,014.8	3,627.5	4,046.1	4,590.4	4,895.0	N.A.
Central & South America	308.2	405.4	497.2	626.6	781.9	908.7	N.A.
Western Europe	2,154.7	2,448.7	2,696.5	2,873.5	3,211.1	3,494.7	N.A.
Eurasia	1,294.0	1,545.0	1,636.1	1,226.0	1,205.3	1,327.3	N.A.
Middle East	91.4	165.0	225.1	318.8	434.7	602.7	N.A.
Africa	189.0	251.8	307.3	354.2	417.1	533.2	N.A.
Asia & Oceania	1,268.1	1,646.5	2,333.1	3,179.4	3,978.7	5,589.1	N.A.

Notes: **1.** Preliminary **2.** Includes crude oil and natural gas plant liquids **3.** Includes conventional thermal electric, hydroelectric, nuclear, geothermal, solar, and waste electric power **Source:** Energy Information Administration, *International Energy Annual, 2007* (2008).

day, forcing America to import more than 13 million barrels of petroleum each day. No other country consumes even half as much oil as the United States. China was second in world consumption with 7.6 million barrels, followed by Japan (5.0 million barrels), Russia (2.9 million), and Germany (2.5 million). Saudi Arabia, the world's largest petroleum producer, consumed 2.3 million barrels per day.

Dry natural gas World production of dry natural gas continued to set all-time highs; in 2006, production was nearly 104 trillion cubic feet. Russia is the world's largest producer of natural gas (23.1 trillion cubic feet, or 23 percent of the world total in 2007), followed by the United States (19.3 trillion cubic feet). The United States consumed 23.1 trillion cubic feet of natural gas in 2007, while Russia consumed 16.7 trillion cubic feet.

Coal World coal production declined during the late 1990's but has increased steadily since 2000 and exceeded 7.0 billion short tons in 2007. China continues to lead the world in production, with more than 2.8 billion short tons per year. The United States, the world leader until 1987, produced just over 1.1 billion short tons in 2007. Together, the U.S.

and China account for half the world's production. They also accounted for the bulk of coal consumption in 2007. China consumed 1.42 billion short tons (27 percent of world consumption) and the U.S. consumed 1.07 million short tons (20 percent).

Hydroelectric power Generation of hydroelectric power worldwide increased 1.9 percent between 2001 and 2002, to a total of 2.63 trillion kilowatthours (kWh). Canada (315 billion kWh), China (309 billion kWh), and Brazil (282 billion kWh) together produced more than a third of the worldwide total. They were also the three biggest users of hydroelectric power, together making up 34 percent of world consumption. U.S. production increased dramatically, from 209 billion kWh in 2001 to 255 billion kWh in 2002.

Nuclear electric power World generation of nuclear electric power nearly quadrupled between 1980 and 2001 from 684.4 billion to 2.5 trillion kWh. In 2002, the U.S. alone produced more nuclear power (780.1 billion kWh) than the entire world total in 1980. France (414.9 billion kWh) and Japan (295.1 billion kWh) followed the U.S. in total nuclear production in 2002, as well as in the total number of reactors.

World Energy Consumption, by Type and Region, 1980–2004

Energy Type and Region	1980	1990	1995	2000	2003	2004
Crude oil (thousand barrels/day)	**63,107.6**	**66,576.0**	**70,017.8**	**76,945.9**	**80,098.8**	**82,594.7**
North America	20,203.8	20,495.0	21,369.3	23,771.8	24,250.3	25,003.4
Central & South America	3,613.4	3,760.6	4,459.1	5,230.0	5,243.4	5,384.0
Western Europe	14,322.0	13,306.2	14,160.7	14,667.8	14,950.6	16,307.8
Eastern Europe & Former U.S.S.R.	10,707.0	9,731.6	5,707.2	5,095.5	5,407.9	4,105.8
Middle East	2,058.1	3,494.2	4,159.0	4,775.6	5,288.1	5,662.0
Africa	1,474.1	2,069.6	2,251.6	2,507.4	2,702.9	2,790.6
Asia & Oceania	10,729.1	13,718.8	17,910.9	20,897.8	22,255.5	23,341.0
Dry Natural Gas (trillion cubic feet)	**52,890**	**73,370**	**78,642**	**88,208**	**95,504**	**99,665**
North America	22,559	22,470	26,040	27,683	27,410	27,597
Central & South America	1,241	2,024	2,581	3,304	3,820	4,077
Western Europe	8,665	10,496	12,761	15,126	16,427	19,897
Eastern Europe & Former U.S.S.R.	15,856	27,825	23,043	22,802	24,970	23,388
Middle East	1,311	3,599	4,735	6,822	7,862	8,613
Africa	735	1,351	1,689	2,038	2,554	2,622
Asia & Oceania	2,523	5,605	7,790	10,433	12,462	13,472
Coal (million short tons)	**4,126.48**	**5,269.29**	**5,115.68**	**5,082.54**	**5,439.33**	**6,098.78**
North America	749.33	972.17	1,032.86	1,168.91	1,183.97	1,182.53
Central & South America	19.40	26.54	32.94	37.10	35.07	38.21
Western Europe	937.45	1,037.19	737.53	717.21	712.54	N.A.
Eastern Europe & Former U.S.S.R.	1,225.11	1,289.06	855.11	724.04	717.52	N.A.
Middle East	1.08	5.68	9.28	13.84	15.55	16.27
Africa	112.50	151.70	174.90	189.56	202.60	205.83
Asia & Oceania	1,081.61	1,786.93	2,273.06	2,231.89	2,572.08	3,190.25
Hydroelectric power (billion kWh)	**1,722.84**	**2,151.72**	**2,461.29**	**2,651.76**	**2,654.37**	**2,746.88**
North America	546.91	609.97	670.65	663.04	627.94	627.61
Central & South America	201.49	365.13	460.75	546.05	561.42	577.08
Western Europe	431.68	453.42	508.49	554.90	483.74	543.56
Eastern Europe & Former U.S.S.R.	210.36	251.72	268.14	258.04	267.80	233.09
Middle East	9.62	12.54	15.39	14.19	22.53	14.11
Africa	60.07	54.82	58.87	73.96	84.96	87.43
Asia & Oceania	262.70	404.14	478.99	541.60	605.98	664.00
Nuclear power (billion kWh)	**684.38**	**1,908.81**	**2,210.04**	**2,450.31**	**2,523.11**	**2,619.18**
North America	287.00	648.89	774.38	830.86	844.49	883.13
Central & South America	2.22	8.97	9.46	10.93	20.43	18.91
Western Europe	219.25	711.29	797.01	850.39	882.96	967.52
Eastern Europe & Former U.S.S.R.	83.19	251.28	224.26	268.32	304.98	236.71
Middle East	0	0	0	0	0	0
Africa	0	8.45	11.30	13.01	12.66	14.28
Asia & Oceania	92.73	279.93	393.64	476.80	457.58	498.62

Source: Energy Information Administration, *International Energy Annual, 2004* (2005).

Top 10 Producers of Primary Energy, by Source, 2007

Petroleum	Thousand barrels/day	Dry Natural Gas	Trillion cubic ft	Coal	Million short tons
Saudi Arabia	10,247.0	Russia	23.1	China	2,804.0
Russia	9,875.8	United States	19.3	United States	1,145.6
United States	8,456.7	Canada	6.6	India	528.5
Iran	4,033.3	Iran	4.0	Australia	428.4
China	3,901.0	Norway	3.3	Russia	346.7
Mexico	3,501.4	Algeria	3.0	South Africa	282.6
Canada	3,424.6	Netherlands	2.7	Germany	227.8
United Arab Emirates	2,947.7	Saudi Arabia	2.7	Indonesia	179.9
Venezuela	2,666.5	United Kingdom	2.6	Poland	162.0
Kuwait	2,613.2	China	2.5	Kazakhstan	103.2

Source: U.S. Dept of Energy, *International Energy Annual, 2007* (2008).

U.S. and World Per Capita Energy Consumption, 1980–2005 (Million Btu)

	1980	1985	1990	1995	2000	2005
United States	343.0	320.8	338.4	342.0	350.6	340.5
North America	285.4	266.8	277.5	279.6	285.8	280.3
Central & South America	39.5	38.1	40.7	45.2	49.7	52.2
Europe	135.5	134.8	137.2	134.5	140.4	146.4
Eurasia	175.7	200.4	211.4	146.5	141.3	160.4
Middle East	62.3	75.5	84.1	92.2	104.1	124.7
Africa	14.4	15.6	15.2	15.0	15.0	16.1
Asia & Oceania	19.9	21.9	25.2	29.9	31.6	41.0
World average	63.8	63.7	65.9	64.3	65.6	71.8

Source: Energy Information Administration, *International Energy Annual, 2005* (2008).

Highest/Lowest Per Capita Total Energy Consumption, 2005 (Million Btu)

Highest per capita areas		Lowest per capita areas	
Gibraltar	2,026.5	Chad	0.3
Virgin Islands, U.S.	1,977.6	Afghanistan	0.6
Qatar	1,000.4	Cambodia	0.6
Netherlands Antilles	678.0	Mali	1.0
Bahrain	665.8	Burundi	1.0
Trinidad and Tobago	613.1	Ethiopia	1.2
United Arab Emirates	563.6	Somalia	1.2
Kuwait	498.3	Rwanda	1.3
Iceland	489.6	Central African Republic	1.3

Note: Per capita information not availbable for the following areas: Falkland Islands, French Guiana, Martinique, Reunion, Timor, Niue, Wake Island. **Source:** Energy Information Administration, *International Energy Annual, 2005* (2007).

World Crude Oil Production, 1960–2007 (million barrels per day)

Country	1960	1970	1980	1990	2000	2005	2007[4]
Organization of Petroleum Exporting Countries (OPEC)[1]	**8.70**	**23.30**	**26.61**	**23.20**	**29.26**	**32.94**	**32.18**
Iran	1.07	3.83	1.66	3.09	3.70	4.14	3.91
Iraq	0.97	1.55	2.51	2.04	2.57	1.88	2.09
Kuwait	1.69	2.99	1.66	1.18	2.08	2.53	2.46
Nigeria	0.02	1.08	2.06	1.81	2.16	2.63	2.35
Saudi Arabia	1.31	3.80	9.90	6.41	8.40	9.55	8.72
United Arab Emirates	0.00	0.78	1.71	2.12	2.37	2.54	2.60
Venezuela	2.85	3.71	2.17	2.14	3.16	2.56	2.43
Non-OPEC countries[1]	**12.29**	**22.59**	**32.99**	**37.37**	**39.10**	**42.36**	**41.09**
Canada	0.52	1.26	1.44	1.55	1.98	2.37	2.61
China	0.10	0.60	2.11	2.77	3.25	3.61	3.73
Mexico	0.27	0.49	1.94	2.55	3.01	3.33	3.08
Norway	0.00	0.00	0.53	1.70	3.20	2.70	2.27
Russia[2]	2.91	6.99	11.71	10.98	6.48	9.04	9.44
United Kingdom	(3)	(3)	1.62	1.82	2.28	1.65	1.50
United States	7.04	9.64	8.60	7.36	5.82	5.18	5.10
Total world[1]	**20.99**	**45.89**	**59.60**	**60.57**	**68.34**	**73.81**	**73.27**

Notes: 1. Includes other countries not shown separately. In addition to those listed separately, current OPEC members are: Algeria, Indonesia, Libya, and Qatar. **2.** Figures for Russia before 1995 refer to the former Soviet Union. **3.** Fewer than 5,000 barrels per day. **4.** Preliminary. **Source:** U.S. Dept. of Energy, *Monthly Energy Review.* (2008)

Leading Suppliers of U.S. Oil, 1990–2007

The United States imports about half of the oil it consumes, or more than 13 million barrels a day. Since 1993, the U.S. has imported more of its oil from non-OPEC countries than from OPEC countries.

Country	U.S. imports, (thousand barrels/day)		
	1990	2000	2007
Canada	934	1,807	2,455
Saudi Arabia	1,339	1,572	1,485
Mexico	755	1,373	1,532
Venezuela	1,025	1,546	1,361
Nigeria	800	896	1,134
United Kingdom	189	366	277
Iraq	518	620	484
Total OPEC countries	4,296	5,203	5,980
Non-OPEC countries	3,721	6,257	7,489
Total imports	**8,018**	**11,459**	**13,468**

Source: Energy Information Administration (2008).

World Crude Oil Reserves, 1980–2007

Country	Reserves (billion barrels)		
	1980	2003	2007
1. Saudi Arabia	166.5	261.8	261.9
2. Canada	N.A.	180.0	179.2
3. Iran	58.0	89.7	136.3
4. Iraq	31.0	112.5	115.0
5. United Arab Emirates	29.4	97.8	97.8
6. Kuwait	68.5	96.5	101.5
7. Venezuela	17.9	77.8	80.0
8. Russia	N.A.	60.0	60.0
9. Libya	23.5	29.5	41.5
10. Nigeria	17.4	24.0	36.2
World Total	**644.9**	**1,213.1**	**1,316.7**

Source: Energy Information Administration, International Energy Annual, 2005 (2008).

World Nuclear Power Generation, by Region and Country

Region and country	Generation (billion killowatthours)						Operable reactors in 2008
	1980	1990	1995	2000	2004	2005	
North America	**287.00**	**648.89**	**774.38**	**830.86**	**883.13**	**879.69**	**124**
Canada	35.88	69.24	92.95	69.16	85.87	87.44	18
Mexico	0	2.79	8.02	7.81	8.73	10.27	2
United States	251.12	576.86	673.40	753.89	788.53	781.99	104
Central & South America	**2.22**	**8.97**	**9.46**	**10.93**	**18.91**	**16.27**	**4**
Argentina	2.22	7.03	7.07	5.99	7.31	6.37	2
Brazil	0	1.94	2.39	4.94	11.6	9.90	2
Europe	**229.56**	**761.26**	**849.22**	**953.74**	**967.52**	**957.27**	**150**
Belgium	11.91	40.59	39.29	45.75	45.80	45.22	7
Bulgaria	5.81	13.53	16.40	17.27	15.60	17.34	2
Czech Republic	N.A.	N.A.	11.62	12.91	25.01	23.59	6
Finland	6.63	18.26	18.26	21.36	21.55	22.10	4
France	63.42	298.38	358.37	394.40	425.83	428.95	59
Germany[1]	N.A.	N.A.	145.44	161.13	158.97	154.85	17
Hungary	0	13.04	13.32	13.47	11.32	13.14	4
Netherlands	3.95	3.33	3.82	3.73	3.63	3.80	1
Romania	0	0	0	5.23	5.27	5.28	2
Slovakia	N.A.	N.A.	10.87	15.67	16.81	16.84	5
Slovenia	N.A.	N.A.	4.56	4.55	5.21	5.61	1
Spain	5.19	51.56	52.68	59.10	60.43	54.66	8
Sweden	25.33	64.78	66.44	54.45	73.43	68.63	10
Switzerland	12.88	22.42	23.65	25.12	25.61	22.17	5
United Kingdom	32.29	62.46	84.52	80.81	73.68	75.17	19
Eurasia	**83.19**	**251.28**	**224.26**	**268.32**	**236.71**	**235.83**	**48**
Armenia	N.A.	N.A.	0	1.84	2.21	2.50	1
Lithuania	N.A.	N.A.	10.64	8.42	14.35	9.82	1
Russia	N.A.	N.A.	94.34	122.46	137.47	140.22	31
Ukraine	N.A.	N.A.	66.98	71.06	82.69	83.29	15
Middle East	**0**	**0**	**0**	**0**	**0**	**0**	**0**
Africa	**0**	**8.45**	**11.30**	**13.01**	**14.28**	**12.24**	**2**
South Africa	0	8.45	11.30	13.01	14.28	12.24	2
Asia & Oceania	**92.73**	**279.93**	**393.64**	**476.80**	**498.62**	**524.27**	**111**
China	0	0	12.38	15.90	47.95	50.33	11
India	3.00	5.61	6.46	14.06	15.04	15.73	17
Japan	78.64	192.16	276.69	305.95	271.58	278.39	55
Korea, South	3.28	50.24	63.68	103.52	124.18	139.44	20
Pakistan	0.002	0.36	0.50	0.38	1.93	2.41	2
Taiwan	7.81	31.55	33.93	37.00	37.94	37.97	6
World Total[2]	**684.38**	**1,908.81**	**2,210.04**	**2,450.31**	**2,619.18**	**2,625.57**	**440**

Notes: Net generation; does not include energy consumed by the generating unit. 1. Data before 1995 includes both the former East Germany and West Germany. 2. Totals include other countries not shown separately. Sources: Energy Information Administration, International Energy Annual, 2005 (2007) and International Atomic Energy Agency, Power Reactor Information System (2008).

The Global Military Situation

With the end of the Cold War, the world entered a period of demilitarization marked by steady declines in global military spending and the ranks of active-duty military personnel. Beginning in 2001, however, several factors contributed to modest growth in overall defense spending that was expected to accelerate in succeeding years. This new phase in global military affairs was signaled by the U.S. commitment to strengthening what the administration of President George W. Bush characterized as an aging, underinvested armed forces; the rise in international terrorism and antiterrorist campaigns; the wars in Afghanistan and later Iraq; and ongoing regional conflicts.

As a candidate for the U.S. presidency in 2000, President Bush had advocated a modernization of U.S. defense forces, better wages for military personnel, and a higher standard of readiness. The terrorist attacks of September 11, 2001, and Bush's declaration of war against global terrorism at once reinforced those priorities and marked a major shift in national strategic policy. The war on terrorism would be the cornerstone of U.S. foreign relations and international diplomacy, as well as the guiding principle of its military affairs. The U.S. action in Afghanistan and heightened military readiness everywhere forced budget increases of tens of billions of dollars annually, contributing to a return to deficit spending. The 2003 war on Iraq was financed by Congressionally approved off-budget funding that also ran into tens of billions of dollars.

According to the Stockholm International Peace Research Institute, global defense spending in 2006 totaled $1.158 trillion—an increase of 40.2 percent over the $825.7 billion spent in 2000, and a 3 percent decline from the $1.193 trillion spent at the close of the cold war in 1998.

The ranks of the world's active-duty military personnel have increased yearly since 2001, however the are still below Cold War levels. In mid-2008, according to London-based International Institute for Strategic Studies (IISS), active-duty military personnel totaled 23.9 million worldwide, up 3.5 million from 2001 but down from 28 million in 1985. The largest active-duty military forces are from China (2.1 million), the United States (1.5 million), India (1.3 million), and North Korea (1.1 million).

Collectively reluctant to follow the U.S. lead in military buildup after 2001, the European NATO nations continued their gradual decrease in troop size. By 2006, European NATO nations had 2.26 million active-duty military personnel, down by about 140,000 since 2000.

The latest worldwide totals, however, conceal notable regional differences and shifts in military priorities. Strategic interventions on the part of the United States and NATO allies; concern over the spread of chemical, biological, and nuclear weapons; antiterrorist initiatives; and local conflicts yielded have a major redistribution of military resources—even before the 2003 Iraq War.

The United States led the military buildup with 41.3 percent of global spending in 2006. U.S. defense spending approached $536 billion and represented 4.0 percent of G.D.P. By comparison, the rest of NATO spent 1.74 percent of G.D.P on defense, a collective $268 billion. The non-NATO Eu-

ropean nations, excluding Russia, spent a combined $21.2 billion (1.16 percent of G.D.P.), down nearly $2 billion from 2001. The notable exception to both trends was Russia, which increased its 2006 defense outlay by more than 30 percent from 2000, to $70.0 billion.

In other regions of the world, political developments and ongoing security issues fueled rises in military commitment. In the Middle East and North Africa, ongoing U.S. action in Iraq and Afghanistan, and a heightened sense of alert in Iran, Saudi Arabia, and elsewhere contributed to an increase in defense expenditure in 2006, to $81.8 billion from $66.7 billion in 2001.

In Central and South Asia combined national spending on defense increased in 2006, to $29.8 billion from $22.1 billion in 2001. In East Asia and Australasia, estimated military spending increased 82.6 percent from 2001, to $241.4 billion. Ongoing tensions between North and South Korea and between China and Taiwan forced sharp increases. In Central America, South America and the Caribbean, economic difficulties squeezed defense spending, which increased 21.8 percent from 2001 to 2006, to just under $39 billion.

▶NUCLEAR AND CHEMICAL WEAPONS

The demise of the Soviet Union and compliance with disarmament agreements has resulted in large-scale reductions in the global nuclear arsenal. Although the precise size of national nuclear stockpiles and number of deployment vehicles remain official secrets, treaty compliance protocols and estimates from a variety of sources provide some reliable figures for the major nuclear powers. The arsenals of more recent members of the nuclear-weapons "community," such as Israel, India and Pakistan, are less known. By common estimates, the total number of nuclear warheads in the world declined by 100 percent in about 15 years—from approximately 70,000 in the mid-1980's to fewer than 35,000 by 2001–02. After 2001 information about nuclear stockpiles became classified.

Moreover, less than half of the world's warhead

Strategic Missile Forces and Nuclear Stockpiles at the End of the Cold War, 2001[1]			
Country	ICBMs[2]	SLBMs/ SSBNs[3]	Estimated Total Deployed Strategic Nuclear Warheads
United States	550	432/18	6,500
Russia	740	280/17	5,600
China	20+	12/1	200–250
France	—	64/4	470
Great Britain	—	58/4	190
Total	1,300+	846/44	13,000

Notes: 1. Current stockpile information unavailable after 2001. 2. Intercontinental Ballistic Missiles. 2. Submarine-Launched Ballistic Missiles and nuclear-fueled ballistic-missile submarines. **Source:** *The Military Balance, 2001/2002,* The International Institute for Strategic Studies; Center for Strategic and International Studies; Natural Resources Defense Council.

stockpile is operational. The five major nuclear powers—the United States, Russia, China, France and Great Britain—had a combined 13,000 deployed nuclear warheads in 2001. The U.S. accounted for a reported 6,500 of these, and Russia accounted for an estimated 5,600, down 4,600 from three years earlier.

The first years of the new century brought notable progress and changes in the course of global nuclear disarmament. The destruction of stockpiles in Ukraine, Belarus and Kazakhstan, mandated by treaty, was completed by year-end 2001. The United States and Russia, meanwhile, began SALT III talks in 2000, shortly after approval by the Duma (Russian parliament) of SALT II. But the U.S. still had not approved SALT II, which would reduce the deployed missile stockpiles of both nations to 3,500 by 2007, and had rejected the Comprehensive Test Ban Treaty (CTBT), which would prohibit nuclear testing.

The direction of nuclear disarmament took a new turn in 2001 with the installation of the Bush administration. To protect against future attack by outlaw nuclear nations, Bush called for the development of a space-based national missile defense (NMD) system. China, Russia, and even European allies expressed grave misgivings, fearing that such an initiative could undermine international stability and risk starting a new arms race. Building NMD, moreover, would violate the 1972 ABM treaty, the cornerstone of cold-war arms control.

Bush openly disavowed the ABM treaty in 2001, calling it a relic of the cold war, and the lack of U.S. interest in rescuing SALT II raised further questions about Bush's commitment to the spirit and goals of nuclear disarmament. The administration's strategy of leapfrogging Salt II and ABM, however, became clear in 2002, as it reached agreement with Russia on what Bush called "the most dramatic nuclear arms reduction in history." The Treaty of Moscow, called for a 65 percent cut in each nation's store of strategic warheads over ten years—from about 6,000 to between 1,700 and 2,200. The accord also called for mutual efforts in developing a missile defense shield. The U.S. Senate ratified the treaty in March 2003 and the Russian Duma in May.

At the same time, however, new threats to national security in 2003 led the Pentagon to begin discussing the prospect of developing a new stockpile of "low-yield" nuclear weapons, or "mininukes," and the Department of Energy proposed Congressional repeal of a nine-year ban on the development of such weapons. The first months of the year also saw a new round nuclear-capable missile tests by India and Pakistan, carried out against a backdrop of mounting political tensions.

In August 2003, in compliance with a long-standing international treaty, the United States began destroying its own stockpile of cold-war-era chemical weapons.

▶ CONVENTIONAL ARMS SALES

Worldwide sales of conventional (non-nuclear) arms declined nearly $5.5 billion between 2000 and 2006. The United States remained the largest arms dealer, with some 41.9 percent of the world total in 2006. Still, U.S. sales of $16.9 billion were $4.0 billion (24 percent) lower in 2006 than in 2000. Russia, the second-biggest dealer with $8.7 billion, was up $700 million. Nearly every other major supplier—France, Germany, China—also showed modest increases. One notable exception is Great Britain, which increased arms sales by $2.4 billion in the same period.

Developing nations remained the largest worldwide market for weapons from 1999–2006, accounting for about 66.4 percent of all arms transfer agreements. India is the leading purchaser of conventional arms among developing countries, totaling $22.4 billion in purchases from 1999–2006. Since 2003, he Near East has been the world's largest conventional arms market, and accounted for 46.6 percent ($46.7 billion) of all arms transfer agreements with developing nations between 2003–2006.

Largest armed forces, 2008

	Number in armed forces (thousands)	Estimated reservists (thousands)	2006 Expenditure (millions)
China	2,105	800	$121,872
United States	1,498	1,083	535,943
India	1,288	1,155	22,428
North Korea	1,106	4,700	N.A.
Russia	1,027	20,000	70,000
South Korea	687	4,500	24,645
Pakistan	619	0	4,156
Iran	545	0	7,160
Turkey	510	379	11,630

Source: *The Military Balance 2008*, The International Institute for Strategic Studies.

Arms Transfer Agreements with the World, by Supplier, 1999–2006

	1999	2000	2001	2002	2003	2004	2005	2006	TOTAL 1999-2006
United States	$14,225	$20,983	$13,371	$14,822	$16,147	$13,634	$13,457	$16,905	$123,543
Russia	6,299	8,041	6,518	6,466	4,994	5,809	7,488	8,700	54,316
France	1,976	5,521	4,889	567	2,775	2,367	8,320	500	26,915
United Kingdom	1,853	720	698	794	666	6,885	2,912	3,100	17,628
China	3,582	720	1,397	454	555	753	2,600	800	10,860
Germany	4,940	1,440	1,397	1,134	1,665	1,829	1,768	1,900	16,073
Italy	865	240	1,280	454	666	645	1,456	900	6,506
All Other European	7,040	4,921	3,143	4,991	2,331	6,992	6,032	5,200	40,649
All Others	2,594	3,000	3,026	2,382	1,887	2,797	2,288	2,300	20,274
TOTAL	43,372	45,587	35,720	32,063	31,685	41,710	46,322	40,305	316,764

Note: In millions of constant 2006 U.S. dollars. Source: Congressional Research Service, *Conventional Arms Transfers to Developing Nations, 1999-2006* (2007).

The Global Economy

(Note: for definitions of G.D.P., G.N.P., etc. see Part II, The U.S. Economy)

The unprecedented global economic expansion that marked the late 1990s and first six years of the 21st century started to lose speed in the second half of 2007, especially in the U.S., where the housing and mortgage market crises continued to ripple throughout other industries. Growth in western Europe also decelerated, though Japan was more resilient, according to the International Monetary Fund. Strong demand from emerging economies fueled a boom in the commodities markets, notably oil and biofuels. Developing nations such as China, India, and Brazil have so far remained relatively unscathed by the global slowdown. But by mid-2008 an ever deepening financial crisis reverberated around the world, causing governments to bail out banks and other institutions. (See "Major News Stories.")

The I.M.F. projects worldwide output growth of about only about 3.7 percent for 2008 (see the accompanying table), and expects that rate to stay unchanged in 2009. That's about the same steady growth rate the global economy experienced between 1983 and 1985. But the credit markets' effect on liquidity and the volatility of the equity and currency markets have the I.M.F. predicting a 25 percent chance of a global recession in 2009.

▶ THE HIERARCHY OF NATIONS

Most contemporary analyses of the global economy begin with the assumption that the nations

G.N.P. Per Capita, by World Regions, 2001-07

	G.N.P. per capita		
Region	2001	2006	2007
East Asia & Pacific	$900	$1,863	$2,180
Eastern Europe & Central Asia	1,970	4,796	6,051
Latin America & Caribbean	3,580	4,767	5,540
Middle East & North Africa	2,220	2,481	2,794
South Asia	450	766	880
Sub-Saharan Africa	460	842	952
Western Europe, U.S. Japan, and other high-income areas	20,680	36,487	37,566
World	**$5,120**	**$7,439**	**$7,958**

Source: The World Bank, The World Bank Atlas 2008.

World G.N.P. Per Capita, by Type of Economy, 2007

More than 70 percent of the world's 6.6 billion people live in low-income or lower middle income economies, according to these World Bank statistics, while only 16 percent of the world's population lives in high-income economies.

Type of Economy	Population	G.N.P. per capita
High-income	1,056,334,000	$37,566
Upper-middle	822,877,000	6,987
Lower-middle	3,437,092,000	1,887
Low-income	1,295,737,000	578
Total	**6,612,040,000**	**$7,958**

Source: The World Bank, The World Bank Atlas 2008.

Change in World Economic Output, 1986-2008

	Annual percent change			
Category	1989-98	2000	2007	2008[1]
World Total	**2.9%**	**4.7%**	**4.9%**	**3.7%**
Advanced economies	**2.7**	**3.9**	**2.7**	**1.3**
United States	3.1	3.7	2.2	0.5
European Union	—	3.8	2.6	1.4
Japan	1.5	2.9	2.1	1.4
Other advanced economies	3.2	5.9	3.9	2.5
Other emerging market and developing economies	**3.2%**	**5.9%**	**7.9%**	**6.7%**
Africa	2.3	3.5	6.2	6.3
Central & Eastern Europe	1.2	4.9	5.8	4.4
Commonwealth of Independent States[2]	—	9.1	8.5	7.0
Developing Asia	7.2	6.9	9.7	8.2
Middle East	4.3	5.4	5.8	6.1
Western Hemisphere	2.9	3.9	3.1	1.8

Note: Output is the value of production minus the cost of inputs by all businesses. 1. Projection. 2. Includes Mongolia for reasons of geography. Source: International Monetary Fund, World Economic Outlook, Statistical Appendix, April, 2008.

Countries With Highest and Lowest G.N.P. Per Capita, 2007

Country	G.N.P. per capita	Country	G.N.P. per capita
Highest		**Lowest**	
Norway	$76,450	Gambia	$ 85
Luxembourg	75,880	Burundi	110
Switzerland	59,880	Congo, Dem. Rep.	140
Denmark	54,910	Liberia	150
Iceland	54,100	Guinea-Bissau	200
Ireland	48,140	Ethiopia	220
Sweden	46,060	Eritrea	230
United States	46,040	Malawi	250
Netherlands	45,820	Sierra Leone	260
Finland	44,400	Niger	280
United Kingdom	42,740	Madagascar	320
Austria	42,700	Mozambique	320
Belgium	40,710	Rwanda	320
Canada	39,420	Nepal	340
Germany	38,860	Uganda	340
France[1]	38,500	Zimbabwe	340
Japan	37,670	Togo	360
Australia	35,960	Central African Rep.	380
Italy	33,540	Guinea	400
Singapore	32,470	Tanzania[2]	400
Kuwait	31,640	Burkina Faso	430
Hong Kong	31,610	Tajikistan	460
Greece	29,630	Bangladesh	470
Spain	29,450	Mali	500
New Zealand	28,780	Cambodia	540
Brunei	26,930	Chad	540
Cyprus	24,940	Haiti	560
Israel	21,900	Benin	570
Slovenia	20,960	Laos	580
South Korea	19,690	Ghana	590

Note: Rankings based only on countries reporting G.N.P. per capita to The World Bank. 1. Includes overseas French territories. 2. Mainland only.
Source: The World Bank, The World Bank Atlas 2008.

of the world are divided into two basic categories, developed and developing. The developed ones are those with the highest G.N.P. figures, and are characterized by high per capita income, low rates of population growth and illiteracy, as well as having a low proportion of their labor force in agriculture and/or mining.

The wealthiest nations are at the center of the global economy and are responsible for promoting international trade, for helping to finance development in the poorer countries, and for maintaining a stable economic world. They attempt to do this through several organizations including:

Group of Seven/Eight (G-8): a loosely knit group of the largest economic powers who meet once a year to discuss policy in what has become a well-publicized media event. **Members:** Canada, France, Germany, Italy, Japan, Russia, U.K., U.S. The European Union also participates in G-8 summits.

Organization of Economic Cooperation and Development (OECD) HQ: 2 rue André Pascal, F-75775 Paris Cedex 16, France. OECD Washington Center, 2001 L St. NW, Washington D.C. 20036. **www.oecdwash.org.** Estab. 1961, . . . to help member countries promote economic growth, employment, and improved standards of living through the coordination of policy (and) . . . to help promote the sound and harmonious development of the world economy and improve the lot of the developing countries, particularly the poorest. **Members (30):** Australia, Austria, Belgium, Canada, Czech Republic, Denmark, Finland, France, Germany, Greece,

Net Foreign Direct Investment in Developing Countries, 1990–2007

Region and country	Billions of U.S. dollars					
	1990	1995	2000	2005	2006	2007[1]
All developing countries	**$24.5**	**$104.0**	**$165.5**	**$288.5**	**$367.5**	**$470.8**
By region						
East Asia and the Pacific	$105.1	$50.8	$45.2	$104.2	$105.0	$115.2
Europe and Central Asia	33.3	14.6	24.8	72.2	124.6	131.9
Latin America and the Caribbean	81.2	30.2	79.5	70.4	70.5	102.2
Middle East and North Africa	7.4	0.9	4.8	14.4	27.5	30.1
South Asia	5.4	2.9	4.4	10.0	22.9	28.0
Sub-Saharan Africa	12.1	4.5	6.8	17.3	17.1	27.4
10 leading nations, 2007						
China	$3.5	$35.8	$38.4	$79.1	$78.1	$84.0
Russia	N.A.	2.1	2.7	12.9	30.8	52.5
Brazil	1.0	4.9	32.8	15.2	18.8	34.6
Mexico	2.6	9.5	17.9	19.9	19.2	23.2
Turkey	N.A.	N.A.	1.0	9.8	20.1	22.0
India	N.A.	N.A.	3.6	6.7	17.5	21.0
Poland	0.1	3.7	9.3	10.4	19.2	17.6
Chile	0.6	3.0	4.9	6.7	0.0	14.5
Ukraine	N.A.	N.A.	0.6	7.8	5.6	9.9
Thailand	N.A.	N.A.	3.4	8.0	9.0	9.6

1. Estimate. **Source:** The World Bank, *Global Development Finance (2008)*.

Total External Debt by Region and Nation, 1970–2006 (billions of dollars)

Region and nation	1970	1980	1990	2000	2005	2006[1]
All developing countries	**$70.2**	**$579.6**	**$1,421.6**	**$2,283.9**	**$2,800.4**	**$2,983.7**
By Region						
East Asia and the Pacific	$8.6	$64.6	$239.0	$498.0	$614.1	$660.0
Europe and Central Asia	5.0	75.6	217.9	511.0	822.7	1,047.0
Latin America and the Caribbean	32.6	257.4	475.4	758.7	746.9	734.5
Middle East and North Africa	4.8	83.4	182.9	145.2	148.9	141.3
South Asia	12.3	37.8	129.5	160.0	191.3	227.3
Sub-Saharan Africa	6.9	60.8	176.9	211.0	216.2	173.5
10 most indebted nations, 2006						
China	N.A.	N.A.	$55.3	$145.7	$281.6	$322.8
Russian Federation	N.A.	N.A.	59.3	160.0	229.1	251.1
Turkey	$2.7	$19.1	49.4	117.3	169.3	207.9
Brazil	5.7	71.5	120.0	239.2	187.3	194.1
Mexico	7.0	57.4	104.4	150.3	167.9	160.7
India	8.4	20.7	83.6	99.1	123.1	153.1
Indonesia	4.5	20.9	69.9	144.4	130.7	131.0
Poland	N.A.	N.A.	49.4	65.8	98.8	125.8
Argentina	5.8	27.2	62.2	147.5	133.0	122.2
Hungary	N.A.	N.A.	N.A.	29.5	66.1	107.7

Note: 1. Estimate. **Source:** The World Bank, *Global Development Finance (2008)*.

U.S. Merchandise Trade Partners, 2007 (millions of dollars)

Country	U.S. exports to	U.S. imports from	U.S. net balance of trade
TOTAL[1]	$1,148,481	$1,967,853	$-819,372
Belgium	25,153	15,284	9,869
France	27,133	41,544	-14,411
Germany	49,025	94,280	-45,255
Ireland	8,997	30,483	-21,486
Italy	13,893	35,027	-21,134
Netherlands	32,670	18,371	14,299
United Kingdom	48,733	56,367	-7,634
Canada	249,712	320,323	-70,611
Brazil	24,497	25,650	-1,153
Mexico	135,962	213,552	-77,590
Venezuela	10,193	39,910	-29,717
China	65,073	321,685	-256,612
Japan	60,898	146,037	-85,139
Malaysia	11,587	32,640	-21,053
South Korea	33,646	47,547	-13,901
Singapore	25,874	18,423	7,451
Taiwan	25,961	38,489	-12,528
Nigeria	2,788	32,770	-29,982

Note: 1. Includes other countries not shown separately. **Source:** U.S. Dept. of Commerce, *U.S. International Transactions,* June 17, 2008.

Hungary, Iceland, Ireland, Italy, Japan, Luxembourg, Mexico, Netherlands, New Zealand, Norway, Poland, Portugal, Slovakia, South Korea, Spain, Sweden, Switzerland, Turkey, U.K., U.S.

The International Monetary Fund (I.M.F.) and The World Bank   Both of these organizations are specialized agencies of the United Nations (see the separate section on the U.N. below) charged with making loans to nations having trouble with debt (I.M.F.) or for long-term growth and development among poorer nations (World Bank).

I.M.F. Classification of Countries
Advanced economies (31): Australia, Austria, Belgium, Canada, Cyprus, Denmark, Finland, France, Germany, Greece, Hong Kong, Iceland, Ireland, Israel, Italy, Japan, Korea, Luxembourg, Malta, Netherlands, New Zealand, Norway, Portugal, Singapore, Slovenia, Spain, Sweden, Switzerland, Taiwan, United Kingdom, the United States.

Other emerging market and developing countries (142): This group includes all other member countries except those non-I.M.F. members (such as Afghanistan) and countries that don't provide data (such as San Marino).

World's Leading Exporters and Importers in Merchandise Trade, 2006

Rank and country	Value 2006 (billions)	Share of world trade	Change in value, 2005-06	Rank and country	Value 2006 (billions)	Share of world trade	Change in value, 2005-06
EXPORTERS				**IMPORTERS**			
1. Germany	$1,112.0	9.2%	15%	1. United States	$1,919.4	15.5%	11%
2. United States	1,038.3	8.6	15	2. Germany	908.6	7.3	17
3. China	968.9	8.0	27	3. China	791.5	6.4	20
4. Japan	649.9	5.4	9	4. United Kingdom	619.4	5.0	21
5. France	490.4	4.1	6	5. Japan	579.6	4.7	13
6. Netherlands	462.4	3.8	14	6. France	534.9	4.3	6
7. United Kingdom	448.3	3.7	17	7. Italy	437.4	3.5	14
8. Italy	410.6	3.4	10	8. Netherlands	416.4	3.4	14
9. Canada	389.5	3.2	8	9. Canada	357.7	2.9	11
10. Belgium	369.2	3.1	10	10. Belgium	353.7	2.9	11
11. South Korea	325.5	2.7	14	11. Hong Kong[1]	335.8	2.7	12
12. Hong Kong[1]	322.7	2.7	10	12. Spain	316.4	2.5	10
13. Russian Federation	304.5	2.5	25	13. South Korea	309.4	2.5	18
14. Singapore[1]	271.8	2.2	18	14. Mexico	268.2	2.2	15
15. Mexico	250.4	2.1	17	15. Singapore[1]	238.7	1.9	19
16. Taipei, Chinese	223.8	1.9	13	16. Taiwan	203.0	1.6	11
17. Saudi Arabia	209.5	1.7	16	17. India	174.8	1.4	26
18. Spain	205.5	1.7	7	18. Russian Federation[3]	163.9	1.3	31
19. Malaysia	160.7	1.3	14	19. Switzerland	141.4	1.1	12
20. Switzerland	147.5	1.2	13	20. Austria	140.3	1.1	10
21. Sweden	147.4	1.2	13	21. Australia	139.3	1.1	11
22. Austria	140.4	1.2	12	22. Turkey	138.3	1.1	18
23. United Arab Emirates	139.4	1.2	19	23. Malaysia	131.2	1.1	14
24. Brazil	137.5	1.1	16	24. Thailand	128.6	1.0	9
25. Thailand	130.8	1.1	19	25. Sweden	126.7	1.0	14
26. Australia	123.3	1.0	16	26. Poland	126.0	1.0	24
27. Norway	121.5	1.0	17	27. United Arab Emirates	97.8	0.8	15
28. India	120.3	1.0	21	28. Brazil	95.9	0.8	24
29. Ireland	111.1	0.9	1	29. Czech Republic	93.2	0.8	22
30. Poland	110.3	0.9	23	30. Denmark	86.3	0.7	14
World Total[1,2]	**$12,083.0**	**100.0%**	**15%**	**World Total[1,2]**	**$12,413.0**	**100.0%**	**14%**

Notes: 1. Includes significant re-exports or imports for re-export. 2. Includes other countries not shown separately. 3. Imports are valued as freight on board. **Source:** World Trade Organization, *International Trade Statistics 2007* (2008). www.wto.org

►INTERNATIONAL FINANCE–BASIC CONCEPTS

Exchange rates Because countries have their own currencies, trade between them also involves exchanging or trading currencies. The *exchange rate* between currencies represents the ratio at which they can be exchanged or the price of one currency in terms of the other. For example, if the exchange rate between the British pound and the U.S. dollar is $1.50, then one British pound can be purchased at that price.

The exchange rate for almost all world currencies is now determined by the market. The exchange rate of a currency rises or appreciates when the demand for it rises and/or the supply falls. This may happen because foreign buyers want to buy more of a nation's goods or because consumers within the country decide to buy fewer imports. It may also happen because the country reduces its money supply. Finally, the central banks of countries can manipulate their exchange rates slightly by buying and selling their own and other currencies (see also Part II: The Federal Reserve).

The gold standard Before World War I, exchange rates for world currencies were fixed, artificially, by tying them to a certain amount of gold—$32, for example, might equal one ounce of gold. Central banks would then buy and sell gold in order to equalize supply and demand for the currencies and maintain the fixed exchange rates. For this reason, the central banks maintained enormous gold stockpiles, like the one the U.S. had at Fort Knox. People therefore referred to currencies as being backed by gold. Long-term changes in trading relationships and in the demand for various currencies eventually made the fixed exchange rates of the gold standard impossible to support. In 1944, the Bretton Woods agreement established the U.S. dollar as the world standard, but the U.S. still backed its dollars with gold and used gold to settle its debts. After 1973, the U.S. abandoned that role, and most of the world's exchange rates were set by the market.

Balance of payments The balance of payments account is the list of transactions between a country and the rest of the world. This account has three parts: *the current account:* a record of exports and imports of goods (e.g. oil, clothing) and services (e.g. tourism); *the capital account:* a record of exports and imports of assets such as bank loans and corporate stock purchases; and *the official-reserves account:* a record of a country's sales and purchases of official reserve assets at the central bank.

Balance of trade When a country imports goods from another country worth more than the value of its exports to it, there is said to be a

Foreign Exchange Rates: Currency Units Per Dollar, 1975–2008

Country/currency	1975	1990	1995	2000	2006	2007	2008[1]
Australia/dollar	$ 0.77	$ 1.28	$ 1.35	$ 1.72	$1.33	$1.19	$1.06
Austria/schilling [2]	17.44	11.33	10.08	N.A.	N.A.	N.A.	N.A.
Belgium/franc [2]	36.80	33.42	29.47	N.A.	N.A.	N.A.	N.A.
Brazil/real	N.A.	N.A.	N.A.	1.83	2.17	1.94	1.63
Canada/dollar	1.02	1.17	1.37	1.49	1.13	1.07	1.02
China/yuan	N.A.	4.79	8.37	8.28	7.97	7.61	6.89
Denmark/krone	5.75	6.19	5.60	8.10	5.94	5.44	4.82
European Community/euro	N.A.	N.A.	0.78	1.08	0.80	0.73	0.65
Finland/markka [2]	3.67	3.83	4.38	N.A.	N.A.	N.A.	N.A.
France/franc [2]	4.29	5.45	4.99	N.A.	N.A.	N.A.	N.A.
Germany/deutsche mark [2]	2.46	1.62	1.43	N.A.	N.A.	N.A.	N.A.
Greece/drachma[2]	32.30	158.59	231.68	365.92	N.A.	N.A.	N.A.
Hong Kong/dollar	4.94	7.79	7.74	7.79	7.77	7.80	7.81
India/rupee	8.40	17.49	32.41	45.00	45.19	41.20	42.93
Ireland/pound [2]	0.45	0.60	0.62	N.A.	N.A.	N.A.	N.A.
Italy/lira [2]	653.10	1,198.27	1,629.45	N.A.	N.A.	N.A.	N.A.
Japan/yen	296.79	145.00	93.96	107.80	116.31	117.76	108.19
Malaysia/ringgit	2.40	2.70	2.51	3.80	3.67	3.44	3.27
Mexico/peso	12.64	2,813.00	6.45	9.46	10.91	10.93	10.31
Netherlands/guilder [2]	2.53	1.82	1.60	N.A.	N.A.	N.A.	N.A.
New Zealand/dollar	0.82	1.68	1.52	2.19	1.54	1.35	1.33
Norway/krone	5.23	6.26	6.34	8.81	6.41	5.86	5.18
Portugal/escudo [2]	25.51	142.70	149.88	N.A.	N.A.	N.A.	N.A.
Singapore/dollar	2.37	1.81	1.42	1.72	1.59	1.51	1.37
South Africa/rand	0.74	2.59	3.63	6.95	6.77	7.05	8.10
South Korea/won	484.00	710.64	772.69	1,130.90	954.32	928.97	1,038.50
Spain/peseta [2]	57.43	101.96	124.64	N.A.	N.A.	N.A.	N.A.
Sri Lanka/rupee	6.98	40.08	51.05	76.96	103.94	110.62	107.82
Sweden/krona	4.15	5.92	7.14	9.17	7.37	6.76	6.04
Switzerland/franc	2.58	1.39	1.18	1.69	1.25	1.20	1.04
Taiwan/dollar	38.00	26.92	26.50	31.26	32.50	32.85	30.38
Thailand/baht	N.A.	N.A.	24.92	40.21	37.88	32.20	33.24
United Kingdom/pound	0.45	0.56	0.64	0.65	0.54	0.50	0.51
Venezuela/bolivar	N.A.	N.A.	174.85	680.52	2,144.60	2,144.60	2,144.60

Note: Averages of certified noon buying rates in New York for cable transfers. **1.** Figures are for June 16, 2008**. 2.** Country converted its currency to euros as of January 3, 2001. A euro is worth 13.76 Austrian schillings, 40.34 Belgian francs, 5.95 Finnish markkas, 6.56 French francs, 1.96 German marks, 340.75 Greek drachmas, 0.79 Irish pounds, 1,936.27 Italian lire, 2.20 Netherlands guilders, 200.48 Portuguese escudos, or 166.39 Spanish pesetas. **Source:** Federal Reserve Bulletin, monthly.

deficit in the balance of trade between the countries. Changes in exchange rates tend to equalize the supply and demand for currencies and the balance of trade; in the above case, the exchange rate for the first country's currency should fall relative to the second country's, reducing imports by making them more expensive and encouraging exports by making them cheaper. But this equalization may take a long time to occur since consumers and producers in the two countries must change their behavior. And central banks may want to slow the pace at which exchange rates adjust to slow the effects on trading sectors within their economies.

The balance of trade is an important issue because it indicates something about how a nation's economy is changing and, ultimately, about its competitiveness vis-à-vis other countries. A rising balance of trade deficit indicates that an economy is not able to sell its goods abroad and that consumers are favoring imports over domestically produced goods.

As the U.S. economy has outsourced manufacturing jobs overseas, the U.S. trade deficit has skyrocketed. In 1980, the deficit was $19.4 billion; by 2000, it had increased to $375 billion, or nearly 20 times that amount. And in 2007, the deficit was more 700 billion dollars. The entire U.S. trade deficit is in the manufactured goods sector; the U.S. actually runs a surplus in the services sector. U.S. exports of goods have not kept up with imports in part because the relative strength of the dollar makes U.S. goods more expensive for foreign nations to buy, while people in America have more money to spend on cheap imports.

U.S. International Trade Balance (millions of U.S. dollars) 1960–2007

	Exports		Imports		Balance		
Year	Goods[1]	Services[2]	Goods[1]	Services[2]	Goods[1]	Services[2]	Total
1960	$19,650	$6,290	$14,758	$7,674	$4,892	$-1,385	$3,508
1970	42,469	14,171	39,866	14,520	2,603	-349	2,254
1980	224,250	47,584	249,750	41,491	-25,500	6,093	-19,407
1990	387,401	147,832	498,435	117,659	-111,034	30,173	-80,861
1995	575,204	218,521	749,374	139,420	-174,170	79,101	-95,069
2000	771,994	298,603	1,224,408	223,748	-452,414	74,855	-377,559
2003	713,415	304,342	1,257,121	250,365	-550,892	53,977	-496,915
2004	807,516	349,734	1,469,704	292,247	-669,578	57,487	-612,091
2005	894,631	389,122	1,681,780	313,540	-787,149	75,582	-711,567
2006	1,023,109	433,905	1,861,380	348,918	-838,270	84,987	-753,283
2007	1,148,481	497,245	1,967,853	378,130	-819,373	119,115	-700,258

Note: The balance is equal to exports minus imports. 1. Adjusted, excluding military. 2. Includes some military goods. Source U.S. Bureau of Economic Analysis, Foreign Trade Division, *U.S. International Transactions, Table 1.* www.bea.doc.gov

10 Largest U.S. Merchandise Imports and Exports, 1990–2003

	Volume (millions)				
Rank, Product Group	1990	1995	2000	2002	2003
TOTAL TOP TEN EXPORTS	**$213,249**	**$324,510**	**$473,256**	**$407,507**	**$412,733**
1. Electrical machinery and appliances	31,554	65,638	110,095	82,657	85,910
2. Motor vehicles	30,524	49,222	59,992	60,329	63,130
3. Transportation equipment	32,346	27,720	43,399	46,148	42,510
4. Office and A.D.P. machines	27,766	41,947	57,595	39,744	41,054
5. Miscellaneous manufactured articles	20,903	28,515	35,538	33,226	34,621
6. Power generating machinery	15,885	22,430	34,345	34,381	33,642
7. General industrial machinery	16,032	25,148	34,455	31,839	32,183
8. Professional scientific instruments	12,601	19,372	32,326	29,210	30,977
9. Specialized machinery	15,737	24,286	32,529	25,091	25,000
10. Telecommunications equipment	9,901	20,332	32,980	24,882	23,706
TOTAL TOP TEN IMPORTS	**$258,293**	**$420,911**	**$768,423**	**$719,152**	**$773,076**
1. Motor vehicles	73,017	100,254	161,682	168,173	172,578
2. Petroleum	N.A.	N.A.	117,174	101,152	129,600
3. Electrical machinery and appliances	33,601	75,169	108,813	81,288	82,545
4. Office and A.D.P. machines	26,917	62,824	92,165	76,970	80,826
5. Telecommunications equipment	22,288	34,384	70,487	66,268	71,137
6. Apparel and clothing	25,533	39,526	64,296	63,810	68,162
7. Miscellaneous manufactured articles	25,028	36,467	56,718	62,044	64,401
8. General industrial machinery	14,484	24,113	34,709	35,201	38,467
9. Organic chemicals	N.A.	13,325	28,563	30,213	32,876
10. Power generating machinery	14,591	20,486	33,815	34,032	32,485

Note: In current U.S. dollars. Source: U.S. Dept. of Commerce, International Trade Administration, *U.S. Foreign Trade Highlights 2003* (2004). www.ita.doc.gov/td/industry/otea/usfth/aggregate/H03T22.html

►GLOBAL CAPITAL MOVEMENT

The current dynamic interaction among these very disparate economies—aided greatly by the technological revolution—has set in motion an unprecedented global movement of capital from the wealthiest nations to developing ones. Because holders of capital always seek greater returns on their investments, they will put their money in economies that show potential growth; if they own or run corporations, they will look for ways to reduce the costs of manufacturing, especially labor costs, so they realize a greater profit. By investing in foreign companies or by establishing their businesses in foreign nations, the power of capital can rapidly transform the economies of poorer nations while rearranging the patterns of daily life for millions.

Foreign Direct Investment (F.D.I) is investment by private companies of one nation in the territory of another nation. The investment can be in an existing enterprise of the host nation or the building of new facilities for the investing foreign company (which would then be known as a multinational enterprise). The amount of money flowing from the wealthy nations to the developing ones in this way has increased from $24.5 billion in 1990 to an estimated $270.8 billion in 2007.

Portfolio Investment is investing in the stocks and bonds of foreign nations. In March 1994, U.S. holdings of foreign securities totaled $870 billion, according to the U.S. Treasury Dept. That number more than doubled, to $1.76 trillion, by December 1997, and jumped to $2.95 trillion in December 2003. Globalization has caused portfolio investment to double yet again, reaching $5.9 trillion by the end of 2006. Of this amount, $4.3 trillion was invested in equities (stocks) and $1.3 trillion was invested in long-term debt (bonds).

►INTERNATIONAL TRADE

International trade takes place because some nations have an advantage in producing certain kinds of products either because they have a comparative wealth of resources (capital, labor, natural resources) or more efficient production techniques. Even an economy with the most efficient technology has a limit on its resources, and rather than using them to produce all variety of products, it concentrates its resources on what it makes most efficiently. It then trades that good for other commodities, importing those that it produces least efficiently. As a result, all countries are better off because specialization results in the expansion of the total supply of goods, and the cost of acquiring them then falls.

Just which commodities a country will export and import depends on the relative prices of the factors used in production. A country like India has abundant labor and low wages. It therefore exports labor-intensive products such as garments. A country like Canada, which has abundant natural resources, specializes in agriculture and raw materials. Countries such as Canada and India then import goods for which the factors of production are in relatively short supply.

Of course, there are political reasons why countries do not completely specialize their production. No country, for example, wants to import all of its military equipment for fear that supplies would be cut off in the event of international conflict. Similarly, even inefficient producers, such as farmers in Japan, where land is scarce and expensive, may have political power that forces their governments to subsidize them.

U.S. Exports and Imports in Services, by Type, 1986–2007 (millions)

Category	1986	1990	1995	2000	2006	2007
SERVICES EXPORTS, TOTAL	**$77,545**	**$137,232**	**$203,060**	**$284,027**	**$415,321**	**$479,980**
Travel	20,385	43,007	63,395	82,400	85,720	96,712
Passenger fares	5,582	15,298	18,909	20,687	22,036	25,586
Other transportation	15,438	22,042	26,081	29,803	46,323	51,586
Royalties and license fees	8,113	16,634	30,289	43,233	72,191	82,614
Other private services[1]	28,027	40,251	64,386	107,904	189,050	223,483
Education	3,495	5,126	7,515	10,348	14,645	15,732
Financial	3,301	4,417	7,029	16,026	47,439	58,266
Insurance	1,385	230	588	3,631	10,095	10,286
Telecommunications	1,827	2,735	3,228	3,884	7,278	8,283
Business, professional, & technical	4,813	7,752	16,078	25,319	89,692	107,675
SERVICES IMPORTS, TOTAL	**$64,731**	**$98,210**	**$126,754**	**$207,392**	**$313,865**	**$341,126**
Travel	25,913	37,349	44,916	64,705	72,104	76,167
Passenger fares	6,505	10,531	14,663	24,274	27,501	28,486
Other transportation	17,766	24,966	27,034	41,425	65,262	67,050
Royalties and license fees	1,401	3,135	6,919	16,468	23,777	25,048
Other private services[1]	13,146	22,229	33,222	60,520	125,221	144,375
Education	433	658	1,125	2,032	4,465	4,523
Financial	1,769	2,475	2,472	4,840	14,242	18,928
Insurance	2,200	1,910	3,272	11,284	37,373	42,761
Telecommunications	3,253	5,583	7,305	5,429	6,367	7,334
Business, professional, & technical	1,303	2,093	4,822	9,130	61,068	68,763

Note: 1. Includes other services not shown separately. The dramatic differences in Other Private Services beginning in 2006 result from a change in accounting methods. **Source:** U.S. Bureau of Economic Analysis, Foreign Trade Division, *U.S. International Transactions,* Table 3a, June 17, 2008. www.bea.doc.gov.

Tariffs and Quotas One way to protect a country's own producers, especially where they are inefficient compared with the international competition, is with import tariffs—taxes on goods that are produced abroad. Import tariffs raise the price of imports relative to domestic alternatives and discourage demand for the former. If one country is the sole importer or even the main importer of another's exports, it is possible that an import tariff will simply force the exporter to cut its selling price (in order to keep the price to consumers—including the tariff—from rising sharply and cutting off demand). In this case, the exporter pays virtually the whole cost of the tariff. If, on the other hand, the importer badly needs the import and there are few substitutes, raising the tariff simply raises the costs to one's own consumers. Critics of U.S. trade policy have pointed out that because Japan has become virtually the sole supplier of many consumer electronic products in the U.S., any tariffs against these products would simply raise their prices and fuel U.S. inflation.

Import quotas attempt to achieve a restriction on imports without the price rises associated with tariffs by setting direct limits on the number of items imported. So-called trade wars start when one country imposes a tariff on imports from a second country, and the latter responds with tariffs of its own against the first country. The arguments presented above about the benefits of trade have led to efforts to restrict the use of tariffs and maintain free trade, i.e. trade without any restrictions. Economists argue that unrestricted trade will always promote economic growth by forcing domestic prices to reflect world prices, thereby encouraging the efficient allocation of resources. Over the last 50 years, i.e. since the end of World War II, many of the leading nations have made a strong and continuous effort to lower or eliminate tariffs, first regionally, then around the world. The most successful regional organization has been the European Union, which has encouraged the formation of many other such alliances in all parts of the world.

Global trade has grown rapidly over the last decade, in large part because of the General Agreement on Tariffs and Trade (GATT) and its successor organization, the World Trade Organization (WTO).

GATT The General Agreement on Tariffs and Trade was first established in 1948. In an attempt to regulate the world's trade, the representatives of 23 leading nations agreed to find ways to lower tariffs, lower quotas, and to make free trade, i.e. trade without restrictions of any kind, their final goal. The United Nations provided headquarters for the group in Geneva, Switzerland. Over a period of almost 50 years the most important trading nations met regularly to discuss specific trade matters and to continue to remove restrictions from trade. Each series of negotiations, called rounds, lasted several years. By 1975 tariffs on manufactured goods had been reduced from 40 percent to 10 percent and world trade more than tripled. By the 1980's, however, the nature of world trade had changed. In 1986 the so-called Uruguay Round of GATT (now with 92 nations represented) addressed these and other issues over a period of eight years. The results—lowering of tariffs of all kind, banning quotas, and protecting copyrights and patents—added an estimated $500 billion annually to the global economy.

World Trade Organization Potentially the most important accomplishment of the 1994 GATT Agreement was the establishment of the World Trade Organization (W.T.O.), a permanent institution with real power to oversee trade agreements, enforce trade rules, and settle disputes. When it was approved by the U.S. Congress (Jan. 1, 1995), the organization became a reality, with 110 members. The basic principles of the W.T.O., derived from the GATT negotiations are the encouragement of fair competition and increased access to markets as well as the development of trade without discrimination (MFN, most favored nation status, i.e. no nation will be given preferential trading terms). In 2003 the W.T.O. failed to reach agreement on the reduction of farm subsidies from the governments of wealthy nations, a vital issue for farmers in developing nations. But in July 2004 the organization succeeded in putting together the framework of an agreement that by 2006 would see the U.S. and other wealthy nations cut subsidies by 20 percent. But in 2008 talks collapsed and were broken off without a deal; again agricultural subsidies were the key sticking points. **HQ:** Centre William Rappard, 154 rue de Lausanne, CH-1211 Geneva 21, Switzerland. (41-22) 739 51 11. **Internet Address: www.wto.org Membership:** (152) Albania, Angola, Antigua and Barbuda, Argentina, Armenia, Australia, Austria, Bahrain, Bangladesh, Barbados, Belgium, Belize, Benin, Bolivia, Botswana, Brazil, Brunei Darussalam, Bulgaria, Burkina Faso, Burundi, Cambodia, Cameroon, Canada, Central African Republic, Chad, Chile, China, Colombia, Congo, Congo (Democratic Rep.), Costa Rica, Croatia, Cuba, Cyprus, Czech Republic, Denmark, Djibouti, Dominica, Dominican Republic, Ecuador, Egypt, El Salvador, Estonia, E.U, Fiji, Finland, France, Gabon, The Gambia, Georgia, Germany, Ghana, Greece, Grenada, Guatemala, Guinea, Guinea Bissau, Guyana, Haiti, Honduras, Hong Kong, Hungary, Iceland, India, Indonesia, Ireland, Israel, Italy, Ivory Coast, Jamaica, Japan, Jordan, Kenya, Kuwait, Kyrgyzstan, Latvia, Lesotho, Liechtenstein, Lithuania, Luxembourg, Macao, Macedonia, Madagascar, Malawi, Malaysia, Maldives, Mali, Malta, Mauritania, Mauritius, Mexico, Moldova, Mongolia, Morocco, Mozambique, Myanmar, Namibia, Nepal, Netherlands, New Zealand, Nicaragua, Niger, Nigeria, Norway, Oman, Pakistan, Panama, Papua New Guinea, Paraguay, Peru, Philippines, Poland, Portugal, Qatar, Romania, Rwanda, Saint Kitts & Nevis, Saint Lucia, Saint Vincent & the Grenadines, Saudi Arabia, Senegal, Sierra Leone, Singapore, Slovak Republic, Slovenia, Solomon Islands, South Africa, South Korea, Spain, Sri Lanka, Suriname, Swaziland, Sweden, Switzerland, Tanzania, Taiwan, Thailand, Togo, Tonga, Trinidad & Tobago, Tunisia, Turkey, Uganda, Ukraine, United Arab Emirates, United Kingdom, United States, Uruguay, Venezuela, Vietnam, Zambia, Zimbabwe. **Observers and applicants:** (30): Afghanistan, Algeria, Andorra, Azerbaijan, Bahamas, Belarus, Bhutan, Bosnia & Herzegovina, Cape Verde, Equatorial Guinea, Ethiopia, Holy See (Vatican), Iran, Iraq, Kazakhstan, Laos, Lebanon, Libya, Montenegro, Russian Federation, Samoa, São Tome & Principe, Serbia, Seychelles, Sudan, Tajikistan, Uzbekistan, Vanuatu, Yemen. *(With the exception of the Holy See, observers must start* *accession negotiations within five years of becoming observers.)*

▶ EUROPEAN UNION

In 2005, the 48th year of its founding, the European Union had achieved success beyond the wildest dreams of its founders. It was now an enormous economic superpower, a gigantic market of over 425 million people in 25 nations with even more nations eager to join. During the previous decade its leaders had succeeded, despite dire predictions, in introducing almost seamlessly a new common currency called the euro which quickly took root throughout Europe and in world markets. Finally the E.U. had integrated many of the countries of post-Communist east-central Europe.

Origins Out of the wreckage of World War II, with generous American Marshall Plan aid after 1948, western Europe commenced reconstruction; by 1954, several economic miracles occurred. Yet without economic integration, the recoveries of the separate nations involved duplications, inefficiencies, diminished competition, and the threats of local gluts and shortages. A small sign of what might be achieved was Benelux, the customs union between Belgium, the Netherlands and Luxembourg, constructed even before war's end in 1944 and a going concern by 1948 despite the very unequal status of the three economies.

On May 9, 1950, France's foreign minister, Robert Schuman, proposed that German and French coal and steel production (the sinews of war) be placed under a supra-national, not inter-governmental, high authority; the West German chancellor, Konrad Adenauer, responded positively that very evening. By May 1952, ratification of the six-nation European Coal and Steel Community was complete, with Italy and the Benelux countries joining the French and Germans. The dramatic successes of the ECSC led the six toward broader integration, with negotiations culminating in the March 1957 Treaties of Rome which established the European Economic Community (EEC) and the European Atomic Energy Commission (Euratom).

The EEC was designed to reduce and eventually abolish all tariffs among the six; to establish a single external tariff for the Community; and to foster the free movement of not only goods but of labor and capital as well. Euratom was intended for the common peaceful development of nuclear power, though common action proved subsequently difficult to agree on. In 1958 the United Kingdom, which had refused to join the original negotiations, proposed that the EEC be expanded into an Atlantic free-trade area, but France, under her new president, Charles de Gaulle, exercised the veto. The rebuff led Britain with Portugal, Austria, Switzerland and the Scandinavian kingdoms to form in 1959 the European Free Trade Association. The EFTA's successes were real but no match for the burgeoning EEC. So in 1961 Britain sought EEC membership. But de Gaulle, fearing American influence and objecting to the special terms that Britain sought for Commonwealth countries, again exercised the veto.

At the same time, de Gaulle was pushing for agricultural integration to match the EEC's industrial unity: the huge German market beckoned for France's chronic farm surpluses, yet Germany hesitated to sacrifice her own farmers in return for cheaper food. In fact, a serious crisis impended since each of the Six had its own system of protectionist duties, farm subsidies and crop controls. But the Dutch (Mansholt) proposals met with relatively easy and rapid agreement. The Common Agricultural Policy of 1962 eventually established a highly bureaucratized, centrally financed common market with managed prices, common duties upon imports, and subsidies for exports.

The European Community (E.C.) With agricultural integration, the stage was set for the Brussels treaty of 1965 (often called the The Second Treaty of Rome), which founded the European Community. The earlier three communities (ECSC, EEC and Euratom) were merged into one and were provided with a four-part structure of Commission, Council, Parliament and Court.

It was this refounded E.C. that the United Kingdom was at last permitted to join in 1973 (after another Gaullist veto in 1967). As in its earlier attempts, it was accompanied by Ireland, Denmark and Norway (though Norwegian voters subsequently rejected admission in a referendum). The Nine subsequently became the Twelve with the admission of Greece (1981), Spain and Portugal (1986).

Twenty years after the Brussels Treaty, with the accession of Jacques Delors as president of the European Commission, the E.C. received new impetus toward what the Treaty of Rome had envisioned: a single market free of all barriers to the free movement of goods, services, capital and labor. The first result was the Single European Act of 1987, an unwieldy compendium of almost 300 rules and directives to bring about by 1992 a Europe without frontiers. Even a decade later, its full meaning remains unclear, although both families and giant corporations have been able to hunt for bargains across national borders, tax and interest rates have been leveled, and trans-national re-

The European Union

Year admitted	Member countries
1957	Belgium, France, Germany, Italy, Luxembourg, Netherlands
1973	Denmark, Ireland, United Kingdom
1981	Greece
1986	Portugal, Spain
1995	Austria, Finland, Sweden
2004	Cyprus, Czech Republic, Estonia, Hungary, Latvia, Lithuania, Malta, Poland, Slovakia, Slovenia
2007	Bulgaria, Romania
Applicants	Croatia, Former Yugoslav Republic of Macedonia, Turkey

gional ties have developed. The abolition of capital controls in 1990 has proven decisive in the movement toward monetary union, the second result of the Delors presidency (and of the strong support given by Helmut Kohl's Germany).

The European Union (E.U.) In December 1991, the E.C. approved its third foundational treaty, the Treaty of Maastricht. Its three pillars were: monetary union, common foreign and security policies, and cooperation in justice and home affairs. The latter two pillars are intergovernmental, not supranational affairs, and have not been dealt with since 1991, as the E.U.'s clumsy responses to the Bosnian and Albanian crises attest.

Following the simple idea that a single market requires a single currency, the Maastricht Treaty established a three-stage (1991, 1994, 1997) creation of the *European Monetary Union* (EMU). During the first two stages, the E.U. members were to converge according to five criteria: inflation rates, interest rates, currency exchange, rate stability (variation within 2.25 percent), budget deficits (less than 3 percent of G.D.P.), and public indebtedness (a debt-to-G.D.P. ratio of less than 60 percent). During the second stage would occur the transition from central bank financing of government spending to creation of the European Central Bank. With the third stage, the European Central Bank would propose and carry out the E.U.'s monetary policies and the euro would circulate as bank money—all preparatory to the actual introduction of the monetary union.

A tone of unreality attended attempts to establish the EMU. When Danish voters rejected Maastricht in a June 1992 referendum (unanimous approval being required for the treaty to take force), the E.U., at the time still called the E.C., permitted Denmark a sort of *à la carte* membership: Denmark could ratify while opting out of the single currency (and other treaty matters). Danish voters in May 1993 thereupon reversed themselves and approved the treaty. German ratification in November 1993 brought the treaty into effect. But between those two votes, the exchange rate variation was altered from 2.25 percent to 15 percent lest the French withdraw from the pact.

It was this oddly flexible E.U. that Austria, Finland and Sweden joined on January 1, 1995. The Norwegian government had sought membership and been approved, but Norwegian voters, as they had in 1973, said no.

The European Monetary Union On Jan. 1, 1999, the E.U. introduced the euro. Initially well received in world financial markets, the euro sagged over the next six months, losing almost 20 percent of its value against the dollar. One reason for the flop was the E.U.'s decision to permit Italy's budget deficit to substantially exceed the target 2 percent of GDP; one member's excessive spend-

Hourly Compensation Costs in U.S. Dollars For Production Workers, Selected Countries, 1975–2006

Country	1975	1985	1990	1995	2000	2005	2006
Australia	$5.60	$8.44	$13.09	$15.36	$14.41	$25.11	$26.14
Austria	4.50	8.87	17.91	25.26	19.12	29.36	30.46
Belgium	5.77	11.74	17.85	25.67	20.13	30.79	31.85
Brazil	N.A.	N.A.	N.A.	N.A.	3.50	4.16	4.91
Canada	6.11	8.87	16.33	16.50	16.48	23.98	25.74
Czech Republic	N.A.	N.A.	N.A.	2.63	3.01	6.04	6.77
Denmark	6.24	10.77	18.35	25.28	21.43	34.45	35.45
Finland	4.63	8.30	21.15	24.31	17.84	28.38	29.90
France	4.50	8.90	15.36	19.26	15.43	24.00	24.90
Germany[1]	N.A.	N.A.	N.A.	30.10	22.67	33.34	34.21
Hong Kong	0.75	1.50	3.22	4.80	5.45	5.65	5.78
Hungary	N.A.	N.A.	N.A.	2.69	2.74	6.13	6.29
Ireland	3.06	6.02	11.77	13.75	13.28	24.15	25.96
Israel	2.02	3.41	7.69	9.41	11.41	12.34	12.98
Italy	4.64	8.09	17.28	15.69	14.47	24.23	25.07
Japan	2.97	5.46	12.59	23.47	21.93	21.54	20.20
Korea	0.32	0.95	3.70	7.28	8.23	12.74	14.72
Luxembourg	6.22	11.51	16.00	23.56	17.41	27.26	27.74
Mexico	1.46	2.20	1.57	1.70	2.07	2.64	2.75
Netherlands	6.58	12.05	17.98	24.03	19.35	31.80	32.34
New Zealand	3.28	5.44	8.48	10.35	8.38	14.97	14.47
Norway	6.90	11.80	21.76	24.84	22.56	39.17	41.05
Poland	N.A.	N.A.	N.A.	N.A.	2.81	4.51	4.99
Portugal	1.52	1.98	3.59	5.09	4.49	7.27	7.65
Singapore	0.83	1.53	3.74	7.57	7.30	7.30	8.55
Spain	2.52	5.86	11.30	12.70	10.66	17.92	18.83
Sri Lanka	0.28	0.22	0.35	0.48	0.48	0.54	—
Sweden	7.14	12.44	20.81	21.68	20.68	30.46	31.80
Switzerland	6.03	10.96	20.63	28.90	20.95	30.50	30.67
Taiwan	0.38	1.03	3.91	5.99	6.19	6.42	6.43
United Kingdom	3.35	7.52	12.61	13.79	16.84	25.72	27.10
United States	$6.16	$9.63	$14.81	$17.17	$19.65	$23.81	$23.82

Note: Hourly compensation includes wages, premiums, bonuses, vacation, holidays and other leave, insurance, and benefit plans.
1. Prior to 1991, data for Germany were for West Germany. **Source:** U.S. Bureau of Labor Statistics, *International Comparisons of Hourly Compensation Costs for Production Workers in Manufacturing*, January, 2008.

ing was dragging the whole currency down. By September, it had lost about 27 percent of its value against the dollar, prompting voters in Denmark to reject the new currency and instead keep their krone.

On Jan. 1, 2002, 50 billion new euro coins and 14.5 billion euro notes went into circulation in the 12 member countries, and on Feb. 28, 2002, all other currencies were withdrawn from circulation in the member nations. The two-month overlap period caused more than a little bit of confusion throughout Europe, but it bolstered the value of the euro to about even with the U.S. dollar. Since then, the euro has continuously outpaced the dollar. In 2008, it was trading above $1.50 (See the accompanying table)

Expansion and Constitution In 2004 the E.U. expanded southward and eastward to include (the Greek part of) Cyprus, the Czech Republic, Estonia, Hungary, Latvia, Lithuania, Malta, Poland, Slovakia and Slovenia. The 10 additional countries make the E.U. truly One Europe, some 450 million people with an economy about the size of that of the U.S. While the average G.D.P. of the new states is less that half that of the earlier 15, their rate of growth is noticeably higher, not least because their corporate income tax rates are, on average, one-third lower, which encourages capital flow eastward. But the greatest contrast is in the agricultural sector.

The addition of the new states poses a possible nightmare for E.U. farm subsidies, which already account for half of the E.U. budget. By the terms of an Oct. 2002 agreement, the new members received 25 percent of the older states' subsidies until 2007, when the subsidy increased to 40 percent; full parity is achieved in 2013. The aggregate expenditure on farm subsidies will be allowed to rise no more than 1 percent per year between 2007 and 2013. In June 2003, the E.U.'s agricultural ministers agreed to begin a reform of the Common Agricultural Policy, planning to sever the link between subsidies and production, linking them instead to farm size.

On June 17-18, 2004, the Heads of State and Government adopted the Treaty establishing a Constitution for Europe, which would have replaced all existing treaties with a single document. Among its notable innovations were: 1) a written bill of rights; 2) a single foreign minister; 3) introduction of majority voting in many policy areas such as energy, agriculture and immigration (while maintaining unanimity in such areas as taxation and foreign policy. However, France and

the Netherlands both rejected the Constitution, thus nixing its potential for ratification. Romania and Bulgaria joined the E.U. in 2007.

The 2007 Treaty of Lisbon did not revisit the idea of a constitution; instead, it focused on making the E.U. more democratic, more efficient, and more transparent. In addition to clearly defining the relationship between the Union and its member states, it explicitly recognized—for the first time—the ability of a member to withdraw from the Union.

Additional information about the European Union (in 11 languages) can be found at the E.U. Web server. The address is http://europa.eu.

Structure of the E.U.
The Commission is composed of 27 commissioners, one appointed by each member country. The Commission supervises implementation of E.U. treaties, initiates and implements E.U. policy, applies E.U. law in member states, transacts negotiations with nonmember states, manages E.U. funds and budgets, and acts as the international mouthpiece of the E.U., enabling the member states to speak with one voice in international forums like the W.T.O. The Commission's term of office expires October 31, 2009; José Manuel Barroso of Portugal is the current president.

The Council of the European Union consists of one minister from each of the 27 member governments. It is the chief decision-making body of the E.U., passing legislation on the major issues affecting all members. Each country takes the presidency for six months. Voting strength is weighted by population. Germany, France, Italy and the United Kingdom, for example, each have 29 votes, while Malta has 3. The Council meets in Brussels.

The European Parliament The 785 deputies of the European Parliament are elected directly by the citizens of the individual countries. The Parliament oversees the E.U. budget and passes on Commission proposals to the Council of Ministers. The Parliament also passes on new applications to the E.U. Deputies are elected to five-year terms.

The Court of Justice is the court of last resort for the E.U., interpreting E.U. treaties and legislation and hearing complaints about member-government violations. The Court also resolves differences between E.U. legislation and national laws. The 27 justices are appointed by the member governments and serve six-year terms.

Unemployment Rates in Leading Developed Nations, 1960–2007									
Nation	1960	1970	1980	1990	1995	2000	2005	2006	2007
Australia[1]	1.6%	1.6%	6.1%	6.7%	8.2%	6.3%	5.1%	4.8%	4.4%
Canada	6.5	5.7	7.3	7.7	8.6	6.1	6.0	5.5	5.3
France	1.5	2.5	6.5	8.6	11.3	9.1	9.6	9.5	8.6
Germany[2]	1.1	0.5	2.8	5.0	8.2	7.8	11.2	10.4	8.7
Italy	3.7	3.2	4.4	7.0	11.3	10.2	7.8	6.9	6.2
Japan	1.7	1.2	2.0	2.1	3.2	4.8	4.5	4.2	3.9
Netherlands	N.A.	N.A.	6.0	7.6	7.1	3.0	4.8	3.9	3.2
Sweden[1]	1.7	1.5	2.0	1.8	9.1	5.8	7.7	7.0	6.1
United Kingdom	2.2	3.1	6.9	7.1	8.7	5.5	4.9	5.5	5.4
United States	5.5	4.9	7.1	5.6	5.6	5.5	5.1	4.6	4.6

Note: Seasonally adjusted. 1. Data for 1960 are estimated. 2. Data for Germany before 1991 refer to the former West Germany.
Source: U.S. Bureau of Labor Statistics. ftp.bls.gov/pub/special.requests/ForeignLabor/lfcompendiumt02.txt

The Economic and Social Committee

The Economic and Social Committee is composed of 344 members representing labor, farmers and consumer groups, and serves as the bridge between the EU and the general citizenry. No decisions on economic and social policy can be made without consulting the Committee. Voting strength on the Committee is weighted by population, with Germany, France, Italy, and the United Kingdom having the most votes.

▶ MAJOR REGIONAL TRADING GROUPS

Africa

Common Market for Eastern and Southern Africa (COMESA): Ben Bella Road. Box 30051, Lusaka, Zambia. www.comesa.int. **Founded:** 1994. **Purpose:** To create an environment for foreign and domestic investment by developing rational production and marketing structures. Help to maintain peace and stability among member states. **Members:** (19) Burundi, Comoros, D.R. Congo, Djibouti, Egypt, Eritrea, Ethiopia, Kenya, Libya, Madagascar, Malawi, Mauritius, Rwanda, Seychelles, Sudan, Swaziland, Uganda, Zambia, Zimbabwe.

Economic Community of West African States (ECOWAS): 60 Yakubu Gowon Crescent, Asokoro District, P.M.B. 401, Abuja, Nigeria. www.ecowas.int. **Founded:** 1975. **Purpose:** to promote economic activity, particularly industry, transport, telecommunications, energy, agriculture, natural resources, commerce, monetary and financial matters, and social and cultural issues. **Members:** (15) Benin, Burkina Faso, Cape Verde, Gambia, Ghana, Guinea, Guinea-Bissau, Ivory Coast, Liberia, Mali, Niger, Nigeria, Senegal, Sierra Leone, Togo.

Southern African Development Community (SADC): Private Bag 0095, Gaborone, Botswana. www.sadc.int. **Founded:** 1992. **Purpose:** To promote regional economic development and integration. **Members:** (14) Angola, Botswana, Democratic Republic of Congo, Lesotho, Madagascar, Malawi, Mauritius, Mozambique, Namibia, South Africa, Swaziland, Tanzania, Zambia, Zimbabwe.

Asia

Asia Pacific Economic Cooperation (APEC): 35 Heng Mui Terrace, Singapore 119616, Singapore. www.apec.org. **Founded:** 1989. **Purpose:** alliance of nations seeking to promote trade and investment in the Pacific Basin. **Members:** (21) Australia, Brunei, Canada, Chile, China, Hong Kong, Indonesia, Japan, Malaysia, Mexico, New Zealand, Papua New Guinea, Peru, Philippines, Russia, Singapore, South Korea, Taiwan, Thailand, United States, Vietnam.

Association of South East Asian Nations (ASEAN): P.O. Box 2072, 70 A Jalan Sisingamangaraja, Jakarta 12110, Indonesia. www.aseansec.org. **Founded:** 1967. **Purpose:** to promote political and economic cooperation among states in region by coordinating policies in trade, transportation, communications, agriculture, science, finance and culture. **Members:** (10) Brunei, Cambodia, Indonesia, Laos, Malaysia, Myanmar, Philippines, Singapore, Thailand, Vietnam.

World's 50 Largest Banking Companies by Assets, 2006

Rank, Company, City	Assets (millions)	Rank, Company, City	Assets (millions)
1. UBS AG, Zurich	$1,961,327	24. Dexia, Brussells	$747,045
2. Barclays PLC, London	1,949,167	25. Rabobank, Utrecht, Netherlands	732,757
3. BNP Paribas, Paris	1,898,186	26. Groupe Caisse d'Epargne, Paris	710,801
4. Citigroup Inc., New York	1,884,318	27. Wachovia Corp., Charlotte, N.C.	707,121
5. HSBC Holdings, PLC London	1,857,520	28. China Construction	697,445
6. Royal Bank of Scotland Group PLC, Edinburgh	1,705,044	Bank Corp., Beijing	
		29. Agricultural Bank of China, Beijing	684,349
7. Credit Agricole SA, Paris	1,662,600	30. Bank of China Ltd., Beijing	679,572
8. Mitsubishi UFJ Financial Group, Tokyo	1,585,767	31. Lloyds TSB Group PLC, London	672,404
		32. HVB Group, Munich	666,923
9. Deutsche Bank AG, Frankfurt	1,480,984	33. Dresdner Bank, Frankfurt	654,928
10. Bank of America Corp., Charlotte, N.C.	1,459,737	34. Credit Mutuel, Paris	635,685
		35. Natixis, Paris	604,366
11. JPMorgan Chase & Co., New York	1,351,520	36. Norinchukin Bank, Tokyo	602,645
12. ABN Amro Holding NV, Amsterdam	1,297,604	37. BBV Argentaria SA Bilbao, Spain	536,972
13. Mizuho Financial Group Inc., Tokyo	1,269,600	38. MetLife, New York	527,715
14. Societe Generale, Paris	1,261,478	39. Danske Bank A/S, Copenhagen	484,515
15. ING Bank, Amsterdam	1,178,697	40. Wells Fargo & Co., San Francisco	481,996
16. HBOS PLC, Edinburgh	1,156,614	41. Royal Bank of Canada, Toronto	477,432
17. Banco Santander Central Hispano SA, Madrid	1,088,015	42. Nordea Bank AB, Stockholm	457,134
		43. KBC Groupe SA, Brussells	428,485
18. Unicredito Italiano Spa, Milan	1,077,209	44. Groupe Banques Populaires, Paris	402,090
19. Credit Suisse Group, Zurich	1,025,111	45. Intesa Sanpaolo, Milan	383,085
20. Fortis NV, Brussells	1,020,098	46. SanPaolo IMI Turin, Italy	380,022
21. Industrial and Commercial Bank of China (ICBC), Beijing	962,969	47. WestLB, Dusseldorf, Germany	376,656
		48. National Australia Bank Ltd., Melbourne	360,563
22. Sumitomo Mitsui Financial Group, Tokyo	901,711		
		49. Toronto-Dominion Bank, Toronto	349,714
23. Commerzbank AG, Frankfurt	795,900	50. Washington Mutual Inc., Seattle	346,288

Note: The financial upheaval of 2008 resulted in the merger or dissolution of many of these banks. **Source:** *American Banker*, October 4, 2007.

The Americas
Caribbean Community and Common Market (CARICOM) HQ: Bank of Guyana Building, P.O. Box 10827, 1 Avenue of the Republic, Georgetown, Guyana. www.caricom.org **Founded:** 1973. **Purpose:** to create greater unity in Caribbean, and to formulate policies and cooperation in services such as education, health, labor matters and foreign policy. **Members:** (15) Antigua and Barbuda, Bahamas, Barbados, Belize, Dominica, Grenada, Guyana, Haiti, Jamaica, Montserrat, Saint Kitts and Nevis, Saint Lucia, Saint Vincent and the Grenadines, Suriname, Trinidad and Tobago.

Central American Common Market (CACM) HQ: c/o SIECA, Apart Postal 1237, 4a Avenida 10-25, Zona 14, Guatemala 01901, Guatemala. www.sice.oas.org **Founded:** 1961. **Purpose:** to promote the establishment of a Central American Common Market and to liberalize trade with other nations including the U.S. **Members:** (5) Costa Rica, El Salvador, Guatemala, Honduras, Nicaragua.

Mercado Comun del Cono Sur (MERCOSUR) HQ: Dr.   Luis   Peria   1992,   piso   1,

The *Fortune* 100 World's Largest Industrial Corporations, 2007

2007 Rank, Company, Country (2006 Rank)	Sales (millions)	2007 Rank, Company, Country (2006 Rank)	Sales (millions)
1. Wal-Mart Stores, U.S (1)	$378,799	51. Tesco, U.K (55)	$94,703
2. Exxon Mobil, U.S (2)	372,824	52. E.ON, Germany (53)	94,356
3. Royal Dutch/Shell Group, Netherlands (3)	355,782	53. Verizon Communications, U.S (39)	93,775
		54. Nippon Telegraph & Telephone, Japan (40)	93,527
4. B.P., U.K. (4)	291,438	55. Deutsche Post, Germany (57)	90,472
5. Toyota Motor, Japan (6)	230,201	56. Metro, Germany (62)	90,267
6. Chevron, U.S (7)	210,783	57. Nestlé, Switzerland (56)	89,630
7. I.N.G. Group, Netherlands (13)	201,516	58. Santander Central Hispano Group, Spain (75)	89,295
8. Total, France (10)	187,280		
9. General Motors, U.S (5)	182,347	59. Statoil, Norway (78)	89,224
10. ConocoPhillips, U.S (9)	178,558	60. Cardinal Health, U.S (51)	88,364
11. Daimler, Germany (8)	177,167	61. Goldman Sachs Group, U.S. (72)	87,968
12. General Electric, U.S (11)	176,656	62. Morgan Stanley, U.S. (61)	87,879
13. Ford Motor Company, U.S (12)	172,468	63. Petrobrás, Brazil (62)	87,735
14. Fortis, U.S (20)	164,877	64. Deutsche Telekom, Germany (60)	85,570
15. AXA, France (15)	162,762	65. Home Depot, U.S (44)	84,740
16. Sinopec, China (17)	159,260	66. Peugeot, France (68)	82,965
17. Citigroup, U.S (14)	159,229	67. LG, South Korea (73)	82,096
18. Volkswagen, Germany (16)	149,054	68. Électricité De France, France (63)	81,629
19. Dexia Group, Belgium (36)	147,648	69. Aviva, U.K (50)	81,317
20. H.S.B.C. Holdings, U.K (22)	146,500	70. Barclays, U.K. (83)	80,347
21. B.N.P. Paribas, France (25)	140,726	71. Fiat, Italy (84)	80,112
22. Allianz, Germany (19)	140,618	72. Matsushita Electric, Japan (59)	79,412
23. Crédit Agricole, France (18)	138,155	73. B.A.S.F., Germany (81)	79,322
24. State Grid, China (29)	132,885	74. Credit Suisse, Switzerland (47)	78,206
25. China National Petroleum, China (24)	129,798	75. Sony, Japan (69)	77,682
26. Deutsche Bank, Germany (35)	122,644	76. Telefonica, Spain (77)	77,254
27. ENI, Italy [1] (26)	120,565	77. UniCredit Group, Italy (97)	77,030
28. Bank of America, U.S (21)	119,190	78. B.M.W., Germany (88)	76,675
29. AT&T, U.S. (86)	118,928	79. Procter & Gamble, U.S (74)	76,476
30. Berkshire Hathaway, U.S (33)	118,245	80. CVS Caremark, U.S. (142)	76,330
31. UBS, Switzerland (27)	117,206	81. UnitedHealth Group, U.S. (66)	75,431
32. J.P. Morgan Chase, U.S (31)	116,353	82. Hyundai Motor, South Korea (76)	74,900
33. Carrefour, France (32)	115,585	83. U.S. Postal Service, U.S.[1] (64)	74,778
34. Assicurazioni Generali, Italy (30)	113,813	84. France Télécom, France (82)	72,488
35. American Intl. Group, U.S (23)	110,064	85. Vodafone, U.K (95)	71,202
36. Royal Bank of Scotland, U.K (54)	108,392	86. SK Holdings, Japan (98)	70,717
37. Siemens, Germany (28)	106,444	87. Kroger, U.S (80)	70,235
38. Samsung Electronics, S. Korea (46)	106,006	88. Nokia, Finland (119)	69,886
39. ArcelorMittal, Luxembourg (99)	105,216	89. ThyssenKrupp, Germany (101)	68,799
40. Honda Motor, Japan (37)	105,102	90. Lukoil, Russia (110)	67,205
41. Hewlett-Packard, U.S (41)	104,286	91. Toshiba, Japan (91)	67,145
42. Pemex, Mexico (34)	103,960	92. Repsol YPF, Spain (90)	67,006
43. Société Générale, France (49)	103,443	93. Boeing, U.S (87)	66,387
44. McKesson, U.S (38)	101,703	94. Prudential, U.S (79)	66,358
45. H.B.O.S., U.K. (58)	100,267	95. Petronas, Malaysia (121)	66,218
46. I.B.M., U.S (42)	98,786	96. AmerisourceBergen, U.S (89)	66,074
47. Gazprom, Russia (52)	98,642	97. Suez, France (105)	64,982
48. Hitachi, Japan (48)	98,306	98. Munich RE Group, Germany (100)	64,774
49. Valero Energy, U.S (43)	96,758	99. Costco Wholesale, U.S (94)	64,400
50. Nissan Motor, Japan (45)	94,782	100. Merrill Lynch, U.S. (70)	64,217

Note: 1. Government-owned. **Source:** *Fortune*, July 21, 2000. Reprinted by permission.

Montivideo, Uruguay 11.200. www.mercosur.int.msweb **Founded:** 1991 (established 1995). **Purpose:** free trade area and a customs union, and to negotiate free trade agreements with other Latin American countries that will eventually produce a Latin American Free Trade Area (LAFTA). **Members:** (4) Argentina, Brazil, Paraguay, Uruguay. **Associate Members:** (6) Bolivia, Chile, Colombia, Ecuador, Peru, Venezuela. **North American Free Trade Agreement (NAFTA) Founded:** 1994. **Purpose:** to remove all barriers to trade among the three nations. **Members:** (3) Canada, Mexico, U.S.

World Economic Indicators, 2007

Country	G.N.P. (millions of U.S. dollars) 2007	G.N.P. per capita (in U.S. dollars) 2007	Real growth rate 1980-91	Real growth rate 1990-2001	Average inflation rate 2006	Agriculture's share in G.D.P. 1970	Agriculture's share in G.D.P. 2004	Net private capital flows (millions) 2006[1]	Foreign direct investment as percent of G.D.P. 2006
Afghanistan	$10,137	—	—	5%					
Albania	10,456	$3,290	—	—	2%	—	24%	$264	3.13%
Algeria	122,465	3,620	-0.8%	—	4	10%	9	—	1.06
Angola	43,635	2,560	—	5	37	45	9	-256	-3.97
Antigua & Barbuda	977	11,520	3.8			—	—	112	—
Argentina	238,853	6,050	-1.5	11	4	13	10	289	2.58
Armenia	7,925	2,640	2.1	2	8	N.A.	23	255	5.27
Australia	755,795	35,960	1.2	3	2	6	—	79,383	-4.70
Austria	355,088	42,700	2.1	6	2	7	1	73,435	2.96
Azerbaijan	21,872	2,550	0.4	4	7	N.A.	12	585	13.37
Bahamas	--		1.3	12	1	—	—	—	—
Bahrain	14,022	19,350	-3.8	6	—	—	—	9,383	—
Bangladesh	75,047	470	1.9	13	3	55	21	803	1.34
Barbados			1.3	4	1	11	—	—	—
Belarus	40,897	4,220	3.3	10	18	N.A.	11	266	1.03
Belgium	432,540	40,710	2.1	8	2	4	1	44,185	8.62
Belize	1,157	3,800	2.5	3	3	—	—	138	11.41
Benin	5,120	570	-1.1	3	1	49	36	87	0.49
Bhutan	1,166	1,770	6.8	5	5	—	—	—	0.09
Bolivia	11,964	1,260	-2.0	4	4	17	15	-126	-2.96
Bosnia & Herzegovina	14,051	3,580	N.A.	2	—	N.A.	11	519	3.01
Botswana	10,991	5,840	5.8	7	7	33	2	755	2.70
Brazil	1,133,030	5,910	0.4	4	7	12	10	21,102	1.91
Brunei	10,287	26,930	—	10		—	—	—	—
Bulgaria	35,062	4,590	1.7	12	6	—	11	1,226	9.81
Burkina Faso	6,384	430	1.3	4	-0	44	30	—	0.38
Burundi	923	110	1.4	5	13	71	51	—	0.07
Cambodia	7,858	540	—	3	4	—	32	380	6.13
Cameroon	19,447	1,050	-0.9	13	—	31	44	218	0.11
Canada	1,300,025	39,420	2.1	15	2	—	—	49,657	3.07
Cape Verde	1,287	2,430	2.2	10	-2	—	6	54	5.54
Central African Rep.	1,667	380	-1.5	3	-2	35	55	—	0.44
Chad	5,760	540	3.8	—	-5	43	—	—	12.89
Chile	138,630	8,350	1.7	3	1	7	3	9,993	5.78
China	3,120,891	2,360	7.8	2	4	35	13	115,201	3.54
Colombia	149,934	3,250	1.2	2	6	25	11	7,228	8.48
Comoros	425	680	-1.0	3	—	—	41	—	0.26
Congo, Dem. Republic	8,573	140	-0.2	2	4	18	—	—	5.66
Congo Republic	5,797	1,540	-1.6	8	2	16	6	710	14.22
Costa Rica	24,831	5,560	1.0	3	12	23	8	1,920	4.30
Croatia	46,426	10,460	N.A.	7	2	N.A.	8	1,437	4.57
Cuba	—	—	N.A.	7					
Cyprus	19,617	24,940	4.9	5	2	—	—	3,894	7.26
Czech Republic[2]	149,378	14,450	0.4	19	3	—	3	13,289	4.12
Denmark	299,804	54,910	2.1	12	1	—	2	47,997	2.02
Djibouti	908	1,090	—	6	—	—	—	—	3.20
Dominica	310	4,250	4.7	8	2	—	—	25	9.19
Dominican Republic	34,611	3,550	-0.2	5	51	20	11	1,092	3.47
East Timor	1,604	1,510	—	—	—	—	31	—	—
Ecuador	41,148	3,080	-0.3	—	3	24	7	2,240	4.51
Egypt	119,405	1,580	2.0	5	11	29	15	8,871	6.02
El Salvador	19,520	2,850	-0.3	—	4	28	9	292	3.05
Equatorial Guinea	6,527	12,860	3.4	11	—	—	—	—	57.58
Eritrea	1,108	230	—	2	—	—	15	—	1.17
Estonia	17,706	13,200	2.1	3	3	N.A.	4	1,899	22.87
Ethiopia	17,565	220	-1.6	6	3	56	46	265	2.37
Fiji	3,189	3,800	0.0	1.7	3	29	—	—	-0.14

Country	G.N.P. (millions of U.S. dollars) 2007	G.N.P. per capita (in U.S. dollars) 2007	Real growth rate 1980-91	Real growth rate 1990-2001	Average inflation rate 2006	Agriculture's share in G.D.P. 1970	Agriculture's share in G.D.P. 2004	Net private capital flows (millions) 2006[1]	Foreign direct investment as percent of G.D.P. 2006
Finland	$234,833	$44,400	2.5%	2.6%	1%	—	3%	$28,912	2.06%
France[3]	2,447,090	38,500	1.8	1.5	2	—	2	401,678	3.32
Gabon	8,876	6,670	-4.2	-0.1	8	17%	8	352	3.72
Gambia	544	85	-0.1	0.1	4	33	31	51	11.26
Georgia	9,337	2,120	2.2	-5.5	8	N.A.	17	528	7.03
Germany[4]	3,197,029	38,860	2.2	1.2	0	3	1	497,423	1.15
Ghana	13,905	590	-0.3	1.9	15	47	37	106	0.99
Greece	331,658	29,630	1.2	2.0	3	18	6	54,683	0.28
Grenada	505	4,670	5.3	2.9	3	—	8	34	5.56
Guatemala	32,585	2,440	-1.8	1.4	6	—	22	207	0.66
Guinea	3,722	400	—	1.6	38	—	24	-14	3.10
Guinea-Bissau	331	200	1.3	-1.3	-4	47	62	8	3.32
Guyana	959	1,300	-4.2	1.6	8	19	31	128	9.76
Haiti	5,366	560	-2.4	-2.5	13	—	27	9	0.22
Honduras	11,339	1,600	-0.7	0.3	5	32	—	468	5.60
Hong Kong	218,910	31,610	—	2.1	0	0	—	43,061	20.20
Hungary	116,303	11,570	0.7	2.1	4	18	—	12,027	5.89
Iceland	16,826	54,100	1.3	2.1	9	—	—	16,958	15.63
India	1,069,427	950	3.3	4.0	6	47	21	11,476	0.82
Indonesia	373,125	1,650	3.9	2.3	14	45	15	8,587	1.83
Iran	246,544	3,470	-1.1	2.0	11	19	10	—	0.02
Iraq	—	—	—	—	—	17	—	—	—
Ireland	210,168	48,140	2.2	6.8	3	—	—	318,484	-14.73
Israel	157,065	21,900	1.8	2.0	2	—	—	15,766	4.52
Italy	1,991,284	33,540	2.1	1.4	2	8	2	251,355	1.11
Ivory Coast	17,543	910	-3.4	0.1	6	40	22	344	1.63
Jamaica	9,923	3,710	-0.3	-0.5	6	7	5	3,268	7.13
Japan	4,813,341	37,670	3.7	1.0	-1	6	—	337,301	0.07
Jordan	16,282	2,850	-3.3	0.9	6	10	2	1,519	12.05
Kazakhstan	78,281	5,060	0.9	-1.9	22	N.A.	8	8,502	3.46
Kenya	25,559	680	0.3	-0.6	7	33	26	72	0.11
Kiribati	120	1,170	0.5	0.6	2	—	—	—	—
Korea, South	955,802	19,690	8.8	4.7	0	26	3	27,478	0.55
Kuwait	80,221	31,640	—	-1.0	—	0	—	2,157	0.31
Kyrgyzstan	3,099	590	2.1	-3.9	9	N.A.	36	46	1.74
Laos	3,413	580	1.2	3.9	5	—	46	—	0.96
Latvia	22,595	9,930	2.8	-1.0	11	N.A.	4	1,021	4.61
Lebanon	23,651	5,770	—	3.6	6	9	6	2,910	11.72
Lesotho	2,007	1,000	0.0	2.1	4	35	17	91	6.34
Liberia	554	150	—	3.5	12	24	—	—	35.37
Libya	55,473	9,010	—	—	15	2	—	1,303	—
Lithuania	33,472	9,920	2.5	-1.6	7	N.A.	6	2,008	4.03
Luxembourg	36,420	75,880	3.8	4.2	6	4	0	575,901	301.32
Macedonia	7,052	3,460	N.A.	-0.9	3	N.A.	13	331	1.73
Madagascar	6,331	320	-2.4	-0.6	11	30	28	28	0.57
Malawi	3,506	250	0.1	1.5	19	44	39	5	0.14
Malaysia	173,705	6,540	2.9	3.9	4	29	9	-1,276	3.04
Maldives	977	3,200	6.7	2.5	0	—	—	9	1.24
Mali	6,136	500	0.1	1.6	4	61	35	104	3.00
Malta	6,216	15,310	3.8	3.8	3	7	—	3,211	—
Marshall Islands	204	3,070	—	-3.5	4	N.A.	—	—	—
Mauritania	2,636	840	-1.8	1.2	30	29	18	—	6.22
Mauritius	6,878	5,450	6.1	3.9	4	16	6	59	0.62
Mexico	878,020	8,340	-0.5	1.5	4	12	4	22,486	2.44
Micronesia	274	2,470	N.A.	-1.3	4	N.A.	—	—	—
Moldova	4,323	1,260e	1.8	-8.2	13	N.A.	21	194	6.81
Mongolia	3,362	1,290	—	0.0	23	—	20	45	9.69
Montenegro[5]	3,109	5,180	-1.4	—	3	18	18	—	5.65
Morocco	69,352	2,250	1.6	0.7	2	20	15	1,586	3.01
Mozambique	6,787	320	-3.6	4.3	6	—	21	196	1.63
Myanmar	—	—	—	5.7	—	38	—	213	—
Namibia	6,970	3,360	-1.5	2.2	9	—	9	402	—
Nepal	9,660	340	2.1	2.4	7	67	40	2	0.03
Netherlands	750,526	45,820	1.5	2.3	2	6	2	140,521	6.47
New Zealand	121,708	28,780	0.2	2.0	1	—	—	4,178	1.81
Nicaragua	5,519	980	-4.6	-0.1	11	25	19	233	4.92
Niger	3,992	280	-4.1	-0.9	1	65	—	18	0.35

Country	G.N.P. (millions of U.S. dollars) 2007	G.N.P. per capita (in U.S. dollars) 2007	G.N.P. per capita Real growth rate 1980-91	G.N.P. per capita Real growth rate 1990-2001	Average inflation rate 2006	Agriculture's share in G.D.P. 1970	Agriculture's share in G.D.P. 2004	Net private capital flows (millions) 2006[1]	Foreign direct investment as percent of G.D.P. 2006
Nigeria	$137,091	$930	-1.7%	-0.3%	8%	40%	16%	$-855	2.03%
Norway	360,036	76,450	2.2	2.9	7	6	1	55,099	1.11
Oman	27,887	11,120	4.5	0.6	—	16	1	808	0.82
Pakistan	141,009	870	3.2	1.2	9	37	22	2,872	1.97
Palau	167	8,210	—	—	3	—	—	—	—
Panama	18,423	5,510	-1.8	2.1	2	15	7	2,393	6.64
Papua New Guinea	5,400	850	-0.7	1.0	10	37	—	-1	0.68
Paraguay	10,225	1,670	-0.8	-0.6	11	32	27	57	0.87
Peru	96,241	3,450	-2.6	2.4	7	19	10	5,920	3.17
Philippines	142,623	1,620	-1.2	1.0	5	30	13	6,111	1.14
Poland	374,633	9,840	0.5	4.4	1	—	3	24,202	3.17
Portugal	201,079	18,950	2.7	2.6	3	—	3	38,039	1.75
Qatar	—	—	-10.9	—	—	—	—	—	—
Romania	132,502	6,150	-0.1	-0.1	10	—	14	7,741	6.73
Russia	1,070,999	7,560	1.3	-3.5	16	N.A.	5	12,063	1.98
Rwanda	3,072	320	-2.6	-1.3	9	62	40	8	0.37
Saint Kitts and Nevis	470	9,630	5.8	3.9	5	—	—	35	10.40
Saint Lucia	929	5,530	2.9	0.7	-2	—	—	114	13.06
Saint Vincent and the Grenadines	507	4,210	5.2	2.5	—	—	8	87	12.93
Samoa	454	2,430	5.1	2.0	5	—	13	-5	-0.90
São Tomé and Principe	138	870	-3.5	-0.6	20	37	17	3	9.92
Saudi Arabia	373,490	15,440	-4.2	-1.1	6	6	3	45,662	—
Senegal	10,170	820	0.0	1.1	3	24	16	112	0.66
Serbia[5]	34,969	4,730d	-1.4	—	16	18	18	—	5.65
Seychelles	762	8,960	2.5	0.1	2	—	2	75	11.88
Sierra Leone	1,537	260	-1.3	-6.6	14	28	—	66	4.91
Singapore	148,992	32,470	4.9	4.4	0	2	0	37,247	17.19
Slovak Republic	63,324	11,730	N.A.	1.9	3	N.A.	3	1,446	4.11
Slovenia	42,306	20,960	N.A.	3.0	2	N.A.	—	2,113	1.57
Solomon Islands	363	730	3.5	-1.4	7	—	—	—	-0.27
Somalia	—	—	—	—	—	59	—	—	—
South Africa	274,009	5,760	0.9	0.2	7	8	3	11,831	2.61
Spain	1,321,756	29,450	2.9	2.2	4	—	3	272,524	2.03
Sri Lanka	30,785	1,540	2.5	3.6	10	28	17	-257	1.16
Sudan	37,031	960	-2.4	3.2	7	43	39	2,254	8.37
Suriname	2,166	4,730	-4.5	2.6	13	7	—	25	—
Swaziland	2,951	2,580	3.1	0.1	6	33	12	5	-0.59
Sweden	421,342	46,060	1.7	1.7	2	—	1	13,237	2.99
Switzerland	452,121	59,880	1.6	0.3	1	—	—	22,192	4.20
Syria	34,993	1,760	-2.1	1.9	9	20	23	427	1.62
Tajikistan	3,103	460	-0.1	-9.9	20	N.A.	24	54	2.36
Tanzania[6]	16,287	400	-1.1	0.4	6	41	44	475	3.91
Thailand	217,348	3,400	5.9	3.0	5	26	10	13,293	2.56
Togo	2,383	360	-1.7	-0.6	-0	34	41	122	0.12
Tonga	233	2,320	1.5	2.1	7	—	28	—	2.12
Trinidad and Tobago	18,795	14,100	-5.2	2.9	8	5	0	1,813	7.66
Tunisia	32,820	3,200	1.2	3.1	3	20	12	725	2.52
Turkey	592,850	8,020	2.9	1.7	11	30	12	24,630	2.70
Turkmenistan	—	—	0.7	-6.1	—	N.A.	—	—	0.76
Uganda	10,469	340	3.3	3.6	7	54	32	245	2.95
Ukraine	118,445	2,550	2.3	-7.4	14	—	12	10,290	9.42
United Arab Emirates	—	—	-5.8	-1.6	—	—	2	—	7.22
United Kingdom	2,608,513	42,740	2.6	2.5	2	—	1	576,487	7.22
United States	13,886,472	46,040	2.1	2.1	3	3	—	-1,189,353	0.88
Uruguay	21,186	6,380	-0.4	2.1	7	13	11	978	4.23
Uzbekistan	19,721	730	0.8	-1.5	22	N.A.	31	—	0.33
Vanuatu	417	1,840	-0.2	-1.1	0	—	—	13	3.89
Venezuela	201,146	7,320	-1.5	-0.6	17	6	—	5,516	2.11
Vietnam	67,236	790	—	6.0	7	—	21	1,139	3.73
Yemen	19,421	870	—	2.4	13	52	13	-251	-1.76
Zambia	9,479	800	-2.9	-1.7	12	11	20	—	3.56
Zimbabwe	4,466	340	0.2	-0.2	—	15	17	—	3.05

Note: The World Bank reports data on Gross National Income (GNI) rather than Gross National Product (GNP). Some figures are for years other than those specified. **1.** Data are shown for low and middle income countries only. **2.** Data for years before 1990 refer to Czechoslovakia. **3.** Data includes French Guiana, Guadeloupe, Martinique, and Réunion. **4.** Data for years before 1990 refer to West Germany. **5.** Data before 2006 refer to the former Yugoslavia. **6.** Data refers to mainland Tanzania only.
Source: The World Bank, *The World Bank Atlas* (2008).

Nations of the World

The following section presents major facts about all the nations of the world, including statistics on each nation's geography, people, government, economy, and written text describing highlights of the country's history.

The commonly used name for each country is listed first, followed by the formal name. A list of colonial and other former names is found in the following section, "Territories of the World." Geographical descriptions are listed in both miles and kilometers, and the latitude and longitude of most islands are given.

Sources of information include the annual *World Factbook* published by the Central Intelligence Agency of the United States, the United Nations, the U.S. Bureau of the Census, and the U.S. Department of State. Names of heads of government are from the United Nations official protocol office and are valid as of September 2008.

▶ AFGHANISTAN

- **GEOGRAPHY Location:** landlocked country in southwestern Asia. **Boundaries:** Turkmenistan to NW, Tajikistan to N, China to NE, Pakistan to E and S, Iran to W. **Total area:** 250,000 sq. mi. (647,500 sq km). **Coastline:** none. **Comparative area:** slightly smaller than Texas. **Land use:** 12% arable land; negl. % permanent crops; 88% other. **Major cities:** Kabul (capital), Qandahar; Herat Mazar-i-Sharif; Jalalabad.
- **PEOPLE Population:** 32,738,376 (July 2008 est.). **Nationality:** noun—Afghan(s); adjective—Afghan. **Ethnic groups:** 42% Pashtun, 27% Tajik, 9% Hazara, 9% Uzbek. **Languages:** 50% Afghan Persian (Dari), 35% Pashtu, 11% Turkic langs. (primarily Uzbek and Turkmen), 4% minor langs. (30, primarily Balochi and Pashai); much bilingualism. **Religions:** 80% Sunni Muslim, 19% Shi'a Muslim, 1% other.

GOVERNMENT Type: Islamic Republic. **Independence:** Aug. 19, 1919 (from U.K.). **Constitution:** In progress. **National holiday:** Independence Day, Aug.19. **Heads of government:** Hamid Karzai, president (since December 2004).

- **ECONOMY Monetary unit:** afghani. **Budget:** (2007 est.) *income:* 300 mil.; *expend.:* 715 mil. **G.D.P.:** $35 bil., $1,000 per capita (2007 est.). **Chief crops:** wheat, opium, fruits, nuts, karakul pelts; wool, mutton. **Natural resources:** natural gas, crude oil, coal, copper, talc. **Major industries:** small-scale production of textiles, soap, furniture, shoes, fertilizer, and cement; hand-woven carpets; natural gas, coal, and copper. **Labor force:** 80% agriculture and animal husbandry, 10% services, 10% industry (2004 est.). **Exports:** $247 mil. (2006); opium, fruits and nuts, hand-woven carpets, wool, and cotton. **Imports:** $3.8 bil. (2006); food supplies, petroleum products. **Major trading partners:** (2006) *exports:* 22.8% India, 21.7% Pakistan, 15.2% U.S., 6.5% U.K., 4.4% Finland; *imports:* 37.9% Pakistan, 12% U.S., 7.2% Germany, 5.1% India.

Mountainous and landlocked, Afghanistan has been a crossroads of trans-Asian trade and conquest since antiquity. A part of the Persian Empire, Bactria was conquered by Alexander the Great, and became independent in the third century B.C.

before falling to the Parthians in the next century. In the seventh century A.D., a flourishing Buddhist civilization there fell to Islamic conquests. Genghis Khan overthrew the 11th-century empire of Mahmud of Gazni in the early 13th century, and Afghanistan was the center of Tamerlane's empire in the late 14th century. Thereafter, the region was divided among various tribes and petty kingdoms.

Modern Afghan history began with the establishment of a united emirate by Ahmed Shah Durrani in 1747. In the 19th century, Russia and Great Britain contested domination of Afghanistan. The British Afghan Wars of 1838-42 and 1878-80 left Afghanistan unconquered but within Britain's sphere of influence. Afghanistan achieved full independence from Britain in 1919 under Amanullah Khan, who proclaimed himself king in 1926. Modern reforms were instituted by Amanullah and his successors Mohammed Nadir Shah (1929-33) and Mohammed Zahir Shah (1933-73).

The monarchy fell to a military coup in 1973, and Mohammed Daud Khan established a republic. In 1978 pro-Soviet leftists seized power, and, ostensibly at the government's invitation, Soviet troops invaded Afghanistan in Dec. 1979 to put down widespread revolts against Communist rule. In the ensuing civil war, the government's forces and their Soviet allies (with an eventual troop strength of more than 100,000) controlled the cities and main transportation routes, but guerrilla forces contested the countryside. In 1988 the Soviet Union began a withdrawal of its troops, completed by February 1989. The rebel factions failed to achieve a united front and the pro-Soviet government held on until Apr. 15, 1992, and rebel troops entered Kabul. A respected religious leader, Sibghatullah Mujaddidi, was named interim president, with the backing of a coalition but Gulbaddin Hekmatyar, leader of the fundamentalist Hizbe Islami faction, declined to join, and fighting broke out around Kabul.

On June 28 Mujaddidi turned over his power to the Leadership Council, which then elected Burhanuddin Rabbani as president. Fighting for control of Kabul continued between forces loyal to the Rabbani government and those backing Hekmatyar. Other factions later joined the fighting, and Kabul was subjected to continual rocket attacks in late 1992 and into the spring of 1993. Hekmatyar was named prime minister in an attempt to make peace. Fighting broke out again in early 1994 with Rabbani's followers getting the upper hand after fierce battles in Kabul.

By early 1995, the U.N. had brokered a scheme uniting the nine major factions in a council to which Rabbani would turn over power. But it was quickly undone by the emergence of a fundamentalist Islamic militia called the Taliban, 20,000 strong and composed of students from the Islamic schools. Taliban forces took over most of the country and established a fundamentalist regime based on Islamic law. In Oct. 1996, three remaining groups of opposition forces formed a loose Northern Alliance and kept up sporadic fighting; but by 1999 the Taliban controlled over 90 percent of Afghanistan's territory.

The Taliban began to enforce a strict Muslim code of behavior. In 2001, the U.N. reported a drop in opium poppies grown in Afghanistan (producer of 75 percent of the world's opium). A second ban, in Feb. 2001, on all statues in the country led to the destruction in March of 1,400-year-old Buddhist cliff carvings in the region of Bamiyan, despite a wave of world protest. In Sept. 2001 Afghanistan became the focus of world attention when the U.S. demanded the Taliban turn over the terrorist leaders suspected of plotting the attack on the World Trade Center.

The Anglo-American air strikes that began Oct. 7 led to the fall (Nov. 13) of Kabul to the Northern Alliance. The interim government under Hamid Karzai organized a Grand Council of about 1,600 members which elected Karzai to lead a transitional government until elections in 2004. In Aug. 2003, NATO forces took command of the international peacekeepers. In Jan. 2004 the National Assembly approved a new constitution but renewed attacks by the Taliban made elections impossible until Oct. 2004 when Karzai won over 15 other candidates. Ever-increasing violence—some of it brought on by the Taliban—continued throughout 2005-06 so that the U.S. asked NATO to take over the fight in the south against the Taliban and the druglords. By 2007 nearly 50,000 NATO troops were fighting the Taliban resurgence with modest success. (See "Major News Stories.")

▶ ALBANIA
Republic of Albania

• **GEOGRAPHY Location:** southeastern Europe. **Boundaries:** Yugoslavia to N, Macedonia to E, Greece to S, and Adriatic and Ionian Seas (parts of Mediterranean Sea) to W. **Total area:** 11,100 sq. mi. (28,750 sq km). **Coastline:** 225 mi. (362 km). **Comparative area:** slightly smaller than Maryland. **Land use:** 21% arable land; 4% permanent crops; 75% other. **Major cities:** Tiranë (Tirana; capital); Durrës (Durazzo); Elbasan; Shkodër (Scutari); Vlorë (Vlonë or Valona).

PEOPLE Population: 3,619,778 (July 2008 est.). **Nationality:** noun—Albanian(s); adjective—Albanian. **Ethnic groups:** 95% Albanian, 3% Greek, 2% Vlach, Gypsy, Serb, and Bulgarian. **Languages:** Albanian (Tosk is official dialect), Greek, Vlach, Romani, Slavic dialects. **Religions:** 70% Muslim, 20% Albanian Orthodox, 10% Roman Catholic (all churches and mosques were closed in 1967 and religious observances prohibited; in November 1990, Albania began allowing private religious practice).

GOVERNMENT Type: emerging democracy. **Independence:** Nov. 28, 1912 (from Ottoman Empire). **Constitution:** Nov. 28, 1998. **National holiday:** Independence Day, Nov. 28. **Heads of Government:** Bamir Topi, president (since July 2007); Sali Berisha, prime minister (since Aug. 2005). **Structure:** executive—president, prime minister, Council of Ministers; legislative—unicameral People's Assembly; judicial—Supreme Court.

ECONOMY Monetary unit: lek. **Budget:** (2007 est.) *income:* $2.8 bil.; *expend.:* $3.1 bil. **G.D.P.:** $11.2 bil., $5,500 per capita (2007 est.). **Chief crops:** vegetables, wheat, potatoes, fruits, sugar beets, corn. **Natural resources:** crude oil, natural gas, coal, chromium, copper. **Major industries:** food processing, textiles and clothing, lumber. **Labor force:** 1.09 mil., including 352,000 emigrant workers (2006 est.); 58% agriculture, 15% industry,

27% services. **Exports:** $425 mil. (f.o.b., 2003 est.); textiles, footwear, asphalt, metals and ores, electricity, crude oil, vegetables, fruits, tobacco. **Imports:** $3.42 bil. (f.o.b., 2007 est.); machinery, consumer goods, grains. **Major trading partners:** (2006) *exports:* 67.6% Italy, 5.8% Serbia & Montenegro, 5.4% Greece; *imports:* 31.9% Italy, 17.7% Greece, 8.1% Turkey, 5.7% Germany.

The city of Epidamnus (Durrës) was colonized by Greeks from Corinth and Corcyra in 625 B.C. Later the Roman province of Illyricum, Albania was a much-coveted area after the fall of Rome and was in turn ruled by Byzantines, Normans, Venetians, Slavs, and the kings of Naples. Under the leadership of Skanderbeg (1405-68), Albania repelled repeated Turkish invasions. But Albania was part of the Ottoman Empire from 1478 until 1912. Ottoman rule succeeded in converting most of the populace to Islam (with Catholic minorities in the north and Greek Orthodox in the south) but did not destroy the Albanian sense of national identity, based on ties of tribe, clan, and family.

Independence came in 1912 as a result of the First Balkan War, when Austria-Hungary and Italy fostered the creation of an Albanian state. Albania emerged from the war in a state of near-anarchy. With Yugoslav support, Ahmed Zogu became president of the republic in 1924 and proclaimed himself King Zog I in 1928.

In 1939 Italy invaded and annexed Albania. During World War II, partisan resistance was dominated by Communist forces under the leadership of Enver Hoxha. In 1944 Hoxha seized control of the government. A socialist republic was established in 1946: foreigners were expelled and their assets nationalized; churches were closed; agriculture and industry were collectivized. Albania under Hoxha became one of the world's most thoroughly totalitarian states.

A doctrinaire Stalinist, Hoxha broke with Khrushchev's Soviet Union in 1961 and became a client state of China. But with liberalization in China after 1977, Hoxha broke that link as well. Albania became almost totally isolated from world affairs.

Hoxha died in 1985 and was succeeded as president and first secretary of the Albanian Communist party by Ramiz Alia. In 1990, Alia eased restrictions on religion, tourism, and foreign investment, and allowed the formation of an opposition Democratic party. But he scheduled elections to the National Assembly for 1991, before awareness had spread of the old regime's faltering power. The Communists carried the rural districts and formed a coalition government with the Democrats, who carried the cities.

In 1992, the Democrats completed the rout of the Communists, winning 92 of the 140 seats in the Assembly, and replacing Alia with Sali Berisha, a heart surgeon. But by the end of the year, factions within the Democratic party were already complaining about Pres. Berisha's "autocratic rule." Meanwhile, anarchy plagued much of the country, with food riots in the cities and armed brigandage in the countryside. E.C. and U.N. grants helped pay for needed imports and Italy provided invaluable assistance to the Albanian police forces. By 1993, zones of law and order were being established, churches were reopening, and 90 percent of farming had been privatized. But in November 1994, voters rejected (54-42) a new constitution proposed by Pres. Berisha.

In 1996 Berisha's Democratic Party won a major electoral victory amidst complaints of fraud, but he and his followers were driven from office in 1997 after a series of pryamid schemes collapsed ruining the finances of tens of thousands of families. Violence and looting occured in many areas and a multi-national force of 7,000 was sent in to help restore order. The Socialists (formerly Communists) returned to power under Fatos Nano. In the spring of 1998 NATO advisors began to train Albania's tiny army as ethnic Albanians in the Kosovo province of Yugoslavia began a violent rebellion. Yugoslavia's suppression of the rebellion drove thousands of ethnic Albanians out of Kosovo into Albania. Amidst this further tumult, internal struggles continued between supporters of the Democratic Party and the Socialists, erupting into serious violence in Sept. 1998. Though Nano resigned as prime minister late in 1998, he returned in 2002 and the economy improved despite widespread corruption. In July 2005, in Albania's first free election, Berisha's Democrats won a small majority but could not take power until protests over election fraud ceased in late August.

▶ ALGERIA
People's Democratic Republic of Algeria
● **Geography** **Location:** northern coast of Africa. **Boundaries:** Mediterranean Sea to N, Tunisia and Libya to E, Mali and Niger to S, Morocco, Western Sahara, Mauritania to W. **Total area:** 919,591 sq. mi. (2,381,740 sq km). **Coastline:** 620 mi. (998 km). **Comparative area:** slightly less than 3.5 times size of Texas. **Land use:** 3% arable land; negl. % permanent crops; 97% other. **Major cities:** Algiers (capital); Oran; Constantine; Annaba; Blida.
● **People** **Population:** 33,769,669 (July 2008 est.). **Nationality:** noun—Algerian(s); adjective—Algerian. **Ethnic groups:** 99% Arab-Berber, less than 1% European. **Languages:** Arabic (official), French, Berber dialects. **Religions:** 99% Sunni Muslim (state religion), 1% Christian and Jewish.
● **Government** **Type:** republic. **Independence:** July 5, 1962 (from France). **Constitution:** Nov. 19, 1976, effective Nov. 22, 1976. **National holiday:** Revolution Day, Nov. 1. **Heads of Government:** Abdelaziz Bouteflika, head of state (since Apr. 1999), M. Ahmed Ouyahia, prime minister (since June 2008). **Structure:** executive; bicameral legislature; judicial—Supreme Court.
● **Economy** **Monetary unit:** Algerian dinar. **Budget:** (2007 est.) *income:* $58.5 bil.; *expend.:* $41.35 bil. **G.D.P.:** $268.9 bil., $8,100 per capita (2007 est.). **Chief crops:** wheat, barley, oats, grapes, olives. **Natural resources:** crude oil, natural gas, iron ore, phosphates, uranium. **Major industries:** petroleum, light industries, natural gas, mining. **Labor force:** 9.4 mil. (2007 est.); 32% government, 14% agriculture, 13.4% construction and public works, 15% trade (2003 est.). **Exports:** $63.3 bil. (f.o.b., 2007 est.); petroleum and natural gas. **Imports:** $26.08 bil. (f.o.b., 2007 est.); capital goods, food, beverages, consumer goods. **Major trading partners:** (2006) *exports:* 27% U.S., 17% Italy, 9.7% Spain, 8.8% France, 8.1% Canada, 4.3% Belgium. *imports:* 22% France, 8.6% Italy, 8.5% China, 5.9% Germany, 5.9% Spain, 4.8% U.S., 4.5% Turkey.

From around 3000 B.C. nomadic ancestors of the Berbers inhabited Algeria, as the expanding Sahara desert displaced prehistoric grasslands and forests. The Phoenicians established trading centers in the Mediterranean coastal plain around 1200 B.C. Those centers were taken over by the Romans beginning around 200 B.C. With Roman support the Berber chief Masinissa formed the kingdom of Numidia in what is now northern Algeria. From 46 B.C. to about A.D. 640, the area was controlled successively by the Romans, Germanic Vandal tribes, and the Byzantine Empire.

In the eighth century A.D., the Islamic conquests spread Arab culture to Numidia. Most of the Berbers converted to Islam. The blend of Berber and Arab culture in Algeria gave rise to a flourishing and rich Islamic civilization in the coastal plain, while Tuareg and other nomadic peoples controlled the sparsely inhabited interior.

Around 1500 the Christian kingdom of Spain captured Algiers and other coastal cities. In 1518 Barbarossa, a Turkish sea captain, captured Algiers and drove the Spanish out. In so doing, he joined Algeria to the expanding Turkish Ottoman Empire. Piracy became a key source of income for the Ottoman cities of Algeria. In the early 1800's, France, along with England and the U.S., began military operations to suppress piracy in the Mediterranean. In 1830 France invaded Algeria, putting an end to Ottoman rule and establishing their own administration. Algeria was ruled as part of France itself. Many French settlers (colons) migrated to Algeria. Both they and the native Algerians were considered citizens of France, but the colons were granted substantial political and economic advantages over the indigenous population.

In 1847 a rebellion led by Abd-al-Qadir, a powerful Muslim leader, was suppressed by the French. In 1848, all of Algeria was conquered by the French and legally confirmed as part of France. During World War II, many Algerians joined the Free French, hoping that their display of loyalty would be rewarded with greater self-rule after the war. Those hopes were disappointed, as French administration was resumed in 1945.

In 1954 the Front de Liberation Nationale (FLN) began a guerrilla war against the French in Algeria. They were opposed by French police and military forces and by the Secret Army Organization (OAS), an underground movement of colons who favored continued French rule. In 1958, French president Charles de Gaulle established a policy designed to prepare Algeria for self-rule.

Algerian independence was proclaimed on July 3, 1962; a million colons fled to France. A power struggle within the new Algerian government was resolved when Ahmed Ben Bella became the country's first premier in 1963. In 1965 Ben Bella was deposed by Col. Houari Boumidienne, who ruled as the head of a military government. In 1967 Algeria declared war on Israel, broke with the West, and established close relations with the U.S.S.R. Since the early 1970's, relations with the West, and particularly with France, have improved (mainly because of oil).

The first free, multiparty elections were held on June 12, 1990. The Islamic Salvation Front, which advocates turning Algeria into an Islamic Republic, won overwhelming control of local assemblies. In 1991 it won 188 seats in Parliament out of 231 up for election and seemed poised to win control of the government when the army interceded to keep the old power structure in place. On June 19, 1992, Pres. Mohammed Boudiaf was assassinated, presumably by Islamic fundamentalists. The military's High Security Council, knowing the Islamic parties would win any free election, postponed a return to democracy. In January 1994 the High Security Council replaced the collective presidency of the High State Council with Gen.

Liamine Zeroual. November 1995 saw the first contested presidential election since 1962, with Gen. Zeroual winning over 60 percent of the vote as major opposition groups boycotted the election. Elections in June 1997 produced Algeria's first mutli-party parliament since 1962, but the ruling military council still remained in control and in August Islamic fundamentalists killed over 300 in one night of terror. These vicious assasinations continued into 1998 with hundreds more having their throats cut over several nights. Civil strife and assassinations claimed the lives of over 40,000. In Sept. 1998 Gen. Zeroual announced that elections would be held in Feb. 1999 and he would not be a candidate.

By the time the elections were held in April, all candidates had withdrawn from the race save one, the army-backed Abdelaziz Bouteflika. His new government reached an accord with the rebel Islamic Salvation Front: in return for the end of the uprising, Pres. Bouteflika pledged to release thousands of militant Islamic prisoners on July 5, Algeria's national holiday, and to submit the peace agreement to a referendum. In Sept., 98 percent of voters favored the agreement that gave amnesty to militants who surrendered. When the amnesty period ended (Jan. 2000), the government claimed that 80 percent of the rebels had surrendered—probably an exaggeration—then commenced a major army offensive against remaining rebels, now organized as the "Armed Islamic Group" (GIA). While the GIA remained unconquered into 2002, the government was mending fences with the Berber people (who constitute about 1/3 of Algeria's population), recognizing their Tamazight language as a legal language. The FLN won 199 seats in the 389-seat National Assembly and in April 2004, Pres. Bouteflika became Algeria's first democratically re-elected president, winning a suspiciously large (84 percent) share of the vote.

Two powerful terrorist attacks in April, 2007, were attributed to a wing of Al Qaeda that wishes to establish an Islamic theocracy, and which has threatened to attack inside France as well. In Aug. 2008, two days of bombing killed 60 people.

▶ ANDORRA
Principality of Andorra
• **Geography Location:** Pyrenees Mountains, southwestern Europe. **Boundaries:** France to N and E, Spain to S and W. **Total area:** 174 sq. mi. (450 sq km). **Coastline:** none. **Comparative area:** 2.5 times size of Washington, D.C. **Land use:** 2% arable land; 0% permanent crops; 98% other. **Major cities:** Andorra la Vella (capital).
• **People Population:** 72,413 (July 2008 est.). **Nationality:** noun—Andorran(s); adjective—Andorran. **Ethnic groups:** 43% Spanish, 33% Andorran, 11% Portuguese, 7% French, 6% other. **Languages:** Catalan (official); many also speak some French and Castilian. **Religions:** virtually all Roman Catholic.
• **Government Type:** parliamentary democracy (since March 1993) that retains as head of state a co-principality; the two princes are the president of France and Spanish bishop of Seo de Urgel, who are represented locally by officials called veguers. **Independence:** 1278. **Constitution:** March 1993. **National holiday:** Mare de Deu de Meritxell, Sept. 8. **Heads of Government:** French co-prince Nicolas Sarkozy, president of France (since 2007) and Spanish co-prince Episcopal

Msgr. Joan Enric Vives Sicília (since May 2003); Albert Pintat, prime minister (since May 2005). **Structure:** executive—co-princes, executive council; unicameral legislature; judiciary—Supreme Court at Perpignan, France.
• **Economy Monetary unit:** euro. **Budget:** (2005) *income:* $333.5 mil.; *expend.:* $386.6 mil. **G.D.P.:** $2.77 bil., $38,800 per capita (2005 est.). **Chief crops:** sheep raising; small quantities of tobacco, rye, wheat, barley, oats, and vegetables. **Natural resources:** hydropower, mineral water, timber, iron ore, lead. **Major industries:** tourism (particularly skiing), cattle raising, timber, tobacco, banking. **Labor force:** 42,420. (2005 est.). **Exports:** $148.7 mil. (f.o.b., 2005); tobacco products, furniture. **Imports:** $1.879 bil. (2005). **Major trading partners:** (2006) *exports:* 17% France, 59.5% Spain; *imports:* 21.1% France, 53.2% Spain.

Set high in the Pyrenees, the tiny state of Andorra has been both a medieval relic and a modern capitalist land. Since 1278 Andorra has owed feudal allegiance to two co-rulers, the bishop of Seo de Urgel in Spain and, now, the president of France. Until 1993, Andorra had no constitution, so the exact rights of the corulers remained vague. Foreign affairs were handled by France.

Andorra's traditional economic mainstay had been the "transshipment of goods" (i.e., smuggling) between France and Spain. Andorra attracts tourists drawn by bargain shopping, and it is a banking center. Spain's 1986 entry into the E.U. led Andorra to seek a customs union with the E.U. The March 1990 treaty was Andorra's first in over 700 years. In the same year, the co-princes introduced Andorra's first penal code and a sales tax, soon followed by the adoption of the E.U.'s external tariff. In March 1993 voters—of whom there are only 9,123—adopted a modern constitution that will reduce the power of the co-princes and establish a government of three branches that will have authority to tax and to make foreign policy. In 1997 Premier Molne's party won a majority of seats in the General Council ending the coalition government.

▶ ANGOLA
Republic of Angola
• **Geography Location:** southwestern Africa. **Boundaries:** Zaire to N and NE, Zambia to E, Namibia to S, South Atlantic Ocean to W; Cabinda district separated from rest of country by Congo to N, Zaire to S. **Total area:** 481,352 sq. mi. (1,246,700 sq km). **Coastline:** 994 mi. (1,600 km). **Comparative area:** slightly less than twice size of Texas. **Land use:** 2% arable land; negl. % permanent crops; 97% other. **Major cities:** Luanda (capital); Huambo (Nova Lisboa); Lobito; Benguela; Lubango (São da Bandeira).
• **People Population:** 12,531,357 (July 2008 est.). **Nationality:** noun—Angolan(s); adjective—Angolan. **Ethnic groups:** 37% Ovimbundu, 25% Kimbundu, 13% Bakongo, 2% Mestiço, 1% European, 22% other. **Languages:** Portuguese (official), Bantu and other African languages. **Religions:** 47% indigenous beliefs, 38% Roman Catholic, 15% Protestant.
• **Government Type:** republic, multiparty presidential regime. **Independence:** Nov. 11, 1975 (from Portugal). **Constitution:** Nov. 11, 1975 (last revised Aug. 26, 1992). **National holiday:** Independence Day, Nov. 11. **Heads of Government:** José Eduardo dos Santos, president

(since Sept. 1979). **Structure:** executive; unicameral legislature; judiciary.
• **ECONOMY Monetary unit:** kwanza. **Budget:** (2007 est.) *income:* $18.58 bil.; *expend.:* $15.7 bil. **G.D.P.:** $80.95 bil., $6,500 per capita (2007 est.). **Chief crops:** bananas, sugarcane, coffee, sisal, corn, cotton, manioc (tapioca), vegetables. **Natural resources:** petroleum, diamonds, iron ore, phosphates, copper. **Major industries:** petroleum, mining (diamonds, iron ore, phosphates), food processing. **Labor force:** 6.6 mil. (2007 est.); 85% agriculture, 15% industry. **Exports:** $43.23 bil. (f.o.b., 2007 est.); oil, diamonds, petroleum products, gas, coffee. **Imports:** $11.41 bil. (f.o.b., 2007 est.); machinery, electrical equipment, vehicles and spare parts, medicines, food, textiles; substantial military deliveries. **Major trading partners:** (2006) *exports:* 38% U.S., 34% China, 6% Taiwan; *imports:* 15% U.S., 15% Portugal, 10% South Korea, 9% China, 7% South Africa.

Bantu peoples have occupied Angola for 2,000 years. Portuguese explorers searching for a sea route to India founded Luanda (1575) and Benguela (1617). Portugal, in alliance with the Angolan kingdom of Bakongo, engaged in an extensive trade of slaves to Brazil—3 million in 300 years.

In the late 19th century, Angola was organized as a Portuguese colony, sometimes called Portuguese West Africa. Portuguese settlers dominated local government, and trade, organized plantation-style cultivation of cotton, palm oil, bananas, and coffee. A railroad was built to transport exports of metal from the Katanga region of the Belgian Congo (now Zaire) to the coast.

By the 1950's non-Portuguese Angolans began to agitate for independence. The National Front spearheaded the liberation movement. Guerrilla warfare began in 1961, with several feuding factions fighting the Portuguese. Following the Portuguese revolution of 1974, factional warfare intensified and most Portuguese settlers fled the country. Independence came on Nov. 11, 1975.

Civil war between the National Front, the Popular Movement for the Liberation of Angola (MPLA), and the National Union for the Total Independence of Angola (UNITA) led, in 1976, to the victory of the MPLA, which organized a Marxist state with Soviet backing and Cuban technical support including 37,000 soldiers. Large portions of the country remained in the hands of UNITA, which continued the civil war with Chinese and American support through the 1980's.

Direct clashes between Angolan and South African troops occurred during the 1980's, as Angola gave shelter to SWAPO guerrilla forces seeking independence for Namibia. Cuban troops withdrew from Angola in 1991, and a cease-fire between the government and UNITA was also concluded. While agreeing to recognize the dos Santos government, UNITA called for elections to be held by Sept. 1992, Angola's first since 1975.

In the elections, MPLA's candidate, José Eduardo dos Santos, decisively defeated UNITA's leader, Jonas Savimbi, but Savimbi's refusal to honor the results led to renewed fighting. The presence of thousands of U.N. peacekeepers from Feb. 1994 until Feb. 1999 made little dent in the continuing struggle which claimed perhaps 100,000 lives. The government succeeded, in 2000, in taking two diamond-mining provinces as well as the town of Cazombo from UNITA, capping the year with an offer of amnesty. But it was not until after Savimbi's death in a gun battle in Feb. 2002 that UNITA could be brought to sign a cease-fire in April. After 27 years of civil war, with one million or more killed and four million displaced, peace finally took hold. Pres. dos Santos pledged elections but they were delayed until Sept. 2008 when the governing party, MPLA, won a landslide victory in a peaceful way. Angola has joined Nigeria as Africa's leading oil producer.

▶ ANTIGUA AND BARBUDA

• **GEOGRAPHY Location:** eastern Caribbean Sea approximately 300 mi. (480 km) SE of Puerto Rico. Antigua 17°06'N, 61°50'W; Barbuda 17°38'N, 61°48'W. **Boundaries:** Atlantic Ocean to N and E, Caribbean Sea to S and W. **Total area:** 170 sq. mi. (440 sq km). **Coastline:** 95 mi. (153 km). **Comparative area:** 2.5 times size of Washington, D.C. **Land use:** 18% arable land; 0% permanent crops; 82% other. **Major cities:** St. John's (capital).
• **PEOPLE Population:** 69,842 (July 2008 est.). **Nationality:** noun—Antiguan(s), Barbudan(s); adjective—Antiguan, Barbudan. **Ethnic groups:** almost entirely of black African origin; some of British, Portuguese, Lebanese, and Syrian origin. **Languages:** English (official), local dialects. **Religions:** Anglican (predominant), other Protestant sects, some Roman Catholic.
• **GOVERNMENT Type:** constitutional monarchy with U.K.-style parliament. **Independence:** Nov. 1, 1981 (from U.K.). **Constitution:** Nov. 1, 1981. **National holiday:** Independence Day, Nov. 1. **Heads of Government:** Dr. James B. Carlisle, governor-general (since June 1993); Winston Baldwin Spencer, prime minister (since Mar. 2004). **Structure:** executive—governor general, prime minister, and cabinet; bicameral legislature; judiciary—East Caribbean Supreme Court.
• **ECONOMY Monetary unit:** East Caribbean dollar. **Budget:** (2000 est.) *income:* $123.7 mil.; *expend.:* $145.9 mil. **G.D.P.:** $1.189 bil., $10,900 per capita (2007 est.). **Chief crops:** cotton, fruits and vegetables, sugar. **Natural resources:** negl.; pleasant climate fosters tourism. **Major industries:** tourism, construction, light manufacturing (clothing, alcohol, household appliances). **Labor force:** 30,000 (1991); 93% industry and services, 7% agriculture; 11% unemployment (2001 est.). **Exports:** $84.3 mil. (2007); petroleum products, manufactures, machinery and transportation equipment, food and live animals. **Imports:** $522.8 mil. (2007); food and live animals, machinery and transport equipment, manufactures, chemicals, oil. **Major trading partners:** (2006) *exports:* 34% Spain, 21% Germany, 8% Italy, 6% Singapore; *imports:* 21% U.S., 16% China, 13% Germany, 13% Singapore, 6% Spain.

Columbus visited and claimed Antigua for Spain in 1493. It was settled by the British in 1632, who grew tobacco, and later sugar. The island's economy was hobbled by abolition of slavery in 1834, a succession of natural disasters in the 1840's, and the closing of the Royal Dockyard in 1854. Today, tourism is a mainstay of the economy, fostered by the ruling Antigua Labor Party, which won its sixth consecutive parliamentary victory in March 1999. But its second economic mainstay, offshore banking, has been shaken by a U.S. Treasury warning in April 1999 that lax standards make it susceptible to money-laundering. In March 2004 the 10-year government of Lester Bird fell to the United Progressive Party.

▶ARGENTINA
Argentine Republic
• **GEOGRAPHY** **Location:** southern South America. **Boundaries:** Bolivia, Paraguay, Brazil to N.; Uruguay, South Atlantic Ocean to E.; Chile to W. **Total area:** 1,068,298 sq. mi. (2,766,890 sq km) (figures exclude Falkland Islands and Antarctic territory claimed by Argentina). **Coastline:** 3,099 mi. (4,989 km). **Comparative area:** slightly less than three-tenths the size of the United States. **Land use:** 9% arable land; 1% permanent crops; 90% other. **Major cities:** Buenos Aires (capital); Córdoba; La Matanza; Rosario; Morón.
• **PEOPLE** **Population:** 40,677,348 (July 2008 est.). **Nationality:** noun—Argentine(s); adjective—Argentine. **Ethnic groups:** 97% white, 3% mestizo, Indian, and other nonwhite groups. **Languages:** Spanish (official), English, Italian, German, French. **Religions:** 92% Roman Catholic (less than 20% practicing), 2% Protestant, 2% Jewish, 4% other.
• **GOVERNMENT** **Type:** republic. **Independence:** July 9, 1816 (from Spain). **Constitution:** May 1, 1853 (revised Aug. 1994). **National holiday:** Revolution Day, May 25. **Head of Government:** Cristina Fernandez De Kirchner, president (since Dec. 2007). **Structure:** executive; bicameral legislature; judiciary.
• **ECONOMY** **Monetary unit:** argentine peso. **Budget:** (2007 est.) *income:* $48.99 bil.; *expend.:* $46.87 bil. **G.D.P.:** $523.7 bil., $13,000 per capita (2007 est.). **Chief crops:** wheat, corn, soybeans. **Natural resources:** fertile plains of the pampas, lead, zinc, tin, copper, iron ore, petroleum. **Major industries:** food processing (especially meat packing), motor vehicles, consumer durables. **Labor force:** 16.1 mil. note - urban areas only (2007 est.); 76% services, 23% industry, 1% agriculture; 8.9% unemployment (2007 est.). **Exports:** $54.6 bil. (f.o.b., 2007 est.); edible oils, cereals, feed, motor vehicles. **Imports:** $40.26 bil. (f.o.b., 2007 est.); motor vehicles and parts, chemicals, plastics. **Major trading partners:** (2006) *exports:* 17.5% Brazil, 8.9% U.S., 9.5% Chile, 7.5% China; *imports:* 34.8% Brazil, 12.6% U.S., 4.5% Germany.

The indigenous nomads of the area around the river La Plata resisted Spanish intrusion, which began with the first founding of Buenos Aires by Pedro de Mendoza in 1536. Argentina was part of Spain's Viceroyalty of Peru until reforms in the Bourbon dynasty and a need to defend against Portuguese encroachment from Brazil led to the formation of the Viceroyalty of La Plata, including Argentina, Bolivia, Paraguay, and Uruguay, in 1776. Following the relaxation of trade restrictions two years later, Buenos Aires grew from a small town to a city of 50,000 by 1800. A provisional junta of the Provinces of Río de la Plata was established in 1810 after the Napoleonic occupation of Spain, and in 1816 the United Provinces of the Río de la Plata declared their independence.

After independence the question of political relations among the United Provinces was settled by a federalist solution in which the provinces dissolved into a number of practically independent republics. In 1824, a constituent assembly created the office of president, first held by Bernardino Rivadavia. However, the failure to ratify a workable constitution caused Rivadavia to resign.

Juan Manuel de Rosas became governor of Buenos Aires in 1829 and presided over the construction of a federal agreement between the provinces in 1831. Rosas governed Buenos Aires with an iron hand until his expulsion in 1852. The other provinces formed the Argentine Federation, based on a federal constitution of 1853, but Buenos Aires refused to join. Buenos Aires and the Argentine Federation entered into war (1859-1861) but reached an agreement on the inclusion of Buenos Aires in the Argentine Republic in 1862.

Argentina joined Brazil and Uruguay in a war (1865-70) against Paraguay. During the latter part of the 1870's, the government took the initiative against the indigenous populations of Patagonia and Tierra del Fuego, which were partitioned with Chile. Immigration from Europe, especially Spain and Italy, resulted in enormous growth. In 1869, there were 2 million inhabitants; by 1914, 8 million; by 1955, 19 million; and by 1990, 32 million.

The Argentine military, led by Lt. Gen. José F. Uriburu, ousted the civilian government of the Radical party in 1930 with the intention of following the European model of politics. In 1946 Juan Domingo Perón won the presidential election and constructed a populist political alliance that included workers, industrialists, and the armed forces. The Perón-inspired populist ideology of *justicialismo* included extension of the franchise to women and redistribution of income to workers and the poor. Perón's charismatic wife, Eva, led the effort to distribute goods to the poor through the Social Aid Foundation.

Tied in with Perón's populist strategy was his policy of nationalist economic development, whereby state-led development was financed by capital from the old export-agricultural elite and politically supported through populism. The Perón government incurred great expense to gain control over foreign-owned economic infrastructure, including railway systems, telephone companies, and dock facilities. A number of events led to Perón's downfall in 1955. The market for Argentine goods deteriorated and as Perón shifted his strategy to encourage foreign investment and impose economic austerity, repression against the political opposition grew. The death of Eva Perón in 1952 robbed Perón of an important political resource, and when the government challenged the Catholic church on a number of issues, the military ousted Perón.

After a brief period of military rule, Arturo Frondizi of the "Intransigent" faction of the Radical party won the presidency in 1958. The military repeatedly attempted to keep the Perónistas from returning to power. In 1962 the military forced Frondizi to annul Perónist victories in provincial elections and removed him from office. Pres. Arturo Illia was ousted from office in 1966.

A military regime led by a series of Argentine officers was established during 1966-73. Extreme violence by factions on the Left and Right led the military to accept Perón's return in 1973. Perón died in 1974, and his third wife, Isabel, replaced him but the military removed her in 1976 in the midst of economic and political upheaval.

Determined to deal with what they saw as a leftist threat, the armed forces launched what was later called the "dirty war," during which up to 20,000 people disappeared and were never heard from again. The authoritarian government collapsed after the 1982 Falkland/Malvinas Islands War against Britain led to the resignation of the junta and the holding of elections. Raúl Alfonsín, of the Radical Union party, was elected president in 1983. In 1989, he was succeeded by Carlos Saúl Menem, who agreed to take office early, in the midst of an economic crisis during which inflation reached 3,000 percent and foreign debt $58 billion.

Menem encouraged free enterprise and good relations with the U.S. Government controls on foreign investment and trade were relaxed, and the government sold off many state enterprises. In 1993 Argentina's 11-year debt crisis officially ended, and by 1995 inflation was down to 4 percent. As Argentina's economy began to flourish, Menem was reelected, and his party won majorities in both houses of the legislature and control of half of Argentina's provincial governments.

But in May 1997, violent protests erupted in several major cities, as unemployment rose to nearly 20 percent. The Peronistas lost control of the Chamber of Deputies, for the first time since 1983, to a left-wing coalition known as The Alliance. Presidential elections in 1999 brought the first-ever Peronista defeat, as Alliance's Fernando de la Rúa defeated Eduardo Duhalde.

Throughout 2000, the rather fragile Alliance managed to move gingerly to fight corruption, to reform certain privileges of organized labor, and to balance the federal and state budgets. This was sufficient to gain a pledge from the I.M.F. and other international lenders for a $40 billion bailout, but by the middle of 2001 the recession had grown worse and the government put a severe austerity plan in place. Strikes and rioting at last drove de la Rua to resign in December, and his successor resigned after only a week. A second interim president, but with a two-year term, was chosen by Parliament: Senator Duhalde. His decoupling of the peso from the dollar and its subsequent devaluation brought some relief but no solution.Only a January 2003 roll-over by the I.M.F. prevented a third major default.

In the 2003 presidential election Menem withdrew from the run-off, leaving the presidency to Duhalde's protege, Nestor Kirchner, who presided over the largest default in I.M.F. history. But he was able to negotiate a refinancing of $21 bil. of debt with the I.M.F. and inflation fell quickly and G.D.P. grew for the first time in four years. Over the next two years the economy grew rapidly and inflation fell to 5 percent. By 2007, a full recovery seemed in full swing with unemployment at 10 percent and annual growth at 9 percent. Kirchner's wife, Cristina, was the surprise Peronist candidate for president and in 2007 won an overwhelming majority.

▶ ARMENIA
Republic of Armenia
● **GEOGRAPHY Location:** southwest Transcaucasia between Europe and Asia. **Boundaries:** Georgia to N, Azerbaijan to E, Iran to S, Turkey to W. Nakhichevan Autonomous Republic, an Azerbaijan territory, is an enclave within Armenian territory. **Total area:** 11,506 sq. mi. (29,800 sq km). **Coastline:** none. **Comparative area:** slightly smaller than Maryland. **Land use:** 18% arable land; 2% permanent crops; 80% other. **Major cities:** (1990 est.) Yerevan (capital) 1,202,000; Kumayri (formerly Leninakan) 123,000; Kirovakan 76,000.
● **PEOPLE Population:** 2,968,586 (July 2008 est.). **Nationality:** noun—Armenian(s); adjective—Armenian. **Ethnic groups:** 98% Armenian, 1.3% Yezidi, .8% Russian and other. **Languages:** 98% Armenian, 1% Russian, 1% Yezidi. **Religions:** 95%

Armenian Apostolic, 4% other Christian, 1% Yezidi.
● **GOVERNMENT Type:** republic. **Independence:** Sept. 21, 1991 (from U.S.S.R.). **Constitution:** July 5, 1995. **National holiday:** Independence Day, Sept. 21. **Heads of Government:** Serzh Sargsian, president (since April 2008); Tigran Sargsian, prime minister (since April 2008). **Structure:** executive; unicameral legislatiure; judiciary.
● **ECONOMY Monetary unit:** dram. **Budget:** (2007 est.) *income:* $1.65 bil.; *expend.:*$1.65 bil. **GDP:** $16.83 bil., $5,700 per capita (2007 est.). **Chief crops:** fruit (especially wine grapes), vegetables, livestock. **Natural resources:** small deposits of gold and copper. **Major industries:** Industrial machinery, electrical equipment, tires, textiles (much of industry). **Labor force:** 1.2 mil. (2007). **Exports:** $1.16 bil. (f.o.b., 2007 est.); diamonds, mineral products, foodstuffs. **Imports:** $3.28 bil. (f.o.b., 2007 est.); natural gas, petroleum, tobacco products, foodstuffs. **Major trading partners:** (2006) *exports:* 18.3% Germany, 14.1% Netherlands, 13.3% Belgium, 13.1% Russia, 7% Israel, 6.1% U.S., 5.1% Georgia, 4.9% Iran; *imports:* 21.8% Russia, 7.8% Ukraine, 7.6% Belgium, 7.1% Turkmenistan, 6.1% Italy, 5.7% Germany, 5.7% Iran, 4.8% Israel, 4.5% U.S., 4.1% Georgia.

Armenia, a small landlocked country just south of the great Caucasus mountain range, is but a fragment of ancient Armenia, one of the world's oldest civilizations dating back to the sixth century B.C. In about A.D. 300, Armenia adopted Christianity, which today is still an important component of Armenian national identity. Because Armenia forms part of a land bridge between the Black and the Caspian Seas, and between Turks and Slavs, it has long been overrun and controlled by the Byzantine, Arab, Ottoman, Mongol, and Russian Empires. In 1236 the Tatar and Mongol invasion spelled the end of Armenia as a separate state. In 1639, after the conclusion of a major war between Turkey and Iran, the territory of Armenia was partitioned. By the end of the 17th century, czarist Russia was also involved in Armenia, and in 1828 eastern Armenia was ceded to the Russian empire by the Treaty of Turkmenchai.

During the First World War, those Armenians living in the western part of the country under Ottoman rule were increasingly subjected to persecution by the Turks. In April 1915, the Turks forcibly removed the Armenians from the border area, during which more than a million of them either starved or were killed. In 1918, an Armenian republic emerged as the Russian empire collapsed, but this entity was short-lived, as Turkey, Russia, and later Britain fought for control. Finally, the Soviet Red Army moved into the territory and on Nov. 29, 1920, declared it a Soviet republic. Armenia was made part of the Transcaucasian Soviet Federal Socialist Republic of the U.S.S.R. in 1922, and in 1936, it became one of the Soviet Union's constituent union republics.

Armenian Christians have been subjected to many years of persecution by various invaders, causing a great diaspora of Armenians, especially to the United States and Europe. This large expatriate community has helped Armenia from abroad through difficult times.

Since 1988, Armenia's most pressing issue has been the war over Nagorno-Karabakh, the Armenian Christian enclave of Muslim Azerbaijan. Fighting broke out when 180,000 ethnic Armenians in Azerbaijan demanded that their homeland become part of Armenia. The war continued even as both nations declared their independence from the Soviet Union (Armenia on Sept. 23, 1991; Azerbaijan a month later). In October 1991, Levon Ter-Petrossian was elected president of independent Armenia, and in December, Armenia was one of 11 former Soviet republics to sign the Alma-Ata Declaration, creating the Commonwealth of Independent States. Since independence, Armenia has remained committed to the war over Nagorno-Karabakh, even though it has hindered the functioning of the stagnant Armenian economy.

In 1995, a new "strong president" constitution was approved by 68 percent in a referendum and Pres. Ter-Petrossian's six-party Republic Coalition carried a majority of seats in the first elections for the 190-seat National Assembly. He was reelected in 1996 but resigned in February 1998 in a dispute over policy toward Nagorno-Karabakh with his hard-line premier Robert Kocharian. In March, Kocharian easily won the presidential election over Soviet-era ruler Karen Demirchyan. In October 1999, gunmen entered Parliament, murdering premier Vazgen Sargissian and seven others. President Kocharian named Sargissian's brother, Aram, a political neophyte, as new premier. In March 2003, Kocharian was elected to a second five-year term as president, taking over 60% of the disputed vote; in May, his coalition won 70 of 131 parliamentary seats.

▶ AUSTRALIA
Commonwealth of Australia

● **GEOGRAPHY** **Location:** continent of Australia, between Indian and Pacific Oceans. **Boundaries:** nearest neighbor is Papua New Guinea, to N. **Total area:** 2,967,897 sq. mi. (7,686,850 sq km). **Coastline:** 16,010 mi. (25,760 km). **Comparative area:** slightly smaller than U.S. **Land use:** 7% arable land; negl. % permanent crops; 93% other. **Major cities:** Canberra (capital); Sydney; Melbourne; Brisbane; Perth.

● **PEOPLE** **Population:** 20,600,856 (July 2008 est.). **Nationality:** noun—Australian(s); adjective—Australian. **Ethnic groups:** 92% Caucasian, 7% Asian, 1% aboriginal and other. **Languages:** English, Chinese, Italian, native langs. **Religions:** 20.5% Anglican, 26.4% Roman Catholic, 20.5% other Christian, 3.5% non-Christian, 1.5% Muslim, 2% Buddhist, 15.3% none.

● **GOVERNMENT** **Type:** federal parliamentary democracy. **Independence:** Jan. 1, 1901 (from federation of U.K. colonies). **Constitution:** July 9, 1900; effective Jan. 1, 1901. **National holiday:** Australia Day, Jan. 26. **Heads of Government:** Michael Jeffery, governor general (since June 2003); Kevin Rudd, prime minister (since Dec. 2007). **Structure:** executive—governor general (appointed by the Queen), prime minister, and cabinet; bicameral legislature; independent judiciary.

● **ECONOMY** **Monetary unit:** Australian dollar. **Budget:** (2007 est.) *income:* $312 bil.; *expend.:* $299.6 bil. **G.D.P.:** $766.8 bil.; $35,700 per capita (2007 est.). **Chief crops:** wheat, barley, sugarcane, fruits; cattle. **Natural resources:** bauxite, coal, iron ore, copper, tin. **Major industries:** mining, industrial and transportation equipment, food processing. **Labor force:** 10.9 mil. (2007); 73% services, 22% industry, 5% agriculture, 4.4% unemployment (2007). **Exports:** $139.4 bil. (f.o.b., 2007 est.); coal, gold, meat, wool. **Imports:** $152.7 bil. (f.o.b., 2007 est.); machinery and transport equipment, computers and office machines,

telecommunication equipment and parts. **Major trading partners:** (2006) *exports:* 19% Japan, 12% China, 8% South Korea, 6% U.S., 5.5% India, 5.5% New Zealand, 5% U.K.; *imports:* 14% China, 14% U.S., 18% Japan, 6% Singapore, 5% Germany.

The continent-nation of Australia is distinguished by its geographical isolation and by the unique flora and fauna that isolation fostered. The ancestors of today's aborigines arrived from Southeast Asia as much as 40,000 years ago. Thereafter, aborigine culture evolved in isolation except for some contact between the peoples of the northern coast and New Guinea. Australia was first sighted by Europeans at the beginning of the 17th century. In the 18th century, it was visited by the Dutch, who named it New Holland. The eastern coast was systematically explored in 1770 by Capt. James Cook, who claimed it for Great Britain.

British settlement began in 1788, with the landing of about 700 convicts near Sydney. Australia remained a penal colony during the first half of the 19th century, during which time the continent was explored and separate colonies established. Aboriginal populations were displaced and in some areas (most notably the island Tasmania) totally exterminated. Discovery of gold in Victoria in 1851 created a gold rush that greatly accelerated immigration. By 1900, the three mainstays of the Australian economy—livestock, mining, and wheat growing—were firmly established.

In 1901, a commonwealth was established consisting of a confederation of the various states except for the Northern Territory, which was added in 1911. The British Crown was represented by an appointed governor-general; the national government today is a parliamentary system, but much local authority resides in the separate states. Comprehensive social welfare legislation was passed by the state and national governments soon after the commonwealth's formation.

Australian troops fought with distinction in both world wars. A Japanese threat to Australia in 1942 was averted by Allied victory in the Battle of the Coral Sea. Australia and the United States are firm allies, and Australian troops joined U.S. forces in Korea, Vietnam, the Persian Gulf War and the invasion of Iraq. Australia administers several external island groups and claims territory in Antarctica.

The abandonment of discriminatory immigration practices in 1973 led to a new wave of immigration, particularly from Asia. Australian economic ties to Asia and the Pacific Rim have expanded considerably; new exploitation of mineral resources has in many cases been accomplished with Japanese investment and export contracts to Japan.

After 10 years in office, Prime Minister Bob Hawke was ousted by his own Labour party in 1991 and replaced by Paul Keating. Keating's government was reelected in 1993 elections, despite a persistent economic slump. But continued high spending and taxes took their toll, and in 1996, 13 years of Labour rule ended. A coalition of the more conservative Liberal and Nationalist parties captured 94 of 148 seats in the House of Representatives. The popular Liberal party leader John Howard became the new prime minister.

Australia's Constitutional Convention voted (in Feb. 1998) to proclaim Australia a republic, severing its residual ties to the British Crown. But in a 1999 referendum, voters rejected the republic 55 to 45 percent. With respect to aboriginal claims to Australian land, the government carried a Native

Title Bill in July 1998, giving Australia's state governments authority to rule on the issue.

Howard and the Liberal-Nationalist coalition gained a third straight term in Nov. 2001 elections, although Labour gained control of every state government. The Howard government's decision to participate in the Iraq war brought a (purely symbolic) vote of "no confidence" in the Senate; the real "no confidence" vote in the House failed by 82-63. By April 2003 Australian troops were already withdrawing, refusing to take part in any peacekeeping force. In Nov. 2007, Kevin Rudd led the Labor Party to a convincing victory ending a decade of Conservative rule.

▶ AUSTRIA
Republic of Austria

• **GEOGRAPHY Location:** landlocked country in central Europe. **Boundaries:** Germany and Czech Republic to N, Hungary and Slovak Republic to E, Slovenia and Italy to S, Switzerland and Liechtenstein to W. **Total area:** 32,377 sq. mi. (83,858 sq km). **Coastline:** none. **Comparative area:** slightly smaller than Maine. **Land use:** 17% arable land; 1% permanent crops; 82% other. **Major cities:** Vienna (capital); Graz; Linz; Salzburg; Innsbruck.

• **PEOPLE Population:** 8,205,533 (July 2008 est.). **Nationality:** noun—Austrian(s); adjective—Austrian. **Ethnic groups:** 91% Austrian, 4% former Yugoslavs, 1.6% Turks, 1% German. **Languages:** German, Turkish, Croatian (official in Burgenland). **Religions:** 73% Roman Catholic, 5% Protestant, 22% Muslim and other.

• **GOVERNMENT Type:** federal republic. **Constitution:** 1920; revised 1929; reinstated May 1945. **National holiday:** National Day, Oct. 26. **Heads of Government:** Dr. Heinz Fischer, president (since July 2004); Alfred Gusenbauer, chancellor (since Jan. 2007). **Structure:** executive; bicameral legislature; directly elected president whose functions are largely representational; independent federal judiciary.

• **ECONOMY Monetary unit:** euro. **Budget:** (2007 est.) *income:* $176.4 bil.; *expend.:* $178.3 bil. **G.D.P.:** $319.7 bil., $39,000 per capita (2007 est.). **Chief crops:** grain, fruits, potatoes, sugar beets. **Natural resources:** iron ore, crude oil, timber, magnesite, lead. **Major industries:** construction machinery, vehicles and parts, food. **Labor force:** 3.56 mil. (2007); 70% services, 30% industry and crafts, 2% agriculture and forestry; 4.3% unemployment (2007 est.). **Exports:** (2007 est.) $158.3 bil.; machinery and equipment, paper and cardboard, metal goods. **Imports:** (2007 est.) $157.4 bil.; vehicles, machinery and equipment, apparel, metal goods. **Major trading partners:** (2006) *exports:* 30% Germany, 9% Italy, 6% U.S., 5% Switzerland; *imports:* 46% Germany, 7% Italy, 4.5% Switzerland, 4% Netherlands.

The Celtic tribes in what is now Austria were conquered by Rome under Emperor Augustus. After the fall of Rome, it was overrun by Huns, Lombards, Ostrogoths, and Bavarians. In 788 it was incorporated into the empire of Charlemagne. From the 9th to the 13th century, its territory was divided among a variety of feudal domains. In the late 13th century, Austria was reunited under Rudolph I of Habsburg, whose dynasty became synonymous with Austrian history for the next seven centuries. Rudolph's successors steadily enlarged their domain by conquest and marital diplomacy until, by the reign of Charles V (1500-

58), they ruled not only the Holy Roman Empire (encompassing most of central Europe) but also the Netherlands, Spain, and all of its colonies.

After the reign of Charles V, the Habsburg Empire was split into two branches, one governing Spain, the other the Holy Roman Empire. Habsburg power in Germany declined after the Thirty Years' War (1618-48) but was affirmed in the Danube valley after the defeat of the Turkish siege of Vienna in 1683 and the subsequent reconquest of Hungary from the Turks. The marriage of Maria Teresa to Francis of Lorraine gave rise to the House of Habsburg-Lorraine in 1745. In 1804 the Austrian empire was founded, and two years later, the defunct Holy Roman Empire was abolished. The Ausgleich ("compromise") of 1867 transformed the empire into the Dual Monarchy of Austria-Hungary.

In 1914 the assassination of Archduke Franz Ferdinand, the heir to the Austrian throne, led to the outbreak of World War I, which resulted in a wholesale redrawing of national boundaries in Central Europe. Austria emerged as a small Alpine republic, with about 12 percent of the territory of the old Dual Monarchy. The new republic faced a severe postwar economic crisis, as well as a political stalemate between the Christian Social party and the Social Democratic party, each with the support of about half of the electorate, and each with its own paramilitary organization.

In 1933, as Hitler's National Socialists rose to power in Germany, Austrian Chancellor Engelbert Dollfuss, leader of the Christian Social party, instituted rule by decree and began building a corporate state modeled on Italian fascism. His attempt to disarm the Social Democratic militia led to civil war. The government triumphed, but Dollfuss was assassinated in an attempted coup by Austrian Nazis in July 1934. Hitler finally forced Austrian union with Germany (the Anschluss) in 1938, after which Austria was considered a part of Greater Germany.

Conquered by American and Soviet troops early in 1945, Austria was divided into French, British, American, and Russian zones of occupation after World War II. But the occupying powers permitted the formation of a unified national government, formed in November 1945 and recognized by the Western powers in 1946. The occupation ended in 1955 with the signing of the Austrian State Treaty. The four powers withdrew their forces, and Austria pledged itself to a policy of permanent neutrality, with no foreign military alliances.

The coalition government continued to 1966, when the People's party under Josef Klaus gained a parliamentary majority. In 1970 the Socialist party under Bruno Kreisky came to power. Socialist dominance continued until 1983, when the Socialists had to form a coalition with the right-wing Freedom party in order to stay in power. Kreisky resigned and was succeeded by Fred Sinowatz. From 1986 to 1997, a "Grand Coalition" of the Socialist and People's Parties governed Austria under Socialist Chancellor Franz Vranitzky. In ten years, the government cautiously privatized state-owned enterprises of the mild Austrian form of socialism, while tourism, a highly developed maunfacturing sector, and substantial petroleum reserves contributed to the country's prosperity. The government dramatically cut taxes and began promoting regional trade with the newly-independent states of East-Central Europe. On Jan. 1, 1995, Austria entered the European Union.

Tensions arising from unemployment and immigration of "economic refugees" from Asia and Africa as well as from Eastern Europe led to the amending of Austria's asylum law, consideration of immigration quotas, and the growing strength of the right-wing Freedom Party. The desire to meet the E.U.'s single currency standards led to welfare spending cuts which provoked further voter dissatisfaction. In Oct. 1996 Austrian voters (participating for the first time in European Parliament elections), gave Freedom Party candidates, who were opposed to Austria's participation in EMU, 27.6 percent of their votes, while Socialists garnered only 29.1 percent and the People's Party took 29.6 percent.

Chancellor Vranitzky resigned in Jan. 1997 and was succeeded by Socialist Finance Minister Viktor Klima. In the Oct. 1999 elections to the National Council, the Social Democrats received only one-third of the votes, while the People's Party and the Freedom Party each took 27 percent. When it proved impossible to reconstruct the "Grand Coalition," the latter two parties, together controlling 104 of 183 seats, formed their own coalition government, with Wolfgang Schuessel of the People's Party as chancellor.

With the Freedom Party entering the Austrian government, the other 14 E.U. governments cut off diplomatic contacts, as did Israel and the U.S. The E.U. lifted the sanctions after their investigative panel reported the superiority of Austria's treatment of immigrants; subsequently, the Freedom Party's share of the vote has shown slippage. In Nov. 2002 parliamentary elections, the party garnered but 10 percent of the vote while Chancellor Schuessel's People's Party won a surprising 43 percent. In Feb. 2003 a new People's-Freedom government was formed which lasted until 2006 when the Social Democrats won a narrow victory and Alfred Gusenbauer became chancellor with immigration still the leading issue.

▶ AZERBAIJAN
Azerbaijani Republic

● **GEOGRAPHY   Location:** southern Transcaucasia between Europe and Asia. **Boundaries:** Georgia to NW, Russian Federation to N, Caspian Sea to E, Iran to S, Armenia to SW. Nakhichevan Autonomous Republic (ASSR) is part of Azerbaijan although it is inside Armenian territory. **Total land area:** 33,436 sq. mi. (86,600 sq km). **Coastline:** Caspian Sea. **Comparative area:** about the size of Maine. **Land use:** 19% arable land; 3% permanent crops; 78% other. **Major cities:** (1990 est.) Baku (capital) 1,149,000; Gyanja (formerly Kirovabad) 281,000; Sumgait 235,000.
● **PEOPLE   Population—**8,177,717 (July 2008 est.). **Nationality:** noun—Azerbaijani(s) or Azeri(s); adjective—Azerbaijani. **Ethnic groups:** 91% Azeri, 2.2% Dagestani Peoples, 1.8% Russian, 1.5% Armenian, 3.9% other. **Languages:** 90.3% Azeri, 2.2% Lezgi, 1.8% Russian, 1.5% Armenian, 4.3% other. **Religions:** 93.4% Muslim, 2.5% Russian Orthodox, 2.3% Armenian Orthodox, 1.8% other.
● **GOVERNMENT   Type:** republic. **Independence:** Aug. 30, 1991 (from U.S.S.R.). **Constitution:** Nov. 12, 1995. **National holiday:** May 28. **Heads of Government:** Ilham Aliyev, president (since Oct. 2003); Artur Rasizadeh, prime minister (since Nov. 2003). **Structure:** executive; unicameral legislature; judiciary.
● **ECONOMY   Monetary unit:** manat. **Budget:** (2007 est.) *income:* $6.75 bil.; *expend.:* $8.36 bil. **G.D.P.:** $31.07 bil., $9,000 per capita (2007 est.).

Chief crops: cotton, tea, tobacco, grain, fruit. **Natural resources:** petroleum, natural gas, iron ore. **Major industries:** petroleum and natural gas, construction materials, chemicals. **Labor force:** 5.243 mil. (2007). **Exports:** $19.53 bil. (f.o.b., 2007 est.); oil, gas, oil field equipment, textiles, cotton. **Imports:** $6.38 bil. (f.o.b., 2007 est.); machinery and parts, foodstuffs, metals. **Major trading partners:** (2006) *exports:* 45% Italy, 11% Israel, 6% Turkey, 6% France, 5% Russia, 5% Iran, 5% Georgia. *imports:* 22% Russia, 9% U.K., 8% Germany, 7% Turkey, 7% Turkmenistan, 6% Ukraine, 4% China.

The territory of present-day Azerbaijan has been inhabited since Paleolithic times. The name Azerbaijan is derived (via Arabic and Turkish) from Atropates (a vassal of Alexander III of Macedonia), who founded an independent state here in the fourth century B.C. The population of Azerbaijan is approximately seven million, but nearly seven million additional Azeris with the same language and faith live across the border in Iran.

For much of its history, the territory of Azerbaijan, home to an indigenous nomadic people, has been occupied by Persians, Muslim Arabs, Turkic tribes from Mongolia, Ottoman Turks, Mongols, and in the 18th century, Russians. The capital city of Baku was an important outlet on the Volga River-Caspian Sea route; under Peter the Great, the Russians occupied Baku and Derbent, and for a while controlled the Caspian Sea. Command of this territory shifted between Ottomans, Persians, and Russians in the 18th and 19th centuries, with the Russians ultimately establishing military rule by 1828 with the Treaty of Turkmenchai. This treaty ceded the southern half of the country to Persia and the northern half to Russia.

Under the Russians, Azerbaijan became an industrial center. In 1883 the Russians finished building the Transcaucasian Railway, which linked Baku with the Black Sea coast and central Russia and made Baku one of the most important industrial hubs in the Russian empire. Baku became a revolutionary center around the turn of the century. In 1918 an independent republic was formed, but in 1920 it was overthrown by the Soviet Red Army, and in April 1920 the Azerbaijan Soviet Socialist Republic (SSR) was proclaimed. Two years later, it was joined with the Armenian and Georgian SSRs to form the Transcaucasian Soviet Federal Socialist Republic; in 1936, however, the three again became separate union republics.

While a Soviet republic, Azerbaijan was industrialized, its agriculture collectivized, and religious persecution was severe. It also entered into a war in 1988 with neighboring Armenia over the Nagorno-Karabakh region, which is largely populated with ethnic Armenians but lies within Azerbaijani territory. The local council of Nagorno-Karabakh petitioned the Armenian and Azerbaijani Supreme Soviets to transfer the region to Armenia in 1988, but Azerbaijan refused, spurring a war that lasts to this day.

In Jan. 1990, attacks on Communist party buildings and against Armenians in Azerbaijan precipitated a brutal Soviet Army intervention to restore order. A state of emergency was declared, and the first secretary of the Communist party was replaced by Ayaz Mutalibov. He was elected president in Sept. 1991, and on Oct. 18, 1991, Azerbaijan's Supreme Soviet declared the country's independence. On Dec. 21, 1991, Azerbaijan joined 10 other former Soviet republics in forming the Commonwealth of Independent States.

After the dissolution of the U.S.S.R., Azerbaijan had problems consolidating its own future. In 1992, Pres. Mutalibov was forced from office. His successor was in turn driven out of office by armed rebels after the fighting in Nagorno-Karabakh turned decisively in Armenia's favor. He was replaced by Heydar Aliyev, a former Communist party boss, in 1993. Aliyev survived two coup attempts and the country's flagging fortunes in Nagorno-Karabakh to complete a $7.4 billion deal with western companies to develop oil fields in the Caspian Sea in 1994. In parliamentary elections in 1995, Aliyev's New Azerbaijan party won 70 percent of the vote, amidst charges of vote-rigging. And in 1996, Aliyev negotiated an agreement to transport oil from the Caspian Sea via pipeline (through Chechnya) to the Russian port of Novorossiysk. The pipeline opened Nov. 12, 1997, soon after Aliyev met with Pres. Clinton in Washington to sign a treaty.

In Oct. 1998, presidential elections which were boycotted by opposition parties, and which European monitors declared to be seriously irregular, gave Aliyev 76 percent of the vote. In parliamentary elections in Nov. 2000, his New Azerbaijan Party carried 70 percent of the vote, to no one's surprise. The ailing president, in Sept. 2002, oversaw the start of construction on a major oil pipeline from the Caspian through Georgia to Turkey and signed a treaty with Russia regularizing the Caspian border. But he was unable to prevent a presidential election in the secessionist, ethnically Armenian province of Nagorno-Karabakh. In 2003 he appointed his son, Ilham, premier and when illness forced him to withdraw from the the presidential race, Ilham was elected with 77 percent of the vote. The new oil pipeline to Turkey was opened helping to spur the economy. In Nov. 2005 Ilham was re-elected but international monitors said fraud and abuse were widespread, and this charge was repeated in 2006 parliamentary elections.

▶ **BAHAMAS**
Commonwealth of The Bahamas
• **GEOGRAPHY Location:** nearly 700 islands in an archipelago that extends 590 mi. (950 km) SE-NW between Florida and Haiti. Nassau 25°05'N, 77°20'W. **Boundaries:** western Atlantic Ocean to N, E, S, and W. **Total land area:** 5,382 sq. mi. (13,940 sq km). **Coastline:** 2,200 mi. (3,542 km). **Comparative area:** slightly larger than Connecticut. **Land use:** 1% arable land; negl. % permanent crops; 99% other. **Major cities:** Nassau (capital).
• **PEOPLE Population:** 307,451 (July 2008 est.). **Nationality:** noun—Bahamian(s); adjective—Bahamian. **Ethnic groups:** 85% black, 12% white, 3% Asian & Hispanic. **Languages:** English, some Creole among Haitian immigrants. **Religions:** 35% Baptist, 15% Anglican, 14% Roman Catholic, 8% Pentecostal, 5% Church of God, 4% Methodist, 15% other Christian.
• **GOVERNMENT Type:** constituional parliamentary democracy. **Independence:** July 10, 1973 (from U.K.). **Constitution:** July 10, 1973. **National holiday:** National Day, July 10. **Heads of Government:** Arthur D. Hanna, governor-general (since Feb. 2006); Hubert Ingraham, prime minister (since May 2007). **Structure:** executive—governor general (appointed by queen); bicameral legislature; judiciary.

• **ECONOMY Monetary unit:** Bahamian dollar. **Budget:** (2007 est.) *income:* $1.03 bil.; *expend.:* $1.03 bil. **G.D.P.:** $6.93 bil., $22,700 per capita (2007 est.). **Chief crops:** citrus fruits, vegetables; poultry. **Natural resources:** salt, aragonite, timber. **Major industries:** tourism, banking, cement. **Labor force:** 181,900 (2006); 50% tourism, 40% other services, 5% industry, 5% agriculture; 6.9% unemployment (2001 est.). **Exports:** $674 mil. (2006 est.); pharmaceuticals, cement, rum, crawfish. **Imports:** $2.4 bil. (2006 est.); foodstuffs, manufactured goods, crude oil. **Major trading partners:** (2006) *exports:* 22% Spain, 20% U.S., 14% Poland, 13% Germany, 6% U.K., 5% Guatemala. *imports:* 25% U.S., 16% Brazil, 13% Japan, 8% South Korea, 6% Spain.

Christopher Columbus made his first landfall in the Americas in the Bahamas Oct. 12, 1492. Though the Spanish never settled the islands, they enslaved and removed to Hispaniola 40,000 of the indigenous Arawaks by 1508. Their shallow seas (baja mar) made the islands a haven for pirates in the 17th century—as well as during the Civil War, Prohibition, and for drug smugglers today. British colonization of the Bahamas began in 1629 and continued slowly over the next two centuries.

Tourism has been the mainstay of the economy in this century, but high unemployment is a continuing problem. Parliament relaxed restrictions on offshore banking to stem the flight of international capital prompted by allegations of government corruption and involvement in drug trafficking. In 1992 the government of Prime Minister Lynden Pindling was defeated after 25 years in office, largely because of corruption charges. The Progressive Liberal Party remained in power for many years, but was defeated in 2007 by the Free National Movement party.

▶ **BAHRAIN**
Kingdom of Bahrain
• **GEOGRAPHY Location:** group of 35 islands in western Persian Gulf. Manama 26°17'N, 50°33'E. **Boundaries:** Saudi Arabia about 15 mi. (24 km) to W and Qatar about 17 mi. (28 km) to SE. **Total land area:** 239 sq. mi. (620 sq km). **Coastline:** 161 mi. (259 km). **Comparative area:** slightly less than 3.5 times size of Washington, D.C. **Land use:** 4.35% arable land; 4.35% permanent crops; 91.3% other. **Major cities:** Manama (capital); Muharraq Town.
• **PEOPLE Population:** 718,306 (July 2008 est.). **Nationality:** noun—Bahraini(s); adjective—Bahraini. **Ethnic groups:** 62.4% Bahraini, 37.6 non-Bahraini. **Languages:** Arabic, English, Farsi, Urdu. **Religions:** 81.2% Muslim (Shi'a and Sunni), 9% Christian, 9.8% other.
• **GOVERNMENT Type:** constitutional monarchy. **Independence:** Aug. 15, 1971 (from U.K.). **Constitution:** adopted late Dec. 2000. **National holiday:** Dec. 16. **Heads of Government:** Hamad Bin Isa Al-Khalifa, amir (since Jan. 2002); Khalifa bin Salman, prime minister (since 1971). **Structure:** executive—amir is traditional arab monarch, appoints cabinet led by prime minister; legislative—amir dissolved National Assembly (Aug. 1975), appointed Advisory Council Dec. 1992; independent judiciary.
• **ECONOMY Monetary unit:** Bahraini dinar. **Budget:** (2007 est.) *income:* $6.05 bil.; *expend.:* $5.08 bil. **G.D.P.:** $16.9 bil., $34,700 per capita (2004 est.). **Chief crops:** not self-sufficient in food production; produces some fruits and vegetables; engages in shrimping and fishing. **Natural**

resources: oil, associated and nonassociated natural gas, fish. **Major industries:** petroleum processing and refining, aluminum smelting, offshore banking. **Labor force:** 363,000 (2007 est.); 79% industry, commerce and service (note: 44% of 15-64 age group is non-national). **Exports:** $13.16 bil. (f.o.b. 2007); petroleum, aluminum. **Imports:** $9.78 bil. (f.o.b., 2007). **Major trading partners:** (2006) *exports:* 3.2% Saudi Arabia, 3% U.S., 2.3% Japan. *note* - data exclude oil exports; *imports:* 37.2% Saudi Arabia, 6.8% Japan, 6.2% U.S., 6.1% U.K., 6% Germany, 4.2% United Arab Emirates.

Bahrain has been an entrepôt of trade between Arabia and India since the second millenium B.C. The Portuguese fortified Bahrain in the 16th century but were driven out by the Persian shah Abbas I early in the 17th century. At the end of the 18th century, it became an Arab sheikhdom within the Ottoman Empire. Bahrain entered into treaty relations with Great Britain in 1820 and became a British protectorate in 1861. After British forces withdrew from the gulf, the nation became an independent emirate, in August 1971, under Amir Isa bin Sulman al-Khalifa, who had come to the throne in 1961. The U.S. has maintained a large military base here for many years and is currently home to the Fifth Fleet.

Oil reserves—first discovered in 1932—were depleted by the mid-1970's. The economy diversified to include oil refining, aluminum smelting, international banking, and shipping. Bahrain has close relations with Saudi Arabia; a causeway permits direct communication between them.

In June 1995 social and political unrest caused by uneven distribution of wealth, high unemployment, and a repressive government erupted into serious rioting. Protests by the Shiite majority began again in early 1996; a government crackdown led to the arrest of over 600 dissidents. Bahrain's family-run, Sunni Muslim government continued with the March 1999 death of its founding emir and his replacement with his son, Hamad bin Isa al-Khalifa. The new emir, in Feb. 2001, fostered a trio of reform measures: extending amnesty to 400 political prisoners and repatriation to 100 exiles; repealing the State Security Law and abolishing the State Security Court, both of which had been designed to quash Shiite unrest; and sponsoring a referendum which approved (by 98 percent) the restoration of a parliament, the founding of an independent judiciary, and the extension of the right to vote to women. Then, in Feb. 2002, Sheik Hamad declared the state to be a constitutional monarchy, the Kingdom of Bahrain, with himself as king. Municipal elections were successfully held in May, with elections for the lower house of the legislature in Oct. giving Sunni candidates 19 of 40 seats. In Nov. the King appointed the upper house, including six women and one Jew.

▶BANGLADESH
People's Republic of Bangladesh
• **GEOGRAPHY Location:** southern Asia. **Boundaries:** India to N, E, and W; Myanmar to E, Bay of Bengal to S. **Total land area:** 55,598 sq. mi. (144,000 sq km). **Coastline:** 360 mi. (580 km). **Comparative area:** between Arkansas and Wisconsin. **Land use:** 61% arable land; 2% permanent crops; 37% other. **Major cities:** Dhaka (formerly Dacca) (capital) ; Chittagong; Khulna; Rajshahi; Barisal.

• **PEOPLE Population:** 153,546,901 (July 2008 est.). **Nationality:** noun—Bangladeshi(s); adjective—Bangladesh. **Ethnic groups:** 98% Bengali, tribal groups, non-Bengali Muslims. **Languages:** Bangla (official); English widely used. **Religions:** 83% Muslim, 16% Hindu, 1% Buddhist, Christian, and other.
• **GOVERNMENT Type:** parliamentary democracy. **Independence:** Dec. 16, 1971 (from Pakistan). **Constitution:** Nov. 4, 1972, effective Dec. 16, 1972, suspended following coup of Mar. 24, 1982, restored Nov. 10, 1986; amended many times. **National holiday:** March 26, Independence Day. **Heads of Government:** Iajuddin Ahmed, president (since Sept. 2002); Fakhruddin Ahmed, chief adviser to Caretaker Government (since Jan. 2007). **Structure:** executive—president appoints prime minister and Advisory Council; unicameral legislature dissolved by president following elections on Feb. 15, 1996 and named caretaker prime minister; judiciary.
• **ECONOMY Monetary unit:** taka. **Budget:** (2007 est.) *income:* $7.08 bil.; *expend.:* $9.64 bil. **G.D.P.:** $209.2 bil., $1,400 per capita (2007 est.). **Chief crops:** large-scale subsistence farming, heavily dependent on monsoon rain; main crops are jute, rice, wheat, tea, sugarcane, and potatoes. **Natural resources:** natural gas, arable land, timber. **Major industries:** jute manufactures, cotton textiles, tea processing. **Labor force:** 69.4 mil. (2007 est.); extensive export of labor to Saudi Arabia, UAE, and Oman; 63% agriculture, 26% services, 11% industry and mining. **Exports:** $11.25 bil. (2007); garments, jute, leather, seafood. **Imports:** $14.91 bil. (2007); machinery, chemicals, iron and steel, textiles. **Major trading partners:** (2006) *exports:* 24.9% U.S., 12.8% Germany, 9.8% U.K., 5% France; *imports:* 17.7% China, 12.5% India, 7.9% Kuwait, 5.5% Singapore, 4.1% Hong Kong.

Located on the alluvial plain of the Ganges River northeast of India, Bengal was ruled by Buddhist kings from the eighth to 12th centuries. Conquered by Muslim invaders around 1200, many inhabitants converted to Islam and Bengal became part of the Moghul Empire in the 16th century. The British East India Company established a settlement in 1642, and by 1750 all of Bengal was under British rule. The diverse agricultural economy became dominated by export crops of opium and jute, while rice was grown in the fertile delta.

With Indian independence in 1947, Bengal was partitioned along religious lines, Hindu West Bengal (including Calcutta) remaining with India and Muslim East Bengal becoming the eastern province of Pakistan. In the elections of 1971, the Bengali Awami League gained control of Pakistan's National Assembly. Seating of the new National Assembly was postponed, and riots broke out in East Pakistan. Troops from West Pakistan were sent to quell the riots on May 25; the following day East Pakistan declared its independence as Bangladesh. Civil war followed; 10 million refugees fled to India. Following Indian intervention, Pakistan acknowledged Bangladesh's independence on Dec. 15.

Bangladesh has consistently been one of the world's poorest countries, plagued by violent political instability, military coups, overpopulation, and frequent catastrophic floods (including one in 1975 that killed half a million people). The first president, Sheik Mujibur Rahman, was assassinated in 1975. Lt. Gen. Hossain Mohammad Ershad, who seized power in a coup in March

1982, was elected president in 1986, but resigned in 1990 in the face of opposition unrest.

In 1991, the Bangladesh Nationalist party (BNP) of Begum Khaleda Zia (widow of former president Ziaur Rahman, who was assassinated in 1981) won 138 of 330 parliamentary seats running on a platform of free enterprise and an Islamic state. In 1991, the constitution was amended to put the prime minister in charge of the government.

In 1994, nearly 150 opposition members of Parliament resigned en masse, eliciting a promise from Prime Minister Zia to hold general elections in June 1996. In those elections, the Awami League, led by Sheik Hasina Wazed, returned to power for the first time since 1975, when the military massacred most of her family, including her father, Pres. Sheik Mujibur Rahman. In 1998, fifteen were convicted and sentenced to death for their role in the assassinations. Zia's call for nation-wide protest strike went unanswered, but her BNP (in Jan. 1999) was one of three parties, with General Ershad's Jatiya and the Moslem Jamaat-e-Islami, to form a bloc seeking to force early elections upon prime minister Hasina. After completing Bangladesh's first-ever five-year term, premier Hasina and her Awami League faced the voters in Oct. 2001 only to be buried in a surprise landslide victory by former premier Khaleda Zia and her Nationalist party coalition. As Zia's term ran out in Oct. 2006, she appointed a caretaker government to run the elections but the opposition protested her choice. By Jan. 2007, as the election approached, cries of fraud and increased violence forced the interim president to declare a state of emergency and the military essentially took power. In April, Sheikh Hasina Wazed and more than 50 people connected to her politically were charged with murder; Zia was under virtual house arrest and her son in jail charged with extortion. The government tried to exile both women and when that failed they accused both of misrule. Elections were expected at the end of 2008.

▶ BARBADOS

• **Geography** **Location:** easternmost of Caribbean islands, about 200 mi. (320 km) NE of Trinidad. Bridgetown 13°06'N, 59°36'W. **Boundaries:** Atlantic Ocean. **Total land area:** 166 sq. mi. (430 sq km). **Coastline:** 60 mi. (97 km). **Comparative area:** slightly less than 2.5 times size of Washington, D.C. **Land use:** 37% arable land; 2% permanent crops; 61% other. **Major cities:** Bridgetown (capital).
• **People** **Population:** 281,968 (July 2008 est.). **Nationality:** noun—Barbadian(s); adjective—Barbadian. **Ethnic groups:** 90% black, 4% white, 6% Asian and mixed. **Languages:** English. **Religions:** 67% Protestant, 4% Roman Catholic, 29% none or other.
• **Government** **Type:** parliamentary democracy recognizing Queen Elizabeth II as chief of state. **Independence:** Nov. 30, 1966 (from U.K.). **Constitution:** Nov. 30, 1966. **National holiday:** Independence Day, Nov. 30. **Heads of Government:** Sir Clifford Husbands, governor general (since June 1996); David Thompson, prime minister (since Jan. 2008). **Structure:** executive—governor general (appointed by the queen) prime minister; bicameral legislature; judiciary.
• **Economy** **Monetary unit:** Barbadian dollar. **Budget:** (2000 est.) *income:* $847 mil.; *expend.:*

$886 mil. **G.D.P.:** $5.53 bil., $19,700 per capita (2007 est.). **Chief crops:** sugarcane, vegetables, cotton. **Natural resources:** crude oil, fish, natural gas. **Major industries:** tourism, sugar, light manufacturing. **Labor force:** 128,500 (2001 est.); 75% services, 15% industry, 10% agriculture. **Exports:** $385 mil. (2006 est.); sugar and molasses, rum, other foods and beverages, chemicals. **Imports:** $1.586 bil. (2006 est.); consumer goods, machinery, foodstuffs. **Major trading partners:** (2006) *exports:* 43.2% CARICOM, 27.6% U.S. *imports:* 37.7% U.S., 22.6% CARICOM, 5.9% U.K.

Barbados is the only Caribbean island not to have changed hands prior to independence. Although the Spanish removed virtually all the indigenous Arawaks of Barbados by the mid1500's, the island was not claimed until the British arrived in the 1620's. Tobacco, cotton, and sugarcane—harvested by slaves until 1833—were mainstays of the economy. The 1966 constitution mandates the promotion of economic equality among Barbadians, and the country was fairly prosperous relative to other Caribbean states until the mid-1990s, when declining tourism and record-low sugar production have had serious adverse effects. Still, the Barbados Labor Party retained its popularity, winning 26 of the parliament's 28 seats in Jan. 1999 elections. The economy revived as new hotels and housing complexes created jobs and increased tourism.

▶ BELARUS
Republic of Belarus

• **Geography** **Location:** northeastern Europe. **Boundaries:** Lithuania and Latvia to N, Russian Federation to NE and E, Ukraine to S, Poland to W, Lithuania and Latvia to NW. **Total land area:** 80,154 sq. mi. (207,600 sq km). **Coastline:** none. **Comparative area:** slightly smaller than Kansas. **Land use:** 30% arable land; 1% permanent crops; 69% other. **Major cities:** Minsk (capital); Gomel (Homel); Mahilou (Mogilev); Vitebsk; Grodno.
• **People** **Population:** 9,685,768 (July 2008 est.). **Nationality:** noun—Belarusian(s); adjective—Belarusian. **Ethnic groups:** 81.2% Byelorussian, 11.4% Russian, 7.4% Polish, Ukrainian and other. **Languages:** Byelorusian (official), Russian. **Religions:** 80% Eastern Orthodox.
• **Government** **Type:** republic. **Independence:** Aug. 25, 1991 (from U.S.S.R.). **Constitution:** Adopted Nov. 1996. **National holiday:** Independence Day, July 3. **Heads of Government:** Aleksander Lukashenko, president (since July 1994); Sergei Sidorskiy, prime minister (since Dec. 2003). **Structure:** executive—president, prime minister, Council of Ministers; bicameral legislature—most members apointed by the president; judiciary.
• **Economy** **Monetary unit:** Belarusian ruble. **Budget:** (2007 est.) *income:* $15.35 bil.; *expend.:* $16.78 bil. **G.D.P.:** $104.7 bil., $10,200 per capita (2007 est.). **Chief crops:** grain, potatoes, vegetables. **Natural resources:** forest, peat, oil, and natural gas. **Major industries:** tractors, metalworking, heavy-duty vehicles. **Labor force:** 4.3 mil. (2005). **Exports:** $22.91 bil. (f.o.b., 2007); machinery, transport equipment, chemicals, metals. **Imports:** $27.05 bil. (f.o.b., 2007); mineral products, machinery and equipment, metals, chemicals. **Major trading partners:** (2006) *exports:* 34.7% Russia, 17.7% Netherlands, 7.5% U.K., 6.3% Ukraine, 5.2% Poland; *imports:* 58.6% Russia, 7.5% Germany, 5.5% Ukraine.

Belarus, also known as White Russia or Byelorussia, has been inhabited since the seventh century. In the 13th and 14th centuries, present-day Belarus became part of the Grand Duchy of Lithuania, which then became part of Poland in the 16th century. Between 1772 and 1795, Poland was partitioned, which resulted in Belarus becoming part of the Russian empire. After the Bolshevik revolution in 1917, Soviet troops came to Minsk, but they were forced to withdraw in the face of approaching German troops. The Treaty of Brest-Litovsk in March 1918 ceded to Germany most of the territory of Belarus. The same year, an independent Belarusian Democratic Republic was founded, but it had little real power. Once the Germans left, the Soviets easily retook Belarus, and on Jan. 1, 1919, the Belarusian Soviet Socialist Republic (SSR) was proclaimed.

This did not end the divisions of the traditional Belarusian lands. In February 1919 they were merged with Lithuania, but the Poles launched an attack in April of the same year and took both Lithuania and Belarus. In 1920 the Belarusian SSR was re-formed, but it included only the eastern portion of historical Belarusian lands. The Treaty of Riga in March 1921 granted the western territories of Belarus to Poland and the eastern portion to the Russian Federation.

After the Soviets invaded Poland in 1939, the lands that Belarus had lost in 1921 were returned to it. Between 1941 and 1945, the Germans occupied the Belarusian lands, and more than a million lost their lives, including most of the large Jewish population. After the war, the Belarusian SSR was restored with all of its historic lands, and Belarus was finally unified. However, when Stalin redrew the Soviet Union's borders, he included Belarus's capital of Vilnius in Lithuania.

Under Soviet rule, Belarus turned from a mainly agricultural to an industrial land. Large numbers of Belarusians fiercely fought Stalin's collectivization plan in the 1930's, and thousands were killed or deported. Both Stalin's purges of the 1930's and World War II, which devastated both its agriculture and industry, inflicted great losses on Belarus. After the war, Soviet policy in Belarus concentrated on rebuilding its economy and encouraging Russian immigration (Russian replaced Belarusian as the official language).

The Belarusian SSR was one of the more prosperous and stable of the union republics, so Mikhail Gorbachev's policy of glasnost, or openness, in the 1980's was relatively slow to have an impact. In 1987, however, two issues had come to the fore in the Belarusian SSR: the status of the Belarusian language and the ecological dangers of Chernobyl, the famous nuclear reactor that had exploded in nearby Ukraine in 1986, but which dropped almost three-quarters of its fallout on Belarus. In voicing these concerns, the Belarusians formed several new, non-Communist parties that challenged the authority of the ruling Communist party. On July 27, 1990, Belarus declared its sovereignty from the U.S.S.R.

After the fall of the Soviet government, Belarus was one of the strongest supporters of maintaining a union of republics. On Dec. 8, 1991, Belarus, Ukraine, and Russia hosted the talks leading to the Minsk Agreement, which created the Commonwealth of Independent States (CIS)

Pres. Aleaksander Lukashenko fostered closer ties with Russia. A 1995 customs union was expanded by the 1996 Union Treaty to include a common currency, joint tax and legal systems, shared energy and transport networks, and common defense and foreign policies. Lukashenko tightened his dictatorial hold on Belarus with a new constitution (Nov. 1996) which allowed presidential rule by decree and gave Lukashenko power to appoint half the members of the Constitutional Court and 20 of the 64 members of the Council of the Republic, the newly-created upper house of the legislature. In 1997, the U.S. announced it was cutting off $4 mil. in aid.

In July 1999, 35 members of the disbanded parliament designated its former speaker, Semyon Sharetsky, as president. Sharetsky promptly fled to Lithuania for safety but claimed the presidency. October saw large demonstrations in Minsk protesting the disappearance of opposition leaders and the proposed reunion with Russia. That reunion was forestalled by a wary Pres. Yeltsin in Dec. 1999, but Pres. Lukashenko was gratified by his party's sweep of all the seats in Oct. 2000 elections for the Chamber of Representatives in what he described as an "absolutely democratic" vote, a stance he took in the presidential election he won overwhelmingly in Sept. 2004. Protests were vigorous but without effect. In March 2006 elections Lukashenko again won by a large margin and again the E.U. and the U.S. protested. Putin and allies of Russia said the vote was legitimate. Later that year Russia doubled the price of oil and gas and threatened to cut off the supply if the government refused to pay.

▶ BELGIUM
Kingdom of Belgium

• **GEOGRAPHY Location:** northwestern Europe. **Boundaries:** Netherlands to N, Luxembourg and Germany to E, France to S, and North Sea to W. **Total land area:** 11,780 sq. mi. (30,510 sq km). **Coastline:** 40 mi. (64 km). **Comparative area:** slightly larger than Maryland. **Land use:** 25% arable land; 0% permanent crops; 75% other. **Major cities:** Bruxelles (Brussels—capital); Antwerpen (Anvers, Antwerp); Gent (Gand, Ghent); Charleroi; Liège (Luik).
• **PEOPLE Population:** 10,403,951 (July 2008 est.). **Nationality:** noun—Belgian(s); adjective—Belgian. **Ethnic groups:** 58% Fleming, 31% Walloon, 11% mixed or other. **Languages:** 60% Dutch, 40% French, less than 1% German (all three official); legally bilingual (Dutch and French). **Religions:** 75% Roman Catholic, remainder Protestant or other.
• **GOVERNMENT Type:** federal parliamentary democracy under a constitutional monarch. **Independence:** Oct. 4, 1830 (from Netherlands). **Constitution:** Feb. 7, 1831; last revised July 14, 1993. **National holiday:** National Day, July 21. **Heads of Government:** Albert II, king (since Aug. 1993); Yves Leterme, prime minister (since March 2008). **Structure:** executive—king, prime minister, and cabinet; bicameral legislature; independent judiciary.
• **ECONOMY Monetary unit:** euro. **Budget:** (2007 est.) *income:* $217 bil.; *expend.:* $217.4 bil.. **G.D.P.:** $378.9 bil., $36,500 per capita (2007 est.). **Chief crops:** sugar beets, vegetables, fruit, grain. **Natural resources:** coal, natural gas. **Major industries:** engineering, metal products, motor vehicle assembly, processed food, beverages, chemicals. **Labor force:** 5.03 mil. (2007); 73% services, 25% industry; 2% agriculture. **Exports:** $328.1 bil. (f.o.b., 2007); machinery and equipment, chemicals, diamonds. **Imports:** $320.9 bil. (f.o.b., 2007); machinery and equipment, chemicals, metals. **Major trading**

partners: (2006) *exports:* 73% E.U., 8% U.S.; *imports:* 71% E.U., 6% U.S.

The country now known as Belgium was, during the Middle Ages, part of the powerful duchy of Burgundy. By marriage and diplomacy, the "Low Countries" became part of the Habsburg Empire in 1482 (see "Austria"). In a struggle lasting from the late 16th century to the Treaty of Westphalia in 1648, the northern part of that region (Netherlands) became independent, but the southern portion remained part of the Habsburg Empire—under the Spanish branch until 1715, then under the Austrian branch until the French Revolution. The Congress of Vienna attached the lands to an enlarged Kingdom of the Netherlands in 1815.

In 1830 the Belgians revolted against the Dutch, and in 1831 the Treaty of London recognized an independent Kingdom of Belgium. Throughout the 19th century, its unity was precarious, as the country was divided politically between Catholic and Liberal parties, and ethnically between Dutch-speaking Flemings and French-speaking Walloons. In 1885 Belgium became a colonial power in Africa with Leopold II's establishment of the Congo Free State (later the Belgian Congo), which gained independence in 1960 as Zaire.

Belgium was a major battleground during World War I, but its boundaries were reestablished in 1919 by the Treaty of Versailles. When German troops overran Belgium in May 1940, King Leopold III quickly signed an armistice, hoping to placate Hitler and avert further fighting. But the Belgian government fled to England, repudiated the armistice, and joined the Allies. The Germans controlled Belgium until Sept. 1944.

Belgium made a swift postwar recovery. But the political atmosphere was poisoned by the issue of what to do about wartime collaborators up to and including the king. A referendum in 1950 narrowly approved Leopold III's return to the throne, but he was persuaded to abdicate in 1951.

Belgium has a flourishing economy with a modernized industrial sector complemented by tourism and agriculture. The issue of language dominates politics; since the 1960's, Belgium has devolved into a de facto confederation of Flemish-, French-, and German-speaking regions, with Brussels a multilingual region unto itself.

In the May 1995 election, the first under the new decentralized constitution of 1993, the Christian Democrat-Socialist coalition government retained a majority in the Chamber of Representatives. In Aug. 1996, the government was shaken by massive demonstrations against inept police and legal handling of a widespread child prostitution and pornography ring. The "poultry scandal" of early 1999 (the government's tardy reaction to the discovery of dioxin in Belgian meat and dairy products) toppled the coalition of Prime Minister Jean-Luc Dehaene. June 1999 elections to the Chamber of Deputies resulted in a coalition government of Liberals, Socialists and Greens controlling a 19-seat majority under Flemish Liberal premier Guy Verhofstadt. In 2003 Liberals and Socialists formed a coalition government with Verhofstadt still in power. In 2007 he was forced to resign as voters resoundingly voted for a change. But the Flemish leader, Yves Leterme was unable to form a coalition government for more than nine months, and did so in March 2008. Little, however, could be done as the nation seemed on the brink of splitting up along linguistic lines.

▶ **BELIZE**

● **GEOGRAPHY Location:** northeastern coast of Central America. **Boundaries:** Mexico to N, Caribbean Sea to E, Guatemala to S and W. **Total land area:** 8,865 sq. mi. (22,960 sq km). **Coastline:** 240 mi. (386 km). **Comparative area:** between Massachusetts and New Hampshire. **Land use:** 3% arable land; 1% permanent crops; 96% other. **Major cities:** Belmopan (capital); Belize City; Orange Walk; San Ignacio; Corozal.

● **PEOPLE Population:** 301,270 (July 2008 est.). **Nationality:** noun—Belizean(s); adjective—Belizean. **Ethnic groups:** 49% mestizo, 25% Creole, 11% Maya, 6.1% Garifuna. **Languages:** English (official), Spanish, Mayan, Garifuna (Carib). **Religions:** 50% Roman Catholic, 27% Protestant.

● **GOVERNMENT Type:** parliamentary democracy. **Independence:** Sept. 21, 1981 (from U.K.). **Constitution:** Sept. 21, 1981. **National holiday:** Independence Day, Sept. 21. **Heads of Government:** Sir Colville Norbert Young, governor general (since Nov. 1993); Dean Barrow, prime minister (since Feb. 2008). **Structure:** executive—governor general (appointed by Queen Elizabeth II, who is recognized as the head of state), prime minister, cabinet; bicameral legislature; judiciary.

● **ECONOMY Monetary unit:** Belizean dollar. **Budget:** (2007 est.) *income:* $328.5 mil.; *expend.:* $365 mil. **G.D.P.:** $2.336 bil., $7,800 per capita (2007 est.). **Chief crops:** bananas, coca, citrus, sugarcane; cultured shrimp; illegal producer of cannabis for international drug trade. **Natural resources:** arable land potential, timber, fish. **Major industries:** garments, food processing, tourism. **Labor force:** 113,000 (2006 est.); 21.3% agriculture, 13.7% industry, 65% services; shortage of skilled labor and all types of technical personnel; 9.1% unemployment (2007 est.). **Exports:** $437 mil. (f.o.b., 2007 est.); sugar, citrus, bananas, clothing. **Imports:** $670 mil. (f.o.b., 2007 est.); machinery and transportation equipment, manufactured goods, food, fuels, chemicals. **Major trading partners:** (2006) *exports:* 34% U.S., 34% U.K., 4% Cote D'Ivoire; *imports:* 36% U.S., 13% Mexico, 8% Cuba, 7% Guatemala, 4% China.

During the 1700's, Spain held sovereignty over Belize but never attempted to settle it. The British gradually did settle there, however, and in 1862, British Honduras, as it was called, became a Crown colony. Although Britain granted Belize independence in 1981, Guatemala claimed sovereignty over the area until 1992, when it finally recognized Belize's independence. But as British defense forces withdrew in 1994, Guatemala reasserted its old claims but without consequence.

Dean Barrow's opposition United Democratic Party won election in 2008, unseating Said Musa after 10 years.

▶ **BENIN**
Republic of Benin
● **GEOGRAPHY Location:** western coast of Africa. **Boundaries:** Burkina Faso and Niger to N, Nigeria to E, Gulf of Guinea to S, Togo to W. **Total land area:** 43,483 sq. mi. (112,620 sq km). **Coastline:** 75 mi. (121 km). **Comparative area:** between Tennessee and Pennsylvania. **Land use:** 15% arable land; 1% permanent crops; 84% other. **Major cities:** Porto-Novo (capital); Cotonou.

● **PEOPLE Population:** 8,294,941 (July 2008 est.). **Nationality:** noun—Beninese (sing., pl.); adjective— Beninese. **Ethnic groups:** 98.4%

African (predominantly Fon, Adja, Yoruba, Bariba); 1.6% other and European. **Languages:** French (official); Fon and Yoruba in south; at least six major tribal languages in north. **Religions:** 42.8% Christian, 24.4% Muslim, 17.3% Vodoun, 15.5% other.

● **GOVERNMENT Type:** Multiparty democratic republic since Apr. 4, 1991. **Independence:** Aug. 1, 1960 (from France). **Constitution:** Dec. 2, 1990. **National holiday:** National Day, Aug. 1. **Head of Government:** Yayi Boni, head of state (since Apr. 2006). **Structure:** executive—president, executive council; unicameral legislature; judiciary.

● **ECONOMY Monetary unit:** Communauté Financiere Africaine franc. **Budget:** (2007 est.) *income:* $936.9 mil.; *expend.:* $1.23 bil. **G.D.P.:** $12.18 bil., $1,500 per capita (2007 est.). **Chief crops:** corn, cotton, cassava, yams. **Natural resources:** small offshore oil deposits, limestone, marble, timber. **Major industries:** textiles, food processing, beverages. **Labor force:** 5.38 mil. (2007); 33.2% agriculture, 14.5% industry, 52.3% services. **Exports:** $708.7 mil. (f.o.b., 2007); cotton, crude oil, palm products, cocoa. **Imports:** $976.3 mil. (f.o.b., 2007); foodstuffs, beverages, tobacco, petroleum products. **Major trading partners:** (2006) *exports:* India, Italy, China, Indonesia, Thailand; *imports:* China, France, Thailand.

Although the early history of Benin is sketchy, a number of kingdoms had appeared in the region by the 11th century, and it was a center of wealth and power by the 1300's. In the 16th century, the Allada kingdom was founded in the south. In 1625, three brothers divided their power between Allada, Adjatché (Porto Novo), and Abomey. Under Ouegbadja (r. 1645-85) the latter, known as Dahomey, predominated. Much of its wealth derived from contact with Europeans, and especially the slave trade, which continued until 1885.

European contact began with the arrival of the Portuguese in 1485. Although traders and missionaries were established at Ouidah and Porto Novo in the 1500's, European influence remained slight. Dahomey expansion continued well into the 19th century. A commercial treaty with the French was signed in 1842, but relations between Dahomeyans and Europeans soon worsened. Outright hostilities began under Behanzin (r. 1858-89), who was defeated by the French, and in 1893 the French assimilated Abomey, Allada, and Porto Novo into the colony of Dahomey.

Independence from French rule came in 1960, followed by several coups until Mathieu Kerekou came to power in 1972. Kerekou established a Marxist regime, nationalizing large private businesses and abolishing opposition parties.

By December 1989, with the economy in a shambles and most trade conducted on the black market, there were demonstrations calling for Kerekou's resignation. A new constitution was approved in a Nov. 1990 referendum, and Nicéphore Soglo, a former World Bank official, was named prime minister. Soglo defeated the Marxist Kerekou in the 1991 presidential election, and appealed to western nations for a "Marshall Plan" for Africa. But in a rematch four years later, Kerekou regained the presidency. Yet, only three years later, in April elections for the National Assembly, it was Soglo's Renaissance of Benin Party that carried the majority. In March 2001 Kerekou won again over Soglo, this time with 84 percent of the vote. In 2006, neither Kerekou nor Soglo were on the ballot because they were over 70 years old. A development banker, Yayi Boni, won the election handily and turned immediately to economic reforms.

▶ **BHUTAN**
Kingdom of Bhutan
● **GEOGRAPHY Location:** Himalaya Mountains in southern Asia. **Boundaries:** China to N and W, India to S and E. **Total land area:** 18,147 sq. mi. (47,000 sq km). **Coastline:** none. **Comparative area:** between Maryland and West Virginia. **Land use:** 3% arable land; negl. % permanent crops; 97% other. **Major cities:** Timphu (capital).
● **PEOPLE Population:** 682,321 (July 2008 est.). **Nationality:** noun—Bhutanese (sing., pl.); adjective— Bhutanese. **Ethnic groups:** 50% Bhote, 35% ethnic Nepalese, 15% indigenous or migrant tribes. **Languages:** Dzongkha (official), various Tibetan dialects, various Nepalese dialects. **Religions:** 75% Lamaistic Buddhism, 25% Indian- and Nepalese-influenced Hinduism.
● **GOVERNMENT Type:** monarchy; special treaty relationship with India. **Independence:** Aug. 8, 1949 (from India). **Constitution:** no written constitution or bill of rights. **National holiday:** Dec. 17. **Head of Government:** Jigme Singye Wangchuk, king (since July 1972); Lyonchoen J.Y. Thinley, prime minister (since Apr. 2008). **Structure:** executive—king, Royal Advisory Council, Council of Ministers; indirectly elected unicameral National Assembly consisting of 105 village elders, 10 monastic representatives, and 35 designated by the king; judicial—Supreme Court is the king.
● **ECONOMY Monetary unit:** ngultrum, Indian rupee. **Budget:** (2005 est.) *income:* $272 mil.; *expend.:* $350 mil. note - the government of India finances nearly three-fifths of Bhutan's expenditures. **G.D.P.:** $3.503 bil., $1,400 per capita (2006 est.). **Chief crops:** rice, corn, root crops, citrus. **Livestock:** cattle, poultry, pigs, sheep, yaks. **Natural resources:** timber, hydropower, gypsum, calcium carbide. **Major industries:** cement, wood products, fruits. **Labor force:** N.A.; (2007) 24.7% agriculture, 38.1% services, 37.2% industry. **Exports:** $350 mil. (f.o.b., 2006 est.); cardamom, gypsum, timber, handicrafts. **Imports:** $320 mil. (c.i.f., 2006 est.); fuels and lubricants, grain, machinery and parts, vehicles. **Major trading partners:** (2006) *exports:* 54.4% India, 34.6% Hong Kong, 6.9% Bangladesh. *imports:* 76% India, 5.5% Japan, 3.2% Germany.

A Tibetan-style Lamaistic Buddhist theocracy was established in this Himalayan enclave in the 16th century. The region came under the domination of the British raj in India in 1865, and Britain established a protectorate in 1910. A 1949 treaty with India granted independence to Bhutan. The present Druk Gyalpo, or Precious Ruler of the Dragon People, is the fourth in a dynasty dating from 1907. During the early years of his reign, he introduced reforms into this feudal, medieval country by broadening educational opportunities and compelling Buddhist monks to take up social work outside their monasteries.

From 1998 to 1999, King Wangchuk ruled through a rubber-stamp National Assembly, passing a series of laws aimed at driving out Nepalese and Indian settlers even if their families have resided in Bhutan for decades. More than 70,000 refugees have been registered by the U.N. high commissioner for refugees since 1991, and the numbers continue to grow. A "Gorkha Liberation

Movement" has carried out raids in Bhutan from sanctuaries in India and Nepal.

In 1998 King Wangchuk began a second wave of reform, permitting the National Assembly to elect members of the Council of Ministers and even, by two-thirds vote, to call for the King's abdication. 1999 saw a mass amnesty of political prisoners. In late 2007, after 34 years, King Wangchuk announced he was stepping down and that his son, Crown Prince Jigme Kesar Namgyel, would be his successor. In July 2008 a constitution was adopted that established a two-party democracy after nearly a century of absolute monarchy.

▶ BOLIVIA
Republic of Bolivia

• **GEOGRAPHY** **Location:** landlocked country in central South America. **Boundaries:** Brazil to N and E, Paraguay and Argentina to S, Chile and Peru to W. **Total land area:** 424,162 sq. mi. (1,098,580 sq km). **Coastline:** none. **Comparative area:** between Texas and Alaska. **Land use:** 2% arable land; negl. % permanent crops; 98% other. **Major cities:** La Paz (administrative capital); Sucre (legal capital and seat of judiciary); Santa Cruz de la Sierra; Cochabamba; Oruro.
• **PEOPLE** **Population:** 9,247,816 (July 2008 est.). **Nationality:** noun—Bolivian(s); adjective—Bolivian. **Ethnic groups:** 30% Quechua, 25% Aymara, 30% mixed, 15% white. **Languages:** Spanish, Quechua, and Aymara (all official). **Religions:** 95% Roman Catholic; active Protestant minority, especially Methodist.
• **GOVERNMENT** **Type:** republic. **Independence:** Aug, 6, 1825 (from Spain). **Constitution:** Feb. 2, 1967. **National holiday:** Independence Day, Aug. 6. **Head of Government:** Evo Morales, president (since Jan. 2006). **Structure:** executive; bicameral legislature; judiciary.
• **ECONOMY** **Monetary unit:** boliviano. **Budget:** (2007 est.) *income:* $4.1 bil.; *expend.:* $4 bil. **G.D.P.:** $39.78 bil., $4,400 per capita (2007 est.). **Chief crops:** soybeans, coffee, coca, cotton, corn, sugarcane, rice, potatoes. **Natural resources:** tin, natural gas, crude oil, zinc, tungsten. **Major industries:** mining, smelting, petroleum. **Labor force:** 4.79 mil.; 14.5% agriculture, 30.5% industry, 55% services. **Exports:** $4.26 bil. (f.o.b., 2007 est.); soybeans, natural gas, zinc, gold. **Imports:** $3.11 bil. (f.o.b., 2007 est.); capital goods, chemicals, petroleum. **Major trading partners:** (2006) *exports:* 46% Brazil, 11% U.S., 9% Argentina, 7% Colombia. *imports:* 29% Brazil, 16% Argentina, 12% Chile, 9% U.S., 8% Peru.

The Incan Empire conquered the region that is now Bolivia in the 13th century. The Spanish discovered the fabulous silver deposits of the region and established their presence in the area in the cities of Sucre (1538) and Potosí (1545). From the early colonial period on, Bolivia—then called Upper Peru and part of the Viceroyalty of Peru—depended heavily on the export of minerals. The exploitation of tin and later oil and natural gas has had an important economic and political impact on the country's development.

In 1776, Upper Peru was transferred to the new Viceroyalty of La Plata centered in Buenos Aires. Upper Peru began agitating for independence in 1809, but it was not until liberation by Símon Bolívar (for whom the country was renamed) in 1825 that Bolivia became the last Spanish possession in South America to achieve independence. During

1836-39, Peru formed a brief union with Bolivia, until Chile broke up the confederation.

Bolivia has lost much of its original territory to its neighbors. The dictator Mariano Melgarejo sold large chunks of territory from 1865 to 1871. After the War of the Pacific (1879-84), Bolivia lost its access to the sea. And in the 1932-35 Chaco War with Paraguay, Bolivia lost more territory in the east.

Bolivia has suffered from Indian/non-Indian racial and cultural divisions, and political rivalry between the elites from the Potosí region and those from La Paz and Santa Cruz. Conservatives of the silver-mining southern region of Potosí controlled the government until their ouster in 1898 by the Liberal tin interests of the La Paz region, who presided over a period of stable republican politics that lasted until the Great Depression and the Chaco War.

One of the results of the Chaco War was the fragmentation of the Bolivian military into competing factions in the struggle for power between conservative landowners and middle-class reformers. In 1941 the National Revolutionary Movement (MNR) was formed with the aim of transferring control of the country from conservative landowning elites to the middle sectors. The leadership of the movement found itself outpaced by revolts sponsored by workers and peasants; the MNR incorporated these elements into its program. When the 1952 revolution brought the MNR to power, its leadership, which included the future four-time president Victor Paz Estenssoro, embarked on a reformist political program. The military overthrew the MNR in 1964, and civilian rule was not restored until 1982. Paz Estenssoro was again elected to the presidency in 1985. Jaime Paz Zamora, leader of the Movement of the Revolutionary Left, gained the presidency in 1989.

In 1993, MNR candidate Gonzalo Sanchez de Lozada won the presidential election. An advocate of free-market economic reform, as planning minister (1986-88) he had reduced the country's hyperinflation rate from 25,000 percent to 15 percent. Opposition to free-market reforms brought a general strike by the leftist Bolivian Workers' Confederation. The government declared a state of siege in April 1995, and suspended civil liberties. Further privatization plans led to another general strike in 1996, with 50,000 demonstrators in the streets of La Paz. Faced with widespread rioting and looting, the government granted large raises to government employees.

Presidential elections in 1997 led to a run-off (settled in Congress) in which retired general Hugo Banzer Suarez, military dictator from 1971 to 1978, was elected president, pledging to continue economic reforms while ensuring that the poor benefit from the reforms. His government was confronted in April 2000 with nationwide riots over a planned increase in water rates and a general strike by the Workers Confederation. Timely retreats ended the protests. Banzer's resignation in 2001 for reasons of health brought elections in June 2002, with Congress again having to choose between the top two finishers; ex-president Sánchez de Lozada narrowly topped Socialist Evo Morales, head of the coca workers' union. By 2003, general strikes, mass demostrations, and road blocks (occasioned by the government's coca eradication program and proposal for natural gas project) led to Sanchez's resignation and replacement by vice-president Carlos Mesa Gisbert; he too was forced to resign (June 2005) after weeks of violent protests by workers' groups demanding nationalization of the oil and gas industry. Eduardo Rodríguez was chosen as interim president but national elections in Dec. 2005 brought a decisive victory to leftist Evo Morales, a congressman allied with Hugo Chavez and Fidel Castro. In May 2006, Morales ordered the military to occupy the oil and gas fields and gave foreign countries 180 days to renegotiate all existing contracts, which they did.

▶ BOSNIA AND HERZEGOVINA
Republic of Bosnia and Herzegovina
• **GEOGRAPHY Location:** southeastern Europe. **Boundaries:** Croatia to N, W, Yugoslavia to S, E, and SE, Adriatic Sea to SW. **Total land area:** 19,776 sq. mi. (51,233 sq km). **Coastline:** 13 mi. (20 km). **Comparative area:** About half the size of Ohio. **Land use:** 10% arable land; 3% permanent crops; 87% other. **Major cities:** Bosnia: Sarajevo (capital) Banja Luka. Herzegovina: Mostar.
• **PEOPLE Population:** 4,590,310 (July 2008 est.) Note: all population data is subject to considerable error due to dislocations caused by military actions and ethnic cleansing. **Nationality:** noun— Bosnian(s); adjective—Bosnian; noun— Herzegovine(s) or Herzegovinian(s); adjective—Herzegovine or Herzegovinian. **Ethnic groups:** 37% Serb, 48% Bozniak, 14% Croat. **Languages:** Croatian, Serbian, Bosnian. **Religions:** 40% Muslim, 31% Orthodox, 15% Catholic, 4% Protestant, 10% other.
• **GOVERNMENT Type:** emerging democracy. **Independence:** Mar. 1, 1992. **Constitution:** Dayton agreement, signed Dec. 1995, included a new constitution now in force. **National holiday:** National Day, Nov. 25 **Heads of Government:** Nebojsa Radmanovic, president (since Nov. 2006); Nikola Spiric, prime minister (since Feb. 2007). **Structure:** executive— 3-member rotating presidency, prime minister, cabinet; bicameral legislature; judiciary.
• **ECONOMY Monetary unit:** convertible mark. **Budget:** (2007 est.) *income:* $6.95 bil.; *expend.:* $7.09 bil. **G.D.P.:** $29.9 bil.; $6,600 per capita (2007 est.). **Chief crops:** corn, wheat, fruits, vegetables; livestock. **Natural resources:** coal, iron, bauxite, manganese, timber. **Major industries:** steel production, mining, manufacturing, armaments. **Labor force:** 1.026 mil (2002 est.). **Exports:** $3.92 bil. (f.o.b., 2007 est.). **Imports:** $9.29 bil. (f.o.b., 2007 est.). **Major trading partners:** (2006) *exports:* 19.6% Croatia, 16.8% Slovenia, 15.3% Italy, 12.3% Germany, 8.7% Austria, 5.3% Hungary; *imports:* 24% Croatia, 14.5% Germany, 13.2% Slovenia, 10% Italy, 5.9% Austria, 5.2% Hungary.

Bosnia-Herzegovina has been in the middle of European power struggles since the 14th century. Its constantly changing boundaries have meant that its population has always been a hodgepodge of races and ethnicities. The name Bosnia comes from the region's geographic location on the Bosna River; Herzegovina was originally an Austrian border duchy (Herzog means "duke" in German). The two lands were conquered by the Ottoman Empire in the 15th century, Bosnia in 1463, Herzegovina 20 years later. The conquered peoples, united into one administrative district by the Turks, were Roman Catholic Croatians and Orthodox Serbs. Over the centuries, a number of Slavic families, Croatians more than Serbs, gave up their Christianity and adopted the religion of their conquerors: Islam.

A peasant uprising (1875) over Turkish refusal to institute reforms ultimately led to the Russo-Turkish War of 1877-78. In 1878, the Congress of Berlin put Bosnia-Herzegovina under the control of Austria-Hungary. Sarajevo, the capital city, was the birthplace of World War I, where a Serbian nationalist assassinated the Austro-Hungarian archduke Francis Ferdinand in 1914. By 1918, Serbia had annexed Bosnia-Herzegovina and held it until World War II, when Germany incorporated it into the state of Croatia. In 1946, Bosnia-Herzegovina was made one of Yugoslavia's six constituent republics, along with Serbia, Croatia, Slovenia, Montenegro, and Macedonia.

The constant redrawing of Bosnia-Herzegovina's borders has meant that ethnicity in the region came to be based on religion, rather than national origin. Thus a Serb who converted to Roman Catholic Christianity was considered a Croatian, while a Croatian who converted to Eastern Orthodoxy was considered a Serb. And to both groups, converts to Islam appeared to be collaborators with the Ottoman Turks.

Nevertheless, the three ethnic groups coexisted peacefully under the iron hand of president-for-life Marshall Tito (Josip Broz). And even after Tito's death in 1980, his rotating presidency scheme, in which the leaders of each republic took turns serving as "president of the presidency," worked smoothly, as long as Yugoslavia was dominated by communism. At times, the president was a Muslim, the prime minister was a Croatian, and the president of the Assembly was a Serb. But when communism fell in 1989, only Serbia and Montenegro returned Communist governments to power; the other four republics established non- and even anti-Communist governments, and quickly sought to establish political independence from the ultra-Marxist regime of Serbian president Slobodan Milosevic.

Milosevic rigged elections in the provinces of Kosovo and Vojvodina to keep them under Serbian control, but he was unsuccessful in ethnically Serbian areas of Slovenia, Croatia, and Bosnia-Herzegovina. Croatia and Slovenia declared their independence in 1991, forcing Bosnia to choose between independence or a diminished role in a Serb-dominated Yugoslavia.

Bosnia-Herzegovina voted for independence in March 1992. But the mostly Serbian military of the former Yugoslavian army refused to go along with the vote. Led by Radovan Karadzic, they gained control of the region's artillery and proclaimed the existence of the "Serbian Republic of Bosnia-Herzegovina." The siege of Sarajevo began in April, with Serbia waging a ferocious war of "ethnic cleansing," to rid Bosnia of Muslims and Croats. By July 1993, the Serbs had surrounded the city, and despite evidence that the Serbs were raping and torturing Muslims, the Bosnian Parliament in Sept. 1993 rejected a U.N.-sponsored peace plan that would have ended the war.

Several other cease-fire agreements were brokered, but none led to a lasting peace until a 1995 pact brokered by U.S. negotiator Richard Holbrooke, in which the Bosnian Serbs agreed to follow the decisions of Yugoslavia's president Slobodan Milosevic in all peace talks. On Nov. 21, 1995, the presidents of Bosnia-Herzegovina, Croatia, and Serbia met in Dayton, Ohio, to sign a peace accord ending the civil war and dividing Bosnia-Herzegovina into two entities: a Serb republic and a Muslim-Croat federation. The two statelets would be governed by the same legislature and president.

The U.N. sent 60,000 peacekeeping troops in Dec. 1995 to supervise the transition. Elections in Sept. 1996 selected a three-member collective presidency, and a legislature whose 42 members were selected in two separate elections. In Jan. 1997, parliament approved a cabinet with joint (Serb and Muslim) premiers.

Yugoslavia and Bosnia established diplomatic relations in Oct. 1996, with Yugoslavia agreeing to respect Bosnia's boundaries while Bosnia dropped charges of genocide. A new crisis arose when on the same day (March 5, 1999), the West's "High Authority" (under the Dayton Accords) deposed the President of the Serb Republic, who had just been elected, while a Western arbitrator awarded the strategic Sava River town of Brcko to the Moslem-Croat Federation, resulting in the Serb republic's effective withdrawal from Bosnia-Herzegovnia. Through 2000 and 2001 incidents of friction continued, provoking interventions by the High Authority and NATO troops,· which themselves became sources of tension and even riots. In Oct. 2002, elections of bewildering complexity were held: for the three-man presidency, for the federation's parliament, and for the parliaments of the two member republics, with 57 parties taking part. Where true authority lay was made clear in 2003 as Chairman of the Presidency Mirko Sarovic resigned before he could be sacked by the High Commissioner who, in the same month, transferred control of the armed forces from the republics to the central authority. In Nov. 2005 the leaders of Serbian, Croatian and Muslim factors pledged to work toward a new constitution to create a stronger government, and in Sept. 2006, citizens of all three communities held elections and in Feb. 2007, a new prime minister was chosen.

▶BOTSWANA
Republic of Botswana
• **Geography** **Location:** landlocked country in southern Africa. **Boundaries:** Namibia to N and W, Zimbabwe to NE, South Africa to SE and S. **Total land area:** 231,803 sq. mi. (600,370 sq km). **Coastline:** none. **Comparative area:** about size of Texas. **Land use:** 1% arable land; negl.% permanent crops; 99% other. **Major cities:** Gaborone (capital); Francistown; Selebi-Phikwe; Molepolole; Serowe.
• **People** **Population:** 1,842,323 (July 2008 est.). **Nationality:** noun and adjective—Motswana (sing.), Batswana (pl.). **Ethnic groups:** 79% Tswana, 11% Kalanga, 3% Basarwa, 7% other. **Languages:** English (official), Setswana. **Religions:** 20.6% none, 71.6% Christian, 6% Badimo, 1.4% other.
• **Government** **Type:** parliamentary republic. **Independence:** Sept. 30, 1966 (from U.K.). **Constitution:** Mar. 1965, effective Sept. 30, 1966. **National holiday:** Independence Day, Sept. 30. **Head of Government:** Seretse Khama Ian Khama, president (since Apr. 2008). **Structure:** executive; bicameral legislature; judiciary.
• **Economy** **Monetary unit:** pula. **Budget:** (2007 est.) *income:* $4.886 bil.; *expend.:* $3.756 bil. **G.D.P.:** $24.14 bil., $14,700 per capita (2007 est.). **Chief crops:** sorghum, maize, millet, peanuts. **Natural resources:** diamonds, copper, nickel, coal, gold, salt, soda ash. **Major industries:** diamonds, copper, nickel, coal, salt, soda ash, potash. **Labor force:** (2004) 288,400 formal sector employees; 23.8% unemployment (2004 est.). **Exports:** $4.798 bil. (f.o.b., 2007 est.); diamonds, copper and nickel, meat. **Imports:** $2.766 bil. (f.o.b., 2007 est.); foodstuffs, vehicles, textiles, petroleum products. **Major trading partners:** (2006) *exports:* 87% European Free Trade Association (EFTA), 7% South African Customs Union (SACU), 3% Zimbabwe; *imports:* 74% SACU, 17% EFTA, 4% Zimbabwe.

Botswana, occupying a high and relatively arid tableland in southern Africa, was traditionally occupied by diverse groups of farmers, pastoralists, and hunter-gatherers. European missionaries arrived from South Africa in the early 19th century. In the late 19th century, native peoples resisted the encroachment of Afrikaners from the Transvaal; in response the British government established a protectorate in what was then called Bechuanaland in 1886. The southern part of the protectorate was organized as a Crown Colony and ultimately passed under the control of South Africa. During the 20th century, the territory remaining in the protectorate saw a steady evolution of local rule.

In 1920 two advisory councils were established to represent the interests of native and European inhabitants. In 1934 British authorities promulgated regulations establishing the powers and jurisdictions of native chiefs and the functions of native councils and courts. In 1951 a joint (native-European) advisory council was set up, and 10 years later an elected legislature met under the provisions of a new constitution.

In 1963-64 the British government accepted Botswanan proposals for self-government. A new capital was established at Gaborone in February 1965; a new constitution came into effect in the following month, and Botswana became fully independent on Sept. 30, 1966. Since independence, Botswana has been a multiparty, multiracial democracy that has remained untouched by the political turmoil affecting most of its neighbors. In National Assembly elections since 1998, voters have given the Botswana Democratic Party and President Festus Mogae strong margins of victory.

In 2008 Mogae was succeeded by Seretse Khama Ian Khama, son of Botswana's first president.

Botswana is one of the most prosperous countries in Africa. It is the world's largest producer of diamonds; revenues from diamond exports have been wisely managed, leading to significant budgetary surpluses in recent years. Tourism, bolstered by Botswana's large herds of big game, is the country's major nonmining industry. But the nation's AIDS epidemic (30 percent of the adult population was infected with H.I.V.) had threatened to undermine the gains made over the past three decades, until a very advanced treatment program was introduced in 2005.

▶BRAZIL
Federative Republic of Brazil
• **Geography** **Location:** central and northeastern South America. **Boundaries:** Colombia, Venezuela, Guyana, Suriname, French Guiana to N; Atlantic Ocean to E; Uruguay, Argentina, Paraguay to S; Peru, Bolivia to W. **Total land area:** 3,286,475 sq. mi. (8,511,965 sq km). **Coastline:** 4,652 mi. (7,491 km). **Comparative area:** slightly smaller than U.S. **Land use:** 6% arable land; 1% permanent crops; 93% other. **Major cities:** Brasília (capital); São Paulo; Rio de Janeiro; Belo Horizonte; Salvador.

• **PEOPLE** **Population:** 191,908,598 (July 2008 est.). **Nationality:** noun—Brazilian(s); adjective—Brazilian. **Ethnic groups:** Portuguese, Italian, German, Japanese, black, Amerindian; 53.7% white, 38% mixed, 6% black, 1% other. **Languages:** Portuguese (official), Spanish, English, French. **Religions:** 73.6% Roman Catholic, 15.4% Protestant, 2.6% other, 7.4% none.
• **GOVERNMENT** **Type:** federative republic. **Independence:** Sept. 7, 1822 (from Portugal). **Constitution:** Oct. 5, 1988. **National holiday:** Independence Day, Sept. 7. **Head of Government:** Luiz Inácio Lula da Silva, president (since Jan. 2003). **Structure:** strong executive with broad powers; bicameral legislature with growing powers; judiciary.
• **ECONOMY** **Monetary unit:** real. **Budget:** (2007) *income:* $244 bil.; *expend.:* $220 bil. **G.D.P.:** $1.84 tril., $9,700 per capita (2007 est.). **Chief crops:** coffee, soybeans, wheat, rice; beef. **Natural resources:** bauxite, gold, iron ore, manganese, nickel. **Major industries:** textiles and other consumer goods, shoes, chemicals. **Labor force:** 99.5 mil. (2007 est.); 66% services, 20% agriculture, 14% industry (2003 est.); 9.8% unemployment (2007 est.). **Exports:** $159.2 bil. (f.o.b., 2007); iron ore, soybean bran, orange juice, footwear. **Imports:** $115.6 bil. (f.o.b., 2007); capital goods, chemical products, oil, electricity. **Major trading partners:** (2006) *exports:* 17.8% U.S., 6.1% China, 8.5% Argentina, 4.2% Netherlands, 4.1% Germany; *imports:* 16.2% U.S., 8.8% Argentina, 8.7% China, 7.1% Germany, 4.3% Nigeria, 4.2% Japan.

The Portuguese arrived on the coast of what would become Brazil with the expedition of Pedro Alvares Cabral in 1500 and found an indigenous population of semisedentary and nonsedentary cultures. Many of the semisedentary Indians spoke the Tupian language and shared similar cultural features. The Tupians quickly formed economic relationships with the first Europeans, who were interested in the valuable dyewood that was so abundant in Brazil.

The transition of Indian-European economic relations from barter to slavery was given momentum by the introduction of sugar export agriculture, a trend that began in the region in the 1540's. The 1560's saw epidemics of smallpox and measles in the coastal areas, which greatly reduced the indigenous population. Although the European sugar growers initially favored the use of indigenous peoples over imported African slave labor, the shortage of labor resulting from the epidemics led to increasing use of African slave labor by the Portuguese.

The Portuguese vied with other European powers for control of Brazilian territory, and in 1630 the Dutch briefly seized the northeastern sugar-growing area. Brazil's southern regions were underpopulated during the early colonial period, and Portuguese activity was largely limited to cattle raising. With the discovery of gold (1690's) and diamonds (1729), European settlement of the Minas Gerais area in the southeast quickened.

In 1808, the Portuguese royal court escaped Napoleon's armies with the help of the British fleet; the prince regent, Dom João VI, sought refuge in Brazil and made it the seat of the Portuguese empire. Dom João returned to Portugal in 1821, leaving his son Dom Pedro behind as prince regent. In 1822, defying orders to return to Portugal and opposed to the reversion of Brazil to colonial status, Dom Pedro declared Brazil's independence and was crowned emperor. In 1825 an agreement mediated by the British led to Portuguese recognition of Brazil as a separate kingdom.

Dom Pedro became increasingly estranged from his people and began losing control of the Brazilian political situation owing to a continuing series of landowner revolts and to the loss of a war with the United Provinces of Rio de la Plata over what would become Uruguay. In 1831 Dom Pedro abdicated in favor of his five-year-old son, Dom Pedro II; a regency governed Brazil until his accession to the throne in 1840.

The Brazilian empire found itself continually involved in the wars and internal politics of Uruguay, Argentina, and Paraguay in the 1850's and 1860's. The bloody five-year war with Paraguay that began in 1865 resulted in Paraguay's eventual defeat, but the process of the war had important consequences for the future of Brazil: the expansion of military power, the fragmentation of the political party system, and the undermining of the legitimacy of slavery. Slavery was abolished in 1888, and the following year, a military coup overthrew the emperor.

The "Old Republic," which lasted from 1889 to 1930, was a federal system in which much of the political control in Brazilian society was relegated to state-based political networks with local bosses. The presidency was assigned in a de facto rotation system called the "politics of the governors," in which the president's office was controlled by the most important state power networks. The world depression of 1929 hit the Brazilian agricultural export economy hard, and in 1930 the military overthrew the elected president; Getúlio Vargas, a politician from the state of Rio Grande do Sul, took over the presidency.

Vargas centralized power in the presidency. Civil unrest allowed Vargas to declare a state of siege with military backing, and in 1937 established the Estado Novo, a state wherein Vargas had absolute power. The military ousted Vargas in 1945, ushering in the period of the "Second Republic." but Vargas won re-election in 1950; he committed suicide in 1954. Juscelino Kubitschek, elected president in 1955, sought to develop the country and led the way for construction of the new capital of Brasília.

His successor, Jânio da Silva Quadros, resigned in 1961 after only seven months in office, and the presidency passed to populist Vice Pres. João Goulart. The populist mobilization of peasants and workers endorsed by the Goulart government led to his overthrow by the military in 1964.

The Brazilian military governed the country until 1985. Military rule was not maintained in the form of a dictatorship; rather, the military ruled as a more or less cohesive institution. The succession of generals and their technocratic allies attempted to develop the country through a pattern of state-led growth from which civilian politics were excluded. In 1985, Tancredo Neves was elected president, but he died before taking office. José Sarney, the vice presidential candidate, became Brazil's first civilian president since 1964.

Promising to revitalize the economy with a free-market revolution, conservative Fernando Collor de Mello became president in 1990. The military's share of the budget was reduced from 6 to 2.2 percent, and some companies were privatized, but inflation and debt still strained the economy. The

1988 murder of environmental activist Chico Mendes had focused world attention on the rapidly accelerating deforestation of the Amazon River basin. Pres. Collor campaigned actively to halt the destruction and in June 1992 Rio De Janeiro was the site of a U.N.-sponsored conference on development and the environment.

Pres. Collor was forced to resign in Dec. 1992 because of charges he stole or misappropriated over $20 million (after a two-year investigation he was cleared of all charges). His successor, Vice Pres. Itamar Franco, worked to privatize industries and halt inflation, but a new corruption scandal involving at least 18 members of the legislature halted most government activity in 1994.

In presidential elections held in Oct. 1994, former finance minister Fernando Henrique Cardoso ran on an anti-inflation platform and won a landslide victory. The Cardoso government focused on establishing federal control over state banks and supporting land reform for peasants. The rewards were a dramatic drop in both inflation and unemployment and great popularity for Cardoso. In 1997 Congress passed a Constitutional Amendment permitting Cardoso to run for a second term.

In Oct. 1998 Cardoso easily won re-election. Despite an unexpected 1999 devaluation of the *real*, the I.M.F. released the remainder of its 1998 aid package. But Cardoso's popularity plummeted and in 2002 elections leftist Luiz Inacio Lula da Silva swamped Cardoso-backed Jose Serra in the presidential run-off, while his Workers' Party won a plurality in the Chamber of Deputies. The new president surprised everyone by quickly initiating reforms of the social security system and the public workers' pension plan. The economy which had picked up nicely turned tepid in early 2005; then a serious political scandal involving corruption charges brought the government to the brink of dissolution. But Lula survived and won a landslide victory in Oct. 2006 elections.

▶BRUNEI
Negara Brunei Darussalam
• **GEOGRAPHY Location:** southeastern Asia, Kalimantan (Borneo) island. Bandar Seri Begawan 4°56'N, 114°58'E. **Boundaries:** surrounded on landward side by Sarawak, state, of Malaysia; South China Sea to N. **Total land area:** 2,228 sq. mi. (5,770 sq km). **Coastline:** 100 mi. (161 km). **Comparative area:** slightly larger than Delaware. **Land use:** 1% arable land; 1% permanent crops; 98% other. **Major cities:** Bandar Seri Begawan (formerly Brunei Town) (capital); Seria, Kuala Belait, Tutong.
• **PEOPLE Population:** 381,371 (July 2008 est.). **Nationality:** noun—Bruneian(s); adjective—Bruneian. **Ethnic groups:** 67% Malay, 15% Chinese, 6% indigenous, 12% other. **Languages:** Malay (official), English, Chinese. **Religions:** 67% Muslim (official), 13% Buddhist, 10% Christian, 10% indigenous and other.
• **GOVERNMENT Type:** constitutional sultanate. **Independence:** Jan. 1, 1984 (from U.K.). **Constitution:** Sept. 29, 1959 (some provisions suspended since Dec. 1962, others since independence). **National holiday:** National Day, Feb. 23. **Head of Government:** Sir Hassanal Bolkiah Mu'izzaddin Waddaulah, sultan and prime minister (since Aug. 1968). **Structure:** chief of state is sultan; unicameral legislature; judiciary.
• **ECONOMY Monetary unit:** bruneian dollar. **Budget:** (2004 est.) *income:* $3.765 bil.; *expend.:* $4.815 bil. **G.D.P.:** $9.58 bil. (2007 est.), $33,600 per

capita (2005 est.). **Chief crops:** rice, cassava, bananas. **Natural resources:** petroleum, natural gas, timber. **Major Industries:** petroleum, petroleum refining, liquefied natural gas, construction. **Labor force:** 180,400 (2006 est.); 2.9% agriculture, 61.1 industry, 36% services (2003 est.). **Exports:** $6.77 bil. (f.o.b., 2006 est.); crude oil, natural gas, petroleum products. **Imports:** $2 bil. (c.i.f., 2006 est.); machinery and transport equipment, manufactured goods, foodstuffs, chemicals. **Major trading partners:** (2006) *exports:* 30.5% Japan, 19.9% Indonesia, 14.9% South Korea, 11.5% Australia, 7.7% U.S.; *imports:* 31.4% Singapore, 18.4% Malaysia, 8% U.K., 5.5% Japan, 5.4% China, 4.5% Thailand.

The Islamic sultanate of Brunei became dominant in northern Borneo in the 16th century but declined in power after the 17th century under pressure from the Dutch and other foreign powers. An Anglo-Dutch agreement of 1824 assigned North Borneo to Great Britain's sphere of influence in Asia. In 1841 a British adventurer, James Brooke, aided the sultan of Brunei in putting down a rebellion and was rewarded by being given the province of Sarawak, comprising more than half of the sultanate's area. Britain established a protectorate over Sabah, the eastern portion of Brunei, in 1881. That left the sultan with a tiny realm on the Brunei River, which was ultimately placed under British protection in 1888. The discovery of Southeast Asia's richest oilfield in Brunei and its offshore waters made the sultanate an enclave of tremendous wealth from the late 1920's onward.

Following Japanese occupation during World War II, British rule resumed in North Borneo. Sarawak and Sabah became part of Malaysia in 1963. Brunei was granted independence from Great Britain on Dec. 1, 1984. The sultan of Brunei, an absolute monarch, rules from the world's largest royal palace in Bandar Seri Begawan, the nation's capital. The economy is centered almost entirely on petroleum and international banking and investments.

▶BULGARIA
Republic of Bulgaria
• **GEOGRAPHY Location:** southeastern Europe. **Boundaries:** Romania to N, Black Sea to E, Turkey and Greece to S, Macedonia and Yugoslavia to W. **Total land area:** 42,822 sq. mi. (110,910 sq km). **Coastline:** 220 mi. (354 km). **Comparative area:** between Tennessee and Pennsylvania. **Land use:** 39% arable land; 2% permanent crops; 59% other. **Major cities:** Sofia (capital); Plovdiv; Varna; Burges; Ruse.
• **PEOPLE Population:** 7,262,675 (July 2008 est.). **Nationality:** noun—Bulgarian(s); adjective—Bulgarian. **Ethnic groups:** 83.9% Bulgarian, 9.4% Turk, 4.7% Roma, 2% other. **Languages:** Bulgarian, Turkish, Roma. **Religions:** 82.6% Bulgarian Orthodox, 12.2% Muslim, 1.2% Christian, 4% other.
• **GOVERNMENT Type:** parliamentary democracy. **Independence:** March 3, 1878 (from Ottoman Empire). **Constitution:** July 12, 1991. **National holiday:** Independence Day, Mar. 3. **Heads of Government:** Georgi Parvanov, president (since Jan. 2002); Sergei Stanishev, prime minister (since Aug. 2005). **Structure:** executive; unicameral legislature; judiciary.
• **ECONOMY Monetary unit:** lev. **Budget:** (2007 est.) *income:* $16.62 bil.; *expend:* $15.18 bil. **G.D.P.:** $86.73 bil., $11,800 per capita (2007 est.).

Chief crops: vegetables, fruits, tobacco; livestock. **Natural resources:** bauxite, copper, lead, zinc, coal. **Major industries:** machine building and metal working, food processing, chemicals. **Labor force:** 3.44 mil. (2007); 33.6% industry, 8.5% agriculture, 57.9% services. **Exports:** $19.77 bil. (f.o.b., 2007 est.); machinery and equipment, metals and ores, chemicals and plastics, food, textiles. **Imports:** $28.79 bil. (f.o.b., 2007 est.); fuels, minerals, and raw materials; machinery and equipment; food; textiles and apparel. **Major trading partners:** (2006) *exports:* 11.6% Turkey, 10.1% Italy, 9.6% Germany, 8% Greece; *imports:* 15% Germany, 10.6% Italy, 7.2% Turkey, 6.3% Greece, 5% China, 4.9% France, 4.5% Romania.

Turkic Bulgars arrived at the west shore of the Black Sea in the seventh century, mingling with the indigenous Slavic population. The Bulgars accepted Eastern Orthodox Christianity in the ninth century and were conquered and incorporated into the Byzantine Empire by Basil II in the late 10th century. With the decline of Byzantium, Bulgaria became independent, but it was conquered by the Ottoman Turks in 1396 and remained part of the Ottoman Empire for the next 500 years.

In the Treaty of San Stefano, ending the Russo-Turkish War in 1878, a Bulgarian state was promised that was to stretch from the Adriatic to the Black Sea. But the Great Powers would not permit so large a Russian client state, and instead the Berlin Conference of 1878 sanctioned a much smaller Bulgarian state, under a German dynasty with the Ottoman sultan as nominal overlord. Bulgaria gained full independence in 1908.

The Balkan Wars of 1912 and 1913 led to a reduction of Bulgarian territory, and after World War I, Bulgaria, which had been allied with the Central Powers, lost its Aegean Coastline to Greece. A series of weak parliamentary governments under King Boris III (r. 1918-43) ended when the king established a dictatorship in 1935. Bulgaria joined the Axis powers in 1941 and declared war against the Western powers but not against Russia.

Russian troops entered Bulgaria in 1944 and organized a Communist government. The boy-king Simeon II remained on the throne until 1946, when the monarchy was abolished by a popular referendum. The People's Republic of Bulgaria was established in 1947.

Until the end of World War II, Bulgaria was a peasant society, with 80 percent of the population engaged in agriculture; industrial development was rudimentary. The People's Republic established a planned economy on the Soviet model; Russian credits and trade agreements permitted a rapid industrialization focused on machinery and equipment for export.

In 1954 Todor Zhivkov became first secretary of the Bulgarian Communist party. He served as premier in the 1960's and president from 1971 to 1990. In the 1960's Zhivkov promoted decentralization and responsiveness to market forces, but with the 1968 Russian invasion of Czechoslovakia, he returned the economy to central planning, collective farming, and giant state-industrial enterprises. In October 1985 Zhivkov met with Gorbachev and reforms based on Gorbachev's "self-management" policies were instituted.

Democratic reform began with Zhivkov's resignation in Nov. 1989. There followed a year of popular unrest and political turmoil with a succession of changes in the ruling hierarchy, culminating in the election of Zheliu Zhelev of the reform Union of Democratic Forces as president (Bulgaria's first non-Communist leader in 40 years), and the appointment in 1990 of Dimitar Popov as premier of a coalition government dominated by the Socialist (formerly Communist) party.

Elections in October 1991 ended the Socialist grip on power, as the Union of Democratic Forces formed a government under Philip Dimitrov. But within a year the government was bankrupt, inflation at 30 percent and unemployment 40 percent, and Dimitrov's government was ousted by Parliament. Lyuben Berov, an economic adviser to Zhelev, came to power for two years and then he was ousted in elections (Dec. 1994) by the Socialists, led by Zhan Videnov.

Under the Videnov-Zhelev "gridlock," matters only grew worse, with a food crisis developing atop growing unemployment and 300 percent inflation in 1996. Protests and riots marked the latter half of 1996, and in the Nov. presidential elections, the UDF candidate, Peter Stoyanov (who defeated Zhelev in a party primary) won easily. And in the April 1997 elections to parliament, the UDF coalition took 137 seats to the Socialists 58. With the promise of economic reform, the I.M.F. and the E.U. provided large new grants.

The new prime minister, Ivan Kostov, commenced some serious reforms of the all-but-insolvent economy, reforms that were on the one hand painful and on the other not radical enough to rid the economy of state control. Bulgaria's last king, Simeon II, founded a political party which in parliamentary elections won half the seats and transformed the one-time king into the Republic's new prime minister who pushed Bulgaria into NATO and later the E.U. In 2005, his party was forced into a coalition with the socialist party led by Sergei Stanishev.

▶ BURKINA FASO

● **GEOGRAPHY Location:** landlocked country in western Africa. **Boundaries:** Mali to N and W, Niger to E, Benin, Togo, Ghana, Ivory Coast to S. **Total land area:** 105,869 sq. mi. (274,200 sq km). **Coastline:** none. **Comparative area:** between Colorado and Nevada. **Land use:** 12% arable land; negl.% permanent crops; 88% other. **Major cities:** Ouagadougou (capital); Bobo-Dioulasso; Koudougou; Ouahigouya; Banfora.

● **PEOPLE Population:** 15,264,735 (July 2008 est.). **Nationality:** noun—Burkinabe (sing., pl.); adjective—Burkinabe. **Ethnic groups:** over 40% Mossi; Gurunsi, Senufo, Lobi, Bobo, Mande, Fulani. **Languages:** French (official); native African languages spoken by 90% of population. **Religions:** 50% Muslim, 40% indigenous beliefs, 10% Christian (mainly Roman Catholic).

● **GOVERNMENT Type:** parliamentary. **Independence:** Aug. 5, 1960 (from France). **Constitution:** June 2, 1991. **National holiday:** Republic Day, Dec. 11. **Heads of Government:** Blaise Compaore, president (since Dec. 1991); Tertius Zongo, prime minister (since June 2007). **Structure:** executive; bicameral legislature; judiciary.

● **ECONOMY Monetary unit:** Communaué Financière Africaine (CFA) franc. **Budget:** (2007 est.) *income:* $1.31 bil.; *expend.:* $1.76 bil. **G.D.P.:**

$17.5 bil., $1,200 per capita (2007 est.). **Chief crops:** peanuts, shea nuts, sesame, cotton. **Natural resources:** manganese, limestone, marble; small deposits of gold, antimony, copper, nickel, bauxite. **Major industries:** cotton, beverages, agricultural processing. **Labor force:** 5 mil. (2003); 90% agriculture; a large part of male labor force migrates to neighboring countries for seasonal employment. **Exports:** $676 mil. (f.o.b., 2007 est.); cotton, gold, animal products. **Imports:** $1.39 bil. (f.o.b., 2007 est.); machinery, food products, petroleum. **Major trading partners:** (2006) *exports:* 42% China, 14% Singapore, 6% Ghana, 5% Thailand, 4% Nigeria; *imports:* 26% Cote D'Ivoire, 23% France, 7% Togo.

The Mossi empire dominated the area of what is now Burkina Faso, a landlocked nation in western Africa with few natural resources and poor agricultural conditions, from as early as the 11th century. They ruled the region, often resisting Muslim invaders, until modern times.

The region was hardly visited by Europeans before the 1880's, but by 1896 the French had captured the Mossi capital city of Ouagadougou and established a protectorate over the area. The French created Upper Volta in 1919, naming it for the upper basin of the Volta River. Upper Volta became a self-governing state with the French Overseas Community in 1958 and gained independence Aug. 5, 1960.

After a brief period of military rule, the nation ratified a new constitution on June 14, 1970, and made a peaceful transition to civilian rule based on the French model. In 1980 the constitution was overthrown and a military government was set up. There was another coup on Aug. 4, 1983, and a government was established patterned after the Libyan government of Muammar al-Qaddafi. On Aug. 14, 1984, Upper Volta officially changed its name to Burkina Faso.

Two attempted coups against the government of Capt. Blaise Compaore, in September and December 1989, were put down and the leaders executed. In 1992, as president, Compaore convened a National Reconciliation Forum followed by legislative elections that resulted in a new prime minister. In 1994 the World Bank reported significant economic progress in this desperately poor country. Compaore won two more elections, the last in 2005.

▶ BURUNDI
Republic of Burundi

• GEOGRAPHY **Location:** landlocked country on northeastern shore of Lake Tanganyika in central Africa. **Boundaries:** Rwanda to N, Tanzania to E and S, Zaire to W. **Total land area:** 10,745 sq. mi. (27,830 sq km). **Coastline:** none. **Comparative area:** slightly larger than Maryland. **Land use:** 30% arable land; 13% permanent crops; 57% other. **Major cities:** Bujumbura (capital); Gitega. • PEOPLE **Population:** 8,691,005 (July 2008 est.). **Nationality:** noun—Burundian(s); adjective—Burundi. **Ethnic groups:** 85% Hutu (Bantu), 14% Tutsi (Hamitic), 1% Twa (Pygmy), 3,000 Europeans, 2,000 South Asians. **Languages:** Kirundi and French (both official), Swahili (along Lake Tanganyika and in Bujumbura area). **Religions:** 67% Christian (62% Roman Catholic, 5% Protestant), 23% indigenous beliefs, 10% Muslim. • GOVERNMENT **Type:** republic. **Independence:** July 1, 1962 (from U.N. trusteeship under Belgian administration). **Constitution:** Mar. 13, 1992. **National holiday:** Independence Day, July 1. **Heads of Government:** Pierre Nkurunziza, president (since June, 2005); **Structure:** executive; unicameral legislature; judiciary. (Note: a military government took office during a 1996 coup, but the new leadership has not been officially recognized.) • ECONOMY **Monetary unit:** Burundi franc. **Budget:** (2007 est.) *income:* $259.4 mil; *expend.:* $331.8 mil. **G.D.P.:** $6.39 bil., $800 per capita (2007 est.). **Chief crops:** coffee, cotton, tea, corn, sorghum. **Natural resources:** nickel, uranium, rare earth oxide, peat, cobalt. **Major industries:** light consumer goods such as blankets, shoes, soap; assembly of imported components; public works construction. **Labor force:** (2002 est.) 2.99 mil.; 93% agriculture, 7% other. **Exports:** $74.17 mil. (f.o.b., 2007); coffee, tea, cotton, hides. **Imports:** $340.2 mil. (f.o.b., 2007); capital goods, petroleum products, foodstuffs. **Major trading partners:** (2006) *exports:* 33.7% Switzerland, 12.2% U.K., 8.5% Pakistan, 5.3% Rwanda, 4.2% Egypt; *imports:* 12.6% Saudi Arabia, 8.2% Kenya, 7.8% Japan, 4.7% Russia, 4.6% U.K., 4.4% France, 4.4% China.

Burundi's population is divided between two ethnic groups, the majority Hutu and the minority, but politically powerful, Tutsi. The Hutu were the original settlers of the country and practiced agriculture; the cattle-herding Tutsi arrived several hundred years ago and established a form of feudal overlordship over the Hutu. The traditional government was monarchical, with a king (mwami) chosen from among a group of aristocratic families (ganwa).

European exploration of Burundi began in 1858, and the territory was incorporated into German East Africa in 1899. Following World War I, the League of Nations (1923) awarded Burundi, along with neighboring Rwanda, to Belgium as a mandated territory. Belgian rule over the Territory of Ruanda-Urundi, as it was then called, continued under a U.N. trusteeship after World War II.

Burundi became independent on July 1, 1962, as a constitutional monarchy under the traditional mwami. The country rapidly lapsed into political chaos. In 1966 Capt. Michel Micombero overthrew the monarchy and proclaimed a republic. A Hutu rebellion in 1972 against Tutsi political domination left 10,000 Tutsi dead; Tutsi reprisals in 1972-73 resulted in the slaughter of 150,000 Hutu. The Micombero government was overthrown in a bloodless coup, and on Nov. 1, 1976, Lt. Col. Jean-Baptiste Bagaza took control of the government.

Bagaza was overthrown in Sept. 1987, and his successor, Maj. Pierre Buyoya, proclaimed a policy of nonalignment, seeking closer links with the West, while maintaining relations with Libya and the eastern bloc. Domestically, the government pledged to eradicate Bagaza's record of persecution of the Catholic church (62 percent of Burundians are Catholic) and to seek ethnic reconciliation between Hutu and Tutsi, but renewed outbreaks of ethnic violence occurred in 1988. Buyoya led the country to its first free presidential elections in June 1993. Melchior Ndadaye, a Hutu, defeated Buyoya by a wide margin.

But in Oct. 1993 Ndadaye was assassinated, as was his Hutu successor (April 1994). The succeeding regime of Hutu president Ntibantunganya, unsuccesful in forming a stable, ethnically balanced goverment, was overturned in a military coup (July 1996) which dissolved parliament, outlawed all political parties, and named Pierre Buyoya to return as president. Vowing yet another return to democracy after the end of civil war, Buyoya faced economic sanctions by the Organization of African Unity. Meanwhile, the complicated civil war was only worsened by Zaire's attempt to expel almost half a million Tutsi (the Banyamulenge people, settled south on Lake Kivi since the 18th century) in 1996. The Tutsi succesful self defense had the paradoxical effect of driving yet more Hutu (50,000) into Burundi—and almost half a million more into neighboring Rwanda.

The civil war continued into 2000, with at least 200,000 dead, with 350,000 Hutu rebels "regrouped" into 50 camps, and with Burundian army involvement (unadmitted) in the Congo conflict. A promising peace accord, brokered by Nelson Mandela in Aug. 2000, collapsed in Feb. 2001 as the capital of Bujumbura fell to Hutu rebels. Government forces re-took it on March 1, and another accord again forged by Mandela was signed by all parties in July 2001. Based on a power-sharing arrangement for three years the new 14 Hutu/12 Tutsi cabinet began ruling Nov. 1. A year later (Dec. 2002) the rebel group "Force for the Defense of Democracy" signed a truce with the government and in April 2003 when (as agreed) Hutu Domitien Ndayizeye was sworn in as president. Yet in July rebels attacked the capital of Bujumbara, while fighting continued in provincial villages as the civil war entered its eleventh year. Sporadic peace talks continued into 2004 but a brutal attack by a rebel group on a Tutsi refugee camp made peace seem a distant reality. Elections were held finally in 2005 and Pierre Nkurunziza, a rebel leader, won the presidency and an uneasy peace settled in for over two years with help from 3,000 U.N. peacekeepers.

▶ **CAMBODIA**
Kingdom of Cambodia
● **GEOGRAPHY** **Location:** on Indochinese peninsula in Southeast Asia. **Boundaries:** Thailand to W and N, Laos to N, Gulf of Thailand to S, Vietnam to E. **Total land area:** 69,900 sq. mi. (181,040 sq km). **Coastline:** 275 mi. (443 km). **Comparative area:** between Missouri and Oklahoma. **Land use:** 21% arable land; 1 % permanent crops; 78% other. **Major cities:** Phnom Penh (capital).
● **PEOPLE** **Population:** 14,241,640 (July 2008 est.). **Nationality:** noun—Cambodian(s); adjective—Cambodian. **Ethnic groups:** 90% Khmer (Cambodian), 5% Vietnamese, 1% Chinese, 4% other minorities. **Languages:** Khmer (official), French, English. **Religions:** 95% Theravada Buddhism.
● **GOVERNMENT** **Type:** multiparty liberal democracy under a constitutional monarchy. **Independence:** November 9, 1953 (from France). **Constitution:** promulgated Sept. 21, 1993. **National holiday:** Independence Day, November 9. **Heads of Government:** Norodom Sihamoni, king (since Oct. 2004); Hun Sen, prime minister (since Nov. 1998). **Structure:** executive; bicameral legislature; judiciary.
● **ECONOMY** **Monetary unit:** riel. **Budget:** (2007 est.) *income:* $915.5 mil.; *expend.:* $1.101 bil. **G.D.P.:** $25.79 bil., $1,800 per capita (2007 est.). **Chief crops:** rice, rubber, corn, vegetables. **Natural resources:** timber, gemstones, some iron ore,

manganese, phosphates, hydropower potential. **Major industries:** garments, rice milling, fishing, wood and wood products. **Labor force:** 7 mil.; 75% agriculture (2007 est.). **Exports:** $4.1 bil. (f.o.b., 2007 est.); timber, garments, rubber, soybeans, sesame. **Imports:** $5.3 bil. (f.o.b., 2007 est.); cigarettes, gold, construction materials, petroleum products. **Major trading partners:** (2006) *exports:* 53% U.S., 15% Hong Kong, 7% Germany, 4% U.K. *imports:* 18% Hong Kong, 18% China, 14% Thailand, 13% Taiwan, 9% Vietnam, 5% Singapore, 5% South Korea, 4% Japan.

The dominant power in Indochina from the Eighth through the 13th centuries, the Khmer Empire encompassed present-day Cambodia and much of western Thailand, southern Laos, and central and southern Vietnam. It built magnificent Buddhist temple cities at Angkor Wat and Angkor Thon. From the 14th century onward, the Khmer Empire came under increasing pressure from the expansionist Vietnamese state of Annam, which absorbed the territories east of the Mekong River. In the 18th century, the kingdom of Siam (Thailand) annexed three western provinces of the Khmer Empire. The remaining Khmer territory became the French protectorate of Cambodia in 1863, and a French colony as part of the Union of Indochina in 1887. In 1907 France forced Siam to return some territory to Cambodia.

During World War II, Cambodia was occupied by Japan from 1942 to 1945, when French control was restored. After the French defeat in Indochina, Cambodia became independent in 1953 under Prince Norodom Sihanouk, who had ascended the throne in 1941. In 1960 Sihanouk was named head of state under a constitutional monarchy. Shaken by the Vietnam War in the 1960's, Cambodia broke relations with the United States in 1965 because of South Vietnamese incursions across the border. In 1969 relations were restored when Sihanouk charged North Vietnam with arming the Khmer Rouge Cambodian Communist rebels. In the same year, American planes began secret bombing raids in Cambodia. In 1970 Sihanouk was ousted by a coup led by pro-U.S. Gen. Lon Nol; the monarchy was abolished, and Prince Sihanouk went into exile.

In April 1975 the Khmer Rouge, led by Pol Pot, captured the capital, Phnom Penh, and established a new government, the Kampuchean People's Republic. In an ensuing reign of terror, an estimated 3 million people died and hundreds of thousands more fled to refugee camps in Thailand. In 1978, Vietnamese troops invaded, capturing Phnom Penh on Jan. 7, 1979, and installing a new government led by Heng Samrin. The Kampuchean People's Republic continued to be recognized as the legal government of Cambodia in the United Nations and by most non-Soviet-bloc nations. A coalition dominated by the Khmer Rouge resisted the Vietnamese takeover, but by 1985 almost all of the country was under Vietnamese control with the Communist Party's Hun Sen as Prime Minister.

Most Vietnamese troops withdrew in 1989, and Prince Sihanouk emerged as the leader of a coalition of antigovernment forces. Starting in late 1988 conferences including representatives from all Cambodian factions were held to forge a political settlement to end the 20-year-old civil war. A peace agreement was signed on Oct. 23, 1991, providing for a cease-fire under U.N. supervision, the disarmament of all military factions, the formation of a coalition government, and the scheduling of a national election.

Despite bloody efforts by Khmer Rouge forces to disrupt the planned election, Cambodians went to the polls in large numbers on May 23, 1993. The Royalist party emerged with about 42 percent of the vote, ousting Hun Sen's Cambodian People's party. Hun Sen agreed to take part in a coalition cabinet as "second premier," with Sihanouk's son, Prince Ranariddh, as "first premier." Sihanouk took the title "king." In Jan. 1994, the united government went on the offensive and captured the Khmer Rouge stronghold of Pailin, driving 3,000 troops and 20,000 civilians into Thailand. Sihanouk succesfully negotiated international loans for rebuilding the country.

The coaltion government proved ineffective due to the inherent rivalry between the prince and Hun Sen, both of whom built up their security forces. When the Khmer Rouge leadership split in mid-1997, with Pol Pot either assasinated or imprisoned, Hun Sen seized the moment and his forces attacked those of his co-ruler's and drove the prince into exile. New elections were held in July 1998 and Hun Sen emerged victorious but agreed to form a coalition government. Hun Sen became "sole premier" with 12 cabinet posts while Ranariddh became President of the Assembly with 11 cabinet posts. In 1998, the last Khmer Rouge troops surrendered, and by March 1999, most of the remaining Khmer Rouge leaders had surrendered or were captured. In Jan. 2001 the Senate and National Assembly approved Hun Sen's agreement with the U.N. for an international tribunal to try the mass murderers. Elections in July 2003 gave Hun Sen's People's Party almost 50 percent of the vote.

▶CAMEROON
Republic of Cameroon

• **GEOGRAPHY Location:** western coast of central Africa. **Boundaries:** Nigeria to NW, Chad to NE, Central African Republic to E, Congo to SE, Gabon, Equatorial Guinea to S, Gulf of Guinea to W. **Total land area:** 183,568 sq. mi. (475,440 sq km). **Coastline:** 250 mi. (402 km). **Comparative area:** slightly larger than California. **Land use:** 13% arable land; 3% permanent crops; 84% other. **Major cities:** Yaoundé (capital); Douala; Nkongsamba (and environs); Maroua (and environs).

• **PEOPLE Population:** 18,467,692 (July 2008 est.). **Nationality:** noun—Cameroonian(s); adjective—Cameroonian. **Ethnic groups:** 31% Cameroon Highlanders, 19% Equatorial Bantu, 11% Kirdi, 10% Fulani, 8% Northwestern Bantu, 7% Eastern Nigritic, 13% other African; less than 1% non-African. **Languages:** English and French (both official); 24 major African language groups. **Religions:** 40% indigenous beliefs, 40% Christian, 20% Muslim.

• **GOVERNMENT Type:** unitary republic; multiparty presidential regime. **Independence:** Jan. 1, 1960 (from U.N. trusteeship under French administration). **Constitution:** May 20, 1972. **National holiday:** Republic Day, May 20. **Heads of Government:** Paul Biya, president (since Nov. 1982); Ephraim Inoni, prime minister (since Dec. 2004). **Structure:** executive; unicameral legislature; judiciary.

• **ECONOMY Monetary unit:** Communauté Financière Africaine franc. **Budget:** (2007 est.) **income:** $4.14 bil.; **expend.:** $3.3 bil. **G.D.P.:** $40.01 bil., $2,300 per capita (2007 est.). **Chief crops:** coffee, cocoa, cotton, rubber. **Natural resources:** crude oil, bauxite, iron ore, timber, hydropower potential. **Major industries:** crude oil production and refining, food processing. **Labor force:** 6.7 mil (2007); 70% agriculture, 13% industry and transport, 17% other services. **Exports:** $3.705 bil. (f.o.b., 2007 est.); crude oil and petroleum products, lumber, cocoa beans, aluminum. **Imports:** $3.632 bil. (f.o.b., 2007 est.); machines and electrical equipment, transport equipment, fuel, food. **Major trading partners:** (2006) *exports:* 21.4% Spain, 15.4% Italy, 11.6% France, 7.3% South Korea, 5.7% U.S.; *imports:* 23.6% France, 13.2% Nigeria, 7.2% China, 6.1% Belgium, 4.5% U.S.

Cameroon was settled by the Sao people about 1,000 years ago. In later times others, including the Bamileke, Bassa, Douala, and Fulani, migrated into the region. Portuguese trading stations were established along the coast beginning in the 15th century, and between 1500 and the early 19th century, the population was severely depleted by the slave trade in the hands of various European nations. European rivalries for domination in Cameroon were settled temporarily in 1884 when Germany established a protectorate.

British and French troops invaded German Cameroon during World War I, and following the war the League of Nations divided the protectorate into two mandated territories—French in the eastern sector and British in the west. French Cameroon rejected the Vichy government in World War II and became an important African base for Charles de Gaulle's Free French. In 1946 British and French rule in Cameroon was reaffirmed under U.N. trusteeships.

In 1958 the French trusteeship was abolished, and the Republic of Cameroon became independent on Jan. 1, 1960. In February 1961 a U.N.-supervised plebiscite was held in British Cameroon, allowing the people of that region to choose between union with Nigeria and union with the Republic of Cameroon. The northern two-thirds of the British territory elected union with Nigeria; the southern portion joined the Republic of Cameroon on Oct. 1, 1961, to form the Federal Republic of Cameroon. In 1972 the federal structure was abolished by a national referendum, and the United Republic of Cameroon was established. In 1984 the nation's name reverted to the Republic of Cameroon.

During the federal period, Cameroon had a multiparty political system, with party divisions coinciding with the old distinctions between west and east Cameroon. In 1966 all political parties were amalgamated to form the Cameroon National Union, which, with various changes in name, has dominated the political life of Cameroon ever since. In 1980 Pres. Ahidjo, the long-time political leader of Cameroon, was elected without opposition to a fifth five-year term in office. He resigned in 1982 and was replaced by Prime Minister Paul Biya, who was re-elected in his own right in 1984. He instituted political reforms whereby multiple candidates ran for office within the structure of the country's single-party system. In 1992 he was elected president in the nation's first multiparty elections. His closest rival was put under house arrest.

The economy of Cameroon is based primarily on agriculture; it is self-sufficient in food and exports coffee, cocoa, rubber, cotton, palm oil, and timber. Oil is the principal export, however, accounting for 60 percent of export earnings.

▶ CANADA

- **GEOGRAPHY Location:** northern North America (excluding Alaska and Greenland); second largest country in the world. **Boundaries:** Arctic Ocean to N, Greenland to NE across Baffin Bay, Atlantic Ocean to E, United States to S, Pacific Ocean and Alaska to W. **Total land area:** 3,851,794 sq. mi. (9,976,140 sq km). **Coastline:** 151,492 mi. (243,791 km). **Comparative area:** slightly larger than U.S. **Land use:** 5% arable land; negl.% permanent crops, 95% other. **Major cities:** Ottawa (capital), Toronto; Montréal; Vancouver; Edmonton.
- **PEOPLE Population:** 33,212,696 (July 2008 est.). **Nationality:** noun—Canadian(s); adjective—Canadian. **Ethnic groups:** 28% British Isles origin, 23% French origin, 15% other European, 2% Amerindian, 6% other, mostly Asian, Arab, African. **Languages:** 59.3% English, 23.2% French (both official). **Religions:** 42.6% Roman Catholic, 23.3% Protestant, 14.1% other, 16% none.
- **GOVERNMENT Type:** confederation with parliamentary democracy. **Independence:** July 1, 1867 (from U.K.). **Constitution:** amended British North America Act of 1867 transferred power and rights to Canada, Apr. 17, 1982; charter of rights and unwritten customs. **National holiday:** Canada Day, July 1. **Heads of Government:** Stephen Harper, prime minister (since Feb. 2006); Adrienne Clarkson, governor-general (since Oct. 1999). **Structure:** executive—cabinet collectively responsible to House of Commons and headed by prime minister; legislative—bicameral Parliament with queen represented by governor general, Senate, and House of Commons; judiciary—judges appointed by governor general with Supreme Court as highest tribunal.
- **ECONOMY Monetary unit:** Canadian dollar. **Budget:** (2007 est.) *income:* $565.8 bil.; *expend.:* $551.2 bil. **G.D.P.:** $1.27 tril., $38,200 per capita (2007 est.). **Chief crops:** grain (principally wheat), oilseeds, tobacco. **Natural resources:** iron ore, nickel, zinc, copper, gold, lead. **Major industries:** processed and unprocessed minerals, food products, wood and paper products. **Labor force:** 17.9 mil.; 2.1% agriculture, 28.8% industry, 69.1% services. **Exports:** $440.1 bil. (f.o.b., 2007 est.); motor vehicles and parts, wood pulp, timber, petroleum. **Imports:** $394.4 bil. (f.o.b., 2007 est.); machinery and equipment, petroleum, chemicals, motor vehicles. **Major trading partners:** (2006) *exports:* 81.6% U.S., 2.3% U.K., 2.1% Japan; *imports:* 54.9% U.S., 8.7% China, 4% Mexico.

Canada is geographically the second-largest country in the world, but most of its territory is very sparsely settled. The vast majority of the country's 32 million people live in a narrow band along the border with the U.S. Despite a long tradition of national independence, Canada's history has been dominated by relations with Great Britain, the U.S., and, to a lesser extent, France.

Canada's earliest inhabitants arrived via the Bering land bridge from Asia around 15,000 years ago and diversified to form the various Inuit (Eskimo), Northwest Indian, Plains Indian, and forest Indian cultures that still contribute significantly to Canada's national identity. The earliest-known European settlers of Canada were Vikings, who established a short-lived colony in Newfoundland around A.D. 1000. Other European explorers made numerous voyages to Canada during the 16th century, stimulated by Canada's rich resources of fish, forest products, and furs.

The first permanent European settlement in Canada was the French trading station at Quebec, founded by Samuel de Champlain in 1608. Fur traders rapidly spread into the interior along the St. Lawrence River and the Great Lakes; European diseases, particularly smallpox, decimated Native American populations as the explorers advanced. In 1663 New France was organized as a French Crown Colony, and royal governors replaced private commercial interests in governing Quebec.

The Hudson Bay Company was chartered by the British Crown in 1670, inaugurating a long period of commercial and territorial rivalry in Canada between Britain and France. In general, France sought to expand New France northward and westward, while Britain sought to expand its domination southward and westward from Hudson Bay. French and British interests clashed directly along the Atlantic coast, where both British and French settlements were established. Local and regional wars between the French and the British were endemic in Canada throughout the 17th and 18th centuries; each side enlisted Native American allies. These wars were often inconclusive, but in Queen Anne's War (1702-13), Britain gained a significant advantage by winning control of Acadia and Newfoundland, and by driving the French from Hudson Bay.

The French and Indian Wars of 1756-63, a North American extension of Europe's Seven Years' War, proved to be the decisive turning point in the Anglo-French rivalry in Canada. Prior to the outbreak of full-scale war, in 1755 the British deported some 7,000-10,000 French settlers from Acadia, in Nova Scotia, to the West Indies; many later settled in Louisiana. When war broke out in Europe in 1756, Britain employed its superior sea power to cut New France off from Europe and captured Quebec in the Battle of the Plains of Abraham in 1759. Montreal capitulated in 1760, leaving Britain in control of New France.

Faced with the problem of governing New France's large French population (which far outnumbered Canada's English-speaking population), the British in 1774 passed the Quebec Act, which recognized the territory's legal code and system of land tenure, and granted legal status to the Roman Catholic church. The act also extended Canadian territory south to the Ohio River, enraging the 13 American colonies and helping to fuel the American Revolution.

During the American Revolution, nearly 40,000 loyalists fled to Canada from the rebellious colonies, establishing English-speaking settlements in New Brunswick and western Quebec. Friction between English- and French-speaking Canadians led the British in 1791 to divide Canada (west of the Atlantic maritime provinces) into two provinces, Upper Canada and Lower Canada. Each was granted a legislature; Upper Canada's was based on British institutions, Lower Canada's retained the French forms established by the Quebec Act of 1774.

During the War of 1812 between Great Britain and the U.S., Canada became a battleground; Toronto was captured and pillaged by the Americans in 1813. Many Americans hoped to expand the territory of the U.S. at the expense of Canada, or even to entice Canada into a continental American union, but Canadians, whether English- or

French-speaking, showed no enthusiasm for joining the U.S. A small British garrison, with the support of Native American irregular forces, kept the Americans at bay. The Convention of 1818 established the border between Canada and the U.S. at latitude 49° north, as far west as the Rocky Mountains, and provided for joint U.S.-British control of Oregon (i.e., the entire Columbia River basin).

Following the War of 1812, British authorities encouraged British immigration to Canada, and between 1815 and 1855, one million Britons answered the call. This immigration radically altered Canada's ethnic balance, making French-speaking Canadians a minority population for the first time. The francophones of Lower Canada, hemmed in on all sides by English speakers, rose in rebellion under the leadership of the Parti Patriote in 1837-38. Lord Durham recommended in 1839 that Canada be united under a single government, and the Union of Canada was enacted in 1841. This move did not, however, quell the growing nationalism of French Canadians.

War with the U.S. threatened in 1844, as the U.S. claimed the entire Columbia River basin north to 54°40' ("fifty-four forty or fight"). But diplomacy triumphed in the end: In 1846 the boundary at 49° was extended westward to the Pacific Ocean. Meanwhile, gold was discovered in British Columbia in 1856, leading to a gold rush and a substantial increase in the population of western Canada.

Growing trade between Canada and the U.S. and the development of a continental system of railroads in both Canada and the U.S. in the 1850s, led to a relative decline in British influence in Canada. The American Civil War had the indirect effect of prompting Canadians to seek self-government in a federal union. Previously, there had been little contact between the Canadas and the maritime provinces, while the vast territories of the west were still privately administered by the Hudson Bay Company. A federal union was forged in a series of conferences beginning in 1864, and the federation of Quebec, Ontario, Nova Scotia, and New Brunswick was recognized by the British North America Act of July 1, 1867.

The Dominion of Canada thus established in 1867 became a self-governing entity within the British Empire; Sir J.A. Macdonald became Canada's first prime minister (1867-73). The dominion rapidly expanded. In 1869 it purchased the western territories of the Hudson Bay Company, and in 1870, in response to a rebellion of French-speaking Métis in Manitoba, Manitoba was granted provincial status within the federation. In 1871 the union of British Columbia with Canada was secured with the promise of a transcontinental railway; the Canadian Pacific Railway was completed in 1885. Prince Edward Island joined the federation in 1873, but neighboring Newfoundland remained a British colony outside the Canadian federation until 1949.

A second francophone rebellion broke out in Saskatchewan in 1885. Its leader, Louis Riel, was executed and became a symbol of French Canadian grievances against the English-speaking majority. Wilfred Laurier became Canada's first francophone prime minister in 1896, but he was unable to solve the problem of the rights of Catholics and French-speakers outside Quebec. Legislation restricting those rights had already been enacted in Manitoba in 1890.

The Klondike Gold Rush of 1897-98 brought Canada worldwide attention and indirectly helped promote the settlement of rich agricultural lands in the Canadian west. Immigrants to the prairie region came not only from eastern Canada, but also from Germany, Scandinavia, and the Ukraine. Japanese farmers and Chinese railroad and mining workers settled west of the Rockies, further increasing Canada's ethnic diversity, though Asian immigrants were denied citizenship. Alberta and Saskatchewan were granted provincial status in 1905; the Yukon Territory and the Northwest Territories continued to be governed by controllers appointed by the federal government and patrolled by the famous Royal Canadian Mounted Police.

Urbanization and industrialization were stimulated in the early 20th century by the exploitation of extensive mineral resources in western Canada and in northern Quebec, and by the development of hydroelectric projects and transportation facilities throughout the country. The long-lived Laurier government fell in 1911, when his proposal for free trade with the U.S. evoked widespread fears that Canada's nascent industries would suffer without protective tariffs.

Laurier's Conservative successor, Robert Borden, sent Canadian troops to fight in World War I in 1914 and bolstered Canada's war efforts in Europe through national conscription in 1917. The distinguished performance of Canada's armed forces in the war bought the country renewed international respect. Borden's wartime English-speaking Conservative-Liberal coalition collapsed in 1921. He was succeeded by the Liberal leader William L. Mackenzie King, who was to be Canada's prime minister for over 20 years (1921-30, 1935-48). He skillfully managed the economic prosperity of the 1920's, which saw the establishment in Canada of branch plants of many American industrial firms.

The Statute of Westminster, which created the British Commonwealth in 1931, had the effect of granting full self-government to Canada within the Commonwealth. The economic collapse of the 1930's brought both industrial depression and a drought-induced agricultural crisis. Efforts to deal with unemployment, land foreclosures, and other economic ills fell to the provincial governments, which were not up to the task.

Canada's recovery from the Great Depression was stimulated by the advent of World War II, which Canada entered in 1939. Although the war brought price controls, rationing, and other emergency measures, the overall effect of the war was to strengthen all sectors of Canada's economy and to enhance Canada's international status as a leading military and industrial power. A Liberal electoral victory of 1945 gave Mackenzie King a renewed mandate for the postwar era.

The two decades following the war saw the gradual expansion of federal financial responsibility for national welfare measures, including pensions, unemployment insurance, and comprehensive medical care, though the administration of such programs remained a provincial matter. These developments coincided with an increase in urbanization and industrialization in the major centers of Vancouver, Toronto, and Montreal. Formal "equalization payments" were enacted in the 1950's to reduce economic disparities between rich and poor provinces. The early stages of these developments played a part in persuading Newfoundland to join the federation as Canada's 10th province in 1949.

A landslide Conservative victory in 1958 brought John Diefenbaker to the prime ministership, but the Conservatives proved unable to offer a coherent political program and were ousted in the elections of 1963, which returned the Liberals to power. Canadian politics since the 1960's have been marked by increasing regionalization; the Liberal party is based largely in the east, while the New Democratic party, organized in 1961, has little support east of Ontario. The Conservatives offer a broad but insecure national alternative.

The language issue continues to divide Canada politically and ideologically. The rise of an aggressive Quebecois nationalism in the 1960's led directly to the Liberal prime ministership of Pierre Trudeau, a Quebecois known as a supporter of a strong federal constitution. Trudeau's efforts toward conciliation and for constitutional guarantees for Quebec within a strong federal structure proved unavailing, however. In 1970 he invoked the War Measures Act to send troops to Quebec to put down a wave of separatist terrorism.

The 1976 electoral victory in Quebec of the Parti Québécois under René Lévesque provoked fears that Quebec would secede from Canada. Lévesque's plan for a separate "sovereignty-association" status for Quebec was rejected by a popular referendum in 1980, but only because of Trudeau's pledge to seek full autonomy for Canada in order to secure constitutional protection for Quebec's special interests.

In 1981, Canada's provincial governments reached agreement on proposals for constitutional change. The result was the passage by the British Parliament of the Canada Act, which came into effect on Apr. 17, 1982, granting full independence and constitutional autonomy to Canada and severing its last colonial ties to the British government. Canada's new 1982 Constitution more clearly delineated the powers of the federal and provincial governments, provided for Supreme Court review of legislation, and included a Charter of Rights to protect civil liberties.

A nationwide recession contributed to the defeat of Trudeau's Liberal government and to the election of the Conservative party leader Brian Mulroney (also a native of Quebec) as prime minister in 1984. The Mulroney government encouraged foreign investment and privatization as a means of revitalizing Canada's economy. But its most significant achievement was the negotiation and passage, in 1988-89, of a free-trade agreement with the U.S. (that also came to include Mexico).

The Meech Lake Agreement, containing a number of articles clarifying the 1982 Constitution, was worked out between Mulroney and Quebec's Liberal premier Robert Bourassa, along with the leaders of Canada's nine other provinces, and signed on June 23, 1987. Its provisions enhanced the power of the provinces; a key provision gave constitutional protection to Quebec's efforts to remain a "distinct society," linguistically and culturally French. But the aggressive measures of the Quebec government to eradicate the use of English in the public affairs of the province provoked a backlash against bilingualism. The Meech Lake Agreement failed to become law when the legislatures of Newfoundland and Manitoba declined to ratify it by the June 23, 1990, deadline. Canada plunged into the most serious constitutional crisis in its history.

An alternative agreement to restructure the federal government and give more power to the 10 provincial governments met initial opposition in Quebec, and was decisively defeated in a national referendum, leaving the nation to deal once again with the awkward status quo.

In 1992, the North American Free Trade Association (NAFTA) with the U.S. and Mexico was finalized, bringing a large increase in trade, especially with the U.S. Mulroney resigned in 1993 and the Progressive Conservative party chose Kim Campbell to lead the government, the first woman to do so. In the 1993 general election, the Conservatives were routed by Jean Chrétien and the Liberals. The new government announced plans in early 1995 to cut the budget deficit through higher taxes and spending cuts on health care and social programs. Although they accomplished this goal, many Canadians were disconcerted because of high unemployment and a decrease in benefits. Chretien was also vulnerable on the problem of Quebec because he and the Liberal Party seemed to favor giving special status to the French province, where in 1995 a separatist referendum was only narrowly defeated. In 1997 elections, the Liberals lost 19 seats, but still held a slim majority. The issue of separatism rose again in Aug. 1998 when the Supreme Court ruled that a referendum on Quebec secession would be invalid without negotiations on the terms with both the provinces and the federation as a whole.

On April 1, 1999 the government officially created a new Arctic territory called Nunavut which is governed solely by the Inuit tribe (called Eskimos in Alaska and Greenland). In Nov. 2000 Chretien's Liberals won their third consecutive victory by a very large margin. The thorny issue of Quebec independence reached a settlement in April 2003 provincial elections in Quebec as the Liberals won 76 of 125 seats, denying another term to the Parti Quebecois, which carried 45 seats.

In 2002 Canada joined with the U.S. to fight the war in Afghanistan, but in 2003, Chretien refused to join the U.S.-led invasion of Iraq. In June elections, 2004 the Liberals fell short of gaining a majority and Paul Martin, Chretien's successor, formed a minority government, the first in Canada since 1980. A serious corruption scandal nearly toppled the government but Martin held on till elections in Jan. 2006 brought the government down and Stephen Harper's Conservative party took power, but also as a minority government.

▶ **CAPE VERDE**
Republic of Cape Verde
● **GEOGRAPHY Location:** archipelago of 15 islands in Atlantic Ocean, off northern Africa. **Boundaries:** Senegal about 300 mi. (500 km) to E. **Total land area:** 1,556 sq. mi. (4,030 sq km). **Coastline:** 600 mi. (965 km). **Comparative area:** slightly larger than Rhode Island. **Land use:** 11% arable land; 1. % permanent crops; 89% other. **Major cities:** Cidade de Praia (capital). ● **PEOPLE Population:** 426,998 (July 2008 est.). **Nationality:** noun—Cape Verdean(s); adjective—Cape Verdean. **Ethnic groups:** 71% Creole (mulatto), 28% African, 1% European. **Languages:** Portuguese and Crioulo (blend of Portuguese and West African). **Religions:** Roman Catholicism fused with indigenous beliefs, Protestantism. ● **GOVERNMENT Type:** republic. **Independence:** July 5, 1975 (from Portugal). **Constitution:** Sept. 25, 1992. **National holiday:** Independence Day, July 5. **Heads of Government:** Pedro Verona Rodrigues Pires, president (since Mar. 2001); José Maria Neves, prime minister (since Feb. 2001). **Structure:** executive; unicameral legislature; judiciary.

• **ECONOMY** **Monetary unit:** Cape Verdean escudo. **Budget:** (2007 est.) *income:* $444.7 mil.; *expend.:* $496 mil. **G.D.P.:** $3.71 mil., $7,000 per capita (2007 est.). **Chief crops:** bananas, corn, beans. **Natural resources:** salt, basalt rock, pozzolana, limestone, kaolin, fish. **Major industries:** food and beverages, fish processing, salt mining. **Labor force:** 120,600 (1990 est); 9.3% agriculture, 73.9% services, 16.9% industry (1990); 21% unemployment (2000 est.). **Exports:** $100.2 mil. (f.o.b., 2007 est.); shoes, garments, fish, bananas. **Imports:** $727.1 mil. (f.o.b., 2007 est.); foodstuffs, consumer goods, industrial products. **Major trading partners:** (2006) *exports:* 44.2% Spain, 21.7% Portugal, 12.6% Netherlands, 4.6% Morocco; *imports:* 41.1% Portugal, 10.6% Netherlands, 6.5% Spain, 5.4% Italy, 5.2% Cote D'Ivoire, 4.8% Brazil.

In 1462 the Portuguese founded the first European city in the tropics at Ribeira Grande on Santiago, one of the 15 islands that compose the Republic of Cape Verde. Located 385 miles off the west coast of Africa, the Cape Verde Islands prospered during the slave trade in the 16th century and later served as supply stations on sea routes and trading lanes. The rise of whaling in the 19th century led to contact with the U.S., as American ships recruited crews from the islands. The United States set up an American consulate, headquarters for the U.S. Navy African Squadron, and a transatlantic cable station in the islands.

Portugal changed the status of the archipelago from colony to overseas province in 1951; in 1956, citizens of Cape Verde and Portuguese Guinea organized the African Party for the Independence of Guinea-Bissau and Cape Verde (PAIGC) to petition Portugal to improve living conditions. Beginning as a clandestine organization, the PAIGC became an overt political movement on the islands after the 1974 revolution in Portugal. An agreement between the PAIGC and Portugal, providing for a transitional government, paved the way for full independence in 1975.

In 1980 the PAIGC became the PAICV, which remained the "supreme expression" of Cape Verdeans' political will until the opposition party, Movement for Democracy, won a parliamentary majority in the nation's first multiparty elections in Jan. 1991. The new government instituted free market reforms, including privatization of industries. Voters approved of the reforms, giving the Movement for Democracy 50 of the 72 seats in Parliament in Dec. 1995 elections. Ten years of rule by the Movement for Democracy ended in 2001 as the opposition won a majority in the legislature and elected their candidate, Pedro Pires, as president. He won reelection in 2006.

▶ CENTRAL AFRICAN REPUBLIC

• **GEOGRAPHY** **Location:** landlocked country in central Africa. **Boundaries:** Chad to N, Sudan to E, Zaire, Congo to S, Cameroon to W. **Total land area:** 240,533 sq. mi. (622,980 sq km). **Coastline:** none. **Comparative area:** slightly smaller than Texas. **Land use:** 3% arable land; negl.% permanent crops; 97% other. **Major cities:** Bangui (capital); Berbérati; Bouar.
• **PEOPLE** **Population:** 4,434,873 (July 2008 est.). **Nationality:** noun—Central African(s); adjective— Central African. **Ethnic groups:** 33% Baya, 27% Banda, 13% Mandija, 10% Sara, 7% Mboum, 4% M'Baka; 2% other. **Languages:** French (official), Sangho (lingua franca and national language), tribal languages. **Religions:** 35% indigenous beliefs, 25% Protestant, 25% Roman Catholic, 15% Muslim; indigenous beliefs and practices strongly influence Christian majority.
• **GOVERNMENT** **Type:** republic. **Independence:** Aug. 13, 1960 (from France). **Constitution:** Adopted Jan. 7, 1995. **National holiday:** Republic Day, Dec. 1. **Heads of Government:** François Bozize, head of state (since March, 2003); Faustin-Archange Touadera, prime minister (since Jan., 2008). **Structure:** executive; unicameral legislature; judiciary.
• **ECONOMY** **Monetary unit:** Communauté Financière Africaine (CFA) franc. **Budget:** (2007 est.) *income:* $250 mil.; *expend.:* $273 bil. **G.D.P.:** $3.101 bil., $700 per capita (2007 est.). **Chief crops:** cotton, coffee, tobacco. **Natural resources:** diamonds, uranium, timber, gold, oil. **Major industries:** sawmills, breweries, diamond mining. **Labor force:** 1.857 mil (2006 est.); 55% agriculture, 25% services, 20% industry. **Exports:** $146.7 mil. (f.o.b., 2007 est.); diamonds, timber, cotton, coffee, tobacco. **Imports:** $237.3 mil. (f.o.b., 2007); food, textiles, petroleum products, machinery, electrical equipment, motor vehicles. **Major trading partners:** (2006) *exports:* 31% Belgium, 11% Spain, 8% Indonesia, 8% France, 7% China; *imports:* 15% France, 15% Netherlands, 9% U.S., 9% Cameroon.

A landlocked country in Africa's central region, the Central African Republic is one of the least-developed countries in the world. Most of its people are farmers, and the nation has little manufacturing, few reliable roads, and no railroad. Europeans first came to the area in the early 1800's in their search for slaves, but it was not until 1889 that the French established an outpost as the current capital city of Bangui. The region was organized as the territory of Ubangi-Shari five years later. In 1910 it was incorporated into French Equitorial Africa along with what are now the countries of Chad, the Congo, and Gabon.

The country was granted internal self government by the French under its present name in 1958 and became a member of the French Overseas Community. Independence was achieved on Aug. 13, 1960. The first prime minister, Barthelemy Boganda, was killed in an airplane crash in 1959 and was succeeded by his nephew, David Dacko. Dacko was elected to a seven-year term in January 1964, but an army coup in 1966 overthrew his government. The head of the army, Jean-Bedel Bokassa, was installed as president. Named president for life in 1972, in 1976 Bokassa declared himself emperor and changed the name of the country to the Central African Empire.

Dacko returned to power in 1979, however, and Bokassa went into exile. The name of the country was changed back to the Central African Republic. A multiparty political system was reinstated in March 1981, but army officers threw Dacko out of office again six months later and banned all political parties. Opposition parties were legalized in 1991, and Bokassa was released shortly before elections in 1993, elections that made Ange Félix Patassé president. He tried to reduce the army's power but met with rebellions requiring the intervention of peacekeepers from neighboring states. Patassé was overturned in March 2003 by fired army head General Francois Bozize who suspended the constitution and proclaimed himself president. In 2005 Bozize won the presidential election although complaints about the process were numerous.

►CHAD
Republic of Chad

• **GEOGRAPHY   Location:** landlocked country in north central Africa. **Boundaries:** Libya to N, Sudan to E, Central African Republic to S, Cameroon, Nigeria to SE, Niger to W. **Total land area:** 495,753 sq. mi. (1,284,000 sq km). **Coastline:** none. **Comparative area:** between Texas and Alaska. **Land use:** 3% arable land; negl. % permanent crops; 97% other. **Major cities:** N'Djamena (capital; Sarh; Moundou; Abéché.

• **PEOPLE   Population:** 10,111,337 (July 2008 est.). **Nationality:** noun—Chadian(s); adjective—Chadian. **Ethnic groups:** Sara, Arab, Mayo-Kebbi, Kanem-Bornou, Ouaddai, Hadjarai, Tandjile, Gorane, Fritri-Batha. **Languages:** French and Arabic (both official); Sara and Sango in south; more than 120 different languages and dialects. **Religions:** 51% Muslim, 35% Christian, 7% Animist, 7% other.

• **GOVERNMENT   Type:** republic. **Independence:** Aug. 11, 1960 (from France). **Constitution:** Mar. 31, 1996. **National holiday:** Independence Day, Aug. 11. **Heads of Government:** Idriss Deby, president (since Dec. 1990); Youssof Sateh Abbas, prime minister (since April 2008). **Structure:** executive; unicameral legislature; judiciary.

• **ECONOMY   Monetary unit:** Communauté Financière Africaine (CFA) franc. **Budget:** (2007 est.) *income:* $1.889 bil.; *expend.:* $1.473 mil.; **G.D.P.:** $15.95 bil., $1,600 per capita (2007 est.). **Chief crops:** cotton, sorghum, millet, peanuts. **Natural resources:** small quantities of crude oil (unexploited but exploitation beginning), uranium, natron (sodium carbonate), kaolin, fish (Lake Chad). **Major industries:** oil, cotton textile mills, slaughterhouses, brewery, natron. **Labor force:** 3.75 mil (2006); 22.2% agriculture, 47.2% industry, 30.6% services. **Exports:** $4.219 bil. (f.o.b., 2007 est.); cotton, cattle, textiles. **Imports:** $1.149 bil. (f.o.b., 2007 est.); machinery and transport equipment, industrial goods, petroleum products, foodstuffs. **Major trading partners:** (2006) *exports:* 81% U.S., 10% China, 2% South Korea; *imports:* 18.6% France, 17.6% Cameroon, 12.5% U.S., 7.4% Germany, 5% Saudi Arabia, 5% Belgium.

The Sao and other ancient peoples built centers of civilization near Lake Chad that flourished for many centuries until they were displaced by the medieval kingdoms of Kanem-Bornu, Baguirmi, and Ouaddai. From about 1400 onward, Chad became a meeting ground between the Muslim cultures of the Sahara and the Sahel and the black African societies of the tropics. Between 1500 and 1800, Arab slave raiders were active around Lake Chad, supplying slaves for European traders on Africa's west coast.

French military forces reached Chad from West Africa in 1891 and fought a series of battles over the next two decades with the Arab rulers of the region. A French governorship of Chad was established in 1905 (based in Brazzaville, the Congo), but the country was not brought entirely under French control until 1914. Chad was incorporated into the federation of French Equatorial Africa in 1910 and was organized as a colony within the federation in 1920.

French Equatorial Africa was dissolved in 1959, and Chad became an autonomous member of the French Community. Full independence followed on Aug. 11, 1960; François Tombalbage became Chad's first president. In 1965 the Muslim northern and eastern parts of the country rebelled against the southern-led government; despite the aid of French troops, the government was unable to suppress the rebellion, and a long civil war ensued.

Tombalbage was overthrown in 1975 in a military coup led by Gen. Felix Malloum. Efforts to broaden the composition of the national government broke down, and in 1979 Prime Minister Hissein Habre broke with the government and led northern forces against the national army. A cease-fire was negotiated under international auspices, and a National Unity Transitional Government (GUNT) was installed in 1979, but civil war broke out again in 1980. Pres. Goukouni Oueddei sought Libyan aid in restoring order; a contingent of 7,000 Libyan troops occupied the country until 1981. They were replaced by an international peacekeeping force organized by the Organization of African Unity.

Civil war broke out again in 1982, and northern forces occupied the capital. A new republican government under the presidency of Hissein Habre was proclaimed on June 7. OAU forces withdrew, and Habre's government soon controlled all of the country except for a few northern areas held by GUNT. In 1983 GUNT launched a counterattack and regained some territory with the aid of Libyan forces. French and Zairian troops were sent to aid Habre's forces. In Sept. 1984 France and Libya agreed to the withdrawal of all foreign forces from Chad, but Libyan forces remained. GUNT forces controlled the country north of the 16th parallel; Libyan forces occupied the Aozou Strip, along the border, with the apparent intention of annexing it to Libya.

Between 1984 and 1986 Habre persuaded most Chadean dissident forces to rejoin the national government, and in Nov. 1986 he launched a campaign to recapture the north. The Chadean forces won a series of victories, and in May 1988 Libya's Col. Qaddafi declared an end to the 20-year war with Chad.

In Nov. 1990, forces led by renegade Gen. Idriss Deby launched attacks from Sudan and ousted Pres. Habre Deby, who favored multiparty democracy, proclaimed a provisional government and suspended the constitution. A national charter calling for a new constitution and elections to be held within 30 months came into force in March 1991. Deby functioned as president after that, suppressing two attempted coups in 1992, and legalizing opposition parties. Deby's "Higher Transitional Council" remained in command until presidential elections were held in 1996, which Deby won. He was reelected in 2001 and 2006. Fighting between the government and a rebel group has continued since 1998. In 2003, Chad became an oil-producing nation with a pipeline linked to terminals on the Atlantic Ocean. With oil money comes corruption, and Chad succumbed quickly. In 2006 Chad cut ties with Sudan for its support of rebel movements to bring down the Deby government.

►CHILE
Republic of Chile

• **GEOGRAPHY   Location:** South Pacific coast of South America. **Boundaries:** Peru, Bolivia to N, Argentina to E, Pacific Ocean to W. **Total land area:** 292,259 sq. mi. (756,950 sq km). **Coastline:** 3,999 mi. (6,435 km). **Comparative area:** slightly larger than Texas. **Land use:** 3% arable land; negl. % permanent crops; 97% other. **Major cities:** Gran

Santiago (capital); Viña del Mar; Concepción; Valparaíso; Temuco.

• **PEOPLE** **Population:** 16,454,143 (July 2008 est.). **Nationality:** noun—Chilean(s); adjective—Chilean. **Ethnic groups:** 95% white and white Amerindian, 3% Amerindian, 2% other. **Languages:** Spanish (official), English, Mapudungun, German. **Religions:** 70% Roman Catholic, 15.1% Evangelical, 1.1% Jehovah Witness, 4.6% other, 8.3% none.

• **GOVERNMENT** **Type:** republic. **Independence:** Sept. 18, 1810 (from Spain). **Constitution:** Sept. 11, 1980, effective Mar. 11, 1981; modified by public referendum on July 30, 1989. **National holiday:** Independence Day, Sept. 18. **Head of Government:** Michele Bachelet, president (since Mar. 2006). **Structure:** executive; bicameral legislature; judiciary.

• **ECONOMY** **Monetary unit:** Chilean peso. **Budget:** (2007 est.) *income:* $44.44 bil.; *expend.:* $31.36 bil. **G.D.P.:** $234.4 bil., $14,400 per capita (2007 est.). **Chief crops:** wheat, corn, grapes, beans, sugar beets. **Natural resources:** copper, timber, iron ore, nitrates, precious metals. **Major industries:** copper, other minerals, foodstuffs, fish processing. **Labor force:** 6.97 mil. (2007); 63% services, 23.4% industry and commerce, 13.6% agriculture, forestry, fishing (2003); 7% unemployment (2007 est.). **Exports:** $66.43 bil. (f.o.b., 2007); copper, fish and fishmeal, other metals and minerals. **Imports:** $41.8 bil. (f.o.b., 2007); consumer goods, chemicals, motor vehicles, fuels. **Major trading partners:** (2006) *exports:* 15.6% U.S., 10.5% Japan, 8.6% China, 6% South Korea; *imports:* 15.6% U.S., 12.6% Argentina, 11.8% Brazil, 9.7% China.

Before the arrival of Europeans in the mid 1530's, indigenous habitation of the territory that would become Chile included the Araucanian population in the south and peoples under the influence of the Inca Empire in the north.

The Spanish founded the cities of Valparaíso in 1536, Santiago in 1541, and Concepción in 1550. Chile was under the authority of the Viceroyalty of Peru, established in 1544. Between 1810 and 1818, fortunes of the Chilean independence movement ebbed and flowed, culminating in the victory of Bernardo O'Higgins and the separatist forces in 1817. Independence was finally achieved in 1818.

From 1818 to 1833, Chile underwent a period of political instability due to power struggles among elite Chilean families. In 1833 a strong presidential-dominant constitution was written under the influence of leading political figure Diego Portales that set the form of government in Chile until 1891. Chile expanded its territory at the expense of Peru and Bolivia, first in a war with the Peruvian-Bolivian Confederation (1836-39) and later as a result of the War of the Pacific (1879-83).

A civil war was fought in 1890-91 between forces of the president, José Balmaceda, and the Chilean Congress over the issue of the limits of presidential authority. The defeat of the presidential forces led to the establishment of a congressional-dominant parliamentary system. The checks on policy initiative resulting from the parliamentary system left government deadlocked in the face of mounting social and political problems arising at the turn of the century. The occurrence of a number of bloody strike actions crystallized political debate around social issues such as better wages and working conditions. The immobilized parliamentary system was unable to respond to these problems. In 1925, when Congress failed to allocate funds for military pay, the forces overthrew the parliamentary government.

A new constitution was drawn up that same year that moved governmental structure toward presidential dominance. Nevertheless, political instability continued until 1933, when the new constitution was implemented. The Chilean balance of political power from 1958 until 1973 remained almost equally divided among parties representing the right, the center, and the left of the political spectrum. In order to prevent an electoral victory for the leftist parties, forces on the right allied themselves with the centrist Christian Democrats in the 1964 election, and this resulted in the victory of Christian Democratic presidential candidate Eduardo Frei Montalva.

The program of the Christian Democrats included agrarian reform and attempts to organize Chile's urban poor. It was believed that these stances would benefit the Christian Democrats at the polls in the 1970 presidential election. As in 1958, the 1970 election fielded three presidential candidates who represented the political right, center, and left. The leftist Popular Unity coalition candidate, Dr. Salvador Allende Gossens, won with 36.3 percent of the vote, but only after bitter debate did Congress recognize Allende's victory.

The Allende government nationalized the foreign-owned copper industry, but an international boycott of Chilean copper imposed in retaliation for this action seriously hurt the country's economy. The government also nationalized the coal and steel industries as well as 60 percent of private banking. The Popular Unity government found itself unable to control peasant seizures of land and factory takeovers by workers. The copper embargo, land and factory seizures, government subsidies to the poor for basic goods, and runaway inflation resulted in a deterioration of the national economy that particularly affected the middle classes. Members of congress from the center and right had hoped to gain enough seats in the 1973 elections to impeach Allende, but instead the Popular Unity made impressive electoral gains. In order to bolster the legitimacy of the Popular Unity administration in the eyes of political opponents, Allende resorted to inclusion of military officers in the government.

On Sept. 11, 1973, segments of the military led by commanders of three of Chile's four armed forces took control of the government, killing Allende in the process. Gen. Augusto Pinochet Ugarte emerged as the new president. The junta announced the arrest of some 13,000 persons, many of whom then lost their lives in a wave of brutal repression. (Mass graves were discovered in the desert in 1990, and in 1991 a commission reported that between 1973 and 1990, more than 2,000 people were killed by the government.) In March 1974 the dictatorship published its Declaration of Principles, which included a laissez-faire economic orientation, anti-Marxism, and nationalism.

A new constitution was approved by plebiscite in 1980. The two-phase evolution of Chile's political structure included an authoritarian "transitional period" between 1980 and 1989 and implementation of a new political structure thereafter. The constitution created a presidential system with very extensive executive powers and a "guardian" role for the military.

In an Oct. 1988 plebiscite, Chileans rejected continuation of Pinochet rule and called for an end to the dictatorship. On Dec. 14, 1989, Patricio Aylwin Azocar of the Christian Democratic party (one of a 17-party alliance) was elected president with over 55 percent of the vote; he took office in March 1990, ending 17 years of military dictatorship. He was succeeded by Eduardo Frei Ruiz-Tagle in March 1994.

In the following years, Chile's economy expanded, as exports increased, and its large external debt was reduced. Although exports were still dominated by copper, other minerals and manufactures gained in importance. In 1996, Chile joined Mercosur, a free trade agreement among six of the largest South American nations. In 1997 the U.S. agreed to sell Chile advanced fighter jets, ending a 20-year ban.

In March 1998 Gen. Pinochet resigned as head of the armed forces after 25 years and was sworn in as senator-for-life. In Oct., while in Britain, Pinochet was arrested after Spain sought his extradition for the murder of Spanish citizens. A long legal minuet ended in Jan. 2000 when Britain's Home Secretary declared Pinochet unfit to stand trial. Only days later, in a run-off presidential election, the candidate of the center-left Concertacion Coalition, Ricardo Lagos Escobar, took 51.3 percent of the vote. Though Lagos was the first Socialist president since Allende, he supported a market economy. In 2003 Chile and the U.S. signed a free trade agreement eliminating tariffs on 85 percent of all goods and economic growth rose dramticaly.

In 2006, Chile's first woman president, Michelle Bachelet, took office as head of a coalition government headed again by Concertacion. Enormous protests by hundreds of thousands of students over education reform marred her first year in office.

▶ **CHINA**
People's Republic of China
● **GEOGRAPHY   Location:** covers vast area of eastern Asia. **Boundaries:** Russia, Mongolia to N; N. Korea to NE; Pacific Ocean to E; India, Nepal, Bhutan, Myanmar, Laos, and Vietnam to S; Afghanistan and Pakistan to W., Kazakhstan, Kyrgyzstan, and Tajikistan to NW. **Total land area:** 3,705,392 sq. mi. (9,596,960 sq km). **Coastline:** 9,112 mi. (14,500 km). **Comparative area:** between coterminous U.S. and Canada. **Land use:** 13% arable land;1% permanent crops, 86% other. **Major cities:** Beijing (capital); Shanghai; Tianjin; Shenyang; Wuhan; Chengdu; Xi'an.
● **PEOPLE   Population:** 1,330,044,605 (July 2008 est.). **Nationality:** noun—Chinese (sing., pl.); adjective—Chinese. **Ethnic groups:** 91.9% Han Chinese; 8.1% Zhuang, Uygur, Hui, Yi, Tibetan, Miao, Manchu, Mongol, Buyi, Korean, and numerous others. **Languages:** Standard Chinese or Mandarin (Putonghua based on the Beijing dialect); Yue (Cantonese), Wu (Shanghainese), Minbei (Fuzhou), Minnan (Hokkien-Taiwanese), Xiang, Gan, Hakka dialects, and minority langs. (see "Ethnic groups" above). **Religions:** officially atheist, but traditionally pragmatic and eclectic; Taoism, Buddhism, 1-2% Muslim, 3-4% Christian.
● **GOVERNMENT   Type:** Communist state. **Constitution:** Dec. 4, 1982. **National holiday:** National Day, Oct. 1, (1949) **Heads of Government:** Hu jintao, president (since Mar. 15, 2003); Wen Jiabao, prime minister (since Mar. 16, 2003). **Structure:** executive; unicameral legislature; judiciary.
● **ECONOMY   Monetary unit:** yuan. **Budget:** (2007 est.) *income:* $640.6 bil.; *expend.:* $634.6 bil.

G.D.P.: $7.04 tril., $5,300 per capita (2007 est.). **Chief crops:** rice, potatoes, sorghum, peanuts. **Natural resources:** coal, iron ore, crude oil, mercury, tin; world's largest hydropower potential. **Major industries:** iron, steel, coal. **Labor force:** 803.3 mil. (2007 est.); 11.7% agriculture and forestry, 49.2% industry, 39.1% services. **Exports:** $1.221 tril. (f.o.b., 2007); machinery and equipment, textiles, clothing. **Imports:** $9.147 bil. (f.o.b., 2007); machinery and equipment, chemicals, plastics, iron and steel. **Major trading partners:** (2006) *exports:* Hong Kong, U.S., Japan, Germany, South Korea; *imports:* Japan, U.S., Taiwan, South Korea, Germany.

China is one of the world's oldest civilizations. Dynastic rule in the North China Plain began around 2000 B.C. The unifying Qin (221 B.C.) and Han (206 B.C.) dynasties greatly expanded the territory of the empire and established the basic pattern of imperial bureaucratic government that would endure until the beginning of the 20th century. Major dynasties during that period include the Han (206 B.C.—A.D. 220), Tang (618-907), Song (960-1279), Yuan or Mongol (1279-1368), Ming (1368- 1644), and Qing (1644-1911).

By the late 18th century, the Qing dynasty faced increasingly dangerous problems of explosive population growth, bureaucratic stagnation, and trade pressure from the West. Opium—introduced by Great Britain to balance its trade in tea, silk, porcelain, and other goods—created severe social problems. Western demands for free trade resulted in the Opium War (1839-42), in which China was humiliatingly defeated by the British. The treaties of Nanjing (1842) and Tianjin (1858) opened China to Western merchants and missionaries and created foreign-ruled enclaves on Chinese soil. At the same time, the Taiping Rebellion and other popular uprisings led to the deaths of at least 20 million Chinese between 1850 and 1870.

Such reform efforts as the Self-Strengthening Movement (1870's) and the 1898 Reform Movement proved inadequate to the task of strengthening and modernizing China's dynastic government. Japan, modernizing rapidly after the Meiji Restoration of 1868, joined the race for commercial access to China, decisively winning the Sino-Japanese War of 1894-95. The antiforeign Boxer Uprising of 1900 was put down by a joint foreign military force, dealing a mortal blow to Qing rule. On Oct. 10, 1911, the dynasty fell to a coalition of forces led by the veteran revolutionary nationalist Sun Yat-sen.

China's first attempt at republican government, under Pres. Yuan Shikai and subsequent presidents, quickly degenerated into factionalism and warlord control in the provinces. In 1915 Japan successfully demanded further concessions, provoking public outcries. When news reached China on May 4, 1919, that the Treaty of Versailles granted Japan all of Germany's former concessions in China, students rioted throughout the country, demanding reforms and modernization (the May Fourth Movement). Sun Yat-sen's Nationalist party (Kuomintang, or KMT) and the Chinese Communist party (CCP, founded in 1921 by Mao Zedong) joined forces in 1922 in an attempt to create a second republican revolution.

Sun Yat-sen died in 1925. His successor, Chiang Kai-shek, consolidated KMT forces in Guangzhou and mounted the Northern Expedition (1927-29) to defeat or co-opt the various provincial warlords and reunify the country. Chiang then turned on his Communist allies. A series of failed Communist uprisings and KMT anti-Communist extermination campaigns between 1927 and 1934 nearly wiped out the CCP. Remnants of the party broke out of encirclement in Jiangxi Province in 1934 and undertook the 6,000-mile Long March to a secure base in Yan'an, Shanxi Province. There, under Mao, Zhou Enlai, and Zhu De, the CCP recovered its strength. In the Xi'an Incident of December 1936, Chiang was kidnapped by mutinous KMT allies and forced at gunpoint to agree to forming a United Front with the CCP against Japan.

Meanwhile Japan continued its penetration of China, with the assassination of Manchurian warlord and KMT ally Jiang Zuolin in 1928, the invasion of Manchuria on Sept. 18, 1931, and the establishment of the puppet state of Manchuguo in 1934. On July 7, 1937, fighting erupted between Japanese and Chinese troops near Beijing. The Japanese rapidly moved south to the Yangtse Valley, bombing and capturing Shanghai. The Nationalist capital at Nanjing fell in November 1937, amid widespread atrocities against civilians. The KMT army and government retreated to a wartime capital at Chongqing. The remainder of World War II in China was largely a stalemate, with Japan occupying most of the country. KMT-held areas opposed the Japanese with conventional forces (supported, after 1941, by the Americans), while the Communists harassed the Japanese with guerrilla tactics.

At the end of World War II, American forces ensured that the KMT would receive Japan's surrender throughout most of China, giving the Nationalists a commanding position while U.S. general George Marshall attempted to mediate the creation of a KMT-CCP coalition government. That effort failed, and civil war broke out. The KMT advantage was dissipated by ruinous inflation, corruption, mismanagement, and military ineffectiveness. At the end of 1947, with the Communist forces making continual advances, the United States pulled out of China. After losing several major battles throughout 1948-49, KMT forces retreated to Taiwan; in Beijing, Mao Zedong proclaimed the establishment of the People's Republic of China (PRC) on Oct. 1, 1949.

With U.S. backing, the Republic of China established a temporary capital at Taipei and continued to claim sovereignty over all of China, retaining China's seat in the U.N. The PRC was quickly granted diplomatic recognition by Soviet bloc nations and some Western nations, notably Great Britain, but was effectively isolated in most international affairs by American support for Nationalist China. Chinese troops entered the Korean War in November 1950, as U.N. forces approached the Sino-Korean border at the Yalu River. This direct confrontation between China and the United States forestalled any possibility of normal contacts for more than two decades.

Within China the CCP rapidly consolidated its control of the country and began rebuilding the nation after decades of warfare. Priority was given to land reform. Land was confiscated from landlords and returned to peasant ownership; landlords and other "class enemies" were tried and condemned by People's Courts set up under party auspices. Under the first five-year plan (1953), peasants were urged to set up rural cooperatives, while industrial recovery began with Soviet assistance. Artists, writers, and intellectuals were ordered to devote themselves to the service of the party and the nation. In 1956 Mao announced

a policy of "let a hundred flowers bloom, let a hundred schools of thought contend," inviting criticism of the party and government. He was shocked by the vigor of the criticism; many critics were sent to labor camps in the ensuing Anti-Rightist Campaign of 1957.

Angered by the arrogance of Soviet advisers and by Soviet refusal to share nuclear weapons technology with China, Mao broke with the Soviet Union and expelled all Soviet personnel in 1958. At the same time, he announced the policy of the Great Leap Forward, under which China was to make progress on all fronts without outside aid. Huge rural communes took the place of peasant smallholdings and cooperatives, and agriculture was placed under the direction of centralized planning. In industry, labor and enthusiasm were expected to make up for a shortage of capital and technical expertise. The Great Leap was a catastrophic failure, causing widespread famine and social dislocation, as Mao admitted in a forced self-criticism in 1960. Mao withdrew into the background as a group of party pragmatists led by Liu Shaoqi assumed power in the early 1960's.

In foreign affairs Chinese shelling of the Nationalist-held offshore islands of Quemoy and Matsu in 1958 led to a crisis in the Taiwan Straits, patrolled by the U.S. Seventh Fleet to prevent a recurrence of China's civil war. A rebellion in Tibet in 1959 was suppressed with much bloodshed, and the dalai lama fled to India. Chinese troop movements into Tibet contributed to the outbreak in 1960 of a border war with India. Throughout the 1960's China worried about being drawn into the Vietnam War.

In late 1965 Mao made a bid to return to full power. His vehicle was the Great Proletarian Cultural Revolution, formally launched in 1966. Shock troops of teenage Red Guards were used to attack the entrenched party bureaucracy; Liu Shaoqi was placed under house arrest, and other prominent officials, including Deng Xiaoping, were exiled to rural areas. By 1968 internal disorder was so great that the military intervened to restore control in many areas. Most established organs of power were replaced under the Cultural Revolution by Revolutionary Committees; intellectuals, technical workers, and bureaucrats were severely persecuted. In 1971 Mao's second-in-command, Marshal Lin Biao, staged an abortive coup and died while attempting to flee the country. With Mao increasingly old and ill, most of his power was exercised by his wife, Jiang Qing, and her associates. Her rival, Premier Zhou Enlai, attempted to maintain orderly government functions in the face of this turmoil.

The 1968 Soviet invasion of Czechoslovakia convinced Mao that the U.S.S.R. was a greater threat to China than America, and he quietly encouraged the growth of better relations with the U.S. With tacit American approval, the PRC replaced the Republic of China (Taiwan) in the U.N. on Oct. 25, 1971. During Feb. 21-28, 1972, U.S. president Richard Nixon visited China. The Shanghai Communiqué, issued at the end of that visit, clarified the positions of both sides and paved the way for the resumption of U.S.-China relations short of formal diplomatic recognition.

Zhou Enlai died in January 1976, and Deng Xiaoping became acting premier. In April 1976 a rally in Beijing commemorating Zhou's birthday was dispersed by police on orders from Jiang Qing, and a riot ensued. Deng was dismissed from office. But when Mao died on Sept. 9, 1976, Deng reemerged as China's paramount leader. Jiang Qing and three associates were arrested along with many of their allies. Labeled the Gang of Four, Jiang Qing's clique was blamed for all the ills of the Cultural Revolution; they were tried and convicted for crimes against the state in 1981.

China's post-Mao transformation took a decisive turn in 1978, with the announcement of the policy of the Four Modernizations (agriculture, industry, science and technology, and defense). Foreign investment and technology transfer were encouraged, and thousands of students were sent to study abroad. In the winter of 1978-79, the authorities tolerated the public posting of written critiques of the government ("Democracy Wall"). Deng consolidated power in his own hands, still acting behind the scenes; Deng's allies Hu Yaobang and Zhao Ziyang were promoted to leadership of the party and government in 1982.

On Jan. 1, 1979, China and the United States entered into formal diplomatic relations; the United States rescinded its recognition of the Republic of China as China's legal government but maintained separate nongovernmental relations with the ROC under the Taiwan Relations Act. China's relations with Vietnam deteriorated in 1978 following Vietnam's invasion of Cambodia. In February 1979, China attempted, with little success, to "teach Vietnam a lesson" in a brief but violent border war. A conflict with Great Britain was resolved in 1984 as both sides agreed that Hong Kong would be returned to Chinese sovereignty, but with considerable local autonomy, in 1997. Relations with the Soviet Union remained strained, China insisting that no improvement could come before the U.S.S.R. reduced its troop concentrations on the Sino-Soviet border, withdrew from Afghanistan, and pressured Vietnam into withdrawing from Cambodia. China's overall foreign-policy stance in the post-Mao era has been low-key and nonconfrontational.

In the 1980's, China achieved spectacular improvements in agricultural production through dismantling rural communes and returning land to individual peasant holdings under long-term leases. Small-scale private enterprise has been encouraged in both rural and urban areas. Within the overall context of reform, factions of relatively more conservative and reformist leaders have coexisted uneasily. A conservative drive against "spiritual pollution" in 1986 was quickly blunted by Deng, but in January 1987, the reformist party-secretary Hu Yaobang was ousted after student demonstrations calling for more democracy. The CCP 12th Party Congress in Oct. 1987 named the reformist Zhao Ziyang as party secretary, and the conservative pragmatist Li Peng as premier.

In April 1989 student demonstrators in Beijing mourning the death of Hu Yaobang launched a general movement for greater democracy. Demonstrators began a hunger strike and disrupted a summit visit by Soviet president Gorbachev. Martial law was proclaimed in May as demonstrations spread to other cities. Troops opened fire in Tienanmen Square on June 3-4, killing hundreds of demonstrators. In the aftermath, Zhao Ziyang was replaced as party secretary by Jiang Zemin, thousands of protesters and suspected dissidents were arrested (and an unknown number executed), and hard-liners in the government took firm control of the country.

World opinion was outraged by the Tienanmen incident; the United States and many other countries instituted sanctions against China, tourism plummeted, and the economy went into general decline. International trade resumed during 1989-90, and the U.S. renewed China's most-favored-nation status in June 1990 after several hundred dissidents were released from prison.

China strove to put Tienanmen Square behind it by holding speedy trials of those charged in connection with demonstrations. The government also made overtures to the former U.S.S.R., and from its permanent seat on the U.N. Security Council supported coalition efforts against Iraq in the Persian Gulf conflict. Economic sanctions were lifted by Western governments in 1991. China continued to pursue its economic reform policies while repressing all signs of political dissent. While national politics, seemed torpid and adrift, the private-sector economy continued to grow vigorously. In 1992-93 runaway growth made China's economy the world's fourth-largest. This resulted in higher wages and increased consumer spending, but also widening income disparities, increased corruption, theft, etc.

Deng's long-expected death, in 1997, produced little immediate effect on the Chinese leadership, except for a new crackdown as leaders competed to seem tough on dissent. But the transition of power to Jiang Zemin, 71, went smoothly.

Domestic affairs in general were overshadowed by national jubilation over the return of Hong Kong to Chinese sovreignty on July 1, 1997. (Macao would follow, in December 1999, after 442 years as a Portuguese colony.) Pres. Clinton made a long state visit in 1998 and appeared on Chinese TV criticizing China for human rights abuses and urged Mr. Jiang to open Chinese society. Undismayed, the Chinese government proceeded to crush the fledgling China Democracy Party, sentencing three of its leaders to long prison terms for subversion. In Feb. 1999, new missiles menaced Taiwan; tensions grew worse in July when Taiwan's president said publicly that his country was a separate Chinese state.

In the face of not only these issues but also the newer "human rights" issue of China's ban on and persecution of the Falun Gong religious movement, the U.S. reached a trade agreement with China at the end of 1999 (as had Japan in July). In 2001 China signed a 20-year Friendship Treaty with Russia, the first since the end of the Cold War; it pledged peaceful settlement of border disputes and coordination against threats of aggression.

In Nov. 2002 the 16th Communist Party Congress named Hu Jintao as Party Secretary, replacing Jiang Zemin, and the National People's Congress formally ratified the Party decisions. Jiang remains as chairman of the Central Military Commission and unofficial eminence grise.

From 2005-2008 China's economy continued its extraordinary expansion through exports of everything from steel to textiles. Free trade agreements with ASEAN nations including Japan and Korea strengthened China's claim to regional leadership. Warnings to Taiwan continued, military spending increased and Russia joined China in military excercises. (See "Major News Stories.")

▶ **COLOMBIA**
Republic of Colombia
● **GEOGRAPHY Location:** northwestern coast of South America. **Boundaries:** Caribbean Sea to N,

Venezuela, Brazil to E, Peru, Ecuador to S, Panama, Pacific Ocean to W. **Total land area:** 439,734 sq. mi. (1,138,910 sq km). **Coastline:** 1,992 mi. (3,208 km). **Comparative area:** between Texas and Alaska. **Land use:** 2% arable land; 2% permanent crops;96% other. **Major cities:** Bogotá (capital); Cali; Medellín; Cartagena.

• **PEOPLE   Population:** 45,013,674 (July 2008 est.). **Nationality:** noun—Colombian(s); adjective—Colombian. **Ethnic groups:** 58% mestizo, 20% white, 14% mulatto, 4% black, 4% other. **Languages:** Spanish. **Religions:** 90% Roman Catholic.

• **GOVERNMENT   Type:** republic; executive branch dominates government structure. **Independence:** July 20, 1810 (from Spain). **Constitution:** July 5, 1991. **National holiday:** Independence Day, July 20. **Head of Government:** Álvaro Uribe Vélez, president (since Aug. 2002). **Structure:** executive; bicameral legislature; judiciary.

• **ECONOMY   Monetary unit:** Colombian peso. **Budget:** (2007 est.) *income:* $64.02 bil.; *expend.:* $64.35 bil. **G.D.P.:** $320.4 bil., $7,200 per capita (2007 est.). **Chief crops:** coffee, flowers, bananas, rice; illegal producer of coca and cannabis for international drug trade. **Natural resources:** crude oil, natural gas, coal, iron ore, nickel. **Major industries:** textiles, food processing, oil. **Labor force:** 20.65 mil. (2007 est.); 58.5% services, 22.7% agriculture, 18.7% industry (2000); 10.6% unemployment (2007 est.). **Exports:** $28.39 bil. (f.o.b., 2007 est.); petroleum, coffee, coal, bananas, flowers. **Imports:** $30.83 bil. (f.o.b., 2007 est.); industrial equipment, transportation equipment, consumer goods, chemicals. **Major trading partners:** (2006) *exports:* 35.8% U.S., 11.4% Venezuela, 5.4% Ecuador; *imports:* 26.8% U.S., 8.6% Brazil, 8.5% Mexico, 6% China, 5.6% Venezuela, 4.1% Japan.

The territory that is now Colombia was home to various cultures prior to the arrival of Europeans. The Chibcha population of the Andean region might have numbered about one million prior to European contact. Portions of the area that make up modern Colombia fell under the authority of the Inca Empire.

In 1538 the colony of New Granada was established with its capital at Bogotá, and for most of the period up until 1740, the area was within the jurisdiction of the Viceroyalty of Peru. In that year a new viceroyalty was established that included modern-day Colombia, Ecuador, Panama, and Venezuela. During the wars of independence against Spain, forces under Simón Bolívar were victorious over the royalists at the Battle of Boyacá in 1819, and the region gained independence in 1821.

Colombian territory was a part of the federation of Gran Colombia until the collapse of the federal arrangement in 1830. Thereafter, the country—called New Granada—remained a separate political entity (which included the area of Panama). By the 1850's a federal system had been adopted by the country. But this arrangement rapidly disintegrated, and the practically semisovereign states were involved in a constant struggle with the central government for autonomy. The effort to define the political structure was largely resolved with the constitution of 1886, which ended federalist regional autonomy and made Colombia a unitary republic.

Colombian political struggle since the 1850's had been characterized by a rivalry between two groups that coalesced into the Liberal and Conservative parties. During much of the 19th cen-

tury, the Liberal-Conservative ideological battle was influenced to a great extent by the definition of the role of the Roman Catholic church in political and social life. The 1887-88 Concordat gave the church "official protection," while the state was given authority over public education. The settlement left a central position for the church in Colombian society that was not substantially altered by the Concordat of 1942.

The Liberal-Conservative struggle led to at least six civil wars, which often ended in interparty compromise. A struggle in 1854 involved the issue of the future direction of the country's economic development and was followed by a settlement among elites. The Liberal-Conservative war of 1860-63 led to a Liberal victory and a period of Liberal political hegemony that lasted until 1886. The period of Conservative rule from 1886 until 1930 was punctuated by the "War of a Thousand Days" (1899-1902), in which the Conservatives defeated the Liberals. In 1903 the Colombian government rejected a U.S. offer for construction of a canal in Panama. Panama (backed by the U.S.) revolted against the Colombian government, ending in the separation of Panama from Colombia.

The world depression of 1929 disrupted both the economy and the politics of Colombia. The loss of popularity of the ruling Conservatives due to both the economic collapse and their brutal repression of the labor movement led to a Liberal victory in 1930. A new civil war between peasants loyal to the two parties also broke out that year. By 1934 Liberal president Alfonso López Pumarejo had inaugurated his "Revolution on the March" program of socioeconomic reform.

During the 1946 presidential election, Conservatives won the presidency with a minority of the overall vote, defeating a split Liberal party. Armed conflict originally instigated by the two party elites erupted. This marked the beginning of La Violencia (1948-57) during which more than 200,000 people died. In the summer of 1957, leaders of the Liberal and Conservative parties reached an agreement on constitutional reform in an attempt to end the violence. The agreement, known as the National Front, was to be in force for 16 years and included provisions for regular alternation of the presidency between the parties, as well as an accord on equal staffing of all political positions by both parties. The Liberal and Conservative parties agreed they alone would monopolize the arena of legitimate political competition for the 16-year period. The agreement held up until 1968 constitutional revisions allowed for other political groups to be officially recognized.

The emergence of terrorist and paramilitary groups on both the right and left—some with ties to the drug trade—in the 1960's and 1970's weakened the two-party power-sharing monopoly. In March 1990, one of the most notorious left-wing groups, M-19, elected to lay down its arms and enter the political mainstream and immediately captured 19 of 70 seats in a constitutional convention called to rewrite the constitution. Other groups followed suit in 1991.

Throughout the 1980's, narco-terrorists murdered government officials, journalists, and innocent bystanders with impunity. Despite the assassination of four presidential candidates prior to the 1990 election, the Liberal party's César Gaviria Trujillo won the election campaigning against the drug traffickers. In 1994 another Liberal party president (Ernesto Samper Pizano) took office pledging to continue the fight. Samper also promised to invest billions of dollars to improve the infrastructure with money from the newly discovered Cusiana oil field.

In the summer of 1995, the Samper government arrested three of the top seven members of the Cali drug cartel; by Sept. 1996, all seven had been apprehended. Meanwhile, Samper faced accusations that he knew of $6 million contributed by the Cali cartel. Formal charges instituted by Prosecutor General Valdivieso in Feb. 1996 were found groundless by the legislature's Accusations Committee. Still, the United States, which had decertified Colombia as a drug-war partner in March, revoked Samper's visa even as Colombian farmers protested government anti-coca and -poppy programs. In 1997 radical leftist terrorist groups began a wave of murders, kidnappings, and other violence against local government officials, and in 1998 attacked and defeated an army battalion. The election of Conservative Andres Pastrana in June 1998 held out promise of victory in the drug war despite violent outbursts during the remainder of 1998 and early 1999. Government meetings with FARC, the principal rebel group, and National Peace Council meetings with ELN, the second major insurgent group, continued into mid-1999. On Dec. 20, FARC announced a ceasefire (the first since 1984) until January 10. When, on Jan. 11, 2000, FARC forces attacked four towns, the Clinton administration approved a two-year aid package to Colombia of $1.4 billion.

Pastrana's patience gave out in 2002 and he again sent jets and ground troops against FARC, but too late to prevent independent ex-Liberal Álvaro Uribe Vélez from winning the May 2002 presidential election. In 2003 the war entered its 35th year but Uribe's policy of "democratic security"—driving FARC from its strongholds, and pardoning many who wished to leave—had some good effects. In 2005, however, the paramilitaries again went on the attack and peace talks were again started. Uribe won reelection in a landslide in May 2006 and with U.S. aid was able to stifle the violence somewhat.

▶COMOROS
Union of Comoros Islands
● **GEOGRAPHY Location:** part of archipelago in Mozambique Channel; three main islands, Njazidja, Nzwami, and Mwali (formerly Grande-Comore, Anjouan, and Mohéli). Moroni, Njazidja Is., 11°40'S, 43°16'E. **Boundaries:** between Madagascar and southeast Africa. **Total land area:** 838 sq. mi. (2,170 sq. km). **Coastline:** 211 mi. (340 km). **Comparative area:** slightly more than 12 times size of Washington, D.C. **Land use:** 35% arable land; 18% permanent crops; 47% other. **Major cities:** Moroni (capital); Mutsamudu; Fomboni. ● **PEOPLE Population:** 731,775 (July 2008 est.). **Nationality:** noun—Comoran(s); adjective—Comoran. **Ethnic groups:** Antalote, Cafre, Makoa, Oimatsaha, Sakalava. **Languages:** Arabic and French (both official), Shikomoro (a blend of Swahili and Arabic). **Religions:** 98% Sunni Muslim, 2% Roman Catholic. ● **GOVERNMENT Type:** independent republic. **Independence:** July 6, 1975 (from France). Independence Day, July 6. **Heads of Government:** Ahmed Abdallah Sambi, head of state (since May 2006). **Structure:** executive; bicameral legislature; judiciary.

● **ECONOMY Monetary unit:** Comoran franc. **Budget:** (2001 est.) *income:* $27.6 mil.; *expend.:* N.A. **G.D.P.:** $436 mil., $600 per capita (2007 est.). **Chief crops:** vanilla, cloves, perfume essences. **Natural resources:** negligible. **Major industries:** tourism, perfume distillation. **Labor force:** 144,500 (1996); 80% agriculture; 20% services. **Exports:** $32 mil. (f.o.b., 2006 est.); vanilla, ylang-ylang, cloves, perfume oils. **Imports:** $143 mil. (f.o.b., 2006 est.); rice and other foodstuffs, consumer goods, petroleum products, cement. **Major trading partners:** (2006) *exports:* 36% Netherlands, 18.3% France, 12.8% Italy, 7.8% Singapore, 5% Turkey, 4.6% U.S.; *imports:* 24.8% France, 9.9% U.A.E., 6.4% South Africa, 6.3% Pakistan, 5% Kenya, 4.8% China, 4.4% India, 4.2% Italy.

Comoros is part of an archipelago composed of four prominent islands (the fourth, Mayotte, is a French dependency) and several smaller islands. Numerous groups from Africa, Europe, and Asia invaded the islands over the centuries. Shirazi Arabs introduced Islam to Comoros around the turn of the 16th century, and the French established colonial rule over the archipelago between 1841 and 1912 and developed a plantation-based economy. The islands remained a French territory until 1961 when political autonomy was granted. Comoros gained independence in 1975. Overthrown by foreign mercenaries in 1975, Pres. Ahmed Abdallah Abderemane returned to power in 1978 and helped establish the country's first constitution. In Nov. 1989 he was assassinated by a small group of rebels who quickly dispersed under pressure from the French government. A new constitution was approved in 1992, and the country's first democratic elections were held in Nov. 1992. An attempt, begun in 1997, by the islands of Anjouan and Moheli to gain independence or at least autonomy led to an army coup in April 1999 and Anjouan's claim of independence in Jan. 2000, a claim he soon renounced.

Much of the nation's soil is laden with lava, making it unsuitable for farming, especially on the island of Njazidja (Grand Comore), which is dominated by Mount Kartala, an active volcano. Poor transportation links between the islands and a harsh cyclone season add further to the country's problems. In an effort to end the series of coup attempts (over 20 since 1975), Comoros adopted a new constitution in Dec. 2001, which provides for a rotating presidency among the four islands in four-year terms, as well as a separate president and more autonomy for each of the four islands.

▶CONGO
Democratic Republic of the Congo (formerly Zaire)
● **GEOGRAPHY Location:** equatorial country in central Africa. **Boundaries:** Central African Republic, Sudan to N, Uganda, Rwanda, Burundi, Tanzania to E, Zambia to S, Angola to SW, Atlantic Ocean, Cabinda district of Angola, Congo to W. **Total land area:** 905,564 sq. mi. (2,345,410 sq km). **Coastline:** 23 mi. (37 km). **Comparative area:** about 1.5 times size of Alaska. **Land use:** 3% arable land; 1% permanent crops; 96% other. **Major cities:** (Kinshasa (capital); Lubumbashi (Elizabethville); Mbuji-Mayi (Bakwanga); Kananga (Luluabourg); Kisangani (Stanleyville). ● **PEOPLE Population:** 66,514,506 (July 2008 est.). **Nationality:** noun—Zairian(s); adjective—Zairian. **Ethnic groups:** 45% of the people belong to one of four largest groups—Mongo, Luba, Kongo (all Bantu), and Mangbetu-Azande; over

200 other ethnic groups. **Languages:** French (official), Lingala, Kingwana, Kikongo, Tshiluba. **Religions:** 50% Roman Catholic, 20% Protestant, 10% Kimbanguist, 10% Muslim, 10% other syncretic sects and traditional beliefs.

• **GOVERNMENT Type:** republic. **Independence:** June 30, 1960 (from Belgium). **Constitution:** Feb. 2006. **National holiday:** Independence Day, Nov. 24. **Heads of Government:** Joseph Kabila, president (since Jan. 2001); Antoine Gizenga, prime minister (since Feb. 2007). **Structure:** executive—president elected for five-year term; legislative—500-member National Assembly; judiciary.

• **ECONOMY Monetary unit:** zaire. **Budget:** (2006 est.) *income*: $700 mil. *expend.*: $2 bil. **G.D.P.:** $19.07 bil., $300 per capita (2007 est.). **Chief crops:** coffee, sugar, palm oil, rubber, tea. **Natural resources:** cobalt, copper, cadmium, crude oil, industrial and gem diamonds. **Major industries:** mining, mineral processing, consumer products (incl. textiles, footwear, cigarettes). **Labor force:** 15 mil (2006 est.); 55% agriculture, 11% industry, 34% services. **Exports:** $1.587 bil. (f.o.b., 2006 est.); diamonds, copper, coffee, cobalt, crude oil. **Imports:** $2.263 bil. (f.o.b., 2006 est.); foodstuffs, mining and other machinery, transport equipment, fuels. **Major trading partners:** (2006) *exports*: 29.4% Belgium, 21.1% China, 12.3% Brazil, 7.8% Chile, 7.2% Finland, 4.9% U.S.; *imports:* 17.7% South Africa, 10.9% Belgium, 8.5% France, 8.1% Zimbabwe, 6.9% Zambia, 6.8% Kenya, 4.4% Cote D'Ivoire.

Pygmies were probably the earliest inhabitants of the Congo region, followed much later by Bantu and Nilotic peoples. By the eighth century A.D., a number of well-established kingdoms and empires occupied the lower reaches of the Congo (now Zaire) River and the coastal plain; these included Kongo (Bakongo), Kuba, Luba, and Lunda.

Portuguese explorers and merchants arrived along the coast in the 1480's and initially traded with these kingdoms on a basis of relative equality; an indigenous Catholic church became established. Soon, however, the Portuguese established a slave trade that brought turmoil and decline to the native states. Europeans did not penetrate the interior of Zaire until the 19th century, but the slave trade (partly in Arab hands, in inland regions) had repercussions everywhere.

Henry Stanley descended the Congo River from east to west in 1876, opening the area for further exploration. In 1878 Stanley was engaged by King Leopold II of Belgium to establish Belgian trading stations along the river. King Leopold established the Congo Free State in 1885, not as a Belgian colony but as a personal possession of which he was king as well as chief stockholder.

The management corporation that ran the Free State abolished slavery but instituted a harsh regime that reduced native peoples to a condition of involuntary servitude. Forced labor and harsh suppression of rebellion resulted in the deaths of unnumbered thousands. Protests against these conditions, led by Great Britain and the U. S., led to the transformation of the Free State into the colony of the Belgian Congo in 1908.

By the 1920's the Belgian Congo had become a major producer of copper, diamonds, gold, rubber, palm oil, and other commodities. Railroads were developed to bring these goods to market. River navigation on the Congo was also developed. All mining, plantation agriculture, industry,

and administration was in Belgian hands with no native participation in government.

In the 1950's agitation for increased native participation in government led, in 1957, to elections for local councils. In 1959 rioting against Belgian rule broke out. Elections were held on May 31 in anticipation of independence. Joseph Kasavubu became president, and Patrice Lumumba, head of the Congolese National Movement, became prime minister. On June 30, 1960, Belgium granted independence to the Congo; many Europeans fled the country. On July 4 the army mutinied, and on July 11 the southern province of Katanga (now Shaba), under the leadership of Moise Tshombe, seceded from the Congo and declared its independence. Belgium sent troops to quell the disorder.

On Aug. 9 the U.N. called on Belgium to withdraw its troops. Kasavubu removed Lumumba as prime minister. Lumumba, with the backing of Ghana, fought for control. He fled to Stanleyville (now Kisangani) but was kidnapped in January 1961 and taken to Katanga, where he was murdered, apparently with U.S. and Belgian complicity. Fighting continued in Katanga, where Tshombe's regime was supported by European mercenaries and opposed by U.N. peacekeeping forces. The Katangan rebellion ended in late 1963; rebels fled to Angola, and U.N. forces were withdrawn in June 1964. In a surprising political settlement, Tshombe became president of the Congo on June 30. On Sept. 7 leftist rebels attempted to establish a "people's republic" based in Stanleyville. Tshombe again resorted to the use of mercenaries and many white settlers, as well as Congolese, were killed in fighting and terrorist atrocities. The rebellion ended in July 1965. In Nov. 1965 Tshombe was deposed in a military coup led by Joseph Mobutu, whose government took steps to reduce European influence.

In 1971 Mobutu changed the country's name to Zaire and also changed the name of Leopoldville to Kinshasa. In 1972 he ordered all Zairians with European names to change them to African names; he became Mobutu Sese Seko. Attempts in 1974 to force foreign investors to sell their holdings to Zairians brought economic disruption, and foreign investors were invited back in 1977.

In 1977 rebellion broke out in Katanga; the government put down the rebellion with the aid of France, Egypt, and Morocco. The rebels fled to Angola, but the province's rich mining economy was again disrupted. Although Congo is rich with minerals, forest products, hydroelectric potential, and agriculture, most of these natural resources remain undeveloped and the country was impoverished by the nearly unprecedented corruption of the Mobutu regime. Rival leaders attempted to organize opposition to the Mobutu government in late 1987 and 1988, but most were arrested or driven into exile.

In June 1991, Mobutu agreed to draft a new constitution and end a 20-year ban on multiparty elections. Étiene Tshisekedi was elected prime minister by a national conference in 1992, but Mobutu fired him in 1993. France and Belgium dispatched troops to protect their nationals and together with the U.S. demanded that Mobutu transfer power to Tshisekedi. Mobutu did not comply, and as his nation's economy sank, he continued to live in luxury, protected by the army and police. In May, 1997, Mobutu was driven from office by the army of Laurent Kabila, who immediately changed the name of the country to Congo.

In the summer of 1998 a new military rebellion began—a rebellion joined by Uganda and Rwanda. By June 1999, a cease-fire seemed near, one that would involve the U.N. and the Organization of African Unity as peacemakers with a mandate to disarm the rebels. The cease-fire came in July 1999, but was not signed by the rebels, only by the six outside states. And an August split in the rebel group brought Rwanda and Uganda to war with each other, each supporting its "own" rebel faction. In 2000 Rwanda proved victorious over Uganda; and by June, the U.N. security council decided that peacekeepers would not be sent.

In Jan. 2001, Pres. Kabila was shot to death by a bodyguard; the (appointed) parliament chose his son, Joseph, as new president. Peace negotiations continued, on and off, through 2003, when Congo reached a series of peace accords with Rwanda,Uganda, and two main rebel groups. A transitional government of President Kabila and four vice presidents ruled until 2006 when elections in July were to bring a new government. Kabila won 45 percent of the vote, thereby forcing a run-off. The U.N. was forced to send troops to stop the violence between rival parties, but in Oct. 2006, Kabila won the presidency. A National Assembly, and local leaders and legislatures were also elected.

▶ CONGO, REPUBLIC OF THE

• **GEOGRAPHY Location:** equatorial country on western coast of Africa. **Boundaries:** Cameroon to NW, Central African Republic to NE, Zaire to E and S, Angolan district of Cabinda to S, Gulf of Guinea to SW, Gabon to W. **Total land area:** 132,046 sq. mi. (342,000 sq km). **Coastline:** 105 mi. (169 km). **Comparative area:** between New Mexico and Montana. **Land use:** 1 % arable land; negl.% permanent crops; 99% other. **Major cities:** Brazzaville (capital); Pointe-Noire; Pool; Bouenza; Cuvette.

• **PEOPLE Population:** 3,903,318 (July 2008 est.). **Nationality:** noun—Congolese (sing., pl.); adjective—Congolese or Congo. **Ethnic groups:** 48% Kongo, 20% Sangha, 17% Teke, 12% M'Bochi; about 8,500 Europeans (may be half that number following 1997 civil war). **Languages:** French (official); many African languages with Lingala and Kikongo most widely used. **Religions:** 50% Christian, 48% Animist, 2% Muslim.

• **GOVERNMENT Type:** republic. **Independence:** Aug. 15, 1960 (from France). **Constitution:** Approved by referendum Jan. 2002. **National holiday:** National Day, Aug. 15. **Heads of Government:** Denis Sassou Nguesso, president (since 1997). **Structure:** executive; bicameral legislature; judiciary.

• **ECONOMY Monetary unit:** Communauté Financière Africaine (CFA) franc. **Budget:** (2007 est.) *income:* $3.369 mil.; *expend.:* $2.104 bil. **G.D.P.:** $13.97 bil., $3,700 per capita (2007 est.). **Chief crops:** cassava, sugar, rice. **Natural resources:** petroleum, timber, potash, lead, zinc. **Major industries:** crude oil, cement, sawmills. **Labor force:** 79,100 (1985); 75% agriculture, 25% commerce, industry, government. **Exports:** $6.455 bil. (f.o.b., 2007); petroleum, lumber, plywood. **Imports:** $1.724 bil. (f.o.b., 2007); petroleum products, capital equipment, construction materials. **Major trading partners:** (2006) *exports:* 36% U.S., 31.4% China, 10% Taiwan, 8% South Korea; *imports:*

23.5% France, 13.2% China, 7.6% U.S., 7% India, 5.6% Italy, 5.3% Belgium.

About 1,500 years ago, the lower reaches of the Congo River formed the focus of a number of well-organized states. The Kongo and Ndonga flourished south of the river; north of the river, in what is now the Congo, the Loango, Teke, and Bobangi were dominant. Some of these states were weakened beginning in the 16th century by the Portuguese slave trade, although the Loango benefited from it through the 19th century.

With the weakening of Portuguese power, the French became the dominant European power in western Africa. In 1883 they established a protectorate over the Teke kingdom, which they renamed Middle Congo. The treaty with the Teke king was concluded by Pierre Savorgnan de Brazza, for whom the capital was named.

In 1910 the French confederated their protectorates of Gabon, Middle Congo, Ubangi-Shari (later the Central African Republic), and Chad to form French Equatorial Africa. The territory became an important base of Free French activity during World War II, in acknowledgment of which Gen. Charles de Gaulle granted French citizenship to the territory's inhabitants in 1946, and local power was devolved upon advisory assemblies. The Republic of the Congo attained full autonomy upon the dissolution of the confederation of French Equatorial Africa in 1959, and the nation gained full independence on Apr. 15, 1960.

In 1963 Pres. Fulbert Youlou was driven from office by violent labor unrest; the military took control and installed a provisional civilian government led by Alphonse Massamba-Debat, who was elected president for a five-year term.

In 1968 Massamba-Debat was overthrown in a military coup and replaced by Capt. Marien Ngouabi, who in 1969 reorganized the Congo as a People's Republic. Despite its Marxist-Leninist stance, Congo remained strongly linked to France, its main source of trade, aid, and foreign investment. Ngouabi was assassinated in 1977 and replaced by a military committee of the Congolese Labor party led by Gen. Joachim Yhomby-Opango, who resigned and was arrested for treason in 1979. He was succeeded by Denis Sassou-Nguesso, who was reelected to a third five-year term in 1989.

In 1990, Congo began a relatively smooth transition to multiparty democracy and opposition parties were legalized as of Jan. 1, 1991. Pascal Lissouba was elected president in Aug. 1992. In June 1997, however, heavy fighting erupted in Brazzaville when Lissouba tried to have his rival, Sassou-Nguesso, arrested just weeks before a new election on the grounds that Sassou-Nguesso was planning a coup. He was and he succeeded, with oil money to buy arms and pay off rivals until by April 2001 a sort of peace and stability ensued, enough to elicit an E.U. loan. But ethnic civil war again broke out in June 2002 and lasted until March 2003. Elections in 2007 seemed odd since the ruling party won 90 percent of the seats in parliament.

▶ COSTA RICA
Republic of Costa Rica

• **GEOGRAPHY Location:** Central American isthmus. **Boundaries:** Nicaragua to N, Caribbean Sea to E, Panama to S, and Pacific Ocean to W. **Total land area:** 19,730 sq. mi. (51,100 sq km). **Coastline:** 801 mi. (1,290 km). **Comparative area:** slightly smaller than West Virginia. **Land use:** 4% arable land; 5% permanent crops; 91% other. **Major cities**: San José (capital); Alajuela; Cartago; Puntarenas; Heredia.

• **PEOPLE** **Population:** 4,195,914 (July 2008 est.). **Nationality:** noun—Costa Rican(s); adjective—Costa Rican. **Ethnic groups:** 94% white (including mestizo), 3% black, 1% Amerindian, 1% Chinese. **Languages:** Spanish (official), Jamaican dialect of English spoken around Puerto Limón. **Religions:** 76.3% Roman Catholic, 13.7% Evangelical Protestant, other Protestant, Jehovah's Witness.

• **GOVERNMENT** **Type:** democratic republic. **Independence:** Sept. 15, 1821 (from Spain). **Constitution:** Nov. 7, 1949. **National holiday:** Independence Day, Sept. 15. **Head of Government:** Oscar Arias, president (since May 2006). **Structure:** executive; unicameral legislature; judiciary.

• **ECONOMY** **Monetary unit:** Costa Rican colón. **Budget:** (2007 est.) *income:* $3.57 bil.; *expend.:* $3.84 bil. **G.D.P.:** $55.95 bil., $13,500 per capita (2007 est.). **Chief crops:** coffee, bananas, sugarcane, corn, rice, cocoa. **Natural resources:** hydropower potential. **Major industries:** microprocessors, food processing, textiles, clothing, construction materials. **Labor force:** 1.946 mil. (2007 est.); 22% industry, 20% agriculture, 58% services; 5.5% unemployment (2007 est.). **Exports:** $9.23 bil. (f.o.b., 2007 est.); manufactured products, coffee, bananas, textiles, sugar. **Imports:** $11.84 bil. (f.o.b. 2007 est.); raw materials, consumer goods, capital equipment. **Major trading partners:** *exports:* U.S., Netherlands, China, U.K., Mexico; *imports:* U.S., China, Brazil, Mexico, Venezuela, Japan, Ireland.

Costa Rica was under the jurisdiction of the Spanish colonial kingdom of Guatemala until it broke with Spain in 1821, along with other parts of Central America. With the collapse of the United Provinces of Central America in 1838, Costa Rica became an independent republic, and the country held its first democratic elections in 1889.

An attempt at electoral fraud in 1948 led to a brief civil war, which was won by the National Liberation forces under "Don Pepé" Jose Figueres Ferrer. The Costa Rican army was subsequently abolished. In the 1980's, under Pres. Oscar Arias Sánchez, Costa Rica vigorously promoted the settlement of civil strife in Nicaragua and El Salvador and he was awarded the 1987 Nobel Peace Prize for his Central American peace plan.

Subsequent governments focused on economic matters. In 1994 Jose Maria Figueres Olsen, son of "Don Pepé," was elected president. But out-of-control public spending brought new debt and inflation. In 1998 Miguel Ángel Rodriguez captured the presidency, and his Social Christian Unity party carried an absolute majority in the Legislative Assembly. In 2002 the same party's candidate, Abel Pacheco, won the presidency. In 2005 a corruption scandal that revealed three previous presidents had bilked the government and taken bribes from foreign companies rocked the political stability of a nation proud of its standing as a model in the region. In 2006, the people elected a winner of the Nobel Peace Prize, Oscar Arias. A free trade deal with the U.S. was narrowly approved in 2007.

▶ **COTE D'IVOIRE**
(see Ivory Coast)

▶ **CROATIA**
Republic of Croatia
• **GEOGRAPHY** **Location:** southeastern Europe. **Boundaries:** Slovenia and Hungary to N, Yu-

goslavia and Bosnia and Herzegovina to E, Adriatic Sea to S, Slovenia to W. **Total land area:** 21,024 sq. mi. (56,538 sq km). **Coastline:** 1,105 mi. (1,778 km). **Comparative area:** Slightly smaller than West Virginia. **Land use:** 24% arable land; 2% permanent crops; 74% other. **Major cities:** Zagreb (capital); Split; Rijeka; Osijek; Zadar.

• **PEOPLE** **Population:** 4,491,543 (July 2008 est.). **Nationality:** noun—Croat(s); adjective—Croatian. **Ethnic groups:** 90% Croat, 5% Serb, 0.5% Bosniak. **Languages:** 96% Croatian. **Religions:** 87.8% Catholic, 4.4% Orthodox, 1.3% Slavic Muslim.

• **GOVERNMENT** **Type:** presidential/parliamentary democracy. **Independence:** June 25, 1991. **Constitution:** Dec. 22, 1990. **National holiday:** Statehood Day, May 30. **Heads of Government:** Stjepan Mesić, president (since Feb. 2000); Ivo Sanader, prime minister (since Dec. 2003). **Structure:** executive; bicameral legislature; judiciary.

• **ECONOMY** **Monetary unit:** Croatian kuna. **Budget:** (2007 est.) *income:* $22.46 bil. *expend.:* $23.85 bil. **G.D.P.:** $69.44 bil.; $15,500 per capita (2007 est.). **Chief crops:** wheat, corn, sugar beets, sunflowers, alfalfa. **Natural resources:** oil, coal, bauxite, low-grade iron ore, calcium. **Major industries:** chemicals and plastics, machine tools, fabricated metal, electronics, pig iron and rolled steel products. **Labor force:** 1.714 mil. (2007 est.); industry and mining, government, agriculture. **Exports:** $12.11 bil. (f.o.b., 2007); textiles, foodstuffs, fuels, chemicals. **Imports:** $25.78 bil. (f.o.b., 2007); machinery and transport equipment, chemicals, food and live animals, fuels and lubricants. **Major trading partners:** (2006) *exports:* 19.3% Italy, 13.9% Bosnia & Herzegovina, 10.2% Germany, 8.4% Slovenai, 6.2% Austria; *imports:* 16.1% Italy, 14.4% Germany, 10.1% Russia, 6.2% China, 6% Slovenai, 5.3% Austria.

Croatia is one of Europe's most ancient states, King Tomaslav having created an independent Catholic realm in 924. In the sixth century the Croats, led by their eponymous chieftain Chrovatos, had migrated to the old Roman province of Illyricum, south of the Danube, where they dwelt in practical independence of the Byzantine Empire. Pope Gregory VII sent a papal crown, and therewith international recognition, to King Zvonimir (1076-89), but the king's death spelt the demise of the native dynasty. In 1102 Hungary's king Kalman was recognized as king of Croatia as well, in a dynastic union in which Croatia retained its own nobility and institutions. From the 14th century, Croatia (along with Hungary and Serbia) formed Europe's bulwark against the Ottoman Empire. After the Turkish victory at Mohacs (1526), the Hungarian and Croatian crowns were added to the Habsburg dynasty. Escaping Turkish sway, Croatia became controlled by Austrian military authorities as the frontier district against the Ottomans.

With the proclamation of the Austrian Empire in 1804, amalgamating the Habsburg possessions into one unified state, the estates of Croatia resisted the royal absolutism, stressing their autonomous status and ties to the Hungarian kingdom, but to slight avail, even after the Croat army of Baron Josip Jellacid proved essential in suppressing the Hungarian revolt of 1848. However, after the 1867 Ausleich ("compromise"), which established a practically independent Hungary within the Dual Monarchy, a further compromise (Nagoda) in the following year recognized Croatian autonomy within the Hungarian realm.

When the Habsburg monarchy collapsed during World War I, Croatia joined the new Yugoslavia, but since that state proved to be no federation but rather a greater Serbia, Croatia resisted Serbian dominance. And after the ferocious ethnic hostility provoked a royal dictatorship in 1929, Ante Pavelic formed the Ustase, a terrorist organization similar to and having ties with the Macedonian IMRO, with the aim of attaining Croatian independence. Just a week before the outbreak of World War II, Croatia was again granted autonomy, but with Hitler's 1941 conquest and dismemberment of Yugoslavia, an "Independent Croat State" was established under Italian protection. While Aimone, Duke of Spoleto was proclaimed king of Croatia under the preposterous name of Tomaslov II, he had the good sense never to enter "his" kingdom, whose governance was left to Pavelic and the Ustase. An "ethnic cleansing" of Croatia commenced, in which perhaps 100,000 Serbs and Jews lost their lives. Since the "chetniks" of Gen. Mihajlovic were Serbs and royalists, anti-Ustase Croats had nowhere to turn but to the Communist "partisans" of Tito (himself a Croat). Postwar vengeance against Tito's enemies, especially the Ustase, was severe but short-lived and Croatia in 1946 became one of the "republics" of the reconstituted Yugoslavia.

With Croatia's June 1991 secession from Yugoslavia, Serbian militias backed by the Yugoslavian army seized about one-third of Croatian territory, but by mid-1995 Croat forces had regained almost all of its land. President Franjo Tudjman also fostered the Muslim-Croat Federation in Bosnia to preserve a sort of Bosnian independence. The Yugoslav-Croat war came to an end in September 1996 with the establishment of diplomatic relations in which Yugoslavia recognized Croatia's boundaries, leaving ethnic Serbs in the lurch. And in Jan. 1998, a U.N. decision returned eastern Slavonia, part of historic Croatia captured by Serb militias in 1991, to Croatia.

Having won a third presidential term in January 1997, despite a stagnant economy, widespread corruption and complaints of autocracy, Tudjman succumbed to stomach cancer in Dec. 1999. Within a month, a six-party opposition coalition had captured 94 of 152 parliamentary seats, with Social Democrat Ivica Racan named premier. In a February 2000 presidential run-off, Stipe Mesic took over 56 percent of the votes, but by 2003 the Croatian Democratic Union returned to power with pledges of leading Croatia into NATO and the E.U. In 2007, changes to the constitution shifted power to the legislature and prime minister Ivo Sanader's conservative HD2 Party won a majority in Nov. 2007.

▶CUBA
Republic of Cuba
• GEOGRAPHY Location: largest island in Caribbean Sea, about 100 mi. (160 km) S of Florida. Boundaries: North Atlantic Ocean to N, Windward Passage to E, Caribbean Sea to S, Yucatan Channel to W. Total land area: 42,803 sq. mi. (110,860 sq km). Coastline: 2,319 mi. (3,735 km). Comparative area: between Tennessee and Pennsylvania. Land use: 33% arable land; 8% permanent crops; 59% other. Major cities: Havana (capital); Santiago de Cuba; Camagüey; Holguín; Guantánamo.
• PEOPLE Population: 11,423,952 (July 2008 est.). Nationality: noun—Cuban(s); adjective—Cuban. Ethnic groups: 51% mulatto, 37% white, 11% black, 1% Chinese. Languages: Spanish. Religions: at least 85% Roman Catholic before Castro assumed power.
• GOVERNMENT Type: Communist state. Independence: Dec. 10, 1898 (from Spain; administered by the U.S. from 1898 to 1902). Constitution: Feb. 24, 1976. National holiday: Independence Day, Dec. 10. Head of Government: Gen. Raul Castro Ruz, president of council of state and president of council of ministers (since Feb. 2008). Structure: executive; unicameral legislature; controlled judiciary.
• ECONOMY Monetary unit: Cuban peso and Convertible peso. Budget: (2007 est.) income: $35.01 bil.; expend.: $36.73 bil. G.D.P.: $51.11 bil., $4,500 per capita (2007 est.). Chief crops: sugar cane, tobacco, citrus, coffee, rice. Natural resources: cobalt, nickel, iron ore, copper, manganese. Major industries: sugar, petroleum, food and tobacco processing. Labor force: 4.85 mil. (2007); 20% agriculture, 19.4% industry, 60.6% services. Exports: $3.23 bil. (f.o.b., 2007 est.); sugar, nickel, shellfish, tobacco. Imports: $10.86 bil. (f.o.b., 2007 est.); petroleum, food, machinery, chemicals. Major trading partners: (2006) exports: 21.8% Netherlands, 21.6% Canada, 18.7% China, 5.9% Spain; imports: 26.6% Venezueal, 15.6% China, 9.8% Spain, 6.4% Germany, 5.6% Cananda, 4.4% Italy, 4.3% U.S.

At the time of Christopher Columbus's arrival in 1492, Cuba was home to Arawak, Ciboney, and Guanahatabey Indian people. Cuba served as a launching point for Spanish conquests in the Americas, and the early- 19th-century wars of independence that swept the rest of Spanish America did not overthrow the imposing Spanish garrison there. Slavery was abolished in 1886, but Spanish colonialism lingered until the 1890's.

Spanish control of the island began to deteriorate in the late 1860's with the beginning of the "Ten Years War" (1868-78). Under the terms of the 1898 Treaty of Paris, which ended the Cuban-U.S.-Spanish War, Cuba became a U.S. protectorate. The U.S.-sponsored Platt Amendment (1901) to the new Cuban constitution gave the United States the right to intervene in Cuban affairs.

Corruption and political repression plagued Cuban politics during the first half of the 20th century. Gerardo Machado won election to the presidency in 1925, but quickly turned his administration into a dictatorship that lasted until his ouster by a progressive coalition of students and labor in 1933. The "revolution" of 1933 installed Ramón Grau San Martín as the new head of the government, but the U.S. supported Grau's ouster, and army sergeant Fulgencio Batista replaced him. Batista ruled the country either directly or indirectly for the next quarter century.

In 1953 Fidel Castro Ruz led a failed attack on the Moncada army barracks in Santiago. In Dec. 1956 Fidel and Raúl Castro, Argentine physician Ernesto "Che" Guevara, and 79 others returned to Cuba and waged a guerrilla campaign against the government. Batista's military failed to defeat the guerrillas, and in the wake of increasing demonstrations of public antipathy for his government, the dictator fled the country. The Communist Fidelistas took control Jan. 1, 1959.

By mid-1959, revolutionary tribunals had tried and executed more than 500 political "enemies." The leaders announced an agrarian reform, and by 1960 the nationalization of the economy was in full swing. In 1961 U.S.-Cuban diplomatic relations were severed, and the U.S.-sponsored Bay of Pigs invasion by Cuban exiles failed. In 1962 the Cuban missile crisis brought the world to the brink of nuclear war when U.S. spy planes uncovered Soviet intentions to place nuclear weapons on the island. The Soviets agreed to the withdrawal of missiles in exchange for a U.S. pledge not to invade Cuba.

In its active foreign policy, Cuba provided assistance to a number of left-wing regimes in Africa and Latin America, most notably its military presence in Angola from 1975 to 1991. With the collapse of the Soviet Union in 1991, Cuba lost huge subsidies, forcing its economy into a downward spiral. In 1994, the worsening economy and a growing dissatisfaction with the Castro government fueled migration of Cubans to U.S. shores. With thousands of refugees arriving in Florida each day—aboard boats, homemade rafts, ferries—the U.S. and Cuba negotiated an agreement in which the United States would increase annual acceptance levels of Cuban immigrants to 20,000 in return for Cuba's promise to curb illegal migration.

Tensions flared between the U.S. and Cuba on Feb. 24, 1996, when Cuban MiGs shot down two private jets operating out of Miami. The U.S. responded by tightening economic sanctions, with penalties for foreigners investing in Cuba. Castro called for a renewed commitment to Marxism and met with Pope John Paul II who visited Cuba in 1999 and publicly confronted Castro on issues of freedom and religious liberty. But the regime remains changeless. In January 2003 "elections," 609 candidates ran unopposed for 609 National Assembly seats. In March, 78 dissidents and independent journalists were arrested; in April all 78 were found guilty in closed trials and given sentences of 6 to 28 years. In Aug. 2006 Castro underwent surgery and turned power over to his brother Raoul who became the official ruler in 2008.

▶ **CYPRUS**
Republic of Cyprus
• **GEOGRAPHY Location:** eastern Mediterranean Sea. Nicosia 35°11'N, 33°23'E. **Boundaries:** 62 mi. (100 km) S of Turkey, Syria to E. **Total land area:** 3,571 sq. mi. (9,250 sq km). **Coastline:** 403 mi. (648 km). **Comparative area:** between Delaware and Connecticut. **Land use:** 11% arable land; 5% permanent crops; 84% other. **Major cities:** Nicosia (capital); Limassol; Larnaca; Famagusta; Phaphos.
• **PEOPLE Population:** 792,604 (July 2008 est.). **Nationality:** noun—Cypriot(s); adjective—Cypriot. **Ethnic groups:** 77% Greek, 18% Turk, 5% other. **Languages:** Greek, Turkish, English. **Religions:** 78% Greek Orthodox, 18% Muslim.
• **GOVERNMENT Type:** republic. **Independence:** Aug. 16, 1960 (from U.K.). **Constitution:** Aug. 16, 1960; negotiations have been held intermittently to create basis for new or revised constitution to govern the island and relations between Greek and Turkish Cypriots. **National holiday:** Independence Day, Oct. 1. **Heads of Government:** Dimitris Christofias, president (since Feb., 2008). **Structure:** republic. note - A separation of the Greek and Turkish communities began in 1963. The island was admitted to the EU in 2004, and the election of one Cypriot president in 2008 encouraged the two sides to reopen unification talks.
• **ECONOMY Monetary unit:** euro. **Budget:** (2007 est.) *income:* $10.2 bil *expend.:* $9.9 bil **G.D.P.:** $21.41 bil., $27,100 per capita. (2007 est.). **Chief

crops: potatoes, citrus, vegetables, barley, grapes. **Natural resources:** copper, pyrites, asbestos, gypsum, timber. **Major industries:** food, beverages, textiles, chemicals. **Labor force:** (2007) 377,400; 8.5% agriculture, 20.5% industry, 71% services (2006). **Exports:** $1.58 bil. (2007 est.); citrus, potatoes, grapes, textiles. **Imports:** $7.698 bil. (2007 est.); consumer goods, petroleum and lubricants, foodstuffs, minerals, chemicals. **Major trading partners:** (2006) *exports:* 15.1% U.K., 14.2% Greece, 7.7% France, 4.9% Germany, 4.2% U.A.E.; *imports:* 17.6% Greece, 11.4% Italy, 9% Germany, 8.9% U.K., 6.3% Israel, 4.3% France, 4.2% China.

Recent excavations on Cyprus indicate a human presence at least 10,000 years ago. Mycenean (Greek) culture flourished in the second millenium B.C. Phoenicians colonized the island in the 10th century B.C., and it remained a major entrepôt for eastern Mediterranean trade. Annexed to Rome in 58 B.C. it was later part of the Byzantine Empire until the English Richard I (Lion Hearted) established a crusader state in A.D. 1191. The Lusignan dynasty ruled until 1489, when Cyprus was annexed by Venice. It was subsequently conquered by the Ottoman Empire in 1571.

In 1878 the Congress of Berlin placed Cyprus under British administration. In 1914 it was annexed outright by Great Britain and was made a British colony in 1925. From 1945 to 1948, the British used Cyprus as a detention area for "illegal" Jewish immigrants to Palestine.

After 1947 the Greek Cypriot community continued its long-standing agitation for union (enosis) with Greece, a policy strongly opposed by the Turkish Cypriot community. Communal violence broke out in 1954-55. In 1960 Cyprus was granted full independence under an agreement that forbade either enosis or partition and included guarantees of the rights of both Greeks and Turks. Attempts by the president, Archbishop Makarios, to alter the constitution to favor the Greek majority provoked further communal clashes in 1964, when a U.N. peacekeeping force was sent to the island. On July 15, 1974, a military coup by officers favoring union with Greece deposed the Makarios government. On July 20 Turkey invaded Cyprus and, after the collapse of cease-fire talks in August, occupied the northern two-fifths of the island. In 1975 the Turkish government announced a de facto partition of Cyprus; the northern territory was proclaimed the Turkish Federated State of Cyprus, under Pres. Rauf Denktash.

Makarios returned as president of the Republic of Cyprus, which was thus reduced in size, and remained in office until his death in 1977. He was succeeded by Spyros Kyprianou. Some 200,000 Greek Cypriots were expelled from the Turkish sector to the Republic; many Turks fled from the Republic to the Turkish sector. With a return of political stability, renewed foreign investment, and a customs union negotiated with the EEC, the Republic's economy has prospered, led by agriculture, light manufacturing, and tourism.

The 1998 decision of the E.U. to invite Cyprus to apply for membership and to deny Turkey's application heightened tensions. In June, both Greece and Turkey sent aircraft to Cyprus and the newly-reelected government of Pres. Clerides sought anti-aircraft missiles from Russia. But by December Cyprus had cancelled plans for deployment, at the urging of Greek Premier Simitis. With the peaceful resolution of so serious a crisis, it became possible for Greek-Turkish relations (the key to reunification of Cyprus) to improve, as they did in the January 2000 accords on the Aegean environment, immigration, tourism and the like. Reunification talks continued through March 2003 but to no avail. So the E.U.'s treaty with Cyprus, signed in April 2003, concerns only the Greek portion of the island. Turkish Cyprus opened its border in April, while Greek Cyprus dropped its trade sanctions raising hopes for reunification. But a referendum in 2004 saw the Greeks overwhemingly rejecting the idea while the Turks voted strongly for it. By 2008, however, new leaders in Turkey and Greece began meaningful talks to end the nation's division.

▶ **CZECH REPUBLIC**
● **GEOGRAPHY Location:** Central Europe. **Boundaries:** Poland to N, Slovakia to E, Austria to S, Germany to W. **Total land area:** 30,387 sq. mi. (78,703 sq km). **Coastline:** none. **Comparative area:** about the size of South Carolina. **Land use:** 40% arable land; 3% permanent crops; 57% other. **Major cities:** Prague (capital); Brno; Ostrava; Pilsen (Plzen); Olomouc.
● **PEOPLE Population:** 10,220,911 (July 2008 est.). **Nationality:** noun—Czech; adjective—Czech. **Ethnic groups:** 90.4% Czech, 3.4% Moravian, 1.9% Slovak. **Languages:** Czech. **Religions:** 59% unaffiliated, 26.8% Roman Catholic, 2.1% Protestant.
● **GOVERNMENT Type:** parliamentary democracy. **Independence:** Oct. 29, 1918 (from Austro-Hungarian Empire); Jan. 2, 1993 (from Czechoslovakia). **Constitution:** Jan. 1, 1993. **National holiday:** Founding of the Republic, Oct. 28. **Heads of Government:** Václav Klaus, president (since Mar. 7, 2003), Mirek Topolánek, prime minister (since Jan. 2007). **Structure:** executive; bicameral legislature; judiciary.
● **ECONOMY Monetary unit:** koruna. **Budget:** (2007 est.) *income:* $69.49 bil., *expend.:* $75.8 bil. **G.D.P.:** $249.1 bil., $24,400 per capita (2007 est.). **Chief crops:** wheat, rye, barley, oats, corn, potatoes. **Natural resources:** coal, kaolin, clay, graphite. **Major industries:** fuels, metallurgy, machines. **Labor force:** (2007) 5.35 mil.; 37.6% industry, 58.3% services, 4.1% agriculture. **Exports:** $113 bil., (f.o.b., 2007); manufactured goods, machinery and equipment, chemicals. **Imports:** $109.89 bil. (f.o.b., 2007); machinery and equipment, manufactured goods, chemicals. **Major trading partners:** (2006) *exports:* 30.9% Germany, 8.8% Slovakia, 6% Poland, 5.3% France, 5% U.K., 4.9% Italy, 4.6% Austria; *imports:* 32% Germany, 6.8% Netherlands, 6.4% Slovakia, 6.3% Poland, 5.1% China, 5% Austria, 4.4% Russia, 4.4% Italy, 4.1% France.

A Moravian empire, Christianized by Cyril and Methodius, existed in the ninth century until destroyed by the Magyars. From the 10th through the 14th century, Bohemia and Moravia, "lands of the crown of St. Vaclav," formed an independent kingdom within the Holy Roman Empire under the Czech Premsylid dynasty. In 1526 the crown lands came under Habsburg rule, a rule that lasted until World War I.

They were the richest crown lands of the Austro-Hungarian Empire. Prosperous agriculture in the central plains and mineral wealth in the hill country were supplemented in the 19th century by industrial development led by urban middle classes, who were largely German and Jewish.

With the crumbling of the Habsburg monarchy during the war, a new multinational state of Czechoslovakia emerged, founded by Eduard Beneš and Thomas Masaryk, in which the Czechs (only 45% of the population) ruled over Germans, Slovaks, Magyars, Poles, and Ukranians. Yet it was the most democratic state in Central Europe.

Following the Munich Pact of September 1938, Hitler annexed the German-speaking regions of the "Sudetenland," and in 1939 he established a "protectorate" over the Czech lands, while Slovakia became a self-governing satellite republic. With the collapse of Hitler's Reich, Czechoslovakia was reestablished (except for the Carpatho-Ukraine, which it was compelled to cede to the U.S.S.R.) with Beneš again as president and a socialist government, independent but pro-Soviet. Three million Germans were expelled, with tens of thousands killed either in mob violence or after hasty trials before "Special People's Courts." In 1948 a Communist coup forced Beneš to resign; he was replaced by the Communist leader Klement Gottwald. Jan Masaryk, the foreign minister, committed suicide or was murdered. Purges and persecutions followed.

With Stalin's death in 1953, Gottwald was replaced as party first secretary by Stalinist hardliner Antonin Novotny, who also became president in 1957. In 1968 Novotny was replaced as first secretary by a Slovak liberal, Alexander Dubcek. Czechoslovakia suddenly was in the vanguard of communist reform. The new regime abolished censorship, denounced Stalin, decentralized economic decision-making, and granted real power to the National Assembly.

The brief "Prague Spring" ended in Aug. 1968, when Warsaw Pact troops invaded. In 1969 Dubcek was replaced by Gustáv Husak. The party was purged, censorship restored, dissent repressed, and the centralized economy restored.

The 1970's brought inflation and economic stagnation but produced no change in policy. The rise of the Solidarity movement in Poland in the early 1980's provoked a backlash of preventive repression in Czechoslovakia, aimed especially at Charter 77, a human-rights organization, and at the Catholic church.

The pro-democracy movement began in earnest in October 1989, inspired by a lack of confidence in Communist rule and by reform movements throughout Eastern Europe. The resignation of Communist leaders throughout December culminated in the parliamentary election of Václav Havel, a dissident playwright and head of a loose coalition of opposition groups called Civic Forum, as president, and the vindicated Alexander Dubcek as chairman of Parliament.

Despite severe economic difficulties, revelations of state security abuses, environmental pollution, and other problems inherited from the Communist era, Czechoslovakia's "Velvet Revolution" seemed a resounding political and popular success. In 1990 Soviet troops left and Civic Forum and its Slovakian ally, Public Against Violence, won 47% of the vote in parliamentary elections, against 14 percent for the Communists and 12 percent for the Christian Democrats. Vaclav Havel was elected president, and Marian Calfa became prime minister.

But Slovak-Czech resentments and Slovakia's economic distress led to a separation of the two republics, effective Jan. 1, 1993. In June 1996, the first elections in the new Czech Republic gave 99 (out of 200) seats to the three-party center-right coalition (led by Prime Minister Vaclav Klaus and President Havel) which had guided the Czech Republic's successful transition to a market economy. After several years of prosperity, the Republic fell on hard times in 1997, and Klaus introduced austerity measures. Revelations of campaign finance irregularities brought Klaus' resignation in 1997. In the subsequent 1998 elections, the Social Democrats won a plurality of seats and, with the Civic Democrats' agreement, formed a minority government for the next four years. The budget adopted in 1999 included the republic's first planned deficit as the nagging recession continued, with little economic growth forecast and unemployment rising to 9.5 percent. In the 2002 elections, the Social Democrats won a plurality but no majority in the Chamber of Deputies, necessitating a coalition with the Christian Democratic Union/Freedom Party and Vladimir Spidla remaining prime minister and Vaclav Klaus becoming president. In June, a referendum of Czech voters approved E.U. membership with a 77 percent "yes" vote. Spidla was forced to resign in 2004 when his party did poorly in elections for the E.U. parliament. The government remained fractured through 2007 as coalitions came and went with very little accomplished.

▶ **DENMARK**
Kingdom of Denmark
● **GEOGRAPHY Location:** northern Europe. **Boundaries:** Skagerrak channel to N, Baltic Sea to E, Germany to S, North Sea to W. **Total land area:** 16,629 sq. mi. (43,070 sq km). **Coastline:** 2,100 mi. (3,379 km). **Comparative area:** between Maryland and West Virginia. **Land use:** 56% arable land; negl. % permanent crops; 44% other. **Major cities:** København (Copenhagen—capital); Århus (Aarhus); Odense; Alborg (Aalborg); Esbjerg.
● **PEOPLE Population:** 5,484,723 (July 2008 est.). **Nationality:** noun Dane(s); adjective—Danish. **Ethnic groups:** Scandinavian, Inuit, Faeroese, German. **Languages:** Danish, Faroese, English, Greenlandic (Eskimo dialect); small German-speaking minority. **Religions:** 95% Evangelical Lutheran, Protestant and Roman Catholic, Muslim.
● **GOVERNMENT Type:** constitutional monarchy. **Constitution:** June 5, 1953. **National holiday:** Constitution Day, Apr. 16. **Heads of Government:** Margrethe II, queen (since Jan. 1972); Anders Fogh Rasmussen, prime minister (since Nov. 2001). **Structure:** executive power vested in Crown, exercised by cabinet responsible to Parliament; unicameral legislature; Supreme Court.
● **ECONOMY Monetary unit:** Danish krone. **Budget:** (2007 est.) *income:* $167.9 bil.; *expend.:* $156.1 bil. **G.D.P.:** $204.6 bil., $37,400 per capita (2007 est.). **Chief crops:** grain, potatoes; meat, dairy; fish. **Natural resources:** crude oil, natural gas, fish, salt, limestone. **Major industries:** food processing, machinery and equipment, textiles, clothing. **Labor force:** 2.9 mil.; 76% services, 21% industry; 3% agriculture (2004) 5.1% unemployment (2002). **Exports:** $102.1 bil. (f.o.b., 2007); machinery and instruments, meat and meat products, fuels, dairy products. **Imports:** $101.3 bil. (f.o.b., 2007); machinery and equipment, petroleum, chemicals, grain and foodstuffs. **Major trading partners:** (2006) *exports:* 17.3% Germany, 14.1% Sweden, 8.7% U.K., 6.2% U.S.; *imports:* 21.4% Germany, 14.2% Sweden, 6.5% Norway, 6.3% Netherlands.

Scandinavian by history, not geography, Denmark in the 11th century, under its second Christian king, Canute, ruled a great northern empire including Greenland, Iceland, the Faeroe Islands, Great Britain, and Norway. By 1387 Britain was long independent, but Denmark added Sweden and Finland to its domain. Yet it was never a great power. Its kings never really controlled the nobility, while in foreign affairs it was dominated by the Hansa, the league of German trading cities.

In the 16th century Denmark had to recognize the independence of Sweden and Finland. In the 19th century it lost Norway (to Sweden in 1814) and Schleswig-Holstein (to Prussia in 1864). In the 20th century Denmark sold the Virgin Islands to the United States in 1914 and had to recognize Iceland's independence in 1944.

In the 19th century, Denmark was transformed from a poor peasant society to one of Europe's richest agricultural nations by means of reforms that established agricultural cooperatives and emphasized intensive specialization in the production of dairy products and pork. These products remain a mainstay of the Danish economy.

Denmark remained neutral during World War I. In 1939 Denmark signed a 10-year nonaggression pact with Germany, but Germany nevertheless invaded Denmark in April 1940; the country surrendered without a fight. In 1941 Denmark's ambassador in Washington transferred defense of Greenland to the United States, and much of Denmark's merchant fleet joined the Allied war effort. Denmark was placed under German martial law in August 1943 and was treated as an enemy nation. Danish resistance succeeded in evacuating 7,000 Jews to neutral Sweden. Denmark was liberated by British troops in May 1945.

Denmark became a U.N. member in 1946 and a founding member of NATO in 1949. By the latter year, the postwar recovery was complete, with industrial levels exceeding those of the prewar period. High taxes, unemployment, and inflation remained problems, but the economy was aided by the growth of trade with West Germany.

In 1953 the king assented to a constitutional reform that abolished the upper house of the legislature, leaving the Folketing as the sole legislative body. Proportional representation meant that it was impossible for any party to gain a parliamentary majority, so Denmark is always governed by coalition regimes. In the postwar period, these normally have been led by the Social Democrats.

In the 1950's Denmark adopted a characteristically Scandinavian program of free enterprise, high taxes, and extensive social welfare systems. A high rate of economic growth, spurred by agricultural exports, continued throughout the 1960's. Denmark joined the E.C. in 1972. The 1970's brought economic difficulties, as Danish oil exploration in the North Sea yielded disappointing results, and inflation reached double digits.

The elections of 1982 installed Denmark's first Conservative government since 1905. A Conservative four-party coalition formed in 1984 remained in office until 1993 when Prime Minister Schlüter resigned over charges of misleading the Folketing about restrictions on the immigration of Tamil refugees. Social Democrat Poul Nyrup Rasmussen formed a coalition government with only a one-seat majority.

The general revival of the world economy in the 1980's coupled with government austerity measures led to renewed growth and lowered infla tion. In 1986 Danish voters renewed their commitment to the E.C., but in the June 1992 referendum on the Maastricht Treaty—providing for common defense and foreign policy as well as a common currency and central bank—Denmark said "no." The E.U. quickly made concessions that guaranteed Denmark's right to opt out of any common E.U. citizenship, police force, defense policy, or judicial arrangement. In May 1993 Danish voters approved this different version of the treaty. In Sept. 2000 a referendum on the euro was defeated and later the Danes said they would not be part of the E.U.'s army. In Nov. 2001 Folketing elections, the Liberal Party, for the first time since 1920, outpolled the Social Democrats and the Liberal coalition organized a new government of the right under premier Anders Fogh Rasmussen. Within a week they had carried stronger immigration-control measures—the principal issue in the campaign.

In 2006 a Danish publication caused an international incident when it published cartoons belittling Islam resulting in massive demonstrations around the world. In Nov. 2007 Rasmussen's party was reelected.

▶ **DJIBOUTI**
Republic of Djibouti
● **GEOGRAPHY Location:** northeastern Africa. **Boundaries:** Red Sea to N, Gulf of Aden to E, Somalia to SE, Ethiopia to S, W, and NW. **Total land area:** 8,494 sq. mi. (22,000 sq km). **Coastline:** 195 mi. (314 km). **Comparative area:** between Massachusetts and New Hampshire. **Land use:** 0% arable land; 0% permanent crops; 100% other. **Major cities:** Djibouti (capital); Dikhil, Ali-Sabieh, Tadjourah, Obock.
● **PEOPLE Population:** 506,221 (July 2008 est.). **Nationality:** noun—Djiboutian(s); adjective—Djiboutian. **Ethnic groups:** 60% Somali, 35% Afar, 5% French, Arab, Ethiopian, and Italian. **Languages:** French and Arabic (official); Somali and Afar widely used. **Religions:** 94% Muslim, 6% Christian.
● **GOVERNMENT Type:** republic. **Independence:** June 27, 1977 (from France). **Constitution:** Sep. 4, 1992. **National holiday:** Independence Day, June 27. **Heads of Government:** Ismail Omar Guelleh, president (since May 1999); Deletia Mohamed Deletia, prime minister (since Mar. 2001). **Structure:** executive; unicameral legislature; judiciary.
● **ECONOMY Monetary unit:** Djiboutian franc. **Budget:** (1999 est.) *income:* $135 mil., *expend.:* $182 mil. **G.D.P.:** $1.878 mil., $1,000 per capita (2006 est.). **Chief crops:** limited fruits and vegetables; goats, sheep, camels. **Natural resources:** geothermal areas. **Major industries:** limited to a few small-scale enterprises, such as construction and agricultural processing. **Labor force:** 282,000 (2000 est.); 75% agriculture, 14% services, 11% industry; 59% unemployment urban, 83% unemployment rural (2007 est.). **Exports:** $340 mil. (f.o.b., 2006 est.); hides and skins and transit of coffee. **Imports:** $1.55 bil. (f.o.b., 2006 est.); foods, beverages, transport equipment, chemicals, petroleum. **Major trading partners:** (2006) *exports:* 66.2% Somalia, 21.4% Ethiopia, 3.4% Yemen; *imports:* 21.4% Saudi Arabia, 17.9% India, 11% China, 4.6% Ethiopia.

This small, arid region on the Horn of Africa near the southern mouth of the Red Sea became the object of British-French rivalry with the opening of the Suez Canal in 1869. The French sphere of influence, called French Somaliland, was affirmed by agreements with Ethiopia in 1897, 1945,

and 1954. In the early 20th century, the French constructed a railroad from Addis Ababa to Djibouti, adding to the colony's strategic value.

French and Italian forces clashed at the border of Ethiopia and French Somaliland with the Italian invasion of Ethiopia in the 1930's. During World War II, the territorial administration at first sided with the Vichy government but in December 1942 established ties with the Free French and the Allies.

The colony was reorganized in 1957 and in 1958 became, by referendum, a French Overseas Territory. In July 1967 its name was changed to the Territory of the Afars and Issas. Growing nationalist sentiment led to a referendum in favor of complete independence. The Republic of Djibouti became independent on June 27, 1977. Hassan Aptidon ruled as president until 1999. Civil war had broken out between the Issas and Afars in the early 1990s that did not end until 2001. But in 1999, multiparty elections were held for the first time and Ismail Omar Guelleh was elected, then reelected in 2005. In 2008 a long-standing border dispute with Eritrea turned violent for a brief time. Djibouti's strategic location has led to the placement of the only U.S. military base in sub-Saharan Africa.

▶ **DOMINICA**
Commonwealth of Dominica
● **GEOGRAPHY Location:** eastern Caribbean Sea, between Guadeloupe to N and Martinique to S. Roseau 15°18'N, 61°23'W. **Boundaries:** Dominica Passage to N, Atlantic Ocean to E, Martinique Passage to S, Caribbean Sea to W. **Total land area:** 290 sq. mi. (750 sq km). **Coastline:** 92 mi. (148 km). **Comparative area:** slightly more than four times size of Washington, D.C. **Land use:** 4% arable land; 16% permanent crops; 80% other. **Major cities:** Roseau (capital).
● **PEOPLE Population:** 72,514 (July 2008 est.) **Nationality:** noun—Dominican(s); adjective—Dominican. **Ethnic groups:** black, Carib Amerindians, mixed, European, Syrian. **Languages:** English (official), French patois. **Religions:** 61.4% Roman Catholic, 6% Seventh Day Adventist, 23.4% other Christian, 1.3% Rastafarian, 6.1% none.
● **GOVERNMENT Type:** parliamentary democracy. **Independence:** Nov. 3, 1978 (from U.K.). **Constitution:** Nov. 3, 1978. **National holiday:** Independence Day, Nov. 3. **Heads of Government:** Nicholas Orville Liverpool, president (since Oct. 2003); Roosevelt Skerrit, prime minister (since Jan. 2004). **Structure:** executive; unicameral legislature; judiciary—East Caribbean Supreme Court.
● **ECONOMY Monetary unit:** East Caribbean (EC) dollar. **Budget:** (2001 est.). *income:* $73.9 mil.; *expend.:* $84.4 mil. **G.D.P.:** $485 mil. (2006), $3,800 per capita (2005 est.). **Chief crops:** bananas, citrus, mangoes; forestry and fisheries. **Natural resources:** timber, hydropower, arable land. **Major industries:** soap, coconut oil, tourism. **Labor force:** 25,000 (2000); 40% agriculture, 32% industry and commerce, 28% services; 23% unemployment (2000 est.). **Exports:** $94 mil. (2006 est.); bananas, soap, bay oil. **Imports:** $296 mil. (2006 est.); manufactured goods, machinery and equipment, foodstuffs. **Major trading partners:** (2006) *exports:* 24.8% U.K., 12.3% Jamaica, 9.8% Antigua & Barbuda, 8.3% Guyana, 7.9% China; *imports:* 25.3% U.S., 22.7% China, 13.8% Trinidad & Tobago, 4.8% South Korea.

Pre-Columbian Dominica was a stronghold of Carib Indians, who had expelled the Arawaks in the 14th century, and today it is the only island in the Caribbean with a native Carib population. Dominica was visited by Columbus on his second American voyage; but though frequented by Spanish ships, it was not settled until French missionaries arrived in the 1630's. Carib resistance was so strong that the French and British agreed to consider the island neutral territory, until it passed under British control in 1763.

Later it was administratively joined to the Leeward and then the Windward Islands, and then became part of the West Indies Federation. It entered into political association with the United Kingdom in 1967. In 1978 Dominica gained independence from Britain. Prime Minister Mary Eugenia Charles's Freedom party has held power since 1980 on a program of economic reconstruction. Hurricanes in 1979-80 largely destroyed the island's agriculture. The government of Prime Minister Mary Eugenia Charles's Freedom party implemented a program of economic reconstruction and diversification after the disaster. In 1992 it began a controversial policy of granting citizenship to businessmen, Asians in particular, in exchange for investment in Dominica's economy. In 1995, Charles resigned after 15 years in office. The United Workers party took 11 of 21 seats in parliamentary elections and named its leader, Edison James, the new prime minister. But Jan. 2000 Assembly elections produced a coalition of the Labor and Freedom Parties, as the United Workers went again into opposition. Labor Party leader Roosevelt "Rosie" Douglas was named prime minister, but he died unexpectedly, leaving Pierre Charles to serve as acting prime minister.

▶ DOMINICAN REPUBLIC
• **GEOGRAPHY Location:** eastern Hispaniola, in Caribbean Sea. Santo Domingo 19°30′N, 70°42′W. **Boundaries:** North Atlantic to N, Mona Passage to E, Caribbean Sea to S, Haiti to W. **Total land area:** 18,815 sq. mi. (48,730 sq km). **Coastline:** 800 mi. (1,288 km). **Comparative area:** slightly more than four times size of Washington, D.C. **Land use:** 21% arable land; 10% permanent crops; 69% other. **Major cities:** Santo Domingo (capital); Santiago de los Caballeros; La Romana; San Pedro de Macorís; San Francisco de Macorís.
• **PEOPLE   Population:** 9,507,133 (July 2008 est.). **Nationality:** noun—Dominican(s); adjective— Dominican. **Ethnic groups:** 73% mixed, 16% white, 11% black. **Languages:** Spanish. **Religions:** 95% Roman Catholic.
• **GOVERNMENT Type:** representative democracy. **Independence:** Feb. 27, 1844 (from Haiti). **Constitution:** Nov. 28, 1966. **National holiday:** Independence Day, Feb. 27. **Head of Government:** Leonel Fernández Reyna, president (since Aug. 2004). **Structure:** executive; bicameral legislature; judiciary.
• **ECONOMY Monetary unit:** Dominican peso. **Budget:** (2007 est.) *income:* $7.014 bil.; *expend.:* $6.985 bil. **G.D.P.:** $85.4 bil., $9,200 per capita (2007 est.). **Chief crops:** sugarcane, coffee, cotton, cocoa, tobacco; cattle, pigs. **Natural resources:** nickel, bauxite, gold, silver. **Major industries:** tourism, sugar processing, mining. **Labor force:** 3.986 mil. (2007 est.); 58.7% services and government, 24.3% industry, 17% agriculture. **Exports:** $6.881 bil. (f.o.b., 2007); ferronickel, sugar, gold, coffee. **Imports:** $12.89 bil. (f.o.b., 2007); foodstuffs, petroleum, cotton, fabrics, chemicals. **Major trading partners:** (2006) *exports:* 72.7% U.S., 3.2% U.K., 2.4% Belgium; *imports:* 46.9% U.S., 8.4% Venezuela, 6.3% Colombia, 5.7% Mexico.

The Dominican Republic takes up the eastern two-thirds of the island of Hispaniola, which it shares with Haiti. Christopher Columbus visited the island in 1492, and Santo Domingo is the oldest continually inhabited European settlement in the Americas, with the oldest cathedral, hospital, and monastery in the Western Hemisphere.

Western Hispaniola (Haiti) was ceded to France in 1697, and the eastern part of the island in 1795. Liberated with the Haitian slave revolts of 1801, it fell under Haitian rule from 1804 to 1808 (when it reverted to Spanish rule), and again from 1822 to 1844. It was again occupied by Spain from 1861 to 1865. Under Ulises Heureux (1882-99), the Dominican Republic enjoyed a period of independence and prosperity. The U.S. occupied the Dominican Republic between 1916 and 1924. In 1930 Rafael Trujillo set up a dictatorship lasting 31 years. Dominican political strife triggered another U.S. invasion (1965-66) to end the revolution. Reformist party candidate Joaquín Balaguer, president from 1966 to 1978, regained the presidency in 1986, was reelected in 1990, and again (at age 87) in 1994, but only for two years, a compromise arranged in the face of charges of election fraud.

The 1996 elections resulted in a runoff between Haitian-born Jose Pena Gomez and Leonel Fernandez—both center-left in politics, both committed to economic privatization. Fernandez was the winner. But even the small and halting steps towards economic reform provoked strikes by labor unions and students over low wages, chronic water and electric outages. The death in May 1998 of Pena one week before legislative elections added a sentimental boost to real opposition. His Dominican Revolutionary Party captured large majorities in both the Senate and Chamber of Deputies. And in May 2000, for the first time, the party's candidate for president won, Hipolito Mejia. At 93, Balaguer tried one more time but finished third, defeated in 2004 by former president Fernandez who won again in 2008.

▶ EAST TIMOR
(see Timor-Leste)

▶ ECUADOR
Republic of Ecuador
• **GEOGRAPHY Location:** northwestern South America. **Boundaries:** Colombia to N, Peru to E and S, Pacific Ocean to W. **Total land area:** 109,483 sq. mi. (283,560 sq km); incl. Galapagos Islands, 0°45′S, 90°19′W. **Coastline:** 1,389 mi. (2,237 km). **Comparative area:** between Colorado and Nevada. **Land use:** 6% arable land; 5% permanent crops; 89% other. **Major cities:** Quito (capital); Guayaquil; Cuenca; Machala; Portoviejo.
• **PEOPLE   Population:** 13,927,650 (July 2008 est.). **Nationality:** noun—Ecuadorian(s); adjective— Ecuadorian. **Ethnic groups:** 65% mestizo, 25% Amerindian, 7% Spanish, 3% black. **Languages:** Spanish (official), Amerindian languages, especially Quechua. **Religions:** 95% Roman Catholic.
• **GOVERNMENT Type:** republic. **Independence:** May 24, 1822 (from Spain). **Constitution:** Aug. 10, 1998. **National holiday:** Independence Day, Aug. 10. **Head of Government:** Rafael Correa, president (since Jan. 2007). **Structure:** executive; unicameral legislature; independent judiciary.
• **ECONOMY Monetary unit:** U.S. dollar. **Budget:** (2007 est.) *income:* $13.1 bil.; *expend.:* $11.3 bil. **G.D.P.:** $98.28 bil., $7,100 per capita (2007 est.). **Chief crops:** bananas, coffee, cocoa, rice; cattle,

sheep, pigs. **Natural resources:** petroleum, fish, timber. **Major industries:** petroleum, food processing, textiles. **Labor force:** 4.55 mil. (urban) (2007); 8% agriculture, 68% services, 24% industry; 9.8% unemployment (2007 est.). **Exports:** $13.3 bil. (f.o.b., 2007 est.); petroleum, bananas, shrimp. **Imports:** $13 bil. (f.o.b., 2007 est.); transport equipment, consumer goods, vehicles, machinery. **Major trading partners:** (2006) *exports:* 53.6% U.S., 8.2% Peru, 5.6% Colombia, 4.4% Chile; *imports:* 23.1% U.S., 13.3% Colombia, 7.3% Brazil, 4% Panama.

The Inca Empire maintained control over the territory that is now Ecuador until the arrival of Spanish conqueror Francisco Pizarro in 1532. The Spanish conquistadores quickly dismantled the indigenous political structure, which had been weakened by a series of wars between the Inca chief Atahualpa and his half brother Huáscar. The Spaniards arrived in the Quito region in 1533 and established the city of Guayaquil shortly thereafter. The administrative center of Spanish rule was originally established through the viceroyalty of Peru in 1544, and an audiencia (a regional high court under the nominal authority of the viceroy) was established at Quito in 1563. Administrative control of the region was transferred to Bogotá and the viceroyalty of New Granada in 1718.

The local junta of Quito ousted the audiencia in 1809, but they did not achieve independence for the region until after the military victory of the rebel forces over the royalists at the battle of Pichincha in 1822. Ecuador formed a part of the Confederation of Gran Colombia until the confederation's collapse in 1830. The leader of the forces for independence, Gen. Juan José Flores, removed the country from the Gran Colombian confederation and ruled as dictator until his ouster in 1845. A political rivalry existed between the Liberals of Guayaquil and the Conservatives of Quito, but Conservative dominance of the government lasted until 1895.

During the rule of Conservative president Gabriel García Moreno (1861-75), the Roman Catholic church gained a central place in the political and cultural life of the country. García Moreno tied citizenship requirements to Catholic religious affiliation, brought in the Jesuits to "purify" the country through education, and dedicated the country to the Sacred Heart of Jesus. He was assassinated in 1875.

In 1895 the Radical Liberal (anticlerical) party seized power and held it until 1944. José María Velasco Ibarra, in and out of power until 1972, dominated the political scene. Political stability within the country had much to do with the state of the economy. The traditional reliance on cacao production was superseded in the 1950's by a "banana boom," and the discovery of large oil deposits by U.S. corporations in the 1960's led to a shift toward reliance on oil revenues by the 70's.

In 1988 Rodrigo Borja, of the Democratic Left party (ID), was elected to the presidency. In 1992 conservative Sixto Durán Ballén, an advocate of free market reforms, won the presidency and immediately moved to eliminate government subsidies and encourage foreign investment.

Duran's successor in 1996 was the bizarre Abdala Bucaram Ortiz, who was removed by Congress in Feb. 1997 for "mental incapacity." Not until July of 1998 was normality restored with the election of Quito mayor Jamil Mahuad Witt. While his austerity measures provoked widespread discontent, Congress passed most of the measures and the 50-year-long border dispute with Peru was peaceably settled in 1998. In Sept. 1999, Ecuador defaulted on part of its international debt, and Witt was overturned in a brief army coup in Jan. 2000; his vice-president, Gustavo Noboa, was installed as president, a change ratified by Congress. In March, Witt's plan to replace the *sucre* with the U.S. dollar as the national currency was adopted (though it had been the occasion of his overthrow). The 2002 presidential election was won by the somewhat leftist Lucio Gutierrez Borbua, a former army colonel and one of the leaders in the 2002 coup, Ecuador's sixth president in seven years. In April 2005 he was forced to flee the country after dissolving the Supreme Court led to large protests.

Over the next year the vice president tried to lead the country but constant protests by indigenous Indian groups paralyzed the government. National elections in late 2006 brought a U.S.-educated leftwing economist, Rafael Correa, to power and he immediately called for radical changes in the constitution, weakened the power of congress, and set out to strengthen the oil industry.

▶EGYPT
Arab Republic of Egypt

● **GEOGRAPHY Location:** northeastern Africa and Asia (Sinai peninsula). **Boundaries:** Mediterranean Sea to N, Israel to NE, Red Sea to E, Sudan to S, and Libya to W. **Total land area:** 386,660 sq. mi. (1,001,450 sq km). **Coastline:** 1,523 mi. (2,450 km). **Comparative area:** slightly more than three times the size of New Mexico. **Land use:** 3% arable land; 0% permanent crops; 97% other. **Major cities:** Cairo (capital); El-Iskandriyah (Alexandria); Giza; Shoubra el-kheima; Port Said.

● **PEOPLE Population:** 81,713,517 (July 2008 est.). **Nationality:** noun—Egyptian(s); adjective—Egyptian. **Ethnic groups:** 99% Eastern Hamitic stock. **Languages:** Arabic (official), English and French widely understood by educated classes. **Religions:** 94% Muslim (mostly Sunni), 6% Coptic Christian and other.

● **GOVERNMENT Type:** republic. **Independence:** Feb. 28, 1922 (from U.K.). **Constitution:** Sept. 11, 1971. **National holiday:** Anniversary of the Revolution, July 23. **Heads of Government:** Mohammed Hosni Mubarak, president (since 1981); Ahmed Nazif, prime minister (since 2005). **Structure:** executive—president nominated by parliament which is validated by popular referendum; bicameral legislature; judiciary.

● **ECONOMY Monetary unit:** Egyptian pound. **Budget:** (2007 est.) *income:* $37.47 bil.; *expend.:* $44.48 bil. **G.D.P.:** $431.9 bil., $5,400 per capita (2007 est.). **Chief crops:** cotton, rice, corn, wheat, beans, fruit, vegetables; cattle, water buffalo, sheep, goats. **Natural resources:** crude oil, natural gas, iron ore, phosphates, manganese. **Major industries:** textiles, food processing, tourism. **Labor force:** 22.49 mil. (2007 est.); 32% agriculture, 51% services, including government, 17% industry (2001); 10.1% unemployment (2007 est.). **Exports:** $27.42 bil. (f.o.b., 2007 est.); crude oil and petroleum products, cotton yarn, raw cotton, textiles, metal products, chemicals. **Imports:** $40.48 bil. (f.o.b., 2007 est.); machinery and equipment, foods, fertilizers, wood products, durable consumer goods, capital goods. **Major trading partners:** (2006) *exports:* 9.9% U.S., 9.7% Italy, 7.8% Spain, 5.6% Syria, 5% Saudi Arabia, 4.7% U.K.; *im-*

ports: 11.8% U.S., 9.7% China, 6.5% Italy, 6.4% Germany, 4.8% Saudi Arabia.

Civilization began in the fertile valley of the Nile River around 5000 B.C. In about 3200 B.C., King Menes established the first of many dynasties of pharaohs that unified the country from the Nile Delta to Upper Egypt, creating a distinctive ancient civilization of great wealth and cultural brilliance.

The last pharaonic dynasty was overthrown by the Persians in 341 B.C. The Persians in turn were replaced by the Alexandrian and Ptolemaic Greek dynasties and then by the Roman Empire. Egypt was part of the Byzantine Empire from the third to the seventh centuries A.D., when it was conquered by the Arab Islamic expansion. Arab rule was ended around 1250 when the Mameluke dynasty, established control. The Mamelukes were defeated by the Turks in 1517, and Egypt was incorporated into the Ottoman Empire.

The Suez Canal was built by a French corporation during 1859-69 but was taken over by the British in 1875. This, together with the expansion of the British Empire in East Africa and the Sudan, led to the establishment of de facto British rule in Egypt in 1882, although Egypt remained nominally part of the Ottoman Empire until 1914. A British protectorate in Egypt was established in that year, replaced by a League of Nations Mandate in 1922. The autonomy of the Egyptian monarchy was strengthened in an Anglo-Egyptian treaty of 1936, but Great Britain continued to maintain military forces in Egypt and controlled the Sudan as an Anglo-Egyptian condominium.

Egypt saw heavy fighting between British and Axis forces during WWII. After the war, a nationalist movement gained strength. The 1936 treaty was abrogated by Egypt in 1951. An uprising of the Society of Free Officers on July 23, 1952, forced King Farouk to abdicate. A republic was proclaimed on June 18, 1953. Lt. Col. Gamal Abdel Nasser became premier in 1954 and president in 1956.

British troops were withdrawn from the Suez Canal zone in June 1956. On July 26, 1956, Egypt announced the nationalization of the canal. Israel invaded the Sinai Peninsula at the end of October 1956. France and Great Britain landed troops and bombed Egyptian positions; a cease-fire went into effect under U.N. supervision on Nov. 17. A U.N. peacekeeping force patrolled the border between Egypt and Israel from 1957 to 1967. Egypt and Syria joined together as the United Arab Republic in 1958. Later joined by Yemen, the union was dissolved in 1961.

Increasing Soviet involvement in Egypt was confirmed with its aid to Egypt in the construction of the Aswan High Dam. The dam, completed in 1971, provides both irrigation and hydropower but at the cost of extensive environmental damage.

A full-scale war with Israel broke out on June 5, 1967. The Six-Day War ended on June 10 with Israel in full control of Gaza and the Sinai peninsula to the banks of the Suez Canal. Sporadic fighting between Egyptian and Israeli forces continued throughout 1969-70. The Suez Canal remained closed to shipping until 1975.

Nasser died in 1970 and was succeeded by Vice Pres. Anwar Sadat, who concluded a treaty of friendship with the U.S.S.R., but expelled all Soviet troops and advisers in 1972. On Oct. 6, 1973, Egyptian forces crossed the Suez Canal and attacked Israeli positions in the Sinai (Syrian forces also attacked Israeli positions in the Golan Heights). Israel drove back the attackers, and the Yom Kippur War ended in a cease-fire on Oct. 24.

In 1974 Sadat's government became increasingly friendly to the West, welcoming foreign investment and American aid. In 1974 and 1975 disengagement accords were signed with Israel, providing for the return of the Sinai to Egypt in stages. In November 1977 Sadat visited Jerusalem as a gesture of peace, and a peace treaty between Israel and Egypt was signed (after a series of talks mediated by Pres. Jimmy Carter) on Mar. 26, 1979. Formal diplomatic relations were established in 1982. Egypt was suspended from the Arab League—it was readmitted in 1989—and attacked by Libyan forces on several occasions along the Egyptian-Libyan border.

Popular unrest fomented by the Muslim Brotherhood in Sept. 1981 led to a military crackdown. Pres. Sadat was assassinated by members of a military conspiracy on Oct. 6, 1981, and was succeeded by Vice Pres. Mohammed Hosni Mubarak. The government has remained on friendly terms with Israel and the U.S. and has gradually improved relations with the rest of the Arab world. During the Persian Gulf War, it was a staunch member of the anti-Iraq coalition, in return for which the U.S. forgave $7 billion in debt.

Through the 1990's Egypt was troubled by bombings and assassinations by Moslem extremist groups such as Islamic Group and Islamic Jihad (the latter claiming to have killed Sadat). But late in the decade, government crackdowns seem to have been effective; Islamic Group in March 1999 announced a permanent cease-fire. In Sept. 1999 Murabarak ran virtually unopposed, winning a fourth six-year term. In 2005, however, presumably under pressure from the U.S. he allowed opposition candidates although the outcome was never in doubt. Even changes to the constitution in 2007 could not loosen his grip on power.

▶ **EL SALVADOR**
Republic of El Salvador
● **GEOGRAPHY Location:** Pacific coast of Central America. **Boundaries:** Honduras to N and E, Pacific Ocean to S, Guatemala to W. **Total land area:** 8,124 sq. mi. (21,040 sq km). **Coastline:** 191 mi. (307 km). **Comparative area:** about size of Massachusetts. **Land use:** 27% arable land; 12% permanent crops; 61% other. **Major cities:** San Salvador (capital); Soyapango; Santa Ana; San Miguel; Mejicanos.
● **PEOPLE Population:** 7,066,403 (July 2008 est.). **Nationality:** noun—Salvadoran(s); adjective— Salvadoran. **Ethnic groups:** 90% mestizo, 1% Amerindian, 9% white. **Languages:** Spanish, Nahua (among some Amerindians). **Religions:** 83% Roman Catholic; extensive activity by Protestant groups throughout country.
● **GOVERNMENT Type:** republic. **Independence:** Sept. 15, 1821 (from Spain). **Constitution:** Dec. 23, 1983. **National holiday:** Independence Day, Sept. 15. **Head of Government:** Elias Antonio Saca González, president (since June 2004). **Structure:** executive; unicameral legislature; judiciary.
● **ECONOMY Monetary unit:** U.S. dollar. **Budget:** (2007 est.) *income:* $3.46 bil.; *expend.:* $3.61 bil. **G.D.P.:** $35.97 bil., $5,200 per capita (2007 est.). **Chief crops:** coffee, sugarcane, corn; beef, dairy; shrimp. **Natural resources:** hydropower and geothermal power, crude oil. **Major industries:** food processing, beverages, petroleum. **Labor force:** 2.87 mil. (2007); 19% agriculture, 58% services,

23% industry. **Exports:** $3.98 bil. (f.o.b., 2007); offshore assembly exports, coffee, sugarcane, shrimp. **Imports:** $8.667 bil. (f.o.b., 2007); raw materials, consumer goods, foodstuffs, capital goods. **Major trading partners:** (2006) *exports:* 49.5% U.S., 14.4% Guatemala, 8.8% Honduras, 5% Nicaragua; *imports:* 32.2% U.S., 9.3% Guatemala, 7.4% Mexico, 6.3% Germany, 4.7% China.

A number of Indian tribes, of which the Pipil were dominant, originally inhabited the area now called El Salvador. The native population resisted the first attempt at Spanish colonization, begun in 1524, for almost 15 years. In 1821 El Salvador gained its independence from Spain, first as a jurisdiction under the Mexican empire and two years later as a member of the United Provinces of Central America. The Central American Federation collapsed in 1838, and in 1840 El Salvador emerged from a bloody two-year struggle as an independent republic.

The Salvadoran economy was dominated by coffee production from the 1860's onward, and a series of laws in the 1880's allowed for concentration of both land ownership and political power in the hands of a coffee oligarchy. In 1931 a reformist president won election, but the military subsequently dismissed him. A revolt ensued (1932) in which 10,000 to 20,000 Salvadorans—mostly peasants—were killed. The result of the massacre, which was called La Matanza, was a period of relative political stability that lasted until the 1970's.

In 1979 a political coup led by a group of junior military officers overthrew Pres. Gen. Carlos Humberto Romero. Owing to the polarization between conservative and reformist political groups, the first two civilian-military juntas resigned as a result of their failure to have their programs implemented by the military. A third government, which included Christian Democrat José Napoleón Duarte, took over on Mar. 5, 1980, on the basis of an armed forces' pledge to carry out an agrarian reform program. In 1980 the coalition of opposition political organizations became the Democratic Revolutionary Front (FDR), and five revolutionary military organizations consolidated under the banner of the Farabundo Marti Front for National Liberation (FMLN). Six social-democratic political leaders were assassinated in November 1980, further cementing the political opposition around the FMLN-FDR coalition.

A three-part agrarian reform program was initiated in 1980 in El Salvador, but the central part of the program—to redistribute most of the land involved in export agriculture—was dropped as a result of opposition from the agricultural elite.

In March 1982 elections for a constituent assembly, a majority of seats went to the rightist ARENA coalition. In December 1983 a new constitution went into effect, and in 1984 Christian Democrat José Napoleón Duarte assumed the presidency.

In 1989, Alfredo Cristiani of the conservative Alliance for National Renovation was elected president. On Nov. 11, 1989, FMLN guerrillas launched a new offensive that lasted for several weeks before fading away. The government's failure to prosecute military officers implicated in the murder of six Jesuit priests shortly thereafter jeopardized U.S. military aid, which totaled $6 billion between 1979 and 1992.

In January 1992, the government signed a peace treaty with the FMLN and the 12-year civil war, in which 70,000 people died, officially ended on December 15. The treaty called for the military to cut its forces by almost half (to 31,000 soldiers), and for the FMLN to lay down its arms and become a political party. A U.N.-sponsored Truth Commission found that 85 percent of all human-rights violations during the war were attributable to the Salvadoran army, security forces, or intelligence-unit death squads. Although the legislature narrowly passed a general amnesty for public officials, military officers, and political party leaders linked to human rights violations in March of 1993, the United States tried to link further military aid to the dismissal of the worst offenders in the military.

In the March 1994 elections, ARENA's candidate Armando Calderon Sol was elected president. ARENA also carried half the seats in the National Assembly. In the 1997 mid-term election, FMLN made a vary strong showing running virtually even with ARENA on the national level. In the March 1999 elections, ARENA and the FMLN carried almost the same number of seats in the National Assembly, but in the presidential election, ARENA easily won for the third straight time, their candidate (Francisco Flores Perez) gaining 51 percent of the vote. In 2004 ARENA again won by a large margin.

▶ **EQUATORIAL GUINEA**
Republic of Equatorial Guinea
● **GEOGRAPHY   Location:** mainland territory of Río Muni in western Africa and five inhabited islands: Bioko (3°45'N, 8°50'E), Corisco, Great Elobey, Small Elobey, and Pagalu (Annabon). **Boundaries:** Cameroon to N, Gabon to E and S, Gulf of Guinea to W. **Total land area:** 10,830 sq. mi. (28,050 sq km). **Coastline:** 184 mi. (296 km). **Comparative area:** slightly larger than Maryland. **Land use:** 5% arable land; 4% permanent crops; 91% other. **Major cities:** Malabo (capital); Bata.
● **PEOPLE   Population:** 616,459 (July 2008 est.). **Nationality:** noun—Equatorial Guinean(s); adjective— Equatorial Guinean. **Ethnic groups:** Fang, Bubi, Mdowe, Annobon, Bujeba. **Languages:** Spanish (official); pidgin English, Fang. **Religions:** Christian, predominantly Roman Catholic; indigenous practices.
● **GOVERNMENT   Type:** republic. **Independence:** Oct. 12, 1968 (from Spain). **Constitution:** Nov. 17, 1991. **National holiday:** Independence Day, Oct. 12. **Heads of Government:** Col. Teodoro Obiang Nguema Mbasogo, president (since Aug. 1979); Ignacio M. Tang, prime minister (since May 2008). **Structure:** executive; unicameral legislature; judiciary.
● **ECONOMY   Monetary unit:** Communauté Financière Africaine (CFA) franc. **Budget:** (2007 est.) *income:* $4.849 mil.; *expend.:* $2.481 mil. **G.D.P.:** $25.69 bil., $44,100 per capita (2007 est.). **Chief crops:** coffee, cocoa, rice, yams; livestock; timber. **Natural resources:** timber, crude oil, small unexploited deposits of gold, manganese, uranium. **Major industries:** petroleum, fishing, sawmilling. **Labor force:** NA; 30% unemployment. **Exports:** $10.03 bil. (f.o.b., 2007 est.); petroleum, timber, cocoa. **Imports:** $3.22 bil. (f.o.b., 2007); petroleum, foodstuffs, beverages, clothing, machinery. **Major trading partners:** (2006) *exports:* 30.9% China, 22.2% U.S., 12.6% Spain, 10.6% Taiwan, 6.1% Portugal; *imports:* 37.7% U.S., 9.8% Spain, 7.9% Cote D'Ivoire, 6.1% France, 6.1% South Korea, 5.8% U.K., 5% Italy.

Equatorial Guinea consists of the Mbini River basin on the West African coast, and a number of offshore islands, chiefly Bioko and Pagalu (Annobón). Indigenous Pygmies were displaced beginning in the 17th century by migrations of various peoples that now inhabit the coastal region and by the Fang, who comprise 80 percent of the present population.

Bioko was discovered in 1473 by the Portuguese explorer Fernando Po, and until modern times the island bore his name. Portugal controlled the islands and adjacent mainland, exploiting them for the slave trade, until 1778 when the territory was ceded to Spain. Equatorial Guinea remained underdeveloped because of conflicting territorial claims and a lack of Spanish investment. Eventually, however, a plantation system was developed for the cultivation of cocoa, particularly on Bioko, using workers imported from Nigeria.

In 1959 the Spanish territories in the Gulf of Guinea were given status equivalent to a province of Spain. Investment in education, health care facilities, and other social programs, combined with the flourishing plantation economy, made the territory one of the most prosperous and best educated in West Africa. Local autonomy came in 1963, full independence in 1968.

Francisco Macias Nguema was elected Equatorial Guinea's first president in 1968. In 1970 he dissolved all opposition parties and declared a one-party state, and in 1972 proclaimed himself president for life and commenced rule by decree. During the next seven years, a reign of terror resulted in the death or exile of one-third of the country's people. Nigerian workers, along with other foreigners, were expelled from the country in 1976; without their labor and technical skills, the economy was quickly ruined.

Macias Nguema was overthrown in August 1979 in a military coup led by his nephew, Lt. Col. Teodoro Obiang Nguema Mbasogo. Macias Nguema was tried and executed a month later. The new leader moved to reduce Soviet influence and to improve relations with Spain. A new constitution was approved in a referendum in August 1982 and again in 1991, the latter calling for a multiparty political system. Nguema, however, retains firm control. Economic prospects have improved with the discovery of oil reserves estimated at over 65 million barrels a year.

▶ ERITREA
State of Eritrea
● **GEOGRAPHY** **Location:** Horn of Africa (central-eastern Africa). **Boundaries:** Sudan to N and W, Red Sea to E, Djibouti and Ethiopia to S. **Total land area:** 46,842 sq. mi. (121,320 sq km). **Coastline:** 680 mi. (1,094 km) on Red Sea. **Comparative area:** about the size of New York. **Land use:** 4% arable land, negl.% permanent crops, 96% other. **Major cities:** Asmara (capital), Asseb, Massawa, Keren.
● **PEOPLE** **Population:** 5,028,475 (July 2008 est.). **Nationality:** noun—Eritrean(s); adjective—Eritrean. **Ethnic groups:** 50% Tigrinya, 40% Tigre and Kunama, 4% Afar, 3% Saho. **Languages:** Afar, Amharic, Arabic, Tigre and Kunama, Tigrinya, minor ethnic group languages. **Religions:** Muslim, Coptic Christian, Roman Catholic, Protestant. ● **GOVERNMENT** **Type:** transitional government. **Independence:** May 24, 1993 (from Ethiopia). **Constitution:** promulgated May 1997. **National holiday:** Independence Day, May 24. **Head of Government:** Isaias Afwerki, president (since May

1993). **Structure:** executive; unicameral legislature; judiciary.
● **ECONOMY** **Monetary unit:** birr. **Budget :** (2007 est.) *income:* $232.7 mil.; *expend.:* $467.6 mil. **G.D.P.:** $4.75 bil; $1,000 per capita (2007 est.). **Chief crops:** sorghum, lentils, vegetables; livestock; fish. **Natural resources:** gold, potash, zinc, copper. **Major industries:** food processing, beverages, clothing and textiles. **Labor force:** N.A.; 80% agriculture, 20% industry and services (2004 est.). **Exports:** $16.82 mil. (f.o.b., 2007); livestock, sorghum, textiles. **Imports:** $565.9 mil. (f.o.b., 2007); processed goods, machinery, petroleum products. **Major trading partners:** (2006) *exports:* 26.7% Italy, 13.8% France, 8.2% Australia, 7.9% Sudan, 7.8% U.S., 6.2% China, 5.5% Saudi Arabia, 5.2% Jordan; *imports:* 15.8% Italy, 15.7% Saudi Arabia, 15.6% China, 6.7% Netherlands, 6.2% Turkey.

In May 1993, after 30 years of fighting, leaders of the Eritrean People's Liberation Front (EPLF) formally declared this small area of north and northeast Ethiopia to be an independent state. Ethiopia, along with the U.S., the Sudan, and several other states, quickly recognized the authority of the new transitional government led by Issaias Afwerki, former head of the liberation movement.

During the early 20th century, the region of Eritrea was an outpost of the Italian empire, but it came under British rule during World War II. The British made Eritrea part of Ethiopia when independence was granted in 1952. The secessionist movement began immediately, first against Haile Selassie, then in the 1970's and '80's against the Marxist Mengistu Haile Mariam, who was finally driven from office by other forces in 1991. The new government quickly made peace with the Eritrean rebels, who promised continued access to the sea after independence became a fact. Late in 1995 Eritrea began to contest with Yemen control of Greater Hanish Island at the mouth of the Red Sea, a struggle serious enough to elicit U.N. mediation. Further troubles broke out in May 1998 when a small skirmish over the border with Ethiopia escalated into major military clashes in June. The U.S. was attempting to mediate. The bloody border war continued, with much loss of life on both sides, into 2000 until June 18 when Eritrean and Ethiopian foreign ministers signed a cease-fire restoring the borders of May 1998. Both countries in April 2002 accepted the Hague Court of Arbitration's definition of the disputed 620-mile border, but animosity between the two nations never dissipated. In 2006, Eritrea's government helped to arm Islamic militants in Somalia, forcing Ethiopia to send troops to stop them from seizing power and destabilizing the region.

▶ ESTONIA
Republic of Estonia
● **GEOGRAPHY** **Location:** northeastern Europe. **Boundaries:** Gulf of Finland to N and NE, Russia Federation to SE, Latvia to SW, Baltic Sea to NW. **Total land area:** 17,413 sq. mi. (45,100 sq km). **Coastline:** Gulf of Finland. **Comparative area:** about twice the size of New Hampshire. **Land use:** 27% arable land; 0% permanent crops; 73% other. **Major cities:** Tallinn (capital); Tartu; Narva; Kohtla-Järve; Pärnu.
● **PEOPLE** **Population:** 1,307,605 (July 2008 est.). **Nationality:** noun—Estonian(s); adjective—Estonian. **Ethnic groups:** 67.9% Estonian, 25.6% Russian, 2.1% Ukrainian. **Languages:** Estonian

(official), Russian, Ukrainian, English, Finnish, other. **Religions:** Lutheran, Orthodox Christian, others.

● **GOVERNMENT Type:** parliamentary democracy. **Independence:** Sep. 6, 1991. **Constitution:** June 28, 1992. **National holiday:** Independence Day, Feb. 24. **Heads of Government:** Toomas Ives, president (since Oct. 2006); Andrus Ansip, prime minister (since Apr. 2007). **Structure:** executive; unicameral legislature; judiciary.

● **ECONOMY Monetary unit:** Estonian kroon. **Budget:** (2007) *income:* $7.67 bil.; *expend.:* $7.02 bil. **G.D.P.:** $29.35 bil., $21,800 per capita (2007 est.). **Chief crops:** potatoes, vegetables, fruit; livestock and dairy products; fish. **Natural resources:** oil shale (world's number two producer), peat, phosphorites. **Major industries:** oil shale processing, shipbuilding, phosphates. **Labor force:** 688,000 (2007 est.); 11% agriculture, 20% industry, 69% services. **Exports:** $11.31 bil. (f.o.b., 2007); 33% machinery and equipment, 15% wood and paper, 14% textiles, 8% food products. **Imports:** $14.71 bil. (f.o.b., 2007); 31% machinery and equipment, 13% chemical products. **Major trading partners:** (2006) *exports:* 17.9% Finland, 13.2% Sweden, 11.4% Latvia, 8.9% Russia, 5.8% Lithuania, 5.2% Germany, 4.1% U.S.; *imports:* 15.9% Finland, 12.8% Germany, 10.1% Sweden, 10% Russia, 7.6% Latvia, 6.9% Lithuania, 4.5% Poland.

Ethnic and linguistic "cousins" of the Finns, the Ests acquired their own independent state only in the 20th century. Previously they had been "colonized" by the Danes (who founded the capital, Tallinn), then in the 13th century by the Teutonic Knights, in the 16th century by the Swedes (who brought the Lutheran Reformation), in the 17th century by the Poles, and in the 18th century by the Russians. Through all these regimes the German element predominated, the "Baltic barons" forming a territorial aristocracy with German burghers ruling the towns. The Ests were restricted to farming, normally as serfs, with serfdom not abolished until 1819.

With that abolition there began a cultural revival with the study of folklore, the collecting of folk songs, the compilation of the national epic, Kalevipoeg, published between 1857 and 1861, and the circulation of newspapers in the Estonian language. Political expression of this revived national spirit came with the 1918 Treaty of Brest-Litovsk in which the new Soviet Union recognized the independence of Estonia. By 1920 Estonia was fully independent, under its own constitution adopted on June 15 of that year.

A radical land reform dispossessed German landowners of large estates, which were distributed to peasants. Dangers from extremists of Left (Communists) and Right ("liberators") were averted by the strong presidency of Constantice Päts, but the Hitler-Stalin Pact of 1939 spelled the end of Estonian independence. Allotted to Stalin's sphere of influence, Estonia was forced to accept Soviet garrisons larger than its national army in 1939, and 65,000 Germans were "repatriated" (after 700 years) to the Third Reich. Rigged elections in 1940 led to a government that "requested" incorporation into the U.S.S.R., an annexation never recognized by the U.S.

There followed nationalization of private property, amalgamation of Estonia's national forces into the Red Army, and a reign of terror against former political leaders and religious and cultural organizations. During and after the war the Es-

tonian people suffered enormous losses through death in battle, murder, flight, and deportation.

Estonia's return to freedom began Mar. 30, 1990, when a freely elected government declared its intention to secede. Violence provoked by Russian "black berets," mass demonstrations, defiance of Gorbachev's economic sanctions and his January 1991 military crackdown, all marked stages toward the Kremlin's recognition in Sept. 1991 of Estonian independence.

Elections in Sept. 1992 produced a divided Parliament, with the majority a center-right coalition led by the Fatherland Alliance. Parliament chose as president Lennart Meri, a nationalist and devotee of free markets. The effective disenfranchisement of 40 percent of the population, mostly Russians, through laws requiring citizenship since 1940, provoked Russian ire. But by 1994 the law was modified and Russian troops left.

In 1995, parliamentary elections brought into power a far-left alliance of parties led by the Coalition Party (the Communists' new name). In the 1999 parliamentary elections, a coalition of three center-right parties regained control of the legislature. Free-marketeer Mart Laar became Prime Minister for the second time. Interparty squabbling brought the coalition down in 2001 and Parliament elected former Finance Minister Siim Kallas to succeed Laar. In 2003 a new center-right party, Res Publica, led a coalition government under Julian Parts into office. In May 2004 Estonia became a member of the E.U. and was one of the fastest growing economies in Europe until the slowdown of 2008.

▶**ETHIOPIA**
Federal Democratic Republic of Ethiopia
● **GEOGRAPHY Location:** Horn of Africa (central eastern Africa). **Boundaries:** Eritrea to N, Djibouti and Somalia to E, Kenya to S, Sudan to W. **Total land area:** 435,184 sq. mi. (1,127,127 sq km). **Coastline:** none. **Comparative area:** somewhat smaller than Alaska. **Land use:** 10% arable land; 1% permanent crops; 89% other. **Major cities:** Addis Ababa (New Flower); Dire Dawa; Harar; Gondar; Nazret.

● **PEOPLE Population:** 78,254,090 (July 2008 est.). **Nationality:** noun—Ethiopian(s); adjective—Ethiopian. **Ethnic groups:** 40% Oromo, 32% Amhara and Tigrean, 9% Sidamo, 6% Shankella. **Languages:** Amharic, Tigrinya, Orominga, Guaraginga, Somali, Arabic, English (major foreign language taught in schools). **Religions:** 61% Christian, 33% Muslim, 4.6% traditional.

● **GOVERNMENT Type:** federal republic. **Independence:** oldest independent country in Africa and one of oldest in the world—at least 2,000 years. **Constitution:** Dec. 1994. **National holiday:** May 28. **Heads of Government:** Girma Wolde Giorgis, president (since Nov. 2001); Meles Zenawi, prime minister (since Aug. 1995). **Structure:** executive; bicameral legislature; judiciary.

● **ECONOMY Monetary unit:** birr. **Budget:** (2007 est.) *income:* $2.944 bil.; *expend.:* $3.683 bil. **G.D.P.:** $55.07 bil., $700 per capita (2007 est.). **Chief crops:** cereals, pulses, coffee, oilseed; hides, cattle. **Natural resources:** small reserves of gold, platinum, copper, potash. **Major industries:** food processing, beverages, textiles. **Labor force:** 27.27 million (1999); 80% agriculture and animal husbandry, 12% government and services, 8% industry. **Exports:** $1.2 bil. (f.o.b., 2007 est.); coffee, leather products, gold, oilseeds. **Imports:** $4.54 bil. (f.o.b., 2007); food and live animals, petroleum, chemicals, machinery. **Major trading partners:** (2006) *exports:* 12.8% Germany, 10.6% China, 7.5% Japan, 6.8% U.S., 5.9% Saudi Arabia, 5.8% Djibouti; *imports:* 18% Saudi Arabia, 11.3% China, 8.1% India, 5.1% Italy, 4.1% Germany.

Ethiopia played an important role in the Red Sea trade of the classical world and was mentioned by the Greek historian Herodotus in the fifth century B.C. According to legend, the Ethiopian monarchy was founded by Melelik I, son of Israel's King Solomon and the Queen of Sheba (Sab'a, i.e., North Yemen). Coptic Christianity became Ethiopia's dominant religion in the fourth century A.D. Ethiopia successfully resisted Islamic invasions in the seventh century except in areas along the Red Sea coast but was cut off from the rest of the Christian world by the Islamic states of North Africa and the Middle East.

Portugal established forts and trading stations on the Red Sea coast beginning in 1493, strengthening their domination of trade in the Indian Ocean. The Portuguese also sponsored Roman Catholic missionaries but with little success. A century of religious strife ended with the expulsion of all foreign missionaries in the 1630's. Ethiopia successfully resisted an attempted Italian invasion in 1880.

Ethiopia began to emerge into the modern world under Melelik II (r. 1889-1913). A period of instability after his death ended with the accession in 1930 of Haile Selassie. Italy invaded again in 1936 and soon conquered the entire country. Protests by the League of Nations had no effect; Haile Selassie fled to exile in England. The Italians were driven out during World War II by British and Ethiopian forces, and Haile Selassie returned to his throne.

Civil unrest broke out in February 1974, and Haile Selassie was deposed on Sept. 13, 1974. A coalition of urban elites and the armed forces took over, abolishing the monarchy in 1975 and curbing the power of the Coptic church. Land reform was instituted, and a socialist state proclaimed. In 1977-78 a period of "red terror" resulted in the arrest and execution of thousands of the regime's opponents. A provisional military council, the Dergue, was confirmed in power under Col. Mengistu Haile-Mariam's leadership.

A military assistance agreement in 1976 between Ethiopia and the U.S.S.R. ended an earlier military relationship with the U.S.; American military advisers were expelled. In 1977 Somalia, taking advantage of Ethiopia's shifting military situation, attacked across the Ogaden desert, aiming to restore certain disputed areas of Ethiopia to Somalia. A massive infusion of Soviet arms and Cuban troops expelled the Somalis in March 1978, but border clashes continued thereafter.

After the expulsion of the Italians during World War II, the province of Eritrea, under a U.N. plan, was to have become autonomous in a federation with Ethiopia. Instead, Eritrea was made a province of the Ethiopian Empire in 1962. A coalition of Marxist and non-Marxist liberation forces—most prominent among them the Eritrean People's Liberation Front (EPLF)— resisted the annexation from the beginning. By the spring of 1991, Eritrean forces had gained control of all of Eritrea, including Ethiopia's outlets to the sea.

Another rebel group, the Ethiopian People's Revolutionary Democratic Front (EPRDF), sought autonomy for Tigre, a northern region between Ethiopia and Eritrea. In February 1991, the EPRDF launched a major offensive, forcing Mengistu Haile Mariam's flight, a week before scheduled cease-fire talks were to start in London. The talks proceeded quickly under the auspices of the United States, and rebel forces under the leadership of the EPRDF entered Addis Ababa virtually unopposed at the end of May.

Years of civil war and devastating famines left Ethiopia in shambles. A transition government was installed to draft a constitution in July 1991, and acknowledged Eritrean independence without incident. But the country's first multiparty elections in June 1992 were so badly handled that the powerful OLF withdrew from the government.

In June 1994, the EPRDF won 484 of the 547 seats in the Constituent Assembly, which by November had drawn up a constitution for a parliamentary government over nine partially autonomous regions. But most opposition parties boycotted the country's first multiparty elections under the new constitution, resulting in decisive victories by the EPRDF, and its leader Meles Zenawi, who became premier.

A small border war with Eritrea in May-June 1998 threatened the fragile political structure. By early 1999, the small war had ballooned into a major conflict with thousands of soldiers on each side struggling for control of some barren borderland near the outpost of Badme. It ended with a cease-fire, signed by the Ethiopian and Eritrean foreign ministers in June 2000, restoring the May 1998 borders. In May 2002 both countries accepted the Hague Court of Arbitration's delineation of the boundary.

In May 2005 a legislative election was marred by charges of fraud that led to violence and 22 deaths, followed by the arrest and imprisonment of hundreds of opposition leaders. Street protests have been stopped with violence and the government has been strongly criticized by the international community. In 2007, Ethiopia sent a large number of troops to Somalia to successfully stop Islamic militants from securing power.

▶ **FIJI**
Republic of Fiji
● **GEOGRAPHY** **Location:** more than 300 islands (100 inhabited), in South Pacific Ocean. Suva 18°08'S, 178°25'E. **Boundaries:** South Pacific Ocean to N, S, and W; Koro Sea to E; nearest neighbor is Vanuatu, about 600 mi. (1,000 km) to W. **Total area:** 7,054 sq. mi. (18,270 sq km). **Coastline:** 702 mi. (1,129 km). **Comparative area:** slightly smaller than New Jersey. **Land use:** 11% arable land; 5% permanent crops; 84% other. **Major cities:** Suva (capital); Lautoka.
● **PEOPLE** **Population:** 931,741 (July 2008 est.). **Nationality:** noun—Fijian(s); adjective—Fijian. **Ethnic groups:** 55% Fijian, 38% Indian, 8% other. **Languages:** English (official), Fijian, Hindustani. **Religions:** 53% Christian, 34% Hindu, 7% Muslim; Fijians are mainly Christian, Indians are Hindu with Muslim minority.
● **GOVERNMENT** **Type:** republic. **Independence:** Oct. 10, 1970 (from U.K.). **Constitution:** new constitution to allow a non-ethnic Fijian to become prime minister was signed by the president on July 25, 1997 and came into force July 28, 1998. **National holiday:** Independence Day, Oct. 10. **Heads of Government:** Ratu Josefa Iloilo, head of state (since July 2000); Josai V. Bainimarama, prime minister (since Jan. 2007). **Structure:** executive; bicameral legislature; judiciary.
● **ECONOMY** **Monetary unit:** Fijian dollar. **Budget:** (2006 est.) *income:* $1.363 bil.; *expend.:* $1.376 bil. **G.D.P.:** $5.079 bil., $5,500 per capita

(2007 est.). **Chief crops:** sugar cane, coconuts, cassava; cattle, pigs, horses; fish. **Natural resources:** timber, fish, gold, copper, offshore oil potential. **Major industries:** sugar, tourism, copra. **Labor force:** 117,500 (2006); 70% agriculture, 30% services & industry (2001). **Exports:** $1.202 bil. (f.o.b., 2006); sugar, clothing, gold, processed fish. **Imports:** $3.12 bil. (f.o.b., 2006); machinery and transport equipment, petroleum products, food, chemicals. **Major trading partners:** (2006) *exports:* 16.8% U.S., 13.9% Australia, 13.5% U.K., 5.3% Japan, 4.7% Samoa, 4.1% Tonga; *imports:* 28.8% Singapore, 23.3% Australia, 16.8% New Zealand, 4.7% China.

First reported to the West by the Dutch navigator Abel Tasman in 1643, the Fiji Islands were annexed as a British Crown Colony in 1874. Between 1879 and 1916, large numbers of Indian indentured laborers were imported to work on sugar plantations; eventually the original Melanesian inhabitants were outnumbered by persons of Indian descent. Fiji became an independent parliamentary democracy on Oct. 10, 1970, with most land ownership and political power vested in the Fijian minority. A parliamentary election in 1987 brought the Indian party to power; the elected government was ousted in a military coup, and Lt. Col. Sitiveni Rabuka assumed control of the government on May 21, 1987. On June 2, 1992, he was sworn in as prime minister under a new constitution that guarantees a majority of seats for ethnic Fijians in the national legislature. He was reelected as the head of a coalition government in Feb. 1994.

Yet another constitution (1997) restored Indian political rights, and elections in May 1999 led to formation of a government with Fiji's first Indian prime minister, Mahendra Chaudhry. But in May 2000 a hostage crisis/coup led to the formation in July of an all-new, all-Fijian government which satisfied no one. Elections in 2001 resolved little: the (ethnic Fijian) Fiji United Party won a narrow victory over the (ethnic Indian) Fiji Labour Party but prime minister Laisenia Qarase appointed only one Indian to his cabinet. Although reelected in 2006, a military coup at the end of the year brought Commodore Josaia V. Bainimarama to power and he became prime minister.

▶ FINLAND
Republic of Finland
● **GEOGRAPHY Location:** northern Europe. **Boundaries:** Norway to N, Russian Federation to E, Baltic Sea to S, Gulf of Bothnia, Sweden to W. **Total area:** 130,127 sq. mi. (337,030 sq km). **Coastline:** 700 mi. (1,126 km) excluding islands and coastal indentations. **Comparative area:** slightly smaller than Montana. **Land use:** 7% arable land; 0% permanent crops; 93% other. **Major cities:** Helsinki (capital); Espoo; Tampere; Vantaa; Turku. ● **PEOPLE Population:** 5,244,749 (July 2008 est.). **Nationality:** noun—Finn(s); adjective—Finnish. **Ethnic groups:** 93% Finn, 6% Swede; Sami, Roma, Tatar. **Languages:** 91.5% Finnish, 5.5% Swedish (both official); small Sami- and Russian-speaking minorities. **Religions:** 82.5% Lutheran Church of Finland, 1.1% Orthodox, 1.1% other Christian, 15.1% none. ● **GOVERNMENT Type:** republic. **Independence:** Dec. 6, 1917 (from Russia). **Constitution:** Mar. 1, 2000. **National holiday:** Independence Day, Dec. 6. **Heads of Government:** Tarja Halonen, president (since Mar. 2000); Matti Vanhanen, prime

minister (since Apr. 2007). **Structure:** executive; unicameral legislature; judiciary.
● **ECONOMY Monetary unit:** euro. **Budget:** (2007 est.) *income:* $62.02 bil.; *expend.:* $58.16 bil. **G.D.P.:** $185.9 bil., $35,500 per capita (2007 est.). **Chief crops:** cereals, sugar beets, potatoes; dairy, cattle; fish. **Natural resources:** timber, copper, zinc, iron ore, silver. **Major industries:** metal manufacturing, shipbuilding, forestry and wood processing (pulp, paper), copper refining. **Labor force:** 2.68 mil. (2007 est.); 2.6% agriculture, 32.3% industry, 65.1% services; 6.9% unemployment (2007). **Exports:** $104.9 bil. (f.o.b., 2007); machinery, chemicals, paper and pulp. **Imports:** $81.54 bil. (f.o.b., 2007); foodstuffs, petroleum and petroleum products, chemicals, transport equipment. **Major trading partners:** (2006) *exports:* 11% Germany, 11% Sweden, 10% Russia, 7% U.K., 6% U.S., 5% Netherlands; *imports:* 16% Germany, 14% Russia, 14% Sweden, 7% Netherlands, 5% China, 5% U.K., 4% Denmark.

The Finns originated in the Ural Mountains, and their language is akin to Hungarian and closely similar to Estonian. Migrating from western Siberia to what is now Finland in the eighth century, they drove the indigenous Lapps to northernmost Scandinavia. Finland was conquered and Christianized by the Swedes in the 12th century and in the 16th century became a Swedish grand duchy. Ethnic Swedes make up about 7 percent of the present population. Finland was frequently a battleground in wars between Sweden and Russia; about one-third of the population perished in a war-induced famine in 1696. In 1721 Sweden ceded the province of Viborg to Russia, and all of Finland was taken over by Russia in 1809.

Under the Russians the czars became simultaneously grand dukes of Finland and ruled it as a semiautonomous province. Attempts to "Russify" Finland in the later 19th century provoked great popular resistance. When the Russian empire and then the Russian Republic fell in the 1917 Revolution, Finland lapsed into a fierce civil war between Communists and non-Communists. The "whites" under Baron Gustaf Mannerheim were the victors, and Finland became an independent country for the first time in its history.

In 1939 the U.S.S.R. attacked the Finnish Republic; Finland's resistance in the "Winter War" was heroic but unavailing. Defeated, it was forced to cede Western Keralia to the U.S.S.R. After the German invasion of Russia in 1941, fighting between Finland and Russia resumed; England, but not America, declared war on Finland as a cocombatant with Germany. Russia again defeated Finland in 1944 and obliged the Finns to wage war against the German occupying army in northern Finland; much of the country was devastated.

The terms of the 1944 armistice between Finland and the U.S.S.R. were very harsh: Finland ceded the Petsamo region to the Soviet Union, and thus was cut off from the Barents Sea; the Porkkala peninsula was leased to the Soviets for 50 years, and reparations amounting to 80 percent of Finland's exports were paid in kind. Soviet pressure forced Finland to reject Marshall Plan aid after World War II, but Finland benefited indirectly from the rapid postwar recovery of the Scandinavian region. The gross national product returned to prewar levels by 1947.

Finland's economy had traditionally been centered on timber and other forest products, including pulp and paper, and on small-scale, highly productive agriculture. In the postwar period, industrial development was emphasized; the production of heavy machinery became the country's leading industry.

In 1948 the Finns signed a mutual defense pact with the U.S.S.R., renewed in 1955, 1970, and 1983. Finland's presidents, Juho Paasikivi (1946-56), Urho Kekkonen (1956-81), and Mauno Koivisto (1982-94), although conservative and nationalistic, realized that the country's independence required the avoidance of any appearance of anti-Soviet moves in foreign policy. With the establishment of good Soviet-Finnish relations, the Porkkala peninsula was returned to Finland in 1956. Finland joined the Nordic Council and the United Nations in 1955. It became an associate member of the European Free Trade Association in 1961 and a full member in 1985.

With a strong presidency providing stability despite revolving-door coalition governments in the Eduskunta (parliament), and a prudent foreign policy in the shadow of the U.S.S.R., Finland preserved its free economy and civil liberties. The U.S.S.R.'s collapse struck a heavy blow to Finland's economy; through the 1980's 15-25 percent of Finland's exports had gone to the Soviet Union. Unemployment, recession and currency devaluation were constant reminders of these changes.

In politics the U.S.S.R.'s demise brought a rightward shift, with the first nonsocialist coalition government in 25 years being elected in April 1991 under Esko Aho of the Center party as prime minister. 1994 saw Finland's first direct election of a president with Social Democrat Martti Ahtisaari carrying 54 percent of the vote. In March, the E.U. voted to accept Finland as a member in 1995. Prime Minister Aho announced that Finland would join NATO's "partnership for peace" but not as a step to full membership, preferring to maintain Finland's neutrality.

The Finnish electorate and Parliament approved membership in the E.U. in late 1994. But years of recession and high unemployment led to the toppling of the Center party government in 1995 as the Social Democrats emerged as Finland's largest party, with Paavo Lipponen as prime minister. Presidential elections in 2000 gave victory to Social Democrat Tarja Halonen (Finland's first woman president) over ex-premier and Center Party candidate, Esko Aho. In June 2003, newly-installed prime minister Anneli Jaatteenmaki, who had just led her Center Party in March to a slender victory in parliamentary elections, resigned in a scandal in which she was accused of misusing leaked documents during the election campaign, alleging that Social Democrat Prime Minister Lipponen supported the war against Iraq. Defense Minister Matti Vanhanen replaced her.

▶FRANCE
French Republic

● **GEOGRAPHY Location:** western Europe. **Boundaries:** English Channel to N, Belgium, Luxembourg, Germany, Switzerland, Italy to E, Mediterranean Sea, Spain to S, Atlantic Ocean to W. **Total area:** 176,460 sq. mi. (547,030 sq km). **Coastline:** 2,130 mi. (3,427 km). **Comparative area:** slightly less than twice the size of Colorado. **Land use:** 33% arable land; 2% permanent crops; 65% other. **Major cities:** Paris (capital); Marseille (Marseilles); Lyon (Lyons); Toulouse; Nice.
● **PEOPLE Population:** 64,057,790 (July 2008 est.). **Nationality:** noun—Frenchman (men), French-

woman (women); adjective—French. **Ethnic groups:** Celtic and Latin with Teutonic, Slavic, North African, Indochinese, and Basque minorities. **Languages:** French (100% of population); rapidly declining regional dialects (Provençal, Breton, Alsatian, Corsican, Catalan, Basque, Flemish). **Religions:** 83-88% Roman Catholic, 2% Protestant, 1% Jewish, 5-10% Muslim (North African workers), 4% unaffiliated.
● **GOVERNMENT Type:** republic. **Constitution:** Sept. 28, 1958, amended concerning election of president in 1962. **National holiday:** Bastille Day, July 14. **Heads of Government:** Nicolas Sarkozy, president (since May 2007); François Fillon, prime minister (since May 2007). **Structure:** executive; bicameral legislature; judiciary.
● **ECONOMY Monetary unit:** euro. **Budget:** (2007 est.) *income:* $1.311 tril.; *expend.:* $1.372 tril. **G.D.P.:** $2.067 trillion, $33,800 per capita (2007 est.). **Chief crops:** cereals, sugarbeets, potatoes, wine grapes (western Europe's foremost producer); beef, dairy products; fish. **Natural resources:** coal, iron ore, bauxite, fish, timber. **Major industries:** steel, machinery, chemicals, automobiles. **Labor force:** 27.76 mil. (2007); 77.3% services, 20.7% industry, 2% agriculture; 8% unemployment (2007 est.). **Exports:** $558.9 bil. (f.o.b., 2007 est.); machinery and transport equipment, chemicals, foodstuffs, agricultural products, iron and steel products. **Imports:** $601.4 bil. (f.o.b., 2007 est.); crude petroleum, machinery and equipment, vehicles, aircraft, chemicals, iron and steel products. **Major trading partners:** (2006) *exports:* 15.6% Germany, 9.6% Spain, 8.9% Italy, 8.3% U,K., 7.3% Belgium, 6.6% U.S., 4% Netherlands; *imports:* 18.9% Germany, 11.1% Belgium, 8.4% Italy, 7% Spain, 6.8% Netherlands, 6.6% U.K., 4.6% U.S.

Pre-Roman France, known as Gaul, was populated by Celtic tribes. The Mediterranean coast, colonized by Phoenician and Greek traders, was conquered by Rome in the second century B.C. The Roman conquest of all of Gaul was carried out by Julius Caesar between 58 and 51 B.C. Gaul became a prosperous and thoroughly Latinized province of the Roman Empire and Christianity was introduced in the first century A.D.

Barbarian invaders including Visigoths, Franks, and Burgundii swept through France in the fifth century. In 486 Clovis, chief of the Franks, unified the country, accepted Christianity, and established the Merovingian dynasty. France was invaded by Muslim Saracens in the seventh century, but in 732 Charles Martel defeated the Saracens. His son, Pepin the Short, overthrew the last Merovingian ruler in 751 and proclaimed himself king. Pepin's son, Charlemagne, greatly expanded his kingdom and was crowned emperor of the West by the pope in 800.

Ninth-century Viking invasions greatly weakened the power of the Carolingians and France broke up into estates, some of them effectively independent countries, ruled by great aristocrats. Among the most important were the duke- doms of Aquitaine and Burgundy and the counties of Flanders, Blois, and Anjou. In 911 the Vikings, who had repeatedly raided the Atlantic coast of France, established the duchy of Normandy.

In 987 the Carolingian dynasty died out in France (although it survived in the Holy Roman Empire) and was replaced by a new line, the Capetians. Steadily expanding in both territory and power from their base in Paris, the Capetians solidified the foundations of the French monarchy. Paris became a great monastic and university city as well as a center of trade and manufacturing. Under the crusader-king Louis IX (St. Louis), France also became an international power.

During the 14th century, the Black Death, peasant rebellions, and the beginning of the Hundred Years' War (1337-1453) with England further weakened the French monarchy. The Norman conquest of England in 1066 had entwined the fortunes of the French and English monarchies, and with the Capetian line in decline, England pursued its claims in France. Henry V of England defeated the French at Agincourt in 1415, and in 1420 Charles IV made Henry heir to the throne of France. Henry's forces were defeated by French armies inspired by Joan of Arc, and in 1429 his claim to the French throne was overturned. In 1435 Burgundy allied itself with France, and in 1453 the English were driven out of France, except for an enclave at Calais.

Louis XI completed the consolidation of France under the French monarchy. France prospered as a center of commerce, industry, agriculture, learning, and culture throughout the 16th century but was disrupted by religious civil wars stemming from the Reformation. The Protestant Henry of Navarre, heir to the throne, was obliged to accept Catholicism before being crowned in 1594; he became founder of the Bourbon monarchy.

The consolidation of power under a highly centralized monarchy continued under Henry's heirs. With a foreign policy shaped by the powerful prime ministers Cardinal Richelieu and Cardinal Mazarin, France under Louis XIII and Louis XIV enhanced its stature in Europe by defeating the Habsburgs in the Thirty Years' War (1618-48). Louis XIV—the Sun King—moved the court from Paris to his new palace at Versailles and presided over the wealthiest and most powerful monarchy in Europe. His persecution of the Huguenots resulted in a great emigration of Protestants from France. A grand alliance of European states thwarted France's expansionist aims on the continent, but France became a major colonial power in North America, controlling Canada and Louisiana (including most of the Mississippi-Missouri valley), and pursued overseas ventures in Africa and Asia as well.

In the mid-18th century, France was weakened internationally by the expensive and fruitless Wars of the Austrian Succession and the Seven Years' War. Under the Treaty of Paris (1763), France ceded control of Canada to Great Britain. The Enlightenment made France a world center of intellectual activity but also led to the questioning of the political and social bases of the French monarchy. An increasingly wealthy but powerless bourgeoisie chafed under the restrictions of an archaic socioeconomic order.

France under Louis XVI supported the American colonies in the Revolutionary War, incurring a large public debt in the process. Combined with unrestrained extravagance on the part of the court and the aristocracy, poverty increased among the rural peasantry and the urban working class, while the bourgeoisie demanded a greater voice in government. These trends came to a head with the storming of the Bastille on July 14, 1789; soon thereafter, the Estates-General took control of the country, and France was in the throes of revolution. Revolutionary leaders at first allowed Louis XVI to remain on the throne in a limited monarchy,

but the king and Marie Antoinette were subsequently tried for treason and executed in 1793. Thousands died during the Reign of Terror which continued until July 1794, ending with the execution of its primary architects, Augustin Robespierre and Georges Danton. The Directory, with five heads of each division of government (1795-99), failed to maintain public order and suffered military reverses in foreign wars in which successive revolutionary governments had been embroiled since 1792. On Nov. 9, 1799, the Directory was overthrown by the Consulate, with Napoleon Bonaparte named first consul.

Napoleon proclaimed himself emperor of France in 1804. He transformed French law through the Code Napoleon and initially expanded the French empire in Europe and the Middle East. Suffering repeated reverses against British naval forces and disastrous losses in his 1812 invasion of Russia, Napoleon was defeated by the British under Wellington at Waterloo in 1815, and the French empire collapsed.

France restored its monarchy in 1815 but not its monarchical absolutism. Charles X, successor to Louis XVIII, was ousted in a coup d'état in 1830 and replaced by the liberal Louis Philippe. The monarchy came to an end in the wave of popular revolt that swept France, along with most of Europe, in 1848; Louis Napoleon (nephew of Bonaparte) became president of the Second Republic. In 1852 he created the Second Empire, ruling as Napoleon III and presiding over a court that set the standards of fashion for the wealthy bourgeois society of 19th-century Europe.

During the 19th century, France again became a major colonial power, acquiring important possessions in North and West Africa and Indochina. It also became a world leader in art, science, and literature and began its slow transformation into a major industrial power. Politically, however, France suffered from endemic weakness. The Second Empire ended disastrously with defeat in the Franco-Prussian War of 1870-71; the Paris Commune, formed during that war, was overthrown with great bloodshed. The Third Republic (1871-1914), despite the glittering pleasures of the Belle Epoque and France's prestige as a world power, was shaken by the Dreyfus Affair of 1894-1906.

France joined with Great Britain and Russia in forming the Triple Entente of 1907, a defensive agreement against the Triple Alliance of Germany, Italy, and the Austro-Hungarian empire. During World War I—in effect a war between these two alliances—France suffered millions of casualties and severe damage in the north. Although its role as a leader of the victorious alliance was confirmed at the Versailles Conference of 1919, France was seriously weakened by the war and played a diminished role as a world power.

France suffered badly in the world depression of the 1930's and could muster neither political nor military energy to offer effective opposition to the rise of Nazi Germany and fascist Italy. France was a participant in the Munich Agreement of 1938, which sealed the fate of central Europe. When World War II broke out in 1939, Hitler initially held off his attack on France, but when it came in May-June 1940, France was swiftly and ignominiously defeated.

During World War II, northern France was under German occupation, while in the south a collaborationist, semifascistic state was organized, with its capital at Vichy. Meanwhile, in London,

Gen. Charles de Gaulle rallied the Free French forces, which fought on the Allied side in various campaigns. After the liberation of Paris a "provisional government" of various Resistance groups combined with de Gaulle's supporters drew up a constitution for the Fourth French Republic.

Although it suffered from inherent political weaknesses and often failed to provide stable cabinets, the Fourth Republic presided over postwar recovery, aided by the Marshall Plan; it promoted a mixed socialist-free enterprise economy and instituted social reforms such as women's suffrage and social security. It also led the way toward a united Europe, playing a leading role in the organization of the EEC in 1957. France became a founding member of NATO in 1949.

The Fourth Republic was unable, however, to withstand the strains of the dismantling of France's empire during the postwar wave of decolonization. France's recovery of Indochina in 1945 set off a war of national liberation there that lasted until France withdrew from the colony in 1954. Morocco and Tunisia won their independence in 1956; in Algeria, regarded as part of France itself, France fought on against Front de Liberation Nationale (FLN) rebels.

The Algerian War seriously polarized French public opinion, and, threatened with an army coup, the National Assembly voted in 1958 to grant Pres. Charles de Gaulle emergency powers for six months. De Gaulle outmaneuvered his army backers and negotiated to turn Algeria over to the FLN, a process completed in 1962. Meanwhile he also restored order at home and presided over the drafting of a new constitution that created the Fifth Republic in 1958.

The new constitution created a strong presidency, with powers to name the premier and the Council of Ministers and to preside over their meetings. The legislature was required to give priority to government initiatives and lacked authority over national defense, education, labor, and local government. Under the governments of premiers Michel Debré and Georges Pompidou, the Gaullist regime further advanced modernization of French industry and greatly benefited French agriculture by expanding the Common Market to include agricultural goods.

De Gaulle followed an independent foreign policy, pursuing European integration as well as closer relations with the Communist bloc and the Third World. He blocked British entry into the Common Market; developed an independent nuclear force, refusing to sign nuclear test-ban and nonproliferation treaties; pursued a historic rapprochement with Germany; recognized the People's Republic of China; established a leading French role in the former French colonies of Africa; and withdrew French forces from the NATO military command.

Reelected president in 1965, after a runoff election against the Socialist-Communist alliance candidate François Mitterrand, de Gaulle continued his independent policy until student riots in early 1968 provoked police repression, which led to further popular support for the students, especially in Paris. De Gaulle dissolved the National Assembly and, in an emotional campaign on behalf of national stability, won a large electoral majority. In 1969, however, following minor political reverses, de Gaulle resigned as president.

The elections of June 1969 gave the presidency to former premier Georges Pompidou, who died in office in April 1974. He was succeeded by the Independent Republican Valery Giscard d'Estaing, who served until May 1981. During these years the Gaullist heritage was developed and consolidated. In foreign policy the movement toward European unity continued with the development of the European Parliament and, in a reversal of policy in 1973, French support for British membership in the EEC. The economic shock of the OPEC price rises of 1973-74 led to a decision to stress new industrial ventures in high-technology fields, symbolized by the Anglo-French Concorde supersonic transport.

The 1970's were years of social ferment, with a relaxation of divorce laws and the legalization of contraception advertisements and abortion, and a decline in church membership and attendance. In 1978 disillusionment stemming from inflation and social difficulties under Giscard d'Estaing brought about a leftist electoral victory for the first time under the Fifth Republic.

The Gaullist era came to an end in 1981, when Socialist François Mitterrand defeated Giscard in a presidential election. He dissolved the National Assembly and led his party to an absolute majority. Socialist premier Pierre Mauroy formed a government which pursued an aggressive program of nationalization of banks and major industries and reform of local government. Continued economic difficulties led to a loss of popular support for Mitterrand's policies. In the elections of 1986, Jacques Chirac's coalition of Gaullists and Giscardists won an almost absolute majority in the National Assembly, and Chirac became premier—the first time since 1958 that the president and the premier were of opposing parties. An accommodation was worked out in which Mitterrand concentrated on foreign affairs, and Chirac on domestic matters. Mitterrand oversaw a restoration of French military cooperation with NATO.

At home Chirac and his party reversed Mitterrand's policy of nationalization, cut taxes, and brought about a significant reduction in the inflation rate. Chirac ran for president against Mitterrand in 1988 but was defeated. Mitterrand's reelection with over 54 percent of the vote carried his Socialist party to a near majority in the assembly, where they constructed a coalition government. Persistent 9 percent unemployment and the growing appeal of Jean-Marie Le Pen's antiimmigrant National Front brought a cabinet shake-up in May 1991 and the designation of France's first female premier, Edith Cresson.

But the shake-up did nothing to stem voter dissatisfaction with the governing Socialists. Elections to regional councils in 1992 saw the Socialist vote drop to 18 percent, but not to the benefit of the center-right coalition Union for France, which gained only one-third of the vote. The National Front and the two rival "green" parties together gained 28 percent of the vote.

Even the formidable Mitterrand could not prevent the Socialist rout in the March 1993 assembly elections. The Rally for France won the most lopsided victory in the republic's history, carrying 460 (of 577) seats while the left took only 93. Rejecting calls for his resignation, Mitterrand vowed to stay on until 1995, when his unprecedented 14-year presidency ended as Jacques Chirac won over Lionel Jospin.

Pledged to tax and spending cuts and continued dismantling of state enterprises, Chirac met with limited success as unemployment reached its highest level ever. A giant truckers' strike blocked French highways without government action, and cutting social welfare spending (to meet the E.U.'s Euro conditions) proved elusive. So, seeking a public mandate for France's participation in the Euro, Chirac dissolved the Assembly a year early. But the result was yet another French "cohabitation": the left coalition took 319 seats and Lionel Jospin became prime minister.

Jospin's run for the presidency ended in embarrassment as he finished third to Pres. Chirac and Jean-Marie LePen, Chirac polling 82 percent in the run-off. Chirac's right wing coalition took 355 of the National Assembly's 577 seats, promising to support "law and order," cut taxes, and privatize the elephantine state pension system. In 2003 Chirac played a leading role in condemning the U.S.-led invasion of Iraq. In 2004 he led the controversial but very popular movement to ban all religious clothing in schools (Muslim head scarves, yarmulkas, large crosses). Chirac's party was humiliated when the E.U. constitution was rejected by a wide margin in 2005, setting the stage for a center-right victory in 2007 led by Nicolas Sarkozy, the new president whose supporters also won a solid majority in the legislature. He immediately sought closer ties with the U.S. and voiced strong support for NATO expansion. (See "Major News Stories.")

▶ **GABON**
Gabonese Republic
• **GEOGRAPHY   Location:** western coast of Africa. **Boundaries:** Equatorial Guinea to NW, Cameroon to N, Congo to E and S, Atlantic Ocean to W. **Total area:** 103,348 sq. mi. (267,670 sq km). **Coastline:** 550 mi. (885 km). **Comparative area:** slightly smaller than Colorado. **Land use:** 1% arable land; 1% permanent crops; 98% other. **Major cities:** Libreville (capital); Port-Gentil; Masuku.
• **PEOPLE   Population:** 1,485,832 (July 2008 est.). **Nationality:** noun—Gabonese (sing., pl.); adjective—Gabonese. **Ethnic groups:** Bantu tribes, including four major tribal groupings (Fang, Nzebi, Obamba, Bapounou); 154,000 other Africans and Europeans, including 10,700 French and 11,000 of dual nationality. **Languages:** French (official), Fang, Myene, Bateke, Bapounou/Eschira, Bandjabi. **Religions:** 55-75% Christian, less than 1% Muslim; Animist.
• **GOVERNMENT   Type:** republic; multi-party presidential regime since 1990. **Independence:** Aug. 17, 1960 (from France). **Constitution:** Mar. 14, 1991 **National holidays:** Founding of the Gabonese Democratic Party, Mar. 12 (1968). **Heads of Government:** El Hadj Omar Bongo Ondimba, president (since Dec. 1967); Jean Eyeghe Ndong, prime minister (since Jan. 2006). **Structure:** executive; bicameral legislature; independent judiciary.
• **ECONOMY   Monetary unit:** Communauté Financière Africaine (CFA) franc. **Budget:** (2007 est.) **income:** $3.353 bil.; **expend.:** $2.283 bil. **G.D.P.:** $20.09 bil., $13,800 per capita (2007 est.). **Chief crops:** coffee, cocoa, sugar; rubber; wood; cattle; fishing. **Natural resources:** crude oil, manganese, uranium, gold, timber, iron ore. **Major industries:** petroleum, manganese, food, beverages. **Labor force:** 582,000; 60% agriculture, 15% industry, 25% services; 21% unemployment (2006). **Exports:** $6.856 bil. (f.o.b., 2007 est.); 77% crude oil, wood, manganese. **Imports:** $1.951 bil. (f.o.b., 2007 est.); machinery and equipment, foodstuffs, chemicals,

petroleum products, construction materials. **Major trading partners:** (2006) **exports:** 27.6% U.S., 15.9% China, 7.8% France, 5.4% Trinidad & Tobago, 4.3% Thailand; **imports:** 35.4% France, 7.6% U.S., 5.5% Netherlands, 4.5% Cameroon, 4.3% Belgium.

Gabon, an equatorial nation largely covered by dense rain forest, is inhabited by a highly diverse mixture of people who migrated into the region over the course of the past 700 years; the now-dominant Fang arrived during the 19th century. The first Europeans to reach the area were the Portuguese in the 15th century; they were followed by Dutch, French, and British traders in the 16th century. All engaged in the slave trade.

France established an informal protectorate in 1839-41 and set about suppressing the slave trade. In 1849 a group of freed slaves settled near the American mission station at Baraka and renamed the town Libreville. France established a colonial administration in 1903 and in 1910 made it part of French Equatorial Africa. The territory became an important base of Free French activity during World War II, and in 1946 Gen. Charles de Gaulle granted French citizenship to the territory's inhabitants, and local power was devolved upon advisory assemblies. Gabon became fully independent on Aug. 17, 1960.

Gabon has remained politically stable under its 1961 constitution. Gabon's first president, Leon M'Ba, was briefly deposed by a military coup in 1964 but quickly reinstated with the aid of French troops. He died in 1967 and was succeeded by the vice president, Omar Bongo who combined all political parties into the Gabonese Democratic party in 1968; he was elected president in his own right in 1975, was reelected in each subsequent election through 1998 (which he won with a highly dubious 67 percent). Despite initial resistance from the government, Gabon has recently made the transition to multiparty democracy, thereby attracting more foreign investment. Bongo's Gabonese Democratic party remains in power.

Although its per capita income is much higher than almost every African nation, there is substantial income inequality and a good deal of poverty in Gabon.

▶ **THE GAMBIA**
Republic of The Gambia
• **GEOGRAPHY   Location:** narrow territory around Gambia River on northwestern coast of Africa. **Boundaries:** Senegal to N, E, and S, Atlantic Ocean to W. **Total area:** 4,363 sq. mi. (11,300 sq km). **Coastline:** 50 mi. (80 km). **Comparative area:** slightly less than twice the size of Delaware. **Land use:** 20% arable land; 1% permanent crops;79% other. **Major cities:** Banjul (capital); Kombo St. Mary (surrounding urban area).
• **PEOPLE   Population:** 1,735,464 (July 2008 est.). **Nationality:** noun—Gambian(s); adjective—Gambian. **Ethnic groups:** 42% Mandinka, 18% Fula, 16% Wolof, 10% Jola, 9% Serahuli, 1% non-African. **Languages:** English (official), Mandinka, Wolof, Fula, and others. **Religions:** 90% Muslim, 9% Christian, 1% indigenous beliefs.
• **GOVERNMENT   Type:** republic under multiparty democratic rule. **Independence:** Feb. 18, 1965 (from U.K.). **Constitution:** Apr. 24, 1970, (suspended July 1994); rewritten, approved and reestablished in Jan. 1997. **National holiday:** Independence Day, Feb. 18. **Head of Government:** Colonel Yahya Jammeh, president (since July

1994). **Structure:** following the coup on July 22, 1994 all elective officers were dissolved; military leaders have promised to return control to a democratically-elected government.

● ECONOMY **Monetary unit:** dalasi. **Budget:** (2007 est.) *income:* $160.4 mil.; *expend.:* $165.7 mil. **G.D.P.:** $1.338 bil., $800 per capita (2007 est.). **Chief crops:** peanuts, millet, sorghum, rice, maize; cattle, goats, sheep. **Natural resources:** fish. **Major industries:** agricultural processing, tourism, beverages. **Labor force:** 400,000; 75% agriculture, 19% industry, commerce, and services, 6.1% government. **Exports:** $147.7 mil. (f.o.b., 2007); peanuts and peanut products, fish, cotton. **Imports:** $276 mil. (f.o.b., 2007 est.); foodstuffs, manufacturing, raw materials. **Major trading partners:** (2006) *exports:* 38.6% India, 15.9% U.K., 7.9% Indonesia, 7% France, 4.6% Italy; *imports:* 25.2% China, 11.3% Senegal, 8.1% Cote d'Ivoire, 6.6% Brazil, 4.5% Netherlands, 4% U.K.

Thirty miles across at its widest point, and 295 miles long, the serpentine republic of The Gambia was gerrymandered into being out of competing French and British colonial interests. Once the westernmost part of the kingdom of Mali, The Gambia was visited by the Portuguese in 1455. In 1588, they sold British traders exclusive rights to the Gambia River, and in 1660 British merchants established a trading fort. England and France struggled for 200 years to gain political and economic control over the territory, but in 1783 the French ceded to Great Britain possession of The Gambia. Its present boundaries were established in 1889 when it became a British Crown Colony. Between 1901 and 1906, legislative councils were established to encourage self-government, and slavery was abolished.

After World War II the country moved quickly toward constitutional government, achieving independence as a constitutional monarchy within the British Commonwealth of Nations in 1965. The Gambia became a republic on Apr. 24, 1970, and it had the same president, Sir Dawda K. Jawara, until 1994.

In 1994, Yahya Jammeh, a 29-year-old lieutenant fresh from a military police training course in the United States, led a bloodless coup deposing the government of Pres. Jawara. Jammeh pledged to restore civilian government "as soon as we have set things right." Later that year the United Kingdom, the United States, and the European Union cut off all economic and military aid pending a return to democracy. Pres. Jammeh was reelected Oct. 2001 in a vote deemed fair by outside observers. He granted amnesty to Jawara, who returned from exile in 2002. Jammeh was reelected in 2006.

▶ GEORGIA

● GEOGRAPHY **Location:** west and central Transcaucasia between Asia and Europe. **Boundaries:** Russian Federation to N and E, Azerbaijan, Armenia to S, Turkey to SW, Black Sea to W. **Total area:** 26,911 sq. mi. (69,700 sq km). **Coastline:** Black Sea. **Comparative area:** slightly smaller than South Carolina. **Land use:** 11% arable land; 4% permanent crops; 85% other. **Major cities:** Tbilisi (capital); Kutaisi; Rustavi; Batumi; Sukhumi.

● PEOPLE **Population:** 4,630,841 (July 2008 est.). **Nationality:** noun—Georgian(s); adjective— Georgian. **Ethnic groups:** 83.8% Georgian, 6.5% Azeri, 5.7% Armenian, 1.5% Russian, 2.5% other. **Languages:** 71% Georgian (official), 9% Russian, 7% Armenian, 6% Azeri; note - Abkhaz is the official language in Abkhazia. **Religions:** 84% Orthodox, 10% Muslim, 4% Armenian Apostolic, 3% other.

● GOVERNMENT **Type:** republic. **Independence:** Apr. 9, 1991 (from Soviet Union). **Constitution:** Oct. 17, 1995. **National holiday:** Independence Day, May 26. **Heads of Government:** Mikheil Saakoshili, president (since 2003); Lado Gurgenidze, prime minister (since Nov. 2007). **Structure:** executive; unicameral legislature; judiciary.

● ECONOMY **Monetary unit:** lari. **Budget:** (2007 est.) *income:* $3.68 bil; *expend.:* $3.006 bil. **G.D.P.:** $19.65 bil., $4,200 per capita (2007 est.). **Chief crops:** citrus, grapes, tea, vegetables. **Natural resources:** forests, hydropower, manganese. **Major industries:** steel, aircraft, machine tools. **Labor force:** 2.02 mil. (2007); 55.6% agriculture, 35.5% services, 8.9% industry; 13.6% unemployment (2006 est.). **Exports:** $1.24 bil. (2007); citrus fruits, tea, wine. **Imports:** $5.2 bil. (2007); fuel, grain and other foods, machinery and parts. **Major trading partners:** (2006) *exports:* 12.6% Turkey, 10.9% U.S., 7.9% Azerbaijan, 5.9% Armenia, 5.8% U.K., 4.9% Bulgaria, 4.8% Ukraine, 4.7% Russia, 4.4% Turkmenistan; *imports:* 14.1% Turkey, 13.1% Russia, 8.5% Ukraine, 7.4% Azerbaijan, 6.8% Germany, 5% U.S., 4.6% Bulgaria.

Georgia is a land of rugged natural beauty, renowned for its famous war heroes and its hospitality. Georgia's most famous son, Iosif Djugashvili, known as Josef Stalin, was born in the mountain village of Gori in 1879. The name of Georgia derives from the Persian name for the native people, Gorj.

An independent state was founded in the fourth century B.C. following the conquest of the Persian Empire by Alexander III. Christianity became the state religion in the 4th century A.D. Both the Georgian language and the capital city of Tbilisi date from the fifth century A.D. The Georgian people began to develop feudal states in the sixth century. Georgia's later history, however, is one of almost continuous foreign domination. In the 12th century, Georgia gained independence from the Persian Empire, but it came under Mongol rule in 1236. For centuries Georgia was a battleground between Turks and Persians, and the territory was ultimately divided into principalities, some under the control of Persia and some under Turkey. In 1801, the Persian principalities were absorbed into the Russian empire, and by the end of the century the remaining Georgian state under Turkish domination was annexed to Russia.

Once the Russian Empire collapsed in 1917 with the Bolshevik revolution, independent Georgia was proclaimed in May 1918. Although the Soviet Union and Georgia signed a treaty in May 1920 agreeing on their respective borders, the Soviet Red Army came into Georgia and forcibly incorporated it into the Soviet Union as a Socialist republic in early 1921. In 1922 it was made part of the Transcaucasian Soviet Federal Socialist Republic with Armenia and Azerbaijan, and in 1936 it became one of the U.S.S.R.'s union republics.

The Georgians have always been fiercely nationalistic, even in the face of the U.S.S.R.'s "one Soviet people" policy. Georgian pride was evident from the first demonstrations against "russification" in 1956, and again in 1978 when the rewritten U.S.S.R. constitution attempted to weaken the status of Georgian language. In 1988, during Gorbachev's policy of "glasnost," or openness, great numbers of Georgians began to call for sovereignty.

Even as Georgia fought for its independence from the U.S.S.R., the autonomous provinces of Abkhazia, Adzharia, and South Ossetia began fighting for independence from Georgia. Tensions continue to run high in Adzharia, where allegiances to Islam frighten many in Christian Georgia, and in South Ossetia, which is struggling to end its association with Georgia.

But the greatest conflict raged in Abkhazia, the home region of Zviad Gamsakhurdia, who was elected the country's first president in May 1991, but ousted from office seven months later. Fighting between the Georgian army and troops loyal to Gamsakhurdia continued from 1991 to 1993, resulting in more than 2,000 casualties, including Gamsakhurdia, until Pres. Eduard Shevardnadze persuaded Parliament to give him emergency powers to quell the insurgency.

His political power consolidated, Shevardnadze, a former Soviet official, began to renew ties to Russia. In 1994 he agreed to a cooperation pact to increase Russia's military influence and Parliament ratified Georgia's membership in the Commonwealth of Independent States.

In 1995 Parliament overwhelmingly approved a new "strong president" constitution. And in Nov. 1995 Shevardnadze easily won election to a new five-year term, while his two-party coalition captured close to 80 percent of the seats in Parliament. But continued instability in Abkhazia, the presence of Russian troops, and several assasination attempts on Shevardnadze left future development in doubt. Still, Shevardnadze easily won re-election in 2000 and Georgia became the WTO's 137th member. After firing his entire cabinet in Nov. 2001, Shevardnadze announced that U.S. troops (to reach a total of 1,200) were arriving (Apr. 2002) to train Georgian troops in the struggle against Muslim separatists. At the end of 2003, daily non-violent protests against Shevardnadze's autocratic rule led to his resignation. U.S.-educated Mikheil Saakashvili, leader of the National Movement, was overwhelmingly elected president. Constitutional reforms soon followed, but Abkhazia and south Ossetia remained unstable and their defacto governments are supported by Russia. Saakashvili was reelected in Jan. 2008 but by a much smaller margin as his insistence on joining NATO made voters nervous that Russia would react strongly. In August, a Russian military strike quickly overwhelmed Georgian forces and occupied the disputed territories and parts of Georgia. (See "Major News Stories.")

▶ **GERMANY**
Federal Republic of Germany
● **GEOGRAPHY** **Location:** central Europe. **Boundaries:** Denmark, Baltic Sea to N, Poland, Czech Republic to E, Austria, Switzerland to S, France, Luxembourg, Belgium, Netherlands to W, North Sea to NW. **Total area:** 137,803 sq. mi. (356,910 sq km). **Coastline:** 1,385 mi. (2,389 km). **Comparative area:** slightly smaller than Montana. **Land use:** 34% arable land; 1% permanent crops; 65% other. **Major cities:** Berlin (capital); Hamburg; München (Munich); Köln (Cologne); Frankfurt. ● **PEOPLE** **Population:** 82,369,548 (July 2008 est.). **Nationality:** noun—German(s); adjective—German. **Ethnic groups:** 91.5% German, 2.4% Turkish. **Languages:** German. **Religions:** 34%

Protestant, 34% Roman Catholic, 3.7% Muslim, 28.3% unaffiliated or other.
● **GOVERNMENT** **Type:** federal republic. **Constitution:** May 23, 1949; provisional constitution known as Basic Law became constitution of reunited German state Oct. 3, 1990. **National holiday:** German Unity Day, Oct. 3. **Heads of Government:** Horst Köhler, president (since July 2004); Angela Merkel, chancellor (since Nov. 2005). **Structure:** president (titular head of state); bicameral parliament—Bundesrat (Federal Council, upper house), Bundestag (National Assembly, lower house); independent judiciary.
● **ECONOMY** **Monetary unit:** euro. **Budget:** (2007 est.) *income:* $1.465 tril.; *expend.:* $1.477 tril. **G.D.P.:** $2.833 tril., $34,400 per capita (2007 est.). **Chief crops:** wheat, barley, rye, potatoes, sugar beets, fruit; cattle, pigs, poultry. **Natural resources:** iron ore, coal, potash, timber. **Major industries:** among world's largest producers of iron, steel, coal, cement, chemicals, machinery, vehicles, machine tools, electronics, food and beverages; shipbuilding; textiles. **Labor force:** 43.63 mil. (2007 est.); 33.4% industry, 2.8% agriculture, 63.8% services. **Exports:** $1.361 tril. (f.o.b., 2007 est.); machinery, vehicles, chemicals. **Imports:** $1.121 bil. (f.o.b., 2007 est.); machinery, vehicles, chemicals, foodstuffs. **Major trading partners:** (2006) *exports:* 9.5% France, 8.7% U.S., 7.3% U.K., 6.7% Italy, 6.3% Netherlands, 5.6% Austria, 5.2% Belgium, 4.7% Spain; *imports:* 11.8% Netherlands, 8.5% France, 7.2% Belgium, 5.9% China, 5.7% U.K., 5.6% Italy, 5.3% U.S., 4.3% Austria.

The ancient tribes of Germany resisted Roman conquest with mixed success. German federated troops served in the Roman legions, and Germanic invasions contributed to the fall of Rome. Most of Germany was united within the empire of Charlemagne. Divided among his three sons in 843, the empire's eastern regions became the heart of the Germanies. The Holy Roman Empire, founded in 962, gave some unity to the politically fragmented German territories, but its boundaries included more than Germany, and some Germans remained outside it. But that unity was fragile; the Holy Roman emperor was a feudal overlord rather than a ruler, and hundreds of separate political bodies coexisted within the imperial domain. Along the North Sea and Baltic coasts, the Hanseatic League controlled much of the commerce of northern Europe.

With the Reformation in the 16th century, religious divisions added to Germany's existing political fragmentation and local allegiances. The Thirty Years War (1618-48) resulted in the virtual extinction of the Holy Roman Empire and left Germany without even a shadow of unity.

After the Napoleonic Wars, in which much of Germany was conquered by France, the Congress of Vienna (1814-15) sanctioned the creation of a German League to succeed the Holy Roman Empire. The league consisted of 39 states, including five substantial kingdoms and the German parts of the Austrian empire. Prussia, one of the five kingdoms, had already risen to prominence under Frederick the Great in the 18th century. In a series of wars in the mid-19th century, Prussia conquered the other German states; after defeating France in the Franco-Prussian War of 1870-71, Prussia declared the establishment of the German empire. Under its chancellor, Otto von Bismarck, Germany became a major European power in the late 19th century, with a booming industrial economy, flourishing agriculture, a small colonial empire, and growing military might.

The German Empire reached its height under Kaiser Wilhelm II on the eve of World War I. Germany's disastrous defeat in that war was compounded by the harsh terms of the Treaty of Versailles (1919), which stripped Germany of its colonial empire, and returned part of Schleswig to Denmark, Alsace-Lorraine to France, and part of Prussia to Poland.

The Weimar Republic, established in 1919, gradually overcame economic difficulties, including ruinous inflation, to achieve a measure of recovery in the 1920's. The republic was disrupted by labor strife, political fragmentation, and the rise of armed extremist political movements on both left and right. After the onset of the world economic depression in 1929, Adolf Hitler's National Socialist movement gained increasing power, both at the polls and through open thuggery against its opponents. Hitler's appointment as chancellor in 1933 effectively put an end to the Weimar Republic as a functioning democracy.

The onset of World War II in Europe was presaged by Hitler's annexation of Austria and Czechoslovakia in 1938 and precipitated by the German invasion of Poland in 1939. Early military successes gave Germany control of most of Europe, but the eventual victory of the Allied powers in 1945 left the country exhausted and in ruins. Much of the Jewish population of Germany, and of other territories under German control, had been killed during the Holocaust. German cities were reduced to rubble, and a quarter of the country's homes were uninhabitable. Famine and fuel shortages added to the general misery.

Politically, Germany had essentially ceased to exist in 1945. The Allies divided the country into four zones of occupation, with a similar four-part division of Berlin. As the Cold War rift between the Western powers and the U.S.S.R. intensified during the late 1940's, so too the division of Germany hardened. In 1948 the U.S.S.R. imposed a blockade on West Berlin; the city was supplied by a massive airlift from the West for several months. In 1949 two Germanies were created: the German Democratic Republic in the Russian zone in the east, and the Federal Republic of Germany in the Allied zone in the west.

The Federal Republic was largely the creation of one man, Konrad Adenauer. A veteran pre-Hitler politician, he founded the Federation of Christian Democratic Parties (CDU-CSU) in 1945, and as president of the Parliamentary Council formed during the occupation, he virtually wrote the new constitution for West Germany. In the first elections held in the Federal Republic (August 1949), the "bourgeois coalition" led by the CDU-CSU won a parliamentary majority in the Bundestag, and Adenauer became chancellor, a post he held for 14 years. In 1951 the Western powers granted the new state autonomy in foreign affairs, and recognized its full sovereignty in 1954.

Even before the fighting in Germany subsided in 1945, the Soviet Air Force brought Walter Ulbricht, the exiled leader of the German Communist party, back to the U.S.S.R.'s zone of occupation in Germany. Backed by 20 Soviet divisions, Ulbricht and the party commenced the communization of the eastern zone. After local and state elections embarrassed the Communists, Stalin and Ulbricht forced all other parties into the National Front. With no other electoral lists permitted, voters gave a 99.7 percent approval to the National Front in the first elections to East Germany's "People's Chamber" in 1950.

While Ulbricht attempted to collectivize agriculture and plan industrial development in the eastern zone, the Soviet Union extracted heavy reparations payments, bringing on an acute economic crisis. In June 1953, shortly after Stalin's death, strikes and riots erupted. The U.S.S.R. renounced further reparation payments and declared East Germany a sovereign state.

In foreign affairs Adenauer relied heavily on friendship with the United States and reconciliation with France. He also supported European integration: In 1951 West Germany joined both the Council of Europe and the Coal and Steel Community. West Germany was admitted to NATO in 1955 and in 1957 became one of the six founding members of the EEC.

In domestic affairs the political alliance between Adenauer and Ludwig Erhard led to political stability and the creation of a marketdriven economy. With a currency reform program and Marshall Plan aid in place by 1948 under occupation administration, the stage was set for Germany's "economic miracle" of the 1950's. Between 1949 and 1964, industrial production increased by 60 percent and gross national product tripled, while unemployment fell to 1 percent, even as millions of refugees from East Germany were integrated into the West German economy.

In 1963 Erhard succeeded Adenauer as chancellor. Economic growth slowed to an annual 3 percent rate, but West Germany was already one of Europe's strongest economic powers, even providing jobs for hundreds of thousands of "guest workers" from southern Europe and Turkey.

By 1963 East Germany had become the second-largest industrial power in Eastern Europe, and in 1968 it surpassed Czechoslovakia in output. A significant shift of labor to industry reduced the farm population to under 20 percent of total population by 1960. Though farming became mechanized, it remained relatively inefficient.

Although East Germany enjoyed prestige within the Eastern bloc as an industrial power, the steady stream of emigrants to West Germany told a different story. After a renewed collectivization policy was implemented in 1960, the stream became a flood, and East Germany responded by building the Berlin Wall. The wall was a visible sign of political failure, but it did slow the stream of emigration to a trickle.

Erhard resigned in 1966 when his coalition fell apart over the issue of a planned tax increase. He was succeeded by Kurt Kiesinger, who presided over a historic "great coalition" of Christian Democrats and Social Democrats. Under Willi Brandt (who served as deputy chancellor and foreign minister), the Social Democrats had shifted their orientation from a Marxist party to a reformist, market-oriented stance.

Elections in 1969 produced a majority for the coalition headed by the Social Democrats who governed until 1982. Brandt succeeded Kiesinger and pursued an Ostpolitik ("opening to the east"), regularizing relations with East Germany, signing a nonaggression pact with the U.S.S.R., and recognizing the border between East Germany and Poland. But domestically, West Germany suffered serious dislocations from the OPEC oil price increases of the early 1970's; inflation reached almost 8 percent. Revelations that a Brandt aide was an East German spy led to his replacement as chancellor by Helmut Schmidt in 1974.

Schmidt continued Brandt's eastern policy but also pursued improved relations with the West. Economic difficulties persisted, however, and Schmidt's government fell in 1982. The Christian Democrats returned to power under chancellor Helmut Kohl. The improvement of the world economy in the 1980's led to economic recovery, boosting Kohl's popularity. In East Germany an aging Ulbricht was replaced in May 1971 as party first secretary by Erich Honecker, who also became head of state in 1976. Honecker completed state ownership of all industry in 1972.

After Brandt's Ostpolitik, the two Germanies grew closer, at least economically. East Germany's trade with West Germany gave it access to the EC. However, East Germany resisted Mikhail Gorbachev's reform policies in the 1980's, trying to establish itself as a model of old-style communism in Eastern Europe. In the fall of 1989 tens of thousands of East Germans fled to West Germany through Hungary and Czechoslovakia, triggering a series of dramatic demonstrations and the dismantling of the Berlin Wall in October. Honecker's government collapsed as the momentum for unification became unstoppable. In March 1990 Christian Democrat Lothar de Maizière was elected prime minister on a unification platform.

In July an economic and fiscal union of the Germanies was completed, and in September the victorious wartime allies (the U.S., U.S.S.R., U.K., and France) agreed to a peace treaty that paved the way for political unification. On October 3, six regions of the former East Germany entered the Federal Republic as member states; eleven days later the Christian Democrats won elections in five of them, the Social Democrats winning one.

In December 1990, all-German elections to the Bundestag were held for the first time in 58 years. The CDU-CSU and the Free Democrats won 398 seats, the Social Democrats 239. Helmut Kohl was sworn in as chancellor Jan. 17, 1991. In June Parliament voted to move the capital back to Berlin.

In the years following unification, euphoria gave way to sober realism; economic restructuring would take many years, because the economy of East Germany proved to be in even worse shape than anyone had imagined. Related to these economic woes was the wave of violent attacks by radical nationalists and neo-Nazi gangs upon immigrants and asylum seekers (who numbered over 2 million). In 1993 the government banned several violent groups and amended Germany's liberal asylum law to prevent refugees seeking economic betterment from entering the country.

In the Bundestag elections of 1994, the Kohl coalition (CDU, CSU, and FD)maintained its majority over the opposition, led by the Social Democrats. Kohl was reelected chancellor, for a fourth time, as the economy remained strong. By 1996, however, unemployment was at an all-time postwar high and the Kohl government announced that the budget deficit required sweeping spending cuts, especially in social welfare programs. The economy worsened in 1997 and rebounded in 1998 but not enough to give Kohl another electoral victory as he lost to the Social Democrats and their leader, Gerhard Schröder.

The Bundestag approved new Chancellor Schröder's "red-green" cabinet whose personnel and program appeared further left than Schröder.

By March 1999, finance minister LaFontaine, an old-style SD, had been replaced by "moderate" Hans Eichel, financial markets responding positively. The government coalition lost control of the state government of Hesse, thereby losing its majority in the Bundesrat, the upper house whose members are elected by the states, dooming the government's plan to loosen citizenship restrictions. Schröder's attempts to introduce an austerity budget led to further electoral setbacks in state elections in 1999.

The large Christian Democratic advances in state and municipal elections were brought to a halt with the revelations, at the end of 1999, of massive illegal contributions to the CDs over the years 1982–1998, leading to heavy fines and the ruin of the reputations of numerous CD politicians, preeminently of former chancellor Helmut Kohl. In return for a fine of 300,000 marks, prosecutors dropped charges against Kohl in 2001. In November the Schröder government narrowly (336-330) survived a vote of confidence over sending 4,000 troops to Afghanistan, but Schröder won re-election in Sept. 2002 in large part because of his opposition to a U.S. strike at Iraq. In 2003, faced with an enduring recession, growing unemployment and budget deficits, Schroeder proposed a reform package to cut unemployment benefits and government pensions, ease job-protection regulations and the Social Democrats grudgingly agreed to back him. The reforms passed in 2004 despite Schröeder's falling approval ratings, but the dye was cast and in the 2005 elections he lost out to Angela Merkel whose integrity was unassailable.

▶ GHANA
Republic of Ghana

● **GEOGRAPHY** **Location:** western Africa. **Boundaries:** Burkina Faso to N, Togo to E, Gulf of Guinea to S, Ivory Coast to W. **Total area:** 92,100 sq. mi. (238,540 sq km). **Coastline:** 335 mi. (539 km). **Comparative area:** slightly smaller than Oregon. **Land use:** 16% arable land; 7% permanent crops; 77% other. **Major cities:** Accra (capital); Kumasi; Tamale; Tema; Sekondi-Takoradi.

● **PEOPLE** **Population:** 23,382,848 (July 2008 est.). **Nationality:** noun—Ghanaian(s); adjective— Ghanaian. **Ethnic groups:** 98.5% black African (major groups— Akan, Moshi-Dagomba, Ewe, Ga, Mole-Dagbon), 1.5% European and other. **Languages:** English (official), Akan, Moshi-Dagomba, Ewe, Ga. **Religions:** 68.8% Christian, 15.9% Muslim, 8.5% traditional, 6.1% none.

● **GOVERNMENT** **Type:** constitutional democracy. **Independence:** Mar. 6, 1957 (from U.K.). **Constitution:** Apr. 28, 1992. **National holiday:** Independence Day, Mar. 6. **Head of Government:** John Agyekum Kufuor (since Jan. 2001). **Structure:** executive; unicameral legislature; judiciary.

● **ECONOMY** **Monetary unit:** new cedi. **Budget:** (2007 est.) *income:* $4.347 bil.; *expend.:* $5.197 bil. **G.D.P.:** $31.23 bil., $1,400 per capita (2007 est.). **Chief crops:** cocoa, rice, coffee, timber. **Natural resources:** gold, timber, industrial diamonds, bauxite, manganese. **Major industries:** mining, lumbering, light manufacturing. **Labor force:** 11.29 million (2007); 56% agriculture and fishing, 15% industry, 29% services (2005); 11% unemployed (2000). **Exports:** $4.194 bil. (f.o.b., 2007); gold, cocoa, timber, tuna. **Imports:** $8.073 bil. (f.o.b., 2007); capital equipment, petroleum, consumer goods, food. **Major trading partners:**

(2006) *exports:* 11.3% Netherlands, 8.7% U.K., 6.7% U.S., 5.7% Spain, 5.2% Belgium, 4.4% France; *imports:* 16.7% Nigeria, 13% China, 5.7% U.K., 4.7% Belgium, 4.7% U.S., 4.1% South Africa, 4.1% France.

The connection between modern Ghana and the 10th century Ghana empire of southern Mali is obscure. In the 13th century, the Akan around the city of Kumasi were trading gold and other commodities with the Mande to the north. The number of competing states in the region grew rapidly after European contact. The Asante empire began in the early 17th century under Osei Tutu. By 1750 it controlled the northern part of Ghana, and by 1820 it had brought the coastal Fante empire under its control.

The Portuguese first explored the area, on Africa's west coast, in 1471, naming it the Gold Coast because of its gold deposits and its reserves of "black gold"—slaves. In the 16th and 17th centuries, the British, Danes, and Dutch established slave trading posts there, which is where most American slaves came from. The slave trade ended in the 1850's, and the British gained control of the Gold Coast, making it a protectorate in 1871 and a colony in 1886. Great Britain gave the colony a new constitution in 1946 under which Africans held a majority of seats in the legislature. Kwame Nkrumah became prime minister of the colony in 1952 and the first prime minister of the nation when it became independent in 1960.

At independence, Ghana boasted Africa's largest man-made deep-water port and the most productive gold mine in the world, and it was the second largest producer of industrial diamonds. Nkrumah began to court Communist bloc nations and exert absolute authority. In January 1964 all opposition parties were outlawed. A military council seized power in February 1966 and ousted Nkrumah.

Civilian governments ran the country briefly, but in 1981, Flt. Lt. Jerry Rawlings took power in a coup and ruled until 2000. Ghana suffered severe economic problems throughout the 1970's and 1980's, and many of Ghana's people left for Nigeria to find work. In 1983 Nigeria returned more than one million of these migrant workers, increasing Ghana's economic woes.

After five years of stagnation, Ghana achieved a 6 percent economic growth rate in 1989 under a World Bank restructuring program. But political unrest remained. A new constitution was approved in an April 1992 referendum, and in November Rawlings received 58 percent of the vote. His National Democratic Congress all but swept the legislative elections due to an opposition boycott. Under the constitution, Rawlings was not permitted to run for a third term and in Dec. 2000 John Kufuor of the opposition New Patriotic Party won the presidency in a run-off election. In June 2007 the government announced the discovery of major offshore oil reserves.

▶ GREAT BRITAIN (see United Kingdom)

▶ GREECE
Hellenic Republic

• **GEOGRAPHY** **Location:** southeastern Europe. **Boundaries:** Albania, Macedonia, Bulgaria to N, Turkey to NE, Aegean Sea to E, Mediterranean Sea to S, Ionian Sea to W, Albania to NW; numerous islands surround mainland. **Total area:** 50,942 sq. mi. (131,940 sq km). **Coastline:** 8,500 mi. (13,676

km). **Comparative area:** slightly smaller than Alabama. **Land use:** 22% arable land; 8% permanent crops; 70% other. **Major cities:** Athinai (Athens, capital); Thessaloniki; Piraeus; Patras; Iraklion. ●**PEOPLE** **Population:** 10,722,816 (July 2008 est.). **Nationality:** noun—Greek(s); adjective—Greek. **Ethnic groups:** 93% Greek, 7% foreign (note: percentages represent citizenship; Greek government does not collect data on ethnicity). **Languages:** Greek (official); English and French widely understood. **Religions:** 98% Greek Orthodox, 1.3% Muslim, 0.7% other.

• **GOVERNMENT** **Type:** parliamentary republic; monarchy rejected by referendum Dec. 8, 1974. **Constitution:** June 11, 1975. **National holiday:** Independence Day, Mar. 25. **Heads of Government:** Constantinos Stephanopoulos, president (since Mar. 1995); Kostas Karamanlis, prime minister (since Mar. 2004). **Structure:** executive—president elected by unicameral legislature; judiciary.

• **ECONOMY** **Monetary unit:** euro. **Budget:** (2007 est.) *income:* $111.9 bil.; *expend.:* $120.7 bil. **G.D.P.:** $326.4 bil., $30,500 per capita (2007 est.). **Chief crops:** wheat, corn, barley, sugar beets, olives; meat, dairy products. **Natural resources:** bauxite, lignite, magnesite, crude oil, marble. **Major industries:** tourism, food and tobacco processing, textiles, chemicals. **Labor force:** 4.94 mil. (2007); 68% services, 12% agriculture, 20% industry (2004); 8.4% unemployment (2007 est.). **Exports:** $25.76 bil. (f.o.b., 2007); manufactured goods, foodstuffs, fuels. **Imports:** $79.92 bil. (c.i.f., 2007); manufactured goods, foodstuffs, fuels. **Major trading partners:** (2006) *exports:* 11.5% Germany, 11.5% Italy, 6.5% Bulgaria, 6.1% U.K., 5.5% Cyprus, 5.2% Turkey, 4.5% France, 4.5% U.S., 4.1% Spain; *imports:* 12.6% Germany, 11.5% Italy, 7.1% Russia, 6% France, 5.2% Netherlands, 4.2% South Korea.

The Bronze Age and Iron Age cultures of Greece evolved to create the most glorious civilization of the ancient world. From the fifth to the third century B.C., the city-states of Greece led the world in art, philosophy, political culture, and science. Greece vied with the Persian Empire for control of Asia Minor and competed with the Phoenicians in maritime commerce in the Mediterranean. Alexander the Great, king of Macedonia, spread Greek civilization widely by conquering much of the Middle East and western Asia, but his empire did not long outlast his death in 323 B.C.

Greece was absorbed into the Roman Empire during the second and first centuries B.C. In the fourth century A.D., with the division of the Roman Empire, Greece became part of the Byzantine (Eastern Roman) Empire. Seven years after the Ottoman Turks captured Constantinople in 1453, they overran Greece and ruled it as part of the Ottoman Empire for 350 years.

Under Ottoman rule, much of the administration of Greece was left in local hands, keeping alive a sense of Greek nationhood and a tradition of Greek leadership, particularly through the clergy of the Greek Orthodox church. Inspired by the French Revolution, a romanticized ideal of the classical past, and the tradition of Greek orthodoxy, in 1821 Greece rebelled against Turkish rule. With the support of England, France, and Russia, Greek independence was won in 1827, although the country included only about half of its present territory.

The Western powers sponsored a monarchical government in Greece, ruled by a German prince. Deposed in a revolt, he was succeeded by King George I, a Danish prince who ruled from 1863 until his assassination in 1913. In the three Balkan Wars of 1912, 1913, and 1914, Greece expanded its borders to reach approximately its present size.

In 1923 a Greek Republic was established, but in 1935 King George II returned, placing government control in the hands of the authoritarian Gen. Ioannis Metaxas. In 1940 Metaxas resisted Italy's attempt to conquer Greece, defeating Mussolini's armies so badly that Hitler sent crack troops to his ally's assistance. The German occupation of Greece was complete by June 1941. The Germans pillaged the country and massacred Jews; their Bulgarian allies colonized Macedonia.

During World War II, resistance grew among both Communist and anti-Communist groups. With the German withdrawal in October 1944, resistance groups battled each other; this led to full-scale civil war by 1946. British, and then American assistance (under the Truman Doctrine), enabled the Greek government to defeat the Communist forces when Stalin refused to intervene. King George II died in 1947, succeeded by his brother, King Paul I. Political instability—16 governments during 1946-52—prevailed until, under American pressure, the Greeks adopted a new constitution.

Until the postwar period, Greece's economy had been dominated by agriculture and livestock raising. Industry was limited largely to textiles and food processing; shipping was the major service industry. Under policies instituted in 1952 by the government of Marshall Alexandros Papagos, the industrial sector led a period of vigorous economic growth lasting into the 1960's. A market-oriented economy, tariff protection for Greek industry, tight internal security, and close ties with the West formed the mainstays of Greek policy.

Greece joined NATO in 1951, as did Turkey. Conflict over Cyprus divided the two nominal allies, however. The failure of the government of Constantine Karamanlis to resolve the Cyprus situation eroded his popularity, and he was replaced in 1964 by George Papandreou, who governed at the head of a left-center coalition. King Constantine, who succeeded his father in 1963, forced Papandreou to resign in 1964, after he and members of his government were accused of various improprieties. A military coup, led by Col. George Papadopoulos, toppled the government in 1967. A countercoup by King Constantine failed, and the king fled the country.

A military dictatorship ruled from 1967 to 1974. Its failed attempt to intervene in Cyprus in 1974 provoked a Turkish invasion of the island and led to the military regime's collapse. Karamanlis headed the government once again and a republic was established with the promulgation of a new constitution in 1975. Karamanlis's New Democracy party again won a majority in 1977 elections.

Greece, an associate member of the EC since 1961, became a full member in 1981. Full military membership in NATO was restored in 1980. In 1981 the Panhellenic Socialist Movement under Andreas Papandreou won a parliamentary majority, renewed in 1984. The left-wing Papandreou government was outspokenly anti-NATO, anti-EC, and anti-American, but its policy was more moderate than its rhetoric, extending even to modest cooperation with Turkey in the Aegean. The Papandreou government was shaken by several pro-Palestinian terrorist incidents in Greece, and by a scandal involving the married Papandreou's relationship with a younger woman.

During 1989-90 Greece struggled through three parliamentary elections in less than a year. In the first two, no major party won a clear victory, leading to weak, short-lived coalition governments. The third, in the spring of 1990, resulted in a slim majority for the New Democracy party (headed by Prime Minister Constantine Mitsotakis) and the apparent decline of Papandreou's stature.

But Papandreou strengthened his grip on power in October 1993, leading his PASOK party to a landslide victory over the New Democrats, as voters expressed their displeasure with Mitsotakis's deficit-cutting "austerity" policies. Papandreou returned to office promising salary and pension increases and a halt to privatization. But serious illness forced him to resign in January 1996. His successor, Costas Simitis, promised to speed up the stalled privatization program, and his new cabinet removed most Papandreou loyalists.

Greece's economy failed to meet the E.U.'s criteria for participating in the European Monetary Union in 1998. New tensions with Turkey over Cyprus, however, threatened to erupt into serious conflict during mid-year. Domestic discontent at what appeared to be Greek assistance in the Turks's capture of Kurdish rebel leader Ocalan in Nairobi led to a shakeup in the Simitis cabinet in Feb. 1999 but in March, government investigators were recommending trials for 18 Greek officials accused of assisting Ocalan's flight from the Turks.

In 1999 and 2000 a series of improvements occurred in Greek-Turkish relations: reciprocal earthquake assistance, agreements on sales of electricity (to Turkey) and water (to Cyprus, both Greek and Turkish, from Turkey) and foreign ministers' accords on crime, immigration, commerce, tourism and the Aegean environment. Greece even agreed to support Turkey's admission to the E.U. In April 2000, in Greece's closest parliamentary elections, PASOK became the first Greek party to win three consecutive elections.

The success of the government's austerity program led the E.U. to approve Greece's joining the E.M.U. in early 2001. This led to a $2 bil. aid package but did not prevent the government from losing power in 2004 to the New Democratic party led by Kostas Karamanlis. He was reelected in 2007 and soon engaged in serious talks with Turkey to end the Cyprus dispute.

▶ GRENADA

● **GEOGRAPHY   Location:** southeastern Caribbean Sea, about 100 mi. (160 km) N of Trinidad. St. George's 12°03'N, 61°45'W. **Boundaries:** Atlantic Ocean to NE, E, and SE.; Caribbean Sea to SW, W, and NW. **Total area:** 131 sq. mi. (340 sq km). **Coastline:** 75 mi. (121 km). **Comparative area:** twice size of Washington, D.C. **Land use:** 6% arable land; 26% permanent crops; 68% other. **Major cities:** St. George's (capital).

● **PEOPLE   Population:** 90,343 (July 2008 est.). **Nationality:** noun—Grenadian(s); adjective—Grenadian. **Ethnic groups:** 83% black, 13% mixed, 5% European and East Indian. **Languages:** English (official), some French patois. **Religions:** 53% Roman Catholic, 13.8% Anglican, 33.2% other Protestant sects.

● **GOVERNMENT   Type:** constitutional monarchy with Westminster-style parliament. **Independence:** Feb. 7, 1974 (from U.K.). **Constitution:** Dec. 19, 1973. **National holiday:** Independence Day, Feb. 7. **Heads of Government:** Sir Daniel C.

Williams, governor-general (since Aug. 1996); Tillman Thomas, prime minister (since July 2008). **Structure:** executive (cabinet led by prime minister); bicameral legislature; judiciary (West Indies Associate States Supreme Court).
● **ECONOMY   Monetary unit:** East Caribbean (EC) dollar. **Budget:** (1997 est.) *income:* $85.8 mil.; *expend.:* $102.1 mil. **G.D.P.:** $982 mil.(2006 est.), $3,900 per capita (2005 est.). **Chief crops:** bananas, cocoa, nutmeg, mace. **Natural resources:** timber, tropical fruit, deep-water harbors. **Major industries:** food and beverages, textiles, light assembly operations. **Labor force:** 42,300 (1996); 62% services, 24% agriculture, 14% industry, 12.5% unemployment. **Exports:** $38 mil. (2006 est.); bananas, cocoa beans, nutmeg. **Imports:** $343 mil. (2006 est.); food, manufactured goods, machinery, chemicals, fuel (1989). **Major trading partners:** (2006) *exports:* 18.8% Santa Lucia, 12.8% Antigua & Barbuda, 11.5% St. Kitts & Nevis, 11.4% Dominica, 11.4% U.S.; *imports:* 33.7% Trinidad & Tobago, 24.2% U.S., 4.3% U.K.

Dominated in the early 1600's by the warlike Carib Indians, Grenada alternated between French and British possession between 1650 and 1783, when British rule was established.

Independence came in 1974. The leftist New Jewel Movement seized power in a 1979 coup, but its leader, Maurice Bishop, was assassinated during a military coup in 1983. Shortly thereafter, the United States invaded and returned power to the governor-general until 1984. Prime Minister Nicholas Braithwaite of the National Democratic Congress party presided over a coalition government from 1990-95, when he was succeeded by George Brizan. In June 1995 the opposition New National party gained an absolute majority in Parliament and designated its leader, Keith Mitchell, as Prime Minister. It won all 18 seats in 1999 and narrowly won again in 2003, but lost in 2008.

▶ GUATEMALA
Republic of Guatemala
● **GEOGRAPHY   Location:** northern part of Central American isthmus. **Boundaries:** Mexico to N and W, Honduras and Belize to E, El Salvador to S. **Total area:** 42,042 sq. mi. (108,890 sq km). **Coastline:** 248 mi. (400 km). **Comparative area:** slightly smaller than Tennessee. **Land use:** 13% arable land; 5% permanent crops; 82% other. **Major cities:** Guatemala City (capital); Quezaltenango; Escuintla; Mazatenango; Puerto Barrios.
● **PEOPLE   Population:** 13,002,206 (July 2008 est.) **Nationality:** noun—Guatemalan(s); adjective—Guatemalan. **Ethnic groups:** 59.4% Ladino (mixed Spanish and Amerindian), 9.1% K'iche, 8.4% Kaqchikel, 7.9% Mam, 6.3% Q'eqhi, 8.6% other Mayan. **Languages:** 60% Spanish, 40% Amerindian languages (23 Amerindian dialects, including Quiche, Cakchiquel, Kekchi). **Religions:** predominantly Roman Catholic, some Protestant and traditional Mayan.
● **GOVERNMENT   Type:** constitutional democratic republic. **Independence:** Sept. 15, 1821 (from Spain). **Constitution:** May 31, 1985, effective Jan. 1986. **National holiday:** Independence Day, Sept. 15. **Head of Government:** Alvaro Colom Caballeros, president (since Jan. 2008). **Structure:** executive; unicameral legislature (113 seats, elected by popular vote to four-year terms); judiciary.
● **ECONOMY   Monetary unit:** quetzal. **Budget:** (2007 est.) *income:* $4.301 bil.; *expend.:* $5.219 bil.

G.D.P.: $67.45 bil., $5,400 per capita (2007 est.). **Chief crops:** sugarcane, corn, bananas; cattle, sheep, pigs. **Natural resources:** crude oil, nickel, rare woods, fish, chicle. **Major industries:** sugar, textiles and clothing, furniture. **Labor force:** 3.958 mil. (2007 est.); 50% agriculture, 15% industry, 35% services; 7.5% unemployment (1999 est.). **Exports:** $7.468 bil. (f.o.b., 2007); coffee, sugar, bananas. **Imports:** $12.67 bil. (f.o.b., 2007); fuel and petroleum products, machinery, grain, fertilizers, motor vehicles. **Major trading partners:** (2006) *exports:* 44.6% U.S., 11.9% El Salvador, 7.2% Honduras, 5.2% Mexico; *imports:* 33.2% U.S., 8.8% Mexico, 6.5% China, 5.3% El Salvador, 4.9% South Korea.

Modern Guatemala was the heart of the Maya civilization that began early in the Christian era and flourished from the fourth to the 10th centuries. From the 11th century on there were two major powers, the Cakchiquel and the Quiché. They were overthrown by the Spanish who invaded from the north in 1524.

The captaincy general of Guatemala was the seat of Spanish military authority in Central America until the 19th century. After an earthquake destroyed Antiqua in 1773, the capital was moved to Guatemala City. Guatemala was the center of the United Provinces of Central America after independence was gained from Spain (1821) and Mexico (1823). The United Provinces collapsed after an uprising by Rafael Carrera, and Guatemala became a separate country in 1838. The Liberal party held power from 1851 to 1944. There was considerable economic development under the repressive regimes of Manuel Estrada Cabrera (1898-1920) and Jorge Ubico (1931-44). Juan José Arévalo was elected president in 1945. He was succeeded, with strong Communist support, by Jacobo Arbenz, who was deposed in 1954 by a U.S.-backed coup led by Col. Carlos Castillo Armas. The military has ruled either directly or indirectly since then, although democratic rule resumed officially in 1986.

A civil war involving the army, right-wing death squads, and the antigovernment guerrilla group, the Guatemalan National Revolutionary Union (URNG) began in 1960 and intensified through the 1980s, resulting in the deaths of 100,000 civilians.

In May 1993, Pres. Jorge Serrano Elias, backed by the military, suspended the constitution in an effort to crack down on labor and student strikes. Eight days later, in the face of overwhelming popular discontent and international protest, the military replaced Serrano with Atty. Gen. for Human Rights Ramiro de Leon Carpio. In March 1994, the URNG and the government reached an agreement to end the 30-year-old civil war, but talks stalled for a year until the two sides could agree on a pact amending the constitution to defend Indian rights. The United States cut off military aid to Guatemala for its failure to prosecute security officers for crimes committed during the civil war.

In January 1996, URNG called a cease-fire during elections, in which Álvaro Arzú Irigoyen won over a candidate backed by the military, The new government purged the military of its corrupt members, and made plans to privatize the economy. The 36-year civil war seemed to end when the last 200 rebels turned in their arms in May 1997.

The April 1998 slaying of a Catholic bishop, a human rights advocate who had authored a report blaming 80 percent of the killings and kidnappings upon the military and right-wing paramilitary forces, remained unsolved a year later, as the lead prosecutor and two successive judges resigned in an atmosphere of threats. In Feb. 1999, an independent report accused the army and paramilitaries of over 90 percent of the civil war abuses.

In May 1999, as the first prosecutions of military and security forces were beginning, Guatemalan voters rejected all the constitutional changes proposed in the 1996 peace. In 1999 elections they gave a majority to the Guatemalan Republican front and overwhelmingly elected its candidate as president. In 2003, however, the more conservative Great National Alliance won both the presidency and a parliamentary majority. A rapid rise in violent crime, much of it caused by the rampant drug trade and police corruption preceded the elections of late 2007, won by businessman Alvaro Colom and his National Unity and Hope Party.

▶ GUINEA
Republic of Guinea
● **GEOGRAPHY Location:** western Africa. **Boundaries**: Guinea-Bissau to NW, Senegal to N, Mali to NE, Ivory Coast to SE, Liberia, Sierra Leone to S, Atlantic Ocean to W. **Total area**: 94,927 sq. mi. (245,860 sq km). **Coastline:** 199 mi. (320 km). **Comparative area:** slightly smaller than Oregon. **Land use:** 4% arable land; 2% permanent crops; 94% other. **Major cities:** Conakry (capital).
● **PEOPLE Population:** 10,211,437 (July 2008 est.). **Nationality:** noun—Guinean(s); adjective—Guinean. **Ethnic groups:** 40% Peuhl, 30% Malinke, 20% Soussou, 10% smaller tribes. **Languages:** French (official), tribal languages. **Religions:** 85% Muslim, 8% Christian, 7% indigenous beliefs.
● **GOVERNMENT Type:** republic. **Independence:** Oct. 2, 1958 (from France). **Constitution:** Dec. 23, 1990. **National holiday:** Independence Day, Oct. 2. **Head of Government:** Lansana Conte, president (since Dec. 1993); Ahmed T. Souraré, prime minister (since May 2008). **Structure:** executive; unicameral legislature; judiciary.
● **ECONOMY Monetary unit:** Guinean franc. **Budget:** (2007 est.) *income:* $382 mil.; *expend.:* $817.4 mil. **G.D.P.:** $9.741 bil., $1,000 per capita (2007 est.). **Chief crops:** rice, coffee, pineapples; cattle, sheep, goats; timber. **Natural resources:** bauxite, iron ore, diamonds, gold, uranium. **Major industries:** bauxite mining, alumina, diamond mining. **Labor force:** 3.7 mil. (2006); 76% agriculture, 24% industry and services. **Exports:** $998 mil. (f.o.b., 2007 est.); bauxite (the world's second largest producer), alumina, diamonds, coffee, fish. **Imports:** $838 mil. (f.o.b., 2007 est.); petroleum products, metals, machinery and transport equipment, foodstuffs, textiles. **Major trading partners:** (2006) *exports:* 11.6% Russia, 9.6% Ukraine, 9% Spain, 8.8% South Korea, 7.7% France, 7.7% U.S., 5.4% Germany, 5.1% Ireland; *imports:* 8.6% China, 8% France, 4.8% Netherlands, 4.4% Belgium.

Guinea was formed out of the remains of a series of empires that flourished in West Africa between the 10th and 15th centuries. Situated to the southwest of the Sahara desert on the west coast of Africa, Guinea was a crossroads of West African trade long before Europeans arrived.

French merchants began trading in what is now Guinea in the early 17th century. France began acquiring land in the area in the mid19th century, and in 1845 the territories were organized as a separate colony. The colony received the name French Guinea in 1893.

Most high political posts were held by Europeans until after World War II. In 1946 French Guinea became a territory in the federation of French West Africa. In September 1958 Guinea became the only French colony to reject membership in the Fifth French Republic, resulting in the severance of political ties with France. The territorial assembly proclaimed Guinean independence on Oct. 2, 1958, and a new government headed by Sékou Touré was formed on the same day.

Touré was adamant in his rejection of French colonialism, severing ties with France (1960-63) and soliciting economic and other assistance from the U.S.S.R., China, and the United States. Touré remained in power until his death in April 1984. Within a week, a military government headed by Gen. Lansana Conte took power and by 1987 had improved relations with France while introducing market mechanisms into the command economy. Conte was elected president in 1993 and in June 1995, in Guinea's first-ever multiparty election, his Unity Progress party took 71 of the 114 legislative seats. He was reelected in 2003, but in 2006 the violent disturbances over corruption and declining economic conditions forced him to make concessions and appoint a prime minister. He has been ailing for years and no clear successor is present so some observers worry about the future.

▶ GUINEA-BISSAU
Republic of Guinea-Bissau
● **GEOGRAPHY Location:** northwestern coast of Africa. **Boundaries**: Senegal to N, Guinea to E and S, Atlantic Ocean to W. **Total area:** 13,946 sq. mi. (36,120 sq km). **Coastline:** 217 mi. (350 km). **Comparative area:** slightly less than three times the size of Connecticut. **Land use:** 11% arable land; 2% permanent crops; 87%% other. **Major cities:** Bissau (capital); Bafatá; Gabú; Mansoa; Catió.
● **PEOPLE Population:** 1,503,182 (July 2008 est.) **Nationality:** noun—Guinean(s); adjective—Guinean. **Ethnic groups:** about 99% African (30% Balanta, 20% Fula, 14% Manjaca, 13% Mandinga, 7% Papel); less than 1% European and mulatto. **Languages:** Portuguese (official), Crioulo, numerous African languages. **Religions:** 50% indigenous beliefs, 45% Muslim, 5% Christian.
● **GOVERNMENT Type:** republic; multi-party since mid-1991. **Independence:** Sept. 24, 1973 (unilaterally declared by Guinea-Bissau); Sept. 10, 1974 (recognized by Portugal). **Constitution:** May 16, 1984, amended May 4, 1991, Dec. 4, 1991, Feb. 26, 1993, June 9, 1993, and 1996. **National holiday:** Independence Day, Sept. 24. **Heads of Government:** João Bernardo Vieira, president (since May 2005); Martinho N'Dafa Cabi, prime minister (since Apr. 2007). **Structure:** executive; unicameral legislature; no judiciary (Ministry of Justice).
● **ECONOMY Monetary unit:** Communauté Financière Africaine (CFA) franc. **Budget:** N.A. **G.D.P.:** $901.2 mil., $600 per capita (2007 est.). **Chief crops:** rice, corn, beans; fishing, forestry. **Natural resources:** fish, timber, phosphates, bauxite, unexploited deposits of petroleum. **Major industries:** agricultural processing, beer, soft drinks. **Labor force:** 480,000; 82% agriculture, 18% industry and services (2000 est.). **Exports:** $133 mil. (f.o.b., 2006 est.); 70% cashews, fish, peanuts. **Imports:** $200 mil. (f.o.b., 2006 est.); foodstuffs, transport equipment, petroleum products. **Major trading partners:** (2006) *exports:* 76.1% India, 18.1% Nigeria,

1.4% Italy; *imports:* 18.7% Portugal, 16.3% Senegal, 13% Italy, 4.5% Pakistan.

The Portuguese began exploring and trading in what is now Guinea-Bissau in the 15th century and in 1630 began to exert administrative control over the territory. The area became the center of the Portuguese slave trade. When the slave trade declined in the 19th century, the coastal port of Bissau became a major commercial center. Later in the 19th century, the Portuguese began to conquer the interior of the territory and in 1879 consolidated the region into a territory called Portuguese Guinea, which in 1952 became an overseas province of Portugal.

A nationalist movement began in 1956 under the leadership of Amilcar Cabral and the African Party for the Independence of Guinea and Cape Verde (PAIGC). Armed insurrection broke out in 1961. By 1972 the PAIGC exerted influence over much of the country. Civilian rule was established in the territory that it controlled, and elections were held for a national assembly. Cabral was assassinated in 1973, but soon after the PAIGC National Assembly declared the independence of Guinea-Bissau from Portugal. Portugal acknowledged the country's new status on Sept. 24, 1973.

The civilian government was overthrown by a military coup in 1980, and the country was run by a Revolutionary Council headed by Brig. Gen. João Bernardo Vieira until a new constitution was adopted in May 1984. Under the new constitution, a new national assembly was selected, and Vieira was elected president in 1984 and 1989. In 1991 the government legalized opposition parties, but presidential elections were postponed.

In June 1998 a former army chief of staff, Ansumane Mane, launched a coup attempt against Vieira who was supported by loyalist troops and the Senegalese army. Hundreds of thousands fled the capital and the surrounding areas as the Senegalese shelled the city. By May 1999, General Mane had driven Vieira to seek asylum with the Portuguese and had installed the leader of the National Popular Assembly, Malan Sanha, as interim president until he was defeated in Jan. 2000 by Kumba Yala (who was overthrown by the army in Sept. 2003). In March 2004 PAIGC won a plurality of seats in the new legislature but failed to capture a majority. In 2005, Vieira was elected president and has brought a modicum of stability.

▶ **GUYANA**
Co-operative Republic of Guyana
● **GEOGRAPHY** **Location:** northeastern South America. **Boundaries:** North Atlantic Ocean to N, Suriname to E, Brazil to S, Venezuela to W. **Total area:** 83,000 sq. mi. (214,970 sq km). **Coastline:** 285 mi. (459 km). **Comparative area:** slightly smaller than Idaho. **Land use:** 2% arable land; negl.% permanent crops; 97% other. **Major cities:** Georgetown (capital).
● **PEOPLE** **Population:** 770,794 (July 2008 est.). **Nationality:** noun—Guyanese (sing., pl.); adjective—Guyanese. **Ethnic groups:** 50% East Indian, 36% black, 7% Amerindian, 7% white, Chinese and mixed. **Languages:** English, Amerindian dialects. **Religions:** 50% Christian, 35% Hindu, 10% Muslim, 5% other.
● **GOVERNMENT** **Type:** republic within Commonwealth. **Independence:** May 26, 1966 (from U.K.). **Constitution:** Oct. 6. 1980. **National holiday:** Republic Day, Feb. 23. **Heads of Government:** Bharrat Jagdeo, executive president (since Aug. 2000);

Samuel Hinds, prime minister (since Feb. 1998). **Structure:** executive—president (appoints and heads cabinet); unicameral legislature; judiciary.
● **ECONOMY** **Monetary unit:** Guyanese dollar. **Budget:** (2007 est.) *income:* $419.4 mil.; *expend.:* $527.4 mil. **G.D.P.:** $4.057 bil., $5,300 per capita (2007 est.). **Chief crops:** sugarcane, rice, wheat; beef, pork, poultry. **Natural resources:** bauxite, gold, diamonds, hardwood timber, shrimp, fish. **Major industries:** bauxite mining, sugar, rice milling. **Labor force:** 418,000 (2001). **Exports:** $499.4 mil. (f.o.b., 2007); sugar, gold, bauxite/alumina, rice, shrimp, molasses. **Imports:** $835.8 mil. (f.o.b., 2007); manufactures, machinery, food, petroleum. **Major trading partners:** (2006) *exports:* 18.8% U.S., 18.4% Canada, 8.7% U.K., 6.5% Portugal, 4.9% Trinidad & Tobago, 4.3% Netherlands, 4.3% Belgium, 4.1% Japan; *imports:* 23% Trinidad & Tobago, 21.3% U.S., 9.7% China, 6.3% Cuba, 4.5% U.K.

Although the region was visited by Europeans in the 15th century, Guyana was only colonized in the early 1600's by the Dutch. Rule in the area was contested by the French and the British, and it became the colony of British Guiana in 1831. After slavery was abolished, indentured servants from the East Indies were brought to work the land, and their descendants are in the majority today.

The People's National Congress was in power from 1964 to 1992, and socialist policies dominated the political landscape. Most of the country's large companies were nationalized, so despite its having the purest bauxite in the world, some gold, and conditions favorable to agriculture, it remains poor, dependent on foreign aid for much of its revenue.

In 1992 Cheddi Jagan of the People's Progressive party won the presidency, but his attempts to privatize the sugar and bauxite industries have failed. In March 1997 Jagan died and Samuel Hinds, the prime minister became president while Jagan's widow took over as prime minister. In the presidential elections in Dec. 1997, Mrs. Jagan won election in her own right, with 56 percent of the vote, but her appointment of Hinds to be Prime Minister did nothing to stop the rioting and demonstrations by followers of the opposition People's National Congress. The PNC represents, principally, black, while the PPP does the same for East Indians. In Aug. 1999, Jagan resigned for health reasons and was succeeded by Bharrat Jagdeo, a 35-year-old Moscow-educated economist who has been elected twice, in 2001 and 2005.

▶ **HAITI**
Republic of Haiti
● **GEOGRAPHY** **Location:** western part of Hispaniola in northern Caribbean Sea. Port-au-Prince 18°33′N, 72°20′W. **Boundaries:** North Atlantic Ocean to N, Dominican Republic to E, Caribbean Sea to S, Windward Passage to W. **Total area:** 10,714 sq. mi. (27,750 sq km). **Coastline:** 1,100 mi. (1,771 km). **Comparative area:** slightly smaller than Maryland. **Land use:** 20% arable land; 13% permanent crops; 67% other. **Major cities:** Port-au-Prince (capital).
● **PEOPLE** **Population:** 8,924,553 (July 2008 est.) **Nationality:** noun—Haitian(s); adjective—Haitian. **Ethnic groups:** 95% black, 5% mulatto and European. **Languages:** French (official, but spoken by only 20% of population); all speak Creole. **Religions:** 80% Roman Catholic, 16% Protestant,

1% none, 3% other; note - roughly half of the population practices voodoo (called vodun).

• **GOVERNMENT Type:** republic. **Independence:** Jan. 1, 1804 (from France). **Constitution:** Mar. 1987, suspended June 1988; return to constitutional rule Oct. 1994. **National Holiday:** Independence Day, Jan. 1. **Heads of Government:** Michéle Pierre-Louis, prime minister (since Sept. 2008). **Structure:** executive; bicameral legislature; judiciary.

• **ECONOMY Monetary unit:** gourde. **Budget:** (2007) *income:* $918.6 mil.; *expend.:* $1.036 bil. **G.D.P.:** $15.82 bil., $1,900 per capita (2007 est.). **Chief crops:** coffee, mangoes, sugarcane, rice, corn, sorghum. **Natural resources:** bauxite, copper, calcium carbonate, gold, marble, hydropower. **Major industries:** sugar refining, textiles, flour milling. **Labor force:** 3.6 mil. (1995); 66% agriculture, 25% services, 9% industry; shortage of skilled labor, unskilled labor abundant; widespread unemployment and underemployment. **Exports:** $554.8 mil. (f.o.b., 2007); light manufactures, coffee, other agriculture. **Imports:** $1.844 bil. (f.o.b., 2007); machines and manufactures, food and beverages, petroleum products. **Major trading partners:** (2006) *exports:* 79.8% U.S., 7.6% Dominican Republic, 3% Canada; *imports:* 46.5% U.S., 11.9% Netherlands, 3.8% Brazil.

The Arawak island of Haiti was discovered by Christopher Columbus, who renamed it Hispaniola, in 1492. In the next century many Arawaks were worked to death or killed by disease. The western third of the island was harassed by French pirates and was ceded to France in 1697. A slave revolt in 1791 led to abolition in 1794, and the island came under French rule the same year. Toussaint Louverture, an ex-slave, became governor-general in 1801, but he was deposed by the French. In 1803 a black army under Jean-Jacques Dessalines (Emperor Jacques I, 1804-6) and Henry Christophe (Henry I, 1806-20) defeated the French in 1803. Independence was declared in 1804. Under Jean-Pierre Boyer (1820-43), Haiti occupied Santo Domingo (which had been restored to Spain in 1808) from 1822 to 1844.

The next century was marked by political instability and an increased U.S. business and military presence in Haitian affairs. From 1905 to 1947, the United States had direct or indirect control of Haitian finances, and from 1915 to 1934 the country was under U.S. military occupation.

François "Papa Doc" Duvalier took power in 1957 and ruled Haiti with a stern hand. In 1971, he transferred power to his son, Jean-Claude (aka "Baby Doc"), whose regime was just as authoritarian. Most of Haiti's wealthy and educated population fled the country, leaving it the poorest and most illiterate nation in the Western Hemisphere.

In 1986, the military ousted Baby Doc, and imposed a succession of short-lived but brutal and incompetent governments. In 1989, Supreme Court Justice Ertha-Pascal Troillot was named interim president, and in 1990, Haiti held its first democratic national elections ever. The winner of those elections was the Rev. Jean-Bertrand Aristide, a 37-year-old Roman Catholic priest. But seven months into his five-year term, Aristide was overthrown in yet another military coup. Aristide fled to the U.S., which refused to recognize the junta and suspended aid to Haiti. But succesive trade embargos by the U.S., Canada, and Western Europe only served to increase hardship. The junta leaders, propped up by Haiti's wealthy elite and by money from drug trafficking, began a campaign of violence against Aristide supporters, killing more than 3,000 of them.

After months of threats, the U.S. invaded on Oct. 15, 1994, forcing the junta's resignation and reinstating Aristide as president. Aristide disbanded the army, replacing it with a civilian police force. In mid-1995, Aristide's three-party coalition, Lavalas Political Organization, won overwhelming victories; in December, the Lavalas candidate, René Préval, took 88 percent in Haiti's first peaceful presidential election since independence.

By 1997 Lavalas and Pres. Préval had split. From June of that year, Haiti was without a government until Jan. 1999 when Préval announced he would rule by decree, and appointed his own prime minister. The U.S. and the U.N. ended their military mission in early 2000. Senate elections were held in May, giving 16 of 17 contested seats to Lavalas candidates. But in run-off elections held in July, opposition candidates and international observers refused to participate because of irregularities in the earlier election. In November, with the opposition and international monitors boycotting, the presidential election returned Aristide with 92 percent, while in remaining run-offs, Lavalas won all 9 Senate races and took 80 percent of the Assembly votes. When in March 2001 Jean-Marie Cherestal was sworn in as prime minister, his cabinet included some opposition members, though the opposition Democratic Convergence coalition had named its own "parallel" president a month earlier. After an attack on the presidential palace by 33 gunmen was thwarted in Dec. 2001, Aristide loyalists meted out savage reprisals to opposition groups. In Feb. 2004 armed groups opposed to Aristide took control of four cities and threatened to kill Aristide (who was taken to Africa by the U.S.). Troops from four nations entered Haiti, the rebels disarmed, and a new government formed under Gerard Latortue. Elections scheduled for Oct. 2005 were cancelled by an upsurge in gang violence. In May of 2006 Rene Preval was elected president in a peaceful election overseen by U.N. troops whose presence has helped end the worst of the violence.

▶ **HOLY SEE**
The Holy See (State of the Vatican City)

• **GEOGRAPHY Location:** entirely within city of Rome, Italy; outside Vatican City, 13 buildings in Rome and Castel Gandolfo (the pope's summer residence) enjoy extraterritorial rights. **Boundaries:** surrounded by Italian territory. **Total area:** 0.17 sq. mi. (0.44 sq km). **Coastline:** none. **Comparative area:** about seven-tenths size of the Mall in Washington, D.C. **Land use:** 0% arable land; 0% permanent crops; 100% other. **Major cities:** Vatican City (capital).

• **PEOPLE Population:** 824 (July 2008 est.). **Nationality:** N.A. **Ethnic groups:** Italians, Swiss, other. **Languages:** Italian, Latin, various other languages. **Religion:** Roman Catholic.

• **GOVERNMENT Type:** monarchical-sacerdotal state. **Independence:** Feb. 11, 1929 (from Italy). **Constitution:** Apostolic Constitution of 1967 (effective Mar. 1, 1968). **Heads of Government:** Pope Benedict XVI, chief of state (since April 2005); Cardinal Tarcisio Bertone, secretary of state (since Sept. 2006). **Structure:** pope possesses full executive, legislative, and judicial powers; he delegates these powers to president of Pontifical Commission, who is subject to pontifical appointment and recall; Secretariat of State and Council of Public Affairs (which handles Vatican diplomacy) and Prefecture of Economic Affairs; College of Cardinals acts as chief papal adviser.

• **ECONOMY Monetary unit:** euro. **Budget:** (2006 est.) *income:* $310 mil.; *expend.:* $307 mil., supported financially by contributions (known as Peter's Pence) from Roman Catholics throughout world; some income derived from sale of Vatican postage stamps and tourist mementos, fees for admission to museums, and sale of publications. **G.D.P.:** N.A. **Chief crops:** N.A. **Natural resources:** N.A. **Major industries:** consists of printing and production of small amount of mosaics and staff uniforms; worldwide banking and financial activities. **Labor force:** N.A.; dignitaries, priests, nuns, guards, and 3,000 lay workers who live outside the Vatican; Vatican City employees are divided into three categories—executives, office workers, and salaried employees. **Exports:** N.A. **Imports:** N.A. **Major trading partners:** N.A.

The Holy See is the smallest sovereign state in the world both in size and in population. It is a remnant of the "Patrimony of St. Peter," the secular state donated to the popes in the eighth century by Pepin the Short, father of Charlemagne. One of the major political powers on the Italian peninsula throughout the Middle Ages and into modern times, the States of the Church were conquered in 1870 by the new kingdom of Italy, which made Rome its capital.

In 1929 Mussolini's government made peace with the papacy in the Lateran Treaty, which recognized the Holy See as an independent state. The treaty was incorporated into the Italian Constitution of 1947. Under the terms of the treaty, the pope is pledged to perpetual neutrality and may intervene in international affairs as a mediator only upon request.

The pope is the sovereign of the Holy See in his capacity as bishop of Rome, and in that capacity, he accepts the credentials of foreign ambassadors assigned to the Holy See. The United States opened diplomatic relations with the Holy See in 1984, following the repeal of an 1867 law forbidding such relations. Pope John Paul II, a native of Poland, has been a source of spiritual leadership especially for Catholics in Eastern Europe. Since the collapse of communism in Eastern Europe, many countries there have renewed diplomatic relations with the Holy See. In a historic breakthrough the Holy See established diplomatic relations with Israel on Dec. 30, 1993.

As sovereign of the Holy See, the pope is an elected absolute monarch who appoints a Pontifical Council to govern the city on his behalf. The council meets only a few times each year. The economy is based on service industries, including printing; its revenues come from museum fees, philatelic sales, and sales of publications.

▶ **HONDURAS**
Republic of Honduras

• **GEOGRAPHY Location:** Central America. **Boundaries:** Caribbean Sea to N, Nicaragua to E, El Salvador, Nicaragua to S, Guatemala, El Salvador to W. **Total area:** 43,278 sq. mi. (112,090 sq km). **Coastline:** 509 mi. (820 km). **Comparative area:** slightly larger than Tennessee. **Land use:** 15% arable land; 3% permanent crops; 82% other. **Major cities:** Tegucigalpa (capital); San Pedro Sula; El Progreso; Danli; Choluteca.

• **PEOPLE Population:** 7,639,327 (July 2008 est.). **Nationality:** noun—Honduran(s); adjective—

Honduran. **Ethnic groups:** 90% mestizo, 7% Amerindian, 2% black, 1% white. **Languages:** Spanish, Amerindian dialects. **Religions:** 97% Roman Catholic, small Protestant minority.

• **GOVERNMENT Type:** democratic constitutional republic. **Independence:** Sept. 15, 1821 (from Spain). **Constitution:** Jan. 11, 1982 (effective Jan. 20, 1982). **National holiday:** Independence Day, Sept. 15. **Head of Government:** José Zelaya Rosales, president (since Jan. 2006). **Structure:** executive—elected president; unicameral legislature (128-seat National Congress); elected judicial branch.

• **ECONOMY Monetary unit:** lempira. **Budget:** (2007 est.) *income:* $2.089 bil.; *expend.:* $2.357 bil. **G.D.P.:** $24.69 bil., $3,300 per capita (2007 est.). **Chief crops:** bananas, coffee, citrus; beef; timber; shrimp. **Natural resources:** timber, gold, silver, copper, lead. **Major industries:** agricultural processing (sugar and coffee), textiles, clothing. **Labor force:** 2.8 mil. (2007); 34% agriculture, 45% services, 21% industry; 27.8% unemployment (2007). **Exports:** $3.924 bil. (f.o.b., 2007 est.); bananas, coffee, shrimp, lobster. **Imports:** $6.798 bil. (f.o.b., 2007 est.); machinery and transport equipment, chemicals, basic manufactures. **Major trading partners:** (2006) *exports:* 70.6% U.S., 3.5% Guatemala, 3.4% El Salvador; *imports:* 53% U.S., 7% Guatemala, 4.5% El Salvador, 4.1% Costa Rica, 4.1% Mexico.

Early in the Christian era, the Mayan civilization extended south to the pre-Columbian city of Copán in what is now northwestern Honduras. The territory was also home to the Lenca Indians and the indigenous people of the Moskitia area.

A silver strike in the 1570's prompted the first major influx of Spanish. The region was also celebrated for its tropical hardwood forests. Although the British controlled the Caribbean coast in the late 1700's, Honduras was a province of the Spanish captaincy of Guatemala. It became a member of the United Provinces of Central America after independence from Spain and Mexico, and an independent republic after the 1838 collapse of the Central American Federation.

Conservatives dominated Honduran politics until the 1870's, when the Liberals came to power and adopted a new constitution that reduced the influence of the church, among other things. Economic development came especially from a number of U.S. firms whose efforts were regarded as exploitative rather than beneficial; in 1912, U.S. president William Taft sent marines to protect U.S. interests.

Political unrest continued until the presidency of Gen. Tiburcio Carías Andino (1932-49), who was followed by a succession of pro-labor presidents. In 1963, a coup led by Col. Osvaldo López Arellano deposed the civilian president, and the military ruled almost uninterrupted until 1982. In 1969, the expulsion of thousands of Salvadoran peasants who had immigrated during the 1950's and 1960's led to the Soccer War with El Salvador. An armistice was negotiated by the OAS.

During the 1980's, Honduras was threatened by civil wars in El Salvador and Nicaragua. Honduran territory was used by Nicaraguan Contras, for which Honduras received substantial U.S. military and other aid. Demobilization of the Contras alleviated tensions between Left and Right, and in Jan. 1994 the new president, Carlos Roberto Reina Idiaquez, took office with the promise of controlling and reducing the power of the military which was more easily accomplished when the U.S. made severe cuts in military aid. In late 1997 the same Liberal Party easily won reelection, maintaining their control of the National Congress, while their candidate, Carlos Roberto Flores, won election as president.

In Oct. 1999, Honduras was devastated by Hurricane Mitch: 7,000 were dead, 600,000 homeless, and 70 percent of its crops destroyed — losses somewhat mitigated by international aid and debt reductions. In Jan. 1999, the legislature unanimously voted to place the autonomous military under civilian control. The Liberal Party was unseated in Nov. 2001 as the National Party elected only its second president since 1981, Ricardo Maduro. In 2006 he was replaced by José Zelaya Rosales.

▶ HUNGARY
Republic of Hungary

• **GEOGRAPHY Location:** landlocked country in eastern Europe. **Boundaries:** Slovakia to N, Ukraine to NE, Romania to E, Yugoslavia to SE, Croatia to SW, Slovenia to W, Austria to NW. **Total area:** 35,919 sq. mi. (93,030 sq km). **Coastline:** none. **Comparative area:** slightly smaller than Indiana. **Land use:** 52% arable land; 3% permanent crops; 45% other. **Major cities:** Budapest (capital); Debrecen; Miskolc; Szeged; Pécs.

• **PEOPLE Population:** 9,930,915 (July 2008 est.). **Nationality:** noun—Hungarian(s); adjective—Hungarian. **Ethnic groups:** 92.3% Hungarian, 1.9% Roma, 5.8% other or unknown. **Languages:** 93.6% Hungarian, 6.4% other. **Religions:** 51.9% Roman Catholic, 15.9% Calvinist, 3% Lutheran, 3.6% other Christian, 14.5% unaffiliated.

• **GOVERNMENT Type:** parliamentary democracy. **Constitution:** Aug. 18, 1949; effective Aug. 20, 1949; revised Oct. 18, 1989; 1997 amendment streamlined judicial system. **National holiday:** St. Stephen's Day, Aug. 20. **Heads of Government:** László Sólyom, president (since Aug 2005); Ferenc Gyurcsány, prime minister (Oct. 2004). **Structure:** executive—president elected by National Assembly; unicameral legislature—National Assembly (elected by direct suffrage); judicial—elected by Parliament.

• **ECONOMY Monetary unit:** forint. **Budget:** (2007 est.) *income:* $62.25 bil.; *expend.:* $69.98 bil. **G.D.P.:** $194.2 bil., $19,500 per capita (2007 est.) **Chief crops:** corn, wheat, sunflower seeds, potatoes, sugar beets; chickens, pigs, cattle. **Natural resources:** bauxite, coal, natural gas, fertile soils. **Major industries:** mining, metallurgy, construction materials. **Labor force:** 4.19 mil. (2007); 64.2% services; 32.4% industry; 3.3% agriculture; 7.1% unemployment (2007). **Exports:** $85.73 bil. (f.o.b., 2007); 57.6% machinery and equipment, 31.0% other manufactures, 7.5% agriculture and food products. **Imports:** $85.99 bil. (f.o.b., 2007); 51% machinery and equipment, 35.3% other manufactures, 8.2% fuels and electricity, 2.9% agricultural and food products, 2.0% raw materials. **Major trading partners:** (2006) *exports:* 29.5% Germany, 5.6% Italy, 5% France, 5% Austria, 4.5% U.K., 4.2% Romania, 4.1% Poland; *imports:* 27.1% Germany, 8.2% Russia, 6.9% China, 6.2% Austria, 4.7% France, 4.6% Italy, 4.3% Netherlands, 4.3% Poland.

The Magyars, a tribe of Central Asian horsemen, terrorized Europe in the ninth century A.D. and settled in the Hungarian plain where, under their chieftain Arpad, they displaced earlier Germanic and Slavic settlers and organized a kingdom in 896. The Hungarians converted to Christianity late in the 10th century, and King Stephen (later St. Stephen) received a royal crown from Pope Sylvester II in 1001.

After the Battle of Mohacs in 1526, most of Hungary fell under Ottoman rule. The Turks were driven out in a series of battles with the Habsburg Holy Roman emperors at the end of the 17th century. Thereafter Hungary was part of the Habsburg Empire until 1867, when the Dual Monarchy of Austria-Hungary was organized, making Hungary independent of Austria in all but finance, the military, and foreign affairs.

During the 18th and 19th centuries, Hungary experienced extensive immigration of Romanians and Slovaks; by 1900 Magyars formed only a bare majority of the population. The pre-World War I economy was largely agricultural. Agriculture-related industry (beet sugar factories, breweries, tanneries, textile mills) developed in the late 19th century, along with some heavy industry.

In the dismemberment of Austria-Hungary following the defeat of the Central Powers in World War I, Hungary surrendered extensive territories to Romania, Yugoslavia, and Czechoslovakia. With the Treaty of Trianon ("Bloody Trianon") in 1920, the country lost 70 percent of its territory and 60 percent of its population; one-third of the Magyar people lived on foreign soil.

Short-lived governments—a republic under Michael Karolyi, and a Bolshevist state under Bela Kun—were replaced in 1920 by a new regime, with Adm. Miklós Horthy serving as regent. The Horthy regime was authoritarian but not fascist; its main objective was the recovery of Hungary's lost territories. Hungary established common cause with Germany in 1938 and 1940, recovering some territory from Czechoslovakia and Romania in the bargain, but at the price of participating in Hitler's war with the Soviet Union. Germany occupied Hungary in 1944 and set up a Hungarian Nazi regime. Late in 1944 the Russian army drove out the Germans and set up their own occupation.

The establishment of a full-scale Soviet-satellite regime was relatively slow. A republic was declared in February 1946, and the non-Communist Zoltan Tildy was elected president. Tildy was forced out in 1947, however, and replaced by the Stalinist dictator, Matias Rakosi. After the death of Stalin in 1953, the moderate Imre Nagy became premier and introduced some economic reforms. Nagy was forced out of office in 1955.

Nikita Khrushchev's denunciation of Stalin in 1956, combined with rising expectations for reforms in Hungary, led to a popular uprising in October 1956. Nagy, backed by the army, formed a coalition government on Oct. 23, proclaimed Hungary's neutrality, ended censorship, opened the borders, and withdrew from the Warsaw Pact. On Nov. 4, Soviet troops launched a massive invasion that crushed the rebellion. The Soviet army installed János Kádár as premier; Nagy was executed. About 200,000 Hungarians fled the country, and many more were imprisoned.

After several years of repressive rule, the Kádár regime announced, in 1963, amnesty for participants in the 1956 rebellion. Stalinists were gradually removed from the government, economic reforms emphasizing profit and productivity were introduced, and trade with the West was expanded. Hungary reluctantly took part in the suppression of Czechoslovakia's "Prague Spring" in 1968. In the same year, it announced the New Economic Mechanism (NEM) policy, ending central economic planning and introducing semifree enterprise under bureaucratic control.

After a brief return to central planning in the 1970's, the NEM was reintroduced in 1979 and expanded in 1982, when Hungary joined the World Bank and the I.M.F. Private ownership of subsidiaries of state-owned enterprises was permitted. In 1987 a pro-Gorbachev premier, Karoly Grosz, took office and in 1988 became head of the Communist party as well.

In 1989 the boundary with Austria was opened, making Hungary a key escape point for refugees from East Germany and Czechoslovakia. Nagy's reburial was attended by 300,000. Free elections were held in 1990, and the Democratic Forum, led by Jozsef Antall, won a plurality and formed a coalition government with the Smallholders and Christian Democratic parties. Having already achieved substantial perestroika-style economic reforms under communism, Hungary was well-placed to make a rapid transition to free enterprise and was seeking admission to the E.U.

Hungarian voters signaled just how painful they found the transition in the 1994 parliamentary elections by giving the Communists (now renamed Socialists) an absolute • majority in Parliament. Privatization moved at a snail's pace, though the new government did appoint a committee to arrange the selling off of about 1,000 state-owned enterprises and soon foreign investment increased faster than anywhere in Central Europe. In 1997 Hungary was one of three eastern European nations invited to apply for admission to NATO and it was admitted in 1999.

Elections in 1998 gave the Socialists only 134 seats (of 386) in Parliament; the new government was formed by Civic Party which won 148 seats of its own, in coalition with the Smallholders and other parties of the right. The 2002 elections returned the Socialists (in coalition with the Free Democrats) to power, toppling the government of Viktor Orban and replacing him with Peter Medgyessy. In a 2003 referendum voters gave 84 percent approval to joining the E.U. In 2004 a business leader, Ferenc Gyurcsány succeeded Medgyessy and was elected again in 2006. Shortly thereafter, political upheaval followed a tape recording of Gyurcsány saying privately that he and his government had lied about the nation's massive debt (10 percent of G.D.P.). Protests, sometimes violent, divided the nation but Gyurcsány's party remained in power.

▶ **ICELAND**
Republic of Iceland
• **GEOGRAPHY Location:** near Arctic Circle in North Atlantic Ocean. Reykjavík 64°09'N, 21°58'W. **Boundaries**: Greenland about 190 mi. (300 km) to NW, Norway about 620 mi. (1,000 km) to E, U.K. 500 mi. (800 km) to S. **Total area**: 39,768 sq. mi. (103,000 sq km). **Coastline:** 3,100 mi. (4,988 km). **Comparative area:** slightly smaller than Kentucky. **Land use:** 1% arable land; 0% permanent crops; 99% other. **Major cities**: Reykjavík (capital). • **PEOPLE Population:** 304,367 (July 2008 est.). **Nationality:** noun—Icelander(s); adjective—Icelandic. **Ethnic groups:** 94% homogeneous mixture of descendants of Norwegians and Celts, 6% of foreign origin. **Languages:** Icelandic (official), English, Nordic languages, German widely spoken. **Religions:** 85.5% Lutheran Church of Iceland, 2.1% Reykjavik Free Church, 2% Roman Catholic, 8% other, 2.4% unaffiliated.

• **GOVERNMENT Type:** constitutional republic. **Independence:** June 17, 1944 (from Denmark). **Constitution:** June 16, 1944; effective June 17, 1944. **National holiday:** Anniversary of the Establishment of the Republic, June 17. **Heads of Government:** Ólafur Ragnar Grímsson, president (since Aug. 1996); Geir Haarde, prime minister (since June 2006). **Structure:** executive power vested in president but exercised by cabinet responsible to Parliament; unicameral legislature; judiciary (Supreme Court justices appointed for life by president).
• **ECONOMY Monetary unit:** Icelandic króna. **Budget:** (2007 est.) *income:* $9.495 bil.; *expend.:* $8.432 bil. **G.D.P.:** $11.89 bil., $39,400 per capita (2007 est.). **Chief crops:** potatoes, turnips; cattle, sheep; fish. **Natural resources:** fish, hydroelectric and geothermal power, diatomite. **Major industries:** fish processing, aluminum smelting, ferrosilicon production. **Labor force:** 180,000 (2007); 71.8% services, 23% industry, 5.1% agriculture (2005); 1% unemployment (2007). **Exports:** $4.569 bil. (f.o.b. 2007); 70% fish and fish products, animal products, aluminum, ferrosilicon, diatomite. **Imports**: $5.777 bil. (f.o.b., 2007); machinery and equipment, petroleum products, foodstuffs, textiles. **Major trading partners:** (2006) *exports:* 16.5% Netherlands, 15.7% U.K., 15% Germany, 10.8% U.S., 6.4% Spain; *imports:* 12.8% U.S., 12.3% Germany, 7.1% Norway, 6.9% Sweden, 61% Denmark, 5.3% U.K., 5.3% China, 4.8% Netherlands, 4.1% Japan.

The volcanic island of Iceland was settled in the ninth century A.D. by Vikings, who established Europe's oldest body of representative government, the Althing, in 930. Christianity was introduced around 1000. In the 13th century, Iceland acknowledged Norwegian rule. In 1380 Denmark, by then in control of all of Scandinavia, conquered Iceland as well. Iceland gained its independence in 1918 but shared a common king, Christian X, with the Danes. During World War II, first British, and then American, troops garrisoned the island; in 1944, with Denmark occupied by the Nazis, Iceland deposed its king and proclaimed itself a republic.

Iceland became a U.N. member in 1946 and a member of NATO in 1949. Lacking its own armed forces, it grudgingly tolerated the presence of an American air base at Keflavik. The republic developed a Scandinavian-style welfare state, with comprehensive social benefits that have produced one of the world's healthiest and best-educated peoples.

Less than 1 percent of Iceland's territory is arable; the island imports grain and vegetables but is self-sufficient in meat and dairy products. Fishing is the principal industry, accounting for 75 percent of exports, 20 percent of G.D.P., and engaging one-seventh of the work force.

Multiparty representation in the Althing has created a trend of government by coalitions or minority cabinets. Politically stable, the republic recently faced economic problems brought on by high taxes, chronic inflation, and a huge national debt. In 1997 and 1998, however, the economy made a strong recovery with G.D.P. growing by 5 percent a year and continuing over a decade.

Iceland maintains close ties with Scandinavia and actively participates in the Nordic Council, but not the E.U., membership in which the government views as harmful to Iceland's all-important fishing industry. In 2006 commercial whaling was resumed.

▶ INDIA
Republic of India

● **GEOGRAPHY Location:** Asian subcontinent, with Himalayan mountain range to N. **Boundaries:** Pakistan to NW; China, Bhutan, Nepal to N; Myanmar to NE; Bangladesh to E (surrounded by Indian territory except for short frontier with Myanmar); Bay of Bengal to E; Sri Lanka to SE across Palk Strait; Arabian Sea to W. **Total area:** 1,269,340 sq. mi. (3,287,590 sq km). **Coastline:** 4,350 mi. (7,000 km). **Comparative area:** slightly more than one-third the size of U.S. **Land use:** 54% arable land; 3% permanent crops; 43% other. **Major cities:** New Delhi (capital); Mumbai (Greater Bombay); Calcutta; Madras; Hyderabad.

● **PEOPLE Population:** 1,147,995,898 (July 2008 est.). **Nationality:** noun—Indian(s); adjective—Indian. **Ethnic groups:** 72% Indo-Aryan, 25% Dravidian, 3% Mongoloid and other. **Languages:** Hindi, English, and 14 other official languages; 24 languages spoken by a million or more persons each; numerous other languages and dialects; Hindi is national language and primary tongue of 30% of the people; English enjoys associate status but is the most important language for national, political, and commercial communication; Hindustani, a variant of Hindi/Urdu, is spoken throughout northern India. **Religions:** 80.5% Hindu, 13.4% Muslim, 2.3% Christian, 1.9% Sikh.

● **GOVERNMENT Type:** federal republic. **Independence:** Aug. 15, 1947 (from U.K.). **Constitution:** Jan. 26, 1950. **National holiday:** Anniversary of the Proclamation of the Republic, Jan. 26. **Heads of Government:** Pratibha Patil, president (since July 2007); Manmohan Singh, prime minister (since May 2004). **Structure:** executive; bicameral parliament—Council of States, 250 members, up to 12 appointed by pres., remainder chosen by regionally elected officials; judiciary.

● **ECONOMY Monetary unit:** Indian rupee. **Budget:** (2007 est.) *income:* $145.2 bil.; *expend.:* $182.4 bil. **G.D.P.:** $2.965 trillion, $2,700 per capita (2007 est.). **Chief crops:** rice, wheat, oilseed, cotton; cattle, water, buffalo, sheep; fish. **Natural resources:** coal (4th largest reserves in world), iron ore, manganese, mica, bauxite. **Major industries:** textiles, chemicals, food processing, steel. **Labor force:** 516.4 mil. (2007 est.); 16.6% agriculture, 55% services, 28.4% industry (2007 est.). **Exports:** $140.8 bil. (f.o.b., 2007 est.); clothing, gems and jewelry, engineering goods, chemicals. **Imports:** $224.1 bil. (f.o.b., 2007 est.); petroleum, machinery, gems, fertilizer. **Major trading partners:** (2006) *exports:* 17% U.S., 8.3% United Arab Emirates, 7.7% China, 4.3% U.K.; *imports:* 8.7% China, 6% U.S., 4.7% Germany, 4.6% Singapore.

Indian civilization is one of the oldest in the world. Neolithic agricultural communities had appeared in the Indus River valley by 3000 B.C. and cities at Harappa and Mohenjo-Daro were founded around 2500 B.C. Around 1500 B.C. Indo-Europeans (Aryans) from Central Asia imposed their religion and political system on the indigenous population and generated population movements toward southern India.

Indo-European civilization was characterized by caste; everyone was a member of one of four fundamental divisions of society: Brahmins, hereditary priests responsible for higher learning and rituals; Ksatrias, warriors and administrators; Vaisas, merchants; and Sudras, farmers and subjugated peoples. At the bottom were casteless people, known later as untouchables.

By the mid-first millennium B.C., Brahminism had declined into a state of religious formalism. That situation prompted two reformations around 600 B.C., the first of which produced the Jain religion; the second, Buddhism. Jainism remained confined largely to India, while Buddhism eventually influenced most of the cultures of Asia, though it died out in India itself. Buddhism was adopted as a state religion by Asoka, third and greatest emperor of the Mauryan empire (325-184 b.c) under which much of India was united for the first time. Following the collapse of the Mauryan empire, Hinduism evolved out of Buddhism, Brahminism, and other local cults and became the dominant religion of India.

South India in the post-Mauryan period was divided into numerous states, the most prominent of which was Chola, a Tamil kingdom in the southeast that had extensive trade connections throughout the Indian Ocean.

The Gupta dynasty (c. A.D. 320-544), based in the Ganges River valley, established its rule over most of northern India and created what is generally regarded as a golden age of north Indian culture, with flourishing cities and significant achievements in art, literature, and science.

In the seventh century, King Sri Harsha created a short-lived feudal empire that united most of the petty states in the upper Ganges valley, while the Chalyuka dynasty dominated southern India. In the early eighth century, the Indus River valley was invaded by Arabs who introduced Islam to the region. The empire of Sri Harsha fell apart, replaced by the petty kingdoms of the Rajputs.

The 11th century saw the ascendency of Islam throughout northern India, which came under the shadow of the empire of Mamud of Ghazni, based in Afghanistan. In 1192 the Ghaznavid general Kutb ud-din Aibak defeated a coalition of Rajput states; in 1206 he founded the Sultanate of Delhi, which in the 13th century held off Mongol invasions in northwestern India and brought all of the subcontinent, except for the southernmost states, under its control. While the rulers of the sultanate were Muslims, most of their subjects remained Hindu.

Internal rebellions combined with the sacking of Delhi by Timur Leng (Tamerlane) in 1398 weakened the Sultanate of Delhi. In 1526 Babur, a descendant of Timur Leng, conquered all of northern India and established the Moghul empire. Under Akbar the Great, the empire flourished; Moghul culture gave rise to new styles of architecture, painting, and music.

In the 17th century, the Moghul emperors were threatened by the Hindu Marathas, whose kingdom on the west-central coast rapidly encompassed most of south India. By the late 18th century, Maratha power had spread to the north, and most of the petty kingdoms of the Moghul empire became part of a Maratha confederacy, owing only nominal allegiance to Delhi. By that time all of India was threatened by the expansion of the European powers.

Vasco da Gama had landed at Calicut in 1498, and in 1510 the Portuguese founded a colony at Goa. Dutch traders competed with the Portuguese during the 16th century, and British and French merchants followed in the 17th century. British trading stations were established at Surat (1612), Bombay (1661), and Calcutta (1690). In the mid-18th century, war broke out between British and French forces in India, and the French were confined to a few small enclaves. The growing instability of the Moghul empire in the face of Marathan and Rajput revolts and the expansion of the southern kingdom of Mysore encouraged the British to seek further control of Indian territory. Robert Clive's victory at Plassey in 1757 brought Orissa, Bihar, and Bengal under British control; British rule was extended to the upper Ganges in 1775. Victory over the maharaja of Mysore in 1792 paved the way for British control over the south.

British parliamentary acts of 1773 and 1784 placed these acquisitions firmly under government control, and in 1803 the Moghul emperor accepted the offer of a protectorate, and British suzerainty in India was assured. After a protracted war, 1812-23, Marathan resistance to British control was broken. The first Anglo-Afghan War, 1838-42, was inconclusive in Afghanistan but led to consolidation of British control of the Punjab.

In 1833 Parliament assumed political control of British interests in South Asia, while private merchants had unrestricted access to the economy. Plantation crops, such as opium and cotton, began to displace agriculture, which made India more dependent on imported goods.

In 1857 Indian troops in the British colonial forces staged a mutiny in north-central India that lasted 14 months. In 1858 the Moghul empire was dissolved, as was the East India Company. The government of India was made directly subject to the British Crown, which exercised control through a viceroy and through the British Colonial Office. Queen Victoria was crowned empress of India in 1877.

British sovereignty in India—the raj—was a patchwork of direct and indirect rule. In general, coastal areas, river valleys, and strategic frontier regions were ruled by British authorities, while interior states continued as British protectorates controlled by British advisers to native princes. In 1861 Indians were appointed to advisory councils of the viceroy and provincial governors.

The Indian National Congress was organized in 1885. In the wake of popular demonstrations in 1905, elections were instituted to choose Indian members of the viceroy's legislative council. Separate electorates were created for the Muslim and Hindu communities, formalizing a divisive force in Indian politics and weakening opposition to British rule. In 1914, with Chinese loss of control in Tibet, India's northern boundary was pushed forward to the McMahon Line, following the highest peaks in the Himalayas. This set the stage for numerous later boundary disputes between China and India, Pakistan, and Burma.

The Government of India Act of 1919 transferred some political power to elected provincial officials but left the appointed British governors firmly in control. In that year Mohandas K. Gandhi organized the first passive-resistance campaigns and was imprisoned. In 1935 the Government of India Act created elected provincial legislatures. In the first elections (1937) the Congress party under Jawaharlal Nehru won control of seven of the 11 provinces. Nehru's goal of a united Indian opposition to British rule was thwarted by Mohammed Ali Jinnah's Muslim League, which demanded the creation of a separate Muslim state.

During World War II, the British military position in South Asia was complicated by calls for Indian independence. An offer of local autonomy, with independence to follow, was spurned by Nehru, and an Indian National army under Subhas Bose fought with the Japanese. Jinnah's call for an independent Pakistan was greatly enhanced by his support of the British.

In 1947, the British raj became two independent nations, predominantly Hindu India and predominantly Muslim Pakistan. Despite its considerable stature in the international community at large, India has been troubled by a number of disputes with its neighbors and separatist movements within its own borders. Following independence hundreds of semiautonomous princely states were brought under control of the central government. The French ceded their remaining trading colonies in the 1950's, and Portugal gave up Goa in 1961. In 1962, India warred with China in a still unresolved dispute over their border along Kashmir and Assam. The state of Bhutan was granted independence in 1971, and in 1974 Sikkim was annexed and its monarchy abolished.

India's most intractable disputes have been with Pakistan. Immediately after independence, Hindus in Pakistan and Muslims in India were set upon by the majority populations; hundreds of thousands were killed, and at least 12 million refugees fled over the border in both directions. On Jan. 30, 1948, Gandhi was assassinated by a Hindu extremist who blamed him for partition.

In granting independence, Britain had divided states of Bengal and Punjab between the two countries, but fighting erupted over the status of Jammu and Kashmir, and a cease-fire line negotiated by the U.N. in 1949 has never been ratified as a formal national boundary. In 1989, separatists in the Indian part of Kashmir began calling for an end to Indian rule, and relations with Pakistan have worsened as India accused its neighbor of providing support for the guerrillas. In 1971, after 10 million refugees poured across its border, India intervened in the Pakistani civil war in an action that prompted an almost immediate cease-fire and the creation of an independent Bangladesh.

India's main separatist movement involves Sikhs in the Punjab who seek the formation of an independent state of Khalistan, but who are thought to be supported by Pakistan. The government is also contending with separatist movements in the northeastern states of Assam.

The British legacy in India included a sizable national elite, well educated and committed to principles of parliamentary democracy. The English language linked the elites of India's linguistically diverse regions, easing minorities' fears of domination by a Hindi-speaking majority. India's economy had seen some industrial development under the British, but its infrastructure was geared to integration in a colonial empire rather than to independence. Port cities, heavy industry, and plantation agriculture coexisted with widespread rural poverty and the years following independence saw a massive migration of the rural poor into overburdened cities.

Under Prime Minister Jawaharlal Nehru, India assumed a leadership role in the world movement of nonaligned nations and followed a policy of neutrality in international affairs. The development of good relations between the United States and Pakistan led to correspondingly difficult U.S.-India relations. In August 1971 India signed a 20-year friendship treaty with the Soviet Union.

Nehru died on May 27, 1964, and was succeeded by Lal Bahadur Shastri. Nehru's daughter, Mrs. Indira Gandhi, was named prime minister on

Jan. 19, 1966. In 1967 the dominant Congress party faced electoral setbacks; in 1969 it split into "Old" and "New" wings. Mrs. Gandhi's New Congress party won control of the legislature.

Faced with protests and strikes after the New Congress party was convicted of voting irregularities in 1975, Mrs. Gandhi declared a state of emergency in June; censorship was imposed, thousands were arrested for political offenses, and various economic-control measures were adopted. An opposition coalition led by the Janata Dal party won a massive victory in parliamentary elections in 1977. Mrs. Gandhi was driven from office, and the state of emergency was annulled. Mrs. Gandhi's party was returned to power in 1980, and she resumed the prime ministership. After an army attack on the Sikhs' Golden Temple in Amritsar, Gandhi was assassinated by Sikh bodyguards in October 1984. She was succeeded in office by her son, Rajiv, who placed the Punjab under direct control of the federal government.

On Dec. 3, 1984, methyl isocyanate gas leaked from a Union Carbide plant in Bhopal, killing over 2,500 people. The accident prompted a broad inquiry into industrial safety standards in India.

In 1989, Rajiv Gandhi's Congress party was voted out of office after people close to the government were accused of taking kickbacks in a government purchase scandal. Gandhi was succeeded by V.P. Singh of the Janata Dal party, whose government collapsed after 11 months over a dispute involving Hindu plans to build a temple on the site of a mosque in Ayodhya. (Hindus contend the mosque was built on the site of Rama's birthplace.) Middle-class Hindus also protested an affirmative action policy to set aside federal jobs for members of lower castes.

Singh was followed by Chandra Shekhar, whose minority government served only with the backing of the Congress party. After a parliamentary boycott by the Congress party instigated by Rajiv Gandhi, Shekhar quit the government in March 1991, agreeing to stay on as a caretaker until the May election. The election, postponed two weeks following the assassination of Gandhi, was won by the Congress party, and P.V. Narasimha Rao became prime minister. The Rao government attempted to foster economic growth by relaxing the centralized planning and controls on international trade and investment.

A rise in Hindu extremist feeling, however, strengthened the hand of the opposition Bharatiya Janata party. On Dec. 6, 1992, a Hindu mob demolished a mosque built several hundred years earlier on a Hindu sacred site in the city of Ayodhya; in the ensuing turmoil, riots broke out in dozens of cities, most notably Bombay, leading to the deaths of hundreds of Muslims at the hands of Hindu attackers. A series of bomb explosions killed hundreds in Bombay on Mar.12, 1993, while dozens more were killed by an explosion in Calcutta four days later. Further riots followed, amid unsubstantiated accusations that Muslims, aided by Pakistan, were responsible for the explosions.

In 1993 separatist movements in Punjab and Assam waned, but violence in Kashmir and Jammu increased dramatically.

The Rao government's economic policies produced good results, but as India's economy strengthened its political stability weakened. The Congress Party continued to lose power to the Hindu Baratiya Janata Party. Congress was defeated in parliamentary elections in May 1996,

ushering in an era of short-lived, weak coalition governments under Pres. K. R. Narayanan. Inder Kumer Gurjal formed a government in April, 1997 that fell in November. The BJP won a plurality of seats in March 1998 elections, but, to govern (under Prime Minister Vajapyee) required a 19-party coalition. Fragile authority need not exclude vigorous policy: it was the BJP coalition that carried out underground tests of five nuclear devices in May, vigorously asserted India's claims in Kashmir, and cut food subsidies as a means of reducing the deficit. It was the latter that dislodged the coalition and in April 1999, Pres. Narayanan dissolved the Lok Sabha, preparatory to India's third election campaign in three years. Perhaps sensing weakness, Muslim insurgents launched attacks against Indian forces in Kashmir. But India retaliated forcefully and peace was restored in July, although India continued to blame Pakistan for the violence. In the election results, the National Democratic Alliance, a 24-party coalition led by the Bharatiya Janata Party, won an absolute majority; so, for the first time in 27 years, an incumbent prime minister won re-election.

On Dec. 13, 2001 an attack on the Parliament in New Delhi by five Pakistan-based terrorists greatly heightened existing tensions between the two countries. While Hindu mobs killed Muslims in Gujarat, Muslim attacks continued, though at a diminished rate in 2002, in Jammu-Kashmir. Upwards of a million troops stood poised on the border with almost daily artillery exchanges. Several terrorist attacks in Kashmir led to U.S. and British diplomatic intervention that eased tensions considerably during 2003. By 2004 serious talks on all issues (including terrorism, nuclear security, and trade) were occuring regularly. In the legislative election a startling victory for the United Progressive Alliance ousted the BJP and brough Manniohan Singh, a Sikh, to the head of the minority government. In 2005 the U.S. formally agreed to provide India with nuclear power expertise despite the presence of nuclear weapons.

India has enjoyed significant domestic and international achievements in the first half-century after independence. The nation's territory was consolidated, and separatist movements in various provinces successfully resisted. The federal parliamentary system has proved workable, and the federal government has established its constitutional right to intervene in state affairs under some conditions. India's armed forces are large, well trained, and well equipped, with nuclear capability. India has maintained watchful, but generally peaceful, relations with two unfriendly neighbors, Pakistan and China. The Green Revolution of the 1970's made the country self-sufficient in food for the first time since the 19th century. The economy has been growing steadily since 2000 as the computer and Internet revolution has provided a huge number of jobs for India's educated middle class.

▶ INDONESIA
Republic of Indonesia

● GEOGRAPHY **Location:** archipelago of about 18,108 islands stretching from Malay peninsula to New Guinea between mainland of Southeast Asia and Australia. Jakarta 6°08'S, 106°45'E. **Boundaries:** land borders with Papua New Guinea, to E of Irian Jaya, and with Malaysian states of Sarawak and Sabah in northern Borneo. **Total area:** 741,097 sq. mi. (1,919,440 sq km). **Coastline:**

34,006 mi. (54,716 km). **Comparative area:** slightly less than three times the size of Texas. **Land use:** 10% arable land; 7% permanent crops; 783% other. **Major cities:** Jakarta (capital); Surabaya; Bandung; Medan; Semarang.
• **PEOPLE Population:** 237,512,355 (July 2008 est.). **Nationality:** noun—Indonesian(s); adjective—Indonesian. **Ethnic groups:** 45% Javanese, 14% Sundanese, 7.5% Madurese, 7.5% coastal Malays. **Languages:** Bahasa Indonesia (modified form of Malay; official); English and Dutch, leading foreign languages; local dialects, most widely spoken of which is Javanese. **Religions:** 86.1% Muslim, 5.7% Protestant, 3% Roman Catholic, 1.8% Hindu, 3.4% other and unspecified.
• **GOVERNMENT Type:** republic. **Independence:** Aug. 17, 1945 (from Netherlands). **Constitution:** Aug. 1945, abrogated by Federal Constitution of 1949 and Provisional Constitution of 1950, restored July 5, 1959. **National holiday:** Independence Day, Aug. 17. **Head of Government:** Susilo Bambang Yudhoyono, president (since Sept. 2004). **Structure:** executive—headed by president who is chief of state and head of cabinet; cabinet selected by president; unicameral legislature (DPR, or House of Representatives) of 500 members (100 appointed, 400 elected); second body (MPR, or People's Consultative Assembly) of 1,000 members includes legislature and 500 other members (chosen by several processes but not directly elected); judicial—Supreme Court Judges appointed by president.
• **ECONOMY Monetary unit:** Indonesian rupiah. **Budget:** (2007 est.) **income:** $88.21 bil.; **expend.:** $95.41 bil. **G.D.P.:** $845.6 bil., $3,400 per capita (2007 est.). **Chief crops:** rice, cassava, peanuts, rubber, cocoa; poultry, pork, beef. **Natural resources:** crude oil, tin, natural gas, nickel, timber. **Major industries:** petroleum and natural gas, textiles, mining. **Labor force:** 108 mil. (2005 est.); 43.3% agriculture, 18% industry, 38.7% services (2004 est.); 9.7% unemployment (2007 est.). **Exports:** $118.4 bil. (f.o.b., 2007); textiles/garments, gas, plywood, rubber. **Imports:** $86.24 bil. (f.o.b., 2007 est.); manufactures, chemicals, foodstuffs, fuels. **Major trading partners:** (2006) **exports:** 19.4% Japan, 11.8% Singapore, 11.5% U.S., 7.7% China, 6.4% South Korea, 4.2% Taiwan; **imports:** 29.6% Singapore, 11.2% China, 8.8% Japan, 5.3% South Korea, 4.8% Malaysia.

The precolonial East Indies consisted of several Islamic and Hindu kingdoms in the western islands and tribal societies in the easterly ones. The Portuguese established trading posts in the 16th century; by the 17th century, control had largely passed to the Dutch East India Company. With the company's bankruptcy in 1799, the Dutch established direct colonial rule. Several 19th-century anticolonial uprisings, though costly to the Dutch, failed to dislodge them. Nationalist sentiment grew in the early 20th century, organized around Islamic groups, the Indonesian Communist party (PKI, founded 1920), and the Indonesian Nationalist party (PNI, founded 1927). Sukarno, founder of the PNI, achieved prominence as a nationalist leader and was jailed by the Dutch.

The Dutch East Indies fell quickly to the Japanese early in 1942. On Aug. 17, 1945, Sukarno proclaimed Indonesia's independence. With British aid, the Dutch returned and tried to reestablish colonial rule; in 1949, threatened with a cutoff of American Marshall Plan aid, they withdrew and acknowledged Indonesia's independent status.

Under Sukarno Indonesia took a leading role in international affairs among the nonaligned nations of the Third World.

In 1963 Indonesia gained control of the last Dutch outpost in the Indies, Irian Jaya (western New Guinea). Sukarno's politics moved steadily to the left, and Indonesia became hostile to the West and friendly with China. The influence of the PKI grew steadily. On Sept. 30, 1965, the army crushed an attempted coup by the PKI, setting off a popular reaction in which several hundred thousand people were killed as suspected Communists. Sukarno was shunted aside, and power devolved to Gen. Suharto, who became president in 1968. The PKI was banned, and Indonesian policy swung sharply in favor of the West.

The economy grew rapidly, aided by oil revenue, timber exports to Japan, and the Green Revolution in rice agriculture. A policy of "transmigration" attempted, with mixed success, to move farmers from overcrowded Java and Bali to underdeveloped areas in Sumatra, Borneo, Sulawesi, and Irian Jaya. In 1975 Indonesia invaded the former Portuguese colony of East Timor, which was annexed in 1976. More than 100,000 East Timorese were killed and the annexation was never recognized internationally.

In the early 1990s declining oil revenues were partly offset by the growth of industry and tourism. Pres. Suharto remained in power, at the head of the Golkar united-front party, and was reelected president for a fifth term in 1993. Despite the most violent campaign in Indonesia's history, the ruling Golkar Party was returned to power with nearly 75 percent of the vote in 1997. But Suharto's regime faced serious problems, including continuing unrest in East Timor and rising public dissatisfaction with the alleged corruption of Suharto's family and close associates. The economy boomed but in 1998 the financial crisis that swept through Asia revealed the hollowness of the Indonesian approach. Strikes, protests, and riots forced Suharto to resign in May and his trusted aide, Vice-Pres. Habibie took power promising reforms and new elections in 1999. Habibie began reforming the banking system, initiated inquiries into Suharto family wealth, and agreed with Portugal to hold a referendum on the status of East Timor. Elections were held in June 1999 with Golkar taking about 25 percent of the votes; an anti-Golkar coalition headed by Sukarno's daughter, Megawati Sukarnoputri, held a plurality. The people of East Timor voted overwhelmingly for independence from Indonesia, leading to violent attacks by militia groups and the sending of U.N. troops.

The Assembly approved the East Timor referendum and elected, not Megawati, but ailing Moslem cleric Abdurrahman Wahid as president, with Megawati as vice president. Under attack for his bumbling governance in a time of crisis, Wahid turned over day-to-day management to Megawati in mid-2000. On July 23, 2001 Wahid was formally impeached and replaced by Megawati. In Feb. 2002 a fragile peace was brokered in the Moluccas between Muslims and Christians. On May 20, East Timor became independent for the first time in 500 years.

In August 2002, the People's Consultative Assembly amended the constitution and established direct election of the president and abolished the military's 38 seats in Parliament. In Oct. terrorists linked to Al Qaeda bombed a Bali nightclub killing 180. In Dec. talks in Geneva with the separatist rebels in Aceh province appeared to have reached success; but in May, 2003 Pres. Megawati declared martial law in Aceh and another army offensive began against the rebels who were driven into the mountains. But serious fighting between Christians and Muslims broke out again in April 2004 in the Moluccas. In July elections Megwati finished second to Suseilo Bamband Yudoyono and lost to him in a run off. A devastating tsunami in Dec. 2004 claimed the lives of more than 100,000 Indonesian people and helped bring about a formal peace treaty with Aceh's rebels in Aug. 2005. Unfortunately another tsunami, an earthquake, and flooding followed in 2006-2007, setting the economy back severely.

▶ IRAN
Islamic Republic of Iran

- **GEOGRAPHY Location:** western Asia. **Boundaries:** Armenia and Azerbaijan to N, Caspian Sea and Turkmenistan to NE, Pakistan and Afghanistan to E, Persian (Arabian) Gulf and Gulf of Oman to S, and Turkey and Iraq to W. **Total area:** 636,294 sq. mi. (1,648,000 sq km). **Coastline:** 1,516 mi. (2,440 km); Iran also borders the Caspian Sea (740 km). **Comparative area:** slightly larger than Alaska. **Land use:** 10% arable land; 1% permanent crops; 89% other. **Major cities:** Tehran (Teheran, capital); Mashad (Meshed); Isfahan (Esfahan); Tabriz; Shiraz.
- **PEOPLE Population:** 65,875,223 (July 2008 est.). **Nationality:** noun—Iranian(s); adjective—Iranian. **Ethnic groups:** 51% Persian, 24% Azerbaijani, 8% Gilaki and Mazandarani, 7% Kurd. **Languages:** 58% Persian, 26% Turkic, 9% Kurdish. **Religions:** 89% Shi'a Muslim; 10% Sunni Muslim; 1% Zoroastrian, Jewish, Christian, and Baha'i.
- **GOVERNMENT Type:** theocratic republic. **Constitution:** Dec. 2-3, 1979; revised 1989 to expand powers of the presidency and eliminate the prime minister. **National holiday:** Islamic Republic Day, April 1. **Head of Government:** Mahmoud Ahmadinejad, president (since Aug. 2005). **Structure:** executive; unicameral legislature (Islamic Consultative Assembly); judicial.
- **ECONOMY Monetary unit:** Iranian rial. **Budget:** (2007 est.) *income:* $64 bil.; *expend.:* $64 bil. **G.D.P.:** $852.6 bil., $12,300 per capita (2007 est.). **Chief crops:** wheat, rice, sugar beets; dairy, wool; caviar. **Natural resources:** petroleum, natural gas, coal, chromium. **Major industries:** petroleum, petrochemicals, textiles. **Labor force:** 28.7 mil. (2006 est.); 25% agriculture, 31% industry, 45% services; 11% unemployment (2007). **Exports:** $76.5 bil. (f.o.b., 2007 est.); 85% petroleum; carpets, fruits, nuts, hides. **Imports:** $61.3 bil. (f.o.b., 2007 est.); machinery, military supplies, metal works, foodstuffs, pharmaceuticals. **Major trading partners:** (2006) *exports:* 14% Japan, 12.8% China, 7.2% Turkey, 6.3% Italy, 6% U.K., 4.6% Netherlands; *imports:* 12.2% Germany, 10.5% China, 9.3% United Arab Emirates, 5.6% France, 5.4% Italy, 5.4% South Korea, 4.4% Russia.

In 549 B.C. Cyrus the Great established the Persian empire by uniting Persia and conquered Babylonia. Alexander the Great conquered Persia in 333 B.C., but the Persians regained their independence after his death. The Persian Sassanian empire, established in A.D. 226, was the principal eastern rival of the Roman Empire. In 641 the Sassanians were defeated by invading Arabs, and Islam replaced the indigenous Zoroastrian religion. Persia reasserted its national identity—though not its political independence—under Islam and became a major center of Shia Muslim culture. In the early 13th century, Persia was conquered by the Mongols, who ruled the country until 1502.

The brilliant Safavid dynasty (1499-1736) was followed by two centuries of decline. During the 19th century, Persia lost control over Afghanistan and the Caucasus, while internal affairs came increasingly under British and Russian control. In 1907 an Anglo-Russian agreement formally divided Persia into spheres of influence. Following World War I, Persia was recognized as an independent nation, but was virtually a British protectorate. The Soviet Union renounced all claims to Persia in 1921.

In 1921 Reza Khan established a military dictatorship and had himself declared a hereditary monarch, Reza Shah Pahlavi, in 1925. In March 1935, the country's name was formally changed to Iran. In 1941 Great Britain, anxious over access to Iran's rich oil fields, charged Iran with pro-Axis activity, occupied Iran, and forced the abdication of Reza Shah in favor of his son, Mohammad Reza Shah Pahlavi.

Under Mohammed Mossadegh the National Front gained power in 1951. Parliament nationalized the oil industry; Britain responded with an economic blockade. The shah was briefly driven from power, but in August 1953, monarchist elements with clandestine British and American support ousted Mossadegh and restored the shah to the throne. The shah pursued a pro-Western policy of modernization and anticommunism and was rewarded with massive military and economic aid. His combination of secular, authoritarian rule and economic and social modernization was popular with the urban business sector but deeply resented by the rural and urban poor. Unrestrained use of the secret police to suppress dissent led to widespread disaffection.

Religiously inspired protests resulted in widespread violence in late 1978. A military government was installed by the shah on Nov. 6, with Prime Minister Shahpur Bakhtiar given sweeping powers. The shah went into exile on Jan. 16, 1979. On Jan. 31 Iran's dominant religious leader, Ayatollah Ruhollah Khomeini, returned to Iran from his exile in France. Government forces were routed by Khomeini's supporters, and Bakhtiar's government fell on Feb. 11. In 1979 clashes took place between rival religious factions, between religious parties and secular leftists, and between the urban middle class and the disenfranchised poor. Thousands were arrested and executed by the religious militia forces.

On Nov. 4, 1979, militants seized the U.S. embassy in Tehran and held 62 Americans hostage, provoking a long international crisis. An American military raid in April 1980 failed in an attempt to free the hostages. The hostages were finally freed on Jan. 21, 1981, minutes after Ronald Reagan's inauguration. The following day Iran's president, Abolhassan Bani-Sadr, was dismissed and the Ayatollah Khomeini took over executive power. A new wave of executions followed, with political moderates and non-Islamic religious believers among the principal victims.

On Sept. 22, 1980, a dispute between Iran and Iraq over the Shatt al-Arab waterway flared into open warfare. The war severely crippled Iran. Estimates on casualties range from 450,000 to over a million dead on both sides, and the war absorbed nearly all Iran's revenue from oil exports, leaving it nearly bankrupt. The U.S. was also drawn into the conflict. In 1986, Reagan-administration officials attempted to secure the release of hostages in Lebanon by trading arms to the Iranians; and on July 3, 1988, an American ship patrolling in the Persian Gulf accidently shot down an Iranian civilian airliner, killing all aboard.

In Sept. 1988, a U.N. initiative led to a cease-fire between Iran and Iraq and to the opening of negotiations to find a permanent settlement to the war. Largely isolated from the world community, Iran's domestic priority was rebuilding the nation's economy. On June 3, 1989, Ayatollah Khomeini died, and Ali-Akbar Rafsanjani assumed the presidency.

In elections held Apr. 10, 1992, supporters of Rafsanjani's moderate policies wrested a parliamentary majority from the radical fundamentalist Islamic factions that had controlled the Iranian Parliament for 13 years. But "moderation" proved elusive, as Rafsanjani's party was subjected to pressure from religious extremists.

Although Iran had condemned the presence of Western troops in the Middle East during the Persian Gulf conflict, it abided by U.N. sanctions against Iraq and grounded Iraqi planes that sought refuge from Allied bombing raids. In 1995 the U.S. accused Iran of beginning a strategic military buildup and forbade all trade with Iran.

Iran has remained mired in economic and political stagnation with evidence of popular discontent for several years. In the 1997 elections the religious authorities gave the voters a genuine choice of presidential candidates and they shockingly chose (in a landslide) a moderate reformist, Mohammed Khatami. Khatami carefully maneuvered for moderate reforms in the face of Islamic clerical opposition, opening non-governmental dialogue with the American "great Satan", quietly replacing provincial governors with reformers, and reining in secret police agents. In Feb. 1999, the religious leaders permitted the first local elections in twenty years: Khatami's new party, swept all 15 seats in the Tehran city council, winning large victories nationwide.

In July 1999, a militant Islamic group attacked pro-democracy students in Tehran, killing several. Student demonstrations against the government erupted in many cities across the country and in Tehran the police dispersed the crowd with severe violence after students attacked buildings and burned cars. Pres. Khatami condemned the riots, leaving questions about the future of reform.

In Feb. 2000 parliamentary elections, voters gave about two-thirds of the seats in the 290-seat Majlis to reformers. But authorities closed most reform newspapers. In June 2001, Khatami won a landslide victory for re-election but his all his reforms were rejected by the Council of Guardians and all demonstrations violently suppressed. In the wake of the Sept. 11th attacks on the U.S., Pres. Bush included Iran in the "axis of evil" that threatened civilization. In 2003 the U.S. accused Iran of trying to develop nuclear weapons. The U.N.'s International Atomic Energy Agency inspected Iran's nuclear program and found no evidence of weapons development, but in 2004 it accused Iran of providing false information and of making reactor parts that could be used to enrich uranium. The U.S. and Europe continued to pressure Iran about its nuclear plans but no action was taken. In June 2005 Mahmoud Ahmadinejad, the popular mayor of Tehran, was elected president and he immediately began attacking Israel's existence, the U.S. occupation of Iraq, and pressing ahead with Iran's search for nuclear power. He has subsequently tempered his speech but the nuclear program continued to develop despite threats of severe sanctions from the U.S. and the E.U. (See "Major News Stories.")

▶ IRAQ
Republic of Iraq

• **GEOGRAPHY** **Location:** western Asia with narrow outlet to Persian (Arabian) Gulf. **Boundaries:** Turkey to N, Iran to E, Saudi Arabia and Kuwait to S, Syria and Jordan to W. **Total area:** 168,754 sq. mi. (437,072 sq km). **Coastline:** 36 mi. (58 km). **Comparative area:** slightly more than twice the size of Idaho. **Land use:** 12% arable land; 1% permanent crops; 87% other. **Major cities:** Baghdad (capital); Basra (Basia); Mosul; Kirkuk.

• **PEOPLE** **Population:** 28,211,181 (July 2008 est.). **Nationality:** noun—Iraqi(s); adjective—Iraqi. **Ethnic groups:** 75-80% Arab, 15-20% Kurdish, 5% Turkoman, Assyrian, and other. **Languages:** Arabic (official), Kurdish (official in Kurdish areas), Assyrian, Armenian. **Religions:** 97% Muslim (60-65% Shi'a, 32-37% Sunni), 3% Christian and other.

• **GOVERNMENT** **Type:** in transition. **Independence:** Oct. 3, 1932 (from League of Nations mandate under British administration). **Constitution:** in transition. **National holiday:** Anniversary of the Revolution, July 17. **Heads of Government:** Jalal Talabani, president (since Apr. 2005); Nuri al-Maliki, prime minister (since May 2006). **Structure:** executive; unicameral legislature (National Assembly)—Kurdish assembly elected in Kurdish areas, but unrecognized by Baghdad.

• **ECONOMY** **Monetary unit:** Iraqi dinar. **Budget:** (2008 est.) *income:* $42.3 bil.; *expend.:* $48.4 bil. **G.D.P.:** $100 bil., $3,600 per capita (2007 est.). **Chief crops:** wheat, barley, rice, cotton; cattle, sheep. **Natural resources:** crude oil, natural gas, phosphates, sulphur. **Major industries:** petroleum, chemicals, textiles, construction materials. **Labor force:** 7.4 mil. (2004); 48% services, 30% agriculture, 22% industry; 18-30% unemployment (2006). **Exports:** $34.04 bil. (2007 est.); crude oil. **Imports:** $23.09 bil. (2007 est.); food, medicine, manufactures. **Major trading partners:** (2006) *exports:* 46.7% U.S., 10.7% Italy, 6.2% Canada; *imports:* 26.5% Syria, 20.5% Turkey, 11.8% U.S., 7.2% Jordan.

The fertile lands of Mesopotamia, between the Tigris and Euphrates rivers, were the site of one of the world's oldest civilizations. The city-states of Sumer were founded before 3000 B.C. and later became the heart of the Babylonian empire. Babylon became subject to the Assyrian empire after 1350 B.C. and was conquered by the Persians under Cyrus and Darius in the mid-sixth century B.C. Mesopotamia remained under the control of various Persian dynasties for the next 1,000 years.

In the seventh century A.D., the region was rapidly incorporated into the expanding Islamic world. The battle of Basra in 656 decisively established Arab control. In 762 the Caliphate, the center of Islamic rule, was moved from Damascus to the newly founded city of Baghdad, near the ruins of ancient Babylon. Mongol invaders sacked Baghdad in 1258 and destroyed its irrigation works; thereafter the region entered a period of long-term decline. Baghdad fell to the Ottoman Turks in 1534, and Iraq remained a province of the Ottoman Empire until the 20th century.

British troops occupied Iraq in 1915, and Great Britain governed the country under a League of

Nations mandate after World War I. A Hashemite monarchy was organized under British protection in 1921. The kingdom of Iraq was granted independence in 1932 but remained closely tied to Great Britain by treaties guaranteeing British interests in petroleum and regional defense. Iraqi oil flowed through British-controlled pipelines traversing Jordan to Haifa (in Israel) and through a French-controlled pipeline traversing Syria.

After 1932 several attempted coups by anti-British factions were put down with the aid of British troops. One such coup in April 1941 sought aid from Italy and Germany; British troops landed at Basra in May and restored the pro-British monarchy. Iraq declared war against the Axis powers in 1943. In 1948 Iraq joined the Arab League and participated in the first Arab-Israeli War. Most of Iraq's 85,000 Jews emigrated to Israel after the war ended.

In 1952 a new agreement with Great Britain gave the Iraq Petroleum Company greater control over the country's oil. While remaining part of the Arab League, Iraq in 1955 broke ties with Egypt and expelled the Soviet ambassador and signed a mutual defense treaty with Turkey.

A pan-Arab revolutionary coup overthrew the monarchy in 1958 and established a republic, reversing Iraq's former pro-Western stance in international affairs. Oil resources were nationalized, and large landholdings were broken up. In 1968 a local branch of the international Ba'ath Socialist party came to power and established rule by decree within the republican framework of government. In 1972 the Soviet Union sent arms and advisers to Iraq. In the 1973 Arab-Israeli War, Iraq sent troops to aid Syrian forces.

Iranian aid to a long-standing Kurdish rebellion in Iraq's northern mountains strained relations between the two countries. The Kurds were defeated in a bloody campaign in 1975, though the rebellion continued, leading to Iraq's bombing of Kurdish villages in 1979 and other incidents.

The execution of 21 alleged Communist conspirators in 1978 disrupted relations between Iraq and the U.S.S.R. Trade relations with the West were resumed. On July 16, 1979, Gen. Saddam Hussein at-Takriti assumed control of the government and purged leftist elements in the Ba'ath movement.

Several months of fighting in 1980 between Iraq and Iran for control of the Shatt al-Arab waterway in southern Iraq led to the outbreak of open warfare on Sept. 22, when each country launched bombing attacks on the other's cities. Warfare quickly spread along the entire Iraq-Iran border. The Iran-Iraq War produced eight years of fierce but generally stalemated fighting, with reports of the use of poison gas by both sides. On June 7, 1981, Israeli war planes destroyed a nuclear reactor near Baghdad, claiming it was capable of producing nuclear weapons. The war spread to the gulf in 1984, as both Iran and Iraq attacked tankers using each other's ports.

On May 17, 1987, the *USS Stark*, an American frigate on station in the gulf, was struck by missiles fired by an Iraqi fighter; 37 American sailors were killed. Iraq claimed that the attack was inadvertent and apologized to the United States. In Sept. 1988, a U.N. conference led to a cease-fire in the Iran-Iraq War. Refugees in Turkey reported that poison gas had been used against Kurdish villages in northeastern Iraq as the Kurdish rebellion there continued. During 1989-90 Iraq's repressive internal policies and arms buildup provoked international criticism. Iraqi agents were caught attempting to smuggle components of nuclear weapons from the U.S. and Great Britain.

On Aug. 2, 1990, 120,000 Iraqi troops invaded and later annexed neighboring Kuwait. The invasion was met with universal disapproval, led by the U.N. Security Council, and U.S. troops were deployed to Saudi Arabia to defend it against a possible invasion. Coalition forces totaled 500,000 troops from 13 countries. After a six-week air war that destroyed most of Iraq's military capabilities and much of the country's infrastructure, Allied ground forces liberated Kuwait and occupied much of southern Iraq in only four days. Emboldened by the proximity of such overwhelming force, Kurds and Shiites in Iraq began a civil war that was put down with surprising speed and resulted in the displacement of hundreds of thousands of refugees to Turkey and Iran.

During 1992 Saddam Hussein solidified his hold on the military and remained in total control of the nation. However, U.N. inspectors discovered his secret plans to build nuclear weapons, and he was forced to destroy the program.

Throughout 1992-93 American warplanes provided protection for Kurdish areas in the north and Shiite Muslim areas in the southern marshlands. U.N. arms inspectors continued to press for access to Iraqi weapons plants and military research centers. On June 19, 1993, American missiles destroyed the Baghdad headquarters of Iraq's military intelligence service, in retaliation for a 1992 Iraq-backed plot to assassinate Pres. George Bush.

In Nov. 1994 Iraq formally recognized the sovereignty and territorial integrity of Kuwait. Nonetheless, the U.N. retained sanctions against Iraq until two conditions were met: destroying its stockpiles of weapons of mass destruction and improving its treatment of minorities. In May 1996 the U.N. agreed to ease sanctions on Iraq, permitting the sale of $2 billion worth of oil to purchase food and medical supplies. In late 1997 Iraq reneged on its agreement to allow U.N. weapons inspectors free access to all sites causing new tension in the region. Hussein's on-again, off-again cooperation with international inspection teams climaxed in the Dec. 1998 U.S./U.K. air strikes against Iraq. U.S. and U.K. patrols in the "no fly" zones regularly clashed with Iraqi MIGs. After the Security Council decision to review all aspects of U.N.-Iraqi relations in Jan. 1999, U.S. influence was further diminished by revelations that its intelligence agents had infiltrated the U.N. Special Commission and used UNSCOM to spy on Iraq. Three compromise recommendations by U.N. panels now met Iraqi rejection in April.

Iraq continuously rejected U.N. arms-monitoring schemes unless sanctions were lifted first. Yet, "oil-for-food" sales continued through 2001. Iraqi overtures (May 2002) and invitations to the U.N. to resume arms inspections came with conditions evoking a negative response and a serious threat of war by the U.S. On March 19, 2003 the U.S., Britain, and several smaller nations launched a devastating attack on Baghdad and in only 43 days took over the country. The ensuing occupation proved less manageable. Although nominal authority was turned over to an interim government in June 2004, the U.S. had 130,000 troops battling Muslim insurgents every day in several regions. By Aug. 2005 nearly 2000 Americans had died, 12,000 had been severely wounded and troops complained openly of lack of body armor. The U.S. pushed for elections in early 2005 and Iraqis turned out in large numbers. A draft constitution drawn up with U.S. guidance did not win Sunni approval but was ratified by the people in Oct. 2005. In December, an election was peacefully held and a 275-member Council of Representatives was put in office. In 2006 the insurgency and the growing violence between the Sunnis and the Shiites exploded. By the end of the year, over 3,000 Americans were dead, 20,000 seriously wounded. By mid-2007 over 2 million Iraqis had left the country and a large percentage were displaced within the country. U.S. casulties passed 4,000 and there seemed no end in sight. Bush and the military then sent in 30,000 additional troops and began to pay large sums of money to Sunni militias and the violence quickly diminshed in a meaningful way. The Iraqi government could not take advantage, however, as now the political infighting intensified. (See "Major News Stories.")

▶ IRELAND

• **GEOGRAPHY   Location:** 26 of 32 counties comprising island of Ireland, in North Atlantic Ocean. Dublin 53°20′N, 6°15′W. **Boundaries:** Northern Ireland (U.K.) to N, Great Britain 50 mi (80 km) to E. **Total area:** 27,135 sq. mi. (70,280 sq km). **Coastline:** 900 mi. (1,448 km). **Comparative area:** slightly larger than W. Virginia. **Land use:** 20% arable land; negl. % permanent crops; 80% other. **Major cities:** Dublin (capital); Cork; Limerick; Galway; Waterford.
• **PEOPLE   Population:** 4,156,119 (July 2008 est.). **Nationality:** noun—Irishman (men), Irishwoman (women), Irish (collective pl.); adjective—Irish. **Ethnic groups:** Celtic, with English minority. **Languages:** Irish (Gaelic) and English (official); English widely spoken. **Religions:** 88.4% Roman Catholic, 3.2% Church of Ireland, 3.2% other, 3.5% none.
• **GOVERNMENT   Type:** republic. **Independence:** Dec. 6, 1921 (from U.K.). **Constitution:** Dec. 29, 1937. **National holiday:** St. Patrick's Day, Mar. 17. **Heads of Government:** Mary McAleese, president (since Oct. 1997); Brian Cowen, prime minister (since May 2008). **Structure:** executive; bicameral parliament (Seanad, Dail); judiciary appointed by president on advice of government.
• **ECONOMY   Monetary unit:** euro. **Budget:** (2008) *income:* $93.85 bil.; *expend.:* $91.07 bil. **G.D.P.:** $187.5 bil., $45,600 per capita (2007 est.) **Chief crops:** turnips, barley, potatoes, sugar beets, wheat; meat, dairy. **Natural resources:** zinc, lead, natural gas, barite, copper. **Major industries:** food products, brewing, textiles, clothing. **Labor force:** 2.21 mil. (2007 est.); 67% services, 27% industry, 6% agriculture (2006); 4.5% unemployment (2001). **Exports:** $124.8 bil. (f.o.b., 2007); chemicals, computers, industrial machinery. **Imports:** $90.34 bil. (f.o.b., 2007 est.); data processing equipment, chemicals, petroleum and petroleum products. **Major trading partners:** (2006) *exports:* 18.7% U.S., 17.9% U.K., 14.4% Belgium, 7.8% Germany, 5.8% France, 4.2% Italy; *imports:* 37.5% U.K., 11.5% U.S., 9.6% Germany, 4.6% Netherlands.

Ireland, a collection of warring Celtic chieftainships, was converted to Christianity by St. Patrick in the fifth century. Over the next two centuries, Ireland became a great center of monastic Christianity, sending missionaries to Scotland, England, and the Continent. While the Roman Empire decayed, Ireland was a center of peace, culture, and learning. Viking invasions in the ninth and 10th centuries caused substantial damage and overturned the rule of the great monasteries and their secular allies. By the time an Irish monarchy was reestablished by Brian Boru in 1014 and the surviving invaders were integrated into Irish society, Ireland had become an isolated, poor backwater on the periphery of Europe.

Trade gave rise to English commercial interests in Ireland and to Henry II's claim to overlordship of Ireland in the 12th century. Henry VIII declared himself king of Ireland and introduced the Reformation there. Large-scale Scottish immigration to Ulster began during the reign of Elizabeth I. Penal laws were applied, banning Catholics from public life and making the Mass an act of treason. A rebellion in 1641 was crushed by Oliver Cromwell, ending with a massacre of thousands of Irish at Drogheda. After William of Orange's "Glorious Revolution" of 1688, the Irish supported James II, who was defeated at the Battle of the Boyne in 1690.

Following these events, British economic sanctions destroyed Ireland's flourishing export trade in wool. "Plantations" were established by British and Scottish Presbyterian landlords and farmers on lands seized from Irish Catholics. Much of the native aristocracy fled into exile, and the Gaelic language declined to near extinction.

A separate Irish Parliament, dominated by the Anglo-Irish establishment, was instituted in 1782, but it had little power. In 1798 a popular uprising led by Wolfe Tone, with inspiration and aid from revolutionary France, was put down with great loss of life. In 1800 Ireland and England were joined by the Act of Union, whereby Ireland was ineffectively represented in the British Parliament. After popular agitation led by Daniel O'Connell, the Catholic Emancipation Act was enacted by Parliament in 1829, though mandatory tithes continued to support the established Anglican church until 1869.

Under absentee landlords, the Irish population was reduced to a subsistence diet based largely on potatoes. When a potato blight struck the country in the 1840's, disaster ensued. Between 1846 and 1851, one million people starved to death, and 1.6 million emigrated, most to America.

In the late 19th century, a home-rule movement under Charles Stewart Parnell won wide popular support. A Home Rule Act finally was passed by Parliament in 1914, but its effect was postponed for the duration of World War I. The Land Purchase Acts of the early 20th century enabled dispossessed peasants to buy land from absentee landlords, creating a rural economic basis for an independent Ireland. The country's economy, based largely on agriculture and pasturage, began to recover. (Industry, principally shipbuilding and textiles, was largely confined to Northern Ireland.)

The postponement of home rule led to the Easter Rebellion of 1916; brutally suppressed, it was followed by the "Troubles," a period of guerrilla warfare lasting to 1920. In that year the Government of Ireland Act established six of Ulster's nine counties as Northern Ireland, an integral part of the United Kingdom but with its own home-rule Parliament. The south's refusal of similar status led to the passage on Dec. 11, 1922, of the Irish Free State Act, by which Ireland became an independent dominion within the British Commonwealth.

The Fine Gael (People of Ireland) party governed until 1932, when Eamon De Valera, as the head of the Fianna Fail (Soldiers of Destiny) party, was elected president, holding that office until 1948. In 1938 the Constitution was revised to sever all connections with the British government except for an "external association" with the British monarchy. The outlawed Irish Republican Army (I.R.A.) pressed for forcible reunification of Ireland and carried out attacks on British interests in both Ireland and Northern Ireland.

Ireland remained neutral during World War II, and its government objected to British military activities in Northern Ireland. But it was generally sympathetic to the Allied war effort, especially after the United States entered the war in 1941.

In 1949 Ireland severed all ties to the British Crown, becoming a fully independent republic. The Fianna Fail won a majority in the republic's first elections, and De Valera became prime minister. In 1954 a coalition government under John Costello took power. De Valera was elected president of the republic in 1959.

During the 1950's, Ireland developed a moderate welfare state with the support of both the Fianna Fail and Fine Gael. In the 1960's attention turned to industrial development: zinc and lead mining, and export-oriented production of textiles, ceramics, and machinery. Ireland was admitted to the E.C. in 1973.

Beginning in the late 1960's, civil rights demonstrations led frequently to civil disorders and an increase in I.R.A. guerrilla activity in the north. While the 1970's were a boom period for the Irish Republic, sectarian violence and terrorism in the north left over 2,500 dead. The 1980's saw the establishment of an Anglo-Irish Intergovernmental Council (1981) and the Hillsborough accords (1985) between the Thatcher government and the Fine Gael-Labour coalition, which gave Ireland a consultative role in Northern Irish disputes.

The government of Charles Haughey, leader of Fianna Fail, elected in 1987, faced economic problems, including high inflation and unemployment, forcing Haughey to form a coalition government in the spring of 1989. After serious losses in June 1991 local elections, and amid charges of corruption, Haughey resigned in 1992. His successor, Albert Reynolds, faced a deep recession with unemployment rates of about 20 percent. In June 1992, a national vote strongly supported the E.C.'s Maastricht Treaty. Reynolds' coalition fell in Nov. 1992, but he created a new coalition between Fianna Fail and Labour.

In 1993, Reynolds and U.K. prime minister John Major announced the "Downing Street Declaration" that Sinn Fein, the political arm of the I.R.A., would be invited to participate in negotiations on Northern Ireland in return for the I.R.A.'s promise to halt terrorism and violence. In 1994, the I.R.A. announced a cease-fire in its 25-year-old effort to expel British troops from Northern Ireland.

Preliminary talks began optimistically, but bogged down over the British demand that the I.R.A. disarm and the I.R.A. demand that Britain withdraw its forces from Ulster. In 1996, the I.R.A. announced an end to the 17-month-old cease-fire less than an hour before setting off a powerful bomb in East London, injuring 100 people. And in June, an even stronger bomb exploded in Manchester, injuring 200 and casting serious doubt on Sinn Fein leader Gerry Adams's ability to control the more militant members of his party.

Meanwhile, Ireland's governing coalition fell in Nov. 1995, and was replaced by an odd coalition with John Bruton of Fine Gael as prime minister. The new government passed legislation permitting Irish doctors to provide information about foreign abortion providers and sponsored a referendum that overturned the consitutional ban on divorce with remarriage. The Dail elections of 1997 brought a new coalition of Fianna Fail and the Progressive Democrats with Fianna Fail's Bertie Ahern as prime minister.

In April 1998 came the breakthrough agreement (overwhelmingly approved in referendums in Northern Ireland and the Republic in May): extensive home rule in a Northern Ireland remaining part of the U.K. with some Republic of Ireland participation and with all paramilitary groups disarmed. When the deadline of Feb. 1, 2000 came and went without the I.R.A. or any other armed group disarming, Great Britain suspended the government that had been functioning for only 10 weeks (since Dec. 2). But when the I.R.A. in May pledged to put its arms "beyond use" and permit inspections, the Ulster Unionist Party accepted and the new government was functioning again by May 29. On July 26, the inspectors reported to Tony Blair that inspections had begun and that arms dumps were secure against use. Yet the refusal of the I.R.A. and other paramilitary groups to disarm led (on July 1, 2001) to the resignation of Protestant leader David Trimble as first minister, once again jeopardizing the peace accord.

But Trimble and the U.U.P. returned with confirmation that the I.R.A. had decommissioned some weapons although any joy was marred by militia violence in Belfast. In the Republic, Fianna Fail became the first ruling party since 1969 to win reelection. In the spring of 2003 the issue of I.R.A. disarmament again caused Britain to suspend the Northern Assembly yet again. Elections in the North in Nov. 2003 proved divisive as Protestant hard liners took the most seats. Trimble stopped negotiating in March 2004. In July 2005 the I.R.A. vowed to end its military struggle for a united Ireland yet Protestants remained skeptical. Finally in May 2007 Gerry Adams of Sinn Fein and the hardline Protestant leader, the Rev. Ian Paisley agreed to work together in governing the province. Bertie Ahern won reelection yet again as Ireland's economy continued its astonishing growth. In 2008, Ahern chose to resign over a problem with his finances.

▶ ISRAEL
State of Israel

● **GEOGRAPHY   Location:** western Asia, on eastern shore of Mediterranean Sea; has outlet to Red Sea via Gulf of Aqaba. **Boundaries:** Lebanon to N, Syria to NE, Jordan to E, Egypt to SW, Mediterranean Sea to W. **Total area:** 8,019 sq. mi. (20,770 sq km). **Coastline:** 170 mi. (273 km). **Comparative area:** slightly smaller than New Jersey. **Land use:** 17% arable land; 4% permanent crops; 79% other. **Major cities:** Jerusalem (capital); Tel Aviv-Jaffa; Haifa; Holon; Petach-Tikva.

● **PEOPLE   Population:** 7,112,359 (July 2008 est.). **Nationality:** noun—Israeli(s); adjective—Israeli. **Ethnic groups:** 76.4% Jewish, 23.6% non-Jewish (mostly Arab). **Languages:** Hebrew (official), Arab (official for Arab minority); English most widely used foreign language. **Religions:** 76.4% Judaism, 16% Islam (mostly Sunni Muslim), 1.7% Arab Christian, 0.4% other Christian, 1.6% Druze, 3.9% unspecified.

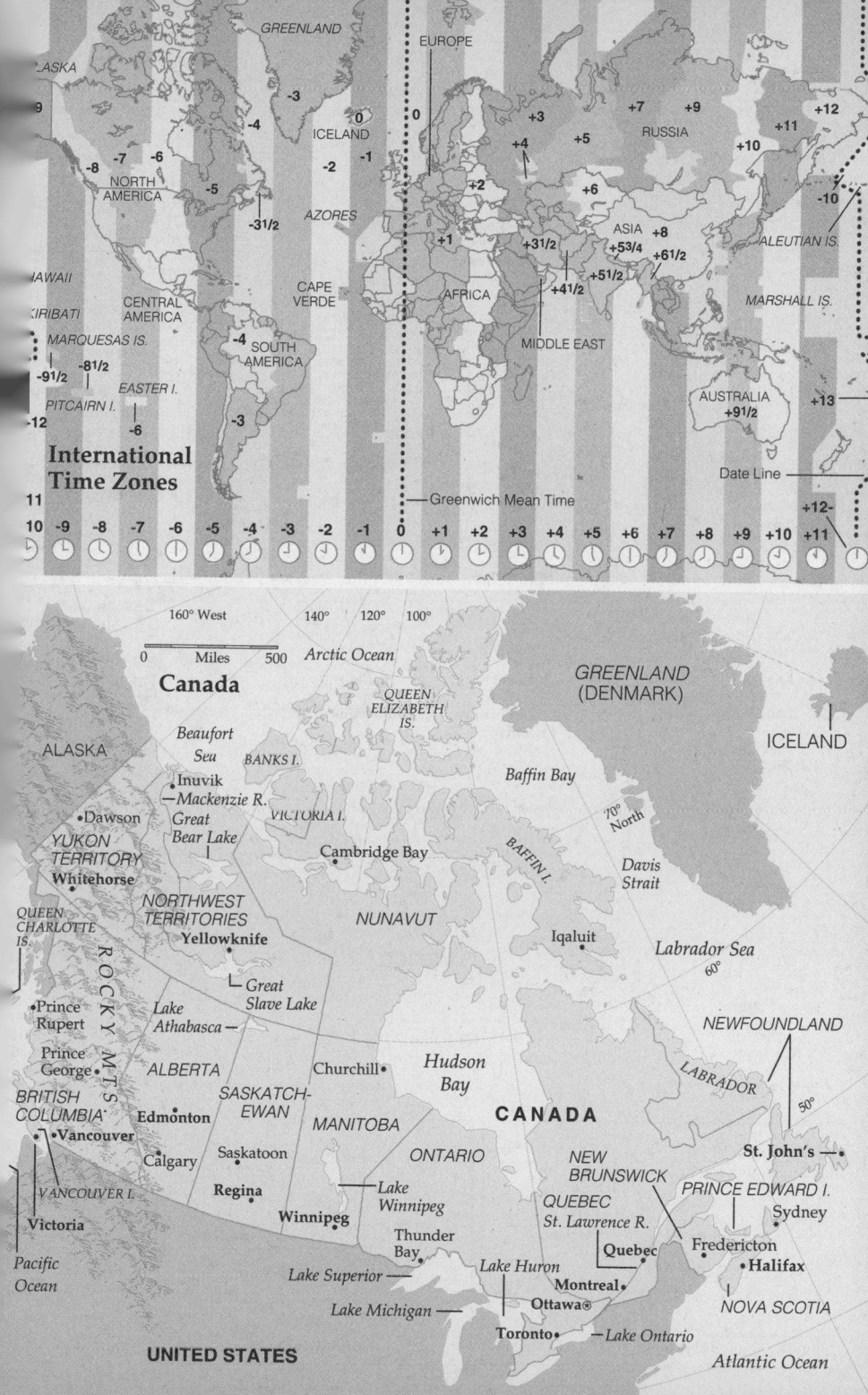

International Time Zones

GREENLAND
EUROPE
-3
0
ICELAND
+3   +7   +9   +12
-4   +4   +5   RUSSIA   +11
-8 -7 -6   +10
NORTH
AMERICA   -5   -2 -1   +2   -10
-31/2   AZORES   +1   +31/2 ASIA +8   ALEUTIAN IS.
                              +53/4
CAPE   +6 +61/2
HAWAII   VERDE
CENTRAL   AFRICA   +41/2 +51/2   MARSHALL IS.
KIRIBATI   AMERICA   -4 SOUTH
MARQUESAS IS.   AMERICA   MIDDLE EAST
-91/2 -81/2
PITCAIRN I. EASTER I.   AUSTRALIA   +13
-12   -6   +91/2
-3

**International
Time Zones**

Date Line

11   — Greenwich Mean Time

| 10 | -9 | -8 | -7 | -6 | -5 | -4 | -3 | -2 | -1 | 0 | +1 | +2 | +3 | +4 | +5 | +6 | +7 | +8 | +9 | +10 | +11 | +12- |

160° West   140°   120°   100°
0   Miles   500   Arctic Ocean

Canada

GREENLAND
(DENMARK)

QUEEN
ELIZABETH
IS.

ICELAND

ALASKA

Beaufort
Sea   BANKS I.   Baffin Bay

Inuvik
Mackenzie R.
Dawson   Great
Bear Lake   VICTORIA I.   70°
YUKON   North
TERRITORY   Cambridge Bay   BAFFIN I.   Davis
Whitehorse   Strait

QUEEN   NORTHWEST
CHARLOTTE   TERRITORIES   NUNAVUT
IS.   Yellowknife   Iqaluit   Labrador Sea   60°

Prince   Great
Rupert   Lake   Slave Lake   NEWFOUNDLAND
Prince   Athabasca   LABRADOR
George   ALBERTA   Churchill   Hudson
BRITISH   SASKATCH-   Bay   50°
COLUMBIA   Edmonton   EWAN   MANITOBA   CANADA   St. John's
Vancouver   ONTARIO   NEW   PRINCE EDWARD I.
Calgary   Saskatoon   BRUNSWICK   Sydney
VANCOUVER I.   Regina   Lake   QUEBEC
Victoria   Winnipeg   Winnipeg   St. Lawrence R.   Fredericton
Pacific   Thunder   Quebec   Halifax
Ocean   Bay   Lake Huron   Montreal   NOVA SCOTIA
Lake Superior   Ottawa
Lake Michigan   Toronto   Lake Ontario   Atlantic Ocean

UNITED STATES

CANADA

Gulf of St. Lawrence

International Falls
MINN.
Grand Rapids
Duluth

Lake Superior

Marquette

Sault Ste. Marie
Lake Huron

Houlton

MAINE • Bangor

Montpelier
Burlington

⊛Augusta
Brunswick

WISCONSIN   MICHIGAN
Minneapolis
Green Bay
Eau Claire
St. Paul
La Crosse
Rochester

Lake Michigan

L. Ontario
Syracuse
Rochester
Buffalo

VT. N.H.

N.Y.

MASS.
CONN.

CAPE COD

40° North

Milwaukee
Madison
Rockford
Chicago
Gary

Grand Rapids
Lansing ⊛
Detroit

L. Erie
Erie

Atlantic Ocean

Kalamazoo
Fort Wayne
South Bend

OHIO
Cleveland
Akron

PENNSYLVANIA
Harrisburg
Pittsburgh

Hagerstown

N.J.
DEL.

Area of detail

R.I.

Waterloo
Dubuque
Des Moines
IOWA
Cedar Rapids
Burlington
Peoria

Springfield
Decatur
Muncie
Columbus
Dayton
Cincinnati
Clarksburg

Wheeling
Washington
D.C.

MD.

Kansas City
Quincy
Columbia
St. Louis
ILLINOIS
Evansville
Frankfort
Louisville

Indianapolis
INDIANA

Huntington
Lexington

Charleston
W.VA.

Richmond
Newport News
Norfolk

Joplin
Jefferson City
MISSOURI
Springfield

Paducah
Bowling Green

KENTUCKY

VIRGINIA
Roanoke
Lynchburg

Greensboro
Durham
Raleigh

NORTH CAROLINA

Fayetteville
ARKANSAS
Fort Smith
Little Rock
Hot Springs
Pine Bluff
Texarkana

Nashville
Memphis
Chattanooga

TENNESSEE
Knoxville
Asheville

Winston-Salem

Charlotte

Fayetteville
Wilmington

Oxford
Decatur
Huntsville
Birmingham
Tuscaloosa

Greenville
Spartanburg

Columbia
SOUTH CAROLINA

United States:
Political

MISSISSIPPI
Monroe
Vicksburg
Shreveport
Jackson
Meridian
ALABAMA
Hattiesburg
LOUISIANA

Atlanta
Augusta
Macon

GEORGIA

Charleston
Savannah
Brunswick

30°

Baton Rouge
Lake Charles
Beaumont
Lafayette
New Orleans

Dothan
Mobile
Biloxi
Pensacola
Montgomery
Albany

Tallahassee ⊛
Panama City
Gainesville
FLORIDA

Jacksonville

Daytona Beach
Orlando

VERMONT
Glens Falls
Rutland
Concord
N.H.
Portland
Portsmouth

Gulf of Mexico

Tampa
St. Petersburg
Sarasota
Fort Myers

West Palm Beach
Fort Lauderdale
Miami

80°

Schenectady
Brattleboro
Albany
Pittsfield
NEW YORK
Springfield

Manchester
Lowell
Boston
MASS.
Worcester
Providence
CONN.
Hartford
R.I.

Key West

Kingston
Binghamton

Newburgh

New London
Newport

90° West

MEXICO

CUBA

20°

Scranton
Paterson
Newark
Allentown
Philadelphia
PA.
Camden

New Haven
New York City
Princeton
Trenton
NEW JERSEY
Atlantic City

Wilmington
Baltimore
Dover
DELAWARE
Annapolis
Salisbury
MARYLAND

70°

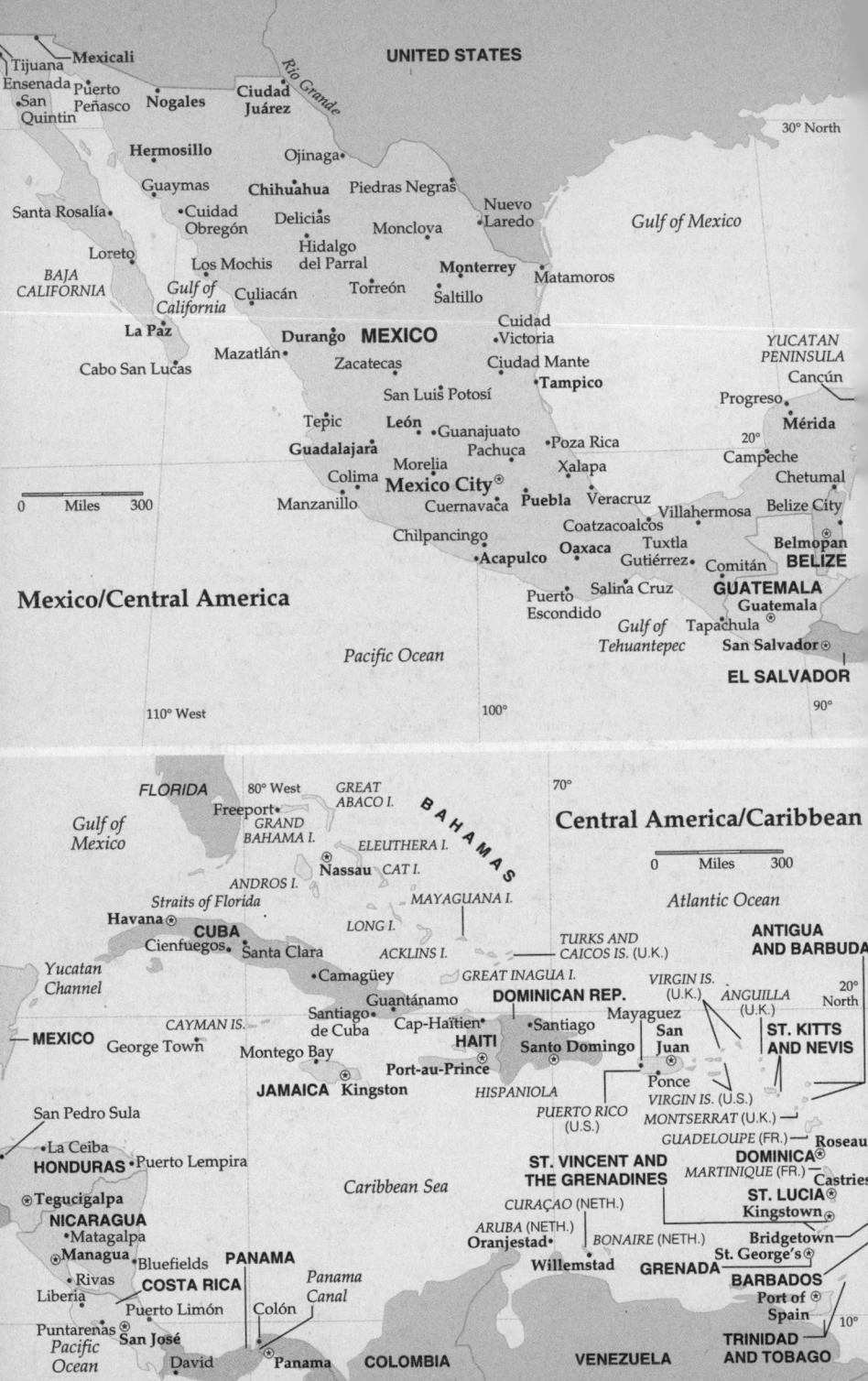

Mexico/Central America

UNITED STATES

Tijuana • Mexicali
Ensenada
San • Puerto • Nogales
Quintin • Peñasco

Rio Grande

Ciudad
Juárez

30° North

Hermosillo • Ojinaga

Guaymas • Chihuahua • Piedras Negras

Santa Rosalía • Cuidad • Delicias • Nuevo
Obregón • Laredo

Loreto • Los Mochis • Hidalgo • Monclova
del Parral

BAJA • Culiacán • Torreón • **Monterrey** • Matamoros
CALIFORNIA *Gulf of* • Saltillo
California

Gulf of Mexico

*YUCATAN
PENINSULA*

La Paz • **Durango** • **MEXICO** • Cuidad
Victoria • Cancún
Mazatlán • Zacatecas • Ciudad Mante • Progreso
Cabo San Lucas • San Luis Potosí • **Tampico** • **Mérida**

Tepic • **León** • Guanajuato • Poza Rica • Campeche
Guadalajara • Pachuca • 20° • Chetumal
Morelia • Xalapa
0 Miles 300 • Colima • **Mexico City** ⊙ • Belize City
Manzanillo • Cuernavaca • **Puebla** • Veracruz • Villahermosa
• Coatzacoalcos • **Belmopan**
Chilpancingo • Oaxaca • Tuxtla • Comitán • **BELIZE**
• **Acapulco** • Gutiérrez
• Salina Cruz • **GUATEMALA**
Puerto • Escondido • **Guatemala** ⊙
Gulf of • Tapachula
Pacific Ocean • *Tehuantepec* • **San Salvador** ⊙
• **EL SALVADOR**

110° West • 100° • 90°

Central America/Caribbean

FLORIDA • 80° West • *GREAT
ABACO I.* • 70°
Gulf of • Freeport • *GRAND
Mexico* • *BAHAMA I.* • *B A H A M A S*
• *ELEUTHERA I.*
ANDROS I. • Nassau • *CAT I.* • 0 Miles 300
Straits of Florida • *MAYAGUANA I.* • Atlantic Ocean
Havana ⊙ • *LONG I.* • **ANTIGUA
CUBA** • *ACKLINS I.* • *TURKS AND* • **AND BARBUDA**
Cienfuegos • Santa Clara • *CAICOS IS.* (U.K.)
Yucatan • Camagüey • *GREAT INAGUA I.* • *VIRGIN IS.* • *ANGUILLA*
Channel • Guantánamo • **DOMINICAN REP.** • (U.K.) • (U.K.)
MEXICO • Santiago • Cap-Haïtien • Santiago • **ST. KITTS
** • *CAYMAN IS.* • de Cuba • Mayaguez • San • **AND NEVIS**
George Town • **HAITI** • Santo Domingo • Juan
Montego Bay • • Ponce
JAMAICA • **Port-au-Prince** • *HISPANIOLA* • *VIRGIN IS.* (U.S.)
San Pedro Sula • Kingston • *PUERTO RICO* • *MONTSERRAT* (U.K.)
• La Ceiba • (U.S.) • *GUADELOUPE* (FR.) • Roseau
HONDURAS • Puerto Lempira • **ST. VINCENT AND** • *MARTINIQUE* (FR.) • **DOMINICA**
Caribbean Sea • **THE GRENADINES** • • Castries
⊙ **Tegucigalpa** • *CURAÇAO* (NETH.) • **ST. LUCIA** ⊙
NICARAGUA • *ARUBA* (NETH.) • *BONAIRE* (NETH.) • Kingstown
• Matagalpa • Oranjestad • • Bridgetown
⊙ **Managua** • Bluefields • **PANAMA** • St. George's ⊙
• Rivas • **COSTA RICA** • Willemstad • **GRENADA** • **BARBADOS**
Liberia • Puerto Limón • *Panama
Canal* • **Panama** • **Port of** ⊙
Puntarenas ⊙ • Colón • Spain • 10°
Pacific • **San José** • David • **Panama** • **COLOMBIA** • **VENEZUELA** • **TRINIDAD
Ocean** • **AND TOBAGO**

Europe

Reykjavik ⊛

ICELAND

Norwegian Sea

Bodo •

60° North

FAROE IS.
(DENMARK)

• **Torshavn**

SHETLAND IS.

Trondheim
Alesund •

SWEDEN

Sundsvall

NORWAY

0   Miles   200

• Lerwick

Bergen

Gavle •

Bergen

ORKNEY IS.

Oslo ⊛

Uppsala •
Stockholm — ⊛

HEBRIDES
Inverness •

Stavanger

SCOTLAND

North Sea

Alborg •
Viborg •

Göteborg

15° West

N. IRELAND
Glasgow • • Edinburgh

Arhus •

Donegal

• Belfast

Sunderland

Vejle •

Copenhagen ⊛

IRELAND

Limerick •   Dublin ⊛
Cork •   Waterford

**UNITED
KINGDOM**

DENMARK

Hamburg •

Liverpool
• **Manchester**
Leeds •

NETHERLANDS

POLAND

WALES   **Birmingham** *ENGLAND*
Leicester •

Amsterdam •

GERMANY

Berlin •

Poznan •

Cardiff •

Ouse R.

The Hague •

*Atlantic
Ocean*

Plymouth •
Portsmouth

London •
Thames R.

• Rotterdam

Essen •

Cologne •

Leipzig •

Elbe R.

English Channel

Brussels •

Bonn •

Rhine R.

Prague •

**CZECH
REP.**

CHANNEL IS. (U.K.) <   • Le Havre

Luxembourg •

Frankfurt •

Brno •

• Brest

Seine R.

LUX.

Nürnberg •

BELGIUM

• Paris

Strasbourg •

Stuttgart •

Bratislava •

45°

Loire R.

Dijon •

Salzburg •

Munich •

Vienna ⊛

Nantes •

FRANCE

Bern ⊛

Zurich •

Vaduz (LIECH.)

AUSTRIA
Graz •

Bay of Biscay

Clermont-Ferrand •

Geneva • **SWITZERLAND**

Ljubljana •

La Coruña •

Bordeaux •

Lyons •

ALPS

Milan •
Po R.

Venice •

Zagreb •

Bilbao •

Bayonne •

SLOVENIA

Porto •

Duero R.

Toulouse •

Genoa •

CROATIA

Coimbra •

Valladolid •

Salamanca •

ANDORRA

PYRENEES
Zaragoza •

Nice •

Marseilles •

MONACO

SAN MARINO

Florence •

*Adriatic
Sea*

PORTUGAL

Ebro R.

Madrid •

Garonne R.

Rhône R.

APENNINES

ITALY

⊛ Lisbon

Tagus R.

Toledo •

Barcelona •

Rome ⊛

Bari —

SPAIN

Valencia •

MALLORCA

CORSICA (FR.)

Naples •

Córdoba •

Palma •

*SARDINIA
(ITALY)*

Guadalquivir R.

*BALEARIC IS.
(SPAIN)*

Palermo •

Seville •
Málaga •

IBIZA

Tyrrhenian Sea

15°

*Strait of
Gibraltar* —

• Gibraltar
(U.K.)

0°

Mediterranean Sea

SICILY
• Catania

MOROCCO

ALGERIA

TUNISIA

MALTA   Valletta

Nations of Former Soviet Union

Miles
0   500

U.K.
GER.
DEN.
NORWAY
SWEDEN
POL.
FINLAND
North Sea
Baltic Sea
Barents Sea
Arctic Circle
Arctic Ocean
Kara Sea
Laptev Sea
East Siberian Sea
Bering Sea

ESTONIA
Tallinn
LATVIA
Riga
LITHUANIA
Vilnius
Kaliningrad **RUSSIA**
BELARUS
Minsk
Pskov · St. Petersburg
Novgorod
Petrozavodsk · Archangel
Murmansk

NOVAYA ZEMLYA
FRANZ JOSEF LAND
NORTH LAND
NEW SIBERIAN IS.

RUSSIA

Smolensk Tver
Moscow
Vologda
Yaroslavl
Kostroma
Ivanovo
Sykty vkar
Vladimir
Nizhniy Kirov
Novgorod
Perm
Kaluga
Tula
Ryazan
Lipetsk
Orel
Tambov
Kursk
Penza
Kazan
Simbirsk
Voronezh
Saratov
Belgorod
Bryansk

MOLDOVA
Chisinau
Lviv
Khmelnitskiy
Kiev
UKRAINE
Dnepropetrovsk
Odessa
Sevastopol
Black Sea
Rostov
Volgograd
Stavropol
Astrakhan
Caspian Sea
Sokhumi
GEORGIA
Tbilisi
ARMENIA
Yerevan
Ganca
AZERBAIJAN
Baku
TURKEY
IRAQ
IRAN

Murmansk
Salekhard
Ob R.
Khanty-Mansiysk
Dudinka · Norilsk
Yenisei R.
Yekaterinburg
Tyumen
Chelyabinsk
Kurgan
Orenburg
Petropavlovsk
Omsk
Irtysh R.
Tomsk
Novosibirsk
Barnaul
Kemerovo
Krasnoyarsk
Abakan
Kyzyl
Oskemen
Semipalatinsk
S I B E R I A
Lena R.
Yakutsk
Lake Baikal
Ulan Ude
Irkutsk
Chita

Kolyma R.
Anadyr
Palana
KAMCHATKA PENINSULA
Petropavlovsk Kamchatskiy
Magadan
Sea of Okhotsk
KURILE IS.
SAKHALIN I.
Yuzhno-Sakhalinsk
Amur R.
Blagoveshchensk
Khabarovsk
Vladivostok
Sea of Japan
JAPAN
NORTH KOREA
SOUTH KOREA
Yellow Sea

MONGOLIA
CHINA

Guryev
Aktyubinsk
KAZAKHSTAN
Astana
Karaganda
Pavlodar
Lake Balkhash
Almaty
Bishkek
KYRGYZSTAN
Dzhambul
Osh
TAJIKISTAN
Dushanbe
Syr Darya R.
Kzyl-Orda
Aral
Aral Sea
Chimbay
Urganch
Bukhoro
Tashkent
Samarkand
UZBEKISTAN
Charjew
TURKMENISTAN
Ashgabat

40° 20° 60° 80° 100° 120° 140° 160°
180° East
80° North
70°
60°
50°

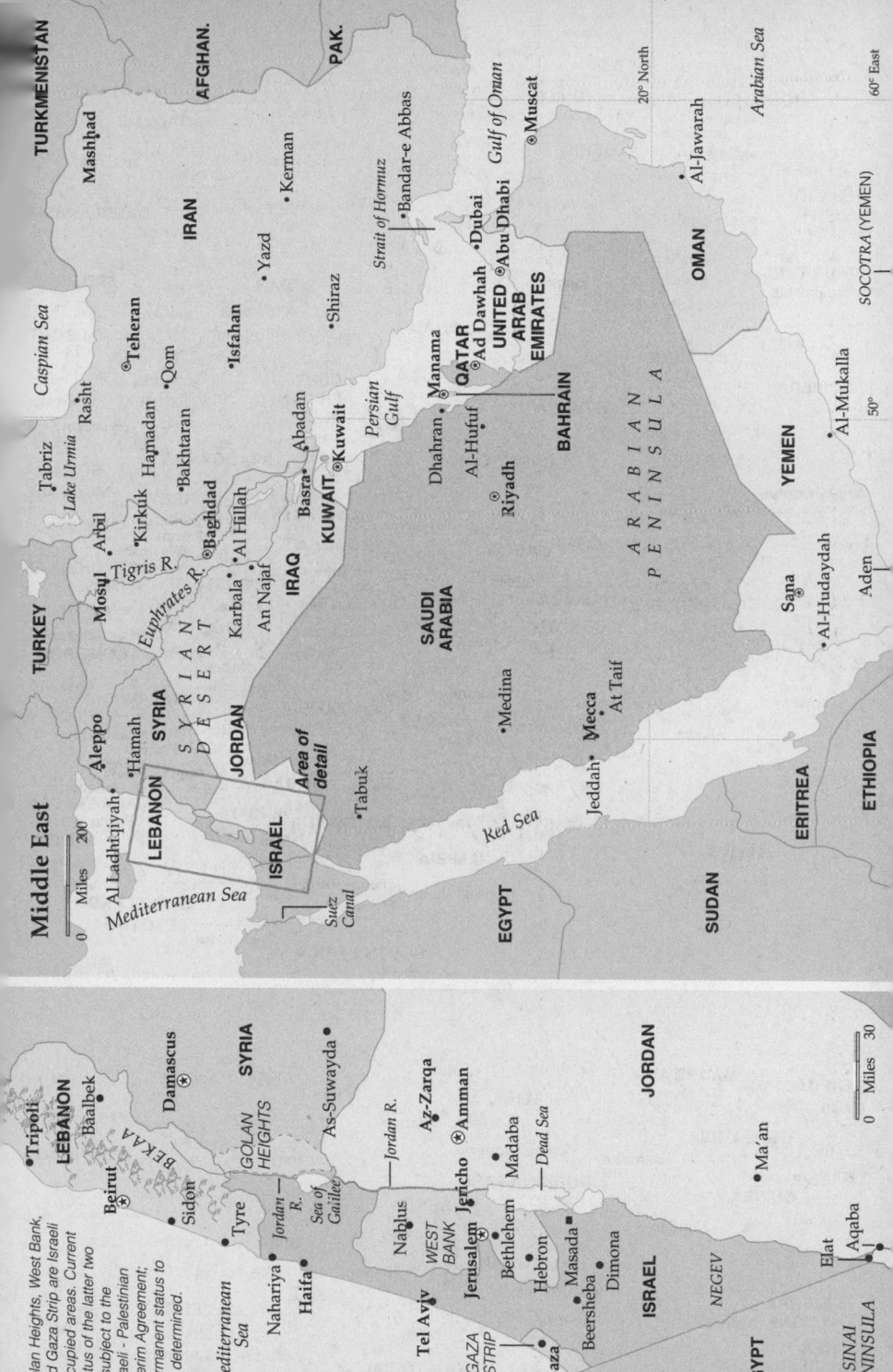

Middle East

0 Miles 200

Golan Heights, West Bank, and Gaza Strip are Israeli occupied areas. Current status of the latter two is subject to the Israeli - Palestinian Interim Agreement; permanent status to be determined.

TURKMENISTAN

AFGHAN.

PAK.

Mashhad

IRAN

Kerman

Teheran

Qom

Yazd

Isfahan

Shiraz

Tabriz

Lake Urmia

Rasht

Caspian Sea

Hamadan

Kirkuk

Bakhtaran

Arbil

Mosul

Tigris R.

Baghdad

Al Hillah

Euphrates R.

Karbala

An Najaf

IRAQ

Basra

Abadan

Persian Gulf

Kuwait

KUWAIT

Dhahran

Al-Hufuf

Riyadh

Strait of Hormuz

Bandar-e Abbas

Gulf of Oman

Dubai

Abu Dhabi

Ad Dawhah

Manama

QATAR

UNITED ARAB EMIRATES

BAHRAIN

Muscat

OMAN

Al-Jawarah

20° North

60° East

Arabian Sea

50°

Al-Mukalla

SOCOTRA (YEMEN)

ARABIAN PENINSULA

SAUDI ARABIA

Medina

Mecca

At Taif

Jeddah

Sana

Al-Hudaydah

Aden

YEMEN

Red Sea

TURKEY

Aleppo

Hamah

SYRIA

S Y R I A N   D E S E R T

JORDAN

Tabuk

Al Ladhiqiyah

LEBANON

ISRAEL

Area of detail

Mediterranean Sea

Suez Canal

EGYPT

SUDAN

ERITREA

ETHIOPIA

(Detail map)

0 Miles 30

Tripoli

LEBANON

Baalbek

Damascus

SYRIA

B E K A A

Beirut

Sidon

Tyre

Nahariya

Haifa

GOLAN HEIGHTS

As-Suwayda

Jordan R.

Sea of Galilee

Az-Zarqa

Amman

JORDAN

Mediterranean Sea

Tel Aviv

Nablus

WEST BANK

Jerusalem

Jericho

Madaba

Dead Sea

Jordan R.

Bethlehem

GAZA STRIP

Gaza

Hebron

Beersheba

Masada

Dimona

Ma'an

ISRAEL

NEGEV

Elat

Aqaba

EGYPT

SINAI PENINSULA

Tangier
Casablanca •Rabat
MOROCCO
Marrakesh
30° North
—CANARY ISLANDS (SPAIN)
•El Aaiun
WESTERN
SAHARA
(MOROCCO)
•Atar
MAURITANIA
⊕Nouakchott

Annaba
Batna •Tunis
Oran Gâfsa •Sfax
Algiers TUNISIA
Ouargla Tripoli
ALGERIA LIBYA
Timimoun
•Reggane
Taoudenni
Tessalit
•Araouane
Djanet

Mediterranean Sea
Benghazi
Misratah
Alexandria
Cairo
Beni Suef•
El-Minya•
Sabhah
Marzuq
Al Jawf
EGYPT
Aswan

LEBANON SYRIA
ISRAEL IRAQ
JORDAN
•Suez KUWAIT
SAUDI ARABIA

MALI
GUINEA
10°

BURKINA
FASO

NIGER
Bilma
Faya-Largeau

Taudenni
Tessalit

NIGERIA

CHAD

Port Sudan
SUDAN Atbara
Khartoum
El Fasher
CENT.
AFRICAN
REP.
Ndele

Asmara
Mekele
Addis
Ababa
Asela•
Goba•

Red
Sea ERITREA

DJIBOUTI
⊕Djibouti
Berbera

ETHIOPIA

CAMEROON

White Nile R.—
Bangassou
Congo R.
Bumba

Wau
Juba

Lake
Victoria
Kisangani

UGANDA
Gulu
Kampala

SOMALIA
Mogadishu

Kismayu

Area of detail

Equator

Mbandaka

Port-Gentil
CONGO
REPUBLIC
Pointe-Noire•

•Libreville
GABON
Brazzaville

CONGO
(ZAIRE)
•Kinshasa
Matadi
Luanda

RWANDA
Bujumbura•
•Kigali
BURUNDI
Lake
Tanganyika—
Kananga

Eldoret
Kisumu•
•Nairobi
KENYA

Tabora
Tanga•
TANZANIA
Kalemie

•Mombasa
ZANZIBAR

Dar es Salaam
COMOROS
⊕Moroni

SEYCHELLES

CABINDA
(ANGOLA)

10°

Atlantic Ocean

•Malange
Huambo•
ANGOLA
Lubango•

Likasi•
•Lubumbashi
ZAMBIA
Lusaka⊕
Mongu•

•Mbeya
Kasama•

MALAWI
Lilongwe⊕
—Zambezi R.

Antsiranana•
•Nampula

20°

Africa

0   Miles   500

Tsumeb•
Walvis Bay•
Windhoek⊕
NAMIBIA
Keetmanshoop•

Maun•
Gaborone⊕
BOTSWANA

ZIMBABWE
Bulawayo•
Harare•

Beira•
MOZAMBIQUE

Antananarivo⊕
MADAGASCAR
Fianarantsoa•
•Tuléar
Tolanaro•

Pietersburg•
Pretoria⊕ Maputo
Johannesburg•
Bloemfontein•
Mbabane⊕
SWAZILAND

30°

Kimberley•
Oudtshoorn
Cape Town⊕
10°   0°

Maseru⊕
SOUTH AFRICA
Umtata•
•Port Elizabeth
10°   20°

Durban
LESOTHO

East London
Indian Ocean

30°   40° East

SENEGAL
—Dakar
⊕
—Banjul
THE GAMBIA
⊕Bissau
GUINEA-
BISSAU

MAURITANIA
Kayes•
⊕Bamako
GUINEA
Conakry⊕
Kankan•
Freetown
⊕
SIERRA
LEONE
Monrovia⊕
GUINEA-
BISSAU
LIBERIA

Timbuktu•
MALI
Niger R.
Ouagadougou•
BURKINA FASO
Korhogo•
Bouaké•
Yamoussoukro•
Man•
IVORY COAST

•Gao

Niamey•

Tamale•
GHANA

Abidjan⊕
Accra⊕

Agadez•
NIGER
Tahoua•
Zinder•
Katsina•
Kaduna•

BENIN
Porto-
Novo
TOGO
Ibadan•
•Lagos
Lomé•
EQUATORIAL
GUINEA

Lake Chad
CHAD

N'Djamena⊕

Maiduguri•

Zaria•
•Abuja

NIGERIA

Moundou•
Bossangoa•

CAMEROON
Ebolowa•
Malabo• Yaoundé⊕

CENT.
AFRICAN
REPUBLIC
Bangui⊕

Pacific Islands/Australia

0 Miles 500

RUSSIA

KAZAKHSTAN

•Hovd
Altay
Ulaanbaatar ⊗

MONGOLIA

Aral Sea

L. Balkhash

•Karamay

Dalandzadagad ▫

•Urumqi

•Hami

G O B I D E S E R T

UZBEKISTAN

KYRGYZSTAN

•Korla

Yumen•

TAJIKISTAN

Kashi⊗ *Yarkant R.*

Tarim R.

CHINA

Yinchuan•

TURKMEN.

TAKLIMAKAN DESERT

•Qiemo

Xining•

Lanzhou•

Mazar-i-Sharif•

•Hotan

Golmud•

Xian—

•Herat

Kabul
⊗

Peshawar•

—Area claimed by India

JAMMU AND KASHMIR

Chongqing•

AFGHANISTAN

Islamabad⊗ •Srinagar

T I B E T

Mianyang•

Kandahar•

Rawalpindi

Chengdu•

Faisalabad• Amritsar•

MOUNT EVEREST

Zigong•

Multan• Lahore•

Brahmaputra R.

PAKISTAN

Yamuna R.

Indus R.

New Delhi•

Ganges R.

NEPAL

HIMALAYAS

Guiyang•

IRAN

Jaipur• Agra•

Katmandu⊗

BHUTAN

Kunming•

Hyderabad•

Kanpur•

Patna•

Nanning—

GREAT INDIAN DESERT

Allahabad•

Ganges R.

Dhaka⊗

MYANMAR

Karachi•

Ahmadabad•

INDIA

Kolkata•

Chitta-
gong

Mandalay•

VIETNAM

LAOS

Hanoi•

Arabian Sea

•Surat

•Nagpur

Godavari R.

BANGLADESH

Chang Mai•

Luang Prabang•

Vinh•

Mumbai•

•Pune

Hyderabad•

Bay of Bengal

Irrawaddy R.

Vientiane⊗

HAINAN

Yangon•

THAILAND

Da Nang—

15° North

ANDAMAN IS. (INDIA)

Bangkok
⊗

Bangalore• •Chennai

Mangalore•

Andaman Sea

CAMBODIA

Dawei•

Phnom Penh
⊗

Madurai•

•Jaffna

Gulf of Thailand

Ho Chi Minh City (Saigon)•

SRI LANKA

NICOBAR IS. (INDIA)

Hat Yai•

Colombo⊗•Kotte

Kota Baharu•

MALAYSIA

Medan• Kuala Lumpur
⊗

⊗ Male

SINGAPORE⊗

SUMATRA

MALDIVES

Equator

•Pontianak
Jambi•

Padang•

Palembang•

INDONESIA

Indian Ocean

Bandar Lampung• Jakarta⊗

Asia/Pacific

Bandung•

JAVA

0 Miles 500

70° East

90°

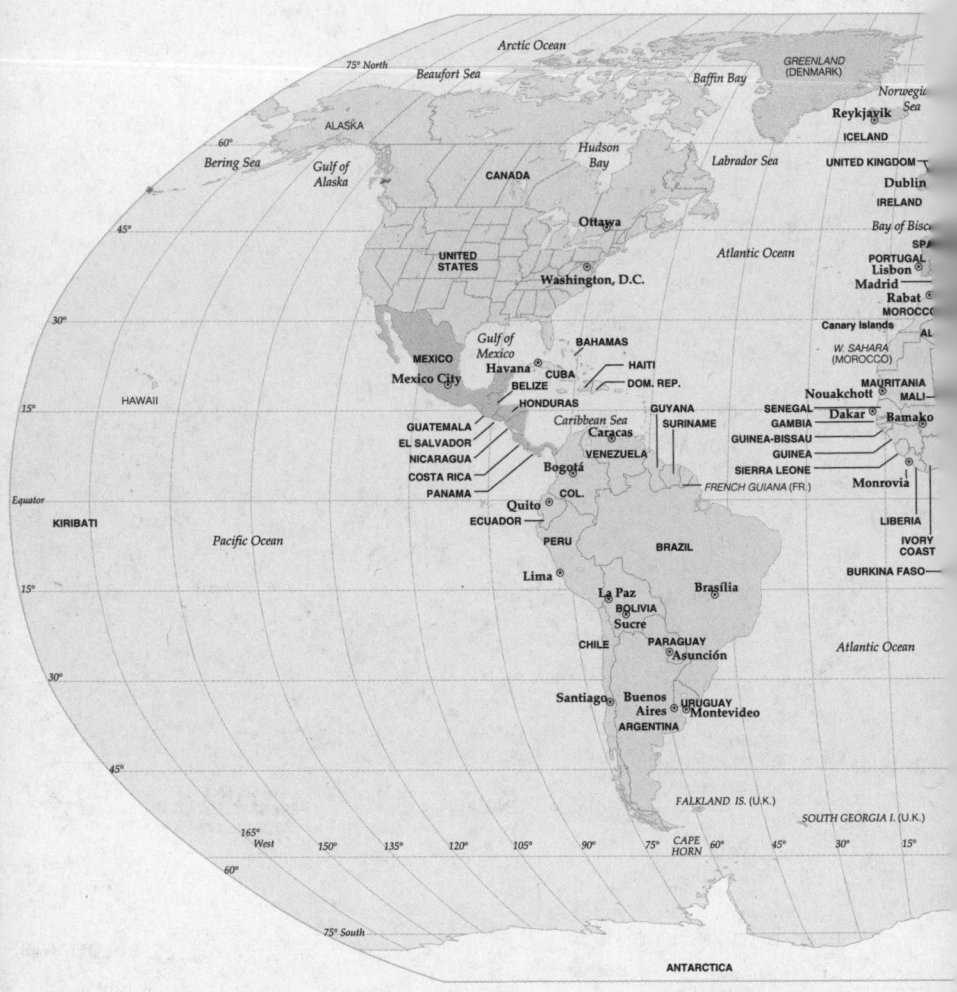

Arctic Ocean

75° North

Beaufort Sea

Baffin Bay

GREENLAND
(DENMARK)

Norwegi
Sea

Reykjavík

ICELAND

ALASKA

60°

Hudson
Bay

Labrador Sea

UNITED KINGDOM

Dublin

Bering Sea

Gulf of
Alaska

CANADA

IRELAND

45°

Bay of Bisce

Ottawa

Atlantic Ocean

SPA

PORTUGAL

UNITED
STATES

Lisbon

Madrid

Washington, D.C.

Rabat

MOROCCO

30°

Gulf of
Mexico

BAHAMAS

Canary Islands

AL

W. SAHARA
(MOROCCO)

MEXICO

Havana

CUBA

HAITI

15°

HAWAII

Mexico City

BELIZE

DOM. REP.

MAURITANIA

Nouakchott

MALI

HONDURAS

GUYANA

SENEGAL

Dakar

Bamako

GUATEMALA

Caribbean Sea

Caracas

SURINAME

GAMBIA

EL SALVADOR

VENEZUELA

GUINEA-BISSAU

GUINEA

NICARAGUA

Bogotá

SIERRA LEONE

Monrovia

COSTA RICA

FRENCH GUIANA (FR.)

PANAMA

COL.

Equator

Quito

KIRIBATI

ECUADOR

LIBERIA

PERU

BRAZIL

IVORY
COAST

Pacific Ocean

BURKINA FASO

15°

Lima

La Paz

Brasília

Santiago

BOLIVIA

Sucre

Atlantic Ocean

30°

CHILE

PARAGUAY

Asunción

Buenos
Aires

URUGUAY

Montevideo

ARGENTINA

45°

FALKLAND IS. (U.K.)

SOUTH GEORGIA I. (U.K.)

165°
West

150°

135°

120°

105°

90°

75°

CAPE
HORN

60°

45°

30°

15°

60°

75° South

ANTARCTICA

Arctic Ocean

75° North

Barents
Sea

SWEDEN

FIN.

WAY

ESTONIA
LATVIA
LITHUANIA

Helsinki

Stockholm
DMARK

Moscow

RUSSIA

Sea of
Okhotsk

60°

Berlin

POL.

BELA.

GEORGIA

KAZAKHSTAN

GER.

Kiev

UKRAINE

ARMENIA

Astana

Ulaanbaatar

45°

aris

3

4

AZERBAIJAN

UZBEKISTAN

MONGOLIA

NORTH
KOREA

don

6

7

9

don

11

8

KYRGYZSTAN

Beijing

Sea of
Japan

Tokyo

Rome

14

TURKMEN.

TAJIKISTAN

CHINA

Seoul

ITALY

17

Ankara

Black Sea

12

13

16

Teheran

Kabul

Islamabad

BHUTAN

JAPAN

30°

Algiers

TURKEY

TUNISIA

Athens

SYRIA

IRAN

New
Delhi

NEPAL

BANGLADESH

SOUTH
KOREA

LEBANON

IRAQ

Baghdad

QATAR

PAK.

AFGH.

THAILAND

TAIWAN

Tripoli

ISRAEL

JORDAN

KUWAIT

LIBYA

Cairo

Red
Sea

SAUDI
ARABIA

UNITED
ARAB
EMIRATES

INDIA

LAOS

South
China Sea

Pacific Ocean

ERIA

EGYPT

Riyadh

MYANMAR

Yangon

Philippine Sea

15°

NIGER

CHAD

ERITREA

OMAN

Arabian
Sea

Bay of
Bengal

VIETNAM

PHILIPPINES

MARSHALL
IS.

NIGERIA

Khartoum

YEMEN

DJIBOUTI

Bangkok

CAMBODIA

CENT.
AF. REP.

SUDAN

Addis Ababa
ETHIOPIA

SRI LANKA

MALDIVES

PALAU

MICRONESIA

CAMEROON

UGANDA

SOMALIA

MALAYSIA

Equator

GABON

Nairobi

KENYA

INDONESIA

Equator

CONGO

RWANDA

SINGAPORE

Java Sea

Dili

PAPUA
NEW GUINEA

TUVALU

CONGO
HEP.

Kinshasa

BURUNDI

Jakarta

EAST TIMOR

Port Moresby

Luanda

Dar es Salaam

SEYCHELLES

Timor Sea

ENIN

TANZANIA

COMOROS

Indian Ocean

15°

GO

ANGOLA

ZAMBIA

Coral Sea

VANUATU

ZIMBABWE

MADAGASCAR

MAURITIUS

FIJI

NAMIBIA

MALAWI

AUSTRALIA

BOTSWANA

MOZAMBIQUE

Pretoria

SWAZILAND

Canberra

30°

SOUTH AFRICA

LESOTHO

| 1. | NETHERLANDS | 10. | SLOVENIA |

| 2. | BELGIUM | 11. | CROATIA |

Tasman Sea

Wellington

CAPE OF
GOOD HOPE

| 3. | CZECH REPUBLIC | 12. | BOSNIA AND |

| 4. | SLOVAKIA | | HERZEGOVINA |

NEW ZEALAND

45°

| 5. | SWITZERLAND | 13. | YUGOSLAVIA |

| 6. | AUSTRIA | 14. | ALBANIA |

| 7. | HUNGARY | 15. | MACEDONIA |

| 8. | ROMANIA | 16. | BULGARIA |

| 9. | MOLDOVA | 17. | GREECE |

15°   30°   45°   60°   75°   90°   105°   120°   135°   150°

165°
East

60°

Southern Ocean

75° South

ANTARCTICA

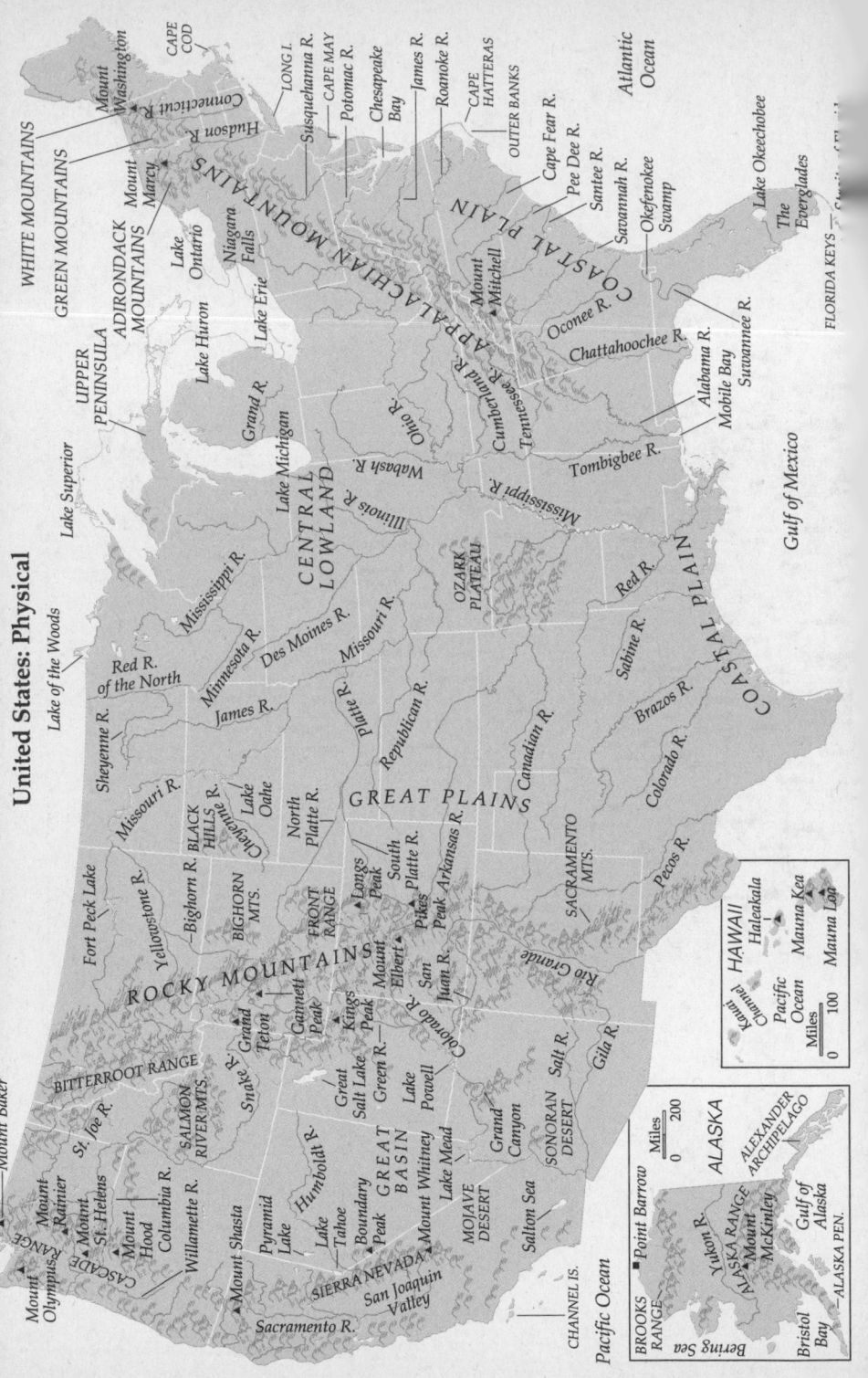

United States: Physical

• **GOVERNMENT   Type:** parliamentary democracy. **Independence:** May 14, 1948 (from League of Nations Mandate under British administration). **Constitution:** no formal constitution; some functions of constitution are filled by Declaration of Establishment (1948), the basic laws of the Knesset (legislature)— relating to the Knesset, Israeli lands, the president, government—and Israeli citizenship law. **National holiday:** Israel declared independence on May 14, 1948; because Jewish calendar is lunar, however, holiday varies from year to year; all major Jewish religious holidays are also observed as national holidays. **Heads of Government:** Dalia Itzik, president (since Jan. 2007); Ehud Olmert, prime minister (since May 2006). **Structure:** executive-president has largely ceremonial functions, except for authority to decide which political leader should try to form ruling coalition following election or fall of previous government, power vested in cabinet; unicameral legislature (Knesset); judiciary-legal system based on combination of English common law, British Mandate regulations, and religious law.

• **ECONOMY   Monetary unit:** new Israeli shekel. **Budget:** (2007 est.) *income:* $57.08 bil.; *expend.:* $57.81 bil. **G.D.P.:** $184.9 bil., $28,800 per capita (2007 est.). **Chief crops:** citrus and other fruits, vegetables, cotton; beef, poultry, dairy products. **Natural resources:** copper, phosphates, bromide, potash, clay. **Major industries:** food processing, diamond cutting and polishing, high-tech projects. **Labor force:** 2.88 mil. (2007 est.); 50% services, 23.7% industry, 18.5% agriculture; 7.6% unemployment (2007 est.). **Exports:** $48.6 bil. (f.o.b., 2007); machinery, software, cut diamonds, chemicals, textiles and clothing. **Imports:** $52.8 bil. (f.o.b., 2007); raw materials, military equipment, investment goods, rough diamonds, oil. **Major trading partners:** (2006) *exports:* 38.4% U.S., 6.5% Belgium, 5.9% Hong Kong; *imports:* 12.4% U.S., 8.2% Belgium, 6.7% Germany, 5.9% Switzerland, 5.1% U.K., 5.1% China.

In ancient times called the Land of Canaan, the region between the Jordan River and the Mediterranean Sea was one of the earliest sites of agricultural civilization in the Middle East. Hebrew exiles from Egypt arrived c. 1200 B.C.; their kingdom, Eretz Israel, was well established by 1000 B.C., with its capital at Jerusalem. The kingdom expanded under Kings Saul and David, who extended domination over the Philistines, a local seafaring people, and established the norms of Jewish religious worship at the great temple of Jerusalem.

After the reign of King Solomon, the kingdom split into two parts, Israel and Judah. Israel was conquered by the Assyrians in 722 B.C., and Judah by the Babylonians in 586 B.C. A locally autonomous state was reestablished under the Persian empire in the fifth century B.C. And in the fourth century B.C., Alexander the Great conquered the region, beginning a period of Hellenizing influence.

A new Jewish state was established in 141 B.C. after the revolt of the Maccabees against hellenic rule, the state falling to the Roman Empire around 70 B.C. Roman rule was exerted through the puppet kings of the Herodian dynasty. Christianity, a messianic religion centering on the teachings of Jesus of Nazareth, was suppressed in Israel by both the Herodian kings and the Jewish priesthood but spread widely in the eastern Mediterranean in the early first century A.D.

A Jewish rebellion against Rome in A.D. 66 was forcibly suppressed, and the temple at Jerusalem was destroyed by the Romans in A.D. 70. Large numbers of Jews were expelled from Judea, beginning the Jewish Diaspora throughout the Roman world and beyond. A second rebellion of Jews in Israel was quelled in A.D. 132.

The territory of the kingdoms of Israel and Judah became generally known as Palestine, after the name of its ancient inhabitants, the Philistines. With the official toleration of Christianity in the Roman Empire under Constantine I (early 4th century), Palestine became a major center of Christian pilgrimage. Politically, Palestine was administered as part of the Byzantine Empire.

Expansion of Islam from Arabia brought Palestine under Islamic rule in 636. Thereafter the region was ruled by the Caliphates of Damascus (661-750) and Baghdad (762-1258). Part of Palestine was captured in 1099 by European Crusaders, who established the short-lived Latin Kingdom of Jerusalem. The region was conquered by the Mongols in 1258; defeat of the Mongols in 1260 at the battle of Ain Jalyut, near Nazareth, prevented a Mongol invasion of Egypt.

Palestine next became part of the Mamluk empire and was incorporated into the Ottoman Empire in 1516. The Ottoman period was one of administrative decline, although the holy places of Judaism, Christianity, and Islam were maintained by local religious authorities.

The emigration of Jews from Europe to the homeland of Israel began around 1870, under the influence of the Zionist movement. Zionism, traceable in part to the thought of Moses Mendelssohn (1729-86), originally emphasized the need to maintain Jewish identity and religious consciousness as well as to promote Jewish assimilation into European culture. By the time of the First World Zionist Congress, convened in Basel by Theodor Herzl in 1897, emphasis had shifted to the need for a specific Jewish homeland. After 1905, under the leadership of Chaim Weizmann, Jewish emigration to Palestine increased.

With the collapse of the Ottoman Empire during World War I, Palestine came under British rule in 1917. In that year the British government issued the Balfour Declaration, committing Britain to aiding the establishment of a Jewish homeland in Palestine. After Britain received a League of Nations Mandate to govern Palestine (as well as Transjordan) in 1923, Jewish immigration into Palestine increased significantly. Faced with rising Palestinian Arab opposition to a further increase in Jewish immigration, Britain reinterpreted the Balfour Declaration in restricted terms and attempted to limit the number of Jewish arrivals.

The crisis lasted until the outbreak of World War II. During the war the Palestinian Jewish community (then about 500,000) generally supported the British war effort, while some Palestinian Arab leaders translated anti-Zionist sentiments into sympathy for the Axis. Despite the horrible revelations about the Holocaust—the systematic killing of six million Jews during the War—in 1946 British authorities refused a recommendation of the Anglo-American Committee of Inquiry that they permit resettlement of 100,000 European Jews in Palestine and they limited further immigration to 2,000 per month. Jewish leaders pressed their cause at the United Nations, while in Palestine, Zionist terrorist organizations waged covert war against the British authorities.

In 1947 a U.N. Special Committee on Palestine, boycotted by Palestinian Arabs, recommended the partition of Palestine into Jewish and Arab sectors, with Jerusalem to be administered under international control. The U.N. adopted the recommendations on Nov. 29, 1947, and the British began to withdraw their forces, while Palestinian Jews and Arabs prepared for war.

On May 14, 1948, the independent state of Israel was established, with its capital at Tel Aviv. On the same day, troops from the Arab League nations attacked Israel. Fighting and cease-fires alternated throughout 1948; Israel lost control of the Old City of Jerusalem but retained the New City, and elsewhere consolidated its territorial control. Separate armistices between Israel and the Arab nations were concluded in 1949; Jordan retained control of the West Bank, and Egypt occupied Gaza. Large numbers of Palestinian Arab refugees departed for camps in Jordan, Lebanon, and Syria, while equally large numbers of Jews from Arab countries resettled in Israel.

Elections to the Knesset (Parliament) were held in Jan. 1949 and resulted in a coalition government. Chaim Weizmann was elected president, and David Ben-Gurion became prime minister. Laws were enacted to ensure religious control of education and civil law and to affirm the "Right of Return" of all Jews to Israel. The role of labor was protected by law, as was the establishment of agricultural collectives (kibbutzim).

Taking advantage of the Suez Crisis involving Great Britain, France, and Egypt, Israel invaded Egypt's Sinai Peninsula on Oct. 29, 1956. Israeli forces withdrew under the terms of a U.N. cease-fire on Nov. 6 but retained control of Gaza.

Throughout this period Israel's population continued to swell with immigrants from Europe, the U.S. and also from the dwindling Jewish communities of the Arab world. Israel's economy, aided by foreign aid and private remittances, grew rapidly, while foreign military aid and the growth of a substantial domestic armaments industry increased its military preparedness.

On May 19, 1967, U.N. peacekeeping forces withdrew from the Egypt-Israel border on the insistence of Egypt's president Gamal Abdel Nasser. Egyptian forces then reoccupied Gaza and closed the Gulf of Aqaba to Israeli shipping. In the Six-Day War, June 5-10, Israel recaptured Gaza, occupied the Sinai Peninsula to the Suez Canal, and captured the West Bank and the Old City of Jerusalem from Jordan and the Golan Heights from Syria. Another U.N.-supervised cease-fire went into effect.

Egypt and Syria, backed by Soviet airlifts, invaded Israel on Yom Kippur, Oct. 6, 1973. Israel, with strong U.S. support, counterattacked, driving back the Syrian forces and crossing the Suez Canal from the Sinai into Egypt. Fighting ceased on Oct. 24, and a disengagement agreement was signed on Jan. 18, 1974. Israeli forces withdrew from the west bank of the Suez Canal and, in stages, from the Sinai Peninsula, completing the withdrawal in 1982.

The government of Prime Minister Golda Meir fell after the Yom Kippur War, and a new coalition took power. A period of domestic and international difficulties followed, with severe inflation in the economy and a marked rise in Palestinian and other terrorist attacks against Israeli targets. Israeli forces repeatedly attacked Palestinian bases in southern Lebanon and aided the Christian militia forces in the Lebanese civil war of 1975-76. On July 3, 1976, Israeli commandos raided the airport at Entebbe, Uganda, to rescue 103 hostages held by Arab and German hijackers.

The 1977 parliamentary elections brought a conservative coalition to power, with Menachem Begin elected prime minister. Egypt's president Anwar Sadat visited Jerusalem in November 1977, and Begin and Sadat met at a conference with U.S. president Jimmy Carter at Camp David in 1979. On Mar. 26, 1979, Egypt and Israel signed a formal peace treaty ending 30 years of war and establishing diplomatic relations between the two nations.

In July 1980 Israel affirmed the transfer of its national capital from Tel Aviv to Jerusalem and the incorporation of the (formerly Jordanian) Old City into Israeli territory. The Israeli government decided in 1980 to promote increased Jewish settlement in the West Bank, provoking protest from Palestinian leaders.

Israeli forces invaded southern Lebanon in March 1978. After a brief occupation, most Israeli forces withdrew and were replaced by a U.N. peacekeeping force, but Israel continued to cooperate with Lebanese Christian militia forces in anti-Palestinian operations.

Israeli and Syrian forces clashed briefly in April 1981. On June 7, 1981, Israeli jets destroyed a nuclear reactor near Baghdad, Iraq, that Israel claimed could have been used to manufacture materials for nuclear weapons. Prime Minister Begin was returned to office in a close election in 1981, and he retired in 1983.

Attacking Palestine Liberation Organization strongholds in Lebanon in May, 1982, Israel mounted a full-scale invasion of Lebanon in June. Israeli and Syrian forces fought in Lebanon's Bekaa Valley but disengaged after a few days. On June 14 Israeli forces surrounded and shelled Beirut, forcing the PLO to evacuate the city. On Sept. 14 Israeli forces occupied West Beirut, following the assassination of the newly elected Lebanese president, Bashir Gemayel. Lebanese Christian militia, with tacit Israeli permission, entered two Palestinian refugee camps at Sabra and Shatila on Sept. 16 and massacred hundreds of civilians, provoking an international outcry against Israel's occupation of Lebanon. Israeli forces withdrew from Lebanon in June 1985, except for a narrow "security zone" along the border. Parliamentary elections in 1984 resulted in a coalition government, with power shared by Likud leader Yitzhak Shamir and Labor leader Shimon Peres.

In December 1987, Palestinian residents of Gaza and the West Bank launched a series of violent demonstrations against Israeli authorities. The *intifada*, or uprising, continued into 1991 in a cycle of protest and police reaction that led to the deaths of hundreds of demonstrators and a crisis of Israeli control in the occupied territories. Tensions were exacerbated by the immigration of hundreds of thousands of Soviet Jews to Israel.

Parliamentary elections in Nov. 1988 continued the Likud-Labor stalemate and brought increased power to the minor religious parties. A new grand-coalition government announced in Jan. 1989, with Yitzhak Shamir as prime minister and Shimon Peres as minister of finance, collapsed in mid-March because of disagreements over an American-backed plan for peace talks with the Palestinians. This plunged the country into a crisis, resolved in June 1990 with the formation of a coalition government of Likud and several right-wing religious parties. Shamir managed to survive several no-confidence votes, and his alliance with religious party Agudat Israel in Nov. solidified his party's power as the Persian Gulf crisis unfolded.

After months of diplomacy spearheaded by the U.S., direct talks between Israel and a (non-PLO) Jordanian-Palestinian joint delegation opened in Washington in December 1991. The talks broke down in stalemate as Israel refused to compromise over the key issue of new Jewish settlements on the West Bank. In the election of June 1992, the Labor party led by Rabin scored an upset victory over Shamir's Likud coalition government. Rabin disclosed that the Shamir government had pursued a deliberate policy of intransigence in the peace talks in order to allow the accelerated West Bank settlement program to continue.

The Palestinian *intifada* gained renewed momentum in Dec. 1992 when Israel deported 400 Palestinians to Lebanon on the grounds that they were responsible for acts of violence. Israel launched a series of air and land attacks on suspected terrorist bases in Lebanon, resulting in many casualties.

The world was stunned only a few weeks later, when on Sept. 13, 1993, Prime Minister Yitzhak Rabin and PLO leader Yasir Arafat signed an agreement in principle for a peace settlement based on Palestinian recognition of Israel's right to exist, and Israel's acceptance of partial self-rule for the Palestinians. Soon, areas in Gaza and the West Bank were under Palestinian control.

By fall of 1995, Israeli troops had begun withdrawing from Palestinian settlements on the West Bank, but a month later an Israeli extremist assassinated Rabin. His successor, Shimon Peres, vowed to continue moves toward peace and moved elections forward from October to May. In early 1996 Israel faced the worst suicide bomber attacks in 20 years: in five days 60 people were dead. Hamas, the Palestinian resistance group, took responsibility for the attacks.

In Israel's first direct election of a prime minister, Likud's hard-line Benjamin Netanyahu narrowly defeated Peres as Israelis chose "security" over "peace." By 1997 the peace process came to a virtual standstill as the Netanyahu government pushed ahead with new settlements in the West Bank and in East Jerusalem. The first sign of a break in the impasse came in June 1998 when Pres. Weizman declared that Netanyahu was undermining peace talks. Negotiations with the Palestinians began anew in July and on Oct. 23, in Washington, Netanyahu and Arafat agreed to the Wye Memorandum by which Israel agreed to surrender about 13 percent of her West Bank holdings. But the Knesset toppled Netanyahu's government and rejected the agreement. Elections in May 1999 brought Ehud Barak, former army chief of staff, to the office of prime minister.

The roller-coaster peace talks between the Barak government and the Palestinians lasted for a year but broke off bitterly (July 25, 2000); what was seen in the Knesset as excessive concessions, especially on Jerusalem, led to the unraveling of Barak's coalition and a call for new elections. In the interim, Israel completed a withdrawal from the security zone it had established in 1978 in Lebanon. In late Sept. renewed violence between Israeli troops and Palestinians forced Barak to resign in December and in Feb. 2001 hard-liner Ariel Sharon won 63 percent of the vote to become prime minister. Nearly 400 people, mainly Pales-

tinians, had died since September and in March began a series of suicide bombings by Palestinians in Israel. The deadly cycle of Palestinian terror-bombings and Israeli reprisals continued without abatement through 2003. Sharon remained firmly in power even after Labor left his coalition forcing new elections in 2003.

In 2004, under pressure from the U.S., Sharon unveiled a plan to remove the settlements from the Gaza Strip while keeping five major ones in the West Bank (to be protected by a 437-mile security wall). In the summer of 2005 all the Gaza settlements were closed down. But at the end of 2005 Sharon suffered a massive stroke and he was replaced by Ehud Olmert. Plans to continue diminishing the number of settlements were put on hold and in July 2006 Israel began a major attack on Hezbollah within Lebanon which ended in a stalemate but with Israel being criticized for the many civilian deaths that resulted. In 2008 a scnadal enveloped Olmert and his government lost all support. (See "Major News Stories")

Palestinian Territories

As a result of the 1993 peace talks sponsored by the U.S., Israel and the P.L.O. signed the Declaration of Principles on Interim Self-Government Arrangements (known as the D.O.P.) which provided for a transitional period of no more than five years of Palestinian self-government in two areas, the Gaza Strip and the West Bank. Israel agreed to transfer some powers to the Palestinian Authority and a Palestinian Legislative Council was elected in 1996. Israel, however, retained control over security in these areas. Several other minor agreements were readied over the next three years but direct negotiations for a permanent settlement did not begin again until 1999. When the talks failed a new *intifada* broke out in Sept. 2000 and, with the onset of suicide bombings, Israel took stern military measures and ended any talk about a permanent settlement of differences.

Over the next five years periodic violence was the norm. Arafat's death in 2005 led to parliamentary elections and the Islamic party known as Hamas won convincingly. In Feb. 2007 a power sharing agreement was reached but a violent power struggle continued and in June Hamas fighters routed those of Fatah as over 150 Palestinians were killed. (See "Major News Stories.")

GAZA STRIP This area (totalling 139 sq. mi. or 360 sq. km.) borders the Mediterranean Sea between Egypt and Israel. Approximately 1.5 million people live here. Israeli settlements were removed by the Sharon government in the summer of 2005. In June 2007 Hamas wrestled control of Gaza from Fatah in a bloody battle that killed more than 100. Major cities include Gaza, Dayr al Balah, Rafah, Khan Yunus, and Abasan.

WEST BANK This area (totalling 2,263 sq. mi. or 5,860 sq. km.) borders Israel and Jordan and includes East Jerusalem and Jerusalem No Man's Land, established after the 1967 war. Approximately 2.6 million people live here including 187,000 Israeli settlers in the West Bank and fewer than 177,000 in East Jerusalem. Major cities include Jericho, Hebron, Bethlehem and Nablus.

▶ ITALY
Italian Republic
● GEOGRAPHY Location: peninsula, extending from southern Europe into Mediterranean Sea,

with a number of adjacent islands, principally Sicily to SW, and Sardinia to W. **Boundaries:** Switzerland and Austria to N, Slovenia to NE, Adriatic Sea to E, Ionian Sea to SE, Mediterranean Sea to W, France to NW. **Total area:** 116,305 sq. mi. (301,230 sq km). **Coastline:** 4,723 mi. (7,600 km). **Comparative area:** slightly larger than Arizona. **Land use:** 28% arable land; 9% permanent crops; 63% other. **Major cities:** Roma (Rome; capital); Milano (Milan); Napoli (Naples); Torino (Turin); Palermo.

●**PEOPLE   Population:** 58,145,321 (July 2008 est.). **Nationality:** noun—Italian(s); adjective—Italian. **Ethnic groups:** primarily Italian, but includes small clusters of German-, French-, and Slovene-Italians in north and Albanian-Italians in south; Sicilians. **Languages:** Italian; parts of Trentino-Alto Adige region (e.g., Bolzano) are predominantly German-speaking; significant French-speaking minority in Valle d'Aosta region; Slovene-speaking minority in Trieste-Gorizia area. **Religions:** predominantly Roman Catholic.

● **GOVERNMENT   Type:** republic. **Constitution:** Jan. 1, 1948. **National holiday:** Anniversary of the Republic, June 2. **Heads of Government:** Giorgio Napolitano, president (since May 2006); Silvio Berlusconi, prime minister (since May 2008). **Structure:** executive—president empowered to dissolve Parliament and call national election; commander of armed forces presides over Supreme Defense Council; otherwise, authority to govern invested in Council of Ministers; bicameral legislature—popularly elected Parliament (315-member Senate, 630-member Chamber of Deputies); judiciary—independent.

● **ECONOMY   Monetary unit:** Italian lira. **Budget:** (2007 est.) *income:* $976 bil.; *expend.:* $1.029 tril. **G.D.P.:** $1.8 tril., $31,000 per capita (2007 est.). **Chief crops:** fruits, vegetables, grapes, potatoes, sugar beets, soybeans, grain, olives; meat and dairy products. **Natural resources:** mercury, potash, marble, sulfur, dwindling natural gas and crude oil reserves. **Major industries:** tourism, machinery and transport equipment, iron, steel, chemicals. **Labor force:** 24.86 mil. (2007 est.); 63% services, 32% industry, 5% agriculture (2001); 6.7% unemployment (2007 est.). **Exports:** $474.8 bil. (f.o.b., 2007); engineering products, textiles and clothing, production machinery, motor vehicles. **Imports:** $483.6 bil. (f.o.b., 2007); engineering products, chemicals, transport equipment, energy products. **Major trading partners:** (2006) *exports:* 13.2% Germany, 11.7% France, 7.6% U.S., 7.3% Spain, 6.1% U.K.; *imports:* 16.7% Germany, 9.2% France, 5.6% Netherlands, 5.2% China, 4.2% Belgium, 4.1% Spain.

Rome became the major power in Italy around 500 B.C., dominating the Etruscans in the north and Greek settlements in the south. The Roman Republic already dominated most of the Mediterranean and western Europe by the time imperial rule was established under Julius Caesar. The empire was divided between Rome and Byzantium in the fourth century A.D. The Roman Empire in the west was severely weakened by Germanic invasions in the fifth century and gradually dissolved, so that Italy became a disunited collection of aristocratic holdings and independent cities.

By the 10th century, the city-states, especially in the north, emerged as major powers, rivaling the Papal States of the central peninsula. Venice and Genoa emerged as major maritime powers during the medieval period, while Florence, Siena, and other cities developed into centers of agricultural and commercial wealth, impelling the successive renaissances of the 12th and 15th centuries. With the rise of the Habsburg empire, the monarchical powers of northern Europe vied for power in Italy, and the peninsula's small states became pawns of France, Spain, and Austria.

At the turn of the 19th century, Napoleon created the short-lived Kingdom of Italy as a French satellite, but after his fall, there was a general return to the old pattern, with Austria dominating the north. Metternich in 1815 called Italy a "geographic expression."

The 19th century saw a growing sense of nationalism. The revolutionary military leader, Giuseppe Garibaldi, and the statesman, Conte Camillo di Cavour, brought about the establishment of the Kingdom of Italy in 1861. The kingdom wrested Venice away from Austria (1866) and absorbed the Papal States in 1870. Although united territorially, the kingdom was divided by conflict between church and state, north and south, modern urban industry versus semifeudal rural poverty. Parliamentary politics under the constitutional monarchy created a regime that was weak and venal, inspiring little popular support.

Italy joined the Allied powers in World War I, but its minor gains in the Peace of Paris scarcely seemed to justify its wartime suffering and one million dead. Postwar economic dislocation, fear of communism, and political disillusionment abetted the rise of fascism. Benito Mussolini took over the Italian government at the invitation of the king in 1922 and soon acquired dictatorial powers. Papal secular authority in Vatican City was reestablished by the Lateran Agreement of 1929. In the late 1920's and early 1930's, Italy appeared to be a major power, defending Austria from Germany, colonizing Ethiopia, supporting Francisco Franco in the Spanish civil war, and joining in an "axis" with Hitler's Germany.

Mussolini was soon eclipsed by Hitler, and Italy was drawn into the disaster of World War II in 1939. Italy annexed Albania and invaded Greece, but that campaign turned into a fiasco from which German troops had to save the Italian army. In 1943 Allied attacks on Italy began; the fascist Grand Council deposed Mussolini, and the king, Victor Emmanuel III, had him arrested. Hitler intervened in September 1943 and began the war in Italy anew, rescuing Mussolini who established another fascist regime in northern Italy, while the legal Italian government in the south switched sides and welcomed Italy's liberation.

The head of the first postwar government was a Christian Democrat, Alcide de Gasperi. The monarchy was abolished by plebiscite in 1946, and the Republic of Italy was established. The north supported the republic, while monarchism retained significant support in the south. This division reflected a roughly accurate generalization that sees Italy as a progressive commercial and industrial north and a backward agricultural/pastoral south. Despite such industrial giants as Fiat and Pirelli, however, Italy's manufacturing has been primarily carried on by medium-size and small firms, while agriculture is characteristic of the whole country. As late as 1956, there were more Italian workers in agriculture than in industry.

In the first elections under the republic, in 1948, the Christian Democrats benefited from American patronage and a split in the ranks of the Left to win a parliamentary majority. Italy accepted Marshall Plan aid and membership in NATO; reintegration into the European mainstream found expression in membership in the Council of Europe and the Coal and Steel Community.

Domestically, reconstruction was the major task, with industrial and agricultural output severely hampered by damage from the war; inflation was rampant and basic social services impaired. The Christian Democrats, normally in Center-Right coalitions in the 1950's and Center-Left coalitions in the 1960's, adopted a policy directed at creating a stable currency, a free market, social welfare programs, and occasional state intervention in the economy. This created an Italian "economic miracle," with industrial production doubling between 1953 and 1961 and an additional 40 percent by 1966, led by steel, automobiles, machinery, and electrical equipment.

In the 1970's the Christian Democrats gradually declined in political influence, normally gaining less than 40 percent of the popular vote while continuing to provide premiers in often short-lived coalition cabinets. Left-wing terrorism became a major national problem. The Christian Democratic leader and former prime minister Aldo Moro was kidnapped and murdered in 1978, and U.S. Brig. Gen./NATO officer James Dozier was kidnapped (and subsequently rescued) in 1981. The government of Bettino Craxi, Italy's first Socialist premier, was severely shaken after it refused to cooperate with the United States in apprehending and trying the hijackers of the Achille Lauro in 1985. Craxi resigned in 1987.

Lacking political unity, Italy's coalition governments—there have been more than 60 since the war—tended to muddle along in the face of slow growth, inflation, and high unemployment. But awareness of Mafia assassinations and revelations of government corruption led to demands for dramatic changes. In April 1993 the electorate overwhelmingly approved reforms that changed the basic elements of Italian political life. The first elections under the reformed system (March 1994) ended half a century of Christian Democrat-led coalition governments. The Christian Democrats, hastily renamed the Italian Popular Party, won only 11 percent of the vote, while the Socialists, normally the second largest party, fell to 2 percent. What replaced the old guard was the right-wing Alliance for Freedom. Wealthy publishing executive Silvio Berlusconi was sworn in as prime minister but his government lasted only five months. Political disputes, union opposition to his austerity budget, and the announcement that magistrates were investigating charges he had bribed tax officials diminished his authority.

Rather than call new elections, Italy's president asked Lamberto Dini to form a new "nonparty" cabinet of businessmen, judges, and professors, a cabinet that won the requisite votes of confidence in the two chambers by Feb.1, 1995. The new government showed surprising staying power, passing its budget and negotiating reform of Italy's bloated pension system with leading trade unions. It even began the politically touchy process of investigating the anticrime magistrates for possible violations of civil rights.

As corruption trials continued, the Dini government survived successive votes of confidence, the last on condition that he resign with the new year, which he did. New elections were not held until April 1996. The left-wing "Olive Tree Coalition," led by the once-Communist "Democratic Party of the Left," trounced the right-wing "Freedom Alliance." Its new prime minister was Professor Romano Prodi of the Popular party. Prodi concentrated on bringing the economy into line so Italy would be eligible for participation in the EMU which, with much manevering, including a stringent austerity budget, and a sudden economic upswing, he did – formal endorsement coming in May 1998. Yet, in October, the Prodi government lost a vote of confidence over budget's cuts in social spending.

The "Olive Tree" government muddled along until the May 2001 elections, convincingly won by the right-wing House of Freedom coalition, spearheaded by Forza Italia, and bringing back Silvio Berlusconi as prime minister. Berlusconi was under indictment for corruption when in June 2003 the legislature granted him immunity until he was out of office but this was later ruled unconstitutional. Prodi returned to power in May 2006 and austerity budgeting became essential as Italy's debt had grown over the past years. But Berlusconi came back in April 2008 to win a solid victory, yet again. (See "Major News Stories.")

▶ IVORY COAST
Republic of Côte d'Ivoire

● **GEOGRAPHY Location:** western coast of Africa. **Boundaries:** Mali and Burkina Faso to N, Ghana to E, Gulf of Guinea to S, Liberia and Guinea to W. **Total area:** 124,502 sq. mi. (322,460 sq km). **Coastline:** 320 mi. (515 km). **Comparative area:** slightly larger than New Mexico. **Land use:** 9% arable land; 14% permanent crops; 77% other. **Major cities:** Yamoussoukro (capital—not recognized by U.S., which recognizes Abidjan); Abidjan; Bouaké.

● **PEOPLE Population:** 18,373,060 (July 2008 est.). **Nationality:** noun—Ivorian(s); adjective—Ivorian. **Ethnic groups:** 41% Akan, 18% Voltaiques or Gur, 17% Northern Mandes, 11% Krous, 10% Southern Mandes, 3% other (including 130,000 Lebanese and 20,000 French). **Languages:** French (official); over 60 African languages and dialects with Dioula most widely spoken. **Religions:** 35-40% Muslim, 20-30%% Christian, 25-40% indigenous beliefs.

● **GOVERNMENT Type:** republic; multiparty presidential regime established 1960. **Independence:** Aug. 7, 1960 (from France). **Constitution:** Nov. 3, 1960. **National holiday:** National Day, Aug. 7. **Heads of Government:** Laurent Gbagbo, president (since Oct. 2000); Guillaume Soro, prime minister (since Apr. 2007). **Structure:** executive—president has broad powers; unicameral legislature—175-member National Assembly; judiciary.

● **ECONOMY Monetary unit:** Communauté Financière Africaine franc. **Budget:** (2007) *income:* $3.196 bil.; *expend.:* $3.806 bil. **G.D.P.:** $32.86 bil., $1,800 per capita (2007 est.). **Chief crops:** coffee, cocoa, bananas, palm oil; cotton, rubber; timber. **Natural resources:** crude oil, diamonds, manganese, iron ore, cobalt. **Major industries:** foodstuffs, wood processing, oil refinery. **Labor force:** 6.907 mil; 68% agriculture; 40-50% unemployment becuase of civil war. **Exports:** $18.5 bil. (f.o.b., 2007 est.); cocoa, coffee, tropical woods. **Imports:** $5.2 bil. (f.o.b., 2007 est.); food, consumer goods, capital goods, fuel. **Major trading partners:** (2006) *exports:* 18.3% France, 9.7% Netherlands, 9.1% U.S., 7.2% Nigeria, 4.2% Germany; *imports:* 25.4% France, 27.6% Nigeria, 4.3% China.

The peoples of the Ivory Coast belong to various tribes that had established small and mutually hostile kingdoms prior to the 18th century. The dominant Baule migrated to the Ivory Coast from Ghana about 200 years ago. European contact began with the Portuguese, who established coastal trading stations in the 15th century. They were followed in rapid succession by the Dutch, British, and finally the French, who landed at Assinie in 1637. Dense tropical forests and a lack of good harbors retarded European exploration.

France established a protectorate over the coastal zone in 1842 and during the remainder of the 19th century expanded its control, by conquest and diplomacy, into the interior. In 1893 the Ivory Coast was organized as a French colony, and in 1904 it was made part of French West Africa.

France's Vichy government controlled French West Africa during World War II and harshly suppressed the region's growing nationalist movements. In 1946 a group of West African leaders, inspired by Félix Houphouet-Boigny, formed the African Democratic Assembly, which later cooperated with the French in the implementation of reforms, including, by 1956, universal suffrage and the formation of locally autonomous assemblies. Complete independence for the Ivory Coast came on Aug. 4, 1960 and Félix Houphouet-Boigny was unanimously elected the first president.

His Democratic party was the only one allowed so Houphouet-Boigny easily won reelection. But even after he liberalized the political process in 1990 he retained control, winning a new five-year term in multiparty elections held in 1990. Under his presidency, the Ivory Coast enjoyed both political stability and economic prosperity.

Houphouet-Boigny died in 1993, and was succeeded by Henri Konan Bedie, president of the National Assembly. Bedie won reelection in 1995, and continued the policies of his predecessor. In Sept. 1999, however, after he ordered the arrest of several hundred members of an opposition party, a military coup led by General Robert Gueï overturned the Bedie government on Christmas Eve 1999. But Gueï's attempt to rig the 2000 elections provoked demonstrations that forced him to flee. Laurent Gbagbo became president.

In Sept. 2002, another coup by Gueï, in which he was killed, precipitated a civil war pitting the Gbagbo government against several rebel movements. French troops, sent to protect foreigners, became involved in the fighting and the negotiating. In March 2003 a power-sharing agreement went into effect with Gbagbo appointing a Muslim premier at the head of a 41-member cabinet representing all factions. But civil war has continued with the government holding power in the south, the rebels in the north until U.N. peacekeepers arrived in late 2004. In 2007 the leader of the rebel forces, Guillaume Soro, was appointed prime minister by Gbagbo to help bring peace.

▶ **JAMAICA**
● **GEOGRAPHY Location:** northern Caribbean Sea. Kingston 17°58′N, 76°48′W. **Boundaries:** Cuba 87 mi. (145 km) to N. **Total area:** 4,243 sq. mi. (10,990 sq km). **Coastline:** 635 mi. (1,022 km). **Comparative area:** slightly smaller than Connecticut. **Land use:** 16% arable land; 9% permanent crops; 75% other. **Major cities:** Kingston (capital); Spanish Town; Montego Bay.
● **PEOPLE Population:** 2,804,332 (July 2008 est.). **Nationality:** noun—Jamaican(s); adjective—Ja-

maican. **Ethnic groups:** 91.2% black, 6.2% mixed, 2.6% other, unknown. **Languages:** English, patois English. **Religions:** 62.5% Protestant, 2.6% Roman Catholic, 14.2% other, 20.9% none.
● **GOVERNMENT Type:** constitutional parliamentary democracy. **Independence:** Aug. 6, 1962 (from U.K.). **Constitution:** Aug. 6, 1962. **National holiday:** Independence Day, first Monday in August. **Heads of Government:** Gov. Gen. Howard F.H. Cooke, governor-general (since Aug. 1991); Bruce Golding, prime minister (since Sept. 2007). **Structure:** cabinet headed by prime minister; bicameral legislature; judiciary follows British tradition under chief justice.
● **ECONOMY Monetary unit:** Jamaican dollar. **Budget:** (2007 est.) *income:* $3.441 bil.; *expend.:* $3.905 bil. **G.D.P.:** $13.47 bil., $4,800 per capita (2007 est.). **Chief crops:** sugarcane, bananas, coffee, citrus, potatoes, vegetables; poultry, goats, milk. **Natural resources:** bauxite, gypsum, limestone. **Major industries:** tourism, bauxite mining, textiles. **Labor force:** 1.255 bil. (2007); 64% services, 17% agriculture, 19% industry; 10.2% unemployment (2007). **Exports:** $2.229 bil. (f.o.b., 2007 est.); alumina, bauxite, sugar, bananas, rum. **Imports:** $5.709 bil. (f.o.b., 2007 est.); machinery and transport equipment, construction materials, fuel; food; chemicals. **Major trading partners:** (2006) *exports:* 30.2% U.S., 15.6% Canada, 15.2% China, 10.3% U.K., 7% Netherlands, 4.6% Norway; *imports:* 39.3% U.S., 13.6% Trinidad & Tobago, 9.5% Venezuela.

Christopher Columbus visited Jamaica in 1494, and the Spanish ruled the island—exterminating the native Arawaks in the process—until it fell to British control in 1655. A haven for buccaneers, by the 18th century Jamaica was a major sugar producer and the site of one of the busiest slave markets in the world. Emancipation of the slaves in 1833 and abolition of tariff protection in 1846 contributed strongly to the subsequent downfall of the plantation economy.

In 1962 the island gained its independence. The country has been plagued by racial and class division set within the context of an underdeveloped economy. Michael Manley of the People's National party became prime minister in 1972. He nationalized some industry and established closer ties with Cuba. Edward Seaga's Jamaica Labour party came to power in 1980 and encouraged more private-sector involvement in developing the economy. Though Manley was reelected to office in 1989, he did not reverse this general trend; in 1992 he was succeeded by Percival James Patterson, who led the People's National party to a landslide victory in violence-marred elections in March 1993. He was reelected in 1997 despite continuing economic problems. In 2006 he was succeeded by Portia Simpson-Miller of the same party, but in 2007, the center-right Jamaica Labour Party took control for the first time after 18 years of People's National Party rule.

▶ **JAPAN**
● **GEOGRAPHY Location:** chain of more than 3,000 islands extending 1,300 mi. (2,200 km) NE to SW between Sea of Japan and western Pacific Ocean; southern Japan about 93 mi. (150 km) E of S. Korea; islands of Hokkaido, Honshu, Shikoku, and Kyushu account for 98% of land area. Tokyo 35°40′N, 139°45′E. **Boundaries:** Sea of Okhotsk to N, Pacific Ocean to E, East China Sea to SW, and Sea of Japan to W. **Total area:** 145,882 sq. mi.

(377,835 sq km). **Coastline:** 18,487 mi. (29,751 km). **Comparative area:** slightly smaller than California. **Land use:** 12% arable land; 1% permanent crops; 87% other. **Major cities:** Tokyo (capital); Yokohama; Osaka; Nagoya; Sapporo.
• **PEOPLE Population:** 127,288,419 (July 2008 est.). **Nationality:** noun—Japanese (sing., pl.); adjective—Japanese. **Ethnic groups:** 99% Japanese, 1% other (mostly Korean). **Languages:** Japanese. **Religions:** most Japanese observe both Shinto and Buddhist rites; about 16% belong to other faiths, including 0.7% Christian.
• **GOVERNMENT Type:** constitutional monarchy. **Constitution:** May 3, 1947. **National holiday:** Birthday of the Emperor, Dec. 23. **Heads of Government:** Akihito, emperor (since Jan. 1989); Taro Aso, prime minister (since Sept. 2008). **Structure:** executive—emperor is symbolic head of state; power is vested in cabinet appointed by prime minister; bicameral legislature; judiciary.
• **ECONOMY Monetary unit:** yen. **Budget:** (2007 est.) *income:* $1.463 tril.; *expend.:* $1.575 tril. **G.D.P.:** $4.417 tril., $33,800 per capita (2007 est.). **Chief crops:** rice, sugar beets, vegetables, fruits; chickens, pigs, cattle; world's largest fish catch. **Natural resources:** negl. mineral resources, fish. **Major industries:** metallurgical and engineering industries, electrical and electronic industries, motor vehicles. **Labor force:** 66.07 mil. (2007); 67.7% services, 27.8% industry. 4.6% agriculture. **Exports:** $665.7 bil. (f.o.b., 2007 est.); semiconductors, office machinery, chemicals, motor vehicles. **Imports:** $571.1 bil. (f.o.b.., 2007); fuels, foodstuffs, chemicals, textiles, office machinery. **Major trading partners:** (2006) *exports:* 22.8% U.S., 14.3% China, 7.8% South Korea, 6.8% Taiwan, 5.8% Hong Kong; *imports:* 20.5% China, 12% U.S., 6.4% Saudi Arabia, 5.5% United Arab Emirates, 4.8% Australia, 4.7% South Korea, 4.2% Indonesia.

Japan's ancient Jomon civilization was displaced by proto-Japanese Yayoi migrants from mainland northeast Asia beginning in the fourth century B.C. In the early Yayoi period, a mounted military aristocracy dominated rice-growing commoners. The shamanic religion of the time was ancestral to Japan's later indigenous religion, Shinto. Yayoi society evolved into the Yamato protostate, c. A.D. 250-500. The Yamato kings were buried in large, elaborate tomb mounds together with haniwa clay sculptures. From the third century A.D., contact with the mainland increased. Korean missionaries introduced Buddhism and Chinese writing in the mid-sixth century. A centralized monarchy developed in the Yamato Plain, central Honshu Island; Prince Shotoku, a great patron of Buddhism, founded the Horyuji and other great temples in the early seventh century. In 710 the Yamato kings established a permanent capital for the first time, at Nara; the city was modeled on the Chinese capital. In 785 the court, split by factionalism and dominated by Nara's large and wealthy Buddhist temples, abandoned the capital; in 794 the new capital at Heian (Kyoto) was completed. The ensuing Heian period was one of the most brilliant in Japanese history. A small civil aristocracy, dominated by the Fujiwara family, drew great wealth from provincial estates and created a metropolitan culture of extreme refinement. From the ninth through the 11th centuries, strong Chinese influences were incorporated into Japanese culture.

In the 12th century the power of the Heian court waned as the influence of the provincial military aristocracy (samurai) grew stronger. In 1156 the capital was seized by the Taira family; in 1185 the Taira were overthrown by their rivals, the Minamoto. The Minamoto established a military government under a shogun (generalissimo) at Kamakura; the emperor remained at Kyoto, stripped of all governmental authority. In Kamakura the Minamoto were soon displaced by their former vassals, the Hojo. During the Kamakura period, the Japanese drew away from Chinese influence in art, architecture, literature, and religion in the process of creating a more distinctively Japanese culture. In 1274 and again in 1281, Mongol invasions were repulsed with the aid of timely typhoons (*kamikaze*, "divine winds").

In the course of a failed attempt at imperial restoration, the Kamakura shogunate was overthrown in the 1330's by the Ashikaga family, which in 1338 established a new shogunal government at Muromachi, a precinct of Kyoto. The Muromachi period saw the flowering of a warrior culture, marked by military virtues as bravery, loyalty, personal honor, and skill with weapons and by adherence to Zen Buddhism and its associated arts (tea ceremony, calligraphy, etc.). With the Onin Wars of the mid-15th century, the Muromachi shogunate lost most of its power, and the country fell into a century of civil war.

The civil wars were brought to an end during the second half of the 16th century by three successive unifiers, Oda Nobunaga, Hideyoshi, and Tokugawa Ieyasu. At the same time, the Jesuit Francis Xavier and his successors established a short-lived Japanese Christian community. Hideyoshi made several attempts (1592-98) to conquer and annex Korea. In 1601 Tokugawa Ieyasu defeated his rivals in the Battle of Sekigahara. He established a shogunal government at Edo (later Tokyo) in 1603; he and his successors formalized the structure of Japanese feudalism, created a rigid class structure, suppressed Christianity, and enforced the isolation of Japan from virtually all outside influence. Some trade with the mainland and a small Dutch trading station at Nagasaki provided Japan's only windows to the outside world for the next 250 years. The Edo period was marked by urbanization and the development of urban culture (Kabuki theater, wood-block prints, etc.) as the merchant class prospered from internal trade.

The Tokugawa shogun's inability to repel the 1854 visit of American commodore Matthew Perry and subsequently to avoid establishing commercial and diplomatic relations with Western nations deeply shocked the samurai class. Patriotic young samurai from Choshu, Satsuma, and other outlying feudal domains began to call for the abolition of the shogunate and the restoration of imperial rule in order to confront the threat of contact with the West. Quickly realizing that isolationism was doomed, the young radicals' program changed from "respect the emperor, expel the barbarians" to "enrich the state, strengthen the military." With the accession of the Meiji emperor in 1868, shogunal government ended.

Under direct imperial rule, feudalism was abolished and a wide-ranging program of military, industrial, commercial, and social modernization was implemented. The Meiji Constitution of 1889 created a constitutional monarchy and a parliamentary system of government. Having avoided domination by Western nations, Japan itself became an imperialist power. Defeating China in the Sino-Japanese War of 1894-95 and Russia in the Russo-Japanese War of 1904-05, Japan gained a dominant position in Manchuria and in Korea, which became a Japanese colony in 1910.

Under the ineffectual Taisho emperor (reigned 1912-26), parliamentary government flourished. Japan sided with the Allied Powers in World War I, and the Treaty of Versailles advanced Japan's international interests, particularly in China. The general prosperity of the 1920's was threatened by the Tokyo earthquake of 1923, by labor strife, and by a stagnant agricultural economy. Militant right-wing nationalism began to play an important role in domestic politics.

During the international economic depression of the early 1930's, right-wing militants gained the upper hand; they assassinated many moderate political figures. Japan invaded Manchuria in 1931 and established the puppet state of Manchuguo in 1934. An attempted military coup in 1936 failed in its immediate objectives but led to the establishment of martial law, under which the Showa emperor (Hirohito; reigned 1926-89) became a pawn of the ultranationalists. An invasion and military takeover of eastern China in 1937 was seen as the first step in the creation of a "Greater East Asian Co-prosperity Sphere," designed to unite Asia under Japanese control.

In 1940 Japan entered the Tripartite Alliance with Italy and Nazi Germany. Japan occupied French Indochina in June 1941, provoking increased Allied resistance to Japanese imperial ambitions. Gen. Hideki Tojo became prime minister in Oct. 1941 and ordered simultaneous preemptive strikes against Pearl Harbor, the Philippines, and Malaya on Dec. 7-8. By mid 1942, Japan controlled most of Southeast Asia and the western Pacific, but American victories at the Battle of the Coral Sea in May 1942 and the Battle of Midway in June 1942 halted Japanese expansion. Thereafter, Japanese forces were steadily pushed back in "island-hopping" campaigns in the central Pacific and along the western Pacific rim, and by Allied counterattacks in Burma. Air attacks on Japan itself culminated in the atomic bombing of Hiroshima and Nagasaki in August 1945.

Following Japan's formal surrender on Sept. 2, 1945, an American army in Japan under Gen. Douglas MacArthur took control of the country. A new constitution was promulgated, relegating the emperor to purely symbolic status, renouncing the use of military force, and guaranteeing the civil rights of citizens. The industrial combines that had lent strength to Japan's empire were partially dismantled. An international tribunal tried many wartime leaders as war criminals in 1948. In 1949 considerable authority was returned to the conservative government of Premier Shigeru Yoshida. Japan served as a base for American forces during the Korean War, 1950-53, greatly accelerating Japan's postwar economic recovery. On Apr. 28, 1952, a peace treaty between Japan and the United States went into effect, ending the Occupation. On Mar. 8, 1954, the two nations signed a mutual defense assistance pact.

Japan was admitted to the United Nations in 1956. The success of Japan's postwar recovery was symbolized by the Tokyo Olympic Games of 1964 and Expo '70 at Osaka. Violent student-protest movements in 1968-69 had no clear political goals and no lasting effect. Politically stable under an unbroken succession of Liberal Democratic party

governments, Japan emerged as a major and steadily expanding world industrial power.

Since the mid-1970's, the balance of trade between Japan and the U.S. has weighed heavily in Japan's favor, occasionally leading to strains in U.S.-Japan relations and American charges that Japan engaged in unfair trade practices. Several times during the 1980's and 1990's, especially when the yen was appreciating rapidly against the dollar, Japan pledged to even the trade balance by improving foreign access to Japan's domestic economy.

Domestically, Japan in the 1980's enjoyed a very high standard of living, marred by the extremely high cost and relatively low quality of housing, and by underinvestment in the public infrastructure. A real estate boom led prices of commercial property in downtown Tokyo to increase as much as 200-fold in the span of a decade. This boom extended to the United States, where the rapidly declining dollar made Japanese investment in the United States especially attractive.

For most of its postwar history, Japan has been essentially a one-party state, run by political professionals of the Liberal Democratic party (LDP) according to a system of consensus. But by the end of the 1980's, the system started to crumble as the regime's widespread corruption was revealed. Prime Minister Noboru Takeshita was force to resign in May 1989 after a bribery scandal. His successor, Sousuke Uno, lasted only two months before resigning in a scandal over his sexual conduct. Public opinion turned sharply against the LDP, which lost control of the upper house of the Diet in July 1989 elections; the Socialist party, led by Takako Doi, posted significant gains.

Uno's successor, Toshiki Kaifu, emerged as an unexpectedly skillful leader who enhanced Japan's international reputation by offering aid to Eastern Europe and the former Soviet Union, and by pledging billions of dollars to support the Persian Gulf War. In Oct. 1991, Kaifu was replaced as LDP chairman by Kiichi Miyazawa, who succeeded in passing legislation authorizing the posting abroad of Japanese troops—for the first time since World War II—for peacekeeping missions in noncombat roles.

An economic slump and political scandals continued to buffet the LDP throughout 1992 and 1993. LDP kingmaker Shin Kanemaru and other party officials resigned after admitting ties to gangsters. The LDP was forced from office in 1993 for the first time in 38 years, and formed successive coalition governments with the Socialist Party and other parties. The weak coalition governments paved the way for an LDP return to power in 1994; the years since have brought continued economic stagnation, bank failures, scandals involving government and business ties to organized crime, and general malaise.

The city of Kobe was hit by a severe earthquake in January, 1995; the government was criticized for ineffective rescue and relief efforts. The country's confidence was further shaken in March, 1995, by a bizarre attack with poison gas in the Tokyo subway, perpetrated by a religious cult, Aum Shinrikyo. Its leader, Shoko Asahara, was eventually arrested and convicted of murder.

Prime Minister Ryutaro Hashimoto, first elected in Jan. 1996, was re-elected leader of the LDP in Sept., 1997. But the Asian economic crisis took a toll on Japan, still in the midst of a long-term recession. In the spring of 1998 a plunge in the value of the yen doomed the Hashimoto government; he resigned and was replaced by party stalwart, Keizo

Obuchi. In 1999 Japan's economy rebounded slightly as the Obuchi government tried desperately to raise the levels of spending throughout the economy. In April 2000, Premier Obuchi suffered a stroke. His successor Yoshiro Mori led the Liberal Democrats to a near majority in parliamentary elections (June 25), forming a coalition government with New Komeito and the Conservatives (a new party, composed of former Liberals). With Mori's resignation in April 2001, the Liberal Democrats selected as their leader, and the lower house named as Prime Minister, Junichiro Koizumi, a man outside the old party "factions" and promising modernizing liberal economic reforms.

Japan's economy grew worse during 2001 and 2002, but rebounded in the following years, and in 2004 foreign direct investment in Japan surged to a record high. Koizumi tried to shake up his party and the nation so when his plan to privatize the post office was defeated in parliament, he called for quick elections in Sept. 2005 which he won in a landslide victory. As his tenure drew to a close, Koizumi strengthened Japan's ties to the U.S. as the economy grew steadily. In 2006, the LDP again won control of the government and elected Shinzo Abe as prime minister. His early popularity faded quickly in light of severe scandals and his aloof manner. After his party suffered a severe defeat in the upper house elections of July, 2007, Abe resigned and was replaced by veteran lawmaker Yasuo Fukuda whose inability to break the political deadlock led to his resignation in Sept. 2008. He was succeeded by Taro Aso, a veteran politician, and the nation's fourth prime minister in two years.

▶ **JORDAN**
Hashemite Kingdom of Jordan
● **GEOGRAPHY Location:** western Asia. **Boundaries:** Syria to N, Iraq to NE, Saudi Arabia to SE, Israel to W. **Total area:** 34,445 sq. mi. (89,213 sq km). **Coastline:** 16 mi. (26 km). **Comparative area:** slightly smaller than Indiana. **Land use:** 3% arable land; 2% permanent crops, 95% other. **Major cities:** Amman (capital); Zarqa; Irbid; Russeita. ● **PEOPLE Population:** 6,198,677 (July 2008 est.). **Nationality:** noun—Jordanian(s); adjective—Jordanian. **Ethnic groups:** 98% Arab, 1% Circassian, 1% Armenian. **Languages:** Arabic (official); English widely understood among upper and middle classes. **Religions:** 92% Sunni Muslim, 6% Christian, 2% other. ● **GOVERNMENT Type:** constitutional monarchy. **Independence:** May 25, 1946 (from League of Nations Mandate under British administration). **Constitution:** Jan. 8, 1952. **National holiday:** Independence Day, May 25. **Heads of Government:** Abdullah Bin Al Hussein, king (since Feb. 1999); Nader al-Dahabi, prime minister (since Nov. 2007). **Structure:** executive—king is chief of state, prime minister and cabinet are appointed by king; bicameral legislature—House of Representatives has been dissolved by the king several times since 1974; House of Notables appointed by the king; judiciary. ● **ECONOMY Monetary unit:** Jordanian dinar. **Budget:** (2007 est.) *income:* $4.999 bil.; *expend.:* $6.449 bil. **G.D.P.:** $28.18 bil., $4,700 per capita (2007 est.) **Chief crops:** wheat, barley, citrus, tomatoes, melons, olives; poultry, goats, sheep. **Natural resources:** phosphates, potash, shale oil. **Major industries:** phosphate mining, petroleum refining, cement. **Labor force:** 1.563 mil (2007); 82.5% services, 12.5% industry, 5% agriculture; 25-30% un-

employment (2001). **Exports:** $6.037 bil. (f.o.b., 2007 est.); phosphates, fertilizers, potash, agricultural products, manufactures. **Imports:** $11.08 bil. (f.o.b., 2007 est.); crude oil, machinery, transport equipment, food, live animals, manufactured goods. **Major trading partners:** (2006) *exports:* 25.2% U.S., 16.9% Iraq, 8% India, 5.8% Saudi Arabia, 4.7% Syria; *imports:* 23.2% Saudi Arabia, 8.3% Germany, 8% China, 5.3% U.S.

The present territory of the Kingdom of Jordan corresponds to the biblical lands of Edom, Gilead, and Moab. The ancient rock city of Petra was the capital of the Edomite and Nabataean kingdoms. The region was incorporated into the Roman Empire, and later the Latin Kingdom of Jerusalem; it was an important early center of Christianity.

In the 630's Jordan became one of the first areas outside Arabia to fall to the expansion of Islam. It became subject to the Caliphate, located at Damascus and later at Baghdad, and in the 11th century became part of the empire of the Seljuk Turks. The Crusades brought European invaders, but with little lasting impact. The Mongols conquered Jordan in the mid-13th century, and it later passed into the control of the Mamluk sultanate. In 1517 Jordan was incorporated into the Ottoman Empire.

Following the post-World War I breakup of the Ottoman Empire, Jordan came under British control as part of a League of Nations Mandate of Palestine. In 1921 Great Britain sponsored the establishment of a monarchy by Abdullah, son of Hussein ibn Ali, ruler of the Hejaz in Arabia. Britain recognized the independence of the Hashemite Kingdom of Transjordan in 1923; a 1928 treaty gave Britain the unrestricted right to station troops in the kingdom.

Transjordan supported the Allies in World War II and was rewarded with full independence in 1946, although strong military ties to Great Britain were maintained. In 1948 the kingdom joined the Arab League, changed its name to Jordan, and joined other Arab states in the first Arab-Israeli War. The war resulted in the occupation by Jordanian troops of the West Bank and the Old City of Jerusalem, which were annexed in 1950. King Hussein I came to the throne on Aug. 11, 1952. All British military forces were withdrawn from the kingdom in 1957.

Israel recaptured the West Bank and the Old City of Jerusalem in the Six-Day War of 1967, and large numbers of Palestinian refugees fled to Jordan. Jordan played no substantial role in the 1974 Arab-Israeli War. In 1974 Jordan accepted the decision of an Arab summit conference designating the Palestine Liberation Organization the sole representative of Palestinians in the West Bank. Jordan's role as a front-line opponent of Israel won it a large annual subvention from Arab oil states; King Hussein's reputation as an Arab moderate led to significant American support.

King Hussein strongly opposed the 1979 Camp David Accords and the Egypt-Israeli peace treaty; Jordan broke off diplomatic relations with Egypt in March 1979 but resumed full relations in 1984.

In July 1981 King Hussein, charging the Palestine Liberation Organization with subversion, forced the withdrawal of PLO troops and political headquarters from Jordan. While some hoped that Hussein would represent the Palestinians in talks with Israel, in 1988 the king flatly rejected any such role, implied that the PLO should declare an independent state on the West Bank and in the Gaza Strip, and declared that a settlement would require talks between Israel and the PLO.

The Persian Gulf War had a drastic impact on Jordan's economy. King Hussein actively backed Iraq, thus jeopardizing direct aid from Kuwait and Saudi Arabia. But the historic peace treaty signed with Israel in October 1994 restored Hussein's standing while returning some territory taken in the 1967 war. In August 1998, while in the U.S. for medical care, King Hussein made a dramatic visit to the PLO-Israeli talks to appeal for a settlement. Back in Jordan, Hussein deposed his brother Hassan as Crown Prince, swearing in his eldest son Abdullah instead. Twelve days later (Feb. 7), the king died. The new king, Abdullah, pledged to continue his father's policies, asking the current cabinet to stay on. King Abdullah moved cautiously against radical Muslim groups (winning Israeli praise) and restructured the army command in 1999. He has maintained a low profile throughout the turmoil in Israel and Iraq.

▶KAZAKHSTAN
Republic of Kazakhstan
• **GEOGRAPHY Location:** central Asia. **Boundaries:** Russian Federation to N and NE, China to SE, Kyrgystan, Uzbekistan, and Turkmenistan to S, Caspian Sea to W. **Total area:** 1,049,151 sq. mi. (2,717,300 sq km). **Coastline:** 1,441 mi. (2,320 km) on Caspian Sea. **Comparative area:** slightly less than four times the size of Texas. **Land use:** 11% arable cropland; 1% permanent crops; 88% other. **Major cities:** Astana (capital); Almaty (formerly Alma-Ata); Karaganda. • **PEOPLE Population:** 15,340,533 (July 2008 est.). **Nationality:** noun—Kazakhstani(s); adjective—Kazakhstani. **Ethnic groups:** 53.4% Kazakh, 30% Russian, 3.7% Ukrainian, 2.5% Uzbek. **Languages:** 64.4 Kazakh (state language); 95% Russian (official, used in everyday business). **Religions:** 47% Muslim, 44% Russian Orthodox, 2% Protestant. • **GOVERNMENT Type:** republic. **Independence:** Dec. 16, 1991 (from the Soviet Union). **Constitution:** Jan 28, 1993. **National holiday:** Day of the Republic, Oct. 25. **Heads of Government:** Nursultan A. Nazarbaev, president (since Dec. 1991); Kaim Massimov, prime minister (since Jan. 2007). **Structure:** executive—president, prime minister, Council of Ministers; bicameral legislature; judicial. •
• **ECONOMY Monetary unit:** tenge. **Budget:** (2007 est.) *income:* $21.49 bil.; *expend.:* $22.31 bil. **G.D.P.:** $161.5 bil., $10,400 per capita (2007 est.). **Chief crops:** grains, cotton; wool, meat. **Natural resources:** major deposits of petroleum, natural gas, coal, iron ore, manganese. **Major industries:** oil, coal, iron ore, manganese. **Labor force:** 8.156 mil. (2007); 49.8% services, 32.2% agriculture, 18% industry (2005); 8.8% unemployment (2002). **Exports:** $44.88 bil. (f.o.b., 2007 est.); oil, ferrous and nonferrous metals, chemicals, grain, wool. **Imports:** $29.91 bil. (f.o.b., 2007 est.); machinery and parts, industrial materials, oil and gas. **Major trading partners:** (2006) *exports:* 12.4% Germany, 11.6% Russia, 10.9% China, 10.5% Italy, 7.6% France, 4.9% Romania; *imports:* 36.4% Russia, 19.3% China, 7.4% Germany.

Kazakhstan, the largest nation in central Asia, is a land of deserts and plateaus stretching across the rolling tablelands of the Eurasian landmass; approximately 20 percent is mountainous. The Kazakhs are descended from Mongol and Turkic tribes who settled in the area known as Kazakhstan about the 1st century B.C. In the sixth century A.D.

the area formed part of the Turkish Khaganate, a loose federation of nomadic tribes, and in the seventh to ninth centuries Islam became established among the settled population. Although the Mongols ruled the area from 1219 to 1447, the Turkish subjects of the Mongol Horde were to play a decisive role in the future of the region.

In the 15th century, the Kazakhs emerged as a distinct people, but by the 17th century, due to internecine fighting, the Kazakhs split into three nomadic federations, known as the Larger, the Middle, and the Lesser Hordes. In the mid-17th century, the Mongols began to invade the region, and the Kazakhs, not being unified enough to repel them, sought protection from the Russians. By the mid-18th century, the Kazakh lands were completely under Russian control. With the freeing of serfs in 1861 in Russia, Kazakhstan experienced its first major influx of Russian and Ukrainian peasants, who were given Kazakh lands. Resentment over this grew until the Kazakhs rebelled against Russian rule in 1916. The Russians brutally repressed the uprising, but not before thousands of Kazakhs and many Russians were killed.

After the 1917 Communist revolution in Russia, a civil war ensued in Kazakhstan, from which the Bolsheviks emerged victorious. The Kazakh territory was incorporated into Russia in 1920, granted "autonomous" status in 1925, and in 1936 it formally became one of the U.S.S.R.'s union republics. Kazakhstan was industrialized, but it suffered enormously from the U.S.S.R.'s policies. In the 1930's, the traditionally nomadic Kazakh people were forcibly settled on collectivized farms, and more than a million died of starvation. In the 1950's, Khrushchev's failed "Virgin Lands" scheme and the Soviet government's repeated nuclear tests wreaked environmental havoc on Kazakhstan. As a result of years of Soviet economic development programs, the rate of Russian and Ukrainian immigration into Kazakhstan greatly increased. By 1979, 41 percent of Kazakhstan's population was Russian.

Under Mikhail Gorbachev's policy of glasnost, or openness, in the 1980's, the corrupt Communist party leader of Kazakhstan and Brezhnev crony Dinmukhamed Kunayev was deposed. He was ultimately replaced by Nursultan Nazarbayev, an ethnic Kazakh, who was elected in April 1990 to the new post of president.

Kazakhstan declared its independence in March 1991 and joined the Commonwealth of Independent States in December. It has pursued closer economic but not political ties with Russia and Belarus. The May 1995 customs union among the three was expanded in March 1996 to include coordination of agricultural and industrial policies and the establishment of joint transport, energy and information systems, with Kyrgystan added as a fourth member. Kazakhstan took part (April 1996) in a five-power non-agression treaty with Russia, China, Kyrgyzstan, and Tajikistan which was extended a year later to include reduction of military forces in border areas. The last remaining Soviet-era nuclear missle was detonated underground in May 1995 and the last ballistic missle silo was torn down in September 1996. In Feb. 1997 the supposedly tame legislature refused to ratify a Russian lease of four nuclear test sites in Kazakhstan.

Independent Kazakhstan's first presidential election was held in December 1991 with Nazarbayev the only candidate. An April 1995 referendum cancelled the 1996 election and extended Nazarbayev's term to 2000 with a gratifying 95 percent "yes" vote; and in August of the year 89 percent approved a new "strong president" constitution, making the president head of the Supreme Court and permitting him to dissolve parliament at will. Nazarbayev had already dissolved parliament in March 1995, a parliament in which his supporters held two-thirds of the seats, but whose pace of economic reform displeased him. He ruled by decree until new elections late in 1995 and early in 1996.

Kazakhstan's economic future is tied to its enormous untapped gas and oil reserves, perhaps 25 billion barrels. In April 1996, Kazakhstan, Russia and Oman established a consortium with eight oil companies to build a 900-mile pipeline linking the Tengiz fields with Russia's Black Sea port of Novorossiyak. And in July of that year, the I.M.F. chipped in with a loan of $446 million.

In 1998 the capital was moved— ostensibly for security reasons—from Almaty to remote Akmola, which was renamed Astana, a word meaning "capital" in Kazakh. In July, Navarbayev signed a pact with Russia, settling the thorny question of dividing the northern Caspian Sea (with its petroleum riches). But with falling world oil prices, the Kazakh economy stalled, bringing Nazarbayev to call for presidential elections 18 months early, elections he not surprisingly won handily, this time with 80 percent of the votes, in January 1999. Over the next years he solidified his hold on the government and made several lucrative energy deals. As the price of oil rose to near record levels the future grew ever more promising.

▶ **KENYA**
Republic of Kenya
● **GEOGRAPHY Location:** eastern Africa. **Boundaries:** Sudan to NW, Ethiopia to N, Somalia to E, Indian Ocean to SE, Tanzania to SW, Lake Victoria, Uganda to W. **Total area:** 224,962 sq. mi. (582,650 sq km). **Coastline:** 333 mi. (536 km). **Comparative area:** slightly more than twice the size of Nevada. **Land use:** 7% arable land; 1% permanent crops; 92% other. **Major cities:** Nairobi (capital); Mombasa; Nakuru; Kisumu; Thika.
● **PEOPLE Population:** 37,953,838 (July 2008 est.). **Nationality:** noun—Kenyan(s); adjective—Kenyan. **Ethnic groups:** 22% Kikuyu, 14% Luhya, 13% Luo, 12% Kalenjin, 11% Kamba, 6% Kisii, 6% Meru, 15% other African, 1% non-African (Asian, European, and Arab). **Languages:** English and Kiswahili (both official), indigenous languages. **Religions:** 45% Protestant, 35% Roman Catholic, 10% indigenous beliefs, 10% Muslim, 2% other.
● **GOVERNMENT Type:** republic. **Independence:** Dec. 12, 1963 (from U.K.). **Constitution:** Dec. 12, 1963. **National holiday:** Independence Day, Dec. 12. **Head of Government:** Mwai Kibaki, president (since Jan. 1, 2003); Raila Amolo Odinga, prime minister (since Apr. 2008). **Structure:** executive— president and cabinet; unicameral legislature— first multiparty election since repeal of one-party state law in 1991; judiciary.
● **ECONOMY Monetary unit:** Kenyan shilling. **Budget:** (2007 est.) *income:* $5.444 bil.; *expend.:* $6.399 bil. **G.D.P.:** $57.65 bil., $1,600 per capita (2007 est.). **Chief crops:** coffee, tea, corn, wheat, sugarcane; cattle, pork, poultry. **Natural resources:** gold, limestone, soda ash, salt barites. **Major industries:** small-scale consumer goods (plastic, furniture, batteries, textiles, soap, cigarettes, flour), agricultural processing, oil refining. **Labor force:** 11.85 mil. (2005); 75-80% agriculture,

20-25% non-agriculture; 40% unemployment (2001). **Exports:** $3.76 bil. (f.o.b., 2007 est.); tea, coffee, petroleum products. **Imports:** $7.602 bil. (f.o.b., 2007 est.); machinery and transport equipment, consumer goods, petroleum and petroleum products **Major trading partners:** (2006) *exports:* 15.9% Uganda, 10% U.K., 8% U.S., 8% Netherlands, 8% Tanzania, 5% Pakistan; *imports:* 12% United Arab Emirates, 9% India, 8% China, 8% Saudi Arabia, 7% U.S., 6% South Africa, 5% U.K., 5% Japan.

Kenya formed part of an ancient network of trade between the Red Sea and the coast of East Africa as early as the fourth century B.C. Persian and Arab trading posts were established on the coast by the eighth century A.D. At about the same time, the indigenous Cushitic people of Kenya had been joined by Bantu and Nilotic immigrants. Swahili, a mixture of Bantu and Arabic, developed as a language of trade throughout the region.

Portuguese explorers reached Kenya in 1498. Portuguese control of the coastal area ended in 1729, when the region came under the control of the sultans of Oman. British adventurers explored Kenya in the late 19th century. In 1885 the Berlin Conference divided East Africa into European spheres of influence. The British East Africa Company established a protectorate over the coastal region in 1890 and extended its control into the interior in 1895. British settlers established farms, mission stations, and towns, and Kenya was given colonial status in 1920.

During World War II, northern Kenya was briefly occupied by troops from the Italian colony of Ethiopia. After the British reasserted control, Africans were granted the right to participate in local government in 1944.

From 1952 to 1959, a state of emergency was declared in Kenya because of the "Mau Mau" rebellion against British colonial rule. In response to local unrest, British authorities widened African participation in government and Africans were elected to the Legislative Council in 1957.

Kenya became independent on Dec. 12, 1963, and in 1964 assumed the status of a republic within the British Commonwealth. Jomo Kenyatta, a member of the dominant Kikuyu population and leader of the main political party, the Kenya African National Union (KANU), was elected Kenya's first president. A leftist party, the Kenya People's Union (KPU) was organized in 1966, led by Oginga Odinga. In 1969 it was implicated in the assassination of Tom Mboya, a prominent political leader; its leaders were imprisoned and the party dissolved. From 1969 to 1992 KANU was Kenya's sole political party.

Kenyatta died on Aug. 22, 1978, and Vice Pres. Daniel arap Moi succeeded him. In 1982 the constitution was amended to make Kenya a one-party state. Moi was reelected president in 1983 and again in 1988, the latter being the first election conducted without secret ballots. Foreign observers accused the Moi government of widespread human rights abuses. Riots broke out in several cities in 1991, and sporadic ethnic violence cost thousands of lives.

In 1991, Odinga formed the opposition Forum for the Restoration of Democracy (FORD), in direct defiance of the government. With Western aid conditioned on economic reform, political pluralism, and improved human rights, Moi allowed presidential elections to be held in Dec. of 1992.

The three opposition parties split, and Moi was returned to office for a fourth time.

Kenya has traditionally been viewed as the success story of postcolonial Africa, but by the 1990's, widespread government corruption, and economic inefficiency had taken a heavy toll. Tourism has fallen due to the rise in violence, and the economy was further strained by the presence of refugees from Ethiopia, Somalia, and Sudan.

Early in 1994 the government announced reforms aimed at restoring confidence in the economy, including lifting the restrictions on foreign investment. But Pres. Moi's (April 1995) arrest of two leading opposition figures (bringing the total arrested since 1993 to more than 50) led to frustration among his many political enemies. In mid-1997, large demonstrations demanding Moi reform the electoral system in time for Dec. presidential elections were broken up by police with a great amount of violence. In the face of international condemnation Moi agreed to the proposed reforms (July 15), but little progress was made in subsequent meetings between the government and the opposition leaders. In Jan. 1998 Moi barely won reelection. (In an unrelated story, the U.S. embassy was attacked by a terrorist truck-bomb August 7, with 250 deaths.)

In 2002 dissentions within Moi's KANU party obliged him not to run for president; his attempt to name his successor (Uhuru Kenyatta, son of Kenya's "founding father") split the party and allowed the opposition National Alliance Party's candidate Mwai Kibaki to win the Dec. 2002 election. A sweeping anti-corruption campaign followed and over 100 judges were suspended. In 2004 allegations were made against Moi himself and his popularity slowly waned. In April 2008 the opposition leader, Raila Odinga, became prime minister in a power-sharing deal after severe violence followed a divided election in Dec. 2007. Over 1,000 were killed and 300,000 displaced. (See "Major News Stories.")

▶ **KIRIBATI**
Republic of Kiribati
● **GEOGRAPHY   Location:** 33 atolls, in three main groups (E to W: Line Is., Phoenix Is., Gilbert Is.) in mid-Pacific Ocean; about 2,400 mi. (3,870 km) E to W and 1,275 mi. (2,050 km) N to S. Tarawa (Gilberts) 1°30'N, 173°00'E. **Boundaries:** surrounded by Pacific Ocean; nearest neighbors are Nauru to W, and Tuvalu and Tokelau to S. **Total area:** 277 sq. mi. (717 sq km). **Coastline:** 710 mi. (1,143 km). **Comparative area:** four times the size of Washington, D.C. **Land use:** 0% arable land; 51% permanent crops; 49% other. **Major cities:** Tarawa (capital).
● **PEOPLE   Population:** 110,356 (July 2008 est.). **Nationality:** noun—I-Kiribati (sing., pl.); adjective—I-Kiribati. **Ethnic groups:** Micronesian. **Languages:** English (official), Gilbertese. **Religions:** 52% Roman Catholic, 40% Protestant (Congregational), some Seventh-Day Adventist, Church of God, Mormon and Baha'i.
● **GOVERNMENT   Type:** republic. **Independence:** July 12, 1979 (from U.K.). **Constitution:** July 12, 1979. **National holiday:** Independence Day, July 12. **Head of Government:** Anote Tong, president (since July 8, 2003). **Structure:** executive; unicameral legislature; judiciary—all judges appointed by the president.
● **ECONOMY   Monetary unit:** Australian dollar. **Budget:** (2005 est.) *income:* $55.52 mil.; *expend.:*

$59.71 mil. **G.D.P.:** $240 mil.(2006 est.), $1,000 per capita (2004 est.). **Chief crops:** copra; taro, bread fruit, vegetables; fish. **Natural resources:** phosphate (production discontinued in 1979). **Major industries:** fishing and handicrafts. **Labor force:** 7,870 economically active (2001 est.). **Exports:** $17 mil. (f.o.b., 2004 est.); 62% copra, seaweed, fish. **Imports:** $62 mil. (c.i.f., 2004 est.); foodstuffs, machinery and quipment. **Major trading partners:** (2006) *exports:* 22.8% U.S., 21.5% Belgium, 14.3% Japan, 7.8% Samoa, 7.5% Australia, 6.7% Malaysia, 5.6% Taiwan, 4.6% Denmark; *imports:* 33% Australia, 27.1% Fiji, 18.1% Japan, 6.9% New Zealand.

In 1892 the British established a protectorate over the Gilbert Islands, inhabited principally by Micronesians. In 1915 Britain joined the islands administratively with the Polynesian-speaking Ellice Islands to the south to form a British colony, the Gilbert and Ellice Islands (later expanded to include other islands). The Japanese occupied the Gilberts in 1942; in 1943 the Allied forces recaptured them, and Tarawa was the scene of some of the fiercest combat in the Pacific.

In 1971 Britain granted the colony self-rule. The Ellice Islands broke away in 1975, becoming the independent nation of Tuvalu in 1978. On July 12, 1979, the Gilbert Islands became independent as Kiribati. United States claims to portions of the Line and Phoenix islands were settled by a friendship treaty in 1979.

Kiribati's economy is based on subsistence farming and on fishing. Copra exports and the sale of fishing rights (principally to Japan) are the main earners of hard currency. The islands joined the United Nations in late 1999.

▶ **KOREA, NORTH**
Democratic People's Republic of Korea
● **GEOGRAPHY   Location:** northern part of Korean peninsula in eastern Asia. **Boundaries:** China to NW, Sea of Japan to E, Republic of Korea to S, Yellow Sea to SW. **Total area:** 46,541 sq. mi. (120,540 sq km). **Coastline:** 1,551 mi. (2,495 km). **Comparative area:** slightly smaller than Mississippi. **Land use:** 14% arable land; 2% permanent crops; 18% other. **Major cities:** Pyongyang (capital); Hamhung; Chongjin; Sinuju; Kaesong.
● **PEOPLE   Population:** 23,479,089 (July 2008 est.) **Nationality:** noun—Korean(s); adjective—Korean. **Ethnic groups:** racially homogeneous, with a small Chinese community. **Languages:** Korean. **Religions:** Buddhism and Confucianism; autonomous religious activities now almost nonexistent.
● **GOVERNMENT   Type:** authoritarian socialist; one-man dictatorship. **Constitution:** adopted 1948, revised Apr. 1992 and Sept. 1998. **National holiday:** Foundation Day, Sept. 9. **Heads of Government:** Kim Jong Il, president (since Oct. 1994); Pak Pong Ju, prime minister (since Dec. 2003). **Structure:** executive—president is dominant figure in government; Supreme People's Assembly theoretically supervises legislative and judicial functions; State Administration Council (cabinet) oversees ministerial operations.
● **ECONOMY   Monetary unit:** North Korean won. **Budget:** N.A.; **G.D.P.:** $2.22 bil. (2006 est.), $1,900 per capita (2007 est.). **Chief crops:** corn, rice, vegetables; pigs, cattle. **Natural resources:** coal, lead, tungsten, zinc, graphite. **Major industries:** machine building, military products, electric power, chemicals. **Labor force:** 20 mil. (note - estimates vary widely); 37% agricultural, 63% nonagricul-

tural. **Exports:** $1.466 bil. (f.o.b., 2006 est.); minerals, metallurgical products, agricultural and fishery products, manufactures. **Imports:** $2.879 bil. (c.i.f., 2006 est.); petroleum, machinery and equipment, coking coal, grain. **Major trading partners:** *exports:* 32% South Korea, 29% China, 9% Thailand; *imports:* 27% China, 16% South Korea, 9% Thailand, 7% Russia.

(For pre-1945 history, see "Republic of Korea.")

The Soviet Union's declaration of war against Japan in the waning days of World War II strengthened its position in northeast Asia, and particularly in Korea. After Japan's surrender, Korea was arbitrarily divided into zones of Soviet and American occupation, north and south of latitude 38° north. The Korean Communist party (KCP), founded in 1922, had functioned in exile in the U.S.S.R. during the Japanese occupation, and KCP workers were quickly moved into the Soviet zone in 1945.

U.S.-Soviet talks aimed at Korean reunification broke down, and in 1948 the establishment of separate regimes in North and South Korea formalized the postwar occupation zones. The Korean Democratic People's Republic was proclaimed on May 1, 1948. It inherited most of the industrial and hydroelectric power infrastructure built during the Japanese colonial period and enjoyed strong Soviet backing.

On June 25, 1950, North Korean troops crossed the 38th parallel in an effort to force the reunification of Korea under a communist regime. U.N. troops under American leadership came to the defense of the South. (For the Korean War, see "South Korea.") The war was fought to a stalemate, and a truce was signed on July 27, 1953.

Until 1994 North Korea had a single leader throughout its national history: Kim Il Sung, chairman of the KCP from 1945 and president from 1972. Under Kim Il Sung, North Korea was a typically Stalinist Soviet nation, concentrating its economic energies on heavy industry and imposing a strictly regimented political and social life on its citizens. Economic development was supported by aid from the Soviet Union and China. After an impressive program of postwar reconstruction in the 1950's and 1960's, the country fell into economic stagnation.

Relations between North and South Korea were hostile; the North has made numerous attempts to infiltrate and sabotage the South. In 1983, 17 people, including four South Korean cabinet ministers, were killed in Rangoon by a bomb planted by North Korean agents. In 1990 the leaders of both countries held three cordial but unproductive meetings. Much of the goodwill was harmed by the assertions of the U.S. that North Korea was planning to build nuclear weapons.

In August 1992, China, North Korea's long-term ally established diplomatic relations with South Korea, leaving North Korea completely isolated. High-level contacts between North and South Korea continued, but reconciliation talks stalled in 1993 as the issue of North Korean nuclear weapons came to the fore. North Korean leaders refused to allow international arms inspectors access to some facilities and withdrew from the Nuclear Non-Proliferation Treaty. In June 1994 former U.S. president Jimmy Carter met with Kim Il Sung and arranged for a summit meeting with South Korea and for another with Pres. Clinton to resolve the nuclear weapons issue. Kim Il Sung's sudden death in July prevented immediate progress, but in 1995 an agreement was reached that called for North Korea to dismantle its nuclear facilities in exchange for two new reactors from which weapons-grade plutonium is hard to extract. In 1996 severe floods destroyed most of the rice crop, left half a million homeless, and forced North Korea to accept emergency grants of rice from Japan and South Korea.

Continued severe famine spurred North Korea to pursue reconciliation talks with the South, but those talks were repeatedly disrupted by strife over its nuclear-weapons programs, incidents of clandestine landing of northern commandos in the south, and the defection of senior communist officials. In the fall of 1997 Kim Jung Il assumed his father's old position as general secretary of the Worker's Party. U.S. suspicions, voiced in 1998, of a new underground nuclear plant were proven baseless in May of 1999, the Great Leader permitting an inspection in return for food aid. (Estimates of 2.3 million deaths from the famine must have influenced the decision). Talks with South Korea in Beijing were broken off in June 1999 after South Korea sank a North Korean torpedo boat in the Yellow Sea. But talks in Geneva continued with South Korea, China and the U.S., supplemented in March 2000 with secret talks with South Korea, as diplomatic relations were opened with Italy and Australia. The secret talks led, in June, to a Pyongyang visit by South Korea's president Kim. The two pledged themselves to peace and reunification. Family visits across the border ensued.

In 2002, a naval attack in the Yellow Sea, in which a North Korean vessel sank a South Korean patrol boat, seriously eclipsed the "sunshine policy." In Oct. North Korean officials admitted to the U.S. they had been secretly developing nuclear weapons and in Dec. they expelled U.N. monitors. Named as part of the Bush administration "axis of evil" North Korea went into an aggressive mode threatening Japan with attack and continuously asserting its right to develop nuclear weapons. The U.S. and China continued to oppose this and a diplomatic surge helped bring North Korea back to the negotiating table. (See "Major News Stories.")

▶KOREA, SOUTH
Republic of Korea

● **GEOGRAPHY   Location:** southern part of Korean peninsula in eastern Asia. **Boundaries:** North Korea to N, separated by frontier roughly following 38th parallel; Sea of Japan to E, East China Sea to S, and Yellow Sea to W. **Total area:** 38,023 sq. mi. (98,480 sq km). **Coastline:** 1,500 mi. (2,413 km). **Comparative area:** slightly larger than Indiana. **Land use:** 17% arable land; 2% permanent crops; 81% other. **Major cities:** (1995 est.) Seoul (capital) 10,776,201; Pusan 3,802,319; Taegu 2,228,843; Inchon 1,818,293; Kwangju 1,144,695.

● **PEOPLE   Population:** 49,232,844 (July 2008 est.) **Nationality:** noun—Korean(s); adjective—Korean. **Ethnic groups:** homogeneous; small Chinese minority (about 20,000). **Languages:** Korean; English widely taught in high school. **Religions:** 26.3% Christianity, 23.2% Buddhism, 49.3% none.

● **GOVERNMENT   Type:** republic. **Constitution:** Feb. 25, 1988. **National holiday:** Liberation Day, Aug. 15. **Heads of Government:** Lee Myung-bak, president (since Feb. 2008); Han Seung-Soo, prime minister (since Feb. 2008). **Structure:** executive; unicameral legislature (National Assembly); judiciary.

● **ECONOMY   Monetary unit:** South Korean won. **Budget:** (2007 est.) *income:* $269.7 bil.; *expend.:*

$256.6 bil. **G.D.P.:** $1.206 tril., $24,600 per capita (2007 est.). **Chief crops:** rice, root crops, barley, vegetables, fruit; cattle, pigs, chickens, milk, eggs; fish catch of 2.9 mil. metric tons, seventh largest in the world. **Natural resources:** coal, tungsten, graphite, molybdenum. **Major industries:** electronics, automobiles, chemicals, shipbuilding. **Labor force:** 23.99 mil. (2007); 75.2% services, 17.3% industry; 7.5% agriculture, fishing, and forestry; 3.7% unemployment (2005). **Exports:** $371.5 bil. (f.o.b., 2007); electronic and electrical equipment, electrical machinery, steel, automobiles. **Imports:** $356.8 bil. (f.o.b., 2007); machinery, electronics and electronic equipment, oil, steel, transport equipment, textiles. **Major trading partners:** (2006) *exports:* 22% China, 12.5% U.S., 7.1% Japan, 5% Hong Kong; *imports:* 17.7% China, 16% Japan, 10.7% U.S., 5.9% Saudi Arabia, 4.2% United Arab Emirates.

From ancient times Korea has struggled successfully to preserve its national independence. To the native culture—marked by a warrior aristocracy, shamanic religion, and a subject class of rice cultivators—was added, under continuous Chinese influence, a strong adherence to Buddhism and a system of government modeled on Chinese Confucian bureaucratism. The three rival kingdoms of Silla, Paekche, and Koguryo were united, through Chinese intervention, in the seventh century a.d.; unified dynastic rule was maintained thereafter.

The Yi dynasty (1392-1910), when Korea was known as the Kingdom of Choson, was a staunch tributary ally of China under both the Ming (1368-1644) and Qing (1644-1911) dynasties. A Japanese invasion of Korea in 1592 conquered most of the country but was finally repelled by combined Chinese and Korean forces. From the late 17th century to the 1870's, all non-Chinese foreign influence was rigorously excluded.

Korea's isolation, and its status as a Chinese tributary, ended in 1874, when Japan imposed on it the Treaty of Kangwha, guaranteeing Japanese commercial access and other interests. The Sino-Japanese War of 1894-95 was fought primarily over the status of Korea; following Japan's victory in that war, Korea was made a Japanese protectorate and was annexed as a Japanese colony in 1910. A harsh regime was established with the aim of eradicating Korean culture and incorporating Korea entirely into the Japanese empire.

During the colonial period, Korean resistance to the Japanese regime was violently suppressed, but resistance movements survived in exile—notably the Korean Communist party in the Soviet Union and a republican movement in China. During World War II, tens of thousands of Koreans were conscripted as forced laborers to work in Japan and in Japanese-occupied territories.

Following Japan's surrender, Korea was arbitrarily divided into zones of Soviet and American occupation, north and south of 38° north latitude. The dividing line split Korea economically as well as geographically and politically; Korea's industry and hydroelectric power was concentrated in the north, while the south was primarily agricultural. In contrast to well-laid Soviet plans for installing a Communist government in the north (see "North Korea"), American attempts to reunify the country under a republican regime were inept. By 1948 it had become clear that plans for reunification were hopeless. In May of that year, the Republic of Korea was organized in the south, with Dr. Syng-man Rhee as president. The United States withdrew its occupation forces in June 1949.

On June 25, 1950, North Korean troops invaded the south in an apparent attempt to unify the country forcibly under the communist regime. An emergency session of the U.N. Security Council voted to send troops to Korea; the U.S.S.R., having boycotted the session, was unable to exercise its veto on North Korea's behalf. U.N. troops, dominated by American forces and commanded by Gen. Douglas MacArthur, launched a counterattack in September with a landing at Inchon and swept north, reaching the Chinese border by Nov. 20. On Nov. 26 the tide turned again when Chinese troops entered the war, ostensibly to defend the Chinese border but also to aid their North Korean allies in driving the U.N. forces south again. Seoul fell once more on Jan. 4, 1951. In February and March another U.N. counteroffensive drove the combined Chinese and North Korean forces back to the 38th parallel again. Thereafter, the battle lines remained generally stable, although fierce fighting continued at intervals for another two years. On Apr. 11, 1951, Gen. MacArthur was relieved of the Korean command for making unauthorized policy statements and was replaced by Gen. Matthew Ridgway.

Armistice talks began in July 1951 but broke down repeatedly. A truce was signed on July 27, 1953, creating a demilitarized zone along the 38th parallel and establishing a framework for talks on a permanent settlement of the war. Negotiations have continued fruitlessly at the Panmunjom armistice conference headquarters ever since.

Postwar reconstruction, with significant U.S. aid, was overseen by the government of Syngman Rhee. Pres. Rhee resigned in 1960 after a wave of student demonstrations charging him with corruption and undemocratic practices. On May 16, 1961, Gen. Park Chung Hee seized power in a military coup. The military government was given democratic trappings when in 1972 a referendum was passed allowing Gen. Park to run for an unlimited series of six-year presidential terms. Gen. Park was assassinated on Oct. 26, 1979, by the government's chief of intelligence. Gen. Chun Doo Hwan rose to power, continuing the military rule of Gen. Park. Gen. Chun's regime was marked by widespread violent political protests but the economy made great strides. The agrarian country was transformed into a modernized, urban, industrial nation. In 1986 South Korea achieved a favorable balance-of-payments ratio in foreign trade, and the favorable balance increased rapidly, led by exports of automobiles, textiles and clothing, and consumer electronic goods.

After weeks of widespread demonstrations in mid-1987, Gen. Chun agreed to allow direct presidential elections to choose his successor. In the elections, the government candidate, Roh Tae Woo, achieved a plurality over the sharply divided opposition parties. Under Pres. Roh, the political situation calmed, although student demonstrations continued, calling for greater efforts for Korean reunification and protesting the presence of large numbers of American troops.

High-level talks between North and South began in 1990, and an agreement in principle was reached that reunification would take place in the near future, a wish that remains unfulfilled. South Korea was a strong economic power in Asia and North Korea would become increasingly isolated, the establishment of diplomatic relations with China was a clear signal that it would remain so.

Also in 1992, longtime political opposition leader Kim Young Sam won election as South Korea's first postwar civilian president. Although he was initially able to liberalize some aspects of civil rights, the renewed threat of war with North Korea became the overriding preoccupation of the government until late 1994, when an agreement was reached calling for North Korea to dismantle its nuclear facilities in exchange for new reactors.

The ruling Democratic Labor Party was plagued by scandals that hampered its effectiveness. Pres. Kim's predecessor, Pres. Roh, was arrested for bribe-taking, as was his predecessor. Several key businessmen, including Kim's own son, were jailed for corruption. In elections in April 1996 the party lost its parliamentary majority but continued to govern as part of a coalition.

South Korea's economy was battered by the Asian economic crisis of 1997-98, leading to severe hardship for many workers. On Dec. 18, 1997, long-time democracy advocate and dissident Kim Dae Jung was elected. In May 1999 (after promising economic figures suggested a rising G.D.P. and falling unemployment) he was able to reshuffle the cabinet to more closely accord with his "sunshine policy" of reforming the great conglomerate business empires and of improving relations with North Korea. In June talks with the North, held in Beijing, were abbreviated after South Korea sank a North Korean torpedo boat in a fishing grounds dispute in the Yellow Sea. Yet talks in Geneva continued and secret talks began in March 2000, leading to a "summit" in Pyongyang in June between President Kim and Kim Jong Il which promised peace and reunification.

Domestically, financial scandals involving Pres. Kim's son and some of his aides led him to distance himself from the Millenium Party, resigning as its head in Nov. 2001 and from the party itself in May. A June 2002 North Korean naval attack called the "sunshine policy" into serious question. In December's presidential election, the Millennium Democrats' candidate, Rho Moo Hyun, defeated Lee Hoi Chang of the Grand National Party. His inaugural address stressed reconcilation through dialogue in the face of the grave threat of North Korea's nuclear blustering. Roh's opponents pushed through a bill impeaching him in March 2004 and removing him from office until the courts ruled in his favor in May. This helped Roh's supporters to win a majority in the National Assembly. In 2008 businessman Lee Myung-bak was elected by a record margin and his party won control of parliament; leading experts predict success for his programs.

▶ **KUWAIT**
State of Kuwait
• **GEOGRAPHY Location:** northeastern Arabian peninsula. **Boundaries:** Iraq to N, Saudi Arabia to S, Persian Gulf to E. **Total area:** 6,880 sq. mi. (17,820 sq km). **Coastline:** 310 mi. (499 km). **Comparative area:** slightly smaller than New Jersey. **Land use:** negl. % arable land; negl. % permanent crops; 100% other. **Major cities:** Kuwait City (capital); Salmiya; Hawalli; Faranawiya; Abraq Kheetan.
• **PEOPLE Population:** 2,596,799 (July 2008 est.). **Nationality:** noun—Kuwaiti(s);   adjective— Kuwaiti. **Ethnic groups:** 45% Kuwaiti, 35% other Arab, 9% South Asian, 4% Iranian, 7% other. **Languages:** Arabic (official), English widely spoken.

Religions: 85% Muslim (30% Shi'a, 70% Sunni), 15% Christian, Hindu, Parsi, and other.
• **GOVERNMENT Type:** nominal constitutional monarchy. **Independence:** June 19, 1961 (from U.K.). **Constitution:** Nov. 11, 1962 (some provisions suspended since Aug. 29, 1962). **National holiday:** National Day, Feb. 25. **Head of Government:** Sabah al-Ahmad al-Jaber Al-Sabah, emir (since Feb. 7, 2006); Nasser Al-Mohammed Al-Ahmad Al-Sabah, prime minister (since Jan., 2006). **Structure:** executive; unicameral legislature; judiciary.
• **ECONOMY Monetary unit:** Kuwaiti dinar. **Budget:** (2007 est.) *income:* $66.92 bil.; *expend.:* $36.39 bil. **G.D.P.:** $138.6 bil., $55,300 per capita (2007 est.). **Chief crops:** virtually none; extensive fishing; about 75% of potable water must be distilled or imported. **Natural resources:** petroleum, fish, shrimp, natural gas. **Major industries:** petroleum, petrochemicals, desalination. **Labor force:** 1.167 mil. (2007 est.); non-Kuwaitis make up 80% of the work force. **Exports:** $59.57 bil. (f.o.b., 2007 est.); oil and refined products, fertilizers. **Imports:** $17.74 bil. (f.o.b., 2003 est.); food, construction materials, vehicles and parts, clothing. **Major trading partners:** (2006) *exports:* 20.4% Japan, 16.2% South Korea, 10.8% Taiwan, 9.7% Singapore, 9% U.S., 5.3% Netherlands, 4.1% China; *imports:* 14.1% U.S., 7.9% Germany, 7.8% Japan, 6.8% Saudi Arabia, 5.7% China, 5.4% U.K., 4.6% Italy.

Kuwait, at the head of the Persian Gulf, was part of the Abbasid empire from the eighth century and was absorbed into the Ottoman Empire in the late 16th century. It was organized as a principality under the al-Sabah dynasty in 1756, but the Ottomans continued to assert sovereignty. Increasing British influence during the 19th century was formalized in 1899, when Kuwait became a British protectorate.

The discovery of oil, first exported from Kuwait after World War II, rapidly made the principality one of the wealthiest in the Middle East. The British protectorate ended in 1961, when Kuwait gained full independence. The great majority of oil field workers in Kuwait are non-Kuwaiti Arabs, including many Palestinians. Oil revenues have made possible a total welfare state for Kuwaiti citizens, who pay no taxes and enjoy a wide range of free social services.

Kuwait allied itself with Iraq in the Iran-Iraq War of 1980-88; Kuwaiti tankers came under heavy attack from Iranian warships in the gulf. In July 1987, Kuwaiti tankers were reflagged with the U.S. flag and placed under escort of American warships in an operation that continued into 1989. Most of Kuwait's territory is barren but with proven crude oil reserves of 94 bil. barrels other economic endeavors are not needed.

On Aug. 2, 1990, Kuwait was invaded, and later annexed, by Iraq. In February 1991 it was liberated by a coalition of Arab, non-Arab Muslim, and Western nations led by the United States. Much of the country was destroyed or looted by the Iraqis. After its return to power, the ruling al-Sabah family came under strong pressure to institute democratic reforms. Parliamentary elections were held in 1992, and opposition candidates won 30 of 50 seats. The sultan then announced a new cabinet with more nonroyal members than ever before.

A brief war-scare flared up in October 1994 as 20,000 Iraqi Republican Guards were moved to the Kuwaiti border, only to retreat in the face of U.S. military opposition. In November, Iraq formally recognized Kuwait's sovereignty. In Jan. 2006 the long-reigning emir Sheik Jaber al-Ahmad al-Sabah died and was succeeded by the prime minister, Sheik Sabah al-Ahmad al-Sabah.

▶KYRGYZSTAN
Kyrgyz Republic

• **GEOGRAPHY Location:** eastern central Asia. **Boundaries:** Kazakhstan to N and NE, China to SE and S, Tajikistan to SW, Uzbekistan to W. **Total area:** 76,641 sq. mi. (198,500 sq km). **Coastline:** none. **Comparative area:** slightly smaller than South Dakota. **Land use:** 7% arable land; 0% permanent crops; 93% other. **Major cities:** Bishkek (known as Frunze 1926-91) (capital).

• **PEOPLE Population:** 5,356,869 (July 2008 est.). **Nationality:** noun—Kyrgyzstani(s); adjective—Kyrgyzstani. **Ethnic groups:** 52.4% Kirghiz, 18% Russian, 12.9% Uzbek, 2.5% Ukrainian, 2.4% German, 11.8% other. **Languages:** Kirghiz and Russian (both official), Kirghiz is a member of south Turkic language group written in Cyrillic since 1940. **Religions:** 75% Muslim; 20% Russian Orthodox.

• **GOVERNMENT Type:** republic. **Independence:** Aug. 31, 1991 (from Soviet Union). **Constitution:** adopted May 5, 1993. **National holiday:** National Day, Dec. 2; Independence Day, Aug. 31. **Heads of Government:** Kurmanbek Bakiev, president (since Apr. 2005). Almaz S. Atambaev, prime minister (since March 2007). **Structure:** executive—president, prime ministers, Cabinet of Ministers; bicameral legislature; judiciary.

• **ECONOMY Monetary unit:** som. **Budget:** (2007 est.) *income:* $684.4 mil.; *expend.:* $764.1 mil. **G.D.P.:** $10.38 bil., $2,000 per capita (2007 est.). **Chief crops:** wool, tobacco, cotton; sheep, goats, cattle. **Natural resources:** hydroelectric potential; gold; coal, natural gas, petroleum, lead, zinc. **Major industries:** small machinery, textiles, food processing, cement. **Labor force:** 2.7 mil. (2000); 55% agriculture and forest, 30% services, 15% industry and construction. **Exports:** $1.04 bil. (f.o.b., 2007 est.); cotton, wool, meat, tobacco; ferrous and nonferrous metals. **Imports:** $2.509 mil. (f.o.b., 2007 est.); foodstuffs, fuel, machinery. **Major trading partners:** (2006) *exports:* 26.1% Switzerland, 20.4% Kazakhstan, 19.3% Russia, 9.4% Afghanistan, 4.8% China; *imports:* 38.1% Russia, 14.4% China, 11.7% Kazakhstan, 5.7% U.S.

Kyrgyzstan is largely mountainous, dominated by the massive Tien Shan range in the northeast and the Pamir-Alay range in the southwest. Most of the population lives in one of three major valleys, the Fergana, the Chu, and the Talas, since much of the country is permanently ice-capped and covered with glaciers. The Kyrgyz people are mentioned in early Turkic inscriptions that date back at least to the eighth century A.D.

They were one of the great nomadic tribes of central Asia, who until the 10th century settled around the Upper Yenisei River. With the Mongol invasions of the 13th century, they migrated to the areas of the Tien Shan range in present-day Kyrgyzstan, a territory that has been controlled variously by Mongols, Kalmyks, Manchus, the large tribal empire of the Kokand khanate, and the Russians. In the mid-17th century, the Kyrgyz began to be converted to Islam, but the Manchus defeated the Mongols and the Kyrgyz people became Chinese subjects. The Chinese did not interfere with their nomadic life, but in the 19th century they were attacked and came under the control of the khanate of Kokand, during which

time Islam was strengthened. In 1868 the khanate became a Russian protectorate and in 1876, the area was merged into the Russian empire as Fergana region. A large Russian influx followed, and many Kyrgyz migrated to China and Afghanistan.

The period immediately following the 1917 Bolshevik revolution was one of confusion and fighting between the Kyrgyz, the Reds, the Whites, and foreign interventionists. Soviet power was established in 1919, although fighting continued in some parts until 1922. In 1918, Kyrgyzstan was included in the Russian republic's Turkestan Autonomous Soviet Socialist Republic; then, with the National Delimitation of Central Asian Republics in 1924, its name changed to Kara-Kirghiz Autonomous Province. On Dec. 5, 1936, it became a Soviet Socialist Republic (SSR) of the U.S.S.R.

In the 1920's and 1930's, land reform and collectivization ended the traditional nomadic way of life. Kyrgyz nationalists strongly opposed the changes that Soviet rule brought, but the central government won in the end, and the nationalists were repressed. From the 1930's, ethnic Russians held most of the leading Communist party and government positions in the Kyrgyz SSR.

Mikhail Gorbachev's policy of glasnost, or openness, was responsible for the first public discussion of corruption in government, the emergence of a more liberal Kyrgyz press by 1988, and the emergence of opposition parties and ethnic conflicts. In 1990 disputes over housing and land in the Osh region of the crowded Fergana Valley led to violent confrontations between the Kyrgyz and the republic's Uzbeks. Osh had been incorporated into Kyrgyzstan in 1924, even though the majority population was Uzbek, and at various times the Uzbeks had lobbied for the establishment of an autonomous Uzbek region in Osh.

In Feb. 1990 traditional Soviet-style elections brought into office many Communist party officials, and in April the Supreme Soviet elected Absamat Masaliyev, who had been the Kyrgyz republic's Communist party First Secretary. In Oct. 1990, however, largely due to the violence in Osh, Masaliyev did not receive enough Supreme Soviet votes, and the reformer Askar Akayev was elected as president. After the failed coup in Moscow in August 1991, Communist party activities were suspended, although most leaders were still party members. In Dec. 1991 Kyrgyzstan signed the Alma-Ata Declaration that founded the Commonwealth of Independent States.

In 1992, with the help of the I.M.F., Akayev embarked on a radical economic program that included lowering wages, raising prices, and abolishing tariffs with Central Asian neighbors Kazakhstan and Uzbekistan. Although the program initially caused hardship, it proved successful. In 1995, elections, Akayev was elected to a second term with 60 percent of the vote. This came six months after international lenders, led by the World Bank, agreed in June to $680 million in aid.

In 1996 Kyrgyzstan joined the common market among Russia, Belarus, and Kazakhstan as it expanded to include development of common energy, transport and information systems. The government signed a non-aggression pact with Russia, China, Kazakhstan and Tajikistan and in Oct. 2000 Akayev won a third term with 75 percent of the vote and in Feb. 2003 a "Constitutional Referendum" gave him greatly expanded powers. But a popular uprising in March 2005 forced him to flee and Kurmanbek Bakiyev became interim president. In July he won a landslide presidential election and was reelected in 2007.

►LAOS
Lao People's Democratic Republic

● **GEOGRAPHY   Location:** landlocked country in Southeast Asia. **Boundaries:** Myanmar to NW, China to N, Vietnam to E, Cambodia to S, and Thailand to W. **Total area:** 91,429 sq. mi. (236,800 sq km). **Coastline:** none. **Comparative area:** slightly larger than Utah. **Land use:** 3% arable land; negl. % permanent crops; 97% other. **Major cities:** Vientiane (capital); Savannaket; Pakse; Luang Prabang; Saya Bury.
● **PEOPLE   Population:** 6,677,534 (July 2008 est.). **Nationality:** noun—Lao or Laotian (sing. and pl.); adjective—Lao or Laotian. **Ethnic groups:** 68% Lao Loum, 22% Lao Theung, 9% Lao Soung including Hmong and Yao. **Languages:** Lao (official), French, English, ethnic languages. **Religions:** 60% Buddhist, 40% animist and other.
● **GOVERNMENT   Type:** communist state. **Independence:** July 19, 1949 (from France). **Constitution:** Aug. 14, 1991. **National holiday:** Republic Day, Dec. 2. **Heads of Government:** Choummaly Sayasone, president (since June 2006); Bouasone Bouphavanh, prime minister (since June 2006). **Structure:** executive; unicameral legislature; independent judiciary.
● **ECONOMY   Monetary unit:** new kip. **Budget:** (2007 est.) *income:* $470.4 mil.; *expend.:* $643.5 mil. **G.D.P.:** $12.61 bil., $1,900 per capita (2007 est.). **Chief crops:** sweet potatoes, vegetables, coffee, sugarcane, cotton; water buffalo, pigs, cattle, poultry; tobacco. **Natural resources:** tin, timber, gypsum, hydropower potential. **Major industries:** timber, hydropower, tin and gypsum. **Labor force:** 2.1 mil. (2006); 80% agriculture; 2.4% unemployment (2005). **Exports:** $720.9 mil. (f.o.b., 2007 est.); electricity, wood products, coffee, tin. **Imports:** $1.199 bil. (f.o.b., 2007 est.); machinery and equipment, vehicles, fuel. **Major trading partners:** (2006) *exports:* 42.1% Thailand, 9.4% Vietnam, 4% China; *imports:* 68.8% Thailand, 11.3% China, 5.6% Vietnam.

Inhabited by the Thai-speaking Lao people in the river valleys and by Hmong and other tribal people in the highlands, Laos historically had little national cohesion and was dominated by its more powerful neighbors, Siam (Thailand) to the west and Vietnam to the east. In 1893 France forced Siam to recognize Laos as a French protectorate; the country was thereafter incorporated into the French Union of Indochina. Laos was occupied by Japan during World War II but saw little major fighting.

In 1946 Laos was united under the Luang Prabang dynasty and was granted local autonomy as a constitutional monarchy in 1949. During the final phases of the Indochina War against French colonialism in 1953-54, Vietnamese Communist (Vietminh) incursions reinforced the position of the Laotian Communist party (Pathet Lao) in Laotian politics. Following the French withdrawal in December 1954, Laos became an independent nation and was admitted to the United Nations in 1955.

The creation of a coalition government under Prince Souvana Phouma in 1962 temporarily resolved a turbulent political situation; an international agreement signed in Geneva that year guaranteed Laos's neutrality. The Pathet Lao withdrew from the coalition in 1964 and renewed its armed uprising against the government,

with North Vietnamese support. American planes bombed Vietnamese supply lines along the Ho Chi Minh trail, and American agents recruited Hmong tribesmen as irregular troops to attack Pathet Lao positions. The Pathet Lao nevertheless made steady gains, especially after 1970. In 1973, Prince Souvana Phouma ordered a cease-fire, and in 1975 the Pathet Lao took control of the capital, Vientiane. The Lao People's Democratic Republic was proclaimed on Dec. 3, 1975. Large numbers of Hmong and other tribal people fled to Thailand.

Subsequently, Laos was strongly dominated by Vietnam, which stationed significant numbers of troops in the country. In 1989, in Laos's first election since the communist takeover, a Supreme People's Assembly was elected specifically to approve a new constitution, which it did in 1991; the constitution confirmed the Lao People's Revolutionary party as the sole legal political party. Single-party elections in 1992 did little to alter the country's political climate, though observers predicted changes as the Communists began to pass from the scene. In 1997, Laos was admitted to the Association of Southeast Asian Nations. Not until 2006, however, was a non-Communist government elected and the National Assembly appointed a prime minister and cabinet.

►LATVIA
Republic of Latvia

● **GEOGRAPHY   Location:** eastern coast of Baltic Sea in northeastern Europe. **Boundaries:** Baltic Sea to N, Estonia to NE, Russian Federation, Belarus to S, Lithuania to W. **Total area:** 24,749 sq. mi. (64,100 sq km). **Coastline:** Baltic Sea. **Comparative area:** slightly larger than West Virginia. **Land use:** 29% arable land; negl.% permanent crops, 71% other. **Major cities:** Riga (capital); Daugav'pils; Liepāja; Jelgava; Jurmala.
● **PEOPLE   Population:** 2,245,423 (July 2008 est.). **Nationality:** noun—Latvian(s); adjective—Latvian. **Ethnic groups:** 57.7% Latvian, 29.6% Russian, 4.1% Belarussian, 2.7% Ukrainian, 2.5% Polish. **Languages:** Latvian (official), Lithuanian, Russian, other. **Religions:** Lutheran, Roman Catholic, Russian Orthodox.
● **GOVERNMENT   Type:** parliamentary democracy. **Independence:** Aug. 21, 1991 (from Soviet Union). **Constitution:** the 1991 Constitutional Law supplements the 1922 constitution and provides for basic rights and freedoms. **National holiday:** Independence Day, Nov. 18. **Heads of Government:** Vaira Vike-Freiberga, president (since June 2003); Ivars Godmanis, prime minister (since Dec. 2007). **Structure:** executive; unicameral legislature; judiciary.
● **ECONOMY   Monetary unit:** lats. **Budget:** (2007 est.) *income:* $8.975 bil.; *expend:* $8.88 bil. **G.D.P.:** $40.04 bil., $17,700 per capita (2007 est.). **Chief crops:** grain, potatoes, sugar beets, vegetables; meat, milk, eggs; fish. **Natural resources:** minimal; amber, peat, limestone, dolomite. **Major industries:** machine building, metalworking, chemical processing. **Labor force:** 1.136 mil. (2006); 21.3% industry, 3.5% agriculture, 75.2% services (2007); 5.9% unemployment (2007). **Exports:** $7.551 bil. (f.o.b., 2007 est.); timber, textiles, foodstuffs. **Imports:** $13.7 bil. (f.o.b., 2007 est.); fuels, machinery and equipment, chemicals. **Major trading partners:** (2006) *exports:* 14.2% Lithuania, 12.3% Estonia, 11.5% Russia, 9.8% Germany, 7.6% U.K., 6.3% Sweden 4.8% Denmark; *imports:* 15.5% Germany,

12.9% Lithuania, 8% Russia, 7.7% Estonia, 7.2% Poland, 5.7% Finland, 5% Sweden, 4.7% Belarus.

Though the Letts ethnically and linguistically are quite distinct from their northern neighbors the Ests, Latvia's history parallels that of Estonia. German merchants, knights, and missionaries made Latvia a semi-ecclesiastical German colony in the 13th century; in the 16th century Latvia passed under first Swedish, then Lithuanian rule; in the 18th century Peter the Great's Russian empire absorbed the land.

A 19th-century cultural revival, inspired in part by Johann von Herder, a native of Riga, found expression in folkloric societies, archaeological research and the compilation of the epic poem, Lacplesis. Brest-Litovsk, the Soviet Union's 1918 peace treaty with Germany, granted Latvia's political independence for the first time in its history.

The constitution of 1922 established a one-house legislature. To avoid violence between left and right armed extremists, Prime Minister Karlis Umanlis dissolved the Parliament in May 1934 and ruled as dictator until a new constitution that provided for expanded presidential powers and a second house of the legislature, based on the conception of a corporate state, came into existence in 1938 just before the Hitler-Stalin Pact awarded Latvia to the Russian sphere of interest. Stalin garrisoned troops in Latvia, rigged elections, and incorporated the country as a new union republic of the U.S.S.R. in 1940.

For 50 years, harsh Soviet rule continued. The larger cities were Russianized and the highly educated middle and upper-middle classes were deported throughout Russia. Industrialization brought relative prosperity, but the national consciousness was never eradicated.

Mikhail Gorbachev's policy of glasnost, or openness, led to the creation of dissident groups who staged public demonstrations on the anniversaries of the Stalin-Hitler Pact and of the establishment of Latvian independence. After the head of the Latvian Communist party, Boris Pugo was transferred to Moscow, Latvia's Communist party came under the influence of the newly created Latvian Popular Front. With the new political influence of non-Communists, on Sept. 29, 1988, Latvian replaced Russian as the official language.

In March 1990, following Lithuania's example, Latvia announced its intention to secede, survived Gorbachev's January 1991 military crackdown, and after the failed August 1991 coup in Moscow, declared independence.

In 1995 summer elections revealed deep political divisions as the three major parties took half the seats. It was not until December that Andris Skele was able to become prime minister, heading a cabinet containing members of six of Latvia's nine parties. Skele was forced to resign in July 1997 because of corruption charges and over disappointment that the E.U. would not consider Latvia's application until the "second wave." Parliamentary elections in Oct. 1998 resulted in the same degree of party splintering, but Vilis Kristopans was able to form a government. More significantly, in a referendum voters eased the citizenship laws, making it simpler for ethnic Russians (one-third of the population) to become citizens. Coalition discord brought the end of the Kristopanis government in July 1999; the successor government, under Andris Skele collapsed in April 2000, with Andris Berzins as his successor.

In 2002 a four-party center-right coalition government was founded with Einers Repse as prime minister but another minority government was needed yet again in 2003, this time headed by a prime minister from the Green Party, Indulis Emsis. In 2004 Latvia joined the E.U. and NATO, but government stability remained an issue as ministers continued to change on a regular basis.

▶ LEBANON
Lebanese Republic

• **GEOGRAPHY   Location:** western Asia. **Boundaries:** Syria to N and E, Israel to S, Mediterranean Sea to W. **Total area:** 4,015 sq. mi. (10,400 sq km). **Coastline:** 140 mi. (225 km). **Comparative area:** about 0.7 times the size of Connecticut. **Land use:** 18% arable land; 13% permanent crops; 69% other. **Major cities:** Beirut (capital); Tarabulus (Tripoli); Zahleh; Saida (Sidon); Sur (Tyre).

• **PEOPLE   Population:** 3,971,941 (July 2008 est.). **Nationality:** noun—Lebanese (sing., pl.); adjective— Lebanese. **Ethnic groups:** 95% Arab, 4% Armenian, 1% other. **Languages:** Arabic (official), French, Armenian, English. **Religions:** 59.7% Muslim, 39% Christian, 1.3% other.

• **GOVERNMENT   Type:** republic. **Independence:** Nov. 22, 1943 (from League of Nations Mandate under French administration). **Constitution:** May 23, 1926 (amended). **National holiday:** Independence Day, Nov. 22. **Heads of Government:** Michel Suleiman, president (since May 2008); Fouad Siniora, prime minister (since July 2005). **Structure:** executive—by custom, president is Maronite Christian, prime minister is Sunni Muslim, and president of legislature is Shia Muslim; unicameral legislature; judiciary—three courts for civil and commercial cases, one court for civil cases.

• **ECONOMY   Monetary unit:** Lebanese pound. **Budget:** (2007 est.) **income:** $6.116 bil.; **expend.:** $9.421 bil. **G.D.P.:** $40.65 bil., $10,400 per capita (2007 est.). **Chief crops:** citrus, vegetables, potatoes, olives, tobacco, hemp (hashish); sheep, goats. **Natural resources:** limestone, iron ore, salt; water-surplus state in water-deficit region. **Major industries:** banking, food processing, textiles. **Labor force:** 1.5 mil. plus as many as 1 mil. foreign workers (2001 est.); 20% unemployment (2006 est.). **Exports:** 3.099 bil. (f.o.b., 2007 est.); foodstuffs and tobacco, textiles, chemicals, metals. **Imports:** $10 bil. (f.o.b., 2007 est.); foodstuffs, machinery & transport equipment, consumer goods. **Major trading partners:** (2006) **exports:** 26.8% Syria, 12% United Arab Emirates, 6% Switzerland, 5.7% Saudi Arabia, 4.5% Turkey; **imports:** 11.6% Syria, 9.8% Italy, 9.3% U.S., 7.7% France, 6.1% Germany, 5% China, 4.7% Saudi Arabia.

The ancient history of Lebanon is essentially coextensive with that of Syria, of which it was long a part. The port cities of Tripoli, Tyre, and Sidon were important centers of the Phoenician empire. The parallel ranges of the Lebanon and Anti-Lebanon mountains, crowned with the country's famous cedar trees, enclose the fertile Bekaa Valley. The coastal cities became strongholds of early Christianity, later fragmented into numerous sects, including Maronites (Syrian Catholic), Roman Catholic, Greek Orthodox, Syrian Orthodox, and others. The mountains of the south became the center of the Druze sect of Islam, while orthodox Sunni Islam dominated in the Bekaa Valley.

Lebanon came under French influence in the late 18th century, as France claimed the role of protector of Syria's Christian community. France intervened in Lebanon in 1841 and again in 1860 when fighting between Maronite and Druze communities led to the massacre of many Christians. Under pressure from France, the Ottoman Empire granted some local autonomy to the Maronites.

In the dismemberment of the Ottoman Empire after World War I, France was granted a League of Nations Mandate over the Levant States (Lebanon and Syria), ensuring French control of the Iraq Petroleum Company pipeline from Iraq to Tripoli. In 1926 Lebanon became a self-governing republic under the mandate, but internal unrest and anti-French sentiment continued.

In June 1940 the French administration in Lebanon declared its allegiance to the Vichy government. British and Free French forces occupied Lebanon in June 1941 and declared it an independent republic; but France retained control, and full independence did not come until Jan. 1, 1944.

Under a National Covenant in 1943, political power in the Lebanese parliament was apportioned among the nation's various communities. The president was always to be a Maronite Christian, the prime minister a Sunni Muslim. This provided a workable formula for power sharing but also ensured that the national government would always be hostage to the considerable power of separate communities and clans.

The years from the end of World War II to the early 1970's were a brief golden age for Lebanon. Beirut developed into a wealthy, cosmopolitan city, the center of Middle Eastern banking and trade, while agriculture and small-scale industry flourished in the rest of the country. A Syrian-backed Muslim uprising in 1958 had no significant impact; U.S. Marines landed in May 1958 to protect American interests and remained until October. By the late 1960's, however, Lebanon's stability was threatened by PLO attacks on Israel from refugee camps in southern Lebanon and by a shift in the country's demographic balance. Muslims had become a majority in Lebanon by the late 1960's and demanded a revision of the National Covenant, while Maronite Christians continued to cling to their position of political dominance.

Throughout the 1970's, Palestinian raids from Lebanon into Israel brought Israeli retaliatory strikes in southern Lebanon. Israeli troops occupied southern Lebanon in 1978 and again in 1980. The Palestinian-Israeli conflict polarized opinion within Lebanon, inflaming anti-Western feelings among Lebanon's Sunni Muslims.

Civil war broke out in 1975, with Palestinian and leftist Muslim militias battling militias of the Maronite community, the Christian Phalange party, and other groups. More than 60,000 died, and damage ranged into the billions of dollars. Syrian troops intervened in 1976, battling Palestinian forces in an attempt to restore the status quo. Arab League efforts to negotiate a cease-fire produced an unstable peace at the end of 1976, though Syrian troops remained in Lebanon.

Fighting broke out between Syrian forces and Christian militiamen near Zahle on Apr. 1, 1981. Other groups joined the fighting in a general war of each against all. Israel staged commando raids against Palestinian positions in Tyre and Tulin. Israeli air raids on Beirut caused extensive loss of life and property damage. Israel invaded Lebanon in a full-scale assault on June 6, 1982, in an attempt to drive out the PLO. Israeli forces surrounded Beirut and began a heavy bombardment of the city. On Aug. 1, Palestinian forces withdrew from Beirut under international supervision. On Sept. 14 newly elected Pres. Bashir Gemayel, a Maronite Christian, was assassinated; Israeli troops occupied the Muslim quarters of West Beirut in response. With tacit Israeli approval, Christian militiamen invaded two refugee camps and slaughtered hundreds of Palestinian civilians.

Beirut remained a battle zone in 1983, divided by the "Green Line" into Christian and Muslim sectors. Terrorist bombings were common. The U.S., France, Italy, and other Western nations stationed troops in Beirut in an attempt to enforce a cease-fire. Fifty people were killed when a bomb partly destroyed the U.S. embassy on Apr. 18; separate attacks on military installations on Oct. 23 killed 241 U.S. Marines and 58 French soldiers.

Rashid Karami became premier with Syrian support on Apr. 26, 1984. The civil war continued, with fighting among various groups of Christian, Druze, Sunni, Shiite, and Palestinian militias. War between Shiite and Palestinian forces broke out in May 1985. Israeli forces withdrew from most of Lebanon in June, but maintained a "security zone" in the southern part of the country. Premier Karami was assassinated on June 1, 1987, when a bomb destroyed his helicopter.

At an October 1989 Arab League-sponsored meeting, Christian and Muslim leaders agreed on a new national charter. The Taif accord was condemned by Christian militants, led by Gen. Michel Aoun, and Muslim militia leaders. Newly elected Pres. René Mowad, a Syrian-backed Christian, was assassinated on Nov. 22 and succeeded by Elias Hraoui. In 1990, rival Shiite militias—the Syrian-backed Amal and Iranian-backed Party of God—signed an agreement ending three years of fighting. In February 1991 Lebanese troops moved to defend the area for the first time in 13 years and called for Israel to abandon its "security zone" in southern Lebanon. In addition to leaving 150,000 dead, the civil war severely disrupted the economy.

The government of Christian prime minister Omar Karami collapsed in May 1992, after riots protesting economic hardship. New elections were held under Syrian supervision with Hezbollah and other Islamic fundamentalist parties gaining the most seats, in part because the Christian parties called for a boycott. In 1994, as Israeli-Hezbollah skirmishes continued, the government banned the Christian political party, Lebanese Forces, arrested some of its leaders, and stopped all "political" broadcasts not government-controlled. In 1995, Syria-backed premier Rafik Hariri won a second term together with a 2-1 backing in Parliament. His attempts at reform were hindered by repeated skirmishes between Israel and Hezbollah Shiite guerrillas in Israel's "security zone" in southern Lebanon. In April 1996 the fighting escalated as Israel launched 600 airraids and 24,000 artillery shells some of which hit a U.N. refugee camp near Tyre, killing over 100 and wounding 100 more. The U.N. voted 64-2 (with 65 abstaining) to condemn the attack.

By 1997 order had been restored but no peace agreement reached with Israel. With $3 bil. in U.S. and E.U. aid the government set about to rebuild this ravaged land. Deadly skirmishes still occured in the "security zone." In 1998 Lebanon held its first municipal elections in 35 years; no clear pattern emerged. In Oct., the (pro-Syrian) National Assembly unanimously elected General Emile Lahoud as president. He nominated Selim al-Hoss as prime minister after Hariri declined a fourth consecutive government. In 1999 the Israeli-Hezbollah warfare in south Lebanon intensified until, suddenly, Israel withdrew completely (May 24, 2000), accompanied by about 3,000 Christian militiamen of the South Lebanese Army to whom Israel offered haven. In early Sept. Hariri won a decisive victory in parliamentary elections and he adopted an anti-Syrian approach to politics. By 2005 Lebanese feelings towards Syria's powerful military presence had turned vociferous and when Hariri, now out of office; was assassinated (Feb.) mass protests followed demanding the ouster of Pres. Lahoud who was backed by Syria. U.S. opposition to Syria's presence soon forced a withdrawal. In June elections the anti-Syrian groups won a clear majority in parliament and again an assassination of a prominent anti-Syrian figure followed. In July 2006 Israel launched another major military assault against Hezbollah with great destruction to Lebanon's infrastructure. A U.N.-brokered ceasefire has held but Hezbollah's leaders reject U.N. calls for disarming.

In May 2008 a new president, army chief Michel Suleiman, was chosen by parliament after a six-month deadlock. He quickly moved to ease tensions with Syria.

▶ LESOTHO
Kingdom of Lesotho
• **GEOGRAPHY Location:** landlocked country in southern Africa. **Boundaries:** entirely surrounded by South African territory. **Total area:** 11,718 sq. mi. (30,350 sq km). **Coastline:** none. **Comparative area:** slightly smaller than Maryland. **Land use:** 11% arable land; 0% permanent crops; 89% other. **Major cities:** Maseru (capital).
• **PEOPLE Population:** 2,128,180 (July 2008 est.). **Nationality:** noun—Mosotho (sing.), Basotho (pl.); adjective—Basotho. **Ethnic groups:** 99.7% Sotho; 0.3% Europeans, Asians and other. **Languages:** Sesotho (southern Sotho), English (official), Zulu, Xhosa. **Religions:** 80% Christian, 20% indigenous beliefs.
• **GOVERNMENT Type:** parliamentary constitutional monarchy. **Independence:** Oct. 4, 1966 (from U.K.). **Constitution:** Apr. 2, 1993. **National holiday:** Independence Day, Oct. 4. **Heads of Government:** Letsie III, king (since Feb. 1996); Pakalitha Bethuel Mosisili, prime minister (since May 1998). **Structure:** executive—king is chief of state but has no power and can be deposed by College of Chiefs; legislature—bicameral legislature; judiciary.
• **ECONOMY Monetary unit:** loti. **Budget:** (2007 est.) **income:** $951.4 mil.; **expend.:** $855.4 mil. **G.D.P.:** $3.088 bil., $1,500 per capita (2007 est.). **Chief crops:** corn, wheat, pulses, sorghum, barley; livestock. **Natural resources:** some diamonds and other minerals, water, agricultural and grazing land. **Major industries:** tourism, food, beverages. **Labor force:** 838,000 economically active; 86% subsistence agriculture; 35% work in South Africa (2002 est.). **Exports:** $905 mil. (f.o.b., 2007 est.); 75% manufactures, wool and mohair, food and live animals. **Imports:** $1.584 bil. (f.o.b., 2007 est.); food, building materials, vehicles, machinery. **Major trading partners:** (2006) **exports:** 81.9% U.S., 15% Belgium, 1.9% Canada; **imports:** 33.4% Hong Kong, 31.2% China, 7.7% Germany, 7.3% India.

Lesotho, formerly Basutoland, is an independent kingdom surrounded entirely by the Republic of South Africa. The area was sparsely populated by Bushmen until the 16th century when refugees from tribal wars in surrounding areas began to move in, an influx that continued through the 19th century. These immigrants coalesced into a homogenous cultural group, the Basothos.

Under King Moshoeshoe (1823-70), several Basotho groups were consolidated, but much land was lost in a series of wars with South Africa. Moshoeshoe appealed to Queen Victoria for aid, and in 1868 the nation became a British protectorate. Between 1884 and 1959 all executive and legislative authority was in the hands of a British high commissioner. In 1903 a Basotho consultative body was established, and in 1959 a new constitution gave the council power to legislate on internal affairs.

On Oct. 4, 1966, Basutoland achieved full independence as the Kingdom of Lesotho. The first elections after independence, in 1970, were nullified by the ruling Basutoland National party (BNP) when early returns indicated that the party might lose. A state of emergency was declared, the constitution was suspended, and parliament dissolved.

Elections in 1985 were boycotted by opposition parties. In 1986 the BNP government was ousted in a coup. The nation was run by a military council, which in 1990 stripped King Moshoeshoe II of his powers. Military rule ended in April 1993 when Ntsu Mokhehle was elected prime minister and his Basotholand Congress party (BCP) gained all 243 seats in the legislature. King Moshoeshoe II was restored in Jan. 1995 but died a year later in an auto accident. The Traditional College of Chiefs named his son Letsie III as his successor.

Elections in May 1998 kept the ruling party in power with a new prime minister, Pakalitha Mosisili, but the opposition and some outside observers said the elections were dishonest and when pro-opposition army officers mutinied the government pledged new and free elections. These were held in March 2003 and Mosisili and his party returned to power and remains so in 2008. A severe drought caused much suffering in 2007.

▶ LIBERIA
Republic of Liberia
• **GEOGRAPHY Location:** western Africa. **Boundaries:** Sierra Leone, Guinea to N, Ivory Coast to E, Atlantic Ocean to S and W. **Total area:** 43,000 sq. mi. (111,370 sq km). **Coastline:** 360 mi. (579 km). **Comparative area:** slightly larger than Tennessee. **Land use:** 2% arable land; 2% permanent crops; 96% other. **Major cities:** Monrovia (capital).
• **PEOPLE Population:** 3,334,587 (July 2008 est.). **Nationality:** noun—Liberian(s); adjective—Liberian. **Ethnic groups:** 95% indigenous peoples, including Kpelle, Bassa, Gio, Kru, Grebo, Mano, Krahn, Gola, Gbandi, Loma, Kissi, Vai, Bella; 2.5% descendants of repatriated slaves from the U.S. known as Americo-Liberians, 2.5% descendents of repatriated slaves from the Carribean known as Congo-people. **Languages:** 20% English (official); more than 20 languages of Niger-Congo language group. **Religions:** 40% indigenous beliefs, 20% Muslim, 40% Christian.
• **GOVERNMENT Type:** republic. **Independence:** July 26, 1847. **Constitution:** Jan. 6, 1986. **National holiday:** Independence Day, July 26. **Head of Government:** Ellen Johnson Sirleaf, president (since Jan. 2006). **Structure:** executive—president, appointed cabinet; bicameral legislature; judiciary.

• **ECONOMY Monetary unit:** Liberian dollar. **Budget:** N.A. **G.D.P.:** $1.498 bil., $500 per capita (2007 est.). **Chief crops:** rubber, coffee, cocoa, rice, cassava, palm oil, sugarcane; sheep, goats; timber. **Natural resources:** iron ore, timber, diamonds, gold. **Major industries:** rubber processing, palm oil processing, diamonds. **Labor force:** 70% agriculture; 85% unemployment (2000 est.) **Exports:** $1.197 bil. (f.o.b., 2006 est.); diamonds, iron ore, rubber, timber, coffee. **Imports:** $7.143 bil. (f.o.b., 2006 est.); fuels, chemicals, machinery, transportation equipment. **Major trading partners:** (2006) *exports:* 40.1% Germany, 12% South Africa, 11.7% Poland, 8.5% U.S., 8.2% Spain; *imports:* 43.2% South Korea, 15% Singapore, 12.8% Japan, 8.2% China.

Liberia was populated by migrants from the north and east beginning in the 12th century, but it remained relatively isolated from the remainder of West Africa and was not incorporated into any of the region's premodern kingdoms and empires. Portuguese explorers first reached the Liberian coast in 1461 to be followed by other European traders. Until the 19th century, Liberia was largely ignored by the world except for a small-scale coastal trade in slaves and forest products.

In 1816 the U.S. Congress granted a charter to the American Colonization Society, ACS, a private organization dedicated to the African repatriation of freed slaves. The first settlers landed in 1822 at the town that was later to become Monrovia. In 1838 the settlers organized the Commonwealth of Liberia under a governor appointed by the ACS. The commonwealth declared its independence as the Republic of Liberia in 1847 and adopted a constitution modeled after that of the United States. The new government, Africa's first independent republic, was granted diplomatic recognition by Great Britain in 1848, France in 1852, and the United States in 1862.

Bolstered by the moral backing of the U.S., Liberia in its first 100 years of independence succeeded in fending off British and French attempts to encroach on its territory from their neighboring colonies. Although descendants of freed American slaves are a minority in Liberia's ethnically diverse population, they have consistently dominated the country's political life.

William V.S. Tubman was elected president in 1944 and served until his death in 1971, successfully steering Liberia through the post War age of African nationalism and decolonization. He was succeeded by William R. Tolbert, Jr. On Apr. 12, 1980, Tolbert was deposed in a military coup led by Master Sgt. Samuel K. Doe. Doe suspended the constitution and imposed martial law but pledged a new constitution by 1985.

Presidential elections were held on Oct. 15, 1985, under the terms of a provisional constitution that for the first time enacted universal suffrage. Doe was elected and his party won 80 percent of the seats in the legislature. Despite allegations of fraud that led to a violent but unsuccessful coup attempt in November 1985, the Second Republic, under the new constitution, was inaugurated on Jan. 6, 1986.

On Dec. 24, 1989, about 150 antigovernment guerrillas of the National Patriotic Forces of Liberia (NPFL), led by Charles Taylor, crossed the border from the Ivory Coast. The fighting degenerated into ethnic warfare between the Krahn and Mandingo, in support of the government, and the Gio and Mano, who supported the rebels. Prince Johnson split from Taylor's forces and took up fighting both government troops and Taylor. A peacekeeping force of the Economic Community of West African States (ECOWAS) landed on Monrovia on Aug. 24 to mediate a cease-fire and prepare for free elections. On Sept. 10 Pres. Doe was killed by Prince Johnson, but a cease-fire was not agreed upon until Nov. 28, 1990.

From 1990 to 1992 Charles Taylor solidified his hold on the country despite the establishment of a government (under Amos Sawyer) in Monrovia by the West African States. By 1993 the government and ECOWAS forces succeeded in containing Taylor's forces. In 1994 an interim coalition government representing the country's three major factions came into power as peace talks began. Elections were scheduled for Nov. 1995 but extensive fighting broke out continually through the end of 1996. Over 150,000 had died up to then.

In early 1997 ECOWAS, led by a Nigeria, helped to restore order and arrange for elections in July. Charles Taylor won a landslide victory. Doubts arose about domestic peace when Taylor attempted to arrest opposition militia leader Roosevelt Johnson; 50 died in the fighting as Johnson fled to the U.S. Embassy for safety. In early 1999, Taylor faced broad international condemnation for Liberia's aid to rebels in Sierra Leone. But the U.N. agreed to place international monitors along Liberia's border with Sierra Leone. In return for Pres. Taylor's support for the RUF rebels in Sierra Leone, he controlled their illegal diamond trade, skimming as much as 90 percent of the profit.

In Aug. 2003 Taylor was forced into exile by ECOWAS and international pressure. An interim government was set up but riots in Dec. 2003 delayed the international effort to bring needed aid to the nation. But it was not until late 2005 that elections could be held, but they were won by a U.S.-educated economist, Ellen Johnson-Sirleaf, Africa's first elected woman head-of-state.

▶ LIBYA
Socialist People's Libyan Arab Jamahiriya
• **GEOGRAPHY Location:** along Mediterranean coast of North Africa. **Boundaries:** Mediterranean Sea to N, Egypt to E, Sudan to SE, Niger, Chad to S, Tunisia, Algeria to W. **Total area:** 679,359 sq. mi. (1,759,540 sq km). **Coastline:** 1,100 mi. (1,770 km). **Comparative area:** slightly larger than Alaska. **Land use:** 1% arable land; 0% permanent crops; 99% other. **Major cities:** in Jan. 1987, Col. Qaddafi designated Hun, a town 404 mi. (650 km) SE of Tripoli, as administrative capital of country; Tripoli; Benghazi; Misurata.
• **PEOPLE Population:** 6,173,579 (July 2008 est.). **Nationality:** noun—Libyan(s); adjective—Libyan. **Ethnic groups:** 97% Berber and Arab; some Greeks, Maltese, Italians, Egyptians, Pakistanis, Turks, Indians, Tunisians. **Languages:** Arabic, Italian, and English widely understood in major cities. **Religions:** 97% Sunni Muslim.
• **GOVERNMENT Type:** Jamahiriya (a state of the masses) in theory, governed by populace through local councils; in fact, a military dictatorship. **Independence:** Dec. 24, 1951 (from Italy). **Constitution:** Dec. 11, 1969, amended Mar. 2, 1977. **National holiday:** Revolution Day, Sept. 1. **Head of Government:** Col. Muammar al-Qaddafi (no official title; runs country and is treated as chief of state) (since Sept. 1969); Al Baghdadi Ali Al-Mahmoudi, prime minister (since Feb. 2007). **Structure:** officially, paramount political power and authority rests with

General People's Congress, which theoretically functions as a parliament with a cabinet called General People's Committee; elections are indirect. ● ECONOMY **Monetary unit:** Libyan dinar. **Budget:** (2007 est.) *income:* $39.62 bil.; *expend.:* $19.51 bil. **G.D.P.:** $78.79 bil., $13,100 per capita (2007 est.) **Chief crops:** wheat, barley, olives, dates, citrus fruits; meat, eggs. **Natural resources:** crude oil, natural gas, gypsum. **Major industries:** petroleum, food processing, textiles. **Labor force:** 1.82 mil.; 23% industry, 59% services, 17% agriculture. **Exports:** $36.37 bil. (f.o.b., 2007 est.); petroleum. **Imports:** $15.35 bil. (f.o.b., 2007 est.) machinery and transport equipment, food. **Major trading partners:** (2006) *exports:* 36.7% Italy, 14.3% Germany, 8.7% Spain, 6.1% U.S., 5.6% France, 5.3% Turkey; *imports:* 18.9% Italy, 7.9% Germany, 7.5% China, 6.3% Tunisia, 5.8% France, 5.2% Turkey, 4.7% U.S., 4.3% South Korea, 4% U.K.

The coastal cities of Libya played an important cultural and commercial role in the Mediterranean in antiquity and were prized possessions of numerous empires. The Libyan coast was successively ruled by Phoenicians, Carthaginians, Berbers, Romans, and Vandals before being incorporated into the Byzantine Empire in the fourth century A.D.; nomadic tribes in the interior were beyond the reach of any government. The Islamic conquests of the seventh and eighth centuries brought Libya into the Muslim world.

Libya was incorporated into the Ottoman Empire shortly after the Ottoman conquest of Egypt in 1517 and was ruled by local Ottoman vassals until 1835 when direct Ottoman government was established. In 1911 Libya was invaded and conquered by Italy. After World War I, local resistance to Italian colonial rule was led by King Idris I, Emir of Cyrenaica. British troops drove Italian and German forces from Libya in 1943. King Idris returned from exile in 1944. Following World War II, most of Libya was ruled as a British protectorate with a smaller portion under French administration.

Libya became an independent constitutional monarchy on Dec. 24, 1951. In 1959 significant oil reserves were discovered, rapidly transforming Libya from one of the poorest states in North Africa to one of the wealthiest.

A military coup on Sept. 1, 1969, led by Col. Muammar al-Qaddafi, deposed the monarchy and declared the establishment of the Libyan Arab Republic. Qaddafi moved rapidly to nationalize foreign assets, expel foreign troops, and close foreign libraries and cultural centers. He also assumed full dictatorial powers under a political system that gives equal weight to Islamic law and his own political philosophy. Popular participation in elections is mandatory, although no government organization outside Qaddafi and his circle of advisers exerts any real authority.

Libya has given strong political and financial aid to various radical Palestinian groups and other enemies of Israel, sponsoring terrorist activities throughout Europe and the Middle East in support of the Palestinian cause. Numerous anti-Qaddafi Libyan exiles were assassinated in Europe. Libya also engaged in sporadic military campaigns against Egypt and the Sudan.

Relations between Libya and the U.S. were very hostile in the 1980's. On May 6, 1981, the U.S. closed the Libyan "People's Bureau" (embassy) in Washington. On Aug. 2, 1981, U.S. jets shot down two attacking Libyan warplanes during U.S. naval exercises in the Gulf of Sidra, which Libya claims as national waters. In 1986 the United States imposed economic sanctions on Libya, ordered all Americans to leave the country, and froze Libyan assets in the U.S. Another clash in March 1986 ended with the loss of two Libyan ships.

On Apr. 5, 1986, Libyan-sponsored terrorists bombed a nightclub in West Berlin, killing two U.S. soldiers; in response, American bombers attacked Tripoli and Benghazi on Apr. 14 in an apparent attempt to kill Col. Qaddafi himself. In 1990, investigators announced they had linked Libyan agents to the bombing of a Pan Am Jet over Lockerbie, Scotland, in 1988.

In January 1989 an international outcry arose when a West German company admitted selling equipment to Libya for a chemical weapons plant. Qaddafi's difficulties with the Western powers continued in 1992, as they demanded he release the suspected terrorists in the Lockerbie bombing. The U.N. imposed sanctions on Libya, including a prohibition on sales of military equipment and a ban on all flights in and out of the country. In Sept. 1995 Qaddafi began the expulsion of the 30,000 Palestinians in Libya, provoking fighting between Libyan security forces and Islamic militants. In 1997 as the Vatican announced that it would establish diplomatic relations, the U.S. listed Libya as one of several nations sponsoring terrorism.

Elaborate diplomatic maneuvers led to President Qaddafi's handing over (April, 1999) two Libyans for trial in the 1988 bombing of Pan Am flight 103. U.N. sanctions were suspended but the U.S. announced that its anti-terrorism sanctions would continue. In Jan. 2001 the Pan Am 103 trial ended with one conviction (with life imprisonment) and one acquittal. Qaddafi denounced the conviction but in 2003 Libya accepted responsibility and agreed to pay victims' families $2.7 bil. In Dec. 2003 Libya suddenly announced its willingness to stop all biological, chemical, and nuclear weapons development and to sign the Nuclear Nonproliferation Treaty. The U.S. soon ended all sanctions, reestablished diplomatic relations and began to purchase Libyan oil.

▶ **LIECHTENSTEIN**
Principality of Liechtenstein
● GEOGRAPHY **Location:** landlocked country in central Europe. **Boundaries:** Austria to N and E, Switzerland to S and W. **Total area:** 62 sq. mi. (160 sq km). **Coastline:** none. **Comparative area:** about 0.9 times the size of Washington, D.C. **Land use:** 25% arable land; 0% permanent crops; 75% other. **Major cities:** Väduz (capital); Schaan; Balzers; Triesen; Eschen.
● PEOPLE **Population:** 34,498 (July 2008 est.). **Nationality:** noun—Liechtensteiner(s); adjective—Liechtenstein. **Ethnic groups:** 86% Alemannic, 14% Italian, Turkish and other. **Languages:** German (official), Alemannic dialect. **Religions:** 76.2% Roman Catholic, 7.0% Protestant.
● GOVERNMENT **Type:** hereditary constitutional monarchy. **Independence:** Jan 23, 1719. **Constitution:** Oct. 5, 1921. **National holiday:** Assumption Day, Aug. 15. **Heads of Government:** Hans-Adam II, prince (since Nov. 1989); Otmar Hasler, prime minister (since Apr. 2001). **Structure:** executive—hereditary prince; unicameral legislature; judiciary—independent.
● ECONOMY **Monetary unit:** Swiss franc. **Budget:** N.A. **G.D.P.:** $1.786 bil. (2001 est.), $25,000 per capita (1999 est.). **Chief Crops:** wheat, barley, maize, potatoes; livestock, dairy products. **Natural resources:** hydroelectric potential. **Major in-**

dustries: electronics, metal manufacturing, tourism. **Labor force:** 29,000 of which 19,000 are foreign workers (mostly from Switzerland and Austria) (2001 est.); 54% services, 43.9% industry, 2.1% agriculture (2005); 1.3% unemployment (2002). **Exports:** $2.47 bil. (f.o.b., 1996 est.); small specialty machinery, dental products, stamps, hardware, pottery. **Imports:** $917.3 mil. (c.i.f., 1996 est.); machinery, metal goods, textiles, foodstuffs, motor vehicles. **Major trading partners:** (2006) *exports:* 62.6% E.U., 18.9% U.S., 15.7% Switzerland; *imports:* E.U. countries, Switzerland.

The alpine principality of Liechtenstein, bordered by Austria and Switzerland, is a remnant of the Holy Roman Empire, an ancient constitutional monarchy with a modern industrial economy. The current dynasty was established in 1699; Prince Franz Josef II came to the throne in 1938, yielding his executive powers to his heir apparent, Hans Adam, in 1984.

Liechtenstein was tied to the Austro-Hungarian monarchy until 1918. Since then it has remained in a customs union with Switzerland, which also handles its foreign affairs. The single-chamber diet, the Landtag is elected by universal suffrage, women having won the right to vote in 1984. For almost 60 years the government was a coalition of the conservcative Progressive Citizens Party and the liberal Fatherland Union. Since April, 1997 Premier Mario Frick has governed with a cabinet of his own Fatherland Union with the PCP in opposition. Liechtenstein joined the U.N. in 1990.

A referendum in 2003 amended the constitution giving the prince authority to dismiss the government and veto legislation; citizens gained the right to vote "no confidence" in the prince. Liechtenstein is a corporate haven, with some 25,000 corporations maintaining nominal headquarters there. Foreign workers constitute about 40 percent of the work force.

▶ **LITHUANIA**
Republic of Lithuania
● **GEOGRAPHY Location:** eastern coast of Baltic Sea in northeastern Europe. **Boundaries:** Latvia to N, Belarus to E and SE, Poland to SW, Russian Federation (Kaliningrad) to W, Baltic Sea to NW. **Total area:** 25,174 sq. mi. (65,200 sq km). **Coastline:** Baltic Sea. **Comparative area:** slightly larger than West Virginia. **Land use:** 45% arable land; 1% permanent crops; 54% other. **Major cities:** Vilnius (capital); Kaunas; Klaipeda; Siauliai; Panevezys.
● **PEOPLE Population:** 3,565,205 (July 2008 est.). **Nationality:** noun—Lithuanian(s); adjective—Lithuanian. **Ethnic groups:** 83.4% Lithuanian, 6.3% Russian, 6.7% Polish. **Languages:** Lithuanian (official), Russian, Polish. **Religions:** primarily Roman Catholic, also Lutheran, Russian Orthodox, Protestant, evangelical Christian Baptist, Islam, Judaism.
● **GOVERNMENT Type:** parliamentary democracy. **Independence:** Sept. 6, 1991 (from Soviet Union). **Constitution:** Oct. 25, 1992. **National holiday:** Statehood Day, Feb. 16. **Heads of Government:** Valdas Adamkus, president (since July 2004); Gediminas Kirkilas, prime minister (since July 2006). **Structure:** executive; unicameral legislature; judiciary.
● **ECONOMY Monetary unit:** litas. **Budget:** (2007 est.). *income:* $12.36 bil.; *expend.:* $12.54 bil. **G.D.P.:** $59.59 bil., $16,700 per capita (2007 est.). **Chief crops:** grain, potatoes, sugar beets, vegetables; meat, milk, eggs; fish; flax fiber. **Natural resources:** peat. **Major industries:** machine

building, metalworking, food processing. **Labor force:** 1.587 mil. (2007 est.); 56% services, 28.2% industry, 15.8% agriculture (2004 est.); 5.7% unemployment (2007 est.). **Exports:** $17.09 bil. (f.o.b., 2007); 22% machinery and equipment, 15% mineral products, 12% chemicals. **Imports:** $22.64 bil. (f.o.b., 2007); 18% machinery and equipment, 16% mineral products, 10% chemicals. **Major trading partners:** (2006) *exports:* 12.8% Russia, 11.1% Latvia, 8.6% Germany, 6.5% Estonia, 6.1% Poland, 4.8% Netherlands, 4.5% Sweden, 4.4% U.K., 4.3% U.S., 4.2% Denmark; *imports:* 24.3% Russia, 14.9% Germany, 9.5% Poland, 4.8% Latvia.

Lithuanians and Latvians are closely related peoples whose languages are quite similar. But their histories, at least until 1795, were radically different. Fierce warriors able to stem the German tide during the Middle Ages, the Lithuanians repeatedly defeated the Teutonic knights, defending their independence and retaining their own religion.

In the 14th century, under Grand Duke Gediminas and his sons, Lithuania conquered White Russia (Belarus) and Ukraine and extended the dynasty from the Baltic almost to the Black Sea. The completion of Gediminas's policies came in 1386 when his grandson Jogaila was baptized, married the Polish heiress Jadwiga, and was crowned king of Poland under the title Wladislaw II, thereby creating the Poland-Lithuania Commonwealth. A condition of the union was that Lithuania had to adopt Christianity, which it did in 1387.

With the Third Partition of Poland in 1795, Lithuania was absorbed into Russia. The upper and educated classes took part in Poland's anti–Russian rebellions in 1830 and 1863. After the latter, the Russians required Lithuanians to use the Russian alphabet instead of the Latin as a move to stop any national renaissance; but after 1883 literature smuggled into the czarist empire from Prussia and secret Lithuanian schools and societies kept alive a national identity based on ethnic, religious, and linguistic grounds rather than on the medieval and Renaissance traditions of political independence.

In Jan. 1921 the victorious allies of World War I acknowledged a new Lithuanian republic in the Soviet-German Treaty of Brest-Litovsk of March 1918. Formal recognition came in 1922. The territory of Memel (Klaipeda in Lithuanian), separated from Germany in the Treaty of Versailles, was seized in Jan. 1923 and organized as an autonomous unit of the new republic. The city itself was largely German, but its countryside was Lithuanian and it was Lithuania's only possible outlet to the sea. With the historic capital Vilnius annexed by the new Polish state, the de facto capital became the university city of Kaunas.

Danger from communists and fascists led the army to dispense with Parliament in Dec. 1926; an authoritarian regime under Pres. Antana Smetona followed. In 1939 Lithuania was doomed by the 1939 Nazi-Soviet Pact. In June 1940 the Soviet Army invaded Lithuania and a Soviet-approved "people's government" was formed. After an election in which only pro-Soviet candidates were permitted to run, the Lithuanian Soviet Socialist Republic was proclaimed on July 21, 1940.

Thousands of Lithuanians fled westward, while other thousands disappeared into Siberia. Stalin returned Vilnius (from Poland) and Klaipeda (which Hitler had taken) to Lithuania and fostered industrialization, which elevated living standards above most of the U.S.S.R. A high Lithuanian birth rate enabled the country to resist "Russification" more easily than Latvia or Estonia.

Mikhail Gorbachev's policy of glasnost, or openness, spurred the strong Lithuanian nationalist and dissident movement into action. It began with a public discussion of the "secret protocols" of the 1939 Nazi-Soviet Pact, which had permitted the U.S.S.R. to annex Lithuania and which the Soviet government long had denied existed. In 1987 the Soviet government tolerated demonstrations in Vilnius, but by Feb. 1988, Soviet troops prevented the Lithuanians from celebrating their 70th year of independence. The Soviet stance resulted in the founding of the new Lithuanian Movement for Reconstruction (Sajudis), which became the main political vehicle for Lithuanian independence from the U.S.S.R.

On Mar. 11, 1990, Lithuania declared its independence, and in response the Soviets began an economic blockade. On Jan. 13, 1991, the world watched as Soviet paratroopers and tanks attacked the radio and television centers, beginning a standoff between the Soviets and the Lithuanians that lasted until Sept. 6, 1991, when the U.S.S.R. recognized Lithuanian independence.

After independence, Lithuania struggled to break a political deadlock caused by its lack of a constitution. In November 1992 free elections were held. The Democratic Labor party (the renamed Communists) gained 47 percent of the vote and 77 seats in Parliament, while Sajudis gained only 22 percent of the vote and 28 seats. In February 1993 the Democratic Labor candidate, Algirdas Brazauskas, handily won the presidential election with 61 percent of the vote.

The last Soviet troops left Lithuanian soil Aug. 31, 1993 and the government moved on a path to a free economy and worked for good relations with Russia and the other former Soviet states. In 1996 the Communists were routed and the Homeland Union party took control of the government. Over the next few years Lithuania followed strict fiscal and monetary policies thereby attracting over $1 bil. in foreign investment and strong G.D.P. growth of 6 to 7 percent. In 1997–1998 presidential elections, Valdas Adamkus won a close victory. While Oct. 2000 elections brought a center-right coalition to power, led by Rolandas Paksas, squabbles over tax-cutting and privatization of utilities broke the coalition in June. The upshot on July 3 was the return of Lithuania's last Communist dictator, Algirdas Brazauskas, as premier. Paksas became president in 2003 and voters gave 90 percent approval to joining the E.U. But Paksas was impeached in April 2004 for corruption and Adamkus was reelected.

Lithuania was admitted to the E.U. in 2004, but political instability continued and a new government, the 14th since independence, was elected in 2006 with corruption still the major issue.

▶ LUXEMBOURG
Grand Duchy of Luxembourg

● **GEOGRAPHY   Location:** landlocked country in western Europe. **Boundaries:** Belgium to N and W, Germany to E, France to S. **Total area:** 998 sq. mi. (2,586 sq km). **Coastline:** none. **Comparative area:** slightly smaller than Rhode Island. **Land use:** 25% arable land; 0% permanent crops; 75% other. **Major cities:** (Luxembourg-Ville (capital); Esch-sur-Alzette; Differdange; Dudelange.

● **PEOPLE   Population:** 486,006 (July 2008 est.). **Nationality:** noun—Luxembourger(s);   adjec-

tive—Luxembourg. **Ethnic groups:** Celtic base, with French and German blend; also, guest and worker residents from Portugal, Italy, and other European countries. **Languages:** Luxembourgish, German, French (both administrative languages), English. **Religions:** 87% Roman Catholic, 13% Protestant, Jewish, Muslim.

● **GOVERNMENT   Type:** constitutional monarchy. **Independence:** 1839 **Constitution:** Oct. 17, 1868, occasional revisions. **National holiday:** Grand Duke's birthday, National Day, June 23. **Heads of Government:** Henri de Luxembourg, grand duke (since Oct. 2000); Jean-Claude Juncker, prime minister (since Aug. 1999). **Structure:** executive—prime minister appointed by Grand Duke but responsible to parliament; unicameral legislature—Chamber of Deputies, appointed for appointed for five-year term; judiciary.

● **ECONOMY   Monetary unit:** euro. **Budget:** (2007 est.) *income:* $14.29 bil.; *expend.:* $13.92 bil. **G.D.P.:** $38.79 bil., $80,800 per capita (2007 est.). **Chief crops:** barley, oats, potatoes, wheat, fruits, wine grapes; livestock products. **Natural resources:** iron ore (no longer exploited). **Major industries:** banking, iron and steel, food processing. **Labor force:** 262,000, of whom 87,400 are foreign (2000); 86% services, 13% industry, 1% agriculture (2004). **Exports:** $19.58 bil. (f.o.b., 2007); finished steel products, chemicals, rubber products, glass, aluminum. **Imports:** $26.85 bil. (c.i.f., 2007); minerals, metals, foodstuffs, machinery, quality consumer goods. **Major trading partners:** (2006) *exports:* 19% Germany, 16% France, 10% Italy, 10% U.K., 9% Belgium, 5% Spain, 5% Netherlands; *imports:* 26% Belgium, 20% Germany, 17% China, 9% France, 6% U.K., 4% Netherlands.

One of hundreds of small principalities in the Holy Roman Empire, Luxembourg joined the German league when the empire was abolished in 1806. It shared a monarchy with the Netherlands, but the two countries remained distinct under a single sovereign. In 1831 Luxembourg lost its French-speaking territory to Belgium. The Treaty of London granted sovereignty to Luxembourg in 1867. When King William III died in 1890, different rules of succession severed the dual monarchy; Queen Wilhelmina succeeded him in the Netherlands, while Adolf of Nassau became grand duke of Luxembourg. The nation's full independence dates from that event.

During the 19th century, Luxembourg developed a balanced modern economy, with prosperous small farms being complemented by industry, particularly mining and steel production. As late as 1970, steel accounted for over 25 percent of the nation's G.D.P. and five-eighths of export earnings, although rising international competition has led to a decline since then.

Luxembourg was overrun by Germany during World War I and again in May 1940, in the early stages of World War II. Archduchess Charlotte fled to London and returned with the Allied armed forces in 1944. The constitutional monarchy has enjoyed political stability since the war, with the Christian Social party normally the senior partner in a three-way coalition.

Luxembourg formed a customs union with Belgium in 1921 and joined the Benelux (Belgium, Netherlands, Luxembourg) union even before World War II had ended. A founding member of the United Nations in 1945, Luxembourg abandoned its traditional neutrality in 1948 and joined NATO in 1949. It was a founding member of the

EEC under the 1956 Treaty of Rome and is now home to numerous European Union institutions. International banking accounts for over half of its gross national product. The country's chief problem is a shrinking and aging citizenry. After 35 years Grand Duke John abdicated in 2000, succeeded by his son Henri.

▶ MACEDONIA
The Former Yugoslav Republic of Macedonia

• **GEOGRAPHY Location:** southern part of the Balkan Peninsula. **Boundaries:** Serbia to N, Bulgaria to E, Greece to S, Albania to W, Yugoslavia to NE and N. **Total area:** 9,781 sq. mi. (25,333 sq km.). **Coastline:** none. **Comparative area:** slightly larger than Vermont. **Land use:** 24% arable land; 2% permanent crops; 74% other. **Major cities:** Skopje (Skoplje or, in Turkish, Uskub); Bitola; Kumanovo; Tetovo.

• **PEOPLE Population:** 2,061,315 (July 2008 est.). **Nationality:** noun—Macedonian(s); adj.—Macedonian. **Ethnic groups:** 64.2% Macedonian, 25.1% Albanian, 3.9% Turkish, 1.8% Serb, 7% other (includes gypsies). **Languages:** 66.5% Macedonian (official), 25.1% Albanian, 3% Turkish, 3% Serbo-Croatian, 3% other. **Religions:** 64.7% Macedonian Orthodox, 33.3% Muslim, 3% other.

• **GOVERNMENT Type:** parliamentary democracy. **Independence:** Sept. 8, 1991 (from Yugoslavia). **Constitution:** Nov. 17, 1991. **National holiday:** Independence Day, Sept. 8. **Heads of Government:** Branko Crvenkovski, president (since May 2004); , Vlado Buckovski, prime minister (since Dec. 2004). **Structure:** executive; unicameral legislature; judiciary.

• **ECONOMY Monetary unit:** denar. **Budget:** (2007 est.) **income:** $2.674 bil.; **expend.:** $2.625 bil. **G.D.P.:** $17.26 bil.; $8,400 per capita (2007 est.). **Chief crops:** rice, tobacco, wheat, corn, millet; beef, pork, poultry, mutton. **Natural resources:** chrome, lead, marble, zinc. **Major industries:** metallurgy and metal processing, chemicals, textiles, timber. **Labor force:** 906,900 mil. (2007 est.); 50% services, 30% industry, 20% agriculture (2007); 37% unemployed (2002 est.). **Exports:** $3.356 bil. (f.o.b., 2007 est.); food, beverage, tobacco, machinery and transport equipment, other manufactured goods. **Imports:** $5.228 bil. (f.o.b., 2007 est.); machinery and transport equipment, chemicals, fuels. **Major trading partners:** (2006) **exports:** 23% Serbia & Montenegro, 15.6% Germany, 15.1% Greece, 10% Italy, 5.4% Bulgaria, 5.2% Croatia; **imports:** 15% Russia, 10% Germany, 9% Greece, 7.5% Serbia & Montenegro, 6.7% Bulgaria, 6% Italy.

Located at the center of the Balkan peninsula, Macedonia is an epitome of the entire region in its history and ethnic complexity as well. While there is a Macedonian language (a Slavic tongue more akin to Bulgarian than to Serbo-Croatian and codified in grammar and orthography only after World War II), the question of whether or not there is a Macedonian nation is contested: to Serbians, Macedonians are "south Serbs"; to Greeks, they are "Slavophone Greeks"; to Bulgars, they are kindred people, ethnic "cousins."

In any case, Macedonians are not related to the classical people of King Philip and Alexander the Great. Their realm had become a Roman province by 146 B.C. and remained part of the Byzantine Empire even after being invaded and settled by Slavic peoples in the sixth and seventh centuries. Contested in the Middle Ages by the Byzantine, Bulgarian, and Serbian empires, Macedonia fell at last to the Ottoman Turks in 1371. Well into the 19th century its population called itself "Christian" or "Slav," while Greek served as the language of culture and business until a literary awakening associated with folk songs and heroic poetry brought a Macedonian consciousness. This found significant political expression with the formation in 1893 of the IMRO (Internal Macedonian Revolutionary Organization) that sought to unify all non-Turks—Bulgars, Greeks, Albanians, Vlacha—in an independent state and which did not shrink from terrorism and revolution.

The peace treaties of Paris concluding World War I divided Macedonia among three states: Greece, Bulgaria, and the newly created Yugoslavia. IMRO turned against Serbian dominance in Yugoslavia and filled the 1930's with violent struggles against "denationalization." Bulgarian claims to Macedonia led that state to ally with Hitler's Germany and to occupy Macedonia in 1941. With the victory of Tito's partisans and the reconstruction of the Yugoslav state as a federation of Communist "republics," a Macedonian People's Republic was established in 1946.

After Tito's death in 1980, Macedonia took part in the "collegial rule" whereby the presidency of Yugoslavia rotated annually among the republics. But as the separate republics declared independence in 1991 and civil war began, Macedonia declared its own independence in Jan. 1992. Greece's opposition to the new nation's name and flag—as menaces to the northern Greek province of the same name—prevented international recognition until a 1995 agreement between the two countries. Under the pact, Macedonia removed an ancient Greek symbol from its flag and changed its constitution so as to remove any suggestion of a claim on Greek Macedonia. With U.N. recognition came both U.N. "peacekeeping forces" to patrol the frontier with rump Yugoslavia and the painful need to comply with the U.N. embargo against Serbia. An April 1996 treaty with Yugoslavia resolved border questions.

Elections in 1998 saw the ruling Social Democrats ousted by the right-wing Coalition for Changes which organized a government under Ljuplo Georgievski. In April, NATO pledged to defend Macedonia from Yugoslav incursions in the latter's struggle again Albanian separatists in Kosovo. Refugees from Kosovo flooded Macedonia, straining its humanitarian capacities. The decision of "founding" president Gligorov not to seek a second term brought presidential elections (Oct.–Dec. 1999) won by Boris Trajkovski of the governing coalition. In March 2001 ethnic Albanians rose up to fight for equal rights, taking over one-third of the country. A cease-fire in August and NATO intervention led to a peaceful settlement. In Sept. 2002 elections, the ruling party lost to a coalition that included Ali Ahmeti, leader of the guerilla uprising and on the U.S. terrorist list. In Feb. 2004 Pres. Trajkovski was killed in a plane crash and Prime Minister Crvenkovski was elected president in April but tension remained and in Dec. 2004 Parliament chose Vlado Buckovski as Prime Minister who pledged he would bring the country into NATO and eventually the E.U. A center-right party won the 2006 and 2008 elections.

▶MADAGASCAR
Republic of Madagascar
● **GEOGRAPHY   Location:** off southeast Africa in western Indian Ocean. Antananarivo: 18°52′S, 47°30′E. **Boundaries:** about 300 mi. (500 km) E of Mozambique. **Total area:** 226,656 sq. mi. (587,040 sq km). **Coastline:** 3,000 mi. (4,828 km). **Comparative area:** slightly less than twice the size of Arizona. **Land use:** 4% arable land; 1% permanent crops; 95% other. **Major cities:** Antananarivo (capital); Antsirabé; Toamasina (Tamatave); Fianarantsoa; Mahajanga (Majunga).
● **PEOPLE   Population:** 20,042,551 (July 2008 est.). **Nationality:** noun—Malagasy (sing., pl.); adjective— Malagasy. **Ethnic groups:** highlanders of predominantly Malayo-Indonesian origin (Merina and related Betsileo); coastal peoples collectively termed Cotiers, with mixed African, Malayo-Indonesian, and Arab ancestry (Betsimisaraka, Tsimihety, Antaisaka, Sakalava); French, Indian, Creole, Comoran. **Languages:** French and Malagasy (both official). **Religions:** 52% indigenous beliefs, 41% Christian, 7% Muslim.
● **GOVERNMENT   Type:** republic. **Independence:** June 26, 1960 (from France). **Constitution:** Aug. 19, 1992. **National holiday:** Independence Day, June 26. **Heads of Government:** Marc Ravalomanana, president (since Apr. 2002); Charles Rabemananjara, premier (since Oct. 2007). **Structure:** executive; unicameral legislature, scheduled to become bicameral—two-thirds of upper house will be filled from directly elected regional assemblies, rest by presidential appointment; judiciary.
● **ECONOMY   Monetary unit:** Malagasy franc. **Budget:** (2007 est.) *income:* $1.22 bil; *expend.:* $1.55 bil. **G.D.P.:** $19.95 bil., $1,000 per capita (2007 est.). **Chief crops:** coffee, vanilla, cloves, sugar; livestock. **Natural resources:** graphite, chromite, coal, bauxite, salt. **Major industries:** agricultural processing (meat canneries, soap factories, brewery, tanneries, sugar refining), light consumer goods industries (textiles, glassware), cement. **Labor force:** (2000) 7.3 mil. **Exports:** $1.027 bil. (f.o.b., 2007 est.); coffee, vanilla, cloves, shellfish, sugar, petroleum products. **Imports:** $2.005 mil. (f.o.b., 2007); 30% intermediate manufactures, capital goods, petroleum, consumer goods, food. **Major trading partners:** (2006) *exports:* 32.1% France, 25.3% U.S., 6.1% Germany, 5% Italy, 4.1% U.K.; *imports:* 14.5% France, 12% China, 9.3% Iran, 5.6% Mauritius, 4.7% Hong Kong.

The largest island nation, and fourth largest island in the world, Madagascar was settled by Malayo-Indonesian migrants some 2,000 years ago. Although later waves of African and Arab migrants were absorbed into the population, to a large extent it is still ethnically and culturally Asian. A Portuguese attempt to colonize the island in the 16th century failed, and during the 18th and 19th centuries, a unified kingdom backed by the British ruled the country. Foreign interests—largely British and French—developed extensive coffee plantations, and the French made Madagascar a protectorate in 1885 and a colony in 1896.

During World War II Madagascar sided with the Free French, and French colonial rule was reestablished after the war. The Malagasy Republic was founded as an independent nation on June 26, 1960. A coup in 1972 brought a repressive anti-French government to power.

A new federal constitution was approved in 1992, and in 1993 elections, Albert Zafy defeated the 17-year incumbent Didier Ratsiraka for the presidency, but the results were reversed in 1997 and Ratsiraka immediately set out to cut inflation, and renegotiate the nation's many foreign loans. The presidential election of 2001 turned into (except for the bloodshed) an opera bouffa, as neither incumbent Didier Ratsiraka nor challenger Marc Ravalomanana would concede defeat and each set up his own government. The military successes of troops loyal to Ravalomanana led to Ratsiraka's July 5 flight to the Seychelles. Corruption was so prevalent that Ratsiraka and others were sent to prison in 2003. In 2007, the I Love Madagascar Party won parliamentary elections.

Madagascar's wildlife (a mixture of African species and others of domestic evolution) and its isolation make it of unique scientific interest. (In 1990, scientists discovered the smallest mammal known to science: the dwarf lemur.) But some 75 percent of the population live in poverty, which has been worsened by frequent cyclones.

▶MALAWI
Republic of Malawi
● **GEOGRAPHY   Location:** landlocked country in southern central Africa. **Boundaries:** Tanzania to N, Mozambique to E, S, and SW; Zambia to W; Lake Malawi forms much of eastern boundary. **Total area:** 45,745 sq. mi. (118,480 sq km). **Coastline:** none. **Comparative area:** slightly smaller than Pennsylvania. **Land use:** 20% arable land; 1% permanent crops; 79% other. **Major cities:** Lilongwe (capital); Blantyre.
● **PEOPLE   Population:** 13,931,831 (July 2008 est.). **Nationality:** noun—Malawian(s); adjective— Malawian. **Ethnic groups:** Chewa, Nyanja, Tumbuko, Yao, Lomwe, Sena, Tonga, Ngoni, Asian, European. **Languages:** English and Chichewa (both official); Tombuka and other regional languages. **Religions:** 55% Protestant, 20% Roman Catholic, 20% Muslim, 3% indigenous beliefs.
● **GOVERNMENT   Type:** multiparty democracy. **Independence:** July 6, 1964 (from U.K.). **Constitution:** May 18, 1994. **National holiday:** Republic Day, July 6. **Head of Government:** Bingu Wa Mutharika, president (since May 2004). **Structure:** executive; legislature—National Assembly of 193 members elected to five-year terms; judiciary.
● **ECONOMY   Monetary unit:** Malawian kwacha. **Budget:** (2007 est.) *income:* $1.082 bil.; *expend.:* $1.142 bil. **G.D.P.:** $10.47 bil., $800 per capita (2007 est.). **Chief crops:** tobacco, tea, sugar, cotton; cattle, goats. **Natural resources:** limestone; hydropower; unexploited deposits of uranium, coal, bauxite. **Major industries:** agricultural processing (tea, tobacco, sugar), sawmilling, cement. **Labor force:** 4.5 mil. (2001 est.); 86% agriculture. **Exports:** $657 mil. (f.o.b., 2007); tobacco, tea, sugar, coffee, wood products. **Imports:** $892 mil. (f.o.b., 2007); food, petroleum products, semimanufactures, consumer goods. **Major trading partners:** (2006) *exports:* 12.6% South Africa, 9.7% Germany, 9.6% Egypt, 9.5% U.S, 8.5% Zimbabwe, 5.4% Russia, 4.4% Netherlands; *imports:* 33.9% South Africa, 8% India, 7.6% Zambia, 6.3% U.S., 5.7% Tanzania, 4.5% Germany, 4.2% China.

Malawi derives its name from the Maravi, a Bantu people who settled in the region in the 13th century and whose descendants, the Chewas, make up a significant segment of the current population. In the 1830's the Ngoni, driven from what is now South Africa by the Zulus, arrived in the area around Lake Nyasa. The arrival of the Scottish missionary David Livingstone in 1859 led to the establishment of the British-controlled Nyasaland Protectorate in 1891. In 1953 Nyasaland formed a federation with Northern and Southern Rhodesia (Zambia and Zimbabwe) and began to organize an independence movement. The fight for independence was led by Dr. H. Kamuzu Banda, an expatriate who assumed the presidency of the Nyasaland African Congress, later the Malawi Congress party, upon his return in 1958. The British granted Nyasaland self-governing status in 1962, and Banda was elected prime minister the following year. Malawi achieved full independence under its present name in 1964.

Banda soon introduced one-party rule and had himself declared president for life in 1971. All dissent was crushed while corruption and nepotism strangled the economy, leaving Malawi's citizens among the poorest in the world. By 1990 internal unrest and the decline of Banda's popularity (he was now in his 90's) rapidly led to change. In 1992 a series of violent strikes by workers in the two largest cities resulted in more than 35 deaths. In June 1993 Malawians voted 2 to 1 to institute a multiparty system and in May 1994 Banda lost his nation's only free election in 30 years to Bakili Muluzi's United Democratic Front (UDF). Corruption remained the nation's major problem through several successive leaders.

▶ **MALAYSIA**
● **GEOGRAPHY Location:** 13 states in Southeast Asia; 11 are in Peninsular Malaysia and two, Sabah and Sarawak, lie about 400 mi. (640 km) across South China Sea on northern coast of island of Borneo (Kalimantan). **Boundaries:** Peninsular Malaysia—Thailand to N, South China Sea to E, island of Singapore to S across Johor Strait, and Indonesian island of Sumatra to W across Strait of Malacca; Sabah and Sarawak—South China Sea to NW, Sulu Sea to NE, Celebes Sea to E, Indonesia to S; Brunei is enclosed within Sarawak on coast of South China Sea. **Total area:** 127,317 sq. mi. (329,750 sq km). **Coastline:** 2,905 mi. (4,675 km). **Comparative area:** slightly larger than New Mexico. **Land use:** 6% arable land; 18% permanent crops; 76% other. **Major cities:** Kuala Lumpur (capital); Ipoh; Johor Baharu; Meleka (Malacca); Petaling Jaya.
● **PEOPLE Population:** 25,274,133 (July 2008 est.) **Nationality:** noun—Malaysian(s); adjective—Malaysian. **Ethnic groups:** 50.4% Malay, 23.7% Chinese, 11% indigenous, 7.1% Indian, 7.8% other. **Languages:** Bahasa Melayu (official); English, Chinese dialects, Tamil, Telugu, Malayalam, Panjabi, Thai; note – in addition, in East Malaysia several indigenous languages are spoken, the largest of which are Iban and Kadazan. **Religions:** Islam, Buddhism, Daoism, Hinduism, Christianity, other traditional Chinese religions.
● **GOVERNMENT Type:** constitutional monarchy; Peninsular Malaysian states—hereditary rulers in all but Meleka and Penang, where governors are appointed by Malaysian government, with powers of state governments limited by federal constitution; Sabah—self-governing state, holding 20 seats in House of Representatives, with foreign affairs, defense, internal security, and other powers delegated to federal government; Sarawak—self-governing state, which holds 24 seats in House of Representatives, with foreign affairs, defense, internal security, and other powers delegated to federal government. **Independence:** Aug. 31, 1957 (from U.K.). **Constitution:** Aug. 31, 1957, amended Sept. 16, 1963, when Federation of Malaya became Federation of Malaysia. **National holiday:** National Day, Aug. 31. **Heads of Government:** Sultan Sirajuddin ibni Al-Marhum Tuanku Syed Putra Jamalullail, king (since Dec. 2001); Abdullah Ahmad Badawi, prime minister (since Oct. 2003). **Structure:** executive—paramount ruler chosen by and from the nine state rulers for five-year term; bicameral legislature; judiciary.
● **ECONOMY Monetary unit:** Malaysian ringgit. **Budget:** (2007 est.) *income:* $41.01 bil. *expend.:* $46.96 bil. **G.D.P.:** $357.9 bil., $14,400 per capita (2007 est.). **Chief crops:** Peninsular Malaysia—natural rubber, palm oil, rice; Sabah—mainly subsistence, main crops are rubber, timber, coconut, rice; Sarawak—rubber, timber, pepper. **Natural resources:** tin, crude oil, timber, copper, iron ore. **Major industries:** Peninsular Malaysia—rubber and oil-palm processing and manufacturing, light manufacturing industry, electronics; Sabah—logging, petroleum production; Sarawak—agriculture processing, petroleum production and refining, logging. **Labor force:** 10.91 mil. (2007 est.); 51% services, 36% industry, 13% agriculture (2005); 3.1% unemployment (2007). **Exports:** $169.9 bil. (2007 est.); electronic equipment, petroleum products, palm oil, wood products, rubber, textiles. **Imports:** $132.7 bil. (2007 est.); machinery and equipment, chemicals, food. **Major trading partners:** (2006) *exports:* 18.8% U.S., 15.4% Singapore, 8.9% Japan, 7.2% China, 5.3% Thailand, 4.9% Hong Kong; *imports:* 13.3% Japan, 12.6% U.S., 12.2% China, 11.7% Singapore, 5.5% Thailand, 5.5% Taiwan, 5.4% South Korea.

From ancient times a group of petty principalities in the southern part of the Malay Peninsula, bordering the Strait of Malacca, maintained extensive ties of maritime commerce throughout Southeast Asia. The early Malay states were Hindu, under Indian influence; with the rise of the Kingdom of Malacca in the 15th century, conversion to Islam was widespread. European influence in the Spice Islands began in the 16th century; the Portuguese, initially dominant, gave way to the Dutch, who seized Malacca in 1641.

British influence grew during the 18th century, with the founding of a trading settlement at Penang in 1789. Singapore was founded in 1819, and the Dutch ceded Malacca to Britain in 1824. By a series of treaties in the late 19th century, the various Malay states became British protectorates; Britain controlled the entire southern peninsula after 1909. Under British rule, commercial tin mining and the establishment of extensive rubber plantations led to the importation of many Indian and Chinese laborers; eventually ethnic Chinese dominated Malaya's domestic economy.

Japan overran Malaya by February 1942. Following World War II, the various Malay states (except Singapore) organized into a federation, which replaced the confusing prewar regime of federated and unfederated protectorates. A Communist rebellion disrupted the country throughout the early 1950's. Following the suppression of the Communist movement, elections were held in mid-1955 for a home-rule government. The elections brought the Alliance party of Tungku Abdul Rahman to power, and the Federation of Malaya became independent in 1957.

The nation expanded on Sept. 16, 1963, with the creation of Malaysia, incorporating the Federation of Malaya as well as Singapore and the former British colonies of North Borneo (thereafter called Sabah) and Sarawak. Singapore seceded in 1965 and became an independent nation.

Malaysia was ruled from 1981 to 2003 by the coalition government of Mahathir Mohamad, who has transformed the country from an agriculture-based economy to one of the fastest-growing economies in Asia. The country sustained annual growth rates of 8 percent through the 1980's. In 1995 Malaysia received $5.8 bil. in foreign direct investment, the most in East Asia. The Asian financial crisis of 1997-98 hit Malaysia very hard as the currency and stockmarkets declined steeply.

Facing Malaysia's first recession in 13 years, Mahathir announced that the free market system had proven a failure and dismissed his finance minister, Anwar Ibrahim in Sept. 1998. Arrested and beaten by police, Anwar faced charges of sodomy and corruption and in 1999 he was found guilty and sentenced to six years in prison. His wife, Azizah Ismail announced a new opposition National Justice Party. But when elections were suddenly called in November, her new party took only five of the 193 seats, as Mahathir's National Front carried 148. Mahathir announced in 2002, that after 21 years, he would resign effective Oct. 25; deputy P.M. Abdullah Badawi had been groomed to succeed and in March 2004 won the election handily. But by 2008 the nation seemed ready for a change from the repressive policies of the National Front. In August, Anwar won a landslide victory for a seat in parliament.

▶ **MALDIVES**
Republic of Maldives
• **GEOGRAPHY Location:** chain of more than 1,200 small coral islands (about 220 inhabited), 475 mi. (764 km) from N to S and 80 mi. (207 km) from W to E in Indian Ocean; northernmost atoll about 370 mi. (960 km) southwest of India. Malé 4°00'N, 73°28'E. **Boundaries:** Laccadive Sea to NE, Arabian Sea to N, Indian Ocean to S and W. **Total area:** 116 sq. mi. (300 sq km). **Coastline:** 400 mi. (644 km). **Comparative area:** about 1.7 times size of Washington, D.C. **Land use:** 3% arable land; 7% permanent crops; 90% other. **Major cities:** Malé (capital).
• **PEOPLE Population:** 379,174 (July 2008 est.). **Nationality:** noun—Maldivian(s); adjective— Maldivian. **Ethnic groups:** South Indian, Sinhalese, and Arab. **Languages:** Maldivian Divehi (dialect of Sinhala; script derived from Arabic); English spoken by most government officials. **Religions:** Sunni Muslim.
• **GOVERNMENT Type:** republic. **Independence:** July 26, 1965 (from U.K.). **Constitution:** Adopted Jan. 1998. **National holiday:** Independence Day, July 26. **Head of Government:** Maumoon Abdul Gayoom, president (since Nov. 1978). **Structure:** executive; unicameral legislature; judiciary.
• **ECONOMY Monetary unit:** rufiyaa. **Budget:** (2006 est.) *income:* $508 mil.; *expend.:* $671 mil. **G.D.P.:** $2.839 bil. (2006 est.), $3,900 per capita (2002 est.). **Chief crops:** coconut, corn, sweet potatoes; fishing. **Natural resources:** fish. **Major industries:** fishing, tourism, shipbuilding, some coconut processing. **Labor force:** 101,300 (2004 est.); 77% services, 16% agriculture, 7% industry (2006 est.). **Exports:** $167 mil. (f.o.b., 2006 est.); fish, clothing. **Imports:** $930 mil. (f.o.b., 2006 est.); intermediate and capital goods, consumer goods, petroleum products. **Major trading partners:** (2006) *exports:* 33.1% Thailand, 14.3% U.K., 11.9%

Sri Lanka, 10.3% Japan, 6.9% France, 6.1% Algeria; *imports:* 23.2% Singapore, 15.8% United Arab Emirates, 11.1% India, 7.9% Malaysia, 6.9% Thailand, 5.6% Sri Lanka.

The small sultanate of the Maldive Islands, with an Islamic population of Sinhalese descent, was made a British protectorate in 1887. The islands' tiny area and poor soil limited development; fishing and fish processing are the main industries, and copra (dried coconut meat for coconut oil) is the only significant crop. The Maldives became an independent nation on July 26, 1965. In 1968 the sultanate was abolished and replaced by a republic. Since independence, tourism has become economically important and now accounts for 18 percent of the G.D.P. Protests over the concentration of development on the island of Malé in recent years have led to political unrest in the other islands, while attempts to address the basic needs of those islands have strained the nation's tiny economic base.

The current president, Maumoon Abdul Gayoom, was elected to office in 1978 and subsequently reelected every time. An attempted coup against the Gayoom government on Nov. 4, 1988, was put down with the intervention of Indian troops. The 2004 tsunami killed hundreds and did severe structural damage. The first multiparty elections for president were scheduled for Oct. 2008.

▶ **MALI**
Republic of Mali
• **GEOGRAPHY Location:** northwestern Africa. **Boundaries:** Algeria to N, Niger to E, Burkina Faso, Ivory Coast, Guinea to S, Senegal and Mauritania to W. **Total area:** 478,765 sq. mi. (1,240,000 sq km). **Coastline:** none. **Comparative area:** slightly less than twice the size of Texas. **Land use:** 4% arable land; negl. % permanent crops; 96% other. **Major cities:** Bamako (capital); Ségou; Mopti; Sikasso; Kayes.
• **PEOPLE Population:** 12,324,029 (July 2008 est.) **Nationality:** noun—Malian(s); adjective— Malian. **Ethnic groups:** 50% Mande (Bambara, Malinke, Soninke), 17% Peul, 12% Voltaic, 6% Songhai, 10% Tuareg and Moor. **Languages:** French (official); Bambara spoken by 80% of population. **Religions:** 90% Muslim, 9% indigenous beliefs, 1% Christian.
• **GOVERNMENT Type:** republic. **Independence:** Sept. 22, 1960 (from France). **Constitution:** Jan. 12, 1992. **National holiday:** Anniversary of the Proclamation of the Republic, Sept. 22. **Heads of Government:** Amadou Toumani Touré, president (since June 2002); Modibo Sidibe, prime minister (since Sept. 2007). **Structure:** executive; unicameral legislature; judiciary.
• **ECONOMY Monetary unit:** Communauté Financière Africaine (CFA) franc. **Budget:** (2006 est.) *income:* $1.5 bil.; *expend.:* $1.8 bil. **G.D.P.:** $14.18 bil., $1,200 per capita (2007 est.). **Chief crops:** cotton, millet, rice, corn; goats, sheep, cattle. **Natural resources:** gold, phosphates, kaolin, salt, limestone, uranium; bauxite, iron ore, manganese, tin, and copper deposits are known but not exploited. **Major industries:** small local consumer goods and food processing, construction, phosphate, gold. **Labor force:** 5.4 mil; 80% agriculture, 19% services. **Exports:** $294 mil. (f.o.b., 2006 est.); cotton, livestock, gold. **Imports:** $2.358 bil. (f.o.b., 2006 est.); machinery and equipment, foodstuffs, construction materials, petroleum. **Major trading partners:** (2006) *exports:* 26.8% China, 24.9% Ger-

many, 7.1% Thailand, 4.9% Taiwan, 4% Bangladesh; *imports:* 12.8% France, 12.2% Senegal, 10.5% Cote d'Ivoire.

Mali has been a center of West African civilization for over 4,000 years. Iron Age civilizations flourished on the middle reaches of the Niger River from about 200 B.C. The kingdom of Ghana arose about A.D. 750 on the strength of the gold trade with North African Berbers. Ghana was overthrown by the Muslim Almoravids, who ruled only 11 years, though Islam remained a major influence from that time. From 1200 to 1400, the Kingdom of Mali was dominant in the region and was renowned throughout Islam and even in Christian Europe for its wealth and power; when Mansa Musa's retinue stopped in Cairo en route to Mecca, it carried so much gold that the price of gold fell 20 percent. By the end of the 14th century, the Mali empire had been eclipsed by the Songhai (Soyinka) empire, centered on the Niger River cities of Gao and Timbuktu.

The Songhai empire collapsed after Timbuktu was sacked by Moroccans in 1591. It fragmented into a series of smaller states, and power shifted from the desert fringe back to the Niger valley, bringing with it a further spread of Islam.

French exploration of Mali led to conquest in 1896 and the creation of the colony of French Sudan in 1898, governed from Dakar, Senegal. Timbuktu declined in importance, and Bamako became the country's principal urban center.

Malians were granted French citizenship and limited self-rule in 1946. In 1958 the territory became autonomous within the French Overseas Community. In 1959, with French support, the French Sudan and Senegal formed the Federation of Mali, which became independent on June 20, 1960. Senegal seceded from the federation almost immediately, and Mali became an independent republic on Sept. 22, 1960. Modibo Keita was elected the country's first president.

Keita's program of radical control of society and the economy by the central government provoked discontent, and he was overthrown in 1968 by military officers led by Lt. Moussa Traore. Traore's Military Committee of National Liberation ruled until 1979 when it was reorganized under a new constitution as the Malian People's Democratic Union. Traore was ousted in a 1991 coup and a transitional government under a civilian prime minister, Soumana Sacko, set up multiparty elections for June 1992. Alpha Konaré was elected president and his Alliance for Democracy in Mali party won 76 of 116 legislative seats. In 1995, the government reached an agreement in its longstanding dispute with the ethnic Tuareg nomads in the northern part of the country.

Pres. Konaré's government succeeded in reviving the economy (cotton and gold production rank among the top in Africa) and winning praise from the World Bank. Political opposition, though small, turned violent in 1997 and caused a cancellation of the results of elections in April. Opposition parties claimed the government had fixed the elections and boycotted new ones held in May that gave Konare victory. Konare bowed to a constitutional provision barring a third term and voters in May 2002 gave 65 percent of the votes to Amadou Toure who was reelected in 2007.

▶ **MALTA**
Republic of Malta
● **GEOGRAPHY   Location:** archipelago (largest islands are Malta, Gozo, and Comino) in central Mediterranean. Valletta 35°54'N, 14°32'E. **Boundaries:** Sicily 58 mi. (93 km) to N, Libya 180 mi. (290 km) to S, Tunisia to W. **Total area:** 124 sq. mi. (320 sq km). **Coastline:** 87 mi. (140 km). **Comparative area:** slightly less than twice the size of Washington, D.C. **Land use:** 31% arable land; 3% permanent crops; 66% other. **Major cities:** Valletta (capital), Birkirkara, Qormi, Sliema.

● **PEOPLE   Population:** 403,532 (July 2008 est.) **Nationality:** noun—Maltese (sing., pl.); adjective—Maltese. **Ethnic groups:** Maltese (descendants of ancient Carthaginians and Phoenicians, with strong elements of Italian and other Mediterranean stock) **Languages:** Maltese and English (both official). **Religions:** 98% Roman Catholic.

● **GOVERNMENT   Type:** parliamentary democracy. **Independence:** Sept. 21, 1964 (from U.K.). **Constitution:** Dec. 13, 1974. **National holiday:** Independence Day, Sept. 21. **Heads of Government:** Edward Fenech-Adami, president (since Apr. 2004); Lawrence Gonzi, prime minister (since Mar. 2004). **Structure:** executive; unicameral legislature—seats are given to largest popular party to ensure a majority, usually 65; judiciary.

● **ECONOMY   Monetary unit:** euro. **Budget:** (2007 est.) *income:* $3.316 bil.; *expend.:* $3.368 bil. **G.D.P.:** $9.342 bil., $23,200 per capita (2007 est.). **Chief crops:** potatoes, cauliflower, grapes, wheat, barley; milk, pork, poultry. **Natural resources:** limestone, salt. **Major industries:** tourism, electronics, ship repair yard, construction. **Labor force:** 164,000 (2006); 22% industry, 75% services, 3% agriculture; 6.8% unemployment (2005). **Exports:** $3.403 bil. (f.o.b., 2007); machinery and transport equipment, manufactures. **Imports:** $4.212 bil. (f.o.b., 2007); machinery and transport equipment, manufactured goods; food, drink and tobacco. **Major trading partners:** (2006) *exports:* 215.3% France, 13.2% Singapore, 13% U.S., 12.5% Germany, 9.5% U.K., 4.9% Japan, 4.2% Hong Kong; *imports:* 28% Italy, 10.5% U.K., 8.7% France, 7.6% Germany, 6.8% Singapore, 5.6% U.S.

Malta, an ancient crossroads of Mediterranean trade, was ruled successively by Phoenicians, Carthaginians, Greeks, Romans, and Byzantines before being conquered by Islamic Saracens from North Africa in the ninth century. In 1090 the Norman kings of Sicily conquered it and made it a way station for the First Crusade. In 1530 Charles V gave the island to the Knights Hospitalers (the Knights of Malta). The island withstood a siege by the Ottoman Turks in 1565 and fell only to Napoleon in 1798.

Malta came under British rule in 1800, and was annexed in 1814. Limited self-rule was granted under the constitutions of 1921 and 1939. During World War II, Malta suffered devastating air raids by German and Italian forces; the entire population was awarded the George Cross for bravery.

In 1964 Malta was granted independence within the British Commonwealth, with Elizabeth II as its sovereign. Abrogating its mutual defense treaty with Great Britain in 1971, the Maltese government severed all ties to the British Crown, becoming a fully independent republic. British forces withdrew from the island in 1979.

Malta was governed by the leftist, anticlerical, and neutralist Labour party from 1971 to 1987, whose leader, the ardent nationalist Dominic Mintoff, was prime minister from 1971 to 1984, succeeded by Mifsud Bonnici. In 1997 the Catholic and pro-Western Nationalist party won a popular electoral majority but not a majority in Parliament. Under a 1987 constitutional amendment, it was granted sufficient extra seats in Parliament to allow it to organize a government under Prime Minister Eddie Fenech Adami.

The Nationalist party ruled for nine years until in 1996 elections the Labour party won a slim majority, but returned to power in Sept. 1998 with Adami returning as prime minister. In 2003 voters approved a move to enter the E.U. which it did in 2004.

▶MARSHALL ISLANDS
Republic of the Marshall Islands

• **GEOGRAPHY   Location:** two groups of islands, the Ratak and Ralik chains, comprising 31 atolls in western Pacific. Majuro 7°09′N, 171°12′E. **Boundaries:** Guam about 1,300 mi. (2,100 km) to NW, Hawaii about 2,000 mi. (3,200 km) to NE, Kiribati to S, Federated States of Micronesia to W. **Total area:** 70 sq. mi. (181 sq km). **Coastline:** 230 (370 km). **Comparative area:** about the size of Washington, D.C. **Land use:** 17% arable land; 0% permanent crops; 83% other. **Major cities:** Majuro (capital).

• **PEOPLE   Population:** 63,174 (July 2008 est.). **Nationality:** noun—Marshallese; adjective—Marshallese. **Ethnic groups:** Micronesian. **Languages:** English (official), two major Marshallese dialects from Malayo-Polynesian family, Japanese. **Religions:** Christian, mostly Protestant.

• **GOVERNMENT   Type:** constitutional government in free association with U.S.; Compact of Free Association entered into force Oct. 21, 1986. **Independence:** Oct. 21, 1986 (from U.S.-administered U.N. trusteeship). **Constitution:** May 1, 1979. **National holiday:** Proclamation of the Republic of the Marshall Islands, May 1. **Head of Government:** Litokwa Tomeing, president (since Jan. 2008). **Structure:** executive; unicameral legislature; judiciary.

• **ECONOMY   Monetary unit:** U.S. dollar. **Budget:** (1999) *income:* $42 mil.; *expend:* $40 mil. **G.D.P.:** $115 mil., $2,900 per capita (2005 est.). **Chief crops:** coconuts, cacao, taro, breadfruit, fruits; pigs, chickens. **Natural resources:** phosphate deposits, marine products, deep seabed minerals. **Major industries:** copra, fish, tourism. **Labor force:** 28,698. **Exports:** $9 mil. (f.o.b., 2000 est.); coconut oil, fish, trochus shells. **Imports:** $54 mil. (c.i.f., 2000 est.); foodstuffs, machinery and equipment, fuels, beverages and tobacco. **Major trading partners:** (2006) *exports:* U.S., Japan, Australia, China; *imports:* U.S., Japan, Australia, NZ, Singapore, Fiji, China, Philippines.

The Marshall Islands, part of the geographic region known as Micronesia, are made up of 31 atolls of the Ratak (Sunrise) and Ralik (Sunset) chains located between 4° and 14°N and 160° and 173°E. Although claimed by Spain in 1592, the islands were left undisturbed by the Spanish empire for 300 years. In 1885, Germany took over the administration on the islands of Jaluit and Ebon. At that time copra (dried coconut meat) trade was the primary industry. Japan assumed control of the Marshalls at the beginning of World War I and held them until 1944, when Allied forces occupied the islands. In 1947 the islands were included in the U.N. Trust Territory of the Pacific and placed under U.S. administration. In 1946 the U.S. government resettled the inhabitants of Bikini and Enewetak in order to begin nuclear tests, which continued through 1958. Residents began returning to Enewetak in 1980; but the estimated cost of a complete clean-up of Bikini is $100 million.

▶MAURITANIA
Islamic Republic of Mauritania

• **GEOGRAPHY   Location:** northwestern Africa. **Boundaries:** territory of Western Sahara to N, Algeria to NE, Mali to E and S, Senegal to S, Atlantic Ocean to W. **Total area:** 397,954 sq. mi. (1,030,700 sq km). **Coastline:** 469 mi. (754 km). **Comparative area:** slightly larger than three times the size of New Mexico. **Land use:** negl. % arable land; negl. % permanent crops; 99% other. **Major cities:** Nouakchott (capital); Nouadhibou (Port Etienne); Kaédi; Zouérate; Rosso.

• **PEOPLE   Population:** 3,364,940 (July 2008 est.). **Nationality:** noun—Mauritanian(s); adjective—Mauritanian. **Ethnic groups:** 40% mixed Maur/black, 30% Maur, 30% black. **Languages:** Hassaniya Arabic (official), Wolof (official), Pular, Soninke, French. **Religions:** 100% Muslim.

• **GOVERNMENT   Type:** republic. **Independence:** Nov. 28, 1960 (from France). **Constitution:** July 12, 1991. **National holiday:** Independence Day, Nov. 28. **Heads of Government:** Ould Cheikh Abdellahi, president (since Apr. 2007); Yahya Ould Ahmed El Waghef, prime minister (since May 2007). **Structure:** executive; bicameral legislature; judiciary.

• **ECONOMY   Monetary unit:** ouguiya. **Budget:** (2002 est.) *income:* $421 mil.; *expend:* $378 mil. **G.D.P.:** $5.818 bil., $1,800 per capita (2007 est.) **Chief crops:** dates, millet, sorghum; cattle, sheep; fish. **Natural resources:** iron ore, gypsum, fish, copper, phosphate. **Major industries:** fish processing, mining of iron ore and gypsum. **Labor force:** 786,000 (2001 est.); 50% agriculture, 40% services, 10% industry and commerce; 21% unemployment (1999). **Exports:** $1.395 bil. (f.o.b., 2006); fish and fish products, iron ore, gold. **Imports:** $1.475 bil. (f.o.b., 2006); machinery and equipment, foodstuffs, consumer goods, petroleum products, capital goods. **Major trading partners:** (2006) *exports:* 26.1% China, 11.7% Italy, 10.5% France, 6.9% Spain, 6.8% Belgium, 5.4% Japan, 4.6% Cote d'Ivoire; *imports:* 11.9% France, 8.1% China, 6.8% Belgium, 6.7% U.S., 5.9% Italy, 5.7% Spain, 5.5% Brazil.

The population of Mauritania is divided between an Arab and Berber majority in the north and various black African peoples in the south. From the ninth through the 15th centuries, southern Mauritania was part of the kingdoms of, successively, Ghana, Mali, and Sanghay. In the 1050's, a puritanical Muslim sect, the Almoravids conquered Ghana, Morocco, Western Algeria, and Spain; they were eclipsed in the next century.

Portuguese trade on the Mauritania coast began in the early 15th century; the Portuguese remained dominant until about 1600 when their control was contested by the British, French, and Dutch. France established a protectorate in 1903, and the area was made a French colony in 1920.

In 1958 Mauritania became a self-governing republic within the French Overseas Community. In 1959 Mokhtar Ould Daddah was elected prime minister, and the country became fully independent on Nov. 28, 1960. A new constitution was adopted in 1961, establishing a presidential form of government. The four major political parties were combined into a single party in 1965.

Morocco claimed Mauritania as part of its sphere of influence; after talks about unifying the two countries broke down, Morocco recognized Mauritanian independence in 1970. Spain relinquished its claim to the Spanish Sahara in 1976.

The southern part of that territory was annexed by Mauritania, while the larger northern section was annexed by Morocco. Rebels of the Polisario Front proclaimed the independent state of Western Sahara, and in 1980 Mauritania relinquished its claims to its portion of the Western Sahara, signed a treaty with Polisario, and resumed relations with Algeria, Polisario's chief backer.

In 1978 Ould Daddah was removed from office in a military coup and was replaced as president by Lt. Col. Haidalla. He in turn was overthrown on Dec. 12, 1984, by Chief of Staff Maaouya Ould Sid' Ahmed Taya. Taya normalized relations with Morocco and held regional and local elections in 1986 and 1987 in a first step toward the restoration of democracy.

Border incidents erupted between Mauritania and Senegal in 1989 and Mauritania expelled 40,000 black Senegalese workers. Racial and religious strife has severely hampered the country's economy. Taya introduced multiparty elections in 1991 and a new constitution was approved; Taya and his Democratic and Social Republican party won the presidency and control of the legislature in 1992 and again in 1997. In the run-up to the 2003 elections, Taya had several top leaders arrested, but he won two-thirds of the vote in a suspicious election. In 2005, however, a military junta overthrew him and in the first honest elections in 2007 a civilian government was installed under Pres. Ould Abdellahi. But he too was ousted by the military in Aug. 2008 and Gen. Mohamed Ould Aziz declared himself president.

▶MAURITIUS
Republic of Mauritius
• **Geography Location:** southwestern Indian Ocean. Port Louis 20°09′S, 57°29′E. **Boundaries:** nearest neighbor is Réunion to SW. **Total area:** 718 sq. mi. (1,860 sq km). **Coastline:** 110 mi. (177 km). **Comparative area:** almost 11 times the size of Washington D.C.. **Land use:** 49% arable land; 3% permanent crops; 48% other. **Major cities:** Port Louis (capital); Beau Bassin/Rose Hill; Vacoas-Phoenix; Curepipe; Quatre Bornes.
• **People Population:** 1,274,189 (July 2008 est.). **Nationality:** noun—Mauritian(s); adjective—Mauritian. **Ethnic groups:** 68% Indo-Mauritian, 27% Creole, 3% Sino-Mauritian, 2% Franco-Mauritian. **Languages:** English (official), Creole, French, Hindi, Urdu, Hakka, Bojpoori. **Religions:** 52% Hindu, 28.3% Christian (mostly Roman Catholic with a few Anglicans), 16.6% Muslim.
• **Government Type:** parliamentary democracy. **Independence:** Mar. 12, 1968 (from U.K.). **Constitution:** Mar. 12, 1968, amended Mar. 12, 1992. **National holiday:** Independence Day, Mar. 12. **Heads of Government:** Aneerood Jugnauth, president (since Oct. 2003); Navinchandra Ramgoolam, prime minister (since Mar. 2008). **Structure:** executive; unicameral legislature; judiciary.
• **Economy Monetary unit:** Mauritian rupee. **Budget:** (2007 est.) *income:* $1.34 bil.; *expend.:* $1.642 bil. **G.D.P.:** $14.9 bil., $11,900 per capita (2007 est.). **Chief crops:** sugarcane, tea, corn, potatoes; cattle, goats; fish. **Natural resources:** arable land, fish. **Major industries:** food processing (largely sugar milling), textiles, and wearing apparel. **Labor force:** 552,700 (2007); 51% services, 30% industry, 9% agriculture. **Exports:** $2.475 bil. (f.o.b., 2007); clothing and textiles, sugar. **Imports:** $3.627 bil. (f.o.b., 2007); manufac-

tured goods, capital equipment, foodstuffs, petroleum products, chemicals. **Major trading partners:** (2006) *exports:* 32.5% U.K., 15.1% France, 11.4% United Arab Emirates, 8.3% U.S., 4.8% Madagascar; *imports:* 14.3% France, 13.6% India, 8.6% China, 7.3% South Africa.

The volcanic island of Mauritius and its seven smaller neighbors lie about 500 miles east of Madagascar and 2,400 miles southwest of India. They were uninhabited when discovered by the Dutch in 1507. Following sporadic Dutch settlement in the 17th century, the French took over in 1721, establishing sugarcane plantations worked by slaves imported from Africa. Mauritius was captured by the British in 1810. Following the abolition of slavery in the British Empire (1834), Indian workers were imported to labor in the cane fields. A majority of the population is of Indian descent. On Mar. 12, 1968, Mauritius became an independent parliamentary democracy within the British Commonwealth. In 1992 it became a republic and the National Assembly elected Cassam Uteem as the country's first president.

In December 1995 the opposition party of Navinchandra Ramgoolam won 65.2 percent of the votes, and captured all 60 seats in Parliament defeating Anerood Jugnauth, PM for 13 years. These results were reversed in Sept. 2000.

Although sugar remains an important element in the economy, textile manufacturing and tourism have helped to make Mauritius one of the strongest economies in Africa.

▶MEXICO
United Mexican States
• **Geography Location:** southernmost state in North America. **Boundaries:** U.S. to N, Gulf of Mexico to E, Belize and Guatemala to S, Pacific Ocean to W. **Total area:** 761,603 sq. mi. (1,972,550 sq km). **Coastline:** 5,798 mi. (9,329 km). **Comparative area:** slightly less than three times the size of Texas. **Land use:** 13% arable land; 1% permanent crops;86% other. **Major cities:** Ciudad de México (Mexico City) (capital); Guadalajara; Netzahualcóyotl; Monterrey; Heróica Puebla de Zaragoza (Puebla).
• **People Population:** 109,955,400 (July 2008 est.). **Nationality:** noun—Mexican(s); adjective—Mexican. **Ethnic groups:** 60% mestizo, 30% Amerindian or predominantly Amerindian, 9% white, 1% other. **Languages:** Spanish, various Mayan, Nahuatl, and other regional indigenous languages. **Religions:** 76.5% Roman Catholic, 6.3% Protestant, 0.3% other, 13.8% unspecified, 3.1% none.
• **Government Type:** federal republic. **Independence:** Sept. 16, 1810 (from Spain). **Constitution:** Feb. 5, 1917. **National holiday:** Independence Day, Sept. 16. **Head of Government:** Felipe Calderon, president (since 2006). **Structure:** dominant executive; bicameral legislature (National Congress—Senate, Federal Chamber of Deputies); Supreme Court.
• **Economy Monetary unit:** peso. **Budget:** (2007 est.) *income:* $209.2 bil.; *expend.:* $209.2 bil. **G.D.P.:** $1.353 tril., $12,500 per capita (2005 est.). **Chief crops:** corn, wheat, soybeans, rice, beans, cotton, coffee, fruit, tomatoes; beef, poultry, dairy products; wood products. **Natural resources:** crude oil, silver, copper, gold, lead. **Major industries:** food and beverages, tobacco, chemicals. **Labor force:** 45.38 mil. (2007); 58% services; 18% agriculture, forestry, hunting, fishing; 24% indus-

try; 3.6% unemployment (2005), plus considerable underemployment. **Exports:** $267.5 bil. (f.o.b., 2007); crude oil, oil products, coffee, silver, engines, cotton. **Imports:** $279.3 bil. (f.o.b., 2007); metal manufactures, agricultural machinery, electrical equipment. **Major trading partners:** (2006) *exports:* 84.7% U.S., 2.1% Canada, 1.3% Spain; *imports:* 50.9% U.S., 9.5% China, 6% Japan, 4.2% South Korea.

The pre-Columbian history of indigenous Mexican cultures is very rich and includes the high civilizations of the Olmecs, Mayas, Toltecs, and Aztecs, in addition to numerous nomadic cultures. In 1519 Hernán Cortés and several hundred Spanish soldiers entered Tenochtitlán (now Mexico City). A two-year campaign against the Aztecs under Montezuma II ended with the Spanish capture of the city. The Viceroyalty of New Spain—with its center at Mexico City—was proclaimed in 1535. At its height it encompassed the lands from California to Panama, Florida, Spain's Caribbean holdings, and the Philippines.

As was the case with the rest of Spanish America, the movement for independence in New Spain coincided with the weakening of the authority of the Spanish Crown as a result of the Napoleonic takeover of Spain in 1808. In 1810 Miguel Hidalgo led a failed uprising and was executed. Following in Hidalgo's footsteps, José María Morelos led another uprising in the south, and he in turn was captured and put to death. Agustín de Iturbide, leader of the royalist forces, defected to the side of those struggling for independence in 1821. Envisioning independent Mexico as a monarchy, military groups proclaimed Iturbide emperor of Mexico in 1822.

The Mexican empire did not last long, and the Central American counties seceded after Iturbide's ouster by Antonio de Santa Anna in 1823. A republic was declared and Guadalupe Victoria was the first president (1824-29). In 1836, Texas seceded from Mexico in a revolution that cost Santa Anna the presidency. Between 1845 and 1848, Mexico fought the United States over U.S. annexation of Texas, and in 1847 U.S. troops occupied Mexico City. Under the Treaty of Guadalupe Hidalgo (1848), Mexico sold about half its territory—including California, Nevada, Utah, most of Arizona, and parts of New Mexico, Colorado, and Wyoming to the United States—for $15 million.

Santa Anna ruled again, as dictator, from 1853 to 1855, before being toppled by the liberal movement, La Reforma. A new constitution was proclaimed in 1857, but Conservatives declared it void. Following the War of Reform (1858-61), France, Britain, and Spain all claimed compensation for destruction of their nations' property, and in 1862 they landed troops at Veracruz. Britain and Spain withdrew, but Napoleon III attempted to establish a dependent empire in Mexico and installed Archduke Ferdinand Maximilian of Austria on the Mexican throne in 1864. In the face of Mexican resistance and U.S. threats, France ended its Mexican adventure, and in 1867 Maximilian was captured and executed by Liberal forces.

Benito Juárez, who served as provisional president during the War of Reform, was a major force behind the liberal movement called La Reforma, which stressed the promotion of capitalism and the destruction of what were seen as vestiges of feudalism in Mexico. Juárez won a third presidential term in 1871 but died in office and was succeeded in office by Sebastián Lerdo de Tejada,

who was in turn overthrown by Gen. Porfirio Díaz. During the stable dictatorship known as the Porfiriato (1876-1911), Mexico experienced economic growth, though wealthy landowners and the church benefited at the expense of the poor.

The Mexican Revolution began in 1910 after Porfirio Díaz had his electoral opponent, Francisco I. Madero, jailed. Madero formulated his Plan of San Luis Potosí, calling for armed resistance. Rebellions broke out in the northern state of Chihuahua under the leadership of Pancho Villa and in the southern state of Morelos led by Emiliano Zapata. The two states soon came under rebel control, and in 1911 Díaz left Mexico. Madero was elected president, but his failure to carry through promised reforms resulted in the continuation of the rebellion.

Backed by the U.S., Gen. Victoriano Huerta overthrew Madero in 1913. But the fighting continued, and Huerta lost the support of the U.S. and was forced from office by Zapata, Villa, and Venustiano Carranza, who became president (1914-20). Zapata and Villa continued their resistance, but by 1916 Gen. Alvaro Obregón had driven Villa back to Chihuahua and Zapata's armies had been contained. Carranza called for the election of delegates to a constitutional convention in 1916, and by the following year, the progressive Mexican Constitution of 1917 was in place.

Obregón deposed Carranza in 1920 and served as president until 1924. He was reelected to succeed Plutarco Elías Calles in 1928 but was assassinated before he could take office. In 1929 Calles founded the National Revolutionary party, which became the Institutional Revolutionary party (PRI) in 1946.

Lázaro Cárdenas won the presidency in 1934, sending Calles into exile. This, coupled with Cárdenas's decision to remove himself from politics at the end of his term, greatly stabilized the institutional structure created by the Mexican Revolution. Cárdenas was the last of the "revolutionary" leaders to make good on the promises to labor and the peasantry. He presided over extensive redistribution of land and in 1938 reorganized the ruling party into four constituencies: peasants, labor, the military, and the middle class. Cárdenas also used the national ownership of subsoil rights enshrined in the Mexican constitution to nationalize U.S. oil companies.

The political movement of Mexican presidents since Cárdenas has been away from its peasant and labor constituencies toward business and the popular sector, beginning with Miguel Alemán's election in 1946.

The PRI's stability was seriously challenged in the 1980's as a result of the economic crisis stemming from the severe decline in the price of oil. Mexico borrowed heavily from foreign creditors during the 1970's on the expectation that oil prices would remain high. The debt problem led to cutbacks in government spending, a catastrophic drop in the value of the currency, and capital and human flight out of the country. It also nearly caused the PRI's downfall. Carlos Salinas de Gortari, the PRI's candidate in the 1988 presidential election, won by one of the narrowest margins ever in a contest widely believed to have been rigged.

Pres. Salinas pursued economic reform and lobbied for passage of the North American Free Trade Agreement with the U.S. and Canada, which promised to bring more jobs and increases in capital investment. But the very day NAFTA went into effect, Jan. 2, 1994, a guerrilla group of poor Indians calling itself the Zapata Army of National Liberation declared war against the government and began fighting government troops in the southern state of Chiapas under the leadership of "Subcomandante Marcos."

The (unrelated) assassination of the PRI presidential candidate at a campaign stop in Tiajuana led Salinas to appoint the campaign manager Ernesto Zedillo, a member of the PRI's reform-minded wing, as the PRI's presidential candidate (over the objections of the "old guard"). With just over 50 percent of the vote (the lowest majority ever for the PRI), Zedillo won the 1994 election. The immediate crisis he faced was the collapse of the peso, which declined by 40 percent in two months. In 1995, in exchange for austere economic measures, the I.M.F. and U.S. offered an enormous bail-out aid package with Mexican oil revenues as collateral. By June 1996 Mexico managed the early repayment of $4.7 billion to the U.S. by privately refinancing the debt.

Zedillo was successful with the situation in Chiapas, arranging 1996 peace talks with the rebels to end fighting and increase Indian autonomy. The appearance of a similar group (the Popular Revolutionary army) in the state of Guerrero began troubles which continued into 1997.

The July 1997 elections saw the PRI lose its majority in the Chamber of Deputies, as it carried only 39 percent of the vote. In March 1999, Pres. Zedillo broke with tradition by not nominating a successor. Democracy entered the PRI itself with primary elections won by Francisco Labastida. But in the July 2000 presidential elections, it was the National Action Party (PAN) candidate, Vincente Fox, who triumphed with about 43 percent in a three-way race. The new president's economic reform agenda stalled in the bitterly divided legislature and in 2003 PAN lost seats there making gridlock even worse. In 2006 a contentious presidential election resulted in conservative Felipe Calderon defeating leftist Andres mauel Lopez Obrador, who refused to accept the results, even after an electoral tribunal certified the election.

▶**MICRONESIA**
Federated States of Micronesia
● **GEOGRAPHY   Location:** forms (with Palau) archipelago of Caroline Islands, Ponape (6°52'N, 158°15'E), Yap (9°32'N, 138°08'E), Kosrae (5°19'N, 162°59'E), and Truk (7°22'N, 151°54'E), in western Pacific Ocean. **Boundaries:** Guam to NW, Marshall Islands to E, Papua New Guinea to S, Philippines about 497 mi. (800 km) to W. **Total area:** 271 sq. mi. (702 sq km). **Coastline:** 3,798 (6,112 km). **Comparative area:** about four times size of Washington, D.C. **Land use:** 6% arable land; 46% permanent crops; 48% other. **Major cities:** Palikir (capital).
● **PEOPLE   Population:** 107,665 (July 2008 est.). **Nationality:** noun—Micronesian(s); adjective—Micronesian, Kosrae(s), Pohnpeian(s), Trukese, Yapese. **Ethnic groups:** nine ethnic Micronesian and Polynesian groups. **Languages:** English (official and common language), Trukese, Pohnpeian, Yapese, Kosrean. **Religions:** 50% Roman Catholic, 47% Protestant.
● **GOVERNMENT   Type:** constitutional government in free association with U.S.; Compact of Free Association entered into force Nov. 3, 1986. **Independence:** Nov. 3, 1986 (from U.S.-administered U.N.

Trusteeship). **Constitution:** May 10, 1979. **National holiday:** Constitution Day, May 10. **Head of Government:** Emanuel Mori, president (since May 2007). **Structure:** executive; unicameral legislature; judiciary.
● **ECONOMY   Monetary unit:** U.S. dollar. **Budget:** (2005 est.) *income:* $127.3 mil.; *expend.:* $144.2 mil. **G.D.P.:** $277 mil. (2002 est.), $2,300 per capita (2005 est.). **Chief crops:** black pepper, tropical fruits and vegetables, coconuts, cassava, sweet potatoes; pigs, chickens. **Natural resources:** forests, marine products, deep seabed minerals. **Major industries:** tourism, construction, fish processing. **Labor force:** two-thirds are government employees. **Exports:** $14 mil. (f.o.b., 2004 est.); fish, garments, bananas, black pepper. **Imports:** $132.7 mil. (c.i.f., 2004 est.); food, manufactured goods, machinery and equipment, beverages. **Major trading partners:** (2006) *exports:* U.S., Japan, Guam; *imports:* U.S., Japan, Hong Kong.

The Federated States of Micronesia extend 1,800 miles across an archipelago of the Caroline Islands in the larger island group of Micronesia. Ethnically diverse (there are eight primary languages, not including dialects), the islands are thought to be the first in the Pacific settled by argonauts from the Philippines and Indonesia, in about 1500 B.C. Ferdinand Magellan landed in the Marianas in A.D. 1521, and Spain claimed sovereignty from 1565 to 1899, when the Caroline Islands were sold to Germany. After World War I, the League of Nations mandated the islands to Japan, which developed agriculture (especially sugarcane), mining, and fishing. After World War II, the islands were included in the U.N. Trust Territory of the Pacific and placed under U.S. administration. A compact of free association between Micronesia and the United States was signed in 1986, and Micronesia's trust territory status with the U.N. trusteeship council was dissolved in December 1990.

▶**MOLDOVA**
Republic of Moldova
● **GEOGRAPHY   Location:** southeastern Europe. **Boundaries:** Ukraine to N, E, S, Romania to W. **Total area:** 13,012 sq. mi. (33,700 sq km). **Coastline:** none. **Comparative area:** slightly more than twice the size of Hawaii. **Land use:** 54% arable land; 12% permanent crops; 34% other. **Major cities:** Kishinev (Chisinäu) (capital); Tiraspol; Beltsy (Balti).
● **PEOPLE   Population:** 4,324,450 (July 2008 est.). **Nationality:** noun—Moldovan(s); adjective—Moldovan. **Ethnic groups:** 64.5% Moldovan/Romanian, 13.8% Ukrainian, 13% Russian, 1.5% Jewish, 2% Bulgarian, 5.2% Gaguaz and other. **Languages:** Moldovan (official), based on Romanian, but using a Cyrillic alphabet; Russian, Gagauz. **Religions:** 98% Eastern Orthodox, 1.5% Jewish.
● **GOVERNMENT   Type:** republic. **Independence:** Aug. 27, 1991 (from Soviet Union). **Constitution:** July 28, 1994. **National holiday:** Independence Day, Aug. 27. **Heads of Government:** Vladimir Voronin, president (since Apr. 2001); Zinaidi Greceanii, prime minister (since Mar. 2008). **Structure:** executive; unicameral legislature; judiciary.
● **ECONOMY   Monetary unit:** leu. **Budget:** (2007 est.) *income:* $1.764 bil.; *expend.:* $1.771 bil. **G.D.P.:** $9.999 bil., $2,200 per capita (2007 est.). **Chief crops:** sugar beets, grain, vegetables, wine grapes, other fruit. **Natural resources:** lignites, phosporites, gypsum. **Major industries:** food processing, agricultural machinery, foundry equip-

ment, textiles, chemicals. **Labor force:** 1.333 mil. (2007); 47% services, 41% agriculture, 12% industry (2005 est.); 2.1% unemployment (2007). **Exports:** $1.43 bil. (f.o.b., 2007); foodstuffs, wine, tobacco, textiles, footwear. **Imports:** $3.59 bil. (f.o.b., 2007); oil, gas, coal, steel, machinery. **Major trading partners:** (2006) *exports:* 22.8% Russia, 12.2% Germany, 11.1% Italy, 9.7% Romania, 9.6% Ukraine, 5.7% Belarusse; *imports:* 20.8% Russia, 16.9% Ukraine, 13.4% Romania, 8.7% Germany, 6.1% Italy, 4.4% Poland.

Historical Moldavia, of which present-day Moldova is only a small portion, encompassed territories that are now in Romania and Ukraine (including southern Bessarabia and northern Bukovina). Moldova is a hilly, fertile land, bounded by two great rivers, the Dniester and the Prut, that flow into the Black Sea. Its climate is very favorable to agriculture.

Moldavia was part of Scythia in the first millennium B.C. and later came under the Roman Empire. Lying on the gateway to Europe, it was invaded successively, but came under the control of Kievan Rus between the 10th and 12th centuries A.D., and in the 13th century it was invaded by the Mongolian empire. In the 16th century, eastern Moldavia, or Bessarabia, came under Turkish control but in 1812 was ceded to the Russian empire. Southern Bessarabia (now in Ukraine) was controlled variously by the Russian empire and by Romania, and in 1878 it again became part of Russia. After the Bolsheviks came to power in 1917 and created the U.S.S.R., a Moldavian Autonomous Soviet Socialist Republic (ASSR) was formed on the eastern side of the Dniester River, a territory claimed by Romania but populated by Ukrainians. In June 1940, as a result of the Nazi-Soviet Pact of 1939, Romania was forced to cede Bessarabia and northern Bukovina to the Soviet Union. These lands were made part of the Ukrainian Soviet Socialist Republic (SSR), and the remaining Bessarabian sections were merged with the old Moldavian ASSR to create on Aug. 2, 1940, the Moldavian SSR. Between 1941 and 1944, while Romania and the U.S.S.R. were at war, Bessarabia again became part of Romania, but in 1944 the Soviets reestablished it as a union republic.

While under Soviet control, Moldavians in the new republic were officially differentiated from their counterparts across the border in Romania. In 1940, the Cyrillic alphabet was imposed on the Romanian language; this official language was called "Moldavian." Contacts between the two countries were discouraged, and the U.S.S.R. encouraged Russian and Ukrainian immigration to the Moldavian SSR. While a part of the U.S.S.R., Moldavia created a diversified economy, which was based on agriculture and food processing.

Gorbachev's policy of glasnost, or openness, in the late 1980's gave vent to Moldavian complaints about "Russification" and immigration of non-Moldavians. In Sept. 1989, Romanian, now in a Latin script, was restored as the official language. Glasnost also gave birth to new political parties, the largest of which was the Popular Front of Moldavia, which organized protest demonstrations against Soviet power. Disturbances during the 1989 celebration of Soviet Revolution Day in the capital city of Kishinev led to the dismissal of the Slavic Communist party First Secretary, and his replacement by an ethnic Romanian.

The Communist party was banned in Moldova in 1990, and laws to develop the basics of a multi-party system were adopted in September 1991. Moldova officially declared its independence from the U.S.S.R. on Aug. 27, 1991, and in December, United Front-supported Mircea Snegur was elected president with 98.2% of the votes cast.

At the time Moldova declared its independence, sentiment was strong for reunification with Romania. So strong, in fact, that ethnic Russians and Ukrainians living in the Trans-Dniester region in eastern Moldova, fearing reunification with Romania, declared an independent Trans-Dniester republic, sparking ethnic violence there. But since then, most activity has focused on reestablishing ties with countries from the former U.S.S.R. In 1991, Moldova singed the Alma-Ata Declaration, joining the other former Soviet republics in the Commonwealth of Independent States. And in the country's first parlimantary elections, held in Feb. of 1994, two nationalist parties captured a combined 15 percent of the vote, while the pro-Russian Socialist party won 25 percent, and the Agrarian Democratic Party, led by former Communists, took 45 percent. Then, in a plebiscite held Mar. 6, 1994, an overwhelming majority (90 percent) of voters rejected reunification with Romania in favor of an independent Moldova. Two-thirds of Moldova's 2.3 million eligible voters cast ballots on the plebiscite. Snegur intended to use the referendum result to entice Trans-Dniester to rejoin Moldova.

In late 1996 Snegur lost the presidency to Petro Lucinschi who quickly recognized Trans-Dniester as autonomous within a single state and began a reform program to stimulate the weak economy. A strong Communist showing in 1998 legislative elections made this agenda more difficult to establish. The slow pace of reform led Prime Minister Ion Ciubuc to resign in Feb. 1999 (replaced by Ion Sturza) and Pres. Lucinschi to propose a referendum to increase the constitutional powers of the president, a model more in accord with the other ex-Soviet states.

Elections in Feb. 2001 gave the Communists a majority in parliament which selected Vladimir Voronin as president and Vasile Tarlev as prime minister. They won again in March 2005 but it is hard to know why since 40 percent of the population is forced to look for work abroad. The presence of Russian troops on the border with Ukraine remained a festering problem.

▶MONACO
Principality of Monaco

● **GEOGRAPHY Location:** tiny enclave on Mediterranean coast of France. **Boundaries:** France to N, E, and W; Mediterranean Sea to S. **Total area:** 1.21 sq. mi. (1.95 sq km). **Coastline:** 2.6 mi. (4.1 km). **Comparative area:** about three times size of the Mall in Washington, D.C. **Land use:** 0% arable land; 0% permanent crops; 100% other. **Major cities:** Monaco (capital).

● **PEOPLE Population:** 32,796 (2008 est.). **Nationality:** noun—Monacan(s) or Monegasque(s); adjective—Monacan or Monegasque. **Ethnic groups:** 47% French, 16% Monegasque, 16% Italian, 21% other. **Languages:** French (official), English, Italian, Monegasque. **Religions:** 90% Roman Catholic.

● **GOVERNMENT Type:** constitutional monarchy. **Independence:** 1419. **Constitution:** Dec. 17, 1962. **National holiday:** National Day, Nov. 19. **Head of Government:** Albert II, chief of state (since Apr. 2005); Jean Paul Proust, prime minister (since June 2005). **Structure:** executive—prince, minis-

ter of state (senior French civil servant appointed by prince), and Council of Government as cabinet; unicameral legislature—prince and National Council of 18 members; judiciary—authority delegated by prince to Supreme Tribunal.
• **ECONOMY** **Monetary unit:** euro. **Budget:** (2005 est.) *income:* $863 mil.; *expend:* $920.6 mil. **G.D.P.:** $870 mil., $30,000 per capita (2006 est.). **Chief crops:** N.A. **Natural resources:** none. **Major industries:** Tourism, construction, small-scale industry and consumer products. **Labor force:** (2005 est.) 44,000; 95.1% services, 4.9% industry. **Exports:** 716.3 mil. (2007 est.) **Imports:** 916.1 mil. (2007 est.) **Major trading partners:** full customs integration with France, which collects and rebates Monacan trade duties; also participates in E.U. market system through customs union with France.

Known to Phoenicians and Greeks from the beginning of the first millenium B.C., the history of the port of Monaco is coextensive with that of southeastern France for much of its history. A western colony of the great trading city-state of Genoa in the 13th century, Monaco in 1368 became an independent principality under the rule of the Matignon-Grimaldi family. At various times a protectorate of Spain, France, and Sardinia, it was restored to independence in 1861 by the Franco-Monegasque treaty.

In 1911 Monaco became a constitutional monarchy under the Matignon-Grimaldi dynasty. In 1918 France required the principality to conform to its national interests in all respects; by an agreement of 1919, should the dynasty fail to produce a male heir, Monaco would be absorbed into France. However, the family is allowed to adopt an heir if they so choose. The marriage of Prince Ranier III to the U.S film star Grace Kelly produced an heir apparent for this generation. The constitutional monarchy under its "Most Serene Prince" was essentially a one-party state in which in every election since 1968 the National and Democratic Union won all the seats in the National Council until February 2003 when the Union for Monaco won 21 of the 24 seats with almost 60% of the popular vote. In 1993 Monaco became the smallest member nation of the U.N.

Despite the fame of the Monte Carlo casino, gambling accounts for only 4 percent of the principality's revenues. The principal industry is tourism, followed by light manufacturing. Monaco also supports a prominent institute of oceanography. Land reclamation projects, impelled by a real estate boom, have added about 20 percent to the nation's territory since World War II. Prince Rainer died in 2005 and was succeeded by his son, Albert.

▶ MONGOLIA

• **GEOGRAPHY** **Location:** landlocked country in central Asia. **Boundaries:** Russia to N, China to E, S, and W. **Total area:** 604,247 sq. mi. (1,565,000 sq km). **Coastline:** none. **Comparative area:** slightly larger than Alaska. **Land use:** 1% arable land; 0% permanent crops; 99% other. **Major cities:** Ulan Bator (capital); Darhan; Erdenet.
• **PEOPLE** **Population:** 2,996,081 (2008 est.). **Nationality:** noun—Mongolian(s) adjective—Mongolian. **Ethnic groups:** 94.9% Mongol, 5% Turkic, 0.1% other. **Languages:** Khalkha Mongol used by over 90% of population; Turkic, Russian, Chinese. **Religions:** predominantly Lamaist Buddhist, 4% Muslim, Shamanism and Christian, 40% none.

• **GOVERNMENT** **Type:** republic. **Independence:** Mar. 13, 1921 (from China). **Constitution:** Feb. 12, 1992. **National holiday:** National Day, July 11. **Heads of Government:** Nambar Enkhbayar, president (since Apr. 2005); Bayar Sanj, prime minister (since Nov. 2007). **Structure:** executive; unicameral legislature; judiciary.
• **ECONOMY** **Monetary unit:** tughrik. **Budget:** (2007) *income:* $1.58 bil.; *expend.:* $1.497 bil. **G.D.P.:** $8.448 bil., $2,900 per capita (2004 est.). **Chief crops:** livestock raising predominates; wheat, barley. **Natural resources:** oil, coal, copper, molybdenum, tungsten, phosphates. **Major industries:** copper, processing of animal products, building materials, foods and beverages. **Labor force:** 1.042 mil. (2006); 41% services, 40% industry, 18.8% agriculture. **Exports:** $1.889 bil. (f.o.b., 2007); copper, livestock, animal products, wool, hides, fluorospar, nonferrous metals. **Imports:** $2.117 bil. (c.i.f., 2007); machinery and equipment, fuels, food products, industrial consumer goods, chemicals. **Major trading partners:** (2006) *exports:* 71.7% China, 11.7% Canada, 7.3% U.S.; *imports:* 29.7% Russia, 29.4% China, 11.9% Japan.

Mongols under Genghis Khan conquered most of Eurasia in the early 13th century. The Mongol empire broke up in the mid-14th century, and Mongolia lapsed into tribal disunion and political insignificance. Chinese rule was established thereafter in Inner Mongolia and, in 1691, in Outer Mongolia (a province under local rule). With the 1911 Chinese Revolution, Outer Mongolia unsuccessfully proclaimed its independence from China. The nationalist religious leader, the Bogdo Lama, sought Russian support in 1920. Under the revolutionary leaders Sukhe Bataar and Khorloin Choibalsan, a "provisional people's government" again declared independence in 1921. Sukhe Bataar died in 1923; on Nov. 26, 1924, the Mongolian People's Republic (MPR) was established with Soviet sponsorship. The early years of the republic were marked by repeated Stalinist purges of Mongol revolutionary leaders and by disastrous attempts at centralized planning.

Choibalsan emerged as party leader and was confirmed as premier in 1940. In 1939 Soviet and Mongolian armies prevented a Japanese conquest of Mongolia. In 1945 the Republic of China recognized the MPR; recognition was reaffirmed by the People's Republic of China in 1949. In 1948 the first of a series of five-year plans began to bring industrial and agricultural development to Mongolia, with extensive Soviet aid and support. Choibalsan died in 1952 and was succeeded as premier by Yumjaagiyn Tsedenbal. Following the Sino-Soviet split of 1958, heavy concentrations of Soviet troops and missiles were stationed along the Chinese-Mongolian border. On Oct. 27, 1961, the MPR was admitted to the United Nations and diplomatic relations with various other non-Soviet bloc nations developed gradually. Tsedenbal was ousted in 1984 and replaced by Zhambyn Batmonh as party chairman and by Dumaagiin Sodnom as premier. The MPR established diplomatic relations with the United States in 1987.

Following widespread demonstrations calling for human rights, religious freedom, and an end to special privileges for Communist officials, the Communist party voted to give up its constitutional power in March 1990. In 1992, under the new constitution, elections were held for four-year terms in the new single-chamber Great

Hural: the Communists (now calling themselves the Mongolian People's Revolutionary Party) won 70 of the 76 seats but in the first popular elections for president the following year, acting president Punsalmaagiin Ochirbat, a reformist ex-communist trounced the hardline MPRP candidate, 60%-40%. The resultant political deadlock only exacerbated the economic crisis brought on by severance of Mongolia's old ties with the Soviet bloc, though international aid kept the state afloat.

A coalition of opposition parties, called the Democratic Alliance, won 50 seats in the 1996 elections for the Great Hural (one vote short of veto-proof 2/3), ending the communist rule that began in 1921. But one year of the ill effects of economic reform brought disillusion with the DA and the triumph in 1997 of MPRP chairman Natsagiin Bagabandi over Ochirbat in the presidential election. This second political deadlock was broken in the 2000 Great Hural elections when the MPRP swept 72 seats. The return of the Communists was confirmed a year later with Bagabandi's re-election in 2001. Privatization remained achingly slow. The MPRP lost half its seats in 2004 legislative elections, with the new opposition alliance, Motherland Democratic Coalition, taking 35 of the 76 seats. This dramatic gain did not end the MPRP control of the Great Hural and in the 2005 presidential election the leader of the MPRP won a convincing victory. A state of emergency was declared in July 2008 as police subdued protestors marching against vote-rigging.

▶MONTENEGRO
• **GEOGRAPHY Location:** southeastern Europe between the Adriatic Sea and Serbia. **Boundaries:** Albania, Bosnia and Herzegovina, Croatia, Serbia. **Total area:** 5,415 sq. mi. (14,026 sq km). **Coastline:** 182 mi. (293.5 km). **Comparative area:** slightly smaller than Connecticut. **Land use:** 13.7% arable land; 1% permanent crops; 85.3% other. **Major cities:** Podgorica (capital); Niksic; Pljevlja; Berane.
• **PEOPLE Population:** 678,177 (July 2008 est.). **Nationality:** noun—Montenegrin(s); adjective—Montenegrin. **Ethnic groups:** Montenegrin 43%, Serbian 32%, Bosniak 8%, Albanian 5%, other 12%. **Languages:** Serbian (official; Ijekavian dialect), Bosnian, Albanian, Croatian. **Religions:** Orthodox, Muslim, Roman Catholic.
• **GOVERNMENT Type:** republic. **Independence:** June 3, 2006 (from Serbia and Montenegro). **Constitution:** Oct. 19, 2007. **National holiday:** National Day, July 13. **Heads of Government:** Filip Vujanovic, president (since May 2003); Milo Djukanovic, prime minister (since Feb. 2008). **Structure:** unicameral assembly; judiciary.
• **ECONOMY Monetary unit:** euro. **Budget:** N.A. **G.D.P.:** $26.38 bil.; $3,800 per capita (2006 est.). **Chief crops:** grains, tobacco, potatoes, citrus fruits, olives, grapes. **Natural resources:** bauxite, hydroelectricity. **Major industries:** steelmaking, aluminum, agricultural processing, consumer goods, tourism. **Labor force:** 259,100 (2004 est.); 2% agriculture, 30% industry, 68% services (2004). **Exports:** $171.3 mil. (2003). **Imports:** $601.7 bil. (2003). **Major trading partners:** (2006) *exports:* 84% Switzerland, 6% Italy, 1.3% Bosnia & Herzegovina; *imports:* 10% Greece, 10% Italy, 9.6% Germany, 9.2% Bosnia & Herzegovina.

After existing as an independent monarchy from 1878-1918, Montenegro became a constituent republic of the Socialist Federal Republic of Yugoslavia. When that country dissolved in 1992, Montenegro joined with Serbia to form the Federal Republic of Yugoslavia, and in 2003, became the looser union of Serbia and Montenegro. On May 21, 2006, 55.5 percent of Montenegrins voted voted to sever ties with Serbia, and independence was declared on June 3. By the end of the month, Montenegro had been incorporated as the 192nd member of the U.N. In the following year, the country joined the World Bank, the IMF, and initiated an agreement with the E.U. The first steps were taken to join NATO. To the chagrin of many, Prime Minister Milo Djukanovic resigned in October, 2006, and appointed Zeljko Sturanovic as his successor.

For ancient and 20th century Montenegrin history, see "Serbia."

▶MOROCCO
Kingdom of Morocco
• **GEOGRAPHY Location:** northwestern Africa. **Boundaries:** North Atlantic Ocean to W and NW, Strait of Gibraltar to N, Mediterranean Sea to NE, Algeria to E and SE, Western Sahara to SW. **Total area:** 172,413 sq. mi. (446,550 sq km). **Coastline:** 1,140 mi. (1,835 km). **Comparative area:** slightly larger than California. **Land use:** 20% arable land; 2% permanent crops; 78% other. **Major cities:** Rabat (including Sale; capital); Casablanca; Marrakesh (Marrakesh); Fès (Fez); Oujda.
• **PEOPLE Population:** 34,343,219 (July 2008 est.). **Nationality:** noun—Moroccan(s); adjective—Moroccan. **Ethnic groups:** 99.1% Arab-Berber, 0.7% non-Moroccan, 0.2% Jewish. **Languages:** Arabic (official), several Berber dialects; French is language of business, government and diplomacy. **Religions:** 98.7% Muslim, 1.1% Christian, 0.2% Jewish.
• **GOVERNMENT Type:** constitutional monarchy. **Independence:** Mar. 2, 1956 (from France). **Constitution:** Mar. 10, 1972, revised Sept. 4, 1992, amended to create bicameral legislature Sept. 1996. **National holiday:** National Day, July 30. **Heads of Government:** Mohammed VI, king (since July 1999); Abbas El Fassi, prime minister (since Sept. 2007). **Structure:** executive—king has paramount powers; bicameral legislature—two-thirds of members are directly elected and one-third are indirectly elected; judiciary—independent of other branches.
• **ECONOMY Monetary unit:** dirham. **Budget:** (2007 est.) *income:* $19.39 bil.; *expend.:* $21.21 bil. **G.D.P.:** $127 bil., $3,800 per capita (2007 est.). **Chief crops:** cereal farming and livestock raising predominant; barley, wheat, citrus fruit, wine, vegetables; livestock. **Natural resources:** phosphates, iron ore, manganese, lead, zinc, fish, salt. **Major industries:** phosphate rock mining and processing, food processing, leather goods. **Labor force:** 11.35 mil. (2007); 40% agriculture, 45% services, 15% industry (2003); 15% unemployment (2007 est.). **Exports:** $12.73 bil. (f.o.b., 2007 est.); food and beverages, semiprocessed goods, consumer goods. **Imports:** $22.15 bil. (f.o.b., 2007 est.); semiprocessed goods, capital goods, food and beverages, fuel and lubricants. **Major trading partners:** (2006) *exports:* 20.6% Spain, 20.5% France, 4.8% U.K., 4.7% Italy, 4% India; *imports:* 17.5% France, 13.9% Spain, 6.9% Saudi Arabia, 6.9% China, 6.3% Italy, 6% Germany.

Neolithic inhabitants of Morocco were displaced by Berbers around 1000 B.C. Phoenician and Carthaginian settlements were established along the Mediterranean coast. Morocco came under Roman rule around 40 A.D. and was invaded via Spain by Germanic Vandals in the fifth century. The Islamic invasions of the mid-seventh century established Arab rule in Morocco, and most of the indigenous Berbers converted to Islam. Ethnic tension between Berbers and Arabs has been a basic element of Moroccan politics and society ever since.

In the late eighth century, King Idris ibn Adballah united Berbers and Arabs in a monarchy that lasted for 200 years and made the capital city of Fez one of the major religious and cultural centers of the Islamic world. In the 11th century, the Almoravid dynasty from Mauritania conquered Morocco, western Algeria, and Spain. It was ousted by another Muslin sect, the Almohads, led by Ibn Tumart. After about 1200 the tide of Moorish expansion in the Iberian Peninsula turned; in 1492 Ferdinand and Isabella expelled the last Moors from Grenada.

Naval conflict between Morocco, Spain, and Portugal continued in the western Mediterranean and along the Atlantic coast of Africa for several centuries more. In the mid-17th century, Morocco was reunited under the present Alawid dynasty. In the early 19th century, American and British forces combatted Moroccan piracy in the Mediterranean, and Spain established colonies in Tangier in the north and along the Atlantic coast between Morocco and Mauritania.

The attempts of Sultan Hassan I (r. 1873-94) to implement reforms to strengthen Morocco's independence were thwarted by European interests. By the early 20th century, France, securely established in Algeria, began exerting increasing control in Morocco. A multipower conference at Algeciras in 1906 affirmed Moroccan independence but upheld the special rights claimed by Spain and France. The Treaty of Fez, signed in 1912 between France and Sultan Abd-al-Hafidn, ended Moroccan independence by granting the country to France and reaffirming a Spanish sphere of influence in the southwest.

Nationalist unrest and tribal uprisings disrupted French administration in Morocco throughout the 1920's and 1930's. Morocco became a battleground during World War II between the Axis-supported Vichy French government and the Free French and their Allied backers. In 1943 Churchill and Roosevelt met at Casablanca to discuss wartime strategy; in the same year, the Istiqlal (Independence) party was founded to fight for independence from the French in the postwar era.

In 1947 Moroccan liberation forces began open warfare against the French. The exiled Sultan Mohammad V was allowed to return, and France promised independence by 1955.

With the withdrawal of French forces, Morocco became independent on Mar. 2, 1956. Tangier (under international administration since 1923) was incorporated into the newly independent state in October 1956, and the Spanish enclave of Ifni was ceded to Morocco in 1969.

A period of instability ensued after 1957 as newly formed political parties vied for power. King Mohammad I died in 1961 and was succeeded by his son, Hassan II. In 1962 an elected parliamentary government took power under the constitutional monarchy. Political unrest and economic difficulties led to the declaration of states of emergency in 1965 and 1970 and a new constitution in 1977.

Spain withdrew from its former territory of Spanish (now Western) Sahara, a phosphate-rich desert territory on Morocco's southern border, in Feb. 1976. On Apr. 14, 1976, Morocco annexed the northern two-thirds of the territory, while Mauritania claimed the remainder. The Polisario Spanish Saharan liberation movement, backed by Algeria and Libya, conducted guerrilla operations against Moroccan and Mauritanian forces. In 1979 Mauritania gave up its claims, and Morocco claimed the entire region.

In 1987, Morocco completed construction of a 2,000-mile sand wall completely enclosing Western Sahara. Polisario forces control much of the Western Saharan countryside, while Morocco holds the cities and towns. In May 1987 a Moroccan-Algerian summit was held under the sponsorship of Saudi Arabia, which offered King Hassan $260 million to rebuild Morocco's war-torn economy in return for allowing a self-determination referendum in the Western Sahara. The king refused. By mid-1992 the situation was resolved as Polisario's leaders accepted an offer of amnesty, leaving the Moroccan government in possession of the territory although U.N. sponsored negotiations have failed to produce a settlement.

The Persian Gulf crisis made an already weak economy weaker, and riots during a general strike protesting low wages and poor job prospects in Fez left 100 dead and hundreds more injured in 1991. Although Morocco was an active member of the Allied coalition against Iraq, Moroccans also staged huge demonstrations in support of Saddam Hussein at the height of the war.

In 1992, demands of Muslim fundamentalist factions for greater political power threatened the stability of King Hassan II's government. In a gesture toward political reform, parliamentary elections were held in June 1993, but the results never posed any immediate challenge to the monarchy.

In March 1998 the king appointed Morocco's first opposition-led government, a coalition of seven political parties. Hassan died in July 1999 and was succeeded by his son Mohammed VI. A government trial balloon on women's rights produced a protest rally of 500,000 in March 2000. In may 2003, five simultaneous suicide bombings rocked Casablanca.

►MOZAMBIQUE
Republic of Mozambique

● **GEOGRAPHY** **Location:** eastern coast of Africa. **Boundaries:** Zambia and Malawi to NW, Tanzania to N, Indian Ocean to E and SE, South Africa and Swaziland to SW, Zimbabwe to W. **Total area:** 309,494 sq. mi. (801,590 sq km). **Coastline:** 1,535 mi. (2,470 km). **Comparative area:** slightly less than twice size of California. **Land use:** 4% arable land; negl. % permanent crops; 96% other. **Major cities:** Maputo (capital).
● **PEOPLE** **Population:** 21,284,701 (July 2008 est.). **Nationality:** noun—Mozambican(s); adjective—Mozambican. **Ethnic groups:** 99.66% indigenous tribal groups (Shangaan, Chokwe, Manyika, Sena, Makua, and others). **Languages:** Portuguese (official), indigenous languages. **Religions:** 50% indigenous beliefs, 30% Christian, 20% Muslim.
● **GOVERNMENT** **Type:** republic. **Independence:** June 25, 1975 (from Portugal). **Constitution:** Nov. 30, 1990. **National holiday:** Independence Day, June 25. **Heads of Government:** Armando Emilio Guebuza, president (since Feb. 2005); Luísa

Diogo, prime minister (since Feb. 2004.). **Structure:** executive; unicameral legislature; judiciary. ● **ECONOMY Monetary unit:** metical. **Budget:** (2007 est.) *income:* $2.163 bil.; *expend:* $2.623 bil. **G.D.P.:** $17.82 bil., $900 per capita (2007 est.). **Chief crops:** cotton, cashew nuts, sugar, tea; beef, poultry. **Natural resources:** coal, natural gas, titanium. **Major industries:** food and beverages, chemicals (fertilizer, soap, paints), petroleum. **Labor force:** 9.6 mil. (2007 est.); 23% agriculture, 30% industry, 47% services (2007). **Exports:** $2.731 bil. (f.o.b., 2007 est.); shrimp; cashews, cotton, sugar. **Imports:** $3.028 bil. (c.i.f., 2007 est.); food, clothing, farm equipment, petroleum. **Major trading partners:** (2006) *exports:* 59.7% Netherlands, 15.2% South Africa, 3.2% Zimbabwe; *imports:* 36.3% South Africa, 15.6% Netherlands, 3.3% Portugal.

Mozambique has been inhabited since prehistoric times by a variety of Bantu peoples. Portuguese trading stations were established starting in 1505, and Portugal developed an extensive coastal trade in gold and ivory. Mozambique also served as a way station for Portuguese trade to East Asia.

Despite competition from other European nations, Portugal maintained control of the Mozambique coast. Settlement by sizable numbers of Portuguese immigrants began in the late 19th century. Mozambique was organized as a colony, sometimes called Portuguese East Africa, in 1885; boundaries in the interior were defined in 1891.

Economic development of Mozambique in the 20th century remained almost entirely in Portuguese hands. By the 1950's native peoples began to protest Portuguese rule; a rebellion of the Frelimo (Front for the Liberation of Mozambique) guerrilla movement began in 1961. Rebels controlled most of the northern part of the country by 1964. Fighting continued for another decade.

Following the Portuguese revolution of 1974, Portugal agreed to independence for Mozambique, and many Portuguese settlers returned to Portugal, leaving the country bereft of administrative personnel and infrastructure support. Mozambique became fully independent on June 25, 1975. A Marxist Frelimo government took office, with Samora Michel as the country's first president. The new government formed agricultural collectives and nationalized most private land and industry as well as all social services.

In the late 1970's, fighting broke out between Mozambique and Rhodesia. When Rhodesia achieved independence (and changed its name to Zimbabwe) in 1980, relations between the two governments improved. But a rebel movement, Renamo (Mozambique National Resistance), dedicated to overthrowing the Frelimo government grew stronger during the 1980's.

In 1986, following the death of Samora Michel, Joachím Chissanó became president. His government reintroduced some private agriculture, loosened ties to the Eastern bloc, and appealed to the West for economic assistance. In 1987 a U.N.-led relief effort began. In 1989 Mozambique signed a cooperation agreement with South Africa, which cut off its aid to the Renamo insurgents. But fighting continued into 1990.

In Nov. 1990, Mozambique adopted a new constitution widening individual rights and freedoms, including abolition of the death penalty, freedom of the press and speech, and an independent judiciary, as well as establishing multiparty democracy, a presidential regime, and free-market economy. On Oct. 4, 1992, Pres. Chissanó and Renamo leader Afonso Dhlakama signed a ceasefire; the U.N. dispatched 7,500 military and civilian personnel to oversee the disarmament and organize elections.

Mozambique's first multiparty elections were held in Oct. 1994. Pres. Chissanó was elected with 53 percent of the vote while his Frelimo party took 129 of the Parliament's 250 seats. (Renamo carried all but nine of the remaining seats.) Chissano was reelected in Dec. 1999 with Frelimo taking 133 seats.

Mozambique is rich in agricultural land and mineral resources. Nevertheless, years of communism, drought, and civil war have left the country poor and dependent on foreign aid. In 1992 the worst drought in memory brought the nation to a virtual standstill, as an estimated 1.8 million people became dependent on donations of food from outsiders for survival. In recent years the I.M.F. has helped enormously with loans and planning advice but Mozambique remains one of the poorest nations. Devastating floods in March 2000 set back much of the progress that had been made.

▶ MYANMAR
Union of Burma

● **GEOGRAPHY Location:** NW region of Southeast Asia. **Boundaries:** China and Laos to NE, Bangladesh, India to NW, Thailand to SE, Andaman Sea to S, and Bay of Bengal to SW. **Total area:** 261,969 sq. mi. (678,500 sq km). **Coastline:** 1,200 mi. (1,930 km). **Comparative area:** slightly smaller than Texas. **Land use:** 15% arable land; 1% permanent crops; 84% other. **Major cities:** Yangon (formerly Rangoon) (capital); Mandalay; Bassein; Moulmein; Akyab.

● **PEOPLE Population:** 47,758,181 (July 2008 est.). **Nationality:** noun—Burmese (sing., pl.); adjective—Burmese. **Ethnic groups:** 68% Burman, 9% Shan, 7% Karen, 4% Rakhine, 3% Chinese, 2% Mon, 2% Indian, 5% other. **Languages:** Burmese, minority ethnic languages. **Religions:** 89% Buddhist, 4% Muslim, 4% Christian, 1% animist beliefs.

● **GOVERNMENT Type:** military regime. **Independence:** Jan. 4, 1948 (from U.K.). **Constitution:** Jan. 3, 1974; new constitution being drafted. **National holiday:** Independence Day, Jan.4. **Head of Government:** Gen. Than Shwe, chairman State Law and Order Restoration Council (SLORC) (since Apr. 1992); Lt. Gen. Thein Sein, prime minister (since Oct. 2007). **Structure:** executive—military junta controls legislature—last election held in 1990, but never convened; judiciary—not independent, no guarantees.

● **ECONOMY Monetary unit:** kyat. **Budget:** N.A. **G.D.P.:** $91.13 bil., $1,900 per capita (2007 est.). **Chief crops:** paddy rice, corn, oilseeds; hardwood. **Natural resources:** crude oil, timber, tin, copper, tungsten. **Major industries:** agricultural processing, textiles and footwear, wood and wood products. **Labor force:** 24.26 mil. (2007 est.); 70% agriculture, 7% industry, 23% services (2001 est.); **Exports:** $6.6 bil. (f.o.b., 2007); teak, rice, pulses, beans. **Imports:** $2.642 bil. (f.o.b., 2007); machinery, transport equipment, chemicals, food products. **Major trading partners:** (2006) *exports:* 48.8% Thailand, 12.7% India, 5.2% China, 5.2% Japan; *imports:* 35.1% China, 22.1% Thailand, 16.4% Singapore, 4.8% Malaysia.

(Until the summer of 1989 this country was known as Burma.)

Burma, an independent Buddhist monarchy from the 11th century, fell to the Mongol empire in the 13th century, and after the 14th century was a satellite state of China. Anglo-French rivalry over trade left Burma under French influence in the early 19th century, but in a series of three wars (1824-26, 1852, 1885), Great Britain succeeded in bringing all of Burma into the British raj of India. The country became self-governing under a British protectorate in 1937.

Japanese occupation of Burma in early 1942 made the country a major theater of fighting during World War II. The Burma Road, built by the Allies to connect northeastern India with southwestern China, was a key link in bringing supplies to the Chinese Nationalist army during the war.

Burma achieved independence as the Union of Burma on Jan. 4, 1948. Promises of autonomy for ethnic minority regions such as the Shan and Karen States have not been fulfilled, leading to armed separatist movements in those areas ever since. In 1962 a coup led by Gen. Ne Win overthrew the democratic government and established a one-party state under the Burmese Socialist Program party. The party's "Burmese Path to Socialism" resulted in self-imposed international isolation and economic stagnation at home despite the country's potential wealth in agriculture, timber, minerals, and gems.

In July 1988 Ne Win resigned from office in the face of mounting popular demonstrations. A series of short-lived successor governments were unable to restore public order and normal governmental functions; direct military rule was announced in September 1988 as demonstrations continued. In the general election held on May 27, 1990 (the first multiparty free elections in three decades), the opposition National League for Democracy, led by Aung San Suu Kyi, won a decisive victory, but the results of the election were nullified by the State Law and Order Restoration Council (SLORC), and leaders of the elected government were placed under house arrest.

In 1991 the continued political repression in Myanmar was brought to international attention when Aung San Suu Kyi was awarded the Nobel Peace Prize. This helped usher in a period of diminishing repression. A new leader of the ruling military junta, Gen. Than Shwe, began peace talks with the Karen rebels in early 1994, and released Aung San Suu Kyi in July 1995. In 1998, renewed pressure by NLD upon the junta (since Nov. 1997 renamed the State Peace and Development Council) to convene the 1990 parliament brought renewed repression and mass arrests; a committee of NLD delcared itself to be the legal parliament of Myanmar, asserting that all the junta legislation since 1990 was invalid. After releasing Aung from her 14-month arrest in May 2002, the junta "detained" Aung and 19 other NLD members in May 2003. In Sept. 2002 three grandsons of Ne Win and a son-in-law were sentenced to death for treason (an alleged coup attempt); Ne Win himself died shortly after. In 2003 Japan and the U.S. froze aid and banned imports, which led to some NLD leaders being released. Aung has refused freedom until all are free. Protests were forbidden but in Sept. 2007 Buddhist monks took to the streets for two days. In May 2008 a cyclone killed over 100,000 but the junta refused outside aid. (See "Major News Stories.")

▶**NAMIBIA**
Republic of Namibia
● **GEOGRAPHY Location:** southwest Africa. **Boundaries:** Angola to N, Botswana to E, South Africa to S, Atlantic Ocean to W. **Total area:** 318,259 sq. mi. (824,290 sq km). **Coastline:** 976 mi. (1,572 km). **Comparative area:** slightly more than half the size of Alaska. **Land use:** 1% arable land; negl. % permanent crops; 99% other. **Major cities:** Windhoek (capital).
● **PEOPLE Population:** 2,088,669 (2008 est.). **Nationality:** noun—Namibian(s); adjective—Namibian. **Ethnic groups:** 87.5% black, 6% white, 6.5% mixed; 50% of the population belongs to the Ovambo tribe. **Languages:** Afrikaans common language, 32% German, and 7% English (official); several indigenous languages. **Religions:** 80%-90% Christian, 10%-20% indigenous religions.
● **GOVERNMENT Type:** republic. **Independence:** Mar. 21, 1990 (from South Africa). **Constitution:** Feb. 9, 1990. **National holiday:** Independence Day, Mar. 21. **Heads of Government:** H. Pohamba, president (since Mar. 2005); Nahas Angula, prime minister (since Mar. 2005). **Structure:** executive; bicameral legislature; judiciary.
● **ECONOMY Monetary unit:** Namibian dollar. **Budget:** (2007) *income:* $2.561 bil.; *expend.:* $2.483 bil. **G.D.P.:** $10.67 bil., $5,200 per capita (2007 est.). **Chief crops:** millet, sorghum, peanuts; livestock; fish. **Natural resources:** diamonds, copper, uranium, gold, lead. **Major industries:** meat packing, fish processing, dairy products, mining (copper, lead, zinc, diamonds, and uranium). **Labor force:** 660,000 (2007 est.); 47% agriculture, 20% industry and commerce, 33% services; 35% unemployment (1998 est.). **Exports:** $2.87 bil. (f.o.b., 2007 est.); diamonds, copper, gold, zinc, lead, uranium; meat, processed fish. **Imports:** $2.82 bil. (f.o.b., 2007 est.); foodstuffs, petroleum products, machinery and equipment, chemicals. **Major trading partners:** (2006) *exports:* 33.4% South Africa, 4% U.S.; *imports:* 85.2% South Africa, U.S.

The Kalahari desert, on the Namibian plateau, has been inhabited since ancient times by San hunter-gatherers. Various Nama and Bantu peoples migrated into the area more recently. British and Dutch explorers and traders began to penetrate Namibia in the 18th century.

In 1872 Great Britain occupied the area around Walvis Bay and in 1884 annexed it to the Cape Colony. Also in 1884 Germany claimed most of South-West Africa; negotiations between the two powers resulted in German acceptance of Britain's claim of Walvis Bay and British acceptance of Germany's claim to the rest of the coastal region with a sphere of influence in the interior.

During World War I, British troops from South Africa occupied South-West Africa in 1915. In 1920 South Africa received a League of Nations mandate to administer the area. In 1946 when the United Nations succeeded the League, the United Nations proposed that South Africa continue its administration under a U.N. trusteeship. South Africa refused and annexed South-West Africa.

The proposed U.N. trusteeship was revoked by the United Nations in 1966. At the same time, the South-West Africa People's Organization (SWAPO), operating from bases in Zambia and Angola, began guerrilla actions against South African troops in the region. In 1968 the United Nations formally renamed the territory Namibia and appointed an 11-nation council to supervise its affairs and devise a plan leading to independence.

In 1971 the International Court of Justice upheld the U.N.'s authority over Namibia and ruled that South Africa's continued occupation of the territory was illegal. In 1975 South Africa convened the Turnhalle Conference, which proposed a plan for Namibian independence based on the racial-separation principles of apartheid. This was rejected by the U.N. and in 1978 the U.N. Security Council approved Resolution 435, which called for a general cease-fire to be followed by U.N.-supervised elections.

In response, South Africa unilaterally held elections in Namibia, which were boycotted by SWAPO and other African organizations and rejected by the U.N. In 1982 South Africa declared it would enter into talks about the future of Namibia only after Cuban troops were withdrawn from Angola. In 1983 South Africa launched a major military operation against SWAPO forces in Angola.

In October 1984 Angolan president dos Santos agreed to work out a plan for withdrawal of Cuban troops as part of a settlement in Namibia. In June 1985 South Africa granted limited local authority to a Namibian government made up of a coalition of parties, excluding SWAPO. In 1987 South African troops occupied southern Angola (to aid Angolan rebels), and in early 1988, fighting between South African troops and Namibian rebels in northern Namibia and southern Angola intensified.

A new round of talks on the future of Namibia among South Africa, Cuba, and Angola, began in 1988, and the three parties agreed on a plan for Namibian independence and a pullout of Cuban troops from Angola. In Jan. 1989 the Cuban withdrawal from Angola began. On Apr. 1 U.N. Resolution 435 went into effect in Namibia, and a U.N. peacekeeping force arrived to supervise the transition to independence. Elections were held in Nov. 1989: SWAPO leader Sam Nujoma won an overwhelming victory. A Western-style democratic constitution was adopted Feb. 16, 1990, and full independence came on Mar. 21. The first elections under the new constitution were held in Dec. 1994 with SWAPO gaining even stronger control of Parliament. In Dec. 1999 elections, Sam Nujoma won a third term as president with 77 percent of the vote while SWAPO took 76 percent of the votes for the National Assembly. Tourism and mining helped bring a modicum of prosperity in the following years. Nujoma left office in Mar. 2005 and was succeeded by his friend and co-founder of SWAPO in 1965, Hifikepunye Pohamba, who began land reform by confiscating white-owned farms.

▶ NAURU
Republic of Nauru
● GEOGRAPHY Location: central Pacific Ocean (0°32'S, 166°56'E), about 2,800 mi. (4,500 km) southwest of Hawaii. Boundaries: nearest neighbor is Banaba (Ocean Island), in Kiribati, about 185 mi. (300 km) to E. Total area: 8 sq. mi. (21 sq km). Coastline: 19 mi. (30 km). Comparative area: about one-tenth size of Washington, D.C. Land use: 0% arable land; 0% permanent crops; 100% other. Major cities: none as such; government offices in Yaren district.
● PEOPLE Population: 13,770 (2008 est.). Nationality: noun—Nauruan(s) adjective—Nauruan. Ethnic groups: 58% Nauruan, 26% other Pacific Islander, 8% Chinese, 8% European. Languages: Nauruan, a distinct Pacific Island language (offi-

cial); English widely understood and spoken and used for most government and commercial purposes. Religions: Christian (two-thirds Protestant, one-third Catholic).
● GOVERNMENT Type: republic. Independence: Jan. 31, 1968 (from U.N. trusteeship under Australia, New Zealand, and U.K.). Constitution: Jan. 29, 1968. National holiday: Independence Day, Jan. 31. Head of Government: Marcus Stephen, president (since Dec. 2007). Structure: executive—president elected from and by Parliament for unfixed term; unicameral legislature; judiciary.
● ECONOMY Monetary unit: Australian dollar. Budget: (2005 est.) *income:* $13.5 mil.; *expend.:* $13.5 mil. G.D.P.: $60 mil., $5,000 per capita (2005 est.). Chief crops: coconuts. Natural resources: phosphates. Major industries: phosphate mining (about 2 mil. tons per year), financial services, coconuts. Labor force: N.A.; 90% unemployment (2004 est.) Exports: $64,000 (f.o.b., 2005); phosphates. Imports: $20 mil. (c.i.f., 2004); food, fuel, manufactures, building materials, machinery. Major trading partners: (2006) *exports:* 63.7% South Africa, 7.6% South Korea, 6.6% Canada; *imports:* 43.8% South Korea, 36.2% Australia, 5.9% U.S., 4.3% Germany.

Nauru, formerly known as Pleasant Island, is an isolated island lying west of the Gilbert Islands. It became a German protectorate in 1888. After World War I, Nauru was administered by Australia under a League of Nations mandate. It was occupied by Japan throughout World War II. In 1947 it became a U.N. Trust Territory administered by Australia, and on Jan. 31, 1968, an independent republic. Nauru has a parliament of 18 members, who elect a prime minister and a cabinet.

Phosphate deposits used to account for almost all of Nauru's revenues, but reserves are now depleted. Trust funds created with phosphate income have also been spent down, leaving the government near bankruptcy and dependent on Australia for assistance. A campaign to encourage registration of offshore banks and corporations has done little to halt rapid deterioration in housing and services throughout Nauru.

▶ NEPAL
Kingdom of Nepal
● GEOGRAPHY Location: central Asia, in Himalayan mountain range. Boundaries: China to N, India to E, S, and W. Total area: 54,363 sq. mi. (140,800 sq km). Coastline: none. Comparative area: slightly larger than Arkansas. Land use: 20% arable land; negl. % permanent crops; 79% other. Major cities: Kathmandu (capital).
● PEOPLE Population: 29,519,114 (July 2008 est.). Nationality: noun—Nepalese (sing. and pl.); adjective—Nepalese. Ethnic groups: Chhettri, Newars, Indians, Tibetans, Gurungs, Magars, Tamangs, Bhotias, Rais, Limbus, Sherpas. Languages: Nepali (official); 20 other languages divided into numerous dialects. Religions: 80.6% Hindu, 11% Buddhist, 4.2% Muslim; only official Hindu kingdom in world, although no sharp distinction between many Hindu and Buddhist groups.
● GOVERNMENT Type: parliamentary democracy. Constitution: Nov. 9, 1990. National holiday: Birthday of King Gyanendra, July 7. Heads of Government: Pushpa K. Dahal, prime minister (since Aug. 2008). Structure: executive—prime minister appointed by king from leading party in parliament; bicameral legislature—upper house (National Assembly) consists of 60 members, 50

appointed by lower house, 10 by the king; judiciary.

• **ECONOMY Monetary unit:** Nepalese rupee. **Budget:** (2007 est.) *income:* $1.153 bil.; *expend.:* $1.927 bil. **G.D.P.:** $30.66 bil., $1,100 per capita (2007 est.). **Chief crops:** rice, corn, wheat, sugarcane; milk, water buffalo meat. **Natural resources:** quartz, water, timber, hydroelectric potential, scenic beauty. **Major industries:** carpet and textiles, small rice, jute, sugar, and oilseed mills; cigarette and brick factories; tourism. **Labor force:** 11.11 mil. (2006 est.); 76% agriculture, 18% services, 6% industry; 42% unemployment (2004 est.). **Exports:** $830 mil. (f.o.b., 2006) (does not include unrecorded border trade with India); clothing, carpets, leather goods, jute goods, grain. **Imports:** $2.398 bil. (f.o.b., 2006); gold, petroleum products, fertilizer, machinery. **Major trading partners:** (2006) *exports:* 68% India, 12% U.S., 4% Germany; *imports:* 62% India, 4% China, 3% Indonesia.

The birthplace of Gautama Buddha (c. 600 B.C.), Nepal was for many centuries a collection of petty principalities, inhabited by various Tibeto-Burman peoples who mostly practiced Lamaistic Buddhism. In 1769 the country's three geographical zones—floodplain, foothills, and high mountains—were united under the Gurkhas, who made Hinduism the country's official religion. Nepal established treaty relations with Great Britain in 1792 and fought a border war with British India in 1814-16, but it was never incorporated into the British Empire.

A revolution in 1950 overthrew a government of heriditary rulers that had overthrown the Shah dynasty in the 19th century. King Tribuhavan (a Shah) was restored and tried to introduce democratic reforms, but his son Mahendra dissolved Parliament and introduced a tiered system of town, district, and national councils. Road and air links to India, Pakistan, and Tibet were improved, and Nepal began to emerge from its customary isolation. The successful climb of Mt. Everest by Sir Edmund Hillary and Tenzing Norgay in 1953 focused international attention on Nepal.

Mahendra was succeeded in 1972 by his son, Birendra. Antigovernment demonstrations in 1990 led to the shooting deaths of 63 civilians, so Birendra lifted a 30-year-old ban on political parties and ordered the constitution rewritten to establish multiparty democracy and human rights as essentials of the political system. The king retains control of the military and is still head of state.

The Nepali Congress Party formed the first government in 1991, but after 1994 a series of brief coalitions, often including the Communist Party, governed Nepal until the May 1999 elections permitted the Nepali Congress Party to govern without a coalition. But prime minister Krishna Prasad Bhattarai proved too ill to deal with Nepal's depressed economy and with the Maoist guerrilla force ("People's War") afflicting Nepal since 1996; he resigned in March 2000 to be replaced by Giriji Prasad Koirala.

On June 1, 2001 Crown Prince Dipendra murdered his parents and eight other members of the royal family, after which he shot himself. His uncle became King Gyanendra. In the turmoil, the Maoist rebels increased their depredations. The accession of Sher Bahadur Deuba as prime minister in July 2001 brought a harder line against the Maoist rebels: no negotiations before surrender. In Oct. 2002, King Gyanendra suspended the constitution, appointed Lokendra Chand as interim prime minis-

ter to open dialogue with the Maoists. Secret talks and quickly-broken truces led nowhere. Chand resigned in May 2002 with the rebels holding about 40 percent of the country. Surya Bahadur Thapa replaced him, only to resign in May 2004. In Feb. 2005 Gyandera seized power and cracked down on all dissent as he vowed to end the Maoist rebellion, but in April 2006, after weeks of angry pro-democracy protests, the king handed back power to parliament. In June, the Maoist rebels agreed to lay down their arms and joined the government in 2007. In May 2008 the monarchy was abolished and in August parliament elected Maoist leader Prachanda to be prime minister. (See "Major News Stories.")

▶ **NETHERLANDS**
Kingdom of The Netherlands
• **GEOGRAPHY Location:** western Europe. **Boundaries:** North Sea to N and W, Germany to E, Belgium to S. **Total area:** 14,413 sq. mi. (37,330 sq km). **Coastline:** 280 mi. (451 km). **Comparative area:** slightly less than twice the size of New Jersey. **Land use:** 27% arable land; 0% permanent crops; 73% other. **Major cities:** Amsterdam (capital); Rotterdam; The Hague; Utrecht; Eindhoven. The Hague is the seat of government.

• **PEOPLE Population:** 16,645,313 (July 2008 est.). **Nationality:** noun—Dutchman (men), Dutchwoman (women); adjective—Dutch. **Ethnic groups:** 83% Dutch, 17% other (9% of which are Moroccans, Turks, Antilleans, Surinamese and Indonesians). **Languages:** Dutch, Frisian (official); English widely spoken. **Religions:** 31% Roman Catholic, 21% Protestant, 40% unaffiliated, 3% Muslim.

• **GOVERNMENT Type:** constitutional monarchy. **Independence:** 1579 (from Spain). **Constitution:** 1814; last amended Feb. 17, 1983. **National holiday:** Queen's Day, Apr. 30. **Heads of Government:** Beatrix Wilhelmina Armgard, queen (since Apr. 1980); Dr. Jan Peter Balkenende, prime minister (since July 2002). **Structure:** executive—queen is constitutional monarch, prime minister is head of government; bicameral parliament; independent judiciary.

• **ECONOMY Monetary unit:** euro. **Budget:** (2007 est.) *income:* $302.8 bil.; *expend.:* $352.3 bil. **G.D.P.:** $638.9 bil., $38,600 per capita (2007 est.). **Chief crops:** grains, potatoes, sugar beets; livestock. **Natural recources:** natural gas, crude oil, fertile soil. **Major industries:** agro-industries, metal and engineering products, electrical machinery and equipment. **Labor force:** 7.5 mil. (2007 est.); 76% services, 21% industry, 3% agriculture (2005); 4.1% unemployment (2007). **Exports:** $465.3 bil. (f.o.b., 2007); machinery and equipment, chemicals, fuels, food and tobacco. **Imports:** $402.4 bil. (c.i.f., 2007 est.); machinery and transport equipment, chemicals, foodstuffs, fuels, clothing. **Major trading partners:** (2006) *exports:* 25.5% Germany, 14% Belgium, 8.9% U.K., 8.6% France, 5.1% Italy, 4.5% U.S.; *imports:* 17.1% Germany, 9.4% Belgium, 9.4% China, 7.8% U.S., 5.9% U.K., 5.1% Russia, 4.5% France.

Historically, the name Netherlands referred to the low-lying areas of the Holy Roman Empire near the mouths of the Rhine, Meuse, and Scheldt rivers. The Habsburg emperor Charles V willed these territories to his son Philip II of Spain in 1555, but by the end of the 16th century, the northern provinces—the Union of Utrecht, formed in 1579 by William the Silent, of the House of Orange—won their independence in a war that was both religious (Calvinist vs. Catholic) and constitutional (aristocratic/patrician vs. foreign monarchy). The independence of the Netherlands was recognized in the Treaty of Westphalia, which ended the Thirty Years' War in 1648.

Dutch prosperity, founded on the woolen trade with England, grew tremendously through trade and seafaring under the 17th-century republic. The Netherlands amassed a world empire, including the Indonesian archipelago, the island of Sri Lanka (then Ceylon), South Africa, Suriname, parts of the West Indies, and the Hudson valley in New Amsterdam (later New York); in addition it monopolized Western trade with Japan after 1637.

The Netherlands were incorporated into the Napoleonic empire. At the Congress of Vienna in 1815, a Dutch monarchy was established, which included Belgium until 1830. Land drainage and reclamation programs maintained the prosperity of the country's small-scale agriculture, while trade and colonial revenues were increasingly supplemented by industrial development in the 19th century. Dutch prosperity and the country's strategic position gave the Netherlands extraordinary influence and prestige in European affairs into the 20th century, despite the country's small size. It remained neutral in World War I.

Germany invaded the Netherlands in May 1940, taking control of the country after five days of fighting. Preparing to incorporate Holland into the Third Reich, Hitler installed a Nazi civilian government that ruled through totalitarian exploitation and cooperated in the persecution of Jews. But Queen Wilhelmina and the Dutch government escaped to England and maintained a government-in-exile throughout the war.

The final stages of fighting on the western front inflicted severe damage on the country, while in Asia the recovery of Indonesia from Japan led to a declaration of independence under Sukarno. Marshall Plan aid was intended to support a domestic postwar recovery; an equal amount was spent by the Dutch government in an attempt to recapture control of Indonesia before that country's independence was recognized in 1949.

Devastated by World War II and the loss of its empire, the country faced a bleak future. Forced to turn its attention to recovery at home, the Netherlands worked through the Benelux (Belgium, Netherlands, Luxembourg) union (founded in 1944) and the Common Market to create another European "economic miracle" between the early 1950's and the 1970's. The older bases of the economy—commerce, maritime industry, dairy farming, and flower farming—were expanded and modernized; Rotterdam was rebuilt to become an important port. Newer industries, such as chemicals and oil refining, electronics, and steel, relied on the country's highly skilled and productive labor force to turn imported raw materials into finished high-value exports. A huge impoundment project turned the Zuider Zee into a new province, increasing the country's land area by 10 percent.

This postwar prosperity has been based in large part on political stability. A coalition of the Catholic State party and the Labor (formerly Social Democratic) party governed for 10 years under Premier Willem Drees. After 1958 cabinets normally were formed from coalitions headed by three Christian parties (merged in 1980 to form the United Christian Appeal) or by the Liberal party; all pursued essentially the same policies of free enterprise, comprehensive social welfare programs, high taxation, and social liberalism.

From 1982 to 1989 a coalition of Christian Democrats and Liberals provided a cabinet headed by Prime Minister Ruud Lubbers; after 1989 the coalition has been of Christian Democrats and Labor. In 1994 Wim Kok, head of Labor, became prime minister, the first government to exclude the Christian Democrats since 1945.

Just 10 days before the May 15, 2002 elections, radical libertarian and anti-Muslim newcomer Pim Fortuyn was assassinated by an animal-rights activist. The election proved a nightmare for Kok's center-left coalition: the Christian Democrats topped the polls, followed by Fortuyn's party. These two put together an inexperienced coalition under CD prime minister Jan Peter Balkenende, but it lasted only three months. Balkendale cobbled together a new coalition after 2003 elections.

In May 2005, voters rejected the E.U. constitution, and in 2006 the government again collapsed over immigration. A new coalition took office in Feb. 2007.

▶NEW ZEALAND

● **GEOGRAPHY Location:** South Pacific Ocean about 1,100 mi. (1,750 km) SE of Australia. **Boundaries:** South Pacific Ocean to N, E, and S; Tasman Sea to W. **Total area:** 103,738 sq. mi. (268,680 sq km). **Coastline:** 9,406 mi. (15,134 km). **Comparative area:** about size of Colorado. **Land use:** 6% arable land; 6% permanent crops; 88% other. **Major cities:** Wellington (capital); Auckland; Christchurch; Hamilton; Napier-Hastings. ● **PEOPLE Population:** 4,173,460 (July 2008 est.). **Nationality:** noun—New Zealander(s); adjective— New Zealand. **Ethnic groups:** 70% New Zealand European, 8% Maori, 8% mixed, 4.4% Pacific Islander, 8% Asian and other. **Languages:** English, Maori, sign language (official). **Religions:** 24% Anglican, 18% Presbyterian, 15% Roman Catholic, 5% Methodist, 2% Baptist, 3% other Protestant, 33% none or unspecified. ● **GOVERNMENT Type:** parliamentary democracy. **Independence:** Sept. 26, 1907 (from U.K.). **Constitution:** no formal, written constitution; consists of various documents, including certain acts of U.K. and New Zealand Parliaments. Constitution Act 1986 was to have come into force Jan. 1, 1987, but has not been enacted. **National holiday:** Waitangi Day, Feb. 6. **Heads of Government:** Dame Silvia Cartwright, governor-general (since Apr. 2001); Helen Clark, prime minister (since Dec. 1999). **Structure:** executive—governor-general represents queen, prime minister is head of government; unicameral legislature; judiciary. ● **ECONOMY Monetary unit:** New Zealand dollar. **Budget:** (2007 est.) *income:* $54.36 bil.; *expend.:* $48.51 bil. **G.D.P.:** $112.6 bil., $27,300 per capita (2007 est.). **Chief crops:** wheat, barley, potatoes, fruits; wool, meat, dairy. **Natural resources:** natural gas, iron ore, sand, coal, timber. **Major industries:** food processing, wood and paper products, textiles, aluminum smelting, tourism. **Labor force:** 2.23 mil. (2007); 74% services, 19% industry, 7% agriculture (2006); 3.5% unemployment (2007). **Exports:** $28.12 bil. (f.o.b., 2007 est.); wool, lamb, mutton, beef, fruit, fish. **Imports:** $29.83 bil. (f.o.b., 2007 est.); machinery and equipment, vehicles and aircraft, petroleum, consumer goods, plastics. **Major trading partners:** (2006) *exports:* 20.5% Australia, 13.1% U.S., 10.3% Japan, 5.4% China, 4.9% U.K.; *imports:* 20.5% Australia, 12.3% China,

11.8% U.S., 9.2% Japan, 4.4% Germany, 4.4% Singapore.

New Zealand was settled by Maori voyagers from Polynesia from about the ninth century a.d. The first European to sight it was the Dutch explorer Abel Tasman, in 1642; he named it, but did not take possession. In 1769, Capt. James Cook visited and claimed it for Britain. The first British missionaries arrived in 1814, and New Zealand became a full-fledged British colony in 1841. By the Treaty of Waitangi in 1840, the Maoris recognized Queen Victoria's protection and agreed to admit British settlers; in return, they were guaranteed possession of their lands. But in a series of bloody wars lasting until 1870, the Maoris were displaced from lands devoted to the expanding British settlements.

As a result of their defeat and of introduced diseases, the Maori population dwindled to about 40,000 by the 1890's. Their numbers have since recovered to over 400,000, and in recent decades, the Maoris have become a cohesive culture and significant political force, directly electing several members of Parliament. In 1985, the Waitangi Tribunal was given power to hear Maori claims for repayment for land taken without compensation since the 1840 treaty. Large financial settlements were negotiated by the government.

New Zealand was one of the first nations to introduce universal adult suffrage (1893) and to establish a comprehensive welfare state. Legislation beginning in 1898 regulates labor practices, and mandates universal old-age pensions, public sector medical care, and other social services. Since 1907, the country has been an independent member of the British Commonwealth. The crown is represented by a governor-general; government is drawn from a parliament and headed by a prime minister. Since the 1930's, government has alternated between the National and Labour parties.

New Zealand troops fought on the side of the Allies in both world wars, with U.N. forces in Korea, and with the U.S. in Vietnam. In 1951, New Zealand joined Australia and the U.S. in the ANZUS mutual-defense treaty, but was excluded from it in 1986 after denying port facilities to ships carrying nuclear weapons. New Zealand has also objected strenuously to French testing of nuclear weapons in the South Pacific and pressed for a comprehensive international nuclear test ban treaty.

Upon its election in 1984, the Labour government launched an economic restructuring program to transform the country from a protected agrarian economy to an open free-market economy. This program, continued by the National Party, which regained power in 1990, eliminated government subsidies, cut spending, liberalized imports, deregulated financial markets, reduced tax rates, and deregulated the labor market. The reforms resulted in an expanding and competitive economy with low inflation, and, in 1993-94, the first budget surplus in 18 years. The government responded in 1995 by cutting taxes again. 1996 election results, however, forced the Nationalist Party into coalition with the new populist/zenophobic New Zealand First Party. The new government now had to defer tax cuts, halt sales of state-owned businesses, and increase spending on health and education. The coalition lasted 19 months but the government did not fall as votes of confidence in 1998 and 1999 permitted continuance of a minority government headed by New Zealand's first female prime minister, Jenny Ship-

ley. Nine years of National Party rule ended in 1999 as a coalition government of Labor and Alliance established Helen Clark as prime minister. In June 2001 elections, the Nationalists garnered only 27 seats, their worse showing in their 66-year history. Clark's Labour Party gained 52 seats. Without a formal coalition, an alliance with the Greens yielded exactly 60 of the 120 votes. The Clark government was able to carry out an almost complete severance from the U.K. but in 2005 elections no dramatic change occurred and Clark remained in power with limitations.

▶ **NICARAGUA**
Republic of Nicaragua

● **GEOGRAPHY   Location:** Central American isthmus. **Boundaries:** Honduras to N, Caribbean Sea to E, Costa Rica to S, Pacific Ocean to W. **Total area:** 49,998 sq. mi. (129,494 sq km). **Coastline:** 565 mi. (910 km). **Comparative area:** slightly smaller than New York State. **Land use:** 20% arable land; 2% permanent crops; 78% other. **Major cities:** Managua (capital); León; Granada; Masaya; Chinandega.

● **PEOPLE   Population:** 5,785,846 (2008 est.). **Nationality:** noun—Nicaraguan(s); adjective—Nicaraguan. **Ethnic groups:** 69% mestizo, 17% white, 9% black, 5% Amerindian. **Languages:** Spanish (official); English- and Amerindian-speaking minorities on Atlantic coast. **Religions:** 73% Roman Catholic, 16.5% Protestant 2% other, 8.5% none.

● **GOVERNMENT   Type:** republic. **Independence:** Sept. 15, 1821 (from Spain). **Constitution:** Jan. 9, 1987 with reforms in 1995 and 2000. **National holiday:** Independence Day, Sept. 15. **Head of Government:** Daniel Ortega, president (since Jan. 2007). **Structure:** executive branch; unicameral legislature; judiciary.

● **ECONOMY   Monetary unit:** córdoba. **Budget:** (2007 est.) **income:** $1.027 mil.; **expend.:** $1.336 bil. **G.D.P.:** $18.17 bil., $3,200 per capita (2007 est.). **Chief crops:** cotton, bananas, coffee, sugarcane, rice, corn, beans. **Natural resources:** gold, silver, copper, tungsten, lead. **Major industries:** food processing, chemicals, metal products. **Labor force:** 2.262 mil. (2007); 52% services, 29% agriculture, 19% industry (2006); 5.6% unemployment (2007). **Exports:** $2.235 bil. (f.o.b., 2007 est.); coffee, seafood, cotton, tobacco, sugar, gold, bananas. **Imports:** $3.647 bil. (c.i.f., 2007 est.); consumer goods, machinery and equipment, petroleum products. **Major trading partners:** (2006) *exports:* 65.2% U.S., 6.9% El Salvador, 3.8% Honduras; *imports:* 20.1% U.S., 14% Mexico, 9.4% Venezuela, 6.9% Costa Rica, 5.4% Guatemala, 4.3% China.

Nicaragua gained independence from Spain in 1821 and formed a constituent part of the United Provinces of Central America in 1823. With the dissolution of the federation in 1838, Nicaragua became an independent republic. Throughout the United Provinces, an intra-elite struggle between Liberal and Conservative factions defined the political arena during the early 19th century. Nicaraguan Liberals invited the adventurer William Walker of Tennessee to take their part against their Conservative rivals in 1855. Walker took control of the country in 1856 but was driven out by a combined Central American force the following year.

The Conservatives held power in Nicaragua until 1893, when a planters' revolt brought Liberal José Santos Zelaya to the presidency. Because of Zelaya's intention to pursue an isthmian canal project, the U.S. government intervened in support of a Conservative uprising. The United States sent marines to Nicaragua in 1909, and Zelaya resigned in 1910. The marines occupied the country during 1909-25 and 1926-33.

Refusing to abide by a political settlement between the U.S. government and Nicaraguan Liberal forces in 1927, Augusto César Sandino, led a guerrilla war against U.S. occupation forces. In 1934, Anastasio Somoza García, head of the Nicaraguan National Guard, had Sandino assassinated and took over the presidency in 1937. Somoza and his sons Luis and Anastasio Somoza Debayle controlled Nicaragua until 1979.

A broad coalition of groups led by the Sandinista National Liberation Front (FSLN) overthrew the Somoza dictatorship in 1979. Elections were held in 1984 for the presidency, vice presidency, and a constituent assembly. The Sandinistas won the election for the presidency, captured a working majority in the National Assembly, and wrote a new constitution in 1987.

Between 1981 and 1990, the United States actively, but covertly supported Contra rebels fighting the Sandinista regime in a civil war that cost the country dearly. In 1989, Pres. Daniel Ortega announced elections for early 1990, which he lost in a stunning upset to Violeta Barrios de Chamorro, who headed a 17-party coalition, the United Nicaragua Opposition. Since then, the transition has been relatively peaceful, highlighted by Gen. Humberto Ortega's uneventful transfer of command of the army in 1995, the first peaceful transfer in Nicaragua's history. In late 1996 presidential elections the Liberal Alliance candidate, Arnoldo Alemán, won a decisive victory over former president Daniel Ortega and voters opted for a return to free enterprise and closer ties with the U.S. Limitations on the Aleman government's free enterprising policies were shown by student protests and transport workers' strikes which forced the government to boost university spending and abandon bus line deregulation while cutting back fuel taxes. In Nov. 2000 the Sandinistas and Daniel Ortega were again defeated as Liberal Alliance candidate Enrique Bolanos Geyer carried 54 percent of the presidential vote. At the end of 2006, however, Ortega made a comeback, promising not to make radical changes in economic policy.

▶NIGER
Republic of Niger
● **Geography   Location:** landlocked country in western Africa. **Boundaries:** Algeria and Libya to N, Chad to E, Nigeria to S, Benin, Burkina Faso to SW, Mali to W. **Total area:** 489,189 sq. mi. (1,267,000 sq km). **Coastline:** none. **Comparative area:** slightly less than twice the size of Texas. **Land use:** 4% arable land; 0% permanent crops; 796% other. **Major cities:** Niamey (capital); Zinder; Maradi; Tahoua; Agadez.
● **People   Population:** 13,272,679 (2008 est.). **Nationality:** noun—Nigerien(s); adjective—Nigerien. **Ethnic groups:** 55.4% Hausa, 21% Djerma, Tuareg, Pechl, Kanouri, Manga. **Languages:** French (official), Hausa, Djerma. **Religions:** 80% Muslim, 20% indigenous beliefs and Christians.
● **Government   Type:** republic. **Independence:** Aug. 3, 1960 (from France). **Constitution:** revised May 12, 1996 and July 18, 1999. **National holiday:** Republic Day, Dec. 18. **Heads of Government:** Mamadou Tandja, president (since Dec. 1999); Seyni Oumarou, prime minister (since June 2007).

Structure: executive; unicameral legislature; judiciary.
● **Economy   Monetary unit:** Communauté Financière Africaine (CFA) franc. **Budget:** (2002 est.) *income:* $320 mil.; *expend.:* $320 mil. **G.D.P.:** $8.998 bil., $700 per capita (2007 est.). **Chief crops:** cowpeas, cotton, peanuts, millet, sorghum, cassava, rice; goats, sheep, cattle. **Natural resources:** uranium, coal, iron ore, tin, phosphates. **Major industries:** uranium mining, cement, brick, textiles. **Labor force:** 70,000 receive regular wages or salaries; 90% agriculture; 6% industry and commerce, 4% government. **Exports:** $428 mil. (f.o.b., 2006 est.); uranium ore, livestock, cowpeas, onions. **Imports:** $800 mil. (f.o.b., 2006); consumer goods, primary materials, machinery, vehicles and parts, petroleum, cereals. **Major trading partners:** (2006) *exports:* 35% France, 26% U.S., 18% Nigeria, 11.3% Russia; *imports:* 14.1% U.S., 12% France, 7.8% China, 7.7% Nigeria, 7.7% French Polynesia, 4.9% Cote d'Ivoire.

Most of Niger's territory is dominated by the Sahara and the Sahel (the "shore" of the desert), which have spread southward since prehistoric times. Much of the population lives in the narrow fertile belt south of the Niger River. Much of Niger was incorporated during medieval times in large empires centered in neighboring Mali, Chad, and Nigeria.

In the 18th century, Tuaregs migrating from the northern desert began to form tribal confederations in Niger. They united with local Hausa peoples to wage war against the Fulani empire. In the 19th century, British and German explorers explored the region. In the European rivalry that followed, the French, from bases in Mali and Chad, began to dominate Niger by 1900; Niger became a French colony in 1922, administered from Dakar, Senegal.

In 1946 the people of Niger, in common with other peoples in French Africa, were granted French citizenship, and limited self-rule began. This local autonomy was expanded in 1956, and in 1958 Niger became an autonomous state within the French Overseas Community. Full independence followed on Aug. 3, 1960; Niger maintained close ties to France.

Hamani Diori was elected Niger's first president in 1960, reelected in 1965 and 1970. He was overthrown in 1974 in a military coup led by Lt. Col. Seyni Kountche. In 1987, Pres. Kountche died and was succeeded by Col. Ali Saibou, who was elected president by the Supreme Military Council. The country began moving toward democracy again in 1989, and a new constitution was approved in 1992. Mahame Ousmane was elected president in 1993, but he and prime minister Hama Amadou were ousted in a violent military coup in Jan. 1996. The leader of the coup, Lt. Col. Ibrahim Barré, who criticized Ousmane's handling of the Taureg Liberation Front, became the new president. He survived an assassination attempt in Jan. 1998, but fell to another in April 1999. Junior army officers formed a junta, supported by all the civilian opposition parties, maintaining Ibrahim Mayaki in his post as prime minister. The junta promised a "nine-month transition", and presidential elections were held in Nov. 1999 in which Tandja Mamadou defeated former premier Mohamadou Issoufou. In 2004-05 a sustained drought brought famine and many deaths.

▶ NIGERIA
Federal Republic of Nigeria

• **GEOGRAPHY   Location:** western coast of Africa. **Boundaries:** Niger to N, Cameroon to E, Gulf of Guinea to S, Benin to W. **Total area:** 356,668 sq. mi. (923,770 sq km). **Coastline:** 530 mi. (853 km). **Comparative area:** slightly more than twice the size of California. **Land use:** 31% arable land; 3% permanent crops; 66% other. **Major cities:** Abuja (capital); Lagos; Ibadan; Kano; Ogbomosho.

• **PEOPLE   Population:** 138,283,240 (2008 est.). **Nationality:** noun—Nigerian(s); adjective—Nigerian. **Ethnic groups:** over 50 ethnic groups, inlcuding 29% Hausa and Fulani, 21% Yoruba, 18% Ibo, 10% Ijaw, Kanuri, Ibibio, Tiv. **Languages:** English (official); Hausa, Yoruba, Ibo, Fulani. **Religions:** 50% Muslim, 40% Christian, 10% indigenous beliefs.

• **GOVERNMENT   Type:** republic in transition from military rule. **Independence:** Oct. 1, 1960 (from U.K.). **Constitution:** New constitution adopted in 1999. **National holiday:** Independence Day, Oct. 1. **Head of Government:** Umaru Yar'Adua, president (since May 2007). **Structure:** executive; bicameral legislature; judiciary.

• **ECONOMY   Monetary unit:** naira. **Budget:** (2007 est.) *income:* $20.5 bil.; *expend:* $21.82 bil. **G.D.P.:** $294.8 bil., $2,200 per capita (2007 est.). **Chief crops:** peanuts, cocoa, palm oil, rubber, corn; goats, sheep, cattle, pigs; fish. **Natural resources:** crude oil, tin, columbite, iron ore, coal. **Major industries:** crude oil, coal, tin, columbite; palm oil, peanuts, cotton, rubber; textiles, cement, building materials. **Labor force:** 50.13 mil. (2007 est.); 70% agriculture; 10% industry, 20% services; 5.8% unemployment (2006 est.). **Exports:** $61.81 bil. (f.o.b., 2007); 95% petroleum and petroleum products, cocoa, rubber. **Imports:** $30.35 bil. (f.o.b., 2007); machinery, chemicals, transportation equipment, manufactured goods, food and animals. **Major trading partners:** (2006) *exports:* 48.9% U.S., 8.9% Spain, 7.3% Brazil, 4.2% France; *imports:* 10.7% China, 8.3% U.S., 6.2% Netherlands, 5.8% U.K., 5.6% France, 5.1% Brazil, 4.6% Germany.

The Nok culture of central Nigeria (500-200 B.C.) was one of the richest and most advanced ancient civilizations in western Africa. Around A.D. 1000, the Muslim Kanem civilization expanded into northern Nigeria; by the 14th century, the amalgamated kingdom of Kanem-Bornu took northern Nigeria as its political center, from which it dominated the Sahel and developed trade routes stretching throughout northern Africa and as far as Europe and the Middle East. During the 15th and 16th centuries, the Hausa Songhai empire rose to power. It was overthrown by the Fulani Muslim leader Uthman Dan Fodio, who created the Sokoto caliphate.

Southern Nigeria is dominated by the Yoruba, whose Oyo kingdom, centered at Ife, became a major power by A.D. 1000. Oyo gave rise to the Benin civilization, which flourished from the 15th to the 18th centuries and is famous for its brass, bronze, and ivory sculpture.

The Portuguese established trading stations on the Benin coast in the 15th century; initially, trade relations were cordial, and Benin became well-known in Europe as a powerful and advanced kingdom. With the rise of the slave trade (which began with the cooperation of the Benin kings, who brought slaves from the interior), relations became hostile, and Benin declined under European pressure. The Dutch, British, and other Europeans competed strenuously with Portugal for control of the slave trade, and by the 18th century, most of the coastal region of Nigeria was under British control. By the turn of the 19th century, Britain suppressed the slave trade; slaves captured aboard European ships were transported by the British to Freetown in Sierra Leone.

The British traded with Nigerians for agricultural and forest products and commenced exploration of the Niger River. Lagos came under British control in 1851, and in 1861 Nigeria was made a British colony. Despite native resistance the colony was expanded in 1906 to include territory east of the Niger River, which was called the Protectorate of Southern Nigeria, The two areas were administratively joined in 1914.

During the 1920's Britain began to respond to Nigerian demands for self-rule. In 1946 the colony was divided into three regions, each with an advisory assembly. In 1954 the colony was reorganized as the Nigerian Federation, and the assemblies were given more authority. Sir Akubar Tafawa Balewa became Nigeria's first prime minister.

The 1960's were marked by a struggle for political dominance among the major ethnic groups of Nigeria, including the Ibo (or Igbo), Yoruba, Hausa, and Fulani. Attempts to partition the country on tribal lines for administrative purposes provoked controversy, and charges of corruption and fraud in elections held in 1964 and 1965 led to violence and rioting.

In January 1966 civil war broke out when a group of Ibo army officers overthrew the central government. Prime Minister Balewa was killed, along with many other political leaders. Gen. Johnson Aguiyi-Ironsi, leader of the Ibo forces, took control of the government.

Aguiyi-Ironsi abolished the country's federal structure and set up a strong central government, dominated by the Ibo. Anti-Ibo riots broke out in the north, and many Ibo were massacred. In July 1966 Aguiyi-Ironsi was assassinated by a group of northern army officers. Army Chief of Staff Yakubu Gowon became head of a new military government. In 1967 Gowon reapportioned Nigeria into 12 states. The Eastern Region rejected this plan and seceded from Nigeria to form the independent state of Biafra, provoking a civil war that lasted until January 1970, when Biafra was rejoined with Nigeria. An estimated one million Biafrans, mostly Ibos, died in the war.

Gowon tried to rebuild the Eastern Region and create a harmonious multitribal government, but he was overthrown in a coup in 1975. His successor was assassinated in 1976 and succeeded by Lt. Gen. Olusegun Obasanjo who increased the number of states from 12 to 19 and promised a return to civilian rule. Shehu Shagari was elected president in 1979 and reelected in 1983, but in Dec. 1983 the military again intervened.

Nigeria's crude oil resources fueled the economy and made it attractive for foreign investment. During the 1970's, petroleum exports helped Nigeria recover from the Biafran War. But corruption and overspending of projected petroleum revenues led to an economic crisis in the early 1980's as oil prices collapsed worldwide. Inflation, unemployment, and food shortages led to rioting in major population centers in 1986. And in 1987, religious violence broke out between the Christian south and the Muslim north.

The government of Maj. Gen. Ibrahim Babangida responded by announcing plans for a new constitution, various economic austerity measures, and the restoration of civilian rule by 1992. He also limited the number of political parties and dictated both party platforms in National Assembly elections held in 1992, and in 1993, he annulled the results of the presidential election, which international monitors said would have been won by opposition leader Moshood K. Abiola, who was taken prisoner for the "treason" of declaring himself the election winner. Babangida resigned in Aug. 1993, but his self-appointed successor was ousted in a November 1993 coup by Defense Minister Sani Abacha.

Abacha's tyranny survived until his death in June 1998. A "transitional" military government led by army chief of staff, Abdusalem Abubakar, freed political prisoners (Abiola dying just before his release), held local, state, and national elections (Dec.– Feb.), and turned over power, May 29, 1999 to the first popularly-elected president in 16 years, former general and once military ruler, Olusegun Obasanjo. The new government faced formidable problems: increased Moslem-Christian violence as northern states attempted to impose Sharia (Koranic law); civil disorder and rioting in the face of increased fuel prices.

In July 2000, violence and bloodshed over the imposition of Sharia increased. Attempts to meet I.M.F. loan conditions, such as ending subsidies which kept oil prices low or reducing government payrolls, provoked riots and strikes. Hausa-Yoruba tribal conflict in Lagos left over 100 dead. Amidst religious, ethnic, and economic turmoil, Pres. Obasanjo (the first civilian president after almost 20 years of military rule) won a second term in 2003. But in 2007, a new president, Umaru Yar'Adua, was elected although observers criticized the elections for fraud and corruption.

Nigeria is one of the world's leading suppliers of oil, but the people are among the poorest in Africa. In 2006 rebel forces (MEND) from the oil-producing regions began guerilla attacks on refineries and pipelines. In 2008 they initiated attacks against facilities of the major foreign oil companies.

▶NORWAY
Kingdom of Norway
● **GEOGRAPHY Location:** western Scandinavian peninsula, northern Europe. **Boundaries:** Norwegian Sea to N and W, Russian Federation, Finland to NE, Sweden to E, North Sea to S and W. **Total area:** 125,182 sq. mi. (324,220 sq km). **Coastline:** 13,626 mi. (21,925 km)—2,125 mi. (3,419 km) mainland; 1,500 mi. (2,413 km) large islands; 10,002 mi. (16,093 km) long fjords, numerous small islands, and minor indentations. **Comparative area:** slightly larger than New Mexico. **Land use:** 3% arable land; negl.% permanent crops; n97% other. **Major cities:** Oslo (capital); Bergen; Trondheim; Stavanger; Kristiansand.
● **PEOPLE Population:** 4,644,457 (July 2008 est.). **Nationality:** noun—Norwegian(s); adjective—Norwegian. **Ethnic groups:** Norwegian (Nordic, Alpine, Baltic), 20,000 Lapps (Sami). **Languages:** Norwegian (official), Lapp- and Finnish-speaking minorities. **Religions:** 86% Church of Norway, 1% Pentacostal, 1% Roman Catholic, 2.4% other Christian, 2% Muslim, 8% other.
● **GOVERNMENT Type:** constitutional monarchy. **Independence:** Oct. 26, 1905 (from Sweden). **Constitution:** May 17, 1814, and modified in 1884. **National holiday:** Constitution Day, May 17. **Heads of Government:** Harald V, king (since Jan.

1991); Jens Stoltenberg, prime minister (since Oct. 2005). **Structure:** executive—prime minister heads government; unicameral legislature—for certain purposes, STORTING divides itself into two chambers and elects 25 percent of its members to an upper house; judiciary.
● **ECONOMY Monetary unit:** Norwegian kroner. **Budget:** (2007 est.) *income:* $232.3 bil.; *expend.:* $158.4 bil. **G.D.P.:** $257.4 bil., $55,600 per capita (2007 est.). **Chief crops:** oats, feed grains; beef, milk; fish (among worlds top ten fishing nations). **Natural resources:** crude oil, copper, natural gas, pyrites, nickel. **Major industries:** petroleum and gas, food processing, shipbuilding. **Labor force:** 2.5 mil. (2007 est.); 74% services, 22% industry, 4% agriculture, forestry and fishing; 3.9% unemployment (1999). **Exports:** $136.1 bil. (f.o.b., 2007 est.); petroleum and petroleum products, metals, chemicals, ships, fish. **Imports:** $75.98 bil. (f.o.b., 2007 est.); machinery and equipment, chemicals, metals, foodstuffs. **Major trading partners:** (2006) *exports:* 27% U.K., 12% Germany, 10% Netherlands, 8% France, 6% Sweden, 6% U.S.; *imports:* 15% Sweden, 14% Germany, 7% Denmark, 6% U.K., 6% China, 5% U.S., 4% Netherlands.

The Viking age began in 793 with the sack of Lindisfarne in Ireland. By the 10th century, Norse and Danish Vikings had touched in almost every navigable river of Western Europe from Germany to Spain. In addition to coastal raiding, the Norse were beginning the first open-ocean voyages from Europe, sailing direct to Iceland (800 miles) and even to Greenland (2,200 miles), which they colonized in the 10th century.

At the beginning of the 10th century, Harold I united the petty kingdoms of western Scandinavia and extended his realm as far as the Orkney and Shetland islands. Viking nobles fleeing from his conquests consolidated the Norse duchy of Normandy in France. Christianity was established under Olaf II at the beginning of the 11th century.

Under Magnus VI (1263-80), medieval Norway reached the height of its power and prosperity. Norwegian independence ended with the accession in 1319 of Magnus VII, who was king of Sweden as well. Under the Kalmar Union of 1397, the three kingdoms of Scandinavia were merged under Danish control; Norway ceased to exist as a nation-state and was governed by the Danes for the following four centuries.

In 1814 Denmark, which had sided with France in the Napoleonic wars, was forced by the victorious powers to cede Norway to Sweden. Under Sweden's military control Norway attempted to establish its own monarchy. The attempt failed, but in 1815 Sweden acknowledged the independence of Norway in perpetual union with the Swedish Crown.

Relations between Norway and Sweden remained strained throughout the 19th century. In 1905 the Norwegian legislature, the Storting, declared the union void and deposed Swedish King Oscar II as king of Norway. Sweden acquiesced, and Prince Charles of Denmark was enthroned as king of Norway, ruling as Haakon VII for 52 years.

During the 19th century, large numbers of Norwegians emigrated to North America. A rising tide of cultural nationalism was expressed in the flourishing Norwegian literature and art, and in Arctic exploration. In the 20th century, industrialization, aided by the development of hydroelectric power, began to supplement Norway's traditional economic mainstays of fishing and seafaring.

Norway remained neutral during World War I and was relatively unaffected by the postwar upheavals. Norway attempted to remain neutral in World War II as well but was invaded and occupied by German troops in April 1940. The king and government fled to London and established a government-in-exile. The Norwegian merchant marine fleet was largely transferred to Great Britain and contributed to the Allied cause in the North Atlantic. At home, resistance grew to the collaborationist government of the Fascist leader Vidkun Quisling. As the Nazis retreated in 1945, King Haakon and his government returned home.

Elections in 1945 returned a majority Labor government in the Storting. Labor set about establishing a Scandinavian welfare state, emphasizing privately owned, free-market industry, publicly owned utilities, state planning to ensure ample housing as well as full employment through export-oriented industries, a comprehensive social welfare system, and high taxes.

Norway was a founding member of the United Nations and provided that body with its first secretary-general, Trygve Lie. With the hardening of the Cold War, Norway joined the NATO alliance in 1949. In 1959 Norway became one of the original members of the European Free Trade Association. Through the 1960's industrial development and exports continued to fuel an economic boom that led to great national prosperity and stability.

The 1970's were the decade of oil and gas, with extensive development of North Sea fields. As international energy prices rose, the government's petroleum monopoly, Statoil, seemed to provide an endless source of funds. Because Norway's hydroelectric plants made the country self-sufficient in electric power, almost all of the oil and gas was available for export; by 1981 energy exports amounted to one-third, and by 1985 one-half, of Norway's total exports. The government expanded the welfare state and encouraged large wage increases. Public spending swelled and government debt mounted; meanwhile Norway became an economic hostage to OPEC oil prices.

In the 1981 elections, the Conservative party formed a government for the first time since 1928; its austerity policy of holding down government spending while increasing taxes on consumer goods aroused popular opposition, and the government fell in 1986. The new Socialist coalition government faced even greater drops in oil revenues, combined with labor unrest and continued inflation. But in 1987 Norway negotiated the sale of gas to E.U. countries, and the recovery of energy prices brought a partial return to economic stability and prosperity.

In 1993 the government of Prime Minister Brundtland sought admission to the E.U. On Mar. 29, 1994, the E.U. agreed to admit Norway to membership after long and intricate negotiations limiting Spanish and Portuguese fishing rights in Norwegian waters. But Norweigian voters in a Nov. 1994 referendum rejected E.U. membership. Brundtland resigned in Oct. 1996 and was replaced by Thorbjoern Jagland, but he remained prime minister less than a year. After 1997 elections to the Storting, a right-wing three-party coalition, which controlled only 24 of the 165 seats, formed a government under Christian Democrat Kjell Magne Bondevik. Even Bondevik's three-week leave of absence (to treat depression) in Sept. 1998 failed to shake the stability of Norway's politics. But a March 2000 no-confidence vote toppled the government, replacing it with a Labor-Conservative coalition under Labor's Jens Stoltenberg as prime minister.

Storting elections in Sept. 2001 brought another of western Europe's right-wing victories as Labor made its worst showing since 1924, losing 22 seats. Conservative Kjell Bondevik became Norway's new prime minister. In 2005 Labor rebounded strongly even though Norway's economy was booming because of rising oil prices. Stoltenberg was able to form the first majority government in two decades.

▶ **OMAN**
Sultanate of Oman

• **GEOGRAPHY Location:** southeastern Arabian peninsula. **Boundaries:** Gulf of Oman to N, Arabian Sea to E and S, Yemen to SW, Saudi Arabia to W, United Arab Emirates to NW; detached portion of Oman lies at tip of Musandam peninsula, on Strait of Hormuz. **Total area:** 82,031 sq. mi. (212,460 sq km). **Coastline:** 1,299 mi. (2,092 km). **Comparative area:** slightly smaller than Kansas. **Land use:** 0% arable land; negl. % permanent crops; 100% other. **Major cities:** Muscat (capital); Al-Batinah; Al-Sharquia.

• **PEOPLE Population:** 3,311,640 (July 2008 est.). **Nationality:** noun—Omani(s); adjective—Omani. **Ethnic groups:** Arab, Baluchi, South Asian, African. **Languages:** Arabic (official), English, Baluchi, Urdu, Indian dialects. **Religions:** 75% Ibadhi Muslim, Sunni Muslim, Shi'a Muslim, Hindu.

• **GOVERNMENT Type:** monarchy. **Constitution:** none. **National holiday:** Birthday of the Sultan, Nov. 18. **Head of Government:** Qaboos bin Said, sultan and prime minister (since July 1970). **Structure:** executive—sultan is hereditary monarch; bicameral legislature-advisory powers only; judiciary—traditional Islamic judges in nascent civil court system; supreme court with non-Islamic judges.

• **ECONOMY Monetary unit:** Omani rial. **Budget:** (2007 est.) **income:** $13.82 bil.; **expend.:** $13.67 bil. **G.D.P.:** $61.21 bil., $19,100 per capita (2007 est.). **Chief crops:** dates, limes, bananas, alfalfa, vegetables, cattle, camels; annual fish catch averages 100,000 metric tons. **Natural resources:** crude oil, copper, asbestos, some marble, limestone. **Major industries:** crude oil production and refining, natural gas production, construction. **Labor force:** 920,000 (2002 est.). **Exports:** $22.68 bil. (f.o.b., 2007 est.); petroleum, reexports, fish, metals, textiles. **Imports:** $11 bil. (f.o.b., 2007 est.); machinery, transportation equipment, manufactured goods, food, livestock, lubricants. **Major trading partners:** (2006) **exports:** 23.6% China, 11% Japan, 17.9% South Korea, 10.7% Thailand, 7.7% South Africa, 6.3% United Arab Emirates; **imports:** 22.4% UAE, 16.4% Japan, 8.1% U.S., 5.5% Germany, 4.3% India.

Oman occupies the southeastern corner of Arabia. From ancient times an important center of trade in the Persian Gulf and the Indian Ocean, Oman was dominated by Persia prior to 1750. The principal port, Muscat, was captured by the Portuguese in 1508 and held by them until 1659, when the Ottoman Turks took possession. They were driven out in 1741 by Ahmed ibn Said of Yemen, who consolidated the sultanate of Oman in 1744 and founded the present royal line.

In the early 19th century, Oman was the most powerful state in Arabia, controlling Zanzibar, the southern coast of Iran, and much of Baluchistan (between Pakistan and Iran). Zanzibar was separated from Oman in 1856, and the Persian coast and much of Baluchistan was detached from Oman during the latter half of the 19th century. In 1958 Oman's sole remaining Baluchi possession, the city-state of Gwadar, was ceded to Pakistan in return for a monetary settlement.

Growing British influence was consolidated by the formation of a British protectorate in 1891, reconfirmed in 1951. In the 1950's Britain aided the sultanate in putting down rebellions in the desert interior. The British protectorate ended with Britain's withdrawal from the gulf in 1971. On July 23, 1970, Sultan Said ibn Taimur was overthrown by his son, Sultan Qaboos bin Said, who instituted a national development program and in 1975 defeated a leftist uprising in the western desert.

Petroleum makes up 95 percent of exports. Banking and shipping services are also important. The country is generally barren, with scattered flocks of sheep and camels. In April 1996 Oman joined with Russia and Kazakhstan to establish a consortium with eight oil companies to build a 900 mile pipeline to move oil to Russia's port in the Black Sea. In 2006 a free trade deal with the U.S. was also concluded.

▶ PAKISTAN
Islamic Republic of Pakistan

● **GEOGRAPHY   Location:** southern Asia. **Boundaries:** Afghanistan to N, China to far NE, India to E, Arabian Sea to S, and Iran to W. **Total area:** 310,402 sq. mi. (803,940 sq km). **Coastline:** 650 mi. (1,046 km). **Comparative area:** slightly less than twice the size of California. **Land use:** 28% arable land; 1% permanent crops; 71% other. **Major cities:** Islamabad (capital); Karachi; Lahore; Faisalabad (Lyallpur); Rawalpindi.
● **PEOPLE   Population:** 167,762,040 (July 2008 est.). **Nationality:** noun—Pakistani(s); adjective—Pakistani. **Ethnic groups:** Punjabi, Sindhi, Pashtun (Pathan), Baloch, Muhajir (immigrants from India and their descendants). **Languages:** 48% Punjabi, 12% Sindhi, 10% Siraiki, 8% Pashtu, 8% Urdu (official), 3% Balochi, 2% Hindko, 1% Brahui, English (official and lingua franca of Pakistani elite and most government ministries), 8% Burushaski and other. **Religions:** 97% Muslim (77% Sunni, 20% Shi'a); 3% Christian, Hindu, and other.
● **GOVERNMENT   Type:** federal republic. **Independence:** Aug. 14, 1947 (from U.K.). **Constitution:** Apr. 10, 1973; suspended July 5, 1977; restored Dec. 30, 1985; suspended Oct. 15, 1999, restored Dec. 31, 2002. **National holiday:** Republic Day, Mar. 23. **Heads of Government:** Asif Ali Zardari, president (since Sept. 2008); Syed Yousuf Raza, prime minister (since Mar. 2008). **Structure:** executive—prime minister is head of government; bicameral legislature—dissolved after military takeover; judiciary.
● **ECONOMY   Monetary unit:** Pakistani rupee. **Budget:** (2007 est.) *income:* $23.17 bil.; *expend.:* $29.74 bil. **G.D.P.:** $446.1 bil., $2,600 per capita (2007 est.). **Chief crops:** wheat, rice, sugarcane, cotton; beef, milk, mutton, eggs. **Natural resources:** land, extensive natural gas reserves, limited petroleum, poor quality coal, iron ore. **Major industries:** cotton textiles, food processing. **Labor force:** 49.18 mil.; 42% agriculture, 20% industry, 38% services (2004 est.); 7.5% unemployment (2007 est.); extensive export of labor, mostly to the Middle East, and use of child labor. **Exports:** $20.58 bil. (f.o.b. 2007); cotton, textiles, clothing, rice, leather, carpets. **Imports:** $30.99 bil. (f.o.b. 2007); petroleum, petroleum products, machinery, transportation equipment, cooking oils. **Major trading partners:** (2006) *exports:* 21% U.S., 9% United Arab Emirates, 7.7% Afghanistan, 5.3% China, 5.1% U.K.; *imports:* 13.8% China, 10.5% South Africa, 9.7% United Arab Emirates, 6.5% U.S., 5.7% Japan, 4.7% Kuwait, 4.2% Germany.

Pakistan occupies the heartland of ancient South Asian civilization, in the Indus River valley. Agricultural settlements in that area arose by 3000 B.C., and the great cities at Harappa and Mohenjo-Daro were founded some 500 years later. Indo-European (Aryan) invaders from Central Asia overthrew the ancient civilization around 1500 B.C. and established a new culture that spread throughout Pakistan and northern India. Brahmanism, the religious culture of the early Indo-European invaders, gave rise to Buddhism and Jainism around the sixth century B.C., and evolved into Hinduism in the early centuries A.D. The Indus valley was incorporated into the empire of Alexander the Great, c. 350 B.C., and then into the Mauryan empire of Asoka, which by the third century B.C. controlled all of South Asia except for the southernmost portion of India.

Under various rulers the Indus Valley and the areas to its northwest were a great center of Buddhist culture until the beginning of the eighth century, when the area fell to Muslim Arab invaders. Thereafter, Islam was firmly established throughout the region. But Baluchistan and the Northwest Frontier region became culturally allied to the Persian civilization of Iran and Afghanistan, while Sind and the Punjab were more closely akin to the culture of northern India.

Northern Pakistan was incorporated into the empire of Mahmud of Gazni in the 11th century, and fell to the Mongols in the 13th century. The Indus River became the boundary between the Mongol Inkhanate of Persia and the sultanate of Delhi. The region was conquered by Timur Leng at the end of the 14th century, and after the fall of the Timurid empire was divided between the kingdoms of Sind and Multan, in southern and central Pakistan, and the sultanate of Delhi, in the Punjab. All of Pakistan and northern India was reunited after 1526, when the conquests of Babur established the Mogul empire.

The expansion of British power in India during the 18th century left Pakistan largely untouched; the area was divided among various states, including Sind, the Punjab, Kashmir, and the western reaches of Rajputana. In the first half of the 19th century, British rule extended to the northwest; after the defeat of the Indian Mutiny of 1857, the entire Indus valley came under British rule. Sind and the Punjab were ruled directly by the British, while the native states were ruled as British protectorates.

From the beginning of the 20th century, various nationalist movements arose throughout British India. The Muslim League, under the leadership of Mohammad Ali Jinnah after 1916, advocated greater popular political participation, dominion status for India, and a strong Muslim voice in Indian administration. Muslims and Hindus were allied in the Non-Cooperation movement of the 1920's, but the alliance soon broke down and degenerated into communal frictions. With growing power of the Congress party in Hindu areas and Gandhi's civil disobedience movement in the 1930's, Jinnah's Muslim League charted an increasingly separate course and called for the creation of a separate Muslim state in 1940.

With the British withdrawal from India in 1947, Hindus in the Muslim majority areas of the Indus valley and in East Bengal fled to Hindu northern India, while Muslims in Hindu areas fled in the opposite direction. These massive population movements were accompanied by widespread violence leading to the loss of hundreds of thousands of lives. Jinnah, the father of modern Pakistan, died in 1948. Pakistan, encompassing Sind, the Punjab, Baluchistan, the Northwest Frontier Territories, part of Jammu and Kashmir, and adjacent areas in the west and East Bengal in the east, was granted dominion status within the British Commonwealth in 1947, becoming an independent republic in 1956.

Pakistan joined the Central Treaty Organization and became allied with the West, in contrast to the Soviet-leaning nonalignment of India. In 1958 Gen. Mohammad Ayub Khan seized power in a coup; he was elected president in 1960 and re-elected in 1965. Following border clashes with India in 1962, Pakistan entered into friendly relations with China, which also had engaged in border warfare with India. Ayub Khan resigned as president in early 1969 after failing to put down widespread demonstrations in East Pakistan. A new government was formed under Gen. Yahya Khan, and martial law was declared. A parliamentary victory by the East Pakistani Awami League in December 1970 led to civil war and the secession of East Pakistan in 1971 (see "Bangladesh").

India's intervention on behalf of East Bengal had led to war on a western front with Pakistan. On July 3, 1972, India and Pakistan agreed to a mutual withdrawal of troops and entered into negotiations designed to settle border disputes and other problems. Diplomatic relations between India and Pakistan were resumed in 1976.

The elections of 1970 that had precipitated the civil war also brought Zulfikar Ali Bhutto to the presidency. He remained in office until July 1977, when he was overthrown in a military coup led by Gen. Mohammad Zia ul-Haq. He was convicted of complicity in a 1974 political murder and hanged in April 1979. Under Pres. Zia, Pakistan moved toward the implementation of Islamic law in parallel with the constitutional law of Pakistan's parliamentary system. In 1986 Bhutto's daughter, Benazir Bhutto, returned to Pakistan from exile in Europe to organize opposition parties against Pres. Zia, leading to widespread rioting.

On Aug. 17, 1988, Pres. Zia was killed in an airplane crash. From 1988 to 1999 the position of prime minister alternated between Benazir Bhutto as head of the Pakistan People's Party and Nawaz Sharif as leader of the Muslim League, each accusing the other in turn of tyranny and corruption, amidst endless tension with India over Jammu-Kashmir. The latter struggle lay at the root of the nuclear-test rivalry in May 1998, after which the prime ministers, Vajpayee and Sharif, attempted to lower the political temperature while not appearing to "cave in" to the other. Sharif's July 1999 agreement in Washington D.C. to withdraw support for Muslims in Kashmir made it appear that he was the one to blink first.

Sharif's dismissal of Gen. Pervez Musharraf over the army's support of Kashmir rebels led to a military coup and Sharif's trial on corruption charges which ended with a guilty verdict and life imprisonment. Musharraf pledged a return to civilian rule, but in June 2001 appointed himself president.

Musharraf has had to walk a delicate line after the Sept. 11th attacks on the U.S. Backing the U.S. in Afghanistan, he fired his three top generals for their ties to the Taliban and arrested leaders of demonstrations against the war in Afghanistan. He denounced a murderous Pakistani Muslim attack on the Indian Parliament. In Oct. 2002, Pakistan held its first elections since 1997, with Musharraf's party gaining a plurality. In the same month both India and Pakistan announced troop withdrawals from their borders (though not the Kashmir border). And in May 2003 Musharraf reciprocated India's decision to restore diplomatic and rail links between the two countries. By Feb. 2004, both agreed to a "road map" for comprehensive peace negotiations. Musharraf survived a Dec. 2003 assassination attempt and then agreed to step down as army chief and to remain as president until 2007 elections. But those elections were not scheduled and his popularity continued to wane dramatically, leading to the possibility of an alliance with Benazir Bhutto who returned from exile in Oct. 2007 to run for office. She was assassinated in December, and her husband was later elected after Musharraf resigned. (See "Major News Stories.")

► **PALAU**
Republic of Palau
● **GEOGRAPHY** **Location:** more than 200 islands, in a chain about 400 mi. (650 km) long, in western central Pacific Ocean; Koror 71°21'N, 134°31'E. **Boundaries:** Guam 720 mi. (1,160 km) to NE, Federated States of Micronesia to E, island of New Guinea to S, Philippines 530 mi. (850 km) to NW. **Total area:** 177 sq. mi. (458 sq km). **Coastline:** 944 mi. (1,519 km). **Comparative area:** slightly more than 2.5 times size of Washington, D.C. **Land use:** 22% arable land; 0% permanent crops; 78% other. **Major cities:** Melekeok (capital), Koror, Babelthuap.
● **PEOPLE** **Population:** 21,093 (2008 est.). **Nationality:** noun—Palauan(s); adjective—Palauan. **Ethnic groups:** composite of Polynesian, Malayan, and Melanesian races. **Languages:** English (official) in all 16 states; Palauan (official) in 13 states; Sonsoralese, Angaur, Japanese, Tobi in one state each. **Religions:** Christian (49% Roman Catholic, Seventh-Day Adventist, Jehovah's Witness, the Assembly of God, the Liebenzell Mission, and Latter-Day Saints), 33% Modekngei (indigenous faith).
● **GOVERNMENT** **Type:** constitutional government in free association with the U.S.; the Compact of Free Association entered into force Oct. 1, 1994. **Independence:** Oct. 1, 1994 (from U.S.-administered U.N. Trusteeship). **Constitution:** Jan. 1, 1981. **National holiday:** Constitution Day, July 9. **Heads of Government:** Tommy E. Remengesau, Jr., president (since Jan. 2001). **Structure:** executive—president and vice president popularly elected; legislative—bicameral legislature; judicial—Supreme Court headed by chief justice.
● **ECONOMY** **Monetary unit:** U.S. dollar. **Budget:** (2005 est.) *income:* $72.07 mil.; *expend.:* $72.43 mil. **G.D.P.:** $125 mil., $7,600 per capita (2005 est.). **Chief crops:** coconuts, copra, cassava, sweet potatoes. **Livestock:** N.A. **Natural resources:** forests, minerals (especially gold), marine products, deep-seabed minerals. **Major industries:** tourism, craft items (shell, wood, pearl), some commercial fishing and agriculture. **Labor force:** 9,777 (2005). **Exports:** $5.882 mil. (f.o.b., 2004); trochus, tuna, copra, handicrafts. **Imports:** $107.3 mil. (f.o.b., 2004). **Major trading partners:** (2006) *exports:*

U.S., Japan, Singapore; *imports:* U.S., Singapore, Japan, South Korea.

The first inhabitants of Palau (or Belau) probably arrived from Indonesia and the Philippines about 1500 B.C. The first European to visit the area was Ferdinand Magellan, in 1521. However, it was the British who dominated trade to Palau until 1885, when Pope Leo XIII acknowledged Spain's claims to the Carolines. Spain controlled Palau from 1885 to 1899, when it sold the territory to Germany. The Germans introduced coconut planting and phosphate mining, and introduced sanitary measures that arrested the deadly epidemics of dysentery and influenza, which over 120 years had reduced the population from 40,000 to 4,000.

Japan occupied Palau in 1914, and over the next 30 years increased the mining, agriculture, and fishing industries. In 1938, Palau became a closed military area, and it was the site of heavy fighting during World War II. On July 18, 1947, the United Nations Trusteeship Council placed the Trust Territory of the Pacific Islands, including Palau, under U.S. authority. This trusteeship ended on Oct. 1, 1994, when the Compact of Free Association with the United States (approved by the voters of Palau) went into effect, making Palau an independent country in association with the United States. The United States continues to provide for Palau's defense and to provide aid. In return, the United States has the right to dock military vessels (including nuclear-powered vessels) in the islands for 50 years, and will consult closely on economic and environmental matters.

▶ **PANAMA**
Republic of Panama

● **GEOGRAPHY Location:** southern Central America. **Boundaries:** Caribbean Sea to N, Colombia to E, Pacific Ocean to S, Costa Rica to W. **Total area:** 30,193 sq. mi. (78,200 sq km). **Coastline:** 1,546 mi. (2,490 km). **Comparative area:** slightly smaller than South Carolina. **Land use:** 7% arable land; 2% permanent crops; 91% other. **Major cities:** Panamá (Panama City—capital); Colón; David.
● **PEOPLE Population:** 3,292,693 (2008 est.). **Nationality:** noun—Panamanian(s); adjective— Panamanian. **Ethnic groups:** 70% mestizo, 14% Amerindian and mixed (West Indian), 10% white, 6% Amerindian. **Languages:** Spanish (official), 14% speak English as native tongue; many Panamanians are bilingual. **Religions:** 85% Roman Catholic, 15% Protestant.
● **GOVERNMENT Type:** constitutional democracy. **Independence:** Nov. 3, 1903 (from Colombia); became independent from Spain Nov. 28, 1821. **Constitution:** Oct. 11, 1972, with major reforms adopted in Apr. 1983 and in 1994. **National holiday:** Independence Day, Nov. 3. **Head of Government:** Martin Torrijos, president (since Sept. 2004). **Structure:** executive—president, two vice presidents, cabinet; unicameral legislature; judiciary.
● **ECONOMY Monetary unit:** balboa. **Budget:** (2007) *income:* $5.206 bil.; *expend.:* $5.089 bil. **G.D.P.:** $29.14 bil., $9,000 per capita (2007 est.). **Chief crops:** bananas, rice, sugarcane, coffee, corn; livestock, fishing. **Natural resources:** copper, mahogany forests, shrimp. **Major industries:** manufacturing and construction, petroleum refining, brewing, cement and other construction material. **Labor force:** 1.471 mil. (2007 est.); 15% agriculture, 18% industry, 67% services (2006 est.). **Exports:** $9.662 bil. (f.o.b., 2007 est.); bananas, shrimp, clothing, sugar, coffee. **Imports:**

$12.1 bil. (f.o.b., 2007 est.); capital goods, crude oil, foodstuffs. **Major trading partners:** (2006) *exports:* 39.8% U.S., 8.1% Spain, 6.7% Netherlands, 6.5% Sweden, 4.5% Costa Rica; *imports:* 27% U.S., 10% Netherlands, 5.1% Costa Rica, 4.7% Japan.

The Spanish first arrived in what is now Panama in 1501. Vasco Nuñez de Balboa returned in 1510, and Pedro Arias Dávila founded the City of Panama in 1519. Panama became attached to the viceroyalty of New Granada after 1739 and left the Spanish empire with the rest of New Granada in 1821, becoming a part of Gran Colombia. The first canal company proposing the construction of a transisthmian passageway was formed in 1825-26. The completion of a U.S.-financed railway from Colón to Panama City by 1855 enhanced Panama's importance as a transoceanic passage.

Panamanian nationalists waged a "War of a Thousand Days" against the Bogotá government between 1899 and 1902. In 1903 Panama gained independence from Colombia with U.S. complicity. Within a month Panamanian officials accepted an agreement with the United States that created a canal zone under the control of the U.S. government "in perpetuity," and the Panama Canal was completed and opened in 1914.

Panama experienced protectorate status under U.S. control after independence insofar as the United States "guaranteed the independence" of Panama. The United States explicitly upheld its right of unilateral military intervention in Panama when in 1918 it sent troops there without the permission of the Panamanian government. The 1936 Hull-Alvaro Treaty eliminated protectorate status, and the U.S. dropped its claim to a right of intervention in the cities of Panama and Colón.

In 1968 a power struggle between Pres. Arnulfo Arias and the Panamanian National Guard led to the ouster of the president. A National Guard junta took control of the government, and Col. (later Gen.) Omar Torrijos Herrera became the ruler of the country the following year. In 1972 a new assembly under Torrijos's control offered him the title of Jefe Maximo (chief executive) in addition to drafting a new constitution for the country. Torrijos constructed a populist following through the creation of housing projects, a new labor code, an agrarian reform, and an increase in tax rates imposed on foreign banana-interests.

The Panamanian government and the U.S. concluded a new canal treaty in 1977, the key provisions of which included integration of the Canal Zone with the rest of Panamanian territory and full Panamanian control of the canal in 2000. In 1981 Omar Torrijos died in an air accident.

In 1988 the head of the military and de facto ruler of the country, Gen. Mañuel Noriega, was indicted in the U.S. on narcotics charges. But Noriega refused to submit to demands by the U.S. and by Panamanian president Eric Arturo Delvalle for his resignation. Delvalle was forced to go into hiding. The U.S. responded by freezing Panamanian assets.

In May 1989 Gen. Noriega annulled election results that showed him losing to Guillermo Endara and assumed the role of dictator. After an unsuccessful coup attempt, the United States invaded Panama on December 20, captured Noriega, and brought him to Miami, where he was convicted on narcotics charges. Endara was restored to the presidency and in December 1990 U.S. forces helped put down a rebellion led by Noriega's former chief of the national police.

Endara's government was often accused of corruption but he left power peacefully in 1994. He helped to arrange honest elections that saw U.S.-educated businessman Ernesto Perez Balladares come to power with promises of improving the economy as Panama prepared to take over control of the canal. His free market reforms and a loosening of trade barriers have brought strong growth in G.D.P. An August 1998 referendum turned down (by 64 percent) Perez' seeking a second term. Voters in May 1999 chose Mireya Moscoso de Grubar, widow of three-time president Arnulfo Arias, over Martin Torrijos, son of the dictator who negotiated the 1977 Canal Treaty with the U.S., as Panama's new president. But Torrijos won in May 2004. A free trade deal with the U.S. was signed in 2006.

▶ PAPUA NEW GUINEA
Independent State of Papua New Guinea
● **GEOGRAPHY Location:** eastern section of island of New Guinea and about 600 smaller islands in Bismarck Archipelago (New Britain, New Ireland, and Manus) and northern part of Solomon Islands. Port Moresby 9°30′S, 147°07′E. **Boundaries:** Bismarck Sea to N, Solomon Sea to E, Australia to S, and Indonesia to W. **Total area:** 178,259 sq. mi. (461,690 sq km). **Coastline:** 3,202 mi. (5,152 km). **Comparative area:** slightly larger than California. **Land use:** negl.% arable land; 1% permanent crops; 99% other. **Major cities:** Port Moresby (administrative capital).
● **PEOPLE Population:** 5,931,769 (July 2008 est.). **Nationality:** noun—Papua New Guinean(s); adjective—Papua New Guinean. **Ethnic groups:** predominantly Melanesian and Papuan; some Negrito, Micronesian, and Polynesian. **Languages:** 820 indigenous languages; English spoken by 1%-2%, pidgin English widespread, Motu spoken in Papua region. **Religions:** 22% Roman Catholic, 16% Lutheran, 28% other Christian, 34% indigenous beliefs.
● **GOVERNMENT Type:** parliamentary democracy. **Independence:** Sept. 16, 1975 (from U.N. trusteeship under Australian administration). **Constitution:** Sept. 16, 1975. **National holiday:** Independence Day, Sept. 16. **Heads of Government:** Paulius Matane, governor-general (since June 2004); Sir Michael T. Somare, prime minister (since Aug. 2002). **Structure:** executive—British monarch (represented by governor general), chief of state, prime minister; unicameral legislature; judiciary.
● **ECONOMY Monetary unit:** kina. **Budget:** (2007 est.) *income:* $2.209 bil.; *expend.:* $1.994 bil. **G.D.P.:** $16.56 bil., $2,900 per capita (2007 est.). **Chief crops:** cocoa, coffee, coconuts, rubber, palm kernels; pigs, chickens. **Natural resources:** gold, copper, silver, natural gas, timber. **Major industries:** copra crushing, palmoil processing, plywood processing. **Labor force:** 3.557 mil., 85% agriculture. **Exports:** $4.553 bil. (f.o.b., 2007 est.); gold, copper ore, oil, logs, coffee, palm oil, cocoa, lobster. **Imports:** $2.269 bil. (f.o.b 2007 est.); machinery and transport equipment, manufactured goods, food, fuels, chemicals. **Major trading partners:** (2006) *exports:* 30.2% Australia, 8.2% Japan, 5.7% China; *imports:* 52% Australia, 12.6% Singapore, 5.9% China, 4.3% Japan.

The island of New Guinea, the world's second-largest, was settled thousands of years ago by waves of Papuan and Melanesian migrants who developed large numbers of linguistically diverse and mutually hostile tribes of hunters and small cultivators. In the 19th century, the island was divided between the Dutch (to the west, in what is now the Indonesian province of Irian Jaya), Germany, and the British. The German sector was occupied by Australia in 1914 and administered under a League of Nations mandate after WWI.

Japanese attempts to occupy New Guinea in 1942 met with only partial success. In a series of counteroffensives, the Allies regained control over the entire island by mid-1944.

Beginning in 1949 the former German and British colonies were administered by Australia under a U.N. mandate. The territories were made self-governing in 1973 and achieved full independence as Papua New Guinea on Sept. 16, 1975. The nation maintains close ties with Australia. In 1989 a rebellion on the mineral-rich island of Bougainville closed a large Australian-run copper mine, led to the deaths of many people and frightened away foreign investors.

An inexplicable decision to recognize Taiwan rather than mainland China, made in 1999 by prime minister Bill Skate, brought domestic (as well as Chinese) opposition, Skate's resignation, and the designation of Sir Mekere Morauta as the new prime minister. He immediately reversed the Taiwan agreement. In Feb. 2000 the government began a program of privatizing all state-owned enterprise within three years. In 2002 elections, violence kept the country without a government for three months until three-time prime minister Michael Somare was able to form a government. In recent years Australia has increased aid significantly and is providing police protection to halt continuing violence caused by extreme poverty among 85 percent of the population. Somare won another term in 2007, vowing to fight rampant crime and corruption, and to fight the spread of AIDS.

▶ PARAGUAY
Republic of Paraguay
● **GEOGRAPHY Location:** landlocked country in central South America. **Boundaries:** Bolivia to N, Brazil to E, Argentina to S and W. **Total area:** 157,046 sq. mi. (406,750 sq km). **Coastline:** none. **Comparative area:** slightly smaller than California. **Land use:** 6% arable land; 0% permanent crops; 94% other. **Major cities:** Asunción (capital); Ciudad del Este (formerly Presidente Stroessner); Pedro Juan Caballero; Encarnación; Villarrica.
● **PEOPLE Population:** 6,831,306 (July 2008 est.). **Nationality:** noun—Paraguayan(s); adjective—Paraguayan. **Ethnic groups:** 95% mestizo (mixed white and Amerindian). **Languages:** Spanish (official), Guaraní. **Religions:** 90% Roman Catholic, Mennonite and other Protestant denominations.
● **GOVERNMENT Type:** constitutional republic. **Independence:** May 14, 1811 (from Spain). **Constitution:** June 20, 1992. **National holiday:** Independence Day, May 14. **Head of Government:** Fernando Lugo, president (since Aug., 2008). **Structure:** president heads executive; bicameral legislature (Senate, Chamber of Deputies); judiciary.
● **ECONOMY Monetary unit:** guarani. **Budget:** (2007 est.) *income:* $2.268 bil.; *expend.:* $2.469 bil. **G.D.P.:** $26.55 bil., $4,000 per capita (2007 est.). **Chief crops:** sugarcane, soybeans, cotton, wheat; beef, pork; timber. **Natural resources:** iron ore, manganese, limestone, hydropower, timber. **Major industries:** sugar, cement, textiles, beverages. **Labor force:** 2.735 mil. (2007 est.); 31% agriculture, 17% industry, 52% services (2007); 11.4% unemployment (2007 est.). **Exports:** $6.898 bil. (f.o.b., 2007 est.); cotton, soybeans, timber, vegetable oils, feed, tung oil. **Imports:** $7.012 bil. (f.o.b., 2007 est.); consumer goods, tobacco, raw

materials, fuels. **Major trading partners:** (2006) *exports:* 22% Uruguay, 17.2% Brazil, 11.9% Russia, 8.8% Argentina, 6.9% Chile; *imports:* 27% China, 20% Brazil, 13.6% Argentina, 8.3% Japan, 6.4% U.S.

When Europeans arrived in what is now Paraguay in the early 16th century, they encountered various groups of indigenous peoples. The Spanish entered into alliances with the Tupian semisedentary Guaraní against the nomadic Guaycuru Indians in the west of the region. Asunción, founded in 1537, was little more than a Spanish defense outpost against the Portuguese and a trading stopover between the silver mines of Potosí and Buenos Aires.

From early in the 17th century, the Jesuits established an extensive network of missions in the southern portion of the colony, and a rivalry grew between the Jesuits and the elites of Asunción over who would determine the colony's social and economic structure. The isolation of the settlers from the mainstream of Spanish colonial society combined with the lack of valuable resources led to the evolution of a relatively egalitarian social structure. The political elite of Asunción deposed Spanish authority in 1811, and Paraguayan independence was declared in 1813.

Authoritarian rule marked the period from independence until 1870. José Gaspar Rodríguez de Francia was declared ruler for life in 1816 and remained in power until his death in 1840. A period of political turmoil followed but was resolved in the election of Carlos Antonio López in 1844; in 1857 he was named president for life. López chose his son Francisco Solano López to succeed him in office in 1862. He intervened in a Brazilian attempt to control the fate of Uruguay, beginning the Paraguayan War, or the War of the Triple Alliance (Brazil, Argentina, Uruguay) from 1865 to 1870. The war was catastrophic for Paraguay, reducing the population from 450,000 to 220,000; and Paraguay lost 60,000 square miles of territory while being saddled with a war debt of 19 million gold pesos ($200,000,000), later dropped as unrealistic.

After the war the Colorado and Liberal parties developed, although the real political distinctions were dependent more on individuals and families than political ideology. Colorado-party general Bernardino Caballero, backed by Brazil, was the power behind the scenes of frequent changes in government personnel between 1874 and 1904. The Liberals, backed by Argentina, were in power from 1904 until 1936.

After 18 years of authoritarian military rule, Gen. Alfredo Stroessner, with the backing of Colorado party factions, began his rule in 1954. Stroessner held power until 1989, when Gen. Andrés Rodríguez overthrew him. Nevertheless, the Colorados maintained their hold on the presidency in hotly contested elections in 1993, when Juan Carlos Wasmosy gained 40 percent of the vote. However, a strong showing by the opposition Authentic Radical Liberal Party (PLRA) and National Encounter prevented a Colorado majority in Congress. A complex political struggle between Pres. Wasmosy and Lino Oviedo, one of the generals who overthrew Stroessner, led to Oviedo's imprisonment. His ally, Raul Cubas Grau, won the 1998 election by vowing to have Oviedo share power even from prison. Three days after taking office in August, however, Cubas released the popular general, causing an outburst of hostility among Congressional leaders.

In March 1999, the vice president was assassinated, Congress accusing Cubas and Oviedo. Impeached the next day, Cubas remanded Oviedo to state custody but refused to appear at his own trial in the Senate. Oviedo fled to Argentina, Cubas to Brazil. Congress named the president of the Senate, Luis Gonzalez Macchi, as president. Gonzalez appointed a cabinet with four opposition members among the 10, the first coalition since 1946. A coup attempt by Oviedo allies was foiled in May 2000. Three weeks later, Oviedo was arrested in Brazil.

In Feb. 2003 the senate tried, but failed, to impeach Gonzalez on corruption charges. Still the Colorado party candidate Nicanor Duarte Frutos won the presidential election in April and won high marks for his crackdown on corruption, although crime remains a serious problem, especially a sudden increase in high-profile kidnapping. The presidential election of April 2008 brought down the Colorado party for the first time in decades. The winner, Fernando Lugo, was formerly a priest and a bishop who has promised land reform.

▶ **PERU**
Republic of Peru
● **GEOGRAPHY   Location:** western coast of South America. **Boundaries:** Ecuador, Colombia to N, Brazil, Bolivia to E, Chile to S, Pacific Ocean to W. **Total area:** 496,224 sq. mi. (1,285,220 sq km). **Coastline:** 1,546 mi. (2,414 km). **Comparative area:** slightly smaller than Alaska. **Land use:** 3% arable land; negl. % permanent crops; 97% other. **Major cities:** Lima (capital); Arequipa; Trujillo; Chiclayo; Callao.
● **PEOPLE   Population:** 29,180,899 (July 2008 est.). **Nationality:** noun—Peruvian(s); adjective—Peruvian. **Ethnic groups:** 45% Amerindian, 37% mestizo, 15% white, 3% black, Japanese, Chinese, and other. **Languages:** Spanish and Quechua (official), Aymara. **Religions:** 81% Roman Catholic, 2.7% other Christian, 16% none or other.
● **GOVERNMENT   Type:** constitutional republic. **Independence:** July 28, 1821 (from Spain). **Constitution:** Dec. 31, 1993. **National holiday:** Independence Day, July 28. **Heads of Government:** Alan García Pérez, president (since July 2006); Jorge del Castillo Gálvez, prime minister (since July 2006). **Structure:** executive; unicameral legislature; judiciary.
● **ECONOMY   Monetary unit:** nuevo sol. **Budget:** (2007 est.) *income:* $30.35 bil.; *expend.:* $29.8 bil. **G.D.P.:** $217.5 bil., $7,600 per capita (2007 est.). **Chief crops:** coffee, cotton, sugarcane, rice, poultry, meat, wool; fish. **Natural resources:** copper, silver, gold, petroleum, timber. **Major industries:** mining of metals, petroleum, fishing. **Labor force:** 9.419 mil. (2007); 9% agriculture, 18% industry, 73% services (2001 est.); 9.4% unemployment (2002 est.). **Exports:** $27.14 bil. (f.o.b., 2007 est.); copper, zinc, gold, petroleum. **Imports:** $18.75 bil. (f.o.b., 2007 est.); machinery, transport equipment, foodstuffs, petroleum. **Major trading partners:** *exports:* 24.1% U.S., 9.6% China, 7.1% Switzerland, 6.8% Canada, 6% Chile, 5.2% Japan; *imports:* 16.5% U.S., 10.3% China, 10.3% Brazil, 7.2% Ecuador, 6.1% Colombia, 5.3% Chile.

Peru was the site of the Inca empire. The Incas had extended their control over most of the Andean region by the late 15th century. The civilization was advanced in terms of its ability to provide for the welfare of its subjects and was in possession of sophisticated knowledge in a number of fields, including medicine. By the time of the arrival of the Spanish conqueror Francisco Pizarro in 1532, the empire was already in decline, and a combination of plague and civil war in the decade prior to the appearance of Europeans no doubt made the empire more vulnerable to Spanish conquest. Inca resistance to Spanish domination was not quelled until the execution of Tupac Amarú in 1571. European-borne diseases such as smallpox and measles devastated the Indian population.

Because of the great wealth of precious metals discovered by the Spanish and the adaptability of a sedentary indigenous civilization to the imposition of Spanish imperial control, Peru quickly became a major focal point of Spanish colonialism; they founded Lima in 1535. The viceroyalty of Peru, established in 1544, originally served as the political and administrative nerve center of Spanish colonization of South America. For nearly two centuries, Lima was the seat of power and wealth for the whole region. Peru was "liberated" by Simón Bolívar and José de San Martín in 1821 when Bolívar's army defeated the royalist forces at the battles of Junín and Ayacucho.

In the 40 years after independence, the presidency changed hands 35 times, and the country generated at least 15 different constitutions. Only four of the presidents of the period were constitutionally chosen, and the vast majority were military figures. In 1829 Peru tried and failed to annex Ecuador; in the 1830's an attempt at political federation between Peru and Bolivia collapsed with the Chilean invasion of 1839.

A political movement in favor of civilian rule, the Civilistas, began to organize by the 1860's. Chile defeated Peru in the War of the Pacific (1879-83), and Chileans occupied Lima and its port city of Callao for two years. The Peruvian government was deeply in debt after the war, resulting in the loss of ownership of much of Peru's infrastructure and natural resources to foreigners.

Peru experienced a period of civilian leadership between 1895 and 1930. Pres. Augusto B. Leguía (1908-12, 1919-30) extended his rule in an extraconstitutional manner until 1930, when Col. Luis Sánchez Cerro seized power; he ruled until his assassination in 1933. Gen. Oscar Benavides succeeded Cerro and managed to restore confidence in the economy. In 1939 civilian banker Manuel Prado was elected to the presidency, and the military allowed him to complete his term in office, which expired in 1945. During Prado's administration, Peru went to war with Ecuador and was victorious, seizing a great deal of territory.

Víctor Raúl Haya de la Torre founded Peru's most prominent political party, the American Popular Revolutionary Alliance (APRA), in 1924. As initiated, the party put forward an "anti-imperialist" platform aiming at nationalization of land and reconstruction of society in favor of oppressed people. Haya de la Torre was apparently fraudulently deprived of a presidential electoral victory in 1931. The following year Apristas (APRA supporters) seized Trujillo and killed some military personnel. By way of revenge, the army massacred 6,000 Apristas. The result was a continuing enmity between the Peruvian armed forces and the APRA party lasting until the 1980's. Although APRA clearly had majority support, the party was not allowed to take power until 1985.

The Peruvian military, led by Gen. Juan Velasco Alvarado, seized power in 1968 and embarked upon a course of reform that included the nationalization of Standard Oil's holdings. The Peruvian military took steps to restructure economic and political power by joining the Andean Pact and undermining the power of the traditional agricultural elite in the country by sponsoring an agrarian reform that mobilized the peasants.

The presidency of Peru returned to civilian leadership under Fernando Belaúnde Terry (1980-85). In 1985, the military allowed the APRA presidential candidate, Alan García, to take office. García promised to spend no more than 10 percent of the country's export earnings on payment of Peru's huge outstanding foreign debt and he was popular during his first years in office. But his public support was undermined by a growing insurgency sponsored by the Sendero Luminoso ("Shining Path") Maoist guerrillas and by runaway inflation.

On June 10, 1990, political novice Alberto Fujimori, the son of Japanese immigrants, defeated the well-known writer Mario Vargas Llosa for the presidency. Throughout 1991 and 1992, Shining Path's influence spread, demoralizing and almost paralyzing the government, and at a cost of 25,000 lives. But in April 1992, Fujimori implemented a "zero tolerance" policy toward terrorism, dissolving the legislature and proclaiming martial law. The capture in September of Abimael Guzmán Reynoso, Path's founder-leader, broke the back of the insurgency. The movement lived on, but diminished in numbers.

Meanwhile, economically, Fujimori pursued free-market reforms, taming runaway inflation and privatizing state-run dinosaurs, so that by 1994 the Peruvian economy was growing at a rate of 12 percent, fastest in the world. In April of that year, Fujimoro was elected to a second term with 64 percent of the vote.

The dramatic liberation in April 1997 of 600 prisoners held for ransom in the Japanese ambassador's compound by another radical terrorist group maintained the president's repute. In Nov. 1997, Peru completed negotiations with Ecuador (the treaty being signed in Oct. of 1998) ending a 50-year old border conflict. But all these achievements were accompanied by a rather hamhanded authoritarian streak which cost Fujimori much esteem. In elections for Congress, held in April 2000, his Peru 2000 party carried a plurality of seats but he himself just failed of a majority in the presidential race. A week before the May 28 run-off, his remaining opponent withdrew, claiming the election as a fraud; the final tally brought Fujimori only 51 percent. His July 28 inauguration was marred by serious rioting, with six dead and many public buildings in Lima burnt. While in Japan, Fujimori resigned, but Congress refused to accept, so it could remove him for abandoning office and dereliction of duty.

In June 2001, in a close run-off against former president Alan García, Alejandro Toledo was elected president, the first Indian elected president in Peru's history. He was able to decentralize the government in 2002 and sucessfully prosecute Fujimori's right-hand man, but strikes by teachers and farmers in 2003 led to a state of emergency and the use of troops to bring order. In 2003 Peru joined the free trade group Mercosur, the last Shining Path leader, "Marcelo," was captured, and the Truth and Reconciliation Commission published its report documenting the killings in the 1980's. In a surprising comeback, Alan García won the election of 2006 and began an economic program that helped grow the economy and tame inflation. But his popularity declined as protests in the poorer sections of the country grew in size.

Drug trafficking and organized crime remained serious concerns that García tried to attack.

▶ PHILIPPINES
Republic of the Philippines

• **GEOGRAPHY** **Location:** archipelago of some 7,100 islands about 500 mi. (800 km) off southeastern Asia; about 1,100 mi. (2,800 km) from N to S and 650 mi. (1,684 km) from W to E; Luzon in N and Mindanao in S account for 66% of land area. Manila 14°36'N, 120°59'E. **Boundaries:** Luzon Strait to N, Philippine Sea to E, Celebes Sea to S, Sulu Sea to SW, and South China Sea to W. **Total area:** 115,830 sq. mi. (300,000 sq km). **Coastline:** 22,554 mi. (36,289 km). **Comparative area:** slightly larger than Arizona. **Land use:** 18% arable land; 15% permanent crops; 67% other. **Major cities:** Manila (capital); Quezon City; Davao City; Caloocan City; Cebu City.

• **PEOPLE** **Population:** 92,681,453 (July 2008 est.). **Nationality:** noun—Filipino(s); adjective—Philippine. **Ethnic groups:** 91.5% Christian Malay, 4% Muslim Malay, 1.5% Chinese, 3% other. **Languages:** Pilipino (based on Tagalog) and English (both official). **Religions:** 83% Roman Catholic, 9% Protestant, 5% Muslim, 3% Buddhist and other.

• **GOVERNMENT** **Type:** republic. **Independence:** July 4, 1946 (from U.S.). **Constitution:** Feb. 2, 1987, effective Feb. 11, 1987. **National holiday:** Independence Day, June 12. **Head of Government:** Gloria Macapagal-Arroyo, president (since Jan. 2001). **Structure:** executive; bicameral legislature; judiciary.

• **ECONOMY** **Monetary unit:** Philippine peso. **Budget:** (2007 est.) *income:* $23.96 bil.; *expend.:* $25.24 bil. **G.D.P.:** $298.9 bil., $3,300 per capita (2007 est.). **Chief crops:** rice, corn, coconut, sugarcane, bananas; pork, eggs, beef; fish. **Natural resources:** timber, crude oil, nickel, cobalt, silver. **Major industries:** textiles, pharmaceuticals, chemicals. **Labor force:** 36.22 mil. (2007 est.); 35% agriculture, 50% services, 15% industry (2007 est.); 7.3% unemployment (2007). **Exports:** $48.38 bil. (f.o.b., 2007 est.); electronics and telecommunications, machinery and transport, garments. **Imports:** $53.96 bil. (f.o.b., 2007 est.); raw materials and intermediate goods, capital goods, consumer goods, fuels. **Major trading partners:** (2006) *exports:* 18.3% U.S., 16.5% Japan, 10.1% Netherlands, 9.8% China, 7.8% Hong Kong; *imports:* 16.3% U.S., 13.6% Japan, 8.5% Singapore, 8% Taiwan, 7.1% China, 6.1% South Korea, 5.8% South Africa, 4.1% Malaysia, 4.1% Thailand.

The Philippines were anciently settled by various Malayan peoples in several waves of migration from Southeast Asia. Tribal societies coexisted with petty principalities that had trade links to China, the East Indies, and countries in the Indian Ocean. The Philippines were visited by Magellan (who was killed there) in 1521, and Spanish conquest of the islands began in 1564. The Spanish colonial capital at Manila was founded in 1571 and became a key transit point for trade between Mexico and the Far East. Under Spanish rule a majority of Filipinos became Christian except in the southwestern islands, which remained Muslim. The Spanish period was marked by a torpid colonial administration and a rise in the power and wealth of the Catholic church.

In the late 19th century, a nationalist movement led by José Rizal gained a wide following. In 1896 an armed uprising began, led by Emilio Aguinaldo. The 1898 victory of Adm. George Dewey at the Battle of Manila Bay during the Spanish-American War led Spain to cede the Philippines to the U.S. in return for a payment of $20 million. Expecting immediate independence with U.S. support, Aguinaldo declared the islands a republic. When this was not recognized by the U.S., Aguinaldo led a new war for independence, which was bloodily suppressed by American troops in a six-year campaign, 1899-1905.

American policy in the Philippines combined military control with a desire to encourage home rule leading to independence. In 1935 the Commonwealth of the Philippines was established, with Manuel Quezon as its first president, beginning what was conceived of as a 10-year period of controlled autonomy leading to full independence on July 4, 1946. In November 1941, Quezon was reelected to the presidency. On Dec. 8, 1941, Japan attacked Manila and destroyed the American bases there. American and Filipino troops, after weeks of fierce fighting, evacuated the islands in March 1942. The battle to recapture the Philippines began with the Battle of Leyte Gulf in October 1944 and was completed by July 1945.

In April 1946, Manuel Roxas was elected president of the Commonwealth. Independence came as scheduled on July 4 of that year, with the United States retaining military bases by treaty and establishing a special economic relationship with the Philippines. The leftist Hukbalahap Rebellion, originally a partisan campaign against the Japanese, caused severe difficulties for the new nation until it was finally defeated in military campaigns led by Ramon Magsaysay who was elected to the presidency in November 1953.

The early years of independence were marked by some economic development, but also great economic inequality. Most land was held by huge estates, and the economy depended primarily on plantation crops (sugar, copra), mining, and timber. Villagers fleeing the rural subsistence economy poured into the cities, leading to huge slums and a climate of urban poverty and violence.

In 1966 Ferdinand Marcos was elected president on a reform platform. Overwhelmed in the early 1970's by demonstrations, a new leftist guerrilla movement, and a separatist rebellion by Islamic Moros in Mindinao, Marcos declared martial law on Sept. 21, 1972. On Jan. 17, 1973, Marcos promulgated a new constitution giving unprecedented power to the presidency. His wife, Imelda, began to wield considerable influence, and the climate of unrest, poverty, and corruption worsened throughout the 1970's. Martial law was lifted, however, on Jan. 17, 1981, and Marcos was reelected to a new six-year term as president.

The airport assassination of opposition leader Benigno Aquino on his return to the Philippines on Aug. 21, 1983, led to a new phase in opposition to Marcos's rule. In a bitterly contested presidential election in February 1986, Marcos was officially declared the winner over Aquino's widow, Corazon. Mrs. Aquino also declared herself the winner, and her supporters took to the streets in massive anti-Marcos demonstrations. Deserted by key supporters in the military, church, and middle class, Marcos fled the country on Feb. 25, 1986. Mrs. Aquino took office pledging land reform, a new constitution, and a commission to recover the wealth Marcos had plundered.

Under Pres. Aquino the Philippines remained unsettled. Her former ally, Vice Pres. Salvador Laurel, formed an opposition party. Military and political measures aimed at putting down the Communist insurrection yielded mixed results.

The economy of the Philippines continued to be dependent on U.S. and international assistance, and sentiment against the continued presence of U.S. military bases was strong. Ironically, an eruption of Mount Pinatubo in June 1991 caused massive devastation in Luzon and destroyed Clark Air Base. In September, the national legislature voted not to renew the leases on U.S. military bases.

Aquino declined to run for re-election in 1992. Fidel Ramos won the presidency in a field of strong contenders, including Imelda Marcos. Lifted by a coalition that gave him a controlling majority in both houses of Congress after the 1994 elections, Ramos made "national reconciliation" his priority. In 1994 he proclaimed a cease-fire and amnesty for various insurgencies.

The Philippines' robust economic growth was slowed but not crippled by the Asian economic crisis of 1997-98. Pres. Ramos decided not to seek reelection in 1998; in a crowded field of candidates, Joseph Estrada, a popular actor, won the presidential election of May 11, 1998, but the ruling LAKAS party elected the vice-president and took control of the lower house. A series of hostage crises with Muslim rebels on Mindanao punctuated the year 2000 but became overshadowed by serious bribery charges against Pres. Estrada. As the House of Representatives moved toward impeachment, gigantic demonstrations for and against Estrada brought reminders of the fall of Pres. Marcos. When the Senate in Jan. 2001 suspended the president's trial, the protests expanded to a general strike; and when the heads of the armed forces joined the protests, Estrada's days were through. Vice-president Gloria Macapagal Arroyo was sworn in as Estrada resigned. By May the anti-Estrada coalition controlled the Congress and Estrada was under arrest.

The U.S. war on terrorism arrived here in 2001–02 as 4,000 troops landed in Mindanao to train Phillipine soldiers for the fight against the Abu Sayyaf Muslim insurgency. But the insurgency, along with the Moro Islamic Liberation Front and the (Indonesia-based) Jemaah Islamica, did not abate, despite an additional 3,000 American troops. Pres. Arroyo's re-election campaign against an action-movie star was confirmed in June 2004 by a Congressional Committee.

In July 2005 a tape of Pres. Arroyo talking about ballot tampering with an election official during the last campaign caused her popularity to plummet and led to many calls for her resignation. She survived but her government was severely weakened. In February 2006 her declaration of a state of emergency because of an alleged coup attempt was viewed by many as a means to silencing opposition critics.

▶ POLAND
Republic of Poland

• **GEOGRAPHY** **Location:** eastern Europe. **Boundaries:** Baltic Sea to N, Russia and Lithuania to NE, Belarus and Ukraine to E, Czech Republic and Slovakia to S, Germany to W. **Total area:** 120,726 sq. mi. (312,680 sq km). **Coastline:** 305 mi. (491 km). **Comparative area:** slightly smaller than New Mexico. **Land use:** 46% arable land; 1% permanent crops; 53% other. **Major cities:** Warszawa (Warsaw, capital); Lodz; Krakow (Cracow); Wroclaw; Poznan.

• **PEOPLE** **Population:** 38,500,696 (July 2008 est.). **Nationality:** noun—Pole(s); adjective—Polish. **Ethnic groups:** 96.7% Polish, 1.3% German, 0.6% Ukrainian, 0.5% Byelorussian. **Languages:** Polish. **Religions:** 89.8% Roman Catholic (about 75%

practicing), 5% Eastern Orthodox, Protestant, and other.

• **GOVERNMENT** **Type:** republic. **Independence:** Nov. 11, 1918 (independent republic proclaimed) **Constitution:** Oct. 16, 1997; adopted by the National Assembly on Apr. 2, 1997; passed by national referendum May 23, 1997. **National holiday:** Constitution Day, May 3. **Heads of Government:** Lech Kaczynski, president (since Oct. 2005); Donald Tusk, prime minister (since Nov. 2007). **Structure:** executive—prime minister is head of government; bicameral legislature—2 seats in lower house are constitutionally assigned to ethnic German parties; judiciary.

• **ECONOMY** **Monetary unit:** zloty. **Budget:** (2007 est.) *income:* $80.53 bil.; *expend.:* $88.7 bil. **G.D.P.:** $624.6 bil., $16,200 per capita (2007 est.). **Chief crops:** potatoes, milk, cheese, fruits, vegetables, wheat; poultry and eggs; pork, beef. **Natural resources:** coal, sulfur, copper, natural gas, silver. **Major industries:** machine building, iron and steel, extractive industries. **Labor force:** 17.01 mil. (2007 est.); 22.1% industry and construction, 27.5% agriculture, 50.4% services. **Exports:** $137.9 bil. (f.o.b., 2007); manufactured goods, chemicals; machinery and equipment; food and live animals. **Imports:** $150.7 bil. (f.o.b., 2007); manufactured goods, chemicals; machinery and equipment; mineral fuels. **Major trading partners:** (2006) *exports:* 27.2% Germany, 6.6% Italy, 6.2% France, 5.7% U.K., 5.6% Czech Republic, 4.3% Russia; *imports:* 29% Germany, 9.6% Russia, 6.4% Italy, 5.7% Netherlands, 5.4% France.

The Slavic people known as Polonians accepted Christianity in the second half of the 10th century, during the reign of Duke Mieszko, whose close relationship with the papacy prevented the Holy Roman Empire from absorbing Poland. A strong and united Polish kingdom existed under the Piast dynasty until 1370, when the Anjou king of Hungary succeeded to the throne, followed by his daughter Jadwiga, who in 1386 married the grand duke of Lithuania, thus forming the great Commonwealth of Poland Lithuania.

With the end of the Jagellonian line in 1572, the monarchy became elective. With a large nobility, equaling about 10 percent of the population, the monarchy grew weak, and Poland increasingly was subject to foreign intervention. The rise of the expansionist powers of Sweden, Prussia, Russia, and Austria came in part at the expense of the Poles. Jan Sobieski (1624-96), who ruled Poland as John III, saved Vienna from the Turks and briefly revived the Polish monarchy, but Polish royal power ended with his death. In a series of partitions in 1772, 1793, and 1795, Poland was dismembered and finally obliterated as a state.

Napoleon revived a Polish national entity with the Grand Duchy of Warsaw; with Napoleon's fall, the Congress of Vienna re-created a Kingdom of Poland in 1815, under the rule of the czar of Russia. After 1830 Poland was subjected to systematic Russification. The fall of Russia in World War I led to Poland's revival. The Lithuanian Socialist Jósef Pilsudski led Poland in war against the new Bolshevik government of Russia until, in the 1921 Treaty of Riga, Poland emerged with its boundaries restored to those after the partition of 1793. It was ethnically about 70 percent Polish, a triumph for Polish nationalism but the end of Pilsudski's dream of a federation of northeastern Europe. Poland also had the largest Jewish population of any country in Europe.

With a strong legislature and a weak president, the new state seemed to Pilsudski too weak for its own defense. He became a virtual dictator in 1926 and ruled until his death in 1935. After his death a weak parliamentary government was controlled by military officers; the tentative revival of republicanism was halted by Hitler's and Stalin's aggression in 1939, yet another partition of Poland.

Poland was primarily an agricultural country, and the postwar republic attempted land reform, with some success; about 750,000 new private farm holdings were created by 1938. Mining—of coal and copper—was the principal traditional industrial activity in the 20th century, supplemented by extraction of natural gas. In the mid-1930's shipbuilding and railroad construction led the way toward a modern economy.

World War II commenced in September 1939, with attacks on Poland by Germany and the Soviet Union. The war brought severe destruction to Poland and the extermination of virtually its entire Jewish population. A government-in-exile was established in London, but the Soviet Union broke relations with it in 1943 when it requested a Red Cross investigation into the murder of 14,000 Polish officers whose bodies were discovered in Katyn Forest. (The Soviet government acknowledged responsibility for the massacre in 1990.) The Soviets established a puppet government in Lublin in 1944. In August the Red Army paused in its western advance on the outskirts of Warsaw, permitting the Nazis to obliterate the Polish Home Army. On Jan. 1, 1945, the U.S.S.R. recognized the Lublin regime as Poland's government.

By the time of the Allied Powers Conference at Yalta in February 1945, the Red Army was only 40 miles from Berlin and had total control of Poland. The Allies agreed to Stalin's proposal concerning the eastern boundary of Poland (allowing Russia to incorporate the eastern half of the country) and agreed that the government should be constituted from an enlargement of the Lublin regime. At Potsdam in Aug. 1945, Poland's borders were shifted approximately 200 miles westward from the prewar configuration, becoming once again those of the 10th century. The German population was expelled remorselessly.

The free elections promised in the Yalta Agreement were postponed until 1947, by which time a Communist victory could be assured. In 1948 the Socialists were forcibly merged into the Communist party; in 1949 Premier Boleslaw Bierut requested that Soviet general Konstantin Rokossovski be appointed minister of defense and commander in chief of the Polish army. All cultural periodicals and all writers' and artists' associations were taken over by the Communist party.

But there was little collectivization of Polish agriculture or forced industrialization on the Stalinist model. Intellectuals, bolstered by the Catholic church (which deeply resented a 1953 law requiring government approval for appointment of bishops), questioned the regime with some boldness. In 1956 both Bierut and Party Secretary Minc died, and Wladislaw Gomulka was elected party chairman in Oct. 1956. As Soviet warships sailed through the Baltic toward Poland, Nikita Khrushchev flew to Poland with a delegation of Soviet generals, where Gomulka assured them that Poland would follow the Soviet lead in foreign policy. Distracted by the crisis in Hungary, the Russians left Gomulka in power and even canceled Poland's debt.

For a short time Gomulka permitted cultural and educational freedom, but by 1958 he had reverted to Stalinist form, imposing controls and pursuing a somewhat anti-Semitic Polish nationalism. Gomulka ruled until 1971, when he was replaced as party secretary by Edward Gierek. But moral leadership within Poland had clearly passed to Stefan Cardinal Wyszynski, leader of the increasingly vocal Catholic church; Gierek was forced to improve relations with the church in order to maintain his own credibility as a national leader.

Gierek presided over a decade of increasing unrest and growing discontent. Polish exports of ham and furniture to the West earned some hard currency but could not curb the rising national debt. The most significant event in Poland in the 1970's was the election of Karol Wojtyla, bishop of Krakow, as Pope John Paul II in October 1978. His visit to Poland in 1979 set the stage for the extraordinary events of the 1980's.

Gierek's austerity program of 1980 sent meat prices soaring. Strikes for wage adjustments, especially at the Lenin Shipyards in Gdansk, thrust Lech Walesa, a shipyard worker, into a position of national leadership. Walesa was elected chairman of the national coordinating committee of independent labor unions, Solidarity. Solidarity's demands went far beyond lower prices and higher wages; they included independent labor unions with the right to strike, freedom for political prisoners, and an end to censorship. In September Gierek resigned as party secretary and was replaced by Stanislaw Kania. By December, 40 independent trade unions had been formed, and a "rural Solidarity" movement was growing. In Feb. 1981 Soviet Army general Wojciech Jaruzelski was named prime minister. When in December Solidarity announced plans to hold a referendum on the Jaruzelski regime, martial law was declared; Solidarity leaders were arrested, all its activities banned, and the right to strike was abolished.

But the government was never able to suppress Solidarity as a popular force, and it was legalized in 1989. In 1989 elections Solidarity won 99 of 100 Senate seats and 299 of 460 seats in the lower house, although 65 percent had been reserved for the Communist party. Jaruzelski was elected president by Parliament and Solidarity leader Tadeusz Mazowiecki became prime minister.

The Communist party voted to disband on Jan. 28, 1990, and the Mazowiecki government announced a program of economic reform, winning promises of foreign aid and increased investment from the West. In June 1990, a commission was appointed to draft a new constitution. Jaruzelski resigned in September, and in presidential elections, Walesa, at the head of Solidarity's labor/Catholic faction, defeated Mazowiecki, representing Solidarity's political/technocrat faction.

The new prime minister, Krzysztof Bielecki, continued the reformist policies of curbing inflation and government spending, fostering foreign investment, and privatizing state enterprises. But the shock therapy, with its higher prices and unemployment (even while creating more than a million new jobs), led to disillusionment.

In the first fully free parliamentary elections, held in Oct. 1991, only 42 percent of the voters participated, electing a fragmented 29-party Parliament. Reluctantly, Pres. Walesa named Jan Olszewski as prime minister of a coalition government. The Olszewski coalition collapsed in June 1992, replaced by an equally fragile seven-party coalition led by Hanna Suchocka, Poland's first female prime minister.

Despite high inflation (40 percent) and high unemployment (13 percent), under Poland's "iron lady" the private sector expanded and even the remaining state-owned enterprises responded to market demand, pushing exports from $8 bil. in 1988 to $14 bil. in 1992. And in May 1993, Parliament passed a bill privatizing 600 companies.

Still, at the end of May 1993, the Suchocka government fell, by one vote, to a Solidarity-sponsored no-confidence measure, in protest against her austerity budget. In new elections held in Oct. 1993, the Communist party (now called the Democratic Left Alliance) formed a coalition with the Peasants party to forge a return to power. The Communist prime minister, Josef Oleksy, was joined by his party-mate Aleksander Kwasniewski, who defeated Walesa in presidential elections held in Nov. 1995. A month after the election Oleksy was accused of spying for Russia, and although he protested his innocence, he resigned.

Poland's economy was among the fastest growing in Europe (a 7 percent rise in G.D.P. and billions in direct foreign investment) although inflation ran high. In 1997, a new constitution and invitations to join NATO and eventually the E.U. gave the Poles a reason to believe the future looked very positive. The first elections under the new constitution produced a center-right coalition government. In 1999 Poland joined NATO, finally achieving security against the Russian expansion it always feared.

Bucking western Europe's right-wing electoral tide, Poland's Democratic Left Alliance (the remnants of the Communists and their friends) captured control of the Sjem, garnering a near majority of the 460 seats. Leszek Miller became premier in coalition with the Polish Peasants' Party. In June 2003 voters gave overwhelming approval (77 percent) to joining the E.U. Miller's government fell in May 2004. A new, center right coalition government headed by Lech Kaczynski took power at the end of 2005. He appointed his twin brother, Jaroslaw, to be prime minister (July 2006) to raised eyebrows at home and abroad.

Poland's entry into the E.U. proved a boon to the economy but rejection of the constitution by France and the Netherlands in 2005 was viewed as a sign of fear that cheap labor from Poland, etc. was causing a backlash. About two million Poles have gone to work in other E.U. nations. In 2007, the Kaczynski government began to fall apart as it concentrated on social issues such as abortion and its demand to examine the past records of 700,000 people for ties to the communist regime, soon overruled by the courts. In Aug. 2007, its coalition dissolved and a snap election resulted in a victory for a liberal, pro-E.U. party. In Aug. 2008 an agreement was reached with teh U.S. to put a missile defense system in Poland despite strong Russian protests.

▶ **PORTUGAL**
Portuguese Republic

● GEOGRAPHY **Location:** Iberian Peninsula in southwest Europe; also two archipelagos in Atlantic Ocean: Azores (37°29'N, 25°40'W) and Madeira Islands (32°40'N, 16°55'W). **Boundaries:** Spain to N and E, Atlantic Ocean to S and W. **Total area:** 35,552 sq. mi. (92,080 sq km). **Coastline:** 1,114 mi. (1,793 km). **Comparative area:** slightly smaller than Indiana. **Land use:** 21% arable land; 8% permanent crops; 71% other. **Major cities:** Lisboa (Lisbon, capital); Porto (Oporto); Amadora; Setubal; Coimbra.

● **PEOPLE** **Population:** 10,676,910 (2008 est.). **Nationality:** noun—Portuguese (sing., pl.); adjective—Portuguese. **Ethnic groups:** homogeneous Mediterranean stock; citizens of African descent who immigrated during decolonization number less than 100,000. **Languages:** Portuguese. **Religions:** 85% Roman Catholic, Protestant, 2% other Christian, 4% none.

● **GOVERNMENT** **Type:** parliamentary democracy. **Independence:** Oct. 5, 1910. **Constitution:** Apr. 25, 1976, revised Oct. 1982 and June 1989, Nov. 1992, Sept. 1997. **National holiday:** Day of Portugal, June 10. **Heads of Government:** Anibal Cavaco Silva, president (since March 2006); José Socrates, prime minister (since March 2005). **Structure:** executive—president and prime minister; unicameral legislature-(popularly elected 230-seat Assembly of the Republic); judiciary.

● **ECONOMY** **Monetary unit:** euro. **Budget:** (2007 est.) *income:* $92.35 bil.; *expend.:* $98 bil. **G.D.P.:** $232 bil., $21,800 per capita (2007 est.). **Chief crops:** grains, potatoes, olives, grapes for wine; livestock. **Natural resources:** fish, forests (cork), tungsten, iron ore, uranium ore. **Major industries:** textiles, footwear, wood pulp, paper, cork. **Labor force:** 5.5 mil. (2007); 60% services, 30% industry, 10% agriculture (2007); 4.7% unemployment (2001 est.). **Exports:** $50.72 bil. (f.o.b., 2007 est.); clothing and footwear, machinery, chemicals, cork and paper products, hides. **Imports:** $72.19 bil. (f.o.b., 2007 est.); machinery and transport equipment, chemicals, petroleum, textiles, agricultural products. **Major trading partners:** (2006) *exports:* 26.5% Spain, 12.9% Germany, 12% France, 6.7% U.K., 6.1% U.S.; *imports:* 29% Spain, 13.1% Germany, 8.1% France, 5.6% Italy, 4.4% Netherlands.

Portugal traces its origins back to the warlike Lusitanian tribes of Roman times. The nation-state originated as a county of the kingdom of Leon-Castile, reconquered from the Moors in the 11th century. Portugal won recognition as an independent kingdom in 1143, and conquered Lisbon four years later. In 1267 the Algarve was conquered, and by then Portugal had expanded to its modern boundaries. Except for the period 1580-1640, when it was ruled by the Spanish Habsburgs, the Portuguese dynasty maintained its independence into the 20th century.

Portuguese fishermen had probably frequented the Grand Banks from before the time of Columbus, and the nation's tradition of seafaring gave rise to a world empire in the 15th and 16th centuries. Prince Henry the Navigator (1394-1460) colonized the Azores and the Madeiras and sponsored voyages of exploration along the west coast of Africa. Under his successors, Portugal controlled the west African coast, the shores of the Indian Ocean, and large stretches of southern Asia, as well as, in the Western Hemisphere, Brazil. Yet the rise of the empires of Spain and the Netherlands quickly reduced the Portuguese to second-rank status, leaving only Macao, Goa, and Timor in Asia; Portuguese Guinea (Guinea Bissau), Mozambique, and Angola in Africa; and the great territory of Brazil in Latin America.

In the 19th century, a series of dynastic civil wars weakened the monarchy, allowing Britain to gain control of the country's foreign policy (in addition to the wine trade of Oporto, long in British hands). Brazil declared its independence in 1822.

In 1910 Portugal became the first kingdom in the 20th century to be transformed into a republic. But in the next 15 years, chaos ensued: eight presidents, 44 governments, and a nearcollapse of the economy. Finally, the military established a dictatorship, lasting until recent times. In 1928 the military installed a civilian dictator, a professor of economics, Antonio Salazar. A firm believer in law and order, he managed to control the turbulence of political life and made the escudo one of Europe's most stable currencies, yet he could do nothing to alter Portugal's fundamental poverty. Although he ruled through civilian governments, his essential support always came from the army.

World War II affected Portugal very little. Salazar deftly managed to remain Britain's ally while keeping his country out of the war as a neutral state. In the postwar period, Portugal accepted Marshall Plan aid and became a member of NATO in 1949. Portugal was a founding member of the European Free Trade Association in 1959 and negotiated a special relationship with the EC in 1972 (when its trading partner and ally, Great Britain, joined that body).

Portugal joined the United Nations in 1955, just in time to become embroiled in the worldwide movement for decolonization. Protesting that Portugal had, not colonies, but "overseas provinces," Salazar refused to bow to the pressure of world opinion. In 1961 India forcibly annexed Goa and other Portuguese enclaves on the subcontinent. In the same year, nationalist revolts broke out in Angola, Guinea and Mozambique.

The colonial wars of the 1960's placed a terrible strain on Portugal's economy. Salazar, gravely ill, retired in 1968 and was replaced by Marcelo Caetano. In 1974 Caetano was deposed in a bloodless coup staged by the secret Armed Forces movement. The coup's leader, Antonio de Spinola, after reaching agreements on the independence of most of Portugal's old colonies, resigned as head of government in September 1974. Costa Gomes replaced Spinola, as a Revolutionary Council was instituted. The council survived two coup attempts, one by right-wing soldiers, the other by Communists, and it promulgated a Socialist constitution in 1976. Through a series of unstable governments (16 between 1974 and 1987), the old agrarian estates were expropriated, and banking, insurance, and large industrial concerns were nationalized. The shock of this economic transformation, along with the OPEC price rises, created a recession in the 1970's. In addition Portugal had to absorb a million Portuguese refugees from the former colonies.

Attempts by center-right coalitions in the 1980's to undo the nationalizations of the 1970's were thwarted by vetoes of the Constitutional Tribunal (successor to the Revolutionary Council), even when the free-market Social Democratic party held an absolute majority in the assembly. Portugal entered the EC on Jan. 1, 1986, pledging to reduce tariffs and end agricultural subsidies over a 10-year transitional period.

In 1987 the Social Democrats, running on a platform of spending cuts, privatization of state-owned firms, reversal of agricultural collectivism, and reliance on free enterprise, became the first party since 1974 to win an absolute majority in the legislative assembly. Per capita income tripled over the years 1985-92, so that Portugal was no longer the poorest country in the E.U. The 1992 sale of the huge state-owned Petrogal oil company was a harbinger of a return to free enterprise. In Oct. 1995, Antonio Guterres of the Socialist party displaced the Social Democrats. And in January 1996, Jorge Sampaio won the presidential election, giving Portugal both a Socialist president and prime minister for the first time since democracy was restored.

Portugal's economic stability was ratified in 1998 by the E.U. when the latter approved Portugal's membership in the Monetary Union. G.D.P. growth averaged 3.5 percent through the late 1990's. In Dec. 1999 the colony of Macao was returned to Chinese rule after 442 years. In 2001 Sampaio was easily reelected. But the December loss by the Socialists of numerous municipal elections, including Lisbon and Oporto, led Sampaio to dissolve Parliament. March elections then brought another center-right coalition as the Social Democrats took 102 (of 230) seats, selecting Manual Durao Barroso as prime minister. In 2005 the Socialists won a landslide victory as the economy hit a stalling pattern, and José Socrates became prime minister. His budget cuts aimed at stimulating the economy did not enhance his popularity.

▶ QATAR
State of Qatar

● **GEOGRAPHY Location:** occupies a peninsula projecting northward from Arabian mainland into western part of Persian (Arabian) Gulf. **Boundaries:** Persian Gulf to N, E, and W; Saudi Arabia and United Arab Emirates to S. **Total area:** 4,247 sq. mi. (11,000 sq km). **Coastline:** 350 mi. (563 km). **Comparative area:** slightly smaller than Connecticut. **Land use:** 1% arable land; 0% permanent crops; 99% other. **Major cities:** Doha (capital); Al Rayyan; Al Wakrah.

● **PEOPLE Population:** 928,635 (July 2008 est.). **Nationality:** noun—Qatari(s); adjective—Qatari. **Ethnic groups:** 40% Arab, 18% Pakistani, 18% Indian, 10% Iranian, 14% other. **Languages:** Arabic (official), English commonly used as second language. **Religions:** 95% Muslim.

● **GOVERNMENT Type:** traditional monarchy. **Independence:** Sept. 3, 1971 (from U.K.). **Constitution:** provisional constitution enacted Apr. 19, 1972; permanent constitution approved by referendum Apr. 29, 2003. **National holiday:** Independence Day, Sept. 3. **Head of Government:** Sheikh Hamad bin Jassim bin Jabr Al-Thani (since Apr. 2007). **Structure:** executive—amir is head of government and chief of state; unicameral legislature—consultative, no elections since 1970, members terms extended every four years; judiciary.

● **ECONOMY Monetary unit:** Qatari riyal. **Budget:** (2007 est.) *income:* $23.5 bil.; *expend.:* $19.61 bil. **G.D.P.:** $57.69 bil., $75,900 per capita (2007 est.). **Chief crops:** fruits, vegetables; poultry, dairy products, beef; fish. **Natural resources:** crude oil, natural gas, fish. **Major industries:** crude oil production and refining, fertilizers, petrochemicals. **Labor force:** 638,000 (2007 est.); less than 1% unemployment (2007). **Exports:** $33.28 bil. (f.o.b., 2007 est.); 80% petroleum products, steel, fertilizers. **Imports:** $15.32 bil. (f.o.b., 2007 est.); machinery, consumer goods, food, chemicals. **Major trading partners:** (2006) *exports:* 40% Japan, 16% South Korea, 7% Singapore, 4% Thailand; *imports:* 13% France, 10% Japan, 9% Italy, 9% U.S., 8% Germany, 6% U.K., 6% South Africa, 5% South Korea.

The Qatar peninsula was ruled as part of the sheikhdom of Bahrain from the late 18th century until the mid-19th century. An informal British protectorate was established in 1868; the Ottoman Empire also asserted authority over the sheikhs of Qatar from 1872 to 1916. The Ottomans ceded authority to the British in that year, and a formal British protectorate was organized. When British forces withdrew from the Persian Gulf region in 1971, Qatar entered into negotiations with the emirates of the Trucial Coast to join the federation of the United Arab Emirates. When those negotiations broke down, Qatar declared its independence on Sept. 3, 1971. For over 30 years it has been politically stable under one ruler, Sheik Hamad bin Khalifa al-Thani, although he was deposed by his son in a bloodless coup in June 1995. He has claimed he wants to move the country toward democracy and has called for a free press, limited elections, and allowing women to vote. Much of this was accomplished by 1999, and in 2005 a constitution came into force with elections for some members of parliament scheduled for 2007. These were rescheduled for 2008, but not had happened as of September.

Qatar's economy is dominated by oil, natural gas (Qatar has the world's third largest supply) banking, and shipping services in the port of Doha.

▶ROMANIA
● **Geography   Location:** southeastern Europe. **Boundaries:** Ukraine to N, Moldova to NE, Black Sea to E, Bulgaria to S, Yugoslavia (Serbia) to SW, Hungary to NW. **Total area:** 91,699 sq. mi. (237,500 sq km). **Coastline:** 140 mi. (225 km). **Comparative area:** slightly smaller than Oregon. **Land use:** 41% arable land; 3% permanent crops; 21% meadows and pastures; 29% forest and woodland; 6% other; includes 11% irrigated. **Major cities:** Bucharesti (Bucharest, capital); Constanta; Iasi; Timisoara; Cluj-Napoca.
● **People   Population:** 22,246,862 (July 2008 est.). **Nationality:** noun—Romanian(s); adjective—Romanian. **Ethnic groups:** 89.5% Romanian, 6.6% Hungarian, 2.5% Roma, German, Ukrainian, Russian, Turk, other. **Languages:** Romanian, Hungarian, German. **Religions:** 87% Eastern Orthodox, 6% Roman Catholic, 7% Protestant.
● **Government   Type:** republic. **Independence:** 1881 (from Turkey). **Constitution:** Dec. 8, 1991; republic proclaimed Dec. 30, 1947. **National holiday:** Unification Day, Dec. 1. **Heads of Government:** Traian Basescu, president (since Dec. 2004); Calin Popescu Tariceanu, prime minister (since Dec. 2004). **Structure:** executive; bicameral legislature; judiciary.
● **Economy   Monetary unit:** leu. **Budget:** (2007 est.): *income:* $56.29 bil.; *expend.:* $60.41 bil. **G.D.P.:** $246.7 bil., $11,100 per capita (2007 est.). **Chief crops:** corn, wheat; milk, eggs, meat. **Natural resources:** crude oil (reserves declining), timber, natural gas, coal, iron ore. **Major industries:** mining, timber, construction materials. **Labor force:** 9.35 mil. (2007 est.); 4.1% unemployment (2007). **Exports:** $40.25 bil. (f.o.b., 2007 est.); textiles and footwear, metals and metal products, machinery and equipment. **Imports:** $64.33 bil. (f.o.b., 2007 est.); machinery and equipment, fuels and minerals, chemicals. **Major trading partners:** (2006) *exports:* 18% Italy, 16% Germany, 8% Turkey, 8% France, 5% Hungary, 4% U.K.; *imports:* 15% Germany, 14% Italy, 8% Russia, 6% France, 5% turkey, 4% China.

The Roman province of Dacia was sufficiently Latinized to retain the name of Rome long after the legions withdrew in A.D. 27. Overrun by invading Bulgars in the eighth century, the Romanians retained their Latinate language and orthodox Christianity; Romania remained beyond the borders of the Byzantine Empire but was in close contact with it. The area was conquered by the Mongols in the 13th century and formed the independent principalities of Moldavia and Walachia after the Mongols withdrew.

By the 15th century, Moldavia and Walachia had become vassal states of the Ottoman Empire, though with some local autonomy that permitted retention of orthodox Christianity and the creation of a rich local culture. Attempts at national unity against Ottoman rule in 1601 and 1711 failed; in 1861 the provinces united as an autonomous state under the name Romania, within the Ottoman Empire, under Greek administration. Independence came in 1878.

Romania was for centuries the poorest country in Europe. Thoroughly agricultural, it was a land of unfree peasants working the great estates of landowners who were generally wealthy, usually absentee, and often Greek. The peasants not only paid taxes but also were required to perform feudal labor services for the estate owners.

After enlarging itself at Bulgaria's expense in the Second Balkan War (1913), Romania switched sides three times in World War I, joining the Allies just before the war's end. Its reward was a huge expansion, doubling its territory with lands taken from Austria, Hungary, Russia, and Bulgaria.

The interwar period was one of political turbulence, marked by violence and assassinations. Twice King Carol II went into exile, leaving his throne to his son Prince Michael; the second time was in 1940, when Russia (in accordance with the Hitler-Stalin pact) reclaimed the territories of Bessarabia and northern Bukovina it had lost to Romania in 1920; Hitler required Romania to return about half of Transylvania to Hungary.

During World War II, the pro-Hitler dictator Marshall Ion Antonescu took power, supported by a semifascist "Iron Guard," but when the latter attempted a coup, the military crushed the uprising. Romanian troops participated in Hitler's invasion of Russia in 1941, and the country paid the price in 1944 when Russian troops "liberated" the country, with devastating results.

The country was quickly transformed into a Soviet satellite through rigged elections in which the communist National Democratic Front replaced the Peasant Alliance in power; a People's Republic was proclaimed on Dec. 30, 1947, and King Michael was forced to abdicate. A peace treaty in 1947 confirmed the loss of Bessarabia to Russia but returned Transylvania to Romania.

Under Russian occupation Romania was a virtual Soviet colony. The occupying armies did not leave until after reparation payments were completed in 1958, leaving the dictator Gheorghe Gheorghiu-Dej in power. Despite Council of Mutual Economic Assistance (COMECON) plans for Romania to become a major food supplier to the Soviet bloc, Gheorghiu-Dej pursued industrialization on the Stalinist model, in the process ruining Romanian agriculture while creating large, labor-intensive, and highly inefficient factories. The result was an economic depression; politically, however, it produced a de facto independence for Romania within the Soviet bloc. Russian troops were forbidden on Romanian soil, and Romania declined to participate in COMECON policies.

With the death of Gheorghiu-Dej in 1965, power passed to Nicolae Ceaușescu. He promulgated a new constitution and instituted a series of purges; he became party leader in 1965, prime minister in 1967, and president of the republic in 1974. Ceaușescu continued his predecessor's economic policy, deepening the country's misery; he also pursued a policy of "independence" from the U.S.S.R., refusing to go along with Soviet policies of de-Stalinization and liberalization. Romania's "national communism" was expressed in militant nationalism, coupled with severe repression of ethnic minorities. Hundreds of Hungarian villages were bulldozed in the name of agricultural collectivization.

Ceaușescu's ambitions included the creation of a family dynasty in the Romanian leadership. In 1979 his wife Elena was named first deputy premier and elevated to the Council of Ministers. Her brothers were given important government positions; Ceaușescu's son, despite his reputation as a playboy, was groomed to replace his father.

Romania's transition from Communist rule was sudden and violent. On Dec. 16-18, 1989, demonstrations in Timisoara calling for Ceaușescu's ouster were put down with brute force by the Securitate (secret police), but they spread and citizens and regular army troops fought pitched battles with Securitate forces in Bucharest. Ceaușescu and his wife fled Bucharest but were captured, tried, and executed. The newly organized Council of National Salvation established a provisional government, consisting primarily of anti-Ceaușescu Communists in league with the Romanian army, with former Communist party official Ion Iliescu as president.

The Communist party was outlawed on Jan. 12, 1990. Despite the Council's domination by former Communists, no effective opposition movement emerged, and in hastily called and rigged elections on May 20, Iliescu was elected president and the Council won 233 of 296 seats in the house.

In June 1990, many anti-Communist demonstrators were beaten and several killed by troops and armed miners brought to Bucharest by the government. Calls for Iliescu's resignation and a purge of Communists from government grew. Tensions were aggravated when the government's abrupt move to a market economy resulted in food shortages and price increases.

Continued rioting in 1991 led to the appointment of the non-Communist Theodor Stolojan at the head of a "caretaker" coalition. More or less free elections in 1992 gave the National Salvation Front 28 percent of the seats in Parliament while the opposition Democratic Convention gained 20 percent; Iliescu defeated the Democratic Convention candidate in the presidential election. Both Iliescu and the prime minister he named (Nicolae Vacaroiu) were pledged to slowing the transition to a market economy but by 1994 with inflation at over 250 percent (leading to a massive workers' strike in Feb.) the government agreed to I.M.F.'s demand for increased privatization and fiscal austerity in order to receive a $700 mil. loan. Iliescu's presidency ended in Nov. 1996 with a coalition government headed by Emil Constantinescu immediately forging links to the Romanian Orthodox Church ending decades of official atheism and taking action against corrupt banking officials, businessmen, and politicians. The economy remained in dire straits but in early 1997 loans were secured from the I.M.F. and the World Bank.

Elections in Nov. 1997 were won by Emil Constantinescu of the Democratic Convention party who became president and Victor Ciorbea the prime minister. Inflation and unemployment were falling but G.D.P. growth was lagging and, international default looked likely. I.M.F. demands for restructuring as a condition of further loans produced government plans which included the closing of mines but that in turn produced, in early 1999, widespread protest marches and violence by mine workers.

Parliamentary elections in Nov. 2000 gave a preponderance to the parties of the left, but the presidential election drew greater interest: Ion Iliescu, claiming now to be a reformer and a pro-westerner, carried two-thirds of the vote in the run-off. The nation moved toward closer ties with the West, joining NATO in 2004 and the E.U. in 2007. Corruption in government remained a major problem and led to the election of an outsider, Traian Basecu, as president in 2004, and again in 2007 after attempts to impeach him failed in a public referendum. His reforms to the justice system and of public services were severe but needed for entry into the E.U.

▶ RUSSIA
Russian Federation

● **GEOGRAPHY Location:** northeastern Europe and northern Asia. **Boundaries:** Baltic Sea, Barents Sea, Kara Sea, East Siberian Sea to N, Bering Sea, Sea of Okhotsk, Sea of Japan to E, China, North Korea, Mongolia, Kazakhstan, Caspian Sea, Azerbaijan, Georgia, Black Sea to S, Ukraine, Belarus to W, Latvia, Estonia, Finland, Norway to NW. **Total area:** 6,592,745 sq. mi. (17,075,200 sq. km). **Coastline:** 23,402 mi. (37,653 km). **Comparative area:** slightly less than 1.8 times the size of the United States. **Land use:** 8% arable land, 0% permanent crops, 94% other. **Major cities:** Moscow (capital); St. Petersburg; Nizhnyi Novgorod; Novosibirsk.

● **PEOPLE Population:** 140,702,094 (July 2008 est.). **Nationality:** noun—Russian(s); adjective—Russian. **Ethnic groups:** Russian, Tatar, Ukrainian, Chuvash. **Languages:** Russian, other. **Religions:** Russian Orthodox, Muslim, other.

● **GOVERNMENT Type:** federation. **Independence:** Aug. 24, 1991 (from Soviet Union). **Constitution:** Dec. 12, 1993. **National holiday:** Russia Day, June 12, celebrating first presidential election. **Heads of Government:** Dmitriy Medvedev, president (since May 2008); Vladimir V. Putin, prime minister (since May 2008). **Structure:** executive—president, premier, various advisory bodies; bicameral legislature; judiciary.

● **ECONOMY Monetary unit:** ruble. **Budget:** (2007 est.) *income:* $299 bil..; *expend.:* $262 bil. **G.D.P.:** $2.076 tril., $14,600 per capita (2007 est.). **Chief crops:** grain, sugar beets, vegetables, sunflower seed; meat, milk. **Natural resources:** oil, natural gas, coal, timber. **Major industries:** extraction and processing raw materials, machine building from rolling mills to high-performance aircraft. **Labor force:** 75.1 mil. (2007). **Exports:** $365 bil. (2007 est.); petroleum and petroleum products, natural gas, wood and wood products, coal, metals, chemicals. **Imports:** $260.4 bil. (2007 est.); machinery and equipment, consumer goods, medicines, meat, grain, sugar, semifinished metal products. **Major trading partners:** (2006) *exports:* 12.3% Netherlands, 8.6% Italy, 8.4% Germany, 5.4% China, 5.1% Ukraine, 5% Turkey, 4% Switzerland; *imports:* 14% Germany, 9.7% China, 7% Ukraine,

6% Japan, 5% South Korea, 5% U.S., 4% France, 4% Italy.

Russia is the largest and most powerful of the states to emerge from the former Soviet Union. As the seat of the Soviet empire that existed for over 70 years, the Russians wielded tremendous power both within the U.S.S.R. and in the international sphere. Almost from their emergence as a separate people, the Russians have extended the boundaries of their country to include a wide variety of non-Russian people. Both the Russian Czars and the Bolsheviks who came to power in 1917 have a long history of expansionist policies, which explains why, even today, an important part of the Russian national identity is that of leader of a large empire.

In the ninth century A.D., Viking traders organized a state, which they called Rus, in the river valleys between the Baltic and the Black Seas, centered on the cities of Kiev and Novgorod. In time the Vikings were absorbed into the native Slavic population; in 998 a Ruthenian prince of Kiev accepted Christianity from Constantinople. In the 13th century, Mongols under Genghis Khan and his descendants conquered most of Russia, and the Mongol Golden Horde maintained its power through the 14th century, exercising loose control over Novgorod and Moscow.

From the mid-19th century, Moscow grew to become the center of a new state that gathered in other cities and territories as Mongol power waned. Ivan III (Ivan the Great, 1440-1505) consolidated the power of Moscow; his marriage to a Byzantine princess led him to regard his empire as a third Rome, heir to the religious tradition of Constantinople. His grandson, Ivan IV (Ivan the Terrible, 1530-84), adopted the title czar (from the Latin caesar). He broke the power of the aristocratic boyar class and greatly extended the power of Moscow through military conquest.

Over the next two centuries, Russia carried out a steady program of expansion eastward into Siberia and across the Bering Strait to Alaska, until the empire covered one-sixth of the land surface of the globe. Peter the Great (1672-1725) made Russia a Baltic and Black Sea naval power, brought Russia into the European state system, and instituted a sweeping, if superficial, Westernization of his realm. His new capital at St. Petersburg became one of the most splendid cities in Europe. At the end of the 18th century, Catherine the Great (1729-96) participated with Prussia and Austria in the partitions of Poland, and Russia thereby became a major power in central Europe.

Catherine's grandson Alexander I (1777-1825), member of the grand coalition that defeated Napoleon, was not only czar of Russia but also king of Poland and grand duke of Finland. His troops occupied Paris in 1815. The Russian aristocracy became ardent Francophiles in the 19th century, ignoring growing problems at home. After losing the Crimean War in 1856, Russia began to develop Siberia and the southern territories near the border of Persia. Alaska was sold to the United States in 1867. In a major reform of the agricultural system, serfdom was abolished under Alexander II in 1861, though the newly independent peasantry, organized into agricultural cooperatives, only slowly derived benefits from its freedom. The late 19th century also marked the beginning of modern industrialization in Russia and of extensive development in Siberia, aided by state investment in railroads and mining.

Under the last czar, Nicholas II (1868-1918), Russia was defeated by Japan in a war over Manchuria in 1905. The defeat sparked a naval mutiny and an abortive revolution, which led to the establishment of a constitutional monarchy and other limited political reforms. Further military losses in World War I set the stage for the monarchy's downfall in the revolution of 1917.

The initial revolution of March 1917 brought a relatively moderate socialist (Menshevik) group to power. Its principal leader, Aleksandr Kerensky, organized a republican government and tried to maintain the Russian war effort but failed to gain control of the many contending revolutionary factions of the time. The Germans allowed the radical Bolshevik leader, Vladimir I. Lenin, to return to Russia, where he and his followers organized workers' soviets (councils) hostile to the Menshevik republic. Bolshevik forces occupied Petrograd (St. Petersburg was renamed in 1914) on Nov. 7, 1917 (October in the old Byzantine calendar, hence the name October Revolution), arrested the cabiinet, and put in place a Council of People's Commissars, under Lenin's chairmanship. There followed four years of civil war between Bolshevik, Menshevik, and czarist forces, in the course of which Nicholas II and his family were executed by the Bolsheviks in 1918.

Decreeing land to the peasants, worker management in industry, and repudiation of czarist debts, the Bolsheviks won the survival of their regime by withdrawing from World War I. The 1918 Treaty of Brest-Litovsk, which gained peace with Germany, granted freedom to Finland, the Baltic republics, Poland, Ukraine, and Bessarabia. At the conclusion of the civil war in 1921, the Soviet state was established, with Ukraine reabsorbed into the Soviet Union. The Bolshevik victory also resulted in the creation in 1921 of the Mongolian People's Republic as a close Soviet ally.

The early 1920's are now remembered as a "golden age" of Soviet history. Lenin's New Economic Policy (NEP) allowed some role for market forces and private ownership and led to a brief burst of economic growth. Art, literature, and science flourished in an atmosphere of revolutionary enthusiasm and little censorship.

Lenin died on Jan. 21, 1924, and after a power struggle, was succeeded by Josef Stalin. Stalin supported communist revolutions in China and elsewhere through the Communist International (Comintern) but generally withdrew from foreign engagements in order to concentrate on domestic affairs. Under Lenin, and even more under Stalin, the Communist party established a police state, condemning millions of people to internal exile in the 1920's and consolidating all power in the hands of the state. In 1929 agriculture was forcibly collectivized, leading to the starvation or execution of millions of peasants, while forced industrialization was carried out under a series of five-year plans. Under the guise of socialist revolution, the Russians continued in much the same manner as their czarist heirs. The Bolsheviks forcibly incorporated most of the territories of the old empire, and once in charge, insisted that Russian be the state language and that Russian Communist party officials run the republics.

On the national level, Stalin's chief rival, Leon Trotsky, was expelled from the U.S.S.R. in 1929 (and assassinated by Stalinist agents in Mexico in 1940). Stalin's obsession with eliminating all possible rivals for power led to a series of purges which saw the summary execution of an estimated seven million of presumed "enemies of the state" and the imprisonment in concentration camps of an estimated 12 million more.

Russia's reemergence as a world power was signaled by the signing in Aug. 1939 of the Hitler-Stalin Pact, a nonaggression treaty through which Stalin aimed to recover territories lost in 1918. Poland was partitioned, Bessarabia annexed (as the Moldavian republic), Finland conquered and partitioned, and the Baltic republics absorbed.

When in June 1941 Hitler turned against his ally and invaded Russia, unprepared Russian armies retreated. But Stalin emerged as a national leader in the "Great Patriotic War," restructuring the army and enlisting the support of the Orthodox church and relying on calls to Russian patriotism in rallying the population. In the early winter of 1942, the war changed course as Russia broke the German siege of Stalingrad, and Russian armies began their westward push that would carry them to the Elbe River by April 1945.

By the end of World War II, Stalin had reestablished the old czarist boundaries of Russia, and he had a ring of occupied states along his western boundary and a divided Germany beyond. Over the years 1945-48, he engineered a thorough communization of those occupied states, turning them into Russian satellites.

Stalin died in March 1953. He was succeeded by a collegial form of party and government leadership, from which Nikita Khrushchev, the party chairman, emerged as the paramount figure. In a secret speech to the party leadership in 1956, Khrushchev denounced Stalin for crimes against the party. He announced a set of new policies designed to bring about rapid modernization and consolidated his power when he became premier in 1958. The Khrushchev years brought a small but steady rise in living standards and a "thaw" in police state methods, the KGB (state security police) being brought under party control.

In foreign policy there was a thaw as well. In 1953 the Soviets agreed to an armistice in Korea and tolerated the formation of a more liberal government in Hungary. In 1955 Russia returned the Porkkala peninsula to Finland and agreed to the Austrian State Treaty, which created an independent and neutral Austria. But the limits of disengagement became clear in 1956 with the ruthless Soviet suppression of the Hungarian uprising. A summit conference between Khrushchev and Eisenhower in 1960 led to a propaganda victory for Russia when an American U-2 spy plane was shot down over Russian territory on May 1. And in 1962 Khrushchev tried to install Soviet missiles in Cuba, a reckless adventure from which he had to back down during the Cuban missile crisis.

While on vacation in 1964, Khrushchev was removed from office and replaced as party secretary by Leonid Brezhnev and as premier by Aleksei Kosygin. His failure to deliver on promises for domestic economic growth and his recklessness in foreign affairs seem to have been responsible for his downfall. The new leaders embarked on an ambitious program of military (especially naval) expansion and pressed ahead vigorously with a space program that had begun with the triumphant launching of Sputnik I in 1957.

Under Brezhnev and Kosygin the U.S.S.R. became more aggressive in foreign policy. The severe suppression of Czechoslovakia's "Prague Spring" in 1968 occasioned development of the Brezhnev Doctrine, whereby Russia claimed the right to intervene militarily in any socialist state.

Soviet involvement in the Third World grew, with Russia supporting Vietnam against China; Syria and the PLO against Israel; leftist regimes in Angola, Ethiopia, and elsewhere in Africa; and the Sandinistas in Nicaragua. Cuba emerged as the principal Soviet proxy in supplying troops for leftist causes in the Third World. In 1979 Soviet troops moved into Afghanistan, allegedly at the invitation of its Marxist government, and remained bogged down there for a decade. Under American pressure, Brezhnev permitted the emigration of about 130,000 Jews and 40,000 ethnic Germans.

Domestically, the regime grew more oppressive; censorship was tightened and dissidents sentenced to terms in penal mental institutions. Elitism and nepotism created a self-perpetuating and interlocking network of power at the top, while the nation as a whole stagnated. Brezhnev's death in 1982 brought about a rapid series of leadership transfers. Yuri Andropov, head of the KGB, succeeded Brezhnev as party secretary but died after only 15 months. He was succeeded by Konstantin Chernenko, who died 13 months later. In March 1985 Mikhail Gorbachev became party secretary, ushering in a new era.

Gorbachev first instituted a cautious shake-up of state and party bureaucrats, promoting younger men who were technocrats rather than party professionals. Under the slogan glasnost (openness, candor), censorship was relaxed and policy was openly debated in the press. Jamming of broadcasts from the West was ended. By the end of 1990, freedom of the press and of religion had been approved, and private citizens were given limited rights to own small businesses.

Gorbachev's other slogan, perestroika (restructuring), addressed his aim to boost morale and increase economic efficiency by devolving responsibility for economic decisions away from the party and government and toward industrial and agricultural managers. Perestroika raised expectations but not output; the system remained sluggish, inefficient, and burdened with the vested interests of state planners. The nuclear power plant disaster of Chernobyl in April 1986 and a gas pipeline fire that killed hundreds of passengers in passing railroad trains in June 1989 exemplified the industrial mismanagement against which Gorbachev's policies were aimed. During 1989-91 there were strikes by coal miners, and shortages of food and consumer goods worsened.

In foreign policy Gorbachev pursued arms reduction agreements with the United States and withdrew Soviet forces from Afghanistan. His international stature exceeded that of any previous Soviet leader; but his problems at home made him increasingly unpopular. Foremost among his problems at home concerned the U.S.S.R.'s various ethnic nationalities. The southern Muslim regions of the U.S.S.R. were the scene of turmoil since the anti-Russian riots in Kazakhstan in 1986; in 1988 riots broke out in the Christian republic of Armenia over the status of ethnic Armenians in the neighboring Muslim republic of Azerbaijan. Fighting in Armenia and Azerbaijan worsened in 1989-90, leading to a breakdown of government control in some areas. Ethnic warfare between Uzbeks and Turks in Uzbekistan led to numerous deaths, and sporadic violence in other central Asian republics broke out in 1990.

The Baltic republics of Estonia, Latvia, and Lithuania raised their old national flags, enacted laws giving their native languages priority over Russian, and proclaimed the superiority of local republican law over the laws of the Soviet Union. Lithuania proclaimed its independence from the U.S.S.R. in Dec. 1989, provoking a confrontation with international ramifications; Lithuania finally agreed to postpone its independence in 1990 pending negotiations with the Soviet government. Within the U.S.S.R. itself, the Russian republic elected maverick Boris Yeltsin as president and pressed for greater autonomy; Yeltsin resigned from the Communist party in July 1990.

The total collapse of communist governments in Eastern Europe in 1989-90 added to Gorbachev's problems and led to the dissolution of the Warsaw Pact; the Berlin Wall fell in Nov. 1989; and the Council of Mutual Economic Assistance (COMECON) was dissolved in July 1990. Gorbachev responded by assuming the presidency of the U.S.S.R. and increasing the powers of that office, and he held off challenges to his leadership in 1990-91. Yet defections from the party by both right- and left-wing groups threw the party's future role in the U.S.S.R. itself in doubt. Demonstrations against Gorbachev and the Communist party took place in Moscow and elsewhere as the economy worsened and food supplies dwindled.

In June of 1991, Boris Yeltsin was elected president of the Russian republic in the first direct elections for the post. His stature soared when he rallied opposition to an unsuccessful coup to topple Gorbachev in August. In December 1991 Gorbachev and Yeltsin agreed that the U.S.S.R. would cease to exist as of Jan. 1, 1992.

In early December 1991, Ukraine, Belarus, and the Russian Federation signed the Minsk Agreement that created the Commonwealth of Independent States, and on Dec. 21, Ukraine and 11 other former union republics officially committed themselves to the union by signing the Alma-Ata Declaration. In Feb. 1992 Russian president Yeltsin agreed to begin dismantling the vast arsenal of Russian nuclear weapons, 80 percent of which were on Russia's territory, the rest being scattered across Ukraine, Belarus, and Kazkhstan. While Belarus agreed to allow Russia to control the weapons, Kazakhstan and Ukraine used their weapons as bargaining chips.

Throughout 1992, Pres. Yeltsin took center stage, first signing the historic second Strategic Arms Reduction Treaty (START II) with the U.S. in January, then in April rallying the people to support a referendum on government elections and to approve his policies, and finally in June calling together a Constitutional Assembly to write a new constitution. As the Russian economy continued to founder, however, Yeltsin became the target of attacks by former Communists. In Dec. 1992, Yeltsin barely survived a series of votes in Parliament that would have severely limited his control.

This struggle came to a violent head on Sept. 21, 1993, when Yeltsin declared Parliament dissolved and called for new elections to be held in December; Parliament then voted to impeach Yeltsin and appointed Vice Pres. Aleksandr V. Rutskoi to replace him. Anti-Yeltsin forces called for a national strike and barricaded themselves inside the Parliament building for two weeks. Anti-Yeltsin rallies escalated into serious violence when 10,000 protesters overwhelmed riot police and broke through government barricades, causing Yeltsin to summon military police. The leaders of the revolt surrendered after tanks fired directly on the Parliament building, and were immediately sent to prison. At least 100 people were killed.

In the aftermath, Yeltsin moved quickly to parlay his victory into even greater political power, by banning several opposition parties, firing powerful opponents, and calling for new parliamentary elections. In Nov. 1993 he unveiled the country's first post-Soviet constitution, which centralized power in the executive presidency and limited the powers of the constituent regions. One of these regions, Chechnya, had long threatened secession from Russia and in 1994 its leaders took that action. In Dec. Yeltsin ordered the army to restore government control, but it took months of fighting before Grozny, the rebel capital, fell.

In 1996, unrest by Russia's nationalist faction eroded much of Yeltsin's support, forcing him into a runoff election against the Communist candidate Gennadi Zyuganov in May 1996. But in the runoff, Yeltsin decisively beat back the Communist challenger. In August, Yeltsin formed a cabinet of pro-business technocrats; in the Fall he chucked National Security advisor (and future rival) Lebed, and he agreed to the final withdrawl of Russia's Chechnya brigades.

Yeltsin met Pres. Clinton in Helsinki in March 1997 subsequently agreeing to NATO's eastward expansion in return for NATO's agreement neither to deploy nor to store nuclear weapons there. Economic difficulties reached serious proportions in 1998 and the I.M.F. and the U.S. pledged huge amounts to keep the economy from crumbling. In the spring, Yeltsin replaced many of his ministers with reform-minded bureaucrats. But in the summer, the economy turned down again, and Yeltsin was forced to devalue the ruble. As the economy worsened day-by-day and international lenders refused aid, Russia stood on the brink of collapse.

Even with Mr. Yeltsin's illnesses, personal volatility, and political capriciousness, the I.M.F. and various western investment "Clubs" managed to keep rescheduling Russian debt, so Russia was able to stumble on despite essentially defaulting on loan repayments. The August 1999 appointment of Vladimir Putin as prime minister made him the fifth in 18 months, the third in a row drawn from the secret police. One day after Putin's appointment, insurgents in the Federal Republic of Dagestan, operating out of Chechnya, proclaimed an independent Islamic state; hence, Putin's determination to have it out with Chechnya. Vigorously pursued and very popular, the war went well for Russia and Putin's popularity soared as Grozny fell. Putin triumphed in the March presidential election occasioned by Yeltsin's resignation. Putin consolidated his power and took a leading role in opposing U.S. plans to build a missile shield but cooperating with U.S. determination to end terrorism.

As 2001 drew to a close, three-pronged Russian American talks continued: American would support closer Russian ties with NATO; both would reduce by two-thirds their nuclear arms; and the U.S. would withdraw from the 1972 ABM pact. In July 2002 Russia and China signed a 20-year Friendship Treaty. In Nov. 2002 Russian troops began arriving in Kyrgystan, ostensibly to counter terrorism, but likely also to establish a military presence in the face of U.S. bases in the region. The war in Chechnya took a particularly nasty turn, from the Oct. 2002 Moscow theater hostage crisis to the eight suicide bombings of May-August 2003 which killed over 150.

At the end of 2003 Putin's United Russia party won about half of the seats in the Duma and in March 2004 he was reelected president with 71 percent of the vote. But the Chechen insurgency grew far worse culminating in a horrific slaughter of hundreds, including schoolchildren, in Sept. 2004. Putin never wavered, however, and the insurgency was checked. He also quietly exercised power on the international stage by frequently opposing U.S. policies in the Middle East. Attempts to bring Russia into the W.T.O. in 2006 failed but with hope for the future. Meanwhile Putin doggedly pursued the build-up of Russia's vast energy supplies, bringing income and influence in the region and the world. (See "Major News Stories.")

▶ RWANDA
Rwandese Republic

• **GEOGRAPHY Location:** landlocked country in central Africa. **Boundaries:** Uganda to N, Tanzania to E, Burundi to S, Zaire to W. **Total area:** 10,170 sq. mi. (26,340 sq km). **Coastline:** none. **Comparative area:** slightly smaller than Maryland. **Land use:** 32% arable land; 10% permanent crops; 158% other. **Major cities:** Kigali (capital); Butare; Ruhengeri; Gisenyi.

• **PEOPLE Population:** 10,186,063 (July 2008 est.). **Nationality:** noun—Rwandan(s); adjective—Rwandan. **Ethnic groups:** 84% Hutu, 15% Tutsi, 1% Twa (Pygmoid). **Languages:** Kinyarwanda (official) universal Bantu vernacular, French and English (both official), Kiswahili (Swahili) used in commercial centers. **Religions:** 57% Catholic, 26% Protestant, 11% Adventist, 5% Muslim.

• **GOVERNMENT Type:** republic; presidential system; multiparty system. **Independence:** July 1, 1962 (from U.N. trusteeship under Belgian administration). **Constitution:** May 5, 1995, the Transitional National Assembly adopted a new constitution. **National holiday:** Independence Day, July 1. **Heads of Government:** Paul Kagame, president (since April 2000); Bernard Makuza, prime minister (since March 2000). **Structure:** executive—president; unicameral legislature; judiciary.

• **ECONOMY Monetary unit:** Rwandan franc. **Budget:** (2007 est.) *income:* $702.6 mil.; *expend.:* $779.6 mil. **G.D.P.:** $8.576 bil., $1,000 per capita (2007 est.). **Chief crops:** coffee, tea, pyrethrum, bananas, beans, sorghum, potatoes; livestock. **Natural resources:** gold, cassiterite (tin ore), wolframite (tungsten ore), natural gas, hydropower. **Major industries:** agricultural products, small-scale beverage, soap, furniture industries, cement. **Labor force:** 4.6 mil. (2000); 90% agriculture. **Exports:** $170.8 mil. (f.o.b., 2007 est.); coffee, tea, hides, tin ore. **Imports:** $472.5 mil. (f.o.b., 2007 est.); foodstuffs, machines and equipment, petroleum products, cement and construction material. **Major trading partners:** (2006) *exports:* 10.3% China, 9.7% Germany, 4.3% U.S.; *imports:* 19.6% Kenya, 7.9% Germany, 6.8% Uganda, 5.1% Belgium.

Tutsi cattle-breeders came to Rwanda, in the late 15th century and slowly conquered the native Hutu farmers. The Tutsi established a monarchy, forcing the Hutus into serfdom. Germans were the first Europeans to arrive in Rwanda and declared it a protectorate in 1899. After World War I Belgium was given a League of Nations mandate over the territory, which became a U.N. trusteeship after World War II.

Tutsi traditionalists resisted Belgian attempts in the 1950's to institute democratic institutions. In 1959 the Hutus revolted against the monarchy in a bloody conflict which led to a mass exodus of Tut-

sis. Two years later the Hutus won a U.N.-supervised referendum and were granted internal autonomy by Belgium on Jan. 1, 1962. Full independence came on July 1, 1962. Political unrest led to the overthrow of the government in 1973. Maj. Gen. Juvénal Habyarimana dissolved the National Assembly and banned all political activity.

In 1990 Tutsi refugees in Uganda fought with the army, and by 1993 as many as one million people were displaced. A cease-fire and amnesty paved the way for political reform, and a new constitution allowing for multi-party democracy, separation of powers, and presidential term limits went into effect in June 1992. Proposals to merge the armies of the government (Hutu) and the Tutsi Rwandan Patriotic Front were signed in 1993.

But in April 1994, the Hutu presidents of Rwanda and Burundi were both killed when rocket fire (perhaps launched by Hutu dissidents) shot down their plane as it returned from a peace conference in Tanzania. In renewed civil war, the Hutu dominated army of Rwanda and the Hutu militias were driven by the Tutsi-led Patriotic Front into Zaire, Tanzania, Uganda and Burundi; the Hutus reportedly slaughtered over 500,000 Tutsi and countless Hutu moderates as they went. The result was threefold: a million dead, three million refugees, and a Tutsi-dominated but multi-ethnic "government of national unity".

As the Mobutu regime collapsed in neighboring Zaire, the Zaire military attempted to expel a Tutsi community of 400,000 (the Banyamulenge people) who had been settled south of Lake Kivu since the 18th century. The Tutsi resistance gained support from the Rwandan government (Oct. 1996); thus commenced a de facto war between Rwanda and Zaire. The 500,000 Hutu militiamen and other refugees who, as a result, fled Zaire back to Rwanda joined another half million driven from Tanzania by the Tanzanian army. Yet another wave of killings by Hutu militants had begun in Rwanda. By 1999 the Hutu rebellion was petering out in small but vicious skirmishes and the government of Rwanda was continuing its military aid to insurgents in Congo while attacking Hutu bases in the eastern parts of that country, despite the July cease-fire. In April 2000, Paul Kagame was elected the first Tutsi president of Rwanda, and reelected in 2003.

▶ SAINT KITTS AND NEVIS
Federation of Saint Kitts and Nevis

• **GEOGRAPHY Location:** two islands in eastern Caribbean Sea, about 45 mi. (72 km) NW of Antigua. Nevis 17°08'N, 62°37'W; St. Kitts 17°17'N, 62°43'W. **Boundaries:** Caribbean Sea to N, E, S, and W. **Total area:** 104 sq. mi. (269 sq km). **Coastline:** 84 mi. (135 km). **Comparative area:** 1.5 times the size of Washington, D.C. **Land use:** 17% arable land; 3% permanent crops; 80% other. **Major cities:** Basseterre (capital).

• **PEOPLE Population:** 39,619 (July 2008 est.). **Nationality:** noun—Kittitian(s), Nevisian(s); adjective—Kittitian, Nevisian. **Ethnic groups:** mainly of black African descent. **Languages:** English. **Religions:** Anglican, other Protestant sects, Roman Catholic.

• **GOVERNMENT Type:** constitutional monarchy. **Independence:** Sept. 19, 1983 (from U.K.). **Constitution:** Sept. 19, 1983. **National holiday:** Independence Day, Sept. 19. **Heads of Government:** Cuthbert Sebastian, governor-general (since Jan. 1996); Denzil Douglas, prime minister (since July

1995). **Structure:** executive—cabinet headed by prime minister; unicameral legislature; judiciary—East Caribbean Supreme Court, based on Saint Lucia.

• **ECONOMY   Monetary unit:** East Caribbean (EC) dollar. **Budget:** (2003 est.) *income:* $89.7 mil.; *expend.:* $128.2 mil. **G.D.P.:** $726 mil. (2006 est.), $8,200 per capita (2005 est.). **Chief crops:** sugarcane, rice, yams, vegetables, bananas. **Natural resources:** negl. **Major industries:** sugar processing, tourism, cotton. **Labor force:** 18,170 (1995); 69% services, 31% manufacturing. **Exports:** $84 mil. (2006 est.); machinery, food, electronics, beverages, tobacco. **Imports:** $383 mil. (2006 est.); machinery, manufactures, food, fuel. **Major trading partners:** (2006) *exports:* 62% U.S., 9.4% Canada, 6.6% Netherlands, 5% Azerbaijan; *imports:* 48.9% U.S., 13.1% Trinidad & Tobago, 4.6% Spain, 4.5% U.K.

The French settled St. Kitts in 1627; the English settled Nevis in 1628. In 1783 both became British possessions, and the two islands were united in 1882. Britain granted them independence in 1983. The country's economy is almost entirely based on sugar exports, so when Hurricane Hugo devastated sugar yields in 1990, the welfare of the entire population was affected. The reign of Kennedy Alphonse Simmonds, the only prime minister St. Kitts and Nevis had ever known, ended in July 1995, when Denzil Douglas's opposition Labour party defeated Kennedy's People's Action Movement. March 2000 elections confirmed the change: Labour took eight of the 11 seats, PAN took none. The continued fall of world sugar prices hurt the economy and in 1997 some leaders in Nevis started a movement to separate from St. Kitts because of high taxes. In 1998 a referendum on separation resulted in a majority yes-vote but not the two-thirds necessary.

▶ SAINT LUCIA

• **GEOGRAPHY   Location:** southeastern Caribbean Sea, between Martinique to N and St. Vincent to SW. Castries 14°01'N, 60°59'W. **Boundaries:** St. Lucia Channel to N, Atlantic Ocean to E, St. Vincent Passage to S, Caribbean Sea to W. **Total area:** 239 sq. mi. (620 sq km). **Coastline:** 98 mi. (158 km). **Comparative area:** 3.5 times size of Washington, D.C. **Land use:** 5% arable land; 23% permanent crops; 72% other. **Major cities:** Castries (capital).

• **PEOPLE   Population:** 172,884 (July 2008 est.). **Nationality:** noun—St. Lucian(s); adjective—St. Lucian. **Ethnic groups:** 82.5% black African descent, 11.9% mixed, 2.4% East Indian, 3.1% unspecified. **Languages:** English (official), French patois. **Religions:** 67.5% Roman Catholic, 20% Protestant, 2% Anglican, 2.1% Rastafarian, 4.5% none.

• **GOVERNMENT   Type:** parliamentary democracy. **Independence:** Feb. 22, 1979 (from U.K.). **Constitution:** Feb. 22, 1979. **National holiday:** Independence Day, Feb. 22. **Heads of Government:** Perlette Louisy, governor-general (since Sept. 1997); Stephenson King, prime minister (since Sept. 2007). **Structure:** executive—cabinet headed by prime minister; bicameral legislature—Senate, House of Representatives; judiciary—East Caribbean Supreme Court.

• **ECONOMY   Monetary unit:** East Caribbean (EC) dollar. **Budget:** (2000 est.) *income:* $141.2 mil.; *expend.:* $146.7 mil. **G.D.P.:** $1.179 bil. (2006 est.), $4,800 per capita (2005 est.). **Chief crops:** bananas, coconuts, vegetables, root crops, citrus, cocoa. **Natural resources:** forests, sandy beaches, minerals (pumice), mineral springs, geothermal

potential. **Major industries:** clothing, assembly of electronic components, beverages. **Labor force:** 43,800 (2001 est.); 21.7% agriculture, 53.6% services, 24.7% industry and commerce; 16.7% unemployment (2002). **Exports:** $288 mil. (2006 est.); 41% bananas, clothing, cocoa, vegetables, fruits, coconut oil. **Imports:** $791 mil. (2006 est.); 23% food, 21% manufactured goods, 19% machinery and transport equipment, chemicals, fuels. **Major trading partners:** (2006) *exports:* 69.7% France, 10.2% U.S., 8.8% U.K.; *imports:* 21.1% U.S., 14.9% Trinidad & Tobago, 12.3% Italy, 11.8% France, 7.2% Venezuela, 6.9% U.K., 5.8% Netherlands.

In 1650 the French settled St. Lucia, which was ceded to Britain in 1783. A member of the Federation of the West Indies from 1958 to 1962, St. Lucia became internally self-governing in 1967 but was still under Great Britain's protection. In 1979 St. Lucia gained full independence and now enjoys stable competitive politics. Hurricane Allen destroyed many of the country's banana plantations in 1980, and the economy took years to recover from the disaster. The government of Prime Minister John Compton of the United Workers party worked for agrarian reform and proposed legalizing gambling to stimulate tourism but after 15 years in power lost the 1997 elections to the Labour Party led by Kenny B. Anthony. In 2006, however, Compton won back the prime minister's title but he died in Sept. 2007 and was replaced by Stephenson King.

▶ SAINT VINCENT AND THE GRENADINES

• **GEOGRAPHY   Location:** large island of St. Vincent (13°12'N, 61°14'W) and about 50 smaller islands in southeastern Caribbean Sea about 21 mi. (34 km) SW of St. Lucia and 100 mi. (160 km) W of Barbados. **Boundaries:** St. Vincent Passage to N, Atlantic Ocean to E and SE, Caribbean Sea to SW and W. **Total area:** 131 sq. mi. (340 sq km). **Coastline:** 52 mi. (84 km). **Comparative area:** twice size of Washington, D.C. **Land use:** 10% arable land; 18% permanent crops; 72% other. **Major cities:** Kingstown (capital).

• **PEOPLE   Population:** 118,432 (2008 est.). **Nationality:** noun—St. Vincentian(s) or Vincentian(s); adjective—St. Vincentian or Vincentian. **Ethnic groups:** mainly of black African descent, remainder mixed, with some white, East Indian, and Carib Amerindian. **Languages:** English, French patois. **Religions:** Anglican, Methodist, Roman Catholic, Seventh-Day Adventist.

• **GOVERNMENT   Type:** parliamentary monarchy. **Independence:** Oct. 27, 1979 (from U.K.). **Constitution:** Oct. 27, 1979. **National holiday:** Independence Day, Oct. 27. **Heads of Government:** Frederick Nathaniel Ballantyne, governor-general (since Sept. 2, 2002); Ralph E. Gonsalves, prime minister (since Mar. 2001). **Structure:** executive—prime minister is head of government; bicameral legislature—15-member elected House of Representatives and 6-member appointed Senate; judiciary—East Caribbean Supreme Court.

• **ECONOMY   Monetary unit:** East Caribbean (EC) dollar. **Budget:** (2000 est.) *income:* $94.6 mil.; *expend.:* $85.8 mil. **G.D.P.:** $902 mil., $3,600 per capita (2005 est.). **Chief crops:** bananas, coconuts, sweet potatoes, spices; small numbers of cattle, sheep, pigs, goats; small fish catch used locally. **Natural resources:** negl. **Major industries:** food processing (sugar, flour), cement, furniture. **Labor force:** 67,000 (1984 est.); 26% agriculture,

17% industry, 57% services; 22% unemployed (1997). **Exports:** $193 mil. (2006 est.); 39% bananas, eddoes and dasheen (taro), arrowroot starch, tennis racquets. **Imports:** $578 mil. (2006 est.); foodstuffs, machinery and equipment, chemicals and fertilizers, minerals and fuels. **Major trading partners:** (2006) *exports:* 26.2% France, 21.3% Germany, 18.9% Italy, 7.2% Russia, 6.8% U.K.; *imports:* 17.3% Singapore, 12.1% Trinidad & Tobago, 11.1% U.S., 11% Italy, 9.5% Spain, 4.6% Turkey, 4.4% Germany.

Although ceded to Britain in 1763, St. Vincent was inhabited by the fierce Carib Indians, who continued fighting for control of the island until 1796, when they had all been either killed or deported. Just prior to its independence in 1979, St. Vincent and the Grenadines was a self-governing state in association with Great Britain. It is one of the poorest countries in the West Indies. Several natural disasters have plagued the economy, including a 1979 volcanic eruption and two destructive hurricanes in 1980 and 1986. Prime Minister James Mitchell of the New Democratic party currently governs the country, winning his fourth term after June 1997 elections gave his New Democratic Party a slender one-vote majority in the 15-seat legislature. But March 2001 elections overturned N.D.P. rule as united Labor won 12 of 15 parliamentary seats. The new left-wing government of Ralph Gonsalves has been seeking international accords with Libya and Cuba. He was reelected in 2005.

▶ SAMOA
Formerly Western Samoa
Independent State of Samoa
● **GEOGRAPHY   Location:** two large and seven small islands (five inhabited) in South Pacific Ocean, about 1,500 mi. (2,400 km) NE of New Zealand. Apia 13°49'S, 171°45'W. **Boundaries:** surrounded by Pacific Ocean; nearest neighbor is American Samoa to E. **Total area:** 1,104 sq. mi. (2,860 sq km). **Coastline:** 250 mi. (403 km). **Comparative area:** slightly smaller than Rhode Island. **Land use:** 19% arable land; 24% permanent crops; 57% other. **Major cities:** Apia (capital).
● **PEOPLE   Population:** 217,083 (July 2008 est.). **Nationality:** noun—Samoan(s); adjective—Samoan. **Ethnic groups:** 92.6% Samoan; about 7% Euronesians (persons of European and Polynesian blood), 0.4% Europeans. **Languages:** Samoan (Polynesian), English. **Religions:** 99.7% Christian (about half of population associated with London Missionary Society; includes Congregational, Roman Catholic, Methodist, Latter-Day Saints, Seventh-Day Adventist).
● **GOVERNMENT   Type:** constitutional monarchy under native chief. **Independence:** Jan. 1, 1962 (from U.N. trusteeship administered by New Zealand). **Constitution:** Jan. 1, 1962. **National holiday:** Independence Day, Jun. 1. **Heads of Government:** Tuiatua Tupua Tamasese Efi, head of state (since June 2007); Tuilaepa Sailele Malielegaoi, prime minister (since Nov. 1998). **Structure:** executive—chief of state appoints prime minister; unicameral legislature (47-member Legislative Assembly); judiciary.
● **ECONOMY   Monetary unit:** tala. **Budget:** (2005 est.) *income:* $171.3 mil.; *expend.:* $78.1 mil. **G.D.P.:** $1.218 bil. (2006 est.), $2,100 per capita (2005 est.). **Chief crops:** coconuts, bananas, taro, yams. **Natural resources:** hardwood forests, fish. **Major industries:** timber, tourism, food processing. **Labor force:** 90,000 (2000 est.); 65% agriculture, 30% ser-

vices. **Exports:** $131 mil. (f.o.b., 2006); coconut oil and cream, copra, fish, beer. **Imports:** $324 mil. (f.o.b., 2006); intermediate goods, food, capital goods. **Major trading partners:** (2006) *exports:* 44.1% Australia, 29.9% American Samoa, 11.3% Taiwan; *imports:* 21.5% New Zealand, 14.8% Fiji, 13.2% Singapore, 8.6% Australia, 8.6% Japan, 6.2% U.S., 5% Indonesia, 4.4% China.

The Polynesian island group of Samoa (Navigator's Islands) was partitioned in 1899 between the United States, which had established a naval base at Pago Pago on Tutuila in 1878, and Germany, which organized the westerly islands into a colony in 1894. In 1914 New Zealand troops occupied the German-held islands. New Zealand administered Western Samoa under a League of Nations mandate beginning in 1920 and continued to control the islands as a U.N. Trust Territory after 1945. In 1959 home rule was established under an elected local government. Western Samoa became an independent nation on Jan. 1, 1962. The constitution blends Western parliamentary government and traditional Samoan forms of rule. The parliamentary electorate is limited to the *matai*, heads of extended families; the malai are wholly responsible for local affairs. The local culture is similarly a blend of Samoan tradition with Christianity. The economy is based on subsistence agriculture, forestry, fishing, and tourism.

In November 1998, after 16 years of stable and peaceful rule, Prime Minister Tofilau Eti Alesana resigned for health reasons and was replaced by his deputy, Tuilaepa Sailele Malielegaoi whose Human Rights Protection Party won the next two elections (2001 and 2006). After 45 years on the throne, King Malietoa Tanumafili II died in May 2007, and was succeeded as head of state by Tuiatua Tupua Tamasese Efi in June.

▶ SAN MARINO
Republic of San Marino
● **GEOGRAPHY   Location:** on slopes of Mt. Titano, in the Apennines, within central Italian region of Emilia-Romagna. **Boundaries:** surrounded by Italian territory. **Total area:** 23 sq. mi. (60 sq km). **Coastline:** none. **Comparative area:** about three-tenths size of Washington, D.C. **Land use:** 17% arable land; 0% permanent crops; 83% other. **Major cities:** San Marino (capital).
● **PEOPLE   Population:** 29,973 (July 2008 est.). **Nationality:** noun—Sammarinese (sing., pl.); adjective—Sammarinese. **Ethnic groups:** Sammarinese, Italian. **Languages:** Italian. **Religions:** Roman Catholic.
● **GOVERNMENT   Type:** republic. **Independence:** 301 A.D. **Constitution:** Oct. 8, 1600; electoral law of 1926 serves some of functions of constitution. **National holiday:** Anniversary of the Foundation of the Republic, Sept. 3. **Heads of Government:** Two co-presidents who rule for six months. **Structure:** executive—two captain-regents with six-month terms elected by and from the legislature, actual power wielded by secretary of state for foreign affairs; unicameral legislature—Great and General Council elected by popular vote for five-year terms; judicial—Council of Twelve is supreme judicial body.
● **ECONOMY   Monetary unit:** Euro. **Budget:** (2004 est.) *income:* $709.6 mil.; *expend:* $672.3 mil. **G.D.P.:** $850 mil., $34,100 per capita (2004 est.). **Chief crops:** wheat, grapes, maize, olives; cattle, pigs, horses, meat, cheese, hides. **Natural resources:** building stones. **Major industries:** tourism, textiles, electronics. **Labor force:** 20,470 (2004); 60% ser-

vices, 40% industry, less than 1% agriculture. **Exports:** $1.291 bil (2004 est.) trade data included with Italian statistics; commodity trade consisting primarily of exchanging building stone, lime, wood, chestnuts, wheat, and wine for a wide variety of consumer manufactures. **Imports:** $2.035 bil (2004 est.) see exports. **Major trading partners:** N.A.

The "Most Serene Republic" of San Marino, entirely surrounded by Italy near the city of Rimini, is the oldest republic in the world, with communitarian roots dating to the fourth century a.d. While Piedmont-Sardinia was conquering all of the rest of the Italian peninsula during the period 1860-70, it left San Marino independent; the new kingdom of Italy signed a treaty of friendship and cooperation with the republic in 1862.

Leftist coalitions governed from 1978 through 1986, giving San Marino the only Communist government west of the Soviet bloc. Since 1986 the government has been controlled by a coalition of Communists and Christian Democrats. In 1992 San Marino joined the United Nations.

The economy is balanced between small-scale agriculture (primarily wine grapes and livestock) and industry, including textiles, ceramics, and furniture. Philatelic sales and tourism are important sources of revenue. Lacking extremes of wealth and poverty and with low unemployment, the republic enjoys general prosperity.

▶ SÃO TOMÉ AND PRÍNCIPE
Democratic Republic of Saõ Tomé and Príncipe

• **GEOGRAPHY   Location:** two main islands, São Tomé (0°19′N, 6°43′E) and Príncipe, and Caroço, Pedras, Tinhosas (off Príncipe), and Rolas (off São Tomé), off west coast of Africa. **Boundaries:** west of Gabon in Gulf of Guinea. **Total area:** 371 sq. mi. (960 sq km). **Coastline:** 130 mi. (209 km). **Comparative area:** more than 5.5 times size of Washington, D.C. **Land use:** 2% arable land; 41% permanent crops; 57% other. **Major cities:** São Tomé (capital).

• **PEOPLE   Population:** 206,178 (July 2008 est.). **Nationality:** noun—São Toméan(s); adjective—São Toméan. **Ethnic groups:** mestiço, angolares (descendants of Angolan slaves), forros (descendents of freed slaves), servicais (contract laborers from Angola, Mozambique, and Cape Verde), tongas (children of servicais born on the islands), and Europeans (primarily Portuguese). **Languages:** Portuguese (official). **Religions:** Roman Catholic, Evangelical Protestant, Seventh-Day Adventist, New Apostolic, 20% none.

• **GOVERNMENT   Type:** republic. **Independence:** July 12, 1975 (from Portugal). **Constitution:** Sept. 10, 1990. **National holiday:** Independence Day, July 12. **Heads of Government:** Fradique Bandeira Melo de Menezes, president (since Sept. 2001); Joaquim Branco, prime minister (since June 2008). **Structure:** executive—president assisted by cabinet of ministers; unicameral legislature; judiciary.

• **ECONOMY   Monetary unit:** dobra. **Budget:** (2007 est.) *income:* $74.11 mil.; *expend.:* $57.71 mil. **G.D.P.:** $278 mil. (2006 est.), $1,200 per capita (2003 est.). **Chief crops:** cocoa, copra, coconuts, coffee, palm kernels, bananas, cinnamon, pepper, papaya, beans; poultry, fish. **Natural resources:** fish. **Major industries:** light construction, textiles, soap, beer; fish processing. **Labor force:** most of population engaged in subsistence agriculture and fishing; labor shortages of skilled workers. **Exports:** $4 mil. (f.o.b., 2007 est.); 90% cocoa, copra,

coffee, palm oil. **Imports:** $73 mil. (f.o.b., 2007 est.); machinery and electrical equipment, food products, fuels. **Major trading partners:** (2006) *exports:* 48% Netherlands, 19% Belgium, 9% Portugal; *imports:* 49% Portugal, 20% France, 5% Belgium, 5% U.S.

The islands of São Tomé and Príncipe, located in the Atlantic Ocean 275 and 125 miles, respectively, off the northern coast of Gabon, make up the smallest nation in Africa. They were uninhabited when first discovered by the Portuguese in 1470 but by the mid-1500's became Africa's foremost exporter of sugar. As the sugar market declined, the islands became a major slave-trading center and producer of coffee and cocoa. By 1908 São Tomé was the world's largest cocoa producer.

Portugal did not abolish slavery until 1876, and abusive labor practices continued until well into the 20th century. In 1953 hundreds of workers were killed in clashes with the Portuguese. Soon after, a small number of São Toméans formed the Movement for the Liberation of São Tomé and Príncipe (MLSTP) with its base in Gabon. But the islands did not gain independence until July 12, 1975.

The MLSTP took over after independence and became the country's only official party. By 1986 the country relied on foreign aid for approximately 41 percent of its G.N.P. Although in the past it received military advisers from the former Soviet Union and economic advisers from Cuba, São Tomé and Príncipe has announced a foreign policy based upon nonalignment. Multi-party democracy was introduced in 1991. At the beginning of the new century oil was discovered and shortly later (July 2002) a military junta seized power. Nigeria agreed to build the port and refinery and bids for exploration were taken in 2003. The junta agreed to the return of the president who pledged equitable distribution of oil revenues.

▶ SAUDI ARABIA
Kingdom of Saudi Arabia

• **GEOGRAPHY   Location:** occupies four-fifths of Arabian peninsula in southwestern Asia. **Boundaries:** Jordan, Iraq, and Kuwait to N, Persian Gulf, Qatar, and United Arab Emirates to E, Oman to SE, Yemen to S and SE, Red Sea to W. **Total area:** 756,982 sq. mi. (1,960,582 sq km). **Coastline:** 1,641 mi. (2,640 km). **Comparative area:** slightly more than one-fifth the size of the U.S. **Land use:** 2% arable land; negl. % permanent crops; 98% other. **Major cities:** Riyadh (capital); Jid'dah; Mecca; Taif; Medina.

• **PEOPLE   Population:** 28,161,447 (July 2008 est.). **Nationality:** noun—Saudi(s); adjective—Saudi or Saudi Arabian. **Ethnic groups:** 90% Arab, 10% Afro-Asian. **Languages:** Arabic. **Religions:** 100% Muslim.

• **GOVERNMENT   Type:** monarchy. **Constitution:** none; governed according to Shari'a or Islamic law. **National holiday:** Unification of the Kingdom, Sept. 23. **Head of Government:** Abdullah Bin Abdulaziz al-Saud, king (since Aug. 2005). **Structure:** king rules in consultation with royal family and Council of Ministers; no elected legislature; Supreme Council of Justice.

• **ECONOMY   Monetary unit:** Saudi riyal. **Budget:** (2007 est.) *income:* $193.7 bil.; *expend.:* $122.2 bil. **G.D.P.:** $572.2 bil., $20,700 per capita (2007 est.). **Chief crops:** wheat, barley, tomatoes, melons, dates, citrus; mutton, chickens, eggs, milk. **Natural resources:** crude oil, natural gas, iron ore, gold, copper. **Major industries:** crude oil production, petroleum refining, basic petrochemicals. **Labor force:** 6.488 mil. (2007); 25% industry, 63% services, 12% agriculture. **Exports:** $215 bil. (f.o.b., 2007); 90% petroleum and petroleum products. **Imports:** $82.77 bil. (f.o.b., 2007); machinery and equipment, foodstuffs, chemicals, motor vehicles, textiles. **Major trading partners:** (2006) *exports:* 17.7% Japan, 15.8% U.S. 9% South Korea, 7.2% China, 4.6% Taiwan, 4.4% Singapore; *imports:* 12.2% U.S., 9.1% Germany, 7.9% China, 7.3% Japan, 4.8% U.K., 4.8% Italy, 4.1% South Korea.

In ancient times various cultures flourished in the Arabian peninsula, particularly along the western rim, in cities devoted to trade between the Gulf of Aden and the eastern Mediterranean, and in such agricultural and trading centers as Yemen and Oman. Cultural and political unity was lacking, however, until the rise of Mohammed, the prophet of Islam. In A.D. 622 Mohammed fled from Mecca, the center of Arabian paganism, to the nearby city of Medina; the Islamic era dates from that year. Preaching from Medina, Mohammed gained converts to Islam throughout Arabia. His army captured Mecca in 630, converting its sacred shrine, the Kaaba, to an Islamic place of worship. By 632, when Mohammed died, all of Arabia was unified under Islamic rule.

In 661 the Caliphate, the ruling body of early Islam, moved from Medina to Damascus. Thereafter Arabia was nominally unified under Islamic rule—but in practice was usually divided among various principalities in the arable areas and trading centers, and under tribal rule in the arid interior. Mecca fell to the Ottoman Empire in 1517, but Ottoman control of Arabia was never complete. The rise of the Wahabi sect of Islam in the 18th century posed a challenge to Ottoman rule. In the 19th century, the Saud family rose to leadership in the Wahabi movement and established a kingdom in Nejd, the central region of Arabia, with a capital at Riyadh.

In 1902 Ibn Saud (1880-1953) consolidated his family's control at Riyadh and in 1912-13 led a new Wahabi revolt against the Ottoman Turks. During World War I, the British aided Ibn Saud's rebellion in the Nejd, along with that of Ibn Saud's rival Hussein ibn Ali in the Hejaz, in the mountains of western Arabia along the coast of the Red Sea. A British protectorate was established in both regions in 1915, and Great Britain maintained a dominant position in Arabia after World War I.

In 1924 Ibn Saud captured Hussein ibn Ali's capital at Mecca, and he proclaimed himself king of Hejaz in 1926 and of Nejd in 1927. Ibn Saud consolidated his control over the following two years, and his kingdom was formally recognized by Great Britain in 1927. The country was renamed Saudi Arabia in 1932.

Saudi Arabia is an absolute monarchy based on Islamic law; it has no written constitution and no parliament. The king exercises sole authority and rules in consultation with a Council of Ministers. Islamic law is enforced; alcohol is prohibited and the public activities of women severely restricted. The Saudi kings have great power within the Islamic world through their control over the holy cities of Mecca and Medina and their administration of the annual Muslim pilgrimages to those cities.

The discovery of oil in eastern Arabia in the early 1930's rapidly transformed Saudi Arabia from an impoverished nation to a center of great wealth. In 1933 an exclusive concession for the exploitation of Saudi Arabian oil was granted to an American-chartered corporation, the Arabian-American Oil Company (Aramco). For many years wealth remained concentrated in the hands of the Saudi clan, and little change was felt in the desert interior, where Bedouin nomads continued to raise sheep and camels. Large numbers of Yemenis, Palestinians, Pakistanis, and other foreign workers are employed in the oil fields.

Saudi Arabia remained neutral during most of World War II but declared war on the Axis powers in March 1945; in the same year, it became a founding member of both the United Nations and the Arab League.

Ibn Saud became a leader of Arab anti-Zionism and contributed a small contingent of troops to the 1948 Arab-Israeli War. That policy was maintained by Ibn Saud's second son and successor, King Faisal, who instituted a policy of providing large annual subsidies to Egypt and other Arab League states following the 1967 Arab-Israeli War. In 1973 King Faisal sent Saudi units to fight in the Arab-Israeli War of that year. He played a leading role in organizing the 1973-74 Arab oil embargo in an effort to force the United States and its allies to take a harder line with Israel.

King Faisal was assassinated by his nephew, Prince Faisal, on Mar. 25, 1975, and was succeeded by King Khalid. Little change in policy resulted. In 1979 Saudi Arabia denounced the Camp David talks and the Egyptian-Israeli peace treaty and led the Arab League effort to ostracize Egypt within the Arab world.

Saudi Arabia has consistently opposed leftist and radical movements in the Arab world, sending troops to help put down leftist rebellions in North Yemen and Oman in the 1970's. Saudi kings have taken a moderate approach toward relations with the West. Following the transfer of Aramco assets to full Saudi Arabian ownership during 1973-76, Saudi Arabia used its leading position within the Organization of Petroleum Exporting Countries (OPEC) to argue for a policy of stable production and prices.

This moderate policy has been rewarded by the willingness of the U.S., Great Britain, France, and other Western nations to sell arms—including jet fighters, tanks, and other sophisticated weapons—to Saudi Arabia despite Israeli protests.

Saudi Arabia experienced repeated disturbances in the 1980's. Muslim fundamentalist terrorists seized the Grand Mosque at Mecca on Nov. 20, 1979, provoking a crisis for the Saudi monarchy. On July 31, 1987, Iranian pilgrims rioted in Mecca and were fired upon by Saudi security forces; 402 persons died, including 275 Iranians. Iran's Ayatollah Khomeini denounced the Saudi government and said it was unworthy of being the guardian of Islam's sacred shrines.

A longtime supporter of the Palestine Liberation Organization, the Saudi government gave the PLO $850 million during the 1980's, but ceased when the PLO backed Saddam Hussein's invasion of Kuwait in 1990. During the Persian Gulf War, King Fahd granted permission to station U.S. troops in Saudi Arabia to guard against a possible Iraqi attack. The Saudis promised the United States $16.8 billion and Egypt $1.5 billion to defray the costs of the war. Little ground fighting took place on Saudi soil, but massive oil spills threatened the operation of crucial desalination plants in the Persian Gulf.

In 1996 King Fahd, ailing from a 1995 stroke, temporarily ceded power to his legal successor, Crown Prince Abdullah. In June, terrorists bombed an apartment complex in Dhahran, killing 19 American soldiers stationed there and wounding more than 300 people.

U.S.–Saudi relations were greatly strained when the 9/11 attacks were revealed to have been perpetrated by Saudi citizens. In May 2003 terrorist attacks in the form of four suicide bombings occurred in Riyad in two days. In Aug. a U.S. Congressional report on the 9/11 attacks appeared with 28 of its 850 pages deleted by the White House, pages reportedly describing support provided by Saudi government officials to the hijacker-terrorists. In 2005 King Fahd died and Prince Abdullah ascended the throne.

The U.S. occupation of Iraq has strained relations with the Bush Administration. In April 2007, however, the Saudi government uncovered a serious terrorist plot on its own territory, a plot it claimed derived from the war in Iraq.

▶ SENEGAL
Republic of Senegal

• **GEOGRAPHY Location:** northwestern coast of Africa. **Boundaries:** Mauritania to N, Mali to E, Guinea and Guinea-Bissau to S, Atlantic Ocean to W; The Gambia forms narrow enclave extending 200 mi. (320 km) inland from Atlantic coast. **Total area:** 75,749 sq. mi. (196,190 sq km). **Coastline:** 330 mi. (531 km). **Comparative area:** slightly smaller than South Dakota. **Land use:** 12% arable land; negl.% permanent crops; 88% other. **Major cities:** Dakar (capital); Thies; Kaolack.

• **PEOPLE Population:** 12,853,259 (July 2008 est.). **Nationality:** noun—Senegalese (sing., pl.); adjective—Senegalese. **Ethnic groups:** 43.3% Wolof, 23.8% Pular, 14.7% Serer, 3.7% Diola, 3% Mandink, 1.1% Soninke, 1% European and Lebanese. **Languages:** French (official), Wolof, Pulaar, Diola, Mandingo. **Religions:** 94% Muslim, 1% indigenous beliefs, 5% Christian (mostly Roman Catholic).

• **GOVERNMENT Type:** republic under multi-party democratic rule. **Independence:** Apr. 4, 1960 (from France). **Constitution:** a new constitution was adopted Jan. 7, 2001. **National holiday:** Independence Day, Apr. 4. **Heads of Government:** Abdoulaye Wade, president (since Apr. 2000); Cheikh H. Soumaré, prime minister (since Dec. 2007). **Structure:** executive—president; unicameral legislature; judiciary—Constitutional Court, Council of State, Court of Final Appeals, Court of Appeals.

• **ECONOMY Monetary unit:** Communauté Financière Africaine (CFA) franc. **Budget:** (2007 est.) **income:** $2.25 bil.; **expend.:** $2.987 bil. **G.D.P.:** $20.61 bil., $1,700 per capita (2007 est.). **Chief crops:** peanuts, millet, corn, sorghum, rice, cotton, tomotoes, green vegetables; cattle, poultry, pigs; fish. **Natural resources:** fish, phosphates, iron ore. **Major industries:** fishing, agricultural processing, phosphate mining. **Labor force:** 4.85 mil (2007 est.), 77.5% agriculture, 22.5% industry and services; 48% unemployment (2007 est.). **Exports:** $1.725 bil. (f.o.b., 2007); fish, peanuts, petroleum products, phosphates, cotton. **Imports:** $3.673 bil. (f.o.b., 2007); foods and beverages, consumer goods, capital goods, petroleum products. **Major trading partners:** (2006) *exports:* 19.2% Mali, 8.3% France, 5.8% India, 5.3% The Gambia, 5.1% Spain, 4.9% Italy; *imports:* 25.1% France, 5.2% U.K., 4.8% Thailand, 4.5% China, 4% Spain.

Inhabited since ancient times, Senegal was dominated in the 13th and 14th centuries by the Mandingo and Jolof empires. Portuguese traders and explorers arrived in Senegal in the early 15th century and later competed with the British, Dutch, and French for domination in Senegal. The French established a trading station at Saint-Louis in 1659 and maintained possession thereafter, except for the British enclave along the Gambia River.

In the early 19th century, the French began a series of campaigns to bring the entire country under their control; the last independent sultanate surrendered in 1893. Senegal became a French colony in 1920, and Dakar became the capital of French West Africa. Senegal became a major contributor of African troops to the French armed forces.

In 1946 a territorial assembly was established, with a limited electorate and advisory powers, which were gradually expanded in subsequent years. With the creation of the French Community of Nations in 1958, Senegal achieved local self-rule within the community.

In 1959, with the encouragement of France, Senegal and French Sudan (now Mali) formed the Federation of Mali, which became fully independent on June 20, 1960. Senegal seceded from the federation on Aug. 20 and declared itself the Republic of Senegal. Leopold Sedar Senghor became Senegal's first president.

In 1962 Prime Minister Mamdou Dia attempted a coup against the Senghor government; it failed, and Dia was imprisoned. A new constitution was subsequently adopted, strengthening the power of the presidency. Senghor retired from office in 1981 and was succeeded by Adbou Diouf. He encouraged political pluralism and has presided over a generally stable government. Diouf was elected in his own right in 1983 and reelected in 1988. Following the 1988 elections, riots broke out over charges of electoral fraud, and a state of emergency was declared.

Diouf, who has taken a lead in African affairs, was reelected for the third time in 1993, and he consolidated his power so well that in 1998 Parliament passed a law allowing him to become President for life. His involvement in the civil war in Guinea-Bissau, however, caused dissension in the army. His creation of a Senate as "upper house" to the National Assembly meant little for democracy since, with all opposition parties boycotting the election, his Socialist Party carried all 45 seats up for election. So the March 2000 presidential election was a surprise: Abdoulaye Wade of the Democratic Party (who had run four times since 1978) took 60 percent of the vote to become Senegal's third, and first non-Socialist, president. At the end of 2004 he was able to end a small but destructive insurgency demanding autonomy for a small piece of land (Casamance) that has befuddled the nation since the early 1980's.

Although now over 80 years old, Wade ran again in March 2007, and was reelected, though some judged the election unfair. Legislative elections in June were boycotted by groups opposed to Wade.

▶ SERBIA

• **GEOGRAPHY Location:** Southern central Europe. **Boundaries:** Hungary to N, Romania to NE, Bulgaria to E, Macedonia and Albania to S, Adriatic Sea, Bosnia and Herzegovina to W., Croatia to NW. **Total area:** 39,517 sq. mi. (102,350 sq km). **Coastline:** 124 mi. (199 km). **Comparative area:** Slightly smaller than Kentucky. **Land use:** 36% arable; 3% permanent crops, 61% other. **Major cities:** Belgrade (capital); Nis; Kragujevac; Novi Sad; Podoricj.

● **PEOPLE** **Population:** 10,159,046 (July 2008 est.). **Nationality:** noun—Serb(s) and Montenegrin(s); adjective—Serbian and Montenegrin. **Ethnic groups:** 82.9% Serbian, 1% Montenegrin, 4% Hungarian, 13.4% other. **Languages:** 95% Serbian, 5% Albanian. **Religions:** 65% Orthodox, 19% Muslim, 4% Roman Catholic, 1% Protestant, 11% other.

● **GOVERNMENT** **Type:** republic. **Independence:** Proclaimed itself successor to former Socialist Federal Republic of Yugoslavia Apr. 11, 1992. **Constitution:** Oct. 2006. **National holiday:** Republic Day, Nov. 29. **Heads of Government:** Boris Tadic, president (since June 2004); Mirko Cvetković, prime minister (since June 2006); **Structure:** executive—president; bicameral legislature; judiciary—judges elected by legislature.

● **ECONOMY** **Monetary unit:** Yugoslav new dinar. **Budget:** (2007 est.) *income:* $9.6 bil., *expend:* $9.8 bil. **G.D.P.:** $56.89 bil., $7,700 per capita (2007 est.). **Chief crops:** cereal, fruits, vegetables, tobacco, olives; cattle, sheep, goats. **Natural resources:** oil, gas, coal, antimony, copper. **Major industries:** machine building, metallurgy, mining, consumer goods, electronics, petroleum products, chemicals, pharmaceuticals. **Labor force:** 2.9 mil. (2002); 18.8% unemployment (2007 est.). **Exports:** $8.824 bil. (2007); manufactured goods, food and live animals, raw materials. **Imports:** $18.3 bil. (2007); machinery and transport equipment, fuels and lubricants, manufactured goods, chemicals, food and live animals, raw materials. **Major trading partners:** Bosnia and Herzegovnia, Italy, Russia.

The lands that composed Yugoslavia until 1991 were incorporated into the Roman Empire as the province of Illyricum in the first century A.D. Christianity became dominant by A.D. 600. Its nucleus was Serbia, settled in the seventh century by South Slav migrants from the Over and Vistula, and converted to Christianity, in its Eastern Orthodox form, in the ninth century. Twice (in 1077 and again in 1202), the Vatican sent royal crowns to Serbian kings, emphasizing their independence, despite the religious differences. Serbia's medieval zenith came during the reign of Stephen Dushan (1331-55), who subjected Albania, Macedonia, Thessaly, and Epirus to his rule, and who gained the vassalage of Bulgaria in addition. But within 30 years of his death, the Ottoman Turks had overrun his realm, a dominance sealed by the Serbian catastrophe at the Battle of Kosovo (1389). Not until 1878 did Serbia regain independence.

The complexities of Balkan politics occupied European statesmen throughout the late 19th century, and the Balkan Wars of 1912 and 1913 led directly to the outbreak of World War I. After the collapse of the Austro-Hungarian Empire during the war, the multiethnic and multinational state of Yugoslavia was patched together in 1918-19. To Serbia were annexed the old Austro-Hungarian lands of Slovenia and Croatia, as well as the ethnically Croatian and Serbian lands of Bosnia and Herzegovina and Montenegro, Macedonia and Kosovo. The last three were Serbian, Bulgarian, and Albanian in nationality, respectively.

The nationalities coexisted in a state of mutual hostility, provoking a royal dictatorship, instituted by King Alexander in 1929 and enduring after his assassination in 1934. Hitler invaded Yugoslavia in 1941; German troops were welcomed in Croatia as liberators from the Serbs. Resistance began almost immediately, split into two mutually hostile groups: Draza Mihajlovic's Serbian royalist Chetniks, and the Partisans, a group of pan-Yugoslav Communists and non-Serbian anti-German forces led by Tito (a.k.a. Josip Broz). By the end of the war, over 2 million Yugoslavs had died, and 3.5 million were homeless. Backed by both Churchill and Stalin, Tito ruled over a ruined land: the new Federal People's Republic of Yugoslavia.

Tito imposed agricultural collectivization on the Stalinist model, and pushed for the development of industry under state ownership. Politically, harsh repression fell on members of the Chetnik resistance as well as on the Slovene Home Guard and the Croatian Ustasa, But the postwar period of tyranny was short-lived. Tito refused to permit Yugoslavia to become a Soviet satellite; in 1948 he expelled Russian military advisers, and was himself expelled from the Comintern.

In the face of economic pressure and military threats, Tito turned westward. Stalinism yielded to decentralized communism. The 1953 Agrarian Reform Law permitted private agricultural holdings, and 80 percent of the land returned to private ownership; "self-management" rather than central control was encouraged in the industrial sector. Economic growth averaged 7 percent per year for three decades, lifting Yugoslavia into the ranks of the semideveloped countries.

Despite a reconciliation with Khruschev's Soviet Union in 1955-56, Tito continued to chart an independent course, taking a leading role in the Third World Non-Aligned Movement and providing a political and economic alternative model for Eastern Europe. But Yugoslavian nationalism masked the development of separate nationalisms within the Yugoslavian federation.

The country's major ethnic groups (Serbs, Croats, and Muslims) coexisted under Tito's iron hand, and even after Tito's death in 1980, his rotating presidency scheme, in which the leaders of each republic took turns serving as "president of the presidency," worked smoothly. But when communism fell in 1989, only Serbia and Montenegro voted for Communist governments, while the republics of Croatia, Slovenia, Macedonia, and Bosnia-Herzegovina sought independence.

A vicious civil war ensued in which Yugoslavia's Serbian president Slobodan Milosevic sought to keep all ethnically Serbian areas under Serbian control. While Serb militias captured about one-third of Croatia in 1991, the Croatian army won back most of the region in 1995. And Yugoslavia's attempt to keep Bosnia-Herzegovina within a "greater Serbia" failed as well, the failure ratified in the November 1995 "Dayton Accords," which brought NATO peacekeepers to the region. The year 1996 saw the formal end of the civil wars, as Milosevic endorsed treaties guaranteeing the boundaries of Macedonia, Croatia and Bosnia; additionally, a pact with the Albanians of Serbia's Kosovo province permitted Albanian as the language of instruction in Kosovo's schools.

Though Milosevic and his political allies won 84 of 138 seats in Yugoslavia's parliament in Nov. 1996, the political opposition, called Zajedno ("Together"), won control of 14 large cities. The annulments of these results by Yugoslav courts and electoral commissions provoked 11 weeks of popular protests until Milosevic conceded in Feb. 1997. In July, however, Milosevic maneuvered to take back the presidency by receiving a majority of votes in Parliament.

In 1998 ethnic Albanians in the Kosovo province of Serbia launched a terrorist campaign to secede from Serbia and join Albania. The Serbs put down the rebellion with unexpected ferocity. In the winter of 1999 Serbia launched a full-scale attack against Kosovo that drove 700,000 ethnic Albanians from their homes. Despite NATO warnings, Pres. Milosevic continued his ethnic cleansing of Serbia's province and at the end of March NATO began a bombing campaign that lasted 72 days. In June Serbia surrendered and Milosevic agreed to 50,000 NATO troops in Kosovo and the withdrawal of all Yugoslav troops. The U.N. supervised peace was slow to form and soon Serbs were being driven from Kosovo. In 2000 Milosevic managed to maintain his power but his attempt to rig elections in the summer led to mass protests.

In 2000, as NATO troops attempted to defend Serbia proper against Albanian incursions from Kosovo, opposition in Serbia to continuance of the Milosevic regime faced police-state measures. A coalition of 15 parties backed Vojislav Kostunica against Milosevic in the Sept. presidential elections. Hundreds of thousands protested the Milosevic attempts to force a run-off and Kostunica was sworn in Oct. 7. Milosevic was turned over to the U.N. for trial on war-crimes charges. In March 2002 the presidents of Serbia and Montenegro agreed to maintain foreign affairs and defense as the sole bonds in a loose federation. The very name "Yugoslavia" was dropped in favor of "Serbia and Montenegro."

In the 2003 elections in Montenegro, former president Milo Đjukanovic became prime minister of a government favoring independence. In Serbia, ex-president Koštunica became prime minister after the assassination of Djindjic. Boris Tadic was elected president in June 2004. In May 2006, 55.5 percent of Montenegro's voters chose independence from Serbia for their future. The process of separation began immediately, and Montenegro and Serbia became independent states. In Oct. 2006, the Serbian parliament unanimously confirmed a new constitution.

In 2007, Kosovo's bid to become independent was stopped by Russia's refusal to accept that idea but in Feb. 2008, Kosovo declared its independence. Tadic was reelected, and Radovan Karadzic was accused of war crimes, arrested, and sent to the Hague.

▶ SEYCHELLES
Republic of Seychelles
• **GEOGRAPHY Location:** more than 90 widely scattered islands in western Indian Ocean about 1,000 mi. (1,600 km) E of Kenya and Tanzania. Victoria (Mahé Is.) 4°37'S, 55°28'E. **Boundaries:** surrounded by Indian Ocean; nearest neighbor is Madagascar about 130 mi. (210 km) S of southernmost island group. **Total area:** 176 sq. mi. (455 sq km). **Coastline:** 305 mi. (491 km). **Comparative area:** 2.5 times the size of Washington, D.C. **Land use:** 2% arable land; 13% permanent crops; 85% other. **Major cities:** Victoria (capital).
• **PEOPLE Population:** 82,247 (July 2008 est.). **Nationality:** noun—Seychellois (sing., pl.); adjective—Seychelles. **Ethnic groups:** Seychellois (mixture of Asians, Africans, Europeans, Arab, Chinese). **Languages:** English, French (both official); Creole. **Religions:** 82% Roman Catholic, 6% Anglican, 6% other, 1% Muslim, 2% Hindu.
• **GOVERNMENT Type:** republic. **Independence:** June 29, 1976 (from U.K.). **Constitution:** June 18, 1993. **National holiday:** National Day, June 18. **Head of Government:** James A. Michel, president (since Apr. 2004). **Structure:** executive—president; unicameral legislature; judiciary.

• **ECONOMY Monetary unit:** Seychelles rupee. **Budget:** (2007 est.) *income:* $380.4 mil.; *expend.:* $361.2 mil. **G.D.P.:** $1.655 bil., $18,400 per capita (2007 est.). **Chief crops:** coconuts, cinnamon, vanilla, sweet potatoes, cassava, bananas; broiler chickens; tuna fishing (expansion under way). **Natural resources:** fish, copra, cinnamon trees. **Major industries:** tourism is largest industry; processing of coconut and vanilla; fishing. **Labor force:** 39,560 (2006); 23% industry, 74% services, 3% agriculture, forestry, and fishing. **Exports:** $434 mil. (f.o.b., 2007); fish, cinnamon bark, copra, petroleum products (reexports). **Imports:** $721 mil. (f.o.b., 2007); food, petroleum products, machinery, transportation equipment. **Major trading partners:** (2006) *exports:* 25.5% U.K., 17.5% France, 12% Italy, 8.5% Mauritius, 8.3% Japan, 8.2% Spain, 4.3% Netherlands; *imports:* 17.7% Saudi Arabia, 9.7% South Africa, 8.1% Spain, 7.8% France, 7.2% Singapore, 4.8% Italy, 4% U.K.

The Seychelles Islands were occupied by France in the 18th century and seized by Great Britain in 1794. They were administered along with Mauritius until 1903, when the Seychelles became a separate British colony. African and Indian workers were brought in to work in coconut and spice plantations and in guano mining. The present population is of mixed African, Indian, and European descent.

In the post-World War II period, a home-rule government rejected independence as impracticable. At the urging of the Organization of African Unity and the United Nations, the Seychelles declared independence on June 29, 1976. Its first president was ousted in a socialist coup in 1977 led by Prime Minister France Albert René. A new constitution, promulgated in March 1979, formalized one-party Socialist rule. In July 1992 a commission was elected to rewrite the constitution before the end of the year, but the delegates defeated the first results. Rene retired in 2004 and his vice president James Michel took over and was elected in 2006 for five years.

Since independence, the economy of the Seychelles has become heavily dependent on the tourist industry, which accounts for 90 percent of the country's foreign exchange earnings. Fishing accounts for 40 percent of exports.

▶ SIERRA LEONE
Republic of Sierra Leone
• **GEOGRAPHY Location:** west central Africa. **Boundaries:** Guinea to N and E, Liberia to S, Atlantic Ocean to W. **Total area:** 27,699 sq. mi. (71,740 sq km). **Coastline:** 250 mi. (402 km). **Comparative area:** slightly smaller than South Carolina. **Land use:** 7% arable land; 1% permanent crops; 92% other.; **Major cities:** Freetown (capital); Koindu; Bo; Kenema; Makeni.
• **PEOPLE Population:** 6,294,774 (July 2008 est.). **Nationality:** noun—Sierra Leonean(s); adjective—Sierra Leonean. **Ethnic groups:** over 90% African (30% Temne, 30% Mende), 10% creole. **Languages:** English (official); regular use limited to literate minority; principal languages are Mende in south and Temne in north; Krio is language of resettled ex-slave population of Freetown area and is lingua franca. **Religions:** 60% Muslim, 30% indigenous beliefs, 10% Christian.
• **GOVERNMENT Type:** constitutional democracy. **Independence:** Apr. 27, 1961 (from U.K.). **Constitution:** Oct. 1, 1991. **National holiday:** Independence Day, Apr. 27. **Heads of Government:** Ernest

Bai Koroma, president (since Sept. 2007). **Structure:** executive—president; unicameral legislature-68 elected seats, 12 filled by paramount chiefs; judiciary.
● ECONOMY **Monetary unit:** leone. **Budget:** (2000 est.) *income:* $96 mil.; *expend.:* $351 mil. **G.D.P.:** $4.882 bil., $800 per capita (2007 est.). **Chief crops:** palm kernels, coffee, cocoa, rice, palm oil, peanuts; poultry, cattle, sheep, pigs; fish. **Natural resources:** diamonds, titanium ore, bauxite, iron ore, gold. **Major industries:** mining (diamonds, iron ore, bauxite, rutile), small-scale manufacturing (beverages, textiles, cigarettes, footwear), petroleum refinery. **Labor force:** 1.369 mil. (1981); 65% agriculture, 19% industry, 16% services; only small minority, some 65,000, earn wages. **Exports:** $216 mil. (f.o.b., 2006); diamonds, rutile, cocoa, coffee, fish. **Imports:** $560 mil. (f.o.b., 2006); foodstuffs, machinery and equipment, fuels and lubricants. **Major trading partners:** (2006) *exports:* 52% Belgium, 19% U.S., 7% Netherlands; *imports:* 9.3% Cote d'Ivoire, 7.7% U.S., 7% Brazil, 6.7% U.K., 5.5% Netherlands, 4.5% South Africa, 4.3% India, 4.2% France.

Portuguese domination of the Sierra Leone coast began in 1462. English explorers, including Francis Drake, arrived in the late 16th century. Europeans traded for slaves in Sierra Leone, but in 1787 Freetown was founded by the British Sierra Leone Co. as a haven for freed slaves. The settlement was populated by former slaves from Great Britain, North America, and the Caribbean, and later by slaves liberated from slave trading ships by the British navy.

Sierra Leone was reorganized as a British colony in 1808. The ex-slave population, from diverse tribal and national backgrounds, developed an English-speaking Creole culture unique in Africa. Freetown became the center of British colonial administration and trade in West Africa and was the focus of missionary-supported projects in health care and economic development.

The native peoples of Sierra Leone staged numerous rebellions against the British and the Creole elite; resentment focused on the tax system and on the privileges of the English-speaking descendents of ex-slaves. During the 20th century, home rule developed through an elected advisory legislature. In 1951 a constitutional framework had been developed as the basis of decolonization. Sir Milton Margei became chief minister in 1953, and prime minister in 1961. The last ties with the British Crown were cut on Apr. 27, 1961, when Sierra Leone became a republic. A referendum in 1978 created a one-party state. In 1984 and 1985 student and public employee protests against the government led to riots and the restoration of multi-party elections.

In April 1992, Momoh was ousted in a coup by Capt. Valentine Strasser. Despite the country's wealth of natural resources, Strasser's corruption and mismanagement threatened to derail the economy. Strasser was overthrown in Jan. 1996 by army officers who pledged to continue his plan for multi-party elections. Ahmad Tejan Kabbah of the People's party captured close to 60 percent of the votes.

In 1991 Sierra Leone was attacked by a murderous gang led by "rebel" Fodaj Sankoh, calling itself the Revolutionary United Front. By July 1999 it controlled perhaps half of the country, including diamond mines which they looted, then marketed through Liberia's president, Charles Taylor. In May 1997 regular army troops loyal to Major Johnny Paul Koroma briefly overthrew Pres. Kabbah until Nigerian-led west African troops restored Kabbah and assisted against the RUF gang. A July 1999 cease-fire brought four RUF killers into the government and an amnesty for Sankoh. But the RUF did not disarm, and continued the struggle into 2000. Sankoh was captured late in May. In 2001 Parliament, with U.N. and British approval, postponed the scheduled March elections and extended President Kabbah's term for six months. With Sankoh captured, more U.N. troops in the country, and, most importantly, diminished support from Pres. Taylor, RUF began in May to disarm and to release hundreds of its boy-soldiers. But fighting continued in the diamond-rich east.

The July 18, 2001 agreement of the U.N., Sierra Leone, and the RUF rebels was strong enough for the government to declare (Jan. 18, 2002) the 11-year civil war over. On March 4, Foday Sankah was charged with murder; and on May 19 elections brought overwhelming approval to both Pres. Kabbah and his Sierra Leone's People's Party (which gained 83 of the 112 parliamentary seats); 17,000 U.N. troops remained in Sierra Leone until 2005. In 2007, opposition leader Ernest Bai Koroma was elected in a presidential run-off, defeating the Sierra Leone People's Party.

▶SINGAPORE
Republic of Singapore
● GEOGRAPHY **Location:** Singapore Island and some 57 islets off southern Malay peninsula (linked by a causeway). **Boundaries:** Johor Strait to N; Pacific Ocean to E; Strait of Malacca to SW, separating Singapore from Indonesian island of Sumatra; and Indian Ocean to W. **Total area:** 244 sq. mi. (633 sq km). **Coastline:** 120 mi. (193 km). **Comparative area:** slightly more than 3.5 times size of Washington, D.C. **Land use:** 2% arable land; 0% permanent crops; 98% other. **Major cities:** Singapore (capital).
● PEOPLE **Population:** 4,608,167 (July 2008 est.). **Nationality:** noun—Singaporean(s); adjective—Singapore. **Ethnic groups:** 77% Chinese, 14% Malay, 7.9% Indian, 1.4% other. **Languages:** Chinese, Malay, Tamil, and English (all official); Malay (national). **Religions:** majority of Chinese are Buddhists or atheists; Malays nearly all Muslim; minorities include Christians, Hindus, Sikhs, Taoists, Confucianists.
● GOVERNMENT **Type:** parliamentary republic. **Independence:** Aug. 9, 1965 (from Malaysia). **Constitution:** June 3, 1959, amended 1965; based on preindependence State of Singapore constitution. **National holiday:** Aug. 9. **Heads of Government:** S.R. Nathan, president (since Sept. 1999); Lee Hsien Loong, prime minister (since Aug. 2004). **Structure:** executive—ceremonial president, power exercised by prime minister and cabinet; unicameral legislature; judiciary.
● ECONOMY **Monetary unit:** Singapore dollar. **Budget:** (2007 est.) *income:* $27 bil.; *expend.:* $21.5 bil. **G.D.P.:** $228.1 bil., $48,900 per capita (2007 est.). **Chief crops:** rubber, copra, fruits, vegetables; poultry. **Natural resources:** fish, deepwater ports. **Major industries:** financial services, petroleum refining, electronics, oil drilling equipment. **Labor force:** 2.67 mil. (2007 est.); 42% services, 26% industry, 25% other (2006). **Exports:** $450.6 bil. (2007 est.); computer equipment, petroleum products, telecommunications equipment. **Imports:** $396 bil. (2007 est.); machinery and equipment, petroleum, chemicals, foodstuffs. **Major trading partners:** (2006) *exports:*

13% Malaysia, 13% U.S., 10% Hong Kong, 10% China, 9% Indonesia, 6% Japan, 4% Thailand; *imports:* 13% Malaysia, 10% U.S., 11% China, 8% Japan, 6% Taiwan, 6% Indonesia, 4% South Korea.

Singapore was founded in 1819 by Sir Thomas Stamford Raffles on land ceded to the East India Company by the sultanate of Johore (see "Malaysia"). An Anglo-Dutch treaty turned Singapore over to the British Crown in 1824, and eventually it was administered as part of the Straits Settlements. With its excellent harbor, Singapore eclipsed Penang and Malacca as the dominant port for trade through the Straits of Malacca.

Fortified as a bastion of British defense in Southeast Asia, Singapore was overrun by Japanese troops in Feb. 1942. The British reoccupied the city in Sept. 1945 and reorganized it as a British colony in 1946. On June 5, 1959, Singapore became a self-governing parliamentary democracy within the British Commonwealth. Lee Kwan Yew became prime minister. On Sept. 16, 1963, Singapore, along with Malaya, Sarawak, and Sabah, formed the Malaysian Federation. Singapore, ethnically Chinese, was uncomfortable within the Malay-dominated federation and seceded after two years, becoming an independent nation on Aug. 9, 1965.

Independent Singapore has enjoyed orderly, if authoritarian, government, economic growth, and a high standard of living. Still a major port, its economy now encompasses international banking, finance, communications, high-technology manufacturing, and tourism. On Nov. 26, 1990, Lee Kuan Yew, Singapore's only prime minister since independence and the longest serving prime minister in the world, resigned. He was succeeded by Goh Chok Tong, but he remains a force in Singapore's political life.

Measures in 2000 opened up segments of the economy to foreign firms, especially telecommunications and law, while the government ended its monopoly on broadcasting and newspapers. In 2004 Lee Kwan Yew's son, Lee Hsien Loong, chairman of the central bank and deputy prime minister, became prime minister.

▶ SLOVAKIA
Slovak Republic

• **GEOGRAPHY** **Location:** Central Europe. **Boundaries:** Czech Republic and Poland to N, Ukraine to E, Hungary to S, Austria to W. **Total area:** 18,859 sq. mi. (48,845 sq km). **Coastline:** none. **Comparative area:** about twice the size of New Hampshire. **Land use:** 31% arable, 3% permanent crops, 66% other. **Major cities:** Bratislava (capital); Kosice; Nitra; Presov; Banská Bystrica.
• **PEOPLE** **Population:** 5,455,407 (July 2008 est.). **Nationality:** noun—Slovak(s); adjective—Slovak. **Ethnic groups:** 85.7% Slovak, 10.6% Hungarian, 1.6% Roma. **Languages:** Slovak (official), Hungarian. **Religions:** 60.3% Roman Catholic, 9.7% atheist, 8.4% Protestant, 4.1% Orthodox.
• **GOVERNMENT** **Type:** parliamentary democracy. **Independence:** Jan. 1, 1993 (from Czechoslovakia). **Constitution:** Jan. 1, 1993; changed Sept. 1996 to allow direct election of president. **National holiday:** Slovak Constitution Day, Sept. 1. **Heads of Government:** Ivan Gasparovic, president (since June 2004); Robert Fico, prime minister (since July 2006). **Structure:** executive—president, prime minister, Council of Ministers; legislative—unicameral (National Council); judicial—Supreme Court.

• **ECONOMY** **Monetary unit:** euro. **Budget:** (2007 est.) *income:* $33.07 bil.; *expend.:* $35.13 bil. **G.D.P.:** $107.6 bil., $19,800 per capita (2007 est.). **Chief crops:** grains, potatoes, sugar beets, hops, fruit; hogs, cattle, poultry; forest products. **Natural resources:** brown coal and lignite; small amounts of iron ore, copper and manganese ore, salt. **Major industries:** metal working, food, beverages, fuels, chemicals. **Labor force:** 2.661 mil.; 29% industry, 6% agriculture, 9% construction, 56% services (2003); 8.6% unemployment (2007). **Exports:** $55.31 bil. (f.o.b., 2007 est.); 39% machinery and transport equipment; 18% intermediate manufactured goods, 10% miscellaneous manufactured goods. **Imports:** $57.06 bil. (f.o.b., 2007 est.); 38% machinery and transport equipment; 18% intermediate manufactured goods, 13% fuels. **Major trading partners:** (2006) *exports:* 23.5% Germany, 13.8% Czech Republic, 6.5% Italy, 6.2% Poland, 6.1% Hungary, 6.1% Austria, 4.3% France, 4.3% Netherlands; *imports:* 23% Germany, 18.1% Czech Republic, 11.2% Russia, 6.1% Hungary, 5.6% Austria, 5% Poland, 4.4% Italy.

Though the Czech and Slovak languages are similar, the two peoples have always been far apart culturally and historically (much like the Letts and Lithuanians). The ninth-century Moravian Empire has been claimed as heritage by both peoples; but with the Magyar invasion of the Pannonian Plain in the 10th century, the Slovaks passed under Hungarian rule for 1,000 years. When in the 19th century a romantic-nationalist revival occurred, the Slovaks, under the leadership of Ludovit Štúr, decided to use their own language in literature (though some of the most prominent writers in the Czech tongue were of Slovak origin, such as the poet Jan Kollár and the historian P.J. Šafarik). Unlike the Czechs, the Slovaks took no part in the revolutions of 1848. They lacked a native aristocracy; their national leadership came from wealthy peasants, small-town shopkeepers and, above all, their priests.

In the peacemaking at the end of World War I, as the Austro-Hungarian Empire collapsed, the Czech politicians Beneš and Masaryk claimed to speak for the (nonexistent) Czechoslovak nation. They carried the day despite apparent Slovak loyalty to Hungary and even the opposition of Fr. Hlinka's Slovak Populist party to union with the Czechs. The synthetic "nation" of Czechoslovakia was created, governed by a sort of benevolent democratic dictatorship of the Czechs over the other nations. With the Munich crisis of October 1939, Hitler imposed a federal structure giving Slovakia almost complete autonomy in the renamed Czecho-Slovakia; in the following March, when Hitler obliterated Czech independence, an "independent" Slovakia was formed with Hlinka's successor, Magr Tiso, as president.

But under the circumstances independence was illusory. German protection (against Hungarian revisionism) required complete Slovak accord with Reich foreign policy, including declarations of war on Poland (1939) and on the U.S.S.R., the United States, and Great Britain (1941). Domestically, Msgr. Tiso organized a one-party state with anti-Jewish legislation, half unwilling and half unable to resist the expulsion (and eventual extermination) of 60,000 Jews.

The cement for a restored Czechoslovakia after the war was the Communist tyranny imposed in 1948. But the "Velvet Revolution" in 1989 overturned Yalta and brought victory over the Communists. As the Czech premier Václav Klaus pushed for free-market "shock therapy," the Slovak premier Vladimír Meciar defended a slower "Slovak way" to capitalism. Economic differences inflamed by ancient Slovak resentment of the Czech majority led to a much-diminished federal government by the spring of 1992. In the summer the split became the "Velvet Divorce."

In July 1992 Slovak deputies to the federal Parliament blocked the reelection of Václav Havel to the presidency, and the Slovak National Council approved, by a vote of 113 to 24, a declaration of sovereignty. In September the two parliaments agreed to the terms. In accord with a two-to-one ratio of the republics' populations, the military and financial assets of Czechoslovakia were divided. By February only a customs union linked the two parts of the old state.

On Feb. 15, 1993, the Slovak Parliament elected its first president, Michal Kováč, with Meciar, as prime minister. Inflation and high unemployment coupled with a corruption scandal toppled the Meciar government in 1994, but a coalition government including many former Communists restored him as prime minister. In Sept. 1998, a four-party opposition coalition toppled Meciar's regime. Mikuláš Dzurinda became prime minister, heading a government whose principal focus was NATO and E.U. membership.

On May 29, 1999, in Slovakia's first popular rather than parliamentary election of a president, Rudolf Schuster defeated Meciar in a run-off; but in July 2000, the cabinet, with Schuster incapacitated by illness, transferred presidential powers to the prime minister and parliament's speaker. Meciar was arrested on charges of fraud and abuse of power. Dzurinda put together a four-party coalition to stay in office and in May 2003, 93 percent of voters approved, joining the E.U. A new center-left government under Robert Fico took office in 2006.

▶ SLOVENIA
Republic of Slovenia
● **Geography Location:** southeastern Europe. **Boundaries:** Austria to N, Hungary to NE, Croatia to E and S, Adriatic Sea and Italy to W. **Total area:** 7,836 sq. mi. (20,296 sq km). **Coastline:** 20 mi. (32 km). **Comparative area:** Slightly smaller than New Jersey. **Land use:** 11% arable land, 3% permanent crops, 86% other. **Major cities:** Ljubljana (capital); Maribor; Celje; Kranj.
● **People Population:** 2,007,711 (July 2008 est.). **Nationality:** noun—Slovene(s); adjective— Slovenian. **Ethnic groups:** 83.1% Slovene, 1.8% Croat, 2% Serb, 1% Bosniak. **Languages:** 91% Slovenian, 6% Serbo-Croatian. **Religions:** 58% Catholic, 1% Muslim, 27.4% other, 10% none.
● **Government Type:** parliamentary democratic republic. **Independence:** June 25, 1991 (from Yugoslavia). **Constitution:** Dec. 23, 1991. **National holiday:** National Statehood Day, June 25. **Heads of Government:** Danilo Turk, president of the presidency (four other members) (since Dec., 2007); Janez Jansa, prime minister (since Dec. 2004). **Structure:** executive—president, prime minister, cabinet; legislative—unicameral parliament-second chamber has only advisory powers; judicial—Supreme Court, Constitutional Court.
● **Economy Monetary unit:** euro. **Budget:** (2007 est.) *income:* $19.17 bil.; *expend.:* $19.41 bil. **G.D.P.:** $54.79 bil., $27,300 per capita (2007 est.). **Chief crops:** potatoes, hops, wheat, sugar beets, corn, grapes; cattle, sheep, poultry. **Natural re-**

sources: lignite coal, lead, zinc, mercury, uranium. **Major industries:** ferrous metallurgy and rolling mill products, aluminum reduction and rolled products, lead and zinc smelting, electronics, trucks, electric power equipment, wood products, textiles. **Labor force:** 920,000; 64.4% services, 33.5% industry, 2.2% agriculture (2007). **Exports:** $27.01 bil. (f.o.b., 2007); manufactured goods, machinery and transport equipment, chemicals. **Imports:** $30.22 bil. (f.o.b., 2007); machinery and transport equipment, other manufactured goods, chemicals. **Major trading partners:** (2006) *exports:* 20% Germany, 13% Italy, 9% Croatia, 9% Austria, 6% France, 4% Russia; *imports:* 20% Germany, 18% Italy, 12% Austria, 6% France, 5% Croatia.

In the sixth century, as part of the great Slavic migrations out of the Vistula and Oder basins, the Slovene people crossed the Carpathians into the Danube plain, penetrating as far as the eastern Alps. In the eighth and ninth centuries the lands they inhabited were subject to Bavarian colonization as part of the Ostmark (Eastern March) of the Carolingian Empire. It is probable, although contested, that most current Austrians are German-speaking Slovenes while the Slovenes are Slavophone Austrians. In any case, for 1,000 years, Slovene history was Austrian history. Thus, like the Croats, Christianity came in its western (Roman Catholic) form.

Lacking their own nobility and even a burgher class for most of their history, the Slovenes tended to look to their priests for leadership, regularly electing them as their representatives to the Reichstag in Vienna (as they did later to the Skupstina in Belgrade after Slovenia became part of Yugoslavia). The 19th-century rise of a national consciousness, associated with literary collections of legend and folklore, took a special turn in the Slovene case because of Napoleon's conquests. His "province of Illyria" was the first association of the Slovenes with Croats and Serbs and his minister of education there was the Slovene Franciscan Valentin Vodnik, so that Slovene "nationalism" had from a start a "Yugoslav" tinge.

In 1815 the Slovenes were again part of the Austrian Empire and were confirmed in the Ausgleich of 1867 as part of the Austrian, not Hungarian, part of the dual Monarchy. As that monarchy collapsed in World War I, it was the Slovene monsignor Anton Korosec who served as president of "The National Council of the Serbs, Croats, and Slovenes" out of which the new state of Yugoslavia emerged. Though the new Yugoslavia was a highly centralized, unitary state with no provision for Slovene autonomy, certain circumstances brought a kind of privileged position to Slovenia. Their distinct language made Serbian administration a practical impossibility and Serbian struggles against Croat separatism led them to favor the Slovenes to Croatia's north, forestalling any additional separatism there. Moreover, as a part of the long Austrian connection, the Slovenes were better educated and more industrially advanced than any other part of Yugoslavia.

After the interlude of Hitler's break-up of Yugoslavia (in which Slovenia itself was partitioned between Germany and Italy) Slovenia became a constituent "republic" in Tito's reconstructed Yugoslavia and, despite the enduring emnity provoked by the Communist slaughter of the Slovene Domobranci (Home Guard), again assumed a kind of privileged status in Yugoslavia. After the dictator's death in 1980, the Slovene Socialist

Republic took part in the "collegial rule" of Yugoslavia, but with the end of Communist rule in 1990, Slovenia became the first of the republics to secede, in June 1991. After the Slovene militia inflicted a humiliating defeat on the Yugoslav army in July and with E.U. recognition in December, Slovenia became independent for the first time in its history. Forging economic ties with Austria, Hungary, and Italy, it has remained prosperously apart from the debacle to its south.

In Nov. 1996 elections, the center-right coalition calling itself Slovenian Spring captured 45 (of 90) seats in the Parliament with the Liberal Democrats and its allies controlling the other 45. After months of deadlock LD leader Janos Drnovsek was confirmed as prime minister. In 2002 he was elected president and Anton Rop became prime minister. In 2003 voters approved joining both the E.U. and NATO which they did in 2004. A left-leaning president, Danilo Turk, was elected at the end of 2007.

▶ **SOLOMON ISLANDS**
• **GEOGRAPHY Location:** archipelago in South Pacific E of Papua New Guinea. Honiara (Guadalcanal Is.) 9°28′S, 159°57′E. **Boundaries:** South Pacific Ocean to N, E, and S, Solomon Sea to W; nearest neighbor is Santa Cruz Islands to SE. **Total area:** 10,985 sq. mi. (28,450 sq km). **Coastline:** 3,302 mi. (5,313 km). **Comparative area:** slightly smaller than Maryland. **Land use:** 2% arable land; 1% permanent crops; 97% other. **Major cities:** Honiara (capital).
• **PEOPLE Population:** 581,318 (July 2008 est.). **Nationality:** noun—Solomon Islander(s); adjective—Solomon Islander. **Ethnic groups:** 93% Melanesian, 4% Polynesian, 1.5% Micronesian, 0.8% European, 0.3% Chinese. **Languages:** 120 indigenous languages; Melanesian pidgin in much of country is lingua franca; English spoken by 1-2% of population. **Religions:** 34% Anglican, 19% Roman Catholic, 17% Baptist, 11% United (Methodist/Presbyterian), 11% Seventh-Day Adventist, 5% other Protestant, 4% traditional beliefs.
• **GOVERNMENT Type:** parliamentary democracy. **Independence:** July 7, 1978 (from U.K.). **Constitution:** July 7, 1978. **National holiday:** Independence Day, July 7. **Heads of Government:** Nathaniel Waene, governor-general (since July 2004); Derek Sikua, prime minister (since Dec. 2007). **Structure:** executive—authority in governor-general; unicameral legislature; judiciary.
• **ECONOMY Monetary unit:** Solomon Islands dollar. **Budget:** (2003 est.) *income:* $49.7 mil.; *expend.:* 75.1 mil. **G.D.P.:** $800 mil., $600 per capita (2005 est.). **Chief crops:** cocoa, beans, coconuts, palm kernels, rice, potatoes, vegetables, fruits; cattle, pigs; timber; fish. **Natural resources:** fish, forests, gold, bauxite, phosphates. **Major industries:** fish (tuna), mining, timber. **Labor force:** 26,842 (1992 est.); 20% services, 75% agriculture, forestry, and fishing, 5% industry. **Exports:** $237 mil. (f.o.b., 2006 est.); timber, fish, palm oil, cocoa, copra. **Imports:** $256 mil. (f.o.b., 2006 est.); plant and equipment, manufactured goods, food and live animals, fuel. **Major trading partners:** (2006) *exports:* 48% China, 10% South Korea, 9% Japan, 5% Thailand, 4% Italy, 4% Philippines; *imports:* 26% Australia, 24% Singapore, 8% Japan, 5% New Zealand, 4% Fiji, 4% Papua New Guinea.

In 1893 Britain established a protectorate over the South Solomon Islands, including the large islands of Guadalcanal, San Cristoban, and Malata; the protectorate was extended to the smaller easterly islands of the chain in 1898. In 1900 Germany relinquished to Great Britain its claim to the North Solomons, including Choiseul and Santa Isabel; Bougainville Island was retained by Germany (see "Papua New Guinea"). The major islands were occupied by Japan in 1942 and retaken by the Allies in a series of battles in 1943.

The Solomon Islands were made self-governing in January 1976 and became an independent nation on July 7, 1978. The economy is based on subsistence agriculture and fishing. The sale of tuna fishing rights in the surrounding waters gave the nation a favorable balance of payments.

In June 1999 ethnic violence erupted on Guadalcanal against settlers from the island of Malaita. Then, in June 2000, gunmen from the Malaita Eagle Force (MEF) placed the prime minister under house arrest and captured Honiara airport. On the eve of a parliamentary no-confidence vote, prime minister Ulufa'alu resigned June 14. On July 1 parliament elected opposition leader Mannasseh Sogavare to be prime minister. In 2001, a truce between militias brought no disarmament, but Sogavare used foreign aid to buy off the Eagle Force and other politicos. With Dec. 2001 elections, his rule was overturned, Sir Allen Kamekeza becoming prime minister after his People's Alliance won a majority in the legislature. But continued ethnic violence through 2003 led the Pacific Islands Forum to approve a regional force led by Australia to restore law and order. The Australian presence brought peace and a bit of prosperity, but in 2006 serious riots against government corruption forced the prime minister to resign and parliament elected Sogavare again. His tenure was short-lived and Derek Sikua succeded him in Dec. 2007.

▶ **SOMALIA**
• **GEOGRAPHY Location:** eastern coast of Africa. **Boundaries:** short frontier with Djibouti to NW, Gulf of Aden to N, long coastline on Indian Ocean to E, Kenya to SW, Ethiopia to W. **Total area:** 246,201 sq. mi. (637,660 sq km). **Coastline:** 1,880 mi. (3,025 km). **Comparative area:** slightly smaller than Texas. **Land use:** 2% arable land; negl. % permanent crops; 98% other. **Major cities:** Mogadishu (capital); Hargeysa; Kismayo; Merca.
• **PEOPLE Population:** 9,558,666 (July 2008 est.). **Nationality:** adjective—Somali. **Ethnic groups:** 85% Somali, rest mainly Bantu; 30,000 Arabs. **Languages:** Somali (official), Arabic, Italian, English. **Religions:** almost entirely Sunni Muslim.
• **GOVERNMENT Type:** none. **Independence:** July 1, 1960 (from a merger of British Somaliland, which became independent from U.K. June 26, 1960, and Italian Somaliland, which became independent from Italian-administered U.N. trusteeship July 1, 1960, to form the Somali Republic). **Constitution:** Aug. 25, 1979, presidential approval Sept. 23, 1979. **National holiday:** N.A. **Heads of Government:** Abdullahi Yusuf Ahmed, president (since Oct. 2004); Nur H. Hussein, prime minister (since Nov. 2007).
• **ECONOMY Monetary unit:** Somali shilling. **Budget:** N.A. **G.D.P.:** $5.575 bil., $600 per capita (2007 est.). **Chief crops:** bananas, sorghum, corn, mangoes, sugarcane, sesame seeds, beans; cattle, sheep, goats; fishing potential largely unexploited. **Natural resources:** uranium, largely unexploited reserves of iron ore, tin, gypsum, bauxite. **Major industries:** a few small industries, including sugar refining, textiles, petroleum refining. **Labor force:** about 3.7 mil. (1993 est.); very few are skilled laborers; 71% agriculture (pastoral nomadism), 29% industry and services. **Exports:** $300 mil. (f.o.b., 2006 est.); livestock, bananas,

hides, fish. **Imports:** $798 mil. (f.o.b., 2006 est.); manufactures, petroleum products, foodstuffs, construction materials. **Major trading partners:** (2006) *exports:* 49.6% United Arab Emirates, 21.4% Yemen, 5.9% Oman; *imports:* 30.8% Djibouti, 8.5% Brazil, 8.2% India, 8.1% Kenya, 5.5% Oman, 3.2% United Arab Emirates, 5% Yemen.

Arab trading settlements in Somalia were established in the seventh century and gradually evolved into independent sultanates. Portuguese traders established settlements and forts along the coast during the 15th and 16th centuries.

In the early 19th century, Great Britain arranged through local treaties to use harbors along the Somali coast and gained control over the northern part of the country by 1840. The border between Somalia and Ethiopia was demarcated by a treaty between Great Britain and Ethiopia in 1897. In 1885 the sultan of Zanzibar granted commercial advantages to Italy, and in 1897 and 1908 Italy gained control over southern Somalia.

During the early 20th century, an uprising against British rule was led by Mohamed Abdullah. Abdullah was defeated by the British with help from his local rivals but is now regarded as the father of Somali nationalism.

The Italian invasion of Ethiopia in 1936 gave Italy a dominant position in the Horn of Africa. In the early phases of World War II, Italian troops drove the British from British Somaliland, but a 1940 counterattack led to British occupation of all of Somalia by 1941. After World War II, Britain handed over the Ogaden and neighboring territories to Ethiopia.

A U.N. pact of 1949 created an Italian trusteeship in the former Italian Somaliland. Italy terminated its trusteeship and British Somaliland, a U.K. protectorate, achieved independence on June 26, 1960. On July 1 the two entities joined to become Somalia. The new country was plagued by clan-based rivalries, with the Somali Youth League emerging as a unifying national force. In 1969 Maj. Gen. Mohamed Siad Barre took control, and established both a socialist regime and relations with the U.S.S.R.

In 1972 Somali forces began border raids into Ethiopia's Ogaden region, peopled largely by ethnic Somalis. The Somali army invaded the Ogaden in 1977. The Soviet Union switched its support to Ethiopia, and with Soviet aid and Cuban troops, Ethiopia drove back the Somali invasion. Over a million refugees fled from Ethiopia into Somalia. The United States was Somalia's principal source of military and economic aid after 1978.

In May 1988, the Somali National Movement captured a number of cities in the northwest and held them. In the summer of 1990, the United Somali Congress began a peaceful antigovernment movement around Mogadishu. In Dec. 1990, this flared into a brief but bloody civil war that resulted in the ouster of Pres. Barre on Jan. 26. The Somali National Congress proclaimed a provisional government, but it was not recognized either by the United Somali Movement, which threatened secession, or the Somali Patriotic Movement, which controlled much of central and southern Somalia. The continued unrest made it difficult to deliver humanitarian aid despite the efforts of Western governments and nongovernment organizations to do so. An estimated 50,000 people were killed between 1988-90.

Despite U.N. attempts to initiate peace talks, widespread clan and tribal warfare led to a complete breakdown of government authority in 1991-92. A severe drought helped to create over two million refugees, and widespread starvation gripped the nation. Relief workers were prevented by warring armed factions from distributing emergency food supplies. An estimated 300,000 people died in 1991-92.

In Dec. 1992, the United States began Operation Restore Hope, sending 28,000 troops to secure distribution of food and aid. The U.S. presence deterred the factions from further open hostilities and brought warring leaders to the peace table. The U.N. took over the operation but led by the followers of Gen. Mohammed Farah Aidid, Somali renegades ambushed U.S. troops and downed a helicopter leading to a U.S. withdrawal in March 1994. U.N. troops left Mogadishu in 1995.

Clan warfare reignited in March 1995, and in June, Aidid declared himself president for life. However, no country recognized any Somali government and in Aug. 1996 Aidid was shot and killed. His son, a former U.S. Marine, replaced him but brutal clan violence continued. In Dec. 1997 a tentative peace agreement was reached among the major factions. Peace settled in during 1998, helped by flooding that killed 2,000. During the summer of 2000, however, a group of leaders met in Djibouti and formed a new government with Abdikassim Salad Hassan as president. But by March 2001 many warlords met in Ethiopia to form an opposition group and by May new clan warfare erupted. In 2004 a National Assembly was cobbled together and in Oct. elected Abdullahi Yusuf, a career soldier, to be president. But chaos returned in Feb. 2006 as Islamists tried to seize power from the ruling warlords. In Dec., Ethiopia sent in troops to fight with the government and capture Mogadishu. In Feb., the U.N. authorized a peacekeeping mission by the African Union, but they encountered the worst violence in years as a pitched battle between government forces backed by Ethiopian soldiers and Islamist insurgents killed over 1,000 in the capital city. In June, a U.S. warship shelled Al-Qaeda targets but also killed a number of civilians. (See "Major News Stories.")

▶**SOUTH AFRICA**
Republic of South Africa
● **GEOGRAPHY Location:** southern Africa. **Boundaries:** Namibia to NW, Botswana, Zimbabwe to N, Mozambique to NE, Swaziland, Indian Ocean to E, Atlantic Ocean to W; Lesotho entirely surrounded by South African territory. **Total area:** 471,444 sq. mi. (1,221,040 sq km). **Coastline:** 1,739 mi. (2,798 km). **Comparative area:** slighlty less than twice the size of Texas. **Land use:** 12% arable land; 1% permanent crops;87% other. **Major cities:** Cape Town (legislative capital); Pretoria (administrative capital); Johannesburg; Durban; Port Elizabeth.
● **PEOPLE Population:** 43,786,115 (July 2008 est.). **Nationality:** noun—South African(s); adjective—South African. **Ethnic groups:** 79% black, 9.6% white, 2.6% Indian; 8.6% other. **Languages:** Afrikaans, English, Zulu, Xhosa, Sotho, Ndebele, Pedi, Swazi, Tsonga, Venda, Tswana (all official). **Religions:** 68% Christian (most whites and about 60% of blacks), 2% Muslim, 1.5% Hindu (60% of Indians), 28.5% traditional and animistic beliefs.
● **GOVERNMENT Type:** republic. **Independence:** May 31, 1910 (from U.K.). **Constitution:** signed Dec. 10, 1996 by then-President Mandela—being implemented in phases. **National holiday:** Freedom Day, Apr. 27. **Head of Government:** Kgalema Motlanthe, president (since Sept. 2008). **Structure:** executive—president is head of govt. and chairman of cabinet; bicameral legislature—National Assembly, National Council of Provinces; judiciary—courts maintain

substantial independence from government influence.

● ECONOMY   Monetary unit: South African rand. **Budget:** (2007 est.) *Income:* $68.2 bil.; *expend.:* $66.7 bil. **G.D.P.:** $467.6 bil., $10,600 per capita (2007 est.). **Chief crops:** corn, wheat, sugarcane, fruits, vegetables; beef, poultry, mutton, wool, dairy products. **Natural resources:** gold, chromium, antimony, coal, iron ore. **Major industries:** mining (world's largest producer of platinum, gold, chromium), automobile assembly, metalworking. **Labor force:** 20.49 mil. economically active (2007); 65% services, 26% industry, 9% agriculture; 24.2% unemployment (2007 est.). **Exports:** $71.52 bil. (f.o.b., 2007 est.); gold, minerals and metals, food, chemicals. **Imports:** $76.59 bil. (f.o.b., 2007 est.); machinery, chemicals, transport equipment. **Major trading partners:** (2006) *exports:* 12.1% Japan, 11.8% U.S., 9% U.K., 7.6% Germany, 5.3% Netherlands, 4% China; *imports:* 12.6% Germany, 10% China, 7.6% U.S., 6.6% Japan, 5.3% Saudi Arabia, 5% U.K.

South Africa was originally inhabited by San and related peoples. Bantu peoples, including the Zulu and Xhosa, migrated to the region beginning around the 15th century and established large native kingdoms.

The Portuguese explorer Bartholomew Diaz discovered and named the Cape of Good Hope in 1488. The Dutch East India Company established a permanent settlement at Cape Town in 1652, which served as a supply and transshipment point for Dutch trade to the East Indies. It attracted Protestant settlers from throughout Western Europe. In a series of wars, the Xhosa people were expelled from the area under Dutch rule.

Great Britain began to dispute Dutch control of the Cape of Good Hope region in the late 18th century. To escape increasing British hegemony, in 1836 many Dutch farmers undertook the Great Trek, a northward migration to lands not under the control of any European power. These Afrikaner pioneers later became known as Boers (farmers). They came into conflict with the Zulu kingdom that, under King Shaka, had recently widened its dominion in the South African interior. The Zulus were defeated at the Battle of Blood River in 1838, but they retained substantial power and territory for another 40 years.

Great Britain formally took control of the Cape Colony in 1841 and annexed Natal in 1843. The other two Afrikaner provinces, the Orange Free State and the Transvaal, remained free of British control. But when diamonds were discovered in the Orange Free State in 1867 and gold in the Transvaal in 1886, an influx of British miners and entrepreneurs provoked Boer rebellions.

In 1878 the Zulu Kingdom under its last great king, Cetewayo, rebelled against British rule in Natal. British troops attacked Zululand in 1878 and crushed the rebellion in 1879.

The first Anglo-Boer War of 1881-82 led to total British victory. A renewed uprising led to the Boer War of 1899-1902, which was fought with great ferocity between British regular troops and Afrikaner guerrilla forces. The eventual British victory led to the establishment of British rule in all of South Africa and to the formation of the Union of South Africa in 1910. The union became a self-governing state within the British Empire in 1934.

South African politics became dominated by friction between British and Afrikaner whites; no effective black participation in government was permitted. The United South African party, led by Jan C. Smuts, advocated cooperation between the

two groups and led South Africa to join World War II on the Allied side, over the opposition of the pro-Afrikaner Nationalist party.

After the war the Nationalists prevailed and won control of the government in 1948. Racial politics became the country's paramount concern, and the Nationalists introduced the policy of "apartheid" (separateness), under which racial groups were rigidly defined as white, black, Asian (primarily Indian), and colored (mixed ancestry). Each group was to be kept physically separate and develop its own political institutions within defined areas of residence; mixed neighborhoods, intermarriage, and other relations were prohibited. Blacks, in particular, were restricted by "pass laws" that allowed them only temporary access to white areas for employment.

International condemnation of these policies began almost immediately, as India broke relations with South Africa in 1946 over discrimination against Asians, and South Africa became the focus of mounting protest, U.N. resolutions, and international sanctions beginning in the 1960's. On May 31, 1961, South Africa gave up its dominion status and became a republic; its application for membership in the British Commonwealth was withdrawn in the face of strong opposition. The African National Congress (ANC), organized in 1912, was banned by South African authorities. The imprisonment of its leader, Nelson Mandela, provided a focus for black political protest and nationalist aspirations.

Homelands were established under the Promotion of Bantu Self-Government Act of 1959 to further the policy of apartheid by creating separate, but dependent, states for South Africa's blacks. Their form of government was set up in the Black Constitution Act of 1971. The South African government intended that the homelands be regarded as separate nations, but none was ever internationally recognized. The scattered homeland territories comprised only a tiny portion of the total area of South Africa, and tended to include marginal and underdeveloped lands. Residents of the homelands were not considered citizens of South Africa, but rather citizens only of their homeland. As such, they could be considered temporary migrant workers and were therefore ineligible for unemployment and other benefits.

An uprising in Soweto in 1976 was put down by South African armed forces with the loss of hundreds of lives. Pieter Willem Botha was elected president in 1978, pledging to uphold apartheid while seeking solutions to racial problems. In 1983, a majority of white voters approved a new constitution that provided for limited power sharing by coloreds and Asians. Blacks, however, continued to be excluded.

In the early 1980's, South African troops intervened in civil wars in Angola and Mozambique and were deployed to counteract growing proindependence rebellions in Namibia. Within South Africa, terrorism and uprisings led by the African National Union grew in intensity in 1983-84. A state of emergency was declared in 1985, accompanied by renewed political and economic pressure from abroad. In 1986, Bishop Desmond Tutu, a leading black nationalist, addressed the United Nations and called for renewed sanctions. The Botha government announced an end to the pass laws and promised limited black participation in government. Fighting among black groups in 1986-87 further increased domestic tension.

On May 19, 1986, South African troops conducted raids against ANC bases in Zambia, Zimbabwe, and Botswana. A new national state of emergency was declared as strikes and riots marked the 10th anniversary of the Soweto uprising. The U.S. announced measures designed to end American investment in South Africa.

In early 1989, in anticipation of elections to be held in September, various proposals were put forward for constitutional reform. Most called for expanded power sharing but still within the context of defined racial groups. In July 1989 Pres. Botha had an unprecedented meeting with Nelson Mandela, amid strong suggestions that the white government was seeking an accommodation with the antiapartheid leadership. Botha's successor, F.W. de Klerk, continued that policy.

A series of measures in 1989-90 resulted in the partial dismantling of apartheid, against the vehement opposition of the white right wing, but violence between supporters of the ANC and the Zulu Inkatha movement in Natal led to the declaration of a state of emergency in the province.

Mandela was released from prison in the spring of 1990 and received a rapturous welcome from South Africa's blacks, and later made a triumphant tour of Western Europe and North America. His glory was short-lived, however, as the struggle for supremacy again erupted in murder and violence between Mandela's ANC and Mangosuthu Buthelezi's Inkatha Freedom party throughout the latter part of 1990 and 1991.

At the same time, Pres. de Klerk and Parliament continued to move the nation toward the ending of apartheid by repealing 60 years of segregation in hospitals, libraries, schools, and other public institutions. The government also released other political prisoners and completely repealed the legal foundations of apartheid: the Land Acts of 1913 and 1936, the Group Areas Act, and the Population Registration Act. The United States and other countries began lifting trade sanctions against South Africa in the summer of 1991.

In September 1991, de Klerk, Mandela, and Buthelezi, together with 20 smaller antiapartheid groups, signed an accord to end factional violence. De Klerk proposed a new constitution that would provide universal suffrage and create a two-chamber parliament open to all races. The new constitution abolished the black homelands, consolidating them into one large, multiracial South Africa. In March 1992 a referendum of white voters overwhelmingly approved a government proposal to dismantle all forms of apartheid and to conduct talks with black leaders designed to end white-only rule.

The new constitution was approved on Nov. 17, 1993, by all of the country's major political parties, except for Chief Mangosuthu Buthelezi's Zulu-based Inkatha Freedom party, which withheld its support until a week before the country's first-ever multiracial elections in April. More than 22 million voters cast ballots. An overwhelming majority chose the 75-year-old Mandela to lead a coalition government that included de Klerk's National party and Buthelezi's Inkatha Freedom party.

In May 1996 South Africa completed the transition to democracy when it approved a permanent constitution. It created a strong central government, an independent judiciary, and a bill of rights with one of the broadest guarantees of liberty in the world. In addition to freedom of speech, movement, and political activity, the South African Bill of Rights protects rights to adequate food, housing, water, education, and health care. The day after the new constitution was approved, de Klerk and his colleagues in the National party quit their cabinet posts, saying that the government was strong enough to handle "robust opposition."

In 1997 there were riots in Johannesburg suburbs by coloreds against discrimination in favor of blacks, and in March, a mass rally (which turned violent) in Johannesburg by Zulus. Bitter feelings between the Inkatha Freedom Party and Mandela's ANC surfaced again when the Truth and Reconciliation Committee reported testimony linking Inkatha leaders to assassination squads during the apartheid era.

On June 2, 1999, South Africa held its second post-apartheid elections: the ANC won a gigantic victory, taking 266 seats in the 400-seat Assembly. An "alliance" with the one member of the (Indian) Minority Front gave ANC the 2/3 majority that permits it to amend the Constitution. Thabo Mbeki, who replaced Nelson Mandela as party chief in December, was elected unopposed to be his successor as South Africa's president as well. In Dec. 2000 local elections the ANC took only 59 percent and a serious bribery scandal developed over a 1999 $3.5 billion arms deal. And the government's own report of March 2001 highlighted the gravity of South Africa's AIDS crisis. But it took until late 2003 before the government agreed to spend $1.8 bil. to provide free drugs to AIDS sufferers. Elections in 2004 gave the ANC its third landslide win (70 percent of the vote). In early 2008, Mbeki lost his power in the ANC and was replaced by Jacob Zuma who faced corruption charges during the summer. Mbeki resigned the presidency in September 2008, and was replaced by former trade unionist and freedom fighter Kgalema Motlanthe.

South Africa has the continent's most highly developed economy; it is a fully-developed, capitalist industrial-commercial society with manufacturing, mining, agricultural, service, and other sectors. It remains the world's largest producer of gold, a key source of chromium and other strategic metals, and of gem-quality diamonds.

▶ **SPAIN**
Kingdom of Spain

● **GEOGRAPHY Location:** Iberian Peninsula in southwest Europe; Canary Is. off West Africa (28°07'N, 15°26'W). **Boundaries:** Bay of Biscay and France to N; Mediterranean Sea to E; Morocco 19 mi. (30 km) to S, across Strait of Gibraltar; Portugal to W. **Total area:** 194,884 sq. mi. (504,750 sq km). **Coastline:** 3,085 mi. (4,964 km). **Comparative area:** slightly more than twice the size of Oregon. **Land use:** 29% arable land; 10% permanent crops; 261% other. **Major cities:** Madrid (capital); Barcelona; Valencia; Sevilla (Seville); Zaragoza (Saragossa).

● **PEOPLE Population:** 40,491,051 (July 2008 est.). **Nationality:** noun—Spaniard(s); adjective—Spanish. **Ethnic groups:** composite of Mediterranean and Nordic types. **Languages:** 74% Castilian Spanish (official); 17% Catalán, 7% Galician, 2% Basque. **Religions:** 94% Roman Catholic, 6% other.

● **GOVERNMENT Type:** parliamentary monarchy. **Independence:** 1492 (expulsion of Moors and unification). **Constitution:** Dec. 6, 1978, effective Dec. 29, 1978. **National holiday:** Oct. 12. **Heads of Government:** Juan Carlos I, king (since Nov. 1975); José Luis Rodriguez Zapatero, prime minister (since Apr. 2004). **Structure:** executive—king is chief of state, prime minister is head of government; bicameral legislature; judiciary— independent.

● **ECONOMY Monetary unit:** euro. **Budget:** (2007 est.) *income:* $571.1 bil.; *expend.:* $544.9 bil.

G.D.P.: $1.362 tril., $33,700 per capita (2007 est). **Chief crops:** grains, vegetables, olives, wine grapes, sugar beets, citrus; beef, pork, poultry, dairy prodcts; fish. **Natural resources:** coal, lignite, iron ore, uranium, mercury. **Major industries:** textiles, apparel (including footwear), food and beverages, metals and metal manufacturing. **Labor force:** 22.01 mil. (2007); 64.6% services, 30.1% industry, 5.3% agriculture. **Exports:** $248.3 bil. (f.o.b., 2007 est.); cars and trucks, manufactured goods, foodstuffs, other consumer goods. **Imports:** $359.1 bil. (f.o.b., 2007 est.); machinery, transport equipment, fuels, semifinished goods, foodstuffs, consumer goods, chemicals. **Major trading partners:** (2006) *exports:* 18.8% France, 11% Germany, 9% Portugal, 8.6% Italy, 8% U.K., 4.4% U.S.; *imports:* 14.8% Germany, 13.4% France, 8.3% Italy, 5.2% U.K., 4.9% Netherlands, 4.6% China.

Prehistoric Spain was populated by Iberians, Basques, and Celts. Its Mediterranean ports were frequented by Phoenician traders, and part of the country was incorporated into the empire of Carthage. Spain fell under the Roman Empire around 200 B.C.; Roman rule ended when the Visigoths invaded and took control of the Iberian Peninsula in the fifth century. The Visigoths adopted Christianity but were in turn conquered by Moors from northwest Africa in A.D. 711. The Berber/Arab civilization of the Moors produced the most elegant and cultivated culture in medieval Europe, and was an important conduit for the reintroduction of Greek science into Europe in the 12th century.

The Christian reconquest of the Iberian Peninsula began almost immediately after the Moors had established themselves and proceeded slowly but steadily over a period of 750 years. The consolidation of the region's small, contentious Christian kingdoms came with the marital alliance of Ferdinand of Aragon and Isabella of Castile in 1469. Granada, the last Moorish outpost in Spain, fell to the forces of Ferdinand and Isabella in 1492, just as Columbus, with Isabella's sponsorship, was discovering the lands that were to become Spain's New World empire. Under the Inquisition, begun in 1478, Jews were expelled from Spain in 1492, and Muslims in 1502.

Under the Habsburg dynasty (1516-1700), Spain reached the zenith of its power and prestige around the year 1600 (despite the 1588 defeat of the Spanish Armada by England), controlling an empire that embraced nearly all of South America (except Brazil), Central America, Mexico, western North America, the Philippines, and smaller territories in Africa and Asia. But Spain's loss of the Netherlands, endless struggles with the French in Europe and the Turks in the Mediterranean, and relentless inflation caused by imports of New World silver—all took their toll. During the 18th century, the Bourbons ruled a declining but still powerful Spain, until Napoleon installed his brother as king in 1808.

After Napoleon's defeat, the Bourbons returned in 1814, but the loss of the South American colonies, three dynastic wars, and a brief republican interlude after 1868 were all signs of progressive weakness. The crowning blow to Spanish power and prestige was the loss of the Spanish-American War to the United States in 1898, leading to the independence of Cuba and the American takeover of Puerto Rico and the Philippines.

Spain remained neutral in World War I. In 1923 Primo de Rivera established a dictatorship; he was forced out of office by King Alfonso XIII in 1930, but in 1931 the king was forced to abdicate. A re-

public replaced the monarchy. Its volatile mixture of socialism, anticlericalism, and decentralization provoked a right-wing reaction. The government moved to the Right, and in 1934 a miner's strike in Asturia was put down with great bloodshed. A left-wing government was elected in 1936 and deposed in a coup, which led to the terrible Civil War of 1936-39, in which Spain became a battleground for competing world ideologies. The Nationalists, aided by Hitler and Mussolini, defeated the Republicans, aided by Stalin and by leftist volunteers from many countries. Out of the wreckage emerged the dictatorship of the intensely patriotic and Catholic general Francisco Franco.

At the time of the Civil War, Spain was still an agricultural country, with small holdings in the north and great estates in the south. In the Basque country, the mining of iron, copper, and lead provided both exports and a domestic iron and steel industry, which had been the case since the 19th century. In the 20th century, shipbuilding and chemicals were added to the traditional textile industries of the Mediterranean coastal cities. The war largely destroyed this industrial base, which was not rebuilt until the 1950's.

Except for a contingent of troops sent to fight with the German invaders of the Soviet Union, Spain remained precariously neutral during World War II; Franco declined to repay Hitler for his support in the Civil War. But wartime Spain, despite its neutrality, could not muster the resources to undertake national reconstruction.

In postwar Europe, the Franco regime seemed like a remnant of the fascism of the 1930's; Stalin's active hostility led the United Nations to treat Spain as an international pariah. At home Franco represented peace and stability; few Spaniards were willing to risk a return to civil strife by opposing him. Over time the military and Catholic aspects of the regime grew more pronounced, while fascist elements were downplayed. In 1947 the Law of Succession made Spain a monarchy without a king, awaiting the restoration of the throne in the post-Franco era.

The Cold War led to friendlier American relations with Spain and the establishment of American military bases in 1953. U.N. membership followed in 1955. Despite some resultant growth in international trade, Spain's economy lagged, with industrialization barely beginning.

In 1958 Franco turned the direction of the economy over to a group of technocrats, mostly neoliberal members of the Opus Dei lay Catholic order. With U.S. economic and military aid, a growing tourist industry, increased foreign investment, and, especially, freer markets, the economy revived. Older industries like iron, steel, and textiles were rejuvenated, while newer ones, such as chemicals, plastics, automobile assembly, and power plants, were created. Agriculture was increasingly mechanized, and it shifted to export-oriented ranching and horticulture.

In 1967 Franco proclaimed the Organic Law, which, while confirming him as head of state, granted some independence to the Cortes (legislature) and permitted heads of families to vote for some of its delegates. This, along with a relaxation of censorship, softened the growing opposition to the regime among students, labor unions, and regional separatists. In 1969 Prince Juan Carlos was named heir apparent to the Spanish throne.

Franco died in 1975 and was duly succeeded by Juan Carlos. With the new prime minister, Adolfo Suarez, the king worked to liberalize the Franco inheritance: Political parties were legalized; the Cortes was transformed into a bicameral legislature, with both houses elected by universal suffrage; the first elections since 1936 were held; and a new constitution was promulgated—all by 1978.

In 1980, Catalonia and the Basque country were granted home rule, following overwhelming plebiscite victories. In the Basque lands, however, violent terrorist agitation for complete independence continues sporadically.

Under the new monarchy, Spain became a full participant in the affairs of Europe. It joined the Council of Europe in 1977, NATO in 1982, and the E.U. in 1986. The Socialist Workers' party controlled both houses of the Cortes from 1982 to 1996, but the party abandoned both Marxism and labor radicalism. Under Prime Minister Felipe Gonzalez Marquéz, G.D.P. grew by an average of almost 5 percent between 1986 and 1990, and business investment jumped by over 10 percent a year. In 1992, the Summer Olympics in Barcelona and the Universal Exposition in Seville focused world attention on two very different parts of Spain.

Economic growth slowed in 1992, and unemployment reached 22 percent. In 1994, Gonzalez's power eroded when several members of his government were indicted for their involvement with an antiterrorist death squad accused of assassinating 27 Basque separatists during the 1980's. After 10 years of Gonzalez and the Socialists, the May 1996 elections brought the Popular Party and its leader Jose Maria Aznar to power. In July 1998, 12 officials of the Gonzalez government were sentenced to jail for crimes in the anti-Basque "dirty war," although Gonzalez himself was not implicated.

Spain's economy quickly reversed itself and annual growth surpassed three percent, so that Spain was able to meet the criteria for membership in the European Monetary Union.

Somewhat unexpectedly the E.T.A., the Basque terrorist organization, declared on September 16, 1998, a "total and indefinite" cease-fire. But despite talks with the Aznar government and the release of "political prisoners," the E.T.A., in late 1999, resumed its war with car-bombings and assassinations. In March 2000, the Popular Party won an unexpected majority (183 of 350 seats) in the Congreso. In Sept. 2002, two important leaders of E.T.A. were captured in France and government officials believed the group, responsible for over 800 deaths, would be crippled.

On the eve of the March 2004 election, 10 bombs exploded on four Madrid commuter trains killing over 200 with 1400 wounded. The Aznar government immediately blamed E.T.A. but it quickly became clear that it was the work of Islamist terrorists. The elections brought the Socialists to power and the removal of Spanish troops from Iraq. In 2006, E.T.A. declared a cease-fire and Prime Minister Zapatero agreed to peace talks, which were suspended after a car bomb attack at a Madrid airport. In 2008 Zapatero's party won reelection handily. The new cabinet had more women than men for the first time.

▶ SRI LANKA
Democratic Socialist Republic of Sri Lanka

● **GEOGRAPHY** **Location:** Indian Ocean about 50 mi. (80 km) SE of India. Colombo 6°55'N, 79°52'E. **Boundaries:** Palk Strait to N, Bay of Bengal to E, Indian Ocean to S and SW, and Gulf of Mannar to NW. **Total area:** 25,332 sq. mi. (65,610 sq km). **Coastline:** 833 mi. (1,340 km). **Comparative area:** slightly larger than West Virginia. **Land use:** 13% arable land; 16% permanent crops; 71% other.

Major cities: Colombo (capital); Dehiwala-Mount Lavinia; Moratuwa.

● **PEOPLE** **Population:** 21,128,773 (July 2008 est.). **Nationality:** noun—Sri Lankan(s); adjective—Sri Lankan. **Ethnic groups:** 74% Sinhalese; 18% Tamil; 7% Moor; 1% Burgher, Malay, and Veddah. **Languages:** Sinhala (official); Sinhala and Tamil listed as national languages; Sinhala spoken by about 74% of population, Tamil spoken by about 18%; English commonly used in government and spoken by about 10% of population. **Religions:** 70% Buddhist, 15% Hindu, 8% Christian, 7% Muslim. ● **GOVERNMENT** **Type:** republic. **Independence:** Feb. 4, 1948 (from U.K.). **Constitution:** Aug. 16, 1978. **National holiday:** Independence Day, Feb. 4. **Heads of Government:** Mahinda Rajapakse, prime minister (since Apr. 2004). **Structure:** executive—president is head of government and chief of state; unicameral legislature; judiciary—Supreme Court, Court of Appeals.

● **ECONOMY** **Monetary unit:** Sri Lankan rupee. **Budget:** (2007) *income:* $5.379 bil.; *expend.:* $7.611 bil. **G.D.P.:** $83.21 bil., $4,100 per capita (2007 est.). **Chief crops:** rice, sugarcane, grains, pulses, oilseed, roots, spices, coconuts, tea, rubber; milk, eggs, hides, meat. **Natural resources:** limestone, graphite, mineral sands, gems, phosphates. **Major industries:** processing of rubber, tea, coconuts, and other agricultural commodities; cement, petroleum refining. **Labor force:** 7.67 mil. (2007 est.); 40.4% services, 34.3% agriculture, 25.3% industry. **Exports:** $8.357 bil. (f.o.b., 2007); tea, textiles and garments, petroleum products, gems, rubber. **Imports:** $10.68 bil. (f.o.b., 2007 est.); machinery and equipment, textiles, petroleum. **Major trading partners:** (2006) *exports:* 27.6% U.S., 11.3% U.K., 9.3% India, 4.7% Belgium, 4.3% Germany; *imports:* 19.5% India, 10.4% China, 8.7% Singapore, 5.6% Iran, 5% Malaysia, 4.2% Hong Kong, 4% Japan.

The ancient Veddah inhabitants of Sri Lanka were conquered by Sinhalese migrants from northern India in the sixth century B.C. The island's spices and precious stones and its position on the trans-Indian Ocean trade routes made it well known in ancient times. From the third century A.D., Sri Lanka became a major center of Buddhist culture. Despite numerous invasions from India, the island was usually ruled by native kingdoms, but the invasions added a Tamil community to the premodern population.

The Portuguese conquered the coastal areas after 1505 and also introduced Roman Catholicism. The Dutch displaced the Portugese in 1648; the British expelled the Dutch in 1795. Great Britain was the first foreign power to extend its rule over the entire island, with the defeat of the central kingdom of Kandy in 1833. In that year all of Sri Lanka was incorporated into the British Crown colony of Ceylon. Under British rule, tea and rubber plantations were established in the island's interior, and coconut plantations in coastal areas were consolidated under foreign control.

Ceylon became an independent member of the British Commonwealth on Feb. 4, 1948; the Republic of Sri Lanka was proclaimed on May 22, 1972.

Prime Minister W.R.D. Bandaranaike was assassinated on Sept. 25, 1959. His widow, Sirimavo Bandaranaike, leader of the Freedom party, was elected as his successor. In 1962 her government expropriated the property of foreign oil companies. The conservative United National party won a majority in Parliament in 1965 and agreed to pay compensation for the expropriated assets. In May 1970 Mrs. Bandaranaike was again elected prime minister. Leftists secured the nationalization of foreign plantations in the mid-1970's. Mrs. Bandaranaike's party was ousted by the United National party in 1977. Constitutional reform in 1978 aimed at increasing stability by establishing a presidential form of government. Pres. J.R. Jayawardene was elected on Feb. 4, 1978.

But stability has eluded Sri Lanka because of the long struggle between Tamils and the Sinhalese. The political power acquired by the Tamil (mostly Hindu) middle class under the British was deeply resented by the Sinhalese (Buddhist) majority, which after independence slowly eroded Tamil rights. In 1957 the government proposed a Tamil state in a federal union and gave Tamil the status of a national (but not official) language. The pact was not fully implemented, and in the 1970's extremists began agitating for an independent Tamil state. The Tamils' minority status was reaffirmed in the constitution of 1972, the year the oldest insurgent group, the Liberation Tigers or Tamil Tigers, was founded.

In July 1987 Pres. Jayawardene accepted an offer from India's Prime Minister Rajiv Gandhi to supervise a truce in the Jaffna region under which the government pledged to hold a referendum aimed at granting self-rule to Tamil majority areas in the north. The plan failed and Indian troops became bogged down in battling the rebels, while the planned referendum was disrupted by fighting between separatists who demanded total independence for Tamil areas.

At the Sri Lankan government's request, India withdrew its forces in March 1989, and the Tamil Tigers agreed to a cease-fire but this cease-fire broke down with the assassination of both the opposition political leader in April 1993 and Pres. Ranasinghe Pemadasa a month later. In parliamentary elections held in 1994, the People's Alliance ended the United National party's 17-year rule. Prime Minister Chandrika Bandaranaike Kumaratunga won a landslide victory in presidential elections, and appointed her 78-year-old mother, Sirimavo Bandaranaike, as prime minister.

Hours after the new president's inauguration, the Tamil Tigers announced a cease-fire. The truce was formalized in Jan. 1995, but when the government offered a peace plan to divide Sri Lanka into autonomous regions, the Tamil rebels renewed the civil war which by 2000 had cost at least 60,000 lives and displaced at least a million people. Pres. Kumaratunga handily won re-election in Dec. 1999 but on the battlefield the Tamils grew more successful in 2000. A series of failed offensives against the Tigers in 2001 brought government to a halt and the loss of its majority. In Oct. 2001, Pres. Kumaratunga dissolved Parliament; resulting elections brought a three-party United Front to power. A Norway-negotiated truce in Feb. 2002 led to renewed peace talks in Thailand between the new government and the Tigers. But talks went nowhere and Kumaratunga again suspended Parliament in Nov. 2003 and deployed troops in Colombo. In 2004 elections her party won 105 of 225 seats. But the peace held and the tragedy of the Dec. 2004 tsunami (which took 30,000 lives in Sri Lanka) seemed to ease political tensions. In Nov. 2005 Mahinda Rajapakse, a hardliner who opposes power sharing with the Tigers, narrowly won the presidential elections. By Aug. 2006 fierce fighting had begun anew, and continued into the summer of 2007 as the Rajapakse government seemed determined to win at all costs.

▶ **SUDAN**
Republic of the Sudan
• **GEOGRAPHY** **Location:** northeastern Africa. **Boundaries:** Egypt to N, Red Sea, Eritrea, and Ethiopia to E, Kenya, Uganda, and Zaire to S, Central African Republic, Chad and Libya to W. **Total area:** 967,495 sq. mi. (2,505,810 sq km). **Coastline:** 530 mi. (853 km). **Comparative area:** slightly more than one-quarter the size of the U.S. **Land use:** 7% arable land; negl. % permanent crops; 93% other. **Major cities:** Khartoum (capital); Nyala; Shargen-Nil; Port Sudan; Omdurman.
• **PEOPLE** **Population:** 40,218,455 (July 2008 est.). **Nationality:** noun—Sudanese (sing., pl.); adjective—Sudanese. **Ethnic groups:** 52% black, 39% Arab, 6% Beja, 2% foreigners. **Languages:** Arabic (official), Nubian, Ta Bedawie, diverse dialects of Nilotic, Nilo-Hamitic, and Sudanic languages; English; program of Arabization in progress. **Religions:** 70% Sunni Muslim (in north), 25% indigenous beliefs, 5% Christian (mostly in south).
• **GOVERNMENT** **Type:** transitional, previously military junta. **Independence:** Jan. 1, 1956 (from Egypt and U.K.). **Constitution:** Apr. 12, 1973, suspended following coup of Apr. 6, 1985; new constitution implemented June 1998, partially suspended Dec. 12 1999 by President Bashir. **National holiday:** Independence Day, Jan. 1. **Head of Government:** Lt. Gen. Omer Hassan Ahmed Al Bashir, president (since Jan. 1993). **Structure:** executive—president is head of government and chief of state; unicameral legislature; judiciary.
• **ECONOMY** **Monetary unit:** Sudanese pound. **Budget:** (2007 est.) *income:* $9.682 bil.; *expend.:* $11.59 bil. **G.D.P.:** $107.8 bil., $2,500 per capita (2007 est.). **Chief crops:** cotton, peanuts,sorghum, millet, wheat, gum arabic, sesame; sheep. **Natural resources:** petroleum, reserves of iron oil, copper, chromium ore, zinc. **Major industries:** cotton ginning, textiles, cement. **Labor force:** 11 mil. (1996 est.); 80% agriculture, 7% industry and commerce, 13% government; labor shortages for almost all categories of skilled employment. **Exports:** $9.156 bil. (f.o.b., 2007 est.); cotton, sesame, livestock/meat. **Imports:** $8.262 bil. (f.o.b., 2007 est.); foodstuffs, petroleum products, manufactured goods, machinery and equipment, medicines and chemicals, textiles. **Major trading partners:** (2006) *exports:* 48% Japan, 31% China, 3.8% South Korea; *imports:* 18% China, 9% Saudi Arabia, 6% United Arab Emirates, 5% Egypt, 5% Germany, 5% India, 4% France.

The northern Sudan, the ancient land of Nubia, was loosely controlled by Egypt in antiquity and incorporated into the Arab world by the Islamic expansion of the seventh century. The southern Sudan was part of tribal black Africa, under no external control but subject to continual raids by slave traders from the north.

Ottoman Egypt conquered the northern Sudan in 1820-21; British influence in Egypt in the 19th century extended into the Sudan as well. In 1881 Muhammed Ahmed ibn Abdalla, a religious leader known as the Mahdi, united northern and north-central Sudan and led a resistance movement against Anglo-Egyptian control. Khartoum, defended by British general Charles George Gordon, fell in 1885, but the Mahdi died soon thereafter, and his revolt came to an end. An Anglo-Egyptian force under Kitchener regained control in 1898; Anglo-Egyptian joint rule was established in the Sudan in 1899.

Great Britain and Egypt granted self-government and self-determination to the Sudan in 1953, and a Sudanese parliament was seated in 1954. Full independence came in 1956. Gen. Ibrahim

Abboud took power in a bloodless coup in 1958 but was forced to resign after riots in 1964. In 1969 a new military coup installed a ruling Revolutionary Command Council and instituted a socialist regime. The council's leader, Gen. Muhammed Nimeiri, became prime minister. Disputes between Marxists and non-Marxists, and between arabized northerners and black southerners, led to continual difficulties. In 1972 Sudan's three black southern provinces were granted local autonomy. Another attempted coup in 1976 was put down by the Nimeiri government, and hundreds of prominent citizens were executed.

In 1983 attempts by the Nimeiri government to institute Islamic law led to riots in the south and the imposition of a state of emergency in 1984. Popular unrest was exacerbated by drought and famine in 1985. On Apr. 6, 1985, Nimeiri was overthrown in a coup by Gen. Suwar El Dahab. After a brief period of rule by a transitional military council, a civilian cabinet was installed, and free parliamentary elections were held in 1986.

In June 1989 the government was overthrown in a coup led by Lt. Gen. Omar Ahmed al-Bashir. The Bashir government renewed the fight against the southern rebels, and supported the imposition of Islamic law throughout the nation. Within three years the civil service, the military, the judiciary, and the educational system were under the control of Muslims and their political organization, the National Islamic Front headed by Hassan al-Turabi who was also the leader of parliament and the most powerful figure in Sudan. All opposition parties, newspapers, and unions were banned and a stepped up military campaign against christians in the South was launched.

In Oct. 1990, the U.S. government stopped aid to the Sudan, which openly supported Iraq during the Persian Gulf War. In 1991, the U.N. suspended relief efforts to help the estimated 7.1 million Sudanese threatened by famine. In 1993, the U.S. added Sudan to its list of states that sponsor terrorism, and in 1995, the U.N. endorsed an accusation that Sudan was sheltering the Islamic militants who attempted to assassinate Egyptian Pres. Hosni Mubarak. The government in 1995 announced plans to free all political prisoners and to hold national elections in 1996 but an increase in violence against the government by rebels in the south delayed them. In 1997 the government made peace with some rebel factions, promising a referendum on self determination. The main force of the Sudan People's Liberation Army (SPLA), led by John Garang, continued to fight.

Another famine in 1998 brought a ceasefire as aid workers transported huge amounts of food to over 300,000 in the south. In Aug. 1998 the U.S. launched cruise missiles at Khartoum to retaliate for the bombing of its embassies in Kenya and Tanzania and to destroy what it said was a chemical weapons plant. Since July 1998, both the S.P.L.A. and the Sudanese government have declared a series of cease-fires to permit international food relief. The rebels lost some international support as Uganda, Ethiopia and Eritrea became embroiled in wars of their own.

The Sudanese government's "restoration" of a multi-party system at the start of 1999 was met with skepticism by the opposition. In 1999 Pres. Bashir sought some sort of reconciliation with opposition parties and with the southern rebels. In December he struck against Turabi, declaring a state of emergency, dissolving parliament dismissing the entire government, and replacing it with his supporters. In Jan. 2002 a cease-fire and

in July a peace accord signed in Nairobi brought hope at last that the war might end.

In early 2004 S.P.L.A. signed a deal with the government splitting oil wealth 50-50 and the civil war seemed to come to an end. But a war between the Sudan Liberation Army and the Justice and Equity Movement in Darfur led to 70,000 deaths and two million people fled their homes. Over 200,000 refugees settled in Chad. By 2008 the U.N. reported that over 200,000 had been killed and two million displaced.

International outrage helped both sides to a peace agreement in Jan. 2005 and in July Pres. Bashir made rebel leader John Garang his vice president. Garang died in a plane crash shortly thereafter and the peace held, but only for a few months. A peace brokered by the African Union in 2006 also fell apart, but in 2007 the government finally accepted 26,000 U.N. peacekeepers in Darfur. (See "Major News Stories.")

▶ **SURINAME**
Republic of Suriname
● **GEOGRAPHY   Location:** northeastern coast of South America. **Boundaries:** North Atlantic Ocean to N, French Guiana to E, Brazil to S, Guyana to W. **Total area:** 63,039 sq. mi. (163,270 sq km). **Coastline:** 240 mi. (386 km). **Comparative area:** slightly larger than Georgia. **Land use:** negl. % arable land; negl. % permanent crops; 100% other. **Major cities:** Paramaribo (capital).
● **PEOPLE   Population:** 475,996 (July 2008 est.). **Nationality:** noun—Surinamer(s); adjective—Surinamese. **Ethnic groups:** 31% Hindustani (East Indian), 31% Creole (black and mixed), 15% Javanese, 10% black. **Languages:** Dutch (official), English widely spoken, Sranang Tongo (Surinamese, sometimes called Taki-Taki, the native language of Creoles and much of younger population and lingua franca among others), Hindustani, Javanese. **Religions:** 27.4% Hindu, 25.2% Protestant (predominantly Moravian), 22.8% Roman Catholic, 19.6% Muslim.
● **GOVERNMENT   Type:** constitutional democracy. **Constitution:** Sept. 30, 1987. **Independence:** Nov. 25, 1975 (from Netherlands). **National holiday:** Independence Day, Nov. 25. **Heads of Government:** Runaldo Ronald Venetiaan, president (since Aug. 2000); **Structure:** executive—president is chief of state and head of government, Commander in Chief of the National Army maintains significant power; unicameral legislature; judiciary.
● **ECONOMY   Monetary unit:** Surinamese guilder. **Budget:** (2004 est.) *income:* $392.6 mil.; *expend.:* $425.9 mil. **G.D.P.:** $3.449 bil., $7,800 per capita (2007 est.). **Chief crops:** rice, bananas, palm oil, timber. **Natural resources:** timber, hydropower potential, fish, shrimp, bauxite. **Major industries:** bauxite mining, alumina and aluminum production, lumbering. **Labor force:** 156,700; 8% agriculture, 14% industry, 78% services (2004); 17% unemployment (2000). **Exports:** $1.391 bil. (f.o.b., 2006); alumina, aluminum, crude oil, lumber, shrimp and fish, rice, bananas. **Imports:** $1.297 bil. (f.o.b., 2006); capital equipment, petroleum, foodstuffs, cotton, consumer goods. **Major trading partners:** (2006) *exports:* 23% Norway, 16% Canada, 12% U.S., 10% Belgium, 9% France, 7% United Arab Emirates, 4% Iceland; *imports:* 29% U.S., 19% Netherlands, 15% Trinidad & Tobago, 5% Japan, 5% China.

In the early 17th century, the Dutch and English settled Suriname, which became a Dutch colony in 1667. Except for brief episodes of British rule, Suriname remained under Dutch control until its independence in 1975, shifting toward authoritarian military rule in 1980. The military created its own political party (the February 25 movement) and banned opposition organizations. The 1988 National Assembly election of Pres. Ramsewak Shankar ended direct military rule, but the restriction of civil liberties continued.

The Shankar government was overthrown in a bloodless coup led by Cmdr. Ivan Graanoogst in 1990, and civilian rule was restored in 1991 although the former military ruler, Col. Desi Bouterse, who led the coup and remains "Advisor of the State," is apparently still the defacto ruler. In June 1999, after the National Assembly voted "no confidence," President Jules Wijdenbosch agreed to resign—but to remain in office until after the May 2000 National Assembly elections, elections in which Ronald Venetiaan became president. Economic problems plagued the country before and since, but Venetiaan was reelected in 2005.

▶SWAZILAND
Kingdom of Swaziland
• **GEOGRAPHY Location:** landlocked country in southern Africa. **Boundaries:** South Africa to N, SE, S, and W; Mozambique to E. **Total area:** 6,703 sq. mi. (17,360 sq km). **Coastline:** none. **Comparative area:** slightly smaller than New Jersey. **Land use:** 11% arable land; negl. % permanent crops; 89% other. **Major cities:** Mbabane (capital); Manzini.
• **PEOPLE Population:** 1,128,814 (July 2008 est.). **Nationality:** noun—Swazi(s); adjective—Swazi. **Ethnic groups:** 97% African, 3% European. **Languages:** English and siSwati (both official); government business conducted in English. **Religions:** 40% Zionist (mixture of Christianity and indigenous beliefs), 20% Roman Catholic, 10% Muslim, 10% other.
• **GOVERNMENT Type:** monarchy; independent member of Commonwealth. **Independence:** Sept. 6, 1968 (from U.K.). **Constitution:** suspended Apr. 12, 1973; new constitution promulgated Oct. 13, 1978, but not yet formally presented to people. **National holiday:** Somhlolo (Independence) Day, Sept. 6. **Heads of Government:** Mswati III, king (since Apr. 1986); Sibusiso Barnabas Dlamini, prime minister (since Aug. 1996). **Structure:** executive—king is hereditary monarch, appoints prime minister; bicameral legislature (lower house-10 members appointed by king, 55 elected; upper house-20 members appointed by king, 10 elected by lower house); judiciary—judges appointed by king.
• **ECONOMY Monetary unit:** lilangeni. **Budget:** (2007 est.) *income:* $1.216 bil.; *expend.:* $1.15 bil. **G.D.P.:** $5.424 bil., $4,800 per capita (2007 est.). **Chief crops:** sugarcane, maize, cotton, maize, tobacco, rice, citrus fruits; cattle, goats, sheep. **Natural resources:** asbestos, coal, clay, cassiterite, hydropower. **Major industries:** mining (coal and asbestos), wood pulp, sugar. **Labor force:** 300,000; 40% unemployment (2006). **Exports:** $2.169 bil. (f.o.b., 2007); soft drink concentrates, sugar, wood pulp, cotton yarn. **Imports:** $2.31 bil. (f.o.b., 2007); motor vehicles, machinery, transport equipment, foodstuffs, chemicals, petroleum products. **Major trading partners:** (2006) *exports:* 60% South Africa, 9% E.U., 9% U.S., 6% Mozambique; *imports:* 96% South Africa, 1% E.U., 1% Japan.

The Kingdom of Swaziland, a landlocked African country, is surrounded on three sides by South Africa and on the fourth by Mozambique. The Swazi are of Bantu origin. They are believed to have migrated in the late 1700's, under their chief Ngwane II, into what is now southeastern Swazi-

land, finding several different peoples there. Ngwane II and his successors united these tribal clans by the beginning of the 19th century.

Although British and Boer traders began exploring the area in the 1830's, it was not until gold was discovered in the 1880's that settlers began coming in large numbers. They hoodwinked the illiterate Swazi leadership into signing away their rights to the land. The British and Boer governments agreed in 1894 that the Boers would control Swaziland, but power reverted to Great Britain after they defeated the Boers in the Boer War, which ended in 1902. Not until the 1967 did they give Swaziland authority over its internal affairs. Under the Britishauthored constitution, Swaziland gained its independence in September 1968 as a constitutional monarchy led by King Sobhuza II. He set aside the constitution in 1973 and disbanded the legislature. He ruled the country with the aid of a council of conservative ministers and named a committee to write a new constitution that was supposed to be more in keeping with Swazi traditions. A new legislature was created in 1979. The king died in 1982 and was replaced by his 18-year-old son, who took the name King Mswati III, in 1986, and has ruled autocratically ever since. His lavish lifestyle and many wives (13 at last count, with two fiances) have caused protests, but no more.

▶SWEDEN
Kingdom of Sweden
• **GEOGRAPHY Location:** Scandinavian peninsula, northwest Europe. **Boundaries:** Norway to NE and W, Finland to NE, Gulf of Bothnia to E, Baltic Sea to E and S, Skagerrak channel to SW. **Total area:** 173,731 sq. mi. (449,964 sq km). **Coastline:** 2,000 mi. (3,218 km). **Comparative area:** slightly larger than California. **Land use:** 7% arable land; 0% permanent crops; 93% other. **Major cities:** Stockholm (capital); Göteburg (Gothenburg); Malmö; Uppsala; Linköping.
• **PEOPLE Population:** 9,045,389 (July 2008 est.). **Nationality:** noun—Swede(s); adjective—Swedish. **Ethnic groups:** homogeneous white population; small Lappish minority; about 12% foreign-born or first-generation immigrants (Finns, Yugoslavs, Danes, Norwegians, Greeks, Turks). **Languages:** Swedish, small Lapp- and Finnish-speaking minorities. **Religions:** 87% Lutheran, Roman Catholic, Orthodox, Baptist, other.
• **GOVERNMENT Type:** constitutional monarchy. **Constitution:** Jan. 1, 1975. **National holiday:** Day of the Swedish Flag, June 6. **Head of Government:** Carl XVI Gustaf, king (since Nov. 1973); Fredrick Reinfeldt, prime minister (since Sept. 2006). **Structure:** executive—prime minister is head of government; unicameral legislature; judiciary.
• **ECONOMY Monetary unit:** Swedish krona. **Budget:** (2007 est.) *income:* $241.2 bil.; *expend.:* $229.1 bil. **G.D.P.:** $333.1 bil., $36,900 per capita (2007 est.). **Chief crops:** grain, sugar beets, potatoes; meat, milk. **Natural resources:** zinc, iron ore, lead, copper, silver. **Major industries:** iron and steel, precision equipment (bearings, radio and telephone parts, armaments), wood pulp. **Labor force:** 4.66 mil. (2007); 74% services, 24% industry, 2% agriculture. **Exports:** $176.5 bil. (f.o.b., 2007); 35% machinery, motor vehicles, paper products, pulp and wood, iron and steel products. **Imports:** $157.2 bil. (f.o.b., 2007); machinery, petroleum and petroleum products, chemicals, motor vehicles, foodstuffs. **Major trading partners:** (2006) *exports:* 10% Germany, 9% U.S., 9% Norway, 7% U.K., 7% Denmark, 6% Finland, 5% France, 5%

Netherlands, 5% Belgium; *imports:* 17% Germany, 9% Denmark, 8% Norway, 6% U.K., 6% Netherlands, 6% Finland, 4% France, 4% Belgium.

The earliest Swedes, the Svear, conquered and merged with their southern neighbors, the Gotar, by the sixth century. Organized into petty kingdoms, Swedes joined with other Norsemen in the Viking raids of the seventh through 11th centuries; in the 10th century, they began to dominate a trading empire that stretched through Russia to the Black Sea. Christianity was introduced by St. Ansgar in 829 but became fully established only in the 12th century, during the reign of Eric IX, who also conquered Finland. For centuries Sweden warred with its neighbors, Norway and Denmark, for control in the north, and it competed with the German Hanseatic League for control of the Baltic trade.

The Swedish and Norwegian monarchies were merged in 1319 by Magnus VII, and in 1397 Queen Margaret effected the Kalmar Union, which united Sweden, Denmark, and Norway under a single monarchy. Sweden resisted Danish rule, and in 1520 King Christian II responded with the massacre of the Swedish nobility at Stockholm. Sweden then rose against the Danish throne and in 1523 enthroned Gustavus Wasa as Gustavus I, founder of the Swedish monarchy. The Wasa dynasty slowly introduced Lutheran Christianity and in 1604 banned Catholicism.

Sweden became a European champion of Protestantism in the 17th century, intervening against the Habsburgs in the Thirty Years' War. Emerging among the victors after 1648, Sweden successfully waged wars with Denmark and Poland, built a great northern empire, and made the Baltic Sea virtually a Swedish lake. But in the late 17th century and into the 18th, the Russians deprived Sweden of the Baltic's eastern shore and, in 1808, of Finland, while the Prussians drove Sweden from the southern Baltic coast.

The kings of Sweden during the 18th century pursued a pointless despotism that weakened the country politically and socially. Sweden joined the European powers against Napoleon in 1813 and was rewarded with Norway in 1814. In 1905 Norway gained its independence, and Sweden took on its modern boundaries.

Sweden's natural resources—timber, iron ore, and hydroelectric power—were exploited by traditional industries, which supplemented other economic activities (fishing, maritime trade). All provided the basis for industrialization in the 19th and 20th centuries, leading to an economic prosperity that was enhanced by political neutrality.

Sweden's neutrality was largely respected by Hitler during World War II. Through the war Sweden continued to be ruled, under King Gustavus V, by a national coalition government lasting until 1945. Sweden's gross national product (GNP) rose by 20 percent during the war years.

The Social Democratic party dominated the Swedish government after 1936, and again after 1945, lasting until 1976 under the leadership of Tage Erlander. Sweden, like its Scandinavian neighbors, constructed an economy based on free enterprise, public ownership of utilities, exports, social welfare, and high taxes.

A U.N. charter member, Sweden accepted Marshall Plan aid and joined the Council of Europe in 1948. Sweden's plan for a Nordic Defense Alliance failed when Norway and Denmark joined NATO (Sweden refused to join), but the political and economic Nordic Council (Sweden, Norway, Denmark, Iceland, and, after 1956, Finland) was formed in 1952-53. This consultative body backed

the establishment of SAS as the joint national airline of the first three members; coordination of the welfare programs of member states; and abolition of passport controls and controls on the migration of labor within Scandinavia.

Erlander retired in 1969 and was succeeded by Olaf Palme, who pursued a more rigid socialist program. Advocating legislation to make incomes more equal, provoking some labor unrest. When King Gustav VI Adolf died in 1973 the Palme government passed the 1974 Instrument of Government Act, divesting the king of his role as commander in chief and of his right to appoint prime ministers.

Economic growth came to a virtual halt in the 1970's; Sweden's oil import costs rose 700 percent between 1972 and 1979. Consumer prices rose sharply, and labor unrest grew. The Social Democrats were turned out by a conservative coalition in 1976 but returned with a minority cabinet in 1982.

Palme was assassinated in 1986, and he was succeeded by Ingvar Carlsson, whose Social Democratic program focused on a scheme whereby business profits are taxed to fund labor union purchases of sufficient stock to gain labor ownership of private enterprise. Elections (Sept. 1991) unseated Carlsson and the Social Democrats, who had ruled for 53 of the last 59 years. A coalition government of four conservative parties pledged to cut taxes and phase out some welfare programs. But in elections held in Sept. 1994, Carlsson returned to power as voters expressed dissatisfaction with inflation, unemployment, and an enormous public debt, all of which spiraled under the conservative coalition. The Social Democrats fell 13 votes short of a majority in Parliament, however, forcing them to seek the support of the right-centrist Liberal party in a coalition government.

On Jan. 1, 1995, Sweden entered the European Union. In March 1996, Finance Minister Göran Persson succeeded Carlsson as prime minister. In 1998 Sweden announced it would not join the European Monetary Union, and in Sept. elections Persson's Government won enough votes to keep power by pledging more money for social welfare services. More significant for Sweden's future was the 1999 completion of the 10-mile, $2.6 billion bridge over (and under) the Baltic, linking Copenhagen with Malmoe (Sweden's third largest city). On Dec. 17, 1999, after almost 500 years, the Lutheran Church was disestablished. Persson and the Social Democrats won the Sept. 2002 elections. In Sept. 2003 Foreign Minister Anna Lindh was assassinated days before voters rejected participation in the European Monetary Union. In Sept. 2006 Persson was badly defeated in large part over welfare and labor issues. The Moderate party under new prime minister Fredrik Reinfeldt pledged to revitalize the economy.

▶ **SWITZERLAND**
Swiss Confederation
• **GEOGRAPHY Location:** landlocked country in central Europe. **Boundaries:** Germany to N, Austria to E, Italy to S, and France to W. **Total area:** 15,942 sq. mi. (41,290 sq km). **Coastline:** none. **Comparative area:** slightly less than twice the size of New Jersey. **Land use:** 11% arable land; 1% permanent crops; 88% other. **Major cities:** Berne (Bern, capital); Zürich; Basel; Genève (Geneva or Genf); Lausanne.
• **PEOPLE Population:** 7,581,520 (July 2008 est.). **Nationality:** noun—Swiss (sing., pl.); adjective—Swiss. **Ethnic groups:** 65% German, 18% French, 10% Italian, 1% Romansch, 6% other. **Languages:**

63.7% German, 19.2% French, 7.6% Italian (all official); 0.6% Romansch, 8.9% other. **Religions:** 41.8% Catholic, 35.3% Protestant, 4% Muslim. ● **GOVERNMENT Type:** federal republic. **Independence:** Aug. 1, 1291. **Constitution:** May 29, 1874. **National holiday:** Anniversary of the Founding of the Swiss Confederation, Aug. 1. **Head of Government:** Pascal Couchepin, president (since Jan. 2008). **Structure:** executive—president is head of government and chief of state; bicameral legislature—National Council, Council of States; judiciary left chiefly to cantons.
● **ECONOMY Monetary unit:** Swiss franc. **Budget:** (2007 est.) *income:* $155.5 bil.; *expend.:* $154.2 bil. **G.D.P.:** $300.9 bil., $39,800 per capita (2007 est.). **Chief crops:** grains, fruits, vegetables; meat, eggs. **Natural resources:** hydropower potential, timber, salt. **Major industries:** machinery, chemicals, watches. **Labor force:** 3.85 mil.; 72.5% services, 23.7% industry, 3.8% agriculture (2007). **Exports:** $201 bil. (f.o.b., 2007); machinery, chemicals, metals, watches, agricultural products. **Imports:** $189.6 bil. (f.o.b., 2007); machinery, chemicals, vehicles, metals, agricultural products. **Major trading partners:** (2006) *exports:* 19.7% Germany, 11.1% U.S., 8.8% Italy, 8.6% France, 4.8% U.K.; *imports:* 31.7% Germany, 10.6% Italy, 10% France, 6.2% U.S., 4.7% Netherlands, 4.3% Austria.

Switzerland, the Roman province of Helvetia, began to assume its modern form in A.D. 1291, when three independent cantons formed a defensive league against the expansion of Habsburg power. The Swiss League grew to eight cantons in 1353, 13 in 1513, 22 in 1815. The league continues to evolve; it reached its present size of 20 cantons and six half-cantons with the creation of the Canton of Jura in 1979.

The Treaty of Westphalia, which ended the Thirty Years' War in 1648, gave international recognition to the independence of Switzerland from the Holy Roman Empire. Switzerland became a client state of France in the Napoleonic period; the European powers guaranteed Swiss independence and neutrality at the Congress of Vienna in 1815. Constitutional changes in 1848 and 1874 somewhat increased the power of the central government, but the individual cantons cling stubbornly to their independence, helping to ensure stability within a multilingual nation.

The Swiss government consists of an upper house, representing the cantons, and a lower house that is directly elected. No executive can veto, nor court disallow, a bill of the Swiss legislature. Executive power is vested in a seven-member committee chosen by the legislature, with a rotating presidency.

Swiss neutrality is defended by more than simply international guarantees. Switzerland is a highly militarized society; every male is required to serve in the citizen's militia until age 47, keeping an assault rifle and other equipment ready at home. The armed forces are equipped with modern weapons, and military spending amounts to 30 percent of the Swiss federal budget.

Landlocked, with little fertile farmland and lacking both natural resources and a colonial empire, Switzerland was traditionally one of Europe's poorest countries. Until the 19th century, its principal export was mercenaries who supplied military services to any European sovereign who could pay for them. (The pope's Swiss Guard is a remnant of this tradition.) With the spread in the late 18th century of the Romantic movement, Europeans learned to appreciate the Alpine scenery, and a tourist industry was born. It was expanded in the 20th century with the development of

Alpine skiing. Tourism remains a conspicuous, though minor, part of the Swiss economy.

Swiss prosperity came in the 20th century with specialized manufacturing and free trade within the world economy. By 1940 half of the population was engaged in manufacturing, producing products requiring high degrees of skill: processed foods, watches, electrical machinery, engines, fine textiles, and the like.

Neutral in both world wars, Switzerland required no postwar recovery in the 1940's. It capitalized on the restructuring of European politics and economics to expand into the service sector, which now employs half of the work force. Tourism, banking, insurance, and clerical/bureaucratic services to the many international organizations with headquarters in Switzerland help give the nation one of Europe's highest standards of living. Under pressure from the E.C. and the United States, Switzerland agreed to phase out its famous "Form B" (i.e., secret bank accounts).

Referenda at this time brought overwhelming rejection of U.N. membership, and support for restrictive immigration legislation. The most significant political changes were the gradual extension of women's right to vote and the 1993 approval of casino gambling to fund social security.

In 1996 and 1997 the Swiss government, responding to international pressures, appointed a panel to examine what funds in Swiss banks the Nazis might have stolen or that Holocaust victims (or their families) might have deposited and were unable to retrieve. A less than rigorous accounting, however, resulted in several lawsuits which were settled in 1998 with the Swiss banks agreeing to pay $1.2 bil. On Dec. 9, 1998, Social Democrat Ruth Dreifuss became Switzerland's first female and first Jewish president. A June 1999 referendum (carried 70 percent–30 percent) to restrict refugee asylum prefigured a very strong showing in the October National Council elections by the nativist Swiss People's Party which had the largest total vote and won the second largest number of seats.

Recent referenda reflect divisions in Swiss minds over the country's identity and her role in the new Europe. In 2000, 64 percent refused to set a limit (18%) on the number of foreigners residing in Switzerland, and 74 percent refused to begin negotiations for E.U. membership. Yet in July, by a slender margin (50.9 percent), voters approved the arming of Swiss troops serving under international auspices as well as joint training of Swiss soldiers with foreign armies, and in 2002 Switzerland entered the U.N. In 2005, voters approved closer ties with the E.U. In 2008 voters rejected a referendum to limit naturalization of foreigners.

▶ SYRIA
Syrian Arab Republic
● **GEOGRAPHY Location:** western Asia. **Boundaries:** Turkey to N, Iraq to E, Jordan to S, Lebanon and Israel to SW, Mediterranean Sea to W. **Total area:** 71,498 sq. mi. (185,180 sq km). **Coastline:** 193 mi. (193 km). **Comparative area:** slightly larger than North Dakota. **Land use:** 26% arable land; 4% permanent crops; 70% other. **Major cities:** Damascus (capital); Aleppo; Homs; Latakia; Hama.
● **PEOPLE Population:** 19,747,586 (July 2008 est.). **Nationality:** noun—Syrian(s); adjective—Syrian. **Ethnic groups:** 90.3% Arab, 9.7% Kurds, Armenians, and other. **Languages:** Arabic (official), Kurdish, Armenian, Aramaic, Circassian, French. **Religions:** 74% Sunni Muslim; 16% Alawite, Druze, and other Muslim sects; 10% Christian.

• **GOVERNMENT Type:** republic under military regime since Mar. 1963. **Independence:** Apr. 17, 1946 (from League of Nations Mandate under French administration). **Constitution:** Mar. 13, 1973. **National holiday:** National Day, Apr. 17. **Heads of Government:** Dr. Bashar Al-Assad, president (since July 2000); Naji Al-Otari, prime minister (since Sept. 2003). **Structure:** executive powers vested in president and Council of Ministers; unicameral legislature (People's Council); judiciary. • **ECONOMY Monetary unit:** Syrian pound. **Budget:** (2007 est.) **income:** $8.45 bil.; **expend.:** $10.38 bil. **G.D.P.:** $83 bil., $4,300 per capita (2007 est.). **Chief crops:** cotton, wheat, barley, lentils; beef, lamb, eggs, poultry, milk. **Natural resources:** crude oil, phosphates, chrome and manganese ores, asphalt, iron ore. **Major industries:** petroleum, textiles, food processing, beverages. **Labor force:** 5.457 mil. (2007 est.); 66% services, 19% agriculture, 15% industry. **Exports:** $10.58 bil. (f.o.b., 2007 est.); 65% petroleum, 10% textiles, 9% food and live animals. **Imports:** $12.38 bil. (f.o.b., 2007 est.); 21% machinery, 18% foodstuffs/animals, 15% metal and metal products, 10% chemicals. **Major trading partners:** (2006) **exports:** 27.3% Iraq, 12.1% Germany, 9.5% Lebanon, 6.6% Italy, 5.3% Egypt, 4.8% Saudi Arabia; **imports:** 12.3% Saudi Arabia, 7.9% China, 6.2% Egypt, 6% United Arab Emirates, 4.9% Germany, 4.9% Italy, 4.8% Ukraine, 4.5% Iran.

The home of some of the world's most ancient centers of civilization, Syria was successively part of the Hittite, Assyrian, and Persian empires. At various times it was conquered by the Babylonians and the Egyptians. From about 1250 B.C., the coastal cities came under Phoenician rule. Alexander the Great brought Syria into the Hellenic world with his conquests in 332 B.C. After the fall of the Alexandrian empire, Syria came under the domain of the Seleucid empire but was constantly threatened by the Hellenic kingdom of Egypt, based in Alexandria.

In the classical period, Syria embraced a much larger territory than that of the present Syrian nation; it included the entire Levant and parts of present-day Turkey, Iraq, Iran, and Jordan. Greater Syria was conquered by Rome in 63 B.C. Under Roman rule the oasis region of Palmyra grew into a powerful semiautonomous kingdom. With the division of the Roman Empire in the fourth century A.D., Syria became part of the Eastern Roman (Byzantine) Empire. Throughout the Roman and Byzantine periods, the country was an important center of Christianity.

Syria was one of the first areas conquered when Islam began expansion from Arabia; Islamic rule was established by 636. From 661 to 751, Damascus was the center of the Caliphate, the ruling body of the Islamic world. By the late 11th century, the Seljuk Turks had conquered Syria. The large Syrian Christian population welcomed the European Crusaders as liberators from the Turks, but both Christians and Turks were defeated by the Arab general Saladin in the late 12th century. Saladin's rule was followed by that of the Mamluk empire of Egypt. During the Mamluk period, Mongol armies twice invaded Syria, in the mid-13th century and at the turn of the 15th century.

An Ottoman army defeated the Mamluks in Syria in 1516, making Syria part of the Ottoman Empire. In the 18th century, France declared itself the protector of Syria's Christian community against Ottoman abuses. Napoleon invaded Syria in 1799 but withdrew after a brief occupation. In the 1830's Egyptian troops occupied Syria but were forced to withdraw by the European powers.

Syrian nationalist aspirations emerged as the Ottoman Empire began to crumble before World War I. During the war the British encouraged Syrians to rebel against Turkish rule. After World War I, France governed both Syria and Lebanon under a League of Nations mandate. Under French rule, the region was divided into small territorial states along communal lines; Lebanon became independent in 1926. After prolonged negotiations much of Syria was organized into a semiautonomous state in 1930-32.

In June 1940 the French administration in Syria declared its loyalty to the Vichy government. British and Free French forces invaded in June 1941, and an independent Syrian republic was established in September 1941. Separately administered territories were consolidated with the republic over the next two years, and full independence was declared on Jan. 1, 1944; foreign troops did not withdraw, however, until April 1946.

Syria became a founding member of the Arab League and participated in the first Arab-Israeli War in 1948. An armistice with Israel was signed in July 1949. Severe political instability marked the early years of Syrian independence; the government was overthrown by military coups three times in 1949 alone.

Most of Syria's Jews emigrated to Israel before or during 1948, and much of its once-substantial Christian population has emigrated also. Syrian politics remain dominated by communal concerns, however; the Arab majority is divided into Sunni, Shiite, Alawite, and Druze communities.

Syria and Egypt merged as the United Arab Republic in February 1958; Syria seceded from the federation on Sept. 30, 1961. In Mar. 1963 a military coup established the pan-Arab Socialist Baath party in power; all other political parties were abolished. The Baath party leadership is dominated by the minority Alawite community. Pres. Hafez al-Assad took power on Feb. 22, 1971.

In the 1967 Arab-Israeli War (the Six Day War), Israel seized and held the Golan Heights region of Syria, from which Syria had long shelled Israeli communities and military installations. The Golan Heights were incorporated into Israeli territory. Syrian troops aided Palestinian forces fighting government troops in Jordan in September 1970. After the expulsion of Palestinian forces from Jordan in July 1971, Syria broke off relations with Jordan; relations were restored in 1975.

On Oct, 6, 1973, Syrian and Egyptian forces attacked Israel, touching off the the Yom Kippur War. A cease-fire took effect on Oct. 24; Syria failed to regain territory lost to Israel in 1967. Following the 1973 war, Syria became a major recipient of economic aid from the Arab oil states and of military equipment from the Soviet Union.

In 1976 Syrian troops entered Lebanon in an attempt to mediate a civil war there and became enmeshed in that conflict. Major fighting between Syrian troops and Lebanese Christian militiamen broke out in April 1981. On June 6, 1982, Israeli troops invaded Lebanon and engaged Syrian troops in a five-day war in the Bekaa Valley. Following serious losses of aircraft and troops, Syria agreed to a cease-fire with Israel on June 11. Syrian troops continue to occupy parts of Lebanon.

An attempted coup, in February 1982, by the Muslim Brotherhood, led to serious fighting within Syria, but the rebellion was put down; casualties topped 5,000 on both sides.

From the time of the 1973 Arab-Israeli War, Syria adopted a radical stance in Middle Eastern politics, rejecting the 1979 Egyptian-Israeli accord and all other attempts at Arab-Israeli reconciliation. Supporting radical movements within the Palestine Liberation Organization, Syria aided Palestinian militants in driving Yasir Arafat's centrist faction of the PLO from its headquarters in Tripoli in 1983. The government was implicated in various acts of international terrorism in support of Palestinian, Libyan, and Iranian causes.

Syria played a major role in the Lebanese peace process and accommodating a peace settlement between rival Shiite militias. Syria also took part in the anti-Iraq coalition in 1990-91, sending 20,000 troops to Saudi Arabia. Syria in 1994 made serious efforts toward achieving peace in the Middle East, including an offer to normalize relations in exchange for a return of the Golan Heights. But talks were suspended after bombings by the militant Islamic group Hamas.

In Oct. 1998, Syria reached an accord with Turkey; with 10,000 Turkish troops massed on Syria's border, Syria agreed to cease supporting Kurdish rebels. In Feb. 1999, Assad won, with 99.95 percent approval in his sole candidacy, election to a fifth seven-year term as president. A cabinet shake-up in March 2000 produced 22 new members among the 36 under new premier Mohammed Mustafa Zubi just three months before the death of Assad. After his 30 years of rule, the government backed his son (and armed forces commander) Bashar al-Assad, 34. In 2005 Syria was forced to remove all of its security forces from Lebanon after mass demonstrations followed the assassination of a popular Lebanese politcian. In 2007 Israel destroyed a nuclear reactor site in Syria.

▶ **TAIWAN**

• **GEOGRAPHY Location:** one large and several smaller islands about 100 mi. (160 km) off SE coast of mainland China. Taipei 25°03'N, 121°30'E. **Boundaries:** East China Sea to N, Pacific Ocean to E, Bashi Channel to S, and Formosa Strait to W; separated from mainland by Formosa Strait. **Total area:** 13,892 sq. mi. (35,980 sq km). **Coastline:** 900 mi. (1,448 km). **Comparative area:** slightly smaller than Maryland. **Land use:** 24% arable land; 1% permanent crops;75% other. **Major cities:** Taipei (capital); Kaohsiung; Taichung; Tainan; Panchiao.

• **PEOPLE Population:** 22,920,946 (July 2008 est.). **Nationality:** noun—Chinese (sing., pl.); adjective—Chinese. **Ethnic groups:** 84% Taiwanese, 14% mainland Chinese, 2% aborigine. **Languages:** Mandarin Chinese (official); Taiwanese and Hakka dialects also used. **Religions:** 93% mixture of Buddhist, Confucian, and Taoist; 4.5% Christian, 2.5% other.

• **GOVERNMENT Type:** multi-party democratic regime headed by popularly elected president. **Constitution:** Jan. 1, 1947, amended 1992, 1994, and 1997. **National holiday:** National Day, Oct. 10. **Heads of Government:** Chen Shui-bian, president (since March 2004); Chang Chun-hsiung, premier (since Feb. 2004). **Structure:** executive—president appoints premier; two-chamber legislature—Legislative Yuan, National Assembly; judiciary—Judicial Yuan.

• **ECONOMY Monetary unit:** New Taiwan dollar. **Budget:** (2007 est.) *income:* $49 bil.; *expend.:* $5.19 bil. **G.D.P.:** $690.1 bil., $29,800 per capita (2007 est.). **Chief crops:** rice, wheat, corn, soybeans, vegetables, fruit, tea; pigs, poultry, beef, milk; fish. **Natural resources:** small deposits of coal, natural gas, limestone, marble, and asbestos. **Major industries:** electronics, petroleum refining, textiles, clothing, chemicals. **Labor force:** 10.78 mil. (2007 est.); 37% industry, 58% services, 5%

agriculture. **Exports:** $246.7 bil. (f.o.b., 2007); 54% electrical equipment and machinery, metals, textiles, plastics, chemicals, electronic products. **Imports:** $219.3 bil. (c.i.f., 2007); 44.5% machinery and electrical equipment, electronic products, minerals, precision instruments. **Major trading partners:** (2006) *exports:* 24% China, 15% Hong Kong, 13.4% U.S., 6.7% Japan; *imports:* 21% Japan, 12.7% China, 12.2% U.S., 7.1% South Korea, 4.6% Saudi Arabia.

Nominally part of the Chinese empire since the Song dynasty (960-1279), Taiwan was inhabited only by non-Chinese aboriginals before the 17th century. Around 1600 the Portuguese established a trading station on Taiwan; they named the island Ilha Formosa. In 1620 the Dutch built Fort Zeelandia near present-day Tainan, controlling the island until they were driven out by the Chinese pirate-patriot Koxinga (Zheng Chenggong). Remnants of the overthrown Ming dynasty (1368-1644) held out on the island until 1683, when it came under the sway of the Qing dynasty (1644-1911). Thereafter, substantial numbers of farmers from Fujian Province migrated to the fertile western lowlands of the island, driving the aboriginals into the central mountains. The Qing dynasty administered Taiwan as a semiautonomous subprovince of Fujian Province.

Following China's defeat by Japan in the Sino-Japanese War of 1894-95, Taiwan was ceded to Japan as a colony. The Japanese built roads and railroads to exploit Taiwan's resources of rice, timber, and minerals. In 1945, after Japan's defeat in World War II, Taiwan was returned to China.

As the Chinese civil war turned against the Nationalist party of Chiang Kai-shek (see "China"), Nationalist troops began to prepare Taiwan as a base for a retreat from the mainland.

In 1947 Nationalist agents executed several thousand students and others suspected of favoring Taiwan's independence from China. In 1949 approximately two million Nationalist soldiers, government officials, and civilian sympathizers retreated to Taiwan. The relocated Republic of China (ROC) continued to claim to be the legitimate government of all of China, now under Communist control. In addition to Taiwan proper, the Nationalists occupied the P'eng-hu Islands in the Taiwan Straits and the small islands of Quemoy and Matsu just off the coast of Fujian. Recovery of the mainland became a cornerstone of ROC policy, but no serious attempt was made to do so. U.S. policy in the Taiwan Straits was to defend Taiwan against Communist attack but also to keep the two rival governments of China separated.

A successful program of land reform in the early 1950's led to the creation of surplus capital, which fueled the development of an industrial base on the island. Foreign investment from Japan and the United States, and American military and economic aid, also enhanced economic development. By the early 1970's, the island had developed an export-oriented economy, producing textiles, cement, plastics, assembled electronic appliances, and other manufactured goods.

Chiang Kai-shek, president of the Republic of China since 1928, died in 1975 and was succeeded by his son, Chiang Ching-kuo. Under both the Nationalist party (Kuomintang, or KMT) controlled both the ROC and the Taiwan Provincial governments; mainland refugees and their descendants (15% of the population) dominated senior government posts and the military officer corps. Native Taiwanese played the leading role in agriculture, industry, and in local governments.

In 1971 China's seat in the United Nations was taken away from the ROC and awarded to the People's Republic of China, leaving Taiwan in international diplomatic limbo. On Jan. 1, 1979, the United States withdrew its recognition of the ROC and inaugurated mutual diplomatic relations with the People's Republic. Under the Taiwan Relations Act of 1979, nominally nongovernmental relations were maintained between the U.S. and Taiwan through the American Institute in Taipei and Taiwan's Coordination Council in the U.S. Taiwan enjoys a substantial favorable balance of trade with the U.S.

In 1987 Pres. Chiang Ching-kuo began a policy of liberalization when he abolished martial law and allowed non-KMT political parties to function legally. Some barriers to travel and communication with the mainland by ROC citizens were eased, but Taiwan's government continued to rebuff all calls from the mainland for discussions of reunification. Chiang Ching-kuo died in Jan. 1988 and was succeeded by his vice president, Lee Teng-hui. In March 1990, Lee was reelected by the National Assembly in the first election for the office.

The ruling KMT maintained its hold on power in legislative elections in 1992, but the opposition Democratic Progressive party scored a stunning success, tripling its number of legislative seats and bringing the issue of Taiwanese independence to the forefront. Factional rivalry deepened in the KMT, with Pres. Lee's Wisdom Coalition challenged by the New Kuomintang Alliance of Prime Minister (and former general) Hau Pei-tsun. Hau reluctantly resigned on Feb. 3, 1993, to take responsibility for the electoral fiasco, but his faction, with military backing, continued to pose a threat to Pres. Lee's power.

During the campaign for Taiwan's presidential election in March, 1996, China held aggressive military exercises off the coast of Taiwan in an effort to influence the voting; the U.S. sent two aircraft carriers to the area. In a rebuke to Beijing, President Lee, who had campaigned for a more visible international role for Taiwan, was resoundingly re-elected; he was also re-elected as the head of the KMT in August, 1997. The ruling KMT saw its power eroded in local elections as voters protested corruption and economic stagnation related to the Asia-wide economic crises of 1997-98. The KMT rebounded strongly in 1998 elections but tensions rose in 1999 with mainland China, when Pres. Lee's expressed interest in Taiwan's being included in a proposed anti-missile defense of its Asian allies (the "last straw" to Beijing). Later, Lee announced that Taiwan would conduct its relations with China on a "state-to-state" basis, meaning Taiwan was an independent state—to Beijing, an "extremely dangerous step".

In March 2000, the KMT was peacefully voted out of power after 50 years. Chen Shui-Bian of the Democratic-Progressive Party was elected president with only 39 percent of the vote. Political rivalries prevented Chen's party from gaining a significant majority and he barely won reelection in 2004. In 2005 his government met with China and these talks ended in a pledge to seek an end to hostilities, but charges of corruption during 2006 resulted in falling popularity and in 2008 a Nationalist Party president was elected, Ma Ying-jeou, who immediately began the first formal talks with China since 1999.

▶ TAJIKISTAN
Republic of Tajikistan
• GEOGRAPHY   Location: southeast central Asia. Boundaries: Kyrgyzstan to NE, China to E,

Afghanistan to S and SW, Uzbekistan to NW and N. Total area: 55,251 sq. mi. (143,100 sq km). Coastline: none. Comparative area: slightly smaller than Wisconsin. Land use: 6% arable land; 1% permanent crops; 93% other. Major cities: Dushanbe (Stalinabad 1929-61) (capital); Khodzhent (formerly Leninabad).
• PEOPLE   Population: 7,211,884 (July 2008 est.). Nationality: noun—Tajikistani(s); adjective— Tajikistani. Ethnic groups: 64.9% Tajik, 25% Uzbek, 3.5% Russian, 6.6% other. Languages: Tajik (official) is closely related to Farsi (Persian) and was written in Cyrillic script since 1940; Russian widely used in government and business. Religions: 85% Sunni Muslim, 5% Shi'a Muslim.
• GOVERNMENT   Type: republic. Independence: Sept. 9, 1991 (from Soviet Union). Constitution: Nov. 6, 1994. National holiday: National Day, Sept. 9. Heads of Government: Emomali Rakhmonov; head of state (since Nov. 1994); Oqil Oqilov, prime minister (since Nov. 2006). Structure: executive— popularly-elected president appoints prime minister and cabinet; bicameral legislature; judiciary.
• ECONOMY   Monetary unit: Tajikistani ruble. Budget: (2007 est.) income: $700 mil.; expend.: $673 mil. G.D.P.: $11.87 bil., $1,600 per capita (2007 est.). Chief crops: cotton, vegetables, fruit, grain, grapes; cattle, sheep, goats. Natural resources: significant hydropower potential, some petroleum, uranium, mercury, brown coal. Major industries: mineral processing, chemicals, fertilizers, cement. Labor force: 2.1 mil. (2007); 67% agriculture, 8% industry, 25% services. Exports: $1.468 bil. (f.o.b., 2007 est.); cotton, aluminum, electricity, fruits, vegetable oil, textiles. Imports: $2.455 bil. (f.o.b., 2007 est.); fuel, electricity, chemicals, machinery and transport equipment, foodstuffs. Major trading partners: (2006) exports: 40.7% Netherlands, 31.7% Turkey, 5.4% Iran, 4.8% Uzbekistan, 4.7% Russia; imports: 24.6% Russia, 10.8% Kazakhstan, 10.2% Uzbekistan, 8.6% China, 8% Azerbaijan.

Tajikistan is a mountainous country, with over half of its territory above 10,000 feet. Its mountain ranges are the northern and southern Tian Shan and the Pamirs, where the former Soviet Union's highest points of Lenin Peak and Communism Peak are found. The dense river system and the many fertile valleys make habitation possible in such a mountainous country, although the entire territory is prone to earthquakes.

Tajikistan exemplifies the complexities of central Asia, since, unlike other ethnic groups on the region, the Tajiks were not nomadic but sedentary, and their language was Persian, not Turkic. They are a population that somehow escaped the waves of Turkish influence that swept through central Asia. As early as the eighth century a.d., the Tajiks probably formed a distinctive ethnic group, although they have never been a completely independent people. Despite the formation of several semi-independent states in their history, they have always been a small part of the larger Uzbek lands. In the mid-19th century, the Russian empire expanded southward, and the northern Tajik territories came under Russian rule. At the same time, the tribal state known as the Khanate of Bukhara controlled the southern Tajik territories.

In April 1918 northern Tajikistan came under Soviet control and was included in the Turkestan Autonomous Soviet Socialist Republic (ASSR). Three years later, the Red Army took the other regions that had been ruled by Bukhara. There was local opposition to Soviet rule, and the fighting meant that full Soviet authority over all of the area was not established until 1925. When the U.S.S.R.

created the National Delimitation of the Central Asian Republics in 1924, it founded the Tajik ASSR as part of the Uzbck Soviet Socialist Republic (SSR); on Oct. 16, 1929, it became the Tajik SSR.

The Tajiks were fiercely opposed to the policies of land reform and collectivization, and during the ensuing Soviet repression of the 1930's, almost all native Tajiks were replaced by Russians in leading government and party positions. There have been reports of rising Islamic influence and increasing anti-Russian sentiment and even riots during the 1970's, evidence that the animosity toward the Russians that stemmed with its forced incorporation into the U.S.S.R. had not abated since the 1920's. Under Soviet rule, there was some economic and social progress.

However, living standards in Tajikistan are still among the lowest in the former union. Most people continue to live in rural qishlaqs, or settlements, consisting of 200-700 one-family houses built along an irrigation ditch or a river. The country is a major producer of cotton, and its industries are nonferrous metallurgy, cotton processing, fruit canning, and wine making.

Mikhail Gorbachev's glasnost, or openness, policy resulted in a campaign against corruption, a relaxation of censorship in the press, and increased ethnic tensions over alleged discrimination against Tajiks living in Uzbekistan. In June 1989 there were violent clashes between the two groups on the border between the two republics. There were also riots in February 1990 in Dushanbe, when the suggestion that Armenian refugees would be resettled there spurred the local Tajiks into action. Increased freedom of the press has given rise to a growing interest in Iran and Iranian culture, for even though they are closely related, contact between Iran and the Tajiks was severely limited during the Soviet period.

In large part due to the riots, opposition candidates were barred from the March 1990 elections and the Communist party won 94 percent of the seats. After the failed Aug. 1991 coup in Moscow, the Communist party was banned, and the president was forced to resign over his support of the coup. Since then, there have been several Communist party coups, and the party has been banned and reinstated several times. In the presidential elections, former Communist party leader Rakhmon Nabiyev won with 58 percent of the vote. But after a relatively tranquil six months, Islamic fundamentalists, armed allegedly by Iran and Afghanistan, rose up against the Nabiyev regime. Vicious fighting for almost four months led to Nabiyev's resignation at gunpoint and the launching of a fundamentalist government.

In 1992 the pro-Communist forces launched a successful counterattack in which thousands were killed and perhaps 300,000 displaced. Voters in Nov. 1994 approved by referendum a new (highly presidential) constitution with 90 percent of the vote, and elected as president Emomali Rakhmonov with 60 percent. But the civil war of the current, ex-Communist and Russian-backed government against Islamic rebels continues, despite U.N.-mediated cease-fires signed in Sept. 1994 and May 1995. Two renegade military commanders mutinied in Feb. 1996, but called off the coup when Rakhmonov dismissed several senior officials. Sporadic fighting between government troops and several rebel groups continued throughout 1997, and while the government appeared to be taking control, flareups continued into 2000. In Sept. 1999 voters amended the constitution to allow opposition Moslem parties and to extend the presidential term from 5 to 7 years.

In November President Rakhmanov won a new term with 96 percent of the vote. He won again in 2006. Russia's president, Vladmir Putin, established a military presence there in 2003.

▶ TANZANIA
United Republic of Tanzania
● **GEOGRAPHY   Location:** Tanganyika, on eastern coast of Africa, and islands of Zanzibar and Pemba, about 25 mi. (40 km) off Tanganyika coast in Indian Ocean. **Boundaries:** Burundi, Rwanda to NW, Uganda, Kenya to N, Indian Ocean to E, Mozambique, Malawi to S, Zambia to SW, Zaire to W. **Total area:** 364,900 sq. mi. (945,090 sq km). **Coastline:** 885 mi. (1,424 km). **Comparative area:** slightly larger than twice size of California. **Land use:** 4% arable land; 1% permanent crops; 95% other. **Major cities:** Dar es Salaam (capital); Mwanza; Tabora; Mbeya; Tanga.
● **PEOPLE   Population:** 40,213,162 (July 2008 est.). **Nationality:** noun—Tanzanian(s); adjective—Tanzanian. **Ethnic groups:** mainland—99% native Africans of over 130 groups; 1% Asian, European, and Arab; Zanzibar—Arab, native African, mixed Arab and native African. **Languages:** Kiswahili and Swahili and English (all official); English primary language of commerce, administration, higher education; Swahili widely understood, generally used for communication between ethnic groups; first language of most people is one of local languages; primary education generally in Swahili. **Religions:** mainland—30% Christian, 35% Muslim, 35% indigenous beliefs; Zanzibar—almost all Muslim.
● **GOVERNMENT   Type:** republic. **Independence:** Tanganyika became independent Dec. 9, 1961 (from U.N. trusteeship under British administration); Zanzibar became independent Dec. 19, 1963 (from U.K.); Tanganyika united with Zanzibar Apr. 26, 1964. **Constitution:** Apr. 25, 1977, revised Oct. 1984 (Zanzibar has own constitution but remains subject to provisions of union constitution). **National holiday:** Union Day, Apr. 26. **Heads of Government:** Jakaya Kikwete, president (since Dec. 2005); **Structure:** executive—president is head of government and chief of state; unicameral legislature (Zanzibar has its own House of Representatives to make laws especially for Zanzibar; judiciary.
● **ECONOMY   Monetary unit:** Tanzanian shilling. **Budget:** (2007 est.) *income:* $3.124 bil.; *expend.:* $3.549 bil. **G.D.P.:** $43.49 bil., $1,100 per capita (2007 est.). **Chief crops:** cotton, coffee, sisal, vegetables, fruits, grain on mainland; cloves and coconuts on Zanzibar; cattle, sheep, goats. **Natural resources:** hydropower potential, tin, phosphates, iron ore and coal, gemstones. **Major industries:** agricultural processing (sugar, beer, cigarettes, sisal twine), diamond mining, oil refining. **Labor force:** 19.69 mil. (2007 est.); 80% agriculture, 20% industry and commerce. **Exports:** $2.119 bil. (f.o.b., 2007 est.); coffee, manufactured goods, cotton, sisal, cashew nuts, tobacco, cloves. **Imports:** $4.59 bil. (f.o.b., 2007 est.); consumer goods, machinery and transport equipment, crude oil. **Major trading partners:** (2006) *exports:* 8.8% China, 8.8% India, 6.2% Netherlands, 5.3% Japan, 4.2% United Arab Emirates, 4.2% Germany; *imports:* 9.8% South Africa, 9.4% China, 7.8% Kenya, 6.7% India, 5.9% United Arab Emirates, 5.7% Zambia.

Formerly known as Tanganyika, Tanzania's indigenous population includes people of diverse ethnic background, including San, Bantu, and Nilotic peoples. It has been the site of a number of relatively advanced and well-organized societies.

Zanzibar and the neighboring island of Pemba have been a crossroads of trade in East Africa since ancient times. Trade via Zanzibar between the Tanganyika coast and the Middle East, primarily ivory, gold, and iron, dates to the late Roman Empire. The coast was dominated by various Arab and Persian powers, usually based in Zanzibar, from about the eighth century. Zanzibar and Tanganyika were visited by Vasco da Gama in 1498, and Portugal claimed Zanzibar in 1503 and the entire Tanganyika coast in 1506. The Portuguese established coastal trading stations but did not colonize the interior.

The Portuguese were driven from Zanzibar in 1652 by the sultanate of Oman, which soon expelled them from the mainland as well. Under Omani rule, trade in gold, ivory, and gems was supplemented by a sizable slave trade, and the clove plantations of Zanzibar became commercially important. Under Sultan Seyyid Said, the capital of the sultanate of Oman was transferred to Zanzibar in 1824, and Zanzibar became independent of Oman upon his death in 1856.

Both Germany and Great Britain became active in the region in the 19th century. Tanganyika was organized as the colony of German East Africa in 1884, while Zanzibar became a British protectorate in 1890. Tanganyika became a secondary battlefield of World War I, with frequent clashes between German and British troops.

Britain assumed control of Tanganyika in 1920 under a League of Nations Mandate and maintained control under a U.N. trusteeship after 1946. The temperate southern highlands were extensively colonized by British immigrants, and railroads and mines were developed by the British.

Elections for a local legislature were held in Zanzibar in July 1957. The island's politics were dominated by a split between Arab and African residents. Zanzibar became independent on Dec. 19, 1963. In January 1964 an African revolt overthrew the sultan of Zanzibar and resulted in the deaths of thousands of Arab residents and the emigration of many more. Political control shifted to the African party and Abeid Karume became president.

Tanganyika became independent in 1961. Julius K. Nyerere was Tanganyika's dominant political figure. Tanzania was formed from the union of Tanganyika and Zanzibar on April 26, 1964, with Zanzibar retaining local autonomy.

Nyerere advocated an "African socialist" form of development and formed close ties with China. The Tan-Zan Railroad between Dar es Salaam and Lusaka, Zambia was built with Chinese aid between 1970 and 1975. The ruling parties of Tanganyika and Zanzibar were united in 1977 under Nyerere's leadership.

Political tensions eased and Tanzania adopted a more open political structure in the 1980's. Pres. Ali Hassan Mwinyi encouraged free-market economic reforms, including encouragement of foreign investment and strengthened ties with Kenya and Uganda (Tanzania invaded the latter in 1979 in an effort to depose Idi Amin). Tanzania's economy has great potential because of the country's extensive natural resources and one of Africa's best educational systems; literacy in both English and Swahili is relatively high.

In 1992, the Revolutionary party of Tanzania voted in favor of a secular multiparty system, that is one based on neither ethnic nor regional lines. It won the country's first-ever multiparty elections in 1995. Benjamin Mkapa succeeded Mwinyi, who was barred by law from seeking a third term as president.

The elections of Oct. 2000 returned Mkapa to the presidency with 72 percent of the vote while the ruling party carried 167 of the National Assembly's 181 seats; similar results were reported from semi-autonomous Zanzibar. The obviously rigged elections provoked demands for new elections from the opposition's Civic United Front and demonstrations in which over 40 were killed. In 2005, Mkapa was succeeded by a member of the ruling party, Jakaya Kikwete.

▶THAILAND
Kingdom of Thailand

● **GEOGRAPHY Location:** extends southward, along isthmus of Kra, to Malay peninsula, in Southeast Asia. **Boundaries:** Myanmar to W and N, Laos to NE, Cambodia and Gulf of Thailand to E, Malaysia to S, Andaman Sea to SW. **Total area:** 198,456 sq. mi. (514,000 sq km). **Coastline:** 2,001 mi. (3,219 km). **Comparative area:** slightly more than twice the size of Wyoming. **Land use:** 33% arable land; 7% permanent crops; 70% other. **Major cities:** Bangkok (capital); Songkhla; Chon Buri; Nakhon Si Thammarat; Chiang Mai.

● **PEOPLE Population:** 65,493,298 (July 2008 est.). **Nationality:** noun—Thai (sing., pl.); adjective—Thai. **Ethnic groups:** 75% Thai, 14% Chinese, 11% other. **Languages:** Thai; English is secondary language of elite; ethnic and regional dialects. **Religions:** 94.6% Buddhist, 4.6% Muslim, 0.7% Christianity, 0.1% other.

● **GOVERNMENT Type:** constitutional monarchy. **Constitution:** new constitution signed by King Phumiphon Oct. 11, 1997. **National holiday:** Birthday of His Majesty the King, Dec. 5. **Heads of Government:** Bhumibol Adulyadej, king (since June 1946); Somchai Wongsawat, prime minister (since Sept. 2008). **Structure:** executive—king is head of state with nominal powers, prime minister is head of government; bicameral legislature (National Assembly—Senate appointed by king, to be phased into an elected body starting in 2000; elected House of Representatives); judiciary relatively independent except in important political subversion cases.

● **ECONOMY Monetary unit:** baht. **Budget:** (2007 est.) **income:** $43.61 bil. **expend.:** $48.18 bil. **G.D.P.:** $519.9 bil., $8,000 per capita (2007 est.). **Chief crops:** rice, cassava, sugar, corn, rubber, manioc, coconuts, soybean. **Natural resources:** tin, rubber, natural gas, tungsten, tantalum. **Major industries:** tourism, textiles and garments, agricultural processing, beverages; world's second-largest tungsten producer and third-largest tin producer. **Labor force:** 37.12 mil. (2007 est.); 49% agriculture, 14% industry, 37% services including government; 1.7% unemployment (2007). **Exports:** $143.1 bil. (f.o.b., 2007 est.); computers and parts, textiles, rice. **Imports:** $121.9 bil. (f.o.b,. 2007 est.); capital goods, intermediate goods, consumer goods, fuels. **Major trading partners:** (2006) **exports:** 15% U.S., 12.6% Japan, 9% China, 6.4% Singapore, 5.5% Hong Kong, 5.1% Malaysia; **imports:** 20% Japan, 10.6% China, 7.5% U.S., 6.6% Malaysia, 5.5% United Arab Emirates, 4.4% Singapore.

Ethnic Thai migrating south from China after about A.D. 1000 created a number of petty states in the region, most notably the kingdom of Sukhothai. These came under the influence of Indian civilization from the adjacent states of Burma and the Khmer empire, and Buddhism became established as the dominant religion of the Thai. A unified kingdom of Siam was established c. 1350, with its capital at Ayutthaya. Portuguese and other European traders and missionaries were active in Siam after 1511.

In 1767 Ayutthaya was destroyed in a war with Burma. In 1782 the Chakkri dynasty was established at Bangkok and restored the power of the Thai monarchy. By skillfully playing off the European powers against one another, Kings Mongkut (r. 1851-68) and Chulalongkorn (r. 1868-1910) enabled Siam to be the only Southeast Asian nation to escape European colonization or political domination. In a series of treaties with Great Britain and France, however, King Chulalongkorn was forced to renounce Siam's claims to portions of Malaya, Laos, and Cambodia.

Absolute monarchy ended in 1932, when a military coup forced the granting of a constitution. Japanese troops occupied Siam in Dec. 1941. Siam concluded a nominal alliance with Japan in 1942 and declared war on Great Britain and the U.S, while the monarchy secretly supported a strong anti-Japanese resistance movement. A period of postwar political turmoil ended with the accession in 1950 of King Phumiphon, who instituted a reformist and pro-Western policy.

Thai politics since World War II have been democratic but dominated by an oligarchy of military officers and civilians with strong military ties. During the Vietnam War, Thailand was an important staging area for American forces. Since then, U.S. and other foreign investment contributed to significant economic growth.

On Dec. 8, 1990, Prime Minister Chatichai Choonhavan resigned amid charges of corruption. Reappointed by the king the next day, Chatichai was overthrown on Feb. 23 by military forces, who invited former diplomat Anand Panyarachun to serve as interim prime minister. After parliamentary elections in March 1992, Gen. Suchinda Kraprayoon, was named prime minister in a government dominated by the military. Mass demonstrations against the Suchinda government, led by former Bangkok governor Chamlong Srimuang, culminated on May 17-18, when troops fired on demonstrators, causing hundreds of fatalities. The king intervened and Suchinda resigned. Chamlong agreed to call off the demonstrations and Anand Panyarachun was invited to head another transitional government, and Parliament agreed in principle to a new constitution with a provision that the prime minister must be an elected member of Parliament.

Parliamentary elections in 1992 gained a majority for a five-party coalition headed by Chuan Leekpai that managed to govern for almost three years, liberalizing financial arrangements, spending heavily on infrastructure, and bringing Thailand to an 8 percent growth rate in 1994. In elections held in 1995, the Thai Nation party captured the largest number of seats; its leader, Banharn Silpa-Archa, became prime minister but the party lost the 1996 elections and a coalition government led by General Chavalit took over. Only six months later the Thai economy began a steep decline and the currency was devalued in June 1997. The U.S. and the I.M.F. agreed to provide loans to stabalize the economy. Chuan Leekpai returned as prime minister in Nov. 1997 but economic recovery was slow to arrive.

Elections in Jan. 2001 brought a near majority to the Thai Rak Thai party of computer and telecommunications billionaire Thaksin Shinawatra, who was named prime minister but who faced serious legal charges of tax evasion. The Constitutional Court acquitted Thaksin by a vote of 8–7 and with no written opinion issued. In early 2005, shortly after the tsunami devastated parts of Thailand he won a convincing electoral victory. In July he signed an emergency decree that allowed him broad powers to ban public gatherings, detain suspects, etc. all to help fight a growing insurgency. But by 2006 Thaksin was under pressure to resign and in Sept., while he was at the U.N. in New York, the military removed him in a bloodless coup and installed a retired general, Surayud Chulanont, as prime minister, promising a new constitution and election. Thaksin and his party were banned from politics for five years for corruption.

In Aug., 2007, voters strongly approved the new constitution and elections in December Thaksin's party prevailed but Thaksin himself remained in exile. Samak Sundaravej, a Thaksin protege, was elected prime minister. Thaksin returned to face corruption charges but when his wife was convicted of tax evasion (Aug.) they both fled the country. Massive protests against the government began in August and in September a new prime minister was chosen, Thaksin's brother-in-law, Somchai Wongsawat.

▶**TIMOR-LESTE**
Democratic Republic of Timor-Leste

GEOGRAPHY   Location: eastern half of island of Timor. **Boundaries**: Banda Sea to N, Timor Sea to S, Indonesia to W. Coastline: 706 km. **Comparative area:** slightly larger than Connecticut. **Land use:** N.A. **Total land area:** 7,336 sq. mi. (19,000 sq km). **Major cities**: Dili (capital).

People   Population: 1,108,777 (2008 est.). **Nationality:** noun—Timorese; adjective—Timorese. **Ethnic Groups:** Austronesian (Malayo-Polynesian), Papuan, small Chinese minority. **Languages:** Tetum and Portuguese (official); English, Indonesian. **Religions:** 90% Roman Catholic, 4% Muslim, 3% Protestant.

● **GOVERNMENT   Type:** Republic. **Independence:** May 20, 2002 (from Indonesia; Nov. 28, 1975 from Portugal). **Constitution:** March 22, 2002. **National Holiday:** Independence Day: Nov. 28. **Head of Government:** José Ramos-Horta, president (since May 2007); Kay Rala X. Gusmão, prime minister (since Aug. 2007).

● **ECONOMY   Monetary unit:** Indonesian Rupiah. **Budget:** (2007) *income:* $733 mil., *expend.:* $309 mil. **G.D.P.:** $2.215 mil., $2,000 per capita (2007 est.). **Chief crops:** coffee, rice, maize, cassava. **Natural resources:** gold, petroleum, natural gas, manganese, marble. **Major industries:** printing, soap manufacturing, handicrafts, woven cloth. **Labor force:** N.A., 50% unemployment. **Exports:** $10 mil. note - excludes oil. (2005 est.); oil, coffee, sandalwood, marble. **Imports:** $202 mil (2004 est.); mainly food. **Major trading partners:** (2006) *exports:* U.S., Germany, Portugal, Australia, Indonesia; *imports:* N.A.

Early in the sixteenth century, Portuguese traders settled on some of the islands of the Malayan Archipelago, including Timor, and established trading posts there. In 1613 rival traders from the Netherlands settled in western Timor and began the slow process of pushing the Portuguese eastward. (The actual boundary on Timor was not settled by treaty until 1859.) As Dutch, and then British, power waxed through the 17th century, that of Portugal waned, leaving but a handful of fragments, like Goa and Macao and East Timor, of the Portuguese eastern sea empire.

But unlike the Dutch or English, the Portuguese sought to maintain close bonds among economic, political, and religious expansion. A missionary effort made East Timor something of a Catholic enclave amidst the predominantly Muslim Dutch East Indies (and, after 1949, Indonesia). Still, as late as 1975 only about one-third were Catholic; it was the independence struggle that brought the Catholic presence to its current 90 percent.

The leftist coup in Portugal in April 1974, with its socialist, democratic, but above all anti-imperialist ideology, led to the abandonment of East Timor; in Dec. 1975 Indonesia began its brutal conquest and annexation which led to an enduring guerilla warfare and eventually independence. The 1998 fall of Indonesia's dictator Suharto gave space for the 1999 U.N.-sponsored referendum on independence: 78 percent voted "yes." While Muslim militias, aided by segments of the Indonesian armed forces, ravaged the country, a U.N. trusteeship, run principally by Australia and Portugal, readied the new state for independence, finally celebrated May 20, 2002 under its first president, resistance leader José Gusmao. In 2006, a military mutiny toppled the government and Nobel Peace Prize recipient, José Ramos-Horta became prime minister. A 3,000-member U.N. international peacekeeping force was deployed and in 2007 Ramos-Horta was elected president, bringing hope the violence could be stopped. But an assasination attempt against Ramos-Horta disspelled that idea and the U.N. considered extending its mandate.

▶ TOGO
Togolese Republic
• **GEOGRAPHY Location:** western coast of Africa. **Boundaries:** Burkina Faso to N, Benin to E, Gulf of Guinea to S, Ghana to W. **Total area:** 21,927 sq. mi. (56,790 sq km). **Coastline:** 35 mi. (56 km). **Comparative area:** slightly smaller than West Virginia. **Land use:** 41% arable land; 2% permanent crops; 57% other. **Major cities:** Lomé (capital); Sokodé; Kpalimé; Atakpamé; Tsevie.
• **PEOPLE Population:** 5,858,673 (July 2008 est.). **Nationality:** noun—Togolese (sing., pl.); adjective—Togolese. **Ethnic groups:** 37 groups; largest are Ewe, Mina, and Kabre; under 1% European and Syrian-Lebanese. **Languages:** French (both official and language of commerce); Ewe and Mina in south, Dagomba and Kabyè in north. **Religions:** about 51% indigenous beliefs, 29% Christian, 20% Muslim.
• **GOVERNMENT Type:** republic under transition to multiparty democratic rule; **Independence:** Apr. 27, 1960 (from U.N. trusteeship under French administration). **Constitution:** Sept. 27, 1992. **National holiday:** Independence Day, Apr. 27. **Heads of Government:** Faure E. Gnassingbé, president (since May 2005); Komlan Mally, prime minister (since Dec. 2007). **Structure:** executive—president appoints prime minister; unicameral legislature—National Assembly; judiciary.
• **ECONOMY Monetary unit:** Communauté Financière Africaine (CFA) franc. **Budget:** (2007 est.) *income:* $478.1 mil.; *expend.:* $554.1 mil. **G.D.P.:** $5.132 bil., $900 per capita (2007 est.). **Chief crops:** coffee, cocoa, cotton, yams, cassava, corn, beans, rice; meat, fish. **Natural resources:** phosphates, limestone, marble. **Major industries:** phosphate mining, agricultural processing, cement, handicrafts, textiles, beverages. **Labor force:** 1.74 mil. (1996 est.); 65% agriculture, 30% services, 5% industry. **Exports:** $675 mil. (f.o.b., 2007); cotton, phosphates, coffee, cocoa. **Imports:** $1.181 bil. (f.o.b., 2007); machinery and equipment, consumer goods, petroleum products. **Major trading partners:** (2006) *exports:* 16.7% Ghana 14.4% Burkina Faso, 9.1% Benin, 6.1% Belgium, 5.8% Mali, 5.4% Germany, 4.6% India, 4.6% Netherlands; *imports:* 29.8% China, 10.9% U.K., 8.9% France, 6% Netherlands, 5.8% Belgium, 4.6% U.S., 4.2% Estonia.

Ewe-speaking peoples began to migrate into what is now Togo, located on Africa's west coast, early in the 14th century. Portuguese explorers arrived in the late 15th century, turning the coast into a point of departure for slaves captured from nearby villages, and between the 1600's and 1800's, the region became known as the "Slave Coast." Germans started to explore and trade in the region in the mid-19th century and declared a protectorate over the area in 1884. After World War I, however, Britain and France divided the nation between them, Britain receiving the western third, France the eastern two-thirds. The League of Nations confirmed this arrangement, giving mandates to British Togoland (later a part of Ghana) and French Togoland.

In 1956 France made French Togo an autonomous republic but retained control of its foreign affairs, defense, and currency; Nicholas Grunitzky was prime minister. The United Nations rejected this plan and in elections in 1958 advocates of complete independence won control of the legislature. On Apr. 27, 1960, French Togo cut its ties with France and became the fully independent Republic of Togo. Sylvanus Olympio became the new nation's first prime minister. Grunitzky went into exile but returned when Olympio was assassinated in January 1963. He led the new government and oversaw the writing of a new constitution allowing more political freedoms.

In 1967 army officers led by Lt. Col. Gnassingbé Eyadema overthrew Grunitzky, suspended the constitution, and named Eyadema president. In 1990, Eyadema was forced out by democratic reformers, and Kokou J. Koffigoh was elected prime minister by a national conference in 1991. Eyadema resumed the presidency in 1992, but his refusal to embrace multiparty democracy and Koffigoh's weak leadership led to violence and public calls for the ouster of both men. Under a new constitution, ratified in 1992, General Eyadema's party, Rally of the Togolese People, always dominates, with prime ministers coming and going at his pleasure. In 2002, parliament amended the constitution, removing the two-term limit on the presidency and in 2003 Eyadema was elected again. Upon his death on Feb. 5, 2005 the army pushed to have one of his sons, Faure Gnassingbé, proclaimed president and the legislature agreed. But pressure from the African Union and weeks of violent street protests led to elections in April. Gnassingbé was declared the winner and again protests erupted and in 2007 free and fair elections were finally held and the government was reelected so E.U. economic cooperation was restored.

▶ TONGA
Kingdom of Tonga
• **GEOGRAPHY Location:** 172 islands in South Pacific Ocean, 36 permanently inhabited. Nuku'alofa 21°09'S, 175°14'W. **Boundaries:** surrounded by South Pacific Ocean; Fiji is about 400 mi. (650 km) to NW and Western Samoa lies N. **Total area:** 289 sq. mi. (748 sq km). **Coastline:** 260 mi. (419 km). **Comparative area:** four times the size of Washington, D.C. **Land use:** 24% arable land; 43% permanent crops; 33% other. **Major cities:** Nuku'alofa (capital); Tongatapu; Vava'u; Ha'apai; Eua.
• **PEOPLE Population:** 119,009 (July 2008 est.). **Nationality:** noun—Tongan(s); adjective—Ton-

gan. **Ethnic groups:** Polynesian; about 300 Europeans. **Languages:** Tongan, English. **Religions:** Christian (Free Wesleyan Church claims over 30,000 adherents). ● **GOVERNMENT Type:** hereditary constitutional monarchy. **Independence:** June 4, 1970 (from U.K.). **Constitution:** Nov. 4, 1875; revised Jan. 1, 1967. **National holiday:** Independence Day, June 4. **Heads of Government:** King Siaosi Tupou V (since Sept. 2006); Frederick Sevele, premier (since March 2006). **Structure:** executive—king, prime minister, cabinet; unicameral legislature—30-seat Legislative Assembly, 9 elected by popular vote, 12 are for cabinet ministers, 9 reserved for nobles; judiciary—appointed by king. ● **ECONOMY Monetary unit:** pa'anga. **Budget:** (2007 est.) *income:* $80.48 mil.; *expend.:* $109.8 mil. **G.D.P.:** $877 mil. (2006), $2,200 per capita (2005 est.). **Chief crops:** squash, coconut, copra, bananas, vanilla beans, cocoa, coffee, ginger, black pepper, fish. **Natural resources:** fish, fertile soil. **Major industries:** tourism, fishing. **Labor force:** 33,910 (2003 est.); 65% engaged in agriculture. **Exports:** $22 mil. (f.o.b., 2006); squash, fish, vanilla. **Imports:** $139 mil: (f.o.b., 2006); food products, machinery and transport equipment, fuels, chemicals. **Major trading partners:** (2006) *exports:* 39.7% U.S., 27.8% Japan, 8.2% New Zealand, 7.6% South Korea; *imports:* 30.3% Fiji, 27.7% New Zealand, 8.2% U.S., 7.5% Australia, 5.7% France, 4.7% U.K.

The Polynesian islands that now compose Tonga were settled some 3,000 years ago. A highly stratified society evolved; the kings of Tonga dominated much of Polynesia by the 13th century. The islands were visited in 1643 by Abel Tasman, and in 1773 by Capt. James Cook, who named them the Friendly Islands. English missionaries arrived in 1797, and the islands came under British political influence. A code of laws was promulgated in 1862, and a constitutional monarchy established in 1875. A series of treaties with Western powers recognized Tonga's independence, but the kingdom became a British protectorate in 1900.

The islands were outside the Japanese perimeter in the Pacific theater of World War II. On June 4, 1970, the British dissolved their protectorate and the Kingdom of Tonga became independent as a member of the British Commonwealth. King Taufa'ahau Tupou IV came to the throne in 1965 and survived until 2006.

Tonga joined the U.N. in late 1999 and a movement for democratic reform soon followed. In 2006 rioting helped bring changes and elections in 2008 brought a pro-democracy government.

▶TRINIDAD AND TOBAGO
Republic of Trinidad and Tobago
● **GEOGRAPHY Location:** two islands (Port of Spain, Trinidad Is., 10°38'N, 61°31'W; Tobago Is., 11°11'N, 60°45'W) in southeastern Caribbean Sea, off northeastern South America. **Boundaries:** Caribbean Sea to N and W, Atlantic Ocean to E and S. **Total area:** 1,981 sq. mi. (5,130 sq km). **Coastline:** 225 mi. (362 km). **Comparative area:** slightly smaller than Delaware. **Land use:** 15% arable land; 9% permanent crops; 26% other. **Major cities:** Port of Spain (capital); San Fernando; Arima (borough). ● **PEOPLE Population:** 1,047,366 (July 2008 est.). **Nationality:** noun—Trinidadian(s), Tobagonian(s); adjective—Trinidadian, Tobagonian. **Ethnic groups:** 40% Indian, 37.5% African, 20.5% mixed, 2% other. **Languages:** English (official), Hindi, French, Spanish, Chinese. **Religions:** 26% Roman

Catholic, 22.5% Hindu, 7.8% Anglican, 14% other Protestant, 5.8% Muslim. ● **GOVERNMENT Type:** parliamentary democracy. **Independence:** Aug. 31, 1962 (from U.K.). **Constitution:** Aug. 1, 1976. **National holiday:** Independence Day, Aug. 31. **Heads of Government:** George Maxwell Richards, president (since Mar. 2003); Patrick Manning, prime minister (since Jan. 2002). **Structure:** executive—is cabinet led by prime minister; bicameral legislature (elected House of Representatives and appointed Senate); judiciary headed by chief justice and includes court of appeal, high court, and lower courts. ● **ECONOMY Monetary unit:** Trinidad and Tobago dollar. **Budget:** (2007 est.) *income:* $6.415 bil.; *expend.:* $6.214 bil. **G.D.P.:** $22.93 bil., $21,700 per capita (2007 est.). **Chief crops:** sugar, cocoa, coffee, rice, citrus, bananas; poultry. **Natural resources:** crude oil, natural gas, asphalt. **Major industries:** petroleum, chemicals, tourism. **Labor force:** 615,400 (2007 est.); 66% services, 30% industry, 4% agriculture. **Exports:** $14.13 bil. (f.o.b., 2007); petroleum and petroleum products, chemicals, steel products, fertilizer, sugar, cocoa, coffee, citrus, flowers. **Imports:** $6.477 bil. (f.o.b., 2007 est.); machinery, transport equipment, manufactured goods, food, live animals. **Major trading partners:** (2006) *exports:* 50% U.S., 5% Spain, 5% Jamaica; *imports:* 31% U.S., 12% Brazil, 7% Venezuela, 5% Gabon, 4% Colombia.

Trinidad was a possession of Spain from 1498 to 1797, when it was surrendered to the British. England took control of Tobago in 1802. Together the two islands achieved independence from the U.K. in 1962. Prime Minister Arthur Robinson's National Alliance for Reconstruction currently governs the country. Civil and political rights are well respected, and political party competition tends to divide along ethnic (black, East Indian) lines. Agrarian reform designed to create tenable landholdings is a central political issue.

In 1990, militant Muslims seized Prime Minister A.N.R. Robinson and dozens of others in Parliament, paralyzing the government for five days. Peace was restored when the government promised reforms. People's National Movement candidate Carson Charles was elected prime minister in 1991, and in the interest of preserving the peace, he granted the Muslim militants amnesty in 1992. Robinson won the presidential election in 1997 in a landslide. Dec. 2001 elections produced an 18–18 tie between the (Indian-descent) United National Congress and the (African-descent) People's National Movement. Both parties agreed to allow Pres. Robinson to choose. His choice: Patrick Manning of the P.N.M. Under his direction the nation has prospered mainly from sales of natural gas to the U.S., and methanol and ammonia to the world. He was succeeded by Maxwell Richards.

▶TUNISIA
Republic of Tunisia
● **GEOGRAPHY Location:** northern coast of Africa. **Boundaries:** Mediterranean to N and E, Libya to SE, Algeria to W. **Total area:** 63,170 sq. mi. (163,610 sq km); includes land and inland waters. **Coastline:** 714 mi. (1,148 km). **Comparative area:** slightly larger than Georgia. **Land use:** 19% arable land; 13% permanent crops; 68% other. **Major cities:** Tunis (capital); Sfax (Safaqis); Ariana; Ehadhamen; Sousse. ● **PEOPLE Population:** 10,383,577 (July 2008 est.). **Nationality:** noun—Tunisian(s); adjective—Tunisian. **Ethnic groups:** 98% Arab, 1% European, 1% Jewish and other . **Languages:** Arabic (official),

Arabic and French (commerce). **Religions:** 98% Muslim, 1% Christian, 1% Jewish and other.
• **GOVERNMENT Type:** republic. **Independence:** Mar. 20, 1956 (from France). **Constitution:** June 1, 1959, amended July 12, 1988. **National holiday:** Independence Day, Mar. 20. **Heads of Government:** Zine el-Abidine Ben Ali, president (since Nov. 1987); Mohamed Ghannouchi, prime minister (since Nov. 1999). **Structure:** executive dominant; unicameral legislature (Chamber of Deputies) largely advisory; judiciary patterned on French and Koranic systems.
• **ECONOMY Monetary unit:** Tunisian dinar. **Budget:** (2007 est.) *income:* $8.355 bil.; *expend.:* $9.476 bil. **G.D.P.:** $77.16 bil., $7,500 per capita (2007 est.). **Chief crops:** olives, dates, oranges, almonds, grain, sugar beets, grapes; poultry, beef, dairy products. **Natural resources:** crude oil, phosphates, iron ore, lead, zinc. **Major industries:** petroleum, mining (particularly phosphates and iron ore), tourism, textiles. **Labor force:** 3.591 mil.; 55% services, 23% industry, 22% agriculture; 13.9% unemployment (2007 est.); shortage of skilled labor. **Exports:** $14.81 bil. (f.o.b., 2007 est.); hydrocarbons, textiles, agricultural products, phosphates and chemicals. **Imports:** $17.9 bil. (f.o.b., 2007 est.); industrial goods, hydrocarbons, food. **Major trading partners:** (2006) *exports:* 29% France, 20% Italy, 9% Germany, 6% Spain, 5% Libya, 4% U.S.; *imports:* 25% France, 22% Italy, 10% Germany, 5% Spain.

The Phoenicians, an ancient seafaring people from the eastern Mediterranean, founded settlements in Tunisia dating back to 1000 B.C. The most important of these was Carthage, which dominated trade in the central Mediterranean until it was conquered and destroyed by Rome in 146 B.C. Tunisia remained part of the Roman Empire until it was conquered by the Vandals in the mid-fifth century A.D. The Byzantine Empire reconquered Tunisia in the sixth century.

Tunisia became part of the Arab world with the expansion of Islam in the seventh century and soon emerged as a principal center of Islamic culture in North Africa. Tunisia was incorporated into the Ottoman Empire in 1574 and was ruled from Constantinople by Turkish governors, or beys.

With the waning of Ottoman power in the 19th century, Tunisia became a French protectorate in 1881. Nationalist movements began in the early 20th century. During World War II Tunisia was under Vichy French rule and was the scene of fighting between the Axis and Allies in 1942-43. Nationalist unrest resumed when France reestablished its rule in the postwar period. Widespread popular unrest in the early 1950's led to a French grant of self-rule in 1954. Full independence was proclaimed on Mar. 20, 1956; large numbers of French settlers returned to France. The French-sponsored monarchy was abolished in 1957, and the Neo-Destour (New Constitution) party under the leadership of Habib Bourguiba took power. Bourguiba was elected president in 1959 without opposition and was named president for life. Under his rule, political parties ranging from Communist to monarchist flourished, leading to both democratic politics and political confusion.

Relations with France were strained in 1964 when Tunisia nationalized foreign assets but have since improved. The basic thrust of Tunisian government was socialist, with state ownership of principal industries and heavy subsidies of basic commodities. In foreign affairs Tunisia has been closely tied to France and has been a moderate voice within the Arab League.

Popular unrest and labor strife characterized Tunisia's internal situation in the 1980's, as political maneuvering began in anticipation of the end of the Bourguiba era, which came in 1987 when the aged leader was overthrown by Ben Ali. In 1989 new elections were planned as part of a political and economic restructuring. Ben Ali was elected president, twice winning 99 percent of the vote, while his party won virtually all the seats in the National Assembly. In 1994 and 1995, however, the political stability was threatened by radical Muslim groups both from within and from Algeria. Rumors of brutal repression were rife. In Oct. 1999, in Tunisia's first "multiparty" elections, Ben Ali was re-elected president, again with 99.42 percent of the vote while his Constitutional Union Party carried 148 of the 182 parliamentary seats.

Tunisia's economy, though plagued by labor difficulties, has developed rapidly, led by textiles, food processing and other light industry, tourism, phosphate mining, and other mineral processing. The large agricultural sector includes grain, olives, dates, and winter fruits and vegetables for export to Europe. In 1998 the government reached an accord with the E.U. to lower trade barriers.

▶**TURKEY**
Republic of Turkey
• **GEOGRAPHY Location:** partly in southeastern Europe and partly in western Asia. **Boundaries:** Black Sea to N; Georgia and Armenia to NE; Iran to E; Iraq, Syria, Mediterranean Sea to S; Aegean Sea, Greece to W; and Bulgaria to NW. **Total area:** 301,382 sq. mi. (780,580 sq km). **Coastline:** 4,471 mi. (7,200 km). **Comparative area:** slightly larger than Texas. **Land use:** 35% arable land; 3% permanent crops; 62% other. **Major cities:** Ankara (capital); Istanbul; Izmir; Adana; Bursa.
• **PEOPLE Population:** 71,892,807 (July 2008 est.). **Nationality:** noun—Turk(s); adjective—Turkish. **Ethnic groups:** 80% Turkish, 20% Kurdish. **Languages:** Turkish (official), Kurdish, Arabic. **Religions:** 99.8% Muslim (mostly Sunni), 0.2% other (mostly Christian and Jewish).
• **GOVERNMENT Type:** republican parliamentary democracy. **Independence:** Oct. 29, 1923 (from Ottoman Empire). **Constitution:** Nov. 7, 1982. **National holiday:** Independence Day. **Heads of Government:** Abdullah Gul, president (since Aug. 2007); Recep Tayyip Erdogan, prime minister (since Mar. 14, 2003). **Structure:** executive—president empowered to call new elections, promulgate laws (elected for seven-year term); unicameral legislature; independent judiciary.
• **ECONOMY Monetary unit:** Turkish lira. **Budget:** (2007) *income:* $137.8 bil.; *expend.:* $151.9 bil. **G.D.P.:** $667.7 bil., $9,400 per capita (2007 est.). **Chief crops:** cotton, tobacco, grain, olives, sugar beets, pulses, citrus; livestock. **Natural resources:** antimony, coal, chromium, mercury, copper. **Major industries:** textiles, food processing, mining (coal, chromite, copper, boron minerals). **Labor force:** 25.3 mil. (2007 est.); 35.9% agriculture, 41.2% services, 22.8% industry; about 1.2 million Turks work abroad (2004 est.); 9.7% unemployment (2007 est.). **Exports:** $110.5 bil. (f.o.b., 2007 est.); 28% textiles and apparel, 17% foodstuffs, 9% iron and steel products. **Imports:** $156.9 bil. (f.o.b., 2007 est.); 29% machinery, fuels, minerals, foodstuffs. **Major trading partners:** (2006) *exports:* 11.3% Germany, 8% U.K., 7.9% Italy, 6% U.S., 5.4% France, 4.4% Spain; *imports:* 12.8% Russia, 10.6% Germany, 6.9% China, 6.2% Italy, 5.2% France, 4.5% U.S., 4% Iran.

The Hittites, an Indo-European people, created an empire in Anatolia before 2000 B.C. and controlled most of what is modern-day Turkey for nearly 1,000 years. The rise of Troy and other Hellenic city-states on the coast of Asia Minor and the expansion of the Assyrian empire led to the collapse of Hittite power by around 900 B.C. Except for some Hellenic enclaves on the Aegean Coast (Ionia), all of Turkey was incorporated into the Persian empire of Cyrus and Darius in the sixth century B.C. Alexander the Great conquered Turkey, but it returned to Persian rule following the collapse of his empire, c. 300 B.C.

All of Turkey, comprising Thracia, Galatia, Cappadocia, Cilicia, and other provinces, was incorporated into the Roman Empire by the end of the first century A.D. Constantine the Great founded the city of Constantinople on the site of ancient Byzantium in 330 as the empire's eastern capital. Following the decline of the western Roman Empire in the seventh century, Constantinople became the capital of the independent Eastern Roman (Byzantine) Empire. The Byzantine Empire fought off repeated attacks by Arab Islamic forces in the seventh and eighth centuries but lost control of central Anatolia to the Seljuk Turkish rulers of Persia after 1038.

The 13th-century Mongol invasions left Turkey largely untouched but weakened both Byzantine and Seljuk power. At the end of the 13th century, the Ottomans, a small Turkish tribe, expanded from their stronghold in western Anatolia and within a century captured most of Turkey, Bulgaria, and Serbia. Constantinople fell to the Ottomans in 1453. By the middle of the 16th century, the Ottoman Empire extended from southeastern Europe into the Crimea and Iran and included most of the Middle East, Egypt, and Arabia.

At its height the Ottoman Empire was a great world power and a substantial participant in European international relations. But in the 18th century, the empire lost much of its autonomy through unequal treaties with European powers, and throughout the 19th century, parts of the empire were detached and either granted independence or placed under European protection. The Ottoman Empire became the "Sick Man of Europe." A liberal constitution was adopted in 1876 but largely ignored until the Young Turk Rebellion of 1908 forced the sultan to accept its provisions.

Siding with the Central Powers in World War I, the Ottoman Empire lost most of its non-Turkish possessions to the Allies. The Treaty of Sèvres (1920) reduced the Ottoman state to a small part of northern Anatolia. Before the treaty was ratified, however, Kemal Ataturk seized power and regained much territory in a series of campaigns with Soviet assistance. The Treaty of Lausanne (1923) established the present boundaries of Turkey, which was proclaimed a republic. The Caliphate was renounced in 1924, ending the Ottoman claim of leadership in the Islamic world.

The Turkish Republic became officially a secular and multiethnic state. Large numbers of Armenians had been killed or driven from the country in widespread campaigns of persecution in the late 19th and early 20th centuries; after 1923 most Greek and Bulgarian residents were forcibly repatriated. The large minority of Kurds in southeastern Turkey were pressured to abandon their ethnic identity. Today more than 85 percent of the population is Turkish. Islam is widely practiced, but the veil and other Islamic dress are prohibited, as are religious political parties. In 1928 the Latin alphabet was adopted in place of Arabic script for writing Turkish. In 1930 Constantinople was officially renamed Istanbul.

Turkey joined the League of Nations in 1932. A series of treaties in the 1930's made small adjustments to Turkey's borders and confirmed Turkey's status as a European nation. Under Ismet Inonu, who became president upon Ataturk's death in 1938, Turkey remained neutral throughout most of World War II but declared war against Germany in Jan. 1945 and became a founding member of the United Nations at the end of the war. Following World War II, Turkey became a major recipient of American aid under the Truman Doctrine. Turkish troops joined U.N. forces in the Korean War. Continuing the Europe-oriented policy, Turkey joined NATO.

In 1974, long-standing discord with Greece erupted over the status of Cyprus, an independent nation with strong ties to Greece. On July 20, 1974, Turkish troops invaded Cyprus, occupying the northeastern 40 percent of the island. The United States cut off military aid to Turkey in 1975. Turkey forced resettlement of Greek and Turkish Cypriot residents; the Turkish sector seceded from Cyprus and became a Turkish federated state on July 8, 1975. American aid was restored in 1978.

Politically, postwar Turkey has alternated between civil and military governments. In the wake of mounting violence, martial law was imposed in 1978, and a military takeover of the government occurred on Sept. 12, 1980. Civil government was restored in 1983, and martial law lifted in 1984.

Turkey tried to remain aloof from the political turmoil of the Middle East, but it was a crucial member of the anti-Iraq coalition in the Persian Gulf War. It supported the U.N. trade embargo and allowed the Allies to use Turkish bases. The Kurdish problem was aggravated after the war as Turkey tried to offer humanitarian assistance to Kurdish refugees from Iraq without encouraging Kurdish nationalists at home. A continuing insurgency in the southeast led to sporadic but serious violence in 1992-93. Muslim fundamentalists became more active and several violent episodes resulted in deaths and destruction.

Pres. Turgut Özal died in Apr. 1993. He was succeeded as president by Prime Minister Suleyman Demirel. On June 14 the ruling True Path party elected as the new prime minister, Mrs. Tansu Ciller, Turkey's first-ever woman prime minister. While the economy was her first concern (inflation hit 70 percent in 1994), military operations against the Kurdish rebels intensified with the launching of an attack into Iraq by 50,000 Turkish troops who aimed to end guerrilla raids.

The Ciller government collapsed in a corruption scandal, and elections held in Dec. 1995 gave Refah (Welfare), a pro-Islamic political party, its first national victory. The other parties, committed to the long tradition of secularism, refused to form a government with the Welfare party. After months of successive coalition governments, in June 1996 the Welfare party leader, Necmettim Erbakan, became prime minister of Turkey's first openly pro-Islamic government. A year later, he was forced from office by pressure from Turkey's military. In the wake of this de facto military coup, the new prime minister, Mesut Yilmaz, put together a fragile coalition government in July 1997 that closed some Islamic schools and banned traditional Muslim garb while the Supreme Court banned Erbakan from politics for five years.

Violence in Cyprus flared up in 1998 but the E.U.'s rejection of Turkey's application was the most serious event of the year. In 1999 Turkey finally wrung an accord from Syria not to aid Kurd rebels (with 10,000 Turkish troops poised on Syria's border), but the Yilmaz government still lost a vote of confidence on corruption charges. Pres. Demirel asked Bulent Ecevit to form a minority, interim government. The results were splintered, and the president asked Ecevit to stay on as head of a coalition government. Kurdish leader Ocalan was apprehended in Nairobi and, after trial, sentenced to death by hanging. From his cell, Ocalan renounced Kurdish independence and called upon his band to stop fighting.

In Aug. 1999 an earthquake brought great devastation and the loss of thousands of lives. It also brought aid from both the E.U. and Greece; Turkey reciprocated in the September earthquake in Greece. In Feb. 2000 the Kurd leadership renounced all violence. In May, Parliament elected chief justice Ahmet Necdet Sezer president to succeed Demirel. Faced with a mass hunger strike by political prisoners in Dec. 2000, Pres. Sezer announced an amnesty plan to release 72,000. A personal argument between Sezer and Ecevit in 2001 provoked fears of government instability which led to a serious economic crisis as foreign investors pulled out of Turkey and the currency lost one-third of its value. While the I.M.F. signalled its approval of Ecevit's economic reforms in a series of loans, parliament voted to hold new elections in Nov. 2002, 18 months early. Justice and Development (an offshoot of the Islamic Welfare Party) gained 363 of the 550 seats, the first majority government in 15 years. None of the cabinet formed by Abdullah Gul had any public association with Islam. In December, President Sezer first vetoed, then signed a constitutional amendment to allow the party's leader, Recip Erdogan, to run for Parliament. He carried a March 2003 by-election with 85 percent of the vote and was named prime minister. Parliament refused to allow U.S. troops to deploy in preparation for the Iraq invasion.

In June 2003 Parliament, in an attempt to apease E.U. sentiment, voted certain civil rights for Kurds. The military budget was brought under parliamentary control and members of the Kurdish Workers Party (PKK) granted amnesty. In June 2004, however, PKK ended a defacto cease-fire and began sporadic attacks on government troops. In Aug. 2006 two terrorist attacks on tourist areas by Kurdish seperatists revived tensions, and in June 2007, Turkish troops massed on the border of Iraq threatening to invade Kurdistan to halt terrorist attacks but withdrew suddenly.

Turkish politics were roiled in April 2007 elections when the military as well as hundreds of thousands of protesters objected to the election of Abdullah Gul, a religious Muslim as president. Prime Minister Erdogan quickly scheduled elections for July and his party won a very strong victory. Parliament elected Gul president in Aug. 2007. In 2008 parliament approved a measure that could lead to women being allowed to wear head scarves in universities. A case to ban the Islamic Party failed in court.

▶ TURKMENISTAN

● **GEOGRAPHY Location:** southwestern central Asia. **Boundaries:** Kazakhstan to N, Uzbekistan to N and E, Iran to S, Afghanistan to SE, Caspian Sea to W. **Total area:** 188,456 sq. mi. (488,100 sq km). **Coastline:** Caspian Sea. **Comparative area:** slightly larger than California. **Land use:** 4% arable land; 0% permanent crops; 96% other. **Major cities:** Ashkhabad (capital); Chardzou (Carzou).

● **PEOPLE Population:** 5,179,571 (July 2008 est.). **Nationality:** noun—Turkmen; adjective—Turkmen. **Ethnic groups:** 85% Turkmen, 5% Uzbek, 4% Russian, 6% other. **Languages:** 72% Turkmen (official), member of southern Turkic language group written in Cyrillic script since 1940; 12% Russian, 9% Uzbek, ethnic languages. **Religions:** 89% Muslim, 9% Eastern Orthodox, 2% unknown.

● **GOVERNMENT Type:** republic. **Independence:** Oct. 27, 1991 (from Soviet Union). **Constitution:** May 18, 1992. **National holiday:** Independence Day, Oct. 27. **Head of Government:** Gurbanguly Berdymukhammedov, president (since Feb. 2007). **Structure:** executive—president, Council of Ministers; bicameral legislature; judicial—Supreme Court.

● **ECONOMY Monetary unit:** Turkmen manat. **Budget:** (2007 est.) *income:* $1.641 bil; *expend.:* $1.6 bil. **G.D.P.:** $47.37 bil., $9,200 per capita (2007 est.). **Chief crops:** cotton, grain; livestock. **Natural resources:** petroleum, natural gas, coal, sulfur, sodium chloride. **Major industries:** natural gas, oil, petroleum products, textiles. **Labor force:** 2.089 mil. (2004). **Exports:** $8.5 bil. (f.o.b., 2007 est.); 63% oil and gas, 18% cotton. **Imports:** $4.2 bil. (c.i.f., 2007 est.); chemicals, foodstuffs, machinery and parts. **Major trading partners:** (2006) *exports:* 47.7% Ukraine, 16.4% Iran, 5.3% Azerbaijan; *imports:* 15.5% United Arab Emirates, 11.1% Turkey, 9.1% Ukraine, 9% Russia, 7.8% Germany, 7.6% Iran, 6.4% China, 4.5% U.S.

Turkmenistan, long a battleground for warring Asian empires, is bordered on the north by Uzbekistan and Kazakhstan, and on the west by the Caspian Sea. It also has a long international border with Iran and Afghanistan. About 90 percent of Turkmenistan is covered by the Kara Kum (Black Sand) desert, one of the largest in the world, and the southern areas are mountainous and prone to serious earthquakes.

A very remote and sparsely populated country, Turkmenistan has been inhabited since prehistoric times, first by Iranian-speaking people, then by Turkic tribes. In the 10th century A.D., Oghuz tribes (from Mongolia) arrived, bringing Islam with them. Although the Turkmen had emerged as a distinct ethnic group by the 15th century, they were ruled by the Persians in the south and the Uzbek khanates in the north for about 200 years. In the 19th century, Russian expansionism into Turkmen territory had begun, culminating in the Russian victory in the famous 1881 battle of Gok Tepe that killed 150,000 Turkmen.

In 1917 the Bolsheviks unsuccessfully attempted to seize power in Turkmen territory. By Apr. 30, 1918, the Soviets succeeded in creating the Turkestan Autonomous Soviet Socialist Republic (ASSR) as part of the Russian republic, but in July the ASSR was overthrown by nationalist elements with the help of the British. Once the British withdrew, however, the territory of Turkmen fell to the Soviets, and in 1924 the National Delimitation of Central Asian Republics took place. This created several central Asian republics, including the Turkmen Soviet Socialist Republic, which came into being on Oct. 27, 1924.

The nomadic Turkmen people suffered enormously under forced collectivization and the many bloody antireligious campaigns. The purges of Turkmen intelligentsia in the 1930's were widespread. The Soviets undertook a small-scale industrialization campaign in Turkmenistan, but aside from the extraction of natural gas and petroleum, the majority of the population continued to work in agriculture, mainly growing cotton and fruits.

Under Gorbachev, the main issue for Turkmenistan became the environment. Large-scale cotton planting had led to serious environmental and health hazards. The Kara Kum Canal, which carries water from the Amu-Dar'ya to Turkmenistan's arid regions, is one of the main factors leading to the desiccation of the Aral Sea. Turkmenistan's main cultural issue was the status of the Turkmen language, for until May 1990 the official language had been listed as Russian (although only 25% of Turkmen people claimed to speak Russian). Due to its remoteness, Turkmenistan did not become involved in the democratic changes that engaged the other former union republics. Its Communist party dominated and still dominates Turkmen politics, although the Turkmen president, Saparmurat A. Niyazov (1990-2006), stood for popular election and was elected by direct ballot in Oct. 1990 by 98.3 percent of the population. However, the Turkmen government has banned demonstrations, picketing, and strikes, and it censors its media.

Turkmenistan was one of the early supporters of Gorbachev's proposal to form a new Union Treaty. When that led to the 1991 coup in Moscow, the Turkmen Supreme Soviet claimed independence on Oct. 27, 1991. Since then, Turkmenistan has begun to develop political and economic relations with Iran and Turkey. With vast oil and gas reserves Turkmenistan faces a brighter future than it ever expected.

Niyazov was overwhelmingly endorsed in a referendum, held Jan. 15, 1994 extending his mandate until 2002, bypassing a constitutional requirement for the reelection of a president every five years. In 1998 Niyazov visited the U.S., conferring with Pres. Clinton and concluding agreements with several U.S. energy firms to study the possibility of a cross-Caucasian gas pipeline to Turkey and the west (bypassing Iran). In Dec. 1999 the 50-member parliament elected (unanimously) Niyazov president-for-life (as recommended by the People's Council, headed by Niyazov). The cult of personality grew to an incredible state as the Council renamed the month of January after him in 2002. His iron-fisted rule has led the U.S. State Dept. to say he governs in a "Soviet-era authoritarian style." Niyazov was suspected of embezzling huge sums from the gas revenues, as he cuts pensions and benefits. In Dec. 2006, he died suddenly of heart disease at age 66. A special election, heavily influenced by the government, in Feb. 2007, gave 90 percent of the vote to a former aide to Niyazov, Gurbanguly Berdymakhammedov. In July he made a deal with Russia to build a pipeline north of the Caspian Sea to guarentee Russian access to natural gas.

▶ **TUVALU**
• **GEOGRAPHY Location:** group of nine small atolls, about 350 mi. (560 km) from N to S, in South Pacific Ocean. Funafuti 8°30'S, 179°12'E. **Boundaries:** surrounded by South Pacific Ocean; Kiribati to N, Fiji to S, Solomon Islands to W. **Total area:** 10 sq. mi. (26 sq km). **Coastline:** 15 mi. (24 km). **Comparative area:** one-tenth size of Washington, D.C. **Land use:** 0% arable land; 0% permanent crops; 100% other. **Major cities:** Funafuti (capital); Vaitupu; Niutao; Nanumea; Nukufetau. • **PEOPLE Population:** 12,177 (July 2008 est.). **Nationality:** noun—Tuvaluan(s); adjective—Tuvaluan. **Ethnic groups:** 96% Polynesian. **Languages:** Tuvaluan, English. **Religions:** 97% Church of Tuvalu (Congregationalist), 1.4% Seventh-Day Adventists, 1% Baha'i.

• **GOVERNMENT Type:** constitutional monarchy with a parliamentary democracy; began debating republic status in 1992. **Independence:** Oct. 1, 1978 (from U.K.). **Constitution:** Oct. 1, 1978. **National holiday:** Independence Day, Oct. 1. **Heads of Government:** Filoimea Telito, governor-general; Apisai Ielemia, prime minister (since

Aug. 2006). **Structure:** executive—prime minister and cabinet; unicameral legislature—12-member House of Assembly; judicial—high court, chief justice presides over sessions twice a year.

• **ECONOMY Monetary unit:** Tuvaluan dollar or Australian dollar. **Budget:** (2006) *income:* $21.54 mil.; *expend.:* $23.05 mil. **G.D.P.:** $12.2 mil., $1,100 per capita (2002 est.). **Chief crops:** coconuts; fish. **Natural resources:** fish. **Major industries:** fishing, tourism, copra. **Labor force:** 3,615 (2004 est.). **Exports:** $1 mil. (f.o.b., 2004); copra. **Imports:** $12.91 mil. (c.i.f., 2005); food, animals, mineral fuels, machinery, manufactured goods. **Major trading partners:** (2006) *exports:* 60.5% Germany, 20.1% Italy, 6.9% Fiji; *imports:* 46.1% Fiji, 18.9% Japan, 18.2% China, 7.7% Australia, 4.1% New Zealand.

A British protectorate was established in 1892, and the islands were incorporated into the British colony of the Gilbert and Ellice Islands in 1915. The nine principal islands that make up the Ellice group escaped Japanese occupation in World War II and were used as Allied bases in the campaign to recapture the Pacific.

The Gilbert and Ellice Islands colony was granted self-rule in 1971. In 1975 the Ellice Islands, inhabited mainly by Polynesians, seceded from the other (mainly Micronesian) islands of the colony and became independent as Tuvalu on Oct. 1, 1978. (See also "Kiribati.") In a 1979 U.S.-Tuvalu friendship treaty, the United States relinquished claims, based on 19th-century guano mining, to the four southernmost islands, in return for access to World War II military airfields and veto power over other nations' use of the islands for military purposes.

The economy is based on subsistence farming and fishing. Exports include copra and woven palm-leaf products, and hydroponic agriculture and offshore fisheries are being developed. Tuvalu remains heavily dependent on foreign aid, principally from Australia, New Zealand, and the United Kingdom. In 2000, Tuvalu was admitted to the U.N.

▶ **UGANDA**
Republic of Uganda
• **GEOGRAPHY Location:** landlocked equatorial country in eastern Africa. **Boundaries:** Sudan to N, Kenya to E, Tanzania to S, Rwanda to SW, Zaire to W. **Total area:** 91,135 sq. mi. (236,040 sq km). **Coastline:** none. **Comparative area:** slightly smaller than Oregon. **Land use:** 25% arable land; 9% permanent crops; 9% meadows and pastures; 266% other. **Major cities:** Kampala (capital); Jinja; Mbale; Masaka; Gulu. • **PEOPLE Population:** 31,367,972 (July 2008 est.). **Nationality:** noun—Ugandan(s); adjective—Ugandan. **Ethnic groups:** 17% Baganda, 8% Basogo, 8% Iteso, 7% Bakiga, 6% Langi, 6% Rwanda, 5% Bagisu, 4% Acholi, 4% Lugbara, 3% Bunyoro, 2% Karamojong. **Languages:** English (official), Luganda, Swahili, Arabic and other Niger-Congo languages. **Religions:** 33% Roman Catholic, 33% Protestant, 16% Muslim, 18% indigenous beliefs. • **GOVERNMENT Type:** republic. **Independence:** Oct. 9, 1962 (from UK). **Constitution:** Oct. 8, 1995. **National holiday:** Independence Day, Oct. 9. **Heads of Government:** Yoweri Kaguta Museveni, president (since Jan. 1986); Prof. Apolo Nsibambi, prime minister (since Apr. 1999). **Structure:** executive—president is head of government and state; unicameral legislature; judiciary.

• **ECONOMY Monetary unit:** Ugandan shilling. **Budget:** (2007 est.) *income:* $2.298 bil.; *expend.:* $2.562 bil. **G.D.P.:** $31.47 bil., $1,100 per capita (2007 est.). **Chief crops:** coffee, cotton, tobacco; beef, milk, poultry. **Natural resources:** copper, cobalt, limestone, salt. **Major industries:** sugar, brewing, tobacco. **Labor force:** 14.05 mil. (2007 est.); 82% agriculture, 13% services, 5% industry. **Exports:** $1.459 bil. (f.o.b., 2007); coffee, gold, fish. **Imports:** $2.726 bil. (f.o.b., 2007); transportation equipment, petroleum, medical supplies, cereals. **Major trading partners:** (2006) *exports:* 10% Belgium, 9% Netherlands, 8% France, 8% Germany, 6% Rwanda, 5% Sudan; *imports:* 34% Kenya, 9% United Arab Emirates, 7% China, 6% India, 5% South Africa, 4% Japan.

Prior to 1800 Uganda was the site of several important kingdoms, notably Buganda, centered on Kampala on the northern shore of Lake Victoria. After 1830, Arabs from the sultanate of Oman, based in Zanzibar, asserted loose control over the region and dominated its trade. British explorers, seeking the source of the Nile, reached the Lake Victoria region in the mid-19th century. Mission stations were established in 1877; a Muslim rebellion destroyed the missions and occupied Kampala in 1888.

Uganda was brought under the control of the British East Africa Company in 1890, and Britain established a protectorate in 1894 that was expanded to include neighboring territories in 1896. In 1902 some of the protectorate's territory was transferred to Kenya. British immigrants extensively developed the agricultural potential of Uganda's fertile and temperate highlands, establishing large and prosperous farms. Lake Victoria was the scene of naval battles between Great Britain and Germany (established in neighboring Tanganyika) during World War I.

In 1955 the British administration created a local parliamentary government in which both whites and Africans held ministerial office. Talks on the terms for independence began in 1961 and after some difficulty arrived at a formula for a national structure in which Buganda and other traditional kingdoms would retain local autonomy. Several political parties competed for power; the Uganda People's Congress led by Milton Obote became dominant. Uganda became independent within the British Commonwealth on Oct. 9, 1962. Several constitutional changes in the early 1960's led to an end to the autonomy of the kingdoms and the effective concentration of all power in Obote's presidency. In 1967 a new constitution proclaimed Uganda an independent republic.

Obote was overthrown on Jan. 25, 1971, by Idi Amin Dada, commander of Uganda's armed forces. Amin declared himself president, dissolved the Parliament, and assumed absolute powers. In 1972 he expelled Uganda's Asians (primarily people of Indian and Pakistani descent), who controlled most of the country's small-scale commerce. The U.S. broke off diplomatic relations in 1973. In 1976 Amin declared himself president for life. His eight-year reign was marked by extreme violence and persecution of political and tribal opponents; as many as 300,000 may have been killed between 1971 and 1979. The country's prosperous agricultural, mining, and commercial economy was devastated, and its infrastructure, including a good road and rail network and Makerere University, fell into ruins.

On July 3, 1976, Israeli airborne troops landed at Entebbe and rescued 103 hostages who had been captured in a skyjacking carried out by Palestinian and German terrorists. In 1978 Amin, with the aid of Libyan troops, invaded Tanzania. Tanzanian troops countered by invading Uganda; they captured Kampala on Apr. 11, 1979, and drove Amin into exile. Diplomatic relations with the U.S. resumed. Elections in 1981 returned Obote to power. Obote's new regime was marked by repression of opponents and by rebellion in the northern part of the country by the National Resistance Army (NRA) under Yoweri Museveni.

Obote fled into exile in 1985 and was succeeded by Lt. Gen. Basilio Olara-Okello, but the NRA rebellion continued. Kenyan president Daniel arap Moi mediated peace talks between Olara-Okello and the NRA in late 1985; in Jan. 1986 Olara-Okello fled, and Museveni organized a new government. Despite continued insurgencies by rival military factions and a rebellion led by the charismatic religious leader, Alice Lakwena, the Museveni government restored order and, with aid from the World Bank and the I.M.F., began to rebuild Uganda's shattered society.

A constituent assembly was elected in 1994. In 1995, it enacted a new constitution, which extended for five years a ban on political parties, and scheduled presidential elections for 1996, elections Museveni won easily. By 1997 Uganda had the fastest growing economy in Africa and in 1998 Pres. Clinton's visit helped to create interst among foreign investors. In a June 2000 referendum voters extended the "no party" system Museveni advocates. Museveni won re-election as president in 2001 and announced in April that Uganda was withdrawing from the Congo peace accord and its troops were withdrawing also since they had accomplished their aim of defeating the Hutu extremists who threatened Uganda's borders

In 2002 fighting within Uganda intensified against the "Lord's Resistance Army", a militia largely of the Acholi tribe, led by Joseph Kony, seeking to establish a theocracy based upon the Ten Commandments through mass kidnapping, rape, and murder both in northern Uganda and in the Sudan. As of 2008 the situation had not changed.

▶ UKRAINE

● **GEOGRAPHY Location:** east-central Europe. **Boundaries:** Belarus to N, Russian Federation to NE and E, Sea of Azov and Black Sea to S, Moldova and Romania to SW, Hungary, Slovakia, Poland to W. **Total area:** 233,089 sq. mi. (603,700 sq km). **Coastline:** Black Sea. **Comparative area:** slightly smaller than Texas. **Land use:** 57% arable land; 2% permanent crops, 41% other. **Major cities:** Kiev (capital); Kharkov (Kharkiv); Dnepropetrovsk; Donetsk (Donetske); Odessa (Odesa).

● **PEOPLE Population:** 45,994,287 (July 2008 est.). **Nationality:** noun—Ukrainian(s); adjective—Ukrainian. **Ethnic groups:** 78% Ukrainian, 17% Russian, 5% other. **Languages:** Ukrainian, Russian, Romanian, Polish, Hungarian. **Religions:** Ukrainian Orthodox—Moscow Patriarchate, Ukrainian Orthodox—Kiev Patriarchate, Ukrainian Autocephalous Orthodox, Ukrainian Catholic, Protestant; Jewish.

● **GOVERNMENT Type:** republic. **Independence:** Aug. 24, 1991 (from Soviet Union). **Constitution:** June 28, 1996. **National holiday:** Independence Day, Aug. 24. **Heads of Government:** Victor Yuschenko, president (since Jan. 2005); Yuliya Tymoshenko, prime minister (since Dec. 2007). **Structure:** executive—president, Cabinet of Ministers; legislative—Supreme Council (450 deputies); judicial—Supreme Court.

● **ECONOMY Monetary unit:** hryvnia. **Budget:** (2007) *income:* $44.63 bil.; *expend.:* $46.98 bil. **G.D.P.:** $321.3 bil., $6,900 per capita (2007 est.). **Chief crops:** grain, sugar beets, sunflower seeds, vegetables; meat, milk. **Natural resources:** coal, iron ore, manganese, natural gas, oil. **Major industries:** coal, electric power, metals, machinery and transport, chemicals. **Labor force:** 21.63 mil. (2007); 32% industry and construction, 24% agriculture and forestry, 44% services, 32% industry. **Exports:** $46.68 bil. (2007 est.); energy, chemicals, machinery and transport equipment. **Imports:** $54.3 bil. (2007 est.); energy, machinery and parts, transportation equipment, chemicals. **Major trading partners:** (2006) *exports:* 21.3% Russia, 7.1% Turkey, 6.4% Italy, 4.1% U.S.; *imports:* 28.2% Russia, 11.7% Germany, 7.6% Poland, 7% China, 5.7% Turkmenistan.

Ukraine is the center of the original Russian state, known as Kievan Rus, which came into existence in the ninth century A.D. In the 13th and 14th centuries, during the Mongol invasion, Ukraine was controlled by Lithuania and Poland, and in 1654 it first entered the Russian empire. In the latter half of the 17th century, Ukraine was divided, with the eastern regions becoming part of Russia and the western part annexed by Poland; when Poland was subsequently partitioned, the western sections were ceded to Austria.

Until 1917 eastern Ukraine was a province of Russia called "Little Russia," and for two centuries the dominant country tried to Russianize the Ukrainian clergy and upper classes, and ban the Ukrainian language. Nevertheless, secret societies for the study of Ukrainian history, language, and culture formed, and when in the 19th century the Russians exiled Ukrainians to Siberia, modern Ukrainian nationalism was born.

In 1917, when the Russian empire collapsed, Ukrainian nationalists demanded Ukraine's autonomy by establishing a Ukrainian People's Republic, but within a few months, Red Army troops had occupied Ukraine. For the next few years, however, Ukraine was in the middle of the civil war and was even ceded to Germany under the Brest-Litovsk treaty of 1918, but in December 1920 a Ukrainian Soviet Socialist Republic (SSR) was established. Ukraine again was divided under the 1921 Treaty of Riga, which gave western Ukraine to Poland, Czechoslovakia, and Romania, while eastern Ukraine formed the Ukrainian SSR. Ukraine became one of the original members of the U.S.S.R. in December 1922.

The Ukrainians strongly opposed Stalin's policy of forced collectivization of agriculture in the 1930's, and the resulting chaos, famine, and deportation resulted in the deaths of millions of Ukrainians. Likewise, Stalin's great terror of the 1930's hit Ukraine hard, with the first victims being Ukrainian nationalists. World War II largely devastated Ukraine and killed millions of Ukrainians, but as a result of the war, Ukraine regained its old territories from Romania and Poland and was enlarged by the addition of historical Tatar lands in 1954. (The native Tatar inhabitants were forcibly deported to central Asia in the 1940's.)

Mikhail Gorbachev's policy of glasnost was slow to take root in Ukraine, largely because the head of the Communist party in Ukraine was a loyal Brezhnev crony, Vladimir Shcherbitsky. Outwardly, he appeared to agree with Gorbachev's policies, but Ukraine dissidents were still being arrested and cultural groups harassed by secret police. In 1986 a deadly nuclear power explosion at Chernobyl—and Soviet attempts at covering it up—turned international attention to Ukraine and gave rise to a number of new, powerful opposition movements. Rukh (the Ukrainian People's Movement for Restructuring), the most important of these, was founded in Kiev by a prominent group of intellectuals. By 1989 branches of Rukh had been organized in most parts of Ukraine. At the same time, Ukrainian miners became active

in strikes, and the Ukrainian Catholic church and the Ukrainian Orthodox church became politically active. Shcherbitsky's failure to contain these groups led to his dismissal in 1989.

On July 16, 1990, the Ukrainian Supreme Soviet adopted a declaration of sovereignty, and Communist party Secretary Leonid Kravchuk became chairman of the Supreme Soviet. In March 1991 Ukraine participated in the negotiations to form a new union treaty, despite more radical demands by Rukh for complete independence. The Ukrainian Communist party's failure to denounce the attempted coup in Moscow in August 1991 led to significant changes in Ukraine's political situation. After the coup collapsed, the Communist party was banned, and on Aug. 24, 1991, Ukraine adopted a declaration of total independence and Kravchuk was elected president.

Ukraine, Belarus, and the Russian Federation signed the Minsk Agreement that created the Commonwealth of Independent States, and on Dec. 21, Ukraine and 10 other former union republics officially committed themselves to the union by signing the Alma-Ata Declaration.

Potentially dangerous conflicts with Russia remained, however, including control of the powerful Black Sea fleet. Soon after the fall of the Soviet government armed conflict erupted in April 1994, when Russia removed a ship from Odessa laden with marine-research and navigational equipment valued at more than $10 million. A compromise was reached in 1995 that divided the 635-vessel fleet equally, with Russia then buying 32 percent of the ships from the Ukraine and paying rent for use of the naval base at Sevastopol.

The other conflict involved 2,000 nuclear warheads present in Ukraine. In Jan. 1994, Kravchuk, Boris Yeltsin, and Bill Clinton negotiated an agreement to dismantle Ukraine's 175 long-range missiles and more than 1,800 warheads. But Ukraine's Parliament refused to approve the agreement, even after Clinton made a $350 million U.S. aid package conditional on total disarmament. Kravchuk in July 1994 lost the presidential election to reformer Leonid Kuchma. In Nov. Parliament overwhelmingly approved the Nuclear Nonproliferation Treaty and loans from the U.S. and the I.M.F. ensued. The U.S. also pledged $400 million to help dismantle the missiles.

In July 1996 the Rada approved a new "strong president" Constitution which guaranteed rights to own property and to engage in business, abolished local councils ("soviets"), and made Ukrainian the only legal language (although Russian is the language of about one-fifth of the population). The May 1997 Friendship Treaty with Russia settled the Black Sea fleet division, guaranteed Russia's right to rent part of the port facilities of Sevastopol to service the fleet, and confirmed Ukrainian sovereignty over all of Crimea.

In Aug. 1998 the I.M.F. agreed to loans totalling $2.2 bil. to assist the government despite its inability to make reforms. Kuchma easily won re-election in Nov. 1999 and in April 2000 his referendum to expand presidential power was approved. Soon after, Kuchma's authority began to unravel: in November, charges, backed by tape recordings, surfaced that he had connived in the murder of an opposition journalist; the tapes also held evidence of election tampering and bribery. Although Kuchma's future seemed shaky, a coalition government emerged that supported him. Large public protests continued and by late 2004 grew to such an extent that Kuchima tried to rig the presidential elections. An "Orange Revolution" for a new vote and Victor Yuschenko emerged as the solid winner

He proved an ineffective leader but by Aug. 2006 he was forced to cede power to Viktor Yanukovich, a man he once called "a bandit." New elections in Sept. 2007 gave a bit more power to pro-Russian parties, but Yuschenko returned to power with the support of Prime Minister Yulia Tymoshenko. Their government collapsed in Sept. 2008.

▶ UNITED ARAB EMIRATES

● GEOGRAPHY Location: eastern Arabian peninsula. Boundaries: Persian Gulf to N, Gulf of Oman to NE, Oman to E, Saudi Arabia to S and W, short frontier with Qatar to NW. Total area: 31,969 sq. mi. (82,880 sq km). Coastline: 819 mi. (1,318 km). Comparative area: slightly smaller than Maine. Land use: negl.% arable land; negl.% permanent crops; 99% other. Major cities: Abu Dhabi (capital); Dubai; Sharjah.
● PEOPLE Population: 4,621,399 (July 2008 est.). Nationality: noun—Emirati(s); adjective—Emirati. Ethnic groups: 19% Emirati, 23% other Arab and Iranian, 50% South Asian, 8% other expatriates (includes Westerners and East Asians); less than 20% of population are UAE citizens (1982). Languages: Arabic (official), Persian, English, Hindi, Urdu. Religions: 96% Muslim (16% Shia), 4% Christian, Hindu, and other.
● GOVERNMENT Type: federation with specified powers delegated to UAE central government and other powers reserved to member emirates. Independence: Dec. 2, 1971 (from UK). Constitution: Dec. 2, 1971; made permanent 1996. National holiday: National Day, Dec. 2. Heads of Government: Sheikh Khalifa Bin Zayed Al-Nahyan, president (since Nov. 2004); Maktoum al-Maktoum, prime minister (since Oct.1990). Structure: executive—Supreme Council of Rulers (seven members), from which president and vice president are elected; prime minister and Council of Ministers; unicameral legislature—Federal National Council; judicial—Union Supreme Court.
● ECONOMY Monetary unit: Emirian dirham. Budget: (2007 est.) income: $58.15 bil.; expend.: $38.06 bil. G.D.P.: $145.8 bil., $55,200 per capita (2007 est.). Chief crops: dates, vegetables, watermelons; poultry, eggs, dairy products; fish. Natural resources: crude oil, natural gas. Major industries: petroleum, petrochemicals. Labor force: 3.119 mil. (2007 est.); 78% services, 15% industry and commerce, 7% agriculture. Exports: $152.1 bil. (f.o.b., 2007 est.); 45% crude oil, natural gas, re-exports, dried fish, dates. Imports: $94.72 bil. (f.o.b., 2007 est.); manufactured goods, machinery and transport equipment, chemicals, food. Major trading partners: (2006) exports: 25.8% Japan, 9.6% South Korea, 5.9% Thailand, 4.5% India; imports: 11.5% U.S., 11% China, 9.8% India, 6.4% Germany, 5.8% Japan, 5.5% U.K., 4.1% France.

In the 1820's Great Britain established protectorates over seven small sheikhdoms along the gulf coast between Qatar and Oman—Abu Dhabi, Dubai, Sharjah, Ajmar, Fujairah, and Umm al-Qaiwain. The region, which had been known as the Pirate Coast, then was generally referred to as the Trucial Coast or Trucial Oman. Under terms of a treaty in 1892, the sheikhdoms agreed not to enter into relations with any other country.

After Great Britain announced that it would withdraw its forces from the gulf in 1971, the seven sheikhdoms formed a federation and became independent as the United Arab Emirates on Dec. 2, 1971.

Just prior to his invasion of Kuwait in August 1990, Saddam Hussein threatened both the UAE and Kuwait for overproduction of petroleum, and the UAE was an integral part of the Allied coalition against Iraq. In 1995 the government signed a defensive alliance with France, who supplies the army with most of its weapons.

The economy is almost entirely dominated by petroleum. Citizens of the UAE receive extensive social services and enjoy one of the world's highest per capita incomes. The government has embarked on an enormous building program to create modern cities in the desert and has created plans to expand the economy beyond oil.

▶ UNITED KINGDOM
United Kingdom of Great Britain and Northern Ireland

● GEOGRAPHY Location: northwestern Europe, occupying major portion of British Isles. Boundaries: Atlantic Ocean to NW and W, North Sea to E; separated from France by English Channel to S; Republic of Ireland to W. Total area: 94,525 sq. mi. (244,820 sq km). Coastline: 7,723 mi. (12,429 km). Comparative area: slightly smaller than Oregon. Land use: 26% arable land; negl. % permanent crops; 473% other. Major cities: London (capital); Birmingham; Leeds; Glasgow; Sheffield.
● PEOPLE Population: 60,943,912 (July 2008 est.). Nationality: noun—Briton(s), British (collective pl.); adjective—British. Ethnic groups: 83.6% English, 8.6% Scottish, 2.9% Irish, 4.9% Welsh, 1.8% Ulster, 2.8% West Indian, Indian, Pakistani, and other. Languages: English, Welsh (about 26% of population of Wales), Scottish form of Gaelic (about 60,000 in Scotland). Religions: 71.6% Christian, 2.7% Muslim, 1% Hindu, 1.6% other, 23.1% unspecified and none.
● GOVERNMENT Type: constitutional monarchy. Independence: N.A. Constitution: unwritten; partly statutes, partly common law and practice. National holiday: Celebration of the Birthday of the Queen, second Saturday in June. Heads of Government: Elizabeth II, queen (since Feb. 1952); Gordon Brown, prime minister (since June 2007). Structure: executive authority lies with collectively responsible cabinet led by prime minister; legislative authority rests with Parliament (House of Lords, House of Commons); House of Lords is supreme judicial authority and highest court of appeals.
● ECONOMY Monetary unit: British pound. Budget: (2007 est.) income: $1.155 tril.; expend.: $1.237 tril. G.D.P.: $2.147 trillion, $35,300 per capita (2007 est.). Chief crops: cereals, oilseed, potatoes, vegetables; cattle, sheep, poultry; fish. Natural resources: coal, crude oil, natural gas, tin, limestone. Major industries: machinery and transportation equipment, metals, food processing. Labor force: 30.71 mil. (2007); 80.4% services, 18.2% industry, 1.4% agriculture (2006 est.), 4.7% unemployment (2005 est.). Exports: $415.6 bil. (f.o.b., 2007); manufactured goods, machinery, fuels, chemicals. Imports: $595.6 bil. (f.o.b., 2007); manufactured goods, machinery, fuels, foodstuffs. Major trading partners: (2006) exports: 14% U.S., 11% Germany, 10% France, 7% Ireland, 6% Netherlands, 5% Belgium, 5% Spain; imports: 13% Germany, 9% U.S., 7% France, 7% Netherlands, 5% China, 5% Norway, 5% Belgium.

Early megalithic and Iron Age peoples of Britain, primarily Celtic, developed tribal states that were conquered by Roman invaders in A.D. 43. After Roman legions withdrew from Britain in 410, invasions of Jutes, Angles, and Saxons conquered much of England, while Celtic peoples flourished in Wales, Scotland, and especially Ireland. Viking invaders established settlements in the eighth century. A united Saxon kingdom fell to the Norman invasion of William the Conquerer in 1066.

An aristocratic rebellion against the royal absolutism of King John in 1215 led to the royal acceptance of the Magna Carta, guaranteeing legal rights and laying the foundations of parliamentary government. From the 12th to the 15th century, the Plantagenet dynasty ruled England and claimed overlordship over Ireland; Wales was conquered in 1283. The Plantagenets also controlled sizable territories in France.

The Hundred Years' War (1337-1453) cost England its French possessions; the War of the Roses, (1455-85) ended the Plantagenet dynasty and brought Henry Tudor (Henry VII) to the throne. The Tudors gradually centralized royal control by bringing pressure against both the church and the nobility. Henry VIII broke with Rome in 1534 and established the Church of England. Under Elizabeth I, the last of the Tudors, England defeated Spain at sea and laid the foundations of later worldwide English sea power. The English Renaissance began under Elizabeth I (1533-1603) with the works of Shakespeare and continued into the 17th century with Milton and Newton.

The Stuart dynasty was founded by James I (1566-1625), uniting the crowns of England and Scotland in 1603. The English Civil War (1642-49) culminated in the execution of Charles I and the proclamation of the Commonwealth (later the Protectorate) under Oliver Cromwell. The monarchy was restored with Charles II in 1660. In the bloodless Glorious Revolution (1688), James II fled before a Protestant army under the Dutch William of Orange, who married and ruled jointly with James's daughter Mary II. The English Bill of Rights established the supremacy of Parliament and made the government a model of constitutional monarchy.

In the last gasp of the Stuart claimants to the throne, Irish supporters of James II were defeated at the Battle of the Boyne (1690), which temporarily crushed Irish resistance to annexation by England. The United Kingdom was created when Scotland was joined with England in a common Parliament by the Act of Union in 1707. A Scottish uprising led by the Young Pretender, Charles Edward Stuart, was crushed at Culloden Moor in 1745. Ireland was made part of the United Kingdom in 1801.

In the 1700's the United Kingdom became the greatest sea power in the world, controlling an empire that included much of North America and India. Agrarian "enclosures" of the 18th century ruined the peasantry but created an entrepreneurial revolution in agriculture that ultimately led to greatly increased agricultural productivity. The capital created in the process contributed to the success of the Industrial Revolution, which over the next century made England the wealthiest land on earth.

Despite the loss of the 13 colonies after the American Revolution (1775-83), England consolidated its holdings in the Indian subcontinent, Australia and New Zealand, Malaya, Hong Kong, much of eastern Africa from "Cape to Cairo," and elsewhere. Britain's prosperity and moral purpose were embodied in the person of Victoria, Queen of Great Britain and Ireland (1836-1901) and Empress of India (from 1836).

The repeal of the protectionist Corn Laws in 1846 led to an agricultural depression and hastened the migration of labor from the countryside to the industrial cities. The rise of labor activism led in 1906 to laws granting privileged status to trade unions, which organized the Labour party to promote their interests.

Britain's involvement in the Triple Entente with France and Russia ensured its participation in World War I (1914-18) against Germany, Italy, and Austria-Hungary. Victory came at the cost of an entire generation of British youth, but Britain emerged from the war with its empire at a high point, adding Tanganyika, Jordan, Palestine, and Iraq as part of the postwar division of spoils. Most of Ireland became independent in 1921, however, leaving only Northern Ireland as part of the United Kingdom.

Between the two world wars, Britain's navy and air force were the largest in the world, its army the third largest. Yet its industry was aging, the Great Depression hit especially hard in the British Isles, strikes and labor unrest weakened the social fabric, and colonial ties began to weaken in the 1930's. Economic retrenchment led to a failure to rearm in the face of the rising threat of Hitler's Germany and Mussolini's Italy.

The Munich Pact of 1938 gave Hitler a license for war; his invasion of Poland in 1939 forced Britain into the conflict. When Winston Churchill became prime minister in 1940, Britain was under daily air attack and in danger of an invasion by sea, and the country was dependent on American friendship and lend-lease war materials. But 1941 brought alliance with the United States and the Soviet Union, and a slowly turning tide of war leading to victory in 1945. Still, postwar Britain dropped to the second rank of superpowers.

The coalition between the Conservative and Labour parties that had governed Great Britain during the war seemed no longer necessary in 1945 as the war wound down. Labour won a landslide victory in the 1945 elections; Churchill was recalled in the midst of the Potsdam Conference, and Clement Atlee became prime minister. A brief Labour flirtation with the U.S.S.R. quickly ended in the postwar 1940's; England became a founding member of the United Nations and also, in 1949, of NATO. As the Cold War took shape, Britain developed its own nuclear arsenal.

The Labour party nationalized the Bank of England along with railroads, public utilities, and heavy industry. A comprehensive welfare state apparatus was created, including a national health service, unemployment and retirement benefits, and free education at all levels. But Britain was in many respects too poor to afford such changes; in order to cut expenditures, the government hastened the process of withdrawal from colonies and military bases around the world. India was granted independence in 1947, and Palestine, Burma, and Ceylon in 1948-49.

The elections of 1951 brought Churchill back to the prime ministership at the head of a Conservative majority that would last for 13 years. The Conservatives returned steel and trucking to the private sector but in general refrained from undoing the social policies of their Labour predecessors. Economic growth began in the 1950's and held steady at about 2.5 percent per year, a significantly lower rate than in continental Europe; obsolescence, excessive wage and benefit settlements, and a low savings rate all took their toll. The coronation of Elizabeth II in 1953 added a much-needed element of national celebration.

Churchill retired in 1955 and was succeeded by Anthony Eden. Eden's government fell in 1956 over the failed Anglo-French invasion of Suez. Eden's fall in 1957 brought to power Harold Macmillan, who pursued close relations with the United States. Most important, he presided over the transformation of an empire to a commonwealth; in the early 1960's, Ghana, Nigeria, Malaya, Singapore, and numerous other colonies were granted independence and Commonwealth status. Immigrants from the Commonwealth promptly flocked to England, straining housing, social services, and the labor market and creating problems of assimilation that remain unsolved.

Britain under Macmillan was the moving force behind the European Free Trade Association in 1960. In 1961 Britain applied for membership in the EEC, but that application was humiliatingly vetoed by France's Charles de Gaulle in 1963. Macmillan's government fell with the Profumo Scandal of 1963, and Douglas Home became a caretaker prime minister pending new elections.

The 1964 elections brought the Labour party to power under Harold Wilson, whose moderate positions made him unpopular with his own party, especially when he sponsored legislation to ban wildcat strikes. Strikes, wage inflation, the steady growth of the public sector (including renationalization of the steel industry), and the rise of turmoil in Northern Ireland in 1968-69 combined to make public support for Labour evaporate.

The Conservative victory in the 1970 elections brought Edward Heath to the office of prime minister. Promising to cut expenditures and taxes, reward initiative, and curb union power, the Conservatives were able to accomplish none of those aims. Heath's government imposed ineffective wage controls in an attempt to slow inflation and passed the 1971 Industrial Relations Act to regulate unions. When unions defied that act, the government fell. Heath's major achievement was the United Kingdom's admission to the EC in 1973. Continued turmoil in Northern Ireland was met with the abolition of Ulster's Stormount Parliament in 1972 and the imposition of direct British rule.

Wilson returned to the prime ministership in 1974 and retired in 1976, passing on the office to James Callaghan, who governed until 1979 at the head of a Labour-Liberal coalition. The continued power of trade unions was seen in the repeal of the Industrial Relations Act and the extension of union privileges. The left wing of the Labour party brought increasing pressure against defense spending, membership in NATO, and so loudly criticized American involvement in Vietnam.

The OPEC oil price rises of 1972-74 hurt Great Britain in the short run but also encouraged development of oil and gas fields in the North Sea, which made the nation a major petroleum exporter and helped revitalize its economy. Oil exploration in the North Sea also encouraged Scottish nationalism, with some damage to national unity, although in both Scotland and Wales, proposals in 1979 for separate parliaments were soundly defeated by plebiscites.

The 1979 elections brought the Conservatives to power again, behind Margaret Thatcher, Great Britain's (and Europe's) first female prime minister. She proved to be the only British prime minister in modern times to lead her party successfully in three elections. Thatcher's agenda involved undoing much of the course of postwar British history. The first target was inflation, attacked through a freeze on expenditures and reduction of government borrowing. The policy was a success; inflation fell from 18 percent in 1980 to 3 percent in 1989. But the austerity program had a high cost in unemployment, which remained at 14 percent in the mid-1980's. In 1982 national attention turned abruptly to overseas concerns, as Argentina invaded the Falkland ("Malvinas") Islands (only 300 miles east of Argentina), which it had long claimed as Argentine national territory, on Apr. 2. On May 21 British forces launched a counteroffensive, and the invading Argentine forces

surrendered on June 14. The nation's success provoked an upsurge of patriotism that swept Thatcher's party into a second term in 1983.

After the election the government turned to denationalization of industry. Over $30 billion in state property—from industrial giants, such as Britoil and British Gas, to individual apartments in municipal housing projects—was sold to private interests. In 1986 the top income-tax rate dropped from 98 percent to 40 percent. Britain agreed in 1985 to return Hong Kong to Chinese sovereignty in 1997.

The 1987 elections pitted the Conservatives against a weak Labour party that opposed NATO missile deployment in Great Britain, advocating unilateral disarmament and calling for renationalization of industry and a return to higher taxes for the wealthy. The Conservatives easily won their third straight election. By 1989 the "Thatcher Revolution" had produced a decisive long-term economic recovery, but one that was unevenly distributed: the southern part of the country enjoyed an economic boom, while the older industrial cities of the north remained stagnant. In 1990 an economic slowdown and rising inflation led to a strong decline in support for Mrs. Thatcher and her government. She resigned in November 1990.

Thatcher was replaced by Chancellor of the Exchequer John Major, whose greatest challenge has been Britain's role in a united Europe, to which Britain now has a land link via the 31-mile Channel Tunnel (Chunnel), completed in 1994. In the April 1992 elections, the Conservatives, led by Major, won a comfortable 21-seat margin in Parliament despite a recession. Not since the Napoleonic Wars had a British political party been able to form four consecutive governments. Yet only 13 months later Major's ratings in the polls had fallen to 21 percent as the economy stalled and the Conservatives themselves split badly over the E.C.'s Maastricht Treaty. The Conservatives were further beset in 1994 with a series of tabloid scandals and allegations of political corruption concerning arms sales to Iraq and Malaysia. In 1994 the government clumsily handled the news that scientists had concluded that eating English beef could cause the fatal "mad-cow" disease. After insisting that there was no cause for alarm the government was forced to deal with an E.U. boycott.

The parliamentary election of May 1997 ended 18 years of Tory government with Labour winning its largest majority since 1935, 419 seats to the Conservatives 165. The new Prime Minister Tony Blair appointed a cabinet of political moderates. In 1997 Hong Kong was returned to China without incident and in April 1998 the Blair government succeeded in negotiating a settlement in Northern Ireland although problems still remain.

In May 1999 the first elections to the Scottish Parliament and the Welsh Assembly were held. Labour won a plurality in both (over nationalist parties). The two bodies have authority over education, environment, health care, housing, and law enforcement. The Scottish Parliament also possesses authority to tax. In the 2001 elections Blair's Labour Party won a huge victory, taking 413 of 659 seats, the first time Labour had won two consecutive victories. The vote on invading Iraq in 2003 carried overwhelmingly (412-143); yet in the aftermath of victory serious troubles arose for the Blair government over the intelligence accounts used to justify British participation. Blair still won a decisive victory in the 2005 elections but his standing had declined. A terrorist attack in London in July 2005 killed 56 people and wounded hundreds. A year later the authorities arrested and charged 14 Muslim men in a plot to blow up planes headed to the U.S., and in 2007 a car loaded with explosives was crashed into a terminal at Glasgow airport, but with little damage. Tony Blair resigned in July 2007, replaced by Gordon Brown who quickly planned Britain's exit from Iraq. But the economy turned sour in 2008 and the Labor Party suffered its worst local election results in 40 years.

▶UNITED STATES OF AMERICA

● **GEOGRAPHY Location:** 48 conterminous states in North America, between Atlantic and Pacific Oceans; Alaska in northwest North America; Hawaiian Islands in Pacific Ocean about 3,000 miles W of California. **Boundaries:** Canada to N; Atlantic Ocean to E; Gulf of Mexico, Mexico to S; Pacific Ocean to W. Alaska bounded on E by Canada, on S and W by Pacific Ocean, on W and N by Arctic Ocean. **Total area:** 3,717,797 sq. mi. (9,629,091 sq km). **Coastline:** 11,954 mi. (19,924 km). **Comparative area:** slightly larger than Brazil; fourth-largest country. **Land use:** 19% arable land; negl. % permanent crops; 80% other. **Major cities:** Washington, D.C. (capital); New York; Los Angeles; Chicago; Houston; Philadelphia; Miami.
● **PEOPLE Population:** 303,824,646 (July 2008 est.). **Nationality:** noun—American(s); adjective—American. **Ethnic groups:** 81.7% white, 12.9% black, 4.2% Asian, 1% Amerindian or Alaska native, .2% Hawaiian and other Pacific islander. **Languages:** predominantly English; sizable Spanish-speaking minority. **Religions:** 51.3% Protestant, 23.9% Roman Catholic, 4% none, 1% Jewish, 1.7% Mormon, 1.7% Muslim, 10% other.
● **GOVERNMENT Type:** federal republic; strong democratic tradition. **Independence:** July 4, 1776 (from U.K.). **Constitution:** Sept. 17, 1787, effective March 4,1789. **National holiday:** Independence Day, July 4. **Heads of Government:** George W. Bush, president (since Jan. 2001); Richard Cheney, vice president (since Jan. 2001). **Structure:** executive—president, vice president, cabinet; legislative—bicameral Congress (House of Representatives and Senate); judicial—Supreme Court; branches, in principle, independent and maintain balance of power.
● **ECONOMY Monetary unit:** United States dollar **Budget:** (2007) *income:* $2.568 tril.; *expend:* $2.731 tril. **G.D.P.:** $13.86 tril., $46,000 per capita (2007). **Chief crops:** wheat, other grains, corn, fruits, vegetables, cotton; beef, pork, poultry, dairy products; forest products; fish. **Natural resources:** coal, copper, lead, molybdenum, phosphates. **Major industries:** leading industrial power in the world, highly diversified; petroleum, steel, motor vehicles, aerospace, telecommunications, chemicals, electronics, food processing, consumer goods, fishing, lumber, mining. **Labor force:** 153.1 mil. (2007; 76.8% services, 22.6% industry, 0.6% agriculture; 4.6% unemployment (2007). **Exports:** $1.14 tril. (f.o.b., 2007 est.); capital goods, automobiles, industrial supplies and raw materials, consumer goods, agricultural products. **Imports:** $1.987 tril. (f.o.b., 2007 est.); crude oil and refined petroleum, machinery, automobiles, consumer goods, industrial raw materials, food and beverages. **Major trading partners:** (2006) *exports:* 22.2% Canada, 12.9% Mexico, 5.8% Japan, 5.3% China, 4.4% UK; *imports:* 16% Canada, 16% China, 10.4% Mexico, 7.9% Japan, 4.8% Germany.

(For current events and history see Part I: "Major News Stories of the Year," and Part II: "Chronology of American History.")

▶URUGUAY
Oriental Republic of Uruguay

● **GEOGRAPHY Location:** southeastern coast of South America. **Boundaries:** Brazil to N, Atlantic Ocean to E and S, Argentina to W. **Total area:** 68,039 sq. mi. (176,220 sq km). **Coastline:** 410 mi. (660 km). **Comparative area:** slightly smaller than Washington State. **Land use:** 7% arable land; negl. % permanent crops; 93% other. **Major cities:** Montevideo (capital); Salto; Paysandú; Las Piedras; Rivera.
● **PEOPLE Population:** 3,477,778 (July 2008 est.). **Nationality:** noun—Uruguayan(s); adjective—Uruguayan. **Ethnic groups:** 88% white, 8% mestizo, 4% black. **Languages:** Spanish, Portunol, or Brazilero; Portuguese-Spanish mix on the Brazilian frontier. **Religions:** 66% Roman Catholic, 2% Protestant, 1% Jewish, 30% nonprofessing or other (less than half of the adult population attends church regularly).
● **GOVERNMENT Type:** republic. **Independence:** Aug. 25, 1825 (from Brazil). **Constitution:** Nov. 27, 1966; effective Feb. 1967; suspended June 27, 1973; constitutional reforms approved Jan. 7, 1997. **National holiday:** Independence Day, Aug. 25. **Head of Government:** Tabaré Vásquez, president (since Mar. 2005). **Structure:** executive—headed by president; bicameral legislature (Senate and House of Deputies); national judiciary headed by Supreme Court.
● **ECONOMY Monetary unit:** Uruguayan peso. **Budget:** (2007 est.) *income:* $6.6 bil.; *expend.:* $6.3 bil. **G.D.P.:** $37.05 bil., $10,700 per capita (2007 est.). **Chief crops:** wheat, rice, corn, sorghum; livestock; fishing. **Natural resources:** fertile soil, hydropower potential, minor minerals, fisheries. **Major industries:** meat processing, wool and hides, sugar. **Labor force:** 1.5 mil. (2007 est.); 76% services, 9% agriculture, 15% industry; 9.2% unemployment (2007). **Exports:** $4.5 bil. (f.o.b., 2007 est.); wool and textile manufactures, beef and other animal products, rice, fish. **Imports:** $5.5 bil. (f.o.b., 2007 est.); machinery and equipment, vehicles, chemicals, minerals, plastics, oil. **Major trading partners:** (2006) *exports:* 15.1% Brazil, 12.1% U.S., 6.8% Argentina, 6.4% Mexico, 6% China, 5% Germany, 5% Russia; *imports:* 20.4% Argentina, 17.1% Brazil, 8.2% U.S., 7.2% Paraguay, 6.9% China, 4.8% Venezuela, 4.4% Nigeria.

Uruguay was known as the Banda Oriental del Uruguay (Eastern Shore of the Uruguay River) during the colonial period. Although the Spanish first explored the area in 1516, they did not immediately settle there. Instead, the Portuguese founded the Colonia de Sacramento, near Buenos Aires, in 1680. They did not permanently establish the settlement of Montevideo until 1726. Under the leadership of José Gervasio Artigas, Uruguayans fought against both the Portuguese and the junta of Buenos Aires between 1811 and 1814 in an effort to establish their independence; in 1815 they proclaimed the Autonomous Government of the Eastern Provinces.

In 1817 the Portuguese again took control of the region, but Uruguayan nationals ousted them in 1828. A new constitution for the country was promulgated in 1830; however, domestic rivalry among elites soon led to civil war. The two contending factions, Liberals (Colorados) and Conservatives (Blancos), wore red and white armbands, respectively. Civil war continued through the 1840's and 1850's, until the victory of the Colorados in 1865. In the War of the Triple Alliance (1865-70), Uruguay allied itself with Argentina and Brazil against Paraguay. The consequence of the war for Uruguay was independence from the other regional powers.

The Colorado party dominated Uruguayan government from 1865 until 1958. Waves of European immigrants transformed Uruguayan society during the latter half of the 19th century, and by 1880 immigrants made up almost half of the population. The last civil war between the Blancos and the Colorados took place in 1904; the Colorados won victory under Pres. José Batlle y Ordóñez, one of Uruguay's political legends.

Batlle inaugurated a labor and social-welfare reform program that created Latin America's first eight-hour working day as well as progressive legislation on women's rights. Impressed with the Swiss plural executive Federal Council during his stay in Switzerland, Batlle believed such a structure could help Uruguay avoid the Latin American hazard of *caudillismo* (authoritarian rule). He proposed the idea of a plural executive, and a version of the idea became part of the constitution in 1919. The new constitution provided for both a president and a collegial National Council, both of which would make up the executive structure.

In 1933 a military coup by Pres. Gabriel Terra sought to dissolve both the legislature and the National Council and to reestablish the single executive presidential system. He managed this by sponsoring a constituent assembly that drew up a new constitution in 1934. In a 1951 plebiscite, Uruguayan voters approved a return to the plural executive system, and a new constitutional order reflecting this went into effect the following year. The debate over the form of the executive was not over, however; in 1966 the public voted for yet another constitution, which once again established the single president as the executive power.

Uruguay's economy began to falter during the 1950's. This, combined with the expansion of governmental bureaucracy tied to the country's social welfare programs, led to increasing popular discontent. In 1958 the Blancos won two successive victories. A candidate from the conservative wing of the Colorado party, Jorge Pacheco Areco, regained the presidency in 1967, but neither the Blancos nor the Colorados were able to deal with Uruguay's deteriorating economy or with its growing political unrest.

Uruguay's politics became increasingly polarized during the 1960's and into the 1970's. The leftist National Liberation Movement (MLN or Tupamaros), formed in 1967, began urban guerrilla activity that included robbery and kidnapping. The Tupamaros, many of whom were young and middle class, embarrassed government officials and were largely successful in eroding the public image of the civilian government. Tupamaro activity generated violence from the military and police, and as the political situation deteriorated in the early seventies, the government granted the military increasing authority.

By 1973 the military was in control of the country, and they dissolved the Congress. The military allowed Pres. Juan María Bordaberry to remain in office until 1976, at which time they installed Aparicio Méndez in the presidency. It was Bordaberry, however, who proposed the dismantling of the political parties in 1976. Uruguayan military rule was brutally repressive, and the armed forces perpetrated many human rights abuses. By some estimates, the Uruguayan military regime had the world's largest number of political prisoners in proportion to the population.

In 1980, Uruguayans rejected in a plebiscite the army's constitution, which would have amounted to continued de facto military control. So began a slow process in which the military tried to bargain with civilian political elites while promising to restore civilian rule. Finally, in 1984, Colorado party candidate Julio María Sanguinetti won a civilian presidential election.

Sanguinetti approved a general amnesty for the leaders of the military regime, but also had success in attracting foreign investment and righting the Uruguayan economy. He was unseated five years later by National party candidate Luis Alberto Lacalle, who further liberalized trade. But his austerity on social problems led voters to overturn some of his reforms by referendum. In 1994 elections, Sanguinetti won back the presidency. In Nov. 1999 the Colorado candidate, Jorge Batlle, pledged to continue the pro-market reforms of Sanguinetti, defeated in a run-off the (left-wing) Broad Front candidate, Tabaré Vázquez, who had led in the first round. But in 2005 Vásquez won the election on a more centrist platform as the economy had been struggling.

▶ **UZBEKISTAN**
Republic of Uzbekistan

● **GEOGRAPHY Location:** central Asia. **Boundaries:** Kazakhstan to N, NE, and NW, Kyrgyzstan to E, Tajikistan to SE, Afghanistan to S, Turkmenistan to SW and W. **Total area:** 172,741 sq. mi. (447,400 sq km). **Coastline:** Aral Sea. **Comparative area:** slightly larger than California. **Land use:** 11% arable land; 1% permanent crops; 88% other. **Major cities:** Tashkent (capital); Samarkand; Namangan; Andizhan; Bukhara.

● **PEOPLE Population:** 28,268,440 (July 2008 est.). **Nationality:** noun—Uzbekistani(s); adjective—Uzbekistani. **Ethnic groups:** 80% Uzbek, 5.5% Russian, 5% Tajik, 3% Kazakh, 2.5% Karakalpak, 1.5% Tatar. **Languages:** 74.3% Uzbek (official), member of Eastern Turk language group written in Cyrillic script since 1940; 14.2% Russian, 4.4% Tajik, 7.1% other languages. **Religions:** 88% Muslim (mostly Sunnis), 9% Eastern Orthodox, 3% other.

● **GOVERNMENT Type:** republic. **Independence:** Sept. 1, 1991 (from Soviet Union). **Constitution:** Dec. 8, 1992. **National holiday:** Independence Day, Sept. 1. **Heads of Government:** Islam A. Karimov, president (since Dec. 1991); Utkir T. Sultanov, prime minister (since Dec. 1995). **Structure:** executive—president, Cabinet of Ministers; legislative—Supreme Assembly; judicial—Supreme Court.

● **ECONOMY Monetary unit:** som. **Budget:** (2007 est.) *income:* $6.584 bil.; *expend:* $6.652 bil. **G.D.P.:** $62.27 bil., $2,200 per capita (2007 est.). **Chief crops:** cotton, vegetables, fruits, grain; livestock. **Natural resources:** natural gas, coal, petroleum, gold, uranium. **Major industries:** textiles, food processing, machine building, metallurgy, natural gas. **Labor force:** 14.6 mil. (2007). **Exports:** $3.045 bil. (2007); cotton, gold, natural gas, mineral fertilizers, ferrous metals, textiles, food products, autos. **Imports:** $4.57 bil. (2007); machinery and parts, foodstuffs, chemicals, metals. **Major trading partners:** (2006) *exports:* 23.7% Russia, 11.6% Poland, 10.4% China, 7.6% Turkey, 5.9% Kazakhstan, 4.7% Ukraine, 4.3% Bangladesh; *imports:* 27.6% Russia, 15.1% South Korea, 10.3% China, 7.8% Germany, 7.2% Kazakhstan, 4.7% Ukraine, 4.5% Turkey.

Uzbekistan, a land of deserts and steppe, lies in the heart of central Asia. Although the territory has been inhabited since prehistoric times, today's Uzbeks are actually descendants of nomadic Mongol, Iranian, and Turkic tribes who mixed with the populations there beginning in the 13th century A.D. The Uzbeks take their name from Khan Uzbek (1282-1342), the ruler responsible for converting the Mongol Golden Horde (the westernmost part of the Mongolian empire) to Islam. In the 18th and 19th centuries, the tribal states known as the Uzbek khanates of Bukhara, Samarkand, and Kokand were formed. Russian conquest of the Uzbek lands began in the 18th century and was completed in 1876 with the conquering of the khanate of Kokand. The Russian empire quickly built the Transcaucasian Railway to connect it with the region's major cities, thus sealing its hold on the area.

As with Kazakhstan, there was a large influx of Russians into Uzbekistan. Uzbek resentment of Russian immigrants precipitated a riot in 1898 in Andidzhan and again in 1916, when a decree that drafted central Asians into the Army was promulgated. Soviet power was established in 1917 in the city of Tashkent, and after some fighting, the region of Uzbekistan was incorporated as the Turkestan Autonomous Soviet Socialist Republic (ASSR) in April 1918. In October 1924, the Uzbek Soviet Socialist Republic (SSR) came into being.

During 1924-25, the Soviet government initiated the National Delimitation of the Central Asian Republics to create Uzbek national symbols, to develop a new literary language, and to increase literacy among Uzbeks. It also conducted a brutal campaign against Islam and its believers. The Soviets modernized agriculture and industrialized the territory, although the native Uzbek population for the most part continued to live in rural areas and worked harvesting cotton, while the Russian population worked in industry. During World War II, Uzbekistan's industrial base expanded as major factories were moved there to keep them safe from enemy attack.

Mikhail Gorbachev's policy of glasnost, or openness, did not immediately result in political changes in Uzbekistan. In time, Uzbeks became politically active over many of the same issues that affected their Kazakh neighbors, such as the environmental problems causing the drying up of its rivers, the desiccation of the Aral Sea, and the salinization of the soil. They also demanded that Uzbek (and not Russian) be the official language.

In March 1990 the Supreme Soviet elected Islam Karimov as president, and on Aug. 31, 1991, Uzbekistan declared its independence, and joined the Commonwealth of Independent States (CIS).

In Dec. 1991 Islam Karimov won the presidential election, and he moved to reduce Uzbekistan's dependence on Russia. In 1994 he signed an economic free-trade agreement with Kazakhstan and Kyrgyzstan and he banned use of the ruble in order to strengthen the som, Uzbekistan's monetary unit. In Dec. 1994 Karimov's supporters (calling themselves the Democratic party) won an overwhelming majority in Uzbekistan's first parliamentary elections. Since then the country has made a slow but steady economic recovery as Karimov ruled with an iron hand. His human rights abuses were ignored after the 9-11 attacks when the U.S. military set up a large base of operations for the war on terror. In May 2005, however, Karimov's government violently supressed a demonstration killing perhaps 1,000 people. When the U.N. helped the fleeing refugees Karimov ordered the U.S. to leave.

▶ VANUATU
Republic of Vanuatu
● GEOGRAPHY Location: chain of 12 principal and some 60 smaller islands in Pacific Ocean, about 500 mi. (800 km) W of Fiji and 1,100 mi.

(2,800 km) E of Australia. Port Vila 17°45'S, 168°18'E. Boundaries: surrounded by South Pacific Ocean; nearest neighbor is Santa Cruz Islands to N. Total area: 5,699 sq. mi. (14,760 sq km). Coastline: 1,571 mi. (2,528 km). Comparative area: slightly larger than Connecticut. Land use: 3% arable land; 7% permanent crops; 90% other. Major cities: Port Vila (capital).
● PEOPLE Population: 215,446 (July 2008 est.). Nationality: noun—Ni-Vanuatu (sing. and pl.); adjective—Ni-Vanuatu. Ethnic groups: 98.5% Ni-Vanuatu, 1.5% other. Languages: English and French (official); pidgin (known as Bislama or Bichelama). Religions: 36.7% Presbyterian, 15% Anglican, 15% Catholic, 7.6% indigenous beliefs, 6.2% Seventh-Day Adventist, 3.8% Church of Christ, 15.7% other.
● GOVERNMENT Type: republic. Independence: July 30, 1980 (from France and U.K.). Constitution: July 30, 1980. National holiday: Independence Day, July 30. Heads of Government: Kalkot Matas Kelekele, president (since Aug. 2004); Rialuth Serge Vohor, prime minister (since Aug. 2004). Structure: executive—president, prime minister, council of ministers; unicameral legislature; judiciary.
● ECONOMY Monetary unit: vatu. Budget: (2005 est.) income: $78.7 mil. expend.: $72.23 mil. G.D.P.: $739 mil. (2006 est.), $2,900 per capita (2003 est.). Chief crops: copra, coconuts, cocoa, coffee, taro, yams, fruits, vegetables; fish, beef. Natural resources: manganese, hardwood forests, fish. Major industries: food and fish freezing, forestry processing, meat canning. Labor force: 76,410; 65% agriculture, 30% services, 5% industry (2000 est.) Exports: $40 mil. (f.o.b., 2006); copra, beef, cocoa, timber, coffee. Imports: $156 mil. (c.i.f., 2006); machines and vehicles, food and beverages, fuels. Major trading partners: (2006) exports: 59.6% Thailand, 16.8% India, 11.5% Japan; imports: 20.6% Australia, 19.7% Japan, 12.1% Singapore, 8.8% New Zealand, 7.7% Fiji, 7.4% China, 4.3% New Caledonia.

Formerly known as the New Hebrides, Vanuatu is a rugged, volcanic island chain with heavily forested mountains; peaks rise to over 6,000 feet (on Espiritu Santo, the largest island). The people are Melanesians. In 1887 the islands were placed under the administration of an Anglo-French naval commission, becoming a joint Anglo-French colony (condominium) in 1906. The islands escaped Japanese occupation during World War II; they sided with the Free French and were used as bases for Allied campaigns in the Pacific. The New Hebrides were granted independence as Vanuatu on July 30, 1980, with membership in the British Commonwealth. The government is a parliamentary system, complemented by a National Council of Chiefs to decide matters of tradition and customary law.

The economy is based on subsistence agriculture, cattle raising, and fishing. Tourism is developing rapidly, and the sale of long-term tuna-fishing rights, principally to Japan, Australia, and the United States, is an important earner of foreign exchange.

▶ VENEZUELA
Republic of Venezuela
● GEOGRAPHY Location: northern coast of South America. Boundaries: Caribbean Sea to N, Guyana to E, Brazil to S, Colombia to W. Total area: 352,144 sq. mi. (912,050 sq km). Coastline: 1,739 mi. (2,800 km). Comparative area: slightly more than twice the size of California. Land use: 3% arable land; 1% permanent crops; 96% other.

Major cities: Caracas (capital); Maracaibo; Valencia; Maracay; Barquisimeto.

●**PEOPLE　Population**: 26,414,815 (July 2008 est.). **Nationality**: noun—Venezuelan(s); adjective—Venezuelan. **Ethnic groups**: Spanish, Italian, Portuguese, Arab, German, African, indigenous people. **Languages**: Spanish (official), native dialects (spoken by about 200,000 Amerindians in remote interior). **Religions**: 96% nominally Roman Catholic, 2% Protestant.

●**GOVERNMENT　Type**: federal republic. **Independence**: July 5, 1811 (from Spain). **Constitution**: Dec. 30, 1999. **National holiday**: Independence Day, July 5. **Head of Government**: Hugo Chávez Frías, president (since Feb. 1999). **Structure**: executive (president); bicameral legislature (National Congress—Senate, Chamber of Deputies); judiciary.

●**ECONOMY　Monetary unit**: bolívar. **Budget**: (2007 est.) *income*: $63.27 bil.; *expend.*: $68.22 bil. **G.D.P.**: $335 bil., $12,800 per capita (2007 est.). **Chief crops**: corn, sorghum, sugarcane, rice, bananas, vegetables, coffee; beef, pork, milk, eggs; fish. **Natural resources**: crude oil, natural gas, iron ore, gold, bauxite. **Major industries**: petroleum, iron ore mining, construction materials. **Labor force**: 12.5 mil. (2007); 64% services, 23% industry, 13% agriculture; 17% unemployment (2002). **Exports**: $65.94 bil. (f.o.b., 2007 est.); petroleum, bauxite, aluminum, steel, chemicals, agricultural products, basic manufactures. **Imports**: $44.38 bil. (f.o.b., 2007 est.); raw materials, construction materials, machinery and transport equipment. **Major trading partners**: (2006) *exports*: 46.2% U.S., 13.5% Netherlands, 3.2% China; *imports*: 30.6% U.S., 10.2% Colombia, 10.1% Brazil, 5.9% Mexico, 4.9% China, 4.8% Panama.

At the time of European contact in the early 16th century, coastal Venezuela was home to nearly 50,000 semisedentary Indians. Although the region was "discovered" by Christopher Columbus in 1498, European settlement of the area was slow in comparison with the neighboring region of New Granada. The Spaniards explored and exploited Venezuela in the 1520's, searching for gold and pearls.

Early attempts at agriculture by the Spaniards failed until they discovered that the area around Caracas (founded in 1567) could sustain the production of both wheat and cocoa. African slave labor was an important part of the economic structure, and as markets for cocoa expanded, Caracas grew in importance. Venezuela became a captaincy general (an administrative region below the level of viceroyalty) with an audiencia (high court) established at Caracas in 1777-78.

As early as 1797, Venezuelan society was in rebellion against the Spanish empire. A major hindrance to the revolutionary leadership of Simón Bolívar was the need to accommodate both conservative landowners and the pardos, lower class citizens of mixed African and European ancestry.

The wars of independence were particularly destructive in Venezuela, but in 1821 the region achieved independence and became part of the federation of Gran Colombia, which also included New Granada and Ecuador. By 1830 Gran Colombia was in a state of political collapse, and Venezuela became an independent republic.

The military caudillo (leader) José Antonio Páez controlled the country for three decades. With the demise of Páez and his conservative allies in the 1860's, the forces of liberalism under Antonio Guzmán Blanco took over. The Guzmán Blanco era ended during a brief civil war in 1889, won by

Gen. Cipriano Castro, who proceeded to establish his own rule. In 1908 Gen. Juan Vicente Gómez occupied the presidency, and he controlled the politics of Venezuela until his death in 1935.

The shift from dictatorship to democracy began with the Generation of 28, a student movement that organized urban workers and peasants into a viable political opposition. The Generation of 28 later became the modern Democratic Action party. In 1945 a group of young military officers overthrew the conservative dictatorship and supported the Democratic Action group in writing a new democratic constitution. Democratic Action won the elections of 1947, but military elements overthrew the new government the following year. The coup brought Col. Marcos Pérez Jiménez to power until his ouster in 1958.

The election of Democratic Action candidate Romulo Betancourt as president marked the beginning of multiparty democratic politics in Venezuela. The stability of the system owed much to political possibilities provided by the country's petroleum revenues. Venezuela nationalized foreign-owned oil and iron firms in 1975 and 1976, but dependence on petroleum revenues still precipitated economic and political problems for the country in the 1980's. The downturn of the global oil market caused Venezuela's economic base to shrink, and the country's massive foreign debt hindered the expansion of populist political strategies.

The Christian Democrats defeated Democratic Action in 1968 and again in 1978. Pres. Luis Herrera Campíns's administration (1979-84) took the country in a more conservative direction but Democratic Action regained the presidency in 1983 under Jaime Lusinchi.

Venezuela's huge foreign debt in the 1980's led to tight economic controls and a reduction in social spending. The administration of Pres. Carlos Andrés Perez, elected in 1989, began with antigovernment riots in which hundreds died. In Feb. 1992, Latin America's oldest civilian government thwarted an attempted coup by soldiers angered over connections between high-ranking officers and drug traffickers; a second coup in November also failed. But in early 1993, Pres. Perez was suspended after the Senate ordered impeachment proceedings against him on charges he embezzled $17 million from the government; the Congress overwhelmingly elected Sen. Ramon Jose Valasquez Mujica to serve as interim president.

In early 1994 Rafael Caldera became president and immediately faced severe economic problems as the currency depreciated by more than 80 percent. Caldera imposed price and currency controls and suspended several constitutional guarantees. In July 1995, he restored those rights, except along Venezuela's borders with Colombia and Brazil, where crime and economic crises were most severe. Violent anti-government demonstrations continued into 1996 but Caldera persisted in austerity plans that resulted in a $1.4 bil. loan from I.M.F. By early 1997 inflation seemed to be in check and the economy stabilizing although the continuing fall in worldwide oil prices added more pressure for budget cuts. By 1998 Venezuela's economy was caught in the worldwide financial crisis and spinning toward chaos as the presidential election approached.

In the December elections, the two old parties (Christian Democrats and Democratic Action) which had dominated for 40 years all but disappeared. The Patriotic Pole Coalition candidate, Hugo Chavez Frias (who had led the unsuccessful coup in 1992 against Perez) easily triumphed over Henrique

Salas Romer. Two days later stock shares rose 22 percent despite Chavez' calls for redistribution of wealth, privatization of the government oil company and abolition of Congress. Chavez called for a Constitutional Assembly to rewrite the constitution (88 percent voted their approval in April 1999). In elections for the Assembly Chavez's supporters won all but seven of 128 seats. In December the Assembly adopted a new constitution (Venezuela's 26th) whose major features are a unicameral National Assembly and a six-year renewable presidential term.

Elections in Aug. 2000 confirmed Chavez for a new term and "Chavista" dominance of the Assembly. Chavez demanded OPEC cut production and travelled to major oil producers (including Iraq) to make his point. He agreed to sell oil to Castro's Cuba at bargain prices. In Nov. the new National Assembly gave him authority to rule by decree in 37 legislative areas.

But Chavez's excesses (such as decreeing 49 new laws in one day) provoked resistance by both business and labor, both of whom backed an army coup attempt on April 12, 2002. Within 48 hours, however, Chavez was back, the coup undercut by divisions in the armed forces. A general strike, called in Oct. by business and labor groups, became a crisis for the regime when 30,000 oil workers joined. The O.A.S. brokered an agreement that both sides would disarm and recognize a constitutional right to a recall referendum. In Sept. 2003 the National Electoral Council rejected the petition signed by 3.2 million people demanding a recall referendum. After surmounting every legal hurdle, the recall referendum was held on August 16, 2004 and Chavez easily triumphed over a stunned opposition. Since then Chavez has grown more popular by using the nation's oil wealth to improve social services, education, and infrastructure, and by openly challenging U.S. dominance in the region. As he continues to assume more and more power through legal changes, more nations in South America have begun to distance themselves from him. (See "Major News Stories.")

▶ **VIETNAM**
Socialist Republic of Viet Nam
• **GEOGRAPHY Location:** Southeast Asia. **Boundaries:** China to N, Gulf of Tonkin to NE, South China Sea to E, Laos and Cambodia to W. **Total area:** 127,243 sq. mi. (329,560 sq km). **Coastline:** 2,140 mi. (3,444 km) excluding islands. **Comparative area:** slightly larger than New Mexico. **Land use:** 17% arable land; 5% permanent crops; 78% other. **Major cities:** Hanoi (capital); Ho Chi Minh City (formerly Saigon); Haiphong; Da Nang; Long Xuyen.
• **PEOPLE Population:** 86,116,559 (July 2008 est.). **Nationality:** noun—Vietnamese (sing., pl.); adjective—Vietnamese. **Ethnic groups:** 86.2% Kinh, 2% Tay, 1.7% Thai; Muong, Khome, Hoa, Nun, Hmong. **Languages:** Vietnamese (official); French, Chinese, English, Khmer, ethnic langs. (Mon-Khmer and Malayo-Polynesian). **Religions:** Buddhist, Taoist, Roman Catholic, indigenous beliefs, Islam, Protestant, Cao Dai, Hoa Hao.
• **GOVERNMENT Type:** Communist state. **Independence:** Sept. 2, 1945 (from France). **Constitution:** Apr. 15, 1992. **National holiday:** Independence Day, Sept. 2. **Heads of Government:** Nguyen Minh Triet, president, (since June 2006); Nguyen Tan Dung, prime minister (since June 2006). **Structure:** executive—president, prime minister, cabinet; unicameral legislature; judiciary—elected by legislature.

• **ECONOMY Monetary unit:** new dong. **Budget:** (2007 est.) *income:* $18.28 bil.; *expend.:* $19.79 bil. **G.D.P.:** $222.5 bil., $2,600 per capita (2007 est.). **Chief crops:** paddy rice, corn, potatoes, rubber, soybeans, coffee, tea, bananas; poultry, pigs; fish. **Natural resources:** phosphates, coal, manganese, bauxite, chromate. **Major industries:** food processing, textiles, machine building. **Labor force:** 45.73 mil. (2007 est.); 56.8% agriculture, 37% industry. 6.2% services, 2.4% unemployment (2005 est.). **Exports:** $48.3 bil. (f.o.b., 2007 est.); crude oil, marine products, rice, coffee, rubber, tea, garments, shoes. **Imports:** $60.75 bil. (f.o.b., 2007 est.); machinery and equipment, petroleum products, fertilizer, steel products, raw cotton, grain, cement, motorcycles. **Major trading partners:** (2006) *exports:* 21.2% U.S., 12.3% Japan, 9.4% Australia, 5.7% China, 4.5% Germany; *imports:* 17.7% China, 12.9% Singapore, 11.5% Taiwan, 9.8% Japan, 8.4% South Korea, 7.3% Thailand, 4.2% Malaysia.

The southward expansion of the Chinese empire in the first millennium B.C. drove the Vietnamese peoples southward into northern Vietnam (Tonkin). The area came under direct Chinese rule in 111 B.C. Chinese rule endured, with some interruptions, until A.D. 948; thereafter, Vietnam was independent under strong Chinese influence.

The Hindu-Buddhist kingdom of Annam, in central Vietnam, gradually increased in size and power at the expense of Tonkin and the Khmer empire and Champa, to the west and south. In 1558 the kingdom of Annam split, with independent courts established at Hanoi, controlling Tonkin and the Red River valley, and Hue, in central Vietnam. A remnant of the old Champa state remained independent in the Mekong delta in the south. In 1802 the monarchy was reunited, with the court at Hue controlling all of Vietnam and exercising hegemony over Cambodia.

European penetration of the region began in the 16th century; by the early 19th century, France was the dominant foreign power in Indochina. Efforts to establish French military control began in 1858-59 with the establishment of a colony in Cochin China, in southern Vietnam. Campaigns in the Red River valley in 1873 and 1882 were complicated by Chinese intervention and the determined resistance of the Vietnamese court. In 1884 separate protectorates were established in Tonkin and Annam; in 1887 those, along with Cochin China and Cambodia, were combined into the Union of Indochina under French colonial rule. Rubber plantations were established, and rice and timber exports were under French control. A nationalist rebellion under Phan Boi Chau was suppressed in the early 20th century.

Nationalist resistance to French colonialism continued, resulting in the creation in 1939 of the Vietminh, or Independence League. In 1940 Japanese troops occupied French Indochina, with the collaboration of colonial administrators loyal to the Vichy regime. The Vietminh spearheaded anti-Japanese guerrilla resistance and in 1945 forced the abdication of King Bao Dai, head of a pro-Japanese puppet state. In 1945 France reoccupied Indochina; in 1946 the leader of the Vietminh, Ho Chi Minh, became president of a separatist government at Hanoi. France ceded local autonomy to Tonkin and Annam but sought to retain Cochin China as a colony. Fighting between the French and the Vietminh resumed. On July 1, 1949, the French reinstalled Bao Dai as king of Vietnam, and in February 1950 recognized the independence of Vietnam within the French Union. Ho Chi Minh's republican government also claimed control of all of Vietnam.

Fighting between the two rivals culminated in the French defeat at Dienbienphu on May 7, 1954. An armistice was concluded and the country was partitioned at a demilitarized zone at latitude 17° north, the northern part going to the Communist-controlled Vietminh government, the southern to Bao Dai. Nearly one million refugees, fled from the north to the south. An international conference in Geneva agreed that elections would be held throughout Vietnam in 1956. In June 1954 Ngo Dinh Diem became premier of South Vietnam; full sovereignty in the south was transferred by France to the Vietnamese government in Dec. 1954. In October 1955 Diem held elections in the south that resulted in the dismissal of Bao Dai as king and the proclamation of an independent Republic of Vietnam.

The scheduled elections of 1956 were never held. French troops withdrew from South Vietnam in that year. Fighting continued in the south, as the Vietminh-backed National Liberation Front (Vietcong) sought to overthrow the Diem government. On Dec. 31, 1959, the Democratic Republic of Vietnam in the north adopted a new constitution calling for the reunification of the country; northern aid to the Vietcong increased significantly, as did American aid to the south. After 1962 American military advisers increased in number and combat exposure.

In 1963 widespead demonstrations, under Buddhist leadership, led to a coup on Nov. 1-2 in which Diem was deposed and assassinated. A series of short-lived military regimes followed until Sept. 1967, when Nguyen Van Thieu was elected president. U.S. air strikes against North Vietnam began in 1964. In the same year, the flow of troops and supplies from north to south increased. American combat troops entered the war in 1965. Despite U.S.-South Vietnamese superiority in arms and troops, and total control of the air, Vietcong control over the countryside increased. Both Operation Phoenix, in which antigovernment rural leaders were assassinated, and the establishment of fortified strategic hamlets to control the rural population, failed to reverse the tide.

The combined Vietcong-North Vietnamese Tet Offensive in early 1968 resulted in serious losses for South Vietnamese and American forces. The war spread to Laos and to Cambodia, the latter bombed in 1969. American air strikes in North Vietnam were stepped up, and U.S. troop strength reached a maximum of 543,000 in 1969. In July 1969 a series of U.S. troop withdrawals began, and secret talks were initiated in search of a negotiated settlement of the war. Following heavy U.S. bombardment of the north in 1972, a cease-fire agreement was signed in Paris by South Vietnam, North Vietnam, the Vietcong, and the United States on Jan. 27, 1973. It was never implemented, but the American withdrawal continued. In early 1975 South Vietnamese forces collapsed in the face of a series of North Vietnamese-Vietcong offensives. Remaining U.S. personnel were evacuated, and Saigon fell on Apr. 30, 1975. Hundreds of thousands of refugees ("boat people") fled the country over the next decade.

Following the fall of Saigon, the country was occupied by northern troops and administrators. Businesses were nationalized, agriculture collectivized, and tens of thousands of people sent to la-

bor camps for "reeducation." A unified National Assembly met in 1976, and the country was officially reunified on July 2, 1976, under the existing government of the north. Saigon was renamed Ho Chi Minh City. A Soviet naval base was established at the former U.S. base at Cam Ranh Bay.

In 1978 Vietnamese troops occupied Cambodia ousting the government of Pol Pot. In Feb.1979 China launched an unsuccessful attack over its border with Vietnam to display displeasure with the invasion of Cambodia and with the treatment of ethnic Chinese in Vietnam. In 1988 Vietnam pledged to withdraw its troops from Cambodia and completed the withdrawal in Sept. 1989.

Vietnam's communist government ruled through the party's powerful Central Committee; no strong personalities emerged to replace the leaders of the wartime generation. The economy was functioning only at a basic level, with the infrastructure in disrepair and agriculture hampered by excessive collectivization. The collapse of the Soviet Union brought about a drastic reduction of the Soviet aid that had kept the Vietnamese economy afloat. Facing economic ruin, Vietnam's leadership eventually turned a blind eye to individual private enterprise. By 1992 the government was encouraging foreign investment.

Resumption of contacts with the U.S. had been precluded by American insistence that Vietnam account more fully for American prisoners of war and troops missing in action. But high-level talks on the normalization of relations and the Cambodian question opened in 1990, and the success of those negotiations helped to open diplomatic channels between Vietnam and the U.S.

In 1994, Pres. Clinton, satisfied with Vietnam's efforts to account for POWs and MIAs, ended the 19-year U.S. trade embargo; the following day, American firms were operating in Ho Chi Minh City. In July 1995, full diplomatic relations were established and in October Vietnam's National Assembly adopted its first-ever national civil code under the Communist government. The document spelled out rights to land, personal property, inheritances, and raising capital. Close to 90 percent of the Assembly members voted in favor of the code.

In July 2000 the U.S. and Vietnam signed a far-reaching trade agreement. In April 2001, the Central Committee of the Communist Party appointed a new Secretary General, Nong Duc Manh, with the aim of modernizing the economy and ending corruption. By rumor, Nong is an illegitimate son of Ho Chi Minh. In Dec. 2001 Vietnam took two steps toward its goal of joining the W.T.O.: a trade agreement with the U.S. and the granting to private investors equal access to bank credit with the public sector. The Communists had no intention of easing their political control, however, was made clear by the May 2002 "elections" to the National Assembly in which the Communists carried 447 of 498 seats. In June 2005 Prime Minister Phan Van Khai became the first Vietnamese leader to be received by the White House.

The government leadership changed in 2006 and the economy began to expand rapidly. Economic liberalization continued and Vietnam joined the W.T.O. in 2007. By then it was second in economic growth only to China among Asian nations.

▶ **WESTERN SAMOA**
see "Samoa"

►YEMEN
Republic of Yemen
● **GEOGRAPHY Location:** southern shore of Arabian peninsula and southwest corner of Arabian peninsula. **Boundaries:** Saudi Arabia to N, Oman to E, Gulf of Aden to S, Red Sea to W. **Total area:** 203,850 sq. mi. (527,970 sq km). **Coastline:** 1,184 mi. (1,906 km). **Comparative area:** slightly larger than twice the size of Wyoming. **Land use:** 3% arable land; negl. % permanent crops; 97% other. **Major cities:** Sana'a (capital); Aden; Hodeida; Mukalla; Taiz.
● **PEOPLE Population:** 23,013,376 (July 2008 est.). **Nationality:** noun—Yemini(s); adjective—Yemeni. **Ethnic groups:** predominantly Arab; Afro-Arab concentrations in western coastal locations; South Asians in southern regions; small European communities in major metropolitan areas. **Languages:** Arabic. **Religions:** Muslim including Shaf'i (Sunni) and Zaydi (Shia), small numbers of Jewish, Christian, and Hindu.
● **GOVERNMENT Type:** republic. **Independence:** May 22, 1990 (merger of North and South Yemen). **Constitution:** May 16, 1991; amended Sept. 29, 1994 and Feb. 2001. **National holiday:** Proclamation of the Republic, May 22. **Heads of Government:** Ali Abdullah Saleh, president (since May 1994); Ali Mujawar, prime minister (since Apr. 2007). **Structure:** executive—president and cabinet; unicameral legislature; judicial—Supreme Court and lesser courts.
● **ECONOMY Monetary unit:** Yemeni rial. **Budget:** (2007 est.) *income:* $7.902 bil.; *expend:* $8.167 bil. **G.D.P.:** $52.61 bil., $2,400 per capita (2007 est.). **Chief crops:** grain, fruits, vegetables, qat, coffee, cotton; dairy products, poultry, meat; fish. **Natural resources:** petroleum, fish, rocksalt, marble, small deposits of coal. **Major industries:** crude oil, petroleum refining, cotton textiles and leather goods, food processing, handicrafts, aluminum products, cement. **Labor force:** 6.316 mil. (2007 est.)mostly agriculture and herding; also services, construction, industry, commerce. **Exports:** $7.586 bil. (f.o.b., 2007 est.); crude oil, cotton, coffee, dried and salted fish. **Imports:** $6.592 bil., (f.o.b., 2007 est.); food and live animals, machinery and equipment, manufactured goods. **Major trading partners:** (2006) *exports:* 31.4% China, 17.4% India, 16.7% Thailand, 7% South Korea, 6.7% U.S., 4.1% United Arab Emirates; *imports:* 16.4% United Arab Emirates, 12.8% China, 7.7% Saudi Arabia, 5.8% Kuwait, 4.5% Brazil, 4.2% Malaysia, 4% U.S.

Yemen—in ancient times Sheba or Saba—is strategically located in the southwestern corner of the Arabian peninsula, near the southern end of the Red Sea. In biblical times and for many centuries thereafter, Yemen dominated the caravan trade in spices, gold, and other luxury goods from India and Africa to the Middle East.

The Islamic unification of Arabia in 628 resulted in the incorporation of Yemen into Arabia as a whole, but many local uprisings broke out over the course of the following three centuries. In the 10th century, control passed to a line of Yemeni kings who were simultaneously imams of the Zaidi sect of Islam; the Zaidi imams ruled until 1962.

Aden was the most important port of the ancient kingdom of Sheba and retained that status under the Zaidi imams of Yemen. Portuguese activity around Aden began in the 15th century; from the mid-16th century, control of the port was disputed by the Portuguese, the Yemeni kings, the Ottoman Turks, and, later, the British.

In 1839, Aden was made a British Crown Colony; the Hadramaut region of southern Arabia, north and east of Aden, became the British Protectorate of Aden. The colony and protectorate were both administered as part of British India.

Yemen came under the control of the Ottoman Empire from the mid-16th to the mid-17th centuries, and again from 1849 to 1918. The Turks were expelled at the end of World War I, and Yemen became an independent kingdom in 1918. The kingdom's independence was threatened by a Saudi invasion in 1934 and by a 1954 dispute with Great Britain over the status of Aden, which was the key to British military power in the western Indian Ocean and Persian Gulf after India's independence in 1947.

Imam Ahmed came to the throne of Yemen in 1948, following the assassination of his predecessor. Most of Yemen's large Jewish population was evacuated to Israel in 1949-50. A palace coup against the imam in 1955 failed, but after his death in 1962, his successor was quickly ousted and the country was proclaimed the Yemen Arab Republic (North Yemen) under the leadership of Brig. Gen. Abdullah al-Salal.

A struggle for independence began in Aden and the protectorate in 1963, with two rival groups competing for power. The National Liberation Front (NLF) gained the upper hand over the Egyptian-backed Front for the Liberation of Occupied South Yemen, as both groups waged guerrilla war against the British. British forces withdrew in 1967, and South Yemen became independent. The nation's territory included Socotra and adjacent islands off the Horn of Africa, which had been British possessions since 1876.

In 1969 a leftist faction of the NLF seized power, nationalized key industries, and instituted a socialist regime. In the mid-1970's, South Yemeni troops aided leftist guerrillas in Oman, and fought in Ethiopia against Eritrean rebels. Subsequently Pres. Salem Robaye Ali took a more moderate stance and improved relations with Oman and Saudi Arabia. He was overthrown in a coup in June 1978 and executed. The succeeding government was overthrown on Jan. 13, 1986; on Feb. 8, Hasin Said Numan became prime minister.

In North Yemen, civil war between royalist and republican factions lasted until April 1970, when a coalition republican government was formed with the aid of Saudi mediation. Col. Ibrahim al-Hamidi came to power in a military coup in 1974; he was assassinated in 1977. Pres. Ali Abdullah Saleh assumed office in 1978, after the assassination of Pres. al-Gashmi.

Border skirmishes between North Yemen and South Yemen broke out during 1972-73. After several years of uneasy peace, South Yemen launched a full-scale war against the north on Feb. 24, 1979. Arab League pressure quickly led to a truce. Relations improved during the 1980's and North Yemen and South Yemen merged as the Republic of Yemen on May 22, 1990. Ali Abdullah Saleh, president of North Yemen, became the new country's president. San'a was proclaimed the capital of the United Yemen, though Aden remained its most important economic center.

The Gulf War forced the repatriation of tens of thousands of Yemeni workers from Kuwait and other Gulf states; later Saudi Arabia expelled 850,000 more to express its displeasure with Yemen's unenthusiastic stance toward the Gulf War. These repatriations deprived Yemen of a most important source of foreign exchange, and severely damaged the economy.

Yemen held its first general election since unification on Apr. 27, 1993, and a coalition government was formed. In Feb. 1994, fighting began and a full-scale civil war broke out in May. But in July the capture of Aden by government troops ended the conflict and Pres. Saleh has ruled in relative peace since. The first direct presidential electrion was held in Sept. 1999 but the Socialist Party was not allowed to field a candidate so Saleh won easily.

On Oct. 10, 2000, over 50,000 protested in Aden against U.S. support for Israel; two days later, the U.S. destroyer *Cole*, refueling in Aden, was attacked, leaving 17 dead and 39 wounded. The Saleh government permitted F.B.I. attendance at the questioning of witnesses; but the F.B.I. (and Navy) investigators became a new object of attack, by the terrorist "Islamic Army of Aden."

A sporadic insurgency threatens the Saleh government as it tries to cooperate with the huge U.S. military presence in the region.

▶YUGOSLAVIA (SEE SERBIA AND MONTENEGRO)

▶ZAIRE (SEE CONGO, DEMOCRATIC REPUBLIC)

▶ZAMBIA
Republic of Zambia
• **GEOGRAPHY** **Location:** landlocked country in southern central Africa. **Boundaries:** Zaire to N, Tanzania to NE, Malawi to E, Mozambique to SE, Zimbabwe to S, Namibia to SW, Angola to W. **Total area:** 290,583 sq. mi. (752,610 sq km). **Coastline:** none. **Comparative area:** slightly larger than Texas. **Land use:** 7% arable land; negl. % permanent crops; 93% other. **Major cities:** Lusaka (capital); Kitwe; Ndola; Kabwe.
• **PEOPLE** **Population:** 11,669,534 (July 2008 est.). **Nationality:** noun—Zambian(s); adjective—Zambian. **Ethnic groups:** 98.7% African, 1.1% European, 0.2% other. **Languages:** English (official), major vernaculars—Bemba, Kaonda, Lozi, Lunda, Luvale, Nyanja, Tonga, and about 70 indigenous languages. **Religions:** 50-75% Christian, 24-49% Muslim and Hindu, 1% indigenous beliefs.
  Government **Type:** republic. **Independence:** Oct. 24, 1964 (from U.K.). **Constitution:** Aug. 2, 1991. **National holiday:** Independence Day, Oct. 24. **Heads of Government:** Rupiah Banda, acting president (since Aug. 2008). **Structure:** executive—modified presidential system; legislative—unicameral National Assembly; judiciary.
• **ECONOMY** **Monetary unit:** kwacha. **Budget:** (2007 est.) *income:* $2.508 bil.; *expend.:* $2.838 bil. **G.D.P.:** $15.93 bil., $1,400 per capita (2007 est.). **Chief crops:** corn, sorghum, rice, peanuts, sunflower seed, tobacco, cotton, sugarcane, cassava; cattle, goats, pigs, poultry, beef, pork, milk, eggs, hides. **Natural resources:** copper, cobalt, zinc, lead, coal. **Major industries:** copper mining and processing, foodstuffs, construction. **Labor force:** 4.989 mil. (2007 est.) ; 85% agriculture, 9% services, 6% industry. **Exports:** $4.017 bil. (f.o.b., 2007 est.); copper, cobalt, zinc, lead, tobacco. **Imports:** $2.993 bil. (f.o.b., 2007 est.); machinery, transport equipment, foodstuffs, fuels, petroleum products, electricity. **Major trading partners:** (2006) *exports:* 38.4% Switzerland, 21.6% South Africa, 10.3% China, 7.6% U.K., 6.4% Tanzania; *imports:* 47.3% South Africa, 10.4% United Arab Emirates, 5.7% Zimbabwe, 4% Norway.

Bantu peoples—including Luba, Lunda, Ngoni, and others—moved into what is now Zambia between the 15th and the 19th centuries, displacing or absorbing aboriginal populations. Occasional Portuguese explorers from Angola and Mozambique entered the region, and Angolan slave-raiders were active in the late 18th and early 19th centuries, but serious European influence did not begin until the mid-19th century. At that time British missionaries and merchants arrived, most notably David Livingstone and Cecil Rhodes.

Local rulers granted mineral concessions to Rhodes in both Northern and Southern Rhodesia (now Zambia and Zimbabwe). Rhodesia was declared a British sphere of influence in 1888; a British protectorate was established in 1891 and enlarged in 1894-95. The borders of Northern Rhodesia were established in 1911. The country was administered by the British South Africa Co. until 1924, when direct colonial rule began. Large numbers of British settlers arrived and developed farms and ranches and mined the region's substantial copper deposits. A railroad was built linking Northern Rhodesia with Elizabethville in the Belgian Congo (now Lubumbashi, Zaire).

In 1953 Northern and Southern Rhodesia (Zimbabwe) were joined with Nyasaland (now Malawi) to form the Federation of Rhodesia and Nyasaland. The country entered a period of unrest with native peoples demanding greater participation in government, while white settlers clung to their privileged positions.

As the result of an election in 1962, the federation was dissolved. A National Assembly was created on the basis of a broader, multiracial electorate. Northern Rhodesia became independent as the Republic of Zambia on Oct. 24, 1964. Relations between Zambia and white-ruled Rhodesia became strained in 1965 in a dispute over ownership and administration of the railway that spanned both countries. A new constitution was promulgated in 1973, creating a stronger presidency and a unicameral legislature; the United National Independence party was made the sole legal political party. Opposition parties were allowed to form again starting in Dec. 1990.

Pres. Kenneth Kaunda, in office after Zambia's independence, led a moderate government that won the support of both whites and blacks. Zambia's economy did not fare well as the price of copper, the nation's main earner of foreign exchange, declined around the world causing massive foreign debt and labor unrest. The I.M.F. demanded reforms as a condition for future aid, and in 1987 Pres. Kaunda announced a program of economic restructuring. In 1990 his government survived an attempted coup precipitated by a doubling in the price of the staple food, maize meal.

At the end of 1991, Kaunda was defeated by Frederick Chiluba, head of the new Labor party. Chiluba's economic reforms helped Zambia repay more than $1.2 billion in outstanding debt, prompting the I.M.F. to restore its eligibility for international loans. But political problems resurfaced when Chiluba's government found a way to block Kaunda from winning in the 1996 presidential election. Kaunda was shot and wounded by a sniper in Aug. 1997 as he continued to criticize the government. In Oct. 1997 a failed coup attempt by army officers was blamed on Kaunda who was arrested in Dec. and put on trial. He was freed in June and all charges dropped on condition that he leave politics. In March 1999 Zambia's High Court declared him not a citizen. Pres. Chiluba honored his pledge not to run for re-election and the Dec. 2001 election was won by Levy Mwanawasa. The new president began a serious investigation into official corruption and Parliament stripped Chiluba of his immunity and he was arrested in Feb. 2003 on charges of stealing millions of dollars.

Mwanawasa was reelected in 2006 based on the economic stability he established. Foreign investment, especially from China, has helped the economy upward. Mwanawasa's death in June 2008 led to a call for elections in November.

▶ ZIMBABWE
Republic of Zimbabwe

• **GEOGRAPHY   Location:** landlocked country in southern Africa. **Boundaries:** Zambia to NW, Mozambique to E, South Africa to S, Botswana to SW. **Total area:** 150,803 sq. mi. (390,580 sq km). **Coastline:** none. **Comparative area:** slightly larger than Montana. **Land use:** 8% arable land; negl. % permanent crops; 91% other. **Major cities:** Harare (capital); Bulawayo; Chitungwiza; Mutare; Gweru.
• **PEOPLE   Population:** 12,382,920 (July 2008 est.). **Nationality:** noun—Zimbabwean(s); adjective—Zimbabwean. **Ethnic groups:** 98% African (82% Shona, 14% Ndebele, 2% other), 1% white, 1% mixed and Asian. **Languages:** English (official), Shona, Sindebele. **Religions:** 50% syncretic (part Christian, part indigenous beliefs), 25% Christian, 24% indigenous beliefs, 1% Muslim.
• **GOVERNMENT   Type:** parliamentary democracy. **Independence:** Apr. 18, 1980 (from U.K.). **Constitution:** Dec. 21, 1979. **National holiday:** Independence Day, Apr. 18. **Head of Government:** Robert Gabriel Mugabe, president (since Dec. 1987). **Structure:** executive—cabinet led by president; unicameral legislature—120 of 150 members are popularly elected, others appointed; judiciary.
• **ECONOMY   Monetary unit:** Zimbabwean dollar. **Budget:** (2007 est.) *income:* $1.105 bil.; *expend.:* $1.366 bil. **G.D.P.:** $6.186 bil., $500 per capita (2007 est.). **Chief crops:** tobacco, corn, tea, sugarcane, cotton, wheat, coffee, peanuts; cattle, sheep, goats, pigs. **Natural resources:** coal, chromium ore, asbestos, gold, nickel. **Major industries:** mining, steel, clothing and footwear. **Labor force:** 3.998 mil. (2007 est.); 80% unemployment (2005 est.). **Exports:** $1.76 bil. (f.o.b., 2007 est.); 23% tobacco, 14% gold, ferroalloys, cotton. **Imports:** $2.183 bil. (f.o.b., 2007 est.); 39% machinery and transport equipment, 18% manufactures, 15% chemicals, 10% fuels. **Major trading partners:** (2006) *exports:* 24.8% South Africa, 17.6% Democratic Republic of the Congo, 15.7% Botswana, 10.4% U.S.; *imports:* 40.8% South Africa, 29.6% Zambia, 4.9% U.S.

Massive stone structures at Great Zimbabwe give evidence of a sizable urban society that flourished from the ninth to the 13th centuries and dominated Iron Age trade in southeastern Africa. Bantu peoples migrated into the region beginning in the 15th century; the Mashona dominated until the early 19th century, when they were displaced by the Matebele.

Portuguese slave traders from Mozambique were active in Zimbabwe from the 16th to the mid-19th centuries. Mineral concessions were granted to Cecil Rhodes by local rulers in the late 19th century, and the region became a British protectorate in 1888. Salisbury (now Harare) was founded in 1890, and the territory comprising Zimbabwe and Zambia was named Rhodesia in 1895. Rhodesia was governed by the British South Africa Co. until 1923, when it was partitioned into Northern and Southern Rhodesia. Northern Rhodesia became a British colony; Southern Rhodesia, rejecting union with South Africa, became a self-governing (and white-ruled) state within the British Empire.

Southern Rhodesia had been heavily settled by whites from Great Britain, South Africa, and elsewhere, who developed extensive farms and ranches, forest products industries, and rich mines. The country prospered but with little native participation in government. In 1953 Northern Rhodesia, Southern Rhodesia, and Nyasaland were joined in the Federation of Rhodesia and Nyasaland. Increasing agitation for black participation in government, especially in the north and in Nyasaland, led to the dissolution of the federation in 1963; Northern Rhodesia subsequently became independent as Zambia, Nyasaland as Malawi. In 1961 Southern Rhodesia adopted a constitution that guaranteed the continuation of white rule. White resistance to black political demands led to the rise of the Rhodesian Front party, whose leader, Ian D. Smith, became prime minister of Rhodesia (formerly Southern Rhodesia). After British-led negotiations for a biracial political compromise broke down, the Smith government on Nov. 11, 1965, issued a unilateral declaration of independence, which was declared illegal and invalid by the British government. The U.N. condemned the Smith government and imposed economic sanctions, and in May 1968 voted to impose a trade embargo on Rhodesia.

In 1970 a new constitution effectively barred black participation in national politics. By 1974 mounting pressure from other African countries led the Smith government to enter into serious negotiations. Guerrilla warfare pitting black nationalist groups against white settlers and mercenaries raged sporadically, and many white settlers emigrated. A 1977 British-American proposal for majority rule provided the basis for a settlement. An "internal settlement" was announced in April 1978 by Smith and three major nationalist leaders: Bishop Abel Muzorewa, leader of the United African National Congress, the Rev. Ndabaningi Sithole, former leader of the Zimbabwe African National Union (ZANU), and Chief Jeremiah Chirau. The settlement was rejected by the Patriotic Front that united ZANU (now led by Robert Mugabe) and Joshua Nkomo's Zimbabwe African People's Union (ZAPU).

Elections were held in April 1979 and Bishop Muzorewa assumed office on June 1 as prime minister of "Zimbabwe-Rhodesia," but the Patriotic Front continued to oppose the government. On Dec. 10 the "Zimbabwe-Rhodesia" Parliament dissolved itself, and the country reverted briefly to British colonial rule. On Dec. 21 all parties agreed to a cease-fire and to a period of transitional British rule leading to independence.

Elections held in 1980 resulted in a clear majority for Mugabe's ZANU party. Zimbabwe became independent, with Mugabe as prime minister, on April 18. As Mugabe embarked on an ambitious program of national reconstruction, Nkomo became leader of the opposition. Guerrillas linked to ZAPU, with Nkomo's tacit leadership, continued to engage in sporadic warfare against Mugabe's government, and banditry disrupted the countryside. The elections of 1985 increased ZANU's majority in Parliament. In 1987 the constitution was amended to strengthen the presidency and to end the separate role of blacks and whites in government; new elections were held for black members of Parliament to fill seats formerly reserved for whites. Guerrillas renewed attacks on white-owned farms.

In Dec. 1987 Mugabe and Nkomo agreed to merge ZANU and ZAPU (ZANU-PF), creating a de facto one-party state under Mugabe. A presidential election was scheduled for 1996, but in 1995, the Rev. Ndonga Sithole, leader of the opposition Zimbabwe African National Union, was arrested and charged with plotting to kill Mugabe.

Amidst a fuel crisis, 60 percent inflation and 50 percent unemployment, Zimbabwe voters in Feb. 2000 rejected a new constitution granting Mugabe 12 more years and power to seize white farmlands without compensation. But, with government approval, squatters began seizing white farms and preventing the tobacco harvest (30 percent of Zimbabwe's export earnings). June elections gave 57 of 120 seats contested to the opposition, sufficient to block any plan for a new constitution. But throughout 2001 Mugabe continued his plan to seize white-owned farms and began to arrest his political opponents. Court-packing, press controls, prohibition of assemblages, banning of non-governmental election-monitors, arrests of opponents—all preceded March 2002 presidential

elections in which Mugabe claimed 1.7 million votes to 1.3 million for his principal opponent, Morgan Tsuangirai. Torture and rape by the army drove tens of thousands of Tsuangirai's supporters to flight. Mugabe seized further white farms amidst the worst famine in 60 years. A wave of arrests—over 300 members of opposition Movement for Democratic Change, including Tsuangirai, six members of Parliament—followed a weak attempt at a general strike in June 2003.

Unsurprisingly Mugabe easily won reelection in April 2005 and began a violent crackdown against thousands of poor urban dwellers, destroying their shanty-homes and sending them back to rural areas. Economic collapse seemed inevitable by mid-2007 with unemployment over 60 percent and the economy shrunk by half. Not surprisingly then the opposition party won the parliamentary elections in 2008, and their leader, Morgan Tsvangirai won the first round of presidential elections.

Selected Territories of the World

▶ AUSTRALIA

CHRISTMAS ISLAND
Location: eastern Indian Ocean;10°25'S, 105°39'E. **Total area:** 52 sq. mi. (135 sq km), about seven-tenths size of Washington, D.C. **Population:** 361 (July 2005 est.). **Type:** territory of Australia.

COCOS (KEELING) ISLANDS
Location: 27 islands in eastern Indian Ocean.West Island 12°05'S, 96°53'E. **Total area:** 5.4 sq. mi. (14.0 sq km), about 24 times size of the Mall in Washington, D.C. **Population:** 628 (2005 est.). **Type:** territory of Australia.

NORFOLK ISLAND
Location: island in western Pacific Ocean; 29°04'S, 167°57'E. **Total area:** 13.3 sq. mi. (34.6 sq km), about one-fifth size ofWashington, D.C. **Population:** 1,828 (2005 est.). **Type:** territory of Australia.

UNINHABITED TERRITORIES OF AUSTRALIA
Ashmore Is. (12°15'S, 123°05'E); Cartier Is. (12°30'S, 123°30'E); Coral Sea Is. (18°00'S, 158°00'E); Heard Is. (53°00'S, 73°35'E); McDonald Is. (52°29'S, 72°50'E).

▶ DENMARK

FAEROE ISLANDS
Location: group of 18 islands (17 inhabited) in Atlantic Ocean SE of Iceland. Tórshavn 62°02'N, 6°47'W. **Total area:** 541 sq. mi. (1,399 sq km), eight times size of Washington, D.C. **Population:** 46,962 (2005 est.).**Type:** self-governing

GREENLAND
Location: North Atlantic Ocean, largely within Arctic Circle. Godthåb 64°11'N, 51°44'W. **Total area:** 840,000 sq.mi. (2,175,600 sq km); land area 131,931 sq. mi. (341,700 sq km) ice free, slightly more than three times size of Texas. **Population:** 56,375 (2005 est.). **Type:** parliamentary democracy with constitutional monarch.

▶ FRANCE

FRENCH GUIANA
Location: NE coast of South America. **Total area:** 35,135 sq. mi. (91,000 sq km), slightly smaller than Indiana. **Population:** 195,506 (2005 est.). **Type:** overseas department of France.

FRENCH POLYNESIA
Location: five island groups or archipelagoes—Gambier, Marquesas, Society (includes Tahiti and Bora Bora),Tuamotu, and Tubuai (Austral Islands)—in South Pacific Ocean about halfway between South America and Australia. Papeete (Society Is.) 17°32'S, 149°34'W. **Total area:** 2,589 sq. mi. (4,167 sq km), slightly less than one third size of Connecticut. **Population:** 270,485 (2005 est.). **Type:** overseas territory of France.

GUADELOUPE
Location: eastern Caribbean Sea: Guadeloupe 16°00'N, 61°42'W; St. Barthélemy 17°55'N, 63°50'W; Marie Galante 15°57'N, 61°20'W. **Total area:** 687 sq.mi. (1,780 sq km),10 times size of Washington, D.C. **Population:** 448,713 (2005 est.). **Type:** overseas department of France.

NEW CALEDONIA
Location: one large and several smaller islands in western South Pacific. Nouméa 22°16'S, 166°26'E. **Total area:** 7,359 sq. mi. (19,060 sq km), slightly smaller than New Jersey. **Population:** 216,494 (2005 est.). **Type:** overseas territory of France.

MARTINIQUE
Location: eastern Caribbean Sea (14°36'N,. 61°05'W). **Total area:** 425 sq.mi. (1,100 sq km), slightly more than six times size of Washington, D.C. **Population:** 432,900 (2005 est.). **Type:** overseas department of France.

MAYOTTE
Location: Comoros archipelago in eastern Indian Ocean (12°47'S, 45°12'E).**Total area:** 145 sq. mi. (375 sq km), slightly more than twice size ofWashington, D.C. **Population:** 193,633 (2005 est.). **Type:** territorial collectivity of France.

ST. PIERRE AND MIQUELON
Location: North Atlantic off east coast of Canada. St. Pierre 46°46'N, 56°12'W. **Total area:** 93 sq.mi. (242 sq km),1.5 times size of Washington, D.C. **Population:** 7,012 (2005 est.). **Type:** territorial collectivity of France.

WALLIS AND FUTUNA
Location: two island groups (Wallis to NE, Hooru, incl. Futuna Is., to SW) in South Pacific. Mata-Utu (Wallis group) 13°22'S, 176°12'W. **Total area:** 106 sq.mi. (274 sq km). **Population:** 16,025 (2005 est.). **Type:** overseas territory of France.

UNINHABITED TERRITORIES OF FRANCE
Bassas da India (21°25'S, 39°42'E); Clipperton Is. (10°21'N, 109°13'W); Europa Is. (22°20'S, 40°22'E); French Southern and Antarctic Lands (Kerguelen Is. 49°20'S, 69°30'E); Glorioso Is. (11°30'S, 47°20'E); Tromelin Is. (15°52'S, 54°25'E).

▶ MOROCCO
WESTERN SAHARA
Location: northwestern coast of Africa. **Total area:** 102,703 sq. mi. (266,000 sq km), about the size of Colorado. **Population:** 273,008 (2005 est.). **Type:** legal status and sovereignty still unresolved.

▶ NETHERLANDS
ARUBA
Location: southern Caribbean Sea (12°32'N, 70°02'W), off NW Venezuela. **Total area:** 75 sq. mi. (193 sq km), slightly larger than Washington, D.C. **Population:** 71,566 (2005 est.). **Type:** Part of the Netherlands, but full autonomy in internal affairs obtained in 1986 upon separation from Netherlands Antilles; parliamentary democracy.
NETHERLANDS ANTILLES
Location: two island groups in Caribbean Sea, about 500 mi. (800 km) apart. **Total area:** 371 sq. mi. (960 sq km), more than 5 times size of Washington, D.C. **Population:** 219,958 (2005 est.). **Type:** autonomous part of Netherlands; parliamentary.

▶ NEW ZEALAND
COOK ISLANDS
Location: 15 islands (13 inhabited) in South Pacific. Avarua 21°12'S, 159° 46'W. **Total area:** 93 sq. mi. (240 sq km). **Population:** 21,388 (2005 est.). **Type:** self-governing parliamentary democracy in free association with New Zealand; Cook Islands government is fully responsible for internal affairs and has right at any time to move to full independence by unilateral action; New Zealand responsible for external affairs, in consultation with Cook Islands government.
NIUE
Location: coral island in western South Pacific (19°02'S, 169°55'W). **Total area:** 100 sq.mi. (260 sq km), 1.5 times size of Washington, D.C. **Population:** 2,166 (2005 est.). **Type:** self-governing parliamentary democracy territory in free association with New Zealand.
TOKELAU
Location: three atolls (Atafu, Nukunonu, Fakaofo) in South Pacific. Atafu 8°33'S, 172°30'W. **Total area:** 4 sq. mi. (10 sq km), about 17 times size of the Mall in Washington, D.C. **Population:** 1,405 (2005 est.). **Type:** territory of New Zealand.

▶ NORWAY
SVALBARD
Location: nine large and numerous smaller islands in Arctic Ocean. **Total area:** 38,557 sq. mi. (62,049 sq km), slightly smaller than West Virginia. **Population:** 2,701 (2005 est.). **Type:** territory of Norway.
UNINHABITED TERRITORIES OF NORWAY
Bouvet Is. (54°26'S, 3°24'E); Jan Mayen Is. (71°00'N, 8°30'W).

▶ UNITED KINGDOM
ANGUILLA
Location: island in northeastern Caribbean (18°03'N, 63°04'W). **Total area:** 35 sq.mi. (91 sq km), about one-half size of Washington,D.C. **Population:** 13,254 (2005 est.). **Type:** dependent territory of U.K.

BERMUDA
Location: archipelago of about 150 islands, in southernNorth Atlantic Ocean (32° 18'N, 64°47'W). **Total area:** 19 sq. mi. (50 sq km), about three-tenths size of Washington, D.C. **Population:** 65,365 (2005 est.). **Type:** British dependent territory.
BRITISH VIRGIN ISLANDS
Location: more than 40 mountainous islands (15 inhabited) in northeastern Caribbean. City of Road Town (on Tortola Is.), 18°26'N, 64°32'W. **Total area:** 58 sq.mi. (150 sq km), 0.9 times the size of Washington, D.C. **Population:** 22,643 (2005 est.). **Type:** dependent territory of U.K.
GIBRALTAR
Location: narrow peninsula running southward from southwest coast of Spain, to which it is connected by an isthmus. **Total area:** 3 sq.mi. (6.5 sq km), about 11 times size of the Mall in Washington, D.C. **Population:** 27,884 (2005 est.). **Type:** colony of U.K.
MONTSERRAT
(Two years of volcanic eruptions have left the southern half of this small island covered with ash and rock. More than half of its population had fled by mid-1997) **Location:** eastern Caribbean Sea (16°44'N, 62°14'W). **Total area:** 39 sq. mi. (100 sq km), about three-fifths size of Washington, D.C. **Population:** 9,341 (2005 est.); an estimated 8,000 refugees left the island following volcanic activity in 1995; some have returned. **Type:** colony of U.K.
CAYMAN ISLANDS
Location: three main and numerous smaller islands in western Caribbean. George Town (Grand Cayman Is.) 19°20'N, 81°23'W. **Total area:** 100 sq. mi. (260 sq km), 1.5 times size of Washington, D.C. **Population:** 44,270 (2005 est.). **Type:** British dependent territory.
FALKLAND ISLANDS
Location: two large and about 2,000 smaller islands in southwestern Atlantic Ocean. Stanley (East Falkland) 51°45'S, 57° 56'W. **Total area:** 4,699 sq. mi. (12,173 sq km), slightly smaller than Connecticut. **Population:** 2,967 (2005 est.). **Type:** colony of U.K.
PITCAIRN ISLANDS
Location: group of islands (one inhabited) in South Pacific. Pitcairn 25°04'S 130°04'W. **Total area:** 18 sq. mi. (47 sq km), three-tenths size of Washington, D.C. **Population:** 46 (2005 est.). **Type:** colony of U.K.
ST. HELENA
Location: eastern South Atlantic (15°56'S, 5°43'W). Dependencies are Ascension Is. (7°56'S, 14°25'W) 700 mi. to NW, and Tristan da Cunha (37°05'S, 12°17'W) 1,500 mi to SSW. **Total area:** 158 sq. mi. (410 sq km), slightly more than two times size ofWashington, D.C. **Population:** 7,460 (2005 est.). **Type:** dependent territory of U.K.
TURKS AND CAICOS ISLANDS
Location: more than 30 islands forming southeastern end of Bahamas Islands in Caribbean Sea. **Total area:** 166 sq.mi. (430 sq km), 2.5 times size of Washington, D.C. **Population:** 20,556 (2005 est.). **Type:** colony of U.K.
UNINHABITED TERRITORIES OF THE UNITED KINGDOM
British Indian Ocean Territory (Diego Garcia 6°34'S, 72°24'E); South Georgia Is. (54°15'S, 36°45'W); South Orkney Is. (60°35'S, 45°30'W); South Sandwich Is. (56°00'S, 26°30'W); South Shetland Is. (62°00'S, 58°00'W).

The United Nations

▶STRUCTURE

Establishment Pres. Franklin D. Roosevelt coined the name "United Nations," which was first used in the "Declaration by United Nations" of Jan. 1, 1942, during World War II, when representatives of 26 countries pledged their governments to continue fighting together against the Axis Powers. From August to October 1944, representatives of China, the Soviet Union, the United Kingdom and the United States met at Dumbarton Oaks, a mansion in Washington, D.C., to discuss creating an international peacekeeping organization. Out of these meetings came a general outline for the United Nations.

At the United Nations Conference on International Organization, which met at San Francisco from Apr. 25 to June 26, 1945, representatives from 50 countries drew up the United Nations Charter and signed it on June 26, 1945. Poland, not present at the Conference, signed on October 15, 1945, and is considered one of the founding member states.

The United Nations officially came into existence on October 24, 1945, when the charter was ratified by China, France, the Soviet Union, the United Kingdom, and the United States and by a majority of the other signatories.

U.N. Charter Full text of the Charter may be purchased for $3.00 from the United Nations, Sales Section, New York, NY 10017 U.S. The Preamble to the Charter sets forth the hopes for the United Nations: WE THE PEOPLES OF THE UNITED NATIONS DETERMINED

- to save succeeding generations from the scourge of war . . .
- to reaffirm faith in fundamental human rights, in the dignity and worth of the human person, in the equal rights of men and women and of nations large and small . . .
- to establish conditions under which justice and respect for the obligations arising from treaties and other sources of international law can be maintained . . .
- to promote social progress and better standards of life in larger freedom.

AND FOR THESE ENDS

- to practice tolerance and live together in peace with one another as good neighbors
- to unite our strength to maintain international peace and security
- to ensure, by the acceptance of principles and the institution of methods, that armed force shall not be used, save in the common interest
- to employ international machinery for the promotion of the economic and social advancement of all peoples.

HAVE RESOLVED TO COMBINE OUR EFFORTS TO ACCOMPLISH THESE AIMS. Accordingly, our respective Governments, through representatives assembled in the city of San Francisco, who have exhibited their full powers found to be in good and due form, have agreed to the present Charter of the United Nations and do hereby establish an international organization to be known as the United Nations.

Purposes The purposes of the United Nations are set forth in Article 1 of the Charter. They are: 1. To maintain international peace and security. 2. To develop friendly relations among nations based on respect for the principle of equal rights and self-determination of peoples. 3. To cooperate in solving international problems of an economic, social, cultural or humanitarian character, and in promoting respect for human rights and fundamental freedoms for all. 4. To be a center for harmonizing the actions of nations in the attainment of these common ends.

Official languages Originally, there were five official languages of the United Nations: Chinese, English, French, Russian and Spanish. Arabic was added to the General Assembly in 1973, to the Security Council in 1982 and to the Economic and Social Council in 1983. Major United Nations documents and all meetings of the General Assembly, the Security Council and the Economic and Social Council are translated into the six working languages.

United Nations headquarters United Nations, New York, NY 10017 U.S. U.N. headquarters covers a 16-acre site in New York City along the East River from 42nd to 48th Streets. It consists of the interconnected General Assembly, Secretariat and Dag Hammarskjöld Library buildings. Acquisition of the site was made possible by a gift of $8.5 million from John D. Rockefeller, Jr., and one-third of that amount from New York City. In 1951, the 39-story Secretariat building was completed and began functioning as the official home of the United Nations.

Permanent observers to the U.N. at New York headquarters cannot vote and do not have diplomatic privileges or immunities unless connected to the member nation's consulate. They do have free access to the public meetings and distribution of relevant documentation.

Non-member observers are the Holy See and Switzerland.

Intergovernmental and observer organizations: More than 25 organizations have observer status at the U.N. Following is a representative sample: Caribbean Community; Commonwealth of Independent States; Council of Europe; International Federation of Red Cross and Red Crescent Societies; League of Arab States; Organization of African Unity; Organization of American States; Organization of Islamic Conference; Palestine.

PRINCIPAL ORGANS

General Assembly

The Assembly is the world's forum for discussing major issues facing the international community including world peace and security, human rights, global environment, disarmament, health issues including AIDS, and the rights of women and children.

The Assembly consists of all 192 member states, each having one vote. On important issues a two-thirds majority of those present and voting is required; other questions require a simple majority vote. It holds its annual session from September to December, and may call for extra sessions as needed. Its agenda of more than 150 matters for discussion is first dealt with in six main committees: Its agenda of more than 150 matters for discussion is first dealt with in six main committees: First Committee: Disarmament and International Security; Second Committee: Economic and Financial; Third Committee: Social, Humanitarian and Cultural; Fourth Committee: Special Political and De-colonization; Fifth Committee: Administrative and Budgetary; Sixth Committee: Legal. After discussing issues facing the world, it adopts recommendations (called resolutions) but has no power to enforce its decisions (resolutions), except the power of world opinion.

The Assembly considers and approves U.N. budget and assesses member states according to their ability to pay.

Security Council
The Council may investigate any dispute or situation that might lead to international friction, and may recommend methods for adjusting such disputes or terms for their settlement. While other organs of the U.N. make recommendations to governments, the Security Council alone has the power to take decisions that member states are obligated under the Charter to carry out.

The Security Council has 15 members: five permanent members, and the General Assembly elects 10 other members for two-year terms. They are not eligible for immediate re-election. The Council may be called into session at any time, and a representative of each member state must be present at U.N. headquarters at all times.

The five permanent members are China, France, Russia, the United Kingdom and the United States.

The terms of office of each non-permanent member ends on December 31 of the year indicated in parentheses: Belgium (2008), Burkina Faso (2009), Costa Rica (2009), Croatia (2009), Indonesia (2008), Italy (2008), Libya (2009), Panama (2008), South Africa (2008), Vietnam (2009).

Decisions on matters of procedure require the approval of at least nine of the 15 members. Decisions on all other matters also require nine votes, including the concurring votes of all five permanent members. A negative vote by any permanent member on a non-procedural matter is often referred to as the "veto," which results in the rejection of the proposal. A state that is involved in a dispute may not vote.

Economic and Social Council (ECOSOC)
The Council is the principal organ to co-ordinate the economic and social work of the U.N. and its specialized agencies. It makes recommendations and initiates activities relating to world trade, industrialization, natural resources, human rights, the status of women, population, social welfare, education, health and related matters, science and technology and many other economic and social questions.

ECOSOC has 54 members elected for three-year terms by the General Assembly.

International Court of Justice (World Court)
The Court is the judicial organ of the U.N. and sits in The Hague, Netherlands. All U.N. member states are automatically members of the Court. One country that is not a member of the U.N. is party to the Court–Switzerland. The Court is not open to individuals. It issues judgments on all questions that states refer to it and all matters provided for in the U.N. Charter or in treaties or conventions in force. Both the General Assembly and the Security Council can ask the Court for an advisory opinion on any legal question as can other organs of the U.N. or specialized agencies, when authorized to do so by the Assembly.

The Court has dealt with a wide variety of subjects, including territorial rights, the delimitation of territorial waters and continental shelves, fishing jurisdiction, questions of nationality and the right of individuals to asylum, territorial sovereignty, and the right of passage through foreign territory.

The judgment of the Court is final and without appeal. However, a revision may be applied for within ten years from the date of the judgment on the ground of a new decisive factor. If a party rejects the judgment, the other party may take the issue to the Security Council.

Judges: The ICJ has 15 independent judges, of different nationalities, elected by both the General Assembly and the Security Council. Judges hold 9-year terms and may be re-elected. All questions are decided by a majority of the judges present; the president votes only in case of a tie.

Secretariat
The Secretariat services the other organs of the U.N. and administers the programs and policies they develop. Headed by the Secretary-General, it consists of an international staff of more than 25,000 men and women from over 150 countries.

Secretaries-General: The General Assembly elects the Secretary-General to terms of office of five years (they may be re-elected). The Secretary-General, by tradition, does not come from one of the permanent member states of the Security Council–China, France, Russia, UK or the U.S. Those who have served in this post are:

Trygve Lie, Norway, Feb. 1, 1946, to Nov. 10, 1952;

Dag Hammarskjöld, Sweden, Apr. 11, 1953, to Sept. 17, 1961;

U Thant, Burma, Nov. 3, 1961, to Dec. 31, 1971;

Kurt Waldheim, Austria, Jan. 1, 1972, to Dec. 31, 1981;

Javier Perez de Cuellar, Peru Jan. 1, 1982 to Dec. 31, 1991;

Boutros Boutros-Ghali, Egypt, Jan. 1, 1992, to Dec. 31, 1996;

Kofi Annan, Ghana, Jan. 1, 1997 to Dec. 31, 2006.

Ban Ki-Moon, South Korea, Jan. 1, 2007 to present.

▶UNITED NATIONS PROGRAMS
Each U.N. program was created by the General Assembly and reports to it through the Economic and Social Council (ECOSOC). Each member of the U.N. is a member of each Program.

International Research and Training Institute for the Advancement of Women (INSTRAW) Estab.: 1979 (made U.N. program in 1985); **HQ:** Calle Cesar Nicolas Penson, 102-A, Santo Domingo, Dominican Republic. Carries out research, training and information activities worldwide to show and increase women's key role in development.

United Nations Centre for Human Settlements (Habitat) Estab.: 1978; **HQ:** P.O. Box 30030, Nairobi, Kenya. Works to provide models and tools so people can improve their housing. Major concerns are planning, financing and management of human settlements—especially in developing countries.

United Nations Children's Fund (UNICEF) Estab.: 1946; **HQ:** UNICEF House, Three United Nations Plaza, New York, NY 10017, U.S. Provides care for children in developing countries by providing low-cost community-based services in maternal and child health, immunization, breast-feeding, growth monitoring, nutrition, clean water and sanitation, and education.

United Nations Conference on Trade and Development (UNCTAD) Estab.: 1964; **HQ:** Place des Nations, 8-14, Av. de la Paix, 1211 Geneva 10, Switzerland. Works to bring developing countries into global trade by formulating international trade policies, mediating multilateral trade agreements and providing assistance to governments.

United Nations Development Programme (UNDP) Estab.: 1965; **HQ:** One United Nations Plaza, New York, NY 10017, U.S. Coordinates development activities within the U.N. Operates more than 5,000 pro-

U.S. Representatives to the U.N.

The U.S. representative to the U.N. holds the title of Ambassador Extraordinary and Plenipotentiary Permanent Representative and heads the U.S. Mission to the U.N.

Year	Ambassador
1946	Edward R. Stettinius, Jr.
1946–47	Herschel V. Johnson (acting)
1947–53	Warren R. Austin
1953–60	Henry Cabot Lodge, Jr.
1960–61	James J. Wadsworth
1961–65	Adlai E. Stevenson
1965–68	Arthur J. Goldberg
1968	George W. Ball
1968–69	James Russell Wiggins
1969–71	Charles W. Yost
1971–73	George H.W. Bush
1973–75	John A. Scali
1975–76	Daniel P. Moynihan
1976–77	William W. Scranton
1977–79	Andrew Young
1979–81	Donald McHenry
1981–85	Jeane J. Kirkpatrick
1985–89	Vernon A. Walters
1989–92	Thomas J. Pickering
1992–93	Edward J. Perkins
1993–96	Madeleine K. Albright
1997–98	Bill Richardson
1999–2001	Richard C. Holbrooke
2001–2004	John D. Negroponte
2004–2005	John C. Danforth
2005–2007	John R. Bolton
2007-present	Dr. Zalmay Khalilzad

jects in 150 countries and territories to facilitate development in economic and social sectors, including: farming, fishing, forestry, mining, manufacturing, power, transport, communications, housing, trade, health and environmental sanitation, economic planning and public administration.

United Nations Environment Programme (UNEP) Estab.: 1972; **HQ:** United Nations Avenue, Gigiri,P.O. Box 30552, Nairobi, Kenya. Coordinates international environment issues, including international environment conventions, monitors significant changes in environment and coordinates sound environmental practices.

United Nations Fund for Population Activities (UNFPA) Estab.: 1969; **HQ:** 220 E. 42nd Street, New York, NY 10017, U.S. Provides assistance to population programs in developing countries; promotes understanding of key population factors: population growth, fertility, mortality, spatial distribution and migration.

Office of the United Nations High Commissioner for Refugees (UNHCR) Estab.: 1950; **HQ:** Case Postale 2500, CH-1211 Geneve 2 Depot, Switzerland. Provides food, clothing and shelter for refugees and works with governments to establish safe conditions whereby refugees may return home and, when that is not possible, seeks to ensure that refugees receive asylum.

United Nations Institute for Training and Research (UNITAR) Estab: 1965; **HQ:** Palais des Nations, CH1211 Geneva 10, Switzerland. Provides training for members of U.N.'s permanent missions, including courses on international economics, workshops on drafting and negotiating international legal instruments, dispute settlement, and training on peace, security, human rights and humanitarian assistance.

United Nations University (UNU) Estab.: 1973; **HQ:** 53-70 Jingumae 5-chome, Shibuya-ku, Tokyo 150, Japan. UNU has no students of its own, no campus and no faculty. It is an international community of scholars engaged in research operating through worldwide networks of academic research institutions.

World Food Council (WFC) Estab.: 1974; **HQ:** Via delle Terme di Caracalla, 00100 Rome, Italy. Encourages developing countries to adopt a national food strategy whereby they assess their food situation needs, supply, potential for increasing production, storage, processing, transportation and distribution.

World Food Programme (WFP) (Joint program operated by U.N. and Food and Agriculture Organization (FAO) **Estab.:** 1963; **HQ:** Via C.G.Viola 68/70, Parco dei Medici, 00148 Rome, Italy. Provides food to support development activities and in times of emergencies. Operates projects in forestry, soil erosion control, irrigation, land rehabilitation and rural settlements.

▶SPECIALIZED AGENCIES OF THE U.N.

The specialized agencies associated with the United Nations are self-governing, independent organizations that work with the U.N. system and each other through the coordination machinery of the Economic and Social Council (ECOSOC). Each country affiliates with each agency on an individual basis. Membership in an agency is separate from U.N. membership. Nongovernmental organizations (NGOs) having expertise in the area may affiliate with each agency on a separate basis.

Food and Agriculture Organization of the United Nations (FAO) Member States: 189; **Estab.:** Oct. 16, 1945; **HQ:** Via delle Terme di Caracalla, 00100 Rome, Italy. Works to increase output of farmlands, forests and fisheries and to raise nutritional levels. Co-sponsors World Food Programme, which uses food, cash and services donated by member states for emergency situations.

International Atomic Energy Agency (IAEA) Member States: 144; **Estab.:** July 29, 1957; **HQ:** Vienna International Centre, P.O. Box 100, A-1400 Vienna, Austria. (Not regular specialized agency in that it does not report through ECOSOC but directly to General Assembly.) Fosters and guides development of peaceful uses of atomic energy, establishes standards for nuclear safety and environmental protection, aids member countries through technical cooperation, and fosters exchange of information on nuclear energy.

International Civil Aviation Organization (ICAO) Member States: 190; **Estab.:** Apr. 4, 1947; **HQ:** 999 University Street, Montreal, Quebec H3C 5H7, Canada. Works for safer air travel conditions worldwide. Establishes visual and instrument flight rules for pilots and crews; develops aeronautical charts for navigation; co-ordinates aircraft radio frequencies and works with customs procedures.

International Fund for Agricultural Development (IFAD) Member States: 164; **Estab.:** Nov. 30, 1977; **HQ:** Via del Serafico 107, 00142 Rome, Italy. Lends money to peoples in developing countries for agricultural development projects, including livestock, fisheries, processing and storage, irrigation, research and training.

International Labor Organization (ILO) Member States: 175; **Estab.:** 1919, under the Treaty of Versailles; (became U.N. specialized agency Dec. 14, 1946);. **HQ:** 4, route des Morillons, CH-1211 Geneva 22, Switzerland. Promotes social justice for working people everywhere by formulating international policies and programs to help improve working and living conditions; creates international labor standards as guidelines for governments and assists in vocational training, management techniques, occupational safety and health.

International Maritime Organization (IMO) Member States: 167; **Estab.**: Mar. 17, 1958; **HQ**: 4 Albert Embankment, London SE1 SR, England. Works to improve international shipping procedures and encourages highest standards in maritime safety; seeks to prevent and control marine pollution from ships and sets standards for training and certification of seafarers.

International Telecommunication Union (ITU) Member States: 191; **Estab.**: 1865, it became a U.N. specialized agency in Jan. 1949; **HQ**: Place des Nations, 1211 Geneva 20, Switzerland. Coordinates use of radio frequencies, tracks positions assigned by countries to geostationary satellites; coordinates modem and Internet standards.

United Nations Educational, Scientific and Cultural Organization (UNESCO) Member States: 192; **Estab.**: Nov. 4, 1946; **HQ**: 7, Place de Fontenoy, 75007 Paris, France. Promotes literacy through teacher training, building schools, and developing textbooks. Natural science programs include Man and the Biosphere and Intergovernmental Oceanographic Commission. Undertakes study and development of cultures, and conservation of world's inheritance of books, art and monuments.

United Nations Industrial Development Organization (UNIDO) Member States: 172; **Estab.**: 1966 (became U.N. specialized agency Jan. 1, 1986); **HQ**: P.O. Box 300, A-1400 Vienna, Austria. Promotes and accelerates industrialization of developing countries by providing technical assistance, training programs and advisory services.

Universal Postal Union (UPU) Member States: 191; **Estab.**: July 1, 1875 (became U.N. specialized agency July 1, 1948); **HQ**: International Bureau, Case postale 13, 3000 Berne 15, Switzerland. Establishes regulations for smooth exchange of mail worldwide.

World Bank Group Group of five closely related institutions. **HQ**: 1818 H Street, N.W., Washington, D.C. 20433 *International Bank for Reconstruction and Development (IBRD)* **Member States**: 185; **Estab.**: Dec. 27, 1945, to provide loans and technical assistance to developing countries to assist in their reconstruction and development. *International Finance Corporation (IFC)* **Member States:** 179 (Membership is open only to World Bank members.); **Estab.:** July 20, 1956, to stimulate flow of private capital into productive investment in member countries. While closely associated with Bank, IFC is separate legal entity and its funds are distinct from those of Bank. *International Development Association (IDA)* **Member States**: 166; **Estab.**: Sept. 24, 1960. (Affiliate of the Bank, IDA has same directors and staff as Bank.) Lends money to poor countries with interest-free credits. Financial resources are from contributions by donor governments. *Multilateral Investment Guarantee Agency (MIGA)* **Member States**: 171; **Estab.**: 1988. Augments capacity of other insurers through coinsurance or reinsurance, thereby insuring investment in countries restricted or excluded by policies of other insurers.

International Monetary Fund (IMF) Member States: 185; **Estab.**: Dec. 27, 1945; **HQ**: 700 19th Street, N.W., Washington, D.C. 20431. Makes financing available to members in balance-of-payments difficulties and provides technical assistance and training to improve their economic management.

World Health Organization (WHO) Member States: 193; **Estab.**: April 7, 1948; **HQ**: 20, avenue Appia, 1211 Geneva 27, Switzerland. Coordinates programs aimed at solving health problems by working with governments, other U.N. agencies and non-governmental organizations. See "World Health" section.

World Intellectual Property Organization (WIPO) Member States: 184; **Estab.**: 1883, (became U.N. specialized agency Dec. 17, 1974); **HQ**: 34, chemin des Colombettes, 121 Geneva 20, Switzerland. Promotes protection of intellectual property and cooperation in enforcement of agreements on matters such as copyrights, trademarks, industrial designs and patents.

World Meteorological Organization (WMO) Member States: 182; **Estab.**: 1873, (became U.N. specialized agency Mar. 23, 1950); **HQ**: 7 bis Avenue de la Paix, CP 2300, 1211 Geneva 2, Switzerland. Facilitates exchange of weather reports among countries; "World Weather Watch" tracks global weather conditions.

World Tourism Group (WTO) Member States: 150. **Estab.:** 1970; **HQ:** Capitan Haya 42, 28020 Madrid, Spain. Serves as a global forum for tourism policy issues and a practical source of tourism know-how.

▶PEACEKEEPING OPERATIONS

United Nations peacekeeping is the use of multinational forces, under U.N. command, to keep disputing countries or communities from fighting while efforts are made to help them negotiate a solution. It is undertaken only with the agreement of both hostile parties. United Nations Peacekeeping Forces received the Nobel Peace Prize in 1988. As of April 2008, the U.N. had approximately 110,000 personnel in 17 peacekeeping operations consisting of more than 77,000 were troops and military observers, about 11,000 were police personnel, more than 5,000 international civilian personnel, 12,000 local civilian staff and some 2,000 UN Volunteers from over 160 nations. The UN increasingly works in peacekeeping partnerships with other international and regional organizations, such as the African Union (AU) or the European Union (EU). In 2007 UN peacekeeping operated 20 military hospitals and over 230 medical clinics; more than 18,000 vehicles and 210 aircraft, 450 satellite earth stations, 40,000 desktop computers and 2,800 servers, with approximately 3.5 million emails and 2.5 million phone calls routed every month (approximately 1 per second) and an average of 200 video conferences per month. The approved budget for 1 July 2007 to 30 June 2008 is approximately US$6.8 billion. Strength of the following operations is as of April or May 2008.

Africa

African Union/United Nations Hybrid operation in Darfur — UNAMID. Since July 2007. Joint African Union/United Nations Hybrid operation in Darfur to support implementation of Darfur Peace Agreement. **Strength:** 9,563 total uniformed personnel: 7,605 troops, 154 military observers, 1,804 police officers, 446 international civilian personnel, 741 local civilian staff and 148 United Nations Volunteers.

Chad — United Nations Mission in the Central African Republic and Chad — MINURCAT. Since September 2007. In concert with European Union to help create security conditions conducive to a voluntary, secure and sustainable return of refugees and displaced persons. Troop strength not available.

Democratic Republic of the Congo–MONUC– U.N. Organization Mission in the Democratic Republic of the Congo. Since December 1991. Implements

Lusaka Ceasefire agreement. **Strength:** 18,428 total uniformed personnel: 16,66 troops, 699 military observers, 1,063 police; supported by 939 international civilian personnel, 2,110 local civilian staff and 590 UN Volunteers.

Ethiopia and Eritrea – UNMEE – U.N. Mission in Ethiopia and Eritrea. Since July 2000. Monitors cease-fire and assists in observance of security commitments. **Strength:** 328 total uniformed personnel: 240 troops and 81 military observers, 151 international civilian personnel, 194 local civilian staff and 61 United Nations Volunteers.

Ivory Coast – UNOCI – U.N. Operation in Ivory Coast. Since April 2004. A political mission to facilitate implementation by the Ivorian parties of the peace agreement signed by them in Jan. 2003. **Strength:** 9,174 total uniformed personnel: 7,833 troops, 189 military observers; 1,152 police; supported by 406 international civilian personnel, 577 local staff and 295 UN Volunteers.

Liberia – UNMIL – U.N. Mission in Liberia. Since September 2003. Supports the implementation of the ceasefire agreement and the peace process. **Strength:** 3,934 total uniformed personnel: 11,588 troops and 201 military observers; 1,146 police; supported by 506 international civilian personnel, 933 local staff and 245 UN Volunteers.

Sudan – UNMIS – U.N. Mission in the Sudan. Since March 2005. Supports implementation of Comprehensive Peace Agreement signed by Government of Sudan and Sudan People's Liberation Movement/Army on January 9, 2005. **Strength:** 9,924 total uniformed personnel: 8,718 troops, 571 military observers, and 635 police; supported by 757 international civilian personnel, 2,381 local civilian and 2254 UN Volunteers.

Western Sahara – MINURSO – U.N. Mission for the Referendum in Western Sahara. Since April 1991. Monitors cease-fire and is to organize and conduct a referendum which would allow people of Western Sahara to decide the Territory's future status. **Strength:** 230 total uniformed personnel: 20 troops, 6 police officers, 204 military observers; supported by 101 international civilian personnel, 148 local civilian staff and 19 United Nations Volunteers.

Americas

Haiti – MINUSTAH – U.N. Stabilization Mission in Haiti. Since June 2004. Supports the Transitional Government to ensure a secure and stable environment within which the constitutional and political-processes in Haiti can take place. **Strength:** 9,055 total uniformed personnel: 7,174 troops and 1,881 police, supported by 499 international civilian personnel, 1,167 local civilian staff and 206 United Nations Volunteers

Asia

India-Pakistan – UNMOGIP – U.N. Military Observer Group in India and Pakistan. Since 1971. Stationed on both sides of Line of Control to observe cease-fire agreed upon by India and Pakistan under Simla Agreement of July 1972. **Strength:** 45 military observers, supported by 23 international civilian personnel and 48 local civilian staff.

Timor-Leste — United Nations Integrated Mission in Timor-Leste— (UNMIT). Since August 2006. Supports Government in consolidating stability, enhancing a culture of democratic governance, and facilitating political dialogue. Strength: 1,550 uniformed personnel: 1,519 police and 31 military liaison officers; 332 international civilian staff; 796 local civilian personnel; and 126 UN Volunteers.

Europe

Cyprus – UNFICYP – U.N. Peacekeeping Force in Cyprus. Since March 1964. Supervises cease-fire lines, undertakes humanitarian activities. **Strength:** 925 uniformed personnel: 856 troops and 69 police; supported by 39 international civilian personnel and 109 local civilian staff.

Georgia – UNOMIG – U.N. Observer Mission in Georgia. Since August 1993. Supervises 1994 Agreement on Ceasefire and Separation of Forces. **Strength:** 149 total uniformed personnel: 134 military observers and 15 police; supported by 97 international civilian personnel, 183 local civilian staff and 1 UN volunteer.

Kosovo - UNMIK – U.N. Interim Administration Mission in Kosova. Since June 1999. Interim civilian administration supported by European Union and Organization for Security and Co-operation in Europe. **Strength:** 37 military observers; 2,086 civilian police; 562 international civilians; 2,165 local civilians; 188 UN volunteers.

Middle East

Golan Heights – UNDOF – U.N. Disengagement Observer Force. Since June 1974. Maintains an "area of separation" on Golan Heights between Israel and Syria and verifies arms limitation on both sides. **Strength:** 1,046 troops, assisted by 57 military observers; and supported by 38 international civilian personnel and 103 local civilian staff.

Lebanon – UNIFIL – U.N. Interim Force in Lebanon. Since March 1978. To confirm Israeli withdrawal from Lebanon, restore peace and security, help Lebanese government restore its authority. **Strength:** 12,383 military personnel, supported by 312 international civilian and 614 local civilian staff.

Middle East – UNTSO – U.N. Truce Supervision Organization. Since May 1948. First U.N. peacekeeping operation. Monitors cease-fire, supervises armistice agreements, prevents isolated incidents from escalating and assists other U.N. peacekeeping operations in the region. **Strength:** 153 military observers; supported by 103 international civilian personnel and 130 local civilian staff.

▶FURTHER U.N. INFORMATION
http://www.un.org
United Nations Bookstore Room GA-32, New York, NY, 10017; 212-963-7680; 1-800-553-3210; Fax: 212-963-4910.

▶KEY EVENTS IN U.N. HISTORY
1946 (Jan. 10) First session of General Assembly begins at London with 51 member states.

1947 (Nov. 29) General Assembly passes Plan of Partition with Economic Union concerning future government of Palestine; government of Tel Aviv declares State of Israel on May 14, 1948.

1948 (Dec. 10) Universal Declaration of Human Rights adopted by General Assembly.
U.N. pioneers concept of peacekeeping observer missions and peacekeeping forces (1956).

1949 Mediates cease-fire between India and Pakistan, ending two years of fighting over Kashmir.

1950 Security Council calls member states to help South Korea repel invasion by North Korea.
Economic and Social Council adopts Standard International Trade Classification as basis for gathering world trade statistics.

1953 U.N. coordinates first global-census effort to establish Earth's population for first time in history–2.4 billion people.

1955 First of ongoing congresses of criminologists and police officials draws up international principles and standards of criminal justice.

1959 U.N. General Assembly adopts Declaration on the Rights of the Child.

1960 Under de-colonization program, 17 territories become newly independent states; 16 in Africa join U.N.

1962 Secretary-General plays key role in resolving U.S.-Soviet confrontation over issue of nuclear missiles in Cuba.

1963 Security Council calls for arms embargo against South Africa. (Made mandatory in 1972.)

1967 After war erupts in Middle East, Security Council adopts Resolution 242, calling for withdrawal of forces from occupied territories, and recognizes right of all states in area to security.

Mediates settlement of Six-Day Arab-Israeli War.

1970 General Assembly adopts first international agreed-upon set of principles on seabed and ocean floor beyond national jurisdiction. Declares area "common heritage" of humanity.

1972 Security Council orders cease-fire in 17-day-old Middle East War and sends peacekeeping force to prevent further fighting between Israel and Arab states.

1975 U.N. conference at Mexico City launches Decade for Women to begin major effort toward women's equality worldwide.

1979 World Health Organization announces smallpox eradicated from all peoples on earth.

1988 Mediates ending of Iran-Iraq War. Mediates Soviet withdrawal from Afghanistan.

1990 Upon invitation, U.N. monitors demobilization of Nicaraguan rebel forces, and for first time monitors a presidential campaign and election in an independent nation.

Security Council Resolution 678 calls upon member states to restore peace and security in Kuwait by "all necessary means."

Responding to request by Haiti, U.N. supervises election of Haiti's first freely elected president.

1991 Security Council Resolution 687 sets terms of cease-fire in Gulf War and gives U.N. variety of duties to ensure peace.

Secretary-general negotiates cease-fire in 16-year-old civil war in Angola.

Secretary-general negotiates release of last six hostages held in Lebanon.

General Assembly rescinds Resolution 3379 of Nov. 10, 1975, equating Zionism with racism.

1992 Secretary-general completes peace negotiations between government of El Salvador and rebel Farabundo Marti National Liberation Front.

1993 145 nations co-sponsor Convention on Prohibition of the Development, Production, Stockpiling and Use of Chemical Weapons.

Human Rights Commission adopts Resolution 1993/8, first formal statement that declares rape, conducted during war, an international war crime under Geneva Convention.

General Assembly creates post of High Commissioner for Human Rights with power to intervene wherever basic freedoms are suppressed.

1994 Security Council removes South Africa from its agenda, declaring end of apartheid.

Security Council establishes International Tribunal for Rwanda to prosecute persons responsible for genocide and other violations of international humanitarian law.

1995 Secretary-general launches 50th anniversary commemoration. International Tribunal for Former Yugoslavia, established in 1993 to prosecute persons responsible for serious violations of international humanitarian law in former Yugoslavia since 1991, schedules first trials for September with 15 judges from 15 countries.

At request of government of Haiti, U.N. supervises free elections in the country.

1996 Upon request of the government, U.N. supervises free and fair elections in Sierra Leone that changes rule from military regime to democracy.

Hague-based International Criminal Tribunal for the former Yugoslavia begins trial for first war crimes in 50 years. Dusan Tadic, Bosnian Serb charged with torturing and murdering Bosnian Muslims and Croats at Omarska prison camp in Prijedor, Bosnia, in 1992. He is convicted in 1997 and sentenced to 20 years in prison.

1997 U.N. launches CyberSchoolBus to reach tens of thousands of students worldwide; provides lesson plans, global trends, quizzes; on-line Model U.N. discussion is first of its kind to reach 60,000 high schools and college students.

Thirteen nations ask for and receive U.N. assistance in holding their elections, including Algeria, Cambodia, Gambia, Guyana, Haiti, Honduras, Liberia, Mali and Yemen.

1998 1998 U.N. Conference on Rome adopts statute to create Permanent International Criminal Court to try individuals for genocide, war crimes, and crimes against humanity.

1999 Secretary-General issues Global Compact —enlisting businesses to advance universally agreed principles on human rights, labor and environment.

Security Council invests U.N. peacekeeping mission authority over Kosovo territory and people, including all legislative, executive, and judicial administration. First ever cooperation with non-U.N. organizations, including the E.U. and the Organization for Security in Europe.

Economic and Social Council holds first live broadcast of its high-level meeting over the Internet allowing global viewing.

2000 Millennium Summit, the largest single gathering of Heads of State and/or Government, brings 180 presidents, prime ministers and monarchs to the U.N. They issue the Millennium Declaration, which intends to solve humanity's most pressing problems, send every child to school, and deliver millions from poverty by 2015.

2001 (Sept. 28, 2001) Security Council establishes Counter Terrorism Committee and calls on all member states to cooperate in various measures to fight terrorism.

2002 (Jan.) Global Fund to fight AIDS, tuberculosis and malaria is launched.

(July 1) Statute of International Criminal Court enters into force. Anyone who commits any crimes under the Statute after this date will be liable for prosecution by the Court.

(July 1) Statute of International Criminal Court enters into force. Anyone who commits any crimes under the Statute after this date will be liable ffor prosecution by the Court.

2003 (Sept. 8, 9, 10) U.N. conducts first webcast of annual conference for nongovernmental organizations allowing people around the world to view and participate via e-mail. Daily live and on-demand webcasts of many U.N. meetings.

2004 (Aug. 12) Security Council unanimously renews for one more year the U.N. Assistance Mission for Iraq (UNAMI) whose tasks include coordinating various humanitarian operations and helping to organize elections by end of Jan. 2005 and draft a new constitution.

2005 (June 23-24) First General Assembly Hearing: 200 nongovernmental organizations present their ideas to Member States.

(Sept. 14-16) U.N. holds 5-year evaluation of Millennium Development Goals.

2007 (May 4) Intergovernmental Panel on Climate Change (IPCC) releases 4th Assesment Report, produced by 600 authors from 40 countries.

United Nations Member States (192)

Country	Joined U.N.	Country	Joined U.N.	Country	Joined U.N
Afghanistan	1946	Ghana	1957	Pakistan	1947
Albania	1955	Greece	1945	Palau	1994
Algeria	1962	Grenada	1974	Panama	1945
Andorra	1993	Guatemala	1945	Papua New Guinea	1975
Angola	1976	Guinea	1958	Paraguay	1945
Antigua and Barbuda	1981	Guinea-Bissau	1974	Peru	1945
Argentina	1945	Guyana	1966	Philippines	1945
Armenia	1992	Haiti	1945	Poland	1945
Australia	1945	Honduras	1945	Portugal	1955
Austria	1955	Hungary	1955	Qatar	1971
Azerbaijan	1992	Iceland	1946	Moldova	1992
Bahamas	1973	India	1945	Romania	1955
Bahrain	1971	Indonesia	1950	Russian Federation	1945
Bangladesh	1974	Iran	1945	Rwanda	1962
Barbados	1966	Iraq	1945	Saint Kitts and Nevis	1983
Belarus	1945	Ireland	1955	Saint Lucia	1979
Belgium	1945	Israel	1949	Saint Vincent and the	1980
Belize	1981	Italy	1955	Grenadines	
Benin	1960	Ivory Coast	1960	Samoa	1976
Bhutan	1971	Jamaica	1962	San Marino	1992
Bolivia	1945	Japan	1956	São Tome and Principe	1975
Bosnia and Herzegovina	1992	Jordan	1955	Saudi Arabia	1945
Botswana	1966	Kazakhstan	1992	Senegal	1960
Brazil	1945	Kenya	1963	Serbia	2000
Brunei Darussalam	1984	Kiribati	1999	Seychelles	1976
Bulgaria	1955	Kuwait	1963	Sierra Leone	1961
Burkina Faso	1960	Kyrgyzstan	1992	Singapore	1965
Burundi	1962	Laos	1955	Slovakia[2]	1993
Cambodia	1955	Latvia	1991	Slovenia	1992
Cameroon	1960	Lebanon	1945	Solomon Islands	1978
Canada	1945	Lesotho	1966	Somalia	1960
Cape Verde	1975	Liberia	1945	South Africa	1945
Central African Republic	1960	Libya	1955	South Korea	1991
Chad	1960	Liechtenstein	1990	Spain	1955
Chile	1945	Lithuania	1991	Sri Lanka	1955
China	1945	Luxembourg	1945	Sudan	1956
Colombia	1945	Macedonia[3]	1993	Suriname	1975
Comoros	1975	Madagascar	1960	Swaziland	1968
Congo	1960	Malawi	1964	Sweden	1946
Congo, Democratic	1960	Malaysia	1957	Switzerland	2002
Republic of[1]		Maldives	1965	Syria	1945
Costa Rica	1945	Mali	1960	Tanzania	1961
Croatia	1992	Malta	1964	Tajikistan	1992
Cuba	1945	Marshall Islands	1991	Thailand	1946
Cyprus	1960	Mauritania	1961	Togo	1960
Czech Republic[2]	1993	Mauritius	1968	Tonga	1999
Denmark	1945	Mexico	1945	Trinidad and Tobago	1962
Djibouti	1977	Micronesia	1991	Tunisia	1956
Dominica	1978	Monaco	1993	Turkey	1945
Dominican Republic	1945	Mongolia	1961	Turkmenistan	1992
East Timor	2002	Montenegro	2006	Tuvalu	2000
Ecuador	1945	Morocco	1956	Uganda	1962
Egypt	1945	Mozambique	1975	Ukraine	1945
El Salvador	1945	Myanmar	1948	United Arab Emirates	1971
Equatorial Guinea	1968	Namibia	1990	United Kingdom	1945
Eritrea	1993	Nauru	1999	United States	1945
Estonia	1991	Nepal	1955	Uruguay	1945
Ethiopia	1945	Netherlands	1945	Uzbekistan	1992
Fiji	1970	New Zealand	1945	Vanuatu	1981
Finland	1955	Nicaragua	1945	Venezuela	1945
France	1945	Niger	1960	Viet Nam	1977
Gabon	1960	Nigeria	1960	Yemen[4]	1947
Gambia	1965	North Korea	1991	Zambia	1964
Georgia	1992	Norway	1945	Zimbabwe	1980
Germany	1973	Oman	1971		

Notes: 1. Formerly Zaire. 2. Czechoslovakia was an original member of the U.N.; when the nation split into separate Czech and Slovak Republics, both new republics were admitted as member states on Jan. 19, 1993. 3. Provisionally referred to for all purposes within the U.N. as "The former Yugoslav Republic of Macedonia" pending settlement of a difference with Greek Macedonia over the name. 4. Includes the former Democratic Yemen (admitted as a separate member in 1967), which merged with Yemen in 1990. **Source:** United Nations.

Major International Organizations

African Union (AU) *[successor to the Organization of African Unity (OAU)]* **HQ:** P.O. Box 3243, Roosvelt Street, W21K19, Addis Ababa, Ethiopia. **Estab.:** By Constitutive Act at Lone, Togo, July 11, 2000 to achieve greater unity and solidarity between African countries and the peoples of Africa; accelerate political and socio-economic integration of the continent; promote democratic principles and institutions, popular participation and good governance. **Members** (53): Algeria, Angola, Benin, Burkina Faso, Burundi, Cameroon, Cape Verde, Central African Republic, Chad, Comoros, Congo, Congo, Dem. Rep, Côte d´Ivoire, Djibouti, Egypt, Equatorial Guinea, Eritrea, Ethiopia, Gabon, Gambia, Ghana, Guinea Bissau, Guinea Conakry, Kenya, Lesotho, Liberia, Libya, Madagascar, Malawi, Mali, Mauritania, Mauritius, Mozambique, Namibia, Niger, Nigeria, Rwanda, Saharawi Arab Democratic Republic, São Tomé & Príncipe, Senegal, Seychelles, Somalia, South Africa, Sudan, Swaziland, Tanzania, Togo, Tunisia, Uganda, Zambia, Zimbabwe.

Commonwealth HQ: Marlborough House, Pall Mall, London, SW1Y 5HX, UK. **Estab.:** By some members of British Empire through evolutionary process formalized by Statute of Westminster on Dec. 31, 1931. As voluntary association of independent states, Commonwealth has no written constitution and no rigid contractual obligations. Emphasis is on consultation and exchange of views for cooperation, especially in economic affairs, drug trafficking, international terrorism and technical assistance to less developed states. Some countries that were part of British Empire are not part of Commonwealth. **Members** (54): Antigua and Barbuda, Australia, Bahamas, Bangladesh, Barbados, Belize, Botswana, Brunei, Cameroon, Canada, Cyprus, Dominica, Fiji, Gambia, Ghana, Grenada, Guyana, India, Jamaica, Kenya, Kiribati, Lesotho, Malawi, Malaysia, Maldives, Malta, Mauritius, Mozambique, Namibia, Nauru, New Zealand, Nigeria, Papua New Guinea, Saint Kitts and Nevis, Saint Lucia, Saint Vincent and the Grenadines, Samoa, Seychelles, Sierra Leone, Singapore, Solomon Islands, South Africa, Sri Lanka, Swaziland, Tanzania, Tong, Trinidad and Tobago, Tuvalu, Uganda, United Kingdom, Vanuatu, Western Samoa, Zambia, Zimbabwe.

Commonwealth of Independent States (CIS) HQ: Uliza Kirowa 17, Minsk 220000. **Estab.:** Dec. 8, 1991, by Byelorussia (Belarus), Russia, and Ukraine, which dissolved USSR and created CIS. Members agree to broad cooperation, including to cooperate in political, economic, ecological, humanitarian, and cultural fields. **Members** (12): Armenia, Azerbaijan, Belarus, Georgia, Kazakhstan, Kyrgyzstan, Moldova, Russia, Tajikistan, Turkmenistan, Ukraine, Uzbekistan.

European Union (EU, the Common Market), See Part III: "The Global Economy."

League of Arab States (LAS, the Arab League) HQ: Tahrir Square, Cairo, Egypt. **Estab.:** By treaty signed on Mar. 22, 1945 at Cairo, Egypt, to strengthen relations among members in financial, communications, cultural, health, social, nationality and social areas. **Members** (22): Algeria, Bahrain, Comoros, Djibouti, Egypt, Iraq, Jordan, Kuwait, Lebanon, Libya, Mauritania, Morocco, Oman, Palestine Liberation Organization, Qatar, Saudi Arabia, Somalia, Sudan, Syria, Tunisia, United Arab Emirates, Yemen.

North Atlantic Treaty Organization (NATO) HQ: B-1110 Brussels, Belgium. **Estab.:** By North Atlantic Treaty on Aug. 24, 1949, to maintain security among member states. NATO attempted to maintain military balance with countries of the Warsaw Pact: Bulgaria, Czechoslovakia, East Germany, Hungary, Poland, Romania, USSR. Since 1989 security challenges have shifted to possible adverse consequences from serious economic, social, and political difficulties, including ethnic rivalries and territorial disputes, arms proliferation, and terrorism. In 1997, leaders of NATO voted to admit Czech Republic, Hungary and Poland, and their official membership received final approval in 1999. In May 2002, Russia became a participant (but not a full-fledged member) of the organization. Russia is not bound by NATO's collective defense pact, nor will it have a veto over NATO decisions. **Members** (26): Belgium, Bulgaria, Canada, Czech Republic, Denmark, Estonia, France, Germany, Greece, Hungary, Iceland, Italy, Latvia, Lithuania, Luxembourg, Netherlands, Norway, Poland, Portugal, Romania, Slovakia, Slovenia, Spain, Turkey, United Kingdom, U.S.

Organization of American States (OAS) HQ: 1889 F St., NW, Washington, DC 20006-4499, U.S. **Estab.:** By charter signed at Bogotá, Columbia, effective Dec. 13, 1951, to strengthen peace and security on continent, promote cooperation in human rights, education, economic and social development and scientific exchanges, and to seek solutions to political, juridical and economic problems. **Members** (35): Antigua and Barbuda, Argentina, Bahamas, Barbados, Belize, Bolivia, Brazil, Canada, Chile, Colombia, Costa Rica, Cuba (suspended from OAS activities but not membership in 1962), Dominica, Dominican Republic, Ecuador, El Salvador, Grenada, Guatemala, Guyana, Haiti, Honduras, Jamaica, Mexico, Nicaragua, Panama, Paraguay, Peru, Saint Kitts and Nevis, Saint Lucia, Saint Vincent and the Grenadines, Suriname, Trinidad and Tobago, U.S., Uruguay, Venezuela.

Organization of the Petroleum Exporting Countries (OPEC) HQ: Obere Donaustrasse 93, A-1020 Vienna, Austria. **Estab.:** Nov. 14, 1960 by resolution adopted at Baghdad Conference, to coordinate and unify petroleum policies and to stabilize international oil prices to prevent harmful fluctuations. **Members** (11): Algeria, Indonesia, Iran, Iraq, Kuwait, Libya, Nigeria, Qatar, Saudi Arabia, United Arab Emirates, Venezuela.

Organization for Security and Cooperation in Europe (OSCE) HQ: Kärtnerring 5-7, A-1010 Vienna, Austria. **Estab.:** by Final Act of Conference on Security and Cooperation in Europe in 1975. In 1990, CSCE members declared end of "era of confrontation and division of Europe" and beginning of "a new era of democracy, peace and unity." Serves as forum for dialogue, negotiation, cooperation, and direction in shaping new Europe. **Members** (55): Albania, Andorra, Armenia, Austria, Azerbaijan, Belarus, Belgium, Bosnia and Herzegovina, Bulgaria, Canada, Croatia, Cyprus, Czech Republic, Denmark, Estonia, Finland, France, Georgia, Germany, Greece, Holy See, Hungary, Iceland, Ireland, Italy, Kazakhstan, Kyrgyzstan, Latvia, Liechtenstein, Lithuania, Luxembourg, Macedonia, Malta, Moldova, Monaco, Netherlands, Norway, Poland, Portugal, Romania, Russia, San Marino, Slovakia, Slovenia, Spain, Sweden, Switzerland, Tajikistan, Turkmenistan, Ukraine, UK, U.S., Uzbekistan.

ASTRONOMY

Astronomy is the oldest science, but it continues to be at the forefront of scientific thought. The ancients of the Northern Hemisphere knew the skies, probably better than most of us do. They recognized that most stars appear to rise in the east at night and travel in circular paths across the sky, and that a few are wanderers—planets—that move among the other stars. They named the groups of stars that we call constellations and recognized that constellations visible in winter are different from those visible in summer (although some are visible all year). They learned how to find the extremities of the sunrise and built giant stone structures, such as Stonehenge, probably to locate certain of the positions of the Sun or other stars.

In 1609 Galileo introduced the first artificial device for exploring the universe—the astronomical telescope. Even in that first year, he saw wonders the ancients never knew. Since then, we have built larger and better telescopes, devices for detecting radio waves, microwaves, X rays, infrared waves, and gamma rays from space, and have even traveled to our own Moon. We have sent space probes to many of the nearby bodies in space, and these have transmitted television close-ups to Earth.

▶ THE SOLAR SYSTEM

All bodies under the gravitational influence of our local star, the Sun, together with the Sun, form the solar system. The largest bodies, including Earth, are called planets. There have been nine bodies recognized as planets by the International Astronomical Union for over 65 years. In August 2006, however, the Union voted to reduce the status of Pluto to a "dwarf planet," of which there are three.

Often smaller cool bodies, called satellites or moons, orbit a planet. Bodies smaller than planets that orbit the Sun are classed as asteroids if they are rocky or metallic, comets if they are mostly ice and dust, and meteoroids if they are very small. Most comets release gases as they near the heat of the Sun, producing a luminous cloud called a coma and often a long tail. A meteoroid that burns in Earth's atmosphere is a meteor, while one that reaches Earth without burning completely becomes a meteorite.

It is currently believed that the solar system formed when a cloud of gas condensed to form the Sun. Parts of the cloud formed small bodies

Major Events in Astronomy and Space

B.C.
585   Thales of Miletus (Greek: c. 625–c. 547) predicts solar eclipse in Asia Minor.
c. 480   Astronomer Oenopides of Chios (Greek: 5th cent.) discovers that Earth is tilted with respect to Sun.
352   Chinese report "guest star," or supernova, the earliest known sighting.
c. 340   Astronomer Kidinnu (Kidenas; Babylon: c. 379) discovers precession of equinoxes, the apparent change in position of stars caused by Earth's wobbling on its orbit.
c. 300   Chinese astronomers compile star maps.
c. 240   Chinese astronomers observe Halley's comet.
   Eratosthenes of Cyrene (Greek: c.276–c.194) correctly calculates Earth's size.
165   Chinese astronomers notice sunspots.
c. 130   Astronomer Hipparchus of Nicea (Greek: 147–127) correctly determines distance to Moon and rediscovers precession of equinoxes (see 340 B.C.).

A.D.
c. 140   *Almagest* of Ptolemy (Greek: c. 90–168) develops astronomy of solar system in form based on Sun and planets revolving about Earth.
1543   *De Revolutionibus* by Nicholas Copernicus (Polish: 1473–1543) presents convincing arguments that Earth and other planets orbit Sun.
1577   Tycho Brahe (Danish: 1546–1601) proves that comets are visitors from space, not weather phenomena as previously believed.
1592   David Fabricius (German: 1564–1617) discovers star, later named Mira, that gradually disappears; in studying it in 1638, Phocylides Ho-

lawarda recognizes that it appears and reappears on regular basis—the first-known variable star.
1609   Johannes Kepler (German: 1571–1630) discovers that the planets move in elliptical orbits.
1610   Galileo observes Jupiter's moons, phases of Venus, and (although he does not recognize what they are) rings of Saturn.
1611   Several astronomers simultaneously discover sunspots for first time in West.
1671   Giovanni Domenico Cassini (Italian-French: 1625-1712) correctly determines distances of the planets from Sun.
1682   Edmond Halley (English: 1656–1742) describes comet now known by his name and in 1705 correctly predicts its return in 1758.
1718   Halley discovers that stars move with respect to each other.
1755   Immanuel Kant (German: 1724–1804) proposes that many nebulas are actually composed of millions of stars and that solar system formed when giant cloud of dust condensed.
1781   William Herschel (German-English: 1738–1822) discovers planet Uranus.
1785   Herschel demonstrates that Milky Way is disk- or lens-shaped group of many stars, one of which is the Sun.
1801   Guiseppe Piazzi (Italian: 1746–1826) discovers first-known asteroid, Ceres.
1838   Friedrich W. Bessel (German: 1784–1846) determines distance to star other than the Sun.
1846   Johann G. Galle (German: 1812–1910) discovers planet Neptune using predictions of Urbain J.J. Leverrier (French: 1811–77) and John Couch Adams (English: 1819–92).

1924 Edwin Hubble (American: 1889–1953) shows that galaxies are "island universes"—giant aggregations of stars as large as Milky Way.
1929 Hubble finds that universe is expanding.
1930 Clyde Tombaugh (American: 1906–97) discovers planet Pluto.
1931 Karl Jansky (American: 1905–50) discovers that radio waves are coming from space, leading to founding of radio astronomy.
1948 George Gamow (Russian-American: 1904–68), Ralph Alpher (American: 1921–), and Robert Herman (American: 1914–97) develop Big Bang theory of origin of universe.

Jan Hendrik Oort (Dutch: 1900–1992) proposes that comets come from a vast cloud of material orbiting far beyond Pluto; the material is now known as the Oort Cloud.
1957 USSR launches *Sputnik 1*, the first man-made satellite.
1961 Soviet cosmonaut Yuri A. Gagarin (Russian: 1934-68) is first human to orbit Earth.
1962 U.S. space probe *Mariner 2* is first to reach neighborhood of another planet, Venus.
1963 Maarten Schmidt (Dutch-American: 1929–) is first astronomer to recognize a quasar.
1964 Arno Penzias (German-American: 1933–) and Robert Wilson (American: 1936–) find radio waves pervading space, proving to most astronomers that Big Bang actually occurred.
1967 Jocelyn Bell-Burnell (English: 1943–) discovers first-known pulsar while working for Antony Hewish (English: 1924–); Hewish later gets Nobel Prize for discovery.
1969 Neil Armstrong (American: 1930–) and Edwin E. "Buzz" Aldrin (American: 1930–) walk on Moon.
1971 American spacecraft, *Mariner 9,* is first to orbit another planet, Mars.
1975 Soviet space probe transmits pictures from surface of Venus.
1976 U.S. Viking space probes begin transmitting pictures of surface of Mars—unsuccessful in detecting life on planet.
1977 Rings of Uranus are discovered.
1979 U.S. space probe *Voyager 1* discovers that, like Saturn and Uranus, Jupiter has rings.
1980 Alan Guth (American: 1947–) develops theory of inflationary universe, an explanation of how Big Bang occurred.
1981 U.S. introduces reusable spacecraft, the space shuttle.
1987 The explosion of Supernova 1987A, the nearest supernova that has been visible from Earth since 1604, is observed.
1989 U.S. space probe *Voyager 2* flies by Neptune, farthest planet from the Sun at that time, imaging the planet, its rings, and its moons.
1990 The Hubble Space Telescope is launched.
1992 The Magellan Venus orbiter completes mapping 95 percent of the planet's surface with radar.

Observations from the *Cosmic Background Explorer Satellite (COBE)* confirm the Big Bang theory.
1993 Members of the crew of the Space Shuttle *Endeavour* successfully repair the main lens of the Hubble Space Telescope.
1994 Comet Shoemaker-Levy 9, broken into 21 fragments, some nearly half a kilometer in diameter, slams into the far side of Jupiter in July.
1995 Astronomers Michel Mayor (Swiss:) and Didier Queloz (Swiss: 1966–) announce the first planet to orbit an ordinary star other than the Sun.

The Hubble Space Telescope focuses on a single patch of the northern sky long enough to reveal previously unknown objects at great distances from Earth.

The experiment, called the Hubble Deep Field, is repeated for the sky's southern hemisphere in 1998.
1996 Firm evidence is found for a massive black hole at the center of the Milky Way galaxy.
1997 Jupiter's moon Europa is found to have a sea of liquid water beneath a surface of ice crossed by giant fissures; astronomers conclude that it is possible that living organisms could exist in Europa's ocean.

The space probe *Pathfinder* lands safely on Mars on July 4. Pathfinder's rover, Sojourner, leaves the craft and sends to Earth reports of its close-up observation of Martian rocks in what appears to be an ancient flood plain.
1998 Astronomers conclude that there isn't enough matter in the universe to stop expansion; expansion may be accelerated by a small antigravity force.
1999 Two independent teams of astronomers determine that a system of at least three planets orbits the star Upsilon Andromedae.
2000 Studies using the Chandra X-Ray Observatory, a satellite launched in 1999, reveal that the pervasive X-ray background of the universe is caused by black holes that lurk in the hearts of most galaxies.

Permanent occupation of the International Space Station begins on May 19.

Calculations based on the US BOOMERANG (Balloon Observations of Millimetric Extragalactic Radiation and Geophysics) experiment, a balloon-borne study of the cosmic background radiation conducted in 1998, reveal that the universe is flat, not curved.
2001 Timothy Beers (American: 1957–) of Michigan State University and coworkers use uranium-238 to date the oldest stars in the universe at 12.5 billion years (with an uncertainty of 3 billion years), giving the minimum age for the universe.

In February the space probe *NEAR-Shoemaker* lands softly on asteroid 433 Eros, after orbiting it for a year.

The orbit of comet 200 CR-105 is calculated to be distorted as if by the presence of a planet larger than Pluto orbiting far beyond Neptune, now or at some time in the distant past—although the planet could have been Neptune itself if Neptune once occupied an orbit much farther from the Sun.
2002 Kenneth R. Sembach and coworkers report studies based on *FUSE (Far Ultraviolet Spectroscopic Explorer)* satellite observations show that the Milky Way is enveloped in a huge cloud of hot gas that extends almost to the nearest galaxies.

The Martian *Odyssey* space probe determined that a large amount of water, frozen into ice, is just below the surface of both poles of Mars.

NASA Scientists propose that an unusual astronomical object named RXJ1856.6-3754 is a "quark star," a body so dense that the atomic nuclei have broken into constituent up and down quarks as well as some strange quarks.

A dozen unusual radio sources that appear as X patterns formed by giant jets of hot matter and radiation are recognized as the results of pairs of black holes colliding and merging.
2003 Images obtained with NASA's *Wilkinson Microwave Anisotropy Probe* (WMAP) confirm Hubble observations for the age of the universe—13,700,000,000 years—with an accuracy of 1 percent.
2004 The robot Mars rover Opportunity shows that rocks on Mars could only have been formed in the presence of liquid water.
2005 Michael Brown, Chad Trujillo, and David Rabinowitz announce the discovery of a body in the outer solar system later named Eris that is larger than Pluto.

Basic Facts About the Planets

Characteristic	Terrestrial Planets				Gas Giants			
	Mercury	Venus	Earth	Mars	Jupiter	Saturn	Uranus	Neptune
Distance from Sun								
miles (millions)	36.0	67.2	93.0	141.6	483.78	890.75	1,784.86	2,793.0
km (millions)	57.9	108.2	149.6	227.9	778.57	1,433.53	2,872.46	4,495.1
Rotation period	59 days	243 days[1]	23.9 hrs	24.6 hrs	9.925 hrs	10.656 hrs	17.24 hrs	16.1 hrs
Orbital period (days)	88	224.7	365.256	686.98	4,331	10,747	30,589	59,800
Orbital velocity (miles/second)	29.74	21.76	18.51	14.99	8.12	6.02	4.23	3.37
Inclination of axis	0.01	3.39	23.45	25.19	3.13	26.73	97.77	28.32
Equatorial diameter								
miles	3,032	7,521	7,926	4,222	88,846	74,897	31,763	30,775
km	4,879	12,104	12,756	6,794	142,984	120,536	51,118	49,528
In relation to Earth:								
Diameter	38.3%	94.9%	100%	53.3%	1,121%	945%	401%	388%
Mass	5.53%	81.5%	100%	10.7%	31,783%	9,516.2%	1,453.6%	1,714.7%
Gravity	37.8%	90.7%	100%	37.7%	236.4%	91.6%	88.90%	112%
Escape velocity								
miles/second	2.7	6.4	7.0	3.1	37.0	22.1	13.2	14.6
km/second	4.3	10.36	11.186	5.03	59.5	35.5	21.3	23.5
Average surface temperature	332.4°F	867.0°F	59°F	-85°F	-166°F	-220°F	-320°F	-330°F
	166.9°C	463.9°C	15°C	-65°C	-110°C	-140°C	-195°C	-200°C
Planetary satellites	0	0	1	2	63	47	27	13

1. Venus's rotation is retrograde, or opposite the direction of other planets. **Source:** NASA: National Space Science Data Center (NSSDC) http://nssdc.gsfc.nasa.gov

similar to today's asteroids, comets, and meteoroids. Collectively, these small bodies are called planetesimals or planetoids. Early in the history of the solar system, about 4.6 billion years ago or even before, the planetoids frequently crashed into one another. While this sometimes resulted in one or more of the planetoids breaking up, often a small planetoid would stick to a larger one, making it larger still. The end products of this process, it is proposed, are the nine solar-system planets and their moons, along with the existing asteroids, comets, and meteoroids.

The solar system is located in a large system of stars called the Milky Way galaxy. The solar system is 28,000 light-years (defined below) from the center of the Milky Way and 67 light-years from the plane defined by the galactic spiral.

The Terrestrial Planets

In terms of distance from the Sun, these are the first four planets of the solar system—Mercury, Venus, Earth and Mars. Terrestrial planets all have a comparatively high density, a concentration of metallic elements, and hard, rocky surfaces. Earth is the largest of the terrestrial planets but is dwarfed by the enormous sizes of the outer "gas giant" planets (Jupiter, Saturn, Uranus and Neptune). Mercury, Earth and Mars have magnetic fields; Venus does not have a detectable magnetic field. Earth and Venus have thick atmospheres, Mars has a thin atmosphere, and Mercury's atmosphere is almost nonexistent.

Mercury

Main components of atmosphere: 98% helium, 2% hydrogen. Mercury is the planet closest to the Sun and in keeping with its namesake—Mercury, the winged messenger—moves the fastest in its orbit. Usually obscured from view from Earth by the Sun's glare, it is sometimes visible on Earth's horizon just after sunset, when it is called the Evening Star, or just before dawn, when it is called the

Glossary of Planetary Terms

Escape velocity   The speed needed for an object to be propelled from the surface of a planet and not fall back. The escape velocity for Earth is 6.96 miles (11.2 km) per second, thus an object must travel at least that fast, or approximately 7 miles per second, to leave Earth's gravitational influence.

Inclination of axis   The angle that the axis about which a planet rotates makes with the plane defined by its path around the Sun.

Orbital period   The time it takes for a planet to orbit the Sun.

Orbital velocity   The speed of a planet in its path around the Sun.

Rotation period   The time it takes for a planet to rotate once about itself.

Morning Star. About 14 times in each 100 years, Mercury can also be seen crossing directly in front of the Sun's disk.

Mercury was long thought to be the smallest planet, but better measurements of Pluto's size have shown that Pluto is even smaller. The U.S. *Mariner 10* space probe provided the first detailed pictures of Mercury's surface during flybys in 1974 and 1975. *Mariner 10* mapped about 35 percent of the planet's heavily cratered, moonlike surface. In 2004 the *Messenger* space probe to Mercury was launched, expected to orbit the planet starting in 2011.

Mercury is a waterless, airless world that alternately bakes and freezes as it orbits the Sun. Its tenuous atmosphere is thought to be one-trillionth the density of Earth's atmosphere and largely composed of helium. On Mercury's sunlit side temperatures reach 850°F (450°C) and plummet to -300°F (-180°C) on the dark side. These extremes are largely due to Mercury's slow rate of rotation: one single rotation is two-thirds of a Mercury year, or 59 days for a rotation compared to 88 days for a revolution. Mercury's axis is almost perpendicular to its plane of rotation, so any single place on the planet sees dawn only once every 176 days—the planet must rotate three times and go through two of its "years" before a new day dawns.

Mercury's surface is scarred with hundreds of thousands of meteor craters. Many such craters were probably formed during the planetoid showers believed to have occurred soon after the formation of the solar system. Many areas have had the craters smoothed over by ancient lava flows, however. This indicates extensive volcanic activity on Mercury during and after the time of the planetoid showers. The surface is also crisscrossed by huge cliffs, or scarps. These probably formed as Mercury's surface cooled and shrank. Some of the scarps are up to 1.2 miles (1.9 km) high and 932 miles (1,500 km) long.

Mercury is so dense for its size that astronomers think that its rocky outer crust is very thin and that the planet is mostly iron. It probably was once larger. During the early bombardment, it is conjectured that one of the larger planetoids (about a sixth of the size of the early planet) hit Mercury so hard that it blasted most of the rocky crust away.

Venus

Main components of atmosphere: 96.5% carbon dioxide, 3.5% nitrogen. As seen in the night sky from Earth, Venus is second only to the Moon in brightness. Venus, named for the Roman goddess of love, is the planet that passes closest to Earth (24,000,000 mi., or 39,000,000 km). Since it is between Earth and the Sun, Venus, like Mercury, is seen either as the Morning Star or the Evening Star.

Because of its proximity to Earth and its position between Earth and the Sun, Venus became (in 1962) the first planet beyond Earth to be scanned by a space probe in its neighborhood (*Mariner 2*). The pull of the Sun's gravity makes Venus and Mercury "downhill" from the Earth; one must travel against the Sun's gravity to reach other planets. Since 1962 Venus has been visited by numerous U.S. and Soviet spacecraft. Soviet space probes *Venera 13* and *Venera 14* were the first to make a soft landing and send back pictures from the Venusian surface.

The Venusian atmosphere is thick with clouds that have shrouded the planet's surface from view, making the planet somewhat mysterious. The Venusian clouds range from about 28 to 37 miles (45 to 60 km) above the planet's surface and are differentiated into three layers. Droplets of sulfuric acid and water have been identified in the clouds.

The clouds and high level of carbon dioxide in the atmosphere have combined to trap heat in the lower atmosphere of Venus. This is an extreme form of the greenhouse effect and is responsible for high temperatures in the lower atmosphere, 870°F (460°C)—hot enough to melt lead. The atmospheric pressure at the surface is 92 times that of Earth. Radiation of heat from the lower atmosphere is so inefficient that there is little variation of temperature between night and day.

One feature of the Venusian upper atmosphere is markedly different from that of Earth. The atmosphere superrotates on Venus—that is, the atmosphere above the clouds moves 60 times faster than the planet rotates—whereas the Earth and its atmosphere rotate at the same speed. So, high winds and steady upper-atmosphere winds—100 mph (160 km/hr) or faster—are a dominant factor in Venusian weather. But at ground level, winds are calmer, with an average closer to 2 mph (3.6 km/hr).

Soviet space probes that soft-landed on Venus have provided photographs of the planet's surface. Radar maps of 99 percent of the Venusian surface, completed by the U.S. Pioneer spacecraft (from 1978 to 1993), and *Magellan* (from 1989 to 1994), now give a detailed picture of features as small as 350 ft. (100 m) in diameter. More than a thousand Venusian mountains, volcanoes, rifts, basins, impact craters, and other features have been identified.

About 10 percent of the surface is highland terrain, 70 percent rolling uplands, and 20 percent lowland plains. There are two major highland areas: one about half the size of Africa and located in the equatorial region and the other, about the size of Australia, located to the north. The highest mountain on Venus—Maxwell Montes—is in the northern highlands and is higher than Earth's Mt. Everest. Volcanic activity dominates Venus; the planet is covered with volcanic domes and lava channels.

Like Earth, Venus is thought to have an internal structure. The crust, however, is much thicker than that of Earth, perhaps twice as deep on the average, making the crust of Venus about 60 mi. (100 km) thick. Below the crust is a large layer called the mantle; below the mantle is a core thought to be molten nickel-iron, similar to Earth's outer core.

Earth

Main components of atmosphere: 78% nitrogen, 21% oxygen, 1% water, 0.93% argon. Earth is the third planet from the Sun and the only one in the solar system known to harbor life. From space, our planet appears as a bright, blue-and-white sphere—blue because some 70 percent of the surface is covered by water, and white because clouds cover about half the planet's surface.

Earth's atmosphere and composition are discussed in **Earth Science** below. Earth's mass is 6.583×10^{21} tons. $(5.972 \times 10^{21}$ metric tons).

The Moon is Earth's only natural satellite. It is over one-quarter the size of Earth in diameter (2,160 mi. or 3,476 km). At an average distance of 238,000 mi. (380,000 km), it is the brightest object in Earth's nighttime sky. The Moon regularly changes in appearance as seen from Earth. See the discussion of these changes, called "Phases of the Moon," in Part I.

The Moon is slightly egg-shaped, and the same side of the satellite always faces Earth—this side being the elongated small end. As a result, the Moon rotates once during each revolution. The side we do not see is called the far side (not the dark side—all parts of the moon undergo 14 Earth days of light, followed by 14 days of darkness).

Over a decade of exploration of the Moon by space probes was capped by the landing of two U.S. astronauts on the Moon on July 20, 1969. A total of six two-man crews of American astronauts eventually landed on the Moon between 1969 and 1972, and they brought back some 842 pounds (382 kg) of samples of Moon rocks. The world these astronauts found was airless and devoid of life. Temperatures on the Moon range from up to 273°F (134°C) on the bright side to -274°F (-170°C) on the unlighted side.

A mixture of fine powder and broken rock blankets the Moon's surface. The near side also has large regions (called maria, or seas) of solidified lava. The lunar surface is pockmarked with craters up to 56 miles (90 km) across and is broken by huge mountain ranges. Some craters at the poles may contain frozen water in their depths.

Mars

Main components of atmosphere: 95% carbon dioxide, 3% nitrogen, 2% argon. Mars is the outermost of the four terrestrial planets and has a distinctive reddish coloring, coming from iron oxide in the Martian soil. The Romans named the planet after their god of war, and the two irregularly shaped satellites of Mars have been named after the horses—Deimos (terror) and Phobos (fear)—that pulled the war god's chariot. Mars is usually visible in Earth's nighttime sky and is lined up with Earth between it and the Sun once every 780 days, though its closest approach to Earth (33,800,000 mi., or 54,500,000 km) comes at 15- or 17-year intervals; 2003 was the closest approach since 1986.

The so-called canals on Mars—later found to be optical illusions—were first observed by 19th-century astronomers and led to the widespread belief that there was life on Mars. (In 1900 the French Academy offered a prize to the first person to find life on any planet except Mars, presumably because everyone knew that there was life on that planet.) The planet thus became the target of numerous space probes, both U.S. and Soviet, from the early years of interplanetary exploration.

The first successful flyby of Mars was achieved by the U.S. spacecraft *Mariner 4* in 1965. The Soviets became the first to land a probe successfully on the surface of Mars in 1971, but the probe malfunctioned and stopped transmitting after only 20 seconds. It was not until 1976, when the U.S. *Viking 1* and *Viking 2* landers touched down on Mars, that extensive study of the planet from its surface became possible. The *Viking 1* lander continued to function until 1983. *Pathfinder* landed on Mars on July 4, 1997. Using a remote-controlled robot called *Sojourner*, whose travels to Martian rocks were televised, the *Pathfinder* mission reported the details of the weather and geology of Mars.

The big question of whether there is (or was) life on Mars has yet to be answered with certainty. The *Viking* landers conducted three experiments on Martian soil to check for biological processes. Some of the tests yielded positive results, but these could also be explained by the soil chemistry. The lack of other evidence of organic molecules adds to the case against life on Mars.

Orbiting satellites have mapped the entire planet down to a resolution of 500-1,000 ft. (150–300 m). The planet's surface is heavily cratered, and there is extensive evidence of once-active volcanoes. There are also such spectacular features as Olympus Mons (an extinct volcano three times as high as Earth's Mt. Everest); mammoth canyons, one of which is four times deeper than the Grand Canyon; and a gigantic basin (larger than Alaska) in the southern hemisphere that was probably created by a single, huge asteroid. The planet has ice caps at both poles (water ice with some frozen carbon dioxide), and the ice caps advance and recede with changes in the seasons.

But the most intriguing aspect of the Martian surface is that water once flowed there in great quantities. Parts of the terrain apparently have sedimentary origins, and there are many long channels, complete with smaller tributary channels and islands, that extend for hundreds of kilometers. Scientists speculate that Mars once had a much thicker atmosphere, made up of gases vented during volcanic eruptions, which would have made it possible for water in its liquid state to exist on the surface. Martian atmospheric pressure is now so low, however, that surface water would immediately vaporize. It is conjectured that in the past, water flowed through the channels to lowland areas and then sank into the Martian regolith, or upper soil layer, since there is no geologic evidence that standing bodies of water ever existed. In 2002 the orbiting Mars *Odyssey* detected signs of a large amount of water ice just below soil level in the south polar region.

Mars is too small to sustain continual volcanic activity. Its atmosphere apparently thinned out after volcanic activity ceased. Atmospheric pressure is now just seven one-thousandths of that on Earth at sea level, and the predominant gas is carbon dioxide, which is relatively heavy. A small amount of water vapor in the atmosphere is enough to form some clouds, small patches of fog in some valleys, and occasionally even patches of frost. Surface temperatures vary from a high of about 70°F (20°C) during summer at the equator to a low of about -220°F (-140°C) during winter at the poles.

By far the most pronounced feature of Martian weather is dust storms, which regularly engulf the entire planet for a period of several months.

The asteroids

Also called minor planets, the asteroids are very small bodies ranging from less than 1 to 600 miles in diameter. The name asteroid means "starlike" and was given to asteroids because they are so small they appear as points of light (as do stars) even in powerful telescopes. Otherwise, asteroids are not like stars at all.

The first four asteroids were discovered between 1801 and 1807. Today several hundred thousand asteroids are known and a million may exist in all. But the total mass of all known asteroids is less than that of Earth's Moon; only 26 asteroids are more than 130 miles (200 km) in diameter. Many asteroids occur in pairs that orbit each other. Some are thought to be solid bodies, while others may be collections of rocks held together by slight gravitational interactions.

Asteroids are found in several locations. The main belt is between Mars and Jupiter, but many inside the orbit of Mars are known as near-Earth asteroids. Asteroids that are thought to be larger than about 500 feet (150 m) in diameter that may travel as close as about 5 million miles (7.5 million km) to Earth are called potentially hazardous objects (PHOs). There are about 300 known PHOs, but none are expected to impact Earth in the foreseeable future. Two groups in the same orbit as Jupiter are called the Trojans because the larger ones are named for characters from Homer's *Iliad*.

The Outer Planets

Beyond Mars and the asteroid belt lie the five known outer planets of our solar system. Four of these planets—Jupiter, Saturn, Uranus, and Neptune—are the so-called gas giants. Many times larger than the terrestrial planets, these planets are huge, dense balls of hydrogen and other gases. Orbiting beyond them (most of the time) lies the Kuiper belt, a group of large bodies that includes Pluto and that have been called planets, asteroids, and even giant comets. The largest of these Eris, followed in size by Pluto and several known bodies that are nearly as big as Pluto, including 2003 EL612, 2005 FY9, and Sedna.

Jupiter

Main components of atmosphere: 90% hydrogen, 10% helium. Jupiter is the largest planet in the solar system. It has 2.5 times more mass than all the other planets of the solar system together and is 11 times as large as Earth in diameter. Jupiter is so large that scientists believe it almost became a star: as the gases and dust contracted to form the planet, gravitational forces created tremendous pressure and temperature inside the core—perhaps as high as tens of thousands of degrees. But there was not enough mass available to create the temperatures needed to start a fusion reaction such as that of the Sun (above 27,000,000°F, or 15,000,000°C, at the Sun's core); thus Jupiter has been slowly cooling down ever since. Even so, Jupiter still radiates about 2.5 times as much heat as it receives from the Sun.

The first object to reach Jupiter from Earth was *Pioneer 10*. It returned the first close-up pictures of the giant planet in 1973. Subsequently, the more sophisticated space probes *Voyager 1* and *Voyager 2* passed by Jupiter in 1979 and sent back images and more data on the planet. One of the most exciting discoveries by *Voyager 1* was that Jupiter has a faint but extensive ring system that extends almost 186,000 miles (300,000 km) out from the planet's surface. *Galileo* found another faint ring at 1 million miles (1.6 million km) in 1998. A probe from *Galileo* arrived at Jupiter on December 7, 1995, finding winds of 435 mph (700 km/hr) and much less water vapor than expected. Scientists later determined that the probe had arrived in what amounts to a Jovian desert. In September 2003, *Galileo's* mission ended with a final plunge into Jupiter's atmosphere.

Jupiter's thick atmosphere, which may extend above the planetary surface as much as 600 miles (1,000 km), is primarily made up of hydrogen, with some helium and traces of other gases. Because the planet spins so fast (one rotation in just under 10 hours), its clouds tend to form bands that give the planet a striped appearance. Darker bands are called belts, while light ones are zones. Clouds at higher altitudes are carried eastward by jet streams, while those at lower levels are blown westward.

There are numerous eddies and swirls in Jupiter's atmosphere, but none can compare with the Great Red Spot, apparently a massive hurricane (rotating counterclockwise) located in the southern hemisphere near the equator. The Great Red Spot was first observed more than 300 years ago, and this storm continues unabated today. Since 1938 three smaller white ovals have been observed to the south of the Great Red Spot.

Jupiter's cloud tops are extremely cold (about -202°F, or -130°C), but temperatures increase deeper inside the atmosphere. Pressure also increases, and at about 600 miles (1,000 km) below the outermost atmospheric layers, great oceans of liquid hydrogen form Jupiter's surface. These may be some 12,000 miles (20,000 km) deep. Beneath them the hydrogen is so densely compacted it is thought to be in a metallic state. Within this is the core, thought to be an iron and silicate rock ball about the size of Earth.

Jupiter is now known to have 63 moons, many of them quite small (less than 6 miles in diameter). The four largest are the Galilean moons, so called because they were first observed by Galileo. The Galilean moons are Ganymede, Callisto, Europa, and Io—after the Roman god Jupiter's cup-bearer (Ganymede) and three of Jupiter's inamorata. Ganymede is the largest moon in the solar system and is larger even than the planets Pluto and Mercury. It is a huge, cratered ball of ice and may have a core of solid silicate rock with liquid water between the thick ice covering and the core. Callisto, with an orbit outside that of Ganymede, is also covered with ice and is riddled with thousands of craters. Europa, which orbits inside Ganymede, is about the size of our Moon and has a smooth surface marked by networks of cracks. The most interesting of Jupiter's moons are Io, which orbits closest to Jupiter, and Europa.

Io undergoes the most intense volcanic activity known, heated it is thought by tidal energy from orbiting near Jupiter. One giant volcano may have been erupting for the past 19 years. Orange-red patches on Io's mottled surface are apparently molten sulfur beds, but most other parts of Io's surface are cold (about -229°F, or -145°C).

Europa, on the other hand, is covered in ice, but some have speculated that a liquid ocean beneath the ice could contain life. The liquid, which probably contains salts like oceans on Earth, could be heated by the same tidal forces that propel Io's volcanoes.

Saturn

Main components of atmosphere: 90% hydrogen, 3% helium. Saturn is the sixth planet of the solar system and the second largest, after Jupiter. The outermost of the planets that can be identified easily in Earth's nighttime sky with the unaided eye, Saturn has a pale yellowish color and is not nearly so bright as Mars. Saturn's spectacular ring system, which makes it one of the most interesting of the planets, is visible only through a telescope. Its rings are more extensive than those of any other planet.

Like Jupiter, Saturn is composed of densely compacted hydrogen, helium, and other gases. Liquid or metallic hydrogen probably exists underneath the planet's thick atmosphere, and scientists believe there is a solid core of rock about two times the size of Earth at its center. Saturn's high rotational speed (once every 10 hours, 12 minutes) makes it the most oblate (flattened) of all the planets; it is almost 6,800 miles (11,000 km) wider at the equator than on a line through the poles.

Exploration of Saturn began in 1979 with the first fly-by (*Pioneer 11*), but the *Voyager 1* (1980) and *Voyager 2* (1981) missions provided the first detailed look at the planet. Scientists have spent years sifting through the data gathered. Though there were important new findings, many questions about Saturn remain unanswered. The *Cassini-Huygens* probe, which arrived in 2004, should provide many answers.

The *Voyagers* found a huge storm thousands of miles across on Saturn, along with a wide band of extremely high winds—up to 1,000 miles (1,600 km) per hour—at the equator. Winds in this band all travel in the direction of the planet's rotation (unlike bands of wind on Jupiter). The *Voyagers* also discovered a vast hydrogen cloud circling the planet above the equator.

The *Voyagers'* most exciting discoveries concern the planetary rings. Previously, about six different rings had been identified within the ring system, but *Voyager 1* pictures show as many as 1,000 separate rings. Narrow rings can even be seen within the Cassini Division, once thought to be an empty gap between the two major parts of the ring system. Some rings are not circular, and at least two rings are intertwined, or "braided." A strange new phenomenon was also discovered in the rings. *Voyager 1* pictures clearly show dark, radial fingers—"spokes"—moving inside the rings in the direction of rotation. Scientists speculate that they are made of ice crystals.

Voyager 2 pictures show that Saturn has far more than 1,000 rings—perhaps as many as a hundred thousand or more. One of the brightest rings is under 152 meters (500 ft.) thick. *Voyager 2* also found seasonal differences between the planet's two hemispheres and photographed a storm 4,000 miles (6,500 km) wide.

Twelve of Saturn's moons were known before the arrival of the *Voyagers*, and instruments aboard the space probe helped locate five new ones in the 1980s. In 1990 an 18th moon, later named Pan, was located in images made by *Voyager 2*. The discovery of 12 small moons of Saturn, found with ground-based telescopes, was reported in 2002 and another in 2003. Astronomers and *Cassini* observed more since then, bringing the total to 47. Most of Saturn's moons are relatively small and composed of rock and ice. All but one of the small moons are pock-marked by meteor craters, and in some cases the moons appear to have been cracked by collisions with especially large meteors. But *Voyager* pictures show that one moon, Enceladus, is smooth in large regions apparently unmarked by collisions with meteors. Scientists believe that Enceladus is being pulled and stretched by the combined gravities of a nearby moon and Saturn itself. Tidal forces have apparently heated the core of Enceladus and made its surface soft enough to smooth over any craters formed by meteor impacts.

Titan, Saturn's largest moon (3,000 mi., or 4,800 km in diameter) is one of the few moons in the solar system known to have an atmosphere of any substance. Scientists suspect that at least some precursors of life may have formed there. For this reason *Voyager 1* was guided to within about 2,500 miles (4,000 km) of Titan during the Saturn flyby. Though Titan's surface was obscured by dense clouds, Voyager's sensors nevertheless returned a considerable amount of information about the moon and its atmosphere. Titan's atmosphere is composed mostly of nitrogen, like that of Earth, with only a small percentage of methane and carbon monoxide. Atmospheric pressure is at least 1.5 times that on Earth and temperatures range around -294°F (-181°C). Titan in fact appears to be a frozen version of Earth before life evolved.

The possibility of oceans of liquid methane (or of nitrogen or methane rain) on Titan was a matter of considerable controversy for some time after *Voyager 1* investigated the moon. But Titan is "dry," at least in the regions investigated. Pools of liquid methane might still exist in other low-lying regions, but it is unlikely that either methane or nitrogen condenses to liquid form on Titan.

Uranus
Main components of atmosphere: 82% hydrogen, 15% helium, 2% methane. Uranus is the seventh planet in the solar system and the third of the gas giants. The planet is barely visible in Earth's night-time sky (it looks like a faint star) and for that reason, it went undiscovered until 1781.

Nearly the same size as Neptune and only about 5 percent of Jupiter's mass, Uranus is a faintly greenish color, perhaps because its atmosphere contains methane. The planet's axis of rotation is tipped over on its side. Astronomers discovered a system of nine faint rings in 1977, and *Voyager* found two more rings in 1986. There are thought to be 27 moons of Uranus. Among these, Caliban and Sycorax were found in 1997; a still-unnamed moon was noticed in 1999 by a researcher studying a 1986 photograph taken by *Voyager 2*. Three more discovered later in 1999 have been named Prospero, Setebos, and Stephano.

Uranus's atmosphere is very cold (-355°F, or -215°C). No clouds have been observed. Scientists speculate that, as on Jupiter and Saturn, temperatures and pressures increase dramatically down through the outer layer of atmosphere. At some point the hydrogen and helium would be sufficiently compressed to form a liquid or slushy surface "crust." Underneath this crust they believe is a mantle of solidified methane, ammonia, and water; and inside this mantle, a rocky core of silicon and iron about 15 times as massive as Earth. The core is thought to be hot, probably about 12,000°F (7,000°C).

Neptune
Main components of atmosphere: 80% hydrogen, 19% helium, 1% methane. The last of the gas giants, Neptune is the eighth planet in the solar system. It was discovered in 1846 after mathematical calculations based on irregularities in the orbit of Uranus provided astronomers with the correct location of the planet. Neptune, like Uranus, has been surrounded by considerable uncertainty because of its enormous distance from Earth. The 1989 visit by *Voyager 2* contributed greatly to improved understanding of the planet.

Neptune is a pale bluish color, but it has a clear atmosphere, and is very cold at the cloud tops (about -365°F or -220°C).

Scientists believe Neptune has a three-layered structure similar to that of Uranus: a crust of solidified or liquid hydrogen and helium that gradually thins outward into an atmosphere; a mantle of solidified gases and water; and a hot, rocky core (about 12,000°F or 7,000°C) some 15 times as massive as Earth. But one aspect of Neptune remains a mystery. Despite similarities with Uranus, Neptune has been found to radiate 2.7 times as much heat as it receives from the Sun (at a rate of 0.03 microwatts per ton of mass). Uranus, on the other hand, does not emit as much excess heat.

Neptune has 13 known moons, Triton and Nereid, discovered from Earth, six others discovered by *Voyager 2*, three more newly spotted in 2002. Triton is the largest moon and has an atmosphere. Triton is unusual in that it travels in a direction opposite that of Neptune's rotation, suggesting that it has a different origin from the planet. Triton also has volcanic activity: geysers of nitrogen rising as high as five miles (8 km).

Dwarf Planets
From 1930 through the end of the 20th century, the solar system was thought to contain nine planets, the ninth planet being Pluto. In recent years, however, several objects similar to Pluto were discovered in the outer solar system. This caused a rethinking of what makes a planet a planet.

On August 24, 2006, the International Astronomical Union (I.A.U.) for the first time defined the term "planet." In this new definition, a planet is a celestial body that is in orbit around a star, has sufficient mass so that it assumes a nearly round shape, and has cleared its orbit of planetesimals and similar debris. The first eight planets (Mercury through Neptune) meet all three criteria, but Pluto meets only the first two.

Pluto was thus removed from the rank of major planets and reclassified as a dwarf planet. The I.A.U. classifies a dwarf planet as a celestial body that is in orbit around the sun, has sufficient mass so that it assumes a nearly round shape, has not cleared its orbit of planetesimals, and is not a satellite of another similar object. Today there are three recognized dwarf planets: Pluto, Eris, and Ceres.

Pluto

Average distance from Sun: 39.5 AU. *Mass:* 0.002 Earth masses. *Diameter:* 0.18 Earth diameters. *Orbit time:* 248 years. *Rotation time:* 6.4 days. *Main components of atmosphere:* methane and nitrogen (quantities unknown). A ball of frozen gases probably only about the size of Earth's moon, Pluto was discovered in 1930 as a result of an extensive search by Clyde Tombaugh. It was originally thought to be a planet, until that term was redefined by the I.A.U. in 2006. Pluto resides in the Kuiper Belt outside the orbit of Neptune; it's chaotic orbit causes it at times to cross inside Neptune's orbit.

Today Pluto is about as close to the Sun as it ever gets and possesses a thin atmosphere, but it is expected to freeze solid as the planet moves away from the sun. Pluto has one known moon, Charon, discovered in 1978. Charon is about half the size of Pluto. Pluto and Charon rotate and revolve synchronously like a double planet system.

Eris

Average distance from Sun: 67.7 AU. *Mass:* .0027 Earth masses. *Diameter:* 0.19 Earth diameters. *Orbit time:* 557 years. *Rotation time:* not yet known. *Main components of atmosphere:* methane and nitrogen (quantities unknown). Similar in composition to Pluto, Eris is the largest dwarf planet in the solar system and the ninth largest body orbiting the Sun. It was discovered in 2005 by a Mount Palomar-based team of astronomers, led by Michael Brown. Eris has one known moon, Dysnomia. Eris resides in the Kuiper Belt, and is at this time the most distant known body in the solar system; its orbit is more eccentric and tilted than that of its neighbor Pluto.

Ceres

Average distance from Sun: 2.767 AU. *Mass:* 0.00016 Earth masses. *Diameter:* .075 Earth diameters. *Orbit time:* 4.6 years. *Rotation time:* 9 hours. Discovered in 1801 by Giuseppe Piazzi, Ceres is the largest and most massive body in the asteroid belt between Mars and Jupiter. First thought to be a comet, then a large asteroid, Ceres has most recently been classified as a dwarf planet. Unlike other objects in the asteroid belt, Ceres is spherical; it has no discernable atmosphere.

The Sun

Virtually all of the energy used by living things comes from the Sun. The Sun's light causes photosynthesis in green plants, and its heat causes winds. Fossil fuels, such as coal, oil, and natural gas, got their energy originally from photosynthesis, as does wood. Animals derive their energy from plants that photosynthesize, either directly or indirectly. The only natural nonsolar energy sources are nuclear reactions (which also produce geothermal energy), some bacteria that metabolize sulfur, and the tides, which on Earth are produced largely by the Moon, but in part by the Sun.

Because the Sun is a ball of gases, it does not rotate as a whole. The equator rotates in about 25 days, while gas near the poles rotates in about 30 days. The period of rotation at each latitude can be found by observing sunspots, which are magnetic storms. Sunspots appear and disappear in a mysterious 11-year cycle that many think influences weather on Earth, although convincing proof is lacking. Sometimes sunspots disappear for tens of years at a time, as during the period from 1645 to 1715. It may or may not be a coincidence that those years coincided with the "Little Ice Age" in Europe, when temperatures were far below average.

Like Earth, the Sun is composed of various layers. The part we see is called the photosphere. In the Sun's interior, energy is generated when hydrogen in the core fuses to become helium. Above the photosphere is a region of pinkish gases, the chromosphere. Above that is a large halo, visible only in eclipses, called the corona. Particles from the Sun, the solar wind, stream through the solar system, creating among other things auroras on Earth. Strong increases in solar wind during solar flares can interfere with radio communication.

▶ PLANETS OUTSIDE THE SOLAR SYSTEM

A detectable wobble or periodic dimming, observed in about 140 nearby stars, indicated that each such star is orbited by one or more planets, known as "extrasolar planets." The star 55 Cancri is known to have at least four extrasolar planets, and 12 other stars have two or three for a total of about 165 planets. At least two pulsars have planets, and several stars are surrounded by dusty regions that may indicate planet formation.

In 1995 the first planet that orbits an ordinary star other than the Sun was established on the basis of regular changes in the position of the Sunlike star 51 Pegasi, which is nearly 50 light-years from the solar system. This discovery by Michel Mayor (Swiss) and Didier Queloz (Swiss: 1966–) was soon followed by detection of many other or-

Characteristics of the Sun	
Position in solar system	Center
Mean distance from Earth	92,960,000 mi. (149,600,000 km)
Distance from center of Milky Way galaxy	27,710 light-years
Period of rotation	25.45 days at 16° longitude
Inclination (relative to Earth's orbit)	7.25°
Equatorial diameter	865,000 mi. (1,392,000 km)
Diameter relative to Earth	109.2 times
Mass	2.192×10^{27} tons (1.9891×10^{30} kg)
Mass converted to energy each second	9,500 million pounds (4,300 million kg)
Surface gravity relative to Earth's	28 times
Temperature at core	28,280,000°F (15,710,000°C)
Temperature at bottom of photosphere	12,400°F (6,900°C)
Main components	Hydrogen and helium
Present age	4.6 billion years
Expected future life of hydrogen fuel supply	6.4 billion years

The Constellations

Name	Genitive	Abbr.	Translation	Remarks
Andromeda	Andromedae	And	Andromeda	Character in Greek myth
Antlia	Antliae	Ant	Air pump	Named by Nicolas Lacaille in 1750
Apus	Apodis	Aps	Swift, or Bird of Paradise	Named by Johann Bayer in 1603
Aquarius	Aquarii	Aqr	Water Bearer	In zodiac
Aquila	Aquilae	Aql	Eagle	Contains Altair
Ara	Arae	Ara	Altar	Part of the Centaurus group
Aries	Arietis	Ari	Ram	In zodiac
Auriga	Aurigae	Aur	Charioteer	Contains Capella
Boötes	Boötis	Boo	Herdsman	Contains Arcturus
Caelum	Caeli	Cae	Chisel, or graving tool	Lacaille, 1750
Camelopardalis	Camelopardalis	Cam	Giraffe	Named by Jakob Bartsch in 1661
Cancer	Cancri	Cnc	Crab	In zodiac
Canes Venatici	Canum Venaticorum	CVn	Hunting dogs	Named by Johannes Hevelius in 1687
Canis Major	Canis Majoris	CMa	Big Dog	Contains Sirius and Adhara
Canis Minor	Canis Minoris	CMi	Little Dog	Contains Procyon
Capricornus	Capricorni	Cap	Goat	In zodiac
Carina	Carinae	Car	Ship's Keel[1]	Lacaille, 1750; contains Canopus
Cassiopeia	Cassiopeiae	Cas	Cassiopeia	Character in Greek myth
Centaurus	Centauri	Cen	Centaur	Character in Greek myth; contains Rigil Kentaurus and Hadar/Agena
Cepheus	Cephei	Cep	Cepheus	Character in Greek myth
Cetus	Ceti	Cet	Whale	Sea monster slain by Perseus
Chamaeleon	Chamaeleontis	Cha	Chameleon	Bayer, 1603
Circinus	Circini	Cir	Compass	Lacaille, 1750
Columba	Columbae	Col	Dove	Bayer, 1603
Coma Berenices	Comae Berenices	Com	Berenice's Hair	Third Century B.C. Egyptian Queen
Corona Australis	Coronae Australis	CrA	Southern Crown	Also Sagittarius' crown
Corona Borealis	Coronae Borealis	CrB	Northern Crown	Also Ariadne's crown
Corvus	Corvi	Crv	Crow	Companion of Orpheus
Crater	Crateris	Crt	Cup	—
Crux[2]	Crucis	Cru	Southern Cross	Named by Augustine Royer in 1679; Contains Beta Crucis and Acrux
Cygnus	Cygni	Cyg	Swan	Contains Deneb
Delphinus	Delphini	Del	Dolphin	—
Dorado	Doradus	Dor	Goldfish	Bayer, 1603
Draco	Draconis	Dra	Dragon	Dragon slain by Hercules
Equuleus	Equulei	Equ	Little Horse	—
Eridanus	Eridani	Eri	River Eridanus	Contains Achernar
Fornax	Fornacis	For	Furnace	Lacaille, 1750
Gemini	Geminorum	Gem	Twins	In zodiac; contains Pollux
Grus	Gruis	Gru	Crane	Bayer, 1603
Hercules	Herculis	Her	Hercules	Character from Greek myth
Horologium	Horologii	Hor	Clock	Lacaille, 1750.
Hydra[3]	Hydrae	Hya	Hydra	Monster from Greek myth
Hydrus	Hydri	Hyi	Sea serpent	Bayer, 1603
Indus	Indi	Ind	Indian	Bayer, 1603
Lacerta	Lacertae	Lac	Lizard	Hevelius, 1687
Leo	Leonis	Leo	Lion	In zodiac; contains Regulus
Leo Minor	Leonis Minoris	LMi	Little Lion	Hevelius, 1687
Lepus	Leporis	Lep	Hare	Prey of Orion
Libra	Librae	Lib	Scales	In zodiac
Lupus	Lupi	Lup	Wolf	Part of Centaurus group
Lynx	Lyncis	Lyn	Lynx	Hevelius, 1687
Lyra	Lyrae	Lyr	Harp	Contains Vega
Mensa	Mensae	Men	Table (mountain)	Lacaille, 1750
Microscopium	Microscopii	Mic	Microscope	Lacaille, 1750
Monoceros	Monocerotis	Mon	Unicorn	Royer, 1679
Musca	Muscae	Mus	Fly	Bayer, 1603
Norma	Normae	Nor	Carpenter's Square	Lacaille, 1750
Octans	Octantis	Oct	Octant	Lacaille, 1750
Ophiuchus	Ophiuchi	Oph	Serpent Bearer	Character in Greek myth
Orion	Orionis	Ori	The Hunter	Character in Greek myth; contains Rigel, Betelgeuse, and Bellatrix
Pavo	Pavonis	Pav	Peacock	Bayer, 1603
Pegasus	Pegasi	Peg	Pegasus	Winged horse in Greek myth

Name	Genitive	Abbr.	Translation	Remarks
Perseus	Persei	Per	Perseus	Character in Greek myth
Phoenix	Phoenicis	Phe	Phoenix	Bayer, 1603
Pictor	Pictoris	Pic	Easel	Lacaille, 1750
Pisces	Piscium	Psc	Fish	In zodiac
Piscis Austrinus	Piscis Austrin	PsA	Southern Fish	Contains Fomalhaut
Puppis	Puppis	Pup	Ship's Stern[1]	Lacaille, 1750
Pyxis	Pyxidis	Pyx	Ship's Compass[1]	Lacaille, 1750
Reticulum	Reticuli	Ret	Net	Lacaille, 1750
Sagitta	Sagittae	Sge	Arrow	—
Sagittarius	Sagittarii	Sgr	Archer	In zodiac
Scorpius	Scorpii	Sco	Scorpion	In zodiac; contains Antares and Shaula
Sculptor	Sculptoris	Scl	Sculptor	Lacaille, 1750
Scutum	Scuti	Sct	Shield	Hevelius, 1687
Serpens	Serpentis	Ser	Serpent	Snake held by giant Ophiuchus
Sextans	Sextantis	Sex	Sextant	Hevelius, 1687
Taurus	Tauri	Tau	Bull	In zodiac; contains Aldebran and El-nath
Telescopium	Telescopii	Tel	Telescope	Lacaille, 1750
Triangulum	Trianguli	Tri	Triangle	Contains spiral galaxy M33
Triangulum Australe	Trianguli Australis	TrA	Southern Triangle	Bayer, 1603
Tucana	Tucanae	Tuc	Toucan	Bayer, 1603
Ursa Major	Ursae Majoria	UMa	Big Bear	Big Dipper
Ursa Minor	Ursae Minoris	UMi	Little Bear	Little Dipper
Vela	Velorum	Vel	Ship's Sails[1]	Lacaille, 1750
Virgo	Virginis	Vir	Virgin	In zodiac; contains Spica
Volans	Volantis	Vol	Flying Fish	Bayer, 1603
Vulpecula	Vulpeculae	Vul	Little Fox	Hevelius, 1687

1. Formerly part of the constellation Argo Navis, the Argonauts' ship. 2. Smallest constellation. 3. Largest constellation.

dinary stars that move back and forth in space. Such small movements indicate one or more large planets in orbit about the each star. This method works for relatively nearby stars orbited by very large planets—planets about half the size of Saturn to eleven times the size of Jupiter. The planets found generally orbit closer to their stars than the orbit of Mercury about the Sun, although one system discovered in 2001 has two planets in orbits about as far from the star as Mars and Jupiter are from the Sun. Some planets have also been detected as they reduce visible light from their stars by passing between the stars and Earth. In the next few years new equipment for existing telescopes and several newly built telescopes are expected to make it possible to observe smaller extrasolar planets than any found so far.

Changes in the pulses from a pulsar are easier to observe than the exact position of an ordinary star, so the first known extrasolar planet was found at a pulsar. In 1991, Aleksander Wolszczan (American: 1946–) observed that the pulsar PSR 1257+12 regularly changed the timing of its pulses as if being pulled back and forth in space by several bodies in orbit. Calculations since then show that two of the bodies, each about the size of Earth, move in small, swift orbits about the pulsar. A third planet is about the size of Earth's Moon and orbits inside the other two.

As early as 1983, infrared studies from space revealed dust clouds that might be the seeds of planets around such nearby stars as Vega and Fomalhaut. In 2001, astronomers studying a young star in the Orion nebula observed what appear to be larger clumps of dust, the predicted next step in planet building. In 2001 even larger clumps about the star Zeta Leopris—perhaps forming an asteroid belt—were proposed to explain its higher-temperature dust halo.

▶STARS AND THE UNIVERSE

Astronomical Distances

The very large distances between stars and the even larger ones between the vast groups of stars called galaxies are usually expressed in terms of units of length that are peculiar to astronomy. The most familiar is the **light-year,** defined as the distance light travels in a vacuum in a year (approximately 365¼ days). Light travels through a vacuum at the rate of about 186,250 miles per second (exactly 299,792,458 m/s—exact because the meter is defined in terms of the speed of light in a vacuum). A light-year is approximately 5,880 trillion miles (9,460 trillion km).

Astronomers also use a measure even larger than the light-year, the **parsec,** equal to about 3.26 light-years, or about 19,170 trillion miles (30,840 trillion km).

A smaller unit, for measurements within the solar system, is the **astronomical unit,** which is the average distance between the Earth and the Sun, or about 93 million miles (150 million km).

The Constellations

Constellations consist of several bright stars that are treated as a group. Long ago, before recorded history, people began naming these groups. By Sumerian times (3000-2500 B.C.), stories were already being told about how particular constellations were formed. Most of our present knowledge of such stories, however, comes from the ancient Greeks.

One group of constellations has exerted a special influence on human thought, at least since 1500 B.C. As the Sun, Moon, and planets move through the sky, they pass through a group of 12 constellations, called the constellations of the zodiac. The ancient belief that the presence of the Sun in one of these constellations at a person's birth influences happenings on Earth is called astrology.

Today astronomers use constellations for mapping the sky. Each part of the sky is named by a particular constellation. These constellations, especially in the southern hemisphere, may not be traditional ones, but rather, groups of stars as-

25 Brightest Stars: Magnitudes and Distances From Earth

The stars we see in the evening sky differ in how bright they appear because of a combination of two factors: 1) their total energy output, or **luminosity** (directly related to their absolute magnitude) and 2) their distance from Earth. Astronomers refer to this combination of effects as the **apparent magnitude** of a star, a measure of how bright the star appears in the nighttime sky. To separate the two effects, astronomers define **absolute magnitude** as the brightness of a star as measured from a fixed distance. Most of the stars we see in the sky have a large absolute magnitude but are relatively far away. If all the stars were placed the same distance from Earth, Deneb would be the brightest and the Sun would be the faintest (about 250,000 times fainter than Deneb). Note that negative magnitudes are higher than positive magnitudes.

Rank/ Common name	Star name	Apparent magnitude	Absolute magnitude	Distance from Earth (light-years)
1. Sirius	α CMa	-1.44	1.45	8.6
2. Canopus[1]	α Car	-0.62	-5.53	312.6
3. Rigil Kentaurus[2]	α Cen A	-0.28	4.07	4.4
4. Arcturus	α Boo	-0.05	-0.31	36.7
5. Vega	α Lyr	0.03	0.58	25.3
6. Capella	α Aur A	0.08	-0.48	42.2
7. Rigel[1]	β Ori	0.18	-6.69	772.5
8. Procyon	β CMi	0.40	2.68	11.4
9. Achernar	α Eri	0.45	-2.77	143.7
10. Betelgeuse[1]	α Ori	0.45	-5.14	427.3
11. Hadar[1]	β Cen	0.61	-5.42	525.0
12. Altair	α Aql	0.76	2.20	16.8
13. Acrux[1,3]	α Cru	0.77	(3)	320.6
14. Aldebaran	α Tau	0.87	-0.63	65.1
15. Spica	α Vir	0.98	-3.55	262.1
16. Antares[1]	α Sco	1.06	-5.28	603.7
17. Pollux	β Gem	1.16	1.09	33.7
18. Fomalhaut	α PsA	1.17	1.74	25.1
19. Mimosa	β Cru	1.25	-3.92	352.4
20. Deneb[1]	α Cyg	1.25	-8.73	3,227.7
21. Regulus	α Leo	1.36	-0.52	77.5
22. Adhara[1]	ε CMa	1.50	-4.10	430.6
23. Castor[1]	α Gem	1.58	0.59	51.5
24. Gacrux	γ Cru	1.59	-0.56	87.9
25. Shaula[1]	λ Sco	1.62	-5.05	702.6

Note: The magnitudes of many stars on this list vary slightly over time, although for most stars, the variation is quite small. Betelgeuse and Antares have the largest variations (about 1 magnitude). For consistency, median magnitudes are shown for all stars. **1.** Stars more than 300 light-years away have an uncertainty of about 20 percent or more in their distances (and therefore in their absolute magnitudes as well). The distance of Deneb, in particular, may be wrong by half (i.e. only 1,600 light-years away). That would reduce Deneb's absolute magnitude to -7.22, still higher than any other star on this list. **2.** A binary star, with both stars orbiting around each other. They appear to the naked eye to be the same star, with a combined apparent and absolute magnitude. **3.** Acrux appears to the naked eye to be a single star, but in fact, it is the combined light of two stars, each at different distances from Earth. Its absolute magnitude, therefore, is impossible to define. **Source:** NASA.

tronomers have named so that for reference purposes all of the sky is labeled.

Star Names

While astronomers often use the traditional names of stars, most of which come to us from Latin or Arabic sources, they also use another system for naming objects in the sky that is based on constellations. Generally, the brightest star in a particular astronomical constellation is called alpha (α), the next brightest beta (ß), and so on through several letters of the Greek alphabet; then numbers are used. All astronomers' constellations are named in Latin. When astronomers refer to a star within its constellation, they use the genitive case, meaning "of the thing." Thus the constellation Big Dog is officially Canis Major, and Sirius is alpha Canis Majoris, or "alpha of Big Dog," usually abbreviated to αCMa. This means it is the brightest star in the constellation Big Dog (Sirius has long been known as the dog star). Since Sirius is a binary star (see "Binary stars," below), the much brighter main star is officially αCMa A. Further along, numbers are used instead of Greek letters. Numbered stars in the news in the 1990s included 51 Pegasi and 71 Virginis.

Magnitude

The brightness of a star is designated by a number called its magnitude, although the relationship between size and brightness is complicated. When the magnitude system was first developed, by the early Greek astronomers Hipparchus (c. 190–c. 120 B.C.) and Ptolemy (c. 100–c. 170), astronomers did not know the actual distances to stars, so magnitude always referred to brightness as seen from Earth. They classed the brightest stars as the first magnitude and the dimmest they could see as the sixth. These numbers were somewhat arbitrary until 1856, when George Phillips Bond (American: 1825–65) determined that photographs of stars show magnitude in a way that is directly measurable—bright stars appear as larger spots than dim stars in photographs even though all stars appear as points to the naked eye. Astronomers could use accurate measures to compare two stars and thus measure magnitude with mathematical precision. Under Bond's system, stars with a magnitude of 1.00 are exactly 100 times as bright as those with a magnitude of 6.00. On this scale, the very brightest stars have negative magnitudes.

Roughly, each whole number difference in magnitude corresponds to 2.5 times the brightness.

By the time this system was introduced, astronomers already were able to determine the distances of some stars from Earth. Friedrich Wilhelm Bessel was the first to make such a measurement, which he announced in 1838. A closer star appears brighter than a similar star that is farther away. To better understand the relative brightness of stars as they actually are, astronomers imagine viewing all stars from the same distance away. A star's brightness from this distance, which is 10 parsecs or 32.6 light-years, is called its absolute magnitude.

If we could see it clearly, the star Cygnus OB2 #12 would be the brightest star in the Milky Way galaxy (absolute magnitude -9.9), but it is not only far from Earth but also is obscured by dust. The brightest single object known is not a star, but a quasar (see "The Universe," below), BR 1202-07, with an absolute magnitude of about -33. The Sun has the brightest apparent magnitude of any star, -26.8, but its absolute magnitude is only 4.75.

The Universe

Most of the universe was greatly misunderstood until the 20th century. The most common notion from the time of the ancient Greek philosophers until the end of the Middle Ages was that a number of crystal spheres revolved about Earth, and that each of the planets, the Sun, and Earth's Moon occupied one of these spheres. All the stars occupied the farthest sphere. There were only about 6,000 stars known, those visible to the naked eye (and about half of these were south of the equator, so few Europeans had ever seen them).

In 1609 Galileo of Italy turned the first astronomical telescope on the heavens. Galileo's early telescopes were good enough to show that the Milky Way was not merely a whitish band across the sky but consisted of a vast number of stars, far more than the few thousand visible with the naked eye. His observations also disproved the old idea of crystal spheres. People began to speculate about astronomical entities beyond a simple sphere of stars. Not until 1924 were telescopes sufficiently powerful to show that many cloudy patches in the sky consisted of millions of stars far away from the Milky Way. This discovery led to the recognition of the enormous complexity and diversity of the universe.

Big Bang The accepted theory of how the universe began is known as the Big Bang theory, since it proposes that the universe began as something like an explosion, which has caused all parts of the universe to rush away from one another (the expansion of the universe). Evidence for the Big Bang theory includes the discovery of cosmic background radiation, a radiation that seems to come equally from all directions. Cosmic background radiation has the characteristics expected if the universe resulted from a small, dense region exploding.

Binary stars Almost half the stars in the visible universe are actually pairs of stars that orbit each other. Astronomers can sometimes see both stars, but more commonly they recognize that a star is part of a binary because of the influence of the dimmer star's gravitational pull on the other star.

Black holes When a body becomes so dense for its size that not even light can escape the powerful gravitational pull it exerts, it is called a black hole. Black holes were predicted as early as 1784 (by John Michell) and invoked later by various astronomers and physicists to explain many strange astronomical phenomena. Black holes have been observed at the center of many galaxies, including our own Milky Way. Several smaller black holes, thought to be remains of supernova explosions, have also been located.

Brown dwarfs are bodies too small to be stars, but too large to be planets. They glow dimly as a result of energy released by gravitational contraction. A brown dwarf must be between 13 and 80 times the mass of Jupiter. The first brown dwarf to be definitely established orbits the star Gliese 229. Although about 50 times Jupiter's mass, its diameter is about the same as Jupiter's. Since then, a number of brown dwarfs have been located, including some not in orbit about other stars.

Clusters of stars Stars often form together, forming associations of hundreds or thousands or clusters of millions of stars. Open clusters, such as the Pleiades (Seven Sisters), contain several hundred to a thousand stars gathered in an irregular region perhaps tens of light years across. There are about a thousand open clusters in the Milky Way Galaxy. Globular clusters contain millions of stars, most very old, that have formed into a sphere a 100 to 200 light-years in diameter. There are about 125 known globular clusters associated with the Milky Way.

Dwarfs Dwarfs are small stars—the brightest are blue dwarfs, the dimmest red dwarfs. The Sun is a yellow dwarf; there are also white and brown dwarfs.

Expanding universe When Albert Einstein developed his general theory of relativity, he found it predicted that the universe would either expand as if it were exploding, or else collapse. He tried to correct this prediction by inserting a term in his equations to counteract the prediction, but in the 1920s, Edwin Hubble discovered that the universe actually is expanding. It is easier to measure the speed of recession than the distance, so astronomers commonly use the speed at which something is moving away as the measure of its distance from us. Of course, it is not just moving away from us. In the expanding universe, everything is moving away from everything else.

Galaxies are systems of very many stars separated from one another by largely empty space (sometimes galaxies are called island universes). In the 18th century, William Herschel concluded that many cloudy patches of light seen among the stars were actually giant systems of billions of stars, but so far away from Earth as to look like clouds. Better telescopes proved him right in the early 20th century, and these far-off, great masses of stars became known as galaxies, after our own Milky Way, the galaxy that includes the Sun. Observation with large telescopes in the 20th century has revealed two main types of galaxies—spiral and elliptical—although some galaxies are neither (irregular).

Milky Way This is the galaxy to which the Sun and Earth belong; it contains about 100 billion stars. If you are in a place unafflicted with much light pollution, when you look at the night sky, you can see a faint band crossing it. The ancient Greeks named this the Milky Way (galaxy in Greek). Early in the 19th century, William Herschel determined that our Sun was a star in a vast lens-shaped star system, and that the Milky Way was the part of the star system we see from our vantage point inside it. Today, recognizing there are very many other such star systems, scientists often call it the Milky Way galaxy.

Missing mass and dark energy are thought to be the main part of the universe, with ordinary matter forming only 5% of the universe by mass. The evidence is that galaxies rotate in a way that indicates they must be embedded in a gravitational field caused by undetectable matter (*missing mass*) while all galaxies are flying apart with increasing speed caused by some unknown force that opposes gravity (*dark energy*). There are a number of competing theories as to the nature of these entities. The missing mass may consist of slow-moving unknown subatomic particles, while dark energy might be a cosmological constant inherent in the vacuum of empty space.

Nebulae are patches of gas and dust observable in telescopes. Before Herschel discovered that some cloudy patches seen through telescopes were vast collections of stars, all such patches were called nebulae (meaning clouds). Some "clouds" turned out to be galaxies, but many did not. The patches of gas emit light, often by the same mechanism that a fluorescent light does; energy from stars ionizes the gas, which gives off visible light. Some patches of dust also glow, usually reflecting the light of nearby stars. Other patches of dust are opaque or nearly so, blocking out part of the sky. Some of the most striking nebulae consist of glowing gas surrounded by opaque dust or vice versa, which gives the nebula a definite shape, such as the North America Nebula or the Horsehead Nebula. Herschel also studied a class of nebulae that looked to be giant spheres. He correctly concluded that these planetary nebulae were balls of gas produced when a star exploded.

Neutron stars are stars that have collapsed in a violent explosion, such as a supernova, so that the force keeping electrons apart is overcome. All the neutrons and protons can touch, forming the equivalent of a giant atomic nucleus. The star is electrically neutral because of the charge of the collapsed electrons. Such a star may be only a dozen miles in diameter but may have a mass twice that of the Sun.

Novae are stars that seem to appear out of nowhere. Later, they disappear. Early peoples were surprised from time to time by the appearance of a new (nova) star in the sky. Ancient Chinese astronomers called them guest stars. It is now clear that a truly new star does not appear; instead, a dim, existing star suddenly brightens. In early days, before the telescope, the dim stars could not be seen at all, so it looked as if a star came from nowhere. Today we know that there are two different types of "guest stars," and we reserve the name nova for one type and call the other a supernova (see below). The type referred to today as novae are less bright than supernovae and may appear more than once. It is thought that they occur when material from one star in a binary pair falls on the other star, causing it suddenly to flare up.

Pulsars are neutron stars that emit electromagnetic signals from their magnetic poles in a direction that reaches Earth. All neutron stars emit signals and rotate very rapidly (at least when they are first formed; they gradually slow down). These signals form a tight beam. If the beam intersects Earth, a radio telescope observes a fast pulsing on and off. The pulses are so regular that when they were first discovered, they were thought to be the work of extraterrestrial beings.

Quasars are distant sources of great energy. The name quasar is short for Quasi-Stellar Object, and the objects are so called because they seem to

Optical Telescopes

Telescopes were first developed in Holland about 400 years ago. The first telescopes used lenses to gather light and focus it. Later in the 17th century, scientists realized that curved mirrors could also gather and focus light. Since the light did not need to pass through the mirror (as light passes through a lens), mirrors proved to be more efficient than lenses for large telescopes.

Year	Type	Importance
1608	Lens	Hans Lippershey (Dutch: d. ca. 1916) applies for first patent on a telescope
1609	Lens	Galileo builds first astronomical telescopes, eventually reaching 30 power (or 30X enlargement)
1611	Lens	Johannes Kepler introduces convex eyepiece, producing greater power
1663	Mirror	James Gregory (Scottish: 1638-1676) is first to think that reflecting telescope can be made
1668	Mirror	Isaac Newton builds first telescope to use mirror to collect light, rather than lens
1723	Mirror	John Hadley (English: 1682-1744) invents reflecting telescope based on parabola, which concentrates light at a point
1789	Mirror	William Herschel builds telescope with 48-in. (122-cm) mirror, largest for many years
1895	Lens	Alvan Clark (American: 1832-1897) builds what is still world's largest telescope to use lens instead of mirror, 40 in. (102 cm)
1917	Mirror	Hooker Telescope at Mount Wilson in California is put into operation; at the time, it was world's largest (100 in., or 2.5 m)
1930	Combination	Bernard Schmidt (Estonian–German: 1879-1935) makes first telescopes combining lenses and mirrors; they become workhorse of astronomy
1948	Mirror	Hale Telescope (200 in., or 5 m) on Mt. Palomar, Calif., becomes largest and best on Earth
1962	Mirror	Largest telescope devoted to observing the Sun is erected at Kitt Peak in Arizona
1990	Mirror	Hubble Space Telescope (94 in., or 2.4 m) becomes first optical telescope in space
1993	Mirrors	Keck I Telescope in Hawaii uses world's largest mirror, 394 in. (10-m) in diameter; joined on May 8, 1996, with identical Keck II Telescope, both on Mauna Kea volcano
1999	Mirror	Japan's Subaru telescope begins operations on Mauna Kea; its 338-in (8.3m) mirror is the world's largest made from a single piece of glass
1999	Mirror	The Frederick C. Gillett Gemini Telescope (or Gemini North) is a 319-in. (8.0 m) reflector on Mauna Kea, built by a consortium. Its Chilean twin, Gemini South, was dedicated in 2002
1999	Mirror	The Hobby-Eberly Telescope has the world's largest primary mirror—433 inches (11 m)—but only 362 in. (9.2 m) of its surface is available at a time
2000	Mirror	The Very Large Telescope (VLT) of the European Southern Observatory (ESO) in Chile combines four 323-in. (8.2 m) mirrors
2005	Mirror	The Large Binocular Telescope on Mount Graham in Arizona uses two 331-in. (8.4 m) "honeycombed" mirrors on a single mount to collect more light than any other telescope

be about the size and general appearance of stars, but produce far too much energy to be stars. No one knows for sure what they are, but there is some evidence that quasars are caused by black holes in the central part of distant galaxies. The stars in the galaxies cannot be seen because of the great distance, so we see only the central part, which is the quasar.

Red giants are stars that have used their hydrogen fuel and expanded as a result. Young stars "burn" hydrogen in a nuclear fusion process that leads to helium. When a star has consumed the hydrogen in its core, new fusion reactions that start with helium begin, leading to carbon. The new reactions are hotter than the fusion of hydrogen to helium. This added energy causes the hydrogen and helium outside the core to expand. The star is red because the outer layers are relatively cool. When the Sun becomes a red giant in the distant future, it will expand almost to the orbit of Earth, completely engulfing Mercury and Venus, and charring Earth to a cinder.

Stars are bodies of gas large enough to undergo fusion reactions in their core. As a result of the energy produced by fusion, stars emit visible light, as well as electromagnetic radiation at other wavelengths. The Sun is a star. The hotter or larger a star is, the brighter it is.

Superclusters and clusters of galaxies are groups of galaxies associated in space. There may be just a few members of a cluster or as many as thousands. About two dozen galaxies near us form, with the Milky Way, our Local Group. The members of the Local Group also include the Andromeda galaxy and the Large and Small Magellanic Clouds. All are traveling through the universe together. The Local Group is a member of a supercluster of galaxies, called the Local Supercluster, that contains about 100 clusters. Clusters and superclusters are recognized because the average distance within a cluster or a supercluster from one galaxy or cluster to another is much less than the distance to other galaxies or clusters.

Supernovae are explosions of large stars. A supernova explosion is much more dramatic than the brightening of a nova. A supernova reported by Chinese astronomers from A.D. 1054 was visible in the daytime. The remnants of this explosion are known today as the Crab Nebula. At its heart the Crab Nebula has a pulsar, all that is left of the star that exploded.

Variable stars Any star that periodically changes brightness is called a variable (a nova changes brightness but not at regular intervals). The period varies with the cause of the change and the individual star. Some variables are part of a binary system in which one star periodically passes in front of the other. Other kinds of variables are called Mira variables and Cepheid variables, after the first stars known of each type. It is not clear what causes the brightness to vary.

White dwarfs are stars whose cores have collapsed until all the atoms are pressed very close together. A single teaspoonful of the matter in a white dwarf weighs about five tons. The core collapses because a red giant has used all its helium for fuel, but the star is too small to start burning carbon.

Major Accomplishments of Satellites and Space Probes, 1957–2005

While much attention is focused on human beings in space, most of the serious scientific progress has been made by satellites or probes—the general name for space vehicles that neither carry humans nor orbit Earth—that are directed internally or from Earth.

10/4/57 *Sputnik 1* First satellite to orbit Earth (USSR).

11/3/57 *Sputnik 2* Carries Laika, first dog in space; burns in atmosphere 4/14/58.

1/31/58 *Explorer 1* First satellite to detect Van Allen radiation belts; first U.S. satellite.

3/17/58 *Vanguard* Demonstrates Earth is pear-shaped with a bulge in Southern Hemisphere (U.S.).

1/2/59 *Mechta* First space probe to go into orbit around Sun, passing 5,000 mi. from Moon (at which it was aimed) (USSR).

3/3/59 *Pioneer 4* First American probe aimed at Moon; misses and goes into orbit about Sun.

9/12/59 *Lunik 2* First space probe to reach Moon, where it crash-lands (USSR).

10/4/59 *Lunik 3* First space probe to return photographs of far side of Moon (USSR).

4/1/60 *Tiros 1* First weather satellite (U.S.).

6/22/60 *Transit 1-B* First navigational satellite (U.S.).

8/12/60 *Echo 1* First communications satellite—actually a large balloon off which radio signals could be bounced (U.S.).

8/18/60 *Corona* First U.S. spy satellite.

8/19/60 *Sputnik 5* Carries dogs Belka and Streika. Successfully returns them to Earth; 18 orbits.

12/12/61 *Venera 1* First space probe intended to reach another planet—Venus (USSR).

3/7/62 *OSO 1* Orbiting Solar Observatory—first major astronomical satellite (U.S.).

4/23/62 *Ranger 4* First U.S. probe to reach Moon.

4/26/62 *Cosmos 4* First Soviet spy satellite.

7/10/62 *Telstar* First active communications satellite, allowing direct television between Europe and U.S. (U.S.).

8/27/62 *Mariner 2* First space probe to reach vicinity of another planet (Venus) and return scientific information (U.S.).

11/1/62 *Mars 1* First space probe aimed at Mars; contact lost about 66 million mi. from Earth (USSR).

6/26/63 *Syncom 2* First communications satellite to go into synchronous orbit with Earth (U.S.).

7/28/64 *Ranger 7* Returns close-up photographs of Moon, then crashes into it (U.S.).

8/28/64 *Nimbus 1* First weather satellite stabilized so that cameras always point toward Earth (U.S.).

11/28/64 *Mariner 4* Flies by Mars and takes 21 pictures of its surface, successfully transmitting them back to Earth; its closest approach is 6,118 mi. (U.S.).

4/6/65 *Early Bird* First commercial satellite (U.S.).

7/16/65   Proton 1 At 26,896 lbs., it is largest Earth satellite to this date (USSR).

11/16/65   Venera 3 Crash-lands on Venus; first space probe to make physical contact with another planet; radio contact lost before it reaches immediate vicinity of planet (USSR).

11/26/65   A-1 First satellite to be launched by nation other than the USSR or U.S. (France).

12/16/65   Pioneer 6 Launched into solar orbit; still partially functions today (U.S.).

1/31/66   Luna 9 Although main vehicle crashlands, ejected capsule lands safely on Moon and transmits photographs to Earth (USSR).

5/30/66   Surveyor 1 First soft landing of complete vehicle on Moon (U.S.).

3/31/66   Luna 10 First space vehicle to go into orbit about Moon (USSR).

8/10/66   Lunar Orbiter 1 First American space vehicle to go into orbit about Moon.

9/15/68   Zond 5 First Soviet satellite to return to Earth from vicinity of Moon.

2/11/70   Ohsumi First satellite launched by Japan.

4/24/70   Mao 1 First Chinese satellite; it broadcasts song "The East Is Red" once a minute, pausing at the end for other signals.

8/17/70   Venera 7 First Venus probe to return signals from planet's surface (USSR).

9/12/70   Luna 16 First space probe to land on Moon without humans aboard, scoop up samples, and return them to Earth (USSR).

11/10/70   Luna 17 Carries roving vehicle to Moon's surface; vehicle roams for 2 weeks at a time (during daylight), then "sleeps"; as it roams, it returns photos and other data to Earth (USSR).

12/12/70   Uhuru First X-ray satellite telescope (U.S.).

5/28/71   Mars 3 First space probe to soft-land on Mars; it quickly ceases functioning (USSR).

5/30/71   Mariner 9 First space probe to orbit another planet (Mars); returns 7,329 photographs of planet (U.S.).

3/2/72   Pioneer 10 First space probe to study Jupiter and, on June 13, 1983, first to leave solar system (U.S.); contact still maintained as of July 14, 2002.

7/23/72   Landsat 1 First Earth resources satellite (U.S.).

3/6/73   Pioneer 11 First space probe to reach vicinity of Saturn (U.S.).

11/3/73   Mariner 10 First space probe to observe 2 planets, Venus and Mercury, and only probe ever to observe Mercury (U.S.).

12/10/74   Helios First W. German space probe.

6/8/75   Venera 9 Returns first photographs from surface of Venus (U.S.).

8/20/75   Viking 1 First American space probe to soft-land on Mars; returns data until Nov., 1982.

9/20/75   Viking 2 Soft-lands on Mars (U.S.).

8/20/77   Voyager 2 After studying Jupiter and Saturn, it becomes first space probe to reach vicinities of Uranus and Neptune (U.S.).

9/5/77   Voyager 1 Studies Jupiter; becomes first probe to reach vicinity of Saturn, then furthest probe from Sun on Feb. 17, 1998; by 2004 is more than 8.4 billion miles (13.5 billion km) from Earth (U.S.).

1/26/78   IUE International Ultraviolet Explorer — the first astronomical satellite to be placed in geosynchronous orbit; it sends back data until 1996 (European Space Agency, or ESA, U.S.; and Britain).

5/20/78   Pioneer 12 (Venus 1) First space probe to go into orbit about Venus. (U.S.).

6/26/78   Seasat Analyzes ocean currents and ice flow (U.S.).

8/12/78   ISEE-3 Originally the third International Sun-Earth Explorer. Renamed International Cometary Explorer when it is redirected to study tail of comet Giacobini-Zinner in 1983 (U.S.).

12/13/78   HEAO-2 High-Energy Astronomy Observatory (or Einstein Observatory); makes high-resolution X-ray images of the universe (U.S.).

2/24/79   P78-1 Studies solar radiation until purposely shot down by U.S. Air Force 9/13/85

2/14/80   Solar Max Studies solar radiation; after failure in Nov. 1980, it is repaired and relaunched from space shuttle in April 1984; finally pushed to its destruction by massive solar flare, 12/2/89 (U.S.).

1/25/83   IRAS Infrared Astronomical Satellite studies galactic and extragalactic infrared sources and discovers new planets forming (U.S.).

12/15/84   Vega 1 First Soviet mission to study Halley's comet; along the way it drops balloon probe into atmosphere of Venus.

12/21/84   Vega 2 Second Soviet mission to Halley's comet; releases a balloon probe at Venus.

1/7/85   Sakigake First Japanese mission to study Halley's comet (this one from far away).

7/2/85   Giotto Joint European mission to Halley's comet; passes closest to the comet—375 mi. (600 km)—and later is redirected to comet Grigg-Skjellerup, which it passes 7/10/92 at a distance of 125 mi. (200 km).

8/18/85   Suisei Japanese mission to Halley's comet.

2/21/86   SPOT French satellite; photographs surface details of Earth as small as 30 ft. across.

5/4/89   Magellan American probe orbits Venus and maps it in detail with radar.

10/18/89   Galileo After passing near Venus and Earth (twice), it reports on Jupiter's moons before crashing into Jupiter in Sept. 2003. (U.S.).

11/18/89   Cosmic Background Explorer (COBE) Studied cosmic background radiation in hopes of learning cause of galaxy formation.

4/24/90   Hubble Space Telescope Flawed optical telescope placed in orbit about Earth by U.S.; successfully repaired 12/10/93.

10/6/90   Ulysses Studying previously unobserved north and south poles of the Sun (U.S.-ESA).

4/5/91   Compton Gamma Ray Observatory A 17-ton telescope that observed the universe at very short wavelengths until June 4, 2000.

8/31/91   Yohkoh Japanese satellite that reports on X-rays and gamma rays from the Sun.

6/7/92   Extreme Ultraviolet Explorer (EUVE) American satellite studies high range of ultraviolet radiation in universe.

7/3/92   Solar Anomalous and Magnetospheric Particle Explorer (SAMPEX) American satellite that reports on particles in space, including space dust and the solar wind.

7/24/92   Geotail Japanese satellite launched by NASA to study Earth's magnetosphere.

2/9/93   Pegasus 3 Brazilian satellite to monitor environment in Amazonia, launched by Orbital Sciences Corp. of Fairfax, Va.

2/20/93   ASCA Japanese X-ray telescope.

1/25/94   Clementine Joint U.S. military-science mission; maps the moon from lunar orbit and later visits the asteroid Geographos.

11/1/94   WIND Goes into a figure-8 path around the Earth and Moon, studying the solar wind; in 1996, moved to a point in Earth's orbit and orbits the Sun itself, staying in the same relation to the Earth as it revolves, a million miles from Earth.

3/18/95   Infrared Telescope in Space (IRTS) Japan's infrared space telescope surveys 7 percent of the sky over a period of 28 days.

11/17/95   Infrared Space Observatory (ISO) A European Space Agency satellite that extends the work of the earlier IRAS. Nicknamed "Europe's Hubble" (ESA).

12/2/95   Solar and Heliospheric Observatory (SOHO) Studies the sun from an orbit of about 930,000 miles (1.5 million km) from Earth (ESA/U.S.).

12/30/95 *Rossi X-Ray Timing Explorer (XTE)* First U.S. X-ray telescope since 1978; studies X-ray sources in Milky Way including stars, pulsars, and possible black holes.

2/17/96 *Shoemaker Near Earth Asteroid Rendezvous (NEAR-Shoemaker)* First of the new, less-expensive Discovery series of space probes. It passes close to asteroid 253 Mathilde in June 1999. *NEAR* orbits asteroid 433 Eros starting in February 2000, and lands on asteroid on February 12, 2001 (U.S.).

2/24/96 *Polar* Like WIND, Polar is reporting on the interaction of the solar wind and Earth's magnetic field, concentrating especially on the poles. It can take UV images of Earth's auroras and X-ray images of high-speed electrons in the solar wind (U.S.).

4/30/98 *BeppoSAX (Satellite per Astronimica a Raggi X)* This small orbiting observatory studies X-ray-emitting events from outer space. It scores a major triumph when it pinpoints the location of a gamma-ray burster for the first time, showing that these events are the most powerful explosions known (Italy/Netherlands/ESA).

8/21/96 *FAST (Fast Auroral Snapshot)* Smaller, cheaper satellite of the Small-Class Explorer series studies auroras from low-Earth orbit (U.S.).

11/7/96 *Mars Global Surveyor* A probe to Mars orbits the planet and surveys it from space for one Mars year (687 Earth days) starting in March, 1999, after delays caused by a defective solar panel. (U.S.).

12/4/96 *Mars Pathfinder* Bounces to the surface of Mars in the Ares Vallis region on 7/4/97, where it releases a rover named *Sojourner* to report on Martian geology. (U.S.).

8/25/97 *Advanced Composition Explorer (ACE)* Studies solar wind and particles from interstellar space (cosmic rays) as it orbits a stable point where the gravity from the Earth and Sun are in balance (U.S.)

10/15/97 *Cassini-Huygens* Mission to orbit Saturn and study its satellites; *Cassini* is the orbiter that began orbiting Saturn on July 1, 2004, while *Huygens* is a probe that sent close-ups of Titan, Saturn's largest moon, as it parachuted through the atmosphere on January 14, 2005. *Huygens* broadcast additional images for 2.5 hours after landing (U.S./ESA)

4/2/98 *Transition Region and Coronal Explorer (TRACE)* Uses ultraviolet telescope to study magnetism in the Sun's corona from a polar orbit about Earth. (U.S.).

7/4/98 *Nozomi/Planet B* Planned orbit about Mars fails and on December 9, 2003, spacecraft flies by Mars (Japan).

10/24/98 *Deep Space 1* Tests new technologies for space use including ion-propulsion system. (U.S.).

12/5/98 *Submillimeter Wave Astronomy Satellite (SWAS)* Space-based radio telescopes analyze microwaves to study chemical composition of interstellar gas clouds, the homes of new star formation. (U.S.).

2/7/99 *Stardust* First mission intended to return material from a comet; flew within 149 miles (214 km) of comet Wild 2 on January 2, 2004, and gathered samples of particles streaming from the comet. Will radio data and images to Earth in 2004, then return in January 2006 and parachute comet samples and interstellar dust back to Earth. (U.S.).

6/24/99 *Far Ultraviolet Spectroscopic Explorer (FUSE)* Exploring the universe at wavelengths slightly longer than X-rays, FUSE fills a significant gap in coverage of the electromagnetic spectrum (U.S./Canada/France).

7/23/99 *Chandra X-Ray Observatory* Its X-ray telescopes reveal previously unknown details of black holes, white dwarfs, neutron stars, and the X-ray background radiation. (U.S.).

12/10/99 *XXM-Newton* The most powerful X-ray detector ever, XXM-Newton has 3 X-ray telescopes using 58 mirrors each as well as 2 X-ray spectrographs and an optical telescope. Its orbit takes it 1/3 the way to the Moon, giving it long periods for observation of active stars, galaxies, and black holes (ESA).

3/25/2000 *Imager for Magnetopause-to-Aurora Global Exploration (IMAGE)* The first satellite mission dedicated to imaging the Earth's magnetosphere, the region of space controlled by the Earth's magnetic field and containing extremely tenuous plasmas of both solar and terrestrial origin. (U.S.).

7/12/00 and **8/9/00** *Cluster* Four spacecraft that maintain positions as the vertices of a pyramid as they orbit Earth in formation and study the interactions of Earth with the solar wind. (ESA).

10/9/00 *High Energy Transient Explorer (HETE II)* Observes, reports, and locates gamma-ray bursts for follow up by astronomers and surveys X-ray sources across the universe. (U.S., France, Japan, Italy).

4/7/01 *Mars Odyssey* Entered Mars orbit on October 23, 2001; primary mission from Feb. 2002 to Aug. 2004 is to search for water using instruments that recognize certain minerals and that detect hydrogen and also study the amount of radiation present; it will also be a communication relay for other Mars probes to be launched starting in 2003.

6/30/01 *Wilkinson Microwave Anisotropy Probe (MAP)* Mission to measure temperature fluctuations in the cosmic microwave background. From its solar orbit at the L2 Lagrange point, 1 million miles (1.6 million km) from Earth, it has made the first full-sky map of the oldest light in the universe, improving understanding of how and when galaxies formed. (U.S.)

8/8/01 *Genesis* A mission designed to spend three years in solar orbit, collecting particles from the solar wind, and then returning the material to Earth. Although its parachute failed to deploy on 9/8/04, usable data was recovered from the crash site. (U.S.)

12/7/01 *Thermosphere-Ionosphere-Mesosphere-Energetics and Dynamics (TIMED)* Studies influence of Sun and humans on the upper atmosphere. (U.S.).

2/5/02 *Reuven Ramaty High Energy Solar Spectroscopic Imager (RHESSI)* Explores the basic physics of particle acceleration and energy release by solar flares. (U.S.).

3/17/02 *Gravity Recovery and Climate Experiment (GRACE)* Two spacecraft flying in tandem make extremely precise measurements of Earth's gravitational field. (U.S.-Germany).

10/17/2002 *International Gamma-Ray Astrophysics Laboratory (INTEGRAL)* The elongated orbit and sensitive detectors of *INTEGRAL* enable it to study gamma rays from the far reaches of the universe. (ESA/Russia/U.S.)

1/12/2003 *Cosmic Hot Interstellar Plasma Spectrometer (CHIPS)* Studying a poorly monitored wavelength region of the electromagnetic spectrum, *CHIPS* will report on hot gas, dissociated into electrons and nuclei, that occupies our region of space. (U.S.).

4/28/2003 *Galaxy Evolution Explorer (GALEX)* A small satellite studying ultraviolet emissions of nearby galaxies in an effort to uncover the origin and evolution of the universe and how stars are formed. (U.S.).

6/2/2003 *Mars Express* This Mars orbiter launched a small lander toward the Red Planet, but the lander, *Beagle 2*, lost contact after its December 19, 2003, separation from the orbiter. The orbiter is using photography and radar to explore the planet. (ESA/U.S.)

6/10/03 and **7/7/03** *Mars Exploration Rovers Mission* Both rovers—*Spirit* and *Opportunity*—successfully landed on Mars and have been transmitting images and data from their two landing sites. A major discovery is the confirmation that liquid water once existed on Mars' surface. (U.S.).

8/25/03 *Spitzer Space Telescope* One of NASA's "four great observatories" (with Hubble, Chandra, and Compton Gamma-Ray Observatory); a sensitive infrared observatory orbiting Earth. (U.S.).

3/2/04 *Rosetta* A mission to Comet 67 P/Churyumov-Gerasimenko ("67/P" for short) that will take a ten-year

journey, using three gravity assists from Earth and one from Mars, before entering orbit about the 67/P. In November 2014 it will release a probe (named *Philae*) intended to land on the comet. (ESA)
4/20/04 *Gravity Probe – B* A satellite using precise gyroscopes to test Einstein's general relativity prediction of how Earth's presence and rotation warp nearby spacetime. (U.S.)
8/3/04 *MESSENGER* The first space probe intended to orbit the planet Mercury. *MESSENGER* will fly by Earth once, Venus twice, and Mercury three times before settling into orbit about Mercury in March 2011. (U.S.)

1/12/05 *Deep Impact* Successfully blasts a crater in the comet Tempel 1 on July 4, 2005. (U.S.)
8/12/05 *Mars Reconnaissance Orbiter* Entered a low Mars orbit in March 2006; the *MRO* will examine the surface of Mars in great detail. (U.S.)
1/19/06 *New Horizons* First space probe sent to study Pluto and objects in the Kuiper Belt. Scheduled to reach Pluto in 2016 and Kuiper belt in 2018. (U.S.)
12/18/07 *Dawn* First space probe sent to study Ceres, Vesta, and other objects in the belt between Mars and Jupiter. Scheduled to reach Ceres in 2011 and Vesta in 2015.

Spaceflights Carrying People, 1961–August 2007

The space programs of the former Soviet Union and the United States both had dramatic flights by human pilots as an important component, although many scientists felt that most goals of the space program could be achieved without risking lives. The *Vostok*, *Voskhod* and *Soyuz* missions were part of the Soviet program; *Mercury*, *Gemini*, *Apollo*, *Skylab* and the shuttle are part of the U.S. program.

Proving that People Can Venture into Space

4/12/61 *Vostok 1* (1 hr. 48 min.) Yuri A. Gagarin. First spaceflight by human.
5/5/61 *Mercury 3* (15 min.) Alan B. Shepard Jr. Suborbital.
7/21/61 *Mercury 4* (16 min.) Virgil "Gus" Grissom. Suborbital.
8/6/61 *Vostok 2* (25 hrs. 18 min.) Gherman S. Titov. First multiorbit flight; 17 orbits.
2/20/62 *Mercury 6* (5 hrs. 55 min.) John H. Glenn. First orbital flight by American; 3 orbits.
5/24/62 *Mercury 7* (4 hrs. 56 min.) M. Scott Carpenter. 3 orbits.
8/11/62 *Vostok 3* (94 hrs. 24 min.) Andrian G. Nikolayev. 64 orbits; landing by parachute.
8/12/62 *Vostok 4* (70 hrs. 57 min.) Pavel R. Popovitch. Dual launch with *Vostok 3*; 48 orbits.
10/3/62 *Mercury 8* (9 hrs. 13 min.) Walter Schirra. 6 orbits.
5/15/63 *Mercury 9* (34 hrs. 20 min.) Gordon Cooper. 22 orbits.
6/14/63 *Vostok 5* (119 hrs. 6 min.) V. Bikovsky. 81 orbits.
6/16/63 *Vostok 6* (70 hrs. 50 min.) Valentina V. Tereshkova. First woman cosmonaut; 48 orbits; dual launch with *Vostok 5*.
10/12/64 *Voskhod 1* (24 hrs. 17 min.) Vladimir M. Komarov, Konstantin P. Feoktistov, Boris B. Yegorov. First multihuman crew; 3 cosmonauts make 16 orbits.

Planning for Operations in Space

3/18/65 *Voskhod 2* (26 hrs.) A. Leonov, P. Belyayev. First extravehicular activity (EVA) by Leonov (20 min.); 17 orbits.
3/23/65 *Gemini 3* (4 hrs. 53 min.) Virgil "Gus" Grissom, John Young. First American multi-person crew; 3 orbits.
6/3/65 *Gemini 4* (97 hrs. 56 min.) James McDivitt, Edward White II. 62 orbits; first American EVA; first use of personal propulsion unit.
8/21/65 *Gemini 5* (190 hrs. 56 min.) Gordon Cooper, Charles Conrad 120 orbits; demonstrates feasibility of lunar mission; simulated rendezvous.
12/4/65 *Gemini 7* (330 hrs. 35 min.) Frank Borman, James Lovell. 206 orbits; extensions of testing and performance; target for first rendezvous.
12/16/65 *Gemini 6A* (25 hrs. 51 min.) Walter Schirra, Thomas Stafford. 15 orbits; rendezvous with *Gemini 7*.
3/16/66 *Gemini 8* (10 hrs. 42 min.) Neil Armstrong, David Scott. 6.5 orbits; first dual launch and docking; first Pacific landing.

6/3/66 *Gemini 9A* (72 hrs. 21 min. Thomas Stafford, Eugene Cernan. 44 orbits; unable to dock with target vehicle; 2 hrs. 7 min. of EVA.
7/18/66 *Gemini 10* (70 hrs. 47 min.) John Young, Michael Collins. 43 orbits; first dual rendezvous; docking maneuvers, umbilical EVA.
9/12/66 *Gemini 11* (71 hrs. 17 min.) Charles Conrad Jr., Richard Gordon Jr. 44 orbits; rendezvous and docking.
11/11/66 *Gemini 12* (94 hrs. 34 min.) James Lovell, Edwin "Buzz" Aldrin Jr. 59 orbits; final *Gemini* mission; 5 hours of EVA.

To the Moon and Beyond

4/23/67 *Soyuz 1* (26 hrs. 48 min.) Vladimir M. Komarov, 18 orbits; Komarov is killed when parachute fails; first fatality of space program.
10/11/68 *Apollo 7* (260 hrs. 8 min.) Walter Schirra, Donn Eisele, Walter Cunningham. 8 service propulsion firings; 7 live TV sessions with crew; rendezvous with S-IVB stage performed.
10/26/68 *Soyuz 3* (94 hrs. 51 min.) G. Beregovoi. 64 orbits; approaches unpiloted *Soyuz 2* to distance of 650 ft. (198 m).
12/21/68 *Apollo 8* (147 hrs.) Frank Borman, James Lovell, William Anders. First *Saturn-V* propelled flight; first lunar orbital mission (10 orbits); returns lunar photography.
1/14/69 *Soyuz 4* (71 hrs. 14 min.) V. Shatalov, 48 orbits; docks with *Soyuz 5* in first linkup of 2 space vehicles both carrying people.
1/15/69 *Soyuz 5* (72 hrs. 46 min.) B. Volynov, A. Yeliseyev, Y. Khrunov. 3 cosmonauts perform EVA, transferred to *Soyuz 4* in rescue rehearsal.
3/3/69 *Apollo 9* (241 hrs. 1 min.) James McDivitt, David Scott, Russell Schweickart. First flight of all lunar hardware in Earth orbit, incl. lunar module.
5/18/69 *Apollo 10* (192 hrs. 3 min.) Eugene Cernan, John Young, Thomas Stafford. Lunar mission development flight to evaluate lunar module performance in lunar environment; descent to within 50,000 ft. of Moon.
7/16/69 *Apollo 11* (165 hrs. 18 min.) Neil Armstrong, Michael Collins, Edwin "Buzz" Aldrin Jr. First lunar landing (July 20); limited inspection, photography, evaluation, and sampling of lunar soil.
10/11/69 *Soyuz 6* (118 hrs. 42 min.) G. Shonin, V. Kubasov. First triple launch (with *Soyuz 7* and 8).
10/12/69 *Soyuz 7* (118 hrs. 41 min.) A. Filipchenko, V. Volkov, V. Gorbatko. With *Soyuz 6* and 8, conducts experiments in navigation and photography.
10/13/69 *Soyuz 8* (118 hrs. 59 min.) V. Shatalov, A. Yeliseyev. 80 orbits.
11/14/69 *Apollo 12* (244 hrs. 36 min.) Charles Conrad Jr., Richard Gordon Jr., Alan Bean. Second lu-

nar landing; demonstrates point landing capability; samples more area.

4/11/70   Apollo 13 (142 hrs. 55 min.) James Lovell, Fred Haise Jr., John Swigert Jr. Third lunar landing attempt aborted owing to loss of pressure in liquid oxygen in service module and fuel cell failure.

6/2/70   Soyuz 9 (424 hrs. 59 min. [17 days 16 hrs.]) A. Nikolayev, V. Sevastianov. Longest spaceflight to this time.

1/31/71   Apollo 14 (9 days 42 min.) Alan Shepard, Stuart Roosa, Edgar Mitchell. Third lunar landing, returns 98 lbs. of material.

4/23/71   Soyuz 10 (47 hrs. 46 min.) V. Shatalov, A. Yeleseyev, N. Rukavishnikov. Docks with *Salyut 1*, the first space station.

6/6/71   Soyuz 11 (23 days 18 hrs. 22 min.) G. Dobrovolsky, V. Patsayev, V. Volkov. All 3 cosmonauts killed during reentry.

7/26/71   Apollo 15 (12 days 7 hrs. 12 min.) David Scott, Alfred Worden, James Irwin. Fourth lunar landing; first to carry Lunar Roving Vehicle (LRV).

4/16/72   Apollo 16 (11 days 14 hrs. 51 min.) John Young, Ken Mattingly, Charles Duke Jr. Fifth lunar landing; second to carry LRV. Returns 213 lbs. of material.

12/7/72   Apollo 17 (12 days 13 hrs. 52 min.) Eugene Cernan, Ronald Evans, Harrison Schmitt. Last manned lunar landing; third with LRV; total EVA time: 44 hrs. 8 min.; returns 243 lbs. of material.

First Stations in Space

5/25/73   Skylab 2 (28 days 49 min.) Charles. Conrad Jr., Joseph Kerwin, Paul Weitz. First *Skylab* launch; establishes *Skylab Orbital Assembly* in earth orbit; conducts medical and other experiments.

7/29/73   Skylab 3 (59 days 11 hrs. 9 min.) Alan Bean, Owen Garriott, Jack Lousma. Second *Skylab*; crew performs systems and operational tests and thermal shield deployment.

9/27/73   Soyuz 12 (47 hrs. 16 min.) V. Lazarev, O. Makarov. First Soviet spaceflight to carry humans since *Soyuz 11* tragedy.

11/16/73   Skylab 4 (84 days 1 hr. 7 min.) Gerald P. Carr, Edward G. Gibson, William R. Pogue. Services unmanned Saturn workshop; obtains medical data for extending spaceflights.

12/18/73   Soyuz 13 (7 days 20 hrs. 55 min.) P. Klimuk, V. Lebedev. Performs astrophysical and biological experiments.

7/3/74   Soyuz 14 (15 days 17 hrs. 30 min.) P. Popovich, Y. Artyukhin. Crew occupies *Salyut 3* space station; studies Earth resources.

8/26/74   Soyuz 15 (48 hrs. 12 min.) G. Sarafanov, L. Demin. Makes unsuccessful attempt to dock with *Salyut 3*.

12/2/74   Soyuz 16 (5 days 22 hrs. 24 min.) A. Filipchenko, N. Rukavishnikov. Taken to check modifications to *Salyut* system.

1/10/75   Soyuz 17 (29 days 13 hrs. 20 min.) A. Gubarev, G. Grechko. Docks with *Salyut 4;* sets Soviet endurance record.

4/5/75   Soyuz 18A (22 min.) V. Lazarev, O. Makarov. Separation from booster fails, and craft fails to reach orbit, but crew successfully lands in western Siberia.

5/24/75   Soyuz 18B (63 days) P. Klimuk, V. Sevastyanov. Docks with *Salyut 4.*

7/15/75   ASTP (9 days 1 hr. 30 min.) Thomas Stafford, Vance Brand, Donald Slayton. *Apollo-Soyuz Test Project,* cooperative U.S.-Soviet mission.

7/15/75   Soyuz 19 (5 days 23 hrs. 31 min.) A. Leonov, V. Kubasov. Docks with *ASTP,* the U.S. *Apollo* capsule.

The Soviet Study of Human Biology in Space

11/17/75   Soyuz 20 (90 days) No crew. Biological mission; docks with *Salyut 4.*

7/6/76   Soyuz 21 (49 days) B. Volynov, V. Zholobov. Docks with *Salyut 5* and performs Earth resource work.

9/15/76   Soyuz 22 (8 days) V. Bykovsky, V. Aksenov. Takes Earth-resources photographs.

10/14/76   Soyuz 23 (2 days) V. Zudov, V. Rozhdestvensky. Unsuccessful attempt to dock with *Salyut 5*; first landing in water (unplanned) for Soviet program (crew survives).

2/7/77   Soyuz 24 (7 days) V. Gorbatko, Y. Glazkov. Docks with *Salyut 5* for 18 days of experiments.

10/9/77   Soyuz 25 (2 days) V. Kovalyonok, V. Ryumin. Unsuccessful attempt to dock with *Salyut 6.*

12/10/77   Soyuz 26 (96 days) Y. Romanenko, G. Grechko. Docks with *Salyut 6*; crew sets endurance record.

1/10/78   Soyuz 27 (6 days) V. Dzhanibekov, O. Makarov. Carries second crew to dock with *Salyut 6* space station.

3/2/78   Soyuz 28 (8 days) V. Remek, A. Gubarev. Carries third crew to board *Salyut 6*; Remek first non-Russian, non-American in space (Czech).

6/15/78   Soyuz 29 (140 days) V. Kovalyonok, A. Ivanchenkov. Docks with *Salyut 6*; crew sets new endurance record.

6/27/78   Soyuz 30 (8 days) P. Klimuk, M. Hermaszewski. Carries second international crew to *Salyut 6*; first Polish cosmonaut, Hermaszewski.

8/25/78   Soyuz 31 (8 days) V. Bykovsky, S. Jahn. Carries third international crew to *Salyut 6*; first East German, Jahn.

2/25/79   Soyuz 32 (175 days) V. Lyakhov, V. Ryumin. Carries crew to *Salyut 6*; sets new endurance record.

4/10/79   Soyuz 33 (2 days) N. Rukavishnikov, Georgi Ivanov (first Bulgarian). Engine failure prior to docking forces early termination.

6/6/79   Soyuz 34 (74 days) No crew. Launches with no crew; returns with crew from *Salyut 6.*

4/9/80   Soyuz 35 (185 days) V. Ryumin, L. Popov. Carries 2 crew members to *Salyut 6.*

5/26/80   Soyuz 36 (8 days) V. Kubasov, B. Farkas. Carries 2 crew members to *Salyut 6*; crew returns in *Soyuz 35*; first Hungarian, Farkas.

6/5/80   Soyuz T-2 (4 days) Y. Malyshev, V. Aksenov. Test of modified *Soyuz* craft; docks with *Salyut 6.*

7/23/80   Soyuz 37 (8 days) V. Gorbatko, P. Tuan (first Vietnamese in space). Exchanges cosmonauts in *Salyut 6*; returns *Soyuz 35* crew after 185 days in orbit.

9/18/80   Soyuz 38 (8 days) Y. Romanenko, A. Tamayo-Mendez (Cuba). Ferries to *Salyut 6.*

11/27/80   Soyuz T-3 (13 days) L. Kizim, O. Makarov, G. Strekalov. Ferries to *Salyut 6*; first 3-person crew since *Soyuz 11.*

3/12/81   Soyuz T-4 (75 days) V. Kovalyonok, V. Savinykh. Mission to *Salyut 6.*

3/22/81   Soyuz 39 (8 days) V. Dzhanibekov, J. Gurragcha (first Mongolian). Docks with *Salyut 6.*

The Space Shuttle: U.S. Reentry in Space

4/12/81   Columbia (2 days 6 hrs.) John Young, Robert Crippen. First flight of reusable space shuttle; first landing of U.S. spacecraft on land.

5/14/81   Soyuz 40 (8 days) L. Popov, D. Prunariu. First Romanian (Prunariu), in space.

11/12/81   Columbia (2 days 6 hrs.) Joe Engle, Richard Truly. First reuse of space shuttle; ends early due to loss of fuel cell.

3/22/82   Columbia (8 days) Jack Lousma, Gordon Fullerton. Third shuttle flight; payload includes space science experiments.

5/13/82   Soyuz T-5 (211 days) A. Berezovoy, V. Lebedev. First flight to *Salyut 7*; space station equipped to measure body functions.

6/24/82   Soyuz T-6 (8 days) V. Dzhanibekov, J. Chrétien, A. Ivanchenkov. Mission to *Salyut 7*; Soviet/French team; first French cosmonaut, Chrétien.

6/27/82   Columbia (7 days 1 hr.) Ken. Mattingly Henry Hartsfield Jr. Fourth shuttle mission; first landing on hard surface.

8/16/82   Soyuz T-7 (8 days) L. Popov, S. Savitskaya (second Soviet woman in space), A. Serebrov. Mission to *Salyut 7.*

11/11/82   Columbia (5 days 2 hrs.) Vance Brand, Robert Overmyer, Joseph Allen, William Lenoir. First operational mission; first 4-man crew; first deployment of satellites from shuttle.

4/4/83   Challenger (5 days) Paul Weitz, Karol Bobko, Donald Peterson, Story Musgrave. Second shuttle joins fleet; deploys TDRS tracking satellite; first shuttle EVA.

4/20/83   Soyuz T-8 (48 hrs.) V. Titov, G. Strekalov, A. Serebrov. Planned rendezvous with *Salyut 7* fails.

6/18/83   Challenger (6 days) Robert Crippen, Frederick Hauck, John Fabian, Sally Ride, Norman Thagard. First 5-person crew; Ride is first U.S. woman in space; first use of Remote Manipulator Structure ("Arm") to deploy and retrieve satellite.

6/27/83   Soyuz T-9 (150 days) V. Lyakhov, A. Aleksandrov. Crew spends 149 days in *Salyut 7* after *Soyuz 10* fails in relief mission.

8/30/83   Challenger (6 days) Richard Truly, Daniel Brandenstein, William Thornton, Guion Bluford (first black American), Dale Gardner. First night launch. Launches weather/communications satellite for India.

11/28/83   Columbia (10 days) John Young, Brewster Shaw Robert Parker, Owen Garriott, Byron Lichtenberg, Ulf Merbold. Launches *Spacelab;* crew performs experiments in astronomy and medicine.

2/3/84   Challenger (8 days) Vance Brand, Bruce McCandless, Robert Stewart, Ronald McNair, Robert Gibson. Jet-propelled backpacks carry 2 astronauts on first untethered space walks; 2 satellites lost; first landing at Kennedy Space Center.

2/8/84   Soyuz T-10B (237 days) L. Kizim, O. Atkov, V. Solovyev. Mission to *Salyut 7* to repair propulsion system; sets new duration-in-space record for crew.

4/2/84   Soyuz T-11 (8 days) Y. Malyshev, G. Strekalov, R. Sharma. Docks with *Salyut 7*; first Indian cosmonaut, Sharma.

4/6/84   Challenger (7 days) Robert Crippen, Richard Scobee, Terry Hart, George Nelson, James van Hoften. Deploys Long Duration Exposure Facility for experiments in space durability; snares Solar Max satellite; repairs altitude-control system.

7/18/84   Soyuz T-12 (12 days) S. Savitskaya, V. Dzhanibekov, I. Volk. Savitskaya becomes first woman to walk in space.

8/30/84   Discovery (7 days) Henry Hartsfield Jr., Michael Coats, Steven Hawley, Judith Resnik, Richard Mullane, Charles Walker. Third shuttle in fleet; deploys 3 satellites and tests a solar sail.

10/5/84   Challenger (8 days) Robert Crippen, Jon McBride, Kathryn Sullivan, Sally Ride, Marc Garneau, David Leestma, Paul Scully-Power. First Canadian astronaut, Garneau; deploys Earth Radiation Budget Satellite and uses Sir-B radar system to see beneath surface of sand.

11/8/84   Discovery (8 days) Frederick Hauck, David Walker, Anna Fisher, Joseph Allen, Dale Gardner. Salvages two inoperative satellites.

1/24/85   Discovery (4 days) Ken Mattingly, Loren Schriver, James Buchli, Ellison Onizuka, Gary Payton. Secret military mission.

4/12/85   Discovery (7 days) Karol Bobko, Donald Williams, Jake Garn, Charles Walker, Jeffrey Hoffman, David Griggs, Margaret Rhea Seddon. First U.S. senator in space, Garn.

4/29/85   Challenger (7 days) Robert Overmyer, Frederick Gregory, Don Lind, Taylor Wang, Lodewijk van den Berg, Norman Thagard, William Thornton. Carries European Spacelab module.

6/6/85   Soyuz T-13 (112 days) V. Dzhanibekov, V. Savinykh. Successful mission to repair damage to *Salyut 7*, which had suffered power failure.

6/17/85   Discovery (7 days) John Creighton, Shannon Lucid, Steven Nagel, Daniel Brandenstein, John Fabian, Prince Salman al-Saud, Patrick Baudry. First Arabian in space, al-Saud; successfully launches 4 satellites.

7/29/85   Challenger (8 days) Roy Bridges, Anthony England, Karl Henize, Story Musgrave, Gordon Fullerton, Loren Acton, John-David Bartoe. Carries *Spacelab 2*, a group of scientific experiments.

8/27/85   Discovery (7 days) John Lounge, James van Hoften, William Fisher, Joe Engle, Richard Covey. Repairs satellite Syncom 3.

9/17/85   Soyuz T-14 (65 days) V. Vasyutin, A. Volkov, G. Grechko. Takes supplies to *Salyut 7.*

10/3/85   Atlantis (4 days) Karol Bobko, Ronald Grabe, David Hilmers, William Pailes, Robert Stewart. Fourth shuttle.

10/30/85   Challenger (7 days) Henry Hartsfield Jr., Steven Nagel, Bonnie Dunbar, Guion Bluford, Ernst Messerschmid, Reinhard Furrer, Wubbo Ockels. Carries Spacelab 1-D; scientific experiments conducted by Germans.

11/26/85   Atlantis (7 days) Brewster Shaw, Bryan O'Conner, Charles Walker, Rudolfo Neri Vela, Jerry L. Ross, Sherwood C. Spring, Mary Cleave. First Mexican in space, Vela.

1/12/86   Columbia (5 days) Robert Gibson, Charles Bolden Jr., George Nelson, Franklin Chang-Diaz, Steven Hawley, Robert Cenker. First U.S. congressman in space, Nelson.

1/28/86   Challenger (73 seconds) Richard Scobee, Michael Smith, Robert McNair, Ellison Onizuka, Judith Resnik, Gregory Jarvis, Christa McAuliffe. O-rings in solid-fuel boosters wear through, and fuel supply explodes, killing all 6 regular astronauts and schoolteacher McAuliffe.

The First Space Station (Soyuz flight durations N.A.)

2/20/86   Mir Soviet space station, No crew.

3/13/86   Soyuz T-15 V. Solovyev, L. Kizim. First cosmonauts to board *Mir* space station.

2/6/87   Soyuz TM-2 Y. Romanenko, A. Laveykin. Cosmonauts begin marathon tours in space.

7/21/87   Soyuz TM-3 A. Alexandrov, A. Viktorenko, M. Faris. First Syrian in space, Faris.

12/21/87   Soyuz TM-4 V. Titov, M. Manarov, A. Levchenko. Cosmonauts set new record of a year in space, mostly in *Mir* space station: 366 days.

6/7/88   Soyuz TM-5 A. Alexandrov, V. Savinykh. Solovyev. First Bulgarian in space, Alexandrov.

8/29/88   Soyuz TM-6 V. Lyakhov, V. Polyakov, A. Ahad. Ahad first Afghan in space; on 9/6/88 Lyakhov and Ahad are stranded as they attempt to return in *Soyuz TM-5*, but land safely on 9/7/88.

9/29/88   Discovery (4 days) John Lounge, David Hilmers, Frederick Hauck, George Nelson, Richard Covey. Redesigned shuttle makes first flight since the *Challenger* disaster.

11/26/88   Soyuz TM-7 A. Volkov, S. Krikalev, J. Chrétien. *Mir* temporarily abandoned for first time.

12/2/88   Atlantis (4 days) Robert Gibson, Jerry Ross, William Shepherd, Guy Gardner, Richard Mullane. Secret military mission known to have deployed radar spy satellite.

3/13/89   Discovery (5 days) Michael Coats, John Blaha, James Buchli, James Bagian, Robert Springer. Deploys NASA's third relay satellite and tests thermal control system for proposed U.S. space station.

5/4/89   Atlantis (4 days) David Walker, Ronald Grabe, Mary Cleave, Norman Thagard, Mark Lee. Launches probe *Magellan* to map Venus with radar.

8/9/89   Columbia (5 days) Brewster Shaw, Richard Richards, David Leestma, James Adamson, Mark Brown. Secret military mission to launch spy satellite.

9/5/89   Soyuz TM-8 A. Viktorenko, A. Serebrov. Reoccupies *Mir.*

10/18/89   Atlantis (5 days) Donald Williams, Michael McCulley, Shannon Lucid, Franklin Chang-Diaz, Ellen Baker. Launches *Galileo* probe.

11/22/89 *Discovery* (5 days) Frederick Gregory, John Blaha, Story Musgrave, Kathryn Thornton, Manley Lanier Carter Jr. Secret military mission.

1/9/90 *Columbia* (11 days) Daniel Brandenstein, Bonnie Dunbar, Marsha Ivens, David Low, James Wetherbee. Launches communication satellite Syncom IV and retrieves the *Long Duration Exposure Facility* (see 4/6/84).

2/11/90 *Soyuz TM-9* A. Solovyev, A. Balandin. Relieves Viktorenko and Serebrov. Solovyev and Balandin briefly locked out of *Mir* by faulty hatch.

2/28/90 *Atlantis* (4 days) John Creighton, John Caspar, David Hilmers, Richard Mullane, Pierre Thout. Secret military mission.

4/24/90 *Discovery* (5 days) Loren Shriver, Charles Bolden Jr., Bruce McCandless, Steven Hawley, Kathryn Sullivan. Launches Hubble Space Telescope.

8/1/90 *Soyuz TM-10* G. Manakov, G. Strekalov. Replace Solovyev and Balandin.

10/6/90 *Discovery* (4 days) Richard Richards, Robert Cabana, Bruce Melnick, William Shepherd, Thomas Akers. Launches *Ulysses* space probe into solar orbit.

11/15/90 *Atlantis* (5 days) Richard Covey, Frank Culberston Jr., Charles Gemar, Carl Meade, Robert Springer. NASA announces this as last secret military mission.

12/2/90 *Columbia* (9 days) Vance Brand, Guy Gardner, Jeffrey Hoffman, John Lounge, Robert Parker, Samuel Durrance, Ronald Parise. Carries 3 UV and 1 X-ray telescope.

12/2/90 *Soyuz TM-11* V. Afansev, M. Manarov, T. Akiyama. Journalist Akiyama, sponsored by Japanese corporations; others replace Manakov and Strekalov on *Mir*.

4/5/91 *Atlantis* (6 days) Steven Nagel, Kenneth Cameron, Linda Godwin, Jerry Ross, Jerome Apt. Launches 17-ton *Gamma Ray Observatory;* unscheduled spacewalk required to open satellite's antenna properly.

4/28/91 *Discovery* (8 days) Michael Coats, Blaine Hammond Jr., Gregory Harbaugh, Charles Lacy Veach, Guion Bluford Jr., Richard Hieb, Donald McMonagle. Tests detection devices and recovers Star Wars satellite.

5/18/91 *Soyuz TM-12* S. Krikalev, A. Artsebarsky, H. Sharman. Political problems in Soviet Union result in Krikalev's spending an unexpected 313 days in space; Sharman is first Briton in space; returns with Manarov and Afansev.

6/5/91 *Columbia* (9 days) Bryan D. O'Connor, Sidney M. Gutierrez, James P. Bagian, Margaret Rhea Seddon, Francis A. Gaffney, Millie Hughes-Fulford, Tamara E. Jernigan. Performs human and animal space-adaptation experiments.

8/21/91 *Atlantis* (9 days) John Blaha, Michael Baker, Shannon Lucid, David Low, James Adamson. Performs 22 experiments and launches communications satellite.

9/12/91 *Discovery* (5 days) John Creighton, Kenneth Reightler Jr., Mark Brown, James Buchlim, Charles Gemar. Launches upper-atmosphere research satellite.

10/2/91 *Soyuz TM-13* A. Volkov, F. Viehboeck, T. Aubakirov. Viehboeck, first Austrian in space, returns with Artsebarsky and Aubakirov.

11/24/91 *Atlantis* (7 days) Frederick Gregory, Tom Henricks, James Voss, Mario Runco Jr., Story Musgrave, Thomas Hennen. First completely nonsecret military flight; studies how well military installations can be seen from space.

1/22/92 *Discovery* (8 days) Ronald Grabe, Stephen Oswald, Norman Thagard, William Readdy, David Hilmers, Roberta Bondar, Ulf Merbold. Performs experiments as the First International Microgravity Lab.

3/17/92 *Soyuz TM-14* K. Flade, A. Viktorenko, A. Kaleri. On March 25, Flade, a German, returns with Sergei Krikalev and Aleksandr Volkov.

3/24/92 *Atlantis* (9 days) Charles Bolden Jr., Brian Duffy, Kathryn Sullivan, David Leestma, Michael Foale, Byron Lichtenberg, Dirk Frimout. Inaugural flight of Mission to Planet Earth studies Earth's atmosphere and auroras.

5/7/92 *Endeavour* (9 days) Daniel Brandenstein, Kevin Chilton, Thomas Akers, Richard Hieb, Bruce Melnick, Kathryn Thornton, Pierre Thout. The first flight of the replacement for *Challenger* succeeds relaunching an erring communications satellite; first ever 3-person EVA.

6/25/92 *Columbia* (14 days) Richard Richards, Kenneth Bowersox, Bonnie Dunbar, Lawrence DeLucas, Ellen Baker, Eugene Trinh, Carl Meade. Sets record for duration of shuttle mission; carries U.S. Microgravity Laboratory.

7/27/92 *Soyuz TM-15* A. Solovyev, S. Avdeyev, M. Tognini. The third trip by a French astronaut, Tognini, to *Mir*.

7/31/92 *Atlantis* (8 days) Loren Schriver, Andrew Allen, Marsha Ivins, Jeffrey Hoffman, Franklin Chang-Diaz, Claude Nicollier, Franco Mallerba. Launches European Retrievable Carrier (Eureca) satellite. First Swiss astronaut (Nicollier); first Italian (Mallerba).

9/12/92 *Endeavour* (8 days) Robert Gibson, Curtis Brown Jr., Jay Apt, Jan Davis, Mae Carol Jemison, Mark Lee, Mamoru Mohri. First professional Japanese astronaut in space (Mohri); first married couple in space (Lee and Davis); first black female astronaut (Jemison). Japanese-sponsored mission to study biology in space.

10/22/92 *Columbia* (10 days) James Wetherbee, Michael Baker, Glenwood MacLean, Tamara Jernigan, William Shepherd, Charles Lacy Veach. Launches the Italian-made satellite *LAGEOS-2*, to provide information about Earth's gravitational field.

12/2/92 *Discovery* (7 days) Daniel Walker, Robert Cabana, Guion Bluford Jr., James Voss, Michael Clifford. Last scheduled military flight for the space shuttle; future military flights to use disposable rockets. Launches secret military satellite.

1/13/93 *Endeavour* (6 days) John Caspar, Gregory Harbaugh, Donald McMonagle, Susan Helms, Mario Runco Jr. Observes X-rays and launches a TDRS (Tracking and Data Relay Satellite).

1/24/93 *Soyuz TM-16* A. Polishchuk, G. Manakov. Docks with *Mir* on Kristall module, using U.S.-compatible port first developed for the joint Soviet-U.S. mission in 1975; A. Solovyev and S. Avdeyev return after six months aboard *Mir*.

4/8/93 *Discovery* (9 days) Kenneth Cameron, Stephen Oswald, Kenneth Cockrell, Michael Foale, Ellen Ochoa. Launches and retrieves the *Spartan* Sun probe, used to study the solar corona, and observes Earth's ozone layer.

4/26/93 *Columbia* (10 days) Steven Nagel, Tom Henricks, Jerry Ross, Charles Precourt, Bernard Harris Jr., Ulrich Walter, Hans Schlegel. The European Spacelab with two German scientists (Walter and Schlegel) conducts experiments on weightlessness.

6/21/93 *Endeavour* (10 days) Ronald Grabe, Brian Duffy, Donald Low, Peter Wisoff, Nancy Jane Sherlock, Janice Voss. Recovers Europe's *Eureca* satellite; and conducts experiments using a pressurized laboratory called Spacehab.

7/1/93 *Soyuz TM-17* V. Tsiblyev, A. Serebrov, J. Haignere. Haignere is French astronaut who returns with A. Solovyev and S. Andreyev on July 29.

9/12/93 *Discovery* (10 days) Frank Culbertson Jr., William Readdy, James Newman, Daniel Bursch, Carl Walz. Tests equipment and procedures to be used in repairing Hubble Space Telescope; first night landing at Kennedy.

10/18/93 *Columbia* (14 days) John Blaha, Richard Searfoss, William McArthur Jr., Shannon Lucid, Martin Fettman, Margaret Rhea Seddon, David Wolf. Conducts biological experiments on humans and rats; first dissection of animal in space.

12/2/93 *Endeavour* (11 days) Richard Covey, Kenneth Bowersox, Claude Nicollier, Story Musgrave, Thomas Akers, Kathryn Thornton, Jeffrey Hoffman. Repairs defective lens on Hubble Space Telescope.

1/8/94 *Soyuz TM-18* V. Afanasyev, Y. Usachyov, V. Polyakov. Trip planned to last 14 months for Polyakov, but Afanasyev and Usachyov return after six months. Previous *Mir* crew returns to Earth.

The U.S. and Russia Work Together in Space

2/3/94 *Discovery* (8 days) Charles Bolden Jr., Sergei Krikalev, Kenneth Reightler Jr., Jan Davis, Franklin Chang-Diaz, Ronald Sega. Krikalev first Russian on U.S. space shuttle mission.

3/4/94 *Columbia* (14 days) John Caspar, Andrew Allen, Charles Gemar, Marsha Ivins, Pierre Thuot. Develops techniques for use in space-station construction.

4/9/94 *Endeavour* (11 days) Sidney Gutierrez, Kevin Chilton, Michael Clifford, Linda Godwin, Jay Apt, Thomas Jones. Uses radar to map details of Earth in 3-D.

7/1/94 *Soyuz TM-19* Y. Malenchenko, T. Musabayev. Relieves Afanasyev and Usachyov on *Mir*.

7/8/94 *Columbia* (15 days) Robert Cabana, Leroy Chiao, James Halsell Jr., Richard Hieb, Chiaki Naito-Mukai, Donald Thomas, Carl Walz. Orbits Earth 236 times, a new record. First Japanese woman in space (heart surgeon Naito-Mukai).

9/9/94 *Discovery* (11 days) Richard Richards, Blaine Hammond Jr., Susan Helms, Mark Lee, J.M. Lineger, Carl Meade. Conducts laser experiments to measure pollution in atmosphere. Releases and recaptures satellite that collects data on solar wind; Meade and Lee use jet pack for untethered spacewalk.

9/30/94 *Endeavour* (11 days) Michael Baker, Daniel Bursch, Thomas Jones, Steven Smith, Jeff Wisoff, Terrence Wukcytt. The *Space Radar Laboratory* 2 mission is follow-up of nearly identical mission flown in the spring to detect seasonal changes.

10/4/94 *Soyuz TM-20* A. Viktorenko, Y. Kondakova, U. Merbold. Merbold, from the European Space Agency, studies space biology aboard *Mir* and returns to Earth on 11/4/94. Viktorenko and Kondakova relieve Malenchenko and Musabaye on *Mir*.

11/3/94 *Atlantis* (11 days) Curtis Brown, Donald Mc-Monagle, Jean-François Clervoy (from ESA), Scott Parazynski, Joseph Tanner. Third shuttle flight since 1992 to carry the *Atlas* lab (Atmospheric Laboratory for Applications and Science).

2/3/95 *Discovery* (8 days) James Wetherbee, Eileen Collins, Michael Foale, Bernard Harris Jr., Vladimir Titov, Janice Voss. Carries Russian Titov to within 11 m (37 ft.) of *Mir*.

3/2/95 *Endeavour* (17 days) Stephen Oswald, Samuel Durrance, Tamara Jernigan, William Gregory, John Grunsfeld, Wendy Lawrence, Ronald Parise. Carries the lab *Astro* 2, used to study volcanic eruptions on Jupiter's moon Io.

3/14/95 *Soyuz TM-21* N. Thagard, V. Dezhurov, G. Strekalov. Thagard becomes the first U.S. astronaut to live aboard *Mir*; he studies the body's reaction to weightlessness; Polyakov, who returns on 3/22/95, with Kondakova and Viktorenko, sets endurance record of 14.5 months in space.

6/27/95 *Atlantis* (10 days) Robert Gibson, Charles Precourt, Ellen Baker, Gregory Harbaugh, Bonnie Dunbar, Anatoly Solovyev, Nikolai Budarin. Docks with *Mir* for 5 days. Spacelab on Atlantis and Spekter module of *Mir* used for biomedical research. Solovyev and Budarin relieve Thagard, Dezhurov, and Strekalov as crew of *Mir*.

7/13/95 *Discovery* (9 days) Tom Henricks, Kevin Kregel, Nancy Currie, Donald Thomas, Mary Ellen Weber. Launches Tracking and Data Relay Satellite (TDRS) to replace one lost when *Challenger* blew up.

9/3/95 *Soyuz TM-22* T. Reiter (Germany), Y. Gidzenko, S. Avdeyev. Replaces Solovyev and Budarin, who return to Earth 9/11/88.

9/7/95 *Endeavour* (11 days) Michael Gernhart, David Walker, Kenneth Cockrell, James Newman, James Voss. Uses an orbiting shield to produce a vacuum in its wake 10,000 times greater than any found on Earth.

10/20/95 *Columbia* (16 days) Ken Bowersox, Kent Rominger, Kathryn Thornton, Cady Coleman, Michael Lopez-Alegria, Fred Leslie, Albert Sacco Conduct microgravity experiments in Spacelab.

11/12/95 *Atlantis* (8 days) Kenneth Cameron, James Halsell Jr., Jerry Ross, William McArthur Jr., Chris Hadfield (Canada). Changes configuration of *Mir* to make docking easier in future missions.

1/11/96 *Endeavour* (9 days) Brian Duffy, Brent Jett Jr., Leroy Chiao, Winston Scott, Daniel Barry, Koichi Wakata (Japan). Recovers Japanese science-experiment orbiting platform, which had been launched by a Japanese H-2 rocket in March 1995.

2/21/96 *Soyuz TM-23* Y. Onufrienko, Y. Usachev. Relieves *Mir* crew.

2/22/96 *Columbia* (15 days) Nobie Stone, Jeffrey Hoffman, Andrew Allen, Doc Horowitz, Franklin Chang-Diaz, Claude Nicollier (ESA), Maurizio Cheli (ESA), Umberto Guidoni (Italian Space Agency).. Tethered satellite experiment partly successful, but satellite is mysteriously lost from end of tether.

3/22/96 *Atlantis* (9 days) Kevin Childon, Richard Seafoss, Ronald Sega, Michael Clifford, Shannon Lucid, Linda Godwin. Docks with *Mir*. Lucid stays behind on the space station.

5/19/96 *Endeavour* (10 days) John Caspar, Curtis Brown Jr., Daniel Bursch, Mario Runco Jr., Marc Garneau (Canadian), Andrew Thomas. Deploys first inflatable antenna from Spartan satellite. Conducts rendezvous studies of the *PAMS* satellite, a test of a system in which a satellite stabilizes itself without expending rocket fuel.

6/20/96 *Columbia* (17 days) Tom Henricks, Kevin Kregel, Rick Linnehan, Susan Helms, Charles Brady, Jean-Jacques Favier (Canada), Robert Thirsk. Carries the Life/Microgravity Spacelab, to study the effects of space flight on the human body, on rats, and on fish embryos; and SAREX-II.

8/17/96 *Soyuz TM-24* V. Korzun, A. Kaleri, C. Andre-Deshays (France). Korzun and Kaleri relieve Onufrienko and Usachev on *Mir*.

9/16/96 *Atlantis* (10 days) William Readdy, Terrence Wilcutt, Tom Akers, Jay Apt, Carl Walz, John Blaha, Shannon Lucid. Blaha relieves Lucid on *Mir*.

11/19/96 *Columbia* (18 days) Kenneth Cockrell, Kent Rominger, Story Musgrave, Thomas Jones, Tamara Jernigan. Deploys and retrieves *ORFEUS-SPAS*, a satellite gathering data about matter in space between the stars and the WSF-3/Wake Shield Facility, a satellite used in testing a method of producing a high vacuum to be used in manufacturing ultra pure semiconductor devices.

1/12/97 *Atlantis* (10 days) Mike Baker, Brent Jett, Jeff Wisoff, John Grunsfeld, Marsha Ivins, J.M. Linenger, John Blaha. Linenger relieves Blaha on *Mir*.

2/10/97 *Soyuz TM-25* V. Tsbliyev, A. Lazutkin, R. Ewald (Germany), V. Korzun, A. Kaleri. Tsbliyev and Lazutkin relieve Korzun and Kaleri on *Mir*.

2/11/97 *Discovery* (10 days) Ken Bowersox, Scott Horowitz, Joe Tanner, Steve Hawley, Greg Harbaugh, Mark Lee, Steve Smith. Replaces eight instruments in the Hubble Space Telescope and adds two new ones, greatly improving its abilities.

4/4/97 *Columbia* (4 days) Jim Halsell, Susan Still, Janice Voss, Mike Gernhardt, Don Thomas, Roger Crouch, Greg Linteris. Carries the Microgravity Science Lab, but 85 percent of the experiments are canceled because of a problem with the fuel cells.

5/15/97 *Atlantis* (9 days) Charlie Precourt, Eileen Collins, Jean-François Clervoy, Carlos Noriega, Ed Lu, Elena Kondakova (Russia), Mike Foale, Jerry Linenger. Docks with Mir, taking Linenger back to Earth and leaving Foale. Brings needed supplies and replacement equipment to aging *Mir*, which has had problems with fires and failures.

7/1/97 *Columbia* (16 days) James Halsell, Susan Still, Janice Voss, Michael Gernhardt, Donald Thomas, Roger Crouch, Gregory Linteris. Replacement for flight of 4/4/97.

8/7/97 *Discovery* (11 days) Curt Brown, Kent Rominger, Jan Davis, Robert Curbeam, Steve Robinson, Bjarni Tryggvason. In the fourth cooperative German-American scientific mission, various experiments using infrared imagining, lasers, and cryogenic devices are conducted.

9/25/97 *Atlantis* (11 days) James Wetherbee, Mike Bloomfield, Vladimir Titov, Scott Parazynski, Jean-Loup Chrétien, Wendy Lawrence, David Wolf, Michael Foale. Takes Wolf to *Mir*, returns with Foale.

11/19/97 *Columbia* (16 days) Kevin Kregel, Steve Lindsey, Kalpana Chawla, Winston Scott, Takao Doi, Leonid Kadenyuk (first Ukranian to fly aboard a shuttle). Conducts microgravity experiments and attempts to launch *SPARTAN* solar research satellite; when *SPARTAN* malfunctions, astronauts retrieve it for a future attempt on a later flight.

1/22/98 *Endeavour* (9 days) Terrence Wilcutt, Joe Edwards, James Reilly, Michael Anderson, Bonnie Dunbar, Salizhan Sharipov, Andrew Thomas, David Wolf. Thomas relieves Wolf on *Mir*. Performs microgravity experiments with plants and crystals.

4/17/98 *Columbia* (16 days) Richard Searfoss, Scott Altman, Kathryn Hire, Richard Linnehan, Dave Williams, Jay Buckey, James Pawelczyk. Carries the *Neurolab* into space where the effects of space flight on the brains and reproduction of various species of animals and plants are studied.

6/2/98 *Discovery* (10 days) Charles Precourt, Dominic Gorie, Wendy Lawrence, Franklin Chang-Diaz, Janet Kavandi, Andrew Thomas, Valery Victorovitch Ryumin. Final U.S. astronaut mission on *Mir* completed as Thomas is returned to Earth.

11/20/98 *Discovery* (9 days) Curtis Brown Jr., Steven Lindsey, Scott Parazynski, Stephen Robinson, Pedro Duque, Chiaki Mukai, John Glenn. Glenn, first American to orbit Earth in 1962, becomes oldest astronau; studies effects of weightlessness on older humans.

Era of the International Space Station (ISS)

12/04/98 *Endeavour* (12 days) Robert Cabana, Frederick Sturckow, James Newman, Nancy Currie, Jerry Ross, Sergei Konstantinovich Krikalev (Russia). Crew docks with the Russian-built Functional Energy Block Zarya and adds Node-1 (Unity) to begin assembly of the International Space Station.

5/27/99 *Discovery* (10 days) Kent Rominger, Rick Husband, Tamara Jernigan, Ellen Ochoa, Daniel Barry, Julie Payette (Canada), Valery Ivanovich Tokarev (Russia). Brings cargo for outfitting ISS, including Russian cargo crane to be mounted on exterior of Functional Energy Block.

7/22/99 *Columbia* (5 days) Eileen Collins, Jeffrey Ashby, Steven Hawley, Catherine Coleman, Michael Tognini (France). Collins first female commander. Launches Chandra X-ray Observatory.

12/19/99 *Discovery* (8 days) Curtis Brown Jr., Scott Kelly, John Grunsfeld, Michael Foales, Steven Smith, Jean-François Clervoy (France), Claude Nicollier (Switzerland). Captures, services, and re-launches Hubble Space Telescope.

2/11/00 *Endeavour* (11 days) Kevin Kregel, Dominic Gorie, Janet Kavandi, Janice Voss, Gerhard Thiele (German-ESA), Mamoru Mohri (Japan). The Shuttle Radar Topography Mission obtain the most detailed topographical map of the Earth to date.

5/19/00 *Atlantis* (10 days) James Halsell Jr., Scott Horowitz, Susan Helms, Mary Ellen Weber, Jeffrey Williams, James Voss, Yury Usachev (Russian). Carries supplies to ISS. Helms and Usachev remain on ISS as part of first crew.

9/8/00 *Atlantis* (12 days) Terry Wilcutt, Scott Altman, Dan Burbank, Ed Lu, Rick Mastracchio, Yuri Malenchenko (Russia), and Boris Morukov (Russia). Brings supplies to ISS and conducts space walk to perform station maintenance.

10/11/00 *Discovery* (13 days) Brian Duffy, Pamela Melroy, Leroy Chiao, Jeff Wisoff, Michael Lopez-Alegria, William McArthur, Jr., Koichi Wakata (Japan). Brings and installs parts needed for solar arrays, communications, and attitude control for ISS.

10/31/00 *Soyuz TM-31* (139 days) Bill Shepherd, Y. Gidzenko, S. Krikalev. This is Expedition 1, beginning the permanent occupation of ISS.

11/30/00 *Endeavour* (12 days) Brent Jett, Michael Bloomfield, Joseph Tanner, Carlos Noriega, Marc Garneau (Canada). Adds photovoltaic modules to the ISS's solar arrays; brings radiators for cooling photovoltaic cells; activates the S-band communications system.

2/7/01 *Atlantis* (13 days) Kenneth Cockrell, Mark Polansky, Robert Curbeam, Thomas Jones, Marsha Ivins. Installs ISS's "Destiny" laboratory module.

3/8/01 *Discovery* (13 days) Jim Wetherbee, Jim Kelly, Andy Thomas, Paul Richards. Brings Expedition 2 crew (Yury Usachev, James Voss, and Susan Helms) to ISS. Returns Expedition 1 crew (see 10/31/00). Brings additional laboratory equipment.

4/19/01 *Endeavour* (12 days) Kent Rominger, Jeffrey Ashby, Scott Umberto Guidoni (ESA), Scott Parazynski, Chris Hadfield (Canada), Yuri Lonchakov (Russia), John Phillips. Delivers the Italian "Raffaello" module and the Canadian mechanical arm to the ISS.

7/12/01 *Atlantis* (11 days) Steven Lindsey, Charles Hobaugh, Michael Gernhardt, Janet Kavandi, James Reilly. Delivers the Joint Airlock; resolves problems with the Canadian robotic arm.

8/10/01 *Discovery* (12 days) Scott Horowitz, Rick Sturckow, Daniel Barry, Patrick Forrester. Installs the Leonardo Multi-Purpose Module; launches Simplesat, a demonstration satellite built with "off-the-shelf" commercial hardware. Brings Expedition 3 crew (Frank Culbertson, Vladimir Dezhurov, and Mikhail Tyurin). Returns Expedition 2 crew (see 3/8/01).

10/21/01 *Soyuz TM-33* (165 days) Viktor Afanasyev (Russia), Konstantin Kozeev (Russia), Claudie Haignere (ESA). Conducts experiments in materials research, life sciences, meteorological phenomena. Emergency vehicle exchanged; crew returns on *Soyuz TM-32*.

12/5/01 *Endeavour* (12 days) Linda Godwin, Dominic Gorie, Mark Kelly, Daniel Tani. Brings Expedition 4 crew (Yury Onufrienko, Carl Walz, Daniel Bursh) and 3 tons (2.7 metric tons) of equipment and supplies. Returns Expedition 3 crew (see 8/10/01).

3/1/02 *Columbia* (11 days) Scott Altman, Duane Carey, Nancy Currie, John Grunsfeld, Richard Linnehan, Michael Massimino, James Newman. Fourth Hubble Space Telescope servicing mission; during five EVAs installs a new power control unit, new camera, new solar arrays.

4/8/02 *Atlantis* (11 days) Crew: Michael Bloomfield, Stephen Frick, Lee Morin, Ellen Ochoa, Jerry Ross, Steven Smith, Rex Walheim. Delivered and installed central truss segment to ISS, the first of nine parts of the space station's external frame.

4/25/02 *Soyuz TM-34* (11 days) Yuri Gidzenko (Russia), Roberto Vittori (ESA), Mark Shuttleworth (a paying tourist from South Africa). Exchange of *Soyuz* emergency vehicles; crew returned on *Soyuz TM-33*.

6/5/02 *Endeavour* (14 days) Franklin Chang-Diaz, Kenneth Cockrell, Paul Lockhart, Philippe Perrin (France). Delivers Microgravity Science Glovebox, enabling crew to work safely with experiments involving fluids, flames, fumes, etc. Delivers Expedition 5 crew (Peggy Whitson, Valery Korzun, Sergei Treschev), returns Expedition 4 crew (see 12/5/01).

10/7/02 *Atlantis* (11 days) Jeffrey Ashby, Pamela Melroy, David Wolf, Piers Sellers, Sandra Magnus, Fyodor Yurchikhin. Delivers S1 Truss.

10/30/02 *Soyuz TMA-1* (9 days) S. Zaletin, F. De Winne (Belgium), Y. Lonchakov, A. Lazutkin. Test flight of new *Soyuz TMA*. Conducts experiments with Microgravity Science Glovebox. Returns *Soyuz TM-34*.

11/23/02 *Endeavour* (14 days) Jim Wetherbee, Paul Lockhart, Michael Lopez-Alegria, John Herrington. Delivers Expedition 6 crew (Peggy Whitson, Valery Korzun, Sergei Treschev) and parts to improve space station's thermal control system. Returns Expedition 5 crew (see 6/5/02).

1/16/03 *Columbia* (16 days) Rick Husband, Willie McCool, Michael Anderson, Kalpana Chawla, David Brown, Laurel Clark, Ilan Ramon. Shuttle explodes on re-entry, killing all aboard.

4/26/03 *Soyuz TMA-2* Yuri Milanchenko (Russia), Edward Lu. Retrieves Expedition 6 crew (see 11/23/02) trapped aboard ISS as Space Shuttle Program is grounded in wake of *Columbia* disaster.

10/18/03 *Soyuz TMA-3* Alexander Kaleri (Russia), Mike Foale (U.S.), and Pedro Duque (Spain). Foale and Kaleri stay on ISS until Expedition 9 arrives, while Duque, after 8 days of research in space for ESA, returns along with *Expedition 7* crew (see 4/26/03).

10/4/04 *SpaceShipOne* Brian Binnie. In the first nongovernmental spaceflight, *SpaceShipOne* wins privately funded $10M X Prize competition to reach outer space twice in two weeks using same reusable craft.

7/26/05 *Discovery* (14 days) Steve Robinson, Jim Kelly, Andy Thomas, Wendy Lawrence, Charlie Camarda, Eileen Collins and Soichi Noguchi. First return to space after *Columbia* disaster is dogged with falling debris from booster and other problems, but inspection resolves most concerns and a space walk repair corrects others. Astronauts also replace failed main gyroscope on International Space Station.

7/4/06 *Discovery* (12 days) Stephanie Wilson, Michael Fossum, Steven Lindsey, Piers Sellers, Mark Kelly, Thomas Reiter and Lisa Nowak. Performs three spacewalks and services the International Space Station.

9/9/06 *Atlantis* (11 days) Brent Jett, Jr., Christopher Ferguson, Heidemarie Stefanyshyn-Piper, Joe Tanner, Daniel Burbank, and Steven MacLean. Resumes assembly of the International Space Station, and performs three spacewalks

12/9/06 *Discovery* (13 days) Mark Polansky, William Oefelein, Robert Curbeam, Joan Higginbotham, Nicholas Patrick, Christer Fuglesang, and Sunita Williams. Delivers Williams to the Internatioonal Space

Station to replace Thomas Reiter, who had been there since July 2006.

7/8/07 *Atlantis* (14 days) Frederick Sturckow, Lee Archambault, James Reilly II, Patrick Forrester, Steven Swanson, John Olivas. Retrieves Sunita Williams from the International Space Station and continues assembly and repairs to the station.

8/8/07 *Endeavor* (12 days) Alvin Drew, Barbara Morgan, Scott Kelly, Charlie Hobaugh, Tracy Caldwell, Rick Martracchio, and Dave WIlliams. Continues construction of the International Space Station.

10/23/2007 *Discovery* (15 days) Pam Melroy, George Zamka, Scott Parazynski, Doug Wheelock, Stephanie Wilson, Paolo Nespoli, Daniel Tani, and Clay Anderson. Continues construction of the International Space Station.

2/7/2008 *Atlantis* (12 days) Steve Frick, Alan Poindexter, Rex Walheim, Stanley Love, Leland Melvin, Hans Schlegel, Leopold Eyharts, and Daniel Tani. Delivers and installs European Columbus laboratory for International Space Station.

3/11/2008 *Endeavor* (16 days) Dominic Gorie, Gregory Johnson, Richard Linnehan, Garrett Reismann, Robert Behnken, Michael Foreman, and Takao Doi. Delivers Garrett Reismann to the International Space Station, continues construction and ferries Leopold Eyharts back to Earth.

5/31/2008 *Discovery* (15 days) Mark Kelly, Ken Ham, Karen Nyberg, Ronald Garan, Michael Fossum, Akihiko Hoshide, and Gregory Chamitoff. Continues construction of the International Space Station and delivers Gregory Chamitoff to station in exchange for Garrett Reismann.

The International Space Station

The International Space Station began at the end of the Cold War era with separate plans by the United States and Soviet Union. With the collapse of the Soviet Union in 1989-90, plans were altered and Russia joined the American-led effort. Today there are 16 nations supporting the International Space Station (ISS)—the U.S., Russia, Japan, Canada, Italy, Belgium, the Netherlands, Denmark, Norway,

France, Spain, Germany, Sweden, Switzerland, the United Kingdom, and Brazil. Construction of the ISS is in modules, requiring some 45 different space flights to put all the parts in place. The completed space station will weigh about a million pounds (453 metric tons) and be 356 feet (109 m) across by 290 feet (88 m) long. ISS is powered by solar arrays that cover more than half an acre of space.

EARTH SCIENCES

Earth sciences include geology (the study of Earth's rocks and interior), oceanography (the study of ocean water, currents, and the ocean floor), paleontology (the study of fossils and ancient lifeforms), parts of astronomy, and meteorology (the study of the atmosphere, including weather). Except for astronomy and weather, which are covered elsewhere, this section deals with all of these studies.

▶THE EARTH'S COMPOSITION

In their study of the Earth, scientists distinguish a number of distinct layers from the inner core—the center of which is 6,371 km (roughly 4,000 mi.) below the surface—to the farthest limit of the atmosphere, about 1,000 km (600 mi.) above the surface. This section describes these layers, from the innermost to the outermost.

Core The core consists of two parts—one solid, the other liquid—both thought to be a mixture of iron and a lighter element, probably sulfur or oxygen. The solid inner core begins about 5,150 km (3,200 mi.) from the surface, and the liquid outer core at 2,891 km (about 1,800 mi.) from the surface.

Mantle The bulk of the Earth—roughly two-thirds of its mass—is composed of the mantle, which extends from the outer core to within about 80 km (50 mi.) of the Earth's surface below the higher mountains, and to within only 5 to 8 km (3 to 5 mi.) of the Earth's surface below some areas of the oceans. Silicon dioxide constitutes almost half of the mantle, and there is an abundance of magnesium oxide, some iron oxide, and smaller amounts of oxides of other metals. (Although silicon dioxide is known as quartz when found in the Earth's crust, under the heat and pressure of the mantle it may have very different properties from the form we know.) Part of the upper mantle is somewhat fluid and is known as the asthenosphere.

Crust The crust is the outermost solid layer of the Earth. Under the continents, the crust varies from 30 to 80 km (19 to 50 mi.) in thickness, while under the oceans it is generally only 5 to 8 km (3 to 5 mi.) thick. Continental and oceanic crust differ from each other in thickness and composition. Continental crust consists of granite and other relatively light rocks, while oceanic crust is made up chiefly of basalt. The crust is separated from the mantle by the Mohorovičić discontinuity, or Moho. The crust that is accessible to accurate measurements contains the following principal elements:

Element	Percent	Element	Percent
Oxygen	45.6%	Magnesium	2.8%
Silicon	27.3	Sodium	2.3
Aluminum	8.4	Potassium	1.8
Iron	6.2	Hydrogen	1.5
Calcium	4.7	Titanium	0.6

Note: Adds to more than 100% due to independent rounding.

Hydrosphere Water—virtually all of it sea water—covers about 71 percent of the Earth's surface and thereby constitutes a distinct layer of the Earth. Sea water varies in composition from place to place, but on average it is about 3.5 percent salts—that is, evaporating 100 lb. of sea water would yield 3.5 lb. of salt. Sodium chloride (ordinary table salt) constitutes 2.7 percent of sea water, or 77.8 percent of total solids in sea water. The typical composition of solids in sea water is as follows:

Compound	Percent
Sodium chloride	77.8%
Magnesium chloride	10.9
Magnesium sulfide	4.7
Calcium sulfate	3.6
Potassium sulfate	2.5
Calcium carbonate	0.3
Magnesium bromide	0.2
Other compounds	trace

Atmosphere The atmosphere is the gaseous layer that envelopes the Earth. The lower atmosphere consists of the troposphere and the stratosphere. The *troposphere* has an average thickness of about 11 km (7 mi.), although it is only 8 km (5 mi.) at the poles and as much as 16 km (10 mi.) around the equator. Most clouds and weather phenomena occur in this region. The composition of dry air at sea level is: nitrogen, 78.08 percent; oxygen, 20.05

Geologic Time Scale

The history of the planet has been divided by geologists and other earth scientists into periods of varying length based on the fossils found in rock strata. Geologists often speak of the period before 545 million years ago as Precambrian Time. The eras after 545 million years ago are grouped into the Phanerozoic Eon.

Mass extinctions—brief periods when large numbers of species become extinct—often mark the boundaries between geologic time periods. In the greatest such extinction, known as the Final

Permian (250 million years ago), perhaps as many as 80 to 90 percent of all species became extinct in less than a million years. No one knows what causes most mass extinctions, but the Final Cretaceous of 65 million years ago (also called the K-T extinction) and the Final Permian were almost certainly caused by impacts of asteroids. The most recent extinction, at the end of the last ice age (11,000 years ago), may have been caused by human hunting. Some biologists believe that human activities are causing a new mass extinction today as well.

Era or Eon, Period, Epoch	Organisms	Beginning of Interval (millions of years ago)
HADEAN EON	No evidence of life	4,600
ARCHEAN EON	Monerans (bacteria and blue-green algae); Archaea	3,800
PROTEROZOIC EON	Protists, algae, and soft-bodied creatures similar to jellyfish and worms	2,500
PHANEROZOIC EON		
Cambrian period	Tiny fossils with skeletons followed by animals with shells, notably trilobites	542.0
Ordovician period	Brachiopods (shellfish similar to clams), corals, starfish, and some organisms that have no modern counterparts, called sea scorpions and conodonts	488.3
Silurian period	Snails, clams and mussels, ammonoids (similar to the nautilus), jawless fish, sea scorpions, land plants and animals (club mosses, land scorpions); modern groups of algae and fungi	443.7
Devonian period	Spiders, amphibians, jawed fish, lobe-finned fish, sharks, lungfish, and ferns	416.0
Carboniferous period	Insects, land snails, amphibians, early reptiles, sea lilies, giant club mosses, and seed ferns	359.2
Permian period	Mammal-like reptiles and fin-backed reptiles, cycads, ginkgoes, and conifers	289.0
MEZOZOIC ERA		
Triassic period	Marine reptiles (plesiosaurs and ichthyosaurs), crocodiles, frogs, turtles, early mammals, and early dinosaurs	251.0
Jurassic period	Dinosaurs (such as stegosaurs), pterosaurs (such as pterodactyl), early birds, dinoflagellates, diatoms, early flowering plants	199.6
Cretaceous period	Dinosaurs (such as tyrannosaurs, triceratops, and apatosaurs), salamanders, modern bony fishes, mosasaurs (marine lizards), flowering plants, placental and marsupial mammals	145.5
CENOZOIC ERA		
Palaeogene period		
Paleocene epoch	Early primates, early horses, rodents, sycamores	65.8
Eocene epoch	Whales, penguins, roses, bats, camels, early elephants, dogs, cats, weasels	57.8
Oligocene epoch	Deer, pigs, saber-toothed cats, monkeys	36.6
Neogene period		
Miocene epoch	Seals, dolphins, grasses, daisies, asters, sunflowers, lettuce, giraffes, bears, hyenas, early apes	23.03
Pliocene epoch	Apes, *Ardipithecus* and australopithecines (early hominids), *Homo habilis* and *rudolfensis* (first human species), mammoths, giant sloths and armadillos	5.2
Pleistocene epoch	*Homo erectus* and other early human species, modern humans; large mammals such as giant bison and beavers; many kinds of hoofed animals	1.6
Holocene epoch	Modern humans and flora and fauna of today	**0.01 (11,000 years)**

percent; argon, 0.93 percent; and carbon dioxide, 0.03 percent. There are also lesser amounts of neon, helium, krypton, and xenon. These proportions change with altitude, lighter gases being more common at higher altitudes, but they are approximately the same everywhere on Earth at the same altitude. There are also variable quantities of water vapor, dust particles, and other compounds whose proportions change from place to place at the same altitude—fewer dust particles being found over oceans, and less water vapor over deserts. Temperature decreases with altitude in the troposphere.

The *stratosphere* is found between 11 km and 50 km (7-30 mi.) out from the Earth's surface. Temperatures in this region rise slightly as altitude increases, to a maximum of about 0°C (32°F). Virtually coextensive with the stratosphere is the *ozonosphere*, or ozone layer, the region in which most of the atmosphere's ozone is found. Because ozone absorbs most of the sun's ultraviolet radiation, it is vital to the continued existence of life on the planet.

Beyond the stratosphere is the upper atmosphere, or *ionosphere*, so called because it is the layer in which atmospheric gases have been ionized by solar radiation. The ionosphere reflects certain wavelengths back to the surface, making it possible to transmit radio waves around the curve of the Earth. The ionosphere is further divided into the *mesosphere*, between 50 km and 80 km (30-50 mi.), in which the temperature decreases with altitude to -90°C (-130°F); and the *thermosphere*, from about 80 km to 450 km (50-280 mi.), in which the molecular temperature increases to as

Major Discoveries in Earth Sciences

B.C.

c.300   Dicaearchus (Greek: c. 320) develops map of Earth on a sphere using lines of latitude.

A.D.

132   Zhang Heng (Chinese: 78–139) develops first crude seismograph.
1600   William Gilbert (English: 1544–1603) suggests that Earth is giant magnet, which is why magnetic compasses indicate north.
1669   Nicolaus Steno (Niels Stensen; Danish: 1638–86) correctly explains origin of fossils.
1777   Nicolas Desmarest (French: 1725–1815) proposes that the rock basalt starts as lava.
1785   James Hutton (Scottish: 1726–97) explains features of Earth on basis of tiny changes taking place over long periods of time (uniformitarianism).
1795   Baron Georges Cuvier (French: 1769–1832) shows that giant bones found in Meuse River are remains of extinct giant reptile.
1797   Sir James Hall (Scottish: 1761–1832) shows that melted rocks form crystals upon cooling.
1822   Gideon A. Mantell (English: 1790–1852) and his wife, Mary Ann, discover and recognize dinosaur bones as those of a giant, extinct reptile.
1830   Sir Charles Lyell (Scottish: 1797–1875) begins to publish *Principles of Geology,* the work that convinced geologists that Earth is at least several hundred million years old.
1880   John Milne (English: 1850–1913) invents modern seismograph.
1896   Svante A. Arrhenius (Swedish: 1859–1927) calculates that global temperatures will rise with higher levels of carbon dioxide in atmosphere (greenhouse effect).
1902   Léon-Philippe Teisserenc de Bort (French: 1855–1913) discovers the stratosphere.
1906   Richard D. Oldham (English: 1858–1936) establishes existence of Earth's core.
1907   Bertram B. Boltwood (American: 1870–1927) shows that age of rocks containing uranium can be determined by measuring ratio of uranium to lead.
1909   Andrija Mohorovičić (Croatia: 1857–1936) discovers boundary between Earth's crust and mantle, now known as Mohorovičić discontinuity, or "Moho."
1912   Alfred L. Wegener (German: 1880–1930) proposes theory of continental drift, idea that a single continent—Pangaea—split into present-day continents, which have drifted away from each other.
1925   The German *Meteor* expedition discovers Mid-Atlantic Ridge, a giant mountain range in middle of the Atlantic Ocean.

1929   Motonori Matuyama (Japanese: 1884–1958) shows that Earth's magnetic field reverses every few hundred million years.
1958   James A. Van Allen (American: 1914–) discovers belts of radiation that surround Earth in space, now known as Van Allen belts.
1962   Harry H. Hess (American: 1906–69) develops theory of seafloor spreading—oceans become wider as new seafloor is formed at midocean ridges.
1979   American oceanographers discover hot vents in oceans, surrounded by exotic forms of life based on sulfur, not oxygen.
1980   Walter Alvarez (American: 1940–) and coworkers discover geologic layer of iridium in region identified with the demise of the dinosaurs; he attributes both iridium and extinction to a large comet or meteorite striking Earth.
1993   Ice cores from Greenland and Antarctica reveal the record of Earth's climate for the past 250,000 years.
   Weather scientists discover unexpected displays of electromagnetism in Earth's upper atmosphere; the displays are named Sprites, ELVES, and blue jets.
1996   A farmer in Liaoning Province in China discovers a dinosaur whose skin is covered with a feathery down, the first major find at what proves to be an important fossil site that also includes dinosaurs with more highly developed feathers.
   Scientists from the Scripps Institution of Oceanography at San Diego find evidence that life has existed on Earth for at least 3.85 billion years.
1998   Paul F. Hoffman (Canadian: 1941–) of Harvard University proposes that some 200 million years ago the surface of Earth was completely frozen from the poles to the equator, a condition known as "snowball Earth;" computer studies in 2000, indicate that a narrow band at the equator remained unfrozen.
2002   Laboratory studies reveal that Earth's mantle (the layer between the crust and core) could hold five times as much water as is in all the oceans.
2003   Marcelo R. Sánchez-Villagra, Orangel Aguilera, and Inés Horovitz discover in Venezuela the first nearly complete fossil of the rodent *Phoberomys pattersoni*, a guinea-pig relative that at 700 kg (1500 lb) was the largest known rodent, about the size of a bison.
2004   Researchers in China find fossil of the oldest known primate, dated from 55 million years ago.
   Geologists from the University of Utah in Salt Lake City establish that a powerful earthquake can alter the periods of geyser eruptions 2,000 miles (3,100 km) away.

much as 1475°C (2690°F). To spacecraft traveling in the atmosphere, as the space shuttle does, however, the temperature seems cold because the molecules are so widely spaced. Beyond the thermosphere is the *exosphere*, extending to about 1,000 km (600 mi.). In this layer, temperature no longer has the customary meaning. (See also "Global Warming" and "The Ozone Layer.")

▶ THE CHANGING EARTH

Despite its apparent solidity, the crust and interior of the Earth are constantly changing.

Plate tectonics   The earth's outer crust is composed of about 20 lithospheric (or tectonic) plates that move from a few millimeters to several centimeters per year. Hundreds of millions of years ago, these plates formed a continuous landmass known as Pangaea, surrounded by ocean. Eventually the plates separated, until they reached the positions they occupy today.

As plates move away from each other, molten rock emerges from the mantle to form oceanic crust. Where they come together, one plate is usually forced under the other, forming either oceanic trenches or mountain ranges (such as the Himalayas) or both. In a few places, one plate slips by the other along a giant crack called a fault, such as the San Andreas Fault in California. These areas are also the site of greatest volcanic and earthquake activity.

Earthquakes and tsunamis   Most earthquakes are caused when rock on one side of a fault (or crack) in the Earth's crust moves with respect to the rock on the other side of the fault. The motion causes vibrations in the crust that travel through the rock as shock waves. When these reach the surface, they cause it to move in various ways, which is called seismic motion. Small earthquakes that accompany volcanic eruptions are caused by the motion of liquid rock, or magma.

More than 800,000 earthquakes are registered by seismographs each year, but the overwhelming majority go unnoticed. However, large earthquakes are of great concern to many people living in regions of significant seismic activity. Although research on earthquake prediction has yielded no breakthroughs, death and destruction have been reduced somewhat by improvements in construction codes and techniques.

One common side effect of undersea earthquakes is tsunamis—or (incorrectly) tidal waves—against which there is little protection. Tsunamis are caused when an earthquake raises or lowers a section of seabed, thereby producing a wave that, while not generally noticeable at sea, can reach great heights as it approaches land. Similar to and as destructive as tsunamis, harbor waves are generated when a landslide falls into a bay, strait, or other confined body of water causing almost immediate flooding. High waves are also caused by volcanic explosions or collapses, such as the explosion and collapse of Krakatau in 1883.

Volcanoes   are openings in the Earth's crust that emit molten or partially molten rock (lava), various hot gases, and ash. (A volcano is also the mountain formed by solidified lava or ash ejected from the opening.) If the opening is like a crack, it is called a vent. If it is larger and fairly circular, it is called a crater. A caldera is a basin formed by the settling of the top of a volcanic mountain, and it may have several vents or craters on its floor.

Most volcanoes are found where two tectonic plates meet, such as along the famous "Ring of Fire" around the Pacific Ocean. A few, such as the volcanoes of the Hawaiian Islands, appear to be over "hot spots" in the Earth's crust where liquid rock flows upward with sufficient force to burn through the crust.

Although volcanoes are associated with destruction, they have many positive effects. Minerals from deep within the Earth make the land around many volcanoes extremely fertile; volcanoes can create new landforms in the sea; and the study of volcanoes contributes enormously to our understanding of the Earth's interior.

Richter Scale and Effects Near the Epicenter

Note: The epicenter is the point on Earth's surface above the center of the quake

Below 2.5   Not felt except by a very few under specially favorable circumstances.

2.5 to 3.5   Felt only by a few persons at rest, especially on upper floors of buildings.

3.5 to 4.5   At lower levels or further from the quake, it is felt by many people, sometimes quite noticeably indoors, especially on upper floors of buildings, but many people do not recognize as an earthquake. At somewhat higher levels or nearer to the epicenter, during the day the quake is felt indoors by many; outdoors by few. Sensation is like heavy truck striking building. At the highest level, the earth movement is felt by nearly everyone; with many awakened if during the night. Disturbances of trees, telephone poles, and other tall objects sometimes can be noticed.

4.5 to 6.0   Felt by all; many frightened and run outdoors. Some heavy furniture moved; there will be a few instances of fallen plaster or damaged chimneys. Other slight local damage may occur. At higher level, however, everybody runs outdoors. At the upper level, while damage is still negligible in buildings of good design and construction, there can be moderate damage even to well-built ordinary structures; there will be considerable damage to poorly built or badly designed structures.

6.0 to 7.0   A destructive earthquake. Damage may still be slight in specially designed structures, but will be considerable in ordinary substantial buildings, often with partial collapse. Damage will be great in poorly built structures, including collapse of chimneys, factory stacks, columns, monuments, and walls. At the upper level, damage is likely to be considerable even in specially designed structures. Most ordinary buildings will be shifted off foundations. Even the ground will be cracked conspicuously.

7.0 to 8.0   A major earthquake. Worldwide, about 10 of these occur each year. Some well-built wooden structures will be destroyed. Most masonry and frame structures will be destroyed along with their foundations. Ground becomes badly cracked.

8.0 and above   Great earthquakes. These occur once every five to 10 years. Few, if any masonry structures remain standing. Bridges are destroyed. Broad fissures appear in ground. At the highest levels and near the epicenter, damage total. Waves seen on solid ground. Heavy objects thrown upward into air.

Although geologists consider a volcano active if it has shown signs of activity in historic times, it is not usually clear whether a volcano is extinct or only dormant and could be active again. (Thus Tambora, which has not erupted since 1815, is considered active.) Some volcanoes once thought to be extinct have become active, and there are now about 600 volcanoes that are considered active. The accompanying list contains about a fourth of all volcanoes known to have been active in recent years, with special emphasis on volcanoes in the United States and volcanoes that have had famous eruptions.

The destruction caused by volcanoes is usually localized, but their effects can be felt around the world and take many forms. At their worst, volcanoes can blow themselves to pieces, as the island of Thera did about 1650 B.C. More often, volcanic ash blankets an area (as Mt. Vesuvius did at Pompeii), or clouds of hot gases and dust sweep down the side of the volcano poisoning the air. Lava generally moves too slowly to be a menace to people. Even more unpredictable, heat from a volcano can melt glaciers or snowcaps, triggering massive mud slides (as happened in Colombia in 1985) or releasing lakes of boiling water.

▶MEASURING EARTHQUAKES

The size of an earthquake is generally reported in the United States using the Richter scale, a system developed by seismologist Charles Richter (American: 1900-85) in 1935. The Richter scale measures the magnitude of an earthquake, that is, the size of ground waves generated by an earthquake as shown on a measuring device called a seismograph. Each whole number on the scale represents a tenfold increase (or decrease) in magnitude: a magnitude 6 earthquake produces a ground wave 10 times greater than a magnitude 5.

This does not mean, however, that a magnitude 6 earthquake has 10 times the energy as one of magnitude 5. Measuring the actual energy requires instruments placed at the site of the earthquake. Various methods have been developed for inferring energy from magnitude and these suggest that one change in magnitude corresponds to a thirty- to sixtyfold change in energy. Using these proportions, the energy of a magnitude 8 earthquake, a very serious event, can be as much as 1 million to 10 million times as much as that of a magnitude 4 earthquake, one that can be felt but causes almost no damage.

Major Earthquakes, 856–2008

Date	Location and remarks	Estimated deaths	Richter magnitude	Date	Location and remarks	Estimated deaths	Richter magnitude
856	Corinth, Greece	45,000	—	Oct. 28, 1891	Central Japan	7,300	—
Dec. 22, 856	Iran	200,000	—	June 15, 1896	Sanriku and Kamaishi, Japan (tsunami)	26,000	—
Mar. 23, 893	Iran	150,000	—				
1036	Shansi	23,000	—	Apr. 4, 1905	Kangra, India	19,000	8.6
1057	Chihli (Hopeh), China	25,000	—	Apr. 18, 1906	San Francisco, California	3,000	7.7
Aug. 9, 1138	Aleppo, Syria	230,000	—	Aug. 17, 1906	Santiago, Chile	20,000	8.6
1170	Sicily	15,000	—	1907	Tajikistan	40,000	—
1268	Silicia (Turkey)	60,000	—	Dec. 28, 1908	Messina, Sicily	75,000	7.5
Sept. 1290	Chihli, China	100,000	—	Jan. 13, 1916	Avezzano, Italy	29,980	7.5
May 20, 1293	Kamakura, Japan	30,000	—	Dec. 16, 1920	Gansu, China	200,000	8.5
Jan. 26, 1531	Lisbon, Portugal	30,000	—	Sept. 1, 1923	Tokyo/Yokohama, Japan	143,000	8.3
Jan. 23, 1556	Shansi, China	830,000	—	Mar. 7, 1927	Tango, Japan	3,020	7.9
Nov. 1667	Shemakha, Azerbaijan	80,000	—	May 22, 1927	Nan-Shan, China	200,000	8.3
June 7, 1692	Port Royal, Jamaica	30,000	—	Dec. 25, 1932	Gansu, China	70,000	7.6
Jan. 11, 1693	Catania province, Sicily	60,000	—	Mar. 2, 1933	Sanriku, Japan (tsunami)	2,990	8.9
1693	Naples, Italy	93,000	—	Mar. 11, 1933	Long Beach, California	115	6.3
1707	Tsunami hits Japan	30,000	—	Jan. 15, 1934	Bihar, India and Nepal	10,700	8.4
Nov. 18, 1727	Tabriz, Iran	77,000	—	May 30, 1935	Quetta, India (Pakistan)	50,000	7.5
Dec. 30, 1730	Hokkaido Island, Japan	137,000	—	Jan. 25, 1939	Chillan, Chile	30,000	8.3
1731	Beijing, China	100,000	—	Dec. 27, 1939	Erzincan, Turkey	30,000	8.0
Oct. 11, 1737	Calcutta, India	300,000	—	Apr. 1, 1946	Earthquake at Unimak Island, Alaska, causes tsunami striking Hilo, Hawaii	165	7.3
June 7, 1755	Northern Iran	40,000	—				
Nov. 1, 1755	Lisbon, Portugal (earthquake, tsunami)	60,000	8.6				
				Dec. 20, 1946	Tonankai, Japan	1,330	8.4
Feb. 4, 1783	Calabria, Italy	50,000	—	June 28, 1948	Fukui, Japan	5,390	7.3
Feb. 4, 1797	Quito, Ecuador and Cuzco, Peru	41,000	—	Oct. 5, 1948	Ashkabad, Turkmenistan	110,000	7.3
				Aug. 5, 1949	Pelileo, Ecuador	6,000	6.8
Dec. 16, 1811	New Madrid, Missouri	<10	7.7	Aug. 15, 1950	Assam State, India	1,530	8.7
Feb. 7, 1812	New Madrid, Missouri	0	7.9	July 21, 1952	Kern County, California	12	7.5
Sept. 5, 1822	Aleppo (Syria)	22,000	—	June 10-17, 1956	Northern Afghanistan	2,000	7.7
Dec. 28, 1828	Echigo, Japan	30,000	—				
Dec. 24, 1854	Tokai, Japan	3,000	8.4	July 2, 1957	Northern Iran	1,200	7.4
Oct. 1855	Tokyo, Japan	2,000+	—	Dec. 13, 1957	Western Iran	1,130	7.3
Jan. 9, 1857	Fort Tejon, California	1	7.9	Aug. 17, 1959	Hebgen Lake, Montana	28	7.3
1857	East of Naples, Italy	10,000+	—	Feb. 29, 1960	Agadir, Morocco	12,000	5.9
Aug. 13-15, 1868	Peru and Ecuador	40,000	—	May 21-30, 1960	Southern Chile; tsunami strikes various Pacific islands, killing 61 in Hawaii; greatest earthquake ever recorded	5,700	9.5
May 16, 1875	Venezuela and Colombia	16,000	—				
Aug. 31, 1886	Charleston, South Carolina	60	7.6				

Date	Location and remarks	Estimated deaths	Richter magnitude
Sept. 1, 1962	Northwestern Iran	12,230	7.3
Mar. 28, 1964	Southern Alaska	125	9.2
Aug. 19, 1966	Eastern Turkey	2,520	7.1
Aug. 31, 1968	Khurasan, Iran	12,000	7.3
July 25, 1969	Eastern China	3,000	5.9
Jan. 5, 1970	Yunnan Province, China	10,000	7.5
May 31, 1970	Yungay, Ranrahirca, and Huarás, Peru	66,000	7.8
Feb. 9, 1971	San Fernando Valley Calif.	65	6.6
Apr. 10, 1972	Ghir, Iran	5,054	7.1
Dec. 23, 1972	Managua, Nicaragua	5,000	6.2
Dec. 28, 1974	North Pakistan	5,300	6.2
Feb. 4, 1975	Liaoning Province, China (predicted)	10,000	7.4
Sept. 6, 1975	Lice, Turkey	2,300	6.7
Feb. 4, 1976	Guatemala City,	23,000	7.5
June 25, 1976	New Guinea and Irian Jaya, Indonesia	8,000+	7.1
July 27, 1976	Tangshan, China	655,000	8.0
Aug. 16, 1976	Mindanao, Philippines (earthquake and tsunami)	8,000	7.9
Nov. 24, 1976	Eastern Turkey	5,000	7.3
Sept. 16, 1978	Northeast Iran	15,000	7.8
Oct. 10, 1980	Northwestern Algeria	3,500	7.7
Nov. 23, 1980	Southern Italy	3,000	7.2
July 28, 1981	Kerman province, Iran	2,500	7.3
Dec. 13, 1982	Yemen	2,800	6.0
Sept. 19, 1985	Mexico City	9,500	8.1
Oct. 10, 1986	San Salvador, El Salvador	1,000+	5.5
Mar. 6, 1987	Ecuador	1,000+	7.0
Dec. 7, 1988	Armenia	25,000	7.0
Oct. 18, 1989	Loma Prieta, California (Santa Cruz Mountains), destructive in San Francisco and Oakland	63	7.2
June 20, 1990	Caspian Sea, Iran	50,000	7.7
July 16, 1990	Cabanatuan (Luzon I.), Philippines	1,621	7.8
Oct. 21, 1991	India and Nepal	2,000	7.0
Dec. 12, 1992	Flores Island, Indonesia (tsunami)	2,500	7.5
Sept. 29, 1993	Bombay, India	9,748	6.3
Jan. 17, 1994	Northridge, California	61	6.8
Jan. 16, 1995	Near Kobe, Japan	5,502	6.9
May 27, 1995	Sakhalin Island, Russia	1,989	7.5
Feb. 28, 1997	Northwestern Iran	1,000+	6.1
May 10, 1997	Northeastern Iran	1,560	7.5
Feb. 4, 1998	Afghanistan	2,323	6.1
May 30, 1998	Afghanistan-Tajikistan border	4,000	6.9
July 17, 1998	Tsunamis strike Papua, New Guinea	2,183	7.1
Jan. 25, 1999	Armenia, Colombia	1,885	6.4
Aug. 17, 1999	Northwestern Turkey	17,118	7.4
Sept. 20, 1999	Nantou, Taiwan	2,101	7.6
Nov. 12, 1999	Turkey	843	7.5
Jan 13, 2001	El Salvador	844	7.7
Jan. 26, 2001	Southern India	20,005	7.7
Feb. 13, 2001	El Salvador	315	6.6
June 23, 2001	Coast of Peru	74	8.4
Jan. 10, 2002	Near north coast of New Guinea	1	6.7
Mar. 3, 2002	Hindu Kush, Afghanistan	163	7.4
Mar. 25, 2002	Hindu Kush, Afghanistan	1,000	6.1
June 22, 2002	Western Iran	227	6.5
Oct. 31, 2002	Southern Italy	29	5.9
Nov. 1, 2002	Kashmir, India/Pakistan	11	5.4
Nov. 20, 2002	Kashmir, India/Pakistan	19	6.3
Jan. 22, 2003	Colima, Mexico	29	7.6
Feb. 24, 2003	Xingjiang, China	261	6.3
May 1, 2003	Turkey	177	6.4
May 21, 2003	Algeria	2,266	6.8
July 21, 2003	Yunnan, China	16	6.0
Dec. 1, 2003	Kazakhstan-China border	11	6.0
Dec. 22, 2003	Paso Robles, California	2	6.5
Dec. 26, 2003	Iran	43,200	6.6
Jan. 1, 2004	Bali, Indonesia	1	5.8
Feb. 14, 2004	Pakistan	24	5.5
Feb. 16, 2004	Sumatra, Indonesia	5	6.0
Feb. 24, 2004	Burundi	3	4.7
Feb. 24, 2004	Morocco and Spain	628	6.4
Mar. 25, 2004	Turkey	10	5.6
Apr. 5, 2004	Afghanistan	3	6.6
May 28, 2004	Iran	35	6.3
July 1, 2004	Turkey	18	5.4
Dec. 26, 2004	Centered off west coast of Sumatra, but tsunamis strike Sumatra, Sri Lanka, Thailand, and other coastal nations	297,200	9.0
Feb. 22, 2005	Central Iran	612	6.4
Mar. 28, 2005	Nias Island, N. Sumatra	1,203	8.7
Oct. 8, 2005	Islamabad, Pakistan	86,000	7.6
May 26, 2006	Java, Indonesia	5,749	6.3
July 17, 2006	South of Java, Indonesia	730	7.7
Mar. 6, 2007	Southern Sumatra, Indonesia	70	6.4
Apr. 1, 2007	Solomon Islands	54	8.1
Aug. 15, 2007	Near Coast of Peru	514	8.0
May 12, 2008	Eastern Sichuan, China	69,185	7.9

Volcano Eruptions and Landslides, 1628 B.C.–A.D. 2002

Date	Event	Deaths
B.C.		
1628 or 1645	Mediterranean volcanic island of Thera (Santorini) explodes.	N.A.
A.D.		
Aug. 24–26, 79	Mt. Vesuvius, near Naples, Italy, erupts, destroying towns of Pompeii and Herculaneum.	2,000+
260	Mt. Ilopango in El Salvador erupts, apparently destroying the early Maya civilization.	N.A.
Sept. 4, 1618	Landslides hit Chiavenna Valley, Italy.	2,420
Dec. 16, 1631	Mt. Vesuvius erupts.	4,000+
Mar. 25, 1669	Mt. Etna at Catania, Sicily, erupts.	20,000
Jan. 11, 1683	Mt. Etna erupts, accompanied by earthquakes.	60,000
Aug. 11–12, 1772	Mt. Papandayan on Java explodes.	3,000 +
1782	Eruption of Mt. Unzen in Japan causes tidal wave.	15,000
June 1783– Feb. 1784	Laki fissure on Mt. Skaptar, Iceland erupts; poisonous gases kill crops and livestock, and thick haze interrupts fishing on oceans.	9,800
Sept. 2, 1806	Rossberg Peak collapses, causing landslides in Goldau Valley, Switzerland.	500
Apr. 5, 1815	Mt. Tambora on Sumbawa in East Indies begins series of eruptions that kill about 10,000 people; another 50,000 die of famine and disease locally	162,000

Date	Event	Deaths	Date	Event	Deaths
Oct. 8 and 12, 1822	Mt. Galunggung on Java erupts, causing slides of mud and boiling water.	4,000	Apr. 30, 1979	Landslide covers side of Marapi volcano in Sumatra, Indonesia.	82 +
1845	Eruption of Nevada del Ruiz in northern Colombia causes mud slides from melting snow.	1,000	July 18, 1979	Landslide on Mt. Werung causes wave to strike beach areas on Lomblen Island, Indonesia.	539
July 28, 1883	Epomeo volcano on Italian Isle of Ischia erupts, causing destructive earthquakes.	2,000 +	May 18, 1980	Mt. St. Helens volcano erupts in Washington.	61
Aug. 26, 1883	Krakatau volcano in East Indies erupts, producing giant waves that strike nearby islands.	36,000	May 20, 1981	Landslides caused by eruption of Semeru in Java, Indonesia.	252
May 7, 1902	La Soufriére on St. Vincent in West Indies erupts.	1,500–2,000	Mar. 28 and Apr. 3-4, 1982	El Chichón in Chiapas, Mexico, erupts, sending cloud of volcanic ash around world.	2,000
May 8, 1902	Pelée volcano on neighboring Martinique erupts, pouring cloud of flaming gas on city of St. Pierre.	29,000	Aug. 16, 1984	Carbon dioxide emitted by Lake Monoun, Cameroon, spreads in region around lake.	37
Aug. 30, 1902	Mt. Pelée erupts.	2,000	Nov. 13, 1985	Eruption of Nevada del Ruiz in northern Colombia causes massive mud slide covering town of Armero.	25,000
Apr. 18, 1906	Mt. Vesuvius near Naples erupts.	150 +			
1911	Taal volcano, near Manila, Philippines, erupts.	1,300	Aug. 21, 1986	Carbon dioxide from Lake Nyos, Cameroon, spreads through region.	1,700 +
May 1919	Crater lake of Mt. Kelut in Indonesia, boiling from volcanic activity, breaks through side of the mountain.	5,000 +	July 13, 1990	Earthquake triggers landslide in Pamir Mts., Tajikistan, USSR.	40+
1937	Eruption of Rabaul caldera on New Britain, Papua New Guinea.	500 +	Oct. 13, 1990	Geyserlike explosion in the Ahuachapán Geothermal Field, El Salvador, releases wave of carbon dioxide and water.	26
Jan. 15, 1951	Mt. Lamington on New Guinea produces cloud of hot gas and dust, similar to that at Mt. Pelée in 1902 and Mt. St. Helens in 1980.	3,000–5,000	June 3, 1991	Eruption of Mt. Unzen, Kyushu, Japan.	43
			June 9, 1991	Mount Pinatubo erupts, as predicted, in Luzon, Philippines; 358 killed by disease in evacuation camps.	754
Dec. 4, 1951	Mt. Catarman (Hibokhibok) in Philippines releases cloud of hot gas.	500	Jan. 14, 1993	Galeras in Colombia unexpectedly erupts during a scientific workshop, killing six volcanologists who had been on the rim studying the volcano.	9
Sept. 24, 1952	Japanese research ship investigating undersea volcano is destroyed in eruptive event.	29			
Dec. 25, 1953	Dam, created by 1945 eruption of Ruapehu volcano on New Zealand, gives way; avalanche of mud and snow strikes passenger train.	150	Feb. 2, 1993	An unexpected eruption of Mayon on Luzon, Philippines produces a cloud of hot gas and dust that rolls down the slope.	70
Jan. 10, 1962	Landslide on Mt. Huascarán, Peru.	3,000	June 6, 1994	An earthquake at the Volcano Nevada de Huila in Colombia causes mud slides that destroy a dozen villages on its slopes.	650 +
Mar. 14, 1962	Two landslides near Paucartambno Hydroelectric Station in Peru.	204			
Mar. 17-21, 1963	Mt. Agung volcano in Bali, Indonesia, erupts.	1,584	Nov. 22, 1994	Various flows of hot ash and gases down the slope of Merapi volcano on Java in Indonesia kill workers at a water-treatment plant and sweep through villages where superstitious villagers ignored a call to evacuate.	64
Aug. 10, 1963	Landslide in Nepal sweeps villages into Trisuli River.	200			
Oct. 9, 1963	Flood occurs when Valont Dam near Langarone, Italy, overflows as result of landslide into its reservoir.	2,200			
1965	Taal volcano near Manila in the Philippines erupts.	150	Feb. 18, 1997	Mudslide caused by heavy rains destroys two Peruvian villages	300
Aug. 30, 1965	Avalanche near Saas-Fee, Switzerland, from Allalin glacier strikes workers building dam.	40-100	May 5-6, 1998	Mudslides caused by heavy rains pour down Mount Sarno, east of Naples, Italy.	135
1968	Eruption of Arenal in Costa Rica.	78	Oct. 30, 1998	Hurricane Mitch causes landslide on San Cristobal volcano in Nicaragua.	1600
July 22, 1970	Landslide diverts Alaknanda River in India, causing sudden flood.	600	Dec., 1999	Heavy rains cause floods and landslides in northern Venezuela.	20,000
Mar. 18, 1971	Landslide into Lake Yanahuani, creates 60-foot wave that sweeps over Chungar, Peru.	200	Jan. 13, 2001	Landslides triggered by an earthquake near Santa Tecla, El Salvador bury villages,	585
July 29, 1971	Landslide into high lake in Hindu Kush mountains of Afghanistan causes instant flood.	1,000 +	Jan. 17, 2002	Lava flows from eruption of Nyirangongo volcano in the Congo.	45
June 28, 1974	Landslides along Quebrada Blanca Canyon in Eastern Colombia.	200	Mar. 3, 2002	Landslide caused by earthquake in the Hindu Kush region of Afghanistan dams and floods Surkundara Valley.	150
Jan. 10, 1977	Fast-moving stream of lava from volcano near Goma, Zaire, overtakes fleeing residents.	70	Aug. 14, 2002	Landslides from heavy rains bury villages in Yunnan Province, China.	52
Feb. 21, 1979	Sinila volcano in Java, Indonesia	175 +			

Major Active Volcanoes

Volcano	Location	Height (feet above reported sea level)	Last reported eruption
Africa and the Indian Ocean			
Cameroon	Cameroon	13,435	2000
Fogo	Cape Verde Islands	9,281	1995
Karthala	Comoros	7,746	1991
Ol Donyo Lengai	Tanzania	9,482	2002
Piton de la Fournaise	Réunion Island	8,632	2004
Nyamuragira	Zaire	10,033	2004
Nyirangongo	Zaire	11,384	2004
Asia			
Agung	Bali, Indonesia	10,308	1964
Akan	Hokkaido, Japan	4,918	1998
Alaid	Kuril Isl. Russia	7,674	1996
Asama	Honshu, Japan	8,339	2004
Aso	Kyushu, Japan	5,223	1995
Batur	Bali, Indonesia	5,633	2000
Bezymianny	Kamchatka, Russia	9,455	2004
Bulusan	Luzon, Philippines	5,134	1995
Chokai	Honshu, Japan	7,339	1974
Dieng Volc	Java, Indonesia	8,415	1996
Dukono	Halmahera, Indonesia	3,888	2004
Fuji	Honshu, Japan	12,388	1708
Galunggung	Java, Indonesia	7,113	1984
Gamalama	Ternate, Indonesia	5,627	2003
Karangetang	Siau Island, Indonesia	5,853	2003
Karymsky	Kamchatka, Russia	5,039	2004
Kelut	Java, Indonesia	5,679	1990
Kerenci	Sumatra, Indonesia	12,467	2004
Kliuchevskoi	Kamchatka, Russia	15,863	2004
Komaga-take	Hokkaido, Japan	3,740	2000
Koryaksky	Kamchatka, Russia	11,338	1957
Krakatau	Indonesia	2,667	2004
Lewotobi	Flores Isl., Indonesia	5,587	2003
Lokon-Empung	Sulawesi, Indonesia	5,184	2003
Mayon	Luzon, Philippines	8,077	2001
Merapi	Java, Indonesia	9,669	2002
Miyake-jima	Izu Islands, Japan	2,674	2002
Nasu	Honshu, Japan	6,289	1963
Nigata Yake-yama	Honshu, Japan	7,874	1989
On-take	Honshu, Japan	10,049	1980
Peuet Sague	Sumatra, Indonesia	9,190	2000
Pinatubo	Luzon, Philippines	4,875	1993
Raung	Java, Indonesia	10,932	2000
Rinjani	Lombok Island, Indonesia	12,224	1994
Sakura-jima	Kyushu, Japan	3,665	2004
Sangeang Api	Lesser Sunda, Indonesia	6,394	1988
Sarychev Peak	Kuril Islands, Russia	4,908	1989
Semeru	Java, Indonesia	12,060	2004
Shiveluch	Kamchatka, Russia	10,771	2002
Slamet	Java, Indonesia	11,260	1999
Suwanose-jima	Ryukyu Islands, Japan	2,621	2001
Taal	Luzon, Philippines	1,342	1977
Tambora	Sumbawa, Indonesia	9,350	1967
Tengger Caldera	Java, Indonesia	7,641	2001
Tiatia	Kuril Isl., Russia	5,968	1981
Unzen	Kyushu, Japan	4,921	1996
Usu	Hokkaido, Japan	2,398	2001
Europe and the Atlantic Ocean			
Askja	Iceland	4,974	1961
Beerenberg	Jan Mayen Island, Norway	7,470	1985
Etna	Italy	10,991	2001

Volcano	Location	Height (feet above reported sea level)	Last reported eruption
Fogo	Cape Verde Islands	9,281	1995
Grímsvötn	Iceland	5,659	1998
Hekla	Iceland	4,892	2000
Krafla	Iceland	2,133	1984
Stromboli	Italy	3,058	2002
Tristan da Cunha	Tristan da Cunha, U.K.	6,758	2004
Vesuvius	Italy	4,203	1944
North America			
Akutan	Alaska	4,275	1992
Amukta	Alaska	3,497	1997
Atka	Alaska	5,029	1998
Augustine	Alaska	4,108	1986
Baker	Washington	10,777	1880
Carlisle	Alaska	5,315	1828
Cerberus	Alaska	2,539	1987
Cleveland	Alaska	5,676	2001
Colima	Mexico	12,631	2004
Crater Lake	Oregon	8,159	c 2290 B.C.
El Chichon	Mexico	3,773	1982
Fisher	Alaska	3,648	1830
Gareloi	Alaska	5,161	1989
Great Sitkin	Alaska	5,709	1974
Hood	Oregon	11,240	1866
Iliamna	Alaska	10,016	1876
Kagamil	Alaska	2,930	1929
Kanaga	Alaska	4,288	1995
Katmai	Alaska	6,716	1912
Kiska	Alaska	4,003	1990
Lassen Peak	California	10,456	1917
Little Sitkin	Alaska	3,852	1830
Makushin	Alaska	5,905	1995
Martin	Alaska	6,112	1953
Novarupta	Alaska	2,759	1912
Okmok	Alaska	3,520	1997
Parícutin	Mexico	1,500	1952
Pavlof	Alaska	8,264	1997
Pavlof Sister	Alaska	7,027	1786
Popocatépetl	Mexico	17,802	2004
Rainier	Washington	14,409	1825
Redoubt	Alaska	10,197	1990
St. Helens	Washington	8,363	1991
Seguam	Alaska	3,458	1993
Shasta	California	14,163	1786
Shishaldin	Alaska	9,373	1999
South Sister	Oregon	10,357	c 50 B.C.
Spurr	Alaska	11,069	2004
Tanaga	Alaska	5,925	1914
Trident	Alaska	6,115	1975
Veniaminof	Alaska	8,225	1994
Westdahl	Alaska	5,426	1992
Yunaska	Alaska	1,804	1937
Central America and the Caribbean			
Acatenango	Guatemala	13,044	1972
Arenal	Costa Rica	5,436	2004
Cerro Negro	Nicaragua	2,388	1999
Concepción	Nicaragua	5,577	1999
Fuego	Guatemala	12,346	2004
Irazú	Costa Rica	11,260	1994
Izalco	El Salvador	6,398	1966
Masaya	Nicaragua	2,083	2001
Pacaya	Guatemala	8,373	2003
Pelée	Martinique	4,583	1932
Poás	Costa Rica	8,884	1996
Rincón de la Vieja	Costa Rica	6,286	1998

Volcano	Location	Height (feet above sea level)	Last reported eruption
San Cristóbal	Nicaragua	5,725	2002
San Miguel	El Salvador	6,988	1997
Santa María	Guatemala	12,375	2004
Soufrière Hills	Montserrat	3,002	2004
Soufriere St. Vincent	St Vincent and the Grenadines	4,003	1979
Tacaná	Mexico/Guatemala	13,320	1986
Telica	Nicaragua	3,481	2000
South America			
Alcedo	Galápagos Islands, Ecuador	3,707	1993
Azul, Cerro	Galápagos Islands, Ecuador	5,381	1998
Copahué	Chile/Argentina	9,728	2000
Cotopaxi	Ecuador	19,393	1940
Galeras	Colombia	14,029	2004
Guagua Pichincha	Ecuador	15,695	2001
Guallatiri	Chile	19,918	1960
Hudson, Cerro	Chile	6,250	1991
Lascar	Chile	18,346	2003
Llaima	Chile	10,253	1998
Lonquimay	Chile	9,399	1990
Puracé	Colombia	15,256	1977
Reventador	Ecuador	11,686	1976
Ruiz, Nevado del	Colombia	17,457	1991
Sangay	Ecuador	17,159	2002
Tungurahua	Ecuador	16,479	2002
Villarrica	Chile	9,340	2000

Volcano	Location	Height (feet above sea level)	Last reported eruptio
Oceania—Australia, New Zealand, and the Pacific Islands			
Ambrym	Vanuatu	4,377	200·
Bagana	Bougainville Island, Papua New Guinea	5,741	200·
Haleakala c.1790	Hawaii	10,023	
Hualalai	Hawaii	8,277	1801
Karkar	Papua New Guinea	6,033	197S
Kilauea	Hawaii	4,009	2004·
Langila	New Britain, Papua New Guinea	4,363	2002
Lopevei	Vanuatu	4.636	2001
Mauna Loa	Hawaii	13,681	1984
Manam	Papua New Guinea	5,928	2000
Ngauruhoe	North Island, New Zealand	6,489	1977
Pagan	Mariana Islands	1,870	1993
Rabaul	New Britain, Papua New Guinea	2,257	2004
Ruapehu	North Island, New Zealand	9,176	1997
Ulawun	New Britain, Papua New Guinea	7,657	2004
White Island	North Island, New Zealand	1,053	2001
Antarctica			
Big Ben	Heard Island	9,007	1993
Mount Erebus	Ross Island	13,444	2001

CHEMISTRY

Chemistry is concerned with the way substances interact with one another. These interactions are chiefly the result of outer electrons of an atom interacting with the outer electrons of another atom. It has increasingly become clear that the shapes of the various combinations of atoms (called molecules) also affect chemical reactions, and physical chemistry is one of the most vital parts of chemistry today. Another vital branch is biochemistry, the study of the chemistry of molecules in living organisms. Organic chemistry generally deals with chemicals formed by living organisms and other chemicals containing carbon, but it treats them as chemicals outside the organism. Inorganic chemistry is concerned with chemicals that do not contain carbon.

▶THE PERIODIC TABLE
In the 19th century, chemists began to determine how much one atom of an element weighed with respect to another—the atomic weight (also known as the atomic mass and measured in atomic mass units, or amu; in modern chemistry, one amu is equal to one-twelfth the weight of the most common form of carbon atom). The first comprehensive list of atomic weights was prepared by Jöns Jakob Berzelius in 1828. When chemists made lists of elements in the order of atomic weights, they noticed that every seven or eight elements in the list had similar properties. In 1869 Dmitri Mendeleyev boldly interchanged some elements in the list and left blanks for others to make sure the properties matched for every "period" of eight elements. This was the first periodic table. Mendeleyev had only 63 elements to work with, but he correctly predicted three more that would make his list more complete. Today the elements up to 116, with the exceptions of 113 and 115, have been identified. Claims for elements 116 and 118 were made in 1999 by Lawrence Berkeley National Laboratory in California and withdrawn in 2002, but element 116 was produced by the Joint Institute for Nuclear Research, Dubna, Russia, in 2000. Elements 110-112, 114 and 116 have not yet been named.

Early in the 20th century, atoms were discovered to consist of protons and electrons (in 1932 it was discovered that neutrons also are found in atoms). The number of protons is the atomic number, which is a different number for every element from hydrogen (atomic number 1) to the unnamed element 116 (elements 113 and 115 have yet to be synthesized). The periodic table was improved by arranging the elements in order of atomic number instead of atomic weight. This clearly showed where the blanks were.

Each column of the periodic table includes elements with similar properties, although hydrogen in the first column is less typical in this respect. But the other elements in the first column are all soft metals that are highly reactive. Similarly, the

Major Discoveries in Chemistry

B.C.

c. 450 Leucippus of Miletus (Greek: 5th cent.) introduces concept of atom, later expanded upon by his pupil Democritus of Abdera (c. 460–c. 370).

A.D.

1662 Robert Boyle (Anglo-Irish: 1627–91) announces what becomes known as Boyle's law: For gas kept at constant temperature, pressure and volume vary inversely.

1755 Joseph Black (Scottish: 1728–99) discovers carbon dioxide.

1778 Antoine-Laurent Lavoisier (French: 1743–94) discovers that air is mostly mixture of nitrogen and oxygen.

1784 Henry Cavendish (English: 1731–1810) announces water is compound of hydrogen and oxygen.

1789 Lavoisier explicitly states law of conservation of matter: In chemical change, matter is neither created nor destroyed.

1791 Jeremias Benjāmin Richter (German: 1762–1807) shows that acids and bases always neutralize each other in same proportion.

1803 John Dalton (English: 1766–1844) establishes atomic theory of matter.

1811 Amedeo Avogadro (Italian: 1776–1856) proposes that equal volumes of gas at same temperature and pressure contain same number of molecules (Avogadro's law).

1824 Joseph-Louis Gay-Lussac (French: 1778–1850) discovers chemical isomers, chemicals with same formula but different structures.

1828 Friedrich Wöhler (German: 1800–1882) prepares organic compound from inorganic chemicals, showing that life is basically same as other matter.

1859 Gustav Robert Kirchhoff (German: 1824–87) and Robert Wilhelm Bunsen (German: 1811–99) introduce use of spectroscope to identify elements from light they give off when heated.

1869 Dmitry Ivanovich Mendeleyev (Russian: 1834–1907) publishes his first version of periodic table of elements.

1906 Mikhail Tsvett (Russian: 1872–1919) develops paper chromatography, the beginning of modern methods of chemical analysis.

1908 Fritz Haber (German: 1868–1934) develops cheap process for making ammonia from nitrogen in the air.

1962 Neil Bartlett (English: 1932–) creates a compound of xenon, platinum, and fluorine, showing that the noble gases can form compounds.

1984 Dany Schechtman (American) and coworkers discover first quasicrystal, a "crystal" that violates the symmetry rules of all other crystals.

1985 Richard E. Smalley (American: 1943–) and Harry Kroto (English: 1939–) discover buckminsterfullerene, a carbon molecule containing 60 carbon atoms arranged in a geodesic sphere (nicknamed "the bucky ball").

1991 Sumio Iijima (Japanese: 1939–) of NEC Corp. discovers that carbon forms tiny hollow cylinders called nanotubes.

1998 Research on carbon nanotubes shows that they conduct electricity with almost no resistance at room temperature (although they are not superconductors), emit light when carrying an electric current, and can behave either as semiconductors or metals depending on the alignment of atoms in the tube.

2001 Researchers discover that the common mineral calcite (calcium carbonate) tends to segregate left-handed amino acids on one face and right-handed ones on another, suggesting a possible origin for all amino acids in living organisms being left-handed; similarly the handedness of amino acids affects crystal formation in calcite.

2002 Researchers at the University of California, Davis, discover that distributing molecules of gadolinium nitrate through porous silicon creates a form of silicon that explodes like gunpowder when scratched or when exposed to a spark from a low-power battery.

Scientists in Rome create molecules consisting of four nitrogen atoms (molecules of nitrogen in air contain two atoms only.

2003 Takashi Saito of Toyota Central Research and Development Laboratories in Nagukute, Japan, and coworkers produce alloys of titanium that have a low and constant coefficient of expansion and that can be formed easily into desired shapes at room temperature.

2004 Chemists at Cornell University discover a new chemical reaction for splitting nitrogen molecules of the kind found in air, one that operates at the temperature of boiling water at one atmosphere of pressure. Then hydrogen can be added to form ammonia.

---

last column of the table contains the gases that react only minimally. In general, elements are metals on the left side of the table (hydrogen is a metal only under great pressure), becoming mostly nonmetals in the last six columns. These last columns include some elements that are metals, such as aluminum. (A broken, heavy line separates the metals from the nonmetals.)

The row of rare earth elements beginning with lanthanum and the row of actinide elements beginning with actinium do not fit neatly into the rest of the table. Elements from atomic number 57 to 71 are all similar to lanthanum, while elements from atomic number 89 to 103 are similar to actinium. The rare earths are not generally rare, nor do they resemble soil. They are moderately common metals that, because of atomic structure, are very similar chemically. The actinide elements are radioactive metals.

The periodic table as shown here also includes the atomic mass as well as the atomic number.

The atomic mass is a relative number; it shows the weight of an element as compared to the weight of an atom of carbon-12, which is assigned a weight of exactly 12. Most elements occur with several different atomic weights (in addition to carbon-12, for example, there are both carbon-13 and carbon-14; carbon-14 has 6 protons and 8 neutrons and is radioactive. These different forms are called isotopes. In the periodic table, the atomic mass given for most elements is the one that would be found by averaging the different isotopes in the amounts they naturally occur. Carbon is given an atomic mass of 12.01 because there is so much more carbon-12 than there is carbon-13 or carbon-14 in an ordinary sample of carbon. For some radioactive elements, natural abundance is meaningless, since there is no stable form. For these, the atomic mass of the most stable form is given, indicated by putting the atomic mass in parentheses.

THE PERIODIC TABLE OF THE ELEMENTS

Key:
- 6 — atomic number
- C — chemical number
- 12.01 — atomic mass
- Carbon — name of element

Period	IA	IIA alkaline earth metals												IIIA	IVA	VA	VIA	VIIA	O noble gases
1	1 H 1.01 Hydrogen																		2 He 4.00 Helium
2	3 Li 6.94 Lithium	4 Be 9.01 Beryllium												5 B 10.81 Boron	6 C 12.01 Carbon	7 N 14.01 Nitrogen	8 O 16.00 Oxygen	9 F 19.00 Fluorine	10 Ne 20.18 Neon
3	11 Na 22.99 Sodium	12 Mg 24.31 Magnesium	IIIB	IVB	VB	VIB	VIIB	VIII	VIII	VIII	IB	IIB		13 Al 26.98 Aluminum	14 Si 28.09 Silicon	15 P 30.97 Phosphorus	16 S 32.07 Sulfur	17 Cl 35.45 Chlorine	18 Ar 39.95 Argon
4	19 K 39.10 Potassium	20 Ca 40.08 Calcium	21 Sc 44.96 Scandium	22 Ti 47.88 Titanium	23 V 50.94 Vanadium	24 Cr 52.00 Chromium	25 Mn 54.95 Manganese	26 Fe 55.85 Iron	27 Co 58.93 Cobalt	28 Ni 58.70 Nickel	29 Cu 63.55 Copper	30 Zn 65.39 Zinc		31 Ga 69.72 Gallium	32 Ge 72.61 Germanium	33 As 74.92 Arsenic	34 Se 78.96 Selenium	35 Br 79.90 Bromine	36 Kr 83.80 Krypton
5	37 Rb 85.47 Rubidium	38 Sr 87.62 Strontium	39 Y 88.91 Yttrium	40 Zr 91.22 Zirconium	41 Nb 92.91 Niobium	42 Mo 95.94 Molybdenum	43 Tc (98) Technetium	44 Ru 101.07 Ruthenium	45 Rh 102.91 Rhodium	46 Pd 106.4 Palladium	47 Ag 107.87 Silver	48 Cd 112.41 Cadmium		49 In 114.82 Indium	50 Sn 118.71 Tin	51 Sb 121.7 Antimony	52 Te 127.60 Tellurium	53 I 126.90 Iodine	54 Xe 131.29 Xenon
6	55 Cs 132.91 Cesium	56 Ba 137.33 Barium	Lanthanide series (see below)	72 Hf 178.49 Hafnium	73 Ta 180.94 Tantalum	74 W 183.85 Tungsten	75 Re 186.21 Rhenium	76 Os 190.23 Osmium	77 Ir 192.22 Iridium	78 Pt 195.08 Platinum	79 Au 196.97 Gold	80 Hg 200.59 Mercury		81 Tl 204.38 Thallium	82 Pb 207.2 Lead	83 Bi 208.98 Bismuth	84 Po (209) Polonium	85 At (210) Astatine	86 Rn (222) Radon
7	87 Fr (223) Francium	88 Ra 226.03 Radium	Actinide series (see below)	104 Rf (261) Rutherfordium	105 Db (262) Dubnium	106 Sg (263) Seaborgium	107 Bh (262) Bohrium	108 Hs (265) Hassium	109 Mt (266) Meitnerium	110 (269)	111 (272)	112 (277)		113 (287)	114 (281)	115 (291)	116 (292)		

rare earth elements—Lanthanide series

57 La 138.91 Lanthanum	58 Ce 140.12 Cerium	59 Pr 140.91 Praseodymium	60 Nd 144.24 Neodymium	61 Pm (145) Promethium	62 Sm 150.4 Samarium	63 Eu 151.96 Europium	64 Gd 157.25 Gadolinium	65 Tb 158.93 Terbium	66 Dy 162.50 Dysprosium	67 Ho 164.93 Holmium	68 Er 167.26 Erbium	69 Tm 168.93 Thulium	70 Yb 173.04 Ytterbium	71 Lu 174.97 Lutetium

Actinide series

89 Ac 227.03 Actinium	90 Th 232.04 Thorium	91 Pa 231.04 Protactinium	92 U 238.03 Uranium	93 Np 237.05 Neptunium	94 Pu (244) Plutonium	95 Am (243) Americium	96 Cm (247) Curium	97 Bk (247) Berkelium	98 Cf (251) Californium	99 Es (252) Einsteinium	100 Fm (257) Fermium	101 Md (258) Mendelevium	102 No (259) Nobelium	103 Lr (260) Lawrencium

Properties and Discovery of the Elements

All ordinary matter is made from one or more substances called elements (because they cannot be changed by chemical means). Ninety elements are found in nature, and people have created others, for a current total of 114. In this table each of the elements is listed in alphabetical order. The chemical symbol and the atomic number can be used to locate other information about the elements in the periodic table reprinted below. Many elements, known from ancient times, are labeled "prehistoric." Others are given with their first discovery—many elements having been independently rediscovered by others. In the following table, elements 110–12, 114, and 116, as yet unnamed, are listed as "Element 110" and so forth.

Element/Type[1]	Symbol/ Atomic number	Melting point[1]	Boiling point[1]	Derivation of name (Discoverer, Year)
Actinium	Ac	1924°F	5788°F	Greek *aktis*, a ray. (André-Louis Debierne, 1899)
Radioactive metal	89	1051°C	3198°C	
Aluminum	Al	1220°F	4566°F	Latin *alumen*, a substance with astringent taste (Hans
Metal	13	660°C	2519°C	Christian Oersted, 1825)
Americium	Am	2149°F	3652°F	Named for America (Glenn T. Seaborg & coworkers,1944)
Radioactive metal	95	1176°C	2011°C	
Antimony	Sb	1168°F	2889°F	Greek *antimonos*, opposed to solitude; symbol Sb from
Metal	51	631°C	1587°C	Latin *stibium*. (Rhazes, c. 900)
Argon	Ar	-308°F	-303°F	Greek *argus*, neutral inactive. (Sir William Ramsay, 1894)
Gas	18	-189°C	-186°C	
Arsenic[2]	As	N.A.	1117°F	Latin *arsenicum*; folk etymology connects with yellow
Nonmetal	33		603°C	and maleness. (Albertus Magnus, 1250)
Astatine	At	576°F	unk.	Greek *astatos*, unstable. (Emilio Segrè, D.R. Corson, &
Radioactive nonmetal	85	302°C		K.R. MacKenzie, 1940)
Barium	Ba	1341°F	3447°F	Greek *baros*, heavy, because of its dense compounds.
Metal	56	727°C	1897°C	(Humphry Davy, 1808)
Berkelium	Bk	1922°F	unk.	First made at Univ. of California. (Glenn T. Seaborg &
Radioactive metal	97	1050°C		coworkers,1949)
Beryllium	Be	2349°F	4480°F	Latin *beryllus*, Greek beryllos, gem. (Louis-Nicolas
Metal	4	1287°C	2471°C	Vauquelin,1798)
Bismuth	Bi	520°F	2847°F	German *weisse masse*, white mass; changed to *bismat*.
Metal	83	271°C	1564°C	(Claude J. Geoffrey, 1753
Bohrium	Bh	unk.	unk.	Named for Danish physicist Niels Bohr. (Russian
Radioactive metal	107			scientists at Dubna, 1977)
Boron	B	3767°F	7232°F	Arabic *borak* (borax); BORax + carbON. (Joseph-Louis
Nonmetal	5	2075°C	4000°C	Gay-Lussac & Louis-Jacques Thénard, 1808)
Bromine	Br	19°F	138°F	Greek *bromos*, a stench; because of odor of its vapors.
Liquid nonmetal	35	-7°C	59°C	(Antoine-Jérôme Balard, 1826)
Cadmium	Cd	610°F	1413°F	Greek *cadmia*, earthy. (Friedrich Strohmeyer, 1817)
Metal	48	321°C	767°C	
Calcium	Ca	1548°F	2703°F	Latin *calx, calcis*, lime. (Humphry Davy, 1808)
Metal	20	842°C	1484°C	
Californium	Cf	1652°F	unk.	First made at Univ. of California. (Glenn T. Seaborg &
Radioactive metal	98	900°C		coworkers, 1949)
Carbon[2]	C	N.A.	N.A.	Latin *carbo*, coal. (Prehistoric)
Nonmetal	6		3825°C	
Cerium	Ce	1468°F	6229°F	Named for asteroid Ceres, discovered in 1801. (Martin
Rare earth	58	798°C	3443°C	Klaproth, 1803)
Cesium	Cs	84°F	1240°F	Latin *caesius*, bluish gray. (Gustav Kirchhoff & Robert
Metal	55	29°C	671°C	Bunsen, 1860)
Chlorine	Cl	-152°F	-29°F	Greek *chloros*, grass-green; from color of gas. (Humphry
Gas	17	-102°C	-34°C	Davy, 1810)
Chromium	Cr	3465°F	4840°F	Greek *chroma*, color; because many of its compounds
Metal	24	1907°C	2671°C	are colored. (Louis-Nicolas Vauquelin, 1797)
Cobalt	Co	2723°F	5301°F	German *Kobalt*, a goblin. (Georg Brandt, 1735)
Metal	27	1495°C	2927°C	
Copper	Cu	1985°F	4644°F	Latin *cuprum*; for island of Cyprus. (Prehistoric)
Metal	29	1085°C	2562°C	
Curium	Cm	2453°F	5612°F	Named after Pierre and Marie Curie. (Glenn T. Seaborg &
Radioactive metal	96	1345°C	3100°C	coworkers, 1944)
Dubnium	Db	unk.	unk.	Named for the Joint Institute for Nuclear Research at
Radioactive metal	105			Dubna,Russia. (Russian scientists at Dubna, 1967)
Dysprosium	Dy	2574°F	4653°F	Greek *dysprositos*, difficult of access. (Paul-Emile Lecoq
Rare earth	66	1412°C	2567°C	deBoisbaudran, 1886)
Einsteinium	Es	1580°F	unk.	Named after Albert Einstein. (Albert Ghiorso &
Radioactive metal	99	860°C		coworkers, 1952)

Element/Type[1]	Symbol/ Atomic number	Melting point[1]	Boiling point[1]	Derivation of name (Discoverer, Year)
Element 110 Radioactive metal	N.A. 110	unk.	unk.	(Society for Heavy Ion Research, Darmstadt, Germany, 1994)
Element 111 Radioactive metal	N.A. 111	unk.	unk.	(Society for Heavy Ion Research, Darmstadt, Germany, 1994)
Element 112 Radioactive metal	N.A. 112	unk.	unk.	(Society for Heavy Ion Research, Darmstadt, Germany, 1996)
Element 113 Radioactive metal	N.A.	unk.	unk.	(Scientists at Dubna, 2004)
Element 114 Radioactive metal	N.A.	unk.	unk.	(Dubna and Lawrence Livermore, 1998)
Element 115 Radioactive metal	N.A.	unk.	unk.	(Scientists at Dubna, 2004)
Element 116 Radioactive metal	N.A. 116	unk.	unk.	(Scientists at Dubna, 2000)
Erbium Rare earth	Er 68	2784°F 1529°C	5194°F 2868°C	Named for Ytterby, village in Sweden. (Carl Gustav Mosander, 1843)
Europium Rare earth	Eu 63	1512°F 822°C	2784°F 1529°C	Named for Europe. (Eugène-Anatole Demarçay, 1896)
Fermium Radioactive metal	Fm 100	2781°F 1527°C	unk.	Named after Italian physicist Enrico Fermi. (Albert Ghiorso & coworkers, 1952)
Fluorine Gas	F 9	-364°F -220°C	-306°F -188°C	Latin fluere, to flow. (Ferdinand-Frédéric-Henri Moissan, 1886)
Francium Radioactive metal	Fr 87	81°F 27°C	unk.	Named for France. (Marguerite Perey, 1939)
Gadolinium Rare earth	Gd 64	2395°F 1313°C	5923°F 3273°C	Named after gadolinite, mineral named for Johan Gadolin, Finnish chemist. (Jean-Charles Marignac, 1880)
Gallium Metal	Ga 31	86°F 30°C	3999°F 2204°C	Latin Gallia, France; also Latin gallus, a cock—a pun on Lecoq. (Paul-Emile Lecoq de Boisbaudran, 1875)
Germanium Metal	Ge 32	1721°F 938°C	5131°F 2833°C	Named for Germany. (Clemens Winkler, 1886)
Gold Metal	Au 79	1948°F 1064°C	5173°F 2856°C	Anglo-Saxon gold; Sanskrit juel, to shine; symbol from Latin aurum, shining dawn. (Prehistoric)
Hafnium Metal	Hf 72	4051°F 2233°C	8317°F 4603°C	From Hafnia, ancient name of Copenhagen. (Dirk Coster & György Hevesy, 1923)
Hassium Radioactive metal	Hs 108	unk.	unk.	Named for the German province of Hesse, where Darmstadt is located. (Society for Heavy Ion Research, Darmstadt, Germany, 1984)
Helium Gas	He 2	N.A. N.A.	-452°F -269°C	Greek helios, the Sun; first observed in Sun's atmosphere. (Pierre-Jules-César Janssen & Sir Joseph Norman Lockyer, 1868)
Holmium Rare earth	Ho 67	2685°F 1474°C	4892°F 2700°C	From Holmia, Latinized form of Stockholm. (Per Teodor Cleve, 1879)
Hydrogen Gas	H 1	-435°F -259°C	-423°F -253°C	Greek hydor, water, plus gen, forming. (Henry Cavendish, 1766)
Indium Metal	In 49	314°F 157°C	3762°F 2072°C	Latin indicum, indigo. (Ferdinand Reich & Hieronymus Theodor Richter, 1863)
Iodine[2] Nonmetal	I 53	237°F 114°C	364°F 184°C	Greek iodes, violet; from color of its vapor. (Bernard Courtois,1811)
Iridium Metal	Ir 77	4435°F 2446°C	8002°F 4428°C	Greek iris, a rainbow, from changing color of its salts. (Smithson Tennant , 1803)
Iron Metal	Fe 26	2800°F 1538°C	5182°F 2861°C	Anglo-Saxon iren; symbol from Latin ferrum. (Prehistoric)
Krypton[3] Gas	Kr 36	-251°F -157°C	-244°F -153°C	Greek kryptos, hidden. (Alexander Ramsay & Morris William Travers, 1898)
Lanthanum Rare earth	La 57	1684°F 918°C	6267°F 3464°C	Greek lanthanein, to be concealed. (Carl Gustav Mosander, 1839)
Lawrencium Radioactive metal	Lr 103	2961°F 1627°C	unk.	Named after American physicist Ernest Lawrence. (Albert Ghiorso & coworkers, 1961)
Lead Metal	Pb 82	621°F 327°C	3180°F 1749°C	Anglo-Saxon lead; symbol from Latin plumbum. (Prehistoric)
Lithium Metal	Li 3	351°F 181°C	2448°F 1342°C	Greek lithos, stony. (Johann A. Arfvedson, 1817)
Lutetium Rare earth	Lu 71	3025°F 1663°C	6159°F 3404°C	Latin Lutetia, ancient name for Paris. (Georges Urbain, 1907)
Magnesium Metal	Mg 12	1202°F 650°C	1994°F 1090°C	Latin Magnesia, a district in Asia Minor. (Humphry Davy, 1808)
Manganese Metal	Mn 25	2275°F 1246°C	3742°F 2061°C	Latin magnes, magnet; because of confusion with magnetic iron ores. (Johann Gottlieb Gahn, 1774)
Meitnerium Radioactive metal	Mt 109	unk.	unk.	Named for the Austrian-Swedish physicist Lise Meitner. (Society for Heavy Ion Research, Darmstadt, Germany, 1982)

Element/Type[1]	Symbol/ Atomic number	Melting point[1]	Boiling point[1]	Derivation of name (Discoverer, Year)
Mendelevium	Md	1521°F	unk.	Named after Russian chemist Dmitri Mendeléev. (Albert
Radioactive metal	101	827°C		Ghiorso & coworkers, 1955)
Mercury	Hg	-38°F	674°F	Named for Roman god Mercurius; symbol from Latin
Liquid metal	80	-39°C	357°C	*hydrargyrum*. (Prehistoric)
Molybdenum	Mo	4753°F	8382°F	Greek *molybdos*, lead. (Karl Wilhelm Scheele, 1778)
Metal	42	2623°C	4639°C	
Neodymium	Nd	1870°F	5565°F	Greek *neo*, new, plus *didymon*, twin (with the element
Rare earth	60	1021°C	3074°C	praseodymium). (Karl Auer (Baron von Welsbach), 1885)
Neon	Ne	-415°F	-411°F	Greek *neo*, new. (Alexander Ramsay & Morris William
Gas	10	-249°C	-246°C	Travers, 1898)
Neptunium	Np	1191°F	unk.	Named for planet Neptune. (Edwin McMillan & Philip
Radioactive metal	93	644°C		Abelson,1940)
Nickel	Ni	2651°F	5308°F	German *Nickel*, Satan (Old Nick). (Axel Cronstedt, 1751)
Metal	28	1455°C	2931°C	
Niobium	Nb	4491°F	8571°F	Latin *Niobe*, daughter of Tantalus. (Charles Hachett,
Metal	41	2477°C	4744°C	1801)
Nitrogen	N	-346°F	-320°F	Latin, forming *niter*, a compound of nitrogen. (Daniel
Gas	7	-210°C	-196°C	Rutherford, 1772)
Nobelium	No	1521°F	unk.	Named after Alfred Nobel; made at Nobel Institute.
Radioactive metal	102	827°C		(Albert Ghiorso & coworkers, 1958)
Osmium	Os	5491°F	9054°F	Greek *osme*, smell; for malodorousness. (Smithson
Metal	76	3033°C	5012°C	Tennant, 1803)
Oxygen	O	-362°F	-297°F	Greek *oxys*, sharp, plus *gen*, forming; from incorrect
Gas	8	-219°C	-183°C	belief that oxygen forms acids. (Joseph Priestley, 1774)
Palladium	Pd	2831°F	5365°F	Named for Greek goddess Pallas; from asteroid Pallas.
Metal	46	1555°C	2963°C	(William Hyde Wollaston, 1803)
Phosphorus	P	111°F	537°F	Greek *phosphoros*, light-bringer; glows because of rapid .
Nonmetal	15	44°C	281°C	oxidation(Hennig Brand, 1669)
Platinum	Pt	3215°F	6917°F	Diminutive of Spanish *plata*, silver, *platina*. (Antonio de
Metal	78	1768°C	3825°C	Ulloa, 1735)
Plutonium	Pu	1184°F	5842°F	Named for planet Pluto. (Glenn T. Seaborg & coworkers,
Radioactive metal	94	640°C	3228°C	1940)
Polonium	Po	489°F	1764°F	Named by Marie Curie for her native Poland. (Marie &
Radioactive metal	84	254°C	962°C	Pierre Curie, 1898)
Potassium	K	146°F	1398°F	Named for potash, a compound of potassium; symbol
Metal	19	64°C	759°C	from Latin *kalium*. (Humphry Davy, 1807)
Praseodymium	Pr	1708°F	6368°F	Greek *prasios*, green, plus *didymos*, twin (with
Rare earth	59	931°C	3520°C	neodymium). (Karl Auer (Baron von Welsbach), 1885)
Promethium	Pm	1908°F	5432°F	Named for Greek god Prometheus, who stole fire from
Radioactive rare earth	61	1042°C	3000°C	heaven. (J.A. Marinsky, L.E. Glendenin, & C.D.Coryell, 1945)
Protactinium	Pa	2862°F	unk.	Latin *proto*, first, plus actinium, one of the elements.
Radioactive metal	91	1572°C		(Otto Hahn & Lise Meitner, 1918)
Radium	Ra	1292°F	unk.	Latin *radius*, ray. (Marie Curie & Pierre Curie, 1898)
Radioactive metal	88	700°C		
Radon	Rn	-96°F	-79°F	*Radium* plus *on*, as in *neon*. (Friedrich Ernst Dorn, 1900)
Radioactive gas	86	-71°C	-62°C	
Rhenium	Re	5767°F	10105°F	Latin *Rhenus*, Rhine. (Walter Noddack, Ida Tacke, & Otto
Metal	75	3186°C	5596°C	Berg, 1925)
Rhodium	Rh	3567°F	6683°F	Greek *rhodon*, rose; for red color of its salts. (William
Metal	45	1964°C	3695°C	Hyde Wollaston, 1803)
Rubidium	Rb	103°F	1270°F	Latin *rubidus*, red; from red lines in its spectrum. (Gustav
Metal	37	39°C	688°C	Kirchhoff & Robert Bunsen, 1861)
Ruthenium	Ru	4233°F	7502°F	Named for Ruthenia in Urals, where ore was first found.
Metal	44	2334°C	4150°C	(Carl Claus, 1844)
Rutherfordium	Rf	unk.	unk.	Named for the New Zealand-born English physicist Ernest
Radioactive metal	104			Rutherford. (Russian scientists at Dubna, 1964)
Samarium	Sm	1965°F	3261°F	Named for Scandinavian mineral samarskite. (Paul-Emile
Rare earth	62	1074°C	1794°C	Lecoq de Boisbaudran, 1879)
Scandium	Sc	2806°F	5137°F	Named for Scandinavia. (Lars Fredrik Nilson, 1879)
Metal	21	1541°C	2836°C	
Seaborgium	Sg	unk.	unk.	Named for American physicist Glenn T. Seaborg. (Russian
Radioactive metal	106			scientists at Dubna and U.S. team from Berkeley and Lawrence Livermore Laboratories, 1974)
Selenium	Se	429°F	1265°F	Greek *selene*, the Moon. (Jöns Jakob Berzelius, 1818)
Nonmetal	34	221°C	685°C	
Silicon	Si	2577°F	5909°F	Latin *silex*, flint. (Jöns Jakob Berzelius, 1824)
Nonmetal	14	1414°C	3265°C	
Silver	Ag	1763°F	3924°F	Anglo-Saxon *sealfor*; symbol is from Latin *argentum*
Metal	47	962°C	2162°C	(Prehistoric)

Element/Type[1]	Symbol/ Atomic number	Melting point[1]	Boiling point[1]	Derivation of name (Discoverer, Year)
Sodium	Na	208°F	1621°F	English *soda*, a sodium compound; symbol from Latin
Metal	11	98°C	883°C	*natrium* (Humphry Davy, 1807)
Strontium	Sr	1431°F	2520°F	For Strontian, a town in Scotland. (Humphry Davy, 1808)
Metal	38	777°C	1382°C	
Sulfur	S	247°F	832°F	Sanskrit *solvere*, Latin *sulphur*. (Prehistoric)
Nonmetal	16	120°C	445°C	
Tantalum	Ta	5463°F	9856°F	For mythical king Tantalus, condemned to thirst; because
Metal	73	3017°C	5458°C	of its insolubility. (Anders Ekeberg, 1802)
Technetium	Tc	3915°F	7709°F	Greek *technetos*, artificial; first artificial element. (Emilio
Radioactive metal	43	2157°C	4265°C	Segrè,1937)
Tellurium	Te	841°F	1810°F	Latin *tellus*, the Earth. (Franz Joseph Müller, 1782)
Metal	52	450°C	988°C	
Terbium	Tb	2473°F	5846°F	For Ytterby, village in Sweden. (Carl Gustav Mosander,
Rare earth	65	1356°C	3230°C	1843)
Thallium	Tl	579°F	2683°F	Greek *thallos*, a green twig; after color of its spectrum
Metal	81	304°C	1473°C	(William Crookes, 1861)
Thorium	Th	3182°F	8650°F	For Norse god Thor. (Jöns Jakob Berzelius, 1829)
Radioactive metal	90	1750°C	4788°C	
Thulium	Tm	2813°F	3542°F	Greek *Thule*, Greek name for land north of Britain. (Per
Rare earth	69	1545°C	1950°C	Teodor Cleve, 1879)
Tin	Sn	449°F	4716°F	Anglo-Saxon *tin*; symbol from Latin *stannum*. (Prehistoric)
Metal	50	232°C	2602°C	
Titanium	Ti	3034°F	5949°F	For Titans of classical mythology. (William Gregor, 1791)
Metal	22	1668°C	3287°C	
Tungsten	W	6192°F	10,031°F	Swedish *tung sten*, heavy stone; symbol from German
Metal	74	3422°C	5555°C	*Wolfram*. (Fausto and Juan José d'Elhuyar, 1783)
Uranium	U	2075°F	7468°F	For planet Uranus. (Martin Klaproth, 1789)
Radioactive metal	92	1135°C	4131°C	
Vanadium	V	3470°F	6165°F	For Scandinavian goddess Vanadis. (Andrès del Rio,
Metal	23	1910°C	3407°C	1801)
Xenon[3]	Xe	-169°F	-163°F	Greek *xenon*, stranger. (Alexander Ramsay & Morris
Gas	54	-112°C	-108°C	William Travers, 1898)
Ytterbium	Yb	1506°F	2185°F	For Ytterby, a village in Sweden. (George Urbain, 1907)
Rare earth	70	819°C	1196°C	
Yttrium	Y	2772°F	6053°F	For Ytterby, a village in Sweden. (Carl Gustav Mosander,
Rare earth	39	1522°C	3345°C	1843)
Zinc	Zn	787°F	1665°F	German *zink*. (Prehistoric)
Metal	30	420°C	907°C	
Zirconium	Zr	3371°F	7968°F	Arabic *zargun*, gold color. (Martin Klaproth, 1789)
Metal	40	1855°C	4409°C	

1. At a pressure of one atmosphere and, for type, at room temperature. 2. This element sublimes (goes directly from a solid to a gas). 3. Liquefaction also requires great pressure.

PHYSICS

Physics is the basis of the other sciences because it is concerned with the fundamental interactions of matter and energy. The first physicists studied how ordinary objects and very large objects (Moon, planets and stars) moved in response to forces. Their study was extremely successful. Near the end of the 19th century, physicists began to investigate radiation in detail, leading to the discovery of various forms of electromagnetic radiation (of which only forms of light, including infrared and ultraviolet, were known previously) and particles smaller than the atom (subatomic particles, such as the electron and proton). In the 20th century, the study of subatomic particles, called particle physics, became a major branch of the science. Many particle physicists limit their work to the particles in the nucleus of atoms and to the behavior of nuclei. Another major branch, condensed-matter physics, is concerned with the physical behavior of materials—for example, their electrical and magnetic properties. Major successes in condensed-matter physics include development of the transistor and related devices (chips) and superconductivity, a state in which electric currents can be transmitted with no resistance. Today many physicists are also cosmologists, who study how the universe began and is constructed, or astrophysicists, who study processes in stars.

Major Discoveries in Physics

1586 Simon Stevinus (Belgian-Dutch: 1548–1620) shows that two different weights dropped at same time from same height will reach ground at same time.

1604 Galileo (Italian: 1564–1642) announces his discovery that a body falling freely will increase its distance as the square of time.

1663 Blaise Pascal (French: 1623–62) proposes what becomes known as Pascal's law: pressure in fluid is transmitted equally in all directions

1675 Ole Rømer (Danish: 1644–1710) becomes first to measure speed of light, although his value is somewhat too slow by today's standards.

1676 Robert Hooke (English: 1635–1703) discovers what becomes known as Hooke's law: The amount a spring stretches varies directly with its tension.

1678 Christiaan Huygens (Dutch: 1629–95) introduces wave theory of light.

1687 Sir Isaac Newton's (English: 1642–1727) *Principia* is published, containing his laws of motion and theory of gravity.

1746 At least two experimenters in Leyden, the Netherlands, invent method for storing static electricity, which becomes known as Leyden jar.

1752 Benjamin Franklin (American: 1706–90) performs kite experiment, demonstrating that lightning is form of electricity.

1787 Jacques A.C. Charles (French: 1746–1823) discovers what is later known as Charles's law: All gases expand same amount with given rise in temperature; e.g., same rise in temperature that will cause hydrogen to double in volume will also cause air to double in volume.

1791 Luigi Galvani (Italian: 1737–98) announces his discovery that when two different metals touch in frog's muscle, they produce electric current.

1798 Benjamin Thompson, Count von Rumford (American-German: 1753–1814) shows that heat is form of motion.

Henry Cavendish (English: 1731–1810) determines gravitational constant and mass of Earth.

1800 William Herschel (German-English: 1738–1822) announces his discovery of infrared light.

1801 Johann W. Ritter (German: 1776–1810) discovers ultraviolet light.

1802 Thomas Young (English: 1773–1829) develops his wave theory of light.

1820 Hans Christian Oersted (Danish: 1777–1851) discovers that magnetism and electricity are two different manifestations of same force.

André-Marie Ampère (French: 1775–1836) formulates first laws of electromagnetism.

1831 Michael Faraday (English: 1791–1867) in England and Joseph Henry (American: 1797–1878) in U.S. (in 1830) independently discover principle of dynamo.

1842 Julius Robert von Mayer (German: 1814–78) is first scientist to state law of conservation of energy.

1848 William Thompson, Baron Kelvin (Scottish: 1824–1907), proposes concept of absolute zero, the lowest possible temperature (-460°F, or -273°C).

1850 Rudolf J.E. Clausius (German: 1822–88) makes first clear statement of second law of thermodynamics: Energy in closed system tends to degrade into heat.

1873 James Clerk Maxwell (Scottish: 1831–79) publishes complete theory of electromagnetism.

1888 Heinrich P. Hertz (German: 1857–94) produces and detects radio waves.

1895 Wilhelm Konrad Röntgen (German: 1845–1923) discovers X rays.

1896 Henri Becquerel (French: 1852–1908) discovers natural radioactivity.

1897 Sir Joseph John Thomson (English: 1856–1940) discovers electron.

1900 Max K.E.L. Planck (German: 1858–1947) explains behavior of electromagnetic radiation by proposing that there is smallest step a physical process can take, which he names quantum.

1905 Albert Einstein (German-American: 1879–1955) shows that photoelectric effect—ejection of electrons from metal by action of light—can be explained if light has particle nature as well as wave nature.

Einstein shows that motion of small particles in liquid ("Brownian motion") can be explained by assuming that the liquid is made of molecules.

Einstein develops his special theory of relativity and the law $E = mc^2$ (energy equals mass times square of speed of light).

1911 Heike Kamerlingh Onnes (Dutch: 1853–1926) discovers superconductivity.

Ernest Rutherford (British: 1871–1937) discovers the proton.

1915 Einstein completes his general theory of relativity, a theory of gravity more accurate than that of Sir Isaac Newton, and publishes it the following year.

1924 Louis-Victor de Broglie (French: 1892–1987) publishes his theory that particles, such as electrons, also have wave nature.

1925 Wolfgang Pauli (Austrian-American: 1900–1958) discovers exclusion principal: Two electrons or protons described by same numbers (called quantum numbers) cannot exist in same atom.

Werner Karl Heisenberg (German: 1901–76) develops matrix version of quantum mechanics, a mathematical treatment that explains behavior of electrons and protons.

1926 Erwin Schrödinger (Austrian: 1887–1961) develops wave version of quantum mechanics, a different mathematical treatment producing same results as Heisenberg's matrix mechanics.

1927 Heisenberg develops his uncertainty principle: It is impossible to measure accurately position and momentum of electron or proton at same time.

1932 Sir James Chadwick (British: 1891–1974) discovers neutron, a neutral particle about same mass as proton.

Carl D. Anderson (American: 1905–91) discovers positron, a positively charged analog of electron.

Sir John G. Cockcroft (English: 1897–1967) and Ernest Walton (Irish: 1903–95) develop first particle accelerator (often still known as "atom smasher").

1937 Carl Anderson, with other physicists, performs the work that culminates in the discovery of the muon.

1938 Otto Hahn (German: 1870–1968), in experiments interpreted by Lise Meitner (Austrian-Swedish: 1878-1968), splits uranium atom, opening way for nuclear bombs and nuclear power.

1945 Scientists funded by U.S. government and led by J. Robert Oppenheimer (American: 1904–67) detonate first nuclear-fission explosion (atomic bomb).

1947 Cecil Frank Powell (English: 1903–69) and coworkers discover pion, first-known meson, a subatomic particle involved in holding nucleus of atom together.

1955 Owen Chamberlain (American: 1920–) and Emilio Segrè (Italian-American: 1905–89) produce antiprotons, negatively charged analogs of proton.

1956 Clyde Cowan Jr. (American: 1919-74) and Frederick Reines (American: 1918-98) are first to observe neutrino, a subatomic particle with no mass or charge produced in certain forms of radioactive decay.

1957   Experiments by group led by Chien-Shiung Wu (Chinese-American: 1912–97) and quickly confirmed by others show that right and left are distinguished by behavior of electrons emitted in certain forms of radioactivity.

John Bardeen (American: 1908–91), Leon Cooper (American: 1930–), and Bob Schrieffer (American: 1931–) develop a theory explaining superconductivity.

1961   Murray Gell-Mann (American: 1929–) and, independently, Yu'val Ne'eman (Israeli: 1925–) and others develop method of classifying heavy sub-atomic particles that comes to be known as "eight-fold way."

1964   Murray Gell-Mann introduces concept of quarks as components of heavy subatomic particles, such as protons and mesons.

1967   Steven Weinberg (American: 1933–), Abdus Salam (Pakistani-British: 1926–96), and Sheldon Lee Glashow (American: 1932–) independently develop theory that combines electromagnetic force with weak force.

1980   Heinrich Rohrer (Swiss: 1933–) and Gerd Binnig (German: 1947–) invent the scanning tunneling microscope, with which it is possible to produce images of individual atoms on crystal surfaces.

1986   Karl Alexander Müller (Swiss: 1927–) and Johannes Georg Bednorz (German: 1950–) discover first "high-temperature" superconductor.

1995   Physicists at Fermilab in Batavia, Ill., announce the first observations of the sixth and last expected quark, known as top.

Eric Cornell of the U.S. National Institute of Standards and Technology and coworkers produce the first sample of the fifth state of matter, known as a Bose-Einstein Condensate (BEC), in which atoms huddle together in essentially the same place and condition.

Physicists at CERN (the European Laboratory for Particle Physics) produce the first few atoms of antihydrogen, with a positron orbiting an antiproton.

1997   Two groups of physicists, one in Austria and one in Rome, show that it is possible to entangle two particles so that measuring an exact quantum state of one of them will instantly determine the corresponding state of the other across any distance, a phenomenon known as "quantum teleportation."

1998   Scientists working with the Super-Kamiokande neutrino telescope in Japan establish indirectly that the neutrinos must have a nonzero, although small, mass.

2000   An experiment at Fermilab creates and detects the tau neutrino, predicted in 1975.

2001   Physicists at Harvard University and the Harvard-Smithsonian Center for Astrophysics, both in Cambridge, MA, independently stop light completely for brief intervals as it travels through ultracold gases.

The SPring-8 synchrotron particle accelerator in Japan produces the first examples of particles that contain five quarks, termed pentaquarks.

2002   Researchers produce the first antimatter hydrogen gas at CERN in Geneva, trapping positrons and antiprotons which combine to form about 50,000 antihydrogen atoms.

Two independent teams of physicists discover a new form of radioactivity, the simultaneous emission of two protons from iron-45 nuclei.

2003   A thermonuclear device called Z at Sandia National Laboratories in Albuquerque, New Mexico, achieves fusion by using a sudden blast of X rays aimed at a tiny capsule of deuterium to fuse it into tritium and helium, producing 10,000,000,000 neutrons with each blast of X rays.

Two groups independently succeed in creating Bose-Einstein Condensates (BECs) from ultracold molecules.

2004   German material scientists discover a form of supercooled liquid water, high-density liquid water (HDL), which is 17 percent denser than ordinary liquid water at the same pressure and temperature.

Two different groups of researchers succeed in using triplets of entangled ions to transmit characteristics from one atom to another via quantum teleportation.

A type of subatomic particle known as DsJ(2632), a meson containing a strange quark and a charm antiquark, is observed to decay in a manner contrary to the standard model of particle physics.

►THE BASIC LAWS OF PHYSICS

Key Terms

Mass   is a measure of the amount of matter; it is proportional to weight. Near the surface of Earth it is roughly equivalent to weight.

Velocity   measures how an object changes position with time.

Acceleration   is how an object changes velocity with time.

Momentum   is the product of mass and velocity.

Energy   is the ability to do work.

Law of Gravity

The gravitational force between any two objects is proportional to the product of their masses and inversely proportional to the square of the distance between them. If F is the force, G is the number that represents the ratio (the gravitational constant), m and M are the two masses, and r is the distance between the objects:

$$F = \frac{GmM}{r^2}$$

In metric measure, the gravitational constant is 0.0000000000667390 (6.67390 x 10^{-11}) newton m^2/kg^2, so another way of writing the basic law of gravity is

$$F = \frac{0.0000000000667390mM}{r^2}$$

This law implies that objects falling near the surface of Earth will fall with the same rate of acceleration (ignoring drag caused by air). This rate is 32.174 feet per second per second (ft./sec^2), or 9.8 m/sec^2, and is conventionally labeled g. Applying this rate to falling objects gives the velocity, v, and distance, d, after any amount of time, t, in seconds. If the object starts at rest and 32 ft./sec^2 is used as an approximation for g,

$$v = 32t$$
$$d = 16t^2$$

For example, after 3 seconds, a dropped object that is still falling will have a velocity of 32 x 3 = 96 feet per second and will have fallen a distance of 16 x 3^2 = 144 feet.

If the object has an initial velocity v_0 and an initial height above the ground of a, the equations describing the velocity and the distance, d, above the ground (a positive velocity is up and a negative velocity is down) become

$$v = v_0 - 32t$$

and

$$d = -16t^2 + v_0 t + a.$$

After 3 seconds, an object tossed in the air from a height of 6 feet with a velocity of 88 feet per second will reach a speed of 88 - 96 = -8 feet per second, meaning that it has begun to descend, and will have a height of (-16 x 9) + (88 x 3) + 6 = -144 + 264 + 6 = 126 feet above the ground.

The maximum height, H, reached by the object with an initial velocity v_0 and initial height a is

$$H = a + \frac{v_0{}^2}{64}$$

For the object tossed upward at 88 feet per second from a height of 6 feet, the maximum height reached would be $6 + 88^2/64 = 6 + 121 = 127$ feet. Therefore, after 3 seconds, the object has just reached its peak and has fallen back only 1 foot.

Albert Einstein's general theory of relativity introduced laws of gravity more accurate than those just given, which were discovered by Sir Isaac Newton. Newton's gravitational theory is extremely accurate for most practical situations, however. For example, Newton's theory is used to determine how to launch satellites into proper orbits.

Newton's Laws of Motion

Newton's Laws of Motion apply to objects in a vacuum and are not easily observed in the real world, where forces such as friction tend to overwhelm the natural motion of objects. To obtain realistic solutions to problems, however, physicists and engineers begin with Newton's laws and then add in the various forces that also affect motion.

1. *Any object at rest tends to stay at rest. A body in motion moves at the same velocity in a straight line unless acted upon by a force.* This is also known as the law of inertia. Note that this law implies that an object will travel in a curved path only so long as a force is acting on it. When the force is released, the object will travel in a straight line. A weight on a string swung in a circle will travel in a straight line when the string is released, for the string was supplying the force that caused circular motion.

2. *The acceleration of an object is directly proportional to the force acting on it and inversely proportional to the mass of the object.* This law, for an acceleration a, a force F, and a mass m, is more commonly expressed in terms of finding the force when you know the mass and the acceleration. In this form it is written as

$$F = ma.$$

The implication of this law is that a constant force will produce acceleration, which is an increase in velocity. Thus, a rocket, which is propelled by a constant force as long as its fuel is burning, constantly increases in velocity. Even with an infinite supply of fuel, the rocket would eventually cease to increase in velocity, however, because Einstein's other relativity theory, the special theory of relativity, states that no object can exceed the speed of light in a vacuum (see "Conservation of mass-energy" below). Nevertheless, even a small force, constantly applied, can cause a large mass to reach velocities near the speed of light if enough time is allowed.

3. *For every action there is an equal and opposite reaction.*

Conservation Laws

Many results in physics come from various conservation laws. A conservation law is a rule that a certain entity must not change in amount during a certain class of operations. All such conservation laws treat closed systems. Anything added from outside the system could affect the amount of the entity being conserved.

Conservation of momentum   In a closed system, momentum stays the same. This law is equivalent to Newton's third law. Since momentum is the product of mass and velocity, if the mass of a system changes, then the velocity must change. For example, consider a person holding a heavy anchor in a stationary rowboat in the water. The momentum of the system is 0, since the masses have no velocity. Now the person in the rowboat tosses the anchor toward the shore. The momentum of the anchor is now a positive number if velocity toward the shore is measured as positive. To conserve momentum, the rowboat is accelerated in the opposite direction, away from the shore. The positive momentum of the anchor is balanced by the negative momentum of the rowboat and its cargo. In terms of two masses, m and M, and matching velocities v and V,

$$mv = MV$$

Conservation of angular momentum

An object moving in a circle has a special kind of momentum, called angular momentum. As noted above, motion in a circle requires some force. Angular momentum combines mass, velocity, and acceleration (produced by the force). For a body moving in a circle, the acceleration depends on both the speed of the body in its path and the square of the radius of the circle. The product of this speed, the mass, and the square of the radius is the angular momentum of the mass.

In a closed system, angular momentum is conserved. This effect is used by skaters to change their velocity of spinning. Angular momentum is partly determined by the masses of a skater's arms combined with the rate of rotation and the square of the radius to the center of mass of each arm (the point that can represent the total mass of the arm). When skaters bring their arms close to their body, this would tend to reduce the angular momentum, because the center of mass is closer to the body. But, since angular momentum is conserved, the rate of rotation has to increase to compensate for the decreased radius. Because the rate depends on the square of the radius, the rate increases dramatically.

Conservation of mass   *In a closed system, the total amount of mass appears to be conserved in all but nuclear reactions and other extreme conditions.*

Conservation of energy   *In a closed system, energy appears to be conserved in all but nuclear reactions and other extreme conditions.* Energy comes in very many forms: mechanical, chemical, electrical, heat, and so forth. As one form is changed into another (excepting nuclear reactions and extreme conditions), this law guarantees that the total amount remains the same. Thus, when you change the chemical energy of a dry cell into electrical energy and use that to turn a motor, the total amount of energy does not change (although some becomes heat energy— see "Laws of Thermodynamics" below).

Conservation of mass-energy
Einstein discovered that his special theory of relativity implies that energy and mass are related. Consequently, mass and energy by themselves are not conserved, since one can be converted into the other. Mass and energy appear to be conserved in ordinary situations because the effect of Einstein's discovery is very small most of the time. The more general law, then, is the law of conservation of mass-energy: *The total amount of mass and energy must be conserved.* Einstein found the following equation that links mass and energy:

$$E = mc^2$$

In this equation, E is the amount of energy, m is the mass, and c is the speed of light in a vacuum.

One instance of energy changing to mass occurs in Einstein's equation for how the mass increases with velocity. If m_0 is the mass of the object when it is not moving, v is the velocity of the object in relation to an observer who is considered to be at rest, and c is the speed of light in a vacuum, then the mass, m, is given by the equation

$$m = \frac{m_0}{\sqrt{1 - \dfrac{v^2}{c^2}}}$$

This accounts for the rule that no object can exceed the speed of light in a vacuum. As the object approaches this speed, so much of the energy is converted to mass that it cannot continue to accelerate.

In both nuclear fission (splitting of the atomic nucleus) and nuclear fusion (the joining of atomic nuclei, producing the energy of a hydrogen bomb), mass is converted into energy.

Conservation for particles
Many properties associated with atoms and subatomic particles are also conserved. Among them are charge, spin, isospin, and a combination known as CPT for *charge conjugation, parity,* and *time.*

First and Second Laws of Thermodynamics

First law This is the same as the law of conservation of energy. It is a law of thermodynamics, or the movement of heat, because heat must be treated as a form of energy to keep the total amount of energy constant. All bodies contain heat as energy no matter how cold they are, although there is not much heat at temperatures close to absolute zero.

Second law *Heat in a closed system can never travel from a low temperature region to one of higher temperature in a self-sustaining process.* Self-sustaining in this case means a process that does not need energy from outside the system to keep it going. In a refrigerator, heat from the cold inside of the refrigerator is transferred to a warmer room, but energy from outside is required to make the transfer happen, so the process is not self-sustaining.

The second law has many implications. One of them is that no perpetual motion machine can be constructed. Another is that all energy in a closed system eventually becomes heat that is diffused equally throughout the system, so that one can no longer obtain work from the system.

The equations that describe the behavior of heat also can be applied to order and therefore to information. The word *entropy* refers to diffuse heat, disorder, or lack of information. Another form of the second law of thermodynamics is that in a closed system, entropy always increases.

Laws of Current Electricity

Key terms When electrons flow in a conductor, the result is electric current. The amount of current is based on an amount of electric charge called the *coulomb*, which is the charge of about 6.25 quintillion (6.25 x 10^{18}) electrons. When 1 coulomb of charge moves past a point in 1 second, it creates a current of 1 ampere. Just as a stream can carry the same amount of water swiftly through a narrow channel or slowly through a broad channel, the energy of an electric current varies depending on the difference in charge between places along the conductor. This is called *potential difference* and is measured in volts. The voltage is affected by the nature of the conductors. Some substances conduct an electric current much more easily than others. This resistance to the current is measured in ohms. *Electric power* is the rate at which electricity is used.

Ohm's law *Electric current is directly proportional to the potential difference and inversely proportional to resistance.* If you measure current, I, in amperes, potential difference, V, in volts, and resistance, R, in ohms, then the current is equal to the potential difference divided by the resistance.

$$I = \frac{V}{R}$$

Law of electric power If electric power, P, is measured in watts, then the power is equal to the product of the current measured in amperes and the potential difference measured in volts.

$$P = IV$$

Laws of Light and Electromagnetic Radiation

Key terms Light is a part of a general form of radiation known as *electromagnetic waves*, or, when thought of as particles, *photons*. Here, electromagnetic radiation is considered as a wave phenomenon for the most part. The velocity of a wave is how fast the wave travels as a whole. The *wavelength* is the distance between one crest of the wave and the next crest. The *frequency* is how many crests pass a particular location in a unit of time. One crest passing each second is called a hertz.

Law of electromagnetic energy The energy of an electromagnetic wave depends on a small number known as Planck's constant. Measured in joules per hertz (energy per frequency), Planck's constant is 6.67259 x 10^{-34}. *The energy is equal to the product of Planck's constant and the frequency.* Using E for energy, h for Planck's constant, and f for frequency,

$$E = hf$$

When thought of in terms of the particles called photons, the energy of a photon obeys the same law. The law of wave motion and the law of electromagnetic energy can be combined with the speed of light in a vacuum (c) to give

$$E = \frac{hc}{l}$$

The energy of a photon is the product of Planck's constant and the speed of light, divided by the wavelength (l) of the photon.

Inverse-square law All radiation obeys an inverse-square law, which is similar to the law of gravity. *The intensity of the radiation decreases as the inverse of the square of the distance from a point source of radiation.*

Two Basic Laws of Quantum Physics

When one considers effects on very small masses and at very small distances, it is necessary to recognize that objects behave differently from their action at sizes and distances one can observe directly. Since these effects occur in discrete steps based upon Planck's constant times the frequency, called the quantum—which is the size by which energy changes in steps (instead of continuously)—the science of such effects is called quantum physics. Small masses act sometimes like particles and sometimes like waves. Two laws in particular that describe the behavior of small masses are basic and easily stated.

Heisenberg's uncertainty principle *It is impossible to specify completely the position and momentum of a particle, such as an electron, at the same time.*

Pauli's exclusion principle *Two particles of matter cannot be in the same exact state.* Particles of matter include the electron, neutron, and proton. Bosons, particles of force, do not obey Pauli's exclusion principle. (See "Subatomic Particles.")

▶SUBATOMIC PARTICLES

The idea of an atom goes back to the ancient Greek philosophers, who thought that matter was composed of tiny indivisible particles. The concept was put on a scientific basis by John Dalton (English: 1766–1844) in 1803 and became the foundation of chemistry. Nearly a hundred years later, experiments by J.J. Thomson (English: 1856–1940) in 1899 were the first to show that atoms are not indivisible after all. In the past hundred years, physics at almost all levels has been completely revolutionized by the study of the particles that make up atoms or that are smaller than atoms. In the last decades of the 20th century physicists developed the standard model of elementary particles. This model incorporates three of the four fundamental forces in nature, the strong and weak nuclear forces and electromagnetic forces (the other force is gravity). In the model, bosons mediate the forces: gluons, for the strong nuclear force; the photon for electromagnetism, and W and Z particles for the weak nuclear force. Within this model, the weak and electromagnetic forces have been combined into electroweak theory. The standard model has thus far met all experimental challenges, but it has some gaps in addition to the omission of gravity: in particular, the strong and electroweak forces are not completely unified. Theories that attempt to unify the strong and electroweak forces are called Grand Unified Theories (GUTs). Beyond Grand Unified Theories, a great challenge for

physicists is a Theory of Everything (TOE) that would account for all of the fundamental forces in nature. Below is a list of all the most important subatomic particles given in the chronological order of their discovery.

1897 Electron The first subatomic particle to be identified, also by J.J. Thomson, was the electron, a low-mass particle that can be found in the outer reaches of the atom. One property of the electron is charge, the response to electric or magnetic fields. The charge of a single electron is always the same, which is identified as –1 (negative one). Each atom consists of a cloud of electrons around a center of positive charge, which is called the nucleus.

1905 Photon The photon is the particle that carries the electromagnetic force. This concept began with Albert Einstein (German-American: 1879–1955) in 1905, when he established that light acts sometimes as a particle instead of as waves. Although we usually think of the photon as the particle of light, it is also the particle form of radio waves, X-rays, or gamma rays. The mass of the photon is 0.

1911 Proton At least one proton is always found in the nucleus of every atom. The proton has a charge that is the same in size as that of the electron, but responds in the opposite direction to an electric or magnetic field. This charge is +1 (positive one). Each proton is almost 2,000 times as heavy as an electron, or about the same as the mass of a single hydrogen atom.

1924 Bosons While matter is made from subatomic particles, the forces that act on matter are also produced by subatomic particles. The particles that create these forces are collectively called bosons because the mathematics of the behavior of this type of particle was worked out originally by Satyendranath Bose (Indian: 1894–1974) in 1924, although put into final form by Einstein. The observed bosons are the photon, pions, gluons, W particles, and Z particles. Bosons that are predicted, but that have not been observed, include the Higgs particle and the graviton.

1925–26 Quantum Mechanics The basic theory of subatomic particles, called quantum mechanics, was developed in two different forms, in 1925 by Werner Heisenberg (German: 1901–76) and in 1926 by Erwin Schrödinger (Austrian: 1887–1961). Although the two forms appear very different, they produce the same results.

1926 Fermions All the particles that make up matter are called fermions, as opposed to the bosons that create forces. The fermions include all the leptons and quarks as well as the particles made from quarks (see below). Fermions are named for Enrico Fermi (Italian-American: 1901–54), who first worked out the mathematics of their interactions in 1926. Fermions all obey the *Pauli exclusion principle* (see the section on *Basic Laws of Physics*, earlier in this chapter), which means that they occupy a definite space. Two fermions cannot be in the same place at the same time.

1930 Antiparticles When Paul A.M. Dirac (English-American: 1902-84) completed his mathematical version of the theory of the electron in 1930, he observed that one solution to his equations predicted a particle that would be a mirror image of the electron, exactly the same as the electron but with a positive charge instead of negative. The particle, discovered two years later in 1932, was named the positron. The same equations predicted mirror images for all subatomic particles. These particles are called the antiparticles, so another name for positron is antielectron.

1932 Neutron　The neutron is very much like a neutral proton, with just slightly more mass. Neutrons are stable when they are found in atoms, but decay into other particles when left to themselves.

1935 Muon　The muon is now recognized as a high energy analog to the electron with a mass about 200 times that of the electron.

1947 Pion　A pion carries the strong force that holds the nucleus of atoms together, but since each pion appears and disappears almost instantly, the pions are not usually counted as part of the nucleus. (Predicted in 1935.) In the same year that the pion was found, theoreticians were able to work out a comprehensive theory of the electron, called quantum electrodynamics (QED).

1950 Strange particles　Starting in 1950 experimenters observed a number of previously undetected particles that did not behave as particles were expected to do. Because these particles have masses greater than that of the proton and neutron, they were called hyperons. Other unexpected particles, about the size of the pion, were classed as mesons. A classification scheme for the hyperons developed in 1961 helped physicists understand them better, but their essential difference was already labeled "strangeness."

1955 Neutrinos　Neutrinos are thought to be among the most common particles in the universe, but they interact with ordinary matter so weakly that they are very difficult to observe. Predicted in 1930, neutrinos were thought to have no rest mass, but Canadian experiments in 2001 indicate that they have a very small mass equal to less than 10^{-7} of the mass of an electron. Different neutrinos are associated with electrons, muons, and tauons.

1964–95 Quarks　Murray Gell-Mann (American: 1928– .) and several other physicists determined that a way to explain the properties of protons, neutrons, mesons, and hyperons, is to think of the heavy particles as made from combinations of light ones, just as the atom is made from combinations of electrons, protons, and neutrons. The smaller particles are quarks; there are six of them in all. Two quarks, known as up and down, form protons and neutrons. The top quark is the most massive—about as heavy as an atom of gold—and the last to be detected. (First version of theory in 1964, evidence for top quark in 1995.)

1965–73 Gluons　The eight different bosons that produce a force between quarks known as the color force are called gluons. The color force is also the basis of the strong force that holds the nucleus together. Because of the color force, the study of quarks and gluons is today called quantum chromodynamics (QCD).

1974 J/psi particle　Like the strange hyperons, the J/psi particle is a heavy particle that appears at high energies. It also is produced by a different kind of quark, the charm quark. The odd name J/psi comes from the particle having been discovered independently by two investigators, one of whom called it J and the other of whom named it psi.

1983 W and Z particles　The particles that produce the weak force are called W and Z. At high energies, however, the weak force merges with the electromagnetic force, so the W and Z are to some extent analogs to the photon, although they could not be more different, since the photon has a 0 rest mass and both W particles and the single Z particle are very massive.

1995 Antiatoms　Since antiparticles have all the properties of ordinary particles except for being mirror images, it is possible to create an antiatom by combining subatomic antiparticles. This was accomplished in 1995 with the production of a few antiatoms of antihydrogen made by causing an antielectron (positron) to orbit an antiproton.

(Not yet observed) Graviton and Higgs particle
A particle that produces gravitational force by its exchange between all kinds of particles is known as the graviton, but so far it is only known in theory. The Laser Interferometer Gravitational Wave Observatory (LIGO) that began operations in 2000 seeks to observe gravity waves, the wave version of the graviton. The Higgs particle is the main undetected particle of the standard model of subatomic particles. Physicists believe that the Higgs, named after Peter Higgs (English: 1919–) who predicted it in 1964, confers mass to all other particles.

LIFE SCIENCES

While the scientific study of living creatures seems to have begun with Aristotle, there was considerable practical experimentation with living things much earlier, going back to the domestication of a species, the dog, perhaps as early as 14,000 B.C. In the years that followed the Scientific Revolution of the 17th century, the science of biology came to include most of the then-known life sciences: zoology (the study of animals), botany (the study of plants), and taxonomy (the classification of living things). In the 19th century, biology began to fragment into other studies: microbiology (the study of creatures visible only through the microscope), genetics (the study of how traits are inherited), biochemistry (the study of molecules in living things), and so forth. At the same time, different ways of studying living organisms were developed, among them anthropology (the study of human beings), ecology (the study of interactions between different living things and their environment), and ethology (the study of animal behavior).

▶MAJOR GROUPS OF LIVING ORGANISMS
Biologists classify all living things (organisms) according to a system first introduced by Carolus Linnaeus in 1735. At that time Linnaeus and other scientists divided all life forms into two kingdoms: plants and animals. Since then, biologists have learned that there are fundamental differences among organisms that go beyond the differences between plants and animals and have added four kingdoms. The six kingdoms commonly recognized today are: Monera, Archaea, Protists, Fungi, Plants, and Animals.

Following Linnaeus, all classification terms are usually given in Latin. In the following list, English terms are substituted when they are an exact translation—for example, animals instead of Animalia and birds instead of Aves. If there is no exact translation, the Latin form is kept.

Each kingdom is divided into two or more phyla (singular: phylum). Organisms within one phylum are more closely related to one another than to members of other phyla.

The phyla are also divided into parts, which are then further divided, each time on the basis of closer and closer relationships. In descending order of size, the main divisions are as follows:

Kingdom
    Phylum
        Class
            Order
                Family
                    Genus
                        Species

Many biologists add to this list by classifying groups of species with sub- or super-, as in subphylum or superfamily.

By convention, Latin names except for genus and species are given in Roman type; genus and species are italicized.

Kingdom: Monera One-celled organisms with simple cells that lack a membrane around the genetic material. Bacteria do not produce their own food; blue-green algae do.
Phylum: Bacteria (also called Eubacteria)
Phylum: Blue-green algae, also called blue-green bacteria or cyanobacteria
Kingdom: Archaea One-celled organisms, sometimes called Archaeobacteria, that are genetically more like the other kingdoms than they are like the Monera. The Archaea were first discovered as creatures living in hot springs and other high-temperature situations. They were later observed among the one-celled creatures that metabolize chemicals such as methane or sulfur instead of using oxygen. They also have been found in great abundance in the oceans and deep in the Earth's crust.
Kingdom: Protists One-celled or colonial; complex cells that have a membrane around their genetic material; protozoans and slime molds do not produce their own food; all other phyla in this kingdom can.
Phylum: Ciliated protozoans, such as Paramecium
Phylum: Protozoans with flagella, such as the trypanosome that causes African sleeping sickness.
Phylum: Amoebas and similar protozoans
Phylum: Protozoans that have no means of motion during most of their life, such as the plasmodia that cause malaria.
Phylum: Euglenas
Phylum: Golden algae and diatoms
Phylum: Fire or golden brown algae
Phylum: Green algae
Phylum: Brown algae
Phylum: Red algae
Phylum: Slime molds
Kingdom: Fungi One-celled or multicelled; cells have nuclei, which stream between cells, giving the appearance that cells have many nuclei; fungi do not produce their own food.
Phylum: Zygomycetes (e.g., black bread mold)
Phylum: Ascomycetes (includes Penicillium, truffles, yeasts)
Phylum: Basidiomycetes (includes mushrooms)

Kingdom: Plants Multicellular organisms that carry out photosynthesis; cells have nuclei and cell walls.
Phylum: Mosses and liverworts
Phylum: Club mosses
Phylum: Horsetails
Phylum: Ferns
Phylum: Conifers
Phylum: Cone-bearing desert plants
Phylum: Cycads
Phylum: The ginkgo
Phylum: Flowering plants
  Subphylum: Dicots (plants with two seed leaves—e.g., most fruits and vegetables, common flowers, and trees)
  Subphylum: Monocots (plants with a single seed leaf—e.g., onions, lilies, and grasses)
Kingdom: Animals Multicellular organisms that get their food by ingestion; most are able to move from place to place; cells have nuclei but not cell walls.
Phylum: Porifera (sponges)
Phylum: Cnidaria (jellyfish, anemones, corals)
Phylum: Platyhelminthes (flatworms)
Phylum: Nematodes (roundworms)
Phylum: Rotifers (microscopic wormlike or spherical animals)
Phylum: Bryozoa (moss animals)
Phylum: Brachiopods (lampshells)
Phylum: Phoronida (tube worms)
Phylum: Annelids (segmented worms, such as earthworms, leeches)
Phylum: Mollusks (soft-bodied animals with a mantle and foot)
  Class: Chitons
  Class: Bivalves (clams, oysters, mussels)
  Class: Scaphopoda (tooth or tusk shells)
  Class: Gastropods (slugs and snails)
  Class: Cephalopods (octopus, squid)
Phylum: Arthropods (segmented animals with an external skeleton)
  Class: Horseshoe crabs
  Class: Crustaceans (lobsters, crabs, shrimp)
  Class: Arachnids (scorpions, spiders, mites, ticks)
  Class: Insects
  Class: Millipedes and centipedes
Phylum: Cycliophora (known only as a tiny species growing in the mouths of lobsters)
Phylum: Echinoderms (starfish, brittle stars)
Phylum: Hemichordata (acorn worms)
Phylum: Chordates
  Subphylum: Tunicates
  Subphylum: Lancelets
  Subphylum: Vertebrates (animals with backbones)
  Class: Agnatha (lampreys, hagfish)
  Class: Sharks and rays
  Class: Bony fish
  Class: Amphibians
  Class: Reptiles
  Class: Birds
  Class: Mammals
    Subclass: Monotremes (egg-laying mammals)
    Subclass: Marsupials
    Subclass: Placentals
    Order: Insectivores (shrews, moles, hedgehogs)
    Order: Flying lemurs
    Order: Bats
    Order: Primates (lemurs, monkeys, apes, humans)
    Order: Edentates (anteaters, sloths, armadillos)
    Order: Pangolins
    Order: Lagomorphs (rabbits, hares)

Order: Rodents (squirrels, rats, mice, porcupines)
Order: Cetaceans (whales, dolphins)
Order: Carnivores (wolves, cats, bears, raccoons, weasels, badgers, skunks, otters, hyenas)
Order: Seals
Order: The aardvark
Order: Elephants
Order: Hyraxes
Order: Sirenians (dugongs, manatees)
Order: Odd-toed ungulates (horses, tapirs, rhinoceroses)
Order: Even-toed ungulates (pigs, hippopotamuses, camels, deer, giraffes, pronghorns, cattle, goats, sheep)

▶ CLASSIFYING HUMANS

KINGDOM: Animals Organisms that use other organisms for food and that sometimes move rapidly.
PHYLUM: Chordates Animals that are partially supported by a rod of cartilage or bone vertebrae and an internal skeleton.
SUBPHYLUM: Vertebrates Chordates that have vertebrae, such as fish, amphibians, reptiles, birds, and mammals.
CLASS: Mammals Vertebrates that have hair and suckle their young.
ORDER: Primates Mammals that use sight more than scent, have nails instead of claws on grasping hands and feet, are mostly active in daylight, and have relatively large brains.
SUPERFAMILY: Hominoids Primates that are tailless, generally large in size, can climb trees, and have relatively flat faces, such as *Sahelanthropus, Ardipithecus, Kenyapithecus,* australopithecines, and human beings.
FAMILY: Hominids Hominoids that walk upright, have small canines, and large brains; specifically, the australopithecines and human beings.
GENUS: Homo Hominids, with especially large brains, that speak and show other signs of culture; specifically, *Homo habilis, Homo erectus* and related species, and *Homo sapiens.*
SPECIES: *Homo sapiens* Modern human beings.

▶ THE HUMAN GENOME PROJECT

On June 25, 2000, President Clinton, British Prime Minister Tony Blair, and Craig Venter of Celera Genomics jointly announced the completion of decoding all the bases that make up the genes in a human. Many assumed it meant that the Human Genome Project had succeeded in deciphering all human genes. But while the announcement marked a major milestone in biology, decoding the bases was actually just a step along the way. It was not until February 15-16, 2001, that scientists from the International Human Genome Sequencing Consortium and from Celera completed the original goal of the Human Genome Project: releasing lists of all the bases in order. And even then, the lists were still slightly incomplete. Yet to come is the recognition of which bases are identified with which genes, and what the function of each gene is. Also, scientists increasingly recognize that knowledge of genes alone is not the whole story.

Every organism is almost completely described by its own genes, combinations of triplets of four chemical building blocks, called bases, carried on long molecules of a chemical named deoxyribonucleic acid (DNA). Several different DNA molecules are found in every cell. Most human cells have 46 such molecules as the working parts of the chromosomes and additional DNA in small, energy-producing bodies called mitochondria. The total group of all the DNA for an organism is called its genome. The Human Genome Project has been a step-by-step process to determine the complete sequence of the more than 3 billion bases in human DNA, to identify the genes in that sequence and to determine the immediate purpose of each gene. The DNA bases are usually known by their abbreviations, T, G, C, and A; thus, the goal of the project reached in February 2001 was to determine a giant string of the letters T, G, C, and A.

One of the surprises of the list so far has been that there appear to be only 30,000 to 40,000 human genes—fewer than half the number expected before sequencing. Ultimately other questions will need to be resolved, such as how genes interact with one another and with other molecules in the body. It appears the number of proteins encoded in the genes is much greater than the number of genes, so a new goal for researchers is to determine all the proteins—known as the proteome. Another task will be identification of variations from human to human called single-nucleotide polymorphisms (SNPs). Such variations are thought to be behind susceptibility to such complex diseases as cancer, diabetes, cardiovascular syndromes and some types of mental illnesses

The National Center for Human Genome Research was instituted on January 3, 1989, and with the participation of both the U.S. Department of Energy and National Institutes for Health, became the Human Genome Project in 1990. Scientists from the European Union, Japan and China also participate, forming together the International Human Genome Sequencing Consortium. Another group has developed out of this effort that plans to concentrate on the genomes of disease-causing organisms, primarily bacteria.

Along the way, the genomes of organisms other than human have been sequenced. Celera achieved the first, the small bacterium *Haemophilus influenzae,* in 1995. Since then, bacteria that cause syphilis, chlamydia, tuberculosis, cholera and staph infections, among some 60 different bacteria, have all had their genomes sequenced. In 1996 the gene of yeast, a more complex organism, was added to the list.

Scientists then targeted commonly used experimental organisms. Teams from the U.S. and Britain completed the genome of the first animal, *Caenorhabditis elegans,* a nematode worm, at the end of 1998. Celera concentrated on the fruit fly, *Drosophila melanogaster,* and established its sequence of 1.8 billion bases by September 9, 1999. In plants, the first success came at the end of 2000 with the mustard *Arabidopsis thaliana,* the common laboratory plant for botanists. In October, 2001, sequencing of the genome of the Japanese puffer fish was finished, the first fish. Scientists have proceeded to sequence the genomes of common laboratory animals, such as the mouse, rat, and chimpanzee, as well as the genomes of species important in agriculture, such as rice and the honeybee. By 2005, the number of species sequenced had reached well over a hundred. Mammals chosen for sequencing in the next few years are intended to reflect genetic diversity: an elephant, the domestic cat, a rabbit, the hedgehog, the guinea pig, the common shrew, an armadillo, and a tenrec, the last a hedgehog-like creature from Madagascar, which may be more closely related to elephants than to European hedgehogs.

Major Discoveries in Life Sciences

B.C.

c.9000   Agricultural Revolution starts in Near East with domestication of sheep and goats in Persia (Iran) and Afghanistan and of pigs in Anatolia (Turkey); and cultivation of wheat in Canaan (Israel and Jordan).

c.8000   Agricultural Revolution starts independently in what are now Peru, Central America, and Indochina.

c.350   Aristotle (Greek: 384–322 B.C.) classifies known animals in system that will continue to be used until 1735.

A.D.

1648   Jan Baptista van Helmont (Flemish: 1580–1644) shows that plants do not obtain large amounts of material for their growth from soil.

1665   Robert Hooke (English: 1635–1703) observes and names the cell.

1668   Francesco Redi (Italian: 1626–97) shows that maggots in meat do not arise spontaneously but are hatched from flies' eggs.

1669   Anton van Leeuwenhoek (Dutch: 1632–1723) discovers microorganisms—creatures too small to see with naked eye—and recognizes that sperm are part of reproduction.

1683   Leeuwenhoek is first to observe bacteria.

1735   Carolus Linnaeus (Carl Linné; Swedish: 1707–78) introduces system in use today for classifying plants and animals.

1779   Jan Ingenhousz (Dutch: 1730–99) discovers that plants release oxygen when exposed to sunlight and they consume carbon dioxide; this is first step in understanding photosynthesis.

1839   Theodor A.H. Schwann (German: 1810–82), building on work of Matthias Jakob Schleiden (German: 1804–81) in 1838, develops cell theory of life.

1856   First skeleton of what we now call Neandertals is found in cave in Neander Valley, near Düsseldorf (Germany).

Louis Pasteur (French: 1822–95) discovers that fermentation is caused by microorganisms.

1858   Charles R. Darwin (English: 1809–82) and Alfred R. Wallace (English: 1823–1913) announce their theory of evolution by natural selection to the Linnean Society.

1859   Darwin publishes *On the Origin of Species*.

1865   Gregor Johann Mendel's (Austrian: 1822–84) theory of dominant and recessive genes is published in obscure local journal.

1868   Workers building road in France discover skeletons of first-known Cro-Magnons in cave.

1894   Eugène Dubois (Dutch: 1858–1940) announces discovery of "Java ape-man," now known to be first specimen of *Homo erectus*.

1898   Mosaic disease of tobacco plants is recognized as being caused by virus, the first identification of a virus.

1900   Three different biologists rediscover laws of genetics originally found by Mendel.

1924   Raymond A. Dart (Australian-South African: 1893–1988) identifies first fossil of an australopithecine, a close relative of early humans.

1953   James D. Watson (American: 1928–) and Francis Crick (English: 1916–) determine structure of DNA, the basis of heredity.

1961   Louis S.B. Leakey (English: 1903–72) and Mary D. Leakey (English: 1913–96) discover a previously unknown ancestor of humans, *Homo habilis*, in the Olduvai Gorge of northern Tanzania.

Marshall W. Nirenberg (American: 1927–) learns to read one of the "letters" of genetic code.

1973   Stanley Cohen (American: 1922–) and Herbert Boyer (American: 1936–) put specific gene into bacterium, the first instance of true genetic engineering.

1974   Donald C. Johanson (American: 1943–) and coworkers discover Lucy in Afar region of Ethiopia, the nearly complete skeleton—but not the skull—of *Australopithecus afarensis*, an early relative of humans (more than 3 million years old).

1995   César Milstein (Argentine-English: 1927–) announces discovery of how to produce monoclonal antibodies, highly specific chemicals that can be made to react with particular proteins or other chemicals in the body.

1980   Martin Cline (American: 1934–) and coworkers succeed in transferring functioning gene from one mouse to another.

1983   Kary B. Mullis (American: 1945–) invents the use of the polymerase chain reaction to make copies of DNA sequences, a vital tool in finding specific genes.

1988   The complete developmental history of every cell in the nematode *Caenorhabditis elegans* published.

1994   Gen Suwa (Japanese), discovers the first fossil of *Ardipithecus ramidus*, the oldest known hominid, in Ethiopia.

1995   Craig Venter (American: 1946–) of the Institute for Genomic Research publishes the complete base sequences for all the genes of a free-living organism, the bacterium *Haemophilus influenzae*.

1997   Ian Wilmut (English: 1944–) succeeds in cloning a sheep from a cell from an adult ewe.

Svante Pääbo of the University of Munich, Germany, and coworkers clone DNA from the first discovered Neanderthal fossil and compare the DNA to that of modern humans. They conclude that the Neandertal is a different species from our own.

1998   Elizabeth Gould and co-workers at Princeton University demonstrate that adult monkeys continue to grow new brain cells, a feat previously thought impossible for adult primates.

1999   Berhane Asfaw (Ethiopian: 1954-) and coworkers announce the discovery in Ethiopia of fossils of a new hominid species, *Australopithecus garhi* ("surprising southern ape").

2000   Tools are found at a Cactus Hill site in Virginia from 15,000 years ago, tending to disprove the theory that early Americans reached the continent through Alaska about 12,000 years ago.

The Human Genome Project and Celera Genomics announce jointly that they have developed a rough draft of the entire human genetic sequence.

2001   Meave G. Leakey (English-Kenyan: 1942-) of the National Museums of Kenya in Nairobi discovers the skull of a 3.5-million-year-old human ancestor, which she names *Kenyanthropus platyops* ("flat-faced man from Kenya").

2002   For the first time in 87 years, a new order of insects is recognized (similar to Lepidoptera for butterflies and moths). Mantophasmatodea includes two genera and three species, popularly named gladiators, each somewhat like a cross between a mantis and a grasshopper.

Michel Brunet and Martin Pickford discover in Chad the oldest hominid fossil found so far, the skull of *Sahelanthropus tchadensis*, who lived 6 to 7 million years ago in a setting of woods broken with patches of savanna.

2003   Tim White and coworkers in Ethiopia announce they have found skulls of the earliest modern humans known, dating from between 154,000 and 160,000 years ago, which they term the subspecies *H. sapiens idaltu* ("elder wise man").

2004   Teams led by Peter Brown and Michael J. Morwood discover a new species of human, *Homo floriensis*, which lived on Flores Island (Indonesia) from at least 36,000 B.C. until 10,000 B.C, making it contemporary with modern *H. sapiens*. It appears to be a dwarfed form of *H. erectus*, reduced in size by its island habitat, as was a dwarf elephant species from the same period on the island. Scientists nicknamed the species "the hobbit," after the small creatures in *The Lord of the Rings*. Hobbits are thought to have preyed on the small elephants. This claim has been called into question recently.

EVOLUTION OF THE HUMAN FAMILY

New fossil finds since the start of 2000 have extended our knowledge of the ancestry of humans deep into the past. Anthropologists continue to argue as to the meaning of specific fossils; and new tools, such as DNA analysis, provide another framework for primate evolution. Several indicators now point to the first primate developing some 85 million years ago, long before the first fossil identified as a primate. The higher primates (monkeys, apes and humans), long thought to have evolved in Africa, may instead have split from the tarsier group in Asia.

Eosimis c. 45 million years ago. Central and eastern China. Evidence from fossils announced in 2000 strongly suggests that *Eosimis*, a small creature thought previously to be a tarsier, walked on all fours on tops of branches as monkeys do, which implies that it was a higher primate, the earliest known.

Catopithecus c. 40 million years ago. Egypt. For those anthropologists who think higher primates arose in Africa and that *Eosimis* is a tarsier ancestor, *Catopithecus* is the earliest representative of the higher primates.

Aegyptopithecus c. 35 million years ago. Egypt. A small, monkey-like, fruit-eating creature about the size of a house cat, *Aegyptopithecus* is sometimes called the "dawn ape" and may be the earliest known ancestor of the hominoids.

Afropithecus and Proconsul c. 15 to 20 million years ago. East Africa. Several different early apes lived in Africa and Asia about this time. Opinion is divided on whether *Afropithecus* or *Proconsul* is the ancestor to the hominids; other apes of this time are ancestral to gorillas and orangutans.

Sahelanthropus tchadensis c. 6 to 7 million years ago. Chad. Discovered by Ahounta Djimdoumalbaye and Michel Brunet on July 19, 2001, this is the earliest known hominid, combining a flat human-looking face with a brain the size of a chimpanzee's. It lived in a mixed region of woods and savanna near a large lake.

Orrorin tugenensis c. 6 million years ago. Kenya (Tugen Hills). Twelve fossils, including fragments of limb bone and jawbones as well as a few teeth, were found in 2000 by a French expedition headed by Brigette Senut and Martin Pickford. The name means "original man of Tugen," for the discoverers claim that this is the ancestor to the human line.

Ardipithecus ramidus kadabba c. 5.5 million year ago. Ethiopia (Middle Awash River Valley). Announced in 2001, these fossils include a jawbone with teeth, hand and foot bones, and fragments of other bones. The team was led by Ethiopians Yohannes Haile-Selassie and Giday WoldeGabriel. The discoverers label this as a subspecies of *Ardipithecus* (see below), but are not sure whether *Ardipithecus* is ancestral to australopithecines and humans or to chimpanzees.

Ardipithecus ramidus c. 4.4 million years ago. Ethiopia. Discovered in 1994 at Aramis, Ethiopia, *A. ramidus* lived in woodlands mixed with patches of savanna, rather than in the true savanna thought before this discovery to have been the home of ancestors to humans.

Australopithecus anamensis c. 4.2 to 3.9 million years ago. Northern Kenya (Lake Turkana region) These fossils, discovered in 1993 by Meave G. Leakey and Alan Walker, indicate that *A. anamensis* could walk upright on two legs.

Kenyapithecus platyops c. 3.5 to 3.3 million years ago. Kenya. Skull found in 2001 by Meave G. Leakey and coworkers and identified as a new genus. Leakey also thinks that some fossils previously identified as *Homo rudolfensis* may belong to *Kenyapithecus* genus.

Australopithecus afarensis "Lucy" and "The First Family" c. 3.6 to 2.9 million years ago. Ethiopia and East Africa. Many think *A. afarensis* is on the direct line to modern humans. A trail of footprints in volcanic ash at Laetoli, Tanzania, made by *A. afarensis* demonstrates that it walked upright.

Australopithecus africanus. c. 3 to 2 million years ago. South Africa First nonhuman hominid to be discovered, in 1924, although few anthropologists accepted it until the 1950s. Walked upright and, while large brained for a primate, had a brain that was much smaller than early *Homo* species. Thought to be on direct line to *Homo*.

Paranthropus (Australopithecus) aethiopicus c. 2.7 to 2.3 million years ago. East Africa. Thought to be the link between *A. africanus* and three "robust" species that many assign to the genus *Paranthropus* while others consider them australopithecines.

Australopithecus garhi c. 2.5 million years ago. Ethiopia. Fossils are found at same site as butchered animals and primitive stone tools, raising possibility that australopithecines used tools found at various early sites.

Homo habilis c. 2.5 to 1.5 million years ago. Tanzania and South Africa—possibly Central Eurasia (Georgia). Earliest known species of our own genus. *H. habilis* ("Handy Man") named for tools found at sites near fossil sites, although tools also could have been made by australopithecines whose contemporaneous fossils are also found nearby.

Homo rudolfensis c. 2.4 to 1.5 million years ago. Kenya. A different member of genus *Homo* that lived in the same general region at the same time as *H. habilis*.

Paranthropus (Australopithecus) robustus and P. bosei c. 2.3 to 1.4 million years ago. Although the *Paranthropus* line is now extinct, these robust hominids were successful contemporaries of *Homo* for about a million years.

Homo ergaster c. 1.8 to 1.4 million years ago. Africa and Central Eurasia (Georgia). Fossils once classed as African *H. erectus* are now often called *H. ergaster* ("Work Man"). Probable ancestor of *H. sapiens*.

Homo erectus "Java Ape Man" and "Peking Man" c. 1.6 million to 40,000 years ago. Africa, Asia and Europe. This maker of hand axes and user of fire has often been thought to be the immediate ancestor of *H. sapiens*, but the last groups of *H. erectus* ("Upright Man") were contemporaries of our species.

Homo heidelbergensis c. 600,000 years ago to 120,000 years ago. Europe and North Africa. Some early members of this group, perhaps those in Spain or North Africa sometimes called *Homo antecessor*, appear to be ancestor to the Neanderthals.

Homo neanderthalensis c. 200,000 years ago to 30,000 years ago. Europe and the Near East. This species was successful in the Ice Age, but became extinct shortly after *H. sapiens* spread across Europe. Although DNA studies indicate that *H. neanderthalis* and *H. sapiens* are different species, a few fossils have mixed characteristics that many think implies breeding across species lines.

Homo florsiensis "the hobbit" c. 38,000 years ago to 12,000 years ago—perhaps until recent times. Flores Island, Indonesia. At 3 feet tall, *H. florsiensis* was smaller than a modern pygmy, but made sophisticated stone tools and may have used fire.

Homo sapiens c. 160,000 years ago to present. Worldwide. The earliest, *H. sapiens idaltu* and other "archaic" humans, lived in Africa. DNA evidence suggests that about 100,000 years ago they spread into Asia and Europe. By 30,000 years ago they were the only remaining hominid (although some authorities include chimpanzees, and perhaps the gorilla, in the hominids).

Elements in a 150-Pound Person

Element/Weight	Use by the body	Element/Weight	Use by the body
Oxygen 97.5 lbs	Part of all major nutrients, which make up tissues of the body, but also vital to production of energy in the form of elemental oxygen obtained from air.	0.3 lbs	transport messages from the body to cells; helps regulate electrical activity.
Carbon 27.0 lbs	Essential element for life—most compounds based on carbon are called organic, meaning "from life." An essential part of proteins, carbohydrates, and fats, the building blocks of human cells	Sodium 0.165 lbs	Required by vertebrates to control fluid pressure in cells.
		Magnesium 0.06 lbs	Required by both plants (it is in chlorophyll) and animals. In humans, works with enzymes to speed chemical reactions, is involved in transmission of messages between nerves, and has a role in bone structure.
Hydrogen 15.0 lbs	Part of each of major nutrients, and thus a building block of every cell. Unlike oxygen, has no part in respiration.		
Nitrogen 4.5 lbs	Essential part of proteins, DNA, and RNA, the compounds most active in controlling cells; most of the body's functions depend on nitrogen compounds at one stage or another.	Iron 0.006 lbs	Essential for carrying oxygen to cells and carbon dioxide waste away. Lack of iron causes anemia.
		Cobalt 0.00024 lbs	Part of vitamin B12, found in meats and dairy products; its exact role in the body is not well understood.
Calcium 3.0 lbs	Mostly locked into hard compounds that form nonliving parts of bone. One of principal messengers between cells, telling them when to act and when to stay quiet.	Copper 0.00023 lbs	Helps form red blood cells, maintain nervous system, and regulate cholesterol levels.
Phosphorus 1.8 lbs	Important element in bone building, but, like calcium, has another role: it is essential in producing energy in cell.	Manganese 0.00020 lbs	Aids in bone formation, helps regulate nervous system, and is part of sex hormones.
Potassium 0.3 lbs	Regulates contraction of muscle cells (and some other cell functions) along with sodium. Potassium is involved with muscle contractions and general maintenance of pressure a cell exerts on its covering membrane.	Iodine 0.00006 lbs	Part of thyroid hormone that controls rate at which food is burned for energy.
		Zinc trace	Needed for some enzymes, for proper sex development, in healing wounds, for sense of taste, and for normal sperm count.
Sulfur 0.3 lbs	Essential to most forms of life. An important constituent of proteins.	Fluorine trace	Strengthens teeth and bones.
Chlorine	Used in form of chloride ions to	Chromium trace	Used in metabolism of sugar and the regulation of fats.
		Selenium trace	In small amounts, may reduce cell damage and promote growth.

Note: In addition, the body contains trace amounts of boron, aluminum, vanadium, molybdenum, and silicon. Their roles, however, are not fully understood.

MATHEMATICS

Strictly speaking, mathematics is not considered a science but a separate branch of learning on its own. Because the use of mathematics has been so important to science, however, it is generally treated along with sciences.

Mathematics consists of a set of abstract symbols and of rules for manipulating them, along with the results of that manipulation. Because of this, some have classified mathematics as a kind of language, while others view it as a kind of game. Many mathematicians believe there is a much deeper reality than those classifications, but it is one that is very difficult to explain. Even when mathematics is treated as a game, the results seem to be strongly connected to the real world.

The 20th century was an era of impressive progress in many fields of mathematics and statistics (see the discoveries listed in Milestones), and this progress continues today. Applied methods of statistical inference ("confidence intervals" and other techniques) based on the work of Sir

R.A. Fisher (British, 1890-1962) and others have been highly developed and widely applied, through computer programs, in the sciences, engineering, and social sciences. There have also been dramatic advances in the ancient science of geometry, such as the development of fractal geometry (Benoit Mandelbrot, French-American, b. Poland, 1924-), in which patterns of smaller parts (such as a coastline seen very close up) relate in complex ways to the same coastline seen from a distance. Encryption methods have developed rapidly, spurred by the need to protect information sent by the Internet. An important class of such methods is based on the use of prime numbers (numbers divisible only by 1 and themselves). The largest prime identified as of August 2002 is $(2^{13,466,917})$-1, a number with more than 4 million digits. Another area in which important advances have been made is in computerizing numerical techniques for solving the equations in weather forecasting models, a use of mathematics that affects everyone's life. These and many other modern developments in mathematics and statistics mean that, while students today study some math that is thousands of years old—Greek geometry; and some that is hundreds of years old—the calculus of Leibniz and Newton; they also study, and their lives are affected by, up-to-date mathematical techniques embodied in powerful computational packages.

▶ COMMONLY USED MATHEMATICAL FORMULAS

Most formulas needed in solving everyday problems are collected below, with special emphasis on formulas relating to measurements, as these are used in everything from sewing to building a house. However, some important formulas from algebra, graphing, and trigonometry are at the end. Additional formulas can also be found in "Basic Laws of Physics."

General

The **distance** d, given the rate r and the time t:

$$d = rt$$

Length

The **perimeter (distance around)** p **of any polygon** (closed plane figure with straight sides that do not cross), given the lengths of the sides a, b, c, and so forth:

$$p = a + b + c + \ldots$$

Perimeter p **of a rectangle**, given the length l and the width w:

$$p = 2l + 2w$$

Perimeter p **of a square**, given the length of a side s:

$$p = 4s$$

Circumference (distance around) C **of a circle**, given the diameter d (distance across) or the radius r (distance from the center to the circle):

$$C = \pi d$$
$$\text{or } C = 2\pi r$$

The number π is an infinite decimal that begins $3.14159\ldots$, which is often approximated as either 3.14 or as $\frac{22}{7}$.

Area

In each of the following, the area (amount of surface) is A. For three-dimensional figures, A is the total surface area.

Rectangle, given the length l and the width w:

$$A = lw.$$

Square, given the length of a side s:

$$A = s^2$$

Circle, given the radius r:

$$A = \pi r^2$$

Triangle, given the base b and the height h:

$$A = \tfrac{1}{2} bh$$

Right triangle, given the lengths a and b of the two sides (legs) that form the right angle:

$$A = \tfrac{1}{2} ab$$

Parallelogram, given the base b and the height h:

$$A = bh$$

Trapezoid, given the two bases B and b and the height h:

$$A = \tfrac{1}{2} h(B + b)$$

Kite, given the lengths of the two diagonals D and d:

$$A = \tfrac{1}{2} Dd$$

Regular polygon (polygon with all sides of equal length and all angles of equal measure), given the perimeter p and the apothem a (the distance from the center of the regular polygon to one of its sides):

$$A = \tfrac{1}{2} ap$$

Equilateral triangle (all sides the same length), given the length of a side s:

$$A = \frac{s^2\sqrt{3}}{4}$$

Heron's formula Any **triangle**, given half the length of the perimeter (the semiperimeter) s and the lengths of the sides a, b, and c:

$$A = \sqrt{s(s-a)(s-b)(s-c)}$$

Right circular cylinder (a cylinder with a circular region as its base whose sides make a right angle with the base), given the radius r of the base and the height h of the cylinder:

$$A = 2\pi r(h + r)$$

Right circular cone (a cone with a circular region as its base and whose altitude makes a right angle with the base), given the radius r of the base and the slant height l of the cone (the shortest distance from the tip of the cone to the circle of the base):

$$A = \pi r(l + r)$$

Sphere, given the radius r:

$$A = 4\pi r^2$$

Volume

In each of the following, the volume (space enclosed) is V.

Cube, given the length of an edge e:

$$V = e^3$$

Right rectangular prism (box), given the length l, the width w, and the height h:

$$V = lwh$$

Prism, given the area of the base B and the height h:

$$V = Bh$$

Right circular cylinder, given the radius r of the base and the height h:

$$V = \pi r^2 h$$

Right circular cone, given the radius r of the base and the height h:

$$V = \tfrac{1}{3} \pi r^2 h$$

Pyramid, given the area of the base B and the height h:

$$V = \tfrac{1}{3} Bh$$

Sphere, given the radius r:

$$V = \tfrac{4}{3} \pi r^3$$

Algebra

If a, b, and x are any numbers or variables ("unknowns"):

$$(a + b)^2 = a^2 + 2ab + b^2$$
$$(a - b)^2 = a^2 - 2ab + b^2$$
$$x^2 - a^2 = (x + a)(x - a)$$
$$x^3 - a^3 = (x - a)(x^2 + ax + a^2)$$
$$x^3 + a^3 = (x + a)(x^2 - ax + a^2)$$

Milestones in the History of Mathematics

B.C.

c. 30,000 People in Europe begin using scratches or notches to record numbers.

c. 3500 Egyptians develop numeration system that can record very large numbers, with different symbols for ones, tens, hundreds, etc.

c. 2400 A numeration system based on place value (similar to Hindu-Arabic system) is introduced in Mesopotamia.

c. 2000 Mesopotamian mathematicians learn how to solve quadratic equations.

c. 1900 Mesopotamian mathematicians discover what we now call the Pythagorean theorem: The sum of the squares of the legs of a right triangle equals the square of the hypotenuse.

c. 470 Mathematician Hippasus of Metapontum (Greek: c. 500) discovers dodecahedron, a regular solid with 12 faces.

c. 450 Pythagoreans show that some lengths, such as the diagonal of a 1 x 1 square ($\sqrt{2}$), cannot be measured exactly using a side as a unit.

c. 300 Euclid's (Greek: c. 300) *Elements* shows that virtually all parts of mathematics known at the time can be proved from short list of assumptions.

c. 260 In Central America, Maya develop numeration system based on place value.

c. 250 Archimedes (Greek: c. 287–212) establishes important theorems about volumes of solids, calculates an excellent approximation of π, and develops a system for representing very large whole numbers.

c. 230 Apollonius of Perga (Greek: c. 262–190) writes *Conics*, an analysis of such curves as parabola, ellipse, and hyperbola.

A.D.

876 The first-known use of a symbol for zero as a number occurs in India.

c. 1100 Poet, mathematician, and astronomer Omar Khayyám (Persian: 1048-c. 1131) develops geometric methods for solving cubic equations.

1321 Levi ben Gershom (Gersonides; French: 1288–1344) is first to use mathematical induction.

c.1515 Scipione del Ferro (Italian: 1465–1526) discovers algebraic method for solving one form of cubic equations.

1536 Niccolò Tartaglia (Italian: 1499–1557) solves two types of cubic equations.

1545 Girolamo Cardano's (Italian: 1501–76) *Ars Magna* contains Lodovico Ferrari's (Italian: 1522–65) complete solution of the quartic, and a complete solution of the cubic based on Tartaglia's work.

1572 Rafael Bombelli (Italian: 1526–c. 1573) uses complex numbers to solve equations.

1614 John Napier (Scottish: 1550–1617) describes logarithms.

1637 René Descartes (French: 1596–1650) publishes first account of analytic geometry; also discovered by Pierre de Fermat (French: 1601–65).

1639 Gérard Desargues (French: 1591–1661) introduces projective geometry.

1654 Blaise Pascal (French: 1623–62) and Pierre de Fermat develop basic laws of probability.

1666 Sir Isaac Newton (English: 1642–1727) describes his invention of the calculus but does not have it published at this time.

1684 Gottfried Wilhelm Leibniz (German: 1646–1716) publishes first account of his independent discovery of the calculus.

1799 Karl Friedrich Gauss (German: 1777–1855) proves fundamental theorem of algebra, which is that every polynomial equation has solution.

Paolo Ruffini (Italian: 1765–1822) offers first proof that not all polynomial equations of fifth degree can be solved by algebraic methods.

1826 Nikolai Ivanovich Lobachevski (Russian: 1793–1856) gives first public address concerning non-Euclidean geometry.

1877 Georg F.L.P. Cantor (German: 1845–1918) shows that number of points in a line segment is same as number in interior of a square.

1882 Ferdinand von Lindemann (German: 1852–1939) proves that the circle cannot be squared with straightedge and compass.

1892 Cantor proves there are at least two types of infinities—specifically, that infinity of real numbers (including all infinite decimals) is bigger than infinity of counting numbers (1, 2, 3, . . .).

1900 David Hilbert (German: 1862–1943) proposes his famous list of 23 unsolved problems.

1931 Kurt Gödel (Austrian-American: 1906–78) shows that mathematical systems are either *incomplete* or *inconsistent*: *incomplete* if not all true theorems can be proved from within the system, or *inconsistent* if two contradictory theorems can be proved.

1936 Independently, Alan M. Turing (English: 1912–54) and Alonzo Church (American: 1903–95) discover there is no single infallible method for proving whether a mathematical statement in mathematics is true or false.

1948 Claude E. Shannon (American: 1916–2001) publishes his work on information theory, a general approach to handling communications.

1976 In first major computer-assisted proof, it is shown that any map can be colored with four colors in such a way that no two regions of the same color share common border.

1995 Andrew Wiles (English-American: 1953-) publishes a corrected version of his 1993 proof that the equation $x^n + y^n = z^n$ has no solution for n greater than 2 when x, y, and z are counting numbers—known as Fermat's last theorem.

1998 Thomas C. Hales of the University of Michigan uses a computer to establish that Johannes Kepler's 1611 conjecture that stacking spheres in a face-centered cubic pattern results in the densest concentration of spheres.

2003 Daniel A. Goldston of San Jose (California) State University and Cem Y. Yildirim of Bogaziçi University in Istanbul prove that for any rational number greater than zero there are an infinite number of prime pairs closer to each other than that fraction of the average spacing of prime numbers.

Grigori (Grisha) Perelman of the Steklov Institute in St. Petersburg proves a generalization of the Poincaré conjecture, the oldest unproved conjecture in topology; it can be expressed as saying that the equivalent to a sphere--that is, the "skin" of a ball--in the four dimensions is the only three-dimensional figure that completely surrounds its inner space and has no holes.

2004 Ben Green of the University of British Columbia in Vancouver and Terence Tao of the University of California, Los Angeles, prove that there are an infinite number of arithmetic sequences of prime numbers for any specific finite length of terms. Arithmetic sequences are progressions with the same difference between terms, such as 5, 11, 17, 23, 29, in which the difference is 6; the length of this sequence for primes is 5 terms, since the next number in the sequence, 35, is not a prime.

If a, b, c, and d are any numbers or variables except that neither b nor d can be zero:

$$a/b + c/d = (ad + bc)/bd$$
$$a/b - c/d = (ad - bc)/bd$$
$$a/b \times c/d = ac/bd$$
$$a/b \div c/d = ad/bc \ (c \neq 0)$$

Quadratic formula for the solutions of a second degree polynomial equation in one variable of the form $ax^2 + bx + c = 0$:

$$x = \frac{-b \pm \sqrt{b^2 - 4ac}}{2a}$$

Laws of exponents, given that a, b, x, and y are numbers or variables:

$$a^x a^y = a^{x+y}$$
$$(a^x)^y = a^{xy}$$
$$(ab)^x = a^x b^x$$
$$(a/b)^x = a^x/b^x$$
$$a^x/a^y = a^{x-y}$$
$$a^{-x} = \frac{1}{a^x}$$
$$a^0 = 1$$
$$a^1 = a$$

Laws of logarithms, given that a, b, x, and y are positive numbers, c is any real number, and $a \neq 1$, $b \neq 1$.

$$\log_a (xy) = \log_a x + \log_a y$$
$$\log_a 1/x = - \log_a x$$
$$\log_a (x/y) = \log_a x - \log_a y$$
$$\log_a (x^c) = c \log_a x$$
$$\log_b x = (\log_a x)/(\log_a b)$$
$$\log_a 1 = 0$$
$$\log_a a = 1$$
$$a^{\log_a x} = x$$
$$\log_a (a^c) = c$$

Graphs

In a rectangular (Cartesian) coordinate plane, where the horizontal axis is x and the vertical axis is y:
Slope of a line, m, given two particular points (x_1, y_1) and (x_2, y_2) *where* $x_1 \neq x_2$:

$$m = (y_2 - y_1)/(x_2 - x_1)$$

Point-slope equation of a line, given the slope m and a point on the nonvertical line (x_1, y_1):

$$y - y_1 = m(x - x_1)$$

Slope-intercept equation of a line, given the slope m and the y-intercept b (the number on the y axis where the line crosses the y axis):

$$y = mx + b$$

Distance d between any two points, (x_1, y_1) and (x_2, y_2):

$$d = \sqrt{(x_2 - x_1)^2 + (y_2 - y_1)^2}$$

Trigonometry

In a **right triangle** whose two shorter sides (or legs) are a and b, opposite angles A and B respectively, and whose longest side (or hypotenuse, always the side opposite the right angle, C) is c:
Pythagorean theorem:

$$c^2 = a^2 + b^2$$

Trigonometric functions:

sine: $\sin A = a/c$
cosine: $\cos A = b/c$
tangent: $\tan A = a/b$
cotangent: $\cot A = b/a$
secant: $\sec A = c/b$
cosecant: $\csc A = c/a$

In any triangle labeled such that side a is opposite angle A, side b is opposite angle B, and side is opposite angle C:

Angle sum:

$$A + B + C = 180°$$

Fractions, Decimals, and Percents

To find the equivalent of a fraction in decimal form, divide the numerator (top number) by the denominator (bottom number). To change from a decimal to a percent, multiply by 100. To change from a percent to a decimal, divide by 100.

Fraction	Decimal	Percent
1/16	0.0625	6.25%
1/8 (= 2/16)	0.125	12.5
3/16	0.1875	18.75
1/4 (= 2/8; = 4/16)	0.25	25.0
5/16	0.3125	31.25
1/3	0.3 . . .	33 1/3
3/8 (= 6/16)	0.375	37.5
7/16	0.4375	43.75
1/2 (= 2/4; = 4/8; = 8/16)	0.5	50.0
9/16	0.5625	56.25
5/8 (= 10/16)	0.625	62.5
2/3	0.6 . . .	66 2/3
11/16	0.6875	68.75
3/4 (= 6/8; = 12/16)	0.75	75.0
13/16	0.8125	81.25
7/8 (= 14/16)	0.875	87.5
15/16	0.9375	93.75
1 (=2/2;=4/4;=8/8;=16/16)	1.0	100.0

Large Numbers

There are two primary naming systems for large numbers. The United States and France (among others) use one system, while Germany and Great Britain use the other. (Googol and googolplex, invented by the nephew of mathematician and author Edward Kasner, are rarely used outside the United States.) (See also "Standard Weights and Measures.")

Number of zeroes after 1	American name	British name
6	million	million
9	billion	milliard
12	trillion	billion
15	quadrillion	1,000 billion
18	quintillion	trillion
21	sextillion	1,000 trillion
24	septillion	quadrillion
27	octillion	1,000 quadrillion
30	nonillion	quintillion
33	decillion	1,000 quintillion
100	googol	googol
googol	googolplex	googolplex

Law of sines:

$$(sin\ A)/a = (sin\ B)/b = (sin\ C)/c$$

Law of cosines:

$$c^2 = a^2 + b^2 - 2ab\ cos\ C$$

If x is any real number or a measure of an angle in degrees, the following statements are true:

Defining trigonometric identities:

$$tan\ x = sin\ x/cos\ x \qquad csc\ x = 1/sin\ x$$
$$cot\ x = cos\ x/sin\ x \qquad cot\ x = 1/tan\ x$$
$$sec\ x = 1/cos\ x$$

Trigonometric identities of symmetry:

$$sin\ (-x) = - sin\ x \qquad cos\ (-x) = cos\ x$$

$$tan\ (-x) = - tan\ x \qquad cot\ (-x) = - cot\ x$$
$$sec\ (-x) = sec\ x \qquad csc\ (-x) = - csc\ x$$

Pythagorean identities:

$$sin^2\ x + cos^2\ x = 1$$
$$tan^2\ x + 1 = sec^2\ x$$
$$cot^2\ x + 1 = csc^2\ x$$

Sum and difference formulas: If x and y are any two real numbers or measures of angles:

$$sin\ (x + y) = sin\ x\ cos\ y + cos\ x\ sin\ y$$
$$cos\ (x + y) = cos\ x\ cos\ y - sin\ x\ sin\ y$$
$$tan\ (x + y) = (tan\ x + tan\ y)/(1 - tan\ x\ tan\ y)$$
$$sin\ (x - y) = sin\ x\ cos\ y - cos\ x\ sin\ y$$
$$cos\ (x - y) = cos\ x\ cos\ y + sin\ x\ sin\ y$$
$$tan\ (x - y) = (tan\ x - tan\ y)/(1 + tan\ x\ tan\ y)$$

Prefixes Used in the International System of Units (SI)

Prefix	Abbreviation	Factor by which unit is multipled	Scientific Notation
Yotta-	Y	1,000,000,000,000,000,000,000,000	10^{24}
Zetta-	Z	1,000,000,000,000,000,000,000	10^{21}
Exa-	E	1,000,000,000,000,000,000	10^{18}
Peta-	P	1,000,000,000,000,000	10^{15}
Tera-	T	1,000,000,000,000	10^{12}
Giga-	G	1,000,000,000	10^{9}
Mega-	M	1,000,000	10^{6}
Kilo-	k	1,000	10^{3}
Hecto-	h	100	10^{2}
Deka-	da	10	10^{1}
Deci-	d	0.1	10^{-1}
Centi-	c	0.01	10^{-2}
Milli-	m	0.001	10^{-3}
Micro-	μ	0.000 001	10^{-6}
Nano-	n	0.000 000 001	10^{-9}
Pico-	p	0.000 000 000 001	10^{-12}
Femto-	f	0.000 000 000 000 001	10^{-15}
Atto-	a	0.000 000 000 000 000 001	10^{-18}
Zepto-	z	0.000 000 000 000 000 000 001	10^{-21}
Yocto-	y	0.000 000 000 000 000 000 000 001	10^{-24}

STANDARD WEIGHTS & MEASURES

▶ SYSTEMS OF MEASUREMENT

There are two widely used measurement systems. Most of the world uses a system known as the metric system, or the International System, abbreviated SI from *Système Internationale*, its name in French. The United States continues to use a system called U.S. customary measure, which derives from (and differs from) the British imperial series of weights and measures. From time to time, our government has taken steps to change from the customary system to the International System, but these efforts have had limited success. Metric measure is legal in the United States, but nearly everyone continues to use the customary system in everyday use. The International System is generally used in scientific pursuits and increasingly in international trade.

The following tables show first the U.S. customary system, then the International System, and finally some important conversion factors between the two.

Length or Distance
U.S. customary system

1 foot (ft.)	=	12 inches
1 yard (yd.)	=	3 feet = 36 inches
1 rod (rd.)	=	5.5 yards = 16.5 feet
1 furlong (fur.)	=	40 rods = 220 yards
		=660 feet
1 mile (mi.)	=	8 furlongs
	=	1,760 yards = 5,280 feet

An international nautical mile has been defined as 6,076.1155 feet.

International System

The basic unit for length is the meter, which is slightly longer than the customary yard. Other units of length are decimal subdivisions or multiples of the meter.

1 decimeter (dm)	=	10 centimeters
	=	0.1 meter
1 centimeter (cm)	=	0.01 meter
1 millimeter (mm)	=	0.1 centimeter
	=	0.001 meter
1 micrometer (μm)	=	0.001 millimeter
	=	0.0001 centimeter
	=	0.000001 meter
1 angstrom (Å)	=	0.0001 micrometers
	=	0.0000001 milimeter

1 dekameter (dam)	=	10 meters
1 hectometer (hm)	=	10 dekameters
		100 meters
1 kilometer	=	10 hectometers
	=	100 dekameters
	=	1,000 meters

Conversions

In 1959 the relationship between between customary and international measures of length was officially defined as follows:

0.0254 meter (exactly)	=	1 inch
0.0245 meter x 12	=	0.3048 meter
	=	1 international foot

This definition, which makes many conversions simple, defines a foot that is shorter (by about 6 parts in 10 million) than the survey foot, which had earlier been defined as exactly 1200/3937, or 0.3048006, meter.

Following the international foot standard, the major equivalents are as listed below:

1 in.	= 2.54 cm	= 0.0254 m
1 ft.	= 30.48 cm	= .3048 m
1 yd.	= 91.44 cm	= 0.9144 m
1 mi.	= 1,609.344 m	= 1.609344 km
1 cm	= 0.3937 in.	
1 m	= 1.093613 yd.	= 3.28084 ft.
1 km	= 0.62137 mi.	

Area
U.S. customary system

Areas are derived from lengths as follows:

1 square foot	=	144 square inches
1 square yard	=	9 sq. ft.
1 square rod (rd.^{2})	=	30.25 square yards
	=	272.25 square feet
1 acre	=	160 square rods
	=	4,840 square yards
	=	43,560 sq. ft.
1 square mile	=	640 acres
1 section	=	1 mile square
1 township	=	6 miles square
	=	36 square miles

Simplified Conversion Table (alphabetical order)

To convert	to	multiply by:
centimeters	feet	0.0328
centimeters	inches	0.3937
cubic cm	cubic in.	0.061
cubic feet	cubic m	0.0283
degrees	radians	0.0175
feet	cm	30.5
feet	meters	0.305
gallons	liters	3.785
gallon of water	pound of water	8.3
grams	ounces	0.035
inches	cm	2.54
kilograms	pounds	2.2
kilometers	feet	3,281
kilometers	miles	0.62
knots	mi./hr.	1.15
liters	gallons	0.264
liters	pints	2.1
meters	feet	3.28
miles	km	1.61
ounces	grams	28.35
pounds	kg	0.454

International System

1 sq. millimeter (mm^2)	=	1,000,000 sq. micrometers
1 sq. centimeter (cm^2)	=	100 mm^2
1 sq. decimeter (dm^2)	=	100 cm^2
1 sq. meter (m^2)	=	10,000 cm^2
1 are (a)	=	100 m^2
1 hectare (ha)	=	100 ares
	=	10,000 m^2
1 sq kilometer (km^2)	=	100 hectares
	=	1,000,000 m^2

Conversions

1 square inch	=	6.4516 cm^2
1 square foot	=	929.0304 cm^2
	=	0.09290304 m^2
1 square yard	=	8,361.2736 cm^2
	=	0.83612736 m^2
1 acre	=	4,046.8564 m^2
	=	0.40468564 hectares
1 square mile	=	2,589,988.11 m^2
	=	258.998811 hectares
	=	2.58998811 km^2
1 cm^2	=	0.1550003 sq. in.
1 m^2	=	1,550.003 sq. in.
	=	10.76391 sq. ft.
	=	1.195990 sq. yds.
1 hectare	=	107,639.1 sq. ft.
	=	11,959.90 sq. yds.
	=	2.4710538 acres
1 km^2	=	247.10538 acres
	=	0.3861006 sq. miles

Cubic Measure
U.S. customary system

1 cu foot (ft.^{3})	=	1,728 cubic inches (in.^{3})
1 cubic yard (yd.^{3})	=	27 cubic feet (ft.^{3})

International System

1 cubic centimeter (cm^3)	=	1,000 cubic millimeters (mm^3)
1 cubic decimeter (dm^3)	=	1,000 cubic centimeters (cm^3)
1 cubic meter (m^3)	=	1,000 cubic decimeters (dm^3)
	=	1,000,000 cubic centimeters (cm^3)

Cubic centimeter is sometimes abbreviated cc and is used in fluid measure interchangeably with milliliter (ml).

Conversions

1 in.^{3}	=	16.387064 cm^3
1 ft.^{3}	=	28.316846592 cm^3
	=	0.028316847 cm^3
1 yd.^{3}	=	764,554.857984 cm^3
	=	0.764554858 m^3
1 cm^3	=	0.06102374 in.^{3}
1 m^3	=	61,023.74 in.^{3}
	=	35.31467 ft.^{3}
	=	1.307951 yd.^{3}

Fluid Volume
U.S. customary system

A gallon is equal to 231 cubic inches of liquid or capacity.

1 tablespoon (tbs.)	=	3 teaspoons (tsp.)
	=	0.5 fluid ounce (fl. oz.)
1 cup	=	8 fl. oz.
1 pint (pt.)	=	2 cups = 16 fl. oz.
1 quart (qt.)	=	2 pt. = 4 cups
	=	32 fl. oz.
1 gallon (gal.)	=	4 qt. = 8 pt. = 16 cups
1 bushel (bu.)	=	8 gal. = 32 qt.

International System

Fluid-volume measurements are directly tied to cubic measure. One milliliter of fluid occupies a volume of 1 cubic centimeter. A liter of fluid (slightly more than the customary quart) occupies a volume of 1 cubic decimeter, or 1,000 cubic centimeters.

1 centiliter (cL)	=	10 mililiters (mL)
1 deciliter	=	10 cl = 100 mL
1 liter (L)	=	10 dl = 1,000 mL
1 dekaliter (daL)	=	10 L
1 hectoliter (hL)	=	10 daL = 100 L
1 kiloliter (kL)	=	10 hl = 1,000 L

Conversions

1 fluid ounce	=	29.573528 mL	= 0.02957 L
1 cup	=	236.588 mL	= 0.236588 L
1 pint	=	473.176 mL	= 0.473176 L
1 quart	=	946.3529 mL	= 0.9463529 L
1 gallon	=	3,785.41 mL	= 3.78541 L
1 milliliter	=	0.0338 fluid ounce	
1 liter	=	33.814 fluid ounces	
		=4.2268 cups	= 2.113 pints
		=1.0567 quarts	= 0.264 gallon

Dry Volume
Conversions

1 pint, dry	=	33.600 cu. in.	= 0.551 L
1 quart, dry	=	67.201 cu. in.	= 1.101 L

Mass & Weight

Mass and weight are often confused. Mass is a measure of the quantity of matter in an object and does not vary with changes in altitude or in gravitational force (as on the Moon or another planet). Weight, on the other hand, is a measure of the force of gravity on an object and so does change with altitude or gravitational force.

U.S. customary system

In customary measure it is more common to measure weight than mass. The most common customary system of weight is avoirdupois:

1 pound (lb.)	–	16 ounces (oz.)
1 (short) hundred-weight (cwt.)	=	100 lb.
1 (short) ton	=	20 hundredweights
	=	2,000 lb.
1 long hundred-weight	=	112 lb.
1 long ton	=	20 long hundredweights
	=	2,240 lb.

A different system called troy weight is used to weigh precious metals. In troy weight the ounce is slightly larger than in avoirdupois, but there are only 12 ounces to the troy pound.

International System

Instead of weight, the International System uses measures of mass. The original basic unit was the gram, which was defined as the mass of 1 milliliter (= 1 cm3) of water at 4 degrees Celsius (about 39ºF). Today the official measure of mass is a specific metal object defined as the standard kilogram.

1 centigram (cg)	=	10 milligrams (mg)
1 decigram (dg)	=	10 cg = 100 mg
1 gram (g)	=	10 dg = 100 cg = 1000 mg
1 kilogram (kg)	=	10 hectograms (hg)
	=	100 dekagrams (dag)
	=	1,000 g
1 metric ton (t)	=	1000 kg

Conversions

Since mass and weight are identical at standard conditions (sea level on Earth), grams and other International System units of mass are often used as measures of weight or converted into customary units of weight. Under standard conditions:

1 ounce	=	28.3495 grams
1 pound	=	453.59 grams
	=	0.45359 kilogram
1 short ton	=	907.18 kilograms
	=	0.907 metric ton
1 milligram	=	0.000035 ounce
1 gram	=	0.03527 ounce
1 kilogram	=	35.27 ounces
	=	2.2046 pounds
1 metric ton	=	2,204.6 pounds
	=	1.1023 short tons

Time
Customary and International System

The International System in 1967 adopted a second that is based on the microwaves emitted by the vibrations of hot cesium atoms. A second (abbreviated sec. in customary usage, s in SI usage) is the time it takes the atoms to vibrate exactly 9,192,631,770 times. In the customary measure of time, the day is divided into 24 hours, the hour into 60 minutes, and the minute into 60 seconds. Since the Earth's rotation is gradually slowing, scientists must periodically add a second to a day to keep the year in sequence with their clocks. The change is so small that for almost all practical purposes an International System second and a customary second are the same.

Decimal fractions of time are used to measure smaller time intervals:

millisecond (ms)	=	0.001 second (10^{-3})
microsecond (μs)	=	0.000001 second (10^{-6})
nanosecond (ns)	=	0.000000001 second (10^{-9})
picosecond (ps)	=	0.000000000001 second (10^{-12})

Temperature
U.S. customary system

In the U.S, temperature is usually measured in degrees Fahrenheit: water freezes at 32°F and boils at 212°F. The basis of the Fahrenheit scale was 0°F, the coldest temperature that its originator, G.D. Fahrenheit (1686–1736), could obtain under laboratory conditions.

International System

The Swedish astronomer Anders Celsius (1701–44) devised the temperature scale that bears his name in 1742. On the Celsius scale, water freezes at 0°C and boils at 100°C. Very low temperatures are measured on the Kelvin scale, named for William Thomson, Baron Kelvin (1824–1907). It is also called the absolute scale because absolute zero— 0°K (-273.15° C)—is the temperature at which no body can give up heat. The interval of a degree Kelvin equals the interval of a degree Celsius. At very high temperatures, differences between the Kelvin and Celsius scales are insignificant.

Conversions

Fahrenheit to Celsius: Subtract 32 from the temperature and multiply the difference by 5; then divide the product by 9. The formula is:

$$C = \tfrac{5}{9} (F\text{-}32)$$

Fahrenheit and Celsius Temperature Conversions

You can **roughly** convert a Celsius temperature to Fahrenheit by doubling the number and adding 30. For example, 20°C Celsius is approximately 70°F. (Conversely, subtract 30 from Fahrenheit temperature and divide by two for a Celsius temperature.) For a closer equivalent, consult the table below.

Celsius	Fahrenheit	Fahrenheit	Celsius
-45° = -49°		-45° = -42.8°	
-40° = -40°		-40° = -40.0°	
-35° = -31°		-35° = -37.2°	
-30° = -22°		-30° = -34.4°	
-25° = -13°		-25° = -31.7°	
-20° = -4°		-20° = -28.9°	
-15° = 5°		-15° = -26.1°	
-10° = 14°		-10° = -23.3°	
-5° = 23°		-5° = -20.6°	
0° = 32°		0° = -17.8°	
5° = 41°		5° = -15.0°	
10° = 50°		10° = -12.2°	
15° = 59°		15° = -9.4°	
20° = 68°		20° = -6.7°	
25° = 77°		25° = -3.9°	
30° = 86°		30° = -1.1°	
35° = 95°		32° = 0.0°	
40° = 104°		35° = 1.7°	
45° = 113°		40° = 4.4°	
50° = 122°		45° = 7.2°	
55° = 131°		50° = 10.0°	
60° = 140°		55° = 12.8°	
65° = 149°		60° = 15.6°	
70° = 158°		65° = 18.3°	
75° = 167°		70° = 21.1°	
80° = 176°		75° = 23.9°	
85° = 185°		80° = 26.7°	
90° = 194°		85° = 29.4°	
95° = 203°		90° = 32.2°	
100° = 212°		95° = 35.0°	
125° = 257°		100° = 37.8°	
150° = 302°		105° = 40.6°	
175° = 347°		110° = 43.3°	
200° = 392°		212° = 100.0°	
225° = 437°		225° = 107.2°	
250° = 482°		250° = 121.1°	
275° = 527°		275° = 135.0°	
300° = 572°		300° = 148.9°	
325° = 617°		325° = 162.8°	
350° = 662°		350° = 176.7°	
375° = 707°		375° = 190.6°	
400° = 752°		400° = 204.4°	
425° = 797°		425° = 218.3°	
450° = 842°		450° = 232.2°	
475° = 887°		475° = 246.1°	

Celsius to Fahrenheit: Multiply the temperature by 1.8 (or $\frac{9}{5}$), then add 32. The formula is: $F = \frac{9}{5} C + 32$
Celsius to Kelvin: Add 273.15 to the temperature The formula is: $K = C + 273.15$

Force, Work/Energy, Power
U.S. customary system
The foot/pound/second system of reckoning includes the following units:

Kelvin, Celsius, and Fahrenheit Equivalents

Characteristic	K	C°	F°
Absolute zero	0	-273.15°	-459.7°
Freezing point, water	273.15	0°	32°
Traditional human body temperature	310.15	37°	98.6°
Boiling point, water	373.15	100°	212°

slug = the mass to which a force of 1 poundal will give an acceleration of 1 foot per second per second (= approximately 32.17 lbs.)
poundal = fundamental unit of force
foot-pound = the work done when a force of 1 poundal produces a movement of 1 foot
foot-pound/second = the unit of power equal to 1 foot/pound per second

Another common unit of power is horsepower, which is equal to 550 foot-pounds per second.

Thermal work or energy is often measured in British thermal units (Btu). One Btu is defined as the energy required to increase the temperature of 1 pound of water by 1 degree Fahrenheit. The Btu is equal to about 0.778 foot-pound.

International System
In physics, compound measurements of force, work or energy, and power are essential. There are two parallel systems using International System units: the centimeter/gram/second system (cgs) is used for small measurements, and the meter/kilogram/second system (mks) is used for larger measurements. The mks system is the official one for SI. They are described below.

Measurement of force
cgs unit   dyne (dy)   The force required to accelerate a mass of 1 g 1 cm/s² (cm/s^2 means "centimeter per second per second")
mks unit   newton (N)   The force required to accelerate a mass of 1 kg 1 m/s²

Measurement of work or energy
cgs unit   erg   The dyne-centimeter, i.e., the work done when a force of 1 dy produces a movement of 1 cm
mks unit   joule (j)   The newton-meter, i.e., the work done when a force of 1 N produces a movement of 1 m (=10,000,000 ergs)

Heat energy is also measured using the calorie (cal), which is defined as the energy required to increase the temperature of 1 cubic centimeter (1 ml) of water by 1 degree C. One calorie is equal to about 4.184 joules. The kilocalorie (Kcal or Cal) is equal to 1,000 calories and is the unit in which the energy values of food are measured. This more familiar unit, also commonly referred to as a Calorie, is equal to about 4,184 joules.

Measurement of power

cgs unit	erg/second	A rate of 1 erg per second
mks unit	watt (W)	The joule/second, i.e., a rate of 1 joule per second

Conversions
Measurement of force

1 poundal	=	13,889 dynes
	=	0.13889 newtons
1 dyne	=	0.000072 poundals
1 newton	=	7.2 poundals

Measurement of work or energy

1 foot-pound	=	1,356 joules
British thermal unit	=	1,055 joules
	=	252 calories
1 joule	=	0.0007374 ft.-lbs.
1 calorie	=	0.003968 Btu
1 Kilocalorie	=	3.968 Btu

Measurement of power

1 foot-pound/second	=	1.3564 watts
1 horsepower	=	746 watts
	=	0.746 kilowatts
1 watt	=	0.73725 ft-lb/sec.
	=	0.00134 horsepower
1 kilowatt	=	737.25 ft.-lb./sec.
	=	1.34 horsepower

Electrical Measure

Originally, the basic unit of quantity in electricity was the coulomb. A coulomb is equal to the passage of 6.25×10^{18} electrons past a given point in an electrical system.

The unit of electrical flow is the ampere, which is equal to a coulomb/second, i.e., the flow of 1 coulomb per second. The ampere is analogous in electrical measure to a unit of flow such as gallons-per-minute in physical measure. In SI, the ampere is taken as the basic unit.

The unit for measuring electrical potential energy is the volt, which is defined as 1 joule/coulomb, i.e., 1 joule of energy per coulomb of electricity. The volt is analogous to a measure of pressure in a water system.

The unit for measuring electrical power is the watt as defined in the previous section. Power in watts (P) is the product of the electrical flow in amperes (I) and the potential electrical energy in volts (E):

$$P = IE.$$

Since the watt is such a small unit for practical applications, the kilowatt (= 1,000 watts) is often used. A kilowatt-hour is the power of 1,000 watts over an hour's time.

The unit for measuring electrical resistance is the ohm, which is the resistance offered by a circuit to the flow of 1 ampere being driven by the force of 1 volt. It is derived from Ohm's law, which defines the relationship between flow or current (amperes), potential energy (volts), and resistance (ohms). It states that the current in amperes (I) is proportional to potential energy in volts (E) and inversely proportional to resistance in ohms (R). Thus, when voltage and resistance are known, amperage can be calculated by the simple formula

$$I = \frac{E}{R}$$

Measure of Angles and Arcs

Angles are measured by systems based on arcs (portions) of circles. Arcs of a circle can be measured by length, but they are also often measured by angles. In the latter case, the measure of the arc is the same as the measure of an angle whose vertex is at the center of the circle and whose sides pass through the ends of the arc. Such an angle is said to be subtended by the arc.

The most commonly used angle measure is degree measure. One degree is the angle subtended by an arc that is 1/360 of a circle. This is an ancient system of measurement probably originally developed by Sumerian astronomers. These astronomers used a numeration system based on 60 ($60 \times 6 = 360$), as well as a 360-day year. They divided the day into 12 equal periods of 30 smaller periods each ($12 \times 30 = 360$) and used roughly the same system for dividing the circle. Even when different years and numeration systems were adopted by later societies, astronomers continued to use a variation of the Sumerian system for angles.

1 degree (1°)	=	60 minutes (60')
	=	3,600 seconds (3,600")
1 minute	=	60 seconds

When two lines are perpendicular to each other, they form four angles of the same size, which are called right angles. Two right angles make up a line, which in this context is considered a straight angle.

1 right angle = 90°
1 straight angle = 180°

While this system is workable for most purposes, it is artificial. Mathematicians discovered that using a natural system of angle measurement produces results that make better sense in mathematical and many scientific applications. This system is called radian measure. Radian measure is considered a supplement to SI. One radian is the measure of the angle subtended by an arc of a circle that is exactly as long as the radius of the circle.

1 radian = about 57° 17' 45"

The circumference, C, of a circle is given by the formula $C = 2\pi r$, where π is a number (approximately 3.14159) and r is the radius. Therefore, a semicircle whose radius is 1 is π units long, which implies that there are π radians in a straight angle. Many of the angles commonly encountered are measured in multiples of π radians:

0° = 0 radians	90° = π/2 radians
30° = π/6 radians	180° = π radians
45° = π/4 radians	270° = 3π/2 radians
60° = π/3 radians	360° = 2π radians

To convert from radians to degrees, use the formula $t\ radians = (180/\pi)\ t°$. To convert from degrees to radians, use the formula

$$w° = (\pi/180)w \text{ radians.}$$

The U.S. artillery uses the mil to measure angles. A mil is the angle subtended by an arc that is 1/6400 of a circle.

1 mil = 0.05625° = 3' 22.5"
1 mil = almost 0.001 radian

The Environment

The modern environmental movement in the United States dates from Earth Day 1970 (April 22), when the American public first began to take stock of the ecological devastation going on around them. Then there were no pollution controls on cars; people and municipalities dumped untreated sewage into the nation's rivers, some of which were so saturated with chemical waste that they actually caught fire; and industrial cities were routinely shrouded with thick acrid smoke.

Many of these problems have been effectively addressed and dramatically diminished. Today the Environmental Protection Agency (EPA), established in 1970, routinely monitors air quality at thousands of sites around the country. Toxic emissions from smokestacks at smelters, factories, and garbage incinerators have been sharply reduced. Mandatory pollution control standards on automobiles have led to an overwhelming drop in lead emissions. Recycling as a way of reducing solid waste has taken hold in cities and towns throughout the country. Many people, however, oppose strong environmental safeguards on economic and other grounds, making it difficult to improve and enforce regulations. Growing population pressures also create environmental threats, particularly to natural habitats, arable soil, and drinking water supplies.

▶ GLOBAL WARMING

Most climatologists are convinced that over the past century the Earth has begun to warm significantly—about 1.1°F (0.6°C)—and that at its current rate, it is likely to warm as much as 3° to 7°F (1.5° to 4°C) by the year 2100 (as compared to 1990). Analyses of data such as tree rings, ice cores, growth of corals, and historical records indicate that in the Northern Hemisphere it is likely that the 1990s were the warmest decade, and 1998 the warmest year, in the past 1,000 years. Globally, the Earth's average surface temperature in 1998 was the highest since thermometer records were first kept in the mid-19th century, as the effects of El Niño heightened the underlying warming trend. If global temperatures continue to increase, the potential devastation is staggering. Worldwide temperatures have risen only 9°F (5°C) since the end of the last ice age 12,000 years ago. Additional warming could cause melting of polar ice caps, setting off a chain of events that begins with a rise in sea level worldwide and could end with the destruction of water supplies, forests, and agriculture in many parts of the world.

Global warming occurs when certain gases in the atmosphere prevent sunlight from being reflected from the Earth. Ordinarily, sunlight that reaches the surface of the Earth is partly absorbed and partly reflected. The absorbed light heats the surface and is later emitted from the surface as infrared radiation. Gases that are not transparent to infrared radiation (carbon dioxide is one) collect this heat and keep it in the atmosphere, hence their name, greenhouse gases. The Earth's atmosphere is only 0.03 percent carbon dioxide, but combined with other gases, this is enough to trap 30 percent of the reflected heat (the rest is radiated out to space), and maintain the Earth's average temperature at about 59°F (15°C).

The most authoritative studies have been those of the Intergovernmental Panel on Climate Change (IPCC), a group of several thousand scientists commissioned by the United Nations. In its most recent report in 2007, the IPCC concluded that "the evidence of global warming is now unequivocal," and that the major contributor is human activity. With this report, the debate over human influence is essentially over for most scientists and policy makers, and the important issues now relate to the development and implementation of policies toward change.

The increased presence of carbon dioxide is due primarily to the burning of carbon fuels including oil, coal, and natural gas, as well as burning trees for deforestation. CFCs, now being phased out by many countries, are used as aerosols, in air-conditioning units, and in various industrial processes. Methane is emitted by decomposing organic wastes, natural-gas leaks, and fermenting rice paddies. The primary sources of nitrogen oxides are automobile exhaust and industrial smoke stacks. At a December 1997 conference in Kyoto, Japan, representatives of more than 150 countries reached tentative agreement to reduce greenhouse gases an average of 5 percent worldwide (from 1990 levels) by the year 2010. By September 2003, most of the world's industrialized nations had ratified the Protocol. In late 2004 Russia ratified the treaty, paving the way for it to come into force on February 16, 2005.

President Bush refused to ratify the agreement, even though a 2002 report from his own administration warned that American ecosystems were in imminent danger of being destroyed by human activity. One notable American initiative is the U.S. Mayors Climate Change Agreement (2005), which as of 2007 had more than 500 signatories, who strive to have their cities reduce GHG emissions by amounts equal or better than the targets in the Kyoto Protocol.

Global warming produces complex and interrelated effects that could under some scenarios spell environmental disaster. Some of the elements of global warming are:

Weather patterns Climatologists think that higher global temperatures and changing precipitation patterns are already disrupting local weather in places around the world. For example, the IPCC (2007) reports that more intense precipitation events (storms) have increased over most land areas, and that more intense droughts have been observed in many areas. The U.S. National Climatic Data Center in Asheville, NC reports that Northern Hemisphere snow cover has been below normal since 1987, and that extreme extratropical cyclone activity over the North Atlantic has increased since 1988.

Changed weather patterns can have a severe impact on crops and other forms of vegetation, as well as on the animals that depend on them. Rising temperatures also enable insects and fungal pests to migrate to previously unaffected regions. Long-lived plants, however, such as trees, spread much more slowly in the face of climate change.

Warming patterns Although global warming will cause an increase in average world temperatures, this increase is not expected to be uniform. In general, climatologists expect greater warming during winter months and at high latitudes (closer to the poles than to the equator). Some places will experience more severe effects than others. For example, the number of +95°F days in Rio de Janeiro

Major Events in the History of the Environment

1775 Percival Pott observes that chimney sweeps develop cancer as a result of their contact with soot, the first recognition of environmental factors on cancer.

1864 George Perkins Marsh (American: 1801-81) publishes *Man and Nature*, the first textbook on conservation and the first detailed study of human influence on the environment.

1872 Robert Angus Smith (Scottish: 1817-84) describes acid rain.

1885 Yellowstone, world's first national park, opens.

1892 Canada establishes first national park at Banff, Alberta.

1895 Svante Arrhenius (Swedish, 1859-1927) is the first person to investigate effect of increasing carbon dioxide in the atmosphere on global climate.

1903 John Muir (Scottish-American: 1838-1914) founds the Sierra Club.

1905 U.S. president Theodore Roosevelt opens the first national refuge, Pelican Island in Florida, to protect nesting sites of brown pelicans.

U.S. Forest Service established.

National Audubon Society founded.

1911 Canada, Japan, Russia, and the United States sign treaty to limit the harvest of northern fur seals.

1916 National Park Service established.

1928 Boulder Canyon project (Hoover Dam) authorized to bring irrigation, electric power, and flood control system to western United States.

1933 Tennessee Valley Authority created to develop the Tennessee River for flood control, navigation, electric power, agriculture, and forestry.

1939 Paul Müller (Swiss: 1899-1965) discovers insecticidal properties of DDT.

1952 Smog blamed for 4,000 deaths in London.

1955 Link between exposure to asbestos and lung cancer established.

1957 Nuclear wastes stored by the Soviet Union in a remote mountain region of the Urals explode; radioactive contamination affects thousands of square miles; several villages permanently evacuated.

1961 Investigations in Scandinavia and the U.S. Adirondacks confirm that acid rain kills some species living in lakes.

1962 *Silent Spring* by Rachel Carson (American: 1907-64) attacks pesticide use and stimulates major environmental movement.

1963 Congress passes first Clean Air Act, allocating $95 million to local, state, and national air pollution control efforts.

1964 Congress passes Wilderness Act, setting up the National Wilderness Preservation System.

1965 Congress passes Highway Beautification Act, banning many highway billboards.

Congress passes Water Quality Act, giving federal government power to set water standards.

Congress passes the Solid Waste Disposal Act, its first major solid waste legislation.

1966 Congress passes Rare and Endangered Species Act.

1967 S. Manabe and R.T. Wetherald predict that increased amounts of carbon dioxide in the atmosphere will lead to global warming.

1968 Congress passes Wild and Scenic Rivers Act, identifying areas of scenic beauty for preservation and recreation.

1970 First Earth Day celebrated on April 22.

Environmental Protection Agency created.

1972 Congress passes Clean Water Act, forbidding discharges of pollutants into navigable waters.

Oregon passes the nation's first bottle recycling law.

The EPA bars registration and interstate sales of DDT because of its persistence in the environment and accumulation in the food chain.

1973 Representatives of 80 nations sign the Convention of International Trade in Endangered Species of Wild Fauna and Flora, which prohibits commercial trade in 375 endangered species of wild animals.

1974 F. Sherwood Rowland and Mario Molinas warn that chlorofluorocarbons (CFCs) are destroying the ozone layer.

1976 Congress passes Toxic Substances Control Act to control hazardous industrial chemicals.

1978 Community of Love Canal, near Niagara, N.Y., evacuated after hazardous waste dumps are uncovered. EPA declares site safe in 1990.

1979 Nuclear reactor at Three Mile Island, near Harrisburg, Pa., suffers partial meltdown; radiation confined to reactor dome.

1980 Congress passes Comprehensive Environmental Response, Compensation and Liability Act (the "Superfund") to clean up hazardous waste sites.

1984 More than 2,000 die and thousands more are injured by toxic gas from an accident at the U.S.-owned Union Carbide plant in Bhopal, India.

1985 British scientists discover that a "hole" in the ozone layer develops over Antarctica each winter.

The U.S. sets up a Conservation Reserve Program to remove environmentally sensitive farmland from agricultural use.

1986 A worldwide ban on whaling begins.

Chernobyl nuclear reactor number 4 explodes and burns, causing 31 deaths within days, shortening the lives of thousands, and forcing the evacuation of hundreds of square miles in Soviet Ukraine for an unknown length of time.

1988 The U.S. Ocean Dumping Ban Act mandates an end to ocean dumping of industrial waste and sewage sludge.

1989 Exxon *Valdez* grounds, leaking 35,000 tons of oil into Prince William Sound, Alaska.

Thirteen industrial nations agree to halt production of CFCs by the year 2000.

1992 Representatives from 178 countries attend the first Earth Summit in Rio de Janeiro, where they sign treaties pledging to increase the diversity of animal and plant species and to halt global warming.

1994 U.S. Fish and Wildlife Service recommends that status of American bald eagle be reduced from "endangered" to "threatened" in most of the U.S..

1995 The United Nations Working Group I of the Intergovernmental Panel on Climate Change endorses global warming, reporting that "the balance of evidence suggests that there is a discernible human influence on global climate."

1996 The U.S. National Oceanic and Atmospheric Administration reports that measurements show that a global campaign to lower production of chemicals that damage the ozone layer has succeeded and that by 2010 the ozone layer will have begun to recover and by 2050 the Antarctic ozone "hole" will have closed.

1997 Representatives from more than 150 countries meet in Kyoto, Japan, where they agree to reduce emissions of greenhouse gases 5.2 percent worldwide by 2010.

2001 The Intergovernmental Panel on Climate Change (IPCC) reports that there is new and stronger evidence that most of the warming in the last half century is due to human activities.

2002 The United Nations World Summit on Sustainable Development in Johannesburg, South Africa, agrees on a program of sustainable development to reduce poverty while protecting the earth's natural resources.

2005 Thought extinct since 1944, the ivory-billed woodpecker is sighted in the swamps of Arkansas.

2007 The IPCC reports that global warming is unequivocal, and is influenced by human activity.

would increase tenfold, from 5 to 52 days. Rome would go from 6 to 55 days and Tokyo from 5 to 41.

Higher temperatures have an even more dire effect than increased numbers of hot days. Increased heat expands the volume of ocean water, and also increases flows to the oceans through melting of glaciers and ice caps, leading to a rise in sea level.

Sea level rise Climatologists generally expect the sea level to rise between 3.4 inches and almost three feet (.09 to .88 meters) by the end of this century (as compared to 1990). Generally speaking, a rise in sea level would be uniform, both geographically and seasonally, because sea level is a global phenomenon. The impact of such a rise, however, would vary greatly from place to place. A three-foot (1 m) rise would inundate 7,000 square miles (18,000 km^2) of dry land—an area the size of Massachusetts—in the United States, mostly in the Southeast. It would also destroy a comparable area of coastal wetlands, erode recreational beaches 100 to 200 meters, exacerbate coastal flooding, and increase the salinity of aquifers and estuaries. It is likely that the people of an industrialized continental nation such as the United States could sustain the population shifts caused by such climatic changes. However, an estimated one-third of the world's population—about 1.75 billion people, today—lives within 40 miles of the sea, mostly along low-lying floodplains and estuaries. How the low-lying Bangladesh or the island nations of the Pacific can or will respond to such forces is impossible to see.

Increasing global temperatures will be accompanied by rising sea levels. The most recent (2007) estimates are that sea levels will rise by between 7 and 23 inches (.18 and .59 meters) by the end of the 21st century (as compared with 1980-1999). These estimates exclude future rapid changes in ice flows, which are difficult to model.) Sea levels will rise for two reasons: warming directly expands the volume of existing seawater and causes melting of land ice, which increases the total amount of water in the oceans. The effective rise in sea level in any region, given global changes, also depends on local factors such as land subsidence.

▶ **THE OZONE LAYER**

There are two distinct problems associated with the chemical ozone (O$_3$): ground-level ozone, the main component of smog (discussed under "Air Pollution," below), and stratospheric ozone. The primary difference between the two problems is that at ground level there is too much ozone, while in the stratosphere there is not enough.

The problem of stratospheric ozone depletion is closely related to global warming in that the chlorofluorocarbons (see below) that are its principal cause are greenhouse gases, but the science is different. Stratospheric ozone (sometimes referred to as upper-atmosphere or atmospheric ozone) absorbs most of the Sun's ultraviolet radiation. A significant reduction of the ozone layer would lead to sharp increases in the incidence of skin cancer and cataracts in humans. It is also thought that there would be serious losses of small ocean algae, which produce oxygen and break down carbon dioxide, and of bacteria important to crop production.

Complex natural forces are continually at work creating and destroying ozone in the atmosphere. This involves first the breakdown of individual molecules of oxygen (O$_2$) into atomic oxygen (O), through the absorption of ultraviolet radiation. In turn, each atomic oxygen normally combines with an additional molecule of O$_2$ to form ozone (O$_3$). Destruction of ozone can be caused by the occasional recombination of ozone with atomic oxygen to form two molecules of O$_2$. As long as the Earth's sunlit atmosphere contains molecular oxygen, as it has for more than one billion years, ozone will be maintained in this dynamic balance.

In 1974, scientists saw the first suggestion that a group of chemicals known as chlorofluorocarbons (CFCs) was destroying the ozone balance by adding chlorine to the atmosphere. Chemically inert, nontoxic, and easily liquefied, CFCs were developed in the 1930s as an ammonia substitute for use in refrigeration, but their use became widespread in air conditioning, packaging and insulation, as a solvent for cleaning electronic circuit boards, and as an aerosol propellant.

It is this very absence of chemical reactivity that makes CFCs so dangerous to the ozone layer. Unlike less inert compounds, CFCs are not destroyed or removed in the lower atmosphere by rain, oxidation, or sunlight, where their lifetimes have been estimated to be between 75 and 110 years. Instead they drift into the upper atmosphere, where their chlorine components are released into the atmosphere under the effects of ultraviolet radiation. Almost all of these freed chlorine atoms find and react with the ozone, creating chlorine monoxide and molecular oxygen. In a subsequent reaction, the chlorine monoxide releases its oxygen atom to form a second molecule of oxygen, and the chlorine atom is freed once again to repeat the process. Through this continuing cycle of reactions, each chlorine atom can destroy about 100,000 molecules of ozone before the chain reaction ends. In the Antarctic, ice crystals in the air speed up reactions, producing an "ozone hole," a region of extremely low levels of atmospheric ozone, over the south polar region during the Antarctic winter. A system of cold winds called the Antarctic Vortex amplifies this effect. NASA reported that the average size of the ozone hole over the period of September 21-30, 2006, was the largest on record, at 10.6 million square miles (27.5 million km^2); and the hole on September 24, 2006, equaled the previous single-day record of 11.4 million square miles (29.5 million km^2) on September 9, 2000.

To combat ozone depletion, there have been stringent reductions in CFC use. The United States, Russia, Japan, and the nations of the European Union have eliminated CFC use and production, and there are further agreements for developing countries. Even so, adverse effects on the ozone layer from human-produced CFCs will likely continue until at least 2020.

▶ **AIR POLLUTION**

Although we tend to think of air pollution as a local problem, studies reported in 1995 demonstrate that there are widespread effects. Air pollution, they report, is so pervasive in industrial regions of northeastern North America, central Europe, and eastern Asia that it partly blocks sunlight, counteracting global warming with regional cooling. The basic law dealing with air pollution is the Clean Air Act of 1990, which directs the U.S. Environmental Protection Agency (EPA) to set standards for air quality.

The Clean Air Interstate Rule of 2005 (CAIR) addresses power plant emissions in 29 eastern states plus the District of Columbia. When fully implemented, CAIR will reduce SO$_2$ emissions in these states by over 70 percent and NO_x emissions by over 60 percent from 2003 levels.

The EPA monitors air quality at about 3,000 sites for six pollutants: particulate matter (soot and dust), sulfur dioxide, carbon monoxide (mostly from automobiles), nitrogen oxides, lead, and ozone. In addition to health concerns, the effects of air pollution on vegetation, materials, and visibility are monitored.

From 1990 to 2006, air quality had improved for each of the six criteria, and emissions had decreased as well. This isn't to say that there isn't work to be done; in 2006, about 103 million people lived in countries with pollution levels above the National Ambient Air Quality Standards. The main pollutants are discussed here.

Particulate matter (PM_{10})   The EPA measures particulate matter with an aerodynamic diameter smaller than 10 micrometers down to 2.5 micrometers. This includes dust, dirt, soot, smoke, and liquid droplets directly emitted into the air from factories, power plants, cars, construction sites, fires, and natural erosion, as well as particles formed in the atmosphere by condensation or transformation of emitted gases such as sulfur dioxide and volatile organic compounds.

Particulate matter is responsible for most adverse health effects in the lower regions of the respiratory tract. People with chronic obstructive pulmonary or cardiovascular disease, individuals with influenza, asthmatics, the elderly, and children are especially sensitive.

Sulfur dioxide (SO_2)   Ambient sulfur dioxide comes mostly from stationary-source coal and oil combustion, refineries, pulp and paper mills, and nonferrous smelters. The health hazards associated with exposure to SO_2 include impaired breathing, respiratory illness, alterations in the lungs' defenses, and aggravation of existing respiratory and cardiovascular disease. Those most sensitive to SO_2 include asthmatics and people with chronic lung disease or cardiovascular

Unhealthy Days in Selected Metropolitan Areas, 1991-2005

To measure air quality in urban areas, the Environmental Protection Agency has developed an indicator called the Air Quality Index (AQI, formerly the Pollutant Standard Index, PSI). The AQI integrates into a single number emission levels of five major pollutants: particulate matter (PM_{10}). Sulfur Dioxide (SO_2), carbon monoxide (CO), ground level ozone (O_3) and nitrogen dioxide (NO_2). An AQI of 0-50 reflects good air, 51-100 denotes moderate air, and an AQI of over 100 is classified as unhealthy (201-300 signifies very unhealthy air; 301-500 is hazardous). The following chart lists the number of days in which the AQI exceeded 100 in metropolitan areas.

Metropolitan area (no. of trend sites)	Number of Unhealthy Days							
	1991	1995	1996	1998	1999	2000	2003	2005
Riverside-San Bernardino, Calif. (47)	154	125	118	96	123	145	138	106
Bakersfield, Calif. (27)	113	107	110	78	144	132	141	90
Fresno, Calif. (19)	83	61	70	67	133	131	127	64
Los Angeles-Long Beach, Calif. (56)	168	113	94	56	56	87	88	80
Houston, Texas (29)	36	66	28	38	52	42	31	40
Knoxville, Tenn. (16)	10	26	21	54	66	41	14	18
Sacramento, Calif. (39)	44	41	44	29	69	45	22	53
Ventura, Calif. (21)	87	66	62	29	24	31	20	12
Atlanta, Ga. (21)	23	36	28	2	67	34	11	19
Memphis, Tenn.-Ark.-Miss. (15)	9	21	19	27	35	24	8	15
Philadelphia, Pa.-N.J. (44)	49	38	38	37	32	22	20	27
Baltimore, Md. (20)	50	36	28	51	40	19	20	27
Nashville, Tenn. (18)	12	26	23	30	36	19	7	11
New Orleans, La. (12)	2	20	8	7	18	17	8	5
St. Louis, Mo.-Ill. (55)	24	38	23	24	31	18	13	35
San Diego, Calif. (36)	67	48	31	33	33	31	20	9
New York, N.Y. (19)	49	21	14	18	25	19	14	16
Washington, D.C.-Md.-Va.-W.V. (46)	48	32	18	47	39	11	12	23
Phoenix-Mesa, Ariz. (25)	11	22	15	14	10	10	9	19
Cleveland-Lorain-Elyria, Ohio (42)	23	27	19	22	40	22	17	28
Cincinnati, Ohio-Ky.-Ind. (16)	19	19	10	13	16	14	10	20
Indianapolis, Ind. (25)	12	21	16	19	24	5	11	20
Pittsburgh, Pa. (57)	21	27	12	39	40	29	37	48
Detroit, Mich. (33)	27	14	13	17	20	15	19	25
El Paso, Texas (19)	7	3	6	6	5	4	7	6
Oakland, Calif. (30)	4	12	11	12	17	12	7	5
Denver, Colo. (32)	6	5	2	9	5	3	5	2
Milwaukee-Waukesha, Wis. (20)	24	14	5	12	19	5	9	18
Boston, Mass.-N.H. (21)	13	7	4	8	10	1	6	10
Seattle-Bellevue-Everett, Wash. (13)	4	2	6	3	6	7	2	1
Chicago, Ill. (51)	25	24	7	12	19	2	10	23
Las Vegas, Nev.-Ariz. (15)	0	3	14	5	8	2	5	10
Miami, Fla. (16)	1	2	1	8	7	2	1	1
Minneapolis-St.Paul, Minn.-Wis. (27)	2	5	0	1	1	2	1	6
San Francisco, Calif. (16)	0	2	0	0	10	4	0	2

Note: Figures reflect data from selected EPA trend sites. Number of unhealthy days recorded by all active EPA monitoring sites may be slightly higher in some cities. **Source:** Environmental Protection Agency, *National Air Quality and Emissions Trends Report 2005* (2007). www.epa.gov/airtrends

disease, children, and the elderly. Sulfur dioxide also damages leaves on trees and crops and it is an agent of acid rain.

Carbon monoxide (CO) Carbon monoxide is a colorless, odorless, and poisonous gas produced by incomplete burning of carbon in fuels. Carbon monoxide enters the bloodstream and disrupts delivery of oxygen to the body's organs and tissues. The health threat from carbon monoxide is serious for those who suffer from cardiovascular diseases. Healthy individuals are also affected, and exposure to elevated carbon monoxide levels is associated with impairment of visual perception and manual dexterity.

Federal regulations have succeeded in cleaning up much of the carbon monoxide pollution that plagued the U.S. in the 1980s. In 1990, 26 metropolitan areas exceeded the National Ambient Air Quality Standards for carbon monoxide at least once. Los Angeles exceeded the standard a whopping 47 times, while Las Vegas exceeded it 17 times. But in 1998, only six metropolitan areas exceeded the standard more than once. In 2000, only three cities exceeded the standard: Calexico, Calif. (2 times), Los Angeles-Long Beach, Calif (2 times), and Fairbanks, Alaska (1 time).

Nitrogen oxides (NO$_x$) These highly reactive gases play a major role, together with volatile or-

ganic compounds, in the formation of ozone. Nitrogen oxides form when fuel is burned at high temperatures. When released into the atmosphere, they are one of the major causes of smog. The two major emissions sources are cars and trucks, and stationary fuel-combustion sources such as electric-utility and industrial boilers.

Nitrogen oxides can irritate the lungs and lower resistance to respiratory infections such as influenza. Prolonged exposure to higher than normal concentrations can cause pulmonary angina. Nitrogen dioxide (NO$_2$) is also an agent of acid rain and plays a key role in nitrogen loading of forests and ecosystems. Over the past decade, Los Angeles is the only urban area that has consistently recorded violations of the EPA's annual NO$_2$ standards. Many other urban areas violate the EPA's standards on occasional hot summer days, when the Sun cooks hydrocarbons and nitrogen oxides, thus producing smog.

Ozone (O$_3$) Ground-level ozone is a colorless gas and the main component of smog. Unlike most other air pollutants, ozone is not emitted by factories or automobiles, but is formed by the interaction of volatile organic compounds (VOCs) and nitrous oxide. These reactions are stimulated by sunlight and temperature so that peak ozone levels occur typically during the warmer times of year. The severity of a smog problem in a given lo-

Emissions Estimates for EPA-Monitored Pollutants, 1970–2005 (millions of tons)

Year	Carbon monoxide (CO)	Nitrogen oxides[3] (NO$_x$)	Volatile organic compounds	Sulfur dioxide (SO$_2$)	Particulate matter (PM$_{10}$)	Lead (Pb)
1970	197.3	26.9	33.7	31.2	12.2	0.221
1975	184.0	26.4	30.2	28.0	7.0	0.160
1980	177.8	27.1	30.1	25.9	6.2	0.074
1985[1]	169.6	25.8	26.9	23.3	3.6	0.022
1990	143.6	25.2	23.1	23.1	3.2	0.005
1995	120.0	24.7	21.6	18.6	3.1	0.004
2000[1]	102.4	22.3	16.9	16.3	2.3	0.003
2005[2]	89.0	19.0	16.0	15.0	2.0	0.003

Note: Particulate matter totals before 1990 do not include estimates for fugitive dust, which arises from construction activities, mining and quarrying and paved road resuspension. It is the leading source of PM$_{10}$ emissions. 1. In 1985 and 1996 the EPA refined its methods for estimating emissions. 2. Preliminary. 3. Prior to 1990, include small percentage of emissions from fires. **Source:** Environmental Protection Agency, *Average Annual Emissions, All Criteria Pollutants*, August 2007.

Emissions Estimates for EPA-Monitored Pollutants By Source, 1970–2003 (thousand short tons)

Source	Carbon monoxide (CO) 1970	2003	Nitrogen oxides (NO$_x$) 1970	2003	Volatile organic compounds 1970	2003	Sulfur dioxide (SO$_2$) 1970	2003	Particulate matter (PM$_{10}$) 1970	2003
Fuel Combustion										
Electric utility	237	530	4,900	4,458	30	56	17,398	10,929	1,775	683
Industrial	770	1377	4,325	2,775	150	170	4,568	2,227	641	317
Other	3,625	3003	836	729	541	878	1,490	596	455	461
Chemical & Allied Processing	3,397	329	271	102	1,341	218	591	329	235	51
Metals Processing	3,644	1,422	77	91	394	72	4,775	285	1,316	141
Petroleum & Related Industries	2,179	138	240	137	1,194	380	881	323	286	38
Other Industrial Processes	620	634	187	504	270	412	846	426	5,832	410
Solvent Utilization	N.A.	73	N.A.	7	7,174	4,562	N.A.	2	N.A.	17
Storage and Transport	N.A.	241	N.A.	16	1,954	1,178	N.A.	6	N.A.	86
Waste Disposal & Recycling	7,059	1,854	440	137	1,984	427	8	32	999	386
On-Road Vehicles	163,231	58,807	12,624	7,381	16,910	4,428	273	256	480	187
Non-Road Sources	11,371	24,447	2,652	4,103	1,616	2,572	278	443	164	308
Miscellaneous[1]	7,909	14,033	330	289	1,101	704	110	88	839	19,854
Total	204,043	93,706	26,805	20,492	34,659	15,429	31,218	15,848	13,023	24,942

Note: Some columns may not sum due to independent rounding. 1. Miscellaneous includes PM$_{10}$ natural sources like fugitive dust, which arises from construction activities, mining and quarrying and paved road resuspension. It is the leading source of PM$_{10}$ emissions. **Source:** Environmental Protection Agency, August 2004. www.epa.gov/airtrends.

ale is directly related to the temperature and ultraviolet radiation intensity in that area. While the problems associated with ozone depletion (see "The Ozone Layer," above) and ground-level ozone are usually viewed separately, it is worth noting that as upper-atmosphere ozone is depleted, more ultraviolet radiation reaches the Earth and stimulates the production of ozone/smog.

Both VOCs and nitrous oxide are emitted by transportation and industrial sources as diverse as autos, chemical manufacturing, dry cleaners, paint shops, and other solvent-using industries. High levels of ozone affect people with impaired respiratory systems, such as asthmatics, and exposure to relatively low concentrations of ozone for only a few hours has been found to significantly reduce lung function in normal, healthy people during exercise. This is generally accompanied by symptoms including chest pain, coughing, sneezing, and pulmonary congestion. Ozone is also responsible each year for several billion dollars worth of domestic crop yield losses, and it causes noticeable damage to leaves in many crops and species of trees.

Lead (Pb) People can be exposed to lead via air, diet, and ingestion of lead in soil and dust. Lead accumulates in the body in blood, bone, and soft tissue, and because it is not readily excreted, it also affects the kidneys, nervous system, and blood-forming organs. Excessive exposure to lead may cause seizures, mental retardation, and/or behavioral disorders. Even at low doses, lead exposure is harmful; infants and children are especially susceptible to low doses of lead and often suffer central nervous system damage.

Lead gasoline additives, nonferrous smelters, and battery plants are the most significant contributors to atmospheric lead emissions. The decline in the share of lead emissions from internal-combustion engines of all kinds is due primarily to the introduction of unleaded gasoline in 1975, for use in automobiles equipped with catalytic control devices, which reduce emissions of carbon monoxide, VOCs, and nitrogen oxides. Today more than 99.8 percent of the lead once added to gasoline in the United States has been removed.

Air pollution worldwide The worst air pollution is undoubtedly in Asia. According to the World Health Organization, more than 1.5 million Asians die each year from the effects of air pollution alone, and another half million die from water pollution.

Anything over 100 micrograms of particles per cubic meter of air is considered dangerous, yet in cities like Taiyuan, China, and Delhi, India, the levels routinely top 500 micrograms. The threat is compounded by the fact that so many people in these areas cook indoors with coal briquettes. Particles in the air are a major cause of respiratory ailments in Asia; such ailments are a leading cause of death in China.

▶ACID RAIN

Acid rain refers to acidic precipitation of all kinds, including rain, snow, and fog, as well as acidic dust particles. The main component of acid rain is sulfuric acid, a product of reactions of sulfur dioxide released by industrial and power plants fueled by coal or oil. Another major agent of acid rain is nitrogen oxides, which form nitric acid and which are found in motor vehicle exhaust and in emissions from industrial plants that burn any fuel at high temperatures. Burning vegetation also produces nitric acid, as well as formic acid and acetic acid. Acid rain can travel great distances from its source: 10 percent to 80 percent increases in acidity have been detected as far away as 2,500 miles from a source.

Acid rain has been implicated in the destruction of lakes, the weathering of man-made structures, and the death of trees, crops, and animals. When acid rain ends up in lakes, it can increase the level of acidity to such an extent that the lake loses its ability to buffer the acidity with alkaline chemicals from the surrounding soil and rocks. How quickly this occurs is to some extent determined by the nature of the surrounding soil, which means that lakes in some regions are more vulnerable to the effects of acid rain than others. As lakes become more acidic, small invertebrates

World Carbon Dioxide Emissions from Consumption and Flaring of Fossil Fuels, 1992–2004

2004 Rank, Country	Millions of metric tons	
	1992	2004
1. U.S.	5,068.01	5,912.21
2. China	2,421.74	4,707.28
3. Russia	2,009.96	1,684.84
4. Japan	1,048.58	1,262.10
5. India	654.37	1,112.84
6. Germany	883.82	862.23
7. Canada	483.27	587.98
8. United Kingdom	571.86	579.68
9. South Korea	289.94	496.76
10. Italy	411.21	484.98

Note: 1 metric ton is equal to 2,204.62 pounds. **Source:** U.S. Dept. of Energy, Energy Information Administration, *International Energy Annual*, (2007).

Ozone in Metropolitan Areas, 2001–2005

The **Air Quality Index (AQI)** is used to determine the amount of pollution in the air for a specific area. It can be measured by any variable of pollution. The following metropolitan areas had the most number of days in 2005 that their AQI ozone levels exceeded 100, and are ranked accordingly.

Metropolitan area	Average number of days exceeding standards		
	2001	2003	2005
Riverside-San Bernardino, California	92	101	81
Bakersfield, California	85	116	54
Fresno, California	92	96	29
Sacramento, California	35	32	29
Houston, Texas	26	30	28
Baltimore, Maryland	26	10	23
Fort Worth-Arlington, Texas	17	22	22
Los Angeles-Long Beach, California	29	61	22
Philadelphia, Pennsylvania-New Jersey	27	13	20
St. Louis, Missouri-Illinois	14	9	20

Source: Environmental Protection Agency Office of Air and Radiation, *Ozone Emissions in Selected Metropolitan Areas*

die off. This begins a reaction up the food chain: as the smallest organisms disappear, the food supply for larger vertebrates such as fish and frogs is depleted. Because lakes are not closed ecosystems, the demise of these organisms also affects land dwellers that depend on them, directly or indirectly, for survival.

A 1999 federal study revealed that regulation has succeeded in reducing harmful levels of sulfur dioxide in the air, but that the problem remains serious. At current rates, more than half of the 2,800 lakes in the Adirondacks will be too acidic to support life by the year 2040. The study also concludes that the San Gabriel Mountains near Los Angeles are already "saturated" with nitrogen, meaning that excess nitrogen is seeping into the surrounding waters.

▶ WATER POLLUTION

Although the bad effect of air pollution on health was suspected even earlier, the first proven environmental cause of illness was water pollution. In England, a famous demonstration by physician John Snow in 1854 showed that removing the handle of a pump could reduce the incidence of cholera by depriving people living near a contaminated well from using the water. Chlorine used for water purification was already known at that time, and by the 20th century most major cities in the United States provided treated water.

Problems not directly connected to health also were recognized in the 19th century. Mining in California was, in some locations, polluting the water supply so greatly that crops could not be grown; a law against using water in extracting ores was instituted in the state in 1884. Industrial water pollution was also recognized, although not stopped. Five years after Dr. Snow's famous demonstration, a new source of water pollution was introduced when the first oil well was drilled.

The 20th century brought with it additional forms of water pollution. A series of revolutions in agriculture included use of artificial fertilizers, introduction of long-lasting pesticides, and concentration of animal wastes. Each change also introduced new forms of water pollution from runoff—water from rain or snow that fails to sink into the soil. "Point sources," such as sewage pipes and factory waste ponds, were now supplemented with the "nonpoint sources" of farming.

In 1999, the EPA released its first ever national index on the quality of the nation's 2,111 watersheds. The index asserts that 21 percent of the watersheds have serious problems, including fish-consumption advisories, pollution, and loss of wetlands. Another 36 percent are of only moderate quality.

The 1972 Clean Water Act was intended to solve many of the nation's water pollution problems, but it has been only partially effective in doing so. In 1972, only about a third of the nation's rivers were safe for fishing and swimming. That number improved to more than 50 percent during the 1970s and 1980s, but by 1998, the levels of pollution had crept back up again. The primary cause was no longer industrial pollution, residue from mining, and untreated sewage; instead, nonpoint sources from runoff, both agricultural and municipal, had taken over as the older point sources were eliminated.

Drinking Water

Americans have for many years taken their drinking water for granted. But despite this complacency, there are many threats to the water supply. These include biological threats to health from contamination, dangerous chemicals in the water supply from a variety of sources, and toxic elements introduced by water treatment or defects in plumbing. A related problem is that high water levels during storms overwhelm both industrial and municipal water treatment. This last source is somewhat more easily controlled than other nonpoint pollution, and revisions of the Clean Water Act in 1987, which went into effect in 1992, attack this problem for urban runoff at the city and county levels.

The Safe Drinking Water Act Amendments of 1996 further strengthened and expanded drinking water protections. They increased standards for microbial contamination such as cryptosporidium, which has been the source of several disease outbreaks, including a 1993 instance in Milwaukee, in which more than 100 people died.

Many municipal water supply systems regularly are found to contain levels of bacterial contamination that exceed EPA standards. Most, but not all, bacterial contamination stems from the use of surface waters—rivers, lakes, and reservoirs. The other major source of water is groundwater—subsurface water contained for the most part in small cavities, or pores, in rock or soil. One common way to obtain unpolluted groundwater is to dig deep wells that find "fossil" water that has been at those levels for thousands of years. This source, however, is not renewable. Most shallow wells obtain their water from groundwater that recently was surface water and therefore subject to greater contamination.

Groundwater pollution is especially difficult to remedy. Almost all solutions are expensive and, in many cases, not feasible at any price. Such remedies include pumping detoxification agents into the ground or treating the water before use.

Groundwater can be contaminated by industrial pollutants stored or released in ways that put them in contact with the water supply; by leakage from underground storage of volatile chemicals, such as gasoline, cleaning fluid, or petroleum; and by seepage into the soil of agricultural pesticides. A privately funded review of federal and state water tests by the Environmental Working Group reported in 1994 that the water supplies used by 14.1 million Americans contain agricultural pesticides in amounts that would be banned if these levels were found in food.

Formerly one of the main sources of ground water contamination had been municipal landfills, but most of these are now sealed with clay liners to prevent seepage; and truly hazardous chemicals, such as mercury or lead from batteries or volatile organic compounds, are banned from landfills.

Some drinking water pollution takes place between the time the water comes from the well or from a surface source and the time it leaves faucets. Even though water from municipal plants is kept lead-free, service pipes, home plumbing, and some brass fixtures can leach lead into water, especially hot water. People who depend on private wells can have additional problems, as most of the pumps sold in recent years contain lead in brass or bronze parts. Lead from plumbing or from pumps can be flushed from drinking or cooking water by letting the water run before use, but for water supplied by submerged pumps in deep wells, it may be necessary to run water for as long as 10 minutes to get to the lead-free supply.

Even municipal treatment of drinking water is suspected of potentially dangerous side effects. About 70 percent of all Americans drink water

Major Ship Oil Spills

Date	Ship Name	Location	Oil Lost (metric tons)
1979	Atlantic Empress	off Tobago, West Indies	287,000
1991	ABT Summer	700 nautical miles off Angola	260,000
1983	Castillo de Bellver	off Saldanha Bay, South Africa	252,000
1978	Amoco Cadiz	off Brittany, France	223,000
1991	Haven	Genoa, Italy	144,000
1988	Odyssey	700 nautical miles off Nova Scotia	132,000
1967	Torrey Canyon	Scilly Isles, UK	119,000
1972	Sea Star	Gulf of Oman	115,000
1976	Urquiola	La Coruna, Spain	100,000
1977	Hawaiian Patriot	300 nautical miles off Honolulu	95,000
1979	Independenta	Bosphorus, Turkey	95,000
2002	Prestige	sea off northern Spain	63,000

Note: One metric ton = 1.1 U.S. tons. Some spills did not impact coastlines, which is why some ship names are unfamiliar to the general public. The Exxon Valdez (1989) spill is estimated to be number 35 in the list of large spills. **Source:** International Tanker Owners Pollution Federation.

that has been disinfected by chlorination. But chlorine can react with organic material in water to form compounds such as chloroform that have been implicated in causing cancer in rats and mice. Except possibly for persons who have some reason for extra caution, however, the benefits of chlorination far outweigh any known danger.

In 2002, the World Health Organization estimated that 1.1 billion people (17 percent worldwide) lacked access to safe drinking water.

Ocean Pollution

Pollution of the oceans disturbs marine ecosystems. It is thought to be the trigger for the algal growth that has all but eliminated the scallop fishery in Long Island Sound, for example. Other ocean fisheries in protected bays and sounds have also been damaged by pollution.

Ocean pollution from oil is primarily noted by the public when an oil well at sea is damaged or when an oil-carrying ship leaks large amounts of oil into the sea as a result of an accident like the 1989 Exxon *Valdez* disaster. Despite this perception, most oil pollution in the ocean actually comes from municipal and industrial runoff, cleaning of ships' bilges or tanks, and other routine events.

Ocean pollution is often in evidence on beaches. Tar balls from oil spills, plastic, and sometimes sewage wash up on beaches. Occasionally beaches have to be closed because of high bacteria counts in the water, making swimming hazardous.

Plastic, which generally does not break down in the ocean, is a hazard to larger organisms, such as endangered sea turtles. An international treaty prohibits disposal of plastic wastes that can kill or maim creatures that become entangled, but the treaty is very difficult to enforce.

▶ SOLID WASTE

Many areas of the United States continue to face serious problems in safely and effectively managing the garbage they generate. As a nation, we are generating more trash than ever before, and as the generation of municipal solid waste (MSW) increases, the capacity to handle it is decreasing. Municipal solid waste is distinct from industrial wastes produced by factories, tailings from mines, construction and demolition waste, sludge from sewage treatment, and junked machinery.

Disposing of Solid Waste The average person disposed of 4.5 pounds of solid waste each day in 2005, up significantly from 1960, when per

person disposal was 2.7 pounds. This waste consists of paper (34.2 percent), yard trimmings (13.1 percent), food scraps (11.7 percent), plastics (11.9 percent), metals (7.6 percent), rubber, leather, and textiles (7.3 percent), glass (5.2 percent), wood (5.7 percent), and other materials (3.4 percent). There are four primary methods of dealing with this waste: putting it in landfills, incinerating it, recycling it, and composting. But a fifth option, source reduction, may be the most effective way of reducing the nation's volume of MSW, which totals nearly 250 million tons per year.

Landfills By far the greatest amount of MSW is sent to MSW landfills, of which there were 1,654 in 2005, a drop from nearly 8,000 in 1988. However, it is important to note that while the number of landfills has decreased, the average size has increased. Landfills are the cheapest method of disposing of MSW but they pose a number of environmental problems. Because most landfills are dry, they preserve garbage by cutting it off from the rotting influences of air and moisture. Even biodegradable materials do not decay; newspapers 40 years old can still be read and hot dogs thrown out years before look more or less unchanged.

EPA regulations favor dry landfills for two reasons. As biodegradation in wet landfills occurs there is a buildup of hazardous methane gas, and contaminated water leaching out of landfills (leachate) can pollute the surrounding groundwater. But wet landfills have their supporters, who argue that by enhancing decay, a landfill's biological life can be compressed from 40-to-50 years to 5-to-10 years. Since landfills can contain hundreds of hazardous chemicals, they require continuous monitoring anyway; so shortening their active biological life can yield significant savings. Moreover, by decreasing the volume of trash through biodegradation, landfills can be kept open longer. This is important because some estimates indicate that 80 percent of the nation's landfills will be closed within 20 years, and people are increasingly adamant about not having landfills in their communities, which makes it harder to site new landfills.

Incineration/combustion One popular method of disposing of municipal waste used to be simply to burn it. In the 1940s there were approximately 700 municipal incinerators in the United States. Despite the efficiency with which they reduced the volume of waste, they stank, their stacks emitted sizable particles of ash, and they produced noxious gases. For these aesthetic rather than environmental reasons, their numbers declined dramatically in the 1950s. By the time of the Clean Air Act of 1970, there were only 67 incinerators still in operation—most with no energy recovery and no air pollution controls.

Incinerator use increased in the 1980s and early 1990s as space for landfills became scarce, and as the energy produced by incineration became a valuable commodity. But in May, 1994, the U.S. Supreme Court ruled that waste from incinerators had to be treated as toxic on the same basis as any other waste.

In that same month, the Court ruled that localities could not prevent landfills from taking waste away from incinerators if the landfills offered better bargains. Because landfill was usually cheaper, few chose to incinerate their waste, and few municipalities could afford to subsidize the cost of incinerators. Within six months of the Court's decision, plans for 77 proposed incinerators were canceled.

In 2007, 14 percent of solid waste was incinerated. There were 88 combustors in the U.S. with energy recovery capabilities, and which were able to incinerate up to 99,000 tons of waste per day.

Recycling/composting Recycling and composting recovered 32 percent (79 million tons) of waste generated in 2005. Recycling rates in 2005 reached 50 percent for paper and paperboard, 62 percent for yard trimmings, 44.8 percent for aluminum beer and soft drink containers, and 99 percent for automobile batteries. By 2005, almost 9,000 curbside recycling programs had sprouted up across the nation, and about 500 material recovery facilities had been established to process the collected materials.

Recycling and composting also have the potential to generate revenues from the sale of secondary materials. According to the EPA, material recycled in 1996 had a value of $3.6 billion; with a 35 percent recycling rate, the value of material recycled in 2005 would be $5.2 billion. Costs of recycling are still high, but these are expected to decline as recycling programs mature and become fully integrated with the total MSW management system.

Yet some recycling is a money-losing proposition for municipalities, and one of the most successful recycling programs, for aluminum cans, depends in large part on the deposit programs run by many states. The first such "bottle bill" was passed in Oregon in 1971, and although many states have followed suit, no state program offers a recycling program for plastic water bottles. In 2007, the Container Recycling Institute estimated that 18 million barrels of crude-oil equivalent were needed to replace the bottles that were trashed in 2005. In one average year, Americans drink more than 30 billion single-serving bottles of water.

Source reduction Many experts believe that the key to solving the municipal waste problem is source reduction—minimizing the volume of products used and the toxins they contain, and extending their lives in use. Removal of toxins enhances the safety of recycling, landfilling, and combustion, while volume reduction helps to extend the capacity of existing waste systems.

A broad variety of products and packaging that reduce waste and save money have been developed. By reducing the textured design on napkins, for example, the McDonald's Corporation found that it could fit 23 percent more napkins into a shipping container, saving 294,000 pounds of corrugated cardboard and 150 truckload shipment annually. Containers and packaging represented approximately 28 percent of the materials source reduced in 2000. More than 55 million tons of waste were source reduced in the U.S. in 2000, and to keep the program alive, in 2007 the EPA offered cooperative agreements that award $15,000 or more in programmatic funds.

In 2007, the first bill to limit the use of plastic bags in grocery and drug stores was passed in San Francisco. Similar bag-banning measures were being considered in Boston, Baltimore, Portland, and Steamboat Springs, Colo. Other initiatives include the introduction of a state bill in New York that would require businesses to reduce their use of plastic bags by 50 percent by 2010.

▶ HAZARDOUS WASTE

Superfund In 1980, Congress enacted the Comprehensive Environmental Response, Compensation, and Liability Act (CERCLA), better known as the Superfund, a $1.6 billion, five-year program to clean up thousands of hazardous waste sites. The fund was renewed in 1986 by the Superfund Amendments and Reauthorization Act (SARA). The EPA, which administers the Superfund, estimated in 2006 that one in four Americans lived within 4 miles of a toxic waste site.

The EPA evaluates hazardous waste sites for their levels of soil and water contamination, the mobility of toxins, and their proximity to human food supplies. (Contamination of petroleum, however, is excluded from this evaluation.) It then ranks the sites on a numerically based system that factors in risks to groundwater, surface water, and air. The highest ranking sites are placed on the EPA's National Priorities List (NPL). CERCLA also allows states and territories to designate one top-priority site regardless of its score; there are several such sites that would not make the NPL on the basis of their numerical score alone.

Once the EPA deems a site a national priority, it can take two types of action. It can remove the hazard in an emergency action limited to one year and/or $2 million. Or it can try to compel the individual or company responsible for the problem to provide a long-term solution.

In 2003, the EPA reported that Congress appropriates nearly $1.3 billion each year to address Superfund contamination. While the total number of sites needing cleanup is decreasing, the EPA is now addressing bigger, more complex sites. More than half of all the sites have been cleaned up and progress is being made at the others. In August, 2007, the first military-base Superfund cleanup was privatized in California.

Nuclear Waste Nuclear waste in the United States comes from nuclear weapons production facilities, nuclear power plants, medical equipment (primarily used in radiation treatments), industrial sources of radioactivity used as a more powerful alternative to X rays, and residues from uranium mining. Nuclear waste is often grouped into two categories, labeled "low-level" and "high-level." Low-level waste is slightly radioactive, often from exposure to a high-level source. High-level waste is often grouped as either civilian, mainly spent fuel from nuclear reactors, or military, wastes produced in the manufacture of nuclear weapons.

The problem with nuclear waste is that it is radioactive and can remain that way for years—in some cases, thousands of years. Early methods of disposal included dumping the wastes at sea and suspending them in a liquid or in cement and injecting the radioactive combination into wells. The United States was among the signatories of a 1976 international convention banning ocean dumping and stopped deep-well injection in 1984.

Current plans call for consortiums of states to develop sites for storage of low-level wastes. One such "temporary" site is in Barnwell County, S.C., which has handled low-level waste for 37 states since 1970. Meanwhile, the federal government continues to search for suitable sites for storage of high-level wastes from nuclear power plants and for very long-lived radioactive materials from weapons production. For the time being, these wastes remain on the sites where they were generated.

In 1998, the EPA certified the Department of Energy's Waste Isolation Pilot Plan in Carlsbad, N.M., the nation's first deep-underground facility for disposal of transuranic waste generated from defense activities. (Transuranic wastes consist primarily of sludges, tools, rags, glassware, and protective clothing that has been contaminated with radioactive elements from weapons production.) The facility is approximately 2,100 feet (640 meters) underground in excavated, natural salt formations. The first shipment of transuranic waste was delivered to the facility in March of 1999. By 2010, shipments from 23 military waste sites from across the nation to this site will reduce

Superfund Hazardous Waste Sites, 1981–2005

Date	Number of sites	Date	Number of sites
Oct. 23, 1981[1]	115	Feb. 23, 1994	1,190
Dec. 30, 1982[1]	418	Sept. 29, 1995	1,232
Sept. 8, 1983	406	June 17, 1996	1,227
Oct. 15, 1984	538	April, 1997	1,208
June 10, 1986	703	Feb. 1998	1,197
July 22, 1987	802	July 22, 1999	1,226
Oct. 4, 1989	981	July 31, 2000	1,236
Feb. 21, 1990	1,081	March 2002	1,223
Feb. 11, 1991	1,189	Sept. 2003	1,233
Feb., 1992	1,183	Sept. 23, 2004	1,244
May 10, 1993	1,201	July 1, 2005	1,241

1. Proposed sites only. Final sites not calculated until release of first National Priorities list in 1983. **Source:** Environmental Protection Agency, National Priorities List. www.epa.gov/superfund/sites

States with the Most NPL Hazardous Waste Sites, 2005

State	Nonfederal	Federal	Total
New Jersey	105	8	113
Pennsylvania	88	6	94
California	69	24	93
New York	85	4	89
Michigan	66	0	66
Florida	44	6	50
Washington	33	13	46
Texas	38	4	42
Illinois	37	4	41
Wisconsin	38	0	38

Source: Environmental Protection Agency, National Priorities List (July 1, 2005). www.epa.gov/superfund/sites

the number of Americans living within 50 miles of nuclear waste from 61 million to 4 million. Of course, the 113,000 people living within 50 miles of Carlsbad (as well as many New Mexicans beyond that radius) were understandably opposed, and fought its operation since the site was first proposed in 1974.

The Nuclear Regulatory Commission is the agency charged with monitoring the disposal of waste generated by civilian-operated nuclear reactors. However, most of the nuclear waste in the United States is the by-product of the federal government's nuclear weapons programs. Disposal and monitoring of this waste—which includes millions of cubic yards of contaminated soil and other debris at more than 100 sites in 32 states and the Marshall Islands—is the responsibility of the Department of Energy, the Department of Defense, the Nuclear Waste Technical Review Board, and the Office of the Nuclear Waste Negotiator. Total cost of the cleanup could be about $300-$400 billion over 30 years.

The difficulty of resolving nuclear waste disposal issues is illustrated by the saga of Yucca Mountain, Nevada, which was approved by Congress in 2002 as the nation's first long-term geologic repository for spent nuclear fuel and high-level radioactive waste. If the Nuclear Regulatory Commission grants the site a license, Yucca Mountain could begin accepting waste in 2025, with closure and decommissioning slated to begin in 2125. In the meantime, the site (about 100 miles northwest of Las Vegas) has been the subject of fierce opposition not only in Nevada, but also in states along proposed transportation routes for nuclear waste. The NRC released the Yucca Mountain plan for final review in February, 2007.

▶ HABITATS

The place where a species lives and its surroundings, both living and non-living, is called a habitat. Broadly speaking, habitats include forests, grasslands, deserts, tundra, and wetlands. But there are many specific types of habitats within each of these categories. The habitat of a giant panda, for example, is a bamboo forest in China, not a pine forest in Canada; that of a tuna is the open ocean, not a Florida lake.

When a species' habitat is destroyed or altered, the species may suffer dramatic population declines. For example, because so much of North America's native grasslands have been replaced by farms and other developments, many songbirds have been left without homes and food, and their populations have decreased. Similarly, destruction of China's bamboo forests threaten the giant panda with extinction.

When a species becomes extinct, the Earth's biodiversity is diminished. Biodiversity is all the organisms in the world or in a particular habitat, including all their individual variations. Loss of biodiversity affects humans as well as the threatened species. For example, all major food crops depend on new genetic material from the wild to remain healthy and productive. Noted the 1992 U.N. Earth Summit report, "Our planet's essential goods and services depend on the variety and variability of genes, species, populations and ecosystems."

The major reasons for loss of biological diversity are habitat destruction and modification, overhunting and overfishing, climate change, pollution, and the introduction of so-called alien species (non-native species, such as African tulip trees in Hawaii and Amazon water hyacinths in Africa's Lake Victoria; native species often are unable to compete with the introduced species).

▶ RAIN FORESTS

Rain forests are defined as forests that grow in regions that receive more than 70 inches (1.8 meters) of rain each year. Some rain forests occur in temperate places, such as southern Chile or the northwest coast of North America, but the majority are found in the tropics. Tropical rain forests cover more than 2 billion acres (0.8 billion hectares) or about 7 percent of the Earth's land surface.' They are found in Central and South America, equatorial Africa, Southeast Asia, and northeastern Australia.

It is estimated that the world may be losing more than 49 million acres (20 million hectares) of tropical forest each year. As the 2000s began, Brazil was losing 12.5-22.5 million acres (5-9 million hectares) of rain forest annually; India was losing 3.7 million acres (1.5 million hectares); and Indonesia was losing 2.2 million acres (0.9 million hectares). Other countries experiencing rapid losses included Myanmar, Costa Rica, Sri Lanka, Vietnam, Thailand, the Philippines, and Ghana.

Tropical rain forests are lush habitats, filled with a greater variety of organisms than any other type of habitat. According to a U.S. National Academy of Sciences report, a typical patch of rain forest covering four square miles (10.4 km²) contains 750 species of trees, 750 species of other plants, 125 species of mammals, 400 species of birds, 100 species of reptiles, and 60 species of amphibians.

The dominant plants in a tropical rain forest are broad-leaved evergreens, while Northern Hemisphere temperate rain forests are filled with needle-leaved conifers. In both, the tallest trees form a dense canopy high above the forest floor. Vines climb up the trees in search of sunlight. In a tropical rain forest, nonparasitic plants grow high in the canopy, using the large trees as perches. In both types of forest, the floor is in deep shade; comparatively few shrubs and grasses grow there.

The rich plant life supports food chains that include many of the world's most spectacular animals: brightly colored frogs, fierce harpy eagles, agile monkeys, powerful tigers, slow-moving sloths, and huge columns of army ants, among many others.

While the diversity of plant life in rain forests is rich, the soil generally is not. The lush plants take up so much of the nutrients in rain forests that little is left for the soil below. A study of a rain forest in Venezuela found that 75 percent of the nutrients were in living organisms like plants and trees, 17 percent were in debris, and only 8 percent were in the soil. When an organism dies and decomposes in a rain forest, the nutrients in its cells are quickly absorbed by nearby plants.

Deforestation has many sources. Individuals often cut down rain forest trees to clear land on which to raise crops and build ranches. But erosion and poor soil fertility soon make these farms and ranches worthless. Large commercial operations deforest vast areas for lumber, paper, and other products, much of which are exported to pay debts owed to foreign governments and banks. Development projects such as roads, hydroelectric dams, and mines also destroy large areas of rain forest.

▶ WETLANDS

A wetland is a location other than a river, lake, or open ocean in which the soil for at least part of the year contains as much water as it will hold (the soil is saturated with water). Saturated soil often slows decomposition of organic matter, resulting in a thin mud or muck, or in the decayed plant remains known as peat. Common names for wetlands include: **Potholes**, which are dry land most of the year, but seasonally become shallow ponds; **Tidal flats**, which are underwater at high tide but become muddy land at low tide; **Permafrost**, which is saturated soil that is frozen most of the year at the surface, and year-round below the surface; **Bogs**, which contain saturated soil and organic material all year, but have little or no standing water; **Marshes,** which contain standing shallow water and low vegetation; and **Swamps,** where trees grow on small hillocks surrounded by standing water. Often these informal categories overlap in a given wetland.

Wetlands produce numerous invaluable benefits. They provide a natural means of flood control, absorbing water from nearby rivers and lakes during periods of high runoff. This buffers the impact of storms and reduces shoreline erosion, thereby protecting against the loss of life and property. And by filtering out pollutants and trapping sediment, wetlands help maintain water quality.

Wetlands are the nurseries for many fish, almost all amphibians, and various birds and mammals. For instance, coastal wetlands are spawning grounds and nurseries for more than two-thirds of U.S. commercial fisheries, a $10 billion a year industry.

Despite all the benefits associated with wetlands, the definition of what is and is not a wetland is still a bone of contention among environmentalists (who would like to preserve the swampy areas), developers (who would like to drain them and erect housing complexes), and farmers (who would like to divert the water to their crops). In 1987, the U.S. Army Corp. of Engineers defined a wetland as "any ground that has mucky or peat-based soils, nourishes specific plant life, and is saturated with water at least seven days a year." Partisans on all sides of the issue have sought since then to modify that definition. Since colonial days, the contiguous United States has lost 53 percent of its wetlands.

The majority of the nation's wetlands are located in Alaska (170 to 200 million acres). Ohio, Indiana, Iowa, and California have lost the greatest percentage of their wetlands, but the wet states of Florida and Louisiana have lost the greatest total number of acres of wetlands.

A report released from the Association of State Wetland Managers in 2006 stated that between 1998 and 2004, 191,750 acres of wetlands were gained in total, due mostly to the efforts of the U.S. Fish and Wildlife Service Coastal Program that in 2007 boasted nearly 90 projects across the country to restore destroyed habitats. Tidal salt marshes and shrub swamps, however, continue to be lost at significant levels.

ENDANGERED SPECIES

A species is a specific kind of organism, such as the common earthworm, the daffodil, the American opossum, or the human. There are about 1.75

million known species of all kinds, including plants, microorganisms, mammals, and fish. This is thought to represent no more than about 10 percent of all species. (And if the results of some surveys of rain forest canopies in Panama are correct, there may be as many as 30 million insect species alone.) Since life developed more than 600 million years ago, innumerable species have appeared and become extinct. Today, biological diversity faces a rate of species destruction greater than any since the mass extinctions of the dinosaurs 65 million years ago.

Animal and plant species are threatened on a number of fronts. Their natural habitats face destruction through deforestation, wetlands loss, and urban sprawl, and are also affected by processes that derive from global warming such as shifting climate and vegetation zones. Another problem is the shift to "monocultures" in agriculture, producing only one strain of crop for food. Some types of environments present special vulnerabilities. As an example, islands have small populations, limited habitats, and allow the introduction of new (alien) species easily

International controls

The U.S. Endangered Species Act of 1966 is the chief bulwark protecting species in the United States. The United States is also a signatory to international treaties that protect species. The Convention on International Trade in Endangered Species of Wild Fauna and Flora (CITES) has been in force since 1975. Signed by more than 120 nations, it lists species for which international trade in the live organisms, meat, lumber, or other parts of species is banned or restricted. While smugglers are thought to violate CITES restrictions regularly in what is believed to be a $5 billion annual illegal trade, CITES continues to be one of the main forces in species preservation.

Supplementing the CITES bans on international acts against species is the Convention on

Endangered and Threatened Species, 2005

Group	Endangered		Threatened		Total Listed
	U.S.	Foreign	U.S.	Foreign	
Mammals	68	251	10	20	349
Birds	77	175	13	6	271
Reptiles	14	64	22	16	116
Amphibians	11	8	10	1	30
Fishes	71	11	43	1	126
Clams	62	2	8	0	72
Snails	21	1	11	0	33
Insects	35	4	9	0	48
Arachnids	12	0	0	0	12
Crustaceans	18	0	3	0	21
Total Animals	**389**	**516**	**129**	**44**	**1078**
Flowering Plants	571	1	144	0	716
Conifers & Cycads	2	0	1	2	5
Ferns and Allies	24	0	2	0	26
Lichens	2	0	0	0	2
Total Plants	**599**	**1**	**147**	**2**	**749**
Total Species	**988**	**517**	**276**	**46**	**1827**

Note: Separate populations of a species, listed both as endangered and threatened, are with few exeptions, tallied only once, for the endangered population only. (For details, see source.) Figures are as of Aug.. 04, 2005.
Source: U.S. Fish and Wildlife Service, Box Score of U.S. List of Endangered and Threatened Species, http:/ecos.fws.gov

Biodiversity, agreed to at the 1992 Earth Summit in Rio de Janeiro. Ratified by 161 countries (though not the U.S.), this treaty commits nations to protect and preserve species and habitats within their own borders.

Other international treaties affect more limited interests. The International Whaling Commission, with 40 members currently, has been in business since 1949. The commission has probably saved whales from extinction with its near-total ban on whaling since the late 1980s. Other groups, such as the 10-nation Inter-American Tropical Tuna Commission, are modeled on the whaling group. Despite this moratorium, however, Norway and Japan have each killed hundreds of whales annually since the early 1990s; Norway, for example, authorized the killing of 425 minke whales in 1996. In 2003, Iceland began its first whale hunt in 14 years, claiming a scientific need to study the stomach contents of minke whales to measure their effect on important local fish stocks, but in August, 2007 it was announced that Iceland would stop this practice.

To reverse the trend toward species extinction, governments around the world have set aside a total of about 425 million hectares (about 16.4 million square miles) of protected lands in about 3,500 parks and preserves. In addition, many countries try to identify and improve the status of species threatened with extinction.

The efforts come none too soon. The World Conservation Union's list of threatened species of animals and plants worldwide, the "Red List" (www.redlist.org), contained 16,119 species of threatened plants and animals in 2006. These include 20 percent (one in four) of mammalian species, and 12 percent (1 in 8) of bird species. Indonesia, India, Brazil and China are among the countries with the most threatened mammals and birds; plant species are declining rapidly in South and Central America, Central and West Africa, and Southeast Asia. The list includes 8,390 threatened plants, but because only a small percentage (about 2 percent) of plant species have been evaluated for threat the number actually endangered is believed to be much larger. The number of critically endangered mammal species went from 184 to 162 from 2003 to 2006, and the number of critically endangered bird species when from 182 to 181 over the same period, but the number of critically endangered fish species increased dramatically from 162 to 253, primarily because of long-line fisheries.

▶ SELECTED ENDANGERED MAMMALS OF THE WORLD

Although the list of endangered species includes plants and animals of every type, it is the growing group of endangered mammals that have been of special interest and concern to both conservationists and the general public. The World Conservation Union Red List of Endangered Animals indicated in 2004 that 1,101 mammals are considered threatened: 587 are listed as vulnerable, 352 as endangered, and 162 as critically endangered. The "critically endangered," a term indicating that a species' numbers have declined by at least 80 percent, include:

Bandicoot, eastern barred   *(Perameles gunnii nova)* Range: Australia
Bat, Bulmer's fruit   *(Aproteles bulmerae)* Range: Papua New Guinea
Bat, Pemba flying-fox   *(Pteropus voeltzkowi)* Range: Tanzania

Bear, Baluchistan (*Ursus thibetanus gedrosianus*) Range: Iran, Pakistan
Chinchilla, short-tailed (*Chinchilla brevicaudata*) Range: Andes of South America
Cougar, Eastern (*puma concolor couguar*) Range: Canada, U.S.
Deer, Pere David's (*Elaphurus davidianus*) Range: China
Gazelle, acacia (*Gazella gazella acaciae*) Range: Israel
Gazelle, Przewalski's (*Procapra przewalskii*) Range: China
Gibbon, silvery (*Hylobates moloch*) Range: Indonesia
Goat, Chiltan (*Capra aegagrus chialtanensis*) Range: Pakistan
Hog, pygmy (*Sus salvanius*) Range: Himalayas of Asia
Hutia, large-eared (*Mesocapromys auritus*) Range: Cuba
Lemur, golden bamboo (*Hapalemur aureus*) Range: Madagascar
Leopard, North African (*Panthera pardus panthera*) Range: North Africa
Mole, Juliana's golden (*Amblysomus julianae*) Range: South Africa
Monkey, Northern brown howling (*Alouata guariba guariba*) Range: Brazil
Pika, Helan Shan (*Ochotona helanshanensis*) Range: China
Potoroo, Gilbert's (*Potorous gilbertii*) Range: Australia
Pronghorn, Baja California (*Antilocapra americana peninsularis*) Range: Mexico
Rabbit, Omiltemi (*Sylvilagus insonus*) Range: Mexico
Rhinoceros, black (*Diceros bicornis*) Range: Subsaharan Africa
Rhinoceros, Javan (*Rhinoceros sondaicus*) Range: Southeast Asia
Seal, Mediterranean monk (*Monachus monachus*) Range: Mediterranean and Black Sea
Shrew, Gansu (*Sorex cansulus*) Range: China
Sika, Ryukyu (*Cervus nippon keramae*) Range: China, Japan
Tamarin, black-faced lion (*Leontopithecus caissara*) Range: Brazil
Tamarin, golden lion (*Leontopithecus rosalia*) Range: Brazil
Tiger, Amur (*Panthera tigris altaica*) Range: Northeast Asia
Tiger, South China (*Panthera tigris amoyensis*) Range: China
Titi, northern Bahian blond (*Callicebus barbarabrownae*) Range: Brazil
Vaquita (*Phocoena sinus*) Range: eastern central Pacific

Wombat, northern hairy-nosed (*Lasiorhinus krefftii*) Range: Australia

▶ ENDANGERED ANIMALS IN THE UNITED STATES

Although the world's attention is often on large endangered mammals from Africa or the oceans, the United States is home to hundreds of endangered species and subspecies. A subspecies, sometimes called a race, is a local population of a given animal that has some distinctive trait, such as size or color, that sets it apart from the main species.

In the United States, species are classified as threatened or endangered by the U.S. Fish and Wildlife service in accordance with the 1973 Endangered Species Act. The list of endangered species maintained by the Department of the Interior goes back to the original Endangered Species Act of 1966. The first list of endangered species, in March 1967, included 78 species. Today's list contains more than 375 endangered animals and close to 600 endangered plants. Species listed are protected in various ways, most specifically by a prohibition against killing them. Also, a critical habitat can be protected against change if the change would contribute to species extinction. The animals and plants listed (www.endangered.fws.gov) range from the large and well-known, such as the Whooping Crane (*Grus americana*) and the Florida Panther (*Felis concolor coryi*), to the small and little-known plants and animals that are nonetheless important for the maintenance of the environment.

Since the Endangered and Threatened Wildlife and Plants listing was started in 1967, several listed species have become extinct, including the Tecopa pupfish (*Cyprinodon nevadensis calidae*, 1982), the blue pike (*Stizostedion vitreum glaucum*, 1983), the Santa Barbara song sparrow (*Melospiza melodia graminea*, 1983), Sampson's pearly mussel (*Epioblasma* (=*Dysnomia*) *sampsoni*, 1984), and the dusky seaside sparrow (*Ammodramus* (=*Ammospiza*) *maritimus nigrescens*, 1990).

There have also been success stories: several species listed as either threatened or endangered have recovered sufficiently to be removed from the list, including the Brown Pelican (*Pelecanus occidentalis*, 1985), and the American Alligator (*Alligator mississippiensis*, 1987). Perhaps the most visible success has been the recovery of bald eagle populations, which had been severely threatened by the effects of the pesticide DDT in the food chain. (DDT is now banned in the United States.) Other causes included loss of habitat and lead in shot in waterfowl carcasses on which eagles and other birds of prey feed (the use of lead shot has been phased out in the U.S.) The bald eagle has not yet been delisted, but this step has been proposed.

Endangered and Threatened Species in the U.S., 1980–2005

| Year | Endangered | | | Threatened | | | Total Species |
	Animals	Plants	Total	Animals	Plants	Total	
1980	174	50	224	48	9	57	281
1985	207	93	300	59	25	84	384
1990	263	179	442	93	61	154	596
1995	324	432	756	113	93	206	962
2000	368	593	961	129	142	271	1,232
2003	388	599	987	129	147	276	1,263
2005[1]	389	599	988	129	147	276	1,264

1. As of August 4, 2005. Source: U.S. Fish and Wildlife Service, U.S. Species listed per Calendar Year, 1980-present. http://endangered.fws.gov/stats/count.

Technology

Major Discoveries in the History of Technology

(See also "Chronology of Information Processing" in "Computers" and "Satellites and Space Probes" and "Spaceflights Carrying People" in "Astronomy")

B.C.

2,400,000   Ancestors of human beings begin to manufacture stone tools.

1,000,000   Ancestors of human beings learn to control fire.

90,000   People from the Katranda culture in what is now Congo make barbed bone points, probably for use in harpoons.

25,000   People in what is now the Czech Republic begin weaving cloth.

23,000   Bow and arrow developed in Mediterranean regions of Europe and Africa.

10,000   The Jomon culture of Japan makes the first known pottery.

5000   Egyptians start mining and smelting copper ore.

3500   Potter's wheel and (shortly after) wheeled vehicles appear in Mesopotamia.

2900   Great Pyramid of Giza and first form of Stonehenge (a ditch and bank) are built.

2000   Interior bathrooms are built in palaces in Crete.

1500   Earliest glass vessels used in Egypt.

522   Eupalinus of Megara (Greek: 6th cent.) constructs 3,600-ft. tunnel on Samos to supply water from one side of Mt. Castro to other.

290   Pharos lighthouse at Alexandria is built.

260   Archimedes (Greek: c. 287–212 B.C.) develops mathematical descriptions of the lever and other simple machines.

200   Romans develop concrete.

140   Chinese start making paper but do not use it for writing.

100   In Illyria (now Yugoslavia and Albania), water-powered mills are introduced.

A.D.

c. 1   Chinese invent centerline rudder for ships and magnetic compass; neither found in West for 1,000 years.

190   Chinese develop porcelain.

600   First windmills are built in what is now Iran.

704   Between 704 and 751, Chinese start printing with woodblocks.

1040   Chinese develop gunpowder.

1041   Between 1041 and 1048, Chinese inventor Bi Sheng develops movable type.

1190   First-known reference to a compass in Europe.

1267   Book written by Roger Bacon (English: c. 1220–92) in 1267 mentions eyeglasses to correct far-sightedness.

1288   First-known gun, a small cannon, made in China.

1310   Mechanical clocks driven by weights begin to appear in Europe.

c. 1440   Johannes Gutenberg (German: c. 1398–1468) reinvents printing with movable type.

1450   Nicholas of Cusa (German: 1401–64) develops eyeglasses for the nearsighted.

1555   Georg Bauer (Georgius Agricola; German: 1494-1555) writes *De re metallica*, a handbook of mining techniques.

c. 1590   Compound microscope (using two lenses) developed in Holland.

1608   Telescope developed in Holland, probably by Hans Lippershey (German-Dutch: c. 1570–1619).

1620   Cornelis Jacobszoon Drebbel (Dutch: 1572–1633) builds first navigable submarine.

1643   Evangelista Torricelli (Italian: 1608–47) makes first barometer, thereby producing first vacuum known to science.

1654   Christiaan Huygens (Dutch: 1629–95) develops pendulum clock.

1658   Robert Hooke (English: 1635–1703) invents balance spring for watches.

1698   Thomas Savery (English: c. 1650–1715) patents the "Miner's Friend," first practical steam engine.

1701   Jethro Tull (English: 1674–1741), possibly inspired by Chinese devices, invents device for planting seeds called a seed drill.

1709   Daniel Gabriel Fahrenheit (German-Dutch: 1686–1736) invents alcohol thermometer; 1714, mercury thermometer.

1733   John Kay (English: 1704–64) invents flying-shuttle loom, which, along with the steam engine and improvements in making iron, is a key to the start of Industrial Revolution.

1751   Benjamin Huntsman (English: 1704–76) invents crucible process for casting steel.

1762   John Harrison (English: 1693–1776) designs a marine chronometer (clock) accurate enough to enable navigators to calculate longitude at sea.

1764   James Hargreaves (English: 1720–78) introduces spinning jenny, a machine that spins from 8 to 120 threads at once.

1765   James Watt (Scottish: 1736–1819) builds model of his improved steam engine.

1769   Sir Richard Arkwright (English: 1732–92) patents the water frame, a spinning machine that complements spinning jenny.

1783   Joseph-Michel and Jacques-Etienne Montgolfier (French: 1740-1810; 1745–99) develop first hot air balloon. Jacques A.C. Charles (French: 1746–1823) builds first hydrogen balloon.

1785   Edmund Cartwright (English: 1743–1823) invents first form of the power loom.

1792   William Murdock (Scottish: 1754–1839) is first to use coal gas for lighting.

1793   Eli Whitney (American: 1765–1825) invents cotton gin, a machine for separating cotton fibers from seeds.

1800   Alessandro G.A.A. Volta (Italian: 1745–1827) invents first form of chemical battery for producing electric current.

1804   Nicolas-François Appert (French: c. 1750–1841) develops canning as means of preserving food.

1807   Robert Fulton (American: 1765–1815) introduces first commercially successful steamboat.

1816   Sir David Brewster (Scottish: 1781–1868) invents kaleidoscope.

1822   Joseph N. Niepce (French: 1765–1833) produces earliest form of the photograph.

1823   Charles Macintosh (Scottish: 1766–1843) patents a waterproof fabric.

1825   George Stephenson (English: 1781–1848) develops first steam-powered locomotive to carry both passengers and freight.

1835   William Henry Fox Talbot (English: 1800–77) invents photographic negative using silver chloride, essentially how black-and-white pictures are made today.

1837   Samuel Finley Breese Morse (American: 1791–1872) patents first commercially successful version of the telegraph.

1839 Louis J.M. Daguerre (French: 1789–1851) announces his process for making photographs, which come to be called daguerreotypes.

Charles Goodyear (American: 1800–60) discovers how to make rubber resistant to heat and cold, a process called vulcanization.

1842 Sir John Bennet Lawes (English: 1814–99) patents manufacture of superphosphate, the first manufactured fertilizer.

1843 Isambard Kingdom Brunel's (English: 1806–59) *Great Britain* is first iron-hulled screw-propellor ship to cross the Atlantic.

1846 Elias Howe (American: 1819–67) patents lock-stitch sewing machine.

Richard March Hoe (American: 1812–96) invents rotary printing press.

1851 Isaac Merrit Singer (American: 1811–75) patents continuous-stitch sewing machine.

1852 Elisha Graves Otis (American: 1811–61) installs first elevator incorporating safety device that prevents cage from falling if the cable breaks.

1856 Henry Bessemer (English: 1813–98) develops method of making inexpensive steel (Bessemer process).

1859 Edwin L. Drake (American: 1819–80) drills first oil well, in Titusville, Pa.

1862 Richard Jordan Gatling (American: 1818–1903) invents first form of machine gun.

1866 Robert Whitehead (English: 1823–1905) invents naval torpedo. Georges Leclanché (French: 1839–82) develops first form of dry cell for producing electricity.

1867 Latham Sholes (American: 1819–90) and two others invent first practical typewriter.

1869 Hippolyte Mège Mouriés (French: 1817–80) patents margarine.

1866 Cyrus W. Field (U.S.: 1819–92) succeeds in laying the Trans-Atlantic Cable under the Atlantic Ocean, connecting Europe to America by telegraph wire.

1874 Joseph Farwell Glidden (American: 1813–1906) invents the kind of barbed wire used today.

1876 Alexander Graham Bell (Scottish-American: 1847–1922) invents telephone.

Karl von Linde (German: 1842–1934) invents first practical refrigerator.

1877 Nikolaus A. Otto (German: 1832–91) invents type of internal combustion engine still used in most automobiles.

Thomas Alva Edison (U.S.: 1847–1931) invents phonograph, which uses a tinfoil-covered cylinder.

1878 Louis-Marie-Hilaire Bernigaud (French: 1839–1924) develops rayon.

Carl Gustaf Patrik de Laval (Swedish: 1845–1913) invents turbine operated centrifugal cream separator.

1879 Edison and Sir Joseph W. Swan (English: 1828–1914) independently discover how to make practical electric lights.

1885 Karl Benz (German: 1844–1929) builds precursor of modern automobile.

Rover Safety Bicycle, built in England, is first bicycle with essentially modern features.

1886 George Westinghouse (American: 1846–1914) invents air brake for railroad cars.

1888 Emile Berliner (German: 1851–1929) invents phonograph disk.

John B. Dunlop (Scottish: 1840–1921) patents air-filled tire.

George Eastman (American: 1854–1932) develops first camera using roll film.

1889 Gustave Eiffel (French: 1832–1923) builds his famous tower in Paris; at 993 ft., it is tallest freestanding structure of the time.

1893 Rudolf Diesel (German: 1858–1913) describes diesel engine.

1895 First public showing of a motion picture, "Workers Leaving the Lumière Factory" by Auguste and Louis Lumière (French: 1862–1954; 1864–1948) in Paris.

Guglielmo Marconi (Italian: 1874–1937) transmits signals for a mile with his wireless telegraph (a precursor of radio) near Bologna, Italy.

1897 Karl Ferdinand Braun (German: 1850–1918) invents cathode-ray tube oscilloscope.

1898 Valdemar Poulsen (Danish: 1869–1942) invents magnetic wire recorder, the precursor to the modern tape recorder.

1902 Willis H. Carrier (American: 1876–1950) invents air conditioning.

1903 Orville and Wilbur Wright (American: 1871–1948; 1867–1912) fly the first successful airplane at Kitty Hawk, N.C.

1904 John Fleming (English: 1849–1945) develops first vacuum tube, a device for changing alternating current to direct.

1907 Lee De Forest (American: 1873–1961) patents Audion vacuum tube, a device for magnifying weak electronic signals.

1908 Henry Ford (American: 1863–1947) introduces Model T, the first affordable automobile.

1909 Leo Baekeland (Belgian-American: 1863–1944) patents Bakelite, the first truly successful plastic.

1912 Reginald Aubrey Fessenden (Canadian-American: 1866–1932) develops heterodyne circuit, an important improvement in radio reception.

1917 Clarence Birdseye (American: 1886–1956) develops freezing as a means of preserving food.

1919 Sir Arthur W. Brown (British: 1886–1948) and Sir John W. Alcock (British: 1892–1919) make first transatlantic flight, Newfoundland to Ireland.

1924 Vladimir Kosma Zworykin (Russian-American: 1889–1982) develops iconoscope, the beginning of modern television.

1929 Robert H. Goddard (American: 1882–1945) launches first instrumented, liquid-fueled rocket.

1930 Sir Frank Whittle (British: 1907–96) patents jet engine.

1931 Ernst A.F. Ruska (German: 1906–88) builds first electron microscope.

1934 Wallace Hume Carothers (American: 1896–1937) invents nylon, first marketed in 1938.

1935 Sir Robert Alexander Watson-Watt (Scottish: 1892-1973) begins work on radio detection and ranging (radar).

1937 Chester F. Carlson (American: 1906–68) invents xerography, the first method of photocopying.

1939 Paul H. Müller (Swiss: 1899–1965) discovers that DDT is potent and long-lasting insecticide.

Igor I. Sikorsky (Russian-American: 1889–1972) designs and flies first helicopter developed for mass production.

1940 Peter Carl Goldmark (Hungarian-American: 1906–77) demonstrates first successful color television system.

1941 John Rex Whinfield (British: 1901–66) invents Dacron.

1942 Enrico Fermi (Italian-American: 1901–54) builds first nuclear reactor.

1947 Dennis Gabor (Hungarian-British: 1900–79) develops holography, a method of recording and displaying a three-dimensional object.

1948 Goldmark develops the 33⅓ rpm long-playing phonograph record.

Georges de Mestral (Swiss: 1908–90) invents Velcro, patented in 1955.

John Bardeen (American: 1908–91), Walter H. Brattain (American: 1902–87), and William B. Shockley (English-American: 1910-89) invent the transistor.

1957 Gordon Gould (American: 1920–2005) develops basic idea for the laser, which he succeeds in patenting in 1986 after long struggle.

The Soviet spacecraft *Sputnik 1* becomes the first satellite to orbit Earth.

1958 United States opens first experimental nuclear power plant.
1959 First industrial robot is marketed.
1962 First active communications satellite, Telstar, goes into orbit.
1963 Audiocassettes introduced.
1964 Touch-tone telephones introduced.
1966 Engineers at ITT demonstrate fiber optics as a method of transmitting data.
1968 The first supersonic airliner, the Soviet Tupolev TU-144, is demonstrated on Dec. 31.
1969 ATMs and bar-code scanners introduced.
1970 Boeing 747 jets go into service.
1975 IBM introduces first laser printer.
1982 Compact disc players introduced.
1984 Motorola introduces first commercial version of cellular phone in U.S.
1989 The U.S. Defense Department launches the first satellite in the Global Positioning System.
1990 Leigh T. Canham (British) develops a method for producing light from stimulated silicon.
1991 Woo Paik and coworkers produce the first prototype of digital high-definition television.
1994 Channel Tunnel, also known as the Chunnel, connecting England and France beneath the English Channel, is officially opened.

Charles K. Rhodes of the University of Chicago develops an X-ray-emitting laser.
1995 Scientists at Los Alamos National Laboratory in New Mexico develop a flexible tape that is superconducting at the temperature of liquid nitrogen (about −325°F).

A group led by Junji Kido of Yamagata Univ. in Japan combines three different diode layers, including a blue-emitting diode that is a major advance of its own, to make white light.

Competing groups agree on standards for the Digital Video Disc (DVD), an improved compact disc that can store a complete motion picture on a disc the size of a CD.
1997 Dolly, the first cloned sheep, is born.
1998 John A. Turner and Oscar Khaselev of the U.S. National Renewable Energy Laboratory in Golden, Colo. develop a solar cell that can split water into hydrogen and oxygen.
2001 The first succesful operation to insert an AbioCor fully self-contained artificial heart is performed.

The first draft of the complete human genome is announced.
2007 U.S. and Australian defense programs annouce the successful flight of a hypersonic scramjet, which reached a speed of Mach 10.

National Inventors Hall of Fame

In 1973 the U.S. National Council of Patent Law Associations (now the National Council of Intellectual Property Law) began the practice of naming inventors who hold U.S. patents to the National Inventors Hall of Fame. Although many of those honored have many patents, the committee selects one patent for each inventor (or group of inventors) as the occasion for the award, which they identify by the title of the original patent application. When an invention is the work of more than one person, the description of the invention is given only for one inventor. The date at the end of each of the following entries denotes the year of induction. The Hall is located in Akron, Ohio.

National Inventors Hall Of Fame Inductees

Field/Invention	Inventor	Born–Died	Inducted
AGRICULTURE			
Automated Sugar Refining	Norbert Rillieux	1806–1894	2004
Breakfast Cereal	John Harvey Kellogg	1852–1943	2006
Food Preservatives	Lloyd Hall	1894–1971	2004
Frozen Foods	Clarence Birdseye	1886–1956	2005
Glyphosate Herbicide (Roundup®)	John Franz	b.1929	2007
Improvement in Concentration of Milk	Gail Borden, Jr.	1801–1874	2006
Modern Beehive	Lorenzo Lorraine Langstroth	1810–1895	2007
Pasteurization	Louis Pasteur	1822–1895	1978
Peach and fruit varieties	Luther Burbank	1849–1926	1986
Plow	John Deere	1804–1886	1989
Products Using Peanuts And Sweet Potatoes	George Washington Carver	1864–1943	1990
Reaper	Cyrus Mccormick	1809–1894	1976
ARTS AND LEISURE			
Ballpoint Pen	Laszlo Josef Biro	1899–1985	2007
Board Game	Milton Bradley	1836–1911	2006
Cast-Iron Piano Frame	Alpheus Babcock	1785–1842	2007
Flexible Flyer Shield Toboggan	Samuel Allen Leeds	1841–1918	2007
Improvement In Clock Manufacture	Eli Terry	1772–1852	2007
Improvements To Fountain Pen	Lewis Waterman	1837–1901	2006
Model Railroad	Joshua Cowen	1877–1965	2007
Solid-Body Electric Guitar	Les Paul	b.1915	2005
Zamboni Machine	Frank Zamboni	1901–1988	2007
ASTRONOMY			
Far Electrograph Ultraviolet Camera	George R. Carruthers	b.1939	2003
Improvements To Telescope	Ambrose Swasey	1846–1937	2006
Satellite Servicing Techniques	Frank Cepollina	b.1936	2003
BIOTECH			
Recombinant DNA technology	Herb Boyer	b.1936	2001
	and Stan Cohen	b.1935	2001

Field/Invention	Inventor	Born-Died	Inducted
CHEMISTRY			
Apparatus For Testing Acidity	Arnold O. Beckman	1900–2004	1987
Bromine	Herbert Henry Dow	1866–1930	1983
Lyophilized Reaction Mixtures	Emmett W. Chapelle	b.1925	2007
Molecular Sieves	Edith Flanigen	b.1929	2004
Process Of Producing Ammonia	Karl Bosch	1884–1940	2006
COMMUNICATIONS			
Audion Amplifier	Lee DeForest	1873–1961	1977
Automatic Telephone-Exchange	Almon Strowger	1829–1908	2006
Automatic Typesetting	John Raphael Rogers	1856–1934	2007
Automobile Radio	William P. Lear	1902–1978	1993
Cathode Ray Tube	Vladimir Kosma Zworykin	1889–1982	1977
Charge-Coupled Device (Ccd)	Willard Sterling Boyle	b.1924	2006
Color Photography	Leopold Godowsky, Jr	1900–1983	2005
	and Leopold Mannes	1899–1964	2005
Communications Satellite	John Pierce	1910–2002	2003
High Resolution Image-Scanning Radar	Robert H. Rines	b. 1922	1994
Dictaphone	Charles Tainter	1854–1940	2006
Dolby Noise Reduction	Ray Dolby	b.1933	2004
Double-Cylinder Printing-Process	Richard March Hoe	1812–1886	2006
Electric Lamp	Thomas Alva Edison	1847–1931	1973
Foil Electret Microphone	James Edward West	b. 1931	1999
	and Gerhard M. Sessler	b. 1931	1999
High Frequency Alternator	Ernst Alexanderson	1878–1975	1983
Kurzweil Reading Machine	Raymond Kurzweil	b. 1948	2002
Localizer Antenna System	Andrew Alford	1904–1992	1983
LP Record	Peter Carl Goldmark	1906–1977	2007
Machine For Producing Printing Bars	Ottmar Mergenthaler	1854–1999	1982
Magnetic Recording.	S. Joseph Begun	1905–1995	1998
Apparatus For Coating Plates For Use In Photography	George Eastman	1854–1932	1977
Method And Means Of Magnetic Recording	Marvin Camras	1916–1995	1985
Method Of Receiving High Frequency Oscillations	Edwin Howard Armstrong	1890–1954	1980
Microphone And Gramophone	Emile Berliner	1851–1929	1994
Modern Photocopier	Robert Gundlach	b.1926	2005
Multiplane Camera	Walt Disney	1901–1966	2000
Negative Feedback Amplifier	Harold Stephen Black	1898–1983	1981
Optical Character Recognition (Ocr)	Jacob Rabinow	1910–1999	2005
Photo Composing Machine	Louis Marius Moyroud	b. 1914	1985
	and René Alphonse Higonnet	1902–1983	1985
Photographic Product Comprising A Rupturable Container Carrying Photographic Processing Liquid	Edwin Herbert Land	1909–1991	1977
Picture Projector	Auguste Lumiere	1852–1954	2007
	and Louis Lumiere	1864–1948	2007
Railway Telegraphy	Granville Woods	1856–1910	2006
Spin Stabilized Synchronous Communications Satellite	Harold Rosen	b.1926	2003
Telautograph	Elisha Gray	1835–1901	2007
Telegraph Signals	Samuel F. B. Morse	1791–1872	1975
Telegraphy	Alexander Graham Bell	1874–1922	1974
Television Receiver	Louis W. Parker	1906–1993	1988
Television System	Philo Taylor Farnsworth	1906–1971	1984
Transmitting Electrical Signals	Guglielmo Marconi	1874–1937	1975
Variable Frequency Oscillation Generator	William R. Hewlett	1913–2001	1992
Videotape Recorder	Charles P. Ginsburg	1920–1992	1990
Wireless Radio Communication	Reginald Aubrey Fessenden	1866–1932	2000
Wireless Telegraphy	Oliver Joseph Lodge	1851–1940	2007
Electrophotography C	Chester F. Carlson	1906–1968	1981
Stroboscope	Harold E. Edgerton	1903–1990	1986
COMPUTING AND ELECTRONICS			
Calculating Machine	William Seward Burroughs	1855–98	1987
Charge-Coupled Device (CCD)	George Smith	b.1930	2006
Complex Computer	George R. Stibitz	1904–95	1983
Computer Mouse	Douglas Engelbart	b.1925	1998
Differential Analyzer	Vannevar Bush	1890–1974	2004
Dynamic Random Access Memory	Robert H. Dennard	b.1932	1997
Eniac Data Translating Device	John Mauchly	1907–1980	2002
	and John Presper Eckert, Jr.	1919–1995	2002
Ethernet	Robert Metcalfe	b.1946	2007
Field Effect Device With Insulated Gate	Robert A. Bower	b.1936	1997
Magnetron and Semiconductor Laser	Robert N. Hall	b.1919	1994
Improved Magnetic Core Memory	Kenneth H. Olsen	b.1926	1990
Liquid-Crystal Display (LCD)	James L. Fergason	b.1934	1998

Field/Invention	Inventor	Born-Died	Inducted
Magnetic Disc Storage	John Joseph Lynott	1921–1994	2007
	and Willliam Goddard	1913–1997	2007
Magnetic Pulse Controlling Device	An Wang	1920–1990	1988
Microcomputer With Bus Control Means For	Dennis Moeller	b.1950	1997
Peripheral Devices	and Mark Dean	b.1957	1997
Microprocessor	Federico Faggin	b.1941	1996
	and Stanley Mazor	b.1941	1996
Microprocessor Concept And Architecture	Marcian Edward "Ted" Hoff, Jr.	b.1937	1996
Miniaturiized Electronic Circuits	Jack S. Kilby	b.1923	1982
Random Access Memory (RAM)	Jay W. Forrester	b.1918	1979
Packet Switching	Donald Watt Davies	1924–2000	2006
Packetized Ensemble Modem	Paul Baran	b.1926	2007
Personal Computer	Steve Wozniak	b.1950	2000
Pulse Code Modulation (PCM)	Claude Shannon	1916–2001	2004
	and Bernard Oliver	1916–1995	2004
Semiconductor Device-And-Lead Structure	Robert N. Noyce	1927–1990	1983
Storage And Processing Of Numerical Data	Herman Hollerith	1869–1929	1990
Supercomputer	Seymour Cray	1925–1996	1997
Transistor	John Bardeen	1908–1991	1974
	Walter H. Brattain	1902–1987	1974
	and William Bradford Shockley	1910–1989	1974
Transmission Control Protocol/Internet	Robert Elliot Kahn	b.1938	2006
Protocol (TCP/IP)	and Vinton Gray Cerf	b.1943	2006

INDUSTRY

Field/Invention	Inventor	Born-Died	Inducted
Adhesive Tape	Richard Gurley Drew	1988–1980	2007
Air Conditioner	Willis Haviland Carrier	1876–1950	1985
Apparatus For Handling Ore	George H. Hulett	1846–1923	2006
Automatic Elevator Doors	Alexander Miles	1838–?	2007
Bessemer Steel Process	Henry Bessemer	1813–1898	2002
Bottle Cap	William Painter	1838–1906	2006
Buckeye Mower Machine	Lewis Miller	1829–1899	2006
Carbon Filament For Lightbulbs	Lewis Latimer	1848–1928	2006
Catalytic Cracking Of Hydrocarbons With A	Charles J. Plank	1915–1989	1979
Crystalline Zeolite Catalyst Composite	and Edward J. Rosinski	1921–2000	1979
Catalytic Cracking Of Petroleum	Eugene J. Houdry	1892–1962	1990
Ceramic Substrate For Catalytic Converters	Irwin Lachman	b.1930	2002
	Ronald Lewis	b.1936	2002
	and Rodney Bagley	b.1934	2002
Construction Of Iron Buildings	James Bogardus	1800–1874	2007
Cotton Gin	Eli Whitney	1765–1825	1974
Direct-Current (D/C) Dynamo	Zénobe Théophile Gramme	1826–1901	2006
Dishwasher	Josephine Garis Cochran	1839–1913	2006
Electric Transformer	William Stanley	1858–1916	1995
Electric-Arc Lamp	Elihu Thomson	1853–1937	2006
Electrostatic Precipitator	Frederick G. Cottrell	1877–1948	1992
Escalator	Charles D. Seeberger	1857–1931	2007
	and Jesse Wilford Reno	1861–1947	2007
Fiberglass	John Thomas	1907–1991	2006
	and Russell Games Slayter	1896–1964	2006
Fire Hydrant	Birdsill Holly, Jr.	1820–1894	2006
Fluid Catalytic Cracking	Eger V. Murphree	1898–1962	1999
	Homer Z. Martin	1910–1993	1999
	and Donald L. Campbell	1904–2002	1999
Fluorescent Light	Edmund Germer	1901–1987	1996
Foot Measuring Device	Charles F. Brannock	1903–1992	2007
Gas Mask, Three-Way Traffic Signal	Garrett Morgan	1887–1963	2005
Gas Optical Maser	Ali Javan	b.1926	2006
Glass Shaping Machine	Michael Joseph Owens	1859–1923	2007
Glass Tile	Louis Comfort Tiffany	1848–1933	2007
High-Voltage Induction Coil	Charles Page	1812–1868	2006
Hydroelectric Waterwheel	Lester Pelton	1829–1908	2006
Ice-Cream Freezer, And Many Others	Beulah Louise Henry	1887–1973	2006
Improvement In Boring-Mills	William Sellers	1824–1905	2007
Improvement In Electromagnetic Alarm-Bells	Moses Gerrish Farmer	1820–1893	2006
Improvement In Hoisting Apparatus	Elisha Graves Otis	1811–1861	1988
Improvement In Rock-Drills	Simon Ingersoll	1818–1984	2006
Improvements In Weaving Looms	George Crompton	1829–1886	2007
Incandescent Electric Lamp	Irving Langmuir	1881–1957	1989
Machine For Crushing Stone	Eli Whitney Blake	1795–1886	2007
Manufacture Of Aluminum	Charles Martin Hall	1863–1914	1976
Maser	Arthur Schawlow	1921–1999	1996

Field/Invention	Inventor	Born-Died	Inducted
Mason Jar	John Mason	1832–1902	2006
Neon Tubing	Georges Claude	1870–1960	2007
Numerical Control Of Machine Tools	John T. Parsons	1913–2007	1993
Optically Pumped Laser Amplifiers	Gordon Gould	1920–2005	1991
Paper Bag Manufacturing	Margaret Knight	1838–1914	2006
Portable Vacuum Cleaner	James Spangler	1848–1915	2006
Portable Voltometer	Edward Weston	1850–1936	2006
Power-Loom	Erastus Brigham Bigelow	1814–1879	2006
Process For Making Malleable Cast Iron	Seth Boyden	1788–1870	2006
Prodution Of Ammonia	Fritz Haber	1868–1934	2006
Propellor	John Ericsson	1803–1889	1993
Revolving Door	Theophilus Van Kannel	1841–1919	2007
Ruby Laser Systems	Theodore Harold Maiman	b.1927	1984
Safety Pin	Walter Hunt	1796–1859	2006
Safety Razor	King Camp Gillette	1855–1932	2007
Sewing Machine	Elias Howe	1819–1867	2004
Shoe Lasting-Machine	Jan Matzeliger	1852–1889	2006
Signal Flare	Martha Coston	1826–1904	2006
Steam Engine	John Stevens	1749–1838	2006
Stock Ticker	Edward Augustin Calahan	1838–1912	2006
System Of Electric Arc Lighting	Charles Francis Brush	1849–1929	2006
System Of Electrical Distribution	Charles Proteus Steinmetz	1865–1923	1977
Traction Engine	Benjamin Holt	1849–1920	2006
Typewriter	Christopher L. Sholes	1819–1890	2001
Vacuum Tube	William D. Coolidge	1873–1974	1975
Water Tube Steam Boiler	George H. Babcock	1832–1893	1997
	and Stephen Wilcox, Jr.	1830–1893	1997
Water-Powered Cotton Mill	Samual Slater	1768–1835	2007
Weaving Straw With Silk Or Thread	Mary Dixon Kies	1752–1837	2006
Yale Lock	Linus Yale, Jr.	1821–1868	2006
Zig-Zag Stitch Sewing Machine	Helen Blanchard	1840–1922	2006
Zipper	Gideon Sundback	1880–1954	2006

MATERIALS

Field/Invention	Inventor	Born-Died	Inducted
Barbed Wire	Joseph Glidden		2006
Carborundum	Edward Acheson	1856–1931	1997
Celluloid	John Wesley Hyatt	1837–1920	2006
Cellophane	Jacques Brandenberger		2006
Coaxial Cable	Lloyd Espenscheid	1889–1986	2006
	and Herman A. Affel	1893–1972	2006
Diamine-Dicarboxylic Acid Salts And Process Of Preparing Same And Synthetic Fiber	Wallace Hume Carothers	1896–1937	1984
Dynamite	Alfred Nobel	1833–1896	1998
Fiberglas	Dale Kleist	1909–1998	2006
Film Structure And Method Of Preparation	Katharine Burr Blodgett	1989–1979	2007
Fused Silica And Silicones	J. Franklin Hyde	1903–1999	2000
Kevlar	Stephanie Kwolek	b. 1923	1995
Manufacture of Titanium	William Justin Kroll	1889–1973	2000
Optical Fiber	Robert D. Maurer	b. 1924	1993
	Donald Keck	b. 1941	1993
	and Peter C. Schultz	b. 1942	1993
Polymers	Paul Hogan	b. 1919	2001
	and Robert L. Banks	1921–1989	2001
Polytetrafluoroethylene (Gore-Tex®)	Robert W. Gore	b.1937	2006
Polyurethane	Donald Fletcher Holmes	1910–1980	1991
	and W.E. "Butch" Hanford	b. 1908	1991
PVC Plastisols	Waldo Semon	1898–1999	
Scotchgard™	Samuel Smith	1927–2005	2001
	and Patsy Sherman	b. 1930	2001
Superglue	Harry Coover	1919–1996	2004
Synthetic Resins (Bakelite)	Leo Hendrik Baekeland	1863–1944	1978
Synthetic Rubber (Neoprene)	Julius A. Nieuwland	1878–1936	1996
Tetrafluoroethylene Polymers	Roy J. Plunkett	1910–1994	1985
Velcro®	George De Mestral	1907–1990	

MEDICINE

Field/Invention	Inventor	Born-Died	Inducted
Ambulatory Insulin Pump	Dean Kamen	b.1951	2005
Aspirin	Felix Hoffmann	1868–1946	2002
Automated DNA Sequencing	Leroy Hood	b.1938	2007
Bifurcated Vaccination Needle	Benjamin A. Rubin	b. 1917	1992
Captopril	Miguel Angel Ondetti	1930–2004	2007
	and Wayne Cushman	1939–2000	2007
CAT Scan	Godfrey Hounsfield	1919–2004	2007
Cimetidine (Tagamet®)	C. Robin Ganellin	b. 1934	1990

Field/Invention	Inventor	Born-Died	Inducted
	John C. Emmet	b. 1938	1990
	and Graham J. Durant	b. 1934	1990
Controlled Release Of Macromolecules	Robert Samuel Langer, Jr.	b.1948	2006
Dip-And-Read Tests For Urinalysis	Alfred Free	1913–2000	2000
	and Helen Murray Free	b. 1923	2000
DNA-Blocking Drugs	Gertrude b. Elion	1918–1999	1991
Echo-Planar Imaging (EPI)	Peter Mansfield	b.1933	2007
Embolectomy Catheter	Thomas J. Fogarty	b. 1934	2001
Excimer Laser Surgery (LASIK)	Rangaswamy Srinivasan	b. 1929	2002
	James Wynne	b. 1943	2002
	and Samuel Blum	b. 1920	2002
Expandable Intravascular Stent	Julio Palmaz	b.1945	2006
Fluorescein isothiocyanate (FITC)	Robert J. Seiwald	b.1925	1995
	and Joseph H. Burckhalter	1912–2004	1995
Genetic Fingerprinting	Alec Jeffreys	b.1950	2005
Heart-Lung Machine	John Gibbon	1903–1973	2004
Hepatitis A, B Vaccines; MMR Vaccine	Maurice Ralph Hilleman	1919–2005	2007
Hepatitis B Vaccine	Irving Millman	b. 1923	1993
	and Baruch S. Blumberg	b. 1925	1993
Implantable Defibrillator	Alois Langer	b. 1945	2002
	M. Stephen Heilman	b. 1933	2002
	Michel Mirowski	1924–90	2002
	and Morton Mower	b. 1933	2002
Insulin	Charles Best	1099–1978	2004
	Frederick Banting	1891–1941	2004
	and James Collip	1982–1965	2004
Iron Lung	Philip Drinker	1894–1972	2007
Isolation Of Vitamin B (Thiamine)	Robert R. Williams	1886–1965	1991
Magnetic Resonance Imaging (MRI)	Raymond V. Damadian	b. 1936	1989
Means For Counting Particles Suspended In A Fluid	Wallace Coulter	1913–1998	2004
Medical Cardiac Pacemaker	Wilson Greatbatch	b. 1919	1986
Medical Respirators	Forrest Bird	b. 1921	1995
Method For Production Of Penicillin	Andrew J. Moyer	1899–1959	1987
Novocain	Alfred Einhorn	1856–1917	2007
Nuclear Magnetic Resonance Imaging (NMR)	Paul Christian Lauterbur	1929–2007	2007
Nystatin	Elizabeth Lee Hazen	1885–1975	1994
	and Rachel Fuller Brown	1898–1980	1994
Oral Contraceptives	Carl Djerassi	b. 1923	1978
Oral Contraceptives (Enovid)	Gregory Pincus	1903–1967	2006
	and Frank B. Colton	1923–2003	1988
Pentothal	Donalee L. Tabern	1900–1974	1986
	and Ernest H. Volwiler	1893–1992	1986
Phacoemulsification Cataract Removal Procedure	Charles Kelman	1930–2004	2004
Pill Form for Medicine	William Eurastus Upjhon	1863–1932	2006
Polymerase Chain Reaction	Kary Banks Mullis	b. 1944	1998
Prednisone And Prednisolone	Arthur Nobile	1920–2004	2007
Prozac	Bryan B. Molloy	1939–2004	1999
	and Klaus K. Schmiegel	b. 1939	1999
Riboflavin And Sulfaquinoxaline	Max Tishler	1906–1984	1982
Scanning Tunneling Microscope	Heinrich Rohrer	b. 1933	1994
Semi-Synthetic Penicillin	John C. Sheehan	1915–1992	1995
Soft Contact Lens	Otto Wichterle	1913–1998	2007
Soft-Shell Mushroom-Shaped Heart	Willem J. Kolff	b. 1911	1985
Streptomycin	Selman Waksman	1888–1973	2005
Synthesis Of Cortisone And Other Hormones	Percy F. Julian	1899–1975	1990
Test To Diagnose HIV Infection	Luc Montagnier	b.1932	2004
	and Robert Gallo	b.1937	2004
Tetracycline	Lloyd H. Conover	b. 1923	1992
Treating Pregene Compounds	Lewis Hastings Sarett	1917–1999	1980
Valium	Leo H. Sternbach	1908–2005	2005
Whole-Body CAT Scanner	Robert S. Ledley	b. 1926	1990
NAVIGATION			
Altimeter	Paul Kollsman	1900–1982	2003
Control Mechanism For Rocket Apparatus	Robert Hutchings Goddard	1882–1945	1979
Global Positioning System (GPS)	Bradford Parkinson	b.1935	2004
	and Ivan Getting	1912–2003	2004
Gyroscopic Equipment	Charles Stark Draper	1901–87	1983
Radar	Percy L. Spencer	1894–1970	1999
Ship's Gyroscopic Compass	Elmer A. Sperry	1860–1930	1991
PHYSICS			
Electron Lens Correction Device	James Hillier	1915–2007	
Hydrometer	Joseph Saxton	1799–1873	2006

Field/Invention	Inventor	Born-Died	Inducted
Masers	Charles Hard Townes	b. 1915–	1976
Method And Apparatus For The Acceleration Of Ions	Ernest Orlando Lawrence	1901–58	1982
Neutronic Reactor	Enrico Fermi	1901–54	1976
Nuclear Reactor	Leo Szilard	1898–1964	1996
Plutonium Isolation	Genn T. Seaborg	1912–1999	2005
Radio Distance And Direction Indicator	Luis Walter Alvarez	1911–88	1978
Radio Frequency Mass Spectrometer	Willard H. Bennett	1903–1987	1991
Scanning Tunneling Microscope,	Gerd Karl Binnig	b. 1947	1994
TRANSPORTATION			
3-Point Safety Belt	Nils Bohlin	1920–2002	2002
Airplane Stall Warning Device	Leonard M. Greene	1918–2006	1991
Automatic Railroad Car Coupler	Andrew Jackson Beard	1849–1921	2006
Automobile Brakes	Louis Renault	1877–1944	2007
Cable Car	Andrew Smith Hallidie	1836–1900	2006
Combustion Motor	Wilhelm Maybach	1846–1929	2007
Electric Railway System	Frank Sprague	1857–1934	2006
Electro-Magnetic Motor	Nikola Tesla	1857–1943	1975
Engine Starting Devices And Ignition System	Charles Franklin Kettering	1875–1958	1980
Ethyl Gasoline	Thomas Midgley, Jr.	1889–1944	2003
Flight Simulator	Edwin A. Link	1904–1981	2003
Fluid Catalytic Cracking	Charles W. Tyson	1900–1977	1999
Flying Machine	Orville Wright	1871–1948	1975
	and Wilbur Wright	1867–1912	1975
Flying Wing Plane; All-Metal High-Wing Monocoque Airplane (Vega)	John Northrop	1895–1981	2003
Gas Motor Engine	Nikolaus August Otto	1832–1891	1981
Ground Proximity Warning System	C. Donald Bateman	b.1932	2005
Helicopter Controls	Igor I. Sikorsky	1889–1972	1987
High Pressure Steam Engine	Oliver Evans	1755–1819	2001
Hydroaeroplane	Glenn Curtis	1878–1930	2003
Improved Velocipede	Thomas Pickering	1831–1895	2007
Improvement In Electric Rail Signals	Thomas Seavey Hall	1827–1880	2007
Improvement In Gas–Motor Engines	Gottlieb Daimler	1834–1900	2006
Improvement In India-Rubber Fabrics	Charles Goodyear	1800–1860	1976
Improvement In Lubricators For Steam-Engines	Elijah J. Mccoy	1844–1929	2001
Improvement In Valve Gears For Steam-Engines	George Henry Corliss	1817–1888	2006
Improvements To Diesel Engine	Alexander Winton	1860–1932	2006
Internal Combustion Engine	Rudolf Diesel	1858–1913	1976
Iron Truss Bridge	Squire Whipple	1804–1888	2007
Jet Engine	Hans J.P. Von Ohain	1911–1998	2003
	and Sir Frank Whittle	1907–1996	2003
Manufacture Of Gasoline	William Meriam Burton	1865–1954	1984
Modern Rubber Tire	Harvey S. Firestone	1868–1938	2006
Outboard Motor	Ole Evinrude	1877–1934	2007
Pneumatic Tire	John Dunlop	1840–1921	2006
Pullman Car	George Pullman	1831–1897	2006
Retractable Landing Gear; Folding Wing	Leroy Grumman	1895–1982	2003
Rotor Control Mechanism For Rotary Aircraft	Charles Kaman	b.1919	2003
Small Fan - Jet Engine	Sam Williams	b.1921	2003
Space Capsule Design	Maxime Faget	1921–2004	2003
Steam Locomotive	Matthias Baldwin	1795–1886	2005
Steamboat	John Fitch	1743–1798	2006
	and Robert Fulton	1765–1815	2006
Steam-Boiler Firebox	Peter Cooper	1791–1883	2006
Steam-Powered Brake Devices	George Westinghouse	1846–1914	1989
Supercritical Wing	Richard Whitcomb	b.1921	2003
Suspension Bridge	John Roebling	1806–1869	2004
Tapered Roller Bearing	Henry Timken	1831–1909	1998
Thrust Bearing	Albert Kingsbury	1983–1943	2007
Transmission Mechanism	Henry Ford	1863–1947	1982
Traveling-Grate Furnace	Eckley Brinton Coxe	1839–1895	2006
Turbo Jet	Theodore Von Kármán	1881–1963	2003
Valve For Steam-Engines	Frederick Sickels	1819–1895	2007
Vehicle Air Conditioning	Frederick Mckinley Jones	1893–1961	2007
Zeppelin	Ferdinand Von Zeppelin	1838–1917	2006
WEAPONS & MILITARY			
Breech-Loading Firearm	John Moses Browning	1855–1926	2007
Improvement To Firearms	Samuel Colt	1814–1862	2006
Maxim Gun	Hiram Maxim	1840–1916	2006
Submarine	John Phillip Holland	1840–1914	2007

Source: National Inventors Hall of Fame.

Utility Patents Granted, 1901–2006

Utility patents, also known as patents for inventions, are issued for the invention of or improvement to a new and useful process, machine, manufacture, or composition of matter. They allow their owners to prohibit others from making, using or selling the invention for up to 17 years from the date of the grant. Utility patents represent about 90 percent of all patents. The other 10 percent are divided among plant patents, for a new and distinct, invented, or discovered asexually reproduced plant; and design patents, for a new, original, and ornamental design for an article of manufacture. Design patents last only 14 years.

Year	Total patents granted	U.S. ownership			Foreign ownership		
		Corporations	Government[1]	Individuals	Corporations	Government	Individuals
1901	25,546	4,370	N.A.	20,896[2]	280	N.A.	(2)
1921	37,798	9,860	N.A.	27,098[2]	840	N.A.	(2)
1930	45,226	19,700	N.A.	23,726[2]	1,800	N.A.	(2)
1940	42,238	22,165	40	17,627[2]	2,406	N.A.	(2)
1950	43,040	21,782	622	18,960[2]	1,660	N.A.	(2)
1960	47,170	28,187	1,244	13,069[2]	4,670	N.A.	(2)
1970	64,427	36,896	1,726	13,511[2]	12,294	N.A.	(2)
1980	61,819	27,640	1,237	9,956	18,874	254	3,858
1990	90,365	36,094	983	12,542	35,548	423	4,775
2000	157,494	70,884	928	16,129	63,182	104	6,267
2001	166,037	74,325	957	15,205	68,943	92	6,515
2002	167,333	74,161	907	14,116	71,663	112	6,374
2003	169,028	75,329	881	13,538	73,099	85	6,096
2004	164,291	73,022	842	12,172	74,637	79	5,400
2005	143,806	65,207	698	10,358	63,114	58	4,371
2006	173,771	78,925	792	11,857	77,373	51	4,773

Note: 1. Excludes patents issued to Alien Property Custodian until 1942. **2.** Patents issued to foreign individuals before 1980 are included with U.S. individuals. **Source:** Department of Commerce, Patent and Trademark Office, *All Technologies Report*, (March, 2007).

COMPUTERS

A computer is a machine for storing and processing information. It converts any information that it receives into a binary code—a string of signals, in which each signal is either 1 or 0. The basic working component of a computer is a series of switches, each of which can be set either "off" or "on" and thus represent 1 or 0 in the binary system. The history of computers is, to some extent, a history of the switching devices that have been used to represent 1 and 0. Early computers were based on mechanical switches; computers based on electronic switches proved much faster. These fall into three main categories: vacuum tubes, transistors, and integrated circuits.

The relative size and power of these three types are so disparate that it is almost impossible to compare them; there is no single scale against which they can be measured. In 1946 the ENIAC (Electronic Numerical Integrator and Calculator)—which occupied 2,000 square feet, weighed 50 tons, and used 18,000 vacuum tubes—could perform about 10,000 multiplications per second and had an internal memory capacity of 200 decimal digits, or about 20 words. The newest personal computers in 2005 could carry out more than 4 billion operations per second and store more than 400 billion bits of information. The world's fastest supercomputer, developed in Japan, could reach speeds of 35,600 gigaflops (billions of operations per second). Innovations in microprocessor and storage technologies promise quantum leaps in the speed and data capacity of the common computer.

▶ A GLOSSARY OF COMPUTER TERMS

Application A computer *program* designed for a specific task or use, like word procesing, accounting, or missile guidance.

Artificial intelligence (AI) The underlying assumption of artificial intelligence is that machines can be programmed to perform human functions. The primary AI functions are *expert systems*, programs that contain a body of knowledge (contributed by experts) that the machine can draw on to solve specific types of problems; *natural language interfaces* that make it possible for users to access a computer's database with commands entered in ordinary written or spoken language (for example, "Give me a list of countries bordering the Atlantic Ocean"); *speech recognition, speech synthesis, and optical recognition systems* that enable computers to understand spoken commands, make speech, and interpret visible images (such as bar codes on retail goods); and *robotics*, machines whose design and systems enable them to imitate complex "eye-hand" coordination of humans.

ASCII (American Standard Code for Information Interchange) Computers work with numbers, not letters. ASCII is the numerical code used by personal computers. While many programs also use special codes of their own, data from one computer to another are best transmitted in "pure ASCII."

Baud rate A transmission rate used in sending data from one computer to another, with a baud approximately equal to one *bit* per second. Rates must be the same between *modems* for data to be transmitted.

Bit In the binary system, a bit (binary digit) is either of the digits 0 or 1. It is the basic unit for storing data, with "off" representing 0 and "on" representing 1.

Blog Short for "web log," a web page that contains a publicly accessible personal journal.

Buffer Any memory location where data can be stored temporarily while the computer is doing something else; specifically, a memory location in the computer, in a printer, or in a separate storage device (*peripheral*) that stores a file being printed so that the computer is not tied up waiting for the printing to finish.

Bug An error in a *software* program or the *hardware*.

Byte A group of eight bits that together represent one character, whether alphabetic, numeric, or other. A byte is the smallest accessible unit in a computer's memory.

Cathode ray tube (CRT) The display device, or *monitor*, similar to a television screen, used with most desktop computers.

CD-ROM A Compact Disc ("CD") used as a Read-Only-Memory ("ROM"). The CD, essentially the same as an audio CD, stores data in a form readable by a laser, resulting in a storage device of great capacity and quick accessibility.

Central processing unit (CPU) The group of circuits that directs the entire computer system by (1) interpreting and executing *program* instruction and (2) coordinating the interaction of input, output, and storage devices.

Computer-aided design (CAD), engineering (CAE) and manufacturing (CAM) Systems that automate many complex tasks such as drafting, computation, or repetitive actions.

Cursor A marker on the computer display that shows which region of the screen is active.

Database Either a *program* for arranging facts in the computer and retrieving them (the computer equivalent of a filing system) or a *file* set up by such a system. Databases may be stored on a standalone computer or network server and accessed online.

Directory An area or data structure in which information is stored regarding the location and contents of files or file structures.

Disk drive A mechanism for retrieving information stored on a magnetic disk. The drive rotates the disk at high speed and "reads" the data with a magnetic head similar to those used in tape recorders.

DVD Digital Versatile Disc, an improvement on the CD-ROM that is capable of storing an entire motion picture.

DOS Acronym for Disk Operating System and shorthand for MS-DOS, the standard operating system for 16-bit and most 32-bit IBM and IBM-compatible PCs.

File Any group of data treated as a single entity by the computer, such as a word processor document, a *program*, or a *database*.

Firewall A dedicated computer or software with special security features to safeguard a network server from damage by authorized or unauthorized users.

Floppy disk A thin, flexible magnetic disk encased in a protective jacket. On the disk's surface are a number of "tracks" on which data may be recorded in the form of magnetic spots.

GHz Gigahertz, now the standard measure of speed used for a *microprocessor*; 1 GHz equals 1 billion electrical cycles per second. Personal computers today typically come with 1.5–2.5 GHz chips.

Gigabyte (G) One billion *bytes*.

Graphical user interface (GUI) A system that uses icons (symbols) seen on the screen to represent available functions. These icons are generally manipulated by a mouse and/or a keyboard. This approach contrasts with the more traditional method of using typed commands.

Groupware Network programming that enables groups of users to work together by providing communication, workflow and task-sharing functions.

Hard disk A sealed cartridge containing magnetic storage disk(s) that holds much more memory—up to more than 100 *gigabytes*—than *floppy disks*. Usually a hard disk is built into the computer, but it can be a peripheral.

Hardware The physical equipment, as opposed to the programs and procedures, used in data processing. It covers not only computers themselves but also *peripherals* (see "Software").

Host The computer used to run programs and store files for remote users or in a LAN.

Icon A graphic symbol on the display screen that represents a file, peripheral, or some other object or function; for example, scissors are generally used to indicate cut-and-paste editing.

Integrated circuit An entire electronic circuit contained on one piece of material. Originally, electronic components (transistors, capacitors, etc.) were placed on a metal chassis and wired together. The first integrated circuit began with a single board (originally plastic), onto which strips of conducting material were sprayed. Electronic components could then be inserted directly onto the board (see "Silicon chip").

Kilobyte (K) A unit of measure for data storage or transmission equivalent to 1,024 bytes, but often rounded to 1,000.

Laptop A portable computer small enough to operate in one's lap. Generally a laptop weighs less than 15 pounds and uses a *liquid crystal display* monitor rather than a *cathode ray tube*.

Liquid crystal display (LCD) A type of flat-panel display monitor used in *laptop computers*.

Local area networks (LANs) Systems that allow users to connect PCs to one another or to *minicomputers* or *mainframes*.

Mainframe computer Generally the largest, fastest, and most expensive kind of computer, usually costing millions of dollars and requiring special cooling. Mainframe computers can accommodate hundreds of simultaneous users and normally are run around the clock; typically they are owned by large companies.

Massively parallel A form of computer architecture that uses hundreds or thousands of inexpensive *microprocessors* to perform many operations simultaneously.

Megabyte (M) One million *bytes*.

Menu-driven A *program* that uses a number of "menus," or lists of possible activities from which the operator chooses in order to activate the appropriate commands. This is the alternative to a command-driven program, for which the operator must remember a number of commands in order to tell the computer what to do.

MHz Megahertz, a measure of microprocessing speed; 1 MHz equals 1 million electrical cycles per second.

Microprocessor A complete central processing unit assembled on one single silicon chip.

MIPS (million instructions per second) A measure of computer processing speed.

Modem (modulator-demodulator) A device capable of converting a digital (computer-compatible) signal to an analog signal, which can be transmitted via a telephone line, reconverted, and then "read" by another computer.

Monitor   The display device on a computer, similar to a television screen.

Motherboard   The largest printed circuit board in a computer, housing the CPU chip and controlling circuitry.

Mouse   A small box connected by cable to a computer and featuring one or more button-style switches. When moved around a desk, the mouse causes a symbol on the computer screen to make corresponding movements. By selecting items on the screen and pressing a button on the mouse, the user can perform certain functions much more quickly than by typing commands on the keyboard.

Network   An interconnected group of computers that can exchange information or work together on different parts of the same problem.

Notebook   A type of full-function portable computer that uses miniaturized components, weighs about 4-6 pounds, and can be carried in a briefcase.

Operating system   A sequence of programming codes that instructs a computer about its various parts and peripherals and how to operate them. Operating systems deal only with the workings of the *hardware* and are separate from *software* programs.

Peripheral   A device connected to the computer that provides communication or auxiliary functions. There are three types of peripherals: input devices, such as keyboards; output devices, such as *monitors* and printers; and storage devices, such as magnetic discs.

Personal computer   A computer used by an individual at home or in the office.

Platform   A fundamental layer of software required to make other systems run—used interchangeably with operating system, the most common type of platform. The Internet, local networks, Web browsers, and Java are all frequently viewed as platforms.

Program   As a noun, a prepared set of instructions for the computer, often with provisions for the operator to choose among various options. As a verb, to create such a set of instructions.

Random-access memory (RAM)   A temporary storage space in which data may be held on a chip rather than being stored on disk or tape. The contents of RAM may be accessed or altered at any time during a session, but will be lost when the computer is turned off (see "Read-only memory").

Read-only memory (ROM)   A type of *chip* memory, the contents of which have been permanently recorded in a computer by the manufacturer and cannot be altered by the user (see "Random access memory").

RISC chip   Reduced Instruction Set Computer chip, such as the Apple-IBM Power PC chip, which gains speed by using fewer instructions than the more familiar Complex Instruction Set chip.

RSS   Short for RDF Site Summary, Rich Site Summary or Really Simple Syndication; a format for syndicating web content, used most commonly with news sites and *blogs*.

Server   The central computer in a network, providing a service or data access to client computers on the network.

Software   The *programs* and procedures, as opposed to the physical equipment, used in data processing (see "Hardware").

Spreadsheet   A *program* that performs mathematical operations on numbers arranged in large arrays; used mainly for accounting and other record keeping.

Supercomputer   The fastest of the *mainframe* class of computers, usually used for complex scientific calculations.

Terabyte (TB)   One trillion *bytes*.

Transistor   A small piece of semiconducting material (material that conducts electricity better than, say, wood but not as well as metal). Flows of electrons within the transistor can be controlled, enabling it to act as an electronic "switching" device. In other words, it can record information in the form of an "on" or an "off" signal. Early transistors were about one-hundredth the size of *vacuum tubes*, required very little energy, and generated no heat.

UNIX   A multi-user, multitasking operating system designed to run on a wide variety of computers, from microcomputers to mainframes.

Virus   A computer program segment or string of code that can attach itself to another program or file, reproduce itself, and spread from one computer to another. Viruses can destroy or change data and in other ways sabotage computer systems.

Window   A portion of the screen display used to view simultaneously a different part of the file in use or a part of a different file than the one in use.

Workstation   High-performance *computers* with advanced graphics capabilities designed for use by scientists and engineers.

Personal Computer Sales, 1985–2007

Year	Unit sales[1] (thousands)	Dollar sales[1] (millions)	Average unit price
1985	3,200	$2,175	$700
1990	4,000	4,187	1,050
1995	8,400	12,600	1,500
1997	11,000	15,950	1,450
1998	12,800	16,640	1,300
1999	14,900	16,390	1,100
2000	16,400	16,400	1,000
2002	N.A.	12,609	N.A.
2004	N.A.	18,233	N.A.
2006	N.A.	19,666	N.A.
2007[1]	N.A.	20,264	N.A.

Note: 1. Sales to dealers.
Source: U.S. Census Bureau, Statistical Abstract 2006 (2007).

Computer and Internet Users, 1995–2006

	Computer Users 2000	Computer Users 2006	Internet Users 2000	Internet Users 2006
Percent by age				
18-29	83%	84%	82%	83%
30-49	81	84	80	82
50-64	72	74	68	70
65+	31	35	28	33
Percent by education				
Less than high school	36%	38%	35%	36%
High school graduate	63	63	59	59
Some college	81	87	80	84
College graduate	90	92	88	91
All adults	71%	73%	69%	70%

Source: U.S. Census Bureau, *Statistical Abstract 2007* (2008).

Chronology of Information Processing

B.C.
500   Bead-and-wire abacus in use in Egypt.**A.D.**
200   Computing trays in use in China and Japan.
1340   Double-entry bookkeeping originates in Lombardy.
c. 1621   Mathematician William Oughtred (English: 1574–1660) invents slide rule.
1642   Blaise Pascal (French: 1623–62) invents "pascaline"—the first calculating machine, capable of addition and subtraction.
1679   Gottfried Wilhelm Leibniz (German: 1646–1716) perfects binary system of notation that eventually will be used by all computers; also develops improved version of pascaline, capable of multiplication and division.
1801   Joseph-Marie Jacquard (French: 1752–1834) uses punched cards to control operation of his mechanical loom—precursor of cards used in early data-storage systems.
1822   Charles Babbage (English: 1792–1871) designs and builds prototype of "Difference Engine" for calculating logarithms.
1833   Babbage designs "Analytical Engine," a computing machine featuring printed card input, memory, and printed output, and capable of being programmed to perform different tasks. Forerunner of modern computer, it never goes beyond design stage.
1847   George Boole (English: 1815–64) publishes *Mathematical Analysis of Logic*, which treats logic as a branch of mathematics (Boolean Algebra).
1853   Pehr Georg Scheutz and his son Edvard G.R. Scheutz (Swedish: 1785–1873; 1821–81) complete version of Babbage's Difference Engine.
1886   William S. Burroughs (American: 1855–98) develops first commercially successful mechanical adding machine.
1887   U.S. Census Bureau holds competition for device to speed up computation of census information; Herman Hollerith (American: 1860–1929) designs winning tabulating machine. His Tabulating Machine Co. (founded 1911) becomes IBM in 1924.
1890   Hollerith's electromechanical machine processes U.S. Census results in six weeks—one-third the time taken in 1880.
1894   Otto Steiger develops "Millionaire," the first commercially successful machine capable of direct multiplication, as opposed to multiplication by repeated addition.
1931   Vannevar Bush (American: 1890–1974) completes "differential analyser," first computing machine to use electronic components (vacuum tubes in which values could be stored as voltages).
1936   Mathematician Alan M. Turing (English: 1912–54) publishes "On Computable Numbers," which describes hypothetical computer with infinite storage capacity, capable of performing any conceivable calculation.
1937   John V. Atanasoff (American: 1903–1995) starts work on first electronic computer.
1938   Konrad Zuse (German: 1910–95) builds "Z1," the first computing machine to use binary, instead of decimal, method of operation. Other features include keyboard to input information and system of electric bulbs to signal results of calculations.
1939   Atanasoff and Clifford Berry complete ABC device, first digital computer.
1940   Zuse's Z2 machine introduces electromagnetic relays (as used in telephone switching gear) to store numbers.

First Generation: Vacuum Tubes
1943   British government uses first fully electronic computer to crack German military codes. Designed by Turing, "Colossus" uses 2,000 vacuum tubes to perform calculations and digest information at rate of 5,000 characters per second.

1944   Completion of "Harvard Mark I," designed by Howard H. Aiken (American: 1900–1973) and built by IBM. Vast, over 50 ft. long, it was obsolete almost immediately because it used electromagnetic relays rather than vacuum tubes.
1946   At the University of Pennsylvania, the ENIAC (Electronic Numerical Integrator and Calculator) multiplies five-digit number by itself 5,000 times in half a second. Designed by J. Presper Eckert, Jr. (American: 1919–) and John W. Mauchly (American: 1907–80) to calculate ballistic trajectories, ENIAC occupies 2,000 sq. ft., weighs 50 tons, uses 18,000 vacuum tubes, and can store about 20 words in its memory.

John von Neumann (Hungarian-American: 1903–57) publishes paper suggesting that instructions given to computer—"programs"—can themselves be stored by computer in numerical form.

First use of term *bit* to mean binary digit.
1948   "Mark I," designed by Tom Kilburn (English: 1921–2001) and Sir Frederic C. Williams (English: 1911–77) at Manchester University, England, is first computer to utilize von Neumann's concept of stored programs.

John Bardeen (American: 1908–91), Walter H. Brattain (American: 1902–87), and William B. Shockley (English-American: 1910–89) invent the transistor, which will eventually replace vacuum tube and make computers faster.

IBM, Bell Telephone, and Sperry-Rand each begin production of commercial computers.

First chess-playing computer built at M.I.T.
1950   Eckert and Mauchly's EDVAC (Electronic Discrete Variable Automatic Computer) is first to use magnetic disks for storage.
1951   Lyons Tea Shop Co. in England uses specially designed computer ("LEO") to perform routine administrative functions.

Eckert and Mauchly's UNIVAC (Universal Automatic Computer) is installed at U.S. Bureau of Census. UNIVAC uses magnetic tape for input and becomes first commercially successful machine, selling over 50 models.
1952   One hour after polls close, CBS television network uses UNIVAC to predict Eisenhower's landslide victory in U.S. presidential election. Prediction was based on less than 10 percent of the votes.
1953   First high-speed printer linked to a computer.

IBM introduces its first stored-program computer, the vacuum-tube-based "701."
1956   First use of term artificial intelligence.

Second Generation: Transistors
1958   Control Data Corp. introduces first fully transistorized computer, the CDC 1604, designed by Seymour Cray (American: 1925–1996).

Jack St. C. Kilby (American: 1923–2005) of Texas Instruments and Robert Noyce (American: 1927–90) of Intel Corp. independently produce first integrated circuits.
1959   First commercially marketed program.

IBM markets its first transistorized computers.
1960   The PDP-1, developed by Digital Equipment Corp., is the first commercial computer to use a keyboard and monitor instead of punched cards.

Introduction of removable magnetic disks for data storage.

Third Generation: Integrated Circuits
1965   IBM markets its first integrated-circuit based computer, the 360.

Digital Equipment Corp. markets the first minicomputer, the PDP-8.
1969   Graduate student Alan Kay, later to become top designer with Apple Computer Co., writes doctoral thesis describing hypothetical "personal computer."

ARPANET, the first part of the Internet, is set up to ink Defense Department contractors.

1970 Lexitron introduces first word processor, a computer designed specifically to handle written text. It features a cathode ray tube (CRT) terminal, as used in television sets, to display information.

Floppy disk is introduced for data storage.

1971 Intel Corp. announces first microprocessor, several integrated circuits contained on one silicon chip.

First electronic pocket calculator produced by Texas Instruments; it weighs about 2½ lbs. and costs about $150.

1973 Introduction of "bit-mapped" monitor capable of high-resolution graphics display.

Xerox markets first hand-held "mouse," a timesaving device for giving commands to computer.

Intel introduces 8080 microprocessor, which will become the central processing unit (CPU) of several microcomputers.

1975 First personal computer, the MITS Altair 8800, is marketed in kit form, with memory of 256 bytes.

Cray Research (founded 1972) announces the Cray-1 supercomputer, capable of 100 million operations per second.

1976 Apple Computer Co. founded by Stephen Wozniak and Steven Jobs (American: 1955–) in the Jobs family garage; first Apple "boards" (self-assembly personal computer kits) go on sale.

1977 Apple markets Apple II—the first widely accepted personal computer. Commodore and Tandy also begin to sell personal computers.

Microsoft Corp. founded by Bill Gates and Paul Allen.

1978 Hayes Microcomputer Products introduces Micromodem 100, the first microcomputer-compatible modem.

1979 Micropro International releases WordStar word processing program for personal computers.

1980 Microsoft adapts the UNIX operating system for use with microcomputers; paves way for personal computers to begin performing tasks associated with larger machines.

1981 IBM introduces its first personal computer, the IBM PC. Using operating system called PC-DOS, developed by Microsoft, it almost immediately becomes the industry standard.

Ashton-Tate introduces dBASE II, the first popular database program for microcomputers.

1982 Microsoft introduces MS-DOS, a version of the PC-DOS operating system designed for IBM PC; allows other manufacturers to produce copies ("clones") of the IBM machine.

Compaq announces its first portable computer (IBM-compatible).

1983 Apple introduces Apple IIe and "Lisa."

First IBM-compatible "laptop" computer introduced by Gavilan Corp.

Lotus Development Corp. introduces 1-2-3, a best-selling program for managing business spreadsheets.

Introduction of optical (laser-readable) disks.

1984 Apple introduces Macintosh. With list price of $2,495, it includes Apple's first "Mac" software programs, MacWrite (for text) and MacPaint (for graphics). Fifty thousand are sold within three months. IBM markets the PC AT (Advanced Technology) model.

1985 Apple's LaserWriter printer and Aldus Corp.'s PageMaker program usher in age of desktop publishing.

Introduction of erasable optical storage disks.

Toshiba markets first widely used laptop computer.

Cray 2 supercomputer is capable of 1.2 billion operations per second.

1986 IBM announces OS/2, a new operating system that allows personal computers to run several programs simultaneously (called multitasking).

1987 Apple introduces Macintosh SE and Macintosh II. IBM introduces Personal System/2 (PS/2), features of which include high-resolution VGA (Video Graphics Array) display.

1988 Computer security becomes an urgent issue when a "worm" program penetrates thousands of systems on Internet information network.

Motorola announces new microprocessor, the 88000, a 32-bit RISC (Reduced Instruction Set Computer) chip.

First IBM PS/2 "clones" announced.

IBM and Sears launch Prodigy, an on-line service enabling subscribers with a computer and modem to access a central information bank.

Parallel processing technique introduced that utilizes many inexpensive microprocessors to perform a large number of operations simultaneously.

1989 Intel announces the iPSC/860 chip, containing one million transistors; designed to give a microcomputer the power and speed normally associated with supercomputers.

IBM announces production of commercial quantities of four-megabyte chips.

First portable computers with color liquid crystal displays (LCDs) announced.

1990 Software writer Tim Berners-Lee writes the program for the World Wide Web to make the Internet easier to use for physicists at CERN in Geneva.

1991 The Thinking Machines Inc. CM-200 massively parallel supercomputer can perform 9.03 billion calculations per second.

1993 Intel begins shipping the Pentium chip with 3.1 million transistors on it; it operates twice as fast as the best previous Intel chip for personal computers.

Electrical engineers from the Univ. of Colorado claim the first fully optical computer that can store, transmit, and process data entirely in the form of light, with no electron intermediaries.

1994 Apple introduces the first personal computers to use the Power PC RISC Chip.

1995 Microsoft introduces its Windows 95 operating system software, featuring an improved interface and better multimedia support.

1997 In a six-game match, the IBM RS/6000 SP supercomputer (known as Deep Blue) defeats world chess champion Garry Kasparov, the first time a computer has beaten a player of this caliber.

Intel introduces a Pentium chip with MMX technology, enhancing multimedia capabilities on a PC.

1999 The total number of Internet users in the U.S. tops 100 million.

2000 The new century begins with minimal disruption from the much-feared Y2K programming bug.

Household penetration of personal computers in the United States surpasses 50 percent.

A U.S. federal circuit court judge finds the software giant Microsoft in violation of antitrust laws and orders the company broken up into two parts. Microsoft appeals.

2001 The U.S. high-tech industry hits hard times. The investment "bubble" in dot.com companies bursts, forcing numerous Web ventures to shut down. PC sales decline for the first time in decades. Still, the number of Internet users continues to climb, reaching 143 million—or 54 percent of the population.

A federal district judge issues an injunction against Napster, Inc., to halt the free exchange of copyright-protected music on the company's popular Internet site. Napster is later acquired by the German-based media giant Bertelsmann.

Microsoft and the U.S. Justice Department reach a settlement in their antitrust dispute by which the software company will be left intact in exchange for specific restrictions on anticompetitive behavior.

2002 A new Japanese supercomputer, called Earth Simulator, achieves a processing speed of 35,600 gigaflops (billions of calculations per second) — five times faster than its closest competitor.

TELECOMMUNICATIONS

Over the course of barely two decades, innovations in data transfer and information processing technologies have combined with increased satellite access, the spread of fiber optic cable, and the explosive growth of the Internet to fuel a communications revolution in North America, Europe, and the industrialized nations of Asia. The proliferation of cellular phones, mobile radio phones, paging services, and personal communication systems (PCS) has greatly expanded the communications capabilities of both consumers and business in terms of speed, accessibility, and cost.

For the telecommunications industry itself—including service providers, equipment manufacturers, and other support services—the enormous growth and promise of the late 1990s is returning after a brief slow between 2000 and 2002. In 2003, overall industry growth began to pick up. The total U.S. marketplace in 2006, according to the Telecommunications Industry Association (TIA), generated revenues of an estimated $944.7 billion, a 10.2 percent increase over 2005 (following 9.5 percent growth in 2004, 6.6 percent growth in 2001). Of total 2006 revenues, $324.7 billion derived from calling services—local exchange access, toll service, and wireless service. The transition from conventional land-line usage wireless usage continues, as reflected by a 13. percent rise in wireless service revenues, to $134. billion. Equipment manufacturers and softwar developers saw revenues recover slowly after drop of 11.7 percent in 2002, rising by 8.9 percent in 2006, to $180.4 billion.

The TIA estimated growth for the U.S. telecommunications industry in 2006 at nearly 10.2 per cent. The increase in service revenues, however, i expected to lag that of the industry as a whole and of wireless services most drastically, in the foreseeable future-to the great advantage of con sumers. Continued expansion of the Interne user base and competitive pricing in the long-dis

Largest U.S. Telecommunications Companies, 2006

Rank, Company	Access lines ('000s)	Operating revenues (millions)	Change in revenues, 2005-06
1. AT&T	66,470	$63,055	+34.5 %
2. Verizon	45,100	88,144	+26.8
3. Alltel	14,899	7,884	+19.9
4. Qwest	13,795	13,923	–
5. Sprint Nextel	N.A.	41,028	+42.5

Source: U.S. Federal Communications Commission, *Statistics of Communications Common Carriers* (annual); annual reports.

U.S. Telecommunications Marketplace, 2000–2006 (millions of dollars)

Service	2000	2003	2004	2005	2006[1]
Total Transport Services	$283,600	$287,630	$298,254	$310,824	$324,656
Local Exchange Services	118,795	121,994	120,694	118,470	116,826
Toll Service	109,615	76,707	74,294	73,780	73,060
Wireless Services	55,190	88,929	103,266	118,574	134,770
Specialized Services	2,721	4,720	5,450	6,200	7,090
Support Services	176,200	264,500	300,700	345,900	402,300
Equipment and Software	167,672	137,620	157,153	165,695	180,393
Industry Total[2]	$641,996	$687,887	$720,500	$769,491	$944,711

Notes: **1.** Estimated. **2.** Installation charges included in both support services and equipment but only once in industry total.
Source: Telecommunications Industry Association (Arlington, Va.), *2006 Telecommunications Market Review and Forecast.* Reprinted by permission.

U.S. Telephone Systems, 1985–2001

Year	1985	1990	1995	1999	2000	2001
Local Exchange Carriers						
Carriers	55	51	53	52	52	52
Access lines (millions)	112	130	166	228	245	253
Business (millions)	31	36	46	57	58	54
Residential (millions)	79	89	101	115	115	112
Other (millions)	2	6	19	53	72	87
Local calls (billions)	365	402	484	554	537	515
Local service revenues (billions)	$32	$46	$52	$58	$60	$58
Long-Distance Carriers						
Carriers	N.A.	325	583	N.A.	700+	700+
Toll calls (billions)	N.A.	63	94	102	106	98
Toll service revenues (billions)	$43	$52	$74	$99	$100	$91
International Service						
U.S.-billed calls (millions)	411	984	2,821	5,215	5,269	5,627
U.S.-billed minutes (billions)	3.4	8.0	15.9	28.0	28.2	29.2
U.S.-billed revenues (billions)	$3.5	$8.0	$14.0	$14.4	14.5	$14.1

Source: U.S. Federal Communications Commission, *Statistics of Communications Common Carriers* (annual).

ance market have steadily increased consumer demand for conventional phone service, even as usage has declined. As of year-end 2001, the total number of U.S. residential and business access lines exceeded 253 million, a nearly 11 percent rise from 1999. This did not even include the rapidly growing wireless segment. At the same time, however, Americans placed 515 billion landline local calls in 2001 (down from 537 billion from 2000), generating an estimated $58 billion in revenues (down $2 billion). The decline in number of calls was due, in large part, to the transition of many home Internet users to broadband wireless alternatives. The rise in local call rates cannot be expected to be reversed until the much-dis-

cussed deregulation of local phone service becomes a reality.

As wireless communications transform the telecommunications market, statistics such as the number of local and long distance calls Americans make each year, or the average rate of a long distance call, are becoming harder for organizations such as the FCC to track. As new technologies become widely used, different ways of defining growth and consumer preferences are emerging.

Wireless Communications By far the most rapid growth in the telecommunications service industry has come in the wireless segment. From 1995 through 2006, the total wireless market more than quadrupled in size, from $25.4 billion to more than $133 billion. Cellular phones continue to account for a majority of wireless service spending, but personal communications systems (PCSs)-handheld devices with fax capability and Internet access-and other equipment are expected to gain share. Some analysts expect wireless usage to account for half of all U.S. telecom service revenues within a few years.

From 1990 to 2005, the number of subscribers to a cellular phone system jumped from 5.3 million to an estimated 207.9 million. Service revenues skyrocketed from $4.5 billion at the beginning of the 1990s to about $113.5 billion in 2005. The one-year increase was 11 percent from 102.1 billion, following 17 percent in 2002 and 24 percent in 2001, and the explosion was expected to continue in coming years.

The paging and messaging market, which grew impressively throughout the 1990s, began to shrink in 2000 and has continued to do so. With cellular

Wireless Communication Services Spending in U.S.,1997-2006 (in millions)

Year	Wireless Telephony	Paging	Total
1998	32,207	5,304	37,511
1999	40,018	4,692	44,710
2000	52,466	2,724	55,190
2002	76,508	1,540	78,103
2003	87,624	1,230	88,929
2004	102,121	1,005	103,266
2005	117,284	960	118,574
2006[1]	133,416	944	134,770

Note: 1. Projected. **Source:** Telecommunications Industry Association. *2005 Telecommunications Market Review and Forecast.*

Cellular Telephone Industry Growth in the U.S., 1990-2005

Year	Systems	Subscriber	Cell sites[1]	Employees	Service revenue (millions)	Average monthly bill
1990	751	5,283,000	5,616	21,382	$4,548	$80.90
1995	1,627	33,786,000	22,683	68,165	19,081	51.00
1998	3,073	69,209,321	65,887	134,754	33,133	39.43
2000	2,440	109,478,031	104,288	188,449	52,466	45.27
2001	2,587	128,374,512	127,540	203,589	65,316	47.37
2002	2,846	140,766,842	139,338	192,410	76,508	48.40
2003	3,123	158,721,981	162,986	205,629	87,624	49.91
2004	N.A.	182,140,362	175,725	226,016	102,121	50.64
2005	N.A.	207,896,198	183,689	233,067	113,538	49.98

1. A cell site is the basic geographic unit of a cellular system. A city or county is divided into smaller cells, each of which is equipped with a low-powered radio transmitter/receiver. The cells can vary in size depending on terrain, capacity, demands, etc. By controlling the transmission power, the radio frequencies assigned to one cell can be limited to the boundaries of that cell. When a cellular telephone moves from one cell to another, a computer at the switching office monitors the movement and transfers the phone call to the new cell and another radio frequency. **Source:** CTIA–The Wireless Association, annual wireless industry survey.

U.S. Paging and Messaging Market, 1990-2006

Year	Subscribers (millions)	Annual Percent Increase	Total Spending (millions)	Annual Percent Increase	Average Monthly Spending	Annual Percent Change
1990	9.9	22.2%	$1,744	17.8%	$14.68	-3.7%
1995	34.5	31.2	3,841	18.8	9.28	-9.4
1998	48.0	2.1	4,896	4.6	8.50	2.4
1999	45.0	-6.3	4,671	-4.6	8.65	1.8
2000	30.0	-33.3	3,168	-32.2	8.80	1.7
2002	14.1	-21.7	1,565	-19.5	9.25	2.8
2003	11.2	-20.6	1,284	-18.0	9.55	3.2
2004	9.1	-18.8	1,005	-18.3	9.20	0.5
2005	8.7	-4.4	960	-4.4	10.15	0.0
2006[1]	8.5	-2.3	944	-1.8	9.25	0.5

1. Projected. **Source:** Telecommunications Industry Association, *2006 Telecommunications Market Review and Forecast.* Reprinted by permission.

telephones serving the needs of many pager users, the number of paging/messaging subscribers (estimated at 8.5 million in 2006) has fallen to less than a quarter of the number that subscribed in 1999 (45 million).

New forms of wireless communication promise even greater versatility and broader usage. Personal communication systems, which transmit cellular calls digitally, provide superior reception. They allow users to download information from the Internet or a corporate data network right to wireless, phones. Local multipoint distributions systems are also expected to see rapid implementation.

Satellites The wireless revolution in telecommunications has been made possible, in large part, by the bandwidth capacity of geostationary satellites orbiting the Earth. As of 2002, more than 250 U.S. and European communications satellites were in place. But with launchings proceeding at record pace—reaching 40 in 2000—commercial satellite bandwidth began to exceed demand, and the number of commercial launchings declined to only 16 in 2001. The industry rebounded well in 2002, however, with more than 30 new satellites placed in orbit and a similar number expected in 2003. About 95 percent of commercial launchings are communications satellites, and about 85 percent are geostationary. As of Sept. 2004, approximately 280 U.S. and 175 non-U.S. European commercial communications satellites were in place

Growth in residential broadband service likely to be dominated by the cable industry—: suggested by the failures of various global sate lite-system ventures—but many analysts conti ued to predict a key role for satellites in the futur Digital radio may prove to be another major cor sumer electronics market served by satellite.

Telecom Industry Competition for the burgeon ing wireless market, declining prices for long-dis tance service, an excess of optic fiber capacit turbulence in the investment market, and im proper or questionable accounting practices mad the period 2000-2002 one of the most difficult eve for the U.S. telecom industry. Virtually every majo company faced a squeeze on profits and declinin share prices. In 2002, the Dow Jones Telecommuni cations Index fell a whopping 36 percent. Five o the eight largest U.S. phone companies showed de clines in annual operating revenue and net in come. WorldCom, after revelations of gros accounting errors, declared bankruptcy in July 2002—the biggest company (in terms of corporate assets) ever to do so. In April 2003, the company filed a reorganization plan with the U.S. Bankruptcy Court and announced that it was changing its name to MCI and moving its headquarters to Ashburn, Virginia—followed shortly by charges from competitors that it had inappropriately handled access fees.

U.S. Consumer Telecommunications Market, 1990–2006

Product	1990	1995	2000	2003	2004	2006[1]
Total Unit Shipments (millions)	**55.9**	**81.5**	**134.5**	**144.9**	—	—
Corded telephone	22.0	25.8	29.7	22.1	17.4	14.4
Cordless telephone	10.1	19.5	39.0	40.3	37.6	33.6
Cellular/PCS handset	8.7	15.9	43.2	58.2	—	—
Answering machine	13.6	17.5	19.9	22.5	24.1	25.7
Home fax machine	1.5	2.8	2.7	2.1	1.8	1.0
Total Dollar Sales (millions)	**$8,686**	**$8,501**	**$10,722**	**$10,362**	—	—
Corded telephone	765	668	463	307	311	284
Cordless telephone	1,170	1,913	1,953	1,585	1,418	1,204
Cellular/PCS handset	4,698	3,578	6,696	6,470	—	—
Answering machine	953	1,242	1,132	1,392	1,465	1,362
Home fax machine	1,100	1,100	463	356	223	104

Note: 1. Projected. **Source:** Telecommunications Industry Association (Arlington, Va.), *2006 Telecommunications Market Review and Forecast.*

Percent of U.S. Homes with Telecommunications Equipment, 1990–2002

Product	1990	1995	1997	1998	1999	2000	2001	2002
Telephone answering device	31%	54%	65%	69%	72%	74%	77%	78%
Cordless telephone	25	52	66	70	75	78	81	81
Home computer	23	22	40	42	48	54	58	60
Fax and/or fax modems	N.A.	16	19	25	38	51	55	56
Wireless telephone	N.A.	20	34	39	44	51	59	66

Note: As of January of each year.
Source: Telecommunications Industry Association (Arlington, Va.); *MultiMedia Telecommunications Market Review and Forecast* (2002).

Televisions, Telephones, and Computers per Capita, by Selected Nation, 2003 (number per 1,000 people)

Nation	Cable television subscribers (2003)	Television sets (2003)	Telephone main lines (2003)	Cellular phone subscribers (2003)	Personal computers (2003)
Algeria	—	114	69	46	8
Argentina	165	326	219[2]	178	82
Australia	72	731	542	720	601
Austria	127	621	480	879	374
Belgium	370	543	494	786	318
Brazil	14	349	223	264	75
Bulgaria	93	453[4]	368[2]	333	52
Canada	253	691	629	417	487
Chile	46	494	230[2]	428	119
China	69	312	209	214	28
Colombia	14[4]	286	200	141	49
Cuba	—	251	51[3]	2	24
Czech Republic	94	538	360	965	177
Denmark	201	859	669	887	577
Dominican Republic	—	—	115[2]	271	—
Ecuador	34	225	119[2]	184	32
Egypt	—	231	127	85	29
Finland	192	678	488	901	442
France	55	632	566	696	347
Germany	246	637	659	785	485
Ghana	0	53	14	36	4
Greece	475	519	454	780	82
Guatemala	—	145	71[2]	132	14
Honduras	8[4]	122	48[2]	49	15
Hungary	160	475	361	676	108
India	39	83	46	25	7
Indonesia	0	153	372	55	12
Iran	—	171	220	51	91
Iraq	—	834	30[1]	—[2]	—
Ireland	160	395	486	844	421
Israel	184	330	453[2]	955	243
Italy	1	494[4]	484	1,018	231
Jamaica	—	374	169[2]	533	54
Japan	167	731	558[2]	680	302
Korea, South	132	363	472	694	558
Kuwait	—	418	198	578	161
Lebanon	30	357	199[2]	227	100
Malaysia	—	202	182	442	167
Mexico	25	282	147[2]	255	83
Morocco	—	167	41	243	20
Netherlands	392	553	614	768	467
New Zealand	7	557	448[2]	648	414
Norway	185	884	734[2]	909	528
Pakistan	0	150	27	2	4
Panama	—	194	129[2]	268	38
Peru	17	149	67	106	43
Philippines	31	173	42[2]	191	28
Poland	91	422	319	451	142
Portugal	108	413	414	904	134
Puerto Rico	91	339	—	209[2]	—
Romania	121	379[4]	205	329	97
Russia	43	538[4]	242	120	89
Saudi Arabia	—	265	155	321	138
Singapore	73	300	463[2]	796	622
South Africa	—	159	107	364	73
Spain	15	564	429	916	196
Sweden	224	965	736[2]	889	621
Switzerland	369	552	744[2]	843	709
Syria	—	172	123[2]	24	29
Taiwan	—	—	590[2]	1,108	—
Thailand	2	300	106	260	40
Turkey	14	319	277	408	43
United Kingdom	64	950	591[2]	841	406
United States	256	938	621	543	660
Uruguay	—	530[4]	280[2]	193	110
Venezuela	40	186	112[2]	256	61

Notes: 1. 1999 figures. **2.** 2002 figures. **3.** 2001 figures. **4.** 2000 figures. **Source:** International Telecommunications Union, *World Telecommunication Report 2003*; The World Bank, *World Development Indicators*.

THE INTERNET

The Internet, an intricate global web of hundreds of thousands of computer networks linked by conventional telephone lines (and now such high-speed alternatives as cable modem and DSL), was created by the U.S. Defense Department in 1969 as a faster way for agencies to share information and as an emergency means of communications in case more traditional means were cut off. But the potential for consumer Internet use didn't occur until the 1980s, when the National Science Foundation created equipment that would allow other computer networks to connect to the government's larger network. From there, commercial services such as CompuServe, Prodigy, and America Online tapped into the ever-growing network and brought a wealth of information to anybody with a computer, a modem, and the monthly fee. In 1993 some three million people worldwide were connected to the Internet. By mid-2007, the total number of users was approaching 1.2 billion.

Today, the Internet is the world's largest communications network. The number of names registered in the *domain name system*—Web sites of commercial enterprises, public institutions, and private individuals—exceeded 50 million by 2003. The networks and switches that make up the Internet carry data around the world in seconds, and link even the most remote user to a vast wealth of resources. The most popular network on the Internet is the *World Wide Web* (WWW, or simply, "the Web"), created in 1989 by CERN, the European Particle Physics Lab in Geneva and made available on the Internet in Aug. 1991. In 1993, the creation of software (Mosaic) that displayed the Internet in a format that resembled a magazine with text and graphics dramatically increased Net usage. In 1994, the Netscape browser came on the market, and since then, the Internet has become hugely popular, as computer users found they could navigate the Web quickly and easily.

In just a few short years, the Internet and the Web have quite literally transformed the way millions of people go about their daily lives. Everything from mundane tasks like banking or ordering tickets to more eventful activities like searching for a job or a date, planning a vacation, or buying a house, can all be done sitting in front of a computer. Physicians, lawyers, real estate agents and marketing specialists, among others, can get vital public documents and other information over the Net. Meanwhile, businesses can market products, purchase materials and services, and carry out other essential activities. For ordinary users, e-mail is by far the most popular online activity. As of 2005, more than half of the U.S. population used it regularly. Worldwide, more than 10 billion messages a day were being sent. If overhyped and overinvested in the 1990s, the Internet remains the fastest-growing and most versatile resource in media history.

Who Uses the Internet?

Almost unheard of before 1990, the Internet has entered the vocabulary of most Americans and the homes of a large number of them. Because Internet use is decentralized and almost completely

U.S. Web Usage Snapshot, August 2008

Monthly Average Usage	Home	Work
Sessions/Visits Per Person	36	64
Domains Visited Per Person	65	120
PC Time Per Person	37:35:52	81:14:08
Duration of a Web Page Viewed	00:00:51	00:00:57
Active Online Users Estimate[1]	153.1 mil.	67.6 mil.
Total Online Users Estimate[2]	220.9 mil.	71.5 mil.

Note: 1. Individuals browsing or actively engaging web applications, IM, or web data sources. 2. Average total of all users connected at any time. Source: Nielsen/NetRatings

U.S. Top 10 Parent Internet Companies, August 2008

Accessed from Work	Audience[1] ('000s)	Reach[2] (%)	Avg. Visit Time
Google	59,095	87.45	02:18:12
Microsoft	58,216	86.15	02:24:38
Yahoo!	50,498	74.72	03:23:20
Time Warner	41,419	61.29	03:12:38
News Corp. Online	32,015	47.37	01:03:54
InterActiveCorp	31,618	46.79	00:20:21
eBay	31,575	46.72	01:55:13
Amazon	28,245	41.80	00:24:59
Wikimedia Foundation	28,181	41.70	00:17:05
Turner Network	27,536	40.75	00:40:55

Accessed from Home	Audience[1] ('000s)	Reach[2] (%)	Avg. Visit Time
Google	111,724	72.95	01:11:29
Microsoft	102,460	66.90	01:36:44
Yahoo!	96,523	63.03	02:22:37
Time Warner	78,004	50.93	02:40:28
News Corp. Online	62,031	40.51	01:50:48
InterActiveCorp	47,885	31.27	00:16:37
eBay	47,085	30.75	01:15:42
Amazon	39,552	25.83	00:19:39
Apple Computer	36,485	23.82	01:00:50
Wikimedia Foundation	36,252	23.67	00:18:20

Note: 1. Unique individuals. 2. Percent of all online users.
Source: Nielsen/NetRatings

Internet Users Worldwide, June 2007

Region	Users (millions)
Asia	436.8
Europe	321.9
North America	232.7
Latin America/Caribbean	110.0
Middle East	19.5
Oceania/Australia	18.9
Africa	33.5
World Total	1,173.1

Source: Internet World Stats.

Guide to Select Domain Name Suffixes

Suffix	Used by
.aero	Air transport industry (Reserved)
.biz	Businesses (alternative to .com)
.com	Commercial entities
.coop	Business cooperatives (Reserved)
.edu	Educational institutions
.gov	Government bodies (at any level)
.info	General use (alternative to .com)
.museum	Museums (Reserved)
.name	Private individuals for personal sites
.net	Internet-related institutions
.org	Nonprofit organizations
.pro	Professionals

Note: Note: "Reserved for" domains are sponsored by an organization that represents the specific domain community and is responsible for policies concerning those sites. Unsponsored domains operate under policies established by the global Internet community through ICANN.

unregulated, statistics on the number of users are difficult to verify and vary significantly among reporting services. By most accounts, however, the number of regular Internet users in the United States reached 50 million in 1998, about five years after the medium became viable for ordinary consumers. That narrow time frame easily eclipsed the 10 years for cable TV, 13 for television, and 38 for radio. And the user base continues to expand rapidly. A rapid increase from 2000 to 2005 put the number of U.S. Internet users at more than 200 million—nearly 68 percent of the total population. Even as evidence began to suggest that users were spending less time online, overall traffic continued to rise.

As the user base has expanded, the demographic profile of the average user has changed. According to several surveys, disparities in gender, age, income, education level, and race between Net users and non-users have continued to shrink. Children and teenagers still use the Internet more than any other age group. As of late 2001, according to a government study, 65 percent of 10–13 year-olds and 75 percent of 14–17 year-olds had Internet access. The median age of the average user, however, rose to 34. The gender gap also continued to close, as women surpassed men as a percentage of the over-18 user base (51 percent–49 percent) for the first time. Disparities remained in Internet access by income level; 86 percent of individuals with a family income of $75,000 or more had access, compared with only 12.7 percent of those with a family income under $15,000—but the latter group grew faster than the former. Likewise, access among blacks and Hispanics grew faster than among whites (33 percent and 30 percent versus 20 percent, respectively), though whites still accounted for 76 percent of users. The highest growth rate among types of households was single mothers with children.

In addition to the increases in the user base and overall traffic—and partly responsible for those increases—have come improvements in the means of access. As of late 2003, some 70 percent of U.S. Internet households still accessed the Net by telephone dial-up service, but such high-speed alternatives as cable modem and DSL (Digital Subscription Line) were growing rapidly. In 2005, Forrester Research predicted that 71 million U.S. households would connect to the Internet via broadband by 2010.

▶ THE WORLD WIDE WEB

The World Wide Web is a vast network of information within the Internet, which uses a hypertext system for quickly transmitting graphics, sound and video over phone lines. To read the information, users must have a *browser* (such as Netscape Navigator or Microsoft Internet Explorer). Because the hypertext system arranges information based on its relationship to other information rather than in linear or alphabetical order, the Web allows users to find information quickly, especially if they don't know exactly what they're looking for. Each piece of information, or *Web page*, can be connected to one or more other pages via a *link*. For example, the U.S. Census Bureau's Web site (www.census.gov) provides thousands of data tables produced by the Department of Commerce, and is also linked to data from 70 other government agencies.

The Web is divided into zones, which organize pages according to the type of information generally contained within them. There is of course some overlap, but generally, Web pages of educational institutions end in .edu; government Web pages end in .gov; Web pages of Internet-related institutions end in .net; commercial entities end with .com; and other organizations end with .org. In an attempt to relieve overcrowding in the .com and .net areas, the ICANN (Internet Corporation for Assigned Names and Numbers), the official governing body for domain names, created seven new suffixes (or TLDs, "Top-Level Domains") for use beginning in 2001: .aero, .biz, .coop, .info, .museum, .name, and .pro.

Growth of the Web It is becoming increasingly easy for companies, organizations, and even individuals to create their own Web sites. Millions of institutions, groups, and individuals have done so, resulting in such dramatic growth that the Web's 50 million sites in 2003 contained an estimated 6-8 billion pages (up to double the previous year's total) with 10K-20K of data per page. With so many sites throughout cyberspace, surfers would find it close to impossible to find what they were looking for without a *search engine*. Like a librarian who knows where in the library to find valuable information, search engines look through countless Web pages and create an index of what appears on each one. If you're looking for the rules of badminton, you can ask the search engine to sift hundreds of thousands of Web pages for the word badminton and it will return a list of Web pages that mention badminton. Google, MetaCrawler, AltaVista, and such newcomers as Teoma and WiseNut are some of the most popular search engines.

As the Internet has emerged as a mass medium, the major online service providers, search services, and other Web companies have competed ever more vigorously for user "audience." To attract the greatest number of visitors on a regular basis, many Web sites have expanded from their core services and established broad-based *portals*—whole arrays of services (such as e-mail, search, special-interest forums and bulletin boards, and chat rooms), information (news, weather, stock reports, reference resources), and links to other useful sites, all accessible from a single home page.

Business on the Web The increasing sophistication of both technology and users have made the World Wide Web a major and rapidly expanding business medium. No longer just a vehicle for publishing brochures and annual reports, the Web has emerged as a low-cost sales channel for producers of goods and services and as a highly convenient purchasing vehicle for end users.

Beginning late in 2000, however, a measure of reality came to the Internet industry, as the sky-high valuations of online ventures came back to earth, investors began demanding profitability, and a number of sites were simply shut down. Yet, while forecasts of e-commerce growth were scaled back, analysts reported strong increases.

A vast majority of all e-commerce is conducted between businesses, as the Internet has helped cut transaction costs, locate surplus or low-cost goods, and otherwise increase efficiencies. According to the research firm eMarketer, world-wide business-to-business net revenues were expected to reach $1.4 trillion in 2003, of which about half would be generated in the United States. The global figure was projected to nearly double in 2004, to $2.7 trillion, with the U.S. total exceeding $1 trillion.

Retail online purchasing, more familiar to the average consumer, suffered more severe setbacks in the dot-com shakeout, as numerous Net vendors were forced out of business. But reports of the death of online business-to-consumer merchandising were also premature. Retailers would be forced to show profits, but consumers continued to increase online spending. According to Jupiter Media Metrix, online retail revenues in the U.S. would reach $51.7 billion in 2003, up more than 50 percent from two years earlier, and were expected to reach $105 billion—or about 5 percent of all U.S. retail spending—in 2007. Jupiter estimated that some 97 million consumers, or nearly 60 percent of the total online population, would make an electronic purchase in 2003. The rate was only expected to increase as users become more comfortable with making online transactions. Travel, computers and consumer electronics, and books and music are the leading online retail categories.

One of the innovative and increasingly popular forms of e-commerce is online auctioning, which enables consumers to bid from their home computers on product offerings from private owners or original manufacturers and service providers. eBay, the largest person-to-person online trading community, claimed tens of millions of registered traders around the world and generated more than $23 billion in gross merchandise sales in 2003.

Few industries have undergone more radical and rapid change as a consequence of online commerce than stock brokerage and financial services. Round-the-clock access, lower service fees, and push-button immediacy have made it easier, cheaper, and faster for ordinary consumers to buy stock or apply for a loan directly online.

Advertising on the Web

Much as it has evolved as a communications and information medium, the World Wide Web, like television and and radio, has also emerged as a major vehicle of commercial advertising. The ads come in the form of banners, pop-up windows, and other Web-page design elements. E-mail has also proven to be viable as an advertising medium, giving birth to the next generation of direct-mail marketing.

The U.S. economic slowdown and shakeout in the dot-com industry in 2000-2002 slowed the growth of Internet advertising, but the rate of increase over the short life of the medium still far exceeded that of any other. And robust increases were expected in the years to come. Media analysts estimated global online ad spending in 2002 at $5-$6.0 billion, a significant decline from the previous year. .

Privacy and Intellectual Property Rights

As the popularity and purchasing power of the Internet have grown, and as monitoring tools have improved, many people have perceived a growing threat to their personal privacy. Software that tracks usage habits, network database technology, and the ability to transmit vast amounts of data have made it possible to collect and share detailed information about the browsing habits, interests and hobbies, buying patterns, financial history, and contact information of ordinary Internet-using citizens. The U.S. Congress in 2002 and 2003 considered various legislative measures to protect privacy and combat identity theft in the online environment.

In a similar vein, the data-sharing power of the Internet has undermined traditional protections for proprietary information and copyright materials. The issue came to the fore in 2000-2001, as the music industry successfully sued Napster.com, which enabled Web site visitors to swap MP3 music files of popular commercial recordings for free. But as millions of users continued to pirate digital songs, music and games through online file-sharing systems, copyright protection and intellectual property rights on the Internet loomed as major long-term issues.

▶ A GLOSSARY OF COMMONLY USED INTERNET TERMS

Account   Permission to use a computer on a network, or an access agreement with an Internet provider

Address   The location of an Internet host. An e-mail   address   might   take   the   form johndoe@xyz.com; a web address might look like www.xyztech.com. See also URL.

Applet   A small program, typically embedded in an Web page, that a user can quickly download and launch, thus enhancing the Web page's content.

Bandwidth   The amount of data, graphics, sound, and other information that can be transmitted through cyberspace at a certain time. Bandwidth is measured in kilobits per second (kbps). Most telephone modems have a bandwidth of 56 kbps (or simply 56k), though *cable modems* and *DSL* can offer bandwidths of more than 1 megabit per second (mbps).

Blog   Short for "weblog." A diary-like Web site, usually containing the personal thoughts of the site's owner as well as links to other sites of interest.

Bookmark   A browser feature (called "Favorites" in Microsoft Explorer) that stores a pointer to a Web site for easy access.

Browser   A program that translates the hypertext markup language of the World Wide Web into languages ordinary people can understand. Netscape and Microsoft Internet Explorer are the two most common Web browsers.

Cable Modem   A high-speed, broadband Internet connection via cable TV lines; services often include a selection of localized content.

Cache   (Pronounced "cash") The place on a hard drive where a Web browser stores images a user has downloaded off the Internet. If the user wants to see the same Web page again, the browser loads it from the cache rather than retrieve it again from the Internet.

Chat line "talk" An electronic forum in which Internet users can communicate with each other online.

Cookie A small piece of information that a Web *browser* picks up from another site and stores. Such bits of information can be read and altered by another site, thereby making it possible to identify users who have been to the site before. Cookies allow you to add items to your "shopping cart" as you browse several pages in a virtual shopping mall.

Cyberspace An all-encompassing term for the digital world of computer networks.

Domain The identifying portion of an Internet address (which follows the @ in an e-mail address. Domain names are followed by a period and a zone that indicates the type of organization. Commercial entities end with *.com*; Educational institutions end with *.edu*; government bodies end with *.gov*; and other organizations end with *.org*.

Download A way to transfer files, graphics, or other information from the Internet to your computer. HTTP and FTP are the most common downloading methods.

DSL Digital Subscription Line, a high-speed Internet connection that uses the ultra-high frequency portion of ordinary telephone lines, allowing users to send and receive voice and data on the same line at the same time.

Emoticon A cluster of punctuation marks commonly used in online chat, postings and e-mail to signify a facial expression or emotional response. For example, :-) represents a smile, and :-(a frown.

Encryption A method of encoding files so only the recipient can read the information. Encryption is necessary for transmitting secure data like credit card numbers over computer networks.

FAQs Frequently Asked Questions. This is generally the first place to stop on a newsgroup or a Web site. It has the answers to the most common questions and indicators of where to go to find the answers to less frequently asked questions.

FTP File Transfer Protocol, the easiest way to download files not on the World Wide Web.

Freeware Free software available over the Internet. This is in contrast with *shareware*, which is available freely, but usually asks the user to send payment for using the software.

GIF Graphic Interchange Format (pronounced "jif"), a common file format for image files; best-suited for nonphotographic material.

Home page The first or main page of a Web site.

HTML HyperText Markup Language, the high-speed computer language used to create documents on the World Wide Web (WWW). To read documents written in HTML, one must have a browser.

HTTP HyperText Transport Protocol, the easiest way to transfer World Wide Web pages from one computer to another.

Hyperlink A connection between two tagged elements in a Web page, or separate sites, that makes it possible to click from one to the other.

Hypertext A system of organizing information based on its relationship to other information, rather than linear or alphabetical orders. Hypertext allows users to *link* related Web pages and to store information in more than one place. For example, in a hypertext almanac, the winners of the National Book Awards could be accessed either through the section on books or on awards.

Intranet A network of computers accessible only by members of the network, often members of one firm. Also known as an internal network.

ISDN Integrated Services Digital Network, a digital type of phone service that permits higher speed transmission of data than conventional phone lines. ISDN lines operate as fast as 128 kilobytes per second (kbps), compared with 28.8 or 56 kbps for the fastest modems.

ISP Internet Service Provider, a company that provides end-user access to the Internet via its central computers and local access lines. America Online (AOL), Earthlink, and Erols are some popular ISPs.

Java A computer language developed by Sun Microsystems that produces programs that run on almost any computer or operating system. Its compatibility and ease of use make it popular for for developing *applets*, tiny applications that can be sent quickly over the World Wide Web.

JPEG Joint Photographic Experts Group, a common file format for photographic images.

Link A hypertext connection that allows a user to jump from one Internet site to another by pointing and clicking. On the World Wide Web, links are often underlined or highlighted.

MIDI Musical Instrument Digital Interface, a file format for high-quality sound.

Mirror site An identical backup site that serves as an alternative for a busy web host.

MPEG Motion Picture Experts Group, a file format for high-quality video in small file sizes.

Newsgroups Discussion forums on the Internet, arranged by category of special interest. To read, respond to, or post information on a newsgroup, you must have a program known as a Newsreader.

Push technology Technology that pushes information onto a user's computer rather than requiring the user to navigate the Internet and "pull" the information from another computer network. E-mail and newsgroups are simple examples of push technology.

Search engine A tool used to look up Web pages. Also known as an index or a directory. Yahoo!, Excite, Lycos, and AltaVista are some of the most popular search engines.

Server The central computer in a network, providing a service or data access to client computers on that network. Frequently, a Web server is dedicated to a specific function, such as e-mail.

Shareware An honor system in which providers make their programs freely accessible over the Internet, with the understanding that those who use them will send payment to the provider after using them. See also *freeware.*

Spam Junk e-mail. As a verb, it means to send thousands of copies of a junk e-mail message.

Thumbnail A tiny picture on a Web page which, when clicked, is replaced by a larger version of the same image.

URL Uniform Resource Locator, the address that identifies a Web page to a browser. Also known as a Web address.

Usenet A system of thousands of newsgroups.

Web page An HTML file, containing text, graphics, and/or mini-applications, viewed with a Web *browser.*

Web site An organized, linked collection of *Web* pages stored on an Internet *server* and read using a Web *browser.* The opening page of a site is called a *home page.*

WebTV A commercial service that accesses the World Wide Web through a television and cable TV wires rather than through a computer and phone wires.

WWW The World Wide Web, or simply the Web, a vast network of information, particularly business, commercial, and government resources, that uses a hypertext system for quickly transmitting graphics, sound, and video over phone, cable TV, and fiber optic lines, allowing easy navigation among related subjects.

XML   eXtensible Markup Language, a universal format for structured documents and data transmitted on the Web. XML is a "metalanguage," a system used for defining and creating specialized languages such as HTML.

Zip file   A file that has been compressed for simpler transmission over the Internet. To read a ZIP file, you need a program to decompress the file, such as PKUNZIP or WinZip.

▶ A FIELD GUIDE TO SEARCHING THE WEB

To search the Web successfully, you need to pick the right engine and learn how to use it. Few people understand the fundamental difference between search engines and Web directories. The former use software agents called "spiders" or "crawlers" to index contents of individual Web pages, then follow links to other pages. Web directories such as Yahoo are compiled by humans who classify sites under topical headings. Most search sites now offer both options, along with information and other services, but topical directories that accompany powerful search engines may be weak, and vice-versa. Moreover, the various search engines themselves operate differently.

The first step in conducting an effective search is to pick an appropriate search site for the job. For a general search, a strong Web directory such as Yahoo or Look Smart is a good place to start. A directory-style search provides two ways to research broad topics: dive through a list of broad topics by clicking on the appropriate links or fill out a search box to find listings.

But directory searches are less effective when looking for specific information—things like the author of a book, the complete text of the Declaration of Independence or research on drug treatments for a medical condition. For this kind of information, search engines like Google and Alta Vista are the way to go. Because they search an index of keywords drawn by spiders from millions of Web pages, the chances are greater that they will find obscure terms in obscure Web pages.

There's a third kind of search site, one that includes popular sites like Metacrawler, Ask Jeeves and Dogpile. These sites—also called metasearch tools—issue search requests to fistfuls of other Web search sites. When Google, Excite, Alta Vista and the like return their results, the metasearch site collects them onto a single Web page for display.

Because no two search sites index exactly the same set of Web pages, metasearch tools give you a wider scope of results—but it's worth remembering that more does not necessarily equal better. What really counts is relevant results that are sorted in a relevant order. And that's the rub.

Simply picking one or two or three types of sites to search from is no guarantee of good results. Brad Hill, the author of World Wide Web Searching for Dummies (IDG), says most search sites deliver too much information. "Search engines do a good job on indexing," he said. "But because of that, they deliver more than you want."

So when you're faced with several hundred thousand results over dozens of pages, what should you do? "Don't go past the first page of results," Hill said. "If it doesn't have something of interest, you've probably entered the wrong search string."

Most people could get much more relevant results with a few simple tricks for constructing a search "string"—the words you enter in the search box. The most obvious is to type in several relevant words instead of just one or two. In general, the fewer words you enter, the more general your results will be.

AllTheWeb (www.alltheweb.com)   A lesser known but superior search engine with a database of more than 2.1 billion indexed Web documents. Its "advanced search" option is a little difficult but well worth mastering.

Alta Vista (www.altavista.com)   A powerful, highly rated search engine with a database of more than 600 million indexed documents. Accurate, well-integrated search results. The portal also includes a modest topical directory, links, tools, and services.

Ask (www.ask.com)   A highly user-friendly metasearch site, with natural language querying and a basic subject directory. It helps you narrow your search through simple questions and simultaneously searches other engines for relevant Web pages. Results are organized under "Web," "News," and "Shopping" tabs. Ask Jeeves for Kids is also available from the home page.

Dogpile (www.dogpile.com)   The most popular Internet metasearch site, Dogpile combs through about 15 search engines and directories. Results are sorted by the engine that found them.

Google (www.google.com)   The leading general Internet search engine, consistently a leader in user preference surveys and trade reviews. Fast and reliable, with more than 1.5 billion indexed documents. Known for yielding high-relevance results and few broken links.

MSN Live Search (www.live.com)   The most frequently visited Internet search service, MSN Search uses the powerful Inktomi engine and database, and the LookSmart subject directory. The basic search screen presents limited options, but "Advanced Search" offers a number of useful functions.

Yahoo! (www.yahoo.com)   One of the world's most popular portals and by all accounts the best directory index for broad general topics, Yahoo! features a comprehensive, hierarchical listing of selected sites—with limited ability to search the contents of individual pages. Reliable and easy to use, Yahoo! remains an excellent choice for basic research while offering a slate of customizable services.

▶ A WEB SITE DIRECTORY

The Internet provides users with an ever-expanding world of information and online services in virtually every field of interest. Along with the popular *search engines* and portals described above, the sites listed below may provide the beginnings of your personal index. Explore the sites yourself and add the ones you like to the "Bookmarks" or "Favorites" list in your *browser*.

Computer/Communication Services

CNET (www.cnet.com) An informative and well-designed technology portal. Product reviews, industry news, extensive selection of downloads.

eFax (www.efax.com) A free service that provides private fax numbers. Receive faxes by e-mail; send or forward them for a fee.

ICQ (wcb.icq.com) Free downloads for global private chat. Leave messages, alert friends to when you're online. Millions of subscribers.

TalkCity (www.talkcity.com) Chat, scheduled chat events, forums, member home pages, celebrity events—a Web community.

ZD Net (www.zdnet.com) Sponsored by Ziff-Davis Interactive, connects to a large worldwide network of computer sites and magazine; also has links, search, shareware. Now part of CNET.

Entertainment and Learning

Broadcast.com (broadcast.com) Live TV and radio broadcasts, CD jukebox of over 1,000 albums, movie trailers, audio books, and more. RealPlayer plug-in available. Now part of the Yahoo network.

Discovery.com (www.discovery.com) Fun, adventure, and learning for children and adults, from the producers of The Discovery Channel.

Disney.com (disney.go.com) Features games and activities for kids, content for parents, shopping for Disney merchandise.

eHow (www.howto.com) More than 15,000 how-to-solutions for day-to-day living in easy, step-by-step instructions. Organized in 14 categories and 120 subcategories.

Electronic Zoo (netvet.wustl.edu/e-zoo.htm) A virtual zoological garden, with extensive animal information, online magazines, links, user groups, and multimedia galore.

How Stuff Works (www.howstuffworks.com) Engaging, clear, informative explanations of common devices and instruments, digital technologies, the human body, natural phenomena.

The Internet Movie Database (www.imbd.com) The biggest and best film resource on the Web, covering more than 200,000 movies, extensive filmographies, and hundreds of thousands of biographical profiles.

NASA (www.nasa.gov) The largest repository of space-related information on the Net. Rich in photos and the latest scoop on current and future missions, astronauts, etc.

National Geographic (www.nationalgeographic.com) Magazine articles, virtual museum exhibits, a mini-encyclopedia, and more, for kids and adults.

PBS Online (www.pbs.org) Educational and entertaining media presentations, transcripts, quizzes, learning guides, and more, based on public television programs and documentaries.

Smithsonian Institution (www.si.edu) "America's attic" comes to the Net. A vast and compelling collection of artifacts, exhibitions, special media presentations, research materials, and links to affiliated museums.

Spinner (www.spinner.com) Self-proclaimed "First and Largest Internet Music Service." Offers a RealAudio-based player, 150+ music channels, and 375,000 songs.

Family and Health

Genealogy.com (www.genealogy.com) Type in a name, begin your search. Take classes, post queries, find links to other sites. A great place to start a family tree. Subscription.

Healthfinder (www.healthfinder.gov) U.S. government site with thousands of documents, well-organized interface, medical news, databases, and links. A useful gateway.

Health Risk Assessment (www.youfirst.com) Tools and information for in-depth personal health assessment; create a confidential personal profile.

SeniorNet (www.seniornet.com) Online services and information for people over 50. Classes, chat, and more.

WebMD (www.webmd.com) Leader in providing services that help consumers, physicians, and health plans navigate the health care system. Medscape.com, accessible from the main page, provides in-depth clinical information.

Finance and Investment

E*Trade (www.etrade.com) The first and leading Internet trading/investment firm. Includes personalized portfolio management and news.

The Motley Fool (www.fool.com) Free, easy-to-understand financial information, including timely stock updates, portfolio tracker, and investor chat boards.

MSN MoneyCentral (moneycentral.msn.com) Portfolio management, stock screening, investment tracking and advice, financial headlines, real-time stock tracker, 401(k) planner, and more.

Quicken.com (quicken.com) Personal finance site, featuring interactive tools to help with insurance, home-loan, tax-preparation, investment, and retirement-planning needs.

TheStreet.com (thestreet.com) Extensive online financial information, including daily market analysis and real-time stock ticker.

General Information/Reference

About.com (www.about.com) A rich portal site and comprehensive Web directory for everyday use. More than 50,000 subjects and 1 million links to Net resources—well organized.

Britannica.com (www.britannica.com) The entire encyclopedia free, with links to related magazine articles and hundreds of thousands of Web sites.

FreeTranslation.com (www.freetranslation.com) Uses the Transparent Language translation engine for free translation of documents or Web pages—English, French, German, Italian, Portuguese, and Spanish.

OneLookDictionaries (www.onelook.com) Access to over 700 general and specialized dictionaries.

Virtual Reference Desk (refdesk.com) Vast collection of links to general and topical information sites.

Government

FedStats (www.fedstats.gov) A full range of statistics and information from more than 100 U.S. federal agencies.

Internal Revenue Service (www.irs.gov) Tax forms and instructions, advice, online filing.

The Library of Congress (www.loc.gov) Photos, documents, online exhibits, legislation text, and other resources make this site valuable for serious research or casual enjoyment.

Stamps.com (www.stamps.com) Users download software that allows them to print metered postage stickers from their desktop printers and pay for the cost of postage with a credit card account.

Thomas (thomas.loc.gov) Authoritative, in-depth information on federal legislation, a service of the Library of Congress.

U.S. Census Bureau (www.census.gov) Authoritative, extensive information on U.S. population, demographics, economy, industry and agriculture, education, law enforcement, etc.

The White House (www.whitehouse.gov) Write to the president, read documents and policy statements, take a tour, browse the archives, etc.

Jobs/Career Development

Career Builder (www.careerbuilder.com) Leading career management site for job seekers and employers.

HotJobs (www.hotjobs.com) Thousands of registered recruiters and over 500,000 resumes; no head-hunters allowed.

Jobs.com (www.jobs.com) Local job search, resume posting. Extensive listings.

Monster.com (www.monster.com) Online employment services, including job searches by location, a resume database available to recruiters, and online job application. Includes resources for freelancers.

News

ABCNews.com (www.abcnews.com) Headlines, online-only features, videos, instant polls, abundant links. Deep coverage with frequent updates.

BBC Online (www.bbc.co.uk) The vast international resources of BBC's news organization. World news with a unique perspective.

CNN Interactive (cnn.com) Late-breaking news and background: multimedia galleries, in-depth analysis, polls, searchable background material, links. Includes the CNNfn financial news network, and CNNSI, sports coverage with *Sports Illustrated*.

MSNBC (www.msnbc.com) The most interactive of all the news sites. Includes a personalized news page and compelling polls, chats, and discussions.

The New York Times (www.nytimes.com) Most of the daily paper is available online, as are extensive archives.

Shopping/Auctions

Alibris (www.alibris.com) Locate use, rare, and hard-to-find books. Millions of titles from a worldwide network of dealers.

Amazon.com (www.amazon.com) The "granddaddy" of consumer online shopping sites, it began with books, then moved into music, video, consumer electronics, and toys. Deep discounts.

CarsDirect (www.carsdirect.com) The leading direct online automobile buying service. Research, price, order, insure, and finance for virtually every make, model, and style of car available in the U.S.

Cooking.com (www.cooking.com) Top shopping site for chefs, offering a huge assortment of cookware, accessories, and specialty foods.

Dealtime (www.dealtime.com) A free online comparison-shopping service that lets you compare products, prices, and stores across the Web. Find the best deal for whatever you're looking for.

eBay (www.ebay.com) The largest online auction site, with millions of items at all times.

MSN CarPoint (www.carpoint.msn.com) Online car shopping service, with 2,000 affiliated dealers and 100,000 used car listings. Personal Auto Pages for tracking your car's service schedule.

Priceline.com (www.priceline.com) A popular buying service that asks you what you're willing to pay and seeks providers. Great for airline tickets, car rentals, hotel rooms and other products.

Ticketmaster (www.ticketmaster.com) One of most visited sites on the Web. Order tickets to concerts, sports competitions, and other events—more than 350,000 a year. Includes special deals.

uBid (www.ubid.com) A central (not person-to-person) online auction house. Great deals on discontinued consumer electronics and computing equipment and more typical auction items.

Sports and Games

CBS SportsLine (cbs.sportsline.com) In-depth, comprehensive, up-to-the-minute coverage. News, multimedia features, personalized information, live celebrity chats, forums, calendars and numerous links.

ESPN.com (msn.espn.go.com) Scores, stories, stats, schedules, standings, video, sound. Up-to-the minute analyses and features. GameCast lets you follow games on your screen as they happen.

Games Domain (www.gamesdomain.com) One of the Net's largest shareware directory sites, plus reviews, tips, contests, walkthroughs, industry news, and more.

GameSpot (gamespot.com) From ZDNet, a favorite with PC gaming enthusiasts—news, reviews, previews, free demo downloads, and more.

The Sporting News (www.sportingnews.com) Hardcore, in-depth coverage. Analysis by 30 well-known columnists. Abundant stats and links, with customizable team/score reporting.

Sportspages.com (www.sportspages.com) Fresh links to the world's best sports pages.

Travel and Weather

Expedia.com (expedia.com) Makes travel planning easy, from research to booking. Find special deals and unique vacations ideas on the Travel Network. Includes mapping features and a staff of travel agents.

Frommer's Online (www.frommers.com) Based on the popular book series, ideal for planning a low-cost excursion. Includes activity suggestions, guidebooks, message boards, and booking links.

National Park Service: ParkNet (www.nps.gov) Click on "Visit Your Parks" link for detailed maps and general information on the U.S. national parks.

National Weather Service (www.nws.noaa.gov) World, national, and regional forecasts—daily and long-term. Includes maps, satellite imagery, specialized data, and abundant links.

Smarter Living (www.smarterliving.com) A free online community dedicated to helping people save time and money on travel. Posts fare sales, special deals, and promotions. Members are eligible for special discounts on airfares, hotels, and more.

Travelocity.com (www.travelocity.com) Owned by Sabre Group, which maintains the largest worldwide reservation system. Best current fares and packages, e-mail and pager bulletins.

Mapquest.com (www.mapquest.com) Interactive maps and driving directions, customized mapping, and travel information for businesses and consumers.

Weather Channel (www.weather.com) The leading commercial weather site, and one of the most popular on the Web. Detailed national and local forecasts, with special details relating to travel, health, recreation, and special event locations. Comprehensive.

Academy Awards 1928–2007

The "Oscars" are officially known as the Academy of Motion Picture Arts and Sciences Awards. They were inaugurated in 1928 as part of Hollywood's drive to improve its less-than-respectable image. Academy librarian and eventual executive director Margaret Herrick remarked that the statuette looked like her uncle Oscar, and the nickname has stuck ever since. Membership in the Academy (currently over 3,000) is by invitation only, with members divided into 13 branches. Each branch selects up to five nominees for awards in its area of expertise; the entire membership makes "Best Film" nominations and then votes on all the categories. Major awards are shown in the chart. Awards for Best Cinematography and for Best Foreign Language Film are shown in a separate table. Best Actors and directors are named for films winning Best Picture except where otherwise indicated.

Year	Best picture	Best director	Best actor	Best actress	Best supporting actor	Best supporting actress
1928	Wings	Frank Borzage, Seventh Heaven Lewis Milestone, Two Arabian Knights	Emil Jannings, The Way of All Flesh, The Last Command	Janet Gaynor, Seventh Heaven, Sunrise, Street Angel	No Awards Given	No Awards Given
1929	The Broadway Melody	Frank Lloyd, The Divine Lady	Warner Baxter, In Old Arizona	Mary Pickford, Coquette	No Awards Given	No Awards Given
1930	All Quiet on the Western Front	Lewis Milestone	George Arliss, Disraeli	Norma Shearer, The Divorcee	No Awards Given	No Awards Given
1931	Cimarron	Norman Taurog, Skippy	Lionel Barrymore, A Free Soul	Marie Dressler, Min and Bill	No Awards Given	No Awards Given
1932	Grand Hotel	Frank Borzage, Bad Girl	Wallace Beery, The Champ Fredric March, Dr. Jekyll and Mr. Hyde	Helen Hayes, The Sin of Madelon Claudet	No Awards Given	No Awards Given
1933	Cavalcade	Frank Lloyd	Charles Laughton, The Private Life of Henry VIII	Katharine Hepburn, Morning Glory	No Awards Given	No Awards Given
1934	It Happened One Night	Frank Capra	Clark Gable	Claudette Colbert	No Awards Given	No Awards Given
1935	Mutiny on the Bounty	John Ford, The Informer	Victor McLaglen, The Informer	Bette Davis, Dangerous	No Awards Given	No Awards Given
1936	The Great Ziegfeld	Frank Capra, Mr. Deeds Goes to Town	Paul Muni, The Story of Louis Pasteur	Luise Rainer	Walter Brennan, Come and Get It	Gale Sondergaard, Anthony Adverse
1937	The Life of Emile Zola	Leo McCarey, The Awful Truth	Spencer Tracy, Captains Courageous	Luise Rainer, The Good Earth	Joseph Schildkraut	Alice Brady, In Old Chicago
1938	You Can't Take It With You	Frank Capra	Spencer Tracy, Boys Town	Bette Davis, Jezebel	Walter Brennan, Kentucky	Fay Bainter, Jezebel
1939	Gone With the Wind	Victor Fleming	Robert Donat, Goodbye, Mr. Chips	Vivien Leigh	Thomas Mitchell, Stagecoach	Hattie McDaniel
1940	Rebecca	John Ford, The Grapes of Wrath	James Stewart, The Philadelphia Story	Ginger Rogers, Kitty Foyle	Walter Brennan, The Westerner	Jane Darwell, The Grapes of Wrath
1941	How Green Was My Valley	John Ford	Gary Cooper, Sergeant York	Joan Fontaine, Suspicion	Donald Crisp	Mary Astor, The Great Lie
1942	Mrs. Miniver	William Wyler	James Cagney, Yankee Doodle Dandy	Greer Garson	Van Heflin, Johnny Eager	Teresa Wright
1943	Casablanca	Michael Curtiz	Paul Lukas, Watch On The Rhine	Jennifer Jones, The Song of Bernadette	Charles Coburn, The More the Merrier	Katina Paxinou, For Whom the Bell Tolls

Year	Best picture	Best director	Best actor	Best actress	Best supporting actor	Best supporting actress
1944	Going My Way	Leo McCarey	Bing Crosby	Ingrid Bergman, Gaslight	Barry Fitzgerald	Ethel Barrymore, None But the Lonely Heart
1945	The Lost Weekend	Billy Wilder	Ray Milland	Joan Crawford, Mildred Pierce	James Dunn, A Tree Grows in Brooklyn	Anne Revere, National Velvet
1946	The Best Years of Our Lives	William Wyler	Fredric March	Olivia De Havilland, To Each His Own	Harold Russell	Anne Baxter, The Razor's Edge
1947	Gentleman's Agreement	Elia Kazan	Ronald Colman, A Double Life	Loretta Young, The Farmer's Daughter	Edmund Gwenn, Miracle on 34th Street	Celeste Holm
1948	Hamlet	John Huston, The Treasure of the Sierra Madre	Laurence Olivier	Jane Wyman, Johnny Belinda	Walter Huston, The Treasure of the Sierra Madre	Claire Trevor, Key Largo
1949	All the King's Men	Joseph L. Mankiewicz, A Letter to Three Wives	Broderick Crawford	Olivia De Havilland, The Heiress	Dean Jagger, Twelve O'Clock High	Mercedes McCambridge
1950	All About Eve	Joseph L. Mankiewicz	José Ferrer, Cyrano de Bergerac	Judy Holliday, Born Yesterday	George Sanders	Josephine Hull, Harvey
1951	An American in Paris	George Stevens, A Place in the Sun	Humphrey Bogart, The African Queen	Vivien Leigh, A Streetcar Named Desire	Karl Malden, A Streetcar Named Desire	Kim Hunter, A Streetcar Named Desire
1952	The Greatest Show on Earth	John Ford, The Quiet Man	Gary Cooper, High Noon	Shirley Booth, Come Back, Little Sheba	Anthony Quinn, Viva Zapata!	Gloria Grahame, The Bad and the Beautiful
1953	From Here to Eternity	Fred Zinnemann	William Holden, Stalag 17	Audrey Hepburn, Roman Holiday	Frank Sinatra	Donna Reed
1954	On the Waterfront	Elia Kazan	Marlon Brando	Grace Kelly, The Country Girl	Edmond O'Brien, The Barefoot Contessa	Eva Marie Saint
1955	Marty	Delbert Mann	Ernest Borgnine	Anna Magnani, The Rose Tattoo	Jack Lemmon, Mister Roberts	Jo Van Fleet, East of Eden
1956	Around the World in 80 Days	George Stevens, Giant	Yul Brynner, The King And I	Ingrid Bergman, Anastasia	Anthony Quinn, Lust for Life	Dorothy Malone Written on the Wind
1957	The Bridge on the River Kwai	David Lean	Alec Guinness	Joanne Woodward, The Three Faces of Eve	Red Buttons, Sayonara	Miyoshi Umeki, Sayonara
1958	Gigi	Vincente Minnelli	David Niven, Separate Tables	Susan Hayward, I Want to Live!	Burl Ives, The Big Country	Wendy Hiller, Separate Tables
1959	Ben-Hur	William Wyler	Charlton Heston	Simone Signoret, Room at the Top	Hugh Griffith	Shelley Winters, The Diary of Anne Frank
1960	The Apartment	Billy Wilder	Burt Lancaster, Elmer Gantry	Elizabeth Taylor, Butterfield 8	Peter Ustinov, Spartacus	Shirley Jones, Elmer Gantry
1961	West Side Story	Jerome Robbins, Robert Wise	Maximilian Schell, Judgment At Nuremberg	Sophia Loren, Two Women	George Chakiris	Rita Moreno
1962	Lawrence of Arabia	David Lean	Gregory Peck, To Kill a Mockingbird	Anne Bancroft, The Miracle Worker	Ed Begley, Sweet Bird of Youth	Patty Duke, The Miracle Worker
1963	Tom Jones	Tony Richardson	Sidney Poitier, Lilies of the Field	Patricia Neal, Hud	Melvyn Douglas, Hud	Margaret Rutherford, The V.I.P.s
1964	My Fair Lady	George Cukor	Rex Harrison	Julie Andrews, Mary Poppins	Peter Ustinov, Topkapi	Lila Kedrova, Zorba the Greek
1965	The Sound of Music	Robert Wise	Lee Marvin, Cat Ballou	Julie Christie, Darling	Martin Balsam, A Thousand Clowns	Shelley Winters, A Patch of Blue
1966	A Man for All Seasons	Fred Zinnemann	Paul Scofield	Elizabeth Taylor, Who's Afraid of Virginia Woolf?	Walter Matthau, The Fortune Cookie	Sandy Dennis, Who's Afraid of Virginia Woolf?

Year	Best picture	Best director	Best actor	Best actress	Best supporting actor	Best supporting actress
1967	In the Heat of the Night	Mike Nichols, The Graduate	Rod Steiger	Katharine Hepburn, Guess Who's Coming to Dinner	George Kennedy, Cool Hand Luke	Estelle Parsons, Bonnie and Clyde
1968	Oliver!	Carol Reed	Cliff Robertson, Charly	Katharine Hepburn, The Lion in Winter; Barbra Streisand, Funny Girl	Jack Albertson, The Subject Was Roses	Ruth Gordon, Rosemary's Baby
1969	Midnight Cowboy	John Schlesinger	John Wayne, True Grit	Maggie Smith, The Prime of Miss Jean Brodie	Gig Young, They Shoot Horses, Don't They?	Goldie Hawn, Cactus Flower
1970	Patton	Franklin J. Schaffner	George C. Scott	Glenda Jackson, Women in Love	John Mills, Ryan's Daughter	Helen Hayes, Airport
1971	The French Connection	William Friedkin	Gene Hackman	Jane Fonda, Klute	Ben Johnson, The Last Picture Show	Cloris Leachman, The Last Picture Show
1972	The Godfather	Bob Fosse, Cabaret	Marlon Brando	Liza Minnelli, Cabaret	Joel Grey, Cabaret	Eileen Heckart, Butterflies Are Free
1973	The Sting	George Roy Hill	Jack Lemmon, Save the Tiger	Glenda Jackson, A Touch of Class	John Houseman, The Paper Chase	Tatum O'Neal, Paper Moon
1974	The Godfather, Part II	Francis Ford Coppola	Art Carney, Harry And Tonto	Ellen Burstyn, Alice Doesn't Live Here Anymore	Robert De Niro	Ingrid Bergman, Murder on the Orient Express
1975	One Flew Over the Cuckoo's Nest	Milos Forman	Jack Nicholson	Louise Fletcher	George Burns, The Sunshine Boys	Lee Grant, Shampoo
1976	Rocky	John G. Avildsen	Peter Finch, Network	Faye Dunaway, Network	Jason Robards, All the President's Men	Beatrice Straight, Network
1977	Annie Hall	Woody Allen	Richard Dreyfuss, The Goodbye Girl	Diane Keaton	Jason Robards, Julia	Vanessa Redgrave, Julia
1978	The Deer Hunter	Michael Cimino	Jon Voight, Coming Home	Jane Fonda, Coming Home	Christopher Walken	Maggie Smith, California Suite
1979	Kramer vs. Kramer	Robert Benton	Dustin Hoffman	Sally Field, Norma Rae	Melvyn Douglas, Being There	Meryl Streep
1980	Ordinary People	Robert Redford	Robert De Niro, Raging Bull	Sissy Spacek, Coal Miner's Daughter	Timothy Hutton, Ordinary People	Mary Steenburgen, Melvin and Howard
1981	Chariots of Fire	Warren Beatty, Reds	Henry Fonda, On Golden Pond	Katharine Hepburn, On Golden Pond	John Gielgud, Arthur	Maureen Stapleton, Reds
1982	Gandhi	Richard Attenborough	Ben Kingsley	Meryl Streep, Sophie's Choice	Louis Gossett Jr., An Officer and a Gentleman	Jessica Lange, Tootsie
1983	Terms of Endearment	James L. Brooks	Robert Duvall, Tender Mercies	Shirley MacLaine	Jack Nicholson, Terms of Endearment	Linda Hunt, The Year of Living Dangerously
1984	Amadeus	Milos Forman	F. Murray Abraham	Sally Field, Places in the Heart	Haing S. Ngor, The Killing Fields	Peggy Ashcroft, A Passage to India
1985	Out of Africa	Sydney Pollack	William Hurt, Kiss of the Spider Woman	Geraldine Page, The Trip to Bountiful	Don Ameche, Cocoon	Anjelica Huston, Prizzi's Honor
1986	Platoon	Oliver Stone	Paul Newman, The Color of Money	Marlee Matlin, Children of a Lesser God	Michael Caine, Hannah and Her Sisters	Dianne Wiest, Hannah and Her Sisters
1987	The Last Emperor	Bernardo Bertolucci	Michael Douglas, Wall Street	Cher, Moonstruck	Sean Connery, The Untouchables	Olympia Dukakis, Moonstruck
1988	Rain Man	Barry Levinson	Dustin Hoffman	Jodie Foster, The Accused	Kevin Kline, A Fish Called Wanda	Geena Davis, The Accidental Tourist

Year	Best picture	Best director	Best actor	Best actress	Best supporting actor	Best supporting actress
1989	Driving Miss Daisy	Oliver Stone, Born on the Fourth of July	Daniel Day-Lewis, My Left Foot	Jessica Tandy	Denzel Washington, Glory	Brenda Fricker, My Left Foot
1990	Dances with Wolves	Kevin Costner	Jeremy Irons, Reversal of Fortune	Kathy Bates, Misery	Joe Pesci, Goodfellas	Whoopi Goldberg, Ghost
1991	The Silence of the Lambs	Jonathan Demme	Anthony Hopkins	Jodie Foster	Jack Palance, City Slickers	Mercedes Ruehl, The Fisher King
1992	Unforgiven	Clint Eastwood	Al Pacino, Scent of a Woman	Emma Thompson, Howards End	Gene Hackman	Marisa Tomei, My Cousin Vinny
1993	Schindler's List	Steven Spielberg	Tom Hanks, Philadelphia	Holly Hunter, The Piano	Tommy Lee Jones, The Fugitive	Anna Paquin, The Piano
1994	Forrest Gump	Robert Zemeckis	Tom Hanks	Jessica Lange, Blue Sky	Martin Landau, Ed Wood	Dianne Wiest, Bullets Over Broadway
1995	Braveheart	Mel Gibson	Nicolas Cage, Leaving Las Vegas	Susan Sarandon, Dead Man Walking	Kevin Spacey, The Usual Suspects	Mira Sorvino, Mighty Aphrodite
1996	The English Patient	Anthony Minghella	Geoffrey Rush, Shine	Frances McDormand, Fargo	Cuba Gooding Jr., Jerry Maguire	Juliette Binoche
1997	Titanic	James Cameron	Jack Nicholson, As Good as it Gets	Helen Hunt, As Good as it Gets	Robin Williams, Good Will Hunting	Kim Basinger, L.A. Confidential
1998	Shakespeare in Love	Steven Spielberg, Saving Private Ryan	Roberto Benigni, Life is Beautiful	Gwyneth Paltrow	James Coburn, Affliction	Judi Dench
1999	American Beauty	Sam Mendes	Kevin Spacey	Hilary Swank, Boys Don't Cry	Michael Caine, The Cider House Rules	Angelina Jolie, Girl, Interrupted
2000	Gladiator	Steven Soderbergh, Traffic	Russell Crowe	Julia Roberts, Erin Brockovich	Benicio Del Toro, Traffic	Marcia Gay Harden, Pollock
2001	A Beautiful Mind	Ron Howard	Denzel Washington, Training Day	Halle Berry, Monsters Ball	Jim Broadbent, Iris	Jennifer Connelly
2002	Chicago	Roman Polanski, The Pianist	Adrien Brody, The Pianist	Nicole Kidman, The Hours	Chris Cooper, Adaptation	Catherine Zeta-Jones
2003	The Lord of the Rings: The Return of the King	Peter Jackson	Sean Penn, Mystic River	Charlize Theron, Monster	Tim Robbins, Mystic River	Renee Zellweger, Cold Mountain
2004	Million Dollar Baby	Clint Eastwood	Jamie Foxx, Ray	Hilary Swank	Morgan Freeman	Cate Blanchett, The Aviator
2005	Crash	Ang Lee, Brokeback Mountain	Philip Seymour Hoffman, Capote	Reese Witherspoon, Walk the Line	George Clooney, Syriana	Rachel Weisz, The Constant Gardener
2006	The Departed	Martin Scorsese	Forest Whitaker, The Last King of Scotland	Helen Mirren, The Queen	Alan Arkin, Little Miss Sunshine	Jennifer Hudson, Dreamgirls
2007	No Country for Old Men	Joel and Ethan Coen	Daniel Day-Lewis, There Will Be Blood	Marion Cotillard, La Vie en Rose	Javier Bardem	Tilda Swinton, Michael Clayton

Source: Academy of Motion Picture Arts & Sciences. www.oscar.org

American Film Institute Life Achievement Awards, 1973–2008

Awarded to individuals whose "talent has fundamentally advanced the art of American film or television . . . and whose work has withstood the test of time."

Year	Recipient	Year	Recipient	Year	Recipient	Year	Recipient
1973	John Ford	1982	Frank Capra	1991	Kirk Douglas	2000	Harrison Ford
1974	James Cagney	1983	John Huston	1992	Sidney Poitier	2001	Barbra Streisand
1975	Orson Welles	1984	Lillian Gish	1993	Elizabeth Taylor	2002	Tom Hanks
1976	William Wyler	1985	Gene Kelly	1994	Jack Nicholson	2003	Robert De Niro
1977	Henry Fonda	1986	Billy Wilder	1995	Steven Spielberg	2004	Meryl Streep
1978	Bette Davis	1987	Barbara Stanwyck	1996	Clint Eastwood	2005	George Lucas
1979	Alfred Hitchcock	1988	Jack Lemmon	1997	Martin Scorsese	2006	Sir Sean Connery
1980	James Stewart	1989	Gregory Peck	1998	Robert Wise	2007	Al Pacino
1981	Fred Astaire	1990	David Lean	1999	Dustin Hoffman	2008	Warren Beatty

Source: American Film Institute. www.afi.com

Academy Awards for Cinematography, 1928–2007

Year	Cinematographer, Film	Year	Cinematographer, Film
1928	Charles Rosher, Karl Struss, *Sunrise*	1961	Eugene Shuftan, *The Hustler*
1929	Clyde DeVinna, *White Shadows, In the South Seas*		Daniel L. Fapp, *West Side Story*
		1962	Jean Bourgoin, Walter Wottitz, *The Longest Day*
1930	Joseph T. Rucker, Willard Van Der Veer, *With Byrd at the South Pole*		Freddie Young, *Lawrence of Arabia*
		1963	James Wong Howe, *Hud*
1931	Floyd Crosby, *Tabu*		Leon Shamroy, *Cleopatra*
1932	Lee Garmes, *Shanghai Express*	1964	Walter Lassally, *Zorba the Greek*
1933	Charles Bryant Lang Jr., *A Farewell to Arms*		Harry Stradling, *My Fair Lady*
1934	Victor Milner, *Cleopatra*	1965	Ernest Laszlo, *Ship of Fools*
1935	Hal Mohr, *A Midsummer Night's Dream*		Freddie Young, *Dr. Zhivago*
1936	Gaetano Gaudio, *Anthony Adverse*	1966	Haskell Wexler, *Who's Afraid of Virginia Woolf?*
1937	Karl Freund, *The Good Earth*		Ted Moore, *A Man for All Seasons*
1938	Joseph Ruttenberg, *The Great Waltz*	1967	Burnett Guffey, *Bonnie and Clyde*
1939	Gregg Toland, *Wuthering Heights*	1968	Pasqualino De Santis, *Romeo and Juliet*
	Ernest Haller, Ray Rennahan, *Gone With the Wind*	1969	Conrad L. Hall, *Butch Cassidy and the Sundance Kid*
1940	George Barnes, *Rebecca*	1970	Freddie Young, *Ryan's Daughter*
	George Perinal, *Thief of Baghdad*	1971	Oswald Morris, *Fiddler on the Roof*
1941	Arthur Miller, *How Green Was My Valley*	1972	Geoffrey Unsworth, *Cabaret*
	Ernest Palmer, Ray Rennahan, *Blood and Sand*	1973	Sven Nykvist, *Cries and Whispers*
1942	Joseph Ruttenberg, *Mrs. Miniver*	1974	Fred Koenekamp, Joseph Biroc, *The Towering Inferno*
	Leon Shamroy, *The Black Swan*		
1943	Arthur Miller, *The Song of Bernadette*	1975	John Alcott, *Barry Lyndon*
	Hal Mohr, W. Howard Greene, *The Phantom of the Opera*	1976	Haskell Wexler, *Bound for Glory*
		1977	Vilmos Zsigmond, *Close Encounters of the Third Kind*
1944	Joseph LaShelle, *Laura*		
	Leon Shamroy, *Wilson*	1978	Nestor Almendros, *Days of Heaven*
1945	Harry Stradling, *The Picture of Dorian Gray*	1979	Vittorio Storaro, *Apocalypse Now*
	Leon Shamroy, *Leave Her to Heaven*	1980	Geoffrey Unsworth, Ghislain Cloquet, *Tess*
1946	Arthur Miller, *Anna and the King of Siam*	1981	Vittorio Storaro, *Reds*
	Charles Rosher, Leonard Smith, Arthur Arling, *The Yearling*	1982	Billy Williams, Ronnie Taylor, *Gandhi*
1947	Guy Green, *Great Expectations*	1983	Sven Nykvist, *Fanny & Alexander*
1948	William Daniels, *The Naked City*	1984	Chris Menges, *The Killing Fields*
	Joseph Valentine, William V. Skall, Winton Hoch, *Joan of Arc*	1985	David Watkin, *Out of Africa*
		1986	Chris Menges, *The Mission*
1949	Paul C. Vogel, *Battleground*	1987	Vittorio Storaro, *The Last Emperor*
	Winton Hoch, *She Wore a Yellow Ribbon*	1988	Peter Biziou, *Mississippi Burning*
1950	Robert Krasker, *The Third Man*	1989	Freddie Francis, *Glory*
	Robert Surtees, *King Solomon's Mines*	1990	Dean Semler, *Dances With Wolves*
1951	William C. Mellor, *A Place in the Sun*	1991	Robert Richardson, *JFK*
	Alfred Gilks, John Alton (ballet), *An American in Paris*	1992	Philippe Rousselot, *A River Runs Through It*
		1993	Janusz Kaminski, *Schindler's List*
1952	Robert Surtees, *The Bad and the Beautiful*	1994	John Toll, *Legends of the Fall*
	Winton Hoch, Archie Stout, *The Quiet Man*	1995	John Toll, *Braveheart*
1953	Burnett Guffey, *From Here to Eternity*	1996	John Seale, *The English Patient*
	Loyal Griggs, *Shane*	1997	Russell Carpenter, *Titanic*
1954	Boris Kaufman, *On the Waterfront*	1998	Janusz Kaminski, *Saving Private Ryan*
	Milton Krasner, *Three Coins in the Fountain*	1999	Conrad L. Hall, *American Beauty*
1955	James Wong Howe, *The Rose Tattoo*	2000	Peter Pau, *Crouching Tiger, Hidden Dragon*
	Robert Burks, *To Catch a Thief*	2001	Andrew Lesnie, *The Lord of the Rings: The Fellowship of the Ring*
1956	Joseph Ruttenberg, *Sombody Up There Likes Me*		
	Lionel Lindon, *Around the World in 80 Days*	2002	Conrad L. Hall, *Road to Perdition* (posthumous)
1957	Jack Hildyard, *The Bridge on the River Kwai*	2003	Russell Boyd, *Master and Commander: The Far Side of the World*
1958	Sam Leavitt, *The Defiant Ones*		
	Joseph Ruttenberg, *Gigi*	2004	Robert Richardson, *The Aviator*
1959	William C. Mellor, *The Diary of Anne Frank*	2005	Dion Beebe, *Memoirs of a Geisha*
	Robert L. Surtees, *Ben-Hur*	2006	Guillermo Navarro, *Pan's Labyrinth*
1960	Freddie Francis, *Sons and Lovers*	2007	Robert Elswit, *There Will Be Blood*
	Russell Metty, *Spartacus*		

Source: Academy of Motion Picture Arts & Sciences. www.oscar.org

Academy Awards for Best Foreign Language Film, 1956–2007

Year	Film, Country, Director	Year	Film, Country, Director
1956	*La Strada,* Italy, Federico Fellini	1959	*Black Orpheus,* France/Italy/Brazil, Marcel Camus
1957	*The Nights of Cabiria,* Italy, Federico Fellini		
1958	*Mon Oncle,* France, Jacques Tati	1960	*The Virgin Spring,* Sweden, Ingmar Bergman

Year	Film, Country, Director	Year	Film, Country, Director
1961	*Through A Glass Darkly*, Sweden, Ingmar Bergman	1983	*Fanny and Alexander*, Sweden, Ingmar Bergman
1962	*Sundays and Cybele*, France, Serge Bourgignon	1984	*Dangerous Moves*, France, Richard Dembo
1963	*8½*, Italy, Federico Fellini	1985	*The Official Story*, Argentina, Luis Puenzo
1964	*Yesterday, Today, and Tomorrow*, Italy/France, Vittorio de Sica	1986	*The Assault*, Netherlands, Fons Rademakers
1965	*The Shop on Main Street*, Czechoslovakia, Jan Kadar	1987	*Babette's Feast*, Denmark, Gabriel Axel
1966	*A Man and a Woman*, France, Claude Lelouch	1988	*Pelle the Conqueror*, Denmark, Bille August
1967	*Closely Watched Trains*, Czechoslovakia, Jiri Menzel	1989	*Cinema Paradiso*, Italy, Giuseppe Tornatore
1968	*War and Peace*, USSR, Sergei Bondarchuk	1990	*Journey of Hope*, Switzerland, Xavier Koller
1969	*Z*, France/Algeria, Constantin Costa-Gavras	1991	*Mediterraneo*, Italy, Gabriel Salvatores
1970	*Investigation of a Citizen Above Suspicion*, Italy, Elio Petri	1992	*Indochine*, France, Regis Wargnier
1971	*The Garden of the Finzi-Continis*, Italy, Vittorio de Sica	1993	*Belle Époque*, Spain, Fernando Trueba
1972	*The Discreet Charm of the Bourgeoisie*, France, Luis Buñuel	1994	*Burnt by the Sun*, Russia, Nikita Mikhalkov
1973	*Day For Night*, France/Italy, François Truffaut	1995	*Antonia's Line*, Netherlands, Marlene Gorris
1974	*Amarcord*, Italy/France, Federico Fellini	1996	*Kolya*, Czech Republic, Jan Sverak
1975	*Dersu Uzala*, USSR/Japan, Akira Kurosawa	1997	*Character*, Netherlands, Mike van Diem
1976	*Black and White in Color*, France/Switzerland/ IvoryCoast, Jean-Jacques Annaud	1998	*Life is Beautiful*, Italy, Roberto Benigni
1977	*Madame Rosa*, France, Moshe Mizrahi	1999	*All About My Mother*, Spain, Pedro Almodóvar
1978	*Get Out Your Handkerchiefs*, France, Bertrand Blier	2000	*Crouching Tiger, Hidden Dragon*, China, Ang Lee
1979	*The Tin Drum*, Germany, Volker Scholondorff	2001	*No Man's Land*, Bosnia & Herzegovina, Danis Tanovic
1980	*Moscow Does Not Believe in Tears*, USSR, Vladimir Menshov	2002	*Nowhere in Africa*, Germany, Caroline Link
1981	*Mephisto*, Austria/Germany/Hungary, Istvan Szabo	2003	*The Barbarian Invasions*, Canada, Denys Arcand
1982	*To Begin Again*, Spain, Jose Luis Garcia	2004	*The Sea Inside*, Alejandro Amenábar
		2005	*Tsotsi*, South Africa, Gavin Hood
		2006	*The Lives of Others*, Germany, Florian Henckel von Donnersmarck
		2007	*The Counterfeiters*, Austria, Stefan Ruzowitzky

Source: Academy of Motion Picture Arts & Sciences. www.oscar.org

Cannes Film Festival *Palme d'Or* Awards, 1946–2008

Year	Film and director	Year	Film and director
1946	*La Bataille du Rail*, René Clément[1]	1980	*Kagemusha*, Akira Kurosawa
1949[2]	*The Third Man*, Carol Reed	1981	*Man of Iron*, Andrzej Wajda
1951	*Miracle in Milan*, Vittorio De Sica	1982	*Missing*, Costa-Gavras
	Miss Julie, Alf Sjöberg		*Yol*, Yilmar Güney
1952	*Two Cents Worth of Hope*, Renato Castellani	1983	*The Ballad of Narayama*, Shohei Imamura
	Othello, Orson Welles	1984	*Paris, Texas*, Wim Wenders
1953	*The Wages of Fear*, Georges Clouzot	1985	*When Father Was Away on Business*, Emir Kusturica
1954	*Gate of Hell*, Teinosuke Kinugasa		
1955	*Marty*, Delbert Mann	1986	*The Mission*, Roland Joffé
1956	*The Silent World*, Jacques Cousteau, Louis Malle	1987	*Under Satan's Sun*, Maurice Pialat
1957	*Friendly Persuasion*, William Wyler	1988	*Pelle the Conqueror*, Bille August
1958	*The Cranes are Flying*, Mikhail Kalatozov	1989	*Sex, Lies and Videotape*, Steven Soderbergh
1959	*Black Orpheus*, Marcel Camus		
1960	*La Dolce Vita*, Federico Fellini	1990	*Wild at Heart*, David Lynch
1961	*Viridiana*, Luis Buñuel	1991	*Barton Fink*, Joel Coen
1962	*The Given Word*, Anselmo Duarte	1992	*The Best Intentions*, Bille August
1963	*The Leopard*, Luchino Visconti	1993	*The Piano*, Jane Campion
1964	*The Umbrellas of Cherbourg*, Jacques Demy		*Farewell My Concubine*, Chen Kaige
1965	*The Knack, and How to Get It*, Richard Lester	1994	*Pulp Fiction*, Quentin Tarantino
1966	*A Man and a Woman*, Claude Lelouch	1995	*Underground*, Emir Kusturica
1967	*Blow-Up*, Michelangelo Antonioni	1996	*Secrets and Lies*, Mike Leigh
1969	*If . . .*, Lindsay Anderson	1997	*Taste of Cherries*, Abbas Kiarostami
1970	*M*A*S*H*, Robert Altman		*Unagi (The Eel)*, Shohei Imamura
1971	*The Go-Between*, Joseph Losey	1998	*Eternity and a Day*, Theo Angelopoulos
1972	*The Working Class Goes to Heaven*, Elio Petri	1999	*Rosetta*, Jean-Pierre and Luc Dardenne
	The Mattei Affair, Francesco Rosi	2000	*Dancer in the Dark*, Lars von Trier
1973	*Scarecrow*, Jerry Schatzberg	2001	*The Son's Room*, Nanni Moretti
	The Hireling, Alan Bridges	2002	*The Pianist*, Roman Polanski
1974	*The Conversation*, Francis Ford Coppola	2003	*Elephant*, Gus Van Sant
1975	*Chronique des Années de Braise*, M. Lakhdar Hamina	2004	*Fahrenheit 9/11*, Michael Moore
		2005	*L'enfant*, Jean-Pierre and Luc Dardenne
1976	*Taxi Driver*, Martin Scorsese	2006	*The Wind that Shakes the Barley*, Ken Loach
1977	*Padre Padrone*, Paolo and Vittorio Taviani		
1978	*The Tree of Wooden Clogs*, Ermanno Olmi	2007	*4 Months, 3 Weeks and 2 Days*, Cristian Mungiu
1979	*The Tin Drum*, Volker Schlöndorff	2008	*The Class (Entre Les Murs)*, Laurent Cantet

1. Winner of the International Jury Prize. **2.** In 1947, there was no "best film" award; prizes were given instead to outstanding works in several categories, including "Psychological and Love Films," "Adventure and Police Films," and so on. The festival was cancelled in 1948 and 1950. **Source:** www.festival-cannes.fr

The Emmy Awards, 1951–2008

The Academy of Television Arts and Sciences, formed in 1946, presented the first Emmy Awards in 1949. The number and names of awards have changed over the years, but since 1965, the Academy has recognized an outstanding comedy and drama, as well as an actor and an actress in a comedy and in a drama.

Year	Comedy	Drama	Comedy Actor	Comedy Actress	Drama Actor	Drama Actress
1951	The Red Skelton Show (CBS)	Studio One (CBS)	Sid Caesar (NBC)	Imogene Coca (NBC)	(1)	(1)
1952	I Love Lucy (CBS)	Robert Montgomery Presents (NBC)	Thomas Mitchell	Helen Hayes	(1)	(1)
1953	I Love Lucy (CBS)	The U.S. Steel Hour (ABC)	Donald O'Connor, Colgate Comedy Hour (NBC)	Eve Arden, Our Miss Brooks (CBS)	(1)	(1)
1954	Make Room for Daddy (ABC)	The U.S. Steel Hour (ABC)	Danny Thomas, Make Room for Daddy (ABC)	Loretta Young, The Loretta Young Show (NBC)	(1)	(1)
1955	The Phil Silvers Show (CBS)	Producers' Showcase (NBC)	Phil Silvers, The Phil Silvers Show (CBS)	Lucille Ball, I Love Lucy (CBS)	(1)	(1)
1956	The Phil Silvers Show (CBS)	Requiem for a Heavyweight (CBS)	Sid Caesar, Caesar's Hour (NBC)	Nanette Fabray, Caesar's Hour (NBC)	Robert Young, Father Knows Best (NBC)	Loretta Young, The Loretta Young Show (NBC)
1957	The Phil Silvers Show (CBS)	Gunsmoke (CBS)	Robert Young, Father Knows Best (NBC)	Jane Wyatt, Father Knows Best (NBC)	(1)	(1)
1958 –59	The Jack Benny Show (CBS)	(2)	Jack Benny, The Jack Benny Show (CBS)	Jane Wyatt, Father Knows Best (NBC and CBS)	Raymond Burr, Perry Mason (CBS)	Loretta Young, The Loretta Young Show (NBC)
1959 –60	"Art Carney Special" (NBC)	Playhouse 90 (CBS)	Robert Stack, The Untouchables (ABC)	Jane Wyatt, Father Knows Best (CBS)	(1)	(1)
1960 –61	The Jack Benny Show (CBS)	"Macbeth," Hallmark Hall of Fame (NBC)	Raymond Burr, Perry Mason (CBS)	Barbara Stanwyck, The Barbara Stanwyck Show (NBC)	(1)	(1)
1961 –62	The Bob Newhart Show (CBS)	The Defenders (CBS)	E.G. Marshall, The Defenders (CBS)	Shirley Booth, Hazel (NBC)	(1)	(1)
1962 –63	The Dick Van Dyke Show (CBS)	The Defenders (CBS)	E.G. Marshall, The Defenders	Shirley Booth, Hazel (NBC) (CBS)	(1)	(1)
1963 –64	The Dick Van Dyke Show (CBS)	The Defenders (CBS)	Dick Van Dyke, The Dick Van Dyke Show (CBS)	Mary Tyler Moore, The Dick Van Dyke Show (CBS)	(1)	(1)
1964 –65	(3)	(3)	(3)	(3)	(3)	(3)
1965 –66	The Dick Van Dyke Show (CBS)	The Fugitive (ABC)	Dick Van Dyke, The Dick Van Dyke Show (CBS)	Mary Tyler Moore, The Dick Van Dyke Show (CBS)	Bill Cosby, I Spy (NBC)	Barbara Stanwyck, The Big Valley (ABC)
1966 –67	The Monkees (NBC)	Mission: Impossible (CBS)	Don Adams, Get Smart (NBC)	Lucille Ball, The Lucy Show (CBS)	Bill Cosby, I Spy (NBC)	Barbara Bain, Mission: Impossible (CBS)
1967 –68	Get Smart (NBC)	Mission: Impossible (CBS)	Don Adams, Get Smart (NBC)	Lucille Ball, The Lucy Show (CBS)	Bill Cosby, I Spy (NBC)	Barbara Bain, Mission: Impossible (CBS)
1968 –69	Get Smart (NBC)	NET Playhouse (NET)	Don Adams, Get Smart (NBC)	Hope Lange, The Ghost and Mrs. Muir (NBC)	Carl Betz, Judd for the Defense (ABC)	Barbara Bain, Mission: Impossible (CBS)
1969 –70	My World & Welcome to It (NBC)	Marcus Welby, M.D. (ABC)	William Windom, My World & Welcome to It (NBC)	Hope Lange, The Ghost and Mrs. Muir (ABC)	Robert Young, Marcus Welby, M.D. (ABC)	Susan Hampshire The Forsyte Saga (NET)
1970 –71	All in the Family (CBS)	The Senator (segment), The Bold Ones (NBC)	Jack Klugman, The Odd Couple (ABC)	Jean Stapleton, All in the Family (CBS)	Hal Holbrook, The Senator (segment), The Bold Ones (NBC)	Susan Hampshire, The First Churchills (PBS)

Year	Comedy	Drama	Comedy Actor	Comedy Actress	Drama Actor	Drama Actress
1971 –72	All in the Family (CBS)	"Elizabeth R"[4] (PBS)	Carroll O'Connor All in the Family (CBS)	Jean Stapleton, All in the Family (CBS)	Peter Falk, Columbo (NBC)	Glenda Jackson, "Elizabeth R"[4] (PBS)
1972 –73	All in the Family (CBS)	The Waltons (CBS)	Jack Klugman, The Odd Couple (ABC)	Mary Tyler Moore, The Mary Tyler Moore Show (CBS)	Richard Thomas, The Waltons (CBS)	Michael Learned, The Waltons (CBS)
1973 –74	M*A*S*H (CBS)	"Upstairs, Downstairs"[4] (PBS)	Alan Alda, M*A*S*H (CBS)	Mary Tyler Moore, The Mary Tyler Moore Show (CBS)	Telly Savalas, Kojak (CBS)	Michael Learned, The Waltons (CBS)
1974 –75	The Mary Tyler Moore Show (CBS)	"Upstairs, Downstairs"[4] (PBS)	Tony Randall, The Odd Couple (ABC)	Valerie Harper, Rhoda (CBS)	Robert Blake, Baretta (ABC)	Jean Marsh, "Upstairs, Downstairs"[4] (PBS)
1975 –76	The Mary Tyler Moore Show (CBS)	Police Story (NBC)	Jack Albertson, Chico & the Man (NBC)	Mary Tyler Moore, The Mary Tyler Moore Show (CBS)	Peter Falk, Columbo (NBC)	Michael Learned, The Waltons (CBS)
1977 –78	All in the Family (CBS)	The Rockford Files (NBC)	Carroll O'Connor, All in the Family (CBS)	Jean Stapleton, All in the Family (CBS)	Edward Asner, Lou Grant (CBS)	Sada Thompson, Family (ABC)
1978 –79	Taxi (ABC)	Lou Grant (CBS)	Carroll O'Connor, All in the Family (CBS)	Ruth Gordon, Taxi (ABC)	Ron Leibman, Kaz (CBS)	Mariette Hartley, The Incredible Hulk (CBS)
1979 –80	Taxi (ABC)	Lou Grant (CBS)	Richard Mulligan, Soap (ABC)	Cathryn Damon, Soap (ABC)	Ed Asner, Lou Grant (CBS)	Barbara Bel Geddes, Dallas (CBS)
1980 –81	Taxi (ABC)	Hill Street Blues (NBC)	Judd Hirsch, Taxi (ABC)	Isabel Sanford, The Jeffersons (CBS)	Daniel Travanti, Hill Street Blues (NBC)	Barbara Babcock Hill Street Blues (NBC)
1981 –82	Barney Miller (ABC)	Hill Street Blues (NBC)	Alan Alda, M*A*S*H (CBS)	Carol Kane, Taxi (ABC)	Daniel Travanti, Hill Street Blues (NBC)	Michael Learned, Nurse (CBS)
1982 –83	Cheers (NBC)	Hill Street Blues (NBC)	Judd Hirsch, Taxi (NBC)	Shelley Long, Cheers (NBC)	Ed Flanders, St. Elsewhere (NBC)	Tyne Daly, Cagney & Lacey (CBS)
1983 –84	Cheers (NBC)	Hill Street Blues (NBC)	John Ritter, Three's Company (ABC)	Jane Curtin, Kate & Allie (CBS)	Tom Selleck, Magnum P.I. (CBS)	Tyne Daly, Cagney & Lacey (CBS)
1984 –85	The Cosby Show (NBC)	Cagney & Lacey (CBS)	Robert Guillaume, Benson (ABC)	Jane Curtin, Kate & Allie (CBS)	William Daniels, St. Elsewhere (NBC)	Tyne Daly, Cagney & Lacey (CBS)
1985 –86	The Golden Girls (NBC)	Cagney & Lacey (CBS)	Michael J. Fox, Family Ties (NBC)	Betty White, The Golden Girls (NBC)	William Daniels, St. Elsewhere (NBC)	Sharon Gless, Cagney & Lacey (CBS)
1986 –87	The Golden Girls (NBC)	L.A. Law (NBC)	Michael J. Fox, Family Ties (NBC)	Rue McClanahan, The Golden Girls (NBC)	Bruce Willis, Moonlighting (ABC)	Sharon Gless, Cagney & Lacey (CBS)
1987 –88	The Wonder Years (ABC)	thirtysomething (ABC)	Michael J. Fox, Family Ties (NBC)	Beatrice Arthur, The Golden Girls (NBC)	Richard Kiley, A Year in the Life (NBC)	Tyne Daly, Cagney & Lacey (CBS)
1988 –89	Cheers (NBC)	L.A. Law (NBC)	Richard Mulligan, Empty Nest (NBC)	Candice Bergen, Murphy Brown (CBS)	Carroll O'Connor, In the Heat of the Night (NBC)	Dana Delany, China Beach (ABC)
1989 –90	Murphy Brown (CBS)	L.A. Law (NBC)	Ted Danson, Cheers (NBC)	Candice Bergen, Murphy Brown (CBS)	Peter Falk, Columbo (ABC)	Patricia Wettig, thirtysomething (ABC)
1990 –91	Cheers (NBC)	L.A. Law (NBC)	Burt Reynolds, Evening Shade (CBS)	Kirstie Alley, Cheers (NBC)	James Earl Jones, Gabriel's Fire (ABC)	Patricia Wettig, thirtysomething (ABC)
1991 –92	Murphy Brown (CBS)	Northern Exposure (CBS)	Craig T. Nelson, Coach (ABC)	Candice Bergen, Murphy Brown (CBS)	Christopher Lloyd, Avonlea (Disney)	Dana Delany, China Beach (ABC)
1992 –93	Seinfeld (NBC)	Picket Fences (CBS)	Ted Danson, Cheers (NBC)	Roseanne Arnold, Roseanne (ABC)	Tom Skerritt, Picket Fences (CBS)	Kathy Baker, Picket Fences (CBS)
1993 –94	Frasier (NBC)	Picket Fences (CBS)	Kelsey Grammer, Frasier (NBC)	Candice Bergen, Murphy Brown (CBS)	Dennis Franz, NYPD Blue (ABC)	Sela Ward, Sisters (NBC)
1994 –95	Frasier (NBC)	NYPD Blue (ABC)	Kelsey Grammer, Frasier (NBC)	Candice Bergen, Murphy Brown (CBS)	Mandy Patinkin, Chicago Hope (CBS)	Kathy Baker, Picket Fences (CBS)
1995 –96	Frasier (NBC)	E.R. (NBC)	John Lithgow, Third Rock From the Sun (NBC)	Helen Hunt, Mad About You (NBC)	Dennis Franz, NYPD Blue (ABC)	Kathy Baker, Picket Fences (CBS)

Year	Comedy	Drama	Comedy Actor	Comedy Actress	Drama Actor	Drama Actress
1996 –97	Frasier (NBC)	Law & Order (NBC)	John Lithgow, Third Rock From the Sun (NBC)	Helen Hunt, Mad About You (NBC)	Dennis Franz, NYPD Blue (ABC)	Gillian Anderson, The X-Files (FOX)
1997 –98	Frasier (NBC)	The Practice (ABC)	Kelsey Grammer, Frasier (NBC)	Helen Hunt, Mad About You (NBC)	Andre Braugher, Homicide (NBC)	Christine Lahti, Chicago Hope (CBS)
1998 –99	Ally McBeal (FOX)	The Practice (ABC)	John Lithgow, Third Rock From the Sun (NBC)	Helen Hunt, Mad About You (NBC)	Dennis Franz, NYPD Blue (ABC)	Edie Falco, The Sopranos (HBO)
1999 –2000	Will and Grace (NBC)	The West Wing (NBC)	Michael J. Fox, Spin City (ABC)	Patricia Heaton, Everybody Loves Raymond (CBS)	James Gandolfini, The Sopranos (HBO)	Sela Ward, Once and Again (ABC)
2000 –01	Sex and the City (HBO)	The West Wing (NBC)	Eric McCormack, Will and Grace (NBC)	Patricia Heaton, Everybody Loves Raymond (CBS)	James Gandolfini, The Sopranos (HBO)	Edie Falco, The Sopranos (HBO)
2001 –02	Friends (NBC)	The West Wing (NBC)	Ray Romano, Everybody Loves Raymond (CBS)	Jennifer Aniston, Friends (NBC)	Michael Chiklis, The Shield (FX)	Allison Janney, The West Wing (NBC)
2002 –03	Everybody Loves Raymond (CBS)	The West Wing (NBC)	Tony Shalhoub, Monk (USA)	Debra Messing, Will & Grace (NBC)	James Gandolfini, The Sopranos (HBO)	Edie Falco, The Sopranos (HBO)
2003 –04	Arrested Development (Fox)	The Sopranos (HBO)	Kelsey Grammer, Frasier (NBC)	Sara Jessica Parker, Sex and the City (HBO)	James Spader, The Practice (ABC)	Allison Janney, The West Wing (NBC)
2004 –05	Everybody Loves Raymond (CBS)	Lost (ABC)	Tony Shalhoub, Monk (USA)	Felicity Huffman, Desperate Housewives (ABC)	James Spader, Boston Legal (ABC)	Patricia Arquette, Medium (NBC)
2005 –06	The Office (NBC)	24 (Fox)	Tony Shaloub, Monk (USA)	Julia-Louise Dreyfus, The New Adventures of Old Christine (CBS)	Kiefer Sutherland, 24 (Fox)	Mariska Hargitay, Law & Order: SVU (NBC)
2006 -07	30 Rock (NBC)	The Sopranos (HBO)	Ricky Gervais, Extras (HBO)	America Ferrera, Ugly Betty (ABC)	James Spader, Boston Legal (ABC)	Sally Field, Brothers and Sisters (ABC)
2007 -08	30 Rock (NBC)	Mad Men (AMC)	Alec Baldwin, 30 Rock (NBC)	Tina Fey, 30 Rock (NBC)	Bryan Cranston, Breaking Bad (AMC)	Glenn Close, Damages (FX)

Notes: 1. Before 1965, the Academy did always not give separate awards for comedy and drama. **2.** *Playhouse 90* (CBS) was best drama of one hour or longer; *Alcoa-Goodyear Theatre* (NBC) was best drama of less than one hour. **3.** In 1964, the Academy gave acting awards to Dick Van Dyke for *The Dick Van Dyke Show* (CBS), Lynn Fontaine and Alfred Lunt for "The Magnificent Yankee" *Hallmark Hall of Fame* (NBC), and Barbra Streisand for *My Name is Barbra* (CBS). It also gave Achievements in Entertainment awards to these programs. **4.** Masterpiece Theatre series.
Source: Academy of Television Arts and Sciences. www.emmys.tv

Emmy Awards for Variety Shows, 1951–2008

Year	Show	Year	Show
1951	Your Show of Shows (NBC)	1980–81	"Lily: Sold Out "(CBS)
1952	Your Show of Shows (NBC)	1981–82	"Night of 100 Stars" (ABC)
1953	Omnibus (CBS)	1982–83	"Motown 25: Yesterday, Today, Forever" (NBC)
1954	Disneyland (ABC)	1983–84	"The 6th Annual Kennedy Center Honors" (CBS)
1955	The Ed Sullivan Show (CBS)	1984–85	"Motown Returns to the Apollo" (NBC)
1956	Caesar's Hour (NBC)	1985–86	"The Kennedy Center Honors" (CBS)
1957	The Dinah Shore Show (NBC)	1986–87	"The 1987 Tony Awards" (CBS)
1958–59	The Dinah Shore Chevy Show (NBC)	1987–88	"Irving Berlin's 100th Birthday Celebration" (CBS)
1959–60	"The Fabulous '50s" (CBS)	1988–89	The Tracey Ullman Show (FOX)
1960–61	"Astaire Time" (NBC)	1989–90	In Living Color (FOX)
1961–62	The Garry Moore Show (CBS)	1990–91	"The 63rd Annual Academy Awards" (ABC)
1962–63	The Andy Williams Show (NBC)	1991–92	The Tonight Show Starring Johnny Carson (NBC)
1963–64	The Danny Kaye Show (CBS)	1992–93	Saturday Night Live (NBC)
1964–65	My Name is Barbra (CBS)	1993–94	Late Show with David Letterman (CBS)
1965–66	The Andy Williams Show (NBC)	1994–95	The Tonight Show with Jay Leno (NBC)
1966–67	The Andy Williams Show (NBC)	1995–96	Dennis Miller Live (HBO)
1967–68	Rowan & Martin's Laugh-In (NBC)	1996–97	Tracey Takes On . . . (HBO)
1968–69	Rowan & Martin's Laugh-In (NBC)	1997–98	Late Show with David Letterman (CBS)
1969–70	The David Frost Show (syndicated)	1998–99	Late Show with David Letterman (CBS)
1970–71	The Flip Wilson Show (NBC)	1999–00	Late Show with David Letterman (CBS)
1971–72	Music: The Carol Burnett Show (CBS) Talk: The Dick Cavett Show (ABC)	2000–01	Late Show with David Letterman (CBS)
1972–73	The Julie Andrews Hour (ABC)	2001–02	Late Show with David Letterman (CBS)
1973–74	The Carol Burnett Show (CBS)	2002–03	The Daily Show With Jon Stewart (Comedy Central)
1974–75	The Carol Burnett Show (CBS)	2003–04	The Daily Show With Jon Stewart (Comedy Central)
1975–76	NBC's Saturday Night (NBC)	2004–05	The Daily Show With Jon Stewart (Comedy Central)
1976–77	Van Dyke & Company (NBC)	2005–06	The Daily Show With Jon Stewart (Comedy Central)
1977–78	The Muppet Show (syndicated)	2006–07	The Daily Show With Jon Stewart (Comedy Central)
1978–79	"Steve & Eydie Celebrate Irving Berlin" (NBC)	2007–08	The Daily Show With Jon Stewart (Comedy Central)
1979–80	"IBM Presents Baryshnikov on B'way" (ABC)		

Source: Academy of Television Arts and Sciences. www.emmys.tv

The Tony Awards, 1947–2008

The Tony Awards are presented by the American Theatre Wing for achievement in the Broadway theater. Named for Antoinette Perry, an actress, producer, director, and chairman of the American Theatre Wing who died in 1946, the Tonys were first presented in 1947. The major writing, composing, and acting awards for each year are listed below.

PLAYS

Year	Best Play, Author	Best Actor, Play	Best Actress, Play
1947	no award	José Ferrer, *Cyrano de Bergerac*	Ingrid Bergman, *Joan of Lorraine*
		Fredric March, *Years Ago*	Helen Hayes, *Happy Birthday*
1948	*Mister Roberts,* Thomas Heggen and Joshua Logan	Henry Fonda, *Mister Roberts* Paul Kelly, *Command Decision* Basil Rathbone, *The Heiress*	Judith Anderson, *Medea;* Katharine Cornell, *Antony and Cleopatra;* Jessica Tandy, *A Streetcar Named Desire*
1949	*Death of a Salesman,* Arthur Miller	Rex Harrison, *Anne of the Thousand Days*	Martita Hunt, *The Madwoman of Chaillot*
1950	*The Cocktail Party,* T. S. Eliot	Sidney Blackmer, *Come Back, Little Sheba*	Shirley Booth, *Come Back, Little Sheba*
1951	*The Rose Tattoo,* Tennessee Williams	Claude Rains, *Darkness at Noon*	Uta Hagen, *The Country Girl*
1952	*The Fourposter,* Jan de Hartog	José Ferrer, *The Shrike*	Julie Harris, *I Am a Camera*
1953	*The Crucible,* Arthur Miller	Tom Ewell, *The Seven Year Itch*	Shirley Booth, *Time of the Cuckoo*
1954	*The Teahouse of the August Moon,* John Patrick	David Wayne, *The Teahouse of the August Moon*	Audrey Hepburn, *Ondine*
1955	*The Desperate Hours,* Joseph Hayes	Alfred Lunt, *Quadrille*	Nancy Kelly, *The Bad Seed*
1956	*The Diary of Anne Frank,* Frances Goodrich and Albert Hackett	Paul Muni, *Inherit the Wind*	Julie Harris, *The Lark*
1957	*Long Day's Journey Into Night,* Eugene O'Neill	Fredric March, *Long Day's Journey Into Night*	Margaret Leighton, *Separate Tables*
1958	*Sunrise at Campobello,* Dore Schary	Ralph Bellamy, *Sunrise at Campobello*	Helen Hayes, *Time Remembered*
1959	*J.B.,* Archibald Macleish	Jason Robards, *The Disenchanted*	Gertrude Berg, *A Majority of One*
1960	*The Miracle Worker,* William Gibson	Melvyn Douglas, *The Best Man*	Anne Bancroft, *The Miracle Worker*
1961	*Becket,* Jean Anouilh	Zero Mostel, *Rhinoceros*	Joan Plowright, *A Taste of Honey*
1962	*A Man for All Seasons,* Robert Bolt	Paul Scofield, *A Man for All Seasons*	Margaret Leighton, *Night of the Iguana*
1963	*Who's Afraid of Virginia Woolf,* Edward Albee	Arthur Hill, *Who's Afraid of Virginia Woolf*	Uta Hagen, *Who's Afraid of Virginia Woolf*
1964	*Luther,* John Osborne	Alec Guiness, *Dylan*	Sandy Dennis, *Any Wednesday*
1965	*The Subject Was Roses,* Frank Gilroy	Walter Matthau, *The Odd Couple*	Irene Worth, *Tiny Alice*
1966	*Marat/Sade,* Peter Weiss	Hal Holbrook, *Mark Twain Tonight!*	Rosemary Harris, *The Lion in Winter*
1967	*The Homecoming,* Harold Pinter	Paul Rogers, *The Homecoming*	Beryl Reid, *The Killing of Sister George*
1968	*Rosencrantz and Guildenstern Are Dead,* Tom Stoppard	Martin Balsam, *You Know I Can't Hear You When the Water's Running*	Zoe Caldwell, *The Prime of Miss Jean Brodie*
1969	*The Great White Hope,* Howard Sackler	James Earl Jones, *The Great White Hope*	Julie Harris, *Forty Carats*
1970	*Borstal Boy,* Frank McMahon	Fritz Weaver, *Child's Play*	Tammy Grimes, *Private Lives* (R)
1971	*Sleuth,* Anthony Shaffer	Brian Bedford, *The School for Wives*	Maureen Stapleton, *Gingerbread Lady*
1972	*Sticks and Bones,* David Rabe	Cliff Gorman, *Lenny*	Sada Thompson, *Twigs*
1973	*That Championship Season,* Jason Miller	Alan Bates, *Butley*	Julie Harris, *The Last of Mrs. Lincoln*
1974	*The River Niger,* Joseph A. Walker	Michael Moriarty, *Find Your Way Home*	Colleen Dewhurst, *A Moon for the Misbegotten* (R)
1975	*Equus,* Peter Shaffer	John Kani, *Sizwe Banzi Is Dead* Winston Ntshona, *The Island*	Ellen Burstyn, *Same Time, Next Year*
1976	*Travesties,* Tom Stoppard	John Wood, *Travesties*	Irene Worth, *Sweet Bird of Youth* (R)
1977	*The Shadow Box,* Michael Cristofer	Al Pacino, *The Basic Training of Pavlo Hummel*	Julie Harris, *The Belle of Amherst*
1978	*Da,* Hugh Leonard	Barnard Hughes, *Da*	Jessica Tandy, *The Gin Game*
1979	*The Elephant Man,* Bernard Pomerance	Tom Conti, *Whose Life Is It Anyway?*	Constance Cummings, *Wings* Carole Shelley, *The Elephant Man*
1980	*Children of a Lesser God,* Mark Medoff	John Rubinstein, *Children of a Lesser God*	Phyllis Frelich, *Children of a Lesser God*
1981	*Amadeus,* Peter Shaffer	Ian McKellen, *Amadeus*	Jane Lapotaire, *Piaf*
1982	*The Life and Adventures of Nicholas Nickleby,* David Edgar	Roger Rees, *The Life and Adventures of Nicholas Nickleby*	Zoe Caldwell, *Medea* (R)

Year	Best Play	Best Actor	Best Actress
1983	Torch Song Trilogy, Harvey Fierstein	Harvey Fierstein, Torch Song Trilogy	Jessica Tandy, Foxfire
1984	The Real Thing, Tom Stoppard	Jeremy Irons, The Real Thing	Glenn Close, The Real Thing
1985	Biloxi Blues, Neil Simon	Derek Jacobi, Much Ado About Nothing (R)	Stockard Channing, Joe Egg (R)
1986	I'm Not Rappaport, Herb Gardner	Judd Hirsch, I'm Not Rappaport	Lily Tomlin, The Search for Signs of Intelligent Life in the Universe
1987	Fences, August Wilson	James Earl Jones, Fences	Linda Lavin, Broadway Bound
1988	M. Butterfly, David Henry Hwang	Ron Silver, Speed-The-Plow	Joan Allen, Burn This
1989	The Heidi Chronicles, Wendy Wasserstein	Philip Bosco, Lend Me a Tenor	Pauline Collins, Shirley Valentine
1990	The Grapes of Wrath, Frank Galati	Robert Morse, Tru	Maggie Smith, Lettice and Lovage
1991	Lost in Yonkers, Neil Simon	Nigel Hawthorne, Shadowlands	Mercedes Ruhl, Lost in Yonkers
1992	Dancing at Lughnasa, Brian Friel	Judd Hirsch, Conversations with My Father	Glenn Close, Death and the Maiden
1993	Angels in America: Millennium Approaches, Tony Kushner	Ron Leibman, Angels in America: Millennium Approaches	Madeline Kahn, The Sisters Rosensweig
1994	Angels in America: Perestroika, Tony Kushner	Stephen Spinella, Angels in America: Perestroika	Diana Rigg, Medea (R)
1995	Love! Valour! Compassion!, Terrence McNally	Ralph Fiennes, Hamlet	Cherry Jones, The Heiress
1996	Master Class, Terrence McNally	George Grizzard, A Delicate Balance (R)	Zoe Caldwell, Master Class
1997	Last Night of Ballyhoo, Alfred Uhry	Christopher Plummer, Barrymore	Janet McTeer, A Doll's House
1998	Art, Yasmina Reza	Anthony La Paglia, A View From the Bridge	Marie Mullen, The Beauty Queen of Leenane
1999	Side Man, Warren Leight	Brian Dennehy, Death of a Salesman	Judi Dench, Amy's View
2000	Copenhagen, Michael Frayn	Stephen Dillane, The Real Thing	Jennifer Ehle, The Real Thing
2001	Proof, David Auburn	Richard Easton, The Invention of Love	Mary-Louise Parker, Proof
2002	The Goat or Who Is Sylvia?, Edward Albee	Alan Bates, Fortune's Fool	Lindsay Duncan, Private Lives
2003	Take Me Out, Richard Greenberg	Brian Dennehy, Long Day's Journey Into Night	Vanessa Redgrave, Long Day's Journey Into Night
2004	I Am My Own Wife, Doug Wright	Jefferson Mays, I Am My Own Wife	Phylicia Rashad, A Raisin in the Sun
2005	Doubt, John Patrick Shanley	Bill Irwin, Who's Afraid of Virginia Woolf?	Cherry Jones, Doubt
2006	The History Boys, Alan Bennett	Richard Griffiths, The History Boys	Cynthia Nixon, Rabbit Hole
2007	The Coast of Utopia, Tom Stoppard	Frank Langella, Frost/Nixon	Julie White, The Little Dog Laughed
2008	August: Osage County, Tracy Letts	Mark Rylance, Boeing-Boeing (R)	Deanna Dunagan, August: Osage County

MUSICALS

Year	Best Musical, Composer	Best Actor, Musical	Best Actress, Musical
1947	no award	no award	no award
1948	no award	Paul Hartman, Angel in the Wings	Grace Hartman, Angel in the Wings
1949	Kiss Me Kate, Cole Porter (M&L)	Ray Bolger, Where's Charley?	Nanette Fabray, Love Life
1950	South Pacific, Richard Rodgers (M), Oscar Hammerstein (L)	Ezio Pinza, South Pacific	Mary Martin, South Pacific
1951	Guys and Dolls, Frank Loesser (M&L)	Robert Alda, Guys and Dolls	Ethel Merman, Call Me Madam
1952	The King and I, Richard Rodgers (M), Oscar Hammerstein (L)	Phil Silvers, Top Banana	Gertrude Lawrence, The King and I
1953	Wonderful Town, Leonard Bernstein (M), Betty Comden and Adolph Green (L)	Thomas Mitchell, Hazel Flagg	Rosalind Russell, Wonderful Town
1954	Kismet, Alexander Borodin (M), adapted by Robert Wright and George Forrest (L)	Alfred Drake, Kismet	Dolores Gray, Carnival in Flanders
1955	The Pajama Game, Richard Adler and Jerry Ross (M&L)	Walter Slezak, Fanny	Mary Martin, Peter Pan
1956	Damn Yankees, Richard Adler and Jerry Ross (M&L)	Ray Walston, Damn Yankees	Gwen Verdon, Damn Yankees
1957	My Fair Lady, Frederick Loewe (M), Alan Jay Lerner (L)	Rex Harrison, My Fair Lady	Judy Holliday, Bells Are Ringing

Year	Best Musical	Best Actor	Best Actress
1958	*The Music Man,* Meredith Willson (M&L)	Robert Preston, *The Music Man*	(tie) Thelma Ritter, Gwen Verdon, *New Girl in Town*
1959	*Redhead,* Albert Hague (M), Dorothy Fields (L)	Richard Kiley, *Redhead*	Gwen Verdon, *Redhead*
1960	(tie) *Fiorello,* Jerry Bock (M), Sheldon Harnick (L); *The Sound of Music,* Richard Rodgers (M), Oscar Hammerstein (L)	Jackie Gleason, *Take Me Along*	Mary Martin, *The Sound of Music*
1961	*Bye, Bye, Birdie,* Charles Strouse (M), Lee Adams (L)	Richard Burton, *Camelot*	Elizabeth Seal, *Irma la Douce*
1962	*How to Succeed in Business Without Really Trying,* Frank Loesser (M&L)	Robert Morse, *How to Succeed in Business Without Really Trying*	(tie) Anna Maria Alberghetti, *Carnival;* Diahann Carroll, *No Strings*
1963	*A Funny Thing Happened on the Way to the Forum,* Stephen Sondheim (M&L)	Zero Mostel, *A Funny Thing Happened on the Way to the Forum,*	Vivien Leigh, *Tovarich*
1964	*Hello, Dolly!* Jerry Herman (M&L)	Bert Lahr, *Foxy*	Carol Channing, *Hello, Dolly!*
1965	*Fiddler on the Roof,* Jerry Bock (M), Sheldon Harnick (L)	Zero Mostel, *Fiddler on the Roof*	Liza Minnelli, *Flora, the Red Menace*
1966	*Man of La Mancha,* Mitch Leigh (M), Joe Darion (L)	Richard Kiley, *Man of La Mancha*	Angela Lansbury, *Mame*
1967	*Cabaret,* John Kander (M), Fred Ebb (L)	Robert Preston, *I Do! I Do!*	Barbara Harris, *The Apple Tree*
1968	*Hallelujah, Baby!* Jule Styne (M), Betty Comden & Adolph Green (L)	Robert Goulet, *The Happy Time*	Patricia Routledge, *Darling of the Day* Leslie Uggams, *Hallelujah, Baby!*
1969	*1776,* Sherman Edwards (M&L)	Jerry Orbach, *Promises, Promises*	Angela Lansbury, *Dear World*
1970	*Applause,* Charles Strouse (M), Lee Adams (L)	Cleavon Little, *Purlie*	Lauren Bacall, *Applause*
1971	*Company,* Stephen Sondheim (M&L)	Hal Linden, *The Rothschilds*	Helen Gallagher, *No, No Nannette* (R)
1972	*Two Gentlemen of Verona* [best score: *Follies,* Stephen Sondheim (M&L)]	Phil Silvers, *A Funny Thing Happened on the Way to the Forum* (R)	Alexis Smith, *Follies*
1973	*A Little Night Music,* Stephen Sondheim (M&L)	Ben Vereen, *Pippin*	Glynis Johns, *A Little Night Music*
1974	*Raisin,* [best score: *Gigi,* Frederick Loewe (M), Alan Jay Lerner (L)]	Christopher Plummer, *Cyrano*	Virginia Capers, *Raisin*
1975	*The Wiz,* Charlie Smalls (M&L)	John Cullum, *Shenandoah*	Angela Lansbury, *Gypsy* (R)
1976	*A Chorus Line,* Marvin Hamlisch (M), Edward Kleban (L)	George Rose, *My Fair Lady* (R)	Donna McKechnie, *A Chorus Line*
1977	*Annie,* Charles Strouse (M), Martin Charnin (L)	Barry Bostwick, *The Robber Bridegroom*	Dorothy Loudon, *Annie*
1978	*Ain't Misbehavin'* [best score: *On the Twentieth Century,* Cy Coleman (M) Betty Comden and Adolph Green (L)]	John Cullum, *On the Twentieth Century*	Liza Minnelli, *The Act*
1979	*Sweeney Todd,* Stephen Sondheim	Len Cariou, *Sweeney Todd*	Angela Lansbury, *Sweeney Todd*
1980	*Evita,* Andrew Lloyd Webber (M), Tim Rice (L)	Jim Dale, *Barnum*	Patti LuPone, *Evita*
1981	*42nd Street,* [best score: *Woman of the Year,* John Kander (M), Fred Ebb (L)]	Kevin Kline, *The Pirates of Penzance*	Lauren Bacall, *Woman of the Year*
1982	*Nine,* Maury Yeston (M&L)	Ben Harney, *Dreamgirls*	Jennifer Holliday, *Dreamgirls*
1983	*Cats,* Andrew Lloyd Webber (M), T.S. Eliot (L)	Tommy Tune, *My One and Only*	Natalia Makarova, *On Your Toes*
1984	*La Cage Aux Folles,* Jerry Herman (M&L)	George Hearn, *La Cage Aux Folles*	Chita Rivera, *The Rink*
1985	*Big River,* Roger Miller (M&L)	No award	No award
1986	*The Mystery of Edwin Drood,* Rupert Holmes (M&L)	George Rose, *The Mystery of Edwin Drood*	Bernadette Peters, *Song and Dance*
1987	*Les Misérables,* Claude-Michel Schönberg (M); Herbert Kretzmer & Alain Boublil (L)	Robert Lindsay, *Me and My Girl*	Maryann Plunkett, *Me and My Girl*
1988	*The Phantom of the Opera* [best score: *Into the Woods,* Stephen Sondheim (M&L)]	Michael Crawford, *The Phantom of the Opera*	Joanna Gleason, *Into the Woods*
1989	*Jerome Robbins' Broadway* [best score: no award]	Jason Alexander, *Jerome Robbins' Broadway*	Ruth Brown, *Black and Blue*
1990	*City of Angels,* Cy Coleman (M) David Zippel (L)	James Naughton, *City of Angels*	Tyne Daly, *Gypsy* (R)
1991	*The Will Rogers Follies,* Cy Coleman (M); Betty Comden and Adolph Green (L)	Jonathan Pryce, *Miss Saigon*	Lea Salonga, *Miss Saigon*

ar	Best Musical	Best Actor	Best Actress
992	*Crazy for You,* [best score: *Falsettos,* William Finn (M&L)]	Gregory Hines, *Jelly's Last Jam*	Faith Prince, *Guys and Dolls* (R)
993	*Kiss of the Spider Woman* [best score: (tie) *Kiss of the Spider Woman,* John Kander (M) and Fred Ebb (L)' *Tommy,* Pete Townshend (M&L)]	Brent Carver, *Kiss of the Spider Woman*	Chita Rivera, *Kiss of the Spider Woman*
994	*Passion,* Stephen Sondheim (M&L)	Boyd Gaines, *She Loves Me* (R)	Donna Murphy, *Passion*
995	*Sunset Boulevard,* Andrew Lloyd Webber (M&L)	Matthew Broderick, *How to Succeed in Business Without Really Trying* (R)	Glenn Close, *Sunset Boulevard*
1996	*Rent,* Jonathan Larson (M&L)	Nathan Lane, *A Funny Thing Happened on the Way to the Forum* (R)	Donna Murphy, *The King and I* (R)
1997	*Titanic,* Maury Yeston (M&L)	James McNaughton, *Chicago* (R)	Bebe Neuwirth, *Chicago* (R)
1998	*The Lion King,* [best score: *Ragtime,* Stephen Flaherty & Lynn Ahrens (M&L)]	Alan Cumming, *Cabaret* (R)	Natasha Richardson, *Cabaret* (R)
1999	*Fosse,* [best score: *Parade,* Jason Robert Brown (M&L)]	Martin Short, *Little Me*	Bernadette Peters, *Annie Get Your Gun* (R)
2000	*Contact* [best score: *Aida,* Elton John (M) and Tim Rice (L)]	Brian Stokes Mitchell, *Kiss Me Kate*	Heather Headley, *Aida*
2001	*The Producers,* Mel Brooks (M&L)	Nathan Lane, *The Producers*	Christine Ebersole, *42nd Street* (R)
2002	*Thoroughly Modern Millie,* [best score: *Urinetown: The Musical,* Mark Hollmann (M); Mark Hollman and Greg Kotis (L)]	John Lithgow, *Sweet Smell of Success*	Sutton Foster, *Thoroughly Modern Millie*
2003	*Hairspray,* Scott Whittman, Marc Shaiman (M&L)	Harvey Fierstein, *Hairspray*	Marissa Jaret Winokur, *Hairspray*
2004	*Avenue Q,* Robert Lopez and Jeff Marx (M&L)	Hugh Jackman, *The Boy From Oz*	Idina Menzel, *Wicked*
2005	*Monty Python's Spamalot,* John Du Prez, Eric Idle (M&L)	Norbert Leo Butz, *Dirty Rotten Scoundrels*	Victoria Clark, *The Light in the Piazza*
2006	*Jersey Boys,* Bob Gaudio (M) Bob Crewe (L)	John Lloyd Young, *Jersey Boys*	LaChanze, *The Color Purple*
2007	*Spring Awakening,* Duncan Sheik (M)	David Hyde Pierce, *Curtains*	Christine Ebersole, *Grey Gardens*
2008	*In the Heights,* Lin-Manuel Miranda (M&L)	Paolo Szot, *South Pacific* (R)	Patti LuPone, *Gypsy* (R)

Note: Since 1971 "Musical" and "Score" have been separate categories. The winner of the Tony for Best Musical usually wins the award for Best Score, except where otherwise indicated. **M** = music; **L** = lyrics, **R** = revival. **Source:** American Theatre Wing. www.tonys.org

The Grammys, 1958–2007

The "Grammys" are officially known as the National Academy of Recording Arts and Sciences Awards. Winners (in almost 70 categories) are selected yearly by the 6,000 or so voting members of the academy.

"Best Vocal Performance" awards were phased out in 1968. From that year on, awards listed are "Best Pop Vocal Performance" (male and female), except indicated.

Year	Record of the year	Album of the year	Song of the year	Best male vocal performance	Best female vocal performance
1958	Domenico Modugno, *Nel Blu Dipinto di Blu (Volare)*	Henry Mancini, *The Music from Peter Gunn*	Domenico Modugno, "Nel Blu Dipinto di Blu *(Volare)*"	Perry Como, *Catch a Falling Star*	Ella Fitzgerald, *Ella Fitzgerald Sings the Irving Berlin Songbook*[2]
1959	Bobby Darin, *Mack the Knife*	Frank Sinatra, *Come Dance with Me*	Jimmy Driftwood, "The Battle of New Orleans"	Frank Sinatra, *Come Dance with Me*	Ella Fitzgerald, *But Not for Me*
1960	Percy Faith, *Theme from a Summer Place*	Bob Newhart, *Button-Down Mind*	Ernest Gold, "Theme from Exodus"	Ray Charles, *Georgia on My Mind*	Ella Fitzgerald, *Mack the Knife*
1961	Henry Mancini, *Moon River*	Judy Garland, *Judy at Carnegie Hall*	Henry Mancini, Johnny Mercer, "Moon River"	Jack Jones, *Lollipops and Roses*	Judy Garland, *Judy at Carnegie Hall*[2]
1962	Tony Bennett, *I Left My Heart in San Francisco*	Vaughn Meader, *The First Family*	Leslie Bricusse, Anthony Newley, "What Kind of Fool Am I?"	Tony Bennett, *I Left My Heart in San Francisco*[2]	Ella Fitzgerald, *Ella Swings Brightly with Nelson Riddle*[2]
1963	Henry Mancini, *The Days of Wine and Roses*	Barbra Streisand, *The Barbra Streisand Album*	Henry Mancini, Johnny Mercer, "The Days of Wine and Roses"	Jack Jones, *Wives and Lovers*	Barbra Streisand, *The Barbra Streisand Album*[2]
1964	Stan Getz, Astrud Gilberto, *The Girl from Ipanema*	Stan Getz, Astrud Gilberto, *Getz/Gilberto*	Jerry Herman, "Hello, Dolly!"	Louis Armstrong, *Hello, Dolly!*	Barbra Streisand, *People*

Year	Record of the year	Album of the year	Song of the year	Best male vocal performance	Best female vocal performance
1965	Herb Alpert & the Tijuana Brass, A Taste of Honey	Frank Sinatra, September of My Years	Paul Francis Webster, Johnny Mandel, "The Shadow of Your Smile"	Frank Sinatra, It Was a Very Good Year	Barbra Streisand, My Name is Barbra[2]
1966	Frank Sinatra, Strangers in the Night	Frank Sinatra, A Man and His Music	John Lennon, Paul McCartney, "Michelle"	Frank Sinatra, Strangers in the Night	Eydie Gorme, If He Walked into My Life
1967	5th Dimension, Up, Up and Away	The Beatles, Sgt. Pepper's Lonely Hearts Club Band	Jim Webb, "Up, Up, and Away"	Glen Campbell, By the Time I Get to Phoenix	Bobbie Gentry, Ode to Billie Joe
1968	Simon & Garfunkel, Mrs. Robinson	Glen Campbell, By the Time I Get to Phoenix	Bobby Russell, "Little Green Apples"	Jose Feliciano,[3] Light My Fire	Dionne Warwick,[3] Do You Know the Way to San Jose?
1969	5th Dimension, Aquarius/Let the Sunshine In	Blood, Sweat & Tears, Blood, Sweat & Tears	Joe South, "Games People Play"	Harry Nilsson,[4] Everybody's Talkin'	Peggy Lee,[4] Is That All There Is?
1970	Simon & Garfunkel, Mrs. Robinson	Simon & Garfunkel, Bridge over Troubled Water	Paul Simon, "Bridge over Troubled Water"	Ray Stevens,[4] Everything is Beautiful	Dionne Warwick,[4] I'll Never Fall in Love Again[2]
1971	Carole King, It's Too Late	Carole King, Tapestry	Carole King, "You've Got a Friend"	James Taylor,[5] You've Got a Friend	Carole King,[5] Tapestry[2]
1972	Roberta Flack, The First Time Ever I Saw Your Face	George Harrison, Ravi Shankar, Bob Dylan et al, Concert for Bangladesh	Ewan McColl, "The First Time Ever I Saw Your Face"	Harry Nilsson, Without You	Helen Reddy, I Am Woman
1973	Roberta Flack, Killing Me Softly with His Song	Stevie Wonder, Innervisions	Norman Gimbel, Charles Fox, "Killing Me Softly with His Song"	Stevie Wonder, You Are the Sunshine of My Life	Roberta Flack, Killing Me Softly with His Song
1974	Olivia Newton-John, I Honestly Love You	Stevie Wonder, Fulfillingness' First Finale	Marilyn & Alan Bergman, Marvin Hamlisch, "The Way We Were"	Stevie Wonder, Fulfillingness' First Finale[2]	Olivia Newton-John, I Honestly Love You
1975	Captain & Tennille, Love Will Keep Us Together	Paul Simon, Still Crazy After All These Years	Stephen Sondheim, "Send in the Clowns"	Paul Simon, Still Crazy after All These Years[2]	Janis Ian, At Seventeen
1976	George Benson, This Masquerade	Stevie Wonder, Songs in the Key of Life	Bruce Johnston, "I Write the Songs"	Stevie Wonder, Songs in the Key of Life[2]	Linda Ronstadt, Hasten Down the Wind[2]
1977	The Eagles, Hotel California	Fleetwood Mac, Rumours	Barbra Streisand, Paul Williams, "Evergreen"	James Taylor, Handy Man	Barbra Streisand, Evergreen
1978	Billy Joel, Just the Way You Are	Various artists, Saturday Night Fever	Billy Joel, "Just the Way You Are"	Barry Manilow, Copacabana (At the Copa)	Anne Murray, You Needed Me
1979	The Doobie Brothers, What a Fool Believes	Billy Joel, 52nd Street	Kenny Loggins, Michael McDonald, "What a Fool Believes"	Billy Joel, 52nd Street[2]	Dionne Warwick, I'll Never Love This Way Again
1980	Christopher Cross, Sailing	Christopher Cross, Christopher Cross	Christopher Cross, "Sailing"	Kenny Loggins, This Is It	Bette Midler, The Rose
1981	Kim Carnes, Bette Davis Eyes	John Lennon/Yoko Ono, Double Fantasy	Donna Weiss, Jackie DeShannon, "Bette Davis Eyes"	Al Jarreau, Breakin' Away[2]	Lena Horne, The Lady and Her Music Live on Broadway[2]
1982	Toto, Rosanna	Toto, Toto IV	Johnny Christopher, Mark James, Wayne Carson, "Always on My Mind"	Lionel Richie, Truly	Melissa Manchester, You Should Hear How She Talks About You
1983	Michael Jackson, Beat It	Michael Jackson, Thriller	Sting, "Every Breath You Take"	Michael Jackson, Thriller[2]	Irene Cara, Flashdance . . . What a Feeling
1984	Tina Turner, What's Love Got to Do with It?	Lionel Richie, Can't Slow Down	Graham Lyle, Terry Britten, "What's Love Got to Do with It?"	Phil Collins, Against All Odds (Take a Look at Me Now)	Tina Turner, What's Love Got to Do with It?
1985	USA for Africa, We Are the World	Phil Collins, No Jacket Required	Michael Jackson, Lionel Richie, "We Are the World"	Phil Collins, No Jacket Required[2]	Whitney Houston, Saving All My Love for You

Year	Record of the year	Album of the year	Song of the year	Best male vocal performance	Best female vocal performance
1986	Steve Winwood, *Higher Love*	Paul Simon, *Graceland*	Various artists, "That's What Friends Are For"	Steve Winwood, *Higher Love*	Barbra Streisand, *The Broadway Album²*
1987	Paul Simon, *Graceland*	U2, *The Joshua Tree*	Linda Ronstadt, James Ingram, "Somewhere Out There"	Sting, *Bring on the Night²*	Whitney Houston, *I Wanna Dance with Somebody (Who Loves Me)*
1988	Bobby McFerrin, *Don't Worry, Be Happy*	George Michael, *Faith*	Bobby McFerrin, "Don't Worry, Be Happy"	Bobby McFerrin, *Don't Worry, Be Happy*	Tracy Chapman, *Fast Car*
1989	Bette Midler, *Wind Beneath My Wings*	Bonnie Rait, *Nick of Time*	Bette Midler, "Wind Beneath My Wings"	Michael Bolton, *How Am I Supposed to Live Without You*	Bonnie Raitt, *Nick of Time*
1990	Phil Collins, *Another Day in Paradise*	Quincy Jones, *Back on the Block*	Julie Gold, "From a Distance"	Roy Orbison, *Oh, Pretty Woman*	Mariah Carey, *Vision of Love*
1991	Natalie Cole, *Unforgettable*	Natalie Cole, *Unforgettable*	Irving Gordon, "Unforgettable"	Michael Bolton, *When a Man Loves a Woman*	Bonnie Raitt, *Something to Talk About*
1992	Eric Clapton, *Tears in Heaven*	Eric Clapton, *Unplugged*	Eric Clapton, "Tears in Heaven"	Eric Clapton, *Tears in Heaven*	k.d. Lang, *Constant Craving*
1993	Whitney Houston, *I Will Always Love You*	Whitney Houston, *The Bodyguard*	Alan Menken and Tim Rice, " A Whole New World" (Aladdin's Theme)"	Sting, *If I Ever Lose My Faith in You*	Whitney Houston, *I Will Always Love You*
1994	Sheryl *Crow, All I Wanna Do*	Tony Bennett, *MTV Unplugged*	Bruce Springsteen, "Streets of Philadelphia"	Elton John, *Can You Feel the Love Tonight*	Sheryl Crow, *All I Wanna Do*
1995	Seal, *Kiss From a Rose*	Alanis Morissette, *Jagged Little Pill*	Seal, "Kiss From a Rose"	Seal, *Kiss From a Rose*	Annie Lennox, *No More "I Love Yous"*
1996	Eric Clapton, *Change the World*	Celine Dion, *Falling Into You*	Wayne Kirkpatrick and Tommy Sims, "Change the World"	Eric Clapton, *Change the World*	Toni Braxton, *Unbreak My Heart*
1997	Shawn Colvin, *Sunny Came Home*	Bob Dylan, *Time Out of Mind*	Shawn Colvin and John Leventhal, "Sunny Came Home"	Elton John, *Candle in the Wind, 1997*	Sarah McLachlan, *Building a Mystery*
1998	Celine Dion, *My Heart Will Go On*	Lauryn Hill, *The Miseducation of Lauryn Hill*	James Horner and Will Jennings, "My Heart Will Go On"	Eric Clapton, *My Father's Eyes*	Celine Dion, *My Heart Will Go On*
1999	Santana, *Smooth*	Santana, *Supernatural*	Itaal Shur and Rob Thomas, "Smooth"	Sting, *Brand New Day*	Sara McLachlan, *I Will Remember You*
2000	U2, *Beautiful Day*	Steely Dan, *Two Against Nature*	U2 "Beautiful Day"	Sting, *She Walks This Earth*	Macy Gray, *I Try*
2001	U2, *Walk On*	Various artists, *O Brother, Where Art Thou?*	Alicia Keys, "Fallin'"	James Taylor, *Don't Let Me Be Lonely Tonight*	Nelly Furtado, *I'm Like a Bird*
2002	Norah Jones, *Don't Know Why*	Norah Jones, *Come Away With Me*	Norah Jones, "Don't Know Why"	John Mayer, *Your Body is a Wonderland*	Norah Jones, *Don't Know Why*
2003	Coldplay *Clocks*	Outkast, *Speakerboxxx/ The Love Below*	Luther Vandross and Richard Marx, "Dance with My Father"	Justin Timberlake, *Cry Me A River*	Christina Aguilera *Beautiful*
2004	Ray Charles & Norah Jones, *Here We Go Again*	Ray Charles & Various Artists, *Genius Loves Company*	John Mayer, "Daughters"	John Mayer *Daughters*	Norah Jones, *Sunrise*
2005	Green Day, *Boulevard of Broken Dreams*	U2, *How to Dismantle an Atomic Bomb*	U2, "Sometimes You Can't Make It on Your Own"	Stevie Wonder, *From the Bottom of My Heart*	Kelly Clarkson, *Since U Been Gone*
2006	Dixie Chicks, *Not Ready to Make Nice*	Dixie Chicks, *Taking the Long Way*	Dixie Chicks, "Not Ready to Make Nice"	John Mayer, *Waiting on the World to Change*	Christina Aguilera, *Ain't No Other Man*
2007	Amy Winehouse, *Rehab*	Herbie Hancock, *River: The Joni Letters*	Amy Winehouse, "Rehab"	Justin Timberlake, *What Goes Around Comes Around*	Amy Winehouse, *Rehab*

Notes: 1. Awarded to the composer, rather than the performer, of the song. **2.** Awarded for an album, rather than an individual song. **3.** Award given for "Best Contemporary Pop Vocal Performance." **4.** Award given for "Best Vocal Performance Contemporary." **5.** From 1971 on, all awards are for "Best Pop Vocal Performance."   **Source:** National Academy of Recording Arts and Sciences; www.grammys.com

MTV Video Music Awards, 1984–2008

Each year MTV Networks recognizes outstanding achievement in the field of video music with the MTV Video Music Awards. In addition to those listed below, there are categories for rap, heavy metal and dance videos, as well as achievement in choreography, cinematography, and direction. In 2007, the categories were changed so that the artist who won the category could win for multiple videos.

Year	Best video	Best male video	Best female video	Best group video	Best new artist
1984	The Cars, *You Might Think*	David Bowie, *China Girl*	Cyndi Lauper, *Girls Just Want to Have Fun*	ZZ Top, *Legs*	Eurythmics, *Sweet Dreams (are Made of This)*
1985	Don Henley, *The Boys of Summer*	Bruce Springsteen, *I'm on Fire*	Tina Turner, *What's Love Got to Do With It?*	USA for Africa, *We Are the World*	til' tuesday, *Voices Carry*
1986	Dire Straits, *Money for Nothing*	Robert Palmer, *Addicted to Love*	Whitney Houston, *How Will I Know?*	Dire Straits, *Money for Nothing*	a-Ha, *Take On Me*
1987	Peter Gabriel, *Sledgehammer*	Peter Gabriel, *Sledgehammer*	Madonna, *Papa Don't Preach*	Talking Heads, *Wild Wild Life*	Crowded House, *Don't Dream it's Over*
1988	INXS, *Need You Tonight/Mediate*	Prince, *U Got the Look*	Suzanne Vega, *Luka*	INXS, *Need You Tonight/Mediate*	Guns N' Roses, *Welcome to the Jungle*
1989	Neil Young, *This Note's for You*	Elvis Costello, *Veronica*	Paula Abdul, *Straight Up*	Living Color, *Cult of Personality*	Living Color, *Cult of Personality*
1990	Sinead O'Connor, *Nothing Compares to You*	Don Henley, *End of the Innocence*	Sinead O'Connor, *Nothing Compares to You*	B-52s, *Love Shack*	Michael Penn, *No Myth*
1991	R.E.M., *Losing My Religion*	Chris Isaak, *Wicked Game*	Janet Jackson, *Love Will Never Do Without You*	R.E.M., *Losing My Religion*	Jesus Jones, *Right Here, Right Now*
1992	Van Halen, *Right Now*	Eric Clapton, *Tears in Heaven*	Annie Lennox, *Why*	U2, *Even Better Than the Real Thing*	Nirvana, *Smells Like Teen Spirit*
1993	Pearl Jam, *Jeremy*	Lenny Kravitz, *Are You Gonna Go My Way*	k.d. lang, *Constant Craving*	Pearl Jam, *Jeremy*	Stone Temple Pilots, *Plush*
1994	Aerosmith, *Cryin'*	Tom Petty and the Heartbreakers, *Mary Jane's Last Dance*	Janet Jackson, *If*	Aerosmith, *Cryin'*	Counting Crows, *Mr. Jones*
1995	TLC, *Waterfalls*	Tom Petty and the Heartbreakers, *You Don't Know How it Feels*	Madonna, *Take a Bow*	TLC, *Waterfalls*	Hootie & the Blowfish, *Hold My Hand*
1996	Smashing Pumpkins, *Tonight, Tonight*	Beck, *Where It's At*	Alanis Morissette, *Ironic*	Foo Fighters, *Big Me*	Alanis Morissette, *Ironic*
1997	Jamiroquai, *Virtual Insanity*	Beck, *Devil's Haircut*	Jewel, *You Were Meant For Me*	No Doubt, *Don't Speak*	Fiona Apple, *Sleep to Dream*
1998	Madonna, *Ray of Light*	Will Smith, *Just the Two of Us*	Madonna, *Ray of Light*	Backstreet Boys, *Everybody (Backstreet's Back)*	Natalie Imbruglia, *Torn*
1999	Lauryn Hill, *Doo-Wop*	Will Smith, *Miami*	Lauryn Hill, *Doo-Wop*	TLC, *No Scrubs*	Eminem, *My Name Is*
2000	Eminem, *The Real Slim Shady*	Eminem, *The Real Slim Shady*	Aaliyah, *Try Again*	Blink-182, *All The Small Things*	Macy Gray, *I Try*
2001	Various artists, *Lady Marmalade*	Moby, *South Side*	Eve, *Let Me Blow Ya Mind*	'N SYNC, *Pop*	Alicia Keys, *Fallin'*
2002	Eminem, *Without Me*	Eminem, *Without Me*	Pink, *Get The Party Started*	No Doubt, *Hey Baby*	Avril Lavigne *Complicated*
2003	Missy Elliott, *Work It*	Justin Timberlake, *Cry Me a River*	Beyonce Knowles, *Crazy in Love*	Coldplay, *The Scientist*	50 Cent, *In Da Club*
2004	Outkast, *Hey Ya*	Usher, *Yeah*	Beyonce, *Naughty Girl*	No Doubt, *It's My Life*	Maroon 5, *This Love*
2005	Green Day, *Boulevard of Broken Dreams*	Kanye West, *Jesus Walks*	Kelly Clarkson, *Since U Been Gone*	Green Day, *Boulevard of Broken Dreams*	The Killers, *Mr. Brightside*
2006	Panic! At the Disco, *I Write Sins Not Tragedies*	James Blunt, *You're Beautiful*	Kelly Clarkson, *Because of You*	The All-American Rejects, *Move Along*	Avenged Sevenfold, *Bat Country*
2007	Rihanna, *Umbrella*	Justin Timberlake, *Let Me Talk To You, SexyBack, What Goes Around Comes Around, Love Stoned*	Fergie, *Big Girls Don't Cry, Glamorous, Fergalicious*	Fall Out Boy, *This Ain't A Scene, It's An Arms Race, Thanks For the Memories, The Take Over, The Break's Over*	Gym Class Heroes, *Cupid's Chokehold, Clothes Off*
2008	Britney Spears, *Piece of Me*	Chris Brown, *With You*	Britney Spears, *Piece of Me*	(1)	Tokio Hotel, *Ready, Set, Go!*

1. Category discontinued after 2007. **Source:** Press Department, MTV Networks. **www.mtv.com.**

The National Book Awards, 1950–2007

The National Book Awards are given annually for outstanding literary works by American citizens. The number of prizes awarded has varied, including categories such as poetry, fiction, biography, science, philosophy, religion, and history.

FICTION

Year	Author, Title
1950	Nelson Algren, *The Man with the Golden Arm*
1951	William Faulkner, *The Collected Stories*
1952	James Jones, *From Here to Eternity*
1953	Ralph Ellison, *Invisible Man*
1954	Saul Bellow, *The Adventures of Augie March*
1955	William Faulkner, *A Fable*
1956	John O'Hara, *Ten North Frederick*
1957	Wright Morris, *Field of Vision*
1958	John Cheever, *The Wapshot Chronicle*
1959	Bernard Malamud, *The Magic Barrel*
1960	Philip Roth, *Goodbye, Columbus*
1961	Conrad Richter, *The Waters of Kronos*
1962	Walker Percy, *The Moviegoer*
1963	J. F. Powers, *Morte d'Urban*
1964	John Updike, *The Centaur*
1965	Saul Bellow, *Herzog*
1966	Katherine Anne Porter, *The Collected Stories*
1967	Bernard Malamud, *The Fixer*
1968	Thornton Wilder, *The Eighth Day*
1969	Jerzy Kosinski, *Steps*
1970	Joyce Carol Oates, *Them*
1971	Saul Bellow, *Mr. Sammler's Planet*
1972	Flannery O'Connor, *The Complete Stories*
1973	John Barth, *Chimera*
1974	Thomas Pynchon, *Gravity's Rainbow*
	Isaac Bashevis Singer, *A Crown of Feathers & Other Stories*
1975	Robert Stone, *Dog Soldiers*
	Thomas Williams, *The Hair of Harold Roux*
1976	William Gaddis, *JR*
1977	Wallace Stegner, *The Spectator Bird*
1978	Mary Lee Settle, *Blood Ties*
1979	Tim O'Brien, *Going After Cacciato*
1980	William Styron, *Sophie's Choice*
1981	Wright Morris, *Plains Song*
1982	John Updike, *Rabbit Is Rich*
1983	Alice Walker, *The Color Purple*
1984	Ellen Gilchrist, *Victory Over Japan*
1985	Don DeLillo, *White Noise*
1986	E. L. Doctorow, *World's Fair*
1987	Larry Heinemann, *Paco's Story*
1988	Pete Dexter, *Paris Trout*
1989	John Casey, *Spartina*
1990	Charles Johnson, *Middle Passage*
1991	Norman Rush, *Mating*
1992	Cormac McCarthy, *All the Pretty Horses*
1993	E. Annie Proulx, *The Shipping News*
1994	William Gaddis, *A Frolic of His Own*
1995	Philip Roth, *Sabbath's Theater*
1996	Andrea Barrett, *Ship Fever and Other Stories*
1997	Charles Frazier, *Cold Mountain*
1998	Alice McDermott, *Charming Billy*
1999	Ha Jin, *Waiting*
2000	Susan Sontag, *In America*
2001	Jonathan Franzen, *The Corrections*
2002	Julia Glass, *Three Junes*
2003	Shirley Hazzard, *The Great Fire*
2004	Lily Tuck, *The News from Paraguay*
2005	William T. Vollmann, *Europe Central*
2006	Richard Powers, *The Echo Maker*
2007	Denis Johnson, *Tree of Smoke*

POETRY

Year	Author, Title
1950	William Carlos Williams, *Paterson: Book III* and *Selected Poems*
1951	Wallace Stevens, *The Auroras of Autumn*
1952	Marianne Moore, *Collected Poems*
1953	Archibald MacLeish, *Collected Poems 1917–52*
1954	Conrad Aiken, *Collected Poems*
1955	Wallace Stevens, *The Collected Poems*
1956	W. H. Auden, *The Shield of Achilles*
1957	Richard Wilbur, *Things of this World*
1958	Robert Penn Warren, *Promises: Poems, 1954–56*
1959	Theodore Roethke, *Words for the Wind*
1960	Robert J. Lowell, *Life Studies*
1961	Randall Jarrell, *The Woman at the Washington Zoo*
1962	Alan Dugan, *Poems*
1963	William Stafford, *Traveling Through the Dark*
1964	John Crowe Ransom, *Selected Poems*
1965	Theodore Roethke, *The Far Field*
1966	James Dickey, *Buckdancer's Choice*
1967	James Merrill, *Nights and Days*
1968	Robert Bly, *The Light Around the Body*
1969	John Berryman, *His Toy, His Dream, His Rest*
1970	Elizabeth Bishop, *The Complete Poems*
1971	Mona Van Duyn, *To See, To Take*
1972	Howard Moss, *Selected Poems*
1973	A. R. Ammons, *Collected Poems: 1951–71*
1974	Allen Ginsberg, *The Fall of America: Poems of These States, 1965–71*
	Adrienne Rich, *Diving into the Wreck: Poems, 1971–72*
1975	Marilyn Hacker, *Presentation Piece*
1976	John Ashbery, *Self-Portrait in a Convex Mirror*
1977	Richard Eberhart, *Collected Poems, 1930–1976*
1978	Howard Nemerov, *The Collected Poems*
1979	James Merrill, *Mirabell: Books of Number*
1980	Philip Levine, *Ashes*
1981	Lisel Mueller, *The Need to Hold Still*
1982	William Bronk, *Life Supports*
1983	Galway Kinnell, *Selected Poems*
1984	Charles Wright, *Country Music*
1991	Philip Levine, *What Work Is*
1992	Mary Oliver, *New and Selected Poems*
1993	A. R. Ammons, *Garbage*
1994	James Tate, *Worshipful Company of Fletchers*
1995	Stanley Kunitz, *Passing Through*
1996	Hayden Carruth, *Scrambled Eggs and Whiskey: Poems 1991–1995*
1997	William Meredith, *Effort at Speech*
1998	Gerald Stern, *This Time*
1999	Ai, *New and Selected Poems*
2000	Lucille Clifton, *Blessing the Boats*
2001	Alan Dugan, *Poems Seven: New and Complete Poetry*
2002	Ruth Stone, *In the Next Galaxy*
2003	C.K. Williams, *The Singing*
2004	Jean Valentine, *Door in the Mountain*
2005	W.S. Merwin, *Migration: New and Selected Poems*
2006	Nathaniel Mackey, *Splay Anthem*
2007	Robert Hass, *Time and Materials*

NONFICTION

Year	Author, Title	Year	Author, Title
1950	Ralph L. Rusk, *Ralph Waldo Emerson*	1982	Tracy Kidder, *The Soul of a New Machine*
1951	Newton Arvin, *Herman Melville*	1983	Fox Butterfield, *China: Alive in the Bitter Sea*
1952	Rachel Carson, *The Sea Around Us*	1984	Robert V. Remini, *Andrew Jackson and the Course of American Democracy, 1833–45*
1953	Bernard De Voto, *Course of Empire*		
1954	Bruce Catton, *A Stillness at Appomattox*	1985	J. Anthony Lukas, *Common Ground: A Turbulent Decade in the Lives of Three American Families*
1955	Joseph Wood Krutch, *The Measure of Man*		
1956	Herbert Kubly, *An American in Italy*	1986	Barry Lopez, *Arctic Dreams*
1957	George F. Kennan, *Russia Leaves the War*	1987	Richard Rhodes, *The Making of the Atom Bomb*
1958	Catherine Drinker Bowen, *The Lion and the Throne*	1988	Neil Sheehan, *A Bright and Shining Lie: John Paul Vann and America in Vietnam*
1959	J. Christopher Herold, *Mistress to an Age*	1989	Thomas L. Friedman, *From Beirut to Jerusalem*
1960	Richard Ellman, *James Joyce*	1990	Ron Chernow, *The House of Morgan*
1961	William L. Shirer, *The Rise and Fall of the Third Reich*	1991	Orlando Patterson, *Freedom*
		1992	Paul Monette, *Becoming a Man: Half a Life*
1962	Lewis Mumford, *The City in History*	1993	Gore Vidal, *United States: Essays 1952-1992*
1963	Leon Edel, *Henry James,* vols. 2 and 3	1994	Sherwin B. Nuland, *How We Die: Reflections on Life's Final Chapter*
1964	Aileen Ward, *John Keats: The Making of a Poet*		
1965	Louis Fisher, *The Life of Lenin*	1995	Tina Rosenberg, *The Haunted Land: Facing Europe's Ghosts After Communism*
1966	Arthur M. Schlesinger Jr., *A Thousand Days: JFK in the White House*		
		1996	James Carroll, *An American Requiem: God, My Father and the War That Came Between Us*
1967	Justin Kaplan, *Mr. Clemens and Mark Twain*		
1968	Jonathan Kozol, *Death at an Early Age*	1997	Joseph J. Ellis, *American Sphinx: The Character of Thomas Jefferson*
1969	Norman Mailer, *The Armies of the Night*		
1970	Lillian Hellman, *An Unfinished Woman, a Memoir*	1998	Edward Ball, *Slaves in the Family*
		1999	John W. Dower, *Embracing Defeat: Japan in the Wake of World War II*
1971	James MacGregor Burns, *Roosevelt: The Soldier of Freedom*		
		2000	Nathaniel Philbrick, *In the Heart of the Sea: The Tragedy of the Whaleship Essex*
1972	Joseph P. Lash, *Eleanor and Franklin*		
1973	Frances Fitzgerald, *Fire in the Lake: The Vietnamese and the Americans in Vietnam*	2001	Andrew Solomon, *The Noonday Demon: An Atlas of Depression*
1974	Pauline Kael, *Deeper into the Movies*	2002	Robert A. Caro, *Master of the Senate: The Years of Lyndon Johnson*
1975	Richard B. Sewall, *The Life of Emily Dickinson*		
	Lewis Thomas, *The Lives of a Cell*	2003	Carlos Eire, *Waiting for Snow in Havana: Confessions of a Cuban Boy*
1976	Paul Fussell, *The Great War and Modern Memory*		
1977	Bruno Bettelheim, *The Uses of Enchantment: The Meaning and Importance of Fairy Tales*	2004	Kevin Boyle, *Arc of Justice: A Saga of Race, Civil Rights, and Murder in the Jazz Age*
1978	Walter Jackson Bate, *Samuel Johnson*	2005	Joan Didion, *The Year of Magical Thinking*
1979	Arthur M. Schlesinger Jr., *Robert Kennedy and His Times*	2006	Timothy Egan, *The Worst Hard Time: The Untold Story of Those Who Survived the Great American Dust Bowl*
1980	Tom Wolfe, *The Right Stuff*		
1981	Maxine Hong Kingston, *China Men*	2007	Tim Weiner, *Legacy of Ashes: The History of the CIA*

YOUNG PEOPLE'S LITERATURE

Year	Author, Title	Year	Author, Title
1996	Victor Martinez, *Parrot in the Oven: Mi Vida*	2003	Polly Horvath, *The Canning Season*
1997	Han Nolan, *Dancing on the Edge*	2004	Pete Hautman, *Godless*
1998	Louis Sachar, *Holes*	2005	Jeanne Birdsall, *The Penderwicks*
1999	Kimberly Willis Holtt, *When Zachary Beaver Came to Town*	2006	M.T. Anderson, *The Astonishing Life of Octavian Nothing, Traitor to the Nation, Vol. 1: The Pox Party*
2000	Gloria Whelan, *Homeless Bird*		
2001	Virginia Eumer Wolff, *True Believer*	2007	Sherman Alexie, *The Absolutely True Diary of a Part-time Indian*
2002	Nancy Farmer, *The House of the Scorpion*		

Note: No award was given in poetry from 1985 to 1990. **Source:** National Book Awards, Inc. www.nationalbook.org

Bollingen Prize for Poetry, 1949–2007

First awarded annually, and biennially since 1965, the Bollingen Prize is offered by Yale University to an American citizen for a distinguished book of poetry, or in recognition of a poet's entire achievement.

Year	Recipient	Year	Recipient	Year	Recipient	Year	Recipient
1949	Ezra Pound	1958	e.e. cummings	1973	James Merrill	1991	Laura Riding Jackson
1950	Wallace Stevens	1959	Theodore Roethke	1975	A. R. Ammons		Donald Justice
1951	John Crowe Ransom	1960	Delmore Schwartz	1977	David Ignatow	1993	Mark Strand
		1961	Ivor Winters	1979	W. S. Merwin	1995	Kenneth Koch
1952	Marianne Moore	1962	Richard Eberhart	1981	May Swenson	1997	Gary Snyder
1953	Archibald MacLeish		John Hall Wheelock		Howard Nemerov	1999	Robert W. Creeley
	William Carlos Williams	1963	Robert Frost	1983	Anthony E. Hecht	2001	Louise Glück
		1965	Horace Gregory		John Hollander	2003	Adrienne Rich
1954	W. H. Auden	1967	Robert Penn Warren	1985	John Ashbery	2005	Jay Wright
1955	Leonie Adams	1969	John Berryman		Fred Chappel	2007	Frank Bidart
	Louise Bogan		Karl Shapiro	1987	Stanley Kunitz		
1956	Conrad Aiken	1971	Richard Wilbur	1989	Edgar Bowers	**Source:** Yale University.
1957	Allen Tate		Mona Van Duyn				

The National Book Critics Circle Award, 1975–2007

Selected by a 24-member board of critics (who serve 3-year terms) from around the country; books are often recommended to the board by the more than 500 general members of the Circle.

FICTION

Year	Author, Title	Year	Author, Title
1975	E.L. Doctorow, *Ragtime*	1992	Cormac McCarthy, *All the Pretty Horses*
1976	John Gardner, *October Light*	1993	Ernest J. Gaines, *A Lesson Before Dying*
1977	Toni Morrison, *Song of Solomon*	1994	Carol Shields, *The Stone Diaries*
1978	John Cheever, *The Stories of John Cheever*	1995	Stanley Elkin[1], *Mrs. Ted Bliss*
1979	Thomas Flanagan, *The Year of the French*	1996	Gina Berriault, *Women in Their Beds*
1980	Shirley Hazzard, *The Transit of Venus*	1997	Penelope Fitzgerald, *The Blue Flower*
1981	John Updike, *Rabbit is Rich*	1998	Alice Munro, *The Love of a Good Woman*
1982	Stanley Elkin, *George Mills*	1999	Jonathan Lethem, *Motherless Brooklyn*
1983	William Kennedy, *Ironweed*	2000	Jim Crace, *Being Dead*
1984	Louise Erdrich, *Love Medicine*	2001	W.G. Sebald, *Austerlitz*
1985	Anne Tyler, *The Accidental Tourist*	2002	Ian McEwan, *Atonement*
1986	Reynolds Price, *Kate Vaiden*	2003	Edward P. Jones, *The Known World*
1987	Phillip Roth, *The Counterlife*	2004	Marilynne Robinson, *Gilead*
1988	Bharati Mukherjee, *The Middleman and Other Stories*	2005	E.L. Doctorow, *The March*
1989	E.L. Doctorow, *Billy Bathgate*	2006	Kiran Desai, *The Inheritance of Loss*
1990	John Updike, *Rabbit at Rest*	2007	Junot Díaz, *The Brief Wondrous Life of Oscar Wao*
1991	Jane Smiley, *A Thousand Acres*		

GENERAL NONFICTION

Year	Author, Title	Year	Author, Title
1975	R.W.B. Lewis, *Edith Wharton*	1994	Lynn H. Nicholas, *The Rape of Europa: The Fate of Europe's Treasures in the Third Reich and the Second World War*
1976	Maxine Hong Kingston, *The Woman Warrior: Memoirs of a Girlhood Among Ghosts*	1995	Jonathan Harr, *A Civil Action*
1977	Walter Jackson Bate, *Samuel Johnson*	1996	Jonathan Raban, *Bad Land: An American Romance*
1978	Maureen Howard, *Facts of Life*		
1979	Telford Taylor, *Munich: The Price of Peace*	1997	Anne Fadiman, *The Spirit Catches You and You Fall Down*
1980	Ronald Steel, *Walter Lippmann and the American Century*	1998	Philip Gourevitch, *We Wish to Inform You That Tomorrow We Will Be Killed With Our Families*
1981	Stephen Jay Gould, *The Mismeasure of Man*		
1982	Robert A. Caro, *The Path of Power: The Years of Lyndon Johnson*	1999	Jonathan Weiner, *Time, Love, and Memory, A Great Biologist and His Quest for the Origins of Behavior*
1983	Seymour M. Hersh, *The Price of Power: Kissinger and the Nixon White House*	2000	Ted Conover, *Newjack: Guarding Sing Sing*
1984	Freeman Dyson, *Weapons and Hope*	2001	Nicholson Baker, *Double Fold: Libraries and the Assault on Paper*
1985	J. Anthony Lukas, *Common Ground: A Turbulent Decade in the Lives of Three Americans*	2002	Samantha Power, *A Problem From Hell: America and the Age of Genocide*
1986	John W. Dower, *War Without Mercy: Race and Power in the Pacific War*	2003	Paul Hendrickson, *Sons of Mississippi*
1987	Richard Rhodes, *The Making of the Atomic Bomb*	2004	Diarmaid MacCulloch, *The Reformation: A History*
1988	Taylor Branch, *Parting the Waters: America in the King Years, 1954–63*	2005	Svetlana Alexievich, *Voices From Chernobyl: The Oral History of a Nuclear Disaster*
1989	Michael Dorris, *The Broken Cord*		
1990	Shelby Steele, *The Content of Our Character: A New Vision of Race in America*	2006	Simon Schama, *Rough Crossings: Britain, the Slaves, and the American Revolution*
1991	Susan Faludi, *Backlash*	2007	Harriet Washington, *Medical Apartheid: The Dark History of Medical Experiments on Black Americans from Colonial Times to the Present*
1992	Norman Maclean, *Young Men and Fire*		
1993	Alan Lomax, *The Land Where Blues Began*		

BIOGRAPHY/AUTOBIOGRAPHY

Year	Author, Title	Year	Author, Title
1983	Joyce Johnson, *Minor Characters*	1998	Sylvia Nasar, *A Beautiful Mind*
1984	Joseph Frank, *Dostoevsky: The Years of Ordeal. 1850–1859*	1999	Henry Wiencek, *The Hairstons: An American Family in Black and White*
1985	Leon Edel, *Henry James: A Life*	2000	Herbert P. Bix, *Hirohito and the Making of Modern Japan*
1986	Theodore Rosengarten, *Tombee: Portrait of a Cotton Planter*	2001	Adam Sisman, *Boswell's Presumptuous Task: The Making of the Life of Dr. Johnson*
1987	Donald R. Howard, *Chaucer: His Life, His Works, His World*	2002	Janet Browne, *Charles Darwin: The Power of Place, Vol. II*
1988	Richard Ellman, *Oscar Wilde*	2003	William Taubman, *Khrushchev: The Man and His Era*
1989	Geoffrey C. Ward, *A First-Class Temperament: The Emergence of Franklin Roosevelt*	2004	Mark Stevens and Annalyn Swan, *De Kooning: An American Master*
1990	Robert A. Caro, *Means of Ascent: The Years of Lyndon Johnson, Vol. 2*	2005	Kai Bird and Martin J. Sherwin, *Prometheus: The Triumph and Tragedy of J. Robert Oppenheimer*
1991	Philip Roth, *Patrimony*	2006	Julie Phillips, *James Tiptree, Jr.: The Double Life of Alice B. Sheldon*
1992	Carol Brightman, *Writing Dangerously: Mary McCarthy and Her World*		Daniel Mendelsohn, *The Lost: A Search for Six Million*
1993	Edmund White, *Genet*	2007	Tim Jeal, *Stanley, the Impossible Life of Africa's Greatest Explorer*
1994	Mikal Gilmore, *Shot in the Heart*		Edwidge Danticat, *Brother, I'm Dying*
1995	Robert Polito, *Savage Art: A Biography of Jim Thompson*		
1996	Frank McCourt, *Angela's Ashes*		
1997	James Tobin, *Ernie Pyle's War: America's Eyewitness to World War II*		

POETRY

Year	Author, Title	Year	Author, Title
1975	John Ashbery, *Self-Portrait in a Convex Mirror*	1990	Amy Gerstler, *Bitter Angel*
1976	Elizabeth Bishop, *Geography III*	1991	Albert Goldbarth, *Heaven and Earth*
1977	Robert Lowell, *Day by Day*	1992	Hayden Carruth, *Collected Shorter Poems*
1978	L.E. Sissman, *Hello Darkness: The Collected Poems of L.E. Sissman*	1993	Mark Doty, *My Alexandria*
		1994	Mark Rudman, *Rider*
1979	Philip Levine, *Ashes and Seven Years from Somewhere*	1995	William Matthews, *Time & Money*
		1996	Robert Hass, *Sun Under Wood*
1980	Frederick Seidel, *Sunrise*	1997	Charles Wright, *Black Zodiac*
1981	A.R. Ammons, *A Coast of Trees*	1998	Marie Ponsot, *The Bird Catcher*
1982	Katha Pollitt, *Antarctic Traveler*	1999	Ruth Stone, *Ordinary Words*
1983	James Merrill, *The Changing Light at Sandover*	2000	Judy Jordan, *Carolina Ghost Woods*
		2001	Albert Goldbarth, *Saving Lives*
1984	Sharon Olds, *The Dead and the Living*	2002	B.H. Fairchild, *Early Occult Memory Systems of the Lower Midwest*
1985	Louise Gluck, *The Triumph of Achilles*	2003	Susan Stewart, *Columbarium*
1986	Edward Hirsch, *Wild Gratitude*	2004	Adrienne Rich, *The School Among the Ruins*
1987	C.K. Williams, *Flesh and Blood*	2005	Jack Gilbert, *Refusing Heaven*
1988	Donald Hall, *The One Day*	2006	Troy Jollimore, *Tom Thomson in Purgatory*
1989	Rodney Jones, *Transparent Gestures*	2007	Mary Jo Blang, *Elegy*

CRITICISM

Year	Author, Title	Year	Author, Title
1975	Paul Fussell, *The Great War and Modern Memory*	1991	Lawrence L. Langer, *Holocaust Testimonies*
		1992	Garry Wills, *Lincoln At Gettysburg: The Words That Remade America*
1976	Bruno Bettelheim, *The Uses of Enchantment: The Meaning and Importance of Fairy Tales*	1993	John Dizikes, *Opera in America*
		1994	Gerald Early, *The Culture of Bruising: Essays on Prizefighting, Literature and Modern American Culture*
1977	Susan Sontag, *On Photography*		
1978	Meyer Schapiro, *Modern Art: 19th and 20th Centuries, Selected Papers*	1995	Robert Darnton, *The Forbidden Best-Sellers of Pre-Revolutionary France*
1979	Elaine Pagels, *The Gnostic Gospels*	1996	William Gass, *Finding a Form*
1980	Helen Vendler, *Part of Nature, Part of Us: Modern American Poets*	1997	Mario Vargas Llosa, *Making Waves*
		1998	Gary Giddins, *Visions of Jazz*
1981	Virgil Thompson, *A Virgil Thompson Reader*	1999	Jorge Luis Borges[1], *Selected Non-Fictions*
1982	Gore Vidal, *The Second American Revolution and Other Essays, 1976–82*	2000	Cynthia Ozick, *Quarrel & Quandary*
		2001	Martin Amis, *The War Against Cliché: Essays and Reviews, 1971–2000*
1983	John Updike, *Hugging the Shore*		
1984	Robert Hass, *Twentieth Century Pleasures: Prose on Poetry*	2002	William H. Gass, *Tests of Time*
		2003	Rebecca Solnit, *River of Shadows: Eadweard Muybridge and the Technological Wild West*
1985	William H. Gass, *Habitations of the Word: Essays*	2004	Patrick Neate, *Where You're At: Notes from the Frontline of a Hip-Hop Plane*
1986	Joseph Brodsky, *Less Than One: Selected Essays*	2005	William Logan, *The Undiscovered Country: Poetry in the Age of Tin*
1987	Edwin Denby, *Dance Writings*		
1988	Clifford Geertz, *Works and Lives: The Anthropologist as Author*	2006	Lawrence Weschler, *Everything that Rises: A Book of Convergences*
1989	John Clive, *Not by Fact Alone: Essays on the Writing and Reading of History*	2007	Alex Ross, *The Rest is Noise: Listening to the Twentieth Century*
1990	Arthur C. Danto, *Encounters and Reflections: Art in the Historical Present*		

1. Awarded posthumously. **Source:** The National Book Critics Circle. www.bookcritics.org

The Newbery Medal, 1922–2008

he Newbery Medal, presented by the American Library Association, is awarded annually to the author of the most distinguished contribution to American literature for children. The award is named in honor of John Newbery (1713–67), the first English publisher of books for children.

Year	Author, Title	Year	Author, Title
922	Willem Van Loon, *The Story of Mankind*	1967	Irene Hunt, *Up a Road Slowly*
923	Hugh Lofting, *The Voyages of Doctor Dolittle*	1968	E.L. Konigsburg, *From the Mixed-up Files of Mrs. Basil E. Frankweiler*
924	Charles Hawes, *The Dark Frigate*	1969	Lloyd Alexander, *The High King*
925	Charles Finger, *Tales from Silver Lands*	1970	William H. Armstrong, *Sounder*
926	Arthur Bowie Chrisman, *Shen of the Sea*	1971	Betsy Byars, *Summer of the Swans*
1927	Will James, *Smoky, The Cowhorse*	1972	Robert C. O'Brien, *Mrs. Frisby and the Rats of NIMH*
1928	Dhan Gopal Mukerji, *Gayneck, The Story of a Pigeon*	1973	Joan George, *Julie of the Wolves*
1929	Eric P. Kelly, *The Trumpeter of Krakow*	1974	Paula Fox, *The Slave Dancer*
1930	Rachel Field, *Hitty, Her First Hundred Years*	1975	Virginia Hamilton, *M.C. Higgins the Great*
1931	Elizabeth Coatsworth, *The Cat Who Went to Heaven*	1976	Susan Cooper, *The Grey King*
1932	Laura Adams Armer, *Waterless Mountain*	1977	Mildred D. Taylor, *Roll of Thunder, Hear My Cry*
1933	Elizabeth Foreman Lewis, *Young Fu of the Upper Yangtze*	1978	Katherine Paterson, *Bridge to Terabithia*
1934	Cornelia Meigs, *Invincible Louisa*	1979	Ellen Raskin, *The Westing Game*
1935	Monica Shannon, *Dobry*	1980	Joan Blos, *A Gathering of Days: A New England Girl's Journal, 1830–32*
1936	Carol Brink, *Caddie Woodlawn*	1981	Katherine Paterson, *Jacob Have I Loved*
1937	Ruth Sawyer, *Roller Skates*	1982	Nancy Willard, *A Visit to William Blake's Inn: Poems for Innocent and Experienced Travelers*
1938	Kate Seredy, *The White Stag*		
1939	Elizabeth Enright, *Thimble Summer*	1983	Cynthia Voigt, *Dicey's Song*
1940	James Daugherty, *Daniel Boone*	1984	Beverly Cleary, *Dear Mr. Henshaw*
1941	Armstrong Sperry, *Call It Courage*	1985	Robin McKinley, *The Hero and the Crown*
1942	Walter D. Edmonds, *The Matchlock Gun*	1986	Patricia MacLachlan, *Sarah, Plain and Tall*
1943	Elizabeth Janet Gray, *Adam of the Road*	1987	Sid Fleischman, *The Whipping Boy*
1944	Esther Forbes, *Johnny Tremain*	1988	Russell Freedman, *Lincoln: A Photobiography*
1945	Robert Lawson, *Rabbit Hill*	1989	Paul Fleischman, *Joyful Noise: Poems for Two Voices*
1946	Lois Lenski, *Strawberry Girl*		
1947	Carolyn Sherwin Bailey, *Miss Hickory*	1990	Lois Lowry, *Number the Stars*
1948	William Pène du Bois, *The 21 Balloons*	1991	Jerry Spinelli, *Maniac Magee*
1949	Marguerite Henry, *King of the Wind*	1992	Phyllis Reynolds Naylor, *Shiloh*
1950	Marguerite de Angeli, *The Door in the Wall*	1993	Cynthia Rylant, *Missing May*
1951	Elizabeth Yates, *Amos Fortune, Free Man*	1994	Lois Lowry, *The Giver*
1952	Eleanor Estes, *Ginger Pye*	1995	Sharon Creech, *Walk Two Moons*
1953	Ann Nolan Clark, *Secret of the Andes*	1996	Karen Cushman, *The Midwife's Apprentice*
1954	Joseph Krumgold, *. . . And Now Miguel*	1997	Elaine Konigsburg, *The View From Saturday*
1955	Meindert DeJong, *The Wheel on the School*	1998	Karen Hesse, *Out of the Dust*
1956	Jean Lee Latham, *Carry On, Mr. Bowditch*	1999	Louis Sachar, *Holes*
1957	Virginia Sorensen, *Miracles on Maple Hill*	2000	Christopher Paul Curtis, *Bud, Not Buddy*
1958	Harold Keith, *Rifles for Watie*	2001	Richard Peck, *A Year Down Yonder*
1959	Elizabeth George Speare, *The Witch of Blackbird Pond*	2002	Linda Sue Park, *A Single Shard*
1960	Joseph Krumgold, *Onion John*	2003	Avi, *Crispin: The Cross of Lead*
1961	Scott O'Dell, *Island of the Blue Dolphins*	2004	Kate DiCamillo, *The Tale of Despereaux*
1962	Elizabeth George Speare, *The Bronze Bow*	2005	Cynthia Kadohata, *Kira-Kira*
1963	Madeleine L'Engle, *A Wrinkle in Time*	2006	Lynne Rae Perkins, *Criss Cross*
1964	Emily Cheney Neville, *It's Like This, Cat*	2007	Susan Patron, *The Higher Power of Lucky*
1965	Maia Wojciechowska, *Shadow of a Bull*	2008	Laura Amy Schlitz, *Good Masters! Sweet Ladies! Voices from a Medieval Village*
1966	Elizabeth Borten de Trevino, *I, Juan de Pareja*		

Source: American Library Association. www.ala.org

The Caldecott Medal, 1938–2008

The Caldecott Medal, presented by the American Library Association, is awarded annually to the illustrator of the most distinguished picture book for children published in the United States during the preceding year. The award is named in honor of the English illustrator Randolph Caldecott (1846–1886). In cases where only one name is given, the book was written and illustrated by the same person.

Year	Illustrator/Author/Title	Year	Illustrator/Author/Title
1938	Dorothy Lathrop; Helen Dean Fish, *Animals of the Bible*	1972	Nonny Hogrogian, *One Fine Day*
1939	Thomas Handforth, *Mei Li*	1973	Blair Lent; retold by Arlene Mosel, *The Funny Little Woman*
1940	Ingri and Edgar Parin d'Aulaire, *Abraham Lincoln*	1974	Margot Zemach; Harve Zemach, *Duffy and the Devil*
1941	Robert Lawson, *They Were Strong and Good*	1975	Gerald McDermott, *Arrow to the Sun*
1942	Robert McCloskey, *Make Way for Ducklings*	1976	Leo and Diane Dillon; retold by Verna Aardema, *Why Mosquitoes Buzz in People's Ears*
1943	Virginia Lee Burton, *The Little House*		
1944	Louis Slobodkin; James Thurber, *Many Moons*		
1945	Elizabeth Orton Jones; Rachel Jones, *Prayer for a Child*	1977	Leo & Diane Dillon; Margaret Musgrove, *Ashanti to Zulu: African Traditions*
1946	Maude and Miska Petersham, *The Rooster Crows* (traditional Mother Goose)	1978	Peter Spier, *Noah's Ark*
		1979	Paul Goble, *The Girl Who Loved Wild Horses*
1947	Leonard Weisgard; Golden MacDonald, *The Little Island*	1980	Barbara Cooney; Donald Hall, *Ox-Cart Man*
		1981	Arnold Lobel, *Fables*
1948	Roger Duvoisin; Alvin Tresselt, *White Snow, Bright Snow*	1982	Chris Van Allsburg, *Jumanji*
		1983	Marcia Brown, *Shadow*
1949	Bert and Elmer Hader, *The Big Snow*	1984	Martin and Alice Provensen, *The Glorious Flight*
1950	Leo Politi, *Song of the Swallows*		
1951	Katherine Milhous, *The Egg Tree*	1985	Trina Schart Hyman, *Saint George and the Dragon*
1952	Nicolas Mordvinoff; Will Mordvinoff, *Finders Keepers*		
		1986	Chris Van Allsburg, *The Polar Express*
1953	Lynd Ward, *The Biggest Bear*	1987	Richard Egielski; Arthur Yorinks, *Hey, Al*
1954	Ludwig Bemelmans, *Madeline's Rescue*	1988	John Schoenherr, *Owl Moon*
1955	Marcia Brown; Charles Perault, *Cinderella, or the Little Glass Slipper*	1989	Stephen Gammell; Karen Ackerman, *Song and Dance Man*
1956	Feodor Rojankovsky; John Langstaff, *Frog Went A-Courtin'*	1990	Ed Young, *Lon Po Po: A Red-Riding Hood Story from China*
1957	Marc Simont; Janice May Udry, *A Tree is Nice*	1991	David Macaulay, *Black and White*
1958	Robert McCloskey, *Time of Wonder*	1992	David Wiesner, *Tuesday*
1959	Barbara Cooney (adapted from Geoffrey Chaucer), *Chanticleer and the Fox*	1993	Emily Arnold McCully, *Mirette on the High Wire*
1960	Marie Hall Ets and Aurora Labastida, *Nine Days to Christmas*	1994	Allen Say, *Grandfather's Journey*
		1995	David Diaz; Eve Bunting, *Smoky Night*
1961	Nicolas Sidjakov; Ruth Robbins, *Baboushka and the Three Kings*	1996	Peggy Rathman, *Officer Buckle and Gloria*
		1997	David Wisniewski, *Golem*
1962	Marcia Brown, *Once a Mouse . . .*	1998	Paul O. Zelinsky, *Rapunzel*
1963	Ezra Jack Keats, *The Snowy Day*	1999	Mary Azarian; Jacqueline Briggs Martin, *Snowflake Bentley*
1964	Maurice Sendak, *Where the Wild Things Are*		
1965	Beni Montresor; Beatrice Schenk de Regniers, *May I Bring a Friend?*	2000	Simms Taback, *Joseph Had a Little Overcoat*
		2001	David Small, *So You Want to Be President?*
1966	Nonny Hogrogian; Sorche Nic Leodhas, *Always Room for One More*	2002	David Wiesner, *The Three Pigs*
		2003	Eric Rohmann, *My Friend Rabbit*
1967	Evaline Ness, *Sam, Bangs & Moonshine*	2004	Mordicai Gerstein, *The Man Who Walked Between the Towers*
1968	Ed Emberley; Barbara Emberley, *Drummer Hoff*		
		2005	Kevin Henkes, *Kitten's First Full Moon*
1969	Uri Shulevitz; Arthur Ransome, *The Fool of the World and the Flying Ship*	2006	Norton Juster, *The Hello, Goodbye Window*
		2007	David Wiesner, *Flotsam*
1970	William Steig, *Sylvester and the Magic Pebble*	2008	Brian Selznick, *The Invention of Hugo Cabret*
1971	Gail E. Haley, *A Story—A Story*		

Source: American Library Association. **www.ala.org**

American Institute of Architects Gold Medalists, 1907–2008

The AIA medal recognizes outstanding lifetime achievement in architecture. It is not awarded every year.

Year	Medalist, Country	Year	Medalist, Country
1907	Sir Aston Webb, U.K.	1967	Wallace K. Harrison, U.S.
1909	Charles Follen McKim, U.S.	1968	Marcel Breuer, U.S.
1911	George B. Post, U.S.	1969	William Wilson Wurster, U.S.
1914	Jean Louis Pascal, France	1970	Richard Buckminster Fuller, U.S.
1922	Victor Laloux, France	1971	Louis I. Kahn, U.S.
1923	Henry Bacon, U.S.	1972	Pietro Belluschi, U.S.
1925	Bertram Grosvenor Goodhue, U.S.	1977	Richard Joseph Neutra, U.S.[1]
1925	Sir Edwin Landseer Lutyens, London	1978	Philip Johnson, U.S.
1927	Howard Van Doren Shaw, U.S.	1979	Ieoh Ming Pei, U.S.
1929	Milton Bennett Medary, U.S.	1981	Josep Lluis Sert, U.S.
1933	Ragnar Ostberg, Stockholm	1982	Romaldo Giurgola, U.S.
1938	Paul Philippe Cret, U.S.	1983	Nathaniel A. Owings, U.S.
1944	Louis Henri Sullivan, U.S.	1985	William Caudill, U.S.[1]
1947	Eliel Saarinen, U.S.	1986	Arthur Erickson, Canada
1948	Charles Donagh Maginnis, U.S.	1989	Joseph Esherick, U.S.
1949	Frank Lloyd Wright, U.S.	1990	Fay Jones, U.S.
1950	Sir Patrick Abercrombie, U.K.	1991	Charles Willard Moore, U.S.
1951	Bernard Ralph Maybeck, U.S.	1992	Benjamin Thompson, U.S.
1952	Auguste Perret, France	1993	Kevin Roche, U.S.
1953	William Adams Delano, U.S.		Thomas Jefferson, U.S.[1]
1955	Willem Marinus Dudock, Netherlands	1994	Sir Norman Foster, U.K.
1956	Clarence S. Stein, U.S.	1995	Cesar Pelli, U.S.
1957	Louis Skidmore, U.S.	1997	Richard Meier, U.S.
1957	Ralph Walker, U.S.	1998	No Award
1958	John Wellborn Root, U.S.	1999	Frank Gehry, U.S.
1959	Walter Gropius, U.S.	2000	Ricardo Legorreta, Mexico
1960	Ludwig Mies van der Rohe, U.S.	2001	Michael Graves, U.S.
1961	Le Corbusier (Charles Edouard Jeanneret-Gris), France	2002	Tadao Ando, Japan
		2004	Samuel Mockbee, U.S.[1]
1962	Eero Saarinen, U.S.[1]	2005	Santiago Calatrava, Spain
1963	Alvar Aalto, Finland	2006	Antoine Predock, U.S.
1964	Pier Luigi Nervi, Italy	2007	Edward Larrabee Barnes, U.S.
1966	Kenzo Tange, Japan	2008	Renzo Piano, Italy

1. Awarded posthumously. **Source:** American Institute of Architects. www.aia.org

Pritzker Prize Winners, 1979–2008

Recognized as the most prestigious award in architecture, the Pritzker Prize is given annually by the Hyatt Hotel Foundation, and is named for its chairman, Jay Pritzker.

Year	Medalist, Country	Year	Medalist, Country
1979	Philip Johnson, U.S.	1994	Christian de Portzamparc, France
1980	Luis Barragan, Mexico	1995	Tadao Ando, Japan
1981	James Stirling, U.K.	1996	Rafael Moneo, Spain
1982	Kevin Roche, U.S.	1997	Sverre Fehn, Norway
1983	I.M. Pei, U.S.	1998	Renzo Piano, Italy
1984	Richard Meier, U.S.	1999	Norman Foster, U.K.
1985	Hans Hollein, Austria	2000	Rem Koolhaas, Netherlands
1986	Gottfried Boehm, Germany	2001	Jacques Herzog, Switzerland
1987	Kenzo Tange, Japan		Pierre de Meuron, Switzerland
1988	Gordon Bunshaft, U.S.	2002	Glenn Murcutt, Australia
	Oscar Niemeyer, Brazil	2003	Jørn Utzon, Denmark
1989	Frank O. Gehry, U.S.	2004	Zaha Hadid, Iraq-U.K.
1990	Aldo Rossi, Italy	2005	Thom Mayne, U.S.
1991	Robert Venturi, U.S.	2006	Paulo Mendes de Rocha, Brazil
1992	Alvaro Siza, Portugal	2007	Richard Rogers, U.K.
1993	Fumihiko Maki, Japan	2008	Jean Nouvel, France

Source: Hyatt Hotel Foundation. www.pritzkerprize.com

Templeton Prize Winners, 1973–2008

Believing that religion had been unfairly excluded from consideration for Nobel Prizes, Tennessee-born financier John Marks Templeton in 1972 established the Templeton Prize for "those who seek new and different paths in advancing the world's understanding of God and/or spirituality." Templeton decreed that the monetary value of his prize should always exceed that of the Nobel Prize. The 2004 Prize was worth 795,000 pounds sterling (more than $ million U.S.).

Year	Recipient
1973	**Mother Teresa**, for aiding the children of Calcutta.
1974	**Brother Roger**, founder of the Taize Community for orphaned children in France.
1975	**Sarvepalli Radhakrishnan**, Pres. of India (1962–67), and Oxford Prof. of Eastern Religions and Ethics.
1976	**Leon Joseph Cardinal Suenens**, Archbishop of Malines-Brussels.
1977	**Chiara Lubich**, founder of Italy's Focolare Movement.
1978	**Thomas F. Torrance**, Moderator of the Church of Scotland.
1979	**Rev. Nikkyo Niwano**, founder of Rissho Kosei-Kai (Japan), World Conference on Religion and Peace.
1980	**Ralph Wendell Burhoe**, founder and editor of *Zygon, Journal of Religion and Science*.
1981	**Dame Cecily Saunders**, founder of the Hospice and Palliative Care Movement.
1982	**The Rev. Billy Graham**, televangelist.
1983	**Aleksandr Solzhenitsyn**, Soviet dissident.
1984	**The Rev. Michael Bourdeaux**, founder of Keston College in England.
1985	**Sir Alister Hardy**, founder of the Sir Alister Hardy Research Centre at Oxford.
1986	**The Rev. James McCord**, Chancellor of the Center of Theological Inquiry in Princeton, N.J.
1987	**The Rev. Stanley L. Jaki**, professor of Astrophysics at Seton Hall University, N.J.
1988	**Dr. Inamullah Khan**, founder of Modern World Muslim Congress in Karachi, Pakistan.
1989	**The very Rev. Lord MacLeod**, founder of the Iona Community; and **Professor Carl Friedrich von Weizsacker**.
1990	**Baba Amte**, Hindu lawyer, and **L. Charles Birch**, Prof. of Biology at the University of Sydney.
1991	**Lord Jakobovits**, Chief Rabbi of Great Britain (1967–91).
1992	**Rev. Dr. Kyung-Chik Han**, founder of Seoul Young Nak Presbyterian Church.
1993	**Charles W. Colson**, founder of the Prison Fellowship and Special Counsel to Pres. Nixon
1994	**Michael Novak**, writer, professor, diplomat
1995	**Paul Charles William Davies**, physicist.
1996	**William R. "Bill" Bright**, founder of Campus Crusade for Christ.
1997	**Pandurang Shastri Athavale**, founder of Bhagavad Gita–based self-study known as *swadhyaya*.
1998	**Sir Sigmund Sternberg**, Hungarian-born British philanthropist.
1999	**Ian Barbour**, professor emeritus at Carleton College in Northfield, Minn.
2000	**Freeman J. Dyson**, Princeton Univ. physicist.
2001	**Arthur Peacocke**, Founder of the Society of Ordained Scientists (S.O.Sc.).
2002	**John C. Polkinghorne**, mathematical physicist and Anglican priest.
2003	**Holmes Rolston III**, Presbyterian minister.
2004	**George F. R. Ellis**, cosmologist
2005	**Charles Townes**, American scientist
2006	**John D. Barrow**, cosmologist
2007	**Charles Taylor**, Canadian philosopher
2008	**Michael Heller**, Polish priest and philosopher

Source: John Marks Templeton Foundation. www.templetonprize.org.

Fields Medal Winners, 1936–2006

The Fields Medal, named for Canadian mathematician J. D. Fields, is often described as the Nobel Prize for Mathematics. In agreement with Fields's wish that the awards recognize both existing work and the promise of future achievement, the medals are awarded to mathematicians no older than 40. Since 1950, medals have been awarded every four years.

Year	Winners
1936	**Lars Ahlfors**, Harvard Univ.; **Jesse Douglas**, MIT
1950	**Laurent Schwartz**, Universite de Nancy; **Atle Selberg**, Princeton/IAS
1954	**Kunihiko Kodaira**, Princeton Univ.; **Jean-Pierre Serre**, College de France
1958	**Klaus Roth**, Univ. of London; **Rene Thom**, Univ. of Strasbourg
1962	**Lars Hormander**, Univ. of Stockholm; **John Milnor**, Princeton Univ.
1966	**Michael Atiyah**, Oxford Univ.; **Paul Cohen**, Stanford Univ.; **Alex Grothendieck**, Univ. of Paris; **Stephen Smale**, Univ. of California
1970	**Alan Baker**, Cambridge Univ.; **Heisuke Hironaka**, Harvard Univ.; **Serge Novikov**, Moscow Univ.; **John Thompson**, Univ. of Chicago
1974	**Enrico Bombieri**, Univ. of Pisa; **David Mumford**, Harvard Univ.
1978	**Pierre Deligne**, IHES; **Charles Fefferman**, Princeton Univ.; **Gregori Margulis**, Moscow Univ.; **Daniel Quillen**, MIT
1982	**Alain Connes**, IHES; **William Thurston**, Princeton Univ.; **Shing-Tung Yau**, IAS
1986	**Simon Donaldson**, Oxford Univ.; **Gerd Faltings**, Princeton Univ.; **Michael Freedman**, Univ. of California at San Diego
1990	**Vladimir Drinfeld**, Phys.Inst.Kharkov; **Vaughan Jones**, Univ. of California; **Shigefumi Mori**, Univ. of Kyoto; **Edward Witten**, Princeton/IAS
1994	**Pierre-Louis Lions**, Universite de Paris-Dauphine; **Jean-Chrisophe Yoccoz**, Universite de Paris-Sud; **Jean Bourgain**, Princeton/IAS; **Efim Zelmanov**, Univ. of Wisconsin
1998	**Richard E. Borcherds**, Cambridge Univ.; **William T. Gowers**, Cambridge Univ.; **Maxim Kontsevich**, IHES and Rutgers Univ.; **Curtis T. McMullen**, Harvard Univ.
2002	**Laurent Lafforgue**, IHES; **Vladimir Voevodsky**, Princeton/IAS
2006	**Andrei Okounov**, Princeton; **Terence Tao**, UCLA; **Wendelin Werner**, Univ. de Paris- South; **Grigori Perelman**, who declined the medal.

Note: IAS=Institute of Advanced Study. IHES=Institut des Hautes Etudes Scientifiques.
Source: Fields Institute for Research in Mathematical Sciences. www.fields.toronto.edu

Pulitzer Prizes

PULITZER PRIZES IN JOURNALISM

The Pulitzer Prize for Reporting is the oldest prize given in journalism and was first awarded in 1917 together with the Pulitzer Prizes for History and Biography. The changing nature and public perception of reporting can be seen in the various categories established over the years. Originally, the prize recognized excellence irrespective of the journalist's beat; it could be local, national or international, and it could be either reporting for a deadline or investigative reporting carried out over a longer period. Over the years, the number of categories has expanded to cover the great variety of reporting and writing contained in modern daily newspapers.

Source: Columbia University. www.pulitzer.org

Public Service, 1918–2008

Year	Paper, Distinction
1918	*New York Times,* Reports, documents, and speeches relating to World War I.
1919	*Milwaukee Journal,* Campaign for Americanism.
1920	No award
1921	*Boston Post,* Articles exposing operations and leading to arrest of Charles Ponzi.
1922	*New York World,* Articles exposing operations of Ku Klux Klan.
1923	*Memphis Commercial Appeal,* News and cartoons about Ku Klux Klan.
1924	*New York World,* Exposure of Florida peonage evil.
1925	No award
1926	*Columbus (Ga.) Enquirer Sun,* Articles decrying Ku Klux Klan, dishonest public officials, lynching, and a law barring the teaching of evolution.
1927	*Canton (Ohio) Daily News,* Articles about collusion between city government and organized crime, resulting in assassination of editor, Don R. Mellett.
1928	*Indianapolis Times,* Exposure of political corruption in Indiana.
1929	*New York Evening World,* Campaign to correct evil and corruption in administration of justice.
1930	No award
1931	*Atlanta Constitution,* Municipal graft exposure leading to convictions.
1932	*Indianapolis News,* Campaign to eliminate waste in city management and reduce tax levy.
1933	*New York World-Telegram,* Series of articles on veterans' relief, real estate bond evil, and articles exposing lottery schemes of fraternal organizations.
1934	*Medford (Oreg.) Mail Tribune,* Campaign against unscrupulous politicians in Jackson County, Oreg.
1935	*Sacramento Bee,* Campaign against political machine influence in appointment of two federal judges in Nevada.
1936	*Cedar Rapids Gazette,* Crusade against corruption and misgovernment in state of Iowa.
1937	*St. Louis Post-Dispatch,* Exposure of registration fraud in St. Louis, resulting in invalidation of more than 40,000 fraudulent ballots and appointment of new election board.
1938	*Bismarck (N.D.) Tribune,* News reports and editorials entitled "Self Help in the Dust Bowl."
1939	*Miami Daily News,* Campaign for recall of Miami City Commission.
1940	*Waterbury (Conn.) Republican & American,* Campaign exposing municipal graft.
1941	*St. Louis Post-Dispatch,* Campaign against city smoke nuisance.
1942	*Los Angeles Times,* Campaign resulting in clarification and confirmation of freedom of press rights for all American newspapers.
1943	*Omaha (Nebr.) World-Herald,* Campaign for collection of scrap metal for war effort.
1944	*New York Times,* Survey of teaching of American history.
1945	*Detroit Free Press,* Investigation of legislative graft and corruption at Lansing, Mich.
1946	*Scranton (Pa.) Times,* Fifteen-year investigation of judicial practices in U.S. District Court, resulting in removal of the district judge and indictment of many others.
1947	*Baltimore Sun,* Series of articles by Howard M. Norton dealing with administration of unemployment compensation in Maryland, resulting in 93 criminal convictions and/or guilty pleas.
1948	*St. Louis Post-Dispatch,* Coverage of Centralia, Ill. mine disaster and follow-up articles resulting in reforms in mine safety laws and regulations.
1949	*Nebraska State Journal,* Campaign establishing "Nebraska All-Star Primary" that called attention to issues early in presidential campaign.
1950	*Chicago Daily News* and *St. Louis Post-Dispatch,* Work of George Thiem and Roy J. Harris, respectively, in exposing presence of 37 Illinois newspapermen on an Illinois state payroll.
1951	*Miami Herald* and *Brooklyn Eagle,* Crime reporting during the year.
1952	*St. Louis Post-Dispatch,* Investigation and disclosures of corruption in Internal Revenue Bureau and other government departments.
1953	*Whiteville (N.C.) News Reporter* and *Tabor City (N.C.) Tribune,* Campaign against Ku Klux Klan, culminating in the conviction of more than 100 Klansman and an end to terrorism in their communities.
1954	*Newsday (Garden City, N.Y.),* Exposé of New York State's racetrack scandals and labor racketeering, leading to imprisonment of racketeer William C. DeKooonig Sr.
1955	*Columbus (Ga.) Ledger* and *Sunday Ledger-Enquirer,* News coverage and editorial attack on corruption in neighboring Phenix City, leading to destruction of racket-ridden city government.
1956	*Watsonville (Calif.) Register-Pajaronion,* Exposure of corruption in public office leading to resignation of a district attorney and conviction of one of his associates.
1957	*Chicago Daily News,* Exposure of $2.5 million fraud in office of Illinois state auditor, resulting in his conviction.
1958	*Arkansas Gazette,* Civic leadership, journalistic responsibility, and moral courage during school integration crisis.
1959	*Utica Observer-Dispatch* and *Utica Daily Press (N.Y.),* Campaign against corruption, gambling, and vice.
1960	*Los Angeles Times,* Attack on narcotics traffic; reporting of Gene Sherman, which led to opening of negotiations between U.S. and Mexico to halt the flow of illegal drugs into California and other border states.
1961	*Amarillo (Tex.) Globe-Times,* Exposure of lax law enforcement resulting in punitive action sweeping officials from their posts and creating election of reform slate.

1962 *Panama City* (Fla.) *News-Herald,* Three-year campaign against entrenched power and corruption, resulting in reforms in Panama City and Bay County.

1963 *Chicago Daily News,* Articles calling public attention to providing birth control services in public health programs.

1964 *St. Petersburg Times,* Investigation of illegal activity within Florida Turnpike Authority, resulting in major reorganization of the state's road construction program.

1965 *Hutchinson* (Kans.) *News,* Campaign for more equitable reapportionment of Kansas legislature.

1966 *Boston Globe,* Campaign to prevent confirmation of Francis X. Morrissey as federal district judge in Massachusetts.

1967 *Louisville Courier Journal* and *Milwaukee Journal,* Campaign to control Kentucky strip-mining industry; campaign to stiffen water pollution laws in Wisconsin.

1968 *Riverside* (Calif.) *Press-Enterprise,* Exposure of corruption in courts in connection with handling of property and estates of an Indian tribe in California.

1969 *Los Angeles Times,* Exposure of wrongdoing within Los Angeles city government commissions, resulting in criminal convictions, resignations, and sweeping reforms.

1970 *Newsday* (Garden City, N.Y.), Three-year investigation and exposure of secret land deals in eastern Long Island, leading to criminal convictions, resignations, and discharges among public and political officials.

1971 *Winston-Salem Journal and Sentinel,* Coverage of environmental problems, as exemplified by campaign to block a strip-mining operation that would have caused irreparable damage to northwest North Carolina hill country.

1972 *New York Times,* Publication of Pentagon Papers.

1973 *Washington Post,* Investigation of Watergate.

1974 *Newsday* (Garden City, N.Y.), Definitive report on illicit narcotics traffic in U.S. and abroad, entitled "The Heroin Trail."

1975 *Boston Globe,* Coverage of Boston school desegregation crisis.

1976 *Anchorage Daily News,* Disclosures of impact and influence of Teamsters Union on Alaska's economy and politics.

1977 *Lufkin* (Tex.) *News,* Obituary of local men who died in Marine training camp, which grew into investigation of that death and fundamental reform in Marine Corps' recruiting and training practices.

1978 *Philadelphia Inquirer,* Series of articles showing abuses of power by Philadelphia police.

1979 *Point Reyes* (Calif.) *Light,* Investigation of Synanon.

1980 *Gannett News Service,* Series on financial contributions to Pauline Fathers.

1981 *Charlotte Observer,* Series called "Brown Lung: A Case of Deadly Neglect."

1982 *Detroit News,* Series exposing U.S. Navy's cover-up of circumstances surrounding deaths of seamen aboard ship and leading to significant reforms in naval procedures.

1983 *Jackson* (Miss.) *Clarion-Ledger,* Campaign supporting Gov. Winter in his legislative battle for reform of Mississippi's public education system.

1984 *Los Angeles Times,* In-depth examination of southern California's growing Latino community.

1985 *Fort Worth Star-Telegram,* Reporting by Mark J. Thompson revealing that nearly 250 U.S. servicemen died because of a design problem in helicopters built by Bell Helicopter.

1986 *Denver Post,* In-depth study of "missing children," revealing that most are involved in custody disputes or are runaways.

1987 *Pittsburgh Press,* Reporting by Andrew Schneider and Matthew Brelis, revealing inadequacy of FAA's medical screening of airline pilots, and leading to reform.

1988 *Charlotte Observer,* Revealing misuse of funds by the PTL television ministry, despite massive campaign by PTL to discredit the newspaper.

1989 *Anchorage Daily News,* Series revealing high incidence of alcoholism and suicide among Native Alaskans.

1990 *Philadelphia Inquirer,* Series by Gilbert M. Gaul disclosing shortcomings in federal regulation of the nation's blood banks.

Washington (N.C.) *Daily News,* Series by Betty Gray and Mike Voss revealing contamination of the municipal water supply in the town of 9,000 and the eight-year cover-up by elected officials.

1991 *Des Moines Register,* Series by Jane Schorer about a rape and its aftermath that reopened debate over whether rape victims should be identified by name.

1992 *Sacramento Bee,* Series by Tom Knudson about pollution, overdevelopment and overpopulation along the Sierra Nevada mountain range.

1993 *Miami Herald,* Helping readers cope with Hurricane Andrew's devastation and for showing "how lax zoning, inspection and building codes had contributed to the destruction."

1994 *Akron Beacon Journal,* Two-part examination of race relations.

1995 *Virgin Islands Daily News,* Ten-part series on crime that examined crime on the islands and ultimately led to major reforms.

1996 *Raleigh News and Observer,* Stories revealing how agricultural corporations, unfettered by government regulation, were elbowing out small family hog farms and polluting the environment in the process.

1997 *New Orleans Times-Picayune,* Series analyzing the environmental, commercial, political, and social conditions that threaten the world's fish supply. It affected changes in Federal fisheries laws.

1998 *Grand Forks* (N.D.) *Herald,* Coverage of the blizzard, flood, and fire that devastated the city and the newspaper's own plant.

1999 *Washington Post,* Series that identified and analyzed patterns of reckless gunplay by city police officers who had little training or supervision.

2000 *Washington Post,* Series by Katherine Boo about gross mistreatment of mentally retarded patients in District of Columbia group homes.

2001 *The Oregonian* (Portland, Ore.), Series on inefficiency, misconduct and other systemic problems in the Immigration and Naturalization Service.

2002 *New York Times,* "A Nation Challenged," a special section published regularly after the Sept. 11 terrorist attacks.

2003 *The Boston Globe,* Coverage of sexual abuse by priests.

2004 *New York Times,* Work of David Barstow and Lowell Bergman that relentlessly examined death and injury among American workers and exposed employers who break basic safety rules.

2005 *Los Angeles Times,* For its exhaustively researched series exposing deadly medical problems and racial injustice at a major public hospital.

2006 *Times-Picayune (New Orleans)* Multi-faceted coverage of Hurricane Katrina.

Sun Herald (Miss.), Comprehensive coverage of Hurricane Katrina.

2007 *Wall Street Journal* for its probe into backdated stock options for business executives that triggered the ouster of top officials, and widespread change in corporate America.

2008 *The Washington Post,* work of Dana Priest, Anne Hull and photographer Michel du Cille in exposing mistreatment of wounded veterans at Walter Reed Hospital, producing reforms by federal officials.

Pulitzer Prizes for National Reporting, 1942–2008

Year	Winner, Newspaper	Year	Winner, Newspaper
1942	Louis Stark, *New York Times*	1975	Donald L. Bartlett and James B. Steele, *Philadelphia Inquirer*
1943	No award	1976	James Risser, *Des Moines Register*
1944	Dewey L. Fleming, *Baltimore Sun*	1977	Walter Mears, Associated Press
1945	James B. Reston, *New York Times*	1978	Gaylord D. Shaw, *Los Angeles Times*
1946	Edward A. Harris, *St. Louis Post-Dispatch*	1979	James Risser, *Des Moines Register*
1947	Edward T. Folliard, *Washington Post*	1980	Bette Swenson Orsini and Charles Stafford, *St. Petersburg Times*
1948	Bert Andrews, *New York Herald Tribune* Nat S. Finney, *Minneapolis Tribune*	1981	John M Crewdson, *New York Times*
1949	C.P. Trussell, *New York Times*	1982	Rick Atkinson, *Kansas City Times*
1950	Edwin O. Guthman, *Seattle Times*	1983	Staff, *Boston Globe*
1951	No award[1]	1984	John Noble Wilford, *New York Times*
1952	Anthony Leviero, *New York Times*	1985	Thomas J. Knudson, *Des Moines Register*
1953	Don Whitehead, Associated Press	1986	Arthur Howe, *Philadelphia Inquirer*
1954	Richard Wilson, *Des Moines Register and Tribune*		Craig Flournoy and George Rodrigues, *Dallas Morning News*
1955	Anthony Lewis, *Washington Daily News*	1987	Staff, *Miami Herald*
1956	Charles L. Bartlett, *Chattanooga Times*		Staff, *New York Times*
1957	James B. Reston, *New York Times*	1988	Tim Weiner, *Philadelphia Inquirer*
1958	Relman Morin, Associated Press	1989	Donald L. Bartlett and James B. Steele, *Philadelphia Inquirer*
	Clark Mollenhoff, *Des Moines Register and Tribune*	1990	Ross Anderson, Bill Dietrich, Mary Ann Gwinn, and Eric Nalder, *Seattle Times*
1959	Howard Van Smith, *Miami News*	1991	Marji Lundstrom and Rochelle Sharpe, Gannet News Service
1960	Vance Trimble, Scripps-Howard Newspaper Alliance	1992	Jeff Taylor and Mike McGraw, *Kansas City Star*
1961	Edward R. Cony, *Wall Street Journal*	1993	David Maraniss, *Washington Post*
1962	Nathan G. Caldwell and Gene S. Graham, *Nashville Tennessean*	1994	Eileen Welsome, *Albuquerque Tribune*
1963	Anthony Lewis, *New York Times*	1995	Tony Horwitz, *Wall Street Journal*
1964	Merriman Smith, United Press International	1996	Alix M. Freedman, *Wall Street Journal*
1965	Louis M. Kohlmeier, *Wall Street Journal*	1997	Staff, *Wall Street Journal*
1966	Haynes Johnson, *Washington Evening Star*	1998	Russell Carollo and Jeff Nesmith, *Dayton (Ohio) Daily News*
1967	Stanley Penn and Monroe Karmin, *Wall Street Journal*	1999	Staff, *New York Times*
1968	Howard James, *Christian Science Monitor* Nathan K. (Nick) Kotz, *Des Moines Register* and *Minneapolis Tribune*	2000	Staff, *Wall Street Journal*
		2001	Staff, *New York Times*
1969	Robert Cahn, *Christian Science Monitor*	2002	Staff, *Washington Post*
1970	William J. Eaton, *Chicago Daily News*	2003	Alan Miller and Kevin Sack, *Los Angeles Times*
1971	Lucinda Franks and Thomas Powers, United Press International	2004	Staff, *Los Angeles Times*
1972	Jack Anderson, (Syndicated columnist)	2005	Walt Bogdanich, *New York Times*
1973	Robert Boyd and Clark Hoyt, Knight Newspapers	2006	James Risen and Eric Lichtblau, *New York Times;* Staffs, *San Diego Union Tribune* and *Copley News Service*
1974	James R. Polk, *Washington Star-News* Jack White, *Providence Journal and Evening Bulletin*	2007	Charlie Savage, *Boston Globe*
		2008	Jo Becker and Barton Gellman, *The Washington Post*

1. The board decided that Arthur Krock of The *New York Times* deserved the prize but he could not accept because he was a board member.

Pulitzer Prizes for International Reporting, 1942–2008

Year	Winner, Newspaper	Year	Winner, Newspaper
1942	Lawrence Edmund Allen, Associated Press	1956	William Randolph Hearst Jr., Kingsbury Smith, Frank Conniff, Int'l News Service
1943	Ira Wolfert, North American Newspaper Alliance, Inc.	1957	Russell Jones, United Press
1944	Daniel DeLuce, Associated Press	1958	Staff, *New York Times*
1945	Mark S. Watson, *Baltimore Sun*	1959	Joseph Martin and Philip Santora, *New York Daily News*
1946	Homer William Bigart, *New York Herald Tribune*	1960	A.M. Rosenthal, *New York Times*
1947	Eddy Gilmore, Associated Press	1961	Lynn Heinzerling, Associated Press
1948	Paul W. Ward, *Baltimore Sun*	1962	Walter Lippmann, *New York Herald Tribune Syndicate*
1949	Price Day, *Baltimore Sun*	1963	Hal Hendrix, *Miami News*
1950	Edmund Stevens, *Christian Science Monitor*	1964	Malcolm W. Browne, Associated Press David Halberstam, *New York Times*
1951	Keyes Beech, *Chicago Daily News*	1965	J. A. Livingston, *Philadelphia Bulletin*
	Homer William Bigart, *New York Herald Tribune*	1966	Peter Arnett, Associated Press
	Marguerite Higgins, *New York Herald Tribune*	1967	R. John Hughes, *Christian Science Monitor*
	Relman Morin, Associated Press	1968	Alfred Friendly, *Washington Post*
	Fred Sparks, *Chicago Daily News*	1969	William Tuohy, *Los Angeles Times*
	Don Whitehead, Associated Press	1970	Seymour M. Hersh, Dispatch News Service
1952	John M. Hightower, Associated Press	1971	Jimmie Lee Hoagland, *Washington Post*
1953	Austin Wehrwien, *Milwaukee Journal*		
1954	Jim G. Lucas, Scripps-Howard		
1955	Harrison E. Salisbury, *New York Times*		

Year	Winner, Newspaper	Year	Winner, Newspaper
1972	Peter R. Kann, *Wall Street Journal*	1990	Nicholas D. Kristof and Sheryl WuDunn, *New York Times*
1973	Max Frankel, *New York Times*		
1974	Hedrick Smith, *New York Times*	1991	Caryle Murphy, *Washington Post*
1975	William Mullen (reporter), Ovie Carter (photographer), *Chicago Tribune*		Serge Schmemann, *New York Times*
		1992	Patrick J. Sloyan, *Newsday* (Garden City, N.Y.)
1976	Sydney H. Schanberg, *New York Times*	1993	John F. Burns, *New York Times*
1977	No award		Roy Gutman, *Newsday* (Garden City, N.Y.)
1978	Henry Kamm, *New York Times*	1994	Team of reporters, *Dallas Morning News*
1979	Richard Ben Cramer, *Philadelphia Inquirer*	1995	Mark Fritz, *Associated Press*
1980	Joel Brinkley (reporter), Jay Mather (photographer), *Louisville Courier-Journal*	1996	David Rohde, *Christian Science Monitor*
		1997	John F. Burns, *New York Times*
1981	Shirley Christian, *Miami Herald*	1998	Staff, *New York Times*
1982	John Darnton, *New York Times*	1999	Staff, *Wall Street Journal*
1983	Thomas L. Friedman, *New York Times*	2000	Mark Schoofs, *Village Voice* (N.Y. City)
	Loren Jenkins, *Washington Post*	2001	Ian Johnson, *Wall Street Journal*
1984	Karen Elliott House, *Wall Street Journal*		Paul Salopek, *Chicago Tribune*
1985	Josh Friedman and Dennis Bell (reporters) and Ozier Muhammad (photographer), *Newsday* (Garden City, N.Y.)	2002	Barry Bearak, *New York Times*
		2003	Kevin Sullivan and Mary Jordan, *Washington Post*
		2004	Anthony Shadid, *Washington Post*
1986	Lewis M. Simons, Pete Carey, and Katherine Ellison, *San Jose Mercury News*	2005	Kim Murphy, *Los Angeles Times*
			Dele Olojede, *Newsday* (Long Island, N.Y.)
1987	Michael Parks, *Los Angeles Times*	2006	Joseph Kahn and Jim Yardley, *New York Times*
1988	Thomas L. Friedman, *New York Times*		
1989	Glenn Frankel, *Washington Post*	2007	Staff, *Wall Street Journal*
	Bill Keller, *New York Times*	2008	Steve Fainaru, *The Washington Post*

Pulitzer Prizes for Editorial Writing, 1917–2008

Year	Winner, Newspaper	Year	Winner, Newspaper
1917	*Lusitania* editorial article, *New York Tribune*	1950	Carl M. Saunders, *Jackson* (Mich.) *Citizen Patriot*
1918	War editorials and articles, *Louisville Courier Journal*		
		1951	William Harry Fitzpatrick, *New Orleans States*
1919	No award		
1920	Harvey E. Newbranch, *Evening World Herald*	1952	Louis LaCoss, *St. Louis Globe Democrat*
1921	No award	1953	Vermont Connecticut Royster, *Wall Street Journal*
1922	Frank M. O'Brien, *New York Herald*		
1923	William Allen White, *Emporia (Kans.) Gazette*	1954	Don Murray, *Boston Herald*
1924[1]	Coolidge editorial, *Boston Herald*	1955	Royce Howes, *Detroit Free Press*
1925	"Plight of the South" editorial, *Charleston (S.C.) News and Courier*	1956	Lauren K. Soth, *Des Moines Register and Tribune*
1926	Edward M. Kingsbury, *New York Times*	1957	Buford Boone, *Tuscaloosa News*
1927	F. Lauriston Bullard, *Boston Herald*	1958	Harry S. Ashmore, *Arkansas Gazette*
1928	Grover Cleveland Hall, *Montgomery Advertiser*	1959	Ralph McGill, *Atlanta Constitution*
		1960	Lenoir Chambers, *Norfolk Virginian-Pilot*
1929	Louis Isaac Jaffe, *Norfolk Virginian-Pilot*	1961	William J. Dorvillier, *San Juan* (Puerto Rico) *Star*
1930	No award		
1931	Charles S. Ryckman, *Fremont* (Nebr.) *Tribune*	1962	Thomas M. Storke, *Santa Barbara* (Calif.) *News Press*
1932	No award		
1933	series of editorials, *Kansas City Star*	1963	Ira B. Harkey Jr., *Pascagoula* (Miss.) *U. Chronicle*
1934	E.P. Chase, *Atlantic* (Iowa) *News-Telegraph*		
1935	No award	1964	Hazel Brannon Smith, *Lexington* (Miss.) *Advertiser*
1936	Felix Morley, *Washington Post*		
	George B. Parker, *Scripps-Howard Newspapers*	1965	John R. Harrison, *Gainesville* (Fla.) *Daily Sun*
		1966	Robert Lasch, *St. Louis Post-Dispatch*
1937	John W. Owens, *Baltimore Sun*	1967	Eugene Patterson, *Atlanta Constitution*
1938	William Wesley Waymack, *Des Moines Register and Tribune*	1968	John S. Knight, *Knight Newspapers*
		1969	Paul Greenberg, *Pine Bluff* (Ark.) *Commercial*
1939	Ronald G. Callvert, *Portland Oregonian*		
1940	Bart Howard, *St. Louis Post-Dispatch*	1970	Philip L. Geyelin, *Washington Post*
1941	Reuben Maury, *New York Daily News*	1971	Horance G. Davis Jr., *Gainesville* (Fla.) *Daily Sun*
1942	Geoffrey Parsons, *New York Herald Tribune*		
1943	Forrest W. Seymour, *Des Moines Register and Tribune*	1972	John Strohmeyer, *Bethlehem* (Pa.) *Globe-Times*
		1973	Roger B. Linscott, *Berkshire Eagle* (Pittsfield, Mass.)
1944	Henry J. Haskell, *Kansas City Star*		
1945	George W. Potter, *Providence Journal-Bulletin*	1974	F. Gilman Spencer, *Trentonian* (Trenton, N.J.)
		1975	John D. Maurice, *Charleston* (W.V.) *Daily Mail*
1946	Hodding Carter, *Delta Democrat-Times* (Greenville, Miss.)	1976	Philip P. Kerby, *Los Angeles Times*
		1977	Warren L. Lerude, Foster Church and Norman F. Cardoza, *Reno Evening Gazette and Nevada State Journal*
1947	William H. Grimes, *Wall Street Journal*		
1948	Virginius Dabney, *Richmond Times-Dispatch*		
1949	John H. Crider, *Boston Herald*	1978	Meg Greenfield, *Washington Post*
	Herbert Elliston, *Washington Post*	1979	Edwin M. Yoder Jr., *Washington Star*

Year	Winner, Newspaper	Year	Winner, Newspaper
1980	Robert L. Bartley, *Wall Street Journal*	1995	Jeffrey Good, *St. Petersburg Times*
1981	No award	1996	Robert B. Semple, Jr., *New York Times*
1982	Jack Rosenthal, *New York Times*	1997	Michael G. Gartner, *Daily Tribune* (Ames, IA)
1983	Editorial Board, *Miami Herald*	1998	Bernard L. Stein, *Riverdale* (N.Y.) *Press*
1984	Albert Scardino, *Georgia Gazette*	1999	Editorial Board, *N.Y. Daily News*
1985	Richard Aregood, *Philadelphia Daily News*	2000	John C. Bersia, *Orlando Sentinel*
1986	Jack Fuller, *Chicago Tribune*	2001	David Moats, *Rutland* (Vt.) *Herald*
1987	Jonathan Freedman, *San Diego Tribune*	2002	Alex Raksin and Bob Sipchen, *Los Angeles Times*
1988	Jane Healy, *Orlando Sentinel*		
1989	Lois Wille, *Chicago Tribune*	2003	Cornelia Grumman, *Chicago Tribune*
1990	Thomas J. Hylton, *Pottstown* (Pa.) *Mercury*	2004	William R. Stall, *Los Angeles Times*
1991	Ron Casey, Harold Jackson, and Joey Kennedy, *Birmingham News*	2005	Tom Philp, *Sacramento Bee*
		2006	Rick Attig and Doug Bates, *Oregonian*
1992	Maria Henson, *Lexington Herald-Leader*	2007	Arthur Browne, Beverly Weintraub and Heidi Evans, *N. Y. Daily News*
1993	No award		
1994	R. Bruce Dold, *Chicago Tribune*	2008	No award

1. A special prize was awarded to the widow of the late Frank I. Cobb of *The New York World* in recognition of his lifetime of editorial writing and service.

Pulitzer Prizes for Editorial Cartooning, 1922–2008

Year	Winner, Newspaper	Year	Winner, Newspaper
1922	Rollin Kirby, *New York World*	1967	Patrick Oliphant, *Denver Post*
1923	No award	1968	Eugene Gray Payne, *Charlotte Observer*
1924	Jay Norwood Darling, *Des Moines Register and Tribune*	1969	John Fischetti, *Chicago Daily News*
		1970	Thomas F. Darcy, *Newsday* (Garden City, N.Y.)
1925	Rollin Kirby, *New York World*		
1926	Daniel R. Fitzpatrick, *St. Louis Post-Dispatch*	1971	Paul Conrad, *Los Angeles Times*
1927	Nelson Harding, *Brooklyn Daily Eagle*	1972	Jeffrey K. MacNelly, *Richmond News-Leader*
1928	Nelson Harding, *Brooklyn Daily Eagle*	1973	No award
1929	Rollin Kirby, *New York World*	1974	Paul Szep, *Boston Globe*
1930	Charles R. Macauley, *Brooklyn Daily Eagle*	1975	Garry Trudeau, Universal Press Syndicate
1931	Edmund Duffy, *Baltimore Sun*	1976	Tony Auth, *Philadelphia Inquirer*
1932	John T. McCutcheon, *Chicago Tribune*	1977	Paul Szep, *Boston Globe*
1933	H.M. Talburt, *Washington Daily News*	1978	Jeffrey K. MacNelly, *Richmond News-Leader*
1934	Edmund Duffy, *Baltimore Sun*	1979	Herbert L. Block (Herblock), *Washington Post*
1935	Ross A. Lewis, *Milwaukee Journal*	1980	Don Wright, *Miami News*
1936	No award	1981	Mike Peters, *Dayton* (Ohio) *Daily News*
1937	C.D. Batchelor, *New York Daily News*	1982	Ben Sargent, *Austin* (Tex.) *American-Statesman*
1938	Vaughn Shoemaker , *Chicago Daily News*		
1939	Charles G. Werner, *Daily Oklahoman*	1983	Richard Locher, *Chicago Tribune*
1940	Edmund Duffy, *Baltimore Sun*	1984	Paul Conrad, *Los Angeles Times*
1941	Jacob Burck, *Chicago Times*	1985	Jeff MacNelly , *Chicago Tribune*
1942	Herbert L. Block (Herblock), NEA Service	1986	Jules Feiffer, *Village Voice* (New York City)
1943	Jay Norwood Darling, *Des Moines Register and Tribune*	1987	Berke Breathed, Washington Post Writers Group
1944	Clifford K. Berryman, *Washington Evening Star*	1988	Doug Marlette, *Atlanta Constitution* and *Charlotte Observer*
1945	Sergeant Bill Mauldin, United Feature Syndicate, Inc	1989	Jack Higgins, *Chicago Sun-Times*
		1990	Tom Toles, *Buffalo News*
1946	Bruce Alexander Russell, *Los Angeles Times*	1991	Jim Borgman, *Cincinnati Enquirer*
1947	Vaughn Shoemaker , *Chicago Daily News*	1992	Signe Wilkinson, *Philadelphia Daily News*
1948	Reuben L. Goldberg, *New York Sun*	1993	Stephen R. Benson, *Arizona Republic*
1949	Lute Pease, *Newark Evening News*	1994	Michael P. Ramirez, *Commercial Appeal* (Memphis)
1950	James T. Berryman, *Washington Evening Star*		
1951	Reg Manning, *Arizona Republic*	1995	Mike Luckovich, *Atlanta Constitution*
1952	Fred L. Packer, *New York Mirror*	1996	Jim Morin, *Miami Herald*
1953	Edward D. Kuekes, *Cleveland Plain Dealer*	1997	Walt Handelsman, *New Orleans Times-Picayune*
1954	Herbert L. Block (Herblock), *Washington Post & Times Herald*		
		1998	Stephen P. Breen, *Asbury Park* (N.J.) *Press*
1955	Daniel R. Fitzpatrick, *St. Louis Post-Dispatch*	1999	David Horsey, *Seattle Post-Intelligencer*
1956	Robert York, *Lousiville Times*	2000	Joel Pett, *Lexington Herald-Leader*
1957	Tom Little, *Nashville Tennessean*	2001	Ann Telnaes, *Los Angeles Times Syndicate*
1958	Bruce M. Shanks, *Buffalo Evening News*	2002	Clay Bennett, *Christian Science Monitor*
1959	Bill Mauldin, *St. Louis Post-Dispatch*	2003	David Horsey, *Seattle Post-Intelligencer*
1960	No award	2004	Matt Davies, *White Plains* (N.Y.) *Journal News*
1961	Carey Orr, *Chicago Tribune*		
1962	Edmund S. Valtman, *Hartford Times*	2005	Nick Anderson, *Courier-Journal* (Louisville, Ky.)
1963	Frank Miller, *Des Moines Register*	2006	Mike Luckovich, *Atlanta Journal-Constitution*
1964	Paul Conrad, *Denver Post*	2007	Walt Handelsman, *Newsday* (Long Island, NY)
1965	No award	2008	Michael Ramirez, *Investor's Business Daily*
1966	Don Wright, *Miami News*		

Pulitzer Prizes for Photography

PHOTOGRAPHY, 1942–67

Year	Winner, Newspaper	Year	Winner, Newspaper
1942	Milton Brooks, *Detroit News*	1955	John L. Gaunt Jr., *Los Angeles Times*
1943	Frank Noel, Associated Press	1956	Photography staff, *New York Daily News*
1944	Frank Filan, Associated Press	1957	Harry A. Trask, *Boston Traveler*
	Earle L. Bunker, *World-Herald* (Omaha, Neb.)	1958	William C. Beall, *Washington Daily News*
1945	Joe Rosenthal, Associated Press	1959	William Seaman, *Minneapolis Star*
1946	No award	1960	Andrew Lopez, United Press International
1947	Arnold Hardy, Amateur; photo distributed by Associated Press	1961	Yasushi Nago, *Manichi* (Tokyo); photo distributed by United Press International
1948	Frank Cushing, *Boston Traveler*	1962	Paul Vathis, Associated Press
1949	Nathaniel Fein, *New York Herald Tribune*	1963	Hector Rondon, *La Republica* (Caracas, Venezuela); photo distributed by Associated Press
1950	Bill Crouch, *Oakland Tribune*		
1951	Max Desfor, Associated Press		
1952	John Robinson and Don Ultang, *Des Moines Register and Tribune*	1964	Robert H. Jackson, *Dallas Times-Herald*
		1965	Horst Faas, Associated Press
1953	William M. Gallagher, *Flint* (Mich.) *Journal*	1966	Kyoichi Sawada, United Press International
1954	Mrs. Walter M. Schau, Amateur; photo published by *Akron Beacon Journal*	1967	Jack R. Thornell, Associated Press

SPOT NEWS PHOTOGRAPHY: 1968–1999

1968	Rocco Morabito, *Jacksonville Journal*
1969	Edward T. Adams, Associated Press
1970	Steve Starr, Associated Press
1971	John Paul Filo, *Valley Daily News* and *Daily Dispatch*, (New Kensington, Pa.)
1972	Horst Faas and Michael Laurent, Associated Press
1973	Hyunh Cong Ut, Associated Press
1974	Anthony K. Roberts, freelancer , Beverly Hills, Calif.
1975	Gerald H. Gay, *Seattle Times*
1976	Stanley Forman, *Boston Herald American*
1977	Neal Ulevich, Associated Press
	Stanley Forman, *Boston Herald American*
1978	John H. Blair, United Press International
1979	Thomas J. Kelly III, *Pottstown* (Pa.) *Mercury*
1980	Unnamed photographer, United Press Int'l
1981	Larry C. Price, *Fort Worth Star-Telegram*
1982	Ron Edmonds, Associated Press
1983	Bill Foley, Associated Press
1984	Stan Grossfeld, *Boston Globe*
1985	Photography Staff, *Register* (Santa Ana, Calif.)
1986	Carol Guzy and Michael duCille, *Miami Herald*
1987	Kim Komenich, *San Francisco Examiner*
1988	Scott Shaw, *Odessa* (Tex.) *American*
1989	Ron Olshwanger, freelancer, *St. Louis Post-Dispatch*
1990	Photography Staff, *Oakland Tribune*
1991	Greg Marinovich, Associated Press
1992	Photography Staff, Associated Press
1993	William Snyder and Ken Geiger, *Dallas Morning News*
1994	Paul Watson, *Toronto Star*
1995	Carol Guzy, *Washington Post*
1996	Charles Porter 4th, freelancer, Associated Press
1997	Annie Wells, *Press Democrat* (Santa Rosa, Calif.)
1998	Martha Rial, *Pittsburgh Post-Gazette*
1999	John McConnico, Associated Press

BREAKING NEWS PHOTOGRAPHY: 2000–2008

2000	Photography Staff, *Rocky Mountain News*
2001	Alan Diaz, Associated Press
2002	Staff, *New York Times*
2003	Staff, *Rocky Mountain News*
2004	David Leeson and Cheryl Diaz Meyer, *Dallas Morning News*
2005	Staff, Associated Press
2006	Staff, *Dallas Morning News*
2007	Oded Balilty, Associated Press
2008	Adrees Latif, Reuters

FEATURE PHOTOGRAPHY: 1968–2008

1968	Toshio Sakai, United Press International
1969	Moneta Sleet Jr., *Ebony* Magazine
1970	Dallas Kinney, *Palm Beach Post* (West Palm Beach, Fla.)
1971	Jack Dykinga, *Chicago Sun-Times*
1972	Dave Kennerly, United Press International
1973	Brian Lanker, *Topeka Capital-Journal*
1974	Slava Veder, Associated Press
1975	Matthew Lewis, *Washington Post*
1976	Photography Staff, *Louisville Courier Journal and Times*
1977	Robin Hood, *Chattanooga News-Free Press*
1978	J. Ross Baughman, Associated Press
1979	Photography Staff, *Boston Herald American*
1980	Erwin H. Hagler, *Dallas Times Herald*
1981	Taro M. Yamasaki, *Detroit Free Press*
1982	John H. White, *Chicago Sun-Times*
1983	James B. Dickman, *Dallas Times Herald*
1984	Anthony Suau, *Denver Post*
1985	Stan Grossfeld, *Boston Globe*
	Larry C. Price, *Philadelphia Inquirer*
1986	Tom Gralish, *Philadelphia Inquirer*
1987	David Peterson, *Des Moines Register*
1988	Michael duCille, *Miami Herald*
1989	Manny Crisostomo, *Detroit Free Press*
1990	David C. Turnley, *Detroit Free Press*
1991	William Snyder, *Dallas Morning News*
1992	John Kaplan, *Pittsburgh Post-Gazette*, Block Newspapers
1993	Staff, Associated Press
1994	Kevin Carter, freelancer, *New York Times*
1995	Staff, Associated Press
1996	Stephanie Welsh, freelancer, Newhouse News Service
1997	Alexander Zemlianichenko, Associated Press
1998	Clarence Williams, *Los Angeles Times*
1999	Susan Walsh, Associated Press
2000	Carol Guzy, Michael S. Williamson and Lucian Perkins, *Washington Post*
2001	Matt Rainey, *Star-Ledger* (Newark, N.J.)
2002	Staff, *New York Times*
2003	Don Bartletti, *Los Angeles Times*
2004	Carolyn Cole, *Los Angeles Times*
2005	Deanne Fitzmaurice, *San Francisco Chronicle*
2006	Todd Heisler, *Rocky Mountain News* (Denver, Colo.)
2007	Renee C. Byer, *Sacramento Bee*
2008	Preston Gannaway, *Concord* (N.H.) *Monitor*

Pulitzer Prizes for Commentary, 1970–2008

Year	Winner, Newspaper	Year	Winner, Newspaper
1970	Marquis W. Childs, *St. Louis Post-Dispatch*	1988	Dave Barry, *Miami Herald*
1971	William A. Caldwell, *The Record* (Hackensack, N.J.)	1989	Clarence Page, *Chicago Tribune*
		1990	Jim Murray, *Los Angeles Times*
1972	Mike Royko, *Chicago Daily News*	1991	Jim Hoagland, *Washington Post*
1973	David S. Broder, *Washington Post*	1992	Anna Quindlen, *New York Times*
1974	Edwin A. Roberts Jr., *National Observer*	1993	Liz Balmaseda, *Miami Herald*
1975	Mary McGrory, *Washington Star*	1994	William Raspberry, *Washington Post*
1976	Walter (Red) Smith, *New York Times*	1995	Jim Dwyer, *New York Newsday*
1977	George F. Will, Washington Post Writers Group	1996	E.R. Shipp, *New York Daily News*
		1997	Eileen McNamara, *Boston Globe*
1978	William Safire, *New York Times*	1998	Mike McAlary, *New York Daily News*
1979	Russell Baker, *New York Times*	1999	Maureen Dowd, *New York Times*
1980	Ellen H. Goodman, *Boston Globe*	2000	Paul A. Gigot, *Wall Street Journal*
1981	Dave Anderson, *New York Times*	2001	Dorothy Rabinowitz, *Wall Street Journal*
1982	Art Buchwald, *Los Angeles Times* Syndicate	2002	Thomas Friedman, *New York Times*
1983	Claude Sitton, *Raleigh* (N.C.) *News & Observer*	2003	Colbert I. King, *Washington Post*
		2004	Leonard Pitts Jr., *Miami Herald*
1984	Vermont Royster, *Wall Street Journal*	2005	Connie Schultz, *Cleveland Plain Dealer*
1985	Murray Kempton, *Newsday* (Garden City, N.Y.)	2006	Nicholas D. Kristof, *New York Times*
1986	Jimmy Breslin, *New York Daily News*	2007	Cynthia Tucker, *Atlanta Journal-Constitution*
1987	Charles Krauthammer, *Washington Post*	2008	Steven Pearlstein, *The Washington Post*

Pulitzer Prizes for Criticism, 1970–2008

Year	Winner, Newspaper	Year	Winner, Newspaper
1970	Ada Louise Huxtable, *New York Times*	1990	Allan Temko, *San Francisco Chronicle*
1971	Harold C. Schonberg, *New York Times*	1991	David Shaw, *Los Angeles Times*
1972	Frank Peters, *St. Louis Post-Dispatch*	1992	No award
1973	Ronald Powers, *Chicago Sun-Times*	1993	Michael Dirda, *Washington Post*
1974	Emily Genauer, *Newsday* Syndicate	1994	Lloyd Schwartz, *Boston Phoenix*
1975	Roger Ebert, *Chicago Sun-Times*	1995	Margo Jefferson, *New York Times*
1976	Alan M. Kriegsman, *Washington Post*	1996	Robert Campbell, *Boston Globe*
1977	William McPherson, *Washington Post*	1997	Tim Page, *Washington Post*
1978	Walter Kerr, *New York Times*	1998	Michiko Kakutani, *New York Times*
1979	Paul Gapp, *Chicago Tribune*	1999	Blair Kamin, *Chicago Tribune*
1980	William A. Henry III, *Boston Globe*	2000	Henry Allen, *Washington Post*
1981	Jonathan Yardley, *Washington Star*	2001	Gail Caldwell, *Boston Globe*
1982	Martin Bernheimer, *Los Angeles Times*	2002	Justin Davidson, *Newsday* (Long Island, N.Y.)
1983	Manuela Hoelterhoff, *Wall Street Journal*		
1984	Paul Goldberger, *New York Times*	2003	Stephen Hunter, *Washington Post*
1985	Howard Rosenberg, *Los Angeles Times*	2004	Dan Neil, *Los Angeles Times*
1986	Donal Henahan, *New York Times*	2005	Joe Morgenstern, *Wall Street Journal*
1987	Richard Eder, *Los Angeles Times*	2006	Robin Givhan, *Washington Post*
1988	Tom Shales, *Washington Post*	2007	Jonathan Gold, *LA Weekly*
1989	Michael Skube, *Raleigh (N.C.) News and Observer*	2008	Mark Feeney, *Boston Globe*

Pulitzer Prizes for Feature Writing, 1979–2008

Year	Winner, Newspaper	Year	Winner, Newspaper
1979	Jon D. Franklin, *Baltimore Evening Sun*	1993	George Lardner, Jr., *Washington Post*
1980	Madeline Blais, *Miami Herald*	1994	Isabel Wilkerson, *New York Times*
1981	Teresa Carpenter, *Village Voice* (New York)	1995	Ron Suskind, *Wall Street Journal*
1982	Saul Pett, Associated Press	1996	Rick Bragg, *New York Times*
1983	Nan Robertson, *New York Times*	1997	Lisa Pollak, *Baltimore Sun*
1984	Peter Mark Rinearson, *Seattle Times*	1998	Thomas French, *St. Petersburg Times*
1985	Alice Steinbach, *Baltimore Sun*	1999	Angelo B. Henderson, *Wall Street Journal*
1986	John Camp, *St. Paul Pioneer Press Dispatch*	2000	J.R. Moehringer, *Los Angeles Times*
1987	Steve Twomey, *Philadelphia Inquirer*	2001	Tom Hallman Jr., *Oregonian* (Portland, Ore.)
1988	Jacqui Banaszynski, *St. Paul* (Minn.) *Pioneer Press Dispatch*	2002	Barry Siegel, *Los Angeles Times*
		2003	Sonia Nazario, *Los Angeles Times*
1989	David Zucchino, *Philadelphia Inquirer*	2004	No award
1990	Dave Curtin, *Colorado Springs Gazette Telegram*	2005	Julia Keller, *Chicago Tribune*
		2006	Jim Sheeler, *Rocky Mountain News* (Denver, Colo.)
1991	Sheryl James, *St. Petersburg Times*		
1992	Howell Raines, *New York Times*	2007	Andrea Elliott, *New York Times*
		2008	Gene Weingarten, *The Washington Post*

Pulitzer Prizes for Local Reporting, 1991–2008

Year	Winner, Newspaper	Year	Winner, Newspaper
1991	Natalie Angier, *New York Times*	1999	Chuck Philips and Michael A. Hiltzik, *Los Angeles Times*
1992	Deborah Blum, *Sacramento* (Calif.) *Bee*		
1993	Paul Ingrassia and Joseph B. White, *Wall Street Journal*	2000	George Dohrmann, *St. Paul Pioneer Press*
		2001	David Cay Johnston, *New York Times*
1994	Eric Freedman and Jim Mitzelfeld, *Detroit News*	2002	Gretchen Morgenson, *New York Times*
		2003	Diane K. Sugg, *Baltimore Sun*
1995	David Shribman, *Boston Globe*	2004	Daniel Golden, *Wall Street Journal*
1996	Bob Keeler, *Newsday* (Garden City, N.Y.)	2005	Amy Dockser Marcus, *Wall Street Journal*
1997	Byron Acohido, *Seattle Times*	2006	Dana Priest, *Washington Post*
1998	Linda Greenhouse, *New York Times*	2007	Debbie Cenziper, *Miami Times*
		2008	David Umhoefer, *Milwaukee Journal Sentinel*

Note: Until 2006, this category was called "Beat Reporting".

Pulitzer Prizes for Explanatory Reporting, 1985–2008

Year	Winner, Newspaper	Year	Winner, Newspaper
1985	Jon Franklin, *Baltimore Evening Sun*	1997	Michael Vitez, April Saul, and Ron Cortes, *Philadelphia Inquirer*
1986	Staff, *New York Times*		
1987	Jeff Lyon and Peter Gorner, *Chicago Tribune*	1998	Paul Salopek, *Chicago Tribune*
1988	Daniel Hertzberg and James B. Stewart, *Wall Street Journal*	1999	Richard Read, *Oregonian*
		2000	Eric Newhouse, *Great Falls* (Mont.) *Tribune*
1989	David Hanners, William Snyder, and Karen Blessen, *Dallas Morning News*	2001	Staff, *Chicago Tribune*
		2002	Staff, *New York Times*
1990	David A. Vise and Steve Coll, *Washington Post*	2003	Staff, *Wall Street Journal*
		2004	Kevin Helliker and Thomas M. Burton, *Wall Street Journal*
1991	Susan C. Faludi, *Wall Street Journal*		
1992	Robert S. Capers and Eric Lipton, *Hartford* (Conn.) *Courant*	2005	Gareth Cook, *Boston Globe*
		2006	David Finkel, *Washington Post*
1993	Mike Toner, *Atlanta Journal-Constitution*	2007	Kenneth R. Weiss, Usha Lee McFarling (reporters), and Rick Loomis (photographer), *Los Angeles Times*
1994	Ronald Kotulak, *Chicago Tribune*		
1995	Leon Dash and Lucian Perkins, *Washington Post*		
1996	Laurie Garrett, *Newsday*	2008	Amy Harmon, *New York Times*

Note: From 1985 to 1997 this category was called "Explanatory Journalism".

Pulitzer Prizes for Investigative Reporting, 1985–2008

Year	Winner, Newspaper	Year	Winner, Newspaper
1985	William K. Marimow, *Philadelphia Inquirer*	1996	Staff, *Orange County Register*
	Lucy Morgan and Jack Reed, *St. Petersburg* (Fla.) *Times*	1997	Eric Nalder, Deborah Nelson and Alex Tizon, *Seattle Times*
1986	Jeffrey A. Marx and Michael M. York, *Lexington* (Ky.) *Herald Leader*	1998	Gary Cohn and Will Englund, *Baltimore Sun*
		1999	Staff, *Miami Herald*
1987	John Woestendiek, *Philadelphia Inquirer*; Daniel R. Biddle, H.G. Bissinger and Frederic N. Tulsky, *Philadelphia Inquirer*	2000	Sang-Hun Choe, Charles J. Hanley and Martha Mendoza, Associated Press
		2001	David Willman, *Los Angeles Times*
1988	Dean Baquet, William Gaines and Ann Marie Lipinski, *Chicago Tribune*	2002	Sari Horowitz, Scott Higham and Sarah Cohen, *Washington Post*
1989	Bill Dedman, *Atlanta Journal and Constitution*	2003	Clifford J. Levy, *New York Times*
		2004	Michael D. Sallah, Mitch Weiss and Joe Mahr, *The Blade* (Toledo, Ohio)
1990	Lou Kilzer and Chris Ison, *Star Tribune* (Minneapolis-St. Paul)	2005	Nigel Jaquiss, *Willamette Week* (Portland, Ore.)
1991	Joseph T. Hallinan and Susan M. Headden, *Indianapolis Star*	2006	Susan Schmidt, James V. Grimaldi and R. Jeffrey Smith, *Washington Post*
1992	Lorraine Adams and Dan Malone, *Dallas Morning News*	2007	Brett Blackledge, *The Birmingham* (Ala.) *Times*
1993	Jeff Brazil and Steve Berry, *Orlando Sentinel*	2008	Staff, *Chicago Tribune* and Jake Hooker and Walter Bogdanich, *The New York Times*
1994	Staff, *Providence Journal-Bulletin*		
1995	Brian Donovan and Stephanie Saul, *Newsday*		

Pulitzer Prizes for Breaking News Reporting, 1998–2008

Year	Winner, Newspaper	Year	Winner, Newspaper
1998	Staff, *Los Angeles Times*	2004	Staff, *Los Angeles Times*
1999	Staff, *Hartford Courant*	2005	Staff, Associated Press
2000	Staff, *Denver Post*	2006	Staff, *Times-Picayune* (New Orleans)
2001	Staff, *Miami Herald*	2007	Staff, *The Oregonian* (Portland)
2002	Staff, *Wall Street Journal*	2008	Staff, *The Washington Post*
2003	Staff, *Eagle-Tribune* (Lawrence, Mass.)		

Special Awards and Citations

Year	Winner, Newspaper	Year	Winner, Newspaper
1930	William O. Dapping, *Auburn* (N.Y.) *Citizen*, Prison reporting	1951	Cyrus L. Sulzberger, *New York Times*, Interview with Archbishop Stepinac
1938	*Edmonton* (Alberta) *Journal*, Freedom of the Press editorials	1952	Max Kase, *New York Journal-American*, Corruption in basketball
1941	*New York Times*, Foreign news reporting	1953	*New York Times*, Sunday *Review of the Week* section
1944	Byron Price, Director of the Office of Censorship, Creation and administration of newspaper and radio codes.	1958	Walter Lippman, *New York Herald Tribune*, Lifetime achievement
1944	Mrs. William Allen White, Services to Advisory Board Graduate School of Journalism, Columbia Univ.	1964	Gannett Newspapers, "Road to Integration" program
1945	American press cartographers, Maps of war fronts	1976	Professor John Hohenberg, Administration of Pulitzer Prizes
1947	Columbia University and Graduate School of Journalism, Governing Pulitzer Prize awards	1978	Richard Lee Strout, *Christian Science Monitor*, Lifetime achievement
1947	*St. Louis Post Dispatch*, Adherence to ideals of journalism	1987	Joseph Pulitzer Jr., Lifetime services to Pulitzer Board
1948	Dr. Frank Diehl Fackenthal, Interest and Service	1996	Herb Caen, *San Francisco Chronicle*, Lifetime achievement

PULITZER PRIZES IN LETTERS

Source: Columbia University. www.pulitzer.org

The Pulitzer Prize for Fiction, 1918–2008

Year	Author, Title	Year	Author, Title
1918	Ernest Poole, *His Family*	1955	William Faulkner, *A Fable*
1919	Booth Tarkington, *The Magnificent Ambersons*	1956	MacKinlay Kantor, *Andersonville*
1920	No award	1957	No award
1921	Edith Wharton, *The Age of Innocence*	1958	James Agee, *A Death in the Family*
1922	Booth Tarkington, *Alice Adams*	1959	Robert Lewis Taylor, *The Travels of Jaimie McPheeters*
1923	Willa Cather, *One of Ours*		
1924	Margaret Wilson, *The Able McLaughlins*	1960	Allen Drury, *Advise and Consent*
1925	Edna Ferber, *So Big*	1961	Harper Lee, *To Kill a Mockingbird*
1926	Sinclair Lewis, *Arrowsmith*	1962	Edwin O'Connor, *The Edge of Sadness*
1927	Louis Bromfield, *Early Autumn*	1963	William Faulkner, *The Reivers*
1928	Thornton Wilder, *The Bridge of San Luis Rey*	1964	No award
1929	Julia Peterkin, *Scarlet Sister Mary*	1965	Shirley Ann Grau, *The Keepers of the House*
1930	Oliver LaFarge, *Laughing Boy*	1966	Katherine Anne Porter, *Collected Stories*
1931	Margaret Ayer Barnes, *Years of Grace*	1967	Bernard Malamud, *The Fixer*
1932	Pearl S. Buck, *The Good Earth*	1968	William Styron, *The Confessions of Nat Turner*
1933	T.S. Stribling, *The Store*		
1934	Caroline Miller, *Lamb in His Bosom*	1969	N. Scott Momaday, *House Made of Dawn*
1935	Josephine Winslow Johnson, *Now in November*	1970	Jean Stafford, *Collected Stories*
		1971	No award
1936	Harold L. Davis, *Honey in the Horn*	1972	Wallace Stegner, *Angle of Repose*
1937	Margaret Mitchell, *Gone With the Wind*	1973	Eudora Welty, *The Optimist's Daughter*
1938	John Phillips Marquand, *The Late George Apley*	1974	No award
		1975	Michael Shaara, *The Killer Angels*
1939	Marjorie Kinnan Rawlings, *The Yearling*	1976	Saul Bellow, *Humboldt's Gift*
1940	John Steinbeck, *The Grapes of Wrath*	1977	No award
1941	No award	1978	James Alan McPherson, *Elbow Room*
1942	Ellen Glasgow, *In This Our Life*	1979	John Cheever, *The Stories of John Cheever*
1943	Upton Sinclair, *Dragon's Teeth*	1980	Norman Mailer, *The Executioner's Song*
1944	Martin Flavin, *Journey in the Dark*	1981	John Kennedy Toole[2], *A Confederacy of Dunces*
1945	John Hersey, *A Bell for Adano*		
1946	No award	1982	John Updike, *Rabbit Is Rich*
1947	Robert Penn Warren, *All the King's Men*	1983	Alice Walker, *The Color Purple*
1948[1]	James A. Michener, *Tales of the South Pacific*	1984	William Kennedy, *Ironweed*
		1985	Alison Lurie, *Foreign Affairs*
1949	James Gould Cozzens, *Guard of Honor*	1986	Larry McMurtry, *Lonesome Dove*
1950	A.B. Guthrie Jr., *The Way West*	1987	Peter Taylor, *A Summons to Memphis*
1951	Conrad Richter, *The Town*	1988	Toni Morrison, *Beloved*
1952	Herman Wouk, *The Caine Mutiny*	1989	Anne Tyler, *Breathing Lessons*
1953	Ernest Hemingway, *The Old Man and the Sea*	1990	Oscar Hijuelos, *The Mambo Kings Play Songs of Love*
1954	No award		

Year	Author, Title	Year	Author, Title
1991	John Updike, *Rabbit at Rest*	2000	Jhumpa Lahiri, *Interpreter of Maladies*
1992	Jane Smiley, *A Thousand Acres*	2001	Michael Chabon, *The Amazing Adventures of Kavalier & Clay*
1993	Robert Olen Butler, *A Good Scent From a Strange Mountain*	2002	Richard Russo, *Empire Falls*
1994	E. Annie Proulx, *The Shipping News*	2003	Jeffrey Eugenides, *Middlesex*
1995	Carol Shields, *The Stone Diaries*	2004	Edward P. Jones, *The Known World*
1996	Richard Ford, *Independence Day*	2005	Marilynne Robinson, *Gilead*
1997	Steven Millhauser, *Martin Dressler: The Tale of an American Dreamer*	2006	Geraldine Brooks, *March*
1998	Philip Roth, *American Pastoral*	2007	Cormac McCarthy, *The Road*
1999	Michael Cunningham, *The Hours*	2008	Junot Díaz, *The Brief Wondrous Life of Oscar Wao*

1. In 1948, the name of the category was changed from "The Novel" to "Fiction." 2. Awarded posthumously.

The Pulitzer Prize for Drama, 1918–2008

Year	Author, Title	Year	Author, Title
1918	Jesse Lynch Williams, *Why Marry?*	1962	Frank Loesser and Abe Burrows, *How to Succeed in Business Without Really Trying*
1919	No award		
1920	Eugene O'Neill, *Beyond the Horizon*	1963	No award
1921	Zona Gale, *Miss Lulu Bett*	1964	No award
1922	Eugene O'Neill, *Anna Christie*	1965	Frank D. Gilroy, *The Subject Was Roses*
1923	Owen Davis, *Icebound*	1966	No award
1924	Hatcher Hughes, *Hell-Bent Fer Heaven*	1967	Edward Albee, *A Delicate Balance*
1925	Sidney Howard, *They Knew What They Wanted*	1968	No award
1926	George Kelly, *Craig's Wife*	1969	Howard Sackler, *The Great White Hope*
1927	Paul Green, *In Abraham's Bosom*	1970	Charles Gordone, *No Place to Be Somebody*
1928	Eugene O'Neill, *Strange Interlude*		
1929	Elmer L. Rice, *Street Scene*	1971	Paul Zindel, *The Effect of Gamma Rays on Man-in-the-Moon Marigolds*
1930	Marc Connelly, *The Green Pastures*		
1931	Susan Glaspell, *Alison's House*	1972	No award
1932	George S. Kaufman, Morrie Ryskind, and Ira Gershwin, *Of Thee I Sing*	1973	Jason Miller, *That Championship Season*
		1974	No award
1933	Maxwell Anderson, *Both Your Houses*	1975	Edward Albee, *Seascape*
1934	Sidney Kingsley, *Men in White*	1976	Michael Bennett; Nicholas Dante & James Kirkwood (book); Marvin Hamlisch (music); and Edward Kleban (lyrics), *A Chorus Line*
1935	Zoe Akins, *The Old Maid*		
1936	Robert E. Sherwood, *Idiot's Delight*		
1937	Moss Hart and George S. Kaufman, *You Can't Take It With You*	1977	Michael Cristofer, *The Shadow Box*
		1978	Donald L. Coburn, *The Gin Game*
1938	Thornton Wilder, *Our Town*	1979	Sam Shepard, *Buried Child*
1939	Robert E. Sherwood, *Abe Lincoln in Illinois*	1980	Lanford Wilson, *Talley's Folly*
1940	William Saroyan, *The Time of Your Life*	1981	Beth Henley, *Crimes of the Heart*
1941	Robert E. Sherwood, *There Shall Be no Night*	1982	Charles Fuller, *A Soldier's Play*
1942	No award	1983	Marsha Norman, *'night Mother*
1943	Thornton Wilder, *The Skin of Our Teeth*	1984	David Mamet, *Glengarry Glen Ross*
1944	No award	1985	Stephen Sondheim (music and lyrics); James Lapine (book), *Sunday in the Park With George*
1945	Mary Chase, *Harvey*		
1946	Russel Crouse and Howard Lindsay, *State of the Union*		
		1986	No award
1947	No award	1987	August Wilson, *Fences*
1948	Tennessee Williams, *A Streetcar Named Desire*	1988	Alfred Uhry, *Driving Miss Daisy*
		1989	Wendy Wasserstein, *The Heidi Chronicles*
1949	Arthur Miller, *Death of a Salesman*	1990	August Wilson, *The Piano Lesson*
1950	Richard Rodgers, Oscar Hammerstein II, and Joshua Logan, *South Pacific*	1991	Neil Simon, *Lost in Yonkers*
		1992	Robert Schenkkan, *The Kentucky Cycle*
1951	No award	1993	Tony Kushner, *Angels in America: Millennium Approaches*
1952	Joseph Kramm, *The Shrike*		
1953	William Inge, *Picnic*	1994	Edward Albee, *Three Tall Women*
1954	John Patrick, *The Teahouse of the August Moon*	1995	Horton Foote, *The Young Man From Atlanta*
		1996	Jonathan Larson, *Rent*
1955	Tennessee Williams, *Cat on a Hot Tin Roof*	1997	No award
1956	Albert Hackett and Frances Goodrich, *The Diary of Anne Frank*	1998	Paula Vogel, *How I Learned to Drive*
		1999	Margaret Edson, *Wit*
1957	Eugene O'Neill, *Long Day's Journey Into Night*	2000	Donald Margulies, *Dinner With Friends*
		2001	David Auburn, *Proof*
1958	Ketti Frings, *Look Homeward, Angel*	2002	Suzan-Lori Parks, *Topdog/Underdog*
1959	Archibald MacLeish, *J.B.*	2003	Nilo Cruz, *Anna In the Tropics*
1960	Jerome Weidman and George Abbott (book); Jerry Bock (music); and Sheldon Harnick (lyrics), *Fiorello!*	2004	Doug Wright, *I Am My Own Wife*
		2005	John Patrick Shanley, *Doubt*
		2006	No award
1961	Tad Mosel, *All the Way Home*	2007	David Lindsay-Abaire, *Rabbit Hole*
		2008	Tracy Letts, *August: Osage County*

The Pulitzer Prize for Biography/Autobiography, 1917–2008

Year	Author, Title	Year	Author, Title
1917	Laura E. Richards and Maude Howe Elliott, with Florence Howe Hall, *Julia Ward Howe*	1959	Arthur Walworth, *Woodrow Wilson, American Prophet*
1918	William Cabell Bruce, *Benjamin Franklin, Self-Revealed*	1960	Samuel Eliot Morison, *John Paul Jones*
1919	Henry Adams, *The Education of Henry Adams*	1961	David Donald, *Charles Sumner and the Coming of the Civil War*
1920	Albert J. Beveridge, *The Life of John Marshall*	1962	No award
1921	Edward Bok, *The Americanization of Edward Bok*	1963	Leon Edel, *Henry James*
		1964	Walter Jackson Bate, *John Keats*
1922	Hamlin Garland, *A Daughter of the Middle Border*	1965	Ernest Samuels, *Henry Adams*
1923	Burton J. Hendrick, *The Life and Letters of Walter H. Page*	1966	Arthur M. Schlesinger Jr., *A Thousand Days*
		1967	Justin Kaplan, *Mr. Clemens and Mark Twain*
1924	Michael Idvorsky Pupin, *From Immigrant to Inventor*	1968	George F. Kennan, *Memoirs*
1925	M.A. DeWolfe Howe, *Barrett Wendell and His Letter*	1969	Benjamin Lawrence Reid, *The Man From New York: John Quinn and His Friends*
1926	Harvey Cushing, *The Life of Sir William Osler*	1970	T. Harry Williams, *Huey Long*
1927	Emory Holloway, *Whitman*	1971	Lawrance Thompson, *Robert Frost*
1928	Charles Edward Russell, *The American Orchestra and Theodore Thomas*	1972	Joseph P. Lash, *Eleanor and Franklin*
		1973	W.A. Swanberg, *Luce and His Empire*
1929	Burton J. Hendrick, *The Training of an American. The Earlier Life and Letters of Walter H.Page*	1974	Louis Sheaffer, *O'Neill, Son and Artist*
		1975	Robert A. Caro, *The Power Broker*
1930	Marquis James, *The Raven*	1976	R.W.B. Lewis, *Edith Wharton: A Biography*
1931	Henry James, *Charles W. Eliot*	1977	John E. Mack, *A Prince of Our Disorder: The Life of T.E. Lawrence*
1932	Henry F. Pringle, *Theodore Roosevelt*		
1933	Allan Nevins, *Grover Cleveland*	1978	Walter Jackson Bate, *Samuel Johnson*
1934	Tyler Dennett, *John Hay*	1979	Leonard Baker, *Days of Sorrow and Pain*
1935	Douglas S. Freeman, *R.E. Lee*	1980	Edmund Morris, *The Rise of Theodore Roosevelt*
1936	Ralph Barton Perry, *The Thought and Character of William James*		
1937	Allan Nevins, *Hamilton Fish*	1981	Robert K. Massie, *Peter the Great*
1938	Odell Shepard, *Pedlar's Progress*; Marquis James, *Andrew Jackson*	1982	William S. McFeely, *Grant: A Biography*
		1983	Russell Baker, *Growing Up*
1939	Carl Van Doren, *Benjamin Franklin*	1984	Louis R. Harlan, *Booker T. Washington*
1940	Ray Stannard Baker, *Woodrow Wilson, Life and Letters*, vols. 7 & 8	1985	Kenneth Silverman, *The Life and Times of Cotton Mather*
1941	Ola Elizabeth Winslow, *Jonathan Edwards*	1986	Elizabeth Frank, *Louise Bogan: A Portrait*
1942	Forrest Wilson, *Crusader in Crinoline*	1987	David J. Garrow, *Bearing the Cross: Martin Luther King, Jr. and the Southern Christian Leadership Conference*
1943	Samuel Eliot Morison, *Admiral of the Ocean Sea*		
1944	Carleton Mabee, *The American Leonardo: The Life of Samuel F.B. Morse*	1988	David Herbert Donald, *Look Homeward: A Life of Thomas Wolfe*
		1989	Richard Ellmann[1], *Oscar Wilde*
1945	Russell Blaine Nye, *George Bancroft*	1990	Sebastian de Grazia, *Machiavelli in Hell*
1946	Linnie Marsh Wolfe, *Son of the Wilderness*	1991	Steven Naifeh, Gregory White Smith, *Jackson Pollock*
1947	William Allen White, *The Autobiography of William Allen White*		
1948	Margaret Clapp, *Forgotten First Citizen: John Bigelow*	1992	Lewis B. Puller Jr., *Fortunate Son*
		1993	David McCullough, *Truman*
1949	Robert E. Sherwood, *Roosevelt and Hopkins*	1994	David Levering Lewis, *W.E.B. DuBois*
1950	Samuel Flagg Bemis, *John Quincy Adams and the Foundations of American Foreign Policy*	1995	Joan D. Hedrick, *Harriet Beecher Stowe*
		1996	Jack Miles, *God: A Biography*
		1997	Frank McCourt, *Angela's Ashes*
1951	Margaret Louise Coit, *John C. Calhoun*	1998	Katharine Graham, *Personal History*
1952	Merlo J. Pusey, *Charles Evan Hughes*	1999	A. Scott Berg, *Lindbergh*
1953	David J. Mays, *Edmund Pendleton 1721–1803*	2000	Stacy Schiff, *Véra (Mrs. Vladimir Nabokov)*
		2001	David Levering Lewis, *W.E.B. DuBois (vol. 2)*
1954	Charles A. Lindbergh, *The Spirit of St. Louis*	2002	David McCullough, *John Adams*
1955	William S. White, *The Taft Story*	2003	Robert A. Caro, *Master of the Senate*
1956	Talbot Faulkner Hamlin, *Benjamin Henry Latrobe*	2004	William Taubman, *Khrushchev: The Man and His Era*
1957	John F. Kennedy, *Profiles in Courage*	2005	Mark Stevens and Annalyn Swan, *De Kooning: An American Master*
1958	Douglas Southall Freeman[1], John Alexander Carroll, Mary Wells Ashworth, *George Washington*, vols. 1–4; and vol. 7, written after Dr. Freeman's death in 1953.	2006	Kai Bird and Martin J. Sherwin, *American Prometheus: The Triumph and Tragedy of J. Robert Oppenheimer*
		2007	Debby Applegate, *The Most Famous Man in America*
		2008	John Matteson, *Eden's Outcasts: The Story of Lousia May Alcott and Her Father*

1. Awarded posthumously.

The Pulitzer Prize for History, 1917–2008

Year	Author, Title	Year	Author, Title
1917	J.J. Jusserand, *With Americans of Past and Present Days*	1958	Bray Hammond, *Banks and Politics in America*
1918	James Ford Rhodes, *A History of the Civil War*	1959	Leonard D. White, with Miss Jean Schneider, *The Republican Era: 1869–1901*
1920	Justin H. Smith, *The War with Mexico*	1960	Margaret Leech, *In the Days of McKinley*
1921	William Sowden Sims, with Burton J. Hendrick, *The Victory at Sea*	1961	Herbert Feis, *Between War and Peace: The Potsdam Conference*
1922	James Truslow Adams, *The Founding of New England*	1962	Lawrence H. Gipson, *The Triumphant Empire: Thunder Clouds in the West*
1923	Charles Warren, *The Supreme Court in United States History*	1963	Constance McLaughlin Green, *Washington, Village and Capital, 1800–1878*
1924	Charles Howard McIlwain, *The American Revolution*	1964	Sumner Chilton Powell, *Puritan Village*
1925	Frederic L. Paxson, *A History of the American Frontier*	1965	Irwin Unger, *The Greenback Era*
		1966	Perry Miller[1], *Life of the Mind in America*
1926	Edward Channing, *The History of the United States*	1967	William H. Goetzmann, *Exploration and Empire*
1927	Samuel Flagg Bemis, *Pinckney's Treaty*	1968	Bernard Bailyn, *The Ideological Origins of the American Revolution*
1928	Vernon Louis Parrington, *Main Currents in American Thought*	1969	Leonard W. Levy, *Origins of the Fifth Amendment*
1929	Fred Albert Shannon, *The Organization and Administration of the Union Army, 1861–1865*	1970	Dean Acheson, *Present at the Creation*
1930	Claude H. Van Tyne, *The War of Independence*	1971	James MacGregor Burns, *Roosevelt, The Soldier of Freedom*
1931	Bernadotte E. Schmitt, *The Coming of the War: 1914*	1972	Carl N. Degler, *Neither Black Nor White*
		1973	Michael Kammen, *People of Paradox*
1932	John J. Pershing, *My Experiences in the World War*	1974	Daniel J. Boorstin, *The Americans: The Democratic Experience*
1933	Frederick J. Turner, *The Significance of Sections in American History*	1975	Dumas Malone, *Jefferson and His Time*
1934	Herbert Agar, *The People's Choice*	1976	Paul Horgan, *Lamy of Santa Fe*
1935	Charles McLean Andrews, *The Colonial Period of American History*	1977	David M. Potter[1] *The Impending Crisis*
1936	Andrew C. McLaughlin, *The Constitutional History of the United States*	1978	Alfred D. Chandler Jr., *The Visible Hand: The Managerial Revolution in American Business*
1937	Van Wyck Brooks, *The Flowering of New England*	1979	Don E. Fehrenbacher, *The Dred Scott Case*
1938	Paul Herman Buck, *The Road to Reunion 1856–1900*	1980	Leon F. Litwack, *Been in the Storm So Long*
		1981	Lawrence A. Cremin, *American Education*
1939	Frank Luther Mott, *A History of American Magazines*	1982	C. Vann Woodward (ed.), *Mary Chesnut's Civil War*
1940	Carl Sandburg, *Abraham Lincoln: The War Years*	1983	Rhys L. Isaac, *The Transformation of Virginia, 1740–1790*
1941	Marcus Lee Hansen, *The Atlantic Migration, 1607–1860*	1985	Thomas K. McCraw, *Prophets of Regulation*
1942	Margaret Leech, *Reveille in Washington*	1986	Walter A. McDougall, *. . .the Heavens and the Earth*
1943	Esther Forbes, *Paul Revere and the World He Lived In*	1987	Bernard Bailyn, *Voyagers to the West*
1944	Merle Curti, *The Growth of American Thought*	1988	Robert V. Bruce, *The Launching of Modern American Science 1846–1876*
1945	Stephen Bonsal, *Unfinished Business*	1989	Taylor Branch, *Parting the Waters*
1946	Arthur Meier Schlesinger Jr., *The Age of Jackson*		James M. McPherson, *Battle Cry of Freedom: The Civil War Era*
1947	James Phinney Baxter III, *Scientists Against Time*	1990	Stanley Karnow, *In Our Image*
1948	Bernard DeVoto, *Across the Wide Missouri*	1991	Laurel Thatcher Ulrich, *A Midwife's Tale*
1949	Roy Franklin Nichols, *The Disruption of American Democracy*	1992	Mark E. Neely Jr., *The Fate of Liberty*
		1993	Gordon S. Wood, *The Radicalism of the American Revolution*
1950	Oliver W. Larkin, *Art and Life in America*	1995	Doris Kearns Goodwin, *No Ordinary Time: Franklin and Eleanor Roosevelt*
1951	R. Carlyle Buley, *The Old Northwest*	1996	Alan Taylor, *William Cooper's Town*
1952	Oscar Handlin, *The Uprooted*	1997	Jack N. Rakove, *Original Meanings: Politics and Ideas in the Making of the Constitution*
1953	George Dangerfield, *The Era of Good Feelings*		
1954	Bruce Catton, *A Stillness at Appomattox*	1998	Edward J. Larson, *Summer for the Gods: The Scopes Trial and America's Continuing Debate Over Science and Religion*
1955	Paul Horgan, *Great River: The Rio Grande in North American History*	1999	Edwin G. Burrows and Mike Wallace, *Gotham: A History of New York City to 1898*
1956	Richard Hofstadter, *The Age of Reform*	2000	David M. Kennedy, *Freedom From Fear: The American People in Depression and War*
1957	George F. Kennan, *Russia Leaves the War: Soviet American Relations, 1917–1920*		

Year	Author, Title	Year	Author, Title
2001	Joseph P. Ellis, *Founding Brothers: The Revolutionary Generation*	2005	David Hackett Fisher, *Washington's Crossing*
2002	Louis Menand, *The Metaphysical Club: A Story of Ideas in America*	2006	David M. Oshinsky, *Polio: An American Story*
2003	Rick Atkinson, *An Army at Dawn: The War in North Africa, 1942–1943*	2007	Gene Roberts and Hank Klibanoff, *The Race Beat*
2004	Steven Hahn, *A Nation Under Our Feet: Black Political Struggles in the Rural South from Slavery to the Great Migration*	2008	David Walker Howe, *What God Hath Wrought: The Transformation of America, 1815-1848*

Notes: No award given in 1919, 1984, or 1994. **1.** Awarded posthumously.

The Pulitzer Prize for Poetry, 1922–2008

Pulitzer Prizes in poetry were first awarded in 1922. The Poetry Society awarded prizes in 1918 to Sara Teasdale for *Love Songs*, and in 1919 to Margaret Widdemer for *Old Road to Paradise* and to Carl Sandburg for *Corn Huskers*.

Year	Author, Title	Year	Author, Title
1922	Edward Arlington Robinson, *Collected Poems*	1964	Louis Simpson, *At the End of the Open Road*
1923	Edna St. Vincent Millay, *The Ballad of the Harp-Weaver; A Few Figs from Thistles; Eight Sonnets in American Poetry, 1922, A Miscellany*	1965	John Berryman, *77 Dream Songs*
		1966	Richard Eberhart, *Selected Poems*
		1967	Anne Sexton, *Live or Die*
1924	Robert Frost, *New Hampshire: A Poem with Notes and Grace Notes*	1968	Anthony Hecht, *The Hard Hours*
		1969	George Oppen, *Of Being Numerous*
1925	Edward Arlington Robinson, *The Man Who Died Twice*	1970	Richard Howard, *Untitled Subjects*
		1971	William S. Merwin, *The Carrier of Ladders*
1926	Amy Lowell[1], *What's O'Clock*	1972	James Wright , *Collected Poems*
1927	Leonora Speyer, *Fiddler's Farewell*	1973	Maxine Kumin, *Up Country*
1928	Edward Arlington Robinson, *Tristram*	1974	Robert Lowell, *The Dolphins*
1929	Stephen Vincent Benét, *John Brown's Body*	1975	Gary Snyder, *Turtle Island*
1930	Conrad Aiken, *Selected Poems*	1976	John Ashbery, *Self-Portrait in a Convex Mirror*
1931	Robert Frost, *Collected Poems*		
1932	George Dillon, *The Flowering Stone*	1977	James Merrill, *Divine Comedies*
1933	Archibald MacLeish, *Conquistador*	1978	Howard Nemerov, *Collected Poems*
1934	Robert Hillyer, *Collected Verse*	1979	Robert Penn Warren, *Now and Then*
1935	Audrey Wurdemann, *Bright Ambush*	1980	Donald Justice, *Selected Poems*
1936	Robert P. Tristram Coffin, *Strange Holiness*	1981	James Schuyler, *The Morning of the Poem*
1937	Robert Frost, *A Further Range*	1982	Sylvia Plath[1], *The Collected Poems*
1938	Marya Zaturenska, *Cold Morning Sky*	1983	Galway Kinnell, *Selected Poems*
1939	John Gould Fletcher, *Selected Poems*	1984	Mary Oliver, *American Primitive*
1940	Mark Van Doren, *Collected Poems*	1985	Carolyn Kizer, *Yin*
1941	Leonard Bacon, *Sunderland Capture*	1986	Henry Taylor, *The Flying Change*
1942	William Rose Benét, *The Dust Which Is God*	1987	Rita Dove, *Thomas and Beulah*
1943	Robert Frost, *A Witness Tree*	1988	William Meredith, *Partial Accounts: New and Selected Poems*
1944	Stephen Vincent Benét[1], *Western Star*		
1945	Karl Shapiro, *V-Letter and Other Poems*	1989	Richard Wilbur, *New and Collected Poems*
1947	Robert Lowell, *Lord Weary's Castle*	1990	Charles Simic, *The World Doesn't End*
1948	W.H. Auden, *The Age of Anxiety*	1991	Mona Van Duyn, *Near Changes*
1949	Peter Viereck, *Terror and Decorum*	1992	James Tate, *Selected Poems*
1950	Gwendolyn Brooks, *Annie Allen*	1993	Louise Glück, *The Wild Iris*
1951	Carl Sandburg, *Complete Poems*	1994	Yusef Komunyakaa, *Neon Vernacular*
1952	Marianne Moore, *Collected Poems*	1995	Philip Levine, *Simple Truth*
1953	Archibald MacLeish, *Collected Poems 1917–1952*	1996	Jorie Graham, *The Dream of the Unified Field*
1954	Theodore Roethke, *The Waking*	1997	Lisel Mueller, *Alive Together: New and Selected Poems*
1955	Wallace Stevens, *Collected Poems*		
1956	Elizabeth Bishop, *Poems—North & South*	1998	Charles Wright, *Black Zodiac*
1957	Richard Wilbur, *Things of This World*	1999	Mark Strand, *Blizzard of One*
1958	Robert Penn Warren, *Promises: Poems 1954-1956*	2000	C.K. Williams, *Repair*
		2001	Stephen Dunn, *Different Hours*
		2002	Carl Dennis, *Practical Gods*
1959	Stanley Kunitz, *Selected Poems 1928–1958*	2003	Paul Muldoon, *Moy Sand and Gravel*
1960	W.D. Snodgrass, *Heart's Needle*	2004	Franz Wright, *Walking to Martha's Vineyard*
1961	Phyllis McGinley, *Times Three: Selected Verse From Three Decades*	2005	Ted Kooser, *Delights and Shadows*
		2006	Claudia Emerson, *Late Wife*
1962	Alan Dugan, *Poems*	2007	Natasha Trethewey, *Native Guard*
1963	William Carlos Williams[1], *Pictures from Breughel*	2008	Robert Hass, *Time and Materials*

Note: No award given in 1946. **1.** Awarded posthumously.

The Pulitzer Prize for General Nonfiction, 1962–2008

Year	Author, Title	Year	Author, Title
1962	Theodore H. White, *The Making of the President, 1960*	1986	Joseph Lelyveld, *Move Your Shadow* J. Anthony Lukas, *Common Ground*
1963	Barbara W. Tuchman, *The Guns of August*	1987	David K. Shipler, *Arab and Jew*
1964	Richard Hofstadter, *Anti-Intellectualism in American Life*	1988	Richard Rhodes, *The Making of the Atomic Bomb*
1965	Howard Mumford Jones, *O Strange New World*	1989	Neil Sheehan, *A Bright and Shining Lie*
1966	Edwin Way Teal, *Wandering Through Winter*	1990	Dale Maharidge, Michael Williamson, *And Their Children After Them*
1967	David Brion Davis, *The Problem of Slavery in Western Culture*	1991	Bert Holldobler, Edward O. Wilson, *The Ants*
1968	Will and Ariel Durant, *Rousseau and Revolution*	1992	Daniel Yergin, *The Prize: The Epic Quest for Oil, Money and Power.*
1969	René Jules Dubos, *So Human An Animal* Norman Mailer, *The Armies of the Night*	1993	Garry Wills, *Lincoln at Gettysburg*
1970	Erik H. Erikson, *Gandhi's Truth*	1994	David Remnick, *Lenin's Tomb: The Last Days of the Soviet Empire*
1971	John Toland, *The Rising Sun*	1995	Jonathan Weiner, *The Beak of the Finch*
1972	Barbara W. Tuchman, *Stilwell and the American Experience in China, 1911–45*	1996	Tina Rosenberg, *The Haunted Land*
1973	Robert Coles, *Children of Crisis, vols.2 & 3* Frances Fitzgerald, *Fire in the Lake*	1997	Richard Kluger, *Ashes to Ashes*
1974	Ernest Becker[1], *The Denial of Death*	1998	Jared Diamond, *Guns, Germs, and Steel: The Fates of Human Societies*
1975	Annie Dillard, *Pilgrim at Tinker Creek*	1999	John McPhee, *Annals of the Former World*
1976	Robert N. Butler, *Why Survive? Being Old in America*	2000	John W. Dower, *Embracing Defeat: Japan in the Wake of World War II*
1977	William N. Warner, *Beautiful Swimmers*	2001	Herbert P. Bix, *Hirohito and the Making of Modern Japan*
1978	Carl Sagan, *The Dragons of Eden*	2002	Diane McWhorter, *Carry Me Home: Birmingham, Alabama, the Climactic Battle of the Civil Rights Revolution*
1979	Edward O. Wilson, *On Human Nature*		
1980	Douglas R. Hofstadter, *Gödel, Escher, Bach: an Eternal Golden Braid*	2003	Samantha Power, *"A Problem From Hell": America and the Age of Genocide*
1981	Carl E. Schorske, *Fin-de Siècle Vienna: Politics and Culture*	2004	Anne Applebaum, *Gulag: A History*
		2005	Steve Coll, *Ghost Wars*
1982	Tracy Kidder, *The Soul of A New Machine*	2006	Caroline Elkins, *Imperial Reckoning: The Untold Story of Britain's Gulag in Kenya*
1983	Susan Sheehan, *Is There No Place on Earth for Me?*	2007	Lawrence Wright, *The Looming Tower*
1984	Paul Starr, *The Social Transformation of American Medicine*	2008	Saul Friedländer, *The Years of Extermination: Nazi Germany and the Jews*
1985	Studs Terkel, *The Good War*		

1. Awarded posthumously.

The Pulitzer Prize for Music, 1943–2008

Year	Author, Title	Year	Author, Title
1943	William Schuman, Secular Cantata No. 2, *A Free Song*	1959	John LaMontaine, Concerto for Piano and Orchestra
1944	Howard Hanson, Symphony No. 4, Opus 34	1960	Elliott Carter, Second String Quartet
1945	Aaron Copland, *Appalachian Spring*	1961	Walter Piston, Symphony No. 7
1946	Leo Sowerby, *The Canticle of the Sun*	1962	Robert Ward, *The Crucible* (opera)
1947	Charles Ives, Symphony No. 3	1963	Samuel Barber, Piano Concerto No. 1
1948	Walter Piston, Symphony No. 3	1964	No award
1949	Virgil Thomson, Music for the film, *Louisiana Story*	1965	No award
		1966	Leslie Bassett, Variations for Orchestra
1950	Gian-Carlo Menotti, Music for the opera *The Consul*	1967	Leon Kirchner, Quartet No. 3
		1968	George Crumb, *Echoes of Time and the River* orchestral suite
1951	Douglas S. Moore, Music for the opera, *Giants in the Earth*	1969	Karel Husa, String Quartet No. 3
1952	Gail Kubik, *Symphony Concertante*	1970	Charles Wuorinen, *Time's Encomium*
1953	No award	1971	Mario Davidovsky, Synchronisms No. 6 for Piano and Electronic Sound
1954	Quincy Porter, Concerto for Two Pianos and Orchestra	1972	Jacob Druckman, *Windows*
1955	Gian-Carlo Menotti, *The Saint of Bleecker Street* (opera)	1973	Elliott Carter, String Quartet No. 3
		1974	Donald Martino, *Notturno* (chamber music)
1956	Ernest Toch, Symphony No. 3	1975	Dominick Argento, *From the Diary of Virginia Woolf*
1957	Norman Dello Joio, *Meditations on Ecclesiastes*		
1958	Samuel Barber, *Vanessa* (opera)	1976	Ned Rorem, *Air Music: Ten Etudes for Orchestra*

Year	Author, Title	Year	Author, Title
1977	Richard Wernick, *Visions of Terror and Wonder*	1993	Christopher Rouse, *Trombone Concerto*
1978	Michael Colgrass, *Deja Vu* for Percussion Quartet and Orchestra	1994	Gunther Schuller, *Of Reminiscences and Reflections*
1979	Joseph Schwantner, *Aftertones of Infinity*	1995	Morton Gould, *Stringmusic*
1980	David Del Tredici, *In Memory of a Summer Day*	1996	George Walker, *Lilacs*
1981	No award	1997	Wynton Marsalis, *Blood on the Fields*
1982	Roger Sessions, Concerto for Orchestra	1998	Aaron Jay Kernis, *String Quartet No.2*
1983	Ellen Taaffe Zwilich, Symphony No. 1	1999	Melinda Wagner, *Concerto for Flute, Strings, and Percussion*
1984	Bernard Rands, "Canti del Sole" for Tenor and Orchestra	2000	Lewis Spratalan, *Life is a Dream, Opera in Three Acts: Act II, Convert Version*
1985	Stephen Albert, Symphony *RiverRun*	2001	John Corigliano, *Symphony No. 2 for String Orchestra*
1986	George Perle, Wind Quintet IV	2002	Henry Brant, *Ice Field*
1987	John Harbison, *The Flight Into Egypt*	2003	John Adams, *On the Transmigration of Souls*
1988	William Bolcom, 12 New Etudes for Piano	2004	Paul Moravec, *Tempest Fantasy*
1989	Roger Reynolds, *Whispers Out of Time*	2005	Steven Stucky, *Second Concerto for Orchestra*
1990	Mel Powell, *Duplicates: A Concerto for Two Pianos and Orchestra*	2006	Yehudi Wyner, *Piano Concerto: 'Chiavi in Mano'*
1991	Shulamitt Ran, *Symphony*	2007	Ornette Coleman, *Sound Grammar*
1992	Wayne Peterson, *The Face of the Night, The Heart of the Dark*	2008	David Lang, *The Little Match Girl Passion*

Pulitzer Special Citations

	SPECIAL CITATIONS IN LETTERS		SPECIAL CITATIONS IN MUSIC
Year	Recipient	Year	Recipient
1957	Kenneth Roberts, for his historical novels	1974	Roger Sessions, Lifetime achievement
1960	Garret Mattingly, *The Defeat of the Spanish Armada*	1976	Scott Joplin[1], Contributions to American music
1961	Publishers, *The American Heritage Picture History of the Civil War*	1982	Milton Babbitt, Lifetime achievement
1973	James Flexner, *George Washington,* vols. 1–4	1985	William Schuman, Lifetime achievement
1977	Alex Haley, *Roots*	1998	George Gershwin[1], Contributions to American music
1978	E.B. White, Lifetime achievement		
1984	Theodore Seuss Geisel (Dr. Seuss), Lifetime achievement	1999	Edward "Duke" Ellington[1], Contributions to American music
1992	Art Speigelman, *Maus*	2008	Bob Dylan, profound impact on American culture
1944	Richard Rodgers and Oscar Hammerstein II, *Oklahoma!*		

Note: 1. Awarded posthumously.   Source: Columbia University. www.pulitzer.org

The Nobel Prizes

First awarded in 1901, the Nobel Prizes were established through a bequest of $9.2 million from Alfred Bernhard Nobel (1833–1896), a Swedish chemical engineer and the inventor of dynamite and other explosives, and by a gift from the Bank of Sweden. Nobel's will directed that the interest from the fund be divided annually among people who have made significant discoveries or inventions in the fields of chemistry, physics, and physiology or medicine, as well as to that author who has "produced in the field of literature the most outstanding work of an idealistic tendency," and to that individual or group that has "done the most or the best work for fraternity between nations, for the abolition or reduction of standing armies and for the holding and promotion of peace congresses." In 1968, the 300th anniversary of the Bank of Sweden, an additional prize for outstanding work in the economic sciences was established; it was first granted the following year.

Today, all of the prizes are funded with the help of the Bank of Sweden. Final decisions are made for physics, chemistry and economics by the Royal Swedish Academy of Sciences, Stockholm; for physiology or medicine by the Nobel Assembly at the Karolinska Institute, Stockholm; for literature by the Swedish Academy, Stockholm; and for peace by the Norwegian Nobel Committee, Oslo.

The prizes are awarded annually on December 10, the anniversary of Nobel's death. The peace prize is presented in Oslo and other awards are given in Stockholm, by the king of Sweden. The amount of each prize varies according to the interest from the fund. In 2008, the award was worth 10 million Swedish kronar (approximately $1.41 million), up from $362,500 in 1987. No prizes were awarded between 1940 and 1942.

Nobel Peace Prize Recipients

1901 Jean-Henri Dunant (Switzerland) Founder of International Committee of the Red Cross; **Frédéric Passy** (France) Founder of first French peace society.
1902 Elie Ducommun (Switzerland) Director of Permanent International Peace Bureau; **Charles Albert Gobat** (Switzerland) Secretary-General of Inter-Parliamentary Union.
1903 Sir William R. Cremer (U.K.) Founder of International Arbitration League.
1904 Institute of International Law Founded in 1873.
1905 Baroness Bertha S.F. von Suttner (Austria) Author of antiwar novel *Lay Down Your Arms.*
1906 Theodore Roosevelt (U.S.) President; mediated Russo-Japanese War.
1907 Ernesto T. Moneta (Italy) Founder of Lombard League of Peace; **Louis Renault** (France) Professor of International Law at Hague Peace Conference.
1908 Klas P. Arnoldson (Sweden) Founder of Swedish Peace and Arbitration League; **Fredrik Bajer** (Denmark) Writer and peace activist, Danish parliament member.
1909 Auguste M.F. Beernaert (Belgium) Prime minister and peace activist; **Paul H.B.B. D'Estournelles de Constant** (Baron Constant de Rebecque) (France) Founder of French parliamentary group for voluntary arbitration.
1910 Permanent International Peace Bureau Founded 1891.
1911 Tobias M.C. Asser (Netherlands) A founder of Institute of International Law; **Alfred H. Fried** (Austria) Journalist and founder of many peace publications.
1912 Elihu Root (U.S.) Former Secretary of state and originator of several arbitration treaties.
1913 Henri Lafontaine (Belgium) President of Permanent International Peace Bureau in Bern.
1914–1916 No awards given.
1917 International Committee of the Red Cross Founded 1863.
1918 No award.
1919 Woodrow Wilson (U.S.) President; instrumental in establishing League of Nations.
1920 Léon Victor A. Bourgeois (France) Drafted framework for League of Nations.
1921 Karl H. Branting (Sweden) Prime minister and pacifist; **Christian L. Lange** (Norway) A founder of Inter-Parliamentary Union.
1922 Fridtjof Nansen (Norway) Scientist; explorer; originator of "Nansen passports." for refugees.
1923–24 No award.
1925 Sir Austen Chamberlain (U.K.) Foreign secretary; worked for Locarno Pact; **Charles G. Dawes** (U.S.) Vice president; drafted Dawes Plan settling German reparations issue.
1926 Aristide Briand (France) and **Gustav Stresemann** (Germany) Creators of Locarno Pact.
1927 Ferdinand Buisson (France) Human rights advocate; **Ludwig Quidde** (Germany) Peace activist.
1928 No award.
1929 Frank B. Kellogg (U.S.) Former Secretary of state; a creator of Kellogg-Briand Pact.
1930 L.O. Nathan Söderblom (Sweden) Archbishop; leader in the ecumenical movement.
1931 Jane Addams (U.S.) President of Women's International League for Peace and Freedom; **Nicholas M. Butler** (U.S.) Promoter of Kellogg-Briand Pact.
1932 No award.
1933 Sir Norman Angell (Ralph Lane) (U.K.) Author of antiwar book *The Great Illusion.*
1934 Arthur Henderson (U.K.) President of League of Nations World Disarmament Conference 1932.
1935 Carol von Ossietzky (Germany) Journalist and pacifist.

1936 Carlos Saavedra Lamas (Argentina) Secretary of state; president of League of Nations and mediator in conflict between Paraguay and Bolivia.
1937 Lord Edgar Algernon R.G. Cecil (U.K.) An architect of League of Nations.
1938 Nansen International Office for Refugees Founded 1921.
1939–1943 No awards given.
1944 International Committee of the Red Cross Founded 1863.
1945 Cordell Hull (U.S.) Former Secretary of state; instrumental in creating United Nations.
1946 Emily G. Balch (U.S.) Leader of international women's movement for peace; **John R. Mott** (U.S.) Leader of Christian ecumenical movement.
1947 The Friends Service Council (U.K.) and **The American Friends Service Committee** (U.S.) (The Quakers).
1948 No award.
1949 Lord John Boyd Orr (U.K.) Nutritionist; worked to eliminate world hunger.
1950 Ralph Bunche (U.S.) Mediator in Middle East war.
1951 Léon Jouhaux (France) Advocate of improved working-class conditions.
1952 Albert Schweitzer (France) Missionary surgeon/founder of Lambarene Hospital in Africa.
1953 George C. Marshall (U.S.) General; originator of Marshall Plan, which provided recovery loans and technical aid to Europe after World War II.
1954 Office of the U.N. High Commissioner for Refugees for their aid work for European refugees.
1955–1956 No awards given.
1957 Lester B. Pearson (Canada) Former Secretary of state; worked to resolve Suez Canal Crisis of 1956.
1958 Georges Pire (Belgium) Dominican priest and leader of relief organization for refugees, l'Europe du Coeur au Service du Monde.
1959 Philip J. Noel-Baker (U.K.) Lifelong worker for international peace through disarmament.
1960 Albert J. Lutuli (South Africa) President of the African National Congress; led peaceful resistance to apartheid.
1961 Dag Hammarskjöld (Sweden) United Nations Secretary General; worked for peace in the Congo.
1962 Linus C. Pauling (U.S.) Chemist; warned against dangers of radioactive fallout in nuclear weapons testing and war.
1963 International Committee of the Red Cross and League of Red Cross Societies
1964 Martin Luther King, Jr. (U.S.) Leader of American civil rights movement.
1965 United Nations Children's Fund (UNICEF).
1966–1967 No awards given.
1968 René Cassin (France) President of European Court for Human Rights.
1969 International Labour Organization United Nations agency involved in improving worldwide working and social conditions.
1970 Norman Borlaug (U.S.) Agricultural scientist and developer of high-yield grains credited with helping to alleviate world hunger.
1971 Willy Brandt (Federal Republic of Germany) Chancellor; champion of East-West détente.
1972 No award
1973 Henry A. Kissinger (U.S.) Secretary of state and **Le Duc Tho** (Democratic Republic of Viet Nam) Foreign minister; negotiated Vietnam cease-fire agreement. Mr. Tho declined the prize.
1974 Seán MacBride (Ireland) President of International Peace Bureau and United Nations commissioner for Namibia; **Eisaku Sato** (Japan) Prime

minister of Japan and campaigner against nuclear weapons.

1975   Andrei Sakharov (USSR) Nuclear physicist and human rights campaigner.

1976   Betty Williams and Mairead Corrigan (Northern Ireland) Founder of Northern Ireland Peace Movement.

1977   Amnesty International for human rights work.

1978   Anwar el-Sadat (Egypt) President, and **Menachem Begin** (Israel) Prime minister; negotiated Israeli-Egyptian peace accord.

1979   Mother Teresa (India) Worker for the poor in Calcutta.

1980   Adolfo Pérez Esquivel (Argentina) Architect, sculptor, and human rights leader.

1981   Office of the United Nations High Commissioner for Refugees for aid work with Asian refugees.

1982   Alva Myrdal (Sweden) and **Alfonso Garcia Robles** (Mexico) Campaigners for disarmament.

1983   Lech Walesa (Poland) Leader of the Solidarity trade union federation.

1984   Desmond M. Tutu (South Africa) Bishop of Johannesburg; a leader of the anti-apartheid movement.

1985   International Physicians for the Prevention of Nuclear War Organization jointly headed by a Soviet and an American doctor.

1986   Elie Wiesel (U.S.) Writer on the Holocaust and Nazi death camp survivor.

1987   Oscar Arias Sánchez (Costa Rica) President of Costa Rica; creator of a peace plan for Central America.

1988   United Nations Peacekeeping Forces

1989   Dalai Lama (Tibet) Exiled religious and political leader of Tibet for his nonviolent campaign to end China's domination of his country.

1990   Mikhail Gorbachev (USSR) President of the Soviet Union, "for his role in the peace process which today characterizes important parts of the international community."

1991   Aung San Suu Kyi (Myanmar), leader of opposition National League for Democracy (under house arrest at the time) "for her nonviolent struggle for democracy and human rights."

1992   Rigoberta Menchú (Guatemala) A Quiché Indian and an outspoken advocate of human rights during the civil war in her country.

1993   Pres. F. W. de Klerk of South Africa and **Nelson Mandela,** black leader of the opposition African National Congress, for negotiating an end to the apartheid policies of the state and their collaboration on the formation of a democracy not based on race.

1994   Yitzhak Rabin (Israel) Prime Minister, **Shimon Peres** (Israel) Foreign Minister, and **Yasir Arafat,** leader of the Palestinian Liberation Organization, for negotiating the historic peace pact allowing Palestinian self-rule in the West Bank and Gaza Strip.

1995   Joseph Rotblat (U.K. b. Poland) and his **Pugwash Conferences on Science and World Affairs.** A former Manhattan Project physicist, Rotblat spent 40 years campaigning to eliminate nuclear weapons.

1996   Bishop Carlos Ximenes Belo (Australia, b. East Timor) and **Jose Ramos-Horta** (East Timor) for "sustained and self-sacrificing contributions for a small but oppressed people" in East Timor, a former Portuguese colony invaded by Indonesia in the 1970s.

1997   The International Campaign to Ban Landmines and its 47-year-old coordinator, **Jody Williams** (U.S.), for their efforts to outlaw land mines worldwide. The Nobel committee admitted that it was openly trying to persuade the U.S. to sign the international treaty banning landmines.

1998   John Hume (Ireland) and **David Trimble** (Ireland) the leaders of the largest Roman Catholic and Protestant political parties in Northern Ireland, who brought about the April 1998 peace agreement.

1999   Doctors Without Borders (Médecins Sans Frontières), whose independence and rapid intervention have helped " to form bodies of public opinion opposed to violations and abuses of power."

2000   Kim Dae Jung, President of South Korea, "for his work for democracy and human rights in South Korea and in East Asia in general, and for peace and reconciliation with North Korea in particular."

2001   United Nations and its Secretary General **Kofi Annan,** (Ghana), in equal portions, for "their work for a better organized and more peaceful world."

2002   Jimmy Carter, (U.S.) "for his decades of untiring effort to find peaceful solutions to international conflicts, to advance democracy and human rights, and to promote economic and social development." In presenting the award to Carter, the Nobel Committee expressly stated its opposition to the Bush Administration's rush to war in the Persian Gulf.

2003   Shirin Ebadi (Iran), "for her efforts for democracy and human rights," especially in the struggle for the rights of women and children.

2004   Wangari Maathai (Kenya), "for her contribution to sustainable development, democracy and peace."

2005   International Atomic Energy Agency (IAEA) and **Mohamed El Barodei** (Egypt) "for their efforts to prevent nuclear energy from being used for military purposes and to ensure that nuclear energy for peaceful purposes is used in the safest possible way."

2006   Muhammad Yunus (Bangladesh) and **Grameen Bank** "for their efforts to create economic and social development from below."

2007   Intergovernmental Panel on Climate Change and **Albert Arnold Gore, Jr.** (U.S.) "for their efforts to build up and disseminate greater knowledge about man-made climate change."

Nobel Prizes in Physiology or Medicine

1901   Emil A. von Behring (Germany) Marburg Univ. "for his work on serum therapy, especially its application against diphtheria, by which he has opened a new road in the domain of medical science and thereby placed in the hands of the physician a victorious weapon against illness and deaths."

1902   Sir Ronald Ross (U.K.) University College "for his work on malaria, by which he has shown how it enters the organism and thereby has laid the foundation for successful research on this disease and methods of combating it."

1903   Niels R. Finsen (Denmark) Finsen Medical Light Institute "in recognition of his contribution to the treatment of diseases, especially lupus vulgaris, with concentrated light radiation, whereby he has opened a new avenue for medical science."

1904   Ivan P. Pavlov (Russia) Military Medical Academy "in recognition of his work on the physiology of digestion."

1905   Robert Koch (Germany) Institute for Infectious Diseases "for his investigations and discoveries in relation to tuberculosis."

1906   Camillio Golgi (Italy) Pavia Univ., and **Santiago Ramon Y Cajal** (Spain) Madrid Univ. for "their work on the structure of the nervous system."

1907   Charles L.A. Laveran (France) Institute Pasteur "in recognition of his work on the role played by protozoa in causing diseases."

1908   Il'ja I. Mecnikov (Russia) Institut Pasteur (Paris), and **Paul Ehrlich** (Germany) Goettingen Univ. and Royal Institute for Experimental Therapy "in recognition of their work on immunity."

1909   Emil R. Kocher (Switzerland) Berne Univ. "for his work on the physiology, pathology, and surgery for the thyroid gland."

1910   Albrecht Kossel (Germany) Heidelberg Univ. "in recognition of the contributions to our knowledge of cell chemistry made through his work on proteins, including the nucleic substances."

1911   Allvar Gullstrand (Sweden) Uppsala Univ. "for his work on the dioptrics of the eye."

1912   Alexis Carrel (France) Rockefeller Institute for Medical Research (New York) "in recognition of his work on vascular suture and the transplantation of blood vessels and organs."

1913   Charles R. Richet (France) Sorbonne Univ. "in recognition of his work on anaphylaxis."

1914   Robert Bárány (Austria) Vienna Univ. "for his work on the physiology and pathology of the vestibular apparatus."

1915–1918   No awards

1919   Jules Bordet (Belgium) Brussels Univ. "for his discoveries relating to immunity."

1920   Schack A.S. Krogh (Denmark) Copenhagen Univ. "for his discoveries of the capillary motor regulating mechanism."

1921   No award

1922   Sir Archibald V. Hill (U.K.) London Univ. "for his discovery relating to the production of heat in the muscle"; **Otto F. Meyerhof** (Germany) Kiel Univ. "for his discovery of the fixed relationship between the consumption of oxygen and the metabolism of lactic acid in the muscle."

1923   Sir Frederick G. Banting (Canada) Toronto Univ. and **John J.R. Macleod** (Canada) Toronto Univ. "for the discovery of insulin."

1924   Willem Einthoven (Netherlands) Leyden Univ. "for his discovery of the mechanism of the electrocardiogram."

1925   No award

1926   Johannes A.G. Fibiger (Denmark) Copenhagen Univ. "for his discovery of the Spiroptera carcinoma."

1927   Julius Wagner-Jauegg (Austria) Vienna Univ. "for his discovery of the therapeutic value of malaria inoculation in the treatment of dementia paralytica."

1928   Charles J.H. Nicolle (France) Institut Pasteur "for his work on typhus."

1929   Christiaan Eijkman (Netherlands) Utrecht Univ. "for his discovery of the antineuritic vitamin"; **Sir Frederick G. Hopkins** (U.K.) Cambridge Univ. "for his discovery of the growth-stimulating vitamins."

1930   Karl Landsteiner (Austria) Rockefeller Institute of Medical Research (New York) "for his discovery of human blood groups."

1931   Otto H. Warburg (Germany) Kaiser-Wilhelm Institut "for his discovery of the nature and mode of action of the respiratory enzyme."

1932   Sir Charles S. Sherrington (U.K.) Oxford Univ. and **Lord Edgar D. Adrian** (U.K.) Cambridge Univ. "for their discoveries regarding the functions of neurons."

1933   Thomas H. Morgan (U.S.) California Institute of Technology "for his discoveries concerning the role played by the chromosome in heredity."

1934   George H. Whipple (U.S.) Rochester Univ. **George R. Minot** (U.S.) Harvard Univ., and **William P. Murphy** (U.S.) Harvard Univ. "for their discoveries concerning liver therapy in cases of anaemia."

1935   Hans Spemann (Germany) Univ. of Freiburg "for his discovery of the organizer effect in embryonic development."

1936   Sir Henry H. Dale (U.K.) National Institute for Medical Research, and **Otto Loewi** (Austria) Graz Univ. "for their discoveries relating to chemical transmission of nerve impulses."

1937   Albert von Szent-Györgyi Nagyrapolt (Hungary) Szeged Univ. "for his discoveries in connection with the biological combustion processes, with special reference to vitamin C and the catalysis of fumaric acid."

1938   Corneille J.F. Heymans (Belgium) Ghent Univ. "for the discovery of the role played by the sinus and aortic mechanisms in the regulation of respiration."

1939   Gerhard Domagk (Germany) Munster Univ. for "discovery of the antibacterial effects of prontosil."

1940–1942   No awards given.

1943   Henrik C.P. Dam (Denmark) Polytechnic Institut "for his discovery of vitamin K"; **Edward A. Doisy** (U.S.) St. Louis Univ. "for his discovery of the chemical nature of vitamin K."

1944   Joseph Erlanger (U.S.) Washington Univ. and **Herbert S. Gasser** (U.S.) Rockefeller Institute for Medical Research "for their discoveries relating to the highly differentiated functions of single nerve fibers."

1945   Sir Alexander Fleming (U.K.) London Univ., **Sir Ernst B. Chain** (U.K.) Oxford Univ., and **Lord Howard W. Florey** (U.K.) Oxford Univ. "for their discovery of penicillin and its curative effect in various infectious diseases."

1946   Hermann J. Muller (U.S.) Indiana Univ. "for his discovery of the production of mutations by means of X-ray irradiation."

1947   Carl F. Cori (U.S.) Washington Univ. and his wife **Gerty T. Cori** (U.S.) Washington Univ. "for their discovery of the course of the catalytic conversion of glycogen"; **Bernardo A. Houssay** (Argentina) Institute of Biology and Experimental Medicine "for his discovery of the part played by the hormone of the anterior pituitary lobe in the metabolism of sugar."

1948   Paul H. Müller (Switzerland) Laboratory of the J.R. Geigy Dye-Factory Co. "for his discovery of the high efficiency of DDT as a contact poison against several arthropods."

1949   Walter R. Hess (Switzerland) Zurich Univ. "for his discovery of the functional organization of the interbrain as a coordinator of the activities of the internal organs; **Antonio Caetano de Abreu F.E. Moniz** (Portugal) Univ. of Lisbon "for his discovery of the therapeutic value of leucotomy in certain psychoses."

1950   Edward C. Kendall (U.S.) Mayo Clinic, **Tadeus Reichstein** (Switzerland) Basel Univ., and **Philip S. Hench** (U.S.) Mayo Clinic "for their discoveries relating to the hormones of the adrenal cortex, their structure, and biological effects."

1951   Max Theiler (Union of South Africa) Laboratories Division of Medicine and Public Health, Rockefeller Foundation (New York) "for his discoveries concerning yellow fever and how to combat it."

1952   Selman A. Waksman (U.S.) Rutgers Univ. "for his discovery of streptomycin, the first antibiotic effective against tuberculosis."

1953   Sir Hans A. Krebs (U.K., b. Germany) Sheffield Univ. "for his discovery of the citric acid cycle"; **Fritz A. Lipmann** (U.S., b. Germany) Harvard Medical School and Massachusetts General Hospital "for his discovery of coenzyme A and its importance for intermediary metabolism."

1954 John F. Enders (U.S.) Harvard Medical School and Research Division of Infectious Diseases, Children's Medical Center; **Thomas H. Weller** (U.S.) Research Division of Infectious Diseases, Children's Medical Center; and **Frederick C. Robbins** (U.S.) Western Reserve Univ. "for their discovery of the ability of poliomyelitis viruses to grow in cultures of various types of tissue."

1955 Axel H.T. Theorell (Sweden) Nobel Medical Institute "for his discoveries concerning the nature and mode of action of oxidation enzymes."

1956 Andre F. Cournand (U.S., b. France) Cardio-Pulmonary Laboratory, Columbia Univ. Division. Bellevue Hospital; **Werner Forssman** (Germany) Mainz Univ. and Bad Kreuznach; and **Dickinson W. Richards** (U.S.) Columbia Univ. "for their discoveries concerning heart catheterization and pathological changes in the circulatory system."

1957 Daniel Bovet (Italy, b. Switzerland) Chief Institute of Public Health "for his discoveries relating to synthetic compounds that inhibit the action of certain body substances, and especially their action on the vascular system and the skeletal muscles."

1958 George W. Beadle (U.S.) California Institute of Technology, and **Edward L. Tatum** (U.S.) Rockefeller Institute for Medical Research "for their discovery that genes act by regulating definite chemical events;" **Joshua Lederberg** (U.S.) Wisconsin Univ. "for his discoveries concerning genetic recombination and the organization of the genetic material of bacteria."

1959 Severo Ochoa (U.S.) New York Univ. College of Medicine, and **Arthur Kornberg** (U.S.) Stanford Univ. "for their discovery of the mechanisms in the biological synthesis of ribonucleic acid and deoxyribonucleic acid."

1960 Sir Frank M. Burnet (Australia) Walter and Eliza Hall Institute for Medical Research, and **Sir Peter B. Medawar** (U.K.) Univ. College "for discovery of acquired immunological tolerance."

1961 Georg von Békésy (U.S., b. Hungary) Harvard Univ. "for his discoveries of the physical mechanism of stimulation within the cochlea."

1962 Francis H.C. Crick (U.K.) Institute of Molecular Biology, **James D. Watson** (U.S.) Harvard Univ., and **Maurice H.F. Wilkins** (U.K.) University of London "for their discoveries concerning the molecular structure of nuclear acids and its significance for information transfer in living material."

1963 Sir John E. Eccles (Australia) Australian National Univ. **Sir Alan L. Hodgkin** (U.K.) Cambridge Univ., and **Sir Andrew F. Huxley** (U.K.) Univ. of London for their discoveries concerning the ionic mechanisms involved in excitation and inhibition in the peripheral and central portions of the nerve cell membrane."

1964 Konrad Block (U.S., b. Germany) Harvard Univ. and **Feodor Lymen** (Germany) Max-Planck-Institut fur Zellchemie "for their discoveries concerning the mechanism and regulation of the cholesterol and fatty acid metabolism."

1965 Francois Jacob (France), **André Lwoff** (France), and **Jacques Monod** (France), all from the Institut Pasteur "for their discoveries concerning genetic control of enzyme and virus synthesis."

1966 Peyton Rous (U.S.) Rockefeller Univ. "for his discovery of tumor-inducing viruses"; **Charles B. Huggins** (U.S.) Ben May Laboratory for Cancer Research, Univ. of Chicago "for his discoveries concerning hormonal treatment of prostatic cancer."

1967 Ragnar Granit (Sweden, b. Finland) Karolinska Institutet, **Haldan K. Hartline** (U.S.) Rockefeller Univ., and **George Wald** (U.S.) Harvard Univ. "for

their discoveries concerning the primary physiological and chemical visual processes in the eye."

1968 Robert W. Holley (U.S.) Cornell Univ., **Har G. Khorana** (U.S., b. India) Univ. of Wisconsin, and **Marshall W. Nirenberg** (U.S.) National Institutes of Health "for their interpretation of the genetic code and its functions in protein synthesis."

1969 Max Delbrück (U.S., b. Germany) California Institute of Technology, **Alfred D. Hershey** (U.S.) Carnegie Institution of Washington, and **Salvador Luria** (U.S., b. Italy) M.I.T. for their discoveries concerning the replication mechanism and the genetic structure of viruses."

1970 Sir Bernard Katz (U.K.) University College, **Ulf von Euler** (Sweden) Karolinska Institutet, and **Julius Axelrod** (U.S.) National Institutes of Health "for their discoveries concerning the humoral transmittors in the nerve terminals and the mechanism for their storage, release, and inactivation."

1971 Earl W. Sutherland, Jr. (U.S.) Vanderbilt Univ. "for his discoveries concerning the mechanisms of the action of hormones."

1972 Gerald M. Edelman (U.S.) Rockefeller Univ. and **Rodney R. Porter** (U.K.) Oxford Univ. "for their discoveries concerning the chemical structure of antibodies."

1973 Karl von Frisch (W. Germany) Zoologisches Institut der Universitat Munchen; **Konrad Lorenz** (Austria) Osterreichische Akademie der Wissenschaften, Institut fur vergleichende Verhaltensforschung, and **Nikolaas Tinbergen** (U.K.) University Museum for their discoveries concerning organization and elicitation of individual and social behavior patterns."

1974 Albert Claude (Belgium) Université Catholique de Louvain, **Christian de Duve** (Belgium) Rockefeller Univ. (New York), and **George E. Palade** (U.S., b. Romania) Yale Univ. "for their discoveries concerning the structural and functional organization of the cell."

1975 David Baltimore (U.S.) M.I.T., **Renato Dulbecco** (U.S., b. Italy) Imperial Cancer Research Fund Laboratory (London), and **Howard M. Temin** (U.S.) Univ. of Wisconsin "for their discoveries concerning the interaction between tumor viruses and the genetic material of the cell."

1976 Baruch S. Blumberg (U.S.) Institute for Cancer Research, and **D. Carleton Gajdusek** (U.S.) National Institutes of Health "for their discoveries concerning new mechanism for the origin and dissemination of infectious diseases."

1977 Roger Guillemin (U.S., b. France) Salk Institute, and **Andrew V. Schally** (U.S., b. Poland) Veterans Administration Hospital, New Orleans "for their discoveries concerning the peptide hormone production of the brain"; **Rosalyn Yalow** (U.S.) Veterans Administration Hospital, Bronx "for the development of radioimmunoassays of peptide hormones."

1978 Werner Arber (Switzerland) Biozentrum der Universitat, **Daniel Nathans** (U.S.) John Hopkins Univ., and **Hamilton O. Smith** (U.S.) John Hopkins Univ. "for the discovery of restriction enzymes and their application to problems of molecular genetics."

1979 Alan M. Cormack (U.S., b. South Africa) Tufts Univ., and **Sir Godfrey N. Hounsfield** (U.K.) Central Research Laboratories, EMI, "for the development of computer assisted tomography."

1980 Baruj Benacerraf (U.S., b. Venezuela) Harvard Medical School; **Jean Dausset** (France) Université de Paris, Laboratoire Immuno-Hemetologie; and **George D. Snell** (U.S.) Jackson Laboratory "for their discoveries concerning genetically determined structures on the cell surface that regulate immunological reactions."

1981   Roger W. Sperry (U.S.) California Institute of Technology "for his discoveries concerning the functional specialization of the cerebral hemispheres"; **David H. Hubel** (U.S., b. Canada) Harvard Medical School, and **Torsten T. Wiesel** (Sweden) Harvard Medical School "for their discoveries concerning information processing in the visual system."

1982   Sune K. Bergström (Sweden) Karolinska Institute, **Bengt I. Samuelsson** (Sweden) Karolinska Institute, and **Sir John R. Vane** (U.K.) Wellcome Research Laboratories "for their discoveries concerning prostaglandins and related biologically active substances."

1983   Barbara McClintock (U.S.) Cold Spring Harbor Laboratory "for her discovery of mobile genetic elements."

1984   Niels K. Jerne (Denmark) and **Georges J.F. Köhler** (W. Germany) of the Basel Institute for Immunology; and **César Milstein** (U.K. and Argentina) Medical Research Council Laboratory of Molecular Biology (Cambridge) for theories concerning the specificity in development and controls of the immune system and the discovery of the principle for production of monoclonal antibodies."

1985   Michael S. Brown (U.S.), and **Joseph L. Goldstein** (U.S.) both of the Univ. of Texas Health Science Center at Dallas "for their discoveries concerning the regulation of cholesterol metabolism."

1986   Stanley Cohen (U.S.) Vanderbilt Univ., and **Rita Levi-Montalcini** (Italy and U.S.) Institute of Cell Biology of the C.N.R. (Rome) "for their discoveries of growth factors."

1987   Susumu Tonegawa (U.S.) MIT "for discovery of the genetic principle for generation of antibody diversity."

1988   Sir James W. Black (U.K.) King's College Hospital Medical School, **Gertrude B. Elion** (U.S.) Welcome Research Laboratories, and **George H. Hitchings** (U.S.) Wellcome Research Laboratories "for their discoveries of Important Principles for Drug Treatment."

1989   J. Michael Bishop and **Harold E. Varmus** (U.S.) Univ. of California, San Francisco "for their discovery of the Cellular Origin of Retroviral Oncogenes."

1990   Joseph E. Murray (U.S.) Brigham and Women's Hospital (Boston) who performed the first kidney transplant (1954), and **E. Donnall Thomas** (U.S.), Fred Hutchinson Cancer Research Center (Seattle), who performed the first successful bone marrow transplant between two people who were not twins (1979).

1991   Erwin Neher (Germany) Max-Planck Institute for Biophysical Chemistry, Göttingen, and **Bert Sakmann** (Germany) Max-Planck Institute for Medical Research, Heidelberg, for establishing existence of ion channels by developing technique that allows detection of "incredibly small electrical currents that pass through a single ion channel."

1992   Edmond H. Fischer (U.S.) and **Edwin G. Krebs** (U.S.), both of the Univ. of Washington for a discovery in the 1950s of a regulatory mechanism in almost all human cells linked to some cancers, to the rejection of transplanted organs, and many other processes.

1993   Richard J. Roberts (U.K.), New England Bio Labs, and **Phillip A. Sharp** (U.S.), MIT, for their discovery in the 1970s that the composition of genes is of several segments, which led to gene splicing and to a better understanding of hereditary diseases and cancer.

1994   Alfred G. Gilman (U.S.) Univ. of Texas Southwestern Medical Center, and **Martin Rodbell** (U.S.) National Institute of Environmental Health Sciences, for their discovery of natural substances known as G-proteins and for showing how they help cells respond to stimuli like light and odors.

1995   Edward B. Lewis (U.S.) California Institute of Technology, **Eric F. Wieschaus** (U.S.) Princeton Univ., and **Christiane Nüsslein-Volhard** (Germany) Max-Planck Institute in Tübingen, for their discovery of how genes control structural development of the body. Their research, performed on fruit flies, helps explain birth defects in humans.

1996   Peter C. Doherty (Australia) St. Jude's Medical Center in Memphis, and **Rolf Zinkernagel** (Switzerland) University of Zurich, "for their discoveries concerning the specificity of the cell mediated immune defense." Their work explained how the immune system recognizes and kills virus-infected cells.

1997   Stanley B. Prusiner (U.S.), Univ. of California, "for his discovery of Prions," disease-causing proteins that can be linked to degenerative brain diseases.

1998   Robert F. Furchgott (U.S.), SUNY Health Science Center; **Louis J. Ignarro** (U.S.), UCLA School of Medicine; and **Ferid Murad** (U.S.), Univ. of Texas, ""for their discoveries concerning nitric oxide as a signalling molecule in the cardiovascular system."

1999   Günter Blobel (U.S., b. Germany), Rockefeller Univ. "for the discovery that proteins have intrinsic signals that govern their transport and localization in the cel." Blobel found that many hereditary diseases are caused by mistakes in these signals.

2000   Arvid Carlsson (Sweden), Univ. of Gothenburg; **Paul Greengard** (U.S.), Rockefeller Univ., N.Y.; and **Eric Kandel** (U.S.), Columbia Univ., "for their discoveries concerning signal transduction in the nervous system," leading to greater understanding of neurological and psychiatric diseases like Parkinson's.

2001   Leland H. Hartwell (U.S.), Fred Hutchinson Cancer Research Center, Seattle, and **R. Timothy Hunt** (U.K.) and **Sir Paul M. Nurse** (U.K.), both of the Imperial Cancer Research Fund, London, "for their discoveries of key regulators of the cell cycle," which may lead to cures for irregular cell growth patterns like cancer.

2002   Sydney Brenner, (U.K.), Molecular Sciences Institute, **H. Robert Horvitz,** (U.S.), M.I.T., and **John E. Sulston,** (U.K.), Wellcome Trust Sanger Institute "for their discoveries concerning genetic regulation of organ development and programmed cell death." Their work has given scientists insights into cancer and the ways bacteria and viruses invade human cells.

2003   Paul C. Lauterbur(U.S.), Univ. of Illinois and **Peter Mansfield** (U.K.), Univ. of Nottingham School of Physics, "For their discoveries concerning magnetic resonancce imaging (MRIs)."

2004   Richard Axel (U.S.) and **Linda B. Buck** (U.S.), both of the Howard Hughes Medical Institute, for their discoveries of "odorant receptors and the organization of the olfactory system."

2005   Barry J. Marshall and **J. Robin Warren** (Australia) "for their discovery of the bacterium *Helicobacter pylori* and its role in gastritis and peptic ulcer disease."

2006   Andrew Z. Fire and **Craig C. Mello** (U.S.) "for their discovery of RNA interference—gene silencing by double-stranded RNA."

2007   Mario R. Capecchi (U.S. ,b. Italy) Univ. of Utah, **Sir Martin J. Evans** (U.K.) Cardiff Univ., and **Oliver Smithies** (U.S., b. U.K.) Univ. of North Carolina at Chapel Hill "for their discoveries of principles for introducing specific gene modifications in mice by the use of embryonic stem cells."

Nobel Prizes in Economic Sciences

1969 **Ragnar Frisch** (Norway) Oslo Univ. and **Jan Tinbergen** (Netherlands) Netherlands School of Economics "for having developed and applied dynamic models for the analysis of economic processes."

1970 **Paul A. Samuelson** (U.S.) M.I.T. "for the scientific work through which he has developed static and dynamic economic theory and...contributed to raising the level of analysis in economic science."

1971 **Simon Kuznets** (U.S.) Harvard Univ. "for his empirically founded interpretation of economic growth which has led to new and deepened insight into the economic and social structure and process of development."

1972 **Sir John R. Hicks** (U.K.) All Souls College, and **Kenneth J. Arrow** (U.S.) Harvard Univ. "for their pioneering contributions to general economic equilibrium theory and welfare theory."

1973 **Wassily Leontief** (U.S.) Harvard Univ. "for the development of the input-output method and for its application to important economic problems."

1974 **Gunnar Mydal** (Sweden), **Friedrich A. von Hayek** (U.K.) "for their pioneering work in the theory of money and economic fluctuations and for their penetrating analysis of the interdependence of economic, social and institutional phenomena."

1975 **Leonid Kantorovich** (USSR) Academy of Sciences, and **Tjalling C. Koopmans** (U.S.) Yale Univ. "for their contributions to the theory of optimum allocation of resources."

1976 **Milton Friedman** (U.S.) Univ. of Chicago for "achievements in the fields of consumption analysis, monetary history and theory. . ."

1977 **Bertil Ohlin** (Sweden) Stockholm School of Economics, and **James E. Meade** (U.K.) Cambridge Univ. "for their pathbreaking contribution to the theory of international trade and international capital movements."

1978 **Herbert A. Simon** (U.S.) Carnegie-Mellon Univ. "for his pioneering research into the decision-making process within economic organizations."

1979 **Theodore W. Schultz** (U.S.) Univ. of Chicago, and **Sir Arthur Lewis** (U.K.) Princeton Univ. "for their pioneering research into economic development research with particular consideration of the problems of developing countries."

1980 **Lawrence R. Klein** (U.S.) Univ. of Pennsylvania "for the creation of econometric models and their application to the analysis of economic fluctuations and economic policies."

1981 **James Tobin** (U.S.) Yale Univ. "for his analysis of financial markets and their relations to expenditure decisions, employment, production, and prices."

1982 **George J. Stigler** (U.S.) Univ. of Chicago "for his seminal studies of industrial structures, functioning markets, and causes and effects of public regulation."

1983 **Gerard Debreu** (U.S.) Univ. of California, "for having incorporated new analytical methods into economic theory and for his rigorous reformulation of the theory of general equilbrium."

1984 **Sir Richard Stone** (U.K.) Cambridge Univ. "for having made fundamental contributions to the development of systems of national accounts and hence greatly improved [sic]the basis for empirical economic analysis."

1985 **Franco Modigliani** (U.S.) M.I.T. "for his pioneering analyses of saving and of financial markets."

1986 **James M Buchanan Jr.** (U.S.) Center for Study of Public Choice "for his development of the contractual and constitutional bases for the theory of economic and political decision-making."

1987 **Robert M. Solow** (U.S.) M.I.T. "for his contributions to the theory of economic growth."

1988 **Maurice Allais** (France) Centre d'analyse économique "for his pioneering contributions to the theory of markets and efficient utilization of resources.

1989 **Trygve Haavelmo** (Norway) Univ. of Oslo "for his clarification of the probability theory foundations of econometircs and his analyses of simultaneous economic structures."

1990 **Harry Markowitz** (U.S.) Baruch College (of the City Univ. of New York, for his Portfolio Theory; **William F. Sharpe** (U.S.) Stanford Univ., for his Capital Asset Pricing Model, and **Merton Miller** (U.S.) Univ. of Chicago, for his work on the Miller-Modigliani Theory. Together, their work revolutionized the financial/business industries.

1991 **Ronald H. Coase** (U.K.) Univ. of Chicago Law School, for his work on the role of firms in the economy and on social cost of industry, notably his articles "The Theory of the Firm" (1937) and "The Problem of Social Cost" (1960).

1992 **Gary S. Becker** (U.S.), Univ. of Chicago, for "having extended the domain of economic theory to aspects of human behavior . . ." including crime, family life, and racial bias.

1993 **Robert W. Fogel** (U.S.), Univ. of Chicago, and **Douglass C. North** (U.S.), Washington Univ., for "applying economic theory and quarantine methods to historical puzzles." Fogel's work on slavery as an efficient economic system caused great controversy.

1994 **John F. Nash** (U.S.) Princeton Univ., **John C. Harsanyi** (U.S., b. Hungary) Univ. of California, and **Reinhard Selten** (Germany) Univ. of Bonn, for their separate contributions to the field of game theory, which is used to predict how information and competition affect economic outcomes.

1995 **Robert E. Lucas, Jr.** (U.S.) Univ. of Chicago, "the economist who has had the greatest influence on macroeconomic research since 1970." His work challenges the Keynesian belief that the government is able to fine-tune the economy.

1996 **James A. Mirrlees** (U.K.) Cambridge Univ. and **William Vickrey** (U.S., b. Canada), Columbia Univ. for "their fundamental contributions to the economic theory of incentives." Their theories have been used in designing more efficient tax codes and eliciting the highest bids at auctions.

1997 **Robert Merton** (U.S.), Harvard University, and **Myron Scholes** (U.S.), Stanford University, for their work in creating "a pioneering formula for the valuation of stock options" and other derivatives. The Nobel committee cited their research as one of the principal reasons for the success of the derivatives markets.

1998 **Amartya Sen** (India), Cambridge Univ. and Harvard Univ., for his work on human rights, poverty, and inequality that has changed the way governments deal with famines, and for restoring "an ethical dimension to the discussion of vital economics problems."

1999 **Robert A. Mundell** (U.S.,b. Canada), Columbia University, "for his analysis of monetary and fiscal policy under different exchange rate regimes and his analysis of optimum currency areas."

2000 **James J. Heckman** (U.S.), Univ. of Chicago "for his development of theory and methods for analyzing selective samples," and **Daniel L. McFadden** (U.S.), Univ. of California, "for his development of theory and methods for analyzing discrete choice."

2001 **George A. Akerlof** (U.S.) Univ. of California, **A. Michael Spence** (U.S.), Stanford Univ., and **Joseph E. Stiglitz** (U.S.), Columbia Univ. "for their analyses of markets with asymmetric information."

Their work has applications in situations ranging from the elderly's inability to find low-cost medical insurance to the prices charged for used cars.

2002 Daniel Kahneman, (U.S. and Israel), Princeton University and **Vernon L. Smith,** (U.S.), George Mason University, whose achievements break new ground in incorporating experimental methods into the study of economics.

2003 Robert F. Engle, (U.S.), New York University, and **Clive W. Granger,** (U.K.), for "methods of analyzing economic time series with common trends (cointegration), allowing researchers to compare data across inconsistent time periods.

2004 Finn E. Kydland (Norway), Carnegie-Mellon University and University of California at Santa Barbara; and **Edward C. Prescott** (U.S.), Arizona State

University and Federal Reserve Bank of Minneapolis; "for their contributions to dynamic macroeconomics: the time consistency of economic policy and the driving forces behind business cycles."

2005 Robert J. Aumann (Israel) and **Thomas C. Schelling** (U.S.) "for having enhanced our understanding of conflict and cooperation through game theory analysis."

2006 Edmund S. Phelps (U.S.) "for his analysis of intertemporal tradeoffs in macroeconomic policy"

2007 Leonid Hurwicz (U.S., b. Russia) Univ. of Minnesota, **Eric S. Maskin** (U.S.) Institute for Advanced Study, and **Roger B. Myerson** (U.S.) Univ. of Chicago "for having laid the foundations of mechanism design theory."

Nobel Prizes in Chemistry

1901 Jacobus H. Van't Hoff (Netherlands) Berlin Univ. (Germany) for "the extraordinary services he has rendered by the discovery of the laws of chemical dynamics and osmotic pressure in solutions."

1902 Hermann E. Fischer (Germany) "in recognition of the extraordinary services he has rendered by his work on sugar and purine synthesis."

1903 Svante A. Arrhenius (Sweden) Stockholm Univ. "in recognition of the extraordinary services he has rendered to the advancement of chemistry by his electrolytic theory of dissociation."

1904 Sir William Ramsay (U.K.) London Univ. "in recognition of his services in the discovery of the inert gaseous elements in air; and his determination of their place in the periodic system."

1905 Johann F.W.A. von Baeyer (Germany) Munich Univ. "in recognition of his services in the advancement of organic chemistry and the chemical industry, through his work on organic dyes and hydroaromatic compounds."

1906 Henri Moissan (France) Sorbonne Univ. "in recognition of the great services rendered by him in his investigation and isolation of the element fluorine, and for the adoption in the service of science of the electric furnace called after him."

1907 Eduard Buchner (Germany) Agricultural College "for his biochemical researches and his discovery of cell-free fermentation."

1908 Lord Ernest Rutherfold (U.K.) Victoria Univ. "for his investigation into the disintegration of the elements, and the chemistry of radioactive substances."

1909 Wilhelm Ostwald (Germany) Leipzig Univ. "in recognition of his work on catalysis, and for his investigations into the fundamental principles governing chemical equilibria and rates of reaction."

1910 Otto Wallach (Germany) Goettingen Univ. "in recognition of his services to organic chemistry and the chemical industry by his pioneer work in the field of alicyclic compounds."

1911 Marie Curie (France) Sorbonne Univ. "in recognition of her services to the advancement of chemistry by the discovery of the elements radium and polonium, by the isolation of radium and the study of the nature and compounds of this remarkable element."

1912 Victor Grignard (France) Nancy Univ. "for the discovery of the so-called Grignard reagent, which in recent years has greatly advanced the progress of organic chemistry"; **Paul Sabatier** (France) Toulouse Univ., "for his method of hydrogenating organic compounds in the presence of finely disintegrated metals whereby the progress of organic chemistry has been greatly advanced in recent years."

1913 Alfred Werner (Switzerland) Zurich Univ. "in recognition of his work on the linkage of atoms in molecules by which he has thrown new light on earlier investigations and opened up new fields of research especially in inorganic chemistry."

1914 Theodore W. Richards (U.S.) Harvard Univ. for "his accurate determinations of the atomic weight of a large number of chemical elements."

1915 Richard M. Willstätter (Germany) Munich Univ. "for his researches on plant pigments, especially chlorophyll."

1916–1917 No awards given.

1918 Fritz Haber (Germany) Kaiser-Wilhelm Institut "for the synthesis of ammonia from its elements.

1919 No award

1920 Walther H. Nernst (Germany) Berlin Univ. "in recognition of his work in thermochemistry."

1921 Frederick Soddy (U.K.) Oxford Univ. "for his contributions to our knowledge of the chemistry of radioactive substances, and his investigations into the origin and nature of isotopes."

1922 Francis W. Aston (U.K.) Cambridge Univ. "for his discovery, by means of his mass spectrograph, of isotopes in a large number of nonradioactive elements, and for his enunciation of the whole-number rule."

1923 Fritz Pregl (Austria) Graz Univ. "for his invention of the method of microanalysis of organic substances."

1924 No award

1925 Richard A. Zsigmondy (Germany) Goettingen Univ. "for his demonstration of the heterogeneous nature of colloid solutions."

1926 The (Theodor) Svedberg (Sweden) Uppsala Univ. "for his work on disperse systems."

1927 Heinrich O. Wieland (Germany) Munich Univ. "for his investigations of the constitution of the bile acids and related substances."

1928 Adolf O.R. Windaus (Germany) Goettingen Univ. "for the services rendered through his research into the constitution of the sterols and their connection with the vitamins."

1929 Sir Arthur Harden (U.K.) London Univ., Hans K.A. von Euler-Chelpin (Sweden) "for their investigations on the fermentation of sugar and fermentative enzymes."

1930 Hans Fischer (Germany) Institute of Technology "for his researches into the constitution of haemin and chlorophyll, and especially for his synthesis of haemin."

1931 Carl Bosch (Germany) Heidelberg Univ. I.G. Farbenindustrie A.G., and **Fredrich Bergius** (Germany) Heidelberg Univ. and I.G. Farbenindustrie A.G. for "their contributions to the invention and development of chemical high pressure methods."

1932 Irving Langmuir (U.S.) General Electric Co., "for his discoveries and investigations in surface chemistry."

1933 No award

1934 Harold C. Urey (U.S.) Columbia Univ. "for his discovery of heavy hydrogen."

1935 Frédéric Joliot (France) Institut du Radium and his wife, **Iréne Joliot-Curie,** (France) Institut du

adium "in recognition of their synthesis of new ra-
oactive elements."

936 Petrus (Peter) J.W. Debye (Netherlands)
erlin Univ. and Kaiser-Wilhelm-Institut (now Max-
lanck-Institut) "for his contributions to our knowl-
dge of molecular structure through his
nvestigations on dipole moments and on the dif-
raction of X-rays and electrons in gases."

1937 Sir Walter N. Haworth (U.K.) Birmingham
Jniv. "for his investigations on carbohydrates and
itamin C"; **Paul Karrer** (Switzerland) Zurich Univ.
for his investigations on carotenoids, flavins, and
vitamins A and B-2."

1938 Richard Kuhn (Germany) Heidelberg Univ.
and Kaiser-Wilhelm-Institut (now Max-Planck-Insti-
ut) "for his work on carotenoids and vitamins.
(Compelled by the authorities of his country to decline the award, but later received diploma and
medal.)

1939 Adolf F.J. Butenandt (Germany) Berlin Univ.
and Kaiser-Wilhelm-Institut (now Max-Planck-Institut) "for his work on sex hormones. (Compelled by
his country to decline the award, but later received
diploma and medal); **Leopold Ruzicka** (Switzerland)
Federal Institute of Technology "for his work on
polymethylenes and higher terpenes."

1940–1942   No awards

1943 George de Hevesy (Hungary) Stockholm
Univ. "for his work on the use of isotopes as tracers
in the study of chemical processes."

1944 Otto Hahn (Germany) Kaiser-Wilhelm-Institut (now Max-Planck-Institut) "for his discovery of
the fission of heavy nuclei."

1945 Artturi I. Virtanen (Finland) Helsinki Univ.
"for his research and inventions in agricultural and
nutrition chemistry, especially for his fodder preservation method."

1946 James B. Sumner (U.S.) Cornell Univ. "for
his discovery that enzymes can be crystallized";
John H. Northrop (U.S.) Rockefeller Institute for
Medical Research "for their preparation of enzymes
and virus proteins in a pure form."

1947 Sir Robert Robinson (U.K.) Oxford Univ.
"for his investigations on plant products of biological importance, especially alkaloids."

1948 Arne W.K. Tiselius (Sweden) Uppsala Univ.
"for his research on electrophoresis and adsorption
analysis, especially for his discoveries concerning
the complex nature of the serum proteins."

1949 William F. Giauque (U.S.) Univ. of California, "for his contributions in the field of chemical
thermodynamics, particularly concerning the behavior of substances at extremely low temperatures."

1950 Otto P.H. Diels (Germany) Kiel Univ. and
Kurt Alder (Germany) Cologne Univ. "for their discovery and development of the diene synthesis."

1951 Edwin M. McMillan (U.S.) and **Glenn T.
Seaborg** (U.S.) both of Univ. of California, "for their
discoveries in the chemistry of the transuranium
elements."

1952 Archer J.P. Martin (U.K.) Nations Institute
for Medical Research, and **Richard L.M. Synge**
(U.K.) Rowett Research Institute (Scotland) "for their
invention of partition chromatography."

1953 Herman Staudinger (Germany) State Research
Institute for Macromolecular Chemistry "for his discoveries in the field of macromolecular chemistry."

1954 Linus C. Pauling (U.S.) California Institute of
Technology "for his research into the nature of the
chemical bond and its application to the elucidation
of the structure of complex substances."

1955 Vincent du Vigneaud (U.S.) Cornell Univ.
"for his work on biochemically important sulphur
compounds, especially for the first synthesis of a
polypeptide hormone."

1956 Sir Cyril N. Hinshelwood (U.K.) Oxford
Univ. and **Nikolaj N. Semenov** (USSR) Institute for

Chemical Physics of the Academy of Sciences of the
USSR "for their researches into the mechanism of
chemical reactions."

1957 Lord Alexander R. Todd (U.K.) Cambridge
Univ. "for his work on nucleotides and nucleotide
co-enzymes."

1958 Frederick Sanger (U.K.) Cambridge Univ.
"for his work on the structure of proteins, especially
that of insulin."

1959 Jaroslav Heyrovsky (Czechoslovakia) Po-
laro-Institute of the Czechoslovakia Academy of Science for his discovery and development of the
polarographic methods of analysis."

1960 Willard F. Libby (U.S.) Univ. of California,
Los Angeles "for his method to use carbon-14 for
age determination in archaeology, geology, geophysics, and other branches of science."

1961 Melvin Calvin (U.S.) Univ. of California, for
research on carbon dioxide assimilation in plants."

1962 Max F. Perutz (U.K.) Laboratory of Molecular Biology, and **Sir John C. Kendrew** (U.K.) Laboratory of Molecular Biology, "for their studies on the
structures of globular proteins."

1963 Karl Ziegler (Germany) Max-Planck-Institute
for Carbon Research, and **Giulio Natta** (Italy) Institute of Technology "for their discoveries in the field
of the chemistry and technology of high polymers."

1964 Dorothy C. Hodgkin (U.K.) Royal Society,
Oxford Univ. "for her determinations by X-ray techniques of the structures of important biochemical
substances."

1965 Robert B. Woodward (U.S.) Harvard Univ.
"for his outstanding achievements in the art of organic synthesis."

1966 Robert S. Mulliken (U.S.) Univ. of Chicago
"for his fundamental work concerning chemical
bonds and the electronic structure of molecules by
the molecular orbital method."

1967 Manfred Eigen (W. Germany) Max-Planck-
Institut, **Ronald G.W. Norrish** (U.K.) Institute of
Physical Chemistry, and **Sir George Porter** (U.K.) The
Royal Institution "for their studies of extremely fast
chemical reactions, effected by disturbing the equi-
librium by means of very short pulses of energy."

1968 Lars Onsager (U.S.) Yale Univ. "for the discovery of the reciprocal relations bearing his name,
which are fundamental for the thermodynamics of
irreversible processes."

1969 Sir Derek H.R. Barton (U.K.) Imperial College of Science and Technology, and **Odd Hassel**
(Norway) Kjemisk Institut "for their contributions to
the development of the concept of conformation
and its application in chemistry."

1970 Luis F. Leloir (Argentina) Institute for Biochemical Research for his discovery of sugar nucleotides and their role in the biosynthesis of
carbohydrates."

1971 Gerhard Herzberg (Canada) National Research Council of Canada "for his contributions to
the knowledge of electronic structure and geometry
of molecules, particularly free radicals."

1972 Christian B. Anfinsen (U.S.) National Institutes of Health "for his work on ribonuclease, especially concerning the connection between the
amino acid sequence and the biologically active
conformation"; **Stanford Moore** (U.S.) Rockefeller
Univ. and **William H. Stein** (U.S.) Rockefeller Univ.
"for their contribution to the understanding of the
connection between chemical structure and catalytic activity of the active center of the ribonuclease
molecule."

1973 Ernst O. Fischer (W. Germany) Technical
Univ. of Munich, and **Sir Geoffrey Wilkinson** (U.K.)
Imperial College "for their pioneering work, performed independently, on the chemistry of the
organometallic, so-called sandwich compounds."

1974   Paul J. Flory (U.S.) Stanford Univ. "for his fundamental achievements, both theoretical and experimental, in the physical chemistry of the macromolecules."

1975   Sir John W. Cornforth (Australia and U.K.) Univ. of Sussex "for his work on the stereo-chemistry of enzyme-catalyzed reactions"; **Vladimir Prelog** (Switzerland) Eidgenossische Technische Hochschule "for his research into the sterochemistry of organic molecules and reactions."

1976   William N. Lipscomb (U.S.) Harvard Univ. "for his studies on the structure of boranes illuminating problems of chemical bonding."

1977   Ilya Prigogine (Belgium) Université Libre de Bruxelles, (Univ. of Texas, U.S.) "for his contributions to nonequilibrium thermodynamics, particularly the theory of dissipative structures."

1978   Peter D. Mitchell (U.K.) Glynn Research Laboratories "for his contribution to the understanding of biological energy transfer through the formulation of the chemiosmotic theory."

1979   Herbert C. Brown (U.S.) Purdue Univ., and **Georg Wittig** (Germany) Univ. of Heidelberg "for their development of the use of boron-and-phosphorus-containing compounds, respectively, into important reagents in organic synthesis."

1980   Paul Berg (U.S.) Stanford Univ. "for his fundamental studies of the biochemistry of nucleic acids, with particular regard to recombinant-DNA"; **Walter Gilbert** (U.S.) Biological Laboratories, and **Frederick Sanger** (U.K.) MRC Laboratory of Molecular Biology "for their contributions concerning the determination of base sequences in nucleic acids."

1981   Kenichi Fukui (Japan) Kyoto Univ. and **Roald Hoffman** (U.S.) Cornell Univ. "for their theories, developed independently, concerning the course of chemical reactions."

1982   Aaron Klug (U.K.) MRC Laboratory of Molecular Biology "for his development of crystallographic electron microscopy and his structural elucidation of biologically important nucleic acid-protein complexes."

1983   Henry Taube (U.S.) Stanford Univ. "for his work on the mechanisms of electron transfer reactions, especially in metal complexes."

1984   Robert B. Merrifield (U.S.) Rockefeller Univ. "for his development of methodology for chemical synthesis on solid matrix."

1985   Herbert A. Hauptman (U.S.) Medical Foundation of Buffalo, and **Jerome Karle** (U.S.) U.S. Naval Research Laboratory "for their outstanding achievements in the development of direct methods for the determination of crystal structures."

1986   Dudley R. Herschbach (U.S.) Harvard Univ., **Yuan T. Lee** (U.S.) Univ. of California, and **John C. Polanyi** (Canada) Univ. of Toronto, "for their contributions concerning the dynamics of chemical elementary processes."

1987   Donald J. Cram (U.S.) University of California, Los Angeles, **Jean-Marie Lehn** (France) Université Louis Pasteur, and **Charles J. Pedersen** (U.S.) Du Pont Laboratory "for their development and use of molecules with structure-specific interactions with high selectivity."

1988   Johann Deisenhofer (U.S.) Howard Hughes Medical Institute, Robert Huber (W. Germany) Max-Planck-Institut, and **Hartmut Michel** (W. Germany) Max-Planck-Institut, "for their determination of the three-dimensional structure of a photosynthetic reaction centre."

1989   Sidney Altman (U.S.) Yale Univ., and **Thomas Cech** (U.S.) Univ. of Colorado for their separate discoveries of the catalytic properties of RNA.

1990   Elias James Corey (U.S.) Harvard Univ. for developing new ways to synthesize complex molecules ordinarily found in nature, work that has contributed to "the high standard of living and health and the longevity enjoyed at least in the Western world."

1991   Richard R. Ernst (Switzerland) Eidgenössische Technische Hochschule, Zurich, for his work in refining nuclear magnetic resonance spectroscopy for use in chemical analysis.

1992   Rudolph A. Marcus (U.S., b. Canada), Cal Tech., for his mathematical explanation of chemical interactions involving the transfer of electrons between molecules.

1993   Kary B. Mullis (U.S.) for his discovery, in the 1970s, of the polymerase chain reaction (PCR) that allowed scientists to make trillions of copies of DNA. **Michael Smith** (Canada), Univ. of British Columbia, for developing the technique that alters the code of organic molecules that will facilitate new medical therapies and plants that resist disease.

1994   George A. Olah (U.S., b. Hungary) Univ. of Southern California, for his discovery of new ways of breaking apart and rebuilding carbon and hydrogen compounds. He opened a wholly new field of hydrocarbon research, leading to improved fuels based on coal, methane, and petroleum.

1995   F. Sherwood Roland (U.S.) Univ. of California-Irvine, **Mario Molina** (U.S.) M.I.T., and **Paul Crutzen** (Netherlands) Max Planck Institute for Chemistry in Mainz, Germany, for their pioneering work in explaining how production and use of refrigerants and other chlorofluorocarbons deplete the ozone layer.

1996   Robert F. Curl, Jr., (U.S.) and **Richard E. Smalley** (U.S.), of Rice Univ. and **Harold W. Kroto** (U.K.) of Univ. of Sussex, for their 1985 discovery of buckminsterfullerene, or "buckyballs." Their work opened an entirely new branch of chemistry and gve scientists a greater understanding on how nature bonds carbon atoms together.

1997   Paul D. Boyer (U.S.), UCLA and **John E. Walker** (U.K.), Medical Research Council Laboratory of Molecular Biology, for demonstrating how all living things create adenosine triphosphate, a tiny molecule that stores energy and builds proteins, transmits nerve impulses, and contracts muscles. **Jens C. Skou** (Denmark), Aarhus Univ., for his discovery of sodium-potassium-stimulated adenosine triphosphate, an enzyme that maintains the balance of sodium and potassium ions in living cells.

1998   Walter Kohn (U.S., b. Austria), Univ. of California, Santa Barbara; **John A. Pople** (U.S., b U.K.), Northwestern Univ. Their achievements helped extend the mathematics of quantum mechanics to predicting specific chemical reactions and designing molecules for use in medicine and other applications.

1999   Ahmed H. Zewail (U.S., b. Egypt), CalTech, "for showing that it is possible with rapid laser technique to see how atoms in a molecule move during a chemical reaction."

2000   Alan J. Heeger (U.S.), Univ. of California at Santa Barbara; **Alan G. MacDiarmid** (U.S.), Univ. of Pennsylvania; and **Hideki Shirakawa** (Japan), Univ. of Tsukuba, for their discovery and development of a plastic that conducts electricity like a metal and may be used to increase the speed and decrease the size of computers.

2001   William S. Knowles (U.S.) and **Ryoji Noyori**, (Japan), Nagoya Univ. "for their work on chirally catalysed hydrogenation reactions." **K. Barry Sharpless** (U.S.), Scripps Research Institute, "for his work on chirally catalysed oxidation reactions," making possible the development of new drugs, insecticides, and flavoring and sweetening agents.

2002 John B. Fenn, (U.S.), Virginia Commonwealth Univ. and **Koichi Tanaka,** (Japan), Shimadzu Corporation; and **Kurt Wüthrich,** (Switzerland), Swiss Federal Institute of Technology Zürich, and The Scripps Research Institute, "for the development of methods for identification and structure analyses of biological macromolecules," through achievements in the fields of mass spectrometry and nuclear magnetic resonance spectrometry.

2003 Peter Agre, (U.S.), Johns Hopkins Univ., for discovering water channels in cell membranes; **Koichi Tanaka,** (U.S.) Rockefeller Univ., forr "Structural and mechanistic studies of ion channels.. Their

discoveries clariefied how salt and water are transported in and out of the body.

2004 Aaron Ciechanover (Israel) and **Avram Hershko** (Israel, b. Hungary) of the Israel Institute of Technology, Haifa, and **Irwin Rose** (U.S.), University of California at Irvine, "for the discovery of ubiquitin-mediated protein degradation."

2005 Yves Chauvin (France), **Robert H. Grubbs** (U.S.), and **Richard R.Schrock** (U.S.) "for the development of the metathesis method in organic synthesis."

2006 Roger D. Kornberg (U.S.) "for his studies of the molecular basis of eukaryotic transcription."

2007 Gerhard Ertl (Germany) Fritz-Haber-Institut der Max-Planck-Gesellschaft in Berlin, Germany "for his studies of chemical processes on solid surfaces."

Nobel Prizes in Physics

1901 Wilhelm C. Röntgen (Germany) Munich Univ. "in recognition of the extraordinary services he has rendered by the discovery of remarkable rays subsequently named after him."

1902 Hendrik A. Lorentz (Netherlands) Leyden Univ., and **Pieter Zeeman** (Netherlands) Amsterdam Univ. "in recognition of the extraordinary service they rendered by their researches into the influence of magnetism upon radiation phenomena."

1903 Antoine H. Becquerel (France) Ecole Polytechnique "in recognition of the extraordinary services he has rendered by the discovery of spontaneous radioactivity"; **Pierre Curie** (France) Municipal School of Industrial Physics and Chemistry and his wife, **Marie Curie,** (France, b. Poland) "in recognition of the extraordinary services they have rendered by their joint researches on the radiation phenomena discovered by Professor Henri Becquerel."

1904 Lord Rayleigh (John W. Strutt) (U.K.) Royal Institution of U.K. "for his investigations of the densities of the most important gases and for his discovery of argon in connection with these studies."

1905 Philipp E.A. Lenard (Germany) Kiel Univ. "for his work on cathode rays."

1906 Sir Joseph J. Thomas (U.K.) Cambridge Univ. "in recognition of the great merits of his theoretical and experimental investigations on the conduction of electricity by gases."

1907 Albert A. Michelson (U.S.) Univ. of Chicago "for his optical precision instruments and the spectroscopic and meteorological investigations carried out with their aid."

1908 Gabriel Lippman (France) Sorbonne Univ. "for his method of reproducing colours photographically based on the phenomenon of interference."

1909 Guglielmo Marconi (Italy) Marconi Wireless Telegraph Co., Ltd., and **Carl F. Braun** (Germany) Strasbourg Univ. "in recognition of their contributions to the development of wireless telegraphy."

1910 Johannes D. van der Waals (Netherlands) Amsterdam Univ. "for his work on the equation of state for gases and liquids."

1911 Wilhelm Wiein (Germany) Würzburg Univ. "for his discoveries regarding the laws governing the radiation of heat."

1912 Nils G. Dalén (Sweden) Swedish Gas-Accumulator Co. "for his invention of automatic regulators for use in conjunction with gas accumulators for illuminating lighthouses and buoys."

1913 Heike Kamerlingh-Onnes (Netherlands) Leyden Univ. "for his investigations on the properties of matter at low temperatures which led, inter alia, to the production of liquid helium."

1914 Max von Laue (Germany) Frankfurt-am-Main Univ. "for his discovery of the diffraction of X-rays by crystals."

1915 Sir William Henry Bragg (U.K.) London Univ. and his son **Sir William Lawrence Bragg** (U.K.) Victoria Univ. "for their services in the analysis of crystal structure by means of X-rays."

1916 No award.

1917 Charles G. Barkla (U.K.) Edinburgh Univ. "for his discovery of the characteristic Röntgen radiation of the elements."

1918 Max K.E.L. Planck (Germany) Berlin Univ. "in recognition of the services he rendered to the advancement of Physics by his discovery of energy quanta."

1919 Johannes Stark (Germany) Greifswald Univ. "for his discovery of the Doppler effect in canal rays and the splitting of spectral lines in electric fields."

1920 Charles E. Guillaume (Switzerland) International Bureau of Weights and Measurers "in recognition of the service he has rendered to precision measurements in physics by his discovery of anomalies in nickel steel alloys."

1921 Albert Einstein (Germany) Kaiser-Wilhelm-Institut für Physik (now Max-Panck-Institut) "for his services to theoretical physics, and especially for his discovery of the law of the photoelectric effect."

1922 Niels Bohr (Denmark) Copenhagen Univ. "for his services in the investigation of the structure of atoms and of the radiation emanating from them."

1923 Robert A. Millikan (U.S.) California Institute of Technology) "for his work on the elementary charge of electricity and on the photoelectric effect."

1924 Karl M.G. Siegbahn (Sweden) Uppsala Univ. "for his discoveries and research in the field of X-ray spectroscopy."

1925 James Franck (Germany) Goettingen Univ., and **Gustav Hertz** (Germany) Halle Univ. "for their discovery of the laws of governing the impact of an electron upon an atom."

1926 Jean B. Perrin (France) Sorbonne Univ. "for his work on the discontinuous structure of matter, and especially for his discovery of sedimentation equilibrium."

1927 Arthur H. Compton (U.S.) Univ. of Chicago "for his discovery of the effect named after him"; **Charles T.R. Wilson** (U.K.) Cambridge Univ. "for his method of making the paths of electrically charged particles visible by condensation of vapor."

1928 Sir Own W. Richardson (U.K.) London Univ. "for his work on the thermionic phenomenon and especially for the discovery of the law named after him."

1929 Prince Louis-Victor de Broglie (France) Sorbonne Univ. "for his discovery of the wave nature of electrons."

1930 Sir Chandrasekhara V. Raman (India) Calcutta Univ. "for his work on the scattering of light and for the discovery of the effect names after him."

1931 No award.

1932 Werner Heisenberg (Germany) Leipzig Univ. "for the creation of quantum mechanics, the application of which, has, inter alia, led to the discovery of the allotropic forms of hydrogen."

1933 Edwin Schrödinger (Austria) Berlin Univ. and **Paul A.M. Dirac** (U.K.) Cambridge Univ. "for the discovery of new productive forms of atomic theory."

1934 No award

1935 Sir James Chadwick (U.K.) Liverpool Univ. "for his discovery of the neutron."

1936 Victor F. Hess (Austria) Innsbruck Univ. "for his discovery of cosmic radiation"; **Carl D. Anderson** (U.S.) California Institute of Technology "for his discovery of the positron."

1937 Clinton J. Davisson (U.S.) Bell Telephone Laboratories, and **Sir George P. Thomson** (U.K.) London Univ. "for their experimental discovery of the diffraction of electrons by crystals."

1938 Enrico Fermi (Italy) Rome Univ. "for his demonstration of the existence of new radioactive elements produced by neutron irradiation, and for his related discovery of nuclear reactions brought about by slow neutrons."

1939 Ernest O. Lawrence (U.S.) Univ. of California, Berkeley "for the invention and development of the cyclotron and for results obtained with it, especially with regard to artificial radioactive elements."

1940–1942 No awards given.

1943 Otto Stern (U.S.) Carnegie Institute of Technology "for his contribution to the development of the molecular ray method and his discovery of the magnetic moment of the proton."

1944 Isidor I. Rabi (U.S.) Columbia Univ. "for his resonance method for recording the magnetic properties of atomic nuclei."

1945 Wolfgang Pauli (Austria) Princeton Univ. "for the discovery of the Exclusion Principle, also called the Pauli Principle."

1946 Percy W. Bridgman (U.S.) Harvard Univ. "for the invention of an apparatus to produce extremely high pressures, and for the discoveries he made therewith in the field of high-pressure physics."

1947 Sir Edward V. Appleton (U.K.) Dept. of Scientific and Industrial Research "for his investigations of the physics of the upper atmosphere, especially the so-called Appleton layer."

1948 Lord Patrick M.S. Blackett (U.K.) Victoria Univ. "for his development of the Wilson cloud chamber method, and his discoveries therewith in the fields of nuclear physics and cosmic radiation."

1949 Hideki Yukawa (Japan) Kyoto Imperial Univ. "for his prediction of the existence of mesons on the basis of theoretical work on nuclear forces."

1950 Cecil F. Powell (U.K.) Bristol Univ. "for his development of the photographic method of studying nuclear processes and his discoveries regarding mesons made with this method."

1951 Sir John D. Cockcroft (U.K.) Atomic Energy Research Establishment, and **Ernest T.S. Walton** (Ireland) Dublin Univ. "for their pioneer work on the transmutation of atomic nuclei by artificially accelerated atomic particles."

1952 Felix Block (U.S.) Stanford Univ., and **Edward M. Purcell** (U.S.) Harvard Univ. "for their development of new methods for nuclear magnetic precision measurements and discoveries in connection therewith."

1953 Frits (Frederik) Zernike (Netherlands) Groningern Univ. "for his demonstration of the phase contrast method, especially for his invention of the phase contrast microscope."

1954 Max Born (U.K.) Edinburgh Univ. "for his fundamental research in quantum mechanics, especially for his statistical interpretation of the wavefunction"; **Walther Bothe** (Germany) Heidelbery Univ., Max-Planck-Institut "for the coincidence method and his discoveries made therewith."

1955 Willis E. Lamb (U.S.) Stanford Univ. "for his discoveries concerning the fine structure of the hydrogen spectrum"; **Polykarp Kusch** (U.S.) Columbia Univ. "for his precision determination of the magnetic moment of the electron."

1956 William Shockley (U.S.) Semiconductor Laboratory of Beckman Instruments, Inc., **John Bardeen** (U.S.) Univ. of Illinois, and **Walter H. Brattain** (U.S.) Bell Telephone Laboratories for research on semiconductors and discovery of "the transistor effect."

1957 Chen N. Yang (China) Institute for Advanced Study (Princeton, N.J.) and **Tsung-Dao Lee** (China) Columbia Univ. "for their penetrating investigation of the so-called parity laws which has led to important discoveries regarding the elementary particles."

1958 Pavel A. Cherenkov (USSR) Physics Institute of USSR Academy of Sciences, **Il'jà M.Frank** (USSR) Academy of Sciences, and **Igor J. Tamm** (USSR) Univ. of Moscow and Physics Institute of USSR Academy of Sciences "for their discovery and the interpretation of the Cherenkov effect."

1959 Emillio G. Segrè (U.S.) Univ. of California, Berkeley, and **Owen Chamberlain** (U.S.) Univ. of California, Berkeley "for their discovery of the antiproton."

1960 Donald A. Glaser (U.S.) Univ. of California, Berkeley "for the invention of the bubble chamber."

1961 Robert Hofstadter (U.S.) Stanford Univ. "for his pioneering studies of electron scattering in atomic nuclei and for his thereby achieved discoveries concerning the structure of the nucleons"; **Rudolf L. Mössbauer** (Germany) Technische Hochschule (Munich), and California Institute of Technology "for his researches concerning the resonance absorption of gamma radiation and his discovery in this connection of the effect which bears his name."

1962 Lev D. Landau (USSR) Academy of Sciences "for his pioneering theories for condensed matter, especially liquid helium."

1963 Eugene P. Wigner (U.S.) Princeton Univ. "for his contributions to the theory of the atomic nucleus and the elementary particles, particularly through the discovery and application of fundamental symmetry principles"; **Maria Goeppert-Mayer** (U.S.) Univ. of California, La Jolla, and **J. Hans D. Jensen** (Germany) Univ. of Heidelberg "for their discoveries concerning nuclear shell structure."

1964 Charles H. Townes (U.S.) M.I.T., **Nikolai G. Basov** (USSR) Lebedev Institute for Physics, and **Aleksandre M. Prochorov** (USSR) Lebedev Institute for Physics "for fundamental work in the field of quantum electronics, which has led to the construction of oscillators and amplifiers based on the maser-laser-principle."

1965 Schin'ichiro Tomonaga (Japan) Toyko Univ., **Julian Schwinger** (U.S.) Harvard Univ., and **Richard P. Feynman** (U.S.) California Institute of Technology "for their fundamental work in quantum electrodynamcis, with deep-ploughing consequences for the physics of elementary particles."

1966 Alfred Kastier (France) Ecole Normale Supérieure, Université de Paris "for the discovery and development of optical methods for studying hertzian resonance in atoms."

1967 Hans A. Bethe (U.S.) Cornell Univ. "for his contributions to the theory of nuclear reactions, especially his discoveries concerning the energy production in stars."

1968 Luis W. Alvarez (U.S.) Univ. of California, Berkeley "for his decisive contributions to elementary particle physics, in particular the discovery of a large number of resonance states, made possible through his development of the technique of using hydrogen bubble chamber and data analysis."

1969 Murray Gell-Mann (U.S.) California Institute of Technology "for his contributions and discoveries concerning the classification of elementary particles and their interactions."

1970 Hannes Alfvén (Sweden) Royal Institute of Technology "for fundamental work and discoveries in magneto-hydrodynamics with fruitful applications in different parts of plasma physics"; **Louis Neel** (France) Univ. of Grenoble "for fundamental work and discoveries concerning antiferromagnetism and ferrimagetism which have led to important applications in solid-state physics."

1971 Dennis Gabor (U.K.) Imperial College of Science and Technology "for his invention and development of the holographic method."

1972 John Bardeen (U.S.) Univ. of Illinois, **Leon N. Cooper** (U.S.) Brown Univ., and J. **Robert Schrieffer** (U.S.) Univ. of Pennsylvania "for their jointly developed theory of superconductivity, usually called the BCS-theory."

1973 Leo Esaki (Japan) IBM Thomas J. Watson Research Center (New York), and **Ivar Giaever** (U.S.) General Electric Co. "for their experimental discoveries regarding tunneling phenomena in semiconductors and superconductors, respectively"; **Brian D. Josephson** (U.K.) Cambridge Univ. "for his theoretical predictions of the properties of a supercurrent through a tunnel barrier, in particular those phenomena which are generally known as the Josephson effects."

1974 Sir Martin Ryle (U.K.) and **Antony Hewish** (U.K.), both of Cambridge Univ., "for their pioneering research in radio astrophysics: Ryle for his observations and inventions, in particular of the aperture synthesis technique, and Hewish for his decisive role in the discovery of pulsars."

1975 Aage Bohr (Denmark) Niels Bohr Institute, **Ben Mottelson** (Denmark) Nordita, and **James Rainwater** (U.S.) Columbia Univ. "for the discovery of the connection between collective motion and particle motion in atomic nuclei and the development of the theory of the structure of the atomic nucleus based on this connection."

1976 Burton Richter (U.S.) Stanford Linear Accelerator Center, and **Samuel C.C. Ting** (U.S.) M.I.T. "for their pioneering work in the discovery of a heavy elementary particle of a new kind."

1977 Philip W. Anderson (U.S.) Bell Laboratories, **Sir Nevill F. Mott** (U.K.) Cambridge Univ. and **John H. van Vleck** (U.S.) Harvard Univ. "for their fundamental theoretical investigations of the electronic structure of magnetic and disordered systems."

1978 Peter L. Kapitsa (USSR) Academy of Sciences "for his basic inventions and discoveries in the area of low-temperature physics, **Arno A. Penzias** (U.S.) Bell Laboratories, and **Robert W. Wilson** (U.S.) Bell Laboratories "for their discovery of cosmic microwave background radiation."

1979 Sheldon L. Glashow (U.S.) Lyman Laboratory, Harvard Univ., **Abdus Salam** (Pakistan) International Centre for Theoretical Physics (Italy) and Imperial College of Science and Technology (London), and **Steven Weinberg** (U.S.) Harvard Univ. "for their contributions to the theory of the unified weak and electromagnetic interaction between elementary particles, including, inter alia, the predictions of the weak neutral current."

1980 James W. Cronin (U.S.) Univ. of Chicago, and **Val L. Fitch** (U.S.) Princeton Univ. "for the dis-covery of violations of fundamental symmetry principles in the decay of neutral K-mesons."

1981 Nicolaas Bloembergen (U.S.) Harvard Univ., and **Arthur L. Schawlow** (U.S.) Stanford Univ. "for their contributions to the development of laser spectroscopy"; **Kai M. Siegbahn** (Sweden) Uppsala Univ. "for his contribution to the development of high-resolution electron spectroscopy."

1982 Kenneth G. Wilson (U.S.) Cornell Univ. "for his theory for critical phenomena in connection with phase transitions."

1983 Subrahmanyan Chandrasekhar (U.S.) Univ. of Chicago "for his theoretical studies of the physical processes of importance to the structure and evolution of the stars"; **William A. Fowler** (U.S.) California Institute of Technology for his "studies of the nuclear reactions of importance in the formation of the chemical elements in the universe."

1984 Carlo Rubbia (Italy) CERN (Switzerland), and **Simon van der Meer** (Netherlands) CERN (Switzerland) "for their decisive contributions to the discovery of the field particles W and Z, communicators of weak interaction."

1985 Klaus von Klitzing (W. Germany) Max-Planck-Institut for Solid State Research "for the discovery of the quantized Hall effect."

1986 Ernst Ruska (W. Germany) Fritz-Haber-Institut der Max-Planck-Gesellschaft "for his fundamental work in electron optics, and for the design of the first electron microscope"; **Gerd Binnig** (W. Germany) IBM Zurich Research Laboratory and **Heinrich Rohrer** (Switzerland) IBM Zurich Research Laboratory "for their design of the scanning tunneling microscope."

1987 Georg J. Bednorz (Switzerland) IBM Zurich research Laboratory, and **Dr. K. Alex Müller** (Switzerland) IBM Zurich Research Laboratory "for the discovery of new superconducting materials."

1988 Leon M. Lederman (U.S.) Fermi National Accelerator Laboratory, **Melvin Schwartz** (U.S.) Digital Pathways, Inc., and **Jack Steinberger** (Switzerland) "for the neutrino beam method and the demonstration of the doublet structure of the leptons through the discovery of the muon neutrino."

1989 Norman R. Ramsey (U.S.) Harvard Univ. "for the invention of the separated oscillatory fields method and its use in . . . atomic clocks"; **Hans G. Dehmelt** (U.S.) Univ. of Washington, and **Wolfgang Paul** (W. Germany) Univ. of Bonn "for the development of the ion trap technique," which allows detailed study of subatomic particles."

1990 Richard E. Taylor (Can.), Stanford U.; **Jerome I. Friedman** (U.S.) MIT; and **Henry W. Kendall** (U.S.) MIT, whose experiments between 1967 and 1973 confirmed the existence of quarks, the fundamental building blocks of matter.

1991 Pierre-Gilles de Gennes (France), Collège de France, Paris, for his discoveries about the ordering of molecules in a variety of substances but especially liquid crystals, where his work has helped in understanding superconductivity.

1992 George Charpak (France, b. Poland), affiliated with CERN, the accelerator complex, where he developed electronic detectors that traced the paths of subatomic particles with lightning speed.

1993 Joseph H. Taylor (U.S.), Princeton Univ., and **Russel A. Hulse** (U.S.), Princeton Plasma Physics Laboratory, for their discovery of a binary pulsar and their later success in measuring its pulse rate.

1994 Clifford G. Shull (U.S.) MIT, and **Bertram N. Brockhouse** (Canada) McMaster Univ., for experiments in the 1940s and '50s that exploited the penetrating power of low-energy neutron beams produced by nuclear reactors. Neutron beams are widely used to explore the atomic structure of matter.

1995 Martin L. Perl (U.S.) Stanford Univ. Linear Accelerator Center, and **Frederick Reines** (U.S.) Los Alamos National Laboratory, for their separate discoveries of "two of nature's most remarkable subatomic particles," Perl's discovery of the tau in the 1970's and Reines's discovery of the neutrino in the 1950's.

1996   Robert C. Richardson (U.S.) and **David M. Lee** (U.S.) of Cornell Univ., and **Douglas S. Osheroff** (U.S.) Stanford Univ., for their 1972 discovery of superfluiditiy in a rare form of helium which may offer insights into the formation of galaxies.

1997   Steven Chu (U.S.) Stanford Univ., **Claude Cohen-Tannoudji** (France), Collège de France, and **William D. Phillips** (U.S.), National Institute of Standards and Technology, for development of a method to trap individual atoms, which allow them to be studied in greater detail.

1998   Robert B. Laughlin (U.S.), Stanford Univ., **Horst L. Störmer** (U.S.), Bell Laboratories; **Daniel Tsui** (U.S.), Princeton Univ., for their discovery of the fractional quantum Hall effect, the culmination of studies of magnetic fields dating back to 1897.

1999   Gerardus 't Hooft (Netherlands), Univ. of Utrecht, and **Martinus J.G. Veltman** (Netherlands) Univ. of Michigan, for placing the theory of particle physics on firm mathematical ground.

2000   Jack S. Kilby (U.S.), Texas Instruments, for his contribution to the invention of the integrated circuit, a.k.a. the computer chip; **Zhores I. Alferov** (Russia), A.F. Ioffe Physico-Technical Institute, St. Petersburg, and **Herbert Kroemer,** (U.S.), Univ. of California at Santa Barbara, for their invention of components called heterostructures, which are used in high-speed electronic devices.

2001   Eric A. Cornell (U.S.) and **Carl E. Wieman** (U.S.) both of the Joint Institute for Laboratory Astrophysics, Boulder, Colo., and **Wolfgang Ketterle** (Germany), M.I.T., "for the achievement of Bose-Einstein condensation in dilute gases of alkali atoms, and for early fundamental studies of the properties of the condensates."

2002   Raymond Davis Jr., (U.S.), Univ. of Pennsylvania and **Masatoshi Koshiba,** (Japan), Univ. of Tokyo; and **Riccardo Giacconi,** (U.S., B. Italy), Univ. of Milan, "for pioneering contributions to astrophysics." Davis and Koshiba's work led to the detection of cosmic neutrinos, Giacconi built the first X-ray telescopes.

2003   Alexei Abrikosov (U.S. and Russia), Argonne (Illinois) National Laboratory, **Vitaly L. Ginzburg** (Russia), P.N. Ledbedev Physical Institute, Moscow, and **Anthony J. Leggett** (U.S. and U.K.), Univ. of Illinois, for their "pioneering contributions to the theory of superconductors and superfluids."

2004   David J. Gross (U.S.), Kavli Institute for Theoretical Physics, University of California at Santa Barbara; **H. David Politzer** (U.S.), California Institute of Technology; and **Frank Wilczek** (U.S.), M.I.T., "for their discovery of asymptotic freedom in the theory of strong interaction."

2005   Roy T. Glauber (U.S.) "for his contribution to the quantum theory of optical coherence." **John L. Hall** (U.S.) and **Theodor W. Hänsch** (Germany) " for their contributions to the development of laser-based precision spectroscopy, including the optical frequency comb technique."

2006   John C. Mather and **George F. Smoot** (U.S.) "for their discovery of the blackbody form and anisotropy of the cosmic microwave background radiation."

2007   Albert Fert (France) Université Paris-Sud in Orsay, France and **Peter Grünberg** (Germany) Forschungszentrum Jülich in Jülich, Germany "for the discovery of Giant Magnetoresistance."

Nobel Prizes in Literature

1901   Sully Prudhomme (pen name of René F.A. Prudhomme) (France) "in special recognition of his poetic composition."

1902   Christian M.T. Mommsen (Germany) "the greatest living master of the art of historical writing, with special reference to his monumental work, *A History of Rome.*

1903   Bjørstjerne M. Bjørnson (Norway) for "his noble, magnificent, and versatile poetry which has always been distinguished by both the freshness of its inspiration and the rare purity of its spirit."

1904   Frédéric Mistral (France) "in recognition of the fresh originality and true inspiration of his poetic production, which faithfully reflects the natural scenery and native spirit of his people, and, in addition, his significant work as a Provençal philologist." **José Echegaray y Eizaguirre** (Spain) "in recognition of the numerous and brilliant compositions which, in an individual and original manner, have revived the great traditions of the Spanish drama."

1905   Henryk Sienkiewicz (Poland) "because of his outstanding merits as an epic writer."

1906   Giosué Carducci (Italy) "as a tribute to the creative energy, freshness of style, and lyrical force which characterize his poetic masterpieces."

1907   Rudyard Kipling (U.K.) "in consideration of the power of observation, originality of imagination, virility of ideas, and remarkable talent for narration which characterize the creations of this world-famous author."

1908   Rudolf C. Eucken (Germany) "in recognition of his earnest search for truth, his penetrating power of thought, his wide range of vision, and the warmth and strength in presentation. . ."

1909   Selma O.L. Lagerlöf (Sweden) "in appreciation of the lofty idealism, vivid imagination, and spiritual perception that characterize her writings."

1910   Paul J.L. Heyse (Germany) "as a tribute to the consummate artistry, permeated with idealism, which he has demonstrated during his long productive career as lyric poet, dramatist, novelist, and writer of world-renowned short stories."

1911   Count Maurice (Mooris) P.M.B. Maeterlinck (Belgium) "in appreciation of his many-sided literary activities, and especially of his dramatic works, which are distinguished by a wealth of imagination and by a poetic fancy."

1912   Gerhart J.R. Hauptmann (Germany) "primarily in recognition of his fruitful, varied, and outstanding production in the realm of dramatic art."

1913   Rabindranath Tagore (India) "because of his profoundly sensitive, fresh, and beautiful verse, by which, with consummate skill, he has made his poetic thought, expressed in his own English words, a part of the literature of the West."

1914   No award

1915   Romain Rolland (France) "as a tribute to the lofty idealism of his literary production and to the sympathy and love of truth with which he has described different types of human beings."

1916   Carl G.V. von Heidenstam (Sweden) "in recognition of his significance as the leading representative of a new era in our literature."

1917   Karl A. Gjellerup (Denmark) "for his varied and rich poetry, which is inspired by lofty ideals"; **Henrik Pontoppidan** (Denmark) "for his authentic descriptions of presentday life in Denmark."

1918   No award

919   Carl F.G. Spitteler (Switzerland) "in special ppreciation of his epic, *Olympian Spring.*"
920   Knut P. Hamsun (Norway) "for his monumental work, *Growth of the Soil.*"
921   Anatole France *(pen name of Jacques A. Thibault)* (France) "in recognition of his brilliant literary achievements, characterized as they are by a nobility of style, a profound human sympathy, grace, and a true Gallic temperament."
922   Jacinto Benavente (Spain) "for the happy manner in which he has continued the illustrious traditions of the Spanish drama."
1923   William Butler Yeats (Ireland) "for his always inspired poetry, which in a highly artistic form gives expression to the spirit of a whole nation."
1924   Wladyslaw S. Reymont (pen name of Reyment) (Poland) "for his great national epic, *The Peasants.*"
1925   George Bernard Shaw (U.K.) "for his work which is marked by both idealism and humanity, its stimulating satire often being infused with a singular poetic beauty."
1926   Grazia Deledda (pen name of Grazia Madesani (Italy) "for her idealistically inspired writings, which picture the life on her native island and with depth and sympathy deal with human problems."
1927   Henri Bergson (France) "in recognition of his rich and vitalizing ideas."
1928   Sigrid Undset (Norway) "principally for her powerful descriptions of Northern life during the Middle Ages."
1929   Thomas Mann (Germany) "principally for his great novel *Buddenbrooks.*"
1930   Sinclair Lewis (U.S.) "for his vigorous and graphic art of description and his ability to create, with wit and humor, new types of characters."
1931   Erik A. Karlfeldt (Sweden) for his poetry.
1932   John Galsworthy (U.K.) "for his distinguished art of narration which takes its highest form in *The Forsyte Saga.*"
1933   Ivan A. Bunin (stateless domicile in France) "for the strict artistry with which he has carried on the classical Russian traditions in prose writing."
1934   Luigi Pirandello (Italy) "for his bold and ingenious revival of dramatic art."
1935   No award
1936   Eugene G. O'Neill (U.S.) "for the power, honesty, and deep-felt emotions of his dramatic works, which embody an original concept of tragedy."
1937   Roger Martin du Gard (France) "for the artistic power and truth with which he has depicted human conflict as well as some fundamental aspects of contemporary life in his novel-cycle *Les Thibault.*"
1938   Pearl Buck (pen name of Pearl Walsh) (U.S.) "for her rich and truly epic descriptions of peasant life in China and for her biographical masterpieces."
1939   Frans E. Sillanpää (Finland) "for his deep understanding of his country's peasantry and the exquisite art with which he has portrayed their way of life and their relationship with Nature."
1940–1943   No awards given.
1944   Johannes V. Jensen (Denmark) "for the rare strength and fertility of his poetic imagination."
1945   Gabriela Mistral (pen name of Lucila Godoy y Alcayaga) (Chile) "for her lyric poetry which, has made her name a symbol of the idealistic aspirations of the entire Latin American world."
1946   Hermann Hesse (Switzerland) "for his inspired writings which exemplify the classical humanitarian ideals and high qualities of style."
1947   André P.G. Gide (France) "for his writings in which human problems and conditions have been presented with a fearless love of truth and keen psychological insight."
1948   Thomas S. Eliot (U.K.) for his "outstanding, pioneer contribution to present-day poetry."

1949   William Faulkner (U.S.) ":for his powerful and artistically unique contribution to the modern American novel."
1950   Earl (Bertrand) Russell (U.K.) "in recognition of his varied and significant writings in which he champions humanitarian ideals and freedom of thought."
1951   Pär Fabian Lägerkvist (Sweden) "for the artistic vigour and true independence of mind with which he endeavours in his poetry to find answers to the eternal questions confronting mankind."
1952   François Mauriac (France) "for the deep spiritual insight and the artistic intensity with which he has in his novels penetrated the drama of human life."
1953   Sir Winston L.S. Churchill (U.K.) "for his mastery of historical and biographical description as well as for brilliant oratory in defending exalted human values."
1954   Ernest M. Hemingway (U.S.) "for his mastery of the art of narrative, most recently demonstrated in *The Old Man and the Sea,* and for the influence that he has exerted on contemporary style."
1955   Halldór K. Laxness (Iceland) "for his vivid epic power which has renewed the great narrative art of Iceland."
1956   Juan R. Jiménez (Puerto Rico, b. Spain) "for his lyrical poetry, which in Spanish language constitutes an example of high spirit and artistic purity."
1957   Albert Camus (France) "for his important literary production, which with clearsighted earnestness illuminates the problems of the human conscience in our times."
1958   Boris L. Pasternak (USSR) "for his important achievement both in contemporary lyrical poetry and in the field of the great Russian epic tradition." (Declined the prize.)
1959   Salvatore Quasimodo (Italy) "for his lyrical poetry, which with classical fire expresses the tragic experience of life in our own times."
1960   Saint-John Perse (pen name of Alexis Léger) (France) "for the soaring flight and the evocative imagery of his poetry which in a visionary fashion reflects the conditions of our time."
1961   Ivo Andric (Yugoslavia) "for the epic force with which he has traced themes and depicted human destinies drawn from the history of his country."
1962   John Steinbeck (U.S.) "for his realistic and imaginative writings, combining as they do sympathetic humour and keen social perception."
1963   Giorgos Seferis (pen name of Giorgos Seferiadis) (Greece) "for his eminent lyrical writing, inspired by a deep feeling for the Hellenic world of culture."
1964   Jean-Paul Sartre (France) "for his work which, rich in ideas and filled with the spirit of freedom and the quest for truth, has exerted a far-reaching influence on our age." (Declined the prize.)
1965   Michail A. Sholokhov (U.S.S.R.) "for the artistic power and integrity with which, in his epic of the Don, he has given expression to a historic phase in the life of the Russian people."
1966   Shmuel U. Agnon (Israel) "for his profoundly characteristic narrative art with motifs from the life of the Jewish people; **Nelly Sachs** (Germany, domiciled in Sweden) " for her outstanding lyrical and dramatic writing, which interprets Israel's destiny with touching strength."
1967   Miguel A. Asturias (Guatemala) "for his vivid literary achievement, deep-rooted in the national traits and traditions of Indian peoples of Latin America."
1968   Yasunari Kawabata (Japan) "for his narrative mastery, which with great sensibility expresses the essence of the Japanese mind."

1969   Samuel Beckett (Ireland) "for his writing, which—in new forms for the novel and drama—in the destitution of modern man acquires its elevation."

1970   Alexander Solzhenitsyn (USSR) "for the ethical force with which he has pursued the indispensable traditions of Russian literature."

1971   Pablo Neruda (pen name of Neftalí Ricardo Reyes Basoalto) (Chile) "for a poetry that brings alive a continent's destiny and dreams."

1972   Heinrich Böll (West Germany) "for his writing which through its combination of a broad perspective on his time and a sensitive skill in characterization has contributed to a renewal of German literature."

1973   Patrick White (Australia, b. U.K.) "for an epic and psychological narrative art which has introduced a new continent into literature."

1974   Eyvind Johnson (Sweden) "for a narrative art, far-seeing in lands and ages, in the service of freedom"; **Harry Martinson** (Sweden) "for writings that catch the dewdrop and reflect the cosmos."

1975   Eugenio Montale (Italy) "for his distinctive poetry which, with great artistic sensitivity, has interpreted human values under the sign of an outlook on life with no illusions."

1976   Saul Bellow (U.S.) "for the human understanding and subtle analysis of contemporary culture."

1977   Vincente Aleixandre (Spain) "for a creative poetic writing which illuminates man's condition in the cosmos and in present-day society, at the same time representing the great renewal of the traditions of Spanish poetry between the wars."

1978   Isaac Bashevis Singer (U.S., b. Poland) "for his impassioned narrative art which, with roots in a Polish-Jewish cultural tradition, brings universal human conditions to life."

1979   Odysseus Elytis (pen name of Odysseus Alepoudhelis) (Greece) "for his poetry, which against the background of Greek tradition, depicts man's struggle for freedom and creativeness."

1980   Czeslaw Milosz (U.S. and Poland) "who with uncompromising clear-sightedness voices man's exposed condition in a world of severe conflicts."

1981   Elias Canetti (U.K., b. Bulgaria) "for writings marked by a broad outlook, a wealth of ideas, and artistic power."

1982   Gabriel García Marquez (Colombia) "for his novels and short stories, in which the fantastic and the realistic are combined in a richly composed world of imagination, reflecting a continent's life and conflicts."

1983   William Golding (U.K.) "for his novels, which illuminate the human condition in the world of today."

1984   Jaroslav Seifert (Czechoslovakia) "for his poetry which, endowed with freshness, sensuality, and rich inventiveness, provides a liberating image of the indomitable spirit and versatility of man."

1985   Claude Simon (France) "who in his novel combines the poet's and the painter's creativeness with a deepened awareness of time in the depiction of the human condition."

1986   Wole Soyinka (Nigeria) "who in a wide cultural perspective and with poetic overtones fashions the drama of existence."

1987   Joseph Brodsky (U.S., b. U.S.S.R.) "for his all-embracing authorship imbued with clarity of thought and poetic intensity."

1988   Naguib Mahfouz (Egypt) "who through works rich in nuance, has formed an Arabian narrative art that applies to all mankind."

1989   Camilo José Cela (Spain) a novelist whose "rich and inventive prose, forms a challenging vision of man's vulnerability." His most famous work is *The Family of Pascual Duarte* (1942).

1990   Octavio Paz (Mexico) poet and social essayist. Volumes include *The Labyrinth of Solitude* (1950), *Sunstone* (1957), and *Sor Juana: Or, th* *Traps of Faith* (1990).

1991   Nadine Gordimer (South Africa) for her "i_ volvement on behalf of literature and free speech _ a police state where censorship and persecution _ books and people exist."

1992   Derek Walcott (West Indies, b. St. Lucia_ poet and playwright whose works evoke the cultur_ diversity of the Carribean "but through them h_ speaks to each and every one of us."

1993   Toni Morrison (U.S.), whose novels abou_ racial prejudice are "characterized by visionar_ force and poetic import."

1994   Kenzaburo Oe (Japan), best known for hi_ accounts of the atomic bombing of Hiroshima. The poetic force of his writing "creates an imagine_ world where life and myth condense to form a dis_ concerting picture of the human predicament."

1995   Seamus Heaney (Ireland), poet and essayist, "for works of lyrical beauty and ethical depth, which exalt everyday miracles and the living past."

1996   Wislawa Szymborska (Poland), a poet whose work contemplates the oddities of daily life.

1997   Dario Fo, (Italy), a leftist playwright, best known for biting political satires (*Can't Pay, Won't Pay* and *Accidental Death of an Anarchist*), which brought threats of censure and condemnation from the Italian government and the Catholic Church.

1998   José Saramago (Portugal), for his richly imaginative works that often use the supernatural and irrational to address questions of faith. Best known novels include: *Baltasar and Blimunda* (1982), *The Year of the Death of Ricardo Reis* (1984).

1999   Günter Grass (Germany) "whose frolicsome black fables portray the forgotten face of history." His epic 1959 novel, *The Tin Drum* addressed the uncomfortable issue of the German national identity through the Nazi era.

2000   Gao Xingjian (France, b. China), one of the most important Chinese dramatists of the 20th century, whose most significant works have been banned in China since the 1980s.

2001   V.S. Naipaul (U.K., b. Trinidad) His fiction, including *A House for Mr. Biswas* (1961) and *The Enigma of Arrival* (1987) is often highly autobiographical, exploring the challenges faced by postcolonial societies like his ancestral home of India.

2002   Imre Kertész, (Hungary) "for writing that upholds the fragile experience of the individual against the barbaric arbitrariness of history." His most important work is *Fateless*, a novel about a man who, like Kertész himself, is forced to spend his youth in a concentration camp.

2003   J.M. Coetzee (South Africa) "who in innumerable guises portrays the surprising involvement of the outsider." His novels have often focused on apartheid; first author to win the Booker Prize twice, for *Life and Times for Michael K.* (1983) and *Disgrace* (1999).

2004   Elfriede Jelinek (Austria), "for her musical flow of voices and counter-voices in novels and plays that with extraordinary linguistic zeal reveal the absurdity of society's clichés and their subjugating power." Her best-known novel is the semi-autobiographical *The Piano Teacher*, which was translated into English in 1988.

2005   Harold Pinter (U.K.) "who in his plays uncovers the precipice under everyday prattle and forces entry into oppression's closed rooms."

2006   Orhan Pamuk (Turkey) "who in the quest for the melancholic soul of his native city has discovered new symbols for the clash and interlacing of cultures."

2007   Doris Lessing (U.K., b. Persia), "that epicist of the female experience, who with skepticism, fire and visionary power has subjected a divided civilization to scrutiny."

THE NCAA

National Collegiate Athletic Association (NCAA)
One NCAA Place
700 W. Washington St.
Indianapolis, Ind. 46204
(317) 917–6222
www.ncaa.org

The NCAA acts as the governing body of intercollegiate athletics, setting the playing rules for each sport, and eligibility standards for athletes.

COLLEGE FOOTBALL

NCAA National Football Champions

For many years, college football selected its national champion through an arcane structure of bowl games and two press association polls (one of coaches, the other of writers), which often did not agree with each other, creating co-champions and arguments about which was the better team.

In 1998, the NCAA adopted the Bowl Alliance, in which the top two teams (as determined by the same two polls) meet in a national championship game that rotates annually among the Rose, Fiesta, Orange, and Sugar Bowls. But in 2003, three teams finished the season with only one loss. Louisiana State defeated Oklahoma in the National Championship game, but the Associated Press poll of writers gave its top ranking to USC, which had been denied the chance to play in the title game.

Year	Team	Year	Team	Year	Team
1936	Minnesota	1960	Minnesota	1984	B.Y.U.
1937	Pittsburgh	1961	Alabama	1985	Oklahoma
1938	T.C.U.	1962	U.S.C.	1986	Penn State
1939	Texas A&M	1963	Texas	1987	Miami (Fla.)
1940	Minnesota	1964	Alabama	1988	Notre Dame
1941	Minnesota	1965	Alabama and Michigan St.	1989	Miami (Fla.)
1942	Ohio State	1966	Notre Dame	1990	Colo. and Georgia Tech
1943	Notre Dame	1967	U.S.C.	1991	Miami and Washington
1944	Army	1968	Ohio State	1992	Alabama
1945	Army	1969	Texas	1993	Florida State
1946	Notre Dame	1970	Nebraska and Texas	1994	Nebraska
1947	Notre Dame	1971	Nebraska	1995	Nebraska
1948	Michigan	1972	U.S.C.	1996	Florida
1949	Notre Dame	1973	Notre Dame and Alabama	1997	Michigan and Nebraska
1950	Oklahoma	1974	U.S.C. and Oklahoma	1998	Tennessee
1951	Tennessee	1975	Oklahoma	1999	Florida State
1952	Michigan St.	1976	Pittsburgh	2000	Oklahoma
1953	Maryland	1977	Notre Dame	2001	Miami (Fla.)
1954	Ohio State and U.C.L.A.	1978	Alabama and U.S.C.	2002	Ohio State
1955	Oklahoma	1979	Alabama	2003	Louisiana State and U.S.C.
1956	Oklahoma	1980	Georgia	2004	U.S.C.
1957	Auburn and Ohio State	1981	Clemson	2005	Texas
1958	Louisiana St.	1982	Penn State	2006	Florida
1959	Syracuse	1983	Miami (Fla.)	2007	Louisiana State

Source: NCAA.

NCAA National Championship Game Results, 1998–2007

Year	Bowl	Score	Year	Bowl	Score
1998	Fiesta	Tennessee 23, Florida State, 16	2003	Sugar	Louisiana State 21, Oklahoma 14
1999	Sugar	Florida State 46, Virginia Tech 29	2004	Orange	U.S.C. 55, Oklahoma 19
2000	Orange	Oklahoma 13, Florida State 2	2005	Rose	Texas 41, U.S.C. 38
2001	Rose	Miami (Fla.) 37, Nebraska 14	2006	BCS	Florida 41, Ohio State 14
2002	Fiesta	Ohio State 31, Miami (Fla.) 24 (2OT)	2007	BCS	LSU 38, Ohio State 24

Note: The National Championship game is played in January of the following year. Years shown refer to the year of the championship.

NCAA Football-Major Bowl Games, 1902–2008

ROSE BOWL (Pasadena, California)

Year	Result	Year	Result
1902	Michigan 49, Stanford 0	1962	Minnesota 21, U.C.L.A. 3
1916	Washington St. 14, Brown 0	1963	U.S.C. 42, Wisconsin 37
1917	Oregon 14, Pennsylvania 0	1964	Illinois 17, Washington 7
1918	Mare Island 19, Camp Lewis 7	1965	Michigan 34, Oregon State7
1919	Great Lakes 17, Mare Island 0	1966	U.C.L.A. 14, Michigan State 12
1920	Harvard 7, Oregon 6	1967	Purdue 14, U.S.C. 13
1921	California 28, Ohio State 0	1968	U.S.C. 14, Indiana 3
1922	Washington and Jefferson 0, Cal. 0	1969	Ohio State 27, U.S.C. 16
1923	U.S.C. 14, Penn State 3	1970	U.S.C. 10, Michigan 3
1924	Navy 14, Washington 14	1971	Stanford 27, Ohio State 17
1925	Notre Dame 27, Stanford 10	1972	Stanford 13, Michigan 12
1926	Alabama 20, Washington 19	1973	U.S.C. 42, Ohio State 17
1927	Alabama 7, Stanford 7	1974	Ohio State 42, U.S.C. 21
1928	Stanford 7, Pittsburgh 6	1975	U.S.C.18, Ohio State 17
1929	Georgia Tech 8, California 7	1976	U.C.L.A. 23, Ohio State 10
1930	U.S.C. 47, Pittsburgh 14	1977	U.S.C. 14, Michigan 6
1931	Alabama 24, Washington State 0	1978	Washington 27, Michigan 20
1932	U.S.C. 21, Tulane 12	1979	U.S.C. 17, Michigan 10
1933	U.S.C. 35, Pittsburgh 0	1980	U.S.C. 17, Ohio State 16
1934	Columbia 7, Stanford 0	1981	Michigan 23, Washington 6
1935	Alabama 29, Stanford 13	1982	Washington 28, Iowa 0
1936	Stanford 7, Southern Methodist 0	1983	U.C.L.A. 24, Michigan 14
1937	Pittsburgh 21, Washington 0	1984	U.C.L.A. 45, Illinois 9
1938	California 13, Alabama 0	1985	U.S.C. 20, Ohio State 17
1939	U.S.C. 7, Duke 0	1986	U.C.L.A. 45, Iowa 28
1940	U.S.C. 14, Tennessee 0	1987	Arizona State 22, Michigan 15
1941	Stanford 21, Nebraska 13	1988	Michigan State 20, U.S.C. 17
1942	Oregon State 20, Duke 16 (at Durham)	1989	Michigan 22, U.S.C. 14
1943	Georgia 9, U.C.L.A. 0	1990	U.S.C. 17, Michigan 10
1944	U.S.C. 29, Washington 0	1991	Washington 46, Iowa 34
1945	U.S.C. 25, Tennessee 0	1992	Washington 34, Michigan 14
1946	Alabama 34, U.S.C. 14	1993	Michigan 38, Washington 31,
1947	Illinois 45, U.C.L.A. 14	1994	Wisconsin 21, U.C.L.A. 16
1948	Michigan 49, U.S.C. 0	1995	Penn State 38, Oregon 20
1949	Northwestern 20, California 14	1996	U.S.C. 41, Northwestern 32
1950	Ohio State 17, California 14	1997	Ohio State 20, Arizona State 17
1951	Michigan 14, California 6	1998	Michigan 21, Washington State 16
1952	Illinois 40, Stanford 7	1999	Wisconsin 38, U.C.L.A. 31
1953	U.S.C. 7, Wisconsin 0	2000	Wisconsin 17, Stanford 9
1954	Michigan State 28, U.C.L.A. 20	2001	Washington 34, Purdue 24
1955	Ohio State 20, U.S.C. 7	2002	Miami (Fla.) 37, Nebraska 14
1956	Michigan State 17, U.C.L.A. 14	2003	Oklahoma 34, Washington St. 14
1957	Iowa 35, Oregon State 19	2004	U.S.C. 28, Michigan 14
1958	Ohio State 10, Oregon 7	2005	Texas 38, Michigan 37
1959	Iowa 38, California 12	2006	Texas 41, U.S.C. 38
1960	Washington 44, Wisconsin 8	2007	U.S.C. 32, Michigan 18
1961	Washington 17, Minnesota 7	2008	U.S.C. 49, Illinios 17

Year	ORANGE BOWL, Miami, Florida	SUGAR BOWL, New Orleans	COTTON BOWL, Dallas
1935	Bucknell 26, Miami (Fla.) 0	Tulane 20, Temple 14	—
1936	Catholic U. 20, Mississippi 19	Texas Christian 3, L.S.U. 2	—
1937	Duquesne 13, Mississippi St. 12	Santa Clara 21, L.S.U. 14	T.C.U. 16, Marquette 6
1938	Auburn 6, Michigan State 0	Santa Clara 6, L.S.U. 0	Rice 28, Colorado 14
1939	Tennessee 17, Oklahoma 0	T.C.U. 15, Carnegie Tech 7	St. Mary's 20, Texas Tech 13
1940	Georgia Tech 21, Missouri 7	Texas A&M 14, Tulane 13	Clemson 6, Boston College 3
1941	Mississippi St. 14, Georgetown 7	Boston College 19, Tennessee 13	Texas A&M 13, Fordham 12
1942	Georgia 40, Texas Christian 26	Fordham 2, Missouri 0	Alabama 29, Texas A&M 21
1943	Alabama 37, Boston College 21	Tennessee 14, Tulsa 7	Texas 14, Georgia Tech 7
1944	Louisiana St. 19, Texas A&M 14	Georgia Tech 20, Tulsa 18	Texas 7, Randolph Field 7
1945	Tulsa 26, Georgia Tech 12	Duke 29, Alabama 26	Oklahoma A&M 34, T.C.U. 0
1946	Miami (Fla.)13, Holy Cross 6	Okla. A&M 33, St. Mary's Co. 13	Texas 40, Missouri 27
1947	Rice 8, Tennessee 0	Georgia 20, North Carolina 10	Arkansas 0, Louisiana State 0
1948	Georgia Tech 20, Kansas 14	Texas 27, Alabama 7	S.M.U. 13, Penn State 13
1949	Texas 41, Georgia 28	Oklahoma 14, North Carolina 6	S.M.U. 21, Oregon 13
1950	Santa Clara 21, Kentucky 13	Oklahoma 35, Louisiana State 0	Rice 27, North Carolina 13
1951	Clemson 15, Miami (Fla.)14	Kentucky 13, Oklahoma 7	Tennessee 20, Texas 14
1952	Georgia Tech 20, Baylor 14	Maryland 28, Tennessee 13	Kentucky 20, Texas Christian 7
1953	Alabama 61, Syracuse 6	Georgia Tech 24, Mississippi 7	Texas 16, Tennessee 0

Year	ORANGE BOWL, Miami, Florida	SUGAR BOWL, New Orleans	COTTON BOWL, Dallas
1954	Oklahoma 7, Maryland 0	Georgia Tech 42, W. Virginia 19	Rice 28, Alabama 0
1955	Duke 34, Nebraska 7	Navy 21, Mississippi 0	Georgia Tech 14, Arkansas 6
1956	Oklahoma 20, Maryland 6	Georgia Tech 7, Pittsburgh 0	Mississippi 14, Texas Christian 13
1957	Colorado 27, Clemson 21	Baylor 13, Tennessee 7	Texas Christian 28, Syracuse 27
1958	Oklahoma 48, Duke 21	Mississippi 39, Texas 7	Navy 20, Rice 7
1959	Oklahoma 21, Syracuse 6	Louisiana State 7, Clemson 0	Texas Christian 0, Air Force 0
1960	Georgia 14, Missouri 0	Mississippi 21, L.S.U. 0	Syracuse 23, Texas 14
1961	Missouri 21, Navy 14	Mississippi 14, Rice 6	Duke 7, Arkansas 6
1962	Louisiana State 25, Colorado 7	Alabama 10, Arkansas 3	Texas 12, Mississippi 7
1963	Alabama 17, Oklahoma 0	Mississippi 17, Arkansas 13	Louisiana State 13, Texas 0
1964	Nebraska 13, Auburn 7	Alabama 12, Mississippi 7	Texas 28, Navy 6
1965	Texas 21, Alabama 17	Louisiana State 13, Syracuse 10	Arkansas 10, Nebraska 7
1966	Alabama 39, Nebraska 28	Missouri 20, Florida 18	Louisiana State 14, Arkansas 7
1967	Florida 27, Georgia Tech 12	Alabama 34, Nebraska 7	Georgia 24, S.M.U. 9
1968	Oklahoma 26, Tennessee 24	L.S.U. 20, Wyoming 13	Texas A&M 20, Alabama 16
1969	Penn State 15, Kansas 14	Arkansas 16, Georgia 2	Texas 36, Tennessee 13
1970	Penn State 10, Missouri 3	Mississippi 27, Arkansas 22	Texas 21, Notre Dame 17
1971	Nebraska 17, Louisiana State 12	Tennessee 34, Air Force 13	Notre Dame 24, Texas 11
1972	Nebraska 38, Alabama 6	Oklahoma 40, Auburn 22	Penn State 30, Texas 6
1973	Nebraska 40, Notre Dame 6	Oklahoma 14, Penn State 0	Texas 17, Alabama 13
1974	Penn State 16, Louisiana State 9	Notre Dame 24, Alabama 23	Nebraska 19, Texas 3
1975	Notre Dame 13, Alabama 11	Nebraska 13, Florida 10	Penn State 41, Baylor 20
1976	Oklahoma 14, Michigan 6	Alabama 13, Penn State 6	Arkansas 31, Georgia 10
1977	Ohio State 27, Colorado 10	Pittsburgh 27, Georgia 3	Houston 30, Maryland 21
1978	Arkansas 31, Oklahoma 6	Alabama 35, Ohio State 6	Notre Dame 38, Texas 10
1979	Oklahoma 31, Nebraska 24	Alabama 14, Penn State	Notre Dame 35, Houston 34
1980	Oklahoma 24, Florida State 7	Alabama 24, Arkansas 9	Houston 17, Nebraska 14
1981	Oklahoma 18, Florida State 17	Georgia 17, Notre Dame 10	Alabama 30, Baylor 2
1982	Clemson 22, Nebraska 15	Pittsburgh 24, Georgia 20	Texas 14, Alabama 12
1983	Nebraska 21, L.S.U. 20	Penn State 27, Georgia 23	S.M.U. 7, Pittsburgh 3
1984	Miami (Fla.) 31, Nebraska 30	Auburn 9, Michigan 7	Georgia 10, Texas 9
1985	Washington 28, Oklahoma 17	Nebraska 28, Louisiana State 10	Boston College 45, Houston 28
1986	Oklahoma 25, Penn State 10	Tennessee 35, Miami (Fla.) 7	Texas A&M 36, Auburn 16
1987	Oklahoma 42, Arkansas 8	Nebraska 30, Louisiana State 15	Ohio State 28, Texas A&M 12
1988	Miami (Fla.) 20, Oklahoma 14	Syracuse 16, Auburn 16	Texas A&M 35, Notre Dame 10
1989	Miami (Fla.) 23, Nebraska 3	Florida State 13, Auburn 7	U.C.L.A. 17, Arkansas 3
1990	Notre Dame 21, Colorado 6	Miami (Fla.) 33, Alabama 25	Tennessee 31, Arkansas 27
1991	Colorado 10, Notre Dame 9	Tennessee 23, Virginia 22	Miami (Fla.) 46, Texas 3
1992	Miami (Fla.) 22, Nebraska 0	Notre Dame 39, Florida 28	Florida St. 10, Texas A&M 2
1993	Florida State 27, Nebraska 14	Alabama 34, Miami 13	Notre Dame 28, Texas A&M 3
1994	Florida State 18, Nebraska 16	Florida 41, West Virginia 7	Notre Dame 24, Texas A&M 21
1995	Nebraska 24, Miami 17	Florida State 23, Florida 17	U.S.C. 55, Texas Tech 14
1996	Florida St. 31, Notre Dame 26	Virginia Tech 28, Texas 10	Colorado 38, Oregon 6
1997	Nebraska 41, Virginia Tech 21	Florida 52, Florida State 20	B.Y.U. 19, Kansas State 15
1998	Nebraska 42, Tennessee 17	Florida State 31, Ohio State 14	U.C.L.A. 29, Texas A&M 23
1999	Florida 31, Syracuse 10	Ohio State 24, Texas A&M 14	Texas 38, Mississippi State 11
2000	Michigan 35, Alabama 34	Florida State 46, Virginia Tech 29	Arkansas 27, Texas 6
2001	Oklahoma 13, Florida State 2	Miami 37, Florida 20	Kansas St. 35, Tennessee 21
2002	Florida 56, Maryland 23	Louisiana State 47, Illinois 34	Oklahoma 10, Arkansas 3
2003	U.S.C. 38, Iowa 17	Georgia 26, Florida State 13	Texas 35, Louisiana State 20
2004	Miami (Fla.) 16, Florida St. 14	Louisiana St. 21, Oklahoma 14	Mississippi 31, Oklahoma St. 28
2005	U.S.C. 55, Oklahoma 19	Auburn 16, Virginia Tech 13	Tennessee 38, Texas A&M 7
2006	Penn State 26, Florida State 23	West Virginia 38, Georgia 35	Alabama 13, Texas Tech 10
2007	Louisville 24, Wake Forest 13	L.S.U. 41, Notre Dame 14	Auburn 17, Nebraska 14
2008	Kansas 24, Virginia Tech 21	Georgia 41, Hawaii 10	Missouri 38, Arkansas 7

NCAA Football Career Leaders

Player, Team	PASSING, Career yards						
	Years	Att.	Comp.	Int.	Pct.	Yards	TD
Timmy Chang, Hawaii	2000-2004	2,436	1,388	80	.570	17,072	117
Ty Detmer, Brigham Young	1988-1991	1,530	958	65	.626	15,031	121
Philip Rivers, North Carolina St.	2000-2003	1,710	1,147	34	.671	13,484	95
Tim Rattay, Louisiana Tech	1997-1999	1,552	1,015	35	.654	12,746	115
Luke McCown, Louisiana Tech	2000-2003	1,775	1,063	62	.599	12,666	87
Chris Redman, Louisville	1996-1999	1,679	1,031	51	.614	12,541	84
Kliff Kingsbury, Texas Tech	1999-2002	1,883	1,231	40	.654	12,429	95
Byron Leftwich, Marshall	1998-2002	1,442	939	28	.651	11,903	89
David Greene, Georgia	2001-2004	1,440	849	32	.590	11,528	72
Gino Guidugli, Cincinnati	2001-2004	1,556	880	48	.566	11,453	78

CAREER POINTS (Nonkickers)

Player, Team	Years	TDs	Pts.
Travis Prentice, Miami (Ohio)	1996-99	78	468
Ricky Williams, Texas	1995-98	75	452
Taureen Henderson, Texas Tech	2002-05	69	414
Brock Forsey, Boise State	1999-02	68	408
Cedric Benson, Texas	2001-04	67	404
Anthony Thompson, Indiana	1968-69	65	394
Ron Dayne, Wisconsin	1996-99	63	378
Marshall Faulk, San Diego St.	1991-93	62	376
Eric Crouch, Nebraska	1998-01	59	374
DeAngelo Williams, Memphis	2002-05	60	362

CAREER POINTS (Kickers)

Player, Team	Years	PAT	FG	Pts.
Roman Anderson, Houston	1988-91	213	70	423
Billy Bennett, Georgia	2000-03	148	87	409
Carlos Huerta, Miami (Fla.)	1988-91	178	73	397
Jason Elam, Hawaii	1988-92	158	79	395
Derek Schmidt, Florida St.	1984-87	174	73	393
Nick Novak, Maryland	2001-04	153	80	393
Kris Brown, Nebraska	1995-98	217	57	388
Xavier Beitia, Florida St.	2001-04	174	67	375
Jeff Hall, Tennessee	1995-98	188	61	371
Shayne Graham, Virginia Tech	1996-99	167	68	371

RUSHING, Career yards

Player, Team	Years	Carries	Yards
Ron Dayne, Wisconsin	1996-99	1,115	6,397
Ricky Williams, Texas	1995-98	1,011	6,279
Tony Dorsett, Pittsburgh	1973-76	1,074	6,082
DeAngelo Williams, Memphis	2002-05	969	6,026
Charles White, U.S.C.	1976-79	1,023	5,598
Travis Prentice, Miami (Ohio)	1996-99	1,138	5,596
Cedric Benson, Texas	2001-04	1,112	5,540
LaDainian Tomlinson, TCU	1997-00	907	5,263
Herschel Walker, Georgia	1980-82	994	5,259
Archie Griffin, Ohio State	1972-75	845	5,177

RECEIVING, Career catches

Player, Team	Years	Catches	Yards
Taylor Stubblefield, Purdue	2001-04	316	3,433
Josh Davis, Marshall	2001-04	306	3,889
Taureen Henderson, Texas Tech	2002-05	303	2,058
Arnold Jackson, Louisville	1997-00	300	3,670
Trevor Insley, Nevada	1996-99	298	5,005
Geoff Noisy, Nevada	1995-98	295	4,249
Rashaun Woods, Oklahoma St.	2000-03	293	4,412
Troy Edwards, Lousiana Tech.	1996-98	280	4,352
Darius Watts, Marshall	2000-03	272	4,031
Aaron Turner, Pacific (Calif.)	1988-91	266	4,345

Heisman Memorial Trophy

Year	Player	College	Pos.	Year	Player	College	Pos.
1935	Jay Berwanger	Chicago	HB	1972	Johnny Rodgers	Nebraska	WR
1936	Larry Kelley	Yale	E	1973	John Cappelletti	Penn State	RB
1937	Clint Frank	Yale	HB	1974	Archie Griffin	Ohio State	RB
1938	Davey O'Brien	Texas Christian	QB	1975	Archie Griffin	Ohio State	RB
1939	Nile Kinnick	Iowa	HB	1976	Tony Dorsett	Pittsburgh	RB
1940	Tom Harmon	Michigan	HB	1977	Earl Campbell	Texas	RB
1941	Bruce Smith	Minnesota	HB	1978	Billy Sims	Oklahoma	RB
1942	Frank Sinkwich	Georgia	HB	1979	Charles White	U.S.C.	RB
1943	Angelo Bertelli	Notre Dame	QB	1980	George Rogers	South Carolina	RB
1944	Les Horvath	Ohio State	QB	1981	Marcus Allen	U.S.C.	RB
1945	Doc Blanchard	Army	FB	1982	Herschel Walker	Georgia	RB
1946	Glenn Davis	Army	HB	1983	Mike Rozier	Nebraska	RB
1947	John Lujack	Notre Dame	QB	1984	Doug Flutie	Boston College	QB
1948	Doak Walker	S.M.U.	HB	1985	Bo Jackson	Auburn	RB
1949	Leon Hart	Notre Dame	E	1986	Vinny Testaverde	Miami (Fla.)	QB
1950	Vic Janowicz	Ohio State	HB	1987	Tim Brown	Notre Dame	WR
1951	Dick Kazmaier	Princeton	HB	1988	Barry Sanders	Oklahoma State	RB
1952	Billy Vessels	Oklahoma	HB	1989	Andre Ware	Houston	QB
1953	John Lattner	Notre Dame	HB	1990	Ty Detmer	Brigham Young	QB
1954	Alan Ameche	Wisconsin	FB	1991	Desmond Howard	Michigan	WR
1955	Howard Cassady	Ohio State	HB	1992	Gino Toretta	Miami (Fla.)	QB
1956	Paul Hornung	Notre Dame	QB	1993	Charlie Ward	Florida State	QB
1957	John David Crow	Texas A&M	HB	1994	Rashaan Salaam	Colorado	RB
1958	Pete Dawkins	Army	HB	1995	Eddie George	Ohio State	RB
1959	Billy Cannon	Louisiana State	HB	1996	Danny Wuerffel	Florida	QB
1960	Joe Bellino	Navy	HB	1997	Charles Woodson	Michigan	CB
1961	Ernie Davis	Syracuse	HB	1998	Ricky Williams	Texas	TB
1962	Terry Baker	Orgeon State	QB	1999	Ron Dayne	Wisconsin	TB
1963	Roger Staubach	Navy	QB	2000	Chris Weinke	Florida State	QB
1964	John Huarte	Notre Dame	QB	2001	Eric Crouch	Nebraska	QB
1965	Mike Garrett	U.S.C.	HB	2002	Carson Palmer	U.S.C.	QB
1966	Steve Spurrier	Florida	QB	2003	Jason White	Oklahoma	QB
1967	Gary Beban	U.C.L.A.	QB	2004	Matt Leinart	U.S.C.	QB
1968	O.J. Simpson	U.S.C.	HB	2005	Reggie Bush	U.S.C.	RB
1969	Steve Owens	Oklahoma	HB	2006	Troy Smith	Ohio State	QB
1970	Jim Plunkett	Stanford	QB	2007	Tim Tebow	Florida	QB
1971	Pat Sullivan	Auburn	QB				

COLLEGE BASKETBALL

NCAA Division I Men's Basketball Championship Final Four Results

Year	Champion	Score	Runner-up	Third place	Fourth place	Champion coach
1939	Oregon	46–33	Ohio State	Oklahoma[1]	Villanova[1]	Howard Hobson
1940	Indiana	60–42	Kansas	Duquesne[1]	U.S.C.[1]	Branch McCracken
1941	Wisconsin	39–34	Washington St.	Pittsburgh[1]	Arkansas[1]	Harold Foster
1942	Stanford	53–38	Dartmouth	Colorado[1]	Kentucky[1]	Everett Dean
1943	Wyoming	46–34	Georgetown	Texas[1]	DePaul[1]	Everett Shelton
1944	Utah	42–40[2]	Dartmouth	Iowa State[1]	Ohio State[1]	Vadal Peterson
1945	Oklahoma State	49–45	N.Y.U.	Arkansas[1]	Ohio State[1]	Henry Iba
1946	Oklahoma State	43–40	North Carolina	Ohio St.	California	Henry Iba
1947	Holy Cross	58–47	Oklahoma	Texas	C.C.N.Y.	Alvin Julian
1948	Kentucky	58–42	Baylor	Holy Cross	Kansas State	Adolph Rupp
1949	Kentucky	46–36	Oklahoma State	Illinois	Oregon State	Adolph Rupp
1950	C.C.N.Y.	71–68	Bradley	North Carolina State	Baylor	Nat Holman
1951	Kentucky	68–58	Kansas State	Illinois	Oklahoma State	Aldolph Rupp
1952	Kansas	80–63	St. John's	Illinois	Santa Clara	Forrest Allen
1953	Indiana	69–68	Kansas	Washington	Louisiana State	Branch McCracken
1954	LaSalle	92–76	Bradley	Penn State	U.S.C.	Kenneth Loeffler
1955	San Francisco	77–63	La Salle	Colorado	Iowa	Phil Woolpert
1956	San Francisco	83–71	Iowa	Temple	Southern Methodist	Phil Woolpert
1957	North Carolina	54–53[3]	Kansas	San Francisco	Michigan State	Frank McGuire
1958	Kentucky	84–72	Seattle	Temple	Kansas State	Adolph Rupp
1959	California	71–70	West Virginia	Cincinnati	Louisville	Pete Newell
1960	Ohio State	75–55	California	Cincinnati	N.Y.U.	Fred Taylor
1961	Cincinnati	70–65[2]	Ohio State	St. Joe's[4]	Utah	Edwin Jucker
1962	Cincinnati	71–59	Ohio State	Wake Forest	U.C.L.A.	Edwin Jucker
1963	Loyola (Ill.)	60–58[2]	Cincinnati	Duke	Utah	George Ireland
1964	U.C.L.A.	98–83	Duke	Michigan	Kansas State	John Wooden
1965	U.C.L.A.	91–80	Michigan	Princeton	Wichita State	John Wooden
1966	U.T.E.P.	72–65	Kentucky	Duke	Utah	Don Haskins
1967	U.C.L.A.	79–64	Dayton	Houston	North Carolina	John Wooden
1968	U.C.L.A.	78–55	North Carolina	Ohio State	Houston	John Wooden
1969	U.C.L.A.	92–72	Purdue	Drake	North Carolina	John Wooden
1970	U.C.L.A.	80–69	Jacksonville	New Mexico St.	St. Bonaventure	John Wooden
1971	U.C.L.A.	68–62	Villanova[4]	Western Kentucky[4]	Kansas	John Wooden
1972	U.C.L.A.	81–76	Florida State	North Carolina	Louisville	John Wooden
1973	U.C.L.A.	87–66	Memphis State	Indiana	Providence	John Wooden
1974	North Carolina State	76–64	Marquette	U.C.L.A.	Kansas	Norm Sloan
1975	U.C.L.A.	92–85	Kentucky	Louisville	Syracuse	John Wooden
1976	Indiana	86–68	Michigan	U.C.L.A.	Rutgers	Bob Knight
1977	Marquette	67–59	North Carolina	U.N.L.V.	U.N.C. Charlotte	Al McGuire
1978	Kentucky	94–88	Duke	Arkansas	Notre Dame	Joe Hall
1979	Michigan State	75–64	Indiana State	DePaul	Pennsylvania	Jud Heathcote
1980	Louisville	59–54	U.C.L.A.[4]	Purdue	Iowa	Denny Crum
1981	Indiana	63–50	North Carolina	Virginia	Louisiana State	Bob Knight
1982	North Carolina	63–62	Georgetown	Houston[1]	Louisville[1]	Dean Smith
1983	North Carolina State	54–52	Houston	Georgia[1]	Louisville[1]	Jim Valvano
1984	Georgetown	84–75	Houston	Kentucky[1]	Virginia[1]	John Thompson
1985	Villanova	66–64	Georgetown	St. John's[1]	Memphis[1,4]	Rollie Massimino
1986	Louisville	72–69	Duke	Kansas[1]	Louisiana State[1]	Denny Crum
1987	Indiana	74–73	Syracuse	U.N.L.V.[1]	Providence[1]	Bob Knight
1988	Kansas	83–79	Oklahoma	Arizona[1]	Duke[1]	Larry Brown
1989	Michigan	80–79[2]	Seton Hall	Illinois[1]	Duke[1]	Steve Fisher
1990	U.N.L.V.	103–73	Duke	Georgia Tech[1]	Arkansas[1]	Jerry Tarkanian
1991	Duke	72–65	Kansas	U.N.L.V.[1]	North Carolina[1]	Mike Krzyzewski
1992	Duke	71–51	Michigan	Cincinnati[1]	Indiana[1]	Mike Krzyzewski
1993	North Carolina	77–71	Michigan	Kansas[1]	Kentucky[1]	Dean Smith
1994	Arkansas	76–70	Duke	Arizona[1]	Florida[1]	Nolan Richardson
1995	U.C.L.A.	89–78	Arkansas	North Carolina[1]	Oklahoma State[1]	Jim Harrick
1996	Kentucky	76–67	Syracuse	Massachusetts[1,4]	Mississippi State[1]	Rick Pitino
1997	Arizona	84–79	Kentucky	Minnesota[1]	North Carolina[1]	Lute Olson
1998	Kentucky	78–69	Utah	North Carolina[1]	Stanford[1]	Tubby Smith
1999	Connecticut	77–74	Duke	Michigan State[1]	Ohio State[1]	Jim Calhoun
2000	Michigan State	89–76	Florida	North Carolina[1]	Wisconsin[1]	Tom Izzo
2001	Duke	82–72	Arizona	Maryland[1]	Michigan State[1]	Mike Krzyzewski
2002	Maryland	64–52	Indiana	Kansas[1]	Oklahoma[1]	Gary Williams
2003	Syracuse	81–78	Kansas	Marquette[1]	Texas[1]	Jim Boeheim
2004	Connecticut	82–73	Georgia Tech	Duke[1]	Oklahoma State[1]	Jim Calhoun
2005	North Carolina	75–70	Illinois	Michigan State[1]	Louisville[1]	Roy Williams
2006	Florida	73–57	U.C.L.A.	George Mason[1]	L.S.U[1]	Billy Donovan
2007	Florida	84–75	Ohio State	Georgetown[1]	U.C.L.A.[1]	Billy Donovan
2008	Kansas	75–68[2]	Memphis	U.N.C	U.C.L.A	Bill Self

1. Tied for third place. 2. Overtime. 3. Triple overtime. 4. Later declared ineligible.

NCAA Basketball Career Leaders

Player, Team	POINTS
Pete Maravich, Louisiana State	3,667
Freeman Williams, Portland State	3,249
Lionel Simmons, LaSalle	3,217
Alphonso Ford, Mississippi Valley	3,165
Harry Kelly, Texas Southern	3,066
Keydren Clark, St. Peter's	3,058
Hersey Hawkins, Bradley	3,008
Oscar Robertson, Cincinnati	2,973
Danny Manning, Kansas	2,951
Alfredrick Hughes, Loyola (Ill.)	2,914

Player, Team	REBOUNDS
Tom Gola, LaSalle	2,201
Joe Holup, George Washington	2,030
Charlie Slack, Marshall	1,916
Ed Conlin, Fordham	1,884
Dickie Hemric, Wake Forest	1,802
Paul Silas, Creighton	1,751
Art Quimby, Connecticut	1,716
Jerry Harper, Alabama	1,688
Jeff Cohen, William and Mary	1,679
Steve Hamilton, Morehead State	1,675

Player, Team	ASSISTS
Bobby Hurley, Duke	1,076
Chris Corchiani, North Carolina State	1,038
Ed Cota, North Carolina	1,030
Keith Jennings, East Tennessee St.	983
Steve Blake, Maryland	972
Sherman Douglas, Syracuse	960
Tony Miller, Marquette	956
Aaron Miles, Kansas	954
Greg Anthony, Portland/U.N.L.V.	950
Doug Gottlieb, Notre Dame/Oklahoma State	947

National Invitation Tournament Champions

Year	Champion	Year	Champion
1938	Temple	1973	Virginia Tech
1939	Long Island	1974	Purdue
1940	Colorado	1975	Princeton
1941	Long Island	1976	Kentucky
1942	West Virginia	1977	St. Bonaventure
1943	St. John's	1978	Texas
1944	St. John's	1979	Indiana
1945	DePaul	1980	Virginia
1946	Kentucky	1981	Tulsa
1947	Utah	1982	Bradley
1948	St. Louis	1983	Fresno State
1949	San Francisco	1984	Michigan
1950	City College of New York	1985	U.C.L.A.
		1986	Ohio State
1951	Brigham Young	1987	So. Mississippi
1952	LaSalle	1988	Connecticut
1953	Seton Hall	1989	St. John's
1954	Holy Cross	1990	Vanderbilt
1955	Duquesne	1991	Stanford
1956	Louisville	1992	Virginia
1957	Bradley	1993	Minnesota
1958	Xavier (Ohio)	1994	Villanova
1959	St. John's	1995	Virginia Tech
1960	Bradley	1996	Nebraska
1961	Providence	1997	Michigan
1962	Dayton	1998	Minnesota
1963	Providence	1999	California
1964	Bradley	2000	Wake Forest
1965	St. John's	2001	Tulsa
1966	Brigham Young	2002	Memphis
1967	Southern Illinois	2003	St. John's
1968	Dayton	2004	Michigan
1969	Temple	2005	South Carolina
1970	Marquette	2006	South Carolina
1971	North Carolina	2007	West Virginia
1972	Maryland	2008	Ohio State

NCAA Division I Women's Basketball Championship Results

Year	Champion	Score	Runner-up	Coach	Outstanding player
1982	Louisiana Tech	76-62	Cheyney	Sonja Hogg	Janice Lawrence
1983	U.S.C.	69-67	Louisiana Tech	Linda Sharp	Cheryl Miller
1984	U.S.C.	72-61	Tennessee	Linda Sharp	Cheryl Miller
1985	Old Dominion	70-65	Georgia	Marianne Stanley	Tracy Claxton
1986	Texas	97-81	U.S.C.	Jody Conradt	Clarissa Davis
1987	Tennessee	67-44	Louisiana Tech	Pat Summitt	Tonya Edwards
1988	Louisiana Tech	56-54	Auburn	Leon Barmore	Erica Westbrooks
1989	Tennessee	76-60	Auburn	Pat Summitt	Brigitte Gordon
1990	Stanford	88-81	Auburn	Tara VanderVeer	Jennifer Azzi
1991	Tennessee	70-67	Virginia	Pat Summitt	Dawn Staley
1992	Stanford	78-62	Western Kentucky	Tara VanderVeer	Molly Goodenbour
1993	Texas Tech	84-82	Ohio State	Marcia Sharp	Sheryl Swoopes
1994	North Carolina	60-59	Louisiana Tech	Sylvia Hatchell	Charlotte Smith
1995	Connecticut	70-64	Tennessee	Geno Auriemma	Rebecca Lobo
1996	Tennessee	83-65	Georgia	Pat Summitt	Michelle Marciniak
1997	Tennessee	68-59	Old Dominion	Pat Summitt	Chamique Holdsclaw
1998	Tennessee	93-75	Louisiana Tech	Pat Summitt	Chamique Holdsclaw
1999	Purdue	62-45	Duke	Carolyn Peck	Ukari Figgs
2000	Connecticut	71-52	Tennessee	Geno Auriemma	Shea Ralph
2001	Notre Dame	68-66	Purdue	Muffet McGraw	Ruth Riley
2002	Connecticut	82-70	Oklahoma	Geno Auriemma	Swin Cash
2003	Connecticut	73-68	Tennessee	Geno Auriemma	Diana Taurasi
2004	Connecticut	70-61	Tennessee	Geno Auriemma	Diana Taurasi
2005	Baylor	84-62	Michigan State	Kim Mulkey-Robertson	Sophia Young
2006	Maryland	78-75	Duke	Brenda Frese	Laura Harper
2007	Tennessee	59-46	Rutgers	Pat Summitt	Candace Parker
2008	Tennessee	64-48	Stanford	Pat Summitt	Candace Parker

NCAA CHAMPIONS IN OTHER SPORTS

Men's Sports

CROSS COUNTRY
1938 Indiana
1939 Michigan State
1940 Indiana
1941 Rhode Island
1942 Indiana
1943 No Meet
1944 Drake
1945 Drake
1946 Drake
1947 Penn State
1948 Michigan State
1949 Michigan State
1950 Penn State
1951 Syracuse
1952 Michigan State
1953 Kansas
1954 Oklahoma St.
1955 Michigan State
1956 Michigan State
1957 Notre Dame
1958 Michigan State
1959 Michigan State
1960 Houston
1961 Oregon State
1962 San Jose State
1963 San Jose State
1964 Western Michigan
1965 Western Michigan
1966 Villanova
1967 Villanova
1968 Villanova
1969 U.T.E.P
1970 Villanova
1971 Oregon
1972 Tennessee
1973 Oregon
1974 Oregon
1975 U.T.E.P
1976 U.T.E.P
1977 Oregon
1978 U.T.E.P
1979 U.T.E.P
1980 U.T.E.P
1981 U.T.E.P
1982 Wisconsin
1983 Vacated
1984 Arkansas
1985 Wisconsin
1986 Arkansas
1987 Arkansas
1988 Wisconsin
1989 Iowa State
1990 Arkansas
1991 Arkansas
1992 Arkansas
1993 Arkansas
1994 Iowa State
1995 Arkansas
1996 Stanford
1997 Stanford
1998 Arkansas
1999 Arkansas
2000 Arkansas
2001 Colorado
2002 Stanford
2003 Stanford
2004 Colorado
2005 Wisconsin
2006 Colorado
2007 Oregon

SOCCER
1959 St. Louis
1960 St. Louis
1961 West Chester
1962 St. Louis
1963 St. Louis
1964 Navy
1965 St. Louis
1966 San Franciso
1967 St. Louis, Michigan State
1968 Maryland. Michigan State
1969 St. Louis
1970 St. Louis
1971 Vacated
1972 St. Louis
1973 St. Louis
1974 Howard
1975 San Francisco
1976 San Francisco
1977 Hartwick
1978 Vacated
1979 So. Ill. Univ at Edwardsville
1980 San Francisco
1981 Connecticut
1982 Indiana
1983 Indiana
1984 Clemson
1985 U.C.L.A.
1986 Duke
1987 Clemson
1988 Indiana
1989 Santa Clara, Virginia
1990 U.C.L.A.
1991 Virginia
1992 Virginia
1993 Virginia
1994 Virginia
1995 Wisconsin
1996 St. John's (N.Y.)
1997 U.C.L.A.
1998 Indiana
1999 Indiana
2000 Connecticut
2001 North Carolina
2002 U.C.L.A.
2003 Indiana
2004 Indiana
2005 Maryland
2006 U.C. Santa Barbara
2007 U.S.C

WATER POLO
1969 U.C.L.A.
1970 UC Irvine
1971 U.C.L.A.
1972 U.C.L.A.
1973 California
1974 California
1975 California
1976 Stanford
1977 California
1978 Stanford

1979 U.C. Santa Barbara
1980 Stanford
1981 Stanford
1982 U.C. Irvine
1983 California
1984 California
1985 Stanford
1986 Stanford
1987 California
1988 California
1989 California
1990 California
1991 California
1992 California
1993 Stanford
1994 Stanford
1995 U.C.L.A.
1996 U.C.L.A.
1997 Pepperdine
1998 U.S.C.
1999 U.C.L.A.
2000 U.C.L.A.
2001 Stanford
2002 Stanford
2003 U.S.C.
2004 U.S.C.
2005 U.S.C.
2006 California
2007 U.C.L.A.
2008 U.C.L.A

FENCING[1]
1941 Northwestern
1942 Ohio State
1943 No Meet
1944 No Meet
1945 No Meet
1946 No Meet
1947 N.Y.U.
1948 C.C.N.Y.
1949 Army, Rutgers
1950 Navy
1951 Columbia
1952 Columbia
1953 Pennsylvania
1954 Columbia, N.Y.U.
1955 Columbia
1956 Illinois
1957 N.Y.U.
1958 Illinois
1959 Navy
1960 N.Y.U.
1961 N.Y.U.
1962 Navy
1963 Columbia
1964 Princeton
1965 Columbia
1966 N.Y.U.
1967 N.Y.U.
1968 Columbia
1969 Pennsylvania
1970 N.Y.U.
1971 N.Y.U., Columbia
1972 Detroit
1973 N.Y.U.
1974 N.Y.U.
1975 Wayne State

1976 N.Y.U.
1977 Notre Dame
1978 Notre Dame
1979 Wayne State
1980 Wayne State
1981 Pennsylvania
1982 Wayne State
1983 Wayne State
1984 Wayne State
1985 Wayne State
1986 Notre Dame
1987 Columbia
1988 Columbia
1989 Columbia

1. For results after 1989, see "Men's and Women's Sports."

GYMNASTICS
1938 Chicago
1939 Illinois
1940 Illinois
1941 Illinois
1942 Illinois
1943-47 No Meet
1948 Penn State
1949 Temple
1950 Illinois
1951 Florida State
1952 Florida State
1953 Penn State
1954 Penn State
1955 Illinois
1956 Illinois
1957 Penn State
1958 Illinois, Michigan State
1959 Penn State
1960 Penn State
1961 Penn State
1962 U.S.C.
1963 Michigan
1964 So. Illinois
1965 Penn State
1966 So. Illinois
1967 So. Illinois
1968 California
1969 Iowa
1970 Michigan
1971 Iowa State
1972 So. Illinois
1973 Iowa State
1974 Iowa State
1975 California
1976 Penn State
1977 Indiana State, Oklahoma
1978 Oklahoma
1979 Nebraska
1980 Nebraska
1981 Nebraska
1982 Nebraska
1983 Nebraska
1984 U.C.L.A.
1985 Ohio State
1986 Arizona State
1987 U.C.L.A.
1988 Nebraska
1989 Illinois

1990 Nebraska
1991 Oklahoma
1992 Stanford
1993 Stanford
1994 Nebraska
1995 Stanford
1996 Ohio State
1997 California
1998 California
1999 Michigan
2000 Penn State
2001 Ohio State
2002 Oklahoma
2003 Oklahoma
2004 Penn State
2005 Oklahoma
2006 Oklahoma
2007 Penn State
2008 Oklahoma

ICE HOCKEY
1948 Michigan
1949 Boston College
1950 Colorado College
1951 Michigan
1952 Michigan
1953 Michigan
1954 Rensselaer
1955 Michigan
1956 Michigan
1957 Colorado College
1958 Denver
1959 North Dakota
1960 Denver
1961 Denver
1962 Michigan Tech.
1963 North Dakota
1964 Michigan
1965 Michigan Tech
1966 Michigan St.
1967 Cornell
1968 Denver
1969 Denver
1970 Cornell
1971 Boston Univ.
1972 Boston Univ.
1973 Wisconsin
1974 Minnesota
1975 Michigan Tech
1976 Minnesota
1977 Wisconsin
1978 Boston Univ.
1979 Minnesota
1980 North Dakota
1981 Wisconsin
1982 North Dakota
1983 Wisconsin
1984 Bowling Green
1985 Rensselaer
1986 Michigan St.
1987 North Dakota
1988 Lake Superior State
1989 Harvard
1990 Wisconsin
1991 N. Michigan
1992 Lake Superior State

1993 Maine	1996 Texas	1990 Oklahoma St.	1929 Ohio State	2005 Arkansas
1994 Lake Superior State	1997 Auburn	1991 Iowa	1930 U.S.C.	2006 Florida St.
1995 Boston Univ.	1998 Stanford	1992 Iowa	1931 U.S.C.	2007 Florida St.
1996 Michigan	1999 Auburn	1993 Iowa	1932 Indiana	2008 Florida St.
1997 North Dakota	2000 Texas	1994 Oklahoma St.	1933 Louisiana St.	
1998 Michigan	2001 Texas	1995 Iowa	1934 Stanford	**BASEBALL**
1999 Maine	2002 Texas	1996 Iowa	1935 U.S.C.	1947 California
2000 North Dakota	2003 Auburn	1997 Iowa	1936 U.S.C.	1948 U.S.C.
2001 Boston Coll.	2004 Auburn	1998 Iowa	1937 U.S.C.	1949 Texas
2002 Minnesota	2005 Auburn	1999 Iowa	1938 U.S.C.	1950 Texas
2003 Minnesota	2006 Auburn	2000 Iowa	1939 U.S.C.	1951 Oklahoma
2004 Denver	2007 Auburn	2001 Minnesota	1940 U.S.C.	1952 Holy Cross
2005 Denver	2008 Arizona	2002 Minnesota	1941 U.S.C.	1953 Michigan
2006 Wisconsin		2003 Oklahoma	1942 U.S.C.	1954 Missouri
2007 Michigan St.	**WRESTLING**	2004 Oklahoma St.	1943 U.S.C.	1955 Wake Forest
2008 Boston Coll.	1928 Oklahoma St.[1]	2005 Oklahoma	1944 Illinois	1956 Minnesota
	1929 Oklahoma St.[1]	2006 Oklahoma St.	1945 Navy	1957 California
SWIMMING	1930 Oklahoma St.[1]	2007 Minnesota	1946 Illinois	1958 U.S.C.
1937 Michigan	1931 Oklahoma St.[1]	2008 Iowa	1947 Illinois	1959 Oklahoma St.
1938 Michigan	1932 Indiana		1948 Minnesota	1960 Minnesota
1939 Michigan	1933 Iowa State,[1]	**1.** Unofficial champions.	1949 U.S.C.	1961 U.S.C.
1940 Michigan	Oklahoma St.[1]		1950 U.S.C.	1962 Michigan
1941 Michigan	1934 Oklahoma St.	**INDOOR TRACK**	1951 U.S.C.	1963 U.S.C.
1942 Yale	1935 Oklahoma St.	1965 Missouri	1952 U.S.C.	1964 Minnesota
1943 Ohio State	1936 Oklahoma	1966 Kansas	1953 U.S.C.	1965 Arizona St.
1944 Yale	1937 Oklahoma St.	1967 U.S.C.	1954 U.S.C.	1966 Ohio State
1945 Ohio State	1938 Oklahoma St.	1968 Villanova	1955 U.S.C.	1967 Arizona St.
1946 Ohio State	1939 Oklahoma St.	1969 Kansas	1956 U.C.L.A.	1968 U.S.C.
1947 Ohio State	1940 Oklahoma St.	1970 Kansas	1957 Villanova	1969 Arizona St.
1948 Michigan	1941 Oklahoma St.	1971 Villanova	1958 U.S.C.	1970 U.S.C.
1949 Ohio State	1942 Oklahoma St.	1972 U.S.C.	1959 Kansas	1971 U.S.C.
1950 Ohio State	1943 No Match	1973 Manhattan	1960 Kansas	1972 U.S.C.
1951 Yale	1944 No Match	1974 U.T.E.P	1961 U.S.C.	1973 U.S.C.
1952 Ohio State	1945 No Match	1975 U.T.E.P	1962 Oregon	1974 U.S.C.
1953 Yale	1946 Oklahoma St.	1976 U.T.E.P	1963 U.S.C.	1975 Texas
1954 Ohio State	1947 Cornell College	1977 Washington St.	1964 Oregon	1976 Arizona
1955 Ohio State	1948 Oklahoma St.	1978 U.T.E.P	1965 Oregon and	1977 Arizona St.
1956 Ohio State	1949 Oklahoma St.	1979 Villanova	U.S.C.	1978 U.S.C.
1957 Michigan	1950 Northern Iowa	1980 U.T.E.P	1966 U.C.L.A.	1979 Cal State—
1958 Michigan	1951 Oklahoma	1981 U.T.E.P	1967 U.S.C.	Fullerton
1959 Michigan	1952 Oklahoma	1982 U.T.E.P	1968 U.S.C.	1980 Arizona
1960 U.S.C.	1953 Penn State	1983 S.M.U.	1969 San Jose St.	1981 Arizona St.
1961 Michigan	1954 Oklahoma St.	1984 Arkansas	1970 BYU, Kansas	1982 Miami (Fla.)
1962 Ohio State	1955 Oklahoma St.	1985 Arkansas	1971 U.C.L.A.	1983 Texas
1963 U.S.C.	1956 Oklahoma St.	1986 Arkansas	1972 U.C.L.A.	1984 Cal State—
1964 U.S.C.	1957 Oklahoma	1987 Arkansas	1973 U.C.L.A.	Fullerton
1965 U.S.C.	1958 Oklahoma St.	1988 Arkansas	1974 Tennessee	1985 Miami (Fla.)
1966 U.S.C.	1959 Oklahoma St.	1989 Arkansas	1975 U.T.E.P	1986 Arizona
1967 Stanford	1960 Oklahoma	1990 Arkansas	1976 U.S.C.	1987 Stanford
1968 Indiana	1961 Oklahoma St.	1991 Arkansas	1977 Arizona St.	1988 Stanford
1969 Indiana	1962 Oklahoma St.	1992 Arkansas	1978 U.C.L.A. and	1989 Wichita St.
1970 Indiana	1963 Oklahoma	1993 Arkansas	U.T.E.P	1990 Georgia
1971 Indiana	1964 Oklahoma St.	1994 Arkansas	1979 U.T.E.P	1991 Louisiana St.
1972 Indiana	1965 Iowa State	1995 Arkansas	1980 U.T.E.P	1992 Pepperdine
1973 Indiana	1966 Oklahoma St.	1996 George Mason	1981 U.T.E.P	1993 Louisiana St.
1974 U.S.C.	1967 Michigan St.	1997 Arkansas	1982 U.T.E.P	1994 Oklahoma
1975 U.S.C.	1968 Oklahoma St.	1998 Arkansas	1983 SMU	1995 Cal State—
1976 U.S.C.	1969 Iowa State	1999 Arkansas	1984 Oregon	Fullerton
1977 U.S.C.	1970 Iowa State	2000 Arkansas	1985 Arkansas	1996 Louisiana St.
1978 Tennessee	1971 Oklahoma St.	2001 Louisiana St.	1986 S.M.U.	1997 Louisiana St.
1979 California	1972 Iowa State	2002 Tennessee	1987 U.C.L.A.	1998 U.S.C.
1980 California	1973 Iowa State	2003 Arkansas	1988 U.C.L.A.	1999 Miama (Fla.)
1981 Texas	1974 Oklahoma	2004 Louisiana St.	1989 Louisiana St.	2000 Louisiana St.
1982 U.C.L.A.	1975 Iowa	2005 Arkansas	1990 Louisiana St.	2001 Miami (Fla.)
1983 Florida	1976 Iowa	2006 Arkansas	1991 Tennessee	2002 Texas
1984 Florida	1977 Iowa State	2007 Wisconsin	1992 Arkansas	2003 Rice
1985 Stanford	1978 Iowa	2008 Wisconsin	1993 Arkansas	2004 Cal State—
1986 Stanford	1979 Iowa		1994 Arkansas	Fullerton
1987 Stanford	1980 Iowa	**OUTDOOR TRACK**	1995 Arkansas	2005 Texas
1988 Texas	1981 Iowa	1921 Illinois	1996 Arkansas	2006 Oregon St.
1989 Texas	1982 Iowa	1922 California	1997 Arkansas	2007 Oregon St.
1990 Texas	1983 Iowa	1923 Michigan	1998 Arkansas	2008 Fresno St.
1991 Texas	1984 Iowa	1924 No Meet	1999 Arkansas	
1992 Stanford	1985 Iowa	1925 Stanford	2000 Stanford	**GOLF**
1993 Stanford	1986 Iowa	1926 U.S.C.	2001 Tennessee	1897 Yale
1994 Stanford	1987 Iowa State	1927 Illinois	2002 Louisiana St.	1898 Harvard (spr),
1995 Michigan	1988 Arizona St.	1928 Stanford	2003 Arkansas	Yale (fall)
	1989 Oklahoma St.		2004 Arkansas	1899 Harvard

1900 No tourney
1901 Harvard
1902 Yale (spring)
1903 Harvard
1904 Harvard
1905 Yale
1906 Yale
1907 Yale
1908 Yale
1909 Yale
1910 Yale
1911 Yale
1912 Yale
1913 Yale
1914 Princeton
1915 Yale
1916 Princeton
1917 No tourney
1918 No tourney
1919 Princeton
1920 Princeton
1921 Dartmouth
1922 Princeton
1923 Princeton
1924 Yale
1925 Yale
1926 Yale
1927 Princeton
1928 Princeton
1929 Princeton
1930 Princeton
1931 Yale
1932 Yale
1933 Yale
1934 Michigan
1935 Michigan
1936 Yale
1937 Princeton
1938 Stanford
1939 Stanford
1940 Louisiana St., Princeton,
1941 Stanford
1942 Louisiana St., Stanford
1943 Yale
1944 Notre Dame
1945 Ohio State
1946 Stanford
1947 Louisiana St.
1948 San Jose St.
1949 North Texas
1950 North Texas

1951 North Texas
1952 North Texas
1953 Stanford
1954 S.M.U.
1955 Louisiana St.
1956 Houston
1957 Houston
1958 Houston
1959 Houston
1960 Houston
1961 Purdue
1962 Houston
1963 Oklahoma St.
1964 Houston
1965 Houston
1966 Houston
1967 Houston
1968 Florida
1969 Houston
1970 Houston
1971 Texas
1972 Texas
1973 Florida
1974 Wake Forest
1975 Wake Forest
1976 Oklahoma
1977 Houston
1978 Oklahoma St.
1979 Ohio State
1980 Oklahoma St.
1981 B.Y.U.
1982 Houston
1983 Oklahoma St.
1984 Houston
1985 Houston
1986 Wake Forest
1987 Oklahoma St.
1988 U.C.L.A.
1989 Oklahoma
1990 Arizona
1991 Oklahoma St.
1992 Arizona
1993 Florida
1994 Stanford
1995 Oklahoma St.
1996 Arizona St.
1997 Pepperdine
1998 U.N.L.V.
1999 Georgia
2000 Oklahoma St.
2001 Florida
2002 Minnesota
2003 Clemson

2003 California
2004 Georgia
2006 Oklahoma St.
2007 Stanford
2008 U.C.L.A

LACROSSE

1971 Cornell
1972 Virginia
1973 Maryland
1974 Johns Hopkins
1975 Maryland
1976 Cornell
1977 Cornell
1978 Johns Hopkins
1979 Johns Hopkins
1980 Johns Hopkins
1981 North Carolina
1982 North Carolina
1983 Syracuse
1984 Johns Hopkins
1985 Johns Hopkins
1986 North Carolina
1987 Johns Hopkins
1988 Syracuse
1989 Syracuse
1990 Syracuse
1991 North Carolina
1992 Princeton
1993 Princeton
1994 Princeton
1995 Syracuse
1996 Princeton
1997 Princeton
1998 Princeton
1999 Virginia
2000 Syracuse
2001 Princeton
2002 Syracuse
2003 Virginia
2004 Syracuse
2005 Johns Hopkins
2006 Virginia
2007 Johns Hopkins
2008 Syracuse

TENNIS

1946 U.S.C.
1947 William and Mary
1948 William and Mary
1949 San Francisco

1950 U.C.L.A.
1951 U.S.C.
1952 U.C.L.A.
1953 U.C.L.A.
1954 U.C.L.A.
1955 U.S.C.
1956 U.C.L.A.
1957 Michigan
1958 U.S.C.
1959 Notre Dame, Tulane
1960 U.C.L.A.
1961 U.C.L.A.
1962 U.S.C.
1963 U.S.C.
1964 U.S.C.
1965 U.C.L.A.
1966 U.S.C.
1967 U.S.C.
1968 U.S.C.
1969 U.S.C.
1970 U.C.L.A.
1971 U.C.L.A.
1972 Trinity (Tex.)
1973 Stanford
1974 Stanford
1975 U.C.L.A.
1976 U.S.C., U.C.L.A.
1977 Stanford
1978 Stanford
1979 U.C.L.A.
1980 Stanford
1981 Stanford
1982 U.C.L.A.
1983 Stanford
1984 U.C.L.A.
1985 Georgia
1986 Stanford
1987 Georgia
1988 Stanford
1989 Stanford
1990 Stanford
1991 U.S.C.
1992 Stanford
1993 U.S.C.
1994 U.S.C.
1995 Stanford
1996 Stanford
1997 Stanford
1998 Stanford
1999 Georgia

2000 Stanford
2001 Georgia
2002 U.S.C.
2003 Illinois
2003 Illinois
2004 Baylor
2005 U.C.L.A.
2006 Pepperdine
2007 Georgia
2008 Georgia

VOLLEYBALL

1970 U.C.L.A.
1971 U.C.L.A.
1972 U.C.L.A.
1973 San Diego St.
1974 U.C.L.A.
1975 U.C.L.A.
1976 U.C.L.A.
1977 U.S.C.
1978 Pepperdine
1979 U.C.L.A.
1980 U.S.C.
1981 U.C.L.A.
1982 U.C.L.A.
1983 U.C.L.A.
1984 U.C.L.A.
1985 Pepperdine
1986 Pepperdine
1987 U.C.L.A.
1988 U.S.C.
1989 U.C.L.A.
1990 U.S.C.
1991 Cal State—Long Beach
1992 Pepperdine
1993 U.C.L.A.
1994 Penn State
1995 U.C.L.A.
1996 U.C.L.A.
1997 Stanford
1998 U.C.L.A.
1999 B.Y.U.
2000 B.Y.U.
2001 B.Y.U.
2002 Hawaii
2003 Lewis
2004 B.Y.U.
2005 Pepperdine
2006 U.C.L.A.
2007 U.C. Irvine
2008 Penn State

Men's and Women's Sports

FENCING

1990 Penn State
1991 Penn State
1992 Columbia
1993 Columbia
1994 Notre Dame
1995 Penn State
1996 Penn State
1997 Penn State
1998 Penn State
1999 Penn State
2000 Penn State
2001 St. John's (N.Y.)
2002 Penn State
2003 Notre Dame
2004 Ohio State
2004 Notre Dame
2005 Notre Dame
2006 Harvard
2007 Penn State
2008 Ohio State

RIFLE

1954 Seattle
1955 Dartmouth
1956 Dartmouth
1957 Colorado
1958 Denver
1959 Denver
1960 Denver
1961 Middlebury
1962 Colorado
1963 Colorado
1964 Dartmouth
1965 Utah
1966 W. Colorado
1967 Wyoming
1968 Denver
1969 Dartmouth
1970 Dartmouth
1971 Colorado
1972 Denver
1973 Wyoming
1974 Wyoming
1975 Vermont
1976 Colorado
1977 Wyoming
1978 Wyoming
1979 Utah
1980 Tennessee Tech
1981 Tennessee Tech
1982 Tennessee Tech
1983 West Virginia
1984 West Virginia
1985 Murray State
1986 West Virginia
1987 Murray State
1988 West Virginia
1989 West Virginia
1990 West Virginia
1991 West Virginia
1992 West Virginia
1993 West Virginia
1994 Alaska Fairbanks
1995 West Virginia
1996 West Virginia
1997 West Virginia
1998 West Virginia
1999 Alaska Fairbanks
2000 Alaska Fairbanks
2001 Alaska Fairbanks
2002 Alaska Fairbanks
2003 Alaska Fairbanks
2004 Alaska Fairbanks
2005 U.S. Military Academy
2006 Alaska Fairbanks
2007 Alaska Fairbanks

SKIING

1954 Denver
1955 Denver
1956 Denver
1957 Denver
1958 Dartmouth
1959 Colorado
1960 Colorado
1961 Denver

1962	Denver	1972	Colorado	1982	Colorado	1992	Vermont	2002	Denver
1963	Denver	1973	Colorado	1983	Utah	1993	Utah	2003	Utah
1964	Denver	1974	Colorado	1984	Utah	1994	Vermont	2004	New Mexico
1965	Denver	1975	Colorado	1985	Wyoming	1995	Colorado	2005	Denver
1966	Denver	1976	Dartmouth	1986	Utah	1996	Utah	2006	Colorado
1967	Denver	1977	Colorado	1987	Utah	1997	Utah	2007	Dartmouth
1968	Wyoming	1978	Colorado	1988	Utah	1998	Colorado	2008	Denver
1969	Denver	1979	Colorado	1989	Vermont	1999	Colorado		
1970	Denver	1980	Vermont	1990	Vermont	2000	Denver		
1971	Denver	1981	Utah	1991	Colorado	2001	Denver		

Women's Sports

Year	Cross-Country	Field Hockey	Soccer	Volleyball	Indoor Track	Outdoor Track	Golf
1981	Virginia	Connecticut	N.A.	U.S.C.	N.A.	N.A.	N.A.
1982	Virginia	Old Dominion	North Carolina	Hawaii	N.A.	U.C.L.A.	Tulsa
1983	Oregon	Old Dominion	North Carolina	Hawaii	Nebraska	U.C.L.A.	T.C.U.
1984	Wisconsin	Old Dominion	North Carolina	U.C.L.A.	Nebraska	Florida State	Miami (Fla.)
1985	Wisconsin	Connecticut	George Mason	Pacific	Florida State	Oregon	Florida
1986	Texas	Iowa	North Carolina	Pacific	Texas	Texas	Florida
1987	Oregon	Maryland	North Carolina	Hawaii	Louisiana St.	Louisiana St.	San Jose St.
1988	Kentucky	Old Dominion	North Carolina	Texas	Texas	Louisiana St.	Tulsa
1989	Villanova	North Carolina	North Carolina	Cal St. Long Bch.	Louisiana St.	Louisiana St.	San Jose St.
1990	Villanova	Old Dominion	North Carolina	U.C.L.A.	Texas	Louisiana St.	Arizona St.
1991	Villanova	Old Dominion	North Carolina	U.C.L.A.	Louisiana St.	Louisiana St.	U.C.L.A.
1992	Villanova	Old Dominion	North Carolina	Stanford	Florida	Louisiana St.	San Jose St.
1993	Villanova	Maryland	North Carolina	Long Beach St.	Louisiana St.	Louisiana St.	Arizona St.
1994	Villanova	James Madison	North Carolina	Stanford	Louisiana St.	Louisiana St.	Arizona St.
1995	Providence	North Carolina	Notre Dame	Nebraska	Louisiana St.	Louisiana St.	Arizona St.
1996	Stanford	North Carolina	North Carolina	Stanford	Louisiana St.	Louisiana St.	Arizona
1997	B.Y.U.	North Carolina	North Carolina	Stanford	Louisiana St.	Louisiana St.	Arizona St.
1998	Villanova	Old Dominion	Florida	Long Beach St.	Texas	Texas	Arizona St.
1999	B.Y.U.	Maryland	North Carolina	Penn State	Texas	Texas	Duke
2000	Colorado	Old Dominion	North Carolina	Nebraska	U.C.L.A.	Louisiana St.	Arizona
2001	B.Y.U.	Michigan	Santa Clara	Stanford	U.C.L.A.	U.S.C.	Georgia
2002	B.Y.U.	Wake Forest	Portland	U.S.C.	Louisiana St.	South Carolina	Duke
2003	Stanford	Wake Forest	North Carolina	U.S.C.	Louisiana St.	Louisiana St.	U.S.C.
2004	Colorado	Wake Forest	Notre Dame	Stanford	Louisiana St.	U.C.L.A.	U.C.L.A.
2005	Stanford	Maryland	Portland	Washington	Texas	Texas	N. Mexico
2006	Stanford	Maryland	North Carolina	Nebraska	Texas	Auburn	Duke
2007	Stanford	North Carolina	U.S.C.	Penn State	Arizona St.	Arizona St.	Duke
2008					Arizona St.	Louisiana St.	U.S.C.

Year	Gymnastics	Lacrosse	Softball	Swimming	Tennis	Fencing[1]		
1982	Utah	Massachusetts	U.C.L.A.	Florida	Stanford	N.A.		
1983	Utah	Delaware	Texas A&M	Stanford	U.S.C.	Wayne State		
1984	Utah	Temple	U.C.L.A.	Texas	Stanford	Penn State		
1985	Utah	New Hampshire	U.C.L.A.	Texas	U.S.C.	Yale		
1986	Utah	Maryland	Cal State Fullerton	Texas	Stanford	Yale		
1987	Georgia	Penn State	Texas A&M	Texas	Stanford	Pennsylvania		
1988	Alabama	Temple	U.C.L.A.	Texas	Stanford	Notre Dame		
1989	Georgia	Penn State	U.C.L.A.	Stanford	Stanford	Wayne State		
1990	Utah	Harvard	U.C.L.A.	Texas	Stanford	Wayne State		
1991	Alabama	Virginia	Arizona	Texas	Stanford			
1992	Utah	Maryland	U.C.L.A.	Stanford	Florida			
1993	Georgia	Virginia	Arizona	Stanford	Texas			
1994	Utah	Princeton	Arizona	Stanford	Georgia			
1995	Utah	Maryland	U.C.L.A.	Stanford	Texas			
1996	Alabama	Maryland	Arizona	Stanford	Florida			
1997	U.C.L.A.	Maryland	Arizona	U.S.C.	Stanford			
1998	Georgia	Maryland	Fresno State	Stanford	Florida			
1999	Georgia	Maryland	U.C.L.A.	Georgia	Stanford			
2000	U.C.L.A.	Maryland	Oklahoma	Georgia	Georgia	Water Polo	Ice Hockey	
2001	U.C.L.A.	Maryland	Arizona	Georgia	Stanford	U.C.L.A.	Minn.Duluth	
2002	Alabama	Princeton	California	Auburn	Stanford	Stanford	Minn.Duluth	
2003	U.C.L.A.	Princeton	U.C.L.A.	Auburn	Florida	U.C.L.A.	Minn.Duluth	
2004	U.C.L.A.	Virginia	U.C.L.A.	Auburn	Stanford	U.S.C.	Minnesota	
2005	Georgia	Northwestern	Michigan	Georgia	Stanford	U.C.L.A.	Minnesota	
2006	Georgia	Northwestern	Arizona	Auburn	Stanford	U.C.L.A.	Wisconsin	
2007	Georgia	Northwestern	Arizona	Auburn	Georgia Tech	U.C.L.A.	Wisconsin	
2008	Georgia	Northwestern	Arizona State	Arizona	U.C.L.A.	U.C.L.A.	Minn.Duluth	

Note: 1. Since 1990, the NCAA has recognized a joint fencing champion. See "Men's and Women's Sports" above.

International Sports

YACHTING: THE AMERICA'S CUP

n 1851, the Royal Yacht Squadron presented a hundred guinea cup" to the winning yacht in a race around the Isle of Wight in the English Channel. The cup was won by the U.S. schooner *America* and thereafter became known as the America's Cup. In 24 challenges over the next 132 years the cup remained in the hands of U.S. yachtsmen.

In 2003, Switzerland became the first landlocked country to win the cup, when *Alinghi* defeated Team New Zealand 5-0 in Auckland.

The America's Cup, 1851–2007

Year	Winner	Loser	Year	Winner	Loser
1851	America, U.S.	Aurora, England	1962	Weatherly, U.S.	Gretel, Australia
1870	Magic, U.S.	Cambria, England	1964	Constellation, U.S.	Sovereign, Britain
1871	Columbia, U.S.	Livonia, England	1970	Intrepid, U.S.	Gretel II, Australia
1876	Madeline, U.S.	Countess of Dufferin, Canada	1974	Courageous, U.S.	Southern Cross, Australia
1881	Mischief, U.S.	Atalanta, Canada	1977	Courageous, U.S.	Australia, Australia
1885	Puritan, U.S.	Genesta, Britain	1980	Freedom, U.S.	Australia, Australia
1886	Mayflower, U.S.	Galatea, Britain	1983	Australia II, Australia	Liberty, U.S.
1887	Volunteer, U.S.	Thistle, Scotland	1987	Stars & Stripes, U.S.	Kookaburra III, Australia
1893	Vigilant, U.S.	Valkyrie II, Britain	1988	Stars & Stripes, U.S.	KZ, New Zealand
1895	Defender, U.S.	Valkyrie III, Britain	1992	America3, U.S.	Il Moro di Venezia, Italy
1899	Columbia, U.S.	Shamrock, Ireland	1995	Black Magic, New Zealand	Young America, U.S.
1901	Columbia, U.S.	Shamrock II, Ireland			
1903	Reliance, U.S.	Shamrock III, Ireland	2000	Team New Zealand, New Zealand	Prada, Italy
1920	Resolute, U.S.	Shamrock IV, Ireland			
1930	Enterprise, U.S.	Shamrock V, Ireland	2003	Alinghi, Switzerland	Team New Zealand, New Zealand
1934	Rainbow, U.S.	Endeavour, Britain			
1937	Ranger, U.S.	Endeavour II, Britain	2007	Alinghi, Switzerland	Emirates Team New Zealand, New Zealand
1958	Columbia, U.S.	Sceptre, Britain			

SOCCER: THE WORLD CUP

The World Cup, modern soccer's crowning event, is staged every four years by the Federation Internationale de Football Association (FIFA). Players represent their home country, regardless of where they regularly play. Millions attend the Cup's many contests, and the televised final is viewed by over a billion people worldwide. In 2006 Germany was the host country.

The World Cup, 1930–2006

Year	Final Score	Leading scorer, country (goals)	Host country	Participating nations
1930	Uruguay 4, Argentina 2	Stabile, Argentina (8)	Uruguay	13
1934	Italy 2, Czechoslovakia 1 (OT)	Conen, Germany; Nejedly, Czechoslovakia; Schiavo, Italy (4)	Italy	31
1938	Italy 4, Hungary 2	Leonidas, Brazil (8)	France	36
1942	No tournament—World War II			
1946	No tournament—World War II			
1950	Uruguay 2, Brazil 1	Ademir, Brazil (7)	Brazil	33
1954	West Germany 3, Hungary 2	Kocsis, Hungary (11)	Switzerland	38
1958	Brazil 5, Sweden 2	Fontaine, France (13)	Sweden	53
1962	Brazil 3, Czechoslovakia 1	Jerkovic, Yugoslavia (5)	Chile	56
1966	England 4, West Germany 2 (OT)	Eusebio, Portugal (9)	England	71
1970	Brazil 4, Italy 1	Muller, West Germany (10)	Mexico	71
1974	West Germany 2, Netherlands 1	Lato, Poland (7)	West Germany	98
1978	Argentina 3, Netherlands 1 (OT)	Kempes, Argentina (6)	Argentina	106
1982	Italy 3, West Germany 1	Rossi, Italy (6)	Spain	109
1986	Argentina 3, West Germany 2	Lineker, England (6)	Mexico	121
1990	West Germany 1, Argentina 0	Schilacci, Italy (6)	Italy	112
1994	Brazil 0, Italy 0 (OT)[1]	Stoichkov, Bulgaria (6)	United States	144
1998	France 3, Brazil 0	Suker, Croatia (6)	France	173
2002	Brazil 2, Germany 0	Ronaldo, Brazil (8)	S. Korea/Japan	198
2006	Italy 1, France 1 (OT)[2]	Miroslav Klose, Germany (5)	Germany	198

Notes: 1. Brazil won 3-2 on penalty kicks. **2.** Italy won 5-3 on penalty kicks. **Source:** FIFA.

2006 World Cup, First Round

Group A	Wins-Losses-Ties	Points
Germany	3-0-0	9
Ecuador	2-1-0	6
Poland	1-2-0	3
Costa Rica	0-3-0	0

Germany 4, Costa Rica 2   Ecuador 2, Poland 0
Germany 1, Poland 0 Ecuador 3, Costa Rica 0 Italy 1, U
Germany 3, Ecuador 0   Poland 2, Costa Rica 1

Group B	Wins-Losses-Ties	Points
England	2-0-1	7
Sweden	1-0-2	5
Paraguay	1-2-0	3
Trinidad & Tobago	0-2-1	1

England 1, Paraguay 0 Trinidad & Tobago 0, Sweden 0
Trinidad & Tobago 0 Sweden 1, Paraguay 0 Brazil 2, Australia
2   Paraguay 2, Trinidad & Tobago 0

Group C	Wins-Losses-Ties	Points
Argentina	2-0-1	7
Netherlands	2-0-1	7
Ivory Coast	1-2-0	3
Serbia & Montenegro	0-3-0	0

Argentina 2, Ivory Coast 1 Neth. 1, Serb & Monte, 0
Argentina 6, Serb & Monte 0 Neth. 2, Ivory Coast 1
Argentina 0, Netherlands 0 Ivory Coast 3, Serb & Monte 0

Group D	Wins-Losses-Ties	Points
Portugal	3-0-0	9
Mexico	1-1-1	4
Angola	0-1-2	2
Iran	0-0-1	1

Portugal 1, Angola 0   Mexico 3, Iran 1
Portugal 2, Iran 0   Mexico 0, Angola 0
Portugal 2, Mexico 1   Angola 1, Iran 1

Group E	Wins-Losses-Ties	Points
Italy	2-0-1	7
Ghana	2-1-0	6
Czech Republic	1-2-0	3
U.S.A.	0-2-1	1

Italy 2, Ghana 0   Czech Republic 3, U.S.A 0
.A. 1   Ghana 2, Czech Republic 0
Italy 2, Czech Republic 0   Ghana 2, U.S.A. 1

Group F	Wins-Losses-Ties	Points
Brazil	3-0-0	9
Australia	1-1-1	4
Croatia	0-1-2	2
Japan	0-2-1	1

Brazil 1, Croatia 0   Australia 3, Japan 1 England 2,
Croatia 0, Japan 1 England 2, Sweden
Australia 2, Croatia 2   Brazil 4, Japan 1

Group G	Wins-Losses-Ties	Points
Switzerland	2-0-1	7
France	1-0-2	5
South Korea	1-1-1	4
Togo	0-2-1	1

Switzerland 0, France 0   S.Korea 2, Togo 1
France 1, South Korea 1   Switzerland 2, Togo 0
France 2, Togo 0   Switzerland 2, South Korea 0

Group H	Wins-Losses-Ties	Points
Spain	3-0-0	9
Ukraine	2-1-0	6
Tunisia	0-2-1	1
Saudi Arabia	0-2-1	1

Spain 4, Ukraine 0   Tunisia 2, Saudi Arabia 2
Spain 3, Tunisia 1   Ukraine 4, Saudi Arabia 0
Spain 1, Sudi Arabia 0   Ukraine 1, Tunisia 0

Note: A win is worth three points and a tie is worth one point. The top two teams in each group advance to the second round.

2006 World Cup, Second Round

Germany 2
Germany 1(OT)[2]
Sweden 0
Germany 0
Argentina 2 (OT)
Argentina 1
Mexico 1
Italy 1
Italy 3
Australia 0
Italy 2 (OT)
Ukraine 0 (OT)[1]
Ukraine 0
Switzerland 0

Semifinals

Italy 1   France 1[4]

World Cup Final

Semifinals

England 0
England 1
Ecuador 0
Portugal 0
Portugal 1
Portugal 0
(OT)[3]
Netherlands 0
France 1
Brazil 3
Brazil 0
Ghana 0
France 3
France 1
Spain 1

Third Place Game
Germany 3   Portugal 1

Notes: 1. Ukraine beat Switzerland 3-0 on penalties. **2.** Germany beat Argentina 4-2 on penalties. **3.** Portugal beat England 3-1 on penalties. **4.** Italy won on penalties, 5-3.

The Women's World Cup, 2007

he 2007 tournament was held in China, returning to the place of the first FIFA Women's World Cup in 1991. In spite of time differences, both Germany and Brazil set new records for television coverage, and Germany took home the title for the second straight time. Brazil finished second with the U.S. following, and although its team finished fourth, Norway received the FIFA fair play award. FIFA.com users voted Brazilian Marta's goal in hte semi-final game the Goal of the Tournament, and Brazil the most entertaining team.

FIRST ROUND

Group A	Wins-Losses-Draws	Points	Group B	Wins-Losses-Draws	Points
Germany	2-0-1	7	United States	2-0-1	7
England	1-0-2	5	North Korea	1-1-1	4
Japan	1-1-1	4	Sweden	1-1-1	4
Argentina	0-3-0	0	Nigeria	0-2-1	1

Germany 11, Argentina, 0	England 0, Germany 0	U.S. 2, North Korea 2	North Korea 2, Nigeria 0
Japan 2, England 2	Germany 2, Japan 0	Nigeria 1, Sweden 1	Nigeria 0, U.S. 1
Argentina 0, Japan 1	England 6, Argentina 1	Sweden 0, U.S. 2	North Korea 1, Sweden 2

Group C	Wins-Losses-Draws	Points	Group D	Wins-Losses-Draws	Points
Norway	2-0-1	7	Brazil	3-0-0	9
Australia	1-0-2	5	China	2-1-0	6
Canada	1-1-1	4	Denmark	1-2-0	3
Ghana	0-3-0	0	New Zealand	0-3-0	0

Ghana 1, Australia 4	Australia 1, Norway 1	New Zealand 0, Brazil 5	Brazil 4, China 0
Norway 2, Canada 1	Norway 7, Ghana 2	China 3, Denmark 2	China 2, New Zealand 0
Canada 4, Ghana 0	Australia 2, Canada 2	Denmark 2, New Zealand 0	Brazil 1, Denmark 0

Note: A win is worth three points, and a tie is worth one point. The top two teams in each group advance to the second round.

2007 Women's World Cup, Second Round

Germany 3

Semifinals   Germany 3

N. Korea 0

Semifinals   U.S. 0

U.S. 3

England 0

World Cup Final
Germany 2   Brazil 0

Norway 1

Norway 0

China 0

Brazil 3

Brazil 4

Australia 2

Third Place Game
U.S. 4   Norway 1

CYCLING

The Tour de France

Year	Champion	Year	Champion	Year	Champion	Year	Champion
1903	Maurice Garin	1907	Lucien Petit-Breton	1911	Gustave Garrigou	1919	Firmin Lambot
1904	Henri Cornet	1908	Lucien Petit-Breton	1912	Odile Defraye	1920	Philippe Thijs
1905	Louis Trousselier	1909	Francois Faber	1913	Philippe Thijs	1921	Leon Scieur
1906	Rene Pottier	1910	Octave Lapize	1914	Philippe Thijs	1922	Firmin Lambot

Year	Champion	Year	Champion	Year	Champion	Year	Champion
1923	Henri Pelissier	1950	Ferdi Kubler	1969	Eddy Merckx	1989	Greg LeMond
1924	Lucien Petit-Breton	1951	Hugo Koblet	1970	Eddy Merckx	1990	Greg LeMond
1925	Ottavio Bottecchia	1952	Fausto Coppi	1971	Eddy Merckx	1991	Miguel Indurain
1926	Lucien Buysse	1953	Louison Bobet	1972	Eddy Merckx	1992	Miguel Indurain
1927	Nicolas Frantz	1954	Louison Bobet	1973	Luis Ocana	1993	Miguel Indurain
1928	Nicolas Frantz	1955	Louison Bobet	1974	Eddy Merckx	1994	Miguel Indurain
1929	Maurice Dewaele	1956	Roger Walkowiak	1975	Bernard Thevenet	1995	Miguel Indurain
1930	Andre Leducq	1957	Jacques Anquetil	1976	Lucien Van Impe	1996	Bjarne Riis
1931	Antonin Magne	1958	Charly Gaul	1977	Bernard Thevenet	1997	Jan Ullrich
1932	Andre Leducq	1959	Federico Bahamontes	1978	Bernard Hinault	1998	Marco Pantini
1933	Georges Speicher			1979	Bernard Hinault	1999	Lance Armstrong
1934	Antonin Magne	1960	Gastone Nencini	1980	Joop Zoetemelk	2000	Lance Armstrong
1935	Romain Maes	1961	Jacques Anquetil	1981	Bernard Hinault	2001	Lance Armstrong
1936	Sylvere Maes	1962	Jacques Anquetil	1982	Bernard Hinault	2002	Lance Armstrong
1937	Roger Lapebie	1963	Jacques Anquetil	1983	Laurent Fignon	2003	Lance Armstrong
1938	Gino Bartali	1964	Jacques Anquetil	1984	Laurent Fignon	2004	Lance Armstrong
1939	Sylvere Maes	1965	Felice Gimondi	1985	Bernard Hinault	2005	Lance Armstrong
1947	Jean Robic	1966	Lucien Aimar	1986	Greg LeMond	2006	Oscar Pereiro[1]
1948	Gino Bartali	1967	Roger Pingeon	1987	Stephen Roche	2007	Alberto Contador
1949	Fausto Coppi	1968	Jan Janssen	1988	Pedro Delgado	2008	Carlos Sastre

Note: 1. Floyd Landis, initially declared champion, was disqualified after testing positive for illegal substance.

CHESS

World and U.S. Chess Champions

WORLD CHESS CHAMPIONS

Year	Champion, Countrry
1886	Wilhelm Steinitz, Austria
1894	Emanuel Lasker, Germany
1921	José R. Capablanca, Cuba
1927	Alexander Alekhine, France
1935	Max Euwe, Netherlands
1937	Alexander Alekhine, France
1948	Mikhail Botvinnik, USSR
1957	Vassily Smyslov, USSR
1958	Mikhail Botvinnik, USSR
1960	Mikhail Tal, USSR
1961	Mikhail Botvinnik, USSR
1963	Tigran Petrosian, USSR
1969	Boris Spassky, USSR
1972	Bobby Fischer, USA
1975	Anatoly Karpov, USSR
1985	Garry Kasparov, USSR/Russia
1993	Anatoly Karpov[1], Russia
1999	Alex Khalifman, Russia
2000	Visawanthan Anand, India
2002	Ruslan Ponomariov, Ukraine
2004	Rustam Kasimdzhanov, Uzbekistan
2005	Veselin Topalov, Bulgaria
2006	Vladmir Kramnik, Russia
2007	Viswanathan Anand, India

U.S. CHESS CHAMPIONS

Year	Champion	Year	Champion
1845–57	Charles Henry Stanley		Larry Christiansen, Roman Dzindzichashvili
1857–71	Paul Morphy	1984–85	Lev Alburt
1871–90	Capt. George Mackenzie	1986	Yasser Seirawan
1890–91	Jackson Showalter	1987	Joel Benjamin, Nick deFirmian
1891–94	Solomon Lipschutz	1988	Michael Wilder
1894	Jackson Showalter	1989	Roman Dzindzichashvili, Stuart Rachels, Yasser Seirawan
1894–95	Albert Hodges		
1895–97	Jackson Showalter		
1897–1906	Harry Nelson Pillsbury	1990	Lev Alburt
1906–09	Jackson Showalter	1991	Gata Kamsky
1909–36	Frank J. Marshall	1992	Patrick Wolff
1936–42	Samuel Reshevsky	1993	Alexander Shabalov, Alex Yermolinsky
1944	Arnold Denker		
1946	Samuel Reshevsky	1994	Boris Gulko
1948	Herman Steiner	1995	Nick deFirmian, Alexander Ivanov, Patrick Wolf
1951–52	Larry Evans		
1954	Arthur Bisguier		
1957–61	Bobby Fischer	1996	Alex Yermolinski
1961–62	Larry Evans	1997	Joel Benjamin
1962–66	Bobby Fischer	1998	Nick deFirmian
1968	Larry Evans	1999	Boris Gulko
1969	Samuel Reshevksy	2000	Joel Benjamin
1972	Robert Byrne	2001	Joel Benjamin, Yasser Seirawan, Alexander Shabalov
1973	John Grefe, Lubomir Kavalek		
1974–77	Walter Browne	2002	Larry Christiansen
1978	Lubomir Kavalek	2003	Alexander Shabalov
1980	Walter Browne, Larry Evans, Larry Christiansen	2004	Hikaru Nakamura
		2006	Alexander Onischuk (men) Anna Zatonskih (women)
1981	Walter Browne, Yasser Seirawan	2007	Alexander Shabalov (men) Irina Krush (women)
1983	Walter Browne,		

Note: Chess championships are not held every year. 1. In 1993, Kasparov vacated his World Chess Federation (FIDE) championship, whereupon FIDE awarded the title to Karpov. Source: U.S. Chess Federation.

FIGURE SKATING

U.S. and World Figure Skating Champions

	U.S. Champions		World Champions	
Year	Men	Women	Men, Country	Women, Country
1952	Richard Button	Tenley Albright	Richard Button, U.S.	Jacqueline du Bief, France
1953	Hayes Jenkins	Tenley Albright	Hayes Jenkins, U.S.	Tenley Albright, U.S.
1954	Hayes Jenkins	Tenley Albright	Hayes Jenkins, U.S.	Gundi Busch, W. Germany
1955	Hayes Jenkins	Tenley Albright	Hayes Jenkins, U.S.	Tenley Albright, U.S.
1956	Hayes Jenkins	Tenley Albright	Hayes Jenkins, U.S.	Carol Heiss, U.S.
1957	Dave Jenkins	Carol Heiss	Dave Jenkins, U.S.	Carol Heiss, U.S.
1958	Dave Jenkins	Carol Heiss	Dave Jenkins, U.S.	Carol Heiss, U.S.
1959	Dave Jenkins	Carol Heiss	Dave Jenkins, U.S.	Carol Heiss, U.S.
1960	Dave Jenkins	Carol Heiss	Alain Giletti, France	Carol Heiss, U.S.
1961	Bradley Lord	Laurence Owen	No champion	No champion
1962	Monty Hoyt	Barbara Roles Pursley	Don Jackson, Canada	Sjoukje Dijkstra, Netherlands
1963	Tommy Litz	Lorraine Hanlon	Don McPherson, Canada	Sjoukje Dijkstra, Netherlands
1964	Scott Allen	Peggy Fleming	Manfred Schnelldorfer, West Germany	Sjoukje Dijkstra, Netherlands
1965	Gary Visconti	Peggy Fleming	Alain Calmat, France	Petra Burka, Canada
1966	Scott Allen	Peggy Fleming	Emmerich Danzer, Austria	Peggy Fleming, U.S.
1967	Gary Visconti	Peggy Fleming	Emmerich Danzer, Austria	Peggy Fleming, U.S.
1968	Tim Wood	Peggy Fleming	Emmerich Danzer, Austria	Peggy Fleming, U.S.
1969	Tim Wood	Janet Lynn	Tim Wood, U.S.	Gabriele Seyfert, E. Germany
1970	Tim Wood	Janet Lynn	Tim Wood, U.S.	Gabriele Seyfert, E. Germany
1971	John Misha Petkevich	Janet Lynn	Ondrej Nepela, Czechoslovakia	Beatrix Schuba, Austria
1972	Ken Shelley	Janet Lynn	Ondrej Nepela, Czechoslovakia	Beatrix Schuba, Austria
1973	Gordon McKellen Jr.	Janet Lynn	Ondrej Nepela, Czechoslovakia	Karen Magnussen, Canada
1974	Gordon McKellen Jr.	Dorothy Hamill	Jan Hoffmann, E. Germany	Christine Errath, E. Germany
1975	Gordon McKellen Jr.	Dorothy Hamill	Sergei Volkov, USSR	Dianne de Leeuw, Netherlands/U.S.
1976	Terry Kubicka	Dorothy Hamill	John Curry, Great Britain	Dorothy Hamill, U.S.
1977	Charles Tickner	Linda Fratianne	Vladimir Kovalev, USSR	Linda Fratianne, U.S.
1978	Charles Tickner	Linda Fratianne	Charles Tickner, U.S.	Anett Potzsch, E. Germany
1979	Charles Tickner	Linda Fratianne	Vladimir Kovalev, USSR	Linda Fratianne, U.S.
1980	Charles Tickner	Linda Fratianne	Jan Hoffmann, E. Germany	Anett Potzsch, E. Germany
1981	Scott Hamilton	Elaine Zayak	Scott Hamilton, U.S.	Denise Biellmann, Switzerland
1982	Scott Hamilton	Rosalynn Sumners	Scott Hamilton, U.S.	Elaine Zayak, U.S.
1983	Scott Hamilton	Rosalynn Sumners	Scott Hamilton, U.S.	Rosalynn Sumners, U.S.
1984	Scott Hamilton	Rosalynn Sumners	Scott Hamilton, U.S.	Katarina Witt, E. Germany
1985	Brian Boitano	Tiffany Chin	Aleksandr Fadeev, USSR	Katarina Witt, E. Germany
1986	Brian Boitano	Debi Thomas	Brian Boitano, U.S.	Debi Thomas, U.S.
1987	Brian Boitano	Jill Trenary	Brian Orser, Canada	Katarina Witt, E. Germany
1988	Brian Boitano	Debi Thomas	Brian Boitano, U.S.	Katarina Witt, E. Germany
1989	Christopher Bowman	Jill Trenary	Kurt Browning, Canada	Midori Ito, Japan
1990	Todd Eldredge	Jill Trenary	Kurt Browning, Canada	Jill Trenary, U.S.
1991	Todd Eldredge	Tonya Harding	Kurt Browning, Canada	Kristi Yamaguchi, U.S.
1992	Christopher Bowman	Kristi Yamaguchi	Victor Petrenko, Russia	Kristi Yamaguchi, U.S.
1993	Scott Davis	Nancy Kerrigan	Kurt Browning, Canada	Oksana Baiul, Ukraine
1994	Scott Davis	Tonya Harding[1]	Elvis Stojko, Canada	Yuka Sato, Japan
1995	Todd Eldredge	Nicole Bobek	Elvis Stojko, Canada	Lu Chen, China
1996	Rudy Galindo	Michelle Kwan	Todd Eldredge, U.S.	Michelle Kwan, U.S.
1997	Todd Eldredge	Tara Lipinski	Elvis Stojko, Canada	Tara Lipinski, U.S.
1998	Todd Eldredge	Michelle Kwan	Alexi Yagudin, Russia	Michelle Kwan, U.S.
1999	Michael Weiss	Michelle Kwan	Alexi Yagudin, Russia	Maria Butyrskaya, Russia
2000	Michael Weiss	Michelle Kwan	Alexi Yagudin, Russia	Michelle Kwan, U.S.
2001	Tim Goebel	Michelle Kwan	Evgeni Plushenko, Russia	Michelle Kwan, U.S.
2002	Tim Goebel	Michelle Kwan	Alexi Yagudin, Russia	Irina Slutskaya, Russia
2003	Michael Weiss	Michelle Kwan	Evgeni Plushenko, Russia	Michelle Kwan, U.S.
2004	Johnny Weir	Michelle Kwan	Evgeni Plushenko, Russia	Shizuka Arakawa, Japan
2005	Johnny Weir	Michelle Kwan	Stephane Lambiel, Switz.	Irina Slutskaya, Russia
2006	Johnny Weir	Sasha Cohen	Stephane Lambiel, Switz.	Kimmie Meissner, U.S.
2007	Evan Lysacek	Kimmie Meissner	Brian Joubert, France	Miki Ando, Japan
2008	Evan Lysacek	Mirai Nagasu	Jeffrey Buttle, Canada	Mao Asada, Japan

1. Later stripped of title. **Source:** U.S. Figure Skating Association.

MARATHON RUNNING

Marathons are 26 miles, 385 yards long, the distance purportedly run by the Athenian messenger who announced his city-state's victory over the Persian Empire on the Plains of Marathon in 490 B.C. The oldest U.S. marathon covers a route from Hopkinton, Mass. to Boston.

Boston Marathon Champions

MEN'S CHAMPIONS

Year	Winner	Time	Year	Winner	Time	Year	Winner	Time
1897	John J. McDermott	2:55:10	1935	John A. Kelley	2:32:07	1970	Ron Hill	2:10:30
1898	Ronald J. McDonald	2:42:00	1936	Ellison M. (Tarzan)	2:33:40	1971	Alavaro Mejia	2:18:45
1899	Lawrence J. Brignolia	2:54:38		Brown		1972	Olavi Suomalainen	2:15:39
1900	James J. Caffrey	2:39:44	1937	Walter Young	2:33:20	1973	Jon Anderson	2:16:03
1901	James J. Caffrey	2:29:23	1938	Leslie Pawson	2:35:34	1974	Neil Cusack	2:13:39
1902	Samuel A. Mellor	2:43:12	1939	Ellison M. (Tarzan)	2:28:51	1975	Bill Rodgers	2:09:55
1903	John C. Lorden	2:41:29		Brown		1976	Jack Fultz	2:20:19
1904	Michael Spring	2:38:04	1940	Gerard Cote	2:33:20	1977	Jerome Drayton	2:14:46
1905	Fred Lorz	2:38:25	1941	Leslie Pawson	2:30:38	1978	Bill Rodgers	2:10:13
1906	Timothy Ford	2:45:45	1942	Bernard Joe Smith	2:26:51	1979	Bill Rodgers	2:09:27
1907	Thomas Longboat	2:24:24	1943	Gerard Cote	2:28:25	1980	Bill Rodgers	2:12:11
1908	Thomas P. Morrissey	2:25:43	1944	Gerard Cote	2:31:50	1981	Toshihiko Seko	2:09:26
1909	Henri Renaud	2:53:36	1945	John A. Kelley	2:30:40	1982	Alberto Salazar	2:08:52
1910	Fred L. Cameron	2:28:52	1946	Stylianos Kyriakides	2:29:27	1983	Gregory A. Meyer	2:09:00
1911	Clarence H. DeMar	2:21:39	1947	Yun Bok Suh	2:25:39	1984	Geoff Smith	2:10:34
1912	Michael J. Ryan	2:21:18	1948	Gerard Cote	2:31:02	1985	Geoff Smith	2:14:05
1913	Fritz Carlson	2:25:14	1949	Karle Leandersson	2:31:50	1986	Robert de Castella	2:07:51
1914	James Duffy	2:25:01	1950	Kee Yong Ham	2:32:39	1987	Toshihiko Seko	2:11:50
1915	Edouard Fabre	2:31:41	1951	Shigeki Tanaka	2:27:45	1988	Ibrahim Hussein	2:08:43
1916	Arthur V. Roth	2:27:16	1952	Doroteo Flores	2:31:53	1989	Abebe Mekonnen	2:09:06
1917	William K. Kennedy	2:28:37	1953	Keizo Yamada	2:18:51	1990	Gelindo Bordin	2:08:20
1918	Service team race		1954	Veikko L. Karvonen	2:20:39	1991	Ibrahim Hussein	2:11:06
	won by Camp Devens		1955	Hideo Hamamura	2:18:22	1992	Ibrahim Hussein	2:08:14
1919	Carl W. A. Linder	2:29:13	1956	Antti Viskari	2:14:14	1993	Cosmas N'Deti	2:09:33
1920	Peter Trivoulidas	2:29:31	1957	John J. Delley	2:20:05	1994	Cosmas N'Deti	2:07:15
1921	Frank Zuna	2:18:57	1958	Franjo Mihalic	2:25:54	1995	Cosmas N'Deti	2:09:22
1922	Clarence H. DeMar	2:18:10	1959	Eino Oksanen	2:22:42	1996	Moses Tanui	2:09:16
1923	Clarence H. DeMar	2:23:37	1960	Paavo Kotila	2:20:54	1997	Lameck Aguta	2:10:34
1924	Clarence H. DeMar	2:29:40	1961	Eino Oksanen	2:23:39	1998	Moses Tanui	2:07:34
1925	Charles L. Mellor	2:33:00	1962	Eino Oksanen	2:23:48	1999	Joseph Chebet	2:09:52
1926	John C. Miles	2:25:40	1963	Aurele	2:18:58	2000	Elijah Lagat	2:09:47
1927	Clarence H. DeMar	2:40:22		Vandendriessche		2001	Lee Bong-ju	2:09:43
1928	Clarence H. DeMar	2:37:07	1964	Aurele	2:19:59	2002	Rodgers Rop	2:09:02
1929	John C. Miles	2:33:08		Vandendriessche		2003	Robert Cheruiyot	2:10:11
1930	Clarence H. DeMar	2:34:48	1965	Morio Shigematsu	2:16:33	2004	Timothy Cherigat	2:10:37
1931	James P. Henigan	2:46:45	1966	Kenji Kimihara	2:17:11	2005	Hailu Negussie	2:11:45
1932	Paul deBruyn	2:33:36	1967	David McKenzie	2:15:45	2006	Robert Cheruiyot	2:07:14
1933	Leslie Pawson	2:33:01	1968	Ambrose Burfoot	2:22:17	2007	Robert Cheruiyot	2:14:13
1934	Dave Komonen	2:32:53	1969	Yoshiaki Unetani	2:13:49	2008	Robert Cheruiyot	2:07:46

WOMEN'S CHAMPIONS

Year	Winner	Time	Year	Winner	Time	Year	Winner	Time
1972	Nina Kuscsik	3:10:26	1985	Lisa Larsen-	2:34:06	1997	Fatuma Roba	2:28:03
1973	Jacqueline Hansen	3:05:59		Weidenbach		1998	Fatuma Roba	2:23:21
1974	Miki Gorman	2:47:11	1986	Ingrid Kristiansen	2:24:55	1999	Fatuma Roba	2:23:25
1975	Liane Winter	2:42:24	1987	Rosa Mota	2:25:21	2000	Catherine Ndereba	2:26:11
1976	Kim Merritt	2:47:10	1988	Rosa Mota	2:24:30	2001	Catherine Ndereba	2:21:50
1977	Miki Gorman	2:46:22	1989	Ingrid Kristiansen	2:24:33	2002	Margaret Okayo	2:20:43
1978	Gayle Barron	2:44:52	1990	Rosa Mota	2:25:24	2003	Svetlana Zakharova	2:25:20
1979	Joan Benoit	2:35:15	1991	Wanda Panfil	2:24:18	2004	Catherine Ndereba	2:24:27
1980	Jacqueline Gareau	2:34:28	1992	Olga Markova	2:23:43	2005	Catherine Ndereba	2:25:13
1981	Allison Roe	2:26:46	1993	Olga Markova	2:25:27	2006	Rita Jeptoo	2:23:38
1982	Charlotte Teske	2:29:33	1994	Uta Pippig	2:21:45	2007	Lidiya Grigoryeva	2:29:18
1983	Joan Benoit	2:22:43	1995	Uta Pippig	2:25:11	2008	Dire Tune	2:25:25
1984	Lorraine Moller	2:29:28	1996	Uta Pippig	2:27:12			

New York Marathon Champions

Year	Winner	Time	Year	Winner	Time	Year	Winner	Time
	MEN		1996	Giacomo Leone	2:10:09	1982	Grete Waitz	2:27:14
1970	Gary Muhrcke	2:31:39	1997	John Kagwe	2:08:12	1983	Grete Waitz	2:27:00
1971	Norman Higgins	2:22:55	1998	John Kagwe	2:08:45	1984	Grete Waitz	2:29:30
1972	Sheldon Karlin	2:27:53	1999	Joseph Chebet	2:09:14	1985	Grete Waitz	2:28:34
1973	Tom Fleming	2:21:55	2000	Abdelkhader	2:10:09	1986	Grete Waitz	2:28:06
1974	Norbert Sander	2:26:31		el-Mouaziz		1987	Priscilla Welch	2:30:17
1975	Tom Fleming	2:19:27	2001	Tesfaye Jifar	2:07:43	1988	Grete Waitz	2:28:07
1976	Bill Rodgers	2:10:10	2002	Rodgers Rop	2:08:07	1989	Ingrid Kristiansen	2:25:30
1977	Bill Rodgers	2:11:28	2003	Martin Lel	2:10:30	1990	Wanda Panfil	2:30:45
1978	Bill Rodgers	2:12:12	2004	Hendrik Ramaala	2:09:28	1991	Liz McColgan	2:27:32
1979	Bill Rodgers	2:11:42	2005	Paul Tergat	2:09:30	1992	Lisa Ondieki	2:24:40
1980	Alberto Salazar	2:09:41	2006	Marilson Gomes	2:09:58	1993	Uta Pippig	2:26:24
1981	Alberto Salazar	2:08:13		dos Santos		1994	Tegla Loroupe	2:27:37
1982	Alberto Salazar	2:09:29	2007	Martin Lel	2:09:04	1995	Tegla Loroupe	2:28:06
1983	Rod Dixon	2:08:59		**WOMEN**		1996	Anuta Catuna	2:28:18
1984	Orlando Pizzolato	2:14:53	1970	No Finisher	—	1997	Franziska	2:28:43
1985	Orlando Pizzolato	2:11:34	1971	Beth Bonner	2:55:22		Rochat-Moser	
1986	Gianni Poli	2:11:06	1972	Nina Kuscsik	3:08:42	1998	Franca Fiacconi	2:25:17
1987	Ibrahim Hussein	2:11:01	1973	Nina Kuscsik	2:57:08	1999	Adriana Fernandez	2:25:06
1988	Steve Jones	2:08:20	1974	Katherine Switzer	3:07:29	2000	Lyudmila Petrova	2:25:45
1989	Jumo Ikangaa	2:08:01	1975	Kim Merritt	2:46:15	2001	Margaret Okayo	2:24:21
1990	Douglas Waikihuri	2:12:39	1976	Miki Gorman	2:39:11	2002	Joyce Chepchumba	2:25:56
1991	Salvador Garcia	2:09:28	1977	Miki Gorman	2:43:10	2003	Margaret Okayo	2:22:31
1992	Willie Mtolo	2:09:29	1978	Grete Waitz	2:32:30	2004	Paula Radcliffe	2:23:10
1993	Andres Espinosa	2:10:04	1979	Grete Waitz	2:27:33	2005	Jelena Prokopcuka	2:24:41
1994	German Silva	2:11:21	1980	Grete Waitz	2:25:41	2006	Jelena Prokopcuka	2:25:05
1995	German Silva	2:11:00	1981	Allison Roe	2:25:29	2007	Paula Radcliffe	2:23:09

TRACK AND FIELD

Track and Field World Records (as of September 24, 2008)

These are the recognized records of the IAAF (International Amateur Athletic Federation). All walk records must have been made on a track, and all relay records must be made by teams composed of individuals from the same country. Indoor records must be performed on tracks no larger than 200m in circumference, and the meet must be subject to drug testing. Awards awaiting ratification are not shown.

MEN'S OUTDOOR TRACK RECORDS				WOMEN'S OUTDOOR TRACK RECORDS			
Event	(min./sec.)	Record holder (country)	Date	Event	(min./sec.)	Record holder (country)	Date
100 m	9.69	Usain Bolt (Jamaica)	8/16/08	100 m	10.49	Florence Griffith Joyner (U.S.)	7/16/88
200 m	19.30	Usain Bolt (Jamaica)	8/20/08				
400 m	43.18	Michael Johnson (U.S.)	8/26/99	200 m	21.34	Florence Griffith Joyner (U.S.)	9/29/88
800 m	1:41.11	Wilson Kipketer (Denmark)	8/24/97				
1,000 m	2:11.96	Noah Ngeny (Kenya)	9/5/99	400 m	47.60	Marita Koch (E. Germany)	10/6/85
1,500 m	3:26:00	Hicham el-Guerrouj (Morocco)	7/14/98	800 m	1:53.28	Jarmila Kratochvilova (Czechoslovakia)	7/26/83
Mile	3:43.13	Hicham el-Guerrouj (Morocco)	7/7/99	1,000 m	2:28.98	Svetlana Masterkova (Russia)	8/23/96
2,000 m	4:44.79	Hicham el-Guerrouj (Morocco)	9/7/99	1,500 m	3:50.46	Yunxia Qu (China)	9/11/93
				Mile	4:12.56	Svetlana Masterkova (Russia)	8/14/96
3,000 m	7:20.67	Daniel Komen (Kenya)	9/1/96				
Steeple-chase	7:53.63	Saif Saaeed Shaheen (Qatar)	9/3/04	2,000 m	5:25.35	Sonia O'Sullivan (Ireland)	7/8/94
				3,000 m	8:06.11	Junxia Wang (China)	9/13/93
5,000 m	12:37.35	Kenenisa Bekele (Ethiopia)	5/31/04	5,000 m	14:11.15	Tirunesh Dibaba (Ethiopia)	6/6/08
10,000 m	26:17.53	Kenenisa Bekele (Ethiopia)	8/26/05	10,000 m	29:31.78	Junxia Wang (China)	9/8/93
				Marathon	2:15:25	Paula Radcliffe (U.K.)	4/13/03[1]
Marathon	2:04:26	Haile Gebrselassie (Ethiopia)	9/30/07	100 m hurdl.	12.21	Yordanka Donkova (Bulgaria)	8/20/88
110 m hurd.	12.87	Dayron Robles (Cuba)	6/12/08	400 m hurdl.	52.34	Yuliya Pechonkina (Russia)	8/8/03
400 m hurd.	46.78	Kevin Young (U.S.)	8/6/92	10 km walk	41:56.23	Nadezhda Ryashkina (USSR)	7/4/90
20 km walk	1:17:25.60	Bernardo Segura (Mexico)	5/7/94	20 km walk	1:26.52	Olimpiada Ivanova (Russia)	9/6/01
50 km walk	3:40:57.90	Thierry Toutain (France)	9/29/96	4 x 100 m	41.37	East Germany	10/6/85
4 x 100 m	37.10	Jamaica	8/22/08	4 x 200 m	1:27.46	United States	4/29/00
4 x 200 m	1:18.68	Santa Monica Track Club	4/17/94	4 x 400 m	3:15.17	Soviet Union	10/1/88
4 x 400 m	2:54.20	United States	7/22/98				

1. Radcliffe also made this time 9/26/99.

MEN'S OUTDOOR FIELD EVENTS

Event	Meters	Ft./In.	Record holder (country)	Date
High jump	2.45	8 ft., 0.5 in.	Javier Sotomayor (Cuba)	7/27/93
Pole vault	6.14	20 ft., 1.75 in.	Sergey Bubka (Ukraine)	7/31/94
Long jump	8.95	29 ft., 4.5 in.	Mike Powell (United States)	8/30/91
Triple jump	18.29	60 ft., 0 in.	Jonathan Edwards (Great Britain)	8/7/95
Shot put	23.12	75 ft., 10.25 in.	Randy Barnes (United States)	5/20/90
Discus	74.08	243 ft., 0 in.	Jurgen Schult (East Germany)	6/6/86
Hammer	86.74	284 ft., 7 in.	Yuriy Syedikh (USSR)	8/30/86
Javelin	98.48	323 ft., 1 in.	Jan Zelezny (Czech Republic)	5/25/96
Decathlon	9,026 points		Roman Sebrle (Czech Republic)	5/27/01

WOMEN'S OUTDOOR FIELD EVENTS

Event	Meters	Ft./In.	Record holder (country)	Date
High jump	2.09	6 ft., 10.25 in.	Stefka Kostadinova (Bulgaria)	8/30/87
Pole vault	5.05	16 ft., 5.6 in.	Yelena Isinbayeva (Russia)	8/18/08
Long jump	7.52	24 ft., 8.25 in.	Galina Chistyakova (USSR)	6/11/88
Triple jump	15.50	50 ft., 10.25 in.	Inessa Kravets (Ukraine)	8/10/95
Shot put	22.63	74 ft., 3 in.	Natalya Lisovskaya (USSR)	6/7/87
Discus	76.80	252 ft., 0 in.	Gabriele Reinsch (East Germany)	7/9/88
Hammer	78.61	258 ft., 0 in.	Tatyana Lysenko (Russia)	5/26/07
Javelin	71.70	235 ft., 2.8 in.	Osleidys Menéndez (Cuba)	8/14/05
Heptathalon	7,291 points		Jackie Joyner-Kersee (United States)	9/24/88

MEN'S INDOOR TRACK EVENTS

Event	(min./sec.)	Record holder (country)	Date
50 m	5.56	Donovan Bailey (Canada)	2/9/96
60 m	6.39	Maurice Greene (U.S.)	2/3/98
200 m	19.92	Frank Fredericks (Namibia)	2/18/96
400 m	44.57	Kerron Clement (U.S.)	3/12/05
800 m	1:42.67	Wilson Kipketer (Denmark)	3/9/97
1,000 m	2:14.96	Wilson Kipketer (Denmark)	2/20/00
1,500 m	3:31.18	Hicham el-Guerrouj (Morocco)	2/2/97
Mile	3:48.45	Hicham el-Guerrouj (Morocco)	2/12/97
3,000 m	7:24.90	Daniel Komen (Kenya)	2/6/98
5,000 m	12:49.60	Kenenisa Bekele (Ethiopia)	2/20/04
50 m hurdles	6.25	Mark McKoy (Canada)	3/5/86
60 m hurdles	7.30	Colin Jackson (Great Britain)	3/6/94
5,000 m walk	18:07.08	Mikhail Shchennikov (Russia)	2/14/95
4 x 200 m	1:22.11	Great Britain	3/3/91
4 x 400 m	3:02.83	United States	3/7/99
4 x 800 m	7:13.94	United States	2/6/00

WOMEN'S INDOOR TRACK EVENTS

Event	(min./sec.)	Record holder (country)	Date
50 m	5.96	Irina Privalova (Russia)	2/9/95
60 m	6.92	Irina Privalova (Russia)	2/9/95
200 m	21.87	Merlene Ottey (Jamaica)	2/13/93
400 m	49.59	Jarmila Kratochvilova (Czechoslovakia)	3/7/82
800 m	1:55.82	Jolanda Ceplak (Slovakia)	3/3/02
1,000 m	2:30.94	Maria Mutola (Mozambique)	2/25/99
1,500 m	3:58.28	Yelena Soboleva (Russia)	2/18/06
Mile	4:17.14	Doina Melinte (Romania)	2/9/90
3,000 m	8:23:72	Meseret Defar (Ethiopia)	2/3/07
5,000 m	14:27.42	Tirunesh Dibaba (Ethiopia)	1/27/07
50 m hurdles	6.58	Cornelia Oschkenat (East Germany)	2/20/88
60 m hurdles	7.68	Susanna Kallur (Sweden)	2/10/08
3,000 m walk	11:40.33	Claudia Stef (Romania)	1/30/99
4 x 200 m	1:32.41	Russia	1/29/05
4 x 400 m	3:23.37	Russia	1/28/06
4 x 800 m	8:14.53	Russia	2/10/08

MEN'S INDOOR FIELD EVENTS

Event	Meters	Ft./In.	Record holder (country)	Date
High jump	2.43	7ft., 11.5 in.	Javier Sotomayor (Cuba)	3/4/89
Pole vault	6.15	20 ft., 2 in.	Sergey Bubka (Ukraine)	2/21/93
Long jump	8.79	28 ft., 10.25 in.	Carl Lewis (United States)	1/27/84
Triple jump	17.83	58 ft., 6 in.	Aliecer Urrutia (Cuba)	3/1/97
Shot put	22.66	74 ft., 4.25 in.	Randy Barnes (United States)	1/20/89
Heptathlon	6,476 points		Dan O' Brien (United States)	3/14/93

WOMEN'S INDOOR FIELD EVENTS

Event	Meters	Ft./In.	Record holder (country)	Date
High jump	2.08	6 ft., 9.9 in.	Kajsa Bergqvist (Sweden)	2/4/06
Pole vault	4.95	16 ft., 2.88 in.	Yelena Isinbayeva (Russia)	2/16/08
Long jump	7.37	24 ft., 2.25 in.	Heike Drechsler (East Germany)	2/13/88
Triple jump	15.36	50 ft., 4.75 in.	Tatyana Lebedeva (Russia)	3/6/04
Shot put	22.50	73 ft., 10 in.	Helena Fibingerova (Czech.)	2/19/77
Pentathlon	4,991 points		Irina Belova (Unified Team)	2/15/92

Source: International Amateur Athletic Federation.

Olympic Sports

The 2008 Summer Olympic Games at Beijing, China
August 8-24, 2008

Event	Gold medal winner, country	Silver medal winner, country	Bronze medal winner,country
SWIMMING—MEN			
50m Freestyle	Cesar Cielo Filho, Brazil(OR)	Amaury Leveaux, France	Alain Bernard, France
100m Freestyle	Alain Bernard, France	Eamon Sullivan, Australia	Jason Lezak, U.S./
		Cesar Cielo Filho, Brazil	
200m Freestyle	Michael Phelps, U.S.(WR)	Park Tae-Hwan, South Korea	Peter Vanderkaay, U.S.
400m Freestyle	Park Tae-Hwan, South Korea	Zhang Lin, China	Larsen Jensen, U.S
1500m Freestyle	Oussama Mellouli, Tunisia	Grant Hackett, Australia	Ryan Cochrane, Canada
100m Backstroke	Aaron Peirsol, U.S.(WR)	Matt Grevers, U.S.	Arkady Vyatchanin, Russia/
			Hayden Stoekel, Australia
200m Backstroke	Ryan Lochte, U.S.	Aaron Peirsol, U.S.	Arkady Vyatchanin, Russia
100m Breaststroke	Kosuke Kitajima, Japan(WR)	Alexander Dale Oen, Netherl.	Hughes Duboscq, France
200m Breaststroke	Kosuke Kitajima, Japan(OR)	Brenton Rickard, Australia	Hughes Duboscq, France
100m Butterfly	Michael Phelps, U.S.(OR)	Milorad Cavic, Serbia	Andrew Lauterstein, Australia
200m Butterfly	Michael Phelps, U.S.(WR)	Laszlo Cseh, Hungary	Takeshi Matsuda, Japan
200m Medley	Michael Phelps, U.S.(WR)	Laszlo Cseh, Hungary	Ryan Lochte, U.S.
400m Medley	Michael Phelps, U.S.(WR)	Laszlo Cseh, Hungary	Ryan Lochte, U.S.
4x100m Freestyle	U.S.(WR)	France	Australia
4x200m Freestyle	U.S.(WR)	Russia	Australia
4x100m Medley	U.S.(WR)	Australia	Japan
Platform Diving	Matthew Mitcham, Australia	Zhou Luxin, China	Gleb Galperin, Russia
Springboard Diving	He Chong, China	Alexandre Despatie, Canada	Qin Kai, China
SWIMMING—WOMEN			
50m Freestyle	Britta Steffen, Germany(OR)	Dara Torres, U.S.	Cate Campbell, Australia
100m Freestyle	Britta Steffen, Germany(OR)	Libby Trickett, Australia	Natalie Coughlin, U.S.
200m Freestyle	Federica Pellegrini, Italy(WR)	Sara Isakovic	Pang Jiaying, China
400m Freestyle	Rebecca Adlington, Gr. Brit.	Katie Hoff, U.S.	Joanne Jackson, Great Britain
800m Freestyle	Rebecca Adlington, Gr. Brtit.(WR)	Alessia Filippi, Italy	Lotte Friis, Denmark
100m Backstroke	Natalie Coughlin, U.S.	Kirsty Coventry, Zimbabwe	Margaret Hoelzer, U.S.
200m Backstroke	Kirsty Coventry, Zimbabwe(WR)	Margaret Hoelzer, U.S.	Reiko Nakamura, Japan
100m Breaststroke	Leisel Jones, Australia(OR)	Rebecca Soni, U.S.	Mirna Jukic
200m Breaststroke	Rebecca Soni, U.S.(WR)	Leisel Jones, Australia	Sara Nordenstam, Norway
100m Butterfly	Libby Trickett, Australia	Christine Magnuson, U.S.	Jessicah Schipper, Australia
200m Butterfly	Liu Zige, China(WR)	Jiao Liuyang, China	Jessicah Schipper, Australia
200m Medley	Stephanie Rice, Australia(WR)	Kirsty Coventry, Zimbabwe	Natalie Coughlin, U.S.
400m Medley	Stephanie Rice, Australia(WR)	Kirsty Coventry, Zimbabwe	Katie Hoff, U.S.
4x100m Freestyle	Netherlands	U.S.	Australia
4x200m Freestyle	Australia	China	U.S.
4x100m Medley	Australia	U.S.	China
Platform Diving	Chen Ruolin, China	Emilie Heymans, Canada	Wang Xin, China
Springboard Diving	Jingjing Guo, China	Yuliya Pakhalina, Russia	Wu Minxia, China
TRACK & FIELD—MEN			
100 Meter Dash	Usain Bolt, Jamaica(WR)	Richard Thompson, Trin.Tob.	Walter Dix, U.S.
200 Meters	Usain Bolt, Jamaica(WR)	Shawn Crawford, U.S.	Walter Dix, U.S.
400 Meters	LaShawn Merritt, U.S.	Jeremy Wariner, U.S.	David Neville, U.S.
800 Meters	Wilfred Bungei, Kenya	Ismail Ahmed Ismail, Sudan	Alfred Kirwa Yego, Kenya
1,500 Meters	Rashid Ramzi, Bahrain	Asbel Kipruto Kiprop, Kenya	Nicholas Willis, New Zeal.
5,000 Meters	Kenenisa Bekele, Ethiopia(OR)	Eliud Kipchoge, Kenya	Edwin Cheruiyot Soi, Kenya
10,000 Meters	Kenenisa Bekele, Ethiopia(OR)	Sileshi Sihine, Ethiopia	Micah Kogo, Kenya
Marathon	Samuel Kamau Wanjiru, Ken.(OR)	Jaouad Gharib, Morocco	Tsegay Kebede, Ethiopia
110-Meter Hurdles	Dayron Robles, Cuba	David Payne, U.S.	David Oliver, U.S.
400-Meter Hurdles	Angelo Taylor, U.S.	Kerron Clement, U.S.	Bershawn Jackson, U.S.
3,000-Meter	Brimin Kiprop	Mahiedine	Richard Kipkemboi
Steeplechase	Kipruto, Kenya	Mekhissi-Benabbad, France	Mateelong, Kenya
20km Walk	Valeriy Borchin, Russia	Jefferson Perez, Ecuador	Jared Tallent, Australia
50km Walk	Alex Schwazer, Italy	Jared Tallent, Australia	Denis Nizhegorodov, Russia,
4x100-Meter Relay	Jamaica(WR)	Trinidad and Tobago	Japan
4x400-Meter Relay	U.S.(OR)	Bahamas	Russia
Discus Throw	Gerd Kanter, Estonia	Piotr Malachowski, Poland	Virgilijus Alekna, Lithuania
Hammer Throw	Primoz Kozmus	Vadim Devyatovskiy, Belarus	Ican Tsikhan, Belarus
High Jump	Andrey Silnov, Russia	Germaine Mason, Gr.Britain	Yaroslav Rybakov, Russia
Javelin	Andreas Thorkildsen, Nor.(OR)	Ainars Kovals, Latvia	Tero Pitkamaki, Finland
Long Jump	Irving Saladino, Panama	Khotso Mokoena, So. Africa	Ibrahim Camejo, Cuba
Triple Jump	Nelson Evora, Portugal	Phillips Idowu, Great Britain	Leevan Sands, Bahamas
Pole Vault	Steve Hooker, Australia(OR)	Evgeny Lukyanenko, Russia	Denys Yurchenko, Ukraine
Shot Put	Tomasz Majewski, Poland	Christian Cantwell, U.S.	Andrei Mikhnevich, Belarus
Deacathlon	Bryan Clay, U.S.	Andrei Krauchanka, Belarus	Leonel Suarez, Cuba

Event	Gold medal winner, country	Silver medal winner, country	Bronze medal winner,country
TRACK & FIELD—WOMEN			
100 Meter Dash	Shelly-Ann Fraser, Jamaica	Sherron Simpson, Jamaica	Kerron Stewart, Jamaica
200 Meters	Veronica Campbell-Brown, Jam.	Allyson Felix, U.S.	Kerron Stewart, Jamaica
400 Meters	Christine Ohuruogu, Gr. Br.	Shericka Williams, Jamaica	Sanya Richards, U.S.
800 Meters	Pamela Jelimo, Kenya	Janeth Jepkosgei Busienei, Ken.	Hasna Benhassi, Morocco
1,500 Meters	Nancy Jebet Langat, Kenya	Iryna Lishchynska, Ukraine	Nataliya Tobias, Ukraine
5,000 Meters	Tirunesh Dibaba, Ethiopia	Elvan Abeylegesse, Turkey	Meseret Defar, Ethiopia
10,000 Meters	Tirunesh Dibaba, Ethiopia(OR)	Elvan Abeylegesse, Turkey	Shalane Flanagan, U.S.
Marathon	Constantina Tomescu, Romania	Catherine Ndereba, Kenya	Zhou Chunxiu, China
100m Hurdles	Dawn Harper, U.S.	Sally McLellan, Australia	Priscilla Lopes-Schliep, Canada
400m Hurdles	Melaine Walker, Jamaica(OR)	Sheena Tosta, U.S.	Tasha Danvers, Great Britain
3,000m Steeplechase	Gulnara Galkina-Samitova, Russia(WR)	Eunice Jepkorir, Kenya	Yekaterina Volkova, Russia
20km Walk	Olga Kaniskina, Russia	Kjersti Tysse Platzer, Norway	Elisa Riguado, Italy
4x100m Relay	Russia	Belgium	Nigeria
4x400m Relay	U.S.	Russia	Jamaica
Discus Throw	Stephanie Brown Trafton, U.S.	Yarelis Barrios, Cuba	Olena Antonova, Ukraine
Hammer Throw	Aksana Miankova, Belarus(OR)	Yipsi Moreno, Cuba	Zhang Wenxiu, China
High Jump	Tia Hellebaut, Belgium	Blanca Vlasic, Croatia	Anna Chicherova, Russia
Javelin	Barbora Spotakova, Czech Rep.	Mariya Abakumova, Russia	Christina Obergfoll
Long Jump	Maurren Higa Maggi, Brazil	Tatyana Lebedeva, Russia	Blessing Okagbare, Nigeria
Triple Jump	Francoise Mbango Etone, Cameroon(OR)	Tatyana Lebedeva, Russia	Hrysopiyi Devetzi, Greece
Pole Vault	Elena Isinbaeva, Russia(WR)	Jennifer Stuczynski, U.S.	Svetlana Feofanova, Russia
Shot Put	Valerie Vili, New Zealand	Natallia Mikhnevich, Belarus	Nadzeya Astapchuk, Belarus
Pentathlon/ Heptathlon	Natalia Dobrynska, Ukraine	Hyleas Fountain U.S.	Tatyana Chernova, Russia
GYMNASTICS-MEN			
All-Around	Yang Wei, China	Kohei Uchimura, Japan	Benoit Caranobe, France
Floor Exercises	Zou Kai, China	Gervasio Deferr, Spain	Anton Golotsutskov, Russia
Horizontal Bar	Zou Kai, China	Jonathan Horton, U.S.	Fabian Humbuchen, Germany
Parallel Bars	Li Xiaopeng, China	Yoo Won-Chul, South Korea	Anton Fokin, Uzbekistan
Pommel Horse	Xiao Qin, China	Filip Ude, Croatia	Louis Smith, Great Britain
Rings	Chen Yibing, China	Yang Wei, China	Oleksandr Vorobiov, Ukraine
Vault	Leszek Blanik, Poland	Thomas Bouhail, France	Anton Golotsutskov, Russia
Team Combined	China	Japan	U.S.
GYMNASTICS-WOMEN			
All-Around	Nastia Liukin, U.S.	Shawn Johnson, U.S.	Yang Yilin, China
Balance Beam	Shawn Johnson, U.S.	Nastia Liukin, U.S	Cheng Fei, China
Floor Exercises	Sandra Izbasa, Romania	Shawn Johnson, U.S.	Nastia Liukin, U.S
Uneven Bars	He Kexin, China	Nastia Liukin, U.S	Yang Yilin, China
Vault	Hong Un Jong, North Korea	Oksana Chusovitina, Germany	Cheng Fei, China
Team Combined	China	U.S.	Romania
BOXING			
Lt. Flyweight (106 lb)	Zou Shiming, China	Purevdorjiin, Mongolia	Paddy Barnes, Ireland/ Yampier Hernandez, Cuba
Flyweight (112 pounds)	Somjit Jongjohor, Thailand	Andry Laffita, Cuba	Georgy Balakshin, Russia/ Vincenzo Picardi, Italy
Bantamweight[1] (119 Pounds)	Enkhbatyn Badar-Uugan, Mongolia/Yankiel Leon, Cuba/Bruno Julie, Mauritius/Veaceslav Gojan, Moldova		
Featherweight[2] (125 pounds)	Vasyl Lomachenko, Ukraine	Khedafi Djelkhir, France/Yakup Kilic, Turkey/Shahin Imranov, Azerbaijan	
Lightweight (132 pounds)	Alexey Tishchenko, Russia	Daouda Sow, France	Hrachik Javakhyan, Armenia/ Yordenis Ugas, Cuba
Lt. Welterweight (139 pounds)	Manuel Feliz Diaz, Dom. Rep.	Manus Boonjumnong, Thailand	Roniel Iglesias, Cuba/Alexis Vastine, France
Welterweight (147 pounds)	Bakhyt Sarsekbayev, Kazakh.	Carlos Banteaux Suarez, Cuba	Hanati Silamu, China/Kim Jung-Joo, South Korea
Middleweight (165 pounds)	James DeGale, Great Britain	Emilio Correa, Cuba	Darren Sutherland, Ireland/ Vijender Kumar, India
Lt. Heavyweight (178 pounds)	Zhang Xiaoping, China	Kenneth Egan, Ireland	Tony Jeffries, Great Britain/ Yerkebuian Shynaliyev, Kazakh.
Heavyweight (201 pounds)	Rakhim Chakhkiev, Russia	Clemente Russo, Italy	Osmay Acosta, Cuba/ Deoontay Wilder, U.S.
Super Heavywt (unlimited)	Roberto Cammarelle, Italy	Zhang Zhilei, China	Vyacheslav Glazkov, Ukraine/David Price, Gr. Br.
TEAM SPORTS			
Baseball	South Korea	Cuba	U.S.
Basketball-Men	U.S.	Spain	Argentina
Basketball-Women	U.S.	Australia	Russia
Soccer-Men	Argentina	Nigeria	Brazil
Soccer-Women	U.S.	Brazil	Germany
Softball	Japan	U.S.	Australia
Volleyball-Men	U.S.	Brazil	Russia
Volleyball-Women	Brazil	U.S.	China
Water Polo-Men	Hungary	U.S.	Serbia

Notes: WR= world record OR=Olympic record1. Badar-Uugan, Leon, Julie, and Gojan tied for gold. 2. Djelkhir, Kilic, and Imranov tied for silver.

Medal Count by Nation, 2008 Summer Olympics

Country	Gold	Silver	Bronze	Total	Country	Gold	Silver	Bronze	Total	Country	Gold	Silver	Bronze	Total
United States	36	38	36	110	Argentina	2	0	4	6	Belgium	1	1	0	2
China	51	21	28	100	Armenia	0	0	6	6	Colombia	0	1	1	2
Russia	23	21	28	72	Czech Republic	3	3	0	6	Dominican Rep.	1	1	0	2
Great Britain	19	13	15	47	Slovakia	3	2	1	6	Estonia	1	1	0	2
Australia	14	15	17	46	Georgia	3	0	3	6	Kyrgyzstan	0	1	1	2
Germany	16	10	15	41	North Korea	2	1	3	6	Morocco	0	1	1	2
France	7	16	17	40	Switzerland	2	0	4	6	Portugal	1	1	0	2
South Korea	13	10	8	31	Uzbekistan	1	2	3	6	Iran	1	0	1	2
Italy	8	10	10	28	Bulgaria	1	1	3	5	Tajikistan	0	1	1	2
Ukraine	7	5	15	27	Croatia	0	2	3	5	Trin. and Tobago	0	2	0	2
Japan	9	6	10	25	Indonesia	1	1	3	5	Bahrain	1	0	0	1
Cuba	2	11	11	24	Lithuania	0	2	3	5	Cameroon	1	0	0	1
Belarus	4	5	10	19	Slovenia	1	2	2	5	Afghanistan	0	0	1	1
Canada	3	9	6	18	Sweden	0	4	1	5	Chile	0	1	0	1
Spain	5	10	3	18	Chinese Taipei	0	0	4	4	Ecuador	0	1	0	1
Netherlands	7	5	4	16	Finland	1	1	2	4	Egypt	0	0	1	1
Brazil	3	4	8	15	Greece	0	2	2	4	Israel	0	0	1	1
Kenya	5	5	4	14	Mongolia	2	2	0	4	Iceland	0	1	0	1
Kazakhstan	2	4	7	13	Nigeria	0	1	3	4	Malaysia	0	1	0	1
Jamaica	6	3	2	11	Thailand	2	2	0	4	Mauritius	0	0	1	1
Hungary	3	5	2	10	Zimbabwe	1	3	0	4	Moldova	0	0	1	1
Norway	3	5	2	10	Austria	0	1	2	3	Panama	1	0	0	1
Poland	3	6	1	10	India	1	0	2	3	South Africa	0	1	0	1
New Zealand	3	1	5	9	Ireland	0	1	2	3	Singapore	0	1	0	1
Romania	4	1	3	8	Latvia	1	1	1	3	Sudan	0	1	0	1
Turkey	1	4	3	8	Mexico	2	0	1	3	Togo	0	0	1	1
Azerbaijan	1	2	4	7	Serbia	0	1	2	3	Tunisia	1	0	0	1
Denmark	2	2	3	7	Algeria	0	1	1	2	Venezuela	0	0	1	1
Ethiopia	4	1	2	7	Bahamas	0	1	1	2	Vietnam	0	1	0	1

SUMMER OLYMPIC CHAMPIONS

Swimming and Diving, Men

50m Freestyle

Year	Champion	Time
1904	Zoltán Halmay, Hungary	0:28.00
1988	Matt Biondi, U.S.	0:22.14
1992	Aleksandr Popov, Unified Team	0:21.91
1996	Aleksandr Popov, Russia	0:22.13
2000	(tie) Anthony Ervin, U.S/Gary Hall Jr., U.S.	0:21.98
2004	Gary Hall Jr., U.S.	0:21.93

100m Freestyle

Year	Champion	Time
1896	Alfréd Hajós, Hungary	1:22.20
1904	Zoltán Halmay, Hungary (100 yds.)	1:02.80
1908	Charles Daniels, U.S.	1:05.60
1912	Duke Paoa Kahanamoku, U.S.	1:03.40
1920	Duke Paoa Kahanamoku, U.S.	1:00.40
1924	Johnny Weissmuller, U.S.	0:59.00
1928	Johnny Weissmuller, U.S.	0:58.60
1932	Yasuji Miyazaki, Japan	0:58.20
1936	Ferenc Csík, Hungary	0:57.60
1948	Walter Ris, U.S.	0:57.30
1952	Clarke Scholes, U.S.	0:57.40
1956	Jon Henricks, Australia	0:55.40
1960	John Devitt, Australia	0:55.20
1964	Donald Schollander, U.S.	0:53.40
1968	Michael Wenden, Australia	0:52.20
1972	Mark Spitz, U.S.	0:51.22
1976	Jim Montgomery, U.S.	0:49.99
1980	Jörg Woithe, East Germany	0:50.40
1984	Rowdy Gaines, U.S.	0:49.80
1988	Matt Biondi, U.S.	0:48.63
1992	Aleksandr Popov, Unified Team	0:49.02
1996	Aleksandr Popov, Russia	0:48.74
2000	Pieter van den Hoogenband, Netherlands	0:48.30
2004	Pieter van den Hoogenband, Netherlands	0:48.71

200m Freestyle

Year	Champion	Time
1900	Frederick Lane, Austria	2:25.20
1904	Charles Daniels, U.S.	2:44.20
1968	Michael Wenden, Australia	1:55.20
1972	Mark Spitz, U.S.	1:52.78
1976	Bruce Furniss, U.S.	1:50.29
1980	Sergei Kopliakov, U.S.S.R.	1:49.81
1984	Michael Gross, West Germany	1:47.44
1988	Duncan Armstrong, Australia	1:47.25
1992	Evgueni Sadovyi, Unified Team	1:46.70
1996	Danyon Loader, New Zealand	1:47.63
2000	Pieter van den Hoogenband, Netherlands	1:45.35
2004	Ian Thorpe, Australia	1:44.71

400m Freestyle

Year	Champion	Time
1896	Paul Neumann, Austria (500m)	8:12.60
1904	Charles Daniels, U.S. (440 yds.)	6:16.20
1908	Henry Taylor, Great Britain (440 yds.)	5:36.80
1912	George Hodgson, Canada	5:24.40
1920	Norman Ross, U.S.	5:26.80
1924	Johnny Weissmuller, U.S.	5:04.20
1928	Alberto Zorilla, Argentina	5:01.60
1932	Clarence "Buster" Crabbe, U.S.	4:48.40
1936	Jack Medica, U.S.	4:44.50
1948	William Smith, U.S.	4:41.00
1952	Jean Boiteux, France	4:30.70
1956	Murray Rose, Australia	4:27.30
1960	Murray Rose, Australia	4:18.30
1964	Donald Schollander, U.S.	4:12.20
1968	Michael Burton, U.S.	4:09.00
1972	Bradford Cooper, Australia	4:00.27
1976	Brian Goodell, U.S.	3:51.93
1980	Vladimir Salnikov, U.S.S.R.	3:51.31
1984	George DiCarlo, U.S.	3:51.23
1988	Ewe Dassler, East Germany	3:46.95
1992	Evgueni Sadovyi, Unified Team	3:45.00
1996	Danyon Loader, New Zealand	3:47.97
2000	Ian Thorpe, Australia	3:40.59
2004	Ian Thorpe, Australia	3:43.10

1,500m Freestyle

Year	Champion	Time
1896	Alfréd Hajós, Hungary (1,200m)	18:22.20
1900	John Arthur Jarvis, Great Britain (1,000m)	13:40.20
1904	Emil Rausch, Germany (1,609m)	27:18.20
1908	Henry Taylor, Great Britain	22:48.40
1912	George Hodgson, Canada	22:00.00
1920	Norman Ross, U.S.	22:23.20
1924	Andrew "Boy" Charlton, Australia	20:06.60
1928	Arne Borg, Sweden	19:51.80
1932	Kusuo Kitamura, Japan	19:12.40
1936	Noboru Terada, Japan	19:13.70
1948	James McLane, U.S.	19:18.50
1952	Ford Konno, U.S.	18:30.30
1956	Murray Rose, Australia	17:58.90
1960	John Konrads, Australia	17:19.60
1964	Robert Windle, Australia	17:01.70
1968	Michael Burton, U.S.	16:38.90
1972	Michael Burton, U.S.	15:52.58

1976	Brian Goodell, U.S.	15:02.40
1980	Vladimir Salnikov, U.S.S.R.	14:58.27
1984	Michael O'Brien, U.S.	15:05.20
1988	Vladimir Salnikov, U.S.S.R.	15:00.40
1992	Kieren Perkins, Australia	14:43.48
1996	Kieren Perkins, Australia	14:56.40
2000	Grant Hackett, Australia	14:48.33
2004	Grant Hackett, Australia	14:43.40

100m Backstroke   **Time**

1904	Walter Brack, Germany (100yds)	1:16.80
1908	Arno Bieberstein, Germany	1:24.60
1912	Harry Hebner, U.S.	1:21.20
1920	Warren Paoa Kealoha, U.S.	1:15.20
1924	Warren Paoa Kealoha, U.S.	1:13.20
1928	George Kojac, U.S.	1:08.20
1932	Masaji Kiyokawa, Japan	1:08.60
1936	Adolf Kiefer, U.S.	1:05.90
1948	Allen Stack, U.S.	1:06.40
1952	Yoshinobu Oyakawa, U.S.	1:05.40
1956	David Theile, Australia	1:02.20
1960	David Theile, Australia	1:01.90
1964	Not held	
1968	Roland Matthes, East Germany	0:58.70
1972	Roland Matthes, East Germany	0:56.58
1976	John Naber, U.S.	0:55.49
1980	Bengt Baron, Sweden	0:56.33
1984	Richard Carey, U.S.	0:55.79
1988	Daichi Suzuki, Japan	0:55.05
1992	Mark Tewksbury, Canada	0:53.98
1996	Jeff Rouse, U.S.	0:54:10
2000	Lenny Krayzelburg, United States	0:53.72
2004	Aaron Piersol, U.S.	0:54.06

200m Backstroke   **Time**

1900	Ernst Hoppenberg, Germany	2:47.00
1964	Jed Graef, U.S.	2:10.30
1968	Roland Matthes, East Germany	2:09.60
1972	Roland Matthes, East Germany	2:02.82
1976	John Naber, U.S.	1:59.19
1980	Sándor Wladár, Hungary	2:01.93
1984	Richard Carey, U.S.	2:00.23
1988	Igor Poliansky, U.S.S.R.	1:59.37
1992	Martin Zubero, Spain	1:58.47
1996	Brad Bridgewater, U.S.	1:58.54
2000	Lenny Krayzelburg, United States	1:56.76
2004	Aaron Piersol, U.S.	1:54.95

100m Breaststroke   **Time**

1968	Donald McKenzie, U.S.	1:07.70
1972	Nobutaka Taguchi, Japan	1:04.94
1976	John Hencken, U.S.	1:03.11
1980	Duncan Goodhew, Great Britain	1:03.44
1984	Steve Lundquist, U.S.	1:01.65
1988	Adrian Moorhouse, Great Britain	1:02.04
1992	Nelson Diebel, U.S.	1:01.50
1996	Fred Deburghgraeve, Belgium	1:00.65
2000	Domenico Fioravanti, Italy	1:00.46
2004	Kosuke Kitajima, Japan	1:00.08

200m Breaststroke   **Time**

1908	Frederick Holman, Great Britain	3:09.20
1912	Walter Bathe, Germany	3:01.80
1920	Haken Malmroth, Sweden	3:04.40
1924	Robert Skelton, U.S.	2:56.60
1928	Yoshiyuki Tsuruta, Japan	2:48.80
1932	Yoshiyuki Tsuruta, Japan	2:45.40
1936	Tetsuo Hamuro, Japan	2:41.50
1948	Joseph Verdeur, U.S.	2:39.30
1952	John Davies, Australia	2:34.40
1956	Masaru Furukawa, Japan	2:34.70
1960	William Mulliken, U.S.	2:37.40
1964	Ian O'Brien, Australia	2:27.80
1968	Felipe Muñoz, Mexico	2:28.70
1972	John Hencken, U.S.	2:21.55
1976	David Wilkie, Great Britain	2:15.11
1980	Robertas Zhulpa, U.S.S.R.	2:15.85
1984	Victor Davis, Canada	2:13.34
1988	Jozsef Szabo, Hungary	2:13.52
1992	Mike Barrowman, U.S.	2:10.16
1996	Norbert Rozsa, Hungary	2:12.57
2000	Domenico Fioravanti, Italy	2:10.87
2004	Kosuke Kitajima, Japan	2:09.44

100m Butterfly   **Time**

1968	Douglas Russell, U.S.	0:55.90
1972	Mark Spitz, U.S.	0:54.27
1976	Matt Vogel, U.S.	0:54.35
1980	Par Arvidsson, Sweden	0:54.92
1984	Michael Gross, West Germany	0:53.08
1988	Anthony Nesty, Suriname	0:53.00
1992	Pablo Morales, U.S.	0:53.32
1996	Denis Pankratov, Russia	0:52.27
2000	Lars Froelander, Sweden	0:52.00

2004	Michael Phelps, U.S.	0:51.2

200m Butterfly   **Tim**

1956	William Yorzyk, U.S.	2:19.3
1960	Michael Troy, U.S.	2:12.8
1964	Kevin Berry, Australia	2:06.6
1968	Carl Robie, U.S.	2:08.7
1972	Mark Spitz, U.S.	2:00.7
1976	Mike Bruner, U.S.	1:59.2
1980	Sergei Fesenko, U.S.S.R.	1:59.76
1984	Jon Sieben, Australia	1:57.04
1988	Michael Gross, West Germany	1:56.94
1992	Mel Stewart, U.S.	1:56.26
1996	Denis Pankratov, Russia	1:56.51
2000	Tom Malchow, United States	1:55.35
2004	Michael Phelps, U.S.	1:54.04

200m Individual Medley   **Time**

1968	Charles Hickcox, U.S.	2:12.00
1972	Gunnar Larsson, Sweden	2:07.17
1984	Alex Baumann, Canada	2:01.42
1988	Tamas Darnyi, Hungary	2:00.17
1992	Tamas Darnyi, Hungary	2:00.76
1996	Attila Czene, Hungary	1:59.91
2000	Massimiliano Rosolino, Italy	1:58.98
2004	Michael Phelps, U.S.	1:57.14

400m Individual Medley   **Time**

1964	Richard W. Roth, U.S.	4:45.40
1968	Charles Hickcox, U.S.	4:48.40
1972	Gunnar Larsson, Sweden	4:31.98
1976	Rod Strachan, U.S.	4:23.68
1980	Aleksandr Sidorenko, U.S.S.R.	4:22.89
1984	Alex Baumann, Canada	4:17.41
1988	Tamas Darnyi, Hungary	4:14.75
1992	Tamas Darnyi, Hungary	4:14.23
1996	Tom Dolan, U.S.	4:14.90
2000	Tom Dolan, U.S.	4:11.76
2004	Michael Phelps, U.S.	4:08.26

4x100m Freestyle Relay   **Time**

1964	U.S.	3:33.20
1992	U.S.	3:16.74
1968	U.S.	3:31.70
1996	U.S.	3:15.41
1972	U.S.	3:26.42
2000	Australia	3:13.67
1984	U.S.	3:19.03
2004	South Africa	3:13.17
1988	U.S.	3:16.53

4x200m Freestyle Relay   **Time**

1908	Great Britain	10:55.60
1964	U.S.	7:52.10
1912	Australia	10:11.60
1968	U.S.	7:52.33
1920	U.S.	10:04.40
1972	U.S.	7:35.78
1924	U.S.	9:53.40
1976	U.S.	7:23.22
1928	U.S.	9:36.20
1980	U.S.S.R.	7:23.50
1932	Japan	8:58.40
1984	U.S.	7:15.69
1936	Japan	8:51.50
1988	U.S.	7:12.69
1948	U.S.	8:46.00
1992	Unified Team	7:11.95
1952	U.S.	8:31.10
1996	U.S.	7:14.84
1956	Australia	8:23.60
2000	Australia	7:07.05
1960	U.S.	8:10.20
2004	U.S.	7:07.33

4x100m Medley Relay   **Time**

1960	U.S.	4:05.40
1984	U.S.	3:39.30
1964	U.S.	3:58.40
1988	U.S.	3:36.93
1968	U.S.	3:54.90
1992	U.S.	3:36.93
1972	U.S.	3:48.16
1996	U.S.	3:34.84
1976	U.S.	3:42.22
2000	U.S.	3:33.73
1980	Australia	3:45.70
2004	U.S.	3:30.68

Platform Diving

1904	George E. Sheldon, U.S.	1932	Harold Smith, U.S.
1908	Hjalmar Johansson, Swed.	1936	Marshall Wayne, U.S.
1912	Erik Adlerz, Sweden	1948	Dr. Samuel Lee, U.S.
1920	Clarence Pinkston, U.S.	1952	Dr. Samuel Lee, U.S.
1924	Albert C. White, U.S.	1956	Joaquin Capilla Perez, Mex.
1928	Pete DesJardins, U.S.	1960	Robert Webster, U.S.

964	Robert Webster, U.S.	2000	Liang Tian, China	1936	Richard Degener, U.S.
968	Klaus Dibiasi, Italy	2004	Jia Hu, China	1948	Bruce Harlan, U.S.
972	Klaus Dibiasi, Italy		**Springboard Diving**	1952	David Browning, U.S.
976	Klaus Dibiasi, Italy	1900	Albert Zürner, Germany	1956	Robert L. Clotworthy, U.S.
980	Falk Hoffmann, E.Germany	1912	Paul Günther, Germany	1960	Gary Tobian, U.S.
984	Gregory Louganis, U.S.	1920	Louis Kuehn, U.S.	1964	Kenneth R. Sitzberger, U.S.
988	Gregory Louganis, U.S.	1924	Albert C. White, U.S.	1968	Bernard Wrightson, U.S.
992	Sun Shuwei, China	1928	Pete Desjardins, U.S.	1972	Vladimir Vasin, U.S.S.R.
996	Xiong Ni, China	1932	Michael Galitzen, U.S.	1976	Philip Boggs, U.S.

1980	Aleksandr Portnov, U.S.S.R.
1984	Gregory Louganis, U.S.
1988	Gregory Louganis, U.S.
1992	Mark Lenzi, U.S.
1996	Dmitri Sautin, Russia
2000	Xiong Ni, China
2004	Bo Peng, China

Swimming and Diving, Women

50m Freestyle		**Time**
1988	Kristin Otto, E. Germany	0:25.49
1992	Yang Wenji, China	0:24.79
1996	Amy Van Dyken, U.S.	0:24.87
2000	Inge de Bruijn, Netherlands	0:24.32
2004	Inge de Bruijn, Netherlands	0:24.58
100m Freestyle		**Time**
1912	Fanny Durack, Australia	1:22.20
1920	Ethelda Bleibtrey, U.S.	1:13.60
1924	Ethel Lackie, U.S.	1:12.40
1928	Albina Osipowich, U.S.	1:11.00
1932	Helene Madison, U.S.	1:06.80
1936	Rie Mastenbroek, Netherlands	1:05.90
1948	Greta Andersen, Denmark	1:06.30
1952	Katalin Szoke, Hungary	1:06.80
1956	Dawn Fraser, Australia	1:02.00
1960	Dawn Fraser, Australia	1:01.20
1964	Dawn Fraser, Australia	0:59.50
1968	Jan Henne, U.S.	1:00.00
1972	Sandra Neilson, U.S.	0:58.59
1976	Kornelia Ender, East Germany	0:55.65
1980	Barbara Krause, East Germany	0:54.79
1984	Nancy Hogshead, U.S.	0:55.92
1988	Kristin Otto, East Germany	0:54.93
1992	Zhuang Yong, China	0:54.65
1996	Le Jingyi, China	0:54.50
2000	Inge de Bruijn, Netherlands	0:53.83
2004	Jodie Henry, Australia	0:53.84
200m Freestyle		**Time**
1968	Deborah Meyer, U.S.	2:10.50
1972	Shane Gould, Australia	2:03.56
1976	Kornelia Ender, East Germany	1:59.26
1980	Barbara Krause, East Germany	1:58.33
1984	Mary Wayte, U.S.	1:59.23
1988	Heike Friederich, East Germany	1:57.65
1992	Nicole Haislett, U.S.	1:57.90
1996	Claudia Poll, Costa Rica	1:58.16
2000	Susie O'Neill, Australia	1:58.24
2004	Camelia Potec, Romania	1:58.03
400m Freestyle		**Time**
1920	Ethelda Bleibtrey, U.S. (300 m)	4:34.00
1924	Martha Norelius, U.S.	6:02.20
1928	Martha Norelius, U.S.	5:42.80
1932	Helene Madison, U.S.	5:28.50
1936	Hendrika "Rie" Mastenbroek, Netherlands	5:26.40
1948	Ann Curtis, U.S.	5:17.80
1952	Valeria Gyenge, Hungary	5:12.10
1956	Lorraine Crapp, Australia	4:54.60
1960	S. Chris Von Saltza, U.S.	4:50.60
1964	Virginia Duenkel, U.S.	4:43.30
1968	Deborah Meyer, U.S.	4:31.80
1972	Shane Gould, Australia	4:19.44
1976	Petra Thümer, East Germany	4:09.89
1980	Ines Diers, East Germany	4:08.76
1984	Tiffany Cohen, U.S.	4:07.10
1988	Janet Evans, U.S.	4:03.85
1992	Dagmar Hase, Germany	4:07.18
1996	Michelle Smith, Ireland	4:07.25
2000	Brooke Bennett, U.S.	4:05.80
2004	Laure Manaudou, France	4:05.34
800m Freestyle		**Time**
1968	Deborah Meyer, U.S.	9:24.00
1972	Keena Rothhammer, U.S.	8:53.68
1976	Petra Thümer, East Germany	8:37.14
1980	Michelle Ford, Australia	8:28.90
1984	Tiffany Cohen, U.S.	8:24.95
1988	Janet Evans, U.S.	8:20.20
1992	Janet Evans, U.S.	8:25.52
1996	Brooke Bennett, U.S.	8:27.89
2000	Brooke Bennett, U.S.	8:19.67
2004	Ai Shibata, Japan	8:24.54
100m Backstroke		**Time**
1924	Sybil Bauer, U.S.	1:23.20
1928	Maria Braun, Netherlands	1:22.00
1932	Eleanor Holm, U.S.	1:19.40

1936	Nida Senff, Netherlands	1:18.90
1948	Karen Harup, Denmark	1:14.40
1952	Joan Harrison, South Africa	1:14.30
1956	Judy Grinham, Great Britain	1:12.90
1960	Lynn Burke, U.S.	1:09.30
1964	Cathy Ferguson, U.S.	1:07.70
1968	Kaye Hall, U.S.	1:06.20
1972	Melissa Belote, U.S.	1:05.78
1976	Ulrike Richter, East Germany	1:01.83
1980	Rica Reinisch, East Germany	1:00.86
1984	Theresa Andrews, U.S.	1:02.55
1988	Kristin Otto, East Germany	1:00.89
1992	Krisztina Egerszegi, Hungary	1:00.68
1996	Beth Botsford, U.S.	1:01.19
2000	Diana Mocanu, Romania	1:00.21
2004	Natalie Coughlin, U.S.	1:00.37
200m Backstroke		**Time**
1968	Lillian "Pokey" Watson, U.S.	2:24.80
1972	Melissa Belote, U.S.	2:19.19
1976	Ulrike Richter, East Germany	2:13.43
1980	Rica Reinisch, East Germany	2:11.77
1984	Jolanda de Rover, Netherlands	2:12.38
1988	Krisztina Egerszegi, Hungary	2:09.29
1992	Krisztina Egerszegi, Hungary	2:07.06
1996	Krisztina Egerszegi, Hungary	2:07.83
2000	Diana Mocanu, Romania	2:08.16
2004	Kirsty Coventry, Zimbabwe	2:09.19
100m Breaststroke		**Time**
1972	Catherine Carr, U.S.	1:13.58
1976	Hannelore Anke, East Germany	1:11.16
1980	Ute Geweniger, East Germany	1:10.22
1984	Petra van Staveren, Netherlands	1:09.88
1988	Tania Dangalakova, Bulgaria	1:07.95
1992	Elena Roudkovskaia, Unified Team	1:08.00
1996	Penny Heyns, South Africa	1:07.73
2000	Megan Quann, U.S.	1:07.05
2004	Xuejan Luo, China	1:06.64
200m Breaststroke		**Time**
1924	Lucy Morton, Great Britain	3:33.20
1928	Hilde Schrader, Germany	3:12.60
1932	Clare Dennis, Australia	3:06.30
1936	Hideko Maehata, Japan	3:03.60
1948	Nelly van Vliet, Netherlands	2:57.20
1952	Eva Szekely, Hungary	2:51.70
1956	Ursula Happe, Germany	2:53.10
1960	Anita Lonsbrough, Great Britain	2:49.50
1964	Galina Prozumenshikova, U.S.S.R.	2:46.40
1968	Sharon Wichman, U.S.	2:44.40
1972	Beverley Whitfield, Australia	2:41.71
1976	Marina Koshevaia, U.S.S.R.	2:33.35
1980	Lina Kaciusyte, U.S.S.R.	2:29.54
1984	Anne Ottenbrite, Canada	2:30.38
1988	Silke Hoerner, East Germany	2:26.71
1992	Kyoko Iwasaki, Japan	2:26.65
1996	Penny Heyns, South Africa	2:25.41
2000	Agnes Kovacs, Hungary	2:24.35
2004	Amanda Beard, U.S.	2:23.37
100m Butterfly		**Time**
1956	Shelly Mann, U.S.	1:11.00
1960	Carolyn Schuler, U.S.	1:09.50
1964	Sharon Stouder, U.S.	1:04.70
1968	Lynnette McClements, Australia	1:05.50
1972	Mayumi Aoki, Japan	1:03.34
1976	Kornelia Ender, East Germany	1:00.13
1980	Caren Metschuck, East Germany	1:00.42
1984	Mary T. Meagher, U.S.	0:59.26
1988	Kristin Otto, East Germany	0:59.00
1992	Qian Hong, China	0:58.62
1996	Amy Van Dyken, U.S.	0:59.13
2000	Inge de Bruijn, Netherlands	0:56.61
2004	Petria Thomas, Australia	0:57.72
200m Butterfly		**Time**
1968	Ada Kok, Netherlands	2:24.70
1972	Karen Moe, U.S.	2:15.57
1976	Andrea Pollack, East Germany	2:11.41

1980	Ines Geissler, East Germany	2:10.44
1984	Mary T. Meagher, U.S.	2:06.90
1988	Kathleen Nord, East Germany	2:09.51
1992	Summer Sanders, U.S.	2:08.67
1996	Susan O'Neill, Australia	2:07.76
2000	Misty Hyman, U.S.	2:05.88
2004	Otylia Jedrzejczak, Poland	2:06.05
200m Individual Medley		**Time**
1968	Claudia Kolb, U.S.	2:24.70
1972	Shane Gould, Australia	2:23.07
1984	Tracy Caulkins, U.S.	2:12.64
1988	Daniela Hunger, East Germany	2:12.59
1992	Lin Li, China	2:11.65
1996	Michelle Smith, Ireland	2:13.93
2000	Yana Klochkova, Ukraine	2:10.68
2004	Yana Klochkova, Ukraine	2:11.14
400m Individual Medley		**Time**
1964	Donna De Varona, U.S.	5:18.70
1968	Claudia Kolb, U.S.	5:08.50
1972	Gail Neall, Australia	5:02.97
1976	Ulrike Tauber, East Germany	4:42.77
1980	Petra Schneider, East Germany	4:36.29
1984	Tracy Caulkins, U.S.	4:39.24
1988	Janet Evans, U.S.	4:37.76
1992	Krisztina Egerszegi, Hungary	4:36.54
1996	Michelle Smith, Ireland	4:39.18
2000	Yana Klochkova, Ukraine	4:33.59
2004	Yana Klochkova, Ukraine	4:34.83
4x100m Freestyle Relay		**Time**
1912	Great Britain	5:52.80
1968	U.S.	4:02.50
1920	U.S.	5:11.60
1972	U.S.	3:55.19
1924	U.S.	4:58.80
1976	U.S.	3:44.82
1928	U.S.	4:47.60
1980	E. Germany	3:42.71
1932	U.S.	4:38.00
1984	U.S.	3:43.43
1938	Netherlands	4:36.00
1988	E. Germany	3:40.63
1948	U.S.	4:29.20
1992	U.S.	3:39.46
1952	Hungary	4:24.40
1996	U.S.	3:39.29
1956	Australia	4:17.10
2000	U.S.	3:36.61

1960	U.S.	4:08.9
2004	Australia	3:35.9
1964	U.S.	4:03.8
4x200m Freestyle Relay		**Time**
1996	U.S.	7:59.8
2004	U.S.	7:53.4
2000	U.S.	7:57.8
4x100m Medley Relay		**Time**
1960	U.S.	4:41.10
1984	U.S.	4:08.34
1964	U.S.	4:33.96
1988	E. Germany	4:03.74
1968	U.S.	4:28.30
1992	U.S.	4:02.54
1972	U.S.	4:20.75
1996	U.S.	4:02.88
1976	E. Germany	4:07.95
2000	U.S.	3:58.30
1980	E. Germany	4:06.67
2004	Australia	3:57.32

Platform Diving

1912	Greta Johansson, Sweden	1968	Milena Duchkova,
1920	Stefani Fryland-Clausen,		Czechoslovakia,
	Denmark	1972	Ulrika Knape, Sweden
1924	Caroline Smith, U.S.	1976	Elena Vaytsekhovskaya,
1928	Elizabeth Becker Pinkston,		U.S.S.R.
	U.S.	1980	Martina Jäschke,
1932	Dorothy Poynton, U.S.		E. Germany
		1984	Zhou Jihong, China
1936	Dorothy Poynton Hill, U.S	1988	Xu Yahmei, China
1948	Victoria Draves, U.S.	1992	Fu Mingxia, China
1952	Patricia McCormick, U.S.	1996	Fu Mingxia, China
1956	Patricia McCormick, U.S.	2000	Laura Wilkinson, U.S.
1960	Ingrid Krämer, E. Germany	2004	Chantelle Newbery, Australia
1964	Lesley Bush, U.S.		

Springboard Diving

1920	Aileen Riggin, U.S.	1968	Sue Gossick, U.S.
1924	Elizabeth Becker, U.S.	1972	Micki King, U.S.
1928	Helen Meany, U.S.	1976	Jennifer Chandler, U.S.
1932	Georgia Coleman, U.S.	1980	Irina Kalinina, U.S.S.R.
1936	Marjorie Gestring, U.S.	1984	Sylvie Bernier, Canada
1948	Victoria Draves, U.S.	1988	Gao Min, China
1952	Patricia McCormick, U.S.	1992	Gao Min, China
1956	Patricia McCormick, U.S.	1996	Fu Mingxia, China
1960	Ingrid Kramer, Germany	2000	Fu Mingxia, China
1964	Ingrid Kramer, E. Germany	2004	Jingjing Guo, China

Track and Field, Men

	100 Meter Dash	**Time**
1896	Thomas E. Burke, U.S.	12.00
1900	Francis W. Jarvis, U.S.	11.00
1904	Archie Hahn, U.S.	11.00
1908	Reginald E. Walker, South Africa	10.80
1912	Ralph C. Craig, U.S.	10.80
1920	Charles W. Paddock, U.S.	10.80
1924	Harold M. Abrahams, Great Britain	10.60
1928	Percy Williams, Canada	10.80
1932	Eddie Tolan, U.S.	10.30
1936	Jesse Owens, U.S.	10.30
1948	Harrison Dillard, U.S.	10.30
1952	Lindy J. Remigino, U.S.	10.40
1956	Bobby J. Morrow, U.S.	10.50
1960	Armin Hary, Germany	10.20
1964	Robert L. Hayes, U.S.	10.00
1968	James Hines, U.S.	9.95
1972	Valery Borzov, U.S.S.R.	10.14
1976	Hasely Crawford, Trinidad & Tobago	10.06
1980	Allan Wells, Great Britain	10.25
1984	Carl Lewis, U.S.	9.99
1988	Carl Lewis, U.S.	9.92
1992	Linford Christie, Great Britain	9.96
1996	Donovan Bailey, Canada	9.84
2000	Maurice Greene, U.S.	9.87
2004	Justin Gatlin, U.S.	9.85
	200 Meters	**Time**
1900	John W.B. Tewksbury, U.S.	22.20
1904	Archie Hahn, U.S.	21.60
1908	Robert Kerr, Canada	22.60
1912	Ralph C. Craig, U.S.	21.70
1920	Allen Woodring, U.S.	22.00
1924	Jackson V. Scholz, U.S.	21.60
1928	Percy Williams, Canada	21.80
1932	Eddie Tolan, U.S.	21.20
1936	Jesse Owens, U.S.	20.70

1948	Melvin Patton, U.S.	21.10
1952	Andrew W. Stanfield, U.S.	20.70
1956	Bobby J. Morrow, U.S.	20.60
1960	Livio Berruti, Italy	20.50
1964	Henry Carr, U.S.	20.30
1968	Tommie Smith, U.S.	19.83
1972	Valery Borzov, U.S.S.R.	20.00
1976	Donald Quarrie, Jamaica	20.23
1980	Pietro Mennea, Italy	20.19
1984	Carl Lewis, U.S.	19.80
1988	Joe DeLoach, U.S.	19.75
1992	Mike Marsh, U.S.	20.01
1996	Michael Johnson, U.S.	19.32
2000	Konstantinos Kenteris, Greece	20.09
2004	Shawn Crawford, U.S.	19.79
400 Meters		**Time**
1896	Thomas E. Burke, U.S.	54.20
1900	Maxey Long, U.S.	49.40
1904	Harry I. Hillman, U.S.	49.20
1908	Wyndham Halswelle, Great Britain	50.00
1912	Charles D. Reidpath, U.S.	48.20
1920	Bevil G.D. Rudd, South Africa	49.60
1924	Eric H. Liddel, Great Britain	47.60
1928	Ray Barbuti, U.S.	47.80
1932	William A. Carr, U.S.	46.20
1936	Archie Williams, U.S.	46.50
1948	Arthur Wint, Jamaica	46.20
1952	George Rhoden, Jamaica	45.90
1956	Charles L. Jenkins, U.S.	46.70
1960	Otis Davis, U.S.	44.90
1964	Michael D. Larrabee, U.S.	45.10
1968	Lee Evans, U.S.	43.86
1972	Vince Matthews, U.S.	44.66
1976	Alberto Juantorena, Cuba	44.26
1980	Viktor Markin, U.S.S.R.	44.60
1984	Alonzo Babers, U.S.	44.27

'88	Steven Lewis, U.S.	43.87
'92	Quincy Watts, U.S.	43.50
'96	Michael Johnson, U.S.	43.49
'00	Michael Johnson, U.S.	43.84
'04	Jeremy Wariner, U.S.	44.00
800 Meters		**Time**
'96	Edwin H. Flack, Australia	2:11.00
'00	Alfred E. Tysoe, Great Britain	2:01.20
'04	James D. Lightbody, U.S.	1:56.00
'08	Melvin W. Sheppard, U.S.	1:52.80
'12	Ted Meredith, U.S.	1:51.90
'20	Albert G. Hill, Great Britain	1:53.40
'24	Douglas G.A. Lowe, Great Britain	1:52.40
'28	Douglas G.A. Lowe, Great Britain	1:51.80
'32	Thomas Hampson, Great Britain	1:49.70
'36	John Woodruff, U.S.	1:52.90
'48	Malvin Whitfield, U.S.	1:49.20
'52	Malvin Whitfield, U.S.	1:49.20
'56	Thomas W. Courtney, U.S.	1:47.70
'60	Peter Snell, New Zealand	1:46.30
'64	Peter Snell, New Zealand	1:45.10
'68	Ralph Doubell, Australia	1:44.30
'72	Dave Wottle, U.S.	1:45.90
'76	Alberto Juantorena, Cuba	1:43.50
1980	Steven Ovett, Great Britain	1:45.40
1984	Joaquim Cruz, Brazil	1:43.00
1988	Paul Ereng, Kenya	1:43.45
1992	William Tanui, Kenya	1:43.66
1996	Vebjoern Rodal, Norway	1:42.59
2000	Nils Schumann, Germany	1:45.08
2004	Yuriy Borzakovskiy, Russia	1:44.45
1,500 Meters		**Time**
'96	Edwin H. Flack, Australia	4:33.20
1900	Charles Bennett, Great Britain	4:06.20
1904	James D. Lightbody, U.S.	4:05.40
1908	Melvin W. Sheppard, U.S.	4:03.40
1912	Arnold N.S. Jackson, Great Britain	3:56.80
1920	Albert G. Hill, Great Britain	4:01.80
1924	Paavo Nurmi, Finland	3:53.60
1928	Harry E. Larva, Finland	3:53.20
1932	Luigi Beccali, Italy	3:51.20
1936	Jack Lovelock, New Zealand	3:47.80
1948	Henry Eriksson, Sweden	3:49.80
1952	Josy Barthel, Luxembourg	3:45.10
1956	Ronald Delany, Ireland	3:41.20
1960	Herbert Elliott, Australia	3:35.60
1964	Peter Snell, New Zealand	3:38.10
1968	Kipchoge Keino, Kenya	3:34.90
1972	Pekka Vasala, Finland	3:36.30
1976	John Walker, New Zealand	3:39.17
1980	Sebastian Coe, Great Britain	3:38.40
1984	Sebastian Coe, Great Britain	3:32.53
1988	Peter Rono, Kenya	3:35.96
1992	Fermin Cacho Ruiz, Spain	3:40.12
1996	Noureddine Morceli, Algeria	3:35.78
2000	Noah Ngeny, Kenya	3:32.07
2004	Hicham El Guerrouj, Morocco	3:34.18
5,000 Meters		**Time**
1912	Johannes Kolehmainen, Finland	14:36.60
1920	Joseph Guillemot, France	14:55.60
1924	Paavo Nurmi, Finland	14:31.20
1928	Ville Ritola, Finland	14:38.00
1932	Lauri Lehtinen, Finland	14:30.00
1936	Gunnar Höckert, Finland	14:22.20
1948	Gaston Reiff, Belgium	14:17.60
1952	Emil Zátopek, Czechoslovakia	14:06.60
1956	Vladimir Kuts, U.S.S.R.	13:39.60
1960	Murray Halberg, New Zealand	13:43.40
1964	Robert K. Schul, U.S.	13:48.80
1968	Mohamed Gammoudi, Tunisia	14:05.00
1972	Lasse Viren, Finland	13:26.40
1976	Lasse Viren, Finland	13:24.76
1980	Miruts Yifter, Ethiopia	13:21.00
1984	Said Aouita, Morocco	13:05.59
1988	John Ngugi, Kenya	13:11.70
1992	Dieter Baumann, Germany	13:12.52
1996	Venuste Niyongabo, Burundi	13:07.97
2000	Millon Wolde, Ethiopia	13:35.49
2004	Hicham El Guerrouj, Morocco	13:14.39
10,000 Meters		**Time**
1912	Johannes Kolehmainen, Finland	31:20.80
1920	Paavo Nurmi, Finland	31:45.80
1924	Ville Ritola, Finland	30:23.20
1928	Paavo Nurmi, Finland	30:18.80
1932	Janusz Kusocinski, Poland	30:11.40
1936	Ilmari Salminen, Finland	30:15.40
1948	Emil Zatopek, Czechoslovakia	29:59.60
1952	Emil Zatopek, Czechoslovakia	29:17.00
1956	Vladimir Kuts, U.S.S.R.	28:45.60
1960	Pyotr Bolotnikov, U.S.S.R.	28:32.20
1964	William Mills, U.S.	28:24.40
1968	Naftali Temu, Kenya	29:27.40
1972	Lasse Viren, Finland	27:38.40
1976	Lasse Viren, Finland	27:40.38
1980	Miruts Yifter, Ethiopia	27:42.70
1984	Alberto Cova, Italy	27:47.54
1988	Brahim Boutaib, Morocco	27:21.46
1992	Khalid Skah, Morocco	27:46.70
1996	Haile Gebrselassie, Ethiopia	27:07.34
2000	Haile Gebrselassie, Ethiopia	27:18.20
2004	Kenenisa Bekele, Ethiopia	27:05.10
Marathon		**Time**
1896	Spiridon Louis, Greece	2:58:50.00
1900	Michel Theato, France	2:59:45.00
1904	Thomas J. Hicks, U.S.	3:28:63.00
1908	John J. Hayes, U.S.	2:55:18.40
1912	Kenneth McArthur, South Africa	2:36:54.80
1920	Johannes Kolehmainen, Finland	2:32:35.80
1924	Albin Stenroos, Finland	2:41:22.60
1928	Boughéra El Ouafi, France	2:32:57.00
1932	Juan Carlos Zabala, Argentina	2:31:36.00
1936	Kitei Son, Japan	2:29:19.20
1948	Delfo Cabrera, Argentina	2:34:51.60
1952	Emil Zátopek, Czechoslovakia	2:23:03.20
1956	Alain Mimoun O'Kacha, France	2:25:00.00
1960	Abebe Bikila, Ethiopia	2:15:16.20
1964	Abebe Bikila, Ethiopia	2:12:11.20
1968	Mamo Wolde, Ethiopia	2:20:26.40
1972	Frank Shorter, U.S.	2:12:19.80
1976	Waldemar Cierpinski, East Germany	2:09:55.00
1980	Waldemar Cierpinski, East Germany	2:11:03.00
1984	Carlos Lopes, Portugal	2:09:21.00
1988	Gelindo Bordin, Italy	2:10:32.00
1992	Young-Cho Hwang, S. Korea	2:13:23.00
1996	Josia Thugwane, South Africa	2:12:36.00
2000	Gezahgne Abera, Ethiopia	2:10:11.00
2004	Stefano Baldini, Italy	2:10.55.00
110-Meter Hurdles		**Time**
1896	Thomas P. Curtis, U.S.	17.60
1900	Alvin E. Kraenzlein, U.S.	15.40
1904	Frederick W. Schule, U.S.	16.00
1908	Forrest Smithson, U.S.	15.00
1912	Frederick W. Kelley, U.S.	15.10
1920	Earl J. Thomson, Canada	14.80
1924	Daniel C. Kinsey, U.S.	15.00
1928	Sydney Atkinson, South Africa	14.80
1932	George Saling, U.S.	14.60
1936	Forrest Towns, U.S.	14.20
1948	William Porter, U.S.	13.90
1952	Harrison Dillard, U.S.	13.70
1956	Lee Q. Calhoun, U.S.	13.50
1960	Lee Q. Calhoun, U.S.	13.80
1964	Hayes W. Jones, U.S.	13.60
1968	Willie Davenport, U.S.	13.30
1972	Rod Milburn, U.S.	13.24
1976	Guy Drut, France	13.30
1980	Thomas Munkelt, East Germany	13.39
1984	Roger Kingdom, U.S.	13.20
1988	Roger Kingdom, U.S.	12.98
1992	Mark McKoy, Canada	13.12
1996	Allen Johnson, U.S.	12.95
2000	Anier Garcia, Cuba	13.00
2004	Xiang Liu, China	12.91
400-Meter Hurdles		**Time**
1900	John W. B. Tewksbury, U.S.	57.60
1904	Harry L. Hillman, U.S.	53.00
1908	Charles J. Bacon, U.S.	55.00
1920	Frank F. Loomis, U.S.	54.00
1924	F. Morgan Taylor, U.S.	52.60
1928	David Burghley, Great Britain	53.40
1932	Robert Tisdall, Ireland	51.70
1936	Glenn Hardin, U.S.	52.40
1948	Roy Cochran, U.S.	51.10
1952	Charles Moore, U.S.	50.80
1956	Glenn A. Davis, U.S.	50.10
1960	Glenn A. Davis, U.S.	49.30
1964	Warren "Rex" Cawley, U.S.	49.60
1968	David Hemery, Great Britain	48.12
1972	John Akii-Bua, Uganda	47.82
1976	Edwin Moses, U.S.	47.64
1980	Volker Beck, East Germany	48.70
1984	Edwin Moses, U.S.	47.75
1988	Andre Phillips, U.S.	47.19
1992	Kevin Young, U.S.	46.78
1996	Derrick Adkins, United States	47.55
2000	Angelo Taylor, U.S.	47.50

2004	Felix Sanchez, Dominican Republic	47.63

3,000-Meter Steeplechase — Time

1900	George Orton, Canada/U.S.	7:34.40
1904	James Lightbody, U.S.	7:39.60
1908	Arthur Russell, Great Britain	10:47.80
1920	Percy Hodge, Great Britain	10:00.40
1924	Ville Ritola, Finland	9:33.60
1928	Toivo A. Loukola, Finland	9:21.80
1932	Volmari Iso-Hollo, Finland	10:33.40
	(3,460m—extra lap by official error)	
1936	Volmari Iso-Hollo, Finland	9:03.80
1948	Thore Sjöstrand, Sweden	9:04.60
1952	Horace Ashenfelter, U.S.	8:45.40
1956	Chris Brasher, Great Britain	8:41.20
1960	Zdzislaw Krzyszkowiak, Poland	8:34.20
1964	Gaston Roelants, Belgium	8:30.80
1968	Amos Biwott, Kenya	8:51.00
1972	Kipchoge Keino, Kenya	8:23.60
1976	Anders Gärderud, Sweden	8:08.20
1980	Bronislaw Malinowski, Poland	8:09.70
1984	Julius Korir, Kenya	8:11.80
1988	Julius Kariuki, Kenya	8:05.51
1992	Matthew Birer, Kenya	8:08.84
1996	Joseph Keter, Kenya	8:07.12
2000	Reuben Kosgei, Kenya	8:21.43
2004	Ezekiel Kemboi, Kenya	8:05.81

20km Walk

2004	Ivano Brugnetti, Italy	1:19:40

50km Walk

2004	Robert Korzeniowski, Poland	3:38:46

4x100-Meter Relay — Time

1912	Great Britain	42.40
1968	U.S.	38.20
1920	U.S.	42.20
1972	U.S.	38.19
1924	U.S.	41.00
1976	U.S.	38.33
1928	U.S.	41.00
1980	U.S.S.R.	38.26
1932	U.S.	40.00
1984	U.S.	37.83
1936	U.S.	39.80
1988	U.S.S.R.	38.19
1948	U.S.	40.60
1992	U.S.	37.40
1952	U.S.	40.10
1996	Canada	37.69
1956	U.S.	39.50
2000	U.S.	37.61
1960	W. Germany	39.50
2004	Great Britain	38.07
1964	U.S.	39.00

4x400-Meter Relay — Time

1908	U.S.	3:29.40
1964	U.S.	3:00.70
1912	U.S.	3:16.60
1968	U.S.	2:56.16
1920	Great Britain	3:22.20
1972	Kenya	2:59.80
1924	U.S.	3:16.00
1976	U.S.	2:58.65
1928	U.S.	3:14.20
1980	U.S.S.R.	3:01.10
1932	U.S.	3:08.20
1984	U.S.	2:57.91
1936	Great Britain	3:09.00
1988	U.S.	2:56.16
1948	U.S.	3:10.40
1992	U.S.	2:55.74
1952	Jamaica	3:03.90
1996	U.S.	2:55.99
1956	U.S.	3:04.80
2000	U.S.	2:56.35
1960	U.S.	3:02.20
2004	U.S.	2:55.91

Discus Throw — Distance

1896	Robert Garrett, U.S.	95' 7½"
1900	Rezsö Bauer, Hungary	118'3"
1904	Martin Sheridan, U.S.	128'10½"
1908	Martin Sheridan, U.S.	134'2"
1912	Armas Taipale, Finland	148'3"
1920	Elmer Niklander, Finland	146'7"
1924	Bud Houser, U.S.	151'4"
1928	Bud Houser, U.S.	155'3"
1932	John Anderson, U.S.	162'4"
1936	W. Kenneth Carpenter, U.S.	165'7"

1948	Adolfo Consolini, Italy	173'
1952	Sim Iness, U.S.	180'
1956	Al Oerter, U.S.	184'1
1960	Al Oerter, U.S.	194'
1964	Al Oerter, U.S.	200'
1968	Al Oerter, U.S.	212'
1972	Ludvik Danek, Czechoslovakia	211'
1976	Mac Wilkins, U.S.	221'.
1980	Viktor Rashuplin, U.S.S.R.	218'
1984	Rolf Danneberg, West Germany	218'
1988	Jurgen Schult, East Germany	225'9½
1992	Romas Ubartas, Lithuania	213'8
1996	Lars Riedel, Germany	227' 8
2000	Virgilijus Alekna, Lithuania	227' 4
2004	Virgilijus Alekna, Lithuania	229'3

Hammer Throw — Distance

1900	John Flanagan, U.S.	163'1
1904	John Flanagan, U.S.	168'1
1908	John Flanagan, U.S.	170'4
1912	Matthew McGrath, U.S.	179'7
1920	Patrick Ryan, U.S.	173'5
1924	Frederick Tootell, U.S.	174'10
1928	Patrick O'Callaghan, Ireland	168'7
1932	Patrick O'Callaghan, Ireland	176'11
1936	Karl Hein, Germany	185'4
1948	Imre Nemeth, Hungary	183'11
1952	Jozsef Csermak, Hungary	197'11
1956	Harold V. Connolly, U.S.	207'3
1960	Vasiliy Rudenkov, U.S.S.R.	220'2
1964	Romuald Klim, U.S.S.R.	228'10"
1968	Gyula Zsivotzky, Hungary	240'8"
1972	Anatoly Bondarchuk, U.S.S.R.	247'8"
1976	Yuri Sedykh, U.S.S.R.	254'4"
1980	Yuri Sedykh, U.S.S.R.	268'4"
1984	Juha Tiainen, Finland	256'2"
1988	Sergei Litinov, U.S.S.R.	278'2½"
1992	Andrei Abduvaliyev, Unified Team	270'9"
1996	Balazs Kiss, Hungary	266'6"
2000	Szymon Ziolkowski, Poland	262'6"
2004	Koji Murofushi, Japan	272'0"

High Jump — Height

1896	Ellery Clark, U.S.	5'11¼"
1900	Irving K. Baxter, U.S.	6'2¾"
1904	Samuel Jones, U.S.	5'11"
1908	Harry Porter, U.S.	6'3"
1912	Alma Richards, U.S.	6'4"
1920	Richmond Landon, U.S.	6'4"
1924	Harold Osborn, U.S.	6'6"
1928	Robert W. King, U.S.	6'4½"
1932	Duncan McNaughton, Canada	6'5½"
1936	Cornelius Johnson, U.S.	6'8"
1948	John Winter, Australia	6'6"
1952	Walter Davis, U.S.	6'8½"
1956	Charles E. Dumas, U.S.	6'11½"
1960	Robert Shavlakadze, U.S.S.R.	7'1"
1964	Valery Brumel, U.S.S.R.	7'1¾"
1968	Richard Fosbury, U.S.	7'4¼"
1972	Juri Tarmak, U.S.S.R.	7'3¾"
1976	Jacek Wszola, Poland	7'4½"
1980	Gerd Wessig, East Germany	7'8¾"
1984	Dietmar Mogenburg, West Germany	7'8½"
1988	Guennadi Avdeenko, U.S.S.R.	7'9½"
1992	Javier Sotomayor, Cuba	7'8"
1996	Charles Austin, U.S.	7' 10"
2000	Sergey Kliugin, Russia	7' 9"
2004	Stefan Holm, Sweden	7'8"

Javelin — Distance

1908	Erik Lemming, Sweden	179'10"
1912	Erik Lemming, Sweden	198'11"
1920	Jonni Myyra, Finland	215'10"
1924	Jonni Myyra, Finland	206'7"
1928	Erik Lundquist, Sweden	218'6"
1932	Matti Jarvinen, Finland	238'6"
1936	Gerhard Stock, Germany	235'8"
1948	Kai Tapio Rautavaara, Finland	228'10"
1952	Cyrus Young, U.S.	242'1"
1956	Egil Danielson, Norway	281'2"
1960	Viktor Tsibulenko, U.S.S.R.	277'8"
1964	Pauli Nevala, Finland	271'2"
1968	Janis Lusis, U.S.S.R.	295'7"
1972	Klaus Wolfemann, West Germany	296'10"
1976	Miklos Nemeth, Hungary	310'4"
1980	Dainis Kula, U.S.S.R.	299'2"
1984	Arto Harkonen, Finland	284'8"
1988	Tapio Korjus, Finland	276'6"
1992	Jan Zelezny, Czechoslovakia	294'2"
1996	Jan Zelezny, Czech Republic	289'3"
2000	Jan Zelezny, Czech Republic	295'10"

2004	Andreas Thorkildsen, Norway	283'9"

	Long Jump	Distance
1896	Ellery Clark, U.S.	20' 10"
1900	Alvin Kraenzlein, U.S.	23'6¾"
1904	Meyer Prinstein, U.S.	24'1"
1908	Frank Irons, U.S.	24'6½"
1912	Albert Gutterson, U.S.	24'11¼"
1920	William Pettersson, Sweden	23'5½"
1924	De Hart Hubbard, U.S.	24'5"
1928	Edward Hamm, U.S.	25'4"
1932	Edward Gordon, U.S.	25'¾"
1936	Jesse Owens, U.S.	26'5½"
1948	Willie Steel, U.S.	25'8"
1952	Jerome Biffle, U.S.	24'10"
1956	Gregory C. Bell, U.S.	25'8¼"
1960	Ralph H. Boston, U.S.	26'7¾"
1964	Lynn Davies, Great Britain	26'5¾"
1968	Robert Beamon, U.S.	29'2½"
1972	Randy Williams, U.S.	27'½"
1976	Arnie Robinson, U.S.	27'4¾"
1980	Lutz Bombrowski, East Germany	28'¼"
1984	Carl Lewis, U.S.	28'¼"
1988	Carl Lewis, U.S.	28'7¼"
1992	Carl Lewis, U.S.	28'5½"
1996	Carl Lewis, U.S.	27'10¾"
2000	Ivan Pedroso, Cuba	28'1"
2004	Dwight Phillips, United States	28'2"

	Pole Vault	Height
1896	William W. Hoyt, U.S.	10'10"
1900	Irving K. Baxter, U.S.	10'10"
1904	Charles E. Dvorak, U.S.	11'5¾"
1908	Albert C. Gilbert, U.S.; Edward T. Cook Jr., U.S.	12'2"
1912	Harry S. Babcock, U.S.	12'11½"
1920	Frank K. Foss, U.S.	13'5"
1924	Lee S. Barnes, U.S.	12'11½"
1928	Sabin W. Carr, U.S.	13'9¼"
1932	William Miller, U.S.	14'1¾"
1936	Earle Meadows, U.S.	14'3¼"
1948	O. Guinn Smith, U.S.	14'1¼"
1952	Robert Richards, U.S.	14'11"
1956	Robert Richards, U.S.	14'11½"
1960	Donald Bragg, U.S.	15'5"
1964	Fred M. Hansen, U.S.	16'8¾"
1968	Robert Seagren, U.S.	17'8½"
1972	Wolfgang Nordwig, East Germany	18'½"
1976	Tadeusz Slusarki, Poland	18'½"
1980	Wladyslaw Kozakiewicz, Poland	18'11½"
1984	Pierre Quinon, France	18'10¼"
1988	Sergei Bubka, U.S.S.R.	19'9¼"
1992	Maksim Tarassov, Unified Team	19'0¼"
1996	Jean Galfiore, France	19'5¼"
2000	Nick Hysong, U.S.	19'4"
2004	Timothy Mack, United States	19'6"

	Shot Put	Distance
1896	Robert Garrett, U.S.	36'9¾"
1900	Richard Sheldon, U.S.	46'3¼"
1904	Ralph Rose, U.S.	48'7"
1908	Ralph Rose, U.S.	46'7½"
1912	Patrick McDonald, U.S.	50'4"
1920	Ville Porhola, Finland	48'7¼"
1924	Bud Houser, U.S.	49'2¼"
1928	John Kuck, U.S.	52'¾"
1932	Leo Sexton, U.S.	52'6"
1936	Hans Woellke, Germany	53'1¾"
1948	Wilbur Thompson, U.S.	56'2"

1952	Parry O'Brien, Jr., U.S.	57'1½"
1956	Parry O'Brien, Jr., U.S.	60'11¼"
1960	William Nieder, U.S.	64'6¾"
1964	Dallas C. Long, U.S.	66'8½"
1968	James Randel Matson, U.S.	67'4¾"
1972	Wladyslaw Komar, Poland	69'6"
1976	Udo Beyer, East Germany	69'6¾"
1980	Vladimir Kiselyov, U.S.S.R.	70'½"
1984	Alessandro Andrei, Italy	69'9"
1988	Ulf Timmermann, East Germany	73'8¾"
1992	Mike Stulce, U.S.	71'2½"
1996	Randy Barnes, United States	70' 11"
2000	Arsi Harju, Finland	69' 10"
2004	Yuriy Bilonog, Ukraine	69'5"

	Triple Jump	Distance
1896	James B. Connolly, U.S.	44' 11¾"
1900	Myer Prinstein, U.S.	47'5¾"
1904	Myer Prinstein, U.S.	47'1"
1908	Timothy Ahearne, Great Britain	48'11¼"
1912	Gustaf Lindblom, Sweden	48'5¼"
1920	Vilho Tuulos, Finland	47'7"
1924	Anthony Winter, Australia	50'11¼"
1928	Mikio Oda, Japan	49'11"
1932	Chuhei Nambu, Japan	51'7"
1936	Naoto Tajima, Japan	52'6"
1948	Arne Ahman, Sweden	50'6¼"
1952	Adhemar da Silva, Brazil	53'2¾"
1956	Adhemar da Silva, Brazil	53'7¾"
1960	Jozef Schmidt, Poland	55'2"
1964	Jozef Schmidt, Poland	55'3½"
1968	Viktor Saneyev, U.S.S.R.	57'¾"
1972	Viktor Saneyev, U.S.S.R.	56'11¼"
1976	Viktor Saneyev, U.S.S.R.	56'8¾"
1980	Jaak Uudmae, U.S.S.R.	56'11¼"
1984	Al Joyner, U.S.	56'7½"
1988	Hristo Markov, Bulgaria	57'9¼"
1992	Mike Conley, U.S.	57'10¼"
1996	Kenny Harrison, United States	59'4¼"
2000	Jonathan Edwards, Great Britain	58'1"
2004	Christian Olsson, Sweden	58'4"

	Decathlon	Points[1]
1904	Thomas Kiely, Ireland	6,036.00
1912	Jim Thorpe, U.S.[2]	8,412.00
1920	Helge Lovland, Norway	6,803.00
1924	Harold Osborn, U.S.	7,710.77
1928	Paavo Yrjola, Finland	8,053.29
1932	James Bausch, U.S.	8,462.23
1936	Glenn Morris, U.S.	7,900.00
1948	Robert Mathias, U.S.	7,139.00
1952	Robert Mathias, U.S.	7,887.00
1956	Milton G. Campbell, U.S.	7,937.00
1960	Rafer Johnson, U.S.	8,392.00
1964	Willi Holdorf, West Germany	7,887.00
1968	Bill Toomey, U.S.	8,193.00
1972	Nikolai Avilov, U.S.S.R.	8,454.00
1976	Bruce Jenner, U.S.	8,617.00
1980	Daley Thompson, Great Britain	8,495.00
1984	Daley Thompson, Great Britain	8,798.00
1988	Christian Schenk, East Germany	8,488.00
1992	Robert Zmelik, Czechoslovakia	8,611.00
1996	Dan O'Brien, U.S.	8,824.00
2000	Erki Nool, Estonia	8,641.00
2004	Roman Sebrle, Czech Republic	8,893.00

Track and Field, Women

	100-Meter Dash	Time
1928	Elizabeth Robinson, U.S.	12.20
1932	Stanislawa Walasiewicz, Poland	11.90
1936	Helen Stephens, U.S.	11.50
1948	Fanny Blankers-Koen, Netherlands	11.90
1952	Marjorie Jackson, Australia	11.50
1956	Betty Cuthbert, Australia	11.50
1960	Wilma Rudolph, U.S.	11.00
1964	Wyomia Tyus, U.S.	11.40
1968	Wyomia Tyus, U.S.	11.00
1972	Renate Stecher, East Germany	11.07
1976	Annegret Richter, West Germany	11.08
1980	Lyudmila Kondratyeva, U.S.S.R.	11.06
1984	Evelyn Ashford, U.S.	10.97
1988	Florence Griffith-Joyner, U.S.	10.54
1992	Gail Devers, U.S.	10.82
1996	Gail Devers, U.S.	10.94

2000	Marion Jones, U.S.	10.75
2004	Yuliya Nesterenko, Belarus	10.93

	200 Meters	Time
1948	Fanny Blankers-Koen, Netherlands	24.40
1952	Marjorie Jackson, Australia	23.70
1956	Betty Cuthbert, Australia	23.40
1960	Wilma Rudolph, U.S.	24.00
1964	Edith McGuire, U.S.	23.00
1968	Irena Kirszenstein Szewinska, Poland	22.50
1972	Renate Stecher, East Germany	22.40
1976	Bärbel Eckert, East Germany	22.37
1980	Bärbel Wöckel (Eckert), East Germany	22.03
1984	Valerie Brisco-Hooks, U.S.	21.81
1988	Florence Griffith-Joyner, U.S.	21.34
1992	Gwen Torrence, U.S.	21.81
1996	Marie-Jose Perec, France	22.12
2000	Marion Jones, U.S.	21.84

2004	Veronica Campbell, Jamaica	22.05
400 Meters		**Time**
1964	Betty Cuthbert, Australia	52.00
1968	Colette Besson, France	52.00
1972	Monika Zehrt, East Germany	51.08
1976	Irena Kirszenstein Szewinska, Poland	49.29
1980	Marita Koch, East Germany	48.88
1984	Valerie Brisco-Hooks, U.S.	48.83
1988	Olga Bryzgina, U.S.S.R.	48.65
1992	Marie-Jose Perec, France	48.83
1996	Marie-Jose Perec, France	48.25
2000	Cathy Freeman, Australia	49.11
2004	Tonique Williams-Darling, Bahamas	49.41
800 Meters		**Time**
1928	Linda Radke-Batschauer, Germany	2:16.80
1960	Lyudmila Shevcova-Lysenko, U.S.S.R.	2:04.30
1964	Ann Packer, Great Britain	2:01.10
1968	Madeline Manning, U.S.	2:00.90
1972	Hildegard Falck, West Germany	1:58.55
1976	Tatyana Kazankina, U.S.S.R.	1:54.94
1980	Nadezhda Olizarenko, U.S.S.R.	1:53.42
1984	Doina Melinte, Romania	1:57.60
1988	Sigrun Wodars, East Germany	1:56.10
1992	Ellen Van Langen, Netherlands	1:55.54
1996	Svetlana Masterkova, Russia	1:57.73
2000	Maria Mutola, Mozambique	1:56.15
2004	Kelly Holmes, Great Britain	1:56.38
1,500 Meters		**Time**
1972	Lyudmila Bragina, U.S.S.R.	4:01.40
1976	Tatyana Kazankina, U.S.S.R.	4:05.48
1980	Tatyana Kazankina, U.S.S.R.	3:56.60
1984	Gabrielle Dorio, Italy	4:03.25
1988	Paula Ivan, Romania	3:53.96
1992	Hassiba Boulmerka, Algeria	3:55.30
1996	Svetlana Masterkova, Russia	4:00.83
2000	Nouria Merah-Bbenida, Algeria	4:05.10
2004	Kelly Holmes, Great Britain	3:57.90
3,000 Meters		**Time**
1984	Maricica Puica, Romania	8:35.96
1988	Tatyana Samolenko, U.S.S.R.	8:26.53
1992	Elena Romanova, Unified Team	8:46.04
5,000 Meters		**Time**
1996	Wang Junxia, China	14:59.88
2000	Gabriela Szabo, Romania	14:40.79
2004	Meseret Defar, Ethiopia	14:45.65
10,000 Meters		**Time**
1988	Olga Boldarenko, U.S.S.R.	31:44.69
1992	Derartu Tulu, Ethiopia	31:06.02
1996	Fernanda Ribeiro, Portugal	31:01.64
2000	Derartu Tulu, Ethiopia	30:17.49
2004	Huina Xing, China	30:24.36
Marathon		**Time**
1984	Joan Benoit, U.S.	2:24.52
1988	Rosa Mota, Portugal	2:25.40
1992	Valentina Yegorova, Unified Team	2:32.41
1996	Fatuma Roba, Ethiopia	2:26:05
2000	Naoko Takahashi, Japan	2:23:14
2004	Mizuki Noguchi, Japan	2:26:20
100-Meter Hurdles[1]		**Time**
1932	Babe Didrikson, U.S.	11.70
1936	Trebisonda Valla, Italy	11.70
1948	Fanny Blankers-Koen, Netherlands	11.20
1952	Shirley Strickland, Australia	10.90
1956	Shirley Strickland, Australia	10.70
1960	Irina Press, U.S.S.R.	10.80
1964	Karin Balzer, East Germany	10.50
1968	Maureen Caird, Australia	10.30
1972	Annelie Erhardt, East Germany	12.59
1976	Johanna Schaller, East Germany	12.77
1980	Vera Komisova, U.S.S.R.	12.56
1984	Benita Fitzgerald-Brown, U.S.	12.84
1988	Jordanka Donkova, Bulgaria	12.38
1992	Paraskevi Patoulidou, Greece	12.64
1996	Ludmila Engquist, Sweden	12.58
2000	Olga Shishigina, Kazakhstan	12.65
2004	Joanna Hayes, United States	12.37
400-Meter Hurdles		**Time**
1984	Nawal El Moutawakel, Morocco	54.61
1988	Debra Flintoff-King, Australia	53.17
1992	Sally Gunnell, Great Britain	53.23
1996	Deon Hemmings, Jamaica	52.82
2000	Irina Privalova, Russia	53.02
2004	Fani Halkia, Greece	52.82

4x100-Meter Relay		**Time**			
1928	Canada	48.40	1972	W. Germany	42.81
1932	U.S.	46.90	1976	E. Germany	42.55
1936	U.S.	46.90	1980	E. Germany	41.60
1948	Netherlands	47.50	1984	U.S.	41.65
1952	U.S.	45.90	1988	U.S.	41.98
1956	Australia	44.50	1992	U.S.	42.11
1960	U.S.	44.50	1996	U.S.	41.95
1964	Poland	43.60	2000	Bahamas	41.95
1968	U.S.	42.80	2004	Jamaica	41.73

4x400-Meter Relay		**Time**			
1972	E. Germany	3:23.00	1992	Unified Team	3:20.20
1976	E. Germany	3:19.23	1996	U.S.	3:20.91
1980	U.S.S.R.	3:20.20	2000	U.S.	3:22.62
1984	U.S.	3:18.29	2004	U.S.	3:19.01
1988	U.S.S.R.	3:15.18			

Discus Throw		**Distance**
1928	Halina Konopacka, Poland	129'11¾"
1932	Lillian Copeland, U.S.	133'2"
1936	Gisela Mauermayer, Germany	156'3"
1948	Micheline Ostermeyer, France	137'6"
1952	Nina Romaschkova, U.S.S.R.	168'8"
1956	Olga Fikotová, Czechoslovakia	176'1"
1960	Nina Ponomareva, U.S.S.R.	180'9"
1964	Tamara Press, U.S.S.R.	187'10"
1968	Lia Manoliu, Romania	191'2"
1972	Faina Melnik, U.S.S.R.	218'7"
1976	Evelin Schlaak, East Germany	226'4"
1980	Evelin Jahl (Schlaak), East Germany	229'6"
1984	Ria Stalman, Netherlands	214'5"
1988	Martina Hellmann, East Germany	237'2¼"
1992	Maritz Marten, Cuba	229'10"
1996	Ilke Wyludda, Germany	228'6"
2000	Ellina Zvereva, Belarus	224'5"
2004	Natalya Sadova, Russia	219'10"
Hammer Throw		**Distance**
2000	Kamila Skolimowska, Poland	233'6"
2004	Olga Kuzenkova, Russia	246'1"
High Jump		**Height**
1928	Ethel Catherwood, Canada	5'2½"
1932	Jean Shiley, U.S.	5'5¼"
1936	Ibolya Csak, Hungary	5'3"
1948	Alice Coachman, U.S.	5'6"
1952	Esther Brand, South Africa	5'5¾"
1956	Mildred McDaniel, U.S.	5'9¼"
1960	Iolanda Balas, Romania	6'0¾"
1964	Iolanda Balas, Romania	6'2¾"
1968	Miloslava Rezkova, Czechoslovakia	5'11½"
1972	Ulrika Meyfarth, West Germany	6'3½"
1976	Rosemarie Ackermann, East Germany	6'4"
1980	Sara Simeoni, Italy	6'5½"
1984	Ulrike Meyfarth, West Germany	6'7½"
1988	Louise Ritter, U.S.	6'8"
1992	Heike Henkel, Germany	6'7½"
1996	Stefka Kostadinova, Bulgaria	6'8¾"
2000	Yelena Yelesina, Russia	6'7"
2004	Yelena Slesarenko, Russia	6'9"
Javelin		**Distance**
1932	Babe Didriksen, U.S.	143'4"
1936	Tilly Fleischer, Germany	148'3"
1948	Herma Bauma, Austria	149'6"
1952	Dana Zatopekova, Czechoslovakia	165'7"
1956	Inessa Janzeme, U.S.S.R.	176'8"
1960	Elvira Ozolina, U.S.S.R.	183'8"
1964	Mihaela Penes, Romania	198'7"
1968	Angela Nemeth, Hungary	198'0"
1972	Ruth Fuchs, East Germany	209'7"
1976	Ruth Fuchs, East Germany	216'4"
1980	Maria Colon Rueñes, Cuba	224'5"
1984	Theresa Sanderson, Great Britain	228'2"
1988	Petra Felke, East Germany	245'0"
1992	Silke Renke, Germany	224'2"
1996	Heli Rantanen, Finland	222'11"
2000	Trine Hattestad, Norway	226'1"
2004	Osleidys Menendez, Cuba	234'8"
Long Jump		**Distance**
1948	Olga Gyarmati, Hungary	18'8¼"
1952	Yvette Williams, New Zealand	20'5¾"
1956	Elizbieta Krzesinska, Poland	20'10"
1960	Vyera Krepkina, U.S.S.R.	20'10¾"
1964	Mary Rand, Great Britain	22'2¼"
1968	Viorica Viscopoleanu, Romania	22'4½"
1972	Heidemarie Rosendahl, West Germany	22'3"
1976	Angela Voigt, East Germany	22'2¾"
1980	Tatiana Kolpakova, U.S.S.R.	23'0¾"
1984	Anisoara Cusmir-Stanciu, Romania	22'10"
1988	Jackie Joyner-Kersee, U.S.	24'3½"
1992	Heike Drechsler, Germany	23'5¼"
1996	Chioma Ajunwa, Nigeria	23'4½"

2000	Heike Drechsler, Germany	22'9"
2004	Tatyana Lebedeva, Russia	23'2"
Pole Vault		**Distance**
2000	Stacy Dragila, U.S.	15'1"
2004	Yelena Isinbayeva, Russia	16'1"
Shot Put		**Distance**
1948	Micheline Ostermeyer, France	45'1½"
1952	Galina Zybina, U.S.S.R.	50'1¾"
1956	Tamara Tyshkevich, U.S.S.R.	54'5"
1960	Tamara Press, U.S.S.R.	56'10"
1964	Tamara Press, U.S.S.R.	59'6¼"
1968	Margitta Gummel, East Germany	64'4"
1972	Nadezhda Chizhova, U.S.S.R.	69'0"
1976	Ivanka Hristova, Bulgaria	69'5¼"
1980	Ilona Slupianek, East Germany	73'6¼"
1984	Claudia Losch, West Germany	67'2¼"
1988	Natalya Lisovskaya, U.S.S.R.	72'11½"
1992	Svetlana Krivaleva, Unified Team	69'1¼"
1996	Astrid Kumbernuss, Germany	67'5½"
2000	Yanina Korolchik, Belarus	67'5"

2004	Yumileidi Cumba, Cuba	64'3"
Triple Jump		**Distance**
1996	Inessa Kravets, Ukraine	50'3½"
2000	Tereza Marinova, Bulgaria	49'10"
2004	Francoise Mbango Etone, Cameroon	50'2"
Pentathlon/Heptathlon[2]		**Points**
1964	Irina Press, U.S.S.R.	5,246
1968	Ingrid Becker, West Germany	5,098
1972	Mary Peters, Great Britain	4,801
1976	Siegrun Siegl, East Germany	4,745
1980	Nadezhda Tkachenko, U.S.S.R.	5,083
1984	Glynis Nunn, Australia	6,390
1988	Jackie Joyner-Kersee, U.S.	7,215
1992	Jackie Joyner-Kersee, U.S.	7,044
1996	Ghada Shouaa, Syria	6,780
2000	Denise Lewis, Great Britain	6,584
2004	Carolina Kluft, Sweden	6,952

1. 80 meters until 1972. 2. In 1984, two additional events were added: the 800-meter run and the javelin throw.

Gymnastics

Men's All-Around
1900	Gustave Sandras, France
1904	Julius Lenhart, Austria
1908	Alberto Braglia, Italy
1912	Alberto Braglia, Italy
1920	Giorgio Zampori, Italy
1924	Leon Stukelj, Yugoslavia
1928	Georges Miez, Switzerland
1932	Romeo Neri, Italy
1936	Alfred Schwarzmann, Germany
1948	Veikko Huhtanen, Finland
1952	Viktor Chukarin, U.S.S.R.
1956	Viktor Chukarin, U.S.S.R.
1960	Boris Shakhlin, U.S.S.R.
1964	Yukio Endo, Japan
1968	Sawao Kato, Japan
1972	Sawao Kato, Japan
1976	Nikolai Andrianov, U.S.S.R.
1980	Aleksandr Dityatin, U.S.S.R.
1984	Koji Gushiken, Japan
1988	Vladimir Artemov, U.S.S.R.
1992	Vitali Scherbo, Unified Team
1996	Li Xiaoshuang, China
2000	Alexei Nemov, Russia
2004	Paul Hamm, U.S.

Men's Floor Exercises
1932	István Pelle, Hungary
1936	Georges Miez, Switzerland
1948	Ferenc Pataki, Hungary
1952	K. William Thoresson, Sweden
1956	Valentin Muratov, U.S.S.R.
1960	Nobuyuki Aihara, Japan
1964	Franco Menichelli, Italy
1968	Sawao Kato, Japan
1972	Nikolai Andrianov, U.S.S.R.
1976	Nikolai Andrianov, U.S.S.R.
1980	Roland Brückner, E. Germany
1984	Li Ning, China
1988	Sergei Kharikov, U.S.S.R.
1992	Xiaoshuang Li, China
1996	Ioannis Melissanidis, Greece
2000	Igors Vihrovs, Latvia
2004	Kyle Shewfelt, Canada

Men's Horizontal Bar
1896	Herman Weingärtner, Germany
1904	Anton Heida, U.S.
	Edward Hennig, U.S. (tie)
1924	Leon Stukelj, Yugoslavia
1928	Georges Miez
1932	Dallas Bixler, U.S.
1936	Aleksanteri Saarvala, Finland
1948	Josef Stalder, Switzerland
1952	Jack Günthard, Switzerland
1956	Takashi Ono, Japan
1960	Takashi Ono, Japan
1964	Boris Shakhlin, U.S.S.R.
1968	Akinori Nakayama, Japan
1972	Mitsuo Tsukahara, Japan
1976	Mitsuo Tsukahara, Japan
1980	Stoyan Deltchev, Bulgaria
1984	Shinji Morisue, Japan
1988	Vladimir Artemov, U.S.S.R.
	Valeri Lioukine, U.S.S.R. (tie)

1992	Trent Dimas, U.S.
1996	Andreas Wecker, Germany
2000	Alexei Nemov, Russia
2004	Igor Cassina, Italy

Men's Parallel Bars
1896	Alfred Flatow, Germany
1904	George Eyser, U.S.
1924	August Güttinger, Switzerland
1928	Ladislav Vácha, Czechoslovakia
1932	Romeo Neri, Italy
1936	Konrad Frey, Germany
1948	Michael Reusch, Switzerland
1952	Hans Eugster, Switzerland
1956	Viktor Chukarin, U.S.S.R.
1960	Boris Shakhlin, U.S.S.R.
1964	Yukio Endo, Japan
1968	Akinori Nakayama, Japan
1972	Sawao Koto, Japan
1976	Sawao Koto, Japan
1980	Aleksandr Tkachyov, U.S.S.R.
1984	Bart Conner, U.S.
1988	Vladimir Artemov, U.S.S.R.
1992	Vitali Scherbo, Unified Team
1996	Rustam Sharipov, Ukraine
2000	Xiaopeng Li, China
2004	Valeri Goncharov, Ukraine

Men's Pommel Horse
1896	Jules Zutter, Switzerland
1904	Anton Heida, U.S.
1924	Josef Wilhelm, Switzerland
1928	Hermann Hänggi, Switzerland
1932	István Pelle, Hungary
1936	Konrad Frey, Germany
1948	Paavo Aaltonen, Finland
1952	Viktor Chukarin, U.S.S.R.
1956	Boris Shakhlin, U.S.S.R.
1960	Eugene Ekman, Finland
1964	Miroslav Cerar, Yugoslavia
1968	Miroslav Cerar, Yugoslavia
1972	Viktor Klimenko, U.S.S.R.
1976	Zoltán Magyar, Hungary
1980	Zoltán Magyar, Hungary
1984	Li Ning, China
1988	Lyubomir Gueraskov, Bulgaria
	Dmitri Bilozertchev, U.S.S.R.
	Zsolt Borkai, Hungary
1992	Vitali Scherbo, Unified Team
	Gil Su Pae, North Korea
1996	Li Donghua, Switzerland
2000	Alexandre Moskalenko, Russia
2004	Haibin Teng, China

Men's Rings
1896	Ioannis Mitropoulos, Greece
1904	Hermann Glass, U.S.
1924	Francesco Martino, Italy
1928	Leon Stukelj, Yugoslavia
1932	George Gulack, U.S.
1936	Alois Hudec, Czechoslovakia
1948	Karl Frei, Switzerland
1952	Grant Shaginyan, U.S.S.R.
1956	Albert Azaryan, U.S.S.R.
1960	Albert Azaryan, U.S.S.R.
1964	Takuji Haytta, Japan

1968	Akinori Nakayama, Japan
1972	Akinori Nakayama, Japan
1976	Nikolai Andrianov, U.S.S.R.
1980	Aleksandr Dityatin, U.S.S.R.
1984	Koji Gushiken, Japan
1988	Holger Behrendt, E. Germany
	Dmitri Bilozertchev, U.S.S.R.
1992	Vitali Scherbo, Unified Team
1996	Yuri Chechi, Italy
2000	Szilveszter Csollany, Hungary
2004	Dimosthenis Tampakos, Greece

Men's Vault
1896	Karl Schumann, Germany
1904	George Eyser, U.S.
	Anton Heida, U.S. (tie)
1924	Frank Kriz, U.S.
1928	Eugen Mack, Switzerland
1932	Savino Guglielmetti, Italy
1936	Alfred Schwarzmann, Germany
1948	Paavo Aaltonen, Finland
1952	Viktor Chukarin, U.S.S.R.
1956	Helmut Bantz, West Germany
1960	Takashi Ono, Japan
1964	Haruhiro Yamashita, Japan
1968	Mikhail Voronin, U.S.S.R.
1972	Klaus Köste, East Germany
1976	Nikolai Andrianov, U.S.S.R.
1980	Nikolai Andrianov, U.S.S.R.
1984	Lou Yun, China
1988	Lou Yun, China
1992	Vitali Scherbo, Unified Team
1996	Alexei Nemov, Russia
2000	Gervasio Deferr, Spain
2004	Gervasio Deferr, Spain

Men's Team Combined
1908	Sweden	1972 Japan
1912	Italy	1976 Japan
1920	Italy	1980 U.S.S.R.
1928	Switzerland	1984 United
1932	Italy	States
1936	Germany	1988 U.S.S.R.
1948	Finland	1992 U.S.S.R.
1952	U.S.S.R.	Team
1956	U.S.S.R.	1996 Russia
1960	Japan	2000 China
1964	Japan	2004 Japan
1968	Japan	

Women's All-Around
1952	Maria Gorokhovskaya, USSR
1956	Larissa Latynina, USSR
1960	Larissa Latynina, USSR
1964	Vera Cáslavská, Czechoslovakia
1968	Vera Cáslavská, Czechoslovakia
1972	Lyudmila Tourischeva, USSR
1976	Nadia Comaneci, Romania
1980	Yelena Davydova, USSR
1984	Mary Lou Retton, U.S.
1988	Elena Shushunova, USSR
1992	Tatiana Goutsou, Unified Team
1996	Lilia Popkopayeva, Ukraine
2000	Simona Amanar, Romania
2004	Carly Patterson, U.S.

Women's Balance Beam
1952 Nina Bocharova, U.S.S.R.
1956 Agnes Keleti, Hungary
1960 Eva Bosáková, Czechoslovakia
1964 Vera Cáslavská, Czechoslovakia
1968 Natalya Kuchinskaya, U.S.S.R.
1972 Olga Korbut, U.S.S.R.
1976 Nadia Comaneci, Romania
1980 Nadia Comaneci, Romania
1984 Simona Pauca, Romania
1988 Daniela Silivas, Romania
1992 Tatiana Lyssenko, UnifiedTeam
1996 Shannon Miller, United States
2000 Xuan Liu, China
2004 Catalina Ponor, Romania

Women's Floor Exercises
1952 Agnes Keleti, Hungary
1956 Agnes Keleti, Hungary
1960 Larissa Latynina, U.S.S.R.
1964 Larissa Latynina, U.S.S.R.
1968 Vera Cáslavská, Czechoslovakia
1972 Olga Korbut, U.S.S.R.
1976 Nelli Kim, U.S.S.R.
1980 Nadia Comaneci, Rom.

1984 Ecaterina Szabó, Romania
1988 Daniela Silivas, Romania
1992 Lavina Milosovici, Rom.
1996 Lillia Podkopayeva, Ukraine
2000 Elena Zamolodtchikova, Russia
2004 Catalina Ponor, Romania

Women's Uneven Bars
1952 Margit Korondi, Hungary
1956 Agnes Keleti, Hungary
1960 Polina Astakhova, U.S.S.R.
1964 Polina Astakhova, U.S.S.R.
1968 Vera Cáslavská, Czechoslovakia
1972 Karin Janz, East Germany
1976 Nadia Comaneci, Romania
1980 Maxi Gnauck, East Germany
1984 Ma Yanhong, China
1988 Daniela Silivas, Romania
1992 Li Lu, China
1996 Svetlana Khorkina, Russia
2000 Svetlana Khorkina, Russia
2004 Emilie Lepennec, France

Women's Vault
1952 Yekaterina Kalinchuk
1956 Larissa Latynina, U.S.S.R.

1960 Margarita Nikolayeva, U.S.S.R.
1964 Vera Cáslavská, Czechoslovakia
1968 Vera Cáslavská, Czechoslovakia
1972 Karin Janz, East Germany
1976 Nelli Kim, U.S.S.R.
1980 Natalya Shaposhnikova, U.S.S.R.
1984 Ecaterina Szabó, Romania
1988 Svetlana Boguinskaya, U.S.S.R.
1992 Henrietta Onodi, Hungary
      Lavinia Milosovici, Romania
1996 Simona Amanar, Romania
2000 Elena Zamolodtchikova, Russia
2004 Monica Rosu, Romania

Women's Team Combined

1928	Holland	1976	U.S.S.R.
1936	W. Germany	1980	U.S.S.R.
1948	Czecho-	1984	Romania
	slovakia	1988	U.S.S.R.
1952	U.S.S.R.	1992	Unified
1956	U.S.S.R.		Team
1960	U.S.S.R.	1996	United
1964	U.S.S.R.		States
1968	U.S.S.R.	2000	Romania
1972	U.S.S.R.	2004	Romania

Boxing

Light Flyweight (106 pounds)
1968 Francisco Rodriguez,
      Venezuela
1972 Gyorgy Gedo, Hungary
1976 Jorge Hernandez, Cuba
1980 Shamil Sabyrov, U.S.S.R.
1984 Paul Gonzalez, U.S.
1988 Ivailo Hristov, Bulgaria
1992 Rogelio Marcelo, Cuba
1996 Daniel Petrov, Bulgaria
2000 Brahim Asloum, France
2004 Yan Bhartelemy Varela, Cuba

Flyweight (112 pounds)
1904 George Finnegan, U.S.
1920 Frank Genaro, U.S.
1924 Fidel LaBarba, U.S.
1928 Antal Kocsis, Hungary
1932 Istvan Enekes, Hungary
1936 Willy Kaiser, Germany
1948 Pascual Perez, Argentina
1952 Nathan Brooks, U.S.
1956 Terence Spinks, Great Britain
1960 Gyula Torok, Hungary
1964 Fernando Atzori, Italy
1968 Ricardo Delgado, Mexico
1972 Georgi Kostadinov, Bulgaria
1976 Leo Randolph, U.S.
1980 Petr Lesov, Bulgaria
1984 Steven McCrory, U.S.
1988 Kwang-Sun Kim, South Korea
1992 Su Choi-Choi, North Korea
1996 Maikro Romero, Cuba
2000 Wijan Ponlid, Thailand
2004 Yuriorkis Gamboa Toledano,
      Cuba

Bantamweight (119 pounds)
1904 Oliver Kirk, U.S.
1908 Henry Thomas, Great Britain
1920 Clarence Walker, South Africa
1924 William Smith, South Africa
1928 Vittorio Tamagnini, Italy
1932 Horace Gwynne, Canada
1936 Ulderico Sergo, Italy
1948 Tibor Csik, Hungary
1952 Pentti Hamalainen, Finland
1956 Wolfgang Behrendt, E. Germany
1960 Oleg Grigoryev, U.S.S.R.
1964 Takao Sakurai, Japan
1968 Valeri Sokolov, U.S.S.R.
1972 Orlando Martinez, Cuba
1976 Yong-Jo Gu, North Korea
1980 Juan Hernandez, Cuba
1984 Maurizo Stecca, Italy
1988 Kennedy McKinney, U.S.
1992 Joel Casamayor, Cuba
1996 Istvan Kovacs, Hungary
2000 Guillermo Rigondeaux Ortiz,
      Cuba
2004 Guillermo Rigondeaux Ortiz,
      Cuba

Featherweight (125 pounds)
1904 Oliver Kirk, U.S.

1908 Richard Gunn, Great Britain
1920 Paul Fritsch, France
1924 John "Jackie" Fields, U.S.
1928 Lambertus "Bep" van Klaveren,
      Netherlands
1932 Carmelo Robledo, Argentina
1936 Oscar Casanovas, Argentina
1948 Ernesto Formenti, Italy
1952 Jan Zachara, Czechoslovakia
1956 Vladimir Safronov, U.S.S.R.
1960 Francesco Musso, Italy
1964 Stanislav Stepashkin, U.S.S.R.
1968 Antonio Roldan, Mexico
1972 Boris Kuznetsov, U.S.S.R.
1976 Angel Herrara, Cuba
1980 Rudi Fink, East Germany
1984 Meldrick Taylor, U.S.
1988 Giovanni Parisi, Italy
1992 Andreas Tews, Germany
1996 Somluck Kamsing, Thailand
2000 Bekzat Sattarkhanov,
      Kazakhstan
2004 Alexei Tichtchenko, Russia

Lightweight (132 pounds)
1904 Harry Spanger, U.S.
1908 Frederick Grace, Great Britain
1920 Samuel Mosberg, U.S.
1924 Hans Nielsen, Denmark
1928 Carlo Orlandi, Italy
1932 Lawrence Stevens, South Africa
1936 Imre Harangi, Hungary
1948 Gerald Dreyer, South Africa
1952 Aureliano Bolognesi, Italy
1956 Richard McTaggart,
      Great Britain
1960 Kazimierz Pazdzior, Poland
1964 Jozef Grudzien, Poland
1968 Ronald Harris, U.S.
1972 Jan Szczepanski, Poland
1976 Howard Davis, U.S.
1980 Angel Herrera, Cuba
1984 Pernell Whitaker, U.S.
1988 Andreas Zuelow, E. Germany
1992 Oscar De La Hoya, U.S.
1996 Hocine Soltani, Algeria
2000 Mario Kindelán, Cuba
2004 Mario Cesar Kindelan Mesa,
      Cuba

Light Welterweight (139 pounds)
1952 Charles Adkins, U.S.
1956 Vladimir Yengibaryan,
      U.S.S.R.
1960 Bohumil Nemecek,
      Czechoslovakia
1964 Jerzy Kulej, Poland
1968 Jerzy Kulej, Poland
1972 Ray Seales, U.S.
1976 Ray Leonard, U.S.
1980 Parizio Oliva, Italy
1984 Jerry Page, U.S.
1988 Viatcheslav Janovski,
      U.S.S.R.
1992 Hector Vinent, Cuba

1996 Hector Vinent, Cuba
2000 Mahamadkadyz Abdullaev,
      Uzbekistan
2004 Manus Boonjumnong, Thailand

Welterweight (147 pounds)
1904 Albert Young, U.S.
1920 Albert "Bert" Schneider, Canada
1924 Jean Delarge, Belguim
1928 Edward Morgan, New Zealand
1932 Edward Flynn, U.S.
1936 Sten Suvio, Finland
1948 Julius Torma, Czechoslovakia
1952 Zygmunt Chychla, Poland
1956 Nicolae Linca, Romania
1960 Giovanni Benvenuti, Italy
1964 Marian Kaspryzk, Poland
1968 Manfred Wolke, East Germany
1972 Emilio Correa, Cuba
1976 Jochen Bachfeld, E. Germany
1980 Andres Aldama, Cuba
1984 Mark Breland, U.S.
1988 Robert Wangila, Kenya
1992 Michael Carruth, Ireland
1996 Oleg Saitov, Russia
2000 Oleg Saitov, Russia
2004 Bakhtiyar Artayev, Kazakhstan

Light Middleweight (156 pounds)
1952 Laszlo Papp, Hungary
1956 Laszlo Papp, Hungary
1960 Wilbert McClure, U.S.
1964 Boris Lagutin, U.S.S.R.
1968 Boris Lagutin, U.S.S.R.
1972 Dieter Kottysch, W.Germany
1976 Jerzy Rybicki, Poland
1980 Armando Martinez, Cuba
1984 Frank Tate, U.S.
1988 Si-Hun Park, South Korea
1992 Juan Lemus, Cuba
1996 David Reid, U.S.
2000 Yermakhan Ibraimov,
      Kazakhstan
2004 Discontinued

Middleweight (165 pounds)
1904 Charles Mayer, U.S.
1908 John Douglas, Great Britain
1920 Harry Mallin, Great Britain
1924 Harry Mallin, Great Britain
1928 Piero Toscani, Italy
1932 Carmen Barth U.S.
1936 Jean Despeaux, France
1948 Laszlo Papp, Hungary
1952 Floyd Patterson, U.S.
1956 Gennady Schatkov,
      U.S.S.R.
1960 Edward Crook, U.S.
1964 Valeri Popenchenko,
      U.S.S.R.
1968 Christopher Finnegan, Gr. Br.
1972 Vyacheslav Lemeschev,
      U.S.S.R.
1976 Michael Spinks, U.S.
1980 Jose Gomez, Cuba

34 Joon-Sup Shin, South Korea
88 Henry Maske, East Germany
92 Ariel Hernandez, Cuba
96 Ariel Hernandez, Cuba
00 Jorge Gutiérrez, Cuba
04 Gaydarbek Gaydarbekov, Russia

ht Heavyweight (178 pounds)
20 Edward Eagan, U.S.
24 Harry Mitchell, Great Britain
28 Victor Avendanno, Argentina
32 David Carstens, South Africa
36 Roger Michelot, France
48 George Hunter, South Africa
52 Norvel Lee, U.S.
56 James Boyd, U.S.
60 Cassius Clay, U.S.
64 Cosimo Pinto, Italy
68 Dan Pozniak, U.S.S.R.
72 Mate Parlov, Yugoslavia
76 Leon Spinks, U.S.
80 Slobodan Kacar, Yugoslavia

1984 Anton Josipovic, Yugoslavia
1988 Andrew Maynard, U.S.
1992 Torsten May, Germany
1996 Vassili Jirov, Kazakstan
2000 Aleksandr Lebziak, Russia
2004 Andre Ward, U.S.

Heavyweight (201 pounds)
1904 Samuel Berger, U.S.
1908 A.L. Oldham, Great Britain
1920 Ronald Rawson, Great Britain
1924 Otto von Porat, Norway
1928 Arturo Rodriguez Jurado, Argentina
1932 Santiago Lovell, Argentina
1936 Herbert Runge, Germany
1948 Rafael Iglesias, Argentina
1952 H. Edward Sanders, U.S.
1956 Peter Rademacher, U.S.
1960 Franco De Piccoli, Italy
1964 Joe Frazier, U.S.
1968 George Foreman, U.S.

1972 Teofilo Stevenson, Cuba
1976 Teofilo Stevenson, Cuba
1980 Teofilo Stevenson, Cuba
1984 Henry Tillman, U.S.
1988 Ray Mercer, U.S.
1992 Felix Savon, Cuba
1996 Felix Savon, Cuba
2000 Felix Savon, Cuba
2004 Odlanier Solis Fonte, Cuba

Super Heavyweight (Unlimited)
1984 Tyrell Biggs, U.S.
1988 Lennox Lewis, Canada
1992 Roberto Balado, Cuba
1996 Wladimir Klitschko, Ukraine
2000 Audley Harrison, Great Britain
2004 Alexander Povetkin, Russia

Team Sports

BASEBALL
1988 U.S.
1992 Cuba
1996 Cuba
2000 U.S.
2004 Cuba

BASKETBALL
Men
1936 U.S.
1948 U.S.
1952 U.S.
1956 U.S.
1960 U.S.
1964 U.S.
1968 U.S.
1972 U.S.S.R.
1976 U.S.
1980 Yugoslavia
1984 U.S.
1988 U.S.S.R.
1992 U.S.
1996 U.S.
2000 U.S.
2004 Argentina

Women
1976 U.S.S.R.
1980 U.S.S.R.
1984 U.S.
1988 U.S.
1992 Unified Team
1996 U.S.
2000 U.S.
2004 U.S.

SOCCER
Men
1900 Great Britain
1904 Canada
1908 Great Britain
1912 Great Britain
1920 Belgium
1924 Uruguay
1928 Uruguay
1936 Italy
1948 Sweden
1952 Hungary
1956 U.S.S.R.
1960 Yugoslavia
1964 Hungary
1968 Hungary

1972 Poland
1976 E. Germany
1980 Czechoslovakia
1984 France
1988 U.S.S.R.
1992 Spain
1996 Nigeria
2000 Cameroon
2004 Argentina

Women
1996 U.S.
2000 Norway
2004 U.S.

SOFTBALL
1996 U.S.
2000 U.S.
2004 U.S.

VOLLEYBALL
Men
1964 U.S.S.R.
1968 U.S.S.R.
1972 Japan
1976 Poland
1980 U.S.S.R.
1984 U.S.

1988 U.S.
1992 Brazil
1996 Netherlands
2000 Yugoslavia
2004 Brazil

Women
1964 Japan
1968 U.S.S.R.
1972 U.S.S.R.
1976 Japan
1980 U.S.S.R.
1984 China
1988 U.S.S.R.
1992 Cuba
1996 Cuba
2000 Cuba
2004 China

WATER POLO
Men
1900 Great Britain
1904 U.S.
1908 Great Britain
1912 Great Britain
1920 Great Britain/Ireland

1924 France
1928 Germany
1932 Hungary
1936 Hungary
1948 Italy
1952 Hungary
1956 Hungary
1960 Italy
1964 Hungary
1968 Yugoslavia
1972 U.S.S.R.
1976 Hungary
1980 U.S.S.R.
1984 Yugoslavia
1988 Yugoslavia
1992 Italy
1996 Spain
2000 Hungary
2004 Hungary

Women
2000 Australia
2004 Italy

The Summer Olympics

Olympiad	Year	Place	Competitors		Nations represented	Events
			Men	Women		
I	1896	Athens, Greece	245	—	14	43
II	1900	Paris, France	1,206	19	24	87
III	1904	St. Louis, U.S.	681	8	13	94
IV	1908	London, U.K.	1,999	36	22	109
V	1912	Stockholm, Sweden	2,490	57	28	102
VI	1916	Berlin, Germany	— Canceled due to War —			
VII	1920	Antwerp, Belgium	2,591	78	29	154
VIII	1924	Paris, France	2,956	136	44	126
IX	1928	Amsterdam, Holland	2,724	290	46	109
X	1932	Los Angeles, U.S.	1,281	127	37	116
XI	1936	Berlin, Germany	3,738	328	49	129
XII	1940	Tokyo, Japan	— Canceled due to War —			
XIII	1944	London, Great Britain	— Canceled due to War —			
XIV	1948	London, Great Britain	3,714	385	59	136
XV	1952	Helsinki, Finland	4,407	518	69	149
XVI	1956	Melbourne, Australia	2,813	371	67	145
XVII	1960	Rome, Italy	4,738	610	83	150
XVIII	1964	Tokyo, Japan	4,457	683	93	163
XIX	1968	Mexico City, Mexico	4,750	780	112	172
XX	1972	Munich, W. Germany	6,065	1,058	121	195
XXI	1976	Montreal, Canada	4,781	1,247	92	198
XXII	1980	Moscow, U.S.S.R.	4,093	1,124	80	203
XXIII	1984	Los Angeles, U.S.	5,230	1,567	140	221
XXIV	1988	Seoul, South Korea	6,279	2,186	159	237
XXV	1992	Barcelona, Spain	6,659	2,708	169	257
XXVI	1996	Atlanta, U.S.	6,797	3,523	197	271
XXVII	2000	Sydney, Australia	6,582	4,069	199	300
XXVII	2004	Athens, Greece	11,099 total		202	301
XXIX	2008	Beijing, China	10,500		205	302
XXX	2012	London, England				

WINTER OLYMPIC CHAMPIONS

Alpine Skiing (Men)

Downhill	Time
1948 Henri Oreiller, France	2:55.00
1952 Zeno Colo, Italy	2:30.80
1956 Anton Sailer, Austria	2:52.20
1960 Jean Vuarnet, France	2:06.00
1964 Egon Zimmerman, Austria	2:18.16
1968 Jean-Claude Killy, France	1:59.85
1972 Bernhard Russi, Switzerland	1:51.43
1976 Franz Klammer, Austria	1:45.73
1980 Leonhard Stock, Austria	1:45.50
1984 William Johnson, United States	1:45.59
1988 Pirmin Zurbriggen, Switzerland	1:59.63
1992 Patrick Ortlieb, Austria	1:50.37
1994 Tommy Moe, United States	1:45.75
1998 Jean-Luc Cretier, France	1:50.11
2002 Fritz Strobl, Austria	1:39.13
2006 Antoine Deneriaz, France	1:48.80

Slalom	Time
1948 Edi Reinalter, Switzerland	2:10.30
1952 Othmar Schneider, Austria	2:00.00
1956 Anton Sailer, Austria	3:14.70
1960 Ernst Hinterseer, Austria	2:08.90
1964 Josef Stiegler, Austria	2:11.13
1968 Jean Claude Killy, France	1:39.73
1972 Francisco Fernandez Ochoa, Spain	1:39.73
1976 Piero Gros, Italy	2:03.29
1980 Ingemar Stenmark, Sweden	1:44.26
1984 Philip Mahre, United States	1:39.41
1988 Alberto Tomba, Italy	1:39.47
1992 Finn Christian Jagge, Norway	1:44.39
1994 Thomas Stangassinger	2:02.02
1998 Hans-Petter Buraas, Norway	1:49.31
2002 Jean-Pierre Vidal, France	1:41.06
2006 Benjamin Raich, Austria	

1. Race shortened by weather conditions

Giant Slalom	Time
1952 Stein Eriksen, Norway	2:25.00
1956 Anton Sailer, Austria	3:00.10
1960 Roger Staub, Switzerland	1:48.30
1964 Francois Bonlieu, France	1:46.71
1968 Jean Claude Killy, France	3:29.28
1972 Gustavo Thöni, Italy	3:09.62
1976 Heini Hemmi, Switzerland	3:26.97
1980 Ingemar Stenmark, Sweden	2:40.74
1984 Max Julen, Switzerland	2:41.18
1988 Alberto Tomba, Italy	2:06.37
1992 Alberto Tomba, Italy	2:06.98
1994 Markus Wasmeier, Germany	2:52.46
1998 Hermann Maier, Austria	2:38.51
2002 Stephan Eberharter, Austria	2:23.28
2006 Benjamin Raich, Austria	2:35.00

Super Giant Slalom	Time
1988 Frank Piccard, France	1:39.66
1992 Kjetil Andre Aamodt, Norway	1:13.04
1994 Markus Wasmeier, Germany	1:32.53
1998 Hermann Maier, Austria	1:34.82
2002 Kjetil Andre Aamodt, Norway	1:21.58
2006 Kjetil Andre Aamodt, Norway	1:30.65

Combined (Downhill/Slalom)
1988 Hubert Strolz, Austria
1992 Josef Polig, Italy
1994 Lasse Kjus, Norway
1998 Mario Reiter, Austria
2002 Kjetil Andre Aamodt, Norway
2006 Ted Ligety, United States

Alpine Skiing (Women)

Downhill	Time
1948 Hedi Schlunegger, Switzerland	2:28.30
1952 Trude Jochum-Beiser, Austria	1:47.10
1956 Madeleine Berthod, Switzerland	1:40.70
1960 Heidi Biebl, Germany	1:37.60
1964 Christl Haas, Austria	1:55.39
1968 Olga Pall, Austria	1:40.87
1972 Marie-Theres Nadig, Switzerland	1:36.68
1976 Rosi Mittermaier, West Germany	1:46.16
1980 Annemarie Moser-Pröll, Austria	1:37.52
1984 Michela Figini, Switzerland	1:13.36[1]
1988 Marina Kiehl, West Germany	1:25.86
1992 Kerrin Lee-Gartner, Canada	1:52.55
1994 Katja Seizinger, Germany	1:35.93
1998 Katja Seizinger, Germany	1:28.89
2002 Carole Montillet, France	1:39.56
2006 Michaela Dorfmeister, Austria	1:56.49

Slalom	Time
1948 Gretchen Fraser, United States	1:57.20
1952 Andrea Mead Lawrence, U.S.	2:10.60
1956 Renée Colliard, Switzerland	1:52.30
1960 Anne Heggtveigt, Canada	1:49.60
1964 Christine Goitschel, France	1:29.86

		Time
1968	Marielle Goitschel, France	1:25.86
1972	Barbara Cochran, United States	1:31.24
1976	Rosi Mittermaier, West Germany	1:30.54
1980	Hanni Wenzel, Liechtenstein	1:25.09
1984	Paoletta Magoni, Italy	1:36.47
1988	Vreni Schneider, Switzerland	1:36.69
1992	Petra Kronberger, Austria	1:32.68
1994	Vreni Schneider, Switzerland	1:56.01
1998	Hilde Gerg, Germany	1:32.40
2002	Janica Kostelic, Croatia	1:46.10
2006	Anja Paerson, Sweden	1:29.04

Giant Slalom		Time
1952	Andrea Mead Lawrence, U.S.	2:06.80
1956	Ossi Reichert, Germany	1.56.50
1960	Yvonne Rüegg, Switzerland	1:39.90
1964	Marielle Goitschel, France	1:52.24
1968	Nancy Greene, Canada	1:51.97
1972	Marie-Theres Nadig, Switzerland	1:29.90
1976	Kathy Kreiner, Canada	1:29.13
1980	Hanni Wenzel, Liechtenstein	2:41.66
1984	Debbie Armstrong, United States	2:20.98
1988	Vreni Schneider, Switzerland	2:06.49
1992	Pernilla Wiberg, Sweden	2:12.74

994	Deborah Compagnoni, Italy	2:30.97
998	Deborah Compagnoni, Italy	2:50.59
002	Janica Kostelic, Croatia	2:30.01
006	Julia Mancuso, U.S.	2:09.19

uper Giant Slalom **Time**

988	Sigrid Wolf, Austria	1:19.03
992	Deborah Compagnoni, Italy	1:21.22
994	Diann Roffe-Steinrotter, U.S.	1:22.15
998	Picabo Street, United States	1:18.02

2002	Daniela Ceccarelli, Italy	1:13.59
2006	Michaela Dorfmeister, Austria	1:32.47

Combined (Downhill/Slalom)

1988	Anita Wachter, Austria
1992	Petra Kronberger, Austria
1994	Pernilla Wiberg, Sweden
1998	Katja Seizinger, Germany
2002	Janica Kostelic, Croatia
2006	Janica Kostelic, Croatia

Biathlon (Cross-country skiing and riflery)

Men's 10-Kilometer (6.2 Miles) **Time**

1980	Frank Ulrich, East Germany	32:10.69
1984	Eirik Kvalfoss, Norway	30:53.80
1988	Frank-Peter Roetsch, E. Germany	25:08.10
1992	Mark Kirchner, Germany	26:02.30
1994	Sergei Tchepikov, Russia	28:07.00
1998	Ole Bjorndalen, Norway	27:16.20
2002	Ole Einar Bjoerndalen, Norway	24:51.30
2006	Sven Fischer, Germany	26:11.60

Men's 20-Kilometer (12.4 miles) **Time**

1960	Klas Lestander, Sweden	1:33:21.60
1964	Vladimir Melanin, U.S.S.R.	1:20:26.80
1968	Magnar Solberg, Norway	1:13:45.90
1972	Magnar Solberg, Norway	1:15:55.50
1976	Nikolai Kruglov, U.S.S.R.	1:14:12.26
1980	Anatoli Alabyev, U.S.S.R.	1:08:16.31
1984	Peter Angerer, West Germany	1:11:52.70
1988	Frank-Peter Roetsch, E. Germany	0:56:33.33
1992	Evgueni Redkine, Unified Team	0:57:34.04
1994	Sergei Tarasov, Russia	0:57:25.30
1998	Halvard Hanevold, Norway	0:56:16.40
2002	Ole Einar Bjoerndalen, Norway	0:51:03.30
2006	Michael Greis, Germany	0:54:23.00

Men's 4x7.5 Kilometer (18.6 mile) Relay [1] **Time**

1968	U.S.S.R., Norway, Sweden	2:13:02.40
1972	U.S.S.R., Finland, East Germany	1:51:44.92
1976	U.S.S.R., Finland, East Germany	1:57:55.64

1980	U.S.S.R., E. Germany, W. Germany	1:34:03.27
1984	U.S.S.R., Norway, West Germany	1:38:51.70
1988	U.S.S.R., West Germany, Italy	1:22:30.00
1992	Germany, Unified Team, Sweden	1:24:43.50
1994	Germany, Russia, France	1:30:22.10
1998	Germany, Norway, Russia	1:19:43.30
2002	Norway, Germany, France	1:23:42.30
2006	Germany, Russia, France	1:21:51.5

Women's 7.5 Kilometer (4.6 miles) **Time**

1992	Anfissa Restzova, Unified Team	24:29.2
1994	Myriam Bedard, Canada	26:08.8
1998	Galina Kukleva, Russia	23:08.0
2002	Kati Wilhelm, Germany	20:41.4
2006	Florence Baverel-Robert, France	22:31.4

Women's 15 Kilometer (9.3 miles) **Time**

1992	Antje Misersky	51:47.2
1994	Myriam Bedard, Canada	52:06.6
1998	Yekaterina Dafovska, Bulgaria	54:52.0
2002	Andrea Henkel, Germany	47:29.1
2006	Svetlana Ishmouratova, Russia	49:24.1

Women's 4x7.5 Kilometer (18.6 miles) Relay[2] **Time**

1992	France, Germany, Unified Team[2]	1:15:55.6
1994	Russia, Germany, France	1:47:19.5
1998	Germany, Russia, Norway	1:40:13.6
2002	Germany, Norway, Russia	1:27:55.0
2006	Russia, Germany, France	1:16:12.5

Nordic Skiing and Jumping (Men)

10-Kilometer (6.2 Miles) Pursuit method **Time**

1992	Vegard Ulvang, Norway	27:36.00
1994	Bjorn Dahlie, Norway	24:20.10
1998	Bjorn Dahlie, Norway	27:24.50
2002	Frode Estil, Norway	26:20.40

15-Kilometer (9.3 Miles) Cross-Country[1] **Time**

1924	Thorleif Haug, Norway	1:14:31.00
1928	Johan Gröttumsbraaten, Norway	1:37:01.00
1932	Sven Utterstrom, Sweden	1:23:07.00
1936	Erik-August Larsson, Sweden	1:14:38.00
1948	Martin Lundström, Sweden	1:13:50.70
1952	Hallgeir Brenden, Norway	1:01:34.00
1956	Hallgeir Brenden, Norway	0:49:39.00
1960	Hakon Brusveen, Norway	0:51:55.50
1964	Eero Mäntyranta, Finland	0:50:54.10
1968	Harald Grönningen, Norway	0:47:54.20
1972	Sven-Ake Lundbäck, Sweden	0:45:28.24
1976	Nikolai Bazhukov, U.S.S.R.	0:43:58.47
1980	Thomas Wassberg, Sweden	0:41:57.63
1984	Gunde Svan, Sweden	0:41:25.60
1988	Mikhail Deviatiarov, U.S.S.R.	0:41:18.90
2002	Andrus Veerpalu, Estonia	0:37:07.40
2006	Andrus Veerpalu, Estonia	0:38:01.30

30-Kilometer (18.6 Miles) Cross-Country **Time**

1956	Veikko Hakulinen, Finland	1:44:06.00
1960	Sixten Jernberg, Sweden	1:51:03.90
1964	Eero Mäntyranta, Finland	1:30:50.70
1968	Franco Nones, Italy	1:35:39.20
1972	Vyacheslav Vedenin, U.S.S.R.	1:36:31.15
1976	Sergei Saveliev, U.S.S.R.	1:30:29.38

1980	Nikolai Zimyatov, U.S.S.R.	1:27:02.80
1984	Nikolai Zimyatov, U.S.S.R.	1:28:56.30
1988	Aleksei Prokourorov, U.S.S.R.	1:24:26.30
1992	Vegard Ulvang, Norway	1:22:27.80
1994	Thomas Alsgaard, Norway	1:12:26.40
1998	Mika Myllylae, Finland	1:33:55.80
2002	Johann Muehlegg, Spain	1:09:28.90
2006	Eugeni Dementiev, Russia	1:17:00.80

50-Kilometer (31.2 Miles) Cross-Country **Time**

1924	Thorleif Haug, Norway	3:44:32.00
1928	Per Erik Hedlund, Sweden	4:52:03.00
1932	Veli Saarinen, Finland	4:28:00.00
1936	Elis Viklund, Sweden	3:30:11.00
1948	Nils Karlsson, Sweden	3:47:48.00
1952	Veikko Hakulinen, Finland	3:33:33.00
1956	Sixten Jernberg, Sweden	2:50:27.00
1960	Kalevi Hamalainen, Finland	2:59:06.30
1964	Sixten Jernberg, Sweden	2:43:52.60
1968	Ole Ellefsaeter, Norway	2:28:45.80
1972	Pål Tyldum, Norway	2:43:14.75
1976	Ivar Formo, Norway	2:37:30.05
1980	Nikolai Zimyatov, U.S.S.R.	2:27:24.60
1984	Thomas Wassberg, Sweden	2:15:55.80
1988	Gunde Svan, Sweden	2:04:30.90
1992	Bjorn Dahlie, Norway	2:03:41.50
1994	Vladimir Smirnov, Kazakhstan	2:07:20.30
1998	Bjorn Dahlie, Norway	2:05:08.20
2002	Mikhail Ivanov, Russia	2:06:20.80
2006	Giorgi di Centa, Italy	2:06:11.80

40-Kilometer (24.8 Miles) Relay (4x10 km)

		Time
1936	Finland, Norway, Sweden	2:41:33.00
1948	Sweden, Finland, Norway	2:32:08.00
1952	Finland, Norway, Sweden	2:20:16.00
1956	U.S.S.R., Finland Sweden	2:15:30.00
1960	Finland, Norway, U.S.S.R.	2:18:45.60
1964	Sweden, Finland, U.S.S.R.	2:18:34.60
1968	Norway, Sweden, Finland	2:08:33.50
1972	U.S.S.R., Norway, Switzerland	2:04:47.94
1976	Finland, Norway, U.S.S.R.	2:07:59.72
1980	U.S.S.R., Norway, Finland	1:57:03.46
1984	Sweden, U.S.S.R., Finland	1:55:06.30
1988	Sweden, U.S.S.R., Czechoslovakia	1:43:58.60
1992	Norway, Italy, Finland	1:39:26.00
1994	Italy, Norway, Finland	1:41:15.00
1998	Norway, Italy, Finland	1:40:55.70
2002	Norway, Italy, Germany	1:32:45.50
2006	Italy, Germany, Sweden	1:43:45.70

Nordic Combined
(15 km Cross-Country and 90-Meter Ski Jump[2])

1924	Thorleif Haug, Norway
1928	Johan Gröttumsbraaten, Norway
1932	Johan Gröttumsbraaten, Norway
1946	Oddbjörn Hagen, Norway
1952	Simon Slåttvik, Norway
1956	Sverre Stenersen, Norway
1960	George Thoma, West Germany
1964	Tormod Knutsen, Norway
1968	Franz Keller, West Germany
1972	Ulrich Wehling, East Germany
1976	Ulrich Wehling, East Germany
1980	Ulrich Wehling, East Germany
1984	Torn Sandberg, Norway
1988	Hippolyt Kempf Switzerland
1992	Fabrice Guy, France
1994	Fred Lundberg, Norway
1998	Bjarte Engen Vik, Norway
2002	Samppa Lajunen, Finland
2006	Georg Hettich, Germany

Nordic Combined, Team

1988	W. Germany, Switzerland, Austria
1992	Japan, Norway, Austria
1994	Japan, Norway, Switzerland
1998	Norway, Finland, France
2002	Finland, Germany, Austria
2006	Austria, Germany, Finland

90-Meter (293.5 ft.) Jump[2]

		Points
1964	Veikko Kankkonen, Finland	229.9
1968	Jiri Raska, Czechoslovakia	216.5
1972	Yukio Kasaya, Japan	244.2
1976	Hans-Georg Aschenbach, E. Germany	252.0
1980	Anton Innauer, Austria	266.3
1984	Jens Weissflog, East Germany	215.2
1988	Matti Nykänen, Finland	229.1
1992	Ernst Vettori, Austria	222.8
1994	Espen Bredesen, Norway	282.00
1998	Jani Soininen, Finland	234.50
2002	Simon Ammann, Switzerland	269.00
2006	Lars Bystoel, Norway	266.50

120-Meter (393.7 ft.) Jump[3]

		Points
1924	Jacob Tullin Thambs, Norway	18.960
1928	Alf Andersen, Norway	19.208
1932	Birger Ruud, Norway	228.10
1936	Birger Ruud, Norway	232.00
1948	Petter Hugsted, Norway	228.10
1952	Arnfinn Bergmann, Norway	226.00
1956	Antti Hyvarinen, Finland	227.00
1960	Helmut Recknagel, Germany	227.20
1964	Toralf Engan, Norway	230.70
1968	Vladimir Beloussov, U.S.S.R.	231.30
1972	Wojiech Fortuna, Poland	219.90
1976	Karl Schnabl, Austria	234.80
1980	Jouko Tormanen, Finland	271.00
1984	Matti Nykänen, Finland	231.20
1988	Matti Nykänen, Finland	224.00
1992	Toni Nieminen, Finland	239.50
1994	Jens Weissflog, Germany	274.50
1998	Kazuyoshi Funaki, Japan	272.30
2002	Simon Ammann, Switzerland	281.40
2006	Thomas Morgenstern, Austria	276.90

120-Meter (393.7 ft.) Jump, Team[3]

		Points
1988	Finland, Yugoslavia, Norway	634.40
1992	Finland, Austria, Czechoslovakia	644.40
1994	Germany, Japan, Austria	970.10
1998	Japan, Germany, Austria	933.00
2002	Germany, Finland, Slovenia	974.10
2006	Austria, Finland, Norway	984.00

1. 18-kilometers until 1956. Event not scheduled from 1992-1998. 2. 70 meters until 1992. 3. 90 meter until 1992.

Nordic Skiing (Women)

5-Kilometer (3.1 Miles) Cross-Country[1]

		Time
1964	Claudia Boyarskikh, U.S.S.R.	17:50.50
1968	Toini Gustafsson, Sweden	16:45.20
1972	Galina Kulakova, U.S.S.R.	17:00.50
1976	Helena Takalo, Finland	15:48.69
1980	Raisa Smetanina, U.S.S.R.	15:06.92
1984	Marja-Liisa Hämäläinen, Finland	17:04.00
1988	Marjo Matikainen, Finland	15:04.00
1992	Marjut Lukkarinen, Finland	14:13.80
1994	Lyubov Egorova, Russia	14:08.80
1998	Larissa Lazutina, Russia	17:39.90
2002	Olga Danilova, Russia	24:52.10

10-Kilometer (6.2 Miles) Cross-Country[2]

		Time
1952	Lydia Wideman, Finland	41:40.00
1956	Lyubov Kosyreva, U.S.S.R.	38:11.00
1960	Maria Gusakova, U.S.S.R.	39:46.60
1964	Claudia Boyarskikh, U.S.S.R.	40:24.30
1968	Toini Gustafsson, Sweden	36:46.50
1972	Galina Kolakova, U.S.S.R.	34:17.82
1976	Raisa Smetanina, U.S.S.R.	30:31.54
1980	Barbara Petzold, East Germany	30:31.54
1984	Marja-Liisa Hämäläinen, Finland	31:44.20
1988	Vida Ventsene, U.S.S.R.	30:08.20
2002	Bente Skari, Norway	28:05.60
2006	Kristina Smigun, Estonia	27:51.50

15-Kilometer (9.3 Miles) Cross-Country

		Time
1992	Lyubov Egorova, Unified Team	42:20.8
1994	Manuela Di Centa, Italy	39:44.5
1998	Olga Danilova, Russia	46:55.4
2002	Stefania Belmondo, Italy	39:54.4
2006	Kristina Smigun, Estonia	42:48.7

30-Kilometer (18.6 Miles) Cross-Country[3]

		Time
1984	Marja Liisa Hämäläinen, Finland	1:01:45.0
1988	Tamara Tikhonova, U.S.S.R.	0:55:53.6
1992	Stefania Belmondo, Italy	1:22:30.1
1994	Manuela Di Centa, Italy	1:25:41.6
1998	Yuliya Chepalova, Russia	1:22:01.5
2002	Gabriella Paruzzi, Italy	1:30:57.1
2006	Katerina Neumannova, Czech Rep.	1:22:25.4

20-Kilometer (12.4 Miles) Cross-Country Relay[4] (4x5Km)

1956	Finland, U.S.S.R., Sweden	1:09.01.00
1960	Sweden, U.S.S.R., Finland	1:04.21.00
1964	U.S.S.R., Sweden, Finland	0:59:20.00
1968	Norway, Sweden, U.S.S.R.	0:57:30.00
1972	U.S.S.R., Finland, Norway	0:48:46.15
1976	U.S.S.R., Finland, E. Germany	1:07:49.75
1980	East Germany, U.S.S.R., Norway	1:02:11.10
1984	Norway, Czechoslovakia, Finland	1:06:49.70
1988	U.S.S.R., Norway, Finland	0:59:51.10
1992	Unified Team, Norway, Italy	0:59:34.80
1994	Russia, Norway, Italy	0:57:12.50
1998	Russia, Norway, Italy	0:55:13.50
2002	Germany, Norway, Switzerland	0:49:30.60
2006	Russia, Germany, Italy	0:54:47.70

1. Pursuit method in 2002. 2. Event not scheduled from 1992-98. 3. 20 Km until 1992. 4. 15 km (3 x 5 km) until 1976.

Bobsled

Two Man	Time	Four Man	Time
1932 U.S.	8:14.74	1924 Switzerland	5:45.54
1936 U.S.	5:29.29	1928 U.S.	3:20.50
1948 Switzerland	5:29.20	1932 U.S.	7:53.68
1952 Germany	5:24.54	1936 Switzerland	5:19.85
1956 Italy	5:30.14	1948 U.S.	5:20.10
1964 Great Britain	4:21.90	1952 Germany	5:07.84
1968 Italy	4:41.54	1956 Switzerland	5:10.44
1972 W. Germany	4:57.07	1964 Canada	4:14.46
1976 E. Germany	3:44.42	1968 Italy	2:17.39
1980 Switzerland	4:09.36	1972 Switzerland	4:43.07
1984 E. Germany	3:25.56	1976 E. Germany	3:40.43
		1988 U.S.S.R.	3:54.19
		1992 Switzerland	4:03.26
		1994 Switzerland	3:30.81
		1998 Canada, Italy	3:37.24
		2002 Germany	3:10.11
		2006 Germany	3:34.38

			Time
1980 E. Germany	3:59.42		
1984 E. Germany	3:20.22		
1988 Switzerland	3:47.51		
1992 Austria	3:53.90		
1994 Germany	3:27.78		
1998 Germany	2:39.41		
2002 Germany	3:07.51		
2006 Germany	3:40.42		

Two-Woman	Time
2002 U.S.	1:37.76
2006 Germany	3:49.98

Luge

Singles (Men)		Time
1964	Thomas Köhler, East Germany	3:26.77
1968	Manfred Schmid, Austria	2:52.48
1972	Wolfgang Scheidel, East Germany	3:27.58
1976	Dettlef Günther, East Germany	3:27.68
1980	Bernhard Glass, East Germany	2:54.79
1984	Paul Hildgartner, Italy	3:04.25
1988	Jens Mueller, East Germany	3:05.54
1992	Georg Hackl, Germany	3:02.36
1994	Georg Hackl, Germany	3:21.57
1998	Georg Hackl, Germany	3:18.44
2002	Armin Zoeggeler, Italy	2:57.94
2006	Armin Zoeggeler, Italy	3:26.09

Singles (Women)		Time
1964	Ortrun Enderlein, East Germany	3:24.67
1968	Erica Lechner, Italy	2:28.66
1972	Anna M. Müller, East Germany	2:59.18
1976	Margit Schumann, East Germany	2:50.62
1980	Vera Zozulya, U.S.S.R.	2:36.53
1984	Steffi Martin, East Germany	2:46.57

		Time
1988	Steffi Walter (Martin), East Germany	3:03.97
1992	Doris Neuner, Austria	3:06.69
1994	Gerda Weissensteiner, Italy	3:15.52
1998	Silke Kraushaar, Germany	3:23.78
2002	Sylke Otto, Germany	2:52.46
2006	Sylke Otto, Germany	3:07.98

Doubles (Men until 2002, mixed after)		Time
1964	Austria	1:41.62
1968	East Germany	1:31.94
1972	(tie) Italy, East Germany	1:28.35
1976	East Germany	1:25.60
1980	East Germany	1:19.33
1984	West Germany	1:23.62
1988	East Germany	1:31.94
1992	Germany	1:32.05
1994	Italy	1:36.72
1998	Germany	1:41.10
2002	Germany	1:26.08
2006	Austria	1:34.50

Ice Hockey- Men

Year	Gold, Silver, Bronze
1920	Canada, United States Czechoslovakia
1924	Canada, United States, Great Britain
1928	Canada, Sweden, Switzerland
1932	Canada, United States, Germany
1936	Great Britain, Canada, United States
1948	Canada, Czechoslovakia, Switzerland
1952	Canada, United States, Sweden
1956	U.S.S.R., United States, Canada
1960	U.S., Canada, U.S.S.R.
1964	U.S.S.R., Sweden, Czechoslovakia
1968	U.S.S.R., Czechoslovakia, Canada

Year	Gold, Silver, Bronze
1972	U.S.S.R., United States, Czechoslovakia
1976	U.S.S.R., Czechoslovakia, West Germany
1980	U.S., U.S.S.R., Sweden
1984	U.S.S.R., Czechoslovakia, Sweden
1988	U.S.S.R., Finland, Sweden
1992	Unified Team, Canada, Czechoslovakia
1994	Sweden, Canada, Finland
1998	Czech Republic, Russia, Finland
2002	Canada, United States, Russia
2006	Sweden, Finland, Czech Republic

Figure Skating

MEN

1908	Ulrich Salchow, Sweden
1920	Gillis Grafstrom, Sweden
1924	Gillis Grafstrom Sweden
1928	Gillis Grafstrom, Sweden
1932	Karl Schafer, Austria
1936	Karl Schafer, Austria
1948	Richard Button, United States
1952	Richard Button, United States
1956	Hayes Alan Jenkins, United States
1960	David W. Jenkins, United States
1964	Manfred Schnelldorfer, Germany
1968	Wolfgang Schwartz, Austria
1972	Ondrej Nepela, Czechoslovakia
1976	John Curry, Great Britain

1980	Robin Cousins, Great Britain
1984	Scott Hamilton, United States
1988	Brian Boitano, United States
1992	Viktor Petrenko, Unified Team
1994	Aleksei Urmanov, Russia
1998	Ilya Kulik, Russia
2002	Alexei Yagudin, Russia
2006	Evgeni Plushenko, Russia

WOMEN

1908	Madge Syers, Great Britain
1920	Magda Julin-Mauroy, Sweden
1924	Herma von Szabo-Planck, Austria
1928	Sonja Henie, Norway
1932	Sonja Henie, Norway
1936	Sonja Henie, Norway

1948	Barbara Ann Scott, Canada
1952	Jeanette Altwegg, Great Britain
1956	Tenley Albright, United States
1960	Carol Heiss, United States
1964	Sjoukje Dijkstra, Netherlands
1968	Peggy Fleming, United States
1972	Beatrix Schuba, Austria
1976	Dorothy Hamill, United States
1980	Annett Pötzsch, East Germany
1984	Katarina Witt, East Germany
1988	Katarina Witt, East Germany
1992	Kristi Yamaguchi, United States
1994	Oksana Baiul, Ukraine
1998	Tara Lipinski, United States
2002	Sarah Hughes, United States
2006	Shizuka Arakawa, Japan

PAIRS

1908	Germany—Anna Hubler, Heinrich Burger
1920	Finland—Ludovika & Walter Jakobsson
1924	Austria—Helene Engelman, Alfred Berger
1928	France—Andree Joly, Pierre Brunet
1932	France—Andree & Pierre Brunet
1936	Germany—Maxie Herber, Ernst Baier
1948	Belgium—Micheline Lannoy, Pierre Baugniet
1952	Germany—Ria & Paul Falk
1956	Austria—Elisabeth Schwartz, Kurt Oppelt
1960	Canada—Barbara Wagner, Robert Paul
1964	U.S.S.R.—Ludmila Beloussova, Oleg Protopopov

1968	U.S.S.R.—Ludmila Beloussova, Oleg Protopopov
1972	U.S.S.R.—Irina Rodnina, Alexei Ulanov
1976	U.S.S.R.—Irina Rodnina, Aleksandr Zaitsev
1980	U.S.S.R.—Irina Rodnina, Aleksandr Zaitsev
1984	U.S.S.R.—Elena Valova, Oleg Vassiliev
1988	U.S.S.R.—Ekaterina Gordeeva, Sergei Grinkov
1992	Unified Team—Natalya Mishkutienok, Artur Dmitriev
1994	Russia—Ekaterina Gordeeva, Sergei Grinkov
1998	Russia—Oksana Kazakova, Artur Dmitriev
2002	tie Canada—Jamie Sale, David Pelletier and Russia—Elena Berezhnaya, Anton Sikharulidze
2006	Russia—Tatiana Totmianina, Maxim Marinin

ICE DANCING

1976	U.S.S.R.—Lyudmila Pakhomova, Aleksandr Gorhkov
1980	U.S.S.R.—Natalia Linichuk, Gennadi Karponosov
1984	Great Britain—Jayne Torvill, Christopher Dean
1988	U.S.S.R.—Natalia Bestemianova, Andrei Bukin
1992	Unified Team—Marina Kimova, Sergei Ponomarenko
1994	Russia—Pasha Grishuk, Yevgeny Platov,
1998	Russia—Pasha Grishuk, Yevgeny Platov
2002	France—Marina Anissina, Gwendal Peizerat
2006	Russoa—Tatiana Navka, Roman Kostomarov

Speed Skating, Men

500 Meters (1,641 Ft.)	Time
1924 Charles Jewtraw, U.S	0:44.00
1928 Clas Thunberg, Finland	0:43.40
Bernst Evensen, Norway (tie)	
1932 John A. Shea, United States	0:43.40
1936 Ivar Ballangrud, Norway	0:43.40
1948 Finn Helgesen, Norway	0:43.10
1952 Ken Henry, United States	0:43.20
1956 Yevgeny Grishin, U.S.S.R.	0:40.20
1960 Yevgeny Grishin, U.S.S.R.	0:40.20
1964 Terry McDermott, United States	0:40.10
1968 Erhard Keller, West Germany	0.40.30
1972 Erhard Keller, West Germany	0.39.44
1976 Yergeny Kulikov, U.S.S.R.	0:39.17
1980 Eric Heiden, United States	0:38.03
1984 Sergei Fokichev, U.S.S.R.	0:38.19
1988 Uwe-Jens Mey, East Germany	0:36.45
1992 Uwe-Jens Mey, Germany	0:37.14
1994 Aleksandr Golubev, Russia	0:36.33
1998[1] Hiroyasu Shimizu, Japan	1:11.35
2002 Casey Fitzrandolph United States	1:09.23
2006 Joey Cheek, United States	1:09.76
1,000 Meters (3,281 Ft.)	Time
1976 Peter Mueller, United States	1:19.32
1980 Eric Heiden, United States	1:15.18
1984 Gaétan Boucher, Canada	1:15.80
1988 Nikolai Guiliaev, U.S.S.R.	1:13.03
1992 Olaf Zinke, Germany	1:14.85
1994 Dan Jansen, United States	1:12.43
1998 Ids Postma, Netherlands	1:10.64
2002 Gerard van Velde Netherlands	1:07.18
2006 Shani Davis, United States	1:08.89
1,500 Meters (4,922 Ft.)	Time
1924 Clas Thunberg, Finland	2:20.80
1928 Clas Thunberg, Finland	2:21.10
1932 John A. Shea, United States	2:57.50
1936 Charles Mathisen, Norway	2:19.20
1948 Sverre Farstad, Norway	2:17.60
1952 Hjalmar Andersen, Norway	2:20.40
1956 Yevgeni Grishin	2:08.60
Yuri Mikhailov, U.S.S.R. (tie)	

1960 Roald Aas, Norway	2:10.40
Yevgeni Grishin, U.S.S.R. (tie)	
1964 Ants Anston, U.S.S.R.	2:10.30
1968 Cornelis Verkerk, Netherlands	2:03.40
1972 Ard Schenk, Netherlands	2:02.96
1976 Jan Egil Storholt, Norway	1:59.38
1980 Eric Heiden, United States	1:55.44
1984 Gaétan Boucher, Canada	1:58.36
1988 Andre Hoffmann, East Germany	1:52.06
1992 Johann Olav Koss, Norway	1:54.81
1994 Johann Olav Koss, Norway	1:51.29
1998 Aadne Sondral, Norway	1:47.87
2002 Derek Parra United States	1:43.95
2006 Enrico Fabris, Italy	1:45.97
5,000 Meters (16,405 Ft.)	Time
1924 Clas Thunberg, Finland	8:39.00
1928 Ivar Ballangrud, Norway	8:50.50
1932 Irving Jaffee, United States	9:40.80
1936 Ivar Ballangrud, Norway	8:19.60
1948 Reidar Liaklev, Norway	8:29.40
1952 Hjalmar Andersen, Norway	8:10.60
1956 Boris Shilkov, U.S.S.R.	7:48.70
1960 Viktor Kosichkin, U.S.S.R.	7:51.30
1964 Knut Johannesen, Norway	7:38.40
1968 F. Anton Maier, Norway	7:22.40
1972 Ard Schenk, Netherlands	7:23.61
1976 Sten Stensen, Norway	7:24.48
1980 Eric Heiden, United States	7:02.29
1984 Sven Tomas Gustafson, Sweden	7:12.28
1988 Tomas Gustafson, Sweden	6:44.63
1992 Geir Karlstad, Sweden	6:59.97
1994 Johann Olav Koss, Norway	6:34.96
1998 Gianni Romme, Netherlands	6:22.20
2002 Jochem Uytdehaage Netherlands	6:14.66
2006 Chad Hedrick, United States	6:14.68
10,000 Meters (32,810 Ft.)	Time
1924 Julien Skutnabb, Finland	18:04.80
1928 (ice thawed, event cancelled)	
1932 Irving Jaffee, United States	19:13.60
1936 Ivan Ballangrud, Norway	17:24.30
1948 Ake Seyffarth, Sweden	17:26.30

952	Hjalmar Andersen, Norway	16:45.80		1992	Bart Veldkamp, Netherlands	14:12.12
956	Sigvard Ericsson, Sweden	16:35.90		1994	Johann Olav Koss, Norway	13:30.55
960	Knut Johannessen, Norway	15:46.60		1998	Gianni Romme, Netherlands	13:15.33
964	Jonny Nilsson, Sweden	15:50.10		2002	Jochem Uytdehaage Netherlands	12:58.92
968	Johnny Hoeglin, Sweden	15:23.60		2006	Bob de Jong, Netherlands	13:01.57
972	Ard Schenk, Netherlands	15:01.35		**Team Pursuit**		
976	Piet Kleine, Netherlands	14:50.59		2006	Italy	
980	Eric Heiden, United States	14:28.13				
984	Igor Malikov, U.S.S.R.	14:39.90				
988	Tomas Gustafson, Sweden	13:48.20				

Speed Skating, Women

500 Meters (1,641 Ft.)		**Time**		1976	Galina Stepanskaya, U.S.S.R.	2:16.58
1960	Helga Haase, Germany	0:45.90		1980	Annie Borchink, Netherlands	2:10.95
1964	Lydia Skoblikova, U.S.S.R.	0:45.00		1984	Karin Enke, East Germany	2:03.42
1968	Ludmila Titova, U.S.S.R.	0:46.10		1988	Yvonne Van Gennip, Netherlands	2:00.68
1972	Anne Henning, United States	0:43.30		1992	Jacqueline Boerner, Germany	2:05.87
1976	Sheila Young, United States	0:42.76		1994	Emese Hunyady, Austria	2:02.19
1980	Karin Enke, East Germany	0:41.78		1998	Marianne Timmer, Netherlands	1:57.58
1984	Christa Rothenburger, East Germany	0:41.02		2002	Anni Friesinger, Germany	1:54.02
1988	Bonnie Blair, United States	0:39.10		2006	Cindy Klassen, Canada	1:55.27
1992	Bonnie Blair, United States	0:40.33		**3,000 Meters (9,843 Ft.)**		**Time**
1994	Bonnie Blair, United States.	0:39.25		1960	Lydia Skoblikova, U.S.S.R.	5:14.30
1998[1]	Catriona Le May-Doan, Canada	1:16.60		1964	Lydia Skoblikova, U.S.S.R.	5:14.90
2002	Catriona Le May Doan, Canada	1:14.75		1968	Johanna Schut, Netherlands	4:56.20
2006	Svetlana Zhurova, Russia	1:16.57		1972	Christina Baas-Kaiser, Netherlands	4:52.14
1,000 Meters (3,281 Ft.)		**Time**		1976	Tatiana Averina, U.S.S.R.	4:45.19
1960	Klara Guseva, U.S.S.R.	1:34.10		1980	Bjoerg Eva Jensen, Norway	4:32.13
1964	Lydia Skoblikova, U.S.S.R.	1:33.20		1984	Andrea Schöne, East Germany	4:24.79
1968	Carolina Geijssen, Netherlands	1:32.60		1988	Yvonne Van Gennip, Netherlands	4:11.94
1972	Monika Pflug, West Germany	1:31.40		1992	Gunda Niemann, Germany	4:19.90
1976	Tatiana Averina, U.S.S.R.	1:28.43		1994	Svetlana Bazhanova, Russia	4:17.43
1980	Natalia Petruseva, U.S.S.R.	1:24.10		1998	Gunda Niemann-Stirnemann,	4:07.29
1984	Karin Enke, East Germany	1:21.61			Germany	
1988	Christa Rothenburger, E.Germany	1:17.65		2002	Claudia Pechstein, Germany	3:57.70
1992	Bonnie Blair, United States	1:21.90		2006	Ireen Wust, Netherlands	4:02.43
1994	Bonnie Blair, United States	1:18.74		**5,000 Meters (16,405 Ft.)**		**Time**
1998	Marianne Timmer, Netherlands	1:16.51		1988	Yvonne Van Gennip, Netherlands	7:14.13
2002	Chris Witty, United States	1:13.83		1992	Gunda Niemann, Germany	7:31.57
2006	Marianne Timmer, Netherlands	1:16.05		1994	Claudia Pechstein, Germany	7:14.37
1,500 Meters (4,922 Ft.)		**Time**		1998	Claudia Pechstein, Germany	6:59.61
1960	Lydia Skoblikova, U.S.S.R.	2:25.20		2002	Claudia Pechstein, Germany	6:46.91
1964	Lydia Skoblikova, U.S.S.R.	2:22.60		2006	Clara Hughes, Canada	6:59.07
1968	Kaija Mustonen, Finland	2:22.40		**Team Pursuit**		
1972	Dianne Holum, United States	2:20.80		2006	Germany	

1. Scoring system changed in 1998. Total is combined time from two performances.

The Winter Olympics

Olympiad	Year	Place	Competitors		Nations represented	Events
			Men	Women		
I	1924	Chamonix, France	245	13	16	16
II	1928	St. Moritz, Switzerland	438	26	25	14
III	1932	Lake Placid, N.Y., U.S.	231	21	17	14
IV	1936	Garmisch-Partenkirchen, Germany	588	80	28	17
V	1948	St. Moritz, Switzerland	592	77	28	22
VI	1952	Oslo, Norway	585	109	30	22
VII	1956	Cortina D'Ampezzo, Italy	688	132	32	24
VIII	1960	Squaw Valley, Calif., U.S.	522	143	30	27
IX	1964	Innsbruck, Austria	891	200	36	34
X	1968	Grenoble, France	947	211	37	35
XI	1972	Sapporo, Japan	800	206	35	35
XII	1976	Innsbruck, Austria	892	231	37	37
XIII	1980	Lake Placid, N.Y., U.S.	839	233	37	38
XIV	1984	Sarajevo, Yugoslavia	1,000	274	49	39
XV	1988	Calgary, Canada	1,110	313	57	46
XVI	1992	Albertville, France	1,313	488	64	57
XVII	1994	Lillehammer, Norway	1,217	522	67	61
XVIII	1998	Nagano, Japan	1,488	814	72	68
XIX	2002	Salt Lake City, Utah, U.S.	1,513	886	77	78
XX	2006	Torino, Italy	1,627	1,006	80	84

Source: International Olympic Committee.

PROFESSIONAL SPORTS

AUTOMOBILE RACING

A number of U.S. states and cities banned automobile racing on public roads during the early 1900s, leading to the development of closed-circuit courses. The Indianapolis Motor Speedway, a 2.5 mile macadam oval, was built in 1909. It was paved with brick in 1911, when the first Indy 500 was run. The American Automobile Association, troubled by a series of fatal crashes, stopped sanctioning races in 1956, whereupon the United States Auto Club (USAC) took over the Indy 500.

Indianapolis 500 Winners, 1911–2008

Year	Winner	Time	MPH	Year	Winner	Time	MPH
Under AAA Sanction				1962	Roger Ward	3:33:50	140.293
1911	Ray Harroun	6:42.08	74.602	1963	Parnelli Jones	3:29:35	143.137
1912	Joe Dawson	6:21.06	78.719	1964	A.J. Foyt, Jr.	3:23:35	147.350
1913	Juses Goux	6:35:05	75.933	1965	Jim Clark	3:19:05	150.686
1914	Rene Thomas	6:03:45	82.474	1966	Graham Hill	3:27:52	144.317
1915	Ralph DePalma	5:33:55	89.840	1967	A.J. Foyt, Jr.	3:18:14	151.207
1916	Dario Resta	3:34:17[1]	84.001	1968	Bobby Unser	3:16:13	152.882
1919	Howard Wilcox	5:40:42	88.050	1969	Mario Andretti	3:11:14	156.867
1920	Gaston Chevrolet	5:38:32	88.618	1970	Al Unser	3:12:37	155.749
1921	Tommy Milton	5:34:34	89.621	1971	Al Unser	3:10:11	157.735
1922	Jimmy Murphy	5:17:30	94.484	1972	Mark Donohue	3:04:05	162.962
1923	Tommy Milton	5:29:50	90.954	1973	Gordon Johncock	2:05:26[4]	159.036
1924	L.L. Corum, Joe Boyer	5:05:23	98.234	1974	Johnny Rutherford	3:09:10	158.589
1925	Peter DePaolo	4:56:39	101.127	1975	Bobby Unser	2:54:55[5]	149.213
1926	Peter Lockhart	4:10:14[2]	95.904	1976	Johnny Rutherford	1:42:52[6]	148.725
1927	George Souders	5:07:33	97.545	1977	A.J. Foyt, Jr.	3:05:57	161.331
1928	Louis Meyer	5:01:33	99.482	1978	Al Unser	3:05:54	161.363
1929	Ray Keech	5:07:25	97.585	1979	Rick Mears	3:08:47	158.899
1930	Billy Arnold	4:58:39	100.448	1980	Johnny Rutherford	3:29:59	142.862
1931	Louis Schneider	5:10:27	96.629	1981	Bobby Unser	3:35:41	139.084
1932	Fred Frame	4:48:03	104.144	1982	Gordon Johncock	3:05:09	162.029
1933	Louis Meyer	4:48:00	104.162	1983	Tom Sneva	3:05:03	162.117
1934	William Cummings	4:46:05	104.863	1984	Rick Mears	3:30:21	163.612
1935	Kelly Petillo	4:42:22	106.240	1985	Danny Sullivan	3:16:06	152.982
1936	Louis Meyer	4:35:03	109.069	1986	Bobby Rahal	2:55:43	170.722
1937	Wilbur Shaw	4:24:07	113.580	1987	Al Unser	3:04:59	162.175
1938	Floyd Roberts	4:15:58	117.200	1988	Rick Mears	3:27:10	144.809
1939	Wilbur Shaw	4:20:47	115.035	1989	Emerson Fittipaldi	2:59:01	167.581
1940	Wilbur Shaw	4:22:31	114.277	1990	Arie Luyendyk	2:41:18	185.984[7]
1941	Floyd Davis, Mauri Rose	4:20:36	115.117	1991	Rick Mears	2:50:01	176.457
1946	George Robson	4:21:16	114.820	1992	Al Unser, Jr.	3:43:05	134.477
1947	Mauri Rose	4:17:52	116.338	1993	Emerson Fittipaldi	3:10:50	157.207
1948	Mauri Rose	4:10:23	119.814	1994	Al Unser, Jr.	3:06:29	160.872
1949	Bill Holland	4:07:15	121.327	1995	Jacques Villeneuve	3:15:18	153.616
1950	Johnnie Parsons	2:46:55[3]	124.002	1996	Buddy Lazier	3:22:46	147.956
1951	Lee Wallard	3:57:38	126.244	1997	Arie Luyendyk	3:25:43	145.827
1952	Troy Tuttman	3:52:41	128.922	1998	Eddie Cheever	3:26:40	145.155
1953	Bill Vukovich	3:53:01	128.740	1999	Kenny Brack	3:15:51	153.176
1954	Bill Vukovich	3:49:17	130.840	2000	Juan Montoya	2:58:59	167.607
1955	Bob Sweikert	3:53:59	128.209	2001	Helio Castroneves	3:31.54	141.574
Under USAC Sanction				2002	Helio Castroneves	3:00:11	166.499
1956	Pat Flaherty	3:53.28	128.490	2003	Gil de Ferran	3:11:57	156.291
1957	Sam Hanks	3:41.14	135.601	2004	Buddy Rice	3:14:55[8]	138.518
1958	Jim Bryan	3:44:13	133.791	2005	Dan Wheldon	3:10:21	157.603
1959	Rodger Ward	3:40:49	135.857	2006	Sam Hornish, Jr.	3:10:58	157.085
1960	Jim Rathmann	3:36:11	138.767	2007	Dario Franchitti[9]	2:44:03	151.774
1961	A.J. Foyt, Jr.	3:35:37	139.131	2008	Scott Dixon	3:28:57	143.567

Notes: 1. 300 miles (scheduled). **2.** 400 miles (rain). **3.** 345 miles (rain). **4.** 332.5 miles (rain). **5.** 435 miles (rain). **6.** 255 miles (rain). **7.** Track record. **8.** 450 miles (rain) **9.** 415 miles (rain)   **Source:** Indianapolis Motor Speedway Hall of Fame and Museum.

Daytona 500 Winners, 1959–2008

Year	Winner	Year	Winner
959	Lee Petty	1984	Cale Yarborough
1960	Junior Johnson	1985	Bill Elliott
1961	Marvin Panch	1986	Geoff Bodine
1962	Fireball Roberts	1987	Bill Elliott
1963	Tiny Lund	1988	Bobby Allison
1964	Richard Petty	1989	Darrell Waltrip
1965	Fred Lorenzen	1990	Derrike Cope
1966	Richard Petty	1991	Ernie Irvan
1967	Mario Andretti	1992	Davey Allison
1968	Cale Yarborough	1993	Dale Jarrett
1969	LeeRoy Yarbrough	1994	Sterling Marlin
1970	Pete Hamilton	1995	Sterling Marlin
1971	Richard Petty	1996	Dale Jarrett
1972	A.J. Foyt, Jr.	1997	Jeff Gordon
1973	Richard Petty	1998	Dale Earnhardt
1974	Richard Petty	1999	Jeff Gordon
1975	Benny Parsons	2000	Dale Jarrett
1976	David Pearson	2001	Michael Waltrip
1977	Cale Yarborough	2002	Ward Burton
1978	Bobby Allison	2003	Michael Waltrip
1979	Richard Petty	2004	Dale Earnhardt Jr.
1980	Buddy Baker	2005	Jeff Gordon
1981	Richard Petty	2006	Jimmie Johnson
1982	Bobby Allison	2007	Kevin Harvick
1983	Cale Yarborough	2008	Ryan Newman

NASCAR Champions, 1959–2007

Year	Winner	Year	Winner
1959	Lee Petty	1984	Terry Labonte
1960	Rex White	1985	Darrell Waltrip
1961	Ned Jarrett	1986	Dale Earnhardt
1962	Joe Weatherly	1987	Dale Earnhardt
1963	Joe Weatherly	1988	Bill Elliott
1964	Richard Petty	1989	Rusty Wallace
1965	Ned Jarrett	1990	Dale Earnhardt
1966	David Pearson	1991	Dale Earnhardt
1967	Richard Petty	1992	Alan Kulwicki
1968	David Pearson	1993	Dale Earnhardt
1969	David Pearson	1994	Dale Earnhardt
1970	Bobby Isaac	1995	Jeff Gordon
1971	Richard Petty	1996	Terry Labonte
1972	Richard Petty	1997	Jeff Gordon
1973	Benny Parsons	1998	Jeff Gordon
1974	Richard Petty	1999	Dale Jarrett
1975	Richard Petty	2000	Bobby Labonte
1976	Cale Yarborough	2001	Jeff Gordon
1977	Cale Yarborough	2002	Tony Stewart
1978	Cale Yarborough	2003	Matt Kenseth
1979	Richard Petty	2004	Kurt Busch
1980	Dale Earnhardt	2005	Tony Stewart
1981	Darrell Waltrip	2006	Jimmie Johnson
1982	Darrell Waltrip	2007	Jimmie Johnson
1983	Bobby Allison		

BOWLING

PBA Leading Money Winners, 1959–2007

Year	Name	Amount	Year	Name	Amount	Year	Name	Amount
1959	Dick Weber	$ 7,672	1977	Mark Roth	$105,583	1994	Norm Duke	$273,753
1960	Don Carter	22,525	1978	Mark Roth	134,500	1995	Mike Aulby	219,792
1961	Dick Weber	26,280	1979	Mark Roth	124,517	1996	Walter Ray. Williams Jr,	241,330
1962	Don Carter	49,972	1980	Wayne Webb	116,700			
1963	Dick Weber	46,333	1981	Earl Anthony	164,735	1997	Walter Ray. Williams Jr,	240,544
1964	Bob Strampe	33,592	1982	Earl Anthony	134,760			
1965	Dick Weber	47,675	1983	Earl Anthony	135,605	1998	Walter Ray Williams Jr.	238,225
1966	Wayne Zahn	54,720	1984	Mark Roth	158,712			
1967	Dave Davis	54,165	1985	Mike Aulby	201,200	1999	Parker Bohn III	240,912
1968	Jim Stefanich	67,375	1986	Walter Ray Williams Jr.	145,550	2000	Norm Duke	136,900
1969	Billy Hardwick	64,160				2001	Parker Bohn III	245,200
1970	Mike McGrath	52,049	1987	Pete Weber	179,516	2003	Walter Ray Williams Jr.	419,700
1971	Johnny Petraglia	85,065	1988	Brian Voss	225,485			
1972	Don Johnson	56,648	1989	Mike Aulby	298,237	2004	Mika Koivuniemi	238,590
1973	Don McCune	69,000	1990	Aurelio Monacelli	204,775	2005	Patrick Allen	350,740
1974	Earl Anthony	99,585	1991	David Ozio	225,585	2006	Tommy Jones	301,700
1975	Earl Anthony	107,585	1992	Marc McDowell	174,215	2007	Doug Kent	200,530
1976	Earl Anthony	110,833	1993	Walter Ray. Williams Jr	296,370			

Note: Since 2001, the PBA season has started in October and ended in March of the year shown. **Source:** Professional Bowlers Association.

Professional Women's Bowling Association, 2007 Leaders

The **Professional Women's Bowling Association** canceled its 2003 fall tour due to lack of funds. In August 2004 the PWBA was bought out by the Women's International Bowling Congress.

Singles			Doubles			Teams		
Rank, Bowler		**Points**	**Rank, Bowler**		**Points**	**Rank, Bowler**		**Points**
1. Lil Holguin		683	1. K. Little, C. Reynolds		1222	1. Ladies on The Roll I		2819
2. LaVonnie Giles		677	2. R. Graham, L. Sills		1204	2. VA FL Friends		2798
3. Veronica Minotti		676	3. M. Mangold, J. Schaub		1195	3. It's All About Us		2777
4. Daisy Amey		660	4. P. Amschler, V. Moores		1191	4. Flavor GA Style		2756
5. Paula Gibson		656	5. B. Brockman, K. Wiesterlee		1184	5. Rollin' Along		2744

Note: Championship standings. **Source:** Professional Women's Bowling Association.

BOXING

Although many governing bodies now issue and certify their own boxing championships, the fourmost widely accepted are the World Boxing Association (WBA), World Boxing Council (WBC), the International Boxing Federation (IBF), and the World Boxing Organization (WBO). Years given indicate the year the championship belt changed hands in a title bout. Champions who were awarded belts without a championship bout are not shown. Current champions (as of August 1, 2007) are shown in **boldface type.**

Heavyweights (over 190 lbs.)

Year	Name	Year	Name	Year	Name
1885	John L. Sullivan	1965	Ernie Terrell (WBA)	1992	Riddick Bowe
1892	James J. Corbett	1967	Muhammad Ali (unifies	1993	Evander Holyfield (WBA, IBF)
1897	Robert Fitzsimmons		world title)	1994	George Foreman (WBA, IBF),
1899	James J. Jeffries	1968	Jimmy Ellis (WBA)		Bruce Seldon
1905	Marvin Hart	1970	Joe Frazier (unifies world title)		(WBA), Frank Bruno[1] (WBC)
1906	Tommy Burns	1973	George Foreman	1996	Mike Tyson (WBC), Michael
1908	Jack Johnson	1974	Muhammad Ali		Moorer (IBF), Mike Tyson (WBA),
1915	Jess Willard	1978	Leon Spinks, Larry Holmes[1],		Evander Holyfield (WBA)
1919	Jack Dempsey		Muhammad Ali[1] (WBA)	1997	Lennox Lewis (WBC), Evander
1926	Gene Tunney[1]	1979	John Tate (WBA)		Holyfield (IBF)
1928–30	vacant	1980	Mike Weaver (WBA)	1999	Lennox Lewis (WBA[1], IBF)
1930	Max Schmeling	1982	Michael Dokes (WBA)	2001	Hasim Rahman (WBC, IBF),
1932	Jack Sharkey	1983	Gerrie Coetzee (WBA)		John Ruiz (WBA),
1933	Primo Carnera	1984	Tim Witherspoon (WBC),		Lennox Lewis (WBC, IBF)
1934	Max Baer		Pinklon Thomas (WBC),	2002	Chris Byrd (IBF)
1935	James J. Braddock		Greg Page (WBA)	2003	Roy Jones Jr. (WBA)
1937	Joe Louis[1]	1985	Tony Tubbs (WBA)	2004	Vitaly Klitschko (WBC)
1949	Ezzard Charles	1986	Tim Witherspoon (WBA),		John Ruiz (WBA)
1951	Jersey Joe Walcott		Trevor Berbick (WBC),	2005	Hasim Rahman (WBC)
1952	Rocky Marciano[1]		Mike Tyson (WBC), James		Nicolay Valuev (WBA)
1956	Floyd Patterson		"Bonecrusher" Smith (WBA)	2006	**Wladimir Klitschko (IBF)**
1959	Ingemar Johansson	1987	Mike Tyson (WBA), Tony		**Oleg Maskaev (WBC)**
1960	Floyd Patterson		Tucker (IBF)	2007	Ruslan Chagaev (WBA)
1962	Sonny Liston	1990	Buster Douglas (unifies world		Sultan Ibragimov (WBO)
1964	Cassius Clay[1]		title), Evander Holyfield	2008	**Ruslan Chagaev (WBA)**
	(Muhammad Ali)				**Wladimir Klitschko (WBO)**

Light Heavyweights (169–175 lbs.)

Year	Name	Year	Name	Year	Name
1903	Jack Root, George	1974	John Conteh (WBC), Victor	1990	Dennis Andries (WBC)
	Gardner		Galindez (WBA)	1991	Thomas Hearns (WBA),
1903	Bob Fitzsimmons	1977	Miguel Angel Cuello (WBC)		Jeff Harding (WBC)
1905	Philadelphia Jack	1978	Mate Parlov (WBC), Mike	1992	Iran Barkley[1] (WBA),
	O'Brien		Rossman (WBA), Marvin		Virgil Hill (WBA)
1912	Jack Dillon		Johnson (WBC)	1993	Henry Maske (IBF)
1916	Battling Levinsky	1979	Matthew Franklin (Matthew	1994	Mike McCallum (WBC)
1920	George Carpentier		Saad Muhammad) (WBC),	1995	Fabrice Tiozzo (WBC)
1922	Battling Siki		Marvin Johnson (WBA)	1996	Roy Jones Jr.[1] (WBC),
1923	Mike McTigue	1980	Eddie Gregory (Eddie		Virgil Hill[1] (IBF),
1925	Paul Berlenbach		Mustafa Muhammad)	1997	William Guthrie (IBF), Dar-
1926	Jack Delaney		(WBA)		iusz Michalczewski[1] (WBA),
1927	Tommy Loughran	1981	Michael Spinks (WBA),		Lou Del Valle (WBA)
1930	Maxey Rosenbloom		Dwight Braxton (Dwight	1998	Reggie Johnson (IBF),
1934	Bob Olin		Muhammad Qawi) (WBC)		Graciano Rocchigiani
1935	John Henry Lewis	1983	Michael Spinks (unifies		(WBC), Roy Jones Jr. (WBA,
1939	Billy Conn		world title)	1999	Roy Jones Jr. (IBF)
1941	Gus Lesnevich	1985	J.B. Williamson (WBC),	2003	Antonio Tarver (WBC, IBF)
1948	Freddie Mills		Slobodan Kacar (IBF)	2004	**Zsolt Erdei (WBO)**, Fabrice
1950	Joey Maxim	1986	Marvin Johnson (WBA),		Tiozzo (WBA), Tomasz
1952	Archie Moore		Dennis Andries (WBC),		Adamek (WBC)
1962	Harold Johnson		Bobby Czyz (IBF)	2005	**Clinton Woods (IBF)**
1963	Willie Pastrano	1987	Thomas Hearns[1] (WBC),	2006	Silvio Branco (WBA)
1965	Jose Torres		Leslie Stewart (WBA), Virgil	2007	Stripe Davis (WBA), Chad
1966	Dick Tiger		Hill (WBA), Prince Charles		Dawson (WBC)
1968	Bob Foster		Williams (IBF), Don	2008	**Danny Green (WBA), Chad**
1971	Vicente Rondon (WBA)		Lalonde (WBC)		**Dawson (WBC)**
1972	Bob Foster (unifies world	1988	Sugar Ray Leonard (WBC)		
	title)	1989	Dennis Andries (WBC),		
			Jeff Harding (WBC)		

Note: WBC = World Boxing Council. WBA = World Boxing Association. IBF = International Boxing Federation.

Middleweights (155–160 lbs.)

Year	Name	Year	Name	Year	Name
1884	Jack Dempsey		Turpin, Sugar Ray Robinson[1]	1990	Julian Jackson (WBC), James Toney[1] (IBF)
1891	Bob Fitzsimmons[1]	1953	Bobo Olson	1991	Reggie Johnson[1] (WBA)
1897	Kid McCoy[1], Tommy Ryan[1]	1955	Sugar Ray Robinson	1993	Gerald McClellan[1] (WBC), Roy Jones[1] (IBF), John David Jackson (WBA)
1907	Stanley Ketchel	1957	Gene Fullmer (NBA), Sugar Ray Robinson, Carmen Basilio	1994	Jorge Castro (WBA)
1908	Billy Papke, Stanley Ketchel[1]	1958	Sugar Ray Robinson	1995	Julian Jackson (WBC), Bernard Hopkins (IBF), Quincy Taylor (WBC), Shinij Takehara (WBA)
1911	Vacant	1960	Paul Pender		
1913	Frank Klaus, George Chip	1961	Terry Downes		
1914	Al McCoy	1962	Paul Pender	1996	Keith Holmes (WBC), William Joppy (WBA)
1917	Mike O'Dowd	1963	Dick Tiger	1997	Julio Cesar Green (WBA)
1920	Johnny Wilson	1963	Joey Giardello	1998	William Joppy (WBA), Hassine Cherifi (WBC)
1921	William Bryan Downey[1]	1965	Dick Tiger	1999	Keith Holmes (WBC)
1923	Harry Greb	1966	Emile Griffith	2001	Felix Trinidad (WBA), Bernard Hopkins (WBA, WBC)
1926	Tiger Flowers, Mickey Walker	1967	Nino Benvenuti, Emile Griffith		
1931	Gorilla Jones	1968	Nino Benvenuti	2005	Jermain Taylor (WBA, WBC, WBO), Arthur Abraham (IBF)
1932	Marcel Thil	1970	Carlos Monzon		
1937	Fred Apostoli	1977	Rodrigo Valdez		
1939	Ceferino Garcia	1978	Hugo Corro	2006	Javier Castillejo (WBA)
1940	Ken Overlin	1979	Vito Antuofermo	2007	Felix Sturm (WBA)
1941	Billy Soose[1], Tony Zale	1980	Alan Minter, Marvin Hagler[1]	2008	Kelly Pavlik (WBC)
1947	Rocky Graziano	1987	Ray Leonard[1] (WBC), Frank Tate (IBF), Sumbu Kalambay (WBA), Thomas Hearns (WBC)		
1948	Tony Zale, Marcel Cerdan	1988	Iran Barkley (WBC), Michael Nunn (IBF)		
1949	Jake LaMotta	1989	Roberto Duran[1] (WBC), Mike McCallum[1] (WBA)		
1951	Sugar Ray Robinson, Randy				

Welterweights (141–147 lbs.)

Year	Name	Year	Name	Year	Name
1888	Paddy Duffy	1935	Barney Ross	1988	Simon Brown[1] (IBF), Thomas Molinares[1] (WBA)
1892	Mysterious Billy Smith	1938	Henry Armstrong	1989	Marlon Starling (WBC), Mark Breland (WBA)
1894	Tommy Ryan[1]	1940	Fritzie Zivic	1990	Aaron Davis (WBA), Maurice Blocker (WBC)
1896	Kid McCoy[1]	1941	Fred Cochrane	1991	Meldrick Taylor (WBA), Simon Brown (WBC), Maurice Blocker (IBF), Buddy McGirt (WBC)
1898	Mysterious Billy Smith	1946	Marty Servo[1], Ray Robinson[1]		
1900	Matty Matthews, Eddie Connolly, Rube Ferns, Matty Matthews	1951	Kid Gavilan	1992	Crisanto Espana (WBA)
		1954	Johnny Saxton	1993	Pernell Whitaker (WBC), Felix Trinidad (IBF)
1901	Rube Ferns, Joe Walcott	1955	Tony De Marco, Carmen Basilio	1994	Ike Quartey[1] (WBA)
1904	Dixie Kid[1]	1956	Johnny Saxton, Carmen Basilio	1997	Oscar de la Hoya (WBC)
1906	Honey Mellody	1957	Carmen Basilio[1]	1998	James Page (WBA)
1907	Frank Mantell	1958	Virgil Akins, Don Jordan	1999	Felix Trinidad[1] (WBC), Rawl Frank (IBF)
1908	Harry Lewis[1]	1960	Benny Paret	2000	Vernon Forrest (IBF), Oscar de la Hoya (WBC), Shane Mosley (WBC)
1911–13	Vacant	1961	Emile Griffith, Benny Paret		
1914	Waldemar Holberg, Tom McCormick, Matt Wells	1962	Emile Griffith	2001	Andrew Lewis (WBA)
		1963	Luis Rodriguez, Emile Griffith[1]	2002	Vernon Forrest[1] (IBF), Michele Piccirillo (IBF), Ricardo Mayorga (WBA), Vernon Forrest (WBC), Antiono Margarito (WBO)
1915	Mike Glover, Jack Britton, Ted (Kid) Lewis	1966	Curtis Cokes		
		1969	Jose Napoles		
1916	Jack Britton	1970	Billy Backus	2003	Ricardo Mayorga (unifies world title), Cory Spinks
1917	Ted (Kid) Lewis	1971	Jose Napoles		
1919	Jack Britton	1975	Angel Espada (WBA), John Stracey (WBC)	2005	Zab Judah (WBC, IBF), Luis Collazo (WBA)
1922	Mickey Walker	1976	Carlos Palomino (WBC), Jose Cuevas (WBA)	2006	Carlos Baldomir (WBC), Floyd Mayweather (WBC), Ricky Hatton (WBA)
1926	Pete Latzo	1979	Wilfredo Benitez (WBC), Sugar Ray Leonard (WBC)		
1927	Joe Dundee			2007	Paul Williams (WBO)
1929	Jackie Fields	1980	Roberto Duran (WBC), Thomas Hearns (WBA), Sugar Ray Leonard (WBC)	2008	Paul Williams (WBO)
1930	Young Jack Thompson, Tommy Freeman				
1931	Young Jack Thompson, Lou Brouillard	1981	Sugar Ray Leonard[1] (unifies world title)		
1932	Jackie Fields	1983	Donald Curry (WBA), Milton McCrory (WBC)		
1933	Young Corbett, Jimmy McLarnin	1985	Donald Curry (unifies world title)		
1934	Barney Ross, Jimmy McLarnin	1986	Lloyd Honeyghan[1]		
		1987	Mark Breland (WBA), Marlon Starling (WBA), Jorge Vaca (WBC)		

Lightweights (131–135 lbs.)

Year	Name	Year	Name	Year	Name
1896	Jack McAuliffe[1], Kid Lavigne	1955	Bud Smith	1989	Edwin Rosario (WBA), Pernell Whitaker (WBC)
1899	Frank Erne	1956	Joe Brown	1990	Juan Nazario (WBA),
1902	Joe Gans[1]	1962	Carlos Ortiz		Pernell Whitaker[1]
1904	Jimmy Britt	1965	Ismael Laguna, Carlos Ortiz		(unifies world title)
1905	Battling Nelson	1968	Teo Cruz	1991	Vacant
1906	Joe Gans	1969	Mando Ramos	1992	Tony Lopez (WBA)
1908	Battling Nelson	1970	Ismael Laguna, Ken Buchanan[1]	1993	Fred Pendleton (IBF),
1910	Ad Wolgast	1971	Pedro Carrasco (WBC)		Dingaan Thobela (WBA),
1912	Willie Ritchie	1972	Mando Ramos (WBC),		Orzubek Nazarov (WBA)
1914	Freddie Welsh		Roberto Duran[1] (WBA)	1994	Rafael Ruelas (IBF)
1917	Benny Leonard[1]		Chango Carmona (WBC),	1995	Oscar de la Hoya[1] (IBF),
1925	Jimmy Goodrich, Rocky Kansas		Rodolfo Gonzalez (WBC)		Phillip Holiday (IBF)
1926	Sammy Mandell	1974	Ishimatsu Suzuki (WBC)	1996	Jean-Baptiste Mendy (WBC)
1930	Al Singer, Tony Canzoneri	1976	Esteban De Jesus[1] (WBC)	1997	Steve Johnston (WBC), Shane Mosley[1] (IBF)
1933	Barney Ross[1]	1979	Jim Watt (WBC), Ernesto España (WBA)	1998	Jean-Baptiste Mendy (WBA),
1935	Tony Canzoneri	1980	Hilmer Kenty (WBA)		Cesar Bazan (WBC)
1936	Lou Ambers	1981	Sean O'Grady (WBA), Alexis	1999	Julian Lorcy Fra (WBA), Steve
1938	Henry Armstrong		Arguello (WBC), Claude Noel		Johnston (WBC), Stefano Zoff
1939	Lou Ambers		(WBA), Arturo Frias (WBA)		(WBA), Paul Spadafora[1] (IBF),
1940	Lew Jenkins	1982	Ray Mancini (WBA)		Gilberto Serrano (WBA)
1941	Sammy Angott	1983	Edwin Rosario (WBC)	2000	Jose Luis Castillo (W,BC)
1942	Beau Jack	1984	Charlie (Choo Choo) Brown	2001	Raul Balbi (WBA)
1943	Bob Montgomery, Beau Jack		(IBF), Livingstone Bramble (WBA), Jose Luis Ramirez (WBC)	2002	Floyd Mayweather (WBC), Leonard Dorin (WBA)
1944	Bob Montgomery, Juan Zurita	1985	Jimmy Paul (IBF), Hector Camacho[1] (WBC)	2004	Julio Diaz(IBF), Lakva Sim (WBA), Jose Luis Castillo (WBC),
1945	Ike Williams	1986	Edwin Rosario (WBA), Greg Haugen (IBF)		Javier Jauregui (IBF)
1951	Jimmy Carter	1987	Vinny Pazienza (IBF),	2005	Diego Corrales (WBC)
1952	Lauro Salas, Jimmy Carter		Jose Luis Ramirez (WBC), Julio Cesar Chavez[1] (WBA)		Juan Diaz (WBA) Jesus Chavez (IBF)
1954	Paddy De Marco, Jimmy Carter	1988	Greg Haugen (IBF), Julio Cesar Chavez[1] (WBC)	2007	Julio Diaz (IBF)
		1989	Pernell Whitaker (IBF),	2008	**Nate Campbell (WBA, WBO, IBF), David Diaz (WBC)**

Featherweights (123–126 lbs.)

Year	Name	Year	Name	Year	Name
1900	Terry McGovern, Young Corbett[1]	1970	Vicente Saldivar (WBC), Kuniaki Shibata (WBC)	1993	Tom Johnson (IBF), Goyo Vargas
1901	Abe Attell	1971	Antonio Gomez (WBA		(WBC), Kevin Kelley (WBC),
1904	Tommy Sullivan[1]	1972	Clemente Sanchez (WBC),		Eloy Rojas (WBA)
1906	Abe Attell		Ernesto Marcel[1] (WBA),	1995	Alejandro Gonzalez (WBC),
1912	Johnny Kilbane		Jose Legra (WBC)		Manuel Medina (WBC),
1923	Eugene Criqui, Johnny Dundee[1]	1973	Eder Jofre[1] (WBC)		Luisito Espinosa (WBC)
1925	Kid Kaplan[1]	1974	Ruben Olivares (WBA), Bobby Chacon (WBC),	1996	Wilfredo Vasquez[1] (WBA)
1927	Benny Bass, Ton Canzoneri		Alexis Arguello[1] (WBA)	1997	Naseem Hamed (IBF), Hector Lizarraga (IBF)
1928	Andre Routis	1975	Ruben Olivares (WBC), David Kotey (WBC)	1998	Fred Norwood (WBA), Manuel Medina (IBF),
1929	Battling Battalino[1]	1976	Danny Lopez (WBC)		Antonio Cermeño Ven (WBA)
1932	Tommy Paul	1977	Rafael Ortega (WBA), Cecillio Lastra (WBA)	1999	Cesar Soto (WBC), Luisito Espinosa (WBC), Paul Ingle (IBF),
1933	Freddie Miller	1978	Eusebio Pedrosa (WBA)		Fred Norwood (WBA)
1936	Petey Sarron	1980	Salvador Sanchez[1] (WBC)	2000	Guty Espadas (WBC),
1937	Henry Armstrong[1]	1982	Juan LaPorte (WBC)		Derrick Gainer (WBA)
1938	Joey Archibald	1984	Min Keun Oh (IBF), Wilfredo Gomez (WBC),	2001	Frankie Toledo (IBF), Manuel Medina (IBF), Erik Morales[1](WBC)
1940	Harry Jeffra, Joey Archibald		Azumah Nelson (WBC)	2002	Johnny Tapia (IBF), Manuel Medina (IBF), Scott Harrison
1941	Chalky Wright	1985	Barry McGuigan (WBA), Ki Yung Chung[1] (IBF)		(WBO)
1942	Wilie Pep	1986	Steve Cruz (WBA)	2003	Juan Marquez (IBF), Chris John
1948	Sandy Saddler	1987	Antonio Esparragoza (WBA)		(WBA)
1949	Willie Pep	1988	Calvin Grove (IBF), Jeff Fenech[1]	2004	In-Jin Chi (WBC)
1950	Sandy Saddler[1]		(WBC), Jorge Paez (IBF)	2006	**Rudolfo Lopez (WBC)**, Eric
1957	Hogan (Kid) Bassey	1990	Marcos Villasana (WBC)		Aiken (IBF)
1959	Davey Moore	1991	Yung Kyun Park (WBA)	2007	Robert Guerrero (IBF)
1963	Sugar Ramos	1992	Troy Dorsey (IBF), Manuel Medina	2008	**Chris John (WBA), Steven**
1964	Vicente Saldivar[1]		(IBF), Paul Hodkinson (WBC)		**Luevano (WBO), Robert**
1968	Jose Legra[1] (WBA), Shojo Saijo (WBA)				**Guerrero (IBF)**
1969	Johnny Famechon (WBC)				

1. Stripped of title or abandoned belt.   **Source:** International Boxing Hall of Fame.

GOLF

THE FOUR MAJOR TOURNAMENTS

o golfer has ever won the four major tournaments—the Masters, the U.S. Open, the British Open, and the PGA—in the same calendar year. he players to come closest were Ben Hogan, who won the first three tournaments in 1953, and Tiger Woods, who won them consecutively, but not in the same calendar year –he won the last hree in 2000 and the Masters in 2001. Five players have won each of the four majors at least once over their entire careers: Hogan, Woods, Jack Nicklaus, Gary Player, and Gene Sarazen. Woods and Nicklaus won each at least three times.

The Senior Tour began with two tournaments in 1980, which offered a total of $250,000 in prize money to qualified PGA members over the age of 50. By 1984, the tour had spiralled to 24 tournaments with prize money totalling $5 million. The arrival in 1990 of Jack Nicklaus and Lee Trevino on the senior tour helped propel the 50-and-over tour to unprecedented popularity, surpassing the Ladies' Professional Tour in both prize money and television ratings.

The Masters

Year	Winner	Year	Winner	Year	Winner	Year	Winner
1934	Horton Smith	1953	Ben Hogan	1972	Jack Nicklaus	1991	Ian Woosnam
1935	Gene Sarazen	1954	Sam Snead	1973	Tommy Aaron	1992	Fred Couples
1936	Horton Smith	1955	Cary Middlecoff	1974	Gary Player	1993	Bernhard Langer
1937	Byron Nelson	1956	Jack Burke Jr.	1975	Jack Nicklaus	1994	José María Olazábal
1938	Henry Picard	1957	Doug Ford	1976	Ray Floyd	1995	Ben Crenshaw
1939	Ralph Guldahl	1958	Arnold Palmer	1977	Tom Watson	1996	Nick Faldo
1940	Jimmy Demaret	1959	Art Wall Jr.	1978	Gary Player	1997	Tiger Woods
1941	Craig Wood	1960	Arnold Palmer	1979	Fuzzy Zoeller	1998	Mark O'Meara
1942	Byron Nelson	1961	Gary Player	1980	Seve Ballesteros	1999	José María Olazábal
1943	Not held	1962	Arnold Palmer	1981	Tom Watson	2000	Vijay Singh
1944	Not held	1963	Jack Nicklaus	1982	Craig Stadler	2001	Tiger Woods
1945	Not held	1964	Arnold Palmer	1983	Seve Ballesteros	2002	Tiger Woods
1946	Herman Keiser	1965	Jack Nicklaus	1984	Ben Crenshaw	2003	Mike Weir
1947	Jimmy Demaret	1966	Jack Nicklaus	1985	Bernhard Langer	2004	Phil Mickelson
1948	Claude Harman	1967	Gay Brewer Jr.	1986	Jack Nicklaus	2005	Tiger Woods
1949	Sam Snead	1968	Bob Goalby	1987	Larry Mize	2006	Phil Mickelson
1950	Jimmy Demaret	1969	George Archer	1988	Sandy Lyle	2007	Zach Johnson
1951	Ben Hogan	1970	Billy Casper	1989	Nick Faldo	2008	Tiger Woods
1952	Sam Snead	1971	Charles Coody	1990	Nick Faldo		

The U.S. Open Championship

Year	Winner	Year	Winner	Year	Winner	Year	Winner
1895	Horace Rawlins	1924	Cyril Walker	1953	Ben Hogan	1982	Tom Watson
1896	James Foulis	1925	W. MacFarlane	1954	Ed Furgol	1983	Larry Nelson
1897	Joe Lloyd	1926	Robert T. Jones Jr.	1955	Jack Fleck	1984	Fuzzy Zoeller
1898	Fred Herd	1927	Tommy Armour	1956	Cary Middlecoff	1985	Andy North
1899	Willie Smith	1928	Johnny Farrell	1957	Dick Mayer	1986	Ray Floyd
1900	Harry Vardon	1929	Robert T. Jones Jr.	1958	Tommy Bolt	1987	Scott Simpson
1901	Willie Anderson	1930	Robert T. Jones Jr.	1959	Billy Casper	1988	Curtis Strange
1902	Laurie Auchterlonie	1931	Billy Burke	1960	Arnold Palmer	1989	Curtis Strange
1903	Willie Anderson	1932	Gene Sarazen	1961	Gene Littler	1990	Hale Irwin
1904	Willie Anderson	1933	Johnny Goodman	1962	Jack Nicklaus	1991	Payne Stewart
1905	Willie Anderson	1934	Olin Dutra	1963	Julius Boros	1992	Tom Kite
1906	Alex Smith	1935	Sam Parks, Jr.	1964	Ken Venturi	1993	Lee Janzen
1907	Alex Ross	1936	Tony Manero	1965	Gary Player	1994	Ernie Els
1908	Fred McLeod	1937	Ralph Guldahl	1966	Billy Casper	1995	Corey Pavin
1909	George Sargent	1938	Ralph Guldahl	1967	Jack Nicklaus	1996	Steve Jones
1910	Alex Smith	1939	Byron Nelson	1968	Lee Trevino	1997	Ernie Els
1911	John McDermott	1940	Lawson Little	1969	Orville Moody	1998	Lee Janzen
1912	John McDermott	1941	Craig Wood	1970	Tony Jacklin	1999	Payne Stewart
1913	Francis Ouimet	1942	Not held	1971	Lee Trevino	2000	Tiger Woods
1914	Walter Hagen	1943	Not held	1972	Jack Nicklaus	2001	Retief Goosen
1915	Jerome Travers	1944	Not held	1973	Johnny Miller	2002	Tiger Woods
1916	Charles Evans Jr.	1945	Not held	1974	Hale Irwin	2003	Jim Furyk
1917	Not held	1946	Lloyd Mangrum	1975	Lou Graham	2004	Retief Goosen
1918	Not held	1947	Lew Worsham	1976	Jerry Pate	2005	Michael Campbell
1919	Walter Hagen	1948	Ben Hogan	1977	Hubert Green	2006	Geoff Ogilvy
1920	Edward Ray	1949	Cary Middlecoff	1978	Andy North	2007	Angel Cabrera
1921	James M. Barnes	1950	Ben Hogan	1979	Hale Irwin	2008	Tiger Woods
1922	Gene Sarazen	1951	Ben Hogan	1980	Jack Nicklaus		
1923	Robert T. Jones Jr.	1952	Julius Boros	1981	David Graham		

The British Open

Year	Winner	Year	Winner	Year	Winner	Year	Winner
1860	Willie Park	1895	John H. Taylor	1934	Henry Cotton	1973	Tom Weiskopf
1861	Tom Morris Sr.	1896	Harry Vardon	1935	Alfred Perry	1974	Gary Player
1862	Tom Morris Sr.	1897	Harold H. Hilton	1936	Alfred Padgham	1975	Tom Watson
1863	Willie Park	1898	Harry Vardon	1937	Henry Cotton	1976	Johnny Miller
1864	Tom Morris Sr.	1899	Harry Vardon	1938	R.A. Whitcombe	1977	Tom Watson
1865	Andrew Strath	1900	John H. Taylor	1939	Richard Burton	1978	Jack Nicklaus
1866	Willie Park	1901	James Braid	1940	Not held	1979	Seve Ballesteros
1867	Tom Morris Sr.	1902	Alexander Herd	–45		1980	Tom Watson
1868	Tom Morris Jr.	1903	Harry Vardon	1946	Sam Snead	1981	Bill Rogers
1869	Tom Morris Jr.	1904	Jack White	1947	Fred Daly	1982	Tom Watson
1870	Tom Morris Jr.	1905	James Braid	1948	Henry Cotton	1983	Tom Watson
1871	Not held	1906	James Braid	1949	Bobby Locke	1984	Seve Ballesteros
1872	Tom Morris Jr.	1907	Arnaud Massy	1950	Bobby Locke	1985	Sandy Lyle
1873	Tom Kidd	1908	James Braid	1951	Max Faulkner	1986	Greg Norman
1874	Mungo Park	1909	John H. Taylor	1952	Bobby Locke	1987	Nick Faldo
1875	Willie Park	1910	James Braid	1953	Ben Hogan	1988	Seve Ballesteros
1876	Bob Martin	1911	Harry Vardon	1954	Peter Thomson	1989	Mark Calcavecchia
1877	Jamie Anderson	1912	Edward (Ted) Ray	1955	Peter Thomson	1990	Nick Faldo
1878	Jamie Anderson	1913	John H. Taylor	1956	Peter Thomson	1991	Ian Baker-Finch
1879	Jamie Anderson	1914	Harry Vardon	1957	Bobby Locke	1992	Nick Faldo
1880	Robert Ferguson	1915	Not held	1958	Peter Thomson	1993	Greg Norman
1881	Robert Ferguson	–19		1959	Gary Player	1994	Nick Price
1882	Robert Ferguson	1920	George Duncan	1960	Kel Nagle	1995	John Daly
1883	Willie Fernie	1921	Jock Hutchison	1961	Arnold Palmer	1996	Tom Lehman
1884	Jack Simpson	1922	Walter Hagen	1962	Arnold Palmer	1997	Justin Leonard
1885	Bob Martin	1923	Arthur G. Havers	1963	Bob Charles	1998	Mark O'Meara
1886	David Brown	1924	Walter Hagen	1964	Tony Lema	1999	Paul Lawrie
1887	Willie Park Jr.	1925	James M. Barnes	1965	Peter Thomson	2000	Tiger Woods
1888	Jack Burns	1926	Robert T. Jones Jr.	1966	Jack Nicklaus	2001	David Duval
1889	Willie Park Jr.	1927	Robert T. Jones Jr.	1967	Roberto	2002	Ernie Els
1890	John Ball	1928	Walter Hagen		DeVicenzo	2003	Ben Curtis
1891	Hugh Kirkaldy	1929	Walter Hagen	1968	Gary Player	2004	Todd Hamilton
1892	Harold H. Hilton[1]	1930	Robert T. Jones Jr.	1969	Tony Jacklin	2005	Tiger Woods
1893	William	1931	Tommy D. Armour	1970	Jack Nicklaus	2006	Tiger Woods
	Auchterlonie	1932	Gene Sarazen	1971	Lee Trevino	2007	Padraig Harrington
1894	John H. Taylor	1933	Denny Shute	1972	Lee Trevino	2008	Padraig Harrington

PGA Championship

Year	Winner	Year	Winner	Year	Winner	Year	Winner
1916	James M. Barnes	1940	Byron Nelson	1964	Bobby Nichols	1988	Jeff Sluman
1917	Not held	1941	Vic Ghezzi	1965	Dave Marr	1989	Payne Stewart
1918	Not held	1942	Sam Snead	1966	Al Geiberger	1990	Wayne Grady
1919	James M. Barnes	1943	Not held	1967	Don January	1991	John Daly
1920	Jock Hutchison	1944	Bob Hamilton	1968	Julius Boros	1992	Nick Price
1921	Walter Hagen	1945	Byron Nelson	1969	Ray Floyd	1993	Paul Azinger
1922	Gene Sarazen	1946	Ben Hogan	1970	Dave Stockton	1994	Nick Price
1923	Gene Sarazen	1947	Jim Ferrier	1971	Jack Nicklaus	1995	Steve Elkington
1924	Walter Hagen	1948	Ben Hogan	1972	Gary Player	1996	Mark Brooks
1925	Walter Hagen	1949	Sam Snead	1973	Jack Nicklaus	1997	Davis Love III
1926	Walter Hagen	1950	Chandler Harper	1974	Lee Trevino	1998	Vijay Singh
1927	Walter Hagen	1951	Sam Snead	1975	Jack Nicklaus	1999	Tiger Woods
1928	Leo Diegel	1952	Jim Turnesa	1976	Dave Stockton	2000	Tiger Woods
1929	Leo Diegel	1953	Walter Burkemo	1977	Lanny Wadkins	2001	David Toms
1930	Tommy Armour	1954	Chick Harbert	1978	John Mahaffey	2002	Rich Beem
1931	Tom Creavy	1955	Doug Ford	1979	David Graham	2003	Shaun Micheel
1932	Olin Dutra	1956	Jack Burke	1980	Jack Nicklaus	2004	Vijay Singh
1933	Gene Sarazen	1957	Lionel Hebert	1981	Larry Nelson	2005	Phil Mickelson
1934	Paul Runyan	1958	Dow Finsterwald	1982	Raymond Floyd	2006	Tiger Woods
1935	Johnny Revolta	1959	Bob Rosburg	1983	Hal Sutton	2007	Tiger Woods
1936	Denny Shute	1960	Jay Hebert	1984	Lee Trevino	2008	Padraig Harrington
1937	Denny Shute	1961	Jerry Barber	1985	Hubert Green		
1938	Paul Runyan	1962	Gary Player	1986	Bob Tway		
1939	Henry Picard	1963	Jack Nicklaus	1987	Larry Nelson		

PGA Leading Money Winners, 1934–2007

Year	Name	Winnings	Year	Name	Winnings	Year	Name	Winnings
934	Paul Runyan	$6,767	1959	Art Wall	$53,167	1984	Tom Watson	$476,260
935	Johnny Revolta	9,543	1960	Arnold Palmer	75,262	1985	Curtis Strange	542,321
936	Horton Smith	7,682	1961	Gary Player	64,540	1986	Greg Norman	653,296
937	Harry Cooper	14,138	1962	Arnold Palmer	81,448	1987	Curtis Strange	925,941
938	Sam Snead	19,534	1963	Arnold Palmer	128,230	1988	Curtis Strange	1,147,644
939	Henry Picard	10,303	1964	Jack Nicklaus	113,284	1989	Tom Kite	1,395,278
940	Ben Hogan	10,655	1965	Jack Nicklaus	140,752	1990	Greg Norman	1,165,477
1941	Ben Hogan	18,358	1966	Billy Casper	121,944	1991	Corey Pavin	979,430
1942	Ben Hogan	13,143	1967	Jack Nicklaus	188,998	1992	Fred Couples	1,344,188
1943	No statistics compiled		1968	Billy Casper	205,168	1993	Nick Price	1,478,557
1944	Byron Nelson	37,967[1]	1969	Frank Beard	164,707	1994	Nick Price	1,499,927
1945	Byron Nelson	63,335[1]	1970	Lee Trevino	157,037	1995	Greg Norman	1,654,959
1946	Ben Hogan	42,556	1971	Jack Nicklaus	244,490	1996	Tom Lehman	1,780,159
1947	Jimmy Demaret	27,936	1972	Jack Nicklaus	320,542	1997	Tiger Woods	2,066,833
1948	Ben Hogan	32,112	1973	Jack Nicklaus	308,362	1998	David Duval	2,591,031
1949	Sam Snead	31,593	1974	Johnny Miller	353,021	1999	Tiger Woods	6,616,585
1950	Sam Snead	35,758	1975	Jack Nicklaus	298,149	2000	Tiger Woods	9,188,321
1951	Lloyd Mangrum	26,088	1976	Jack Nicklaus	266,438	2001	Tiger Woods	5,687,777
1952	Julius Boros	37,032	1977	Tom Watson	310,653	2002	Tiger Woods	6,912,625
1953	Lew Worsham	34,002	1978	Tom Watson	362,428	2003	Vijay Singh	7,573,907
1954	Bob Toski	65,819	1979	Tom Watson	462,636	2004	Vijay Singh	10,905,166
1955	Julius Boros	63,121	1980	Tom Watson	530,808	2005	Tiger Woods	10,628,024
1956	Ted Kroll	72,835	1981	Tom Kite	375,698	2006	Tiger Woods	9,941,563
1957	Dick Mayer	65,835	1982	Craig Stadler	446,462	2007	Tiger Woods	10,867,052
1958	Arnold Palmer	42,607	1983	Hal Sutton	426,668			

1. Paid in War Bonds. **Source:** Professional Golfers' Association. www.pgatour.com

PGA Leading Money Winners, 2008 and Career

2007			Career					
Rank, Golfer		**Earnings**	**Rank, Golfer**		**Earnings**	**Rank, Golfer**		**Earnings**
1. Tiger Woods		$10,867,052	**1.** Tiger Woods		$81,004,376	**11.** Mark Calcavecchia		22,969,846
2. Phil Mickelson		5,819,988	**2.** Vijay Singh		56,434,235	**12.** Stuart Appleby		22,032,786
3. Vijay Singh		4,728,376	**3.** Phil Mickelson		49,206,296	**13.** Mike Weir		22,019,610
4. Steve Stricker		4,663,077	**4.** Jim Furyk		36,955,143	**14.** Sergio Garcia		21,850,717
5. K.J. Choi		4,587,859	**5.** Davis Love III		35,861,958	**15.** Scott Verplank		21,736,392
			6. Ernie Els		32,499,673	**16.** Fred Funk		20,887,449
			7. David Toms		28,365,366	**17.** Nick Price		20,563,108
			8. Justin Leonard		26,063,865	**18.** Tom Lehman		20,269,230
			9. Kenny Perry		24,013,749	**19.** Fred Couples		19,990,822
			10. Stewart Cink		23,593,205	**20.** Chris Demarco		19,821,453

Note: As of June 8, 2008. **Source:** Professional Golfers' Association. www.pga.com

LPGA Leading Money Winners, 1956–2007

Year	Player	Winnings	Year	Player	Winnings	Year	Player	Winnings
1956	Marlene Hagge	$20,235	1974	JoAnne Carner	87,094	1992	Dottie Mochrie	693,335
1957	Patty Berg	16,272	1975	Sandra Palmer	76,374	1993	Betsy King	595,992
1958	Beverly Hanson	12,629	1976	Judy T. Rankin	150,734	1994	Laura Davies	687,201
1959	Betsy Rawls	26,774	1977	Judy T. Rankin	122,890	1995	Annika Sorenstam	666,533
1960	Louise Suggs	16,892	1978	Nancy Lopez	189,813	1996	Karrie Webb	1,002,000
1961	Mickey Wright	22,238	1979	Nancy Lopez	197,488	1997	Annika Sorenstam	1,236,789
1962	Mickey Wright	21,654	1980	Beth Daniel	231,000	1998	Annika Sorenstam	1,092,748
1963	Mickey Wright	31,269	1981	Beth Daniel	206,977	1999	Karrie Webb	1,591,959
1964	Mickey Wright	29,800	1982	JoAnne Carner	310,399	2000	Karrie Webb	1,876,853
1965	Kathy Whitworth	28,658	1983	JoAnne Carner	291,404	2001	Annika Sorenstam	2,105,868
1966	Kathy Whitworth	33,517	1984	Betsy King	266,771	2002	Annika Sorenstam	2,863,904
1967	Kathy Whitworth	32,937	1985	Nancy Lopez	416,472	2003	Annika Sorenstam	2,029,506
1968	Kathy Whitworth	48,379	1986	Pat Bradley	492,021	2004	Annika Sorenstam	2,544,707
1969	Carol Mann	49,152	1987	Ayako Okamoto	466,034	2005	Annika Sorenstam	2,588,240
1970	Kathy Whitworth	30,235	1988	Sherri Turner	350,851	2006	Lorena Ochoa	2,592,872
1971	Kathy Whitworth	41,181	1989	Betsy King	654,132	2007	Lorena Ochoa	4,364,994
1972	Kathy Whitworth	65,063	1990	Beth Daniel	$863,578			
1973	Kathy Whitworth	$82,864	1991	Pat Bradley	763,118			

Source: Ladies Professional Golfers' Association. www.lpga.com.

LPGA Leading Money Winners, 2007 and Career

2007		Career		Career	
Rank, Golfer	Earnings	Rank, Golfer	Earnings	Rank, Golfer	Earnings
1. Lorena Ochoa	$4,364,994	1. Annika Sorenstam	$20,837,280	11. Cristie Kerr	7,830,051
2. Suzann Pettersen	1,802,400	2. Karrie Webb	13,457,025	12. Betsy King	7,637,621
3. Paula Creamer	1,384,798	3. Juli Inkster	11,701,376	13. Dottie Popper	6,827,284
4. Mi Hyun Kim	1,273,848	4. Lorena Ochoa	10,434,216	14. Lorie Kane	6,644,027
5. Seon Hwa Lee	1,100,198	5. Se Ri Pak	9,787,077	15. Pat Hurst	5,911,397
6. Cristie Kerr	1,098,921	6. Meg Mallon	8,885,694	16. Pat Bradley	5,755,951
7. Jeong Jang	1,038,598	7. Beth Daniel	8,755,733	17. Liselotte Neumann	5,734,653
8. Angela Park	983,922	8. Rosie Jones	8,355,068	18. Kelly Robbins	5,621,742
9. Morgan Pressel	972,452	9. Laura Davies	8,168,615	19. Sherri Steinhauer	5,617,672
10. Jee Young Lee	966,256	10. Mi Hyun Kim	6,827,284	20. Patty Sheehan	5,513,409

Source: Ladies Professional Golfers' Association. www.lpga.com.

U.S. Women's Grand Slam Champions, 1972–2008

Year	Kraft-Nabisco Championship	LPGA Championship	U.S. Women's Open	du Maurier Classic[1]
1972		Kathy Ahern	Susie Berning	
1973		Mary Mills	Susie Berning	
1974		Sandra Haynie	Sandra Haynie	
1975		Kathy Whitworth	Sandra Palmer	
1976		Betty Burfeindt	JoAnne Carner	
1977		Chako Higuchi	Hollis Stacy	
1978		Nancy Lopez	Hollis Stacy	
1979		Donna Caponi	Jerilyn Britz	Amy Alcott
1980		Sally Little	Amy Alcott	Pat Bradley
1981		Donna Caponi	Pat Bradley	Jan Stephenson
1982		Jan Stephenson	Janet Anderson	Sandra Haynie
1983	Amy Alcott	Patty Sheehan	Jan Stephenson	Hollis Stacy
1984	Juli Inkster	Patty Sheehan	Hollis Stacy	Juli Inkster
1985	Alice Miller	Nancy Lopez	Kathy Baker	Pat Bradley
1986	Pat Bradley	Pat Bradley	Jane Geddes	Pat Bradley
1987	Betsy King	Jane Geddes	Laura Davies	Jody Rosenthal
1988	Amy Alcott	Sherri Turner	Liselotte Neumann	Sally Little
1989	Juli Inkster	Nancy Lopez	Betsy King	Tammie Green
1990	Betsy King	Beth Daniel	Betsy King	Cathy Johnston
1991	Amy Alcott	Meg Mallon	Meg Mallon	Nancy Scranton
1992	Dottie Pepper	Betsy King	Patty Sheehan	Sherri Steinhauer
1993	Helen Alfredsson	Patty Sheehan	Lauri Merten	Brandie Burton
1994	Donna Andrews	Laura Davies	Patty Sheehan	Martha Nause
1995	Nanci Bowen	Kelly Robbins	Annika Sorenstam	Jenny Lidback
1996	Patty Sheehan	Laura Davies	Annika Sorenstam	Laura Davies
1997	Betsy King	Chris Johnson	Alison Nicholas	Colleen Walker
1998	Pat Hurst	Se Ri Pak	Se Ri Pak	Brandie Burton
1999	Dottie Pepper	Juli Inkster	Juli Inkster	Karrie Webb
2000	Karrie Webb	Juli Inkster	Karrie Webb	Meg Mallon
				Women's British Open[1]
2001	Annika Sorenstam	Karrie Webb	Karrie Webb	Se Ri Pak
2002	Annika Sorenstam	Se Ri Pak	Juli Inkster	Karrie Webb
2003	Patricia Meunier-Lebouc	Annika Sorenstam	Hilary Lunke	Annika Sorenstam
2004	Grace Park	Annika Sorenstam	Meg Mallon	Karen Stupples
2005	Annika Sorenstam	Annika Sorenstam	Birdie Kim	Jeong Jang
2006	Karrie Webb	Se Ri Pak	Annika Sorenstam	Sherri Steinhauer
2007	Morgan Pressel	Suzann Pettersson	Cristie Kerr	Lorena Ochoa
2008	Lorena Ochoa	Yani Tseng		

Note: 1. The Women's British Open replaced the duMaurier Classic as the fourth major in 2001. **Source:** LPGA

U.S. Women's Open Champions, 1946–71

Year	Champion	Year	Champion	Year	Champion	Year	Champion
1946	Patty Berg	1953	Betsy Rawls	1960	Betsy Rawls	1966	Sandra Spuzich
1947	Betty Jameson	1954	Babe Zaharias	1961	Mickey Wright	1967	Catherine LaCoste
1948	Babe Zaharias	1955	Fay Crocker	1962	Murle Breer	1968	Susie Berning
1949	Louise Suggs	1956	Kathy Cornelius	1963	Mary Mills	1969	Donna Caponi
1950	Babe Zaharias	1957	Betsy Rawls	1964	Mickey Wright	1970	Donna Caponi
1951	Betsy Rawls	1958	Mickey Wright	1965	Carol Mann	1971	JoAnne Carner
1952	Louise Suggs	1959	Mickey Wright				

TENNIS

►THE GRAND SLAM CHAMPIONSHIPS

The four tournaments that constitute the Grand Slam are the Australian, French, Wimbledon (officially known as the All-England Club's Lawn Tennis Championships), and U.S. championships. A challenge round system, in which the defending champion automatically qualified for the following year's final, was used at Wimbledon from 1877-1921 and at the U.S. Championships from 1884-1911. Prior to 1925, the French Open was restricted to members of French clubs, and from 1941-45, it was closed to all foreigners. Wimbledon, the French, and U.S. Championships became open to amateurs and pros in 1968; the Australian championships joined the open era a year later. Five players have achieved the Grand Slam, winning all four championships in the same year: Don Budge (1938), Maureen Connolly (with straight set victories in all four finals in 1953), Rod Laver (1962 and 1969), Margaret Court (1970) and Steffi Graf (1988). Martina Navratilova (1983-84) and Serena Williams (2002-03) have won the four tournaments consecutively, but not in the same calendar year.

Men's Grand Slam Champions, 1920-2008

Year	Australian Champion	French Champion	Wimbledon Champion	U.S. Champion
1920	Pat O'Hara Wood	—	Bill Tilden	Bill Tilden
1921	Rhys H. Gemmell	—	Bill Tilden	Bill Tilden
1922	Pat O'Hara Wood	—	Gerald L. Patterson	Bill Tilden
1923	Pat O'Hara Wood	—	William M. Johnston	Bill Tilden
1924	James Anderson	—	Jean Borotra	Bill Tilden
1925	James Anderson	Rene Lacoste	Rene Lacoste	Bill Tilden
1926	John Hawkes	Henri Cochet	Jean Borotra	Rene Lacoste
1927	Gerald Patterson	Rene Lacoste	Henri Cochet	Rene Lacoste
1928	Jean Borotra	Henri Cochet	Rene Lacoste	Henri Cochet
1929	John C. Gregory	Rene Lacoste	Henri Cochet	Bill Tilden
1930	Gar Moon	Henri Cochet	Bill Tilden	John H. Doeg
1931	Jack Crawford	Jean Borotra	Sidney B. Wood Jr.	H. Ellsworth Vines
1932	Jack Crawford	Henri Cochet	Ellsworth Vines	H. Ellsworth Vines
1933	Jack Crawford	John H. Crawford	Jack Crawford	Fred Perry
1934	Fred J. Perry	Gottfried von Cramm	Fred Perry	Fred Perry
1935	Jack Crawford	Fred J. Perry	Fred Perry	Wilmer L. Allison
1936	Adrian Quist	Gottfried von Cramm	Fred Perry	Fred Perry
1937	Vivian B. McGrath	Henner Henkel	Don Budge	Don Budge
1938[1]	Don Budge	Don Budge	Don Budge	Don Budge
1939	John Bromwich	W. Donald McNeill	Bobby Riggs	Bobby Riggs
1940	Adrian Quist	No competition	Not Held	Donald McNeill
1941	Foreigners excluded	Bernard Destremau	Not Held	Bobby Riggs
1942	Foreigners excluded	Bernard Destremau	Not Held	Frederick Schroeder
1943	Foreigners excluded	Yvon Petra	Not Held	Joseph R. Hunt
1944	Foreigners excluded	Yvon Petra	Not Held	Frank Parker
1945	Foreigners excluded	Yvon Petra	Not Held	Frank Parker
1946	John Bromwich	Marcel Bernard	Yvon Petra	Jack Kramer
1947	Dinny Pails	Joseph Asboth	Jack Kramer	Jack Kramer
1948	Adrian Quist	Frank Parker	Bob Falkenburg	Pancho Gonzales
1949	Frank Sedgman	Frank Parker	Ted Schroeder	Pancho Gonzales
1950	Frank Sedgman	Budge Patty	Budge Patty	Arthur Larsen
1951	Richard Savitt	Jaroslav Drobny	Dick Savitt	Frank Sedgman
1952	Ken McGregor	Jaroslav Drobny	Frank Sedgman	Frank Sedgman
1953	Ken Rosewall	Ken Rosewall	Vic Seixas	Tony Trabert
1954	Mervyn Rose	Tony Trabert	Jaroslav Drobny	E. Victor Seixas Jr.
1955	Ken Rosewall	Tony Trabert	Tony Trabert	Tony Trabert
1956	Lew Hoad	Lew Hoad	Lew Hoad	Ken Rosewall
1957	Ashley Cooper	Sven Davidson	Lew Hoad	Malcolm Anderson
1958	Ashley Cooper	Mervyn Rose	Ashley Cooper	Ashley J. Cooper
1959	Alex Olmedo	Nicola Pietrangeli	Alex Olmedo	Neale Fraser
1960	Rod Laver	Nicola Pietrangeli	Neale Fraser	Neale Fraser
1961	Roy Emerson	Manuel Santana	Rod Laver	Roy Emerson
1962[1]	Rod Laver	Rod Laver	Rod Laver	Rod Laver
1963	Roy Emerson	Roy Emerson	Chuck McKinley	Rafael Osuna
1964	Roy Emerson	Manuel Santana	Roy Emerson	Roy Emerson
1965	Roy Emerson	Fred Stolle	Roy Emerson	Manuel Santana
1966	Roy Emerson	Tony Roche	Manuel Santana	Fred Stolle
1967	Roy Emerson	Roy Emerson	John Newcombe	John Newcombe
1968	Bill Bowrey	Ken Rosewall	Rod Laver	Arthur Ashe
1969[1]	Rod Laver	Rod Laver	Rod Laver	Rod Laver
1970	Arthur Ashe	Jan Kodes	John Newcombe	Ken Rosewall

Year	Australian Champion	French Champion	Wimbledon Champion	U.S. Champion
1971	Ken Rosewall	Jan Kodes	John Newcombe	Stan Smith
1972	Ken Rosewall	Andres Gimeno	Stan Smith	Ilie Nastase
1973	John Newcombe	Ilie Nastase	Jan Kodes	John Newcombe
1974	Jimmy Connors	Bjorn Borg	Jimmy Connors	Jimmy Connors
1975	John Newcombe	Bjorn Borg	Arthur Ashe	Manuel Orantes
1976	Mark Edmondson	Adriano Panatta	Bjorn Borg	Jimmy Connors
1977	Roscoe Tanner[2] Vitas Gerulaitis[2]	Guillermo Vilas	Bjorn Borg	Guillermo Vilas
1978	Guillermo Vilas	Bjorn Borg	Bjorn Borg	Jimmy Connors
1979	Guillermo Vilas	Bjorn Borg	Bjorn Borg	John McEnroe
1980	Brian Teacher	Bjorn Borg	Bjorn Borg	John McEnroe
1981	Johan Kriek	Bjorn Borg	John McEnroe	John McEnroe
1982	Johan Kriek	Mats Wilander	Jimmy Connors	Jimmy Connors
1983	Mats Wilander	Yannick Noah	John McEnroe	Jimmy Connors
1984	Mats Wilander	Ivan Lendl	John McEnroe	John McEnroe
1985	Stefan Edberg	Mats Wilander	Boris Becker	Ivan Lendl
1986	Moved to Jan. 1987	Ivan Lendl	Boris Becker	Ivan Lendl
1987	Stefan Edberg	Ivan Lendl	Pat Cash	Ivan Lendl
1988	Mats Wilander	Mats Wilander	Stefan Edberg	Mats Wilander
1989	Ivan Lendl	Michael Chang	Boris Becker	Boris Becker
1990	Ivan Lendl	Andrés Gomez	Stefan Edberg	Pete Sampras
1991	Boris Becker	Jim Courier	Michael Stich	Stefan Edberg
1992	Jim Courier	Jim Courier	Andre Agassi	Stefan Edberg
1993	Jim Courier	Sergi Bruguera	Pete Sampras	Pete Sampras
1994	Pete Sampras	Sergi Bruguera	Pete Sampras	Andre Agassi
1995	Andre Agassi	Thomas Muster	Pete Sampras	Pete Sampras
1996	Boris Becker	Yevgeny Kafelnikov	Richard Krajicek	Pete Sampras
1997	Pete Sampras	Gustavo Kuerten	Pete Sampras	Patrick Rafter
1998	Petr Korda	Carlos Moya	Pete Sampras	Patrick Rafter
1999	Yevgeny Kafelnikov	Andre Agassi	Pete Sampras	Andre Agassi
2000	Andre Agassi	Gustavo Kuerten	Pete Sampras	Marat Safin
2001	Andre Agassi	Gustavo Kuerten	Goran Ivanisevic	Lleyton Hewitt
2002	Thomas Johansson	Albert Costa	Lleyton Hewitt	Pete Sampras
2003	Andre Agassi	Juan Carlos Ferrero	Roger Federer	Andy Roddick
2004	Roger Federer	Gaston Gaudio	Roger Federer	Roger Federer
2005	Marat Safin	Rafael Nadal	Roger Federer	Roger Federer
2006	Roger Federer	Rafael Nadal	Roger Federer	Roger Federer
2007	Roger Federer	Rafael Nadal	Roger Federer	Roger Federer
2008	Novak Djokovic	Rafael Nadal	Rafael Nadal	Roger Federer

Note: 1. Grand Slam winner. 2. Two tournaments were held in 1977, the first in January, the second in December.

Women's Grand Slam Champions, 1920–2008

Year	Australian Champion	French Champion	Wimbledon Champion	U.S. Champion
1920	Not held	Suzanne Lenglen	Suzanne Lenglen	Molla Bjurstedt Mallory
1921	Not held	Suzanne Lenglen	Suzanne Lenglen	Molla Bjurstedt Mallory
1922	Margaret Molesworth	Suzanne Lenglen	Suzanne Lenglen	Molla Bjurstedt Mallory
1923	Margaret Molesworth	Suzanne Lenglen	Suzanne Lenglen	Helen Wills
1924	Sylvia Lance	Diddie Vlasto	Kathleen McKane	Helen Wills
1925	Daphne Akhurst	Suzanne Lenglen	Suzanne Lenglen	Helen Wills
1926	Daphne Akhurst	Suzanne Lenglen	Kathleen McKane Godfree	Molla Bjurstedt Mallory
1927	Edna Boyd	Kea Bouman	Helen Wills	Helen Wills
1928	Daphne Akhurst	Helen Wills	Helen Wills	Helen Wills
1929	Daphne Akhurst	Helen Wills	Helen Wills	Helen Wills
1930	Daphne Akhurst	Helen Wills Moody	Helen Wills Moody	Betty Nuthall
1931	Coral Buttsworth	Cilly Aussem	Cilly Aussem	Helen Wills Moody
1932	Coral Buttsworth	Helen Wills Moody	Helen Wills Moody	Helen Jacobs
1933	Joan Hartigan	Margaret Scriven	Helen Wills Moody	Helen Jacobs
1934	Joan Hartigan	Margaret Scriven	Dorothy Round	Helen Jacobs
1935	Dorothy Round	Hilde Sperling	Helen Wills Moody	Helen Jacobs
1936	Joan Hartigan	Hilde Sperling	Helen Jacobs	Alice Marble
1937	Nancye Wynne Bolton	Hilde Sperling	Dorothy Round	Anita Lizane
1938	Dorothy Bundy	Simone Mathieu	Helen Wills Moody	Alice Marble
1939	Emily Westacott	Simone Mathieu	Alice Marble	Alice Marble
1940	Nancye Wynne Bolton	Not Held	Not Held	Alice Marble
1941	Not Held	Not Held	Not Held	Sarah Palfrey Cooke
1942	Not Held	Not Held	Not Held	Pauline Betz
1943	Not Held	Not Held	Not Held	Pauline Betz
1944	Not Held	Not Held	Not Held	Pauline Betz Cooke

Year	Australian Champion	French Champion	Wimbledon Champion	U.S. Champion
1945	Not Held	Not Held	Not Held	Sarah Palfrey Cooke
1946	Nancye Wynne Bolton	Margaret Osborne	Pauline Betz	Pauline Betz
1947	Nancye Wynne Bolton	Patricia Todd	Margaret Osborne	Louise Brough
1948	Nancye Wynne Bolton	Nelly Landry	Louise Brough	Margaret Osborne duPont
1949	Doris Hart	Margaret Osborne duPont	Louise Brough	Margaret Osborne duPont
1950	Louise Brough	Doris Hart	Louise Brough	Margaret Osborne duPont
1951	Nancye Wynne Bolton	Shirley Fry	Doris Hart	Maureen Connolly
1952	Thelma Long	Doris Hart	Maureen Connolly	Maureen Connolly
1953[1]	Maureen Connolly	Maureen Connolly	Maureen Connolly	Maureen Connolly
1954	Thelma Long	Maureen Connolly	Maureen Connolly	Doris Hart
1955	Beryl Penrose	Angela Mortimer	Louise Brough	Doris Hart
1956	Mary Carter	Althea Gibson	Shirley Fry	Shirley Fry
1957	Shirley Fry	Shirley Bloomer	Althea Gibson	Althea Gibson
1958	Angela Mortimer	Zsuzsi Kormoczy	Althea Gibson	Althea Gibson
1959	Mary Carter Reitano	Christine Truman	Maria Bueno	Maria Bueno
1960	Margaret Smith	Darlene Hard	Maria Bueno	Darlene Hard
1961	Margaret Smith	Ann Haydon	Angela Mortimer	Darlene Hard
1962	Margaret Smith	Margaret Smith	Karen Hantze Susman	Margaret Smith
1963	Margaret Smith	Lesley Turner	Margaret Smith	Maria Bueno
1964	Margaret Smith	Margaret Smith	Maria Bueno	Maria Bueno
1965	Margaret Smith	Lesley Turner	Margaret Smith	Margaret Smith
1966	Margaret Smith	Ann Jones	Billie Jean King	Maria Bueno
1967	Nancy Richey	Francoise Durr	Billie Jean King	Billie Jean King
1968	Billie Jean King	Nancy Richey	Billie Jean King	Virginia Wade
1969	Margaret Smith Court	Margaret Smith Court	Ann Jones	Margaret Smith Court
1970[1]	Margaret Smith Court	Margaret Smith Court	Margaret Smith Court	Margaret Smith Court
1971	Margaret Smith Court	Evonne Goolagong	Evonne Goolagong	Billie Jean King
1972	Virginia Wade	Billie Jean King	Billie Jean King	Billie Jean King
1973	Margaret Smith Court	Margaret Smith Court	Billie Jean King	Margaret Smith Court
1974	Evonne Goolagong	Chris Evert	Chris Evert	Billie Jean King
1975	Evonne Goolagong	Chris Evert	Billie Jean King	Chris Evert
1976	Evonne Goolagong Cawley	Sue Barker	Chris Evert	Chris Evert
1977	Kerry Melville Reid[2] Evonne Goolagong Cawley[2]	Mima Jasuovec	Virginia Wade	Chris Evert
1978	Chris O'Neil	Virginia Ruzici	Martina Navratilova	Chris Evert
1979	Barbara Jordan	Chris Evert Lloyd	Martina Navratilova	Tracy Austin
1980	Hana Mandlikova	Chris Evert Lloyd	Evonne Goolagong Cawley	Chris Evert Lloyd
1981	Martina Navratilova	Hana Mandlikova	Chris Evert Lloyd	Tracy Austin
1982	Chris Evert Lloyd	Martina Navratilova	Martina Navratilova	Chris Evert Lloyd
1983	Martina Navratilova	Chris Evert Lloyd	Martina Navratilova	Martina Navratilova
1984	Chris Evert Lloyd	Martina Navratilova	Martina Navratilova	Martina Navratilova
1985	Martina Navratilova	Chris Evert Lloyd	Martina Navratilova	Hana Mandlikova
1986	Moved to Jan. 1987	Chris Evert Lloyd	Martina Navratilova	Martina Navratilova
1987	Hana Mandlikova	Steffi Graf	Martina Navratilova	Martina Navratilova
1988[1]	Steffi Graf	Steffi Graf	Steffi Graf	Steffi Graf
1989	Steffi Graf	Arantxa Sanchez	Steffi Graf	Steffi Graf
1990	Steffi Graf	Monica Seles	Martina Navratilova	Gabriela Sabatini
1991	Monica Seles	Monica Seles	Steffi Graf	Monica Seles
1992	Monica Seles	Monica Seles	Steffi Graf	Monica Seles
1993	Monica Seles	Steffi Graf	Steffi Graf	Steffi Graf
1994	Steffi Graf	Arantxa Sánchez Vicario	Conchita Martinez	Arantxa Sánchez Vicario
1995	Mary Pierce	Steffi Graf	Steffi Graf	Steffi Graf
1996	Monica Seles	Steffi Graf	Steffi Graf	Steffi Graf
1997	Martina Hingis	Iva Majoli	Martina Hingis	Martina Hingis
1998	Martina Hingis	Arantxa Sánchez Vicario	Jana Novotna	Lindsay Davenport
1999	Martina Hingis	Steffi Graf	Lindsay Davenport	Serena Williams
2000	Lindsay Davenport	Mary Pierce	Venus Williams	Venus Williams
2001	Jennifer Capriati	Jennifer Capriati	Venus Williams	Venus Williams
2002	Jennifer Capriati	Serena Williams	Serena Williams	Serena Williams
2003	Serena Williams	Justine Henin-Hardenne	Serena Williams	Justine Henin-Hardenne
2004	Justine Henin-Hardenne	Anastasia Myskina	Maria Sharapova	Svetlana Kuznetsova
2005	Serena Williams	Justine Henin-Hardenne	Venus Williams	Kim Clijsters
2006	Amelie Mauresmo	Justine Henin-Hardenne	Amelie Mauresmo	Maria Sharapova
2007	Serena Williams	Justine Henin	Venus Williams	Justine Henin
2008	Maria Sharapova	Ana Ivanovic	Venus Williams	Serena Williams

1. Grand Slam winner. 2. Two tournaments were held in 1977, the first in January, the second in December.

THOROUGHBRED RACING

Thoroughbred Horse of the Year (Eclipse Award)

Year	Horse	Year	Horse	Year	Horse	Year	Horse
1936	Granville	1954	Native Dancer	1972	Secretariat	1990	Criminal Type
1937	War Admiral	1955	Nashua	1973	Secretariat	1991	Black Tie Affair
1938	Seabiscuit	1956	Swaps	1974	Forego	1992	A.P. Indy
1939	Challedon	1957	Bold Ruler	1975	Forego	1993	Kotashaan
1940	Challedon	1958	Round Table	1976	Forego	1994	Holy Bull
1941	Whirlaway	1959	Sword Dancer	1977	Seattle Slew	1995	Cigar
1942	Whirlaway	1960	Kelso	1978	Affirmed	1996	Cigar
1943	Count Fleet	1961	Kelso	1979	Affirmed	1997	Favorite Trick
1944	Twilight Tear	1962	Kelso	1980	Spectacular Bid	1998	Skip Away
1945	Busher	1963	Kelso	1981	John Henry	1999	Charismatic
1946	Assault	1964	Kelso	1982	Conquistador Cielo	2000	Tiznow
1947	Armed	1965	Moccasin	1983	All Along	2001	Point Given
1948	Citation	1966	Buckpasser	1984	John Henry	2002	Azeri
1949	Capot	1967	Damascus	1985	Spend a Buck	2003	Mineshaft
1950	Hill Prince	1968	Dr. Fager	1986	Lady's Secret	2004	Ghostzapper
1951	Counterpoint	1969	Arts and Letters	1987	Ferdinand	2005	Saint Liam
1952	Native Dancer	1970	Personality	1988	Alysheba	2006	Invasor
1953	Tom Fool	1971	Ack Ack	1989	Sunday Silence	2007	Curlin

Source: The Jockey Club

The Triple Crown Winners

Only 11 horses have won the Kentucky Derby, the Preakness, and the Belmont Stakes in the same year.

Year	Horse	Year	Horse	Year	Horse	Year	Horse
1919	Sir Barton	1937	War Admiral	1946	Assault	1977	Seattle Slew
1930	Gallant Fox	1941	Whirlaway	1948	Citation	1978	Affirmed
1935	Omaha	1943	Count Fleet	1973	Secretariat		

The Breeders' Cup

Thoroughbred racing's richest, most glamorous, and most exciting day of the year attracts the finest horses in the world for record purses as high as $5 million. The site changes from year to year.

Year	Winner	Jockey	Time	Year	Winner	Jockey	Time
Juvenile ($1.5 million, 1 1/16 miles)				**Juvenile Fillies ($2 million, 1 1/16 miles)**			
1984[1]	Chief's Crown	D. MacBeth	1:36.1	1984[1]	Outstandingly	W. Guerra	1:37.4
1985[1]	Tasso	L. Pincay Jr.	1:36.1	1985[1]	Twilight Ridge	J. Velasquez	1:35.4
1986	Capote	L. Pincay Jr.	1:43.4	1986	Brave Raj	P. Valenzuela	1:43.1
1987[1]	Success Express	J. Santos	1:35.1	1987[1]	Epitome	P. Day	1:36.2
1988[1]	Is It True	L. Pincay Jr.	1:36.3	1988	Open Mind	A. Cordero Jr.	1:46.3
1989	Rhythm	C. Perret	1:43.3	1989	Go For Wand	R. Romero	1:44.1
1990	Fly So Free	J. Santos	1:43.2	1990	Meadow Star	J. Santos	1:44.0
1991	Arazi	P. Valenzuela	1:44.78	1991	Pleasant Stage	E. Delahoussaye	1:46.48
1992	Gilded Time	C. McCarron	1:43.43	1992	Eliza	P. Valenzuela	1:42.93
1993	Brocco	G. Stevens	1:42.99	1993	Phone Chatter	L. Pincay Jr.	1:43.08
1994	Timber Country	P. Day	1:44.55	1994	Flanders	P. Day	1:45.28
1995	Unbridled's Song	M. Smith	1:41.60	1995	My Flag	J. Bailey	1:42.55
1996	Boston Harbor	J. Bailey	1:43.40	1996	Storm Song	C. Perret	1:43.60
1997	Favorite Trick	P. Day	1:41.47	1997	Countess Diana	S. Sellers	1:42.11
1998	Answer Lively	J. Bailey	1:44.00	1998	Silverbulletday	G. Stevens	1:43.68
1999	Anees	G. Stevens	1:42.29	1999	Cash Run	J. Bailey	1:36.32
2000	Macho Uno	J. Bailey	1:42.05	2000	Caressing	J. Velasquez	1:42.77
2001	Johannesburg	M. Kinane	1:42.27	2001	Tempera	D. Flores	1:41.49
2002	Vindication	M. Smith	1:49.61	2002	Storm Flag Flying	J. Velasquez	1:49.60
2003	Action This Day	D. Flores	1:43.62	2003	Halfbridled	J. Krone	1:42.75
2004	Wilko	F. Dettorri	1:42.09	2004	Sweet Catomine	C. Nakatani	1:41.65
2005	Folklore	E. Prado	1:43.85	2005	Stevie Wonderboy	G. Gomez	1:41.64
2006	Street Sense	C. Borel	1:42.59	2006	Dreaming of Anna	R. Douglas	1:43.81
2007	War Pass	C. Velasquez	1:42.76	2007	Indian Blessing	G. Gomez	1:44.73

Sprint ($2 million, 6 furlongs)

Year	Winner	Jockey	Time
1984	Eillo	C. Perret	1:10.1
1985	Precisionist	C. McCarron	1:08.2
1986	Smile	J. Vasquez	1:08.2
1987	Very Subtle	P. Valenzuela	1:08.4
1988	Gulch	A. Cordero Jr.	1:10.2
1989	Dancing Spree	A. Cordero Jr.	1:09.0
1990	Safely Kept	C. Perret	1:09.3
1991	Sheik Albadou	P. Eddery	1:09.36
1992	30 Slews	E. Delahoussaye	1:08.21
1993	Cardmania	E. Delahoussaye	1:08.76
1994	Cherokee Run	M. Smith	1:09.54
1995	Desert Stormer	K. Desormeaux	1:09.14
1996	Lit de Justice	C. Nakatani	1:08.60
1997	Elmhurst	C. Nakatani	1:08.01
1998	Reraise	C. Nakatani	1:09.07
1999	Artax	J. Chavez	1:07.89
2000	Kona Gold	A. Solis	1:07.77
2001	Squirtle Squirt	J. Bailey	1:08.41
2002	Orientate	J. Bailey	1:08.89
2003	Cajun Beat	C. Velasquez	1:07.95
2004	Speightstown	J. Velasquez	1:09.11
2005	Silver Train	E. Prado	1:08.86
2006	Thor's Echo	C. Nakatani	1:08.80
2007	Midnight Lute	G. Gomez	1:09.18

Mile ($2 million, 1 mile, turf)

Year	Winner	Jockey	Time
1984	Royal Heroine	F. Toro	1:32.3
1985	Cozzene	W. Guerra	1:35.0
1986	Last Tycoon	Y. Saint-Martin	1:35.1
1987	Miesque	F. Head	1:32.4
1988	Miesque	F. Head	1:38.3
1989	Steinlen	J. Santos	1:37.1
1990	Royal Academy	L. Piggott	1:35.1
1991	Opening Verse	P. Valenzuela	1:37.59
1992	Lure	M. Smith	1:32.90
1993	Lure	M. Smith	1:33.58
1994	Barathea	L. Dettori	1:34.50
1995	Ridgewood Pearl	J. Murtagh	1:43.65
1996	Da Hoss	G. Stevens	1:35.80
1997	Spinning World	C. Asmussen	1:32.77
1998	Da Hoss	J. Velazquez	1:35.27
1999	Silic	C. Nakatani	1:34.26
2000	War Chant	G. Stevens	1:34.67
2001	Val Royal	J. Valdivia Jr.	1:32.05
2002	Domedriver	T. Thulliez	1:36.92
2003	Six Perfections	J. Bailey	1:33.86
2004	Singletary	D. Flores	1:36.90
2005	Artie Schiller	G. Gomez	1:36.10
2006	Miesque's Approval	E. Castro	1:34.75
2007	Kip Deville	C. Velasquez	1:39.78

Distaff ($2 million, 1⅛ miles)

Year	Winner	Jockey	Time
1984[2]	Princess Rooney	E. Delahoussaye	2:02.2
1985[2]	Life's Magic	A. Cordero Jr.	2:02.0
1986[2]	Lady's Secret	P. Day	2:01.1
1987[2]	Sacahuista	R. Romero	2:02.4
1988	Personal Ensign	R. Romero	1:52.0
1989	Bayakoa	L. Pincay Jr.	1:47.2
1990	Bayakoa	L. Pincay Jr.	1:49.1
1991	Dance Smartly	P. Day	1:50.95
1992	Paseana	C. McCarron	1:48.17
1993	Hollywood Wildcat	E. Delahoussaye	1:48.35
1994	One Dreamer	G. Stevens	1:50.70
1995	Inside Information	M. Smith	1:46.15
1996	Jewel Princess	C. Nakatani	1:48.40
1997	Ajina	M. Smith	1:47.20
1998	Escena	G. Stevens	1:49.89
1999	Beautiful Pleasure	J. Chavez	1:47.56
2000	Spain	V. Espinoza	1:47.66
2001	Unbridled Elaine	P. Day	1:49.21
2002	Azeri	M. Smith	1:48.64
2003	Adoration	P. Valenzuela	1:49.17
2004	Ashado	J. Velasquez	1:48.26
2005	Pleasant Home	J. Velasquez	1:48.34
2006	Round Pond	E. Prado	1:50.50
2007	Ginger Punch	R. Bejarano	1:50.11

Turf ($3 milion, 1½ miles)

Year	Winner	Jockey	Time
1984	Lashkari	Y. Saint-Martin	2:25.1
1985	Pebbles	P. Eddery	2:27.0
1986	Manila	J. Santos	2:25.2
1987	Theatrical	P. Day	2:24.2
1988	Great Communicator	R. Sibille	2:35.1
1989	Prized	E. Delahoussaye	2:28.0
1990	In the Wings	G. Stevens	2:29.3
1991	Miss Alleged	E. Legrix	2:30.95
1992	Fraise	P. Valenzuela	2:24.08
1993	Kotashaan	K. Desormeaux	2:25.16
1994	Tikkanen	M. Smith	2:26.50
1995	Northern Spur	C. McCarron	2:42.07
1996	Pilsudski	W. Swinburn	2:30.20
1997	Chief Bearhart	J. Santos	2:23.92
1998	Buck's Boy	S. Sellers	2:28.74
1999	Daylami	L. Dettori	2:24.73
2000	Kalanisi	J. Murtagh	2:26.96
2001	Fantastic Light	L. Dettori	2:24.36
2002	High Chaparral	M. Kinane	2:30.14
2003	High Chaparral	M. Kinane	2:24.24
	Johar	A Solis	dead heat
2004	Better Talk Now	R. Dominguez	2:29.70
2005	Shirocco	C. Soumillon	2:29.30
2006	Red Rocks	F. Dettori	2:27.32
2007	English Channel	J. Velasquez	2:35.96

Classic ($5 million, 1¼ miles)

Year	Winner	Jockey	Time
1984	Wild Again	P. Day	2:03.2
1985	Proud Truth	J. Velasquez	2:00.4
1986	Skywalker	L. Pincay Jr.	2:00.2
1987	Ferdinand	B. Shoemaker	2:01.2
1988	Alysheba	C. McCarron	2:04.4
1989	Sunday Silence	C. McCarron	2:00.1
1990	Unbridled	P. Day	2:02.1
1991	Black Tie Affair	J. Bailey	2:02.95
1992	A.P. Indy	E. Delahoussaye	2:00.20
1993	Arcangues	J. Bailey	2:00.83
1994	Concern	P. Day	2:02.41
1995	Cigar	J. Bailey	1:59.58
1996	Alphabet Soup	C. McCarron	2:01.00
1997	Skip Away	M. Smith	1:59.16
1998	Awesome Again	P. Day	2:02.16
1999	Cat Thief	P. Day	1:59.52
2000	Tiznow	C. McCarron	2:00.75
2001	Tiznow	C. McCarron	2:00.62
2002	Volponi	J. Santos	2:01.39
2003	Pleasantly Perfect	A. Solis	1:59.88
2004	Ghostzapper	J. Castellano	1:59.02
2005	Saint Liam	J. Bailey	2:01.49
2006	Invasor	F. Jara	2:02.18
2007	Curlin	R. Albarado	2:00.59

Fillies and Mares Turf ($2 million, 1¼ miles)

Year	Winner	Jockey	Time
1999	Soaring Softly	J. Bailey	2:13.89
2000	Perfect Sting	J. Bailey	2:13.07
2001	Banks Hill	O. Peslier	2:00.36
2002	Starine	J. Velasquez	2:03.57
2003	Islington	K. Fallon	1:59.13
2004	Ouija Board	K. Fallon	2:18.25
2005	Intercontinental	R. Bejarano	2:02.34
2006	Ouija Board	L. Dettori	2:14.55
2007	Lahudood	A. Garcia	2:22.75

BREEDERS' CUP LOCATIONS

Year	Location	Year	Location
1984	Hollywood	1997	Hollywood
1985	Aqueduct	1998	Churchill Downs
1986	Santa Anita	1999	Gulfstream
1987	Hollywood	2000	Churchill Downs
1988	Churchill Downs	2001	Belmont Park
1989	Gulfstream	2002	Arlington Park
1990	Belmont Park	2003	Santa Anita
1991	Churchill Downs	2004	Lone Star Park
1992	Gulfstream	2005	Belmont Park
1993	Santa Anita	2006	Churchill Downs
1994	Churchill Downs	2007	Monmouth Park
1995	Belmont Park	2008	Santa Anita
1996	Woodbine		

Note: Before 1991, decimals refer to fifths of a second. 1. One mile. 2. 1¼ miles

Kentucky Derby, 1875–2008

"The Run for the Roses," is the first leg of racing's Triple Crown for three-year-olds. It is always on the first Saturday in May. The distance was 1½ miles until 1896, 1¼ miles thereafter. **Site: Churchill Downs**, Louisville

Year	Horse	Jockey	Time	Year	Horse	Jockey	Time
1875	Aristides	O. Lewis	2:37¾	1942	Shut Out	W. D. Write	2:04.2
1876	Vagrant	R. Swim	2:38¼	1943	**Count Fleet**	J. Longden	2:04.0
1877	Baden-Baden	W. Walker	2:38.0	1944	Pensive	C. McCreary	2:04.1
1878	Day Star	J. Carter	2:37¼	1945	Hoop Jr.	E. Arcaro	2:07.0
1879	Lord Murphy	C. Shauer	2:37.0	1946	**Assault**	W. Mehrtens	2:06.3
1880	Fonso	G. Lewis	2:37½	1947	Jet Pilot	E. Guerin	2:06.3
1881	Hindoo	J. McLaughlin	2:40.0	1948	**Citation**	E. Arcaro	2:05.2
1882	Apollo	B. Hurd	2:40¼	1949	Ponder	S. Brooks	2:04.1
1883	Leonatus	W. Donohue	2:43.0	1950	Middleground	W. Boland	2:01.3
1884	Buchanan	I. Murphy	2:40¼	1951	Count Turf	C. McCreary	2:02.3
1885	Joe Cotton	E. Henderson	2:37¼	1952	Hill Gail	E. Arcaro	2:01.3
1886	Ben Ali	P. Duffy	2:36½	1953	Dark Star	H. Moreno	2:02.0
1887	Montrose	I. Lewis	2:39¼	1954	Determine	R. York	2:03.0
1888	MacBeth II	G. Covington	2:38¼	1955	Swaps	W. Shoemaker	2:01.4
1889	Spokane	T. Kiley	2:34½	1956	Needles	D. Erb	2:03.2
1890	Riley	I. Murphy	2:45.0	1957	Iron Liege	W. Hartack	2:02.1
1891	Kingman	I. Murphy	2:52¼	1958	Tim Tam	I. Valenzuela	2:05.0
1892	Azra	A. Clayton	2:41½	1959	Tommy Lee	W. Shoemaker	2:02.1
1893	Lookout	E. Kunze	2:39¼	1960	Venetian Way	W. Hartack	2:02.2
1894	Chant	F. Goodale	2:41.0	1961	Carry Back	J. Sellers	2:04.0
1895	Halma	J. Perkins	2:37½	1962	Decidedly	W. Hartack	2:00.2
1896	Ben Brush	W. Simms	2:07¾	1963	Chateaugay	B. Baeza	2:01.4
1897	Typhoon II	F. Garner	2:12½	1964	Northern Dancer	W. Hartack	2:00.0
1898	Plaudit	W. Simms	2:09.0	1965	Lucky Debonair	W. Shoemaker	2:01.1
1899	Manuel	F. Taral	2:12.0	1966	Kauai King	D. Brumfield	2:02.0
1900	Lieut.Gibson	J. Boland	2:06¼	1967	Proud Clarion	R. Ussery	2:00.3
1900	Lieut. Gibson	J. Boland	2:06¼	1968	Forward Pass[1]	R. Ussery	2:02.1
1901	His Eminence	J. Winkfield	2:07¾	1969	Majestic Prince	W. Hartack	2:01.4
1902	Alan-a-Dale	J. Winkfield	2:08¼	1970	Dust Commander	M. Manganello	2:03.2
1903	Judge Himes	H. Booker	2:09.0	1971	Canonero II	G. Avila	2:03.1
1904	Elwood	F. Prior	2:08½	1972	Riva Ridge	R. Turcotte	2:01.4
1905	Agile	J. Martin	2:10¾	1973	**Secretariat**[2]	R. Turcotte	1:59.2
1906	Sir Huon	R. Troxler	2:08.4	1974	Cannonade	A. Cordero	2:04.0
1907	Pink Star	A. Minder	2:12.3	1975	Foolish Pleasure	J. Vasquez	2:02.0
1908	Stone Street	A. Pickens	2:15.1	1976	Bold Forbes	A. Cordero	2:01.3
1909	Wintergreen	V. Powers	2:08.1	1977	**Seattle Slew**	J. Cruguet	2:02.1
1910	Donau	F. Herbert	2:06.2	1978	**Affirmed**	S. Cauthen	2:01.1
1911	Meridan	G. Archibald	2:05.0	1979	Spectacular Bid	R. Franklin	2:02.2
1912	Worth	C. H. Shilling	2:09.2	1980	Genuine Risk	J. Vasquez	2:02.0
1913	Donerail	R. Goose	2:04.4	1981	Pleasant Colony	J. Velasquez	2:02.0
1914	Old Rosebud	J. McCabe	2:03.2	1982	Gato Del Sol	E. Delahoussaye	2:02.2
1915	Regret	J. Notter	2:05.2	1983	Sunny's Halo	E. Delahoussaye	2:02.1
1916	George Smith	J. Loftus	2:04.3	1984	Swale	L. Pincay	2:02.2
1917	Omar Khayyam	C. Borel	2:04.0	1985	Spend A Buck	A. Cordero	2:00.1
1918	Exterminator	W. Knapp	2:10.4	1986	Ferdinand	W. Shoemaker	2:02.4
1919	**Sir Barton**	J. Loftus	2:09.4	1987	Alysheba	C. McCarron	2:03.2
1920	Paul Jones	T. Rice	2:09.0	1988	Winning Colors	G. Stevens	2:02.2
1921	Behave Yourself	C. Thompson	2:04.1	1989	Sunday Silence	P. Valenzuela	2:05.0
1922	Morvich	A. Johnson	2:04.3	1990	Unbridled	C. Perret	2:02.0
1923	Zev	E. Sande	2:05.2	1991	Strike the Gold	C. Antley	2:03.0
1924	Black Gold	J. D. Mooney	2:05.1	1992	Lil E. Tee	P.Day	2:03.0
1925	Flying Ebony	E. Sande	2:07.3	1993	Sea Hero	J. Bailey	2:02.42
1926	Bubbling Over	A. Johnson	2:03.4	1994	Go for Gin	C. McCarron	2:03.72
1927	Whiskery	L. McAtee	2:06.0	1995	Thunder Gulch	G. Stevens	2:01.27
1928	Reigh Count	C. Lang	2:10.2	1996	Grindstone	J. Bailey	2:01.60
1929	Clyde Van Dusen	L. McAtee	2:10.4	1997	Silver Charm	G. Stevens	2:02.44
1930	**Gallant Fox**	E. Sande	2:07.3	1998	Real Quiet	K. Desormeaux	2:02.38
1931	Twenty Grand	C. Kurtsinger	2:01.4	1999	Charismatic	C. Antley	2:03.29
1932	Burgoo King	E. James	2:05.1	2000	Fusaichi Pegasus	K. Desormeaux	2:01.12
1933	Brokers Tip	D. Meade	2:06.4	2001	Monarchos	J. Chavez	1:59.97
1934	Cavalcade	M. Garner	2:04.0	2002	War Emblem	V. Espinoza	2:01.13
1935	**Omaha**	W. Saunders	2:05.0	2003	Funny Cide	J. Santos	2:01.19
1936	Bold Venture	I. Hanford	2:03.3	2004	Smarty Jones	S. Elliott	2:04.06
1937	**War Admiral**	C. Kurtsinger	2:03.1	2005	Giacomo	M. Smith	2:02.75
1938	Lawrin	E. Arcaro	2:04.4	2006	Barbaro	E. Prado	2:01.36
1939	Johnston	J. Stout	2:03.2	2007	Street Sense	C. Borel	2:02.17
1940	Gallahadion	C. Bierman	2:05.0	2008	Big Brown	K.Desormeaux	2:01.82
1941	**Whirlaway**	E. Arcaro	2:01.2				

Note: Names in bold indicate Triple Crown winners. Before 1993, decimals refer to fifths of a second. 1. In 1968, Dancer's Image finished first, but was later disqualified from the purse money, and Forward Pass was declared winner. 2. Record. **Source:** *Daily Racing Form.*

Preakness Stakes Winners 1873–2008

The Preakness was first run in 1873. The distance varied from 1 mile 70 yards to 1½ miles until 1925, when it was standardized at 1³⁄₁₆ miles. The race was not held 1891-93 **Site: Pimlico Racetrack,** Baltimore, Maryland.

Year	Horse	Jockey	Time	Year	Horse	Jockey	Time
1873	Survivor	G. Barbee	2:43.0	1942	Alsab	B. James	1:57.0
1874	Culpepper	Donohue	2:56½	1943	**Count Fleet**	J. Longden	1:57.2
1875	Tom Ochiltree	L. Hughes	2:43½	1944	Pensive	C. McCreary	1:59.1
1876	Shirley	Barbee	2:44¾	1945	Polynesian	W. D. Wright	1:58.4
1877	Cloverbrook	Holloway	2:45½	1946	**Assault**	W. Mehrtens	2:01.2
1878	Duke of Magenta	Holloway	2:41¾	1947	Faultless	D. Dodson	1:59.0
1879	Harold	Hughes	2:40½	1948	**Citation**	E. Arcaro	2:02.2
1880	Grenada	L. Hughes	2:40½	1949	Capot	T. Atkinson	1:56.0
1881	Saunterer	Costello	2:40½	1950	Hill Prince	E. Arcaro	1:59.1
1882	Vanguard	Costello	2:44½	1951	Bold	E. Arcaro	1:56.2
1883	Jacobus	Barbee	2:42½	1952	Blue Man	C. McCreary	1:57.2
1884	Knight of Ellerslie	Fisher	2:39½	1953	Native Dancer	E. Guerin	1:57.4
1885	Tecumseh	M. McLaughlin	2:49.0	1954	Hasty Road	J. Adams	1:57.2
1886	The Bard	Fisher	2:45.0	1955	Nashua	E. Arcaro	1:54.3
1887	Dunboyne	W. Donohue	2:39½	1956	Fabius	W. Hartack	1:58.2
1888	Refund	Littlefield	2:49.0	1957	Bold Ruler	E. Arcaro	1:56.1
1889	Buddhist	Anderson	2:17½	1958	Tim Tam	I. Valenzuela	1:57.1
1890	Montague	W. Martin	2:36¾	1959	Royal Orbit	W. Harmatz	1:57.0
1894	Assignee	F. Taral	1:49¼	1960	Bally Ache	R. Ussery	1:57.3
1895	Belmar	F. Taral	1:50½	1961	Carry Back	J. Sellers	1:57.3
1896	Margrave	H. Griffin	1:51.0	1962	Greek Money	J. L. Rotz	1:56.1
1897	Paul Kauver	Thorpe	1:51¼	1963	Candy Spots	W. Shoemaker	1:56.1
1898	Sly Fox	W. Simms	1:49¾	1964	Northern Dancer	W. Hartack	1:56.4
1899	Half Time	R. Clawson	1:47.0	1965	Tom Rolfe	R. Turncotte	1:56.1
1900	Hindus	H. Spencer	1:48.2	1966	Kauai King	D. Brumfield	1:55.2
1901	The Parader	F. Landry	1:47.1	1967	Damascus	W. Shoemaker	1:55.1
1902	Old England	L. Jackson	1:45.4	1968	Forward Pass	I. Valenzuela	1:56.4
1903	Flocarline	W. Gannon	1:44.4	1969	Majestic Prince	W. Hartack	1:55.3
1904	Bryn Mawr	E. Hildebrand	1:44.1	1970	Personality	E. Belmonte	1:56.1
1905	Cairngorm	W. Davis	1:45.4	1971	Canonero II	G. Avila	1:54.0
1906	Whimsical	W. Miller	1:45.0	1972	Bee Bee Bee	E. Nelson	1:55.3
1907	Don Enrique	G. Mountain	1:45.2	1973	**Secretariat**	R. Turcotte	1:54.2
1908	Royal Tourist	E. Dugan	1:46.2	1974	Little Current	M. Rivera	1:54.3
1909	Effendi	W. Doyle	1:39.4	1975	Master Derby	D. McHargue	1:56.2
1910	Layminister	R. Estep	1:40.3	1976	Elocutionist	J. Lively	1:55.0
1911	Watervale	E. Dugan	1:51.0	1977	**Seattle Slew**	J. Cruguet	1:54.2
1912	Colonel Holloway	C. Turner	1:56.3	1978	**Affirmed**	S. Cauthen	1:54.2
1913	Buskin	J. Butwell	1:53.2	1979	Spectacular Bid	R. Franklin	1:54.1
1914	Holiday	A. Schuttinger	1:53.4	1980	Codex	A. Cordero	1:54.1
1915	Rhine Maiden	D. Hoffman	1:58.0	1981	Pleasant Colony	J. Velasquez	1:54.3
1916	Damrosch	L. McAtee	1:54.4	1982	Aloma's Ruler	J. Kaenel	1:55.2
1917	Kalitan	E. Haynes	1:54.2	1983	Deputed Testamony	D. Miller	1:55.2
1918	Jack Hare Jr.	C. Peak	1:53.2	1984	Gate Dancer	A. Cordero	1:53.3
	War Cloud	J. Loftus	1:53.3	1985	Tank's Prospect	P. Day	1:53.2
1919	**Sir Barton**	J. Loftus	1:53.0	1986	Snow Chief	A. Solls	1:54.4
1920	Man o'War	C. Kummer	1:51.3	1987	Alysheba	C. McCarron	1:55.4
1921	Broomspun	F. Coltiletti	1:54.1	1988	Risen Star	E. Delahoussaye	1:56.1
1922	Pillory	L. Morris	1:51.3	1989	Sunday Silence	P. Valenzuela	1:53.4
1923	Vigil	B. Marinelli	1:53.3	1990	Summer Squall	P. Day	1:53.3
1924	Nellie Morse	J. Merimee	1:57.1	1991	Hansel	J. Bailey	1:54.0
1925	Coventry	C. Kummer	1:59.0	1992	Pine Bluff	C. McCarron	1:55.3
1926	Display	J. Maiben	1:59.4	1993	Prairie Bayou	M. Smith	1:56.3
1927	Bostonian	A. Abel	2:01.3	1994	Tabasco Cat	P. Day	1:56.2
1928	Victorian	R. Workman	2:00.1	1995	Timber Country	P. Day	1:54.2
1929	Dr. Freeland	L. Schaefer	2:01.3	1996	Louis Quatorze	P. Day	1:52.2
1930	**Gallant Fox**	E. Sande	2:00.3	1997	Silver Charm	G. Stevens	1:54.4
1931	Mate	G. Ellis	1:59.0	1998	Real Quiet	K. Desormeaux	1:54.75
1932	Burgoo King	E. James	1:59.4	1999	Charismatic	C. Antley	1:55.32
1933	Head Play	C. Kurtsinger	2:02.0	2000	Red Bullet	J. Bailey	1:56.04
1934	High Quest	R. Jones	1:58.1	2001	Point Given	G. Stevens	1:56.51
1935	**Omaha**	W. Saunders	1:58.2	2002	War Emblem	V. Espinoza	1:56.36
1936	Bold Venture	G. Woolf	1:59.0	2003	Funny Cide	J. Santos	1:55.61
1937	**War Admiral**	C. Kurtsinger	1:58.2	2004	Smarty Jones	S. Elliott	1:55.59
1938	Dauber	M. Peters	1:59.4	2005	Afleet Alex	J. Rose	1:55.04
1939	Challedon	G. Seabo	1:59.4	2006	Bernardini	J. Castellano	1:54.65
1940	Bimelech	F. A. Smith	1:58.3	2007	Curlin	R. Albarado	1:53.46
1941	**Whirlaway**	E. Arcaro	1:58.4	2008	Big Brown	K. Desormeaux	1:54.86

Note: Names in **bold** indicate Triple Crown winners. Before 1998, decimals refer to fifths of a second. **Source:** *Daily Racing Form.*

Belmont Stakes Winners 1880–2008

The Belmont Stakes was first run in 1867. The distance of the race varied from 1 1/18 miles to 1 5/8 miles until 1926, when it was standardized at 1 1/2 miles. **Site: Belmont Park,** New York. (The race was held at Jerome Park prior to 1890, at Morris Park from 1890 to 1904, at Aqueduct from 1963 to 1967.)

Year	Horse	Jockey	Time	Year	Horse	Jockey	Time
1880	Grenada	L. Hughes	2:47.0	1945	Pavot	E. Arcaro	2:30.1
1881	Saunterer	T. Costello	2:47.0	1946	**Assault**	W. Mehrtens	2:30.4
1882	Forester	J. McLaughlin	2:43.0	1947	Phalanx	R. Donoso	2:29.2
1883	George Kinney	J. McLaughlin	2:42.2	1948	**Citation**	E. Arcaro	2:28.1
1884	Panique	J. McLaughlin	2:42.0	1949	Capot	T. Atkinson	2:30.1
1885	Tyrant	P. Duffy	2:43.0	1950	Middleground	W. Boland	2:28.3
1886	Inspector B.	J. McLaughlin	2:41.0	1951	Counterpoint	D. Gorman	2:29.0
1887	Hanover	J. McLaughlin	2:43.2	1952	One Count	E. Arcaro	2:30.1
1888	Sir Dixon	J. McLaughlin	2:40.2	1953	Native Dancer	E. Guerin	2:28.3
1889	Eric	W. Hayward	2:47.0	1954	High Gun	E. Guerin	2:30.4
1890	Burlington	S. Barnes	2:07.6	1955	Nashua	E. Arcaro	2:29.0
1891	Foxford	E. Garrison	2:08.6	1956	Needles	D. Erb	2:29.4
1892	Patron	W. Hayward	2:17.0	1957	Gallant Man	W. Shoemaker	2:26.3
1893	Comanche	W. Simms	1:53.2	1958	Cavan	P. Anderson	2:30.1
1894	Henry of Navarre	W. Simms	1:56.2	1959	Sword Dancer	W. Shoemaker	2:28.2
1895	Belmar	F. Taral	2:11.2	1960	Celtic Ash	W. Hartack	2:29.3
1896	Hastings	H. Griffin	2:24.2	1961	Sherluck	B. Baeza	2:29.1
1897	Scottish Chieftain	J. Scherrer	2:32.2	1962	Jaipur	W. Shoemaker	2:28.4
1898	Bowling Brook	F. Littlefield	2:32.0	1963	Chateaugay	B. Baeza	2:30.1
1899	Jean Bereaud	R.R. Clawson	2:23.0	1964	Quadrangle	M. Ycaza	2:28.2
1900	Ildrim	N. Turner	2:21½	1965	Hail To All	J. Sellers	2:28.2
1901	Commando	H. Spencer	2:21.0	1966	Amberoid	W. Boland	2:29.3
1902	Masterman	J. Bullman	2:22½	1967	Damascus	W. Shoemaker	2:28.4
1903	Africander	J. Bullman	2:23.1	1968	Stage Door Johnny	H. Gustines	2:27.1
1904	Delhi	G. Odom	2:06.3	1969	Arts and Letters	B. Baeza	2:28.4
1905	Tanya	E. Hildebrand	2:08.0	1970	High Echelon	J. L. Rotz	2:34.0
1906	Burgomaster	L. Lyne	2:20.0	1971	Pass Catcher	W. Blum	2:30.2
1907	Peter Pan	G. Mountain	No Time	1972	Riva Ridge	R. Turcotte	2:28.0
1908	Colin	J. Notter	No Time	1973	**Secretariat**	R. Turcotte	2:24.0
1909	Joe Madden	E. Dugan	2:21.3	1974	Little Current	M. Rivera	2:29.1
1910	Sweep	J. Butwell	2:22.0	1975	Avatar	W. Shoemaker	2:28.1
1911–12	Not run			1976	Bold Forbes	A. Cordero	2:29.0
1913	Prince Eugene	R. Troxler	2:18.0	1977	**Seattle Slew**	Jean Cruguet	2:29.3
1914	Luke McLuke	M. Buxton	2:20.0	1978	**Affirmed**	S. Cauthen	2:26.4
1915	The Finn	G. Byrne	2:18.2	1979	Coastal	R. Hernandez	2:28.3
1916	Friar Rock	E. Haynes	2:22.0	1980	Temperance Hill	E. Maple	2:29.4
1917	Hourless	J. Butwell	2:17.4	1981	Summing	G. Martens	2:29.0
1918	Johren	F. Robinson	2:20.2	1982	Conquistador Cielo	L. Pincay	2:28.1
1919	**Sir Barton**	J. Loftus	2:17.2	1983	Caveat	L. Pincay	2:27.4
1920	Man o'War	C. Kummer	2:14.1	1984	Swale	L. Pincay	2:27.1
1921	Grey Lag	E. Sande	2:16.4	1985	Creme Fraiche	E. Maple	2:27.0
1922	Pillory	C. H. Miller	2:18.4	1986	Danzig Connection	C. McCarron	2:29.4
1923	Zev	E. Sande	2:19.0	1987	Bet Twice	C. Perret	2:28.1
1924	Mad Play	E. Sande	2:18.4	1988	Risen Star	E. Delahoussaye	2:26.1
1925	American Flag	A. Johnson	2:16.4	1989	Easy Goer	P. Day	2:26.0
1926	Crusader	A. Johnson	2:32.1	1990	Go and Go	M. Kinane	2:27.1
1927	Chance Shot	E. Sande	2:32.2	1991	Hansel	J. Bailey	2:28.0
1928	Vito	C. Kummer	2:33.1	1992	A.P. Indy	E. Delahoussaye	2:26.0
1929	Blue Larkspur	M. Garner	2:32.4	1993	Colonial Affair	J. Krone	2:29.4
1930	**Gallant Fox**	E. Sande	2:31.1	1994	Tabasco Cat	P. Day	2:26.4
1931	Twenty Grand	C. Kurtsinger	2:29.3	1995	Thunder Gulch	G. Stevens	2:32.0
1932	Faireno	T. Malley	2:32.4	1996	Editor's Note	R. Douglas	2:28.4
1933	Hurryoff	M. Garner	2:32.3	1997	Touch Gold	C. McCarron	2:28.4
1934	Peace Chance	W. D. Wright	2:29.5	1998	Victory Gallop	G. Stevens	2:29.16
1935	**Omaha**	W. Saunders	2:30.3	1999	Lemon Drop Kid	J. Santos	2:27.88
1936	Granville	J. Stout	2:30.0	2000	Commendable	P. Day	2:31.19
1937	**War Admiral**	C. Kurtsinger	2:28.3	2001	Point Given	G. Stevens	2:26.56
1938	Pasteurized	J. Stout	2:29.2	2002	Sarava	E. Prado	2:29.71
1939	Johnstown	J. Stout	2:29.2	2003	Empire Maker	J. Bailey	2:28.26
1940	Bimelech	F. A. Smith	2:29.3	2004	Birdstone	E. Prado	2:27.50
1941	**Whirlaway**	E. Arcaro	2:31.0	2005	Afleet Alex	J. Rose	2:28.75
1942	Shut Out	E. Arcaro	2:29.1	2006	Jazil	F. Jara	2:27.86
1943	**Count Fleet**	J. Longden	2:28.1	2007	Rags to Riches	J.R. Velazquez	2:28.74
1944	Bounding Home	G. L. Smith	2:32.1	2008	Da' Tara	A. Garcia	2:29.65

Note: Names in **bold** indicate Triple Crown winners. Before 1998, decimals refer to fifths of a second. **Source:** *Daily Racing Form.*

FOOTBALL

National Football League
280 Park Avenue
New York, NY 10017
(212) 450-2000

www.nfl.com
Commissioner: Roger Goodell
Founded 1920.
Number of Teams: 32

2007 NFL Regular Season Final Standings

AMERICAN FOOTBALL CONFERENCE

AFC East	W-L	AFC North	W-L	AFC South	W-L	AFC West	W-L
New England*	16-0	Pittsburgh*	10-6				
Buffalo	7-9	Cleveland	10-6				
NY Jets	4-12	Cincinnati	7-9				
Miami	1-15	Baltimore	5-11				
AFC South	W-L	AFC West	W-L				
Indianapolis*	13-3	San Diego*	11-5				
Jacksonville+	11-5	Denver	7-9				
Tennessee+	10-6	Kansas City	4-12				
Houston	8-8	Oakland	4-12				

NATIONAL FOOTBALL CONFERENCE

NFC East	W-L	NFC North	W-L
Dallas*	13-3	Green Bay*	13-3
NY Giants+	10-6	Minnesota	8-8
Washington+	9-7	Detroit	7-9
Philadelphia	8-8	Chicago	7-9
NFC South	**W-L**	**NFC West**	**W-L**
Tampa Bay*	9-7	Seattle*	10-6
Carolina	7-9	Arizona	8-8
New Orleans	7-9	San Francisco	5-11
Atlanta	4-12	St. Louis	3-13

Note: *Division Winner +Wild Card

2006 NFL Post-Season Playoff Results

AFC Wild Card Playoff
Jacksonville 31, Pittsburgh 29
San Diego 17, Tennessee 6
AFC Divisional Playoff
New England 31, Jacksonville 20
San Diego 28, Indianapolis 24
AFC Championship Game
New England 21, San Diego 12

NFC Wild Card Playoff
Seattle 35, Washington 14
NY Giants 24, Tampa Bay 14
NFC Divisional Playoff
Green Bay 42, Seattle 20
NY Giants 21, Dallas 17
NFC Championship Game
NY Giants 23, Green Bay 20 (OT)

Super Bowl XLII at University of Phoenix Stadium, February 3, 2008
NY Giants 17, New England 14

NFL First Round Draft Choices, 2008

Team	Selection, Position	School	Team	Selection, Position	School
1. Miami	Jake Long, OT	Michigan	12. Denver	Ryan Clady, OT	Boise State
2. St. Louis	Chris Long, DE	Virginia	13. Carolina	Jonathan Stewart, RB	Oregon
3. Atlanta	Matt Ryan, QB	Boston Coll.	14. Chicago	Chris Williams, OT	Vanderbilt
4. Oakland	Darren McFadden, RB	Arkansas	15. Kansas City[4]	Branden Albert, OG	Virginia
5. Kansas City	Glenn Dorsey, DT	LSU	16. Arizona	Dominique Rogers-Cromartie, CB	Tenn. State
6. NY Jets	Vernon Gholston, DE	Ohio State			
7. New Orleans[1]	Sedrick Ellis, DT	USC	17. Detroit[5]	Gosder Cherilus, OT	BostonColl.
8. Jacksonville[2]	Derrick Harvey, DE	Florida	18. Baltimore[6]	Joe Flacco, QB	Delaware
9. Cincinnati	Keith Rivers, LB	USC	19. Carolina[7]	Jeff Otah, OT	Pittsburgh
10. New England[3]	Jerod Mayo, LB	Tennessee	20. Tampa Bay	Aqip Talib, CB	Kansas
11. Buffalo	Leodis McKelvin, CB	Troy			

Notes: 1. From San Francisco through New England **2.** From Baltimore **3.** From New Orleans **4.** From Detroit **5.** From Minnesota through Kansas City **6.** From Houston **7.** From Philadelphia **Source:** National Football League

NFL Leaders, 2007

AFC Rushing

Player, Team	Yds	Att	Avg	TD	Long
1. LaDainian Tomlinson, SD	1474	315	4.7	15	49
2. Willie Parker, PIT	1316	321	4.1	2	32
3. Jamal Lewis, CLE	1304	298	4.4	9	66
4. Willis McGahee, BAL	1207	294	4.1	7	46
5. Fred Taylor, JAC	1202	223	5.4	5	80
6. Thomas Jones, NYJ	1119	310	3.6	1	36
7. Marshawn Lynch, BUF	1115	280	4.0	7	56
8. LenDale White, TEN	1110	303	3.7	7	28
9. Joseph Addai, IND	1072	261	4.1	12	23
10. Justin Fargas, OAK	1009	222	4.5	4	48

NFC Rushing

Player, Team	Yds	Att	Avg	TD	Long
1. Adrian Peterson, MIN	1341	238	5.6	12	73
2. Brian Westbrook, PHI	1333	278	4.8	7	36
3. Clinton Portis, WAS	1262	325	3.9	11	32
4. Edgerrin James, ARI	1222	324	3.8	7	27
5. Frank Gore, SF	1102	260	4.2	5	43
6. Brandon Jacobs, NYJ	1009	202	5.0	4	43
7. Steven Jackson, STL	1002	237	4.2	5	54
8. Marion Barber, DAL	975	204	4.8	10	54
9. Ryan Grant, GB	956	188	5.1	8	66
10. Earnest Graham, TB	898	222	4.0	10	28

AFC Receiving

Player, Team	Rec	Yds	Avg	TD	Long
1. Reggie Wayne, IND	104	1510	14.5	10	64
2. Randy Moss, NE	98	1493	15.2	23	65
3. Chad Johnson, CIN	93	1440	15.5	8	70
4. Brandon Marshall, DEN	102	1325	13.0	7	68
5. Braylon Edwards, CLE	80	1289	16.1	16	78
6. Wes Welker, NE	112	1175	10.5	8	42
7. Tony Gonzalez, KC	99	1172	11.8	5	31
8. T.J. Houshmandzadeh, CIN	112	1143	10.2	12	42
9. Jerricho Cotchery, NYJ	82	1130	13.8	2	50
10. Kellen Winslow, CLE	82	1106	13.5	5	49

NFC Receiving

Player, Team	Rec	Yds	Avg	TD	Long
1. Larry Fitzgerald, ARI	100	1409	14.1	10	48
2. Terrell Owens, DAL	81	1355	16.7	15	52
3. Roddy White, ATL	83	1202	14.5	6	69
M. Colston, NO	98	1202	12.3	11	45
5. Torry Holt, STL	93	1189	12.8	7	40
6. Bobby Engram, SEA	94	1147	12.2	6	49
7. Jason Witten, DAL	96	1145	11.9	7	53
8. Kevin Curtis, PHI	77	1110	14.4	6	75
9. Donald Driver, GB	82	1048	12.8	2	47
10. Plaxico Burress, NYG	70	1025	14.6	12	60

AFC PASSER RATING

Player, Team	Yds	Att	Cmp	TDs	Ints	Long	Rating
1. Tom Brady, NE	4806	578	398	50	8	69	117.2
2. Ben Roethlisberger, PIT	3154	404	264	32	11	83	104.1
3. David Garrard, JAC	2509	404	264	18	3	59	102.2
4. Peyton Manning, IND	4040	515	337	31	14	73	98.0
5. Jay Cutler, DEN	3497	467	297	20	14	68	88.1
6. Matt Schaub, HOU	2241	189	192	9	9	77	87.2
7. Carson Palmer, CIN	4131	575	373	26	20	70	86.7
8. Chad Pennington, NYJ	1765	260	179	10	9	57	86.1
9. Sage Rosenfels, HOU	1684	240	154	15	12	53	84.8
10. Derek Anderson, CLE	3787	527	298	29	19	78	82.5

NFC PASSER RATING

Player, Team	Yds	Att	Cmp	TDs	Ints	Long	Rating
1. Tony Romo, DAL	4211	520	335	36	19	59	97.4
2. Brett Favre, GB	4155	535	356	28	15	82	95.7
3. Jeff Garcia, TB	2440	327	209	13	4	69	94.6
4. Matt Hasselbeck, SEA	3966	562	352	28	12	65	91.4
5. Donovan McNabb, PHI	3324	473	291	19	7	75	89.9
6. Kurt Warner, ARI	3417	451	281	27	17	62	89.8
7. Drew Brees, NO	4423	652	440	28	18	58	89.4
8. Jon Kitna, DET	4068	561	355	18	20	91	80.9
9. Jason Campbell, WAS	2700	417	250	12	11	54	77.6
10. Joey Harrington, ATL	2215	348	215	7	8	69	77.2

Source: National Football League. www.nfl.com

NFL Number One Draft Picks, 1936–2008

Year	Player	Team	Pos.	College
1936	Jay Berwanger	Philadelphia Eagles	RB	Chicago
1937	Sam Francis	Philadelphia Eagles	RB	Nebraska
1938	Corbett Davis	Cleveland Rams	RB	Indiana
1939	Charles Aldrich	Chicago Cardinals	OL	Texas Christian

ar	Player	Team	Pos.	College
940	George Cafego	Chicago Cardinals	QB	Tennessee
941	Tom Harmon	Chicago Bears	RB	Michigan
942	Bill Dudley	Pittsburgh Steelers	RB	Virginia
943	Frank Sinkwich	Detroit Lions	RB	Georgia
944	Angelo Bertelli	Boston Yanks	QB	Notre Dame
945	Charley Trippi	Chicago Cardinals	RB	Georgia
946	Frank Dancewicz	Boston Yanks	QB	Notre Dame
947	Bob Fenimore	Chicago Bears	RB	Oklahoma A&M
1948	Harry Gilmer	Washington Redskins	QB	Alabama
949	Chuck Bednarik	Philadelphia Eagles	OL	Pennsylvania
1950	Leon Hart	Detroit Lions	E	Notre Dame
1951	Kyle Rote	New York Giants	E/K	Southern Methodist
1952	Bill Wade	Los Angeles Rams	QB	Vanderbilt
1953	Harry Babcock	San Francisco 49ers	E	Georgia
1954	Bobby Garrett	Cleveland Browns	QB	Stanford
1955	George Shaw	Baltimore Colts	QB	Oregon
1956	Gary Glick	Pittsburgh Steelers	QB	Colorado State
1957	Paul Hornung	Green Bay Packers	RB	Notre Dame
1958	King Hill	St. Louis Cardinals	QB	Rice
1959	Randy Duncan	Green Bay Packers	QB	Iowa
1960	Billy Cannon	Los Angeles Rams	RB	Louisiana State
1961	Tommy Mason	Minnesota Vikings	RB	Tulane
1962	Ernie Davis	Washington Redskins	RB	Syracuse
1963	Terry Baker	Los Angeles Rams	QB	Oregon State
1964	Dave Parks	San Francisco 49ers	E	Texas Tech.
1965	Tucker Frederickson	New York Giants	RB	Auburn
1966	Tommy Nobis	Atlanta Falcons	LB	Texas
1967	Bubba Smith	Baltimore Colts	DL	Michigan State
1968	Ron Yary	Minnesota Vikings	OL	U.S.C.
1969	O.J. Simpson	Buffalo Bills	RB	U.S.C.
1970	Terry Bradshaw	Pittsburgh Steelers	QB	Louisiana Tech.
1971	Jim Plunkett	Boston Patriots	QB	Stanford
1972	Walt Patulski	Buffalo Bills	DL	Notre Dame
1973	John Matuszak	Houston Oilers	DL	Tampa
1974	Ed Jones	Dallas Cowboys	DL	Tampa
1975	Steve Bartkowski	Atlanta Falcons	QB	California
1976	Lee Roy Selmon	Tampa Bay Buccaneers	DL	Oklahoma
1977	Ricky Bell	Tampa Bay Buccaneers	RB	U.S.C.
1978	Earl Campbell	Houston Oilers	RB	Texas
1979	Tom Cousineau	Buffalo Bills	LB	Ohio State
1980	Billy Sims	Detroit Lions	RB	Oklahoma
1981	George Rogers	New Orleans Saints	RB	South Carolina
1982	Kenneth Sims	New England Patriots	DL	Texas
1983	John Elway	Baltimore Colts[1]	QB	Stanford
1984	Irving Fryar	New England Patriots	WR	Nebraska
1985	Bruce Smith	Buffalo Bills	DL	Virginia Tech.
1986	Bo Jackson	Tampa Bay Buccaneers	RB	Auburn
1987	Vinny Testaverde	Tampa Bay Buccaneers	QB	Miami
1988	Aundray Bruce	Atlanta Falcons	LB	Auburn
1989	Troy Aikman	Dallas Cowboys	QB	U.C.L.A.
1990	Jeff George	Indianapolis Colts	QB	Illinois
1991	Russell Maryland	Dallas Cowboys	DT	Miami (Fla.)
1992	Steve Emtman	Indianapolis Colts	DT	Washington
1993	Drew Bledsoe	New England Patriots	QB	Washington State
1994	Dan Wilkinson	Cincinnati Bengals	DT	Ohio State
1995	Ki-Jana Carter	Cincinnati Bengals	RB	Penn State
1996	Keyshawn Johnson	New York Jets	WR	Southern California
1997	Orlando Pace	St. Louis Rams	OT	Ohio State
1998	Peyton Manning	Indianapolis Colts	QB	Tennessee
1999	Tim Couch	Cleveland Browns	QB	Kentucky
2000	Courtney Brown	Cleveland Browns	DL	Penn State
2001	Michael Vick	Atlanta Falcons	QB	Virginia Tech
2002	David Carr	Houston Texans	QB	Fresno State
2003	Carson Palmer	Cincinnati Bengals	QB	U.S.C.
2004	Eli Manning	San Diego Chargers[2]	QB	Mississippi
2005	Alex Smith	San Francisco 49ers	QB	Utah
2006	Mario Williams	Houston Texans	DE	N.C. State
2007	JaMarcus Russell	Oakland Raiders	QB	Louisiana State
2008	Jake Long	Miami Dolphins	OT	Michigan

1. Baltimore traded Elway to Denver. 2. San Diego traded the rights to Manning to the New York Giants for draft picks.

The Sporting News' NFL Rookie of the Year, 1955–2007

Year	Player	Pos.	Team	Year	Player	Pos.	Team
1955	Alan Ameche	FB	Baltimore Colts	1979 NFC:	Ottis Anderson	RB	St. Louis Cardinals
1956	J.C. Caroline	HB	Chicago Bears	AFC:	Jerry Butler	WR	Buffalo Bills
1957	Jim Brown	FB	Cleveland Browns	1980	Billy Sims	RB	Detroit Lions
1958	Bobby Mitchell	HB	Cleveland Browns	1981	George Rogers	RB	New England Patrio
1959	Nick Pietrosante	FB	Detroit Lions	1982	Marcus Allen	RB	Los Angeles Raider
1960	Gail Codgill	E	Detroit Lions	1983	Dan Marino	QB	Miami Dolphins
1961	Mike Ditka	E	Chicago Bears	1984	Louis Lipps	WR	Pittsburgh Steelers
1962	Ronnie Bull	HB	Chicago Bears	1985	Eddie Brown	WR	Cincinnati Bengals
1963	Paul Flatley	WR	Minnesota Vikings	1986	Rueben Mayes	RB	New Orleans Saint
1964	Charley Taylor	HB	Washington Redskins	1987	Robert Awalt	TE	St. Louis Cardinals
1965	Gale Sayers	RB	Chicago Bears	1988	Keith Jackson	TE	Philadelphia Eagles
1966	Tommy Nobis	LB	Atlanta Falcons	1989	Barry Sanders	RB	Detroit Lions
1967	Mel Farr	RB	Detroit Lions	1990	Richmond Webb	OL	Miami Dolphins
1968	Earl McCullouch	WR	Detroit Lions	1991	Mike Croel	LB	Denver Broncos
1969	Calvin Hill	RB	Dallas Cowboys	1992	Santana Dotson	DE	Tampa Bay Buccaneers
1970 NFC:	Bruce Taylor	CB	San Francisco 49ers	1993	Jerome Bettis	RB	Los Angeles Rams
AFC:	Dennis Shaw	QB	Buffalo Bills	1994	Marshall Faulk	RB	Indianapolis Colts
1971 NFC:	John Brockington	RB	Green Bay Packers	1995	Curtis Martin	RB	New England
AFC:	Jim Plunkett	QB	New England Patriots	1996	Eddie George	RB	Houston Oilers
1972 NFC:	Chester Marcol	PK	Green Bay Packers	1997	Warrick Dunn	RB	Tampa Bay Buccaneers
AFC:	Franco Harris	RB	Pittsburgh Steelers	1998	Randy Moss	WR	Minnesota Vikings
1973 NFC:	Chuck Foreman	RB	Minnestoa Vikings	1999	Edgerrin James	RB	Indianapolis Colts
AFC:	Boobie Clark	RB	Cincinnati Bengals	2000	Brian Urlacher	LB	Chicago Bears
1974 NFC:	Wilbur Jackson	RB	San Francisco 49ers	2001	Kendrell Bell	LB	Pittsburgh Steelers
AFC:	Don Woods	RB	San Diego Chargers	2002	Clinton Portis	RB	Denver Broncos
1975 NFC:	Steve Bartkowski	QB	Atlanta Falcons	2003	Anquan Boldin	WR	Arizona Cardinals
AFC:	Robert Brazile	LB	Houston Oilers	2004	Ben Roethlisberger	QB	Pittsburgh Steelers
1976 NFC:	Sammy White	WR	Minnesota Vikings	2005	Shawne Merriman	LB	San Diego Chargers
AFC:	Mike Haynes	CB	New England Patriots	2006	Vince Young	QB	Tennessee Titans
1977 NFC:	Tony Dorsett	RB	Dallas Cowboys	2007 Off:	Adrian Peterson	RB	Minnesota Vikings
AFC:	A.J. Duhe	DT	Miami Dolphins	Def:	Patrick Willis	LB	San Francisco 49ers
1978 NFC:	Al Baker	DE	Detroit Lions				
AFC:	Earl Campbell	RB	Houston Oilers				

Note: From 1970–79, separate players were chosen for each conference. Source: The Sporting News.

NFL Most Valuable Player, 1957–2007

Year	Player,	Pos.	Team	Year	Player,	Pos.	Team
1957	Jim Brown	RB	Cleveland Browns	1983	Joe Theismann	QB	Washington Redskins
1958	Gino Marchetti	DE	Baltimore Colts	1984	Dan Marino	QB	Miami Dolphins
1959	Charley Conerly	QB	New York Giants	1985	Marcus Allen	RB	Los Angeles Raiders
1960	Norm Van Brocklin	QB	Philadelphia Eagles	1986	Lawrence Taylor	LB	New York Giants
	Joe Schmidt	LB	Detroit Lions	1987	John Elway	QB	Denver Broncos
1961	Paul Hornung	RB	Green Bay Packers	1988	Boomer Esiason	QB	Cincinnati Bengals
1962	Jim Taylor	RB	Green Bay Packers	1989	Joe Montana	QB	San Francisco 49ers
1963	Y.A. Tittle	QB	New York Giants	1990	Joe Montana	QB	San Francisco 49ers
1964	Johnny Unitas	QB	Baltimore Colts	1991	Thurman Thomas	RB	Buffalo Bills
1965	Jim Brown	RB	Cleveland Browns	1992	Steve Young	QB	San Francisco 49ers
1966	Bart Starr	QB	Green Bay Packers	1993	Emmitt Smith	RB	Dallas Cowboys
1967	Johnny Unitas	QB	Baltimore Colts	1994	Steve Young	QB	San Francisco 49ers
1968	Earl Morrall	QB	Baltimore Colts	1995	Brett Favre	QB	Green Bay Packers
1969	Roman Gabriel	QB	Los Angeles Rams	1996	Brett Favre	QB	Green Bay Packers
1970	John Brodie	QB	San Francisco 49ers	1997	Brett Favre	QB	Green Bay Packers
1971	Alan Page	DT	Minnesota Vikings		Barry Sanders	RB	Detroit Lions
1972	Larry Brown	RB	Washington Redskins	1998	Terrell Davis	RB	Denver Broncos
1973	O.J. Simpson	RB	Buffalo Bills	1999	Kurt Warner	QB	St. Louis Rams
1974	Ken Stabler	QB	Oakland Raiders	2000	Marshall Faulk	RB	St. Louis Rams
1975	Fran Tarkenton	QB	Minnesota Vikings	2001	Kurt Warner	QB	St. Louis Rams
1976	Bert Jones	RB	Baltimore Colts	2002	Rich Gannon	QB	Oakland Raiders
1977	Walter Payton	RB	Chicago Bears	2003	Peyton Manning	QB	Indianapolis Colts
1978	Terry Bradshaw	QB	Pittsburgh Steelers		Steve McNair	QB	Tennesse Titans
1979	Earl Campbell	RB	Houston Oilers	2004	Peyton Manning	QB	Indianapolis Colts
1980	Brian Sipe	QB	Cleveland Browns	2005	Shaun Alexander	RB	Seattle Seahawks
1981	Ken Anderson	QB	Cincinnati Bengals	2006	LaDainian Tomlinson	RB	San Diego Chargers
1982	Mark Moseley	PK	Washington Redskins	2007	Tom Brady	QB	New England Patriots

Source: National Football League

All-Time Pro Football Records

SCORING (Total Points)

	Years	Points	Touchdowns	PATs	Field Goals
1. MORTEN ANDERSON	25	2,544	0	849	565
2. Gary Anderson	23	2,434	0	798	520
3. George Blanda	26	2,002	9	943	335
4. MATT STOVER	17	1,822	0	517	435
5. JOHN CARNEY	20	1,812	0	537	425
6. JASON ELAM	16	1,786	0	316	490
7. Norm Johnson	18	1,736	0	638	366
8. Nick Lowery	18	1,711	0	562	383
9. Jan Stenerud	19	1,699	0	580	373
10. JASON HANSON	17	1,659	0	504	385

RUSHING

	Years	Rushes	Yards	Avg.	TD
1. Emmitt Smith	15	4,409	18,355	4.2	164
2. Walter Payton	13	3,838	16,726	4.4	110
3. Barry Sanders	10	3,062	15,269	5.0	99
4. Curtis Martin	11	3,518	14,101	4.0	90
5. Jerome Bettis	13	3,479	13,662	3.9	91
6. Eric Dickerson	11	2,996	13,259	4.4	90
7. Tony Dorsett	12	2,936	12,739	4.3	77
8. Jim Brown	9	2,359	12,312	5.2	106
9. Marshall Faulk	12	2,836	12,279	4.3	100
10. Marcus Allen	16	3,022	12,243	4.1	123

RECEPTIONS

	Years	Recep.	Yards	Avg.	TD
1. Jerry Rice	20	1,549	22,895	14.8	197
2. Cris Carter	16	1,101	13,899	12.6	130
3. Tim Brown	17	1,094	14,934	13.7	100
4. MARVIN HARRISON	12	1,042	13,944	13.4	123
5. Andre Reed	16	951	13,198	13.9	87
6. ISAAC BRUCE	15	942	14,109	15.0	84
7. Art Monk	16	940	12,721	13.5	68
8. KEENAN McCARDELL	16	883	11,373	12.9	63
9. TERRELL OWENS	12	882	13,070	14.8	129
10. Jimmy Smith	12	862	12,287	14.3	67

PASSER RATING

(minimum 6 years in NFL)

	Years	Attempts	Completions	Yards	TDs	Interceptions	Rating
1. Steve Young	15	4,149	2,667	33,124	232	107	96.8
2. PEYTON MANNING	10	4,890	3,131	37,586	275	139	94.4
2. KURT WARNER	10	2,508	1,645	20,591	125	83	93.8
4. Joe Montana	15	5,391	3,409	40,551	273	139	92.3
5. MARC BULGER	7	2,106	1,357	16,233	95	59	91.3
6. Daunte Culpepper	9	2,741	1,759	21,091	137	89	90.8
7. CHAD PENNINGTON	8	1,659	1,080	11,973	72	46	89.3
8. TOM BRADY	8	3,064	1,896	21,564	147	78	88.4
9. DREW BREES	7	2,363	1,481	16,766	106	64	87.6
10. TRENT GREEN	14	3,527	2,143	26,963	157	101	87.5

All-Time Passes Completed

1. BRETT FAVRE	5,377
2. Dan Marino	4,967
3. John Elway	4,123
4. Warren Moon	3,988
5. Drew Bledsoe	3,839
6. Vinny Testaverde	3,787
7. Fran Tarkenton	3,686
8. PEYTON MANNING	3,454
9. Joe Montana	3,409
10. Dan Fouts	3,297
11. Dave Krieg	3,105
12. Boomer Esiason	2,969
13. KERRY COLLINS	2,918
14. Troy Aikman	2,898
15. Jim Kelly	2,874

All-Time Yards Passing

1. BRETT FAVRE	61,655
2. Dan Marino	61,361
3. John Elway	51,475
4. Warren Moon	49,325
5. Fran Tarkenton	47,003
6. Vinny Testaverde	46,233
7. Drew Bledsoe	44,611
8. Dan Fouts	43,040
9. PEYTON MANNING	41,531
10. Joe Montana	40,551
11. Johnny Unitas	40,239
12. Dave Krieg	38,147
13. Boomer Esiason	37,920
14. Jim Kelly	35,467
15. Jim Everett	34,837

All-Time Touchdown Passes

1. BRETT FAVRE	442
2. Dan Marino	420
3. Fran Tarkenton	342
4. PEYTON MANNING	306
5. John Elway	300
6. Warren Moon	291
7. Johnny Unitas	290
8. Vinny Testaverde	275
9. Joe Montana	273
10. Dave Krieg	261
11. Sonny Jurgensen	255
12. Dan Fouts	254
13. Drew Bledsoe	251
14. Boomer Esiason	247
15. John Hadl	244

Note: Through end of 2007 season. Players active in 2008 in CAPS.

NFL Champions, 1921–66

Year	Team (record)	Year	Team (record)	Year	Team (record)
1921	Chicago Staleys[1] (10-1-1)	1937	Washington Redskins (8-3-0)	1952	Detroit Lions (9-3-0)
1922	Canton Bulldogs (10-0-2)	1938	New York Giants (8-2-1)	1953	Detroit Lions (10-2-0)
1923	Canton Bulldogs (11-0-1)	1939	Green Bay Packers (9-2-0)	1954	Cleveland Browns (9-3-0)
1924	Cleveland Bulldogs[2] (7-1-1)	1940	Chicago Bears (8-3-0)	1955	Cleveland Browns (9-2-1)
1925	Chicago Cardinals (11-2-1)	1941	Chicago Bears (10-1-1)	1956	New York Giants (8-3-1)
1926	Frankford Yellowjackets (14-1-1)	1942	Washington Redskins (10-1-1)	1957	Detroit Lions (8-4-0)
1927	New York Giants (11-1-1)	1943	Chicago Bears (8-1-1)	1958	Baltimore Colts (9-3-0)
1928	Providence Steam Roller (8-1-2)	1944	Green Bay Packers (8-2-0)	1959	Baltimore Colts (9-3-0)
1929	Green Bay Packers (12-0-1)	1945	Cleveland Rams (9-1-0)	1960	Philadelphia Eagles (10-2-0)
1930	Green Bay Packers (10-3-1)	1946	Chicago Bears (8-2-1)	1961	Green Bay Packers (11-3-0)
1931	Green Bay Packers (12-2-0)	1947	Chicago Cardinals (9-3-0)	1962	Green Bay Packers (13-1-0)
1932	Chicago Bears (7-1-6)	1948	Philadelphia Eagles (9-2-1	1963	Chicago Bears (11-1-2)
1933	Chicago Bears (10-2-1)	1949	Philadelphia Eagles (11-1-0)	1964	Cleveland Browns (10-3-1)
1934	New York Giants (8-5-0)	1950	Cleveland Browns (10-2-0)	1965	Green Bay Packers (10-3-1)
1935	Detroit Lions (7-3-2)	1951	Los Angeles Rams (8-4-0)	1966	Green Bay Packers (12-2-0)
1936	Green Bay Packers (10-1-1)				

1. Later called the Chicago Bears. 2. Franchise moved from Canton.

Super Bowl Results

SUPER BOWL I
Jan. 15, 1967, Memorial Coliseum, Los Angeles
Green Bay Packers 35 Kansas City Chiefs 10
Green Bay's Max McGee was a surprise star, filling in for ailing Boyd Dowler. McGee had caught only four passes all year, but in Super Bowl I he caught seven for 138 yards and two touchdowns. Quarterback Bart Starr was the game's MVP, as he completed 16 of 23 passes for 250 yards and two touchdowns. Green Bay broke open the game with three second-half touchdowns, the first of which was set up by safety Willie Wood's 45-yard interception return.

SUPER BOWL II
Jan. 14, 1968, Orange Bowl, Miami
Green Bay Packers 33 Oakland Raiders 14
Bart Starr again dominated proceedings with 13 completions in 24 attempts, for 202 yards and a touchdown, winning his second straight MVP award. The Pack attack was in control all the way after building a 16–7 halftime lead. Don Chandler kicked four field goals and all-pro cornerback Herb Adderley capped the Green Bay scoring with a 60-yard interception return.

SUPER BOWL III
Jan. 12, 1969, Orange Bowl, Miami
New York Jets 16 Baltimore Colts 7
Quarterback Joe Namath guaranteed victory before the game and then he and the upstart AFL Jets easily dispatched the heavily favored Colts. Namath won MVP honors by completing 17 of 28 passes for 206 yards and directing a steady attack that racked up 337 total yards. Three times in the first half, the Jet defense intercepted Colts quarterback Earl Morrall, who was playing for an injured Johnny Unitas. With the Jets ahead 13–0 in the third quarter, Unitas came off the bench and later orchestrated Baltimore's sole touchdown.

SUPER BOWL IV
Jan. 11, 1970, Tulane Stadium, New Orleans
Kansas City Chiefs 23 Minnesota Vikings 7
MVP quarterback Len Dawson called a nearly flawless game for Kansas City, completing 12 of 17 passes and hitting Otis Taylor on a 46-yard pass for the final Chiefs touchdown. The Kansas City defense limited Minnesota's strong rushing game to 67 yards and had three interceptions and two

fumble recoveries. The second consecutive victory by an AFL team proved that AFL teams could compete with NFL franchises, and assured a smooth merger between the two leagues.

SUPER BOWL V
Jan. 17, 1971, Orange Bowl, Miami
Baltimore Colts 16 Dallas Cowboys 13
Rookie Jim O'Brien's 32-yard field goal in the closing seconds broke a 13–13 tie and gave the Colts their first Super Bowl victory. Dallas led 13–6 at halftime, but two Colt interceptions set up a Baltimore touchdown and O'Brien's crucial kick. Baltimore's first touchdown came when a Johnny Unitas pass caromed off receiver Eddie Hinton's fingertips, bounced off Dallas defensive back Mel Renfro, and finally settled into the grasp of tight end John Mackey, who went 47 yards for the score. Dallas linebacker Chuck Howley was the MVP, the only time the MVP came from the losing team.

SUPER BOWL VI
Jan. 16, 1972, Tulane Stadium, New Orleans
Dallas Cowboys 24 Miami Dolphins 3
The Cowboys rushed for 252 yards and their defense limited the Dolphins to 185 total yards and no touchdowns. Dallas converted Chuck Howley's recovery of Larry Csonka's first fumble of the season into a 3–0 advantage. At halftime, Dallas led 10–3. An eight-play, 71-yard march made it a 17–3 game. Cowboys' quarterback Roger Staubach was voted MVP for his 12 completions in 19 attempts, 119 yards passing and two touchdowns.

SUPER BOWL VII
Jan. 14, 1973, Memorial Coliseum, Los Angeles
Miami Dolphins 14 Washington Redskins 7
In a game that wasn't as close as the score, the Dolphins thoroughly dominated the Redskins to complete the NFL's only undefeated season. Quarterback Bob Griese hit Paul Warfield for 18 yards, then delivered a 28-yard strike to Howard Twilley for the Dolphins' first score. Just before the half, Dolphins linebacker Nick Buoniconti intercepted a Billy Kilmer pass and returned it to the Washington 27, setting up Miami's second touchdown. Safety Jake Scott led the Dolphin defense with two interceptions (one in the end zone killing a Redskin scoring drive) and was the MVP. The Redskins' sole touchdown resulted when Dol-

phin kicker Garo Yepremian tried to turn a botched field goal into a forward pass. Washington's Mike Bass picked the ball out of the air and returned it 49 yards for the score.

SUPER BOWL VIII
Jan. 13, 1974, Rice Stadium, Houston
Miami Dolphins 24   Minnesota Vikings 7
Miami scored on its first two possessions, on 62- and 56-yard marches. The initial 10-play drive was climaxed by a Larry Csonka touchdown bolt through right guard. Four plays later, Miami's Jim Kiick burst one yard through the middle for the second touchdown. By halftime Miami led 17–0. The Dolphins defense held off the Vikings on a crucial fourth-and-one play from the Miami 6-yard-line when middle linebacker Nick Buoniconti jarred the ball loose from Minnesota running back Oscar Reed and Jake Scott recovered for Miami. Csonka rushed 33 times for 145 yards, winning the MVP.

SUPER BOWL IX
Jan, 12, 1975, Tulane Stadium, New Orleans
Pittsburgh Steelers 16   Minnesota 6
Steeler Dwight White tackled Minnesota quarterback Fran Tarkenton in the end zone for a safety to put the Steelers on the board in the second quarter. They took advantage of another break in the second half, when Minnesota's Bill Brown fumbled the kickoff and Marv Kellum recovered for Pittsburgh on the Vikings' 30. From there, Franco Harris carried three straight times for the game's first touchdown. Minnesota blocked a Bobby Walden punt and Terry Brown recovered the ball for a touchdown to cut the lead to 9–6, but the Steelers roared back with a 66-yard march, climaxed by Terry Bradshaw's 4-yard scoring pass to Larry Brown. Pittsburgh's defense controlled the game, permitting Minnesota only 119 yards total offense. Franco Harris rushed 34 times for 158 yards to win MVP honors. .

SUPER BOWL X
Jan. 18, 1976, Orange Bowl, Miami
Pittsburgh Steelers 21   Dallas Cowboys 17
Steeler quarterback Terry Bradshaw hurled a 64-yard touchdown pass to Lynn Swann to win the game, while the Steel Curtain defense stopped the Cowboys' last rally with an end-zone interception in the game's final play. It was a battle of quarterbacks with Bradshaw and Cowboy Roger Staubach each hurling two touchdowns. Swann earned MVP honors with 161 yards on four receptions. The Steelers blasted out in front with a 14-point fourth quarter.

SUPER BOWL XI
Jan. 9, 1977, Rose Bowl, Pasadena,California
Oakland Raiders 32   Minnesota Vikings 14
A record 81 million TV viewers watched the Raiders gain a record-breaking 429 yards, including running back Clarence Davis' 137 yards rushing. Wide receiver Fred Biletnikoff made four key receptions, which earned him the game's MVP trophy. Oakland scored on three successive possessions in the second quarter to build a 16–0 halftime lead. Minnesota's Fran Tarkenton passed for a touchdown in the third to cut the deficit, but two fourth-quarter interceptions clinched the title for the Raiders. One set up Pete Banaszak's second touchdown run, the other resulted in cornerback Willie Brown's 75-yard interception return.

SUPER BOWL XII
Jan. 15, 1978, Louisiana Superdome, New Orleans
Dallas Cowboys 27   Denver Broncos 10
The TV audience climbed to 102 million, as Dallas converted two interceptions into 10 points and a 13–0 halftime lead. Butch Johnson made a spectacular diving catch in the end zone of a Roger

Staubach pass to make it 20–3. Dallas clinched the victory when running back Robert Newhouse threw a 29-yard touchdown pass to Golden Richards. Co-MVP's Harvey Martin and Randy White led the Cowboys' defense, which recovered four fumbles and intercepted four passes.

SUPER BOWL XIII
Jan, 21, 1979, Orange Bowl, Miami
Pittsburgh Steelers 35   Dallas Cowboys 31
MVP Terry Bradshaw hurled four touchdown passes to lead the Steelers to victory, making them the first team to win three Super Bowls. Bradshaw completed 17 of 30 passes for 318 yards. In the fourth quarter, the Steelers broke open the contest with two touchdowns in 19 seconds. Franco Harris rambled 22 yards up the middle to put Pittsburgh in front 28–17. The Steelers got the ball right back when Randy White fumbled the kickoff and Dennis Winston recovered. On first down, Bradshaw hit Lynn Swann with an 18-yard scoring pass to boost the lead to 35–17. The Cowboys came back with a Roger Staubach touchdown pass to Billy Joe DuPree and then recovered an onside kick, which led to another Staubach touchdown pass, this time to Butch Johnson. But Rocky Bleier smothered an onside kick with 17 seconds remaining to seal the victory.

SUPER BOWL XIV
Jan. 20, 1980, Rose Bowl, Pasadena, California
Pittsburgh Steelers 31   Los Angeles Rams 19
It was all Terry Bradshaw again as he completed 14 of 21 passes for 309 records, and set two passing records as the Steelers became the first team to win four Super Bowls. Despite three interceptions by the Rams, Bradshaw brought the Steelers back from behind twice in the second half. On Pittsburgh's first possession of the final period, Bradshaw lofted a 73-yard scoring pass to John Stallworth to put the Steelers in front to stay, 24–19. Franco Harris scored on a one-yard run later to seal the verdict. Bradshaw was the MVP for the second straight Super Bowl.

SUPER BOWL XV
Jan. 25, 1981, Louisiana Superdome, New Orleans
Oakland Raiders 27   Philadelphia Eagles 10
Jim Plunkett threw three touchdown passes, including an 80-yarder to Kenny King, to give Oakland a decisive 14-0 advantage nine seconds before halftime. Oakland linebacker Rod Martin intercepted three passes as the Raiders completely stifled Eagle quarterback Ron Jaworski's offense. Jaworski managed an 8-yard touchdown pass in the fourth quarter, but the issue had been decided by Plunkett, who completed 13 of the 21 pass attempts for 261 yards and was named MVP.

SUPER BOWL XVI
Jan. 24, 1982, Pontiac Silverdome, Pontiac, Mich. .
San Francisco 49ers 26   Cincinnati Bengals 21
The 49ers led 20-0 at halftime, but barely hung on for the win. Ray Wersching kicked four field goals for San Francisco and quarterback Joe Montana engineered two touchdown drives, passing for one and scoring the other himself on a one-yard dive. The Bengals rebounded in the second half as quarterback Ken Anderson ran in a touchdown and passed for another. With 16 seconds remaining, the Bengals scored again, on a 3-yard pass to Dan Ross, but couldn't get the ball back a final time. Ross set a Super Bowl record with 11 receptions for 104 yards. Montana, the MVP, completed 14 of 22 passes for 157 yards.

SUPER BOWL XVII
Jan. 30, 1983, Rose Bowl, Pasadena, California

Washington Redskins 27 Miami Dolphins 17
Washington fullback John Riggins carried the ball for 166 yards on 38 carries to lead Washington to their first NFL title since 1942. Riggins, the MVP, and quarterback Joe Theismann, who passed 23 times for 15 completions, 143 yards, and two touchdowns paced the Redskins to 400 total yards of offense. Riggin's 43-yard touchdown run on fourth-and-one was the gamebreaker.

SUPER BOWL XVIII
Jan. 22, 1984, Tampa Stadium, Tampa, Florida
Los Angeles Raiders 38 Washington Redskins 9
This hopelessly lopsided victory set records. Raider reserve linebacker Jack Squirek intercepted a Joe Theismann pass at the Redskins five-yard line and ran the ball in for a touchdown with seven seconds left in the first half. Raiders' Marcus Allen rushed for 191 yards on 20 carries, including two touchdowns, one on a 74-yard run. Allen was voted game MVP.

SUPER BOWL XIX
Jan. 20, 1985, Stanford Stadium, Stanford, Calif.
San Francisco 49ers 38 Miami Dolphins 16
The Dolphins led 10-7 at the end of the first quarter, but 49er running back Roger Craig came back with three touchdowns. Joe Montana dominated the game with an MVP performance: 24 of 35 passes for 331 yards and three touchdowns. He also rushed five times for 59 yards and a touchdown. Craig had 58 yards on 15 carries and caught seven passes for 77 yards. Wendell Tyler rushed 13 times for 65 yards, as San Francisco's running game racked up 211 yards..

SUPER BOWL XX
Jan. 26, 1986, Louisiana Superdome, New Orleans
Chicago Bears 46 New England Patriots 10
The Patriots took a quick 3-0 lead on Tony Franklin's 36-yard field goal with 1:19 elapsed in the first period. But the Bears rebounded by mauling the Pats. Chicago tied the record for sacks (7), and limited the Pats to 7 yards rushing. Total yardage at intermission told the story: Chicago 236, New England -19. The Bears ran up a fat 23–3 lead in the first half. In the second, the Bears marched 96 yards in nine plays, capped by quarterback Jim McMahon's one-yard rush for a touchdown. Bears defensive end Richard Dent won the MVP after contributing 1½ sacks, and leading the ferocious Chicago defense.

SUPER BOWL XXI
Jan. 25, 1987, Rose Bowl, Pasadena, California
New York Giants 39 Denver Broncos 20
The Broncos held a 10–9 lead at halftime, backed by the passing of John Elway, who capped a 58 yard scoring drive on six plays with a four yard touchdown run. But in the second half, the Giants' defense took over, sacking Elway in his end zone for a safety. The Broncos had a first and goal, but failed to score on three plays and a field goal attempt. After that the Giants' offense rebounded, scoring 30 points in the second half. Giant quarterback Phil Simms passed for 268 yards and three touchdowns, and was named MVP.

SUPER BOWL XXII
Jan 31, 1988, Jack Murphy Stadium, San Diego
Washington Redskins 42 Denver Broncos 10
The Broncos led early as John Elway hurled a 56-yard touchdown pass to wide receiver Ricky Nattiel on the Broncos' first play from scrimmage. But the Redskins erupted for 35 points on five straight possessions. Redskins' quarterback Doug Williams led the assault, hurling four touchdown passes, including 80- and 50-yarders to wide receiver Rick

Sanders. Washington scored five touchdowns in 18 plays in 5:47 of possession. MVP Williams completed 18 of 29 passes for 340 yards. Rookie running back Timmy Smith ran 22 times for 204 yards.

SUPER BOWL XXIII
Jan. 22, 1989, Joe Robbie Stadium, Miami
San Francisco 49ers 20 Cincinnati Bengals 16
San Francisco became the first NFC team to win three Super Bowls by defeating the Bengals in a rematch of Super Bowl XVI. Even though San Francisco held an advantage in total yards (453 vs. 229), they found themselves trailing when Jim Breech's field goal gave Cincinnati a 16–13 lead with 3:20 left in the game. The 49ers started their winning drive at their own 8-yard line. Over the next 11 plays, they drove 92 yards to the winning score, a 10-yard touchdown pass from Joe Montana to John Taylor with 34 seconds left.

SUPER BOWL XXIII
Jan. 28,1990, Louisiana Superdome, New Orleans
San Francisco 49ers 55 Denver Broncos 10
San Francisco demolished the Broncos and became the first team to repeat as champions since the 1979–80 Steelers. Quarterback Joe Montana orchestrated the 49ers' offense, completing 22 of 29 passes for 297 yards and five touchdowns, en route to winning the MVP. Montana raised his record to 122 straight Super Bowl pass attempts without an interception. His primary receiver was Jerry Rice, who hauled in seven passes for 148 yards and three touchdowns. Running backs Tom Rathman and Roger Craig ran for three more touchdowns. Meanwhile, the 49er defense completely dominated Denver's offense, limiting them to 167 total yards, sacking quarterback John Elway six times and intercepting two passes.

SUPER BOWL XXV
Jan. 27, 1991, Tampa Stadium, Tampa, Florida
New York Giants 20 Buffalo Bills 19
The Giants edged the Bills in a nearly error-free game that was decided only when the Bills' Scott Norwood missed a field goal with eight seconds to play. Backup QB Jeff Hostetler and running back Ottis Anderson led the Giants' ball-control offense, holding the ball for a stunning 40:33. Anderson carried 21 times for 102 yards and was the MVP. After falling behind 12–3, the Giants defense slowed Buffalo's "hurry-up" offense, surrounding Jim Kelly's receivers with extra defensive backs and linebackers. Kelly completed 18 of 30 passes for 205 yards, but couldn't convert crucial third down opportunities.

SUPER BOWL XXVI
Jan. 26, 1992, The Metrodome, Minneapolis
Washington Redskins 37 Buffalo Bills 24
Washington jumped out to a 17-0 lead in the first half and never looked back. MVP quarterback Mark Rypien completed 18 of 33 passes for 292 yards and two touchdowns. Meanwhile, the blitzing Redskin defense intercepted Buffalo quarterback Jim Kelly four times and sacked him five times. In all, Kelly threw a record 58 passes, 30 of which went incomplete. Brad Edwards, Washington's free safety, had two interceptions and broke up five passes; linebacker Wilber Marshall forced two fumbles.

SUPER BOWL XXVII
Jan. 31, 1993, Rose Bowl, Pasadena, California
Dallas Cowboys 52 Buffalo Bills 17
Buffalo lost its third straight Super Bowl and the second consecutive rout. The game's turning point came early in the second quarter, when Buffalo drove inside the Dallas five-yard-line twice

it came away with only three points, and lost quarterback Jim Kelly to injury. Inspired by its defense's two goal line stands, the Cowboys' offense, which had been fairly inept up to this point, came ive for a long scoring drive. The Bills fumbled on eir first play from scrimmage on the ensuing 'ive, and one play later, the Cowboys had scored gain, this time on a strike from Troy Aikman to ichael Irvin, giving Dallas a 28–10 halftime lead. ikman passed for four touchdowns and was amed MVP.

SUPER BOWL XXVIII
Jan. 30, 1994, Georgia Dome, Atlanta
Dallas Cowboys 30   Buffalo Bills 13
uffalo became the first team in U.S. professional ports history to lose four consecutive championship games. The Bills led 13–6 at halftime on hurman Thomas's 37 yards rushing and 54- and 8-yard field goals by Steve Christie. But Thomas umbled on the opening drive of the second half nd Dallas safety James Washington returned it 46 yards for a touchdown. Dallas then drove the length of the field on its next drive, with running back Emmitt Smith grinding out 61 yards. The Cowboys added another touchdown and a field goal to secure the victory. Smith, the league's regular season MVP, was named MVP of the Super Bowl as well.

SUPER BOWL XXIX
Jan. 29, 1995, Joe Robbie Stadium, Miami
San Francisco 49ers 49   San Diego Chargers 26
Favored by 20 points, (the largest margin in Super Bowl history), San Francisco scored early and often to capture a fifth Super Bowl championship. On the third play from scrimmage, Steve Young found Jerry Rice wide open inside the San Diego 10-yard line. Young then won six touchdowns and ran for 49 yards, making him the 49ers' leading rusher as well. Rice and running back Ricky Watters each scored three touchdowns. Young was named MVP for his 24-for-36, 325 yard performance.

SUPER BOWL XXX
Jan. 28, 1996, Sun Devil Stadium, Tempe, Ariz.
Dallas Cowboys 27   Pittsburgh Steelers 17
Dallas scored on its first three possessions, but failed to dominate the game, and led only 13–7 at halftime. In the second half, the Steelers threatened to close the gap, but quarterback Neil O'Donnell stunted the drive by throwing an interception to Cowboy cornerback Larry Brown. Pittsburgh rallied again in the fourth quarter to cut Dallas' lead to 20–17. But O'Donnell threw another interception to Brown, who returned it to the Steeler 6-yard line, setting up the Cowboys' final touchdown. Brown was the obvious MVP choice.

SUPER BOWL XXXI
Jan. 26, 1997, Louisiana Superdome, New Orleans,
Green Bay Packers 35   New England Patriots 21
Packer quarterback Bret Favre hit Andre Rison for a 54-yard touchdown pass on Green Bay's second play from scrimmage, but the Patriots rallied for a 14-10 first quarter lead. The Packers recaptured the lead with a 17-points in the second quarter. In the second half, New England running back Curtis Martin scored to cut the lead to 27-21, but Desmond Howard returned the ensuing kickoff 99 yards for a touchdown. Howard's 154 yards on four kickoff returns and 90 yards on six punt returns earned him MVP honors.

SUPER BOWL XXXII
Jan. 25, 1998, Qualcomm Stadium, San Diego,
Denver Broncos 31   Green Bay Packers 24
The victory was Denver's first in five tries, and the AFC's first in 13 years. With the game tied at 24 late in the fourth quarter, Denver took over at midfield.

A penalty and a pass moved the Broncos closer, and then running back Terrell Davis ran 17 yards to the one-yard-line. On the next play, he punched it in for his third touchdown. With less than two minutes left, the Packers drove into Denver territory but could not convert a 4th and 6. Davis earned MVP honors for his 30 carries, 157 yards, and three touchdowns.

SUPER BOWL XXXIII
Jan. 31, 1999, Pro Player Stadium, Miami
Denver Broncos 34   Atlanta Falcons 19
Denver quarterback John Elway completed 18 of 29 passes for 336 yards and MVP honors, as the Broncos cruised to their second straight Super Bowl victory. Broncos running back Terrell Davis added 102 yards rushing, and cornerback Darrien Gordon had interception returns of 50 and 58 yards, each setting up a Denver touchdown. Despite driving deep into Denver territory several times, Atlanta could not crack the end zone until the fourth quarter, when the outcome was already decided.

SUPER BOWL XXXIV
Jan. 30, 2000, Georgia Dome, Atlanta
St. Louis Rams 23   Tennessee Titans 16
St. Louis dominated the first half, moving at will into Tennessee territory, but came away with only three field goals to show for it. The Rams extended their lead to 16-0 in the third quarter before the Titans put together three long scoring drives that tied the game with 2:12 remaining. On the very next play from scrimmage, quarterback Kurt Warner hit Isaac Bruce for a 73-yard touchdown pass. With time running out, Tennessee quarterback Steve McNair engineered an 87-yard drive, but his last completion to Kevin Dyson left the Titans a yard short of a game-tying touchdown as time expired. Warner was named MVP on the strength of his 414 yards passing.

SUPER BOWL XXXV
Jan. 28, 2001, Raymond James Stadium, Tampa
Baltimore Ravens 34   New York Giants 7
Baltimore's vaunted defense pitched a shutout, as the Giants' only points came on special teams. Jermaine Lewis's 34-yard punt return set up Baltimore's first touchdown in the first quarter, and Duane Starks's interception return gave the Ravens a 17-0 lead late in the third quarter. Ron Dixon returned the ensuing kickoff 97 yards for the Giants to cut the score to 17-7, but Lewis put the game out of reach on the very next play with an 84-yard kickoff return of his own. Middle linebacker Ray Lewis, the heart and soul of the Ravens defense, was the MVP.

SUPER BOWL XXXVI
Feb. 3, 2002, Louisiana Superdome, New Orleans
New England Patriots 20   St. Louis Rams 17
The Patriots, a 14-point underdog to the high-flying St. Louis offense, shocked the football world twice. First, they capitalized on three Ram turnovers to jump out to a 17-3 lead after three quarters. Then, after giving up the tying touchdown with 1:21 left in the game, New England marched 53 yards with no timeouts to set up Adam Vinatieri's game-winning 48-yard field goal. Patriots quarterback Tom Brady completed his Cinderella season by completing five passes in eight attempts in the final drive, and was named MVP.

SUPER BOWL XXXVII
Jan. 26, 2003, Qualcomm Stadium, San Diego
Tampa Bay Buccaneers 48   Oakland Raiders 21
The Buccaneers' defense dominated, intercepting five passes and returning three of them for touch-

downs, and sacking Oakland quarterback Rich Gannon five times. Tampa Bay piled up 34 unanswered points on the strength of Michael Pittman's 124 rushing yards and Joe Jurevicius' 78 receiving yards. The Raiders rallied for two touchdowns in the fourth quarter, but the Bucs dashed any hopes of a comeback by returning two interceptions for touchdowns. Dexter Jackson, who had the first two interceptions, was the MVP.

SUPER BOWL XXXVIII
Feb. 1, 2004, Reliant Stadium, Houston
New England Patriots 32   Carolina Panthers 29
Just as he did two years earlier, Adam Vinatieri kicked a tie-breaking field goal in the final seconds. Defense dominated for much of the game, which remained scoreless until the final 5:29 of the first half. Carolina took a 22-21 lead on an 85-yard pass from Jake Delhomme to Muesin Mohammed, let the Patriots go up 29-22, and then tied the game at 29-29. With 1:08 remaining, New England drove down the field again, setting up Vinatieri's 41-yard kick. Patriot's quarterback Tom Brady, who threw for 354 yards, was the MVP again.

SUPER BOWL XXXIX
Feb. 6, 2005, Alltel Stadium, Jacksonville, Florida
New England Patriots 24   Philadelphia Eagles 21
For the third time in four years the Patriots won the Super Bowl matching the achievement of the Dallas Cowboys in the early 1990's. Quarterback Tom Brady was a standout again completing 22 of 33 passes, 11 of them to the game's MVP Deion Branch. On defense safety Rodney Harrison had two interceptions off Eagles' quarterback Donovan McNabb who otherwise played well, throwing for 357 yards and three touchdowns. A highlight was the play of All-Pro Eagles' wide receiver, Terrell Owens, who broke his leg and tore a ligament only seven weeks before but caught nine passes for 122 yards playing in 62 of 72 offensive snaps.

SUPER BOWL XL
February 5, 2006, Ford Field, Detroit
Pittsburgh Steelers 21 Seattle Seahawks 10
The Steelers relied on big plays to set up or score all three of their touchdowns, including a 75-yard touchdown run by RB Willie Parker to open the second half, followed by an end around pass from Antwaan Randle El to fellow wide receiver Hines Ward in the fourth quarter. The game also serve as a farewell for Steelers RB Jerome Bettis, a Detro native who retired as the fifth-leading rusher NFL history. With the victory, Pittsburgh joined th San Francisco 49ers and the Dallas Cowboys as th only franchises to win five Super Bowls.

SUPER BOWL XLI
February 4, 2007, Dolphin Stadium, Miami
Indianapolis Colts 29, Chicago Bears 17
Led by MVP quarterback Peyton Manning, th Colts' steady offense wore down the Bears to wi the first Super Bowl ever played in the rain. Despit three turnovers, a botched extra point attempt, an a missed chip-shot field goal attempt by Adan Vinatieri, the Colts still managed to take a 16-1 lead by half-time. The Colts intercepted Bear quarterback Rex Grossman twice in the fourth quarter to nail down the victory, Kelvin Hayden returning the first one 56 yards for the game's fina touchdown. Indianapolis's Tony Dungy and Chicago's Lovie Smith were the first African-Americans to coach in a Super Bowl; Dungy became the first African-American to win a Super Bowl.

SUPER BOWL XLII
February 3, 2008 at University of Phoenix Stadium, Phoenix
New York Giants 17, New England Patriots 14
In one of the greatest upsets in sports history Eli Manning led the Giants to a 17-14 win in Super Bowl XLII, marching his team 83 yards on a final scoring drive to stun the heavily favored Patriots—and shatter New England's unbeaten season. The Patriots much-vaunted offense never seemed to find a rhythm, and led by only 7-3 going into the final quarter. New York finally scored a touchdown with 11:05 left to take the lead, but New England responded with their own, going ahead by 14-10 with only 2:42 remaining. The scene was now set for one of the most dramatic Super Bowl plays of all time: with 1:15 left to go, Eli Manning escaped what looked like a certain sack and completed an improbable 32-yard pass to a leaping David Tyree, who managed to pin the ball to his helmet as he fell to the turf. Four plays later Manning hit Plaxico Burress in the end zone for the winning score. Super Bowl XLII was the most-watched NFL championship game of all time with 97.5 million viewers in the US.

Pro Football Hall of Fame Members

Alphabetical listing of the members of the Professional Football Hall of Fame. Listing includes enshrinee's name, year of enshrinement, position, and the teams he played for.

Herb Adderley (1980) CB, Packers, Cowboys.
Troy Aikman (2006) QB, Cowboys.
Lance Alworth (1978) WR, Chargers, Cowboys.
George Allen (2002) Coach, Rams, Redskins.
Marcus Allen (2003) RB, Raiders, Chiefs.
Doug Atkins (1982) DE, Browns, Bears, Saints.
Morris (Red) Badgro (1981) E, Yankees, Giants, Dodgers.
Lem Barney (1992) CB, Lions.
Cliff Battles (1968) RB, QB, Braves, Redskins.
Sammy Baugh (1963) QB, Redskins.
Chuck Bednarik (1967) C, LB, Eagles.
Bert Bell (1963 Charter) Commissioner, NFL. Founder/coach, Eagles, Steelers.
Bobby Bell (1983) LB, DE, Chiefs.
Raymond Berry (1973) E, Colts.
Elvin Bethea (2003) DE, Oilers
Charles W. Bidwill, Sr. (1967) Owner/president, Cardinals.
Fred Biletnikoff (1988) WR, Raiders.

George Blanda (1981) QB, PK, Bears, Colts, Oilers, Raiders.
Mel Blount (1989) CB, Steelers.
Terry Bradshaw (1989) QB, Steelers.
Bob Brown (2004) T, Eagles, Rams, Raiders
Jim Brown (1971) FB, Browns.
Paul E. Brown (1967) Coach, General Manager, Browns, Bengals.
Roosevelt Brown (1975) OT, Giants.
Willie Brown (1984) CB, Broncos, Raiders.
Buck Buchanan (1990) DT, Chiefs.
Nick Buoniconti (2001) LB, Patriots, Dolphins.
Dick Butkus (1979) LB, Bears.
Earl Campbell (1991) RB, Oilers, Saints.
Tony Canadeo (1974) RB, Packers.
Joe Carr (1963) NFL President.
Harry Carson (2006) LB, Giants.
Dave Casper (2002) TE, Raiders, Oilers, Vikings.
Guy Chamberlin (1965) E, Bulldogs, Staleys, Yellowjackets, Cardinals. Coach, Bulldogs, Yellowjackets, Cardinals.

Joe Montana (2000) QB, 49ers, Chiefs.
Warren Moon (2006) QB, Edmonton Eskimos (CFL),Oilers, Vikings, Seahawks, Chiefs.
Lenny Moore (1975) WR, RB, Colts.
Marion Motley (1968) RB, Browns, Steelers.
Mike Munchak (2001) G, Oilers.
Anthony Muñoz (1998) T, Bengals.
George Musso (1982) OT, G, Bears.
Bronko Nagurski (1963) RB, Bears.
Joe Namath (1985) QB, Jets, Rams.
Earle (Greasy) Neale (1969) Coach, Eagles.
Ernie Nevers (1963) RB, Eskimos, Cardinals.
Ozzie Newsome (1999) TE, Browns.
Ray Nitschke (1978) LB, Packers.
Chuck Noll (1993) Coach, Steelers.
Leo Nomellini (1969) DT, 49ers.
Merlin Olsen (1982) DT, Rams.
Jim Otto (1980) C, Raiders.
Steve Owen (1966) T, Cowboys, Giants. Coach, Giants.
Alan Page (1988) DT, Vikings, Bears.
Clarence (Ace) Parker (1972) QB, Dodgers, Yankees.
Jim Parker (1973) OL, Colts.
Walter Payton (1993) RB, Bears.
Joe Perry (1969) RB, 49ers, Colts.
Pete Pihos (1970) E, Eagles.
Fritz Pollard (2005) HB, Pros/Indians, Badgers, Cadamounts, Steam Roller.
Hugh (Shorty) Ray (1966) Supervisor of Officials.
Dan Reeves (1967) Owner, Rams.
Mel Renfro (1996), CB, Cowboys.
John Riggins (1992) RB, Jets, Redskins.
Jim Ringo (1981) C, Packers, Eagles.
Andy Robustelli (1971) DE, Rams, Giants.
Art Rooney (1964) Founder, President, Pirates, Steelers.
Dan Rooney (2000) President, Steelers.
Pete Rozelle (1985) Commissioner, NFL.
Bob St. Clair (1990) OT, 49ers.
Barry Sanders (2004) RB, Lions.
Charlie Sanders (2007) TE, Lions.
Gale Sayers (1977) RB, Bears.
Joe Schmidt (1973) LB, Lions. Coach, Lions.
Tex Schramm (1991) GM, Cowboys.
Lee Roy Selmon (1995) DE, Buccaneers.
Billy Shaw (1999) OG, Bills.
Art Shell (1989) OT, Raiders.
Don Shula (1997) Coach, Colts, Dolphins.
Mike Singletary (1998) LB, Bears.
O.J. Simpson (1985) RB, Bills, 49ers.

Jackie Slater (2001) OT, Rams.
Jackie Smith (1994) TE, Cardinals, Cowboys.
John Stallworth (2002) WR, Steelers.
Bart Starr (1977) QB, Packers.
Roger Staubach, (1985) QB, Cowboys.
Ernie Stautner (1969) DT, Steelers.
Jan Stenerud (1991) PK, Chiefs, Packers, Vikings.
Dwight Stephenson (1998) C, Dolphins.
Hank Stram (2003) Coach, Texans, Chiefs, Saints.
Ken Strong (1967) RB, Stapletons, Giants, Yankees.
Joe Stydahar (1967) OT, Bears.
Lynn Swann (2001) WR, Steelers.
Fran Tarkenton (1986) QB, Giants, Vikings.
Charley Taylor (1984) WR, RB, Redskins.
Jim Taylor (1976) RB, Packers, Saints.
Lawrence Taylor (1999) LB, Giants.
Emmitt Thomas (2008) CB, Chiefs.
Thurman Thomas (2007) RB, Bills, Browns.
Jim Thorpe (1963) RB, Bulldogs, Indians, Maroons, Independents, Giants, Bulldogs, Cardinals.
Andre Tippett (2008) LB, Patriots
Y.A. Tittle (1971) QB, Colts 49ers, Giants.
George Trafton (1964) C, Staleys, Bears.
Charley Trippi (1968) RB, QB, Cardinals.
Emlen Tunnell (1967) DB, Giants, Packers.
Clyde (Bulldog) Turner (1966) C, LB, Bears.
Johnny Unitas (1979) QB, Colts, Chargers.
Gene Upshaw (1987) G, Raiders.
Norm Van Brocklin (1971) QB, Rams, Eagles.
Steve Van Buren (1965) RB, Eagles.
Doak Walker (1986) HB, Lions.
Bill Walsh (1993) Coach, 49ers.
Paul Warfield (1983) WR, Browns, Dolphins.
Bob Waterfield(1965) QB, Coach, Rams.
Mike Webster (1997) C, Steelers.
Roger Wehrli (2007) CB, Cardinals.
Arnie Weinmeister, (1984) DT, Yankees, Giants.
Randy White (1994) DT, Cowboys.
Reggie White (2006) DE, Eagles, Packers.
Dave Wilcox (2000) LB, 49ers.
Bill Willis (1977) G, MG, Browns.
Larry Wilson (1978) DB, Cardinals.
Kellen Winslow (1995) TE, Chargers.
Alex Wojciechowicz (1968) C, LB, Lions, Eagles.
Willie Wood (1989) S, Packers.
Rayfield Wright (2006) OT, Cowboys.
Ron Yary (2001) OT, Vikings.
Steve Young (2005) QB, Buccaneers, 49ers.
Jack Youngblood (2001) DE, Rams.
Gary Zimmerman (2008) T, Vikings, Broncos.

BASKETBALL

National Basketball Association

Olympic Tower
645 Fifth Avenue
New York, NY 10022
(212) 826-7000

www.nba.com
Commissioner: David Stern
Founded: 1946
Number of teams: 30

Dr. James Naismith invented basketball in 1891, only after his indoor versions of lacrosse, rugby, and soccer proved too violent for the intended use in a YMCA fitness program. Yet even his "noncontact" amateur sport proved too rough for many YMCAs, which dropped basketball. Teams were forced to rent halls; they charged an admission fee to pay the rent, and split any leftover cash among the players.

The first pro game was played in 1896 in Trenton, N.J., and by 1898, the fledgling National Basketball League (NBL) and several others were organized. The Buffalo Germans were the first powerhouse, winning 792 games against only 86 losses from 1895 to 1925. In 1914, the New York Celtics (later renamed the Original Celtics) were organized, playing a "modern" style of basketball using zone defenses, the fast break, and a pivot man.

Other "ethnic" teams dominated in the 1930's, including the Philadelphia SPHAs (South Philadelphia Hebrew Association) under Eddy Gottlieb, and the black barnstorming New York Rens. The Basketball Association of America was formed in 1946 by hockey arena managers seeking additional tenants. In 1949, it merged with the NBL to form the modern NBA.

The American Basketball Association, an alternative pro league known for its three-point shots and its red, white and blue ball, lasted for nine seasons (1968–76) and featured such future NBA All-Stars as Julius Erving and Artis Gilmore. When the league folded after the 1975–76 season, four of its teams, the Denver Nuggets, Indiana Pacers, New York (now New Jersey) Nets, and San Antonio Spurs were admitted into the NBA.

NBA Final Standings, 2007–08

EASTERN CONFERENCE	W-L	Pct.	Home	Away
Atlantic Division				
Boston (1)	66-16	.805	35-6	31-10
Toronto (6)	41-41	.500	25-16	27-14
Philadelphia (7)	40-42	.488	22-19	18-23
New Jersey	34-48	.415	21-20	13-28
New York	23-59	.280	15-26	8-33
Central Division				
Detroit (2)	59-23	.720	34-7	25-16
Cleveland (4)	45-37	.549	27-14	18-23
Indiana	36-46	.439	21-20	15-26
Chicago	33-49	.402	20-21	13-28
Milwaukee	26-56	.317	19-22	7-34
Southeast Division				
Orlando (3)	52-30	.634	25-16	27-14
Washington (5)	43-39	.524	25-16	18-23
Atlanta (8)	37-45	.451	25-16	12-29
Charlotte	32-50	.390	21-20	11-30
Miami	15-67	.183	9-32	6-35

WESTERN CONFERENCE	W-L	Pct.	Home	Away
Northwest Division				
Utah (4)	54-28	.659	37-4	17-24
Denver (8)	50-32	.610	33-8	17-24
Portland	41-41	.500	28-13	13-28
Minnesota	22-60	.269	15-26	7-34
Seattle	20-62	.244	13-28	7-34
Southwest Division				
New Orleans (2)	56-26	.683	30-11	26-15
San Antonio (3)	56-26	.683	34-7	22-19
Houston (5)	55-27	.671	31-10	24-17
Dallas (7)	51-31	.622	34-7	17-24
Memphis	22-60	.269	14-27	8-33
Pacific Division				
Los Angeles Lakers (1)	57-25	.695	30-11	27-14
Phoenix (6)	55-27	.671	30-11	25-16
Golden State	48-34	.585	27-14	21-20
Sacramento	38-44	.463	26-15	12-29
Los Angeles Clippers	23-59	.280	13-28	10-31

Note: The numbers in parentheses reflect the team's seed for the playoffs. **Source:** NBA.

NBA Playoff Results, 2008

FIRST ROUND

EASTERN CONFERENCE
Boston 4, Atlanta 3
Detroit 4, Philadelphia 2
Orlando 4, Toronto 1
Cleveland 5, Washington 2

WESTERN CONFERENCE
L.A. Lakers 4, Denver 0
New Orleans 4, Dallas 1
San Antonio 4, Phoenix 1
Utah 5, Houston 2

CONFERENCE SEMIFINALS

EASTERN CONFERENCE
Detroit 4, Orlando 1
Boston 4, Cleveland 3

WESTERN CONFERENCE
New Orleans 3, San Antionio 4
Los Angeles 4, Utah 3

CONFERENCE FINALS

EASTERN CONFERENCE
Boston 4, Detroit 2

WESTERN CONFERENCE
Los Angeles 4, San Antonio 1

NBA CHAMPIONSHIP FINALS

Boston Celtics defeat Los Angeles Lakers, 4 games to 2

Game 1: Boston 98, Los Angeles 88
Game 2: Boston 108, Los Angeles 102
Game 3: Los Angeles 87, Boston 81
Game 4: Boston 97, Los Angeles 91
Game 5: Los Angeles 103, Boston 98
Game 6: Boston 131, Los Angeles 92

2008 NBA First Round Draft Picks

Rank, Team	Player, Position, College/Country
1. Bulls	Derrick Rose, G, Memphis
2. Heat	Michael Beasley, F, Kansas St.
3. Timberwolves	O.J. Mayo, G, USC (to Memphis)
4. Supersonics	Russell Westbrook, G, UCLA
5. Grizzlies	Kevin Love, F, UCLA (to Minnesota)
6. Knicks	Danilo Gallinari, F, Italy
7. Clippers	Eric Gordon, G, Indiana
8. Bucks	Joe Alexander, F, West Virginia
9. Bobcats	D.J. Augustin, G, Texas
10. Nets	Brook Lopez, C, Stanford

Rank, Team	Player, Position, College/Country
11. Pacers	Jerryd Bayless, G, Arizona
12. Kings	Jason Thompson, F, Rider
13. Trail Blazers	Brandon Rush, F, Kansas
14. Warriors	Anthony Randolph, F, LSU
15. Suns	Robin Lopez, F, Stanford (from Atlanta)
16. 76ers	Marreese Speights, F, Florida
17. Raptors	Roy Hibbert, C, Georgetown
18. Wizards	JaVale McGee, C, Nevada
19. Cavaliers	J.J. Hickson, F, N.C. State
20. Bobcats	Alexis Ajinca, C, France (from Denver)

NBA Leaders, 2007–08

Scoring	G	Avg.
LeBron James, Cleveland	75	30.0
Kobe Bryant, L.A. Lakers	82	28.3
Allen Iverson, Denver	82	26.4
Carmelo Anthony, Denver	77	25.7
Amare Stoudemire, Phoenix	79	25.2
Kevin Martin, Sacramento	61	23.7
Dirk Nowitzki	77	23.6
Michael Redd, Milwaukee	72	22.7
Richard Jefferson, N.J.	82	22.6
Chris Bosh, Toronto	67	22.3

Rebounds	G	Reb.	Avg.
Dwight Howard, Orlando	82	1,161	14.2
Marcus Camby, Denver	79	1,037	13.1
Tyson Chandler, New Orleans	79	928	11.7
Tim Duncan, San Antonio	78	881	11.3
Al Jefferson, Minnesota	82	911	11.1

Assists	G	No.	Avg.
Chris Paul, New Orleans	80	925	11.6
Steve Nash, Phoenix	81	898	11.1
Deron Williams, Utah	82	862	10.5
Jason Kidd, NJ/Dallas	80	806	10.1
Jose Calderon, Toronto	82	678	8.3

Blocked Shots	G.	No.	Avg.
Marcus Camby, Denver	79	285	3.61
Josh Smith, Atlanta	81	227	2.80
Chris Kaman, L.A. Clippers	56	155	2.77
Samuel Dalembert, Phila.	82	269	2.34
Dwight Howard, Orlando	82	176	2.15

Steals	G.	No.	Avg.
Chris Paul, New Orleans	80	217	2.71
Ron Artest, Sacramento	57	133	2.33
Baron Davis, Golden State	82	191	2.33
Caron Butler, Washington	58	128	2.21
Gerald Wallace, Charlotte	62	131	2.11

Field Goal Percentage	FGM	FGA	Pct.
Andris Biedrins, Golden State	340	543	.626
Tyson Chandler, New Orleans	377	605	.623
Dwight Howard, Orlando	583	974	.599
Shaquille O'Neal, Mia/Phoenix	331	558	.593
Amare Stoudemire, Phoenix	714	1211	.590

Free Throw Percentage	FTM	FTA	Pct.
Peja Stojakovic, New Orleans	130	140	.929
Chauncey Billups, Detroit	401	437	.918
Ben Gordon, Chicago	266	293	.908
Ray Allen, Boston	215	237	.907
Steve Nash, Phoenix	222	245	.906

3-Pt. FG Percentage	FGM	FGA	Pct.
Jason Kapono, Toronto	57	118	.483
Steve Nash, Phoenix	179	381	.470
James Jones, Portland	91	205	.444
Peja Stojakovic, New Orleans	231	524	.441
Daniel Gibson, Cleveland	118	268	.440

Minutes Per Game	G	Min.	Avg.
Allen Iverson, Denver	82	3428	41.8
Joe Johnson, Atlanta	82	3342	40.8
LeBron James, Cleveland	75	3028	40.4
Caron Butler, Washington	58	2317	39.9
Jamal Crawford, New York	80	3193	39.9

WNBA Final Standings and Playoffs, 2008

EASTERN CONFERENCE TEAM	W-L	WESTERN CONFERENCE TEAM	W-L
Detroit	22-12	San Antonio	24-10
Connecticut	21-13	Seattle	22-12
New York	19-15	Los Angeles	20-14
Indiana	17-17	Sacramento	18-16
Chicago	12-22	Houston	17-17
Washington	10-24	Phoenix	16-18
Atlanta	4-30	Minnesota	16-18

CONFERENCE SEMI-FINALS

Eastern:
Detroit 2, Indiana 1
New York 2, Connecticut 1

Western:
San Antonio 2, Sacramento 1
Los Angeles 2, Seattle 1

CONFERENCE FINALS

Eastern:
Detroit 2, New York 1

Western:
San Antonio 2, Los Angeles 1

WNBA CHAMPIONSHIP
San Antonio Silver Stars 3, Detroit Shock 0

Note: The top four teams in each division made the playoffs. **Source:** WNBA. www.wnba.com.

NBA World Championship Series

Year	Winner	Loser	Games	Year	Winner	Loser	Games
1947	Philadelphia Warriors	Chicago Stags	4-1	1977	Portland Trail Blazers	Philadelphia 76ers	4-2
1948	Baltimore Bullets	Philadelphia Warriors	4-2	1978	Washington Bullets	Seattle SuperSonics	4-3
1949	Minneapolis Lakers	Washington Capitols	4-2	1979	Seattle SuperSonics	Washington Bullets	4-1
1950	Minneapolis Lakers	Syracuse Nationals	4-2	1980	Los Angeles Lakers	Philadelphia 76ers	4-2
1951	Rochester Royals	New York Knicks	4-3	1981	Boston Celtics	Houston Rockets	4-2
1952	Minneapolis Lakers	New York Knicks	4-3	1982	Los Angeles Lakers	Philadelphia 76ers	4-2
1953	Minneapolis Lakers	New York Knicks	4-1	1983	Philadelphia 76ers	Los Angeles Lakers	4-0
1954	Minneapolis Lakers	Syracuse Nationals	4-3	1984	Boston Celtics	Los Angeles Lakers	4-3
1955	Syracuse Nationals	Fort Wayne Pistons	4-3	1985	Los Angeles Lakers	Boston Celtics	4-2
1956	Philadelphia Warriors	Fort Wayne Pistons	4-1	1986	Boston Celtics	Houston Rockets	4-2
1957	Boston Celtics	St. Louis Hawks	4-3	1987	Los Angeles Lakers	Boston Celtics	4-2
1958	St. Louis Hawks	Boston Celtics	4-2	1988	Los Angeles Lakers	Detroit Pistons	4-3
1959	Boston Celtics	Minneapolis Lakers	4-0	1989	Detroit Pistons	Los Angeles Lakers	4-0
1960	Boston Celtics	St. Louis Hawks	4-3	1990	Detroit Pistons	Portland Trail Blazers	4-1
1961	Boston Celtics	St. Louis Hawks	4-1	1991	Chicago Bulls	Los Angeles Lakers	4-1
1962	Boston Celtics	Los Angeles Lakers	4-3	1992	Chicago Bulls	Portland Trail Blazers	4-2
1963	Boston Celtics	Los Angeles Lakers	4-2	1993	Chicago Bulls	Phoenix Suns	4-2
1964	Boston Celtics	San Francisco Warriors	4-1	1994	Houston Rockets	New York Knicks	4-3
1965	Boston Celtics	Los Angeles Lakers	4-1	1995	Houston Rockets	Orlando Magic	4-0
1966	Boston Celtics	Los Angeles Lakers	4-3	1996	Chicago Bulls	Seattle SuperSonics	4-2
1967	Philadelphia	San Francisco Warriors	4-2	1997	Chicago Bulls	Utah Jazz	4-2
1968	Boston Celtics	Los Angeles Lakers	4-2	1998	Chicago Bulls	Utah Jazz	4-2
1969	Boston Celtics	Los Angeles Lakers	4-3	1999	San Antonio Spurs	New York Knicks	4-1
1970	New York Knicks	Los Angeles Lakers	4-3	2000	Los Angeles Lakers	Indiana Pacers	4-2
1971	Milwaukee Bucks	Baltimore Bullets	4-0	2001	Los Angeles Lakers	Philadelphia 76ers	4-1
1972	Los Angeles Lakers	New York Knicks	4-1	2002	Los Angeles Lakers	New Jersey Nets	4-0
1973	New York Knicks	Los Angeles Lakers	4-1	2003	San Antonio Spurs	New Jersey Nets	4-2
1974	Boston Celtics	Milwaukee Bucks	4-3	2004	Detroit Pistons	Los Angeles Lakers	4-1
1975	Golden State Warriors	Washington Bullets	4-0	2005	San Antonio Spurs	Detroit Pistons	4-3
1976	Boston Celtics	Phoenix Suns	4-2	2006	Miami Heat	Dallas Mavericks	4-2
				2007	San Antonio Spurs	Cleveland Cavaliers	4-0

NBA All-Time Career Leaders

Games		Points		Scoring average (min. 400 games)	
Robert Parish	1,611	Kareem Abdul-Jabbar	38,387	Michael Jordan	30.1
Kareem Abdul-Jabbar	1,560	Karl Malone	36,928	Wilt Chamberlain	30.1
John Stockton	1,504	Michael Jordan	32,292	Allen Iverson[1]	27.7
Karl Malone	1,476	Wilt Chamberlain	31,419	Elgin Baylor	27.4
Kevin Willis	1,419	Moses Malone	27,409	Jerry West	27.0
Reggie Miller	1,389	Elvin Hayes	27,313	Bob Pettit	26.4
Clifford Robinson[1]	1,380	Hakeem Olajuwon	26,946	George Gervin	26.2
Gary Payton	1,335	Oscar Robertson	26,710	Karl Malone	26.2
Moses Malone	1,329	Dominique Wilkins	26,668	Oscar Robertson	25.7
Buck Williams	1,307	John Havlicek	26,395	Shaquille O'Neal[1]	25.2

Assists		Rebounds		Free throw percentage (min. 1,200 made)	
John Stockton	15,806	Wilt Chamberlain	23,924	Mark Price	.904
Mark Jackson	10,334	Bill Russell	21,620	Rick Barry[1]	.900
Magic Johnson	10,141	Kareem Abdul-Jabbar	17,440	Steve Nash[1]	.897
Oscar Robertson	9,887	Elvin Hayes	16,279	Peja Stojakovic[1]	.894
Isiah Thomas	9,061	Moses Malone	16,212	Calvin Murphy	.892
Jason Kidd	9,497	Karl Malone	14,968	Scott Skiles	.889
Isiah Thomas	9,061	Robert Parish	14,715	Ray Allen	.889
Gary Payton[1]	8,996	Nate Thurmond	14,464	Reggie Miller	.888
Rod Strickland	7,987	Walt Bellamy	14,241	Chauncey Billups	.886
Maurice Cheeks	7,392	Wes Unseld	13,769	Larry Bird	.884

Note: Does not include statistics compiled in the ABA. Totals are as of the end of 2007–08 season. 1. Player active in 2007–08.
Source: NBA. www.nba.com

NBA Most Valuable Players, 1955–2007

Year	Most Valuable Player	Team	Year	Most Valuable Player	Team
1955–56	Bob Pettit	St. Louis Hawks	1981–82	Moses Malone	Houston Rockets
1956–57	Bob Cousy	Boston Celtics	1982–83	Moses Malone	Philadelphia 76ers
1957–58	Bill Russell	Boston Celtics	1983–84	Larry Bird	Boston Celtics
1958–59	Bob Pettit	St. Louis Hawks	1984–85	Larry Bird	Boston Celtics
1959–60	Wilt Chamberlain	Philadelphia Warriors	1985–86	Larry Bird	Boston Celtics
1960–61	Bill Russell	Boston Celtics	1986–87	Magic Johnson	Los Angeles Lakers
1961–62	Bill Russell	Boston Celtics	1987–88	Michael Jordan	Chicago Bulls
1962–63	Bill Russell	Boston Celtics	1988–89	Magic Johnson	Los Angeles Lakers
1963–64	Oscar Robertson	Cincinnati Royals	1989–90	Magic Johnson	Los Angeles Lakers
1964–65	Bill Russell	Boston Celtics	1990–91	Michael Jordan	Chicago Bulls
1965–66	Wilt Chamberlain	Philadelphia 76ers	1991–92	Michael Jordan	Chicago Bulls
1966–67	Wilt Chamberlain	Philadelphia 76ers	1992–93	Charles Barkley	Phoenix Suns
1967–68	Wilt Chamberlain	Philadelphia 76ers	1993–94	Hakeem Olajuwon	Houston Rockets
1968–69	Wes Unseld	Baltimore Bullets	1994–95	David Robinson	San Antonio Spurs
1969–70	Willis Reed	New York Knicks	1995–96	Michael Jordan	Chicago Bulls
1970–71	Kareem Abdul-Jabbar	Milwaukee Bucks	1996–97	Karl Malone	Utah Jazz
1971–72	Kareem Abdul-Jabbar	Milwaukee Bucks	1997–98	Michael Jordan	Chicago Bulls
1972–73	Dave Cowens	Boston Celtics	1998–99	Karl Malone	Utah Jazz
1973–74	Kareem Abdul-Jabbar	Milwaukee Bucks	1999–00	Shaquille O'Neal	Los Angeles Lakers
1974–75	Bob McAdoo	Buffalo Braves	2000–01	Allen Iverson	Philadelphia 76ers
1975–76	Kareem Abdul-Jabbar	Los Angeles Lakers	2001–02	Tim Duncan	San Antonio Spurs
1976–77	Kareem Abdul-Jabbar	Los Angeles Lakers	2002–03	Tim Duncan	San Antonio Spurs
1977–78	Bill Walton	Portland Trail Blazers	2003–04	Kevin Garnett	Minn. Timberwolves
1978–79	Moses Malone	Houston Rockets	2004–05	Steve Nash	Phoenix Suns
1979–80	Kareem Abdul-Jabbar	Los Angeles Lakers	2005–06	Steve Nash	Phoenix Suns
1980–81	Julius Erving	Philadelphia 76ers	2006–07	Dirk Nowitzki	Dallas Mavericks

NBA Rookies of the Year, 1952–2007

Year	Rookie of the Year	Team	Year	Rookie of the Year	Team
1952–53	Don Meineke	Fort Wayne Pistons	1980–81	Darrell Griffith	Utah Jazz
1953–54	Ray Felix	Baltimore Bullets	1981–82	Buck Williams	New Jersey Nets
1954–55	Bob Pettit	Milwaukee Hawks	1982–83	Terry Cummings	San Diego Clippers
1955–56	Maurice Stokes	Rochester Royals	1983–84	Ralph Sampson	Houston Rockets
1956–57	Tom Heinsohn	Boston Celtics	1984–85	Michael Jordan	Chicago Bulls
1957–58	Woody Sauldsberry	Philadelphia Warriors	1985–86	Patrick Ewing	New York Knicks
1958–59	Elgin Baylor	Minneapolis Lakers	1986–87	Chuck Person	Indiana Pacers
1959–60	Wilt Chamberlain	Philadelphia Warriors	1987–88	Mark Jackson	New York Knicks
1960–61	Oscar Robertson	Cincinnati Royals	1988–89	Mitch Richmond	Golden State Warriors
1961–62	Walt Bellamy	Chicago Packers	1989–90	David Robinson	San Antonio Spurs
1962–63	Terry Dischinger	Chicago Zephyrs	1990–91	Derrick Coleman	New Jersey Nets
1963–64	Jerry Lucas	Cincinnati Royals	1991–92	Larry Johnson	Charlotte Hornets
1964–65	Willis Reed	New York Knicks	1992–93	Shaquille O'Neal	Orlando Magic
1965–66	Rick Barry	San Francisco Warriors	1993–94	Chris Webber	Golden State Warriors
1966–67	Dave Bing	Detroit Pistons	1994–95	Grant Hill	Detroit Pistons
1967–68	Earl Monroe	Baltimore Bullets		Jason Kidd	Dallas Mavericks
1968–69	Wes Unseld	Baltimore Bullets	1995–96	Damon Stoudamire	Toronto Raptors
1969–70	Kareem Abdul-Jabbar	Milwaukee Bucks	1996–97	Allen Iverson	Philadelphia 76ers
1970–71	Dave Cowens	Boston Celtics	1997–98	Tim Duncan	San Antonio Spurs
	Geoff Petrie	Portland Trail Blazers	1998–99	Vince Carter	Toronto Raptors
1971–72	Sidney Wicks	Portland Trail Blazers	1999–00	Elton Brand	Chicago Bulls
1972–73	Bob McAdoo	Buffalo Braves		Steve Francis	Houston Rockets
1973–74	Ernie DiGregorio	Buffalo Braves	2000–01	Mike Miller	Orlando Magic
1974–75	Keith Wilkes	Golden State Warriors	2001–02	Pau Gasol	Memphis Grizzlies
1975–76	Alvin Adams	Phoenix Suns	2002–03	Amaré Stoudamire	Phoenix Suns
1976–77	Adrian Dantley	Buffalo Braves	2003–04	LeBron James	Cleveland Cavaliers
1977–78	Walter Davis	Phoenix Suns	2004–05	Emeka Okfor	Charlotte Bobcats
1978–79	Phil Ford	Kansas City Kings	2005–06	Chris Paul	N.O./Ok. Hornets
1979–80	Larry Bird	Boston Celtics	2006–07	Brandon Roy	Portland Trail Blazers

Naismith Memorial Basketball Hall of Fame

The Basketball Hall of Fame elected its first members (including Dr. James Naismith, the game's originator) in 1959, but it did not have a physical home until February 17, 1968. In 1985 the Hall of Fame moved to larger quarters in Springfield, Mass. The Basketball Hall of Fame includes players from all basketball levels, including college, women's, and foreign leagues. Career statistics are given only for players who played some portion of their career in the NBA.

Player (Year Elected)	Games	Points	FG%	FT%	Rebs.	Assts.
Archibald, Nate (Tiny) (1991)	876	16,481	.467	.810	2,046	6,476
Averaged 18.8 ppg over 13 seasons; six–time All-Star.						
Arizin, Paul J. (1977)	713	16,266	.421	.810	6,129	1,665
NBA scoring leader in 1952 (25.4 ppg) and 1957 (25.6 ppg).						
Barkley, Charles (2006)	1,073	23,757	.541	.735	12,546	4,215
11-time All-Star, MVP in 1993, two-time Olympicgold medalist.						
Barry, Rick (1987)	794	18,395	.449	.900	5,168	4,017
(ABA Statistics)	226	6,884	.477	.880	1,695	935
NBA all-time free-throw percentage leader.						
Baylor, Elgin (1976)	846	23,149	.431	.780	11,463	3,650
Named to NBA All-Star First Team 10 times.						
Bellamy, Walt (1993)	1,043	20,941	.516	.632	14,241	2,544
NBA Rookie of the Year in 1962.						
Bing, Dave (1990)	901	18,327	.441	.775	3,420	5,397
NBA Rookie of the Year 1967, MVP 1976.						
Bird, Larry (1998)	897	21,791	.496	.886	8,974	5,695
NBA Rookie of the Year 1980. NBA MVP 1984, 1985, and 1986. 12-time All-star.						
Bradley, Bill (1982)	742	9,217	.448	.840	2,533	2,363
Averaged 30.2 ppg in 83 games at Princeton University.						
Chamberlain, Wilt (1978)	1045	31,419	.540	.511	23,924	4,643
Holds NBA single-game records for points (100) and rebounds (55); led league in scoring 1959-66.						
Cousy, Bob (1970)	924	16,960	.375	.803	4,786	6,955
Led NBA in assists eight consecutive seasons (1953-60).						
Cowens, Dave (1991)	766	13,516	.460	.783	10,444	2,950
Seven-time All-star; three-time All-defensive team.						
Cunningham, Billy (1986)	654	13,626	.446	.720	6,638	2,625
(ABA Statistics)	116	2,684	.483	.791	1,343	680
Coached Philadelphia 76ers to 454-196 record in eight years.						
Davies, Bob (1969)	462	6,594	.378	.759	980[1]	2,050
NBL MVP, 1947	(NBL)[2]	107	1177		.747	
DeBusschere, Dave (1982)	875	14,053	.432	.699	9,618	2,497
NBA All-Defensive team six consecutive seasons (1969-74)						
Drexler, Clyde (2004)	1,086	22,195	.472	.788	6,677	6,125
Nine-time All-Star; led Houston Cougars to Final Four in 1982 and 1983.						
Dumars, Joe (2006)	1,018	16,401	.460	.843	2,203	4,612
Six-time All-Star, four times on NBA All-Defensive team.						
English, Alex (1997)	1,193	25,613	.507	.832	6,538	4,351
Eight-time all-star; Averaged 21.5 points per game over 15 seasons.						
Erving, Julius (Dr. J) (1993)	836	18,364	.507	.777	5,601	3,224
(ABA Statistics)	407	11,662	.504	.778	4,924	1,952
ABA MVP 1974-76; NBA MVP, 1981.						
Frazier, Walt (Clyde) (1987)	825	15,581	.490	.786	4,830	5,040
NBA All-Defensive team seven consecutive seasons (1969-75).						
Fulks, Joe (1977)	489	8,003	.302	.766	1,382[1]	587
NBA scoring leader in 1947 (23.2 ppg)						
Gallatin, Harry (1991)	682	8,843	.398	.773	6,684	1,208
Seven-time All-Star						
Gervin, George (Iceman) (1996)	791	20,708	.511	.844	3,607	2,214
(ABA Statistics)	269	5,887	.480	.831	1,995	584
All-NBA team five years in a row (1978-82).						
Gola, Tom (1975)	698	7,871	.431	.760	5,605	2,953
One of only two major-college players with over 2,000 points and 2,000 rebounds in career.						
Goodrich, Gail (1996)	1,031	19,181	.456	.807	3,279	4,805
Scored 42 points in 1965 NCAA Final; averaged 18.6 points per game over 14 years in NBA.						
Greer, Harold (Hal) (1981)	1,122	21,586	.452	.801	5,665	4,540
Scored 19 points in one quarter of 1968 All-Star game						
Hagan, Cliff (1977)	746	13,447	.450	.798	5,019	2,236
(ABA Statistics)	94	1,423	.496	.807	436	398
Helped St. Louis to 1958 championship with 27.7 ppg in playoffs.						
Havlicek, John J. (Hondo) (1983)	1,270	26,395	.439	.815	8,007	6,114
Averaged 20.8 ppg; Member of 8 NBA championship teams.						
Hawkins, Connie (1992)	499	8,233	.467	.785	3,971	2,052
(ABA Statistics)	117	3,295	.515	.765	1,479	504
Four-time All-Star; ABA MVP 1969.						
Hayes, Elvin (1990)	1,303	27,313	.452	.670	16,279	2,398
Led league in scoring (1969) and rebounds per game (1970,1974).						

Player (Year Elected)	Games	Points	FG%	FT%	Rebs.	Assts.
Heinsohn, Tom (1986)	654	12,194	.405	.790	5,749	1,318
Played for eight NBA championship teams and coached two others.						
Houbregs, Robert J. (1987)	281	2,611	.404	.721	1,552	500
NCAA Player of the Year, 1953.						
Issel, Dan (1993)	718	14,659	.506	.797	5,707	1,804
(ABA Statistics)	500	12,823	.488	.786	5,426	1,103
Averaged 33.7 points per game in senior year at Kentucky, 1969-70.						
Jabbar, Kareem Abdul (1995)	1,560	38,387	.559	.721	17,440	5,660
Six-time NBA MVP. All-time NBA leader in scoring, games, minutes, field goals.						
Jeannette, Buddy (1994) (BAA-NBA)	139	997	.341	.781	N.A.	287
Won NBL MVP three times.						
Johnson, Earvin (Magic) (2002)	906	17,707	.520	.848	6,559	10,141
Led Lakers to five NBA championships; 3-time NBA MVP (1987, 1989, 1990); 12-time All-Star.						
Johnston, Neil (1990)	516	10,023	.444	.768	5,856	1,269
Named to four straight all-NBA First Teams (1953-56).						
Jones, K.C. (1989)	676	5,011	.387	.647	2,399	2,908
High scorer in 1955 NCAA finals (24 pts); held Tom Gola scoreless for 21 mins.						
Jones, Sam (1983)	871	15,411	.456	.803	4,305	2,209
Member of 10 NBA championship teams.						
Lanier, Bob (1992)	959	19,248	.514	.767	9,698	3,007
Eight-time All-Star; NBA MVP, 1974.						
Lloyd, Earl (2003)	560	4,682	.356	.750	3,609	810
First African-American to play in a NBA game, 1950.						
Lovellette, Clyde (1988)	704	11,947	.443	.756	6,663	1,165
Three-time All-American at University of Kansas (1950-52).						
Lucas, Jerry Ray (Luke) (1979)	829	14,053	.499	.783	12,942	2,730
NBA Rookie of the Year and field-goal percentage leader (.527) in 1964.						
Macauley, Edward (Easy Ed) (1960)	641	11,234	.436	.761	2,079	1,667
NBA All-Star Game MVP, 1951						
Malone, Moses (2001)	1,329	27,409	.491	.769	16,212	1,796
Three-time MVP, 12-time All-Star. Averaged 20 points per game 11 straight seasons.						
Maravich, Pete (Pistol) (1987)	658	15,948	.441	.820	2,747	3,563
NCAA career record holder for points scored (3667) and scoring avg. (44.2 ppg).						
Martin, Slater (1981)	745	7,337	.364	.762	2,302[1]	3,160
Played in seven straight All-Star Games, 1953-59.						
McAdoo, Bob (2000)	852	18,787	.503	.754	8,048	1,951
NBA Rookie of the Year (1973); led league in scoring 1974, 1975, and 1976.						
McGuire, Dick (1993)	738	5,921	.389	.644	2,784	4,205
Averaged 8.0 ppg.						
McHale, Kevin (1999)	971	17,335	.554	.798	7,122	1,670
Seven-time All-Star; won Sixth Man Award twice; won 3 NBA Championships: 1981, 1984, 1986.						
Mikan, George L. (1959)	439	10,156	.404	.782	4,167[1]	1,245
Three-time NBA scoring leader (1949, 1950, 1952).						
Mikkelson, Vern (1995)	699	10,063	.403	.766	5,940[1]	1,515
Six-time NBA All-Star; won 4 NBA Championships: 1950, 1952, 1953, & 1954.						
Monroe, Earl (The Pearl) (1990)	926	17,454	.464	.807	2,796	3,594
NBA Rookie of the Year, 1968.						
Murphy, Calvin (1993)	1,002	17,949	.482	.892	2,103	4,402
Set single-season free throw percentage record with .958 in 1980-81.						
Parish, Robert (2003)	1,611	23,334	.537	.721	14,715	2,180
Nine-time NBA All-Star (1981-87, 1990-91). Won 3 NBA Championships (1981, 1984, & 1986).						
Petrovic, Drazen (2002)	290	4,461	.506	.841	669	701
Averaged 15.4 ppg and 43.7% from 3-pt range over 4 years before being killed in auto accident.						
Pettit, Bob (1970)	792	20,880	.436	.761	12,849	2,369
Led NBA in scoring (25.7 ppg) and rebounds (1164) in 1956.						
Phillip, Andy (1961)	701	6,384	.368	.695	2,395[1]	3,759
Led NBA in assists, 1951 and 1952.						
Pollard, Jim (1977)	438	5,762	.360	.750	2,487[1]	1,417
Started four NBA All-Star Games.						
Ramsey, Frank (1981)	623	8,378	.402	.804	3,410	1,136
Member of seven NBA championship teams.						
Reed, Willis (1981)	650	12,183	.476	.747	8,414	1,186
1970 NBA Most Valuable Player, All-Star Game MVP and Playoff MVP.						
Risen, Arnie (1998)	637	7,633	.381	.699	5,011	1,058
Three-time NBA All-star (1953, 1954,and 1955).						
Robertson, Oscar (1979)	1,040	26,710	.485	.838	7,804	9,887
NBA MVP 1964; Member of All-NBA First team, 1961-69.						
Russell, Bill (1974)	963	14,522	.440	.561	21,620	4,100
Five-time NBA Most Valuable Player; 32 rebounds in one half vs. Philadelphia, 1957.						
Schayes, Adolph (Dolph) (1972)	996	18,438	.380	.849	11,256[1]	3,072
NBA Coach of the Year (1966).						

Player (Year Elected)	Games	Points	FG%	FT%	Rebs.	Assts.
Sharman, Bill (1974)	711	12,665	.426	.883	2,779	2,101
Led NBA in free-throw percentage seven seasons.						
Stokes, Maurice (2004)	202	3,315	.351	.698	3,492	1,062
Rookie of the Year (1955-56; killed in freak accident after three NBA seasons.						
Thomas, Isiah, (2000)	979	18,822	.452	.759	3,478	9,061
NBA Rookie of the Year (1982); 12-time All-Star; MVP of the 1990 Finals.						
Thompson, David (1996)	509	11,264	.504	.778	1,921	1,631
(ABA Statistics)	83	2,158	.515	.794	525	308
NCAA player of the year 1974 and 1975; ABA Rookie of the Year, 1976.						
Thurmond, Nate (1984)	964	14,437	.421	.667	14,464	2,575
1,000+ rebounds 1964-69, 1970-73.						
Twyman, Jack (1982)	23	15,840	.450	.778	5,421	1,969
Led NBA in field-goal percentage, 1958 (.452).						
Unseld, Wes (1988)	984	10,624	.509	.633	13,769	3,822
Named NBA Most Valuable Player and Rookie of the Year in same year (1969).						
Walton, Bill (1993)	468	6,215	.521	.660	4,923	1,590
MVP in 1976.						
Wanzer, Robert (1987)	502	5,891	.388	.800	1,652[1]	1,575
Free-throw percentage leader, 1952 (.904).						
West, Jerry Alan (1979)	932	25,192	.474	.814	5,376	6,238
NBA MVP in 1970; .805 free throw percentage in 13 years in the playoffs.						
Worthy, James (2003)	926	16,320	.521	.769	4,707	2,791
MVP of 1988 NBA Finals. Won three NBA titles with L.A. Lakers (1985, 1987, and 1988).						
Wilkins, Dominique (2006)	1,074	26,668	.461	.811	7,169	2,677
Nine-time All-Star, All-NBA first team in 1986.						
Wilkens, Lenny (1989)	1,077	17,772	.432	.774	5,030	7,211
600+ assists 6 consecutive seasons.						
Yardley, George (1996)	472	9,063	.422	.780	4,220	815
First player in NBA history to score 2,000 points in a season.						

Note: All statistics for NBA career unless otherwise noted. NBL = National Basketball League. ABA = American Basketball Association. NCAA (National Collegiate Athletic Association) 1. Does not include seasons played prior to 1950-51 when the NBA first began keeping statistics for rebounds. 2. The National Basketball League did not keep statistics for field-goal percentage, rebounds, or assists.

COACHES AND CONTRIBUTORS

Anderson, W. Harold 1984
Auerbach, Arnold J. "Red" 1968
Auriemma, Geno 2006
Barry, Justin "Sam" 1978
Blood, Ernest A. 1960
Boeheim, Jim 2005
Brown, Hubie 2005
Brown, Larry 2002
Calhoun, Jim 2005
Cann, Howard G. 1967
Carlson, Dr. H. Clifford 1959
Carnesecca, Lou 1992
Carnevale, Ben 1969
Carril, Pete 1997
Case, Everett 1981
Chaney, John 2001
Conradt, Jody 1998
Crum, Denny 1994
Daly, Chuck, 1994
Dean, Everett S. 1966
Diddle, Edgar A. 1971
Drake, Bruce 1972
Gaines, Clarence 1981
Gamba, Sandro 2006
Gardner, James H. "Jack" 1983
Gavitt, David 2006
Gill, Amory T. "Slats" 1967
Gunter, Sue 2005
Hannum, Alex 1998
Harshman, Marv 1984
Haskins, Don 1997
Hickey, Edgar S. 1978
Hobson, Howard A. 1965
Holzman, William "Red" 1985-86
Iba, Henry P. "Hank" 1968
Jackson, Phil 2007

Julian, Alvin "Doggie" 1967
Keaney, Frank W. 1960
Keogan, George E. 1961
Knight, Bob 1991
Krzyzewski, Mike 2001
Kundla, John 1995
Lambert, Ward L. 1960
Litwack, Harry 1975
Loeffler, Kenneth D. 1964
Lonborg, Arthur C. 1972
McCutchan, Arad A. 1980
McGuire, Al 1992
McGuire, Frank J. 1976
Meanwell, Dr. Walter E. 1959
Meyer, Raymond J. 1978
Miller, Ralph 1987
Moore, Billie 1999
Nikolic, Aleksandar 1998
Olson, Lute 2002
Ramsay, Jack 1992
Rupp, Adolph F. 1968
Sachs, Leonard D. 1961
Sharman, Bill, 2004
Shelton, Everett F. 1979
Smith, Dean 1982
Summitt, Pat, 2000
Taylor, Fred R. 1985-86
Teague, Bertha 1984
Thompson, John 1999
Wade, L. Margaret 1984
Watts, Stanley H. 1985-86
Wilkens, Lenny 1998
Wooden, John R. 1972
Woolpert, Phil 1992
Wootten, Morgan 2000

ICE HOCKEY

National Hockey League
www.nhl.com **Commissioner: Gary Bettman**
No. of Teams: 30 **Founded: 1917**

In September 2004, franchise owners locked out their players upon the expiration of the collective bargaining agreement. NHL Commissioner Gary Bettman claimed that salary arbitration, expensive signing bonuses for rookies, and the lack of a salary cap or luxury tax had caused the league to lose close to $500 million over the previous two seasons, although he never acknowledged the owners' responsibility for this situation. After months of negotiation the entire season was cancelled in February 2005. An agreement was finally reached in June as the players accepted a salary cap that would guarantee large salaries only to the older players.

The Stanley Cup

The oldest trophy competed for by professional athletes in North America, the Stanley Cup was donated by Frederick Arthur, Lord Stanley of Preston, in 1893. Lord Stanley purchased the trophy for 10 guineas (about $50) for presentation to the amateur hockey champions of Canada. Since 1910, when the National Hockey Association took possession of the Stanley Cup, the trophy has been the symbol of professional hockey supremacy. The National Hockey League took exclusive control of the cup in 1946, and now awards it annually to the team that wins the league's best-of-seven final playoff series.

Season	Champion	Finalist	GP in final	Season	Champion	Finalist	GP in final
1917–18	Toronto Arenas	Vancouver Millionaires	5	1962–63	Toronto Maple Leafs	Detroit Red Wings	5
1918–19	No decision[1]	No decision	5	1963–64	Toronto Maple Leafs	Detroit Red Wings	7
1919–20	Ottawa Senators	Seattle Millionaires	5	1964–65	Montreal Canadiens	Chicago Blackhawks	7
1920–21	Ottawa Senators	Vancouver Millionaires	5	1965–66	Montreal Canadiens	Detroit Red Wings	6
1921–22	Toronto St. Pats	Vancouver Millionaires	5	1966–67	Toronto Maple Leafs	Montreal Canadiens	6
1922–23	Ottawa Senators	Edmonton	2	1967–68	Montreal Canadiens	St. Louis Blues	4
1923–24	Montreal Canadiens	Calgary	2	1968–69	Montreal Canadiens	St. Louis Blues	4
1924–25	Victoria Cougars	Montreal Canadiens	4	1969–70	Boston Bruins	St. Louis Blues	4
1925–26	Montreal Maroons	Victoria Cougars	4	1970–71	Montreal Canadiens	Chicago Blackhawks	7
1926–27	Ottawa Senators	Boston Bruins	2	1971–72	Boston Bruins	New York Rangers	6
1927–28	New York Rangers	Montreal Canadiens	5	1972–73	Montreal Canadiens	Chicago Blackhawks	6
1928–29	Boston Bruins	New York Rangers	2	1973–74	Philadelphia Flyers	Boston Bruins	6
1929–30	Montreal Canadiens	Boston Bruins	2	1974–75	Philadelphia Flyers	Buffalo Sabres	6
1930–31	Montreal Canadiens	Chicago Blackhawks	5	1975–76	Montreal Canadiens	Philadelphia Flyers	4
1931–32	Toronto Maple Leafs	New York Rangers	3	1976–77	Montreal Canadiens	Boston Bruins	4
1932–33	New York Rangers	Toronto Maple Leafs	3	1977–78	Montreal Canadiens	Boston Bruins	6
1933–34	Chicago Blackhawks	Detroit Red Wings	4	1978–79	Montreal Canadiens	New York Rangers	5
1934–35	Montreal Maroons	Toronto Maple Leafs	3	1979–80	New York Islanders	Philadelphia Flyers	6
1935–36	Detroit Red Wings	Toronto Maple Leafs	4	1980–81	New York Islanders	Minnesota North Stars	5
1936–37	Detroit Red Wings	New York Rangers	5	1981–82	New York Islanders	Vancouver Canucks	4
1937–38	Chicago Blackhawks	Toronto Maple Leafs	4	1982–83	New York Islanders	Edmonton Oilers	4
1938–39	Boston Bruins	Toronto Maple Leafs	5	1983–84	Edmonton Oilers	New York Islanders	5
1939–40	New York Rangers	Toronto Maple Leafs	6	1984–85	Edmonton Oilers	Philadelphia Flyers	5
1940–41	Boston Bruins	Detroit Red Wings	4	1985–86	Montreal Canadiens	Calgary Flames	5
1941–42	Toronto Maple Leafs	Detroit Red Wings	7	1986–87	Edmonton Oilers	Philadelphia Flyers	7
1942–43	Detroit Red Wings	Boston Bruins	4	1987–88	Edmonton Oilers	Boston Bruins	4
1943–44	Montreal Canadiens	Chicago Blackhawks	4	1988–89	Calgary Flames	Montreal Canadiens	6
1944–45	Toronto Maple Leafs	Detroit Red Wings	7	1989–90	Edmonton Oilers	Boston Bruins	5
1945–46	Montreal Canadiens	Boston Bruins	5	1990–91	Pittsburgh Penguins	Minnesota North Stars	5
1946–47	Toronto Maple Leafs	Montreal Canadiens	6	1991–92	Pittsburgh Penguins	Chicago Blackhawks	4
1947–48	Toronto Maple Leafs	Detroit Red Wings	4	1992–93	Montreal Canadiens	Los Angeles Kings	5
1948–49	Toronto Maple Leafs	Detroit Red Wings	4	1993–94	New York Rangers	Vancouver Canucks	7
1949–50	Detroit Red Wings	New York Rangers	7	1994–95[2]	New Jersey Devils	Detroit Red Wings	4
1950–51	Toronto Maple Leafs	Montreal Canadiens	5	1995–96	Colorado Avalanche	Florida Panthers	4
1951–52	Detroit Red Wings	Montreal Canadiens	4	1996–97	Detroit Red Wings	Philadelphia Flyers	4
1952–53	Montreal Canadiens	Boston Bruins	5	1997–98	Detroit Red Wings	Washington Capitals	4
1953–54	Detroit Red Wings	Montreal Canadiens	7	1998–99	Dallas Stars	Buffalo Sabres	6
1954–55	Detroit Red Wings	Montreal Canadiens	7	1999–00	New Jersey Devils	Dallas Stars	6
1955–56	Montreal Canadiens	Detroit Red Wings	5	2000–01	Colorado Avalanche	New Jersey Devils	7
1956–57	Montreal Canadiens	Boston Bruins	5	2001–02	Detroit Red Wings	Carolina Hurricanes	5
1957–58	Montreal Canadiens	Boston Bruins	6	2002–03	New Jersey Devils	Anaheim Mighty Ducks	7
1958–59	Montreal Canadiens	Toronto Maple Leafs	5	2003–04	Tampa Bay Lightning	Calgary Flames	7
1959–60	Montreal Canadiens	Toronto Maple Leafs	4	2005–06[3]	Carolina Hurricanes	Edmonton Oilers	7
1960–61	Chicago Blackhawks	Detroit Red Wings	6	2006–07	Anaheim Ducks	Ottawa Senators	5
1961–62	Toronto Maple Leafs	Chicago Blackhawks	6	2007–08	Detroit Red Wings	Pittsburgh Penguins	6

Notes: 1. In the spring of 1919 the Montreal Canadiens traveled to Seattle to meet Seattle, champs of the Pacific Coast Hockey League. After five games had been played—teams were tied at 2 wins and 1 tie—the series was called off by the local Department of Health because of the influenza epidemic. 2. Strike-shortened season. 3. The 2004-05 season was canceled due to labor disagreement. **Source:** National Hockey League.

NHL Standings, 2007–08

EASTERN CONFERENCE

Northeast Division	W	L	OT	Pts.
Montreal	47	25	10	104
Ottawa	43	31	8	94
Boston	41	29	12	94
Buffalo	39	31	12	90
Toronto	36	35	11	83

Atlantic Division	W	L	OT	Pts.
Pittsburgh	47	27	8	102
New Jersey	46	29	7	99
NY Rangers	42	27	13	97
Philadelphia	42	29	11	95
NY Islanders	35	38	9	79

Southeast Division	W	L	OT	Pts.
Washington	43	31	8	94
Carolina	43	33	6	92
Florida	38	35	9	85
Atlanta	34	40	8	76
Tampa Bay	31	42	9	71

WESTERN CONFERENCE

Central Division	W	L	OT	Pts.
Detroit	54	21	7	115
Nashville	41	32	9	91
Chicago	40	34	8	88
Columbus	34	36	12	80
St. Louis	33	36	13	79

Northwest Division	W	L	OT	Pts.
Minnesota	44	28	10	98
Colorado	44	31	7	95
Calgary	42	30	10	94
Edmonton	41	35	6	88
Vancouver	39	33	10	88

Pacific Divison	W	L	OT	Pts.
San Jose	49	23	10	108
Anaheim	47	27	8	102
Dallas	45	30	7	97
Phoenix	38	37	7	83
Los Angeles	32	43	7	71

Stanley Cup Playoffs, 2007–08

(All rounds are seven-game series)

EASTERN CONFERENCE

ROUND 1

Montreal Canadiens 4, Boston Bruins 3
Pittsburgh Penguins 4, Ottawa Senators 0
Philadelphia Flyers 4, Washington Capitols 3
NY Rangers 4, NJ Devils 1

ROUND 2

Philadelphia Flyers 4, Montreal Canadiens 1
Pittsburgh Penguins 4, NY Rangers 1

CONFERENCE CHAMPIONSHIPS

Pittsburgh Penguins 4, Philadelphia Flyers 1

WESTERN CONFERENCE

ROUND 1

Detroit Red Wings 4, Nashville Predators 2
San Jose Sharks 4, Calgary Flames 3
Colorado Avalanche 4, Minnesota Wild 2
Dallas Stars 4, Anaheim Ducks 2

ROUND 2

Detroit Red Wings 4, Colorado Avalanche 0
Dallas Stars 4, San Jose Sharks 2

CONFERENCE CHAMPIONSHIPS

Detroit Red Wings 4, Dallas Stars 2

STANLEY CUP CHAMPIONSHIP
Detroit Red Wings 4, Pittsburgh Penguins 2

Top Scorers, 2007–08

Player, Team	POINTS
Alexander Ovechkin, Wash.	112
Evgeni Malkin, Pittsburgh	106
Jarome Iginla, Calgary	98
Pavel Datsyuk, Detroit	97
Joe Thornton, San Jose	96
Henrik Zetterberg, Detroit	92
Vincent Lecavalier, Tampa Bay	92
Jason Spezza, Ottawa	92
Daniel Alfredsson, Ottawa	89
Ilya Kovalchuk, Atlanta	87

Player, Team	GOALS
Alexander Ovechkin, Wash.	65
Ilya Kovalchuk, Atlanta	52
Jarome Iginla, Calgary	50
Evgeni Malkin, Pittsburgh	47
Henrik Zetterberg, Detroit	43
Brad Boyes, St. Louis	43
Marian Gaborik, Minnesota	42
Dany Heatley, Ottawa	41
Vincent Lecavalier, Tampa Bay	40
Daniel Alfredsson, Ottawa	40

PLAYER, TEAM	Assists
Joe Thornton, San Jose	67
Pavel Datsyuk, Detroit	66
Marc Savard, Boston	63
Henrik Sedin, Vancouver	61
Nicklas Lidstrom, Detroit	60
Evgeni Malkin, Pittsburgh	59
Jason Spezza, Ottawa	58
Martin St. Louis, Tampa Bay	58
Ryan Getzlaf, Anaheim	58
Mike Ribeiro, Dallas	56

Source: National Hockey League

Top 10 All-Time NHL Scoring Leaders

Player	Seasons	GOALS Games	Goals	Goals/ Game	Player	Seasons	ASSISTS Games	Assists	Assists/ Game
Wayne Gretzky	20	1,487	894	.601	Wayne Gretzky	20	1,487	1,963	1.320
Gordie Howe	26	1,767	801	.453	Ron Francis	23	1,731	1,249	.722
Brett Hull	19	1,264	741	.586	Mark Messier	25	1,756	1,193	.679
Marcel Dionne	18	1,348	731	.542	Ray Bourque	22	1,612	1,169	.725
Phil Esposito	18	1,282	717	.559	Paul Coffey	21	1,409	1,135	.806
Mike Gartner	19	1,432	708	.494	Adam Oates	19	1,337	1,079	.807
Mark Messier	25	1,756	694	.395	Steve Yzerman	23	1,514	1,063	.702
Steve Yzerman	23	1,514	692	.457	Gordie Howe	26	1,767	1,049	.594
Mario Lemieux	22	915	690	.754	Marcel Dionne	18	1,348	1,040	.772
Luc Robitaille	20	1,431	668	.467	Mario Lemieux	22	915	1,033	1.129

POINTS

Player	Seasons	Games	Goals	Assists	Points	Player	Seasons	Games	Goals	Assists	Points
Wayne Gretzky	20	1,487	894	1,963	2,857	Steve Yzerman	23	1,514	692	1,063	1,755
Mark Messier	25	1,756	694	1,193	1,887	Mario Lemieux	22	915	690	1,033	1,723
Gordie Howe	26	1,767	801	1,049	1,850	Joe Sakic	22	1,363	623	1,006	1,629
Ron Francis	23	1,731	549	1,249	1,798	Jaromir Jagr	19	1,273	646	953	1,599
Marcel Dionne	18	1,348	731	1,040	1,771	Phil Esposito	18	1,282	717	873	1,590

Note: As of end of 2007–08 season.

Art Ross Trophy Winners, 1918–2008

The Art Ross Trophy goes to the player who leads the league in scoring at the end of the regular season.

Season	Player, Team	Season	Player, Team	Season	Player, Team
1918	Joe Malone, Montreal	1945	Elmer Lach, Montreal	1978	Guy Lafleur, Montreal
1919	Newsy Lalonde, Montreal	1946	Max Bentley, Chicago	1979	Bryan Trottier, New York Islanders
1920	Joe Malone, Quebec	1947	Max Bentley, Chicago		
1921	Newsy Lalonde, Montreal	1948	Elmer Lach, Montreal	1980	Marcel Dionne, Los Angeles
1922	Punch Broadbent, Ottawa	1949	Roy Conacher, Chicago	1981	Wayne Gretzky, Edmonton
1923	Babe Dye, Toronto	1950	Ted Lindsay, Detroit	1982	Wayne Gretzky, Edmonton
1924	Cy Denneny, Ottawa	1951	Gordie Howe, Detroit	1983	Wayne Gretzky, Edmonton
1925	Babe Dye, Toronto	1952	Gordie Howe, Detroit	1984	Wayne Gretzky, Edmonton
1926	Nels Stewart, Montreal Maroons	1953	Gordie Howe, Detroit	1985	Wayne Gretzky, Edmonton
		1954	Gordie Howe, Detroit	1986	Wayne Gretzky, Edmonton
1927	Bill Cook, New York Rangers	1955	Bernie Geoffrion, Montreal	1987	Wayne Gretzky, Edmonton
		1956	Jean Béliveau, Montreal	1988	Mario Lemieux, Pittsburgh
1928	Howie Morenz, Montreal	1957	Gordie Howe, Detroit	1989	Mario Lemieux, Pittsburgh
1929	Ace Bailey, Toronto	1958	Dickie Moore, Montreal	1990	Wayne Gretzky, Los Angeles
1930	Cooney Weiland, Boston	1959	Dickie Moore, Montreal	1991	Wayne Gretzky, Los Angeles
1931	Howie Morenz, Montreal	1960	Bobby Hull, Chicago	1992	Mario Lemieux, Pittsburgh
1932	Harvey Jackson, Toronto	1961	Bernie Geoffrion, Montreal	1993	Mario Lemieux, Pittsburgh
1933	Bill Cook, New York Rangers	1962	Bobby Hull, Chicago	1994	Wayne Gretzky, Los Angeles
		1963	Gordie Howe, Detroit	1995	Jaromir Jagr, Pittsburgh
1934	Charlie Conacher, Toronto	1964	Stan Mikita, Chicago	1996	Mario Lemieux, Pittsburgh
1935	Charlie Conacher, Toronto	1965	Stan Mikita, Chicago	1997	Mario Lemieux, Pittsburgh
1936	Dave Shriner, New York Americans	1966	Bobby Hull, Chicago	1998	Jaromir Jagr, Pittsburgh
		1967	Stan Mikita, Chicago	1999	Jaromir Jagr, Pittsburgh
1937	Dave Shriner, New York Americans	1968	Stan Mikita, Chicago	2000	Jaromir Jagr, Pittsburgh
		1969	Phil Esposito, Boston	2001	Jaromir Jagr, Pittsburgh
1938	Gordie Drillon, Toronto	1970	Bobby Orr, Boston	2002	Jarome Iginla , Calgary
1939	Toe Blake, Montreal	1971	Phil Esposito, Boston	2003	Peter Forsberg, Colorado
1940	Milt Schmidt, Boston	1972	Phil Esposito, Boston	2004	Martin St. Louis, Tampa Bay
1941	Bill Cowley, Boston	1973	Phil Esposito, Boston	2006	Joe Thornton, San Jose
1942	Bryan Hextall, New York Rangers	1974	Phil Esposito, Boston	2007	Sidney Crosby, Pittsburgh
		1975	Bobby Orr, Boston	2008	Alexander Ovechkin, Wash.
1943	Doug Bentley, Chicago	1976	Guy Lafleur, Montreal		
1944	Herbie Cain, Boston	1977	Guy Lafleur, Montreal		

Hart Trophy Winners, 1924–2008

The league's most valuable player is chosen by a poll of the Professional Hockey Writers' Association.

Season	Player, Team	Season	Player, Team	Season	Player, Team
1924	Frank Nighbor, Ottawa Senators	1949	Sid Abel, Detroit	1979	Bryan Trottier, New York Islanders
1925	Billy Burch, New York Americans	1950	Charlie Rayner, New York Rangers	1980	Wayne Gretzky, Edmonton
1926	Nels Stewart, Montreal Maroons	1951	Milt Schmidt, Boston	1981	Wayne Gretzky, Edmonton
1927	Herb Gardiner, Montreal	1952	Gordie Howe, Detroit	1982	Wayne Gretzky, Edmonton
1928	Howie Morenz, Montreal	1953	Gordie Howe, Detroit	1983	Wayne Gretzky, Edmonton
1929	Roy Worters, New York Americans	1954	Al Rollins, Toronto	1984	Wayne Gretzky, Edmonton
1930	Nels Stewart, Montreal Maroons	1955	Ted Kennedy, Toronto	1985	Wayne Gretzky, Edmonton
		1956	Jean Béliveau, Montreal	1986	Wayne Gretzky, Edmonton
1931	Howie Morenz, Montreal	1957	Gordie Howe, Detroit	1987	Wayne Gretzky, Edmonton
1932	Howie Morenz, Montreal	1958	Gordie Howe, Detroit	1988	Mario Lemieux, Pittsburgh
1933	Eddie Shore, Boston	1959	Andy Bathgate, New York Rangers	1989	Wayne Gretzky, Los Angeles
1934	Aurel Joliat, Montreal			1990	Mark Messier, Edmonton
1935	Eddie Shore, Boston	1960	Gordie Howe, Detroit	1991	Bret Hull, St. Louis
1936	Eddie Shore, Boston	1961	Bernie Geoffrion, Montreal	1992	Mark Messier, New York Rangers
1937	Babe Siebert, Montreal	1962	Jacques Plante, Montreal		
1938	Eddie Shore, Boston	1963	Gordie Howe, Detroit	1993	Mario Lemieux, Pittsburgh
1939	Toe Blake, Montreal	1964	Jean Béliveau, Montreal	1994	Sergei Fedorov, Detroit
1940	Ebbie Goodfellow, Detroit	1965	Bobby Hull, Chicago	1995	Eric Lindros, Philadelphia
1941	Bill Cowley, Boston	1966	Bobby Hull, Chicago	1996	Mario Lemieux, Pittsburgh
1942	Tom Anderson, New York Americans	1967	Stan Mikita, Chicago	1997	Dominik Hasek, Buffalo
		1968	Stan Mikita, Chicago	1998	Dominik Hasek, Buffalo
1943	Bill Cowley, Boston	1969	Phil Esposito, Boston	1999	Jaromir Jagr, Pittsburgh
1944	Babe Pratt, Toronto	1970	Bobby Orr, Boston	2000	Chris Pronger, St. Louis
1945	Elmer Lach, Montreal	1971	Bobby Orr, Boston	2001	Joe Sakic, Colorado
1946	Max Bentley, Toronto	1972	Bobby Orr, Boston	2002	Jose Theodore, Montreal
1947	Maurice Richard, Montreal	1973	Bobby Clarke, Philadelphia	2003	Peter Forsberg, Colorado
1948	Buddy O'Connor, New York Rangers	1974	Phil Esposito, Boston	2004	Martin St. Louis, Tampa Bay
		1975	Bobby Clarke, Philadelphia	2006	Joe Thornton, San Jose
		1976	Bobby Clarke, Philadelphia	2007	Sidney Crosby, Pittsburgh
		1977	Guy Lafleur, Montreal	2008	Alexander Ovechkin, Wash.
		1978	Guy Lafleur, Montreal		

Conn Smythe Trophy Winners, 1965–2008

The Conn Smythe Trophy is awarded to the most valuable player in the playoffs.

Season	Player, Team	Season	Player, Team
1965	Jean Béliveau, Montreal	1987	Ron Hextall, Philadelphia
1966	Roger Crozier, Detroit	1988	Wayne Gretzky, Edmonton
1967	Dave Keon, Toronto	1989	Al MacInnis, Calgary
1968	Glenn Hall, St. Louis	1990	Bill Ranford, Edmonton
1969	Serge Savard, Montreal	1991	Mario Lemieux, Pittsburgh
1970	Bobby Orr, Boston	1992	Mario Lemieux, Pittsburgh
1971	Ken Dryden, Montreal	1993	Patrick Roy, Montreal
1972	Bobby Orr, Boston	1994	Brian Leetch, New York Rangers
1973	Yvan Cournoyer, Montreal	1995	Claude Lemieux, New Jersey
1974	Bernie Parent, Philadelphia	1996	Joe Sakic, Colorado
1975	Bernie Parent, Philadelphia	1997	Mike Vernon, Detroit
1976	Reggie Leach, Philadelphia	1998	Steve Yzerman, Detroit
1977	Guy Lafleur, Montreal	1999	Joe Nieuwendyk, Dallas
1978	Larry Robinson, Montreal	2000	Scott Stevens, New Jersey
1979	Bob Gainey, Montreal	2001	Patrick Roy, Colorado
1980	Bryan Trottier, New York Islanders	2002	Nicklas Lidstrom, Detroit
1981	Butch Goring, New York Islanders	2003	Jean Sebastien Giguere, Anaheim
1982	Mike Bossy, New York Islanders	2004	Brad Richards, Tampa Bay
1983	Bill Smith, New York Islanders	2006	Cam Ward, Carolina
1984	Mark Messier, Edmonton	2007	Scott Neidermayer, Anaheim
1985	Wayne Gretzky, Edmonton	2008	Henrik Zetterberg, Detroit
1986	Patrick Roy, Montreal		

James Norris Memorial Trophy, 1954–2008

The league's best defenseman is chosen by the Pro Hockey Writers' Association.

Season	Player, Team	Season	Player, Team	Season	Player, Team
1954	Red Kelly, Detroit	1972	Bobby Orr, Boston	1990	Ray Bourque, Boston
1955	Doug Harvey, Montreal	1973	Bobby Orr, Boston	1991	Ray Bourque, Boston
1956	Doug Harvey, Montreal	1974	Bobby Orr, Boston	1992	Brian Leetch, N.Y. Rangers
1957	Doug Harvey, Montreal	1975	Bobby Orr, Boston	1993	Chris Chelios, Chicago
1958	Doug Harvey, Montreal	1976	Denis Potvin, N.Y. Islanders	1994	Ray Bourque, Boston
1959	Tom Johnson, Montreal	1977	Larry Robinson, Montreal	1995	Paul Coffey, Detroit
1960	Doug Harvey, Montreal	1978	Denis Potvin, N.Y. Islanders	1996	Chris Chelios, Chicago
1961	Doug Harvey, Montreal	1979	Denis Potvin, N.Y. Islanders	1997	Brian Leetch, N.Y. Rangers
1962	Doug Harvey, N.Y. Rangers	1980	Larry Robinson, Montreal	1998	Rob Blake, Los Angeles
1963	Pierre Pilote, Chicago	1981	Randy Carlyle, Pittsburgh	1999	Al MacInnis, St. Louis
1964	Pierre Pilote, Chicago	1982	Doug Wilson, Chicago	2000	Chris Pronger, St. Louis
1965	Pierre Pilote, Chicago	1983	Rod Langway, Washington	2001	Nicklas Lidstrom, Detroit
1966	Jacques Laperrière, Montreal	1984	Rod Langway, Washington	2002	Nicklas Lidstrom, Detroit
1967	Harry Howell, N.Y. Rangers	1985	Paul Coffey, Edmonton	2003	Nicklas Lidstrom, Detroit
1968	Bobby Orr, Boston	1986	Paul Coffey, Edmonton	2004	Scott Niedermayer, N. J.
1969	Bobby Orr, Boston	1987	Ray Bourque, Boston	2006	Nicklas Lindstrom, Detroit
1970	Bobby Orr, Boston	1988	Ray Bourque, Boston	2007	Nicklas Lindstrom, Detroit
1971	Bobby Orr, Boston	1989	Chris Chelios, Montreal	2008	Nicklas Lindstrom, Detroit

Vezina Trophy Winners, 1927–2008

The Vezina Trophy is awarded to the league's best goalkeeper and is selected by a poll of the league's general managers.

Season	Player	Team	Season	Player	Team
1927	George Hainsworth	Montreal	1969	Jacques Plante/Glenn Hall	St. Louis
1928	George Hainsworth	Montreal	1970	Tony Esposito	Chicago
1929	George Hainsworth	Montreal	1971	Ed Giacomin/Gilles Villemure	N.Y. Rangers
1930	Tiny Thompson	Boston	1972	Tony Esposito/Gary Smith	Chicago
1931	Roy Worters	N.Y. Americans	1973	Ken Dryden	Montreal
1932	Charlie Gardiner	Chicago	1974	Bernie Parent	Philadelphia
1933	Tiny Thompson	Boston		Tony Esposito	Chicago
1934	Charlie Gardiner	Chicago	1975	Bernie Parent	Philadelphia
1935	Lorne Chabot	Chicago	1976	Ken Dryden	Montreal
1936	Tiny Thompson	Boston	1977	Ken Dryden/Michel Larocque	Montreal
1937	Normie Smith	Detroit	1978	Ken Dryden/Michel Larocque	Montreal
1938	Tiny Thompson	Boston	1979	Ken Dryden/Michel Larocque	Montreal
1939	Frank Brimsek	Boston	1980	Bob Sauvé/Don Edwards	Buffalo
1940	Dave Kerr	N.Y. Rangers	1981	Richard Sevigny/Denis	Montreal
1941	Turk Broda	Toronto		Herron/ Michel Larocque	
1942	Frank Brimsek	Boston	1982	Bill Smith	N.Y. Islanders
1943	Johnny Mowers	Detroit	1983	Pete Peeters	Boston
1944	Bill Durnan	Montreal	1984	Tom Barrasso	Buffalo
1945	Bill Durnan	Montreal	1985	Pele Lindbergh	Philadelphia
1946	Bill Durnan	Montreal	1986	John Vanbiesbrouck	N.Y. Rangers
1947	Bill Durnan	Montreal	1987	Ron Hextall	Philadelphia
1948	Turk Broda	Toronto	1988	Grant Fuhr	Edmonton
1949	Bill Durnan	Montreal	1989	Patrick Roy	Montreal
1950	Bill Durnan	Montreal	1990	Patrick Roy	Montreal
1951	Al Rollins	Toronto	1991	Ed Belfour	Chicago
1952	Terry Sawchuk	Detroit	1992	Patrick Roy	Montreal
1953	Terry Sawchuk	Detroit	1993	Ed Belfour	Chicago
1954	Harry Lumley	Toronto	1994	Dominik Hasek	Buffalo
1955	Terry Sawchuk	Detroit	1995	Dominik Hasek	Buffalo
1956	Jacques Plante	Montreal	1996	Jim Carey	Washington
1957	Jacques Plante	Montreal	1997	Dominik Hasek	Buffalo
1958	Jacques Plante	Montreal	1998	Dominik Hasek	Buffalo
1959	Jacques Plante	Montreal	1999	Dominik Hasek	Buffalo
1960	Jacques Plante	Montreal	2000	Olaf Kolzig	Washington
1961	Johnny Bower	Toronto	2001	Dominik Hasek	Buffalo
1962	Jacques Plante	Montreal	2002	Jose Theodore	Montreal
1963	Glenn Hall	Chicago	2003	Martin Brodeur	New Jersey
1964	Charlie Hodge	Montreal	2004	Martin Brodeur	New Jersey
1965	Terry Sawchuk/Johnny Bower	Toronto	2006	Miikka Kiprusoff	Calgary
1966	Lorne Worsley/Charlie Hodge	Montreal	2007	Martin Brodeur	New Jersey
1967	Glenn Hall/ Denis Dejordy	Chicago	2008	Martin Brodeur	New Jersey
1968	Lorne Worsley/Rogie Vachon	Montreal			

Calder Memorial Trophy Winners, 1933–2008

The NHL rookie of the year is chosen by the Professional Hockey Writers' Association.

Season	Player, Team	Season	Player, Team	Season	Player, Team
1933	Carl Voss, Detroit	1955	Ed Litzenberger, Chicago	1981	Peter Stastny, Quebec
1934	Russ Blinko, Montreal Maroons	1956	Glenn Hall, Detroit	1982	Dale Hawerchuk, Winnipeg
		1957	Larry Regan, Boston	1983	Steve Larmer, Chicago
1935	Dave Schriner, New York Americans	1958	Frank Mahovlich, Toronto	1984	Tom Barrasso, Buffalo
		1959	Ralph Backsrom, Montreal	1985	Mario Lemieux, Pittsburgh
1936	Mike Karakas, Chicago	1960	Bill Hay, Chicago	1986	Gary Suter, Calgary
1937	Syl Apps, Toronto	1961	Dave Keon, Toronto	1987	Luc Robitaille, Los Angeles
1938	Cully Dahlstrom, Chicago	1962	Bobby Rousseau, Montreal	1988	Joe Nieuwendyk, Calgary
1939	Frank Brimsek, Boston	1963	Kent Douglas, Toronto	1989	Brian Leetch, New York
1940	Kilby MacDonald, New York Rangers	1964	Jacques Laperrière, Montreal Canadiens		Rangers
				1990	Sergei Makarov, Calgary
1941	Johnny Quilty, Montreal	1965	Roger Crozier, Detroit	1991	Ed Belfour, Chicago
1942	Grant Warwick, New York Rangers	1966	Brit Selby, Toronto	1992	Pavel Bure, Vancouver
		1967	Bobby Orr, Boston	1993	Teemu Selanne, Winnipeg
1943	Gaye Stewart, Toronto	1968	Derek Sanderson, Boston	1994	Martin Brodeur, New Jersey
1944	Gus Bodnar, Toronto	1969	Danny Grant, Minnesota	1995	Petr Forsberg, Quebec
1945	Frank McCool, Toronto	1970	Tony Esposito, Chicago	1996	Daniel Alfredsson, Ottawa
1946	Edgar Laprade, New York Rangers	1971	Gilbert Perreault, Buffalo	1997	Bryan Berard, New York Islanders
		1972	Ken Dryden, Montreal		
1947	Howie Meeker, Toronto	1973	Steve Vickers, New York Rangers	1998	Sergei Samsonov, Boston
1948	Jim McFadden, Detroit			1999	Chris Drury, Colorado
1949	Pentti Lund, New York Rangers	1974	Denis Potvin, New York Islanders	2000	Scott Gomez, New Jersey
				2001	Evgeni Nabokov, San Jose
1950	Jack Gelineau, Boston	1975	Eric Vail, Atlanta	2002	Dany Heatley, Atlanta
1951	Terry Sawchuk, Detroit	1976	Bryan Trottier, New York Islanders	2003	Barret Jackman, St. Louis
1952	Bernie Geoffrion, Montreal Canadiens	1977	Willie Plett, Atlanta	2004	Andrew Raycroft, Boston
1953	Lorne Worsley, New York Rangers	1978	Mike Bossy, New York Islanders	2006	Alexander Ovechkin, Washington
1954	Camille Henry, New York Rangers	1979	Bobby Smith, Minnesota	2007	Evgeni Malkin, Pittsburgh
		1980	Ray Bourque, Boston	2008	Patrick Kane, Chicago

BASEBALL

MAJOR LEAGUE BASEBALL

245 Park Avenue
New York, N.Y. 10167
(212)-931-7800

www.mlb.com
Number of teams: 30
Commissioner: Allan "Bud" Selig

▶THE 2008 BASEBALL SEASON

The 2008 baseball season resembled 2007 in many ways. Going into the last week of the season, five teams were vying for two final playoff spots, and, as in 2007, the New York Mets lost their bid to reach the playoffs on the final day of the season (even if their collapse was not quite as dramatic and precipitous as it had been the year before). The Milwaukee Brewers reached the NLDS by beating the Cubs in the last regular-season game of 2008, marking the first time since 1982 that the franchise would play in October. In the American League, the Chicago White Sox and the Minnesota Twins played their 163rd game of the year to determine the AL Wild Card team: Chicago's Jim Thome propelled the Sox to a date with Tampa Bay in the ALDS by blasting a 7th inning homer to give them a 1-0 victory. 2008 was also the first year since 1996 that the New York

Yankees did not play in the postseason, a failure fueled in large part by the Tampa Bay Rays who surprised the baseball world by capturing the AL East title.

In 2008, several milestones were reached, including Ken Griffey, Jr. joining the elite 600 Club and ending the season with a career 611 home runs; Alex Rodriguez moving to number 12 on the all-time home run list at only 33 years of age; and Randy Johnson rocketing ahead of Roger Clemens to second place on the list of career strikeout leaders, fanning his 4,789th batter in his final start of the season. Sadly, in 2008 was the last-ever game in the venerable Yankee Stadium, and the final game at not-quite-as-venerable Shea Stadium a few miles away in Queens.

2008 American League Standings

Region	W	L	PCT	GB	Home	Away	DIV	Streak
East								
Tampa Bay	97	65	.599	---	57-24	40-41	43-29	Won 1
x-Boston	95	67	.586	2	56-25	39-42	38-34	Won 1
NY Yankees	89	73	.549	8	48-33	41-40	40-32	Lost 1
Toronto	86	76	.531	11	47-34	39-42	37-35	Won 1
Baltimore	68	93	.422	28 1/2	37-43	31-50	22-50	Lost 1
Central								
Chicago WSox	89	74	.546	---	54-28	35-46	44-29	Won 3
Minnesota	88	75	.540	1	53-28	35-47	43-30	Lost 1
Cleveland	81	81	.500	7	45-36	36-45	36-36	Lost 1
Kansas City	75	87	.463	13	38-43	37-44	31-41	Lost 1
Detroit	74	88	.457	14	40-41	34-47	27-45	Lost 2
West								
LA Angels	100	62	.617	---	50-31	50-31	36-21	Won 1
Texas	79	83	.488	21	40-41	39-42	30-27	Lost 1
Oakland	75	86	.466	24 1/2	43-38	32-48	26-31	Lost 5
Seattle	61	101	.377	39	35-46	26-55	22-35	Won 3

Note: x = clinched playoff berth

Final 2008 AL Team Statistics - Batting

Team	AVG	G	AB	R	OR	H	TB	2B	3B	HR	GS	RBI
Texas	.283	162	5728	901	967	1619	2647	376	35	194	8	867
Boston	.280	162	5596	845	694	1565	2503	353	33	173	6	807
Minnesota	.279	163	5641	829	745	1572	2301	298	49	111	4	791
NY Yankees	.271	162	5572	789	727	1512	2381	289	20	180	7	758
Detroit	.271	162	5641	821	857	1529	2504	293	41	200	6	780
Kansas City	.269	162	5608	691	781	1507	2226	303	28	120	2	650
LA Angels	.268	162	5540	765	697	1486	2287	274	25	159	4	721
Baltimore	.267	161	5559	782	869	1486	2384	322	30	172	3	750
Seattle	.265	162	5643	671	811	1498	2195	285	20	124	3	631
Toronto	.264	162	5503	714	610	1453	2198	303	32	126	7	681
Chicago WSox	.263	163	5553	811	729	1458	2485	296	13	235	12	785
Cleveland	.262	162	5543	805	761	1455	2351	339	22	171	3	772
Tampa Bay	.260	162	5541	774	671	1443	2341	284	37	180	5	735
Oakland	.242	161	5451	646	690	1318	2009	270	23	125	2	610

Final 2008 AL Team Statistics - Pitching

Team	W	L	ERA	G	CG	SHO	REL	SV	IP	H
Toronto	86	76	3.49	162	15	13	421	44	1446.2	1330
Tampa Bay	97	65	3.82	162	7	12	448	52	1457.2	1349
LA Angels	100	62	3.99	162	7	10	383	66	1451.1	1455
Boston	95	67	4.01	162	5	16	466	47	1446.1	1369
Oakland	75	86	4.01	161	4	7	441	33	1435.0	1364
Chicago WSox	89	74	4.06	163	4	10	463	34	1457.2	1471
Minnesota	88	75	4.16	163	5	10	485	42	1459.0	1568
NY Yankees	89	73	4.28	162	1	11	475	42	1441.2	1478
Cleveland	81	81	4.45	162	10	13	399	31	1437.0	1530
Kansas City	75	87	4.48	162	2	8	439	44	1445.2	1473
Seattle	61	101	4.73	162	4	4	469	36	1435.1	1544
Detroit	74	88	4.90	162	1	2	440	34	1445.0	1541
Baltimore	68	93	5.13	161	4	4	492	35	1422.0	1538
Texas	79	83	5.37	162	6	8	457	36	1442.0	1647

2008 National League Standings

Region	W	L	PCT	GB	Home	Away	DIV	Streak
East								
Philadelphia	92	70	.568	---	48-33	44-37	41-31	Won 3
NY Mets	89	73	.549	3	48-33	41-40	40-32	Lost 1
Florida	84	77	.522	7 1/2	45-36	39-41	40-31	Won 1
Atlanta	72	90	.444	20	43-38	29-52	31-41	Lost 1
Washington	59	102	.366	32 1/2	34-46	25-56	27-44	Lost 4
Central								
Chicago Cubs	97	64	.602	---	55-26	42-38	48-33	Lost 1
x-Milwaukee	90	72	.556	7 1/2	49-32	41-40	47-32	Won 1
Houston	86	75	.534	11	47-33	39-42	43-35	Won 1
St. Louis	86	76	.531	11 1/2	46-35	40-41	36-41	Won 6
Cincinnati	74	88	.457	23 1/2	43-38	31-50	31-47	Lost 5
Pittsburgh	67	95	.414	30 1/2	39-42	28-53	32-49	Won 1
West								
Los Angeles	84	78	.519	---	48-33	36-45	40-32	Lost 1
Arizona	82	80	.506	2	48-33	34-47	44-28	Won 3
Colorado	74	88	.457	10	43-38	31-50	31-41	Lost 3
San Francisco	72	90	.444	12	37-44	35-46	36-36	Won 1
San Diego	63	99	.389	21	35-46	28-53	29-43	Lost 1

Note: x = clinched playoff berth

Final 2008 NL Team Statistics - Batting

Team	AVG	G	AB	R	OR	H	TB	2B	3B	HR	GS	RBI
St. Louis	.281	162	5636	779	725	1585	2442	283	26	174	4	744
Chicago Cubs	.278	161	5588	855	671	1552	2475	329	21	184	7	811
Atlanta	.270	162	5604	753	778	1514	2286	316	33	130	2	721
NY Mets	.266	162	5606	799	715	1491	2357	274	38	172	4	751
Los Angeles	.264	162	5506	700	648	1455	2195	271	29	137	1	659
Colorado	.263	162	5557	747	822	1462	2308	310	28	160	4	714
Houston	.263	161	5451	712	743	1432	2261	284	22	167	6	684
San Francisco	.262	162	5543	640	759	1452	2119	311	37	94	1	606
Pittsburgh	.258	162	5628	735	884	1454	2269	314	21	153	3	705
Philadelphia	.255	162	5509	799	680	1407	2412	291	36	214	2	762
Florida	.254	161	5499	770	767	1397	2379	302	28	208	4	741
Milwaukee	.253	162	5535	750	689	1398	2386	324	35	198	1	722
Washington	.251	161	5491	641	825	1376	2048	269	26	117	4	608
Arizona	.251	162	5409	720	706	1355	2244	318	47	159	3	683
San Diego	.250	162	5568	637	764	1390	2170	264	27	154	1	615
Cincinnati	.247	162	5465	704	800	1351	2229	269	24	187	5	677

Final 2008 NL Team Statistics - Pitching

Team	W	L	ERA	G	CG	SHO	REL	SV	IP	H
Los Angeles	84	78	3.68	162	5	11	461	35	1447.1	1381
Milwaukee	90	72	3.85	162	12	10	445	45	1455.2	1415
Chicago Cubs	97	64	3.87	161	2	8	478	44	1450.2	1329
Philadelphia	92	70	3.88	162	4	11	468	47	1449.2	1444
Arizona	82	80	3.98	162	6	9	444	39	1434.2	1403
NY Mets	89	73	4.07	162	5	12	557	43	1464.1	1415
St. Louis	86	76	4.19	162	2	7	506	42	1454.0	1517
Houston	86	75	4.36	161	4	13	488	48	1425.1	1453
San Francisco	72	90	4.38	162	4	12	478	41	1442.0	1416
San Diego	63	99	4.41	162	3	6	491	30	1458.1	1466
Florida	84	77	4.43	161	2	8	511	36	1435.1	1421
Atlanta	72	90	4.46	162	2	7	545	26	1440.2	1439
Cincinnati	74	88	4.55	162	2	6	507	34	1442.1	1542
Washington	59	102	4.66	161	2	8	517	28	1434.0	1496
Colorado	74	88	4.77	162	3	8	485	36	1446.0	1547
Pittsburgh	67	95	5.08	162	3	7	497	34	1455.0	1631

Note: As of Sept 28, 2008.

Major League Baseball All-Time Career Leaders

Hits (3,000 or more)
1. Pete Rose	4,256
2. Ty Cobb	4,191
3. Hank Aaron	3,771
4. Stan Musial	3,630
5. Tris Speaker	3,514
6. Carl Yastrzemski	3,419
7. Cap Anson	3,418
8. Honus Wagner	3,415
9. Paul Molitor	3,319
10. Eddie Collins	3,315
11. Willie Mays	3,283
12. Eddie Murray	3,255
13. Nap Lajoie	3,242
14. Cal Ripken Jr.	3,184
15. George Brett	3,154
16. Paul Waner	3,152
17. Robin Yount	3,142
18. Tony Gwynn	3,141
19. Dave Winfield	3,110
20. Craig Biggio	3,060
21. Rickey Henderson	3,055
22. Rod Carew	3,053
23. Lou Brock	3,023
24. Rafael Palmeiro	3,020
25. Wade Boggs	3,010

Home Runs
1. Barry Bonds[1]	762
2. Hank Aaron	755
3. Babe Ruth	714
4. Willie Mays	660
5. Ken Griffey	611
6. Sammy Sosa[1]	609
7. Frank Robinson	586
8. Mark McGwire	583
9. Harmon Killebrew	573
10. Rafael Palmeiro	569
11. Reggie Jackson	563
12. Alex Rodriguez[1]	553
13. Mike Schmidt	548
14. Jim Thome[1]	540
15. Mickey Mantle	536
16. Jimmie Foxx	534
17. Manny Ramirez	527
18. Willie McCovey	521
18. Ted Williams	521
18. Frank Thomas[1]	521
12. Ernie Banks	512
12. Eddie Mathews	512
23. Mel Ott	511
24. Eddie Murray	504
25. Gary Sheffield	499

Runs Batted In
1. Hank Aaron	2,297
2. Babe Ruth	2,213
3. Cap Anson	2,076
4. Barry Bonds[1]	1,996
5. Lou Gehrig	1,995
6. Stan Musial	1,951
7. Ty Cobb	1,938
8. Jimmie Foxx	1,922
9. Eddie Murray	1,917
10. Willie Mays	1,903

Runs
1. Rickey Henderson	2,295
2. Ty Cobb	2,245
3. Barry Bonds[1]	2,227
4. Babe Ruth	2,174
4. Hank Aaron	2,174
6. Pete Rose	2,165

7. Willie Mays	2,062
8. Cap Anson	1,996
9. Stan Musial	1,949
10. Lou Gehrig	1,888

Average (minimum 5,000 at bats)
1. Ty Cobb	.367
2. Rogers Hornsby	.358
3. Joe Jackson	.356
4. Ed Delahanty	.346
5. Tris Speaker	.345
6. Ted Williams	.344
7. Billy Hamilton	.344
8. Babe Ruth	.342
8. Dan Brouthers	.342
8. Harry Heilmann	.342

Stolen Bases
1. Rickey Henderson	1,406
2. Lou Brock	938
3. Billy Hamilton	912
4. Ty Cobb	892
5. Tim Raines	808
6. Vince Coleman	752
7. Eddie Collins	745
8. Arlie Latham	739
9. Max Carey	738
10. Honus Wagner	722

Total Bases
1. Hank Aaron	6,856
2. Stan Musial	6,134
3. Willie Mays	6,066
4. Barry Bonds[1]	5,976
5. Ty Cobb	5,859
6. Babe Ruth	5,793
7. Pete Rose	5,752
8. Carl Yastrzemski	5,539
9. Eddie Murray	5,397
10. Rafael Palmero	5,388

Slugging Percentage[2]
1. Babe Ruth	.690
2. Ted Williams	.634
3. Lou Gehrig	.632
4. Jimmie Foxx	.609
5. Barry Bonds[1]	.607
6. Hank Greenberg	.605
7. Manny Ramirez[1]	.593
8. Mark McGwire	.588
9. Todd Helton[1]	.583
10. Vladimir Guerrero[1]	.579

Extra Base Hits
1. Hank Aaron	1,477
2. Barry Bonds[1]	1,440
3. Stan Musial	1,377
4. Babe Ruth	1,356
5. Willie Mays	1,323
6. Rafael Palmeiro[1]	1,192
7. Lou Gehrig	1,190
8. Frank Robinson	1,186
9. Carl Yastrzemski	1,157
10. Ken Griffey	1,151

Games Played
1. Pete Rose	3,562
2. Carl Yastrzemski	3,308
3. Hank Aaron	3,298
4. Rickey Henderson	3,081
5. Ty Cobb	3,035
6. Eddie Murray	3,026
7. Stan Musial	3,026
8. Cal Ripken	3,001
9. Willie Mays	2,992
10. Barry Bonds[1]	2,986

Pitching-Wins
1. Cy Young	511
2. Walter Johnson	417
3. Christy Mathewson	373
3. Grover Alexander	373
5. Pud Galvin	365
6. Warren Spahn	363
7. Kid Nichols	361
8. Greg Maddux[1]	355
9. Roger Clemens[1]	354
10. Tim Keefe	342
11. Steve Carlton	329
12. John Clarkson	328
13. Eddie Plank	326
14. Nolan Ryan	324
15. Don Sutton	324
16. Phil Niekro	318
17. Gaylord Perry	314
18. Tom Seaver	311
19. Charles Radbourn	309
20. Mickey Welch	307
21. Tom Glavine	305
22. Lefty Grove	300
22. Early Wynn	300

Strikeouts
1. Nolan Ryan	5,714
2. Randy Johnson[1]	4,789
3. Roger Clemens	4,672
4. Steve Carlton	4,136
5. Bert Blyleven	3,701
6. Tom Seaver	3,640
7. Don Sutton	3,574
8. Gaylord Perry	3,534
9. Walter Johnson	3,508
10. Phil Niekro	3,342

Earned Run Average[3]
1. Ed Walsh	1.82
2. Addie Joss	1.89
3. Al Spalding	2.04
4. Mordecai "Three Finger" Brown	2.06
5. John Ward	2.10
6. Christy Mathewson	2.13
7. Tommy Bond	2.14
8. Rube Waddell	2.16
9. Walter Johnson	2.17
10. Ed Reulbach	2.28

Innings Pitched
1. Cy Young	7,356
2. Pud Galvin	6,003
3. Walter Johnson	5,914
4. Phil Niekro	5,404
5. Nolan Ryan	5,386
6. Gaylord Perry	5,350
7. Don Sutton	5,282
8. Warren Spahn	5,244
9. Steve Carlton	5,217
10. Grover Cleveland Alexander	5,190

Shutouts
1. Walter Johnson	110
2. Grover Cleveland Alexander	90
3. Christy Mathewson	80
4. Cy Young	76
5. Eddie Plank	69
6. Warren Spahn	63
7. Nolan Ryan	61
7. Tom Seaver	61
9. Bert Blyleven	60
10. Don Sutton	58

Note: As of October, 2008. 1. Active during the 2008 season. 2. Total bases divided by minimum 5,000 at-bats. 3. Minimum 2,000 innings pitched. **Source:** Major League Baseball.

Batting Champions 1901–2008

	NATIONAL LEAGUE			AMERICAN LEAGUE		
Year	Name	Team	Avg.	Name	Team	Avg.
1901	Jesse Burkett	St. Louis Cardinals	.382	Nap Lajoie	Philadelphia Athletics	.422
1902	C.H. Beaumont	Pittsburgh Pirates	.357	Ed Delahanty	Washington Senators	.376
1903	Honus Wagner	Pittsburgh Pirates	.355	Nap Lajoie	Cleveland Indians	.355
1904	Honus Wagner	Pittsburgh Pirates	.349	Nap Lajoie	Cleveland Indians	.381
1905	J. Bentley Seymour	Cincinnati Reds	.377	Elmer Flick	Cleveland Indians	.306
1906	Honus Wagner	Pittsburgh Pirates	.339	George Stone	St. Louis Browns	.358
1907	Honus Wagner	Pittsburgh Pirates	.350	Ty Cobb	Detroit Tigers	.350
1908	Honus Wagner	Pittsburgh Pirates	.354	Ty Cobb	Detroit Tigers	.324
1909	Honus Wagner	Pittsburgh Pirates	.339	Ty Cobb	Detroit Tigers	.377
1910	Sherwood Magee	Philadelphia Phillies	.331	Ty Cobb	Detroit Tigers	.385
1911	Honus Wagner	Pittsburgh Pirates	.334	Ty Cobb	Detroit Tigers	.420
1912	Heinie Zimmerman	Chicago Cubs	.372	Ty Cobb	Detroit Tigers	.410
1913	Jake Daubert	Brooklyn Dodgers	.350	Ty Cobb	Detroit Tigers	.390
1914	Jake Daubert	Brooklyn Dodgers	.329	Ty Cobb	Detroit Tigers	.368
1915	Larry Doyle	New York Giants	.320	Ty Cobb	Detroit Tigers	.370
1916	Hal Chase	Cincinnati Reds	.339	Tris Speaker	Cleveland Indians	.386
1917	Edd Roush	Cincinnati Reds	.341	Ty Cobb	Detroit Tigers	.383
1918	Zack Wheat	Brooklyn Dodgers	.335	Ty Cobb	Detroit Tigers	.382
1919	Edd Roush	Cincinnati Reds	.321	Ty Cobb	Detroit Tigers	.407
1920	Rogers Hornsby	St. Louis Cardinals	.370	George Sisler	St. Louis Browns	.407
1921	Rogers Hornsby	St. Louis Cardinals	.397	Harry Heilmann	Detroit Tigers	.394
1922	Rogers Hornsby	St. Louis Cardinals	.401	George Sisler	St. Louis Browns	.420
1923	Rogers Hornsby	St. Louis Cardinals	.384	Harry Heilmann	Detroit Tigers	.403
1924	Rogers Hornsby	St. Louis Cardinals	.424	Babe Ruth	New York Yankees	.378
1925	Rogers Hornsby	St. Louis Cardinals	.403	Harry Heilmann	Detroit Tigers	.393
1926	Bubbles Hargrave	Cincinnati Reds	.353	Heinie Manush	Detroit Tigers	.377
1927	Paul Waner	Pittsburgh Pirates	.380	Harry Heilmann	Detroit Tigers	.398
1928	Rogers Hornsby	Boston Braves	.387	Goose Goslin	Washington Senators	.379
1929	Lefty O'Doul	Philadelphia Phillies	.398	Lew Fonseca	Cleveland Indians	.369
1930	Bill Terry	New York Giants	.401	Al Simmons	Philadelphia Athletics	.381
1931	Chick Hafey[1]	St Louis Cardinals	.349	Al Simmons	Philadelphia Athletics	.390
1932	Lefty O'Doul	Brooklyn Dodgers	.368	Dale Alexander	Detroit-Boston	.367
1933	Chuck Klein	Philadelphia Phillies	.368	Jimmie Foxx	Philadelphia Athletics	.356
1934	Paul Waner	Pittsburgh Pirates	.362	Lou Gehrig	New York Yankees	.363
1935	Arky Vaughan	Pittsburgh Pirates	.385	Buddy Myer	Washington Senators	.349
1936	Paul Waner	Pittsburgh Pirates	.373	Luke Appling	Chicago White Sox	.388
1937	Joe Medwick	St. Louis Cardinals	.374	Charlie Gehringer	Detroit Tigers	.371
1938	Ernie Lombardi	Cincinnati Reds	.342	Jimmie Foxx	Boston Red Sox	.349
1939	Johnny Mize	St. Louis Cardinals	.349	Joe DiMaggio	New York Yankees	.381
1940	Debs Garms	Pittsburgh Pirates	.355	Joe DiMaggio	New York Yankees	.352
1941	Pete Reiser	Brooklyn Dodgers	.343	Ted Williams	Boston Red Sox	.406
1942	Ernie Lombardi	Boston Braves	.330	Ted Williams	Boston Red Sox	.356
1943	Stan Musial	St. Louis Cardinals	.357	Luke Appling	Chicago White Sox	.328
1944	Dixie Walker	Brooklyn Dodgers	.357	Lou Boudreau	Cleveland Indians	.327
1945	Phil Cavarretta	Chicago Cubs	.355	Snuffy Stirnweiss	New York Yankees	.309
1946	Stan Musial	St. Louis Cardinals	.365	Mickey Vernon	Washington Senators	.352
1947	Harry Walker	St. Louis-Philadelphia	.363	Ted Williams	Boston Red Sox	.343
1948	Stan Musial	St. Louis Cardinals	.376	Ted Williams	Boston Red Sox	.369
1949	Jackie Robinson	Brooklyn Dodgers	.342	George Kell	Detroit Tigers	.343
1950	Stan Musial	St. Louis Cardinals	.346	Billy Goodman	Boston Red Sox	.354
1951	Stan Musial	St. Louis Cardinals	.355	Ferris Fain	Philadelphia Athletics	.344
1952	Stan Musial	St. Louis Cardinals	.336	Ferris Fain	Philadelphia Athletics	.327
1953	Carl Furillo	Brooklyn Dodgers	.344	Mickey Vernon	Washington Senators	.337
1954	Willie Mays	New York Giants	.345	Bobby Avila	Cleveland Indians	.341
1955	Richie Ashburn	Philadelphia Phillies	.338	Al Kaline	Detroit Tigers	.340
1956	Hank Aaron	Milwaukee Braves	.328	Mickey Mantle	New York Yankees	.353
1957	Stan Musial	St. Louis Cardinals	.351	Ted Williams	Boston Red Sox	.388
1958	Richie Ashburn	Philadelphia Phillies	.350	Ted Williams	Boston Red Sox	.328
1959	Hank Aaron	Milwaukee Braves	.355	Harvey Kuenn	Detroit Tigers	.353
1960	Dick Groat	Pittsburgh Pirates	.325	Pete Runnels	Boston Red Sox	.320
1961	Roberto Clemente	Pittsburgh Pirates	.351	Norm Cash	Detroit Tigers	.361
1962	Tommy Davis	Los Angeles Dodgers	.346	Pete Runnels	Boston Red Sox	.326
1963	Tommy Davis	Los Angeles Dodgers	.326	Carl Yastrzemski	Boston Red Sox	.321
1964	Roberto Clemente	Pittsburgh Pirates	.339	Tony Oliva	Minnesota Twins	.323
1965	Roberto Clemente	Pittsburgh Pirates	.329	Tony Oliva	Minnesota Twins	.321
1966	Matty Alou	Pittsburgh Pirates	.342	Frank Robinson	Baltimore Orioles	.316
1967	Roberto Clemente	Pittsburgh Pirates	.357	Carl Yastrzemski	Boston Red Sox	.326
1968	Pete Rose	Cincinnati Reds	.335	Carl Yastrzemski	Boston Red Sox	.301
1969	Pete Rose	Cincinnati Reds	.348	Rod Carew	Minnesota Twins	.332
1970	Rico Carty	Atlanta Braves	.366	Alex Johnson	California Angels	.329

	NATIONAL LEAGUE				AMERICAN LEAGUE		
Year	Name	Team	Avg.		Name	Team	Avg
1971	Joe Torre	St. Louis Cardinals	.363		Tony Oliva	Minnesota Twins	.337
1972	Billy Williams	Chicago Cubs	.333		Rod Carew	Minnesota Twins	.318
1973	Pete Rose	Cincinnati Reds	.338		Rod Carew	Minnesota Twins	.350
1974	Ralph Garr	Atlanta Braves	.353		Rod Carew	Minnesota Twins	.364
1975	Bill Madlock	Chicago Cubs	.354		Rod Carew	Minnesota Twins	.359
1976	Bill Madlock	Chicago Cubs	.339		George Brett	Kansas City Royals	.333
1977	Dave Parker	Pittsburgh Pirates	.338		Rod Carew	Minnesota Twins	.388
1978	Dave Parker	Pittsburgh Pirates	.334		Rod Carew	Minnesota Twins	.333
1979	Keith Hernandez	St. Louis Cardinals	.344		Fred Lynn	Boston Red Sox	.333
1980	Bill Buckner	Chicago Cubs	.324		George Brett	Kansas City Royals	.390
1981[2]	Bill Madlock	Pittsburgh Pirates	.341		Carney Lansford	Boston Red Sox	.336
1982	Al Oliver	Montreal Expos	.331		Willie Wilson	Kansas City Royals	.332
1983	Bill Madlock	Pittsburgh Pirates	.323		Wade Boggs	Boston Red Sox	.361
1984	Tony Gwynn	San Diego Padres	.351		Don Mattingly	New York Yankees	.343
1985	Willie McGee	St. Louis Cardinals	.353		Wade Boggs	Boston Red Sox	.368
1986	Tim Raines	Montreal Expos	.334		Wade Boggs	Boston Red Sox	.357
1987	Tony Gwynn	San Diego Padres	.370		Wade Boggs	Boston Red Sox	.363
1988	Tony Gwynn	San Diego Padres	.313		Wade Boggs	Boston Red Sox	.366
1989	Tony Gwynn	San Diego Padres	.336		Kirby Puckett	Minnesota Twins	.339
1990	Willie McGee	St. Louis Cardinals	.335		George Brett	Kansas City Royals	.329
1991	Terry Pendleton	Atlanta Braves	.319		Julio Franco	Texas Rangers	.341
1992	Gary Sheffield	San Diego Padres	.330		Edgar Martinez	Seattle Mariners	.343
1993	Andres Galarraga	Colorado Rockies	.370		John Olerud	Toronto Blue Jays	.363
1994[2]	Tony Gwynn	San Diego Padres	.394		Paul O'Neill	New York Yankees	.359
1995[2]	Tony Gwynn	San Diego Padres	.368		Edgar Martinez	Seattle Mariners	.356
1996	Ellis Burks	Colorado Rockies	.344		Alex Rodriguez	Seattle Mariners	.358
1997	Tony Gwynn	San Diego Padres	.372		Frank Thomas	Chicago White Sox	.347
1998	Larry Walker	Colorado Rockies	.363		Bernie Williams	New York Yankees	.339
1999	Larry Walker	Colorado Rockies	.379		Nomar Garciaparra	Boston Red Sox	.357
2000	Todd Helton	Colorado Rockies	.372		Nomar Garciaparra	Boston Red Sox	.372
2001	Larry Walker	Colorado Rockies	.350		Ichiro Suzuki	Seattle Mariners	.350
2002	Barry Bonds	San Francisco Giants	.370		Manny Ramirez	Boston Red Sox	.349
2003	Albert Pujols	St. Louis Cardinals	.359		Bill Mueller	Boston Red Sox	.326
2004	Barry Bonds	San Francisco Giants	.362		Ichiro Suzuki	Seattle Mariners	.372
2005	Derrek Lee	Chicago Cubs	.335		Michael Young	Texas Rangers	.331
2006	Freddy Sanchez	Pittsburgh Pirates	.344		Joe Mauer	Minnesota Twins	.347
2007	Matt Holliday	Colorado Rockies	.340		Magglio Ordonez	Detroit Tigers	.363
2008	Chipper Jones	Atlanta Braves	.364		Joe Mauer	Minnesota Twins	.330

1. Hafey led with .3489, Bill Terry, N.Y., second with .3486, Jim Bottomley, St. Louis, third with .3482. 2. Strike-shortened season.

Home Run Champions, 1919–2008

	NATIONAL LEAGUE		AMERICAN LEAGUE	
Year	Name, Team	Home Runs	Name, Team	Home Runs
1919	Gavvy Cravath, Philadelphia	12	Babe Ruth, Boston	29
1920	Cy Williams, Philadelphia	15	Babe Ruth, New York	54
1921	George Kelly, New York	23	Babe Ruth, New York	59
1922	Rogers Hornsby, St. Louis	42	Ken Williams, St. Louis	39
1923	Cy Williams, Philadelphia	41	Babe Ruth, New York	41
1924	Jack Fournier, Brooklyn	27	Babe Ruth, New York	46
1925	Rogers Hornsby, St. Louis	39	Bob Meusel, New York	33
1926	Hack Wilson, Chicago	21	Babe Ruth, New York	47
1927	Cy Williams, Philadelphia; Hack Wilson, Chicago	30	Babe Ruth, New York	60
1928	Jim Bottomley, St. Louis; Hack Wilson, Chicago	31	Babe Ruth, New York	54
1929	Chuck Klein, Philadelphia	43	Babe Ruth, New York	46
1930	Hack Wilson, Chicago	56	Babe Ruth, New York	49
1931	Chuck Klein, Philadelphia	31	Lou Gehrig, Babe Ruth, New York	46
1932	Chuck Klein, Philadelphia; Mel Ott, New York	38	Jimmie Foxx, Philadelphia	58
1933	Chuck Klein, Philadelphia	28	Jimmie Foxx, Philadelphia	48
1934	Ripper Collins, St. Louis; Mel Ott, New York	35	Lou Gehrig, New York	49
1935	Wally Berger, Boston	34	Jimmie Foxx, Philadelphia; Hank Greenberg, Detroit	36
1936	Mel Ott, New York	33	Lou Gehrig, New York	49
1937	Joe Medwick, St. Louis; Mel Ott, New York	31	Joe Dimaggio, New York	46
1938	Mel Ott, New York	36	Hank Greenberg, Detroit	58
1939	Johnny Mize, St. Louis	28	Jimmie Foxx, Boston	35
1940	Johnny Mize, St. Louis	43	Hank Greenberg, Detroit	41
1941	Dolph Camilli, Brooklyn	34	Ted Williams, Boston	37
1942	Mel Ott, New York	30	Ted Williams, Boston	36
1943	Bill Nicholson, Chicago	29	Rudy York, Detroit	34

Year	NATIONAL LEAGUE Name, Team	Home Runs	AMERICAN LEAGUE Name, Team	Home Runs
1943	Bill Nicholson, Chicago	29	Rudy York, Detroit	34
1944	Bill Nicholson, Chicago	33	Nick Etten, New York	22
1945	Tommy Holmes, Boston	28	Vern Stephens, St. Louis	24
1946	Ralph Kiner, Pittsburgh	23	Hank Greenberg, Detroit	44
1947	Ralph Kiner, Pittsburgh; Johnny Mize, New York	51	Ted Williams, Boston	32
1948	Ralph Kiner, Pittsburgh; Johnny Mize, New York	40	Joe DiMaggio, New York	39
1949	Ralph Kiner, Pittsburgh	54	Ted Williams, Boston	43
1950	Ralph Kiner, Pittsburgh	47	Al Rosen, Cleveland	37
1951	Ralph Kiner, Pittsburgh	42	Gus Zernial, Chicago-Philadelphia	33
1952	Ralph Kiner, Pittsburgh; Hank Sauer, Chicago	37	Larry Doby, Cleveland	32
1953	Eddie Mathews, Milwaukee	47	Al Rosen, Cleveland	43
1954	Ted Kluszewski, Cincinnati	49	Larry Doby, Cleveland	32
1955	Willie Mays, New York	51	Mickey Mantle, New York	37
1956	Duke Snider, Brooklyn	43	Mickey Mantle, New York	52
1957	Hank Aaron, Milwaukee	44	Roy Sievers, Washington	42
1958	Ernie Banks, Chicago	47	Mickey Mantle, New York	42
1959	Eddie Mathews, Milwaukee	46	Rocky Colavito, Cleveland; Harmon Killebrew, Washington	42
1960	Ernie Banks, Chicago	41	Mickey Mantle, New York	40
1961	Orlando Cepeda, San Francisco	46	Roger Maris, New York	61
1962	Willie Mays, San Francisco	49	Harmon Killebrew, Minnesota	48
1963	Hank Aaron, Milwaukee; Willie McCovey, San Francisco	44	Harmon Killebrew, Minnesota	45
1964	Willie Mays, San Francisco	47	Harmon Killebrew, Minnesota	49
1965	Willie Mays, San Francisco	52	Tony Conigliaro, Boston	32
1966	Hank Aaron, Atlanta	44	Frank Robinson, Baltimore	49
1967	Hank Aaron, Atlanta	39	Harmon Killebrew, Minnesota; Carl Yastrzemski, Boston	44
1968	Willie McCovey, San Francisco	36	Frank Howard, Washington	44
1969	Willie McCovey, San Francisco	45	Harmon Killebrew, Minnesota	49
1970	Johnny Bench, Cincinnati	45	Frank Howard, Washington	44
1971	Willie Stargell, Pittsburgh	48	Bill Melton, Chicago	33
1972	Johnny Bench, Cincinnati	40	Dick Allen, Chicago	37
1973	Willie Stargell, Pittsburgh	44	Reggie Jackson, Oakland	32
1974	Mike Schmidt, Philadelphia	36	Dick Allen, Chicago	32
1975	Mike Schmidt, Philadelphia	38	Reggie Jackson, Oakland; George Scott, Milwaukee	36
1976	Mike Schmidt, Philadelphia	38	Graig Nettles, New York	32
1977	George Foster, Cincinnati	52	Jim Rice, Boston	39
1978	George Foster, Cincinnati	40	Jim Rice, Boston	46
1979	Dave Kingman, Chicago	48	Gorman Thomas, Milwaukee	45
1980	Mike Schmidt, Philadelphia	48	Reggie Jackson, New York; Ben Oglivie, Milwaukee	41
1981[1]	Mike Schmidt, Philadelphia	31	Tony Armas, Boston; Dwight Evans, Boston; Bobby Grich, California; Eddie Murray, Baltimore	22
1982	Dave Kingman, New York	37	Reggie Jackson, California; Gorman Thomas, Milwaukee	39
1983	Mike Schmidt, Philadelphia	40	Jim Rice, Boston	39
1984	Dale Murphy, Atlanta; Mike Schmidt, Philadelphia	36	Tony Armas, Boston	50
1985	Dale Murphy, Atlanta	37	Darrell Evans, Detroit	40
1986	Mike Schmidt, Philadelphia	37	Jesse Barfield, Toronto	40
1987	Andre Dawson, Chicago	49	Mark McGwire, Oakland	49
1988	Darryl Strawberry, New York Mets	39	Jose Canseco, Oakland	42
1989	Kevin Mitchell, San Francisco	47	Fred McGriff, Toronto	36
1990	Ryne Sandberg, Chicago	40	Cecil Fielder, Detroit	51
1991	Howard Johnson, New York Mets	38	Jose Canseco, Oakland	44
1992	Fred McGriff, San Diego	35	Juan González, Texas	43
1993	Barry Bonds, San Francisco	46	Juan González, Texas	46
1994[1]	Matt Williams, San Francisco	43	Ken Griffey Jr., Seattle	40
1995[1]	Dante Bichette, Colorado	40	Albert Belle, Cleveland	50
1996	Andres Galarraga, Colorado	47	Mark McGwire, Oakland	52
1997	Larry Walker, Colorado[2]	49	Ken Griffey Jr., Seattle[2]	56
1998	Mark McGwire, St. Louis	70	Ken Griffey Jr., Seattle	56
1999	Mark McGwire, St. Louis	65	Ken Griffey Jr., Seattle	48
2000	Sammy Sosa, Chicago Cubs	50	Troy Glaus, Anaheim	47
2001	Barry Bonds, San Francisco	73	Alex Rodríguez, Texas	52
2002	Sammy Sosa, Chicago Cubs	49	Alex Rodríguez, Texas	57
2003	Jim Thome, Philadelphia	47	Alex Rodríguez, Texas	47
2004	Adrian Beltré, Los Angeles	48	Manny Ramírez, Boston	43
2005	Andrew Jones, Atlanta	51	Alex Rodriguez, N.Y. Yankees	48
2006	Ryan Howard, Philadelphia	58	David Ortiz, Boston	54
2007	Prince Fielder, Milwaukee Brewers	50	Alex Rodriguez, NY Yankees	54
2008	Ryan Howard, Philadelphia Phillies	48	Miguel Cabrera, Detroit Tigers	37

1. Strike-shortened season 2. Mark McGwire hit 34 home runs with Oakland and 24 with St. Louis for a major-league-leading total of 58.

Rookie of the Year

	NATIONAL LEAGUE			AMERICAN LEAGUE	
Year	Name	Team	Year	Name	Team
1947[1]	Jackie Robinson	Brooklyn Dodgers			
1948[1]	Alvin Dark	Boston Braves			
1949	Don Newcombe	Brooklyn Dodgers			
1950	Sam Jethroe	Boston Braves	1950	Walt Dropo	Boston Red Sox
1951	Willie Mays	New York Giants	1951	Gil McDougald	New York Yankees
1952	Joe Black	Brooklyn Dodgers	1952	Harry Byrd	Philadelphia Athletics
1953	Junior Gilliam	Brooklyn Dodgers	1953	Harvey Kuenn	Detroit Tigers
1954	Wally Moon	St. Louis Cardinals	1954	Bob Grim	New York Yankees
1955	Bill Virdon	St. Louis Cardinals	1955	Herb Score	Cleveland Indians
1956	Frank Robinson	Cincinnati Reds	1956	Luis Aparicio	Chicago White Sox
1957	Jack Sanford	Philadelphia Phillies	1957	Tony Kubek	New York Yankees
1958	Orlando Cepeda	San Francisco Giants	1958	Albie Pearson	Washington Senators
1959	Willie McCovey	San Francisco Giants	1959	Bob Allison	Washington Senators
1960	Frank Howard	Los Angeles Dodgers	1960	Ron Hansen	Baltimore Orioles
1961	Billy Williams	Chicago Cubs	1961	Don Schwall	Boston Red Sox
1962	Ken Hubbs	Chicago Cubs	1962	Tom Tresh	New York Yankees
1963	Pete Rose	Cincinnati Reds	1963	Gary Peters	Chicago White Sox
1964	Richie Allen	Philadelphia Phillies	1964	Tony Oliva	Minnesota Twins
1965	Jim Lefebvre	Los Angeles Dodgers	1965	Curt Blefary	Baltimore Orioles
1966	Tommy Helms	Cincinnati Reds	1966	Tommie Agee	Chicago White Sox
1967	Tom Seaver	New York Mets	1967	Rod Carew	Minnesota Twins
1968	Johnny Bench	Cincinnati Reds	1968	Stan Bahnsen	New York Yankees
1969	Ted Sizemore	Los Angeles Dodgers	1969	Lou Piniella	Kansas City Royals
1970	Carl Morton	Montreal Expos	1970	Thurman Munson	New York Yankees
1971	Earl Williams	Atlanta Braves	1971	Chris Chambliss	Cleveland Indians
1972	Jon Matlack	New York Mets	1972	Carlton Fisk	Boston Red Sox
1973	Gary Matthews	San Francisco Giants	1973	Al Bumbry	Baltimore Orioles
1974	Bake McBride	St. Louis Cardinals	1974	Make Hargrove	Texas Rangers
1975	John Montefusco	San Francisco Giants	1975	Fred Lynn	Boston Red Sox
1976	Pat Zachry	Cincinnati Reds	1976	Mark Fidrych	Detroit Tigers
	Butch Metzger	San Diego Padres	1977	Eddie Murray	Baltimore Orioles
1977	Andre Dawson	Montreal Expos	1978	Lou Whitaker	Detroit Tigers
1978	Bob Horner	Atlanta Braves	1979	John Castino	Minnesota Twins
1979	Rick Sutcliffe	Los Angeles Dodgers		Alfredo Griffin	Toronto Blue Jays
1980	Steve Howe	Los Angeles Dodgers	1980	Joe Charboneau	Cleveland Indians
1981	Fernando Valenzuela	Los Angeles Dodgers	1981	Dave Righetti	New York Yankees
1982	Steve Sax	Los Angeles Dodgers	1982	Cal Ripken Jr.	Baltimore Orioles
1983	Darryl Strawberry	New York Mets	1983	Ron Kittle	Chicago White Sox
1984	Dwight Gooden	New York Mets	1984	Alvin Davis	Seattle Mariners
1985	Vince Coleman	St. Louis Cardinals	1985	Ozzie Guillen	Chicago White Sox
1986	Todd Worrell	St. Louis Cardinals	1986	Jose Canseco	Oakland Athletics
1987	Benito Santiago	San Diego Padres	1987	Mark McGwire	Oakland Athletics
1988	Chris Sabo	Cincinnati Reds	1988	Walt Weiss	Oakland Athletics
1989	Jerome Walton	Chicago Cubs	1989	Greg Olson	Baltimore Orioles
1990	Dave Justice	Atlanta Braves	1990	Sandy Alomar Jr.	Cleveland Indians
1991	Jeff Bagwell	Houston Astros	1991	Chuck Knoblauch	Minnesota Twins
1992	Eric Karros	Los Angeles Dodgers	1992	Pat Listach	Milwaukee Brewers
1993	Mike Piazza	Los Angeles Dodgers	1993	Tim Salmon	California Angels
1994	Raul Mondesi	Los Angeles Dodgers	1994	Bob Hamelin	Kansas City Royals
1995	Hideo Nomo	Los Angeles Dodgers	1995	Marty Cordoba	Minnesota Twins
1996	Todd Hollandsworth	Los Angeles Dodgers	1996	Derek Jeter	New York Yankees
1997	Scott Rolen	Philadelphia Phillies	1997	Nomar Garciaparra	Boston Red Sox
1998	Kerry Wood	Chicago Cubs	1998	Ben Grieve	Oakland Athletics
1999	Scott Williamson	Cincinnati Reds	1999	Carlos Beltran	Kansas City Royals
2000	Rafael Furcal	Atlanta Braves	2000	Kazuhiro Sasaki	Seattle Mariners
2001	Albert Pujols	St. Louis Cardinals	2001	Ichiro Suzuki	Seattle Mariners
2002	Jason Jennings	Colorado Rockies	2002	Eric Hinske	Toronto Blue Jays
2003	Dontrelle Willis	Florida Marlins	2003	Angel Berroa	Kansas City Royals
2004	Jason Bay	Pittsburgh Pirates	2004	Bobby Crosby	Oakland Athletics
2005	Ryan Howard	Philadelphia Phillies	2005	Huston Street	Oakland Athletics
2006	Hanley Ramirez	Florida Marlins	2006	Justin Verlander	Detroit Tigers
2007	Ryan Braun	Milwaukee Brewers	2007	Dustin Pedroia	Boston Red Sox

1. One player selected as Major League Rookie of the Year. Policy of naming a player from each league was inaugurated in 1949.
Source: Baseball Writer's Association.

Cy Young Award Winners

BOTH LEAGUES

Year	Name, Team	W–L	ERA	Year	Name, Team	W–L	ERA
1956	Don Newcombe, Brooklyn Dodgers	27–7	3.06	1962	Don Drysdale, Los Angeles Dodgers	25–9	2.83
1957	Warren Spahn, Milwaukee Braves	21–11	2.69	1963	Sandy Koufax, Los Angeles Dodgers	25–5	1.88
1958	Bob Turley, New York Yankees	21–7	2.97	1964	Dean Chance, Los Angeles Angels	20–9	1.65
1959	Early Wynn, Chicago White Sox	22–10	3.17	1965	Sandy Koufax, Los Angeles Dodgers	26–8	2.04
1960	Vernon Law, Pittsburgh Pirates	20–9	3.08	1966	Sandy Koufax, Los Angeles Dodgers	27–9	1.73
1961	Whitey Ford, New York Yankees	25–4	3.21				

Year	National League Winner, Team	W-L	ERA	American League Winner, Team	W-L	ERA
1967	Mike McCormick, San Francisco Giants	22–10	2.85	Jim Lonborg, Boston Red Sox	22–9	3.16
1968	Bob Gibson, St. Louis Cardinals	22–9	1.12	Denny McLain, Detroit Tigers	31–6	1.96
1969	Tom Seaver, New York Mets	25–7	2.21	Mike Cuellar, Baltimore Orioles	23–11	2.38
1970	Bob Gibson, St. Louis Cardinals	23–7	3.12	Jim Perry, Minnesota Twins	24–12	3.03
1971	Ferguson Jenkins, Chicago Cubs	24–13	2.77	Vida Blue, Oakland Athletics	24–8	1.82
1972	Steve Carlton, Philadelphia Phillies	27–10	1.97	Gaylord Perry, Cleveland Indians	24–16	1.92
1973	Tom Seaver, New York Mets	19–10	2.08	Jim Palmer, Baltimore Orioles	22–9	2.40
1974	Mike Marshall, Los Angeles Dodgers	21 saves	2.42	Catfish Hunter, Oakland Athletics	25–12	2.49
1975	Tom Seaver, New York Mets	22–9	2.38	Jim Palmer, Baltimore Orioles	23–11	2.09
1976	Randy Jones, San Diego Padres	22–14	2.74	Jim Palmer, Baltimore Orioles	22–13	2.51
1977	Steve Carlton, Philadelphia Phillies	23–10	2.64	Sparky Lyle, New York Yankees	26 saves	2.17
1978	Gaylord Perry, San Diego Padres	21–6	2.72	Ron Guidry, New York Yankees	25–3	1.74
1979	Bruce Sutter, Chicago Cubs	37 saves	2.23	Mike Flanagan, Baltimore Orioles	23–9	3.08
1980	Steve Carlton, Philadelphia Phillies	24–9	2.34	Steve Stone, Baltimore Orioles	25–7	3.23
1981[1]	Fernando Valenzuela, Los Angeles Dodgers	13–7	2.48	Rollie Fingers, Milwaukee Brewers	28 saves	1.04
1982	Steve Carlton, Philadelphia Phillies	23–11	3.10	Pete Vuckovich, Milwaukee Brewers	18–6	3.34
1983	John Denny, Philadelphia Phillies	19–6	2.37	LaMarr Hoyt, Chicago White Sox	24–10	3.66
1984	Rick Sutcliffe, Chicago Cubs	20–6	3.64	Willie Hernandez, Detroit Tigers	32 saves	1.92
1985	Dwight Gooden, New York Mets	24–4	1.53	Bret Saberhagen, Kansas City Royals	20–6	2.87
1986	Mike Scott, Houston Astros	18–10	2.22	Roger Clemens, Boston Red Sox	24–4	2.48
1987	Steve Bedrosian, Philadelphia Phillies	40 saves	2.83	Roger Clemens, Boston Red Sox	20–9	2.97
1988	Orel Hershiser, Los Angeles Dodgers	23–8	2.26	Frank Viola, Minnesota Twins	24–7	2.64
1989	Mark Davis, San Diego Padres	44 saves	1.85	Bret Saberhagen, Kansas City Royals	23–6	2.16
1990	Doug Drabek, Pittsburgh Pirates	22–6	2.76	Bob Welch, Oakland Athletics	27–6	3.06
1991	Tom Glavine, Atlanta Braves	20–11	2.55	Roger Clemens, Boston Red Sox	18–10	3.06
1992	Greg Maddux, Chicago Cubs	20–11	2.18	Dennis Eckersley, Oakland Athletics	51 saves	1.91
1993	Greg Maddux, Atlanta Braves	20–10	2.36	Jack McDowell, Chicago White Sox	22–10	3.37
1994[1]	Greg Maddux, Atlanta Braves	16–6	1.56	David Cone, Kansas City Royals	16–5	2.94
1995[1]	Greg Maddux, Atlanta Braves	19–2	1.53	Randy Johnson, Seattle Mariners	18–2	2.48
1996	John Smoltz, Atlanta Braves	24–8	2.94	Pat Hentgen, Toronto Blue Jays	20–10	3.22
1997	Pedro Martínez, Montreal Expos	17–8	1.90	Roger Clemens, Toronto Blue Jays	21–7	2.05
1998	Tom Glavine, Atlanta Braves	20–6	2.47	Roger Clemens, Toronto Blue Jays	20–6	2.65
1999	Randy Johnson, Arizona Diamondbacks	17–9	2.48	Pedro Martínez, Boston Red Sox	23–4	2.07
2000	Randy Johnson, Arizona Diamondbacks	19–7	2.64	Pedro Martínez, Boston Red Sox	18–6	1.74
2001	Randy Johnson, Arizona Diamondbacks	21–6	2.49	Roger Clemens, New York Yankees	20–6	2.65
2002	Randy Johnson, Arizona Diamondbacks	24–5	2.32	Barry Zito, Oakland Athletics	23–5	2.75
2003	Eric Gagné, Los Angeles Dodgers	55 saves	1.20	Roy Halladay, Toronto Blue Jays	22–7	3.25
2004	Roger Clemens, Houston Astros	18–4	2.98	Johan Santana, Minnesota Twins	20–6	2.61
2005	Chris Carpenter, St. Louis Cardinals	21–5	2.83	Bartolo Colon, Los Angeles Angels	21–8	3.48
2006	Brandon Webb, Arizona Diamondbacks	16–8	3.10	Johan Santana, Minnesota Twins	19–6	2.77
2007	Jake Peavey, San Diego Padres	19–6	2.54	C.C. Sabathia, Cleveland Indians	19–7	3.21

Note: Saves, rather than win-loss records, are shown for relievers. 1. Strike-shortened season.

Most Wins by Managers

Manager	Wins	Losses	Pct.	Manager	Wins	Losses	Pct.
1. Connie Mack	3,731	3,948	.486	6. Joe Torre[1]	2,148	1,827	.537
2. John McGraw	2,763	1,984	.586	7. Bucky Harris	2,157	2,218	.493
3. Tony La Russa[1]	2,339	2,034	.535	8. Joe McCarthy	2,125	1,333	.615
4. Bobby Cox[1]	2,221	1,730	.562	9. Walter Alston	2,040	1,613	.558
5. Sparky Anderson	2,194	1,834	.545	10. Leo Durocher	2,008	1,709	.540

Note: 1. Manager active in 2008. **Source:** Major League Baseball.

Most Valuable Player Award Winners

Between 1911 and 1914 the Chalmers Award was given to the player judged to be the most valuable in each league. It was not until 1922 that the American League began to select a league MVP. The National League began to do so as well two years later. By the end of the decade , though both leagues failed to select an MVP. In 1931 th Baseball Writers Association of America began to select the league MVP's and has continued to do so through today.

NATIONAL LEAGUE

Year	Name	Team	HRs	RBIs	Avg.
1911	Frank Schulte	Chicago Cubs	21	121	.300
1912	Larry Doyle	New York Giants	10	90	.330
1913	Jake Daubert	Brooklyn Dodgers	2	52	.350
1914	Johnny Evers	Chicago Cubs	1	40	.279
1924	Dazzy Vance (Pitcher)	Brooklyn Dodgers	28W	6L	2.16 ERA
1925	Rogers Hornsby	St. Louis Cardinals	29	143	.403
1926	Bob O'Farrell	St. Louis Cardinals	7	68	.293
1927	Paul Waner	Pittsburgh Pirates	9	131	.380
1928	Jim Bottomley	St. Louis Cardinals	31	136	.325
1929	Rogers Hornsby	St. Louis Cardinals	39	149	.380
1931	Frankie Frisch	St. Louis Cardinals	4	82	.311
1932	Chuck Klein	Philadelphia Phillies	38	137	.348
1933	Carl Hubbell (Pitcher)	New York Giants	23W	12L	1.66 ERA
1934	Dizzy Dean (Pitcher)	St. Louis Cardinals	30W	7L	2.66 ERA
1935	Gabby Hartnett	Chicago Cubs	13	91	.344
1936	Carl Hubbell (Pitcher)	New York Giants	26W	6L	2.31 ERA
1937	Joe Medwick	St. Louis Cardinals	31	154	.374
1938	Ernie Lombardi	Cincinnati Reds	19	95	.342
1939	Bucky Walters (Pitcher)	Cinncinati Reds	27W	11L	2.29 ERA
1940	Frank McCormick	Cinncinati Reds	19	127	.309
1941	Dolph Camilli	Brooklyn Dodgers	34	120	.285
1942	Mort Cooper (Pitcher)	St. Louis Cardinals	22W	7L	1.78 ERA
1943	Stan Musial	St. Louis Cardinals	13	81	.357
1944	Marty Marion	St. Louis Cardinals	6	63	.267
1945	Phil Cavarretta	Chicago Cubs	6	97	.355
1946	Stan Musial	St. Louis Cardinals	16	103	.365
1947	Bob Elliott	Boston Braves	22	113	.317
1948	Stan Musial	St. Louis Cardinals	39	131	.376
1949	Jackie Robinson	Brooklyn Dodgers	16	124	.342
1950	Jim Konstanty (Pitcher)[1]	Philadelphia Phillies	16W	7L	2.66 ERA
1951	Roy Campanella	Brooklyn Dodgers	33	108	.325
1952	Hank Sauer	Chicago Cubs	37	121	.270
1953	Roy Campanella	Brooklyn Dodgers	41	142	.312
1954	Willie Mays	New York Giants	41	110	.345
1955	Roy Campanella	Brooklyn Dodgers	32	107	.318
1956	Don Newcombe (Pitcher)	Brooklyn Dodgers	27W	7L	3.06 ERA
1957	Hank Aaron	Milwaukee Braves	44	132	.322
1958	Ernie Banks	Chicago Cubs	47	129	.313
1959	Ernie Banks	Chicago Cubs	45	143	.304
1960	Dick Groat	Pittsburgh Pirates	2	50	.325
1961	Frank Robinson	Cincinnati Reds	37	124	.323
1962	Maury Wills	Los Angeles Dodgers	6	48	.299
1963	Sandy Koufax (Pitcher)	Los Angeles Dodgers	25W	5L	1.88 ERA
1964	Ken Boyer	St. Louis Cardinals	24	119	.295
1965	Willie Mays	San Francisco Giants	52	112	.317
1966	Roberto Clemente	Pittsburgh Pirates	29	119	.317
1967	Orlando Cepeda	San Francisco Giants	25	111	.325
1968	Bob Gibson (Pitcher)	St. Louis Cardinals	22W	9L	1.12 ERA
1969	Willie McCovey	San Francisco Giants	45	126	.320
1970	Johnny Bench	Cincinnati Reds	45	148	.293
1971	Joe Torre	St. Louis Cardinals	45	137	.363
1972	Johnny Bench	Cincinnati Reds	40	125	.270
1973	Pete Rose	Cincinnati Reds	5	64	.338
1974	Steve Garvey	Los Angeles Dodgers	21	111	.312
1975	Joe Morgan	Cincinnati Reds	17	94	.327
1976	Joe Morgan	Cincinnati Reds	27	111	.320
1977	George Foster	Cincinnati Reds	52	149	.320
1978	Dave Parker	Pittsburgh Pirates	30	117	.334
1979	Keith Hernandez	St. Louis Cardinals	11	105	.344
	Willie Stargell	Pittsburgh Pirates	32	82	.281
1980	Mike Schmidt	Philadelphia Phillies	48	121	.286

NATIONAL LEAGUE

Year	Name	Team	HRs	RBIs	Avg.
1981	Mike Schmidt[2]	Philadelphia Phillies	31	91	.316
1982	Dale Murphy	Atlanta Braves	36	109	.281
1983	Dale Murphy	Atlanta Braves	36	121	.302
1984	Ryne Sandberg	Chicago Cubs	19	84	.314
1985	Willie McGee	St. Louis Cardinals	10	82	.353
1986	Mike Schmidt	Philadelphia Phillies	37	119	.290
1987	Andre Dawson	Chicago Cubs	49	137	.287
1988	Kirk Gibson	Los Angeles Dodgers	25	76	.290
1989	Kevin Mitchell	San Francisco Giants	47	125	.291
1990	Barry Bonds	Pittsburgh Pirates	33	114	.301
1991	Terry Pendleton	Atlanta Braves	22	86	.319
1992	Barry Bonds	Pittsburgh Pirates	34	103	.311
1993	Barry Bonds	San Francisco Giants	46	123	.336
1994	Jeff Bagwell[2]	Houston Astros	39	116	.368
1995	Barry Larkin[2]	Cincinnati Reds	15	66	.319
1996	Ken Caminiti	San Diego Padres	40	130	.326
1997	Larry Walker	Colorado Rockies	49	130	.366
1998	Sammy Sosa	Chicago Cubs	66	158	.308
1999	Chipper Jones	Atlanta Braves	45	110	.319
2000	Jeff Kent	San Francisco Giants	33	125	.334
2001	Barry Bonds	San Francisco Giants	73	137	.328
2002	Barry Bonds	San Francisco Giants	46	110	.370
2003	Barry Bonds	San Francisco Giants	45	90	.341
2004	Barry Bonds	San Francisco Giants	45	101	.362
2005	Albert Pujols	St. Louis Cardinals	41	117	.330
2006	Ryan Howard	Philadelphia Phillies	58	149	.313
2007	Jimmy Rollins	Philadelphia Phillies	30	94	.296

1. 22 saves in 1950. 2. Strike-shortened season. **Source:** Baseball Writers' Association.

AMERICAN LEAGUE

Year	Player	Team	HRs	RBIs	Avg.
1911	Ty Cobb	Detroit Tigers	8	144	.420
1912	Tris Speaker	Boston Red Sox	10	98	.383
1913	Walter Johnson (Pitcher)	Washington Senators	36W	7L	1.09 ERA
1914	Eddie Collins	Philadelphia Athletics	2	85	.344
1922	George Sisler	St. Louis Browns	8	105	.420
1923	Babe Ruth	New York Yankees	41	131	.393
1924	Walter Johnson (Pitcher)	Washington Senators	23W	7L	2.72 ERA
1925	Roger Peckinpaugh	Washington Senators	4	64	.294
1926	George Burns	Cleveland Indians	4	114	.358
1927	Lou Gehrig	New York Yankees	47	175	.373
1928	Mickey Cochrane	Philadelphia Athletics	10	57	.293
1931	Lefty Grove (Pitcher)	Philadelphia Athletics	31W	4L	2.06 ERA
1932	Jimmie Foxx	Philadelphia Athletics	58	169	.364
1933	Jimmie Foxx	Philadelphia Athletics	48	163	.356
1934	Mickey Cochrane	Detroit Tigers	2	76	.320
1935	Hank Greenberg	Detroit Tigers	36	170	.328
1936	Lou Gehrig	New York Yankees	49	152	.354
1937	Charley Gehringer	Detroit Tigers	14	96	.371
1938	Jimmie Foxx	Boston Red Sox	50	175	.349
1939	Joe DiMaggio	New York Yankees	30	126	.381
1940	Hank Greenberg	Detroit Tigers	30	125	.357
1941	Joe DiMaggio	New York Yankees	30	125	.357
1942	Joe Gordon	New York Yankees	18	103	.322
1943	Spud Chandler (Pitcher)	New York Yankees	20W	4L	1.64 ERA
1944	Hal Newhouser (Pitcher)	Detroit Tigers	29W	9L	2.22 ERA
1945	Hal Newhouser (Pitcher)	Detroit Tigers	25W	9L	1.81 ERA
1946	Ted Williams	Boston Red Sox	38	123	.342
1947	Joe DiMaggio	New York Yankees	20	97	.315
1948	Lou Boudreau	Cleveland Indians	18	106	.355
1949	Ted Williams	Boston Red Sox	43	159	.343
1950	Phil Rizzuto	New York Yankees	7	66	.324
1951	Yogi Berra	New York Yankees	27	88	.294
1952	Bobby Shantz (Pitcher)	Philadelphia Athletics	24W	7L	2.48 ERA
1953	Al Rosen	Cleveland Indians	43	145	.336
1954	Yogi Berra	New York Yankees	22	125	.307
1955	Yogi Berra	New York Yankees	27	108	.272
1956	Mickey Mantle	New York Yankees	52	130	.353

AMERICAN LEAGUE

Year	Player	Team	HRs	RBIs	Avg.
1957	Mickey Mantle	New York Yankees	34	94	.365
1958	Jackie Jensen	Boston Red Sox	35	122	.286
1959	Nelson Fox	Chicago White Sox	2	70	.306
1960	Roger Maris	New York Yankees	39	112	.283
1961	Roger Maris	New York Yankees	61	142	.269
1962	Mickey Mantle	New York Yankees	30	89	.321
1963	Elston Howard	New York Yankees	28	85	.287
1964	Brooks Robinson	Baltimore Orioles	28	118	.317
1965	Zoilo Versalles	Minnesota Twins	19	77	.273
1966	Frank Robinson	Baltimore Orioles	49	122	.316
1967	Carl Yastrzemski	Boston Red Sox	44	121	.326
1968	Denny McLain (Pitcher)	Detroit Tigers	31W	6L	1.96ERA
1969	Harmon Killebrew	Minnesota Twins	49	140	.276
1970	Boog Powell	Baltimore Orioles	35	114	.297
1971	Vida Blue (Pitcher)	Oakland Athletics	24W	8L	1.82ERA
1972	Dick Allen	Chicago White Sox	37	113	.308
1973	Reggie Jackson	Oakland Athletics	32	117	.293
1974	Jeff Burroughs	Texas Rangers	25	118	.301
1975	Fred Lynn	Boston Red Sox	21	105	.331
1976	Thurman Munson	New York Yankees	17	105	.302
1977	Rod Carew	Minnesota Twins	14	100	.388
1978	Jim Rice	Boston Red Sox	46	139	.315
1979	Don Baylor	California Angels	36	139	.296
1980	George Brett	Kansas City Royals	24	118	.390
1981	Rollie Fingers (Pitcher)[1, 2]	Milwaukee Brewers	6W	3L	1.04 ERA
1982	Robin Yount	Milwaukee Brewers	29	114	.331
1983	Cal Ripken Jr.	Baltimore Orioles	27	102	.318
1984	Willie Hernandez (Pitcher)[3]	Detroit Tigers	9W	3L	2.48 ERA
1985	Don Mattingly	New York Yankees	35	145	.324
1986	Roger Clemens (Pitcher)	Boston Red Sox	24W	4L	2.48 ERA
1987	George Bell	Toronto Blue Jays	47	134	.308
1988	Jose Canseco	Oakland Athletics	42	124	.307
1989	Robin Yount	Milwaukee Brewers	21	103	.318
1990	Rickey Henderson	Oakland Athletics	28	61	.325
1991	Cal Ripken Jr.	Baltimore Orioles	34	114	.323
1992	Dennis Eckersley (Pitcher)[4]	Oakland Athletics	7W	1L	1.91 ERA
1993	Frank Thomas	Chicago White Sox	41	128	.317
1994	Frank Thomas[1]	Chicago White Sox	38	101	.353
1995	Mo Vaughn[1]	Boston Red Sox	39	126	.300
1996	Juan González	Texas Rangers	47	144	.314
1997	Ken Griffey Jr.	Seattle Mariners	56	147	.304
1998	Juan González	Texas Rangers	45	157	.318
1999	Iván Rodríguez	Texas Rangers	35	113	.332
2000	Jason Giambi	Oakland Athletics	43	137	.333
2001	Ichiro Suzuki	Seattle Mariners	8	69	.350
2002	Miguel Tejada	Oakland Athletics	34	131	.308
2003	Alex Rodríguez	Texas Rangers	47	118	.298
2004	Vladimir Guerrero	Anaheim Angels	39	126	.337
2005	Alex Rodriguez	New York Yankees	48	130	.321
2006	Justin Morneau	Minnesota Twins	34	130	.321
2007	Alex Rodriguez	New York Yankees	54	156	.314

1. Strike-shortened season. 2. 28 saves in 1981. 3. 32 saves in 1984. 4. 51 saves in 1992. **Source:** Baseball Writers' Association.

Triple Crown Winners

Only 11 players have led their league in home runs, runs batted in, and batting average in one season.

Year	Player	Team	HR	RBI	AVG.
1909	Ty Cobb	Detroit Tigers	9	115	.377
1912	Henry Zimmerman	Chicago Cubs	14	98	.372
1922	Rogers Hornsby	St. Louis Cardinals	42	152	.401
1925	Rogers Hornsby	St. Louis Cardinals	39	143	.403
1933	Chuck Klein	Philadelphia Phillies	28	120	.368
1933	Jimmie Foxx	Philadelphia Athletics	48	163	.356
1934	Lou Gehrig	New York Yankees	49	165	.363
1937	Joe Medwick	St. Louis Cardinals	31	154	.374
1942	Ted Williams	Boston Red Sox	36	137	.356
1947	Ted Williams	Boston Red Sox	32	114	.343
1956	Mickey Mantle	New York Yankees	52	130	.353
1966	Frank Robinson	Baltimore Orioles	49	122	.316
1967	Carl Yastrzemski	Boston Red Sox	44	121	.326

The Baseball Hall of Fame

National Baseball Hall of Fame and Museum
25 Main Street, Cooperstown, NY 13326.
888-HALL-OF-FAME (888-425-5633); www.baseballhalloffame.org
Open every day of the year except Thanksgiving, Christmas and New Year's.
Hours: 9am- 9pm, Memorial Day weekend to Labor Day; 9am-5pm the rest of the year.

The Hall of Fame was established in 1936 and opened in Cooperstown, N.Y. in 1939. From the start, there were two ways to be elected: by receiving 75 percent of the votes cast by the Baseball Writers Association of America or 75 percent of the votes cast by a Committee on Old Timers. In the first year, the writers picked the top five players of the post-1900 era: Ty Cobb, Walter Johnson, Christy Mathewson, Babe Ruth, and Honus Wagner. To be elected, a player must have played at least 10 years in the major leagues and been retired for at least five years. The Committee on Old Timers, originally created to consider 19th Century players, was replaced by a Special Veterans Committee whose scope includes all players retired for a minimum of 25 years who may have been overlooked when they were first eligible. In 1971 a Special Committee on the Negro Leagues was set up to consider ballplayers who played in the old Negro Leagues.

Player/Position/Year Inducted	Games	At Bats	HRs	Avg.	Hits	RBIs
Aaron, Henry (Hank) OF 1982	3,298	12,364	755	.305	3,771	2,297
All-time leader in home runs and RBI						
Anson, Adrian (Cap) 1B 1939	2,523	10,278	97	.333	3,418	2,076
Managed 20 years, 1879-98, winning five pennants						
Aparicio, Luis SS 1984	2,599	10,230	83	.262	2,677	791
Led AL in stolen bases nine years in a row (1955–64)						
Appling, Luke SS 1964	2,422	8,857	45	.310	2,749	1,116
Batted .388 in 1936						
Ashburn, Richie OF 1995	2,189	8,365	29	.308	2,574	586
Hit .300 or more nine times						
Averill, Earl OF 1975	1,669	6,358	238	.318	2,020	1,165
232 hits in 1936.						
Baker, Frank (Home Run) 3B 1955	1,575	5,985	96	.307	1,838	1,013
Batted .363 in six World Series						
Bancroft, Dave SS 1971	1,913	7,182	32	.279	2,004	591
Handled 984 chances in 1922						
Banks, Ernie SS, 1B 1977	2,528	9,421	512	.274	2,583	1,636
Consecutive MVP awards, 1958–59						
Beckley, Jake 1B 1971	2,386	9,527	88	.308	2,931	1,575
244 career triples, mostly in 19th Century						
Bench, Johnny C 1989	2,158	7,658	389	.267	2,048	1,376
Hit .529 in 1976 World Series; NL MVP 1970, 1972						
Berra, Lawrence (Yogi) C, OF 1972	2,120	7,555	358	.285	2,150	1,430
Three MVP awards, 1951, 1954, 1955						
Boggs, Wade 3B 2005	2,432	9,180	118	.328	3,010	1,014
Led AL in batting five times; at least 200 hits in seven consecutive seasons.						
Bottomley, Jim 1B 1974	1,991	7,471	219	.310	2,313	1,422
12 RBI in one game, 1924						
Boudreau, Lou SS 1970	1,646	6,030	68	.295	1,779	789
MVP in 1948; managed 16 years						
Bresnahan, Roger C, OF 1945	1,430	4,478	26	.279	1,251	530
212 stolen bases; first catcher elected to Hall of Fame						
Brett, George 3B, 1B 1999	2,707	10,349	317	.305	3,154	1,595
Hit .300 11 times; 13-time all-star; hit .390 in 1980.						
Brock, Lou OF 1985	2,616	10,332	149	.293	3,023	900
938 stolen bases; batted .391 in three World Series						
Brouthers, Dan 1B 1945	1,673	6,711	106	.342	2,296	1,296
Seven slugging and five batting titles during 19th Century						
Burkett, Jesse OF 1946	2,072	8,430	75	.341	2,873	952
Led NL in batting three times and in hits four times						
Campanella, Roy C 1969	1,215	4,205	242	.276	1,161	856
Three MVP awards, 1951, 1953, 1955						
Carey, Max OF 1961	2,476	9,363	69	.285	2,665	800
738 stolen bases						
Carter, Gary C 2003	2,296	7,971	324	.262	2,092	1,225
11-time All-Star (1975, 1979-88); won three gold gloves						
Cepeda, Orlando 1B 1999	2,124	7,927	379	.297	2,351	1,365
Seven-time All-star; NL MVP 1967; .499 career slugging percentage						
Chance, Frank 1B 1946	1,286	4,295	20	.297	1,274	596
Managed Chicago (NL) to four pennants in five years, 1906–10						
Clarke, Fred OF 1945	2,245	8,588	67	.315	2,708	1,015
223 career triples, hit .300 or better 11 times						
Clemente, Roberto OF 1973	2,433	9,454	240	.317	3,000	1,305
Career average of over 18 outfield assists per season						

Player/Position/Year Inducted	Games	At Bats	HRs	Avg.	Hits	RBIs
Cobb, Ty OF 1936	3,035	11,429	117	.367	4,191	1,938
Batted .320 or better in 23 straight years						
Cochrane, Micky C 1947	1,482	5,169	119	.320	1,652	832
Two MVP awards, 1928 and 1934						
Collins, Eddie 2B 1939	2,826	9,949	47	.333	3,315	1,300
Hit .340 or better 10 times; led AL in fielding nine times						
Collins, Jimmy 3B 1945	1,728	6,796	64	.294	1,997	982
Led NL in home runs, 1898						
Combs, Earle OF 1970	1,454	5,748	58	.325	1,866	629
Averaged 127 runs scored per season						
Connor, Roger 1B 1976	1,998	7,798	136	.318	2,480	1,078
Held all-time HR record before Babe Ruth						
Crawford, Sam OF 1957	2,517	9,580	97	.309	2,964	1,525
312 triples, best ever						
Cronin, Joe SS 1956	2,124	7,579	170	.301	2,285	1,424
MVP in 1930; managed 1933–47						
Cuyler, Hazen (Kiki) OF 1968	1,879	7,161	127	.321	2,299	1,065
Led NL in runs scored twice, stolen bases four times						
Davis, George SS 1998	2,376	9,035	73	.295	2,665	1,435
Hit over .300 nine years in a row (1893–1901)						
Delahanty, Ed IF, OF 1945	1,835	7,505	101	.346	2,596	1,464
Batted .410 in 1899						
Dickey, Bill C 1954	1,789	6,300	202	.313	1,969	1,209
Catcher on eight AL-pennant-winning teams						
DiMaggio, Joe OF 1955	1,736	6,821	361	.325	2,214	1,537
56 game hitting streak in 1941						
Doby, Larry OF 1998	1,533	5,348	253	.283	1,515	969
Led AL in HR twice; seven-time all-star (1949–55); first black man to play in AL						
Doerr, Bobby 2B 1986	1,865	7,093	223	.288	2,042	1,247
Led AL in slugging 1944						
Duffy, Hugh OF 1945	1,736	7,062	103	.328	2,314	1,299
Batted .438 in 1894						
Evers, Johnny 2B 1946	1,783	6,134	12	.270	1,658	538
NL MVP in 1914						
Ewing, Buck C, IF, OF 1939	1,315	5,363	70	.303	1,625	733
Regarded as the greatest player of the 19th Century						
Ferrell, Rick C 1984	1,884	6,028	28	.281	1,692	734
Led AL catchers at times in putouts, assists, fielding average, and double plays						
Fisk, Carlton C 2000	2,499	8,756	376	.269	2,356	1,330
Hit 20 or more home runs 8 times						
Flick, Elmer OF 1963	1,484	5,603	47	.315	1,767	756
Led AL in triples 1905–07						
Fox, Nellie 2B 1997	2,367	9,232	35	.288	2,663	790
Led AL in putouts, 1951–60						
Foxx, Jimmie 1B, 3B 1951	2,317	8,134	534	.325	2,646	1,921
Slugged over .700 three seasons						
Frisch, Frank 2B, 3B 1947	2,311	9,112	105	.316	2,880	1,244
Hit .300 or better 11 years in a row (1921–31)						
Gehrig, Lou 1B 1939	2,164	8,001	493	.340	2,721	1,990
Played in 2,130 consecutive games; first player to hit 4 HRs in one game						
Gehringer, Charlie 2B 1949	2,323	8,860	184	.320	2,839	1,427
60 doubles in 1936						
Goslin, Leon (Goose) OF 1968	2,287	8,655	248	.316	2,735	1,609
100+ RBI 11 years						
Greenberg, Hank 1B 1956	1,394	5,193	331	.313	1,628	1,276
58 home runs in 1938; 63 doubles in 1934						
Gwynn, Tony, OF 2007	2,440	9,288	135	.338	3,141	1,138
Won eight batting titles						
Hafey, Charles (Chick) OF 1971	1,283	4,625	164	.317	1,466	833
NL batting title (.349) in 1931						
Hamilton, Billy OF 1961	1,591	6,269	40	.344	2,159	739
Scored 196 runs in 1894, with a .509 on-base average and 99 stolen bases						
Hartnett, Charles (Gabby) C 1955	1,990	6,432	236	.297	1,912	1,179
Played on four NL pennant winners, managed one						
Heilmann, Harry OF, 1B 1952	2,147	7,787	183	.342	2,660	1,539
Batted .403 in 1923						
Herman, Billy 2B 1975	1,922	7,707	47	.304	2,345	839
57 doubles in 1935						
Hooper, Harry OF 1971	2,308	8,785	75	.281	2,466	817
375 career stolen bases						
Hornsby, Rogers 2B, IF 1942	2,259	8,173	301	.358	2,930	1,584
Batted .424 in 1924; won nine slugging titles						
Jackson, Reggie 1993	2,820	9,864	563	.262	2,584	1,702
Played in 5 World Series and 11 divisional playoffs in 21 years; World Series MVP 1977						
Jackson, Travis SS 1982	1,656	6,086	135	.291	1,768	929
Batted over .300 six times in 1920's and 1930's						

Player/Position/Year Inducted	Games	At Bats	HRs	Avg.	Hits	RBIs
Jennings, Hugh SS 1945	1,285	4,905	18	.312	1,531	840
Batted .398 in 1896						
Kaline, Al OF 1980	2,834	10,116	399	.297	3,007	1,583
3,007 career hits						
Keeler, Willie OF 1939	2,123	8,591	33	.341	2,932	810
Batted .424 in 1897; 495 career stolen bases						
Kell, George 3B 1983	1,795	6,702	78	.306	2,054	870
AL batting champ (.343) in 1949						
Kelley, Joe OF 1971	1,845	7,018	65	.319	2,242	1,193
Averaged 151 runs scored, 1894–96						
Kelly, George 1B 1973	1,622	5,993	148	.297	1,778	1,020
Led NL in RBI, 1920 and 1925						
Kelly, Mike (King) OF, C 1945	1,463	5,923	69	.307	1,820	794
Two batting titles, 1884 and 1886; 315 career stolen bases						
Killebrew, Harmon 1B, 3B, OF 1984	2,435	8,147	573	.256	2,086	1,584
40+ home runs eight years						
Kiner, Ralph OF 1975	1,472	5,205	369	.279	1,451	1,015
Second highest home run per at bat ratio of all-time						
Klein, Chuck OF 1980	1,753	6,486	300	.320	2,076	1,201
44 outfield assists in 1930						
Lajoie, Napoleon 2B 1937	2,480	9,589	82	.338	3,242	1,599
Batted .422 in 1901						
Lazzeri, Tony IF 1991	1,740	6,297	178	.292	1,840	1,191
Batted .300 or better five times; clutch hitter in World Series						
Lindstrom, Fred 3B, OF 1976	1,438	5,611	103	.311	1,747	779
231 hits in 1928						
Lombardi, Ernie C 1986	1,853	5,855	190	.306	1,792	990
Two NL batting titles, 1938 and 1942						
Mantle, Mickey OF 1974	2,401	8,102	536	.298	2,415	1,509
52 home runs in 1956, 54 in 1961						
Manush, Heinie OF 1964	2,009	7,653	110	.330	2,524	1,173
Hit .378 in 1926						
Maranville, Rabbit SS, 2B 1954	2,670	10,078	28	.258	2,605	884
23 year career; hit .308 in two World Series						
Mathews, Eddie 3B 1978	2,388	8,537	512	.271	2,315	1,453
1,444 career walks						
Mays, Willie OF 1979	2,992	10,881	660	.302	3,283	1,903
Slugged over .600 six seasons						
Mazeroski, Bill 2B 2001	2,163	7,775	138	.260	2,016	853
Eight-time gold glove winner. Turned a record 1,706 double plays.						
McCarthy, Tommy OF 1946	1,275	5,128	44	.292	1,496	666
Averaged 122 runs scored, 1888–94						
McCovey, Willie 1B, OF 1986	2,588	8,197	521	.270	2,211	1,555
Hit 18 career grand slams						
McPhee, Bid 2B 2000	2,135	8,291	53	.279	2,250	727
Considered greatest second baseman of the 19th century, though he played without a glove						
Medwick, Joe OF 1968	1,984	7,635	205	.324	2,471	1,383
Won NL triple crown in 1937						
Mize, Johnny 1B 1981	1,884	6,443	359	.312	2,011	1,337
Four-time NL home run champ						
Molitor, Paul DH, 2004	2,683	10,835	234	.306	3,319	1,307
Seven-time All-Star; 1993 World Series MVP						
Morgan, Joe 2B 1990	2,649	9,277	268	.271	2,517	1,133
Won back-to-back MVP Awards (1975–76)						
Murray, Eddie 1B 2003	3,026	11,336	504	.287	3,255	1,917
Third player ever with 3,000 hits and 500 HRs						
Musial, Stan OF, 1B 1969	3,026	10,972	475	.331	3,630	1,951
725 doubles and 177 triples						
O'Rourke, Jim OF 1945	1,774	7,435	51	.310	2,304	830
Batted .300+ eleven times in the 19th Century						
Ott, Mel OF 1951	2,732	9,456	511	.304	2,876	1,860
Averaged 121 RBI 1929–38						
Perez, Tony 1B 2000	2,777	9,778	379	.279	2,732	1,652
His 1,652 RBIs are the most ever by a Latin player						
Puckett, Kirby OF 2001	1,783	7,244	207	.318	2,304	1,085
Led Minnesota Twins to World Series wins in 1987 and 1991; won AL batting title in 1989						
Reese, Harold (Pee Wee) SS 1984	2,166	8,058	126	.269	2,170	885
Finished in the top ten of MVP balloting nine times						
Rice, Sam OF 1963	2,404	9,269	34	.322	2,987	1,078
Only 18 strikeouts per 154 games						
Ripkin, Cal, Jr. SS 2007	3,001	11,551	431	.276	3,184	1,695
Played in record 2,636 consecutive games						
Rizzuto, Phil SS 1994	1,661	5,816	38	.273	1,588	563
AL MVP in 1950; Played in 9 World Series						
Robinson, Brooks 3B 1983	2,896	10,654	268	.267	2,848	1,357
16 consecutive Gold Gloves, 1960–75						

Player/Position/Year Inducted	Games	At Bats	HRs	Avg.	Hits	RBIs
Robinson, Frank OF 1982	2,808	10,006	586	.294	2,943	1,812
MVP in both leagues; AL triple crown in 1966						
Robinson, Jackie 2B 1962	1,382	4,877	137	.311	1,518	734
First black player in MLB; Rookie of the Year 1947; MVP and batting champ 1949						
Roush, Edd OF 1962	1,967	7,363	68	.323	2,376	981
Two NL batting titles, 1917 and 1919						
Ruth, George (Babe) OF, P 1936	2,503	8,399	714	.342	2,873	2,211
Slugged .847 1920–21						
Sandberg, Ryne 2B 2005	2,164	8,385	282	.285	2,386	1,061
Won nine Gold Gloves; ten-time All-Star						
Schalk, Ray C 1955	1,760	5,306	12	.253	1,345	594
176 stolen bases						
Schmidt, Mike 3B 1995	2,404	8,352	548	.267	2,234	1,595
Led NL in homers 8 times; won 10 Gold Gloves						
Schoendienst, Albert (Red) 1989	2,216	8,479	84	.289	2,449	773
Managed Cardinals to two pennants and 1967 World Series crown						
Sewell, Joe SS, 3B 1977	1,902	7,132	49	.312	2,226	1,051
Only 22 strikeouts in his last 2,500 at bats, 1929–33						
Simmons, Al OF 1953	2,215	8,761	307	.334	2,927	1,827
Drove in over 100 runs in each of his first 11 years, 1924–34						
Sisler, George 1B 1939	2,055	8,267	100	.340	2,812	1,175
Batted .400 1920–22						
Slaughter, Enos OF 1985	2,380	7,946	169	.300	2,383	1,304
52 doubles in 1939						
Smith, Ozzie SS 2002	2,573	9,396	28	.262	2,460	793
Won 13 Gold Gloves; 15-time All-Star						
Snider, Edwin (Duke) OF 1980	2,143	7,161	407	.295	2,116	1,333
Averaged 41 home runs, 1953–57						
Speaker, Tris OF 1937	2,789	10,195	117	.345	3,514	1,529
Led AL in doubles eight times						
Stargell, Willie OF, 1B 1988	2,360	7,927	475	.282	2,232	1,540
MVP in 1979						
Terry, Bill 1B 1954	1,721	6,428	154	.341	2,193	1,078
Hit .401 in 1930						
Thompson, Sam OF 1974	1,410	6,005	128	.331	1,986	1,299
166 RBI in 1887, 165 in 1895						
Tinker, Joe SS 1946	1,805	6,441	31	.263	1,695	782
Played in four World Series with Chicago Cubs						
Traynor, Pie 3B 1948	1,941	7,559	58	.320	2,416	1,273
100+ RBI seven years						
Vaughan, Joseph (Arky) SS 1985	1,817	6,622	96	.318	2,103	926
.385 in 1935						
Wagner, Honus SS 1936	2786	10,427	101	.329	3,430	1,732
Eight batting titles, four in a row 1906–09						
Wallace, Bobby SS 1953	2,386	8,652	35	.267	2,314	1,121
Handled 6.1 chances per game at shortstop						
Waner, Lloyd OF 1967	1,992	7,772	28	.316	2,459	598
234 hits in 1929						
Waner, Paul OF 1952	2,549	9,459	112	.333	3,152	1,309
62 doubles in 1932						
Wheat, Zack OF 1959	2,410	9,106	132	.317	2,884	1,261
Batted .375 at age 36 in 1924						
Williams, Billy OF 1987	2,488	9,350	426	.290	2,711	1,475
30+ home runs in five seasons						
Williams, Ted OF 1966	2,292	7,706	521	.344	2,654	1,839
Last .400 hitter in majors, .406 in 1941						
Wilson, Lewis (Hack) OF 1979	1,348	4,760	244	.307	1,461	1,062
56 home runs and 190 RBI in 1930						
Winfield, Dave OF 2001	2,973	11,003	465	.283	3,110	1,833
Member of both the 3,000-hit and 400-home run club.						
Yastrzemski, Carl (Yaz) OF, 1B 1989	3,308	11,988	452	.285	3,419	1,844
Won Triple Crown in 1967; won batting titles in 1963, 1967, and 1968						
Youngs, Ross OF 1972	1,211	4,627	42	.322	1,491	592
Killed at age 30; .398 on-base average in four World Series, 1921–24						
Yount, Robin SS, OF 1999	2,856	11,008	251	.285	3,142	1,406
Won AL MVP awards at shortstop (1982) and center field (1989), the only player ever to do so						

Source: National Baseball Hall of Fame.

Hall of Fame Pitchers

Player/Year Inducted	W	L	ERA	Games	Innings	Strikeouts
Alexander, Grover Cleveland 1938	373	208	2.56	696	5,190	2,198
Won 30 games three years; led NL in ERA five times						
Bender, Charles (Chief) 1953	210	127	2.46	459	3,017	1,711
Led AL in winning percentage three seasons						
Brown, Mordecai (Three-Finger) 1949	239	130	2.06	481	3,172	1,375
1.04 ERA in 1906						
Bunning, Jim 1996	224	184	3.27	591	3,760	2,855
Struck out 1,000 batters in each league						
Carlton, Steve (Lefty) 1994	329	244	3.22	741	5,217	4,136
Four-time Cy Young Award winner (1972, 1977, 1980, 1982)						
Chesbro, Jack 1946	198	132	2.68	392	2,897	1,265
41 wins in 1904						
Clarkson, John 1963	326	177	2.81	531	4,536	2,015
53 wins in 1885, with 623 innings pitched						
Coveleski, Stan 1969	215	142	2.88	450	3,093	981
Led AL in ERA in 1925, 2.84						
Cummings, Williams (Candy) 1939	21	22	2.78	43	372	37
Inventor of the curveball						
Dean, Jay (Dizzy) 1953	150	83	3.03	317	1,966	1,155
30 wins in 1934						
Drysdale, Don 1984	209	166	2.95	518	3,432	2,486
56 2/3 consecutive scoreless innings, 1968						
Eckersley, Dennis 2004	197	171	3.50	1,071	3,286	2,401
Only pitcher with 100 complete games and 100 saves						
Faber, Urban (Red) 1964	254	212	3.15	669	4,088	1,471
Led AL in ERA in 1921 and 1922						
Feller, Bob 1962	266	162	3.25	570	3,827	2,581
Led AL in wins six times, in shutouts seven						
Fingers, Rollie 1992	114	118	2.90	944	1,701	1,299
341 saves over 17 years; AL MVP in 1981						
Ford, Edward (Whitey) 1974	236	106	2.75	498	3,170	1,956
25–4 in 1961, 24–7 in 1963						
Galvin, James (Pud) 1965	365	310	2.85	705	6,003	1,807
46 wins in 1883 and 1884						
Gibson, Bob 1981	251	174	2.91	528	3,885	3,117
1.12 ERA in 1968, seven straight wins in World Series play						
Gomez, Vernon (Lefty) 1972	189	102	3.34	368	2,503	1,468
Led AL in shutouts three years						
Gossage, Richard (Goose) 2008	124	107	3.01	1,002	1,809	1,502
310 career saves						
Grimes, Burleigh 1964	270	212	3.53	617	4,180	1,512
Last legal spitball pitcher, he won 20+ five times						
Grove, Robert (Lefty) 1947	300	141	3.06	616	3,941	2,266
Led AL in ERA nine times, in strikeouts seven						
Haines, Jesse 1970	210	158	3.64	555	3,209	981
Twice led NL in shutouts, 1921 and 1927						
Hoyt, Waite 1969	237	182	3.59	674	3,763	1,206
1.83 in 84 World Series innings						
Hubbell, Carl 1947	253	154	2.97	535	3,589	1,678
26–6 in 1936; 1.66 ERA in 1933						
Hunter, Jim (Catfish) 1987	224	166	3.26	500	3,448	2,012
21 or more wins, 1971–75						
Jenkins, Ferguson 1991	284	226	3.34	664	4,499	3,192
Cy Young Award winner in 1971; three-time all-star						
Johnson, Walter 1936	417	279	2.17	802	5,914	3,508
36-7, 1.14 ERA in 1913						
Joss, Addie 1978	160	97	1.89	286	2,327	920
Averaged 21–11, 1.66 ERA in years 1904–08						
Keefe, Tim 1964	342	225	2.62	600	5,049	2,564
Averaged 37 wins 1883–85						
Koufax, Sandy 1972	165	87	2.76	397	2,324	2,396
95–27, 1.85 ERA for seasons 1963-66						
Lemon, Bob 1976	207	128	3.23	460	2,850	1,277
Won 20 or more seven times						
Lyons, Ted 1955	260	230	3.67	594	4,161	1,073
Pitched 27 shutouts, but never won 20 games						
Marichal, Juan 1983	243	142	2.89	471	3,509	2,303
Only 1.8 walks per nine innings over career						
Marquard, Richard (Rube) 1971	201	177	3.08	536	3,307	1,593
73–23 in years 1911–13						
Mathewson, Christy 1936	373	188	2.13	635	4,780	2,502
79 career shutouts						
McGinnity, Joe 1946	247	144	2.64	466	3,459	1,068
35–8 in 1904, with an ERA of 1.61						

Player/Year Inducted	W	L	ERA	Games	Innings	Strikeouts
Newhouser, Hal 1992	207	150	3.06	488	2,993	1,796
Led AL in victories three years in a row (1944–46)						
Nichols, Charles (Kid) 1949	361	208	2.95	620	5,056	1,873
Won 30 or more games seven times, 1891-94, 1896-98						
Niekro, Phil 1997	318	274	3.35	864	5,404	3,342
Knuckleballer pitched until age 48; five-time all-star						
Palmer, Jim 1990	268	152	2.86	558	3,948	2,212
Won Cy Young Award 1973, 1975, 1976						
Pennock, Herb 1948	240	162	3.61	617	3,558	1,227
162–90 as a New York Yankee, 1923-33						
Perry, Gaylord 1991	314	265	3.10	777	5,352	3,534
Won Cy Young Award in both leagues						
Plank, Eddie 1946	326	194	2.35	623	4,496	2,246
1.32 ERA in seven World Series games						
Radbourn, Charles (Old Hoss) 1939	309	195	2.67	528	4,535	1,830
60–12 in 1884, with 679 innings pitched						
Rixey, Eppa 1963	266	251	3.15	692	4,495	1,350
Won 25 games in 1922						
Roberts, Robin 1976	286	245	3.41	676	4,689	2,357
28–7 in 1952; five-time NL leader in complete games						
Ruffing, Charles (Red) 1967	273	225	3.80	624	4,344	1,987
.645 winning percentage as a New York Yankee						
Rusie, Amos 1977	243	160	3.07	462	3,770	1,957
Won 30+ games three years						
Ryan, Nolan 1999	324	292	3.19	807	5,386	5,714
Threw seven no-hitters; struck out 300 or more six times; struck out 200 or more 15 times						
Seaver, Tom 1992	311	205	2.86	656	4,782	3,640
Won 20 or more games five times; won Cy Young Award 1969, 1973, 1975						
Spahn, Warren 1973	363	245	3.09	750	5,244	2,583
Won 20 or more games 13 times, including 23 at age 42						
Sutter, Bruce 2006	68	71	2.83	661	1042.3	861
Led the National League in saves five times						
Sutton, Don 1998	324	256	3.26	774	5,280	3,574
Won 15 or more games eight years in a row (1969–76)						
Vance, Clarence (Dazzy) 1955	197	140	3.24	442	2,697	2,045
60–15 over two years—1924, 1925						
Waddell, George (Rube) 1946	193	143	2.16	407	2,961	2,316
349 strikeouts in 1904						
Walsh, Ed 1946	195	126	1.82	430	2,964	1,736
40–15 in 1908 with 11 shutouts; all-time ERA leader						
Ward, Monte 1964	161	101	2.10	291	2,462	920
47 wins in 1879; 40 wins in 1880; played 1,825 games as a hitter						
Welch, Mickey 1973	307	210	2.71	565	4,802	1,850
44–11 in 1885						
Wilhelm, Hoyt 1985	143	122	2.52	1,070	2,254	1,610
227 career saves; first relief pitcher elected to Hall of Fame						
Willis, Vic 1995	249	205	2.63	513	3,996	1,651
Won 20 games eight times; 45 complete games in 1902						
Wynn, Early 1972	300	244	3.54	691	4,564	2,334
Led AL in shutouts at age 40 in 1960						
Young, Cy 1937	511	313	2.63	906	7,359	2,799
All-time leader in wins, losses, complete games, and innings pitched						

Negro Leaguers

Bell, James "Cool Papa" 1974
Brown, Ray 2006
Brown, Willard 2006
Charleston, Oscar 1976
Cooper, Andy 2006
Dandridge, Ray 1987
Day, Leon 1995
Dihigo, Martin 1977
Foster, Bill 1996
Gibson, Josh 1972
Grant, Frank 2006
Hill, Pete 2006
Irvin, Monte 1973
Johnson, Judy 1975
Leonard, William "Buck" 1972
Lloyd, Pop 1977
Mackey, Biz 2006
Mendez, Jose 2006
Paige, Satchel 1971
Rogan, "Bullet" Joe 1998
Santop, Louis 2006

Smith, Hilton 2001
Stearnes, Turkey 2000
Suttles, Mule 2006
Taylor, Ben 2006
Torriente, Cristobal 2006
Wells, Willie 1997
Williams, "Smokey Joe", 1999
Wilson, Jud 2006

Managers

Alston, Walter 1983
Anderson, Sparky 2000
Durocher, Leo 1994
Hanlon, Ned 1996
Harris, Bucky 1975
Huggins, Miller 1964
Lasorda, Tommy 1997
Lopez, Al 1977
Mack, Connie 1937
McCarthy, Joe 1957
McGraw, John 1937
McKechnie, Bill 1962
Robinson, Wilbert 1945
Selee, Frank, 1999

Stengel, Casey 1966
Weaver, Earl 1996
Williams, Dick 2008

Umpires

Barlick, Al 1989
Chylak, Nestor, 1999
Conlan, Jocko 1974
Connolly, Tom 1953
Evans, Billy 1973
Hubbard, Cal 1976
Klem, Bill 1953
McGowan, Bill 1992

Pioneers and Executives

Barrow, Ed 1953
Bulkeley, Morgan 1937
Cartwright, Alexander 1938
Chadwick, Henry 1938
Chandler, Happy 1982
Comiskey, Charles 1939
Foster, Andrew (Rube) 1981
Frick, Ford 1970
Giles, Warren 1979

Griffith, Clark 1946
Harridge, William 1972
Hulbert, William 1995
Johnson, Ban 1937
Kuhn, Bowie 2008
Landis, Kenesaw Mountain 1944
MacPhail, Larry 1978
MacPhail, Lee 1998
Manley, Effa 2006
O'Malley, Walter 2008
Pompez, Alex 2006
Posey, Cumberland 2006
Rickey, Branch 1967
Spalding, Albert Goodwill 1939
Veeck, Bill 1991
Weiss, George 1971
White, Sol 2006
Wilkinson, J.L. 2006
Wright, George 1937
Wright, Harry 1953
Yawkey, Tom 1980

The World Series

From 1882-90, the winners of the National League and American Association played each other in a championship series. After the A.A. folded, the top two N.L. clubs played for the "Temple Cup", but the idea never really caught on. The American League began operations in 1901, setting off bidding wars with the National League for the services of star players. Peace was established in 1903; toward the end of that season, the owners of the winning franchises in each league agreed to hold a "World Series" in October. Many were surprised that Boston, from the newer American League, won the title.

There was no agreement to play such a series every year, however, and in 1904 the New York Giants refused to meet the Boston club, probably due to John Mc-Graw's dislike of American League President Ban Johnson. But the baseball public wanted a championship series, and by 1905 Giants owner John Brush proposed rules governing a mandatory series to be played every year. With minute changes, those rules stand to this day.

1903 Boston (A) over Pittsburgh (N), 5-3. The upstart American league emerged victorious in the first World Series, a best of nine affair. The "Pilgrims" (Red Sox) staged one of the greatest comebacks in history by sweeping the final four games. Bill Dineen won three and Cy Young won two for Boston, and held Pirate immortal Honus Wagner to a .222 average.

1904 No series. New York Giant owner John T. Brush and manager John McGraw refused to play the World Champion Boston club, dismissing them as representative of an "inferior league."

1905 New York (N) over Philadelphia (A), 4-1. Every game was a shutout, with Cristy Mathewson throwing three for the Giants. In 27 innings, he allowed 14 hits, struck out 18 and walked one. The Athletics committed five errors in the pivotal Game 3.

1906 Chicago (A) over Chicago (N), 4-2. The first "subway series" was a stunning upset. The "Hitless Wonders" White Sox had batted .230 with 7 home runs during the season, while the Cubs were winning 116 games, still the all-time record. Utilityman George Rohe hit two game-winning triples for the Sox and Ed Walsh pitched two of their wins.

1907 Chicago (N) over Detroit (A), 4-0. The Cubs shut down Ty Cobb, Sam Crawford et al, behind a superb fourman pitching performance, and the hitting of Harry Steinfeldt (.471) and Johnny Evers (.350).

1908 Chicago (N) over Detroit (A), 4-1. Johnny Evers repeated his .350 average of 1907, player-manager Frank Chance hit .421, and outfielder Wildfire Schulte batted .389 in the Cub attack. Ty Cobb led Detroit (.368), to no avail.

1909 Pittsburgh (N) over Detroit (A), 4-3. The Tigers lost their third straight series, as Honus Wagner bested Ty Cobb. The Pirate shortstop hit .333 with six RBI and six stolen bases. Babe Adams pitched in with three complete game victories.

1910 Philadelphia (A) over Chicago (N), 4-1. Connie Mack's infielders combined to bat .364 as the A's rolled to an easy title. Jack Coombs pitched three wins and hit .385.

1911 Philadelphia (A) over New York (N), 4-2. The Athletics beat a strong New York club featuring Christy Mathewson and Rube Marquard. Frank "Home Run" Baker got his nickname from game-winning blasts in Games 2 and 3.

1912 Boston (A) over New York (N), 4-3. This thrill-a-minute series featured an 11-inning tie in Game 2. Errors by Giants Fred Merkle and Fred Snodgrass enabled Boston to score two runs in the bottom of the 10th inning of the final contest.

1913 Philadelphia (A) over New York (N), 4-1. Home Run Baker again hammered Giant pitching, batting .450 with seven RBI. Eddie Collins also starred for the A's, hitting .421 with three stolen bases.

1914 Boston (N) over Philadelphia (A), 4-0. The red-hot "Miracle Braves" swept the heavily favored Athletics, who scored only six runs in the four games. Catcher Hank Gowdy (.545) and second baseman Johnny Evers (.438) led the Boston offense.

1915 Boston (A) over Philadelphia (N), 4-1. The famous Red Sox outfield of Speaker, Lewis, and Hooper combined to bat .364 while Rube Foster pitched two complete game wins. Foster also batted .500 and drove in the winning run in Game 2.

1916 Boston (A) over Brooklyn (N), 4-1. After three one-run games, Boston took charge with 6-2 and 4-1 victories. A young lefthander named Babe Ruth twirled a 14-inning six hitter in Game Two.

1917 Chicago (A) over New York (N), 4-2. The pitching of Red Faber (3-1, 2.33) and the hitting of Eddie Collins, Buck Weaver, and Joe Jackson were too much for the Giants in a sloppy (23 errors) series.

1918 Boston (A) over Chicago (N), 4-2. Every game was a pitchers' duel. The losing Cubs posted a 1.04 ERA over the six games. The Boston staff allowed but nine runs in the series, led by Babe Ruth who extended his consecutive scoreless inning streak to 29 2/3.

1919 Cincinnati (N) over Chicago (A), 5-3. The results of this surprising World Series were declared invalid after eight members of the "Black Sox," including Shoeless Joe Jackson, were accused of throwing games for money. A court later found the Chicago players not guilty (most of them never even received the money from the gamblers with whom they conspired), but commissioner Kenesaw Mountain Landis nonetheless barred them from baseball forever.

1920 Cleveland (A) over Brooklyn (N), 5-2. Game 5 was surely the most freakish in series history. It featured a) the first World Series grand slam (Indians rightfielder Elmer Smith), b) the first World Series home run by a pitcher (Indians Jim Bagby), and c) the first and only unassisted triple play in series action (Indians second baseman Billy Wambsganss).

1921 New York (N) over New York (A), 5-3. Six Giants batted over .300, and their pitchers held Babe Ruth to a .500 slugging average. Giant hurler Jesse Barnes won two games and batted .444.

1922 New York (N) over New York (A), 4-0. The result was said to be final proof that "brains beat brawn." Giant pitching shut down Babe Ruth, allowing only 11 runs in the five contests (one tie).

1923 New York (A) over New York (N), 4-2. The Yankees took the last favor to break the spell of their cross-river rivals, behind Babe Ruth's three homers and .368 average. Casey Stengel hit two home runs for the losers.

1924 Washington (A) over New York (N), 4-3. A 12-inning Game 7, won by Walter Johnson in relief, capped an exciting affair. Player-manager Bucky Harris starred for the Senators (.333, 7 RBIs), as did outfielder Goose Goslin (.344, 7 RBIs).

1925 Pittsburgh (N) over Washington (A), 4-3. Pirate centerfielder Max Carey had 11 hits and three stolen bases, as Pittsburgh became the first team since 1903 to come back from a three games to one deficit.

1926 St. Louis (N) over New York (A), 4-3. Babe Ruth hit three homers in Game 4, but in the seventh inning of Game 7, Grover Cleveland Alexander struck out Tony Lazzeri with the bases loaded, saving the game and the series for the Cardinals.

1927 New York (A) over Pittsburgh (N), 4-0. Generally regarded as the greatest team of all time, the "Murderers' Row" Yankees disposed of the Pirates behind two Babe Ruth homers, plus the pitching of Wilcy Moore, Herb Pennock, and George Pipgrass.

1928 New York (A) over St. Louis (N), 4–0. Another Yankee sweep. Ruth and Lou Gehrig combined to bat .593, with seven home runs and 13 RBI. Waite Hoyt pitched two complete game victories.

1929 Philadelphia (A) over Chicago (N), 4–1. Trailing 8-0 in Game 4, the A's roared back to score 10 runs in the seventh inning. In the next contest, the Mackmen took the series with a three-run ninth inning.

1930 Philadelphia (A) over St. Louis (N), 4–2. Lefty Grove and George Earnshaw pitched well, while Al Simmons, Jimmie Foxx, and Mickey Cochrane combined for 11 extra-base hits. Cardinal regulars batted only .185 in the six games.

1931 St. Louis (N) over Philadelphia (A), 4–3. Cardinal centerfielder Pepper Martin set a record that stood for 33 years with his 12 hits. Martin also stole five bases and hit a home run. Bill Hallahan and Burleigh Grimes combined for a 4-0, 1.25 ERA.

1932 New York (A) over Chicago (N), 4–0. The Yankees completed a streak of 12 straight World Series victories in sweeping the Cubs. Babe Ruth and Lou Gehrig combined to bat .438, with five homers and 14 RBI.

1933 New York (N) over Washington (A), 4–1. Bill Terry's Giants defeated Joe Cronin's Senators in a battle of player-managers. Carl Hubbell won two for New York and did not allow an earned run.

1934 St. Louis (N) over Detroit (A), 4–3. Dizzy and Paul Dean hurled the Cardinals to the title, winning all four Redbird victories. A bad defensive series, with 27 errors and 13 unearned runs.

1935 Detroit (A) over Chicago (N), 4–2. The Cubs won 21 straight games in September, but came up short against Mickey Cochrane's Tigers. Charlie Gehringer and Tommy Bridges starred for Detroit, while Lou Warneke (2–0, 0.54) was superb for the losers.

1936 New York (A) over New York (N), 4–2. Joe McCarthy's "Windowbreakers" hammered Giant pitching for a record 18 runs in Game 2 and 43 runs for the series. Tony Lazzeri and Bill Dickey each drove in five runs in Game 2.

1937 New York (A) over New York (N), 4–1. Lefty Gomez pitched two of the Yankee wins and drove in the winning run with a single in the final game. The Yanks scored seven runs in the sixth inning of Game 1, then coasted to an easy championship.

1938 New York (A) over Chicago (N), 4–0. In a replay of 1932, the Bronx Bombers blew out an overmatched Cub squad. Cub fans are still waiting for their team's first series victory over the Yankees.

1939 New York (A) over Cincinnati (N), 4–0. New York won its fourth straight World Championship the same way they won the first three—easily. Charlie Keller batted .438 with three homers, and scored as many runs as the entire Reds team, eight.

1940 Cincinnati (N) over Detroit (A), 4–3. The Reds repeated as NL champs, then beat the Tigers when Paul Derringer beat Bobo Newsome 2–1 in Game 7. Derringer and Bucky Walters each won two games.

1941 New York (A) over Brooklyn (N), 4–1. With two outs in the ninth inning of Game Four, Dodger catcher Mickey Owen dropped a third strike on Tommy Henrich, allowing him to reach first base. The Yankees then scored four times to win the ballgame, and finished Brooklyn off the next day.

1942 St. Louis (N) over New York (A), 4–1. The Cardinals, winners of 106 games during the regular season, lost Game 1 with the tying run at bat. They then swept four in a row, behind the pitching of Johnny Beazley (2–0, 2.50) and Ernie White's shutout in Game 3.

1943 New York (A) over St. Louis (N), 4–1. In this rematch of the 1942 series, the Yanks held St. Louis to nine runs in the five games. Joe Gordon and Bill Dickey homered, while third baseman Billy Johnson drove in three runs for New York.

1944 St Louis (N) over St. Louis (A), 4–2. In their lone World Series appearance, the Browns struggled valiantly before falling short against a strong Cardinal club left relatively intact by World War II. Ten Browns errors gave the Redbirds seven unearned runs.

1945 Detroit (A) over Chicago (N), 4–3. Tiger ace Hal Newhouser was hit hard in Game 1, but he bounced back to win Games 5 and 7. Doc Cramer (.379) and Hank Greenberg (2 HR, 7 RBIs) led the Detroit offense.

1946 St. Louis (N) over Boston (A), 4–3. Enos Slaughter scored from first on a base-hit by Harry Walker in the eighth inning of Game 7, giving St. Louis its third title in five years. Harry Brecheen won three games for the Cardinals, allowing but one run.

1947 New York (A) over Brooklyn (N), 4–3. Yankee pitcher Bill Bevens had a no-hitter for 8 2/3 innings in Game 4, but lost the game on a double by Cookie Lavagetto. Tommy Henrich (.323) had the game winning RBI in Games 1, 2, and 7.

1948 Cleveland (A) over Boston (N), 4–2. The series featured fine pitching on both sides, including Game 1 when Boston's Johnny Sain beat Bob Feller 1–0. Cleveland's Gene Beardon pitched 10 2/3 scoreless innings.

1949 New York (A) over Brooklyn (N), 4–1. Game 1 was 0–0 until Tommy Henrich led off the bottom of the ninth with a home run off Don Newcombe. Bobby Brown batted .500 with five RBIs.

1950 New York (A) over Philadelphia (N), 4–0. New York struggled to win the first three contests by scores of 1-0, 2-1, and 3–2, in a series that was closer than it looks. The "Whiz Kid" Phillies held the Yanks to a .222 batting average, but managed to win only .203 themselves.

1951 New York (A) over New York (N), 4–2. A tired Giant pitching staff held the Yankees in check for three games, but the AL champs broke out to score 23 runs in the final three. Eddie Lopat (2–0, 0.50) starred for the Yankees.

1952 New York (A) over Brooklyn (N), 4–3. Allie Reynolds and Vic Raschi each won two games, combining for a 1.69 ERA. Johnny Mize hit three homers, and Mickey Mantle and Yogi Berra each hit two. Duke Snider batted .345 with four homers in a losing cause.

1953 New York (A) over Brooklyn (N), 4–2. The Yankees won their fifth straight World Championship as second baseman Billy Martin tied a record with 12 hits. Martin slugged .958 and drove in eight runs.

1954 New York (N) over Cleveland (A), 4–0. The Indians won 111 games during the season. But the Giants, sparked by a spectacular Willie Mays catch in Game 1, went on to beat Cleveland easily. Dusty Rhodes drove in seven runs on two homers and two singles in six at bats.

1955 Brooklyn (N) over New York (A), 4–3. The Dodgers finally won a World Series in their eighth try, behind the pitching of series MVP Johnny Podres (2–0, 1.00). Duke Snider hit four homers in a series for the second time, and Dodger leftfielder Sandy Amoros made a game-saving catch in Game 7.

1956 New York (A) over Brooklyn (N), 4–3. Yankee righthander and series MVP Don Larsen pitched a perfect game in the fifth contest, while Mickey Mantle and Yogi Berra each hit three homers for New York.

1957 Milwaukee (N) over New York (A), 4–3. Lew Burdette won three times for the Braves, allowing but two runs in 27 innings and won the MVP. Milwaukee's hitting was led by Hank Aaron (.393, 3 HR, 7 RBIs).

1958 New York (A) over Milwaukee (N), 4–3. Hank Bauer and Moose Skowron combined for six homers and 15 RBI, as the Bronx Bombers came back from a 3–1 deficit. Yankee pitcher "Bullet" Bob Turley earned MVP honors.

1959 Los Angeles (N) over Chicago (A), 4–2. Los Angeles enjoyed its first World Championship as the transplanted Dodgers prevailed. MVP Larry Sherry had two wins and two saves; Ted Kluszewski of the "Go-Go" Sox hit .391, with three homers and 10 RBI.

1960 Pittsburgh (N) over New York (A), 4–3. Pirate second baseman Bill Mazeroski's home run in the bottom of the ninth in Game 7 capped one of the most exciting contests in history. Ten of the runs in the 10–9 ballgame were scored in the last two innings. Yankee second baseman Bobby Richardson, a hitting star throughout the series, was named MVP.

1961 New York (A) over Cincinnati (N),4–1. Whitey Ford tossed two shutouts in winning the MVP, and the Yankee offense pounded out 16 extra-base hits in the five games. Bobby Richardson (.391) and John Blanchard (.400, 2 HR) starred for New York.

1962 New York (A) over San Francisco (N), 4–3. Ralph Terry's four-hit shutout won the seesaw affair for the Yanks, and earned him the MVP. Whitey Ford completed his series record 33 2/3 consecutive scoreless innings in the first game. Chuck Hiller hit the first National League series grand slam in Game 4.

1963 Los Angeles (N) over New York (A), 4–0. Dodger pitchers held New York to four runs, led by Sandy Koufax's two wins and 23 strikeouts, including a record-breaking 15 in the first game. Koufax was the runaway choice for MVP.

1964 St. Louis (N) over New York (A), 4–3. Ten Yankee home runs were not enough to beat the Cardinals. Bob Gibson was the series MVP, and Tim McCarver (.478) also starred. Highlights included Ken Boyer's game-winning grand slam in Game 4, and Bobby Richardson's record 13 hits.

1965 Los Angeles (N) over Minnesota (A), 4–3. As in 1963, MVP Sandy Koufax again excelled for the Dodgers, allowing only two runs in 24 innings, striking out 29. Jim "Mudcat" Grant won two games and hit a three-run homer for the Twins.

1966 Baltimore (A) over Los Angeles (N), 4–0. The Orioles shone in their first World Series appearance, as their young pitchers did not allow a run after the third inning of Game 1. Slugger Frank Robinson capped a great year with the series MVP award.

1967 St. Louis (N) over Boston (A), 4–3. Bob Gibson pitched three complete game victories, added a home run in Game 7, and was named MVP. Lou Brock batted .414 and stole seven bases, tying Eddie Collins' record and pacing the Cards.

1968 Detroit (A) over St. Louis (N), 4–3. The Cardinals were rolling behind Bob Gibson's record 17 strikeouts in Game 1 and his record seventh straight series win in Game 4. Again Lou Brock joined him in the record books with 13 hits and seven stolen bases. But their feats couldn't stop the Tigers, led by the MVP pitching of Mickey Lolich (3–0, 1.67).

1969 New York (N) over Baltimore (A), 4–1. The Amazin' Mets stunned the baseball world by winning four in a row after dropping Game 1. Their young pitchers held the Orioles to nine runs, aided by great outfield catches by Ron Swoboda and Tommy Agee. Series MVP Donn Clendenon (.357, 3 HR) and Al Weis (.455, 1 HR) led the Met attack.

1970 Baltimore (A) over Cincinnati (N), 4–1. MVP Brooks Robinson almost singlehandedly beat the Reds with spectacular defense at third base and a .429 average with two homers and two doubles. Also chipping in for the Orioles were Paul Blair (.474), Frank Robinson, and Boog Powell (two homers each).

1971 Pittsburgh (N) over Baltimore (A), 4–3. Roberto Clemente played in 14 World Series games and hit safely in every one. Here he batted .414, slugged .759, and won MVP honors. Steve Blass, Nelson Briles, and Bruce Kison won all the Pirate victories with a combined ERA of 0.54.

1972 Oakland (A) over Cincinnati (N), 4–3. A's backup catcher Gene Tenace hit home runs in his first two series at bats, then went on to hit two more, becoming the surprise star. MVP Rollie Fingers relieved in six contests, winning one and saving two.

1973 Oakland (A) over New York (N), 4–3. The Mets had the worst record of any pennant winner ever (82–79), but they lasted till the Game 7 in a sloppy (19 errors) affair. Darold Knowles pitched in all seven games for the A's, saving two. Reggie Jackson slugged his way to his first series MVP award.

1974 Oakland (A) over Los Angeles (N), 4–1. The A's won their third straight Championship behind the two saves and one win of MVP Rollie Fingers. and the hitting of Joe Rudi (.333) and Bert Campaneris (.353).

1975 Cincinnati (N) over Boston (A), 4–3. Five games were decided by one run, including Game 6, a memorable 12-inning contest decided by Carlton Fisk's famous home run. Pete Rose, the heart and soul of the Big Red Machine, hustled his way to MVP honors.

1976 Cincinnati (N) over New York (A), 4–0. The Big Red Machine drove over the Yankees, slugging .522 as a team. Seven Reds hitters batted over .300, led by MVP Johnny Bench's .533 (1.133 slugging average).

1977 New York (A) over Los Angeles (N), 4–2. Reggie Jackson hit five homers, including three in the final game, to equal records set by Babe Ruth, and win his second MVP award. Mike Torrez won two for the Yanks.

1978 New York (A) over Los Angeles (N), 4–2. Shortstop Bucky Dent and backup infielder Brian Doyle batted .417 and .438 respectively, pacing New York in its second straight six-game triumph. Dent was named MVP. In the last four contests, the Yankees outscored L.A. 28–8.

1979 Pittsburgh (N) over Baltimore (A), 4–3. The Pirates overcame a three games to one deficit as Earl Weaver's Orioles waited for three-run homers that never came. Led by Willie "Pops" Stargell (.400, 3 HR) and Phil Garner (.500), Pittsburgh batted .323 as a team. Stargell's leadership of the Pirates' "family" on and off the field earned him MVP honors.

1980 Philadelphia (N) over Kansas City (A), 4–2. The two teams batted .292 in a series decided largely by the relief pitching of Tug McGraw (1–1, 2 saves) vs. Dan Quisenberry (1–2, 1 save). Mike Schmidt took MVP honors with a .381 average and seven RBI.

1981 Los Angeles (N) over New York (A), 4–2. Many observers called this sloppy series a fitting end to this strike-stricken 1981 season. Even the MVP award proved impossible to settle, as Pedro Guerrero, Steve Yeager, and Ron Cey shared the honor.

1982 St. Louis (N) over Milwaukee (A), 4–3. Joaquin Andujar won two games for the Cardinals, and Willie McGee had perhaps the greatest single series game by a rookie, with two homers and two great catches in Game 3. St. Louis' Darrell Porter won MVP honors for his clutch hitting and 5 RBI.

1983 Baltimore (A) over Philadelphia (N), 4–1. The Phillies couldn't hit Orioles' pitching, scoring but nine runs in the five games. Catcher Rick Dempsey hit four doubles and a home run, held the Phils to one stolen base, and was named MVP.

1984 Detroit (A) over San Diego (N), 4–1. The Tigers belted seven homers and backed them up with the pitching of Jack Morris (2–0, 2.00). Sparky Anderson became the first manager to win World Championships in both leagues. Alan Trammell, the Tigers' shortstop, hit two home runs to earn MVP honors.

1985 Kansas City (A) over St. Louis (N), 4–3. The Cards were one inning away from the title, but a disputed call at first base opened the door for the Royals in Game 6. They won that contest, then blew St. Louis away 11–0 in the finale. Bret Saberhagen won two for Kansas City, and the MVP.

1986 New York (N) over Boston (A), 4–3. The Red Sox were one out away from winning it all, when Bob Stanley's wild pitch let in the tying run, and Mookie Wilson's grounder slipped between Bill Buckner's legs to score the winning run in Game 6. MVP Ray Knight hit a tie-breaking homer in Game 7 to send Boston to its fourth straight six-game defeat.

1987 Minnesota (A) over St. Louis (N), 4–3. The Twins won their first championship by taking all four games in at the Metrodome. Cardinal pitching held Minnesota to five runs in the three games in St. Louis, but in Minnesota, the Twins could not be contained, scoring 33 times. Frank Viola (2–1,3.72) was the MVP.

1988 Los Angeles (N) over Oakland (A), 4–1. Series MVP Orel Hershiser (2–0, 17 K's) dazzled the powerful A's. Injured Dodger Kirk Gibson's dramatic two-out home run in the bottom of the ninth in Game 1 set the tone for the unexpected L.A. triumph.

1989 Oakland (A) over San Francisco (N), 4–0. The A's thoroughly dominated a weak Giants' pitching staff, pounding out 32 runs, 44 hits (including nine home runs) in only four games. Series MVP Dave Stewart and reliever Dennis Eckersley led the Oakland staff. This series will be long remembered for the major earthquake that struck the Bay area just before Game 3 and delayed the contest for 12 days.

1990 Cincinnati (N) over Oakland (A), 4–0. Cincinnati dominated the heavily favored A's in a stunning sweep. The Reds hit .317 as a team, while their pitchers, led by MVP José Rijo, held Oakland's vaunted offense to a mere .207 series average. Billy Hatcher broke Babe Ruth's World Series record by hitting .750, with seven consecutive hits and four doubles.

1991 Minnesota (A) over Atlanta (N), 4–3. No team in baseball had ever gone from worst to first. In 1991, it happened for both the Twins and Braves. Five games were decided by one run, three went into extra innings, and four were decided on the last at bat. Jack Morris pitched all 10 innings for Minnesota and earned MVP honors.

1992 Toronto (A) over Atlanta (N), 4–2. The Blue Jays became the first non-American team to win (or play in) the World Series. Dave Winfield's double in the 11th-inning of Game 6 sent the Braves to their second straight World Series defeat. Toronto catcher Pat Borders was the MVP with a .450 average.

1993 Toronto (A) over Philadelphia (N), 4–2. The Blue Jays became the first team since the 1977–78 Yankees to repeat as champions, battering the Phillies for 45 runs (despite a Game 5 shutout). Joe Carter's homer in Game 6 marked only the second time the World Series had ended on a home run (Bill Mazeroski the other in 1960). DH Paul Molitor went 12 for 24 with six extra-base hits to win MVP honors.

1994 World Series canceled. The longest work stoppage in professional sports history, a 232-day dispute over a cap on player salaries, forced the first-ever cancellation of the World Series and playoffs.

1995 Atlanta (N) over Cleveland (A), 4–2. Good pitching beats good hitting as evidenced by this dramatic series. Baseball's best pitching staff (the Braves) held the game's most explosive offense (the Indians) to a .179 average and 19 runs. Five games were decided by one run, including the clincher: a dazzling 1–0 one-hitter by Atlanta's Tom Glavine, the series MVP.

1996 New York (A) over Atlanta (N), 4–2. The Braves shellacked the Yankees 12–1 and 4–0 in the first two games. But the Yankees struck back and won the next four. The turning point was in Game 4, when New York rallied from a 6–0 deficit to win 8–6 in 10 innings. Jim Leyritz provided the crushing blow: a three-run homer off Mark Wohlers to tie the game 6–6. Yankee closer John Wetteland saved all four wins and was the MVP.

1997 Florida (N) over Cleveland (A), 4–3. This sloppy series was marked by porous defense and poor relief pitching. Game 3 alone involved 17 walks and 6 errors. In the 11th, Edgar Renteria singled home the winning run. Florida rookie Liván Hernández, winner of Games 1 and 5, was the MVP.

1998 New York (A) over San Diego (N), 4–0. The Yankees completed one of the greatest seasons in baseball history with a sweep that gave them a combined record of 125–50 and a .714 winning percentage. Homers by Chuck Knoblauch and Tino Martínez helped the Yankees come from behind in Game 1, while Scott Brosius's three-run blast off San Diego closer Trevor Hoffman in Game 3 broke the Padres' back. Brosius, the MVP, hit .471 with two homers.

1999 New York (A) over Atlanta (N), 4–0. The Yankees' World Series winning streak increased to 12 games with their second straight sweep. Atlanta errors opened the door to big innings for New York in Games 1 and 2; the Yankees hit four homers in Game 3 to turn a 5-1 deficit into a 10-inning, 6-5 win. Mariano Rivera, who did not allow a run after July, saved Games 1 and 4, won Game 3 in relief, and took MVP honors.

2000 New York (A) over New York (N), 4–1. Every game of the first Subway Series in 45 years was decided by one or two runs. The Yankees rallied to tie Game 1 in the ninth inning, and won it in the 12th. Derek Jeter hit the first pitch of Game 4 over the center field fence and the Yankees never trailed again. Jeter batted .409 with two homers, and was the MVP.

2001 Arizona (N) over New York (A), 4–3. Curt Schilling and Randy Johnson powered Arizona to a 2-0 lead, but the Yankees came back with three straight one-run victories in New York. In *both* Game 4 *and* Game 5, the Yankees were down to their last out when they rallied with game-tying homers against closer Byung-Hyun Kim (by Tino Martinez and Scott Brosius, respectively). Schilling and Johnson were co-MVPs.

2002 Anaheim (A) over San Francisco (N), 4–3. Anaheim pitched carefully to Barry Bonds, and although he hit .471 with four homers and 13 walks, the batters before and after him hit .276 and .231 respectively, limiting the damage Bonds was able to inflict. The Angels batted .310 as a team, led by MVP third baseman Troy Glaus, who hit .385 with 3 homers and 8 RBIs. With the Giants six outs away from winning it all in Game 6, Glaus's eighth-inning double turned a 5-4 deficit into a 6-5 Anaheim victory.

2003 Florida (N) over New York (A), 4-2. New York's two victories were by both by 6-1 margins, while Florida's wins were by one or two runs. Alex González's walk-off homer in the 12th inning of Game 4 turned the tide for Florida. Brad Penny 2-0 for the Marlins, but he was eclipsed for MVP honors by Josh Beckett, who came back on two days' rest to pitch a Game 6 shutout that clinched it for the Marlins, who have not lost a postseason series in their short history.

2004 Boston (A) over St. Louis (N), 4-0. The Sox swept the powerful Cardinals behind the hitting of MVP Manny Ramirez (.412 average) and the pitching of Curt Schilling, Derek Lowe, and Pedro Martinez.

2005 Chicago (A) over Houston (N), 4-0 The Chicago White Sox used timely hitting and stellar pitching to win the club's first World Series title since 1917. Although the result was a sweep, each game was closely contested: Chicago outscored Houston by only six runs over the four games. In the crucial Game 3, the longest by time in World Series history, the White Sox beat the Astros 7-5 in 14 innings.

2006 St. Louis (N) over Detroit (A), 4-1 In the third championship meeting of these two teams, the 102nd World Series in baseball history, the Cardinals defeated the Tigers in five games, taking the home-field advantage away from Detroit with an emphatic 7-2 victory in Game One. The Tigers entered the Series as favorites after coasting through the division series and the ALCS, while it took the Cardinals a full seven games—and a late inning homer by the unlikely hero Yadier Molina—to put the Mets away in the NLCS. In the final game of the series Jeff Weaver tossed eight brilliant innings and Series MVP David Eckstein drove in the go-ahead run in the Cardinal's 4-2 victory.

2007 Boston (A) over Colorado (N), 4-0 The wild-card Rockies entered the series having won 21 of their previous 22 games, sweeping both the Phillies and Diamondbacks in the Division Series and ALCS en route. The Red Sox greeted them in the Fall Classic with a 13-1 thumping in Fenway Park, and it was never a contest after that. Boston ultimately did some sweeping of their own, eliminating Colorado in four games to claim their second title in three years.

World Series MVP Winners

Year	Name	Team
1955	Johnny Podres	Brooklyn Dodgers
1956	Don Larsen	New York Yankees
1957	Lew Burdette	Milwaukee Braves
1958	Bob Turley	New York Yankees
1959	Larry Sherry	Los Angeles Dodgers
1960	Bobby Richardson	New York Yankees
1961	Whitey Ford	New York Yankees
1962	Ralph Terry	New York Yankees
1963	Sandy Koufax	Los Angeles Dodgers
1964	Bob Gibson	St. Louis Cardinals
1965	Sandy Koufax	Los Angeles Dodgers
1966	Frank Robinson	Baltimore Orioles
1967	Bob Gibson	St. Louis Cardinals
1968	Mickey Lolich	Detroit Tigers
1969	Donn Clendenon	New York Mets
1970	Brooks Robinson	Baltimore Orioles
1971	Roberto Clemente	Pittsburgh Pirates
1972	Gene Tenace	Oakland Athletics
1973	Reggie Jackson	Oakland Athletics
1974	Rollie Fingers	Oakland Athletics
1975	Pete Rose	Cincinnati Reds
1976	Johnny Bench	Cincinnati Reds
1977	Reggie Jackson	New York Yankees
1978	Bucky Dent	New York Yankees
1979	Willie Stargell	Pittsburgh Pirates
1980	Mike Schmidt	Philadelphia Phillies
1981	Ron Cey, Pedro Guerrero, Steve Yeager	Los Angeles Dodgers
1982	Darrell Porter	St. Louis Cardinals
1983	Rick Dempsey	Baltimore Orioles
1984	Alan Trammell	Detroit Tigers
1985	Bret Saberhagen	Kansas City Royals
1986	Ray Knight	New York Mets
1987	Frank Viola	Minnesota Twins
1988	Orel Hershiser	Los Angeles Dodgers
1989	Dave Stewart	Oakland Athletics
1990	José Rijo	Cincinnati Reds
1991	Jack Morris	Minnesota Twins
1992	Pat Borders	Toronto Blue Jays
1993	Paul Molitor	Toronto Blue Jays
1994	No World Series	
1995	Tom Glavine	Atlanta Braves
1996	John Wetteland	New York Yankees
1997	Liván Hernández	Florida Marlins
1998	Scott Brosius	New York Yankees
1999	Mariano Rivera	New York Yankees
2000	Derek Jeter	New York Yankees
2001	Randy Johnson and Curt Schilling	Arizona Diamondbacks
2002	Troy Glaus	Anaheim Angels
2003	Josh Beckett	Florida Marlins
2004	Manny Ramirez	Boston Red Sox
2005	Jermaine Dye	Chicago White Sox
2006	David Eckstein	St. Louis Cardinals
2007	Mike Lowell	Boston Red Sox

All-Star Game Results, 1933–2008

To revive interest in the midsummer classic, Major League Baseball decided in 2003 to award home field advantage in the World Series to the league that wins the All-Star Game.

Year	Winner, Score	Year	Winner, Score
1933	American, 4-2	1969	National, 9-3
1934	American, 9-7	1970	National, 5-4
1935	American, 4-1	1971	American, 6-4
1936	National, 4-3	1972	National, 4-3
1937	American, 8-3	1973	National, 7-1
1938	National, 4-1	1974	National, 7-2
1939	American, 3-1	1975	National, 6-3
1940	National, 4-0	1976	National, 7-1
1941	American, 7-5	1977	National, 7-5
1942	American, 3-1	1978	National, 7-3
1943	American, 5-3	1979	National, 7-6
1944	National, 7-1	1980	National, 4-2
1945	No game [1]	1981	National, 5-4
1946	American, 12-0	1982	National, 4-1
1947	American, 2-1	1983	American, 13-3
1948	American, 5-2	1984	National, 3-1
1949	American, 11-7	1985	National, 6-1
1950	National, 4-3	1986	American, 3-2
1951	National, 8-3	1987	National, 2-0 (10)
1952	National, 3-2	1988	American, 2-1
1953	National, 5-1	1989	American, 5-3
1954	American, 11-9	1990	American, 2-0
1955	National, 6-5	1991	American, 4-2
1956	National, 7-3	1992	American, 13-6
1957	American, 6-5	1993	American, 9-3
1958	American, 4-3	1994	National, 8-7 (10)
1959(1)[2]	National, 5-4	1995	National, 3-2
1959(2)	American, 5-3	1996	National, 6-0
1960(1)	National, 5-3	1997	American, 3-1
1960(2)	National, 6-0	1998	American, 13-8
1961(1)	National, 5-4	1999	American, 4-1
1961(2)	Tie[3], 1-1	2000	American, 6-3
1962(1)	National, 3-1	2001	American, 4-1
1962(2)	American, 9-4	2002	Tie[4], 7-7
1963	National, 5-3	2003	American, 7-6
1964	National, 7-4	2004	American, 9-4
1965	National, 6-5	2005	American, 7-5
1966	National, 2-1	2006	American, 3-2
1967	National, 2-1	2007	American, 5-4
1968	National, 1-0	2008	American, 4-3 (15)

1. Wartime travel restrictions. 2. Two All Star games were played 1959–62. 3. Game was called because of rain after nine innings. 4. Game was called after nine innings because both managers had already used all their pitchers.

Major League Baseball League Championship Series Results

		AMERICAN LEAGUE	
Year	Winner	Loser	MVP
1969	Baltimore Orioles-3	Minnesota Twins-0	
1970	Baltimore Orioles-3	Minnesota Twins-0	
1971	Baltimore Orioles-3	Oakland A's-0	
1972	Oakland Athletics-3	Detroit Tigers-2	
1973	Oakland Athletics-3	Baltimore Orioles-2	
1974	Oakland Athletics-3	Baltimore Orioles-1	
1975	Boston Red Sox-3	Oakland Athletics-0	
1976	New York Yankees-3	Kansas City Royals-2	

AMERICAN LEAGUE (continued)

Year	Winner	Loser	MVP
1977	New York Yankees-3	Kansas City Royals-2	
1978	New York Yankees-3	Kansas City Royals-1	
1979	Baltimore Orioles-3	California Angels-1	
1980	Kansas City Royals-3	New York Yankees-0	Frank White, Kansas City
1981	New York Yankees-3	Oakland Athletics-0	Graig Nettles, New York
1982	Milwaukee Brewers-3	California Angels-2	Fred Lynn, California
1983	Baltimore Orioles-3	Chicago White Sox-1	Mike Boddicker, Baltimore
1984	Detroit Tigers-3	Kansas City Royals-0	Kirk Gibson, Detroit
1985[1]	Kansas City Royals-4	Toronto Blue Jays-3	George Brett, Kansas City
1986	Boston Red Sox-4	California Angels-3	Marty Barrett, Boston
1987	Minnesota Twins-4	Detroit Tigers-1	Gary Gaetti, Minnesota
1988	Oakland Athletics-4	Boston Red Sox-0	Dennis Eckersley, Oakland
1989	Oakland Athletics-4	Toronto Blue Jays-1	Rickey Henderson, Oakland
1990	Oakland Athletics-4	Boston Red Sox-0	Dave Stewart, Oakland
1991	Minnesota Twins-4	Toronto Blue Jays-1	Kirby Puckett, Minnesota
1992	Toronto Blue Jays-4	Oakland Athletics-2	Roberto Alomar, Toronto
1993	Toronto Blue Jays-4	Chicago White Sox-2	Dave Stewart, Toronto
1994	No League Championship Series		
1995	Cleveland Indians-4	Seattle Mariners-2	Orel Hershiser, Cleveland
1996	New York Yankees-4	Baltimore Orioles-1	Bernie Williams, New York
1997	Clevland Indians-4	Baltimore Orioles-2	Marquis Grissom, Cleveland
1998	New York Yankees-4	Cleveland Indians-2	David Wells, New York
1999	New York Yankees-4	Boston Red Sox-1	Orlando Hernández, New York
2000	New York Yankees-4	Seattle Mariners-2	David Justice, New York
2001	New York Yankees-4	Seattle Mariners-1	Andy Pettitte, New York
2002	Anaheim Angels-4	Minnesota Twins-1	Adam Kennedy, Anaheim
2003	New York Yankees-4	Boston Red Sox-3	Mariano Rivera, New York
2004	Boston Red Sox-4	New York Yankees-3	David Ortiz, Boston
2005	Chicago White Sox-4	Los Angeles Angels-1	Paul Konerko, Chicago
2006	Detroit Tigers-4	Oakland Athletics-0	Placido Polanco, Tigers
2007	Boston Red Sox-4	Cleveland Indians-3	Josh Beckett, Red Sox

NATIONAL LEAGUE

Year	Winner	Loser	MVP
1969	New York Mets-3	Atlanta Braves-0	
1970	Cincinnati Reds-3	Pittsburgh Pirates-0	
1971	Pittsburgh Pirates-3	San Francisco Giants-1	
1972	Cincinnati Reds-3	Pittsburgh Pirates-2	
1973	New York Mets-3	Cincinnati Reds-2	
1974	Los Angeles Dodgers-3	Pittsburgh Pirates-1	
1975	Cincinnati Reds-3	Pittsburgh Pirates-0	
1976	Cincinnati Reds-3	Philadelphia Phillies-0	
1977	Los Angeles Dodgers-3	Philadelphia Phillies-1	Dusty Baker, Los Angeles
1978	Los Angeles Dodgers-3	Philadelphia Phillies-1	Steve Garvey, Los Angeles
1979	Pittsburgh Pirates-3	Cincinnati Reds-0	Willie Stargell, Pittsburgh
1980	Philadelphia Phillies-3	Houston Astros-2	Manny Trillo, Philadelphia
1981	Los Angeles Dodgers-3	Montreal Expos-2	Burt Hooton, Los Angeles
1982	St. Louis Cardinals-3	Atlanta Braves-0	Darrell Porter, St. Louis
1983	Philadelphia Phillies-3	Los Angeles Dodgers-1	Gary Mathews, Philadelphia
1984	San Diego Padres-3	Chicago Cubs-2	Steve Garvey, San Diego
1985[1]	St. Louis Cardinals-4	Los Angeles Dodgers-2	Ozzie Smith, St. Louis
1986	New York Mets-4	Houston Astros-2	Mike Scott, Houston
1987	St. Louis Cardinals-4	San Francisco Giants-3	Jeff Leonard, San Francisco
1988	Los Angeles Dodgers-4	New York Mets-3	Orel Hershiser, Los Angeles
1989	San Francisco Giants-4	Chicago Cubs-1	Will Clark, San Francisco
1990	Cincinnati Reds-4	Pittsburgh Pirates-2	Rob Dibble, Rany Myers, Cincinnati
1991	Atlanta Braves-4	Pittsburgh Pirates-3	Steve Avery, Atlanta
1992	Atlanta Braves-4	Pittsburgh Pirates-3	John Smoltz, Atlanta
1993	Philadelphia Phillies-4	Atlanta Braves-2	Curt Schilling, Philadelphia
1994	No League Championship Series		
1995	Atlanta Braves-4	Cincinnati Reds-0	Mike Devereaux, Atlanta
1996	Atlanta Braves-4	St. Louis Cardinals-3	Javier Lopez, Atlanta
1997	Florida Marlins-4	Atlanta Braves-2	Liván Hernández, Florida
1998	San Diego Padres-4	Atlanta Braves-2	Sterling Hitchcock, San Diego
1999	Atlanta Braves-4	New York Mets-2	Eddie Perez, Atlanta
2000	New York Mets-4	St. Louis Cardinals-1	Mike Hampton, New York
2001	Arizona Diamondbacks-4	Atlanta Braves-1	Craig Counsell, Arizona
2002	San Francisco Giants-4	St. Louis Cardinals-1	Benito Santiago, San Francisco
2003	Florida Marlins-4	Chicago Cubs-3	Iván Rodríguez, Florida
2004	St. Louis Cardinals	Houston Astros	Albert Pujols, St. Louis
2005	Houston Astros-4	St. Louis Cardinals-2	Roy Oswalt, Houston
2006	St. Louis Cards-4	N.Y. Mets-3	Jeff Suppan, Cardinals
2007	Colorado Rockies-4	Arizona Diamondbacks-0	Matt Holliday, Rockies

Note: 1. In 1985, the League Championship Series was switched to a best-of-seven format.

2008 Baseball Playoffs

American League | National League

DIVISION SERIES

RED SOX 3, ANGELS 1

Boston Outfielder Jason Bay homered in each of his first two career playoff games as the Red Sox jumped out to a 2-0 lead on the road. The Angels' 12-inning win in Game 3 broke a nine-game postseason losing streak, and was also Los Angeles's first playoff victory over Boston in the last twelve games, but the Red Sox came right back and won the deciding game on a walk-off single by rookie shortstop Jed Lowrie. Starting pitcher Jon Lester gave up only one unearned run over 14 innings in games one and four. Three of the four winning runs in the series were scored in the last inning.

RAYS 3, WHITE SOX 1

Evan Longoria became the second player in major-league history to hit home runs in each of his first two career postseason at-bats as Tampa Bay began its first playoff series ever with a 6-4 victory over the White Sox. Chicago scored two runs and loaded the bases on Scott Kazmir in the first inning of Game 2, but the Rays starter settled down, worked his way out of the inning, and combined with his bullpen to shut out the Sox the rest of the way to go up 2-0. John Danks, making his first start since clinching Chicago's playoff berth in a one-game playoff against the Minnesota Twins, pitched another winning game to help the White Sox stave off elimination in Game 3, but B.J. Upton homered in his first two at bats in game four, leading the Rays to a second 6-2 win and a trip to the League Championship series against the Boston Red Sox.

PHILLIES 3, BREWERS 1

Three big innings for Philadelphia batsmen made the difference in what was otherwise a four-game pitcher's battle between the Phillies and the Brewers. Philadelphia starter Cole Hamels finished with eight innings of shutout pitching to win the opener. In Game 2, Milwaukee ace C. C. Sabathia's workload finally caught up with him. Making his fourth straight start on three-day's rest, Sabathia gave up a grand slam to Shane Victorino and was pulled after only three and two-thirds innings. Milwaukee avoided a sweep by winning Game 3, but the Phillies hit four home runs, two by Pat Burrell, to take the fourth game and the series.

DODGERS 3, CUBS 0

All four of the divisional series got off to 2-0 starts, but the Dodgers were the only team to pull off a sweep, which they did against the team with the best regular-season record in the National League. James Loney's grand slam gave Los Angeles a 4-2 lead in the fifth inning of Game 1, and they never trailed again. In Game 2, each of Chicago's four infielders were charged with an error, and the Dodgers' four unearned runs were enough to win the game by themselves. Loney's two-run first-inning double was all Los Angeles needed to win Game 3. In all, Loney had two of the Dodgers' three game-winning RBIs depite hitting just .214. All three Dodger starters (Derek Lowe, Chad Billingsley, and Hiroki Kuroda) earned wins, posting a combined ERA of 1.42.

LEAGUE CHAMPIONSHIP SERIES

RAYS 4, RED SOX 3

ALCS MVP Matt Garza beat Red Sox ace Jon Lester twice in a row, in games 3 and 7, and Tampa Bay rookie David Price became the first pitcher in major-league history to record his first postseason win and his first postseason save before earning either in a regular-season game. Daisuke Matsuzaka and the Boston bullpen shut out the Rays in Game 1. The two teams combined for seven home runs in Game 2, including two by Red Sox Dustin Pedroia. A sacrifice fly by B. J. Upton won it for Tampa Bay in the 11th. The Rays won games 3 and 4 handily in Boston's Fenway Park and were ahead 7-0 in the seventh inning of Game 5, nine outs away from their first World Series. Tampa Bay starting pitcher Scott Kazmir was replaced after six dominant innings of two-hit, shutout ball, and Boston scored eight runs on nine hits in the final three innings. J. D. Drew followed up his two-run homer in the seventh with a game-winning RBI single in the ninth. The young Tampa Bay team seemed fatally rattled by the meltdown. But they rallied behind the pitching of Garza and Price to tough out a 3-1 victory and trip to the World Series. During the series, the Rays and Red Sox combined for 26 home runs, an ALCS record. Evan Longoria of Tampa Bay homered in four straight games.

PHILLIES 4, DODGERS 1

An error by Los Angeles shortstop, Rafael Furcal, was followed by home runs from Chase Utley and Pat Burrell as Philadelphia scored all their runs in the sixth inning to beat the Dodgers in Game 1. In Game 2, Phillies starting pitcher Brett Myers made a convincing argument against the designated hitter rule with a three-for-three, two-run, three-RBI night at the plate, which did more than his five-inning, five-run pitching performance to earn him the win. Philadelphia continued to score their runs in bunches, plating four each in the second and third innings and none the rest of the game. The Dodgers raked Phillies starter Jaime Moyer for five runs in the first inning and sailed to victory in Game 3. A high inside fastball from Dodger pitcher Hiroki Kuroda to Phillies outfielder Shane Victorino led to a bench-clearing scene in the top of the third inning, but nobody was ejected. A pair of two-run homers by Victorino and Matt Stairs gave Philadelphia a dramatic come-from-behind win in Game 4. Series MVP Cole Hamels notched his second win in the decisive Game 5. Jimmy Rollins led off the game with a home run, and the Phillies put it out of reach in the fifth with two runs off two more Dodger errors.

INDEX

Z